DIRECTORY OF GEOSCIENCE DEPARTMENTS

56th Edition

Christopher M. Keane, Editor

American Geosciences Institute
Alexandria, Virginia

american
geosciences
institute
connecting earth, science, and people

Directory of Geoscience Departments 2021, 56th Edition
Edited by Christopher M. Keane
ISBN-13: 978-0-922152-46-9
ISBN-10: 0-922152-46-9
ISSN: 0364-7811

Typeset in Times New Roman and Arial using Adobe InDesign CC.

Layout and programming: Christopher M. Keane

Advertising: John P. Rasanen

For more information on the American Geosciences Institute and its publications check us out at https://www.americangeosciences.org

Cover: This view of windmills in the Tehachapi, California area shows one of the world's leading wind energy producers. Prevailing northwesterly winds blow through passes in the Tehachapi Mountains that connect the San Joaquin Valley with the Mojave Desert. The best winds occur from March to September, averaging 15-20 miles per hour.

INTRODUCTION

Thank you for purchasing the 56th edition of the Directory of Geoscience Departments. The American Geosciences Institute (AGI) is grateful to all the departments who updated their information and provided additional historical data of enrollments and awarded degrees for their department.

We have continued the enhancements introduced last year, including the expanded list of research specialties to better represent the various areas of research currently conducted in the geosciences, along with information about specific programs and certificates offered by individual programs, and indications of whether programs offered online or blended courses and degree or certificate programs.

This edition includes a listing of U.S. and Canadian student theses and dissertations from 2018 that have been reported to GeoRef Information Services. We would like to thank GeoRef for their diligent work compiling this list for use in this edition.

The data used to compile the directory is provided by the individuals and departments listed. AGI only edits the information for consistency and format. Any errors or omissions most likely reflect the entries of the individuals or the primary department contact. If you identify any issues, please email keane@americangoesciences.org with information about a current responsible contact for the department in question, so that we may further encourage updates to the next edition.

The American Geosciences Institute does not warrant the accuracy of any of the self-reported information, but we do encourage individuals and departments to update the material they believe is out-of-date.

Some basic statistics for the 56th edition of the Directory of Geoscience Departments: 1928 academic departments and programs globally, with 976 of those departments in the United States. Three hundred twenty-four departments in the United States are two-year institutions. There are 18,132 individuals globally identified in the Directory, with 13,369 in the United States and 1401 in Canada.

Christopher M. Keane
Editor

DIRECTORY OF GEOSCIENCE DEPARTMENTS 56th Edition 2021

TABLE OF CONTENTS

USAGE KEY

Degrees Offered
A - Associate's or 2-year degree
B - Bachelor's or equivalent undergraduate degree
M - Master's Degree
D - Doctorate

Basic enrollment and degrees-granted data for the most recent year reported are shown below department information: degree level, enrollment, and degrees granted (in parentheses).

🗍 indicates thesis and dissertations were provided.
● indicates department offers a field camp only for their majors.
○ indicates department offers a field camp with open enrollment.
☒ indicates department does not offer any online courses
▣ indicates department offers blended learning courses
🖱 indicates department offers fully online courses
☑ indicates department offers fully online programs or certificates

The letters following individual faculty listings indicates their research specialties. Capital letters indicate general area, lowercase letters indicate subspecialty. Two or more consecutive lowercase letters refer to multiple subspecialties in the same major focus area referred to by the preceding capital letter.

DEPARTMENTS AND FACULTIES

This section contains a global listing of academic geoscience departments. Universities and colleges in the United States are arranged alphabetically by state. Non-U.S. institutions are listed alphabetically by country following the U.S. section.

All data is as reported by the departments and faculty themselves and current as of March 17, 2021. If you are aware of updates, corrections, or other means to ensure continued improvement of this listing, please email dgd@americangeosciences.org with the appropriate information so that it can be addressed during the next revision.

Alabama

Alabama A&M University

Dept of Biological and Environmental Sciences (A,B,M,D) (2015)
P.O. Box 1208
Normal, AL 35762
p. (256) 372-4214
wubishet.tadesse@aamu.edu
http://www.aamu.edu

Chair:
Anthony Overton

Professor:
Tommy L. Coleman, (D), Iowa State, 1980, So
Florence A. Okafor, (D), Nigeria, 1995, ZnEn
Govind Sharma, (D), Kansas State, 1970, Zn
James W. Shuford, (D), Penn State, 1975, So

Associate Professor:
Monday O. Mbila, (D), Iowa State, 2000, Sd

Secretary:
Martha Palmer

Auburn University

Dept of Crop, Soil & Environmental Sciences (B,M,D) ☒ (2019)
201 Funchess Hall
Auburn University, AL 36849
p. (334) 844-4100
jpb0035@auburn.edu
Programs: Crop and Soil Sciences (B.S.)
Crop, Soil & Environmental Sciences (M.S., M.Ag., Ph.D.)
Enrollment (2006): M: 8 (2) D: 6 (3)

Professor:
Yucheng Feng, (D), Penn State, 1995, SbCb
Elizabeth A. Guertal, (D), Oklahoma State, 1993, Sc
Joey N. Shaw, (D), Georgia, 1997, Sd

Associate Professor:
Gobena E. Huluka, (D), Auburn, 1990, Sc

Assistant Professor:
Audrey V. Gamble, (D), Delaware, 2017, Sc
Thorsten J. Knappenberger, (D), Hohenheim (Germany), 2009, Sp
Rishi Prasad, (D), Florida, 2014, Sb
Di Tian, (D), Florida, 2014, At
Matthew N. Waters, (D), N Carolina, 2007, Gn

Dept of Geosciences (B,M) ●⊘ (2019)
2050 Beard Eaves Coliseum
Auburn, AL 36849
p. (334) 844-4282
apr0022@auburn.edu
http://www.auburn.edu/cosam/departments/geosciences
Enrollment (2016): B: 62 (17) M: 30 (8)

Chair:
Ming-Kuo Lee, (D), Illinois, 1993, HwGe

Professor:
Willis E. Hames, (D), Virginia Tech, 1990, CcGpt
David T. King, Jr., (D), Missouri, 1980, GrZn
Charles E. Savrda, (D), S California, 1986, GdPeGr
Ashraf Uddin, (D), Florida State, 1996, GdoGt
Lorraine W. Wolf, (D), Alaska (Fairbanks), 1989, Ysg
Haibo Zou, (D), Florida State, 1999, CcGiv

Associate Professor:
Phil L. Chaney, (D), Louisiana State, 1999, ZnnZn
Ronald D. Lewis, (D), Texas, 1982, Pi
Luke J. Marzen, (D), Kansas State, 2001, Zir
Karen S. McNeal, (D), Texas A&M, 2007, ZeGeCm
Martin A. Medina Elizalde, (D), California (Santa Barbara), 2007, PeHyCl

Assistant Professor:
Christopher G. Burton, (D), South Carolina, 2012, Zi
Chandana Mitra, (D), Georgia, 2011, ZgAsZi
Stephanie L. Shepherd, (D), Arkansas, 2010, GmZi

Lecturer:
Carmen P. Brysch, (D), Texas State, 2014
John F. Hawkins, (M), Auburn, 2013, GcZeGt

Emeritus:
Robert B. Cook, (D), Georgia, 1971, Eg
Cyrus B. Dawsey, (D), Florida, 1975, Zy

On Leave:
Mark G. Steltenpohl, (D), N Carolina, 1985, Gtc

Dauphin Island Sea Lab

Marine Science Program (M,D) (2015)
P.O. Box 369
101 Bienville Boulevard
Dauphin Island, AL 36528
p. (334) 861-7528
langelo@disl.org
http://www.disl.org/aboutus.html
Department Secretary: Carolyn F. Wood

Director:
William W. Schroeder, (D), Texas A&M, 1971, Og

Professor:
Thomas S. Hopkins, (D), California (San Diego), 1967, Ob

Associate Professor:
Jonathan R. Pennock, (D), Delaware, 1983, Oc

Librarian:
Dennis Patronas, Zn

University of Alabama

Dept of Geological Sciences (B,M,D) O☒ (2020)
Box 870338
201 7th Avenue
Room 2003 Bevill Bldg.
Tuscaloosa, AL 35487-0338
p. (205) 348-5095
geology@geo.ua.edu
http://www.geo.ua.edu
t: @UA_GEOLOGY
Programs: Geology; Marine Science Geology
Enrollment (2020): B: 74 (16) M: 33 (5) D: 28 (4)

Chair:
Delores Robinson, (D), Arizona, 2001, Gc

Adjunct:
Chunmiao Zheng, (D), Wisconsin, 1988, Hw

Professor:
C. Fred T. Andrus, (D), Georgia, 2000, PcGaCs
Ibrahim Çemen, (D), Penn State, 1983, Gct
Rona J. Donahoe, (D), Stanford, 1984, Cl
Harold H. Stowell, (D), Princeton, 1987, GpCcGt
Nick Tew, (D), Alabama, 1999, EoGro
Geoffrey Tick, (D), Arizona, 2003, Hw

Associate Dean of the Graduate School:
Andrew Goodliffe, (D), Hawaii, 1998, YgeGt

Associate Professor:
Natasha T Dimova, (D), Florida State, 2010, HwCcm
Kimberly Genareau, (D), Arizona State, 2009, Gvi
Samantha E. Hansen, (D), California (Santa Cruz), 2007, YsGt
Yuehan Lu, (D), Michigan, 2008, GgOuGe
Alberto Perez-Huerta, (D), Oregon, 2004, PgClGz
Yong Zhang, (D), Nanjing (China), 1998, Hqw

Assistant Professor:
Julia Cartwright, (D), Manchester (UK), 2010, XmgCc
Deborah A. Keene, (D), Georgia, 2002, Gga
Marcello Minzoni, Kansas, 2007, GosEo
Rebecca T. Minzoni, (D), Rice, 2015, GsPme

Alain Plattner, (D), ETH (Switzerland), 2011, YmuYg
Tom S. Tobin, (D), Washington, 2014, PsCsPe
Matthew Wielicki, (D), California (Los Angeles), CcgGt
Michelle Wielicki, (D), Colorado, 2014, CcXgGi
Bo Zhang, (D), Oklahoma, 2014, YeGoEo
Stable Isotope Research Scientist:
W. Joseph Lambert, (D), Alabama, 2010, CsPeCg
Emeritus:
Paul Aharon, (D), Australian Nat, 1980, ClmCq
Donald J. Benson, (D), Cincinnati, 1976, Gd
Richard H. Groshong, Jr., (D), Brown, 1971, Gc
W. Gary Hooks, (D), N Carolina, 1961, Gm
Ernest A. Mancini, (D), Texas A&M, 1974, Gro
Carl W. Stock, (D), N Carolina, 1977, Pi
Geochemical Research Lab Manager:
Sidhartha Bhattacharyya, (D), Alabama, 2010, CatGe

University of South Alabama

Dept of Earth Sciences (B) O⁄🖱 (2018)
5871 USA Dr. N.
Room 136
Mobile, AL 36688-0002
p. (251) 460-6381
dbeebe@southalabama.edu
http://www.usouthal.edu/earthsci
Programs: Geology (B); Geography (B); Meteorology (B); GIS (minor)
Certificates: GIS
Enrollment (2017): B: 20 (20)
Chair:
Sytske K. Kimball, (D), Penn State, 2000, Am
Professor:
Roy Ryder, (D), Florida, 1989, SdZry
Associate Professor:
David T. Allison, (D), Florida State, 1992, Gc
Murlene W. Clark, (D), Florida State, 1983, PiGrg
Carol F. Sawyer, (D), Texas State, 2007, GmZye
Assistant Professor:
Alex Beebe, (D), Clemson, 2013, Ge
William T. Jackson, (D), Alabama, 2017, GsCc
Steven R. Schultze, (D), Michigan State, 2015, At
Wes Terwey, (D), Colorado State, 2007, Am
Instructor:
Karen J. Jordan, (M), Alabama, 2005, Zyr
Andrew Murray, (M), Florida State, 2010, Am
Diana Sturm, (D), Alabama, 2000, GeZge
Emeritus:
Keith G. Blackwell, (D), Texas A&M, 1990, Am
Douglas W. Haywick, (D), James Cook, 1990, Gs
Aaron Williams, (D), Oklahoma, 1971, Am

Dept of Marine Sciences (M,D) (2019)
307 University Drive
Mobile, AL 36688-0002
p. (334) 460-7136
keyser@southalabama.edu
Administrative Assistant: Jan Keyser
Chair:
Sean Powers, (D), Ob
Professor:
Ronald P. Kiene, (D), SUNY (Stony Brook), 1986, Oc
Adjunct Professor:
Douglas W. Haywick, (D), James Cook, 1990, Gs
Erich M. Mueller, (D), Miami, 1983, Ob

University of West Alabama

Dept of Biological & Environmental Sciences (B) ⁄🖱 (2019)
UWA Station 7
Livingston, AL 35470
p. (205) 652-3416
arindsberg@uwa.edu
http://www.uwa.edu/Biological_and_Environmental_Sciences.aspx
Programs: Environmental Science
Director, Black Belt Museum:
James P. Lamb, (B), Alabama, PvePg
Professor:
Andrew K. Rindsberg, (D), Colorado Mines, 1986, PeGePi

Alaska

University of Alaska, Anchorage

Dept of Geological Sciences (B) ● (2016)
3211 Providence Drive
CPISB 101
Anchorage, AK 99508-4670
p. (907) 786-1298
uaa_mns@uaa.alaska.edu
http://www.uaa.alaska.edu/geology/
f: www.facebook.com/UAAGeologicalSciences
t: @UAAGeology
Enrollment (2015): B: 60 (8)
Chair:
Kristine J. Crossen, (D), Washington, 1997, Gl
Professor:
LeeAnn Munk, (D), Ohio State, 2001, Cle
Associate Professor:
Jennifer Aschoff, (D), Colorado Mines, 2008, GrdGo
Donald Matt Reeves, (D), Nevada, 2006, GeHgZn
Term Assistant Professor:
Terry R. Naumann, (D), Idaho, 1998, Gi
Assistant Professor:
Erin Shea, (D), MIT, 2014, CcGcCg
Term Instructor:
Peter J. Oswald, (M), Idaho, Gg
Mark Rivera, (M), New Mexico State, 2000, Gg

University of Alaska, Fairbanks

Alaska Quaternary Center (2015)
907 Yukon Drive
Fairbanks, AK 99775-1200
p. (907) 474-7758
nhbigelow@alaska.edu
https://www.uaf.edu/aqc/
Administrative Assistant: Leicha Welton
Professor:
W. Scott Ambruster, (D), California (Davis), 1981, Zn
Bruce P. Finney, (D), Oregon State, 1987, Ou
David M. Hopkins, (D), Harvard, 1955, Gg
Roger W. Powers, (D), Wisconsin, 1973, Zn
Dan L. Wetzel, (B), Alaska (Fairbanks), 1975, Zn
Research Associate:
Wendy H. Arundale, (D), Michigan State, 1976, Zn
Peter Bowers, (M), Washington State, 1980, Ga
Owen Mason, (D), Alaska, 1990, Ga
Adjunct Professor:
Daniel H. Mann, (D), Washington, 1983, Pe
Geology Librarian:
Judy Triplehorn, Zn

Dept of Civil & Environmental Engineering (2015)
Fairbanks, AK 99775-5900
jlhulsey@alaska.edu

Dept of Geosciences (B,M,D) O⁄🖱 (2019)
1930 Yukon Drive
P.O. Box 755780
Fairbanks, AK 99775-5780
p. (907) 474-7565
pjmccarthy@alaska.edu
http://www.uaf.edu/geology/
Programs: Geoscience; Geology; Geophysics; Earth Science; Geography
Enrollment (2019): B: 94 (10) M: 44 (10) D: 34 (5)
Chair:
Paul McCarthy, (D), Guelph, 1995, GsSaPc
Professor:
Bernard Coakley, (D), Columbia, 1991, Yg
Patrick S. Druckenmiller, (D), Calgary, 2006, Pv
Sarah J. Fowell, (D), Columbia, 1994, Pl
Regine M. Hock, (D), Swiss Fed Inst Tech, 1997, Gl
Jessica F. Larsen, (D), California (Santa Cruz), 1996, Gv
Franz J. Meyer, (D), Tech (Munich), 2004, Zr
Rainer J. Newberry, (D), Stanford, 1980, Em
Vladimir Romanovsky, (D), Alaska (Fairbanks), 1996, Yg
Michael T. Whalen, (D), Syracuse, 1993, Gs

Associate Professor:
Cary de Wit, (D), Kansas, 1997, Zg
Ronni Grapenthin, (D), Yd
Chris Maio, (D), Massachusetts (Boston), 2014, Zy
Dan Mann, (D), Washington, 1983, Zy
Elisabeth S. Nadin, (D), Caltech, 2007, Gtc
Carl Tape, (D), Caltech, 2009, Ys
Assistant Professor:
Sean Regan, (D), Gzx
Instructor:
Jochen E. Mezger, (D), Alberta, 1997, GcpCc
Emeritus:
James E. Beget, (D), Washington, 1981, Gm
Douglas Christensen, (D), Michigan, 1987, Ys
Catherine L. Hanks, (D), Alaska (Fairbanks), 1991, Go
Mary J. Keskinen, (D), Stanford, 1979, Gxz
Kenneth P. Severin, (D), California (Davis), 1987
David B. Stone, (D), Newcastle, 1963, Ym
Donald M. Triplehorn, (D), Illinois, 1961, Gs

Dept of Mining & Geological Engineering (B,M,D) (2020)
P.O. Box 755800
Fairbanks, AK 99775-5800
p. (907) 474-7388
mmdarrow@alaska.edu
http://www.alaska.edu/uaf/cem/ge/
Administrative Assistant: Judy L. Johnson
Enrollment (2011): B: 10 (10) M: 2 (2) D: 2 (2)
Professor:
Sukumar Bandopadhyay, (D), Penn State, 1982, Nm
Gang Chen, (D), Virginia Tech, 1989, Nm
Scott L. Huang, (D), Missouri (Rolla), 1981
Hsing K. Lin, (D), Utah, 1985, Zn
Paul A. Metz, (D), Imperial Coll (UK), 1991
Debsmita Misra, (D), Minnesota, 1994, HwZrNg
Daniel E. Walsh, (D), Alaska (Fairbanks), 1984, Zn
Assistant Professor:
Margaret M. Darrow, (D), Znn
Sabry Sabour Hafez, (D), Nm
Emeritus:
Rajive Ganguli, (D), Kentucky, 1999, Nm

Dept of Petroleum Engineering (2015)
Fairbanks, AK 99775-5880
adandekar@alaska.edu

University of Alaska Museum Earth Science (B,M,D) ○☒ (2020)
Box 756960
Fairbanks, AK 99775-6960
p. (907) 474-7505
psdruckenmiller@alaska.edu
http://www.uaf.edu/museum/collections/earth/
Programs: Geology
Enrollment (2020): M: 2 (1) D: 0 (1)
Curator of Earth Science:
Patrick S. Druckenmiller, (D), Calgary, 2006, Pv

University of Alaska, Southeast

Dept of Natural Sciences ⦸ (2021)
11066 Auke Lake Way
Juneau, AK 99801
p. (907) 796-6580
sanagorski@alaska.edu
https://www.uas.alaska.edu/arts_sciences/naturalsciences/
Programs: Environmental Science B.S.
Environmental Resources B.S.
Environmental Studies B.A.
Assistant Professor:
Sonia Nagorski, (D), Montana, 2001, GgZcCt

Arizona

Arizona State University

School of Earth and Space Exploration (B,M,D) ● (2020)
Box 871404
Tempe, AZ 85287-1404
p. (480) 965-5081
sese@asu.edu
https://sese.asu.edu
f: https://www.facebook.com/SESE.at.ASU
t: @SESEASU
Programs: Earth and Environmental Studies, Earth and Space Exploration, Astrobiology and Biogeosciences, Astrophysics, Exploration Systems Design, Geological Sciences
Enrollment (2019): B: 230 (65) M: 17 (8) D: 73 (15)
Director:
Meenakshi Wadhwa, (D), Washington (St Louis), 1994, Xc
Research Professor:
Laurence Garvie, (D), Bristol, 1991, GzXc
Amy Jurewicz, (D), Stanford, 1986, Xm
Paul Scowen, (D), Rice, 1993, Xa
Lynda Williams, (D), Calgary, 2000, Gb
Mikhail Y. Zolotov, (D), Vernadsky Inst (Russia), 1990, Cg
Professor of Practice:
Catherine Coleman, (D), Massachusetts, 1991, Ze
Professor:
Ariel D. Anbar, (D), Caltech, 1996, CbsXb
Ramon Arrowsmith, (D), Stanford, 1995, GcmGt
Gregory Asner, (D), Colorado, 1997, ZrGmSb
James Bell, (D), Hawaii, 1992, Xg
Judd Bowman, (D), MIT, 2007, Xa
Donald M. Burt, (D), Harvard, 1972, EgCgGz
Peter R. Buseck, (D), Columbia, 1962, Cg
Philip R. Christensen, (D), California (Los Angeles), 1981, Xg
Steven Desch, (D), Illinois, 1998, Xa
Linda Elkins-Tanton, (D), MIT, 2002, Xg
Jack D. Farmer, (D), California (Davis), 1978, Pg
Edward Garnero, (D), Caltech, 1994, Ys
Arjun Heimsath, (D), California (Berkeley), 1999, Gc
Richard Hervig, (D), Chicago, 1979, Cg
Kip V. Hodges, (D), MIT, 1982, CcGtXg
Philip Mauskopf, (D), California (Berkeley), 1997, Xa
Stephen J. Reynolds, (D), Arizona, 1982, GctZe
Mark Robinson, (D), Hawaii, 1993, Xg
Steven Semken, (D), MIT, 1989, ZeGgZg
Thomas G. Sharp, (D), Arizona State, 1990, Gz
Everett Shock, (D), California (Berkeley), 1987, Cg
Sumner Starrfield, (D), California (Los Angeles), 1969, XaZnn
Francis Timmes, (D), California (Santa Cruz), 1992, Xa
James A. Tyburczy, (D), Oregon, 1983, GyzYx
Enrique Vivoni, (D), MIT, 2003, Hg
Ian Walker, (D), Guelph, 2000, Gm
Kelin Whipple, (D), Washington, 1994, Gmt
Rogier Windhorst, (D), Leiden (Neth), 1984, Xa
Research Professor:
Cassandra Bowman, (D), Harvard, 2008, Ze
Steven Ruff, (D), Arizona State, 1998, Xg
David Williams, (D), Alabama, 1998, Xg
Associate Professor:
Nathaniel Butler, (D), MIT, 2003, Xa
Amanda Clarke, (D), Penn State, 2002, Gv
Christopher Groppi, (D), Arizona, 2003, XaZrn
Hilairy E. Hartnett, (D), Washington, 1998, ComOc
Jennifer Patience, (D), California (Los Angeles), 2000, Xa
Evan Scannapieco, (D), California (Berkeley), 2001, Xa
Sang-Heon Shim, (D), Princeton, 2011, Gz
Manoochehr Shirzaei, (D), Potsdam, 2010, Yd
Evgenya Shkolnik, (D), British Columbia, 2004, Xa
Heather Throop, (D), SUNY (Stony Brook), 2002, Cb
Sara Walker, (D), Dartmouth, 2010, Xb
Patrick Young, (D), Arizona, 2004, Xa
Research Professor:
Duane DeVecchio, (D), California (Santa Barbara), 2009, GtmGc
Jordan Okie, (D), New Mexico, 2011, Cb
Devin Schrader, (D), Arizona, 2012, Xm
Assistant Professor:
Melanie Barboni, (D), Lusanne, 2011, Gi
Sanchayeeta Borthakur, (D), Massachusetts, 2010, Xa
Maitrayee Bose, (D), Washington (St Louis), 2011, Xc
Craig Hardgrove, (D), Tennessee, 2011, Xg
Daniel Jacobs, (D), Pennsylvania, 2011, Xa
Mingming Li, (D), Arizona State, 2015, Yg
Michael Line, (D), Caltech, 2013, Xy
Allison Noble, (D), McGill, 2014, Xa
Joseph O'Rourke, (D), Caltech, Xy
Christy Till, (D), MIT, 2011, Gi

Elizabeth Trembath-Reichert, (D), Caltech, 2016, Cb
Alexander Van Engelen, (D), McGill, Xa
Emeritus:
L. Paul Knauth, (D), Caltech, 1979, Cs
Robert F. Lundin, (D), Illinois, 1962, Pm
Edmund Stump, (D), Ohio State, 1976, Gt
Stanley N. Williams, (D), Dartmouth, 1983, Gv

Arizona Western College

Dept of Geosciences (A) (2020)
2020 S. Avenue 8E
Yuma, AZ 85365
p. (928) 317-6000
fred.croxen@azwestern.edu
https://www.azwestern.edu/instruction/science
Programs: Geology (A); Geography (A); Applied Geology (A)
Certificates: GIS Technician, UAS Operator (Unmanned Aerial Systems)
Enrollment (2017): A: 1 (0)
Professor:
Fred W. Croxen III, (M), N Arizona, 1977, HwPvZi
Catherine R. Hill, (M), GgOgHw
Adjunct Professor:
Heather Casares, (M), Ball State, 2019, Gvi
Kelly L. Esslinger, (M), AsOpGg
Maureen Garrett, (M), Mississippi State, 2004, GgeOg
Todd Pinnt, (M), N Arizona, 2017, ZyiZg

Central Arizona College

Div of Science (2015)
Coolidge, AZ 85228
p. (602) 426-4444
diane.beecroft@centralaz.edu
Instructor:
Allan E. Morton, (M), Brigham Young, 1975, Ze

Cochise College

Geology Dept (A) (2016)
901 North Colombo Avenue
Sierra Vista, AZ 85635
p. (520) 515-5425
deakinj@cochise.edu
http://skywalker.cochise.edu/wellerr/aawellerweb.htm
Instructor:
Joann Deakin, (M), Mast, Ggg

Dine' College

Science Dept (A,B) (2017)
#1 Circle Drive
Tsaile, Navajo Nation, AZ 86556
p. (928) 724-6721
cacate@dinecollege.edu
http://www.dinecollege.edu
Chair:
Don Robinson, (D), Maharishi Mgmt
Instructor:
Margaret Mayer, (M), Rhode Island, GeZn

Mesa Community College

Dept of Physical Science (A) (2015)
1833 W. Southern Avenue
Mesa, AZ 85202
p. (480) 461-7015
kelli.santistevan@mesacc.edu
http://www.mesacc.edu/dept/d43/glg/
Professor:
Donna M. Benson, (M), Arizona State, 1996, Gg
Kaatje Kraft, (M), Arizona State, 1999, Gg
Robert S. Leighty, (D), Arizona State, 1997, Zg
Adjunct Professor:
Zack Bowles, (M), Arizona State, Gg
Chloe Branciforte, (M), SD Mines, Gg
Mike Grivois, (M), Texas Christian
Steve Guggino
Jack Kepper
Jill Lockard
Tony Occhiuzzi, (M), Arizona State, Zn
Donna Pollard, (M)
Joanna Scheffler, (M), Washington State, Gg
Melinda Shimizu, (M), Arizona State, 2008, Gg
Carolyn Taylor, (M), Georgia State, Gg
Kelli Wakefield, (M), Arizona State, Gg
Emeritus:
Armand J. Lombard, (M), Arizona, 1977, Gg

Northern Arizona University

Dept of Geography, Planning, and Recreation (B,M) (2020)
P.O. Box 15015
Flagstaff, AZ 86011
p. (928) 523-2650
geog@nau.edu
https://nau.edu/gpr/
f: https://www.facebook.com/NAUGPR
Programs: Parks and Recreation Management Planning, Geography
Certificates: GIS, Planning
Enrollment (2013): B: 39 (15) M: 44 (17)
Park Ranger Training Program Director:
Mark J. Maciha, (M), N Arizona, 2009, ZnnZn
Coordinator, Parks and Recreation Management Program:
Charles Hammersley, (D), New Mexico, 1988, Zn
Associate Professor:
Rebecca D. Hawley, (D), Arizona State, 1994, Zn
Ruihong Huang, (D), Wisconsin (Milwaukee), 2003
Associate Scientist:
Erik Schiefer, (D), British Columbia, 2004, GmZyi
Lecturer - Outdoor Leadership and Education:
Aaron Divine, (M), N Arizona, 2004, ZnnZn
Distance Learning Lecturer:
R. Marieke Taney, (M), N Arizona, 2002, ZnnZn
Senior Lecturer:
Judith Montoya, (M), New Mexico, 1985, Zy
Professor and Chair:
Pamela Foti, (D), Wisconsin, 1988, Zn
Emeritus:
Graydon L. Berlin, (D), Tennessee, 1970, Zr
Robert O. Clark, (D), Denver, 1970, Zn
Carolyn M. Daugherty, (D), Arizona State, 1987, Zn
Leland R. Dexter, (D), Colorado, 1986, Zy
Christina B. Kennedy, (D), Arizona, 1989, Zn
Alan A. Lew, (D), Oregon, 1986, Zgn
Stanley W. Swarts, (D), California (Los Angeles), 1975, Zy
George A. Van Otten, (D), Oregon State, 1977, Zn

Div of Geosciences, School of Earth and Sustainability (B,M,D) O (2019)
P O Box 4099
Building 12, Room 100
625 S Knoles Dr
Flagstaff, AZ 86011-4099
p. 928-523-9333
SES.Admin@nau.edu
https://nau.edu/ses/division-of-geosciences/
Enrollment (2018): B: 120 (32) M: 26 (9)
Professor:
David K. Elliott, (D), Bristol, 1979, Pv
Thomas D. Hoisch, (D), S California, 1985, Gp
Darrell S. Kaufman, (D), Colorado, 1991, Zc
Michael H. Ort, (D), California (Santa Barbara), 1991, Gv
Roderic A. Parnell, (D), Dartmouth, 1982, Cl
Mary R. Reid, (D), MIT, 1987, CucGi
Nancy Riggs, (D), California (Santa Barbara), 1991, Gv
James C. Sample, (D), California (Santa Cruz), 1986, GtClOu
Abraham E. Springer, (D), Ohio State, 1994, Hw
Paul J. Umhoefer, (D), Washington, 1989, Gt
Associate Professor:
Laura Wasylenki, (D), Caltech, 1999, ClOoCs
Assistant Professor:
Nicholas McKay, (D), Arizona, 2012, PcZo
Ryan Porter, (D), Arizona, 2011, YgsGt
Michael E. Smith, (D), Wisconsin, 2007, Gsr
Research Associate:
Joseph E. Hazel, Jr., (M), N Arizona, 1991, Gs
Matthew A. Kaplinski, (M), N Arizona, 1990, Yg

Lecturer:
Lisa Skinner, (M), ZeGvZi
Kelsey Winsor, (D), Wisconsin, 2014, PcGm
Adjunct Professor:
Wendell A. Duffield, (D), Stanford, 1967, Gv
David D. Gillette, (D), S Methodist, 1974, Pv
James Wittke, (D), Texas, 1984, Gi
Emeritus:
Charles W. Barnes, (D), Wisconsin, 1965, GcXg
Ronald C. Blakey, (D), Iowa, 1973, Gr
David S. Brumbaugh, (D), Indiana, 1972, Ys
Ernest M. Duebendorfer, (D), Wyoming, 1986, Gct
Richard F. Holm, (D), Washington, 1969, Gv
James I. Mead, (D), Arizona, 1983, Pg
Larry T. Middleton, (D), Wyoming, 1979, Gs
Paul Morgan, (D), London (UK), 1973, Yh
Business Manager:
Sarah Colby, Zn

Phoenix College

Dept of Physical Sciences (A) (2016)
1202 West Thomas Road
Phoenix, AZ 85013
p. (602) 285-7244
abeer.hamdan@phoenixcollege.edu
Chair:
James J. White, (D), Arizona, 1986
Professor:
Richard Cups, (M), Arizona State, 1983, Gg
Don Speed, (M), Arizona, 1980, Gg

Pima Community College - Community Campus

Geology Dept (2015)
401 North Bonita Ave.
Tucson, AZ 85709-5000
p. (520) 206-4500
wrcavanaugh@pima.edu
http://www.pima.edu

Pima Community College - West Campus

Geology Dept (2015)
2202 West Anklam Rd.
Tucson, AZ 85709-0001
p. (520) 206-4500
jrasmussen@pima.edu
http://www.pima.edu

Prescott College

Dept of Environmental Studies (B) (2015)
220 Grove Avenue
Prescott, AZ 86301
p. (928) 350-2256
eboyer@prescott.edu
http://www.prescott.edu
Professor:
Kurt Refsnider, (D), Colorado, 2012, GmlPe

Scottsdale Community College

Dept of Mathematics and Sciences (2015)
9000 East Chaparral Road
Scottsdale, AZ 85256-2626
p. (480) 423-6111
merry.wilson@scottsdalecc.edu
http://www.scottsdalecc.edu/academics/departments/math-sciences

South Mountain Community College

Geology Program (2015)
7050 South 24th Street
Phoenix, AZ 85042-5806
p. (602) 243-8290
jacqueline.levy@southmountaincc.edu
http://www.southmountaincc.edu/math-science-engineering/program/geology/

University of Arizona

Dept of Geosciences (B,M,D) O (2015)
Gould-Simpson Building
1040 E. Fourth Street
Tucson, AZ 85721-0077
p. (520) 621-6000
bcarrapa@email.arizona.edu
http://www.geo.arizona.edu
Administrative Assistant: Anne Chase
Administrative Assistant: Sylvia Quintero
Enrollment (2006): B: 70 (0) M: 23 (0) D: 52 (0)
Head:
Peter Reiners, (D), Washington, Cg
Professor:
Victor R. Baker, (D), Colorado, 1971, GmXgRh
Mark D. Barton, (D), Chicago, 1981, Eg
Susan L. Beck, (D), Michigan, 1987, YsGt
Richard Bennett, (D), MIT, 1995, YdGt
Jon Chorover, California (Berkeley), 1993, Sc
Andrew S. Cohen, (D), California (Davis), 1982, Ps
Julia E. Cole, (D), Columbia, 1992, PeCsAs
Owen K. Davis, (D), Minnesota, 1981, Pl
Peter G. DeCelles, (D), Indiana, 1984, GtsGc
Robert T. Downs, (D), Virginia Tech, 1992, Gi
Mihai N. Ducea, (D), Caltech, 1998, Gt
Karl W. Flessa, (D), Brown, 1973, PgeGe
Jiba Ganguly, (D), Chicago, 1967, Gx
George E. Gehrels, (D), Caltech, 1986, Gt
Vance T. Holliday, (D), Colorado, 1982, GamSa
Roy A. Johnson, (D), Wyoming, 1984, Ys
A. J. Timothy Jull, (D), Bristol, 1976, CclCg
Paul A. Kapp, (D), California (Los Angeles), 2001, GtcGm
Alfred S. McEwen, (D), Arizona State, 1988, XgGmv
Jonathan T. Overpeck, (D), Brown, 1985, As
Jon D. Pelletier, (D), Cornell, 1997, Gm
Mary Poulton, (D), Arizona, 1990, Ng
Jay Quade, (D), Utah, 1990, Sc
Randall M. Richardson, (D), MIT, 1978, Yg
Joaquin Ruiz, (D), Michigan, 1983, CgcEz
Timothy Swindle, (D), Washington, 1986, Xc
Connie Woodhouse, (D), Arizona, 1996, Pe
Associate Specialist:
Michael A. Crimmins, (D), Arizona, 2004, Zc
Associate Professor:
Barbara Carrapa, (D), Vrije (Amsterdam), 2002, Gs
Joellen Russell, (D), Scripps, 1999, Oc
Eric Seedorff, (D), Stanford, 1987, Eg
Jessica Tierney, (D), Brown, 2010, Co
Marek Zreda, (D), New Mexico Tech, 1994, Cc
Assistant Professor:
Jennifer McIntosh, (D), Michigan, 2004, Hy
Jianjun Yin, (D), Illinois, Og
Lecturer:
Paul Goodman, Washington, 2000, As
Jessica Kapp, (D), California (Los Angeles), Gg
Adjunct Professor:
Robert J. Kamilli, (D), Harvard, 1976, EgmCg
Charles Prewitt, (D), MIT, 1969, Zn
Marc Sbar, (D), Columbia, 1972, Yes
Emeritus:
William B. Bull, (D), Stanford, 1960, Gm
Clement G. Chase, (D), California (San Diego), 1970, Yg
George H. Davis, (D), Michigan, 1971, Gc
William R. Dickinson, (D), Stanford, 1958, Gt
John M. Guilbert, (D), Wisconsin, 1962, Em
DeVerle P. Harris, (D), Penn State, 1965, Eg
C. Vance Haynes, Jr., (D), Arizona, 1965, Ga
Everett H. Lindsay, (D), California (Berkeley), 1967, Pv
Edgar J. McCullough, Jr., (D), Arizona, 1963, Ge
Jonathan Patchett, (D), Edinburgh, 1976
Joseph Schreiber, (D)
Spencer R. Titley, (D), Arizona, 1958, Eg
George Zandt, (D), MIT, 1978, Ys
Researcher:
David Dettman, (D), Michigan, 1994, Cs
Chris J. Eastoe, (D), Tasmania, 1979, CsGg

Dept of Hydrology & Atmospheric Sciences (B,M,D) ● (2015)
226A Harshbarger Building #11
PO Box 210011
Tucson, AZ 85721-0011
p. (520) 621-5082
tmeixner@email.arizona.edu
http://www.hwr.arizona.edu
Administrative Assistant: Erma Santander
Enrollment (2014): B: 0 (2) M: 23 (2) D: 27 (1)
Head:
Thomas Maddock, III, (D), Harvard, 1972, Hq
Regents Professor:
Victor R. Baker, (D), Colorado, 1971, GmXgRh
W. James Shuttleworth, (D), Manchester (UK), 1971, Hs
Director, SAHRA Center:
Juan B. Valdes, (D), MIT, 1976, Hs
Professor:
Paul D. Brooks, (D), Colorado, 1995, Cg
Paul A. Ferre, (D), Waterloo, 1997, Hw
Hoshin V. Gupta, (D), Case Western, 1984, HqZgAs
Thomas Meixner, (D), Arizona, 1999, CgRw
Peter A. Troch, (D), Ghent, 1993, Hs
Tian-Chyi Jim Yeh, (D), New Mexico Tech, 1983, Hq
Marek G. Zreda, (D), New Mexico Tech, 1994, Hw
Associate Professor:
Michael D. Bradley, (D), Michigan, 1971, Zn
Jennifer C. McIntosh, (D), Michigan, 2004, Cg
Associate Director, SAHRA Center:
Gary C. Woodard, (D), Michigan, 1981, Zn
Adjunct Associate Professor:
David C. Goodrich, (D), Arizona, 1990, Hs
Robert H. Webb, (D), Arizona, 1985, Gm
Adjunct Assistant Professor:
James E. Smith, (D), Waterloo, 1995, Hw
Adjunct Professor:
Roger C. Bales, (D), Caltech, 1984, Cg
David Hargis, (D), Arizona, 1979, Hwq
Leo S. Leonhart, (D), Arizona, 1978, Hw
Robert MacNish, (D), Michigan, 1966, Hw
Soroosh Sorooshian, (D), California (Los Angeles), 1978, Hg
Donald W. Young, (D), Arizona, 1994, Zn
Regents Professor:
Shlomo P. Neuman, (D), California (Berkeley), 1968, HwqGq
Chair, Global Change IDP:
Katherine K. Hirschboeck, (D), Arizona, 1985, AtHsRn
Emeritus:
Robert A. Clark, (D), Texas A&M, 1964, Hs
Lucien Duckstein, (D), Colorado State, 1962, Hq
Simon Ince, (D), Iowa, 1953, Hs
Austin Long, (D), Arizona State, 1966, Cl
Ernest T. Smerdon, (D), Missouri State, 1959, Hs
Arthur W. Warrick, (D), Iowa State, 1967, Sp
Peter J. Wierenga, (D), California (Davis), 1968, Sp
Lorne G. Wilson, (D), California (Davis), 1962, Hw
Cooperating Faculty:
Mark L. Brusseau, (D), Florida, 1989, Hw
Jonathan D. Chorover, (D), California (Berkeley), 1993, Cg
Bonnie C. Colby, (D), Wisconsin, 1983, Zn
R. B. Hawkins, (D), Colorado State, 1968, Hs
Kevin E. Lansey, (D), Texas, 1987, Hs
Sharon B. Megdal, (D), Princeton, 1981, Hg
Steven L. Mullen, (D), Washington, 1985, As
Robert G. Varady, (D), Arizona, 1981, Zn
Marvin Waterstone, (D), Rutgers, 1983, Zn

Dept of Mining & Geological Engineering (B,M,D) (2020)
1235 E. James E. Rogers Way
Mines Building, Room 229
PO Box 210012
Tucson, AZ 85721-0012
p. (520) 621-6063
ENGR-Mining@email.arizona.edu
http://www.mge.engineering.arizona.edu
f: https://www.facebook.com/UAMining/
Programs: Mining Engineering, Mining & Geological Engineering
Certificates: Mineral Processing and Extractive Metallurgy Geomechanics and Rock Mechanics, Mine Production & Information Technology, Mining Occupational Health & Safety
Enrollment (2017): B: 71 (26) M: 24 (8) D: 11 (4)
Professor of Practice:
Victor O. Tenorio, (D), Arizona, 2012, Nmx
Director, Lab for Advanced Subsurface Imaging:
Ben K. Sternberg, (D), Wisconsin, 1977, Ye
Professor:
John M. Kemeny, (D), California (Berkeley), 1986, Nr
Interim Head:
Moe Momayez, (D), McGill, NmYxNr
Associate Professor:
Jaeheon Lee, (D), Arizona, 2004, Nx
Jinhong Zhang, (D), Virginia Tech, 2006, Nm
Assistant Professor:
Isabel Barton, (D), Arizona
Kwangmin Kim, (D), Arizona, 2012, NmrNx
Emeritus:
J. Brent Hiskey, (D), Utah, 1973, Nx

Dept of Soil, Water & Environmental Science (B,M,D) ☒ (2019)
PO Box 210038
Shantz 429
Tucson, AZ 85721-0038
p. (520) 621-1646
wrhaley@email.arizona.edu
https://swes.cals.arizona.edu
Programs: Environmental Science, Sustainable Plant Systems, Subsurface science, Soil, plant, atmosphere systems
Head:
Jonathan Chorover, (D), California (Berkeley), 1993, ScClo
Associate Director, SAHRA Center:
Katharine L. Jacobs, (M), California (Berkeley), 1981, Hg
Professor:
Mark L. Brusseau, (D), Florida, 1989, Hw
Kevin Fitzsimmons, (D), Arizona, 1999, Zn
Charles P. Gerba, (D), Miami, 1973, Sb
Martha C. Hawes, (D)
Raina M. Maier, (D), Rutgers, 1988, Zn
Ian L. Pepper, (D), Ohio State, 1975, Zn
Craig Rasmussen, (D), SzGmCl
Charles Sanchez, (D), Iowa State, 1986, Zn
Jeffrey C. Silvertooth, (D), Oklahoma State, 1986, So
Markus Tuller, (D), Zn
James Walworth, (D), Georgia, 1985, Soc
Arthur W. Warrick, (D), Iowa State, 1967, Sp
Associate Professor:
Joan E. Curry, (D), California (Davis), 1992, Sc
Marcel Schaap, (D), So
Assistant Professor:
Karletta Chief, (D), Arizona, 2007, Zn
Associate Research Scientist:
Janick F. Artiola, (D), Arizona, 1980, ScHsCa
Associate Professor of Practice:
Thomas B. Wilson, (D), Zn
Adjunct Professor:
Floyd Adamsen, (D), Colorado State, 1983, So
Paul (Ty) Ferre, (D), So
Jim Yeh, (D), Sp
Emeritus:
Ed Glenn, (D), Hawaii, 1978, Zn
Donald F. Post, (D), Purdue, 1967, Sd
James Riley, (D), Arizona, 1968, Zn
Peter J. Wierenga, (D), California, 1968, Sp
Extension Specialist:
Paul W. Brown, (D), Wisconsin, 1981, Am

Laboratory of Tree Ring Research O (2019)
Bryant Bannister Tree-Ring Bldg
1215 E. Lowell St.
Tucson, AZ 85721
p. (520) 621-1608
webmaster@ltrr.arizona.edu
http://ltrr.arizona.edu/
f: https://www.facebook.com/pages/Laboratory-of-Tree-Ring-Research/112628272090047
t: @TreeRingLabUA
Certificates: Graduate Certificate in Dendrochronology
Professor:
David C. Frank, (D), Bern, 2005
Malcolm K. Hughes, (D), Durham (UK), 1970, Pe
Steven W. Leavitt, (D), Arizona, 1982, Csc

Russ Monson, (D), Washington State, 1982
Associate Professor:
Bryan A. Black, (D), 2003
Paul Sheppard, (D), 1995
Ronald Towner, (D), Arizona, 1997, Gae
Valerie Trouet, (D), KU Leuven, 2004, PeZyAs
Assistant Professor:
Charlotte Pearson, (D), Reading (UK), 2003
Research Associate:
Matthew W. Salzer, (D), Arizona, 2000, PeGav
Christopher H. Guiterman, (D), Arizona, 2016
Kiyomi A. Morino, (D), Arizona, 2008
Emeritus:
Jeffrey S. Dean, (D), Arizona, 1967, Zn
Katherine K. Hirschboeck, (D), Arizona, 1985, AsHsZc
Charles W. Stockton, (D), Arizona, 1971, Hq
Thomas W. Swetnam, (D), Arizona, 1987, Pe
Research Professor:
David M. Meko, (D), Arizona, 1981, Hq
Ramzi Touchan, (D), Arizona, 1991, PcHsAs
Curator, Collections:
Peter Brewer, (D), Reading (UK), 2004
Associate Professor:
Pearce Paul Creasman, (D), Texas A&M, 2008
Assoc. Research Professor:
Irina Panyushkina, (D), Sukachev Inst Forest, 1997
Assistant Research Professor:
Margaret Evans, (D), Arizona, 2003

Lunar and Planetary Laboratory (M,D) (2015)
1629 E. University Boulevard
Tucson, AZ 85721-0092
p. (520) 621-6963
acad_info@lpl.arizona.edu
http://www.lpl.arizona.edu
Head:
Michael J. Drake, (D), Oregon, 1972, Xc
Research Professor:
Martin G. Tomasko, (D), Princeton, 1969, As
Professor:
Erik I. Asphaug, (D), Arizona, 1993, XygXa
Victor R. Baker, (D), Colorado, 1971, XgGmRh
William V. Boynton, (D), Carnegie Mellon, 1971, XcZr
Robert H. Brown, (D), Hawaii, 1982, Xc
Uwe Fink, (D), Penn State, 1965, As
Tom Gehrels, (D), Chicago, 1956, Zn
Richard J. Greenberg, (D), MIT, 1972, Xy
Donald M. Hunten, (D), McGill, 1950, As
Jack R. Jokipii, (D), Caltech, 1965, Xy
Harold P. Larson, (D), Purdue, 1967, Zn
Dante Lauretta, (D), Washington (St Louis), 1997, XcmXg
Jonathan I. Lunine, (D), Caltech, 1985, Xc
Renu Malhotra, (D), Cornell, 1988, Xs
Alfred McEwen, (D), Arizona State, 1988, Xg
Henry J. Melosh, (D), Caltech, 1972, Gt
George H. Rieke, (D), Harvard, 1969, Zn
Timothy D. Swindle, (D), Washington (St Louis), 1986, XmCc
Roger Yelle, (D), Wisconsin, 1984, Zn
Senior Research Scientist:
Lonnie L. Hood, (D), California (Los Angeles), 1979, XyAs
Larry A. Lebofsky, (D), MIT, 1974, ZngXm
Senior Scientist:
Jozsef Kota, (D), Roland Eotvos, 1980, As
David Kring, (D), Harvard, 1989, XcGiXg
Associate Professor:
Caitlin Griffith, (D), SUNY (Stony Brook), 1991, Zn
Robert Kursinski, (D), Caltech, 1997, As
Associate Research Scientist:
Robert S. McMillan, (D), Texas, 1977, ZnnZn
Assistant Professor:
Joe Giacalone, (D), Kansas, 1991, Xy
Adam Showman, (D), Caltech, 1998, Zn
Senior Research Scientist:
Lyle A. Broadfoot, (D), Saskatchewan, 1963, Zr
Jay B. Holberg, (D), California (Berkeley), 1974, As
Bill R. Sandel, (D), Rice, 1972, As
Research Associate:
Alexander Dessler, (D), Duke, 1956, Zn
Ralph Lorenz, (D), Kent (UK), 1994, Xg
Elizabeth Turtle, (D), Arizona, 1998, Xg
Associate Research Scientist:
Peter Smith, (M), Arizona, 1977, Zr
Emeritus:
William B. Hubbard, (D), California (Berkeley), 1967, XyYvAs
John S. Lewis, (D), California (San Diego), 1968, Xcm
Elizabeth Roemer, (D), California (Berkeley), 1955, Zn
Charles P. Sonett, (D), California (Los Angeles), 1954, Yg
Robert G. Strom, (M), Stanford, 1957, Xg
Graduate Secretary:
Mary Guerrieri, Zn

School of Geography and Development (B,M,D) (2015)
Harvill Building
PO Box 210076
Tucson, AZ 85721
p. (520) 621-1652
liverman@email.arizona.edu
http://geography.arizona.edu/
Enrollment (2010): B: 350 (0) M: 20 (0) D: 54 (0)
Director:
Paul Robbins, (D), Clark, 1996
Dean:
John Paul Jones, III, (D), Ohio State, 1984, Zn
Co-Director of the University of Arizona Institute of the Env :
Diana Liverman, (D), California (Los Angeles), 1984
Professor:
Michael E. Bonine, (D), Texas, 1975, Zu
Andrew Comrie, (D), Pennsylvania, 1992, Zy
Sallie A. Marston, (D), Colorado, 1986, Zu
Beth A. Mitchneck, (D), Columbia, 1990, Zn
David A. Plane, (D), Pennsylvania, 1981, Zn
Lecturer:
Dereka Rushbrook, (D), Arizona, 2005
Associate Professor:
Keiron D. Bailey, (D), Kentucky, 2002, Zi
Carl J. Bauer, (D), California (Berkeley), 1995, Hs
Sandy Dall'Erba, (D), Pau, 2004
Elizabeth Oglesby, (D), California (Berkeley), 2002, Zn
Christopher A. Scott, (D), Cornell, 1998, Hw
Willem van Leeuwen, (D), Arizona, 1995, Zy
Marvin Waterstone, (D), Rutgers, 1983, Zn
Margaret Wilder, (D), Arizona, 2002, Zn
Director of GIST:
Christopher Lukinbeal, (D), San Diego State, 2000, Zi
Assistant Professor:
Jeffrey Banister, (D), Arizona, 2010
Gary Christopherson, (D), Arizona, 2000, Zi
Sarah Moore, (D), Kentucky, 2006
Tracey Osborne, (D), California (Berkeley), 2010
Daoqin Tong, (D), Ohio State, 2007, Zi
Adjunct Professor:
Julio Betancourt, (D), Arizona, 1989, Zn
Vance Holliday, (D), Colorado, 1982, Ga
Laura Huntoon, (D), Pennsylvania, 1991, Zn
Charles F. Hutchinson, (D), California (Riverside), 1978, Zr
Miranda Joseph, (D), Stanford, 1995, Zn
Barbara Morehouse, (D), Arizona, 1993, Zn
Thomas W. Swetnam, (D), Arizona, 1987, Zn
Emeritus:
Stephen R. Yool, (D), California (Santa Barbara), 1985, Zri
Director, International Studies-External Affairs:
Wayne Decker, (D), Johns Hopkins, 1979

Arkansas

Arkansas Tech University

Dept of Physical Sciences - Geology (B) (2015)
1701 N. Boulder Ave
McEver Science Building
Russellville, AR 72801
p. (479) 968-0293
jpatton@atu.edu
http://www.atu.edu/physci
Enrollment (2014): B: 44 (10)
Professor:
Cathy Baker, (D), Iowa, 1986, Gg

Associate Professor:
Jason A. Patton, (D), Arkansas, 2008, GgeGc
Assistant Professor:
Genet Duke, (D), SD Mines

Northwest Arkansas Community College

Northwest Arkansas Community College (2015)
One College Drive
Bentonville, AR 72712
p. (479) 631-8661
dandroes@nwacc.edu
http://www.nwacc.edu

University of Arkansas at Little Rock

Dept of Earth Sciences (B) O✓ (2020)
2801 South University Avenue
Little Rock, AR 72204-1099
p. (501) 569-3546
memcmillan@ualr.edu
http://www.ualr.edu/earthsciences/
Programs: Geology (B); Environmental Geology (B)
Enrollment (2020): B: 23 (11)
Chair:
Margaret E. McMillan, (D), Wyoming, 2003, Gm
Professor:
Jeffrey B. Connelly, (D), Tennessee, 1993, GcNg
Associate Professor:
Michael T. DeAngelis, (D), Tennessee, 2011, GpCp
Laura S. Ruhl, (D), Duke, 2012, GeClGb
Assistant Professor:
Rene A. Shroat-Lewis, (D), Tennessee, 2011, PeZe
Instructor:
Joshua C. Spinler, (D), Arizona, 2014, YdGt
Emeritus:
Michael T. Ledbetter, (D), Rhode Island, 1978, Og

University of Arkansas, Fayetteville

Arkansas Water Resources Center (2015)
113 Ozark Hall
Fayetteville, AR 72701
p. (501) 575-4403
haggard@uark.edu
http://www.uark.edu/depts/awrc
Administrative Assistant: Theresa J. Russell
Director:
Kenneth F. Steele, (D), North Carolina, 1971, Cg
Research Associate:
Terry E. Nichols, (D), Chicago, 1973, Zn
Laboratory Director:
Marc A. Nelson, (D), Arkansas, 1992, Cl

Dept of Geosciences (B,M,D) O⊘ (2019)
340 N. Campus Drive
216 Gearhart Hall
Fayetteville, AR 72701
p. (479) 575-3355
geosdept@uark.edu
http://fulbright.uark.edu/departments/geosciences/
f: https://www.facebook.com/uageosciences/0396/
Programs: Earth Science (BS); Geology (BS,MS); Geography (BA,MS); Geosciences (PhD)
Certificates: Geospatial Technologies (UG,G)
Enrollment (2019): B: 121 (39) M: 51 (29) D: 20 (3)
Maurice Storm Endowed Chair:
Christopher Liner, (D), Colorado Mines, 1989, YseGg
University Professor:
William (. Limp, (D), Indiana, 1983, Zfi
Thomas R. Paradise, (D), Arizona State, 1993, GmZyRn
Distinguished Professor:
David W. Stahle, (D), Arizona State, 1990, GeZon
Daniel Sui, (D), Georgia, 1993, Zf
Director of the Center for Advanced Spatial Technologies:
Jackson D. Cothren, (D), Ohio State, 2004, Zir
Professor:
Stephen K. Boss, (D), North Carolina, 1994, RcYgGg
Jason A. Tullis, (D), South Carolina, 2003, ZriZf
Associate Professor:
Mohamed H. Aly, (D), Texas A&M, 2006, Gg
Matthew Covington, (D), California, 2008, HqGmg
Fiona M. Davidson, (D), Nebraska, 1991, Zy
Gregory Dumond, (D), Massachusetts, 2008, GtcGg
Song Feng, (D), Chinese Acad of Sci, 1999, AsZyAm
Adriana Potra, (D), Florida Intl, 2011, EgCcGg
John B. Shaw, (D), Texas, 2013, GsrGg
Celina Suarez, (D), Kansas, 2010, ClPqGg
Assistant Professor:
Linyin Cheng, (D), California (Irvine), Zo
Edward C. Holland, (D), Colorado, unkn, Zy
Andrew P. Lamb, (D), Boise State, 2013, YumYv
Jill A. Marshall, (D), Oregon, 2015, Gm
Glenn R. Sharman, (D), Stanford, 2014, Go
Research Professor:
Phillip D. Hays, (D), Texas A&M, 1996, HwCsGg
Research Associate:
Barry J. Shaulis, (D), Houston, 2013
Instructor:
Paula Anderson, (M), Arkansas, 2012, Gg
Rashauna Hintz, (M), Arkansas, Zu
Henry Turner, III, (D), Arkansas, 2010, GgtGc
Adjunct Professor:
Fred Paillet, (D), Rochester, 1974, YgHw
Emeritus:
John Van Brahana, (D), Missouri, 1973, HwGe
Malcolm K. Cleaveland, (D), Arizona, 1983, PcZc
John C. Dixon, (D), Colorado, 1983, GmXgSo
Margaret J. Guccione, (D), Colorado, 1982, GmaGg
Walter Manger, (D), Iowa, Gr
Richard Smith, N Colorado, Gm
Doy L. Zachry, (D), Texas, 1969, Gr

California

American River College

Dept of Earth Science (A) (2015)
4700 College Oak Drive
Sacramento, CA 95841
p. (916) 484-8107
aubertj@arc.losrios.edu
http://arc.losrios.edu/~earthsci/
Chair:
Melissa H. Levy, (M), E Tennessee State, 1994, GgZgy
Professor:
John E. Aubert, (M), California (Davis), 1994, Zy
Charles E. Thomsen, (M), Cal State (Chico), 1994, Zy
GIS Coordinator:
Hugh H. Howard, (D), Kansas, 2003, Zi
Assistant Professor:
Glenn Jaecks, (D), California (Davis), 2002, GgOgPg
Adjunct:
Paul M. Veisze, (M), California (Berkeley), 1985, Zi
Adjunct Professor:
Terry J. Boroughs, (M), Ohio State, 1992, GgXgCg
Beth Dushman, (M), California (Davis), 2007, Gg
Robert Earle, (M), Zi
Nathan Jennings, (M), Zi
Tom Lupo, (M), Zi
Richard L. Oldham, (M), Nevada, 1972, Gg
Kimberly Olson, (M), Cal State (Chico), 2008, Zye
Steven C. Smith, (M), Cal State (Chico), 1994, ZynZn

Antelope Valley College

Div-Geosciences Prog (2018)
3041 West Avenue K
Lancaster, CA 93536
mpesses@avc.edu
https://www.avc.edu/sites/default/files/catalog/geosciences.pdf
Associate Professor:
Michael Pesses, Zyi
Assistant Professor:
Aurora Burd, (D), Washington, 2013, GgZgYm

Bakersfield College

Physical Science Dept (2015)
1801 Panorama Drive
Bakersfield, CA 93305
p. (661) 395-4391
mbresso@bakersfieldcollege.edu
Acting Chair:
Robert A. Schiffman, (M), California (Santa Barbara), 1971, Ga
Professor:
John C. Lyman, (B), Cal State (San Diego), 1962, Gg
Instructor:
Robert Lewy, (M), Cal State (Bakersfield), 1992, Gx
Michael Oldershaw, (M), California (Davis), 1987, Eo

Cabrillo College

Dept of Geology, Oceanography and Env Sci (A) ⊘ (2017)
6500 Soquel Drive
Aptos, CA 95003
p. (408) 479-6495
daschwar@cabrillo.edu
http://www.cabrillo.edu/academics/earthscience/
Programs: Geology (A); Environmental Science (A)
Enrollment (2015): A: 35 (0)
Chair:
David Schwartz, (M), San Jose State, 1983, Gu

California Institute of Technology 🗍

Div of Geological & Planetary Sciences (B,M,D) ●☒ (2019)
1200 East California Boulevard
MC 170-25
Pasadena, CA 91125
p. (626) 395-6111
shechet@gps.caltech.edu
http://www.gps.caltech.edu
Enrollment (2018): B: 17 (0) D: 112 (0)
Chair:
John P. Grotzinger, (D), Virginia Tech, 1985, GsPeXg
Professor:
Jess F. Adkins, (D), MIT, 1997, Cm
Jean-Paul Ampuero, (D), Paris VII, 2002, Ys
Paul D. Asimow, (D), Caltech, 1997, CpGzy
Jean-Philippe Avouac, (D), Inst Physique du Globe de Paris, 1991, GtYs
Geoffrey A. Blake, (D), Caltech, 1985, Xc
Simona Bordoni, (D), California (Los Angeles), 2007, Op
Michael E. Brown, (D), California (Berkeley), 1994, Xy
Robert W. Clayton, (D), Stanford, 1981, Ys
Bethany L. Ehlmann, (D), Brown, 2010, XgZrGz
John M. Eiler, (D), Wisconsin, 1994, Cg
Kenneth A. Farley, (D), California (San Diego), 1991, Cg
Woodward W. Fischer, (D), Harvard, 2007, Pg
Christian Frankenberg, (D), Ruprecht-Karls Univ, 2005, Zr
Michael C. Gurnis, (D), Australian Nat, 1987, Ys
Thomas H. Heaton, (D), Caltech, 1979, Ne
Andrew P. Ingersoll, (D), Harvard, 1966, As
Jennifer M. Jackson, (D), Illinois, 2005, Gy
Joseph L. Kirschvink, (D), Princeton, 1979, Pg
Heather Knutson, (D), Harvard, 2009, Xg
Shrinivas R. Kulkarni, (D), California (Berkeley), 1983, Xa
Michael P. Lamb, (D), California (Berkeley), 2008, Gm
Nadia Lapusta, (D), Harvard, 2001, GcYs
Jared R. Leadbetter, (D), Michigan State, 1997, Pm
Dianne K. Newman, (D), MIT, 1997, Pg
Victoria Orphan, (D), California (Santa Barbara), 2001, Pg
George R. Rossman, (D), Caltech, 1971, GzCa
Tapio Schneider, (D), Princeton, 2001, AsmZg
Alex L. Sessions, (D), Indiana, 2001, CosCb
Mark Simons, (D), MIT, 1995, Ys
David J. Stevenson, (D), Cornell, 1976, Xy
Joann M. Stock, (D), MIT, 1988, GtcYr
Edward M. Stolper, (D), Harvard, 1979, Cp
Andrew F. Thompson, (D), Scripps, 2006, OpgZc
Victor Tsai, (D), Harvard, 2009, Yg
Paul O. Wennberg, (D), Harvard, 1994, As
Brian P. Wernicke, (D), MIT, 1982, Gtc
Yuk L. Yung, (D), Harvard, 1974, As
Assistant Professor:
Konstantin Batygin, (D), Caltech, 2012, Xg
Zhongwen Zhan, (D), Caltech, 2013, Ys
Research Professor:
Egill Hauksson, (D), Columbia, 1981, YsGtYg
Emeritus:
Arden L. Albee, (D), Harvard, 1957, GizXg
Clarence R. Allen, (D), Caltech, 1954, Ys
Donald S. Burnett, (D), California (Berkeley), 1963, Xc
Charles Elachi, (D), Caltech, 1971, Xg
Peter M. Goldreich, (D), Cornell, 1963, Xy
Donald V. Helmberger, (D), California (San Diego), 1967, Ys
Hiroo Kanamori, (D), Tokyo, 1964, Ysg
Duane O. Muhleman, (D), Harvard, 1963, Xy
Jason B. Saleeby, (D), California (Santa Barbara), 1975, Gc
Leon T. Silver, (D), Caltech, 1955, Cc
Hugh P. Taylor, (D), Caltech, 1959, Cs
Peter J. Wyllie, (D), St Andrews, 1958, Cp

California Lutheran University

Dept of Earth and Environmental Science (B) ☒ (2019)
60 West Olsen Road #3700
Thousand Oaks, CA 91360-2787
p. (805) 493-3264
bilodeau@callutheran.edu
http://www.callutheran.edu/admission/undergraduate/majors/geology/
Programs: Geology (B), Environmental Science (B)
Enrollment (2018): B: 4 (5)
Professor:
William L. Bilodeau, (D), Stanford, 1979, GcsGg
Chair:
Robert Dull, (D)
Assistant Professor:
Megan Fung, (D)
Emeritus:
Linda A. Ritterbush, (D), California (Santa Barbara), 1990, Pi

California Polytechnic State University

Department of Natural Resources Management and Environmental Sciences (B,M) (2015)
One Grand Avenue
San Luis Obispo, CA 93407
p. (805) 756-2261
jstevens@calpoly.edu
http://nres.calpoly.edu
Professor:
Delmar D. Dingus, (D), Oregon State, 1975, So
Brent G. Hallock, (D), California (Davis), 1979, Sf
William L. Preston, (D), Oregon, 1979, Ze
Thomas A. Ruehr, (D), Colorado State, 1975, Sb
Terry L. Smith, (D), Nebraska, 1980, So
Assistant Professor:
Christopher (Chip) S. Appel, (D), Florida, 2001, Sc
Emeritus:
Ronald D. Taskey, (D), Oregon State, 1977, Sf
Administrative Coordinator:
Joan M. Stevens, Zn
Instructional Tech:
Craig Stubler, (B), Cal Poly, 1996, So

Department of Physics (B) ☒ (2019)
1 Grand Ave
180-204
San Luis Obispo, CA 93407
p. (805) 756-2448
geology@calpoly.edu
https://physics.calpoly.edu/geology
Administrative Assistant: Michell Maksoudian
Professor:
Antonio F. Garcia, (D), California (Santa Barbara), 2001, Gmg
John J. Jasbinsek, (D), Wyoming, 2008, YsuHw
Scott Johnston, (D), California (Santa Barbara), 2006, GcpCc
Emeritus:
Lawrence Balthaser, Indiana, 1969
David H. Chipping, (D), Stanford, 1970, Grt
Ken Hoffman, California (Berkeley), NA

California State Polytechnic University, Pomona

Dept of Geological Sciences (B,M) (2020)
3801 West Temple Avenue
Pomona, CA 91768
p. (909) 869-3454
janourse@cpp.edu
https://www.cpp.edu/sci/geological-sciences/
Programs: Geology (B,M)
Administrative Assistant: Monica Baez
Enrollment (2020): B: 115 (21) M: 30 (5)
Chair:
Jonathan A. Nourse, (D), Caltech, 1989, GctEm
Professor:
Jeffrey S. Marshall, (D), Penn State, 2000, GmtHs
Stephen G. Osborn, (D), Arizona, 2010, HwClSp
Jascha Polet, (D), Caltech, 1999, Ysg
Associate Professor:
Nicholas J. Van Buer, (D), Stanford, 2012, GxtGz
Assistant Professor:
Bryan P. Murray, (D), California (Los Angeles), 2013, Gsg
Emeritus:
John A. Klasik, (D), Louisiana State, 1976, Gu
Equipment Technician:
Frank Wille, (B), Cal State (Fullerton), 2009, Zn

California State University, Bakersfield

Dept of Geological Sciences (B,M) ☒ (2021)
9001 Stockdale Hwy, 66 SCI
Bakersfield, CA 93311
p. (661) 654-3027
arathburn@csub.edu
http://www.csub.edu/Geology/
f: https://www.facebook.com/groups/103146842589/
Programs: Geology; Natural Science
Administrative Assistant: Sue Holt
Enrollment (2020): B: 42 (25) M: 14 (9)
Professor:
Anthony E. Rathburn, (D), Duke, PmOoCb
Associate Professor:
Junhua Guo, (D), Missouri, Gs
W Chris Krugh, (D), Swiss Fed Inst Tech, 2008, GcmCc
Assistant Professor:
Mathew Herman, (D), Penn State, 2017, GtYsRn
Katie O'Sullivan, (D), Notre Dame, 2013, GviXg
Anna Paula . Soares Cruz, (D), Federal Fluminense, 2016, CmOoPc
Liaosha Song, (D), West Virginia, 2018, GoYeEo
Lecturer:
Robert Crewdson, (D), Colorado Mines, HwYgCg
Emeritus:
Dirk Baron, (D), Oregon, Hg
Janice Gillespie, (D), Wyoming, GorZi
Robert A. Horton, Jr., (D), Colorado Mines, 1985, GdsGo
Robert M. Negrini, (D), California (Davis), 1986, YmgGn
Department IT Support:
Elizabeth Powers, (B), N Arizona, 1998, Gg

California State University, Chico

Dept of Geological and Environmental Sciences (B,M) ●☒ (2021)
400 W First Street
Chico, CA 95929-0205
p. (530) 898-5262
geos@csuchico.edu
http://www.csuchico.edu/geos/
f: https://www.facebook.com/CSUChicoGEOS/
Programs: Geology, Environmental Science
Certificates: Geology (Minor)
Enrollment (2020): B: 200 (34) M: 14 (6)
Chair:
Todd Greene, (D), Stanford, 2000, Gsr
Professor:
Ann Bykerk-Kauffman, (D), Arizona, 1990, GcZe
Julie Monet, (D), Rutgers, 2006, GgNg
Russell S. Shapiro, (D), California (Santa Barbara), 1998, PgGdXb
Rachel Teasdale, (D), Idaho, 2001, Gv
Associate Professor:
Hannah M. Aird, (D), Duke, 2014, GxEg
Kristen M. Kaczynski, (D), Colorado State, 2015, ZnHg
Sandrine Matiasek, (D), California (Davis), 2015, CqRw
Shane D. Mayor, (D), Wisconsin, 2001, AsZrAp
Lecturer:
Carrie Monohan, (D), Washington, 2004, Hg
Jochen Nuester, (D), Max Planck, 2005, Cm
Emeritus:
Terence T. Kato, (D), California (Los Angeles), 1976, GtcGp

California State University, Dominguez Hills

Earth Sciences (B) ☒ (2018)
1000 E. Victoria Street
NSM B202
Carson, CA 90747
p. (310) 243-3377
cmtrujillo@csudh.edu
Programs: Earth Science (m,B), Geography (m,B)
Certificates: Geotechniques
Enrollment (2014): B: 55 (9)
Chair, Earth Sciences and Geography:
Brendan A. McNulty, (D), California (Santa Cruz), 1996, Gc
Professor:
Rodrick Hay, (D), Arizona State, 1996, Zr
Ashish Sinha, (D), S California, 1997, PeCs
Associate Professor:
John Keyantash, (D), California (Los Angeles), 2001, HgAsZe
Ralph Saunders, (D), Arizona, 1996, Zg
Assistant Professor:
Parveen Chhetri, (D), Texas A&M, 2017, Geg
Lecturer:
Michael H. Ferris, (M), Cal State (Long Beach), 2012, Zr
Emeritus:
David Sigurdson, (D), California (Riverside), 1974, GizEg

California State University, East Bay

Dept of Anthropology, Geography, and Env Studies (2015)
25800 Carlos Bee Blvd
Hayward, CA 94542
p. (510) 885-3193
david.larson@csueastbay.edu
http://class.csueastbay.edu/geography
Chair:
David J. Larson, (D), California (Berkeley), 1994, Zu
Professor:
Scott W. Stine, (D), California (Berkeley), 1987, Gm
Associate Professor:
Karina Garbesi, (D), California (Berkeley), 1994, Cg
Michael D. Lee, (D), London Schl of Econ, 1990, Hg
Gary Li, (D), SUNY (Buffalo), 1997, Zi
David Woo, (D), California (Santa Barbara), 1991, Zr

Dept of Earth & Environmental Sciences (B,M) ● (2019)
25800 Carlos Bee Blvd.
Hayward, CA 94542
p. (510) 885-3486
mitchell.craig@csueastbay.edu
http://www.csueastbay.edu/earth
Programs: Geology (B); Geoscience Education (B); Environmental Science (B); Environmental Geoscience (M); Environmental Health (B)
Certificates: Geology minor
Enrollment (2019): B: 75 (0) M: 12 (0)
Associate Professor and Chair:
Michael S. Massey, (D), Stanford, 2013, ScGeCg
Professor:
Mitchell S. Craig, (D), Georgia Tech, 1990, Yg
Jean E. Moran, (D), Rochester, 1994, HwCl
Jeffery C. Seitz, (D), Virginia Tech, 1994, CgZeGx
Associate Professor:
Luther M. Strayer, (D), Minnesota, 1998, Gc
Assistant Professor:
Patricia Oikawa, (D), Virginia, 2011, SbCoSf
Jose Rosario, (D), Cornell, 2015, PsSaGr

California State University, Fullerton

Dept of Geological Sciences (B,M) ●⃠ (2021)
800 N. State College Boulevard
Geological Sciences, MH 254
Fullerton, CA 92831

p. (657) 278-3882
geology@fullerton.edu
http://www.fullerton.edu/geology/
f: https://www.facebook.com/CalStateFullerton.Geology/
t: @csufgeology
Programs: Geology (B,M), Earth Science (B)
Enrollment (2020): B: 64 (37) M: 4 (8)

Chair:
Adam D. Woods, (D), S California, 1998, GsPe
Professor:
Matthew E. Kirby, (D), Syracuse, 2001, GnPeGg
Associate Professor:
Nicole Bonuso, (D), S California, 2005, Pie
Joe Carlin, (D), Texas A&M, 2013, GuOuGs
W. Richard Laton, (D), W Michigan, 1997, HwGeHy
Sean Loyd, (D), S California, 2010, CgGe
Valbone Memeti, (D), S California, 2009, GivCa
James Parham, (D), California (Berkeley), 2003, PvgGg
Assistant Professor:
Sinan Akciz, (D), MIT, GcRn
Lecturer:
Angela Aranda, (M), Cal State (Fullerton), 2016, Rn
Freddi Jo Bruschke, (D), Gg
Patricia M. Butcher, (M), Utah, 1993, Zeg
Emily A. Hamecher, (D), Caltech, 2013, GgzGi
Wayne G. Henderson, (M), George Washington, 1997, PgGg
Joanna Hynes, (M), Cal State (Fullerton), Gg
Scott Mata, (D), S California, Gg
Carolyn Rath, (M), Cal State (Fullerton), Gg
Kelly R. Ruppert, (M), California (Riverside), 2001, Gg
Emeritus:
Phillip A. Armstrong, (D), Utah, 1996, GcYg
Galen R. Carlson, (D), Zg
Diane Clemens-Knott, (D), Caltech, 1992, Gig
John H. Foster, (D)
Jeffrey R. Knott, (D), California (Riverside), 1998, Gmg
Prem K. Saint, (D), Minnesota, 1973, Hw

California State University, Long Beach

Dept of Geological Sciences (B,M) (2015)
1250 Bellflower Boulevard
Long Beach, CA 90840-3902
p. (562) 985-4809
rfrancis@csulb.edu
http://www.csulb.edu/colleges/cnsm/departments/geology/
Administrative Assistant: Margaret Costello
Enrollment (2009): B: 67 (11) M: 16 (3)

Chair:
Richard J. Behl, (D), California (Santa Cruz), 1992, GsPeGd
Conrey Endowed Chair:
Matthew Becker, (D), Texas, 1996, Hwg
Professor:
Stanley C. Finney, (D), Ohio State, 1977, Psi
Robert D. Francis, (D), California (San Diego), 1980, Co
Roswitha B. Grannell, (D), California (Riverside), 1969, Yv
Jack Green, (D), Columbia, 1953, Gv
Gregory J. Holk, (D), Caltech, 1997, CsGxEm
Nate Onderdonk, (D), California (Santa Barbara), 2003, Gtm
Associate Professor:
Thomas Kelty, (D), California (Los Angeles), 1998, Gc
Assistant Professor:
Lora R. Stevens (Landon), (D), Minnesota, 1997, Gn
Lecturer:
Bruce Perry, (M), Cal State (Long Beach), 1993, Gc
Emeritus:
Kwan M. Chan, (D), Liverpool (UK), 1966, Oc
Paul J. Fritts, (D), Colorado, 1969, Pm
Charles T. Walker, (D), Leeds (UK), 1952, Cl
Robert E. Winchell, (D), Ohio State, 1963, Gz

California State University, Los Angeles

Department of Geosciences and Environment (B,M) O (2016)
5151 State University Drive
Los Angeles, CA 90032
p. (323) 343-2400
smulher@calstatela.edu
http://www.calstatela.edu/academic/geos
Enrollment (2016): B: 65 (0) M: 13 (0)

Department Chair:
Hengchun Ye, (D), Delaware, 1995, ZyHs
Associate Dept Chair:
Steven Mulherin, (D), Ohio State, 1999
Professor:
Qiu Hong-lie, (D), Louisiana State, 1994
Steve LaDochy, (D), Manitoba, 1985, Zn
Pedro C. Ramirez, (D), California (Santa Cruz), 1990, Gs
Associate Dept Chair:
Jennifer M. Garrison, (D), California (Los Angeles), 2004, GiCcGv
Associate Professor:
Andre Ellis, (D), Illinois, 2003, HwCg
Barry Hibbs, (D), Texas, 1993, Hw
Assistant Professor:
Kris Bezdecny, (D), S Florida, 2011, ZniZn
Jingjing Li, (D), California (Irvine), 2013
Instructor:
Yoshie Hagiwara, (M)
Angel Hamane, (D), Pepperdine, 2015, Ze
Adjunct Professor:
Mohammad Hassan Rezaie-Boroon, (D), Erlangen (Germany), 1997, GeCg
Emeritus:
Kim Bishop, (D), S California, 1994, Gc
Ivan P. Colburn, (D), Stanford, 1961, Gs
Robert J. Stull, (D), Washington, 1969, Gi

California State University, Northridge

Dept of Geography and Environmental Studies (B,M) ⃠ (2020)
18111 Nordhoff Street
Northridge, CA 91330-8249
p. (818) 677-3532
geography@csun.edu
http://www.csun.edu/social-behavioral-sciences/geography
Programs: Geography: Standard and GIS (BA/MA); Graduate (MA) GIS (MSc)
Enrollment (2020): B: 127 (33) M: 37 (18)

Professor:
Julie E. Laity, (D), California (Los Angeles), 1982, Zy
Amalie Orme, (D), California (Los Angeles), 1983, Gm
Yifei Sun, (D), SUNY (Buffalo), 2000, Zi
Associate Professor:
Soheil Boroushaki, (D), W Ontario, 2010, Zi
Mario A. Giraldo, (D), Georgia, 2007, ZriZg
Regan Maas, (D), California (Los Angeles), 2010, Zi
Assistant Professor:
Sanchayeeta Adhikari, (D), Florida, 2011, Zi
Luke Drake, (D), Rutgers, 2015, Zi

Dept of Geological Sciences (B,M) ● ☒ (2019)
18111 Nordhoff Street
MD: 8266
Northridge, CA 91330-8266
p. (818) 677-3541
geology@csun.edu
http://www.csun.edu/geology/
Programs: Geology, Geophysics
Administrative Assistant: Mari C. Flores-Garcia
Enrollment (2012): B: 72 (0) M: 23 (0)

Retired:
J. Douglas Yule, (D), Caltech, 1996, Gt
Professor:
Kathleen M. Marsaglia, (D), California (Los Angeles), 1989, Gs
Elena A. Miranda, (D), Wyoming, 2006, Gc
Dayanthie Weeraratne, (D), Carnegie Inst, 2005, Yg
Associate Professor:
M. Robinson Cecil, (D), Arizona, 2009, GiCcGz
Matthew d'Alessio, (D), California (Berkeley), 2004, ZeGt
Richard V. Heermance, (D), California (Santa Barbara), 2007, GrCc
Joshua J. Schwartz, (D), Wyoming, 2007, GiCc
Assistant Professor:
Jennifer Cotton, (D), Michigan, 2013, Pc
Eileen L. Evans, (D), Harvard, 2014, YdGtYg
Priya Ganguli, (D), California (Santa Cruz), 2013
Scott Hauswirth, (D), N Carolina, 2014, HgCg
Julian Lozos, (D), California (Riverside), 2013, YgGt
Emeritus:
Herbert G. Adams, (D), California (Los Angeles), 1971, Ng

Lorence G. Collins, (D), Illinois, 1959, Gzx
George C. Dunne, (D), Rice, 1972, Gc
Vicki A. Pedone, (D), SUNY (Stony Brook), 1990, GdCs
Gerald W. Simila, (D), California (Berkeley), 1979, Yg
Jon R. Sloan, (D), California (Davis), 1980, Pm
Richard L. Squires, (D), Caltech, 1973, Pi

California State University, San Bernardino

Dept of Geological Sciences (B,M) ☒ (2019)
5500 University Parkway
San Bernardino, CA 92407-2397
p. (909) 537-5336
CPalmer@csusb.edu
https://cns.csusb.edu/geology
Administrative Assistant: Christina Palmer
Enrollment (2018): B: 47 (7) M: 5 (0)
Professor:
Sally F. McGill, (D), Caltech, 1992, GtYdGm
Professor:
Joan E. Fryxell, (D), North Carolina, 1984, Gct
Erik Melchiorre, (D), Washington (St Louis), 1997, EmHwCl
Associate Professor:
W. Britt Leatham, (D), Ohio State, 1987, PsmOg
Assistant Professor:
Kerry Cato, (D), Texas A&M, 1991, Ng
Codi Lazar, (D), California (Los Angeles), 2010, Cp
Emeritus:
Louis A. Fernandez, (D), Syracuse, 1969, Gi
Alan L. Smith, (D), California (Berkeley), 1969, GviGz
Cooperating Faculty:
David Maynard, (D), California (Riverside), 1992, Zn
Stuart S. Sumida, (D), California (Los Angeles), 1987, Pv

California State University, Stanislaus

Dept of Physics and Geology (B) ●☒ (2021)
One University Circle
Turlock, CA 95382
p. (209) 667-3466
HFerriz@csustan.edu
https://www.csustan.edu/geology
Programs: Geology (B); Applied Geology (B); Geology (minor)
Enrollment (2020): B: 15 (7)
Program coordinator:
Robert D. Rogers, (D), Texas, 2003, GcmGt
Professor:
Horacio Ferriz, (D), Stanford, 1984, NgHgYe
Mario J. Giaramita, (D), California (Davis), 1989, Gpz
Julia Sankey, (D), Louisiana State, 1998, Pve
Lecturer:
Garry F. Hayes, (M), Nevada (Reno), 1988, Gg
Michael Whittier, (M), Cal State (Stanislaus), 2005, Ggz

Cerritos College

Earth Science Dept (A) O✓ (2021)
11110 E. Alondra Boulevard
Norwalk, CA 90650
p. (562) 860-2451
ddekraker@cerritos.edu
http://www.cerritos.edu/earth-science/
Programs: AS - Geology, AA - Geography
Enrollment (2012): A: 9 (0)
Chair:
Dan DeKraker, (M), Cal State (Fullerton), 2004, ZeOpGg
Professor:
tor b. lacy, (M), Cal State (Long Beach), 2005, GgcGc
Crystal LoVetere, (D), USC, 2012, Zy
Assistant Professor:
Ryan Goode, (D), Cal State (Fullerton), Zc

Chabot College

Div of Mathematics & Science (A) (2015)
25555 Hesperian Boulevard
Hayward, CA 94545
p. (415) 786-6865
kbononcini@chabotcollege.edu
Instructor:
Adolph A. Oliver, (M), Stanford, 1974, Ys

David J. Perry, (M), San Jose State, 1967, Op

Chaffey College

Earth Science/Geology Dept (2015)
5885 Haven Avenue
Rancho Cucamonga, CA 91737-3002
p. (909) 652-6402
henry.shannon@chaffey.edu
http://www.chaffey.edu/mathandscience/
Professor:
Jane Warger, (M), Columbia, 1990, ZgGg

City College of San Francisco

Earth Sciences (A) ✓ (2021)
Box S99
50 Frida Kahlo Way
San Francisco, CA 94112
p. (415) 452-7423
rduncan@ccsf.edu
http://www.ccsf.edu/Earth
Programs: Geography, Geology, Oceanography
Certificates: GIS
Enrollment (2018): A: 10 (1)
Chair:
Ian Duncan, (D), Washington, 2013, Zyi
Professor:
Darrel E. Hess, (M), California (Los Angeles), 1990, Zy
Chris Lewis, (M), California (Berkeley), 1993, GgEmSo
Katryn Wiese, (M), Oregon State, 1992, GiOg
Adjunct Professor:
James Kuwabara, (D), Caltech, 1980, RwOgCg
Elizabeth Proctor, (M), San Francisco State, Zi
Gordon Ye, (M), California (Berkeley), 1993, Zi

College of Marin

Geology Dept (A) (2015)
835 College Ave
SC 192, Phone Ext: 7523
Kentfield, CA 94904
p. (415) 457-8811
dfoss@marin.edu
http://marin.edu/~geology
Professor:
Donald J. Foss, (M), Boise State, 1980, Zg
Emeritus:
James L. Locke, (M), San Jose State, 1971, Zg

College of San Mateo

Geological Sciences (A) ☒ (2019)
1700 W. Hillsdale Blvd.
San Mateo, CA 94402
p. (650) 574-6633
hand@smccd.edu
http://www.collegeofsanmateo.edu/geologicalsciences
Programs: Geological Sciences, Geology
Enrollment (2018): A: 9 (1)
Professor:
Linda M. Hand, (M), Texas A&M, 1988, GgPgOg

College of the Canyons

Dept of Earth, Space, and Environmental Sciences (A) (2015)
26455 Rockwell Canyon Road
Santa Clarita, CA 91355
p. (661) 362-3658
Vincent.Devlahovich@canyons.edu
http://www.canyons.edu/departments/ESES/
Enrollment (2012): A: 4 (0)
Chair:
Vincent A. Devlahovich, (D), Cal State (Northridge), 2012, GgZye
Professor:
Mary Bates, (M), Cal State (Northridge), Zyg

College of the Desert

Dept of Science (A) (2016)
43-500 Monterey Avenue
Palm Desert, CA 92260

p. (760) 776-7272
nmoll@collegeofthedesert.edu
http://www.collegeofthedesert.edu/students/ap/masc/sci/Pages/sciencesphysical.aspx
Enrollment (2013): A: 3 (1)
Professor:
Nancy E. Moll, (D), Washington, 1981, Gge
Adjunct Professor:
Brian Koenig, (M), Arizona, 1978, Gge
Robert Pellenbarg, (D), Delaware, 1976, OcGu

College of the Sequoias

Science Div (A) (2015)
Visalia, CA 93277
p. (209) 730-3812
erich@cos.edu
Chair:
Eric D. Hetherington, (D), Minnesota, 1991, Gc
Emeritus:
John R. Crain, (M), Nevada, 1961, Gg

College of the Siskiyous

Dept of Biological & Physical Sciences (A) (2016)
800 College Avenue
Weed, CA 96094
p. (530) 938-5255
hirt@siskiyous.edu
http://www.siskiyous.edu/instruction/programs/geology/
Enrollment (2015): A: 1 (0)
Instructor:
William H. Hirt, (D), California (Santa Barbara), 1989, Gi

Contra Costa College

Astronomy/Engineering/Geology/Physics Dept (A) (2015)
2600 Misson Bell Drive
San Pablo, CA 94806
p. (510) 235-7800
jsmithson@contracosta.edu
http://www.contracosta.edu/home/programs-departments/engineering/
Professor:
Mary Lewis, Gg
Jayne Smithson, Gg

Cosumnes River College

Dept of Science, Mathematics & Engineering (A) (2015)
8401 Center Parkway
Sacramento, CA 95823
p. (916) 691-7210
MuranaB@crc.losrios.edu
Department Secretary: Sue McCoy
Chair:
Debra Sharkey, (M), California (Davis), 1994, Zy
Assistant Professor:
Hiram Jackson, (M), California (Davis), 1992, Gg
Adjunct Professor:
Gerry Drobny, (M), Washington State, 1981, Gg

Crafton Hills College

Geology Dept (A) ⊘ (2021)
11711 Sand Canyon Road
Yucaipa, CA 92399
p. (909) 794-2161
rihughes@craftonhills.edu
http://www.craftonhills.edu/courses_&_programs/Physical_Science/Geology/
Programs: Geology, Geography, Environmental Science
Enrollment (2020): A: 20 (8)
Professor:
Richard O. Hughes III, (M), Ohio, 1994, GlZe

Cuesta College

Physical Sciences Div (A) (2015)
P. O. Box 8106
San Luis Obispo, CA 93403
p. (805) 546-3230
jgrover@cuesta.edu
http://academic.cuesta.edu/physci/Geology
Enrollment (2014): A: 6 (0)
Professor:
Jeffrey A. Grover, (M), Arizona, 1982, Gg
Debra Stakes, (D), Gg

Cuyamaca College

Dept of Science and Engineering (A) (2015)
900 Rancho San Diego Parkway
El Cajon, CA 92019
p. (619) 660-4345
Glenn.Thurman@gcccd.edu
http://www.cuyamaca.edu/
Instructor:
Lisa Chaddock, Zy
Michael Farrell, Gg
Bryan Miller-Hicks, Gg
Agatha Wein, Gg
Ray Wolcott, Og
Emeritus:
Waverly Ray, Gg

Cypress College

Geology Dept (A) (2015)
9200 Valley View Street
Cypress, CA 90630
p. (714) 484-7153
RArmale@CypressCollege.edu
Professor:
Russell L. Flynn, (M), San Diego State, 1971, Op
Adjunct Professor:
Hank Wadleigh, (B), Cal State (Long Beach), 1957, Gg
Visiting Professor:
Curtis J. Williams, (M), Cal State (Los Angeles), 1996, Gg
Emeritus:
Keith E. Green, (M), S California, 1958, Pg
Altus Simpson, (M), S California, 1958, Go

Diablo Valley College

Div of Physical Sciences (A) (2015)
321 Golf Club Road
Pleasant Hill, CA 94523
p. (925) 685-1230 x46
JHetherington@dvc.edu
http://www.dvc.edu/org/departments/physics/
Chair:
Jean Hetherington, (M), Washington, 1983, Gg

East Los Angeles College

Anthropology, Geography, and Geology (2016)
1301 Avenida Cesar Chavez
Monterey Park, CA 91754
p. (323) 265-8843
grimmejc@elac.edu
http://www.elac.edu/academics/departments/anthrogeo
Chair:
John Grimmer
Gold Creek Coordinator:
Robert West, (D), California (Santa Barbara), 2004, GgmSd

El Camino College

Dept of Earth Sciences (A) (2015)
16007 Crenshaw Blvd.
Torrance, CA 90506
p. (310) 660-3593
jholliday@elcamino.edu
http://www.elcamino.edu/academics/naturalsciences/earth/
Professor:
Jerry Brothen, (M), California (Los Angeles), Zy
Sara Di Fiori, (M), California (Los Angeles), GgOg
Matt Ebiner, (M), California (Los Angeles), Zy
Joseph W. Holliday, (M), Oregon State, 1982, Og
Associate Professor:
Chuck Herzig, (D), California (Riverside), GgOg

Instructor:
Gary Booher, Zg
Robin Bouse, Gg
Charles Dong, Og
Lynn Fielding, Zg
Patricia Neumann, Zg
Douglas Neves, Zg
Jim Noyes, (D), Scripps, Og
Ebenezer Peprah, Zg

Feather River College

Feather River College (A) (2015)
570 Golden Eagle Ave.
Quincy, CA 95971
dlerch@frc.edu
http://www.frc.edu/
Instructor:
Derek Lerch, Zg

Folsom Lake College

Geosciences (A) ● (2015)
10 College Parkway
Folsom, CA 95630
p. (916) 608-6668
pittmaj@flc.losrios.edu
http://www.flc.losrios.edu/Academics/Geology.htm
Enrollment (2015): A: 7 (1)
Professor:
Jason Pittman, (M), Oregon State, 1999, ZgiZi

Fresno City College

Earth & Physical Science Dept (A) ⦸ (2019)
Math, Science & Engineering Div
1101 E. University Avenue
Fresno, CA 93741
p. (559) 442-4600
alexandra.priewisch@fresnocitycollege.edu
Programs: Geology (A)
Enrollment (2018): A: 40 (1)
Instructor:
T. Craig Poole, (M), Cal State (Fresno), 1987, Gg
Alexandra Priewisch, (D), New Mexico, 2014, Gg

Fresno State University

Dept of Earth & Environmental Sciences (B,M) (2015)
2345 E. San Ramon Avenue
MH24
Fresno, CA 93740-8031
p. (559) 278-3086
rdundas@csufresno.edu
http://www.csufresno.edu/ees/
Enrollment (2009): B: 51 (13) M: 30 (5)
Chair:
Stephen D. Lewis, (D), Columbia, 1982, Yg
Professor:
Keith D. Putirka, (D), Columbia, 1997, GviGp
Zhi (Luke) Wang, (D), Leuven (Belgium), 1997, SpHwZi
Associate Professor:
Christopher J. Pluhar, (D), California (Santa Cruz), 2003, GtYmNg
John Wakabayashi, (D), California (Berkeley), GmcGt
Assistant Professor:
Robert G. Dundas, (D), California (Berkeley), 1994, PvGr
Mathieu Richaud, (D), N Illinois, 2006, GusCs
Peter Van de Water, (D), Arizona, GrPbGf
Lecturer:
Jeff Anglen, (M), Texas Tech, 2001, GsdPg
Susan Bratcher, (M), Cal State (Fresno), 2008, Hw
Kerry Workman-Ford, (M), Cal State (Fresno), 2003, Gc
Adjunct Professor:
Jerry DeGraff, (M), Utah State, 1976, Zn
Dong Wang, (D), HwSpZr
Emeritus:
Jon C. Avent
Bruce A. Blackerby, (D), California (Los Angeles), Giz
Roland H. Brady, (D), California (Davis), 1986, NgZuGa
Seymour Mack, YrHgOn
Robert D. Merrill, (D), Texas, 1974, GsmPe

C. John Suen, (D), MIT, 1978, HwCsGe

Fullerton College

Div of Natural Sciences (Geology) (A) ⍻ (2021)
321 E. Chapman Ave
Fullerton, CA 92832
p. (714) 992-7445
rlozinsky@fullcoll.edu
http://natsci.fullcoll.edu/
Programs: AS, AS-T Geology
AS Earth Science
Enrollment (2020): A: 2 (2)
Professor:
William S. Chamberlin, (D), S California, 1989, OgbZe
Richard P. Lozinsky, (D), New Mexico Tech, 1988, GreGm
Marc Willis, (M), Gg
Associate Professor:
Roman DeJesus, (D), Og

Gavilan College

Dept of Physical Sciences (2015)
5055 Santa Theresa Boulevard
Gilroy, CA 95020
p. (408) 848-4701
dwillahan@gavilan.edu
http://www.gavilan.edu/natural_sciences/
Instructor:
Duane Willahan, (M), Santa Fe State, 1992, Gg

Golden West College

Physical Science Program (A) (2015)
15744 Golden West Street
Huntington Beach, CA 92647
p. (714) 892-7711 x51116
msouto@gwc.cccd.edu
http://www.goldenwestcollege.edu/campus/physicalscience.html
Professor:
Ronald C. Gibson, (M), California (Riverside), 1964, Gc
Bernard J. Gilpin, (M), California (Riverside), 1976, Ys

Grossmont College

Dept of Earth Sciences (A) O⍻ (2017)
8800 Grossmont College Drive
El Cajon, CA 92020
p. (619) 644-7887
gary.jacobson@gcccd.edu
https://www.grossmont.edu/academics/programs-departments/earth-sciences/
f: https://www.facebook.com/grossmontearthsciences/
Programs: Geology (A); Geography (A); Oceanography (A)
Professor:
Chris Hill, (D), S California, 2000, GgOg
Instructor:
Gary L. Jacobson, (M), San Diego State, 1982, GucEm

Hartnell College

Div of Math and Science (A) (2015)
411 Central Avenue
Salinas, CA 93901
aramirez@hartnell.edu
http://www.hartnell.edu/academics/math.html
Instructor:
Robert Barminski, (M), Moss Landing Marine Lab, GgOg

Humboldt State University

Dept of Geology (B,M) O☒ (2019)
1 Harpst Street
Arcata, CA 95521-8299
p. (707) 826-3931
geology@humboldt.edu
http://www.humboldt.edu/geology/
Programs: Geology (B); Geoscience (B)
Enrollment (2019): B: 77 (21) M: 7 (0)
Chair:
Brandon L. Browne, (D), Alaska (Fairbanks), 2005, GivZe
Mark Hemphill-Haley, (D), Oregon, 2000, Gt

Assistant Professor:
Laura B. Levy, (D), Dartmouth, 2014, GslPc
Melanie Michalak, (D), California (Santa Cruz), 2013
Jasper Oshun, (D), California (Berkeley), 2015, HyGmg
Research Associate:
Eileen Hemphill-Haley, (D), California (Santa Cruz), 1991, Pm
Harvey M. Kelsey, (D), California (Santa Cruz), 1977, Gmt
Robert C. McPherson, (M), Humboldt State, 1989, Gt
Lecturer:
Amanda R. Admire, (M), Humboldt State, 2013, Zg
Adjunct Professor:
David Bazard, (D), Arizona, 1991
Jason R. Patton, (D), Oregon State, 2014, GuOuGg
Emeritus:
Raymond M. Burke, (D), Colorado, 1976, Gm
Gary A. Carver, (D), Washington, 1972, Gmt
Susan M. Cashman, (D), Washington, 1977, Gc
Lorinda Dengler, (D), California (Berkeley), 1978, Yg
Andre K. Lehre, (D), California (Berkeley), 1982, GmHs
Alistair W. McCrone, (D), Kansas, 1961, Gs
William C. Miller, (D), Tulane, 1984, Pi

Irvine Valley College

Dept of Geology (A) ☒ (2018)
5500 Irvine Center Drive
Irvine, CA 92618
p. (949) 451-5561
astinson@ivc.edu
http://www.ivc.edu
Programs: Geology (A)
Enrollment (2007): A: 20 (5)
Professor:
Amy L. Stinson, (M), San Diego State, 1990, Gc
Adjunct Professor:
Mark Bordelon, (M)
Scott Mata, (D), S California
Doug Neves, (D)
Jim Schneider, (M)

Laney College

Dept of Geography/Geology (A) (2015)
900 Fallon Street
Oakland, CA 94607
p. (510) 464-3233
dwoodrow@peralta.edu
http://www.laney.peralta.edu/apps/comm.asp?Q=30123

Las Positas College

Dept of Geology (A) (2018)
3000 Campus Hill Drive
Livermore, CA 94551
p. (925) 424-1319
rhanna@laspositascollege.edu
http://www.laspositascollege.edu/geology/
Programs: Geology (AS and AS-T)
Certificates: Geology
Enrollment (2018): A: 10 (2)
Instructor:
Ruth L. Hanna, (M), California (Davis), 1988, Gg
Geology Lab Technician:
Carol Edson, Gg

Loma Linda University

Dept of Earth and Biological Sciences (B,M,D) ● (2017)
Loma Linda University
Loma Linda, CA 92350
p. (909) 824-4530
pbuchheim@llu.edu
https://medicine.llu.edu/research/department-earth-and-biological-sciences
f: https://www.facebook.com/lomalindageology
Enrollment (2016): B: 1 (0) M: 1 (4) D: 11 (2)
Professor:
Leonard R. Brand, (D), Cornell, 1970, Pv
Paul Buchheim, (D), Wyoming, 1978, GnsPe
Leroy Leggitt, (D), Loma Linda, 2005, Pi
Senior Scientist:
Benjamin L. Clausen, (D), Colorado, 1987, GiCtYg
Associate Professor:
Kevin Nick, (D), Oklahoma, 1990, GsbGr
Assistant Professor:
Ronald Nalin, (D), Padua, 2006, Gsr
Adjunct Professor:
Raul Esperante, (D), Loma Linda, 2002, Pv

Los Angeles County Museum of Natural History

Research and Collections Branch (2016)
900 Exposition Boulevard
Los Angeles, CA 90007
p. (213) 763-3360
acelesti@nhm.org
https://www.nhm.org/site/research-collections/mineral-sciences
Associate Curator:
Luis M. Chiappe, (D), Buenos Aires, 1992, Pv
Curator:
Kenneth E. Campbell, (D), Florida, 1973, PvGgr
Anthony R. Kampf, (D), Chicago, 1976, Gz
Associate Curator:
Aaron Celestian, (D)
Nathan Smith, (D)
Collections Manager:
Samuel A. McLeod, (D), California (Berkeley), 1981, Pv
Christopher A. Shaw, (M), Cal State (Long Beach), 1981, Pv

Los Angeles Harbor College

Dept of Earth Science (A) (2015)
1111 Figueroa Place
Wilmington, CA 90744
p. (310) 233-4000
munasit@lahc.edu
http://www.lahc.cc.ca.us/
Instructor:
Patricia Kellner, (D), Zg
John Mack, Zg
Tissa Munasinghe, (D), Zg
Melanie Renfrew, (D), Zg
Susan White, Zg

Los Angeles Pierce College

Physics and Planetary Sciences (A) (2015)
6201 Winnetka Ave
Woodland Hills, CA 91371
p. (818) 710-2218
zayacjm@piercecollege.edu
Enrollment (2012): A: 11 (0)
Professor:
John M. Zayac, (M), California (Santa Barbara), 2006, Ggv
Professor:
Jason P. Finley, (M), California (Los Angeles), Am
Stephen C. Lee, (B), Illinois, 1971, Og
W. Craig Meyer, (M), S California, 1973, GeuPm
Adjunct Professor:
Harry Filkorn, (D), Kent State, GgPi
James P. Krohn, (M), S California, 1974, NgGg
Donald Prothero, (D), Columbia, Gg
Emeritus:
Ruth Y. Lebow, (M), Chicago, 1941, Op
Mark L. Powell, (M), Cal State (Northridge), 1967, As
William H. Russell, (M), Cal State (Northridge), 1970, Am
James Y. Vernon, (M), California (Los Angeles), 1951, Am

Los Angeles Southwest College

Geology Dept (A) (2015)
1600 West Imperial Highway
Los Angeles, CA 90047
p. (323) 241-5297
RobertTJ@lasc.edu
http://www.lasc.edu
Chair:
Glenn Yoshida, Gg
Professor:
Paul R. Doose, (D), California (Los Angeles), 1980

Los Angeles Valley College

Earth Science (A) ⌂ (2021)
5800 Fulton Ave.
Valley Glen, CA 91401
p. (818) 778-5566
hamsje@lavc.edu
https://lavc.edu/earthscience
Programs: AS-Transfer Geology, AS Earth Science, AA-Transfer Geography
Enrollment (2020): A: 3 (3)

Chair:
Jacquelyn E. Hams, (M), Cal State (Los Angeles), 1987, GgOuZe

Professor:
Meredith L. Leonard, (M), Cal State (Northridge), AmZei

Academic Senate President:
Donald J. Gauthier, (M), California (Los Angeles), 1993, ZiyAm

Mendocino College

Earth Science (A) ⌂ (2018)
1000 Hensley Creek Road
Ukiah, CA 95482
p. (707) 468-3002
scardimo@mendocino.edu
Programs: Earth Science (A); Natural Resources (A); Geology (A); Geography (A)
Enrollment (2018): A: 74 (3)

Professor:
Steve Cardimona, (D), Texas, 1992, Ys

Merced College

Science, Mathematics & Engineering (A) ☒ (2017)
3600 M Street
Merced, CA 95348
p. (209) 384-6293
kain.d@mccd.edu
http://www.mccd.edu/academics/sme
Programs: Geology

MiraCosta College

Dept of Geography (A) ⌂ (2018)
1 Barnard Drive
Oceanside, CA 92056
lmiller@miracosta.edu
https://www.miracosta.edu/Instruction/Geography/

Chair:
Herschel I. Stern, (D), Oregon, 1988, Zy

Dept of Physical Sciences (A) (2015)
1 Barnard Drive
Oceanside, CA 92056
p. (760) 944-4449 x7738
lmiller@miracosta.edu
https://www.miracosta.edu/Instruction/Geology/

Professor:
Keith H. Meldahl, (D), Arizona, 1990, Gg
Christopher V. Metzler, (D), California (San Diego), 1987, Gg
John Turbeville, GgOg

Adjunct Professor:
Phil Farquharson, Gg

Laboratory Director:
Larry Hernandez, Gg

Modesto Junior College

Dept of Science, Mathematics & Engineering (A) ⊘ (2021)
435 College Avenue
Modesto, CA 95350
p. (209) 575-6172
hayesg@mjc.edu
https://www.mjc.edu/instruction/sme/earthscience.php
Programs: Geology

Professor:
Noah C. Hughes, (M), Montana, 2001, ZgAs

Instructor:
Garry F. Hayes, (M), Nevada (Reno), 1985, Gg

Monterey Peninsula College

Earth Sciences Dept (A) ⌂ (2021)
980 Fremont St.
Monterey, CA 93940
p. (831) 646-4149
ahochstaedter@mpc.edu
http://www.mpc.edu/academics/academic-divisions/physical-science/earth-science-eart
Programs: Geology
Enrollment (2018): A: 1 (1)

Chair:
Alfred Hochstaedter, (D), California (Santa Cruz), 1991, GgOgZg

Moorpark College

Geology Program (A) (2016)
7075 Campus Road
Moorpark, CA 93021
p. (805) 553-4161
rharma@vcccd.edu
http://www.moorparkcollege.edu/geology
Enrollment (2016): A: 24 (2)

Instructor:
Roberta L. Harma, (M), Hawaii, 1982, Gg

Moss Landing Marine Laboratories

CSU Consortium for Marine Sciences (M) O☒ (2018)
8272 Moss Landing Road
Moss Landing, CA 95039
p. (831) 771-4400
jharvey@mlml.calstate.edu
http://www.mlml.calstate.edu
Enrollment (2014): M: 7 (25)

Director:
James T. Harvey, (D), Oregon, 1987, Ob

Librarian:
Joan Parker, (M), California (Los Angeles), 1986, Zn

Professor:
Ivano Aiello, (D), Bologna, 1997, OuGmu
Kenneth H. Coale, (D), California (Santa Cruz), 1988, CtcOc
Jonathan Geller, (D), California (Berkeley), 1988, Zn
Michael Graham, (D), Scripps, 2000, Ob
Nicholas A. Welschmeyer, (D), Washington, 1982, Ob

Research Faculty:
John S. Oliver, (D), Scripps, 1980, Ob

Assistant Professor:
Scott Hamilton, (D), California (Santa Barbara), 2008
Birgitte McDonald, (D)

Research Faculty:
Simona Bartl, (D), California (San Diego), 1989, Zn
Laurence Breaker, (D), Naval Postgrad Sch, 1983, Op
David Ebert, (D), Rhodes, 1990, Zn
Stacy Kim, (D), MIT/WHOI, 1996, Zn
Valerie Loeb, (D), Scripps, 1979, Zn
Richard Starr, (D), Auto de Baja California, 2002, Zn

Emeritus:
Gregor M. Cailliet, (D), California (Santa Barbara), 1972, Zn
Michael Foster, (D), California (Santa Barbara), 1971, Zn
H. Gary Greene, (D), Stanford, 1977, Gu

Diving Safety Officer:
Diana Steller, (D), California (Santa Cruz), 2003, Zn

Mt. San Antonio College

Dept of Earth Sciences & Astronomy (A) (2017)
1100 North Grand Avenue
Walnut, CA 91789
p. (909) 594-5611
cwebb@mtsac.edu
Enrollment (2010): A: 16 (0)

Acting Chair:
Julie Ali-Bray, (M), S California, 1999, Zn

Professor:
Micol Christopher, (D), Caltech, 2007, Zn
Craig A. Webb, (M), Duke, 1996, ZgAmOg

Instructor:
Mark Boryta, (D), New Mexico Tech, 1997
Barbara Grubb, (M), Cal State (Long Beach), 1991, Ps
Larry Mendenhall, (D), Oregon State, 1961, Am

Charles Roberts, (M), Ohio, 1972, Pm
Emeritus:
Hallock J. Bender, (D), San Gabriel, 1959, Gg
John W. Burns, (M), Pittsburgh, 1960, Zn
Damon P. Day, (M), Michigan Tech, 1965, Gg
Ron N. Hartman, (M), Cal State (Los Angeles), 1973, Xm
Kazimierz M. Pohopien, (M), McGill, 1951, Ge
Harold V. Thurman, (M), Cal State (Los Angeles), 1966, Og
Geotechnician:
Mark Koestel, (B), Arizona, 1978, Em

Naval Postgraduate School

Dept of Meteorology (M,D) (2015)
589 Dyer Road
Root Hall, Room 254
Monterey, CA 93943-5114
p. (831) 656-2516
nuss@nps.edu
http://www.nps.edu/Academics/Schools/GSEAS/Departments/Meteorology/
Enrollment (2012): M: 45 (36) D: 9 (2)
Chair:
Wendell A. Nuss, (D), Washington, 1986, Am
Distinguished Professor:
Michael T. Montgomery, (D), Harvard, 1990, AmsZg
Dean:
Philip A. Durkee, (D), Colorado State, 1984, AmZr
Professor:
Patrick A. Harr, (D), Naval Postgrad Sch, 1993, Am
Qing Wang, (D), Penn State, 1993, Am
Associate Professor:
Joshua P. Hacker, (D), British Columbia, 2001, Am
Assistant Professor:
Richard W. Moore, (D), Colorado State, 2004, Am
Barbara V. Scarnato, (D), ETH (Switzerland), 2008, Am
Research Associate:
Hway-Jen Chen, (M), California (Los Angeles), 1993, Am
Paul A. Frederickson, (M), Maryland, 1989, Am
Mary S. Jordan, (M), Naval Postgrad Sch, 1985, Am
Kurt E. Nielsen, (M), Oklahoma, 1988, Am
Andrew Penny, (M), Arizona, 2009, Am
Emeritus:
Robert Haney, (D), California (Los Angeles), 1971, Am
Robert J. Renard, (D), Am
Carlyle H. Wash, (D), Wisconsin, 1978, Am
Forrest Williams, (M), MIT, 1972, Am
Roger T. Williams, (D), California (Los Angeles), 1963, Am
Research Professor:
Kenneth L. Davidson, (D), Michigan, 1970, Am
Peter S. Guest, (D), Naval Postgrad Sch, 1992, Am
Research Associate Professor:
James Thomas Murphree, (D), California (Davis), 1989, Am
NRC Postdoctoral Fellow:
Myung-Sook Park, (D), Am
Distinguished Research Professor:
Russell L. Elsberry, (D), Colorado State, 1968, Am
Distinguished Professor:
Chih-Pei Chang, (D), Washington, 1972, Am
Meteorologist:
Robert L. Creasey, (M), Am

Dept of Oceanography (M,D) ☒ (2019)
833 Dyer Road, Room 328
Monterey, CA 93943-5122
p. (831) 656-2673
pcchu@nps.edu
http://www.nps.edu/Academics/GSEAS/Oceanography/
Enrollment (2014): M: 14 (14) D: 2 (2)
Chair:
Peter C. Chu, (D), Chicago, 1985, OpZr
Professor:
John A. Closi, California (Santa Cruz), 1993
Jamie MacMahan, (D), Florida, 2003, Onp
Jeffrey D. Paduan, (D), Oregon State, 1987, Op
Timour Radko, Florida State, 1997, Op
Assistant Professor:
Derek Olson, (D), Penn State, 2017, Zn
Emeritus:
Robert H. Bourke, (D), Oregon State, 1972, Op
Ching-Sang Chiu, (D), MIT/WHOI, 1985, Op
Curtis A. Collins, (D), Oregon State, 1967, Op
Roland W. Garwood, (D), Washington, 1976, Op
Thomas H. Herbers, (D), California (San Diego), 1990, Op
Timothy P. Stanton, (M), Auckland, 1978, Op
Edward B. Thornton, (D), Florida, 1970, On
Robin T. Tokmakian, (D), Naval Postgrad Sch, 1997, Op
Joseph J. Von Schwind, (D), Texas A&M, 1968, Op
Research Professor:
Wieslaw Maslowski, (D), Alaska (Fairbanks), 1994, Op

Occidental College

Dept of Geology (B) ☒ (2019)
1600 Campus Road
Los Angeles, CA 90041
p. (323) 259-2823
coze@oxy.edu
http://www.oxy.edu/Geology.xml
Administrative Assistant: Elisa Ruiz
Enrollment (2018): B: 33 (0)
Chair:
Christopher Oze, (D), Stanford
Professor:
Scott W. Bogue, (D), California (Santa Cruz), 1982, Ym
Darren J. Larsen, (D), Colorado
Margaret E. Rusmore, (D), Washington, 1985, Gc
James L. Sadd, (D), South Carolina, 1987, ZiGeZr
Related Staff:
Jan Garcia, Zn

Ohlone College

Dept of Geology (A) ⊘ (2018)
43600 Mission Boulevard
Fremont, CA 94539
p. (510) 979-7938
pbelasky@ohlone.edu
http://www.ohlone.edu/instr/geology/
Programs: Geology
Certificates: Geology, Paleobiology, GIS
Professor:
Paul Belasky, (D), California (Los Angeles), 1994, PgqGs

Orange Coast College

Div of Mathematics & Science (A) ☒ (2020)
2701 Fairview Road
Box 5005
Costa Mesa, CA 92626-5005
p. (714) 432-5647
ebender@occ.cccd.edu
http://www.orangecoastcollege.edu/academics/divisions/math_science/geology/Pages/
Programs: Geology; Earth Science
Enrollment (2020): A: 17 (3)
Chair:
E. Erik Bender, (D), S California, 1994, GitGz
Assistant Professor:
Christopher A. Berg, (D), Texas, 2007, GpZeGt
Lecturer:
Michael Van Ry, (M), Cal State (Fullerton), 2010, Gv

Palomar College

Dept of Earth, Space, and Aviation Sciences (A) ☒ (2020)
1140 West Mission Road
San Marcos, CA 92069
p. (760) 744-1150
sfigg@palomar.edu
http://www.palomar.edu/earthscience/
Programs: Geology. Palomar College offers two-degree options. Geology A.S. (Associates) and A.S.-T (geology for transfer)
Enrollment (2014): A: 35 (0)
Professor:
Wing H. Cheung, (D), California (Irvine), 2017, ZiRnZr
Doug Key, (M), San Diego State, Zy
Lisa Yon, (D), Brown, 1994, OgZg

Associate Professor:
Wing Cheung, (M), Indiana, 2007, ZirZy
Sean Figg, (M), N Colorado, 2012, Gg
Mark Lane, (M), San Diego State, 1996, Zn
Assistant Professor:
Steven Crook, (D), Zi
Emeritus:
Jim Pesavento, (D), GgZg

Pasadena City College

Dept of Geology ● (2017)
NAtural Sciences Division
1570 E. Colorado Boulevard
Pasadena, CA 91106
p. (626) 585-7138
naturalsciences@pasadena.edu
http://pasadena.edu/academics/divisions/natural-sciences/areas-of-study/geology.php
Dean, Natural Sciences:
David N. Douglass, (D), Dartmouth, 1987, Ze
Acting Chair:
Martha House, (D), MIT, Gg
Professor:
Elizabeth Nagy-Shadman, (D), Caltech, Gg
Yuet-Ling O'Connor, (D), S California, Ge
Bryan Wilbur, (D), California (Los Angeles), Gg
Instructor:
MIchael Vendrasco, (D), California (Los Angeles)
Emeritus:
Gerald L. Lewis, (M), Cal State (Long Beach), 1965, Ps
Geology Lab Tech:
Debra A. Cantarero, (A), Pasadena City Coll, 2000, Zn

Pomona College

Geology Dept (B) ☒ (2020)
185 East Sixth Street
Claremont, CA 91711-6339
p. (909) 621-8675
LKeala@pomona.edu
http://www.geology.pomona.edu
Programs: Geology
Administrative Assistant: Lori Keala
Enrollment (2018): B: 31 (6)
Chair:
Eric B. Grosfils, (D), Brown, 1996, XgGvq
Professor:
Robert R. Gaines, (D), California (Riverside), 2003, GsClPi
Linda A. Reinen, (D), Brown, 1993, Gct
Associate Professor:
Jade Star Lackey, (D), Wisconsin, 2005, GipCs
Department Technician:
Jonathan Harris

Riverside City College

Dept of Physical Science: Geology (A) (2017)
4800 Magnolia Avenue
Riverside, CA 92506-1299
p. (951) 222-8350
william.phelps@rcc.edu
Enrollment (2016): A: 11 (0)
Assistant Professor:
William Phelps, (D), California (Riverside), 2007, PeOpPg

Sacramento City College

Dept of Physics, Astronomy, & Geology (A) (2021)
3835 Freeport Blvd.
Sacramento, CA 95822
p. (916) 558-2343
stantok@scc.losrios.edu
https://scc.losrios.edu/academics/programs-and-majors/geology
Programs: AS-T (Associate of Science for Transfer) in Geology
Enrollment (2020): A: 18 (0)
Professor:
Kathryn Stanton, (D), California (Davis), 2006, GgPg

Sacramento State University

Dept of Geology (B,M) O (2015)
6000 J Street
Placer Hall
Sacramento, CA 95819-6043
p. (916) 278-6337
geology@csus.edu
http://www.csus.edu/geology/
Enrollment (2010): B: 77 (16) M: 18 (3)
Chair:
Tim C. Horner, (D), Ohio State, 1992, HwGs
Professor:
Kevin J. Cornwell, (D), Nebraska, 1994, GmeHs
David G. Evans, (D), Louisiana State, 1989, HqYg
Lisa Hammersley, (D), California (Berkeley), 2003, Gig
Brian Hausback, (D), California (Berkeley), 1984, Gv
Judith E. Kusnick, (D), California (Davis), 1996, Ze
Lecturer:
Barbara J. Munn, (D), Virginia Tech, 1997, Ggp
Adjunct Professor:
Brian Bergamaschi, (D), Washington, 1995, HwOc
Emeritus:
Diane H. Carlson, (D), Washington State, 1984, Gc
Charles C. Plummer, (D), Washington, 1969, Gp
Greg Wheeler, (D), Washington, Em
Secretary:
Stacy Lindley, (B), California (Sacramento), 2010, Zn
Instructional Support Tech:
Steven W. Rounds, (B), Cal State (Sacramento), 1990, Gg

Saddleback Community College

Dept of Earth and Ocean Sciences (A) ☒ (2018)
28000 Marguerite Parkway
Mission Viejo, CA 92692
p. (949) 582-4820
jrepka@saddleback.edu
http://www.saddleback.edu/mse/geo/
f: https://www.facebook.com/Saddleback-College-Geology-731491460197935/
Enrollment (2015): A: 7 (1)
Chair:
James Repka, (D), California (Santa Cruz), 1998, GgmZe

San Bernardino County Museum

Geological Sciences Div (2015)
2024 Orange Tree Lane
Redlands, CA 92374
p. (909) 307-2669
kspringer@sbcm.sbcounty.gov
http://www.co.san-bernardino.ca.us/museum/
Senior Curator:
Kathleen B. Springer, (M), California (Riverside), Zg
Curator:
J. Chris Sagebiel, (M), Texas, 1998, Pv

San Bernardino Valley College

Earth and Spatial Sciences Program (A) (2019)
701 South Mount Vernon Ave.
San Bernardino, CA 92410
p. (909) 384-8638
theibel@valleycollege.edu
Head:
Todd Heibel, Zyi
Professor:
Stephen H. Sandlin, Zy
Instructor:
Gary M. Croft, Zy
Vanessa Engstrom, Zy
Walter Grossman, Og
Jeffrey Krizek, Zi
William Muir, Og
Solomon Nana Kwaku Nimako, Zi
Edmund Jekwu Ogbuchiekwe, Zy
Lisa Schmidt, Zy
Adjunct Professor:
Donald G. Buchanan, (M), Naval Postgrad Sch, 1975, Og

San Diego State University ▯

Dept of Geological Sciences (B,M,D) ●☒ (2019)
5500 Campanile Drive
San Diego, CA 92182-1020
p. (619) 594-5586
dkimbrough@mail.sdsu.edu
http://www.geology.sdsu.edu
f: https://www.facebook.com/SDSU.Geology
t: @sdsugeology
Administrative Assistant: Irene Occhiello, Pia Parrish
Enrollment (2015): B: 72 (9) M: 25 (12) D: 9 (0)

Chair:
David L. Kimbrough, (D), California (Santa Barbara), 1982, Cc
Associate Dean, Division of Undergraduate Studies:
Stephen A. Schellenberg, (D), S California, 2000, Pe
Professor:
Eric G. Frost, (D), S California, 1983, Zr
Gary H. Girty, (D), Columbia, 1983, Gc
Kim B. Olsen, (D), Utah, 1994, Ye
Thomas K. Rockwell, (D), California (Santa Barbara), 1983, Gm
Senior Scientist:
Barry B. Hanan, (D), Virginia Tech, 1980, Cc
Associate Professor:
Shuo Ma, (D), California (Santa Barbara), 2006, Ys
Kathryn W. Thorbjarnarson, (D), California (Los Angeles), 1990, Hq
Lecturer:
Victor E. Camp, (D), Washington State, 1976, Gv
Kevin Robinson, (M), San Diego State, 1996, Gc
Isabelle Sacramentogrilo, (M), San Diego State, 1999, Gg
Adjunct Professor:
Mario V. Caputo, (D), Cincinnati, 1988, GsdOn
Emeritus:
Patrick L. Abbott, (D), Texas, 1973, Gs
Kathe K. Bertine, (D), Yale, 1970, Cl
Steven M. Day, (D), California (San Diego), 1977, Ys
Clive E. Dorman, (D), Oregon State, 1974, OpAmt
George R. Jiracek, (D), California (Berkeley), 1972, Ye
J. Philip Kern, (D), California (Los Angeles), 1968, Pg
Daniel Krummenacher, (D), Geneva, 1959, Cc
Monte Marshall, (D), Stanford, 1971, YmGtc
Richard H. Miller, (D), California (Los Angeles), 1975, Ps
Gary L. Peterson, (D), Washington, 1963, Gr
Anton D. Ptacek, (D), Washington (St Louis), 1965, Gx

San Francisco State University

Dept of Earth & Climate Sciences (B,M) (2015)
1600 Holloway Avenue TH 509
San Francisco, CA 94132
p. (415) 338-2061
geosci@sfsu.edu
http://tornado.sfsu.edu
Enrollment (2013): B: 56 (0) M: 22 (0)

Chair:
Karen Grove, (D), Stanford, 1989, Gs
Professor:
David P. Dempsey, (D), Washington, 1985, As
Oswaldo Garcia, (D), SUNY (Albany), 1976, As
Mary L. Leech, (D), Stanford, 1999, GptGz
John P. Monteverdi, (D), California (Berkeley), 1977, As
David A. Mustart, (D), Stanford, 1972, GizGv
Raymond Pestrong, (D), Stanford, 1965, Ng
Associate Professor:
John Caskey, (D), Nevada (Reno), 1996, Gc
Petra Dekens, (D), California (Santa Cruz), 2007, Pe
Newell (Toby) Garfield, (D), Rhode Island, 1990, Op
Jason Gurdak, (D), Colorado Mines, 2006, HwCqAt
Leonard Sklar, (D), California (Berkeley), 2003, Gm
Assistant Professor:
Alexander Stine, (D), California (Berkeley), At
Adjunct Professor:
E. Jan Null, (D), California (Davis), 1974, Ge
Emeritus:
Charles E. Bickel, (D), Harvard, 1971, Gx
York T. Mandra, (D), Stanford, 1958, Pg
Erwin Seibel, (D), Michigan, 1972, On
Raymond Sullivan, (D), Glasgow, 1960, Go
Lisa D. White, (D), California (Santa Cruz), 1989, Pg

Geosciences Tech:
Russell McArthur, Zn

San Joaquin Delta College

Dept of Geology (A) (2015)
Stockton, CA 95204
p. (209) 954-5354
gfrost@deltacollege.edu
http://www.deltacollege.edu/div/scimath/geology.html

Professor:
Gina Marie Frost, (D), California (Santa Cruz), Gg

San Jose City College

Dept of Earth and Space Sciences ☒ (2019)
2100 Moorpark Ave
San Jose, CA 95128
p. (408) 288-3716
jessica.smay@sjcc.edu
http://www.sjcc.edu/academics/departments-divisions/physical-sciences

Associate Professor:
Jessica J. Smay, (M), California (Santa Barbara), 2002, ZeGm

San Jose State University ▯

Dept of Geology (B,M) ○☒ (2019)
One Washington Square
San Jose, CA 95192-0102
p. (408) 924-5050
leslie.blum@sjsu.edu
http://www.sjsu.edu/geology/
Enrollment (2009): B: 26 (7) M: 24 (6)

Chair:
Jonathan S. Miller, (D), North Carolina, 1994, GiCc
Professor:
Emmanuel Gabet, (D), California (Santa Barbara), 2002, Gm
Paula Messina, (D), CUNY, 1998, ZeGm
Ellen P. Metzger, (D), Syracuse, 1984, GpZe
Robert B. Miller, (D), Washington, 1980, Gct
June A. Oberdorfer, (D), Hawaii, 1983, HwGeHy
Donald L. Reed, (D), California (San Diego), 1985, GuYg
Assistant Professor:
Kimberly Blisniuk, (D), California (Davis), 2011, Gmt
Carlie Pietsch, (D), S California, 2015, PiePc
Ryan Portner, (D), Macquarie, 2010, Gdv
Emeritus Professor:
David W. Andersen, (D), Utah, 1973, GsCl
Calvin H. Stevens, (D), S California, 1963, PsGrs
John W. Williams, (D), Stanford, 1970, Ng

Santa Barbara City College

Dept of Earth & Planetary Sciences (A) (2015)
721 Cliff Drive
Santa Barbara, CA 93109
p. (805) 965-0581
ebkitao@sbcc.edu

Chair:
Michael A. Robinson, (D), California (Santa Barbara), 2009, ZyiAm
Professor:
Jeffrey W. Meyer, (D), California (Santa Barbara), 1992, GgzGx
Jan Schultz, (M), California (Santa Barbara), 1991, GgePg
Assistant Professor:
William Dinklage, (D), California (Santa Barbara), Gge
Emeritus:
Robert S. Gray, (D), Arizona, 1965, PvGzx

Santa Monica College

Earth Science Dept (A) ○⁄ⓘ (2018)
1900 Pico Blvd.
Santa Monica, CA 90405
p. (310) 434-8652
drake_vicki@smc.edu
http://www.smc.edu/AcademicPrograms/EarthScience/Pages/
Programs: Geography, Geospatial Technologies
Certificates: Geospatial Technologies

Professor:
Pete Morris, (M), Wisconsin, 1999, Zyc

Associate Professor:
Jing Liu, (D), Wisconsin, 2017, ZyiZr
Adjunct Professor:
Alessandro Grippo, (D), Gs

Santa Rosa Junior College

Earth and Space Sciences (A) (2015)
1501 Mendocino Avenue
Santa Rosa, CA 95401-4395
p. (707) 527-4365
dkratzmann@santarosa.edu
http://online.santarosa.edu/presentation/?2992

Santiago Canyon College

Dept of Earth, Space, & Physical Sciences (2015)
8045 East Chapman Avenue
Orange, CA 92869-4512
p. (714) 564-4788
hannes_susan@sccollege.edu
Chair:
Debra A. Brooks, (M), Texas A&M, 1989, Yg
Adjunct Professor:
Gail F. Montwill, (M), Cal State (Los Angeles), 1988, Gg
Lizanne V. Simmons, (B), Brigham Young, 1979, Gr
Amy L. Stinson, (M), San Diego State, 1990, Gc
Adam D. Woods, (D), S California, 1998, Gs

Solano Community College

School of Mathematics and Science (2015)
4000 Suisun Valley Road
Fairfield, CA 94534
p. (707) 864-7211
danielle.widemann@solano.edu
http://www.solano.edu/

Sonoma State University

Dept of Geology (B) ☒ (2017)
1801 East Cotati Avenue
Rohnert Park, CA 94928
p. (707) 664-2334
matty.mookerjee@sonoma.edu
http://www.sonoma.edu/geology/
Enrollment (2017): B: 80 (30)
Department Chair:
Matthew J. James, (D), California (Berkeley), 1987, PiRhPg
Professor:
Matty Mookerjee, (D), Rochester, 2005, GcYgZi
Assistant Professor:
Owen Anfinson, (D), Calgary, 2012, GsdGg
Laura E. Waters, (D), Michigan, 2013, GviGz
Emeritus:
Thomas B. Anderson, (D), Colorado, 1969, GsrGd
Rolfe C. Erickson, (D), Arizona, 1968, Gx
Retired:
Daniel B. Karner, (D), California (Berkeley), 1997, Cc
Instructional Support Technician:
Phillip Mooney, (M), California (Davis), 2010, ZnGc

Stanford University ▯

Dept of Geological and Environmental Sciences (B,M,D) ☒ (2021)
450 Jane Stanford Way Bldg 320
Stanford, CA 94305-2215
p. (650) 723-5002
cbaroni@stanford.edu
http://pangea.stanford.edu/GES/
Enrollment (2010): B: 21 (9) M: 11 (5) D: 45 (8)
Chair:
Kevin Boyce, (D)
Professor:
Jef Caers, (D)
C. Page Chamberlain, (D), Harvard, 1985, Yr
Robert B. Dunbar, (D), California (San Diego), 1981, On
W. Gary Ernst, (D), Johns Hopkins, 1959, Cp
Rodney C. Ewing, (D), Stanford, 1974, GzeCl
Stephan A. Graham, (D), Stanford, 1976, Go
Martin Grove, (D)
George Hilley, (D)
Donald R. Lowe, (D), Illinois, 1967, Gd
Wendy Mao, (D)
Elizabeth L. Miller, (D), Rice, 1977, Gc
Jonathan Payne, (D)
Associate Professor:
Jane Willenbring, (D)
Assistant Professor:
Mathieu Lapôtre, (D)
Andrew Leslie, (D)
Ayla Pamukcu, (D)
Laura Schaefer, (D)
Erik Sperling, (D)
Courtesy Professor:
James O. Leckie, (D), Harvard, 1970, Cl
Emeritus:
Atilla Aydin, (D), Stanford, 1978, Gc
Dennis K. Bird, (D), California (Berkeley), 1978, Cg
Gordon E. Brown, Jr., (D), Virginia Tech, 1970, Gz
Robert G. Coleman, (D), Stanford, 1957, Gi
Robert R. Compton, (D), Stanford, 1949, Gx
John W. Harbaugh, (D), Wisconsin, 1955, Gq
James C. Ingle, Jr., (D), S California, 1966, Pm
Andre G. Journel, (D), Nancy (France), 1977, Gq
Juhn G. Liou, (D), California (Los Angeles), 1970, Gp
Ronald J. P. Lyon, (D), California (Berkeley), 1954, Zr
Gail A. Mahood, (D), California (Berkeley), 1979, Gi
David D. Pollard, (D), Stanford, 1969, Gc
Irwin Remson, (D), Columbia, 1954, Hw
Jonathan F. Stebbins, (D), California (Berkeley), 1983, Cg

Dept of Geophysics (B,M,D) ☒ (2018)
397 Panama Mall
Stanford, CA 94305-2215
p. (650) 497-3498
biondo@stanford.edu
https://earth.stanford.edu/geophysics/
Programs: Geophysics
Enrollment (2018): B: 2 (2) M: 7 (5) D: 76 (19)
Chair:
Howard A. Zebker, (D), Stanford, 1984, Yx
Research Professor:
William L. Ellsworth, (D), MIT, 1978, Ys
Courtesy Associate Professor:
Simon L. Klemperer, (D), Cornell, 1985, GtYes
Professor:
Gregory C. Beroza, (D), MIT, 1989, Ys
Biondo L. Biondi, (D), Stanford, 1990, Ye
Jerry M. Harris, (D), Caltech, 1980, Ys
Rosemary J. Knight, (D), Stanford, 1985, Hy
Paul Segall, (D), Stanford, 1981, Yg
Norman H. Sleep, (D), MIT, 1972, Yg
Mark D. Zoback, (D), Stanford, 1975, Yg
Associate Professor:
Eric M. Dunham, (D), California (Santa Barbara), 2005, Ys
Assistant Professor:
Dustin M. Schroeder, (D), Texas, 2014, Gl
Jenny Suckale, (D), Yg
Tiziana Vanorio, (D), Yx
Adjunct Professor:
Steven Gorelick, Yr
Emeritus:
Jon F. Claerbout, (D), MIT, 1967, Ye
Antony C. Fraser-Smith, (D), Auckland, 1966, Ym
Robert L. Kovach, (D), Caltech, 1962, Ys
Gerald M. Mavko, (D), Stanford, 1977, Yg
Amos M. Nur, (D), MIT, 1969, Yg
Joan Roughgarden, (D), Harvard, 1971, Ob
Department Manager:
Jen Kidwell, Zn

Taft College

Math/Science Div (2015)
29 Emmons Park Drive
Taft, CA 93268
p. (661) 763-7932
ggolling@taftcollege.edu

University of California, Berkeley

Dept of Earth & Planetary Science (B,M,D) (2015)
307 McCone
Berkeley, CA 94720-4767
p. (510) 642-3993
bbuffett@berkeley.edu
http://eps.berkeley.edu
Chair:
Hans-Rudolf Wenk, (D), Zurich, 1965, Gz
Professor:
Walter Alvarez, (D), Princeton, 1967, GrRh
Jillian Banfield, (D), Johns Hopkins, 1990, CoGz
James K. Bishop, (D), MIT/WHOI, 1977, Oc
George H. Brimhall, (D), California (Berkeley), 1972, Eg
Roland Burgmann, (D), Stanford, 1993, GtYd
Donald J. DePaolo, (D), Caltech, 1978, Cc
William E. Dietrich, (D), Washington, 1982, Gm
Inez Fung, (D), MIT, 1977, As
B. Lynn Ingram, (D), Stanford, 1992, Cs
Raymond Jeanloz, (D), Caltech, 1979, Gy
James W. Kirchner, (D), California (Berkeley), 1990, Ge
Michael Manga, (D), Harvard, 1994, GvXyHw
Mark A. Richards, (D), Caltech, 1986, Yg
Barbara A. Romanowicz, (D), Paris, 1979, Ys
Associate Professor:
Kristie Boering, (D), Stanford, 1991, As
Douglas S. Dreger, (D), Caltech, 1992, Ys
Assistant Professor:
Richard M. Allen, (D), Princeton, 2001, Ys
Burkhard Militzer, (D), Illinois (Urbana), 2000, Gy
Adjunct Associate Professor:
David L. Alumbaugh, (D), California (Berkeley), 1993, Ye
Paul Renne, (D), California (Berkeley), 1987, Cc
Adjunct Professor:
Steven Pride, (D), Texas A&M, 1991, Ys
Visiting Professor:
William D. Collins, (D), Chicago, 1988, As
Emeritus:
Mark S. Bukowinski, (D), California (Los Angeles), 1975, Gy
Ian S. Carmichael, (D), London (UK), 1958, Gi
Garniss H. Curtis, (D), California (Berkeley), 1951, Cc
Lane R. Johnson, (D), Caltech, 1966, Ys
Doris Sloan, (D), California (Berkeley), 1981, Pme
Chi-Yuen Wang, (D), Harvard, 1964, Yg

Dept of Environmental Science, Policy and Management (B,M,D) O☒ (2018)
140 Mulford Hall
Berkeley, CA 94720-3110
p. (510) 643-3788
earthy@berkeley.edu
http://espm.berkeley.edu/
Enrollment (2018): B: 200 (200) D: 30 (10)

Dept of Integrative Biology (B,M,D) (2017)
3040 Valley Life Sciences Building #3140
Berkeley, CA 94720-3140
p. (510) 502-5887
johnh@berkeley.edu
http://ib.berkeley.edu/
Curator:
Carole S. Hickman, (D), Stanford, 1975, PgePg
Professor:
F. Stuart Chapin, (D), Stanford, 1973, Pe
William A. Clemens, (D), California (Berkeley), 1960, Pv
Robert J. Full, (D), SUNY (Buffalo), 1984, Pi
Harry W. Green, (D), Tennessee, 1977, Pv
Ned K. Johnson, (D), California (Berkeley), 1961, Pv
Mimi A. R. Koehl, (D), Duke, 1976, Pg
Brent Mishler, (D), Harvard, 1984, Pe
Kevin Padian, (D), Yale, 1980, Pv
Wayne P. Sousa, (D), California (Santa Barbara), 1977, Ob
Associate Professor:
Mary E. Power, (D), Washington, 1981, Pe
Emeritus:
Roy L. Caldwell, (D), Iowa, 1969, Pi
Carole S. Hickman, (D), Stanford, 1975, Pg
William Z. Lidicker, Jr., (D), Illinois, 1957, Pv
David R. Lindberg, (D), California (Santa Cruz), Pi
James L. Patton, (D), Arizona, 1968, Pv
Thomas M. Powell, (D), California (Berkeley), 1970, Op
Montgomery Slatkin, (D), Harvard, 1970, Pg
Glennis Thompson, (D), Melbourne (Australia), 1974, Zn
James W. Valentine, (D), California (Los Angeles), 1958, Pg
David B. Wake, (D), S California, 1964, Pg
Marvalee H. Wake, (D), S California, 1968, Pg

Dept of Materials Science and Engineering (B,M,D) (2015)
577 Evans Hall
Berkeley, CA 94720-1760
p. (510) 642-3801
hfmorrison@berkeley.edu
http://www.mse.berkeley.edu/
Chair:
Robert O. Ritchie, (D), Cambridge, 1973, Zm
Professor:
Alex Becker, (D), McGill, 1963, Yg
George A. Cooper, (D), Cambridge, 1967, Np
Didier deFontaine, (D), Northwestern, 1967, Zm
Lutgard DeJonghe, (D), California (Berkeley), 1970, Zm
Thomas M. Devine, (D), MIT, 1974, Zm
Fiona M. Doyle, (D), Imperial Coll (UK), 1983, Nx
James W. Evans, (D), SUNY (Buffalo), 1970, Nx
Douglas W. Fuerstenau, (D), MIT, 1953, Nx
Andreas Glaeser, (D), MIT, 1981, Zm
Ronald Gronsky, (D), California (Berkeley), 1977, Zm
Eugene Haller, (D), Basel (Switzerland), 1970, Zm
J. W. Morris, Jr., (D), MIT, 1969, Zm
H. Frank Morrison, (D), California (Berkeley), 1967, Yg
T. N. Narasimhan, (D), California (Berkeley), 1975, Hw
Timothy Sands, (D), California (Berkeley), 1984, Zm
Kalanadh V. S. Sastry, (D), California (Berkeley), 1970, Nx
Eicke Weber, (D), Cologne, 1976, Zm
Associate Professor:
Tad W. Patzek, (D), Silesian Tech, 1979, Np
James W. Rector, III, (D), Stanford, 1990, Ys
Assistant Professor:
Daryl Chrzan, (D), California (Berkeley), 1989, Zm
Mauro Ferrari, (D), California (Berkeley), 1989, Zm

GeoEngineering Program (B,M,D) (2015)
Berkeley, CA 94720
p. (510) 642-3157
pestana@ce.berkeley.edu
http://www.ce.berkeley.edu/geo/
Chair:
Lisa Alvarez-Cohen
Professor:
Alex Becker, (D), McGill, 1964, Ye
Huntly Frank Morrison, (D), California (Berkeley), 1967, Ye
Senior Scientist:
Ki Ha Lee, (D), California (Berkeley), 1978, Ye
Assistant Professor:
James W. Rector, (D), Stanford, 1990, Ye

Museum of Paleontology (D) (2016)
1101 Valley Life Sciences Bldg #4780
Berkeley, CA 94720-4780
p. (510) 642-1821
crmarshall@berkeley.edu
http://www.ucmp.berkeley.edu
Enrollment (2016): D: 25 (3)
Professor:
Charles R. Marshall, (D), Chicago, 1989, PqgPi
Curator:
Kevin Padian, (D), Yale, 1980, Pv
Principal Museum Scientist:
Mark B. Goodwin, (D), California (Davis), 2008, Pv
Museum Scientist:
Diane Erwin, (D), Alberta, 1990, Pb
Pat Holroyd, (D), Duke, 1994, Pv
Curator:
Leslea Hlusko, (D), Penn State, 2000, PgZnn
Associate Professor:
Cynthia Looy, (D), Utrecht, 1995, Pb
Assistant Professor:
Seth Finnegan, (D), California (Riverside), 1994, Pig

Curatorial Associate:
Walter Alvarez, (D), Princeton, 1967, Gr
Curator:
Anthony D. Barnosky, (D), Washington, 1983, Pv
William A. Clemens, (D), California (Berkeley), 1960, Pv
David R. Lindberg, (D), California (Santa Cruz), 1983, Pg
Emeritus:
Roy Caldwell, (D), Iowa, 1969, Pg
James W. Valentine, (D), California (Los Angeles), 1958, Pg
Assistant Director:
Lisa D. White, California (Santa Cruz), 1989, ZePim

University of California, Davis

Dept of Earth and Planetary Sciences (B,M,D) ●⦸ (2021)
2119 Earth & Physical Sciences Building
One Shields Ave.
Davis, CA 95616-5270
p. (530) 752-0350
geology@ucdavis.edu
http://geology.ucdavis.edu
f: https://www.facebook.com/pages/Geology-Department-at-UC-Davis/87869598212
Programs: Geology (B,M,D); Marine and Coastal Science (B)
Enrollment (2020): B: 174 (48) M: 9 (2) D: 36 (6)
Chair:
Michael Oskin, (D), Caltech, 2002, GmtGc
Professor:
Magali I. Billen, (D), Caltech, 2001, Yg
Sandra J. Carlson, (D), Michigan, 1986, Pg
Kari M. Cooper, (D), California (Los Angeles), 2001, Gi
Eric S. Cowgill, (D), California (Los Angeles), 2001, Gtc
Tessa M. Hill, (D), California (Santa Barbara), 2004, Pe
Isabel P. Montañez, (D), Virginia Tech, 1990, Gd
Ryosuke Motani, (D), Toronto, 1997, Pv
Sujoy Mukhopadhyay, (D), Caltech, 2002, Cg
David A. Osleger, (D), Virginia Tech, 1990, Pc
Nicholas Pinter, (D), California (Santa Barbara), 1992, Gm
John Rundle, (D), California (Los Angeles), 1976, Yd
Howard J. Spero, (D), California (Santa Barbara), 1986, Cm
Sarah T. Stewart, (D), Caltech, 2002
Dawn Y. Sumner, (D), MIT, 1995, Gs
Geerat J. Vermeij, (D), Yale, 1971, Pe
Qing-zhu Yin, (D), Max Planck, 1995, Cc
Assistant Professor:
David Gold, (D), California (Los Angeles), 2014, Pg
Barbara C. Ratschbacher, (D), S California, 2017, GgCg
Maxwell L. Rudolph, (D), California (Berkeley), 2012, Yg
Research Associate:
Oliver Kreylos, (D), California (Davis), 2003, Ng
Ann D. Russell, (D), Washington, 1994, Cm
Peter Thy, (D), Aarhus (Denmark), 1982, Gx
Burak Yikilmaz, California (Davis), 2010, Gc
Emeritus:
Cathy J. Busby, (D), Princeton, 1983, Gt
Richard Cowen, (D), Cambridge, 1966, Pg
Howard W. Day, (D), Brown, 1971, Gx
John Dewey, (D), London (UK), 1960, Gt
James A. Doyle, (D), Harvard, 1971, Pb
Graham E. Fogg, (D), Texas, 1986, Hw
Charles G. Higgins, (D), California (Berkeley), 1950, Gm
Charles E. Lesher, (D), Harvard, 1985, Gi
James S. McClain, (D), Washington, 1979, Yr
Jeffrey F. Mount, (D), California (Santa Cruz), 1980, Gm
Alexandra Navrotsky, (D), Chicago, 1967, Zm
Sarah M. Roeske, (D), California (Santa Cruz), 1988, GtcGp
James R. Rustad, (D), Minnesota, 1992, Cl
Peter Schiffman, (D), Stanford, 1978, Gp
Donald L. Turcotte, (D), Caltech, 1958, Yg
Robert J. Twiss, (D), Princeton, 1970, Gc
Kenneth L. Verosub, (D), Stanford, 1973, Ym
Robert A. Zierenberg, (D), Wisconsin, 1983, Cs
Chief Administrative Officer:
Corinne Esser, (M), UCD, Zn
Cooperating Faculty:
William H. Casey, (D), Penn State, 1985, Cl

Dept of Land, Air & Water Resources (B,M,D) O☒ (2017)
1110 Plant and Environmental Sciences Building
One Shields Avenue
Davis, CA 95616
p. (530) 752-1130
rjsouthard@ucdavis.edu
http://lawr.ucdavis.edu/
Programs: Atmospheric Science; Hydrology/Hydrologic Science; Environmental Science and Management; Soils and Biogeochemistry
Enrollment (2014): B: 5 (5) M: 54 (19) D: 55 (8)
Specialist in Cooperative Extension:
Thomas Harter, (D), Arizona, 1994, Hg
Toby O'Geen, (D), Idaho, 2002, So
Professor:
Cort Anastasio, (D), Duke, 1994, As
Shu-Hua Chen, (D), Purdue, 1999, ZrAsm
Randy A. Dahlgren, (D), Washington, 1987, So
Graham E. Fogg, (D), Texas, 1986, Hw
Richard Grotjahn, (D), Florida State, 1979, As
Peter J. Hernes, (D), Washington, 1999, Hg
Jan W. Hopmans, (D), Auburn, So
William R. Horwath, (D), Michigan State, 1993, Sob
Louise E. Jackson, (D), Washington, 1982, So
Terrence R. Nathan, (D), SUNY (Albany), 1985, Asm
Kate Scow, (D), Cornell, 1988, So
Randal J. Southard, (D), North Carolina State, 1983, So
Susan L. Ustin, (D), California (Davis), 1983, Zr
Associate Professor:
Ian C. Faloona, (D), Penn State, 2001, AscAp
Ben Houlton, (D), Princeton, So
Sanjai Parikh, (D), Arizona, So
20% Cooperative Extension:
Samuel Sandoval Solis, (D), Texas, 2011, Hg
Assistant Professor:
Yufang Jin, (D), Boston, 2002, Zr
Adjunct Professor:
Travis A. O'Brien, (D), California (Santa Cruz), 2011, AstAp
Minghua Zhang, (D), California (Davis), 1993, Hg
Emeritus:
James H. Richards, (D), Alberta, 1981, So
Asst Proj Scientist:
Michael L. Grieneisen, (D), North Carolina, 1992, Hg
Asst Professional Researcher:
Lucas CR Silva, (D), Guelph, 2011, Sb
Cooperating Faculty:
Daniel Geisseler, (D), California (Davis), 2009, So
Stephen R. Grattan, (D), California (Riverside), 1984, Sp
Richard L. Snyder, (D), Iowa State, 1980, As
Daniele Zaccaria, (D), Utah State, 2011, Hg

Dept of Land, Air & Water Resources - Hydrology Program (B,M,D) ☒ (2020)
1110A Plant Environmental Sciences
One Shields Avenue
Davis, CA 95616-8628
p. (530) 752-3060
thharter@ucdavis.edu
http://lawr.ucdavis.edu/
Programs: B.S. in Hydrology, Soil Sciences, Environmental Science and Management, Atmospheric Sciences. M.S. and Ph.D. in Hydrologic Sciences, Soils and Biogeochemistry, Atmospheric Sciences.
Enrollment (2012): B: 25 (0) M: 16 (0) D: 21 (0)
Groundwater Hydrology Specialist:
Thomas L. Harter, (D), Arizona, 1993, Hw
Professor:
Cort Anastasio, (D), Duke, Acs
Shu-Hua Chen, (D), Purdue, Apm
Mark E. Grismer, (D), Colorado State, 1984, Hw
Peter J. Hernes, (D), Washington, CoHg
William R. Horwath, (D), Michigan State, ScCo
Terry Nathan, SUNY (Albany), AsZc
Toby A. O'Geen, Idaho, Sod
Gregory B. Pasternack, (D), Johns Hopkins, 1998, GmHg
Kyaw Tha Paw U, (D), Yale, Asm
Carlos E. Puente, (D), MIT, 1984, Hqg
Jorge Rodrigues, Michigan State, SbPo
Kate M. Scow, Cornell, Sb
Anthony S. Wexler, (D), Caltech, ZcAsZn
Minghua Zhang, (D), California (Davis), HgEg

Associate Professor:
Majdi Abou Najm, (D), CbSb
Helen E. Dahlke, (D), Cornell, 2011, HgsZi
Yufang Jin, Boston, ZrHg
Isaya Kisekka, Florida, ZuRw
Sanjai Parikh, Arizona, ScbCb
Kerri Steenwerth, Cb
Paul Ullrich, Waterloo, As
Associate Scientist:
Mallika Nocco, Wisconsin, Sp
Kosana Suvocarev, (D), Zaragoza, Asm
Daniele Zaccaria, Utah State (Logan), HgRw
Assistant Professor:
Rebecca Hernandez, (D), Stanford, Zcn
Adele Igel, (D), Colorado State, Asp
Rebecca A. Lybrand, SbCb
Erwan Monier, California (Davis), Atm
Samuel Sandoval, (D), Texas, 2011, Hg
Da Yang, Caltech, Ast
Research Associate:
Victor P. Claassen, (D), California (Davis), So
Daniel Geisseler, (D), California (Davis), Sb
Adjunct Professor:
Laura Foglia, (D), ETH (Switzerland), HwZc
Matthew Igel, (D), Colorado State, Asm

Graduate Group in Hydrologic Sciences (M,D) (2015)
1152 PES
One Shields Ave
Davis, CA 95616
p. (530) 752-1669
lawrgradadvising@ucdavis.edu
http://hydscigrad.ucdavis.edu/
Administrative Assistant: Diane Swindall
Enrollment (2010): M: 14 (1) D: 14 (0)
Chair:
Graham E. Fogg, (D), Texas, 1986, Hy
Professor:
William H. Casey, (D), Pennsylvania, 1985, Cl
Jeannie Darby, (D), Texas, 1988, Hg
Mark E. Grismer, (D), Colorado State, 1984, Hw
Jan W. Hopmans, (D), Auburn, 1985, So
Theodore C. Hsiao, (D), Illinois, 1964, Zn
B. E. Larock, (D), Stanford, 1966, Zn
Jay R. Lund, (D), Washington, 1986, Hs
M. A. Marino, (D), California (Los Angeles), 1972, Hw
James S. McClain, (D), Washington, 1979, Yr
Eldridge M. Moores, (D), Princeton, 1963, Gt
Jeffrey F. Mount, (D), California (Santa Cruz), 1980, Gs
Dennis E. Rolston, (D), California (Davis), 1971, So
K. K. Tanji, (M), California (Davis), 1961, Zn
Wes W. Wallender, (D), Utah State, 1982, Hg
B. C. Weare, (D), SUNY (Buffalo), 1974, As
Associate Professor:
Bruce Kutter, (D), Cambridge, 1983, Ne
Carlos E. Puente, (D), MIT, 1984, Hg
Emeritus:
Robert A. Matthews, (B), California (Berkeley), 1953, Ge

University of California, Irvine

Dept of Earth System Science (B,D) (2015)
School of Physical Sciences
Irvine, CA 92697-3100
p. (949) 824-8794
essinfo@ess.uci.edu
http://www.ess.uci.edu
Enrollment (2013): B: 166 (64) D: 49 (5)
Chair:
Michael L. Goulden, (D), Stanford, 1992, Zg
Advance Professor:
Ellen R. M. Druffel, (D), California (San Diego), 1980, Oc
Professor:
James Famiglietti, (D), Princeton, Hw
Gudrun Magnusdottir, (D), Colorado State, 1989, As
Michael J. Prather, (D), Yale, 1975, As
Eric Rignot, (D), S California, 1991, GlOpZr
Eric S. Saltzman, (D), Rosenstiel, 1986, As
Soroosh Sorooshian, (D), California (Los Angeles), 1978, Hg
Susan E. Trumbore, (D), Columbia, 1989, Sc
Jin-Yi Yu, (D), Washington, AsOpZc
Charles Zender, (D), Colorado, 1996, As
Associate Professor:
Steven J. Davis, (D), Stanford, 2008, GeCsZu
Jefferson Keith Moore, (D), Oregon State, 1999, Op
Francois Primeau, (D), MIT/WHOI, 1998, Op
Assistant Professor:
Claudia Czimczik, (D)
Todd Dupont, (D), Penn State, 2004, Gl
Julie Ferguson, (D), Oxford, 2008, Ze
Kathleen Johnson, (D), California (Berkeley), 2004, Zg
Saewung Kim, (D), Georgia Tech, 2007, As
Adam Martiny, (D), Tech (Denmark), 2003, Ob
Michael Pritchard, (D)
Isabella Velicogna, (D), Trieste, 1999, Zr
Laboratory Director:
John Southon, (D), Auckland, 1976, CcOcPe

University of California, Los Angeles

Dept of Atmospheric and Oceanic Sciences (B,M,D) ☒ (2019)
7127 Math Sciences
Box 951565
Los Angeles, CA 90095
p. (310) 825-1217
paulson@atmos.ucla.edu
http://www.atmos.ucla.edu
f: https://www.facebook.com/AOS.UCLA
Chair:
Suzanne Paulson, (D), Caltech, 1991, As
Professor:
Jacob Bortnik, (D)
Marcelo Chamecki
Gang Chen
Rong Fu
Alex Hall, (D)
Qinbin Li
Kuo Nan Liou, (D), New York, 1970, As
James McWilliams, (D), Harvard, 1971, OgAs
J. David Neelin, (D), Princeton, 1987, As
Jochen P. Stutz, (D), Heidelberg, 1996, As
Tina Treude
Yongkang Xue, (D)
Associate Professor:
Jasper Kok , (D)
Ulli Seibt , (D)
Arahdna Tripati, (D)
Assistant Professor:
Daniele Bianchi , (D)
Rob Eagle
Andrew Stewart, (D)
Lecturer:
Jeffrey Lew, (D), California (Los Angeles), 1985, As
Adjunct Professor:
Yi Chao
Emeritus:
Akio Arakawa, (D), Tokyo, 1961, As
Robert Fovell, (D), Illinois, 1988, As
Michael Ghil, (D), Courant Inst, 1975, As
Lawrence Lyons, (D), California (Los Angeles), 1972, As
Carlos R. Mechoso, (D), Princeton, 1978, As
Richard M. Thorne, (D), MIT, 1968, As
Richard Turco, (D), Illinois, 1971, As

Dept. of Earth, Planetary, and Space Sciences (B,M,D) O☒ (2020)
595 Charles E Young Drive East
3806 Geology Building, Box 951567
Los Angeles, CA 90095-1567
p. 310.825.3880
info@epss.ucla.edu
https://epss.ucla.edu
f: https://www.facebook.com/uclaepss
t: @uclaepss
Programs: Geology (BS); Geology/Engineering Geology (BS); Geophysics (BS); Earth & Environmental Science (BA)
Enrollment (2020): B: 68 (20) M: 3 (11) D: 78 (5)
Chair:
Edwin A. Schauble, (D), Caltech, 2002, Csg

Professor:
Vassilis Angelopoulos, (D), California (Los Angeles), 1993, XyAsYm
Jonathan M. Aurnou, (D), Johns Hopkins, 1999, YgmYx
T. Mark Harrison, (D), Australian Nat, 1981, CcGt
David Jewitt, (D), Caltech, 1983, XyZnn
Abby Kavner, (D), California (Berkeley), 1997, GyYg
Carolina Lithgow-Bertelloni, (D), California (Berkeley), 1994, Yg
Craig E. Manning, (D), Stanford, 1989, GxCp
Jean-Luc Margot, (D), Cornell, 1999, XyYdv
Kevin D. McKeegan, (D), Washington (St Louis), 1987, XcCsc
William I. Newman, (D), Cornell, 1979, Xy
David A. Paige, (D), Caltech, 1985, Xy
Gilles Peltzer, (D), Paris VII, 1987, ZrGt
Christopher T. Russell, (D), California (Los Angeles), 1968, Xy
J. William Schopf, (D), Harvard, 1968, Pg
Lars Stixrude, (D), California (Berkeley), 1991, YgXy
Tina Treude, (D), Max Planck, 2004, ObPgCm
Marco Velli, (D), Pisa, 1985, Yg
An Yin, (D), S California, 1988, Gt
Edward D. Young, (D), S California, 1990, CsXc
Associate Professor:
Caroline Beghein, (D), Utrecht, 2003, Ysg
Lingsen Meng, (D), Caltech, 2012, Ys
Jonathan Mitchell, (D), Chicago, 2007, AsXg
Hilke Schlichting, (D), Caltech, 2009, Xy
Ulrike Seibt, (D), Hamburg, 2003, PgCg
Aradhna Tripati, (D), California (Santa Cruz), 2002, CmPeCs
Assistant Professor:
Mackenzie Day, (D), Caltech, 2017, Ggs
Seulgi Moon, (D), Stanford, 2013, Gm
Adjunct Professor:
Robert C. Newton, (D), California (Los Angeles), 1963, CpGp
Edward J. Rhodes, (D), Oxford, 1990, CcGma
Emeritus:
G. Peter Bird, (D), MIT, 1976, GtYsRn
Paul M. Davis, (D), Queensland, 1974, YsmYg
Wayne A. Dollase, (D), MIT, 1966, Gz
Clarence A. Hall, (D), Stanford, 1956, GgtGe
Raymond V. Ingersoll, (D), Stanford, 1976, Gst
David D. Jackson, (D), MIT, 1969, YsdYg
Isaac R. Kaplan, (D), S California, 1962, Csg
Margaret G. Kivelson, (D), Radcliffe, 1957, Xy
Robert L. McPherron, (D), California (Berkeley), 1968, Xy
Paul M. Merifield, (D), Colorado, 1963, Ng
Bruce Runnegar, (D), Queensland, 1967, Pg
Gerald Schubert, (D), California (Berkeley), 1964, YgXy
Laurence C. Smith, (D), Cornell, 1996, Hs
Raymond J. Walker, (D), California (Los Angeles), 1973, Xy

Inst of Geophysics & Planetary Physics (2015)
3845 Slichter Hall
Los Angeles, CA 90095-1567
p. (310) 825-1664
jnakatsu@igpp.ucla.edu
http://www.igpp.ucla.edu
Professor:
Vassilis Angelopoulos, (D), California (Los Angeles), 1993, Yg
Maha Ashour-Abdalla, (D), Imperial Coll (UK), 1971, Zn
Friedrich H. Busse, (D), Munich, 1967, Zn
Richard E. Dickerson, (D), Minnesota, 1957, Zn
Michael Ghil, (D), New York, 1975, AsYdOp
T. Mark Harrison, (D), Australian Nat, 1980, Cc
Charles F. Kennel, (D), Princeton, 1964, Zn
Margaret G. Kivelson, (D), Radcliffe, 1957, Xy
Robert L. McPherron, (D), California (Berkeley), 1968, Xy
James C. McWilliams, (D), Harvard, 1971, As
Paul H. Roberts, (D), Cambridge, 1967, Ym
Bruce Runnegar, (D), Queensland, 1967, Pg
Christopher T. Russell, (D), California (Los Angeles), 1968, Yg
J. William Schopf, (D), Harvard, 1968, Pg
Gerald Schubert, (D), California (Berkeley), 1964, Yg
Karl O. Stetter, (D), Tech (Munich), 1973, Pg
Richard Turco, (D), Illinois, 1971, As
Raymond J. Walker, (D), California (Los Angeles), 1973, Zn
John T. Wasson, (D), MIT, 1958, Xm
Edward Young, Cg
Senior Scientist:
Stanislav I. Braginsky, (D), Moscow Inst, 1948, Ym
Robert J. Strangeway, (D), London (UK), 1978, Zn
M I. Venkatesan, (D), Madras (India), 1973, Co
Paul Warren, (D), California (Los Angeles), 1979, Xm
Associate Professor:
Abby Kavner, (D), California (Berkeley), 1997, Yg
J. David Neelin, (D), Princeton, 1987, As
Associate Research Scientist:
Jean Berchem, (D), California (Los Angeles), 1986, Zn
Gregory Kallemeyn, (D), California (Los Angeles), 1982, Cg
Frank T. Kyte, (D), California (Los Angeles), 1983, Ct
Alan E. Rubin, (D), New Mexico, 1982, Xm
David Schriver, (D), California (Los Angeles), 1988, Yg
Fred Schwab, (B), California (Los Angeles), 1960, Ys
Assistant Research Scientist:
Kayo Ide, (D), Caltech, 1990, Zg
Krishan Khurana, (D), Durham (UK), 1984, Zn
Robert Richard, (D), California (Los Angeles), 1988, Yg
William Smythe, (D), California (Los Angeles), 1979, Ys
Ferenc D. Varadi, (D), California (Los Angeles), 1989, Zn
Emeritus:
Orson L. Anderson, (D), Utah, 1951, Yx
Paul J. Coleman, Jr., (D), California (Los Angeles), 1966, Gc
Isaac R. Kaplan, (D), S California, 1962, Cg
Leon Knopoff, (D), Caltech, 1949, Ys
Ronald L. Shreve, (D), Caltech, 1958, Gm
Department Manager:
James Nakatsuka, Zn

University of California, Riverside

Department of Earth Sciences (B,M,D) ●⁄ (2019)
Department of Earth Sciences
University of California, Riverside
Riverside, CA 92521
p. (951) 827-3434
david.oglesby@ucr.edu
http://earthsciences.ucr.edu
f: https://www.facebook.com/ucrearthsciences/
Programs: Geology, Earth Sciences, Geophysics
Enrollment (2013): B: 51 (13) M: 15 (8) D: 38 (4)
Chair:
David D. Oglesby, (D), California (Santa Barbara), 1999, Ys
Distinguished Professor:
Timothy W. Lyons, (D), Yale, 1992, CgOcCl
Professor:
Mary L. Droser, (D), S California, 1987, Pg
Nigel C. Hughes, (D), Bristol, 1990, Pg
Gordon D. Love, (D), Strathclyde, 1995, Cog
Richard A. Minnich, (D), California (Los Angeles), 1978, Zy
Andy Ridgwell, (D), E Anglia (UK), 2001, Zn
Peter M. Sadler, (D), Bristol, 1973, GrPs
Associate Professor:
Robert J. Allen, (D), Yale, 2009, As
Andrey Bekker, (D), Virginia Tech, 2001, GsrCg
Gareth J. Funning, (D), Oxford, 2005, YdgYs
Abhijit Ghosh, (D), Washington, 2011, YsGt
Michael A. McKibben, (D), Penn State, 1984, Cg
Assistant Professor:
Nicolas Barth, (D), Otago (NZ), 2013, Gt
Maryjo Brounce, (D), Rhode Island, 2014, Cg
Roby Douilly, (D), Purdue, 2016, YsGtYg
Heather Ford, (D), Brown, 2013, Ys
Sandra Kirtland Turner, (D), Scripps, Cs
Adjunct Assistant Professor:
Katherine J. Kendrick, (D), California (Riverside), 1999, Gm
Thomas A. Scott, (D), California (Berkeley), 1987, Zy
Adjunct Professor:
Elizabeth Cochran, California (Los Angeles), 2005, Ys
Larissa F. Dobrzhinetskaya, (D), Inst of Physics of Earth (Moscow), 1978, Gx
Douglas M. Morton, (D), California (Los Angeles), 1966, Gp
Professor of the Graduate Division:
James H. Dieterich, (D), Yale, 1968, Yg
Emeritus:
Wilfred A. Elders, (D), Durham (UK), 1961, Gi
Michael A. Murphy, (D), California (Los Angeles), 1954, Ps
Stephen K. Park, (D), MIT, 1984, Ym
Michael O. Woodburne, (D), California (Berkeley), 1966, Pv

University of California, San Diego

Scripps Institution of Oceanography (B,M,D) ☒ (2020)
Graduate & Undergraduate Office
9500 Gilman Dr.
Mail Code 0208
La Jolla, CA 92093-0208
p. (858) 534-3206
siodept@sio.ucsd.edu
https://scripps.ucsd.edu/education/
Enrollment (2012): M: 7 (0) D: 62 (13)

Vice Chancellor:
Margaret Leinen, (D), Rhode Island, 1980, OgPe

Professor:
Brian Palenik, (D), MIT/WHOI, 1989, Ob

Director of MPL:
William A. Kuperman, (D), Maryland, 1972, Op

Deputy Director Research:
Douglas H. Bartlett, (D), Illinois, 1985, Ob

Department Vice Chair:
Sarah T. Gille, (D), MIT/WHOI, 1995, Op

Department Chair:
Peter J. S. Franks, (D), MIT/WHOI, 1990, Ob

Professor:
Eric E. Allen, (D), California (San Diego), 2002, Ob
Lihini I. Aluwihare, (D), MIT/WHOI, 1999, Gu
Laurence Armi, (D), California (Berkeley), 1975, Op
Farooq Azam, (D), Czech Acad of Sci, 1968, Ob
Katherine A. Barbeau, (D), MIT/WHOI, 1998, Oc
Adrian Borsa, (D), Scripps, 2005, Hg
Kevin M. Brown, (D), Durham (UK), 1987, Gu
Michael J. Buckingham, (D), Reading (UK), 1971, Op
Ronald S. Burton, (D), Stanford, 1981, Ob
Paterno R. Castillo, (D), Washington (St Louis), 1987, Giu
Paola Cessi, (D), MIT, 1987, Op
Christopher D. Charles, (D), Columbia, 1991, Pe
Catherine G. Constable, (D), California (San Diego), 1987, Ymg
Steven C. Constable, (D), Australian Nat, 1983, Yr
James Day, (D), Durham (UK), Cg
Andrew G. Dickson, (D), Liverpool (UK), 1978, Cm
Neal W. Driscoll, (D), Columbia, 1992, Gu
William H. Fenical, (D), California (Riverside), 1968, Oc
Yuri A. Fialko, (D), Princeton, 1998, YgdGt
Helen A. Fricker, (D), Tasmania, 1999, Yr
Terry Gaasterland, (D), Maryland, 1992, Ob
Jeffrey S. Gee, (D), California (San Diego), 1991, Gu
William H. Gerwick, (D), California (San Diego), 1981, Cm
Carl H. Gibson, (D), Stanford, 1962, No
Vicki Grassian, (D), California (Berkeley), 1987, Cm
Philip A. Hastings, (D), Arizona, 1987, Ob
Myrl C. Hendershott, (D), Harvard, 1966, Op
John A. Hildebrand, (D), Stanford, 1983, Yr
William S. Hodgkiss, Jr., (D), Duke, 1975, No
Ralph F. Keeling, (D), Harvard, 1988, As
Michael R. Landry, (D), Washington, 1976, Ob
Gabi Laske, (D), Karlsruhe, 1993, Ys
James J. Leichter, (D), Stanford, 1997, Ob
Lisa A. Levin, (D), California (San Diego), 1982, Ob
Peter F. Lonsdale, (D), California (San Diego), 1974, Gu
Todd Martz, (D), Montana, 2005, Gg
W. Kendall Melville, (D), Southampton (UK), 1974, Op
J. Bernard H. Minster, (D), Caltech, 1974, Ys
Mario J. Molina, (D), California (Berkeley), 1972, As
Bradley S. Moore, (D), Zurich, 1995, Cm
Joel R. Norris, (D), Washington, 1997, As
Richard D. Norris, (D), Harvard, 1990, Gu
Mark D. Ohman, (D), Washington, 1983, Ob
Anne Pommier, (D), Orleans (France), 2009, Cg
Kimberly A. Prather, (D), California (Davis), 1990, AsCmHg
V. Ramanathan, (D), SUNY (Stony Brook), 1973, As
Dean H. Roemmich, (D), MIT/WHOI, 1980, Op
Gregory W. Rouse, (D), Sydney, 1991, Ob
Daniel L. Rudnick, (D), California (San Diego), 1987, Op
Lynn M. Russell, (D), Caltech, 1995, As
David T. Sandwell, (D), California (Los Angeles), 1981, Yr
Uwe Send, (D), California (San Diego), 1988, Op
Jeffrey P. Severinghaus, (D), Columbia, 1995, Pe
Peter M. Shearer, (D), California (San Diego), 1986, Ysg
Len Srnka, (D), Newcastle upon Tyne, 1974, Ym
Dave Stegman, (D), California (Berkeley), Yd
Dariusz Stramski, (D), Gdansk (Poland), 1985, Op
George Sugihara, (D), Princeton, 1983, Ob
Lynne D. Talley, (D), MIT/WHOI, 1982, OpZc
Lisa Tauxe, (D), Columbia, 1983, Ym
Bradley T. Werner, (D), Caltech, 1987, Gm
William R. Young, (D), MIT/WHOI, 1981, Op

Associate Professor:
Andreas Andersson, (D), Hawaii, 2006, Oc
Jennifer E. Smith, (D), Hawaii, 2003, Obn

Adjunct Professor:
Jay P. Barlow, (D), California (San Diego), 1982, Ob

Emeritus:
Duncan C. Agnew, (D), California (San Diego), 1979, Ys
George E. Backus, (D), Chicago, 1956, YmsOp
Jeffrey L. Bada, (D), California (San Diego), 1968, Co
David M. Checkley, (D), California (San Diego), 1978, Ob
Paul Crutzen, (D), Oc
Joseph R. Curray, (D), Scripps, 1959, Gu
Paul K. Dayton, (D), Washington, 1970, Ob
Leroy M. Dorman, (D), Wisconsin, 1970, Yg
Horst Felbeck, (D), Muenster (Germany), 1979, Ob
Joris M. Gieskes, (D), Manitoba, 1965, Oc
Robert T. Guza, (D), California (San Diego), 1974, On
James W. Hawkins, (D), Washington, 1963, OuGip
Anthony DJ Haymet, (D), Chicago, 1981, OcZgn
Nicholas D. Holland, (D), Stanford, 1965, Ob
Jeremy B. C. Jackson, (D), Yale, 1971, PgePi
Miriam Kastner, (D), Harvard, 1970, CmlCm
Charles F. Kennel, (D), Princeton, 1964, As
Gerald L. Kooyman, (D), Arizona, 1966, Ob
J. Douglas Macdougall, (D), California (San Diego), 1972, Cg
T. Guy Masters, (D), Cambridge, 1979, YsGy
John A. McGowan, (D), California (San Diego), 1960, Ob
Walter H. Munk, (D), Scripps, 1947, Op
William A. Newman, (D), California (Berkeley), 1962, Ob
John A. Orcutt, (D), California (San Diego), 1976, YrsYd
Robert L. Parker, (D), Cambridge, 1966, Ym
Robert Pinkel, (D), California (San Diego), 1974, Op
Richard L. Salmon, (D), California (San Diego), 1976, Op
John G. Sclater, (D), Cambridge, 1966, Yh
Richard C. J. Somerville, (D), New York, 1966, As
Victor D. Vacquier, (D), California (Berkeley), 1968, Ob
Ray F. Weiss, (D), California (San Diego), 1970, Cm
Clinton D. Winant, (D), S California, 1972, On

University of California, Santa Barbara

Dept of Earth Science (B,M,D) ☒ (2019)
Room 1006
Webb Hall
Santa Barbara, CA 93106-9630
p. (805) 893-4688
wyss@geol.ucsb.edu
http://www.geol.ucsb.edu
Enrollment (2012): B: 81 (22) M: 12 (2) D: 36 (3)

Professor:
Stanley M. Awramik, (D), Harvard, 1973, Pg
Jordan F. Clark, (D), Columbia, 1995, ClHg
John Cottle, (D), Oxford, 2007, Gi
Phillip B. Gans, (D), Stanford, 1987, Gt
Bradley R. Hacker, (D), California (Los Angeles), 1998, Gp
Matt Jackson, (D), Cu
Chen Ji, (D), Caltech, 2002, Ys
Edward A. Keller, (D), Purdue, 1973, Gm
David W. Lea, (D), MIT, 1990, PeCm
Lorraine Lisiecki, (D), Brown, 2005, Gn
Francis Macdonald, (D), Harvard, Gg
Susannah Porter, (D), Harvard, 2002, Gn
Roberta Rudnick, (D)
Toshiro Tanimoto, (D), California (Berkeley), 1982, Ys
Bruce H. Tiffney, (D), Harvard, 1977, Pb
David Valentine, (D), Cm
Andre R. Wyss, (D), Columbia, 1989, Pv

Associate Professor:
Robin Matoza, (D), Gv
Alexander Simms, (D), Rice, 2006, GsuGm
Syee Weldeab, (D), Tubingen, 2002, PeCm

Assistant Professor:
Zach Eilon, (D), Colombia, Ys

Kristen Morell, (D)
Morgan Raven, (D), Caltech, Cl
Lecturer:
Matt Rioux, (D), California (Santa Barbara), Cc
Emeritus:
Ralph J. Archuleta, (D), California (San Diego), 1976, Ys
Doug Burbank, (D), Dartmouth, 1982, GmtGs
Frank J. Spera, (D), California (Berkeley), 1977, Gi

Earth Research Institute ☒ (2020)
Mail Code 1100
Santa Barbara, CA 93106-1100
p. (805) 893-8231
director@eri.ucsb.edu
http://eri.ucsb.edu
Administrative Assistant: Kathy J. Scheidemen
Director:
Kelly Caylor, (D), Virginia, 2003, HgZcy
Associate Director:
Susannah Porter, (D), Harvard, 2002, Pg

University of California, Santa Cruz

Center for the Dynamics & Evolution of the Land-Sea Interface (2015)
1156 High Street
Room A234, Earth & Marine Sciences Building
Santa Cruz, CA 95064
p. (831) 459-4089
acr@es.ucsc.edu
Professor:
Robert S. Anderson, (D), Washington, 1986, Gm
Kenneth W. Bruland, (D), California (San Diego), 1974, OcCtm
Margaret L. Delaney, (D), MIT/WHOI, 1983, Oc
Russell Flegal, (D), Oregon State, Cg
Laurel R. Fox, (D), California (Santa Barbara), Zn
Dianne Gifford-Gonzalez, (D), California (Berkeley), Zn
Mark S. Mangel, (D), British Columbia, 1978, Zn
Donald C. Potts, (D), California (Santa Barbara), Ob
Mary W. Silver, (D), California (San Diego), 1971, Ob
Jonathan P. Zehr, (D), California (Davis), 1985, Ob
Associate Professor:
Mark Carr, (D), California (Santa Barbara), Ob
Brent Haddad, (D), California (Berkeley), 1996, Zn
Karen D. Holl, (D), Virginia Tech, 1994, Zu
Christina Ravelo, (D), Columbia, 1991, Cs
Donald R. Smith, (D), California (Santa Cruz), Zn
Assistant Professor:
Don Croll, (D), California (Santa Cruz), Ob
Raphael M. Kudela, (D), S California, 1995, Zr
Margaret A. McManus, (D), Old Dominion, 1996, On

Center for the Origin, Dynamics, & Evolution of Planets (2015)
1156 High Street
Room A234, Earth & Marine Sciences Building
Santa Cruz, CA 95064
p. (831) 459-4089
dkorycan@ucsc.edu
Professor:
Robert S. Anderson, (D), Washington, 1986, Gm
Peter Bodenheimer, (D), California (Berkeley), 1965, Xc
Frank Bridges, (D), California (San Diego), 1968, Yx
Douglas Lin, (D), Cambridge, 1976, Xc
Steven Vogt, (D), Texas, 1978, Xc
Other:
Don Korycansky, (D), California (Santa Cruz), Xc

Earth & Planetary Sciences Dept (B,M,D) ●✓ (2019)
1156 High Street
Earth & Marine Sciences Bldg, Rm A232
Santa Cruz, CA 95064
p. (831) 459-4089
jzachos@ucsc.edu
http://www.eps.ucsc.edu
f: https://www.facebook.com/UcscEPS
t: @EpsUcsc
Programs: Earth Sciences B.S., Earth Sciences B.S.with Environmental Geology, Earth Sciences B.S. with Ocean Sciences, Earth Sciences B.S. with Planetary Sciences, Earth Sciences B.S. with Science Education, Earth Sciences/Anthropology BA, Earth Sciences Minor
Enrollment (2018): B: 220 (55) M: 8 (4) D: 48 (6)
Distinguished Professor, Department Chair:
Quentin Williams, (D), California (Berkeley), 1988, Gy
Distinguished Professor:
Thorne Lay, (D), Caltech, 1983, Ys
Professor:
Emily Brodsky, (D), Caltech, 2001, YsgHw
Patrick Y. Chuang, (D), Caltech, 1999, As
Matthew Clapham, (D), S California, 2006
Andrew T. Fisher, (D), Miami, 1989, Hw
Garry Griggs, (D), Oregon State, 1968, On
Elise Knittle, (D), California (Berkeley), 1988, Gy
Paul L. Koch, (D), Michigan, 1989, Pv
Francis Nimmo, Cambridge, 1996, Xy
Susan Schwartz, (D), Michigan, 1988, Ys
Eli A. Silver, (D), California (San Diego), 1969, Yr
Othmar T. Tobisch, (D), Imperial Coll (UK), 1963, Gct
Slawek Tulaczyk, (D), Caltech, 1998, GlmNg
James Zachos, Rhode Island, 1988, Pc
Associate Professor:
Noah J. Finnegan, (D), Washington, 2007, Gm
Ian Garrick-Bethell, (D), MIT, 2009, Xy
Jeremy Hourigan, (D), Stanford, 2002, Cc
Assistant Professor:
Terrence Blackburn, (D), MIT, 2012, Cc
Nicole Feldl, (D), Washington, 2013, At
Myriam Telus, (D), Hawaii, 2015, Xc
Xi Zhang, (D), Caltech, 2013, AsXy
Margaret Zimmer, (D), Duke, 2017, Hw
Senior Lecturer:
Hilde Schwartz, (D), California (Santa Cruz), 1983, Pv
Emeritus:
Erik Asphaug, (D), Arizona, 1993, Xg
Robert S. Coe, (D), California (Berkeley), 1966, Ym
Robert E. Garrison, (D), Princeton, 1964, Gs
James B. Gill, (D), Australian Nat, 1972, Gi
Leo F. Laporte, (D), Columbia, 1960, Pg
J. Casey Moore, (D), Princeton, 1971, Gc
Lisa C. Sloan, (D), Penn State, 1990, Pe
Graduate Program Advisor:
Jennifer M. Fish, (B), California (Santa Cruz), Zn

Inst of Geophysics & Planetary Physics (2015)
1156 High Street
Earth & Marine Sciences Building, Room A234
Santa Cruz, CA 95064
p. (831) 459-4089
shalevst@gmail.com
http://igpp.ucsc.edu
Director:
Ana Christina Ravelo, (D), OcGe

University of San Diego

Dept of Environmental and Ocean Sciences (B,M) ☒ (2019)
Alcala Park
San Diego, CA 92110
p. (619) 260-4795
eosc@sandiego.edu
https://www.sandiego.edu/cas/environmental-ocean-sciences/
Programs: B.A. Marine Ecology, B.A. Environmental Science, B.A. Environmental Studies, M.S. Environmental and Ocean Science
Chair:
Sarah Gray, (D), California (Santa Cruz), Zn
Professor:
Zhi-Yong Yin, (D), Georgia, Zir
Graduate Director:
Ronald S. Kaufmann, (D), California (San Diego), 1992, Ob
Associate Professor:
Michel A. Boudrias, (D), California (San Diego), 1992, Ob
Bethany O'Shea, (D), New South Wales, 2006, CqGeCt
Nathalie Reyns, (D), North Carolina State
Drew Talley, (D), California (San Diego), 2000, ObZe
Assistant Professor:
Jennifer Prairie, (D), Scripps, Ob
Suzanne Walther, (D), Oregon, GmZi

Adjunct Assistant Professor :
LeeAnna Y. Chapman, (D), North Carolina State, 2017, GeZe
Adjunct Assistant Professor and Field Trip Coordinator:
Elizabeth Baker-Treloar, (M), Scripps, 1995, Geu
Adjunct Assistant Professor :
Eric Cathcart, (M), California (San Diego), 1996, Geg
Andrew Nosal, (D), Scripps, Ob
Steven Searcy, (D), North Carolina State, Ob

University of Southern California

Dept of Earth Sciences (B,M,D) ● ☒ (2020)
3651 Trousdale Parkway
ZHS 117
Los Angeles, CA 90089-0740
p. (213) 740-6106
waite@usc.edu
http://www.usc.edu/dept/earth
Administrative Assistant: Vardui Ter-Simonian, Cynthia H.. Waite
Enrollment (2016): B: 30 (12) M: 0 (1) D: 61 (9)
Chair:
William M. Berelson, (D), S California, 1986, Cm
Research Professor:
David A. Okaya, (D), Stanford, 1985, Ys
Professor:
Jan Amend, (D), California (Berkeley), 1995, ClmCo
Yehuda Ben-Zion, (D), S California, 1990, Ys
David J. Bottjer, (D), Indiana, 1978, Pe
Frank A. Corsetti, (D), California (Santa Barbara), 1998, Gs
James F. Dolan, (D), California (Santa Cruz), 1988, Gt
Douglas E. Hammond, (D), Columbia, 1975, Cm
Heidi B. Houston, (D), Caltech, 1987, YsGt
Thomas H. Jordan, (D), Caltech, 1972, Ys
Steven P. Lund, (D), Minnesota, 1981, Ym
James W. Moffett, (D), Miami, 1986, OcCba
Kenneth Nealson, (D), Chicago, 1969, Pg
Scott R. Paterson, (D), California (Santa Cruz), 1986, Gc
John P. Platt, (D), California (Santa Barbara), 1973, GctGp
Charles G. Sammis, (D), Caltech, 1971, Yg
Sergio Sanudo, (D), California (Santa Cruz), 1993, Pg
Lowell D. Stott, (D), Rhode Island, 1989, Pm
Ta-liang Teng, (D), Caltech, 1966, YsGtYe
John E. Vidale, (D), Caltech, 1986, YsGtYg
Associate Professor:
Julien Emile-Geay, (D), Columbia, 2006, Oc
Sarah Feakins, (D), Columbia, 2006, CoGuCs
A. Joshua (Josh) West, (D), Cambridge, 2007, ClGmHs
Research Associate Professor:
Yong-Gang Li, (D), S California, 1988, Ys
Ellen S. Platzman, (D), ETH (Switzerland), 1990
Emeritus:
Gregory A. Davis, (D), California (Berkeley), 1961, GtcGe
Alfred G. Fischer, (D), Columbia, 1950, Gs
Thomas L. Henyey, (D), Caltech, 1968, Yg
Teh-Lung Ku, (D), Columbia, 1966, CgcGn
Bernard W. Pipkin, (D), Arizona, 1964, Ng

University of the Pacific

Department of Geological & Environmental Sciences (B) ☒ (2020)
3601 Pacific Avenue
Stockton, CA 95211
p. (209) 946-2482
lrademacher@pacific.edu
http://pacific.edu/GESC
f: https://liberalarts.pacific.edu/liberalarts/academics/departments-and-programs/geological-and-environmental-sciences
t: @PacificGESC
Programs: BS in Geological and Environmental Sciences with a concentration in Geology or Environmental Science; BA in Geological and Environmental Sciences; 3+3 (BA+JD) in Geological and Environmental Sciences / Environmental Law
Certificates: Wilderness first aid
Enrollment (2020): B: 35 (16)
Professor:
Thomas Naehr, (D)
Eugene F. Pearson, (D), Wyoming, 1972, GsPgZg
Associate Professor:
Lydia K. Fox, (D), California (Santa Barbara), 1989, GizZe
Laura K. Rademacher, (D), California (Santa Barbara), 2002, ClHySo

Emeritus:
Roger T. Barnett, (D), California (Berkeley), 1973, Zy
J. Curtis Kramer, (D), California (Davis), 1976, Gg

Ventura College

Dept of Geology (2017)
4667 Telegraph Road
Ventura, CA 93003
spalladino@vcccd.edu
Chair:
Luke D. Hall, (M), W Kentucky, 1975, Zy
Assistant Professor:
Steve D. Palladino, (M), California (Santa Barbara), 1994, Zi
Instructor:
William Budke, (M), Cal Poly, 2001, So

Victor Valley College

Victor Valley College (2015)
18422 Bear Valley Road
Victorville, CA 92395
p. (415) 506-0234
carol.delong@vvc.edu
http://www.vvc.edu/

West Valley College

Dept of Geology (A) (2015)
14000 Fruitvale Avenue
Saratoga, CA 95070-5698
p. (408) 741-2437
robert_lopez@westvalley.edu
Instructor:
Harry Shade, (M), Miami (Ohio), 1959, Gg
Emeritus:
Theodore C. Herman, (M), Michigan, 1961, Ze

Whittier College

Environmental Science Program (B) (2015)
Whittier, CA 90608
p. (562) 907-4220
cswift@whittier.edu
http://www.whittier.edu/Academics/EnvironmentalSciences/
Chair:
Cheryl Swift
Visiting Professor:
Andrew H. Wulff, (D), Massachusetts, 1998, Gi
Emeritus:
William B. Wadsworth, (D), Northwestern, 1966, Gi

Colorado

Adams State University

School of Science, Mathematics, and Technology (B) ☒ (2021)
208 Edgemont Blvd
Suite 3060
208 Edgemont Blvd.
Alamosa, CO 81101
p. (719) 587-8614
matt.nehring@adams.edu
https://www.adams.edu/academics/undergraduate/earth-science/
f: https://www.facebook.com/pg/AdamsStateBioGeoOutdoorEd/posts/
Programs: Geology, Physical Geography and Conservation, Science Education (Secondary Teacher Licensure)
Enrollment (2020): B: 14 (2)
Assistant Professor:
Chayan Lahiri, (D), Mississippi, 2018, HwZr

Aims Community College

Dept of Sciences (A) ☒ (2017)
5401 West 20th Street
Greeley, CO 80634
p. (970) 339-6637
jim.stone@aims.edu
http://www.aims.edu/academics/sciences

Instructor:
Jim Stone, Zg

Arapahoe Community College

Geology Program (A) (2015)
5900 South Santa Fe Drive
Littleton, CO 80120
p. (303) 797-5831
henry.weigel@arapahoe.edu
http://www.arapahoe.edu/departments-and-programs/a-z-offerings/geology
Program Chair:
Henry Weigel

Colorado College

Geology Dept (B) ☒ (2019)
14 E Cache La Poudre
Colorado Springs, CO 80903
p. (719) 389-6621
geology@coloradocollege.edu
http://www.coloradocollege.edu/academics/dept/geology
f: https://www.facebook.com/geodept.coloradocollege
Programs: Geology
Enrollment (2018): B: 24 (17)
Professor:
Eric M. Leonard, (D), Colorado, 1981, Gl
Paul M. Myrow, (D), Memorial, 1987, Gsr
Jeffrey B. Noblett, (D), Stanford, 1980, Gxv
Christine S. Siddoway, (D), California (Santa Barbara), 1995, GctGg
Department Chair:
Henry C. Fricke, (D), Michigan, 1997, Cs
Technical Director:
Stephen G. Weaver, (D), Colorado Mines, 1988, Gx

Colorado Mesa University

Dept of Physical & Environmental Sciences (A,B) O (2017)
1100 North Avenue
Grand Junction, CO 81501-3122
p. (970) 248-1993
aaslan@coloradomesa.edu
http://www.coloradomesa.edu/geosciences/
Programs: Geosciences (B); Geology (B); Environmental Geology (B); Secondary Education (B); Geology (A); Geology (minor); Watershed Science (minor); GIST (minor)
Certificates: GIS Technology
Enrollment (2017): B: 75 (15)
Professor:
Andres Aslan, (D), Colorado, 1994, Gm
Rex D. Cole, (D), Utah, 1975, GsrGo
Verner C. Johnson, (D), Tennessee, 1975, Yg
Richard F. Livaccari, (D), New Mexico, 1994, Gc
Gigi A. Richard, (D), Colorado State, 2001, Hsg
Instructor:
Cassandra Fenton, (D), Utah, 2002, CcGmCl
Lecturer:
Lawrence S. Jones, (D), Wyoming, 1996, GsmGr
Adjunct Professor:
William C. Hood, (D), Montana, 1964, Gg
Julia McHugh, (D), Iowa, 2012, Pgv
Dave Wolny, (B), Mesa State, 1992, Ys
Emeritus:
James B. Johnson, (D), Colorado, 1979, Gl
Jack E. Roadifer, (D), Arizona, 1966, Gx

Colorado Mountain College

Geology Div (A) (2015)
3000 County Road 114
Glenwood Springs, CO 81601
p. (303) 945-7481 x263
mhaselhorst2@coloradomtn.edu
Professor:
Garrett E. Zabel, (M), Houston, 1977, Gg

Colorado School of Mines

Department of Chemistry (B,M,D) ☒ (2018)
1012 14th Street, CO 204
Golden, CO 80401
p. (303) 273-3610
chemistry@mines.edu
http://chemistry.mines.edu/
f: https://www.facebook.com/csmchemistry/
t: @MinesChemistry
Enrollment (2016): B: 78 (27) M: 14 (5) D: 52 (10)
Department Head:
Thomas Gennett, (D), Vermont
Professor:
Mark E. Eberhart, (D), MIT, 1983, Zm
Mark Jensen, (D), Florida State, 1994
Daniel M. Knauss, (D), Virginia Tech, 1994
James Ranville, (D), Colorado Mines, Ca
Ryan M. Richards, (D), Michigan State, 2000
Bettina Voelker, (D), Swiss Fed Inst Tech, 1994, Ca
Kim R. Williams, (D), Michigan State, 1986, Ca
David T. Wu, (D), California (Berkeley), 1991, Zn
Associate Professor:
Stephen G. Boyes, (D), New South Wales, 2000
Renee L. Falconer, (D), South Carolina, 1994
Matthew C. Posewitz, (D), Dartmouth, 1995
Mark R. Seger, (D), Colorado State
Alan Sellinger, (D), Michigan, 1997
Angela C. Sower, (D), New Mexico
Assistant Professor:
Allison Caster, (D), California (Berkeley), 2010
Dylan Domaille, (D), California (Berkeley)
Amanda Jameer, (M)
Svitlana Pylypenko, (D), New Mexico, Zmn
Jenifer C. Shafer, (D), Washington State, 2010
Brian G. Trewyn, (D), Iowa State, 2006
Shubham Vyas, (D), Ohio State
Yongan Yang, (D), Chinese Acad of Sci, 1999
Emeritus:
Dean W. Dickerhoof, (D), Illinois, 1961
Donald L. Macalady, (D), Wisconsin, 1969, Cl
Patrick MacCarthy, (D), Cincinnati, 1975, Co
Craig Simmons, (D), SUNY (Stony Brook), 1976, Cp
Kent J. Voorhees, (D), Utah State, 1970, Co
Thomas R. Wildeman, (D), Wisconsin, 1967, Ct

Dept of Geology & Geological Engineering (B,M,D) ●⊘ (2021)
1516 Illinois Street
Golden, CO 80401-1887
p. (303) 273-3800
cmedford@mines.edu
http://geology.mines.edu/
Programs: BS Geology & Geological Engineering, Master of Science (Geology), Master of Science (Geological Engineering) Doctor of Philosophy (Geology), Doctor of Philosophy (Geological Engineering), Master of Engineering (Geological Engineer) (Non-Thesis), Professional Master Degree (Petroleum Reservoir Systems) (Non- Thesis), Professional Master Degree (Mineral Exploration) (Non-Thesis)
Certificates: GIS, Economic Geology, Exploration Methods, Earth Resource Data Science
Enrollment (2019): B: 138 (28) M: 100 (60) D: 70 (9)
Professor:
Wendy Bohrson, (D), California, 1993, Gv
Professor:
David A. Benson, (D), Nevada (Reno), 1998, Hq
Zhaoshan Chang, (D), Peking, 1997, Eg
Wendy J. Harrison, (D), Manchester (UK), 1979, Cl
Yvette D. Kuiper, (D), New Brunswick, 2003, Gc
Alexei Milkov, (D), Texas A&M, 2001, Cg
Thomas Monecke, (D), Germany, 2003, Em
Piret Plink-Bjorklund, (D), Goteborg (Sweden), 1998, Gs
Paul M. Santi, (D), Colorado Mines, 1995, Ng
Kamini Singha, (D), Stanford, 2005, Hw
Stephen A. Sonnenberg, (D), Colorado Mines, 1981, Go
Lesli Wood, (D), Colorado State, 1992, GsoGm
Associate Professor:
Alexis Navarre-Sitchler, (D), Penn State, 2008, Ca
Bruce D. Trudgill, (D), Imperial Coll (UK), 1989, Gc
Wendy W. Zhou, (D), Missouri S&T, 2001, NgZir
Assistant Professor:
Kevin Cannon, (D), Brown, 2017, ZnnZr
Danica Roth, (D), California, 2016, GmYs
Gabriel Walton, (D), Queen's, 2014, NgrYg

Lecturer:
Christian V. Shorey, (D), Iowa, 2002, Gg
Emeritus:
L. Graham Closs, (D), Queen's, 1973, Ce
John B. Curtis, (D), Ohio State, 1989, GoCo
Jerry D. Higgins, (D), Missouri (Rolla), 1980, NxgNt
Keenan Lee, (D), Stanford, 1969, Zr
Eileen P. Poeter, (D), Washington State, 1980, Ng
Samuel B. Romberger, (D), Penn State, 1968, Em
A. Keith Turner, (D), Purdue, 1969, Ng
John E. Warme, (D), California (Los Angeles), 1966, GsPeGu
Robert J. Weimer, (D), Stanford, 1953, Gr
Richard F. Wendlandt, (D), Penn State, 1978, GizCp

Dept of Geophysics (B,M,D) ● (2020)
924 16th Street
Room 283
Golden, CO 80401
p. (303) 273-3451
geophysics@mines.edu
http://geophysics.mines.edu/
f: https://www.facebook.com/MinesGeophysics/
t: @MinesGeophysics
Programs: Geophysical Engineering (B,M,D); Petroleum Reservoir Systems (PSM); Geophysics (M,D); Humanitarian Geophysics (M); Hydrogeophysics (M)
Certificates: 12-credit Certificate Program in Petroleum Geophysics
Enrollment (2017): B: 115 (44) M: 28 (24) D: 44 (4)
C.H. Green Professor of Exploration Geophysics:
Paul Sava, (D), Stanford, 2005, Ye
W. M. Keck Professor of Professional Development Education:
Roel Snieder, (D), Utrecht, 1987, Ye
Vice Provost for External Initiatives and Dean of Earth Resources and Environmental Programs:
John Bradford, (D), Rice, 1999, Yue
Director, Reservoir Characterization Project:
Ali Tura, (D), California (Berkeley), YsNr
Director, Center for Wave Phenomena:
Ilya D. Tsvankin, (D), Moscow State (Russia), 1982, Ye
Director, Center for Gravity, Electrical, and Magnetic Studies:
Yaoguo Li, (D), British Columbia, 1992, Yev
Professor:
Manika Prasad, (D), Kiel, 1990, NrYx
Baker Hughes Chair of Petrophysics and Borehole Geophysics and Associate Dept Head:
Brandon Dugan, (D), Penn State, 2003, GuYrHw
Associate Professor:
Jeffrey Shragge, (D), Stanford, 2009, Ys
Andrei Swidinsky, (D), Toronto, 2011, Ye
Assistant Professor:
Ebru Bozdag, (D), Utrecht, 2009, Ys
Ge Jin, (D), Columbia, 2014, Ye
Matthew Siegfried, (D), Scripps, 2015, ZrGl

Dept of Mining Engineering (B,M,D) ● (2016)
1600 Illinois
Golden, CO 80401
p. (303) 273-3700
pnelson@mines.edu
http://mining.mines.edu/
Enrollment (2015): B: 100 (41) M: 18 (18) D: 14 (6)
Department Head:
Priscilla P. Nelson, (D), Cornell, 1983, NrgNm
Professor:
Kadri Dagdelen, (D), Colorado Mines, 1985, Nm
M. Ugur Ozbay, (D), Witwatersrand, 1988, Nr
Associate Professor:
Mark Kuchta, (D), Lulea Univ of Tech, 1990, Nm
Hugh Miller, (D), Colorado Mines, 1996, Nmg
Masami Nakagawa, (D), Cornell, 1988, Ze
Assistant Professor:
Elizabeth Holley, (D), Colorado Mines, 2012, Eg
Rennie Kaunda, (D), W Michigan, 2007, Nm
Eunhye Kim, (D), Penn State, 2010, NrmNt
Research Professor:
Karl Zipf, (D), Penn State, 1988, Nm
Research Assistant Professor:
Vilem Petr, (D), Colorado Mines, 2000, Nm
Manager of Earth Mechanics Institute:
Brian Asbury, Nr
Research Associate:
Jürgen F. Brune, (D), Tech (Clausthal), 1994, Nm

Colorado State University

Dept of Atmospheric Science (M,D) ☒ (2018)
1371 Campus Delivery
Fort Collins, CO 80523-1371
p. (970) 491-8360
info@atmos.colostate.edu
http://www.atmos.colostate.edu
Programs: Master of Science in Atmospheric Science
Doctorate in Atmospheric Science
Enrollment (2018): M: 34 (12) D: 43 (6)
Head:
Jeffrey L. Collett, Jr., (D), Caltech, 1989, As
Professor:
A. Scott Denning, (D), Colorado State, 1994, AsZg
James Hurrell, (D), Purdue, 1990, As
Sonia M. Kreidenweis, (D), Caltech, 1989, As
Christian D. Kummerow, (D), Minnesota, 1987, Yr
Eric Maloney, (D), Washington, 2000, As
David A. Randall, (D), California (Los Angeles), 1976, As
A.R. Ravishankara, (D), Florida, 1975, AsZg
Steven A. Rutledge, (D), Washington, 1983, As
David W. J. Thompson, (D), Washington, 2000, Yr
Sue van den Heever, (D), Colorado State, 2001, As
Peter Jan van Leeuwen, (D), Delft (Neth), 1992, As
Associate Professor:
Elizabeth A. Barnes, (D), Washington, 2012, As
Michael M. Bell, (D), Naval Postgrad Sch, 2010, As
Christine Chiu, (D), Purdue, 2003, As
Jeff Pierce, (D), Carnegie Mellon, 2008, As
Russ Schumacher, (D), Colorado State, 2008, As
Assistant Professor:
Emily Fischer, (D), Washington, 2010, As
Kristen L. Rasmussen, (D), Washington, 2014, As

Dept of Geosciences (B,M,D) ● (2019)
1482 Campus Delivery
Fort Collins, CO 80523-1482
p. (970) 491-5661
WCNR_GEO_Info@mail.colostate.edu
https://warnercnr.colostate.edu/geosciences/
Programs: Geology (B); Geology, Environmental Geology Concentration (B); Geology, Geophysics Concentration (B); Geology, Hydrogeology Concentration (B); Geosciences (M,D)
Enrollment (2019): B: 110 (33) M: 37 (7) D: 27 (5)
Head:
Richard C. Aster, (D), California (San Diego), 1991, YsGv
Professor:
Sven O. Egenhoff, (D), Tech (Berlin), 2000, Gsu
Judith L. Hannah, (D), California (Davis), 1980, GiCc
Dennis L. Harry, (D), Texas (Dallas), 1989, Yg
Ellen E. Wohl, (D), Arizona, 1988, GmHs
Senior Scientist:
Holly Stein, (D), N Carolina, 1985, Cc
Associate Professor:
Jerry F. Magloughlin, (D), Minnesota, 1993, Gpz
Sara L. Rathburn, (D), Colorado State, 2001, Ggm
John R. Ridley, (D), Edinburgh, 1982, Eg
Michael J. Ronayne, (D), Stanford, 2008, Hwq
William E. Sanford, (D), Cornell, 1992, Hw
Derek L. Schutt, (D), Oregon, 2000, Ysg
Sally J. Sutton, (D), Cincinnati, 1987, GdCl
Assistant Professor:
Sean Gallen, (D), North Carolina State, 2013, GemGt
Daniel McGrath, (D), Colorado, 2013, YuGl
John Singleton, (D), Texas, 2011, Gct
Lisa Stright, (D), Stanford, 2011, GoNpYe
Research Associate:
James R. Chappell, (B), Colorado State, 2000, Ge
Svetoslav Georgiev, (D), ETH (Switzerland), 2008, CcGo
Ronald J. Karpilo, Jr, (M), Denver, 2004, Zy
Stephanie A. O'Meara, (M), Colorado State, 1997, Gc
Trista L. Thornberry-Ehrlich, (M), Colorado State, 2001, GgcGx
Gang Yang, (D), Sci & Tech (China), 2005, CcaCg

Aaron Zimmerman, (M), Colorado State, 2006, Cc
Senior Instructor:
Sean Bryan, (D), Colorado, 2010, Gg
Emeritus:
Eric A. Erslev, (D), Harvard, 1981, GctGg
Frank G. Ethridge, (D), Texas A&M, 1970, Gs
Academic Success Coordinator:
Jill Putman, (M), Georgia, 2009

Community College of Aurora

Dept of Science (2015)
16000 East Centretech Parkway
Aurora, CO 80011
p. (303) 361-7398
Martha.Jackson-Carter@ccaurora.edu
http://www.ccaurora.edu

Denver Museum of Nature & Science

Dept of Earth Sciences ☒ (2019)
2001 Colorado Boulevard
Denver, CO 80205-5798
p. (303) 370-6000
libby.couch@dmns.org
http://www.dmns.org
Director of Earth and Space Sciences Branch, Department Chair of Earth Sciences, Curator of Paleobotany:
Ian Miller, (D), Yale, 2007, PbGg
Tim and Kathryn Ryan Curator of Geology:
James W. Hagadorn, (D), S California, 1998, GgsPg
Preparator:
Natalie Toth, (M), SD Mines, 2010, Pg
Curator of Vertebrate Paleontology:
Tyler Lyson, (D), Yale, 2012, Pv
Joseph Sertich, (D), SUNY (Stony Brook), 2011, Pv
Collections Manager:
Kristen Mackenzie, (M), Oregon, 2013, Zg
Business Specialist:
Libby Couch, Zn

Fort Lewis College

Dept of Geosciences (B) (2015)
1000 Rim Drive
Durango, CO 81301
p. (970) 247-7278
gonzales_d@fortlewis.edu
http://geo.fortlewis.edu
Enrollment (2012): B: 120 (22)
Chair:
David A. Gonzales, (D), Kansas, 1997, Gx
Professor:
James D. Collier, (D), Colorado Mines, 1982, Cg
Gary Gianniny, (D), Wisconsin, 1995, Gs
Kimberly Hannula, (D), Stanford, 1993, GctGp
Ray Kenny, (D), Arizona State, 1991, Gm
Scott White, (D), Utah, 2001, ZirZy
Instructor:
Lauren Heerschap, (M), Colorado, GgEgGt
Adjunct Professor:
Charles Burnham, (D), MIT, 1961, Gz
Mary L. Gillam, (D), Colorado, 1998, Gm
Laboratory Director:
Andrea J. Kirkpatrick,

Front Range Community College - Larimer

Natural Sciences (A) ☒ (2017)
4616 S. Shields Street
Fort Collins, CO 80526
p. (970) 204-8607
stephanie.irwin@frontrange.edu
http://www.frontrange.edu/Academics/Academic-Departments/Larimer-Campus/Natural-Applied-Environment-Science/
Programs: Geology (A)
Instructor:
Andy Caldwell, (M), N Colorado, 1999, Gg
Mike Smith, (M), N Colorado, 1998, GgZe

Front Range Community College - Westminster

Science and Technology (A) 🖱 (2020)
3645 West 112th Avenue
Westminster, CO 80031
p. (303) 404-5279
Angela.Greengarcia@frontrange.edu
https://www.frontrange.edu/programs-and-courses/a-z-program-list/geology
Enrollment (2018): A: 2 (2)

Metropolitan State College of Denver

Earth & Atmospheric Sciences Dept (B) (2015)
P.O. Box 173362, Campus Box 22
Denver, CO 80217-3362
p. (303) 556-3143
jharr115@msudenver.edu
Administrative Assistant: Diane Hollenbeck
Chair:
James M. Cronoble, (D), Colorado Mines, 1977, Gg
Ken Engelbrecht
Professor:
John R. Kilcoyne, (D), Washington, 1973, Zy
Anthony A. Rockwood, (M), Colorado State, 1976, Am
Roberta A. Smilnak, (D), Clark, 1973, Zg
Associate Professor:
Thomas J. Corona, (M), Colorado State, 1978, Am
Assistant Professor:
Robert E. Leitz, (M), California (Berkeley), 1974, Gz
Rafael Moreno, (D), Colorado State, 1992, Zg
Emeritus:
James MacLachlan, (D), Princeton, Gg
H. Dixon Smith, (D), Minnesota, 1960, Zg

Northeastern Junior College

Math, Science, and Health (A) ☒ (2019)
100 College Avenue
Sterling, CO 80751
p. (970) 521-6753
david.coles@njc.edu
http://njc.edu
Programs: Geology Designation

Red Rocks Community College

Geology Program, Science Dept (A) ●☒ (2021)
13300 West Sixth Avenue
Campus Box 20
Lakewood, CO 80228
p. (303) 914-6290
eleanor.camann@rrcc.edu
http://rrcc.edu/geology/
Programs: Geology
Enrollment (2018): A: 5 (6)
Professor:
Eleanor J. Camann, (D), N Carolina, 2005, OnZeGs

United States Air Force Academy

Dept of Economics & Geosciences (B) (2015)
HQ USAFA/DFEG
2354 Fairchild Drive, Suite 6K110
USAF Academy, CO 80840-5701
p. (719) 333-3080
ian.irmischer@usafa.edu
http://www.usafa.edu/df/dfeg/?catname=dfeg
Enrollment (2013): B: 90 (27)
Professor:
Terry W. Haverluk, (D), Minnesota, 1993, Zg
Associate Professor:
Steven J. Gordon, (D), Arizona State, 1999, Gm
Thomas Koehler, (D), Wisconsin, As
Lt Col :
Matthew Tracy, (D), Arizona State, 2008, Zn
Assistant Professor:
Glen Gibson, (D), Virginia Tech, 2012, Zri
Brett Machovina, (D), Denver, 2010, Zir
Evan Palmer, (D), Arizona State, 2014, Zig
Sarah Robinson, (D), Arizona State, GgZi

Instructor:
Scott Dubsky, (M), North Dakota, 2006, ZyGm
Related Staff:
Danny Portillo, (B), Zi

University of Colorado

Dept of Geography (B,M,D) ☒ (2020)
Campus Box 260
Boulder, CO 80309-0260
p. (303) 492-8312
darla.shatto@colorado.edu
http://www.colorado.edu/geography
Programs: Geography
Certificates: GIS and Computational Science (Undergraduate)
Enrollment (2020): B: 168 (58) M: 21 (10) D: 41 (12)
Professor:
Waleed Abdalati, (D), Colorado, 1996, Zr
Peter D. Blanken, (D), British Columbia, 1997, HsAsm
Mark Serreze, (D), Colorado, 1989, As
Associate Professor:
Jennifer K. Balch, (D), Yale, 2008, Zg
Holly R. Barnard, (D), Oregon State, 2009, Hg
Noah Molotch, (D), Arizona, 2004, Hg
Assistant Professor:
Katherine Lininger, (D), Colorado State, 2018, Gm
Emeritus:
John Pitlick, (D), Colorado State, 1988, Gm
Thomas T. Veblen, (D), California (Berkeley), 1975, Zg
Mark W. Williams, (D), California (Santa Barbara), 1990, Zg

Dept of Geological Sciences (B,M,D) (2015)
Campus Box 399
Boulder, CO 80309-0399
p. (303) 492-8141
robert.s.anderson@Colorado.edu
https://www.colorado.edu/geologicalsciences/
Administrative Assistant: Carmen Juszczyk
Enrollment (2014): B: 248 (29) M: 13 (7) D: 45 (10)
Associate Dean:
Mary J. Kraus, (D), Colorado, 1983, GsSa
Professor:
Robert Anderson, (D), Washington, 1986, Gm
David A. Budd, (D), Texas, 1984, GdsEo
Jaelyn J. Eberle, (D), Wyoming, 1996, Pv
G. Lang Farmer, (D), California (Los Angeles), 1983, Cg
Shemin Ge, (D), Johns Hopkins, 1990, HwEoYg
Bruce M. Jakosky, (D), Caltech, 1982, Xg
Craig H. Jones, (D), MIT, 1987, YsGtYg
Gifford H. Miller, (D), Colorado, 1975, GlCc
Stephen J. Mojzsis, (D), California (San Diego), 1997, XcCcGp
Peter Molnar, (D), Columbia, 1970, Gt
Karl J. Mueller, (D), Wyoming, 1992, GtcGm
Anne F. Sheehan, (D), MIT, 1991, YszYe
Joseph R. Smyth, (D), Chicago, 1970, Gz
Charles R. Stern, (D), Chicago, 1973, Gi
Eric E. Tilton, (D), California (Santa Cruz), 1998, Hw
Gregory E. Tucker, (D), Penn State, 1996, GmtGs
Paul Weimer, (D), Texas, 1989, Gor
James W. C. White, (D), Columbia, 1983, CsAt
Associate Professor:
Karen Chin, (D), California (Santa Barbara), 1996, Pg
Rebecca M. Flowers, (D), MIT, 2005, CgcGt
Brian M. Hynek, (D), Washington, 2003, Xg
Thomas M. Marchitto, (D), MIT, 1999, Oc
Dena M. Smith, (D), Arizona, 2000, Pg
Alexis Templeton, (D), Stanford, 2002, ClZaCq
Assistant Professor:
Kevin H. Mahan, (D), Massachusetts, 2005, Gpc
Julio C. Sepúlveda, (D), Bremen, 2008, Co
Instructor:
Lon Abbott, (D), California (Santa Cruz), 1993, GgtGm
Emeritus:
John T. Andrews, (D), Nottingham (UK), 1965, GluGs
William W. Atkinson, Jr., (D), Harvard, 1973, EgmCg
Peter W. Birkeland, (D), Stanford, 1961, Sd
William C. Bradley, (D), Stanford, 1956, Gm
Don L. Eicher, (D), Yale, 1958, Pm
Alexander Goetz, (D), Caltech, 1967, Zr
Edwin E. Larson, (D), Colorado, 1965, Ym
James L. Munoz, (D), Johns Hopkins, 1966, Cp
Peter Robinson, (D), Yale, 1960, Pv
Donald D. Runnells, (D), Harvard, 1964, Cl
Hartmut A. Spetzler, (D), Caltech, 1969, Ys
Theodore R. Walker, (D), Wisconsin, 1952, Gd

Univ of Colorado Museum (2015)
Campus Box 265
Boulder, CO 80309-265
p. (303) 492-6165
karen.chin@colorado.edu
http://cumuseum.colorado.edu/
Associate Professor:
Jaelyn J. Eberle, (D), Wyoming, 1996, Pve
Assistant Professor:
Karen Chin, (D), California (Santa Barbara), 1996, Pg
Research Associate:
Dena M. Smith, (D), Arizona, 2000, PeiPb
Adjunct Curator:
Kenneth Carpenter, Pv
Mary Dawson, Pv
Trihn Dzanh, Pv
Emmett Evanoff, Pi
Jeff Indeck, Pv
Jonathan Marcot, Pv
Greg McDonald, Pv
Karen Sears, Pv
Emeritus:
Judith A. Harris, (D), Cambridge, 1972, Pv
Peter Robinson, (D), Yale, 1960, Pv
Museum Associate:
Emily Bray, Pg
Frank Fisher, Pg
Pat Monaco, Pg
Steve Wallace, Pg
Collection Manager:
Tonia Superchi-Culver, (M), SD Mines, 2001, Pg
Associate Curator, Micropaleontology:
Donald Eicher, (D), Yale, 1958, Pm
Associate Curator, Fossil Primates:
Herbert Covert, Pv

University of Colorado, Denver

Dept of Geography & Environmental Science (2015)
CB 172
P.O. Box 173364
Denver, CO 80217-3364
p. (303) 556-2276
sue.eddleman@ucdenver.edu
Associate Professor:
John W. Wyckoff, (D), Utah, 1980, Zy
Emeritus:
Wesley E. LeMasurier, (D), Stanford, 1965, Gv
Martin G. Lockley, (D), Birmingham (UK), 1977, Pi

University of Denver

Dept of Geography and the Environment (B,M,D) (2019)
2050 E. Iliff Avenue
Boettcher Center West, Room 120
Denver, CO 80208
p. (303) 871-2654
Michael.Keables@du.edu
http://www.du.edu/geography
f: https://www.facebook.com/DUGeography/
Programs: Environmental Science (B); Geography (B,M); Geographic Information Science (M); Geography (D)
Certificates: Geographic Information Systems (G)
Enrollment (2018): B: 198 (34) M: 46 (23) D: 10 (1)
Professor:
Andrew R. Goetz, (D), Ohio State, 1987, Zgu
Paul C. Sutton, (D), California (Santa Barbara), 1999, Zc
Matthew Taylor, (D), Arizona State, 2003, Zc
Teaching Professor:
Hillary Hamann, (D), Colorado, 2002, HgZy
Teaching Associate Professor:
Helen Hazen, (D), Minnesota, 2006, Zy
Erika Trigoso, (D), Oxford, 2010, Zc

Associate Professor:
E. Eric Boschmann, (D), Ohio State, 2008, Zc
J. Michael Daniels, (D), Wisconsin, 2002, GmSp
Michael J. Keables, (D), Wisconsin, 1986, AstAm
Michael W. Kerwin, (D), Colorado, 2000, GgeZc
Jing Li, (D), George Mason, 2012, Zi
Rebecca Powell, (D), California (Santa Barbara), 2006, Zr
Donald G. Sullivan, (D), California (Berkeley), 1988, Pc
Teaching Assistant Professor:
Kristopher Kuzera, (D), San Diego State, 2011, ZyHg
Assistant Professor:
Hanson Nyantakyi-Frimpong, (D), W Ontario, 2014, Zc
Guiming Zhang, (D), Wisconsin, 2018, Zi
Adjunct Professor:
G. Thomas Lavanchy, (D), Denver, 2015, Hg
Michelle Moran-Taylor, (D), Arizona State, 2003, Zn
Martha A. Narey, (D), Denver, 1999, Zg
Sean Tierney, (D), Denver, 2009, Zc
Emeritus:
David Longbrake, (D), Iowa, 1972, Zi
Terrence J. Toy, (D), Denver, 1973, Gm

University of Northern Colorado

Earth and Atmospheric Sciences (B,M) (2020)
Campus Box 100
Greeley, CO 80639
p. (970) 351-2647
timothy.grover@unco.edu
http://esci.unco.edu
Programs: Environmental Earth Sciences (B); Geology (B); Meteorology (B); Secondary Teaching (B); Earth Sciences (M); Environmental Geosciences (PSM)
Certificates: Safety Science Certificate (12 credits), including Industrial Safety course and HAZWOPER certificate (OSHA Hazardous Waste Operations and Emergency Response)
Enrollment (2020): B: 67 (17) M: 7 (4)
Chair:
Timothy W. Grover, (D), Oregon, 1988, GpzGt
Professor:
Steven W. Anderson, (D), Arizona, 1990, GvZeXg
Graham Baird, (D), Minnesota, 2006, GcgGz
Lucinda Shellito, (D), California (Santa Cruz), 2004, AsPeAm
Associate Professor:
Joe T. Elkins, (D), Georgia, 2002, ZeGgCl
Emmett Evanoff, (D), Colorado, 1990, GrPgGs
Wendilyn Flynn, (D), Illinois, 2012, Ams
David G. Lerach, (D), Colorado State, 2012, Ams
Assistant Professor:
Sharon Bywater-Reyes, (D), Montana, 2015, HqsHt
Senior Lecturer:
Byron Straw, (M), N Colorado, 2010, ZeGgl
Adjunct Professor:
Todd A. Dallegge, (D), Alaska (Fairbanks), 2002, GosGr
Emeritus:
Richard D. Dietz, (D), Colorado, 1965, Xg
Kenneth D. Hopkins, (D), Washington, 1976, Gml
William H. Hoyt, (D), Delaware, 1982, OgGsZe
William D. Nesse, (D), Colorado, 1977, Gxz
K. Lee Shropshire, (D), Colorado, 1974, Pg
Other:
Carolyn D. Lambert, (M), Arizona, 2003, Hw
Walter A. Lyons, (D), Chicago, 1970, Asm

Western Colorado University

Geology Program in the Natural and Environmental Sciences Dept (B) O☒ (2019)
1 Western Way
Gunnison, CO 81231
p. (970) 943-2015
dmarchetti@western.edu
http://www.western.edu/geology
Programs: Geology; Petroleum Geology; Geoarchaeology; Environmental Geology, Earth Science Education
Enrollment (2018): B: 46 (14)
Professor:
Robert P. Fillmore, (D), Kansas, 1994, Gs
David W. Marchetti, (D), Utah, 2006, GmClc
Allen L. Stork, (D), California (Santa Cruz), 1984, Giv
Rady Chair:
Bradford R. Burton, (D), Wyoming, 1997, GocGt
Moncrief Chair:
Elizabeth S. Petrie, (D), Utah State, 2014, GcoYe
Lecturer:
Holly Brunkal, (D), Colorado Mines, 2015, NgGm

Connecticut

Central Connecticut State University

Dept of Geography (2015)
New Britain, CT 06050-4010
p. (860) 832-2785
cannatadij@ccsu.edu
http://www.ccsu.edu/geography

Dept of Physics & Earth Sciences (B,M) (2015)
1615 Stanley Street
New Britain, CT 06050-4010
p. (860) 832-2930
antar@ccsu.edu
http://www.physics.ccsu.edu/
Department Secretary: Sandra O'Day
Chair:
Ali A. Antar, (D), Connecticut, Zn
Professor:
Sandra Burns, (D), Connecticut, 1972, Ze
Steven B. Newman, (D), SUNY (Albany), As
Michael Wizevich, (D), Virginia Tech, GsdGm
Associate Professor:
Marsha Bednarski, (D), Connecticut, 1997, Ze
Mark Evans, (D), Pittsburgh, 1989, GciGz
Kristine Larsen, (D), Connecticut, 1988, Xy
Jennifer L. Piatex, (D), Pittsburgh, XgZr
Emeritus:
Charles W. Dimmick, (D), Tulane, 1969, Ge
Related Staff:
R. Craig Robinson, (B), Millersville, 1971, Xy

Eastern Connecticut State University

Environmental Earth Science (B) ● (2021)
83 Windham Street
Willimantic, CT 06226
p. (860) 465-4317
cunninghamw@easternct.edu
https://www.easternct.edu/environmental-earth-science/
f: https://www.facebook.com/groups/181927638678890/
Programs: Environmental Earth Science; Environmental Science, General Earth Science; Sustainable Energy Science
Enrollment (2020): B: 75 (19)
Chair:
Stephen Nathan , (D), Massachusetts, 2005, PmEo
Professor:
Catherine A. Carlson, (D), Michigan State, 1994, Hwg
Dickson Cunningham, (D), Texas, 1993, GtcGx
Peter A. Drzewiecki, (D), Wisconsin, 1996, GrsGd
James A. Hyatt, (D), Queens, 1993, Gml
Associate Professor:
Meredith Metcalf, (D), Connecticut, 2013, ZirHw
Bryan Oakley, (D), Rhode Island, 2012, OnGml
Adjunct Professor:
Heath Carlson, (M), E Connecticut State, 2013, Zg
Lynn-Ann DeLima, (M), S Connecticut State, 2000, Zg
Vishnu R. Khade, (D), Cincinnati, 1987, Zg
Emile Levasseur, (M), Sacred Heart, 1992, Zg
Bruce Morton, (M), Connecticut, 1983, Zg
James Motyka, (M), E Connecticut State, 1987, Zg
Julie Sandeen, (M), Connecticut, 1991
Wesley Winterbottom, (M), Connecticut, 1988, Zg
Emeritus:
Sherman M. Clebnik, (D), Massachusetts, 1975, Gl
Fred Loxsom, (D), Dartmouth, 1969, Zn
Henry I. Snider, (D), New Mexico, 1966, Ge
Roy R. Wilson, (D), Oregon State, 1984, Zi

Middlesex Community College

Div of Science, Allied Health and Engineering (A) ⊘ (2021)
100 Training Hill Road
Middletown, CT 06457
p. (860) 343-5779
MBusa@mxcc.commnet.edu
http://www.mxcc.commnet.edu/Content/Environmental_Science_1.asp
Programs: Physics studies, Chemistry studies, Biology studies
Certificates: Manufacturing Engineering Technology, Computer Engineering Technology

Professor:
Mark Busa, (D), Connecticut, ZgEgYg

Naugatuck Valley Community College

Science, Technology, Engineering, and Mathematics (STEM) (2015)
750 Chase Parkway
Waterbury, CT 06708
p. (203) 596-8690
cdonaldson@nv.edu
http://www.nvcc.commnet.edu

Norwalk Community College

Sciences Deptartment (2015)
188 Richards Avenue
Norwalk, CT 06854
p. (203) 857-7275
mbarber@ncc.commnet.edu
http://www.ncc.commnet.edu/dept/science/

Quinebaug Valley Community College

Dept of Environmental Science (2015)
742 Upper Maple Street
Danielson, CT 06239
p. (860) 412-7230
mphilion@qvcc.edu
http://www.qvcc.commnet.edu

Southern Connecticut State University

Department of Earth Science (B) O⊘ (2020)
501 Crescent Street
New Haven, CT 06515
p. (203) 392-5835
flemingt1@southernct.edu
https://inside.southernct.edu/earth-science
Programs: Geology (BS); Environmental Earth Science (BS); General Earth Science (BS); Earth Science Education (BS); Natural Resources (BS); Natural Hazards; Earth Science (BA)
Enrollment (2014): B: 46 (7)

Professor:
Cynthia R. Coron, (D), Toronto, 1982, Eg
Thomas H. Fleming, (D), Ohio State, 1995, GiCgc

Assistant Professor:
Jennifer Cooper-Boemmels, (D), Connecticut, 2020, GcgOg
Nicholas D. Fedorchuk, (D), Wisconsin (Milwaukee), 2019, GslGg
Dushmantha Jayawickreme, (D), Michigan State, 2008, YgSpNg

Instructor:
Bryan Adinolfi, (M), SUNY (Environ), 2006, GgZg
Christopher Balsley, (M), Wesleyan, 1972, Gg
Daniel Coburn, (M), C Connecticut, 2003, Ze
Yolanda Lee-Gorishti, (M), Connecticut, 2006, GaZe
Julie Rumrill, (M), Vermont, 2009, GgeGl

Emeritus:
John W. Drobnyk, (D), Rutgers, 1962, RhGs
James W. Fullmer, (D), MIT, 1979, AmXa
Robert Radulski, (D), Rhode Island, Og
William Tolley, (M), Syracuse, Gg

University of Connecticut

Dept of Geography (2015)
Storrs, CT 06269-4148
p. (860) 486-2610
cindy.zhang@uconn.edu
https://geography.uconn.edu/

Dept of Geosciences (B,M,D) (2015)
354 Mansfield Road
U-1045
Storrs, CT 06269-1045
p. (860) 486-4432
hren@uconn.edu
http://geosciences.uconn.edu
Enrollment (2012): B: 31 (0) M: 10 (0) D: 7 (0)

Program Director:
Pieter Visscher, (D), Groningen (Neth), 1991, Co

Professor:
Vernon F. Cormier, (D), Columbia, 1976, YsGt
William F. Fitzgerald, (D), MIT/WHOI, 1970, Oc
Gary A. Robbins, (D), Texas A&M, 1983, Hw
Robert M. Thorson, (D), Washington, 1970, Gm

Associate Professor:
Andrew M. Bush, (D), Harvard, 2005, PgqPi
Timothy Byrne, (D), California (Santa Cruz), 1981, Gc
Jean M. Crespi, (D), Colorado, 1985, Gc
Lanbo Liu, (D), Stanford, 1993, Yg

Assistant Professor:
Christophe Dupraz, (D), Fribourg, 1999, Pg
Michael Hren, (D), Stanford, 2007, CslCo
William Ouimet, (D), MIT, 2007, GmZy

Emeritus:
Larry Frankel, (D), Nebraska, 1956, Pm
Alfred J. Frueh, (D), MIT, 1949, Gz
Norman H. Gray, (D), McGill, 1971, Gx
Raymond Joesten, (D), Caltech, 1974, GzZmGp
Homer C. Liese, (D), Utah, 1962, Ct
Anthony R. Philpotts, (D), Cambridge, 1963, Gi

Dept of Marine Sciences (B,M,D) ⊘ (2021)
1080 Shennecossett Road
Groton, CT 06340
p. (860) 405-9152
marinesciences@uconn.edu
http://www.marinesciences.uconn.edu/
Programs: BS and BA - Marine Sciences
MS and PhD - Oceanography
Enrollment (2018): B: 50 (10) M: 9 (0) D: 33 (0)

Head:
J. Evan Ward, (D), Delaware, 1989, Ob

Professor:
Ann Bucklin, (D), California (Berkeley), 1980, Ob
Timothy Byrne, (D), California (Santa Cruz), 1981, Ou
Hans G. Dam, (D), SUNY (Stony Brook), 1989, Ob
Heidi Dierssen, (D), California, 2000, Op
Senjie Lin, (D), SUNY (Stony Brook), 1995, Ob
Robert P. Mason, (D), Connecticut, 1991, OcCtm
George B. McManus, (D), SUNY (Stony Brook), 1986, Ob
James O'Donnell, (D), Delaware, 1986, Op
Craig Tobias, (D), William & Mary, 1999, Oc
Pieter T. Visscher, (D), Groningen (Neth), 1991, Co

Associate Professor:
Hannes Baumann, (D), Hamburg, 2006, Ob
Julie Granger, (D), British Columbia, 2006, Oc
David Lund, (D), MIT/WHOI, 2006, Oc
Annelie Skoog, (D), Goteborg (Sweden), Oc
Penny Vlahos, (D), Massachusetts, 2001, OcGeu
Michael Whitney, (D), Delaware, 2003, Op
Huan Zhang, (D), Tokyo Fisheries, 1995, Ob

Assistant Professor:
Catherine Matassa, (D), Northeastern, 2014, Ob
Cesar Rocha, (D), Scripps, 2018, Op
Leonel Romero, (D), Scripps, 2008, Op
Samantha Siedlecki , (D), Chicago, 2010, On
Jamie Vaudrey, (D), Connecticut, 2007, Ob

Research Associate:
Zofia Baumann, (D), SUNY (Stony Brook), 2011, ObcCm

Emeritus:
Peter Auster, (D), National (Ireland), 2000, Ob
Walter F. Bohlen, (D), MIT/WHOI, 1969, Op
James Edson, (D), Penn State, Op
William F. Fitzgerald, (D), MIT/WHOI, 1970, Oc
Edward C. Monahan, (D), MIT, 1966, AsOp
Sandra Shumway, (D), Coll of North Wales, 1976, Ob

University of New Haven

Dept of Environmental Sciences (B,M) O☒ (2017)
300 Boston Post Rd
West Haven, CT 06516
p. (203) 932-7101
rldavis@newhaven.edu
http://www.newhaven.edu
Programs: Environmental Science (BS, MS), Marine Biology (BS), Marine Affairs (BS), MS in Environmental Science offers concentrations in Environmental Geoscience, Environmental Ecology, GIS, Environmental Health and Management
Certificates: GIS
Enrollment (2016): B: 28 (5) M: 29 (8)

Provost and Senior Vice President of Academic Affairs:
Daniel J. May, (D), California (Santa Barbara), 1986, GtxGe
Coordinator-Graduate Environmental Science:
Roman N. Zajac, (D), Connecticut, 1985, Zni
Professor:
Carmela Cuomo, (D), Yale, CmmGu
R. Laurence Davis, (D), Rochester, 1980, GemHg
Coordinator-Undergraduate Environmental Science:
Kristen Przyborski, (D)
Associate Professor:
Amy L. Carlile, (D), Washington, ObZn
John Kelly, (D), California (Davis), ObZn
Lecturer:
Jean-Paul Simjouw, (D), Old Dominion, 2004, OcCma
Practitioner-in-Residence:
Paul Bartholemew, (D), British Columbia, GeZiGz

Wesleyan University

Dept of Earth & Environmental Sciences (B,M) ☒ (2019)
265 Church Street
Room 455
Middletown, CT 06459-0139
p. (860) 685-2244
vharris@wesleyan.edu
http://www.wesleyan.edu/ees
Programs: Earth & Environmental Sciences
Administrative Assistant: Virginia M. Harris
Enrollment (2019): B: 41 (7) M: 5 (3)

Professor:
Barry Chernoff, (D), Michigan, 1983, Ge
Martha S. Gilmore, (D), Brown, 1997, XgGmZr
Suzanne B. OConnell, (D), Columbia, 1986, GsuGe
Dana Royer, (D), Yale, 2002, PegPb
Johan C. Varekamp, (D), Utrecht, 1979, CgGzv
Chair:
Timothy C.W. Ku, (D), Michigan, 2001, Cl
Associate Professor:
Phillip G. Resor, (D), Stanford, 2003, Gct
Assistant Professor:
James P. Greenwood, (D), Brown, 1997, Xc
University Professor:
Ellen Thomas, (D), Utrecht, 1979, Pm
Assistant Professor of the Practice:
Kim Diver, (D), Syracuse, 2004, ZiyZg
Emeritus:
James T. Gutmann, (D), Stanford, 1972, GviGz
Peter C. Patton, (D), Texas, 1976, Gm
Facilities Manager:
Joel LaBella, (B), S Connecticut, 1987, Zn

Yale University

Dept of Earth and Planetary Sciences (B,D) ☒ (2020)
210 Whitney Avenue
P.O. Box 208109
New Haven, CT 06520-8109
p. (203) 432-3114
rebecca.pocock@yale.edu
http://earth.yale.edu
Enrollment (2019): B: 18 (7) D: 54 (13)

Curator:
Derek E. G Briggs, (D), Cambridge, 1976, PigPg
Professor:
Jay J. Ague, (D), California (Berkeley), 1987, Gx
David Bercovici, (D), California (Los Angeles), 1989, Yg
Ruth E. Blake, (D), Michigan, 1997, Cg
Mark T. Brandon, (D), Washington, 1984, Gc
Derek E G Briggs, (D), Cambridge, 1976, Yg
David A D Evans, (D), Caltech, 1998, YmGt
Alexey V. Fedorov, (D), Scripps, 1997, Op
Jacques Gauthier, (D), California (Berkeley), 1984, Pv
Shun-ichiro Karato, (D), Tokyo, 1977, Gy
Jun Korenaga, (D), MIT, 2000, YgsCg
Maureen D. Long, (D), MIT, 2006, Ysg
Jeffrey J. Park, (D), California (San Diego), 1985, YsZgc
Danny M. Rye, (D), Minnesota, 1972, Cs
Mary-Louise Timmermans, (D), Cambridge, 2000, Oc
John S. Wettlaufer, (D), Washington, 1991, Yg
Senior Research Scientist:
Edward W. Bolton, (D), California (Los Angeles), 1985, GqHqCq
Ellen Thomas, (D), Utrecht, 1979, Pm
Associate Professor:
Noah Planavsky, (D), California (Riverside), 2012, CsbCm
Assistant Professor:
Bhart-Anjan Bhullar, (D), Harvard, 2014
Pincelli Hull, (D), California (San Diego), 2010
Juan Lora, (D), Arizona, 2014, ZoAs
Alan Rooney, (D), Durham (UK), 2011, Cc
Lidya Tarhan, (D), California (Riverside), 2013, PiGsPe
Emeritus:
Robert B. Gordon, (D), Yale, 1955, Nr
Ronald B. Smith, (D), Johns Hopkins, 1975, As
Elisabeth S. Vrba, (D), Cape Town, 1974, Pv
Research Affiliate:
William C. Graustein, (D), Yale, 1981, Cl
Related Staff:
James O. Eckert, (D), Texas A&M, 1988, Gp

Peabody Museum of Natural History ☒ (2021)
PO Box 208118
170 Whitney Avenue
New Haven, CT 06520-8118
p. (203) 432-3752
peabody.director@yale.edu
http://www.peabody.yale.edu/

Emeritus Curator:
Leo W. Buss, (D), Johns Hopkins, 1979, Pi
Elisabeth S. Vrba, (D), Cape Town, 1974, Pvg
Curator:
Jay J. Ague, (D), California (Berkeley), 1987, Gzx
Michael J. Donoghue, (D), Harvard, 1982, Pbg
Jacques A. Gauthier, (D), California (Berkeley), 1984, Pv
Assistant Curator:
Bhart-Anjan Bhullar, (D), Pv
Senior Collections Manager:
Susan H. Butts, (D), Idaho, 2003, PiGsPe
Collections Manager:
Shusheng Hu, (D), Florida, 2006, PblGs
Stefan Nicolescu, (D), Gothenburg, 1998, CtGpz

Delaware

University of Delaware

Dept of Earth Sciences (B,M,D) ●☒ (2021)
103 Penny Hall
Newark, DE 19716
p. (302) 831-2569
jmadsen@udel.edu
https://www.udel.edu/academics/colleges/ceoe/departments/es/
f: https://www.facebook.com/UDCEOE
t: @udceoe
Programs: BS Geological Sciences,BA Geological Sciences, BS Earth Science Education, MS Geological Sciences, PhD Geological Sciences
Enrollment (2020): B: 43 (19) M: 20 (7) D: 14 (2)

Director, DGS, and State Geologist:
David R. Wunsch, (D), Kentucky, 1992, Ge
Acting Chair:
John A. Madsen, (D), Rhode Island, 1987, YrOuZe
Professor:
Eliot A. Atekwana, (D), W Michigan, 1996, CgsCq
Ronald E. Martin, (D), California (Berkeley), 1981, PmePg
Holly A. Michael, (D), MIT, 2005, Hwq
Michael ONeal, (D), Washington, 2005, Gm

James E. Pizzuto, (D), Minnesota, 1982, Gm
Neil C. Sturchio, (D), Washington (St Louis), 1983, ClcCa
Associate Professor:
Clara S. Chan, (D), California (Berkeley), 2006, PoObGz
Susan McGeary, (D), Stanford, 1984, Ze
Adam F. Wallace, (D), Virginia Tech, 2008, ClGzZm
Jessica Warren, (D), MIT/WHOI, 2007, GxCpGt
Assistant Professor:
Chandranath Basak, (D), Florida, 2011, ClOcCs
Colton Lynner, (D), Yale, 2015, GtYsGc
Visiting Professor:
Claire J. O'Neal, (D), Washington, 2005, Ze
Director Emeritus, DGS:
Robert R. Jordan, (D), Bryn Mawr, 1964, Gr
John H. Talley, (M), Franklin and Marshall, 1974, Eg
Emeritus:
Billy P. Glass, (D), Columbia, 1968, XmcGz
Peter B. Leavens, (D), Harvard, 1967, Gz
John F. Wehmiller, (D), Columbia, 1971, Cl
Laboratory Director:
Bill Parnella, (B), Buffalo, 1984, Gg
Cooperating Faculty:
A. Scott Andres, (M), Lehigh, 1984, Hw
Katharina Billups, (D), California (Santa Cruz), 1998, Ou
Laurent E. Cartier, (D), Basel, 2014, Gz
Shreeram Inamdar, (D), Virginia Tech, 1996, Hg
Deb Jaisi, (D), Miami, 2007, Cb
Kendra J. Lynn, (D), Hawaii, 2017, Gi
Thomas E. McKenna, (D), Texas, 1997, Hy
Peter P. McLaughlin, Jr., (D), Louisiana State, 1989, Gr
Jack Puleo, (D), Florida, 2004, Hw
Kelvin W. Ramsey, (D), Delaware, 1988, Gs
William S. Schenck, (M), Delaware, 1997, Gg
Angelia L. Seyfferth, (D), California (Riverside), 2008, Sc
Art Trembanis, (D), Virginia Inst of Marine Sci, 2004, Ou
William J. Ullman, (D), Chicago, 1982, Oc

Dept of Geography ● ☒ (2018)
125 Academy Street
216 Pearson Hall
Newark, DE 19716-2541
p. (302) 831-3218
dlevia@udel.edu
http://www.ceoe.udel.edu/schools-departments/department-of-geography

Oceanography Program (M,D) (2015)
700 Pilottown Road
Lewes, DE 19958
p. (302) 645-4279
kbillups@udel.edu
http://www.ocean.udel.edu
Professor:
Thomas M. Church, (D), California (San Diego), 1970, Cm
Victor Klemas, (D), Braunschweig (Germany), 1965, Zr
George W. Luther, III, (D), Pittsburgh, 1972, Cm
Jonathan H. Sharp, (D), Dalhousie, 1972, Oc
Christopher K. Sommerfield, (D), SUNY (Stony Brook), 1997, OuGsCc
William J. Ullman, (D), Chicago, 1982, Cm
Ferris Webster, (D), MIT, 1961, Op
Xiao-Hai Yan, (D), SUNY (Stony Brook), 1989, Zr
Associate Professor:
Katharina Billups, (D), California (Santa Cruz), 1998, Pe
Douglas C. Miller, (D), Washington, 1985, Ob
Associate Scientist:
Charles H. Culberson, (D), Oregon State, 1972, Oc
Richard T. Field, (D), Delaware, 1994, Og
Assistant Professor:
Matthew J. Oliver, (D), Rutgers, 2006, ObZrOg
Adjunct Professor:
Richard B. Coffin, (D), Delaware, 1986, Zn
James Crease, (D), Cambridge, 1951, Op
Marilyn L. Fogel, (D), Texas, 1977, Oc
Norden E. Huang, (D), Johns Hopkins, 1967, Zn
David E. Krantz, (D), South Carolina, Cs
Kamlesh Lulla, (D), Indiana State, 1963, Zr
Donald B. Nuzzio, (D), Rutgers, 1982, Oc
Manmohan Sarin, (D), Gujarat (India), 1984, Zn
Alain J. Veron, (D), Paris, 1988, Oc
John F. Wehmiller, (D), Columbia, Gu
Emeritus:
Jin Wu, (D), Iowa, 1964, Op

Physical Ocean Science and Engineering (2015)
Lewes, DE 19958
p. (302) 831-6640
carcher@udel.edu
http://www.ceoe.udel.edu/schools-departments/school-of-marine-science-and-policy/pose-program

District of Columbia

Carnegie Institution for Science

Department of Terrestrial Magnetism ☒ (2019)
5241 Broad Branch Road, N.W.
Washington, DC 20015-1305
p. (202) 478-8820
firstinitiallastname@carnegiescience.edu
https://dtm.carnegiescience.edu
Director:
Richard W. Carlson, (D), California (San Diego), 1980, Ccg
Senior Scientist:
Conel M. O'D Alexander, (D), Essex (UK), 1987, Xc
Alan P. Boss, (D), California (Santa Barbara), 1979, Xa
R. Paul Butler, (D), Maryland, 1993, Xa
John E. Chambers, (D), Manchester (UK), 1994, Xa
Peter E. Driscoll, (D), Johns Hopkins, 2010, GtYm
Helene Le Mevel, (D), Wisconsin, 2016, Gv
Larry R. Nittler, (D), Washington (St Louis), 1996, Xc
Diana C. Roman, (D), Oregon, 2004, Gv
Scott S. Sheppard, (D), Hawaii, 2004, Xa
Steven B. Shirey, (D), SUNY (Stony Brook), 1984, CcGiz
Peter E. vanKeken, (D), Utrecht, 1993, GtYsCg
Lara S. Wagner, (D), Arizona, 2005, YsgGt
Alycia J. Weinberger, (D), Caltech, 1998, Xa
Emeritus:
Alan T. Linde, (D), Queensland, 1972, Ys
I. Selwyn Sacks, (D), Witwatersrand, 1961, Ys
Fouad Tera, (D), Vienna, 1962, CcgXm
Senior Research Scientist and SIMS Lab Manager:
Jianhua Wang, (D), Chicago, 1995, Cs
Mass Spectrometry Laboratory Manager:
Timothy D. Mock, (M), Vermont, 1989, Cc
Geochemistry Laboratory Manager:
Mary F. Horan, (M), SUNY (Stony Brook), 1984, Cc
Assistant Controller:
Wan Kim, (M), Yonsei (Seoul), 1989, Zn
Librarian:
Shaun J. Hardy, (M), SUNY (Buffalo), 1987, Zn

Geophysical Laboratory ☒ (2019)
5251 Broad Branch Road, N.W.
Washington, DC 20015-1305
p. (202) 478-8900
mwalter@carnegiescience.edu
https://gl.carnegiescience.edu
Senior Scientist:
Ronald E. Cohen, (D), Harvard, 1985, Gy
Yingwei Fei, (D), CUNY, 1989, Cp
Alexander F. Goncharov, (D), Russian Acad of Sci, 1983, GyYxh
Robert M. Hazen, (D), Harvard, 1975, Gz
Ho-kwang Mao, (D), Rochester, 1968, Yx
Bjorn O. Mysen, (D), Penn State, 1974, Cp
Douglas Rumble, III, (D), Harvard, 1969, Gp
Anat Shahar, (D), California (Los Angeles), 2008, CgYxCs
Andrew Steele, (D), Portsmouth, 1996, Xy
Timothy A. Strobel, (D), Colorado Mines, 2008, Zm
Viktor V. Struzhkin, (D), Moscow Inst, 1991, Gy
Senior Scientist:
T. Neil Irvine, (D), Caltech, 1959, Gi
Research Scientist:
Jinfu Shu, (M), Wuhan, 1981, Yx
Director:
Wesley T. Huntress, Jr., (D), Stanford, 1968, Xc
Research Scientist:
Dionysis Foustoukos, (D), Minnesota, 2005, Cg

Changsheng Zha, (D), Beijing Inst Tech, 1969, YgZm
Acting Director:
George D. Cody, (D), Penn State, 1992, Co
Librarian:
Shaun J. Hardy, (M), SUNY (Buffalo), 1987, Zn

George Washington University

Dept of Geography (B,M) (2019)
2036 H St NW
Washington, DC 20052
p. (202) 994-6185
geog@gwu.edu
https://geography.columbian.gwu.edu/
f: https://www.facebook.com/GWGeography/
Enrollment (2018): B: 60 (0) M: 21 (0)
Chair:
Lisa Benton-Short, (D), Syracuse
Professor:
Elizabeth Chacko, (D), California (Los Angeles), 1997, Zy
Marie D. Price, (D), Syracuse, 1990, Zy
Associate Professor:
Mona Atia, (D), Washington
Ryan Engstrom, (D), San Diego State, Zr
David Rain, (D), Penn State
Nikolay Shiklomanov, (D)
Dmitry Streletskiy, (D)
Assistant Professor:
Ginger Allington, (D), Saint Louis
Melissa Keeley, Tech (Berlin)
Michael Mann, (D)

National Academies of Sciences, Engineering, and Medicine

Board on Earth Sciences and Resources ☒ (2019)
Keck Center-6th Floor
500 5th Street, NW
Washington, DC 20001
p. (202) 334-2744
besr@nas.edu
http://dels.nas.edu/besr
f: https://www.facebook.com/Board-on-Earth-Sciences-and-Resources-260128822801/
t: @NASEM_Earth
Director:
Elizabeth A. Eide, (D), Stanford, 1993, GgoGt
Senior Program Officer:
Sammantha L. Magsino, (M), Florida Intl, 1993, GvNg
Scholar:
Anne M. Linn, (D), California (Los Angeles), 1991, Gs
Senior Program Officer:
Deborah Glickson, (D), Washington, 2007, GutGg

Smithsonian Institution / National Air & Space Museum

Center for Earth & Planetary Studies (2016)
MRC 315, P.O. Box 37012
6th and Independence Ave., SW
Washington, DC 20013-7012
p. (202) 633-2470
irwinr@si.edu
https://airandspace.si.edu/about/organization/staff?tid_1=3
Geophysicist:
Bruce A. Campbell, (D), Hawaii, 1991, Zr
Planetary Geologist:
James R. Zimbelman, (D), Arizona State, 1984, Xg
Geologist:
Robert A. Craddock, (D), Virginia, 1999, Xg
John A. Grant, (D), Brown, 1990, Xg
Rossman P. Irwin, (D), Virginia, 2005
Thomas R. Watters, (D), George Washington, 1985, Xg
Ted A. Maxwell, (D), Utah, 1977, Xg
Program Manager:
Priscilla L. Strain, (B), Smith, 1974, Zr
Photo Librarian:
Rosemary Aiello

Smithsonian Institution / National Museum of Natural History

Dept of Mineral Sciences ☒ (2018)
NHB MRC 119
10th & Constitution Avenue, NW
PO Box 37012
Washington, DC 20013-7012
p. (202) 633-1860
mccoyt@si.edu
http://mineralsciences.si.edu/
Research Geologist:
Jeffrey E. Post, (D), Arizona State, 1981, Gz
Research Geologist:
Benjamin Andrews, (D), Texas, 2009, Gv
Catherine Corrigan, (D), Case Western, 2004, XmcXg
Elizabeth Cottrell, (D), Columbia, 2004, Cp
Glenn J. MacPherson, (D), Princeton, 1981, XcGi
Senior Scientist:
Timothy J. McCoy, (D), Hawaii, 1994, Xmg
Museum Specialist (Labs):
Timothy Gooding, (B), Hampshire Coll, 1990
Museum Specialist (GVP):
Sally K. Sennert, (M), Pittsburgh, 2003, GvZr
Edward Venzke, (M), Minnesota (Duluth), 1993, Gv
Collection Manager:
Cathe Brown, (M), Maryland, 1996, CgGzi
Russell Feather, (B), George Mason, 1982, Gz
Analytical Laboratories - Manager:
Timothy Rose, (M), Maryland, 1991, CaGv
Research Collaborator:
Steve Lynton, (D), Maryland, 2003
Postdoctoral Fellow:
Marion Le Voyer, (D), Blaise Pascal, 2009, Cu
Contract Geologist:
B. Carter Hearn Jr, (D), Johns Hopkins, 1959, Gic
Research Geologist:
Sorena S. Sorensen, (D), California (Los Angeles), 1984, Gp
Contractor:
Christine R. Webb, (B), Penn State, GzgZn
Research Geologist:
Michael A. Wise, (D), Manitoba, 1987, Gz
Museum Specialist (IT):
Adam Mansur, (M), Maryland, 2008, Zf
Management Support:
Phyllis McKenzie, (D), Zn
Collection Manager:
Leslie J. Hale, (B), Maryland, 1989, GgZnRh

Dept of Paleobiology (2015)
Dept. of Paleobiology, MRC121
NMNH, Smithsonian Institution
P.O. Box 37012
Washington, DC 20013-7012
p. (202) 633-1320
huntg@si.edu
https://naturalhistory.si.edu/research/paleobiology
Curator:
Scott L. Wing, (D), Yale, 1981, Pb
Anna K. Behrensmeyer, (D), Harvard, 1973, Pv
William A. DiMichele, (D), Illinois, 1979, Pb
Brian T. Huber, (D), Ohio State, 1988, Pm
Conrad C. Labandeira, (D), Chicago, 1991, Pi
Ian G. Macintyre, (D), McGill, 1967, Gs
Martin A. Buzas, (D), Yale, 1963, Pm
Douglas H. Erwin, (D), California (Santa Barbara), 1985, Pi
Daniel J. Stanley, (D), Grenoble, 1964, Ou
Matthew T. Carrano, (D), Chicago, 1998, Pv
Gene Hunt, (D), Chicago, 2003, Pm
Geologist:
Thomas Dutro, (D), Pi
Bevan French, (D), Xm
John Pojeta, (D), Cincinnati, 1963, Pi
Curator:
Alan H. Cheetham, (D), Columbia, 1959, Pg
Robert Emry, (D), Columbia, 1970, Pv
Clayton E. Ray, (D), Harvard, 1962, Pv
Thomas R. Waller, (D), Columbia, 1966, Pi

Associate Chair & Collections Manager:
Jann W. M. Thompson, (B), George Washington, 1970, Pg

Florida

Broward College

Environmental Science Department (A,B) (2016)
3501 SW Davie Road
Davie, FL 33314
p. (954) 201-6771
jmuza@broward.edu
http://www.broward.edu/academics/programs/environmental/Pages/
Administrative Assistant: Nicki Pickett
Chair:
Valerio Bartolucci, (M), Bologna, Ge
Professor:
Lewis Fox, (D), Delaware, 1981, Oc
Jay P. Muza, (D), Florida State, 1996, OuPmOo
Laura Precedo, (D), Emory, 1993, Oc
Lab Manager:
Lynn A. Curtis, (B), Florida Atlantic, 1997, GgPg

Natural Science Dept (A) (2015)
111 East Las Olas Boulevard
Fort Lauderdale, FL 33301
p. (954) 201-7650
mdugan@broward.edu
Instructor:
Xenia Conquy, (M), Florida Atlantic, Gg
Henri L. Liauw, (M), S Florida, Gg
William Opperman, (M), Florida, Gg

Chipola College

Dept of Natural Science (A) (2015)
3094 Indian Circle
Mariana, FL 32446
p. (850) 526-2761
hiltond@chipola.edu
http://www.chipola.edu/instruct/science
Professor:
Allan Tidwell, (M), Troy State, Zg

Daytona State College

School of Biological and Physical Sciences (A) (2017)
1200 W. International Speedway Blvd.
Daytona Beach, FL 32114
horikas@daytonastate.edu
http://www.daytonastate.edu/CampusDirectory/deptInfo.jsp?dept=SCI
Professor:
Debra W. Woodall, (D), Florida Inst of Tech, GgOg

Eckerd College

Dept of Geosciences (B) ☒ (2019)
Galbraith Marine Science Laboratory
4200 54th Avenue South
St. Petersburg, FL 33711
p. (727) 864-8200
wetzellr@eckerd.edu
https://www.eckerd.edu/marinescience/
Programs: Geosciences, Marine Science
Enrollment (2018): B: 5 (5)
Professor:
Gregg R. Brooks, (D), S Florida, 1986, Gu
Joel B. Thompson, (D), Syracuse, 1989, Pg
Laura R. Wetzel, (D), Washington (St Louis), 1997, YrOuGg

Florida Atlantic University

Dept of Geosciences (B,M,D) O (2019)
777 Glades Road
Boca Raton, FL 33431
p. (561) 297-3250
warburto@fau.edu
http://www.geosciences.fau.edu
Programs: BS Geoscience
MS Geoscience
PhD Geoscience
Certificates: GIS certificate
Advanced GIS certificate
Enrollment (2018): B: 103 (25) M: 27 (8) D: 34 (1)
Chair:
Zhixiao Xie, (D), SUNY (Buffalo), 2002, ZirZy
Director, Florida Center for Environmental Studies:
Colin Polsky, (D), Penn State, 2002, Znc
Associate Provost for Programs and Assessment :
Russell L. Ivy, (D), Florida, 1992, Zn
Professor:
Leonard Berry, (D), Bristol, 1969, Zg
Assistant Chair:
David L. Warburton, (D), Chicago, 1978, CgGe
Associate Professor:
Xavier Comas, (D), Rutgers, 2005, Yg
Maria Fadiman, (D), Texas, 2003, Zn
Scott H. Markwith, (D), Georgia, 2007, Zy
Anton Oleinik, (D), Purdue, 1998, Pi
Tara L. Root, (D), Wisconsin, 2005, Hg
Caiyun Zhang, (D), Texas (Dallas), 2010, Zr
Associate Scientist:
Tobin Hindle, (D), Florida Atlantic, 2006, ZyiZc
Assistant Professor:
Tiffany Roberts M. Briggs, (D), S Florida, 2012, On
Erik Johanson, (D), Tennessee, 2016, RnZy
Weibo Liu, (D), Kansas, 2016, Zi
Instructor:
James Gammack-Clark, (M), Florida Atlantic, 2001, Zri
Emeritus:
Howard Hanson, (D), Miami, 1979, AsOg
Edward J. Petuch, (D), Miami, 1980, Pg
Jorge I. Restrepo, (D), Colorado State, 1987, Hqw
Charles E. Roberts, (D), Penn State, 1991, Zri

Florida Gateway College

Mathematics/Science Div (A,B) (2019)
149 SE College Place
Lake City, FL 32025
p. (386) 752-1822
mustapha.kane@fgc.edu
https://www.fgc.edu/academics/liberal-arts--sciences/math-and-science.aspx
Programs: Geology, Earth Science Education
Professor:
Mustapha Kane, (D), Zg
Instructor:
Avo Oymayan, Zg

Florida Gulf Coast University

Dept of Marine and Earth Sciences ☒ (2020)
10501 FGCU Blvd. S.
Fort Myers, FL 33965
p. (239) 590-1000
jmacdona@fgcu.edu
https://www.fgcu.edu/cas/departments/mes/envirogeobs/
Programs: Environmental Geology BS
Professor:
James H. MacDonald, (D), SUNY (Albany), 2006, GizGt
Michael Savarese, (D), California (Davis)
Department Chair:
Joanne Muller, (D), James Cook
Assistant Professor:
Rachel Rotz, (D), Georgia, 2020, HwGg
Instructor:
Mary Abercrombie, (D), S Florida
Alayde Barbosa, (D)

Florida Institute of Technology

Ocean Engineering and Marine Science (B,M,D) O☒ (2019)
150 West University Boulevard
Melbourne, FL 32901
p. (321) 674-8034
oems@fit.edu
https://www.fit.edu/engineering-and-science/academics-and-learning/ocean-engineering-and-marine-sciences/

f: https://www.facebook.com/pg/FLTechOEMS

Programs: Biological Sciences (D), Conservation Technology (M), Earth Remote Sensing (M), Ecology (M), Environmental Resource Management (M), Environmental Science (B,M,D), Fisheries and Aquaculture (B), General Biology (B), Marine Biology (B,M), Marine Conservation (B), Meteorology (B,M), Ocean Engineering (B,M,D), Oceanography (B,M,D), Sustainability Studies (B)
Enrollment (2014): B: 100 (25) M: 60 (20)

Head:
George A. Maul, (D), Miami, 1974, Op

Professor:
Kevin Johnson, (D), Oregon, 1998, Ob
Steven M. Lazarus, (D), Oklahoma, 1996, As
Geoffrey Swain, (D), Southampton (UK), 1981, Ob
John G. Windsor, Jr., (D), William & Mary, Oc
Gary Zarillo, (D), Georgia, OupOn

Associate Professor:
Charles Bostater, (D), Delaware, 1990, Op

Assistant Professor:
Austin Fox, (D), Florida Inst of Tech, 2015, Oc
Kelli Hunsucker, (D), Florida Inst of Tech, 2013, Ob
Pallav Ray, (D), Miami, 2008, AstZo

Florida International University

Center for the Study of Matter at Extreme Conditions (M,D) (2016)
11200 SW 8th ST
VH 150, CeSMEC
Miami, FL 33199
p. (305) 348-3030
chenj@fiu.edu
http://cesmec.fiu.edu
Enrollment (2012): D: 2 (2)

Director:
Jiuhua Chen, (D), Japan Grad Univ Adv Studies, 1994, Gyz

Emeritus:
Surendra K. Saxena, (D), Uppsala, 1967, Gy

Dept of Earth & Environment (B,M,D) (2015)
Miami, FL 33199
p. (305) 348-2365
geology@fiu.edu
http://www.fiu.edu/orgs/geology
Enrollment (2007): B: 30 (7) M: 11 (5) D: 20 (5)

Chair:
Rene Price, (D), Miami, 2001, HwClRw

Professor:
William T. Anderson, (D), ETH (Switzerland), 2000, CsPcCl
Grenville Draper, (D), West Indies, 1979, GctRh
Rosemary Hickey-Vargas, (D), MIT, 1983, Cg
Jose F. Longoria, (D), Texas (Dallas), 1972, ZeGoe
Florentin J-M.R Maurrasse, (D), Columbia, 1973, PsGsCm
Gautam Sen, (D), Texas (Dallas), 1981, Gi
Michael C. Sukop, (D), Kentucky, 2001, HwqSp
Dean Whitman, (D), Cornell, 1993, YgGet

Associate Professor:
Laurel S. Collins, (D), Yale, 1988, Pg
Michael Gross, (D), Penn State, 1993, Gc
Andrew W. Macfarlane, (D), Harvard, 1989, Em
Shimon Wdowinski, (D), Harvard, 1990, YdGt

Assistant Professor:
Ping Zhu, (D), Miami, 2002, As

Distinguished Research Professor:
Stephen E. Haggerty, (D), London (UK), 1968, GiEgGz
Hugh E. Willoughby, (D), Miami, 1977, As

Lecturer:
Neptune Srimal, (D), Rochester, 1986, Gt

Adjunct Professor:
Jose Antonio Barros, (D), Miami, 1995, Zr
Michael Wacker, (M), Florida Intl, Gg

Research Scientist:
Edward Robinson, (D), London (UK), 1969, Pm

Research Lab Manager:
Diane H. Pirie, (B), Florida Intl, 1980, Gg

Cooperating Faculty:
Gabriel Guitierrez-Alonso, (D), Oviedo, 1992, Gc

Florida State University ❐

Dept of Earth, Ocean, and Atmospheric Science (B,M,D) (2015)
108 Carraway Building
Tallahassee, FL 32306-4100
p. (850) 644-5861
odom@gly.fsu.edu
http://www.gly.fsu.edu
Program Assistant: Tami S. Karl

Chair:
LeRoy A. Odom, (D), N Carolina, 1971, Cg
James F. Tull, (D), Rice, 1973, Gct

Professor:
James B. Cowart, (D), Florida State, 1974, Cc
Lynn M. Dudley, (D), Washington State, 1983, Sc
Philip Froelich, (D), Rhode Island, 1979, Og
Bill X. Hu, (D), Purdue, 1996, Hw
Munir Humayun, (D), Chicago, 1994, XcCgGi
Yang Wang, (D), Utah, 1992, CgsPc

Associate Professor:
Anthony J. Arnold, (D), Harvard, 1983, Pm
Stephen A. Kish, (D), North Carolina, 1983, Eg
William C. Parker, (D), Chicago, 1983, PqeGq
Vincent J. Salters, (D), MIT, 1989, Cg

Assistant Professor:
Jennifer Georgen, (D), MIT/WHOI, 2001, Gu
Ming Ye, (D), Arizona, 2002, Hg

Emeritus:
George W. Devore, (D), Chicago, 1952, Gp
John K. Osmond, (D), Wisconsin, 1954, Cc
Paul C. Ragland, (D), Rice, 1962, Ca
Sherwood W. Wise, Jr, (D), Illinois, 1970, PmGu

Hillsborough Community College

Earth Science (A) (2015)
2112 North 15th St.
Tampa, FL 33605
p. (813) 253-7647
jolney2@hccfl.edu
http://www.hccfl.edu

Instructor:
Marianne O. Caldwell, (D), S Florida, 2012, Ggs
James W. Fatherree, Zg
Thomas M. Klee, (M), S Illinois, 1986, Gg
Jessica L. Olney, (D), N Illinois, 2006, ZgGg
Matthew J. Werhner, (M), Adelphi, 1974, Gg
James F. Wysong, Jr., (M), S Florida, 1989, Am

Adjunct Professor:
Joseph D. Brod, Zg
Kyle M. Champion, Zg
James R. Douthat, Jr., Zg
Van E. Hayes, Zg
James E. MacNeil, Zg
Brian W. Marlowe, Zg
Matthew P. Olney, (D), N Illinois, 2006, ZgGg
Leonard T. Roth, Zg
Norman E. Soash, Zg
Poetchanaporn Tongdee, Zg
Kevan A. Van Cleave, Zg
William V. Wills, Zg

Jacksonville University

Dept of Biology & Marine Science (B,M) ☒ (2020)
2800 University Boulevard North
Jacksonville, FL 32211
p. (904) 256-7302
ngoldbe@ju.edu
Programs: Biology; Marine Science
Enrollment (2018): B: 10 (10)

Chair:
Nisse Goldberg, (D)

Miami Dade College (Kendall Campus)

Chemistry-Physics & Earth Science Dept (A) (2015)
11011 S.W. 104 St.
Room 3291
Miami, FL 33176
p. (305) 237-2492

sorbon@mdc.edu
http://www.mdc.edu/kendall/chmphy/
Enrollment (2010): A: 100 (0)

Assistant Professor:
Michael G. McGauley, (M), Miami, 2003, AmOp

Emeritus:
John M. Steger, (D), Naval Postgrad Sch, 1997, OgAmZg

Miami-Dade College (Wolfson Campus)

Dept of Natural Sciences, Health & Wellness (A) (2017)
300 NE 2nd Avenue
Miami, FL 33132
p. (305) 237-3658
mkraus@mdc.edu
Administrative Assistant: Ileana Baldizon

Professor:
Tony Barros, (D), Miami, 1995, Og
Michael Kaldor, (M), SUNY (Buffalo), 1969, Gg

Palm Beach StateCollege

Environmental Science (A) (2020)
MS #56 4200 Congress Avenue
Lake Worth, FL 33467
p. (561) 868-3475
milesj@palmbeachstate.edu
https://www.palmbeachstate.edu/areasofstudy/AreasofStudy-Environment.aspx
Programs: Environmental Science Technology A.S.
Certificates: Hazardous Materials Specialist College Credit Certificate, Environmental Science Technician College Credit Certificate, HAZWOPER 40-hr Certificate

Pensacola State College

Natural Sciences Department (2015)
1000 Collge Blvd
Pensacola, FL 32504-8998
p. (850) 484-1189
hbc@pensacolastate.edu
https://www.pensacolastate.edu/departments/natural-sciences/
Administrative Assistant: Kimberly LaFlamme

District Academic Department Head:
Edwin Stout

Professor:
Lois Dixon
Brooke L. Towery, (M), Ball State, 1969, Gg
Wayne Wooten
Joseph Zayas

Assistant Professor:
Thor Garber
Timothy Hathaway

Instructor:
Bobby Roberson
Michael Stumpe

Emeritus:
Thomas Gee

Science Lab Specialist:
Darrell Kelly

Saint Petersburg College, Clearwater

Dept of Natural Sciences (A) (2015)
2465 Drew Street
Clearwater, FL 33765
p. (727) 791-2534
Andrasik.Stephen@spcollege.edu
http://www.spcollege.edu/clw/science/

Professor:
Carl Opper, (M), Florida, 1982, Hw

Adjunct Professor:
Neva Duncan Tabb, Am
Hilary Flower, (M), California (Santa Barbara), Gg
Joseph C. Gould, (D), Nova, Gg
Heather L. Judkins, (D), S Florida, Og

Sante Fe Community College

Physical Science Dept (2015)
3000 NW 83rd Street
Gainesville, FL 32606
p. (505) 428-1307
david.johnson@sfcc.edu
http://www.sfcollege.edu

University of Florida

Dept of Geological Sciences (B,M,D) O (2020)
P.O. Box 112120
241 Williamson Hall
1843 Stadium Road
Gainesville, FL 32611-2120
p. (352) 392-2231
info@geology.ufl.edu
http://web.geology.ufl.edu/
Programs: Geology
Certificates: Geology
Enrollment (2020): M: 7 (0) D: 7 (0)

Chair:
David A. Foster, (D), SUNY (Albany), 1989, GtCc

Professor:
Thomas S. Bianchi, (D), Maryland, 1987, Co
Mark Brenner, (D), Florida, 1983, Gn
James E T Channell, (D), Newcastle upon Tyne, 1975, YmGt
Douglas S. Jones, (D), Princeton, 1980, PeiPg
Ellen E. Martin, (D), California (San Diego), 1993, Cl
Jonathan B. Martin, (D), California (San Diego), 1993, ClHg
Joseph G. Meert, (D), 1993, YgGt
Paul A. Mueller, (D), Rice, 1971, CcGit
Michael R. Perfit, (D), Columbia, 1977, Giu
Elizabeth J. Screaton, (D), Lehigh, 1995, Hg

Associate Professor:
Peter N. Adams, (D), California (Santa Cruz), 2004, Gm
Rene Gassmoeller, (D)
John M. Jaeger, (D), SUNY (Stony Brook), 1998, Gs
Raymond Russo, (D), Northwestern, 1990, Yg
Courtney Sprain, (D), California (Berkeley), 2017, CgYg
Amy Williams, (D), California (Davis), 2014, Co
Andrew Zimmerman, (D), William & Mary, 2000, ComSb

Associate Scientist:
Ann L. Heatherington, (D), Washington (St Louis), 1988, CcGti
Kyoungwon Min, (D), California (Berkeley), 2002, Cc

Assistant Professor:
Juliane Dannberg, (D)
Stephen Elardo, (D), New Mexico, 2014, GiXgCp
Robert G. Hatfield, (D), Lancaster, 2008

Research Associate:
Ray G. Thomas, (B), Florida, 1990, Zg

Lecturer:
Anita Marshall, (D)
Matthew C. Smith, (D), Gi
Jim Vogl, (D), California (Santa Barbara), 2000, Gct

Laboratory Director:
Jason H. Curtis, (D), Florida, 1997, Pe
George D. Kamenov, (D), Florida, 2004, CgaEm

Assistant Curator:
Jonathan Bloch, (D), Michigan, 2001, Pv

Cooperating Faculty:
Bruce J. McFadden, (D), Columbia, 1976, Pv

Florida Museum of Natural History (2015)
PO Box 117800
Gainesville, FL 32611-7800
p. (352) 846-2000
bmacfadd@flmnh.ufl.edu
http://www.flmnh.ufl.edu
Administrative Assistant: Pam Dennis

Director:
Douglas S. Jones, (D), Princeton, 1980, Pg

Associate Director:
Graig D. Shaak, (D), Pittsburgh, 1972, Pe

Associate Curator:
David W. Steadman, (D), Arizona, 1982, PvGaPs

Professor:
Steven R. Manchester, (D), Indiana, 1981, PbGs

Senior Scientist:
Roger W. Portell, (B), Florida, 1985, PisPv

Associate Curator:
Bruce J. MacFadden, (D), Columbia, 1976, Pv

Graduate Research Professor:
David L. Dilcher, (D), Yale, 1964, Pb
Research Associate:
David M. Jarzen, (D), Toronto, 1973, Pb
Emeritus:
Sylvia J. Scudder, (M), Florida, 1993, Pg
Other:
Ann S. Cordell, (M), Florida, 1983, Gxa

Soil & Water Science Dept (B,M,D) ☒ (2018)
PO Box 110290
2181 McCarty Hall A
Gainesville, FL 32611-0290
p. (352) 294-3151
krr@ufl.edu
http://soils.ifas.ufl.edu
Chair:
K Ramesh Reddy, (D), Louisiana State, 1976, CbSbc
Professor and Center Director:
Nicholas B. Comerford, (D), SUNY (Syracuse), 1980, Sf
John E. Rechcigl, (D), Virginia Tech, 1986, So
Charley Wesley Wood, (D), So
Professor:
Teri Balser, (D), Soo
Mary E. Collins, (D), Iowa State, 1980, Sd
James H. Graham, Jr., (D), Oregon State, 1980, Sb
Sabine -. Grunwald, (D), Giessen (Germany), 1996, ZiSoZr
Willie G. Harris, Jr., (D), Virginia Tech, 1984, Scd
George J. Hochmuth, (D), Wisconsin, 1980, So
Yuncong Li, (D), Maryland, 1993, Sco
Lena Q. Ma, (D), Colorado State, 1991, Sc
Peter Nkedi-Kizza, (D), California, 1979, Sp
George A. O'Connor, (D), Colorado State, 1970, Sc
Thomas A. Obreza, (D), Florida, 1983, So
Andrew V. Ogram, (D), Tennessee, 1988, Sb
Jerry B. Sartain, (D), North Carolina, 1973, So
Associate Professor:
Zhenli He, (D), Zhejang Ag, 1988, Sc
James W. Jawitz, (D), Florida, 1999, SpHsw
Marc Kramer, (D), So
S Rao Mylavarapu, (D), Clemson, 1996, Sc
Arnold W. Schumann, (D), Georgia, 1997, So
P. Christopher Wilson, (D), Clemson, 1999, So
Assistant Professor:
Mark W. Clark, (D), Florida, 2000, Sf
Samira H. Daroub, (D), Michigan State, 1994, So
Stefan Gerber, (D), So
Patrick Inglett, (D), Florida, 2005, Sf
Cheryl Mackowiak, (D), Utah State, 2001, So
Kelly Morgan, (D), So
Maria Silveira, (D), Sao Paulo, 2003, So
Max Teplitski, (D), Ohio State, 2002, Zn
Gurpal Toor, (D), Lincoln (NZ), 2002, Sc
Alan Wright, (D), Sc
Research Associate Professor:
Vimala D. Nair, (D), Gottingen, 1978, Sc
Ann C. Wilkie, (D), Univ Coll (Ireland), 1984, Sb
Lecturer:
James Bonczek, (D), SoHsg
Susan Curry, (M), ZiSo
Research Assistant Professor:
Todd Osborne, (D), Sf
John Thomas, (D), Sp
Assistant In:
Mengsheng Gao, (D), Zn

University of Miami

Dept of Geography and Regional Studies (2015)
Coral Gables , FL 33124
p. (305) 284-6695
dofuller@miami.edu
http://www.as.miami.edu/geography/

Dept of Geological Sciences (B,M,D) (2017)
1301 Memorial Drive
43 Cox Science Building
Coral Gables, FL 33124
p. (305) 284-4253
ruthgoodin@miami.edu
http://www.as.miami.edu/geology/
Administrative Assistant: Ruth Goodin
Enrollment (2016): B: 37 (7)
Professor:
Larry C. Peterson, (D), Brown, 1984, Gr
Peter Swart
Harold R. Wanless, (D), Johns Hopkins, 1971, GseOn
Senior Lecturer:
Teresa A. Hood, (D), Miami, 1991, Gg
Lecturer:
Peter J. Leech, (D), Georgia Tech, 2013
Ta-Shana A. Taylor, (M), Arizona, 2006, ZePvGe
Emeritus:
David E. Fisher, (D), Florida, 1958, Cs
John R. Southam, (D), Illinois, 1974, Op

Dept of Marine Geosciences (M,D) ☒ (2019)
RSMAS
4600 Rickenbacker Causeway
Miami, FL 33149-1098
p. (305) 421-4662
spurkis@rsmas.miami.edu
https://marine-geosciences.rsmas.miami.edu/
Programs: PhD and MSc in Marine Geosciences
BS Dual major in Marine Science/Geological Sciences, BS in Geological Sciences, BS/MS Marine Geology ,BA in Geological Sciences
Certificates: Applied Carbonate Geology
Enrollment (2019): M: 3 (1) D: 17 (4)
Chair:
Sam J. Purkis, (D), Vrije (Amsterdam), 2004, Gu
Professor:
Falk Amelung, (D), Lous Pasteur, 1996, Zn
Keir Becker, (D), Scripps, 1981, YrGu
Gregor P. Eberli, (D), ETH (Switzerland), 1985, GusYx
Larry C. Peterson, (D), Brown, 1984, GuPcm
Pam Reid, (D), Miami, 1979, Gs
Peter K. Swart, (D), London (UK), 1980, ClPsCs
Scientist:
Donald F. McNeill, (D), Miami, 1989, GsrGu
Associate Professor:
Adam Francis Holt, (D), Los Angeles, 2016
James S. Klaus, (D), Illinois, 2005, Gg
Associate Scientist:
Guoqing Lin, (D), Scripps, 2005, Yg
Ali Pourmand, (D), Tulane, 2005, Cga
Assistant Professor:
Amanda M. Oehlert, (D), Miami, 2014, Gu
Emeritus:
Christopher G.A. Harrison, (D), 1964, Yr
Cooperating Faculty:
Patricia L. Blackwelder, (D), South Carolina, 1976, Pg

University of South Florida

College of Marine Science (M,D) (2017)
140 7th Avenue South
St. Petersburg, FL 33701
p. (727) 553-1130
Mitchum@usf.edu
http://www.marine.usf.edu
Enrollment (2009): M: 30 (13) D: 50 (6)
Distinguished Research Professor:
Robert H. Byrne, (D), Rhode Island, 1974, Cm
John H. Paul, (D), Miami, 1980, Ob
John J. Walsh, (D), Miami, 1969, Ob
Robert H. Weisberg, (D), Rhode Island, 1975, Op
Professor:
Luis H. Garcia-Rubio, (D), McMaster, 1981, Oc
Pamela Hallock-Muller, (D), Hawaii, 1977, OuGsPm
Gary T. Mitchum, (D), Florida State, 1984, Op
Frank E. Muller-Karger, (D), Maryland, 1988, Zr
Joseph J. Torres, (D), California, 1980, Ob
Associate Professor:
Paula G. Coble, (D), MIT/WHOI, 1992, Cm
Kendra Lee Daly, (D), Tennessee, 1995, Ob
Boris Galperin, (D), Israel Inst of Tech, 1982, Op
David J. Hollander, (D), Swiss Fed Inst Tech, 1989, Oc

Mark E. Luther, (D), N Carolina, 1982, Op
David F. Naar, (D), Scripps, 1990, Ou
Ernst B. Peebles, (D), S Florida, 1996, ObCs
Assistant Professor:
Mya Breitbart, (D), California (San Diego), 2006, Ob
Ashanti J. Pyrtle, (D), Texas A&M, 1999, Oc
Research Associate:
Rick Cole, (B), Florida Inst of Tech, 1983, Op
Dwight A. Dieterle, (M), California (San Jose), 1979, Ob
Jeff C. Donovan, (B), Florida, 1985, Op
Debra E. Huffman, (D), S Florida, 1994, Zn
Stanley D. Locker, (D), Rhode Island, 1989, Ou
Wensheng Yao, (D), Miami, 1995, Oc
Research Assistant:
David C. English, (M), Washington, 1983, Op
Adjunct Professor:
Serge Andrefouet, (D), Polynesie Francaise, 1998, OpZr
Bruce Barber, (D), Ob
Leonard Ciaccio, (D)
Thomas Cuba, (D), S Florida, Ob
Christopher D'Elia, (D), Georgia, 1974, Ob
George Denton, (D), Og
Cynthia Heil, (D), S Florida, Ob
Brian Keller, (D)
John Lisle, (D)
Anne Meylan, (D), Florida, 1984, Ob
Terrence Quinn, (D), Ou
Harunur Rashid, (D)
Eugene Shinn, (B), Miami, 1957, Gg
Randy Wells, (D), California (Santa Cruz), 1986, Ob
Emeritus:
Peter R. Betzer, (D), Rhode Island, 1970, Cm
Norman J. Blake, (D), Rhode Island, 1972, Ob
John C. Briggs, (D), Stanford, 1951, Ob
Kendall L. Carder, (D), Oregon State, 1970, Op
Kent A. Fanning, (D), Rhode Island, 1973, OcGu
Albert C. Hine, (D), South Carolina, 1975, Gus
Thomas L. Hopkins, (D), Florida State, 1964, Ob
Harold J. Humm, (D), Duke, 1945, Ob
Edward S. Van Vleet, (D), Rhode Island, 1978, Co
Gabriel A. Vargo, (D), Rhode Island, 1976, Ob

School of Geosciences (B,M,D) O⁄🖱 (2021)
4202 East Fowler Avenue
NES 107
Tampa, FL 33620-5201
p. (813) 974-2236
mrains@usf.edu
http://hennarot.forest.usf.edu/main/depts/geosci/
f: https://www.facebook.com/USFGeosciences
Programs: Geology, Geography, and Environmental Science & Policy
Certificates: GIS, Environmental Science & Policy
Director:
Mark C. Rains, (D), California (Davis), 2002, Hw
Professor:
Fenda Akiwumi, (D), Texas State, 2006, Zy
Jennifer Collins, (D), Univ Coll London, 2002, As
Charles B. Connor, (D), Dartmouth, 1987, Gv
Barnali Dixon, (D), Arkansas, 2001, Zi
Tim Dixon, Scripps, 1979, Yd
Sarah E. Kruse, (D), MIT, 1989, Yg
Steve McNutt, (D), Columbia, 1985, Ys
Ambe njoh, (D), London, 1990, Zn
Petroniu (Bogdan) Onac, (D), Babes-Bolyai, Pc
Matthew Pasek, (D), Arizona, 2006, Cq
Ruiliang Pu, (D), Chinese Acad of Sci, 2000, Zr
Jeffrey G. Ryan, (D), Columbia, 1989, Ct
Joseph (Donny) Smoak, (D), S Carolina, Sf
Ping Wang, (D), S Florida, 1995, Gs
Associate Professor:
Kamal Alsharif, (D), Minnesota, 2004, Rw
Martin Bosman, (D), Kentucky, 1999, Zn
Sylvain Charbonnier, (D), Keele, 2008, Gv
Joni Downs, (D), Florida State, 2008, Zi
Jason Gulley, Florida, 2010, Hw
Gregory Herbert, (D), California (Davis), 2005, Pe
Rebecca Johns, (D), Wisconsin, Zn
Shawn Landry, (D), S Florida, 2013, Zi
Rocco Malservisi, (D), Penn State, 2002, Yd
Richard Mbatu, (D), Oklahoma State, 2006, Zy
Christopher Meindl, (D), Florida, 1996, Hg
Kai Rains, (D), California (Davis), 2006, Sf
Steven Reader, (D), Bristol, 1989, Zi
Phil van Beynen, (D), McMaster, 1998, Pc
Paul Wetmore, (D), S California, 2003, Gc
Assistant Professor:
Zachary Atlas, (D), Miami, 2008, Gi
Jochen Braunmiller, (D), Ys
Yasin Elshorbany, Wuppertal, Ac
Aurelie Germa, (D), Paris-Sud, 2008, Gv
Joeseph Panzik, (D), Yale, 2015, Ym
Yi Qiang, (D), Ghent, 2012, Zi
Mel Rodgers, (D), S Florida, 2013, Gv
Sarah Sheffield, (D), Tennessee, 2017, Pe
Patricia Spellman, (D), Michigan Tech, 2016, Hq
Ran Tao, (D), N Carolina (Charlotte), 2017, Zi
zglenn Thompson, (D), Leeds, 1999, Ys
Research Associate:
Laura Connor, (M), San Antonio, 2000, Zf
Anthony Menicucci, (D), California (Davis), Cs
Instructor:
Seth Cavello, (D), SUNY Buffalo, 2019, Zn
James Ivey, (D), S Florida, 2009, Zy
He (Hannah) Jin, (D), Texas State, 2019, Zi
Thomas C. Juster, (D), S Florida, 1995, Hw
Judy McIlrath, (M), S Florida, 2004, Gg
Connie Mizak, (D), S Florida, 2004, Zy

University of West Florida

Dept of Earth and Environmental Sciences (B,M) ⁄🖱 (2019)
11000 University Parkway
Bldg 13
Pensacola, FL 32514
p. (850) 474-3377
environmental@uwf.edu
http://uwf.edu/cse/departments/earth-and-environmental-sciences/
f: https://www.facebook.com/pages/UWF-Department-of-Environmental-Studies/205988446096964
t: @UWF_EES
Programs: Environmental Science (B,M); GIS Administration (M)
Certificates: GIS (UG,G)
Enrollment (2016): B: 133 (39) M: 40 (6)
Chair:
Matthew C. Schwartz, (D), Delaware, 2002, OcCl
Professor:
Johan Liebens, (D), Michigan State, 1995, So
Associate Professor:
Zhiyong Hu, (D), Georgia, 2003, Zr
Assistant Professor:
John D. Morgan, (D), Florida State, 2010, Zi
Jason Ortegren, (D), North Carolina (Greensboro), 2008, PeZu
Phillip P. Schmutz, (D), Louisiana State, 2014, Gm
Instructor:
Chasidy Hobbs, (M), W Florida, 2005, ZgeZy
Taylor Kirschenfeld, (M), W Florida, 1988, Ob
Adjunct Professor:
Wilbur G. Hugli, (D), W Florida, 2001, As
Hilde Snoeckx, (D), Michigan, 1995, OuZg
Online GIS Program Coordinator:
Amber Bloechle, (M), W Florida, 2007, Zi

Valencia Community College

Valencia Community College (2015)
P.O. Box 3028
Orlando, FL 32802
p. (407) 299-5000
abosley@valenciacollege.edu
http://www.valenciacc.edu

Georgia

Columbus State University

Earth & Space Sciences (B,M) ☒ (2020)
4225 University Avenue
Columbus, GA 31907-5645

p. (706) 507-8091
barineau_clinton@columbusstate.edu
http://ess.columbusstate.edu/
f: https://www.facebook.com/Earth-and-Space-Sciences-at-Columbus-State-University-GA-347767372234/
Programs: AS Engineering Studies
BS Robotics Engineering
BS Earth and Space Sciences with 4 concentrations: Astrophysics and Planetary Geology, Environmental Science, Geology, Secondary Education, MS Natural Sciences with 2 tracks: Environmental Science, Geosciences
Certificates: Robotics
Enrollment (2020): B: 108 (18) M: 12 (0)

Professor:
Clinton I. Barineau, (D), Florida State, 2009, GctGg
Warren Church, (D), Yale, 1996, ZnPcZc
Shawn Cruzen, (D), Nevada, 1997, Xa
Zdeslav Hrepic, (D), Kansas State, 2004, Zn
Troy Keller, (D), Michigan, 1997, RwZc
Shaw Kimberly, (D), Florida State, 1997, Zn
David R. Schwimmer, (D), SUNY (Stony Brook), 1973, Pv
Abiye Seifu, (D), Rensselaer, 1991, Zn
Rosa Williams, (D), Illinois, 1999, Xa

Associate Professor:
Andrew Puckett, (D), Chicago, 2007, Xa

Assistant Professor:
Stacey Sloan Blersch, (D), SUNY (Buffalo), 2016, HsgRw
Lavi Zamstein, (D), Florida, 2009, Zn

Emeritus:
Thomas B. Hanley, (D), Indiana, 1975, Gc

Dalton State Community College

Dept of Natural Sciences (A,B) ☒ (2019)
650 College Drive
Dalton, GA 30720
p. (706) 272-4440
jmjohnson@daltonstate.edu
http://www.daltonstate.edu/natural-sciences

Professor:
Jean M. Johnson, (D), Michigan, 1995, Zg

East Georgia State College

Science & Mathematics (A,B) ☒ (2017)
131 College Circle
Swainsboro, GA 30401
p. (478) 289-2073
wedincamp@ega.edu
http://faculty.ega.edu/facweb/stracher/stracher.html
Enrollment (2015): A: 3 (1)

Professor Emeritus:
Glenn B. Stracher, (D), Nebraska, 1989, GycEc

Emory University

Dept of Environmental Sciences (B) (2019)
Mathematics & Science Center
400 Dowman Drive
Atlanta, GA 30322
p. (404) 727-4216
jwegner@emory.edu
http://www.envs.emory.edu/

Head:
Joy Budensiek, (D)

Chair:
Lance Gunderson, (D), Florida, 1992, Sf

Professor:
William B. Size, (D), Illinois, 1971, GivGa

Associate Professor:
Thomas Gillespie, (D), Florida, 2004, Zn

Assistant Professor:
Tracy Yandle, (D), Indiana, 2001, Ob

Instructor:
Anne M. Hall, (M), Georgia Tech, 1985, Gz

Campus Env Officer:
John Wegner, (D), Carleton, 1995, Sf

Lecturer:
Anthony J. Martin, (D), Georgia, 1991, Pe

Adjunct Professor:
Pamela J. W. Gore, (D), George Washington, 1983, Gs

Senior Lecturer:
Charles W. Hickcox, (D), Rice, 1971, Gg

Emeritus:
Howard R. Cramer, (D), Northwestern, 1954, Pg
Willard H. Grant, (D), Johns Hopkins, 1955, Cg
Lore Ruttan, (D), California (Davis), 1999, Ob

Fort Valley State University

Cooperative Developmental Energy Program ☒ (2017)
Box 5800 FVSU
1005 State University Drive
Fort Valley, GA 31030
p. (912) 825-6454
crumblyi@fvsu.edu
http://www.fvsu.edu/academics/cdep

Director:
Isaac J. Crumbly, (D), North Dakota State, 1970, Zn

Assistant Director:
Jackie Hodges, (B), Georgia Southern, 1983, Zn

Associate Professor:
Aditya Kar, (D), Oklahoma, 1997, Ct

Georgia Highlands College

Div of Science and Physical Education (A,B) (2015)
Main Campus 3175 Hwy 27 South
P.O. Box 1864
Rome, GA 30162
p. (706) 368-7528
bmorris@highlands.edu
http://www.highlands.edu/site/geology

Associate Professor:
Billy Morris, Gg

Instructor:
Tracy Hall, Gg

Georgia Institute of Technology

School of Earth & Atmospheric Sciences (B,M,D) (2020)
311 Ferst Drive
Atlanta, GA 30332-0340
p. (404) 894-3893
greg.huey@eas.gatech.edu
http://www.eas.gatech.edu
Enrollment (2011): B: 63 (21) M: 34 (19) D: 76 (13)

Chair:
Judith A. Curry, (D), Chicago, 1992, AsZrn

Professor:
Annalisa Bracco, (D), Genova (Italy), 2000, OpZnn
Kim M. Cobb, (D), Scripps, 2002, PeCsOg
Felix J. Herrmann, (D), Delft (Neth), 1997, YesZn
Gregory L. Huey, (D), Wisconsin, 1992, As
Ellery D. Ingall, (D), Yale, 1991, CmlOc
Jean Lynch-Stieglitz, (D), Columbia, 1995, OoPcCs
Andrew V. Newman, (D), Northwestern, 2000, YdsYg
Edward Michael Perdue, (D), Georgia Tech, 1973, Co
Irina Sokolik, (D), Russian Acad of Sci, 1989, AsZr
Martial Taillefert, (D), Northwestern, 1997, ClmCa
Rodney J. Weber, (D), Minnesota, 1995, As
Peter J. Webster, (D), MIT, 1972, AsOp

Senior Scientist:
Hai-ru Chang, (D), As
Robert Stickel, (D), Rice, 1979, As
Viatcheslav Tatarskii, (D), As
Hsiang-Jui Wang, (D), Georgia Tech, 1995, As

Associate Professor:
Michael H. Bergin, (D), Carnegie Mellon, 1995, As
Robert X. Black, (D), MIT, 1990, As
Yi Deng, (D), Illinois, 2005, AsZoAm
Emanuele Di Lorenzo, (D), Scripps, 2003, OpZnn
Takamitsu Ito, (D), MIT, 2005
Athanasios Nenes, (D), Caltech, 2002, As
Marc Stieglitz, (D), Columbia, 1995, Hsg
Yuhang Wang, (D), Harvard, 1997, As
James Wray, (D), Cornell, 2010

Assistant Professor:
Josef Dufek, (D), Washington, 2006, GvZnn

Carol M. Paty, (D), Washington, 2006, YmgZn
Zhigang Peng, (D), S California, 2004, YsgZn
Andrew Stack, (D), Wyoming, 2002, Cg

Research Scientist:
Carlos Hoyos, (D), Georgia Tech, 2008, As
Hyemi Kim, (D), As
Jiping Liu, (D), Columbia, As
Chao Luo, (D), Peking, 1990, As
James C. St. John, (D), Georgia Tech, 1997, As
Henian Zhang, (D), As

Adjunct Associate Professor:
Jay Brandes, (D), Washington, Og
Carmen Nappo, (D), Georgia Tech, 1989, As
Valerie Thomas, (D), Cornell, 1987, Zu

Adjunct Assistant Professor:
Karim Sabra, (D), Michigan, 2003, Yg

Adjunct Professor:
Clark R. Alexander, (D), North Carolina State, 1990, Cl
Dominic Assimaki, (D)
Jackson O. Blanton, (D), Oregon State, 1968, Cl
Thomas D. Christina, (D), Caltech, 1989, Cl
James Crawford, (D), Georgia Tech, As
Heidi Cullen, (D), Columbia, Am
Rong Fu, (D)
Leonid Germanovich, (D), Moscow State (Russia), 1982, NrYg
Gary G. Gimmestad, (D), Colorado, 1978, ZrAs
Richard Jahnke, (D), Washington, 1976, Cl
Yongqiang Liu, (D), Am
Joseph Montoya, (D), Harvard, 1990, Cm
Armistead G. Russell, (D), Caltech, 1985, As
Stuart G. Wakeham, (D), Washington, 1976, Co
Herbert L. Windom, (D), California (San Diego), 1968, Cm

Emeritus:
Paul H. Wine, (D), Florida State, 1974, As

Georgia Southern University

Applied Coastal Research Laboratory (2015)
10 Ocean Science Circle
Savannah, GA 31411
p. (912) 598-2329
icps@georgiasouthern.edu
http://cosm.georgiasouthern.edu/icps/acrl/

Director:
Clark R. Alexander, (D), North Carolina State, 1990, OuGsOn

Assistant Professor:
Chester M. Jackson, (D), Georgia, 2010, OnGs

Research Associate:
Michael Robinson, (B), Georgia Southern, 2002, ZiOn

Dept of Geology and Geography (B,M) (2019)
68 Georgia Avenue
Building 201
PO Box 8149
Statesboro, GA 30460-8149
p. (912) 478-5361
jreich@georgiasouthern.edu
https://cosm.georgiasouthern.edu/geo/
Programs: BA Geology, BS Geology, BA Geography, BS Geography, MS Applied Geography
Enrollment (2019): B: 71 (23) M: 6 (0)

Chair:
James S. Reichard, (D), Purdue, 1995, HwGe

Professor:
Wei Tu, (D), Texas A&M, 2004, Zi
Robert Kelly Vance, (D), New Mexico Tech, 1989, GiEgGg

Associate Professor:
Christine Hladik, (D), Georgia, 2012, SbZr
Chester W. Jackson, (D), Georgia, 2010, GsmGu
Jacque L. Kelly, (D), Hawaii, 2012, Cl
Amy E. Potter, (D), Louisiana State, 2011, Zn
Kathlyn M. Smith, (D), Michigan, 2010, Pv
John Van Stan, (D), Delaware, 2012, HgClSb
Robert A. Yarbrough, (D), Georgia, 2006, Zn

Assistant Professor:
Steve N. Guggino, (D), Arizona State, 2012, GgCg
Meimei Lin, (D), Miami, 2015, Zi
Travis Swanson, (D), Texas, 2015, Gsm

Lecturer:
Nicholas Radko, (M), Georgia, 2011, Geg

Emeritus:
Gale A. Bishop, (D), Texas, 1971, Pi
James H. Darrell, (D), Louisiana State, 1973, Pl
Daniel B. Good, (D), Tennessee, 1973, Zn
Dallas D. Rhodes, (D), Syracuse, 1973, Gm
Fredrick J. Rich, (D), Penn State, 1979, Pl

Georgia Southwestern State University

Dept of Geology & Physics (B) (2015)
800 GSW State University Drive
Americus, GA 31709
p. (229) 931-2353
Deborah.Standridge@gsw.edu
http://www.gsw.edu/%7Egeology/
Administrative Assistant: Debbie Standridge

Professor:
Burchard D. Carter, (D), West Virginia, 1981, Pg
Thomas J. Weiland, (D), North Carolina, 1988, Gi

Associate Professor:
Samuel T. Peavy, (D), Virginia Tech, 1997, Yg

Assistant Professor:
Svilen Kostov, (D), CUNY, 1992, Zn

Emeritus:
Daniel D. Arden, (D), California (Berkeley), 1961, Ps
Harland E. Cofer, (D), Illinois, 1957, Gz
John P. Manker, (D), Rice, 1975, Gs

Georgia State University

Dept of Geosciences (B,M,D) O⊘ (2019)
730 Langdale Hall
PO Box 3965
38 Peachtree Center Avenue
Atlanta, GA 30302-3965
p. (404) 413-5750
khankins@gsu.edu
http://geosciences.gsu.edu
f: https://www.facebook.com/gsugeosciences
t: @gsugeos
Programs: B.S. in Geosciences with concentrations in Geography, Urban Studies, Environmental Geosciences, and Geology M.S. in Geosciences with concentrations in Geography, Geology, or Water Science
Certificates: Water Science, GIS, Sustainability
Administrative Assistant: Basirat Lawal
Enrollment (2019): B: 113 (29) M: 48 (22) D: 3 (0)

Chair:
Katherine B. Hankins, (D), Georgia, 2004, Zn

Associate Dean:
Daniel M. Deocampo, (D), Rutgers, 2001, Gsn

Professor:
Jeremy E. Diem, (D), Arizona, 2000, At

Associate Professor:
Hassan A. Babaie, (D), Northwestern, 1984, GcZf
Dajun Dai, (D), S Illinois, 2007, Zi
W. Crawford Elliott, (D), Case Western, 1988, Clc
Nadine Kabengi, (D), Florida, ScClGe
Lawrence M. Kiage, (D), Louisiana State, 2007, ZyPlZr

Assistant Professor:
Sarah Ledford, (D), Syracuse, 2016, HsRw
Richard Milligan, (D), Georgia, 2016, Zn
Luke Pangle, (D), Oregon State, 2013, HqCs

Lecturer:
Armita Davarpanah, (D), Georgia State, 2015, Ggc
Paulo J. Hidalgo, (D), Michigan State, 2011, GivGz
Brian Meyer, (D), Georgia State, 2013, GesHw
Ricardo Nogueira, (D), Louisiana State, 2009, Asm
Christy Visaggi, (D), North Carolina (Wilmington), 2011, PiZe

Adjunct Professor:
J. Marion Wampler, (D), Columbia, 1963, Cc

Emeritus:
Sanford H. Bederman, (D), Minnesota, 1973, Zn
W. Robert Power, (D), Johns Hopkins, 1959, En
Seth E. Rose, (D), Arizona, 1987, Hw

Related Staff:
Atieh Tajik, (M), Georgia State, 2005, Gg

Georgia State University, Perimeter College, Alpharetta Campus

Dept of Life & Earth Sciences (A) ⁂ (2020)
3705 Brookside Parkway
Alpharetta, GA 30022
p. (678) 240-6227
dstewart29@gsu.edu
Programs: Geology
Enrollment (2020): A: 2 (0)
Professor:
Dion C. Stewart, (D), Penn State, 1980, Gzi

Georgia State University, Perimeter College, Clarkston Campus

Dept of Life & Earth Sciences (A) ⊘ (2020)
555 North Indian Creek Drive
Clarkston, GA 30021
p. (678) 891-3754
pgore@gsu.edu
Programs: Geology
Enrollment (2020): A: 4 (0)
Professor:
Pamela J. W. Gore, (D), George Washington, 1983, GsZeGn
Associate Professor:
E. Lynn Zeigler, (M), Emory, 1989, Gdg
Assistant Professor:
Victor J. Ricchezza, (D), S Florida, 2019, Ze
Lecturer:
Stephan D. Fitzpatrick, (M), Georgia, 2011, HwCgSo

Georgia State University, Perimeter College, Decatur Campus

Dept of Life & Earth Sciences (A) ☒ (2020)
3251 Panthersville Road
Decatur, GA 30034-3897
p. 678 891-2641
jjoyner12@gsu.edu
Programs: Geology
Enrollment (2020): A: 1 (0)
Assistant Professor:
Mengist Teklay, (D), Johannes Gutenberg Univ Mainz, 1996, Gg

Georgia State University, Perimeter College, Dunwoody Campus

Dept of Life & Earth Sciences (A) ⁂ (2020)
2101 Womack Road
Dunwoody, GA 30338-4497
p. (770) 274-5050
Programs: Geology
Enrollment (2020): A: 2 (0)
Assistant Professor:
Robin John McDowell, (D), Kentucky, 1992, Gge
Instructor:
Alexander David Ullrich, (M), Florida, 2010, GgZnGu

Georgia State University, Perimeter College, Newton Campus

Dept of Geology (A) (2017)
239 Cedar Lane
Covington, GA 30014
p. (770) 278-1263
Polly.bouker@gpc.edu
http://www.gpc.edu/~newsci/
Associate Professor:
Polly A. Bouker, (M), Georgia, 2006, Gg

Georgia State University, Perimeter College, Online

Dept of Life & Earth Sciences (A) ⁂ (2020)
555 North Indian Creek Drive
Clarkston, GA 30021
p. (678) 212-7577
dballero@gsu.edu
Programs: Geology
Associate Chair :
Deniz Z. A. Ballero, (D), Georgia, 2013, GgPm
Adjunct Professor:
Edward Albin, (D), Georgia, Xm
Jefferson B. Chaumba
Kimberly D. Schulte, (M), Gg
Christine D. Valenti, Gg

Mercer University

Dept of Environmental Engineering (B,M) (2015)
1400 Coleman Avenue
Macon, GA 31207
p. (912) 744-2597
lackey_l@mercer.edu
Department Secretary: Brenda Walraven
Professor:
Bruce D. Dod, (D), S Mississippi, 1973, Zg
Dan R. Quisenberry, (D), World Open, 1980, Zr
Assistant Professor:
Geoffrey W. Hayden, (D), Pennsylvania, 1987, Zm
Robert L. Huffman, (D), Massachusetts, 1985, Zn
Research Associate:
Paul P. Sipiera, (D), Otago (NZ), 1985, Xm
Instructor:
Barbara D. Henley, (M), Mercer, 1978, Gg

Middle Georgia College

Geology Dept (A) (2015)
1100 Second Street
Cochran, GA 31014
dawn.sherry@mga.edu
http://www.mgc.edu
Associate Professor:
Tina Mahaffee, (M), Georgia State, Gg
Assistant Professor:
Daniel Snyder, (D), Iowa, Gg

University of Georgia

Dept of Crop & Soil Science (B,M,D) (2015)
311 Plant Sciences Building
Athens, GA 30602-7272
p. (706) 542-2461
dgs@uga.edu
http://www.cropsoil.uga.edu/
Chair:
Don Shilling
Professor:
Domy C. Adriano, (D), Kansas State, 1970, Sc
Paul M. Bertsch, (D), Kentucky, 1983, Sc
Gary J. Gascho, (D), Michigan State, 1968, Sc
James E. Hook, (D), Penn State, 1975, Sp
Edward T. Kanemasu, (D), Wisconsin, 1969, Sp
David E. Kissel, (D), Kentucky, 1969, Sc
William P. Miller, (D), Virginia Tech, 1981, Sc
David E. Radcliffe, (D), Kentucky, 1984, Sp
William P. Segars, (D), Clemson, 1972, Sc
Larry M. Shuman, (D), Penn State, 1970, Sc
Associate Professor:
Miguel L. Cabrera, (D), Kansas State, 1986, So
Peter G. Hartel, (D), Oregon State, 1984, Sb
Owen C. Plank, (D), Virginia Tech, 1973, Sc
Larry T. West, (D), Texas A&M, 1986, Sd
Assistant Professor:
Glendon H. Harris, (D), Michigan State, 1993, Sb

Dept of Geology (B,M,D) ●⊘ (2021)
210 Field Street
Room 308
Athens, GA 30602
p. (706) 542-2652
geology@uga.edu
http://geology.uga.edu/
Enrollment (2011): B: 69 (9) M: 32 (11) D: 6 (0)
Head:
Paul A. Schroeder, (D), Yale, 1992, GzEnCl
Graduate Coordinator :
Steven M. Holland, (D), Chicago, 1990, Gr

Professor:
Douglas E. Crowe, (D), Wisconsin, 1990, Em
Ervan G. Garrison, (D), Missouri, 1979, GamGn
Robert B. Hawman, (D), Princeton, 1988, YseYu
Valentine A. Nzengung, (D), Georgia Tech, 1993, ClGeCq
L. Bruce Railsback, (D), Illinois, 1989, PcClGd
Sally E. Walker, (D), California (Berkeley), 1988, Pm
Associate Head:
Adam Milewski, (D), W Michigan, 2008, Hw
Assistant Professor:
Charlotte Garing, (D), Montpellier, 2011, Hw
Christian Klimczak, (D), Nevada, 2011, GcmGt
Mattia Pistone , (D), ETH (Switzerland), 2012, Gv
Senior Lecturer:
Marta Patino-Douce, (D), Buenos Aires, 1990, Gi
Lecturer:
Andy Darling, (D), Arizona State, 2016
Adjunct Professor:
Omer Isik Ece
Elizabeth J. Reitz, (D), Florida, 1979, Ga
John Washington, (D), Penn State, 1991
Sandra Whitney , (D), Georgia, Ga
Emeritus:
Gilles O. Allard, (D), Johns Hopkins, 1956, Eg
R. David Dallmeyer, (D), SUNY (Stony Brook), 1972, Gt
John F. Dowd, (D), Yale, 1984, Hy
Raymond Freeman-Lynde, Columbia, 1980, Gu
John Noakes, (D)
Michael F. Roden, (D), MIT, 1982, Gi
Sam Swanson , (D), Stanford, 1974, Gi
David B. Wenner, (D), Caltech, 1971, Cs
James A. Whitney, (D), Stanford, 1972, GivCg
James (Jim) E. Wright, (D), California (Santa Barbara), 1981, Gt

University of West Georgia

Dept of Geosciences (B) (2016)
1601 Maple Street
Callaway Building, Room 148
Carrollton, GA 30118
p. (678) 839-6479
jmayer@westga.edu
http://www.westga.edu/geosci/
Administrative Assistant: Anita M. Bryant
Enrollment (2016): B: 122 (22)
Chair:
James R. Mayer, (D), Texas, 1995, Hw
Professor:
David M. Bush, (D), Duke, 1991, Ou
Curtis L. Hollabaugh, (D), Washington State, 1980, GzCg
Randal L. Kath, (D), SD Mines, 1990, GcNgHg
Jeong C. Seong, (D), Georgia, 1999, Zir
Associate Professor:
Brad Deline, (D), Cincinnati, 2009, Pi
Georgina G. DeWeese, (D), Tennessee, 2007, Zy
Hannes Gerhardt, (D), Arizona, 2007, Zn
Leanna Shea Rose, (D), Florida State, 2008, ZyAsm
Karen S. Tefend, (D), Michigan State, 2005, CgGe
Nathan A. Walter, (D), Florida State, 2005, Zg
Assistant Professor:
Christopher A. Berg, (D), Texas, 2007, Gpi
Jessie Hong, (D), Colorado, 2012, ZieZy
Research Associate:
Randa R. Harris, (M), Tennessee, 2001, Hs
Emeritus:
Timothy M. Chowns, (D), Newcastle, 1968, GsrGg
Thomas J. Crawford, (M), Emory, 1957, Eg
Lab Coordinator:
John D. Congleton, (M), S Methodist, 1990, GeZiHs

Valdosta State University

Dept of Physics, Astronomy & Geosciences (B) (2015)
1500 North Patterson Street
Valdosta, GA 31698-0055
p. (229) 333-5752
echatela@valdosta.edu
http://www.valdosta.edu/phy/
Enrollment (2010): B: 77 (10)
Head:
Edward E. Chatelain, (D), Iowa, 1984, PiGlPv
Professor:
Cecilia S. Barnbaum, (D), California (Los Angeles), 1992, Zn
Frank A. Flaherty, (D), Fordham, 1983, Zn
Martha A. Leake, (D), Arizona, 1982, Xg
Kenneth S. Rumstay, (D), Ohio State, 1984, Znn
Associate Professor:
Can Denizman, (D), Florida, 1998, Hw
Mary A. Fares, (D), Tennessee Tech, 1992, Zn
Judy Grable, (D), Tennessee, 2001, Hs
Mark S. Groszos, (D), Florida State, 1996, GctEg
Michael G. Noll, (D), Kansas, 2000, Zn
Paul C. Vincent, (D), Texas A&M, 2004, Zig
Pre-Engineering Director:
Barry Hojjatie, (D), Florida, 1990, Zm
Assistant Professor:
Jason Allard, (D), Penn State, 2006, AsZg
Instructor:
Perry A. Baskin, (M), Valdosta State, 1972, Zn
Donald Thieme, (D), Georgia, 2003, GaSdGm
Emeritus:
Dennis W. Marks, (D), Michigan, 1970, Zn
Arnold E. Somers, Jr., (D), Virginia Tech, 1975, Zn

Guam

University of Guam

College of Natural and Applied Sciences (B,M) (2015)
Mohammad H. Golabi, PhD
Mangilao, GU 96923
p. (671) 734-9305
mgolabi@uguam.uog.edu
Professor:
Mohammad H. Golabi, (D), Georgia, 1991, SzpSc

Water & Environmental Research Institute of the Western Pacific (M) ☒ (2021)
303 University Drive
UOG Station
Mangilao, GU 96923
p. (671) 735-2685
jjenson@triton.uog.edu
https://weri.uog.edu/
Programs: Environmental Science (M)
Certificates: Groundwater Hydrology
Enrollment (2017): M: 7 (2)
Director:
John W. Jenson, (D), Oregon State, 1993, HwGel
Associate Professor:
Nathan C. Habana, (D), Guam, 2014, Hw
Yuming Wen, (D), Rhode Island, 2004, Zir
Assistant Professor:
Yongsang (Barry) Kim, (D), Purdue, 2008, Hw
Mark A. Lander, (D), Hawaii, 1990, Am
MYEONG-HO (CHRIS) YEO, (D), McGill, 2014, Hwy
Professor of Hydrology:
Leroy F. Heitz, (D), Idaho, Hg
Professor of Geology:
Henry Galt Siegrist, jr, (D), Penn State, 1961, GdzHy
Emeritus:
Gary R. W. Denton, (D), London (UK), 1974, Ob

Hawaii

Honolulu Community College

Natural Sciences (A) (2017)
874 Dillingham Blvd.
Honolulu, HI 96817
p. (808) 845-9488
brill@hawaii.edu
http://libart.honolulu.hawaii.edu/natsci/geology.php
Professor:
Richard C. Brill, Jr., (M), Hawaii, Gg

University of Hawai'i, Hilo

Dept of Geology (B) (2015)
200 W. Kawili Street
Hilo, HI 96720-4091
p. (808) 933-3383
kenhon@hawaii.edu

Chair:
Ken Hon, (D), Colorado, 1987, Gvi
Professor:
Steven P. Lundblad, (D), North Carolina, 1994, GraCz
Jene D. Michaud, (D), Arizona, 1992, HqwGm
Associate Professor:
James L. Anderson, (D), S California, 1987, GctYd
Affiliate Faculty:
Cheryl A. Gansecki, (D), Stanford, 1998, GviZe
Affiliate Faculty:
John P. Lockwood, (D), Princeton, 1966, Gvg
Emeritus:
Joseph B. Halbig, (D), Penn State, 1969, Ca
Cooperating Faculty:
Christina C. Heliker, (M), W Washington, 1984, Gv

University of Hawai'i, Manoa

Dept of Atmospheric Sciences (B,M,D) ☒ (2019)
2525 Correa Road, HIG 350
Honolulu, HI 96822
p. (808) 956-8775
metdept@hawaii.edu
http://www.soest.hawaii.edu/MET
Programs: Atmospheric Sciences BS
- with NWS Forecasting or US Government Track available
- ATMO Minor possible with other Geo-science, Engineering, or Math or Computer Programming degrees. Atmospheric Sciences Masters Plan A & B, Plan A is Thesis track, Plan B is non-thesis track. Requires a general capstone research project., Atmospheric Sciences Ph.D.
Certificates: None at this time
Enrollment (2018): B: 13 (7) M: 17 (7) D: 14 (4)

Chair:
Steven Businger, (D), Washington, 1986, Am
Professor:
Yi-Leng Chen, (D), Illinois, 1980, Asm
Pao-Shin Chu, (D), Wisconsin, 1981, As
Fei Fei Jin, (D), Acad Sinica (Beijing), 1985, AmsZo
Tim Li, (D), Hawaii, 1993, Asm
Bin Wang, (D), Florida State, 1984, Am
Yuqing Wang, (D), Monash, 1995, As
Associate Professor:
Jennifer Small Griswold, (D), California (Santa Cruz), AmZr
Assistant Professor:
Christina Karamperidou, (D), Columbia, 2012, AsZoc
Alison D. Nugent, (D), Yale, 2014, AsZnn
Giuseppe Torri , (D), Imperial Coll (UK), 2012, ApsAm
Jingxia Zhao, (D), California (Los Angeles), 1993, AmmAc

Dept of Earth Sciences (B,M,D) ⃠ (2021)
1680 East-West Road, POST 701
Honolulu, HI 96822
p. (808) 956-7640
earth-chair@soest.hawaii.edu
http://www.soest.hawaii.edu/gg
f: https://www.facebook.com/UHEarthSciences
t: https://twitter.com/uh_earthscience
Programs: Earth Sciences, Environmental Earth Science, Earth and Planetary Sciences
Enrollment (2020): B: 46 (16) M: 26 (14) D: 25 (6)

Chair:
Paul Wessel, (D), Columbia, 1989, Yr
Dean:
Brian Taylor, (D), Columbia, 1982, Gtu
Assoc. Dean:
Charles H. Fletcher, (D), Delaware, 1986, GsOnZu
Professor:
Robert A. Dunn, (D), Oregon, 1999, Yrs
Aly I. El-Kadi, (D), Cornell, 1983, Hw
L. Neil Frazer, (D), Princeton, 1978, Ys
Eric J. Gaidos, (D), MIT, 1996, Pg
Craig R. Glenn, (D), Rhode Island Grad Sch Ocean, 1987, GeCmGs
Julia E. Hammer, (D), Oregon, 1998, GiCpGv
Bruce F. Houghton, (D), Otago (NZ), 1977, Gv
Garrett T. Ito, (D), MIT/WHOI, 1996, YgrGt
Brian N. Popp, (D), Illinois, 1986, Cs
Scott K. Rowland, (D), Hawaii, 1987, Zn
Kenneth H. Rubin, (D), California (San Diego), 1991, CcGvCg
Associate Professor:
Henrietta Dulai, (D), Florida State, 2005, CcHw
Jasper G. Konter, (D), California (San Diego), 2007, CcGiCt
Gregory Ravizza, (D), Yale, 1991, Cm
Kathleen Ruttenberg, (D), Yale, 1990, Cg
Bridget R. Smith-Konter, (D), California (San Diego), 2005, YdXy
Associate Scientist:
Aaron Pietruszka, (D), Hawaii, 2008, Ca
Assistant Professor:
Sloan Coats, (D), Columbia, 2017, Zo
Helen Janiszewski, (D), Columbia, 2017, Ys
Thomas Shea, (D), Hawaii, 2010, Gv
Emeritus:
Michael O. Garcia, (D), California (Los Angeles), 1976, Gi
Kevin T. M. Johnson, (D), MIT, 1990, Gi
Stephen J. Martel, (D), Stanford, 1987, Ng
Ralph Moberly, (D), Princeton, 1956, GutGs
Gregory F. Moore, (D), Cornell, 1977, Gt
John M. Sinton, (D), Otago (NZ), 1976, Gi
Director of Student Services:
Heather Saito, Zn
Cooperating Faculty:
Margo H. Edwards, (D), Columbia, 1992, Gu
Sarah Fagents, (D), Lancaster (UK), 1994, Gv
Luke P. Flynn, (D), Hawaii, 1992, Zr
Patricia B. Fryer, (D), Hawaii, 1981, Gu
Milton A. Garces, (D), California (San Diego), 1995, Ys
Alexander N. Krot, (D), Moscow State (Russia), 1989, Xm
Paul G. Lucey, (D), Hawaii, 1986, Xy
Murli H. Manghnani, (D), Montana State, 1962, Yx
Fernando Martinez, (D), Columbia, 1988, Yr
Floyd W. McCoy, Jr., (D), Harvard, 1974, Gu
Peter J. Mouginis-Mark, (D), Lancaster (UK), 1977, Xg
Shiv K. Sharma, (D), Indian Inst of Tech, 1973, Gx
G. Jeffrey Taylor, (D), Rice, 1970, Xm
Donald M. Thomas, (D), Hawaii, 1977, Ca
Affiliate Graduate Faculty:
Donald A. Swanson, (D), Johns Hopkins, 1964, Gv

Dept of Oceanography (B,M,D) (2015)
1000 Pope Road
Honolulu, HI 96822
p. (808) 956-7633
ocean@soest.hawaii.edu
http://www.soest.hawaii.edu/oceanography/
Administrative Assistant: Kristin Momohara

Professor:
Barbara Bruno, (D), Hawaii, 1994, Ob
Eric H. De Carlo, (D), Hawaii, 1982, Cm
Jeffrey C. Drazen, (D), California (San Diego), 2000, Ob
Eric Firing, (D), MIT, 1978, Op
Pierre J. Flament, (D), California (San Diego), 1986, Op
David Ho, (D), Columbia, 2001, OcCb
David M. Karl, (D), California (San Diego), 1978, Ob
Paul Kemp, (D), Oregon State, 1985, Ob
Rudolf C. Kloosterziel, (D), Utrecht, 1990, Op
Douglas S. Luther, (D), MIT, 1980, Op
Julian P. McCreary, (D), California (San Diego), 1977, Op
Margaret Anne McManus, (D), Old Dominion, 1996, Op
Christopher Measures, (D), Southampton (UK), 1978, Oc
Mark A. Merrifield, (D), California (San Diego), 1989, Op
Michael J. Mottl, (D), Harvard, 1976, OuCgm
Bo Qiu, (D), Kyoto, 1990, Op
Kelvin J. Richards, (D), Southampton (UK), 1978, Op
Kathleen C. Ruttenberg, (D), Yale, Cg
Francis J. Sansone, (D), N Carolina, 1980, Cm
Niklas Schneider, (D), Hawaii, 1992, Og
Craig R. Smith, (D), California (San Diego), 1983, Ob
Grieg F. Steward, (D), California (San Diego), 1996, Ob
Axel Timmermann, (D), Hamburg, 1999, Op
Richard E. Zeebe, (D), Bremen, 1998, Ou
Associate Professor:
Glenn Carter, (D), Washington, 2005, Op

Matthew Church, (D), William & Mary, 2003, Ob
Brian Glazer, (D), Cm
Erica Goetze, (D), California (San Diego), 2004, Ob
Christopher Kelley, (D), Hawaii, 1995, Ob
Gary M. McMurtry, (D), Hawaii, 1979, CaGvu
Brian Powell, (D), Colorado, 2005, Op
Karen E. Selph, (D), Hawaii, 1999, Ob

Affiliate Graduate Faculty:
Allen H. Andrews, (D), Rhodes, 2009, Oc

Emeritus:
Paul K. Bienfang, (D), Hawaii, 1977, Ob
Antony D. Clarke, (D), Washington, 1983, As
Richard W. Grigg, (D), California (San Diego), 1969, Ob
Barry J. Huebert, (D), Northwestern, 1970, OcCg
Yuan-Hui Li, (D), Columbia, 1967, Cm
Roger Lukas, (D), Hawaii, 1981, Op
Fred T. Mackenzie, (D), Lehigh, 1962, CmGes
Lorenz Magaard, (D), Kiel, 1963, Op
Alexander Malahoff, (D), Hawaii, 1965, Cm
Peter Muller, (D), Hamburg, 1974, Op
Jane E. Schoonmaker, (D), Northwestern, 1981, Cm
Stephen V. Smith, (D), Hawaii, 1970, Ou
Richard E. Young, (D), Miami, 1968, Ob

Affiliate Graduate Faculty:
Russell E. Brainard, (D), Naval Postgrad Sch, 1994
Paul G. Falkowski, (D), British Columbia, 1975, Og
Carolyn Jones, (D), Georgia Tech, 2004
Dennis Moore, (D), Harvard, 1968, Og
Jaromir Ruzicka, (D), Tech (Czech), 1963, Zn
John R. Sibert, (D), Columbia, 1968, Ob
Kevin Weng, (D), Stanford, 2007, Ob

Cooperating Faculty:
Marlin J. Atkinson, (D), Hawaii, 1981, Ob
Whitlow W L. Au, (D), Washington State, 1970, Zn
Janet M. Becker, (D), California (San Diego), 1989, Og
Michael Cooney, (D), California (Davis), 1992, Og
Walter Dudley, (D), Hawaii, 1976, Ou
Eric J. Gaidos, (D), MIT, 1996, Yg
Ruth D. Gates, (D), Newcastle (UK), 1990, Ob
Petra H. Lenz, (D), California (Santa Barbara), 1983, Og
Jeffrey J. Polovina, (D), California (Berkeley), 1974, Zn
Brian N. Popp, (D), Illinois, 1986, Cm
Michael S. Rappe, (D), Oregon State, 1997, Og
Florence Thomas, (D), California (Berkeley), 1992, Ob
Robert Toonen, (D), California (Davis), 2001, Ob
John C. Wiltshire, (D), Hawaii, 1983, Og

Windward Community College

Natural Sciences (A) O (2018)
45-720 Kea'ahala Rd.
Kane'ohe, HI 96744
p. (808) 236-9115
fmccoy@hawaii.edu
http://windward.hawaii.edu
Programs: AA in Natural Sciences
Certificates: certificate programs in Natural Science; Sustainability; Marine Science [Marine Option Program])
Enrollment (2018): A: 6 (4)

Professor:
Floyd W. McCoy, (D), Harvard, 1974, GgaGu

Idaho

Boise State University

Dept of Geosciences (B,M,D) ● (2018)
1910 University Drive
Mail Stop 1535
Boise, ID 83725
p. (208) 426-1631
geosciences@boisestate.edu
http://earth.boisestate.edu/
Programs: Geology, Geophysics, Hydrology, Earth Science Education
Certificates: Geographic Information Systems
Administrative Assistant: Liz Johansen
Enrollment (2014): B: 143 (11) M: 29 (6) D: 20 (7)

University Distinguished Professor:
Matthew Kohn, (D), Rensselaer, 1991, CsGpPv

Dean Graduate College:
John R. Pelton, (D), Utah, 1979, YgeYs

Chair:
James P. McNamara, (D), Alaska (Fairbanks), 1997, Hg

Associate Dean/College of Arts & Sciences:
Clyde J. Northrup, (D), MIT, 1996, Gc

Professor:
Shawn Benner, (D), Waterloo, 2000, Clt
Nancy Glenn, (D), Nevada (Reno), 2000, ZrNgZi
Mark D. Schmitz, (D), MIT, 2001, CcaCg

Senior Scientist:
Jim Crowley, (D), Carleton, 1997, Ccg

Associate Professor:
Brittany Brand, (D), Arizona State, 2008, Gsv
Alejandro N. Flores, (D), MIT, 2009, HqAs
Jeffrey Johnson, (D), Washington, 2000, YsGv
Hans-Peter Marshall, (D), Colorado, YxGl
Jennifer L. Pierce, (D), New Mexico, 2004, GmRcZc
David E. Wilkins, (D), Utah, 1997, ZyGm

Assistant Professor:
Ellyn Enderlin, (D), Ohio State, 2013, GlYg
Dylan Mikesell, (D), Boise State, 2012, YsuYx
Qifei iu Niu, (D), Hong Kong, 2014, Ygu
Karen Viskupic, (D), MIT, 2002, ZeGc
Dorsey Wanless, (D), Florida, 2010, Gi

Research Professor:
Lee M. Liberty, (M), Wyoming, 1992, Ys

Adjunct Professor:
Virginia S. Gillerman, (D), California (Berkeley), 1982, Eg

Emeritus Research Professor:
Warren Barrash, (D), Idaho, 1986, HwYxGe

Emeritus:
Paul R. Donaldson, (D), Colorado Mines, 1974, Ye
Kenneth M. Hollenbaugh, (D), Idaho, 1968, Eg
Paul Michaels, (D), Utah, 1993, Ne
Walter S. Snyder, (D), Stanford, 1977, GrcGt
Claude Spinosa, (D), Iowa, 1968, Pi
Charles J. Waag, (D), Arizona, 1968, Gc
Craig M. White, (D), Oregon, 1980, Giv
Monte D. Wilson, (D), Idaho, 1969, Gm
Spencer H. Wood, (D), Caltech, 1975, Gmm

Brigham Young University - Idaho

Dept of Geology (B) ● (2020)
525 South Center Street
Rexburg, ID 83460-0510
p. (208) 496-7670
geologysec@byui.edu
http://www.byui.edu/Geology
Programs: Geology; Earth Science Education; Environmental Geoscience; Geospatial Computing; GeoBusiness and Data Analytics
Certificates: Geospatial Technology
Enrollment (2020): B: 173 (24)

Chair:
Gregory T. Roselle, (D), Wisconsin, 1997, GpCaHg

Professor:
Robert W. Clayton, (D), S California, 1993, GcYgNg
Forest J. Gahn, (D), Michigan, 2004, PggGs
William W. Little, (D), Colorado, 1995, GsdGm
Mark D. Lovell, (M), Idaho, 1999, HyZiGo
Daniel K. Moore, (D), Rensselaer, 1997, GxiCp
Megan Sjoblom, (D), Penn State, 2015, GiZeGe
Julie B. Willis, (D), Utah, 2009, GtcZi

College of Southern Idaho

Dept of Physical Science (A) (2015)
Box 1238
315 Falls Avenue
Twin Falls, ID 83301
p. (208) 732-6400
swillsey@csi.edu
http://physsci.csi.edu/geology/
Enrollment (2013): A: 8 (0)

Professor:
Shawn P. Willsey, (M), N Arizona, 2000, GgcGv

College of Western Idaho

Physical & Agricultural Sciences (A) (2018)
5500 E Opportunity Drive
Nampa, ID 83687
andreaschumaker@cwidaho.cc
http://cwidaho.cc
Programs: Geology; Geography; Biology-Natural Resources
Certificates: GIS
Enrollment (2018): A: 38 (3)
Assistant Professor:
Ander Sundell, (M), Boise State, Ggc

Idaho State University

Department of Geosciences (B,M,D) O☒ (2020)
921 S. 8th Ave STOP 8072
Pocatello, ID 83209-8072
p. (208) 282-3365
geology@isu.edu
http://geology.isu.edu/
f: https://www.facebook.com/idahostategeosciences/
t: @ISUGeoscience
Programs: BA/BS Geology, BA/BS Earth and Environmental Science, BS Earth and Environmental Science - Geospatial Systems
Minor Geology or Geotechnology, MS Geology, MS Geographic Information Science, PhD Geosciences
Enrollment (2020): B: 25 (11) M: 16 (10) D: 7 (0)
GIS Training and Research Center:
Keith Weber, (M), Montana, 2000, Zi
Director, Idaho Museum of Natural History:
Leif Tapanila, (D), Utah, 2005, Pig
Department Chair:
Benjamin T. Crosby, (D), MIT, 2006, GmHsRn
Associate Vice President for Research:
David W. Rodgers, (D), Stanford, 1987, Gct
Professor:
Glenn D. Thackray, (D), Oregon State, 1989, Glm
Associate Professor:
Donna M. Delparte, (D), Calgary, 2008, Zir
Sarah E. Godsey, (D), California (Berkeley), 2009, HgsHq
Shannon E. Kobs-Nawotniak, (D), Buffalo, 2007, Gv
David M. Pearson, (D), Arizona, 2012, Gct
Field Camp Director:
Ryan Anderson, (D), Washington State, 2019, GcCaZe
Assistant Professor & Director of Geotechnologies:
H. Carrie Bottenberg, (D), Missouri S&T, 2012, ZiGtc
Assistant Professor:
Kendra Murray, (D), Arizona, 2016, ClGtm
Emeritus:
Scott S. Hughes, (D), Oregon State, 1983, GvXgGi
Paul K. Link, (D), California (Santa Barbara), 1982, GsgGr
Michael O. McCurry, (D), California (Los Angeles), 1985, Gzv

Lewis-Clark State College

Earth Sciences (B) ☒ (2019)
Div of Natural Science & Mathematics
500 8th Ave
Lewiston, ID 83501
p. (208) 792-2283
klschmidt@lcsc.edu
http://www.lcsc.edu/science/degree-programs/earth-science/
Programs: Earth Science (B), Geochemistry emphasis in Chemistry (B), Earth Science Secondary Education
Certificates: GIS, Geology
Enrollment (2018): B: 13 (3)
Professor:
Keegan L. Schmidt, (D), S California, 2000, Gc

North Idaho College

Dept of Geosciences (A) (2020)
1000 West Garden Avenue
Coeur d'Alene, ID 83814
p. (208) 769-3477
Bill_Richards@nic.edu
https://www.nic.edu/
Programs: Geology
Geography
Enrollment (2020): A: 2 (1)
Associate Professor:
Bill Richards, (M), Kansas State, 1984, GgzZe

University of Idaho

College of Natural Resources (2015)
Moscow, ID 83844-3019
drbecker@uidaho.edu

Dept of Civil & Environmental Engineering (2019)
875 Perimeter Drive - MS 1022
Moscow, ID 83844-1022
sjung@uidaho.edu
Programs: Civil : M. Eng., MS, PhD
Geological Engineering: M Eng, MS
Certificates: N/A
Professor:
SJ Jung, (D), West Virginia, 1989, NrxNr

Dept of Geography (2019)
875 Perimeter Drive MS 3021
Moscow, ID 83844-3021
p. (208) 885-6216
geography@uidaho.edu
https://www.uidaho.edu/sci/geography
f: https://www.facebook.com/groups/502335576777518
t: @GeogUidaho
Programs: Geography (B,M,D)
Certificates: GIS, Climate Change
Professor:
Raymond Dezzani, (D), California, 1996, RhZnn
Jeffrey Hicke, (D), Colorado, 2000, ZcyZn
Karen Humes, (D), Arizona, 1992, ZriZn
Associate Professor:
John Abatzoglou, (D), California, 2006, ZoyZc
Assistant Professor:
Chao Fan, Arizona State, 2016, Zir
Grant Harley, (D), Tennessee, 2012, ZynZn
Haifeng (Felix) Liao, (D), Utah, 2014, ZuiZn
Tom Ptak, (D), Oregon, 2016, Zu
Steven Radil, (D), Illinois, 2011, Zn
Research Scientist:
Katherine Hegewisch, (D), Washington State, 2010, Zo

Dept of Soil and Water Systems (B,M,D) (2015)
Moscow, ID 83844-2339
p. (208) 885-7012
jmaynard@uidaho.edu
https://www.uidaho.edu/cals/soil-and-water-systems
Professor:
Guy Knudsen, (D), Cornell, 1984, Sb
Robert L. Mahler, (D), North Carolina State, 1980, Zn
Daniel G. Strawn, (D), Delaware, 1999, Sc
Associate Professor:
Bradford D. Brown, (D), Utah State, 1985, Zn
Matthew J. Morra, (D), Ohio State, 1986, Sb
Assistant Professor:
Jodi Johnson-Maynard, (D), California (Riverside), 1999, Sd
Paul A. McDaniel, (D), North Carolina State, 1989, Sd

Geological Sciences (B,M,D) O☒ (2019)
875 Perimeter Drive
MS 3022
Moscow, ID 83844-3022
p. (208) 885-6192
geology@uidaho.edu
http://www.uidaho.edu/sci/geology
Enrollment (2018): B: 42 (9) M: 8 (2) D: 8 (2)
Chair:
Leslie L. Baker, (D), Brown, 1996, ClXgGe
Distinguished Professor:
Robert Smith, (D), New Mexico Tech, 1984, Cb
Professor:
Jerry P. Fairley, (D), California (Berkeley), 2000, HwGv
Kenneth F. Sprenke, (D), Alberta, 1983, Ye
Clinical Associate Professor:
Thomas Williams, (D), Maryland, 1994, Gf

Assistant Professor:
Timothy Bartholomaus, (D), Alaska, 2013, Gl
Elizabeth J. Cassel, (D), Stanford, 2010, Gs
Jeffrey Langman, (D), Texas, 2008, ClHws
Eric L. Mittelstaedt, (D), Hawaii, 2008, Yr
Jessica Stanley, (D), Colorado, 2015, Gt
Instructor:
Renee Love, (D), Idaho, 2011, Pg
Malinda Ritts, (D), Stanford, 2009, GsCg
Emeritus University Distinguished Professor:
Mickey E. Gunter, (D), Virginia Tech, 1987, GzEnGb
Emeritus:
Dennis J. Geist, (D), Oregon, 1985, Giv
Peter E. Isaacson, (D), Oregon State, 1974, Psi

Illinois

Augustana College

Department of Geology (B) ☒ (2021)
639 38th St.
Rock Island, IL 61201
p. (309) 794-7318
jeffreystrasser@augustana.edu
https://augustana.edu/academics/areas-of-study/geology
f: https://www.facebook.com/AugustanaGeology/
Programs: B.A. major in geology
Administrative Assistant: Jennifer Milner
Enrollment (2020): B: 26 (4)
Professor:
Jeffrey C. Strasser, (D), Lehigh, 1996, GmlGe
Michael B. Wolf, (D), Caltech, 1992, Gi
Professional Faculty:
Jenny C. Arkle, (D), Cincinnati, 2019, GtmCc
Assistant Professor:
Kelsey M. Arkle, (D), Cincinnati, 2015, PeGsg
Emeritus:
William R. Hammer, (D), Wayne State, 1979, Pv
Assistant Curator:
John Oostenryk
Assistant Curator and Educational Programs Coordinator:
Susan Kornreich Wolf, (B), Hamilton, 1987, Ze

College of Lake County

Earth Science Dept (A) (2017)
19351 W. Washington Steet
Grayslake, IL 60030-1198
p. (847) 543-2504
eng499@clcillinois.edu
http://www.clcillinois.edu/programs/esc/
Professor:
Eric Priest, (M), Creighton, 1986, AmZe
Xiaoming Zhai, (D), California (Davis), 1997, Gp

Eastern Illinois University

Geology and Geography Department (B,M) (2020)
600 Lincoln Avenue
Charleston, IL 61920-3099
p. (217) 581-2626
geoscience@eiu.edu
http://www.eiu.edu/~geoscience/
Programs: Geology (B.S); accelerated B.S Geology/law degree with NIU; Geography (B.S.); Science Teacher Certification (B.S); Geographic Information Systems (MBA, PSM)
Certificates: GISci Graduate Certificate, co-offer Certificate in Public Planning (with Political Science)
Administrative Assistant: Susan Kile
Enrollment (2020): B: 30 (13) M: 11 (1)
Associate Professor:
Diane M. Burns, (D), Wyoming, 2006, GsrGe
Vice President of Academic Affairs:
Jay Gatrell, (D), West Virginia, 1997, Zi
Professor:
Michael W. Cornebise, (D), Tennessee, 2003, Zg
Associate Professor:
James A. Davis, (D), Kansas State, 2001, Zg
Barry J. Kronenfeld, (D), SUNY (Buffalo), 2004, Zi
Christopher R. Laingen, (D), Kansas State, 2009, SfZy
Katherine Lewandowski, (D), Ohio State, 2008, PmcZe
James D. Riley, (D), Illinois, 2013, ZyHsq
David C. Viertel, (D), Texas State, 2008, Zru
Assistant Professor:
Jake R. Crandall, (M), S Illinois (Carbondale), 2015, GzXgEd
Instructor:
Cameron D. Craig, (M), Indiana State, 2003, ZgAm
Emeritus:
Craig A. Chesner, (D), Michigan Tech, 1988, GivGz
Belayet H. Khan, (D), Pittsburgh, 1985, Zy
Betty E. Smith, (D), SUNY (Buffalo), 1994, Zu
James F. Stratton, (D), Indiana, 1975, PgGu

Elgin Community College

Dept of Geology (2015)
1700 Spartan Drive
Elgin, IL 60123
p. (847) 214-7359
agoyal@elgin.edu
http://www.elgin.edu/employeelisting/faculty/
Adjunct Professor:
Mark R. Kuntz, Gg
Timothy M. Millen, (M), N Illinois, 1982, Gg
Joseph E. Peterson, Gg

Field Museum of Natural History

Dept of Geology (2015)
1400 S. Lake Shore Drive
Chicago, IL 60605-2496
p. (312) 665-7621
klawson@fieldmuseum.org
http://www.fieldmuseum.org
Administrative Assistant: Karsten L.. Lawson, Elaine Zeiger
Chair:
Olivier C. Rieppel, (D), Basel (Switzerland), 1978, Pv
Curator, Meteoritics:
Meenakshi Wadhwa, (D), Washington (St Louis), 1994, Xm
Curator, Fossil Fishes:
Lance Grande, (D), CUNY, 1983, Pv
Associate Curator, Fossil Invertebrates:
Scott H. Lidgard, (D), Johns Hopkins, 1984, Pi
Curator, Fossil Amphibians & Reptiles:
John R. Bolt, (D), Chicago, 1968, Pv
Emeritus:
Matthew H. Nitecki, (D), Chicago, 1968, Pi
Bertram G. Woodland, (D), Chicago, 1962, Gp
Associate Curator, Fossil Invertebrates:
Peter J. Wagner, (D), Chicago, 1995, Pi

Harold Washington College

Physcial Science Dept (A) (2015)
30 E. Lake Street
Room 903
Chicago, IL 60601
p. (312) 553-5791
aescuadro@ccc.edu
http://www.ccc.edu/colleges/washington/departments/Pages/Physical-Sciences.aspx
Enrollment (2012): A: 17 (0)

Heartland Community College

Math And Science Div (A) (2015)
2400 Instructional Commons Building
1500 W Raab Road
Normal, IL 61761
p. (309) 268-8640
mark.finley@heartland.edu
http://www.heartland.edu/ms/easc/
Professor:
Robert Dennison, (M), S Mississippi, Zgn
Mark Finley, (M), Iowa State, Gg
Adjunct Professor:
Janet Beach Davis, (B), Illinois (Springfield), Zg
Paul Ritter, (M), E Illinois, Zg
Steven Travers, (M), Illinois State, Zg
Mark Yacucci, (B), Youngstown State, Zg

Illinois Central College

Math, Science, and Engineering Dept (A) (2015)
One College Drive
East Peoria, IL 61611
p. (309) 694-5364
mse@icc.edu
Administrative Assistant: Diane Weber
Professor:
Martin A. Petit, (M), Illinois State, 1967, Ze
Associate Professor:
Cheryl R. Emerson, (M), N Arizona, 1989, Ze
Assistant Professor:
Ed Stermer, (M), Iowa, Zg
Adjunct Professor:
Linda Aylward, (B), Bradley, 1980, Ze
Sean Mulkey, (M), Iowa, 1994, Ze

Illinois State University

Dept of Geography, Geology, and the Environment (B,M)
○⊘ (2020)
101 South School Street
Campus Box 4400
206 Felmley Hall of Science
Normal, IL 61790-4400
p. (309) 438-7649
geo@illinoisstate.edu
https://geo.illinoisstate.edu/
f: https://www.facebook.com/groups/21051078663/
Programs: Geography (BA or BS); Geography Education (BS); Earth and Space Science Education (BS); Environmental Systems and Sustainability (BS) Geology (BS); Hydrogeology (M) Minors in Geography, Geology, and Environmental Studies Certificates: Geographic Information Systems, Hydrogeology Geographic Information Systems
Administrative Assistant: Karen K. Dunton
Enrollment (2020): B: 73 (12) M: 19 (13)
University Professor:
Eric W. Peterson, (D), Missouri, 2002, Hws
Distinguished University Professor:
David H. Malone, (D), Wisconsin, 1994, GcsEg
Chair:
Dagmar Budikova, (D), Calgary, 2001, AsZyi
Professor:
James E. Day, (D), Iowa, 1988, PisPm
John Kostelnick, (D), Kansas, 2006, Zi
Associate Professor:
Catherine M. O'Reilly, (D), Arizona, 2001, HgCgGg
Rex J. Rowley, (D), Kansas, 2009, Zi
Jonathan B. Thayn, (D), Kansas, 2009, Zir
Lisa M. Tranel, (D), Virginia Tech, 2010, Gmt
Assistant Professor:
Tenley Banik, (D), Vanderbilt, 2015, GviCc
Wondwosen M. Seyoum, (D), Georgia, 2016, HwqZr
Adjunct Professor:
Toby J. Dogwiler, (D), Missouri, 2002, Gm
Walton R. Kelly, (D), Virginia, 1993, HgCg
Edward Mehnert, (D), Illinois, 1998, Hg
Andrew Stumpf, (D), New Brunswick, 2001, GgsCg
Steve Van Der Hoven, (D), Utah, 2000, HwSpYg
Emeritus:
Robert S. Nelson, (D), Iowa, 1970, Gm
Coordinator of Academic Services :
Paul A. Meister, (M), Illinois State, 2016, GgHgZn

Illinois Valley Community College

Dept of Geology (A) ☒ (2020)
Natural Sciences, Math, & Business Division
815 North Orlando Smith Road
Oglesby, IL 61348-9692
p. (815) 224-0394
Mike_Phillips@ivcc.edu
https://facultyweb.ivcc.edu/mphillips/
Programs: Geology
Enrollment (2018): A: 2 (2)
Professor:
Michael Phillips, (M), S Illinois, 1990, GgeGm

Kaskaskia College

Life and Physical Sciences Dept (A) (2015)
27210 College Road
Centralia, IL 62801
pvig@kaskaskia.edu
http://www.kaskaskia.edu/LPDept/
Instructor:
Pradeep K. Vig, Gg

Lincoln Land Community College

Math and Sciences (A) (2015)
Springfield, IL 62794-9256
p. (217) 786-4923
dean.butzow@llcc.edu
http://www.llcc.edu/mtsc/Sciences/tabid/3280/
Enrollment (2006): A: 7 (0)
Professor:
Dean G. Butzow, (M), W Michigan, Zy
Instructor:
Samantha Reif, (M), Michigan Tech, Gg

McHenry County College

Earth Science and Geography (A) (2021)
8900 US Hwy 14
Crystal Lake, IL 60012
p. (815) 455-3700
kkramer@mchenry.edu
http://www.mchenry.edu/EarthScience
Instructor:
Theodore Erski, (M), Akron, 1995, ZgEg
Paul Hamill, (M), Wisconsin, AmZg
Kate Kramer, (M), Indiana-Purdue, 2008, GgZg

Moraine Valley Community College

Physical Sciences Dept (A) ☒ (2020)
9000 W. College Pwky
Palos Hills, IL 60465-2478
p. 708-974-5615
syrup@morainevalley.edu
Professor:
Krista A. Syrup, (M), W Michigan, 2002, Cs

Northeastern Illinois University

Dept of Earth Science (B) ●⊘ (2018)
5500 N. St. Louis Avenue
Chicago, IL 60625
p. (773) 442-6050
E-Head@neiu.edu
https://www.neiu.edu/academics/college-of-arts-and-sciences/departments/earth-science
f: https://www.facebook.com/neiuearthscience/
Programs: Earth Science (B)
Administrative Assistant: Lidia Costea
Enrollment (2018): B: 28 (6)
Professor:
Laura L. Sanders, (D), Kent State, 1986, HwGe
Associate Professor:
Elisabet M. Head, (D), GvZrCg
Kenneth M. Voglesonger, (D), Arizona State, 2004, ClGe
Assistant Professor:
Nadja Insel, (D), Michigan, 2011, Gt
Instructor:
Mohammad Fariduddin, (D), N Illinois, 1999, Pe
Rebekah Fitchett, (M), Illinois (Chicago), 2006, GgCg
Jean M. Hemzacek Laukant, (M), N Illinois, 1986, Sc

Northern Illinois University

Dept of Geology and Environmental Geosciences (B,M,D)
○ (2020)
1425 W. Lincoln Hwy
De Kalb, IL 60115-2854
p. (815) 753-1943
askgeology@niu.edu
http://www.niu.edu/geology/
f: https://www.facebook.com/NIU-Geology-and-Environmental-Geosciences-346654145320/?ref=aymt_homepage_panel&eid

=ARAaKxUV4veRGbvNDUVXDD7c6lp2k-JCEuQQs-CNdgA7Y zlE4mAD9EaJKJTiNmFLcJa019c_6zO2seUZ
Programs: B.S. Geology and Environmental Geosciences High School Teacher Licensure in Earth and Space Science Education, M.S. Geology and Environmental Geosciences, Ph.D. Geology and Environmental Geosciences
Administrative Assistant: Lesslie Erickson, Patricia Liberty-Baczek
Enrollment (2020): B: 33 (11) M: 15 (9) D: 6 (0)

Graduate Program Director:
Mark R. Frank, (D), Maryland, 2001, Cp
Chair:
Mark P. Fischer, (D), Penn State, 1994, GcoHy
Professor:
Philip J. Carpenter, (D), New Mexico Tech, 1984, YgHwNg
Melissa E. Lenczewski, (D), Tennessee, 2001, HwGeCo
Ross D. Powell, (D), Ohio State, 1980, GslZc
Reed P. Scherer, (D), Ohio State, 1991, Pm
Associate Professor:
Justin P. Dodd, (D), New Mexico, 2011, Cs
Nicole D. LaDue, (D), Michigan State, 2013, Ze
Nathan D. Stansell, (D), Pittsburg State, 2009, Gl
Assistant Professor:
Megan R.M. Brown, (D), Colorado, 2020, HwRw
Research Associate:
Anna Buczynska, (D), Antwerp (Belgium), 2014, Csa
Guillaume Girard, (D), McGill, 2009, GviCu
Adjunct Professor:
B. Brandon Curry, (D), Illinois, 1995, GelPs
Virginia Naples, (D), Massachusetts, 1980, Pv
Karen Samonds, (D), SUNY (Stony Brook), 2006, Pv
Laboratory Manager:
Joshua Schwartz, (B)

Northwestern University

Earth and Planetary Sciences (B,D) ● ☒ (2021)
2145 Sheridan Rd - TECH-F374
Evanston, IL 60208-3130
p. (847) 491-3238
earth@northwestern.edu
http://www.earth.northwestern.edu/
t: @NU_EARTHSCI
Programs: Earth and Planetary Sciences (B)
Administrative Assistant: Lisa J. Collins
Enrollment (2020): B: 0 (12) D: 25 (3)

Professor:
Matthew T. Hurtgen, (D), Penn State, 2003, GsPgGr
Director of the Environmental Sciences Program:
Andrew D. Jacobson, (D), Michigan, 2001, ClPeCa
Director of Graduate Studies:
Suzan van der Lee, (D), Princeton, 1996, YsxYg
Director of Graduate Admissions:
Steven D. Jacobsen, (D), Colorado, 2001, GyzZm
Professor:
Craig R. Bina, (D), Northwestern, 1987, YgZmGy
Neal E. Blair, (D), Stanford, 1980, CoSbOc
Donna M. Jurdy, (D), Michigan, 1974, YgXyg
Bradley B. Sageman, (D), Colorado, 1991, PsCbPc
Seth Stein, (D), Caltech, 1978, YsdYg
Associate Professor:
Yarrow L. Axford, (D), Colorado, 2007, GnPmi
Assistant Professor:
Daniel E. Horton, (D), Michigan, 2011, AsPeZn
Magdalena Osburn, (D), Caltech, 2013, PoCbs
Radiogenic Lab Manager:
Meagan Ankney, (D), CcqCa
IRMS Lab Manager:
Andrew Masterson, (D), CslCa
Research Associate:
Mitchell Barklage, (D), YgeYs
Director of Undergraduate Studies, Assistant Chair, Assistant Prof. of Instruction:
Patricia A. Beddows, (D), Bristol, 2004, HyGma
Adjunct Professor:
Gilbert Klapper, (D), Iowa, 1962, Pm
Emeritus:
Abraham Lerman, (D), Harvard, 1964, CgGnCm
Emile A. Okal, (D), Caltech, 1978, YsgYr

Oakton Community College

Earth Science (A) ☒ (2019)
1600 E. Golf Road
Des Plaines, IL 60016
p. (847) 376-7042
clandrie@oakton.edu
http://www.oakton.edu/academics/academic_departments/earth_science/

Chair:
Chad Landrie, (D), Illinois (Chicago)
Lecturer:
Richard DiMaio, (M), N Illinois
David LoBue, (M), Kansas
William Tong, (M), NE Illinois
Raymond Wiggers, (B), Purdue
Julie Wulff, (D), Ohio State

Olivet Nazarene University

Dept of Chemistry and Geosciences (B) ☒ (2019)
One University Avenue
Bourbonnais, IL 60914
p. (815) 939-5394
ccarriga@olivet.edu
http://geology.olivet.edu/
f: https://www.facebook.com/pages/Olivet-Nazarene-University-Geosciences/50458842809
Programs: Geology (B.S.), Earth and Space Science (B.A.), Science Education (B.S.), Geography (B.A.), Environmental Science (B.S.).
Enrollment (2018): B: 14 (4)

Acting Director:
Charles W. Carrigan, (D), Michigan, 2005, GzCgGc
Director, Strickler Planetarium:
Stephen Case, (D), Notre Dame, 2014, RhXg
Emeritus:
Max W. Reams, (D), Washington (St Louis), 1968, GsmPg

Prarie State College

Dept of Physical Science, Earth Science Discipline (A) ☒ (2019)
202 S. Halsted St
Chicago Heights, IL 60411
p. (708) 709-3674
lburrough@prairiestate.edu
https://prairiestate.edu/academics/academic-programs/natural-sciences/physical-scienceearth-sciencegeology.aspx
Programs: Associates in Science

Principia College

Biology and Natural Resources Department (B) ☒ (2018)
1 Maybeck Place
Elsah, IL 62028
scott.eckert@principia.edu
http://www.principiacollege.edu/biology-env-studies

Chair:
Scott Eckert, (D), Georgia
Professor:
Greg Bruland, (D), Duke
Christine McAllister, (D), St Louis
Instructor:
John Lovseth, (D), S Illinois, 2018, Zni

Richard J. Daley Community College

Physical Sciences (2015)
7500 South Pulaski Rd
Chciago, IL 60652
p. (773) 838-7636
efuoco@ccc.edu
http://daley.ccc.edu/

Richland Community College

Richland Community College (2015)
One College Park
Decatur, IL 62521
p. (217) 875-7211

jsmith@richland.edu
http://www.richland.edu/

Rock Valley College

Rock Valley College (2015)
3301 North Mulford Road
Rockford, IL 61114
M.Kelley@RockValleyCollege.edu
http://ednet.rockvalleycollege.edu/

Sauk Valley Community College

Earth Science (2015)
173 IL Rt. 2
Dixon, IL 61021
therese.l.wood@svcc.edu
http://www.svcc.edu

South Suburban College

Dept of Physical Science (2015)
15800 South State Street
South Holland, IL 60473
p. (708) 596-2000 x2417
ahelwig@ssc.edu
http://www.ssc.edu

Southern Illinois University Carbondale

Geology Programs (B,M,D) O☒ (2020)
1259 Lincoln Drive, Mailcode 4324
Parkinson 102
Carbondale, IL 62901
p. (618) 453-3351
geology@geo.siu.edu
http://www.geology.siu.edu/
f: https://www.facebook.com/Geology-at-Southern-Illinois-University-191268227586004/
Programs: BA Geology, BS Geology, MA Geology, MS Geology, PhD Geosciences
Administrative Assistant: Dana Wise
Enrollment (2018): B: 30 (14) M: 22 (9) D: 8 (1)

Director:
Justin Schoof, (D), Indiana, 2004

Professor:
Ken B. Anderson, (D), Melbourne (Australia), 1989, Co
Scott E. Ishman, (D), Ohio State, 1990, Pmc
Susan M. Rimmer, (D), Penn State, 1985, EcCgGo
John L. Sexton, (D), Indiana, 1974, Ye

Associate Professor:
James A. Conder, (D), Brown, 2001, Ysr
Steven P. Esling, (D), Iowa, 1983, HwGl
Liliana Lefticariu, (D), N Illinois, 2004, CsbGe
Sally Potter-McIntyre, (D), Utah, 2013, Gs

Assistant Professor:
Harvey Henson, (M), S Illinois, 1989, Yg
Daniel R. Hummer, (D), Penn State, 2010, GzyCu

Research Associate:
William Huggett, (M), S Illinois, 1981, Ec

Emeritus:
Richard Fifarek, (D), Oregon State, 1985, Em
Charles O. Frank, (D), Syracuse, 1973, Gx
Stanley E. Harris, Jr., (D), Iowa, 1947, Ge
John E. Marzolf, (D), California (Los Angeles), 1970, Gs
Paul D. Robinson, (M), S Illinois, 1963, Gz
Jay Zimmerman, Jr., (D), Princeton, 1968, Gc

Southwestern Illinois College - Belleville Campus

Dept of Earth Science (2015)
2500 Carlyle Avenue
Belleville, IL 62221
p. (618) 235-2700
http://www.swic.edu

Southwestern Illinois College - Sam Wolf Granite City Campus

Physical Science (A) (2015)
4950 Maryville Road
Granite City, IL 62040
p. (618) 235-2700
http://www.swic.edu

Professor:
Joy Branlund, (D), Washington (St Louis), 2008, Zg

Triton College

Triton College (2015)
2000 Fifth Ave.
River Grove, IL 60171
p. (708) 456-0300
austinweinstock@triton.edu
http://www.triton.edu

University of Chicago

Dept of the Geophysical Sciences (B,M,D) ☒ (2019)
5734 S. Ellis Avenue
Chicago, IL 60637
p. (773) 702-8101
info@geosci.uchicago.edu
http://geosci.uchicago.edu
Enrollment (2009): B: 20 (9) D: 31 (4)

Professor:
David Archer, (D), Washington, 1990, Yr
Andrew Davis, (D), Yale, 1977, Xc
Michael J. Foote, (D), Chicago, 1989, Pg
John E. Frederick, (D), Colorado, 1975, As
David Jablonski, (D), Yale, 1979, Pi
Susan M. Kidwell, (D), Yale, 1982, GsPe
Douglas R. MacAyeal, (D), Princeton, 1983, Yr
Frank M. Richter, (D), Chicago, 1972, Gt
David B. Rowley, (D), SUNY (Albany), 1983, GtgGc

Associate Professor:
Dion L. Heinz, (D), California (Berkeley), 1986, GyzYx
Noboru Nakamura, (D), Princeton, 1989, As

Assistant Professor:
Fred Ciesla, (D), Arizona, 2003, Xcg
Nicolas Dauphas, (D), Ctr Pétro et Géochimiques, 2002, Xc
Elisabeth Moyer, (D), Caltech, 2001, As
Mark Webster, (D), California (Riverside), 2003, Pi

Emeritus:
Alfred T. Anderson, Jr., (D), Princeton, 1963, Gv
Robert N. Clayton, (D), Caltech, 1955, Cs
Ramesh C. Srivastava, (D), McGill, 1964, AsmAm

Student Services Administrator:
Sarah Lippert, Zn

University of Illinois at Chicago

Dept of Earth and Environmental Sciences (B,M,D) ⃠ (2020)
845 W. Taylor Street
2440 SES
MC 186
Chicago, IL 60607-7059
p. (312) 996-3155
klnagy@uic.edu
http://eaes.uic.edu/
Programs: Earth and Environmental Sciences
Enrollment (2020): B: 100 (17) M: 5 (1) D: 14 (1)

Head:
Kathryn L. Nagy, (D), Texas A&M, 1988, Cg

Professor:
Andrew J. Dombard, (D), Washington (St Louis), 2000, Xy
Fabien Kenig, (D), Orleans (France), 1991, CobOo
Carol A. Stein, (D), Columbia, 1984, Yg

Associate Professor:
Max Berkelhammer, (D), S California, 2010, Cg
DArcy Meyer Dombard, (D), Washington (St Louis), 2004, Pg

Assistant Professor:
Gavin McNicol, (D), California (Berkeley), 2016, Cg
Kimberly Van Meter, (D), Waterloo, 2017, Hs

Adjunct Assistant Professor:
Andrew King, (D), California (San Diego), 2008, Og

Adjunct Professor:
Peter T. Doran, (D), Nevada (Reno), 1996, HswAm
Paul Fenter, (D), Pennsylvania, 1990, Gy
Barry Lesht, (D), Chicago, 1977, Op
Eugene Yan, (D), Ohio State, 1998, Hg
Visiting Assistant Professor:
Andrew Malone, (D), Chicago, 2017, GlAt
Emeritus:
Jean E. Bogner, (D), N Illinois, 1996, ClSbHy
Martin F.J Flower, (D), Manchester (UK), 1971, GiCuGt
Stephen J. Guggenheim, (D), Wisconsin, 1976, Gz
August F. Koster Van Groos, (D), Leiden (Neth), 1966, Cp
Roy E. Plotnick, (D), Chicago, 1983, PgiGq
Kelvin S. Rodolfo, (D), S California, 1967, GueGs
Clinical Associate Professor:
Stefany Sit, (D), Miami, 2013, Ygs
Office Support Specialist:
Minnie O. Jones, Zn
Coordinator of Undergrad Labs:
Lee Falkena, (M), Iowa, 2012, ZeGig
Asst to the Head/Business Manager:
Edna L. Fuentes, (B), Illinois (Chicago), 2004, Zn

University of Illinois, Urbana-Champaign

Dept of Atmospheric Sciences (B,M,D) ●⦸ (2020)
Nat Hist Bldg, Rm 3081, MC-104
1301 W Green Street
Urbana, IL 61801
p. (217) 333-2046
atmos-sci@illinois.edu
http://www.atmos.illinois.edu
f: https://www.facebook.com/dasuiuc/
Programs: Atmospheric Sciences
Administrative Assistant: Tammy R. Warf
Enrollment (2018): B: 71 (17) M: 12 (10) D: 34 (8)
Director:
Robert M. Rauber, (D), Colorado State, 1985, As
Head:
Robert J. Trapp, (D), Oklahoma, 1994, As
Professor:
Larry Di Girolamo, (D), McGill, 1996, Zr
Atul K. Jain, (D), India, 1988, As
Sonia Lasher-Trapp, (D), Oklahoma, 1998, As
Donald J. Wuebbles, (D), California (Davis), 1983, As
Associate Professor:
Francina Dominguez, (D), Illinois, 2007, AsHg
Stephen W. Nesbitt, (D), Utah, 2003, As
Nicole Riemer, (D), Karlsruhe, 2002, As
Zhuo Wang, (D), Hawaii, 2004, As
Assistant Professor:
Deanna A. Hence, (D), Washington, 2011, AsmAp
Cristian (Cristi) Proistosescu, (D), Harvard, 2017, AsGgAp
Ryan Sriver, (D), Purdue, 2008, As
Research Scientist:
Brian Jewett, (D), Illinois, 1996, As
Advisor:
Jessica (Jessie) Choate, (M), Illinois, 2016, Asm
Lecturer:
Donna J. Charlevoix, (M), California (Davis), 1996, As
Emeritus:
Kenneth V. Beard, (D), California (Los Angeles), 1970, As
Mankin Mak, (D), MIT, 1968, As
Walter A. Robinson, (D), Columbia, 1985, As
Robert B. Wilhelmson, (D), Illinois, 1972, As
Teaching Asst Professor:
Alicia Klees, (D), Penn State, 2020, As
Office Manager:
Joe Jeffries, (B)
Clinical Assistant Professor:
Jeffrey Frame, (D), Penn State, 2008, Asm

Dept of Geology (B,M,D) ● (2020)
1301 W Green Street
3081 Natural History Building
Urbana, IL 61801
p. (217) 333-3540
geology@illinois.edu
http://www.geology.illinois.edu
Programs: Geology (B, M, D); Geology and Geophysics (B); Earth Science Teaching (B)
Enrollment (2019): B: 50 (29) M: 2 (2) D: 36 (2)
Threet Professor:
James L. Best, (D), London (UK), 1985, Gs
Johnson Professor:
Gary Parker, (D), Minnesota, 1974, Gm
Head:
Thomas M. Johnson, (D), California (Berkeley), 1995, HwCls
Affiliate Faculty:
Stanley Ambrose, (D), California (Santa Barbara)
Kenneth T. Christensen, (D), Illinois
Marcelo H. Garcia, (D), Minnesota, 1989, Gmu
Bruce Rhoads, (D), Arizona, Gm
Charles J. Werth, (D), Stanford
Professor:
Bruce W. Fouke, (D), SUNY (Stony Brook), 1993, GsdGb
Craig C. Lundstrom, (D), California (Santa Cruz), 1996, Cpg
Gillen D. Wood, (D), Columbia, 2000, Zc
Associate Head:
Stephen P. Altaner, (D), Illinois, 1985, Gz
Affiliate Faculty:
Scott Olson, (D), Illinois
Associate Professor:
Alison M. Anders, (D), Washington, 2005, Gm
Jessica Conroy, (D), Arizona, 2011, Cs
Patricia Gregg, (D), MIT/WHOI, 2008, YgCg
Lijun Liu, (D), Caltech, 2010, YgGtm
Wendy Yang, (D), California (Berkeley), 2010
Affiliate Faculty:
Surangi W. Punyasena, (D), Chicago, 2007, PblPe
Assistant Professor:
Jennifer Druhan, (D), California (Berkeley), 2012, HwCs
Willy Guenthner, (D), Arizona, 2013, GtzCg
Cristian Proistosescu, (D), Harvard, 2017
Lecturer:
Max L. Christie, (D), Penn State, 2017, PgGr
Adjunct Professor:
Ercan Alp, (D), S Illinois, 1984
Kurtis Burmeister, (D), Illinois, 2005
Brandon Curry, Illinois, 1995
Przemyslaw Dera, (D), Mickiewicz (Poland), 2000
Robert J. Finley, (D), South Carolina, 1975, Go
Leon R. Follmer, (D), Illinois, 1970, SaGlm
Hannes E. Leetaru, (D), Illinois, 1997, GoYe
Morris W. Leighton, (D), Chicago, 1951, Eo
M. Scott Wilkerson, (D), Illinois, 1991, Gc
Walgreen Chair Emeritus Professor:
Susan W. Kieffer, (D), Caltech, 1971, Gv
Grim Professor:
Jay D. Bass, (D), SUNY (Stony Brook), 1982, Gy
Feng-Sheng Hu, (D), Washington, 1994, Pe
Grim Emeritus Professor:
Craig M. Bethke, (D), Illinois, 1984, Hw
Emeritus:
Thomas F. Anderson, (D), Columbia, 1967, CslCm
Daniel B. Blake, (D), California (Berkeley), 1966, Pi
Chu-Yung Chen, (D), MIT, 1983, Cg
Wang-Ping Chen, (D), MIT, 1979, YsGt
Donald L. Graf, (D), Columbia, 1950, Cl
Stephen Marshak, (D), Columbia, 1983, Gct
Alberto S. Nieto, (D), Illinois, 1974, Ng
Philip A. Sandberg, (D), Stockholm, 1965, Gd
Xiaodong Song, (D), Caltech, 1994, Ys
Teaching Specialist:
Ann D. Long, (M), Leeds (UK), 1981, Gm
Teaching Assistant Professor:
J. Cory Pettijohn, (D), Boston, 2008, Hg
Research Scientist:
Jonathan H. Tomkin, (D), Australian Nat, 2002, Gm
Research Associate Professor:
Robert A. Sanford, (D), Michigan State, 1996, CbSbPo
Clinical Associate Professor:
Michael A. Stewart, (D), Duke, 2000, Gi

Dept of Natural Resources & Environmental Sciences
(B,M,D) (2015)
W-503 Turner Hall
1102 South Goodwin Avenue

Urbana, IL 61801-4798
p. (217) 333-2770
g-rolfe@uiuc.edu
http://nres.illinois.edu/
Chair:
Jeffrey Brawn
Professor:
Charles W. Boast, (D), Iowa State, 1970, Sp
Mark B. David, (D), New York, 1983, Sf
John J. Hassett, (D), Utah State, 1970, Sc
Robert L. Jones, (D), Illinois, 1962, Sc
Richard L. Mulvaney, (D), Illinois, 1983, Sc
Theodore R. Peck, (D), Wisconsin, 1962, Sc
Joseph W. Stucki, (D), Purdue, 1975, Sc
Associate Professor:
Robert G. Darmody, (D), Maryland, 1980, Sd
Timothy R. Ellsworth, (D), California, 1989, Sp
Kenneth R. Olson, (D), Cornell, 1983, Sc
F. William Simmons, (D), North Carolina State, 1987, Sp
Assistant Professor:
Robert J. M. Hudson, (D), MIT, 1989, Cg
Gregory F. McIsaac, (D), Illinois, 1994, Hs

Waubonsee Community College

Earth Sciences (A) (2020)
Rt. 47 at Waubonsee Dr.
Sugar Grove, IL 60554
p. (630) 466-2783
dvoorhees@waubonsee.edu
https://www.waubonsee.edu/programs-courses/programs-subject/science-technology-engineering-and-mathematics/earth-science
Programs: Geology (A)
Certificates: GIS
Enrollment (2019): A: 5 (2)
Professor:
David H. Voorhees, (M), Rensselaer, 1982, ZgGg
Associate Professor:
Karl Schulze, (M), Texas A&M, 2003, ZgAms
Assistant Professor:
Alfred W. Weiss, (M), S Illinois, 2000, Ziy

Western Illinois University

Department of Geography, Geographic Information Science and Meteorology (2015)
Macomb, IL 61455
p. (309) 298-1648
s-thompson@wiu.edu
http://www.wiu.edu/cas/geography/

Dept of Geology (B) O (2018)
1 University Circle
Macomb, IL 61455
p. (309) 298-1151
geology@wiu.edu
http://www.wiu.edu/cas/geology/
Programs: Geology; Paleontology
Administrative Assistant: Cerese Wright
Enrollment (2017): B: 16 (0)
Professor:
Kyle R. Mayborn, (D), California (Davis), 2000, Gic
Leslie A. Melim, (D), S Methodist, 1991, Gd
Associate Professor:
Steven W. Bennett, (D), Indiana, 1994, Hw
Assistant Professor:
Thomas A. Hegna, (D), Yale, 2012, PigPg
Instructor:
Sara Bennett, (M), Indiana, Gg
Emeritus:
Jack B. Bailey, (D), Illinois, 1975, Pg
Peter L. Calengas, (D), Indiana, 1977, En

Wheaton College

Dept of Geology & Environmental Science (B) ☒ (2019)
501 E. College Ave.
Wheaton, IL 60187
p. (630) 752-5063
geology@wheaton.edu
http://www.wheaton.edu/geology/
Enrollment (2018): B: 20 (6)
Chair:
Stephen O. Moshier, (D), Louisiana State, 1986, Gd
Professor:
Chris Keil, (D), Illinois (Chicago), 1994, Rm
Assistant Professor:
Andrew J. Luhmann, (D), Minnesota, 2011, HwGmCl
Kathryn A. Maneiro, (D), Boston, 2016, CcGic
Instructor:
Lisa Heidlauf, (M), Illinois (Urbana), 1986, Gg
Visiting Professor:
Gilles V. Tagne, (M), Rennes I, 2013, HwZiGe
Emeritus:
James A. Clark, (D), Colorado, 1977, GmYgZi
Jeffrey K. Greenberg, (D), N Carolina, 1978, GicGe

Indiana

Ball State University

Dept of Geography (2015)
Muncie, IN 47306
p. 765-285-1776
turk@bsu.edu
https://www.bsu.edu/academics/collegesanddepartments/geography

Ball State University

Dept of Geology (B,M,D) O (2016)
2000 University Avenue
AR117
Muncie, IN 47306
p. (765) 285-8270
geology@bsu.edu
http://www.bsu.edu/geology
Administrative Assistant: Brenda J. Rathel
Enrollment (2016): B: 47 (8) M: 14 (4) D: 4 (0)
Chair:
Richard H. Fluegeman, (D), Cincinnati, 1987, PmGro
Associate Dean:
Jeffry D. Grigsby, (D), Cincinnati, 1989, GdClGo
Professor:
Kirsten N. Nicholson, (D), Joseph Fourier, 1999, Gi
R. Scott Rice-Snow, (D), Penn State, 1983, Gm
Associate Professor:
Carolyn B. Dowling, (D), Rochester, 2002, HgGeCg
Klaus Neumann, (D), Alabama, 1999, Cl
Assistant Professor:
Shawn J. Malone, (D), Iowa, 2012, GtxGm
Emeritus:
Alan C. Samuelson, (D), Penn State, 1972, Hw
Technician, Environmental Science:
Eric Lange, (M), Ball State, 2014, Cg
Geological Tech:
Michael Kutis, (B), Wisconsin (Platteville), 1989, Gg

College of the Holy Cross

Dept of Geosciences (A,B) ☒ (2018)
P.O. Box 308
Notre Dame, IN 46556
p. (219) 239-8417
smitchel@holycross.edu

DePauw University

Dept of Geosciences (B) ● ☒ (2020)
2 East Hanna Street
Julian Science Center
Greencastle, IN 46135
p. (765) 658-4654
mswilke@depauw.edu
https://www.depauw.edu/academics/departments-programs/geosciences/
f: https://www.facebook.com/DePauwGeosciences/
t: https://twitter.com/depauwgeo
Programs: Geology, Environmental Geoscience, Earth Science
Administrative Assistant: Rachel Curtis

Enrollment (2020): B: 16 (13)
Professor:
Tim D. Cope, (D), Stanford, 2003, GsZiGr
M. Scott Wilkerson, (D), Illinois, 1991, GctZi
Term Professor :
Kenneth L. Brown, (D), Miami (Ohio), 2015, GizGe
Emeritus:
James G. Mills, (D), Michigan State, 1991, Gi
Frederick M. Soster, (D), Case Western, 1984, Gs
Cooperating Faculty:
Jeanette K. Pope, (D), Virginia Tech, 2002, Ge

Earlham College

Geology Dept (B) ☒ (2017)
801 National Road West
Richmond, IN 47374-4095
p. (765) 983-1429
streeme@earlham.edu
http://www.earlham.edu/geology/
Programs: Geology
Enrollment (2017): B: 14 (4)
Associate Professor:
Cynthia M. Fadem, (D), Washington (St Louis), 2009, GaSoCs
Andrew Moore, (D), Washington, 1999, Gm
Meg Streepey Smith, (D), Michigan, 2001, Gt
Emeritus:
Jon W. Branstrator, (D), Cincinnati, 1975, Pg

Hanover College

Dept of Geology (B) (2015)
PO Box 890
Hanover, IN 47243-0890
p. (812) 866-7306
worcestr@hanover.edu
Enrollment (2007): B: 12 (5)
Chair:
Peter A. Worcester, (D), Miami (Ohio), 1976, Gi
Professor:
Kenneth A. Bevis, (D), Oregon State, 1995, GlmGe
Heyo Van Iten, (D), Michigan, 1989, PgHgRn
Emeritus:
Stanley M. Totten, (D), Illinois, 1962, Gl

Indiana State University

Dept of Earth and Environmental Systems (B,M,D) ☒ (2020)
159 Science Building
Terre Haute, IN 47809
p. (812) 237-2444
isu-ees@mail.indstate.edu
https://www.indstate.edu/cas/ees
f: www.facebook.com/isu.ees
Enrollment (2009): B: 87 (13) M: 16 (7) D: 6 (2)
Professor:
Gregory Bierly, (D), Michigan State, Asm
Sandra S. Brake, (D), Colorado Mines, 1989, GeEm
Jennifer C. Latimer, (D), Indiana, 2004, CmGeb
Shawn Phillips, (D), New York, 2001
James Speer, (D), Tennessee, 2001, PeZyGe
Qihao Weng, (D), Georgia, Zru
Associate Professor:
Susan Berta, (D), Oklahoma, 1986, GmZr
Kathleen M. Heath, (D), Utah, 2001, Pb
Nancy J. Obermeyer, (D), Chicago, 1987, Zi
Emeritus:
William Dando, (D)
Prodip K. Dutta, (D), Indiana, 1983, Gs
C. Russell Stafford, (D), Arizona State, 1981, Gam

Indiana University - Purdue University Indianapolis

Dept of Earth Sciences (B,M,D) ● (2020)
723 West Michigan Street
Indianapolis, IN 46202-5132
p. (317) 274-7484
geology@iupui.edu
https://science.iupui.edu/earthsciences
Programs: Geology
Environmental Science
Professor:
Andrew P. Barth, (D), S California, 1989, Gi
Gabriel M. Filippelli, (D), California (Santa Cruz), 1994, CmGb
Pierre-Andre Jacinthe, (D), Ohio State, 1995, Cl
Lin Li, (D), Brown, 2002, ZrXgZg
Kathy J. Licht, (D), Colorado, 1999, Gl
Associate Professor:
Broxton Bird, (D), Pittsburgh, 2009, Gmn
Greg Druschel, (D), Wisconsin, 2002, Cl
William Gilhooly, (D), Virginia, 2006, ClOc
Lixin Wang, (D), Virginia, 2008, HyCl
Assistant Professor:
Catherine Macris, (D), California, 2012, GzCu
Lecturer:
Anna Jessee, (D), Indiana, 2017, GgYg
Jennifer Nelson, (M), Indiana, 2006, Gg
Thomas Rossbach, (D), N Carolina, 1992, GgPg

Indiana University Northwest

Dept of Geosciences (A,B) (2019)
3400 Broadway
Gary, IN 46408
p. (219) 980-6738
zkilibar@iun.edu
https://www.iun.edu/geosciences
Programs: Geology (B); Environmental Science (B)
Enrollment (2017): B: 21 (3)
Chair:
Zoran Kilibarda, (D), Nebraska, 1994, GsmGd
Associate Professor:
Erin Argyilan, (D), Illinois (Chicago), 2004, GeHwAm
Kristin Huysken, (D), Michigan State, 1996, GizGc
Emeritus:
Robert Votaw, (D), PiGrs

Indiana University, Bloomington

Dept of Earth and Atmospheric Sciences (B,M,D) O (2020)
1001 E. Tenth Street
Bloomington, IN 47405
p. (812) 855-5582
geoinfo@indiana.edu
https://earth.indiana.edu/
Programs: Earth Sciences, Atmospheric Sciences, Environmental Geoscience, Environmental Sciences
Certificates: Atmospheric Sciences
Enrollment (2020): B: 51 (10) M: 15 (5) D: 27 (6)
Chair:
P. David Polly, (D), California (Berkeley), 1993, PvgPq
Professor:
Simon C. Brassell, (D), Bristol, 1980, Cob
Michael W. Hamburger, (D), Cornell, 1986, YsGtv
Claudia C. Johnson, (D), Colorado, 1993, Peg
Kaj Johnson, (D), Stanford, 2004, Yg
Juergen Schieber, (D), Oregon, 1985, Gs
Chen Zhu, (D), Johns Hopkins, 1992, CgHg
Assistant Research Scientist:
Shelby Rader, (D), Arizona, 2018, Ct
Senior Scientist:
Chusi Li, (D), Toronto, 1993, EgGiEm
Arndt Schimmelmann, (D), California (Los Angeles), 1985, CsGsPe
Adjunct Associate Professor:
Michael C. Rygel, (D), Dalhousie, 2005, Gg
Associate Professor:
Douglas A. Edmonds, (D), Penn State, 2009, Gsm
Chanh Q. Kieu, (D), Maryland, 2008, As
Jackson K. Njau, (D), Rutgers, 2006, Pv
Brian Yanites, (D), Colorado, 2009, Gm
Associate Scientist:
Edward W. Herrmann, (D), Indiana, 2013, Sa
Jessica Miller-Camp, (D), Iowa, 2015, Pv
Peter Sauer, (D), Colorado, 1997, Pe
Adjunct Associate Professor:
Adam V. Maltese, (D), Virginia, 2008, Ze
Adjunct Assistant Professor:
Page Quinton, (D), Missouri, 2016, Pc
Adam Ward, (D), Penn State, 2011, Hs

Assistant Professor:
Ben Kravitz, (D), Rutgers, 2011, At
Travis O'Brien, (D), California (Santa Cruz), 2011, As
Paul W. Staten, (D), Utah, 2013, As
Andrea L. Stevens-Goddard, (D), Arizona, 2017, Cc
Adjunct Research Scientist:
Jose Luis Antinao-Rojas, (D), Dalhousie, 2009
Lee Florea, (D), S Florida, Hg
Maria D. Mastalerz, (D), Silesian Tech, 1988, Ec
Patrick McLaughlin, (D), Cincinnati, 2006, Ps
Tara M. Smiley, (D), Michigan, 2016, Pe
Todd Thompson, (D), Indiana, 1987, Gg
Senior Lecturer:
Bruce Douglas, (D), Princeton, 1983, Gcg
Erika R. Elswick, (D), Cincinnati, 1998, Cl
Cody Kirkpatrick, (D), Alabama (Huntsville), 2010, As
Emeritus:
Abhijit Basu, (D), Indiana, 1975, Gd
David L. Bish, (D), Penn State, 1977, Gz
James G. Brophy, (D), Johns Hopkins, 1984, Gi
Jeremy D. Dunning, (D), N Carolina, 1978, Yg
Enrique Merino, (D), California (Berkeley), 1973, Cl
Greg A. Olyphant, (D), Iowa, 1979, Hw
Gary L. Pavlis, (D), Washington, 1982, YsGtYe
Lisa M. Pratt, (D), Princeton, 1981, Co
Lee J. Suttner, (D), Wisconsin, 1966, Gd
Robert P. Wintsch, (D), Brown, 1975, GpcGt

School of Public & Environmental Affairs (B,M,D) (2015)
SPEA Building
Bloomington, IN 47408
p. (812) 855-7485
troyer@indiana.edu
http://www.spea.indiana.edu/home/
Geology Librarian:
Christina Sheley, Zn
Chair:
Philip S. Stevens, (D), Harvard, 1990, As
Professor:
Ronald A. Hites, (D), MIT, 1968, Co
Jeffrey R. White, (D), Syracuse, 1984, Hg
Associate Professor:
Diane S. Henshel, (D), Washington, 1987, Zn
Todd Royer, (D), Idaho State, 1999, HsZg
Assistant Professor:
Vicky J. Meretsky, (D), Arizona, 1995, Sf
Flynn W. Picardal, (D), Arizona, 1992, So
Lecturer:
Melissa Clark, (M), Indiana, 1999, SfZg

Indiana University, Indianapolis

Dept of Geography (A,B) (2015)
213 Cavanaugh Hall
Indianapolis, IN 46202
p. (317) 274-8877
tbrother@iupui.edu
http://www.iupui.edu/~geogdept/
Chair:
Jeffey S. Wilson, (D), Indiana State, 1998, Zy
Professor:
F. L. Bein, (D), Florida, 1974, Zy
Associate Professor:
Timothy S. Brothers, (D), California (Los Angeles), 1985, Zy
Catherine J. Souch, (D), British Columbia, 1990, Gm

Purdue University

Dept of Earth, Atmospheric, and Planetary Sciences (B,M,D) (2017)
550 Stadium Mall Drive
West Lafayette, IN 47907-2051
p. (765) 494-3258
eas-info@purdue.edu
http://www.eaps.purdue.edu
Enrollment (2014): M: 13 (13) D: 58 (6)
Department Head:
Indrajeet Chaubey, (D), Oklahoma State, 1997, Hg
University Distinguished Professor:
H. Jay Melosh, (D), Caltech, 1972, XmgXy
Distinguished Professor:
John Cushman, (D), Iowa State, 1978, Sp
Paul B. Shepson, (D), Penn State, 1982, As
Director:
Douglas R. Schmitt, (D), Caltech, 1987, YxNrYe
Associate Department Head:
Darryl E. Granger, (D), California (Berkeley), 1996, As
Harshvardhan, (D), SUNY (Stony Brook), 1976, As
Professor:
Ernest M. Agee, (D), Missouri, 1968, As
Lawrence W. Braile, (D), Utah, 1973, Ys
Maarten de Hoop, (D), Delft (Neth), 1992, Gq
Timothy R. Filley, (D), Penn State, 1997, Co
Andrew M. Freed, (D), Arizona, 1998, Gg
Andrei Gabrielov, (D), Moscow State (Russia), 1973, Ys
Alexander Gluhovsky, (D), USSR Acad of Sci, 1973, As
Jon M. Harbor, (D), Washington, 1990, GmlGe
Robert L. Nowack, (D), MIT, 1985, Ys
James G. Ogg, (D), Scripps, 1981, PsGsYm
Kenneth D. Ridgway, (D), Rochester, 1992, Gs
Daniel P. Shepardson, (D), Iowa, 1990, Ze
Yuch-Ning Shieh, (D), Caltech, 1968, CsGpv
Wen-Yih Sun, (D), Chicago, 1975, AsZoAm
Terry R. West, (D), Purdue, 1966, Ng
Qianlai Zhuang, (D), Alaska (Fairbanks), As
William J. Zinsmeister, (D), California (Riverside), 1974, Ps
Indiana State Climatologist:
Dev Niyogi, (D), North Carolina State, 2000, As
Associate Professor:
Chris Andronicos, (D), Princeton, 1999, Gg
Michael Baldwin, (D), Oklahoma, 2003, As
Lucy M. Flesch, (D), SUNY (Stony Brook), 2002, Yg
Hersh Gilbert, (D), Colorado, 2001, Ys
Nathaniel A. Lifton, (D), Arizona, 1997, GmCc
Greg Michalski, (D), California (San Diego), 2003, CsGeAs
Wen-wen Tung, (D), California (Los Angeles), 2002, As
Assistant Professor:
Julie Elliott, (D), Alaska (Fairbanks), 2011, Yd
Marty Frisbee, (D), New Mexico Tech, 2010, Hws
Saad Haq, (D), SUNY (Stony Brook), 2004, Gt
Briony Horgan, (D), Cornell, 2010, XgZr
David Minton, (D), Arizona, 2009, Xg
Lisa Welp, (D), Caltech, 2006, Cs
Yutian Wu, (D), Columbia, 2011, As
Emeritus:
William J. Hinze, (D), Wisconsin, 1957, YevGt
Arvid M. Johnson, (D), Penn State, 1965, Gc
Gerald H. Krockover, (D), Iowa, 1970, Ze
Darrell I. Leap, (D), Penn State, 1974, Hy
Phillip J. Smith, (D), Wisconsin, 1967, As
Thomas M. Tharp, (D), Wisconsin, 1978, Nm
Dayton G. Vincent, (D), MIT, 1969, As

University of Notre Dame

Dept of Civil & Environmental Engineering & Earth Sciences
(B,M,D) ☒ (2018)
156 Fitzpatrick Hall
Notre Dame, IN 46556
p. (219) 631-5380
ceees@nd.edu
http://www.nd.edu/~ceees
Programs: Environmental Earth Sciences; Environmental Science with a Concentration in Earth Sciences
Certificates: Earth Sciences (minor)
Chair:
Joannes J. Westerink, (D), MIT, 1984, On
Professor:
Peter C. Burns, (D), Manitoba, 1994, Gz
Jeremy B. Fein, (D), Northwestern, 1989, Cl
Joe Fernando, (D), Johns Hopkins, 1983, As
Clive R. Neal, (D), Leeds (UK), 1985, Gi
Associate Professor:
Diogo Bolster, (D), California (San Diego), 2007, Hw
Andrew Kennedy, (D), Monash, 1998, On
Tony Simonetti, (D), Carleton, 1994, Ct
Assistant Professor:
Melissa Berke, (D), Minnesota, 2011, Cs
Alan Hamlet, (D), Washington, 2006, Hs

Amy E. Hixon, (D), Clemson, 2013, ClqCc
Marc Muller, (D), Rw
David Richter, (D), Stanford, 2011, As
Instructor:
Stephanie Simonetti, (D), McGill, 2002, Zn

University of Southern Indiana

Dept of Geology & Physics (B) (2021)
8600 University Boulevard
Evansville, IN 47712
p. (812) 464-1701
wselliott@usi.edu
http://www.usi.edu/science/geology-and-physics/
Programs: Environmental Science; Geology
Administrative Assistant: Kim E.. Schauss
Enrollment (2020): B: 46 (9)
Chair:
William S. Elliott, Jr., (D), Indiana, 2002, GsrCl
Professor:
Joseph A. DiPietro, (D), Oregon State, 1990, GcpGm
Paul K. Doss, (D), N Illinois, 1991, HwGeZu
Associate Professor:
James Durbin, (D), Nebraska, 1999, Gm
Tony Maria, (D), Rhode Island, 2000, Gv
Instructor:
Carrie L. Wright, (M), Wright State, 2006, Ze
Emeritus:
Norman R. King, (D), Indiana, 1973, Gr

Iowa

Cornell College

Dept of Geology (B) ●☒ (2021)
600 First Street SW
Mount Vernon, IA 52314
p. (319) 895-4306
rdenniston@cornellcollege.edu
http://www.cornellcollege.edu/geology
Programs: Geology
Enrollment (2020): B: 15 (10)
Professor:
Rhawn F. Denniston, (D), Iowa, 2000, GeCs
Emily O. Walsh, (D), California (Santa Barbara), 2003, GptCc
Assistant Professor:
Drew Muscente, (D), Virginia Tech, 2017, PgGs

Drake University

Dept of Environmental Science and Policy (B) (2015)
Des Moines, IA 50311
p. (515) 271-2803
thomas.rosburg@drake.edu

Iowa State University of Science & Technology

Dept of Agronomy (B,M,D) (2015)
2101 Agronomy Hall
Ames, IA 50011-1010
p. (515) 294-1360
agron@iastate.edu
http://www.agron.iastate.edu/
Department Secretary: Pam Hinderaker
Director:
Dennis R. Keeney, (D), Iowa, 1965, So
Chair:
Kendall Lamkey, (D), Iowa State, 1985
Professor:
Raymond W. Arritt, (D), Colorado State, 1985, As
Richard E. Carlson, (D), Iowa State, 1971, Am
Richard M. Cruse, (D), Minnesota, 1978, So
V. P. (Bill) Evangelou, (D), California (Davis), 1981, Sc
William J. Gutowski, (D), MIT, 1984, Am
Robert Horton, (D), New Mexico State, 1981, Sp
Douglas L. Karlen, (D), Kansas State, 1978, So
Randy J. Killorn, (D), Idaho, 1983, So
Thomas B. Moorman, (D), Washington State, 1983, So
Jonathan A. Sandor, (D), California (Berkeley), 1983, Sd
Eugene S. Takle, (D), Iowa State, 1971, Asm
Elwynn Taylor, (D), Washington (St Louis), 1970, As
Michael L. Thompson, (D), Ohio State, 1980, Sc
Regis D. Voss, (D), Iowa State, 1962, So
Douglas N. Yarger, (D), Arizona, 1967, As
Associate Professor:
Cynthia Cambardella, (D), Colorado, 1991, So
Thomas A. Kaspar, (D), Iowa State, 1982, So
David A. Laird, (D), Iowa State, 1987, Sc
Antonio W. Mallarino, (D), Iowa State, 1991, So
Assistant Professor:
Lee Burras, (D), Ohio State, 1992, Sd
Larry Halverson, (D), Wisconsin, 1991, So
Stanley J. Henning, (D), Oregon State, 1975, So
Thomas A. Polito, (D), Iowa State, 1987, So
Associate Dean, College of Agriculture:
Gerald A. Miller, (D), Iowa State, 1974, SdoGm
Emeritus:
Thomas E. Loynachan, (D), North Carolina State, 1975, So
Geology Librarian:
Peter A. Peterson, (D), Illinois, 1953, Zn

Dept of Geological & Atmospheric Sciences (B,M,D) O⊘ (2019)
253 Science I
2237 Osborn Drive
Ames, IA 50011-3212
p. (515) 294-4477
geology@iastate.edu
http://www.ge-at.iastate.edu/
f: https://www.facebook.com/ISUgeology
Programs: Geology; Earth Science, Meteorology
Administrative Assistant: DeAnn M. Frisk
Enrollment (2018): B: 136 (43) M: 26 (8) D: 22 (4)
Chair:
Sven S. Morgan, (D), Virginia Tech, 1998, Gc
Professor:
Igor A. Beresnev, (D), USSR Acad of Sci, 1986, YgsYe
Cinzia C. Cervato, (D), ETH (Switzerland), 1990, GgZe
William A. Gallus, (D), Colorado State, 1993, As
William J. Gutowski, (D), MIT, 1984, ZoAtZc
Neal R. Iverson, (D), Minnesota, 1989, Gl
William W. Simpkins, (D), Wisconsin, 1989, HwGlCs
Paul G. Spry, (D), Toronto, 1984, Em
Xiaoqing Wu, (D), California (Los Angeles), 1992, As
Associate Professor:
Kristie Franz, (D), California (Irvine), 2006, Hs
Chris Harding, (D), Houston, 2001, Gq
Alan D. Wanamaker, (D), Maine, 2007, CsPeOg
Assistant Professor:
Beth E. Caissie, (D), Massachusetts, 2012, Pe
Alex Gonzalez, (D), Colorado State, 2015, As
Jacqueline Reber, (D), Oslo, 2012, Gct
Yuyu Zhou, (D), Rhode Island, 2008, Zyi
Senior Lecturer:
James V. Aanstoos, (D), Purdue, 1996, ZrAs
Jane P. Dawson, (D), New Mexico, 1995, Gp
David M. Flory, (M), Iowa State, 2003, AmsZn
Lecturer:
Rachindra Mawalagedara, (D), Nebraska, 2013, As
Aaron R. Wood, (D), Michigan, 2009, PvGrs
Adjunct Professor:
Michael R. Burkart, (D), Iowa, 1976, Hy
Emeritus:
Tsing-Chang Chen, (D), Michigan, 1975, As
Robert Cody, (D), Colorado, 1968, Gz
Carl E. Jacobson, (D), California (Los Angeles), 1980, GtcGp
Karl E. Seifert, (D), Wisconsin, 1963, Ct
Eugene S. Takle, (D), Iowa State, 1971, As
Carl F. Vondra, (D), Nebraska, 1963, Gr
Kenneth E. Windom, (D), Penn State, 1976, Cp
Douglas N. Yarger, (D), Arizona, 1967, As
Lab Equipment Specialist:
Alison Whale, (M), Iowa State, 2018

Scott Community College

Environmental Science (2015)
500 Belmont Road
Bettendorf, IA 52722
p. 563-441-4001

eiccinfo@eicc.edu
http://www.eicc.edu

University of Iowa

Earth & Environmental Sciences (B,M,D) ●⃠ (2021)
115 Trowbridge Hall
123 N. Capitol Street
Iowa City, IA 52242
p. (319) 335-1818
geology@uiowa.edu
http://clas.uiowa.edu/ees/
f: https://www.facebook.com/UIowaGeoscience
Programs: Geoscience, BA, BS, MS, PhD, Environmental Sciences, BA, BS
Administrative Assistant: Angela Bellew
Enrollment (2020): B: 180 (57) M: 16 (3) D: 13 (4)

Chair:
David W. Peate, (D), Open (UK), 1989, GiCa
Professor:
Jonathan M. Adrain, (D), Alberta, 1993, Pi
Christopher A. Brochu, (D), Texas, 1997, Pv
Charles T. Foster Jr., (D), Johns Hopkins, 1975, GptGg
Jane A. Gilotti, (D), Johns Hopkins, 1987, GctGp
William C. McClelland, (D), Arizona, 1990, GtCcGc
Mark K. Reagan, (D), California (Santa Cruz), 1987, Gi
Associate Professor:
Bradley D. Cramer, (D), Ohio State, 2009, GrPsGs
Jeffrey A. Dorale, (D), Minnesota, 2001, CsPc
Emily Finzel, (D), Purdue, 2010, GstEo
Frank H. Weirich, (D), Toronto, 1982, Gm
Assistant Professor:
Jessica R. Meyer, (D), Guelph, 2013, Hw
Lecturer:
Mary Kosloski, (D), Cornell, 2012, Pig
Benjamin Swanson, (D), New Mexico, 2012, Gme
Kate Tierney, (D), Ohio State, 2010, GrCsGg
Adjunct Associate Professor:
William Barnhart, (D), Cornell, 2013, YdsGt
Ingrid Ukstins, (D), Royal Holloway (UK), 2003, GviXg
Brian J. Witzke, (D), Iowa, 1981, GrPsg
Kathleen Woida, (D), Iowa, 1991, So
Adjunct Assistant Professor:
Raymond R. Anderson, (D), Iowa, 1992, Gr
Rhawn F. Denniston, (D), Iowa, 2000, Cs
Keith E. Schilling, (D), Iowa, 2009, Hgs
Emily O. Walsh, (D), California (Santa Barbara), 2003, GptCc
Adjunct Professor:
Leon Aden, (M), Iowa, 1982, Go
Neil P. Bernstein, (D), Minnesota, 1982, Ge
Emeritus:
Richard G. Baker, (D), Colorado, 1969, PebPc
E. Arthur Bettis III, (D), Iowa, 1995, SdGmSa
Ann F. Budd, (D), Johns Hopkins, 1978, Pgi
Robert S. Carmichael, (D), Pittsburgh, 1967, YexGg
Lon D. Drake, (D), Ohio State, 1968, Hy
Philip H. Heckel, (D), Rice, 1966, GrPsGd
George R. McCormick, (D), Ohio State, 1964, GzEmCa
Holmes A. Semken, Jr., (D), Michigan, 1965, Pv
You-Kuan Zhang, (D), Arizona, 1990, Hw
Rock Lab Manager:
Matthew J. Wortel, (M), Iowa, 2007, Gx
Collections Manager, Paleontology:
Tiffany S. Adrain, (M), Iowa, 2003, Pg

University of Northern Iowa

Dept of Earth and Environmental Sciences (B) ⃠ (2020)
121 Latham Hall
Cedar Falls, IA 50614-0335
p. (319) 273-2759
siobahn.morgan@uni.edu
http://www.earth.uni.edu/
f: https://www.facebook.com/pages/University-of-Northern-Iowa-Earth-and-Environmental-Science/56860203682
t: @uni_earthsci
Programs: Earth Science; Earth Science Teaching; Environmental Sciences, Environmental Resource Management
Administrative Assistant: Noel Graff
Enrollment (2020): B: 68 (22)

Head:
Siobahn M. Morgan, (D), Washington, 1991, Xa
Professor:
Alan C. Czarnetzki, (D), Wisconsin, 1992, Am
Chad E. Heinzel, (D), N Illinois, 2005, GmaSa
Thomas A. Hockey, (D), New Mexico State, 1988, Zn
Mohammad Z. Iqbal, (D), Indiana, 1994, Hw
Associate Professor:
Kyle R. Gray, (D), Akron, 2009, ZeGg
Alexa Sedlacek, (D), Ohio State, 2013, CsGr
Xinhua Shen, (D), Colorado State, 2011, Asm
Instructor:
Aaron Spurr, (M), N Iowa, 1997, Zeg
Emeritus:
Wayne I. Anderson, (D), Iowa, 1964, Pg
Lynn A. Brant, (D), Penn State, 1980, Gn
Timothy M. Cooney, (D), N Colorado, 1976, Ze
Walter E. De Kock, (D), Ohio State, 1972, Ze
Kenneth J. De Nault, (D), Stanford, 1974, Gz
James C. Walters, (D), Rutgers, 1975, Gm
Lab Tech:
Steven J. Smith, (M), N Iowa, 2000, Zg

Kansas

Emporia State University

Earth Science Program (B,M) O (2021)
1 Kellogg Circle
Emporia, KS 66801-5087
p. (620) 341-5330
mmorales@emporia.edu
http://www.emporia.edu/earthsci/
Programs: Master's degree in Earth Science and Undergraduate degrees in Earth Science
Certificates: GIS
Enrollment (2018): B: 19 (9) M: 15 (5)

Professor:
Marcia K. Schulmeister, (D), Kansas, 2000, HwClGe
Richard O. Sleezer, (D), Kansas, 2001, ZiSdHs
Associate Professor:
Michael A. Morales, (D), California (Berkeley), 1987, PvGrg
Assistant Professor:
Alivia J. Allison, (D), Missouri (Kansas City), 2013, GgaGm
Paul Zunkel, (D), Texas State, 2017, AmZig
Emeritus:
James S. Aber, (D), Kansas, 1978, Gl
Paul L. Johnston, (M), Kansas, 1959, Gg
Kenneth W. Thompson, (D), Iowa State, 1991, Ze

Fort Hays State University

Department of Geosciences (B,M) O (2020)
600 Park Street
Tomanek Hall
Hays, KS 67601-4099
p. (785) 628-5389
geosciences@fhsu.edu
http://www.fhsu.edu/geo
f: https://www.facebook.com/GeoFHSU/
t: @GeoFHSU
Programs: Geology, Geography, Geographic Information Systems, Environmental Geosciences
Certificates: Geographic Information Systems, Museum Studies, Crime Mapping and Analysis
Administrative Assistant: Patricia Duffey
Enrollment (2019): B: 152 (27) M: 22 (6)

Emeritus:
Kenneth R. Neuhauser, (D), South Carolina, 1973, GceGs
Paul Phillips, (D), Kansas, 1977, Zen
Richard J. Zakrzewski, (D), Michigan, 1968, PvsPe
Professor:
Richard Lisichenko, (D), Kansas State, 2000, Zie
Interim Chair, Geosciences & Curator, Sternberg Museum:
Laura E. Wilson, (D), Colorado, 2012, PvePg
Associate Professor:
Hendratta N. Ali, (D), Oklahoma State, 2010, GogYs
Tom Schafer, (D), Kansas State, 2000, ZyiRn

Assistant Professor:
Henry Agbogun, (D), New Brunswick, 2012, GgYg
Keith A. Bremer, (D), Texas State, 2011, ZuiZn
Jonathan B. Sumrall, (D), Mississippi State, 2013, GgxZn
Instructor:
Eamonn Coveney, (M), Fort Hays State, 2006, Zyn
William H. Heimann, (M), Fort Hays State, 1987, HgwGm
Kara Kuntz, (M), Kansas State, 1990, Zn
Jami J. Seirer, (M), Montana, 2015, ZriZn
Jeanne L. Sumrall, (D), Mississippi State, 2015, Zgn
Cooperating Faculty (Emeritus) Paleobiology:
Joseph R. Thomasson, (D), Iowa State, 1976, Pb
Dean, College of Science Technology and Mathematics:
P. Grady Dixon, (D), Arizona State, 2005, AmZyAs

Johnson County Community College

Science Division (A) (2021)
12345 College Blvd
Overland Park, KS 66210
p. (913) 469-3826
mwisgird@jccc.edu
http://www.jccc.edu/academics/math-science
Enrollment (2015): A: 7 (2)
Professor:
Lynne Beatty, (M), S Illinois, 1985, GgZy
Assistant Professor:
John P. Harty, (D), Zy
Adjunct Professor:
Bruce Frederick, (D), Gg
John Maher, (D), Maryland, 1999, Zy

Kansas State University

Dept of Agronomy (B,M,D) (2016)
2004 Throckmorton
Manhattan, KS 66506
p. (785) 532-6101
agronomy@ksu.edu
http://www.agronomy.k-state.edu/
f: https://www.facebook.com/kstate.agronomy
t: @KStateAgron
Enrollment (2014): B: 70 (33) M: 41 (9) D: 43 (10)
Deparment Head:
Gary M. Pierzynski, (D), Ohio State, 1989, Sc
Professor:
Stewart Duncan, (D), Kansas State, 1991, So
Walter H. Fick, (D), Texas Tech, 1978, Sf
Dale Fjell, (D), Kansas State, 1982, So
Allan Fritz, (D), Kansas State, 1994, So
Mary Beth Kirkham, (D), Wisconsin, Sp
Gerard J. Kluitenberg, (D), Iowa State, 1989, Sp
David Mengel, (D), Purdue, 1975, So
Clenton E. Owensby, (D), Kansas State, 1969, Sf
Dallas Peterson, (D), North Dakota State, 1987, So
Vara Prasad, (D), Reading (UK), 1999, So
Michel D. Ransom, (D), Ohio State, 1984, SdcGm
Chuck W. Rice, (D), Kentucky, 1983, Sb
Bill T. Schapaugh, (D), Purdue, 1979, So
Alan Schlegel, (D), Purdue, 1985, So
Phillip Stahlman, (D), Wyoming, 1989, So
Curtis Thompson, (D), Idaho, 1993, So
Steve M. Welch, (D), Michigan State, 1977, Sp
Associate Professor:
Ignacio Ciampitti, (D), Purdue, 2012, So
Gary Cramer, (D), Nebraska, 1998, So
Ganga Hettiarachchi, (D), Kansas State, 2000, Sc
John Holman, (D), Idaho, 2005, So
Doo-Hong Min, (D), Maryland, 1998, So
Nathan Nelson, (D), North Carolina State, 2004, So
DeAnn Presley, (D), Kansas State, 2007, So
Kraig Roozeboom, (D), Kansas State, 2006, So
Dorivar Ruiz-Diaz, (D), Iowa State, 2007, So
Gretchen Sassenrath, (D), Illinois, 1988, So
Tesfaye Tesso, (D), Kansas State, 2002, So
Assistant Professor:
Eric Adee, (D), Wisconsin, 1993, So
Lucas Haag, (D), Kansas State, 2013, So
Mithila Jugulam, (D), Guelph, 2004, So
Xiaomao Lin, (D), Nebraska, 1999, Zn
Colby Moorberg, (D), North Carolina, 2014, So
Geoffrey Morris, (D), Chicago, 2007, So
Augustine Obour, (D), Florida, 2010, So
Ram Perumal, (D), Tamil Nadu Ag, 1993, So
Eduardo Santos, (D), Guelph, 2011, So
Peter Tomlinson, (D), Arkansas, 2006, So
Guorong Zhang, (D), North Dakota State, 2007, So
Emeritus:
Mark Claassen, (D), Iowa State, 1971, So
Bill Eberle, (D), Illinois, 1973, SoZu
Stan Ehler, (D), Missouri, 1975, So
Barney Gordon, (D), South Dakota, 1990, So
Keith Janssen, (D), Michigan State, 1973, So
George Liang, (D), Wisconsin, 1965, So
Gerry L. Posler, (D), Iowa State, 1969, Sf
Kevin Price, (D), Utah, 1987, Zr
David Regehr, (D), Illinois, 1975, So
Jim Shroyer, (D), Iowa State, 1980, So
Loyd Stone, (D), South Dakota, 1973, Sp
Steve J. Thien, (D), Purdue, 1971, Sc
Richard Vanderlip, (D), So
D.A. Whitney, (D), Iowa State, 1966, So
Agronomist:
Doug Shoup, (D), Kansas State, 2006, So
Librarian:
Nancy William, (N), Zn

Dept of Geology (B,M) (2015)
108 Thompson Hall
Manhattan, KS 66506-3201
p. (785) 532-6724
rocknrat@ksu.edu
http://www.k-state.edu/geology/
Administrative Assistant: Lori Page-Willyard
Enrollment (2013): B: 69 (15) M: 27 (5)
Department Head:
Pamela D. Kempton, (D), S Methodist, 1984, GiCtc
Professor:
Sambhudas Chaudhuri, (D), Ohio State, 1966, GeoCc
Associate Professor:
Allen W. Archer, (D), Indiana, 1983, Gr
Matthew E. Brueseke, (D), Miami (Ohio), 2006, GitGv
Abdelmoneam E. Raef, (D), AGH (Poland), 2001, YesZr
Matthew W. Totten, (D), Oklahoma, 1992, Gso
Assistant Professor:
Saugata Datta, (D), W Ontario, 2001, ClHwGe
Keith B. Miller, (D), Rochester, 1988, Pe
Joel Q.G. Spencer, (D), Glasgow, 1996, CcGs
Emeritus:
Robert L. Cullers, (D), Wisconsin, 1971, Ct
Charles G. Oviatt, (D), Utah, 1984, Gm
Ronald R. West, (D), Oklahoma, 1970, PgeGs

University of Kansas

Dept of Geology (B,M,D) O (2021)
1414 Naismith Dr
Room 254
Ritchie Hall
Lawrence, KS 66045-7613
p. (785) 864-4974
geology@ku.edu
http://geo.ku.edu/
f: https://www.facebook.com/KUGeology
Programs: BA, BS, MS, PhD in Geology
Professional Science MS in Environmental Geology
Certificates: Environmental Geology
Enrollment (2013): B: 72 (14) M: 50 (17) D: 34 (9)
Union Pacific Distinguished Professor:
J. Douglas Walker, (D), MIT, 1985, Gc
Ritchie Distinguished Professor:
Michael D. Blum, (D), Texas, 1997, GsrGm
Professor and Chair:
Jennifer A. Roberts, (D), Texas, 2000, Cbl
Gulf-Hedberg Distinguished Professor:
Paul A. Selden, (D), Cambridge, 1979, Pig
Distinguished Professor:
Robert H. Goldstein, (D), Wisconsin, 1986, Gs

Courtesy Professor:
Rolfe Mandel, (D), Kansas, 1991, Gam
Professor:
J. F. Devlin, (D), Waterloo, 1994, Hw
David A. Fowle, (D), Notre Dame, 2000, Cb
Evan K. Franseen, (D), Wisconsin, 1989, Gd
Luis A. Gonzalez, (D), Michigan, 1989, CsGd
Stephen T. Hasiotis, (D), Colorado, 1997, Pe
Mary C. Hill, (D), Princeton, 1985, HgqHw
Gwendolyn L. Macpherson, (D), Texas, 1989, Hw
Gene Rankey, (D), Kansas, 1996, GsrGu
Michael H. Taylor, (D), California (Los Angeles), 2004, GtmZr
George P. Tsoflias, (D), Texas, 1999, YgeGe
Associate Professor:
Craig Marshall, (D), Tech (Australia), 2001, GzZmXb
Andreas Möller, (D), Christian-Albrechts (Germany), 1996, Gt
Alison Olcott Marshall, (D), S California, 2006, PgCoPo
Leigh Stearns, (D), Maine, 2008, GlZrf
Anthony W. Walton, (D), Texas, 1972, GsEoGv
Associate Scientist:
Diane Kamola, (D), Georgia, 1989, Gs
Randy Stotler, (D), Waterloo, 2008, Hw
Assistant Professor:
Noah McLean, (D), MIT, 2012, CcGq
Chi Zhang, (D), Rutgers, 2012, YgxYu
Courtesy Professor:
John H. Doveton, (D), Edinburgh, 1969, Gq
William C. Johnson, (D), Wisconsin, 1976, Grm
Leonard Krishtalka, (D), Kansas, 1976, Pv
Bruce S. Lieberman, (D), Columbia, 1994, Pgi
Gregory A. Ludvigson, (D), Iowa, 1988, Gs
Richard D. Miller, (M), Kansas, 1983, Ye
Edith Taylor, (D), Ohio State, 1983, Pb
W. Lynn Watney, (D), Kansas, 1985, Gr
Donald O. Whittemore, (D), Penn State, 1973, Cl
Courtesy Associate Professor:
Geoff Bohling, (D), Kansas, 1999, Hw
Gaisheng Liu, (D), Alabama, 2004, Hg
Courtesy Assistant Professor:
Andrea Brookfield, (D), Waterloo, 2009, Hw
Jon Smith, (D), Kansas, 2008, GsPe
Adjunct Professor:
Timothy R. Carr, (D), Wisconsin, 1981, Go
John Gosse, (D), Lehigh, 1994, Gm
Emeritus:
Ernest E. Angino, (D), Kansas, 1961, Cl
Ross A. Black, (D), Wyoming, 1989, Ye
Wakefield Dort, Jr., (D), Stanford, 1955, Gm
Gisela Dreschoff, (D), Tech (Braunschweig), 1972, Ce
Paul Enos, (D), Yale, 1965, GsdGu
Lee C. Gerhard, (D), Kansas, 1964, GsoGd
Carl D. McElwee, (D), Kansas, 1970, HgYg
Richard A. Robison, (D), Texas, 1962, PiGr
Albert J. Rowell, (D), Leeds (UK), 1953, Pi
Don W. Steeples, (D), Stanford, 1975, YseGe
W. Randall Van Schmus, (D), California (Los Angeles), 1964, Cc

Wichita State University

Dept of Geology (B,M) (2015)
1845 Fairmount
Wichita, KS 67260-0027
p. (316) 978-3140
bill.bischoff@wichita.edu
https://www.wichita.edu/academics/fairmount_college_of_liberal_arts_and_sciences/geology/
Administrative Assistant: K. L. Smith
Chair:
William C. Parcell, (D), Alabama, 2000, Gr
Professor:
William D. Bischoff, (D), Northwestern, 1985, Cl
John C. Gries, (D), Texas, 1970, Gt
Salvatore J. Mazzullo, (D), Rensselaer, 1974, Go
Associate Professor:
Collette D. Burke, (D), Wisconsin (Milwaukee), 1983, Pm
Assistant Professor:
Hongsheng Cao, (D), Florida State, 2001, Cl
Wan Yang, (D), Texas, 1999, Gs
Lecturer:
Toni K. Jackman, (M), Wichita State, 1984, Ge
David L. Schaffer, (B), Utah, 1982, Am
Emeritus:
James N. Gundersen, (D), Minnesota, 1958, Ga
Daniel F. Merriam, (D), Kansas, 1961, Gr
Peter G. Sutterlin, (D), Northwestern, 1958, Gd

Kentucky

Alice Lloyd College

Div of Natural Sciences & Mathematics (2015)
Pippa Passes, KY 41844-9701
p. (606) 368-2101 x5405
paulyeary@alc.edu
https://www.alc.edu/academics/natural-science-and-mathematics/

Bluegrass Community and Technical College

Environmental Science Technology Program (2015)
470 Cooper Dr
Lexington, KY 40506
p. (859) 246-6448
tracy.knowles@kctcs.edu
https://bluegrass.kctcs.edu/education-training/program-finder/environmental-science-technology.aspx

Eastern Kentucky University

Dept of Geosciences (B) (2019)
521 Lancaster Avenue
Science 2234
Richmond, KY 40475-3102
p. (859) 622-1273
melissa.dieckmann@eku.edu
http://www.geosciences.eku.edu
f:https://www.facebook.com/EKU-Geosciences-447266678713162
Programs: B.S. Environmental and Applied Geology, B.S. Geographic Information Science
Certificates: GIS Certificate
Enrollment (2018): B: 61 (20)
Chair:
Melissa S. Dieckmann, (D), Notre Dame, 1995, ZeCl
Professor:
Walter S. Borowski, (D), North Carolina, 1998, GsrOu
Alice Jones, (D), Ohio State, 1998, Zyn
John C. White, (D), Baylor, 2002, GiCgt
Donald M. Yow, (D), South Carolina, 2003, AtZye
Associate Professor:
F. Tyler Huffman, (D), Connecticut, 2006, Zi
Kelly Watson, (D), Florida State, 2012, ZriZn
Assistant Professor:
Jonathan Malzone, (D), Buffalo, 2015, HwgGm
Instructor:
Cory BlackEagle, (M), E Kentucky, 1989, HwZg
Ann Harris, (D), Kentucky, 2018, GgZy
Sung Bae Jeon, (D), Zy
Craig Webb, (M), W Kentucky, 1994, Zyn
Peter Worcester, (D), Miami, 1977, GgOuZe
Senior Lecturer:
Glenn A. Campbell, (M), Marshall, 1995, Zy
Emeritus:
Gary L. Kuhnhenn, (D), Illinois, 1976, GgZe
David Zurick, (D), Hawaii, 1986, Zn

Morehead State University

Dept of Earth and Space Sciences (B) (2015)
235 Martindale Drive
Morehead, KY 40351
p. (606) 783-2381
c.mason@moreheadstate.edu
http://www.moreheadstate.edu/physsci/
Administrative Assistant: Amanda Holbrook
Enrollment (2014): B: 40 (4)
Department Chair:
Benjamin K. Malphrus, (D), West Virginia, 1990

Professor:
Charles E. Mason, (M), George Washington, 1981, PiGrs
Associate Professor:
Marshall Chapman, (D), Massachusetts, 1996, Gv
Eric Jerde, (D), California (Los Angeles), 1991, Cg
Jennifer O'Keefe, (D), Kentucky, 2008, PlEcZe
Steven K. Reid, (D), Texas A&M, 1991, GsoGe

Murray State University

Dept of Earth and Environmental Sciences (B,M) O (2019)
334 Blackburn Science Building
Murray, KY 42071
p. (270) 809-2591
qzhang@murraystate.edu
http://murraystate.edu/ees
f: https://www.facebook.com/murraystateees/
t: @MurrayStateEES
Programs: BS Tracks: Geology, Earth Science Education, Environmental Science, Geography & GIS, Archaeology
MS Concentrations: Environmental Geology, Geoinformatics, Watershed Science, Archaeology
Certificates: GIS, Geospatial Data Science (graduate)
Enrollment (2012): B: 44 (9) M: 8 (4)
Chair:
Qiaofeng (Robin) Zhang, (D), W Ontario, 2002, ZirZu
Professor:
Haluk Cetin, (D), Purdue, 1993, ZrGe
Associate Professor:
Anthony L. Ortmann, (D), Tulane, 2007, GaYg
Assistant Professor:
Bassil El Masri, (D), Indiana, 2011, Zc
Sung-ho Hong, (D), New Mexico Tech, 2008, HyGe
Gary E. Stinchcomb, (D), Baylor, 2012, Ge
Marcie Venter, (D), Kentucky, Ga
Lecturer:
Jane L. Benson, (M), Murray State, 1986, Zi
Michael R. Busby, (M), Murray State, 1996, Zi

Northern Kentucky University

Dept of Geology (B) O (2017)
204H Natural Sciences Center
Highland Heights, KY 41099
p. (859) 572-5309
rockawayj@nku.edu
http://nku.edu/
Programs: Geology; Earth Science Education
Certificates: GIS
Enrollment (2017): B: 30 (60)
Associate Professor:
Janet Bertog, (D), Cincinnati, 2002, Gd
John D. Rockaway, (D), Purdue, 1968, Ng
Assistant Professor:
Trent Garrison, (D), Kentucky, 2015, GeHwEc
Lecturer:
Sarah E. Johnson, (M), Purdue, 1997, GmNgZi

Owensboro Community and Technical College

Owensboro Community and Technical College (2015)
4800 New Hartford Road
Owensboro, KY 42303
http://www.owensboro.kctcs.edu/

University of Kentucky

Dept of Earth and Environmental Sciences (B,M,D) O (2018)
101 Slone Research Building
121 Washington St.
Lexington, KY 40506-0053
p. (859) 257-3758
ewoolery@uky.edu
http://ees.as.uky.edu
Programs: Geological Sciences
Enrollment (2018): B: 47 (12) M: 24 (5) D: 14 (2)
Chair:
David P. Moecher, (D), Michigan, 1988, GxtCg
Professor:
Frank R. Ettensohn, (D), Illinois, 1975, PsGdPi
William C. Haneberg, (D), Cincinnati, 1989, NgZi
James C. Hower, (D), Penn State, 1978, Ec
Dhananjay Ravat, (D), Purdue, 1989, YgmYv
Edward W. Woolery, (D), Kentucky, 1998, Ys
Associate Professor:
Alan E. Fryar, (D), Alberta, 1992, HwGeCl
Kevin M. Yeager, (D), Texas A&M, 2002, GsCmc
Assistant Professor:
John R. Bowersox, (D), S Florida, 2006, God
Andrea M. Erhardt, (D), Stanford, 2013, CgsCm
Rebecca Freeman, (D), Tulane, 2011, GrPi
Michael M. McGlue, (D), Arizona, 2011, GnrGm
Keely A. O'Farrell, Toronto, 2013, Ygd
Ryan Thigpen, (D), Virginia Tech, 2009, Gtc
Research Associate:
Jordan S. Munizzi, (D), W Ontario, 2018, Cs
Instructor:
Summer Brown, (M), Virginia Tech, 2010, GgZei
Lecturer:
Kent Ratajeski, (D), North Carolina, 1999, Gi
Adjunct Professor:
Cortland F. Eble, (D), West Virginia, 1988, Pl
Stephen F. Greb, (D), Kentucky, 1992, GsEcGr
Hickman B. John, (D), Kentucky, 2011, Gto
Thomas M. Parris, (D), California (Santa Barbara), 1998, Cg
Zhenming Wang, (D), Kentucky, 1998, YsNeRn
Junfeng Zhu, (D), Arizona, 2005
Emeritus:
William H. Blackburn, (D), MIT, 1967, GxCg
Bruce R. Moore, (D), Melbourne (Australia), 1967, Gd
Kieran D. O'Hara, (D), Brown, 1984, GcCg
Lyle V. A. Sendlein, (D), Iowa State, 1964, Hw
Ronald L. Street, (D), St Louis, 1975, Ys
Laboratory Director:
Peter J. Idstein, (M), E Kentucky, 1992, Gg

Dept of Mining Engineering (B,M,D) (2015)
230 Mining & Mineral Resources Building
Lexington, KY 40506-0107
p. (859) 257-8026
rick.honaker@uky.edu
http://www.engr.uky.edu/mng/
t: @UK_Mining
Enrollment (2015): B: 125 (36) M: 14 (7) D: 17 (3)
Chair:
Rick Honkaer, (D), Virginia Tech, 1992, Nm
Professor:
Zach Agioutantis, (D), Virginia Tech, 1987, NrmEc
Braden Lusk, (D), Missouri (Rolla), 2006, Nm
Thomas Novak, (D), Penn State, 1984, Nm
Joseph Sottile, Jr., (D), Penn State, 1991, Nm
Assistant Professor:
Kyle Perry , (D), Kentucky, 2010, Nr
Jhon Silva-Castro, (D), Kentucky, 2012, Nm
William Chad Wedding, (D), Kentucky, 2014, Nm
Emeritus:
Kot F. Unrug, (D), Acad Mining-Metallurgy, 1966, Nr
Andrew M. Wala, (D), Acad Mining-Metallurgy, 1972, Nm

Western Kentucky University

Dept of Geography & Geology (B,M) O (2019)
1906 College Heights Blvd
#31066
Bowling Green, KY 42101-1066
p. (270) 745-4555
fred.siewers@wku.edu
http://www.wku.edu/geoweb
Programs: Geology, Geography, Meteorology, GIS
Certificates: GIS, grad and undergrad
Enrollment (2016): B: 110 (33) M: 25 (9)
Chair:
Fredrick D. Siewers, (D), Illinois, 1995, GsPiZc
Professor:
Catherine Algeo, (D), Louisiana State, 1997, Zi
Stuart A. Foster, (D), Ohio State, 1988, At
Margaret Gripshover, (D), Tennessee, Zy
Christopher Groves, (D), Virginia, 1993, Hg
David J. Keeling, (D), Oregon, 1992, Zg

Michael May, (D), Indiana, 1993, Ge
Jun Yan, (D), Buffalo, 2004, Zi
Associate Professor:
Josh Durkee, (D), Georgia, 2008, AsZy
Xingang Fan, (D), Lanzhou, As
M. Royhan Gani, (D), Texas (Dallas), 2005, GsrGg
Nahid Gani, (D), Texas (Dallas), Gc
Greg Goodrich, (D), Arizona State, 2005, Ast
Jason Polk, (D), S Florida, Gm
Andrew Wulff, (D), Massachusetts, 1993, Gv
Associate Scientist:
Leslie North, (D), S Florida, Zg
Instructor:
William Blackburn, (M), W Kentucky, 2002, Zy
Kevin Cary, (M), W Kentucky, 2000, Zi
Margaret Crowder, (D), W Kentucky, 2012, Ze
Scott Dobler, (M), Bowling Green, 1996, As
Patricia Kambesis, (D), Mississippi State, 2014, ZigHw
Instructor:
Amy Nemon, (M), W Kentucky, 2005, Zig
Emeritus:
Nicholas Crawford, (D), Clark, 1977, Hg

Louisiana

Centenary College of Louisiana

Dept of Geology (B) ☒ (2021)
2911 Centenary Boulevard
Shreveport, LA 71104
p. (318) 869-5234
dbieler@centenary.edu
Programs: Geology (B)
Enrollment (2020): B: 7 (6)
Professor:
David B. Bieler, (D), Illinois, 1983, GtrYe
Scott K. Vetter, (D), South Carolina, 1989, Gi

Delgado Community College

Science & Math Div (A) (2015)
615 City Park Avenue
New Orleans, LA 70119
p. (504) 671-6480
jadams@dcc.edu
http://www.dcc.edu/divisions/sciencemath/
Professor:
Jacqueline Wood, (M), New Orleans, Gg

Louisiana State University

Dept of Geography & Anthropology (B,M,D) (2015)
227 Howe-Russell Geoscience Complex
Baton Rouge, LA 70803
p. (225) 578-5942
gachair@lsu.edu
http://www.ga.lsu.edu
Enrollment (2006): B: 54 (23) M: 12 (6) D: 22 (7)
Chair:
Kevin Robbins
Professor:
Patrick A. Hesp, (D), Sydney, 1981, Gm
Richard H. Kesel, (D), Maryland, 1971, Hg
Associate Professor:
Steven Namikas, (D), S California, 1999, Gms

Dept of Geology & Geophysics (B,M,D) O☒ (2019)
E235 Howe Russell Kniffen Geoscience Complex
Baton Rouge, LA 70803-4101
p. (225) 578-3353
geology@lsu.edu
http://www.lsu.edu/science/geology/
f: http://www.facebook.com/LSUGeology
t: @LSUGeology
Enrollment (2017): B: 86 (31) M: 28 (16) D: 28 (7)
Chair:
Carol M. Wicks, (D), Virginia, 1992, HwClHy
Professor:
Huiming Bao, (D), Princeton, 1998, CsAcCu
Samuel J. Bentley, (D), SUNY (Stony Brook), 1998, Gu
Peter Clift, (D), Edinburgh, 1993, GsuGo
Peter Doran, (D), Nevada (Reno), 1996, Hws
Barbara L. Dutrow, (D), S Methodist, 1985, Gz
Brooks B. Ellwood, (D), Rhode Island, 1977, Ym
Darrell J. Henry, (D), Wisconsin, 1981, Gp
Associate Professor:
Philip J. Bart, (D), Rice, 1998, Gr
Juan M. Lorenzo, (D), Columbia, 1991, Ys
Sophie Warny, (D), Catholic (Belgium), 1999, Pl
Assistant Professor of Research:
Xiaobin Cao, (D), Chinese Acad of Sci, 2012, Cs
Yongbo Peng, (D), Louisiana State, Cg
Assistant Professor - Professional Practice:
Amy Luther, (D), New Mexico Tech, GcZe
Assistant Professor:
Adam Forte, (D), California (Davis), 2012, Gcm
Achim Herrmann, (D), Penn State, 2005, PeGd
Suniti Karuntillake, (D), Cornell, 2008, Xg
Karen Luttrell, (D), Scripps, Yg
Patricia Persaud, (D), Caltech, Ys
Jianwei Wang, (D), Illinois (Urbana), 2004, ClZmGy
Carol A. Wilson, (D), Boston, 2013, GsOnCc
Guangsheng Zhuang, (D), California (Santa Cruz), 2011, CocGs
Instructor:
Yanxia Ma, (D), Og
Associate Curator, LSU Museum of Natural Science:
Judith A. Schiebout, (D), Texas, 1973, Pv
Emeritus:
Ajoy K. Baksi, (D), Toronto, 1970, Cc
Gary R. Byerly, (D), Michigan State, 1974, Gi
Ray E. Ferrell, Jr., (D), Illinois, 1966, Cl
Jeffrey S. Hanor, (D), Harvard, 1967, Cl
George Hart, (D), Sheffield, 1961, Gg
Clyde Moore, Zn
Jeffrey A. Nunn, (D), Northwestern, 1981, Yg
James E. Roche, (D), Illinois, 1969, Gg
Barun K. Sen Gupta, (D), Indian Inst of Tech, 1963, Pm
Accountant Technician:
Jeanne L. Johnson, Zn

Dept of Oceanography & Coastal Sciences (M,D) (2015)
1002 Energy Coast and Environment Building
Baton Rouge, LA 70803
p. (225) 578-6308
ocean@lsu.edu
http://www.ocean.lsu.edu
Administrative Assistant: Gaynell Gibbs
Enrollment (2010): M: 63 (11) D: 92 (11)
Professor:
Robert P. Gambrell, (D), North Carolina State, 1974, Cg
Paul A. LaRock, (D), Rensselaer, 1968, Ob
Irving A. Mendelssohn, (D), North Carolina State, 1974, Ob
Richard F. Shaw, (D), Maine, 1981, Ob
Robert E. Turner, (D), Georgia, 1974, Ob
Associate Professor:
Donald M. Baltz, (D), California (Davis), 1980, Ob
Robert S. Carney, (D), Oregon State, 1977, Ob
Lawrence J. Rouse, Jr., (D), Louisiana State, 1969, Op
Assistant Professor:
Mark C. Benfield, (D), Texas A&M, 1991, Ob
Adjunct Professor:
Dubravko Justic, (D), Zagreb, 1989, Op
Nancy N. Rabalais, (D), Texas, 1983, Ob
Harry H. Roberts, (D), Louisiana State, 1969, Gs
Paul W. Sammarco, (D), SUNY, 1978, Zn
Nan D. Walker, (D), Cape Town, 1989, Og

School of Plant, Environmental and Soil Sciences (B,M,D) ☒ (2017)
104 M. B. Sturgis Hall
Baton Rouge, LA 70803
p. (225) 578-2110
spess@lsu.edu
http://www.spess.lsu.edu
f: https://www.facebook.com/LsuSchoolOfPlantEnvironmental-SoilSciences/
Programs: Plant, Environmental Management and Soil Sciences (M,D)
Enrollment (2017): B: 3 (0) M: 3 (3) D: 13 (0)

Professor:
Lewis A. Gaston, (D), Florida, 1987, Sc
Hussein M. Selim, (D), Iowa State, 1971, Sp
Maud M. Walsh, (D), Louisiana State, 1989, GeRcZe
Jim Wang, (D), Iowa State, 1990, Szc
Associate Professor:
Brenda S. Tubana, (D), Oklahoma State, 2007, So
Assistant Professor:
Lisa M. Fultz, Texas Tech, 2012, Sb

Louisiana Tech University

Environmental Science Program (B,M) (2015)
600 W. Arizona Street
Ruston, LA 71272
p. (318) 257-3972
campbell@latech.edu
Department Secretary: Connie McKenzie
Chair:
Gary S. Zumwalt, (D), California (Davis), 1976, Pi
Associate Professor:
Maureen McCurdy, (D), Wisconsin, 1990, Hw
Emeritus:
Leo A. Herrmann, (D), Johns Hopkins, 1951, Go

Nicholls State University

Dept of Physical Sciences (2016)
P.O. Box 2022
Thibodaux, LA 70310
p. (985) 448-4502
marguerite.moloney@nicholls.edu
http://www.nicholls.edu/phsc
Assistant Professor:
Marguerite M. Moloney, (M), S Illinois, 2004, GeZnn
Instructor:
Adam Beyer, (M), S Illinois, Gg

Northwestern State University

Dept of Chemistry and Physics (B) (2015)
Natchitoches, LA 71497
p. (318) 357-5501
chem_phys@nsula.edu
http://chemphys.nsula.edu/
Director:
Paul Withey
Professor:
Carol S. Chin, (D)
Kelly Knowlton, (D), Texas A&M, 1991, Gg

South Louisiana Community College

South Louisiana Community College (2015)
320 Devalcourt
Lafayette, LA 70506
p. (337) 521-8983
http://www.slcc.cc.la.us

Tulane University

Dept of Earth and Environmental Sciences (B,M,D) ☒ (2019)
6823 St. Charles Ave.
101 Blessey Hall
New Orleans, LA 70118
p. (504) 865-5198
ees@tulane.edu
http://www.tulane.edu/sse/eens
f: https://www.facebook.com/EENS6823/
Programs: Geology BS, Environmental Earth Science BS, Earth & Env Sciences MS, Earth & Env Sciences PhD
Certificates: GIS
Enrollment (2015): B: 6 (0) M: 0 (2) D: 0 (2)
Chair:
Torbjörn E. Törnqvist, (D), Utrecht, 1993, Gs
Professor:
Mead A. Allison, (D), SUNY (Stony Brook), 1993, Gs
Karen Haley Johannesson, (D), Nevada, 1993, HgCg
Associate Professor:
Nancye H. Dawers, (D), Columbia, 1997, GcoGm
George C. Flowers, (D), California (Berkeley), 1979, Hw
Associate Scientist:
Nicole Gasparini, (D), MIT, 2003, GmHs
Assistant Professor:
Brent M. Goehring, (D), Columbia, 2010, CcGlm
Kyle Martin Straub, (D), MIT, 2007, GgCg
Lecturer:
Jeffrey G. Agnew, (D), Louisiana State, 2008, Pge
Visiting Professor:
Reda Amer, (D), St Louis, 2011, ZirGe
Emeritus:
Stephen A. Nelson, (D), California (Berkeley), 1979, GivRn

University of Louisiana at Lafayette

School of Geosciences (B,M,D) O☒ (2020)
611 McKinley St
Lafayette, LA 70504
p. (337) 482-6468
geosciences@louisiana.edu
https://geos.louisiana.edu/
Programs: Bachelors of Science in Environmental Geology and Petroleum Geology
Master's in Geology
Ph.D. in Earth and Energy Sciences , Bachelors in Environmental Sciences. Master's in Environmental Resource Science
Administrative Assistant: Nadean S.. Bienvenu
Enrollment (2020): B: 80 (20) M: 30 (24) D: 11 (0)
Director:
Eric C. Ferre', (D), Toulouse, 1989, YmGc
Assistant Director:
Durga Poudel, (D), Georgia, 1998, Ge
Professor:
Gary L. Kinsland, (D), Rochester, 1974, YgeGt
Carl Richter, (D), Tubingen, 1990, Ym
Senior Scientist:
James E. Martin, (D), Washington, 1979, PvGg
Resource Facilitator:
Jim Foret, (M), Iowa State, 1971, Ge
Associate Professor:
Timothy W. Duex, (D), Texas, 1983, HgGex
Geology Program Director:
Brian Schubert, (D), SUNY (Binghamton), 2008, Cg
Field Camp Director:
Raphael Gottardi, (D), Minnesota, 2012, Gcp
Assistant Professor:
Katie H. Costigan, (D)
Aubrey Hillman, (D), Pittsburg State, 2015, GneGa
Davide Oppo, (D), Bologna, 2012, Gs
Anna Paltseva, (D), CUNY, 2019, Ge
Jorge Villa, (D), Ohio State, 2014, Ge
Rui Zhang, (D), Houston, 2010, Ye
Instructor:
Kristie Cornell, (M), Louisiana (Lafayette), 2003, Gg
Jennifer E. Hargrave, (D), Oklahoma, 2009, PvGrZe
Emeritus:
Brian E. Lock, (D), Cambridge, 1969, Gs
Laboratory Director:
Yingfeng XU, (D), Tulane, 2004, ZgGe
Adjunct Instructor:
William R. Finley, (M), SW Louisiana, 1975, YsZi
Bernardo Teixeira, (M), Lisbon, 2012, GdrGn

University of Louisiana, Monroe

School of Science, Atmospheric Science Program (B) (2017)
700 University Avenue
Monroe, LA 71209-0550
p. (318) 342-1822
casehanks@ulm.edu
http://www.ulm.edu/atmos/
Enrollment (2012): B: 43 (9)
Associate Dean of Arts and Sciences:
Michael A. Camille, (D), Texas A&M, 1991, Zy
Professor:
Eric A. Pani, (D), Texas Tech, 1987, As
Associate Professor:
M. Sean Chenoweth, (D), Wisconsin (Milwaukee), 2003, GmZir
Department Head:
Anne T. Case Hanks, (D), Georgia Tech, 2008, AsZe

Assistant Professor:
Ken Leppert, (D), Alabama (Huntsville), As
Todd Murphy, (D), Alabama (Huntsville), As
Station Archeologist/Poverty Point:
Diana M. Greenlee, (D), Washington, 2002, GaCo

University of New Orleans

Dept of Earth and Environmental Sciences (B,M,D) ☒ (2021)
2000 Lakeshore Drive
New Orleans, LA 70148
p. (504) 280-6325
igeorgio@uno.edu
http://www.uno.edu/geology/
Professor:
William H. Busch, (D), Oregon State, 1981, Ou
Terry L. Pavlis, (D), Utah, 1982, Gt
Denise J. Reed, (D), Cambridge, 1986, GmOn
A. K. Mostofa Sarwar, (D), Indiana, 1983, Ye
Laura F. Serpa, (D), Cornell, 1986, Ys
William B. Simmons, (D), Michigan, 1973, Gz
Ronald K. Stoessell, (D), California (Berkeley), 1977, Cl
Associate Professor:
Kraig L. Derstler, (D), California (Davis), 1985, PgiPv
Mark A. Kulp, (D), Kentucky, 2000, GrmGs
Assistant Professor:
Christopher D. Parkinson, (D), London (UK), 1991, Gp
Adjunct Professor:
Miles O. Hayes, (D), Texas, 1965, Gs
Karen L. Webber, (D), Rice, 1988, Gv
Michael A. Wise, (D), Manitoba, 1987, Gz
Emeritus:
Gary C. Allen, (D), N Carolina, 1968, Gp
Jacqueline Michel, (D), South Carolina, 1980, Cg

Maine

Bates College

Dept of Earth and Climate Science (B) ☒ (2018)
Carnegie Science Center
44 Campus Avenue
Lewiston, ME 04240-6084
p. (207) 786-6490
bjohnso3@bates.edu
http://www.bates.edu/geology/
f: https://www.facebook.com/groups/243958415633596/
Programs: Geology
Administrative Assistant: Sylvia Deschaine
Enrollment (2018): B: 15 (12)
Chair:
J. Dykstra Eusden, (D), Dartmouth, 1988, Gc
Professor:
Beverly J. Johnson, (D), Colorado, 1995, CsbCl
Michael J. Retelle, (D), Massachusetts, 1985, Gl
Assistant Professor:
Genevieve Robert, (D), Missouri, 2014, CpGiz
Assistant Instructor:
Marita Bryant, (M), Free (Berlin), 1984, Gg
Lecturer:
Raj Saha, (D), N Carolina, 2011
Visiting Professor:
Alice Doughty, Victoria (NZ), 2013, Gl
Emeritus:
Gene A. Clough, (D), Caltech, 1978, Ym

Bowdoin College

Dept of Earth and Oceanographic Science (B) (2015)
6800 College Station
Brunswick, ME 04011
p. (207) 725-3628
croesler@bowdoin.edu
http://www.bowdoin.edu/earth-oceanographic-science/
Administrative Assistant: Marjorie Parker
Enrollment (2014): B: 60 (27)
Rusack Professor of Environmental Studies:
Philip Camill III, (D), Duke, 1999, PebSb
Professor:
Rachel J. Beane, (D), Stanford, 1997, GzxZe
Chair:
Collin Roesler, (D), Washington, 1992, OgpZr
Associate Professor:
Peter D. Lea, (D), Colorado, 1989, Gl
Assistant Professor:
Michéle LaVigne, (D), Rutgers, 2010, OcPe
Emily M. Peterman, (D), California (Santa Barbara), 2009, Gtp
Service Learning Coord/Lab Instr:
Cathryn K. Field, (M), Smith, 2000, Ge
Lab Instructor:
Joanne Urquhart, (M), Dartmouth, 1987, Gge
Associate Professor:
Edward P. Laine, (D), MIT, 1977, Gu

Colby College

Department of Geology (B) ☒ (2020)
5800 Mayflower Hill
Waterville, ME 04901-8858
p. (207) 859-5800
amridky@colby.edu
http://www.colby.edu/geologydept/
Programs: Geology
Administrative Assistant: Alice M. Ridky
Enrollment (2020): B: 10 (9)
Chair:
Walter Sullivan, (D), Wyoming, 2007, Gct
Associate Professor:
Tasha L. Dunn, (D), Tennessee, 2008, XmGiz
Assistant Professor:
Bess Koffman, (D), Maine, 2013, PcClZc
Alejandra C. Ortiz, (D), MIT/WHOI, 2015, Gm
Visiting Professor:
Bruce F. Rueger, (D), Colorado, 2002, PlGg

University of Maine

School of Earth and Climate Sciences (B,M,D) ☒ (2019)
5790 Bryand Global Sciences Center
Orono, ME 04469-5790
p. (207) 581-2152
johnsons@maine.edu
http://www.umaine.edu/earthclimate/
f: https://www.facebook.com/pages/UMaine-School-of-Earth-and-Climate-Sciences/238244500701
Enrollment (2015): B: 42 (6) M: 13 (4) D: 14 (1)
Research Professor:
Edward S. Grew, (D), Harvard, 1971, Gpz
Roger L. Hooke, (D), Caltech, 1965, Gm
Director:
Scott E. Johnson, (D), James Cook, 1989, Gc
Professor:
George H. Denton, (D), Yale, 1965, Gl
Brenda L. Hall, (D), Maine, 1997, Gl
Joseph T. Kelley, (D), Lehigh, 1980, Gua
Peter O. Koons, (D), ETH (Switzerland), 1982, Gt
Karl J. Kreutz, (D), New Hampshire, 1998, Cs
Kirk A. Maasch, (D), Yale, 1989, As
Paul A. Mayewski, (D), Ohio State, 1973, Pe
Aaron E. Putnam, (D), Maine, 2011, Gll
Andrew S. Reeve, (D), Syracuse, 1996, Hw
Associate Professor:
Christopher C. Gerbi, (D), Maine, 2005, Gt
Assistant Professor:
Katherine A. Allen, (D), Columbia, 2013, Gu
Alicia M. Cruz-Uribe, (D), Penn State, 2014, GpCpt
Amanda A. Olsen, (D), Virginia Tech, 2007, Cl
Sean Smith, (D), Johns Hopkins, 2010, Hs
Research Assistant Professor:
Seth W. Campbell, (D), Maine, 2010, Gl
Instructor:
Alice R. Kelley, (D), Maine, 2006, GalGm
Martin G. Yates, (D), Indiana, 1988, EgGzx
Emeritus:
Daniel F. Belknap, (D), Delaware, 1979, GusGa
Harold W. Borns, Jr., (D), Boston, 1959, Gl
Terence J. Hughes, (D), Northwestern, 1968, Gl
Stephen A. Norton, (D), Harvard, 1967, Cl
Research Assistant Professor:
Sean Birkel, (D), Maine, 2010, Gl

School of Marine Sciences (B,M,D) O (2015)
5706 Aubert Hall, Rm 360
Orono, ME 04469-5706
p. (207) 581-4381
fchai@maine.edu
http://www.umaine.edu/marine/
Enrollment (2010): B: 145 (38) M: 56 (0) D: 9 (0)

University of Maine, Farmington

Dept of Geology (B) ☒ (2017)
173 High Street
Farmington, ME 04938
p. (207) 778-7402
dgibson@maine.edu
http://sciences.umf.maine.edu
Programs: Geology (B); Earth and Environmental Science (B)
Enrollment (2017): B: 26 (8)
Professor:
David Gibson, (D), Queen's (Ireland), 1984, GigGz
Douglas N. Reusch, (D), Maine, 1998, GtCgOu
Associate Professor:
Julia F. Daly, (D), Maine, 2002, GmHsGu
Emeritus:
Thomas E. Eastler, (D), Columbia, 1970, GeZrGg

University of Maine, Presque Isle

Div of Mathematics & Science (B) (2015)
181 Main Street
Presque Isle, ME 04769
p. (207) 768-9482
kevin.mccartney@umpi.edu
http://www.umpi.edu/
Department Secretary: Connie Leveque
Chair:
Michael Knopp
Professor:
Kevin McCartney, (D), Florida State, 1988, Pm

Maryland

College of Southern Maryland

Biological and Physical Sciences (A) (2015)
8730 Mitchell Rd
La Plata, MD 20646
p. (301) 934-7841
jenniferh@csmd.edu
http://www.csmd.edu/bio
Professor:
Jean M. Russ, (M), Kutztown, Zey

Community College of Baltimore County, Catonsville

School of Mathematics & Science (A) ☒ (2017)
800 S. Rolling Road
MASH 015B
Catonsville, MD 21228
p. (443) 840-5935
DLudwikoski@ccbcmd.edu
http://www.ccbcmd.edu/math_science/geology.html
Programs: Earth Science; Geology
Certificates: GIS
Administrative Assistant: Annjeannette Black
Enrollment (2015): A: 3 (0)
Associate Professor:
David J. Ludwikoski, (M), Toledo, 1993, ZegZn

Frederick Community College

Science Dept (A) (2018)
7932 Opossumtown Pike
Frederick, MD 21702
p. (301) 846-2510
shsmith@frederick.edu
http://www.frederick.edu/courses_and_programs/dept_science.aspx
Professor:
Natasha Cleveland, (M), Utah, 2001, Zge

Frostburg State University

Dept of Geography (B) (2015)
101 Braddock Rd.
Frostburg, MD 21532
p. (301) 687-4369
jsaku@frostburg.edu
http://www.frostburg.edu/dept/geog/
Administrative Assistant: Gale Yutzy
Enrollment (2010): B: 65 (16)
Chair:
Craig L. Caupp, (D), Utah State, 1986, ZnHs
Professor:
Henry W. Bullamore, (D), Iowa, 1978, Zn
Francis L. Precht, (D), Georgia, 1989, Zy
James C. Saku, (D), Saskatchewan, 1995, Zn
Associate Professor:
Phillip Allen, (D), Coventry (UK), 2005, GmePe
Fritz Kessler, (D), Kansas, 1999, Zr
George W. White, (D), Oregon, 1994, Zn
Assistant Professor:
David L. Arnold, (D), Indiana, 1994, As
Matthew E. Ramspott, (D), Kansas, 2006, Zr

Howard Community College

Science, Engineering, and Technology Division (2015)
10901 Little Patuxent Pkwy
Columbia, MD 21044
p. (443) 518-1000
pturner@howardcc.edu
http://www.howardcc.edu/programs-courses/academics/academic-divisions/science-engineering-technology/sciences/

Johns Hopkins University

Dept of Environmental Health & Engineering (B,M,D) (2015)
313 Ames Hall
34th & Charles Streets
Baltimore, MD 21218-2681
p. (410) 516-7092
mwkarp@jhu.edu
http://www.jhu.edu/dogee
Professor:
William P. Ball, (D), Stanford, 1989, Zn
Edward Bouwer, (D), Stanford, 1982, RwHws
Grace S. Brush, (D), Harvard, 1956, PleGn
Hugh Ellis, (D), Waterloo, 1984, Zn
Steve H. Hanke, (D), Colorado, 1969, Zn
Benjamin F. Hobbs, (D), Cornell, 1983, Zn
A. Lynn Roberts, (D), MIT, 1991, Zn
Erica Schoenberger, (D), California (Berkeley), 1984, Zn
Alan T. Stone, (D), Caltech, 1983, ClSc
Peter W. Wilcock, (D), MIT, 1987, Gm
Associate Professor:
Markus Hilpert, (D), Zn
Assistant Professor:
Kai Loon Chen, (D), Yale, 2008, Zn
Seth Guikema, (D), Stanford, 2003, Zn
Catherine Norman, (D), California (Santa Barbara), 2005, Zn
Lecturer:
Hedy Alavi, (D), Ohio State, 1983, Zn
Emeritus:
John J. Boland, (D), Johns Hopkins, 1973, Zn
Charles R. O'Melia, (D), Michigan, 1963, Zn
Eugene D. Shchukin, (D), Moscow State (Russia), 1958, Zn
Senior Academic Program Coordinator:
Adena Rojas, (M), Zn

The Morton K. Blaustein Dept of Earth & Planetary Sciences (B,M,D) (2015)
3400 N Charles Street
301 Olin Hall
Baltimore, MD 21218
p. (410) 516-7135
jseat@jhu.edu
http://eps.jhu.edu/
Enrollment (2013): D: 33 (5)

Chair:
Thomas W.N. Haine, (D), Southampton (UK), 1993, OpgAs
Professor:
Anand Gnanadesikan, (D), MIT/WHOI, 1994, OpcAs
Peter L. Olson, (D), California (Berkeley), 1977, Yg
Darrell F. Strobel, (D), Harvard, 1969, AsZnn
Dimitri A. Sverjensky, (D), Yale, 1980, Cl
Darryn W. Waugh, (D), Cambridge, 1991, As
Assistant Professor:
Sarah Horst, (D), Arizona, 2011, XaAcXb
Naomi Levin, (D), Utah, 2008, Gs
Kevin Lewis, (D), Caltech, 2009
Benjamin Zaitchik, (D), Yale, 2006, As
Research Professor:
Katalin Szlavecz, (D), Eotvos Lorand, 1981, Pi

Montgomery College

Dept of Physics, Engineering & Geosciences (A) (2015)
51 Mannakee Street
Rockville, MD 20850
p. (301) 279-5230
Muhammad.Kehnemouyi@montgomerycollege.edu
http://www.montgomerycollege.edu/Departments/phengrv/
Administrative Assistant: Mary (Deep) McGregor
Professor:
Alan Cutler, (D), Geology, PgRh
Instructional Laboratory Coordinator for Geosciences:
Kimberly Kelly, (B), Pittsburg State, Zn

St. Charles Community College

4601 Mid Rivers Mall Drive
Cottleville, MD 63376
p. (636) 922-8000
jmatheney-rood@stchas.edu
http://www.stchas.edu/

Towson University

Dept of Physics, Astronomy & Geosciences (B) ☒ (2020)
8000 York Road
Towson, MD 21252-0001
p. (410) 704-3020
dschaefer@towson.edu
http://wwwnew.towson.edu/physics/geosciences/
Programs: Geology, Earth Space Science (for secondary education majors as well as for science majors), Environmental Science, Physics
Enrollment (2020): B: 66 (12)
Professor:
Rachel J. Burks, (D), Texas, 1985, Gc
Joel Moore, (D), Penn State, 2008, ClsSc
David A. Vanko, (D), Northwestern, 1982, Gxz
Associate Professor:
Wendy Nelson, (D), Penn State, 2009, GiCc
Assistant Professor:
Michelle Casey, (D), Yale, 2011, Pe
Lecturer:
Andrew Hawkins, (D), Virginia Tech, 2017, Pg
Eriks Perkons, (M), Penn State, 2016, Ge

United States Naval Academy

Dept of Oceanography (B) ☒ (2020)
572C Holloway Road
Annapolis, MD 21402-5026
p. (410) 293-6550
natunewi@usna.edu
https://www.usna.edu/Oceanography
f: https://www.facebook.com/usnaoceanography
Administrative Assistant: Ira Ostrowski
Enrollment (2020): B: 133 (32)
Chair:
Cecily N. Steppe, (D), Delaware, 2001, Obp
Professor:
Bradford S. Barrett, (D), Oklahoma, 2007, As
Peter L. Guth, (D), MIT, 1980, GcZiy
CAPT:
Elizabeth R. Sanabia, (D), Naval Postgrad Sch, 2010, Am
Associate Professor:
Gina R. Henderson, (D), Delaware, 2010, As
Andrew C. Muller, (D), Old Dominion, 1999, OpnOu
Joseph P. Smith, (D), Massachusetts (Boston), 2007, CmOg
CDR:
Shawn Gallaher, (D), Naval Postgrad Sch
LCDR:
Matthew Burich, (M)
CDR:
Francis Carmody, (M)
Michael Cornelius, (M)
Allon Turek, (M)
Instructor:
Brianna Tracy, (M)
Related Staff:
Benjamin Hickman, (M)

University of Maryland

Dept of Geographical Studies (2015)
College Park, MD 20742
p. (301) 405-1600
dubayah@umd.edu
https://geog.umd.edu/

Dept of Geology (B,M,D) ☒ (2020)
Geology Building (#237)
8000 Regents Drive
College Park, MD 20742
p. (301) 405-4082
geology@umd.edu
http://www.geol.umd.edu
f: https://www.facebook.com/UMDGeology
Administrative Assistant: Dorothy Brown
Enrollment (2018): B: 54 (12) M: 0 (3) D: 33 (2)
Chair:
Richard J. Walker, (D), SUNY (Stony Brook), 1984, CcXcCg
Affiliate Professor:
Fernando Mirales-Wilhelm, (D)
Raghuram G. Murtugudde, (D), Columbia, 1994, ObZr
Jessica Sunshine, (D), Brown, 1993
Ning Zeng, (D), Arizona, 1994, AsCgGl
Professor:
Michael Brown, (D), Keele, 1975, GxpGt
James Farquhar, (D), Alberta, 1995, Cs
Alan J. Kaufman, (D), Indiana, 1990, Csg
Daniel Lathrop, (D), Texas, 1991, Yg
William F. McDonough, (D), Australian Nat, 1988, Cg
Laurent G.J. Montesi, (D), MIT, 2002, YgXyGt
Wenlu Zhu, (D), SUNY (Stony Brook), 1996, YrNrHg
Senior Research Scientist:
Philip M. Piccoli, (D), Maryland, 1992, Cg
Igor Puchtel, (D), Russian Acad of Sci, 1992, CcgGi
Associate Professor:
Ricardo Arevalo, Jr, (D), Maryland, 2010
Michael N. Evans, (D), Columbia, 1999, PeAsCs
Sujay Kaushal, (D), Colorado, 2003, ZuGeHs
Sarah Penniston-Dorland, (D), Johns Hopkins, 2005, Gp
Karen L. Prestegaard, (D), California (Berkeley), 1982, Hgw
Associate Research Scientist:
Richard Ash, (D), Open, 1990, Ca
Affiliate Assistant Professor:
Derrick Lampkin, (D), GlAsZr
Assistant Professor:
Mong-Han Huang, (D), California (Berkeley), 2017
Vedran Lekic, (D), California (Berkeley), 2009, Ysg
Megan E. Newcombe, (D), Caltech, 2017
Nicholas C. Schmerr, (D), Arizona State, 2008, XyYs
Research Associate:
Jabrane Labidi, (D), Inst Physique du Globe de Paris, 2012, Cg
Research Assistant Scientist:
Katherine R. Bermingham, (D), Muenster (Germany), 2011, XcCcg
Shuiwang Duan, (D), Tulane, 2005, HsZu
Principal Lecturer:
Thomas R. Holtz, Jr., (D), Yale, 1992, PvgPg
John W. Merck, Jr., (D), Texas, 1997, Pv
Lecturer:
Tracey Centorbi, (B), Maryland, 2003, Cg

Adjunct Professor:
Anat Shahar, (D), California (Los Angeles), 2008, CspCa
Adjunct Associate Professor:
Elizabeth Cottrell, (D), Columbia, 2004, CpgGx
Adjunct Professor:
Yingwei Fei, (D), CUNY, 1989, CpGxCg
Jeffrey Plesia, (D)
Deborah Smith, (D), California (San Diego), 1985
Professor Emeritus:
Philip A. Candela, (D), Harvard, 1982, CpgEg
Galt Siegrist, (D)
Emeritus Professor:
Ann G. Wylie, (D), Columbia, 1972, Gz
Emeritus Affiliate Research Professor:
George Helz, (D), Penn State, 1970, HsGeCg
Associate Professor Emeritus:
Peter B. Stifel, (D), Utah, 1964, Pg
Adjunct Professor Emeritus:
Roberta L. Rudnick, (D), Australian Nat, 1988, CgsCt
Faculty Research Assistant:
Todd Karwoski, (B), Maryland, 2005, Gg
Valentina Puchtel, (M), Moscow Geol Prospect Acad, 1983

Dept of Plant Science & Landscape Architecture (B,M,D) (2015)
2102 Plant Sciences Building
College Park, MD 20742-4432
p. (301) 405-4356
asmurphy@umd.edu
http://www.psla.umd.edu/
Professor:
Christopher Walsh, (D), Cornell, 1980, Zn
Associate Professor:
Gary D. Coleman, (D), Nebraska, 1989, Zn
Jack B. Sullivan, (M), Virginia, 1980, Zu
Program Management Specialist:
Kathy Hunt, Zn
Coordinator:
Sue Burk, Zn

Marine-Estuarine-Environmental Sciences Graduate Program (M,D) ☒ (2018)
1213 HJ Patterson Hall
University of Maryland
College Park, MD 20742
p. (301) 405-6938
mees@umd.edu
http://www.mees.umd.edu
Enrollment (2013): M: 6 (0) D: 12 (2)
Professor:
Shenn-Yu Chao, (D), North Carolina State, 1979, Op
Keith N. Eshleman, (D), MIT, 1985, Hg
Thomas R. Fisher, Jr., (D), Duke, 1975, ObZiCl
Patricia M. Gilbert, (D), Harvard, 1982, Ob
Lawrence P. Sanford, (D), MIT, 1984, Op
Diane Stoecker, (D), SUNY (Stony Brook), 1979, Ob
Associate Professor:
William Boicourt, (D), Johns Hopkins, 1973, Op
James Carton, (D), Princeton, 1983, Op
Micheal S. Kearney, (D), Ontario, 1981, Gu
Karen L. Prestegaard, (D), California (Berkeley), 1982, Hw
Research Associate Professor:
Jeffery C. Cornwell, (D), Alaska, 1983, Oc
Assistant Professor:
Mark S. Castro, (D), Virginia, 1991, As
Raleigh Hood, (D), California (San Diego), 1990, Ob
Alba Torrents, (D), Johns Hopkins, 1992, Sb
Research Associate Professor:
Todd M. Kana, (D), Harvard, 1982, Ob

Massachusetts

Amherst College

Dept of Geology (B) ☒ (2020)
P.O. Box 2238
Amherst, MA 01002-5000
p. (413) 542-2233
dbhutton@amherst.edu
https://www.amherst.edu/academiclife/departments/geology
Programs: Bachelor of Arts
Enrollment (2020): B: 11 (0)
Professor:
John T. Cheney, (D), Wisconsin, 1975, Gi
Peter D. Crowley, (D), MIT, 1985, Gc
Tekla A. Harms, (D), Arizona, 1986, Gt
Anna M. Martini, (D), Michigan, 1997, Cl
Associate Professor:
David S. Jones, (D), Harvard, 2009, GsClGr
Assistant Professor:
Victor E. Guevara, (D), Virginia Tech, 2017, GpiGg
Nicholas D. Holschuh, (D), Penn State, 2016, GlYg
Postdoctoral Fellow:
Rachael E. Bernard, (D), Texas, 2018, Gc
Emeritus:
Margery C. Coombs, (D), Columbia, 1971, Pv

Bard College at Simon's Rock

Bard College at Simon's Rock (2015)
84 Alford Rd.
Great Barrington, MA 01230
p. (413) 644-4400
admin@simons-rock.edu
http://www.simons-rock.edu/

Bentley University

Dept of Natural and Applied Sciences (B) ☒ (2020)
175 Forest Street
Waltham, MA 02452-4705
p. (781) 891-2980
dszymanski@bentley.edu
https://www.bentley.edu/academics/departments/natural-and-applied-sciences
Programs: BA in Sustainability Science
Enrollment (2018): B: 1 (0)
Dean of Arts and Sciences:
Rick Oches, (D), Massachusetts, 1994, ZcePe
Professor:
P. Thompson Davis, (D), Colorado, 1980, GlmZc
Associate Professor:
David Szymanski, (D), Michigan State, 2007, GifCg
Lecturer:
George Fishman, (M), Boston, 1993, XgbXc
Nicole Hill, (D), Cornell, 2016, Ge
Betsy Stoner, (D), Florida Intl, 2014, ObPe
Adjunct Professor:
Janette Gartner, (M), Massachusetts, 2000, Hy

Berkshire Community College

Environmental and Life Science Dept (A) (2015)
Pittsfield, MA 01201
p. (413) 236-4601
tflanagan@berkshirecc.edu
Chair:
Clifford D. Myers, (D), Maine, Zn
Professor:
Timothy Flanagan, (M), Antioch, 1983, Zei
Thomas F. Tyning, (M), Zn
Charles E. Weinstein, (M), Wisconsin, Zn
Emeritus:
Richard L. Ferren, (M), Louisiana State, Zn
George Hamilton, (M), North Adams State Coll, Zn
Mary R. Mercuri, (M), Catholic

Boston College

Dept of Earth & Environmental Sciences (B,M,D) ☒ (2021)
140 Commonwealth Avenue
213 Devlin Hall
Chestnut Hill, MA 02467-3809
p. (617) 552-3640
ethan.baxter@bc.edu
https://www.bc.edu/bc-web/schools/mcas/departments/eesc.html
Programs: Geological sciences, Environmental geoscience, Environmental studies
Enrollment (2020): B: 43 (15) M: 14 (8) D: 3 (0)
Chair:
Ethan Baxter, (D), California (Berkeley), 2000, Ccg

Professor:
John E. Ebel, (D), Caltech, 1981, Ys
Gail C. Kineke, (D), Washington, 1993, On
Noah Snyder, (D), MIT, 2001, GgHg
Associate Professor:
Mark Behn, (D), MIT/WHOI, 2002, YgrGt
Alan L. Kafka, (D), SUNY (Stony Brook), 1980, Yg
Seth C. Kruckenberg, (D), Minnesota, 2009, Gct
Tara Pisani-Gareau, (D), California (Santa Cruz), 2008, Ge
Jeremy D. Shakun, (D), Oregon State, 2010, Gg
Assistant Professor:
Hilary I. Palevsky, (D), Washington, 2016, Oc
Xinchen Wang, (D), Princeton, 2016, Cb
Lab Coordinator:
Kenneth G. Galli, (D), Massachusetts, 2003, GsdGg
Adjunct Professor:
Paul K. Strother, (D), Harvard, 1980, PlbPg
Emeritus:
J. Christopher Hepburn, (D), Harvard, 1972, Gpt

Weston Observatory (2015)
381 Concord Road
Weston, MA 02493
p. (617) 552-8300
weston.observatory@bc.edu
http://www.bc.edu/westonobservatory
Director:
Alan L. Kafka, (D), SUNY (Stony Brook), 1980, Ys
Science Education:
Michael Barnett, (D), Indiana, 2003, Ze
Senior Scientist:
John E. Ebel, (D), Caltech, 1981, Yg
Seismology, Seismic Network Development:
Michael Hagerty, (D), California (Santa Cruz), 1998, Ys
Seismic Analyst and Educational Seismologist:
Anastasia Moulis, (M), Boston, 2003, Ys
Research Scientist:
Seth Kruckenberg, (D), Minnesota, 2009, Gc
Research Scientist:
John J. Cipar, (D), Caltech, 1981, Ys
Research Associate:
John H. Beck, (D), Boston, 1998, Pb
Adjunct Professor:
Paul L. Strother, (D), Harvard, 1980, PlbPm
Alfredo Urzua, (D), MIT, 1981, Ng
Visiting Professor:
Vincent Murphy, (M), Boston, 1957, Yg
Emeritus:
J. Christopher Hepburn, (D), Harvard, 1972, Gg
James W. Skehan, (D), Harvard, 1953, Gc

Boston University

Center for Remote Sensing (2015)
685 Commonwealth Avenue
Room 433
Boston, MA 02215
p. (617) 353-9709
crsadmin@bu.edu
https://www.bu.edu/remotesensing/
Administrative Assistant: Emily P. Johnson
Director:
Farouk El-Baz, (D), Missouri (Rolla), 1964, Zr
Professor:
Sucharita Gopal, (D), California (Santa Barbara), 1988, Zi
Alan Strahler, (D), Johns Hopkins, 1969, Zr
Curtis E. Woodcock, (D), California (Santa Barbara), 1986, Zr
Research Associate Professor:
Magaly Koch, (D), Boston, 1993, HyZri
Associate Professor:
Mark A. Friedl, (D), California (Santa Barbara), 1994, Zr
Kenneth L. Kvamme, (D), California (Santa Barbara), 1983, Ga
Guido D. Salvucci, (D), MIT, 1994, Hq
Research Associate Professor:
Cordula Robinson, (D), Univ Coll (UK), 1991, Gm
Crystal Schaaf, (D), Boston, 1994, Zr
Research Associate:
Eman Ghoneim, (D), Southampton (UK), 2002, Gm

Geology Librarian:
Nasim Momen, Zn

Dept of Earth & Environment (B,M,D) (2015)
675 Commonwealth Avenue
Boston, MA 02215
p. (617) 353-2525
earth@bu.edu
http://www.bu.edu/earth/
Enrollment (2015): B: 70 (15) M: 15 (10) D: 50 (8)
Chair:
David R. Marchant, (D), Edinburgh, 1994, Gm
Professor:
Bruce Anderson, (D), Scripps, 1998, AsOp
James Lawford Anderson, (D), Gi
Duncan M. FitzGerald, (D), South Carolina, 1977, OnGsu
Mark Friedl, (D), California (Santa Barbara), 1993, Zr
Sucharita Gopal, California (Santa Barbara), 1988, Zi
Tony Janetos, (D), 1980, Zn
Richard Murray, (D), California (Berkeley), 1991, Cm
Ranga Myneni, (D), Antwerp (Belgium), 1985, Zr
Nathan Phillips, (D), Duke, 1997, Zy
Guido D. Salvucci, (D), MIT, 1994, Hq
Curtis Woodcock, (D), California (Santa Barbara), 1986, Zr
Associate Professor:
Rachel Abercrombie, (D), Reading (UK), 1991, Gt
Michael Dietze, (D), Duke, 2006, SfZr
Sergio Fagherazzi, (D), Padua, 1999, GmOnGs
Robinson Fulweiler, (D), Rhode Island, 2007, Cm
Lucy Hutyra, (D), Harvard, 2007, AsZr
Andrew Kurtz, (D), Cornell, 2000, Clg
Assistant Professor:
Dan Li, (D), Princeton, 2013, HqAs
Christine Regalla, (D), Penn State, 2013, GtcGm
Diane Thompson, Arizona, 2013, ObPe
Research Associate:
Farouk El-Baz, (D), Missouri, 1964, Zr

Bridgewater State University

Dept of Geological Sciences (B) (2018)
Conant Science Building
Bridgewater, MA 02325
p. (508) 531-1390
Brenda.Flint@bridgew.edu
http://www.bridgew.edu/academics/colleges-departments/department-geological-sciences
Programs: Geological Sciences; Environmental Geosciences; Earth Science
Administrative Assistant: Brenda Flint
Enrollment (2017): B: 60 (9)
Chairperson:
Robert D. Cicerone, (D), MIT, 1991, YsgXy
Professor:
Richard L. Enright, (D), Rutgers, 1969, HgZrEg
Michael A. Krol, (D), Lehigh, 1996, GzxGt
Peter J. Saccocia, (D), Minnesota, 1991, CqsCm
Assistant Professor:
Christine M. Brandon, (D), Massachusetts, 2015, Gs
Lecturer:
Joseph Doyle, (M), New Hampshire, Gg
Suzanne R. O'Brien, (M), New Hampshire, 1995, Zg
Michael A. Penzo, (M), SUNY (Binghamton), 1981, Ge

Bristol Community College

Div of Mathematics, Science and Engineering (A) (2015)
777 Elsbree Street
Fall River, MA 02720
p. (508) 678-2811
John.Ahola@bristolcc.edu
Instructor:
John Ahola, Gg

Cape Cod Community College

Environmental Technology Program (2020)
2240 Iyannough Rd
West Barnstable, MA 02668
p. (508) 362-2131 x4468

jalai@capecod.edu
http://www.capecod.edu/web/natsci/env

Fitchburg State University

Earth and Geographic Sciences (B) (2019)
160 Pearl Street
Fitchburg, MA 01420-2697
p. (978) 665-4636
egordon3@fitchburgstate.edu
http://www.fitchburgstate.edu/academics/academic-departments/earth-and-geographic-sciences-dept/
f: https://www.facebook.com/FitchburgStateUniversityEGS
Programs: Environmental and Earth Science; Geographic Science and Technology
Enrollment (2018): B: 43 (5)

Professor:
Jane Huang, (D), Zi

Associate Professor:
Elizabeth S. Gordon, (D), OgAsZg

Assistant Professor:
Elyse Clark, (D), Cq
Reid A. Parsons, (D), XgHs

Hampshire College

School of Natural Science (B) ⊠ (2017)
Amherst, MA 01002
p. (413) 582-5373
sroof@hampshire.edu

Professor:
Steven Roof, (D), Massachusetts, 1995, ZiPe

Associate Professor:
Christina Cianfrani, (D), Vermont, Hg

Harvard University

Dept of Earth and Planetary Sciences (B,D) ●⊠ (2019)
Hoffman Laboratory
20 Oxford Street
Cambridge, MA 02138-2902
p. (617) 495-2351
shaw@eps.harvard.edu
http://www.eps.harvard.edu
f: https://www.facebook.com/Harvard-University-Earth-and-Planetary-Sciences-6322073679/
Programs: Earth and Planetary Sciences
Enrollment (2018): B: 34 (6) D: 58 (10)

Chair:
John Shaw, (D), Princeton, 1993, Gt

Affiliated Faculty with EPS:
Naomi Oreskes, (D), Stanford, 1990, Rh

Professor:
James G. Anderson, (D), Colorado, 1970, As
Jeremy Bloxham, (D), Cambridge, 1985, Yg
Brian F. Farrell, (D), Harvard, 1981, Am
John P. Holdren, (D), Stanford, 1970, Zn
Peter Huybers, (D), MIT, 2004, Pe
Miaki Ishii, (D), Harvard, 2003, Yg
Daniel J. Jacob, (D), Caltech, 1985, As
Stein B. Jacobsen, (D), Caltech, 1980, Cc
David T. Johnston, (D), Maryland, 2007, CgPg
Andrew H. Knoll, (D), Harvard, 1977, Pb
Zhiming Kuang, (D), Caltech, 2003, As
Charles H. Langmuir, (D), SUNY (Stony Brook), 1980, Cg
Scot T. Martin, (D), Caltech, 1995, Cg
James T. McCarthy, (D), Scripps, 1971, Ob
Michael B. McElroy, (D), Queen's, 1962, As
Brendan Meade, (D), MIT, 2004, Yg
Jerry X. Mitrovica, (D), Toronto, 1991, Yg
Ann Pearson, (D), MIT/WHOI, 2000, Cb
James R. Rice, (D), Lehigh, 1964, Ygu
Daniel P. Schrag, (D), California (Berkeley), 1993, Cg
Eli Tziperman, (D), MIT/WHOI, 1987, Op
Steven C. Wofsy, (D), Harvard, 1971, As

Affiliated Faculty with EPS:
Robin Wordsworth, (D), Oxford, 2008, Xg

Assistant Professor:
Marine Denolle, (D), Stanford, 2014, Ys
Rebecca A. Fischer, (D), Chicago, 2015, Gy
Roger Fu, (D), MIT, 2015, YmXym
Kaighin McColl, (D), MIT, 2016, Hg

Visiting Professor:
Carl Wunsch, (D), MIT, 1966, Op

Emeritus:
Charles W. Burnham, (D), MIT, 1961, GzyGe
Paul F. Hoffman, (D), Johns Hopkins, 1970, Gc

Massachusetts Institute of Technology

Dept of Earth, Atmospheric, & Planetary Sciences (B,M,D) ●⊠ (2021)
77 Massachusetts Avenue, 54-918
Cambridge, MA 02139
p. (617) 253-2127
eapsinfo@mit.edu
http://eapsweb.mit.edu/
f: https://www.facebook.com/EAPS.MIT
t: @eapsmit
Programs: Earth, Atmospheric and Planetary Sciences (B, M, D); Atmospheric Science (M,D); Climate Science (M,D); Geology (M, D); Geochemistry (M, D); Geobiology (M, D); Geophysics (M, D); Planetary Sciences (M, D)
Certificates: none
Enrollment (2020): B: 21 (5) M: 0 (5) D: 166 (20)

Vice-President for Research:
Maria T. Zuber, (D), Brown, 1986, Xy

Department Head:
Robert van der Hilst, (D), Utrecht, 1990, Ys

Professor:
Richard P. Binzel, (D), Texas, 1986, Xm
Edward A. Boyle, (D), MIT, 1976, Oc
Kerry A. Emanuel, (D), MIT, 1978, AmRn
Dara Entekhabi, (D), MIT, 1990, Hg
Raffaele Ferrari, (D), Scripps, 2000, OpAsOb
Glenn R. Flierl, (D), Harvard, 1975, Op
Michael Follows, (D), E Angola (UK), 1991, Op
Timothy L. Grove, (D), Harvard, 1976, Gi
Bradford H. Hager, (D), Harvard, 1978, Ys
Thomas A. Herring, (D), MIT, 1983, Yd
Paola M. Malanotte-Rizzoli, (D), California (San Diego), 1978, Op
John C. Marshall, (D), Imperial Coll (UK), 1980, Op
F Dale Morgan, (D), MIT, 1981, Yg
Taylor Perron, (D), California (Berkeley), 2006, Gm
Ronald G. Prinn, (D), MIT, 1971, As
Daniel H. Rothman, (D), Stanford, 1986, Yg
Leigh H. Royden, (D), MIT, 1982, Gt
Sara Seager, (D), Harvard, 1999, Xy
Susan Solomon, (D), California (Berkeley), 1981, As
Roger Summons, (D), New South Wales, 1972, CobCs
Jack Wisdom, (D), Caltech, 1981, Zn

Senior Research Scientist:
William Durham, (D), MIT, 1975, Cg
Michael Fehler, (D), MIT, 1979, Yg
C. Adam Schlosser, (D), Maryland, 1995, As

Principal Research Scientist:
Nilanjan Chatterjee, (D), CUNY, 1989, Cg
Stephanie Dutkiewicz, (D), Rhode Island, 1997, Cm
Eduardo Andrade Lima, (D), Catholic (Brazil), Ym
Nori Nakata, (D), Colorado Mines, 2013
Sai Ravela, (D), Massachusetts, 2002, Zn
Ryan Woosley, (D), Miami, 2012

Associate Professor:
Tanja Bosak, (D), Caltech, 2004, Pg
Kerri Cahoy, (D), Stanford, 2008, Zn
Laurent Demanet, (D), Caltech, 2006, Zn
Gregory Fournier, (D), Connecticut, 2009, Pg
Colette Heald, (D), Harvard, 2005, As
Oliver Jagoutz, (D), ETH (Switzerland), 2004, GitGc
Ruben Juanes, (D), California (Berkeley), 2003, Zn
David McGee, (D), Columbia, 2009, Cl
Paul O'Gorman, (D), Caltech, 2004, As
Shuhei Ono, (D), Penn State, 2001, PgCs
Noelle Selin, (D), Harvard, 2007, As

Assistant Professor:
Andrew Babbin, (D), Princeton, 2014, Cb
Kristin Bergmann, (D), Caltech, 2013, GsCl
Camilla Cattania, (D), GFZ German Res Ctr Geosci, 2015, Ys
Timothy W. Cronin, (D), MIT, 2014, As

Julien de Wit, (D), MIT, 2014, Zn
William Frank, (D), Institut de Physique du Globe de Paris, 2014
Brent Minchew, (D), Caltech, 2016, Yg
Matej Pec, (D), Basel (Switzerland), 2012, Nr
Senior Lecturer:
Lodovica Illari, (D), Imperial Coll (UK), 1982, Am
Emeritus:
B. Clark Burchfiel, (D), Yale, 1961, Gc
Charles C. Counselman, III, (D), 1969
J. Brian Evans, (D), MIT, 1978, Yx
Frederick A. Frey, (D), Wisconsin, 1967, CtGvi
Richard S. Lindzen, (D), Harvard, 1964, Am
Gordon H. Pettengill, (D), California (Berkeley), 1955, Zg
Raymond A. Plumb, (D), Manchester (UK), 1972, As
M. Gene Simmons, (D), Harvard, 1962, Yg
John B. Southard, (D), Harvard, 1966, Gs
Peter H. Stone, (D), Harvard, 1964, As
M Nafi Toksoz, (D), Caltech, 1963, Ys
Carl I. Wunsch, (D), MIT, 1967, Opo
Principal Research Engineer:
Christopher Hill, (D), Zn

Mount Holyoke College

Dept of Geology (B) (2016)
50 College Street
Clapp Laboratory #304
South Hadley, MA 01075-6419
p. (413) 538-2278
rforjwuo@mtholyoke.edu
http://www.mtholyoke.edu/acad/geology
f: https://www.facebook.com/groups/mhcgeoalums/
Administrative Assistant: Rhodaline Forjwuor
Enrollment (2016): B: 22 (14)
Professor:
Steven R. Dunn, (D), Wisconsin, 1989, Gp
Girma Kebbede, (D), Syracuse, 1981, Zy
Mark McMenamin, (D), California (Santa Barbara), 1984, PgGst
Thomas L. Millette, (D), Clark, 1989, ZriGm
Alan Werner, (D), Colorado, 1988, GleGm
Associate Professor:
Michelle J. Markley, (D), Minnesota, 1998, GcgGt
Assistant Professor:
Serin D. Houston, (D), Syracuse, 2012, Zyn
Geoprocessing Lab Manager:
Eugenio J. Marcano, (D), Cornell, 1994, ZiSoZn
Visiting Assistant Professor:
Samuel Tuttle, (D), Boston, 2015, Gq
Emeritus:
Martha M. Godchaux, (D), Oregon, 1969, Gv
Laboratory Director:
Penny M. Taylor, (M), SUNY (Oneonta), 2000, Gg
Geology Technician:
Gerard Marchand, (B), Westfield State, 1990, Gga

Northeastern University

Dept of Marine and Environmental Sciences (B,M,D) ○☒ (2020)
14 Holmes Hall
360 Huntington Ave
Boston, MA 02115
p. (617) 373-3176
environment@neu.edu
http://www.northeastern.edu/mes
Programs: Environmental Science (B); Environmental Studies (B); Ecology, Evolution, and Marine Biology (B), Marine Biology (B,M,D); Ecology (D); Evolution (D)
Enrollment (2018): B: 591 (154) M: 18 (1) D: 65 (13)
Professor:
Joseph Ayers, (D), California (Santa Cruz), 1975, Zn
Richard H. Bailey, (D), N Carolina, 1973, Pi
William Detrich, (D), Yale, Zn
Brian Helmuth, (D), Washington, 1997, OnZcRc
Mark Patterson, (D), Harvard, 1995, Zn
Hanumant Singh, (D), MIT, 1995, Zn
Chair:
Geoffrey Trussell, (D), William & Mary, 1998, Zn
Associate Professor:
Jonathan Grabowski, (D), North Carolina, 2012, GuEg
Malcolm D. Hill, (D), California (Santa Cruz), 1979, ZiGze
Justin Ries, (D), Johns Hopkins, 2005, Cm
Rebeca Rosengaus, (D), Boston, 1993, Zn
Steven Scyphers, (D), S Alabama, 2012, Zn
Aron Stubbins, (D), Newcastle upon Tyne, 2001, CgbZc
Associate Chair:
Jennifer Bowen, (D), Boston, Zn
Assistant Professor:
Loretta Fernandez, (D), MIT, 2010, Co
Tarik Gouhier, (D), McGill, Zn
Randall Hughes, (D), California (Davis), 2006, Zn
David Kimbro, (D), California, Zn
Kathleen Lotterhos, (D), Florida State, 2011, Zn
Amy Mueller, (D), MIT, 2012, Zn
Samuel Munoz, (D), Wisconsin, 2015, GsPcRn
Samuel Scarpino, (D), Texas, Zn
Steve Vollmer, (D), Harvard, Zn
Lecturer:
Daniel C. Douglass, (D), Wisconsin, 2005, GlSdPc
Tara Duffy, (D), SUNY (Stony Brook), Ob
Stephanie Eby, (D), Syracuse, 2010, Zn
Emeritus:
Donald Cheney, (D), S Florida, Zn
Gwilym Jones, (D), Indiana State, Zn
Peter S. Rosen, (D), William & Mary, 1976, OnZu
Martin E. Ross, (D), Idaho, 1978, Gie
Business and Operations Manager:
Elizabeth Magee, Zn
Academic Program Assistant:
Jessica Smith-Japhet

Salem State University

Geological Sciences Dept (B) ○⊘ (2021)
352 Lafayette Street
Salem, MA 01970
p. (978) 542-6282
bhubeny@salemstate.edu
https://www.salemstate.edu/academics/college-arts-and-sciences/geological-science
Programs: Geology, Applied Geosciences: Sustainability, Applied Geosciences: Forensic, Earth Science Education, Earth Studies
Enrollment (2018): B: 50 (17)
Chair:
J Bradford Hubeny, (D), Rhode Island, 2006, GeOnCs
Professor:
Douglas Allen, (D), Minnesota, 2003, CgHsCt
James L. Cullen, (D), Brown, 1984, GsPmOu
Assistant Professor:
Sara Mana, (D), Rutgers, 2013, GciGv
Erkan Toraman, (D), Minnesota, 2014, GpiGt
Emeritus:
Lindley S. Hanson, (D), Boston, 1988, GmgOn
Laboratory Director:
Renee Knudstrup, (B), Ca

Smith College

Dept of Geosciences (B) ☒ (2019)
Clark Science Center
44 College Lane
Northampton, MA 01063
p. (413) 585-3805
aavard@smith.edu
https://www.smith.edu/academics/geosciences
Enrollment (2010): B: 27 (6)
Chair:
Sara B. Pruss, (D), S California, 2004, Pg
Professor:
Bosiljka Glumac, (D), Tennessee, 1997, Gs
Robert M. Newton, (D), Massachusetts, 1978, Gm
Amy L. Rhodes, (D), Dartmouth, 1996, ClGe
Associate Professor:
Jack Loveless, (D), Cornell, 2008, Gtc
Assistant Professor:
Sarah Mazza, (D), Virginia Tech, 2016, Gx
Lecturer:
Mark E. Brandriss, (D), Stanford, 1994, Gx
Emeritus:
John B. Brady, (D), Harvard, 1975, GxzZe

H. Robert Burger, (D), Indiana, 1966, GcYeZi
H. Allen Curran, (D), N Carolina, 1968, Pg
Geoscience Technician:
Michael Vollinger, (B), Massachusetts, 1993

Tufts University

Dept of Earth and Ocean Sciences (B) ☒ (2020)
Lane Hall
2 N Hill Road
Medford, MA 02155
p. (617) 627-3494
anne.gardulski@tufts.edu
http://eos.tufts.edu/
f: https://www.facebook.com/TuftsEOS
Programs: Geological Sciences (B); Environmental Geology (B)
Enrollment (2019): B: 20 (12)
Associate Professor:
Anne F. Gardulski, (D), Syracuse, 1987, GrdGg
Professor:
Grant Garven, (D), British Columbia, 1982, HwqHy
John C. Ridge, (D), Syracuse, 1985, GlnGg
Associate Professor:
Andrew Kemp, (D), Pennsylvania, 2009, OnPmOg
Jill VanTongeren, (D), Columbia, 2010, GiCu
Lecturer:
Noel A. Heim, (D), Georgia, 2008, PgiPs
Emeritus:
Robert L. Reuss, (D), Michigan, 1970, Gzi

University of Massachusetts, Amherst

Dept of Geosciences (B,M,D) ●☒ (2019)
233 Morrill Science Center BLDG2
627 North Pleasant St.
Amherst, MA 01003-9297
p. (413) 545-2286
sburns@geo.umass.edu
http://www.geo.umass.edu/
f: https://www.facebook.com/umassgeo
t: https://twitter.com/umassgeo
Programs: Geology (BS, BA), Earth Systems (BS), Geosciences (MS & PhD), Geography (BA, BS & MS)
Certificates: GIST
Enrollment (2019): B: 77 (27) M: 26 (13) D: 33 (2)
Department Head:
Stephen J. Burns, (D), Duke, 1987, Cs
Distinguished University Professor:
Raymond S. Bradley, (D), Colorado, 1974, As
Professor:
Julie Brigham-Grette, (D), Colorado, 1985, GlPcGu
Michele L. Cooke, (D), Stanford, 1996, Gc
Robert DeConto, (D), Colorado, 1996, As
Piper Gaubatz, (D), California (Berkeley), 1968, Zy
R. Mark Leckie, (D), Colorado, 1984, PmGru
J. Michael Rhodes, (D), Australian Nat, 1970, GviCa
Sheila J. Seaman, (D), New Mexico, 1988, Gi
Michael L. Williams, (D), New Mexico, 1987, Gc
Extension Associate Professor:
Michael Rawlins, (D), New Hampshire, 2006, As
Extension Assistant Professor:
Christine Hatch, (D), California (Santa Cruz), 2007, HwgSp
Associate Extension Professor:
William P. Clement, (D), Wyoming, 1995, Yue
Associate Professor:
David Boutt, (D), New Mexico Tech, 2004, HwqHy
Steven Petsch, (D), Yale, 2000, Col
Stan Stevens, (D), California (Berkeley), 1983, Zy
Eve Vogel, (D), Oregon, 2007, Zy
Jonathan D. Woodruff, (D), MIT, 2008, Gs
Qian Yu, (D), California (Berkeley), 2005, Zri
Research Assistant Professor:
Ambarish Karmalkar, (D), Massachusetts, 2010, As
Brian Yellen, (D), Univ, Gs
Assistant Professor:
Isla Castañeda, (D), Minnesota, 2007, Ca
Haiying Gao, (D), Rhode Island, 2012, Ys
Isaac J. Larsen, (D), Washington, 2013, Gm
Justin Richardson, (D), Dartmouth, 2015, CbSc
Stephen Turner, (D), Harvard, 2015, Giv
Matthew Winnick, Stanford, 2015, Cbq
Research Associate:
Tim Cook, (D), Massachusetts, 2009, Pc
Lab Manager:
Jeff Salacup, (D), Brown, 2014, PcCb
Assistant Professor :
Forrest J. Bowlick, (D), Texas A&M, 2016, ZieZg
Lecturer:
Michael J. Jercinovic, (D), New Mexico, 1988, Gx
Seda Ialap-Ayça, (D), San Diego State, 2018, Zi
Adjunct Professor:
Eileen McGowan, (D), Massachusetts, 2010, Xg
Peter T. Panish, (D), Massachusetts, 1989, Gp
Emeritus:
Laurie L. Brown, (D), Oregon State, 1974, Ymg
Christopher D. Condit, (D), New Mexico, 1984, Gi
James A. Hafner, (D), Michigan, 1970, Zn
William D. McCoy, (D), Colorado, 1981, Zy
George E. McGill, (D), Princeton, 1958, Gc
Stearns A. Morse, (D), McGill, 1962, Gi
Rutherford H. Platt, (D), Chicago, 1971, Zu
Peter Robinson, (D), Harvard, 1963, Gc
Richard W. Wilkie, (D), Washington, 1968, ZynZn
Richard F. Yuretich, (D), Princeton, 1976, Cl
Massachusetts State Geologist:
Stephen B. Mabee, (D), Massachusetts, 1992, GgHw

University of Massachusetts, Boston

School for the Environment (B,M,D) ☒ (2019)
100 Morrissey Boulevard
Boston, MA 02125
p. (617) 287-7440
sfe@umb.edu
http://www.umb.edu/environment
Enrollment (2010): B: 153 (27) M: 22 (12) D: 18 (4)
Dean:
Robyn Hannigan, (D), Rochester, ClmCt
Professor:
Bob Chen, (D), California (San Diego), 1992, CoOc
Zhongping Lee, (D), S Florida, 1994, ZrOg
William Robinson, (D), Northeastern, 1981, Zn
Crystal Schaaf, (D), Boston, 1994, ZrAm
Director for Research, New England Aquarium:
Michael Tlusty, (D), Syracuse, 1996, Ob
Director, Environmental Studies Program:
Alan D. Christian, (D), Miami, 2002, HsGmCs
Associate Professor:
Robert Bowen, (D), S California, 1981, ZnnZn
Ellen Douglas, (D), Tufts, 2002, HwqHy
John Duff, (D), Washington, 1995, ZnnZn
Eugene Gallagher, (D), Washington, 1983, Ob
Juanita Urban-Rich, (D), Memorial, Ob
Assistant Professor:
Jennifer Bowen, (D), Boston, 2005, ObPgZn
Helen Poynton, (D), California (Berkeley), Zn
Research Engineer:
Francesco Peri, (M), Massachusetts (Boston), Zn
Manager, GIS Lab:
Helenmary Hotz, (M), Massachusetts (Boston), Zi
Director, Green Harbors Project:
Anamarija Frankic, (D), Virginia Inst of Marine Sci, Ze

University of Massachusetts, Lowell

Dept of Environmental, Earth, & Atmospheric Sciences (B,M,D) ⃠ (2020)
1 University Avenue
University of Massachusetts
Lowell, MA 01854
p. (978) 934-3903
Erica_Gavin@uml.edu
https://www.uml.edu/sciences/eeas/
f: https://www.facebook.com/Earth.Sciences.UMass.Lowell/
Programs: Geology, Environmental Science, Atmospheric Sci
Enrollment (2020): B: 28 (6) M: 18 (1)
Chair:
Daniel Obrist, (D), Nevada, 2002, As
Professor:
Frank P. Colby, (D), MIT, 1983, Am

G. Nelson Eby, (D), Boston, 1971, CgGiCt
Associate Professor:
Mathew Barlow, (D), Maryland, 1999, As
Juliette Rooney-Varga, (D), ZcRc
Assistant Professor:
Richard M. Gaschnig, (D), Washington State, 2010, CctCa
James Heiss, (D), Delaware, 2017, Hw
Christopher Skinner, (D), Stanford, 2014, At
Kate Swanger, (D), Boston, 2009, Gl
Lecturer:
Lori Weeden, (M), Boston Coll, 2002, GgeGs
Emeritus:
Arnold L. O'Brien, (D), Boston, 1973, Hw

Wellesley College

Dept of Geosciences (B) ☒ (2020)
106 Central Street
Wellesley, MA 02481-8203
p. (781) 283-3151
dbraband@wellesley.edu
http://www.wellesley.edu/Geosciences/
Programs: Geosciences
Administrative Assistant: Carol Gagosian
Enrollment (2020): B: 12 (4)
Chair:
Daniel J. Brabander, (D), Brown, 1997, Cl
Associate Scientist:
Katrin Monecke, (D), ETH (Switzerland), Gsn
Assistant Professor:
Adrian Castro, (D), Rensselaer, 2018, Gp
Emeritus:
James Besancon, (D), MIT, 1975, Hww
David Hawkins, (D), MIT, 1996, Gzi
Margaret D. Thompson, (D), Harvard, 1976, Gc
Instructor:
Kathleen W. Gilbert, (M), Miami, 1995, Cs

Williams College

Dept of Geosciences (B) ☒ (2020)
947 Main Street
Williamstown, MA 01267
p. (413) 597-2221
patricia.e.acosta@williams.edu
http://www.williams.edu/Geoscience
f: https://www.facebook.com/groups/williamsgeosciences
Programs: Geosciences
Administrative Assistant: Patricia E. Acosta
Enrollment (2020): B: 13 (13)
Chair:
Mea S. Cook, (D), MIT/WHOI, 2006, OuGe
Professor:
Ronadh Cox, (D), Stanford, 1993, GsXg
Paul Karabinos, (D), Johns Hopkins, 1981, Gc
Reinhard A. Wobus, (D), Stanford, 1966, GivGz
Associate Professor:
Phoebe A. Cohen, (D), Harvard, 2010, Pgg
Assistant Professor:
Alice Bradley, (D), Colorado, 2016, AtOn
Jose A. Constantine, (D), California (Santa Barbara), 2008, GmZi
Research Associate:
B. Gudveig Baarli, (D), Oslo, 1988, PssPi
Mark E. Brandriss, (D), Stanford, 1993, Gi
Lecturer:
Alex Apotsos, (D), MIT, 2007, Ge
Emeritus:
David P. Dethier, (D), Washington, 1977, Gm
Markes E. Johnson, (D), Chicago, 1977, PseGm
Science Librarian:
Helena F. Warburg, (M), Indiana Sch Lib Sci, 1987, Zn

Woods Hole Oceanographic Institution ❒

Dept of Geology & Geophysics (D) (2018)
Woods Hole, MA 02543-1541
p. (508) 289-2388
mburke@whoi.edu
http://www.whoi.edu/page.do?pid=7145
Administrative Assistant: Maryanne F. Ferreira
Enrollment (2014): D: 26 (0)
Chair:
Robert L. Evans, (D), Cambridge, 1991, Yrr
Senior Scientist:
Mark D. Behn, (D), MIT/WHOI, 2002, Yr
Joan M. Bernhard, (D), California (San Diego), 1990, Cg
Henry J B. Dick, (D), Yale, 1975, GitGc
Jeffrey Donnelly, (D), Brown, 2000, Gu
Daniel J. Fornari, (D), Columbia, 1978, Gu
Chris German, (D), Cambridge, 1988, Gt
Susan E. Humphris, (D), MIT/WHOI, 1977, GuCm
Lloyd D. Keigwin, (D), Rhode Island, 1979, CsGul
Jian Lin, (D), Brown, 1988, Gt
Olivier Marchal, (D), Paris, 1996, Pe
Daniel C. McCorkle, (D), Washington, 1987, Cm
Delia W. Oppo, (D), Columbia, 1989, Pm
Ralph A. Stephen, (D), Cambridge, 1978, Ys
Maurice A. Tivey, (D), Washington, 1988, Yrm
Tenured Associate Scientist:
Andrew Ashton, (D), Duke, 2005, On
Juan Pablo Canales Cisneros, (D), Barcelona, 1997, Yr
Anne L. Cohen, (D), Cape Town, 1993, PecOo
Sarah B. Das, (D), Penn State, 2003, GlAtZg
Virginia Edgcomb, (D), Delaware, 1997, ObZc
Glenn A. Gaetani, (D), MIT, 1996, Gi
Liviu Giosan, (D), SUNY (Stony Brook), 2001, GusPc
Daniel Lizarralde, (D), MIT/WHOI, 1997, Ys
Jeffrey J. McGuire, (D), MIT, 2000, Ys
Robert A. Sohn, (D), California (San Diego), 1996, Yr
S. Adam Soule, (D), Oregon, 2003, Gvu
Associate Scientist:
Weifu Guo, (D), Caltech, 2008, CslPe
Sune G. Nielsen, (D), ETH (Switzerland), 2005, Cs
Assistant Scientist:
Veronique Le Roux, (D), Macquarie, 2008, Gi
Senior Research Specialist:
James E. Broda, (B), Penn State, 1970, Gs
John A. Collins, (D), MIT/WHOI, 1989, Ys
Ann P. McNichol, (D), MIT, 1986, Oc
Mark L. Roberts, (D), Duke, 1988, Yg
Research Specialist:
Jurek Blusztajn, (D), Polish Acad of Sci, 1985, CcGi
Alan R. Gagnon, (B), New Hampshire, 1983, Cs
Li Xu, (D), Xiamen, 1992, Yr
Engineer:
Peter B. Landry, (B), NEIT, 1990, Ca
Research Associate:
Kathryn L. Elder, (B), Massachusetts, 1985, Cs
Kalina D. Gospodinova, (M), MIT/WHOI, 2012, Cm
Joshua D. Hlavenka, (B), N Texas
Peter C. Lemmond, (B), Lehigh, 1978, Zn
Brett Longworth, (M), Massachusetts, 2005, Ou
Brian D. Monteleone, (D), Syracuse, 2000, Cc
Kathryn R. Pietro, (M), California (Davis), 2007, Gu
Adjunct Scientist:
Peter D. Bromirski, (D), Hawaii, 1993
Johnson R. Cann, (D), Cambridge, 1963, Ys
Colin Devey, (D), Oxford, 1986
Javier Escartin, (D), MIT, 1996, Gg
Andrea D. Hawkes, (D), Pennsylvania, 2008
Gregory Hirth, (D), Brown, 1991, Gc
Kuo-Fang (Denner) Huang, (D), Natl Cheng Kung, 2007
Peter B. Kelemen, (D), Washington, 1987, Gi
Yajing Liu, (D), Harvard, 2007
John Maclennan, (D), Cambridge, 2000
Larry Mayer, (D), Scripps, 1979, Gg
Andrew M. McCaig, (D), Cambridge, 1983
Jerry F. McManus, (D), Columbia, 1997, Pe
Uri S. ten Brink, (D), Columbia, 1986, Yg
David Thornalley, (D), Churchill, 2008
Masako Tominaga, (D), Texas A&M, 2009
Oceanographer Emeritus:
Graham S. Giese, (D), Chicago, 1966, On
Steven J. Manganini, (B), Nasson, 1974, Ou
Robert J. Schneider, (D), Tufts, 1968, Cc
Stephen A. Swift, (D), MIT/WHOI, 1986, Yr
Karl F. Von Reden, (D), Hamburg, 1983, Ct
Emeritus:
William A. Berggren, (D), Stockholm, 1962, Ps

Carl O. Bowin, (D), Princeton, 1960, YrGtg
William B. Curry, (D), Brown, 1980, Pm
Stanley R. Hart, (D), MIT, 1960, CgGvCp
Susumu Honjo, (D), Hokkaido, 1961, Ou
George P. Lohmann, (D), Brown, 1972, Pe
David A. Ross, (D), California (San Diego), 1965, GuOg
Hans Schouten, (D), Utrecht, 1970, Yr
Nobumichi Shimizu, (D), Tokyo, 1968, Ca
William G. Thompson, (D), Columbia, 2005, PeCc
Brian E. Tucholke, (D), MIT/WHOI, 1973, Gut
Elazar Uchupi, (D), S California, 1962, Ou
Frank B. Wooding, (B), Harvard, 1965, Yr

Dept of Marine Chemistry & Geochemistry (M,D) ☒ (2020)
360 Woods Hole Road
MS 25
Woods Hole, MA 02543-1541
p. (508) 289-3696
mcg@whoi.edu
http://www.whoi.edu/page.do?pid=7146
Programs: Chemical Oceanography
Administrative Assistant: Linda Cannata, Sheila A. Clifford, Donna Mortimer, Mary Zawoysky
Enrollment (2015): D: 28 (5)
Dept. Administrator:
Mary Murphy
Dept. Chair:
Bernhard Peucker-Ehrenbrink, (D), Max Planck, 1994, CmlHs
Associate Dean:
Margaret K. Tivey, (D), Washington, 1989, Cm
Senior Scientist:
Ken O. Buesseler, (D), MIT/WHOI, 1986, Oc
Matthew A. Charette, (D), Rhode Island, 1998, Cm
Colleen Hansel, (D), Stanford, 2004, Cm
Konrad A. Hughen, (D), Colorado, 1997, Cc
Elizabeth B. Kujawinski, (D), MIT/WHOI, 2000, Oc
Mark D. Kurz, (D), MIT/WHOI, 1982, Cc
Christopher M. Reddy, (D), Rhode Island, 1997, Co
Daniel J. Repeta, (D), MIT/WHOI, 1982, Co
Mak A. Saito, (D), MIT/WHOI, 2001, Oc
Jeffrey S. Seewald, (D), Minnesota, 1990, Cp
Benjamin Van Mooy, (D), Washington, 2003, Oc
Associate Scientist w/Tenure:
Valier Galy, (D), Inst Nat Polytechnique de Lorrain, 2007, Cm
Julie Huber, (D), Washington, 2004, Cm
Frieder Klein, (D), Bremen, 2009, Cm
Z. Aleck Wang, (D), Georgia, 2003, Cm
Scott Wankel, (D), Stanford, 2007, Cm
Associate Scientist:
Amy Apprill, (D), Hawaii, 2009, Ob
David Nicholson, (D), Washington, 2009, Gu
Assistant Scientist:
Peter Barry, (D), California (San Diego), 2012, Cm
Ann Dunlea, (D), Boston, 2016, Cm
Tristan Horner, (D), Oxford, 2012, Cm
Hyewon (Heather) Kim, (D), Columbia, 2017, Cm
Matthew Long, (D), Virginia, 2013, Cm
Adam Subhas
Collin Ward, (D), Michigan, 2015, Cm
Sr. Research Specialist:
Robert K. Nelson, (B), C Connecticut, 1980, Co
Senior Research Specialist (ret.):
Dempsey E. Lott, (M), Florida State, 1973, Oc
Research Specialist:
Heather Benway, (D), Oregon State, 2005, OcCmOo
Helen Fredricks, (D), Plymouth (UK), 2000, Oc
Paul Henderson, (B), Bowling Green, 1997, Cm
Carl G. Johnson, (M), Maine, 1983, Ca
Ivan D. Lima, (D), Miami, 1999, Oc
Krista Longnecker, (D), Oregon State, 2004, Oc
Steven M. Pike, (M), Rhode Island, 1998, Ca
Jennie Rheuban, (M), Virginia, 2013, Oc
Melissa Soule, (D), Oregon, 2007
Research Assistant:
Samual Bowman
Kevin Cahill, (B), Massachusetts, 1999, Cm
Jessica Drysdale, (M), Queens (Ontario), 2011, Oc
Dan Lowenstein, (B), Dartmouth, 2014
Kate Morkeski, (M), Virginia Tech, 2007
Justin Ossolinski
Information Systems Associate:
Adam Shepherd, (B), Northeastern, 2001
Communications Specialist for WHOI SeaGrant:
Stephanie Murphy, (B), California (Santa Cruz), 1985
Research Associate:
Maureen Auro, (M), San Francisco State, 2007
Joshua M. Curtice, (B), Massachusetts, 1992, Cc
Dana Gerlach
Mairead Mahegan, (M), Cal State (Northridge), Ob
Matt McIlvin, (D), Massachusetts, 2004, Oc
Carolyn Miller, (D), Boston, 2006
Dawn Moran, (B), Bridgewater State, 2003, Ob
Margrethe Serres, (D), Wisconsin (Madison), 1995
Gretchen Swarr, (B), Colgate, 2007, Oc
Sean Sylva, (B), Rhode Island, 1997, Oc
Adjunct Scientist:
Scott C. Doney, (D), MIT, 1991, Cm
Tim Eglinton, (D), Newcastle (UK), 1988, Oc
Margaret Estapa, (D), Maine, 2011, Oc
Adjunct Professor:
Minhan Dai, (D), Pierre & Marie Curie, 1995, Cm
Rachel Stanley
Scientist Emeritus:
Michael P. Bacon, (D), MIT/WHOI, 1976, Oc
Werner G. Deuser, (D), Penn State, 1963, CsGsu
John W. Farrington, (D), Rhode Island, 1972, ComOc
William R. Martin, (D), MIT/WHOI, 1985, Oc
Frederick L. Sayles, (D), Manchester (UK), 1968, Oc
Edward R. Sholkovitz, (D), California (San Diego), 1972, Oc
Geoffrey Thompson, (D), Manchester (UK), 1965, Cm
Oliver C. Zafiriou, (D), Johns Hopkins, 1966, Oc
Oceanographer Emeritus:
Cyndy Chandler, (B), SUNY (Geneseo), 1975, Og
Nelson M. Frew, (D), Washington, 1971, Ca
David M. Glover, (D), Alaska, 1985, Oc
Jean K. Whelan, (D), MIT, 1965, Co
Marine Education Specialist:
Grace Simpkins, (M), Alaska, 2000
Communications and Outreach Specialist:
Jeffrey Brodeur

Worcester State University

Earth, Environment and Physics (B) (2018)
486 Chandler Street
Worcester, MA 01602-2597
p. (508) 929-8583
whansen@worcester.edu
http://www.worcester.edu/Earth-Environment-and-Physics/
f: https://www.facebook.com/worcesterstatedeep
Programs: Earth Science Education; Geography; Environmental Science
Enrollment (2018): B: 120 (12)
Professor:
Allison L. Dunn, (D), Harvard, 2006, AsZyHg
William J. Hansen, (D), CUNY, 2002, ZiyZr
Associate Professor:
Patricia A. Benjamin, (D), Clark, 2002, Zg
Douglas E. Kowalewski, (D), Boston, 2009, GmlZy
Assistant Professor:
Nabin Malakar, (D), SUNY (Albany), 2012, Ap
Alexander Tarr, (D), California (Berkeley), 2014, Zg
Instructor:
Mark O. Johnson, (D), Clark, 1993, Zy

Michigan

Adrian College

Geology Dept (A,B) ☒ (2019)
110 S. Madison St.
Adrian, MI 49221
p. (517) 265-5161
tmuntean@adrian.edu
http://adrian.edu/academics/academic-departments/geology/
f: https://www.facebook.com/groups/55153346895/
Programs: Geology, Environmental Geology
Enrollment (2018): B: 14 (4)

Chair:
Thomas Muntean, (D), Nevada, 2012, Gde
Professor:
Sarah L. Hanson, (D), Utah, 1995, Giz

Albion College

Dept of Geological Sciences (B) ○⊘ (2021)
611 E. Porter St.
Albion, MI 49224
p. (517) 629-0312
cmenold@albion.edu
http://www.albion.edu/geology/
Programs: Geology; Earth Science; Earth Science with Secondary Education Certification; Geology with Secondary Education Certification
Certificates: Geology; GIS; Paleontology; Environmental Geology; Earth Science with Secondary Education Certification (minors)
Enrollment (2020): B: 28 (7)
Chair:
Carrie A. Menold, (D), California (Los Angeles), 2006, GpCsGt
Professor:
Beth Z. Lincoln, (D), California (Los Angeles), 1985, Gc
Thomas I. Wilch, (D), New Mexico Tech, 1997, GlvGm
Associate Professor:
Michael McRivette, (D), California (Los Angeles), 2011, GtZir
Assistant Professor:
Joe Lee-Cullin, (D), Michigan State, 2020, Ge
Madeline Marshall, (D), Chicago, 2018, GsPi
Emeritus:
William S. Bartels, (D), Michigan, 1986, Pv
Russell G. Clark, (D), Dartmouth, 1972, GiZi
Lawrence D. Taylor, (D), Ohio State, 1962, Gl

Calvin College

Dept of Geology, Geography & Environmental Studies (B) (2015)
3201 Burton SE
Grand Rapids, MI 49546
p. (616) 526-8415
jbascom@calvin.edu
http://www.calvin.edu/academic/geology/
Enrollment (2012): B: 60 (14)
Chair:
Jason E. VanHorn, (D), Ohio State, 2007, ZirRh
Johnathan Bascom, (D), Iowa, 1989, Zy
Professor:
Henry Aay, (D), Clark, 1978, Zyu
Janel M. Curry, (D), Minnesota, 1985, Zy
Ralph F. Stearley, (D), Michigan, 1990, PvOgRh
Associate Professor:
Deanna van Dijk, (D), Waterloo, 1998, GmOnZy
Assistant Professor:
Kenneth A. Bergwerff, (M), Grand Valley State, 1988, Ze
James Skillen, (D), Cornell, 2006, Zu
Laboratory Manager/Instructor:
Margene Brewer, (M), W Michigan, 1991, ZnGgZn
Emeritus:
Clarence Menninga, (D), Purdue, 1966, CcGg
Gerald K. Van Kooten, (D), California (Santa Barbara), 1980, GoCePi
Davis A. Young, (D), Brown, 1969, GlRhGz

Central Michigan University

Dept of Earth and Atmospheric Sciences (B) 🖱 (2020)
314 Brooks Hall
Mount Pleasant, MI 48859
p. (989) 774-3179
l.d.lemke@cmich.edu
https://www.cmich.edu/colleges/cst/earth_atmos/Pages/
Programs: Geology; Meteorology; Environmental Science
Enrollment (2020): B: 33 (16)
Professor:
Martin Baxter, (D), St Louis, 2006, Ams
Lawrence D. Lemke, (D), Michigan, 2003, HwGer
Mona Sirbescu, (D), Missouri, 2002, GiCup
Associate Professor:
Anthony Chappaz, (D), Quebec, 2008, Cat
Daria Kluver, (D), Delaware, 2011, Asm
Wendy Robertson, (D), Texas, 2014, HwCg
Assistant Professor:
John Allen, (D), Australian Nat, 2013, Ams
Jason Keeler, (D), Illinois, 2015, Am
Natalia Zakharova, (D), Columbia, 2014, YgGe
Lecturer:
Rachael Agardy, (M), Texas A&M, 2005, OuGrs
Maria Mercedes Gonzalez, (D), Nac del Sur (Argentina), 1997, Gig
Adjunct Professor:
Megan Rohrssen, (D), California, 2013, Co
Nicole West, (D), Penn State, 2014, Gm
Emeritus:
Richard Mower, (D), Wisconsin, 1981, Am
Related Staff:
James J. Student, (D), Virginia Tech, 2002, CaGiz

Charles Stewart Mott Community College

Div of Science and Mathematics (A) 🖱 (2020)
1401 East Court St.
Flint, MI 48503
p. (810) 762-0279
sheila.swyrtek@mcc.edu
http://www.mcc.edu/science_math
Professor:
Sheila Swyrtek, (M), Minnesota (Duluth), 1996, Ga

Concordia University

Div of Natural Sciences (A,B,M) ⊘ (2019)
4090 Geddes Road
Ann Arbor, MI 48105-2750
p. (734) 995-7300
James.Refenes@cuaa.edu
Programs: Earth Science Education
Assoc. Prof. Biology:
James L. Refenes, (D), E Michigan, 2016, Ze

Delta College

Dept of Geology (A) (2015)
1961 Delta Road
University Center, MI 48710-0002
p. (989) 686-9252
andreabair@delta.edu
Department Secretary: Barb Jurmanovich
Enrollment (2011): A: 8 (4)
Department Chair:
Timothy L. Clarey, (D), W Michigan, 1996, HwGcPv
Lecturer:
Mary C. Gorte, (M), Rensselaer, 1983, Gs
Emeritus:
Barry A. Carlson, (D), Michigan State, 1974, Yg
Paul A. Catacosinos, (D), Michigan State, 1972, Gr
Cooperating Faculty:
Kevin T. Dehne, (M), E Michigan, 1992, Ze

Eastern Michigan University

Dept of Geography & Geology (B) (2015)
Ypsilanti, MI 48197
p. (743) 487-8589
rsambroo@emich.edu
Head:
Michael Kasenow, (D), W Michigan, 1994, Hg
Richard A. Sambrook, (D)
Professor:
Eugene Jaworski, (D), Louisiana State, 1971, Zr
Carl F. Ojala, (D), Georgia, 1972, As
Constantine N. Raphael, (D), Louisiana State, 1967, Gu
Associate Professor:
Steven T. LoDuca, (D), Rochester, 1990, Pi
Assistant Professor:
Kevin Blake, (D), Wisconsin, 1998, Gl
Michael Bradley, (D), Utah, 1988, Gc
Maria-Serena Poli, (D), Padua, 1995, Pe

Ferris State University

Dept of Physical Sciences ☒ (2019)
ASC-3021
Big Rapids, MI 49307

p. (231) 591-2588
heckf@ferris.edu
https://ferris.edu/arts-sciences/departments/physical-sciences
Programs: None
Certificates: None
Professor:
Frederick R. Heck, (D), Northwestern, 1987, GgZg

Gogebic Community College

Math-Science Div (A) (2015)
E4946 Jackson Rd.
Ironwood, MI 49938
p. (906) 932-4231
admissions@gogebic.edu
http://www.gogebic.edu/academics/Math_Science/
Professor:
Bill Perkis, Gg

Grand Rapids Community College

Physical Sciences Dept (A) (2020)
143 Bostwick Avenue, NE
Grand Rapids, MI 49503
p. (616) 234-4248
jqualls@grcc.edu
http://www.grcc.edu/physicalscience/geology
f: https://www.facebook.com/GRCCphysicalsciences
Programs: Geology, Environmental Studies and Sustainablility
Enrollment (2018): A: 9 (0)
Assistant Professor:
Tari Mattox, (M), N Illinois, 1984, GgvCg

Grand Valley State University

Dept of Geology (B) ⃠ (2019)
1 Campus Drive
118 Padnos Hall
Allendale, MI 49401
p. (616) 331-3728
geodept@gvsu.edu
http://www.gvsu.edu/geology
Programs: Geology; Geology with Environmental Emphasis; Geology-Chemistry
Administrative Assistant: Janet H. Potgeter
Enrollment (2018): B: 100 (23)
Head:
Figen A. Mekik, (D), N Illinois, 1999, GuCm
Professor:
Patrick M. Colgan, (D), Wisconsin, 1996, GmlPe
Stephen R. Mattox, (D), N Illinois, 1992, ZeGv
Virginia L. Peterson, (D), Massachusetts, 1992, GxcGt
Peter J. Wampler, (D), Oregon State, 2004, HsZiGm
John C. Weber, (D), Northwestern, 1995, GctYd
Associate Professor:
Kevin C. Cole, (D), Arizona, 1990, Gz
Peter E. Riemersma, (D), Wisconsin, 1997, Hw
Assistant Professor:
Caitlin N. Callahan, (D), W Michigan, 2013, GgZg
Tara A. Kneeshaw, (D), Texas A&M, 2008, ClGe
Instructor:
Kelly L. Heid, (M), Mississippi State, 2011, Ze
John M. VanRegenmorter, (M), Colorado, 2011, PvGsr
Ian Z. Winkelstern, (D), Michigan, 2018, GsOo
Visiting Professor:
Jeremy C. Gouldey, (D), Northwestern, 2015, CgPeCg
Emeritus:
Thomas E. Hendrix, (D), Wisconsin, 1960, Gc
William J. Neal, (D), Missouri, 1968, GsdGr
Norman W. Ten Brink, (D), Washington, 1971, Gm
Patricia E. Videtich, (D), Brown, 1982, Gd

Henry Ford Community College

Science Div (2015)
Dearborn, MI 48128
p. (313) 845-9632
cjacobs@hfcc.edu

Hope College

Dept of Geological & Environmental Sciences (B) (2020)
P.O. Box 9000
Holland, MI 49422-9000
p. (616) 395-7540
bodenbender@hope.edu
https://hope.edu/academics/geological-environmental-sciences/
Programs: BA in Geology, BS in Geology, Minor in Geology, Minor in Environmental Science, Environmental Science with Concentration in Biology, Environmental Science with Concentration in Chemistry, Environmental Science with Concentration in Geology
Enrollment (2020): B: 16 (5)
Chair:
Brian E. Bodenbender, (D), Michigan, 1994, GsPiGe
Professor:
Jon W. Peterson, (D), Chicago, 1989, Ge
Assistant Professor:
Sarah L. Dean, (D), Rice, 2014, Gc
Michael Philben, (D), S Carolina, 2014, CgScGe
Adjunct Professor:
Suzanne DeVries-Zimmerman, (M), Princeton, 1989, Gge

Jackson College

Dept of Geology & Geography (A,B) (2017)
2111 Emmons Road
Jackson, MI 49201
p. ((51) 7) -787- (Ext. 00 x157)
AlbeeScSteven@jccmi.edu
http://www.jccmi.edu/academics/science/geo
Enrollment (2012): A: 200 (20)
Wilbur L. Dungy Endowed Chair in the Sciences:
Steven R. Albee-Scott, (D), Michigan, 2005, GePeSf

Lake Michigan College

Lake Michigan College (A) (2015)
Napier Avenue Campus
2755 E. Napier Avenue
Benton Harbor, MI 49022
lovett@lakemichigancollege.edu
http://www.lakemichigancollege.edu/index.php?option=com_content&task=view&id=509&Itemid=157
Instructor:
Cole Lovett, (D), W Michigan, 1995, Gg

Lake Superior State University

Geology (B) O ☒ (2019)
650 W. Easterday Avenue
Sault Ste. Marie, MI 49783
p. (906) 635-2267
pkelso@lssu.edu
https://www.lssu.edu/geology/
Programs: B.S. Geology, B.S. Geology - Environmental option
Certificates: GIS, GIS associates degree
Administrative Assistant: Donna White
Enrollment (2018): B: 38 (12)
Professor:
Paul R. Kelso, (D), Minnesota, 1993, YmGct
Assistant Professor:
William (Bill) Houston, (D), Michigan Tech, 2002, Gsg
Hari Kandel, (D), Florida Intl, 2015, HgZi
MaryKathryn (Kat) Rocheford, (D), Iowa, 2014, GeZiGa
Matt Spencer, (D), Penn State, 2005, Gl
Emeritus:
Lewis M. Brown, (D), New Mexico, 1973, PiZe
Science Lab Manager:
Benjamin Southwell, (M), C Michigan, 2012, Zn

Macomb Community College, Center Campus

Dept of Science (Geology) (A) (2015)
44575 Garfield Road
Clinton Township, MI 48038-1139
p. (586) 286-2154
schaferc@macomb.edu
Enrollment (2014): A: 9 (0)
Professor:
Carl M. Schafer, (M), Montana, 1998, Gg

Michigan State University

Dept of Earth and Environmental Sciences (B,M,D) (2018)
288 Farm Lane
East Lansing, MI 48824-1115
p. (517) 355-4626
geosci@msu.edu
https://glg.natsci.msu.edu/
Enrollment (2014): M: 4 (0) D: 20 (0)

Chair:
Ralph E. Taggart, (D), Michigan State, 1971, Pb

Professor:
jiquan Chen, (D), Washington, 1991, Zg
Kazuya Fujita, (D), Northwestern, 1979, Ys
Julie C. Libarkin, (D), Arizona, 1999, Zen
David T. Long, (D), Kansas, 1977, ClGeb
Michael A. Velbel, (D), Yale, 1984, ClGdSc

Associate Professor:
Bruno Basso, (D), Michigan State, 2002, Zn
Danita S. Brandt, (D), Yale, 1985, PiGr
Michael D. Gottfried, (D), Kansas, 1991, Pv
David W. Hyndman, (D), Stanford, 1995, Hy

Assistant Professor:
Tyrone Rooney, (D), Penn State, 2006, Gi
Matt Schrenk, (D), Washington, 2005, Pg
Jay Zarnetske, (D), Oregon State, 2011, Hwg

Michigan Technological University

A. E. Seaman Mineral Museum ☒ (2018)
1404 E. Sharon Avenue
Houghton, MI 49931
p. (906) 487-2572
tjb@mtu.edu
http://www.museum.mtu.edu

Director:
Theodore J. Bornhorst, (D), New Mexico, 1980, EgCgGx

Associate Curator:
Christopher J. Stefano, (D), Michigan, 2010, GzxCg

Dept of Geological & Mining Engineering & Sciences (B,M,D) O☒ (2019)
1400 Townsend Drive
Dow Building, Room 630
Houghton, MI 49931-1295
p. (906) 487-2531
asmirnov@mtu.edu
http://www.mtu.edu/geo
Enrollment (2018): B: 78 (30) M: 39 (5) D: 7 (5)

Chair & Professor:
John S. Gierke, (D), Michigan Tech, 1990, Hy

Provost and Acting Dean, Graduate School:
Jacqueline E. Huntoon, (D), Penn State, 1990, GsZe

Professor:
Simon Carn, (D), Cambridge, 1999, ZrGv
Alex S. Mayer, (D), North Carolina, 1992, Hy
Aleksey V. Smirnov, (D), Rochester, 2002, YmgGt
James R. Wood, (D), Johns Hopkins, 1973, Cl

Associate Professor:
Thomas Oommen, (D), Tufts, 2009, NeZiNg
Gregory P. Waite, (D), Utah, 2004, YsGv
Shiliang Wu, (D), Harvard, 2007, AsCg

Assistant Professor:
Roohollah Askari, (D), Calgary, 2013, YxxNp
Snehamoy Chatterjee, (D), Indian Inst of Tech, 2007, NmGqNx
Chad Deering, (D), Canterbury (NZ), 2009, Ggi

Department Facilities Manager:
Robert Barron, (B), Michigan Tech, 1979, ZgGzi

Lecturer:
Nathan Manser, (D), S Florida, 2015, GeNm

Adjunct Professor and Director, Great Lakes Research Ctr.:
Guy A. Meadows, (D), Purdue, 1977, Gu

Senior Lecturer:
Jeremy Shannon, (D), Michigan Tech, 2006, Gg

Postdoctoral Research Fellow and Temporary Faculty:
Rudiger Escobar-Wolf, (D), Michigan Tech, 2013, Gv

Research Scientist:
Carol Asiala, (B), Michigan Tech, 1985

Cooperating Faculty:
William I. Rose, (D), Dartmouth, 1970, Gv
Roger M. Turpening, (D), Michigan, 1966, Ye

Mott Community College

Science and Mathematics (A) ☒ (2019)
1401 East Court St.
Flint, MI 48503
p. (810) 232-9312
sheila.swyrtek@mcc.edu
http://www.mcc.edu
Enrollment (2015): A: 4 (0)

Professor:
Sheila M. Swyrtek, (M), Minnesota (Duluth), 1997, ZeGa

Muskegon Community College

Dept of Mathematics & Physical Sciences (A) (2016)
221 S. Quarterline Road
Muskegon, MI 49442
p. (231) 777-0289
amber.kumpf@muskegoncc.edu
http://www.muskegoncc.edu/pages/652.asp
Administrative Assistant: Tamera Owens

Instructor:
Amber C. Kumpf, (M), Rhode Island, 2010, GgYrOu

Northwestern Michigan College

Northwestern Michigan College (2015)
1701 East Front Street
Traverse City, MI 49686
p. (231) 995-1000
rhouston@nmc.edu
http://www.nmc.edu

Oakland Community College

Natural Sciences Dept (A) ☒ (2017)
2900 Featherstone Road
Auburn Hills, MI 48326
p. (248) 232-4538
lgkodosk@oaklandcc.edu
Programs: Science (A)

Schoolcraft College

Dept of Geology (A) (2015)
18600 Haggerty Road
Livonia, MI 48151
p. (734) 462-4400
jrexius@schoolcraft.edu

Instructor:
James E. Rexius, (M), E Michigan, 1978, Gl

University of Michigan

Dept of Climate and Space Sciences and Engineering (B,M,D) ☒ (2019)
2455 Hayward
Ann Arbor, MI 48109-2143
p. (734) 615-3583
clasp--um@umich.edu
http://clasp.engin.umich.edu/
f: www.facebook.com/umclasp
t: @umclasp
Programs: Climate & Space Science & Engineering PhD; Applied Climate MEng; Space Engineering MEng; Atmospheric & Space Sciences MS; Climate & Meteorology BSE; Space Sciences & Engineering BSE
Certificates: N/A
Enrollment (2019): B: 30 (7) M: 49 (26) D: 122 (5)

Chair:
Tuija Pulkkinen, (D), Helsinki, 1992, Zn

Professor:
Sushil Atreya, (D), Michigan, ApZy
John Boyd, (D), Harvard, 1976, OpAs
R. Paul Drake, (D), Johns Hopkins
Lennard Fisk, (D), California (San Diego)
Brian Gilchrist, (D), Stanford
Tamas Gombosi, (D), Lóránd Eötvös

Enrico Landi, (D), Florence
Michael Liemohn, (D), Michigan
Mark B. Moldwin, (D), Boston, 1993, XpYz
Joyce Penner, (D), Harvard
Nilton Renno, (D), MIT
Aaron Ridley, (D), Michigan
Richard B. Rood, (D), Florida State, 1982, ZcAsm
Christopher Ruf, (D), Massachusetts
Perry Samson, (D), Wisconsin, 1979, AsZeAm
James Slavin, (D), California (Los Angeles)

Associate Professor:
Jeremy Bassis, (D), Scripps, 2007, GlOgZg
Mark Flanner, (D), California (Irvine)
Xianglei Huang, (D), Caltech
Christiane Jablonowski, (D), Michigan, 2004, AsmZo
Xianzhe Jia, (D), California (Los Angeles)
Justin C. Kasper, (D), MIT, 2003
Susan Lepri, (D), Michigan
Allison Steiner, (D), Georgia Tech
Shasha Zou, (D), California (Los Angeles)

Assistant Professor:
Angel F. Adames-Corraliza, (D), Washington, Ast
Gretchen Keppel-Aleks, (D), Caltech
Eric A. Kort, (D), Harvard
Ashley E. Payne, California (Irvine), 2016, At

Dept of Earth and Environmental Sciences (B,M,D) (2015)
2534 C.C. Little Building
1100 North University Avenue
Ann Arbor, MI 48109-1005
p. (734) 764-1435
mukasa@umich.edu
http://www.lsa.umich.edu/geo/
Administrative Assistant: Robert J. Patterer

Professor:
Tomasz K. Baumiller, (D), Chicago, 1990, Pg
Joel D. Blum, (D), Caltech, 1990, CsaCl
Maria Clara Castro, (D), Paris, 1995, Hy
Daniel C. Fisher, (D), Harvard, 1975, Pi
Stephen E. Kesler, (D), Stanford, 1966, Eg
Rebecca A. Lange, (D), California (Berkeley), 1989, Gi
Kyger C. Lohmann, (D), SUNY (Stony Brook), 1977, CsGsCl
Samuel B. Mukasa, (D), California (Santa Barbara), 1984, Cc
Henry N. Pollack, (D), Michigan, 1963, Yg
Jeroen Ritsema, (D), California (Santa Cruz), 1995, Ysg
Larry J. Ruff, (D), Caltech, 1981, Ys
Gerald R. Smith, (D), Michigan, 1965, Ps
Ben van der Pluijm, (D), New Brunswick, 1984, GcZce
Lynn M. Walter, (D), Miami, 1983, Cl
Youxue Zhang, (D), Columbia, 1989, Cu

Associate Professor:
Udo Becker, (D), Virginia Tech, 1995, Zn
Robyn J. Burnham, (D), Washington, 1987, Pb
Todd A. Ehlers, (D), Utah, 2001, Yg
Nathan A. Niemi, (D), Caltech, 2001, Gtc
Benjamin Passey, (D), Utah, 2007, CsaCl
Christopher J. Poulsen, (D), Penn State, 1999, Pe
Peter J. van Keken, (D), Utrecht, 1989, Yg

Associate Research Scientist:
Shaopeng Huang, (D), Acad Sinica (Beijing), 1990, YhZcGt

Assistant Professor:
Marin Clark, (D), MIT, 2003, Gm
Ingrid Hendy, (D), California (Santa Barbara), 2000, Pg
Jeffrey A. Wilson, (D), Chicago, 1999, Gg

Research Scientist:
Jeffrey C. Alt, (D), Miami, 1984, Ou

Associate Research Scientist:
Chris Hall, (D), Toronto, 1982, Cc
Josep M. Pares, (D), Barcelona, 1988, Ym

Assistant Research Scientist:
James D. Gleason, (D), Arizona, 1994, Cg
Jie Lian, (D), Michigan, 2003, Gz
Mirjam Schaller, (D), Bern, 2001, Gm

Adjunct Assistant Research Scientist:
Roland C. Rouse, (D), Michigan, 1972, Gz

Adjunct Assistant Professor:
Karen L. Webber, (D), Rice, 1988, Gv

Adjunct Professor:
John W. Geissman, (D), Michigan, 1980, Ym
William B. Simmons, (D), Michigan, 1973, Gz

Emeritus:
Charles Beck, (D), Cornell, 1955, Pg
William Farrand, (D), Michigan, 1960, Ga
William C. Kelly, (D), Columbia, 1954, Eg
Philip A. Meyers, (D), Rhode Island, 1972, CoGnu
Theodore C. Moore, (D), California (San Diego), 1968, OuPmc
James O'Neil, (D), Chicago, 1963, Cs
Robert M. Owen, (D), Wisconsin, 1975, CmGu
Donald R. Peacor, (D), MIT, 1962, Gz
David K. Rea, (D), Oregon State, 1974, Gu
Rob Van der Voo, (D), Utrecht, 1969, YmGtc
Bruce H. Wilkinson, (D), Texas, 1973, GseGt

University of Michigan, Dearborn

Dept of Natural Sciences (B,M) (2015)
4901 Evergreen Road
Dearborn, MI 48128
p. (313) 593-5277
kmurray@umd.umich.edu
http://www.umd.umich.edu/?id=570101
Enrollment (2013): B: 30 (4) M: 14 (3)

Acting Chair:
Kent S. Murray, (D), California (Davis), 1981, Hw

Professor:
Don Bord, (D), Dartmouth, 1976, Xy
Jacob A. Napieralski, (D), Purdue, 2005, GmlZi

Associate Professor:
John Riebesell, (D), Chicago, 1975, Zu

Lecturer:
David Matzke, (M), Michigan, 1975, Xy

Adjunct Professor:
Michael Favor, (B), Michigan, 1985, Zn

Washtenaw Community College

Dept of Geology (A) (2015)
4800 E. Huron River Drive
Ann Arbor, MI 48105
p. (734) 677-5111
salbach@wccnet.edu

Head:
Suzanne M. Albach, (M), Mississippi State, 2005, ZegGe

Wayne State University

Geology Dept (B,M) ☒ (2019)
0224 Old Main Building
4831 Cass Avenue
Detroit, MI 48201
p. (313) 577-2506
baskaran@wayne.edu
http://www.clas.wayne.edu/geology/
t: @WSUgeology
Programs: Geology; Environmental Science
Certificates: Hoz
Enrollment (2011): B: 101 (15) M: 9 (1)

Professor:
Jeffrey L. Howard, (D), California (Santa Barbara), 1987, GsScGa

Associate Professor:
Sarah J. BrownLee, (D), California (Berkeley), 2009, GxcGy
Shirley Papuga, (D), Colorado, 2006, Hgs

Assistant Professor:
Scott Burdick, (D), MIT, 2014, Ysg

Instructor:
Walter Pociask, (M), Zn

Lecturer:
Grazyna Sledzinski, (M), Wayne State, 1994, Gg
Felice Sperone, (M), Calabria - Rende (Italy), 2003, GgZr
John M. Zawiskie, (M), Wayne State, 1979, Gg

Adjunct Professor:
Gi-Hoon Hong, (D), Alaska, 1986, OcCcm
Bratton F. John, (D), California (Berkeley), 1997, Cg

Western Michigan University

Dept of Geosciences (B,M,D) O (2018)
1903 W Michigan Ave
Kalamazoo, MI 49008-5241
p. (269) 387-5486

kathryn.wright@wmich.edu
http://www.wmich.edu/geology/
f: https://www.facebook.com/wmugeosciences
Programs: Earth Science (B); Earth Science Education (B); Geochemistry (B); Geology (B); Geophysics (B); Hydrogeology (B); Accelerated MA in Earth Sciences (M), Earth Sciences (M), Geosciences (M, D)
Certificates: Applied Hydrogeology (UG, G)
Enrollment (2015): B: 108 (18) M: 51 (17) D: 12 (4)

Chair:
Mohamed Sultan, (D), Washington, 1984, ZriGe
Dean of the College of Arts and Sciences:
Carla Koretsky, (D), Johns Hopkins, 1998, CglHs
Professor:
Alan E. Kehew, (D), Idaho, 1977, GmlHw
Michelle A. Kominz, (D), Columbia, 1986, OuYgGu
R. V. Krishnamurthy, (D), Phy Res Lab (India), 1984, Cs
Geosciences Specialist and Co-Director of the Hydrogeology Field Course:
Thomas R. Howe III, (M), W Michigan, 2017, HwGem
Co-Director of the Hydrogeology Field Course:
Donald Matthew M. Reeves, (D), Nevada (Reno), 2006, HwqNr
Associate Professor:
Daniel P. Cassidy, (D), Notre Dame, 1995, Hw
Johnson R. Haas, (D), Washington, 1993, Cl
Duane R. Hampton, (D), Colorado State, 1989, HwSpHg
William A. Sauck, (D), Arizona, 1972, YgeYv
Assistant Professor:
Robb Gillespie, (D), SUNY, GsoGm
Stephen E. Kaczmarek, (D), Michigan State, 2005, GdCgGz
Joyashish Thakurta, (D), Indiana, 2008, GiEg
Senior Research Associate and Part-time Instructor:
Andrew Caruthers, (D), British Columbia, 2013, GsCsGr
Director of Michigan Geological Repository for Research and Education and Professor Emeritus:
William B. Harrison, III, (D), Cincinnati, 1974, GsrPg
Teaching Faculty Specialist and Director of CoreKids:
Peter J. Voice, (D), Virginia Tech, 2010, GsZn
Emeritus:
Caryl E. Buchwald, (D), Kansas, 1966, Gg
Technical Director:
Jonathon L. Cooper, (B), W Washington, Gg

Minnesota

Bemidji State University

Center for Environmental, Economic, Earth, & Space Studies (A,B,M) (2017)
#27, 1500 Birchmont Drive NE
Bemidji, MN 56601
p. (218) 755-2783
jeffrey.ueland@bemidjistate.edu
http://www.bemidjistate.edu/academics/departments/ceeess/
Enrollment (2012): B: 109 (17) M: 23 (3)

Professor:
Dragoljub D. Bilanovic, (D), Tech Israel Inst Tech, 1990, GePgCa
Assistant Professor:
Carl Isaacson, (D), Oregon State, 2007, Ge
Miriam Rios-Sanchez, (D), Michigan Tech, 2012, HwZrGg

Carleton College

Dept of Geology (B) ☒ (2020)
One North College Street
Northfield, MN 55057
p. (507) 222-5769
cdavidso@carleton.edu
https://apps.carleton.edu/curricular/geol/
Programs: Geology
Administrative Assistant: Tamara Little
Enrollment (2020): B: 39 (12)

Professor:
Clinton A. Cowan, (D), Queen's, 1992, GsPe
Cameron Davidson, (D), Princeton, 1991, GptCc
Bereket Haileab, (D), Utah, 1994, GxzGi
Sarah J. Titus, (D), Wisconsin, 2006, Gc
Assistant Professor:
Dan Maxbauer, (D), Minnesota, 2017, PcYm
Director, Science Ed Resource Center:
Cathryn A. Manduca, (D), Caltech, 1988, Gi
Charles L. Denison Professor of Geology, Emerita:
Mary E. Savina, (D), California (Berkeley), 1982, Gm

Century College

Earth Science (A) (2021)
3300 Century Avenue North
White Bear Lake, MN 55110
p. (651) 779-3242
joe.osborn@century.edu
http://www.century.edu/futurestudents/programs/pnd.aspx?id=66
Programs: AS in Earth Science
Enrollment (2020): A: 2 (2)

Head:
Joe Osborn, (M), Zg
Instructor:
Jill Bries-Korpik, (M), Zg

Fond du Lac Tribal and Community College

Fond du Lac Tribal and Community College (A) ☒ (2021)
2101 14th Street
Cloquet, MN 55720
http://www.fdltcc.edu/

Gustavus Adolphus College

Dept of Geology (B) ☒ (2021)
800 West College Avenue
St Peter, MN 56082
p. (507) 933-7333
triplett@gustavus.edu
http://www.gustavus.edu/geology
Programs: Geology
Administrative Assistant: Jennifer Kruse
Enrollment (2020): B: 20 (4)

Professor:
Julie K. Bartley, (D), California (Los Angeles), 1994, GsPgo
Chair:
Laura Triplett, (D), Minnesota, 2008, GemCl
Assistant Professor:
Rory McFadden, (D), GxcGz
Emeritus:
James L. Welsh, (D), Wisconsin, 1982, Gxc
Cooperating Faculty:
Daniel Mollner, Zn

Inver Hills Community College

Geology Dept (A) (2015)
2500 East 80th Street
Inver Grove Heights, MN 55076
ewood@inverhills.edu
http://www.inverhills.edu/Departments/Geology/

Instructor:
Jill Bries Korpik, Gg

Itasca Community College

Geography/Geographic Info Systems (GIS) (A) (2016)
1851 East Highway 169
Grand Rapids, MN 55744
p. (218) 322-2364
timothy.fox@itascacc.edu

Instructor:
Mike LeClair
Kenneth Tapp

Lake Superior College

Liberal Arts & Sciences Dept (A) (2015)
2101 Trinity Rd.
Duluth, MN 55811
m.whitehill@lsc.edu
http://www.lsc.edu

Instructor:
Matthew Whitehill, Gg

Macalester College

Geology Department (B) ☒ (2020)
1600 Grand Avenue
St Paul, MN 55105
p. (651) 696-6000
rogers@macalester.edu
http://www.macalester.edu/geology/
Programs: Geology
Enrollment (2020): B: 26 (10)

Chair:
Raymond R. Rogers, (D), Chicago, 1995, GsrPv

Professor:
Kristina A. Curry Rogers, (D), SUNY (Stony Brook), 2001, PveGg
Kelly MacGregor, (D), California (Santa Cruz), 2002, GmlGg

Associate Professor:
Alan Chapman, (D), Caltech, 2011, GctCc
Karl R. Wirth, (D), Cornell, 1991, GiZeGg

Geology Lab Supervisor:
Jeffrey T. Thole, (M), Washington State, 1991, GgCaHw

Minneapolis Community and Technical College

Div of Arts and Sciences (2015)
1501 Hennepin Ave S
Minneapolis, MN 55403
nick.taylor@minneapolis.edu
http://www.minneapolis.edu/academics/artsandsciences.cfm

Minnesota State University

Chemistry and Geology (B) ✍ (2018)
Department of Chemistry and Geology
241 Ford Hall
Mankato, MN 56001
p. (507) 389-1963
christine.cords@mnsu.edu
http://cset.mnsu.edu/chemgeol/programs/geol/
Programs: Geology (B); Earth Science Education (B); Earth Science (B)
Certificates: Environmental Geology

Professor:
Bryce W. Hoppie, (D), California (Santa Cruz), 1996, GeHw
Steven Losh, (D), Yale, 1985, GzxGo

Associate Professor:
Chad Wittkop, (D), Minnesota, GsCgGl

Normandale Community College

Dept of Geography and Geology (A) ✍ (2017)
9700 France Avenue South
Bloomington, MN 55431
p. (952) 358-8668
lindsay.iredale@normandale.edu
http://www.normandale.edu/departments/stem-and-education/geography-and-geology

Instructor:
David J. Berner, (M), Colorado
Douglas J. Claycomb, (D), Texas A&M
Richard P. Dunning, (D), Wisconsin
Carolyn Dykoski, (M), Minnesota
Annia Fayon, (D), Arizona State
Lindsay Iredale, (M), Minnesota
Paul D. Sabourin, (D), Minnesota
Ronald D. Ward, (D), Georgia

Other:
Cary Komoto, (D), Minnesota, 1994, ZnnZn

North Hennepin Community College

Earth & Environmental Science Dept (A) ⦸ (2018)
7411 85th Avenue N.
Brooklyn Park, MN 55445
p. (763) 424-0869
megan.jones@nhcc.edu
http://www.nhcc.edu/academic-programs/academic-departments/geology
Programs: Environmental Science (AS)
Enrollment (2017): A: 1 (0)

Northland Community & Technical College

Liberal Arts Program (2015)
2022 Central Avenue NE
East Grand Forks, MN 56721
p. (218) 683-8694
http://www.northlandcollege.edu

Rochester Community & Technical College

Department of Earth Sciences (2015)
851 30th Ave SE
Rochester, MN 55904
p. (507) 285-7220
John.Tacinelli@rctc.edu
http://www.rctc.edu

Instructor:
John C. Tacinelli, (D), Minnesota, 2000, Gig

Saint Cloud State University

Dept of Atmospheric and Hydrologic Sciences (B) (2015)
720 4th Avenue South
St Cloud, MN 56301-4498
p. (320) 308-3260
arhansen@stcloudstate.edu
http://www.stcloudstate.edu/eas/
Administrative Assistant: Debbie Schlumpberger
Enrollment (2012): B: 119 (31)

Professor:
Anthony R. Hansen, (D), Iowa State, 1981, Am

Professor:
Kate S. Pound, (D), Otago (NZ), 1993, GgZeGd
Robert A. Weisman, (D), SUNY (Albany), 1988, Am

Associate Professor:
Juan J. Fedele, (D), Illinois, 2003, Hg
Jean L. Hoff, (D), North Dakota, 1989, HwZeGg
Rodney Kubesh, (D), Illinois, 1991, Am

Assistant Professor:
Brian J. Billings, (D), Nevada (Reno), 2009, Am

St. Cloud State University

Department of Geography & Planning ✍ (2020)
720 4th Ave S
Stewart Hall 359
St. Cloud, MN 56301-4498
p. (320) 308-3160
geog@stcloudstate.edu
https://www.stcloudstate.edu/geogplan/
Programs: B.A. Geography, M.S. Geography with GIS emphasis
Certificates: Land Surveying

University of Minnesota Duluth

Earth & Environmental Science (B,M) O☒ (2020)
230 Heller Hall
1114 Kirby Drive
Duluth, MN 55812
p. (218) 726-8385
dees@d.umn.edu
http://www.d.umn.edu/dees/
f: https://www.facebook.com/umdees/
Programs: Geological Sciences; Environmental Science; Earth Science
Administrative Assistant: April A. Finkenhoefer
Enrollment (2020): B: 10 (15) M: 9 (6)

Head:
Karen B. Gran, (D), Washington, 2005, Gms

Emeritus:
John C. Green, (D), Harvard, 1960, GieGv
Timothy Holst, (D), Minnesota, GcYnGt
Thomas C. Johnson, (D), California (San Diego), 1975, PcGn
Ronald L. Morton, (D), Carleton, 1976, GvEg

Professor:
Erik T. Brown, (D), MIT, 1990, Og
John W. Goodge, (D), California (Los Angeles), 1987, Gp
Vicki L. Hansen, (D), California (Los Angeles), 1987, GtXgGc
Howard D. Mooers, (D), Minnesota, 1988, GleHw

Emeritus:
James D. Miller, (D), Minnesota, 1986, GiEd
Penelope C. Morton, (D), Carleton, 1982, EgGpCg

Associate Professor:
Christina D. Gallup, (D), Minnesota, 1997, Cct
John B. Swenson, (D), Minnesota, 2000, GrsGm
Nigel J. Wattrus, (D), Minnesota, 1984, Yr
Director of Graduate Studies:
Byron A. Steinman, (D), Pittsburgh, 2011, Gn
Assistant Professor:
Latisha A. Brengman, (D), Tennessee, 2015, Gd
Fred A. Davis, (D), Minnesota, 2012, CpGi
Salli F. Dymond, (D), Minnesota, 2014, Hg
Wendy F. Smythe, (D), Oregon Health & Sci, 2015, Ou

University of Minnesota, Morris

Div of Science & Mathematics (B) (2015)
Geology Discipline
Science Building
600 East 4th Street
Morris, MN 56267
p. (320) 589-6300
geol@mrs.umn.edu
http://www.mrs.umn.edu
Coordinator:
James F. Cotter, (D), Lehigh, 1984, Gl
Professor:
Keith A. Brugger, (D), Minnesota, 1992, GlGm
James B. Van Alstine, (D), North Dakota, 1980, Pg
Emeritus:
Peter M. Whelan, (D), California (Santa Cruz), 1988, Gx

University of Minnesota, Twin Cities

Dept of Civil, Environmental and Geo-Engineering (B,M,D) (2015)
500 Pillsbury Drive SE
Minneapolis, MN 55455
p. (612) 625-5522
cege@umn.edu
http://www.ce.umn.edu/
Enrollment (2010): B: 26 (8) M: 11 (4) D: 49 (2)
Head:
John S. Gulliver, (D), Minnesota, 1980, Hs
Professor:
Emmanuel M. Detournay, (D), Minnesota, 1983, NrpNm
Andrew Drescher, (D), Inst of Fund Tech Res (Poland), 1968, So
Efi Foufoula-Georgiou, (D), Florida, 1985, Hg
Joseph F. Labuz, (D), Northwestern, 1985, Nr
Otto D. Strack, (D), Delft (Neth), 1973, Hw
Vaughan R. Voller, (D), Sunderland, 1980, Zm
Associate Professor:
Randal J. Barnes, (D), Colorado Mines, 1985, Zn
Bojan B. Guzina, (D), Colorado, 1996, Nr
Karl A. Smith, (D), Minnesota, 1980, Nx
Research Associate:
Sonia Mogilevskaya, (D), Russian Acad of Sci, 1987, Ng
Adjunct Professor:
Peter A. Cundall, (D), Nr

Dept of Earth & Environmental Sciences (B,M,D) O☒ (2020)
116 Church Street SE
150 John T. Tate Hall
Minneapolis, MN 55455
p. (612) 624-1333
esci@umn.edu
http://www.esci.umn.edu
t: @UMNEarthScience
Programs: Earth Sciences; Geology; Geophysics; Geobiology; Environmental Sciences; Hydrogeology
Enrollment (2016): B: 48 (15) M: 15 (2) D: 41 (7)
Director, PGC:
Paul Morin, Zn
Head:
Donna L. Whitney, (D), Washington, 1991, Gpt
Teaching Professor:
Kent C. Kirkby, (D), Wisconsin, 1994, Gg
Regents Professor:
R. Lawrence Edwards, (D), Caltech, 1988, Cc
Director, Minnesota Geological Survey:
Harvey Thorleifson, (D), Colorado, 1989, Gg
Director of IRM:
Bruce M. Moskowitz, (D), Minnesota, 1980, Ym
Assoc Director of IRM:
Joshua Feinberg, (D), California (Berkeley), 2005, YmGze
Professor:
David L. Fox, (D), Michigan, 1999, Pg
Marc M. Hirschmann, (D), Washington, 1992, Gi
Emi Ito, (D), Chicago, 1979, ClGnCs
Sally G. Kohlstedt, (D), Illinois, 1972, Rh
Peter Makovicky, (D), Columbia, 2002, Pv
Katsumi Matsumoto, (D), Columbia, 2000, Oc
Samuel Mukasa, (D), Cg
Christopher Paola, (D), MIT/WHOI, 1983, Gs
Vera Pospelova, (D), McGill, 2003, GePl
Justin Revenaugh, (D), MIT, 1989, Ys
William E. Seyfried, Jr., (D), S California, 1977, Cm
Christian P. Teyssier, (D), Monash, 1986, GctGg
Senior Scientist:
Amanda Dillman, (D), Yx
Associate Professor:
Jake Bailey, (D), S California, 2008, Pg
Cara M. Santelli, (D), MIT/WHOI, 2007, Pg
Assistant Professor:
Max Bezada, (D), Rice, 2010, Ys
Anna Graber, (D), Yale, 2016, Rh
Lars N. Hansen, (D), Minnesota, 2012, Yx
Peter Kang, (D), Hg
Crystal Ng, (D), MIT, 2008, Hy
Ikuko Wada, (D), Victoria, 2009, ZnYgGt
Andrew D. Wickert, (D), Colorado, 2014, Gml
Xinyuan Zheng, (D), Oxford, 2014, CsOc
XRCT Lab Manager:
Brian Bagley, (D), Minnesota, 2011, YsZn
Research Associate Professor:
Michael Jackson, (D), Michigan, 1986, Ym
Microprobe Manager:
Anette von der Handt, (D), GiCt
Research Associate:
Dario Bilardello, (D), Lehigh, 2009, Ym
Randy Calcote, (D), Minnesota, 2000, Ple
Hai Cheng, (D), Nanjing (China), 1988, CcPe
Kang Ding, (D), Acad Sinica (Beijing), 1987, Cg
Beverly Flood, (D), Pg
Jed Mosenfelder, (D), Cp
Mark Shapley, Minnesota, 2005, Gn
Ivanka Stefanova, (D), Sofia, 1991, Pl
Alexander Stone, (M), Gn
Chunyang Tan, (D), Zhejiang, 2011, Cm
Mark Zimmerman, (D), Minnesota, 1999, Yx
Adjunct Professor:
James E. Almendinger, (D), Minnesota, 1988, Pe
Val W. Chandler, (D), Purdue, 1977, Ye
Mark B. Edlund, (D), Michigan, 1998, Pe
Daniel R. Engstrom, (D), Minnesota, 1983, Pe
Annia K. Fayon, (D), Arizona State, 1997, Gc
Robert G. Johnson, (D), Iowa State, 1952, Pe
Shenghua Mei, (D), Yx
Kristina Curry Rogers, (D), Pg
Raymond Rogers, (D), Pg
Anthony Runkel, (D), Texas, 1988, Gs
Emeritus:
E. Calvin Alexander, Jr., (D), Missouri (Rolla), 1970, HwCcl
Subir K. Banerjee, (D), Cambridge, 1963, Ym
Roger LeB Hooke, (D), Gl
Peter J. Hudleston, (D), Imperial Coll (UK), 1969, Gc
Karen L. Kleinspehn, (D), Princeton, 1982, Gt
David L. Kohlstedt, (D), Illinois, 1970, YxGzi
Hans Olaf Pfannkuch, (D), Paris, 1962, HwGeRh
James H. Stout, (D), Harvard, 1970, GpzGt
Paul W. Weiblen, (D), Minnesota, 1965, Gi
Student Services:
Jennifer Petrie
Researcher:
Michelle LaRue, (D), Zi
Remote Sensing Specialist:
Cathleen Torres Parisian, (M), Zr
Postdoc:
Joseph Byrnes, (D), Oregon, 2016, Ys
Director, CSDCO:
Anders Noren, Gn

Dept Administrator:
Sharon J. Kressler, (B), Zn
Department Safety Officer:
Scott Alexander, (B), Hw
Curator, LacCore:
Kristina Brady, (M), Minnesota, 2006, Gn
Research Fellow:
Cole Kelleher, (M), Zi
Claire Porter, (M), Zi
Geology Librarian:
Carolyn Rauber, (M), Zn
Coordinator - PGC:
Jonathan Pundsack, Zn
Cooperating Faculty:
Martin O. Saar, (D), California (Berkeley), 2003, Hg

Dept of Soil, Water & Climate (B,M,D) ●⃠ (2019)
1991 Upper Buford Circle
St. Paul, MN 55108-6028
p. (612) 625-8114
crosen@umn.edu
http://www.swac.umn.edu
Programs: Environmental Science, Policy and Management (BS); Land and Atmospheric Science (MS, PhD)
Administrative Assistant: Marjorie J. Bonse
Enrollment (2019): B: 345 (66) M: 16 (6) D: 21 (1)
Head:
Carl J. Rosen, (D), California (Davis), 1983, Sc
Professor:
James C. Bell, (D), Penn State, 1990, SdfZe
Timothy J. Griffis, (D), McMaster, 2000, As
Satish C. Gupta, (D), Utah State, 1972, Sp
Dylan B. Millet, (D), California (Berkeley), 2003, As
David J. Mulla, (D), Purdue, 1983, Sp
Edward A. Nater, (D), California (Davis), 1987, Sd
Michael J. Sadowsky, (D), Hawaii, 1983, Sb
Michael A. Schmitt, (D), Illinois, 1985, Sc
Jeffrey S. Strock, (D), North Carolina State, 1999, So
Brandy M. Toner, (D), California (Berkeley), 2004, ClmSc
Kyungsoo Yoo, (D), California (Berkeley), 2003, Sd
Associate Professor:
Melinda L. Erickson, Minnesota, 2005, Hw
Fabian G. Fernandez, (D), Purdue, 2006, ScbSo
Satoshi Ishii, (D), Minnesota, 2007, SbPg
Daniel E. Kaiser, (D), Iowa State, 2007, Sc
Paulo H. Pagliari, (D), Wisconsin, 2012, Sc
Albert L. Sims, (D), North Carolina State, 1992, Sc
Peter K. Snyder, (D), Wisconsin, 2003, As
Tracy E. Twine, (D), Wisconsin, 2003, As
Assistant Professor:
Anna Cates, (D), Wisconsin, 2018, Sb
Jessica L. M. Gutknecht, (D), Wisconsin, 2007, Sb
Nicolas Jelinski, (D), Minnesota, 2014, SdCs
Yuxin Miao, (D), Minnesota, 2005, ScZf
Vasudha Sharma, (D), Nebraska, 2018, SpHg
Melissa L. Wilson, (D), Minnesota, 2012, Sco
Adjunct Professor:
John M. Baker, (D), Texas A&M, 1987, Sp
Gary Feyereisen, (D), Minnesota, 2005, Sp
Jane M F Johnson, (D), Minnesota, 1995, So
Randall K. Kolka, (D), Minnesota, 1996, So
Pamela J. Rice, (D), Iowa State, 1996, So
Kurt Spokas, (D), Minnesota, 2005, Spo
Rodney T. Venterea, (D), California (Davis), 2000, Sp
Emeritus:
Deborah L. Allan, (D), California (Riverside), 1987, Sb
James L. Anderson, (D), Wisconsin, 1976, Sd
Paul R. Bloom, (D), Cornell, 1978, Sc
H. H. Cheng, (D), Illinois, 1961, Sb
Terence H. Cooper, (D), Michigan State, 1975, Sd
Robert H. Dowdy, (D), Michigan State, 1966, Sc
William C. Koskinen, (D), Washington State, 1980, Sc
John A. Lamb, (D), Nebraska, 1984, Sc
Gary L. Malzer, (D), Purdue, 1973, Sc
Jean-Alex E. Molina, (D), Cornell, 1967, SbCgSo
John F. Moncrief, (D), Wisconsin, 1981, Sp
Gyles W. Randall, (D), Wisconsin, 1972, So
George W. Rehm, (D), Minnesota, 1969, Sc
Michael P. Russelle, (D), Nebraska, 1982, Sc
Mark W. Seeley, (D), Nebraska, 1977, As
Executive Secretary:
Kari A. Jarcho, (B), Zn

University of Saint Thomas

Earth, Environment and Society, Geology Program (B) ●☒ (2020)
OWS 153
2115 Summit Avenue
St Paul, MN 55105
p. (651) 962-5241
tahickson@stthomas.edu
http://www.stthomas.edu/geology/
Programs: Geology BA, BS and Minor
Environmental Science with Geology, Biology, or Chemistry Concentrations
Geography BA, Minor
GIS Minor
Enrollment (2020): B: 14 (7)
Director:
Thomas A. Hickson, (D), Stanford, 1999, GsmGe
Professor:
Melissa A. Lamb, (D), Stanford, 1998, GtcGs
Kevin Theissen, (D), Stanford, GnOg
Associate Professor:
Jeni McDermott, (D), Arizona State, GmHw

Vermilion Community College

Vermilion Community College (2015)
1900 East Camp Street
Ely, MN 55731
p. (218) 235-2173
http://www.vcc.edu/

Winona State University

Dept of Geoscience (B) ☒ (2020)
P.O. Box 5838
Winona, MN 55987
p. (507) 457-5260
geoscience@winona.edu
https://www.winona.edu/geoscience/
f: https://www.facebook.com/GeoscienceWSU
Programs: Geoscience (B); Geology (B); Environmental Science (B); Earth Science Teaching (B)
Enrollment (2020): B: 50 (16)
Professor:
Stephen T. Allard, (D), Wyoming, 2003, GctGx
Jennifer LB Anderson, (D), Brown, 2004, XgYgZe
William L. Beatty, (D), Pittsburgh, 2003, PgiGs
Candace L. Kairies-Beatty, (D), Pittsburgh, 2003, GeClRw
Associate Professor:
Dylan Blumentritt, (D), Minnesota, 2013, HsGm
Emeritus:
John F. Donovan, (D), Cornell, 1963, Eg
Nancy O. Jannik, (D), New Mexico Tech, 1989, Hw
Jamie Ann Meyers, (D), Indiana, 1971, Gsd
Dennis N. Nielsen, (D), North Dakota, 1973, Gm
College Laboratory Services Specialist:
Luke Zwiefelhofer, (B), Wyoming, 2004, Zn

Mississippi

Jackson State University

Chemistry, Physics, and Atmospheric Sciences (B,M,D) ☒ (2017)
1400 J. R. Lynch St.
JSU Box 17660
Jackson, MS 39217
p. (601) 979-7012
mfadavi@jsums.edu
http://www.jsums.edu/cset/phyat.htm
Programs: Physics (B); Chemistry (B); Meteorology (B); Earth System Science (B); Chemistry (M,D)
Enrollment (2014): B: 9 (4)

Millsaps College

Dept of Geosciences (B) O☒ (2018)
Box 150648

1701 North State Street
Jackson, MS 39210
p. (601) 974-1344
galics@millsaps.edu
http://www.millsaps.edu/geology/
Enrollment (2018): B: 8 (5)

Professor:
Stan Galicki, (D), Mississippi, 2002, Ged
James B. Harris, (D), Kentucky, 1992, Ye

Chair:
Zachary A. Musselman, (D), Kentucky, 2006, Gm

Emeritus:
Delbert E. Gann, (D), Missouri Sch of Mines, 1976, Gz

Mississippi State University

Dept of Geosciences (B,M,D) (2015)
P. O. Box 5448
108 Hilbun Hall
East Lee Blvd.
Mississippi State, MS 39762
p. (662) 325-3915
rclary@geosci.msstate.edu
http://www.geosciences.msstate.edu/
f: https://www.facebook.com/MSUGeosciences/
Enrollment (2014): B: 505 (86) M: 224 (103) D: 24 (4)

Professor:
Michael E. Brown, (D), North Carolina, 1999, Am
Brenda L. Kirkland, (D), Louisiana State, 1992, GdEoPo
Darrel W. Schmitz, (D), Texas A&M, 1991, Hw

Associate Professor:
Shrinidhi Ambinakudige, (D), Florida State, 2006, ZiyZr
Renee M. Clary, (D), Louisiana State, 2003, ZePgGe
Jamie Dyer, (D), Georgia, 2005, Am
Andrew Mercer, (D), Oklahoma, 2008, Ams
John C. Rodgers, (D), Georgia, 1999, Zy
Kathleen M. Sherman-Morris, (D), Florida State, 2006, As

Assistant Professor:
Padmanava Dash, (D), Louisiana State, 2011, ZrHg
Christopher Fuhrmann, (D), 2011, As
Rinat Gabitov, (D), Rensselaer, 2005, Cas
Qingmin Meng, (D), Georgia, 2006, Zig
Adam Skarke, (D), Delaware, 2013, GuYrOn
Kim Wood, (D), Arizona, 2012, AsmZr

Research Associate:
Katarzynz Grala, (M), Iowa State, 2004, Zi

Instructor:
Christa M. Haney, (M), Mississippi State, 1999, Am
Amy P. Moe-Hoffman, (M), Colorado, 2002, Zn
John A. Morris, (M), Mississippi State, 2007, ZirAm
Lindsey Morschauser, (M), Mississippi State, Am
Athena Nagel, (D), Mississippi State, 2014, ZgiZr
Greg Nordstrom, (M), Mississippi State, 2007, Am
Tim Wallace, (M), Mississippi State, 1994, Am

Adjunct Professor:
Paul J. Croft, (D), Rutgers, 1991, Am
Patrick J. Fitzpatrick, (D), Colorado State, 1995, Am
James May, (D), Texas A&M, 1988, Hw
Jack C. Pashin, (D), Kentucky, 1990, GoEcGs
Janet E. Simms, (D), Texas A&M, 1991, Yg
Jayaram Veeramony, (D), Delaware, 1999, Og

Emeritus:
John M. Kaye, (D), Louisiana State, 1974, Gg
John E. Mylroie, (D), Rensselaer, 1977, GmHyGs
Charles L. Wax, (D), Louisiana State, 1977, As

Distance Academic Coordinator:
Mary A. Dean

Collection Manager:
Amy P. Moe-Hoffman, (M), Colorado, 2002, PgZe

Business Manager:
Jerri Wright, (B), Mississippi Univ for Women, 1996

Academic Coordinator:
Tina Davis, (M), Mississippi Univ for Women

Related Staff:
Cynthia Bell

University of Mississippi

Dept of Geology & Geological Engineering (B,M,D) ● (2017)
School of Engineering
P.O. Box 1848
120A Carrier Hall
University, MS 38677-1848
p. (662) 915-7498
geology@olemiss.edu
http://www.engineering.olemiss.edu/gge/
Enrollment (2016): B: 301 (45) M: 21 (6) D: 5 (0)

Professor:
Adnan Aydin, (D), Memorial, 1994, NgrYe
Gregg R. Davidson, (D), Arizona, 1995, Hw
Gregory L. Easson, (D), Missouri (Rolla), 1996, Zr
Robert M. Holt, (D), New Mexico Tech, 2000, Hq

Associate Professor:
Louis G. Zachos, (D), Texas, 2008, PiGeNx

Assistant Professor:
Jennifer N. Gifford, (D), Florida, 2013, GtxCg
Andrew M. O'Reilly, (D), Florida, 2012, Hwq
Brian F. Platt, (D), Kansas, 2009, GsPe
Lance D. Yarbrough, (D), Mississippi, 2006, Ng

Instructor:
Inoka Widanagamage, (D), Kent State, 2015, ClGep

Lecturer:
Cathy A. Grace, (M), Mississippi, 1996, Gg

University of Southern Mississippi

Dept of Geography and Geology (B,M,D) O (2018)
118 College Drive, Box 5051
Walker Science Building, Room 127
Hattiesburg, MS 39406
p. (601) 266-4729
david.cochran@usm.edu
http://www.usm.edu/geography-geology
f: https://www.facebook.com/groups/Geography.GeologyUSM/
t: @geousm
Programs: Geology (B, M); Geography (B, M, D)
Certificates: Geographic Information Technologies
Enrollment (2014): B: 114 (19) M: 30 (5) D: 4 (1)

Professor:
Andy Reese, (D), Louisiana State, 2003, Zy

Professor:
Greg Carter, (D), Wyoming, 1985, Zyi
Clifton Dixon, (D), Texas A&M, 1988, Zn
Maurice A. Meylan, (D), Hawaii, 1978, Gu
Mark Miller, (D), Arizona, 1988, Zn
David M. Patrick, (D), Oklahoma, 1972, Ng
Mark Puckett, (D), Alabama, PmiGg

Associate Professor:
Jerry Bass, (D), Texas, 2003, Zn
David Cochran, (D), Kansas, 2005, Zn
Franklin Heitmuller, (D), Texas, 2009, GmsGe
David Holt, (D), Arkansas, 2002, Zyi
Bandana Kar, (D), South Carolina, 2008, Zi
George Raber, (D), South Carolina, 2003, Zi

Assistant Professor:
Jeremy Deans, (D), Texas Tech, 2016, YrGc

Instructor:
Evan Bagley, (M), GgEo
Alyson Brink, (D), Texas Tech, 2016, PgvGg

Gulf Coast Research Laboratory (M,D) O⊘ (2020)
703 E. Beach Drive
Ocean Springs, MS 39564
p. (228) 818-8804
read.hendon@usm.edu
http://gcrl.usm.edu

Director:
Joe Griffitt, (D)

Chair:
Leila Hamdan, (D)

Marine Science (B,M,D) ☒ (2021)
1020 Balch Boulevard
National Aeronautics and Space Administration
Stennis Space Center, MS 39529
p. (228) 688-3177
marine.science@usm.edu
http://www.usm.edu/marine
f:https://www.facebook.com/

SouthernMissDivisionOfMarineScience/
t: @USMMarineSci
Programs: Marine Science; Hydrographic Science; Ocean Eng
Certificates: UMS Certificate Program - Tier 1
UMS Operator Certificate Program - Tier 2
Enrollment (2020): B: 56 (5) M: 26 (16) D: 22 (2)
Associate Director, SOSE, & Associate Professor:
Jerry Wiggert, (D), S California, 1995, Op
Director of the Center for Gulf Studies:
Denis A. Wiesenburg, (D), 1980, Og
Professor:
Stephan Howden, (D), Rhode Island, 1996, Op
Alan M. Shiller, (D), California (San Diego), 1982, OcCtHs
Xiaodong Zhang, (D), Dalhousie, 2002, Op
Associate Professor:
Maarten Buijsman, (D), Utrecht, 2007, Op
Scott P. Milroy, (D), S Florida (St. Petersburg), 2007, Ob
Dmitri Nechaev, (D), Shirshov Inst, 1986, Op
Davin Wallace, (D), Rice, 2010, Ou
Assistant Professor:
Mustafa Kemal Cambazoglu, (D), Georgia Tech, 2009, No
Christopher T. Hayes, (D), 2013, Oc
Anand Devappa Hiroji, (D), 2016, Yd
Kristina Mojica, (D), Amsterdam, 2015, Ob
Gero Nootz, (D), C Florida, 2010, No
Research Faculty:
Leonardo Macelloni, (D), Rome, 2005, Yr
Associate Research Professor:
Arne R. Diercks, (D), S Mississippi, 1995, Ou
Emeritus:
Vernon Asper, (D), MIT, 1986, Og

Missouri

Metropolitan Community College-Blue River

Geology and Geography Program (A) (2015)
20301 E. 78 Highway
Independence, MO 64057-2053
p. (816) 220-6622
benjamin.wolfe@mcckc.edu
http://www.mcckc.edu/progs/geol/geology/overview.asp

Metropolitan Community College-Kansas City

Geology Dept (A) (2015)
3200 Broadway
Kansas City, MO 64111
p. (816) 604-3335
melissa.renfrow@mcckc.edu
http://www.mcckc.edu/programs/geology/
Instructor:
Alice Fuerst, Gg
John Horn, (D), Nebraska, GgZy
Carl Priesendorf, (M), Missouri, 1987, GgZyGe
Laura Veverka, (M), Missouri (Kansas City), Zy
Ben Wolfe, (M), Alaska (Fairbanks), 2001, GgZyg
Adjunct Professor:
Janet Raymer, (M), Missouri S&T, GgEo

Mineral Area College

Science Dept (A) (2020)
5270 Flat River Road
P.O. Box 1000
Park Hills, MO 63601
p. (573) 518-2314
bscheidt@MineralArea.edu
http://www.mineralarea.edu/faculty/academicDepartments/science.aspx
Enrollment (2016): A: 2 (2)
Professor:
Brian Scheidt, (M), S Illinois, Hw

Missouri State University

Dept of Geography, Geology & Planning (B,M) (2018)
901 S. National
Springfield, MO 65897
p. (417) 836-5800
ggp@missouristate.edu
https://geosciences.missouristate.edu
f: https://www.facebook.com/MSUggp/
t: @MSUggp
Programs: https://geosciences.missouristate.edu
Certificates: https://geosciences.missouristate.edu
Administrative Assistant: Tracy Carroll, Deana Gibson
Enrollment (2016): B: 185 (56) M: 38 (8)
Distinguished Professor:
Kevin L. Mickus, (D), Texas (El Paso), 1989, GtYv
Robert T. Pavlowsky, (D), Wisconsin, 1995, Gm
Department Head:
Toby Dogwiler, (D), Missouri, 2002, ZiGmZy
Professor:
Kevin R. Evans, (D), Kansas, 1997, GrsGt
Douglas R. Gouzie, (D), Kentucky, 1986, HwGeCl
Melida Gutierrez, (D), Texas (El Paso), 1992, CgHy
Rajinder S. Jutla, (D), Virginia Tech, 1995, Zn
Jun Luo, (D), Wisconsin (Milwaukee), Zi
Judith Meyer, (D), Wisconsin, 1994, Zn
Xin Miao, (D), California (Berkeley), 2005, Zri
Charles W. Rovey, (D), Wisconsin (Milwaukee), 1990, HyGle
Associate Professor:
Alice (Jill) Black, (D), Missouri, 2003, ZeAsHw
Assistant Professor:
Mario Daoust, (D), McGill, 1992, AtZy
Krista M. Evans, (D), Clemson, 2017, Zn
Ron Malega, (D), Georgia, Zn
Matthew P. McKay, (D), West Virginia, 2015, Gct
Gary Michelfelder, (D), Montana State, 2015, GviCg
David R. Perkins, (D)
Senior Instructor:
Damon Bassett, (M), Missouri, 2003, Gg
Deborah Corcoran, (M), Michigan State, 1980, Zn
Linnea Iantria, (M), George Washington, Zn
Instructor:
Melanie E. Carden-Jessen, (M), Missouri State, 1998, Ze
Emeritus:
David A. Castillon, (D), Michigan State, 1972, Gm
John C. Catau, (D), Michigan State, 1973, Zn
William H. Cheek, (D), Michigan State, 1976, Zn
William Corcoran, (D), Michigan State, 1981, As
Dimitri Ioannides, (D), Rutgers, 1994, Zn
Elias Johnson, (D), Oklahoma, 1977, Zr
Vincent E. Kurtz, (D), Oklahoma, 1960, Ps
Erwin J. Mantei, (D), Missouri (Rolla), 1965, EdGez
Diane M. May, (M), S Illinois (Edwardsville), 1974, Zn
James F. Miller, (D), Wisconsin, 1970, Ps
Thomas D. Moeglin, (D), Nebraska, 1978, Ng
Thomas G. Plymate, (D), Minnesota, 1986, Gx
Paul A. Rollinson, (D), Illinois, 1988, Zn

Missouri University of Science and Technology

Dept of Geology & Geophysics (B,M,D) (2020)
129 McNutt Hall
Rolla, MO 65409-0410
p. (573) 341-4616
borrokd@mst.edu
https://ggpe.mst.edu/academic-programs/geology-and-geophysics/
Programs: Geology and Geophysics and Geological Engineering
Certificates: Petroleum Systems, Geoenvironmental Science and Engineering, Geophysics, Geoanalytics and Geointelligence, Space Resources, Natural Hazards, Subsurface Water Resources
Enrollment (2020): B: 41 (29) M: 14 (6) D: 30 (0)
Professor:
David Borrok, (D), Cl
Stephen Gao, (D), California (Los Angeles), 1995, Yg
Kelly Liu, (D), California (Los Angeles), 1998, Ye
Francisca Oboh-Ikuneobe, (D), Cambridge, 1991, Pg
Wan Yang, (D), Texas, 1995, Gs
Associate Professor:
Andreas Eckert, (D), Yg
John Hogan, (D), Gc
David Wronkiewicz, (D), Cl
Assistant Professor:
Marek Locmelis, (D), Macquarie, 2011, Eg

Jonathan Obrist Farner, (D), Missouri S&T, 2015, Gr
Adjunct Professor:
Cheryl Seeger
Emeritus:
Richard D. Hagni, (D), Missouri, 1962, Em
Robert Laudon

Moberly Area Community College - Columbia Campus

Moberly Area Community College - Columbia Campus (2015)
601 Business Loop 70 West
Columbia, MO 65203
p. (573) 234-1067
SandyAnderson@macc.edu
http://www.macc.edu/

Northwest Missouri State University

Dept of Geology-Geography (B,M) (2015)
800 University Drive
Maryville, MO 64468
p. (660) 562-1723
crater@nwmissouri.edu
Chair:
C. Renee Rohs, (D), Kansas, 2000, Cg
Professor:
Gregory D. Haddock, (D), Idaho, 1996, Zi
Associate Professor:
Theodore L. Goudge, (D), Oklahoma State, 1984, Zy
Assistant Professor:
James Hickey, (D), Dartmouth, 2006, Ge
Ming-Chih Hung, (D), Utah, 2003, Zr
Yanfen Le, (D), Georgia, 2005, Zi
Leah D. Manos, (M), Tennessee, 1997, Zy
Instructor:
Jeffrey Bradley, (M), Oklahoma State, 1991, Zg
Emeritus:
Richard M. Felton, (M), Missouri, 1979, Pg

Ozarks Technical Community College

Physical Sciences (2015)
1001 E. Chestnut Expressway
Springfield, MO 65802
p. (417) 447-8238
ehrichp@otc.edu

Saint Louis University

Earth & Atmospheric Sciences (B,M,D) ☒ (2020)
3642 Lindell Blvd
O'Neil Hall
Room 205
St. Louis, MO 63108
p. (314) 977-3116
linda.warren@slu.edu
http://www.slu.edu/department-of-earth-and-atmospheric-sciences-home
Programs: Geoscience with Concentrations in Geology, Geophysics and Environmental Geoscience
Certificates: GIS
Enrollment (2018): B: 69 (10) M: 7 (4) D: 5 (0)
Chair:
Charles E. Graves, (D), Iowa State, 1988, As
Professor:
David J. Crossley, (D), British Columbia, 1973, YdsXy
Benjamin de Foy, (D), Cambridge, 1998, As
John Encarnacion, (D), Michigan, 1994, Gx
Jack Fishman, (D), As
Daniel M. Hanes, (D), Scripps, 1983, GesGm
Zaitao Pan, (D), Iowa State, 1996, As
Lupei Zhu, (D), Caltech, 1998, YsGt
Associate Professor:
Elizabeth Hasenmueller, (D), Washington (St Louis), 2011, ClHs
Robert W. Pasken, (D), St Louis, 1981, Am
Vasit Sagan, (D), Zi
Linda M. Warren, (D), California (San Diego), 2003, YgsZn
Emeritus:
Robert B. Herrmann, (D), St Louis, 1974, Ys

Systems Engineer:
Eric J. Haug, (M)
Computer/Electronics Tech:
Robert Wurth

University of Missouri

Dept of Geological Sciences (B,M,D) O☒ (2017)
101 Geology Building
Columbia, MO 65211
p. (573) 882-6785
HuckabeyM@missouri.edu
http://geology.missouri.edu/
Administrative Assistant: Marsha Huckabey
Enrollment (2013): B: 60 (7) M: 13 (11) D: 21 (0)
Director of Geology Field Studies:
Miriam Barquero-Molina, (D), Texas, 2009, Gct
Chair:
Kevin L. Shelton, (D), Yale, 1982, EmCs
Alan Whittington, (D), Open (UK), 1997, GivCp
Professor:
Mian Liu, (D), Arizona, 1989, Yg
Kenneth A. MacLeod, (D), Washington, 1992, Pg
Peter I. Nabelek, (D), SUNY (Stony Brook), 1983, GipCu
Eric A. Sandvol, (D), New Mexico State, 1995, Ys
Associate Professor:
Martin S. Appold, (D), Johns Hopkins, 1998, HwEm
Francisco Gomez, (D), Cornell, 1999, Gt
Assistant Professor:
John Huntley, (D), Virginia Tech, 2007, PqgPe
James Schiffbauer, (D), Virginia Tech, 2009, Pgi
Emeritus:
Michael B. Underwood, (D), Cornell, 1984, GsuCt

School of Natural Resources (B,M,D) (2017)
302 Anheuser-Busch Natural Resources Building
Columbia, MO 65211-7250
p. (573) 882-6446
joses@missouri.edu
http://www.snr.missouri.edu/
Enrollment (2012): B: 165 (15) M: 24 (3) D: 13 (0)
Professor:
Stephen H. Anderson, (D), North Carolina State, 1985, Sp
Keith W. Goyne, (D), Penn State, 2003, Sc
Anthony R. Lupo, (D), Purdue, 1995, As
Patrick S. Market, (D), St Louis, 1999, As
Peter P. Motavalli, (D), Cornell, 1989, So
Extension:
Patrick E. Guinan, (D), Missouri, 2004, As
Associate Professor:
Neil I. Fox, (D), Salford (UK), 1998, As
Instructor:
Eric A. Aldrich, (M), Missouri, 2011, As
Adjunct Professor:
Frieda Eivazi, (D), Iowa State, 1980, Sc
Newell R. Kitchen, (D), Colorado State, 1990, So
Robert J. Kremer, (D), Mississippi State, 1981, Sb
Robert N. Lerch, (D), Colorado State, 1990, So
W. Gene Stevens, (D), Mississippi State, 1992, So
Christopher K. Wikle, (D), Iowa State, As
Emeritus:
Robert W. Blanchar, (D), Minnesota, 1964, Sc
James R. Brown, (D), Iowa State, 1963, So
Clark J. Gantzer, (D), Minnesota, 1980, So
Ernest C. Kung, (D), Wisconsin, 1963, As
Randall J. Miles, (D), Texas A&M, 1981, Sd
Stephen E. Mudrick, (D), MIT, 1973, As

University of Missouri, Kansas City

Dept of Geosciences (B,M,D) ●⊘ (2019)
5100 Rockhill Road
Room 420, Robert H. Flarsheim Hall
Kansas City, MO 64110-2499
p. (816) 235-1334
geosciences@umkc.edu
http://cas.umkc.edu/Geosciences/
t: @UMKC_geosci
Programs: Geology (B); Geography (B); Environmental Sci (B)
Certificates: GIS

Enrollment (2018): B: 108 (56) M: 0 (6) D: 26 (2)
Chair:
Wei Ji, (D), Connecticut, 1991, ZriZy
Professor:
Jimmy Adegoke, (D), Penn State, 2000, AsZyr
James B. Murowchick, (D), Penn State, 1984, CgGz
Tina M. Niemi, (D), Stanford, 1992, Gt
Associate Professor:
Caroline P. Davies, (D), Arizona State, 2000, GnZce
Jejung Lee, (D), Northwestern, 2001, GqHw
Assistant Professor:
Alison Graettinger, (D), Pittsburg State, 2012, Gv
Fengpeng Sun, (D), California (Irvine), 2008, ZoiZc
Emeritus:
Raymond M. Coveney Jr, (D), Michigan, 1972, EgmCe
Steven L. Driever, (D), Georgia, 1977, ZnnZn
Richard J. Gentile, (D), Missouri, 1965, GrsNx
Syed E. Hasan, (D), Purdue, 1978, Ng

Washington University in St. Louis

Dept of Earth & Planetary Sciences (B,M,D) ☒ (2020)
Campus Box 1169
Rudolph Hall
1 Brookings Drive
St Louis, MO 63130-4899
p. (314) 935-5610
slava@wustl.edu
http://eps.wustl.edu
f: https://www.facebook.com/WashU.EPSci/
t: @WUSTL_EPS
Programs: Geology; Geochemistry; Geophysics; Geobiology
Administrative Assistant: Katherine M.. Totty
Enrollment (2017): B: 56 (15) M: 0 (3) D: 31 (5)
Chair:
Viatcheslav S. Solomatov, (D), Moscow Inst, 1990, Yg
Rudolph Professor of Earth & Planeary Sciences:
Bradley L. Jolliff, (D), SD Mines, 1987, GxzGi
Robert S. Brookings Distinguished Professor:
Douglas A. Wiens, (D), Northwestern, 1985, YsrYg
James S. McDonnell Distinguished University Professor:
Raymond E. Arvidson, (D), Brown, 1974, Xg
Professor:
Jeffrey G. Catalano, (D), Stanford, 2004, Cl
Robert F. Dymek, (D), Caltech, 1977, GpiGa
M. Bruce Fegley, (D), MIT, 1980, Xc
David A. Fike, (D), MIT, 2007, CsmPg
William B. McKinnon, (D), Caltech, 1981, Xg
Jill D. Pasteris, (D), Yale, 1980, GbzGe
Jennifer R. Smith, (D), Pennsylvania, 2001, Ga
William H. Smith, (D), Princeton, 1966, Xc
Michael E. Wysession, (D), Northwestern, 1991, Ys
Research Professor:
Katharina Lodders-Fegley, (D), Max Planck, 1991, Xc
Alian Wang, (D), Sci/Tech (France), 1987, Ca
Associate Professor:
Alexander S. Bradley, (D), MIT, 2008, CboGg
Philip Skemer, (D), Yale, 2007, GcCp
Assistant Professor:
Bronwen L. Konecky, (D), Brown, 2014, PcGn
Michael J. Krawczynski, (D), MIT, 2011, Cg
Claire C. Masteller, (D), California (Santa Cruz), 2017, Hg
Rita Parai, (D), Harvard, 2014, Cs
Kun Wang, (D), Washington (St Louis), 2013, XcCsXm
Emeritus:
Robert E. Criss, (D), Caltech, 1981, Cs
Research Professor:
Anne M. Hofmeister, (D), Caltech, 1984, YghXa
Distinguished Scientist:
Robert D. Hatcher, Jr., (D), Tennessee, 1965, GtcYm
Administrative Officer:
Robert Gemignani, (M), Notre Dame de Namure, 1998, Zn

Environmental Studies Program (B) (2018)
Box 1169
One Brookings Drive
St. Louis, MO 63130-4899
p. (314) 935-7047
enstadmin@levee.wustl.edu
http://enst.wustl.edu
Administrative Assistant: Barbara Winston
Enrollment (2010): B: 161 (59)
Director:
Jan P. Amend, (D), California (Berkeley), 1995, Co
Professor:
Raymond E. Arvidson, (D), Brown, 1974, Zn
Richard Axelbaum, (D), California (Davis), 1988, Ng
Pratim Biswas, (D), Caltech, 1985, Ng
Robert Blankenship, (D), California (Berkeley), 1975, Zn
Robert E. Criss, (D), Caltech, 1981, CsHqXa
Willem H. Dickhoff, (D), Free (Amsterdam), Zn
Mike Dudukovic, (D), Illinois Inst Tech, 1971, Zn
Robert F. Dymek, (D), Caltech, 2006, Gi
Claude Evans, (D), SUNY (Stony Brook), Zn
Bruce Fegley, (D), MIT, 1980, Xc
T.R. Kidder, (D), Harvard, 1988, Zn
Maxine I. Lipeles, (D), Harvard, 1979, Zn
William R. Lowry, (D), Stanford, 1988, Zn
Jill D. Pasteris, (D), Yale, 1980, Zn
Bruce Petersen, (D), Harvard, Zn
Robert Pollak, (D), MIT, 1964, Zn
Tab Rasmussen, (D), Duke, Zn
Barbara Schaal, (D), Yale, 1974, Zn
Glenn D. Stone, (D), Arizona, 1988, Zn
Robert W. Sussman, (D), Duke, 1972, Zn
Alan R. Templeton, (D), Michigan, 1972, ZicZr
Associate Professor:
Jon M. Chase, (D), Chicago, Zn
Clare Palmer, (D), Zn
Jen R. Smith, (D), Pennsylvania, 2001, Ga
Jay Turner, (D), Washington (St Louis), 1993, Zn
Assistant Professor:
Jeff Catalano, (D), Stanford, 2004, Ca
Geoff Childs, (D), Indiana, Zn
Ellen Damschen, (D), North Carolina State, Zn
Daniel Giammar, (D), Caltech, 2001, Zn
Young-Shin Jun, Harvard, 2005, Zn
Tiffany Knight, (D), Pittsburgh, 2003, Pe
John Orrock, (D), Iowa State, 2004, Zn
Engineering & Science Director:
Beth Martin, (M), Washington (St Louis), 1996, Ng
Geology Librarian:
Clara McLeod, Zn

William Jewell College

Dept of Biology (2015)
Liberty, MO 64068
p. (816) 781-3806 x230
allent@william.jewell.edu
http://www.jewell.edu
Chair:
Tara Allen
Associate Professor:
Charles F. J. Newlon, (M), Missouri, 1962, Zg

Montana

Flathead Valley Community College

Geology and Geography (A) (2020)
777 Grandview Drive
Kalispell, MT 59901
p. (406) 756-3873
aho@fvcc.edu
f: https://www.facebook.com/fvccmt/
t: @fvccmt
Programs: Transfer programs in geology/earth science, geography, environmental science and environmental studies. Also forestry, parks, tourism and recreation management, environmental biology and wildlife biology.
Certificates: AAS or certificates in natural resources conservation and management, geospatial technology and surveying.
Associate Professor:
Anita Ho, (D), Oregon, Gg

Montana State University

Dept of Earth Sciences (B,M,D) O☒ (2019)
P.O. Box 173480
226 Traphagen Hall
Bozeman, MT 59717-3480
p. (406) 994-3331
earth@montana.edu
http://www.montana.edu/wwwes/
Enrollment (2018): B: 228 (45) M: 21 (8) D: 22 (1)

Regents Professor:
Cathy Whitlock, (D), Washington, 1983, Peg

Professor:
Mary Hubbard, (D), MIT, 1988
David R. Lageson, (D), Wyoming, 1980, GctGs
David W. Mogk, (D), Washington, 1984, GpZeGz
Mark L. Skidmore, (D), Alberta, 2001, ClPgGl
David J. Varricchio, (D), Montana State, 1995, Pv
William K. Wyckoff, (D), Syracuse, 1982, Zn

Associate Professor:
Jordy Hendrikx, (D), Canterbury (NZ), 2005, ZnHsAs

Assistant Professor:
Jean Dixon, (D), Dartmouth, 2009, GmScZg
Julia H. Haggerty, (D), Colorado, 2004, Zu
Andrew Laskowski, (D), Arizona, 2016
Jamie McEvoy, (D), Arizona, 2013, Ze
David B. McWethy, (D), Montana State, 2007, PeSb
Madison Myers, (D), Oregon, 2017
Devon Orme, (D), Arizona, 2015
Eric Sproles, (D), Oregon, 2012

Research Assistant Professor:
Frankie Jackson, (D), Montana State, 2007, Pv
Colin Shaw, (D), New Mexico, 2001, GcEmGp

Assistant Teaching Professor:
Christopher Organ, (D), Montana State, 2003

Research Assistant Professor:
David W. Bowen, (D), Colorado, 2001, GroGs

Regents Professor:
John R. Horner, Penn State, 2006, Pv

Dept of Land Resources & Environmental Sciences (B,M,D) (2020)
334 Leon Johnson Hall
P.O. Box 173120
Bozeman, MT 59717-3120
p. (406) 994-7060
lresfrontdesk@montana.edu
http://landresources.montana.edu/
Programs: Environmental Science
Land Rehabilitation
Land Resources & Environmental Sciences
Ecology & Environmental Sciences
Administrative Assistant: Dorie Seymour

Department Head:
Tracy M. Sterling, (D), Wisconsin, 1988, Zn

Professor:
William P. Inskeep, (D), Minnesota, 1985, Sc
Clain Jones, (D), So
Timothy McDermott, (D), Po
Geoff Poole, (D), Hg
John Priscu, (D), Po

Senior Scientist:
John Dore, (D), Hawaii, 1995, Ca

Associate Professor:
Jack Brookshire, (D), Zc
Stephanie Ewing, (D), Sd
Tony Hartshorn, (D), So
Robert Payn, (D), Hg
Scott Powell, (D), Zr

Assistant Professor:
Adam Sigler, (D), Rw

Research Associate:
William Kleindl, (D), Sf
Luke McKay, (D), Po
Ann Marie Reinhold, (D), Montana State, 2014, Hq

Instructor:
Nicholas Fox, (M), Zi
Paul B. Hook, (D), Colorado State, 1992, Sf

Emeritus:
James W. Bauder, (D), Utah State, 1974, Sf
Richard E. Engel, (D), Minnesota, 1983, Sc
Jeffrey Jacobsen, So
Rick L. Lawrence, (D), Oregon State, 1998, Zr
Cliff Montagne, (D), Montana State, 1976, Sd
Gerald A. Nielsen, (D), Wisconsin, 1963, Sd
David M. Ward, (D), Wisconsin, 1975, Po

Montana State University, Billings

Dept of Biological & Physical Sciences (2015)
1500 N. 30th Street
Billings, MT 59101
p. (406) 657-2341 x2028
ccastles@msubillings.edu
http://www.msubillings.edu/cas/sciences

Head:
Stanley Wiatr

Dean:
Tasneem Khaleel, (D), Bangalore, 1970, Pg

Professor:
Matt Benacquista, (D), Montana State, 1989, Xy
Thomas T. Zwick, (D), N Colorado, 1977, Ze

Montana Tech of the University of Montana

Dept of Chemistry & Geochemistry (B,M) (2015)
1300 West Park Street
Butte, MT 59701-8997
p. (406) 496-4207
acox@mtech.edu
https://mtech.edu/gradschool/degreeprograms/geochemistry.html
Department Secretary: Wilma Immonen

Professor:
Douglas A. Coe, (D), Oregon State, 1974, Cg
Douglas A. Drew, (D), Wyoming, 1971, Cg
Donald Stierle, (D), California (Riverside), 1979, Co

Assistant Professor:
Alysia Cox, (D), MIT/WHOI, 2011, CqlCm
John D. Hobbs, (D), New Mexico, 1991, Zn

Research Associate:
Wayne Olmsted, (B), Montana State, 1962, Ca
Andrea Stierle, (D), Montana State, Zn

Instructor:
Stephen R. Parker, (M), Indiana, 1972, Zn

Emeritus:
Frank E. Diebold, (D), Colorado Mines, 1967, Cl
Alexis Volborth, (D), Helsinki, 1954, Ca

Dept of Geological Engineering (B,M) ●☒ (2018)
1300 West Park Street
Butte, MT 59701
p. (406) 496-4262
dconrad@mtech.edu
https://www.mtech.edu/mines-engineering/geological
Programs: Geological Engineering (B, M); Geotechnical (B); Mining Geology (B); Hydrogeology (B, M); Petroleum Geology (B); Geology (M); Hydrogeological Engineering (M)
Enrollment (2018): B: 37 (9) M: 20 (7)

Chair:
Larry N. Smith, (D), New Mexico, 1988, GsmEo

Professor:
Christopher H. Gammons, (D), Penn State, 1988, CgEmCs
Mary M. MacLaughlin, (D), California (Berkeley), 1997, NrgNt
Diane Wolfgram, (D), California (Berkeley), 1977, EgoNm

Associate Professor:
Glenn D. Shaw, (D), California (Merced), 2009, HwCsHs

Geophysical Engineering Department (B,M) O☒ (2019)
1300 West Park Street
Butte, MT 59701
p. (406) 496-4401
mspeece@mtech.edu
https://www.mtech.edu/mines-engineering/geophysical
f: https://www.facebook.com/GeophysicalEngineeringMontanaTech/
Programs: Geophysical Engineering (B,M); Geoscience (M)
Enrollment (2018): B: 15 (5) M: 6 (4)

Head:
Marvin A. Speece, (D), Wyoming, 1992, YeuYs

Associate Professor:
Xiaobing Zhou, (D), Alaska (Fairbanks), 2002, Zr
Assistant Professor:
Trevor Irons, (D), Colorado Mines, Yue
Mohamed Khalil, (D), Giessen, 2002, YeuGe
Emeritus:
Curtis A. Link, (D), Houston, 1993, Ye

Rocky Mountain College

Dept of Geology (B) ☒ (2018)
1511 Poly Drive
Billings, MT 59102
p. (406) 657-1101
kalakayt@rocky.edu
http://www.rocky.edu/academics/academic-programs/undergraduate-majors/geology/
f: https://www.facebook.com/rmcgeology/
Programs: Geology
Geology-Petroleum Systems Concentration
Enrollment (2018): B: 11 (5)
Professor:
Thomas J. Kalakay, (D), Wyoming, 2001, GcpGi
Associate Professor:
Emily Geraghty Ward, (D), Montana, 2007, ZeGc
Derek Sjostrom, (D), Dartmouth, 2002, ClGsHs

Salish Kootenai College

Dept of environmental Science (2015)
58138 US Hwy 93
Ronan, MT 59855
antony_berthelote@skc.edu
http://www.skc.edu

University of Montana

Dept. of Geosciences (B,M,D) (2018)
32 Campus Drive #1296
Missoula, MT 59812-1296
p. (406) 243-2341
bendick@mso.umt.edu
http://www.umt.edu/geosciences
Programs: Geosciences; Geosciences Earth Education; International Field Geosciences
Administrative Assistant: Loreene Skeel
Enrollment (2017): B: 68 (0) M: 16 (0) D: 10 (0)
Chair:
James R. Staub, (D), South Carolina, 1985, GsrEo
Professor:
Joel Harper, (D), Wyoming, 1998, GlZc
Marc S. Hendrix, (D), Stanford, 1992, Gs
Nancy W. Hinman, (D), California (San Diego), 1987, Cgl
James W. Sears, (D), Queens, 1979, GctEg
George D. Stanley, Jr., (D), Kansas, 1977, Pi
Associate Professor:
Julia Baldwin, (D), MIT, 2003, Gp
Rebecca Bendick, (D), Colorado, 2000, Yg
Marco Maneta, (D), Extremadura (Spain), 2006, Hsg
Andrew Wilcox, (D), Colorado State, 2005, Gm
Assistant Professor:
Payton Gardner, (D), Utah, 2009, Hw
Hilary R. Martens, (D), Caltech, 2016, YgsYd
Research Associate:
Michael Hofmann, (D), Montana, 2005, GosGr

University of Montana Western

Environmental Sciences Dept (B) ●⦸ (2020)
710 South Atlantic Street
Dillon, MT 59725-3598
p. (406) 683-7615
rob.thomas@umwestern.edu
https://w.umwestern.edu/department/environmental-sciences/
f: https://www.facebook.com/UMWenvirosciences/
Programs: Environmental Science (B); Environmental Sustainability (B); Earth Science Education (B)
Enrollment (2020): B: 50 (12)
Chair:
Robert C. Thomas, (D), Washington, 1993, GseZe

Professor:
Craig E. Zaspel, (D), Montana State, 1975, Yg
Associate Professor:
Rebekah Levine, (D), New Mexico, 2016, GmHsSd
Spruce W. Schoenemann, (D), Washington, 2015, GeCgs
Assistant Professor:
Arica Crootof, (D), Arizona, 2019, RwcZi
Instructor:
Celine Beaucamp-Stout, (M), Québec, 2010, GctEm
Adjunct Professor:
Heidi Anderson-Folnagy, (D), Idaho, 2011, Gs
Emeritus:
R. Stephen Mock, (D), Montana State, 1989, Ca
Sheila M. Roberts, (D), Calgary, 1996, GeSo

Nebraska

Central Community College

Physical Science (A) (2015)
4500 63rd Street
PO Box 1027
Columbus, NE 68602
p. (402) 562-1216
wadlonhilker@cccneb.edu
https://www.cccneb.edu/physicalscience
Instructor:
Denise Condreay, Zg

Chadron State College

Dept of Geosciences (B,M) O (2019)
1000 Main Street
Chadron, NE 69337
p. (308) 432-6377
mleite@csc.edu
http://www.csc.edu/geoscience
f: https://www.facebook.com/CSCgeoscience/
Programs: Geoscience, Environmental Geoscience
Certificates: Water Resources Management
Administrative Assistant: Stacy Mittleider
Enrollment (2019): B: 16 (0) M: 1 (0)
Professor:
Michael B. Leite, (D), Wyoming, 1992, Gg
Assistant Professor:
Tawny Tibbits, (D), Ggz
Instructor:
Jennifer L. Balmat, (M), Chadron State Coll, 2008, GgZe
Adjunct Professor:
Matthew Tibbits, (D), Gg

Creighton University

Dept of Atmospheric Sciences (B,M) (2015)
2500 California Plaza
Omaha, NE 68178
p. (402) 280-2641
zehnder@creighton.edu
Enrollment (2012): B: 10 (0) M: 3 (0)
Professor:
Joseph A. Zehnder, (D), Chicago, 1986, As
Associate Professor:
Jon M. Schrage, (D), Purdue, 1998, Am
Assistant Professor:
Timothy J. Wagner, (D), Wisconsin, 2011, As
Adjunct Professor:
Richard Ritz, (M), Texas A&M, Am
Emeritus:
Arthur V. Douglas, (D), Arizona, 1976, Zg

University of Nebraska, Kearney

Dept of Geography (B) (2015)
203 Copeland Hall
Kearney, NE 68849
p. (308) 865-8355
combshj@unk.edu
Chair:
Jason Combs, (D), Nebraska, 2000

Professor:
Vijay Boken, (D), Manitoba, 1999
Paul Burger, (D), Oklahoma State, 1997
Jeremy Dillon, (D), Kansas, 2001
Associate Professor:
John Bauer, (D), Kansas, 2006
Instructor:
Nate Eidem, (D), Oregon State, 2011
Matt Engel, (D), Nebraska, 2007

University of Nebraska, Lincoln

Dept of Earth & Atmospheric Sciences (B,M,D) ●☒ (2019)
126 Bessey Hall
Lincoln, NE 68588-0340
p. (402) 472-2663
crowe1@unl.edu
http://eas.unl.edu/
f: https://www.facebook.com/UNLEarthAtmosSci
Programs: Geology (B); Meteorology-Climatology (B); Earth and Atmospheric Sciences (M,D)
Administrative Assistant: Janelle Gerry, Tina M. Schinstock
Enrollment (2018): B: 97 (19) M: 38 (18) D: 20 (2)
Chair:
Clinton M. Rowe, (D), Delaware, 1988, As
Professor:
Mark R. Anderson, (D), Colorado, 1985, As
Christopher R. Fielding, (D), Durham (UK), 1982, Gs
Tracy D. Frank, (D), Michigan, 1996, GssCs
Sherilyn C. Fritz, (D), Minnesota, 1985, Pem
David M. Harwood, (D), Ohio State, 1986, PmGul
Adam L. Houston, (D), Illinois, 2004, Asm
Qi S. Hu, (D), Colorado State, 1992, As
R. M. Joeckel, (D), Iowa, 1993, GrsGm
David K. Watkins, (D), Florida State, 1984, PmGu
Vitaly A. Zlotnik, (D), Natl Inst Hydro Engi Geo (Russia), 1979, HwyHq
Associate Professor:
Caroline M. Burberry, (D), Imperial Coll (UK), 2008, Gct
Richard M. Kettler, (D), Michigan, 1990, Cl
Ross Secord, (D), Michigan, 2004, PvCs
Matthew S. Van Den Broeke, (D), Oklahoma, 2011, AsZr
Peter J. Wagner, (D), Chicago, 1995, PigPq
Karrie A. Weber, (D), Alabama, 2002, PgCl
Assistant Professor:
Lynne J. Elkins, (D), MIT/WHOI, 2009, GivCt
Irina Filina, (D), Texas, 2007, YgGtYe
Erin Haacker, (D), Hw
Research Assistant Professor:
Mindi L. Searls, (D), Washington, 2007, YgGg
Emeritus:
Ronald G. Goble, (D), Toronto, GxEg
Priscilla C. Grew, (D), California (Berkeley), 1967, GpeZe
Mary Anne Holmes, (D), Florida State, 1989, GsOuZn
Robert M. Hunt, (D), Columbia, 1971, Pv
Merlin P. Lawson, (D), Clark, 1973, AmtZr
David B. Loope, (D), Wyoming, 1981, Gsg
Darryll T. Pederson, (D), North Dakota, 1971, Hw
Norman D. Smith, (D), Brown, 1967, Gsm
Michael R. Voorhies, (D), Wyoming, 1966, Pv
Assistant Professor of Practice:
Dawn Kopacz, (D), Ast

School of Natural Resource Sciences (B,M,D) ●☒ (2021)
Hardin Hall
3310 Holdrege Street
Lincoln, NE 68583-0961
p. (402) 472-3471
jcarroll2@unl.edu
http://snr.unl.edu/
Programs: Applied Climate Science, Water Science, Environmental Restoration Science, Environmental Science.
Certificates: GIS
Enrollment (2019): B: 48 (21)
Research Hydrogologist:
Jozsef Szilagyi, (D), California (Davis), 1997, Hw
Quaternary Geologist:
Paul Hanson, (D), Nebraska, 2005, Gm
Nebraska State Geologist/Research Geologist:
R.M. Joeckel, (D), Iowa, 1993, Grs
Hydrogeochemist/Lab Services Director:
Daniel Snow, (D), Nebraska, 1996, Ge
Environmental Biophysicist:
Elizabeth A. Walter-Shea, (D), Nebraska, 1987, As
Earth Systems Scientist:
David C. Gosselin, (D), SD Mines, 1987, Ze
Climatologist:
Michael J. Hayes, (D), Missouri, 1994, As
Agricultural Climatologist:
Qi (Steve) Hu, (D), Colorado State, 1992, As
Nebraska State Climatologist/Applied Climatologist:
Martha D. Shulski, (D), Minnesota, 2002, As
Micrometeorologist:
Andrew E. Suyker, (D), Nebraska, 2000, As
Climatologist:
Tsegaye Tadesse, (D), Nebraska, 2002, ZirAs
Climate Scientist:
Deborah J. Bathke, (D), Ohio State, 2004, AsZe
Pedologist:
Judith Turk, (D), California (Riverside), 2012, Sd
Groundwater Hydrologist:
Troy Gilmore, (D), N Carolina State, 2015, Hw
Groundwater Geologist:
Jesse Korus, (D), Nebraska, 2015, Gs

University of Nebraska, Omaha

Dept of Geography and Geology (B,M) (2019)
6001 Dodge Street
DSC 260
Omaha, NE 68182-0199
p. (402) 554-2662
rshuster@unomaha.edu
http://www.unomaha.edu/college-of-arts-and-sciences/geology/
Programs: Geology, Environmental Science-Earth Science Option, Geography
Certificates: GIS
Administrative Assistant: Brenda Todd
Enrollment (2019): B: 64 (18) M: 20 (8)
Professor:
George F. Engelmann, (D), Columbia, 1978, PvGdr
Harmon D. Maher, Jr., (D), Wisconsin, 1984, GcsGt
Associate Professor:
Bradley Bereitschaft, (D), North Carolina (Greensboro), 2011, Zuy
Ashlee LD Dere, (D), Penn State, 2014, SdGmCl
Robert D. Shuster, (D), Kansas, 1985, GiaZe
Assistant Professor:
Zac Suriano, (D), Delaware, 2018, Atm
Emeritus:
Jeffrey S. Peake, (D), Louisiana State, 1977, ZyAtRm
John F. Shroder, Jr., (D), Utah, 1967, GmlZy

Nevada

College of Southern Nevada - West Charleston Campus

Dept of Physical Sciences (A) (2018)
6375 W. Charleston Blvd.
Las Vegas, NV 89146
p. (702) 651-7475
physic@csn.edu
http://www.csn.edu/pages/2497.asp
Lead Faculty:
Barbara Graham, (M), ZyAm
John E. Keller, (D), S Illinois, 2009, GeHw
Cynthia S. Shroba, (D), Illinois, Gg
Professor:
Patrick D. Clennan, (M), ZyGe
Gale D. Martin, (M), Gg
Instructor:
Douglas Sims, (D), Kingston, 2011, GeSp

Desert Research Institute

Earth & Ecosystems Sciences (2015)
2215 Raggio Parkway
Reno, NV 89512-1095
p. (775) 673-7300

bj@dri.edu
Assistant Research Professor:
Thomas F. Bullard, (D), New Mexico, 1995, Gma
Professor:
John Arnone, (D), Yale, 1988, Pg
Colleen M. Beck, (D), California (Berkeley), 1979, Sa
Christian H. Fritsen, (D), S California, 1996, Pg
Eric McDonald, (D), New Mexico, 1994, Sd
Alison E. Murray, (D), California (Santa Barbara), 1998, Pg
David E. Rhode, (D), Washington, 1987, Pe
Staff Geomorphologist:
Sophie Baker, (M), Dalhousie, 2005, Gm
Associate Research Geomorphologist:
Steven N. Bacon, (M), Humboldt State, 2003, Gm
Associate Professor:
Kenneth D. Adams, (D), Nevada (Reno), 1997, Gm
Thomas F. Bullard, (D), New Mexico, 1995, Gm
Mary Cablk, (D), Oregon State, 1997, Zr
Lynn Fenstermaker, (D), Nevada, 2003, Zr
Giles Marion, (D), California (Berkeley), 1974, Sc
Kenneth C. McGwire, (D), California (Santa Barbara), 1992, Zy
David A. Mouat, (D), Oregon State, 1974, Ge
Assistant Professor:
JoseLuis Antinao, (D), Dalhousie, 2009, Gm
Donald E. Sabol, Jr, (D), Washington, 1991, Zr
GIS/Remote Sensing Scientist:
Timothy B. Minor, (M), California (Santa Barbara), 1982, Zr
Assistant Research Ecologist:
Richard Jasoni, (D), Texas A&M, 1998, So
Archaeological Technician:
David Page, (M), Nevada (Reno), 2008, Ga

Great Basin College

Science Dept (A,B) ⊘ (2018)
1500 College Parkway
Elko, NV 89801
p. (775) 753-2120
caroline.meisner@gbcnv.edu
http://www2.gbcnv.edu/departments/SCI.html
Programs: Associates of Science - Pattern of Study Geosciences
Associates of Science - Natural Resources
Bachelor's of Arts - Natural Resources
Professor:
Caroline Bruno Meisner, (M), Oregon State, 2003, ZgSo

Truckee Meadows Community College

Dept of Physical Sciences (2015)
7000 Dandini Boulevard
Reno, NV 89512
p. (775) 673-7183
loanderson@tmcc.edu
http://www.tmcc.edu/physicalsci/

University of Nevada, Las Vegas

Geoscience Department (B,M,D) ●⁄🖱 (2019)
4505 S. Maryland Parkway
Box 454010
Las Vegas, NV 89154-4010
p. (702) 895-3262
Matthew.Lachniet@unlv.edu
http://geoscience.unlv.edu
f: https://www.facebook.com/UNLVGeoscience/
t: @UNLVGeoscience
Programs: Geology BS, Earth & Environmental Science BS, PhD & MS in Geoscience
Administrative Assistant: Maria I. Rojas, Elizabeth Y. Smith
Enrollment (2016): B: 18 (18) M: 14 (14) D: 0 (3)
Chair:
Terry L. Spell, (D), SUNY (Albany), 1991, CcGvi
Professor:
Brenda J. Buck, (D), New Mexico State, 1996, GbSd
Andrew D. Hanson, (D), Stanford, 1998, Co
Ganqing Jiang, (D), Columbia, 2002, GsClGr
David K. Kreamer, (D), Arizona, 1982, Hw
Matthew S. Lachniet, (D), Syracuse, 2001, PeCs
Rodney V. Metcalf, (D), New Mexico, 1990, Gp
Margaret N. Rees, (D), Kansas, 1984, Gs
Stephen Rowland, (D), California (Santa Cruz), 1978, Pi
Wanda J. Taylor, (D), Utah, 1989, Gc
Michael L. Wells, (D), Cornell, 1991, Gc
Water Resourse Director/ Co-Chair:
Michael J. Nicholl, (D), Nevada (Reno), 1993
Associate Scientist:
Kathleen Zanetti, (M), Idaho, 1997, Gg
Assistant Professor:
Elisabeth M. Hausrath, (D), Penn State, 2007, CgScCl
Associate Chair:
Eugene I. Smith, (D), New Mexico, 1970, Gi
Emeritus:
Jean S. Cline, (D), Virginia Tech, 1990, EmCe
Associate Reseach Professor:
Pamela C. Burnley, (D), California (Davis), 1990, GpyGg

University of Nevada, Reno

Center for Neotectonic Studies (2015)
MS 0169
Reno, NV 89557-0169
p. (775) 784-6067
wesnousky@unr.edu
http://neotectonics.seismo.unr.edu/CNSHome.html
Director:
Steven Wesnousky, (D), Columbia, 1982, Ys

Center for Research in Economic Geology (M,D) ☒ (2020)
Mail Stop 1169
Reno, NV 89557-1169
p. (775) 784-1382
dawnsnell@unr.edu
Administrative Assistant: Dawn Lee Snell
Enrollment (2020): M: 7 (2) D: 6 (4)
Director:
John Muntean, (D), Stanford, Eg

Dept of Geography (B,M,D) ☒ (2021)
Mail Stop 0154
Reno, NV 89557-0154
p. (775) 784-6995
geography@unr.edu
http://www.unr.edu/geography/
Enrollment (2020): B: 53 (16) M: 16 (6) D: 17 (3)
Chair:
Douglas Boyle, (D), Arizona, 2000, Hg
Professor:
Kate Berry, (D), Colorado, 1993, Zy
Jill Heaton, (D), Oregon State, 2001, ZniZy
Scott A. Mensing, (D), California (Berkeley), 1993, Zy
Anne Nolin, (D), California (Santa Barbara), 1993, Hg
Associate Professor:
Thomas Albright, (D), Wisconsin, 2007, Zy
Scott Bassett, (D), Harvard, 2001, Zu
Stephanie McAfee, (D), Arizona, 2009, Zy
Paul White, (D), Brown, 2008, Zn
Assistant Professor:
Jessie Clark, (D), Arizona, 2012, Zu
Adam Csank, (D), Arizona, 2011, Zy
Jia Feng, (D), Michigan State, 2016, Zi
Scott Kelley, (D), Arizona State, 2015, Zi
Casey Lynch, (D), Arizona, 2019, Zn
Kenneth Nussear, (D), Nevada, 2004, Zn
Kerri Jean Ormerod, (D), Arizona, 2015, Zu

Dept of Geological Sciences and Engineering (B,M,D) O⊘ (2020)
1664 N. Virginia St., MS 0172
Reno, NV 89557-0172
p. (775) 784-6050
geology@unr.edu
http://www.unr.edu/geology
Programs: Geology, Hydrogeology, Geophysics Geological Engineering
Dual degree Geology and Secondary Education via NevadaTeach
Enrollment (2020): B: 132 (16) M: 29 (12) D: 20 (1)
Research Professor:
Simon R. Poulson, (D), Penn State, 1990, Cs
Professor:
Wendy M. Calvin, (D), Colorado, 1991, XgZrYg

Paula J. Noble, (D), Texas, 1993, PmGnPs
Scott W. Tyler, (D), Nevada (Reno), 1990, Hw
Robert J. Watters, (D), Imperial Coll (UK), 1972, Nrg
Associate Professor:
Stacia M. Gordon, (D), Minnesota, 2009, Gpz
Scott W. McCoy, (D), Colorado, 2012, GmNg
Assistant Professor:
Wenrong Cao, (D), S California, 2015, Gtc
Michael H. Gardner, (D), California (Berkeley), 2018, NxRn
Kaitlin M. Keegan, (D), Dartmouth, 2014, PcNg
Philipp P. Ruprecht, (D), Washington, 2009, Giv
Joel S. Scheingross, (D), Caltech, 2016, Gsm
Lecturer:
John K. McCormack, (D), Nevada (Reno), 1997, GzEm
Laboratory Director:
Joel DesOrmeau, (D), Nevada (Reno), 2016, Gp
Cooperating Faculty:
John G. Anderson, (D), Columbia, 1976, Ys
Bridget F. Ayling, (D), Australian Nat, 2006, Ce
Geoffrey Blewitt, (D), Caltech, 1986, Yd
Mike Darin, (D), N Arizona, 2019, Gc
James E. Faulds, (D), New Mexico, 1989, Gc
William C. Hammond, (D), Oregon, 2000, Yd
Matthieu Harlaux, (D), Lorraine, France, 2016, Em
Graham Kent, (D), Scripps, 1992, Ys
Rich D. Koehler, (D), Nevada (Reno), 2009, Rn
Corne Kreemer, (D), SUNY (Stony Brook), 2001, Yd
John N. Louie, (D), Caltech, 1987, Ys
John L. Muntean, (D), Stanford, 1998, Em
Lisa L. Stillings, (D), Penn State, 1994, Cl
Steven G. Wesnousky, (D), Columbia, 1982, Ys
Andrew Zuza, (D), California (Los Angeles), 2016, Gc

Dept of Mining Engineering (B,M,D) (2015)
Mail Stop 0173
Reno, NV 89557-0173
p. (775) 784-6961
jameshendrix@unr.edu
http://www.unr.edu/cos/mining/
Administrative Assistant: Carla Scott
Enrollment (2011): B: 66 (5) M: 8 (0) D: 5 (0)
Chair:
Danny L. Taylor, (D), Colorado Mines, 1980, Nm
Professor:
Jaak Daemen, (D), Minnesota, 1975, Nr
George Danko, (D), Budapest, 1985, Nm
Associate Professor:
Carl Nesbitt, (D), Nevada, 1990, Nx
Thom Seal, (D), Idaho, 2004, Nx
Emeritus:
Maurice Feunstenau, (D), Nx
Pierre Mousset-Jones, (D), London (UK), 1988, Nm
Development Technician:
John D. Leland, (M), Stanford, 1983

Graduate Program of Hydrologic Sciences (M,D) (2016)
1664 N. Virginia Street
MS 0186
Reno, NV 89557-0175
p. (775) 784-6221
hydro@unr.edu
http://www.hydro.unr.edu
Enrollment (2015): M: 32 (10) D: 8 (1)
Research Professor:
Kumud Acharya, (D), Saitama, HsGeHq
Kenneth Adams, (D), Nevada (Reno), 1997, Gam
Braimah Apambire, (D)
John J. Arnone, (D), Yale, 1988, Sp
Gayle L. Dana, (D), Nevada (Reno), 1997, Zr
Joseph Grzymski, (D)
Roger Jacobson, (D), Penn State, 1973, Cg
Nick Lancaster, (D), Cambridge, 1977, Gm
Joseph McConnell, (D), Arizona, 1997, Zn
Eric McDonald, (D), New Mexico, 1994, Sp
Alison Murray, (D), California (Santa Barbara), 1998, ObCg
Daniel Obrist, (D), Nevada (Reno), 2002
Simon Poulson, (D), Penn State, 1990, Cls
Associate Director:
Rina Schumer, (D), Nevada (Reno), 2002, HqwGm
Research Professor:
Christian H. Fritsen, (D), S California, 1995, Og
Professor:
Franco Biondi, (D), Arizona, 1994
Wendy Calvin, (D), Colorado, 1991, YgZr
George Danko, (D), Hungarian Acad of Sci, 1985, Hq
Mae Gustin, (D), Arizona, 1988, Cg
David Kreamer, (D), Arizona, 1982, HwGn
John Louie, (D), Caltech, 1987, Yg
Maureen McCarthy, (D)
Paula Noble, (D), Texas, 1993, Gn
Anna Panorska, (D), California (Santa Barbara), 1992
Mark Pinsky, (D)
Greg Pohll, (D), Nevada (Reno), 1996, Hwq
Robert G. Qualls, (D), Georgia, 1989, SoHsSf
Loretta Singletary, (D)
Scott Tyler, (D), Nevada (Reno), 1990, Hg
Mark Walker, (D), Cornell, 1998, Zn
Research Hydrologist:
Brian Andraski, (D), Nevada (Reno)
Senior Scientist:
Richard Niswonger, (D)
Research Hydrogeologist and Civil Engineer:
Dave Decker, (D), Nevada (Reno), Hw
Associate Research Professor:
Marcus Berli, (D), Swiss Fed Inst Tech, Sp
Li Chen, (D), Chinese Acad of Sci
Clay A. Cooper, (D), Nevada (Reno), 1999, HySpHq
Alan Heyvaert, (D), California (Davis), 1998, GnHs
Justin Huntington, (D), Nevada (Reno), 2011, HgZr
Richard Jasoni, (D), Texas A&M
Alexandra Lutz, (D), Nevada (Reno), Hw
Kenneth McGwire, (D), California (Santa Barbara), 1992, Zr
Don Sada, (D)
Rick Susfalk, (D)
Julian Zhu, (D), Dalhousie
Associate Professor:
Sudeep Chandra, (D), California (Davis), 2003, Hs
Keith E. Dennett, (D), Georgia Tech, 1995, Hs
Eric Marchand, (D), Colorado, 2000
Sherman Swanson, (D), Oregon State, 1983, Hs
Aleksey S. Telyakovskiy, (D), Wyoming, 2002, Hqy
Associate Research Professor:
Ronald L. Hershey, (D), Nevada (Reno), 2010, HwCls
Associate Scientist:
Lisa Shevenell, (D), Nevada (Reno), 1990, Hw
Assistant Research Professor:
Rishi Parashar, (D), Purdue, 2008, Hq
Seshadri Rajagopal, (D)
Casey Schmidt, (D)
Assistant Research Hydrogeologist:
Rosemary Carroll, (D), Nevada (Reno), 2010, Hq
Assistant Professor:
Ronald Breitmeyer, (D), Wisconsin, 2011, HwGe
Adrian Harpold, (D), Cornell, 2010, HqsZr
Scott McCoy, (D)
Ben Sullivan, (D)
Paul Verburg, (D), Wageningen (Neth), 1998, SdcSb
Steve G. Wells, (D), Cincinnati, 1976, Zn
Yu (Frank) Yang, (D)
Research Associate:
Ramon Naranjo, (D), Nevada (Reno), 2012, CgHw
Lisa Stillings, (D), Penn State, 1994, Cm
Assistant Research Professor:
Tom Bullard, (D), New Mexico, 1995, Gm
Adjunct Professor:
Jonathan Price, (D)
Jim Thomas, (D), Nevada (Reno), 1996, Cg
Research Professor:
Ken Taylor, (D)
Emeritus:
Dale Johnson, (D)
Wally Miller, (D)
Steve Wheatcraft, (D), Hawaii, 1979, Hw
Cooperating Faculty:
Chris Benedict
Jeanne Chambers, (D), Sf
David Prudic, (D), Nevada (Reno)
Michael R. Rosen, (D), Texas, 1989, Gn

Keirith Snyder, (D)
Mark Weltz, (D)

Great Basin Center for Geothermal Energy (2015)
Mail Stop 0172
1664 N. Virginia St
Reno, NV 89557-0172
p. (775) 784-7018
geothermal@unr.edu
http://www.gbcge.org
Director:
Wendy Calvin, (D), Colorado, 1991, ZrYgXg
Professor:
John Louie, (D), Caltech, 1987, Yse
Research Professor:
James Faulds, (D), New Mexico, 1989, Gc
Research Associate:
Nick Hinz, (M), Nevada (Reno), 2004, Gcg

Mackay School of Earth Sciences and Engineering (Director's Office) ⊠ (2017)
Mail Stop 0168
Reno, NV 89557-0168
p. (775) 784-6987
juliehill@unr.edu
http://www.mines.unr.edu/Mackay/
Administrative Assistant: Julie Hill
Director:
Thom Seal, (D), Idaho, 2004, NxEmNm

Nevada Seismological Lab ⊠ (2018)
Mail Stop 0174
Reno, NV 89557-0174
p. (775) 784-4975
mainofc@seismo.unr.edu
http://www.seismo.unr.edu
Administrative Assistant: Lori McClelland, Erik Williams
Director:
Graham Kent, (D), California (San Diego), 1992, Ys
Professor:
John G. Anderson, (D), Columbia, 1976, Ys
John N. Louie, (D), Caltech, 1987, YesRn
Steve Wesnousky, (D), Columbia, 1982, Ys
Research Associate Professor:
Glenn P. Biasi, (D), Oregon, 1994, Ys
Ileana Tibuleac, (D), S Methodist, 1999, Ys
Assistant Director, Seismic Network Manager & Development Director:
Ken D. Smith, (D), Nevada (Reno), 1991, YsGt
Adjunct Research Associate:
Bill Honjas, (M), Nevada (Reno), Ys
Emeritus Seismic Network Manager:
David H. von Seggern, (D), Penn State, 1982, YsgEo
Emeritus:
James N. Brune, (D), Columbia, 1961, Ys
Development Technician:
Ryan Presser, (A)
Volunteer Adjunct Faculty:
Aasha Pancha, (D), Nevada (Reno), 2007, Ys
Seismic Systems Analyst:
David Slater, (B), Calgary, 1990, Ys
Seismic Records Technician:
Tom Rennie, (D), Nevada (Reno), 2007, Ys
Programmer/Analyst, Seismic Network:
Gabriel Plank, (B), Cornell, 1994, Ys
Network Seismologist:
Diane dePolo, (M), Nevada (Reno), 1989, Ys
Development Technician:
Kent Straley
Associate Engineer:
John Torrisi, (A)

Western Nevada College

Western Nevada College (2015)
2201 West College Parkway
Carson City, NV 89703
p. (775) 445-4442
Winnie.Kortemeier@wnc.edu
http://www.wnc.edu/academics/division/sme/

New Hampshire

Dartmouth College

Dept of Earth Sciences (B,M,D) ⊠ (2018)
227 Fairchild Hall, HB 6105
Hanover, NH 03755
p. (603) 646-9037
phyllis.ford@dartmouth.edu
http://www.dartmouth.edu/~earthsci
f: www.facebook.com/DartmouthEarthSciences
Programs: Earth Sciences (B,M,D)
Enrollment (2018): B: 22 (0) M: 10 (0) D: 15 (0)
Professor:
Xiahong Feng, (D), Case Western, 1991, Cs
Carl E. Renshaw, (D), Stanford, 1993, HgGc
Associate Professor:
Robert L. Hawley, (D), Washington, 2005, Gl
Meredith Kelly, (D), Bern, 2003, Gl
Mukul Sharma, (D), Rochester, Ge
Leslie J. Sonder, (D), Harvard, 1986, Gq
Assistant Professor:
William D. Leavitt, (D), Harvard
Erich C. Osterberg, (D), Maine, 2007, AsCl
Marisa Palucis, (D)
Justin V. Strauss, (D), Harvard, 2015, GsCgGt
Emeritus:
William Brian Dade, (D), Washington, GsHgEo
Gary D. Johnson, (D), Iowa State, 1971, GrdYm
Research Professor:
Brian P. Jackson, (D), Georgia, 1998, CaGeCt

Keene State College

Dept of Geology (B) ⊠ (2019)
Mail Stop 2001
229 Main Street
Keene, NH 03435-2001
p. (603) 358-2553
pnielsen@keene.edu
http://www.keene.edu/academics/programs/geol/
Enrollment (2014): B: 17 (4)
Adjunct Professor:
Charles M. Kerwin, (D), New Hampshire, 2006, Gg
Emeritus:
Steven D. Bill, (D), Case Western, 1982, Pg
Peter A. Nielsen, (D), Alberta, 1977, GxzGc

Plymouth State University

Environmental Science and Policy Program (B,M) ⊘ (2019)
17 High Street
Campus Box 48
Plymouth, NH 03264
p. (603) 536-2573
ladoner@plymouth.edu
http://oz.plymouth.edu/esp
Programs: Environmental Science & Policy BS
Environmental Science & Policy MS, Sustainability minor
Certificates: GIS (offered through our school's Geography program)
Enrollment (2019): M: 6 (3)
Professor:
Eric G. Hoffman, (D), SUNY (Albany), 2000, Am
Undergraduate program coordinator:
Lisa A. Doner, (D), Colorado, 2001, PcGes
Research Assistant Professor and Director of Research at the Mount Washington Observatory:
Eric Kelsey, (D), New Hampshire, 2014, AtsGl
Instructor:
Erik W. Burtis, (M), Montana, 2003, GczGe

University of New Hampshire

Dept of Earth Sciences (B,M,D) ⊘ (2021)
214 James Hall
56 College Road
Durham, NH 03824
p. (603) 862-1718

earth.sciences@unh.edu
http://ceps.unh.edu/earth-sciences
Programs: Earth Sciences; Geochemistry; Geology; Hydrology; Ocean Mapping; Oceanography
Administrative Assistant: Susan E. Clark
Enrollment (2020): B: 56 (14) M: 30 (7) D: 23 (7)

Chair:
Joseph M. Licciardi, (D), Oregon State, 2000, Gl
Research Professor:
Stephen E. Frolking, (D), New Hampshire, 1993, As
Cameron P. Wake, (D), New Hampshire, 1993, Gl
Affiliate Professor:
Christopher E. Parrish, (D), Wisconsin, Zr
Professor:
Julia G. Bryce, (D), California (Santa Barbara), 1998, CgcCb
William C. Clyde, (D), Michigan, 1997, PgYmGs
John E. Hughes-Clarke, (D), Dalhousie, 1988, Og
Joel E. Johnson, (D), Oregon State, 2004, Gus
Joseph M. Licciardi, (D), Oregon State, 2000, Gl
Larry A. Mayer, (D), California (San Diego), 1979, Gu
David C. Mosher, (D), Dalhousie, 1993, Og
James M. Pringle, (D), MIT/WHOI, 1998, Op
Ruth K. Varner, (D), New Hampshire, 2000, Cl
Research Associate Professor:
Jack E. Dibb, (D), SUNY (Binghamton), 1988, AcClAs
Larry G. Ward, (D), South Carolina, 1978, Gu
Associate Professor:
Michael W. Palace, (D), New Hampshire, Zn
Affiliate Research Associate Professor:
Mark A. Fahnestock, (D), Caltech, 1991, Gl
Affiliate Associate Professor:
Joseph Salisbury, Og
Mary D. Stampone, (D), Delaware, 2009, Zy
Associate Professor:
Rosemarie E. Came, (D), MIT/WHOI, 2005, OoZnn
J. Matthew Davis, (D), New Mexico Tech, 1994, HwYh
Jo Laird, (D), Caltech, 1977, Gp
Anne F. Lightbody, (D), MIT, 2007, HgsZn
Thomas C. Lippmann, (D), Oregon State, 1992, Onp
Affiliate Research Assistant Professor:
Alexandra Contosta, (D), New Hampshire, 2011, So
Assistant Professor:
Robert T. Letscher, (D), Rosenstiel, 2012, OcCbZo
Affiliate Research Associate Professor:
Brian Calder, (D), Heriot-Watt, 1997, Og
Affiliate Research Assistant Professor:
Kai Ziervogel, Rostock, 2004, Gu
Affiliate Professor:
Andrew Armstrong, (M), Johns Hopkins, 1991, Zn
Affiliate Professor:
Douglas C. Vandemark, (M), New Hampshire, 2005, Zr
Emeritus:
Franz E. Anderson, (D), Washington, 1967, Yr
Wallace A. Bothner, (D), Wyoming, 1967, Gc
S. Lawrence Dingman, (D), Harvard, 1970, Hq
Henri E. Gaudette, (D), Illinois, 1963, Cc
Theodore C. Loder, (D), Alaska, 1971, Oc
Affiliate Research Scientist III:
Semme Dijkstra, (D), New Brunswick, Og
Affiliate Research Professor:
Erik Hobbie
Affiliate Research Assistant Professor:
Christos Kastrisios, (D), Natl Tech Athens, 2017, Zn
Affiliate Faculty:
Rochelle Wigley, (D), Cape Town, 2005, CgGu

Dept of Natural Resources and the Environment (B,M,D) ☒ (2018)
114 James Hall
56 College Rd
Durham, NH 03824-3589
p. 603-862-1022
wendy.rose@unh.edu
https://colsa.unh.edu/natural-resources-environment
Programs: Environmental Science
Certificates: GIS certificate
Enrollment (2018): B: 70 (25) M: 20 (0) D: 20 (0)

Chair:
Mark Ducey, (D), Zc
Professor:
Russell Congalton, (D), Zi
Serita Frey, (D), Sb
William H. McDowell, (D), HgRw
Scott Ollinger, (D), Zc
Associate Professor:
Stuart Grandy, (D), Sc
Wil Wollheim, (D), Zu
Assistant Professor:
Jessica Ernakovich, (D), Zc
Research Associate:
Adam Wymore, (D), Hg

New Jersey

Bergen Community College

Department of Physical Sciences (2021)
400 Paramus Rd
Paramus, NJ 07652-1508
p. (201) 447-7100
mnotholt@bergen.edu
http://bergen.edu/academics/academic-divisions-departments/physical-science/
Programs: AS in Physics, Chemistry, and Engineering Science.

College of New Jersey

Physics Dept (2017)
2000 Pennington Rd.
Ewing , NJ 08628
p. 609-771-2569
physics@tcnj.edu

Associate Professor:
Margaret Benoit, Penn State, 2005, Ys
Nathan Magee, (D), Penn State, 2006, As
Adjunct Professor:
Thomas Gillespie, (M), Rutgers, 1986, Gc

Kean University

School of Environmental and Sustainability Sciences (B) (2015)
1000 Morris Avenue
Union, NJ 07083-0411
p. (908) 737-3737
fqi@kean.edu
http://www.kean.edu/KU/College-of-Natural-Applied-Health-Sciences
Enrollment (2006): B: 160 (0)

Professor:
Robert Metz, (D), Rensselaer, 1967, Gr
Shing Yoh, (D), Drexel, 1989, Am
Constantine S. Zois, (D), Rutgers, 1980, Am
Executive Director:
Paul J. Croft, (D), Rutgers, 1991, AmsZe
Associate Professor:
Carrie M. Manfrino, (D), Miami, 1995, GuOb
Feng Qi, (D), Wisconsin, 2005, ZiyZg
Assistant Professor:
Kikombo Ngoy, (D), Oregon, 1996, Zy
Lecturer:
William C. Heyniger, (B), Montclair State, 2011, Am
Secretary:
Christina Pacia, (N), Zn

Montclair State University

Dept of Earth & Environmental Studies (B,M) (2015)
1 Normal Avenue
Upper Montclair, NJ 07043
p. (973) 655-4448
ophorid@montclair.edu
http://www.csam.montclair.edu/earth/eesweb

Chair:
Jonathan M. Lincoln, (D), Northwestern, 1990, Gr
Associate Dean, Science & Mathematics:
Michael A. Kruge, (D), California (Berkeley), 1985, Co
Professor:
Mark J. Chopping, (D), Nottingham (UK), 1998, ZriZe
Huan E. Feng, (D), SUNY (Stony Brook), 1997, Cm

Gregory A. Pope, (D), Arizona State, 1994, GmaZy
Harbans Singh, (D), Rutgers, 1973, Zn
William Solecki, (D), Rutgers, 1990, Zu
Rolf Sternberg, (D), Syracuse, 1971, Zn
Robert W. Taylor, (D), St Louis, 1971, Zn
John V. Thiruvathukal, (D), Oregon State, 1968, Yg

Associate Dean:
Duke U. Ophori, (D), Alberta, 1986, Hw

Associate Professor:
Matthew L. Gorring, (D), Cornell, 1997, Gi

Adjunct Professor:
Kathryn Black, (M), Oklahoma, 1966, Zy
Matthew S. Tomaso, (M), Texas, 1995, Ga
Christine Valenti, (M), Montclair State, 1997, Gg

Emeritus:
Barbara De Beus, Zn

Laboratory Director:
Yoko Sato, (M), Montclair State, 2000, Gg

New Jersey City University

Dept of Earth and Environmental Sciences (B) (2015)
Rossey Hall - Room 608
2039 Kennedy Boulevard
Jersey City, NJ 07305-1597
p. (201) 200-3161
lengland@njcu.edu
http://www.njcu.edu/dept/geoscience%5Fgeography/
Enrollment (2006): B: 37 (19)

Chair:
Deborah Freile, (D), Boston, 1992, GseGg

Professor:
Martin Abend, (D), Syracuse, 1955, Zy

Research Associate:
John M. O'Brien, (D), California (Santa Barbara), 1973, Gs

Lecturer:
William W. Montgomery, (D), W Michigan, 1998, Hw

Adjunct Professor:
George Papcun, (M), Ze
Howard Zlotkin, (M), Ze

Emeritus:
John Marchisin, (M), Montclair State, 1965, Gg

Princeton University

Dept of Geosciences (B,D) ☒ (2021)
113 Guyot Hall
Princeton, NJ 08544-1003
p. (609) 258-4101
mrusso@princeton.edu
http://www.geoweb.princeton.edu
f: https://www.facebook.com/GeosciencesPU/
Programs: Environmental Biogeochemistry; Geophysical & Geology; Ocean, Atmosphere & Climate
Administrative Assistant: Mary Rose Russo
Enrollment (2020): B: 21 (16) D: 38 (10)

Chair:
Bess B. Ward, (D), Washington, 1982, ObCb

Associate Chair:
Frederik J. Simons, (D), MIT, 2002, YsdYm

Professor:
Thomas S. Duffy, (D), Caltech, 1992, GyYgZm
Adam C. Maloof, (D), Harvard, 2004, Ym
Satish C B. Myneni, (D), Ohio State, 1995, Sc
Tullis C. Onstott, (D), Princeton, 1980, Pg
Michael Oppenheimer, (D), Chicago, 1970, AsGe
Allan M. Rubin, (D), Stanford, 1988, Yg
Daniel M. Sigman, (D), MIT, 1997, ClsPc
Jeroen Tromp, (D), Princeton, 1992, Yss
Gabriel Vecchi, (D), Washington, 2000, ZoOp

Professional Specialist:
Amal Jayakumar, (D), Goa, 1999, Cm
Sergey Oleynik, (D), Moscow State (Russia), 1999, Cs

Associate Professor:
Stephan A. Fueglistaler, (D), ETH (Switzerland), 2002, As
John A. Higgins, (D), Harvard, 2009, ClPcCs
Blair Schoene, (D), MIT, 2006, Cc

Research Scholar:
Anne Morel-Kraepiel, (D), Princeton, 2001, Em

Assistant Professor:
Ching-Yao Lai, (D), Princeton, 2018, YgZoGl
Laure Resplandy, (D), Sorbonne (France), 2010, Ob
Xinning Zhang, (D), Caltech, 2010, Cb

Academic Lab Manager:
Laurel P. Goodell, (M), Princeton, 1983, ZeGgc
Danielle M. Schmitt, (M), W Michigan, 1999, Ze

Emeritus:
Michael L. Bender, (D), Columbia, 1970, Cg
Lincoln S. Hollister, (D), Caltech, 1966, GptGz
Gerta Keller, (D), Stanford, 1978, Pm
Francois M M. Morel, (D), Caltech, 1971, Cl
S. George H. Philander, (D), Harvard, 1970, Op
Robert A. Phinney, (D), Caltech, 1961, Ys
Jorge L. Sarmiento, (D), Columbia, 1978, Oc

Post Doctoral Research Fellow:
Romain Darnajoux, (D), Sherbrooke, 2015, Cb
Jesse Farmer, (D), Columbia, 2017, Cm
Jessica Lueders-Dumont, (D), Princeton, 2019, Cm
Dario Marconi, (D), Princeton, 2017, Cms

Post Doctoral Research Associate:
Anne-Sofie Ahm, (D), Copenhagen, 2016, ClsPc
Alyssa Anderson, (D), Arizona State, 2019, CcgGz
Etienne Bachmann, (D), Toulouse, 2016, Ys
Stephen Beller, (D), Côte d'Azur, 2017, Ysg
Gregory Davies, (D), Princeton, 2018, Yg
Mathurin Dongmo Wamba, (D), Paris, 2020, YsnYg
Behrooz Ferdowsi, (D), ETH (Switzerland), 2014, Yu
Sirisha Kalidindi, (D), Max Planck, 2019, As
Wenjie Lei, (D), Princeton, 2019, Ys
Renxing Liang, (D), Oklahoma, 2015, Po
Enhui Liao, (D), Delaware, 2017, Op
Qiangcheng Liu, (D), Chinese Acad of Sci, 2016, Yg
Zhaolun Liu, (D), King Abdullah Sci & Tech, 2019, Yg
Ashley Maloney, (D), Washington, 2017, Oc
Jenna L. Pearson, (D), Brown, 2020, Ogp
Lauren N. Pincus, (D), Yale, 2020, CqlCg
Linta Reji, (D), Stanford, 2020, CbPoOb
Melinda Rucks, (D), Stoney Brook, 2019, Gy
Sarah Shackelton, (D), California (San Diego), 2016, Pc
Linhan Shen, (D), Caltech, 2017, Cas
Joel D. Simon, (D), Princeton, 2020, YsgYr
Jingru Sun, (D), Tsinghua, 2018, As
Weiyi Tang, (D), Duke, 2019, CbOcb
Xianhui S. Wan, (D), Xiamen, 2017, Cm
Wenchang Yang, (D), Columbia, 2014, As
Zhendong Zhang, (D), King Abdullah Sci & Tech, 2019, Yg

Laboratory Technician:
Sarah Ward, (B), Carleton, 2019, Zg

Associate Research Scholar:
Hom Nath Gharti, (D), Oslo, 2011, YsdYg

Associate Professional Specialist:
Stefania Gili, (D), Nacl de Córdoba (Argentina), 2014, CgGgCo
Shannon Haynes, (D), West Virginia, 2019, CsOoGg
Dawid Szymanowski, (D), ETH (Switzerland), 2018, CcGiv

Undergraduate/Graduate Coordinator:
Sheryl A. Robas, (A), 1975, Zn

Environmental Engineering & Water Resources Program (B,M,D) ☒ (2018)
E-220 Engineering Quad
Princeton, NJ 08544
p. (609) 258-4655
cee@princeton.edu
https://www.princeton.edu/cee/graduate/programs/eewr/
Programs: Civil and Environmental Engineering (B,M,D); Geosciences (B,M,D)
Enrollment (2018): B: 30 (0) M: 4 (0) D: 40 (0)

Director:
Elie Bou-Zeid, (D), Johns Hopkins, 2005, As

Professor:
Michael A. Celia, (D), Princeton, 1983, Hw
Peter R. Jaffe, (D), Vanderbilt, 1981, SbHgw
James A. Smith, (D), Johns Hopkins, 1981, Hg
Eric F. Wood, (D), MIT, 1974, HgZrHq

Assistant Professor:
Catherine A. Peters, (D), Carnegie Mellon, 1992, Hw

Program in Atmospheric & Oceanic Sciences (D) ☒ (2019)
300 Forrestal Road, Sayre Hall
Princeton, NJ 08540-6654
p. (609) 258-6677
apval@princeton.edu
http://www.princeton.edu/aos/
Enrollment (2018): D: 15 (6)

Professor:
Denise L. Mauzerall, (D), Harvard, 1996, As
Michael Oppenheimer, (D), Chicago
Stephen Pacala, (D), Stanford
James Smith, (D), Johns Hopkins
Gabriel Vecchi, (D), Washington

Senior Scientist:
Isaac Held, (D), Princeton
Syukuro Manabe, (D), Tokyo, 1958, AstPc

Associate Professor:
Stephan Fueglistaler, (D), ETH (Switzerland)
Mark Zondlo, (D), Colorado

Assistant Professor:
Laure Resplandy, 2010

Lecturer:
Thomas Delworth, (D), Wisconsin
Leo Donner, (D), Chicago
Stephen Garner, (D), MIT
Stephen Griffies, (D), Pennsylvania
Robert Hallberg, (D), Washington
Larry Horowitz, (D), Harvard
Sonya Legg, (D), Imperial Coll (UK)
Yi Ming, (D), Princeton
V. Ramaswamy, (D), SUNY (Albany)
Rong Zhang, (D), MIT, Op

Emeritus:
Michael Bender, (D), Columbia
George Mellor, (D), MIT, 1957, Op
Isidoro Orlanski, (D), MIT, 1967, AsZoc
George Philander, (D), Harvard
Jorge L. Sarmiento, (D), Columbia, 1978, Zn

Raritan Valley Community College

Dept of Biology (2015)
118 Lamington Road
Branchburg, NJ 08878
p. (908) 526-1200
marianne.baricevic@raritanval.edu

Rider University

Geological, Environmental, & Marine Sciences (GEMS) (B) ⌂ (2019)
2083 Lawrenceville Road
Lawrenceville, NJ 08648-3099
p. (609) 896-5092
browne@rider.edu
https://www.rider.edu/academics/colleges-schools/college-liberal-arts-education-sciences/science-programs/geological-environment
f: www.facebook.com/riderclas/
t: @RiderCLAS
Programs: Geosciences (B.S.); Environmental Sciences (B.S.); Environmental Studies (B.A.); Marine Sciences (B.S.); Earth Sciences (B.A.), Integrated Sciences and Math (B.A.)
Enrollment (2019): B: 62 (7)

Chair:
Kathleen M. Browne, (D), Miami, 1993, GuZe

Professor:
Jonathan M. Husch, (D), Princeton, 1982, GieXg
Hongbing Sun, (D), Florida State, 1995, HwCgSc

Associate Professor:
Daniel L. Druckenbrod, (D), Virginia, 2003, AtZu
Reed A. Schwimmer, (D), Delaware, 1999, GsOgn
Gabriela W. Smalley, (D), Maryland, 2002, ObcOp

Assistant Professor:
Randy Kertes, (M), Ge

Adjunct Professor:
William B. Gallagher, (D), Pennsylvania, 1990, PvgGr

Emeritus:
Mary Jo Hall, (D), Lehigh, 1981, Gs

Rutgers, The State University of New Jersey

Earth and Planetary Sciences (B,M,D) ⌂ (2019)
Wright Lab
610 Taylor Road
Piscataway, NJ 08854-8066
p. (848) 445-2044
gmtn@eps.rutgers.edu
http://geology.rutgers.edu/
f: https://www.facebook.com/Earth-and-Planetary-Sciences-at-Rutgers-University-187118004101/
Programs: Geological Sciences (B.S.), Geology (B.A.), Environmental Geology (B.S.), Planetary Sciences (B.S.)
Administrative Assistant: Michael Flak, Katanya Myers, Wendy Rodriguez, Tonya Rufus
Enrollment (2018): B: 30 (10) M: 6 (4) D: 23 (0)

Undergraduate Director:
Roy W. Schlische, (D), Columbia, 1990, GctEo

Graduate Program Director:
James D. Wright, (D), Columbia, 1991, CsOuPm

Distinguished Professor:
Gail M. Ashley, (D), British Columbia, 1977, GsmSa
Marie-Pierre Aubry, (D), Marie Curie, Pms
Paul G. Falkowski, (D), British Columbia, 1975, ObCmPe
Dennis V. Kent, (D), Columbia, 1974, YmZcGr
George R. McGhee, Jr., (D), Rochester, 1978, PgqPi
Kenneth G. Miller, (D), MIT/WHOI, 1982, GurPm
Yair Rosenthal, (D), MIT/WHOI, CmlOc

Chair:
Gregory S. Mountain, (D), Columbia, 1981, GuYrGr

Associate Chair:
Ying Fan Reinfelder, (D), Utah State, 1992, HgqGe

Professor:
Craig S. Feibel, (D), Utah, 1988, GrsGa
Mark D. Feigenson, (D), Princeton, 1982, CgGiv
Claude T. Herzberg, (D), Edinburgh, 1975, CpGi
Robert E. Kopp, (D), Caltech, 2007, ZcOoZg
Vadim Levin, (D), Columbia, 1996, Ysg
Robert M. Sherrell, (D), MIT/WHOI, 1991, CmOu
Carl C. Swisher III, (D), California (Berkeley), 1992, Cc
Martha O. Withjack, (D), Brown, 1977, GctEo
Nathan Yee, (D), Notre Dame, 2001, PgCo

Associate Professor:
Juliane Gross, (D), Ruhr (Germany), 2009, Xcm

Assistant Professor:
Sonia M. Tikoo, (D), MIT, 2014, YmXy
Jill A. Van Tongeren, (D), Columbia, 2010, GiCgGt

Research Professor:
Brent D. Turrin, (D), California (Berkeley), 1996, CcGvYm

Assistant Research Professor:
James V. Browning, (D), Rutgers, 1996, GgsGr
Linda Godfrey, (D), Cambridge, 1990, CmlCq
Richard Mortlock, (D), Rutgers, 2017, CgmCs

Co-Director, Rutgers Geology Museum:
Lauren Neitzke Adamo, (D), Rutgers, 2016, GuPmZe

Research Associate:
Don Monteverde, (D), Rutgers, 2008, GruGg
Peter P. Sugarman, (D), Rutgers, 1995, Gr

Lecturer:
Christopher H. Lepre, (D), Rutgers, 2009, YmSaPv

Distinguished Visiting Professor:
William A. Berggren, (D), Stockholm, 1962, PmsPe

Emeritus:
Michael J. Carr, (D), Dartmouth, 1974, Gv
Richard K. Olsson, (D), Princeton, 1958, PmGr
Robert E. Sheridan, (D), Columbia, 1968, YrGu

IT Specialist:
Jason Pappas

Cooperating Faculty:
Jeremy S. Delaney, (D), Belfast, 1978, Xg

Rutgers, The State University of New Jersey, Newark

Dept of Earth & Environmental Sciences (B,M,D) ●⊘ (2017)
101 Warren Street
Smith Hall, room 135
Newark, NJ 07102
p. (973) 353-5100
nicky.agate@rutgers.edu

http://www.ncas.rutgers.edu/ees
Programs: Geology; Geoscience Engineering; Environmental Sciences
Certificates: Environmental Geology (G)
Enrollment (2017): B: 71 (13) M: 3 (0) D: 13 (2)

Chair:
Lee S. Slater, (D), Lancaster (UK), 1997, YeHw

Professor:
Yuan Gao, (D), Rhode Island, 1994, As
Alexander E. Gates, (D), Virginia Tech, 1986, Gc

Associate Research Professor:
Francisco Artigas, Ohio State, Zi

Associate Professor:
Evert J. Elzinga, (D), Delaware, 2000, Sc
Kristina M. Keating, (D), Stanford, 2009, Yug
Adam B. Kustka, (D), SUNY (Stony Brook), 2002, OgCmHs
Dimitrios Ntarlagiannis, (D), Rutgers, 2006, Yu
Ashaki Rouff, (D), SUNY (Stony Brook), 2004, Cl

Assistant Professor:
Mihaela Glamoclija, (D), D'Annunzio (Italy), 2005, PgXgGe

Research Associate:
Judith Robinson, (D), Rutgers, 2015, Yg

Emeritus:
Warren Manspeizer, (D), Rutgers, 1964, Gr
John H. Puffer, (D), Stanford, 1969, GivGe
Andreas H. Vassiliou, (D), Columbia, 1969, Gz

Stockton University

Dept of Environmental Sciences (B,M) ☒ (2019)
Division of Natural Science and Mathematics
101 Vera King Farris Drive
Galloway, NJ 08205
p. (609) 652-4620
jeffrey.webber@stockton.edu
http://intraweb.stockton.edu/eyos/page.cfm?siteID=183&pageID=23

Professor:
Tait Chirenje, (D), Florida, Sc
Weihong Fan, (D), Colorado State, 1993, Zi

Associate Professor:
Daniel Moscovici, (D), Pennsylvania, 2009, Zu
Matthew Severs, (D), Virginia Tech, 2009, Gg

Assistant Professor:
Jessica Favorito, (D), Virginia Tech, 2017, So
Jeffrey Webber, (D), Massachusetts, 2015, Gg
Emma Witt, (D), Kentucky, 2012, Hg

Dept of Geology (B) ●☒ (2020)
101 Vera King Farris Dr
Galloway, NJ 08205
p. 609-626-6857
matthew.severs@stockton.edu
http://intraweb.stockton.edu/eyos/page.cfm?siteID=183&pageID=33
Programs: Geology BS and BA
Enrollment (2020): B: 16 (8)

Associate Professor:
Matthew Rocky Severs, (D), Virginia Tech, 2007, GxCgEg

Assistant Professor:
Jessica Favorito, (D), Virginia Tech
Susanne Moskalski, (D), Delaware, GsOn
Jeffrey R. Webber, (D), Massachusetts, 2016, GcpGt
Emma Witt, (D), Hgs

Emeritus:
Stewart C. Farrell, (D), Massachusetts, 1972, On
Michael J. Hozik, (D), Massachusetts, 1976, GcYmg

William Paterson University

Dept of Environmental Science (B) (2015)
Science Hall
Wayne, NJ 07470
p. (201) 595-2721
beckerm2@wpunj.edu
http://www.wpunj.edu/cosh/departments/environmental-science/
Enrollment (2011): B: 90 (3)

Chairman:
Martin A. Becker, (D), Brooklyn Coll, 1997, PgAm

Professor:
Richard R. Pardi, (D), Pennsylvania, 1983, Cc

Assistant Professor:
Jennifer R. Callanan, (D), Montclair State, 2008, ScGmSz
Karen Swanson, (D), Penn State, 1989, Cc

New Mexico

Eastern New Mexico University

Dept of Physical Sciences (B) ⃠ (2020)
1500 S Ave K
STA 33
Portales, NM 88130
p. (575) 562-2174
jim.constantopoulos@enmu.edu
https://www.enmu.edu/academics/degrees-programs/undergraduate-degree/bachelor/environmental-science
Programs: Environmental Science
Enrollment (2020): B: 25 (3)

Professor:
James T. Constantopoulos, (D), Idaho, 1989, GezGx

Mesalands Community College

Mesalands Dinosaur Museum and Natural Sciences Laboratory (A) O☒ (2019)
911 South Tenth Street
Tucumcari, NM 88401
p. (575) 461-4413
axelh@mesalands.edu
http://www.mesalands.edu/
Programs: Associate of Arts Degree in Natural Sciences, option Paleontology, Associate of Arts Degree in Natural Sciences, option Geology
Enrollment (2018): A: 5 (2)

Instructor:
Axel Hungerbuehler, (D), Bristol, 1998, PvgGg

New Mexico Community College

New Mexico Community College (2015)
525 Buena Vista Dr. SE
Albuquerque, NM 87106
p. (505) 224-3000
pcarman@cnm
http://www.cnm.edu

New Mexico Highlands University

Natural Resources Management Dept (B,M) (2015)
P.O. Box 9000
Las Vegas, NM 87701
p. (505) 454-3000
lindlinej@nmhu.edu
http://www.nmhu.edu/academics/undergraduate/arts_science/natural_resources/
Enrollment (2012): B: 16 (4) M: 6 (1)

Professor:
Jennifer Lindline, (D), Bryn Mawr, 1997, GizZe

Associate Professor:
Michael S. Petronis, (D), New Mexico, 2005, YmGcv

New Mexico Institute of Mining and Technology

Dept of Earth & Environmental Science (B,M,D) O (2019)
801 Leroy Place
Socorro, NM 87801
p. (575) 835-5634
geos.dept@npe.nmt.edu
https://www.nmt.edu/academics/ees/
Programs: B.S. in Earth Science, B.S. in Environmental Science, M.S. in Geology, M.S. in Geochemistry, M.S. in Geophysics, M.S. in Hydrology, Ph.D. in Earth and Environmental Science, Professional Master of Hydrology
Certificates: Graduate Certificate Program in Hydrology
Enrollment (2018): B: 33 (10) M: 36 (16) D: 18 (2)

Professor:
Susan L. Bilek, (D), California (Santa Cruz), 2001, Ys
Peter S. Mozley, (D), California (Santa Barbara), 1988, Gs
Mark A. Person, (D), Johns Hopkins, 1990, HyYhg

Glenn Spinelli, (D), California (Santa Cruz), 2002, Hw
Senior Volcanologist, NMBG:
William C. McIntosh, (D), New Mexico Tech, 1990, Cc
Associate Professor:
Gary Axen, (D), Harvard, 1991, Gct
Daniel Cadol, (D), Colorado State, 2010, HsGe
Bruce I. Harrison, (D), New Mexico, 1992, GmSof
Jolante Van Wijk, (D), Vrije (Amsterdam), 2002, GtoYe
Assistant Professor:
Ronni Grapenthin, (D), Alaska (Fairbanks), 2012, Gv
Daniel Jones, (D), Cb
Ryan Leary, Gs
Kierran Maher, Washington State, Eg
Associate Research Professor:
Mark Murray, (D), MIT, Yds
David B. Reusch, (D), Penn State, 2003, Zn
Dana S. Ulmer-Scholle, (D), S Methodist, 1992, GsdCl
Map Production Coordinator, NMBG:
Phillip Miller
Technical Staff Member, Seimologist:
Charlotte A. Rowe, (D), New Mexico Tech, 2000, Ys
Sr. Geochronologist/Co-Director NM Geochronology Research:
Matthew T. Heizler, (D), California (Los Angeles), 1993, Cc
Senior Scientist:
Robert S. Balch, (D), New Mexico Tech, 1997, Yse
Senior Mineralogist/Economic Geologist/ Director XRD Lab/Curator Mineral Museum:
Virgil L. Lueth, (D), Texas (El Paso), 1988, GzEg
Senior Field Geologist:
Steven M. Cather, (D), Texas, 1986, Gc
Daniel Koning, (M), New Mexico, 1999
Senior Economic Geologist:
Virginia T. McLemore, (D), Texas (El Paso), 1993, Eg
Research Associate, NMBG:
Matthew Zimmerer, New Mexico Tech
Principal Senior Petroleum Geologist:
Ronald F. Broadhead, (M), Cincinnati, 1979, GorGs
Principal Senior Environmental Geologist:
David W. Love, (D), New Mexico, 1980, Ge
Principal Geologist:
Paul W. Bauer, (D), New Mexico Tech, 1988, Gc
Postdoc Fellow, USGS:
Jesus Gomez, New Mexico Tech, 2014
Planetary Protection Officer, NASA:
Catharine A. Conley, (D), Cornell, 1994, Pg
Geophysicist/Field Geologist/Web Information Specialist:
Shari A. Kelley, (D), S Methodist, 1984, Gt
Geologic Mapping Program Manager:
J Michael Timmons, (D), New Mexico, 2004, GctGs
Geochemist & Deputy Director Manger of Electron Microprobe Lab:
Nelia W. Dunbar, (D), New Mexico Tech, 1989, Cg
Emeritus Senior Principal Geophysicist:
Marshall A. Reiter, (D), Virginia Tech, 1969, Yh
Emeritus Senior Field Geologist:
Richard Chamberlin, (D), Colorado Mines, 1980, GcvGg
Emeritus Director and State Geologist:
Charles E. Chapin, (D), Colorado Mines, 1965, Gv
Distinguished Member of Technical Staff:
Vincent C. Tidwell, (D), New Mexico Tech, 1999, Hwq
Cave & Karst Hydrologist:
Lewis Land, (D), North Carolina, 1999, Hy
Assistant Professor of Hydrogeology and Applied Geology, Purdue:
Marty Frisbee, New Mexico Tech, 2010
Assistant Professor:
Nigel J.F. Blamey, (D), New Mexico Tech, 2000, CaeCl
Adjunct Professor:
Denis Cohen
Charles (Jack) Oviatt
Michael Underwood
Emeritus Senior Environmental Geologist:
John W. Hawley, (D), Illinois (Urbana), 1962, GeHwGr
Emeritus:
Antonius J. Budding, (D), Amsterdam
Andrew R. Campbell, (D), Harvard, 1984, CsEmGz
Kent C. Condie, (D), California (San Diego), 1965, Ct
Gerardo W. Gross, (D), Penn State, 1959, Yx
Jan M. H. Hendrickx, (D), New Mexico State, 1984, Hw
David B. Johnson, (D), Iowa, 1978, Ps
Philip R. Kyle, (D), Victoria (NZ), 1976, Giv
Fred M. Phillips, (D), Arizona, 1981, Hw
John W. Schlue, (D), California (Los Angeles), 1975, YsgZg
John L. Wilson, (D), MIT, 1974, Hw

Dept of Mineral Engineering (B,M,D) (2015)
Campus Station
Socorro, NM 87801-9990
p. (505) 835-5345
navid.mojtabai@nmt.edu
http://nmt.edu/academics/mining
Department Secretary: Lucero Joanna
Chair:
Navid Mojtabai, (D), Arizona, 1990, Nr
Professor:
William X. Chavez, Jr., (D), California (Berkeley), 1984, Em
Associate Professor:
Cathrine T. Aimone-Martin, (D), Northwestern, 1982, Ng
Assistant Professor:
Baolin Deng, (D), Johns Hopkins, 1995, Cg
Randal S. Martin, (D), Washington State, 1992, As
Adjunct Professor:
William Haneberg, (D), Cincinnati, 1989, Ng
Per-Anders Persson, (D), Cambridge, 1960, Nr
Ingar F. Walder, (D), New Mexico Tech, 1991, Cl
Emeritus:
George B. Griswold, (D), Arizona, Nx
Kalman I. Oravecz, (D), Witwatersrand, 1967, Nr

New Mexico State University, Alamogordo

New Mexico State University, Alamogordo (2015)
2400 N. Scenic Drive
Alamogordo, NM 88310
hrnmsua@nmsu.edu
http://www.nmsua.edu

New Mexico State University, Grants

Dept of Natural Sciences ☒ (2019)
1500 N Third St
Grants, NM 87020
p. (505) 287-6678
ssgrants@nmsu.edu
http://www.grants.nmsu.edu

New Mexico State University, Las Cruces

Department of Physics (M,D) ☒ (2021)
MSC 3D
P.O. Box 30001
Las Cruces, NM 88003-8001
p. (505) 646-3831
physics@nmsu.edu
http://physics.nmsu.edu
Programs: Physics, Geophysics
Enrollment (2020): D: 1 (0)
Head:
Heinz Nakote, (D), Arizona State, 1991, Zm
Associate Professor:
Thomas M. Hearn, (D), Caltech, 1985, Ys
Assistant Professor:
Lauren Waszek, (D), Cambridge, 2012, Ys
Emeritus:
James F. Ni, (D), Cornell, 1984, YsGtYg

Dept of Geological Sciences (B,M) ●☒ (2019)
MSC 3AB, Box 30001
1255 N. Horseshoe
Gardiner Hall, Room 171
Las Cruces, NM 88003
p. (575) 646-2708
geology@nmsu.edu
http://geology.nmsu.edu/
Programs: Geology (B,M); Geological Sciences (B); Earth and Environmental Systems (B); Earth Science Education (B)
Administrative Assistant: Lee Hubbard
Enrollment (2019): B: 40 (7) M: 17 (5)
Head:
Nancy J. McMillan, (D), S Methodist, 1986, Gi

Professor:
Jeffrey M. Amato, (D), Stanford, 1995, GcCc
Frank C. Ramos, (D), California (Los Angeles), 2000, CcuGi
Assistant Professor:
Reed J. Burgette, (D), Oregon, 2008, Gtc
Brian A. Hampton, (D), Purdue, 2006, Gst
Emily R. Johnson, (D), Oregon, 2008, Gvi

Dept of Plant & Environmental Sciences (A,B,M,D) ⊘ (2021)
Box 30003
Dept. 3Q
Las Cruces, NM 88003-0003
p. (505) 646-3405
mhammitt@nmsu.edu
http://aces.nmsu.edu/academics/pes/
Programs: Agronomy, Environmental Science, Genetics, Horticulture, Soil Science, Turfgrass Science and Management, and interdisciplinary degree program in Water Science and Management
Department Secretary: Paula Ross
Head:
LeRoy A. Daugherty, (D), Cornell, 1975, Sd
Richard Pratt, (D)
Professor:
William C. Lindemann, (D), Minnesota, 1978, Sb
Bobby D. McCaslin, (D), Minnesota, 1974, Sc
Theodore W. Sammis, (D), Arizona, 1974, Sp
Assistant Professor:
Dean Heil, (D), California (Berkeley), 1991, Sc
Tim L. Jones, (D), Washington State, 1989, Sp
H. C. Monger, (D), New Mexico State, 1990, Sa

San Juan College

San Juan College (A) (2019)
4601 College Blvd.
Farmington, NM 87402
p. (505) 566-3325
burrisj@sanjuancollege.edu
http://www.sanjuancollege.edu/geology
Programs: Geology (A)
Enrollment (2019): A: 13 (4)
Professor:
John H. Burris, (D), Michigan State, 2004, GgRhGz

University of New Mexico

Dept of Earth & Planetary Sciences (B,M,D) O☒ (2019)
221 Yale Blvd NE
Northrop Hall, Room 141
MSC03 2040
Albuquerque, NM 87131-0001
p. (505) 277-4204
epsdept@unm.edu
http://eps.unm.edu/
Enrollment (2019): B: 68 (33) M: 12 (17) D: 33 (1)
Chair:
Peter J. Fawcett, (D), Penn State, 1994, Pe
Professor:
Carl A. Agee, (D), Columbia, 1988, Cp
Yemane Asmerom, (D), Arizona, 1988, CcPeCg
Adrian J. Brearley, (D), Manchester (UK), 1984, Gz
Laura J. Crossey, (D), Wyoming, 1985, Cl
Tobias Fischer, (D), Arizona State, 1999, Gv
Joseph Galewsky, (D), California (Santa Cruz), 1996, Am
David J. Gutzler, (D), MIT, 1986, As
Karl E. Karlstrom, (D), Wyoming, 1980, Gt
James J. Papike, (D), Minnesota, 1964, Ca
Louis A. Scuderi, (D), California (Los Angeles), 1984, GmPcGs
Zachary D. Sharp, (D), Michigan, 1987, Cs
Gary S. Weissmann, (D), California (Davis), 1999, HwGsr
Senior Scientist:
Nieu-Viorel Atudorei, (D), Lausanne, 1998, Cs
Victor J. Polyak, (D), Texas Tech, 1998, CcGzm
Associate Professor:
Brandon Schmandt, (D), Oregon, 2011, Yg
Assistant Professor:
Tyler Mackey, (D), California (Davis), 2016, GdPo
Corinne E. Myers, (D), Kansas, 2013, PeqPi
Lindsay Lowe Worthington, (D), Texas, 2010, Yg
Jin Zhang, (D), Illinois, 2014, Gyp
Research Associate:
Frans J.M. Rietmeijer, (D), Utrecht, 1979, Gp
Lecturer:
Aurora Pun, (D), New Mexico, 1996, Ca
Adjunct Professor:
Fraser Goff, (D), California (Santa Cruz), 1977, Cg
Duane M. Moore, (D), Illinois (Urbana), 1963, Sc
Chester J. Weiss, (D), Texas A&M, 1998, Ye
Thomas E. Williamson, (D), New Mexico, 1993, Pv
Emeritus:
Roger Y. Anderson, (D), Stanford, 1960, Gn
Maya Elrick, (D), Virginia Tech, 1990, Gs
Rodney E. Ewing, (D), Stanford, 1974, Gz
John W. Geissman, (D), Michigan, 1980, Ym
Rhian Jones, (D), Manchester (UK), 1986, Gz
Barry S. Kues, (D), Indiana, 1974, Pi
Leslie M. McFadden, (D), Arizona, 1982, Sd
Grant A. Meyer, (D), New Mexico, 1993, Gm
Jane E. Selverstone, (D), MIT, 1985, Gpt
Lee A. Woodward, (D), Washington, 1962, Gc

Institute of Meteoritics (B,M,D) ☒ (2017)
MSC03 2050
1 University of New Mexico
Albuquerque, NM 87131
p. (505) 277-1644
iom@unm.edu
http://meteorite.unm.edu
Administrative Assistant: Beth Ha
Enrollment (2017): M: 1 (1) D: 3 (1)
Professor:
Carl B. Agee, (D), Columbia, 1988, XcGyCp
Senior Scientist III:
Horton E. Newsom, (D), Arizona, 1981, XgcXm
Senior Scientist III:
Charles K. Shearer, Jr., (D), Massachusetts, 1983, Gi
Senior Research Scientist III:
Steven B. Simon, (D), SD Mines, 1988, XmcGi
Assistant Professor:
Jin Zhang, (D), Illinois, 2014, Gy
Senior Scientist:
Karen Ziegler, (D), Reading (UK), 1993, CsXc
Research Scientist III:
Michael N. Spilde, (M), SD Mines, 1987, Gz
Program Manager:
Shannon Clark, Zn

Water Resources Program (2015)
1915 Roma NE, Room 1044
Albuquerque, NM 87131-1217
p. (505) 277-5249
fleckj@unm.edu
http://www.unm.edu/~wrp/
Director:
Michael E. Campana, Zn

University of New Mexico, Gallup

Div of Arts and Sciences (2015)
200 College Road
Gallup, NM 87301
p. (505) 863-7500
pwatt@unm.edu
http://www.gallup.unm.edu/

University of New Mexico, Taos

University of New Mexico - Taos (A,B) ● (2015)
1157 County Road 110
Ranchos de Taos, NM 87557
colnic@unm.edu
http://www.taos.unm.edu
Adjunct Professor:
Deborah Ragland, (D), Gg

Western New Mexico University

Dept of Natural Sciences ☒ (2018)
P.O. Box 680

1000 West College Avenue
Silver City, NM 88062
p. (575) 538-6352
corrie.neighbors@wnmu.edu
http://natsci.wnmu.edu/
Assistant Professor:
Corrie Neighbors, (D), California (Riverside), 2015, Ysr

New York

Adelphi University

Environmental Studies Program (B,M) O☒ (2021)
South Avenue
Garden City, NY 11530
p. (516) 877-4170
bwygal@adelphi.edu
http://environmental-studies.adelphi.edu
t: @mammothunter
Enrollment (2018): B: 30 (7) M: 8 (3)
Associate Professor:
Brian Wygal, (D), Nevada (Reno), 2009, GaRmGe

Adirondack Community College

Science Div (A) (2015)
640 Bay Road
Queensbury, NY 12804
p. (518) 743-2325
minkeld@sunyacc.edu
http://www.sunyacc.edu

Alfred University

Dept of Geology (B) ☒ (2018)
Saxon Drive
Alfred, NY 14802
p. (607) 871-2208
fmuller@alfred.edu
http://ottohmuller.com/ENSweb2008/
Programs: Geology
Enrollment (2018): B: 9 (2)
Professor:
Michele M. Hluchy, (D), Dartmouth, 1988, Cl
Otto H. Muller, (D), Rochester, 1974, Gc

American Museum of Natural History

Dept of Earth & Planetary Sciences ☒ (2020)
Central Park West at 79th Street
New York, NY 10024-5192
p. (212)769-5100
https://www.amnh.org/research/physical-sciences/earth-and-planetary-sciences
Administrative Assistant: Nanette Nicholson
Chair and Curator:
Denton S. Ebel, (D), Purdue, 1993, XmCgZe
Curator:
George E. Harlow, (D), Princeton, 1977, Gz
Associate Curator:
Nathalie Goodkin, (D), MIT/WHOI, 2007
Research Scientist:
Céline Martin, (D), Henri Poincaré, 2009
Nicholas Tailby, (D), Australian Nat, 2014
Senior Museum Specialist:
Saebyul Choe, (B), Bates, 2014
Jamie Newman, (M), Brooklyn Coll, Gg
Museum Specialist:
Sam Alpert, (B), Case Western, 2012, Xm
Keiji Hammond, (B), Northeastern, 2016
Curator Emeritus:
Edmond A. Mathez, (D), Washington, 1981, Gx
Special Projects Staff:
Elizabeth Haussner, (M), Cincinnati, 2016
Andrea Mason, (M), Brooklyn Coll, 2013
Postdoctoral Fellow:
Steven Jaret, (D), SUNY (Stony Brook), 2017
Natalie Umling, (D), South Carolina, 2017

Div of Paleontology (D) (2015)
Central Park West at 79th Street
New York, NY 10024
p. (212) 769-5815
norell@amnh.org
http://paleo.amnh.org/
Administrative Assistant: Judy Galkin
Enrollment (2009): D: 8 (0)
Chair, Professor and Curator:
Mark A. Norell, (D), Yale, 1989, Pv
Provost, Professor and Curator:
Michael J. Novacek, (D), California (Berkeley), 1978, Pv
Professor and Curator:
Niles Eldredge, (D), Columbia, 1969, Pi
Neil H. Landman, (D), Yale, 1982, Pi
John G. Maisey, (D), London (UK), 1974, Pv
Jin Meng, (D), Columbia, 1991, Pv
Dean of the Richard Gilder Graduate School, Professor, and Frick Curator:
John J. Flynn, (D), Columbia, 1983, Pv
Frick Curator Emeritus:
Richard H. Tedford, (D), California (Berkeley), 1960, Pv
Curator Emeritus:
Roger L. Batten, (D), Columbia, 1956, Pi
Eugene S. Gaffney, (D), Columbia, 1969, Pv

Binghamton University

Dept of Geological Sciences and Environmental Studies (B,M,D) ☒ (2019)
PO Box 6000
Binghamton, NY 13902-6000
p. (607) 777-2264
tdesmet@binghamton.edu
http://geology.binghamton.edu
Administrative Assistant: Carol Slavetskas
Enrollment (2012): B: 30 (0) M: 4 (0) D: 12 (0)
Chair:
Tim K. Lowenstein, (D), Johns Hopkins, 1982, Cl
Professor:
Joseph R. Graney, (D), Michigan, 1994, ClGeHs
David M. Jenkins, (D), Chicago, 1980, CpGzp
H. Richard Naslund, (D), Oregon, 1980, Gi
Associate Professor:
Peter L. K. Knuepfer, (D), Arizona, 1984, Gt
Thomas Kulp, (D), Indiana, 2002, Pg
Assistant Professor:
Alex Nikulin, (D), Rutgers, 2011, Ys
Molly Patterson, (D), Victoria (NZ), 2015, CmGl
Jeff Pietras, (D), Wisconsin, 2003, GsEo
Research Associate:
Alan Jones, (D), Purdue, 1964, Ys
Emeritus:
Richard E. Andrus, (D), SUNY (Syracuse), 1974, Sf
Jeffrey S. Barker, (D), Penn State, 1984, Ys
Donald R. Coates, (D), Columbia, 1956, Gm
Robert V. Demicco, (D), Johns Hopkins, 1981, Gs
Steven R. Dickman, (D), California (Berkeley), 1977, Yg
Thomas W. Donnelly, (D), Princeton, 1959, Gg
William D. MacDonald, (D), Princeton, 1965, Gc
Karen M. Salvage, (D), Penn State, 1998, Hw
James E. Sorauf, (D), Kansas, 1962, Pi
Francis T. Wu, (D), Caltech, 1966, Ys
Related Staff:
Michael Hubenthal, (M), SUNY (Binghamton), 2010, ZeYg

Brooklyn College (CUNY)

Dept of Earth and Environmental Science (B,M) ●☒ (2018)
2900 Bedford Avenue
Brooklyn, NY 11210
p. (718) 951-5416
wpowell@brooklyn.cuny.edu
http://depthome.brooklyn.cuny.edu/geology/
Enrollment (2009): B: 24 (5) M: 10 (4) D: 3 (1)
Chair:
Wayne G. Powell, (D), Queen's, 1994, GaCsEm
Chair:
Jennifer Cherrier, OcCmRw
Professor:
John A. Chamberlain, (D), Rochester, 1971, Pg

Zhongqi Cheng, (D), Ohio State, 2001, CaScGe
Constantin Cranganu, (D), Oklahoma, 1997, GoYhHw
Peter Groffman, SbCl
John Marra, (D), Dalhousie, 1977, Ob
David E. Seidemann, (D), Yale, 1975, Cc
Associate Professor:
Stephen U. Aja, (D), Washington State, 1989, Cl
Rebecca Boger, (D), William & Mary, 2002, ZiHs
Assistant Professor:
Brett Branco, (D), Connecticut, 2007, OnHsOg
Kennet Flores, (D), Gpc
Brianne Smith, (D), Hs
Lecturer:
Matt Garb, (M), Brooklyn Coll, Pg
Laboratory Director:
Guillermo Rocha, (M), CUNY, 1994, GgeCg

Broome Community College

Dept of Physical Sciences (A) (2015)
Upper Front Street
Box 1017
Binghamton, NY 13902
p. (607) 778-5000
smithjj@sunybroome.edu
Professor:
Bruce K. Oldfield, (M), SUNY (Binghamton), 1988, Gg
Assistant Professor:
Jason J. Smith, (M), SUNY (Binghamton), 2009, Ggs

Buffalo State College

Earth Sciences and Science Education (B) ●⊘ (2020)
SAMC 160
1300 Elmwood Avenue
Buffalo, NY 14222
p. (716) 878-6731
solargs@buffalostate.edu
https://earthsciences.buffalostate.edu
Programs: Geology; Earth Sciences
Administrative Assistant: Cindy Wong
Enrollment (2020): B: 60 (20)
Professor:
Jill K. Singer, (D), Rice, 1986, GsOp
Planetarium Director:
Kevin K. Williams, (D), Johns Hopkins, 2002, Xg
Chair:
Gary S. Solar, (D), Maryland, 1999, GcpGt
Associate Professor:
Elisa T. Bergslien, (D), SUNY (Buffalo), 2002, ClHw
Kevin K. Williams, (D), Johns Hopkins, 2002, GmXg
Adjunct Professor:
Daniel E. MacIssac, (D), XaZe
Emeritus:
John E. Mack, (D), Fordham, 1971, Xg
Irving Tesmer, (D), Syracuse, Pg

Cayuga Community College

Math and Science (A) (2015)
197 Franklin Street
Auburn, NY 13021
p. (315) 255-1743
waters@cayuga-cc.edu
http://www.cayuga-cc.edu/academics/programs_of_study/math_and_science.php
Professor:
Abu Z. Badruddin, (D), SUNY (Environ), Zi
Raymond F. Leszczynski, (M), SUNY (Albany), 1965, GglGm

City College (CUNY)

Dept of Earth & Atmospheric Sciences (B,M) (2015)
New York, NY 10031
p. (212) 650-6984
kmcdonald2@ccny.cuny.edu
Chair:
Jeffrey Steiner, (D), Stanford, 1970, Cp
Professor:
Stanley Gedzelman, (D), MIT, 1970, As
Edward E. Hindman, (D), Washington, 1975, As

Margaret A. Winslow, (D), Columbia, 1979, Gc
Associate Professor:
Patricia M. Kenyon, (D), Cornell, 1986, Yg
Federica Raia, (D), Naples, 1997, Giv
Pengfei Zhang, (D), Utah, 2000, Hw

Colgate University

Department of Geology (B) ●☒ (2020)
13 Oak Drive
Hamilton, NY 13346
p. (315) 228-7201
http://www.colgate.edu/academics/departments-and-programs/geology
Enrollment (2020): B: 22 (3)
Chair:
William H. Peck, (D), Wisconsin, 2000, GpiCs
Professor:
Karen Harpp, (D), Cornell, 1994, GvCgGi
Amy Leventer, (D), Rice, 1988, Ou
Associate Professor:
Martin Wong, (D), California (Santa Barbara), 2005, Gtc
Assistant Professor:
Aubreya Adams, (D), Penn State, 2010, Yg
Paul Harnik, (D), Chicago, 2009, PieOb
Joseph Levy, (D), Brown, 2009, GlsGm
Senior Lecturer:
Dianne M. Keller, (M), Colgate, 1988, Gz
Alison Koleszar, (D), Oregon State, 2011, GviCu
Emeritus:
Richard April, (D), Massachusetts, 1978, CgGze
James McLelland, (D), Chicago, 1961, Gp
Paul Pinet, (D), Rhode Island, 1972, Ou
Constance M. Soja, (D), Oregon, 1985, PiGs

College of Staten Island/CUNY

Engineering and Environmental Science (A,B) ☒ (2020)
2800 Victory Boulevard
Staten Island, NY 10314-6609
p. 718-982-2800
alan.benimoff@csi.cuny.edu
https://csivc.csi.cuny.edu/geology/files/geo.html
Professor:
Alan I. Benimoff, (D), Lehigh, 1984, GizGp
William J. Fritz, (D), Montana, 1980, Grv
Athanasios Koutavas, (D), Columbia, 2003, PeOg
Lecturer:
Jane L. Alexander, (D), Univ Coll (UK), 1998, GsClt
Adjunct Lecturer:
Imad Harone, (M), CUNY (Staten Island), Gg
Edward Johnson, (M), CUNY (Staten Island), Gg
Vladimir Jovanovic, (M), CUNY (Staten Island), Ge
Adjunct Associate Professor:
Mosbah Kolkas, (D), CUNY, Gg
Adjunct Assistant Professor:
Noureddin Amaach, (D), CUNY, Gg
Rosemary McCall, (D), Gg

Columbia University ▯

Dept of Earth & Environmental Engineering (2015)
Henry Krumb School of Mines
500 West 120 Street
918 Mudd Bldg
New York, NY 10027
p. (212) 894-2905
schlosser@ldeo.columbia.edu
http://www.eee.columbia.edu/
Administrative Assistant: Co'Quesie Gilbert
Department Administrator: Barbara Algin
Acting Chair:
Nickolas J. Themelis, (D), McGill, 1961, Nx
Professor:
Paul F. Duby, (D), Columbia, 1962, Nx
Peter Schlosser, (D), Heidelberg, 1985, Cg
Ponisseril Somasundaran, (D), California (Berkeley), 1964, Nx
Tuncel M. Yegulalp, (D), Columbia, 1968, Nm
Associate Professor:
Ross Bagtzoglou, (D), California (Berkeley), 1990, Hw

Senior Research Scientist:
Roelof Versteeg, (D), Paris VII, 1991, Yg
Adjunct Professor:
Vasilis M. Fthenakis, (D), New York, 1991, As
Emeritus:
Stefan H. Boshkov, (M), Columbia, 1942, Nm
John T. Kuo, (D), Stanford, 1958, Yg
Malcolm T. Wane, (M), Columbia, 1954, Nm

Dept of Earth & Environmental Sciences (B,M,D) ☒ (2019)
P.O. Box 1000
61 Route 9W
Palisades, NY 10964
p. (845) 365-8550
odland@ldeo.columbia.edu
http://eesc.columbia.edu
Programs: Earth and Environmental Sciences
Vice Chair:
Peter B. de Menocal, (D), Columbia, 1991, PeOuCg
Director, Lamont Doherty Earth Observatory:
Sean Solomon, (D), MIT, 1971, Xy
Dir. Graduate Studies:
Goran Ekstrom, (D), Harvard, 1987, Ys
Chair:
Sidney R. Hemming, (D), SUNY (Stony Brook), 1994, CscPe
Professor:
Wallace S. Broecker, (D), Columbia, 1958, CmOcPe
Nicholas Christie-Blick, (D), California (Santa Barbara), 1979, Gst
Joel E. Cohen, (D), Harvard, 1970, Zn
Hugh Ducklow, (D), Harvard, 1977, ObCb
Peter M. Eisenberger, (D), Harvard, 1967, Zn
Steven L. Goldstein, (D), Columbia, 1986, Csg
Arnold L. Gordon, (D), Columbia, 1965, Op
Kevin L. Griffin, (D), Duke, 1994, PbeZn
Peter B. Kelemen, (D), Washington, 1988, GiCg
Jerry F. McManus, (D), Columbia, 1989, PeOu
William H. Menke, (D), Columbia, 1981, YsGvq
John C. Mutter, (D), Columbia, 1982, YrGtYs
Paul E. Olsen, (D), Yale, 1984, PvgGr
Terry A. Plank, (D), Columbia, 1993, GxCg
Lorenzo M. Polvani, (D), MIT, 1988, AmsGq
G. Michael Purdy, (D), Cambridge, 1974, Yr
Peter Schlosser, (D), Heidelberg, 1985, Hw
Adam H. Sobel, (D), MIT, 1998, As
Marc W. Spiegelman, (D), Cambridge, 1989, GqxCg
Martin Stute, (D), Heidelberg, 1989, CsHgGe
Felix Waldhauser, (D), ETH (Switzerland), 1996, YsgGt
Associate Professor:
Sonya Dyhrman, Scripps, 1999, Ob
Arlene M. Fiore, (D), Harvard, 2003, As
Baerbel Hoenisch, (D), Bremen, 2002, PcClm
Meredith Nettles, (D), Harvard, 2005, YsGl
Maria Tolstoy, (D), California (San Diego), 1994, Yr
Assistant Professor:
Ryan P. Abernathey, (D), MIT, 2012, Op
Lecturer:
Alberto Malinverno, (D), Columbia, 1989, Gug
Benjamin S. Orlove, (D), California (Berkeley), 1975, As
Andreas M. Thurnherr, (D), Southampton (UK), 2000, Op
Christopher J. Zappa, (D), Washington, 1999, OpAsZr
Adjunct Professor:
Robert F. Anderson, (D), MIT, 1981, OcCmPe
W. Roger Buck, IV, (D), MIT, 1984, YgGt
John J. Flynn, (D), Columbia, 1983, PvgYm
Alessandra Giannini, (D), Columbia, 2001, AsOpZc
Lisa M. Goddard, (D), Princeton, 1995, AstZc
Arthur L. Lerner-Lam, (D), California (San Diego), 1982, Ys
Douglas G. Martinson, (D), Columbia, 1982, OpGq
Ronald L. Miller, (D), MIT, 1990, As
Mark A. Norell, (D), Yale, 1988, Pv
Dorothy M. Peteet, (D), New York, 1983, PelGn
Andrew W. Robertson, (D), Reading (UK), 1984, As
Joerg Schaefer, (D), ETH (Switzerland), 2000, Cg
Christopher Small, (D), California (San Diego), 1993, ZrYr
Taro Takahashi, (D), Columbia, 1957, OcCg
Mingfang Ting, (D), Princeton, 1990, As
Spahr C. Webb, (D), California (San Diego), 1984, Yrg
Gisela Winckler, (D), Heidelberg, 1998, Cm

Emeritus:
James D. Hays, (D), Columbia, 1964, PemOu
Paul G. Richards, (D), Caltech, 1970, YsZn
Christopher H. Scholz, (D), MIT, 1967, YxNr
H. James Simpson, Jr., (D), Columbia, 1970, Cm
Lynn R. Sykes, (D), Columbia, 1965, YsGtZn
David Walker, (D), Harvard, 1972, CpGzCg
Dir. Academic Admin & Finance:
Sarah K. Odland, (M), Colorado, 1981, Zn
Asst. Director Climate and Society Program:
Cynthia Thomson, (M), Columbia, 2009, Zn

Lamont-Doherty Earth Observatory (M,D) ☒ (2020)
P.O. Box 1000
61 Route 9W
Palisades, NY 10964
p. (845) 359-2900
director@ldeo.columbia.edu
http://www.ldeo.columbia.edu
f: https://www.facebook.com/Lamont.Doherty/
t: @LamontEarth
Programs: M.S. in Sustainability Science; M.A. in Climate and Society
Enrollment (2006): M: 40 (0) D: 83 (6)
William B. Ransford Professor of Earth and Planetary Science, Columbia University:
Sean C. Solomon, (D), MIT, 1971, Xgy
Arthur D. Storke Memorial Professor:
Peter Kelemen, (D), Washington, 1987, Gi
Paul E. Olsen, (D), Yale, 1983, Gm
Professor:
Nicholas Christie-Blick, (D), California (Santa Barbara), 1979, Gs
Peter B. deMenocal, (D), Columbia, 1991, Pe
Hugh W. Ducklow, (D), Harvard, 1977
Goran Ekstrom, (D), Harvard, 1987, Yg
Arlene Fiore, (D), Harvard, 2003, As
Steven Goldstein, (D), Columbia, 1986, Cg
Arnold L. Gordon, (D), Columbia, 1965, Op
Kevin Griffin, (D), Duke, 1994, Zn
Galen McKinley, (D), MIT, 2002, Cg
Jerry McManus, (D), Cm
William H. Menke, (D), Columbia, 1981, Ys
John C. Mutter, (D), Columbia, 1982, Yr
Christopher H. Scholz, (D), MIT, 1967, Ys
Adam Sobel, (D), MIT, 1998, As
Marc Spiegelman, (D), Cambridge, 1989, Ys
Renata Wentzcovitch, California (Berkeley), 1988, Ys
Sr. PGI Research Scientist:
Richard Seager, (D), Columbia, 1990, Am
Senior Research Scientist:
Kerstin Lehnert, (D), Albert-Ludwigs Freiburg, 1989, Gi
Research Scientist:
Robert Newton, (D), Columbia, 2001, Ct
Palisades Geophysical Institute/Lamont Research Professor:
Robin E. Bell, (D), Columbia, 1989, Yr
Lamont Research Professor:
Roger W. Buck, (D), MIT, 1984, Yr
Brendon Buckley, (D), Tasmania, 1997, Pe
Suzana Camargo, (D), Tech (Munich), 1992, As
Steven Chillrud, (D), Columbia, 1995, Cg
Rosanne D'Arrigo, (D), Columbia, 1989, Zn
James Davis, (D), MIT, 1986, Yd
James Gaherty, (D), MIT, 1995, Ys
Joaquim Goes, (D), Nagoya, 1996, Gu
David S. Goldberg, (D), Columbia, 1985, Yr
Won-Young Kim, (D), Uppsala, 1986, Ys
Yochanan Kushnir, (D), Oregon State, 1985, As
Braddock Linsley, (D), New Mexico, 1990, Pe
Alberto Malinverno, (D), Columbia, 1989, Go
Douglas G. Martinson, (D), Columbia, 1982, Op
Joerg Schaefer, (D), Swiss Fed Inst Tech, 2000, Pe
Bruce Shaw, (D), Chicago, 1989, Ys
Christopher Small, (D), California (San Diego), 1993, Zr
Michael Steckler, (D), Columbia, 1980, Yv
Ajit Subramaniam, (D), SUNY (Stony Brook), 1995, ObZr
Marco Tedesco, (D), Italian Nat Res Cncl, 2003, GlZr
Andreas Thurnherr, (D), Southampton (UK), 1999, Op
Mingfang Ting, (D), Princeton, 1990, As
Alexander Van Geen, (D), MIT/WHOI, 1989, Cg

Felix Waldhauser, (D), ETH (Switzerland), 1996, Ys
Gisela Winckler, (D), Heidelberg, 1998, Cg
Xiaojun Yuan, (D), California (San Diego), 1994, Op
Heezen Senior Research Scientist:
Suzanne Carbotte, (D), California (Santa Barbara), 1992, Yr
Ewing LDEO Rsrch Professor:
Edward R. Cook, (D), Arizona, 1985, Hw
Ewing Lamont Research Professor:
Robert F. Anderson, (D), MIT, 1981, Cg
Taro Takahashi, (D), Columbia, 1957, Cm
Deputy Director:
Arthur L. Lerner-Lam, (D), California (San Diego), 1982, Ys
Associate Professor:
Baerbel Hoenisch, (D), Alfred Wegener Inst (Germany), 2002, Cm
Meredith Nettles, (D), Harvard, 2005, YsGl
Lamont Associate Research Professor:
Michela Biasutti, (D), Washington, 2003, Am
Benjamin C. Bostick, (D), Stanford, 2002, Sc
Connie Class, (D), Karlsruhe, 1994, Cg
Benjamin Holtzman, (D), Minnesota, 2003, Ys
Michael Kaplan, (D), Colorado, 1999, Gl
Raymond N. Sambrotto, (D), Alaska, 1983, Ob
David Schaff, (D), Stanford, 2001, Ys
Donna Shillington, (D), Wyoming, 2004, Yr
Jason Smerdon, (D), Michigan, 2004, Pe
Susanne Straub, (D), Kiel, 1991, Gv
Christopher Zappa, (D), Washington, 1999, Op
Assistant Professor:
Ryan Abernathy, (D), MIT, 2012, Og
Roisin Commane, (D), Leeds (UK), 2009, Yr
Special Research Scientist:
Pierre E. Biscaye, (D), Yale, 1964, Cm
Enrico Bonatti, (D), Pisa, 1967, Yr
Dake Chen, (D), SUNY (Stony Brook), 1989, Op
James R. Cochran, (D), Columbia, 1977, Yr
Klaus H. Jacob, (D), Goethe (Frankfurt), 1968, Ys
Stanley Jacobs, (B), MIT, 1962, Op
Paul G. Richards, (D), Caltech, 1970, Ys
William B. F. Ryan, (D), Columbia, 1961, Yr
Leonardo Seeber, (B), Columbia, 1964, Ys
William Smethie, (D), Washington, 1979, Cg
Emeritus:
Mark A. Cane, (D), MIT, 1975, Op
David Walker, (D), Harvard, 1972, Gx
Special Research Scientist:
Mikhail Kogan, (D), Inst of Physics (Moscow), 1977, Yd
Senior Research Scientist:
Andrew Barclay, (D), Oregon, 1998, Ys
Research Scientist:
Victoria Ferrini, (D), SUNY (Stony Brook), 2004, Ou
Helga Gomes, (D), Bombay, 1985, Ob
Gilles Guerin, (D), Columbia, 2000, Gu
Naomi Henderson, (D), Wisconsin, 1987, Yr
Timothy Kenna, (D), MIT/WHOI, 2002, Cg
Frank Nitsche, (D), Alfred Wegener Inst (Germany), 1997, Gu
Lamont Associate Research Professor:
Laia Andreu-Hayles, (D), Barcelona, 2007, Pe
Natalie Boelman, (D), Columbia, 2004, Zn
Timothy Crone, Washington, 2007, Gu
William Joseph D'Andrea, (D), Brown, 2008, Pe
Solange Duhamel, (D), Aix-Maraseille II, Pe
Jonathan E. Nichols, (D), Brown, 2009, Pe
Pratigya J. Polissar, (D), Massachusetts, 2005, Gg
Michael Previdi, (M), Rutgers, 2006, As
Heather M. Savage, (D), Penn State, 2007, Ys
Beizhan Yan, (D), Rensselaer, 2004, Cg
Lamont Assistant Research Professor:
Anne Becel, (D), Inst de Physique du Globe de Paris, 2006, Gu
Einat Lev, (D), MIT, 2009, Gv
Lamont Associate Research Professor:
Timothy T. Creyts, (D), British Columbia, 2007, Gl

Cornell University

Dept of Earth & Atmospheric Sciences (B,M,D) ●☒ (2021)
2122 Snee Hall
Ithaca, NY 14853-1504
p. (607) 255-3474
easinfo@cornell.edu
http://www.eas.cornell.edu/
Programs: Earth and Atmospheric Sciences (B); Atmospheric Science (B,M,PhD); Geological Sciences (M,PhD); Geological Sciences (MEng)
Certificates: Cornell Satellite Remote Sensing Program (Professional Training Certificate Program)
Enrollment (2018): B: 43 (13) M: 3 (1) D: 24 (8)
Wold Family Professor in Environmental Balance for Human Sustainability:
John F.H. Thompson, (D), Toronto, 1982, EmgNx
William and Katherine Snee Professor of Geological Sciences:
Geoffrey A. Abers, (D), MIT, 1989, YsGt
Sidney Kaufman Professor in Geophysics:
Larry D. Brown, (D), Cornell, 1976, Ye
J. Preston Levis Professor of Engineering:
Teresa E. Jordan, (D), Stanford, 1979, GrtPc
Irving Porter Church Professor of Engineering:
Natalie M. Mahowald, (D), MIT, 1996, As
Hunter R. Rawlings III Professor of Paleontology:
Warren D. Allmon, (D), Harvard, 1988, PgePi
Charles L. Pack Professor:
Susan Riha, (D), Washington, 1980, Sf
Professor:
Richard W. Allmendinger, (D), Stanford, 1979, Gc
Stephen J. Colucci, (D), SUNY (Albany), 1982, As
Arthur DeGaetano, (D), Rutgers, 1989, As
Louis A. Derry, (D), Harvard, 1989, Cl
Charles H. Greene, (D), Washington, 1985, Ob
David Hysell, (D), Cornell, 1992, Znr
Matthew E. Pritchard, (D), Caltech, 2003, YdGvl
Sara C. Pryor, (D), E Anglia (UK), 1992, AsZn
William M. White, (D), Rhode Island, 1977, CctCa
Associate Professor:
Esteban Gazel, (D), Rutgers, 2009, CeGiv
Katie M. Keranen, (D), Stanford, 2008, Ys
Rowena B. Lohman, (D), Caltech, 2004, YsZrGt
Assistant Professor:
Toby R. Ault, (D), Arizona, 2011, Am
Sr. Lecturer:
Bruce Monger, (D), Hawaii, 1993, Ob
Senior Lecturer:
Mark Wysocki, (M), Cornell, 1988, As
Adjunct Associate Professor:
Gregory P. Dietl, (D), North Carolina State, 2002, Peg
Adjunct Professor:
Martin J. Evans, (D), Wales, 1985, Eo
Jason Phipps Morgan, (D), Brown, 1985, GvCmPe
Diego Pol, (D), Columbia, 2005, Pv
Robert M. Ross, (D), Harvard, 1990, PgZeGs
Manfred Strecker, (D), Cornell, 1987, Gt
Martyn Unsworth, (D), Cambridge, 1991, Ye
William and Katherine Snee Professor of Geological Sciences:
Suzanne M. Kay, (D), Brown, 1975, GiCuGz
Emeritus:
Muawia Barazangi, (D), Columbia, 1971, YsGt
William A. Bassett, (D), Columbia, 1959, Gz
Lawrence M. Cathles, (D), Princeton, 1971, GqYgEg
John L. Cisne, (D), Chicago, 1973, PgsPe
Bryan L. Isacks, (D), Columbia, 1965, GtYsGm
Daniel E. Karig, (D), California (San Diego), 1970, YrGl
Robert W. Kay, (D), Columbia, 1970, Giz
Warren Knapp, (D), Wisconsin, 1968, As
Frank H. T. Rhodes, (D), Birmingham (UK), 1950, Pi
Daniel Wilks, (D), Oregon, 1986, As
Cooperating Faculty:
Ludmilla Aristilde, (D), California (Berkeley), 2008, Ge
Rebecca J. Barthelmie, (D), As
Oliver H. Gao, (D), California (Davis), 2004, Zn
Alexander G. Hayes, (D), Caltech, 2011, Xg
Peter G. Hess, (D), Ac
Jonathan I. Lunine, (D), Xc
Sturt W. Manning, (D), Cambridge, 1995, Ga
Greg C. McLaskey, (D), California (Berkeley), 2011, Ys
Thomas D. O'Rourke, (D), Illinois, 1975, Ng
Andy L. Ruina, (D), Brown, 1981, Yx
Steven W. Squyres, (D), Cornell, 1981, Xg
Tammo S. Steenhuis, (D), Wisconsin, 1977, Hg
Scott Steinschneider, (D), Rw
Yervant Terzian, (D), Xy

Jefferson W. Tester, (D), MIT, 1971, Ng
Zellman Warhaft, (D), London (UK), 1975, Zn
Max Zhang, (D), California (Davis), 2004, Zn

Institute for the Study of the Continents ☒ (2019)
2122 Snee Hall
Ithaca, NY 14853-1504
p. (607) 255-3474
easinfo@cornell.edu
http://www.eas.cornell.edu/
Enrollment (2010): M: 9 (0) D: 29 (4)

Professor:
Geoffrey A. Abers, (D), MIT, 1989, Ys
Richard W. Allmendinger, (D), Stanford, 1979, Gct
Larry D. Brown, (D), Cornell, 1976, YesGt
Louis A. Derry, (D), Harvard, 1989, Cg
David L. Hysell, (D), Cornell, 1992, Znr
Teresa E. Jordan, (D), Stanford, 1979, GrtZg
Suzanne M. Kay, (D), Brown, 1975, GiCuGt
William M. White, (D), Rhode Island, 1977, Ce

Associate Professor:
Katie M. Keranen, (D), Stanford, 2008, Ys
Rowena B. Lohman, (D), Caltech, 2004, Yg
Matthew E. Pritchard, (D), Caltech, 2003, YdGvl

Assistant Professor:
Greg C. McLaskey, (D), California (Berkeley), 2011, YsNre

Visiting Professor:
Franklin G. Horowitz, (D), Cornell, 1989, YgZnYe

Emeritus:
Muawia Barazangi, (D), Columbia, 1971, Ys
Bryan L. Isacks, (D), Gmt
Robert W. Kay, (D), Columbia, 1970, Gi

Dowling College

Dept of Earth & Marine Sciences (2015)
Oakdale, NY
asmirnov@dowling.edu

Dutchess Community College

Physical Science (A) (2019)
53 Pendell Road
Poughkeepsie, NY 12601
p. (845) 431-8550
rambo@sunydutchess.edu
http://www.sunydutchess.edu/academics/departments/mathematicsphysicalandcomputersciences/
Enrollment (2016): A: 5 (2)

Chair:
Tim Welling, (M), GeSo

Professor:
Mark McConnaughhay, ZgAmEo

Associate Professor:
Susan H. Conrad, GsmHs

Graduate School of the City University of New York

PhD Program in Earth & Environmental Sciences (D) ☒ (2020)
365 Fifth Avenue, Room 4306
New York, NY 10016
p. (212) 817-8240
ees@gc.cuny.edu
http://www.gc.cuny.edu/Page-Elements/Academics-Research-Centers-Initiatives/Doctoral-Programs/Earth-and-Environmental-Sciences
f: https://www.facebook.com/CunyGCEES/
t: @cunygcees
Programs: Environmental and Geological Sciences; Geography
Certificates: GIS
Enrollment (2020): D: 24 (24)

President, CSI:
William Fritz, (D), Montana, Zg

Herbert Kayser Professor:
Samir Ahmed, (D), Univ Coll (UK), Gg

Distinguished Professor:
George Hendrey, (D), Washington, Gg

Discipline Cooordinator of Geology:
Nazul Khandaker, (D), Penn State, Gg

Professor:
Teresa Bandosz, (D), Tech (Cracow), Gge
Homar S. Barcena, (D), New York, Gg
Sunil Bhaskaran, (D), New South Wales, 2003, ZfrZi
Jeffrey Bird, (D), California (Davis), 2001, Sbf
Anthony Carpi, (D), Cornell, Gg
John A. Chamberlain, (D), Rochester, 1971, Pg
Zhongqi (Joshua) Cheng, (D), Ohio State, Zg
Constantin Cranganu, (D), Oklahoma, Zg
Eric Delson, (D), Columbia, 1973, PvqPs
Timothy Eaton, (D), Wisconsin, Gg
Allan Frei, (D), Rutgers, Gg
Alexander Gilerson, (D), Tech, Kazan, Gu
Yuri Gorokhovich, (D), CUNY (Grad Ctr), Gg
Peter Groffman, (D), Georgia, Zg
Carsten Kessler, (D), Muenster (Germany), Gg
Reza M. Khanbilvardi, (D), Penn State, 1983, Hy
Athanasios Koutavas, (D), Columbia, Gg
Nir Krakauer, (D), Caltech, Gg
Tammy Lewis, (D), California (Davis), Gg
Allan Ludman, (D), Pennsylvania, 1969, Gg
Johnny Luo, (D), Columbia, Zg
John Marra, (D), Dalhousie, Zg
Kyle McDonald, (D), Michigan, As
Cecilia M. McHugh, (D), Columbia, 1993, Ou
Fred Moshary, (D), Columbia, Gg
Wenge Ni-Meister, (D), Boston, Gg
Stephen Pekar, (D), Rutgers, Zg
Wayne G. Powell, (D), Queen's, 1994, EmGaCs
David E. Seidemann, (D), Yale, 1976, Cc
Gillian Stewart, (D), SUNY (Stony Brook), Oc
Maria Tzortziou, (D), Maryland, As
Charles Vorosmarty, (D), New Hampshire, Ng
John Waldman, (D), CUNY (Grad Ctr), ObHsZc
William G. Wallace, (D), SUNY (Stony Brook), 1996, Og
Zhengrong Wang, (D), Caltech, Gge
Michael Weisberg, (D), CUNY (Grad Ctr), Zy
Chuixiang Yi, (D), Nanjing (China), Zg
Pengfei Zhang, (D), Utah, Zg

Chairperson, Queens College:
Gregory O'Mullan, (D), Princeton, Zg

Chairperson:
Jennifer Cherrier, (D), Florida State, Zg

Associate Professor:
Stephen U. Aja, (D), Washington State, 1989, Cl
Karin Block, (D), CUNY (Grad Ctr), Ze
Rebecca Boger, (D), Virginia Inst of Marine Sci, Zg
James Booth, (D), Washington, Gge
Brett Branco, (D), Connecticut, Gg
Frank S. Buonaiuto Jr., (D), SUNY (Stony Brook), Ze
Nathalie Goodkin, (D), MIT/WHOI, Gg
Jean Grassman, (D), California (Berkeley), Gg
Dianne I. Greenfield, (D), SUNY (Stony Brook), Gu
Kieren Howard, (D), Tasmania, Ggz
Urs Jans, (D), Swiss Fed Inst Tech, Gg
Patricia M. Kenyon, (D), Cornell, 1986, Yg
Jacob Mey, (D), CUNY (Grad Ctr), Gg
Hamidreza Norouzi, (D), CUNY (Grad Ctr), Gg
Michael Piasecki, (D), Michigan, Gg
Andrew Reinmann, (D), Boston, Gg
Randye Rutberg, (D), Columbia, Gg
Haydee Salmun, (D), Johns Hopkins, Gg
Heather Sloan, (D), Paris, Gg

Assistant Professor:
Benjamin Black, (D), MIT, Mass, As
William Blanford, (D), Arizona, Ze
Cheila Cullen, (D), CUNY (Grad Ctr), Rn
Kennet Flores, (D), Lausann, Zg
Steven Kidder, (D), Caltech, As
David Lindo Atachati, (D), Georgia, Og
Marc-Antoine Longpre, (D), Trinity (Dublin), Zg
Hari Pant, (D), Dalhousie, Zg
Jisun Park, (D), Tokyo Grad Sch Sci, Xm

Adjunct Professor:
Denton Ebel, (D), Purdue, Gg
John T. Flynn, (D), Columbia, Gg
George E. Harlow, (D), Princeton, 1977, Gz

Neil H. Landman, (D), Yale, 1982, Ps
Jin Meng, (D), Columbia, 1991, Pv
Robert P. Nolan, (D), CUNY, 1986, Co

Hamilton College

Geosciences Department (B) ☒ (2020)
198 College Hill Road
Clinton, NY 13323
p. (315) 859-4142
dbailey@hamilton.edu
https://my.hamilton.edu/academics/departments?dept=Geosciences
Programs: Geoscience; Geoarchaeology
Enrollment (2020): B: 20 (13)

Chair:
David G. Bailey, (D), Washington State, 1990, GizGa

Professor:
Cynthia R. Domack, (D), Rice, 1985, Pg
Todd W. Rayne, (D), Wisconsin, 1993, Hy
Barbara J. Tewksbury, (D), Colorado, 1981, Gc

Associate Professor:
Michael L. McCormick, (D), Michigan, 2002, Cb

Assistant Professor:
Catherine C. Beck, (D), Rutgers, 2015, GsnGr

Hartwick College

Dept of Geological and Environmental Sciences (B) (2015)
Johnstone Science Center
1 Hartwick Drive
Oneonta, NY 13820
p. (607) 431-4658
griffingd@hartwick.edu
http://www.hartwick.edu/geology.xml
Administrative Assistant: Nancy Heffernan
Enrollment (2011): B: 28 (9)

Chair:
David H. Griffing, (D), SUNY (Binghamton), 1994, GduGm

Professor Emeritus:
David Hutchison, (D), West Virginia, 1968, GxgGi

Professor:
Eric L. Johnson, (D), SUNY (Binghamton), 1990, GpcGi
Robert C. Titus, (D), Boston, 1974, Ps

Associate Professor:
Zsuzsanna Balogh-Brunstad, (D), Washington State, 2006, ClHgSo

Hobart & William Smith Colleges

Dept of Geoscience (B) ●☒ (2018)
300 Pulteney Street
Geneva, NY 14456
p. (315) 781-3586
geoscience@hws.edu
http://www.hws.edu/academics/geoscience/
f: https://www.facebook.com/geoscience.hws
Programs: Geoscience (B)
Enrollment (2018): B: 31 (21)

Professor:
Nan Crystal Arens, (D), Harvard, 1993, Pg
John D. Halfman, (D), Duke, 1987, GeHsGn
Neil Laird, (D), Illinois, 2001, As

Associate Professor:
Tara M. Curtin, (D), Arizona, 2001, PeGs
David Finkelstein, (D), Illinois (Urbana), 1997, CgbCs
David C. Kendrick, (D), Harvard, 1997, PgGg
Nicholas Metz, (D), SUNY (Albany), 2011, As

Technician:
Barbara Halfman, Zn

Hofstra University

Dept of Geology, Environment and Sustainability (B,M) ☒ (2020)
114 Hofstra University
Hempstead, NY 11549
p. (516) 463-5564
j.b.bennington@hofstra.edu
http://www.hofstra.edu/Academics/Colleges/HCLAS/GEOL/
f: https://www.facebook.com/GESatHU/
Programs: BA / BS Geology
BS Environmental Resources
BA /BS Sustainability Studies
MA Sustainability
Enrollment (2018): B: 50 (10) M: 25 (7)

Professor and Chair:
J Bret Bennington, (D), Virginia Tech, 1994, PeGs

Professor:
Emma Christa Farmer, (D), Columbia, 2005, Ou

Associate Professor:
Antonios Marsellos, (D), SUNY (Albany), 2008, GtqZf

Assistant Professor:
Jase Bernhardt, Penn State, 2016, Ams

Instructor:
Annetta Centrella-Vitale, (M), SUNY (Stony Brook), 1998
Adina Hakimian, (M), CUNY (Queens), 2012, Gg
Steven C. Okulewicz, (M), CUNY (Brooklyn), 1979, CgGue

Adjunct Professor:
Nehru Cherukupalli, (D), Madras (India), 1963, Gg
Sandra J. Garren, (D), S Florida, 2014, Zi
Richard Liebling, (D), Columbia, 1963, Gg

Emeritus:
Charles M. Merguerian, (D), Columbia, 1985, Gc
Dennis Radcliffe, Queens, 1966, Gzx

Hudson Valley Community College

Biology, Chemistry, Physics Dept (2015)
80 Vandenburgh Ave.
Troy, NY 12180
p. (518) 629-7453
p.schaefer@hvcc.edu

Assistant Professor:
Ruth H. Major, (M), Syracuse, 1989, GgRh

Hunter College (CUNY)

Dept of Geography (B,M) 🖱 (2017)
695 Park Avenue
Room 1006 North Building
New York, NY 10021
p. (212) 772-5265
imiyares@hunter.cuny.edu
http://www.geo.hunter.cuny.edu
Programs: Geography; Environmental Studies; Earth Science Education; Geoinformatics (M); Geography (M)
Certificates: GIS
Administrative Assistant: Dana G.. Reimer
Enrollment (2006): B: 135 (30) M: 40 (8)

Chair:
Allan Frei, (D), Rutgers, 1997, AtHgs

Professor:
Sean C. Ahearn, (D), Wisconsin, 1986, Zi
Jochen Albrecht, (D), Vechta (Germany), 1995, ZiyZu
Hongmian Gong, (D), Georgia, 1997, Zn
Ines Miyares, (D), Arizona State, 1994, Zen
Wenge Ni-Meister, (D), Boston, 1997, Zr
Marianna Pavlovskaya, (D), Clark, 1998, Zi
William Solecki, (D), Rutgers, 1990, Zu

Associate Professor:
Frank Buonaiuto, (D), SUNY (Stony Brook), 2003, On
Mohamed Ibrahim, (D), Alberta, 1985, ZgRwZc
Rupal Oza, (D), Rutgers, 1999, Zn
Haydee Salmun, (D), Johns Hopkins, 1989, OpZgAs

Assistant Professor:
Randye L. Rutberg, (D), Columbia, 2000, CmOcZc

Director, SPARs Lab:
Thomas Walter, (M), Miami, 1984, ZyeAm

Lecturer:
Anthony Grande, (M), CUNY (Baruch), 1999, Zn

Adjunct Professor:
Jack Eichenbaum, (D), Michigan, 1972, Zie
Edward Linky, (D), Duquesne Law, 1973, Zn
Teodosia Manecan, (D), Bucharest, 1985, Gp
Faye Melas, (D), CUNY, 1989, Gs
Douglas Williamson, (D), CUNY, 2003, Zi

Emeritus:
Charles A. Heatwole, (D), Michigan State, 1974, Zn
Karl H. Szekielda, (D), Marseille, 1967, Zrg

GeoScience Lab Tech:
Amy Jeu, (M), Minnesota, 2002, Zi

Lehman College (CUNY)

Earth, Environmental and Geospatial Sciences (B) ☒ (2019)
250 Bedford Park Boulevard West
Bronx, NY 10468-1589
p. (718) 960-8660
heather.sloan@lehman.cuny.edu
http://www.lehman.edu/academics/eggs/
Programs: BA in Earth Science, BA in Geography, BS in Environmental Science, MS in GISc
Certificates: Earth Science, GIS
Enrollment (2014): B: 24 (5)
Chair:
Hari Pant, (D), Dalhousie, Cg
Professor:
Irene S. Leung, (D), California (Berkeley), 1969, Gz
Juliana Maantay, (D), Rutgers, Zi
Associate Professor:
Elia Merchado
Heather Sloan, (D), Paris VI, 1993, Yr
Emeritus:
Frederick C. Shaw, (D), Harvard, 1965, Ps

Long Island University, Brooklyn Campus

Dept of Physics (2015)
1 University Plaza
Brooklyn, NY 11201-8423
p. (718) 488-1011
bkln-admissions@liu.edu
http://www.liu.edu/Home/Brooklyn
Professor:
Richard Macomber, (D), Iowa, 1963, Pg
Adjunct Professor:
Richard A. Jackson, (D), Massachusetts, 1980, Gc
Alan Siegelberg, (M), Brooklyn Coll, 1977, Gg
Emeritus:
Samuel R. Kamhi, (D), Columbia, 1963, Gz

Long Island University, C.W. Post Campus

Dept of Biological and Environmental Sciences (B,M) ⃠ (2021)
720 Northern Boulevard
Brookville, NY 11548-1300
p. (516) 299-2318
margaret.boorstein@liu.edu
Programs: Biology BS. Biology Adolescent-ed BS
Our Geography BA, Biology BA, Geology BA and BS, Earth System Sciences BA, Earth Science Adol Ed BS were frozen [no new majors are accepted] by the Administration
Enrollment (2020): B: 3 (0) M: 10 (11)
Chair:
Margaret F. Boorstein, (D), Columbia, 1977, Zg
Associate Professor:
Scott Carlin, (D), Zn
Lillian Hess-Tanguay, (D), CUNY, 1993, Gs
Emeritus:
Robert S. Harrison, (D), Cambridge, 1965, Zy
Heinrich Toots, (D), Wyoming, 1965, Pg

Monroe Community College

Geoscience Dept (A) (2016)
1000 E. Henrietta Road
Rochester, NY 14623
p. (716) 292-2425
jbarone@monroecc.edu
http://www.monroecc.edu/depts/geochem/
Administrative Assistant: Judy Miller
Enrollment (2013): A: 7 (0)
Associate Professor:
Jessica Barone, (M), Ball State, Ge
Michael Boester, (M), Zy
Amanda Colosimo, (M), North Carolina, 2004, Gg
Daniel E. Robertson, (M), Arizona State, 1986, Eg
Assistant Professor:
Jonathan Little, (M), ZyGlZi
Jason Szymanski, (M), GlPe
Instructor:
Heather Pierce, (M), Connecticut, Zyi

Orange County Community College

Dept of Science, Engineering, and Architecture (A) (2015)
115 South Street
Middletown, NY 10940
p. (845) 341-4570
lawrenceobrien@sunyorange.edu
Enrollment (2015): A: 3 (1)
Professor:
Lawrence E. O'Brien, (M), Michigan, 1972, Gg

Pace University, New York Campus

Dept of Chemistry & Physical Sciences (2015)
1 Pace Plaza
New York, NY 10038
p. (212) 346-1502
mshirigarakani@pace.edu
http://www.pace.edu/dyson/academic-departments-and-programs/chemistry-and-physical-sciences---nyc
Department Secretary: Pat Calegari
Chair:
Nigel Yartlett, (D)
Assistant Professor:
Stephen T. Lofthouse, (M), Hunter (CUNY), 1974, Zg
Adjunct Professor:
Anatole Dolgoff, (M), Miami (Ohio), 1960, Zg
William Hansen, (M), Hunter, 1991, As
John Marchisin, (M), Rutgers, 1965, Zg
Nathan Reiss, (D), New York, 1973, As

Paleontological Research Institution

Paleontological Research Instituion ☒ (2019)
1259 Trumansburg Road
Ithaca, NY 14850
p. (607) 273-6623
allmon@priweb.org
http://www.priweb.org
f: https://www.facebook.com/museumoftheearth/
t: @PRInstitution
Director:
Warren D. Allmon, (D), Harvard, 1988, Pg
Education Director:
Robert M. Ross, (D), Harvard, 1990, PgZePc
Director of Collections:
Gregory Dietl, (D), North Carolina State, 2002, Pg
Director of Publications:
Jonathan R. Hendricks, (D), Cornell, 2005, Pig

Queens College (CUNY)

School of Earth & Environmental Sciences (B,M,D) (2015)
65-30 Kissena Boulevard
Flushing, NY 11367
p. (718) 997-3300
gregory.omullan@qc.cuny.edu
http://www.qc.edu/EES
Administrative Assistant: Gladys Sapigao
Enrollment (2012): B: 150 (19) M: 19 (6) D: 11 (2)
Distinguished Professor, Director & Chair:
George Hendrey, (D), Washington, 1973, Zg
Professor:
Nicholas K. Coch, (D), Yale, 1965, GseOu
N. Gary Hemming, (D), SUNY (Stony Brook), 1993, CaOcGg
Allan Ludman, (D), Pennsylvania, 1969, GgtGr
Steven Markowitz, (D), Columbia, 1981, GbZn
Cecilia McHugh, (D), Columbia, 1993, Ou
Alfredo Morabia, (D), Johns Hopkins, 1989, GbZn
Stephen Pekar, (D), Rutgers, 1999, PeGrOu
Gillian Stewart, (D), SUNY (Stony Brook), 2005, OcCmOz
Yan Zheng, (D), Columbia, 1998, CgHwCm
Associate Professor:
Jeffrey Bird, (D), California (Davis), 2001, Sbc
Timothy Eaton, (D), Wisconsin, 2002, HgwGg
Assistant Professor:
Gregory O'Mullan, (D), Princeton, 2005, PgOb
Ashaki Rouff, (D), SUNY (Stony Brook), 2004, Cac
Chuixiang Yi, (D), Nanjing (China), 1991, Asm

Emeritus:
Eugene A. Alexandrov, (D), Columbia, 1959, Eg
Patrick W. G. Brock, (D), Leeds (UK), 1963, Gg
Hannes K. Brueckner, (D), Yale, 1968, GgtCg
Robert M. Finks, (D), Columbia, 1959, Pi
Daniel Habib, (D), Penn State, 1965, Pl
Peter H. Mattson, (D), Princeton, 1957, Gc
Andrew McIntyre, (D), Columbia, 1967, Pe
B. Charlotte Schreiber, (D), Rensselaer, 1974, Gd
David H. Speidel, (D), Penn State, 1964, Cgp
David L. Thurber, (D), Columbia, 1964, Cl

Queensborough Community College

Dept of Biological Sciences and Geology (2015)
222-05 56th Avenue
Bayside, NY 11364
p. (718) 631-6335
MGorelick@qcc.cuny.edu
http://www.qcc.cuny.edu/biologicalsciences/advisors.asp

Rensselaer Polytechnic Institute

Dept of Earth & Environmental Sciences (B,M,D) ☒ (2021)
Science Center 1W19
110 8th Street
Troy, NY 12180-3590
p. (518) 276-6474
ees@rpi.edu
https://science.rpi.edu/earth
Programs: Geology (B,M,D); Hydrogeology (B); Environmental Science (B)
Enrollment (2020): B: 35 (2) M: 4 (2) D: 7 (2)
Head:
Frank S. Spear, (D), California (Los Angeles), 1976, GpCpGc
Professor:
Peter A. Fox, (D), Monash, 1985, GqZig
Steven W. Roecker, (D), MIT, 1981, Yg
Associate Professor:
Miriam E. Katz, (D), Rutgers, 2001, PmeGu
Karyn L. Rogers, (D), Washington, 2006, PgCl
Morgan F. Schaller, (D), Rutgers, 2011, CsPe
Assistant Professor:
Sasha Wagner, (D), Florida Intl, 2015, Cob
Research Associate Professor:
Daniele J. Cherniak, (D), SUNY (Albany), 1990, Gx
Lecturer:
Sarah Cadieux, (D), Indiana, 2015, ZeCb
Emeritus:
E. Bruce Watson, (D), MIT, 1976, CpcCt

Skidmore College

Dept of Geosciences (B) ☒ (2019)
815 North Broadway
Saratoga Springs, NY 12866
p. (518) 580-5190
afrappie@skidmore.edu
https://www.skidmore.edu/geosciences/
Programs: Geosciences
Enrollment (2018): B: 14 (3)
Associate Professor:
Amy Frappier, (D), New Hampshire, 2006, GePe
Kyle K. Nichols, (D), Vermont, 2002, Gm
Visiting Assistant Professor:
Margaret Estapa, (D), Maine, 2011, Oc
Assistant Professor:
Greg Gerbi, (D), MIT/WHOI, OpYg
Victor Guevara, (D), Virginia Tech, 2017, Gp
Instructor:
Jennifer Cholnoky, (M), Rensselaer, 2013, Gg

St. Lawrence University

Department of Geology (B) ●⃠ (2020)
23 Romoda Dr.
Brown Hall
Canton, NY 13617-1475
p. (315) 229-5851
astewart@stlawu.edu
https://www.stlawu.edu/geology
f: https://www.facebook.com/SLUGeology
Programs: Geology
Administrative Assistant: Sherrie Kelly
Enrollment (2020): B: 24 (12)
Professor:
Jeffrey R. Chiarenzelli, (D), Kansas, 1989, GzCg
Antun Husinec, (D), Zagreb, 2002, GsCsGo
Chair:
Alexander K. Stewart, USA (ret), (D), Cincinnati, 2007, GmlHw
Associate Professor:
Judith Nagel-Myers, (D), Muenster (Germany), 2006, PisPe
Research Associate:
George W. Robinson, (D), Queens, 1978, Gz
Emeritus:
J. Mark Erickson, (D), North Dakota, 1971, Pgi
Technician:
Matthew F. Van Brocklin, (M), Akron, 1996, GgZgn

Stony Brook University

Dept of Geosciences (B,M,D) O✓🖱 (2019)
Nicolls Road
Stony Brook, NY 11794-2100
p. (631) 632-8200
brian.phillips@stonybrook.edu
https://www.stonybrook.edu/geosciences
Professor:
Daniel M. Davis, (D), MIT, 1983, Yg
Timothy Glotch, (D), Arizona State, 2004, XgGz
Gilbert N. Hanson, (D), Minnesota, 1964, GgZe
William E. Holt, (D), Arizona, 1989, Ys
Baosheng Li, (D), Stoney Brook, 1996, Yx
Robert C. Lieberman, (D), Columbia, 1969, GyYsx
Scott M. McLennan, (D), Australian Nat, 1981, Cg
Hanna Nekvasil, (D), Penn State, 1986, Cp
John B. Parise, (D), James Cook, 1980, Gz
Brian L. Phillips, (D), Illinois, 1990, GzCl
Richard J. Reeder, (D), California (Berkeley), 1980, ClGz
Martin A. Schoonen, (D), Penn State, 1989, Cl
Donald J. Weidner, (D), MIT, 1972, Gy
Lianxing Wen, (D), Caltech, 1998, Ys
Associate Professor:
Lars Ehm, (D), Christian-Albrechts-Univ Kiel, 2003, Gz
E. Troy Rasbury, (D), SUNY (Stony Brook), 1998, Cc
A. Deanne Rogers, (D), Arizona State, 2005, XgZr
Assistant Professor:
Gregory Henkes, (D), Johns Hopkins, 2014, Cs
Joel A. Hurowitz, (D), Stoney Brook, 2006, Xg
Weisen Shen, (D), Colorado, 2014, Ys
Research Associate:
Michael Sperazza, (D), Montana, 2006, Zn
Lecturer:
Christiane W. Stidham, (D), California (Berkeley), 1999, YgGe
Adjunct Professor:
Robert C. Aller, (D), Yale, 1977, Cm
Henry J. Bokuniewicz, (D), Yale, 1976, Yr
J. Kirk Cochran, (D), Yale, 1979, Oc
Maureen O'Leary, (D), Johns Hopkins, 1997, Pv
Michael T. Vaughan, (D), SUNY (Stony Brook), 1979, Yx
Emeritus:
Donald H. Lindsley, (D), Johns Hopkins, 1961, Cp
Teng-fong Wong, (D), MIT, 1981, Yx
Laboratory Director:
Owen C. Evans, (D), SUNY (Stony Brook), 1994, Cg

Suffolk County Community College, Ammerman Campus

Dept of Physical Science (A) (2016)
533 College Road
Selden, NY 11784
p. (631) 451-4338
butkosd@sunysuffolk.edu
http://depthome.sunysuffolk.edu/Selden/PhysicalScience/
Enrollment (2016): A: 27 (0)
Professor:
Darryl J. Butkos, (M), GgHw
Michael Inglis, (D), Zg
Scott A. Mandia, (M), Penn State, 1990, Amt

Associate Professor:
Matthew Pappas, Zg
Assistant Professor:
Sean Tvelia, (M), SUNY (Stony Brook), Ggl
Adjunct Professor:
Jessica Dutton, Zg
Michael Flanagan, Zg
Philip Harrington, Zg
Margaret Lomaga, Zg
Brian Vorwald, Zg

Sullivan County Community College

Mathematics and Natural Sciences (2015)
112 College Road
Lock Sheldrake, NY 12759
dlewkiewicz@sunysullivan.edu

SUNY Jefferson

Science (2015)
1220 Coffeen Street
Watertown, NY 13601
p. (315) 786-2200
cebeyhoneycutt@sunyjefferson.edu
http://www.sunyjefferson.edu/academics/programs-study/liberal-arts-sciences-mathematics-science

SUNY Potsdam

Department of Geology (B) ☒ (2020)
220 Timerman Hall
44 Pierrepont Avenue
Potsdam, NY 13676
p. (315) 267-2286
rygelmc@potsdam.edu
http://www.potsdam.edu/academics/AAS/Geology/
f: https://www.facebook.com/potsdamgeology/
Programs: Geology, Geographic Information Science
Administrative Assistant: Beth A. Fayette
Enrollment (2020): B: 34 (0)
Professor:
Michael C. Rygel, (D), Dalhousie, 2005, GsrZi
Assistant Professor:
Sara E. Bier, (D), Penn State, 2010, GctGg
Kamal Humagain, (D), Texas Tech, 2016, Zir
Adam Pearson, (D), Delaware, 2015, Gm
Page C. Quinton, (D), Missouri, 2016, PcCsPm
Christian M. Schrader, (D), Georgia, 2009, GiEmGv
Emeritus:
Robert L. Badger, (D), Virginia Tech, 1989, GipGc
Frank A. Revetta, (D), Rochester, 1970, YgGtg

SUNY, Albany

Dept of Atmospheric and Environmental Sciences (B,M,D) (2015)
1400 Washington Avenue
Albany, NY 12222
p. (518) 442-4466
daeschair@albany.edu
http://www.atmos.albany.edu
Chair:
Vincent P. Idone, (D), SUNY (Albany), 1982, As
Professor:
Lance F. Bosart, (D), MIT, 1969, As
Daniel Keyser, (D), Penn State, 1981, As
John E. Molinari, (D), Florida State, 1979, As
Senior Research Professor:
David R. Fitzjarrald, (D), Virginia, 1980, Asm
Richard R. Perez, (D), SUNY (Albany), 1983, As
James J. Schwab, (D), Harvard, 1983, Acs
Christopher J. Walcek, (D), California (Los Angeles), 1983, As
Wei-Chyung Wang, (D), Columbia, 1973, As
Associate Professor:
Robert G. Keesee, (D), Colorado, 1979, As
Christopher D. Thorncroft, (D), Reading (UK), 1988, As
Research Associate:
Stephen S. Howe, (M), Penn State, 1981, Cs
David Knight, (D), Washington, 1987, As

SUNY, Buffalo

Dept of Geology (B,M,D) O⊘ (2021)
126 Cooke Hall
Buffalo, NY 14260
p. (716) 645-3489
geology@buffalo.edu
http://www.geology.buffalo.edu
t: @UBGeology
Programs: BA, BS Geological Sciences, MS, PhD Geological Sciences
Certificates: Graduate: Professional Science Management
Enrollment (2020): B: 34 (30) M: 34 (11) D: 10 (2)
Empire Innovation Professor:
Sophie Nowicki, (D), Univ Coll London, 2007, Gl
Chair:
Beata M. Csatho, (D), Miskolc (Hungary), 1993, GlZrYg
Professor:
Richelle Allen-King, (D), Waterloo, 1991, Cg
Jason P. Briner, (D), Colorado, 2003, Gl
Howard R. Lasker, (D), Chicago, 1978, Gu
Gregory Valentine, (D), California (Santa Barbara), 1988, Gv
Director of Graduate Studies:
Christopher S. Lowry, (D), Wisconsin, 2008, Hw
Associate Professor:
Tracy K. P. Gregg, (D), Arizona State, 1995, Gv
Margarete Jadamec, (D), California (Davis), 2009, GtYgZf
Clinical Assistant Professor:
James Boyle, (D), Buffalo, 2018
Kimberly Meehan, (D), CUNY, 2014, Pe
Assistant Professor:
Mattia de' Michieli Vitturi, (D), Rome, 2004, Gv
Stephan Kolzenburg, (D), Studi di Torino, 2016, Gv
Richard Marinos, (D), Duke, 2018, Sc
Erasmus K. Oware, (D), Clemson, 2014, YgHq
Kristin Poinar, (D), Washington, 2017, Gl
Elizabeth K. Thomas, (D), Brown, 2014, Cos
Adjunct Assistant Professor:
Julio Sepulveda, (D), Bremen, 2008
Nicolas Young, (D), Buffalo, 2012
Adjunct Professor:
Jesse Johnson, (D), Maine, 2002
Corneilus van der Veen, (D), Utrecht, 1986
Professor Emeritus:
Marcus I. Bursik, (D), Caltech, 1989, Gv
SUNY Distinguished Teaching Professor Emeritus:
Charles E. Mitchell, (D), Harvard, 1983, Pg
Emeritus:
Mary Alice Coffroth, (D), Miami, 1988, Gu
Dennis S. Hodge, (D), Wyoming, 1966
Robert D. Jacobi, (D), Columbia, 1980, GctGs
Chester C. Langway, (D), Michigan, 1965, Gl
Michael F. Sheridan, (D), Stanford, 1965, Gv
Research Support Specialist:
Ivan Parmuzin, (M)
Research Professor:
Galina L. Rogova, (D), Moscow State (Russia), 1988, Gq
Anton Schenk, (D), Switzerland (Berne), 1972, Zr
Research Assistant Professor:
Cari Ficken, (D), Duke, 2018, Zc
Andrew Harp, (D), Buffalo, 2018
Samuel Kelley, Buffalo, 2014
Susan Sakimoto, (D), Johns Hopkins, 1995
Ingo Sonder, (D), Wurzburg, 2010, Gv
Laboratory Technician:
Owen Cowling, (M), Buffalo, 2018, Cs
Assistant to Chair:
Alison A. Lagowski, (M), Buffalo, 1996, Zn

SUNY, Cortland

Geology Dept (B,M) (2015)
342 Bowers Hall
PO Box 2000
Cortland, NY 13045
p. (607) 753-2815
gleasong@cortland.edu
http://www.cortland.edu/geology/
Administrative Assistant: Susan K. Nevins
Enrollment (2007): B: 48 (15) M: 8 (6)

Professor:
David J. Barclay, (D), SUNY (Buffalo), 1998, Glm
Christopher P. Cirmo, (D), Syracuse, 1994, Hg
Robert S. Darling, (D), Syracuse, 1992, GzpCp
Associate Professor:
Christopher A. McRoberts, (D), Syracuse, 1994, Pg
Associate Scientist:
Gayle C. Gleason, (D), Brown, 1993, Gct
Lecturer:
Julie L. Barclay, (M), SUNY (Buffalo), 1997, Ggm
Laboratory Director:
John R. Driscoll, (A), Northwest Electronic, 1974, Zn

SUNY, Fredonia

Department of Geology and Environmental Sciences (B) (2016)
280 Central Avenue
Fredonia, NY 14063-1020
p. (716) 673-3303
earth@fredonia.edu
http://www.fredonia.edu/earth
Enrollment (2016): B: 40 (7)
Chair:
Gordon C. Baird, (D), Rochester, 1975, PseGs
Professor:
Gordon C. Baird, (D), Rochester, 1975, GrPgGs
Gary G. Lash, (D), Lehigh, 1980, Gr
Sherri A. Mason, (D), Montana, 2001, ZgGe
Associate Professor:
Ann K. Deakin, (D), SUNY (Buffalo), 1996, ZiGgZr
Instructor:
Kimberly Weborg-Benson, (M), Illinois, 1991, GgAsPg

SUNY, Geneseo

Dept of Geological Sciences (B) (2015)
1 College Circle
ISC 235
Geneseo, NY 14454
p. (585) 245-5291
farthing@geneseo.edu
http://www.geneseo.edu/geology
Administrative Assistant: Diane E. Lounsbury
Enrollment (2015): B: 130 (27)
Professor:
Scott D. Giorgis, (D), Wisconsin, 2003, GctYm
D. Jeffrey Over, (D), Texas Tech, 1990, Ps
Chair:
Benjamin J.C. Laabs, (D), Wisconsin, 2004, GmlGe
Associate Professor:
Dori J. Farthing, (D), Johns Hopkins, 2001, Gz
Amy L. Sheldon, (D), Utah, 2002, Hw
Assistant Professor:
Nicholas H. Warner, (D), Arizona State, 2008, XgGrHg
Emeritus:
Phillip D. Boger, (D), Ohio State, 1976, Cg
William J. Brennan, (D), Colorado, 1968, Gc
Richard B. Hatheway, (D), Cornell, 1969, GxzGp
James W. Scatterday, (D), Ohio State, 1963, Pg
Richard A. Young, (D), Washington (St Louis), 1966, GmXgZr

SUNY, Maritime College

Science Dept (B) (2015)
6 Pennyfield Avenue
Bronx, NY 10465
p. (718) 409-7380
kolszewski@sunymaritime.edu
Enrollment (2009): B: 68 (22)
Chair:
Kathy Olszewski, (D), SUNY (Stony Brook), 1994, Cg
Associate Professor:
Marie deAngelis, (D), Washington, 1989, Oc
Assistant Professor:
Anthony Manzi, (M), Montclair State, Am

SUNY, New Paltz

Geology (B) ☒ (2021)
1 Hawk Drive
New Paltz, NY 12561
p. (845) 257-3760
vollmerf@newpaltz.edu
http://www.newpaltz.edu/geology/
Programs: Geology, Environmental Geoscience, Earth Science Education
Enrollment (2019): B: 45 (11)
Professor:
Frederick W. Vollmer, (D), Minnesota, 1985, GctGx
Professor:
John A. Rayburn, (D), SUNY Binghamton, 2004, Gml
Associate Professor:
Alexander J. Bartholomew, (D), Cincinnati, 2006, GrPi
Shafiul H. Chowdhury, (D), W Michigan, 1999, HwGe
Assistant Professor:
Gordana Garapic, (D), Boston, 2013, Gz
Lecturer:
Kaustubh Patwardhan, (D), Johns Hopkins, 2009, Ggi
Adjunct Professor:
Laurel Mutti, (M), Johns Hopkins, 2004, Gg
Emeritus:
Gilbert J. Brenner, (D), Penn State, 1962, Pl
Alvin S. Konigsberg, (D), Syracuse, 1969, As
Constantine Manos, (D), Illinois, 1963, Gs
Martin S. Rutstein, (D), Brown, 1969, Gz
Related Staff:
Donald R. Hodder, (B), SUNY (Geneseo), 1985, Gg

SUNY, Oneonta

Dept of Earth and Atmospheric Sciences (B) ☒ (2017)
108 Ravine Parkway
209 Sci. #1
Oneonta, NY 13820-4015
p. (607) 436-3707
Lisa.Hoffman@oneonta.edu
http://www.oneonta.edu/academics/earths/
Programs: Geology; Earth Science; Meteorology; Earth Science Education
Enrollment (2017): B: 91 (0)
Chair:
Jerome B. Blechman, (D), Wisconsin, 1979, As
Distinguished Teaching Professor:
James R. Ebert, (D), SUNY (Binghamton), 1984, GrsZe
Associate Professor:
Keith A. Brunstad, (D), Washington State, 2013, GviEg
Leigh M. Fall, (D), Texas A&M, 2010, Pgq
Melissa Godek, (D), Delaware, 2009, AmsZg
Leslie E. Hasbargen, (D), Minnesota, 2003, GmHgZr
Assistant Professor:
Christopher Karmosky, (D), Penn State, 2013, AmsZy
Dr.:
Marta L. Clepper, (D), Kentucky, 2011, ZeGgs
Lecturer:
Kathryn Metcalf, (M), Arizona, 2012, GctGg
Emeritus:
P. Jay Fleisher, (D), Washington State, 1967, GlmGe
Arthur N. Palmer, (D), Indiana, 1969, HgqGm

SUNY, Oswego

Dept of Atmospheric and Geological Sciences (B) (2018)
394 Shineman Science Center
Oswego, NY 13126
p. (315) 312-3065
tomascak@oswego.edu
http://www.oswego.edu/ags
Programs: Geology; Meteorology
Enrollment (2015): B: 160 (25)
Professor:
Alfred J. Stamm, (D), Wisconsin, 1976, Am
Paul B. Tomascak, (D), Maryland, 1995, CgGzi
David W. Valentino, (D), Virginia Tech, 1993, GtcYu
Associate Professor:
Scott Steiger, (D), Texas A&M, 2005, Am
Assistant Professor:
Rachel J. Lee, (D), Pittsburg State, 2013, GvZr
Steven T. Skubis, (D), SUNY (Albany), 1994, Am
Justin Stroup, (D), Dartmouth, 2015, GmHwGe
Michael Veres, (D), Nebraska, 2014, As

Lab/Field Technician:
Richard Frieman, (M), Buffalo, 2016, Gg

SUNY, Plattsburgh

Center for Earth & Environmental Science (B) ☒ (2019)
101 Broad Street
132 Hudson Hall
Plattsburgh, NY 12901
p. (518) 564-2028
cees@plattsburgh.edu
http://www.plattsburgh.edu/cees
f: https://www.facebook.com/SUNYPlattsburghCEES/
Programs: Geology, Environmental Geology, and Earth Science (with a 5 year Ba/MST)
Enrollment (2019): B: 28 (4)

Director:
Edwin A. Romanowicz, (D), Syracuse, 1993, HwGcYu
Professor:
David A. Franzi, (D), Syracuse, 1984, Gl
Associate Professor:
Eric Leibensperger, (D), Harvard, 2011, AsOg
Assistant Professor:
Nancy A. Price, (D), Maine, 2012, GzCgGc
James R. Thomka, (D), Cincinnati, 2015, GsPg
Lecturer:
Patrick Korths, (M), Syracuse, 2006, RwGg

SUNY, Purchase

Environmental Studies (B) ⊘ (2020)
735 Anderson Hill Road
Purchase, NY 10577
p. (914) 251-6646
naturalsciences@purchase.edu
https://www.purchase.edu/academics/environmental-studies/
Programs: Environmental Studies: Ecology and Policy Concentrations
Enrollment (2020): B: 305 (15)

Director of Teaching and Learning Technologies:
Keith Landa, (D), Michigan, 1989, XgbGg
Professor:
George P. Kraemer, (D), California (Los Angeles), 1989, ObnCm
Department Chair:
Ryan W. Taylor, (D), Oregon State, 2006, ZiyZg
Assistant Professor:
Allyson K. Jackson, (D), Oregon State, 2017, ZgcZe

SUNY, Stony Brook

School of Marine and Atmospheric Sciences (B,M,D) (2015)
145 Endeavour Hall
Stony Brook, NY 11794-5000
p. (516) 632-8700
minghua.zhang@stonybrook.edu
http://www.somas.stonybrook.edu

Professor:
Josephine Y. Aller, (D), S California, 1975, ObAs
Edmund K. M. Chang, (D), Princeton, 1993, As
J. Kirk Cochran, (D), Yale, 1979, Oc
Brian Colle, (D), Washington, 1997, As
David O. Conover, (D), Massachusetts, 1981, Ob
Roger D. Flood, (D), MIT/WHOI, 1978, Ou
Marvin A. Geller, (D), MIT, 1969, As
Christopher Gobler, (D), SUNY (Stony Brook), 1999, Ob
Sultan Hameed, (D), Manchester (UK), 1968, As
Darcy J. Lonsdale, (D), Maryland, 1979, Ob
Glenn R. Lopez, (D), SUNY (Stony Brook), 1976, Ob
John E. Mak, (D), California (San Diego), 1992, AsCas
Anne E. McElroy, (D), MIT/WHOI, 1985, ObCb
Ellen K. Pikitch, Indiana, 1983, Ob
Mary I. Scranton, (D), MIT/WHOI, 1977, Oc
R. Lawrence Swanson, (D), Oregon State, 1971, Og
Gordon T. Taylor, (D), S California, 1983, Obc
Minghua Zhang, (D), Inst of Atm Physics, 1987, As
Associate Professor:
Bassem Allam, (D), W Brittany (France), 1998, Ob
Robert A. Armstrong, (D), Minnesota, 1975, Ocb
David Black, (D), Ou
Bruce J. Brownawell, (D), MIT/WHOI, 1986, Oc
Robert M. Cerrato, (D), Yale, 1980, Ob
Jackie Collier, (D), Stanford, 1994, Ob
Michael Frisk, (D), Maryland, 2004
Marat Khairoutdinov, (D), Oklahoma, 1997, As
Daniel A. Knopf, (D), Swiss Fed Inst Tech, 2003, As
Kamazima M. Lwiza, (D), Wales, 1991, Oc
Bradley Peterson, (D), S Alabama, 1998, Ob
Joseph Warren, (D), MIT, 2001, Ob
Robert E. Wilson, (D), Johns Hopkins, 1973, Op
Assistant Science Director, IOCS:
Demian Chapman, (D), Nova Southeastern, 2007
Assistant Professor:
Anthony Dvarskas, (D), Maryland, 2007
Hyemi Kim, (D), Seoul Nat, 2008
Janet Nye, (D), Maryland, 2008, Ob
Christopher Wolfe, (D), Oregon State, 2006, Op
Qingzhi Zhu, (D), Xiamen, 1997, Oc
Faculty Director Semester By The Sea:
Kurt Bretsch, (D), South Carolina, 2005
Lecturer:
Lesley Thorne, (D), Duke, 2010
Research Scientist:
Wuyin Lin, (D), SUNY (Stony Brook), 2002, As
Research Professor:
Charles Flagg, (D), MIT, 1977, Op
Engineer:
Douglas Hill, (D), Columbia, 1977
Ecologist, Author:
Carl Safina, (D), Rutgers, 1987
Director Riverhead Foundation:
Robert A. DiGiovanni, Jr., (M), SUNY (Stony Brook), 2002
Adjunct Professor:
James Ammerman, (D), Scripps, 1983
Paul Bowser, (D), Auburn, 1978, Obb
Carl Brenninkmeijer, (D), Groningen (Neth), 1983
Michael J. Cahill, (D), DePaul, 1978, Zn
Alistair Dove, Queensland, 1999
Anga Engel, Oc
Emmanuelle pales Espinosa, (D), Nante (France), 1999
Mark Fast, (D), Dalhousie, 2005, Ob
Scott Ferson, (D), SUNY (Stony Brook), 1988
Scott Fowler, (D), 1969
Roxanne Karimi, (D), Dartmouth, 2007
Kathryn Kavanagh, (D), James Cook, 1998
Jeffrey Levinton, (D), Yale, 1971, Ob
Yangang Liu, (D), Nevada (Reno), 1998
Stephan Munch, (D), SUNY (Stony Brook), 2002, Ob
John Rapaglia, (D), SUNY (Stony Brook), 2007
Frank J. Roethel, (D), SUNY (Stony Brook), 1981, Oc
Jeffrey Tongue, As
Andrew Vogelmann, (D), Penn State, 1994, As
Duane E. Waliser, (D), As
Douglas W. R. Wallace, (D), Dalhousie, 1985, Oc
Jian Wang, (D), Caltech, 2002, As
Distinguished Professor:
Cindy Lee, (D), California (San Diego), 1975, OcCo
Emeritus:
Dong-Ping Wang, (D), Miami, 1975
Affiliated and Joint Faculty:
Heather L. Lynch, (D), Harvard, 2006
Cooperating Faculty:
Resit Akcakaya, (D), SUNY (Stony Brook), 1989
Stephen Baines, (D), Yale, 1993
Lee K. Koppelman, (D), New York, 1968, On
Dianna K. Padilla, (D), Alberta, 1987, Ob
Sheldon Reaven, (D), California (Berkeley), 1975, Zn

SUNY, The College at Brockport

Dept of the Earth Sciences (B) (2015)
350 New Campus Drive
Brockport, NY 14420-2936
p. (585) 395-2636
earthsci@esc.brockport.edu
http://www.brockport.edu/esc
Enrollment (2012): B: 117 (16)

Associate Professor:
James A. Zollweg, (D), Cornell, 1994, Hs

Professor:
Mark R. Noll, (D), Delaware, 1989, Cl
Associate Professor:
Paul L. Richards, (D), Penn State, 1999, Hg
Scott M. Rochette, (D), St Louis, 1998, Am
Adjunct Professor:
David A. Boehm, (M), SUNY (Buffalo), 2003, Gg
Christine Crafts, (B), SUNY (Brockport), 2000, Am
Jutta S. Dudley, (D), SUNY (Buffalo), 1998, Gg
William G. Glynn, (M), Texas A&M, 1984, Gg
Linda J. Schaffer, (M), SUNY (Brockport), 1988, Ze
Department Secretary:
Lauri A. Kifer, (A), Monroe Comm Coll, 1997, Zn
Emeritus:
Robert W. Adams, (D), Johns Hopkins, 1964, Gs
Whitney J. Autin, (D), Louisiana State, 1989, Gs
John E. Hubbard, (D), Colorado State, 1968, Hg
Richard M. Liebe, (D), Iowa, 1962, Ps
Judy A. Massare, (D), Johns Hopkins, 1983, Pv
John M. Williams, (B), Goshen, As
On Leave:
Robert S. Weinbeck, (D), Iowa State, 1980, As
Systems Administrator:
Thomas M. McDermott, Zn

SUNY, Ulster County Community College

STEM (A) (2017)
Burroughs 105
491 Cottekill Road
Stone Ridge, NY 12484
p. (845) 687-5230
schimmrs@sunyulster.edu
http://people.sunyulster.edu/esc
Programs: Liberal Arts & Sciences (A); Math & Science (A)
Professor:
Steven Schimmrich, (M), SUNY (Albany), 1991, GgZgn
Assistant Professor:
Karen Helgers, (M), SUNY, 1987, GeZgy

Syracuse University

Department of Earth & Environmental Sciences (B,M,D) ⊘ (2020)
204 Heroy Geology Laboratory
Syracuse, NY 13244-1070
p. (315) 443-2672
earadmin@syr.edu
http://earthsciences.syr.edu
f: https://www.facebook.com/EarthSciencesSU/
t: @SUEarthScience
Programs: B.A. in Earth Sciences, B.S. in Earth Sciences, B.A. in Environment Sustainability and Policy, B.S. in Environment Sustainability and Policy, B.A. in Energy and Its Impacts, B.S. in Energy and Its Impacts, M.A. in Earth Sciences, M.S. in Earth Sciences, Ph.D. in Earth Sciences
Enrollment (2019): B: 30 (10) M: 16 (5) D: 27 (5)
Professor:
Jeffrey Karson, (D), SUNY (Albany), 1977, GtcGv
Professor:
Suzanne L. Baldwin, (D), SUNY (Albany), 1988, Cc
Paul G. Fitzgerald, (D), Melbourne (Australia), 1988, GtCc
Linda C. Ivany, (D), Harvard, 1997, PegCs
Zunli Lu, (D), Rochester, 2008, Cg
Cathryn R. Newton, (D), California (Santa Cruz), 1983, Pg
Scott D. Samson, (D), Arizona, 1990, Cc
Christopher A. Scholz, (D), Duke, 1989, Gs
Associate Professor:
Gregory Hoke, (D), Cornell, 2006, ZgGmt
Christopher Junium, (D), Penn State, 2010, CsPeCo
Robert Moucha, (D), Toronto, 2003, GtYeg
Jay Thomas, (D), Virginia Tech, 2003, Gi
Assistant Professor:
Tripti Bhattacharya, (D), California (Berkeley), 2016, Ge
Melissa Chipman, (D), Illinois (Urbana), 2017, GelGn
Samuel Tuttle, (D), Boston, 2015, Ge
Tao Wen, (D), Michigan, 2017, Ge
Instructor:
Daniel Curewitz, (D), Duke, 1999, OgGct
Emeritus:
M. E. Bickford, (D), Illinois, 1960, CcGiz
Donald I. Siegel, (D), Minnesota, 1981, Hw
Other:
Bruce Wilkinson, (D), Texas, 1974, Gs

Union College

Geology Dept (B) (2015)
807 Union Street
Schenectady, NY 12308-3107
p. (518) 388-6770
geology@union.edu
http://www.union.edu/academic_depts/geology/
Administrative Assistant: Deborah A. Klein
Enrollment (2015): B: 40 (15)
Chair:
Donald T. Rodbell, (D), Colorado, 1991, GlmGe
Professor:
John I. Garver, (D), Washington, 1989, GtCcGr
Kurt T. Hollocher, (D), Massachusetts, 1985, GxCga
Associate Professor:
Holli M. Frey, (D), Michigan, 2005, GvCag
David P. Gillikin, (D), Vrije (Brussel), 2005, CsmCl
Lecturer:
Matthew R. Manon, (D), Michigan, 2008, Gp
Anouk Verheyden-Gillikin, (D), Vrije (Brussel), 2004
Emeritus:
George H. Shaw, (D), Washington, 1971, Yx
Related Staff:
William S. Neubeck, (M), SUNY (Binghamton), 1980, Gm

United States Military Academy

Dept of Geography & Environmental Engineering (B) ●☒ (2020)
745 Brewerton Rd
West Point, NY 10996
p. (914) 938-2300
william.wright@westpoint.edu
https://westpoint.edu/academics/academic-departments/geography-and-environmental-engineering
f: https://www.facebook.com/WPGENE
t: usma_gene
Programs: Geospatial Information Science; Geography; Environmental Science; Environmental Engineering
Department Secretary: Jean Keller
Enrollment (2018): B: 80 (19)
LTC (P):
William C. Wright, (D), Florida, 2017, ZriYd
COL:
Christopher E. Oxendine, (D), 2014, ZirZf
Assistant Professor:
Matthew S. O'Banion, (D), Oregon State, 2017, ZrGg

University of Rochester

Dept of Earth & Environmental Sciences (B,M,D) ☒ (2021)
120 Trustee Road
227 Hutchison Hall
Box 270221
Rochester, NY 14620
p. (585) 275-5713
john.kessler@rochester.edu
https://www.sas.rochester.edu/ees/
Chair:
John Kessler, (D), Oc
Professor:
Gautam Mitra, (D), Johns Hopkins, 1977, GctNr
John A. Tarduno, (D), Stanford, 1987, YmGtXm
Associate Professor:
Vasilii Petrenko, (D)
Dustin Trail, (D), Cp
Associate Scientist:
Rory D. Cottrell, (D), Rochester, 2000, Ym
Assistant Professor:
Lee Murray, (D), Ac
Miki Nakajima, (D)
Tolulope Olugboji, (D), Ys
Thomas Weber, (D), Obu
Research Associate:
Chiara Borrelli, (D), Rensselaer, 2014, PmcCb

Lecturer:
Karen Berger, (D)
Adjunct Professor:
Carmala N. Garzione, (D), Arizona, 2000, Gs
Emeritus:
Udo Fehn, (D), Tech (Munich), 1973, GeCgOu
Lawrence W. Lundgren, (D), Yale, 1958, Ge

Utica College

Dept of Geology (B) (2015)
Gordon Science Center
1600 Burrstone Road
Utica, NY 13502
p. (315) 792-3134
skanfoush@utica.edu
https://www.utica.edu/academic/as/geoscience/new/bachelors.cfm
Enrollment (2015): B: 10 (6)
Chair:
Adam Schoonmaker, (D), SUNY (Albany), 2005, GczGx
Associate Professor:
Sharon L. Kanfoush, (D), Florida, 2002, GsOuGn
Adjunct Professor:
Lindsey Geary, (M), Florida State, 2008, Geg
Tiffany McGivern, (M), Utica Coll, 2014, Geg
Emeritus:
Herman Muskatt, (D), Syracuse, 1963, GgrPg

Vassar College

Dept of Earth Science & Geography (B) (2015)
Box 735
124 Raymond Avenue
Poughkeepsie, NY 12604-0735
p. (845) 437-5540
geo@vassar.edu
http://earthscienceandgeography.vassar.edu/
Administrative Assistant: Lois Horst
Enrollment (2015): B: 12 (3)
Chair:
Mary A. Cunningham, (D), Minnesota, 2001, ZiyZu
Professor:
Brian J. Godfrey, (D), California (Berkeley), 1984, Zu
Kirsten M. Menking, (D), California (Santa Cruz), 1995, GmPeGc
Joseph Nevins, (D), California (Los Angeles), Zu
Jill S. Schneiderman, (D), Harvard, 1987, Gs
Jeffrey R. Walker, (D), Dartmouth, 1987, GzScGv
Yu Zhou, (D), Minnesota, 1995, Zun
Lab Technician and Collections Manager:
Richard Jones, (M), California (Santa Cruz), 1996
GIS specialist:
Neil Curri, (B), Zi

York College (CUNY)

Dept of Earth and Physical Sciences (B) O⊘ (2021)
94-20 Guy R. Brewer Blvd
Jamaica, NY 11451
p. (718)262- 2654
nkhandaker@york.cuny.edu
http://www.york.cuny.edu/academics/departments/earth-and-physical-sciences/
f: https://www.facebook.com/groups/787724658666512
Programs: Geology, Environmental Health Science and K7-12 Earth Science Teacher Certification Program
Enrollment (2020): B: 11 (7)
Geology Discipline Coordinator & CUNY Doctoral Faculty in Earth and Environmental Sciences:
Nazrul I. Khandaker, (D), Iowa State, 1991, GdeZe
Emeritus:
Stanley Schleifer, (D), CUNY, 1996, Ge
Chair:
Timothy Paglione, (D), Boston, Xa
Associate Professor:
Ratan K. Dhar, (D), CUNY (Grad Ctr), 2006, Hw
Assistant Professor:
Dawn Roberts-Semple, (D), Rutgers, 2012, Gem
Instructor:
Malek Shami, (M), Brooklyn Coll, 2019, Gcg

Emeritus:
Stephen Lakatos, (D), Rensselaer, 1971, Cc
Arthur P. Loring, (D), New York, 1966, Gm

North Carolina

Appalachian State University

Dept of Geography & Planning (B,M) ☒ (2019)
323 Rankin Science West
ASU Box 32066
Boone, NC 28608-2066
p. (828) 262-3000
schroederk@appstate.edu
http://www.geo.appstate.edu
f: Appalachian State Geography & Planning
t: AppstateGhyPln
Professor:
Jeff Colby, (D), Colorado, 1995, Zi
Michael W. Mayfield, (D), Tennessee, 1984, Hs
Baker Perry, (D), North Carolina, 2006, Zg
Kathleen Schroeder, (D), Minnesota, 1995, Zn
Peter T. Soule, (D), Georgia, 1989, As
Saskia van de Gevel, (D), Tennessee, 2008, Zg
Associate Professor:
Rob Brown, (D), Louisiana State, 2001, Zn
Richard J. Crepeau, (D), California (Irvine), 1995, Zn
Derek Martin , (D), Tennessee
Assistant Professor:
Kara Dempsey, (D)
Elizabeth Shay, (D)
Song Shu, (D), 2019
Johnathan Sugg, (D)
Maggie Sugg, (D)

Dept of Geological and Environmental Sciences (B) O☒ (2019)
PO Box 32067
033 Rankin Science West
Boone, NC 28608-2067
p. (828) 262-3049
earth_env_sci@appstate.edu
http://www.earth.appstate.edu/
Programs: Geology, Environmental Science, Earth/Environmental Science Secondary Education
Enrollment (2019): B: 140 (0)
Chair:
William P. Anderson, (D), North Carolina State, 1999, HwqHs
Professor:
Sarah Carmichael, (D), Johns Hopkins, 2006, GxCgGd
Ellen A. Cowan, (D), N Illinois, 1988, GsmGu
Steven J. Hageman, (D), Illinois, 1992, PieGg
Andrew B. Heckert, (D), New Mexico, 2001, PvgZe
Cynthia M. Liutkus-Pierce, (D), Rutgers, 2005, Gd
Scott T. Marshall, (D), Massachusetts, 2008, YxGc
Associate Professor:
Gabriele M. Casale, (D), Gct
Jamie SF Levine, (D), Texas, 2010, Gzp
Assistant Professor:
William H Armstrong, (D), Colorado, 2017, Glm
Cole T. Edwards, (D), Ohio State, 2015, GsCs
Sarah G. Evans, (D), Colorado, 2017, Hwq
Senior Lecturer:
Laura D. Mallard, (M), Vermont, 2000, GtZe
Lauren H. Waterworth, (M), Texas A&M, 2002, Gcg
Brian W. Zimmer, (M), N Arizona, Gg
Lecturer:
Joey D. Mosteller, (M), Appalachian State, 2009, Gg
Visiting Professor:
Hannah B. Riegel, (D), Camerino (Italy), 2019, Ggc

Asheville-Buncombe Technical Community College

Dept of Chemistry and Physics (A) (2015)
340 Victoria Road
Asheville, NC 28801
p. (828) 254-1921
mfender@abtech.edu
http://www1.abtech.edu/content/arts-and-sciences/

chemistryphysics/chemistry-and-physics-overview
Instructor:
John Bultman, Gg
Adjunct Professor:
Dan Murphy, Gg

Brevard College

Geology Program (B) ☒ (2021)
1 Brevard College Drive
Brevard, NC 28712
p. (828) 884-8377
Programs: None, Brevard eliminated Geology when I retired.
Certificates: None

Cape Fear Community College

Dept of Science (2015)
411 N. Front Street
Wilmington, NC 28401
lerotanz59@cfcc.edu
https://cfcc.edu/associate-in-science/
Chair:
Joy Smoots, (D)

Science Dept (A) (2016)
411 N Front St
Wilmington, NC 28401
p. (910) 362-7674
baparnell251@cfcc.edu
http://cfcc.edu/programs/science/
Enrollment (2016): A: 5 (0)
Instructor:
Alvin L. Coleman, (M), Tennessee, 2008, Gg
Phil Garwood, (D), Edith Cowans (Australia), 1978, Gg

Central Piedmont Community College

Sciences Div (A) (2015)
PO Box 35009
Charlotte, NC 28235
p. (704) 330-6750
David.Privette@cpcc.edu
http://www.cpcc.edu/
Chair:
Steppen Murphy, (M), S Illinois, Gue
Division Director:
David Privette, (M), Georgia, 1978, Zy
Instructor:
Alisa Hylton, (M), Wichita State, Gg

Coastal Carolina University

Dept of Marine Science (2015)
Conway, NC 29528
jguentze@coastal.edu

Duke University

Div of Earth & Ocean Sciences (B,M,D) (2015)
Nicholas School of the Environment and Earth Sciences
Box 90227
Durham, NC 27708-0227
p. (919) 684-5847
bill.chameides@duke.edu
http://www.nicholas.duke.edu/eos
Enrollment (2010): B: 37 (15) D: 21 (0)
Chair:
M. Susan Lozier, (D), Washington, 1989, Op
Professor:
Paul A. Baker, (D), California (San Diego), 1981, PcCgGg
Alan E. Boudreau, (D), Washington, 1986, Gi
Bruce H. Corliss, (D), Rhode Island, 1978, Pm
Peter K. Haff, (D), Virginia, 1970, Zn
Robert B. Jackson, (D), Utah State, 1992, Zn
Emily M. Klein, (D), Columbia, 1988, Gi
A. Bradshaw Murray, (D), Minnesota, 1995, Gm
Lincoln F. Pratson, (D), Columbia, 1993, Gs
Avner Vengosh, (D), Australian Nat, 1990, Hw
Associate Professor:
Nicolas Cassar, (D), Hawaii, 2003, CbOcb
Associate Scientist:
Gary S. Dwyer, (D), Duke, 1996, Gs
Assistant Professor:
Wenhong Li, (D), Georgia Tech, Zn
Lecturer:
Alexander Glass, (D), Illinois (Urbana), 2006, PiGgZe
Adjunct Professor:
David J. Erickson, (D), Rhode Island, 1987
Peter E. Malin, (D), Princeton, 1978, Ys
Bruce F. Molnia, (D), South Carolina, 1972, ZrGlu
Daniel D. Richter, (D), Duke, 1980, So
William H. Schlesinger, (D), Cornell, 1976, Zn
Emeritus:
Richard T. Barber, (D), Stanford, 1967, Ob
Duncan Heron, (D), North Carolina, 1958, Grg
Daniel A. Livingstone, (D), Yale, 1953, Pe
Ronald D. Perkins, (D), Indiana, 1962, Gdo
Orrin H. Pilkey, Jr., (D), Florida State, 1962, Ou
Other:
James S. Clark, (D), Minnesota, 1988, Zn
Mark N. Feinglos, (D), McGill, 1973, Gz
Richard F. Kay, (D), Yale, 1973, Zn

East Carolina University

Dept of Geological Sciences (B,M) O⁄🖱 (2020)
101 Graham Building
Greenville, NC 27858-4353
p. (252) 328-6360
culvers@ecu.edu
http://www.geology.ecu.edu
f: https://www.facebook.com/ecugeology/
t: @Ecugeology
Programs: Geology (B,M)
Certificates: Hydrogeology and Environmental Geology (G)
Administrative Assistant: Emily Griffin, Lauren Morrison
Enrollment (2020): B: 48 (16) M: 21 (7)
Chair:
Stephen J. Culver, (D), Wales, 1976, PmGu
Professor:
David Mallinson, (D), S Florida, 1995, Gu
Siddhartha Mitra, (D), William & Mary, 1997, Co
Stephen Moysey, (D), Stanford, 2005, Hg
Catherine A. Rigsby, (D), California (Santa Cruz), 1989, Gs
Associate Professor:
Adriana Heimann, (D), Iowa State, 2006, GzpGi
Eric M. Horsman, (D), Wisconsin, 2006, GcYgGt
Eduardo Leorri, (D), Basque (Spain), 2003, GsPm
Alex K. Manda, (D), Massachusetts, 2009, HwgHq
Assistant Professor:
Margaret Blome, (D), Arizona, 2012, Ggn
David Farris, (D), S California, 2006, Ggc
Distinguished Research Professor:
Stanley R. Riggs, (D), Montana, 1967, GusGe

Guilford College

Dept of Geology & Earth Science (B) (2016)
5800 West Friendly Avenue
Greensboro, NC 27410-4173
p. (336) 316-2263
ddobson@guilford.edu
http://www.guilford.edu/academics/departments-and-programs/geology/
f: https://www.facebook.com/guilfordgeo/
Enrollment (2016): B: 22 (7)
Professor:
David M. Dobson, (D), Michigan, 1997, GusPc
Marlene McCauley, (D), California (Los Angeles), 1986, Cp
Assistant Professor:
Holly Peterson, (D), British Columbia, 2014, HwGe
Emeritus:
Cyril H. Harvey, (D), Nebraska, 1960, Gr

North Carolina Agricultural & Tech State University

Dept of Natural Resources and Environmental Design (B,M) ⃠ (2018)
1601 E. Market St
Carver Hall Room 238

Greensboro, NC 27411
p. (336) 334-7543
uzo@ncat.edu
Programs: Environmental Studies
Certificates: Certificate In Waste Management
Enrollment (2018): B: 79 (22) M: 13 (7)
Professor:
Godfrey A. Uzochukwu, (D), Nebraska, 1983, Gz
Assistant Professor:
Niroj Aryal, (D), Michigan State, 2015, HsgZi

North Carolina Central University

Department of Environmental, Earth and Geospatial Sciences (B,M) O (2020)
1801 Fayetteville Street
Durham, NC 27707-19765
p. (919) 530-5296
gvlahovic@nccu.edu
http://www.nccu.edu/academics/sc/artsandsciences/geospatialscience
f: https://www.facebook.com/groups/142873172423480/
t: @DEEGS_NCCU
Programs: Environmental and Geographic Sciences (B); Earth Science (M)
Certificates: USGIF Accredited Geospatial Intelligence Certificate (undergraduate and graduate)
Enrollment (2020): B: 37 (9) M: 14 (7)
Professor :
Gordana Vlahovic, (D), North Carolina, 1999, YsZeRn
Professor:
John Bang, (D), Texas (El Paso), GeZa
Associate Professor:
Rakesh Malhotra, (D), Georgia, Zri
Chris McGinn, (D), North Carolina (Greensboro), Zgi
Timothy Mulrooney, (D), North Carolina (Greensboro), Zir
Zhiming Yang, (D), Oklahoma State, Zry
Assistant Professor:
Carresse Gerald, (D), North Carolina A&T, GeZg
Christopher Zarzar, (D), Mississippi State, 2017, At

North Carolina State University

Dept of Marine, Earth & Atmospheric Sciences (B,M,D) O (2020)
P.O. Box 8208
Raleigh, NC 27695-8208
p. (919) 515-3711
meas-grad-program@ncsu.edu
http://www.meas.ncsu.edu
f: https://www.facebook.com/measncsu
t: @ncsumeas
Programs: Geology
Marine Sciences
Meteorology
Natural Resources
Certificates: Climate Change and Society (Graduate Program)
Enrollment (2020): B: 205 (44) M: 27 (7) D: 51 (16)
Head:
Lewis A. Owen, (D), Leicester, 1988, GmtGl
Director of Graduate Programs:
Elana L. Leithold, (D), Washington, 1987, Gs
Professor:
Viney P. Aneja, (D), North Carolina State, 1977, Ac
DelWayne Bohnenstiehl, (D), Columbia, 2002, YrsGt
David B. Eggleston, (D), William & Mary, 1991, Ob
Ruoying He, (D), S Florida, 2002, Op
Gary M. Lackmann, (D), SUNY (Albany), 1995, As
Jay F. Levine, (D)
Jingpu P. Liu, (D), William & Mary, 2001, Gu
David A. McConnell, (D), Texas A&M, 1987, ZeRcGc
Nicholas Meskhidze, (D), Georgia Tech, 2003, As
Helena Mitasova, (D), Slovak Tech, 1987, Zi
Matthew Parker, (D), Colorado State, 2002, Am
Walter Robinson, (D), Columbia, 1985, As
Lian Xie, (D), Miami, 1992, As
Sandra Yuter, (D), Washington, 1996, As
Associate Professor:
Anantha Aiyyer, (D), SUNY (Albany), 2003, As
Paul K. Byrne, (D), Trinity (Dublin), 2010, XgGcZr
Chris Osburn, (D), Lehigh, 2000, Cms
Astrid Schnetzer, (D), Vienna, 2001, Ob
Karl Wegmann, (D), Lehigh, 2008, Gm
Assistant Professor:
Stuart P. Bishop, (D), Rhode Island, 2012, OpGq
Lisa Falk, (D), Columbia, 2014, Zg
Ethan Hyland, (D), Michigan, 2014, GrCsPe
Markus Petters, (D), Wyoming, 2004, As
Arianna Soldati, (D), Missouri, 2018, Gv
Emeritus:
Satyapal S. Arya, (D), Colorado State, 1968, As
David J. DeMaster, (D), Yale, 1979, OcCbc
Ronald V. Fodor, (D), New Mexico, 1972, Gi
John C. Fountain, (D), California (Santa Barbara), 1975, Hw
James P. Hibbard, (D), Cornell, 1988, GctZn
Daniel Kamykowski, (D), California (San Diego), 1973, ObpOc
Charles E. Knowles, (D), Texas A&M, 1970, Op
Sethu S. Raman, (D), Colorado, 1972, As
Allen J. Riordan, (D), Wisconsin, 1977, As
Dale A. Russell, (D), Columbia, 1964, Pv
Fred H. M. Semazzi, (D), Nairobi, 1983, As
Ping-Tung Shaw, (D), MIT/WHOI, 1982, Op
William J. Showers, (D), Hawaii, 1982, Cs
Edward F. Stoddard, (D), California (Los Angeles), 1976, Gp
Charles W. Welby, (D), MIT, 1952, Hw
Donna L. Wolcott, (D), California (Berkeley), 1972, Ob
Thomas G. Wolcott, (D), California (Berkeley), 1971, Ob

Dept of Soil Science (B,M,D) (2015)
Box 7619
Raleigh, NC 27695-7619
p. (919) 515-2655
jeff_mullahey@ncsu.edu
Administrative Assistant: Ashru Shah
Professor:
Aziz Amoozegar, (D), Arizona, 1977, Sp
Stephen W. Broome, (D), North Carolina, 1973, Sf
Donald K. Cassel, (D), California (Davis), 1968, Sp
John L. Havlin, (D), Colorado State, 1983, Sc
Dean L. Hesterberg, (D), California (Riverside), 1988, Sc
Michael T. Hoover, (D), Penn State, 1983, Sd
Greg D. Hoyt, (D), Georgia, 1981, Sb
Daniel W. Israel, (D), Oregon State, 1973, Sb
Harold J. Kleiss, Illinois, 1972, Sd
Deanna L. Osmond, (D), Cornell, 1991, Sb
Wayne P. Robarge, (D), Wisconsin, 1975, Sc
Thomas J. Smyth, (D), North Carolina State, 1981, Sc
Michael J. Vepraskas, (D), Texas A&M, 1980, Sd
Michael G. Wagger, (D), Kansas State, 1983, Sb
Associate Professor:
David A. Crouse, (D), North Carolina State, 1996, Sc
Carl Crozier, (D), North Carolina State, 1992, Sb
David Lindbo, (D), Massachusetts, 1990, Sd
Richard A. McLaughlin, (D), Purdue, 1985, Sc
Jeffrey G. White, (D), Cornell, 1988, SoZri
Assistant Professor:
Alexandria Graves, (D), Virginia Tech, 2003, Sb
Wei Shi, (D), Purdue, Sb
Emeritus:
James W. Gilliam, (D), Mississippi State, 1965, Sb

University of North Carolina, Asheville

Dept of Atmospheric Sciences (B) ● ☒ (2018)
CPO 2450
One University Heights
Asheville, NC 28804-3299
p. (828) 251-6149
chennon@unca.edu
https://atms.unca.edu
f: https://www.facebook.com/uncaweather/
t: @uncaweather
Programs: Atmospheric Sciences
Enrollment (2018): B: 36 (11)
Chair:
Chris Hennon, (D), Ohio State, 2003, AstZn
Professor:
Christopher Godfrey, (D), Oklahoma, 2006, AsZnn
Alex Huang, (D), Purdue, 1984, As
Doug Miller, (D), Purdue, 1996, AsZnn

Environmental Studies (B) ☒ (2020)
1University Heights, CPO 2330
Asheville, NC 28804-8511
p. (828) 251-6441
bmcnamee@unca.edu
http://envr.unca.edu
f: https://www.facebook.com/uncaenvr
Programs: B.S. Environmental Studies, including concentrations in Earth Science, Ecology and Environmental Biology, and Environmental Management and Policy.
Certificates: Sustainability
Enrollment (2020): B: 39 (9)
Professor:
Irene M. Rossell, (D), SUNY (Syracuse), 1995, Zn
Associate Professor:
Delores M. Eggers, (D), N Carolina, 1999, Zn
David P. Gillette, (D), Oklahoma, 2008, Zn
Jackie M. Langille, (D), Tennessee, 2012, GctGe
Brittani D. McNamee, (D), Idaho, 2013, GzEgGe
Jeffrey D. Wilcox, (D), Wisconsin, 2007, HwClGg
Assistant Professor:
Andrew Laughlin, (D), Tulane, Zn
Lecturer:
Jake Hagedorn, (D), Maryland, ABD, SbZun
Alison Ormsby, (D), Antioch New England Grad, Zn
Landon Ward, (M), Virginia Inst of Marine Sci, ZnnZn

University of North Carolina, Chapel Hill

Dept of Geological Sciences (B,M,D) (2019)
CB 3315, Mitchell Hall
Chapel Hill, NC 27599-3315
p. (919) 966-4516
dcoleman@unc.edu
http://www.geosci.unc.edu
t: @geosciUNC
Programs: BA Earth Science, BS Earth Science, BS Environmental Geoscience
Enrollment (2016): B: 66 (21) M: 4 (5) D: 20 (2)
Chair:
Drew S. Coleman, (D), Kansas, 1991, CcGit
Professor:
Jonathan M. Lees, (D), Washington, 1989, YsGv
Associate Professor:
Laura J. Moore, (D), California (Santa Cruz), 1998, Gme
Tamlin M. Pavelsky, (D), California (Los Angeles), 2008, Hg
Kevin G. Stewart, (D), California (Berkeley), 1987, Gc
Donna M. Surge, (D), Michigan, 2001, Pe
Assistant Professor:
Xiaoming Liu, (D), Maryland, 2013, Cgl
Emeritus:
Larry Benninger, (D), Yale
Paul D. Fullagar, (D), Illinois, 1963, CcGaZe
Allen F. Glazner, (D), California (Los Angeles), 1981, GitZf
Daniel A. Textoris, (D), Illinois, 1963, Gd

University of North Carolina, Charlotte

Dept of Geography & Earth Sciences (B,M,D) (2015)
9201 University City Boulevard
Charlotte, NC 28223-0001
p. (704) 687-5973
ges@uncc.edu
http://www.geoearth.uncc.edu/
Enrollment (2010): B: 280 (70) M: 86 (16) D: 32 (8)
Professor:
John F. Bender, (D), SUNY (Stony Brook), 1980, GiCtOu
John A. Diemer, (D), SUNY (Binghamton), 1985, Gs
Associate Professor:
Craig J. Allan, (D), York, 1992, Hg
Andy R. Bobyarchick, (D), SUNY (Albany), 1983, Gc
Scott P. Hippensteel, (D), Delaware, 2000, Gr
Walter Martin, (D), Tennessee, 1984, As
Ross Meentemeyer, (D), North Carolina, 2000, Zi
Assistant Professor:
Manda S. Adams, (D), Wisconsin, 2005, Am
Matt Eastin, (D), Colorado State, 2003, Am
Martha Cary Eppes, (D), New Mexico, 2002, So
Lecturer:
Jake Armour, (M), New Mexico, 2002, GmlGg
Terry Shirley, (M), Penn State, 2003, Asm
Emeritus:
Anne Jefferson, (D), Oregon State, 2006, HgGm
Laboratory Director:
William Garcia, (M), Cincinnati, Pv

University of North Carolina, Pembroke

Geology & Geography Dept (B) (2021)
PO Box 1510
Pembroke, NC 28372-1510
p. (910) 775-4024
geo@uncp.edu
https://www.uncp.edu/departments/geology-and-geography
Programs: Geo-Environmental Studies
Certificates: Geospatial Technologies
Enrollment (2020): B: 26 (7)
Chair:
Martin B. Farley, (D), Penn State, 1987, PlZe
Associate Professor:
Jeff B. Chaumba, (D), Georgia, 2009, GxEgGz
Dennis J. Edgell, (D), Kent State, 1992, As
Assistant Professor:
Madan Maharjan, (D), West Virginia, 2017, Hw
Jesse Rouse, (D), West Virginia, 2018, Zni
Lecturer:
Amy Gross, (M), North Carolina (Wilmington), 2006, Gg
Nathan E. Phillippi, (M), South Dakota State, 2004, Zgi
Emeritus:
Thomas E. Ross, (D), Tennessee, 1977, Zy

University of North Carolina, Wilmington

Dept of Earth and Ocean Sciences (B,M) O (2016)
601 South College Road
Wilmington, NC 28403-5944
p. (910) 962-3490
lynnl@uncw.edu
http://www.uncw.edu/earsci/
Administrative Assistant: Alexis Lee
Enrollment (2007): B: 78 (21) M: 32 (5)
Chair:
Lynn A. Leonard, (D), S Florida, 1993, Gu
Professor:
Michael M. Benedetti, (D), Wisconsin, 2000, GmSaZy
Nancy R. Grindlay, (D), Rhode Island, 1991, Yg
Michael S. Smith, (D), Washington (St Louis), 1990, GzpGa
Associate Professor:
Lewis J. Abrams, (D), Rhode Island, 1992, Gu
David E. Blake, (D), Washington State, 1991, Gp
Douglas W. Gamble, (D), Georgia, 2000, Zy
Joanne N. Halls, (D), South Carolina, 1996, Zi
Eric J. Henry, (D), Arizona, 2001, Hw
Mary E. Hines, (D), Louisiana State, 1992, Zu
Lecturer:
Roger D. Shew, (M), North Carolina, 1979, Eo
Emeritus:
Robert T. Argenbright, (D), California (Berkeley), 1990, Zn
William J. Cleary, (D), South Carolina, 1972, Gu
James A. Dockal, (D), Iowa, 1980, GdcEm
W. Burleigh Harris, (D), North Carolina, 1975, GrdGs
Patricia H. Kelley, (D), Harvard, 1979, Pgi
Paul A. Thayer, (D), North Carolina, 1967, GdoHg
Laboratory Director:
Yvonne Marsan, (B), North Carolina (Wilmington), Zi

Wake Technical Community College

Natural Sciences Dept (2015)
9101 Fayetteville Rd
Raleigh, NC 27603
p. (919) 866-5000
mnbalachander@waketech.edu
http://www.waketech.edu/programs-courses/credit/natural-sciences

Western Carolina University

Dept of Geosciences & Natural Resources (B) ☒ (2018)
Stillwell Building Room 331
Cullowhee, NC 28723-9047
p. (828) 227-7367
mlord@wcu.edu
http://geology.wcu.edu
Enrollment (2015): B: 52 (12)
Head:
Mark L. Lord, (D), North Dakota, 1988, HwGmZe
Whitmire Prof Env Sci:
Jerry R. Miller, (D), S Illinois, 1990, GmeGf
Director Prog Study Dev Shorelines:
Robert S. Young, (D), Duke, 1995, GsOn
Associate Provost:
Brandon E. Schwab, (D), Oregon, 2000, GizGv
Assoc. Dean, Arts & Sciences:
David A. Kinner, (D), Colorado, 2003, HgZe
Associate Professor:
Benjamin R. Tanner, (D), Tennessee, 2005, Cos
Cheryl Waters-Tormey, (D), Wisconsin, 2004, Gct
Assistant Professor:
Amy Fagan, (D), Notre Dame, 2013, GiXg
Frank Forcino, (D), Alberta, 2013, PgZeGr
John P. Gannon, (D), Virginia Tech, 2014, HgSo
Instructor:
Emily Stafford, (D), Alberta, 2014, PgGg
Emeritus:
Steven P. Yurkovich, (D), Brown, 1972, Gx

North Dakota

Dickinson State University

Dept of Natural Science (B) (2015)
Dickinson, ND 58601
p. (701) 227-2114
Michael.Hastings@dickinsonstate.edu
http://www.dsu.nodak.edu/
Chair:
Michael Hastings
Associate Professor:
Larry D. League, (M), Kansas, 1971, Zy

Minot State University

Dept of Geoscience (B) ☒ (2020)
500 University Avenue West
Minot, ND 58707
p. (701) 858-3873
john.webster@minotstateu.edu
http://www.minotstateu.edu/geology/
Programs: Geology; Earth Science Education
Enrollment (2020): B: 20 (2)
Head:
John R. Webster, (D), Indiana, 1992, Giz
Assistant Professor:
Joseph Collette, (D), California (Riverside), 2014, PgGsr
Kathyrn Kilroy, (D), Nevada (Reno), 1992, Hg

North Dakota State University

Dept of Geosciences (B) ⦸ (2020)
NDSU Dept. 2745
P.O. Box 6050
Fargo, ND 58108-6050
p. (701) 231-8455
stephanie.day@ndsu.edu
http://www.ndsu.edu/geosci
f: https://www.facebook.com/NDSUGeosciences
Programs: Geology (B); Geography (minor); Geology (minor); Environmental Geology (minor)
Enrollment (2018): B: 32 (5)
Professor:
Kenneth Lepper, (D), Oklahoma State, 2001, CcGml
Peter Oduor, (D), Missouri (Rolla), 2004, ZiRwZr
Bernhardt Saini-Eidukat, (D), Minnesota, 1991, GxCqEg
Scott A. Wood, (D), Princeton, 1985, Cq
Chair:
Stephanie S. Day, (D), Minnesota, 2012, GmZiu
Associate Professor:
Benjamin J. C. Laabs, (D), Wisconsin, 2004, GlPcGm
Assistant Professor:
Lydia S. Tackett, (D), S California, 2014, PeGsPi
Lecturer:
Jessie L. Rock, (M), North Dakota State, 2009, ZgPcg
Emeritus:
Allan C. Ashworth, (D), Birmingham (UK), 1969, Pe
Donald P. Schwert, (D), Waterloo, 1978, PeGe

Dept of Soil Science (B,M,D) (2015)
Walster Hall
Fargo, ND 58105
p. (701) 231-8690
Thomas.Desutter@ndsu.edu
Administrative Assistant: Jacinda Wollan
Enrollment (2014): B: 18 (0) M: 10 (0) D: 4 (0)
Professor:
Francis Casey, (D), Iowa State, 2000, SpHq
Dave Franzen
Robert J. Goos, (D), Colorado, 1980, Sc
Associate Professor:
Larry J. Cihacek, (D), Iowa State, 1976, Zg
Assistant Professor:
Amitava Chatterjee, Wyoming
Aaron Daigh, (D), Iowa State
Tom DeSutter, (D), Kansas State, So
Ann-Marie Fortuna
David G. Hopkins, (D), North Dakota State, 1997, Sd
Abbey Wick, Wyoming

University of North Dakota

Dept of Geography and Geographic Information Science (B,M) (2020)
221 Centennial Drive
Stop 9020
Grand Forks, ND 58202
p. (701) 777-4246
und.geography@und.edu
http://arts-sciences.und.edu/geography/
f: https://www.facebook.com/groups/91074880028/
Programs: Geography (B,M); Geospatial Technologies (minor); Environmental Studies (BA, BS)
Certificates: GISc (G)
Enrollment (2020): M: 4 (3)
Chair:
Douglas C. Munski, (D), Illinois, 1978, ZeRhZu
Professor:
Bradley C. Rundquist, (D), Kansas State, 2000, ZriZy
Paul Todhunter, (D), California (Los Angeles), 1986, Zy
Gregory S. Vandeberg, (D), Kansas State, 2005, GmZiGl
Associate Professor:
Enru Wang, (D), Washington, 2005, Zgi
Assistant Professor:
Christopher Atkinson, (D), Kansas, 2010, AsZi
Instructor:
Mbongowo J. Mbuh, (D), George Mason, 2015, ZrHs

Harold Hamm School of Geology & Geological Engineering (B,M,D) (2021)
81 Cornell Street
Stop 8358
Grand Forks, ND 58202
p. (701) 777-2248
jaakko.putkonen@UND.edu
http://engineering.und.edu/geology-and-geological-engineering/
Programs: BS, MS, and PhD Geology
BS Earth Science
BS Environmental Geoscience
BS, MS, and PhD Geological Engineering
Certificates: Certificate for Petroleum Geology
Enrollment (2014): B: 78 (0) M: 17 (0) D: 10 (0)
Director:
Jaakko Putkonen, (D), Washington, 1997, Gml
Professor:
William D. Gosnold, (D), S Methodist, 1976, YghCt

Joseph H. Hartman, (D), Minnesota, 1984, Pi
Dexter Perkins, III, (D), Michigan, 1979, Gp

Associate Professor:
I-Hsuan Ho, (D), Iowa, Ng
Ronald K. Matheney, (D), Arizona State, 1989, Cs
Stephan Nordeng, (D), Michigan, Go
Dongmei Wang, (D), China, NgGo

Emeritus:
Nels F. Forsman, (D), North Dakota, 1985, GgXgRh
Philip J. Gerla, (D), Arizona, 1983, Hw
Richard D. LeFever, (D), California (Los Angeles), 1979, GsrGo

Ohio

Ashland University

Dept of Chemistry/Geology/Physics (B) (2019)
401 College Avenue
Ashland, OH 44805
p. (419) 289-5268
rcorbin@ashland.edu
http://www.ashland.edu/departments/geology
f: https://www.facebook.com/Ashland-University-Sciences-314117456597/
t: @ausciences
Programs: Geology (B); Geoscience Technology and Management (B); Geology/Environmental Science (B); Earth Science Education (B)
Enrollment (2018): B: 16 (2)

Professor:
Nigel Brush, (D), California (Los Angeles), 1992, GmdGa

Adjunct Professor:
Tess Holloway, (M), Wright State, 2017, Rn
Amanda L. Kozak, (M), Wright State, Rn
Elizabeth Mazzocco, (M), Ohio State, AsRn
William A. Reinthal, (D), Wisconsin, GzoGg
Mackenzie Taylor, (M), Miami, 2017, RnGg

Bowling Green State University

Dept of Geology (B,M) (2015)
190 Overman Hall
Bowling Green, OH 43403
p. (419) 372-2886
jasnyd@bgsu.edu
https://www.bgsu.edu/arts-and-sciences/earth-environment-and-society/geology.html
Administrative Assistant: Pat A. Wilhelm
Enrollment (2010): B: 29 (13) M: 23 (2)

Professor:
James E. Evans, (D), Washington, 1988, GsHsGe
Charles M. Onasch, (D), Penn State, 1977, Gc
Robert K. Vincent, (D), Michigan, 1973, Yg
Peg M. Yacobucci, (D), Harvard, 1999, Pgi

Associate Professor:
John R. Farver, (D), Brown, 1988, Gy
Enrique Gomezdelcampo, (D), Tennessee, 2003, Ge
Peter Gorsevski, (D), Idaho, 2002, ZirGm
Kurt S. Panter, (D), New Mexico Tech, 1995, Giv
Jeffrey A. Snyder, (D), Ohio State, 1996, Gm

Lecturer:
Nichole Elkins, (M), Georgia, 2002, GaZe
Christopher Pepple, (M), Ze
Paula J. Steinker, (D), Bowling Green, 1982, Pg

Emeritus:
Don C. Steinker, (D), California (Berkeley), 1969, Pg

Department IT:
William Butcher, (B), Rochester, 1972, Gg

Case Western Reserve University

Dept of Earth, Environmental and Planetary Sciences (B,M,D) (2016)
10900 Euclid Avenue
A.W. Smith #112
Cleveland, OH 44106-7216
p. (216) 368-3690
eepsweb@case.edu
http://eeps.case.edu/
Enrollment (2016): B: 15 (0) M: 2 (0) D: 5 (0)

Chair:
James A. Van Orman, (D), MIT, 2000, CgGyCp

Professor:
Steven A. Hauck, II, (D), Washington (St Louis), 2001, XyYgXg
Peter L. McCall, (D), Yale, 1975, Pg
Peter J. Whiting, (D), California (Berkeley), 1990, Gm

Associate Professor:
Mulugeta Alene Araya, (D), Turin
Ralph P. Harvey, (D), Pittsburgh, 1990, Xm
Beverly Z. Saylor, (D), MIT, 1996, Gs

Assistant Professor:
Carlo DeMarchi, (D), Georgia Tech
Zhicheng Jing, (D), Yale, 2010

Adjunct Professor:
Andrew Dombard, (D), Washington, 2000, Xy
Joseph T. Hannibal, (D), Kent State, 1990, Pi
David Saja, (D), Pennsylvania, 1999, Gc

Emeritus:
Gerald Matisoff, (D), Johns Hopkins, 1978, Cbc
Samuel M. Savin, (D), Caltech, 1967, Cs

Cedarville University

Dept of Science and Mathematics (B) (2020)
251 North Main Street
Cedarville, OH 45314
p. (937) 766-7940
trice@cedarville.edu
https://www.cedarville.edu/Academic-Programs/Geology.aspx
f: https://www.facebook.com/cedarvillegeology
Programs: Geology (BS) with two tracks to choose from - Physical Geology (BS) and Geoscience (BS)
Enrollment (2020): B: 20 (0)

Professor:
Mark Gathany, (D), Colorado State, ZiuSb
Steven Gollmer, (D), Purdue, GzAmOg
John H. Whitmore, (D), Loma Linda, 2003, PgGsg

Assistant Professor:
Thomas L. Rice, (M), Colorado Mines, 1987, GemEo

Adjunct Professor:
Steve A. Austin, (D), Penn State, 1979, GsEcGd

Central State University

Intl Center for Water Resources Management (B) ☒ (2019)
C.J. McLin Bldg
Wilberforce, OH 45384
p. (937) 376-6212
knedunuri@centralstate.edu
Enrollment (2017): B: 35 (4)

Chairperson and Director:
Krishna Kumar Nedunuri, (D), Purdue, 1999, HwCaSo

Associate Ditector for Land Grant Research:
Subramania I. Sritharan, (D), Colorado State, 1984, Hg

Professor:
Ramanitharan Kandiah, (D), Tulane, 2004, HqSoZi
Sam Laki, (D), Michigan State, 1992, EgSoHs
Xiaofang Wei, (D), Indiana State, 2008, ZrOgZe

Associate Professor:
De Bonne N. Wishart, (D), Rutgers (Newark), 2008, YgCa
Ning Zhang, (D), West Virginia, 2012, RwEo

Emeritus:
Samuel Okunade, (D), Kent State, 1986, Gm

Cincinnati Museum Center

Geier Collections and Research Center ☒ (2017)
1301 Western Avenue
Cincinnati, OH 45203
p. (513) 287-7000
information@cincymuseum.org
http://www.cincymuseum.org

Associate Vice President:
Glenn W. Storrs, (D), Yale, 1986, PvGgr

Curator:
Brenda Hunda, (D), California (Riverside), 2004, Pi

Research Associate:
Nigel C. Hughes, (D), Bristol, 1990, Pi
Takuya Konishi, (D), Alberta, 2009, Pv
Arnold I. Miller, (D), Chicago, 1986, Pq

Joshua H. Miller, (D), Chicago, 2009, Pe
Andrew Webber, (D), Cincinnati, 2007, Pi

Cleveland Museum of Natural History

Department of Paleobotany & Paleoecology ☒ (2021)
1 Wade Oval Drive
Cleveland, OH 44106-1767
p. (216) 231-4600 (Ext. 3529)
mdonovan@cmnh.org
https://www.cmnh.org/research-collections/paleobotany-paleo-ecology

Dept of Vertebrate Paleontology ☒ (2021)
1 Wade Oval Drive
University Circle
Cleveland, OH 44106-1767
p. (216) 231-4600
vertpaleo@cmnh.org
https://www.cmnh.org/research-collections/vertebrate-paleontology
Head:
Joseph T. Hannibal, (D), Kent State, 1990, PiEn
Collections Manager:
Amanda R. McGee, (M)

Mineralogy ☒ (2020)
1 Wade Oval Drive
University Circle
Cleveland, OH 44106-1767
p. (216) 231-4600
mineralogy@cmnh.org
http://www.cmnh.org/mineralogy
Emeritus:
David Saja, (D), Pennsylvania, 1999, GdcZe

College of Wooster

Dept of Earth Sciences (B) ☒ (2020)
Scovel Hall
944 College Mall
Wooster, OH 44691-2363
p. (330) 263-2380
preeder@wooster.edu
https://www.wooster.edu/departments/earth-sciences/
f: https://www.facebook.com/pages/College-of-Wooster-Geology-Department/143144126437
Programs: Environmental Geoscience or Geology Major
Administrative Assistant: Patrice Reeder
Enrollment (2020): B: 28 (7)
Chair:
Meagen Pollock, (D), Duke, 2007, CuGiv
Professor:
Gregory C. Wiles, (D), SUNY (Buffalo), 1992, Gl
Mark A. Wilson, (D), California (Berkeley), 1982, Pi
Associate Professor:
Shelley Judge, (D), Ohio State, 2007, GtsGc

Cuyahoga Community College - Western Campus

Earth Science (A) (2015)
11000 Pleasant Valley Road
Parma, OH 44130
p. (216) 987-5278
enroll@tri-c.edu
Assistant Professor:
Robert Zaleha, Zg
Instructor:
Carol Fondran, Zg
Joseph M. Lane, Zg
Abby N. Norton-Krane, Zg
Kathryn Sasowsky, Zg
Adjunct Professor:
Gloria CC Britton, (D), ZgGmZn
Jennifer Deka, Zg
John L. Ezerskis, (M), Toledo, 1988, ZgGcHw

Denison University

Dept of Geosciences (B) (2016)
F.W. Olin Science Hall
100 W. College Street
Granville, OH 43023
p. (740) 587-6217
hall@denison.edu
http://www.denison.edu/academics/departments/geosciences/
Administrative Assistant: Jude Hall
Enrollment (2013): B: 9 (9)
Professor:
Tod A. Frolking, (D), Wisconsin, 1985, Zy
David C. Greene, (D), Nevada (Reno), 1995, GctGe
Associate Professor:
David H. Goodwin, (D), Arizona, 2003, PiCs
Assistant Professor:
Erik Klemetti, (D), Oregon State, 2005, GvxGg
Kate E. Tierney, (D), Ohio State, 2010, CgGrZg
Emeritus:
Kennard B. Bork, (D), Indiana, 1967, PiRhGs
Robert J. Malcuit, (D), Michigan State, 1973, Gx

Hocking College

GeoEnvironmental Science Program (2015)
3301 Hocking Parkway
Nelsonville, OH 45764-9704
p. (740) 753-6277
barron-holcombk@hocking.edu
http://www.hocking.edu/programs/geoenvironmental
Professor:
Michael R. Caudill, (D), Tennessee, 1996, GsSaHw
Instructor:
Kimberly S. Caudill, (B), Ohio, 1984, GeZuHw

Kent State University

Dept of Geology (B,M,D) O☒ (2020)
221 McGilvrey Hall
325 South Lincoln Street
Kent, OH 44242
p. (330) 672-2680
geology@kent.edu
http://www.kent.edu/geology/
Enrollment (2015): B: 154 (23) M: 22 (10) D: 9 (3)
Chair:
Daniel K. Holm, (D), Harvard, 1992, Gc
Professor:
David B. Hacker, (D), Kent State, 1998, GcHw
Joseph D. Ortiz, (D), Oregon State, 1995, Gs
Carrie E. Schweitzer, (D), Kent State, 2000, Pi
Alison J. Smith, (D), Brown, 1991, GnPce
Neil A. Wells, (D), Michigan, 1984, Gs
Associate Professor:
Anne J. Jefferson, (D), Oregon State, 2006, HgGmCs
David M. Singer, (D), Stanford, 2008, Gze
Assistant Professor:
Timothy M. Gallagher, (D), Michigan, 2016
Christopher J. Rowan, (D), Southampton (UK), 2006, Gt
Kuldeep Singh, (D), Texas, 2013
Allyson Tessin, (D), Michigan, 2016
Jeremy C. Williams, (D), Massachusetts (Boston), 2014, Cg
Emeritus:
Rodney M. Feldmann, (D), North Dakota, 1967, Pi
Donald F. Palmer, (D), Princeton, 1968, Yg
Abdul Shakoor, (D), Purdue, 1982, Ng
Related Staff:
Merida Keatts, (M), Kent State, 2000, Zn

Kent State University at Stark

Dept of Geology (B) O⁄🖱 (2019)
6000 Frank Avenue NW
North Canton, OH 44720
p. 330-244-3303
cschweit@kent.edu
https://www.kent.edu/geology
Programs: Geology, Earth Science
Administrative Assistant: Debra Stimer
Enrollment (2019): B: 22 (0)
Chair:
Carrie E. Schweitzer, (D), Kent State, 2000, PiGg

Associate Professor:
Eric Taylor, (D), Ohio State, GezZe

Lakeland Community College

Geoscience Dept (A) (2017)
7700 Clocktower Drive
Kirtland, OH 44094
p. (440) 525-7341
dpierce@lakelandcc.edu
http://www.lakelandcc.edu/academic/sh/geol
Professor:
David Pierce, (D), GgHsAm

Marietta College

Dept of Petroleum Engineering & Geology (B) ☒ (2018)
215 Fifth Street
Marietta, OH 45750
p. (740) 376-4775
sch030@marietta.edu
http://w3.marietta.edu/departments/Petroleum_Engineering/
Programs: Geology; Petroleum Engineering; Environmental Engineering
Enrollment (2017): B: 36 (13)
Professor:
David L. Jeffery, (D), Texas A&M, 1996, PsGo
Associate Professor:
Tej P. Gautam, (D), Kent State, 2012, NgGeZi
Instructor:
Wendy Bartlett, (M), Texas A&M, 1980, Goe
Veronica Freeman, (M), Texas (Arlington), 1993, Pg
Visiting Professor:
Paul A. Washington, (D), Connecticut, 1987, Gcs
Administrative Coordinator:
Susan Hiser, (M), Springfield Coll, 1992, Zn

Miami University

Dept of Geology and Environmental Earth Sciences (B,M,D) O⊘ (2021)
250 S,. Patterson Avenue
118 Shideler Hall
Oxford, OH 45056
p. (513) 529-3216
edwardca@MiamiOh.edu
http://www.miamioh.edu/geology
f: https://www.facebook.com/MiamiGeology
t: @geologymiamioh
Programs: Geology (B.A. & B.S.); Environmental Earth Science (B.A.)
Administrative Assistant: Cathy Edwards
Enrollment (2020): B: 159 (31) M: 12 (2) D: 11 (2)
Janet & Elliot Baines Bicentenntial Professor & Chair:
Elisabeth Widom, (D), California (Santa Cruz), 1991, CcGve
Professor:
Michael Brudzinski, (D), Illinois, 2002, Ys
Brian S. Currie, (D), Arizona, 1998, GstGc
Yildirm Dilek, (D), California (Davis), 1989, Gt
Hailiang Dong, (D), Michigan, 1997, Cg
John F. Rakovan, (D), SUNY (Stony Brook), 1996, GzCl
Jason Rech, (D), Arizona, 2001, Gm
Associate Professor (Hamilton Campus:
Mark Krekeler, (D), Illinois (Chicago), 2003, Ge
Associate Professor & Director of IES:
Jonathan Levy, (D), Wisconsin, 1993, Hw
Assistant Professor:
Claire McLeod, (D), Durham (UK), 2012, Gx
Carrie Tyler, (D), Virginia Tech, 2012, Pb
Instructor:
Jill Mignery, (M), Miami, 2004, Zge
Lecturer (Middletown Campus:
Tammie Gerke, (D), Cincinnati, 1995, ClGea
Adjunct Professor:
Patri Larrea, (D), Zaragoza, 2014
Emeritus:
A. Dwight Baldwin, Jr., (D), Stanford, 1966, Hw
Mark R. Boardman, (D), North Carolina, 1978, On
William K. Hart, (D), Case Western, 1982, GivCc
John M. Hughes, (D), Dartmouth, 1981, Gz
Robert G. McWilliams, (D), Washington, 1968, Ps
John K. Pope, (D), Cincinnati, 1966, Pi
Isotope Geochemistry & Mass Spec Lab Mgr:
David C. Kuentz, (M), Texas (Arlington), 1986, Ca
Geochemistry Lab Manager:
Marion Lytle, (D), Rhode Island, 2013
Associate Teaching Professor:
Todd Dupont, (D), Penn State, 2004, Gl
Assistant Teaching Professor:
Maija Sipola, (D), Iowa, 2018, Gg
Accounting Technician:
Gail Burger
Director Limper Geology Museum:
Kendall L. Hauer, (D), Miami (Ohio), 1995, GgZeCg
Cooperating Faculty:
Jerome Bellian, (D), Texas, 2009, Go
Carina Colombi, (D), National (San Juan), 2007, Gr
R. Hays Cummins, (D), Texas A&M, 1984, Ge
J Christophe Haley, (D), Johns Hopkins, 1986, Gt
Hassan Mirnejad, (M), Carleton, 2001, Gx
Hassan Mirnejad, (D), Carleton, 2001, Gx
Monica Rakovan, (D), Miami (Ohio), 2011, Hg
Fara Rasoazanamparany, (D), Miami, 2015

Mount Union College

Dept of Geology (B) (2015)
Alliance, OH 44601
p. (330) 823-3672
graylm@mountunion.edu
http://www.mountunion.edu/gy
Enrollment (2010): B: 8 (2)
Professor:
Lee M. Gray, (D), Rochester, 1985, PgGg
Department Chair:
Mark A. McNaught, (D), Rochester, 1991, Gcg
Adjunct Professor:
Leonard G. Epp, (D), Penn State, 1970, Ob

Muskingum University

Dept of Geology (B) (2016)
163 Stormont Street
New Concord, OH 43762
p. (740) 826-8306
svanhorn@muskingum.edu
http://muskingum.edu/dept/geology
Enrollment (2016): B: 33 (6)
Associate Professor:
Stephen R. Van Horn, (D), Connecticut, 1996, GeZiEo
Associate Professor:
Eric W. Law, (D), Case Western, 1982, Gp
David L. Rodland, (D), Virginia Tech, 2003, PieGr

Northwest State Community College

Div of Arts and Sciences (2015)
22600 State Route 34
Archbold, OH 43502
levans@northweststate.edu
http://www.northweststate.edu

Oberlin College

Dept of Geology (B) (2016)
52 West Lorain Street
Oberlin, OH 44074-1044
p. (440) 775-8350
geology@oberlin.edu
http://new.oberlin.edu/arts-and-sciences/departments/geology/
Enrollment (2016): B: 46 (18)
Chair:
Dennis K. Hubbard, (D), South Carolina, 1977, Gsu
Professor:
Karla M. Parsons-Hubbard, (D), Rochester, 1993, PgGu
Steven F. Wojtal, (D), Johns Hopkins, 1982, Gc
Associate Professor:
F Zeb Page, (D), Michigan, 2005, GpCsg
Assistant Professor:
Amanda H. Schmidt, (D), Washington, 2010, Gm

Visiting Professor:
Andrew J. Horst, (D), Stanford, 2013, Gcg
Emeritus:
Bruce M. Simonson, (D), Johns Hopkins, 1982, GsXmHw
Cooperating Faculty:
Alison Ricker, (M), Rhode Island, 1977, Zn

Ohio State University

Dept of Civil, Environmental & Geodetic Engineering (B,M,D) ☒ (2018)
470 Hitchcock Hall
2070 Neil Avenue
Columbus, OH 43210
p. (612) 292-2771
mackay.49@osu.edu
http://ceg.osu.edu
Programs: Civil Engineering
minor in Survey Engineering
Enrollment (2016): M: 11 (4) D: 8 (2)
Professor and Chair:
Allison A. MacKay, (D), MIT, 1998, Cq
Research Professor:
Charles K. Toth, (D), ZrYdZi
Professor:
Harvey J. Miller, (D), Ohio State, 1991, Zi
Alper Yilmaz, (D), C Florida, 2004, ZfrZu
Assistant Professor:
Rongjun Qin, (D), Zrf
Lei Wang, (D), Ohio State, Zri

Dept of Geography (B,M,D) (2015)
1036 Derby Hall
154 North Oval Mall
Columbus, OH 43210-1361
p. (614) 292-2514
geog_webmaster@osu.edu
http://www.geography.osu.edu/
Chair:
Daniel Sui
Professor:
David H. Bromwich, (D), Wisconsin, 1979, As
Ellen E. Mosley-Thompson, (D), Ohio State, 1979, As
Jeffrey C. Rogers, (D), Colorado, 1979, As
Associate Professor:
Jay S. Holgood, (D), Ohio State, 1984, As
Jialin Lin, (D), SUNY (Stony Brook), 2001, As
Bryan G. Mark, (D), Syracuse, 2001, As
Assistant Professor:
Alvaro Montenegro, (D), Florida State, 2004, OgAsZy
Emeritus:
A. John Arnfield, (D), McMaster, 1973, As
John N. Rayner, (D), Canterbury (NZ), 1965, As

Geography (B,M,D) ☒ (2019)
1036 Derby Hall
154 North Oval Mall
Columbus, OH 43210-1361
p. (614) 292-2514
geog_webmaster@osu.edu
https://geography.osu.edu/
Programs: BA in Geography, BS in Geography, BS in Atmospheric Sciences, MA in Geography, MS in Atmospheric Sciences, PhD in Geography, PhD in Atmospheric Sciences
Associate Professor:
Alvaro Montenegro, (D), Florida State, 2003, AsOg

School of Earth Sciences (B,M,D) O☒ (2019)
275 Mendenhall Lab
125 South Oval Mall
Columbus, OH 43210-1398
p. (614) 292-2721
earthsciences@osu.edu
http://www.earthsciences.osu.edu
f: https://www.facebook.com/OSUGeology/
t: @osuearthscience
Programs: Earth History, Geodetic Science, Solid Earth Dynamics, and Water, Climate, and the Environment
Administrative Assistant: Jill Bryant, Theresa Mooney, Angeletha M. Rogers
Enrollment (2011): M: 36 (16) D: 40 (2)
Undergraduate Coordinator:
Anne E. Carey, (D), Nevada (Reno), 1995, HwCg
School Director:
Matthew R. Saltzman, (D), California (Los Angeles), 1996, GsClg
Ohio Research Scholar:
David R. Cole, (D), Penn State, 1980, CgsZa
Ohio Eminent Scholar:
Michael G. Bevis, (D), Cornell, 1982, Yx
Frank W. Schwartz, (D), Illinois, 1972, Hw
Distinguished University Scholar:
William Berry Lyons, (D), Connecticut, 1979, HwCgZg
CK Shum, (D), Texas, 1982, YdHg
Director, Byrd Polar Research Center:
Ian M. Howat, (D), California (Santa Cruz), 2006, GlZr
Professor:
Douglas E. Alsdorf, (D), Cornell, 1996, HgYg
Loren E. Babcock, (D), Kansas, 1990, Pg
Michael Barton, (D), Manchester (UK), 1975, GiCpt
Yu-Ping Chin, (D), Michigan, 1988, CqHw
Andrea G. Grottoli, (D), Houston, 1998, ObCbOo
Christopher Jekeli, (D), Ohio State, 1981, Ydv
Mark A. Kleffner, (D), Ohio State, 1988, PgsGr
Wendy R. Panero, (D), California (Berkeley), 2001, Yg
Burkhard A. Schaffrin, (D), Bonn, 1983, Yd
Lonnie G. Thompson, (D), Ohio State, 1976, GlZgPc
Design Engineer:
Dana Caccamise, (M)
Senior Scientist:
Junyi Guo
John W. Olesik, (D), Wisconsin, 1982, Ca
Yuchan Yi, (D), Ohio State, 1995, Ydv
Associate Professor:
Ann Cook, (D), Columbia, 2010, GuYg
Ozeas S. Costa, Jr, (D), Plymouth (UK), 2002, CblZu
Thomas Darrah, (D), Rochester, 2009, Cg
Michael T. Durand, (D), California, 2007, HsZr
William Ashley Griffith, (D), Stanford, 2008, GcNr
Motomu Ibaraki, (D), Waterloo, 1994, Hg
Steven K. Lower, (D), Virginia Tech, 2001, PoZa
Alan J. Saalfeld, (D), Maryland, 1993, Zi
Senior Research Associate:
Christopher Gardner, (M)
Research Scientist:
Paolo Gabrielli, (D), LGGE Grenoble, 2004, CtPeGl
Susan A. Welch, (D), Delaware, 1997, ClGeCs
Instructional Lab Supervisor:
Christena Cox, (D), Ohio State, 1994, GeoGc
Assistant Professor:
Joel D. Barker, (D), Alberta, 2007, CblPe
Elizabeth Griffith, (D), Stanford, 2008, CsOoCb
Jill Leonard-Pingel, (D), Scripps, 2012, Pi
Joachim Moortgat, (D), Radboud, 2006, HwNp
Audrey Sawyer, (D), Texas, 2011, HwSpHs
Derek Sawyer, (D), Texas, 2010, YgGoRn
Research Associate:
Gerald Allen, (D), Ohio State, 2011
Chunli Dai, (D), Ohio State, 2015, ZrYg
Renato Frasson, (D), Iowa, 2011, Hg
Siddharth Gautam, (D), Mumbai, 2009
Eric Kendrick, (D), Hawaii
How-wai (Peter) Luk
Anthony Lutton, (D)
Myoung-Jong Noh, (D), Inha, 2011, Zr
Julie Sheets, (D), Ohio State, 1994, Gz
Stephanie Sherman, (D), Ohio State
Museum Curator :
Dale M. Gnidovec, (M), Fort Hays State, 1978, PvGr
Adjunct Professor:
Thomas G. Naymik, (D), Ohio State, 1978, Hw
Visiting Professor:
David Young, (D), California, 2005, GcpCc
Academy Professor:
William I. Ausich, (D), Indiana, 1978, PgGs
Stig M. Bergstrom, (D), Lund (Sweden), 1961, PgGg
David H. Elliot, (D), Birmingham (UK), 1965, GxtGv
Lawrence A. Krissek, (D), Oregon State, 1982, Gsu
Teresa Mensing, (D), Ohio State, 1987, Cg

Ralph R. B. von Frese, (D), Purdue, 1980, Ye
Emeritus:
E. Scott Bair, (D), Penn State, 1980, HwGe
James Bradley
James W. Collinson, (D), Stanford, 1966, PgGsg
Charles E. Corbato, (D), California (Los Angeles), 1960, Ye
Jeffrey J. Daniels, (D), Colorado Mines, 1974, Yg
James W. Downs, (D), Virginia Tech, 1983, Gz
Gunter Faure, (D), MIT, 1961, CgHw
Kenneth A. Foland, (D), Brown, 1972, CcgCs
Charles E. Herdendorf, (D), Ohio State, 1970, OgGuOn
Kenneth Jezek, (D), Wisconsin, 1980, YgPcGl
Garry D. McKenzie, (D), Ohio State, 1968, GmeZe
Ivan Mueller, (D), Ohio State, 1960, YddYv
David Nickey, (D), Penn State, 1966
Hallan C. Noltimier, (D), Newcastle upon Tyne, 1965, YmgGt
Douglas E. Pride, (D), Illinois, 1969, Eg
Richard H. Rapp, (D), Ohio State, 1964, Yd
Rodney T. Tettenhorst, (D), Illinois, 1960, Gz
Russell O. Utgard, (D), Indiana, 1969, YgEnZe
Peter N. Webb, (D), Utrecht, 1966, PmRhGr
Terry J. Wilson, (D), Columbia, 1983, GctGl
Program Coordinator:
Mike Kositzke
Courtesy Appt.:
Bryan Mark
Undergraduate Advisor:
Karen Royce, (D), Ohio State
Space Management Coordinator:
Dan Dunlap
Related Staff:
Christina Millan, (D), Ggc

School of Environment and Natural Resources (B,M,D) (2015)
2021 Coffey Road
Room 210 Koffman Hall
Columbus, OH 43210
p. (614) 292-2265
sullivan.191@osu.edu
http://senr.osu.edu/
Administrative Assistant: Mary Capoccia
Eminent Scholar:
Richard P. Dick, (D), Iowa State, 1986, Sb
Associate Director:
Donald J. Eckert, (D), Ohio State, 1978, Sc
Professor:
Jerry M. Bigham, (D), North Carolina State, 1977, Sd
Frank G. Calhoun, (D), Florida, 1971, Sd
Rattan Lal, (D), Ohio State, 1968, Sp
Associate Professor:
Nicholas T. Basta, (D), Iowa State, 1989, Sc
Edward L. McCoy, (D), Oregon State, 1984, Sp
Brian K. Slater, (D), Wisconsin, 1994, SdZi
Assistant Professor:
Dawn Ferris, (D), Minnesota, 1997, Sf
Emeritus:
Warren A. Dick, (D), Iowa State, 1980, SbCbHs

Ohio University

Geological Sciences (B,M) ●✓ (2020)
316 Clippinger Lab
Athens, OH 45701
p. (740) 593-1101
geological.sciences@ohio.edu
http://www.ohio.edu/geology/
Programs: BS Geological Sciences, BS Environmental Geology, BA Geological Sciences, Minor Geological Sciences, Minor Paleontology
Enrollment (2018): B: 75 (23) M: 22 (9)
Professor:
Daniel Hembree, (D), Kansas, 2005, Pi
Dina L. Lopez, (D), Louisiana State, 1992, CgHwGv
R. Damian Nance, (D), Cambridge, 1978, Gtc
Alycia L. Stigall, (D), Kansas, 2004, Pg
Chair:
Gregory S. Springer, (D), Colorado State, 2002, GmPcGa
Associate Professor:
Eung Seok Lee, (D), Indiana, 1999, Hw
Keith A. Milam, (D), Tennessee, 2006, Xg
Gregory C. Nadon, (D), Toronto, 1991, Gs
Technician & Information Tech:
Timothy A. Grubb, (A), Washington State Comm Coll, 2002
Administrative Associate:
Cheri Sheets, (B), Ohio, 1997

Ohio Wesleyan University

Dept of Geology & Geography (B) ☒ (2019)
61 S. Sandusky Street
Delaware, OH 43015
p. (740) 368-3615
bsmartin@owu.edu
http://geo.owu.edu
Programs: Geology (B.A. and B.S.), Planetary Science, Geography, Environmental Science
Enrollment (2018): B: 26 (10)
Director, Environmental Studies Program:
John B. Krygier, (D), Penn State, 1995, Zi
Chair:
Barton S. Martin, (D), Massachusetts, 1991, GxvCg
Professor:
Keith O. Mann, (D), Iowa, 1987, Pi
Assistant Professor:
Nathanael S. Amador, (D), Penn State, 2015, ZyGlZr
Charles C. Trexler, (D), California (Davis), 2018, Gct
Instructor:
Ashley L. Allen, (M), Wyoming, 2014, Znu
Emeritus:
Karen H. Fryer, (D), Illinois, 1986, GcpGt
Richard D. Fusch, (D), Oregon, 1972, Zu
David H. Hickcox, (D), Oregon, 1979, ZyAm

Shawnee State University

Dept of Natural Sciences (B) ●☒ (2020)
940 Second Street
Portsmouth, OH 45662
p. (740) 351-3395
kshoemaker@shawnee.edu
https://www.shawnee.edu/areas-study/college-arts-sciences/natural-sciences/bachelor-degrees/geology
f: https://www.facebook.com/DeptNaturalSciencesShawneeStateUniversity/
t: @SSU_Science
Programs: Geology
Administrative Assistant: Heather Thacker
Enrollment (2020): B: 16 (2)
Professor:
Kurt A. Shoemaker, (D), Miami (Ohio), 2004, GxzGm
Associate Professor:
Erik B. Larson, (D), Mississippi State, 2014, GmsHg
Other:
Jeffrey A. Bauer, (D), Ohio State, 1987, Ps

University of Akron

Dept of Geosciences (B,M) O✓ (2020)
Akron, OH 44325-4101
p. (330) 972-7630
steer@uakron.edu
http://www.uakron.edu/geology/
Programs: Geology (B,M); Earth Science (B); Environmental Science (B); Environmental Geology (M)
Certificates: Environmental Studies
Administrative Assistant: Lynne Suponcic
Enrollment (2020): B: 91 (11) M: 6 (2)
Professor of Instruction:
John F. Beltz, (M), Akron, 1992, GgRh
Meera Chatterjee, (D), Zy
Professor:
John A. Peck, (D), Rhode Island, 1995, GseGn
Ira D. Sasowsky, (D), Penn State, 1992, HwGmo
David N. Steer, (D), Cornell, 1996, Yes
Associate Professor:
John M. Senko, (D), Oklahoma, 2004, Cg
Assistant Professor of Instruction:
Thomas J. Quick, (M), Akron, 1983, GgCaYe

Assistant Professor:
Caleb Holyoke, (D), Brown, 2005, GcNrYx

University of Akron - Wayne College

University of Akron - Wayne College (2015)
1901 Smucker Road
Orrville, OH 44667
p. (330) 972-8934
WayneCommunityRelations@uakron.edu
http://www.wayne.uakron.edu/

University of Cincinnati

Dept of Geology (B,M,D) ☒ (2018)
500 Geology/Physics Building
P. O. Box 210013
Cincinnati, OH 45221-0013
p. (513) 556-3732
krista.smilek@uc.edu
http://www.artsci.uc.edu/departments/geology.html
Programs: Geology
Enrollment (2018): B: 83 (10) M: 13 (8) D: 17 (2)

Head:
Lewis Owen, (D), Leicester (UK), 1988, GmlGt

Professor:
Thomas J. Algeo, (D), Michigan, 1989, Gs
Carlton E. Brett, (D), Michigan, 1978, Pe
Attila I. Kilinc, (D), Penn State, 1969, CpGvCu
Thomas V. Lowell, (D), SUNY (Buffalo), 1986, Gl

Associate Professor:
Christopher L. Atchison, (D), Ohio State, 2011, Ze
Brooke E. Crowley, (D), California (Santa Cruz), 2009, CsPev
Andrew D. Czaja, (D), California (Los Angeles), 2006, PmCl
Craig Dietsch, (D), Yale, 1985, Gp
Amy Townsend-Small, (D), Texas, 2006, Co
Dylan Ward, (D), Colorado, 2010, GmqZi

Assistant Professor:
Aaron Diefendorf, (D), Penn State, 2010, Co
Joshua H. Miller, (D), Chicago, 2009, PgvPe
Reza Soltanian, (D), Wright State, 2015, Hw
Daniel M. Sturmer, (D), Cal State (Fullerton), 2003, YeGdo
Yurena Yanes, (D), La Laguna (Spain), 2005, PeCsPg

Adjunct Professor:
Brenda R. Hunda, (D), California (Riverside), 2004, Pi
Glenn W. Storrs, (D), Yale, 1986, Pv

Emeritus:
Madeleine Briskin, (D), Brown, 1973, Pe
John E. Grover, (D), Yale, 1972, Gz
Warren D. Huff, (D), Cincinnati, 1963, GzvGr
J. Barry Maynard, (D), Harvard, 1972, Cl
David L. Meyer, (D), Yale, 1971, Pi
Arnold I. Miller, (D), Chicago, 1986, Pi
David Nash, (D), Michigan, 1977, Gm
Paul E. Potter, (D), Chicago, 1952, Gs

University of Dayton

Dept of Geology (B) ● (2016)
300 College Park
SC 179
Dayton, OH 45469-2364
p. (937) 229-3432
dgoldman1@udayton.edu
http://www.udayton.edu/artssciences/geology/
Administrative Assistant: Darla Titus
Enrollment (2016): B: 40 (7)

Chair:
Daniel Goldman, (D), SUNY (Buffalo), 1993, PgqGr

Professor:
Donald Pair, (D), Syracuse, 1991, Gl
Michael R. Sandy, (D), London (UK), 1984, Pi

Associate Professor:
Umesh Haritashya, (D), Indian Inst of Tech, 2005, ZrGm
Andrea M. Koziol, (D), Chicago, 1988, Cp
Allen J. McGrew, (D), Wyoming, 1992, GtcGp
Shuang-Ye Wu, (D), Cambridge, 2000, Zy

Visiting Assistant Professor:
Zelalem Bedaso, (D), S Florida, 2011, CslGs

Adjunct Professor:
Sue Klosterman, (M), Wright State, 2005, Gg
Andrew Rettig, (D), Cincinnati, 2014, Zy

Emeritus:
Charles J. Ritter, (D), Michigan, 1971, Ct

University of Toledo

Dept of Environmental Sciences (B,M,D) ☒ (2020)
2801 W. Bancroft Street
Toledo, OH 43606-3390
p. (419) 530-2009
jonathan.bossenbroek@utoledo.edu
http://www.utoledo.edu/nsm/envsciences/
Administrative Assistant: Shirley Michel
Enrollment (2019): B: 33 (13) M: 4 (2)

Chair:
Timothy G. Fisher, (D), Calgary, 1993, GlmGn

Director, Lake Erie Center :
Thomas Bridgeman, (D), Michigan, 2001, Zn

Dean, Jesup Scott Honors College:
Heidi Appel, (D), Michigan, 1990, Zn

Professor:
Jonathon Bossenbroek, (D), Colorado State, 2004, Zn
Scott Heckathorn, (D), Illinois, 1995, Zn
Christine M. Mayer, (D), Illinois, 1998, Zn
Daryl L. Moorhead, (D), Tennessee, 1985, Zn
William V. Sigler, (D), Purdue, 1999, Zn
Alison L. Spongberg, (D), Texas A&M, 1994, Co
Michael N. Weintraub, California, 2004, Zn

Director, Stranahan Arboretum:
Daryl F. Dwyer, (D), Michigan State, 1986, Zn

Associate Professor:
Richard H. Becker, (D), W Michigan, 2008, ZrHzGe
Mark J. Camp, (D), Ohio State, 1974, PiRhEs
David E. Krantz, (D), South Carolina, 1988, Gs
James Martin-Hayden, (D), Connecticut, 1994, Hq
Song Qian, (D), Duke, 1995, Zn

Assistant Professor:
Kennedy Doro, (D), Tuebingen, 2015, Zn
William Hintz, (D), S Illinois, 2014, Zn
Jeanine Refsnider-Streby, (D), Iowa, 2012, Zn
Trisha Spanbauer, (D), Nebraska, 2015, Zn
Henry Streby, (D), Minnesota, 2010, Zn

Lecturer:
Todd Crail, (D), Toledo, 2012, Zn

Wittenberg University

Dept of Geology (B) ☒ (2019)
P.O. Box 720
Springfield, OH 45501-0720
p. (937) 327-6475
mzaleha@wittenberg.edu
http://www.wittenberg.edu/academics/geology
f: https://www.facebook.com/WittenbergGeology
Programs: B.S. & B.A. in Geology, B.S. & B.A. in Environmental Science, B.A. in Earth Science Education
Enrollment (2018): B: 11 (4)

Professor:
John B. Ritter, (D), Penn State, 1990, Gm

Associate Professor:
Sarah K. Fortner, (D), Ohio State, 2008, ClZeHg
Michael J. Zaleha, (D), SUNY (Binghamton), 1994, Gs

Emeritus:
Katherine L. Bladh, (D), Arizona, 1976, Gi
Kenneth W. Bladh, (D), Arizona, 1978, GzEm
Robert W. Morris, (D), Columbia, 1969, PiGg

Wright State University

Dept of Earth and Environmental Science (B,M) (2015)
3640 Colonel Glenn Highway
260 Brehm Lab
Dayton, OH 45435
p. (937) 775-2201
david.schmidt@wright.edu
http://www.wright.edu/ees/
Enrollment (2010): B: 66 (8) M: 48 (15)

Director of Undergraduate Programs:
David Schmidt, (D), Ohio State, PiGd
Chair:
David F. Dominic, (D), West Virginia, 1988, GsrRc
Professor:
Christopher C. Barton, (D), Yale, 1983, GqYgHq
C. B. Gregor, (D), Utrecht, 1967, Gs
Chad Hammerschmidt, (D), Connecticut, 2005, CmOcCb
Allen G. Hunt, (D), California (Riverside), 1983, GqSpCl
Robert W. Ritzi, Jr., (D), Arizona, 1989, Hw
Associate Professor:
Abinash Agrawal, (D), North Carolina, 1990, ClHwPg
Songlin Cheng, (D), Arizona, 1984, Hw
Ernest C. Hauser, (D), Wisconsin, 1982, YeGtYu
William Slattery, (D), CUNY, 1994, ZeGr
Rebecca Teed, (D), Minnesota, 1999, ZePeGn
Doyle Watts, (D), Michigan, 1979, YeZr
Director of Sustainability:
Huntting (Hunt) Brown, (D), Ge
Emeritus:
Byron Kulander, (D), West Virginia, 1966, Gc
Benjamin H. Richard, (D), Indiana, 1966, Ye
Paul J. Wolfe, (D), Case Western, 1966, Ye

Youngstown State University

Dept of Geological & Environmental Sciences (B,M) (2015)
One University Plaza
2120 Moser Hall
Youngstown, OH 44555
p. (330) 941-3612
amjacobs@ysu.edu
http://www.as.ysu.edu/~geology/
Enrollment (2007): B: 48 (4) M: 21 (1)
Chair:
Jeffrey C. C., (D), Kent State, 1992, EoNgHy
Director, Env Studies Program:
Isam E. Amin, (D), Nevada (Reno), 1987, Hw
Professor:
Raymond E. Beiersdorfer, (D), California (Davis), 1992, Cg
Alan M. Jacobs, (D), Indiana, 1967, Ge
Assistant Professor:
Joseph E. Andrew, (D), Kansas, 2002, Gc
Felicia P. Armstrong, (D), Oklahoma State, 2003, Sb
Shane V. Smith, (D), Washington State, 2005, Gs
Instructor:
Harry Bircher, (M), Youngstown State, 1995, Ge
Brian M. Greene, (D), Kent State, 2001, Ng
Lawrence P. Gurlea, (M), Pennsylvania, 1971, Cg
Engineering Adjunct:
Scott C. Martin, (D), Clarkson, 1984, Ge
Douglas M. Price, (D), Notre Dame, 1988, Cg
Emeritus:
Ann G. Harris, (M), Miami (Ohio), 1958, Ge
Ikram U. Khawaja, (D), Indiana, 1969, Ec
Charles R. Singler, (D), Nebraska, 1969, Gs
Cooperating Faculty:
Thomas P. Diggins, (D), SUNY, 1997, Pg
Carl G. Johnston, (D), Cincinnati, 1992, Pg

Zane State College

Oil and Gas Engineering Technology (A) (2015)
1555 Newark Rd
Zanesville, OH 43701
p. (740) 588-1282
nwelch@zanestate.edu
http://www.zanestate.edu
f: https://www.facebook.com/ZaneStateCollege
t: @ZaneStateC

Oklahoma

Oklahoma City Community College

Physical Sciences (2015)
7777 South May Avenue
Oklahoma City, OK 73159
p. (405) 682-1611
elizabeth.c.eustice@occc.edu
http://www.occc.edu

Oklahoma State University

Boone Pickens School of Geology (B,M,D) O☒ (2021)
105 Noble Research Center
Stillwater, OK 74078-3031
p. (405) 744-6358
sandy.earls@okstate.edu
http://geology.okstate.edu
Administrative Assistant: Sandy Earls
Enrollment (2018): B: 60 (17) M: 48 (15) D: 26 (2)
Head:
Camelia Knapp, (D), Cornell, 2000, GtYgs
Professor:
Mohamed G. Abdelsalam, (D), Texas (Dallas), 1993, GctYg
Michael Grammer, (D), Miami, 1991, GsEoGr
Todd Halihan, (D), Texas, 2000, HwYuRc
James Knapp, (D), MIT, 1989, GcYgs
Jack C. Pashin, (D), Kentucky, 1990, GrcGo
Associate Professor:
Priyank Jaiswal, (D), Yg
Daniel A. Lao, (D), Pittsburgh, 2008, GctGg
James Puckette, (D), Oklahoma State, 1996, Go
Tracy Quan, (D), MIT/WHOI, 2005, Og
Assistant Professor:
Ashley Burkett, (D), Indiana State, 2015, Pme
Ahmed Ismail, (D), Missouri S&T, 2006, Ysu
Natascha Riedinger, (D), Bremen, 2005, CgGu
Javier Vilcaez, (D), Tohoku, 2009, XzNpCl
Tingying Xu, (D), Washington, 2018, Cbq
Visiting Professor:
Mary E. Hileman, (D), Michigan, 1973, GorGd
Emeritus:
Jay M. Gregg, (D), Michigan State, 1982, Gs
Arthur Hounslow, (D), Carleton, 1968, Cl
Douglas Kent, (D), Iowa State, 1969, Hw
Vernon Scott, (D), Utah, 1975, Ze
Gary Stewart, (D), Kansas, 1973, Go
John D. Vitek, (D), Iowa, 1973, Gm
Teaching Assistant Professor:
Brendan Hanger, (D), Australian Nat, 2014, Ggz

Rogers State University

Dept of Mathematics and Physical Sciences (2015)
1701 W. Will Rogers Blvd.
Claremore, OK 74107
p. (918) 343-6812
jgraham@rsu.edu
http://www.rsu.edu

Tulsa Community College

Science and Math (A) (2021)
909 S. Boston Avenue
Tulsa, OK 74119
p. (918) 595-7085
Kelly.E.Allen@tulsacc.edu
http://www.tulsacc.edu
Programs: Geology (AS)
Certificates: GIS
Enrollment (2018): A: 19 (5)
Professor:
Kelly E. Allen, (D), Texas Tech, 2000, ZyiZe
Adjunct Professor:
Douglas Ashe, (M), Oklahoma State, 2018, GgZe
Joshua Florie, (M), Tulsa, 2018, OgGg
Christina Opfer, (M), Tusla, 2015, GgoZe

University of Oklahoma

Mewbourne School of Petroleum & Geological Engineering (B,M,D) (2015)
100 East Boyd Street
Sarkeys Energy Center 1210
Norman, OK 73019-1001
p. (405) 325-2921
mpge@ou.edu
http://mpge.ou.edu/
f: https://www.facebook.com/OUMPGE

t: @ou_mpge
Enrollment (2015): B: 975 (133) M: 101 (25) D: 37 (4)
Director:
Chandra S. Rai, (D), Hawaii, 1977, Np
Graduate Liaison:
Deepak Devegowda, (D), Texas A&M, 2008, Np
Director Natural Gas Engineering & Management:
Suresh Sharma, (D), Oklahoma, 1968, Np
Professor:
Younane Abousleiman, (D), Delaware, 1991, Nr
Ramadan Ahmed, (D), Norwegian Inst of Tech, 2001, Np
Jeff Callard, (D), Louisiana State, 1994, Np
Ahmed Ghassemi, (D), Oklahoma, 1996, Nr
Ben Shiau, (D), Oklahoma, 1995
Carl H. Sondergeld, (D), Cornell, 1977, NpYex
Musharraf Zaman, (D), Bangladesh Univ of Eng and Tech, 1975, Np
Associate Professor:
Mashhad Fahes, (D), Imperial Coll, 2006, Np
Ahmad Jamili, (D), Kansas, 2004, Np
Rouzbeh Moghanloo, (D), Texas, 2012, Np
Maysam Pournik, (D), Texas A&M, 2008, Np
Catalin Teodoriu, (D), Ploiesti, Np
Xingru Wu, (D), Texas, 2006, Np
Assistant Professor:
Siddharth Misra, (D), Texas, 2015, Np
Ahmad Sakhaee-Pour, (D), Texas, 2012, Np
Instructor:
Ilham El-Monier, (D), Texas A&M, 2012, Np
Emeritus:
Faruk Civan, (D), Oklahoma, 1978, Np
Roy M. Knapp, (D), Kansas, 1973, Np
Jean-Claude Roegiers, (D), Minnesota, 1974, Nr
Subhash N. Shah, (D), New Mexico, 1974, Np

School of Geosciences (B,M,D) O☒ (2021)
100 East Boyd
710 Energy Center
Norman, OK 73019-0628
p. (405) 325-3253
geosciences@ou.edu
https://geosciences.ou.edu
Programs: Geology and Geophysics
Enrollment (2020): B: 90 (10) M: 38 (16) D: 34 (10)
Director:
Gerilyn S. Soreghan, (D), Arizona, 1992, GsPcZg
Professor:
Younane N. Abousleiman, (D), Delaware, 1991, Gg
R. Douglas Elmore, (D), Michigan, 1981, GdYm
Andrew S. Elwood Madden, (D), Virginia Tech, 2005, ClZaCb
Megan E. Elwood Madden, (D), Virginia Tech, 2005, ClXgCg
Michael H. Engel, (D), Arizona, 1980, Co
Kurt J. Marfurt, (D), Columbia, 1978, Ys
Matthew J. Pranter, (D), Colorado Mines, Go
Stephen R. Westrop, (D), Toronto, 1984, Pi
Associate Professor:
Xiaowei Chen, (D), California (San Diego), 2013, YsGt
Richard Lupia, (D), Chicago, 1997, Pm
John D. Pigott, (D), Northwestern, 1981, GoYeGd
Michael J. Soreghan, (D), Arizona, 1994, Gs
Barry L. Weaver, (D), Birmingham (UK), 1980, Ct
Assistant Professor:
Heather Bedle, (D), Northwestern, 2008, Yg
Brett Carpenter, (D), Penn State, 2012, Gc
Kato Dee, (D), Colorado Mines, HgCg
Shannon Dulin, (D), Oklahoma, 2014, YmGs
Junle Jiang, (D), California Inst of Technology, 2016, Yg
Xiaolei Liu, (D), Bremen (Germany), 2011, Cg
Emeritus:
Judson L. Ahern, (D), Cornell, 1980, Yg
M. Charles Gilbert, (D), California (Los Angeles), 1965, Cp
Charles W. Harper, Jr., (D), Caltech, 1964, Pi
G. Randy Keller, (D), Texas Tech, 1973, YgGtEo
David London, (D), Arizona State, 1981, CpGiz
Shankar Mitra, (D), Johns Hopkins, 1977, Gc
R. Paul Philp, (D), Sydney, 1972, Co
David W. Stearns, (D), Texas A&M, 1969, Gc

University of Tulsa

Dept of Geosciences (B,M) ☒ (2021)
800 S. Tucker Drive
Tulsa, OK 74104-9700
p. (918) 631-2517
jingyi-chen@utulsa.edu
https://engineering.utulsa.edu/academics/geosciences/
Programs: Geosciences with Geology, Environmental, and Petroleum Engineering Options (B); Geosciences (M)
Administrative Assistant: Ann Archer
Enrollment (2019): B: 24 (10) M: 17 (4)
Decker Dawson Associate Professor of Geophysics:
Jingyi Chen, (D), Chinese Acad of Sci, 2005, Yes
Emeritus:
Janet A. Haggerty, (D), Hawaii, 1982, GudGs
Professor:
Kerry Sublette, (D), Tulsa, 1985, Ge
Associate Professor:
Junran Li, (D), Virginia, 2008, Gme
Assistant Professor:
Christine J. Ruhl, (D), Nevada (Reno), 2016, YsGtc
Professor:
Peter J. Michael, (D), Columbia, 1983, GivGz
Associate Professor:
Dennis R. Kerr, (D), Wisconsin, 1989, GsrGt
Steven L. Roche, (D), Colorado Mines, 1997, YesYg
Applied Associate Professor:
Winton Cornell, (D), Rhode Island, 1987, GivCa
Research Associate:
Robert W. Scott, (D), Kansas, 1967, GsrPi
Bethany P. Theiling, (D), New Mexico, 2012, Cs
Emeritus:
J. Bryan Tapp, (D), Oklahoma, 1983, GceZi

Oregon

Central Oregon Community College

Dept of Science (A) (2015)
2600 NW College Way
Bend, OR 97701
p. (541) 383-7557
breynolds@cocc.edu
http://science.cocc.edu/Programs_Classes/Geology/
Associate Professor:
Robert W. Reynolds, (D), Idaho, 1994, Gv

Oregon State University

College of Earth, Ocean, and Atmospheric Sciences (B,M,D) ●⊘ (2019)
104 CEOAS Administration Building
Corvallis, OR 97331-5503
p. (541) 737-1201
contact@coas.oregonstate.edu
http://ceoas.oregonstate.edu
Programs: Earth Science (B); Environmental Sciences (B); Geography and Geospatial Science (B); Geography (M,D); Geology (M,D); Marine Resource Management (M,D); Ocean, Earth, and Atmospheric Sciences (M,D)
Certificates: GIS (UG); GIS (G), Marine Resource Management (G), Water Conflict Management and Transformation (G)
Enrollment (2018): B: 706 (98) M: 64 (21) D: 67 (14)
Senior Research:
Mitchell Lyle, (D), Oregon State, 1978, GgYg
David Mellinger, Cb
R.S. Yeats Professor of Earthquake Geology and Active Tectonics and Associate Dean for Academic Programs:
Eric Kirby, (D), MIT, 2001, GtmGc
Professor, Associate Dean for Strategic Initiatives, and director of the Oregon Climate Change Research Institute (OCCRI):
Philip Mote, (D), Washington, 1994, AsZg
Exec Dir-Marine Studies Initiative:
Jack A. Barth, (D), MIT, 1987, On
Director-Budget & Fiscal Planning:
Sherman H. Bloomer, (D), California (San Diego), 1982, Gi
Director of Ocean Science Program:
Rob Wheatcroft, (D), Washington, 1990, OgGg

Director of Marine Resource Management Program:
Flaxen D. Conway, (M), Oregon State, 1986, Gu
Director of Geology Program:
Adam J. R Kent, (D), Australian Nat, 1995, GiCga
Director of Geography Program:
Julia A. Jones, (D), Johns Hopkins, 1983, So
Director of Environmental Science Program:
Laurence Becker, (D), California (Berkeley), 1989, Zn
Professor:
Jeffrey R. Barnes, (D), Washington, 1983, As
Kelly Benoit-Bird, (D), Hawaii, 2003, Gu
Edward J. Brook, (D), MIT/WHOI, 1993, ClPeGl
Michael E. Campana, (D), Arizona, 1975, Hg
Lorenzo Ciannelli, (D), Washington, 2002, Og
Frederick (Rick) Colwell, (D), Virginia Tech, 1986, Zn
Byron Crump, (D), Washington, 1999
Shanika de Silva, (D), Open (UK), 1987, Gv
John H. Dilles, (D), Stanford, 1984, Em
Gary D. Egbert, (D), Washington, 1987, Yr
Chris Goldfinger, (D), Oregon State, 1994, Yr
Miguel A. Goni, (D), Washington, 1992, Gu
David W. Graham, (D), MIT, 1987, Cm
Burke R. Hales, Washington, 1995, Oc
Merrick C. Haller, (D), Delaware, 1999, OnZrOp
Robert N. Harris, (D), Utah, 1996, Yhr
Michael Harte, (D), Victoria, 1994, Gu
Anthony Koppers, (D), Free (Amsterdam), 1988, CgGv
Michael Kosro, (D), Scripps, 1985, OpZrOn
Jim Lerczak, (D), Scripps, 2000, Op
Ricardo Letelier, (D), Hawaii, 1994, ObZr
Ricardo P. Matano, (D), Princeton, 1991, OpAs
Andrew J. Meigs, (D), S California, 1995, Gc
James N. Moum, (D), British Columbia, 1984, Op
John L. Nabelek, (D), MIT/WHOI, 1984, GtYs
Jonathan Nash, (D), Oregon State, 2000, Op
Roger L. Nielsen, (D), S Methodist, 1983, GizGv
David Noone, (D), Melbourne (Australia), 2001, AmZg
Clare Reimers, (D), Oregon State, 1982, Oc
Peter Ruggiero, (D), Oregon State, 1997, On
Roger Samelson, (D), Oregon State, 1987, Op
Andreas Schmittner, (D), Bern, 1999, AsYr
Adam Schultz, (D), Washington, 1986, YgmRn
Eric Skyllingstad, (D), Wisconsin, 1986, Am
William D. Smyth, (D), Toronto, 1990, Op
Richard Spinrad, Op
Yvette H. Spitz, (D), Old Dominion, 1995, Yr
Frank J. Tepley, III, (D), California (Los Angeles), 1999, GiCs
Marta E. Torres, (D), Oregon State, 1988, Cm
Anne M. Trehu, (D), MIT/WHOI, 1982, YrsGt
Aaron T. Wolf, (D), Wisconsin, 1992, Hg
Senior Research:
Theodore Durland, (D), Hawaii, 2006, Yg
Brian Haley, (D), Oregon State, 2004, Cs
Haruyoshi Matsumoto
Nicholas Tufillaro, (D), Bryn Mawr, 1990, Cb
Director, Water Resources Graduate Program:
Mary V. Santelmann, (D), Minnesota, 1988, Zy
Director of Atmospheric Science Program:
Karen M. Shell, (D), Scripps, 2004, As
Associate Professor:
Anders Carlson, (D), Oregon State, 2006, GlCt
Patrick Corcoran, 1989
Simon P. de Szoeke, (D), Washington, 2004, OpAs
Hannah Gosnell, (D), Colorado, 2000, Zu
Alexander Kurapov, (D), St Petersburg, 1994, Yr
Stephen Lancaster, (D), MIT, 1999, Hs
Kipp Shearman, (D), Oregon State, 1999, Opn
Emily L. Shroyer, (D), Oregon State, 2009, On
Joseph Stoner, (D), Québec (Montréal), 1995, Gsr
George Waldbusser, (D), Maryland (Baltimore), 2008, Ob
Senior Research:
Christo Buizert, (D), Copenhagen, 2012, Yr
Louise A. Copeman, (D), Memorial, 2011, Zn
Jonathan Fram, (D), California (Berkeley), 2005, Op
Joseph Haxel
W. Todd Jarvis, (D), Oregon State, 2006, Hw
Maria Kavanaugh, Cb
Jennifer L. McKay, (D), British Columbia, 2004, Cm
David Rupp, (D), Oregon State, 2005, AsOp
Jenna Tilt, (D), Washington, 2007, Zu
Assistant Professor:
Kim S. Bernard, (D), Rhodes, 2007
Jessica Creveling, (D), Harvard, 2012, GgsGr
Jennifer Fehrenbacher, (D), N Illinois, 1997, Cm
Jennifer Hutchings, Gl
Lauren W. Juranek, Washington, 2007, Cm
Robert Kennedy, (D), Oregon State, 2004, Zri
Larry O'Neill, (D), Oregon State, 2007, AmOg
Alyssa E. Shiel, (D), British Columbia, 2010, ClsCt
Nick Siler
Andrew Thurber, (D), California (San Diego), 2010, Cb
Jamon Van Den Hoek, (D), Wisconsin, 2012, Zur
James R. Watson, Zy
Justin Wettstein, (D), Washington, 2007, As
Greg Wilson, (D), Oregon State, 2013, Onp
Bo Zhao, (D), Ohio State, 2015, Zi
Senior Instructor:
Lorene Yokoyama Becker, (M), Wisconsin, 1999, Zi
Instructor:
Andrea Allan, (D), Oregon State, 2012, As
Lynette de Silva, (M), Indiana, 2000
Randall A. Keller, (D), Oregon State, 1996, Gu
Randall Milstein, (D), Oregon State, 1994
Rebecca Yalcin, (M), Maine, 2001, Gg
Emeritus:
A. Jon Kimerling, (D), Wisconsin, 1976, Zir
Gary P. Klinkhammer, (D), Rhode Island, 1979, CaHsRw
Robert Lloyd Smith, (D), Oregon State, 1964, OpgZn
Robert S. Yeats, (D), Washington, 1958, GtYsNg
Dean of College of Earth, Ocean, and Atmospheric Sciences and Professor:
Roberta Marinelli, (D), South Carolina, 1991, GuOcGe

Portland Community College - Sylvania Campus

Physical Science Dept (A) O (2017)
12000 SW 49th Ave.
Portland, OR 97219
p. 971-722-8209
mnarayan@pcc.edu
http://www.pcc.edu/programs/geology/
Instructor:
Talal Abdulkareem, (D)
Kali Abel, (M)
Sharon Delcambre, (D), AsOg
Gretchen Gebhardt, (M)
Melinda Hutson, (D), Xm
Hollie Oakes-Miller, (M), Gg
Kristy Schepker, (M)
Steve Todd, Am
Jonathan Weatherford, (M), Gg

Portland State University

Dept of Geology (B,M,D) (2020)
P.O. Box 751
Portland, OR 97207
p. (503) 725-3022
geology@pdx.edu
http://www.pdx.edu/geology
t: @PSUGeology
Programs: Geology
Enrollment (2018): B: 85 (18) M: 31 (7) D: 2 (0)
Acting Chair:
Martin J. Streck, (D), Oregon State, 1994, GivCt
Associate Professor:
John T. Bershaw, (D), Rochester, 2011, GsCsHy
Adam M. Booth, (D), Oregon, 2012, GmZr
Robert Benjamin Perkins, (D), Portland State, 2000, Hq
Alexander (Alex) M. Ruzicka, (D), Arizona, 1996, Xm
Assistant Professor:
Ashley Streig, (D), Oregon, 2014, YsGt
Research Associate:
Richard Hugo, (D), Washington State, 1998, Gy
David Percy, (B), Portland State, 1999, Zi
Adjunct Professor:
Sheila Alfsen, (D), GgPgOu
Matthew Brunengo, (D), Portland State, 2012, GgNgGm
Megan Faust, (D), ZeGr
Frank D. Granshaw, (D), Portland State, 2011, ZnGl

Melinda Hutson, (D), Arizona, 1996, Xmc
William Orr, (D), Michigan State, 1968, GgOg
Erik Shafer, Portland State, 2015, Gg
Barry Walker, (D), Oregon State, 2011, GiCgGv
Emeritus:
Scott F. Burns, (D), Colorado, 1980, Ng
Kenneth M. Cruikshank, (D), Purdue, 1991, Gc
Michael L. Cummings, (D), Wisconsin, 1978, GgHg
Andrew G. Fountain, (D), Washington, 1992, Gl
Paul E. Hammond, (D), Washington, 1963, Gi
Ansel G. Johnson, (D), Stanford, 1973, Ye
Richard E. Thoms, (D), California, 1965, Ps
Cooperating Faculty:
Christina L. Hulbe, (D), Chicago, 1998, Gl

Rogue Community College

Science Dept-Physical Sciences-Geology (2015)
3345 Redwood Highway
Grants Pass, OR 97527
p. (541) 245-7527
jvanbrunt@roguecc.edu
http://learn.roguecc.edu/science/physical.htm

Southern Oregon University

Dept of Geology (B) (2015)
1250 Siskiyou Boulevard
Ashland, OR 97520
p. (541) 552-6479
lane@sou.edu
Administrative Assistant: Susan Koralek
Enrollment (2006): B: 45 (5)
Chair:
Charles L. Lane, (D), California (Los Angeles), 1987, Hg
Dean, Science:
Joseph L. Graf, Jr., (D), Yale, 1975, Em
Professor:
Jad A. D'Allura, (D), California (Davis), 1977, Gc
Associate Professor:
Eric Dittmer, (M), San Jose State, 1972, Gg
Adjunct Professor:
Vernon J. Crawford, (M), Oregon, 1970, Gg
Harry W. Smedes, (D), Washington, 1959, Gi
Richard Ugland, (M), Utah, 1974, Gg
Emeritus:
Monty A. Elliott, (D), Oregon State, 1971, Gr
William B. Purdom, (D), Arizona, 1960, Gx

Southwestern Oregon Community College

Dept of Geology (A) (2020)
1988 Newmark Ave
Coos Bay, OR 97420-2912
p. (541) 888-7216
rmetzger@socc.edu
https://www.socc.edu/geology
Enrollment (2013): A: 2 (0)
Professor:
Ronald A. Metzger, (D), Iowa, 1991, PmZePs

Tillamook Bay Community College

Associate of Science (2015)
2510 First Street
Tillamook, OR 97141
robertpietruszka@tillamookbaycc.edu

Treasure Valley Community College

Career and Technical Education ● ☒ (2018)
650 College Blvd.
Ontario, OR 97914
p. (541) 881-8866
dtinkler@tvcc.cc
http://www.tvcc.cc.or.us/science
f: https://www.facebook.com/profile.php?id=100005312898088
Instructor:
Dorothy Tinkler, (D), Texas Tech, 2003, Zi

University of Oregon

Dept of Earth Sciences (B,M,D) ○⊘ (2021)
1272 University of Oregon
Eugene, OR 97403-1272
p. (541) 346-4573
jroering@uoregon.edu
https://earthsciences.uoregon.edu
Programs: Geology; Earth Science; Geophysics; Paleontology; Environmental Geoscience;
Enrollment (2019): B: 87 (21) M: 6 (7) D: 51 (5)
Lillis Professor of Volcanology:
Josef Dufek, (D), Washington, 2006, Gv
Department Head:
Joshua J. Roering, (D), California (Berkeley), 2000, Gm
Professor:
Ilya N. Bindeman, (D), Chicago, 1998, CsGvCl
Rebecca J. Dorsey, (D), Princeton, 1989, Gr
Samantha Hopkins, (D), California (Berkeley), 2005, Pg
Eugene D. Humphreys, (D), Caltech, 1985, YsGt
Mark H. Reed, (D), California (Berkeley), 1977, CgEm
Alan W. Rempel, (D), Cambridge, 2001, YgNrGl
Gregory J. Retallack, (D), New England, 1978, PbSoGa
Douglas R. Toomey, (D), MIT/WHOI, 1987, YsGt
Paul Wallace, (D), California (Berkeley), 1991, GviCg
Ray J. Weldon, (D), Caltech, 1986, Gc
Associate Professor:
Edward B. Davis, (D), California (Berkeley), 2005, PvePq
Emilie E. Hooft, (D), MIT, 1996, Yr
Qusheng Jin, (D), Illinois (Urbana), 2003, Cg
Leif Karlstrom, (D), California (Berkeley), 2011, Yx
Carol Paty, (D), Washington, 2006
Matthew Polizzotto, (D), Stanford, 2007, CqSc
Dave Sutherland, (D), MIT, 2008, Op
Amanda Thomas, (D), California (Berkeley), 2012, Ys
James Watkins, (D), California (Berkeley), 2010, Cg
Assistant Professor:
Estelle Chaussard, (D), Miami, 2013, Yd
Brittany Erickson, (D), California, 2010, Ygs
Thomas Giachetti, (D), Clermont-Ferrand, 2010, Gvu
Diego Melgar, (D), Scripps, 2014, Yd
Valerie J. Sahakian, (D), Scripps, 2015, Yg
Meredith Townsend, (D), Stanford, 2017, Gv
Instructor:
Marli G. Miller, (D), Washington, 1997, Gc
Emeritus:
A. Dana Johnston, (D), Minnesota, 1983, Cp
Marvin A. Kays, (D), Washington (St Louis), 1960, GpcGt
William N. Orr, (D), Michigan State, 1967, Pm
Norman M. Savage, (D), Sydney, 1968, Pi
Office & Business Manager:
Sandy K. Thoms, (B), Portland State, 1993

Dept of Geography (B,M,D) ⊘ (2020)
107 Condon Hall
1251 University of Oregon
Eugene, OR 97403-1251
p. (541) 346-4555
uogeog@uoregon.edu
http://geography.uoregon.edu
f: https://www.facebook.com/universityoforegongeography/
t: @uogeog
Enrollment (2009): B: 167 (55) M: 22 (9) D: 19 (5)
Department Head:
W. Andrew Marcus, (D), Colorado, 1987
Professor:
Patrick Bartlein, (D), Wisconsin, 1978, Pe
Dan Gavin, (D), Washington, 2000, ZyPle
Amy Lobben, (D), Michigan State, 1999, ZinZn
Patricia McDowell, (D), Wisconsin, 1980, Gm
Alexander Murphy, (D), Chicago, 1987, Zn
Laura Pulido, (D), California (Los Angeles), 1991
Xiaobo Su, (D), Singapore, 2007, Zn
Peter Walker, (M), Oregon, 1966, Zn
Associate Professor:
Daniel Buck, (D), California (Berkeley), 2002, Zn
Shaul Cohen, (D), Chicago, 1991, Zn
Mark Fonstad, (D), Arizona State, 2000, Zy
Lucas Silva, (D), Guelph, 2011

Assistant Research Professor:
Melissa Lucash, (D), SUNY, 2005
Assistant Professor:
Sarah Cooley, (D), Brown, 2020
Carolyn Fish, (D), Penn State, 2018
Leigh Johnson, (D), California (Berkeley), 2011
Henry Hui Luan, (D), Waterloo, 2016
Johnny Ryan, (D), Aberystwyth, 2018
Sr. Instructor:
Nicholas Kohler, (D), Oregon, 2004, Zi
Instructor:
Donald Holtgrieve, (D), Oregon, 1973
Leslie McLees, (D), Oregon, 2012
Emeritus:
Stanton Cook, (D), California (Berkeley), 1960, Zn
Alvin Urquhart, California (Berkeley), 1962, Zn
Ronald Wixman, (D), Columbia, 1978, Zn

Western Oregon University

Earth and Physical Science Dept. (B) ☒ (2019)
345 N. Monmouth Ave.
Monmouth, OR 97361
p. (503) 838-8398
taylors@wou.edu
http://www.wou.edu/earthscience
Programs: B.S. / B.A. Earth Science
Certificates: Minor / Certificate in Geographic Information Sci
Enrollment (2018): B: 50 (10)
Professor:
Jeffrey A. Myers, (D), California (Santa Barbara), 1998, Gs
Stephen B. Taylor, (D), West Virginia, 1999, Gm
Jeffrey H. Templeton, (D), Oregon State, 1998, GivZe
Instructor:
Don Ellingson, (M), W Oregon, 1988, AmZgXg
Matthew Goslin, (M), Oregon State, 1999, Gmg
Jeremiah Oxford, (M), Oregon State, 2006, Zg
Grant Smith, (D), Oregon State, 2012, Zg
Phillip Wade, (M), San Diego State, 1991, Zge

Willamette University

Department of Environmental Science (B) ☒ (2019)
900 State Street
Salem, OR 97301
p. (503) 370-6587
spike@willamette.edu
http://willamette.edu/cla/envs
f: https://www.facebook.com/groups/186102921735448/
Programs: Environmental Science
Enrollment (2018): B: 99 (0)
Chair:
Scott Pike, (D), Georgia, 2000, Gag
Professor:
Karen Arabas, (D), Penn State, 1997, Zn
Endowed Dempsey Chair:
Joe Bowersox, (D), Wisconsin, 1995, Zn
Assistant Professor:
Melinda Butterworth, (D), Arizona, 2015
Katja Meyer, (D), Penn State, 2008

Pennsylvania

Allegheny College

Dept of Geology (B) ☒ (2020)
520 North Main Street
Meadville, PA 16335
p. (814) 332-2350
robrien@allegheny.edu
https://sites.allegheny.edu/geo/
Programs: BA, Geology, BS, Geology, BS, Environmental Geology
Certificates: OSHA 40 hour online safety training
Enrollment (2020): B: 13 (6)
Dept. Chair:
Rachel O'Brien, (D), Washington State, 2000, HwGe
Assistant Professor:
Matthew J. Carter, (D), Minnesota (Twin Cities), 2013, Gct
Kathryn L. Tamulonis, (D), Cornell, 2010, Gsr
Emeritus:
Robert K. Schwartz, (D), Indiana, GsrGt
Currently Provost and Dean of the College:
Ron B. Cole, (D), Rochester, 1993, Gt

Bloomsburg University

Dept of Environmental, Geographical, and Geological Sciences (B) ☒ (2019)
400 East Second Street
Bloomsburg, PA 17815-1301
p. (570) 389-4108
mshepard@bloomu.edu
https://intranet.bloomu.edu/eggs-department
Programs: Professional Geology, Environmental Geoscience, Geography and Planning. Minors in Hydrology, Spatial Analysis and GIS, Geoscience, Geography.
Administrative Assistant: Cheryl Smith
Enrollment (2018): B: 200 (50)
Professor:
John E. Bodenman, (D), Penn State, 1995, Zu
Sandra J. Kehoe-Forutan, (D), Queensland, 1991, Znu
Brett T. McLaurin, (D), Wyoming, 2000, GrsGd
Michael K. Shepard, (D), Washington (St Louis), 1994, XgYgZr
Cynthia Venn, (D), Pittsburgh, 1996, OgClOc
Associate Professor:
Patricia J. Beyer, (D), Arizona State, 1997, HsZyGm
Jeffrey C. Brunskill, (D), SUNY (Buffalo), 2005, ZiAmZy
Jennifer B. Whisner, (D), Tennessee, 2010, GmHw
S. Christopher Whisner, (D), Tennessee, 2005, GciGz
Assistant Professor:
Tina Delahunty, (D), Florida, 2002, Zri
Benjamin Franek, (D), Connecticut, 2013, HsZy
John G. Hintz, (D), Kentucky, 2005, Zin
Adrian Van Rythoven, (D), Toronto, 2012, GxzEg
Dana Xiao, (D), California (Santa Barbara), 2013, Zi

Bryn Mawr College

Dept of Geology (B) ☒ (2020)
101 North Merion Avenue
Bryn Mawr, PA 19010-2899
p. (610) 526-5115
aweil@brynmawr.edu
http://www.brynmawr.edu/geology/
Programs: Geology
Enrollment (2020): B: 22 (7)
Professor:
Arlo B. Weil, (D), Michigan, 2001, GctYm
Associate Professor:
Donald C. Barber, (D), Colorado, 2001, GesOn
Selby Cull-Hearth, (D), Washington, 2011, XgGzx
Pedro J. Marenco, (D), S California, 2007, PgCsPg
Instructor:
Katherine N. Marenco, (D), S California, 2008, PiePg
Emeritus:
Maria Luisa B. Crawford, (D), California (Berkeley), 1965, GxzGp

Bucknell University

Geology and Environmental Geosciencs (B) (2016)
231 O'Leary Center
Lewisburg, PA 17837
p. (570) 577-1382
cdaniel@bucknell.edu
http://www.bucknell.edu/Geology
f: http://www.facebook.com/BucknellGeology
Administrative Assistant: Carilee Dill
Enrollment (2016): B: 36 (7)
Chair:
Christopher G. Daniel, (D), Rensselaer, 1998, Gp
Professor:
Mary Beth Gray, (D), Rochester, 1991, Gc
Carl S. Kirby, (D), Virginia Tech, 1993, Cl
R. Craig Kochel, (D), Texas, 1980, Gm
Jeffrey M. Trop, (D), Purdue, 2000, Gs
Associate Professor:
Ellen K. Herman, (D), Penn State, 2006, Hw
Robert W. Jacob, (D), Brown, 2006, Yg

Emeritus:
Jack C. Allen, (D), Princeton, 1962, GizGe
Edward Cotter, (D), Princeton, 1963, GmPg
Laboratory Director:
Bradley C. Jordan, (M), Rhode Island, 1983, Gg

California University of Pennsylvania

Dept of Earth Sciences (B) (2015)
250 University Avenue
California, PA 15419
p. (724) 938-4180
wickham@calu.edu
http://www.cup.edu/eberly/earthscience
Administrative Assistant: Pamela Higinbotham
Enrollment (2015): B: 195 (25)
Chair:
Thomas Wickham, (D), Penn State, 2000, Zu
Professor:
Kyle Fredrick, (D), SUNY (Buffalo), 2008, GgHgGm
Associate Professor:
Thomas Mueller, (D), Illinois, 1999, Zi
Assistant Professor:
John Confer, (D), Penn State, 1997, Zn
Swarndeep S. Gill, (D), Wyoming, 2002, As
Chad Kauffman, (D), Nebraska, 2000, As
Susan Ryan, (D), Calgary, 2005, Zg

Carnegie Museum of Natural History

Section of Vertebrate Paleontology (2015)
4400 Forbes Avenue
Pittsburgh, PA 15213
p. (412) 622-5782
beardc@carnegiemnh.org
http://www.carnegiemnh.org/vp/
Curator:
K. Christopher Beard, (D), Johns Hopkins, 1989, Pv
Assistant Curator:
Matthew C. Lamanna, (D), Pennsylvania, 2004, PvgPe
Curator:
David S. Berman, (D), California (Los Angeles), 1969, PggPv
Mary R. Dawson, (D), Kansas, 1957, Pv
Preparator:
Dan Pickering, (B), Carnegie Mellon, 1983, Zn
Alan R. Tabrum, (M), SD Mines, 1981, Pv
Norman Wuerthele, (B), Pittsburgh, 1966, Pv
Curator & Associate Director:
Zhexi Luo, (D), California (Berkeley), 1987, Pv
Collections Manager:
Amy C. Henrici, (M), Pittsburgh, 1990, Pv

Clarion University

Dept of Biology and Geosciences (B) O (2019)
840 Wood Street
Clarion, PA 16214
p. (814) 393-2317
cking@clarion.edu
http://www.clarion.edu/BIGS
Programs: B.S. Geology, B.S. Environmental Geoscience, Minors in Geology and Environmental Geoscience
Certificates: GIS
Enrollment (2019): B: 60 (17)
Professor:
Yasser M. Ayad, (D), Montreal, 2000, Zi
Valentine U. James, (D), Texas A&M, ZuRwZn
Anthony J. Vega, (D), Louisiana State, 1994, AtmOp
Craig E. Zamzow, (D), Texas, 1983, Gi
Adjunct Professor:
Sheila Kasar, (D), ZreGe
Shane Smith, (D), Washington State, 2005

Delaware County Community College

STEM (A) (2015)
901 Media Line Road
Media, PA 19063
p. (610) 359-5082
dchilders@dccc.edu
http://www.dccc.edu/
Professor:
Daniel Childers, (D), Delaware, 2014, ZgOuZi
Associate Professor:
Jennifer L. Snyder, (D), W Michigan, 1998, Zg

Dickinson College

Dept of Earth Sciences (B) ☒ (2020)
P.O. Box 1773
Carlisle, PA 17013-2896
p. (717) 245-1355
edwardsb@dickinson.edu
https://www.dickinson.edu/earthsciences
f: https://www.facebook.com/pages/category/Product-Service/Dickinson-College-Department-of-Earth-Sciences-108884862477555/
t: @dsonearthsci
Programs: Earth Sciences (geoscience and environmental geoscience tracks)
Administrative Assistant: Debra Peters
Enrollment (2020): B: 16 (6)
Chair:
Benjamin R. Edwards, (D), British Columbia, 1997, GivCg
Professor:
Marcus M. Key, Jr., (D), Yale, 1988, PiGsa
Associate Professor:
Peter B. Sak, (D), Penn State, 2002, Gcm
Assistant Professor:
Jorden L. Hayes, (D), Wyoming, 2016, Ygs
Alyson M. Thibodeau, (D), Arizona, 2012, CcGaCs
Emeritus:
Jeffery W. Niemitz, (D), S California, 1978, ClOuGn
Noel Potter, Jr., (D), Minnesota, 1969, Gmc
Technician:
Robert Dean, (M), Texas (El Paso), 2004, Gi

Environmental Studies & Environmental Science (2015)
P.O. Box 1773
Carlisle, PA 17013-2896
p. (717) 245-1355
arnoldt@dickinson.edu
Administrative Assistant: Patricia Braught
Associate Professor:
Candie Wilderman, (D), Johns Hopkins, 1984, Hs
Visiting Professor:
Kirsten Hural, (D), Cornell, 1997, Gg

Drexel University

Dept of Biodiversity, Earth & Environmental Science (B,M,D) ☒ (2020)
2024 MacAlister Hall
3250 Chestnut Street
Philadelphia, PA 19104
p. (215) 571-4651
bees@drexel.edu
http://drexel.edu/bees/
f: https://www.facebook.com/groups/DrexelBEES/
Programs: Geoscience; Environmental Science; Environmental Studies
Enrollment (2019): B: 15 (5) D: 5 (0)
Pilsbry Chair of Malacology:
Gary Rosenberg, (D), Harvard, 1989, Pi
Professor:
David Velinsky, (D), Old Dominion, 1987, OcCms
Associate Professor:
Ted Daeschler, (D), Pennsylvania, 1998, PvGgPg
Loyc Vanderkluysen, (D), Hawaii, 2008, GviGz
Assistant Professor:
Marie J. Kurz, (D), Florida, 2013, CqbHw
Amanda Lough, (D), Washington (St Louis), 2014, Ysg
Jocelyn A. Sessa, (D), Penn State, 2009, PeCsPq
Elizabeth Watson, (D), California (Berkeley), Zc
Adjunct Professor:
Mitch Cron, (M), Pennsylvania, 2013, Gge
Stephen Huxta, (M), Pennsylvania, 2017, Gg
Carl Mastropaolo, (M), Drexel, Hw

Edinboro University of Pennsylvania

Dept of Geosciences (B) ☒ (2018)
126 Cooper Hall
230 Scotland Road
Edinboro, PA 16444-0001
p. (814) 732-2529
geosciences@edinboro.edu
http://www.edinboro.edu/academics/schools-and-departments/cshp/departments/geosciences/
f: https://www.facebook.com/pages/Edinboro-University-Geosciences-Department/426407214146067
Programs: Geology (B); Environmental Studies (B); GIS (B)
Enrollment (2017): B: 108 (24)

Chair:
Brian S. Zimmerman, (D), Washington State, 1991, Gzx

Professor:
Baher A. Ghosheh, (D), SUNY (Buffalo), 1988, Zn
David Hurd, (D), Cleveland State, 1997, Zg
Kerry A. Moyer, (D), Penn State, 1993, As
Laurie A. Parendes, (D), Oregon State, 1997, Zn
Joseph F. Reese, (D), Texas, 1995, GctZe
Eric Straffin, (D), Nebraska, 2000, GmsSo
Dale Tshudy, (D), Kent State, 1993, Pi

Associate Professor:
Karen Eisenhart, (D), Colorado, 2004, Zy
Wook Lee, (D), Ohio State, Zi

Assistant Professor:
Richard Deal, (D), South Carolina, 2000, Zi
Tamara Misner, (D), Pittsburg State, 2013, GmHs

Elizabethtown College

Dept of Engineering and Physics (B) ☒ (2019)
One Alpha Drive
Esbenshade Room 160
Elizabethtown, PA 17022-2298
p. (717) 361-1392
mcfaddenj@etown.edu
http://www.etown.edu/PhysicsEngineering.aspx
Administrative Assistant: Jennifer McFadden

Associate Professor:
Michael A. Scanlin, (D), Penn State, Ye

Emeritus:
David Ferruzza, (M), MIT, 1967, AsZn

Franklin and Marshall College

Dept of Earth and Environment (B) ⃠ (2021)
PO Box 3003
Lancaster, PA 17604-3003
p. (717) 358-4133
mbetrone@fandm.edu
http://www.fandm.edu/earth-environment
f: https://www.facebook.com/FM-Department-of-Earth-Environment
t: @FandMENE
Programs: Geosciences, Environmental Science, Environmental Studies majors; minor in Science, Technology and Society
Enrollment (2020): B: 11 (9)

Director, Center for Sustainable Environment:
Sarah Dawson, (D), Utah State, 2008, Zn

Chair of Environmental Science Program:
Andrew P. deWet, (D), Cambridge, 1989, Ge

Chair Department of Earth and Environment:
Christopher J. Williams, (D), Pennsylvania, 2002, PeSb

Professor:
Carol B. de Wet, (D), Cambridge, 1989, GsdGn
Dorothy J. Merritts, (D), Arizona, 1987, Gm
Stanley A. Mertzman, (D), Case Western, 1971, GizZm
James E. Strick, (D), Princeton, 1997, RhGe
Robert C. Walter, (D), Case Western, 1981, Cc

Associate Professor:
Eilzabeth De Santo, (D), Univ Coll (UK), Zn
Zeshan Ismat, (D), Rochester, 2002, Gc

Assistant Professor:
Eve Bratman, (D), American, 2009, Zn
Eric Hirsch, (D), Chicago, Zn

Emeritus:
Robert S. Sternberg, (D), Arizona, 1982, YmGa
Roger D. K. Thomas, (D), Harvard, 1970, PgRh

Laboratory Director:
Emily Wilson, (M), Idaho, 2013, CgGi

Director of F&M Science Outreach & Teaching Professor of Geosciences:
Timothy D. Bechtel, (D), Brown, 1989, GeYg

Gannon University

Earth Science Program (B) (2015)
109 University Square
PMB 3183
Erie, PA 16541
p. (814) 871-7453
homan001@gannon.edu
http://www.gannon.edu/

Assistant Professor:
Johnson Olanrewaju, (D), Penn State, 2002, Cg

Harrisburg Area Community College

Science (A) (2017)
One HACC Drive
Harrisburg, PA 17110
p. 800-222-4222
rkdennis@hacc.edu
http://www.hacc.edu
f: https://www.facebook.com/HACC64
t: @hacc_info
Enrollment (2016): A: 2 (0)

Professor:
James E. Baxter, P.G., (M), Penn State, 1983, GgHwGm

Indiana University of Pennsylvania

Dept of Geography and Regional Planning (2015)
Indiana, PA 15705
p. (724) 357-2250
donaldb@iup.edu
https://www.iup.edu/georegionalplan/

Dept of Geoscience (B) O✓ (2019)
306 Weyandt Hall
Kopchick College Natural Sciences
Indiana, PA 15705
p. (724) 357-2379
geoscience-info@iup.edu
http://www.iup.edu/geoscience
Programs: Geology
Earth and Space Science Education
Enrollment (2019): B: 40 (16)

Chair:
Nicholas Deardorff, (D), Oregon, Gv

Professor:
Karen Rose Cercone, (D), Michigan, 1984, Zeg
Jon C. Lewis, (D), Connecticut, 1998, Gc

Associate Professor:
Kenneth S. Coles, (D), Columbia, 1988, XgZeYg
Katie Farnsworth, (D), Virginia Inst of Marine Sci, 2003, Ong
Gregory Mount, (D), Florida Atlantic, 2014, Hy

Assistant Professor:
Yvonne K. Branan, (D), Michigan Tech, 2007, Gv
Jonathan P. Warnock, (D), N Illinois, 2013, PemPv

Emeritus:
Joseph C. Clark, (D), Stanford, 1966, Gr
Frank W. Hall, (D), Montana, 1969, Gc
Darlene S. Richardson, (D), Columbia, 1974, Gd
Connie J. Sutton, (M), Indiana (Penn), 1968, Ze
John F. Taylor, (D), Missouri, 1984, PsiGs

On Leave:
Steven A. Hovan, (D), Michigan, 1993, Ou

Juniata College

Dept of Environmental Science & Studies (2015)
1700 Moore Street
Huntingdon, PA 16652
yohn@juniata.edu
http://www.juniata.edu/departments/environmental/

Dept of Geology (B) ●☒ (2019)
1700 Moore St
Huntingdon, PA 16652

p. (814) 641-3601
johanesen@juniata.edu
http://www.juniata.edu/academics/departments/geology/
Programs: Geology; Environmental Geology; Earth and Space Science Education
Enrollment (2017): B: 25 (10)

Dept. Chair:
Ryan Mathur, (D), Arizona, 2000, CeYgHw

Associate Professor:
Matthew G. Powell, (D), Johns Hopkins, 2005, PiqPe

Assistant Professor:
Katharine Johanesen, (D), S California, 2011, GzxGc

Research Associate:
Adam J. Ianno, (D), S California, 2015, GgiCu

Emeritus:
Laurence J. Mutti, (D), Harvard, 1978, GxzSc
J. Peter Trexler, (D), Michigan, 1964, Ps
Robert H. Washburn, (D), Columbia, 1966, Gs

Kutztown University of Pennsylvania

Dept of Physical Science (B) ☒ (2018)
Boehm Science Building Room 135
Kutztown, PA 19530
p. (610) 683-4447
simpson@kutztown.edu
http://www.kutztown.edu/acad/geology
Administrative Assistant: Caecilia Holt
Enrollment (2018): B: 35 (11)

Chair:
Edward L. Simpson, (D), Virginia Tech, 1987, Gs

Professor:
Kurt Friehauf, (D), Stanford, 1998, EmCgGx
Laura Sherrod, (D), W Michigan, 2007, YgHwGa
Sarah E. Tindall, (D), Arizona, 2000, Gc

Assistant Professor:
Erin Kraal, (D), California (Santa Cruz), XgGm
Adrienne Oakley, (D), Hawaii, 2009, YrOun
Jacob Sewall, (D), California (Santa Cruz), 2004, GeAs

Lafayette College

Dept of Geology & Environmental Geosciences (B) ☒ (2020)
116 Van Wickle Hall
4 South College Drive
Easton, PA 18042
p. (610) 330-5193
geology@lafayette.edu
http://geology.lafayette.edu
f: @LafayetteGeology
Department Secretary: Rohana Meyerson
Enrollment (2020): B: 37 (14)

Professor:
Dru Germanoski, (D), Colorado State, 1989, Gm
Kira Lawrence, (D), Brown, 2006, Oo

Associate Professor:
Lawrence L. Malinconico, (D), Dartmouth, 1982, YgGcv
David Sunderlin, (D), Chicago, 2004, Gg

Assistant Professor:
Tamara Carley, (D), Vanderbilt, 2014, GviCg

Research Associate:
Mary Ann Malinconico, (D), Columbia, 2002, Eo

Emeritus:
Guy L. Hovis, (D), Harvard, 1971, GzxCg

Laboratory Coordinator:
John R. Wilson, (M), Virginia Tech, 2001, Zi

Lehigh University

Dept of Earth & Environmental Sciences (B,M,D) O☒ (2020)
1 W. Packer Ave.
Bethlehem, PA 18015-3001
p. (610) 758-3660
ahg212@lehigh.edu
http://www.ees.lehigh.edu
f: https://www.facebook.com/LehighEES/
Enrollment (2018): B: 61 (15) M: 8 (3) D: 12 (1)

Department Chair:
Gray E. Bebout, (D), California (Los Angeles), 1989, Gp

Professor:
David J. Anastasio, (D), Johns Hopkins, 1988, Gca
Robert K. Booth, (D), Wyoming, 2003, ZnnPc
Edward B. Evenson, (D), Michigan, 1972, Gl
Kenneth P. Kodama, (D), Stanford, 1978, Ym
Anne S. Meltzer, (D), Rice, 1988, Ys
Frank J. Pazzaglia, (D), Penn State, 1993, Gm
Dork Sahagian, (D), Chicago, 1987, PeGvr
Zicheng Yu, (D), Toronto, 1997, Pe
Peter K. Zeitler, (D), Dartmouth, 1983, Cc

Associate Professor:
Benjamin S. Felzer, (D), Brown, 1995, ZcoZn
Donald P. Morris, (D), Colorado, 1990, Zn
Stephen C. Peters, (D), Michigan, 2001, Cl
Joan Ramage, (D), Cornell, 2001, ZrGlm

Assistant Professor:
Jill I. McDermott, (D), MIT/WHOI, 2015, Cm

Research Associate:
Bruce D. Idleman, (D), SUNY (Albany), 1990, Cc
Joshua Stachnik, (D), Wyoming, 2010, Ys

Emeritus:
Bobb Carson, (D), Washington, 1971, GusGt
Bruce R. Hargreaves, (D), California (Berkeley), 1977, Ob

Lock Haven University

Dept of Geology & Physics (B) ☒ (2018)
301 West Church Street
Lock Haven, PA 17745-2390
p. (570) 484-2048
mkhalequ@lockhaven.edu
Programs: Geology
Administrative Assistant: Denise Rupert
Enrollment (2018): B: 30 (6)

Professor:
Loretta D. Dickson, (D), Connecticut, 2006, GizGe
Md. Khalequzzaman, (D), 1998, HwOnZi

Associate Scientist:
Thomas C. Wynn, (D), Virginia Tech, 2004, GsPiEo

Mansfield University

Dept of Geosciences (A,B) O☒ (2019)
Belknap Hall
Mansfield, PA 16933
p. (570) 662-4613
jdemchak@mansfield.edu
http://geoggeol.mansfield.edu/
Enrollment (2016): A: 10 (6) B: 124 (42)

Chair:
Jennifer Demchak, (D), West Virginia, 2005, Hs

Associate Professor:
Christopher F. Kopf, (D), Massachusetts, 1999, Gcp
Lee Stocks, (D), Kent State, 2010, ZyGgm

Assistant Professor:
Linda Kennedy, (D), North Carolina (Greensboro), 2012, Zy

Mercyhurst University

Dept of Geology (B,M,D) (2015)
501 East 38th Street
Erie, PA 16546
p. (814) 824-2581
rbuyce@mercyhurst.edu
http://mai.mercyhurst.edu
Enrollment (2012): B: 16 (3)

Director:
James M. Adovasio, (D), Utah, 1970, GafGs

Professor:
M. Raymond Buyce, (D), Rensselaer, 1975, GsaOn

Assistant Professor:
Nicholas Lang, (D), Minnesota, 2006, GvXgGc
Scott C. McKenzie, (B), Edinboro, 1976, PgXmZe
Lyman Perscio, (D), New Mexico, 2012, GsSpHg

Adjunct Professor:
Frank Vento, (D), Pittsburg State, 1985, GaSoGm

Millersville University

Dept of Earth Sciences (B,M) (2015)
PO Box 1002

Millersville, PA 17551
p. (717) 872-3289
esci@millersville.edu
http://www.millersville.edu/esci
Enrollment (2010): B: 23 (4)

Chair:
Richard D. Clark, (D), Wyoming, 1987, As

Professor:
Alex J. DeCaria, (D), Maryland, 2000, As
L. Lynn Marquez, (D), Northwestern, 1998, Cg
Sepideh Yalda, (D), St Louis, 1997, As

Associate Professor:
Sam Earman, (D), New Mexico Tech, 2004, HwCsl
Ajoy Kumar, (D), Old Dominion, 1996, OpZr
Jason R. Price, (D), Michigan State, 2003, Gs
Todd D. Sikora, (D), Penn State, 1996, As

Assistant Professor:
Robert Vaillancourt, (D), Rhode Island, 1996, Obc

Instructor:
Joseph Calhoun, (B), Penn State, As
Mary Ann Schlegel, (M), MIT/WHOI, 1998, Og

Professor:
Robert S. Ross, (D), Florida State, 1977, As

Emeritus:
William M. Jordan, (D), Wisconsin, 1965, Gs
Bernard L. Oostdam, (D), Delaware, 1971, Ou
Charles K. Scharnberger, (D), Washington (St Louis), 1971, Gc

Montgomery County Community College

Dept of Science, Technology, Engineering, and Math (A) (2015)
Blue Bell, PA 19422
p. (215) 641-6446
rkuhlman@mc3.edu

Professor:
Robert Kuhlman, (M), Bryn Mawr, 1975, Gg

Instructor:
George Buchanan, (M), Drexel, 1992, Ng

Adjunct Professor:
Laurie Martin-Vermilyea, (D), South Carolina, 1992, Ze
Frank Roberts, (D), Bryn Mawr, 1969, Gp
Kelly C. Spangler, (M), Drexel, 2003
Anthony Stevens, (M), Florida, 1981, Ge

Moravian College

Dept of Physics & Earth Science (B) ☒ (2019)
1200 Main Street
Bethlehem, PA 18018-6650
p. (610) 861-1437
krieblek@moravian.edu
http://www.physics.moravian.edu
Programs: Geology; General Science; Physics
Administrative Assistant: Ann Sywensky
Enrollment (2017): B: 1 (1)

Chair:
Kelly Krieble, (D), Lehigh, 1993, ZnnZn

Pennsylvania State University, Erie

Geoscience Dept (2015)
Erie, PA 16510
p. (814) 898-6277
amf11@psu.edu
http://www.personal.psu.edu/faculty/a/m/amf11/

Chair:
Anthony M. Foyle

Assistant Professor:
Eva Tucker, (M), Cincinnati, 1962, Gg

Pennsylvania State University, Monaca

Dept of Geosciences (B) (2015)
100 University Drive
Monaca, PA 15061
p. (412) 773-3867
jac7@psu.edu
http://www.br.psu.edu/

Assistant Professor:
John A. Ciciarelli, (D), Penn State, 1971, Gg

Pennsylvania State University, University Park

Dept of Geosciences (B,M,D) ● ☒ (2019)
503 Deike Building
University Park, PA 16802-2714
p. (814) 865-6711
demian@psu.edu
http://www.geosc.psu.edu/
Programs: Geosciences BS, Earth Science & Policy BS, Earth Sciences BS, Geosciences MS, PhD
Certificates: Sustainability Certificate, MEd certificate
Administrative Assistant: Amy L.. Homan
Enrollment (2018): B: 133 (0) M: 20 (0) D: 59 (0)

Head:
Demian M. Saffer, (D), California (Santa Cruz), 1999, Hw

Evan Pugh Professor:
Richard B. Alley, (D), Wisconsin, 1987, Gl
James F. Kasting, (D), Michigan, 1979, As

Distinguished Professor:
Katherine H. Freeman, (D), Indiana, 1991, Cos

Director, Earth & Mineral Science Museum:
Russell W. Graham, (D), Texas, 1976, Pv

Director, Earth & Env Systems Inst:
Susan L. Brantley, (D), Princeton, 1987, Cg

Director, Astrobiology Research Center:
Christopher H. House, (D), California (Los Angeles), 1999, Pg

Associate Head, Graduate Programs:
Mark E. Patzkowsky, (D), Chicago, 1992, Pg

Professor:
Charles J. Ammon, (D), Penn State, 1991, Ys
Sridhar Anandakrishnan, (D), Wisconsin, 1990, Ys
David M. Bice, (D), California (Berkeley), 1989, Gg
Timothy J. Bralower, (D), California (San Diego), 1986, Pe
Donald M. Fisher, (D), Brown, 1988, GctZm
Kevin P. Furlong, (D), Utah, 1981, Gt
Tanya Furman, (D), MIT, 1989, GiCu
Peter J. Heaney, (D), Johns Hopkins, 1989, GzClGe
Klaus Keller, (D), Princeton, 2000, Og
Lee R. Kump, (D), S Florida, 1986, ClPeCm
Michael E. Mann, (D), Yale, 1998, As
Chris Marone, (D), Columbia, 1988, Yx
Andrew A. Nyblade, (D), Michigan, 1992, Yg
Peter D. Wilf, (D), Pennsylvania, 1998, Pg

Senior Scientist:
Todd Sowers, (D), Rhode Island, 1991, Cs

(Associate Head for Undergraduate Programs):
Maureen D. Feineman, (D), California (Berkeley), 2004, Cp

Associate Professor:
Matthew S. Fantle, (D), California (Berkeley), 2005, Cs
Elizabeth Hajek, (D), Wyoming, 2009, Gs
Peter C. LaFemina, (D), Miami, 2005, Yd
Jennifer L. Macalady, (D), California (Davis), 2000, PgClSb
Eliza Richardson, (D), MIT, 2002, YsZe

Assistant Professor:
Roman DiBiase, (D), Arizona State, 2011, Gmt
Bradford Foley, (D), Yale, 2014, YgXyGt
Sarah Ivory, (D), Arizona, 2013, Pl
Tess A. Russo, (D), California (Santa Cruz), 2012, Hw
Christelle Wauthier, (D), Liege, 2011, Zn

Emeritus:
Shelton S. Alexander, (D), Caltech, 1963, Ys
Michael A. Arthur, (D), Princeton, 1979, OuClGs
Hubert L. Barnes, (D), Columbia, 1958, CgEmCe
Roger J. Cuffey, (D), Indiana, 1966, PiePv
David H. Eggler, (D), Colorado, 1967, CpGiv
Terry Engelder, (D), Texas A&M, 1973, Nr
David (Duff) P. Gold, (D), McGill, 1963, GcgGx
Earl K. Graham, Jr., (D), Penn State, 1969, Yx
Roy J. Greenfield, (D), MIT, 1965, YgsYu
Albert L. Guber, (D), Illinois, 1962, Pe
Benjamin F. Howell, Jr., (D), Caltech, 1949, Ys
Derrill M. Kerrick, (D), California (Berkeley), 1968, Gp
Hiroshi Ohmoto, (D), Princeton, 1969, Cs
Richard R. Parizek, (D), Illinois, 1961, Hw
Arthur W. Rose, (D), Caltech, 1958, Cge
Rudy L. Slingerland, (D), Penn State, 1977, Gs
Barry Voight, (D), Columbia, 1965, GveGg
William B. White, (D), Penn State, 1962, CgGzy

Dept of Meteorology and Atmospheric Science (B,M,D) (2020)
503 Walker Building
University Park, PA 16802-5013
p. (814) 865-0478
meteodept@meteo.psu.edu
http://www.met.psu.edu
Programs: Meteorology and Atmospheric Science, Dual Title PhD in Climate Science
Certificates: Certificate of Achievement in Weather Forecasting, Graduate Certificate in Weather and Climate Analytics
Professor and Head:
David J. Stensrud, (D), Penn State, 1992, Am
Evan Pugh Professor:
James F. Kasting, (D), Michigan, 1979, AsPc
Distinguished Professor:
William H. Brune, (D), Johns Hopkins, 1978, Am
Michael E. Mann, (D), Yale, 1998, AsZoPc
Director, Institute for Computational and Data Sciences:
Jenni L. Evans, (D), Monash, 1990, Am
Associate Head, Undergraduate Program:
Jon Nese, (D), Penn State, 1989, Am
Associate Head, Graduate Program:
Paul M. Markowski, (D), Oklahoma, 2000
Professor:
Eugene E. Clothiaux, (D), Brown, Am
Kenneth J. Davis, (D), Colorado, 1992, Am
Jose D. Fuentes, (D), Guelph, 1992, As
John Harlim, (D), Maryland, 2006, Am
Jerry Y. Harrington, (D), Colorado State, 1997, Am
Gregory S. Jenkins, (D), Am
Sukyoung Lee, (D), Princeton, 1991, Am
Raymond G. Najjar, (D), Princeton, 1990, OcpAt
Johannes Verlinde, (D), Colorado State, 1992, Am
George S. Young, (D), Colorado State, Am
Associate Professor:
Steven J. Greybush, (D), Maryland, 2011, Am
Matthew R. Kumjian, (D), Oklahoma, 2012, Am
Kelly A. Lombardo, (D), Stoney Brook, 2011, As
Assistant Professor:
Anthony Didlake, Jr., (D), Washington, As
Melissa Gervais, (D), McGill, As
Laifang Li, (D), Duke, 2014, AsZo
Ying Pan, (D), Penn State, 2014, As
Colin Zarzycki, (D), Michigan, 2014, As
Research Assistant:
William F. Ryan, (M), Maryland, 1990, Am
Director of Meteorological Computing:
Chad Bahrmann, (M), North Carolina State, 1997, Am
Research Associate:
Arthur Person, (M), Penn State, 1983, Am
William Syrett, (M), Penn State, 1987, Am
Emeritus:
Peter R. Bannon, (D), Colorado, 1979, Am
Craig F. Bohren, (D), Arizona, 1975, Am
John J. Cahir, (D), Penn State, 1971, Am
Toby N. Carlson, (D), Imperial Coll (UK), 1965, Am
John H. E. Clark, (D), Florida State, 1969, Am
John A. Dutton, (D), Wisconsin, Am
William M. Frank, (D), Colorado State, 1976, Am
Alistair B. Fraser, (D), Imperial Coll (UK), 1968, Am
J. Michael Fritsch, (D), Colorado State, 1978, Am
Charles L. Hosler, (D), Penn State, 1951, Am
Dennis Lamb, (D), Washington, 1970, Am
Nelson L. Seaman, (D), Penn State, 1977, Am
Hampton N. Shirer, (D), Penn State, 1978, Am
David R. Stauffer, (D), Penn State, 1990, Am
Dennis W. Thomson, (D), Wisconsin, 1968, Am
John C. Wyngaard, (D), Penn State, 1967, Am
Associate Dean of Undergraduate Education:
Yvette P. Richardson, (D), Oklahoma, 1999, Ams

Dept of Plant Science (A,B,M,D) (2015)
119 Tyson Building
University Park, PA 16802
p. (814) 865-6541
rpm12@psu.edu
http://plantscience.psu.edu/
Professor:
Jean-Marc Bollag, (D), Basel (Switzerland), 1959, Sb
Edward J. Ciolkosz, (D), Wisconsin, 1967, Sd
Daniel D. Fritton, (D), Iowa State, 1968, Sp
Sridhar Komarneni, (D), Wisconsin, 1973, Sc
Gary W. Petersen, (D), Wisconsin, 1965, Sd
Associate Professor:
Peter J. Landschoot, (D), Rhode Island, 1988, So
Gregory W. Roth, (D), Penn State, 1987, So
Assistant Professor:
Rick L. Day, (D), Penn State, 1991, Zu
Research Associate:
Barry M. Evans, (M), Penn State, 1977, Sd
Adjunct Professor:
Andrew S. Rogowski, (D), Iowa State, 1964, Sp
Lawrence A. Schardt, (D), Penn State, 2000, SoHw

Earth and Mineral Sciences Museum & Art Gallery ☒ (2020)
116 Deike Building
University Park, PA 16802
p. (814) 863-8554
museum@ems.psu.edu
https://museum.ems.psu.edu/
f: https://www.facebook.com/EMSMAAG
t: @emsmaag
Director:
Jane Cook, (D), Wisconsin (Madison), 1998, ZmeZn

John and Willie Leone Family Dept of Energy and Mineral Engineering (B,M,D) ☒ (2018)
110 Hosler Building
University Park, PA 16802
p. (814) 865-3437
eme@ems.psu.edu
http://www.eme.psu.edu/mnge
Program Chair, and Deike Endowed Chair in Mining Engineering:
Jeffery L. Kohler, (D), Penn State, 1982, Nm
Assistant Professor:
Shimin Liu, (D), S Illinois, 2013, Nm

Point Park University

Dept of Environmental Studies (A,B) (2015)
201 Wood Street
Pittsburgh, PA 15222-1994
p. (412) 392-3900
jkudlac@pointpark.edu
http://www.pointpark.edu/Academics/Schools/SchoolofArtsandSciences/Departments/NaturalSciencesandEngineeringTechnology
Administrative Assistant: Roberta T. Gallick
Head:
Mark O. Farrell, (D), Carnegie Mellon, 1978, Zn
Professor:
John J. Kudlac, (D), Pittsburgh, Ng

Shippensburg University

Geography-Earth Science Department (B,M) ● (2021)
1871 Old Main Drive
Shearer Hall 104
Shippensburg, PA 17257
p. (717) 477-1685
tlmyers@ship.edu
https://www.ship.edu/geo-ess/
f: https://www.facebook.com/ShipGeoESS/
Programs: B.Sc. in Geoenvironmental Studies, B.Sc. in Environmental Sustainability, B.Sc. in Geography - GIS, B.S.Ed. Science Education-Earth and Space Science, M.Sc. Geoenvironmental Studies
Certificates: GIS Certificate, GIS Minor, Geography Minor, Marine Science Minor
Administrative Assistant: Tammy Myers
Enrollment (2020): B: 134 (60) M: 26 (16)
Chair:
Christopher J. Woltemade, (D), Wisconsin, 1993, HgRwGm
Professor:
Scott A. Drzyzga, (D), Michigan State, 2007, ZiuGl
Alison E. Feeney, (D), Michigan State, 1998, ZinZn
Thomas P. Feeney, (D), Georgia, 1997, ZyGeHw

Kurtis G. Fuellhart, (D), Penn State, 1998, ZnnZn
Timothy W. Hawkins, (D), Arizona State, 2004, AsmHg
Claire A. Jantz, (D), Maryland, 2005, ZuiZc
Paul G. Marr, (D), Denver, 1996, ZfyZi
George M. Pomeroy, (D), Akron, 1999, ZuyZn
Janet S. Smith, (D), Georgia, 1999, Zi

Associate Professor:
Michael T. Applegarth, (D), Arizona State, 2001, GmZrSo
Sean R. Cornell, (D), Cincinnati, 2008, GgsOn
Joseph T. Zume, (D), Oklahoma, 2007, HgYug

Assistant Professor:
Russell Hedberg, (D), Penn State, 2018, ZiSoZc

Slippery Rock University

Dept of Geography, Geology, and the Environment (B) (2015)
Slippery Rock, PA 16057
p. (724) 738-2048
jack.livingston@sru.edu
https://www.sru.edu/academics/colleges-and-departments/ches/departments/geography-geology-and-the-environment
Administrative Assistant: Bonita L. Vinton
Enrollment (2006): B: 50 (9)

Chair:
Jack Livingston

Professor:
Tamra A. Schiappa, (D), Idaho, 1999, PiGrZe
Michael J. Zieg, (D), Johns Hopkins, 2001, Gi

Associate Professor:
Patrick A. Burkhart, (D), Lehigh, 1994, Hg

Assistant Professor:
Patricia A. Campbell, (D), Pittsburgh, 1994, Gc
Xianfeng Chen, (D), West Virginia, 2005, Zr
Julie A. Snow, (D), Rhode Island, 2002, As
Michael G. Stapleton, (D), Delaware, 1995, So

State Museum of Pennsylvania

Section of Paleontology & Geology (2015)
300 North Street
Harrisburg, PA 17120-0024
p. (717) 783-9897
c-sjasinsk@pa.gov
http://www.statemuseumpa.org/geologyc.html
f: https://www.facebook.com/StateMuseumofPA

Acting Curator:
Steven E. Jasinski, (D), Pennsylvania, pend, PvgPg

Susquehanna University

Dept of Earth & Environmental Sciences (B) (2015)
514 University Ave
Selinsgrove, PA 17870
p. (570) 372-4216
straubk@susqu.edu
http://www.susqu.edu/ees
Enrollment (2009): B: 29 (7)

Chair:
Jennifer M. Elick, (D), Tennessee, 1999, Pe
Katherine H. Straub, (D), Colorado State, 2002, Am

Associate Professor:
Daniel E. Ressler, (D), Iowa State, 1998, Sp
Derek J. Straub, (D), As

Assistant Professor:
Ahmed Lachhab, (D), Iowa, 2006, Hw

Temple University

Earth & Environmental Science (B,M,D) (2019)
1901 N. 13th Street
Beury Hall, Rm. 326
Philadelphia, PA 19122-6081
p. (215) 204-8227
scox@temple.edu
http://www.temple.edu/geology
f: https://www.facebook.com/tu.geology
Programs: BS, Geology, BA, Geology, Minor, Geology, BS, Environmental Science, Masters, Geology, PhD, Geoscience
Certificates: Environmental Professional Training Undergraduate Certificate
Administrative Assistant: Shelah Cox

Chair:
Nicholas Davatzes, (D), Stanford, 2003, GcNrZn

Professor:
David E. Grandstaff, (D), Princeton, 1974, Cl
Jonathan Nyquist, (D), Wisconsin, 1986, Ygu
Laura Toran, (D), Wisconsin, 1986, HwZu

Associate Professor:
Ilya Buynevich, (D), Boston, 2001, GmPeOn
Alexandra K. Davatzes, (D), Stanford, 2007, GsXgZe
Dennis O. Terry, (D), Nebraska, 1998, SaPcGr
Allison Tumarkin-Deratzian, (D), Pennsylvania, 2003, Pv

Assistant Professor:
Steven Chemtob, (D), 2012
Natalie Flynn, (D), Temple, 2015, Gx
Bojeong Kim, (D), GzZa
Atsuhiro Muto, (D), 2010, GlYg
Sujith Ravi, (D), HqZuRw
Jesse Thornburg, (D), Rutgers, 2016, GsPs

Instructor:
Timothy Davis, (M), Temple, 2011, Gg

Emeritus:
George Myers, (D), Yale, 1965, Gz

Asst. Lab Manager/Bldg. Coordinator:
James Ladd, (M)

Thiel College

Dept of Environmental Science (B) (2015)
Greenville, PA 16125
p. (412) 589-2821
areinsel@thiel.edu

Professor:
James H. Barton, (D), N Colorado, 1977, Zy

University of Pennsylvania

Dept of Earth & Environmental Science (B,M,D) (2020)
240 S. 33rd Street
Hayden Hall
Philadelphia, PA 19104-6316
p. (215) 898-5724
earth@sas.upenn.edu
http://www.sas.upenn.edu/earth/
Programs: Undergraduate majors in Earth Science (EASC) and Environmental Studies (ENVS), as well as minors in Environmental Science, Environmental Studies, Geology, and Sustainability and Environmental Management.
Certificates: Various certificates within our professional masters programs; see MES and MSAG websites at: https://www.sas.upenn.edu/earth/graduate/professional-masters-programs
Administrative Assistant: Sally A.. Cardy
Enrollment (2020): B: 30 (19) M: 29 (11) D: 17 (12)

Chair:
Brenda B. Casper, (D), Utah, 1982

Undergraduate Chair:
Alain F. Plante, (D), Alberta, 2001, SboCo

Professor of Practice:
Howard Neukrug, (B), Pennsylvania, 1978, Hs

Distinguished Professor:
Joseph Francisco, (D), MIT, 1983, Ac

Professor:
Reto Gieré, (D), ETH (Switzerland), 1990, GzCgGe
Douglas Jerolmack, (D), MIT, 2006, GmYxHq

Graduate Chair:
David Goldsby, (D), Minnesota, 1997, Yg

Associate Professor:
Irina Marinov, (D), Princeton, 2005, ZoOg

Assistant Professor:
Ileana Pérez-Rodríguez, (D), Rutgers, 2012, Po
Lauren Sallan, (D), Chicago, 2012, PqvPe

Lecturer:
Willig B. Sarah, (D), Pennsylvania, 1988, Ge

Emeritus:
Robert F. Giegengack, Jr., (D), Yale, 1968, Gg
Arthur H. Johnson, (D), Cornell, 1975, So
Hermann W. Pfefferkorn, (D), Muenster (Germany), 1968, PbePs
Stephen P. Phipps, (D), Princeton, 1984, Gc

Laboratory Manager:
David R. Vann, (D), Pennsylvania, 1993, GeSfXm

Teaching Faculty:
Jane Dmochowski, (D), Caltech, 2004, Yg
Gomaa I. Omar, (D), Pennsylvania, 1985, Cc
Education Administrator:
Nicholas Crivaro
Director, Professional Masters Programs:
Yvette Bordeaux, (D), Pennsylvania, 2000, Pg
Department Administrator:
Joan Buccilli
Associate Director:
Maria Andrews, (M)

University of Pittsburgh

Dept of Geology & Environmental Science (B,M,D) ●☒ (2019)
200 SRCC Building
4107 O'Hara Street
Pittsburgh, PA 15260-3332
p. (412) 624-8780
gpsgrad@pitt.edu
http://www.geology.pitt.edu
Enrollment (2018): B: 218 (79) M: 9 (2) D: 24 (7)
Chair:
Josef Werne, (D), Northwestern, 2000, CosGn
Professor:
Mark B. Abbott, (D), Minnesota, 1995, Gs
Emily M. Elliott, (D), Johns Hopkins, 2003, Cbs
William P. Harbert, (D), Stanford, 1987, Ym
Nadine McQuarrie, (D), Arizona, 2001, Gct
Michael S. Ramsey, (D), Arizona State, 1996, Zr
Associate Professor:
Daniel J. Bain, (D), Johns Hopkins, 2004, HgGmZu
Rosemary C. Capo, (D), California (Los Angeles), 1990, Cl
Brian W. Stewart, (D), California (Los Angeles), 1990, CclCq
Assistant Professor:
Eitan Shelef
Brian Thomas
Environmental Reporter, Pittsburgh Post-Gazette:
S. Don Hopey
Instructor:
Emily Collins
Lecturer:
R. Ward Allebach
Danielle Andrews-Brown, (D)
Charles E. Jones, (D), Oxford, 1992, GgsPg
Adjunct Professor:
Matthew C. Lamanna, (D), Pennsylvania, 2004, Pv
Steven C. Latta
John S. Pallister, (D), California (Santa Barbara), 1980, GviGg
Serge Shapiro
Matthew Watson
Emeritus:
Thomas Anderson
Bruce W. Hapke, (D), Cornell, 1962, Xy
Edward G. Lidiak, (D), Rice, 1963, Gi

University of Pittsburgh, Bradford

Dept of Petroleum Technology (A) (2015)
300 Campus Drive
Bradford, PA 16701-2898
p. (814) 362-7569
aap@pitt.edu
http://www.upb.pitt.edu/academics/petroleumtechnology.aspx
Administrative Assistant: Janet Shade
Enrollment (2010): A: 28 (8)
Program Director:
Assad I. Panah, (D), Oklahoma, 1966, GorGc

West Chester University

Dept of Earth and Space Sciences (B,M) ●⊘ (2020)
750 South Church Street
Merion Science Center
West Chester, PA 19383
p. (610) 436-2727
hbosbyshell@wcupa.edu
https://www.wcupa.edu/sciences-mathematics/earthSpace-Sciences/
f:https://www.facebook.com/WCU-Earth-Space-Sciences-143447267219/
Programs: Geoscience (B,M); Earth Systems (B); Geology (B); Earth and Space Science Education (B)
Certificates: GIS (B,M)
Enrollment (2019): B: 85 (16) M: 25 (12)
Professor:
Richard M. Busch, (D), Pittsburgh, 1984, GrPgZe
Marc R. Gagne, (D), Georgia, 1994, Xa
Martin F. Helmke, (D), Iowa State, 2003, HwSdZg
Timothy M. Lutz, (D), Pennsylvania, 1979, Gq
Daria L. Nikitina, (D), Delaware, 2000, Gm
Chair:
Joby Hilliker, (D), Penn State, 2002, Am
Associate Professor:
Howell Bosbyshell, (D), Bryn Mawr, 2001, GcpGt
Karen Schwarz, (D), Arizona State, XaZe
Assistant Professor:
Yong Hoon Kim, (D), South Carolina, 2005, OgZr
Christopher Roemmele, (D), Purdue, 2017, ZeGgZg
Adjunct Professor:
Cynthia V. Hall, (D), Georgia Tech, 2008, Cg
Vicky Helmke, (M), Iowa State, Gg
James "Sandy" Maxwell, (B), Ze
Jamie Vann, (M), CgGg

Wilkes University

Dept of Environmental Engineering & Earth Sciences (B) O☒ (2018)
84 West South Street
Wilkes-Barre, PA 18766
p. (570) 408-4610
sid.halsor@wilkes.edu
http://wilkes.edu/academics/colleges/science-and-engineering/environmental-engineering-earth-sciences/
Programs: Geology; Earth & Environmental Sciences; Environmental Engineering
Certificates: Sustainability
Enrollment (2018): B: 7 (0)
Chair:
Marleen Troy, (D), Drexel, 1989, Ht
Professor:
Dale A. Bruns, (D), Idaho State, 1981, ZirSf
Sid P. Halsor, (D), Michigan Tech, 1989, Giv
Kenneth M. Klemow, (D), SUNY (Syracuse), 1982, Pg
Prahlad N. Murthy, (D), Texas A&M, 1993, AsZnn
Michael A. Steele, (D), Wake Forest, 1988, Pg
Brian E. Whitman, (D), Michigan Tech, 1998, HqwSb
Associate Professor:
Holly Frederick, (D), Penn State, 1999, Sdb
Assistant Professor:
Matthew S. Finkenbinder, (D), Pittsburg State, 2015, GsmGl
Bobak Karimi, (D), Pittsburg State, 2014, GctYg
Lecturer:
Mark A. Kaster, (M), Saint Louis, 1993, Am
Julie McMonagle, (M), Lehigh, 1991, Gge
Emeritus:
James M. Case, (D), Dalhousie, 1979, Ob
Brian T. Redmond, (D), Rensselaer, 1982, GsHwZg

York College of Pennsylvania

Dept of Physical Science (2015)
York, PA 17405
p. (717) 846-7788 x333
jforesma@ycp.edu
Assistant Professor:
William (Bill) Kreiger, (D), Penn State, 1976, GisZg
Adjunct Professor:
Ralph Eisenhart, (M), Penn State, 1994, Gg
Jeri L. Jones, (B), Catawba, 1977, Ga

Puerto Rico

University of Puerto Rico

Dept of Geology (B,M) O⌕ (2020)
PO Box 9000
Mayaguez, PR 00681-9000
p. (787) 265-3845

lizzette.rodriguez1@upr.edu
https://www.uprm.edu/geology/
f: https://www.facebook.com/geologyuprm/
t: @GeologyUPRM
Programs: Geology
Enrollment (2020): B: 115 (16) M: 14 (2)

Director:
Lizzette A. Rodriguez, (D), Michigan Tech, 2007, GviZr

Professor:
Fernando Gilbes, (D), S Florida, 1996, ZrGuZi
James Joyce, (D), Northwestern, 1985, NgGcp
Alberto Lopez, (D), Northwestern, 2006, YdGtYs
Wilson R. Ramirez, (D), Tulane, 2000, GudOu
Hernan Santos, (D), Colorado, 1999, PiGdr

Associate Professor:
Thomas Hudgins, (D), Michigan, 2014, GiCpGv
Kenneth Stephen Hughes, (D), N Carolina State, 2014, Gcm
Elizabeth A. Vanacore, (D), Rice, 2008, YsuYx

Director of Puerto Rico Seismic Network:
Victor Huerfano, (D), Puerto Rico, 2004, YsgGt

Rhode Island

Brown University

Dept of Earth, Environmental and Planetary Sciences (B,M,D) ☒ (2019)
Box 1846, 324 Brook Street
Providence, RI 02912
p. (401) 863-3339
DEEPS@brown.edu
http://www.brown.edu/academics/earth-environmental-planetary-sciences/
f: https://www.facebook.com/BrownGeologicalSciences
t: @BrownGeoSci
Enrollment (2018): B: 0 (12) M: 0 (10) D: 55 (8)

Chair:
Greg Hirth, (D), Brown, 1991, GcyYg

Professor:
Reid F. Cooper, (D), Cornell, 1983, Gy
Karen M. Fischer, (D), MIT, 1988, Ys
Timothy D. Herbert, (D), Princeton, 1987, Pe
Yongsong Huang, (D), Bristol, 1997, Co
Yan Liang, (D), Chicago, 1994, Cp
Amanda H. Lynch, (D), Melbourne (Australia), 1993, AsGe
John F. Mustard, (D), Brown, 1990, Zr
James M. Russell, (D), Minnesota, 2004, Gn
Alberto E. Saal, (D), MIT/WHOI, 2000, CgGi

Senior Scientist:
David Murray, (D), Oregon State, 1987, Ou

Associate Professor of Research:
Steven C. Clemens, (D), Brown, 1990, Ou

Associate Professor:
Colleen Dalton, (D), Harvard, 2007, Ys
Baylor Fox-Kemper, (D), MIT/WHOI, 2003, OpYnAt
Meredith Hastings, (D), Princeton, 2004, As
Christian Huber, (D), California (Berkeley), 2009, Gv
Ralph E. Milliken, (D), Brown, 2006
Stephen Parman, (D), MIT, 2001, CpgCt
Victor Tsai, (D), Ys

Assistant Professor:
Alexander J. Evans, (D)
Jung-Eun Lee, (D), California (Berkeley), 2005

Emeritus:
Donald W. Forsyth, (D), MIT/WHOI, 1974, YrsGt
L. Peter Gromet, (D), Caltech, 1979, Cc
James W. Head, III, (D), Brown, 1969, XgGvt
John F. Hermance, (D), Toronto, 1967, HqZrHw
Paul C. Hess, (D), Harvard, 1968, Gi
E. Marc Parmentier, (D), Cornell, 1975, Yg
Carle M. Pieters, (D), MIT, 1977, Zr
Warren L. Prell, (D), Columbia, 1974, Ou
Malcolm J. Rutherford, (D), Johns Hopkins, 1968, Cp
Peter H. Schultz, (D), Texas, 1972, Xg
Jan A. Tullis, (D), California (Los Angeles), 1971, Gcy
Terry E. Tullis, (D), California (Los Angeles), 1971, Yx
Thompson Webb, III, (D), Wisconsin, 1971, PeIAs

Academic Program Manager:
Patricia M. Davey, (B), Rhode Island Coll, 1986, Zn

Academic Department Manager:
Dina Egge, (M), 2015

Community College of Rhode Island

Dept of Physics and Engineering (Geology & Oceanography Div) (A) ☒ (2020)
400 East Avenue
Warwick, RI 02886
p. (401) 825-2156
kkortz@ccri.edu
http://www.ccri.edu/physics/

Professor:
Emily Burns, (D), Rhode Island, GgOgZi
Karen M. Kortz, (D), Rhode Island, 2009, ZeGg
Paul White, (D), Gg

Associate Professor:
Duayne Rieger, (D), Ys

Assistant Professor:
Roger M. Hart, (M), 2018, Gg

Providence College

Biology Dept (A,B) ⃠ (2019)
1 Cunningham Sq
Providence, RI 02918
p. (401) 865-2150
ctoth@providence.edu
Programs: BA Biology, BS Biology, BA Biology/Secondary Ed, BS Biology/Secondary Ed, BA Biology/Optometry, BS Biology/Optometry, BS Environmental Biology
Certificates: Neuroscience Certificate

Chair:
Charles Toth

Roger Williams University

College of Arts & Sciences (B) (2015)
Bristol, RI 02809
p. (401) 254-3087
jborden@rwu.edu
Department Secretary: Valerie Catalano

Head:
Mark D. Gould, (D), Rhode Island, 1973, Ob

Chair:
Paul Webb

Professor:
Thomas Doty, (D), Rhode Island, 1977, Ob
Richard Heavers, (D), Rhode Island, 1977, Op
Thomas J. Holstein, (D), Brown, 1969, Zn
Martine Villalard-Bohnsack, (D), Rhode Island, 1971, Ob

Assistant Professor:
Tim Scott, (D), SUNY (Stony Brook), 1993, Ob

University of Rhode Island

Dept of Geosciences (B,M,D) ☒ (2019)
9 East Alumni Ave.,
Kingston, RI 02881
p. (401) 874-2265
http://web.uri.edu/geo/
t: @URI_GEO
Programs: Geology; Geological Oceanography
Certificates: Hydrology
Enrollment (2018): B: 42 (8) M: 6 (0) D: 6 (0)

Associate Dean:
Anne I. Veeger, (D), Arizona, 1991, HwCl

Professor:
Thomas B. Boving, (D), Arizona, 1999, Hw
David E. Fastovsky, (D), Wisconsin, 1986, PvGsPs

Chair:
Brian K. Savage, (D), Caltech, 2004, Ys

Associate Professor:
Dawn Cardace, (D), Washington, GpPg
Simon E. Engelhart, (D), Pennsylvania, OnGmYs

Assistant Professor:
Ananya Mallik, (D), Rice, 2014, Gx
Soni M. Pradhanang, (D), HsqHq

Emeritus:
J. Allan Cain, (D), Northwestern, 1962, Gx
O Don Hermes, (D), North Carolina, 1967, Gi

Daniel P. Murray, (D), Brown, 1976, ZeGtp

Graduate School of Oceanography (M,D) (2015)
215 South Ferry Road
Narragansett, RI 02882
p. (401) 874-6222
bcorliss@uri.edu
http://www.gso.uri.edu
Enrollment (2010): M: 41 (12) D: 31 (8)

Research Professor:
Theodore J. Smayda, (D), Oslo, 1967, Ob

Associate Dean:
Mark Wimbush, (D), California (San Diego), 1969, Op

Professor:
Robert D. Ballard, (D), Rhode Island, 1974, Ga
Steven N. Carey, (D), Rhode Island, 1982, Ou
Jeremy S. Collie, (D), MIT/WHOI, 1985, Ob
Peter Cornillon, (D), Cornell, 1973, Op
Steven L. D'Hondt, (D), Princeton, 1989, Ou
Edward G. Durbin, (D), Rhode Island, 1976, Ob
Isaac Ginis, (D), Inst Exp Meteor, 1986, Op
Tetsu Hara, (D), MIT, 1990, Op
Paul E. Hargraves, (D), William & Mary, 1968, Ob
David L. Hebert, (D), Dalhousie, 1988, Op
Christopher Kincaid, (D), Johns Hopkins, 1990, Ou
John King, (D), Minnesota, 1983, Ou
Roger Larson, (D), California (San Diego), 1970, Ou
Margaret Leinen, (D), Rhode Island, 1980, Ou
John T. Merrill, (D), Colorado, 1976, Oc
S. Bradley Moran, (D), Dalhousie, 1991, Oc
Scott W. Nixon, (D), North Carolina, 1970, Ob
Candace Oviatt, (D), Rhode Island, 1967, Ob
Hans Thomas Rossby, (D), MIT, 1966, Op
Lewis Rothstein, (D), Hawaii, 1983, Op
Haraldur Sigurdsson, (D), Durham (UK), 1970, Ou
Jennifer Specker, (D), Oregon State, 1980, Ob
Robert Tyce, (D), California (San Diego), 1976, Ou
D. Randolph Watts, (D), Cornell, 1973, Op
Karen Wishner, (D), California (San Diego), 1979, Ob

Associate Professor:
Brian G. Heikes, (D), Michigan, 1984, As
Yang Shen, (D), Brown, 1994, Ou
David C. Smith, (D), California (San Diego), 1994, Ob

Marine Research Scientist:
Percy Donaghay, (D), Oregon State, 1980, Ob
Kathleen Donohue, (D), Rhode Island, 1996, Op
Alfred K. Hanson, Jr., (D), Rhode Island, 1981, Oc
Barbara K. Sullivan-Watts, (D), Oregon State, 1977, Og

Associate Dean:
John Farrell, (D), Brown, 1991, Ou

Adjunct Professor:
Lawrence J. Buckley, (D), New Hampshire, 1975, Oc
Richard J. Pruell, (D), Rhode Island, 1984, Co
Charles T. Roman, (D), Delaware, 1981, Ob

Marine Research Scientist:
Dian J. Gifford, (D), Dalhousie, 1986, Ob
Robert D. Kenney, (D), Rhode Island, 1984, Ob

Emeritus:
H. Perry Jeffries, (D), Rutgers, 1959, Ob
John A. Knauss, (D), California, 1959, Op
Theodore A. Napora, (D), Yale, 1964, Ob
Michael E. Pilson, (D), California (San Diego), 1964, Oc
James G. Quinn, (D), Connecticut, 1967, Oc
Kenneth A. Rahn, (D), Michigan, 1971, Oc
Saul B. Saila, (D), Cornell, 1952, Ob
Jean-Guy E. Schilling, (D), MIT, 1966, OuCuc
John M. Sieburth, (D), Minnesota, 1954, Ob
Elijah V. Swift, (D), Johns Hopkins, 1967, Ob

South Carolina

Clemson University

Bob Campbell Geology Museum (A,B,M,D) (2015)
140 Discovery Lane
Clemson, SC 29634-0130
p. (864) 656-4602
tsteadm@clemson.edu
http://www.clemson.edu/geomuseum

Director:
Todd A. Steadman, (M), Louisiana State, 1987, ZnnZn

Curator:
David J. Cicimurri, (M), SD Mines, 1998, Pv

Curator:
Christian M. Cicimurri, (M), SD Mines, 1999, Pv

Environmental Engineering and Earth Sciences (B,M) (2015)
321 Calhoun Drive
Room 445 Brackett Hall
Clemson, SC 29634-0919
p. (864) 656-3438
clemson-eees@lists.clemson.edu
http://www.clemson.edu/ces/departments/eees/
Administrative Assistant: Cynthia Rae Gravely
Enrollment (2013): B: 40 (9) M: 8 (6)

Chair:
Tanju Karanfil, (D), Michigan, 1995, NgZnn

Professor:
James W. Castle, (D), Illinois, 1978, GseHw
Ronald W. Falta, (D), California (Berkeley), 1990, Hq
Cindy M. Lee, (D), Colorado Mines, 1990, GeClZe
Lawrence C. Murdoch, (D), Cincinnati, 1991, Hw
Mark Schlautman, (D), Caltech, 1992, ClHgSc

Assistant Professor:
Stephen M.J Moysey, (D), Stanford, 2005, HwYuZe
Brian A. Powell, (D), Clemson, 2004, Cg
Lindsay C. Shuller-Nickles, (D), Michigan, 2010, Gz

Research Associate:
Scott E. Brame, (M), Clemson, 1993, Hw

Lecturer:
Alan B. Coulson, (D), South Carolina, 2009, PgGgCs

Adjunct Professor:
C. Brannon Andersen, (D), Syracuse, 1994, Cl
Christian M. Cicimurri, (M), South Dakota, 1999, Pv
Brian Looney, (D), Minnesota, 1984, Hq
Vaneaton Price, (D), North Carolina, 1969, Ce
Tommy Temples, (D), South Carolina, 1996, GoYg

Emeritus:
Lois B. Krause, (D), Clemson, 1996, Ze
Fred Molz, (D), Stanford, 1970, Sp
John R. Wagner, (D), South Carolina, 1993, ZeGm
Richard D. Warner, (D), Stanford, 1971, Gz

College of Charleston

Dept of Geology & Environmental Geosciences (B,M) ○⊘ (2018)
66 George Street
Charleston, SC 29424
p. (843) 953-5589
callahant@cofc.edu
http://geology.cofc.edu/
f: https://www.facebook.com/Geology.CofC/
t: @AquaTimCal
Programs: Geology
Enrollment (2018): B: 100 (43)

Chair:
Timothy J. Callahan, (D), New Mexico Tech, 2001, Hwq

Associate Professor:
K. Adem Ali, (D), Kent State, 2011, ZrHwNg
Erin K. Beutel, (D), Northwestern, 2000, Gct
John Chadwick, (D), Florida, 2002, GiZrGt
Mitchell W. Colgan, (D), California (Santa Cruz), 1990, PeGe
M. Scott Harris, (D), Delaware, 2000, OnGam
Steven C. Jaumé, (D), Columbia, 1994, Ys
Norman S. Levine, (D), Purdue, 1995, ZiGeNg
Cassandra R. Runyon, (D), Hawaii, 1988, XgSoZe
Leslie R. Sautter, (D), South Carolina, 1990, Ob
Vijay M. Vulava, (D), Swiss Fed Inst Tech, 1998, CgHwSc

Assistant Professor:
Barbara Beckingham, (D), Maryland, 2011, Cl
Theodore R. Them, II, (D), Virginia Tech, 2016, CmOcZc

Emeritus:
James L. Carew, (D), Texas, 1978, PgGd
Michael P. Katuna, (D), N Carolina, 1974, Gus
Robert L. Nusbaum, (D), Missouri (Rolla), 1984, Gz
Alexander W. Ritchie, (D), Texas, 1975, Gc

Laboratory Director:
Robin Humphreys, (M), Charleston, 2000, Ge

Furman University

Earth and Environmental Sciences (B) ☒ (2018)
3300 Poinsett Highway
Greenville, SC 29613
p. (864) 294-2052
nina.anthony@furman.edu
http://ees.furman.edu
Administrative Assistant: Nina Anthony
Enrollment (2018): B: 82 (35)

Chair:
C. Brannon Andersen, (D), Syracuse, 1994, ClGe

Professor:
Geoffrey Habron, (D), Oregon State, 1999, Zn
William A. Ranson, (D), Massachusetts, 1979, GxzGp

Associate Professor:
Weston R. Dripps, (D), Wisconsin, 2003, HwsGe
Suresh Muthukrishnan, (D), Purdue, 2002, ZiGmZr

Assistant Professor:
Karen Allen, (D), Georgia, 2016, Zn
Ruth F. Aronoff, (D), Purdue, 2016, Gc
Matt Cohen, (D), Arizona State, 2015, Zn

Adjunct Professor:
Courtney Quinn, (D), Nebraska, 2012, Zn
Melissa Ranhofer, (D), South Carolina, 2009, Gg

Visiting Research Professor:
Christopher Romanek, (D), Texas A&M, 1991, Cls

Emeritus:
John M. Garihan, (D), Penn State, 1973, Gct
Kenneth A. Sargent, (D), Oklahoma, 1973, Hy

Laboratory Director:
Lori Nelsen, (M), Furman, 2007, Ca

University of South Carolina

School of the Earth, Ocean & Environment (B,M,D) ●⊘ (2019)
701 Sumter St
EWS 617
Columbia, SC 29208
p. (803) 777-4535
khamilton@geol.sc.edu
http://sc.edu/seoe
f: https://www.facebook.com/MarineScienceSC/
Programs: Geological Sciences (B,M,D); Geophysics (B); Marine Science (B,M,D); Environmental Science (B); Environmental Studies (B); Earth & Environmental Resources Management (M,JD);
Enrollment (2017): B: 582 (111) M: 39 (17) D: 39 (6)

Director:
Thomas J. Owens, (D), Utah, 1984, Ys

Research Professor:
Dwayne E. Porter, (D), South Carolina, 1995, OgHsRw

Director of the Belle Baruch Marine Institute:
James Pinckney, (D), South Carolina, 1992, Obn

Associate Dean:
Claudia R. Benitez-Nelson, (D), MIT/WHOI, 1999, OcGe

Professor:
Ron Benner, (D), Georgia, 1984, Ob
Carol Boggs, (D), Texas, 1979, Zn
Subrahmanyam Bulusu, (D), Southampton (UK), 1998, Op
Thomas Lekan, (D), Zn
Joseph Quattro, (D), Rutgers, 1991, Ob
Tammi Richardson, (D), Dalhousie, 1996, Ob
Raymond Torres, (D), California (Berkeley), 1997, Hy
George Voulgaris, (D), Southampton (UK), 1992, OnpOg
Scott M. White, (D), California (Santa Barbara), 2001, YrZr
Alicia M. Wilson, (D), Johns Hopkins, 1999, Hw
Neal Woods, (D), Zn
Gene M. Yogodzinski, (D), Cornell, 1993, GiCuc

Research Professor, Director of Undergraduate Studies:
Gwendelyn Geidel, (D), South Carolina, 1982, HwGeCg

Associate Professor:
David Barbeau, Jr., (D), Arizona, 2003, Gs
Michael Bizimis, (D), Florida State, 2001, GiCg
Andrew L. Leier, (D), Arizona, 2005, Gst
Howie Scher, (D), Florida, 2005, GuCl
Alexander E. Yankovsky, (D), Marine Hydrophysical Inst (Ukraine), 1991, OpnAm
Lori A. Ziolkowski, (D), California (Irvine), 2009, CoOcCs

Assistant Professor:
Jessica Barnes, (D), Zn
Monica Barra, (D), New York, 2019, Zn
Annie Bourbonnais, (D), Victoria, 2012, Oc
Besim Dragovic, (D), Boston, 2013
David E. Fuente, (D), North Carolina, 2017, Zn
R. Dean Hardy, (D), Georgia, 2016
Conor Harrison, (D), Zn
David Kneas, (D), Zn
Susan Q. Lang, (D), Washington, 2006, Oc
Katherine Ryker, (D), North Carolina State, Ze

Research Assistant Professor:
Matthew Kimball, (D), Rutgers, 2008, Ob
Erik Smith, (D), Maryland, 2000, HsOb

Emeritus:
Philip Barnes, (D), Zn
Bruce Coull, (D), Lehigh, 1968, Ob
John Mark Dean, (D), Purdue, 1962, Ob
Robert Feller, (D), Washington, 1977, Ob
Madilyn Fletcher, (D), Univ Coll (Wales), 1975, Ob
James N. Kellogg, (D), Princeton, 1981, Yg
Christopher G. Kendall, (D), Imperial Coll (UK), 1966, Gs
Willard S. Moore, (D), SUNY (Stony Brook), 1969, Cc
W. Edwin Sharp, (D), California (Los Angeles), 1964, Gz
Stephen Stancyk, (D)
Pradeep Talwani, (D), Stanford, 1973, Ys
Sarah A. Woodin, (D), Washington, 1972, Ob
Richard Zingmark, (D)

Research Professor:
Jennifer R. Pournelle, (D), California (San Diego), 2003, GaZuSa

University of South Carolina, Lancaster

University of South Carolina, Lancaster (A) ☒ (2017)
P.O. Box 889
Lancaster, SC 29721
p. (803) 313-7129
martek@mailbox.sc.edu
http://usclancaster.sc.edu

Instructor:
Lynnette Flann Martek, (M), Emporia State, 1994, ZgAm

Winthrop University

Dept of Chemistry, Physics, & Geology (2015)
Sims Science Building
Winthrop University
Rock Hill, SC 29733
p. (803) 323-4949
lammir@winthrop.edu
https://www.winthrop.edu/cas/chemistry/

Chair, Environmental Sciences and Studies Program:
Marsha S. Bollinger, (D), South Carolina, 1986, CmOcCc

Professor:
Irene B. Boland, (D), South Carolina, 1996, GtgZe

Associate Professor:
Gwen M. Daley, (D), Virginia Tech, 1999, PqgGs
Scott P. Werts, (D), Johns Hopkins, 2006, ScbPg

Wofford College

Dept of Geology (2015)
Wofford College
429 North Church Street
Spartanburg, SC 29303-3663
p. (864) 597-4527
fergusonta@wofford.edu
http://www.wofford.edu/geology/

Director:
Terry A. Ferguson, (D), Tennessee, 1988, Ga

South Dakota

Black Hills State University

School of Natural Sciences (B) ●☒ (2019)
1200 University Street, Unit 9008
Spearfish, SD 57799-9008
p. (605) 642-6506
abigail.domagall@bhsu.edu

https://www.bhsu.edu/Academics/Natural-Sciences/Environmental-Physical-Science
f: https://www.facebook.com/EnvPhysSciBHSU/
Programs: Environmental Physical Science, Earth Science minor, Composite Science Education
Enrollment (2018): B: 35 (7)
Professor:
Mark Gabel, (D), Iowa State, 1982, Pb
Associate Professor:
Abigail M S Domagall, (D), SUNY (Buffalo), 2008, GveZe

Oglala Lakota College

Dept of Math, Science & Technology (2015)
P.O. Box 490
Kyle, SD 57755
p. (605) 455-6124
hlagarry@olc.edu
http://www.olc.edu/local_links/smet/

South Dakota School of Mines & Technology

Dept of Atmospheric and Environmental Sciences (B,M,D) (2015)
501 E. St. Joseph Street
Rapid City, SD 57701-3995
p. (605) 394-2291
william.capehart@sdsmt.edu
http://www.ias.sdsmt.edu/
Enrollment (2011): B: 15 (0) M: 14 (3)
Associate Professor:
William J. Capehart, (D), Penn State, 1997, AsZoHq
Donna V. Kliche, (D), SD Mines, 2007, AssAs
P. V. Sundareshwar, (D), South Carolina, 2002, ZeCgSb
Assistant Professor:
Adam French, (D), North Carolina State, 2011, Asm
Lisa Kunza, (D), Wyoming, 2012, HsZe
Instructor:
Darren R. Clabo, (M), SD Mines, 2009, AssAs
Emeritus:
Andrew G. Detwiler, (D), SUNY (Albany), 1980, AspAm
John H. Helsdon, (D), SUNY (Albany), 1979, As
Mark R. Hjelmfelt, (D), Chicago, 1980, As
Paul L. Smith, (D), Carnegie Inst, 1960, As

Dept of Geology & Geological Engineering (B,M,D) O⊘ (2020)
501 E. Saint Joseph St.
Rapid City, SD 57701-3901
p. (605) 394-2461
laurie.anderson@sdsmt.edu
http://geology.sdsmt.edu
f: https://www.facebook.com/SDSMTGeologyGeologicalEngineering
Programs: Geology (B); Geological Engineering (B); Geology and Geological Engineering (M,D); Paleontology (M)
Certificates: Geospatial Technology (UG,G); Petroleum Systems (G)
Administrative Assistant: Cleo J. Heenan
Enrollment (2020): B: 110 (22) M: 23 (10) D: 9 (2)
Field Station Director:
Nuri Uzunlar, (D), SD Mines, 1993, EmCeGc
Department Head; Director Museum of Geology:
Laurie C. Anderson, (D), Wisconsin, 1991, PiePq
Dean of Graduate Education:
Maribeth H. Price, (D), Princeton, 1995, Zir
Professor:
Edward F. Duke, (D), Dartmouth, 1984, GpiZr
Timothy L. Masterlark, (D), Wisconsin, 2000, YdhNr
Larry D. Stetler, (D), Washington State, 1993, NxGsm
Research Scientist:
Roger Nielsen, (D), S Methodist, 1983
William M. Roggenthen, (D), Princeton, 1980, NgYg
Associate Professor:
Kurt W. Katzenstein, (D), Nevada (Reno), 2008, NxtZr
Darrin C. Pagnac, (D), California (Riverside), 2005, PvGrZe
J. Foster Sawyer, (D), SD Mines, 2006, GsoHw
Assistant Professor:
Zeynep O. Baran, (D), Miami, 2012, GcoGt
Sarah W. Keenan, (D), Tennessee, 2014, PvClb
Liangping Li, (D), Polytechnic Univ of Valencia (Spain), 2011, HwqHt
Gokce K. Ustunisik, (D), Cincinnati, 2009, Cp
Kevin M. Ward, (D), Arizona, 2016, YsGtYg
Coordinator and Instructor:
Christopher J. Pellowski, (D), SD Mines, 2012, Gg
Associate Director, Museum of Geology:
Nathaniel Fox, (D), California (Merced), 2020, Pgv
Lecturer:
Curtis V. Price, (M), Dartmouth, 1985, ZifRw
Emeritus:
Phillip Bjork, (M), SD Mines, 1964
Arden D. Davis, (D), SD Mines, 1983, HwNx
James E. Fox, (D), Wyoming, 1972, Gs
James E. Martin, (D), Washington, 1979, Ps
Colin J. Paterson, (D), Otago (NZ), 1978, Eg
Perry H. Rahn, (D), Penn State, 1965, Ng
Preparator and Lab Manager:
Kayleigh Johnson, (M), SD Mines, 2018, Pgv

University of South Dakota

Dept of Earth Sciences & Physics (B) (2015)
414 East Clark Street
Vermillion, SD 57069-2390
p. (605) 677-5649
esci@usd.edu
http://www.usd.edu/earthsciences/
Enrollment (2011): B: 25 (9)
Chair:
Timothy H. Heaton, (D), Harvard, 1988, PvOg
Associate Professor:
Brennan T. Jordan, (D), Oregon State, 2002, GiAm
Mark R. Sweeney, (D), Washington State, 2004, Gms
Instructor:
Jeanne M. Fromm, (M), Idaho State, 1995, GgHs

Tennessee

Austin Peay State University

Geosciences Dept (B) ✆ (2020)
601 College St
Clarksville, TN 37044
p. (931) 221-7454
deibertj@apsu.edu
http://www.apsu.edu/geosciences
Programs: Geosciences
Enrollment (2019): B: 85 (10)
Chair:
Jack Deibert, (D), Wyoming, GsrGo
Professor:
Phyllis A. Camilleri, (D), Wyoming, 1994, Gct
Daniel L. Frederick, (D), Tennessee, 1994, PgGsr
Gregory D. Ridenour, (D), Texas A&M, 1993, HsOgZn
Associate Professor:
Kallina M. Dunkle, (D), Wisconsin, 2012, HwGle
Christopher Gentry, (D), Indiana State, 2008, Ziy
Christine Mathenge, (D), Indiana, 2008, Zcy
Assistant Professor:
Madeline M. Giefer, (D), N Carolina, 2020, ZcrZi
Erik L. Haroldson, (D), Wisconsin, 2016, EdGzCg
Emeritus:
Phillip R. Kemmerly, (D), Oklahoma State, 1973, GmeHg
Laboratory Director:
Randal P. Roberson, (M), Murray State, 2018, Gg
Other:
Richard F. Wheeler, (M), Brigham Young, 1980, Ggo

Middle Tennessee State University

Dept of Geosciences (B,M) ✆ (2020)
Box 9
Davis Science Building
Room 241
Murfreesboro, TN 37132
p. (615) 898-2726
karen.wolfe@mtsu.edu
http://mtsu.edu/geosciences
f: https://www.facebook.com/groups/88868852075/
t: @MTSUGeosciences
Programs: Geology; Earth Science; Earth Science for Teachers;

Physical Geography; Geospatial Analysis; Environmental Sci
Administrative Assistant: Karen M. Wolfe
Enrollment (2019): B: 163 (25) M: 12 (14)
Director:
Zada Law, (M), Wisconsin, 1980, Zin
Chair:
Warner Cribb, (D), Ohio State, 1993, GipGz
Professor:
Mark J. Abolins, (D), Caltech, 1999, Gc
Chair:
Henrique G. Momm, (D), Mississippi, 2008, ZfHqRw
Associate Professor:
Clay D. Harris, (D), Indiana, 1992, Gse
Melissa Lobegeier, (D), James Cook, 2001, Pmg
Assistant Professor:
Jeremy Aber, (D), Kansas State, 2011, Zyi
Joe D. Collins, (D), Texas (El Paso), 2016, Gms
Racha El Kadiri, (D), W Michigan, 2014, Hg
Alisa L. Hass, (D), Tennessee, 2019, AtZy
Instructor:
Laura R. Collins, (M), Mississippi State, 2005, Gg
Lecturer:
Alan Brown, (M), Illinois State, 2005, Gg

Motlow State Community College

Dept of Natural Sciences (A) (2015)
PO Box 8500
Lynchburg, TN 37352-8500
p. (931) 393-1810
lmayo@mscc.edu
http://www.mscc.edu/natural_science/
Instructor:
Lisa L Herring Mayo, (M), Mississippi State, 2000, GgZge

Pellissippi State Community College

Natural and Behavioral Sciences (2015)
10915 Hardin Valley Road
P.O. Box 22990
Knoxville, TN 37801
p. (865) 694-6685
kmbarker1@pstcc.edu
http://www.pstcc.edu
Adjunct Professor:
Peter J. Lemiszki, (D), Tennessee, 1992, GcgZi

Roane State Community College - Oak Ridge

Mathematics and Sciences (Geology) (A) (2015)
276 Patton Lane
Harriman , TN 37748
p. (865) 481-2000
leea@roanestate.edu
http://aclee1234.fortunecity.com
Professor:
Arthur C. Lee, (D), S California, 1994, Ges

Sewanee: University of the South

Dept of Earth and Environmental Systems (B) (2015)
735 University Avenue
Sewanee, TN 37383-1000
p. (931) 598-1271
Sherwood@sewanee.edu
http://www.sewanee.edu/EnvStudies
Chair:
Scott Torreano, (D), Georgia, 1991, Sf
Professor:
Martin A. Knoll, (D), Texas (El Paso), 1988, Hw
Donald B. Potter, Jr., (D), Massachusetts, 1985, Gc
Stephen A. Shaver, (D), Stanford, 1984, Eg
Associate Professor:
C. Ken Smith, (D), Florida, 1996, Sf
Adjunct Professor:
Glendon W. Smalley, (D), Tennessee, 1975, Sf

Tennessee Tech University

Dept of Earth Sciences (B) ⊘ (2020)
PO Box 5062
Cookeville, TN 38505
p. (931) 372-3121
MHarrison@tntech.edu
https://www.tntech.edu/cas/earth/
Programs: Geosciences
Administrative Assistant: Peggy Medlin
Enrollment (2020): B: 49 (12)
Chair:
Evan A. Hart, (D), Tennessee, 2000, Zy
Professor:
Michael J. Harrison, (D), Illinois (Urbana), 2002, Gc
H. Wayne Leimer, (D), Missouri, 1969, Gz
Ping-Chi Li, (D), Iowa, 1992, Zi
Associate Professor:
Joseph Asante, (D), Nevada, 2012, HwZrGe
Jeannette Wolak, (D), Montana State, 2011, Gsr
Assistant Professor:
Lauren Michel, (D), Baylor, 2014, PcSaCl
Adjunct Professor:
Jason E. Duke, (M), Tennessee Tech, 1995, Zi
Emeritus:
Larry W. Knox, (D), Indiana, 1974, Pmg

University of Memphis

Center for Earthquake Research & Information (CERI) (M,D) ⊠ (2020)
3876 Central Avenue, Suite 1
Memphis, TN 38152-3050
p. (901) 678-2007
clangstn@memphis.edu
http://www.memphis.edu/ceri
Programs: M.S. and PhD concentration in Geophysics
Enrollment (2018): M: 9 (2) D: 17 (1)
Director:
Charles A. Langston, (D), Caltech, 1976, Ys
Graduate Coordinator:
Christine A. Powell, (D), Princeton, 1976, Ys
Professor:
Randel Tom Cox, (D), Missouri, 1995, GtcGm
Associate Professor:
Eunseo Choi, (D), Caltech, 2008, Gtq
Assistant Professor:
Thomas H. Goebel, (D), S California, 2013, Yxs
Christodoulos Kyriakopoulos, (D), Bologna, 2011, Yd
Research Professor :
James Dorman, (D), Columbia, 1961, Yse
CERI Founding Director:
Archibald C. Johnston, (D), Colorado, 1979, Ys
Emeritus:
Jer-Ming Chiu, (D), Cornell, 1982, Ys
Research Scientist:
Stephen P. Horton, (D), Nevada (Reno), 1992, Ys
Research Professor :
Chris Cramer, (D), Stanford, 1976, Ys
Robert Smalley, Jr., (D), Cornell, 1988, Yd
Assoc. Research Professor:
Mitchell M. Withers, (D), New Mexico Tech, 1997, Ys
Seismic Network Engineer:
James Bollwerk, (M), Memphis
Research Equipment Technician II:
Chris McGoldrick
David Steiner
Research Equipment Tech II:
Patrick Shivers
Research Associate Technician:
John Parker
Research Associate II:
Kent Moran, (D), Memphis
Holly Withers
Local Technical Support Provider II:
Robert Debula
Deshone Marshall
Local Technical Support Provider I:
James Davis, (D), Memphis, 2013
Director Education & Outreach:
Gary Patterson, (M), Memphis, Gg
Digital Seismic Systems Supervisor:
Steve Brewer, (M), Memphis

Assistant Director Administration & Finance:
Michelle Smith, (B)

Dept of Earth Sciences (B,M,D) (2019)
109 Johnson Hall
488 Patterson Street
Memphis, TN 38152-3550
p. (901) 678-4571 or 678-2177
aahill@memphis.edu
http://memphis.edu/earthsciences/
Programs: Earth Sciences (B, M, D); Geoarchaeology (B); Geography (B, M); Geology (B, M); Archaeology (M); Interdisciplinary Studies (M)
Certificates: GIS (G)
Enrollment (2019): B: 60 (7) M: 23 (13) D: 33 (5)

Chair:
Daniel Larsen, (D), New Mexico, 1994, ClGsHw
Director, Confucius Institute:
Hsiang-Te Kung, (D), Tennessee, 1980, Zy
Professor:
Mervin J. Bartholomew, (D), Virginia Tech, 1971, Gtc
Randel T. Cox, (D), Missouri, 1995, GcmGt
David H. Dye, (D), Washington, 1980, Ga
Arleen A. Hill, (D), South Carolina, 2002, Rn
Esra Ozdenerol, (D), Louisiana State, 2000, Zi
Jose Pujol, (D), Wyoming, 1985, Ye
Roy B. Van Arsdale, (D), Utah, 1979, Gcm
Associate Professor:
Anzhelika Antipova, (D), Louisiana State, 2010, Zg
Dorian Burnette, (D), Arkansas, 2009, Atm
Andrew M. Mickelson, (D), Ohio State, 2002, Ga
Ryan M. Parish, (D), Memphis, 2013, Ga
Assistant Professor:
Youngsang Kwon, (D), SUNY (Buffalo), 2012, Zi
Deborah Leslie, (D), Ohio State, 2013, HwCl
Visiting Professor:
Elizabeth Rhenberg, (D), West Virginia, 2015, Pg
Emeritus:
Phili B. Deboo, (D), Louisiana State, 1963, Pg
Robert W. Deininger, (D), Rice, 1964, Gx
James Dorman, (D), Columbia, 1961, Ys
Archibald C. Johnston, (D), Colorado, 1979, Ys
David N. Lumsden, (D), Illinois (Urbana), 1965, Gd
Instructor/Coordinator:
Julie Johnson, (D), Florida Intl, 2012, Gx

University of Tennessee, Chattanooga

Biology, Geology, and Environmental Science (B) ☒ (2021)
615 McCallie Ave., Dept. 2653
Chattanooga, TN 37403
p. (423) 425-4341
http://www.utc.edu/biology-geology-environmental-science/division-geology/
f: https://www.facebook.com/GeologyatUTC
Programs: Geology:Geology,
Geology: Environmental Geology, Geology: STEM Education
Enrollment (2020): B: 38 (4)

Professor:
Jonathan W. Mies, (D), North Carolina, 1990, GctHg
Associate Professor:
Amy Brock-Hon, (D), Nevada, 2007, GmSc
Assistant Professor:
Stephanie DeVries, (D), HgCq
A K M Azad Hossain, (D), Mississippi, 2008, ZriZg
Ashley Manning-Berg, (D), GsPo
Laboratory Coordinator:
Jason Muhlbauer, (D), UTK, 2021, Gg
Adjunct Professor:
Gregory Brodie, (M), Purdue, 1979, Ge

University of Tennessee, Knoxville

Dept. of Earth & Planetary Sciences (B,M,D) (2020)
602 Strong Hall
1621 Cumberland Ave.
Knoxville, TN 37996-1526
p. (865) 974-2366
eps@utk.edu
https://eps.utk.edu/
f: https://www.facebook.com/UTEPS
Programs: Geology; Environmental Studies
Enrollment (2018): B: 131 (35) M: 21 (9) D: 27 (3)

Interim Head:
Edmund Perfect, (D), Cornell, 1986, SpHwGq
Governors Chair:
Terry C. Hazen, (D), Michigan State, 1973, Po
Professor:
Thomas W. Broadhead, (D), Iowa, 1978, Pi
William M. Dunne, (D), Bristol, 1980, Gc
Annette S. Engel, (D), Texas, 2004, Cl
Christopher Fedo, (D), Virginia Tech, 1994, GsXgCg
Linda Kah, (D), Harvard, 1997, Gs
Larry D. McKay, (D), Waterloo, 1991, HyGe
Michael L. McKinney, (D), Yale, 1985, GePg
Jeffery E. Moersch, (D), Cornell, 1997, XgZr
Associate Professor:
Micah Jessup, (D), Virginia Tech, 2007, Gc
Molly McCanta, (D), Brown, 2004, GiXg
Stephen J. Romaniello, (D), Arizona State, 2012, Cg
Colin Sumrall, (D), Texas, 1997, Pi
Anna Szynkiewicz, (D), Wroclaw, 2004, CslXg
ORNL Joint Faculty:
Elizabeth M. Herndon, (D), Penn State, 2012, Cg
Melanie A. Mayes, (D), Tennessee, 2006, ClGeHw
Assistant Professor:
Nick Dygert, (D), Brown, 2015, Giz
Andrew Steen, (D), North Carolina, 2009, CoOb
Bradley J. Thomson, (D), Brown, 2006, Xg
Lecturer:
Md Iftekhar Alam, (D), Oklahoma State, 2016, Yu
Jake Benner, (M), Utah, 2002, ZePg
Stephanie K. Drumheller-Horton, (D), Iowa, 2012, Pg
Estifanos Haile, (D), Kentucky, 2011, Hy
Adjunct Professor:
Gary G. Bible, (D), Iowa State, 1978, Go
Devon M. Burr, (D), Arizona, 2003, Xg
Emily J. Chin, (D), Rice, 2013, Cu
John M. Cottle, (D), Oxford, 2008, Gt
William E. Doll, (D), Wisconsin, 1983, Ys
Steven G. Driese, (D), Wisconsin, 1982, SaClGs
Joshua P. Emery, (D), Arizona, 2002, Xy
Craig J. Hardgrove, (D), Tennessee, 2011, Xg
Christian Klimczak, (D), Nevada, 2011, Xg
Jasper F. Kok, (D), Michigan, 2009, Ap
Peter J. Lemiszki, (D), Tennessee, 1992, Gc
Claudia I. Mora, (D), Wisconsin, 1988, Cs
Matthew L. Niemiller, (D), Tennessee, 2011, Zn
Tommy J. Phelps, (D), Wisconsin, 1985, Cb
Louise M. Prockter, (D), Brown, 2000, Xg
Ganapathy Shanmugam, (D), Tennessee, 1978, Gs
Ben Thuy, (D), Gottingen, Germany, 2012, Pg
Christina E. Viviano-Beck, (D), Tennessee, 2012, Xg
Steven W. Wilhelm, (D), W Ontario, 1994, Po
Emeritus:
Robert D. Hatcher Jr., (D), Tennessee, 1965, Gct
Theodore C. Labotka, (D), Caltech, 1978, GpCg
Harry Y. McSween, Jr., (D), Harvard, 1977, XcGi
Kula C. Misra, (D), W Ontario, 1973, Eg
Research Professor:
Liyuan Liang, (D), Caltech, 1988, Cb
Robert Riding, (D), Sheffield, UK, Cb

University of Tennessee, Martin

Dept of Agriculture, Geosciences, and Natural Resources (B) (2015)
256 Brehm Hall
Martin, TN 38238
p. (731) 881-7260
mehlhorn@utm.edu
http://www.utm.edu/departments/caas/agnr/geosciences/
Enrollment (2013): B: 29 (13)

Professor:
Paula M. Gale, (D), Arkansas, 1988, SodSc
Michael A. Gibson, (D), Tennessee, 1988, PgiZe
Jefferson S. Rogers, (D), Illinois, 1995, Zn
Robert M. Simpson, (D), Indiana State, 2000, AsmZi

Associate Professor:
Stan P. Dunagan, (D), Tennessee, 1998, GsSa
Assistant Professor:
Thomas A. DePriest, (D), Union (Jackson), 2009, Ze
Benjamin P. Hooks, (D), Maine, 2009, GciNr
Instructor:
Eleanor E. Gardner, (M), Georgia, GgPg
Emeritus:
William T. McCutchen, (M), Berea, 1967, Gg
Robert P. Self, (D), Rice, 1971, Gs
Helmut C. Wenz, (M), W Michigan, 1968, Zn

Vanderbilt University

Earth & Environmental Sciences (B,M,D) ☒ (2021)
2301 Vanderbilt Place
VU Station B 351805
Nashville, TN 37235-1805
p. (615) 322-2976
gale.newton@vanderbilt.edu
http://www.vanderbilt.edu/ees/
f: https://www.facebook.com/groups/393646734010753/
t: @vanderbiltEES
Enrollment (2020): B: 45 (10) D: 17 (2)
Chair:
Steven L. Goodbred, Jr., (D), William & Mary, 1999, GsOn
Professor:
John C. Ayers, (D), Rensselaer, 1991, CgGx
Ralf Bennartz, (D), Free (Berlin), 1997, AsZr
David J. Furbish, (D), Colorado, 1985, GmHg
Guilherme Gualda, (D), Chicago, 2010, GivGz
George Hornberger, (D), Stanford, 1970, HgwHs
Associate Professor:
Larisa R.G DeSantis, (D), Florida, 2009, Pve
Jonathan M. Gilligan, (D), Yale, 1991, ZcRwZu
Jessica L. Oster, (D), California (Davis), 2010, ClsPc
Assistant Professor:
Simon A.F. Darroch, (D), Yale, 2015, PgiPe
Kristen Fauria, (D), California (Berkeley), 2017, GvqYu
Maria Luisa Jorge, (D), Illinois (Chicago), 2007, Pg
Neil P. Kelley, (D), California (Davis), 2012, GgOgPg
Principal Senior Lecturer:
Lily L. Claiborne, (D), Vanderbilt, 2011, GivCg
Daniel J. Morgan, (D), Washington, 2009, GmCc
Emeritus:
Leonard P. Alberstadt, (D), Oklahoma, 1967, Gd
Calvin F. Miller, (D), California (Los Angeles), 1977, Gi
Molly F. Miller, (D), California (Los Angeles), 1977, PeGs
Arthur L. Reesman, (D), Missouri, 1966, Gg
William G. Siesser, (D), Cape Town, 1971, PmGsu

Volunteer State Community College

Volunteer State Community College (2015)
1800 Nashville Pike
Gallatin, TN 37006
p. (615) 230-3294
Clark.Cropper@volstate.edu
http://www.volstate.edu

Walters State Community College

Walters State Community College (2015)
500 South Davy Crockett Parkway
Morristown, TN 37813
p. (423) 585-6764
http://www.ws.edu

Texas

Alamo Colleges, Palo Alto College

Dept of Geology (A) (2015)
1400 W. Villaret Blvd
San Antonio, TX 78224
p. (210) 486-3000
swilkins6@alamo.edu
http://alamo.edu/pac/geology/

Alamo Colleges, San Antonio College

Natural Sciences (2020)
1819 N Main Ave
San Antonio, TX 78212
p. (210) 486-0840
dlambert@alamo.edu
http://alamo.edu/sac/earthsci/
Professor:
Dean Lambert, (D), Texas, Zy
Adjunct Professor:
Dwight Jurena, (M), Renssalear, GgZg
Ryan E. Rudnicki, (D), Penn State, Zy
Charles K. Smith, (M), Texas State, Zy

Alvin Community College

Physcial Science Program (A) (2021)
3110 Mustang Rd
Alvin, TX 77511
p. (281) 756-5670
pobrien@alvincollege.edu
https://www.alvincollege.edu/physical-science/faculty.html
Programs: Physical Sciences
Enrollment (2012): A: 2 (1)
Geology Instructor:
Philip O'Brien, (M), Texas Tech, 2014, Gg

Amarillo College

Dept of Physical Science ☒ (2020)
P.O. Box 447
Amarillo, TX 79178
p. (806) 371-5333
rdhobbs@actx.edu
https://www.actx.edu/pscience/
Enrollment (2009): A: 3 (0)
Professor:
Richard D. Hobbs, (D), Wyoming, 1998, ZrGc
Adjunct Professor:
David Pertl, (M), W Texas A&M, 1984, Go

Angelo State University

Dept of Physics and Geosciences (B) O (2021)
ASU Station #10904
San Angelo, TX 76909
p. (325) 942-2242
joseph.satterfield@angelo.edu
https://www.angelo.edu/departments/physics-geosciences/Geosciences/
Programs: Geosciences (B)
Enrollment (2020): B: 49 (8)
Professor:
Joseph I. Satterfield, (D), Rice, 1995, Gc
Associate Professor:
Heather L. Lehto, (D), S Florida, 2012, GvYsZe
Assistant Professor:
Elizabeth Koeman-Shields, (D), Notre Dame, 2015, CgXg
Instructor:
Jessica Garza, (M), Hawaii, 2011, AmGg
Stephen Shields, (M), Missouri State, 2013, Ggm
Adjunct Professor:
Cary D. Carman, (B), Angelo State, 1999, Hg
Steven Lyons, (D), Hawaii, 1981, Am
Robert Purkiss, (M), Texas Tech, 1991, Gg
Fred L. Wilson, (D), Kansas, 1964, Gm

Austin Community College District

Dept of Earth and Environmental Sciences (A) (2021)
6101 Highland Campus Drive
Austin, TX 78752
p. (512) 223-7157
mshepherd@austincc.edu
http://sites.austincc.edu/ees/
Programs: Environmental Studies (A); Environmental Technology (A); Geology (A)
Certificates: Environmental Technology
Administrative Assistant: Oralia Guerra
Enrollment (2020): A: 227 (12)

Chair:
Mark A. Shepherd, (D), Nebraska (Medical Center), 2015, AsObZn
Associate Dean:
Ronald A. Johns, (D), Texas, 1993, Pi
Professor:
Robert H. Blodgett, (D), Texas, 1990, RnGsZe
Associate Professor:
Heather R. Miller, (D), Texas A&M, 2012, Zeg
Peter J. Wehner, (M), Vanderbilt, 1992, GieXs
Adjunct Professor:
Brittany N. Blomberg, (D), Texas A&M (Corpus Christi), 2015, OnbRn
Peter A. Boone, (D), Texas A&M, 1972, Gro
Thomas W. Brown, (M), Indiana, 1987, Ges
Laura E. Chapa, (M), Texas State, 2014, ZgeZr
M. Jennifer Cooke, (D), Texas, 2005, GmCl
Leslie M. Davis, (M), Florida State, 1986, Op
Meredith Y. Denton-Hedrick, (M), Texas A&M, 1992, ZeYeEo
Maedeh Faraji, (D), Texas, 2007, AsZge
Kusali R. Gamage, (D), Florida, 2005, HyOuPm
Khaled W. Hasan, (D), Texas A&M, 1995, HsZri
Elena K. Keen, (D), Texas A&M (Corpus Christi), 2017
Zackary E. Martin, (M), Texas State, 2006, RwZn
Amy L. Moreland, (D), Texas, 2011, Zge
Ata U. Rahman, (D), Texas Tech, 1987, GgdGe
Fabienne M. Rambaud, (M), Texas, 2005, Eg
Carolyn M. Riess, (M), Texas (El Paso), 1984, GoeGg
Alina A. Satkoski, (M), Syracuse, 2011, GemGg
Raymond M. Slade, Jr., (B), SW Texas, 1971, HgsHq
Paepin K. Starr, (D), Texas State, 2019, GlZrRc
Jason H. Stephens, (D), Texas, 2014, YrGuYe
Anne Turner, (M), Texas, 1986, Hg
Holly Zafian, (M), Texas State, 2011, Ze
Science Laboratory Technician:
Shannon M. Grace, (M), Illinois, 2017, Zn
Amie C. Hammond, (B), Texas, 2014, ZeGg
Sean C. Murphy, (M), Georgia, 1984, EgGpRc
Cooperating Faculty:
David J. Froehlich, (D), Texas, 1996, Pv

Baylor University

Dept of Environmental science (2015)
Waco, TX 76706
p. (254) 710-3406
George_Cobb@baylor.edu
https://www.baylor.edu/environmentalscience/index.php?id=55209

Dept of Geosciences (B,M,D) ●⦸ (2021)
One Bear Place #97354
101 Bagby Ave.
BSB, 4th Floor, Rm. D409
Waco, TX 76798-7354
p. (254) 710-2361
paulette_penney@baylor.edu
http://www.baylor.edu/geosciences
f: https://www.facebook.com/baylorgeosciences
t: @BaylorGeo
Programs: Geology; Geophysics; Earth Science
Administrative Assistant: Janelle Atchley, Jamie J.. Ruth
Enrollment (2020): B: 23 (10) M: 15 (5) D: 26 (5)
W.M. Keck Foundation Professor of Geophysics:
Robert Jay Pulliam, (D), California (Berkeley), 1991, YsgYe
Keck Foundation Prof. of Geophysics:
Jay Pulliam, (D), California (Berkeley), 1991, YsgYe
Associate Graduate Dean for Research and Chair of Dept.:
Steven G. Driese, (D), Wisconsin, 1982, SaClGs
Professor:
Stacy C. Atchley, (D), Nebraska, 1990, GroGo
Vincent S. Cronin, (D), Texas A&M, 1988, GctNg
Stephen I. Dworkin, (D), Texas, 1991, ClGd
Stephen Forman, (D), Colorado, CcPc
Don M. Greene, (D), Oklahoma, 1980, ZyAm
Lee C. Nordt, (D), Texas A&M, 1996, SdGa
Kenneth Wilkins, (D), Florida, 1982, Pv
Joe C. Yelderman, Jr., (D), Wisconsin, 1983, HwgZu
Graduate Program Director:
Daniel J. Peppe, (D), Yale, 2009, PbcYm
Associate Professor:
William C. Hockaday, (D), Ohio State, 2006, CoaSb
Joseph D. White, (D), Montana, 1998, Zr
Assistant Professor:
Kenneth S. Befus, (D), Texas, 2014, GviGv
Peter B. James, (D), MIT, Ygg
Scott C. James, (D), California (Irvine), 2001, HwGeEo
Elizabeth Petsios, (D), S California, 2016, Pie
Emeritus:
Peter M. Allen, (D), S Methodist, 1977, HgNg
Rena M. Bonem, (D), Oklahoma, 1975, PieOb
John A. Dunbar, (D), Texas, 1989, YgHg
Thomas T. Goforth, (D), S Methodist, 1973, Yg
Don F. Parker, (D), Texas, 1976, Giv
Luminescence Geochronology Research Specialist:
Liliana Marin, (M), Illinois (Chicago), 2005, ZiGgCc
Instrumentation Specialist:
Timothy Meredith
Ren Zhang, (D), McMaster, 2007, Cs
Laboratory Director:
Sharon Browning, (M), Gg
Office Manager:
Paulette Penney, (A), Zn

Blinn College

Agricultural and Natural Science Programs (A) (2017)
902 College Avenue
Brenham, TX 77833
p. (979) 830-4200
cl.metz@blinn.edu
http://www.blinn.edu/natscience
Professor:
Michael Dalman, (M), W Michigan, 1999, Ze
Cheyl L. Metz, (D), Texas A&M, GgOg

Brookhaven College

Science/Math Div - Geology Dept (2017)
3939 Valley View Lane
Farmers Branch, TX 75244
p. (972) 860-4758
LannaBradshaw@dcccd.edu
https://www.brookhavencollege.edu/cd/credit/geology/pages/
Chair:
Lanna K. Bradshaw, (M), Texas A&M, 2000, GgZg

Coastal Bend College

Science Div (A) (2015)
3800 Charco Road
Beeville, TX 78102
p. (361) 354-2423
recowart@coastalbend.edu
http://www.coastalbend.edu/acdem/science/
Enrollment (2011): A: 3 (0)
Instructor:
Danny Burns, (M), Ball State, 1984, Zgn
Richard Cowart, (D), Texas A&M (Corpus Christi), 2008, GeEo

Collin College - Central Park Campus

Deptartment of Geology (A) (2018)
2200 W. University Drive
McKinney, TX 75071
p. (972) 548-6790
bburkett@collin.edu
http://www.collin.edu/geology/
Enrollment (2016): A: 30 (0)
Professor:
Brett Burkett, (M), SUNY (Buffalo), 2008, Gvg
Related Staff:
Shannon Burkett, (M), SUNY (Buffalo), 2005, Gv

Collin College - Preston Ridge Campus

Dept of Geology and Environmental Science (A) (2017)
9700 Wade Boulevard
Frisco, TX 75035
p. (972) 377-1635
smay@collin.edu

Professor:
Heinrich Goetz, (M), Texas A&M, 1997, Ge
Paul Manganelli, (M), Boston Coll, 1998
S Judson May, (D), New Mexico, 1980, GgoGc

Collin College - Spring Creek Campus

Dept of Geology and Environmental Science (A) ⃠ (2017)
2800 E. Spring Creek Parkway
Plano, TX 75074
p. (972) 578-5518
dbabcock@collin.edu
http://www.collin.edu/academics/programs/geology.html
Enrollment (2012): A: 10 (0)
Head:
Daphne H. Babcock, (M), Memphis, 1989, Geg
Professor:
Neal Alexandrowicz, (D)
Patrick Gonsulin-Getty, (D)
Instructor:
Stacey Bilich, (B)

Dallas College

Engineering, Technology, Mathematics, and Sciences (A) O (2021)
1601 S. Lamar St.
Dallas, TX 75215
p. 214-378-1500
dallascollegeacademics@dcccd.edu
https://www.dcccd.edu/cd/schools/stem/pages/
Programs: See link for a full list of course offerings.
https://www1.dcccd.edu/catalog/coursedescriptions/detail.cfm?loc=DCCCD&heading=Geology

Del Mar College

Dept of Natural Sciences (A) (2015)
Corpus Christi, TX 78404
p. (512) 886-1240
jhalcomb@delmar.edu
Professor:
Roger T. Steinberg, (M), Tennessee, 1981, GgoPg
Associate Professor:
Walter V. Kramer, (M), Texas (El Paso), 1970, GgoGx
Emeritus:
Mary S. Thorpe, (M), Baylor, 1966, Ge

El Centro College - Dallas Community College District

Geology Program (A) (2016)
801 Main Street
Dallas, TX 75202
p. (214) 860-2429
nfields@dcccd.edu
http://elcentrocollege.edu/programs/geology
Coordinator:
Nancy Fields, (M), Baylor, Zg
Professor:
Steven McCauley, (M), Mississippi State, GgAm
Bethan Salle, (M), N Colorado, 1999, GgeZg
Adjunct Professor:
Anna F. Banda, (M), Baylor, 2007, GgeGv
David Coffman, (M), Baylor, Gg
Stephanie Coffman, (M), Baylor, Gg
Alice Ruffel, (M), Oklahoma, Gg

El Paso Community College

Dept of Geological Sciences (A) (2021)
P.O. Box 20500
El Paso, TX 79998
p. (915) 831-5161
jvillal6@epcc.edu
https://www.epcc.edu/Academics/Geology
Programs: Associates of Science in Geology
Chair:
Joshua Villalobos, (M), Texas (El Paso), 2001, ZeYgu
Coordinator - Transmountain Campus:
Kathleen Devaney, (D), California (Los Angeles), 1992, Gg
Professor:
Sulaiman Abushagur, (D), Texas (El Paso), 1991, Gg
Assistant Professor:
Tina L. Carrick, (D), Texas (El Paso), 2014, ZeGgYg
Adriana Perez, (M), Texas (El Paso), Gg
Robert Rohbaugh, (M), Texas (El Paso), Ggt
Adjunct Professor:
Brenda Barnes, (D), Texas (El Paso), Gg
Sabrina Canalda, (M), Texas (El Paso), Gg
Emile Couroux, Gg
Kirk Rothemund, Gg

Hardin-Simmons University

Dept of Geology & Environmental Science (B) (2015)
Box 16164
2200 Hickory Street
Abilene, TX 79698-6164
p. (325) 670-1383
wicks@hsutx.edu
http://www.hsutx.edu/academics/undergraduate/holland/geology
Enrollment (2015): B: 20 (5)
Head:
Mark A. Ouimette, (D), Texas (El Paso), 1994, GieGt
Associate Professor:
Marla Potess, (D), Texas Tech, 2011, Zgu
Steven Rosscoe, (D), Texas Tech, 2008, PmGsPs

Hill College

Div of Mathematics and Sciences (Environmental Science) (2018)
112 Lamar
Hillsboro, TX 76645
p. 254-659-7500 or 817 295-7392
rroberts@hillcollege.edu
http://www.hillcollege.edu/academics/Traditional/Math_Science_EdServices/Geology.html
Programs: Associate of Science

Houston Community College System

Geology Dept (A) (2016)
1010 W. Sam Houston Pkwy.N.
Houston, TX 77043
p. (713) 718-5641
dwight.kranz@hccs.edu
http://learningwebsys.hccs.edu/discipline/geology/
Professor:
Dwight S. Kranz, (M), Texas A&M, 1980, Gg

Kilgore College

Dept of Chemistry and Geology (A) (2019)
1100 Broadway
Kilgore, TX 75662
p. (903) 983-8253
pbuchanan@kilgore.edu
Programs: Geology
Enrollment (2016): A: 5 (2)
Instructor:
Paul C. Buchanan, (D), Houston, 1995, GgiXm

Lamar University

Dept of Earth and Space Sciences (B) ☒ (2018)
P.O. Box 10031
Beaumont, TX 77710
p. (409) 880-8236
jim.jordan@lamar.edu
http://ess.lamar.edu
Professor:
Jim L. Jordan, (D), Rice, 1975, XcgXm
Roger W. Cooper, (D), Minnesota, 1978, Gi
Donald E. Owen, (D), Kansas, 1963, Gr
James W. Westgate, (D), Texas, 1988, Pev
Associate Professor:
Joseph M. Kruger, (D), Arizona, 1991, YgGgZi
Instructor:
Bennetta Schmidt, (D), Gg
Adjunct Professor:
Mark Adams, (M), Houston (Clear Lake), Xg

Cynthia L. Parish, (M), Lamar, 2004, Gg
Carla M. Tucker, (M), Texas, 1990, Hw
Laboratory Coordinator:
Karen M. Woods, (B), Lamar, 1991, Zg

Laredo College

Dept of Natural Sciences (2020)
West End Washington Street
Laredo, TX 78040
p. (956) 721-5195
glenn.blaylock@laredo.edu
http://www.laredo.edu/cms/LCC/Instruction/Divisions/Sciences/Natural_Sciences/Science/
Professor:
Glenn W. Blaylock, (M), Brigham Young, 1998, Ggv

Lee College

Dept of Physical Sciences (A) (2017)
P. O.Box 818
Baytown, TX 77522
p. (281) 425-6552
jdobberstine@lee.edu
Enrollment (2016): A: 2 (0)
Professor:
Sharon Gabel, (D), SUNY, 1991, GseGg

Lonestar College - CyFair

Geology Dept (2015)
9191 Barker Cypress Road
Cypress, TX 77433
p. (281) 290-3919
michael.r.konvicka@lonestar.edu
http://www.lonestar.edu/geology-dept-cyfair.htm

Lonestar College - Kingwood

Geology Dept (2015)
20000 Kingwood Drive
Kingwood, TX 77339
p. (281) 312-1629
Jean.Whileyman@lonestar.edu
http://www.lonestar.edu/geology-dept-kingwood.htm

Lonestar College - Montgomery

Geology Dept (2017)
3200 College Park Drive
Conroe, TX 77384
p. (936) 273-7077
Michael.J.Sundermann@lonestar.edu
http://www.lonestar.edu/geology-dept-montgomery.htm
Professor:
Nathalie N. Brandes, (M), New Mexico Tech
Cynthia Lawry-Berkins, (D), Texas A&M, 2009, Ges

Lonestar College - North Harris

Geology Dept (2015)
2700 W.W. Thorne Drive
Houston, TX 77073-3499
p. (281) 618-5685
richard.a.owen@lonestar.edu
Enrollment (2007): A: 20 (0)
Head:
Thomas M. C. Hobbs, (M), Texas (El Paso), 1979, Gg
Professor:
Peter E. Price, (M), Kentucky, 1979, Zi
Adjunct Professor:
Penni Major, (M), Gg
Michelle Mc Mahon, (D), Aberdeen, 1993, Go
Victor S. Resnic, (D), Nat Pet Inst (Russia), 1971, Go
Linda C. Tran, (B), Texas A&M, 1999, Zi

Lonestar College - Tomball

Geology Dept (2015)
30555 Tomball Parkway
Tomball, TX 77375
p. (281) 351-3324
David.O.Bary@lonestar.edu
http://www.lonestar.edu/geology-dept-tomball.htm

McLennan Community College

Geology Dept (A) (2015)
1400 College Drive
Waco, TX 76708
p. (254) 299-8442
efagner@mclennan.edu
http://www.mclennan.edu/departments/geol/
Instructor:
Elaine Alexander, Gg

Midland College

Geology (A) (2015)
3600 N. Garfield
Midland, TX 79705
p. (432) 685-4612
agiles@midland.edu
https://www.midland.edu/academics/degrees/stem/geology.php
Enrollment (2011): A: 14 (6)
Associate Professor:
Joan Gawloski, (M), Baylor, GgzGe
Antony Giles, (M), Sul Ross State, 2006, GgvGi
Assistant Professor:
Keonho Kim, (D), GgAmPi
Adjunct Professor:
Karen Waggoner, (D), Texas Tech, GgRhGc

Midwestern State University

Kimbell School of Geosciences (B,M) (2021)
3410 Taft
Wichita Falls, TX 76308
p. (940) 397-4250
geology.program@msutexas.edu
http://www.msutexas.edu/academics/scienceandmath/geosciences
f: https://www.facebook.com/MSUGeosProgram/
t: @KSG_msutexas
Programs: Geology; Environmental Sciences
Enrollment (2020): B: 51 (19) M: 14 (10)
Chair & Prothro Distinguished Associate Professor of Geological Science:
Jonathan D. Price, (D), Oklahoma, 1998, GiCuGz
Robert L. Bolin Distinguished Professor of Petroleum Geology:
W. Scott Meddaugh, (D), Harvard, 1982, GoEgCg
Assistant Professor and Graduate Coordinator:
Andrew Katumwehe, (D), Oklahoma State, 2016, YuvYe
Assistant Professor:
Peyton E. Lisenby, (D), Macquarie, 2017, GmeZi
Anna M. Weiss, (D), Texas, 2019, PcgGs
Emeritus:
Rebecca L. Dodge, (D), Colorado Mines, 1982, Zre
John Kocurko, (D), Texas Tech, 1972, Gs

Odessa College

Dept of Geology, Anthropology & Geography (A) (2015)
201 W. University
Odessa, TX 79762
p. (915) 335-6558
jbolton@odessa.edu
https://catalog.odessa.edu/preview_program.php?catoid=9&poid=1102&returnto=379
Enrollment (2010): A: 1 (1)
Associate Professor:
Gerald B. McAfee, (M), Sul Ross State, 1966, Pi

Paris Junior College

Dept of Science (2015)
2400 Clarksville Street
Paris, TX 75460
p. 903-782-0481
mbarnett@parisjc.edu
http://www.parisjc.edu/index.php/pjc2/directory-index/C208

Rice University

Center for Computational Earth Science (M,D) (2018)
MS-126

PO Box 1892
Houston, TX 77251-1892
p. (713) 348-3574
dmberry@rice.edu
http://earthscience.rice.edu/centers/ccg/
Enrollment (2016): M: 7 (2) D: 335 (4)
Associate Director:
Alan Levander, (D), Stanford, 1984, Ys
Professor:
Richard G. Gordon, (D), Stanford, 1979, YmGtYd
Adrian Lenardic, (D), California (Los Angeles), 1995, Gc
Julia K. Morgan, (D), Cornell, 1993, Gc
Fenglin Niu, (D), Tokyo, 1997, Ysg
Dale S. Sawyer, (D), MIT, 1982, Ys
Colin A. Zelt, (D), British Columbia, 1989, Ys
Assistant Professor:
Helge Gonnermann, (D), California (Berkeley), 2004, Gv

Dept of Civil and Environmental Engineering (M,D) ☒ (2019)
P.O. Box 1892
MS 519
Houston, TX 77251-1892
p. (713) 348-4949
bedient@rice.edu
http://ceve.rice.edu/
Certificates: UG - Bachelor of Science in Civil Engineering, UG - B.A. in Civil and Environmental Engineering, UG - Minor in energy and water sustainability (EWSU), GR - Master of Science (M.S.), Doctor of Philosophy (Ph.D.), Master of Civil and Environmental Engineering (M.C.E.E.)

Dept of Earth, Environmental and Planetary Sciences
(B,M,D) ☒ (2018)
MS 126
PO Box 1892
Houston, TX 77251-1892
p. (713) 348-4880
geol@rice.edu
http://earthscience.rice.edu/
Enrollment (2015): B: 28 (8) M: 45 (18) D: 40 (5)
Chair:
Cin-Ty A. Lee, (D), Harvard, 2001, CgGiv
Professor:
Rajdeep Dasgupta, (D), Minnesota, 2006, GxCg
Gerald R. Dickens, (D), Michigan, 1996, OgCg
Andre W. Droxler, (D), Miami, 1984, Gs
Richard G. Gordon, (D), Stanford, 1979, YmGtYd
Adrian Lenardic, (D), California, 1995, Yg
Alan R. Levander, (D), Stanford, 1984, Ye
Caroline A. Masiello, (D), California (Irvine), 1999, Zn
Julia K. Morgan, (D), Cornell, 1993, GctGv
Fenglin Niu, (D), Tokyo, 1997, YsGt
Dale S. Sawyer, (D), MIT, 1982, Yr
Colin A. Zelt, (D), British Columbia, 1989, Yg
Associate Professor:
Helge Gonnermann, (D), California (Berkeley), 2004, Gv
Assistant Professor:
Sylvia G. Dee, (D), S California, 2015, Zo
Melodie E. French, (D), Texas A&M, 2014, Gc
Jeffrey A. Nittrouer, (D), Texas, 2010, Gms
Kirsten L. Siebach, Caltech, 2016, Xg
Mark Torres, (D), S California, 2015, Cb
Laurence Y. Yeung, (D), Caltech, 2010, CsAsCl
Adjunct Professor:
Vitor Abreu, (D), Rice, 1998, Gg
K. K. Bissada, (D), Washington (St Louis), 1967, Cg
Jeffrey J. Dravis, (D), Rice, 1980, Gs
Paul M. Harris, (D), Miami, 1977, Yr
N Ross Hill, (D), Virginia, 1978
Stephen J. Mackwell, (D), Australian Nat, 1985, Yg
Patrick J. McGovern, (D), MIT, 1996, Xy
David L. Olgaard, (D), MIT, 1985, Yg
Stephanie S. Shipp, (D), Rice, 1999, Ze
Emeritus:
John B. Anderson, (D), Florida State, 1972, Gu
Albert W. Bally, (D), Zurich, 1953, Gg
H. C. Clark, (D), Stanford, 1966, YgGeYu
Dieter Heymann, (D), Amsterdam, 1958, Xm
William P. Leeman, (D), Oregon, 1974, Gi
Andreas Luttge, (D), Tubingen, 1990, Cg
John C. Stormer, Jr., (D), California (Berkeley), 1971, Gi
Manik Talwani, (D), Columbia, 1959, Yr
Peter R. Vail, (D), Northwestern, 1959, Gr
Department Administrator:
Lee Willson, Zn

Saint Mary's University

Dept of Physics and Earth Sciences (2015)
One Camino Santa Maria
San Antonio, TX 78228-8569
p. (210) 436-3235
rcardenas@stmarytx.edu
http://www.stmarytx.edu/acad/physicsandearthscience
Chair:
Paul Nienaber
Professor:
David Fitzgerald, (M), Iowa, 1977, Gd
Associate Professor:
Gene W. Lene, (D), Texas, 1981, Ge

Sam Houston State University

Department of Geography and Geology O✓ (2018)
Huntsville, TX 77341
p. (936) 294-1073
fsm002@shsu.edu
http://www.shsu.edu/academics/geography-geology/gis/graduate.html
Programs: Geography, Geology, GIS
Certificates: GIS
Associate Professor:
Falguni Mukherjee, (D), 2009, Zin

San Antonio Community College

Dept of Chemistry/Earth Sciences/Astronomy (A) (2015)
1300 San Pedro Avenue
CG Rm 207
San Antonio, TX 78212
p. (210) 486-0045
tstaggs@alamo.edu
http://www.alamo.edu/sac/earthsci
Professor:
Dean P. Lambert, (D), Texas, 1992, ZyiZz
Associate Professor:
Anne D. Dietz, (M), Texas A&M (Kingsville), 1989, PgZg
George R. Stanley, (M), Texas (San Antonio), 2006, XzZgRm
David A. Wood, (D), Arizona, 2000, XsZnn
Adjunct Professor:
Thomas Adams, (D), 2011, PvGg
T Scott Girhard, (M), SW Texas State, ZyAm
Robert Janusz, (M), Texas (San Antonio), Gg
Dwight J. Jurena, (M), Rensselaer, 2002, XgYvGz
Ryan E. Rudnicki, (D), Penn State, 1979, Zyr
C. Keith Smith, (M), Texas State, 2005, ZyzZz
Cooperating Faculty:
Steve Dingman, Zn

San Jacinto Community College-Central

Geology Dept (2015)
8060 Spencer Hwy.
Pasadena, TX 77089
p. (281) 998-6150 x1882
Karen.Purpera@sjcd.edu
http://www.sanjac.edu/

San Jacinto Community College-North

Geology Dept (2015)
5800 Uvalde
Houston, TX 77049
p. (281) 998-6150 x7210
susan.starr@sjcd.edu
http://www.sanjac.edu/

San Jacinto Community College-South

Geology Dept (2015)
13735 Beamer Rd.

Houston, TX 77089
p. (281) 998-6150 x4662
Tyler.Olivier@sjcd.edu
http://www.sanjac.edu/

Southern Methodist University

Roy M. Huffington Dept of Earth Sciences (B,M,D) O☒ (2020)
Post Office Box 750395
Dallas, TX 75275-0395
p. (214) 768-2750
geol@smu.edu
https://www.smu.edu/Dedman/Academics/Departments/Earth-Sciences
Programs: Geology, Geophysics
Administrative Assistant: Stephanie L. Schwob
Enrollment (2020): B: 25 (11) M: 11 (1) D: 18 (2)

Chair:
Robert T. Gregory, (D), Caltech, 1981, Cs
Shuler-Foscue Chair in Earth Sciences:
Zhong Lu, (D), Alaska (Fairbanks), 1996, Zr
Albritton Chair in Earth Sciences:
Brian W. Stump, (D), California (Berkeley), 1979, Ys
Professor:
Heather R. DeShon, (D), California (Santa Cruz), 2004, Ysr
Matthew J. Hornbach, (D), Wyoming, 2005, YrhYe
M. Beatrice Magnani, (D), Perugia, 2000, YsGtYe
James E. Quick, (D), Caltech, 1981, Gv
Neil J. Tabor, (D), California (Davis), 2002, SdGs
Crayton J. Yapp, (D), Caltech, 1980, Csl
Hamilton Chair in Earth Sciences:
Stephen J. Arrowsmith, (D), Leeds (UK), 2004, Ys
Associate Scientist:
Christopher T. Hayward, (D), S Methodist, 1997, Ys
Ian J. Richards, (D), Tennessee, 1994, Cs
Assistant Professor:
Rita C. Economos, (D), California (Los Angeles), 2009, CsGc
Adjunct Professor:
Anthony R. Fiorillo, (D), Pennsylvania, 1989, Pv
Matthew Siegler, (D), California (Los Angeles), 2011, YgXy
Alisa Winkler, (D), S Methodist, 1990, Pv
Dale A. Winkler, (D), Texas, 1985, Pv
Emeritus:
David D. Blackwell, (D), Harvard, 1968, Yh
Michael J. Holdaway, (D), California (Berkeley), 1963, Gp
Bonnie F. Jacobs, (D), Arizona, 1983, Pl
Louis L. Jacobs, (D), Arizona, 1977, Pv
Robert L. Laury, (D), Wisconsin, 1966, Gd
John V. Walther, (D), California (Berkeley), 1978, Cg

Stephen F. Austin State University

Dept of Geology (B,M) O (2020)
PO Box 13011 SFA Station
Nacogdoches, TX 75962
p. (936) 468-3701
geology@sfasu.edu
http://www.geology.sfasu.edu/
Programs: B.S. Geology, M.S. Geology
Administrative Assistant: Shana Scott
Enrollment (2020): B: 49 (9) M: 30 (4)

Chair:
Wesley A. Brown, (D), Texas (El Paso), 2004, YgsGt
Professor:
R. LaRell Nielson, (D), Utah, 1981, Grs
Kevin W. Stafford, (D), New Mexico Tech, 2008, Hw
Assistant Professor:
Julie M. Bloxson, (D), Case Western, 2017, Go
Melinda S. Faulkner, (D), Stephen F. Austin, 2016, GeClEg
Liane M. Stevens, (D), Montana, 2015, Gpc
Lab Coordinator:
Wesley L. Turner, (M), Stephen F. Austin, 2016, Gg
Lecturer:
Michael T. Read, (D), Texas (Arlington), 2018, PgGg
Visiting Professor:
Jenny M. Rashall, (D), Texas (Arlington), 2020, GgPg

Sul Ross State University

Dept of Biology, Geology and Physical Sciences (B,M) O☒ (2019)
Box C-64
Alpine, TX 79832
p. (432) 837-8112
measures@sulross.edu
http://www.sulross.edu/BGPS
Programs: Geology, Teacher Certification in Geology
Enrollment (2019): B: 28 (8) M: 21 (4)

Professor:
Elizabeth A. Measures, (D), Idaho, 1992, Gdq
Kevin Urbanczyk, (D), Washington State, 1993, GiZi
Assistant Professor:
Thomas Shiller, (D), Texas Tech, 2017, PvGrd
Lecturer:
Jesse Kelsch, (M), New Mexico, Gct
Emeritus:
David M. Rohr, (D), Oregon State, 1978, PiGd

Tarleton State University

Chemistry, Geosciences and Physics (B,M) ☒ (2019)
Box T-540
Stephenville, TX 76402
p. (254) 968-9143
rmorgan@tarleton.edu
http://www.tarleton.edu/CHGP/
Programs: Geosciences Bachelor's of Science (concentrations in Earth Science, Earth Science with Teacher Certification, Environmental Science, Geology, Petroleum Geology, Hydrogeology, Accelerated bachelor's-to-master's degree), Master's of Science in Geosciences, Master's of Science in Environmental Science
Certificates: GIS
Administrative Assistant: Eva Moody
Enrollment (2018): B: 47 (11) M: 11 (4)

Head:
Ryan Morgan, (D), Baylor, 2015, Pei
Professor:
Stephen W. Field, (D), Massachusetts, 1988, Gz
Assistant Professor:
Catherine Ronck, (D), God
Christopher Saxon, (D), Oklahoma, Gco
Instructor:
Joree Burnett, (M), Tarleton State, 2015, HwGe

Tarrant County College, Northeast Campus

Natural Science Dept (A) (2015)
828 Harwood Road
Hurst, TX 76054
p. (817) 515-6565
marles.mccurdy@tccd.edu
https://www.tccd.edu/academics/tcc-catalog/courses-and-programs/geology/
Enrollment (2011): A: 650 (30)

Associate Professor:
Meena Balakrishnan, (D), GggGg
Kevin M. Barrett, (D), Texas State, 2012, AsZgr
Professor:
Hayden R. Chasteen, (M), NE Louisiana, 1981, GgeGg

Tarrant County College, Southeast Campus

Physical Sciences Dept ☒ (2020)
2100 Southeast Pkwy
Arlington, TX 76018
p. (817) 515-3238
thomas.awtry@tccd.edu
https://www.tccd.edu/academics/
Programs: Associate of Science

Assistant Professor:
Stephanie Mitzman, (M), Texas A&M, 1999, Gg
Instructor:
Samantha Caputi, (M), 1997, Gg
Darren Greenaway, (M), 1997, Gg

Temple College

Temple College (2015)
2600 South First Street

Temple, TX 76504
p. (254) 298-8472
john.mcclain@templejc.edu
http://www.templejc.edu/

Texas A&M University

Center For Tectonophysics (M,D) (2017)
3115 TAMU
Department Geology & Geophysics
College of Geosciences
College Station, TX 77843-3115
p. (979) 845-3296
chesterf@tamu.edu
http://tectono.tamu.edu/
Enrollment (2016): M: 7 (1) D: 13 (1)

Director:
Frederick Chester, (D), Texas A&M, 1988, GcNrYx
Assistant Director:
Andreas Kronenberg, (D), Brown, 1983, GtyGc
Professor:
Judith Chester, (D), Texas A&M, 1992, GcNrGo
Marcelo J. Sanchez, (D), Politecnica de Catalunya, 2004, NtrNx
Associate Professor:
Benchuan Duan, (D), California (Riverside), 2006, YsgGq
David Sparks, (D), Brown, 1992, YdGq
Assistant Professor:
Patrick M. Fulton, (D), Penn State, 2008, YhHyRn
Hiroko Kitajima, (D), Texas A&M, 2010, YxSpGc
Julia S. Reece, (D), Texas, 2011, SpGso

Dept of Atmospheric Sciences (B,M,D) ☒ (2019)
3150 TAMU
College Station, TX 77843-3150
p. (979) 845-7671
sarava@tamu.edu
http://atmo.tamu.edu/
Programs: Meteorology (B); Atmospheric Sciences (M,D)
Enrollment (2018): B: 120 (0) M: 20 (0) D: 20 (0)

Instructional Professor:
Don T. Conlee, (D), Texas A&M, 1994
Distinguished Professor:
Gerald North, (D), 1966, As
Distinguished Professor :
Renyi Zhang, (D), MIT, 1993, As
Department Head:
Ping Yang, (D), Utah, 1995, As
Professor:
Kenneth P. Bowman, (D), Princeton, 1984, Am
Sarah D. Brooks, (D), Colorado, 2002, AsZc
Ping Chang, (D), Princeton, 1988, Op
Andrew E. Dessler, (D), Harvard, 1994, As
John Nielsen-Gammon, (D), MIT, 1990, As
Richard L. Panetta, (D), Wisconsin, 1978, Am
R. Saravanan, (D), Princeton, 1990, As
Courtney Schumacher, (D), Washington, 2003, As
Istvan Szunyogh, (D), Hungarian Acad of Sci, 1994, As
Associate Professor:
Craig Epifanio, (D), Washington, As
Robert Korty, (D), MIT, 2005, As
Gunnar Schade, (D), Johannes-Gutenberg (Germany), 1997, As
Instructional Assistant Professor:
Tim Logan
Assistant Professor:
Christopher J. Nowotarski, (D), Penn State, 2013, Ams
Anita Rapp, (D), Colorado State, 2008, Zr
Yangyang Xu
Adjunct Professor:
Alex Dessler, (D), Duke, 1956, As
Emeritus:
Richard E. Orville, (D), Arizona, 1966, As

Dept of Geography (B,M,D) (2015)
810 Eller O&M Building
3147 TAMU
College Station, TX 77843-3147
p. (979) 845-7141
cbruton@geog.tamu.edu
http://geog.tamu.edu/
Enrollment (2009): B: 156 (40) M: 16 (8) D: 18 (3)

Head:
David M. Cairns, (D), Iowa, 1995, Zy
Professor:
Sarah W. Bednarz, (D), Texas A&M, 1992, Ze
John R. Giardino, (D), Nebraska, 1979, Gm
Andrew G. Klein, (D), Cornell, 1997, ZriGl
Michael R. Waters, (D), Arizona, 1983, Ga
Associate Professor:
Daniel Z. Sui, (D), Goergia, 1993, Zr
Vatche P. Tchakerian, (D), California (Los Angeles), 1989, Gm
Assistant Professor:
Anne Chin, (D), Arizona State, 1994, Gm
Research Associate:
Jean A. Bowman, (M), Rutgers, 1984, Hg
Emeritus:
Robert S. Bednarz, (D), Chicago, 1975, Zeu
Clarissa T. Kimber, (D), Wisconsin, 1969, Zy

Dept of Geology & Geophysics (B,M,D) (2015)
3115 TAMU
College Station, TX 77843-3115
p. (979) 845-2451
mcpope@tamu.edu
http://geoweb.tamu.edu
Enrollment (2012): B: 278 (41) M: 81 (21) D: 66 (5)

Head:
John R. Giardino, (D), Nebraska, 1979, GmNg
Regents Professor:
Mary J. Richardson, (D), MIT, 1980, Op
Professor:
Tom Blasingame, (D), Texas A&M, 1989, Np
Richard L. Carlson, (D), Washington, 1976, YrGty
Frederick M. Chester, (D), Texas A&M, 1988, GcNr
Judith Chester, (D), Texas A&M, 1992, GcNr
Mark Everett, (D), Toronto, 1991, Ym
Richard L. Gibson, Jr., (D), MIT, 1991, Yse
Ethan L. Grossman, (D), S California, 1982, Csl
Andrew Hajash, (D), Texas A&M, 1975, Cp
Bruce Herbert, (D), California (Riverside), 1992, Ge
Andreas Kronenberg, (D), Brown, 1983, GyNr
Franco Marcantonio, (D), Columbia, 1994, Ct
Julie Newman, (D), Rochester, 1993, Gct
Anne Raymond, (D), Chicago, 1983, Pb
William W. Sager, (D), Hawaii, 1979, Ou
David Sparks, (D), Brown, 1992, YgGq
Yuefeng Sun, (D), Columbia, 1994, GoYe
Debbie Thomas, (D), North Carolina, 2002, Ou
Thomas E. Yancey, (D), California (Berkeley), 1971, Pg
Hongbin Zhan, (D), Nevada (Reno), 1996, Hw
Associate Research Professor:
Renald Guillemette, (D), Stanford, 1983, Gz
Associate Professor:
Benchun Duan, (D), California (Riverside), 2006, YsGtYg
Will Lamb, (D), Wisconsin, 1987, GpCpGz
Brent Miller, (D), Dalhousie, 1997, Cc
Julie Newman, (D), Rochester, 1993, Gc
Thomas Olszewski, (D), Penn State, 2000, Pe
Michael Pope, (D), Virginia Tech, 1995, GrCc
Assistant Professor:
Mike Tice, (D), Stanford, 2006, Pg
Assistant Dean :
Eric Riggs, (D), California (Riverside), 2000, Gy
Lecturer:
Alfonso Benavides-Iglesias, (D), Texas A&M, 2007, Ys
Emeritus:
Christopher C. Mathewson, (D), Arizona, 1971, NgHwEg
John D. Vitek, (D), Iowa, 1973, GmZe
Technical Laboratory Director:
Michael Heaney, (D), Texas A&M, 1998, Pg
Dean of College of Geosciences:
Kate Miller, (D), Stanford, 1991, Ys

Dept of Oceanography (B,M,D) (2017)
1204 Eller O&M Blg
MS 3146
College Station, TX 77843-3146
p. (979) 845-7211
syvon-lewis@tamu.edu

http://ocean.tamu.edu
Programs: Oceanography (B, M, D); Ocean Science and Technology (M)
Enrollment (2017): B: 8 (0) M: 22 (10) D: 42 (6)
Director, Texas Sea Grant:
Pamela Plotkin, (D), Texas A&M, 1994, Ob
Interim Dean:
Debbie Thomas, (D), North Carolina, 2002, Ou
Head:
Shari A. Yvon-Lewis, (D), Miami, 1994, Oc
Executive Associate Dean for Research:
Jack G. Baldauf, (D), California (Berkeley), 1984, Ou
Director, Geochemical and Environmental Research Group:
Anthony Knap, (D), Southampton (UK), Oc
Professor:
Rainier MW Amon, (D), Texas, 1995, CbOcb
David A. Brooks, (D), Miami, 1975, Op
Lisa Campbell, (D), SUNY (Stony Brook), 1985, Ob
Ping Chang, (D), Princeton, 1988, Op
Piers Chapman, (D), Univ Coll (N Wales), 1982, OcCm
Steven F. DiMarco, (D), Texas (Dallas), 1991, OpnOg
Wilford D. Gardner, (D), MIT/WHOI, 1978, OugZr
Benjamin S. Giese, (D), Washington, 1989, Op
Gerardo Gold-Bouchot, (D), Ctr Res Adv Stud (Mexico), 1991, OcCm
Norman L. Guinasso, (D), Texas A&M, 1984, Opc
Robert D. Hetland, (D), Florida State, 1999, Op
Alejandro H. Orsi, (D), Texas A&M, 1993, Op
Mary Jo Richardson, (D), MIT/WHOI, 1980, Gu
Gilbert T. Rowe, (D), Duke, 1968, Ob
Peter H. Santschi, (D), Switzerland (Berne), 1975, Oc
Niall C. Slowey, (D), MIT, 1991, Ou
Senior Scientist:
Troy L. Holcombe, (D), Columbia, 1972, OuGcg
Matthew K. Howard, (D), Texas A&M, 1992, Op
Ann E. Jochens, (D), Texas A&M, 1977, Op
Adam Klaus, (D), Hawaii, 1991, Gu
Associate Professor:
Ayal Anis, (D), Oregon State, 1993, Opn
Timothy M. Dellapenna, (D), William & Mary, 1999, Ou
Anja Schulze, (D), Victoria, 2001, Ob
Achim Stoessel, (D), Hamburg, 1990, OpAmGl
Daniel C.O Thornton, (D), Queen Mary (London), 1995, Ob
Associate Scientist:
Steven K. Baum, (D), Texas A&M, 1996, Op
Jose L. Sericano, (D), Texas A&M, 1993, Cm
Assistant Professor:
Jessica N. Fitzsimmons, (D), MIT/WHOI, 2013, OcCta
Henry Potter, (D), Miami, 2014, Op
Kathryn E. F. Shamberger, (D), Washington, 2011, OcZc
Jason B. Sylvan, (D), Rutgers, 2008, ObXb
Chrissy Wiederwohl, (D), Texas A&M, 2012, Op
Yige Zhang, (D), Yale, 2014, Co
Research Associate:
Shinichi Kobara, (D), Texas A&M, Zi
Marion Stoessel, (M), Hamburg, 1985, Op
Zhankun Wang, (D), Massachusetts (Dartmouth), 2009, Op
Distinguished Professor Emeritus:
Robert A. Duce, (D), MIT, 1964, Oc
Worth D. Nowlin, Jr., (D), Texas A&M, 1966, OpZn
Distinguished Professor:
Gerald R. North, (D), Wisconsin, 1966, Am
Director, Texas Sea Grant College Program:
Robert R. Stickney, (D), Florida State, 1971, Ob
Emeritus:
Douglas C. Biggs, (D), MIT/WHOI, 1976, Ob
George A. Jackson, (D), Caltech, 1976, Op
Bobby J. Presley, (D), California, 1969, Oc
Robert H. Stewart, (D), California (San Diego), 1969, Op
Laboratory Director:
Terry L. Wade, (D), Rhode Island, 1978, OcCao

Dept of Soil & Crop Sciences (B,M,D) ☒ (2017)
TAMU 2474
College Station, TX 77843-2474
p. (979) 845-3603
cmorgan@tamu.edu
http://soilcrop.tamu.edu
Programs: Environmental Plant and Soil Science
Certificates: none
Enrollment (2017): B: 32 (15) M: 19 (3) D: 21 (3)
Professor:
David D. Baltensperger, (D), New Mexico State, 1981, PvCbSb
Terry Gentry, (D), Arizona, Sb
Kevin J. McInnes, (D), Kansas State, 1985, Sp
Cristine L. S. Morgan, (D), Wisconsin, 2003, Spd
Tony L. Provin, (D), Purdue, 1995, Sc
Paul Schwab, (D), Colorado State, 1981, Sc
Associate Professor:
Jacqueline A. Aitkenhead-Peterson, (D), New Hampshire, 2000, HsSoGf
Paul DeLaune, (D), Arkansas, 2002, So
Youjun Deng, (D), Texas A&M, 2001, GzSc
Fugen Dou, (D), Texas A&M, 2005, So
Julie Howe, (D), Wisconsin, 2004, Sc
Donald McGahan, (D), California (Davis), 2007, Sdc
Assistant Professor:
Jourdan Bell, Texas A&M, 2014
Katie Lewis, (D), Texas A&M, 2014, Sco
Jake Mowrer, (D), Georgia, 2014, Sc
Haly L. Neely, (D), Texas A&M, 2014, Spd
Anil Somenhally, (D), Texas A&M, 2010, Sb

Texas A&M University, Commerce

Dept of Biological & Environmental Sciences (B,M) (2015)
Commerce, TX 75429
p. (903) 886-5378
DongWon.Choi@tamuc.edu
http://www.tamu-commerce.edu/biology/
Assistant Professor:
Haydn A "Chip" Fox, (D), South Carolina, 1994, HgGe

Texas A&M University, Corpus Christi

Dept of Physical and Environmental Sciences (B) (2017)
6300 Ocean Drive
Corpus Christi, TX 78412
p. (361) 825-6000
Valeriu.Murgulet@tamucc.edu
http://geology.tamucc.edu/
Enrollment (2016): B: 84 (13)
Chair, Dept, Physical and Environmental Sciences:
Richard Coffin, (D), Delaware, 1986, Ouc
Professor:
Jennifer M. Smith-Engle, (D), Georgia, 1983, Gs
Associate Professor:
Thomas H. Naehr, (D), GEOMAR (Kiel), 1996, GuCm
Director, Center for Water Supply Studies:
Dorina Murgulet, (D), Alabama, 2009, Hw
Assistant Professor:
Xinping Hu, (D), Old Dominion, 2007, Oc
Brandi Kiel Reese, (D), Texas A&M, 2011, Obc
Endowed Associate Research Professor:
James Gibeaut, (D), S Florida, 1991, OnZi
Adjunct Professor:
Clinton Randall (R Bissell, (M), Oklahoma State, 1984, GosGr
Erika Locke, (M), California (Los Angeles), 1998, GgoGs
Coordinator, Geology Program:
Valeriu Murgulet, (D), Alabama, 2010, Cg

Environmental Science Program (B,M) (2020)
6300 Ocean Drive
Corpus Christi, TX 78412
p. (361) 825-2814
jennifer.smith-engle@tamucc.edu
http://sci.tamucc.edu/PENS
Programs: Environmental Science
Enrollment (2020): B: 222 (52) M: 18 (9)
Director of National Spill Control School:
Howard Wood, (M), American Military Univ, 2011, ZeHsZn
Program Coordinator:
Jennifer M. Smith-Engle, (D), Georgia, 1983, Gs
Endowed Chair for Socioeconomics:
David Yoskowitz, (D), Texas Tech, 1997, Zn
Endowed Chair for Fisheries and Ocean Health:
Greg Stunz, (D), Texas A&M, 1999, Zn
Endowed Chair for Ecosystems Studies and Modeling:
Paul Montagna, (D), South Carolina, 1983, ObCmHs

Director of Center for Coastal Studies:
Paul Zimba, (D), Mississippi State, 1990, Zn
Chair, Physical and Environmental Sciences Dept.:
Richard Coffin, (D), Delaware, 1986, Oc
Professor:
Fereshteh Billiot, (D), Louisiana State, 2000, Zn
Cherie McCollough, (D), Texas, 2005, Ze
Richard McLaughlin, (D), California (Berkeley), 1997, Zn
Toshiaki Shinoda, (D), Hawaii, 1993, As
Chair, Center for Water Supply Studies:
Dorina Murgulet, (D), Alabama, 2009, Hw
Associate Professor:
Hussain Abdulla, (D), Old Dominion, 2009, Co
Darek Bogucki, (D), S California, 1996, Op
Gregory Buck, (D), Georgia State, 1999, Zn
Kirk Cammerata, (D), Kentucky, 1987, Zn
Jeremy Conkle, (D), Louisiana State, 2010, Zn
Xinping Hu, (D), Old Dominion, 2007, Cms
Patrick Larkin, (D), Texas A&M, 1999, Zn
Riccardo Mozzachiodi, (D), Pisa, 1999, Zn
Jennifer Pollack, (D), South Carolina, 2006, Ob
James Silliman, (D), Michigan, 1998, Co
Michael Starek, (D), Florida, 2008, Zi
Michael Wetz, (D), Oregon State, 2006, Ob
Assistant Professor:
Mohamed Ahmed, (D), W Michigan, 2012, YgZri
Sharon Derrick, (D), Texas A&M, 2001, Zn
Joseph David Felix, (D), Pittsburg State, 2012, Zn
Chuntao Liu, (D), Wyoming, 2003, As
Lindsay O. Prothro, (D), Rice, 2018, GluGs
Kim Withers, (D), Texas A&M, 1994, Zn
Lin Zhang, (D), Rhode Island, 2012, Cs
Research Associate:
Philippe Tissot, (D), Texas A&M, 1994, Zn

Texas A&M University, Kingsville

Dept of Geosciences (B) O (2017)
Campus Box 164
Kingsville, TX 78363
p. (512) 595-3310
kftlm00@tamuk.edu
Enrollment (2016): B: 52 (6)
Professor:
Thomas L. McGehee, (D), Texas (Dallas), 1987, Cl
Assistant Professor:
Mark T. Ford, (D), Oregon State, GxzCg
Brent Hedquist, (D), Arizona State, 2010, ZyAtZi
Veronica I. Sanchez, (D), Houston, GctGm
Robert V. Schneider, (D), Texas (El Paso), 1990, GoYes
Haibin Su, (D), Cincinnati, Zir
Subbarao Yelisetti, (D), Victoria (Canada), 2014, Ygs
Lecturer:
Richard M. Parker, (M), Texas A&M, 2000, GgPg

Texas Christian University

Department of Geological Sciences (B,M) ☒ (2018)
TCU Box 298830
2950 West Bowie
Fort Worth, TX 76129
p. (817) 257-7270
geology@tcu.edu
https://geology.tcu.edu/
Programs: Geology; Applied Geoscience
Administrative Assistant: Krista Scapelli
Enrollment (2016): B: 76 (13) M: 30 (6)
TCU Provost and Academic Vice Chancellor:
R Nowell Donovan, (D), Newcastle upon Tyne, 1972, GdcGt
Professor of Professional Practice:
Richard A. Denne, (D), Louisiana State, 1990, GoPms
Professor:
Richard E. Hanson, (D), Columbia, 1983, GxvGt
John M. Holbrook, (D), Indiana, 1992, Gsr
Chair:
Helge Alsleben, (D), S California, 2005, GctGg
Associate Professor:
Arthur B. Busbey, (D), Chicago, 1982, PgvGr
Xiangyang Xie, (D), Wyoming, 2007, GoEog
Assistant Professor:
Omar R. Harvey, (D), Texas A&M, 2010, GeHwg
Adjunct Professor:
Floyd Henk, Jr., (M), Texas Christian, 1981, Go
Emeritus:
John Breyer, (D), Nebraska, 1977, GsdEo
Professor of Professional Practice:
Milton Enderlin, (M), Texas Christian, 2010, Nr
Tamie Morgan, (M), Texas Christian, 1984, Zi

Texas State University

Dept of Geography (B,M,D) ☒ (2020)
Evans Liberal Arts, Room 139
601 University Drive
San Marcos, TX 78666
p. (512) 245-2170
rd11@txstate.edu
http://www.geo.txstate.edu
Chair:
Richard W. Dixon, (D), Zy

Richard W. Dixon ☒ (2020)
601 University Drive
Evans Liberal Arts Room 139
San Marcos, TX 78666
p. (512) 245-2170
rd11@txstate.edu
https://www.geo.txstate.edu
Programs: Physical Geography (BS), Resource and Environmental Studies (BA, BS, MAG), Geographic Information Science (BA, BS, MAG), Water Resources (BA, BS), Geology (minor), Geography (MS, PhD)
Certificates: Geographic Information Science, Water Resources Policy, Environmental Interpretation
Professor of Practice:
Timothy Loftus, (D), S Illinois (Carbondale), 2000, RwHs
Robert Mace, (D), Texas, 1998, HwgHy
Department Chair:
Yongmei Lu, (D), SUNY (Buffalo), 2001, Zi
Professor:
R. Denise Blanchard, (D), Colorado, 1992, RnmRc
Richard Dixon, (D), Texas A&M, 1996, AsOpRn
Alberto Giordano, (D), Syracuse, 1999, Zi
Jason Julian, (D), N Carolina, 2007, HsRwZc
Oswaldo Muniz-Solari, (D), Tennessee, 1991, Ze
John Tiefenbacher, (D), Rutgers, 1992, Rnm
F Benjamin Zhan, (D), SUNY (Buffalo), 1994, Zi
Associate Professor:
Edwin Chow, (D), S Carolina, 2005, ZiRn
Nathan Currit, (D), Penn State, 2003, ZruZc
Ronald Hagelman III, (D), Texas State, 2001, Rnm
Jennifer Jensen, (D), Idaho, 2009, Zru
Injeong Jo, (D), Texas A&M, 2011, Ze
Kimberly Meitzen, (D), S Carolina, 2011, HsGmZy
Assistant Professor:
Samantha Krause, (D), Texas, 2018, ScHyZc
Yanan Li, (D), Tennessee, 2015, GmCcPc
Alexander Savelyev, (D), Penn State, 2015, Zfi
Yihong Yuan, (D), California (Santa Barbara), 2013, Ze
Senior Lecturer:
Rene Dehon, (D), Texas Tech, 1970, GzxGg
Suzon Jammes, (D), Strasbourg, 2009, GgYg
Christi Townsend, (D), Texas State, 2012, Zy
Dolores van der Kolk, (D), Texas, 2016, Gcg

Texas Tech University

Dept of Geosciences (B,M,D) O (2016)
Box 41053
2500 Broadway
Science 125
Lubbock, TX 79409-1053
p. (806) 834-0497
alison.winton@ttu.edu
http://www.geosciences.ttu.edu
Enrollment (2015): B: 390 (33) M: 48 (21) D: 23 (0)
Chair:
Jeffrey A. Lee, (D), Arizona State, 1990, Zy

Horn Professor:
Sankar Chatterjee, (D), Calcutta, 1970, PvGct
Professor:
George B. Asquith, (D), Wisconsin, 1966, Go
Calvin G. Barnes, (D), Oregon, 1982, Gi
James E. Barrick, (D), Iowa, 1978, Psm
Gary S. Elbow, (D), Pittsburgh, 1972
Juske Horita, (D), Texas A&M, 1997
Thomas M. Lehman, (D), Texas, 1985, Gs
Moira K. Ridley, (D), Nebraska, 1997, CqlZm
John L. Schroeder, (D), Texas Tech, 1999, As
Paul J. Sylvester, (D)
Aaron S. Yoshinobu, (D), S California, 1999, GctGu
Senior Scientist:
Melanie A. Barnes, (D), Texas Tech, 2001, CaGie
Associate Professor:
Eric C. Bruning, (D), Oklahoma, 2008, As
Perry L. Carter, (D), Ohio State, 1998
Harold Gurrola, (D), California (San Diego), 1995, Ys
Callum J. Hetherington, (D), Basel (Switzerland), 2001, GxzCg
Haraldur R. Karlsson, (D), Chicago, 1988, Cl
David W. Leverington, (D), Manitoba, 2001, GmZrXg
Kevin R. Mulligan, (D), Texas A&M, 1997, ZiGmSo
Seiichi Nagihara, (D), Texas, 1992, Zi
Dustin E. Sweet, (D), Oklahoma, 2009, GsdGr
Christopher C. Weiss, (D), Oklahoma, 2004, AssAs
Assistant Professor:
Brian C. Ancell, (D), Washington, 2006, As
Guofeng Cao, (D), California (Santa Barbara), 2011, Zi
Johannes M L Dahl, (D), Ludwig-Maximilians (Germany), 2010, Ams
Song-Lak Kang, (D), Penn State, 2007, AsHg
Instructor:
Steven R. Cobb, As
Linda L. Jones, (M), California (Los Angeles), 1986
Justin E. Weaver, (M), Texas Tech, 1992, As
Professor:
Richard E. Peterson, (D), Missouri, 1971, As
Unit Coordinator:
Alisan C. Sweet, (M), Oklahoma, 2011, Gs
Debra J. Walker
Senior Technician:
James M. Browning, (B), Lamar, 1983, Ggx
Senior Business Assistant:
Alison Winton, (B), Texas Tech, 1992, ZnnZn
Computer Technician:
Darren W. Hedrick
Academic Advisor:
Celeste N. Yoshinobu, (M), San Diego State, 1994

Trinity University

Department of Geosciences (B) ☒ (2020)
One Trinity Place
San Antonio, TX 78212-7200
p. (210) 999-7092
ksurples@trinity.edu
https://www.trinity.edu/academics/departments/geosciences
Programs: Geosciences (B); Earth Systems Science (B)
Enrollment (2020): B: 31 (13)
Chair:
Kathleen D. Surpless, (D), Stanford, 2001, Gst
Professor:
Daniel J. Lehrmann, (D), Kansas, 1993, PiGs
Diane R. Smith, (D), Rice, 1984, Gi
Benjamin E. Surpless, (D), Stanford, 1999, GctGi
Associate Professor:
Glenn C. Kroeger, (D), Stanford, 1987, Yg
Assistant Professor:
Brady A. Ziegler, (D), Virginia Tech, 2018, HwCqGe
Adjunct Professor:
Leslie F. Bleamaster III, (D), S Methodist, 2003, Xg
Visiting Professor:
Kurt Knesel, (D), California (Los Angeles), 1998, Gvi
Emeritus:
Walter Coppinger, (D), Miami (Ohio), 1974, Gcg
Robert L. Freed, (D), Michigan, 1966, Gz
Thomas W. Gardner, (D), Cincinnati, 1978, GmtHg

Tyler Junior College

Dept of Geology (2015)
1327 South Baxter Avenue
Tyler, TX 75701
p. (903) 510-2232
wbec@tjc.edu
http://www.tjc.edu/

University of Houston

Allied Geophysical Laboratories (AGL) (B,M,D) O☒ (2018)
SR1 131C
Houston, TX 77204-4231
p. (713) 743-9150
rrstewart@uh.edu
http://www.agl.uh.edu
Programs: Research and Development in Applied Geophysics especially exploration seismology
Professor:
Robert R. Stewart, (D), MIT, 1983, YesYu

Dept of Earth and Atmospheric Sciences (B,M,D) O☒ (2020)
Science & Research Building 1
3507 Cullen Blvd, Rm. 312
Houston, TX 77204-5007
p. (713) 743-3399
tjlapen@uh.edu
http://www.eas.uh.edu
Administrative Assistant: Edwina Boateng Kumi, Jim Parker, Kirene Ramesar, Anja Wells
Enrollment (2016): B: 413 (69) M: 129 (41) D: 128 (10)
Chair:
Thomas Lapen, (D), Wisconsin, 2005, Gz
Professor:
Alan Brandon, (D), Alberta, 1992, GiCac
John F. Casey, (D), SUNY (Albany), 1980, GtiGu
John P. Castagna, (D), Texas, 1983, Ye
Henry S. Chafetz, (D), Texas, 1970, Gds
Evgeny Chesnokov, (D), Russian Acad of Sci, 1987, YseYx
Peter Copeland, (D), SUNY (Albany), 1990, CcGt
Stuart A. Hall, (D), Newcastle, 1976, Ym
Shuhab D. Khan, (D), Texas (Dallas), 2001, ZrGtYg
Aibing Li, (D), Brown, 2000, Ys
Rosalie F. Maddocks, (D), Kansas, 1965, Pm
Paul Mann, (D), SUNY (Albany), 1983
Michael Murphy, (D), California (Los Angeles), 2000, Gct
Bernhard Rappenglueck, (D), Munich, 1996, As
Arch M. Reid, (D), Pittsburgh, 1964, GizXm
William W. Sager, (D), Hawaii, 1983, GtYrm
Jonathan Snow, (D), MIT/WHOI, 1992, Ca
Robert Stewart, (D), MIT, 1983, Ye
John Suppe, (D), Yale, 1969, Gtc
Robert Talbot, (D), Wisconsin, 1981, ActAm
Arthur B. Weglein, (D), CUNY, 1980, Ye
Hua-Wei Zhou, (D), Caltech, 1989, YseYg
University Distinguished Research Professor:
Fred Hilterman, (D), Colorado Mines, 1970, Ye
Research Professor:
Adry Bissada, (D), Washington, 1967, Co
De-hua Han, (D), Stanford, 1987, Ye
Leon Thomsen, (D), Columbia, 1969, Ye
Research Associate Professor:
Donald Van Niewenhuise, (D), South Carolina, 1978, PsGoPe
Associate Professor:
Regina M. Capuano, (D), Arizona, 1988, HwCqs
William R. Dupre, (D), Stanford, 1975, On
Xun Jiang, (D), Caltech, 2006
Alexander Robinson, (D), California (Los Angeles), 2005, Gc
Guoquan Wang, (D), Inst of Geology (China), 2001
Research Associate Professor:
Yongjun Gao, (D), Goettingen (Germany), 2004, CstCa
Virginia Sisson, (D), Princeton, 1985, Gpt
Instructional Assistant Professor:
Daniel Hauptvogel, (D), CUNY, 2015
Jennifer N. Lytwyn, (D), Houston, 1993, Gi
Assistant Professor:
Emily Beverly, (D), Baylor
Yunsoo Choi, (D), Georgia Tech, 2007

Qi Fu, (D), Minnesota, 2006, CosCa
Joel Saylor, (D), Arizona, 2008
Yuxuan Wang, (D), Harvard, 2005, As
Julia Wellner, (D), Rice, 2001, GslOu
Jonny Wu, (D), Royal Holloway (UK), 2010, GtcGo
Yingcai Zheng, (D), California (Santa Cruz), 2007

Research Scientist:
Tom Bjorklund, (D), Houston, 2002, Gco
Martin Cassidy, (D), Houston, 2005, GoCo
Nikolay Dyaur, (D), Russian Acad of Sci, 1986, Yxs
Xiangshan Li, (D), Tulane, 2000, Asm

Research Professor:
James Lawrence, (D), Caltech, 1970, Cl
Peter Percell, (D), California (Berkeley), 1973, As

Research Associate Professor:
Dale Bird, (D), Houston, 2004
Robert Wiley, (D), Colorado Mines, 1980

Research Assistant Professor:
James Flynn, (M), Houston, 1991
Charlotte Sjunneskog, (D), Uppsala, 2002

Adjunct Professor:
Peter Bartok, (M), SUNY (Buffalo), 1972, GoYeNr

Senior Researcher:
Mike Darnell, (B), Texas A&M, 1974

Postdoctoral Fellow:
Hao Hu, (D), CAS (China), 2015, Ye

Adjunct:
Amy Kelly, (D), MIT, 2009
Gary Morris, (D), Rice, 1995

Researcher:
Min Sun
Ewa Szymczyk
Fuyong Yan

Laboratory Supervisor:
Minako Righter, (D), Grad Univ for Adv Studies, 2006

University of Houston Downtown

Dept of Natural Sciences (2015)
1 Main Street
Houston, TX 77002
p. (713) 221-8015
lyonsp@uhd.edu

Professor:
Glen K. Merrill, (D), Louisiana State, 1968, Pi
Penny A. Morris-Smith, (D), California (Berkeley), 1975

Associate Professor:
Kenneth Johnson, (D), Texas Tech, 1995, GiCac

Lecturer:
Donald S. Musselwhite, (D), 1995

University of North Texas

Dept of Geography (B,M) (2019)
1155 Union Circle #305279
Denton, TX 76203
p. (940) 565-2091
geog@unt.edu
http://www.geography.unt.edu
Certificates: GIS
Administrative Assistant: Tami Deaton

Professor:
Pinliang Dong, (D), New Brunswick, 2003, Zir
C. Reid Ferring, (D), Texas (Dallas), 1993, Ga
Paul F. Hudak, (D), California (Santa Barbara), 1991, Hw
Joseph R. Oppong, (D), Alberta, 1992, Zn
Murray Rice, (D), Saskatchewan, 1995, Zn
Harry F. L. Williams, (D), Simon Fraser, 1989, Gm
Steve Wolverton, (D), N Texas, 2001, Ga

Associate Professor:
Waquar Ahmed, (D), Clark, 2007, Zn
Ipsita Chatterjee, (D), Clark, 2007, Zn
Matthew Fry, (D), Texas, 2008, Zn
Kent M. McGregor, (D), Kansas, 1982, AsZg
Lisa A. Nagaoka, (D), Washington, 2000, Ga
Feifei Pan, (D), Georgia Tech, 2002, Hw
Alexandra Ponette-Gonzalez, (D), Yale, 2011, Zyc
Chetan Tiwari, (D), Iowa, 2008, Zi

Assistant Professor:
Lu Liang, (D), Zi

University of Texas Permian Basin

Geosciences (B,M) O (2020)
4901 E. University Boulevard
Geosciences
Odessa, TX 79762-0001
p. (432) 552-2243
zavada_m@utpb.edu
http://www.utpb.edu/geosciences
Programs: BS Geology with optional concentrations in Petroleum Geology and Environmental Geology. MS Geology with both Thesis and Non-Thesis options.
Enrollment (2018): B: 20 (0)

Chair:
Mike Zavada

Assistant Professor:
Miles Henderson, (D), Tennessee, 2018, GsdGg
Joon Heo, (D), Texas A&M, 2012, Hg
Sumit Verma, (D), Oklahoma, 2015, YeGo
Mohamed Zobaa, (D), Missouri S&T, 2011, PlEoCo

Lecturer:
Robert C. Trentham, (D), Texas (El Paso), 1981, Go

University of Texas Rio Grande Valley

School of Earth, Environmental, and Marine Sciences (2015)
Brownsville, TX 78520
p. (956) 761-2644
abdullah.rahman@utrgv.edu
https://www.utrgv.edu/graduate/for-future-students/graduate-programs/program-requirements/ocean-coastal-and-earth-sciences-ms/in

University of Texas, Arlington

Dept of Earth & Environmental Sciences (B,M,D) O (2017)
Box 19049
500 Yates Street
Arlington, TX 76019
p. (817) 272-2987
geology@uta.edu
http://www.uta.edu/ees/
Enrollment (2014): B: 189 (29) M: 70 (21) D: 28 (3)

Professor:
Asish Basu, (D), California (Davis), 1975, GxCcs
Glen Mattioli, (D), Northwestern, 1987, GitYd
Merlynd K. Nestell, (D), Oregon State, 1966, PmiPs

Associate Professor:
Qinhong (Max) Hu, (D), Arizona, 1995, GoHwNg
Andrew Hunt, (D), Liverpool (UK), 1988, GbCg
Arne M. Winguth, (D), Hamburg, 1997, OpAs

Assistant Professor:
Majie Fan, (D), Arizona, 2009, GstCs
Ashley Griffith, (D), Stanford, 2008, Gct
Liz Griffith, (D), Stanford, 2008, CslCm
Ashanti Johnson, (D), OgGe

Lecturer:
Cornelia Winguth, (D), Hamburg, 1998, GugZm

Adjunct Professor:
John E. Damuth, (D), Columbia, 1973, GusYr
Galina P. Nestell, (D), VSEGEI (Russia), 1990, PmsPi

Emeritus:
Brooks Ellwood, (D), Rhode Island, 1977, Yg
Christopher R. Scotese, (D), Chicago, 1985, Gt
John S. Wickham, (D), Johns Hopkins, 1969, Gco

University of Texas, Austin

Dept of Marine Science (M,D) ● ☒ (2019)
750 Channel View Drive
Port Aransas, TX 78373-5015
p. (361) 749-6711
facsearch@utlists.utexas.edu
http://www.utmsi.utexas.edu
f: www.facebook.com/utmsi
Programs: Marine Science
Enrollment (2015): M: 16 (6) D: 16 (1)

Associate Chair:
Edward J. Buskey, (D), Rhode Island, 1983, Ob

Professor:
Kenneth H. Dunton, (D), Alaska, 1985, Ob
Lee A. Fuiman, (D), Michigan, 1983, Ob
James W. McClelland, (D), Boston, 1998, CgHsCs
Peter Thomas, (D), Leicester (UK), 1977, Ob
Tracy A. Villareal, (D), Rhode Island, 1989, Ob
Associate Professor:
Deana L. Erdner, (D), MIT/WHOI, 1997, Ob
Andrew J. Esbaugh, (D), Queens, 2005, Ob
Zhanfei Liu, (D), SUNY (Stony Brook), 2006, Og
Assistant Professor:
Brett Baker, (D), Michigan, 2014, Ze
Brad Erisman, (D), California (San Diego), 2008, Ob
Amber K. Hardison, (D), William & Mary, 2010, Cm
Lauren A. Yeager, (D), Florida Intl, 2013, Og
Lecturer:
Dong-Ha Min, (D), Scripps, 1999, Og
Emeritus:
Wayne S. Gardner, (D), Wisconsin, 1971, Ob
Gloria J. Holt, (D), Texas A&M, 1976, Ob

Inst for Geophysics (2017)
JJ Pickle Research Campus
10100 Burnet Road, Bldg. 196 (ROC)
Austin, TX 78758
p. (512) 471-6156
utig@ig.utexas.edu
http://www.ig.utexas.edu/
Associate Director:
Ian W. D. Dalziel, (D), Edinburgh, 1963, Gt
Cliff Frohlich, (D), Cornell, 1976, Ys
Research Professor:
Stephen P. Grand, (D), Caltech, 1986, Ys
Yosio Nakamura, (D), Penn State, 1963, Ys
Mrinal K. Sen, (D), Hawaii, 1987, Ye
Professor:
Sean S. Gulick, (D), Lehigh, 1999, YrGtb
Paul L. Stoffa, (D), Columbia, 1974, Ye
Research Scientist:
Gail L. Christeson, (D), MIT/WHOI, 1994, YrsGt
Craig S. Fulthorpe, (D), Northwestern, 1988, Gu
Senior Scientist:
James A. Austin, Jr., (D), MIT/WHOI, 1979, Gut
Nathan L. Bangs, (D), Columbia, 1990, Gu
John A. Goff, (D), MIT/WHOI, 1990, Yr
Charles Jackson, (D), Chicago, 1998, ZoOoAt
Lawrence A. Lawver, (D), California (San Diego), 1976, YrGt
Paul Mann, (D), SUNY (Albany), 1983, Gt
Thomas H. Shipley, (D), Rice, 1975, Yr
Frederick W. Talyor, (D), Cornell, 1979, Pe
Research Scientist:
Donald D. Blankenship, (D), Wisconsin, 1989, Yg
Kirk D. McIntosh, (D), California (Santa Cruz), 1992, Yr
Robert J. Pulliam, (D), California (Berkeley), 1991, Ys
Associate Professor:
Luc L. Lavier, (D), Columbia, 1999, YgGt
Research Associate:
John W. Holt, (D), Caltech, 1997, Ye
David L. Morse, (D), Washington, 1997, Yg
Robert B. Scott, (D), McGill, 1999, Og
Roustam K. Seifoullaev, (D), Baku State, 1979, Ye
Harm Van Avendonk, (D), Scripps, 1998, Yg
Research Professor:
William E. Galloway, (D), Texas, 1971, GsoGr
Emeritus:
Milo M. Backus, (D), MIT, 1956, Ye
Arthur E. Maxwell, (D), Scripps, 1959, Og
Postdoc:
Christina Holland, (D), S Florida, 2003, Og
Matthew Hornbach, (D), Wyoming, 2004, Yg
Timothy Whiteaker, (D), Texas, 2004, Gs
Project Coordinator:
Patricia E. Ganey-Curry, (B), Texas A&M, 1978, Zn
Program Manager:
Katherine K. Ellins, (D), Columbia, 1988, Zn
Related Staff:
Mark Wiederspahn, (B), Bucknell, 1975, Zn

Jackson School of Geosciences (B,M,D) ☒ (2021)
Jackson School of Geosciences
2225 Speedway, Stop C1160
Austin, TX 78712-1692
p. (512) 471-5172
stockli@jsg.utexas.edu
http://www.jsg.utexas.edu
f: https://www.facebook.com/UTJSG
t: @txgeosciences
Enrollment (2019): B: 190 (46) M: 22 (24) D: 140 (14)
Principal Research Scientist:
Patrick Heimbach, (D), Max Planck, 1998, OpGlAs
Director, UTIG:
Demian Saffer, (D), California (Santa Cruz), 1999, Gu
Director, Bureau of Economic Geology:
Scott W. Tinker, (D), Colorado, 1996, Go
Dean, Jackson School of Geosciences:
Claudia Mora, (D), Wisconsin, Gg
Chair, Department of Geological Sciences:
Daniel Stockli, (D), Stanford, 1999, CcGct
Associate Dean for Research, Jackson School:
David Mohrig, (D), Washington, 1994, GsmGr
Professor:
Jay L. Banner, (D), SUNY (Stony Brook), 1986, Cl
Jaime D. Barnes, (D), New Mexico, 2006, CgsCc
Thorsten Becker, (D), Harvard, Yg
Christopher J. Bell, (D), California (Berkeley), 1997, Pv
Philip Bennett, (D), Syracuse, 1988, Hg
Daniel O. Breecker, (D), New Mexico, 2008, ClsSc
Bayani Cardenas, (D), New Mexico Tech, 2006, Hg
Ginny A. Catania, (D), Washington, 2004, Gl
Julia A. Clarke, (D), Yale, 2002, PvgPq
Mark P. Cloos, (D), California (Los Angeles), 1981, Gcx
Kerry H. Cook, (D), North Carolina State, 1984, AsPe
Ian W. D. Dalziel, (D), Edinburgh, 1963, Gt
Peter B. Flemings, (D), Cornell, 1990, Gr
Sergey B. Fomel, (D), Stanford, 2001, YesEo
Rong Fu, (D), Columbia, 1991, As
James E. Gardner, (D), Rhode Island, 1993, Gv
Omar Ghattas, (D), Duke, 1988, ZnYg
Stephen P. Grand, (D), McGill, 1986, Yg
Patrick Heimbach, Max Planck, 1998, Og
Brian Horton, (D), Arizona, 1998, Gs
Charles Kerans, (D), Carleton, 1982, GsrGo
Richard A. Ketcham, (D), Texas, 1995, GgCc
J. Richard Kyle, (D), W Ontario, 1977, EmnCe
John Lassiter, (D), California (Berkeley), 1995, Cc
Luc L. Lavier, (D), Columbia, 1999, Gt
Jung-Fu Lin, (D), Chicago, 2002, GyYm
Sharon Mosher, (D), Illinois, 1978, Gc
Dev Niyogi, (D), North Carolina State, 2000, As
Terry Quinn, (D), Brown, 1989, Pe
Timothy B. Rowe, (D), California (Berkeley), 1987, Pv
Mrinal K. Sen, (D), Hawaii, 1987, Ye
Robert H. Tatham, (D), Columbia, 1975, Yg
Zong-Liang Yang, (D), Macquarie, 1992, AmsHq
Senior Research Scientist:
James A. Austin, Jr., (D), MIT/WHOI, 1979, YrGr
Nathan L. Bangs, (D), Columbia, 1990, Gc
Donald D. Blankenship, (D), Wisconsin, 1989, Gl
Gail L. Christeson, (D), MIT, 1994, Yr
Craig S. Fulthorpe, (D), Northwestern, 1988, GusGr
John A. Goff, (D), MIT, 1990, Gu
Bob A. Hardage, (D), Oklahoma State, 1967, Yes
Susan D. Hovorka, (D), Texas, 1990, Gs
Michael R. Hudec, (D), Wyoming, 1990, Gc
Stephen E. Laubach, (D), Illinois, 1986, GcoNp
Lawrence A. Lawver, (D), Scripps, 1976, Yr
Robert G. Loucks, (D), Texas, 1976, Gso
F. Jerry Lucia, (M), Minnesota, 1954, Eo
Kitty L. Milliken, (D), Texas, 1985, Gd
Jeffrey G. Paine, (D), Texas, 1991, On
Stephen C. Ruppel, (D), Tennessee, 1979, GsrGo
Bridget R. Scanlon, Kentucky, Hg
Thomas H. Shipley, (D), Rice, 1975, Ys
Michael H. Young, (D), Arizona, 1995, SpHwGe
Hongliu Zeng, (D), Texas, 1994, YsGs
Research Scientist:
Peter Eichhubl, (D), California (Santa Barbara), 1997, GcCgNr

Charles S. Jackson, (D), Chicago, 1998, ZoAtOo
Associate Professor:
Elizabeth J. Catlos, (D), California (Los Angeles), 2000, GzCg
Marc A. Hesse, (D), Stanford, 2008, GqoYg
Joel P. Johnson, (D), MIT, 2007, Gs
Rowan Martindale, USC, 2014, PgGs
Timothy M. Shanahan, (D), Arizona, 2007, PeGsCg
Kyle T. Spikes, (D), Stanford, 2008, Ye
Research Scientist:
Xavier Janson, (D), Miami, 2002, Gs
Laura Wallace, (D), California (Santa Cruz), 2002, GtYdZr
Associate Scientist:
Harm J. Van Avendonk, (D), Scripps, 1998, Ys
Assistant Professor:
Timothy Goudge, (D), Brown, 2015, Gs
Ashley Matheny, Ohio State, 2016, Hg
Geeta Persad, Princeton, 2016, As
Daniella Rempe, Hg
Chenguang Sun, (D), Brown, 2014, Gx
Nicola Tisato, (D), ETH, 2013, Yg
Daniel Trugman, (D), California (San Diego), 2017, Yg
Senior Energy Economist:
Gurcan Gulen, (D), Boston Coll, 1996, Ego
Energy Economist:
Svetlana Ikonnikova, (D), Humboldt (Germany), 2007, Ego
Research Associate:
Todd Caldwell, (D), Nevada (Reno), 2011, Sp
Sigrid Clift, (B), Texas, 1989, Zg
Andras Fall, (D), Virginia Tech, 2008, CgGcEg
Peter P. Flaig, (D), Alaska (Fairbanks), 2010, GsrEo
Nicholas W. Hayman, (D), Washington, 2003, Ou
Seyyed Abolfazi Hosseini, (D), Tulsa, 2008, Eo
Farzam Javadpour, (D), Calgary, 2006, NpEo
Carey King, (D), Texas, 2004, Eog
Gang Luo, (D), Missouri, Gtc
Hardie S. Nance, (M), Texas, 1978, Grc
Maria-Aikaterini Nikolinakou, (D), MIT, 2008, Np
Yuko Okumura, (D), Hawaii, 2005, AsZoOp
Cornel Olariu, (D), Texas (Dallas), 2005, Gr
Mariana Olariu, (D), Texas (Dallas), 2007, GruGs
Christopher Omelon, Cg
Diana C. Sava, (D), Stanford, 2004, Yg
Timothy L. Whiteaker, (D), Texas, 2004, Zi
Brad Wolaver, (D), Texas, 2008, HwGe
Changbing Yang, Hw
Christopher K. Zahm, (D), Colorado Mines, 2002, Yg
Mehdi Zeidouni, (D), Calgary, 2011, Eo
Tongwei Zhang, (D), Chinese Acad of Sci, 1999, Cgs
Senior Lecturer:
Mark A. Helper, (D), Texas, 1985, GctXg
Lecturer:
Hillary C. Olson, (D), Stanford, 1988, Ps
Mary F. Poteet, (D), California (Berkeley), 2001, Pg
Adjunct Professor:
Marcus Gary, (D), Texas, 2009, Hgs
Senior Research Scientist:
Clifford A. Frohlich, (D), Cornell, 1976, YsGt
Frederick W. Taylor, (D), Cornell, 1978, GtmGe
Emeritus:
William D. Carlson, (D), California (Los Angeles), 1980, GpzCp
William L. Fisher, (D), Kansas, 1961, GsrGo
Peter T. Flawn, (D), Yale, 1951, Eg
Robert L. Folk, (D), Penn State, 1952, Gd
William E. Galloway, (D), Texas, 1971, Gs
Gary A. Kocurek, (D), Wisconsin, 1980, Gs
Leon E. Long, (D), Columbia, 1959, Cc
Earle F. McBride, (D), Johns Hopkins, 1960, Gd
Yosio none Nakamura, (D), Penn State, 1963, YsGt
John M. Sharp, Jr., (D), Illinois, 1974, HqwGe
Douglas Smith, (D), Caltech, 1969, GipGz
James T. Sprinkle, (D), Harvard, 1971, PigGr
Ronald J. Steel, (D), Glasgow, 1970, Gs
Paul L. Stoffa, (D), Columbia, 1974, Ye
Clark R. Wilson, (D), California (San Diego), 1975, Yg
Research Scientist:
Fred W. McDowell, (D), Columbia, 1966, Cc
Research Associate Professor:
Sean S. Gulick, (M), Lehigh, 1999, Gc

University of Texas, Dallas

Dept of Geosciences (B,M,D) O🖱 (2020)
Mail Stop ROC21
800 W Campbell Rd
Richardson, TX 75083-3021
p. (972) 883-2401
geissman@utdallas.edu
Programs: No full degrees on line
Certificates: None
Enrollment (2020): B: 65 (14) M: 13 (5) D: 29 (5)
Professor and Program :
John Dr. Geissman, (D), Michigan, 1980, GtYm
Director, Center for Lithosphere Studies:
David Lumley, (D), Stanford, 1995, YsrYn
Professor:
John F. Ferguson, (D), S Methodist, 1981, Yg
William I. Manton, (D), Witwatersrand, 1968, Cc
Robert J. Stern, (D), California (San Diego), 1979, Gt
Associate Professor:
Tom H. Brikowski, (D), Arizona, 1987, Hw
Assistant Professor:
Hejun Zhu, (D), Princeton, 2014, Ysx
Research Professor:
Robert B. Finkelman, (D), Maryland, 1980, GbEcCa
Senior Lecturer:
William R. Griffin, (D), Texas (Dallas), 2008, Gg
Ignacio Pujana, (D), Texas (Dallas), 1997, Pm
Retired Professor:
Richard M. Mitterer, (D), Florida State, 1966, ColOc
Emile A. Pessagno, Jr., (D), Princeton, 1960, Pm
Dean C. Presnall, (D), Penn State, 1963, Cp
Retired President and Professor:
Robert H. Rutford, (D), Minnesota, 1969, Gl
Emeritus:
Carlos L. V. Aiken, (D), Arizona, 1976, Yv
George A. McMechan, (M), Toronto, 1972, Ys
Senior Lecturer:
Mortaza X. Pirouz, (D), Geneva, 2013, GcZiGc

Science/Mathematics Education Program (M) (2015)
P. O. Box 830688 FN33
Richardson, TX 75080-9688
p. (972) 883-2496
mont@utdallas.edu
http://www.utdallas.edu/dept/SciMathEd
Professor:
Thomas R. Butts, (D), Michigan State, 1973, Zn
Fred L. Fifer, (D), Vanderbilt, 1973, Zn
Associate Professor:
Cynthia E. Ledbetter, (D), Texas A&M, 1987, Zn
Assistant Professor:
Homer A. Montgomery, (D), Texas (Dallas), 1988, Pg
Mary Urquhart, (D), Colorado, 1999, Xy
Instructor:
Barbara Curry, (M), Texas (Dallas), 1998, Zn

University of Texas, El Paso

Dept of Geological Sciences (B,M,D) O☒ (2019)
500 W. University Avenue
101 Geological Sciences
El Paso, TX 79968-0555
p. (915) 747-5501
jdkubicki@utep.edu
http://science.utep.edu/geology/
Programs: BA Geology, BS Geology, BS Geophysics, BS Geology – Secondary Education Minor – 7-12 Science Certification, BS Environmental Science - Biology Concentration, BS Environmental Science - Chemistry Concentration, BS Environmental Science - Geoscience Concentration, BS Environmental Science - Hydroscience Concentration, BS Environmental Science – Secondary Education Minor – 7 – 12 Science Concentration, BS Geology to MS Geology, BS Geology to MBA, MS Geology, MS Geophysics, MS Environmental Science, PhD Geology
Certificates: Geospatial Information Science and Technology - GIST
Enrollment (2019): B: 185 (27) M: 31 (9) D: 29 (8)
National Seismic Source Facility:
Galen M. Kaip, (D), Texas (El Paso), 1998, Yx

Professor:
James D. Kubicki, (D), Yale, 1989, ClGe
Professor:
Elizabeth Y. Anthony, (D), Arizona, 1986, GiCcGv
Diane I. Doser, (D), Utah, 1984, Ys
Katherine A. Giles, (D), Arizona, 1991, Go
Thomas E. Gill, (D), California (Davis), 1995, GmAsCl
Philip C. Goodell, (D), Harvard, 1970, Ce
Jose M. Hurtado, (D), MIT, 2002, Gt
Richard S. Jarvis, (D), Cambridge, 1975, ZyGmAs
Richard P. Langford, (D), Utah, 1989, Gs
Terry L. Pavlis, (D), Utah, 1982, Gc
Nicholas E. Pingitore, Jr., (D), Brown, 1973, Cl
Laura F. Serpa, (D), Cornell, 1986, Ye
Aaron A. Velasco, (D), California (Santa Cruz), 1993, Yx
Associate Professor:
Lixin Jin, (D), Michigan, 2007, Ge
Marianne Karplus, (D), Stanford, 2012, Ysg
Lin Ma, (D), Michigan, 2008, HgCg
Deana Pennington, (D), Oregon State, 2002, ZyfZe
Assistant Professor:
Benjamin Brunner, (D), ETH (Switzerland), 2003, Cs
Julien Chaput, (D), New Mexico Tech, 2012, GeYes
Hugo A. Gutierrez-Jurado, (D), New Mexico Tech, 2011, HgsHw
Jason Ricketts, (D), New Mexico, 2014, GctGi
Jie Xu, (D), Wisconsin, 2011, ClPoGz
Lecturer:
Vicki Harder, (D), Texas (El Paso), 1997, Gg
Musa Hussein, (D), Texas (El Paso), 2007, YgeYm
Adriana Perez, (D), Texas (El Paso), 2008, Gg
Associate Professor Emeritus:
William Cornell , (D), California (Los Angeles), Gg
Emeritus:
Kenneth F. Clark, (D), New Mexico, 1966, Eg
George Randy Keller , (D), Texas Tech, 1973, Yg
David V. Le Mone, (D), Michigan State, 1964, Ps
Research Assistant Professor :
Steven H. Harder, (D), Texas (El Paso), 1986, Yg

University of Texas, Rio Grande Valley

School of Earth, Environmental and Marine Sciences (B,M) ⊘ (2020)
1201 W. University Drive
ESCNE 2.620
Edinburg, TX 78539
p. (956) 882-5040
juan.l.gonzalez@utrgv.edu
https://www.utrgv.edu/seems/
Programs: BS Environmental Science - Earth and Ocean Sciences Concentration, MS Ocean, Coastal and Earth Sciences, MS Agricultural, Environmental, and Sustainability Sciences
Enrollment (2020): B: 140 (0) M: 32 (0)
Director:
David Hicks, (D), Texas (Arlington), 1999, Ob
Professor:
Carlos Cintra-Buenrostro, (D), Arizona, 2006, PlCsPe
Abdullah F. Rahman, (D), Arizona, 1996, Zr
Associate Professor:
Jude Benavides, (D), Rice, 2005, Hsq
John Breier, (D), Texas, 2006, Cma
Juan L. Gonzalez, (D), Tulane, 2008, GmsGa
Elizabeth Heise, (D), Texas A&M, 2001, OnZeGg
Ruben Mazariegos, (D), Texas A&M, 1993, ZiYe
Assistant Professor:
Chu-Lin Cheng, (D), Iowa State, 2009, HgwHq
Christopher Gabler, (D), Rice, 2012, PeSf
Cheryl Harrison, (D), California (Santa Cruz), 2012, Op
James Kang, (D), N Carolina State, 2007, SpcZu
Engil I. Pereira, (D), California (Davis), 2014, SbZcSo
Amit Raysoni, (D), Texas (El Paso), 2011, Asc
Research Associate:
Lorena Longoria, (B), Texas (Pan American), 2012, Ob
Lecturer:
Sarah M. Hardage, (M), New Orleans, 2004, GmZiGg
Saad Mohamed, (D), Dalhousie
Idua Olunwa, (M), Texas (Dallas), 2009
Adjunct Professor:
James R. Hinthorne, (D), California (Santa Barbara), 1974, GgzCa

University of Texas, San Antonio

Dept of Geological Sciences (B,M) ●⊘ (2020)
One UTSA Circle
San Antonio, TX 78249-0663
p. (210) 458-4455
geosciences@utsa.edu
http://www.utsa.edu/geosci
f: https://www.facebook.com/Dpt-of-Geological-Sciences-UTSA-881208175556941/
Programs: Geology (B,M); Geoinformatics (M)
Certificates: GIS (G) (U)
Enrollment (2017): B: 107 (0) M: 35 (0)

Victoria College

Science, Mathematics, & Physical Education (A) (2015)
2200 E. Red River
Victoria, TX 77901
p. (361)573-3291 (Ext.3432)
Alisha.Stearman@VictoriaCollege.edu
https://www.victoriacollege.edu/sciencemathematicsphysical-education

Wayland Baptist University

Geology Department (B) ● (2018)
1900 W. 7th Street
Plainview, TX 79072
p. (806) 291-1115
walsht@wbu.edu
http://www.wbu.edu/academics/schools/math_and_science/geology/
f: https://www.facebook.com/Wayland-Baptist-University-Geology-Department-198757676854342/
Programs: Geology
Enrollment (2018): B: 4 (1)
Professor:
Don Parker, (D), GivCg
Tim R. Walsh, (D), Texas Tech, 2002, GsPmGo
Assistant Professor:
Mark Bryan, (M), Oklahoma State, 2001, GeoPs

Weatherford College

Weatherford College (2015)
225 College Park Drive
Weatherford, TX 76086
p. (817) 598-6277
http://www.wc.edu

West Texas A&M University

Dept of Life, Earth & Environmental Sciences (B,M) (2015)
P. O. Box 60808, WT Station
Canyon, TX 79016-0001
p. (806) 651-2570
dsissom@wtamu.edu
http://www.wtamu.edu/academics/life-earth-environmental-sciences.aspx
Administrative Assistant: Debi Adams
Enrollment (2013): B: 13 (2)
Chair:
David Sissom, (D), Zn
Professor:
Joseph C. Cepeda, (D), Texas, 1977, GiHw
David B. Parker, (D), Nebraska, 1996, Sbf
William J. Rogers, (D), Texas A&M, 1999, Zn
Gerald E. Schultz, (D), Michigan, 1966, PvGzZg
Associate Professor:
Gary C. Barbee, (D), Texas A&M, 2004, HwSoZi
Instructor:
Cindy D. Meador, (M), W Texas A&M, 1989, Zg
Joe D. Rogers, (M), WTSU (WTAMU), 1987, Ga
William C. Rogers, (M), WTAMU, 2005, Ge
Lynn C. Rosa, (M), Oklahoma, 1984, Zge

Wharton County Junior College - Sugarland Campus

Wharton County Junior College - Sugarland Campus (2015)
14004 University Blvd.
Sugarland, TX 77479
p. (281) 239-1559
dannyg@wcjc.edu
http://www.wcjc.edu

Wharton County Junior College - Wharton Campus

Geology (2015)
911 Boling Highway
Wharton, TX 77488
p. (979) 532-6506
dannyg@wcjc.edu
https://www.wcjc.edu/Programs/math-and-science/geology/

Utah

Brigham Young University

Dept of Geography (B) ☒ (2018)
690 SWKT
Provo, UT 84602
p. (801) 378-3851
geography@byu.edu
http://www.geography.byu.edu/
Programs: Geospatial Science & Technology
Geospatial Intelligence
Environmental Systems
Urban & Regional Planning
Global Studies
Travel and Tourism Studies

Chair:
Ryan R. Jensen, (D), Florida, 2000, Zii

Professor:
Perry J. Hardin, (D), Utah, 1989, Zr
Samuel M. Otterstrom, (D), Louisiana State, 1997, Zu
Matthew J. Shumway, (D), Indiana, 1991, Zn

Associate Professor:
Matthew F. Bekker, (D), Iowa, 2002, Zy
Michael J. Clay, (D), California (Davis), 2005
James A. Davis, (D), Arizona State, 1992, Zn
Jeffrey O. Durrant, (D), Hawaii, 2001, Ge
Chad Emmett, (D), Chicago, 1991, Zn
Clark S. Monson, (D), Hawaii, 2004
Daniel H. Olsen, (D), Waterloo, 2008
Brandon Plewe, (D), Buffalo, 1997

Dept of Geological Sciences (B,M) ●⊘ (2019)
S 389 ESC
Provo, UT 84602
p. (801) 422-3918
geology@byu.edu
http://www.geology.byu.edu
Programs: Geology, Earth Space and Science Education
Enrollment (2019): B: 89 (24) M: 32 (13)

Research Professor:
Michael J. Dorais, (D), Georgia, 1987, Gi

Teaching Professor:
Randall Skinner, (M), Brigham Young, 1996, Gg

Professor:
Barry R. Bickmore, (D), Virginia Tech, 2000, ClGz
Eric H. Christiansen, (D), Arizona State, 1981, GiXgGv
Ron Harris, (D), London (UK), 1989, Gc
Jeffrey D. Keith, (D), Wisconsin, 1982, Eg
John H. McBride, (D), Cornell, 1987, YeGoe
Stephen T. Nelson, (D), California (Los Angeles), 1991, Cs
Jani Radebaugh, (D), Arizona, 2005, XgGvm
Scott M. Ritter, (D), Wisconsin, 1986, Ps

Research Professor:
David G. Tingey, (M), Brigham Young, 1989, Zn

Associate Professor:
Brooks B. Britt, (D), Calgary, 1993, Pg
Gregory T. Carling, (D), Utah, 2012, HwCts

Assistant Professor:
Samuel M. Hudson, (D), Utah, 2008, GosGr

Visiting Professor:
R. William Keach II, (M), Cornell, 1986, YeEoGg

Emeritus:
Myron G. Best, (D), California (Berkeley), Gg
Dana T. Griffen, (D), Virginia Tech, 1976, Gz
Lehi F. Hintze, (D), Columbia, 1951, Pg
Bart J. Kowallis, (D), Wisconsin, 1981, GgCcGz
Alan L. Mayo, (D), Idaho, 1982, Hw
Wade E. Miller, (D), California (Berkeley), 1968, Pv
Thomas H. Morris, (D), Wisconsin, 1986, Gr
R. Paul Nixon, (D), Brigham Young, 1972, Go
Morris S. Petersen, (D), Iowa, 1962, Gso
William R. Phillips, (D), Utah, 1954, Gz

Dept of Plant and Wildlife Sciences (2015)
Provo , UT 84602
p. 801-422-9389
pws-grad-secretary@byu.edu
http://pws.byu.edu/

Salt Lake City Community College-Jordan Campus

Dept of Geosciences (2015)
4600 South Redwood Road
Salt Lake City, UT 84123
p. (801)957-4150
adam.dastrup@slcc.edu
http://www.slcc.edu

Snow College

Dept of Geology (A) (2016)
150 College Ave E
Ephraim, UT 84627
p. (435) 283-7519
renee.faatz@snow.edu
https://www.snow.edu/academics/science_math/geology
f:https://www.facebook.com/Snow-College-Geology-616452215106045/
Enrollment (2016): A: 7 (1)

Chair:
Renee M. Faatz, (M), Ohio State, 1985, Gg

Assistant Professor:
Ted L. Olson, (M), Utah, 1976, Ys

Southern Utah University

Dept of Physical Science (B) O (2019)
351 West University Blvd.
Cedar City, UT 84720
p. (435) 586-7900
jasonkaiser@suu.edu
http://www.suu.edu/geology
f: https://www.facebook.com/SUUGeologyClub
Programs: B.S. in Geology, B.A. in Geosciences
Certificates: GIS
Administrative Assistant: Rhonda Riley
Enrollment (2018): B: 44 (8)

Professor:
Robert L. Eves, (D), Washington State, 1991, CgZeCa

Assistant Professor:
Jason Kaiser, (D), Oregon State, 2014, GzvCg
John S. MacLean, (D), Montana, 2009, GctZe
Grant Shimer, (D), Alaska, Gs

University of Utah

Dept of Atmospheric Sciences (B,M,D) ☒ (2019)
135 S 1460 E, Rm 819
Salt Lake City, UT 84112-0110
p. (801) 581-6136
atmos-info@lists.utah.edu
http://www.atmos.utah.edu
f: www.facebook.com/UUAtmos
t: @UofUATMOS
Programs: Atmospheric Sciences
Enrollment (2018): B: 40 (14) M: 11 (6) D: 23 (2)

Chair:
John Horel, (D), Washington, 1982, AsZf
Professor:
Timothy J. Garrett, (D), Washington, 2000, As
Steven Krueger, (D), California (Los Angeles), 1985, As
John Chun-Han Lin, (D), Harvard, 2003, As
Gerald Mace, (D), Penn State, 1994, As
Zhaoxia Pu, (D), Lanzhou, 1997, As
Jim Steenburgh, (D), Washington, 1995, As
Edward Zipser, (D), Florida State, 1965, As
Associate Professor:
Anna Gannet Hallar, (D), Colorado, 2003, AspAc
Kevin D. Perry, (D), Washington, 1995, As
Thomas Reichler, (D), California (San Diego), 2003, As
Courtenay Strong, (D), Virginia, 2005, As

Dept of Geography (B,M,D) (2015)
260 S. Central Campus Drive
Rm 270
Salt Lake City, UT 84112-9155
p. (801) 581-8218
thomas.kontuly@geog.utah.edu
http://www.geog.utah.edu
Administrative Assistant: Susan Van Roosendaal
Chair:
George F. Hepner, (D), Arizona State, 1979, Zy
Professor:
Donald R. Currey, (D), Kansas, 1969, Gm
Thomas M. Kontuly, (D), Pennsylvania, 1978, Zn
Chung M. Lee, (D), Michigan, 1961, Zu
Assistant Professor:
Thomas J. Cova, (D), California (Santa Barbara), 1999, Zi
Richard R. Forster, (D), Cornell, 1997, Zr
Adjunct Professor:
Jeffrey R. Keaton, (D), Texas A&M, 1988, Zn
Elliott W. Lips, (M), Colorado State, 1990, Gm
Emeritus:
Philip C. Emmi, (D), North Carolina, 1979, Zu
Roger M. Mccoy, (D), Kansas, 1967, Zr
Merrill K. Ridd, (D), Northwestern, 1963, Zr
Professor-Lecturer:
Arthur Hampson, (D), Hawaii, 1980, Zy
Assistant Professor:
Trevor J. Davis, (D), British Columbia, 1999, Zi
Other:
Fred E. May, (D), Virginia Tech, 1976, Zn

Dept of Geology & Geophysics (B,M,D) ●☒ (2020)
Frederick Albert Sutton Building, Rm 383
115 South 1460 East
Salt Lake City, UT 84112-0102
p. (801) 581-7062
gg-info@lists.utah.edu
http://www.earth.utah.edu/
f: https://www.facebook.com/University-of-Utah-Geology-and-Geophysics-361264640646
Programs: Geoscience (emphasis in Geology, Environmental Geoscience, or Geophysics), Geological Engineering, Earth Science Composite Teaching, Earth Science Minor
Certificates: Interdisciplinary Graduate Certificate in Hydrology and Water Resources (can be taken as a non-degree seeking student with a completed Bachelor's degree from an accredited college or university)
Enrollment (2020): B: 91 (45) M: 14 (6) D: 37 (10)
CMES Student Services Director:
Michelle Tuitupou, (M), 2004
Chair:
Thure E. Cerling, (D), California (Berkeley), 1977, ClsZc
Professor Lecturer:
David A. Dinter, (D), MIT, 1994, GtcGu
Director, Seismograph Stations:
Keith Koper, (D), Washington, 1998
Associate Director, Global Change and Sustainability Center:
Brenda Bowen, (D), Gse
Professor:
Gabriel Bowen, (D), California (Santa Cruz), 2003, Cs
Paul D. Brooks, (D), Colorado, 1995, HgCbZg
Marjorie A. Chan, (D), Wisconsin, 1982, Gs
Paul W. Jewell, (D), Princeton, 1989, GmHg
Cari Johnson, (D), Stanford, 2003, Gs
William P. Johnson, (D), Colorado, 1993, Ng
Douglas K. Solomon, (D), Waterloo, 1992, Hw
Tonie van Dam, (D), Yd
Michael S. Zhdanov, (D), Moscow State (Russia), 1968, Ye
Research Associate Professor:
Diego Fernandez, (D), Buenos Aires, 1991, Cg
Marie D. Jackson, (D), Gv
James M. Karner, (D), Xm
Huilian Ma, (D)
Kristine L. Pankow, (D), California, 1999, Ys
James C. Pechmann, (D), Caltech, 1983, YsGt
Chief Curator and Curator of Paleontology (NHMU):
Randall B. Irmis, (D), California (Berkeley), 2008, Sa
Associate Professor Lecturer:
Holly Godsey, (D), Ze
Mark Loewen, (D), Pvg
Associate Professor:
Lauren Birgenheier, (D), Nebraska, 2007, Gso
Fan-Chi Lin, (D), Colorado, 2009, Ygs
Peter C. Lippert, (D), California (Santa Cruz), 2010, YmGtPe
Lowell Miyagi, (D), California (Berkeley), 2009, Gz
Jeffrey Moore, (D), California (Berkeley), 2007, NgrGm
Michael S. Thorne, (D), Arizona State, 2005, YsxYv
Research Assistant Professor:
Amir Allam, (D)
Jamie Farrell, (D), Ys
Richard Fiorella, (D)
Alex Gribenko, (D), Yg
Scott R. Miller, (D)
Assistant Professor:
Kathleen Allabush, (D), Pe
Sarah Lambart, (D), Cpg
Emeritus:
John M. Bartley, (D), MIT, 1981, GciCc
John R. Bowman, (D), Michigan, 1976, Cs
Barbara P. Nash, (D), California (Berkeley), 1971, Gi
Erich U. Petersen, (D), Michigan, 1983, Em

Dept of Mining Engineering (B,M,D) (2015)
135 South 1460 East
Room 313
Salt Lake City, UT 84112-0113
p. (801) 581-7198
mineeng@mines.utah.edu
http://www.mines.utah.edu/mining
Enrollment (2009): B: 48 (11) M: 6 (3) D: 1 (0)
Chair:
Michael G. Nelson, (D), West Virginia, 1989, Nm
Professor:
Michael K. McCarter, (D), Utah, 1972, Nm
William G. Pariseau, (D), Minnesota, 1966, Nr
Adjunct Associate Professor:
Stephen Bessinger, (D), Nm
Associate Professor:
Felipe Calizaya, (D), Colorado Mines, 1985, Nm
Adjunct Associate Professor:
Helmut H. Doelling, (D), Utah, 1964, Gg
Duane L. Whiting, (B), Utah, 1959, Hw
Adjunct Professor:
James Donovan, (D), Virginia Tech, 2003, NmrZr
Krishna P. Sinha, (D), Minnesota, 1979, Nr
Jeffrey Whyatt, (D), Nm
Zavis Zavodni, (D), Nm

Energy & Geoscience Institute (M) ● (2016)
423 Wakara Way
Suite 300
Salt Lake City, UT 84108
p. (801) 581-5126
egidirector@egi.utah.edu
http://www.egi.utah.edu
Director:
Raymond A. Levey, (D), South Carolina, 1981, Eo
Professor:
Richardson B. Allen, (D), Columbia, 1983, GctZi
Alastair Fraser, (D), Edinburgh, Gco
Brian McPherson, (D), Utah, 1996, Ye
Joseph N. Moore, (D), Penn State, 1975, Gv

Michal Nemcok, (D), Comenius Univ (Slovakia), 1991, GctGo
Peter E. Rose, (D), Utah, 1993, Np
Stuart Simmons, (D), Minnesota, 1986, EmCqHg
Rasoul Sorkhabi, (D), Japan, 1991, GctGc
Phillip E. Wannamaker, (D), Utah, 1983, Ye

Scientific Staff :
Julia Kotulova, (D), Komenius (Slovakia), CoGo

Senior Scientist:
Bryony Richards-McClung, (D), Go
Lansing Taylor, (D), Stanford, 1999, Gc
David Thul, (D), Colorado Mines, 2014, Gg

Associate Professor:
Glenn W. Johnson, (D), South Carolina, 1997, Gq
Greg Nash, (D), Utah, Gt
Marylin Segall, (D), 1991, GeOu

Assistant Professor:
Shu Jiang , (D), China Geosciences, GoYsNp
Sudeep Kanungo, (D), Univ Coll (UK), Pms

Research Associate:
Kenneth L. Shaw, (B), British Columbia, 1965, Ye

Instructor:
William Keach, (M), Cornell, 1986, GoYes

Adjunct Professor:
Ian Walton, (D), Manchester (UK), 1972, Gq

Utah State University

Department of Geosciences (B,M,D) (2020)
4505 Old Main Hill
Logan, UT 84322-4505
p. (435) 797-1273
geo@usu.edu
http://geo.usu.edu/
f: https://www.facebook.com/USUGeologyDepartment/
Programs: Geology; Applied Environmental Geoscience; Earth Science Composite Teaching
Enrollment (2020): B: 44 (7) M: 24 (3) D: 3 (1)

Head:
Joel L. Pederson, (D), New Mexico, 1999, Gm

Professor:
Carol M. Dehler, (D), New Mexico, 2001, Gs
James P. Evans, (D), Texas A&M, 1987, Gc
Susanne U. Janecke, (D), Utah, 1991, Gt
Tammy M. Rittenour, (D), Nebraska, 2004, GmCcGa
John W. Shervais, (D), California (Santa Barbara), 1979, Gi

Associate Professor:
Alexis K. Ault, (D), Colorado, 2012, GtCc
Benjamin J. Burger, Colorado, 2009, PvGs
Thomas E. Lachmar, (D), Idaho, 1989, Hw
Anthony R. Lowry, (D), Utah, 1994, YdsGt
Dennis L. Newell, (D), New Mexico, 2007, Cls

Professional Practice:
Kelly K. Bradbury, (D), Utah State, 2012, Gc
Katherine E. Potter, (D), Utah State, 2014, GiZeEg

Assistant Professor:
Evelyn Gannaway Dalton, (D), Texas (El Paso), 2019, GstZe
Donald E. Penman, (D), California (Santa Cruz), 2015, GsCbPc

Emeritus:
Donald W. Fiesinger, (D), Calgary, 1975, Gi
Peter T. Kolesar, (D), California (Riverside), 1973, Cg
W. David Liddell, (D), Michigan, 1979, GsPg
Robert Q. Oaks, Jr., (D), Yale, 1965, GsHwYv

Utah State University Eastern

Dept of Geology (A) ☒ (2018)
451 East 400 North
Price, UT 84501
p. (435) 613-5232
michelle.fleck@usu.edu
Programs: Associate of Science
Enrollment (2017): A: 4 (0)

Associate Professor:
Michelle Cooper Fleck, (D), Wyoming, 2001, GgZy

Utah Valley University

Dept. of Earth Science (A,B) (2020)
800 West University Parkway
MS 179
Orem, UT 84058
p. (801) 863-8582
hornsda@uvu.edu
https://www.uvu.edu/earthscience
f: https://www.facebook.com/groups/uvuearthscience/
Programs: Geology; Geography; Environmental Science; Earth Science Education
Certificates: GIS
Enrollment (2019): B: 144 (0)

Professor:
Michael Bunds, (D), GctRn
Daniel Horns, (D), NgGeRn

Associate Professor:
Joel Bradford, (M), Utah, RwGe
Eddy Cadet, (D), Ge
James Callison, (D), GeSfo
Hilary Hungerford, (D), ZuRw
Daniel Stephen, (D), PiGsPe
Nathan Toke', (D), Arizona State, 2011, GtmZi
Weihong Wang, (D), CmGeZi
Alessandro Zanazzi, (D), CgsPe

Assistant Professor:
Doug Czajka, (D), N Carolina State, 2018
Daren Nelson, (D)
Michael Stearns, (D), California (Santa Barbara), 2014, Gip
Justin White, ZyiZu

Weber State University

Department of Earth and Environmental Sciences (B) (2020)
1415 Edvalson St. Dept 2507
Ogden, UT 84408-2507
p. (801) 626-7139
mmatyjasik@weber.edu
https://www.weber.edu/ees/
f: https://www.facebook.com/WSUGeosciences
Programs: Geology (B); Applied Environmental Geoscience (B); Earth Science Teaching (B)
Certificates: Geospatial Analysis (GIS)
Administrative Assistant: Brooklyn Smout
Enrollment (2020): B: 78 (20)

Chair:
Marek Matyjasik, (D), Kent State, 1997, HwGe

Acting Associate Dean, College of Science:
Richard L. Ford, (D), California (Los Angeles), 1997, GmZeEo

Professor:
Michael W. Hernandez, (D), Utah, 2004, Zir
David J. Matty, (D), Rice, 1984, Gig
W. Adolph Yonkee, (D), Utah, 1990, Gct

Assistant Professor:
Elizabeth A. Balgord, (D), Arizona, 2015, Grt
Carie M. Frantz, (D), S California, 2013, PoCbZn
Ryan J. Frazier, (D), British Columbia, 2016, ZriZc
Caitlin E. Tems, (D), S California, 2016, OoCs

Adjunct Professor:
Amanda L. Gentry, (M), Nevada (Las Vegas), 2016, GgsGg
David Larsen, (M), Brigham Young, Gge
Gregory B. Nielsen, (D), Utah, 2010, Gg

Emeritus:
Jeffrey G. Eaton, (D), Colorado, 1987, PsGs
James R. Wilson, (D), Utah, 1976, Gz

Laboratory Director:
Sara Summers, (M), Notre Dame, 2012, Gg

Vermont

Castleton University

Dept of Natural Sciences (Geology) (B) (2018)
Castleton University
233 South Street
Castleton, VT 05735
p. (802) 468-1238
helen.mango@castleton.edu
http://www.castleton.edu/academics/undergraduate-programs/geology/
Enrollment (2015): B: 12 (3)

Professor:
Timothy W. Grover, (D), Oregon, 1988, GptGc
Helen N. Mango, (D), Dartmouth, 1992, CgGe

Middlebury College

Geology Dept (B) (2016)
276 Bicentennial Hall
Middlebury, VT 05753
p. (802) 443-5029
geology_chair@middlebury.edu
http://www.middlebury.edu/academics/geol
f: https://www.facebook.com/MiddleburyGeology
Administrative Assistant: Eileen Brunetto
Enrollment (2016): B: 30 (15)
Chair:
David P. West, (D), Maine, 1993, Gc
Professor:
Patricia L. Manley, (D), Columbia, 1989, YrGu
Jeffrey S. Munroe, (D), Wisconsin, 2001, Gln
Peter C. Ryan, (D), Dartmouth, 1994, Cl
Assistant Professor:
Will Amidon, (D), Caltech, 2010, CcGmt
Kristina J. Walowski, (D), Oregon, 2015, Gi
Visiting Professor:
Thomas O. Manley, (D), Columbia, 1981, Op

Northern Vermont University-Lyndon

Dept of Atmospheric Sciences (B) ☒ (2018)
1001 College Road
PO Box 919
Lyndonville, VT 05851
p. (802) 626-6225
jason.shafer@northernvermont.edu
http://meteorology.lyndonstate.edu
f: https://www.facebook.com/nvuatm/
t: @lyndonweather
Enrollment (2018): B: 73 (9)
Chair:
Janel Hanrahan, (D), Wisconsin, 2010, AsZoRc
Professor:
Jason Shafer, (D), Utah, 2005, As
Research Associate:
David Siuta, (D), British Columbia, 2017, AsZn
Adjunct Professor:
George Loriot, (D), Connecticut, AsZn
Visiting Professor:
Aaron Preston, (D), Florida State, AsZrAc
Atmospheric Sciences Data Systems Administrator:
Jason Kaiser, (M), Plymouth State, 2013, AsZn

Geology Minor (A,B) (2015)
1001 College Rd
Lyndonville, VT 05851
p. (802) 635-1325
brad.moskowitz@northernvermont.edu
Enrollment (2010): B: 37 (11)
Professor:
Tania S. Bacchus, (D), Maine, 1993, GuAm

Norwich University

Dept of Earth and Environmental Sciences (B) ☒ (2019)
158 Harmon Drive
Northfield, VT 05663
p. (802) 485-2304
rdunn@norwich.edu
https://www.norwich.edu/programs/geology
f: https://www.facebook.com/groups/102347383133958/
Programs: Geology, and Environmental Science
Enrollment (2019): B: 40 (6)
Professor:
Richard K. Dunn, (D), Delaware, 1998, GalGs
Associate Professor:
G. Christopher Koteas, (D), Massachusetts, 2010, GitYh
Assistant Professor:
Laurie Grigg, (D), Oregon, 2000, PeGnZi
Research Associate:
George E. Springston, (M), Massachusetts, 1990, GmZiYg
Lecturer:
John Gartner, (D), Dartmouth, 2015, GmHy
Emeritus:
David S. Westerman, (D), Lehigh, 1972, Gxi

University of Vermont

Dept of Geology (B,M) ☒ (2020)
Delehanty Hall
180 Colchester Avenue
Burlington, VT 05405-0122
p. (802) 656-3396
geology@uvm.edu
http://www.uvm.edu/geology
f: https://www.facebook.com/UVMGeology/
Programs: Geology
Administrative Assistant: Robin Hopps
Administrative Assistant: Srebrenka Mrsic
Enrollment (2015): B: 48 (0) M: 13 (0)
Professor:
Paul R. Bierman, (D), Washington, 1993, GmeCc
John M. Hughes, (D), Dartmouth, 1981, Gz
Keith A. Klepeis, (D), Texas, 1993, Gct
Research Associate Professor:
Andrew W. Schroth, (D), Dartmouth, 2007, ClqCb
Chair:
Andrea Lini, (D), ETH (Switzerland), 1994, CsGn
Associate Professor:
Laura E. Webb, (D), Stanford, 1999, GtCcGc
Assistant Professor:
Julia Perdrial, (D), Strasbourg (France), 2008, ClSc
Nicolas Perdrial, (D), Strasbourg (France), 2007, GezCl
Senior Lecturer:
Stephen F. Wright, (D), Minnesota, 1988, Glc
Emeritus:
David P. Bucke, (D), Oklahoma, 1969, GgdGs
Barry L. Doolan, (D), SUNY (Binghamton), 1970, Gx
John C. Drake, (D), Harvard, 1967, Cl
Charlotte J. Mehrtens, (D), Chicago, 1979, Gs
Senior Research Technician:
Gabriela Mora-Klepeis, (M), Texas, 1992, CacGi

Dept of Plant & Soil Science (B,M,D) (2015)
Jeffords Hall
63 Carrigan Drive
Burlington, VT 05405-1737
p. (802) 656-2630
pss@uvm.edu
http://www.uvm.edu/~pss/

Virginia

Central Virginia Community College

Science, Math, and Engineering (A) (2015)
3506 Wards Road
Lynchburg, VA 24502
p. (434) 832-7707
laubj@cvcc.vccs.edu
http://www.cvcc.vccs.edu/Academics/SME/
Instructor:
Mark Tinsley, Zg

George Mason University

Department of Geography and Geoinformation Science (2015)
Fairfax, VA 22030
p. (703) 993-1210
ggs@gmu.edu
https://cos.gmu.edu/ggs/

Dept of Atmospheric, Oceanic, and Earth Sciences (B,M,D)
O⊘ (2020)
Research Hall 280
Mail Stop 6C5
4400 University Drive
Fairfax, VA 22030-4444
p. (703) 993-5700
ikinter@gmu.edu
https://cos.gmu.edu/aoes/

t: @MasonAOES
Programs: Atmospheric Sciences, Earth Science, Geology, Climate Dynamics
Administrative Assistant: Maria D'Souza, Stephanie O'Neill
Enrollment (2020): B: 85 (21) M: 9 (0) D: 16 (3)
University Professor:
Jagadish Shukla, (D), MIT, 1976, As
Professor:
Timothy DelSole, (D), Harvard, 1993, As
Paul A. Dirmeyer, (D), Maryland, 1992, As
Linda Hinnov, (D), Johns Hopkins, 1994, GrYg
Bohua Huang, (D), Maryland, 1992, Op
Jim Kinter, (D), Princeton, 1984, As
David M. Straus, (D), Cornell, 1977, As
Stacey Verardo, (D), CUNY, 1995, Pei
Associate Professor:
Zafer Boybeyi, (D), North Carolina State, 1993, As
Long S. Chiu, (D), MIT, 1980, AsZrAm
Barry Klinger, (D), MIT/WHOI, 1992, Op
Randolph McBride, (D), Louisiana State, 1997, On
Julia Nord, (D), CUNY (Brooklyn), 1989, Gzg
Cristiana Stan, (D), Colorado State, 2005, As
Daniel Tong, (D), N Carolina State, 2003, Ac
Assistant Professor:
Paul Betka, (D), Texas, 2013, GctGg
Natalie Burls, (D), Cape Town, 2010, AsOp
Geoff Gilleaudeau, (D), Tennessee, 2013, Gs
Giuseppina Kysar Mattietti, (D), George Washington, 2001, GiZeGa
Kathy Pegion, (D), George Mason, 2007, AsOp
Mark Uhen, (D), Michigan, 1996, Pv
University Professor:
Edwin K. Schneider, (D), Harvard, 1976, As
Emeritus:
Richard J. Diecchio, (D), N Carolina, 1980, Gr
Paul S. Schopf, (D), Princeton, 1978, OpAs

Hampton University

Center for Marine & Coastal Environmental Studies (B) (2015)
100 Queen Street
Hampton, VA 23668
p. (757) 727-5783
cas@hamptonu.edu
Enrollment (2010): B: 32 (9)
Chair:
George P. Burbanck, (D), Delaware, 1981, On
Professor:
Benjamin E. Cuker, (D), North Carolina State, 1981, Ob
Associate Professor:
Robert A. Jordan, (D), Michigan, 1970, Ob
Assistant Professor:
Deidre M. Gibson, (D), Georgia, 2000, Ob
Adjunct Faculty:
Emory Morgan, (M), Ze
Related Staff:
Gary Morgan, (B), North Carolina State, 2007, ZnnZn

James Madison University

Dept of Geology & Environmental Science (B) (2015)
MSC 6903
Memorial Hall
Harrisonburg, VA 22807
p. (703) 568-6130
ulansksl@jmu.edu
http://www.jmu.edu/geology/
Department Secretary: Sandra Delawder
Head:
Stanley L. Ulanski, (D), Virginia, 1977, Og
Professor:
Roddy V. Amenta, (D), Bryn Mawr, 1971, Gc
Lynn S. Fichter, (D), Michigan, 1972, Gr
William C. Sherwood, (D), Lehigh, 1961, So
Steven J. Whitmeyer, (D), Boston, 2004, GctZi
Associate Professor:
Steven J. Baedke, (D), Indiana, 1998, Hy
Lewis S. Eaton, (D), Virginia, 1999, Gm
Eric J. Pyle, (D), Georgia, 1995, Ze
Kristen E. St. John, (D), Ohio State, 1998, Ou

Emeritus:
Lance E. Kearns, (D), Delaware, 1977, Gz

Mary Washington College

Dept of Geography (B) (2015)
1301 College Avenue
Fredericksburg, VA 22401-5358
p. (540) 654-1470
jhayob@umw.edu
http://www.mwc.edu/geog
Enrollment (2006): B: 80 (0)
Chair:
Joseph W. Nicholas, (D), Georgia, 1991, Zy
Associate Professor:
Donald N. Rallis, (D), Penn State, 1992, Zn
Assistant Professor:
Dawn S. Bowen, (D), Queen's, 1998, Zn
Stephen P. Hanna, (D), Kentucky, 1997, Zr
Farhang Rouhani, (D), Arizona, 2001, Zn

Mountain Empire Community College

Mountain Empire Community College (2015)
3441 Mountain Empire Road
Big Stone Gap, VA 24219
p. (276) 523-7460
sfritts@mecc.edu
http://www.me.vccs.edu/

Northern Virginia Community College - Alexandria

Geology Program (A) (2017)
5000 Dawes Avenue
Alexandria, VA 22311-5097
p. 703.845.6507
vzabielski@nvcc.edu
http://www.nvcc.edu/campuses-and-centers/alexandria/academic-divisions/science/geology.html
Assistant Dean of Geology:
Victor Zabielski, (D), Brown, 2001, GgOg

Northern Virginia Community College - Annandale

Geology Program (A) (2017)
8333 Little River Turnpike
Annandale, VA 22003
p. (703) 323-3276
bwang@nvcc.edu
http://www.nvcc.edu/campuses-and-centers/annandale/academic-divisions/math-science--engineering/gol.html
Programs: Science (B)
Enrollment (2011): A: 10 (10)
Professor:
Kenneth Rasmussen, (D), North Carolina, 1989, Gus
Assistant Professor:
Callan Bentley, (M), Maryland, 2004, Gg
Shelley Jaye, (M), Wayne State, 1984, Giy

Northern Virginia Community College - Loudoun Campus

Mathematics, Sciences, Technologies and Business Div - Dept of Geology (A) (2018)
21200 Campus Drive
Sterling, VA 20164
p. (703) 450-2612
wbour@nvcc.edu
https://www.nvcc.edu/academics/divisions/mstb
Programs: Associates degree in Science
Associate Professor:
William Bour, (M), George Washington, 1993, Gge
William Straight, (D), North Carolina State, GgPv
Assistant Professor:
Okia Ikwuazorm, (M), Gg

Northern Virginia Community College - Woodbridge

Geology Program (A) ☒ (2018)
2645 College Drive
Woodbridge, VA 22191
p. (703) 878-5614
athimblin@nvcc.edu
http://www.nvcc.edu/woodbridge/divisions/natural.html
Enrollment (2014): A: 6 (1)

Instructor:
Erik Burtis, (M), Montana, GgcGi

Old Dominion University

Dept of Ocean, Earth & Atmospheric Sciences (B,M,D) (2018)
4600 Elkhorn Avenue
Norfolk, VA 23529-0496
p. (757) 683-4285
OEASadmin@odu.edu
http://www.odu.edu/oeas
Programs: BS in Ocean and Earth Sciences; MS in Ocean and Earth Sciences; PhD in Oceanography
Certificates: GIS; Ocean Modeling; Marine Science Technology (scheduled for late 2019)
Enrollment (2018): B: 67 (13)

Professor:
H. Rodger Harvey, (D), 1985, Com

Chair:
Fred C. Dobbs, (D), Florida State, 1987, Ob

Professor:
David J. Burdige, (D), California (San Diego), 1983, OcCbo
Gregory A. Cutter, (D), California (Santa Cruz), 1982, OcCtHs
Eileen E. Hofmann, (D), North Carolina State, 1980, Op
John M. Klinck, (D), Iowa, 1980, Op
Margaret Mulholland, (D), Maryland, 1998, Ob

Associate Professor:
Alexander Bochdansky, (D), Memorial, 1997, Ob
Jennifer Georgen, (D), MIT/WHOI, 2001, Gu
Nora K. Noffke, (D), Oldenburg, 1997, GsPoGu
Matthew Schmidt, (D), California, 2005, Ou
G. Richard Whittecar, Jr., (D), Wisconsin, 1979, GmHwZe

Assistant Professor:
P. Dreux Chappell, (D), MIT/WHOI, 2009, Oc

Emeritus:
Larry P. Atkinson, (D), Dalhousie, 1972, Op
Dennis A. Darby, (D), Wisconsin, 1971, Ou

Patrick Henry Community College

Art, Science, Business, and Technology Dept (A) (2015)
645 Patriot Avenue
Martinsville, VA 24112
cferguson@patrickhenry.edu
http://www.ph.vccs.edu/

Assistant Professor:
Brett Dooley, (M), Virginia Tech, 2005, Gg

Piedmont Virginia Community College

Associate of Science (2015)
501 College Drive
Charlottesville, VA 22902
p. (434) 961-5446
khudson@pvcc.edu
http://www.pvcc.edu/

Radford University

Dept of Geology (B) (2015)
Box 6939
Radford University
Radford, VA 24142
p. (540) 831-5652
geology@radford.edu
http://www.radford.edu/~geol-web
Administrative Assistant: Theresa Gawthrop
Enrollment (2013): B: 62 (12)

Associate Professor:
Jonathan L. Tso, (D), Virginia Tech, 1987, Gcp

Professor:
Rhett B. Herman, (D), Montana State, 1996, YuXaGa
Parvinder S. Sethi, (D), North Carolina State, 1994, Gz
Chester F. Watts, (D), Purdue, 1983, NgrHw

Director, Museum of the Earth Sciences:
Stephen W. Lenhart, (D), Kentucky, 1985, Pgg

Associate Professor:
Elizabeth McClellan, (D), Tennessee, GipGd

Emeritus:
Robert C. Whisonant, (D), Florida State, 1967, GsaGg

Randolph-Macon College

Environmental Studies Program (B) ☒ (2018)
P.O. Box 5005
Ashland, VA 23005
p. (804) 752-3745
mfenster@rmc.edu
http://www.rmc.edu/academics/environmental-studies.aspx
Programs: Environmental Studies major with an Area of Expertise in Geology
Enrollment (2018): B: 31 (15)

Watts Professor of Science:
Michael S. Fenster, (D), Boston, 1995, OnGue

Adjunct Professor:
Charles Saunders, (M), E Carolina, 1990, ZgGrPg

Rappa Hannock Community College

Rappa Hannock Community College (2015)
12745 College Drive
Glenns, VA 23149
p. (804) 435-8970
babdul-malik@rappahannock.edu
http://www.rappahannock.edu

Tidewater Community College

Geophysical Sciences Dept (A) ☒ (2018)
1700 College Crescent
Virginia Beach, VA 23453
p. (757) 822-7089
RClayton@tcc.edu
Programs: Physical and Historical Geology, Oceanography I & II, Earth Science
Certificates: GIS and Remote Sensing

Professor:
Rodney L. Clayton, (D), NCU, 2016, GgOg

Instructor:
Mike Lyle, Gg
John Waugh, Gg

University of Lynchburg

Environmental Sciences, Studies, and Sustainability (B,M) O☒ (2019)
1501 Lakeside Dr.
Lynchburg, VA 24501
p. (434) 544-8415
haiar@lynchburg.edu
https://www.lynchburg.edu/academics/majors-and-minors/environmental-science/
Programs: Environmental Science; Environmental Studies
Enrollment (2019): B: 44 (16)

Professor:
David R. Perault, (D), Oklahoma, 1998, Ge

Associate Professor:
Brooke Haiar, (D), Oklahoma, 2008, PgGeg

University of Mary Washington

Dept of Earth and Environmental Sciences (B) ●⦸ (2020)
1301 College Avenue
Fredericksburg, VA 22401-5358
p. (540) 654-1016
jhayob@umw.edu
http://cas.umw.edu/ees/
f: https://www.facebook.com/UMW-Earth-Environmental-Sciences-259585170726418/?view_public_for=259585170726418
Programs: Geology; Environmental Geology; Environmental Science-Natural Track; Environmental Science-Social Track
Certificates: GIS (through the Geography department)

Enrollment (2020): B: 100 (0)
Chair:
Jodie Hayob, (D), Michigan, 1994, GxzGg
Professor:
Ben O. Kisila, (D), Arkansas, 2002, HsSfZu
Grant R. Woodwell, (D), Yale, 1985, Gc
Associate Professor:
Melanie Szulczewski, (D), Wisconsin, 1999, ScClZg
Charles Whipkey, (D), Pittsburgh, 1999, Cg
Assistant Professor:
Tyler E. Frankel, (D), Maryland, Rw
Pamela Grothe, (D), Georgia Tech, GsOgZc
Instructor:
Sarah A. Morealli, (M), Pittsburg State, 2010, Gg
Adjunct Professor:
John Tippett, (M), Duke, Zn

University of Virginia

Blandy Experimental Farm (2015)
400 Blandy Farm Lane
Boyce, VA 22620
p. (540) 837-1758
Blandy@virginia.edu
http://blandy.virginia.edu/
Director:
David E. Carr, (D), Maryland, 1990, Zn
Associate Director:
Kyle J. Haynes, (D), Louisiana State, 2004, Zn

Dept of Environmental Sciences (B,M,D) ☒ (2020)
Clark Hall
291 McCormick Road
Box 400123
Charlottesville, VA 22904
p. (434) 924-7761
cba4a@virginia.edu
http://www.evsc.as.virginia.edu
Programs: MA, MS and PhD in Environmental Sciences.
Enrollment (2018): B: 170 (91) M: 17 (6) D: 31 (9)
Research Full Professor:
Peter Berg, (D), Tech (Denmark), 1988, So
David E. Carr, (D), Maryland, 1990, Zn
William Keene, (M), Virginia, 1981, As
G. Carleton Ray, (D), Columbia, 1960, Ob
Dept Chair:
Howard E. Epstein, (D), Colorado State, 1997, Zn
Professor:
Lawrence Band, (D), California, 1983
Robert Davis, (D), Delaware, 1988, AsmZy
Stephan F. J DeWekker, (D), British Columbia, 2002, As
Scott Doney, (D), MIT, 1991, Oc
James N. Galloway, (D), California (San Diego), 1972, As
Janet S. Herman, (D), Penn State, 1982, ClHw
Alan D. Howard, (D), Johns Hopkins, 1970, GmXg
Deborah Lawrence, (D), Duke, 1998, ZcoZg
Manuel Lerdau, (D), Stanford, 1994, Zn
Stephen A. Macko, (D), Texas, 1981, CosOc
Karen McGlathery, (D), Cornell, 1992, Ob
Aaron L. Mills, (D), Cornell, 1975, So
Michael L. Pace, (D), Georgia, 1981, Zn
Matthew A. Reidenbach, (D), Stanford, 2004, Hg
Todd M. Scanlon, (D), Virginia, 2002, Hg
Herman H. Shugart, Jr., (D), Georgia, 1971, Zg
David E. Smith, (D), Texas A&M, 1982, Ob
Vivian E. Thomson, (D), Virginia, 1997, Zn
Patricia L. Wiberg, (D), Washington, 1987, Og
Research Associate Professor:
Linda K. Blum, (D), Cornell, 1980, Sb
Kyle J. Haynes, (D), Louisiana State, 2004, Zn
Jennie L. Moody, (D), Michigan, 1986, As
John H. Porter, (D), Virginia, 1988, Zif
Tai Roulston
Associate Professor:
Kevin M. Grise, (D), Colorado State, 2011, As
Thomas M. Smith, (D), Tennessee, 1982, Zg
Research Assistant Professor:
Karen C. Rice, (D), Virginia, 2001, HgCg
Assistant Professor:
Max Castorani, (D), California, 2014
Ajay Limaye
Sally Pusede, (D), California, 2014, As
Kathleen Schiro
Lauren Simkins
Xi Yang, (D), Brown, 2014
Emeritus:
Bruce W. Nelson, (D), Illinois, 1955, Gs
Wallace E. Reed, (D), Chicago, 1967, Zr
William F. Ruddiman, (D), Columbia, 1969, Gu

Shenandoah Watershed Study (B,M,D) (2015)
Department of Environmental Sciences
Clark Hall
Charlottesville, VA 22904
p. (434) 924-3382
tms2v@virginia.edu
http://people.virginia.edu/~swas/POST/scripts/overview.php
Associate Professor:
Todd M. Scanlon, (D), Virginia, 2002, Hgs
Research Scientist:
Ami L. Riscassi, (D), Virginia, 2009

Virginia Coast Reserve Long Term Ecological Research ☒ (2020)
291 McCormick Road
P.O. Box 400123
Charlottesville, VA 22904-4123
p. 434-924-0558
kjm4k@virginia.edu
https://www.vcrlter.virginia.edu
f: https://www.facebook.com/virginia.coast.reserve
t: https://twitter.com/vcrlter
Professor:
Karen J. McGlathery, (D), Cornell, 1992, Obn

University of Virginia's College at Wise

Dept of Natural Science (B) ☒ (2018)
1 College Avenue
Wise, VA 24293
p. (276) 328-0203
maw4v@uvawise.edu
https://www.uvawise.edu/academics/department-natural-sciences/
f: https://www.facebook.com/UVaWiseNaturalSciences
t: @UVaWiseNatSci
Programs: BA in Earth Science
Environmental Science, geology track
Administrative Assistant: Alan West
Instructor:
Robert D. VanGundy, (M), North Carolina, 1983, GeHgZg

Virginia Highlands Community College

Virginia Highlands Community College (2015)
100 VHCC Drive
Abingdon, VA 24212
p. (276)739-2433
jsurber@vhcc.edu
http://www.vhcc.edu

Virginia Polytechnic Institute & State University

Dept of Civil & Environmental Engineering (B,M,D) ☒ (2018)
750 Drillfield Drive
200 Patton Hall
Blacksburg, VA 24061-0105
p. (703) 231-6635
mwiddows@vt.edu
http://www.cee.vt.edu/
Administrative Assistant: Beth Lucas
Graduate Chair:
Mark A. Widdowson, (D), Auburn, HwSpHq
Professor:
Stanley Grant, (D), Caltech, Hs
Jennifer Irish, (D), Delaware, NoOg
Associate Professor:
Randel Dymond, (D), Penn State, HqsZi

Erich Hester, (D), North Carolina, Hsw
Kyle Strom, (D), Iowa, HsGs
Assistant Professor:
Megan Rippy, (D), Scripps, Rw

Dept of Crop & Soil Environmental Sciences (B,M,D) (2017)
240 Smyth Hall
Blacksburg, VA 24061-0404
p. (540) 231-6305
tlthomps@vt.edu
http://www.cses.vt.edu
Department Secretary: Nancy Shields
Head:
John R. Hall, III, (D), Ohio State, 1971, So
Professor:
Marcus M. Alley, (D), Virginia Tech, 1975, Sc
James C. Baker, (D), Virginia Tech, 1978, Sd
Walter L. Daniels, (D), Virginia Tech, 1985, SdGeCg
Stephen J. Donohue, (D), Purdue, 1974, Sc
Gregory K. Evanylo, (D), Georgia, 1982, Sc
Charles Hagedorn, (D), Iowa, 1974, Sb
Gregory L. Mullins, (D), Purdue, 1985, Sc
Raymond B. Reneau, (D), Florida, 1969, Sc
Lucian W. Zelazny, (D), Virginia Tech, 1970, Sc
Associate Professor:
Duane F. Berry, (D), Michigan State, 1984, Sb
Matthew J. Eick, (D), Delaware, 1995, Sc
Naraine Persaud, (D), Florida, 1978, Sp
Assistant Professor:
John M. Galbraith, (D), Cornell, 1997, Sp
Carl E. Zipper, (D), Virginia Tech, 1986, Ze
Adjunct Professor:
Domy C. Adriano, (D), Kansas State, 1970, Sc
V. C. Baligar, (D), Mississippi State, 1975, Sc
Pamela J. Thomas, (D), Virginia Tech, 1998, Sd

Dept of Geography (B,M,D) (2015)
115 Major Williams Hall
Blacksburg, VA 24061-0115
p. (540) 231-7557
carstens@vt.edu
Enrollment (2010): B: 170 (49) M: 17 (9) D: 8 (0)
Head:
Laurence W. Carstensen, (D), North Carolina, 1981, Zi
Professor:
James B. Campbell, (D), Kansas, 1976, Zr
Associate Professor:
Lawrence S. Grossman, (D), Australian Nat, 1979, Zn
Lisa M. Kennedy, (D), Tennessee, Pe
Resler M. Lynn, (D), Texas State, Zy
Instructor:
David Carroll, (M), Mississippi State, Am

Dept of Geosciences (B,M,D) (2020)
4044 Derring Hall
Blacksburg, VA 24061
p. (540) 231-6521
wstevenh@vt.edu
http://www.geos.vt.edu
f: https://www.facebook.com/vtgeosciences/
t: @vtgeosciences
Programs: Six options: Geology, Geophysics, Geochemistry, Environmental and Engineering Geoscience, Paleobiology, and Geoscience Education
Enrollment (2020): B: 73 (19) M: 10 (9) D: 37 (6)
Research Professor:
Martin C. Chapman, (D), Virginia Tech, 1998, Ys
Department Head:
W. Steven Holbrook, (D), Stanford, 1989, Yur
Professor:
Robert J. Bodnar, (D), Penn State, 1985, CgEmGv
Thomas J. Burbey, (D), Nevada (Reno), 1994, HwyZr
Patricia M. Dove, (D), Princeton, 1991, Cl
Kenneth A. Eriksson, (D), Witwatersrand, 1977, Gs
John A. Hole, (D), British Columbia, 1993, Ye
Scott D. King, (D), Caltech, 1990, Yg
Richard D. Law, (D), London (UK), 1981, Gc
Nancy L. Ross, (D), Arizona State, 1985, Gz
Madeline E. Schreiber, (D), Wisconsin, 1999, Hw
James A. Spotila, (D), Caltech, 1998, Gtm
Robert Weiss, (D), Westfalische–Wilhelms, 2005, RnOn
Shuhai Xiao, (D), Harvard, 1998, Pi
Research Associate Professor:
Susanna Werth, (D), Potsdam, 2010, ZrHgYv
Associate Collegiate Professor:
John A. Chermak, (D), Virginia Tech, 1989, ClGeEd
Associate Professor:
Mark Caddick, (D), Cambridge, 2005, GpCa
Benjamin Gill, (D), California (Riverside), 2009, CsPcGs
F. Marc Michel, (D), SUNY (Stony Brook), 2007, ZaGz
Sterling J. Nesbitt, (D), Columbia, 2009, Pv
Brian W. Romans, (D), Stanford, 2008, GsrEo
Manoochehr Shirzaei, (D), Potsdam, 2010, ZrYd
Ying Zhou, (D), Princeton, 2004, Ys
Assistant Professor:
Megan S. Duncan, (D), Rice, 2015, GiCp
Christina Dura, (D), Pennsylvania, 2014, OnRnPm
Ryan M. Pollyea, (D), Idaho, 2012, Hq
D. Sarah Stamps, (D), Purdue, 2013, YdGtRn
Michelle Stocker, (D), Texas, 2013, Pv
Sr. Research Associate:
Jing Zhao, (D), Chinese Acad of Sci, 1997
Research Associate:
Nizhou Han, (D), Iowa State, 1996, Sc
Advanced Instructor:
Neil E. Johnson, (D), Virginia Tech, 1986, GzEg
Adjunct Professor:
James S. Beard, (D), California (Davis), 1985, GiClg
Benedetto DeVivo, (D)
William S. Henika, (M), Virginia, 1969, Ng
Emeritus:
F. Donald Bloss, (D), Chicago, 1951, Gz
G. A. Bollinger, (D), St Louis, 1967, Ys
Cahit Coruh, (D), Istanbul, 1970, YesGt
James R. Craig, (D), Lehigh, 1965, Eg
Jerry Gibbs, (D), Penn State, Gz
Gordon C. Grender, (D), Penn State, 1960, Go
David A. Hewitt, (D), Yale, 1970, Cp
Michael F. Hochella, Jr., (D), Stanford, 1981, ClGze
Wallace D. Lowry, (D), Rochester, 1943, Gc
J. Fred Read, (D), W Australia, 1971, Gs
Paul H. Ribbe, (D), Cambridge, 1963, Gz
A. Krishna Sinha, (D), California (Santa Barbara), 1969, Gt
J. Arthur Snoke, (D), Yale, 1969, Ys
Research Scientist, Stable Isotope Lab Manager:
Rachel E.B. Reid, (D), California (Santa Cruz), 2014, CsPcCb
Research Scientist, Field Operations Lab Manager:
Sean P. Bemis, Oregon, 2010, Gt
Research Associate, Paleontology Lab Manager:
Vicki Yarborough, (B), Texas, 1991, Pv
Research Associate, Microbeam Facility Manager:
Lowell P. Moore, (D), Virginia Tech, 2019, Ca
A/P Faculty:
Gary Glesener, (M), California (Los Angeles), 2016, Ze
Cooperating Faculty:
Edward Lener, (M), Virginia Tech, 1997, Zn

Virginia Wesleyan College

Dept of Earth and Environmental Sciences (B) (2015)
1584 Wesleyan Dr
Norfolk, VA 23502
p. 757.455.3200
emalcolm@vwu.edu
http://www.vwc.edu/earth-and-envirmental-sciences/
f: https://www.facebook.com/vwc.ees
Enrollment (2015): B: 22 (0)
Professor:
John C. Haley, (D), Johns Hopkins, 1986, GgeZi
Associate Professor:
Elizabeth Malcolm, (D), Michigan, 2002, AsCgOg
Garry Noe, (D), California (Riverside), 1982, HsZin

Virginia Western Community College

Geology Dept (A) (2015)
3095 Colonial Avenue
Roanoke, VA 24038
p. (540) 857-7273

abalog-szabo@virginiawestern.edu

Professor:
Anna Balog-Szabo, (D), Virginia Tech, 1996, Gs

Washington & Lee University

Dept of Geology (B) ☒ (2020)
204 West Washington Street
Lexington, VA 24450
p. (540) 458-8800
geology@wlu.edu
http://geology.wlu.edu
Programs: Geology
Administrative Assistant: Sarah Barrash. Wilson
Enrollment (2020): B: 21 (11)

Professor:
Christopher Connors, (D), Princeton, 1999, GcYeGo
Lisa Greer, (D), Miami, 2001, GsPe
David J. Harbor, (D), Colorado State, 1990, Gm
Elizabeth P. Knapp, (D), Virginia, 1997, Cl
Jeffrey Rahl, (D), Yale, 2005, Gt

Assistant Professor:
Margaret Anne Hinkle, (D), Washington (St. Louis), 2015, Cqb

Emeritus:
Frederick Lyon Schwab, (D), Harvard, 1968, Gdg

Laboratory Supervisor:
Emily Flowers Falls, (M), E Kentucky, 2009, Gg

William & Mary

Department of Geology (B) ⦸ (2020)
PO Box 8795
Williamsburg, VA 23187-8795
p. (757) 221-2440
crroex@wm.edu
http://www.wm.edu/as/geology
Programs: B.S. in Geology; B.S. in Environmental Geology
Certificates: GIS
Administrative Assistant: Carol Roe
Enrollment (2020): B: 63 (23)

Chair:
Rowan Lockwood, (D), Chicago, 2001, PgePi

Professor:
Christopher M. Bailey, (D), Johns Hopkins, 1994, Gc
Gregory S. Hancock, (D), California (Santa Cruz), 1998, Gm
R. Heather Macdonald, (D), Wisconsin, 1984, GsZe
Brent E. Owens, (D), Washington (St Louis), 1992, Gx

Associate Professor:
James Kaste, (D), Dartmouth, 2003, ClcSc

Assistant Professor:
Nicholas Balascio, (D), Massachusetts, 2011, ZyGnl

Research Associate:
Carl R. Berquist, Jr., (D), William & Mary, 1986, Ou

Lecturer:
Rebecca Jiron, (D), California (Santa Barbara), 2015, GgsZi
Linda D. Morse, (B), Virginia Tech, 1983, GeZg

Visiting Professor:
Jonathan Kay, (D), Illinois (Chicago), 2017, ZyiGc

Emeritus:
Stephen C. Clement, (D), Cornell, 1964, Gz
P. Geoffrey Feiss, (D), Harvard
Gerald H. Johnson, (D), Indiana, 1965, Pg

School of Marine Science (M,D) ☒ (2021)
Virginia Institute of Marine Science
P. O. Box 1346
Gloucester Point, VA 23062-1246
p. (804) 684-7105
ad-as@vims.edu
http://www.vims.edu
Programs: Biological Sciences, Fisheries Science, Aquatic Health Sciences, Physical Sciences (Physical Oceanography, Chemical Oceanography, Marine Geology)
Enrollment (2020): M: 7 (2) D: 11 (3)

Research Professor:
Jian Shen, (D), William & Mary, 1996, Op

Department Chair:
Carl T. Friedrichs, (D), MIT/WHOI, 1993, On

Professor:
Elizabeth A. Canuel, (D), North Carolina, 1992, Oc
Courtney K. Harris, (D), Virginia, 1999, On
Steven A. Kuehl, (D), North Carolina State, 1985, Ou
Harry Wang, (D), Johns Hopkins, 1983, Op

Research Associate Professor:
William G. Reay, (D), Virginia Tech, 1992, Hg
Y. Joseph Zhang, (D), Wollongong (Australia), 1996, Opn

Associate Professor:
Donglai Gong, (D), Rutgers, 2010, Op
Christopher J. Hein, (D), Boston, 2012, Ou
Matthew L. Kirwan, (D), Duke, 2007, Gm

Assistant Professor:
Amber Hardison, (D), Virginia Inst of Marine Sci, Cm
Pierro Mazzini, (D), Oregon State, 2014, Op

Washington

Bellevue College

Earth and Space Sciences Program (A) (2015)
3000 Landerholm Circle SE
Bellevue, WA 98007
p. (425) 564-3158
kshort@bellevuecollege.edu
http://scidiv.bellevuecollege.edu/

Instructor:
Cary Easterday, (M), GgPg
Gwyn Jones, (M), Gg
Deborah Minium, (M), Gg
Rob Viens, (D), Washington, GgZg

Central Washington University

Dept of Geological Sciences (B,M) ●✇ (2019)
400 East University Way
MS 7418
Ellensburg, WA 98926-7418
p. (509) 963-2701
chair@geology.cwu.edu
http://www.geology.cwu.edu
Programs: Geology (B,M); Environmental Geology (B)
Enrollment (2019): B: 46 (12) M: 19 (6)

Chair:
Chris Mattinson, (D), Stanford, 2006, GpCcGt

Director, PANGA Laboratory:
Timothy I. Melbourne, (D), Caltech, 1998, Yd

Professor:
Lisa L. Ely, (D), Arizona, 1992, Gm
Carey A. Gazis, (D), Caltech, 1994, CsHw

Senior Scientist:
Angela Halfpenny, (D), Liverpool (UK), 2007, Gcz

Associate Professor:
Anne E. Egger, (D), Stanford, 2010, GtZeRn
Audrey Huerta, (D), MIT, 1998, Ygd
Susan Kaspari, (D), Maine, 2007, PcAtGl
Breanyn MacInnes, (D), Washington, 2010, GseGu
Walter Szeliga, (D), Colorado, 2010, YgsYd

GPS Data Analyst:
Marcelo Santillan, (M), Memphis, 2003, Yd

Research Associate:
Paul Winberry, Penn State, 2008, Yg

Science Outreach & Education Coordinator:
Nick Zentner, (M), Idaho State, 1989, Gg

Lecturer:
Keegan Fengler, (M), C Washington, Gg
Winston Norrish, (D), Cincinnati, 1990, GgeGo

Emeritus:
Robert Bentley, (D), Columbia, 1969, Gi
Wendy A. Bohrson, (D), California (Los Angeles), 1993, GivCc
Steven Farkas, (D), New Mexico, 1965, Gs
James R. Hinthorne, (D), California (Santa Barbara), 1974, Ca
Jeffrey Lee, (D), Stanford, 1990, Gct
M. Meghan Miller, (D), Stanford, 1987, Yd
Charles M. Rubin, (D), Caltech, 1990, Gt

Systems Administrator:
Craig Scrivner, (D), Caltech, 1998

Centralia College

Geosciences (A) ⃠ (2019)
600 Centralia College Blvd
Centralia, WA 98531
p. (360) 623-8472
michelle.harris@centralia.edu
http://www.centralia.edu/academics/earthscience
Programs: Geology and Earth Science
Certificates: None
Enrollment (2019): A: 6 (1)
Assistant Professor:
Michelle Harris, (M), Gg
Emeritus:
Patrick T. Pringle, (M), Akron, 1982, ZgGvZn

Eastern Washington University

Dept of Geology (B) O☒ (2018)
140 Science Building
Cheney, WA 99004-2439
p. (509) 359-2286
geology@ewu.edu
https://www.ewu.edu/cstem/departments/geology
Programs: Geology; Environmental Science; Earth and Space Science Education
Enrollment (2017): B: 33 (19)
Chair:
Jennifer A. Thomson, (D), Massachusetts, 1992, Gpz
Professor:
John P. Buchanan, (D), Colorado State, 1985, Hw
Carmen A. Nezat, (D), Michigan, 2006, ClGeSc
Associate Professor:
Richard L. Orndorff, (D), Kent State, 1994, Ge
Assistant Professor:
Chad Pritchard, (D), Washington State, Gct
Lecturer:
Jeanne Case, (M), California (Riverside), Gg
Sharen Keattch, (M), Kent State, 1993, Gg
Emeritus:
Ernest H. Gilmour, (D), Montana, 1967, Pi
Eugene P. Kiver, (D), Wyoming, 1968, Gl
Linda B. McCollum, (D), SUNY (Binghamton), 1980, Pg

Edmonds Community College

Geology (A) (2015)
20000 68th Ave W
Lynnwood, WA 98036
p. (425) 640-1918
mkelly@edcc.edu
http://www.edcc.edu/stem/geology/
Enrollment (2013): A: 4 (0)
Instructor:
Maria Kelly, Zg
Adjunct Professor:
Dylan Ahearn, (D), California (Davis)
Thomas Hamilton, Zg

Everett Community College

Dept of Physical Sciences (A) (2015)
2000 Tower Street
Everett, WA 98201
p. (425) 388-9429
sdamp@everettcc.edu
http://www.everettcc.edu/programs/mathsci/physical/
Instructor:
Steve Grupp, (M), Colorado Mines, GgOg
Adjunct Professor:
Alecia Spooner, Zg

Grays Harbor College

Dept of Geology & Oceanography (A) (2015)
Aberdeen, WA 98520
p. (206) 538-4299
john.hillier@ghc.edu
Professor:
John Hillier, (D), Cornell, ZgCa
Emeritus:
James B. Phipps, (D), Oregon State, 1974, Gu

Green River Community College

Dept of Geology (A) ⍻ (2019)
12401 S.E. 320th
Auburn, WA 98092-3699
p. (253) 833-9111 (Ext. 4248)
khoppe@greenriver.edu
https://www.greenriver.edu/grc/course-descriptions/course-description-detail.aspx?desc=GEOL&deptname=Geology
Programs: AA, AS; & BAS in Natural Resources in Forest Resource Management
Instructor:
Kathryn A. Hoppe, (D), Princeton, 1999, ZgOgPg
Katy Shaw, (M), Washington, ZgOgGg
Adjunct Professor:
Megan Onufer, (M)

Highline College

Physical Sciences Dept/Geology Program (A) ⍻ (2020)
MS 29-3
PO Box 98000
2400 S. 240th St.
Des Moines, WA 98198-9800
p. (206) 878-3710
geology@highline.edu
http://geology.highline.edu/
Enrollment (2018): A: 5 (2)
Instructor:
Eric M. Baer, (D), California (Santa Barbara), 1995, GgvZg
Stephaney Puchalski, (D), Indiana, 2011, PgGg
Jacob Selander, (D), California (Davis)
Michael Valentine, (D), Massachusetts, 1990, Gt
Carla Whittington, (M), Indiana, GgvZg

Lower Columbia College

Earth Sciences (Natural Sciences Dept.) (A) (2015)
P.O. Box 3010
Longview, WA 98632
p. (360) 442-2883
msalisbury@lowercolumbia.edu
https://lowercolumbia.edu/programs/natural-science.php
Professor:
David I. Cordero, (M), Portland State, 1997, Zg

North Seattle Community College, North Campus

Earth Science (2015)
9600 College Way North
Seattle, WA 98103
p. (206) 934-4509
john.figge@seattlecolleges.edu
http://www.northseattle.edu/

Northwest Indian College

Native Environmental Studies (2015)
2522 Kwina Road
Bellingham, WA 98226
p. (360) 392-4256
enorman@nwic.edu
http://www.nwic.edu/degrees-and-certificates/bsnes-bachelors-degree

Olympic College

Mathematics, Engineering, Sciences, and Health Div (A) (2015)
Bremerton, WA 98310
p. (360) 475-7777
SMacias@olympic.edu
http://www.olympic.edu/Students/AcadDivDept/MESH/Sciences/Geology/
Instructor:
Steve E. Macias, (M), Washington, 1996, Gg
Adjunct Professor:
Katie Howard, Gg

Pacific Lutheran University

Dept of Geosciences (B) (2015)
12180 S. Park
Tacoma, WA 98447
p. (253) 535-7378
geos@plu.edu
http://www.plu.edu/geosciences/
Enrollment (2013): B: 52 (11)

Chair:
Jill M. Whitman, (D), California (San Diego), 1989, OuGuZe

Professor:
Duncan Foley, (D), Ohio State, 1978, GeHyZe

Associate Professor:
Rosemary McKenney, (D), Penn State, 1997, Gm
Claire E. Todd, (D), Washington, 2007, Glm

Assistant Professor:
Peter B. Davis, (D), Minnesota, 2008, GcpGz

Peninsula College

Environmental Science (2015)
1502 East Lauridsen Boulevard
Port Angeles, WA 98362
p. (360) 452-9277
jganzhorn@pencol.edu
http://www.pc.ctc.edu

Pierce College

Pierce College (2015)
9401 Farwest Drive SW
Lakewood, WA 98498
p. (253) 964-6676
zayacjm@piercecollege.edu
http://www.piercecollege.edu/departments/physics_planetary_sciences/geology.asp

Seattle Central College

Div of Science & Mathematics (2015)
1701 Broadway
Seattle, WA 98122
p. (206) 587-3858
Nancy.Sola-Llonch2@seattlecolleges.edu
http://seattlecentral.edu/sci-math/

Instructor:
Katie Gagnon, (D), California (San Diego), 2007, OuZg
Joseph M. Hull, (D), Rochester, 1988, Gc

Adjunct Professor:
Michael Harrell, Gg

Shoreline Community College

Geology & Earth Sciences (A) (2015)
16101 Greenwood Avenue North
Seattle, WA 98133
p. (206) 546-4659
eagosta@shoreline.edu
http://www.shoreline.edu/science/geology.htm

Spokane Community College

Dept of Earth Science (2015)
1810 N. Greene Street
Spokane, WA 99217
Andy.Buddington@scc.spokane.edu
http://www.scc.spokane.edu/ArtsSciences/Science/

Tacoma Community College

Dept of Earth Sciences (A) 🖱 (2018)
6501 South 19th Street
Tacoma, WA 98466
p. (253) 566-5060
rhitz@tacomacc.edu
https://www.tacomacc.edu/academics-programs/programs/geology
Programs: Associate of Science with an Earth Sciences Specialization, Associate of Arts
Enrollment (2018): A: 3 (0)

Professor:
Ralph B. Hitz, (D), California (Santa Barbara), 1997, PvSaZi

Adjunct Professor:
Jim McDougall, (D), Zg
James Peet, (D), Washington
Michael Valentine, (D), Zg

University of Puget Sound

Geology Dept (B) ☒ (2019)
1500 N. Warner Street
Tacoma, WA 98416-1048
p. (253) 879-3814
kena@pugetsound.edu
http://www.pugetsound.edu/academics/departments-and-programs/undergraduate/geology/
f: https://www.facebook.com/upsgeology
Programs: B.S in Geology; B.S.in Natural Science
Administrative Assistant: Leslie Levenson
Enrollment (2019): B: 20 (12)

Chair:
Michael J. Valentine, (D), Massachusetts, 1990, YmGc

Professor:
Barry Goldstein, (D), Minnesota, 1985, GlmGs
Jeffrey H. Tepper, (D), Washington, 1991, GiCgGv

Associate Professor:
Kena L. Fox-Dobbs, (D), California (Santa Cruz), 2006, PgCsGe

Instructor:
Ken P. Clark, (M), W Washington, 1989, GgcGi

Emeritus:
Albert A. Eggers, (D), Dartmouth, 1972, Gv

University of Washington

Dept of Atmospheric Sciences (B,M,D) ☒ (2019)
Box 351640
Seattle, WA 98195-1640
p. (206) 543-4250
chair@atmos.washington.edu
http://www.atmos.washington.edu
f: www.facebook.com/UWAtmosSci
t: @UWAtmosSci
Programs: Atmospheric Sciences
Enrollment (2017): B: 73 (18) M: 34 (16) D: 29 (7)

Affiliate Associate Professor:
Philip W. Mote, (D), Washington, 1994, As

Professor:
Cecilia M. Bitz, (D), Washington, 1997, As

Research Associate Professor:
Roger T. Marchand, (D), Virginia Tech, 1997, Ass

Professor:
Thomas P. Ackerman, (D), Washington, 1976, As
Becky Alexander, (D), California (San Diego), 2002, AsCsPe
David S. Battisti, (D), Washington, 1988, As
Christopher S. Bretherton, (D), MIT, 1984, As
Shuyi S. Chen, (D), Penn State, 1990, As
Dale R. Durran, (D), MIT, 1981, As
Qiang Fu, (D), Utah, 1991, As
Gregory J. Hakim, (D), SUNY (Albany), 1997, As
Dennis L. Hartmann, (D), Princeton, 1975, As
Lyatt Jaegle, (D), Caltech, 1996, As
Daniel A. Jaffe, (D), Washington, 1987, As
Clifford F. Mass, (D), Washington, 1978, As
Joel A. Thornton, (D), California (Berkeley), 2002, As
Robert Wood, (D), Manchester (UK), 1997, As

Associate Professor:
Dargan M. Frierson, (D), Princeton, 2005, As
Abigail L. S. Swann, (D), California (Berkeley), 2010, AsZn

Assistant Professor:
Daehyun Kim, (D), Seoul Nat, 2010, As

Adjunct Associate Professor:
Jessica D. Lundquist, (D), Scripps, 2004, As

Adjunct Professor:
Gerard H. Roe, (D), MIT, 1999, As
Eric J. Steig, (D), Washington, 1996, CsGlAs
LuAnne Thompson, (D), MIT, 1990, Og
Ka-Kit Tung, (D), Harvard, 1977, As

Research Professor Emeritus:
James E. Tillman, (M), MIT, As

Emeritus:
Marcia B. Baker, (D), Washington, As
Robert A. Brown, (D), Washington, 1969, As

Joost A. Businger, (D), State (Utrecht), As
Robert J. Charlson, (D), Washington, As
David S. Covert, (D), Washington, 1974, As
Thomas C. Grenfell, (D), Washington, 1972, As
Halstead Harrison, (D), Stanford, 1960, As
Dean A. Hegg, (D), Washington, 1979, As
Robert A. Houze, (D), MIT, 1972, As
Gary A. Maykut, (D), Washington, As
Peter B. Rhines, (D), Trinity Coll (Cambridge), 1967, Op
Edward S. Sarachik, (D), Brandeis, As
John M. Wallace, (D), MIT, 1966, As
Stephen G. Warren, (D), Harvard, 1973, ApGl

Research Associate Professor:
Lynn A. McMurdie, (D), Washington, 1989, As

Research Assistant Professor:
Edward Blanchard, (D), Washington, 2013, As

Affiliate Professor:
James E. Overland, (D), New York, 1973, As
Lawrence F. Radke, (D), Washington, 1968, As
Chidong Zhang, (D), Penn State, 1989, AsmOp

Affiliate Associate Professor:
Timothy S. Bates, (D), Washington, 1992, As
Nicholas A. Bond, (D), Washington, 1986, As
Bradley R. Colman, (D), MIT, 1984, As
Mark T. Stoelinga, (D), Washington, 1993, As

Affiliate Assistant Professor:
Bonnie Light, (D), Washington, 2000, As

Dept of Earth & Space Sciences (B,M,D) ●☒ (2019)
070 Johnson Hall
Box 351310
Seattle, WA 98195-1310
p. (206) 543-1190
essadv@uw.edu
http://www.ess.washington.edu
f: https://www.facebook.com/pages/University-of-Washington-Earth-and-Space-Sciences/132505186787510
t: @UW_ESS
Programs: Earth and Space Sciences, Earth and Space Sciences: Geology, Earth and Space Sciences: Biology, Earth and Space Sciences: Environmental, Earth and Space Sciences: Physics, Applied Geosciences, Geological Sciences, Geophysics
Administrative Assistant: Scott Dakins
Enrollment (2019): B: 172 (81) M: 20 (10) D: 22 (12)

Academic Services:
Noell Bernard-Kingsley, Ze

Chair:
Kenneth C. Creager, (D), California (San Diego), 1984, Ys

Research Professor:
Howard B. Conway, (D), Canterbury (NZ), 1986, Gl
Dale P. Winebrenner, (D), Washington, 1985, GlZr

Pacific Northwest Seismic Network:
Harold Tobin

Affiliate Professor:
Arthur Frankel, (D), Ys
Joan Gomberg, (D), YsGt
Frank I. Gonzalez, (D), Hawaii, 1977, OpRn
Tony Irving, (D), CgXmGi
Richard Sack, (D), CgZn
George Shaw

Affiliate Assistant Professor:
Ralph Haugerud, (D), Zi
Brian L. Sherrod, (D), YsGt

Professor:
George W. Bergantz, (D), Johns Hopkins, 1988, Gi
J. Michael Brown, (D), Minnesota, 1980, Gy
Roger Buick, (D), W Australia, 1986, CbXbPm
David C. Catling, (D), Oxford, 1994, CgAsXb
Bernard Hallet, (D), California (Los Angeles), 1975, Gml
Robert H. Holzworth, (D), California (Berkeley), 1977, XyAsZg
David R. Montgomery, (D), California (Berkeley), 1991, Gm
Bruce K. Nelson, (D), California (Los Angeles), 1985, CcGie
Charles A. Nittrouer, (D), Washington, 1978, GuYr
Mark Richards
Eric J. Steig, (D), Washington, 1996, CsGlAs
Edwin D. Waddington, (D), British Columbia, 1981, Gl
Peter D. Ward, (D), McMaster, 1976, Pg
Stephen G. Warren, (D), Harvard, 1973, AsGl
Robert M. Winglee, (D), Sydney, 1984, XyYx

Research Associate Professor:
Evan H. Abramson, (D), MIT, 1985, Gy
Paul A. Bodin, (D), Colorado, 1992, Ys
Michael P. McCarthy, (D), Washington, 1988, XyYx
Ronald S. Sletten, (D), Washington, 1995, Sob

Research Assistant Professor:
Erika M. Harnett, (D), Washington, 2003, XyGev

Affiliate Associate Professor:
Amit Mushkin, (D), ZrCcGm

Associate Professor:
Rolf E. Aalto, Gms
Derek Booth, Gm
Juliet G. Crider, (D), Stanford, 1998, GcmNr
Drew J. Gorman-Lewis, (D), Notre Dame, 2006, PgCl
Bob Hawley, Gl
Katharine W. Huntington, (D), MIT, 2006, Gt
Seth Moran, Gv
Gerard H. Roe, (D), MIT, 1999, AsGml
David Schmidt, (D), California (Berkeley), 2002, Gt
Ben Smith, GlZr
John O.H Stone, (D), Cambridge, 1986, Cca
Caroline Stromberg, Pbe
Fangzhen Teng, (D), Maryland, 2005, Cg
Jeremy Thomas, ZrXa
Gregory Wilson, (D), California (Berkeley), 2004, Pvg

Research Assistant Professor:
Michelle Koutnik, (D), Washington, 2009, Gll

Adjunct Assistant Professor:
Christian A. Sidor, (D), Chicago, 2000, Pv

Assistant Professor:
Scott Bennett, (D), California (Davis), 2013, YsGtm
Tom Brown, CcAt
Knut Christianson, (D), GlZr
Trenton Cladouhos, Gcg
Cailey Condit
Janice DeCosmo, AtZe
Alison Duvall, (D), Michigan, 2011, GmcGt
T.J. Fudge, (D), Gl
Alex Grant
Alexis Licht, (D), Gsn
Kenichi Matsuoka, Gl
Tom Neumann, Gl
Gregg Petrie, Zr
David Reusch
Erin Wirth, (D), Yale, 2014, YsRn
Tim Ziemba, Xa

Research Associate:
Marc Biundo, Ys
Doug Gibbons, ZeYs
Renate Hartog, Ys
Scott Henderson
Alex Hutko
Abram Jacobsen, Xg
Scott Kuehner, Ggz

Scientific Instructional Designer:
Michael Harrell, (D), Washington, Ze

Senior Lecturer:
Terry W. Swanson, (D), Washington, 1994, CcGe
Kathy G. Troost, (D), Zun

Lecturer:
Brian Collins, Gm
Ruth Martin
Steven Walters, Zir

Adjunct Professor:
David S. Battisti, (D), Washington, 1988, As
John R. Delaney, (D), Arizona, 1977, GuYr
Harlan Paul Johnson, (D), Washington, 1972, Gu
Randy LeVeque, (D), Stanford, 1982, GvYs
Andrea Ogston, Og
John D. Sahr, (D), Cornell, 1990, ZrXym
William S.D Wilcock, (D), MIT, 1992, Gu

Research Professor Emeritus:
Stephen D. Malone, (D), Nevada (Reno), 1972, YsGt
Gary A. Maykut, (D), Washington, 1969, AsGlYr

Research Professor:
Alan R. Gillespie, (D), Caltech, 1982, GmlZr

Research Associate Professor:
Robert I. Odom, (D), Washington, 1980, YrGu

Professor:
Joost Businger, Am
Affiliate Professor:
Brian Atwater, (D), Delaware, 1980, RnGr
Charlotte Schreiber, (D), Gsd
Emeritus:
John B. Adams, (D), Washington, 1961, GcXgZr
Patricia M. Anderson, (D), Brown, 1982, Ple
Marcia B. Baker, (D), Washington, 1971, AsYg
John Booker, (D), California (San Diego), 1968, YmGct
Joanne (Jody) Bourgeois, (D), Wisconsin, 1980, GsrRh
Bob Charlson, As
Eric S. Cheney, (D), Yale, 1964, Eg
Darrel S. Cowan, (D), Stanford, 1972, Gct
Robert S. Crosson, (D), Stanford, 1966, YsGct
Bernard W. Evans, (D), Oxford, 1959, GpzGi
Heidi Houston
Estella Leopold
Ronald T. Merrill, (D), California (Berkeley), 1967, Ygm
George K. Parks, (D), California (Berkeley), 1966, YxXy
Charles F. Raymond, (D), Caltech, 1969, Gl
John M. Rensberger, (D), California (Berkeley), 1967, Pvg
Stewart W. Smith, (D), Caltech, 1961, Ys
Minze Stuiver, (D), Groningen (Neth), 1958, Cc
Brian Swanson, Asp
Joseph A. Vance, (D), Washington, 1957, Gi
Seismology Lab:
Bill Steele, Ys
Senior Computer Specialist:
Harvey Greenberg, (M), Cal State (Chico), 1977, Gml
Postdoctoral Researcher:
Jon Toner, (D)
Other:
Nick Lancaster

School of Oceanography (B,M,D) (2015)
Box 357940
Seattle, WA 98195-7940
p. (206) 543-5060
admin@ocean.washington.edu
http://www.ocean.washington.edu/
Research Professor:
Mark L. Holmes, (D), Washington, 1975, OuGl
Ronald L. Shreve, (D), Caltech, 1959, Yr
Professor:
Knut Aagaard, (D), Washington, 1966, Op
John A. Baross, (D), Washington, 1972, Ob
Roy Carpenter, (D), California (San Diego), 1968, No
William O. Criminale, Jr., (D), Johns Hopkins, 1960, Op
Eric A. D'Asaro, (D), MIT/WHOI, 1980, Op
John R. Delaney, (D), Arizona, 1977, Yr
Jody W. Deming, (D), Maryland, 1981, Ob
Allan H. Devol, (D), Washington, 1975, Oc
Steven R. Emerson, (D), Columbia, 1974, OcCmOg
Charles C. Eriksen, (D), MIT, 1977, Op
Bruce W. Frost, (D), California (San Diego), 1969, Ob
Michael C. Gregg, (D), California (San Diego), 1971, Op
G. Ross Heath, (D), Scripps, 1968, Cm
Barbara M. Hickey, (D), California (San Diego), 1975, Op
H. Paul Johnson, (D), Washington, 1972, Yr
Deborah S. Kelley, (D), Dalhousie, 1990, OuGvp
Marvin D. Lilley, (D), Oregon State, 1983, Ob
Seelye Martin, (D), Johns Hopkins, 1967, Op
James W. Murray, (D), MIT/WHOI, 1973, Oc
Charles A. Nittrouer, (D), Washington, 1978, Ou
Arthur R. M. Nowell, (D), British Columbia, 1975, Ou
Paul D. Quay, (D), Columbia, 1977, Oc
Peter B. Rhines, (D), Cambridge, 1967, Op
Jeffrey E. Richey, (D), California (Davis), 1973, CbHs
Stephen C. Riser, (D), Rhode Island, 1981, Op
Associate Professor:
Virginia E. Armbrust, (D), MIT/WHOI, 1990, Ob
Susan L. Hautala, (D), Washington, 1992, Op
Bruce M. Howe, (D), California (San Diego), 1986, Op
Mitsuhiro Kawase, (D), Princeton, 1986, Op
Richard G. Keil, (D), Delaware, 1991, Oc
Evelyn J. Lessard, (D), Rhode Island, 1984, Ob
Parker MacCready, (D), Washington, Op
LuAnne Thompson, (D), MIT/WHOI, 1990, Op
Mark J. Warner, (D), California (San Diego), 1988, Op
William S. D. Wilcock, (D), MIT/WHOI, 1992, Ou
Kevin L. Williams, (D), Washington State, 1985, Op
Research Assistant Professor:
Miles G. Logsdon, (D), Washington, 1997, Zi
Andrea S. Ogston, (D), Washington, 1997, Ou
Assistant Professor:
Andrew Barclay, (D), Oregon, 1998, Gu
Daniel Grunbaum, (D), Cornell, 1992, Ob
Anitra E. Ingalls, (D), SUNY (Stony Brook), 2002, Oc
Jeffrey D. Parsons, (D), Illinois, 1998, Ou
Gabrielle L. Rocap, (D), MIT/WHOI, 2000, Ob
Senior Lecturer:
Christina M. Emerick, (D), Oregon State, 1985, Ou
Lecturer:
Richard M. Strickland, (M), Washington, 1975, ObgZg
Adjunct Professor:
Rose Ann Cattolico, (D), SUNY (Stony Brook), 1973, Zn
Robert Francis, (D), Washington, 1970, Ob
Barbara B. Krieger-Brockett, (D), Wayne State, 1976, Ob
Ronald T. Merrill, (D), California (Berkeley), 1967, Ym
Edward Sarachik, (D), Brandeis, 1966, As
Robert C. Spindel, (D), Yale, 1971, Op
Emeritus:
George C. Anderson, (D), Washington, 1954, Ob
Karl Banse, (D), Kiel, 1955, Ob
Joe S. Creager, (D), Texas A&M, 1958, Ou
Alyn C. Duxbury, (D), Texas A&M, 1963, On
Terry E. Ewart, (D), Washington, 1965, Op
Richard H. Gammon, (D), Harvard, 1970, Oc
Joyce C. Lewin, (D), Yale, 1953, Ob
Brian T. R. Lewis, (D), Wisconsin, 1970, Yr
Russell E. McDuff, (D), California (San Diego), 1978, OcGu
Dean A. McManus, (D), Kansas, 1959, Ou
Gunnar I. Roden, (M), California (Los Angeles), 1956, Op
David A. Rothrock, (D), Cambridge, 1968, Op
Thomas B. Sanford, (D), MIT, 1967, Op
Richard W. Sternberg, (D), Washington, 1965, Ou
Cooperating Faculty:
Matthew H. Alford, (D), California (San Diego), 1998, Op
Edward T. Baker, (D), Washington, 1973, Ou
Laurie Balistrieri, (M), Washington, 1977, Oc
John Bullister, (D), California (San Diego), 1984, Oc
David A. Butterfield, (D), Washington, 1990, Yr
Glenn A. Cannon, (D), Johns Hopkins, 1969, Op
Meghan F. Cronin, (D), Rhode Island, 1993, Op
Brian D. Dushaw, (D), California (San Diego), 1992, Op
Richard A. Feely, (D), Texas A&M, 1974, Oc
Don E. Harrison, (D), Harvard, 1977, Op
Albert Hermann, (D), Washington, 1988, Op
Robin T. Holcomb, (D), Stanford, 1981, Ou
Gregory C. Johnson, (D), MIT/WHOI, 1990, Op
Peter A. Jumars, (D), California (San Diego), 1974, Ob
Kathryn A. Kelly, (D), California (San Diego), 1983, Op
William S. Kessler, (D), Washington, 1989, Op
Craig M. Lee, (D), Washington, 1995, Op
Michael J. McPhaden, (D), California (San Diego), 1980, Og
Curtis D. Mobley, (D), Maryland, 1977, Ob
Harold O. Mofjeld, (D), Washington, 1970, Op
Dennis W. Moore, (D), Harvard, 1968, Op
James H. Morison, (D), Washington, 1980, Op
Jeffrey Napp, (D), California (San Diego), 1986, Ob
Jan Newton, (D), Washington, 1989, Ob
Jeffrey A. Nystuen, (D), California (San Diego), 1985, Op
Joan M. Oltman-Shay, (D), California, 1986, Op
Mary Jane Perry, (D), California (San Diego), 1974, Ob
Thomas Pratt, (N), Gu
Joseph A. Resing, (D), Hawaii, 1997, Oc
Christopher L. Sabine, (D), Hawaii, 1992, Oc
Randy Shuman, (D), Washington, 1978, Ob
Laurenz A. Thomsen, (D), Kiel, 1992, Ob
Cynthia T. Tynan, (D), California (San Diego), 1993, Ob
Rebecca A. Woodgate, (D), Oxford, 1994, Op

Walla Walla Community College

Walla Walla Community College (2015)
500 Tausick Way
Walla Walla, WA 99362

p. (509) 527-4278
steven.may@wwcc.edu
http://www.wwcc.edu

Washington State University

Dept of Crop & Soil Sciences (B,M,D) (2015)
201 Johnson Hall
P.O. Box 646420
Pullman, WA 99164-6420
p. (509) 335-3475
bc.johnson@wsu.edu
http://css.wsu.edu/
Chair:
Richard Koenig, (D)
Professor:
David F. Bezdicek, (D), Minnesota, 1967, Sb
James B. Harsh, (D), California (Berkeley), 1983, Sc
Shiou Kuo, (D), Maine, 1973, Sc
Thomas A. Lumpkin, (D), Hawaii, 1978, Zn
William L. Pan, (D), North Carolina, 1983, Sb
John P. Reganold, (D), California (Davis), 1980, Soo
Senior Scientist:
Robert G. Stevens, (D), Colorado State, 1971, Sb
Associate Professor:
Joan R. Davenport, (D), Guelph, 1985, Sb
Frank J. Peryea, (D), California, 1983, Sc
Assistant Professor:
Markus Flury, (D), Swiss Fed Inst Tech, 1994, Sp
Adjunct Professor:
Alan J. Busacca, (D), California (Davis), 1982, Sa
Ann C. Kennedy, (D), North Carolina State, 1985, Sb
Robert I. Papendick, (D), South Dakota State, 1962, Sp
Jeffery L. Smith, (D), Washington State, 1983, Sb

Peter Hooper GeoAnalytical Lab (B,M,D) (2021)
School of the Environment
1228 Webster Physical Sciences Building
Washington State University
Pullman, WA 99164-2812
p. (509) 335-1626
jawolff@wsu.edu
https://environment.wsu.edu/facilities/geoanalytical-lab/
Professor:
John A. Wolff, (D), London (UK), 1983, Gi
Research Associate:
Owen K. Neill, (D), Alaska (Fairbanks), 2012, Ca
Emeritus:
Franklin F. Foit, Jr., (D), Michigan, 1968, Gz
Laboratory Manager:
Scott Boroughs, (D), Washington State, 2010, GiCa
Research Technologist:
Charles Knaack, (M), Washington State, 1991, Ca

School of the Environment (B,M,D) ●✓ (2021)
Webster 1228
P.O. Box 642812
Pullman, WA 99164-2812
p. (509) 335-3009
soe@wsu.edu
http://environment.wsu.edu/
Programs: Bachelors of Science degree in Earth and Environmental Sciences:with a major in: Earth Science, Environmental & Ecosystem Sciences; Forest Ecology and Management; Wildlife Ecology and Conservation (Pre-Vet Option)
Enrollment (2009): B: 34 (11) M: 30 (9) D: 11 (5)
Director:
C. Kent Keller, (D), Waterloo, 1987, Hw
Professor:
Stephen Bollens, (D), Washington, 1990, Ob
Matt Carroll, (D), Washington, 1984, Zn
Peter B. Larson, (D), Caltech, 1983, Cs
Jeffrey D. Vervoort, (D), Cornell, 1994, CcaGt
John A. Wolff, (D), Imperial Coll (UK), 1983, Giv
Clinical Associate Professor:
Allyson Beall King, (D), Washington State
Associate Professor:
Sean P. Long , (D), Princeton, 2010, Gc
Clinical Assistant Professor :
Mike Berger , (D), Oregon, 2004
Assistant Professor:
Catherine Cooper, (D), Rice, 2005, Yg
Research Associate:
Scott Boroughs, (D), Washington State, 2010, Gv
Victor A. Valencia, (D), Arizona, 2005, ZgCcEg
Instructor:
Kurt Wilkie, (D)
Adjunct Professor:
Regan L. Patton, (D), Washington State, 1997, Gc
Stephen P. Reidel, (D), Washington State, 1978, GivGt
Dirk Schulze-Makuch, (D), Wisconsin (Milwaukee), 1996, Hw
Emeritus:
Keith Blatner , (D), 1983, Zn
Franklin F. Foit, Jr., (D), Michigan, 1968, Gza
Andrew Ford, (D), Dartmouth, 1975, Zu
Eldon H. Franz, (D), Illinois, 1971, Sf
David R. Gaylord, (D), Wyoming, 1983, Gs
George Hinman
Philip E. Rosenberg, (D), Penn State, 1960, GzCg
A. John Watkinson, (D), Imperial Coll (UK), 1972, Gc
Gary D. Webster, (D), California (Los Angeles), 1966, Pis

Wenatchee Valley College

Earth Sciences (A) (2015)
1300 Fifth Street
Wenatchee, WA 98801
p. (509) 682-6754
rdawes@wvc.edu
https://www.wvc.edu/directory/departments/geology/
Professor:
Ralph Dawes, (D), Washington, 1993, GgeAm
Adjunct Professor:
Kelsay Stanton, (M), W Washington, 2005, GgZe

Western Washington University

Geology Department (B,M) ○⊘ (2020)
516 High Street
Bellingham, WA 98225-9080
p. (360) 650-3582
geology@wwu.edu
https://geology.wwu.edu/
Programs: Geology; Geophysics
Administrative Assistant: Kate Blizzard
Enrollment (2018): B: 156 (57) M: 38 (10)
Chair:
Bernard A. Housen, (D), Michigan, 1994, Ym
Director Honors Program:
Scott R. Linneman, (D), Wyoming, 1990, GmZe
Professor:
Jackie Caplan-Auerbach, (D), Hawaii, Ys
Susan M. DeBari, (D), Stanford, 1991, GxZe
Robert J. Mitchell, (D), Michigan Tech, 1996, Hw
Elizabeth R. Schermer, (D), MIT, 1989, Gt
Associate Professor:
Colin B. Amos, (D), California (Santa Barbara), 2007, Gc
Douglas H. Clark, (D), Washington, 1995, Gl
Pete Stelling, (D), Alaska (Fairbanks), 2003, GxEgGv
Assistant Professor:
Robyn Dahl, (D), California (Riverside), 2015, PiZe
Brady Z. Foreman, (D), Wyoming, 2012, Grs
Sean R. Mulcahy, (D), California (Davis), 2009, GpzGp
Allison Pfeiffer, (D), California (Santa Cruz), 2017
Camilo Ponton, (D), MIT, 2012, CsoPc
Melissa S. Rice, (D), Cornell, 2012, XgGsm
Paleomagnetism Lab Manager:
Cristina Garcia Lasanta, (D), Zaragoza, 2016, YmGtc
Geochemistry Research Associate:
Nicole M. McGowan, (D), Macquarie, 2017, CtaCg
Research Associate:
Russell F. Burmester, (D), Princeton, 1974, Ym
Eric Grossman, (D), Hawaii, 2001, GusGm
George Mustoe, (M), W Washington, 1972, PbCaPo
Charles A. Ross, (D), Yale, 1964, Pm
Brian Rusk, (D), Oregon, 2003
Senior Instructor:
Paul Thomas, (M), W Washington, 1997, Gm

Emeritus:
R. Scott Babcock, (D), Washington, 1970, Cg
Edwin H. Brown, (D), California (Berkeley), 1966, Gp
Don J. Easterbrook, (D), Washington, 1962, GlmGe
David C. Engebretson, (D), Stanford, 1983, Gt
Thor A. Hansen, (D), Yale, 1978, Pg
James L. Talbot, (D), Adelaide, 1962, Gc

Whatcom Community College

Sciences Dept (2018)
237 W. Kellogg Road
Bellingham, WA 98226
tslagle@whatcom.edu
Assistant Professor:
Kaatje Kraft, (D), Arizona State, 2014, Gg
Adjunct Professor:
Bernie Dougan, (M), W Washington, 1990, Gg

Whitman College

Dept of Geology (B) ☒ (2019)
345 Boyer
Walla Walla, WA 99362
p. (509) 527-5225
baderne@whitman.edu
http://www.whitman.edu/geology
Programs: Geology
Administrative Assistant: Patti Moss
Enrollment (2018): B: 40 (19)
Chair:
Kevin R. Pogue, (D), Oregon State, 1993, Gc
Professor:
Patrick K. Spencer, (D), Washington, 1984, Pg
Associate Professor:
Nicholas E. Bader, (D), California (Santa Cruz), 2006, SoHgZi
Kirsten P. Nicolaysen, (D), MIT, 2001, GiCgGa
Assistant Professor:
Lyman P. Persico, (D), New Mexico, 2012, Gm
Emeritus:
Robert J. Carson, (D), Washington, 1970, GmeGl
Geology Technician:
Elliot Broze, (M), Tromsø, 2017, Gg

Yakima Valley College

Dept of Geology (A) (2015)
P. O. Box 22520
16th Ave. & Nob Hill Blvd.
Yakima, WA 98907
p. (509) 575-2350 x2366
dhuycke@yvcc.edu
http://www.yvcc.edu/FutureStudents/AcademicOptions/Programs/PhysicalSciences/Geology/Pages/
Instructor:
David Huycke, (M), Wyoming, 1979, Gg

West Virginia

Concord University

Dept of Physical & Environmental Sciences (B) ●✓ (2020)
1000 Vermillion St.
Athens, WV 24712-1000
p. (304) 384-5327
allenj@concord.edu
https://www.concord.edu/geosci
f: www.facebook.com/ConcordGeoscience/
t: @CUGeology
Programs: Environmental Geoscience
Enrollment (2020): B: 18 (2)
Chair:
Joseph L. Allen, (D), Kentucky, 1994, Gct
Professor:
Alice M. Hawthorne Allen, (D), Indiana, 1998, Xa
Associate Professor:
Stephen C. Kuehn, (D), Washington State, 2002, CaGv
Thomas Saladyga, (D), West Virginia, 2011, Zyi
Assistant Professor:
Aaron C. Paget, (D), Florida State, 2013, ApOpZr

Adjunct Professor:
Alyce Lee, (D), Texas A&M, 2009, Og

Fairmont State University

Natural Sciences (B) ✓ (2020)
1201 Locust Avenue
Fairmont, WV 26554
p. (304) 367-4393
dhemler@fairmontstate.edu
Programs: Earth & Space Science Education
Certificates: Surveying
Enrollment (2017): B: 3 (0)
Coordinator of Geoscience Program:
Deb Hemler, (D), West Virginia, 1997, Ze
Instructor:
Todd I. Ensign, (D), West Virginia, 2017, Ze
Josh Revels, (M), Fairmont State, 2012, Ze
Adjunct Professor:
Ronald McDowell, (D), Gge
Barnes Nugent, (M), Gg

Marshall University

Dept of Geology (B,M) ☒ (2018)
One John Marshall Drive
Huntington, WV 25755
p. (304) 696-6720/(304) 696-6756
geology@marshall.edu
http://marshall.edu/geology
Programs: B.S. Geology, B.A. Geology, M.S. Physical Science, Geology Concentration
Enrollment (2018): B: 26 (10)
Professor:
Ronald L. Martino, (D), Rutgers, 1981, GsrPe
Chair:
William L. Niemann, (D), Missouri (Rolla), 1999, Ng
Associate Professor:
Aley El Shazly, (D), Stanford, 1991, GpiCg
Assistant Professor:
Andrew J. Horst, (D), Syracuse, 2013, GcOgGt

West Virginia University

Dept of Geology & Geography (B,M,D) ●✓ (2019)
330 Brooks Hall
P.O. Box 6300
98 Beechurst Ave.
Morgantown, WV 26506-6300
p. (304) 293-5603
tim.carr@mail.wvu.edu
http://www.geo.wvu.edu
Programs: Geology, Geography, Environmental Sciences
Certificates: GIS
Enrollment (2011): B: 165 (21) M: 45 (10) D: 13 (1)
Chair:
Timothy R. Carr, (D), Wisconsin, 1981, GoYeGg
Professor:
Jaime Toro, (D), Stanford, 1998, GctGo
Dorothy Vesper, (D), Penn State, 2002, Hw
Timothy A. Warner, (D), Purdue, 1992, Zr
Associate Professor:
Kathleen Benison, (D), GrsCm
Dengliang Gao, (D), Duke, 1997, Ye
Shikha Sharma, (D), Lucknow Univ (India), 1998, Csa
Amy L. Weislogel, (D), Stanford, 2006, Gs
Teaching Assistant Professor:
Joe Lebold, (D), West Virginia, 2005, PeGrg
Assistant Professor:
Graham D. M. Andrews, (D), Leicester (UK), 2006, GvtGx
Adjunct Professor:
Katherine Lee Avary, (M), North Carolina, 1978, Go
Bascombe (Mitch) Blake, (D), West Virginia, 2009, GsEcPb
Alan Brown, (D), Louisiana State, 2002, EoYe
Katherine R. Bruner, (D), West Virginia, 1991, Gd
Phillip Dinterman
Jason A. Hubbart, (D), Idaho, 2007, HqgHs
Ronald McDowell, (D), Colorado Mines, 1987, GsPiCe
Paul F. Ziemkiewicz, , (D), Hg

Research Assistant Professor:
Payam Kavousi Ghahfarohki, (D), West Virginia, 2016, Gog
Emeritus:
Joseph J. Donovan, (D), Penn State, 1992, Hq
Thomas W. Kammer, (D), Indiana, 1982, Pi
J. Steven Kite, (D), Wisconsin, Gm
Henry W. Rauch, (D), Penn State, 1972, HwGe
John J. Renton, (D), West Virginia, 1965, Ec
Robert C. Shumaker, (D), Cornell, 1960, Go
Thomas H. Wilson, (D), West Virginia, 1980, YeGcYg

Wisconsin

Beloit College

R.D. Salisbury Dept of Geology (B) ☒ (2020)
700 College Street
Beloit, WI 53511
p. (608) 363-2132
swansons@beloit.edu
http://www.beloit.edu/geology/
f: https://www.facebook.com/groups/47867916990/
Programs: Geology
Environmental Geology
Enrollment (2015): B: 20 (11)
Chair:
Susan K. Swanson, (D), Wisconsin, 2001, HwGm
Associate Professor:
James R. Rougvie, (D), Texas, 1999, GxpGz
James J. Zambito, (D), Cincinnati, 2011, PcGsPg
Emeritus:
Carol Mankiewicz, (D), Wisconsin, 1987, Gs
Carl V. Mendelson, (D), California (Los Angeles), 1981, PmGs

Lawrence University

Department of Geosciences (B) ☒ (2019)
711 E Boldt Way
Appleton, WI 54911
p. (920) 832-6731
knudsena@lawrence.edu
http://www.lawrence.edu/dept/geology/
Administrative Assistant: Ellen c. Walsh
Enrollment (2018): B: 16 (5)
Professor:
Marcia Bjornerud, (D), Wisconsin, 1987, GctRc
Associate Professor:
Jeffrey J. Clark, (D), Johns Hopkins, 1997, Gm
Andrew Knudsen, (D), Idaho, 2002, CgGez
Assistant Professor:
Relena R. Ribbons, (D), Copenhagen, 2017, SbGe
Emeritus:
John C. Palmquist, (D), Iowa, 1961, GcpGg
Theodore W. Ross, (D), Washington State, 1969, Gg
Ronald W. Tank, (D), Indiana, 1962, Ge

Milwaukee Public Museum

Dept of Geology (2015)
800 W. Wells Street
Milwaukee, WI 53233
p. (414) 278-2741
sheehan@mpm.edu
http://www.mpm.edu/collect/geology/geosec-noframes.html
Chair:
Peter M. Sheehan, (D), California (Berkeley), 1971, Pi
Adjunct Professor:
Gary D. Rosenberg, (D), California (Los Angeles), 1972, RhPg

Northland College

Dept of Geosciences (B) ●☒ (2020)
1411 Ellis Avenue
Ashland, WI 54806
p. (715) 682-1852
tfitz@northland.edu
Programs: Geology and Water science
Enrollment (2020): B: 20 (15)
Professor:
Thomas J. Fitz, (D), Delaware, 1999, GgxGc
Assistant Professor:
Cynthia May, (M), Penn State, 2007, ZiyZn
David J. Ullman, (D), Wisconsin, 2013, GlPeGm

Saint Norbert College

Geology Dept (B) ☒ (2021)
100 Grant Street
De Pere, WI 54115
p. (920) 403-3987
tim.flood@snc.edu
http://www.snc.edu
Programs: Geology
Enrollment (2020): B: 12 (12)
Professor:
Tim P. Flood, (D), Michigan State, 1987, GvZe
Nelson R. Ham, (D), Wisconsin, 1994, Gl
Associate Professor:
Rebecca McKean , (D), Nebraska, 2009, GdPgRh

University of Wisconsin Colleges

Dept of Geography & Geology (A) (2016)
UW Sheboygan
1 University Dr
Sheboygan , WI 53081
p. (920) 459-6619
jim.mccluskey@uwc.edu
http://www.uwc.edu/depts/geography-geology
Chair:
Karl Byrand, (D), Maryland, 1999, Zny
Chair/CEO UW Marathon County:
Keith Montgomery, (D), Waterloo, 1986, ZyGg
Professor:
Norlene Emerson, (D), Wisconsin, 2002, GgPiGs
Diann Kiesel, (D), Wisconsin, 1998, GgZyGg
Robert McCallister, (D), Wisconsin, 1996, ZyGgZn
Dean/CEO UW Washington County:
Alan Paul Price, (D), California (Los Angeles), 1998, ZyGmZg
Associate Professor:
Iddrisu Adam, (D), Wilfrid Laurier, 2001, ZynZn
Assistant Professor:
Beth Johnson, (D), N Illinois, 2009, GlRh
James McCluskey, (D), Rutgers, 1987, ZinZn
Miclelle Palma, (D), Georgia, 2012, ZnnZn
Andrew Shears, (D), Kent State, 2011, Zin
Keith West, (D), Wisconsin (Milwaukee), 2007, ZynZn
Instructor:
Sanborn Robert, (M), 1991, GgZyn
Mengist Teklay Berhe
Lecturer:
Jane Fairchild, (M), Wisconsin, 2003, Am
Seth Rankin, (M), Wisconsin (Milwaukee), 1974, ZnnZn
Emeritus:
Thomas Bitner, (M), ZynZn
Richard Cleek, (M), ZnyZn
Garret Deckert, (M), ZynZn
Edwin Dommissee, (M), ZyGgZn
James Heidt, (M), Zn
Kenneth Korb, (D)
Gene E. Musolf, (D), Wisconsin, 1970, Zy
Shamim Naim, (D)
Randall Rohe, (D), Colorado, 1978, ZyGgZn
Leonard Weis, (D)
Barbara Williams, (D)

University of Wisconsin Oshkosh

Geography Department (B) 🖱 (2018)
800 Algoma Blvd
Oshkosh, WI 54901
p. (920) 424-4105
geography@uwosh.edu
https://geography.uwosh.edu/
f: https://www.facebook.com/UWOgeography/
Programs: Geography
Certificates: GIS
Enrollment (2018): B: 32 (14)
Chair:
Angela G. Subulwa, (D), Kansas, 2009, Zn

Associate Dean:
Colin Long, (D), Oregon, 2003, PeZyc
Professor:
Heike C. Alberts, (D), Minnesota, 2003, Zn
John A. Cross, (D), Illinois, 1979, ZyAst
Kazimierz J. Zaniewski, (D), Wisconsin (Milwaukee), 1987, Zn
Associate Professor:
Mamadou Coulibaly, (D), S Illinois, 2004, ZiyHg
Assistant Professor:
Elizabeth Barron, (D), Rutgers, 2010, Zn

University of Wisconsin, Eau Claire

Dept of Geology (B) ☒ (2018)
157 Phillips Hall
Eau Claire, WI 54702-4004
p. (715) 836-3732
steinklm@uwec.edu
http://www.uwec.edu/academic/geology
Administrative Assistant: Lorilie M. Steinke
Enrollment (2011): B: 88 (0)
Chair:
Kent M. Syverson, (D), Wisconsin, 1992, GlEnGe
Professor:
Scott K. Clark, (D), Illinois (Urbana), 2007, Ze
Karen G. Havholm, (D), Texas, 1991, GsZe
Robert L. Hooper, (D), Washington State, 1983, Gz
Phillip D. Ihinger, (D), Caltech, 1991, Gx
J. Brian Mahoney, (D), British Columbia, 1994, GstEg
Assistant Professor:
Robert Lodge, (D), EmCuGv
Sarah A. Vitale, (D), Connecticut, 2017, Hq
Senior Lecturer:
Lori D. Snyder, (M), British Columbia, 1994, Gx

University of Wisconsin, Extension

Dept of Environmental Sciences (2015)
3817 Mineral Point Road
Madison, WI 53705-5100
p. (608) 262-1705
elmo.rawling@uwex.edu
Professor:
John W. Attig, (D), Wisconsin, 1984, Gl
Thomas J. Evans, (D), Wisconsin, 1994, Gg
James M. Robertson, (D), Michigan, 1972, Eg
Associate Professor:
Madeline B. Gotkowitz, (M), New Mexico, 1993, Hw
David J. Hart, (D), Wisconsin, 2000, Hw
Assistant Professor:
Eric C. Carson, (D), Wisconsin, 2003, Gl
Patrick I. McLaughlin, (D), Cincinnati, 2006, Gr
Emeritus:
Lee Clayton, (D), Illinois, 1965, Gl

University of Wisconsin, Fox Valley

Dept of Geography and Geology (2015)
1478 Midway Rd
Menasha, WI 54952
p. (920) 832-2600
joanne.kluessendorf@uwc.edu
http://uwc.edu/depts/geography-geology/geography-geology

University of Wisconsin, Green Bay

Dept. of Natural & Applied Sciences - Geoscience Program (B,M) ☒ (2021)
LS-465
2420 Nicolet Drive
Green Bay, WI 54311
p. (920) 465-2371
luczajj@uwgb.edu
http://www.uwgb.edu/geoscience/
Programs: Geoscience; Earth Science Teaching; Accelerated Emphasis merged with Environmental Science & Policy Masters Program
Enrollment (2020): B: 17 (2) M: 3 (2)
Chair of Geoscience:
John A. Luczaj, (D), Johns Hopkins, 2000, HwGsCl

Professor:
Kevin J. Fermanich, (D), Wisconsin, 1995, SpRwHt
Associate Professor:
Steven J. Meyer, (D), Nebraska, 1990, AsmZg
Assistant Professor:
Kelly Deuerling, (D), Florida, 2016, HySoCq
Shawn Malone, (D), Iowa, 2012, GgpGz
Emeritus:
Steven I. Dutch, (D), Columbia, 1976, GcgGe
Ronald D. Stieglitz, (D), Illinois, 1972, GrlHy

University of Wisconsin, Madison

Center for Limnology (M,D) ☒ (2018)
Hasler Lab
680 N. Park Street
Madison, WI 53706
p. (608)262-3014
mjvanderzand@wisc.edu
https://limnology.wisc.edu/
f: https://www.facebook.com/centerforlimnology/
t: @WiscLimnology
Director:
Jake Vander Zanden, (D), McGill, 1999, On
Chair:
Kenneth Potter, (D), Johns Hopkins, Ng
Professor:
Calvin B. DeWitt, (D), Michigan, 1963, Ob
Linda K. Graham, (D), Michigan, 1975, Ob
John A. Hoopes, (D), MIT, 1965, No
John E. Kutzbach, (D), Wisconsin, 1966, Pe
Joy Zedler, (D), Wisconsin, 1968, Ob
Associate Professor:
Emily Stanley, (D), Arizona State, 1993, Ob
Assistant Professor:
Sarah Hotchkiss, (D), Minnesota, 1998, Ob
Carol Lee, (D), Washington, 1998, Ob
Zheng-yu Liu, (D), MIT, 1991, Op
Katherine McMahon, (D), California (Berkeley), 2002, Ng
Chin Wu, (D), MIT, Ng
Emeritus:
Michael S. Adams, (D), California (Riverside), 1968, Ob
Anders W. Andren, (D), Florida State, 1972, Oc
David E. Armstrong, (D), Wisconsin, 1966, Oc
Steve Carpenter, (D), Wisconsin, 1979, Ob
James F. Kitchell, (D), Colorado, 1970, Ob
William C. Sonzogni, (D), Wisconsin, 1974, Oc

Department of Geography (B,M,D) (2020)
550 N. Park St.
Room 160 Science Hall
Madison, WI 53706
p. (608) 262-2138
mason@geography.wisc.edu
http://www.geography.wisc.edu
f: https://www.facebook.com/UWMadisonGeography/
t: @UWMadisonGeog
Programs: GIS Development (PSM), Geography - MS (incl Physical Geography & Earth System Science focus), Cartography / GIS - MS, Geography - PhD (incl Physical Geography & Earth System Science focus; Cartography/GIS focus)
Certificates: GIS Fundamentals; Advanced GIS
Enrollment (2020): B: 112 (36) M: 16 (3) D: 46 (15)
Professor:
Erika Marin-Spiotta, Cb
Joseph Mason, GmSd
John W. Williams, (D), Brown, 1999, PeZyPl
Assistant Professor:
Christian Andresen, Zy
Ken Keefover-Ring, Zg

Department of Geoscience (B,M,D) ● ⦸ (2018)
1215 West Dayton St
Madison, WI 53706
p. (608) 262-8960
geodept@geology.wisc.edu
http://geoscience.wisc.edu/geoscience/
Programs: Geoscience
Enrollment (2009): B: 58 (17) M: 20 (6) D: 42 (4)

Chair:
D. Charles DeMets, (D), Northwestern, 1988, Ym
Professor:
Alan R. Carroll, (D), Stanford, 1991, Gs
Kurt Feigl, (D), MIT, 1991, Yd
Dante Fratta, (D), Georgia Tech, 1999, Ng
Laurel B. Goodwin, (D), California (Berkeley), 1988, Gc
Clark M. Johnson, (D), Stanford, 1986, CgcCs
D. Clay Kelly, (D), North Carolina, 1999, Pm
Stephen R. Meyers, (D), Northwestern, 2003, PcOoGs
Shanan Peters, (D), Chicago, 2003, Gs
Eric E. Roden, (D), Maryland, 1990, PgSbCl
Bradley S. Singer, (D), Wyoming, 1990, Cc
Clifford H. Thurber, (D), MIT, 1981, YsGv
Basil Tikoff, (D), Minnesota, 1994, Gc
Harold Tobin, (D), California (Santa Cruz), 1995, Yg
John W. Valley, (D), Michigan, 1980, CsGxz
Huifang Xu, (D), Johns Hopkins, 1993, Gz
Senior Scientist:
Brian L. Beard, (D), Wisconsin, 1992, Cc
John Fournelle, (D), Johns Hopkins, 1989, GiZn
Associate Professor:
Michael A. Cardiff, (D), Stanford, 2010, HwYg
Assistant Professor:
Annie Bauer, (D), MIT, 2017, Cca
Chloe Bonamici, (D), Wisconsin, 2013, GxCa
Ken Ferrier, (D), California (Berkeley), 2009, GmZo
Shaun Marcott, (D), Oregon State, 2011, GlPe
Lucas Zoet, (D), Penn State, 2012, GllGm
Emeritus:
Mary P. Anderson, (D), Stanford, 1973, Hw
Jean M. Bahr, (D), Stanford, 1987, Hw
Carl J. Bowser, (D), California (Los Angeles), 1965, Cl
Philip E. Brown, (D), Michigan, 1980, EmGzp
Charles W. Byers, (D), Yale, 1973, Grs
Nikolas I. Christensen, (D), Wisconsin, 1963, Yx
David L. Clark, (D), Iowa, 1957, Pm
Dana H. Geary, (D), Harvard, 1986, Pg
Louis J. Maher, Jr., (D), Minnesota, 1961, Pl
Levi Gordon Medaris, Jr., (D), California, 1966, GipSa
David M. Mickelson, (D), Ohio State, 1971, Glm
Herbert F. Wang, (D), MIT, 1971, YgHwYx
Museum Director:
Richard Slaughter, (D), Iowa, 2001, Pg
Geology Librarian:
Marie Dvorzak, (M), Zn
Related Staff:
David J. Hart, (D), Wisconsin, 2000, Hg
Thomas S. Hooyer, (D), Iowa State, 1999, Hg
David Krabbenhoft, (D), Wisconsin, 1988, ClGeHw
James M. Robertson, (D), Michigan, 1972, Eg
Cooperating Faculty:
Kenneth R. Bradbury, (D), Wisconsin, 1982, Hw

Dept of Atmospheric & Oceanic Sciences (B,M,D) (2016)
1225 W. Dayton Street
Atmospheric, Oceanic & Space Science Building
Madison, WI 53706-1695
p. (608)262-2828
aos@aos.wisc.edu
http://www.aos.wisc.edu
Enrollment (2011): B: 24 (14) M: 32 (9) D: 34 (5)
Chair:
Gregory J. Tripoli, (D), Colorado State, 1986, Am
Affiliate:
Tracey Holloway, (D), Princeton, 2001, AscZn
Professor:
Steven A. Ackerman, (D), Colorado State, 1987, Zr
Ankur R. Desai, (D), Penn State, 2006, Asm
Matthew H. Hitchman, (D), Washington, 1985, As
Zhengyu Liu, (D), MIT, 1991, Op
Jonathan E. Martin, (D), Washington, 1992, Am
Galen McKinley, (D), MIT, 2002, OcpOg
Michael C. Morgan, (D), MIT, 1994, Am
Grant W. Petty, (D), Washington, 1990, AsZrAm
John A. Young, (D), MIT, 1966, AstOp
Senior Scientist:
Edwin W. Eloranta, (D), Wisconsin, 1972, Yr
Affiliate :
Chris Kucharik, (D), Wisconsin, 1997, As
Associate Professor:
Daniel J. Vimont, (D), Washington, 2001, As
Affiliate:
Samuel Stechmann, (D), Courant Inst, 2008, ZnAs
Assistant Professor:
Larissa E. Back, (D), Washington, 2007, As
Tristan S. L'Ecuyer, (D), Colorado State, 2001, As
Adjunct Associate Professor:
Jeffrey R. Key, (D), Colorado, 1988, ZrAs
Adjunct :
Andrew Heidinger, (D), Colorado State, 1998, Zr
Adjunct Professor:
James Kossin, (D), Colorado State, 2000, As
Steven Platnick, (D), Arizona, Zr
Emeritus:
Linda M. Keller, (M), Wisconsin, 1971, As
Francis P. Bretherton, (D), Cambridge, 1961, Zg
Stefan L. Hastenrath, (D), Bonn, 1959, As
Donald R. Johnson, (D), Wisconsin, 1965, As
John E. Kutzbach, (D), Wisconsin, 1966, As
John M. Norman, (D), Wisconsin, 1971, So
Robert A. Ragotzkie, (D), Wisconsin, 1953, Ob
Pao-Kuan Wang, (D), California (Los Angeles), 1978, As
Research Specialist:
Dierk T. Polzin, (B), Wisconsin, As

Dept of Soil Science (B,M,D) (2015)
1525 Observatory Drive
Madison, WI 53706-1299
p. (608) 262-2633
slspeth@wisc.edu
http://www.soils.wisc.edu
Enrollment (2011): B: 34 (4) M: 16 (2) D: 8 (2)
Chair:
William L. Bland, (D), Wisconsin, 1984, Sp
Professor:
Phillip W. Barak, (D), Hebrew, 1988, ScGzRw
William F. Bleam, (D), Cornell, 1984, Sc
James G. Bockheim, (D), Washington, 1972, Sf
William J. Hickey, (D), California (Riverside), 1990, Sb
King-Jau S. Kung, (D), Cornell, 1984, Sp
Birl Lowery, (D), Oregon, 1980, Sp
Frederick W. Madison, (D), Wisconsin, 1972, Sd
J. Mark Powell, (D), Texas A&M, 1989, So
Stephen J. Ventura, (D), Wisconsin, 1989, ZrSo
Associate Professor:
Teri C. Balser, (D), California (Berkeley), 2000, Sb
Nick J. Balster, (D), Idaho, 1999, Sf
Carrie A.M Laboski, (D), Minnesota, 2001, So
Joel A. Pedersen, (D), California (Los Angeles), 2001, So
Assistant Professor:
Matthew D. Ruark, (D), Purdue, 2006, So
Douglas J. Soldat, (D), Cornell, 2007, So
Emeritus:
Larry G. Bundy, (D), Iowa, 1973, So
Robin F. Harris, (D), Wisconsin, 1972, Sb
Philip A. Helmke, (D), Wisconsin, 1971, Sc
Keith A. Kelling, (D), Wisconsin, 1974, So
Wayne R. Kusssow, (D), Wisconsin, 1966, So
Kevin McSweeney, (D), Illinois, 1984, SdaSf
John M. Norman, (D), Wisconsin, 1971, Spo
E. Jerry Tyler, (D), North Carolina, 1975, Sd

Geological Engineering (B,M,D) ●☒ (2021)
1415 Engineering Drive
2205 Engineering Hall
Madison, WI 53706-1691
p. (608) 890-2662
jmtinjum@wisc.edu
http://www.gle.wisc.edu
Programs: Geological Engineering
Enrollment (2018): B: 92 (0) M: 9 (0) D: 5 (0)
Chair:
William J. Likos, (D), Colorado Mines, 2000, NgSp
Professor:
Jean M. Bahr, (D), Stanford, 1987, Hw
Kurt L. Feigl, (D), Gt

Laurel Goodwin, California (Berkeley), 1988
Tracey Holloway, (D), Princeton, As
Steven P. Loheide, (D), Stanford, 2006, HwSp
Clifford Thurber, (D), MIT, 1981, Ysx
Basil Tikoff, (D), Minnesota, 1997, Gc
Chin Wu, (D), MIT, Onp

Associate Professor:
Mike Cardiff, Stanford, 2010, Hw
Dante Fratta, (D), Georgia Tech, 1999, Yx
James M. Tinjum, (D), Wisconsin, 2003, Ng

Assistant Professor:
Greeshma Gadikota, (D), Columbia, 2014, GzCqu
Matt Ginder-Vogel, (D), Stanford, 2006, Sc
Andrea Hicks, (D), Illinois (Chicago), Zn
Hiroki Sone, (D), Stanford, 2012, NrYxGt
Lucas Zoet, (D), Penn State, Gl

Emeritus:
Tuncer B. Edil, (D), Northwestern, 1973, Ng
Bezalel C. Haimson, (D), Minnesota, 1968, Nr
Herbert F. Wang, (D), MIT, 1971, YgHwYx

University of Wisconsin, Milwaukee

Dept of Geosciences (B,M,D) (2020)
P.O. Box 413
Milwaukee, WI 53201-0413
p. (414) 229-4561
geosci-office@uwm.edu
https://uwm.edu/geosciences/
f: https://www.facebook.com/UWMgeosci
Enrollment (2020): B: 91 (20) M: 25 (3) D: 5 (2)

Chair:
John L. Isbell, (D), Ohio State, 1990, Gs

Professor:
Dyanna M. Czeck, (D), Minnesota, 2001, Gc
Timothy J. Grundl, (D), Colorado Mines, 1988, HwCl
Mark T. Harris, (D), Johns Hopkins, 1988, GsrGd
Lindsay J. McHenry, (D), Rutgers, 2004, GzaXg
Keith A. Sverdrup, (D), Scripps, 1981, YsGt

Associate Professor:
Barry I. Cameron, (D), N Illinois, 1998, Gvi
Shangping Xu, (D), Princeton, 2005, Hg

Assistant Professor:
Julie Bowles, (D), California (San Diego), 2005, Ym
Charles Paradis, (D), Tennessee, 2017, Hw

Adjunct Professor:
Stephen Q. Dornbos, (D), S California, 2003, PeiPo
Daniel T. Feinstein, (M), Wisconsin, 1986, Hw
Margaret L. Fraiser, (D), S California, 2005, PiePg

Visiting Assistant Professor:
Victoria McCoy, (D), Yale, 2015, Pb

Emeritus:
Douglas S. Cherkauer, (D), Princeton, 1972, HwGe
William F. Kean, Jr., (D), Pittsburgh, 1972, Ym
Norman P. Lasca, (D), Michigan, 1965, GmlSd
Peter M. Sheehan, (D), California (Berkeley), 1971, Pie

University of Wisconsin, Oshkosh

Geology Dept (B) O☒ (2018)
645 Dempsey Trail
Oshkosh, WI 54901-8649
p. (920) 424-4460
mode@uwosh.edu
http://www.uwosh.edu/geology/
f: http://www.facebook.com/UWOgeology
Programs: Geology; Earth Science Secondary Education
Administrative Assistant: Courtney Maron
Enrollment (2018): B: 40 (15)

Chair:
William N. Mode, (D), Colorado, 1980, Gl

Professor:
Eric E. Hiatt, (D), Colorado, 1997, GsOcGu
Maureen A. Muldoon, (D), Wisconsin, 1999, Hw
Timothy S. Paulsen, (D), Illinois, 1997, Gc
Jennifer M. Wenner, (D), Boston, 2001, Gi

Assistant Professor:
Benjamin W. Hallett, (D), Rensselaer, 2012, Gpx
Joseph E. Peterson, (D), N Illinois, 2010, PgGr

Emeritus:
Norris W. Jones, (D), Virginia Tech, 1968, Gi
Gene L. La Berge, (D), Wisconsin, 1963, Eg
James W. McKee, (D), Louisiana State, 1967, Gr
Brian K. McKnight, (D), Oregon State, 1970, Gdu
Thomas J. Suszek, (M), Minnesota (Duluth), 1991, Gg

Instrumentation Specialist:
James A. Amato, (M), Wisconsin (Milwaukee), 2017, GgZi

University of Wisconsin, Parkside

Dept of Geosciences (B) (2021)
Box 2000
900 Wood Road
Kenosha, WI 53141
p. (262) 595-2744
li@uwp.edu
Programs: Earth Sciences; Environmental Geosciences
Enrollment (2020): B: 24 (8)

Chair:
Li Zhaohui, (D), SUNY (Buffalo), 1994, ClGzHw

Professor:
John D. Skalbeck, (D), Nevada (Reno), HwYgGg

Associate Professor:
Rachel Headley, (D), Washington, 2011, Gl

Research Associate:
Julie Kindelman, (D), Hs

Emeritus:
Gerald A. Fowler, PgGg
Allan F. Schneider, (D), Gl
James H. Shea, (D), Gs

University of Wisconsin, Platteville

Dept of Geography & Geology (B) (2015)
Platteville, WI 53818
p. (608) 342-1791
underwoodc@uwplatt.edu
http://www.uwplatt.edu/geography/

Professor:
Charles W. Collins, (D), Nova, 1985, Gm

Associate Professor:
Richard A. Waugh, (D), Wisconsin, 1995, Gc

Assistant Professor:
Mari A. Vice, (D), S Illinois, 1993, Gd

Emeritus:
William A. Broughton, (B), Wisconsin, 1938, Em
Kenneth A. Shubak, (M), Michigan, 1966, Pi

University of Wisconsin, River Falls

Dept of Plant & Earth Science (B) ☒ (2019)
410 S. Third Street
River Falls, WI 54022
p. (715) 425-3345
holly.dolliver@uwrf.edu
http://www.uwrf.edu/pes/geol/
Program Assistant: Sue Freiermuth
Enrollment (2016): B: 50 (0)

Chair:
Holly A.S. Dolliver, (D), Minnesota, 2007, GmSd

Professor:
Kerry L. Keen, (D), Minnesota, 1992, HwGse
Ian S. Williams, (D), California (Santa Barbara), 1981, Yg

Lecturer:
Kevin Thaisen, (D)

University of Wisconsin, Stevens Point

Dept of Geography and Geology (B,M) (2019)
2001 Fourth Avenue, SCI D332
Stevens Point, WI 54481
p. (715) 346-2629
David.Ozsvath@uwsp.edu
http://www.uwsp.edu/geo/
Programs: Geospatial Sciences (B)
Certificates: GIS
Enrollment (2017): B: 63 (27)

Professor:
Neil C. Heywood, (D), Colorado, 1988, Zy
Eric J. Larson, Oregon State, 2001, Zr

David L. Ozsvath, (D), SUNY (Binghamton), 1985, Hw
Keith W. Rice, (D), Kansas, 1989, Zir
Associate Professor:
Samantha W. Kaplan, (D), Wisconsin, 2003, GnPlGd
Ismaila Odogba, (D), Louisville, 2009, Zui

University of Wisconsin, Superior
Dept of Natural Sciences (B,M) (2015)
PO Box 2000
Belknap & Catlin
Superior, WI 54880
p. (715) 394-8322
natsci@uwsuper.edu
Professor:
William Bajjali, (D), Ottawa, 1994, HwCsg
Associate Professor:
Andy Breckenridge, (D), Minnesota, 2005, GlnGs
Assistant Professor:
Kristin E. Riker-Coleman, (D), Minnesota, 2008, Gg

University of Wisconsin, Whitewater
Geography, Geology, and Environmental Science (B) (2020)
800 W Main Street
Whitewater, WI 53190
p. (262) 472-1071
filipiap@uww.edu
http://www.uww.edu/cls/departments/geography-geology-env-sci
Programs: Geography, Geology, and Environmental Science majors; Geography, Geology, GIS, and Environmental Studies minor.
Certificates: GIS
Enrollment (2020): B: 150 (45)
Professor:
Prajukti Bhattacharyya, (D), Minnesota, 2000, Gce
Eric Compas, (D), Wisconsin, 2008, ZiRw
Rex Hanger, (D), California (Berkeley), 1992, PigGs
Peter Jacobs, (D), Wisconsin, 1994, SdaGm
Dale Splinter, (D), Oklahoma State, 2006, Hs
Associate Professor:
Rocio Duchesne, (D), Montclair State, 2015, Zri
John Frye, (D), Georgia, 2011, AtZr
Jeff Olson, (D), Ohio State, 2013, Ziu
Assistant Professor:
Stephen J. Levas, (D), Ohio State, 2015, CmGe

Wyoming

Casper College
Department of Earth and Environmental Sciences (A) (2019)
School of Science
125 College Drive
Casper, WY 82601
p. (307) 268-2017
mconnely@caspercollege.edu
http://www.caspercollege.edu/geology/
Programs: Geology (A); Environmental Science (A); GIS(A)
Certificates: GIS (A)
Enrollment (2019): A: 5 (3)
Klaenhammer Earth Science Chair:
Melissa Connely, (M), Utah State, 2000, GsPev
Instructor:
Jeff Sun, (M), Texas State, Zi
Kent A. Sundell, (D), California (Santa Barbara), 1985, GgvPv
Beth Wisely, (D), Oregon, 2005, YgHwGc

Central Wyoming College
Earth, Energy, Environment (A) (2015)
2660 Peck Avenue
Riverton, WY 82501
p. (307) 855-2000
jklanche@cwc.edu
http://www.cwc.edu/academics/programs/earthenviron
f: https://www.facebook.com/cwc.edu/
Enrollment (2015): A: 5 (0)
Professor:
Suzanne M. Smaglik, (M), Colorado Mines, 1987, GgZeCg
Assistant Professor:
Jacki Klancher, (M), Zi

Eastern Wyoming College
Eastern Wyoming College (A) (2015)
3200 West C. Street
Torrington, WY 82240
p. (307) 532-8330
bob.creagar@ewc.wy.edu
http://www.ewc.wy.edu/
Instructor:
Christopher Wenzel, (D), Wyoming, 2019, SbfHg

Northwest College
Northwest College (2015)
231 West 6th Street
Powell, WY 82435
p. 307.754.6405
Eric.Atkinson@nwc.edu
http://www.nwc.cc.wy.us/

University of Wyoming
Dept of Geology and Geophysics (B,M,D) ●⊘ (2019)
Dept. 3006
1000 E. University Ave.
Laramie, WY 82071
p. (307) 766-3386
carrick@uwyo.edu
http://www.uwyo.edu/geolgeophys/
Programs: BS in Geology, BA in Earth Science, BS in Environmental Geology and Geohydrology, MS in Geology, MS in Geophysics, PhD in Geology
Enrollment (2015): B: 157 (26) M: 28 (7) D: 31 (2)
Head:
Carrick M. Eggleston, (D), Stanford, 1991, ClqCb
Professor:
Kevin R. Chamberlain, (D), Washington (St Louis), 1990, CcGt
Mark T. Clementz, (D), California (Santa Cruz), 2002, Pg
Carol D. Frost, (D), Cambridge, 1984, CcGit
Neil F. Humphrey, (D), Washington, 1987, GlmYh
Barbara E. John, (D), California (Santa Barbara), 1987, Gci
Subhashis Mallick, (D), Hawaii, 1987, YseYg
James D. Myers, (D), Johns Hopkins, 1979, Gi
Bryan N. Shuman, (D), Brown, 2001, PeGne
Kenneth W.W Sims, (D), California (Berkeley), 1995, CgGvCa
Ye Zhang, (D), Indiana, 2005, HyGeYu
Senior Scientist:
Janet Dewey, (M), Auburn, 1993, CaGg
Susan M. Swapp, (D), Yale, 1982, Gp
Associate Professor:
Michael J. Cheadle, (D), Cambridge, 1989, Yg
Po Chen, (D), S California, 2005, YseYg
Ellen Currano, (D), Penn State, 2008, Pbe
Kenneth G. Dueker, (D), Oregon, 1994, Ys
Dario Grana, (D), Stanford, 2013, Ye
John P. Kaszuba, (D), Colorado Mines, 1997, CgGze
Brandon McElroy, (D), Texas, 2009, GsmGr
Clifford S. Riebe, (D), California (Berkeley), 2000, ClGme
Associate Scientist:
Laura Vietti, (D), Minnesota, 2014, Pv
Assistant Professor:
James Chapman, (D), Arizona, 2018, Gct
Kimberly Lau, (D), Stanford, 2017, Cb
Andrew D. Parsekian, (D), Rutgers, 2011, Yg
Simone Runyon, (D), Arizona, 2017, EdGip
Adjunct Professor:
Vladimir Alvarado, (D), Minnesota, 1996, Np
Eric A. Erslev, (D), Harvard, 1981, GctGg
Peter H. Hennings, (D), Texas, 1991, Gc
Ranie Lynds, (D), Wyoming, 2005, Gsr
Emeritus:
B. Ronald Frost, (D), Washington, 1973, GpiEd
Robert R. Howell, (D), Arizona, 1980, XgZr
Department Secretary:
Deborah Prusia

Western Wyoming Community College

Western Wyoming Community College (2015)
2500 College Drive
Rock Springs, WY 82901
p. (307) 382-1662
dpertermann@westernwyoming.edu
http://www.wwcc.wy.edu/academics/geology/

Algeria

Algerian Petroleum Institute

Algerian Petroleum Institute (B) (2015)
Avenue 1er Novembre
Boumerdes, Skikda, Oran 35000
p. +213 (0) 24 81 90 56
iap@iap.dz
http://www.iap.dz/

Centre Universitaire de Khemis Miliana

Institut de Sciences de la Nature et de la Terre (B) (2015)
Route de Theniet El-Had
Khemis Miliana, Khemis Miliana 44225
p. +213-27-66-42-32
kouben55@hotmail.fr
http://www.cukm.org/

Universite Abou Bekr Belkaid de Tlemcen

Faculté des sciences de la nature et de la vie et sciences de la terre et de l'univers (B) (2015)
BP 119
Tlemcen 13000
p. (+213) 040.91.59.09
webcri@mail.univ-tlemcen.dz
http://snv.univ-tlemcen.dz/

Universite Badji Mokhtar

Faculte des Sciences de la Terre: Amenagement du territoire, Geologie, Hydraulique, Mines (B) (2015)
BP 12
Annaba 23000
d.fst@univ-annaba.dz
http://www.univ-annaba.org/

Universite D'Oran

Faculté des Sciences de la Terre, de la Géographie et de l'Amenagement du Territoire (B) (2015)
Rue du Colonel Lofti
Es-Senia, El-Mnouar, Oran 31000
p. +213 (0) 41 58 19 47
contact@univ-oran.dz
http://www.univ-oran.dz/facultes/F_Terre

Universite de Annaba

Inst of Natural Sciences (2015)
BP 12
El Hadjar
Annaba
http://www.univ-annaba.org/

Universite de Batna

Dept de Sciences de la Terre (B) (2015)
1, Rue Chahid Boukhlouf Mohamed
El Hadi, Batna 5000
p. (+213) 033.86.06.02
recteur@univ-batna.dz
http://www.univ-batna.dz/

Universite de Jijel

Dept de Geologie (B,M,D) (2015)
Ouled Aissa, Jijel
p. +213 (34) 498016
webmaster@univ-jijel.dz
http://www.univ-jijel.dz/

Universite de Mentouri

Dept des Sciences de la Terre/Geologie (B) (2015)
Campus Ahmed Zouaghi
B.P. 325 Route d Ain El Bey
Constantine 25000
p. 213 031 90 38 52
univ-constantine@fr.fm
http://www.umc.edu.dz/fst/

Dept de l'Amenagement du territoire (B) (2015)
Campus Ahmed Zouaghi
B.P. 325 Route d Ain El Bey
Constantine 25000
p. (+213) 31.90.02.07
fstgat@umc.edu.dz
http://www.umc.edu.dz/vf/index.php/recherche-scientifique/annuaire-des-laboratoires/110-faculte-des-sciences-de-la-terre-/398-de

Universite des Sciences et de la Technologie

Inst of Earth Sciences (2015)
Houari Boumediene
B.P. 139 Dar El Beida
Eldjazair

Faculte de Sciences de la Tere, Geographie et Amenagement du Territoire (B) (2015)
USTHB-IST BP 32 El Alia
Bab-Ezzouar Alger 16123
p. (+213) 21247904
aouabadi@usthb.dz
http://www.usthb.dz/fst/

Universite Djillali Liabes Sidi Bel Abbes

Faculte des Sciences de la Nature et de la vie (B) (2015)
BP 89
Sidi Bel Abbes 22000
p. +213 (48) 543018
mbouziani@univ-sba.dz
http://www.univ-sba.dz/

Universite Kasdi Merbah Ouargla

Dept de Geologie (B) (2015)
Route de Ghardaia
Ouargla
p. +213 (29) 712468
info@ouargla-univ.dz
http://193.194.92.30/spip/dept/filiere-hydrocarbures-chimie.htm

Dept des Hydrocarbures (B) (2015)
Route de Ghardaia
Ouargia
p. +213 (29) 712468
info@ouargla-univ.dz
http://www.ouargla-univ.dz/

Universite M'hamed Bouguerra de Boumerdes

Faculte des Hydrocarbures et de la chimie (B) (2015)
Avenue de Ildependance
Boumerdes 35000
p. +213 (24) 816420
doyen_fhc@umbb.dz
http://www.umbb.dz/

Universite Saad Dahlab, Blida

Dept des Sciences de l'Eau et de l'Environnement (B) (2015)
BP 270
Blida 9000
p. +213 (25) 433625
contact@univ-blida.dz
http://www.univ-blida.dz/fac_ingenieur

Angola

Universidade Agostinho Neto

Faculdade de Geologia (B) (2015)
Av. 4 de Fevereiro
No. 7
2 andar
Luanda C. P. 815
p. +244-222-333-816
info@geologia-uan.com
http://www.geologia-uan.com/

Universidade Independente de Angola

Engenharia dos Recursos Naturais e Ambiente (B) (2016)
Rua da Missao
Bairro Morro Bento II - Corimba
Luanda
p. (+244) 222 33 89 70
unia@unia.ao
http://www.unia.ao/curso.php?cr=6
Vice-Rector:
Nuno Nascimento Gomes, (M), Lisbon, 1992, GesGu

Universite de Angola

Dept of Geology (2015)
Avenida 4 de Fevereiro 7
Caixa postal 815-C
Luanda

Argentina

Servicio Geologico Minero Argentino

Servicio Geologico Minero Argentino (2015)
Av. Julio Argentino Roca 651. P.B
Capital Federal
mjanit@mecon.gov.ar
http://www.segemar.gov.ar/

Universidad de Buenos Aires

Departamento de Ciencias Geológicas - FCEN (B,D) O☒ (2018)
Ciudad Universitaria-Pabellón 2
Intendente Güiraldes 2160
Ciudad Autónoma de Buenos Aires C1428EHA
p. (5411) 528-58249
geologia@gl.fcen.uba.ar
http://www.gl.fcen.uba.ar/
Programs: Geology, Paleontology

Universidad Nacional de Catamarca

Facultad de Tecnologia Y Ciencias Aplicadas (2015)
Maximio Victoria No. 55
San Fernando del Valle de Catamarca (470, Catamarca CP 4700
p. (54) 0383-4435 112 int. 112
daa@tecno.unca.edu.ar
http://tecno.unca.edu.ar

Universidad Nacional de Cordoba

Facultad de Ciencias Exactas, Fisicas Y Naturales (2015)
Apartado 35-2060 UCR
San Pedro de Montes de Oca
San Jose, Cordoba
p. +03514332098
geologia@ucr.ac.cr
http://www.geologia.ucr.ac.cr/

Universidad Nacional de Jujuy

Instituto de Geologia y Mineria (2015)
San Salvador de Jujuy , Jujuy
narce@idgym.unju.edu.ar
http://www.idgym.unju.edu.ar/

Universidad Nacional de la Pampa

Dept of Geologia (2015)
Uruguay 151, 6300 Santa Rosa
La Pampa
susanapaccapelo@exactas.unlpam.edu.ar
http://www.exactas.unlpam.edu.ar/

Universidad Nacional de la Patagonia San Juan Bosco

Facultad de Ciencias Naturales (2015)
Comodoro Rivadavia , Chubut
secacademica@unp.edu.ar
http://www.unp.edu.ar/

Universidad Nacional de La Plata

School of Astronomy and Geophysics (2015)
Paseo del Bosque s/n
B1900FWA
p. (0221)-423-6593
academic@fcaglp.unlp.edu.ar
http://www.fcaglp.unlp.edu.ar/

Universidad Nacional de Rio Cuarto

Dept. of Geology (B,M,D) O (2016)
ocampanella@gmail.com
mvillegas@exa.unrc.edu.ar
Rio Cuarto , Cordoba C.P. X5804BYA
p. (0358) 467-6198
webgeo@exa.unrc.edu.ar
http://geo.exa.unrc.edu.ar/
Enrollment (2016): B: 32 (0) M: 5 (0) D: 2 (0)
Associate Professor:
Monica B. Villegas, (M), UNRC, 1995, Gsc
Associate Scientist:
Juan Enrique Otamendi, (D), Nac de Río Cuarto, 2000, CgaCp
Adjunct Professor:
Hector Daniel Origlia, (M), Arizona State, 1999, NgZn

Universidad Nacional de Rio Negro

Dept. of Geology (2015)
Building Perito Moreno - Pacheco 460
General Roca , Rio Negro
sedevallemedio@unrn.edu.ar
http://www.unrn.edu.ar

Universidad Nacional de Salta

Facultad de Ciencias Naturales (2015)
Salta
p. (0387) 425-5413
decnat@unsa.edu.ar
http://naturales.unsa.edu.ar/

Universidad Nacional de San Juan

Facultad de Ciencias Exactas, Físicas y Naturales (2015)
Parque de Mayo
5400 San Juan
comunicacionfcefyn1@gmail.com
http://exactas.unsj.edu.ar/

Universidad Nacional de San Luis

Facultad de Ciencias Exactas, Fisico, Matematicas Y Naturales (2015)
Ejército de los Andes 950
San Luis D5700HHW
p. +54 (2652) 424027
sacadfmn@unsl.edu.ar
http://webfmn.unsl.edu.ar

Universidad Nacional de Tucuman

Facultad de Ciencias Naturales E Instituto Miguel Lillo (D) (2015)
Miguel Lillo 205
S.M. de Tucuman
San Miguel de Tucuman, Tucuman CP4000

p. 0381-4239456
info@csnat.unt.edu.ar
http://www.csnat.unt.edu.ar/

Universidad Nacional del Comahue

Dept of Geology and Petroleum (2015)
School of Engineering
Buenos Aires 1400
Neuquen 18300 , Patagonia
p. +54-299-4490300
sacadfi@uncoma.edu.ar
http://www.uncoma.edu.ar/

Universidad Nacional del Sur

Departamento de Geologia (2015)
San Juan 670
Primer Piso
Bahia Blanca
Buenos Aires 8000
p. 54-(0291)-4595147
secgeo@uns.edu.ar
http://www.uns.edu.ar/

Australia

Australian National University

Research School of Earth Sciences (M,D) ☒ (2020)
142 Mills Rd.
Canberra, ACT 0200
p. +61 2 6125 3406
Director.rses@anu.edu.au
http://rses.anu.edu.au/
Emeritus:
Patrick De Deckker, (D), Adelaide, 1981, GuPmGn

Dept of Earth & Marine Sciences (B,M,D) ☒ (2021)
47 Daley Road
Canberra, ACT 0200
p. 02 6125 2056
director.rses@anu.edu.au
http://rses.anu.edu.au/

Curtin University

Dept of Mining Engineering (B,M,D) (2015)
P. O. Box 597
Kalgoorlie, WA
e.topal@curtin.edu.au

School of Earth and Planetary Sciences (B,M,D) O✓ (2021)
GPO Box U1987
Perth, WA 6845
p. +618 92667968
eps-admin@curtin.edu.au
https://scieng.curtin.edu.au/schools/school-of-earth-and-planetary-sciences/
f: https://www.facebook.com/CurtinEPS
t: @CurtinGeology
Programs: Geology, Earth Sciences, Surveying, GIS, Petroleum Geoscience, Mineral Exploration and Mining Geology
Enrollment (2019): B: 467 (106) M: 128 (47) D: 99 (15)
Head:
Ian Fitzsimons, (D), GptCc
Professor:
David Antoine, (D), ObZrc
Joseph Awange, (D), ZfGqZr
Gretchen Benedix, (D), XgmXc
Phil Bland, (D), XcgXm
Chris Clark, (D), GpCcGt
Chris Elders, (D), GcoGt
Christine Erbe, (D), ObpOg
Katy Evans, (D), GpEmCp
Noreen Evans, (D), CacCl
Will Featherstone, (D), YdvXy
Kliti Grice, (D), CosPc
Fred Jourdan, (D), CcGiXm
Pete Kinny, (D), Cca
Chris Kirkland, (D), Cca
Zheng-Xiang Li, (D), YmGtg
Rob McCauley, (D), ObYr
Alexander Nemchin, (D), CcXc
Steve Reddy, (D), ZaGzCc
Simon Wilde, (D), CcGit
Associate Professor:
Marco Coolen, (D), PoCbPe
Ahmed El-Mowafy, (D), YdZrf
Alexander Gavrilov, (D), YrOb
Tim Johnson, (D), Gpt
Jon Kirby, (D), Ydv
Michael Kuhn, (D), YdvOp
Katarina Miljkovic, (D), Xyg
Nick Timms, (D), GzcXg
Jianhong (Cecilia) Xia, (D), Zi
Senior Lecturer:
Mehrooz Aspandiar, (D), CeZaSa
Milo Barham, (D), Gsg
Dave Belton, (D), Zfr
Alison Blyth, (D), PeCsZc
Sten Claessens, (D), Yd
Ashraf Dewan, (D), RnZof
Petra Helmholz, (D), Zfr
Ivana Ivanova, (D), Zif
Todd Robinson, (D), ZfrZi
Tony Snow, (B), Zn
Dom Wolff-Boenisch, (D), CqGe
Lecturer:
Mick Filmer, (D), YdZrOp
Senior Research Fellow:
Aaron Cavosie, (D), GzCuXm
Alec Duncan, (D), Yr
Paul Johnston, (D), Yd
Iain Parnum, (D), YrOup
Sergei Pisarevskiy, (D), Ym
Vladimir Puzyrev, (D), Ye
Research Fellow:
Luc Doucet, (D), GiCus
Lucy Forman, (D), Xgm
Denis Fougerouse, (D), ZaCcEm
Hugo Olierook, (D), CceEm
Kadija Oubelkheir, (D), Zr
Amy Parker, (D), YdZrRn
Ellie Sansom, (D), Xm
Leonid Shumlyanskyy, (D), CcGiEm
Martin Towner, (D), Xgm
Kan Wang, (D), Yd
Daniel Wilkes, (D), Yr
Research Associate:
Hadrien Devillepoix, (D), Xa
Jack Gillespie, (D), CcGt
Michael Hartnady, (M), Cc
Robert Howie, (D), Xm
Anthony Lagain, (D), Xg
Yebo Liu, (B), Ym
Richard Palmer, (D), Zr
Charlotte Robinson, (D), Ob
Sergio Rojas Hernandez, (D), NrpYe
Alan Scarlett, (D), CbaEo
Lewis Trotter, (M), Zi
Alex Walker, (D), EmGt
Chong Wei, (D), Ob
Adjunct Senior Research Fellow:
Paul Greenwood, (D), CaoCe
Chris Spencer, (D), CcGt
Chris Swain, (D), Yg
Adjunct Senior Lecturer:
Allison Dugdale, (D), EmCe
Adjunct Research Fellow:
Jane Cuneen, (D), GstGc
Lynne Milne, (D), Plb
Matthew Slivkoff, (D), Zr
Adjunct Professor:
Bill Collins, (D), GiCgGt
Bob Pidgeon, (D), Cc
Andrew Putnis, (D), Gz
Greg Smith, (D), GoCoGq
Peter Teunissen, (D), YdZrf

Emeritus Professor:
Merv Lynch, (D), Zr
John Penrose, (D), YrZrOg
Geoff West, (D), Zf
Technical Officer:
Alex Holman, (D), CasCe
Software Developer:
Martin Cupak, (M), Zn
Senior Research Technician:
Malcolm Perry, Og
Senior Research Officer:
Josh Beardmore, (D), Ym
Project Coordinator:
Ben Hartig, (B), Zn
Laboratory Technician:
Peter Hopper, (B), CaEoRw

Dept of Exploration Geophysics (B,M,D) (2017)
GPO Box U1987
Perth, WA 6845
p. +61 8 9266-3565
Geophysics-GeneralEnquiries@curtin.edu.au
http://www.geophysics.curtin.edu.au/
f: https://www.facebook.com/ExplorationGeophysicsCurtinUniversity
t: @CurtinGeophys
Enrollment (2014): B: 27 (13) M: 26 (4) D: 28 (6)
Professor:
Boris Gurevich, (D), Moscow (Russia), 1988, Ye
Anton W. Kepic, (D), British Columbia, 1990, YexYg
Maxim Lebedev, (D), Moscow State (Russia), 1990, YxNr
Senior Lecturer:
Vassily Mikhaltsevitch, (D), Kaliningrad State, 1997, Ye
Andrew Peter Squelch, (D), Nottingham (UK), 1998, NmYeZe
Research Fellow:
Michael Carson, (D), Univ Coll (Dublin), 2000, Yx
Aleksandar Dzunic, (M), Belgrade, 1989, YgsYe
Senior Scientist:
Stephanie Vialle, (D), Paris 7, 2008, YxCqNp
Head of Department:
Andrej Bona, (D), Calgary, 2002, Yx
Associate Professor:
Brett D. Harris, (D), Curtin, 2002, HwYve
Roman Pevzner, (D), Moscow State (Russia), 2004, YxxYz
Milovan Urosevic, (D), Curtin, 1998, YerYx
Lecturer:
Robert Galvin, (D), Curtin, 2006, Ye
Stanislav Glubokovskikh, (D), Lomosov (Moscow), 2012, Yxe
Mahyar Madadi, (D), Inst Adv Studies Basic Sci (Zanjan), 1997, Ye
Andrew Pethick, (D), Curtin, 2013, YevYg
Konstantin Tertyshnikov, (D), Curtin, 2014, Ye
Sasha Ziramov, (M), Belgrade, 2005, Ye
Senior Technical Officer:
Dominic J. Howman, (B), Curtin, 1994, Ye

Federation University Australia

Dept of Geology (B,M,D) ●☒ (2019)
Federation University
P. O. Box 663
Ballarat, VIC 3353
p. 613 53279354
k.dowling@federation.edu.au
Programs: Bachelor of Geosciences

Flinders University

School of the Environment (B,M,D) ● (2017)
GPO Box 2100
Adelaide, SA 5001
p. +61 8 8201 7577
jeanne.young@flinders.edu.au
http://www.flinders.edu.au/science_engineering/environment/
Enrollment (2012): B: 44 (14) M: 15 (5) D: 37 (4)
Professor of Hydrogeology:
Okke Batelaan, (D), Free (Brussels), Hw
Research Fellow:
Peter Cook, (D), Flinders, Hw
ARC Future Fellow:
Adrian Werner, (D), Queensland, Hw
Academic Status:
Nancy Cromar, (D), Napier (UK), Zn
Professor:
Howard Fallowfield, (D), Dundee (UK), Zn
Iain Hay, (D), Washington, 1989, Zyy
Patrick Hesp, (D), Sydney, GmZy
Andrew Millington, (D), Sussex (UK), ZuyZr
Craig Simmons, (D), Adelaide, Hw
Director ARA:
Jorg Hacker, (D), Bonn, ZrAs
Academic Status:
John Edwards, (D), Adelaide, Zn
Andew Love, (D), Hw
Associate Professor:
Erick Bestland, (D), Oregon, GsSa
Beverley Clarke, (D), Adelaide, Zyn
Huade Guan, (D), New Mexico Tech, 2005, HgsHg
Udoy Saikia, (D), Flinders, Zn
DECRA Research Fellow:
Margaret Shanafield, (D), Nevada, Hw
Sessional Lecturer:
Harpinder Sandhu, (D), Lincoln (NZ), Zn
Maria Zotti, Zn
Senior Lecturer:
David Bass, (D), New England, Zy
Kirstin Ross, (D), S Australia, Zn
Adjunct Senior Lecturer:
Simon Benger, (D), Australian Nat, Ziy
John Hutson, (D), Natal, Spc
Vincent Post, (D), Amsterdam, Hw
Adjunct Lecturer:
Stephen Fildes, (M), Adelaide, Zri
Ben van den Akker, (D), Flinders, Zn
Lecturer:
Dylan Irvine, (D), Flinders, Hw
Mark Lethbridge, (D), S Australia, Ziy
Graziela Miot da Silva, (D), Fed Rio Grande do Sul (Brazil), Gug
Michael Taylor, (D), Flinders, Zn
Ilka Wallis, (D), Flinders, HqCg
Harriet Whiley, (D), Flinders, Zn
Academic Status:
Gour Dasvarma, (D), Australian Nat, Zn
Adjunct Professor:
Jim Smith, Zn
Research Fellow:
Eddie Banks, (D), Flinders, Hw
Adjunct Academic Status:
Samantha de Ritter, (M), Flinders, Ze
Academic Status:
Glenn Harrington, (D), Flinders, Hw
Andrew McGrath, (D), ZrAs

Geoscience Australia

Geoscience Australia ☒ (2017)
GPO Box 378
Canberra, ACT 2601
p. +61 2 6249 9111
ref.library@ga.gov.au
http://www.ga.gov.au/
t: @GeoAusLibrary

Government of South Australia - Department for Energy and Mining

Geological Survey of South Australia ☒ (2021)
GPO Box 320
Adelaide, SA 5001
p. +61 8 8463 3000
DEM.customerservices@sa.gov.au
http://www.energymining.sa.gov.au
t: @DEM_sagov

James Cook University

Geosciences (B,M,D) O☒ (2018)
Building 034
College of Science & Engineering
James Cook University
Townsville, QLD 4811

p. 07 4781 6947
eric.roberts@jcu.edu.au
https://www.jcu.edu.au/college-of-science-and-engineering
Enrollment (2016): B: 85 (54) M: 6 (2) D: 25 (7)

Associate Professor:
Eric M. Roberts, (D), Utah, 2005, GsPvCc

Professor:
Michael I. Bird, (D), Australian Nat, 1988, ClsSa

Senior Scientist:
Karen E. Joyce, (D), Quebec, 2005

Associate Professor:
Zhaoshan Chang, (D), Washington State, 2003, EmCce
Carl Spandler, (D), 2005, GxEmCg

Postdoctoral Research Fellow:
Arianne Ford, (D), James Cook, 2008, GqZiEg

Lecturer:
James J. Daniell, (D), Sydney, 2010, GumYr
Jan Marten Huizenga, (D), Vrije (Amsterdam), 1995, GpCgGc
Christa Placzek, (D), Arizona, 2006, CclGe
Ioan Sanislav, (D), James Cook, 2009, GctGp
Peter W. Whitehead, (B), La Trobe, 1986, Ggv

Adjunct Professor:
Robert Henderson, (D), Victoria (NZ), 1967, GtPiGg

Postdoctoral Research Fellow & Lecturer:
Hannah L. Hilbert-Wolf, (D), James Cook, 2016, GsCc

Economic Geology Research Centre (A,B,M,D) ○⊘ (2021)
EGRU
James Cook University
Townsville, QLD 4811
p. +61 7 4781 4726
egru@jcu.edu.au
http://www.jcu.edu.au/economic-geology-research-centre-egru
Programs: Bachelor of Science, Bachelor of Advanced Science, Bachelor of Geology, Bachelor of Science Honours, Bachelor Geology Honours, Diploma of Science, Master of Science, Master of Science (Professional), Doctorate (PhD)
Certificates: Professional Development Training relevant to the minerals industry

La Trobe University

Environmental Geoscience (B,M,D) ⊠ (2018)
Environmental Geoscience
La Trobe University
Victoria 3086
Melbourne, VIC 3086
p. +61 3 9479 1273
john.webb@latrobe.edu.au
http://www.latrobe.edu.au/environmental-geoscience
Programs: Environmental Geoscience
Enrollment (2018): B: 39 (5) D: 6 (1)

Associate Professor:
John A. Webb, (D), Queensland, 1982, GeHwGa

Lecturer:
David Steart, (D), Victoria, 2003, GgPb
Susan Q. White, (D), La Trobe, 2005, GmgGe

Other:
Vincent J. Morand, (D), Sydney, 1987, GgcGt

Macquarie University

Dept of Earth and Planetary Sciences (B,M,D) ○⊠ (2018)
North Ryde
Sydney, NSW 2109
p. 61-2-98508426
eps-admin@mq.edu.au
http://www.eps.mq.edu.au/
f: https://www.facebook.com/MQeps

Department of Environmental Sciences (B,M,D) (2016)
North Ryde, NSW 2109
neil.saintilan@mq.edu.au
http://www.mqu.edu.au/

Monash University

School of Earth, Atmosphere and Environment (B,M,D) ⊠ (2018)
PO Box 28E
Clayton, VIC 3800
p. +61 3 99054884
earth-atmosphere-environment@monash.edu
http://www.earth.monash.edu.au/

Professor:
Peter A. Cawood, (D), Sydney, 1980, GtcGg

New South Wales Resources & Energy

New South Wales Resources & Energy (2017)
NSW Resource & Energy, PO Box 344
Hunter Regional Mail Centre, NSW 2310
p. 1300 736 122
geologicalsurvey.info@trade.nsw.gov.au
http://www.resourcesandenergy.nsw.gov.au/

Queensland University of Technology

School of Earth & Atmospheric Sciences (B,M,D) ●⊘ (2021)
GPO Box 2434
2 George Street
Brisbane, QLD 4001
p. 61 7 3138 2324
sef.easenquiry@qut.edu.au
https://www.qut.edu.au/study/science
f: https://www.facebook.com/QUTEarthScienceUndergraduatePage/
Programs: Bachelor of Science (3 yrs) with majors in Earth Science, Environmental Science; Geology Extension Minor
Climate Science Minor (from 2022)
Enrollment (2020): B: 32 (16) M: 1 (0) D: 12 (2)

Professor:
Zoran Ristovski, (D), Belgrade, 1996, Asp

Distinguished Professor:
Lidia Morawska, (D), Jagiellonian, 1982, Asc
Lidia Morawska, (D), Jagiellonian, 1982, Asc

Professor:
David A. Gust, (D), Australian Nat, 1982, GiCpGt
Balz Kamber, (D), Bern, 1995, GpCgGz

Senior Research Fellow :
Charlotte M. Allen, (D), Virginia Tech, CcaGi

Research Fellow:
Henrietta Cathey, (D), Utah, 2006, Giv

Senior Scientist:
Andrew Fletcher, (D), Queensland, 2003, Zri

Associate Professor:
Scott E. Bryan, (D), Monash, 1999, GitGs

Senior Lecturer:
Craig Sloss, (D), Wollongong (Australia), 2005, GsrGm
Jessica Trofimovs, (D), Monash, 2003, GsvGu

Research Associate:
David Flannery, (D), New South Wales, 2012, PoCaXg

Senior Lecturer:
Graham Johnson, (D), Queensland Tech, 2005, Asp
Branka Miljevic, (D), Queensland Tech, 2010, Acs

Lecturer:
Oliver M. Gaede, (D), W Australia, YeNrYs
Patrick C. Hayman, (D), Monash, 2009, EgGvi
David T. Murphy, (D), Queensland, 2002, CgEgCc
Luke Nothdurft, (D), Queensland Tech, 2009, GdCmGg
Christoph Schrank, (D), Toronto, 2009, GcqGt

Emeritus:
John Rigby, Pb

Analytical Laboratory Coordinator :
Wan-Ping (Sunny) Hu, (D), Canterbury (NZ), Ca

Technician - Geology:
Alex Hepple, (M), Queensland Tech, 2014, ZerGg

Senior Technician - Geology :
Will Stearman, (B), Queensland Tech, 2011, Geg

Southern Cross University

School of Environment, Science & Engineering (A,B,M,D) ○ (2020)
P. O. Box 157
Lismore, NSW 2480
p. +61 2 6620 3766
ese@scu.edu.au
http://scu.edu.au/environment-science-engineering/
f: https://www.facebook.com/scu.sese

Programs: BSc. with four specializations in Earth & Environmental Systems, Marine Systems, Forestry Systems and Regenerative Agriculture
Certificates: Diploma of Science

Chair of Engineering:
Peter J. Coombes, (D), Newcastle, 2002, Hgs

Biogeochemistry:
Bradley Eyre, (D), Queensland Tech, CoGeCs

Professor:
Nicholas J. Ashbolt, (D), Tasmaina, 1985, PoCb
Edward Burton, (D), Southern Cross, 2013, CaHy
Peter Harrison, (D), James Cook, Cm
Renaud Joannes-Boyau, (D), France, CcaCs
Scott Johnston, (D), CaGe
Damien Maher, (D), Sourthern Cross, 2001, GeCs
Amanda Reichelt-Brushett, (D), Southern Cross, Hs

Adjunct:
Graham Jones, (D), James Cook, Ca

Lecturer:
Sumith Pathirana, (D), Kent State, Zr

Emeritus:
Bill Boyd, (D), Glasgow, 1982, Pe

University of Adelaide

School of Earth and Environmental Sciences (2015)
Adelaide, SA 5000
p. +61 8 8303 3999
graham.heinson@adelaide.edu.au
http://www.ees.adelaide.edu.au/

Australian School of Petroleum and Energy Resources (B,M,D) O☒ (2021)
Santos Petroleum Engineering Building
North Terrace
Adelaide, SA 5005
p. 61-8-8313-8000
admin@asp.adelaide.edu.au
https://ecms.adelaide.edu.au/petroleum-engineering/
Programs: Petroleum Geoscience, Petroleum Engineering - Bachelors, Masters and Doctorate
Certificates: Graduate Certificate in Petroleum Geoscience. Graduate Certificate and Graduate Diploma in Petroleum Engineering

Dr:
Kathryn Amos, (D), E Anglia (UK), Gs

Professor:
Pavel Bedrikovetski, (D), Gubkin Russian State Oil and Gas (Moscow), Np

Associate Professor:
Manouchehr Haghighi, (D), S California, Np
Simon Holford, (D), Birmingham, Go

Research Associate:
Alex Badalyan, (D), Grozny State Oil Tech, Np
Sara Borazjani, (D), Adelaide, Np
Themis Carageorgos, (D), Imperial (London), Np
Ulrike Schacht, (D), Kiel, Gd
Carmine Wainman, (D), Adelaide, Grs

Senior Lecturer:
Khalid Amrouch, (D), Pierre & Marie Curie, Gc
Abbas Zeinijahromi, (D), Adelaide, Np

Lecturer:
Mark Bunch, (D), Birmingham, Ye
Maria Gonzalez-Perdomo, (B), Zulia, Np
Alireza Salmachi, (D), Adelaide, Np
Mohammad Sayyafzadeh, (D), Adelaide, Np

Professor - Decision Making:
Stephen Begg, (D), Reading, Eo

Professor:
John Kaldi, (D), Cambridge, Go

Professor :
Peter McCabe, (D), Keele, Go

University of Canberra

Institute for Applied Ecology (2015)
Duanne.White@canberra.edu.au
https://www.canberra.edu.au/research/institutes/iae

Faculty of Science and Technology ☒ (2019)
P. O. Box 1
Belconnen, ACT
George.Cho@canberra.edu.au
http://scides.canberra.edu.au/rehs/

University of Melbourne

School of Earth Sciences (B,M,D) (2016)
Melbourne, VIC 3010
p. +61 3 8344 9866
head@earthsci.unimelb.edu.au
http://www.earthsci.unimelb.edu.au

University of New England

Earth Sciences (A,B,M,D) O (2015)
Armidale, NSW 2351
p. +61-2-67732101
geology@une.edu.au
http://www.une.edu.au/about-une/academic-schools/school-of-environmental-and-rural-science/research/life-earth-and-environment/e

Associate Professor:
John R. Paterson, (D), Macquarie, 2005, PigPs

Lecturer:
Phil R. Bell, (D), Alberta, 2011, PgvPg
Luke Milan, (D), GtcGp
Nancy Vickery, (D), New England, GgeYg

Adjunct Professor:
Ian Metcalfe, (D), Leeds (UK), 1976, PmGtg

Emeritus:
Paul Ashley, (D), Macquarie, EgGeEm
Peter Flood, (D), EcGt

University of New South Wales

School of Biological, Earth & Environmental Sciences (B,M,D) ☒ (2021)
UNSW
Sydney, NSW 2052
p. 61 2 93852961
bees@unsw.edu.au
http://www.bees.unsw.edu.au
Enrollment (2013): B: 80 (24) M: 5 (0) D: 14 (4)

Associate Professor:
David R. Cohen, (D), New South Wales, 1990, Cet

Professor:
Michael Archer, (D), Pv
Andy Baker, (D), HwCs
James Goff, (D), Gsm
Suzanne J. Hand, (D), Pv
Martin van Kranendonk, (D), Queens (Canada), GxPeGd

Associate Professor:
Bryce Kelly, (D), New South Wales, 1995, HwAcGe
Shawn Laffan, (D), Ziy

Dr:
Ian Graham, (D), UTS Sydney, 1995, GxEg

Lecturer:
Catherine Chague-Goff, (D), CgGs

Adjunct Professor:
Derecke Palmer, (D), New South Wales, 2001, Ye

Dr:
Paul G. Lennox, (D), Monash, 1985, GcgZe

Visiting Professor:
Colin R. Ward, (D), New South Wales, 1971, EcGd

University of Newcastle

Discipline of Earth Sciences (B,M,D) O (2015)
School of Environmental & Life Sciences
University Drive
Callaghan, NSW 2308
p. +61 2 4921 8976
name.surname@newcastle.edu.au
http://www.newcastle.edu.au/school/environ-life-science
Enrollment (2014): B: 132 (121) D: 5 (3)

Associate Professor:
Silvia Frisia, (D), Milan (Italy), 1991, ClPeGd
Phil Geary, (D), UWS, HwSoHw
Gregory Hancock, (D), ZiGmm

Lecturer:
Judy Bailey, (D), Newcastle, 1993, Ec
David Boutelier, (D), Gtc
Alistair Hack, (D), GcCgEm
Anthony Kiem, (D), HqAsZi
Bill Landenberger, (D), Newcastle, 1997, GiCg
Danielle Verdon-Kidd, (D), HqAsZi

University of Queensland
School of Earth Sciences (B,M,D) O (2015)
Faculty of Science
Steele Building
Brisbane, QLD 4072
p. +61 7 3365 1180
sees.hos@uq.edu.au
https://sees.uq.edu.au/
Enrollment (2015): B: 106 (57) M: 38 (5) D: 60 (6)

University of South Australia
School of Natural and Built Environments (B) O (2016)
GPO Box 2471
Adelaide, SA 5001
Amie.Albrecht@unisa.edu.au
http://www.unisa.edu.au/it-engineering-and-the-environment/natural-and-built-environments/
Research Fellow:
Juliette Woods, (D), Adelaide, Hwq

University of Sydney
School of Geosciences (A,B,M,D) ⦸ (2021)
Room 348
Madsen Building F09
Sydney, NSW 2006
geosciences.enquiries@sydney.edu.au
https://sydney.edu.au/science/schools/school-of-geosciences.html
f: https://www.facebook.com/sydneyunigeo/
t: @sydneyunigeo
Professor:
Jonathan Aitchison, (D), UNE, 1989, GrtPm
Professor:
Geoffrey L. Clarke, (D), Melbourne (Australia), 1987, Gp
Dietmar Muller, (D), Scripps, 1989, Yrg

University of Tasmania
ARC Center of Excellence in Ore Deposits (M,D) O (2017)
Private Bag 79
Hobart, TAS 7001
steve.calladine@utas.edu.au
http://www.utas.edu.au/codes

School of Earth Sciences (B,M,D) (2015)
Private Bag 79
Hobart, TAS 7001
p. 61 3 6226 2476
Rose.Pongratz@utas.edu.au
http://www.utas.edu.au/earth-sciences/home
Director:
J Bruce Gemmell, (D), Dartmouth, 1987, Eg
Ross R. Large, (D), New England, Eg
Professor:
David R. Cooke, (D), Monash, Eg
Anthony J. Crawford, (D), Melbourne (Australia), 1983, Git
Jocelyn McPhie, (D), New England, Gv
Associate Professor:
Ron F. Berry, (D), Flinders, Gc
Lecturer:
Garry J. Davidson, (D), Tasmania, Cs
Peter J. McGoldrick, (D), Melbourne (Australia), Ce
Anya Reading, (D), Ysg
Michael Roach, (N), Tasmania, Yg

University of Western Australia
School of Earth & Environment (B,M,D) (2015)
M004
35 Stirling Highway
Crawley, WA 6009
p. 6488 1921
enquiry-see@uwa.edu.au
http://www.see.uwa.edu.au/

University of Wollongong
School of Earth & Environmental Sciences (B,M,D) (2018)
Northfields Avenue
Wollongong, NSW 2522
p. 61 2 4221 4419
anutman@uow.edu.au
http://www.uow.edu.au/science/eesc/

Austria

Geological Survey of Austria
Geologische Bundesanstalt von Osterreich ☒ (2020)
Neulinggasse 38, A 1030
Vienna
p. 43-1-712 56 74
office@geologie.ac.at
https://www.geologie.ac.at/

Karl-Franzens-Universitaet Graz
Inst for Earth Science (A,B,M,D) O (2017)
Heinrichstraße 26
Graz 8010
p. +43 316 380-5587
erdwissenschaften@uni-graz.at
http://erdwissenschaften.uni-graz.at/index_en.php
Enrollment (2016): A: 10 (1) B: 40 (35) M: 20 (14) D: 12 (2)

Leopold-Franzens-Universitaet Innsbruck
Inst fuer Geologie (2016)
Innrain 52-f
6020 Innsbruck
p. +43 (0) 512 / 507 - 96125
dekanat-geowiss@uibk.ac.at
http://www.uibk.ac.at/fakultaeten/geo_und_atmosphaerenwissenschaften/

Montan Universitaet
Dept of Applied Geological Sciences and Geophysics (2015)
Inst. for Prospecting
A-8700
Leoben
geologie@mu-leoben.at

Technische Universitaet Graz
Earth Sciences (2015)
Rechbauerstrasse 12
A-8010 Graz
p. +43(0)316 873 6360
martin.dietzel@tugraz.at

University Leoben
Chair of Geology and Economic Geology (B,M,D) ☒ (2021)
Montanuniversitat Leoben
Peter-Tunnerstrasse 5
Leoben A-8700
p. +43 3842 402 6101
geologie@unileoben.ac.at
http://www.unileoben.ac.at/~buero62/geologie/geologie.html
Programs: Applied Geosciences and Geophysics
Enrollment (2018): B: 300 (0) M: 35 (0) D: 4 (0)
Professor:
Frank Melcher, (D), Leoben, 1993, GgEgm
Senior Scientist:
Heinrich Mali, (D), Leoben, GcEgNm
Associate Professor:
Gerd Rantitsch, (D), Graz, Ggq
Assistant Professor:
Phillip Gopon, (D)
Research Associate:
Viktor Erlandsson, (M), Gothenburg, 2018, Gg

University of Innsbruck
Institute of Geology (A,B,M,D) ○☒ (2019)
Innrain 52f
A-6020
Innsbruck 6020
p. +43 512 507-54300
regina.gratzl@uibk.ac.at
http://www.uibk.ac.at/geologie
Programs: Earth Science (Bachelor), Geology (MSc, PhD)

University of Salzburg
Inst fuer Geowissenschaften (2015)
Hellbrunner Strasse 34
A-5020 Salzburg
p. +43-662-8044-5200 oder 5400
geo@sbg.ac.at
http://www.uni-salzburg.at/geo

University of Vienna
Dept of Meteorology and Geophysics (B,M,D) ●☒ (2019)
Althanstrasse 14
A-1090 Vienna
p. 0043 1 4277 53701
img-wien@univie.ac.at
http://imgw.univie.ac.at/en/imgw/
Programs: Master programme "Physics of the Earth", in collaboration between the University of Vienna (Austria) and the Comenius University Bratislava (Slovakia)
Enrollment (2016): B: 40 (30) M: 20 (16) D: 10 (4)
Univ.-Prof.:
Goetz Bokelmann, (D), Princeton, 1992, Ygs
Univ.-Prof.:
Leopold Haimberger, (D), Wien, 1995, Ams

Dept of Geography (2017)
Althanstrasse 14
Vienna A-1090
p. 00431427753401
elisabeth.aufhauser@univie.ac.at
http://www.univie.ac.at/Geologie/
Head:
Thilo Hofmann, (D)

Azerbaijan

Baku State University
Faculty of Geology (2015)
23 Z. Khalilov Street
370145 Baku
m.mahluga@rambler.ru
http://www.ceebd.co.uk/ceeed/un/az/az003.htm

Bangladesh

Jahangirnagar University
Dept of Geological Sciences (2015)
University Campus, Savar, Dhaka
Dhaka
p. 0088 2 7791045-51 (Ext. 1402)
rabiulju@gmail.com
http://www.juniv.edu/home.php?pg=faculty_science

Rajshahi University
Dept of Geology & Mining (2016)
Motihar, Rajshahi
Rajshahi
p. +880 721-750041
chair.geology@ru.ac.bd
http://www.ru.ac.bd/geol

University of Dhaka
Department of Geology (B,M,D) ☒ (2020)
Curzon Hall Campus
Dhaka 1000
p. (880) 2- 966 1920-73 Ext. 7301
geology@du.ac.bd
http://www.du.ac.bd/academic/department_item/GLG
Enrollment (2017): B: 190 (37) M: 85 (31) D: 2 (0)
Chair:
M Aziz Hasan, (D), KTH, Stockholm, 2008, CqHwGg
Professor:
Kazi Matin Ahmed, (D), UK, 1994, HwGgHg

Belgium

Faculte Polytechnique de Mons
Dept of Geology (2015)
Fue de Houdain 9
7000 Mons
yves.quinif@fpms.ac.be

Faculte Univ Catholique de Mons
Dept of Geology (2015)
Chaussee de Binche 151
B-7000 Mons

Facultes Univ Notre Dame de la Paix
Dept Geologie (2015)
Rue de Bruxelles 61
B-5000 Namur
vincent.hallet@fundp.ac.be

Geological Survey of Belgium
Service geologique de Belgique (2015)
Department VII
of the Royal Belgian Institute of Natural Sciences (RBINS)
13, Rue Jenner
1000 Brussels
p. +32 (0)2.788.76.61
bgd@natuurwetenschappen.be
http://www.naturalsciences.be/geology/

Ghent University
Dept of Geology (B,M,D) ●⦸ (2020)
Krijgslaan 281-S8
Gent B-9000
p. +32 9 264 45 94
we13@ugent.be
https://www.ugent.be/we/geologie/nl/nl
f: https://www.facebook.com/GeologieUGent
t: @GeologyUGent
Programs: Geology; Marine and Lacustrine Science and Management; Physical Land Resources
Head:
Marc De Batist, (D), Ghent, 1989, GnuGs
Professor:
Veerle Cnudde, (D), Ghent, 2005, EsHt
Stephen Louwye, (D), Ghent, Pm
Kristine EMT Walraevens, (D), Ghent, 1987, HwCqYu
Associate Professor:
Johan De Grave, (D), Ghent, Cc
David Van Rooij, (D), Ghent, Yr
Thijs Vandenbroucke, (D), Ghent, Ps
Assistant Professor:
Stijn Dewaele, (D), KU Leuven, 2004, EgGzCg
Thomas Hermans, (D), Liege, HwYeu
Maarten Van Daele, (D), Ghent, 2013, GsRn

Katholieke Universiteit Leuven
Dept of Earth and Environmental Science (B,M,D) (2015)
Department of Earth & Environmental Sciences
Redingenstraat 16
B-3000 Leuven-Heverlee
p. (+32) 016 321450
erik.mathjis@ees.kuleaven.be
http://ees.kuleuven.be/
Professor:
Patrick Degryse, (D), GaCeGf
Jan Elsen, (D), Gz

Philippe Muchez, (D), 1988, EmCgGd
Manuel Sintubin, (D), GtcGa
Robert Speijer, (D), Utrecht, 1994, PmcOo
Rudy Swennen, Gso
Associate Professor:
Okke Batelaan, (D), Hw
Sarah Fowler, (D), Gip
Assistant Professor:
Marijke Huysmans, (D), Hw

Earth and Environmental Sciences (B,M,D) ☒ (2020)
Celestijnenlaan 200E PO 2408
Leuven BE-3001
p. +32 16 327580
gert.verstraeten@kuleuven.be
http://ees.kuleuven.be
Programs: Geography; Geology

Universite Catholique de Louvain

Dept of Geology (2015)
Bâtiment Mercator
place Louis Pasteur 3
B-1348 Louvain-la-Neuve
p. (32) 10 47 32 97
monique.descampsl@uclouvain.be
http://www.uclouvain.be/geo.html

Universite de Liege

Dept of Geology (B,M,D) (2015)
Batiment B18 (secretariat)
Sart Tilman
Liege B-4000
p. 32 4 366 22 51
TH.Billen@ulg.ac.be

http://www.ulg.ac.be/geolsed/geologie
Chair:
Frederic P. Boulvain, (D), Brussels, 1990, GdgGs
chargé de cours:
Nathalie Fagel, (D), GsuGe
Hans-Balder Havenith, (D), Liege, Ge
Professor:
Andre-Mathieu Fransolet, (D), Liege, Gz
Emmanuelle Javaux, (D), Dalhousie, 1999, Pl
Jacqueline Vander Auwera, (D), Louvain-la-Neuve, 1988, Giv
Emeritus:
Edouard Poty, (D), Liege, 1981, PiGsPe

Universite Libre de Bruxelles (ULB)

Département des Sciences de la Terre et de l'Env (2015)
50, Ave. F. Roosevelt
Brussels 1050
Julie.Paraire@ulb.ac.be

University of Mons

Dept of Geology and Applied Geology (M,D) O (2016)
rue de Houdain, 9
Mons
gfa@umons.ac.be

Vrije University Brussel

Analytical-Environmental and Geo-Chemistry (D) ☒ (2021)
AMGC-WE-VUB
Faculty of Sciences
Pleinlaan 2
Brussels 1050
p. 0113226293394
phclaeys@vub.be
https://we.vub.ac.be/en/analytical-environmental-and-geo-chemistry
f: https://www.facebook.com/amgcvub/
Enrollment (2017): D: 9 (2)
Head:
Philippe Claeys, (D), California (Davis), 1993, CgaXc

Bolivia

Universidad Mayor de San Andres

Dept of Geology (2015)
P. O. Box 12198
Campus Universitario Cota Cota, Calle 27
La Paz
p. (591-2) 2441983
webmaster@umsa.bo
http://www.geologia.umsa.bo/

Botswana

Geological Survey of Botswana

Geological Survey of Botswana (2015)
Khama One Avenue
Plot 1734
Lobatse
p. +267 5330327
http://www.gov.bw/en/Ministries

University of Botswana

Dept of Geology (B) (2015)
4775 Notwane Rd.
Private Bag UB00704
Gaborone
p. (267)355 2529
geology@mopipi.ub.bw
http://www.ub.bw/home/ac/1/fac/1/dep/79/Geology/

Dept of Environmental Science (B) (2015)
4775 Notwane Road
Private Bag UB 0022
Gaborone
p. (267) 355-0000
Sedilamoya.Pansiri@mopipi.ub.bw
http://www.ub.bw/learning_faculties.cfm?pid=588

Brazil

Federal University of Bahia Geophysics

CPGG (2015)
Salvador
BA
geofisic@ufba.br
http://www/pppg.ufba.br/

Geological Survey of Brazil

Servico Geologico do Brasil (2015)
Av. SGAN- Quadra 603 - conjunto J
Parte A - 1° andar
Brasilia - DF 70830-030
cprmsede@df.cprm.gov.br
http://www.cprm.gov.br/

Universidad Federal de Rio Grande do Sul

Institute de Geociencia (2015)
Avenida Bento Gonçalves, 9500
Porto Alegre, RS - 91.501-970
p. +55 51 3308-6337
igeo@ufrgs.br
http://www.ufrgs.br/english/the-university/institutes-faculties-and-schools/institute-of-geoscience

Universidade de Brasília

Instituto de Geociências (2015)
Campus Universitário Darcy Ribeiro ICC - Ala Central
CEP 70.910-900 - Brasilia DF
Caixa Postal 04465.
CEP 70919-970
p. +61 3307-2433
igd@unb.br
http://www.igd.unb.br/

Universidade de Sao Paulo

Inst de Geociencias (2015)
Rua do Lago
562 Cidade Universitaria
05508-080 São Paulo
p. 63.025.530/0007-08
gmgigc@usp.br
http://www.igc.usp.br/

Inst Oceanografico (2015)
Cidade Universitaria, Av. Prof. Luciano Gualberto, Travessa 3 no 380, 05508-900 Sao Paulo - SP

Universidade do Vale do Rio Dos Sinos

Inst de Geociencias (2015)
Av. Unisinos, 950 - Cristo Rei, 93 000 Sao Leopoldo - RS

Universidade Federal da Bahia

Inst de Geociencias (2015)
Rua Augusto Viana s/n - Canela, 40 410 Salvador - BA
olivia@ufba.br

Universidade Federal de Minas Gerâis

Inst de Geociencias (2015)
Av. Antonio Carlos 6.627
Pampulha , 31 270 Belo Horizont
p. 55(31) 3409-5420
dir@igc.ufmg.br
http://www.igc.ufmg.br/

Universidade Federal de Ouro Preto

Dept de Geologia (2015)
Campus Morro do Cruzeiro
35 400 Ouro Preto
p. (31) 3559-1600
web@degeo.ufop.br
http://www.degeo.ufop.br/

Universidade Federal de Pernambuco

Centro de Tecnologia - Geociencias (2015)
Av. Agamenon Magalhaes s/n - Santo Amaro, 50 000 Recife - PE
p. (81) 2126.8105
secretaria.proacad@ufpe.br
http://www.ufpe.br/proacad/index.php?option=com_content&view=article&id=150&Itemid=138

Universidade Federal do Ceara

Inst de Geociencias (2015)
Av. Da Universidade, 2853 - Benfica, 60 000 Fortaleza - CE

Universidade Federal do Para

Inst. de Geociencias (B,M,D) O⊘ (2018)
Augusto Correa Street, 01
Campus Guamá
Belem, Pará 66075-110
p. +55 91 3201 7107
dirig@ufpa.br
http://www.ig.ufpa.br/
Programs: We have at the Geosciences Institute (IG): bachelor's degree in Geophysics, Geology, Meteorology and Oceanography; Master's and Doctoral's programs in Geophysics, Geology and Geochemistry; Professional Masters in Environmental Sciences, Water Resources, Natural Hazards and Risk Management in the Amazon, Environmental Sciences Teaching; Specialization in Water and Environmental Management, Mine Geology and Open-pit mining, Sedimentary Basin Analysis.

Universidade Federal Fluminense

Dept de Geociencias (2015)
Av. Gal. Milton Tavares de Souza
p. +55 (21) 2629-5951
gge@vm.uff.br
http://www.uff.br/degeografia/

Universidade Federal Rural do Rio de Janeiro

Inst de Geociencias (2015)
Km 47 da Antigua Rodovia Rio/Sao Paulo - Seropedico, 23 460 Itaguai - RJ

University of Campinas Geoscience Institute

Inst de Geosciencias (2019)
Caixa Postal: 6152
13083-970
Campinas
secretaria.prpg@reitoria.unicamp.br
http://www.ige.unicamp.br/

Bulgaria

Bulgarian Academy of Sciences

Geological Institute (D) ☒ (2019)
Acad.G.Bonchev st. bl.24
Sofia 1113
p. +0359 2 8723 563
geolinst@geology.bas.bg
http://www.geology.bas.bg/
Programs: Paleontology and stratigraphy, Geotectonics, Regional Geology, Mineralogy, Petrology, Geochemistry, Lithology, Hydrogeology, Engineering geology,
Professor:
Radoslav Alexandrov Nakov, (D), Geological Inst, 1989, GtEgm
Professor:
Iliana Boncheva, (D)
Professor Dr, DSc:
Kristalina Christova Stoykova, (D), Bulgaria Acad Sci, 2008, PemPi
Professor:
Thomas Noubar Kerestedjian, (D), Bulgaria Acad Sci, 1990, GzeEg

Mining and Geology University

Geology Dept (2015)
Studentski Grad
Sofia 1756
p. 8060221
dekangpf@mgu.bg

Ministry of Environment and Water

Ministry of Environment and Water (2015)
22 Maria Louiza Blvd.
Sofia, 1000
minister@moew.government.bg
http://www.moew.government.bg/

Sofia University St. Kliment Ohridski

Dept of Geology and Paleontology (2016)
1504 Sofia
15 Tsar Osvobodtel Blvd.
Geology of Fossil, Fuel, Organic Petrology, Organic Geochemistry
room 276
gigeor@gea.uni-sofia.bg
http://www.uni-sofia.bg/newweb/faculties/geo/departments/geo

Dept of Cartography & GIS (B,M,D) (2015)
1504 Sofia
15 Tsar Osvobodtel Blvd.
GIS, General Physical Geography, Landscape Ecology, Agroecology
Sofia, Sofia 1504
p. 9308261
popov@gea.uni-sofia.bg
http://www.gis.gea.uni-sofia.bg/

University of Mining and Geology, St. Ivan Rilski

Faculty of Geology (2015)
Studentski grad
1100 Sofia
dekangpf@mgu.bg
http://www.mgu.bg/frame/html

Burkina Faso

Universite de Ouagadougou

L'Unité de Formation et de Recherche en Sciences de la Vie et de la Terre (UFR/SVT) (B) (2015)
03 BP 7021, Ougadougou 03
p. +226 50-30-70-64/65
webmaster@univ-ouaga.bf
http://www.univ-ouaga.bf.html/formations/ufr_SVT/frFormtnsS-VTdip1.html

Burundi

Universite du Burundi

Dept of Earth Sciences (B) ○ (2015)
B.P. 2700
Bujumbura, Burundi
p. 00257 22 22 55 56
webmaster@ub.edu.bi
http://www.ub.edu.bi/

Faculté des Sciences (2015)
B.P. 2700
Bjumbura
p. 0025722222059
http://www.ub.edu.bi/ub-fac6.php

Cameroon

Bamenda University of Science and Technology

Dept of Geology (B) (2015)
PO Box 277
Bamenda, NW Province
p. +237 7726 1789
http://www.bamendauniversity.com/

Universite de Buea

Dept of Geology and Environmental Science (B) (2015)
PO Box 63
Buea, South West Province
p. 237-332-2134
vpktitanji@yahoo.co.uk
http://ubuea.cm/

Universite de Douala

Faculty of Sciences (B,M,D) (2015)
BP 2701
Douala, Cameroun
p. (237) 33 40 75 69
infos.fs@univ-douala.com
http://www.facsciences-univ-douala.cm/index.php/contact

Universite de Dschang

Faculte D'Agronomie et des Sciences Agricoles (B,M) (2017)
POB 96
Dschang
p. (237) 33 45 15 66
agro.50tenair@gmail.com

Universite de Ngaoundere

School of Geology and Mining (B) (2015)
BP 454
Ngaoundere
p. +(237) 225 2767
http://www.univ-ndere.cm/index.php?LANG=EN&ETS=0433A030F35FE61&RUB=E2C0BE24560D78C

Universite de Yaounde 1

Dept des Sciences de la Terre (B) (2015)
BP 812
Yanounde
p. (237) 222 56 60
facsciences@uy1.uninet.cm
http://www.facsciences.uninet.cm/act_aca_dst.html

Canada

Aboriginal Affairs and Northern Development Canada

Mineral Resources Division (2017)
Mineral Resources Division
PO Box 100
Iqaluit, NU X0A 0H0
p. (867) 975-4293
nunavutarchives@aandc.gc.ca
http://nunavutgeoscience.ca/

Acadia University

Dept of Earth and Environmental Science (B,M) ● ☒ (2020)
Huggins Science Hall
12 University Avenue HSH 327
Wolfville, NS B4P 2R6
p. (902) 585-1208
ees@acadiau.ca
http://ees.acadiau.ca/
f: https://www.facebook.com/Acadia-Department-of-Earth-and-Environmental-Science-335568173300748/
Programs: Geology; Environmental Geoscience; Environmental Science
Enrollment (2020): B: 36 (11) M: 7 (0)

Head:
Robert P. Raeside, (D), Calgary, 1982, GptGc

Professor:
Sandra M. Barr, (D), British Columbia, 1973, GitGg
Nelson O'Driscoll, (D), Ottawa, 2003, CgGgZn
Ian S. Spooner, (D), Calgary, 1994, Ge
Clifford R. Stanley, (D), British Columbia, 1988, Cea

Associate Professor:
Alice Cohen, (D), British Columbia, 2011, ZnnZn

Assistant Professor:
Morgan E. Snyder, (D), Calgary, 2019, Gc

Instructor:
David W.A. McMullin, (D), British Columbia, 1991, Ze

Geology Tech:
Pam Frail, Gg

Brandon University

Dept of Geology (B,M) ○ ☒ (2020)
270 18th Street
Brandon, MB R7A 6A9
p. (204) 727-9677
mumin@brandonu.ca
http://www.brandonu.ca/geology
Programs: Geology, Mineral Resources, Energy Resources, Environmental Geoscience, Paleontology
Enrollment (2020): B: 26 (5)

Professor:
Rong-Yu Li, (D), Alberta, 2002, PgmGg
A. Hamid Mumin, (D), W Ontario, 1994, EgGzt
Simon A. J Pattison, (D), McMaster, 1992, GsoGd
Alireza Somarin, (D), New England, 1999, Gig

Emeritus:
Robert K. Springer, (D), California (Davis), 1971, Gi
Harvey R. Young, (D), Queen's, 1973, Gd

Laboratory Director:
Ayat Baig, (M), Lakehead, 2016, EdmEg

Other:
Paul Alexandre, (D), Loraine, 2000, EgCgGz

Brock University

Dept of Earth Sciences (B,M) ● 🖱 (2021)
1812 Sir Isaac Brock Way
St. Catharines, ON L2S 3A1
p. 905 688-5550
earth@brocku.ca
http://www.brocku.ca/mathematics-science/departments-and-centres/earth-sciences
Programs: Earth Sciences; Environmental Geoscience
Enrollment (2020): B: 64 (16) M: 10 (7)

Professor:
Uwe Brand, (D), Ottawa, 1979, ClsAs
Richard J. Cheel, (D), McMaster, 1984, Gs
Frank Fueten, (D), Toronto, 1989, Gc
Martin J. Head, (D), Aberdeen, 1990, Pl
Francine G. McCarthy, (D), Dalhousie, 1992, Pm
John Menzies, (D), Edinburgh, 1976, GlmGs
Associate Professor:
Gregory C. Finn, (D), Memorial, 1989, Gx
Daniel P. McCarthy, (D), Saskatchewan, 1993, Gl
Mariek Schmidt, (D), Oregon State, 2005, GivXg
Adjunct Professor:
Paul Budkewitsch, (M), Toronto, 1990, GeZrHq
Phil McCausland, (D), Gz
Andrew W. Panko, (D), McMaster, 1985, Ge

Cape Breton University

Math, Physics, Geology (B) (2015)
P.O. Box 5300
Sydney, NS B1P 6L2
p. (902) 539-5300
fenton_isenor@cbu.ca
Instructor:
Fenton M. Isenor, (M), Acadia, 2000, GgNgGm
Emeritus:
Erwin L. Zodrow, (D), Pi

Capilano University

Geology Dept (A,B) (2015)
2055 Purcell Way
North Vancouver, BC V7J 3H5
p. (604) 986-1911
sciences@capilanou.ca
http://www.capilanou.ca/programs/geology.html
Head:
Dileep J A Athaide, (M), British Columbia, 1974, GgZge
Professor:
Jennifer Getsinger, (D), British Columbia

Carleton University ❒

Dept of Earth Sciences (B,M,D) ● (2015)
1125 Colonel By Drive
Ottawa, ON K1S 5B6
p. (613) 520-5633
earth.sciences@carleton.ca
http://earthsci.carleton.ca/
f: https://www.facebook.com/pages/Department-of-Earth-Sciences-Carleton-University/510369329037382
t: @ErthSciCarleton
Professor:
Keith Bell, (D), Oxford, 1964, Cc
Brian L. Cousens, (D), California (Santa Barbara), 1990, GiCgc
George R. Dix, (D), Syracuse, 1988, Gsd
James E. Mungall, (D), McGill, 1993, GiEgCg
R. Timothy Patterson, (D), California (Los Angeles), 1986, Pm
Giorgio Ranalli, (D), Illinois, 1970, Yg
Claudia Schroder-Adams, (D), Dalhousie, 1986, Pm
George B. Skippen, (D), Johns Hopkins, 1966, Cg
Richard P. Taylor, (D), Leicester (UK), 1980, Cg
David H. Watkinson, (D), Penn State, 1965, Em
Associate Professor:
Gail M. Atkinson, (D), W Ontario, 1993, Ne
John Blenkinsop, (D), British Columbia, 1972, Cc
Sharon D. Carr, (D), Carleton, 1990, Gt
Fred A. Michel, (D), Waterloo, 1982, Hw
Lecturer:
Ildi Munro, (M), Waterloo, 1975, Pg
Adjunct Professor:
Robert Berman, (D), British Columbia, 1983, Gp
Steve L. Cumbaa, (D), Florida, 1975, Pv
J. Allan Donaldson, (D), Johns Hopkins, 1960, Gs
T. Scott Ercit, (D), Manitoba, 1986, Gz
Harold Gibson, (D), Carleton, 1990, Em
Simon Hanmer, (D), Chelsea (UK), 1977, Gc
Mark D. Hannington, (D), Toronto, 1989, Em
Jarmila Kukalova-Peck, (D), Charles (Prague), 1962, Pi
Dale A. Leckie, (D), McMaster, 1983, Gs
R. R. Rainbird, (D), Western, 1991, Gs
Emeritus:
F. K. North, (D), Oxford, 1951, Go

Dalhousie University ❒

Dept of Earth Sciences (B,M,D) ●☒ (2019)
Halifax, NS B3H 3J5
p. (902) 494-2358
earth.sciences@dal.ca
http://earthsciences.dal.ca
Programs: Earth Sciences (minor,B,M,D); Geography (minor)
Certificates: Geographic Information Science; Materials Science; Science Leadership and Communication
Enrollment (2017): B: 94 (39) M: 24 (9) D: 13 (2)
Chair:
James M. Brenan, (D), Rensselaer, 1990, CptEm
Professor:
John C. Gosse, (D), Lehigh, 1994, CcGmRn
Djordje Grujic, (D), ETH (Switzerland), 1992, Gt
Mladen Nedimovic, (D), Toronto, 2000, Ysg
Grant D. Wach, (D), Oxford, 1993, GorGs
Retired:
Nicholas Culshaw, (D), Ottawa, 1983, Gc
Associate Professor:
Isabelle Coutand, (D), Rennes, Gg
Yana Fedortchouk, (D), Victoria, 2006, CpEdGi
Shannon Sterling, (D), Duke, 2005, HgCbHs
Assistant Professor:
Lawrence Plug, (D), Alaska (Fairbanks), 2000, Gm
Owen Sherwood, (D), Dalhousie, 2006, CsOoGo
Research Associate:
Alan Ruffman, (M), Dalhousie, 1966, Ys
Senior Instructor:
Mike Young, (M), Queens, 2003, GgcGp
Retired:
Charles C. Walls, (M), Dalhousie, 1996, Zi
Instructor:
Richard Cox, (D), Memorial, 1999, GzEdGg
Chris Greene, (D), Ryerson, 2015, Zi
Honorary Research Associate:
Prasanta Mukhopadhyay, (D), Jadavpur, 1971, Ec
Adjunct Professor:
Sandra Barr, (D), British Columbia, 1973, Gx
D. Brown, (B), Dalhousie
John Calder, (D), Dalhousie, 1991, Ec
C. Campbell, (D), Dalhousie
T. Claire, (D), McMaster
D Barrie Clarke, (D), Edinburgh, Gi
M. Deptuck, (D), Dalhousie
Jarda Dostal, (D), McMaster, 1974, Cg
A. Dyke, (D), Colorado
T. J. Fedak, (D), Dalhousie
R. Fensome, (D), Nottingham (UK)
D. Forbes, (D), British Columbia
M. Fowler, (D), Newcastle upon Tyne
D.G. Froese, (D), Calgary
C. Gerbi, (D), Maine
D. Gibson, (D), Simon Fraser
J. Hanley, (D), Toronto
C. Keen, (D), Cambridge
Lisa M. Kellman, (D), Quebec (Montreal), 1998, Cg
Y. Kettanah, (D), Southampton (UK)
E. Kirby, (D), MIT
T. Lakeman, (D), Alberta
M. Lavigne, (D), Yale
K. E. Louden, (D), MIT
J. Marsh, (D), Maine
T. Martel, (D), Dalhousie
Michael Melchin, (D), Western, 1987, Pg
D. Mosher, (D), Dalhousie
Peta J. Mudie, (D), Dalhousie, 1980, Pl
J. E. Mungall, (D), McGill
J. B. Murphy, (D), McGill
J. Brendan Murphy, (D), McGill, 1982, Gx
Michael Parsons, (D), Stanford, Gg
David Piper, (D), Cantab, 1969, Gs
P. Pufhal, (D), British Columbia, 2002
F. W. Richards, (M), Imperial Coll (UK)

D. Risk, (D), Dalhousie
Cliff Shaw, (D), W Ontario
J. Shimeld, (M), Dalhousie
D. W. Simpson, (D), Australian Nat
S. Swinden, (D), Memorial
H. Vincent, (D), Dalhousie
J. Waldron, (D), Edinburgh
C. Warron, (D), Oxford
T. Webster, (D), Dalhousie
D. M. Whipp, (D), Michigan
B. Wilson, (D), Wales

Emeritus:
H.B. S. Cooke, (D), Witwatersrand, 1947, Pv
Martin R. Gibling, (D), Ottawa, 1978, Gs
G. Clinton Milligan, (D), Harvard, 1961, Gc
Peter H. Reynolds, (D), British Columbia
Patrick J.C. Ryall, (D), Dalhousie, 1974, Yg
David B. Scott, (D), Dalhousie, 1977, Pm
Marcos Zentilli, (D), Queen's, 1974, Eg

University Teaching Fellow:
Anne-Marie Ryan, (D), Dalhousie, 2006, GeZeCg

Administrator:
Ann Bannon, (B), Dalhousie, 2001, Zn

Cooperating Faculty:
Christopher Beaumont, (D), Dalhousie, 1973, Ys

Dept of Oceanography (B,M,D) (2018)
Life Sciences Centre
1355 Oxford Street
PO Box 15000
Halifax, NS B3H 4R2
p. (902) 494-3557
oceanography@dal.ca
http://oceanography.dal.ca/
Enrollment (2015): M: 22 (6) D: 31 (2)

Chair:
Paul S. Hill, (D), Washington, 1992, Gs

Professor:
Christopher Beaumont, (D), Dalhousie, 1973, Yg
Bernard P. Boudreau, (D), Yale, 1985, OcCml
Katja Fennel, (D), Rostock, 1998, Ob
Jonathan Grant, (D), South Carolina, 1981, Ob
Alex E. Hay, (D), British Columbia, 1981, OpnGu
Dan Kelley, (D), Dalhousie, 1986, Op
Markus Kienast, (D), British Columbia, 2002, Cs
Hugh MacIntyre, (D), Deleware, 1996, Ob
Anna Metaxas, (D), Dalhousie, 1994, Ob
Jinyu Sheng, (D), Memorial, 1991, Op
Christopher T. Taggart, (D), McGill, 1986, Ob
Helmuth Thomas, (D), Rostock, 1997, Oc
Keith R. Thompson, (D), Liverpool (UK), 1979, Op
Douglas Wallace, (D), Dalhousie, 1985, Oc

Associate Professor:
Tetjana Ross, (D), Manitoba, 2003, Op

Assistant Professor:
Christopher Algar, (D), Dalhousie, 2009, Obc
David R. Barclay, (D), California (San Diego), 2011, OpNo
Carolyn Buchwald, (D), MIT/WHOI, 2013, Oc
Stephanie Kienast, (D), British Columbia, 2002, Gu
Eric Oliver, (D), Dalhousie, 2011, Op

Lecturer:
Barry R. Ruddick, (D), MIT, 1977, Op

Adjunct Professor:
Mark Baumgartner, (D), Oregon, 2002, Ob
Susanne Craig, (D), Strathclyde, 2000, Op
Peter Cranford, (D), Dalhousie, 1998, Ob
Claudio DiBacco, (D), California (San Diego), 1999, Ob
Dale Ellis, (D), McMaster, 1976, Op
Kenneth Frank, (D), Toledo, 1978, Ob
Richard Greatbatch, (D), Cambridge, 1981, Op
David Greenberg, (D), Liverpool (UK), 1975, Op
David Hebert, (D), Dalhousie, 1988, Op
Paul Hines, (D), Bath, 1989, Op
Bruce D. Johnson, (D), Dalhousie, 1979, Oc
Sebastian Krastel, (D), Kiel, 1999, Yr
William K. W. Li, (D), Dalhousie, 1978, Ob
Keith E. Louden, (D), MIT, 1976, Yr
Youyu Lu, (D), Victoria, 1997, Op
Timothy Milligan, (M), Dalhousie, 1997, Gs
David C. Mosher, (D), Dalhousie, 1993, Ou
Andreas Oschlies, (D), Kiel, 1994, Ob
William Perrie, (D), MIT, 1979, OpAm
David J.W. Piper, (D), Cambridge, 1969, GusGo
Harold C. Ritchie, (D), McGill, 1982, Am
Peter C. Smith, (D), MIT/WHOI, 1973, Op
Ulrich Sommer, (D), Vienna, 1977, Ob
Toste Tanhua, (D), Goteborg (Sweden), 1997, Oc

Emeritus:
Anthony J. Bowen, (D), California (San Diego), 1967, On
John J. Cullen, (D), California (San Diego), 1980, Ob
Robert O. Fournier, (D), Rhode Island, 1967, Ob
Marlon R. Lewis, (D), Dalhousie, 1984, Ob
Eric L. Mills, (D), Yale, 1964, ObZnn
Robert M. Moore, (D), Southampton, 1977, Oc

Douglas College

Dept of Earth and Environmental Sciences, Faculty of Science and Technology (A) ● ☒ (2019)
P.O. Box 2503
New Westminster, BC V3L 5B2
p. (604) 527-5400
vigourouxcaillibotn@douglascollege.ca
http://www.douglascollege.ca/programs-courses/faculties/science-technology/earth-and-environmental-sciences
Programs: Earth and Environmental Science (A); Geological Resources Diploma; Environmental Science (A)
Enrollment (2019): A: 39 (0)

Chair:
Nathalie Vigouroux-Caillibot, (D), Simon Fraser, 2011, GviCg
David C. Waddington, (M), Queen's (Canada), 1991, ZgGuEd

Lab Facilitator:
Denis Beausoleil, (M), Victoria, GgZg
Corinne Griffing, (D), Simon Fraser, 2018, GgeGm
Christine Shiels, (M), Saskatchewan, 2017, GgxZg

Instructor:
Reid Staples, (D), Simon Fraser, 2014, GpxGg
Selina Tribe, (D), Simon Fraser, 2004, EgGge
Derek Turner, (D), Simon Fraser, 2014, GemGl

Emeritus:
Michael C. Wilson, (D), Calgary, 1981, GaPgGs

Lakehead University

Geology (B,M) ● ☒ (2018)
955 Oliver Road
Thunder Bay, ON P7B 5E1
p. (807) 343-8461
kristine.carey@lakeheadu.ca
https://www.lakeheadu.ca/academics/departments/geology
f: https://www.facebook.com/lakeheaduniversity
t: @mylakehead
Programs: The Department of Geology offers programs leading to Bachelor and Master of Science degrees. These undergraduate programs are offered in Geology and Earth Science majors. A Geography major combined with a Geology minor and an HBESc in Earth Science are available. Geology and Earth Science programs are also offered concurrently with a BEd from the Department of Undergraduate Studies in Education.
Certificates: None
Administrative Assistant: Kristine M. Carey
Enrollment (2018): B: 60 (26) M: 15 (4)

Chair:
Peter N. Hollings, (D), Saskatchewan, 1998, Eg

Professor:
Philip W. Fralick, (D), Toronto, 1985, Gs
Mary Louise Hill, (D), Princeton, 1985, Gc

Associate Professor:
Andrew G. Conly, (D), Toronto, 2003, EgCgGz
Amanda Diochon, (D), Dalhousie, 2009, Ge
Shannon Zurevinski, (D), Alberta, 2009, Gz

Emeritus:
Manfred M. Kehlenbeck, (D), Queen's, 1971, Gc
Stephen A. Kissin, (D), Toronto, 1974, Em
Edward L. Mercy, (D), Imperial Coll (UK), 1955, Cg
Roger H. Mitchell, (D), McMaster, 1969, Gi

Geology Technician:
Kristi Tavener, Zn
Jonas K. Valiunas, (D), Lakehead, 2017, Zm

CANADA

Geology Technician:
Anne Hammond, (B), Lakehead, 1999, Zn

Laurentian University, Sudbury

Harquail School of Earth Sciences (B,M,D) ●☒ (2019)
Ramsey Lake Road
Sudbury, ON P3E 2C6
p. (705) 675-1151 Ext. 6575
hes@laurentian.ca
http://hes.laurentian.ca/
Administrative Assistant: Roxane J. Mehes
Enrollment (2016): B: 90 (0) M: 66 (0) D: 21 (0)

Director:
Doug Tinkham, (D), Alabama, 2002, Gp

Professor:
Harold L. Gibson, (D), Carleton, 1990, EmGv
Daniel J. Kontak, (D), Queens, 1985, Eg
Bruno Lafrance, (D), New Brunswick, 1990, GcEmGt
Michael Lesher, (D), W Australia, 1984, Em
Andrew M. McDonald, (D), Carleton, 1992, Gz
Jeremy P. Richards, (D), Australian Nat, 1990, EmGiCg
Richard S. Smith, (D), Toronto, Ye
Elizabeth C. Turner, (D), Queen's (Canada), 1999, GrdEm

Associate Professor:
Pedro J. Jugo, (D), Alberta, 2003, EgCpGi
Matthew I. Leybourne, (D), Ottawa, Cg
Michael Schindler, (D), Frankfurt (Germany), Gz

Assistant Professor:
Alessandro Ielpi, (D), Siena, 2013, GsmGr

Emeritus:
Anthony E. Beswick, (D), London (UK), 1965, Gi
Paul Copper, (D), Imperial Coll (UK), 1965, PieZc
Richard James, (D), Manchester (UK), 1967, GpiEm
Reid R. Keays, (D), McMaster, 1968, Em
Darrel Long, (D), W Ontario, 1976, GsaGl
Don H. Rousell, (D), Manitoba, 1965, Gc
Robert E. Whitehead, (D), New Brunswick, 1973, Ce

Other:
Bruce C. Jago, (D), Toronto, 1990, EgCe

Cooperating Faculty:
Phillips C. Thurston, (D), Western, 1981, Zg

Manitoba Museum

Dept. of Geology & Paleontology ☒ (2021)
190 Rupert Avenue
Winnipeg, MB R3B 0N2
p. (204) 956-2830
gyoung@manitobamuseum.ca
http://www.manitobamuseum.ca

Curator:
Graham A. Young, (D), New Brunswick, 1988, PieRc

McGill University

Dept of Earth & Planetary Sciences (B,M,D) ●☒ (2020)
3450 University Street
Room 238
Montreal, QC H3A 0E8
p. (514) 398-6767
kristy.thornton@mcgill.ca
http://www.mcgill.ca/eps
Programs: Geology (B); Planetary Sciences (B); Earth and Planetary Sciences (M,D)
Enrollment (2020): B: 15 (9) M: 24 (6) D: 39 (5)

Chair:
Jeffrey M. McKenzie, (D), Syracuse, 2005, Hw

Professor:
Don Baker, (D), Penn State, 1985, CuGvCp
Eric Galbraith, (D), British Columbia, 2006, Zo
Galen Halverson, (D), Harvard, 2003, GsrCs
Olivia G. Jensen, (D), British Columbia, 1971, Yg
John Stix, (D), Toronto, 1989, Gv
Anthony E. Williams-Jones, (D), Queens, 1973, Ce

Associate Professor:
Nicolas B. Cowan, (D), Washington, 2009, AsXyg
Yajing Liu, (D), Harvard, 2007, Ygs
Jeanne Paquette, (D), SUNY (Stony Brook), 1991, Gz
Christie Rowe, (D), California (Santa Cruz), 2007, GctEm
Vincent van Hinsberg, (D), Bristol, 2006, EgCg

Assistant Professor:
Kim Berlo, (D), Bristol, 2006, Gv
Peter Douglas, (D), Yale, 2014, Cs
Natalya Gomez, (D), Harvard, 2013, Og
James Kirkpatrick, (D), Glasgow, 2008, Gct
Nagissa Mahmoudi, (D), McMaster, 2013, Cb

Earth System Science Faculty Lecturer:
William G. Minarik, (D), Rensselaer, 1993, Cp

Adjunct Professor:
Richard Léveillé, (D), W Ontario, 2000, CgXb
Bjorn Sundby, (D), Bergen (Norway), 1966, Cm

Emeritus:
Jafar Arkani-Hamed, (D), MIT, 1969, Xy
Don Francis, (D), MIT, 1974, Gi
Reinhard Hesse, (D), Tech (Munich), 1964, Gs
Andrew J. Hynes, (D), Cambridge, 1972, Gc
Robert F. Martin, (D), Stanford, 1969, GziEm
Alfonso Mucci, (D), Miami, 1981, CmlOc
Colin Stearn, (D), Yale, Ps

Dept of Mining & Materials Engineering (B,M,D) ☒ (2021)
Rm 125 FDA Building
3450 University Street
Montreal, QC H3A 0E8
p. (514) 398-4986
roussos.dimitrakopoulos@mcgill.ca
http://www.mcgill.ca/minmat/mining
Programs: Mining Engineering

Chair:
Stephen Yue, (D), Leeds (UK), 1979, Nx

Professor:
George Demopoulos, (D), McGill, 1982, Nx
Roussos Dimitrakopoulos, (D), Ecole Polytechnique, 1989, Nm
Raynald Gauvin, (D)
Roderick I. Guthrie, (D), London (UK), 1967, Nx
Ferri Hassani, (D), Nottingham (UK), 1981, Nm
Hani Mitri, (D), Nottingham (UK), 1981, Nm

Associate Professor:
Mathieu Brochu, (D), McGill
Mainul Hasan, (D), McGill, 1987, Nx
Showan Nazhat, (D)
Mihriban Pekguleryuz, (D), McGill

Assistant Professor:
Kirk Bevan, (D), Purdue
Marta Cerruti, (D)
Richard Chromik, (D), SUNY
Nathaniel Quitoriano, (D), MIT
Jun Song, (D), Princeton
Kristian Waters, (D)

Lecturer:
Forence Paray, (D), McGill

Emeritus:
John J. Jonas, (D), Cambridge, 1960, Nx

Dept of Atmospheric & Oceanic Sciences (B,M,D) ☒ (2017)
805 Sherbrooke Street West
Room 945
Montreal, QC H3A 0B9
p. (514) 398-3764
john.gyakum@mcgill.ca
http://www.mcgill.ca/meteo
Administrative Assistant: Lucy Nunez
Enrollment (2017): B: 6 (10) M: 13 (10) D: 31 (5)

Professor:
Parisa A. Ariya, (D), York, 1996, As
Peter Bartello, (D), McGill, 1988, As
John R. Gyakum, (D), MIT, 1981, Am
Man Kong Yau, (D), MIT, 1977, As

Associate Professor:
Frederic Fabry, (D), McGill, 1994, As
Daniel Kirshbaum, (D), Washington, 2005, Asm
David Straub, (D), Washington, 1990, Op
Bruno Tremblay, (D), McGill, Op

Assistant Professor:
Yi Huang, (D), Princeton, 2007, ZrYgAs
Timothy Merlis, (D), Caltech, 2011, Asm
Thomas Colin Preston, (D), Duke, 2011, AsZnn
Andreas Zuend, (D), ETH (Switzerland), 2008, Asm

Adjunct Professor:
Gilbert Brunet, (D), McGill, 1989, Am
Ashu Dastoor, (D), IIT
Luc Fillion, (D), McGill, 1991, Ams
Pavlos Kollias, (D), Miami, 2000, ZrAs
Hai Lin, (D), McGill, 1995, As
Emeritus:
Jacques F. Derome, (D), Michigan, 1968, As
Henry G. Leighton, (D), Alberta, 1968, As
Lawrence A. Mysak, (D), Harvard, 1966, Op
Isztar Zawadzki, (D), McGill, 1972, AsZr

McMaster University

School of Earth, Environment & Society (B,M,D) ●☒ (2020)
1280 Main Street West
General Science Building
Room 206
Hamilton, ON L8S 4K1
p. (905) 525-9140 (Ext. 24535)
geograd@mcmaster.ca
https://www.science.mcmaster.ca/ees/
Programs: Honours Earth & Environmental Sciences; Honours Environmental Sciences; Honours Geography & Environmental Sciences; Honours Biology & Environmental Sciences; Environmental Sciences (B); Geographic Information Systems (minor); Earth & Environmental Sciences (D); Geography (D); Earth & Environmental Sciences (M); Geography (M)
Enrollment (2020): B: 237 (81) M: 43 (16) D: 45 (8)
Director:
K. Bruce Newbold, (D), McMaster, 1994, Ge
Professor:
M. Altaf Arain, (D), Arizona, 1997, Hg
Janok Bhattacharya, (D), McMaster, 1989, Gr
Sean Carey, (D), McMaster, 2000, Hg
Vera Chouinard, (D), McMaster, 1986, Zn
Paulin Coulibaly, (D), Laval, 2000, Hg
Carolyn H. Eyles, (D), Toronto, 1986, GslGm
Karen Kidd, (D), Alberta, 1996, Gu
H. Antonio Paez, (D), Tohoku, 2000, Eg
Edward G. Reinhardt, (D), Carleton, 1996, PmGam
Darren M. Scott, (D), McMaster, 2000, Zi
Gregory F. Slater, (D), Toronto, 2001, Cg
James E. Smith, (D), Waterloo, 1995, Hw
J. Michael Waddington, (D), York, 1995, Pe
Allison M. Williams, (D), York, 1997, Zn
Robert D. Wilton, (D), S California, 1999, Zn
Associate Professor:
Joseph I. Boyce, (D), Toronto, 1997, Zg
Sang-Tae Kim, (D), McGill, 2006, Cg
Gita Ljubicic, (D)
Suzanne Mills, (D), Saskatchewan, 2007, Zn
Maureen Padden, (D), ETH (Switzerland), 2001, CsPc
Niko Yiannakoulias, (D), Alberta, 2006, Ge
Assistant Professor:
Melanie Bedore, (D), Queens, 2010, Zu
Luc Bernier, (D), McMaster, 2007, Cg
Alemu Gonsamo, (D), Helsinki, 2009
Michael Mercier, (D), McMaster, 2004, Zu
Alexander Peace, (D), Durham (UK), 2016
Lecturer:
John MacLachlan, (D), McMaster, 2011, Gs
Adjunct Professor:
Matthew Adams, (D), McMaster, 2015
David Atkinson
Howard Barker, (D), McMaster, 1991
Patricia Beddows, (D), Bristol, 2004
Jing Chen, (D), Reading (UK), 1986, AmZry
Susan J. Elliott, (D), McMaster, 1992, Ge
Beverly Goodman-Tchernov, (D), McMaster, 2006
Peter Kitchen, (D), Ottawa
Chris McLaughlin, (D), McMaster
Hamid Mehmood, (D), Asian Inst Tech, 2012
Nidhi Nagabhatla, (D), ISRO, 2005
Duminda Perera, (D), Kyushu, 2010
Michael Pisaric, (D), Queens, 2001
Manzoor Qadir, (D), Ag, Faisalabad, 1995
Dominique Rissolo, (D), California (Riverside), 2001
James Roy, (D), Waterloo, 2004
Corinne Schuster-Wallace, (D), Wilfred Laurier, 2001
Vladimir Smakhtin, (D), Moscow (Russia), 1984
Matthias Sweet, (D), Pennsylvania, 2012
Lina Taing, (D), Cape Town, 2015
S Martin Taylor, (D), Victoria (Canada), 1974
Shuzen Wang
Lesley A. Warren, (D), Toronto, 1994, CgHg
Amin Yazdani, (D), Waterloo, 2015
University Professor:
John D. Eyles, (D), London (UK), 1983, Ge
Henry P. Schwarcz, (D), Caltech, 1960, Cs
Emeritus:
Andrew F. Burghardt, (D), Wisconsin, 1958
Paul Clifford, (D), London (UK), 1956
James H. Crocket, (D), MIT
Alan P. Dickin, (D), Oxford, 1981, Cc
John J. Drake, (D), McMaster, 1973
Derek C. Ford, (D), Oxford, 1963, GmHwCc
Doug Grundy, (D), Manchester (UK), 1966
Fred L. Hall, (D), MIT, 1975
Richard S. Harris, (D), Queens, 1981, Zu
Leslie J. King, (D), Iowa, 1960
James R. Kramer, (D), Michigan, 1958, Cl
Kao Lee Liaw, (D), Clark, 1972
Gerry V. Middleton, (D), London (UK), 1954
William A. Morris, (D), 1974, Yg
Yorgos Papageorgiou, (D), Ohio State, 1970
W. Jack Rink, (D), Florida State, 1990, CcGam
Michael J. Risk, (D), S California, 1971, Pg
Wayne R. Rouse, (D), McGill, 1968
Roger G. Walker, (D), Oxford, 1964
Ming-Ko Woo, (D), British Columbia, 1972, HgZy

Memorial University of Newfoundland

Dept of Earth Sciences (B,M,D) ☒ (2021)
Alexander Murray Building
St. John's, NL A1B 3X5
p. (709) 864-8142
earthsci@mun.ca
http://www.mun.ca/earthsciences
Professor:
Karem Azmy, (D), Cl
Elliott T. Burden, (D), Calgary, 1982, PlGso
Farquharson Colin, (D), Yg
Gregory R. Dunning, (D), Memorial, 1984, CcGit
John Hanchar, (D), Cg
Aphrodite D. Indares, (D), Montreal, 1989, Gp
Graham Layne, (D), Cg
Duncan McIlroy, (D), Gg
Michael A. Slawinski, (D), Calgary, 1996, Ys
Associate Professor:
Luke Beranek, (D), GgsCc
Tao Cheng, (D), Hw
Charles A. Hurich, (D), Wyoming, 1988, Ys
Alison Leitch, (D), Australian Nat, 1986, Yg
Alison Malcolm, (D), Yg
Penny Morrill, Cg
Assistant Professor:
Michael Babechuk, (D), Cu
John Jamieson, (D), Gu
First Year Lab Instructor:
Amanda Langille, (M), Gg
Emeritus:
Ali E. Aksu, (D), Dalhousie, 1980, Gu
Jeremy Hall, (D), Glasgow, 1971, YsGtYr
Richard N. Hiscott, (D), McMaster, 1977, Gs
Joseph P. Hodych, (D), Toronto, 1971, Ym
Henry Longerich, (D), Indiana, 1967, Cg
Toby C. J. S. Rivers, (D), Ottawa, 1976, Gp
Michael G. Rochester, (D), Utah, 1959, Yg

Memorial University of Newfoundland, Grenfell Campus

Environmental Science Program (B) ●⊘ (2019)
School of Science and Environment
University Drive
Corner Brook, NL A2H 6P9
p. (709) 637-6215

Ian.Warkentin@grenfell.mun.ca
https://www.grenfell.mun.ca/academics-and-research/Pages/school-of-science-and-the-environment/programs/Environmental-Science.as
Programs: Environmental Science
Enrollment (2018): B: 56 (12)

Mount Allison University

Dept of Geography (B,M) (2015)
144 Main Street
Sackville, NB E4L 1A7
p. (506) 364-2326
dlieske@mta.ca
http://www.mta.ca/departments/geography
Associate Professor:
Jeffery W. Ollerhead, (D), Guelph, 1994, Yr
Assistant Professor:
James Xinxia Jiang, (D), Southampton (UK), Gg
Research Associate:
Thomas A. Clair, (D), McMaster, 1991, Hy
Research Professor:
David J. Mossman, (D), Otago (NZ), 1970, EmZn
Emeritus:
Laing Ferguson, (D), Edinburgh, 1960, Pi

Mount Royal University

Dept of Earth and Environmental Sciences (A,B) (2015)
4825 Mount Royal Gate SW
Calgary, AB T3E 6K6
p. (403) 440-6165
ttaylor@mtroyal.ca
http://www.mtroyal.ab.ca/scitech/earth.shtml
Administrative Assistant: Leona Stadnyk
Chair:
Paul Johnston, (D), W Australia, 1986, Pi
Professor:
John Cox, (D), Aberdeen, 1994, EoGsHw
Barbara McNicol, (D), Calgary, 1997, Zg
Associate Professor:
Katherine Boggs, (D), Calgary, 2004, Gt
Pamela MacQuarrie, (M), Calgary, 1988, Zy
Related Staff:
Michael Clark, (B), Adams, 1976, Zg

Natural Resources Canada

Ressources Naturelles Canada (2015)
580 Booth Street , 21st Floor
Ottawa, ON K1A 0E4
debra.tompkinscaron@canada.ca
http://www.nrcan.gc.ca/
Senior Scientist:
Sergey V. Samsonov, (D), Western, 2007, YdZrYg
Other:
Esther Asselin, (M), Laval, 1988, PlGuRh

New Brunswick Department of Natural Resources and Energy Development

New Brunswick Department of Natural Resources and Energy Development ☒ (2020)
Hugh John Flemming Forestry Centre
P.O. Box 6000
Fredericton, NB E3B 5H1
p. (506) 453-3826
geoscience@gnb.ca
http://www.gnb.ca/minerals

Queen's University

Dept of Geological Sciences and Geological Engineering (B,M,D) ● (2017)
#240, Bruce Wing, Miller Hall
36 Union St.
Kingston, ON K7L 3N6
p. (613) 533-2597
geolundergradassistant@queensu.ca
http://www.queensu.ca/geol
Enrollment (2011): B: 232 (47) M: 46 (20) D: 18 (5)
Head:
Jean Hutchinson, (D), Toronto, 1992
Professor:
Mark Diederichs, (D), Toronto, Nr
Georgia Fotopoulos, (D), Calgary, 2003, Yd
Laurent Godin, (D), Carleton, 1999, Gct
Noel P. James, (D), McGill, 1972, Gd
Guy M. Narbonne, (D), Ottawa, 1981, PigGs
Gema Olivo, (D), Québec (Montréal), 1995, Eg
Ronald C. Peterson, (D), Virginia Tech, 1980, Gz
Victoria H. Remenda, (D), Waterloo, 1993, Hw
Associate Professor:
Alexander Braun, (D), Goethe (Frankfurt), 1999, YgdYv
John A. Hanes, (D), Toronto, 1979, Cc
Heather E. Jamieson, (D), Queen's, 1982, Ge
Daniel Layton-Matthews, (D), Toronto, 2006, EgCte
Research Associate:
Doug A. Archibald, (D), Queen's, 1982, Cc
Adjunct Professor:
Rob Harrap, (M), Carleton, 1990, Gc
Emeritus:
Alan H. Clark, (D), Manchester (UK), 1964, Em
Robert W. Dalrymple, (D), McMaster, 1977, Gs
John M. Dixon, (D), Connecticut, 1974, Gct
Herwart Helmstaedt, (D), New Brunswick, 1968, Gc
Raymond A. Price, (D), Princeton, 1958, GtcGe

Royal Ontario Museum

Dept of Palaeobiology (2015)
100 Queen's Park
Toronto, ON M5S 2C6
p. (416) 586-5591
davidru@rom.on.ca
Curator Of Vertebrate Palaeontology:
David C. Evans, (D), Toronto, 2007, PvgPq

Department of Natural History ☒ (2019)
100 Queen's Park
Toronto, ON M5S 2C6
p. (416) 586-5820
ktait@rom.on.ca
Emeritus:
Robert I. Gait, (D), Manitoba, 1967, Gz
Frederick J. Wicks, (D), Oxford, 1969, Gz
Curator:
Kimberly T. Tait, (D), Arizona, 2007, GzyXm

Royal Tyrrell Museum of Palaeontology

Royal Tyrrell Museum of Palaeontology ☒ (2017)
P.O. Box 7500
Drumheller, AB T0J 0Y0
p. (403) 823-7707
tyrrell.info@gov.ab.ca
http://www.tyrrellmuseum.com/
Executive Director:
Andrew G. Neuman, (M), Alberta, 1986, Pv
Director, Preservation and Research:
Donald B. Brinkman, (D), McGill, 1979, Pv
Curator:
David A. Eberth, (D), Toronto, 1987, Gs
James D. Gardner, (D), Alberta, 2000, Pv
Donald Henderson, (D), Bristol, 2000, Pv
Craig Scott, (D), Alberta, 2008, Pv
Curator:
Francois Therrien, (D), Johns Hopkins, 2004, Pv
Post-doctoral fellow:
Caleb Brown, (D), Toronto, 2013, Pv

Saint Francis Xavier University

Dept of Earth Sciences (B,M) (2015)
P.O Box 5000
Antigonish, NS B2G 2W5
p. (902) 867-5109
igreen@stfx.ca
http://sites.stfx.ca/earth_sciences/
Enrollment (2015): B: 11 (15) M: 13 (3)

Professor:
Alan J. Anderson, (D), Queen's, 1990, Gx
Hugo Beltrami, (D), Quebec (Montreal), 1993, YhAs
Lisa M. Kellman, (D), Quebec (Montreal), 1997, CsSo
Michael J. Melchin, (D), Western, 1987, Pi
J. Brendan Murphy, (D), McGill, 1982, Gt
Associate Professor:
Dave A. Risk, (D), Dalhousie, 2006, SoZr
Instructor:
Cindy Murphy, (M), McGill, 1986, Gg
Colette Rennie, (M), Queen's, 1987, Gg
Matthew Schumacher, (M), Waterloo, 2006, Zg
Sid Taylor, (M), Memorial, 1977, Gg

Simon Fraser University

Dept of Earth Sciences (B,M,D) ●⦸ (2021)
8888 University Drive
Burnaby, BC V5A 1S6
p. 778-782-4229
easchair@sfu.ca
http://www.sfu.ca/earth-sciences
Professor:
Diana M. Allen, (D), Carleton, 1996, Hy
Andrew J. Calvert, (D), Cambridge, 1985, Ys
Shahin Dashtgard
Gwenn Flowers, (D), British Columbia, 2000, Gl
H. Daniel (Dan) Gibson, (D), Carleton, 2003, GcCcGp
James A. Mac Eachern, (D), Alberta, 1994, Gs
Dan D. Marshall, (D), Lausanne, 1995, Ca
Douglas Stead, (D), Nottingham (UK), 1984, Ng
Derek J. Thorkelson, (D), Carleton, 1992, Gt
Brent C. Ward, (D), Alberta, 1992, GlmGe
Glyn Williams-Jones, (D), Open (UK), 2001, GvCeYe
Associate Professor:
Dirk Kirste, (D), Calgary, 2001, Cg
Assistant Professor:
Jessica Pilarczyk
Lecturer:
Kevin Cameron, (M), Memorial, 1986, Gg
Roberta Donald, (M), British Columbia, 1984, GsZe
Cindy Hansen
Emeritus:
John J. Clague, (D), British Columbia, 1973, Gl

Universite du Quebec

INRS, centre Eau Terre Environnement (Quebec Geoscience Center) (M,D) ☒ (2019)
490 de la Couronne
Quebec, QC G1K 9A9
p. + (418) 654-4677
info@ete.inrs.ca
http://www.ete.inrs.ca
Programs: PhD in Earth sciences, Master's in Earth Sciences, Professional Master's in Earth Sciences
Professor:
Normand Bergeron, (D), SUNY (Buffalo), 1994, Gm
Monique Bernier, (D), Zr
Fateh Chebana, Hq
Karem Chokmani, Zi
Pierre Francus, (D), 1997, PeGse
Bernard Giroux, Yeg
Erwan Gloaguen, Ye
Lyal B. Harris, GcYg
Marc R. LaFleche, (D), Montpellier II, 1991, Ct
Rene Lefebvre, (D), Laval, 1994, Hw
Richard Martel, (D), Laval, 1996, Hw
Claudio Paniconi, (D), Hw
Pierre-Simon Ross, GvEg
Senior Scientist:
Jean H. Bedard, (D), Montreal, 1985, Gi
Christian Begin, (D), Laval, 1991, PeGmSo
Benoit Dube, (D), Quebec, 1990, Em
Denis Lavoie, (D), Laval, 1988, Gs
Yves Michaud, (D), Laval, 1991, Gm
Michel Parent, (D), W Ontario, 1987, Gl
Didier Henri Perret, (D), Laval, 1995, NgeZu
Research Associate:
Eric Boisvert, (M), Quebec (Montreal), 1994, Zn
Kathleen Lauziere, (M), Quebec, 1989, Gg
Marc R. Luzincourt, (B), Quebec (Montreal), 1982, Cs
Anna Smirnov, (M), Memorial, 1997, Cs
Adjunct Professor:
Geneviève Bordeleau, (D), INRS, Hw
Louise Corriveau, (D), McGill, 1989, EmGpg
Saied Homayouni, (D), Zrf
Damien Pham van Bang, (D), HtOn
Jasmin Raymond, (D), Hy
Renaud Soucy de la Roche, (D), Gc

Universite du Quebec a Chicoutimi

Sciences de la Terre (B,M,D) ●☒ (2019)
555, Boulevard de l'Universite
Chicoutimi, QC G7H 2B1
p. (418) -545- 5011 (Ext. 5202)
sue_sc-terre@uqac.ca
Programs: B.Sc Geology, B.Sc. geological engineering, M.Sc. Earth science and geological engineering, M. Sc. Professional, exploration geology, Ph.D. Earth sciences
Enrollment (2018): B: 55 (13) M: 34 (8) D: 6 (1)
Professor:
Sarah- Jane Barnes, (D), Toronto, 1983, EgGiCt
Paul Bedard, (D), Quebec, 1992, CaGzEg
Romain Chesnaux, (D), École Polytechnique (Canada), 2005, Hw
Damien Gaboury, (D), Quebec, 1999, EmCe
Ali Saeidi, (D), Lorraine INP (France), 2010, Nrm
Edward W. Sawyer, (D), Toronto, 1983, GptGi
Julien Walter, (D), Quebec, 2018, HwqGm
Assistant Professor:
Lucie Mattieu, (D), Trinity (Dublin), 2010, EgmCe
Research Associate:
Silvain Rafini, (D), Quebec (Montreal), 2008, GcHwEg
Instructor:
Denis Cote, (M), Quebec, 1986, GiEgZi
Lecturer:
Dominique Genna, (D), Quebec, 2009, GvEn
Philippe Page, (D), INRS-ETE, 2006, GiCgEm
Adjunct Professor:
Sylvain Raffini, (D), Quebec (Montreal), 2008, GcHw
Emeritus:
Guy Archambault, (D), Nr
Pierre Cousineau, (D), Laval, 1986, Gd
Jayanta Guha, (D), Jadavpur, 1967, Eg
Michael D. Higgins, (D), McGill, 1980, Gi
Alain Rouleau, (D), Waterloo, 1984, Hw
Denis W. Roy, (D), Princeton, 1976, Gc
On Leave:
Real Daigneault, (D), Laval, 1991, GcEgZi
Laboratory Director:
Dany Savard, (M), Quebec, 2010, Ca

Universite du Quebec a Montreal

Département des sciences de la Terre et de l'atmosphere (B,M,D) (2015)
C.P. 8888, succursale Centre-ville
Montreal, QC H3C 3P8
p. +1 514-987-3000
dept.sct@uqam.ca
http://scta.uqam.ca
Administrative Assistant: France Beauchemin
Professor:
Florent Barbecot, (D), Hw
Jean-Pierre Blanchet, (D), Toronto, 1984, Pe
Gilles Couture, (D), British Columbia, 1987, Yg
Fiona Ann Darbyshire, (D), Cambridge, 2000, Ys
Anne de Vernal, (D), Montreal, 1986, Pm
Alessandro Marco Forte, (D), Toronto, 1989, Yg
Pierre Gauthier, (D), McGill, 1988, Am
Eric Girard, (D), McGill, 1999, Am
Normand Goulet, (D), Queen's, 1976, Gc
Cherif Hamzaoui, (D), Alziers, 1980, Yg
Alfred Jaouich, (D), Minnesota, 1975, Sc
Michel Jebrak, (D), Orleans (France), 1984, Eg
Michel Lamothe, (D), W Ontario, 1985, Gl
Rene Laprise, (D), Toronto, 1988, As
Marie Larocque, (D), de Poitiers (France), 1998, Hw
Marc Michel Lucotte, (D), McGill, 1987, Oc

CANADA

Daniele Luigi Pinti, (D), France, 1993, Cs
Martin Roy, (D), Oregon, 1998, Gl
Ross Stevenson, (D), Arizona, 1989, Cg
Laxmi Sushama, (D), Melbourne (Australia), 1999, Hy
Julie Mireille Thériault, (D), McGill, 2009, Zn
Enrico Torlaschi, (D), Ecole Polytechnique (Milan), 1976, Am
Alain Tremblay, (D), Laval, 1989, Gct
David Widory, (D), IPGP, 1999, Cs

Associate Professor:
Sanda Balescu, (D), Free (Brussels), 1988, Pe
Jean Côté, As
Bernard Dugas, As
Stephane Faure, (D), INRS-Georessources, 1995, Gc
Philippe Gachon, (D), Quebec (Montreal), 1999, As
Michel Gauthier, (D), Polytechnique (Montreal), 1982, Eg
Jean-François Helie, (D), Quebec, 2004, Cs
Claude Hillaire-Marcel, (D), Paris VI, 1979, Cs
Jean-Claude Mareschal, (D), Texas A&M, 1975, Yg
Andre Poirier, (D), Quebec (Montreal), 2005, Cs
Gilbert P. Prichonnet, (D), Bordeaux, 1967, Pi
William W. Shilts
Gabriel-Constantin Voicu, (D), Quebec (Montreal), 1995, GcCg

Universite du Quebec a Rimouski

Inst des sciences de la mer de Rimouski (M,D) (2015)
310, Allee des Ursulines
Rimouski, QC G5L 3A1
p. (418) 723- 8617
andre_rochon@qc.ca
http://www.ismer.ca

Director:
Serge Demers, (D), Laval, 1981, Ob

Professor:
Celine Audet, (D), Laval, 1985, Ob
Jean-Claude Brethes, (D), Aix-Marseille, 1978, Ob
Jean-Pierre Gagne, (D), Montreal, 1993, OcCmo
Michel Gosselin, (D), Laval, 1990, Ob
Vladimir G. Koutitonsky, (D), SUNY (Stony Brook), 1985, Op
Jocelyne Pellerin, (D), Laval, 1982, Ob
Emilien Pelletier, (D), McGill, 1983, Oc
Suzanne Roy, (D), Dalhousie, 1986, Ob
Bjorn Sundby, (D), Bergen (Norway), 1966, Oc
Bruno Zakardjian, (D), Paris, 1994, Ob

Universite Laval

Dept de geologie (B,M,D) (2015)
Pavillon Pouliot
Faculte des Sciences et de genie
Ste-Foy, QC G1K 7P4
p. (418) 656-2193
marc.constantin@ggl.ulaval.ca
http://www.ggl.ulaval.ca

Head:
Marc Constantin, (D), Brest, 1995, Gi
Josee Duchesne, (D), Laval, 1993, Gz

Professor:
Georges Beaudoin, (D), Ottawa, 1991, EgGzCa
Richard Fortier, (D), Montreal, 1994, Yg
Paul W. Glover, (D), E Anglia (UK), 1989, Yx
Rejean J. Hebert, (D), Brest, 1985, Gi
Jacques E. Locat, (D), Sherbrooke, 1982, Ng
Fritz Neuweiler, (D), Berlin, 1995, GsdPg
Rene Therrien, (D), Waterloo, 1992, HwGe

Eletron Microprobe Specialist:
Marc Choquette, (D), Laval, 1988, Zn

Associate Scientist:
Pauline Dansereau, (M), Laval, 1988, Gs
Andre Levesque, (B), Laval, 1979, Gz
Pierre Therrien, (M), Laval, 1986, Gq

Research Associate:
Danielle Cloutier, (D), Laval, GeOg

Adjunct Professor:
Benoit Fournier, (D), Laval, 1993, NgZmGg

Technician:
Jean Frenette, (B), Laval, 1985, Gz
Martin Plante, Cg

University of Alberta

Dept of Earth & Atmospheric Sciences (B,M,D) ●☒ (2018)
1-26 Earth Sciences Building
Edmonton, AB T6G 2E3
p. (780) 492-3265
eas@ualberta.ca
http://www.ualberta.ca/EAS/
f: https://www.facebook.com/UofAEarthandAtmosphericSciences-esDepartment
t: @UofA_EAS
Programs: Geology, Environmental Earth Sciences, Human Geography, Urban and Regional Planning, Paleontology
Enrollment (2016): B: 449 (129) M: 0 (17) D: 0 (18)

Chair:
Stephen T. Johnston, (D), Alberta, 1993, GctGg

Professor & Inaugural Director, Planning Program:
Sandeep Agrawal, (D), Zu

Professor:
Robert W. Luth, (D), California (Los Angeles), 1985, Gi
Martin J. Sharp, (D), Aberdeen, 1982, Gl

Canada Research Chair:
Thomas Stachel, (D), Wurzburg, 1991, GiCs

Associate Dean (Research):
Larry M. Heaman, (D), McMaster, 1986, Cc

Associate Chair:
Murray Gingras, (D), North Carolina, 1987, Go
Kurt Konhauser, (D), W Ontario, 1993, Pg

Professor:
Andrew B.G Bush, (D), Toronto, 1995, AsOpPe
Michael W. Caldwell, (D), McGill, 1995, Pv
Octavian Catuneanu, (D), Toronto, 1996, Gs
Thomas Chacko, (D), N Carolina, 1987, Gp
Robert A. Creaser, (D), La Trobe, 1990, Cc
Philippe Erdmer, (D), Queen's, 1982, Gc
Duane Froese, (D), Calgary, 2001, GlmPe
John Gamon, (D), California (Davis), 1989, Zr
Christopher DK Herd, (D), New Mexico, 2001, XcGiCp
Brian Jones, (D), Ottawa, 1974, Ps
Lindsey Leighton, (D), Michigan, 1999, Pi
Hans G. Machel, (D), McGill, 1985, Go
Karlis Muehlenbachs, (D), Chicago, 1971, Cs
Graham Pearson, (D), Leeds (UK), Cec
David Potter, (D), Newcastle upon Tyne, Ye
Gerhard Reuter, (D), McGill, 1985, Am
Benoit Rivard, (D), Washington (St Louis), 1990, Zr
Benjamin J. Rostron, (D), Alberta, 1995, HwGoCg
G. Arturo Sanchez-Azofeifa, (D), New Hampshire, 1996, ZirZg
Bruce Sutherland, (D), Toronto, 1994, Cm
Martyn Unsworth, (D), Cambridge, GtvYe
John W.F Waldron, (D), Edinburgh, 1981, Gc
John D. Wilson, (D), Guelph, 1980, Am
John-Paul Zonneveld, (D), Alberta, 1999, Go

Associate Chair:
Tara McGee, (D), Australian Nat, 1996, Zn

Associate Professor:
Damian Collins, (D), Simon Fraser, 2004, Zn
Theresa D. Garvin, (D), McMaster, 1999, Zn
Nicholas Harris, (D), Stanford, Gso
Jeffrey Kavanaugh, (D), British Columbia, 2001, Ng
Paul Myers, (D), Victoria, 1996, Og

Assistant Professor:
Daniel S. Alessi, (D), Notre Dame, 2009, ClGeHw
Jeff Birchall, (D), Canterbury (NZ), 2013, ZuyZg
Monireh Faramarzi, (D), ETH (Switzerland), 2010, HgwHq
Long Li, (D), Lehigh, 2006, CsGpv
Manish Shirgaokar, (D), Zu
Amrita Singh, (D), California (Irvine), 2015, Zu

Distinguished University Professor:
Nathaniel W. Rutter, (D), Alberta, 1966, Ge

Emeritus:
Ronald A. Burwash, (D), Minnesota, 1955, Gp
Ian A. Campbell, (D), Colorado, 1968, Gm
Brian D. Chatterton, (D), Australian Nat, 1970, Pi
David M. Cruden, (D), London (UK), 1969, Nr
John England, (D), Colorado, 1974, Gml
Leszek A. Kosinski, (D), Warsaw, 1958, Zn
Arleigh H. Laycock, (D), Minnesota, 1957, Hg
Edward P. Lozowski, (D), Toronto, 1970, As
Carl A. Mendoza, (D), Waterloo, 1993, HwSpHq

O.F. George Sitwell, (D), Toronto, 1968, Zn
Peter J. Smith, (D), Edinburgh, 1964, Zn
József Tóth, (D), Utrecht, 1965, Hw
Related Staff:
Robert Summers, (D), Guelph, 2005, Zn

Inst of Geophysical Research (B,M,D) (2015)
Mailstop #615
CEB/Physics
Edmonton, AB T6G 2G7
p. (780) 492-3521
msacchi@ualberta.ca
http://www-geo.phys.ualberta.ca/institute/
Administrative Assistant: Lee Grimard
Professor:
Robert A. Creaser, (D), La Trobe, 1992, Cc
T. Bryant Moodie, (D), Toronto, 1972, Zn
Robert Rankin, (D), North Wales, 1984, Xy
Gerhard W. Reuter, (D), McGill, 1985, As
Wojciech Rozmus, (D), Inst Nuc Res (Poland), Zn
John C. Samson, (D), Alberta, 1971, Xy
Martin J. Sharp, (D), Aberdeen, Gl
John Shaw, (D), Reading (UK), 1969, Gl
Samuel S. Shen, (D), Wisconsin, As
Bruce R. Sutherland, (D), Toronto, 1994, Zn
Gordon E. Swaters, (D), British Columbia, 1985, Op
Richard D. Sydora, (D), Texas, 1985, Xy
Martyn Unsworth, (D), Cambridge, Zn
John D. Wilson, (D), Guelph, 1980, As
Associate Professor:
Andrew B. G. Bush, (D), Toronto, As
Carl Mendoza, (D), Waterloo, 1993, Hw
Benoit Rivard, (D), Washington, 1990, Zr
Ben Rostron, (D), Alberta, Zn
Mauricio D. Sacchi, (D), British Columbia, Ys
Assistant Professor:
Francis Fenrich, (D), Alberta, 1997, Xy
Jeff Gu, (D), Harvard, 2001, Ys
Moritz Heimpel, (D), Johns Hopkins, 1995, Zn
Vadim Kravchinsky, (D), Irkutsk, 1996, Ym
Paul Myers, (D), Victoria, 1992, Op
Emeritus:
Michael E. Evans, (D), Australian Nat, 1969, Ym
Keith D. Hage, (D), Chicago, 1957, As
F. Walter Jones, (D), McGill, 1968, Ym
Edward P. Lozowski, (D), Toronto, 1970, As
Roger D. Morton, (D), Nottingham (UK), 1959, Em
Edo Nyland, (D), California (Los Angeles), 1967, Ys
David Rankin, (D), Alberta, 1960, Ym
Gordon Rostoker, (D), British Columbia, 1966, Xy
T.J.T (Tim) Spanos, (D), Alberta, 1977, YgsEo

University of British Columbia

Dept of Earth, Ocean, and Atmospheric Sciences (B,M,D) O (2015)
2020-2207 Main Mall
Vancouver, BC V6T 1Z4
p. (604) 827-5284
acairns@eos.ubc.ca
http://www.eoas.ubc.ca
Enrollment (2010): B: 361 (105) M: 111 (20) D: 93 (15)
Director, Geological Engineering Program:
Roger D. Beckie, (D), Princeton, 1992, HwCl
Honorary Professor:
Mati Raudsepp, (D), Manitoba, 1984, GzeZm
Dean, Science:
Simon M. Peacock, (D), California (Los Angeles), 1985, GtpYs
Canada Research Chair:
Roger Francois, (D), British Columbia, 1987, Cm
Dominique A.M. Weis, (D), Free (Brussels), 1982, CaGeCu
Professor:
Susan E. Allen, (D), Cambridge, 1988, Op
Raymond J. Andersen, (D), California (San Diego), 1975, Oc
Neil Balmforth, (D), Cambridge, 1990, As
Michael G. Bostock, (D), Australian Nat, 1991, YsGt
R. Marc Bustin, (D), British Columbia, 1979, Ec
Gregory M. Dipple, (D), Johns Hopkins, 1991, Gp
Erik Eberhardt, (D), Saskatchewan, 1998, Ng
Lee A. Groat, (D), Manitoba, 1988, GzEg
Oldrich Hungr, (D), Alberta, 1981, Gm
Mark Jellinek, (D), Australian Nat, 1999, Gg
Catherine L. Johnson, (D), California (San Diego), 1994
Ulrich Mayer, (D), Waterloo, 1999, Nm
James K. Mortensen, (D), California (Santa Barbara), 1983, Cc
Douglas W. Oldenburg, (D), California (Santa Barbara), 1974, Yg
Evgeny Pakhomov, (D), Russian Acad of Sci, 1992, Ob
James Kelly Russell, (D), Calgary, 1984, GviCg
James S. Scoates, (D), Wyoming, 1994, GizGv
Paul L. Smith, (D), McMaster, 1981, Pg
Douw G. Steyn, (D), British Columbia, 1980, Asm
Roland B. Stull, (D), Washington, 1975, As
Curtis Suttle, (D), British Columbia, 1987, Ob
NSERC Industrial Research Chair in Computational Geoscience:
Eldad Haber, (D), British Columbia, 1997, YgZn
Director, MDRU:
Craig J.R. Hart, (D), W Australia, 2004, EmGiCc
Canada Research Chair:
Maria Maldonado, (D), McGill, 1999, Ob
Christian Schoof, (D), Oxford, 2002, Gl
Associate Professor:
Philip Austin, (D), Washington, 1987, As
Kurt A. Grimm, (D), California (Santa Cruz), 1992, Gs
Mark S. Johnson, (D), Cornell, 2005, SpHsq
Lori Kennedy, (D), Texas A&M, 1996, Gc
Maya G. Kopylova, (D), Moscow (Russia), 1990, Gi
Kristin J. Orians, (D), California (Santa Cruz), 1988, Cm
Richard A. Pawlowicz, (D), MIT/WHOI, 1994, Op
Philippe Tortell, (D), Princeton, 2001, Ob
Assistant Professor:
Kenneth A. Hickey, (D), James Cook, 1995, EgGcg
Valentina Radic, (D), Alaska (Fairbanks), 2008, GlAsZg
Honorary Research Associate:
Kevin Kingdon, (M), British Columbia, 1998, Yg
Michael Maxwell, (D), British Columbia, 1986, Yg
Research Associate:
Thomas Bissig, (D), Queens, 2001, EmCg
Farhad Bouzari, (D), Queens, 2003, Eg
Amanda Bustin, (D), Victoria, 2006, YgNg
Philip T. Hammer, (D), California (San Diego), 1991, Ys
Brian Hunt, (D), Tasmania, 2005, Ob
Bruno Kieffer, (D), Grenoble, 2002, Cs
Henryk Modzelewski, (D), British Columbia, 2004, As
Roger Pieters, (D), California (Santa Barbara), Op
Lin-Ping Song, (D), Sichuan (China), 1996, Ng
Dave E. Williams, (D), British Columbia, 1987, Oc
Instructor:
Brett H. Gilley, (M), Simon Fraser, 2003, GsZeRn
Sara Harris, (D), Oregon State, 1998, Ou
Tara Ivanochko, (D), British Columbia, 2004, OoZce
Stuart Sutherland, (D), Leicester (UK), 1992, Pg
Lecturer:
Francis H. M. Jones, (M), British Columbia, 1987, YeZe
Honorary Lecturer:
Dileep Athaide, (M), British Columbia, 1975, Gg
Adjunct Professor:
Robert G. Anderson, (D), Carleton, 1983, Gt
Stephen Billings, (D), Sydney, 1998, Yg
Alex Cannon, (D), British Columbia, 2009, As
Edward Carmack, (D), Washington, 1972, Op
Michael G. G. Foreman, (D), British Columbia, 1984, Op
James Haggart, (D), California (Davis), 1984, PgGr
Catherine J. Hickson, (D), British Columbia, 1987, EgGvZe
Mark Holzer, (D), Simon Fraser, 1990, As
R. Lynn Kirlin, (D), Utah State, 1968, As
Doug McCollor, (D), British Columbia, 2008, Asm
Barry Narod, (D), British Columbia, 1979, Yx
Michael Orchard, (D), Hull, 1975, PgGg
K. Wayne Savigny, (D), Alberta, 1980, Ng
Barbara H. Scott Smith, (D), Edinburgh, 1977, Gz
John F. H. Thompson, (D), Toronto, 1984, Em
Richard E. Thomson, (D), British Columbia, 1971, Op
Richard Tosdal, (D), California (Santa Barbara), 1988, Em
Knut von Salzen, (D), Hamburg, 1997, As
Chi S. Wong, (D), California (San Diego), 1968, Cm
Emeritus:
Mary Lou Bevier, (D), California (Santa Barbara), 1982
Peter M. Bradshaw, (D), Durham (UK), 1965, EgCeGe

Stephen E. Calvert, (D), California (San Diego), 1964, Cm
Richard L. Chase, (D), Princeton, 1963, Gu
Garry K. C. Clarke, (D), Toronto, 1967, Yg
Ronald M. Clowes, (D), Alberta, 1969, Ys
Robert M. Ellis, (D), Alberta, 1964, Ys
William K. Fletcher, (D), Imperial Coll (UK), 1968, Ce
Michael Healey, (D), Aberdeen, 1969, Ob
William W. Hsieh, (D), British Columbia, 1981, OpAs
Alan G. Lewis, (D), Hawaii, 1961, Ob
Stephen G. Pond, (D), British Columbia, 1965, Op
R. Doncaster Russell, (D), Toronto, 1954, Yg
Alastair J. Sinclair, (D), British Columbia, 1964, EmGg
J. Leslie Smith, (D), British Columbia, 1978, Hw
Frank J. R. Taylor, (D), Cape Town, 1965, Ob

Undergraduate Program Coordinator:
Teresa Woodley, Zn
Secretary to the Head:
Selene Chan, (B), British Columbia, 1995, Zn
Office Support:
Alicia Warkentin, Zn
Human Resources Manager:
Cary Thomson, Zn
Graduate Coordinator:
Audrey Van Slyck
Finance Clerk:
Anita Lam, Zn
Kathy Scott, Zn
Director of Resources and Operations:
Renee Haggart, Zn
Computer Department Manager:
John Amor, Zn

Soil Science (B,M,D) O✓ (2018)
2357 Main Mall
Vancouver, BC V6T 1Z4
p. (604) 822-0252
maja.krzic@ubc.ca
http://www.landfood.ubc.ca/academics/graduate/soil-science-msc-phd/
Programs: Soil Science
Enrollment (2018): B: 4 (4) M: 9 (5) D: 11 (1)

Professor:
T. Andrew Black, (D), Wisconsin, 1969, Sp
Christopher Chanway, (D), British Columbia, 1987, Sb
Sue Grayston, (D), Sheffield, 1988, Sb
Cindy Prescott, (D), Calgary, 1988, Sb
Suzanne Simard, (D), Oregon State, 1995, Sb
Associate Professor:
Maja Krzic, (D), British Columbia, 1997, Sf
Assistant Professor:
Sean Smukler, (D), California (Davis), 2008, So
Instructor:
Sandra Brown, (D), British Columbia, 1997, Sp
Emeritus:
Arthur A. Bomke, (D), Illinois, 1972, Sc
Leslie M. Lavkulich, (D), Cornell, 1969, Sd
Hans D. Schreier, (D), British Columbia, 1976, Zg

University of British Columbia, Okanagan Campus

Earth, Environmental and Geographic Sciences ●☒ (2020)
Science 305
1177 Research Road
Kelowna, BC V1V 1V7
p. (250) 807-8757
eegs.okanagan@ubc.ca
https://eegs.ok.ubc.ca/
Programs: Earth and Environmental Sciences
Freshwater Science
Geography
Minor in Geospatial Information Science
Administrative Assistant: Janet Heisler, Christina Morris

Head:
Edward RC Hornibrook, (D), W Ontario, 1997, CbsSc
Forest Renewal BC Chair of Watershed Research:
Xiaohua (Adam) Wei, (D), Northeast Forestry, 1990, HqgSf
Associate Dean, Research, Graduate and Post-doctoral Studies; Director Okanagan Institute for Biodiversity, Resilience, and Ecosystem Services:
Lael Parrot, (D), McGill, 2000, ZgiZf
Professor:
Bernard O. Bauer, (D), Johns Hopkins, 1988, GmOnZy
John D. Greenough, (D), Memorial, 1984, GiCtGa
Ian R. Walker, (D), Simon Fraser, 1988, PeGnHs
Forest Renewal BC Chair of Watershed Research:
David F. Scott, (D), KwaZulu-Natal, 1994, SpHgs
Director, Fipke Laboratory for Trace Element Research:
Kyle Larson, (D), Queens, 2009, GtpCc
Associate Head; Associate Professor of Teaching:
Craig F. Nichol, (D), British Columbia, 2002, HwSpZe
Associate Dean Undergraduate Recruitment, Services, and Success; Associate Professor of Teaching:
Trudy A. Kavanagh, (D), W Ontario, 2000, ZyRcZg
Associate Professor:
Yuan Chen, (D), W Ontario, 1993, EmCeGz
P. Jefferson Curtis, (D), Manitoba, 1991, CbHsRw
Kevin Hanna, (D), Toronto, 1998, ZnRcZu
Michael Pidwirny, (D), Simon Fraser, 1994, AtZyc
Ian Saunders, (D), Simon Fraser, 1990, AtGlZy
Robert R. Young, (D), Calgary, 1995, GlmZy
Assistant Professor:
Mathieu L. Bourbonnais, (D), Victoria, 2018, ZifRn
Emeritus:
Fes De Scally, (D), Waterloo, 1989, RnZyRm
Watershed Management Extension Facilitator:
Marni Turek, (B), Thomson Rivers, 1998, Hg
Laboratory Program Manager:
Stuart J. MacKinnon, (M), Victoria, 2016, ZeRcZg

University of Calgary

Dept of Geoscience (B,M,D) ●☒ (2020)
2500 University Drive NW
ES118
Calgary, AB T2N 1N4
p. (403) 220-5184
geoscience@ucalgary.ca
https://www.geoscience.ucalgary.ca
Programs: BSc Geology Major, BSc Geology Major (Petroleum Geology Concentration), BSc Geology Major Hydrogeology-Environmental Geoscience), BSc Geology Major (Solid Earth), BSc Geophysics Major
Enrollment (2020): M: 78 (7) D: 64 (3)

Acting Head:
Stephen M. Hubbard, (D), Stanford, 2006, Gs
Professor:
Benoit Beauchamp, (D), Calgary, 1987, Pm
Christopher Clarkson, (D), British Columbia, 1998, Eo
David Eaton, (D), Calgary, 1992, Ys
Masaki Hayashi, (D), Waterloo, 1997, HwSp
Charles M. Henderson, (D), Calgary, 1988, Pm
Kristopher Innanen, (D), British Columbia, 2003, Ye
Stephen Larter, (D), Newcastle (UK), 1978
Donald C. Lawton, (D), Auckland, 1979, Ye
David R. Pattison, (D), Edinburgh, 1985, Gp
Cathy Ryan, (D), Waterloo, 1994, Hw
Associate Professor:
Robert Ferguson, (D), Calgary, 2000, Ye
Alan R. Hildebrand, (D), Arizona, 1992, XmgXc
Per Pedersen, (D), Aarhus (Denmark), 1999, Go
Assistant Professor:
Sytle Antao, (D), Stoney Brook, 2006, Gz
Jan Dettmer, (D), Victoria (Australia), 2007, Ys
Eva Enkelmann, (D), 2005, CcGmt
Hersh Gilbert, (D), Colorado, 2001, Ys
Rachel Lauer, (D), Penn State, 2013, Hy
Darla Zelenitsky, (D), Calgary, 2004, Pg
Adjunct Professor:
Stephen E. Grasby, (D), Calgary, 1997, Hw
Thomas F. Moslow, (D), South Carolina, 1980, Co
Senior Instructor:
Jon W. Jones, (D), Calgary, 1972, Gp
Emeritus:
Laurence R. Bentley, (D), Princeton, 1990, Hw
Frederick A. Cook, (D), Cornell, 1980, YeGtYs
Edward D. Ghent, (D), California, 1964, Gp
Terence M. Gordon, (D), Princeton, 1969, Gq

Ian E. Hutcheon, (D), Carleton, 1977, Cl
Federico F. Krause, (D), Calgary, 1979, GsdGo
Edward S. Krebes, (D), Alberta, 1980, Ys
Gary F. Margrave, (D), Alberta, 1981, Ye
James W. Nicholls, (D), California, 1969, Gi
Gerald D. Osborn, (D), California, 1972, Gm
Philip S. Simony, (D), London (UK), 1963, Gc
Ronald J. Spencer, (D), Johns Hopkins, 1981, Cg
Deborah A. Spratt, (D), Johns Hopkins, 1980, Gc
Norman C. Wardlaw, (D), Glasgow, 1960, Go

Interim Dean, Faculty of Sciece:
Bernhard Mayer, (D), LMU Munich, 1993, CslGe

University of Guelph

School of Environmental Sciences (B,M,D) (2015)
Guelph, ON N1G 2W1
p. (519) 824-2052
earnaud@uoguelph.ca
http://www.ses.uoguelph.ca

Director:
Jonathan Newman, (D), Albany, 1990, Zn

Director, Controlled Environment Systems Research Facility:
Michael Dixon, (D), Edinburgh, Zn

Canada Research Chair in Recombinant Antibody Technology:
Christopher C. Hall, (D), Alberta, Zn

Canada Research Chair in Microbial Ecology:
Kari Dunfield, (D), Saskatchewan, 2002, SbZn

Associate Dean, Research, OAC:
Beverley A. Hale, (D), Guelph, 1989, Ct

Associate Dean, Academics, OAC:
Jonathan Schmidt, (D), Toronto, Zn

Professor:
Paul Goodwin, (D), California (Davis), Zn
Andrew Gordon, (D), Alaska (Fairbanks), 1984, Zn
Ernesto Guzman, (D), California (Davis), Zn
Tom Hsiang, (D), Washington, Zn
Hung Lee, (D), McGill, Zn
Stephen Marshall, (D), Guelph, Zn
Gard Otis, (D), Kansas, Zn
Cynthia Scott-Dupree, (D), Simon Fraser, 1986, Zn
Jack Trevors, (D), Waterloo, Zn
R. Paul Voroney, (D), Saskatchewan, 1983, Sb
Claudia Wagner Riddle, (D), Guelph, 1992, Am

Director of the Arboretum:
Shelley Hunt, (D), Guelph, Zn

Dean, OAC:
Rob J. Gordon, (D), Guelph, As

Associate Professor:
Madhur Anand, (D), W Ontario, Zn
Emmanuelle Arnaud, (D), McMaster, 2002, Gls
Susan Glasauer, (D), Tech (Munich), 1995, Pg
Marc Habash, (D), Guelph, Zn
Rebecca Hallett, (D), Simon Fraser, Zn
Richard Heck, (D), Saskatchewan, Sd
John Lauzon, (D), Guelph, So
Ivan O'Halloran, (D), Saskatchewan, 1986, So
Paul Sibley, (D), Waterloo, Zn
Jon Warland, (D), Guelph, 1999, As

Assistant Professor:
Tim Rennie, Zn
Laura Van Eerd, (D), Guelph, Zn
Alan Watson, (M), Guelph, Zn

Instructor:
Neil Rooney, (D), McGill, Zn

Adjunct Professor:
Gary Parkin, (D), Guelph, 1994, HwSp

Emeritus:
George Barron, (D), Iowa State, Zn
Greg J. Boland, (D), Guelph, Zn
Ward Chesworth, (D), McMaster, 1967, ClGe
Les J. Evans, (D), Wales, 1974, Cl
Austin Fletcher, (D), Alberta, Zn
Terry J. Gillespie, (D), Guelph, 1968, Am
Michael J. Goss, (D), Reading (UK), So
Pieter H. Groenevelt, (D), Wageningen (Neth), 1969, Sp
Robert Hall, (D), Melbourne (Australia), Zn
Stewart G. Hilts, (D), Toronto, 1981, Zn
Peter Kevan, (D), Alberta, Zn
Kenneth M. King, (D), Wisconsin, 1956, As
I. Peter Martini, (D), McMaster, 1966, Gsl
Raymond G. McBride, (D), Guelph, 1982, So
Murray H. Miller, (D), Purdue, 1957, So
Kaushik Narinder, Zn
Leonard Ritter, Zn
Keith Solomon, (D), Illinois, Zn
Gerry Stephenson, Zn
George W. Thurtell, (D), Wisconsin, 1965, As
H. Peter Van Straaten, (D), Goettingen (Germany), 1974, EnScCb

University of Lethbridge

Dept of Geography (B,M) (2015)
4401 University Drive
Lethbridge, AB T1K 3M4
p. (403) 329-2225
geography.chair@uleth.ca
http://home.uleth.ca/geo
Administrative Assistant: Margaret Cook

Professor:
Walter E. Aufrecht, (D), Toronto, Zn
Rene W. Barendregt, (D), Queen's (Canada), 1977, Gm
Robert J. Rogerson, (D), Macquarie, 1979, Gm

Associate Professor:
James M. Byrne, (D), Alberta, 1990, Hg
Hester Jiskoot, (D), Leeds (UK), 2000, GlmZy
Thomas Johnston, (D), Waterloo, 1988, Ze
Derek R. Peddle, (D), Waterloo, 1997, Zr

Assistant Professor:
Craig Coburn, (D), Simon Fraser, 2002, Zy
Susan Dakin, (D), Waterloo, 2000, Ze
Stefan Kienzle, (D), Heidelberg, 1993, Zi
Ivan Townshend, (D), Calgary, 1997, Zn
Wei Xu, (D), Guelph, 1998, Zi

Adjunct Professor:
John Dormaar, (D), Alberta, 1961, So
Ron Hall, Zn
Larry Herr, (D), Zn
Daniel L. Johnson, (D), British Columbia, 1983, Zn
Pano George Karkanis, (D), Uppsala, 1966, So
Ross McKenzie, (D), Zn
Anne Smith, (D)
Derald Smith, (D), Zn

Emeritus:
Roy J. Fletcher, (D), Clark, 1968, As
Ian R. MacLachlan, (D), Toronto, 1990, Ze

University of Manitoba

Geological Sciences (B,M,D) O⊘ (2020)
240 Wallace Building
125 Dysart Road
Winnipeg, MB R3T 2N2
p. (204) 474-9371
alfredo.camacho@umanitoba.ca
http://www.umanitoba.ca/geoscience
Administrative Assistant: Brenda Miller
Enrollment (2014): M: 12 (3) D: 8 (2)

Professor:
Anton Chakhmouradian, (D), St Petersburg State (Russia), 1997, GziCg
Nancy Chow, (D), Memorial, 1986, Gs
Robert J. Elias, (D), Cincinnati, 1979, Pi
Mostafa Fayek, (D), Saskatchewan, 1996, Cs
Ian J. Ferguson, (D), Australian Nat, 1988, YemYu
Andrew Frederiksen, (D), British Columbia, 2001, YsGt
Norman M. Halden, (D), Glasgow, 1983, Cg
Frank C. Hawthorne, (D), McMaster, 1973, Gz
William M. Last, (D), Manitoba, 1980, GsnGo
Soren Rysgaard, (D), Aarhus (Denmark), 1995, Gl
Elena Sokolova, (D), Moscow (Russia), 1980, Gz

Senior Scholar:
George S. Clark, (D), Columbia, 1967, Cc
Barbara L. Sherriff, (D), McMaster, 1988, Gz
Allan C. Turnock, (D), Johns Hopkins, 1960, Gp

Associate Professor:
Alfredo Camacho, (D), Australian Nat, 1998, Gt

Assistant Professor:
Genevieve Ali, (D), Montreal, 2010, Hw
Zou Zou Kuzyk, (D), Manitoba, 2009, Cg

Research Associate:
Yassir Abdu, (D), Uppsala, 2004, Gz
Instructor:
Karen Ferreira, (M)
William S. Mandziuk, (M), Manitoba, 1989, Gg
Jeffrey Young, (M), Manitoba, 1992, GcZe
Adjunct Professor:
Scott Anderson, (D), Dalhousie, 1998
Christian Bohm, (D), ETH (Switzerland), 1996, Cg
William Buhay
David Corrigan, (D), Carleton, Gt
Jody Deming, (D), Maryland, 1981, Zn
Michel Houle, (D), Laurentian, 2008, Gv
Brooke Milne, (D), Ga
Vince Palace, (D), Manitoba, 1996
James Reist, (D), Toronto, 1983
Graham A. Young, (D), New Brunswick, 1988, Pi
Emeritus:
William C. Brisbin, (D), California (Los Angeles), 1970, Gc
Robert B. Ferguson, (D), Toronto, 1948, Gz
Wooil M. Moon, (D), British Columbia, 1976, ZrYnOp
James T. Teller, (D), Cincinnati, 1970, Gs
Related Staff:
Neil Ball, (B), Manitoba, 1982, Gz
Laura Bergen, (M), Manitoba, 2013
Mark Cooper, (M), Manitoba, 1997, Gz
Mulu Serzu, (D), Manitoba, 1990, Yg
Ryan Sharpe, (M), Manitoba, 2012
Ravinder Sidhu
Panseok Yang, (D), Memorial, 2002, CaGp
Misuk Yun, (M), Manitoba, 1986, Cs

University of New Brunswick

Dept of Earth Sciences (B,M,D) (2015)
Fredericton, NB E3B 5A3
p. (506) 453-4803
geology@unb.ca
Administrative Secretary: Merrill Ann Beatty
Chair:
Cliff S.J. Shaw, (D), W Ontario, 1994, Giv
Joseph C. White, (D), W Ontario, 1979, Gc
Professor:
Bruce E. Broster, (D), W Ontario, 1982, Gl
John Todd Dunn, (D), Alberta, 1983, Gi
John G. Spray, (D), Cambridge, 1980, GpXgGz
Paul F. Williams, (D), Sydney, 1969, Gc
Associate Professor:
Nicholas J. Susak, (D), Princeton, 1981, CglEm
Assistant Professor:
Karl Butler, (D), British Columbia, 1996, Yg
Research Associate:
James Whitehead, (D), New Brunswick, 1998, Gg
Honorary Research Professor:
Henk W. Van De Poll, (D), Swansea, 1970, Gs
Adjunct Professor:
Richard A. F. Grieve, (D), Toronto, 1970, Xg
David R. Lentz, (D), Ottawa, 1992, Cg
Randall F. Miller, (D), Waterloo, 1984, Pg
Emeritus:
Arnold L. McAllister, (D), McGill, 1950, Em
Geology Librarian:
Eszter Schwenke, Zn

University of New Brunswick Saint John

Dept of Biological Sciences (B,M,D) ⦸ (2021)
PO Box 5050
100 Tucker Park Road
Saint John, NB E2L 4L5
p. (506) 648-5607
lwilson@unbsj.ca
http://www.unbsj.ca/sase/biology/
Programs: Primarily a Biology department, with a Geology minor as an option.
Enrollment (2007): B: 2 (0) M: 1 (0)
Professor:
Lucy A. Wilson, (D), Paris VI, 1986, Ga
Emeritus:
Alan Logan, (D), Durham (UK), 1962, Ob

University of Ottawa

Department of Earth and Environmental Sciences (B,M,D) ●☒ (2021)
STEM Complex
150 Louis Pasteur Pvt
Ottawa, ON K1N 6N5
p. (613)-562-5800 x6870
david.schneider@uOttawa.ca
http://www.science.uottawa.ca/est/eng/welcome.html
Programs: Geology, Geology-Physics, Environmental Geosciences, Environmental Sciences
Enrollment (2020): B: 200 (51) M: 30 (3) D: 26 (2)
Chair:
David Schneider, (D), Lehigh, 2000, GtCcGg
Professor:
Tom A. Al, (D), Waterloo, 1996, HwCgZg
R. William C. Arnott, (D), Alberta, 1987, GsSo
Ian D. Clark, (D), Paris, 1988, HwGel
Danielle Fortin, (D), Quebec, 1992, CblGe
Mark Hannington, (D), Toronto, 1989, Eg
Keiko Hattori, (D), Tokyo, 1977, CgEmGz
Glenn A. Milne, (D), Toronto, 1998, YgAsZg
Associate Professor:
Pascal Audet, (D), British Columbia, 2008, YgGc
Jonathan O'Neil, (D), McGill, 2009, Cgc
Assistant Professor:
Clement Bataille, (D), Utah, 2014, ClGeCs
Brett Walker, (D), California (Santa Cruz), 2010, OgcCc
Lecturer:
Simone Dumas, (D), Ottawa, 2004, GsOg
Adjunct Professor:
Eric De Kemp, (D), Quebec, 2000, ZirZg
Andre Desrochers, (D), Memorial, 1986, Gs
David Andrew Fisher, (D), Copenhagen, 1978, Gl
William K. Fyson, (D), Reading (UK), 1960, Gc
Quentin Gall, (D), Carleton, 1994, GsEmGe
Richard Goulet, (D), Ottawa, 2001, CgPgGe
Jeffrey Wayne Hedenquist, (D), Auckland, 1983, Eg
Dogan Paktunc, (D), Ottawa, 1983, Gz
Pat E. Rasmussen, (D), Waterloo, 1993, GeAsGb
Emeritus:
Jan Veizer, (D), Australian Nat, 1971, Cl

University of Regina

Dept of Geology (B,M,D) ●☒ (2019)
3737 Wascana Parkway
Regina, SK S4S 0A2
p. (306) 585-4147
geology.office@uregina.ca
http://www.uregina.ca/science/geology/
Administrative Assistant: Van Tran
Professor:
Kathryn Bethune, (D), Queens, GcpGt
Guoxiang Chi, (D), Queens, Eg
Ian Coulson, (D), Birmingham (UK), 1996, Gvi
Hairuo Qing, (D), McGill, 1991, GsCg
Associate Professor:
Janis Dale, (D), Queens, Gml
Osman Salad Hersi
Maria Velez, (D), Amsterdam
Adjunct Professor:
Kenneth E. Ashton, (D), Gp
Pier L. Binda, (D), Alberta, 1970, Ge
Donald M. Kent, (D), Alberta, 1968, Gs
Emeritus:
Stephen L. Bend, (D), Newcastle, Gox
Laurence W. Vigrass, (D), Stanford, 1961, Eo

University of Saskatchewan

Dept of Geological Sciences (B,M,D) O-✓ (2019)
114 Science Place
Saskatoon, SK S7N 5E2
p. (306) 966-5683
sam.butler@usask.ca
http://artsandscience.usask.ca/geology/
Programs: Geology; Geophysics; Paleobiology; Environmental

Geoscience
Enrollment (2019): B: 102 (37) M: 35 (11) D: 24 (2)
Head:
Sam Butler, (D), Toronto, 2000, Yg
Professor:
Kevin M. Ansdell, (D), Saskatchewan, 1992, EgCgGt
James F. Basinger, (D), Alberta, 1979, Pb
Luis Buatois, (D), Buenos Aires, 1992, Ps
Graham George, (D), Sussex (UK), 1983, Cg
Chris Holmden, (D), Alberta, 1995, Csc
Gabriela Mangano, (D), Buenos Aires, 1992, PsGs
James B. Merriam, (D), York, 1976, Yg
Igor B. Morozov, (D), Moscow State (Russia), 1985, YsGy
Yuanming Pan, (D), W Ontario, 1990, Gx
William P. Patterson, (D), Michigan, 1995, CsPeGn
Ingrid J. Pickering, (D), Imperial Coll (UK), 1990, CgtZn
Brian R. Pratt, (D), Toronto, 1989, PgGsr
Associate Professor:
Matthew B. Lindsay, (D), Waterloo, 2009, ClGg
Camille Partin, (D), Gtc
Assistant Professor:
Joyce M. McBeth, (D), Manchester (UK), 2007, PgGeSb
Adjunct Professor:
Irvine Annesley, (D), Ottawa, 1989, Gi
Ning Chen, (D), Saskatchewan, 2001, Gz
David Greenwood, (D), Pg
Tom Kotzer, (D), Saskatchewan, 1993, CgEg
Brett Moldovan, (D), Cg
Len Wassenaar, (D), Waterloo, 1990, Hw
Derek A. Wyman, (D), Saskatchewan, 1990, Cg
Emeritus:
William G. E. Caldwell, (D), Glasgow, 1957, Ps
Donald J. Gendzwill, (D), Saskatchewan, 1969, Ye
Zoltan Hajnal, (D), Manitoba, 1970, YsGtc
Jim Hendry, (D), Waterloo, 1984, HwClHy
Robin W. Renaut, (D), London (UK), 1982, Gsn
Mel R. Stauffer, (D), Australian Nat, 1964, Gc

University of Toronto

Dept of Earth Sciences (B,M,D) ●☒ (2017)
Earth Sciences Centre
22 Russell Street
Toronto, ON M5S 3B1
p. (416) 978-3022
welcome@es.utoronto.ca
http://www.es.utoronto.ca
Business Officer: Silvanna Papaleo
Chair:
Russell N. Pysklywec, (D), Toronto, 1998, Yg
Professor:
Nicholas Eyles, (D), Leicester (UK), 1978, Gl
Grant F. Ferris, (D), Guelph, 1985, Gn
Henry C. Halls, (D), Toronto, 1970, Ym
Kenneth W.F. Howard, (D), Birmingham (UK), 1979, Hw
Andrew D. Miall, (D), Ottawa, 1969, Gso
Barbara Sherwood Lollar, (D), Waterloo, 1990, Cs
Director, Jack Satterly Geochronology Lab:
Michael A. Hamilton, (D), Massachusetts, 1993, CcGiCu
Associate Professor:
Bridget Bergquist, (D), MIT, 2004, Cgb
Donald W. Davis, (D), Alberta, 1978, Cc
Grant S. Henderson, (D), W Ontario, 1983, Gz
Qinya Liu, (D), Caltech, 2006, Ygx
Daniel J. Schulze, (D), Texas, 1982, Gi
Assistant Professor:
Carl-Georg Bank, (D), British Columbia, 2002, Zg
Jörg Bollmann, (D), Swiss Fed Inst Tech, 1995, Pm
Xu Chu, (D), Yale, 2015, Gx
Rebecca Ghent, (D), S Methodist, 2002, Zr
Jochen Halfar, (D), Stanford, 1999, Pe
Ulrich B. Wortmann, (D), Tech (Munich), Gg
Zoltan Zajacz, (D), ETH (Switzerland), 2007, Cu
Research Associate:
Colin Bray, (D), Oxford, 1980, Cs
Adjunct Professor:
Jean-Bernard Caron, (D), Toronto, 2005, Pi
John H. McAndrews, (D), Minnesota, 1964, Pl
Emeritus:
G M. Anderson, (D), Toronto, 1961, Cp
Richard C. Bailey, (D), Cambridge, 1970, Yg
J. J. Fawcett, (D), Manchester (UK), 1961, Gp
John Gittins, (D), Cambridge, 1959, GipGz
Anthony J. Naldrett, (D), Queen's, 1964, EmGiCp
Geoffrey Norris, (D), Cambridge, 1964, Pl
Pierre-Yves F. Robin, (D), MIT, 1974, Gc
John C. Rucklidge, (D), Manchester (UK), 1962, Ge
Walfried M. Schwerdtner, (D), Free (Berlin), 1961, GctGq
Steven D. Scott, (D), Penn State, 1968, GuEmCm
Edward T. C. Spooner, (D), Manchester (UK), 1976, En
Peter H. von Bitter, (D), Kansas, 1971, Pm
John A. Westgate, (D), Alberta, 1964, Gl
Frederick J. Wicks, (D), Oxford, 1969, Gz

Dept of Physics, Geophysics Div (B,M,D) (2015)
60 St. George Street
Toronto, ON M5S 1A7
p. (416) 978-5175
cliao@physics.utoronto.ca
http://www.physics.utoronto.ca
Professor:
Bernd Milkereit, (B), Kiel, 1984, Ye
Emeritus:
Richard C. Bailey, (D), Cambridge, 1970, Yg
Richard N. Edwards, (D), Cambridge, 1970, Yr

University of Victoria

School of Earth & Ocean Sciences (B,M,D) O☒ (2018)
P.O. Box 1700
3800 Finnerty Road
Victoria, BC V8W 2Y2
p. (250) 721-6120
seos@uvic.ca
http://www.uvic.ca/science/seos/
Associate Director (SCIENCE) NEPTUNE Canada:
Kim Juniper, (D), Canterbury (NZ), 1982, Ob
Associate Dean of Science:
Kathryn Gillis, (D), Dalhousie, 1987, Gp
Professor:
Dante Canil, (D), Alberta, 1989, Gi
Laurence Coogan, (D), Leicester (UK), Gi
Stanley E. Dosso, (D), British Columbia, 1990, Op
Adam Monahan, (D), British Columbia, 2000, Zn
Thomas F. Pedersen, (D), Edinburgh, 1979, CmOcCs
Vera Pospelova, (D), McGill, 2003, PelOu
George D. Spence, (D), British Columbia, 1984, Ys
Verena Tunnicliffe, (D), Yale, 1980, Ob
Michael J. Whiticar, (D), Kiel, 1978, CosGo
Associate Professor:
Jay Cullen, (D), Rutgers, 2001, Oc
John Dower, (D), Victoria, 1994, Ob
Roberta C. Hamme, (D), Washington, 2003, Oc
Thomas S. James, (D), Princeton, 1991, YdvYg
Jody Klymak, (D), Washington, 2001, Op
Eileen Van Der Flier-Keller, (D), W Ontario, 1985, Cl
Diana Varela, (D), British Columbia, 1998, Ob
Assistant Professor:
Colin Goldblatt, (D), E Anglia (UK), 2008, As
Lucinda Leonard, (D), Victoria, Yg
Adjunct Professor:
Vaughn Barrie, (D), Wales, 1986, Gu
John Cassidy, (D), British Columbia, Ys
James R. Christian, (D), Hawaii, 1995, Obc
Kenneth L. Denman, (D), British Columbia, 1972, Op
Richard K. Dewey, (D), British Columbia, 1987, Opg
Gregory M. Flato, (D), Dartmouth, 1991, As
John C. Fyfe, (D), McGill, 1987, As
Richard J. Hebda, (D), British Columbia, 1977, Pl
Roy D. Hyndman, (D), Australian Nat, 1967, Ys
Stephen T. Johnston, (D), Alberta, 1993, Gc
Victor M. Levson, (D), Alberta, 1995, Gl
David L. Mackas, (D), Dalhousie, 1977, Ob
Norman McFarlane, (D), Michigan, 1974, As
Garry C. Rogers, (D), British Columbia, 1983, Ys
George J. Simandl, (D), Ecole Polytechnique, 1992, En
Richard Thomson, (D), British Columbia, 1971, Og

Kelin Wang, (D), W Ontario, 1989, Yg
Michael Wilmut, (D), Queen's, 1971, Zn
Emeritus:
Christopher R. Barnes, (D), Ottawa, 1964, PmOgPe
Ross N. Chapman, (D), British Columbia, 1975, Op
Christopher J. R. Garrett, (D), Cambridge, 1968, Op
John T. Weaver, (D), Saskatchewan, 1959, Ym
On Leave:
Andrew J. Weaver, (D), British Columbia, 1987, Op
Administrative Officer:
Terry P. Russell, (B), Victoria, 2000, Zn

University of Waterloo

Dept of Earth and Environmental Sciences (B,M,D) ● (2016)
Waterloo, ON N2L 3G1
p. (519) 888-4567, ext. 32069
klalbrec@uwaterloo.ca
https://uwaterloo.ca/earth-environmental-sciences/
Administrative Assistant: Lorraine Albrecht
Chair:
Barry G. Warner, (D)
Professor:
David W. Blowes, (D), Waterloo, 1990, Cg
Mario Coniglio, (D), Memorial, 1985, Gr
Maurice B. Dusseault, (D), Alberta, 1977, Ng
Thomas W. D. Edwards, (D), Waterloo, 1987, Cs
Stephen George Evans, (D), Alberta, 1983, Ng
Shaun K. Frape, (D), Queen's, 1979, Cl
Shoufa Lin, (D), New Brunswick, 1992, Zn
Carol J. Ptacek, (D), Waterloo, 1992, Cg
David L. Rudolph, (D), Waterloo, 1989, Hq
Sherry L. Schiff, (D), Columbia, 1986, Ng
Edward A. Sudicky, (D), Waterloo, 1983, Hw
Philippe Van Cappellen, (D)
Associate Professor:
Anthony E. Endres, (D), British Columbia, 1991, Pe
Walter Illman, (D)
Martin Ross, (D)
Andre Unger, (D), Waterloo, 1995, Hw
Assistant Professor:
Nandita Basu, (D)
Carl Guilmette, (D)
Brian Kendall, (D)
Lingling Wu, (D)
Lecturer:
Eric C. Grunsky, (D)
John Johnson, (D)
Isabelle McMartin, (D)
Brent Wolfe, (D)
Adjunct Professor:
Edward C. Appleyard, (D), Cambridge, 1963, Gp
Gail Atkinson, (D)
James F. Barker, (D), Waterloo, 1979, Co
Steven Berg, (D)
Alec Blyth, (D)
Thomas Bullen, (D)
Lauren Charlet, (D)
John A. Cherry, (D), Illinois, 1966, Hw
Peter Condon, (D)
Rick Devlin
Michael English, (D)
Nicholas Eyles, (D)
John F. Gartner, Zn
John J. Gibson, (D), Waterloo, 1996, Cs
Susan Glasuer, (D)
David Good, (D)
John Gosse, (D)
Douglas Gould, (D)
Norman Halden, (D)
Daniel Hammarlund, (D)
Jens Hartman, (D)
Lin Huang, (D)
Daniel Hunkeler
Hyoun-Tae Hwang, (D)
Richard Jackson, (D)
Sun-Wook Jeen, (D)
Michael Krom, (D)
David R. Lee, (D), Virginia Tech, 1976, Hw
Yuri Leonenko, (D)
John Lin, (D)
Robert Linnen, (D), McGill, 1992, Eg
Benoit Made, (D)
Uli Mayer, (D)
Hossein Memarian, (D)
John Molson
Alan V. Morgan, (D), Birmingham (UK), 1970, Gl
Christopher Neville, (D)
Dogan Paktunc, (D)
Sorab Panday, (D)
Young-Jin Park, (D), Hq
Gary Parkin, (N)
Peter Pehme, (D)
Jennifer Pell, (D)
Richard Peltier, (D)
Terry D. Prowse, (D), Canterbury (NZ), 1981, Cg
William Quinton, (D)
Eric J. Reardon, (D), Penn State, 1974, Cl
Rashid Rehan, (D)
Iain Samson, (D)
Houston C. Saunderson, (N)
James Sloan, (D)
James Smith
John Spoelstra, (D)
Andrew Stumpf, (D)
William Taylor, (D)
Rene Therrien, (D)
Harvey Thorleifson, (D)
Martin Thullner, (D)
Benoit Valley, (D)
Garth Van der Kamp, (D), Amsterdam, 1973, Hw
Jan van der Kruk, (D)
Cees van Staal
Andrea Vander Woude, (D)
Owen L. White, (D), Illinois, 1970, Ng
C. Wolkersdorfer, (D)
Wenjiao Xiao, (D)
Leiming Zhang, (D)
Emeritus:
Emil O. Frind, (D), Toronto, 1971, Hq
Robert W. Gillham, (D), Illinois, 1973, Hq
Paul Karrow, (D), Illinois, 1957, Gl
Research Professor:
Ramon Aravena, (D), Waterloo, 1993, Co
Research Associate Professor:
Will Robertson, (D), Waterloo, 1992, Hw
Other:
Brewster Conant, Hw

University of Windsor

Dept of Earth and Environmental Sciences (B,M,D) (2015)
401 Sunset Avenue
Windsor, ON N9B 3P4
p. (519) 253-3000 x2486
earth@uwindsor.ca
http://www.uwindsor.ca/ees
Administrative Assistant: Sharon Horne
Professor:
Ihsan S. Al-Aasm, (D), Ottawa, 1985, GdClGo
Aaron Fisk, (D), Manitoba, 1998, ObCs
V. Chris Lakhan, (D), Toronto, 1982, ZriOn
Ali Polat, (D), Saskatchewan, 1998, GixCc
Iain M. Samson, (D), Strathclyde, 1983, CgEmGx
Frank -. Simpson, (D), Jagellonian (Krakow), 1968, GsrGe
Alan S. Trenhaile, (D), Wales, 1969, Gm
Associate Professor:
Maria T. Cioppa, (D), Lehigh, 1997, Ym
Joel E. Gagnon, (D), McGill, 2006, CaqEg
Phil A. Graniero, (D), Toronto, 2001, ZinZy
Cyril G. Rodrigues, (D), Carleton, 1980, Pm
Christopher Weisener, (D), South Australia, 2003, CoGePg
Jianwen Yang, (D), Toronto, 1997, HwYg
Instructor:
Denis Tetrault, (D), Western, 2002, Gg
Emeritus:
Brian J. Fryer, (D), MIT, 1971, Cla
Peter P. Hudec, (D), Rensselaer, 1965, NgEmGe

Terence E. Smith, (D), Wales, 1963, Gi
David T. A. Symons, (D), Toronto, 1965, YmGtEm
Andrew Turek, (D), Australian Nat, 1966, Cc

Western University

Dept of Earth Sciences (B,M,D) O☒ (2018)
Biology & Geology Building
Room 1026
1151 Richmond Street North
London, ON N6A 5B7
p. (519) 661-3187
earth-sc@uwo.ca
http://www.uwo.ca/earth/
t: @westernuEarth
Administrative Assistant: Erika Gongora
Enrollment (2016): B: 123 (15) M: 77 (16) D: 54 (8)
Chair:
Patricia Corcoran, (D), Dalhousie, 2001, Gd
Robert Hodder Chair:
Robert Linnen, (D), McGill, 1992, EmCe
NSERC Industrial Research Chair:
Gail M. Atkinson, (D), W Ontario, 1993, YssYs
Joint appointment with Geography, U.W.O.:
Desmond Moser, (D), Queens, 1993, GtCcXg
Industrial Research Chair, Joint Appt Physics & Astronomy, U.W.O:
Gordon R. Osinski, (D), New Brunswick, 2004, XgcGp
Cross-Appt.UWO: Physics&Astronomy:
Sean R. Shieh, (D), Hawaii, 1998, YxGzZm
Cross-Appt.-Home Dept: Physics & Astronomy, UWO:
Peter Brown, (D), W Ontario, 1999, Xym
Canada Research Chair, Cross Appt. Biology&Geography, UWO:
Brian Branfireun, (D), McGill, Ge
Canada Research Chair:
Frederick J. Longstaffe, (D), McMaster, 1978, Cs
(P.Eng.,P.Geo.):
Robert A. Schincariol, (D), Ohio State, 1993, HwsNg
Professor:
Dazhi Jiang, (D), New Brunswick, 1996, GcgGg
Jisuo Jin, (D), Saskatchewan, 1988, Pi
A Guy Plint, (D), Oxford, 1980, Gs
R. Gerhard Pratt, (D), Imperial Coll (UK), 1989, Yeg
Richard A. Secco, (D), W Ontario, 1988, Gy
Industrial Research Chair:
Neil Banerjee, (D), Victoria, 2001, EgCgGx
Cross-Appt.UWO: Physics&Astronomy:
Robert Shcherbakov, (D), Cornell, 2002, YgsYd
Canada Research Chair:
Audrey Bouvier, (D), École Normale Supérieure de Lyon, 2005, Xc
Associate Professor:
Burns A. Cheadle, (D), W Ontario, 1986, Go
Roberta L. Flemming, (D), Queen's (Canada), 1997, GzXmZm
Katsu Goda, (D), Rn
Elizabeth A. Webb, (D), W Ontario, 2000, CslSa
Assistant Professor:
Sheri Molnar, (D), Victoria, 2011, Ys
Catherine Neish, (D), Arizona, 2008, Xg
Cameron J. Tsujita, (D), McMaster, 1995, Pi
Tony Withers, (D), Bristol, 1997, Cp
Research Technician:
Peter Christoffersen, (M), W Ontario
Claire Montera
Research Scientist:
Li Huang, (M), Concordia, 1992, Yr
Research Engineer:
Matthew Bourassa, (D), Xg
Research Associate:
Hadi Ghofrani, (D)
W.S. Fyfe Visiting Scientist- in- Residence:
David Good, (D), McMaster, 1992, Em
Research Associate:
Brian R. Hart, (D), W Ontario, 1995, Ca
Research Adjunct Professor:
Natalie Pietrzak-Renaud, (D), W Ontario, 2011, Eg
Associate Curator of Mineralogy, Royal Ontario Museum/Professor, University of Toronto:
Kim Tait, (D), Arizona, 2007, Xm
Adjunct Professor:
Keith Baron, (D)
Melissa Battler
Rob Carpenter, (D)
Ed Cloutis, (D), Alberta, 1989, Zi
Claudia Cochrane, (M), W Ontario, Go
Yunpeng Dong, (D), Northwest Univ (China), 1997, GtcCg
Richard Grieve, (D), Toronto, 1970, Xg
Matt Izawa, (D), W Ontario, 2012, Gz
Laura Jansen
Peter Lightfoot
Phil JA McCausland, (D), Western, 2002, YmXm
Gero Michel, (D), Harvard, Ys
Sobhi Nasir, (D), Wuerzburg, 1989
Sergey Samsonov
Brenden Smithyman, (D), Ye
Gordon Southam, (D), Guelph, 1990, Pg
Yves Thibault, (D), W Ontario, 1990, Gz
Kristy F. Tiampo, (D), Colorado, 2000, Yd
Livio Tornabene, (D), Tennessee, 2007, XgZr
Lisa Van Loon, (D), Ohio State, 2007, Ca
Emeritus:
Alan Beck, (D), Australian Nat, 1964, Zn
W. Glen E. Caldwell, (D), Glasgow, 1957, Pm
William R. Church, (D), Wales, 1961, Gt
Norman A. Duke, (D), Manitoba, 1983, Eg
Akio Hayatsu, (D), Toronto, 1965, Cc
Stephen R. Hicock, (D), W Ontario, 1980, Gl
Alfred C. Lenz, (D), Princeton, 1959, PiePi
Robert F. Mereu, (D), W Ontario, 1962, Ys
H Wayne Nesbitt, (D), Johns Hopkins, 1975, Cl
H. Currie Palmer, (D), Princeton, 1963, YmGv
Grant M. Young, (D), Glasgow, 1967, GrCgGt
Laboratory Director:
Kim Law, Cs
Wenjun Yong, (D), Yx
Technical Specialist:
Barry Price
Research Technologist:
Jon Jacobs, Gg
Research Technician:
Marc Beauchamp, Ca
Grace Yau
Lab Technician:
Steven Wood
Geoscience Collections Curator:
Alysha McNeil, (D), W Ontario, 2017
Financial Assistant:
Miyako Maekawa
Computer Technician:
Bernie Dunn, Ye
Administrative Officer:
Kristen Harris
Academic Program Coordinator:
Amy N. Wickham, (M), Connecticut, 2016

York University

Earth and Space Science and Engineering (B,M,D) ● (2015)
4700 Keele Street
Toronto, ON M3J 1P3
p. (416) 736-5245
esse@yorku.ca
http://www.yorku.ca/esse
Administrative Assistant: Paola Panaro
Enrollment (2010): B: 100 (38)
Professor:
Qiuming Cheng, (D), Ottawa, 1994, Zi
Christian Haas, (D), Bremen, 1996, Yg
Gary T. Jarvis, (D), Cambridge, 1978, Yg
Ian C. McDade, (D), Belfast, 1979, Zr
Tom McElroy, (D), York, 1985, As
Spiros Pagiatakis, (D), New Brunswick, 1988, Yd
Jinjun Shan, (D)
Peter A. Taylor, (D), Bristol, 1967, As
Chair:
Regina Lee, (D), Toronto, 2000
Associate Professor:
Costas Armenakis, (D), New Brunswick, 1988, Zr
Sunil Bisnath, (D), New Brunswick, 2004
Yongsheng Chen, As

Michael Daly, (D)
Baoxin Hu, (D), Boston, 1998, Zr
Mary Ann Jenkins, (D), Toronto, 1986, As
Gary P. Klaassen, (D), Toronto, 1983, As
Brendan Quine, (D)
Gunho Sohn, (D)
George Vukovich, (D), As
James Whiteway, (D), York, 1994, As

Assistant Professor:
William Colgan, (D), Yg
Mark Gordon, (D), As
John E. Moores, (D), Arizona, 2008

Lecturer:
Hugh Chesser, (M), Toronto, 1987
Franz Newland, (D), Southampton (UK), 2000, Zr
Jian-Guo Wang, (D)

Emeritus:
Keith D. Aldridge, (D), MIT, 1967, YmdYh
John Miller, (D), Saskatchewan, 1969, Zr
Gordon G. Shepherd, (D), Toronto, 1956, AsZrAp
Douglas E. Smylie, (D), Toronto, 1963, Yg
Anthony M. K. Szeto, (D), Australian Nat, 1982, Yg

Cape Verde

Universidade de Cabo Verde

Dept de Ciencia e Tecnologia (M,D) (2018)
Campus de Palmarejo - CP 279
Palmarejo, Praia - Cabo Verde
Praia
Praca Antonio Lereno, Praia CP 379C
p. +238 261 99 01
joao.semedo@docente.unicv.edu.cv
http://www.unicv.edu.cv/dct

Faculdade de Engenharia e Ciencias do Mar (B,M,D) ☒ (2017)
Ribeira de Julião
CP 163
Mindelo, São Vicente CP 163
p. +238 2326561/62
amdelgado@uta.cv
http://www.unicv.edu.cv

Universidade Jean Piaget de Cabo Verde

Ecologia e Desenvolvimento (B) (2015)
Campus Universitario da Cidade da Praia
Praia
p. +238 629085
info@unipiaget.cv
http://www.unipiaget.cv/pdf/cursos/ecdm.pdf

Central African Republic

Universite de Bangui

Dept de Chimie-Biologie-Geologie (B) (2015)
BP 1450
Avenue des Martyrs
Bangui
p. (236) 61 20 05
info@univ-bangui.org
http://www.univ-bangui.org/

Chad

Universite de N'Djamena

Dept de Geologie (B) (2015)
BP 1117
Avenue Mobutu
N'Djamena
sg@undt.info
http://www.undt.info/

Chile

Servicio National de Geologia y Mineria de Chile

Servicio National de Geologia y Mineria de Chile (2015)
Avda Sta Maria Nº 0104
Providence
p. 56-2-7375050
oirs@sernageomin.cl
http://www.sernageomin.cl/

Universidad Austral de Chile

Inst de Geociencias (2015)
Campus "Isla Teja", Casilla 567, Valdivia
p. +56 63 2293861
cienciasdelatierra@uach.cl

Universidad Catolica del Norte

Dept de Ciencias Geologicas (2015)
Avenida Angamos 610, ,
Casilla 1280, Antofagasta
p. (55) 2355968
mbembow@ucn.cl
http://www.ucn.cl/facultades/SitioDeInteres/?cod=2&codItem=110&codPrincipal=1124

Universidad de Chile

Dept de Geologia (2015)
Plaza Ercilla 803, Casilla 13148, Correo 21, Santiago
colegios@ing.uchile.cl

Dept de Geofisica (2015)
Blanco Encalada 2002
Casilla 2777
Santiago
p. (56 2)696 6563
rmunoz@dgf.uchile.cl
http://www.dgf.uchile.cl

Universidad de Concepcion

Inst de Geologia Economica Aplicada (2015)
Barrio Universitario - Victor Lamas 1290
Casilla 4107
Concepcion, Region del Bio-Bio
p. (56) 41 220 44 88
maravenah@udec.cl
http://www.udec.cl/postgrado/?q=node/39&codigo=4161

Dept de Geociencia (2015)
Cabina 13 - Barrio Universitario, Casilla 3-C, 4250-1 Concepcion, Region del Bio-Bio

China

Capital Normal University

College of Resources, Environment and Tourism (2015)
West 3rd Ring Road North 105#
Beijing 100048
p. 86 10 68903321
info@mail.cnu.edu.cn
http://www.cnu.edu.cn

China Geological Survey

China Geological Survey (2015)
24 Huangsi Dajie,
Xicheng District
Beijing 100011
p. +86 10 51632963 51632906
enwebmaster@mail.cgs.gov.cn
http://www.cgs.gov.cn/

China University of Geosciences, Beijing

Geosciences (2015)
No.29, Xueyuan Road,
Haidian District
Beijing 100083

http://www.cugb.edu.cn/EnglishWeb

China University of Geosciences, Wuhan

Faculty of Geosciences (2015)
No. 388, Lumo Road, Hongshan District
Wuhan 430074
p. 86-27-87481030
cugxb@cug.edu.cn
http://en.cug.edu.cn/cug

China University of Mining and Technology, Beijing

College of Geoscience and Surveying Engineering (2015)
Beijing
dcxy@cumtb.edu.cn
http://dcxy.cumtb.edu.cn/

Nanjing University

Dept of Earth Sciences (2015)
22 Hankou Road
Nanjing , Jiangsu
wsj@nju.edu.cn
http://www.nju.edu.cn/cps/site/njueweb/fg

University of Hong Kong

Dept of Earth Sciences (B,M,D) ● ☒ (2021)
James Lee Science Building
Pokfulam Road
Hong Kong
p. (852) 2859 1084
earthsci@hku.hk
http://www.earthsciences.hku.hk
Programs: Geology, Earth System Science

Colombia

EAFIT University

Dept of Geology (2015)
Carrera 49 No. 7 Sur - 50
Medellin
p. 01 8000515 900
contacto@eafit.edu.co

Escuela de Ingenieria de Antioquia

Dept of Geologic Engineering ☒ (2018)
Calle 25 Sur
#42-63 Envigado
Medellin
maria.espinosa68@eia.edu.co
http://www.eia.edu.co/site/index.php/pregrados/programas/ing-geologica.html

Universidad de Santander

Environmental Engineering (B,M) (2015)
Facultad Ingenierias
Cll 70 No. 55-210 Campus Universitario Lagos del Cacique
Bucaramanga, Santander
p. +57 7 6516500
nmantilla@udes.edu.co
http://www.udes.edu.co/programas-profesionales/facultad-ingenierias/ingenieria-ambiental.html

Universidad Industrial de Santander

School of Geology (B,M) ○ (2016)
Cra 27 Calle 9 Ciudad Universitaria
Bucaramanga, Santander 1
p. 57-7-6343457
escgeo@uis.edu.co
http://geologia.uis.edu.co/eisi/

Director:
Juan Diego Colegial Gutierrez, (D), Politecnica de Madrid (Spain), 2004, GeNgZr

Professor:
Luis Carlos Mantilla Figueroa, (D), EgCec

Universidad Nacional de Colombia

Dept de Geociencias (2015)
Carrera 30 No. 45-03, Edificio 224
Calle 45, Cr. 30
Bogota
lhochoag@unal.edu.co

Costa Rica

Universidad de Costa Rica

Escuela Centroamericana de Geologia (B,M) ● ☒ (2020)
Apartado 35-2060 UCR, San Pedro de Montes de Oca, San José
San José
p. 506 25118129
geologia@ucr.ac.cr
http://www.geologia.ucr.ac.cr/
f: https://www.facebook.com/ECG.UCR/
t: @geologiaucr
Programs: Geology (BS)

Director:
Mauricio Manuel Mora Fernández, (D), Savoie (France), 2003

Professor:
Mario Enrique Arias Salguero, (M)
Marco Barahona Palomo, (D)
Guaria Cárdenes Sandí, (D)
Percy Denyer Chavarría, (D)
Lepolt Linkimer Abarca, (D)
Rolando Mora Chinchilla, (M)

Associate Professor:
Elena Badilla Coto, (M)
Oscar Lucke Castro, (D)
María Isabel Sandoval Gutiérrez, (D)

Instructor:
María Cristina Araya , (D), 2020, YdGtYs
Patrick Durán Leiva, (B)
Maximiliano Garnier Villareal, (D), NxYgGg
María del Pilar Madrigal Quesada, (D)
Stephanie Murillo Maikut, (D)
Giovanni Marino Peraldo Huertas, (M)
Vanessa Rojas Herrera, (A)
Paulo Ruiz Cubillo, (D), GvmRn
Luis Guillermo Salazar Mondragón, (M)
César Sequeira Peraza, (D), Rutgers, 2019
Ingrid Vargas Azofeifa, (M)

Croatia

Croatian Geological Survey

Croatian Geological Survey ☒ (2018)
Sachsova 2
P.O.Box 268
Zagreb HR-10000
p. +38516160888
ured@hgi-cgs.hr
http://www.hgi-cgs.hr/
f: https://www.facebook.com/HGI.CGS/

University of Zagreb

Dept of Geology, Faculty of Science (B,M,D) (2015)
Horvatovac 102a
Zagreb HR-10000
p. +38514605960
godsjek@geol.pmf.hr
http://www.geol.pmf.hr
Enrollment (2010): B: 121 (27) M: 28 (11) D: 30 (6)

full professor:
Mladen Juraèiæ, (D), Zagreb, 1987, GueCm

associate professor:
Dražen Balen, (D), Zagreb, 1999, GxpGi

full professor:
Darko Tibljaš, (D), Zagreb, 1996, GzScGx
Vlasta Æosoviæ, (D), Zagreb, 1996, PemPs

emeritus:
Ivan Gušiæ, (D), Zagreb, 1974, GgPsm

Cyprus

Ministry of Agriculture, Rural Development and Environment

Cyprus Geological Survey Department ☒ (2020)
1 Lefkonos Street
Strovolos 2064
p. +357 22409213
director@gsd.moa.gov.cy
http://www.moa.gov.cy/gsd
f: https://www.facebook.com/Cyprus-Geological-Survey-Department-894868840721111
t: @CY_earthquakes

Czech Republic

Charles University

Inst of Hydrogeology, Engineering Geology and Applied Geophysics (2015)
Albertov 6
128 43 Praha 2
fischer@natur.cuni.cz
http://prfdec.natur.cuni.cz/~geophys/ustav/katedra.htm

Institute of Petrology and Structural Geology (B,M,D) (2015)
Albertov 6
Praha 2 128 43
p. 00420-221951524
petrol@natur.cuni.cz
http://petrol.natur.cuni.cz
Enrollment (2012): B: 3 (5) M: 15 (4) D: 15 (0)
Assoc. Prof.:
David Dolejs, (D), 2004, GiCpg
Professor:
Shah Wali Faryad, (D), 1990, GpzGi

Dept of Geophysics (B,M,D) ☒ (2017)
KG MFF UK
V Holesovickach 2
180 00 Prague 8, Czech Republic
Prague 180 00
geo@mff.cuni.cz
http://geo.mff.cuni.cz
Programs: Solid Earth Geophysics (B); Planetary Science (B)
Enrollment (2017): B: 5 (0) M: 3 (0) D: 2 (0)

Czech Geological Survey

Czech Geological Survey ☒ (2021)
Klarov 3
Praha 1 118 21
p. +420 257 089 500
secretar@geology.cz
http://www.geology.cz

Geofond (2015)
Kostelni 26
Prague PSC 170 06
p. +420 234 742 111
jana.kubova@geologycz
http://www.geofond.cz/cz/domu

Masaryk University

Dept of Geological Sciences (B,M,D) O☒ (2018)
Faculty of Science
Kotlarska 2
Brno 611 37
p. +420 549 49 4322
geologie@sci.muni.cz
http://ugv.cz/
f: https://www.facebook.com/chci.byt.geolog
Enrollment (2017): B: 134 (30) M: 80 (35) D: 81 (5)
Head:
Zdenek Losos, (D), Gzy
Professor:
Ondrej Babek, (D), Gds
Jiri Kalvoda, (A), PsePm
Milan Novak, (A), GzpGi
Antonín Prichystal, (A), GgaGv
Associate Professor:
Jan Cenpírek, Gz
Eva Geršlová, Ge
Martin Ivanov, (A), PgiPe
Jaromir Leichmann, (A), GxpGi
Rostislav Melichar, (A), GtcGr
Slavomír Nehyba, (A), GsdGg
Radek Skoda, (A), Masaryk (Czech Republic), 2017, GzZmGi
Marek Slobodnik, (A), GeEg
Josef Zeman, (D), Comenius Univ (Slovakia), 1987, CgpCe
Assistant Professor:
Martin Knizek, (D), NgmNr
Tomas Kuchovsky, (D), Hgy
Tomas Kumpan, Ps
Pavel Pracny, Cg
Adam Ricka, (D), Hgy
Research Associate:
Renata Copjakova, (D), Gz
Lecturer:
Nela Dolakova, (A), Plg
Emeritus:
Rostislav Brzobohaty, (A), PgsPe
Rudolf Musil, (D), Charles (Prague), 1968, PgvGe

Dept of Geological Sciences (2015)
Kotlarska 2
611 37 Brno
Brno 611 37
pechmannova@sci.muni.cz
https://www.muni.cz/en/about-us/organizational-structure/faculty-of-science/315010-deptof-geological-sciences/teaching

Dept of Geography (2015)
Kotlarska 2
611 37 Brno
dobro@sci.muni.cz
http://www.muni.cz/sci/structure/315030.html

Technical University of Ostrava

Faculty of Mining & Geology (2015)
Vysoka Skola Banska v Ostrava
17.listopadu 15/2172
708-33 Ostrava
p. +420 597 325 456
dekan.hgf@vsb.cz
http://www.hgf.vsb.cz/cs

D.R. of Congo

Marien Ngouabi University

Faculty of Science and Technology (B,M,D) O (2015)
Face Square Général Charles De Gaulle
Bacongo
BP:69
Brazzaville, Congo
p. (+242) 06 623 61 22
jm_ouamba@yahoo.fr
http://www.univ-mngb.net/fs/

Universite de Kinshasa

Dept des Sciences de la Terre (B) (2015)
PO Box 190
Kinshasa XI
p. (+243) 82 333 96 93
rectorat@unikin.cd
http://www.unikin.cd

Départements et filières Sciences Agronomiques (B) (2015)
PO Box 190
Kinshas XI
p. +243 89 89 20 507

fbkapuku@hotmail.com
http://www.unikin.cd/ogec/

Universite de Lumumbashi

Faculté des sciences (B) (2015)
BP 1825
Lubumbashi
p. +243 263-22-5403
unilu@unilu.net
http://www.unilu.ac.cd/En/Pages/

Denmark

Aarhus University

Department of Geoscience (B,M,D) ☒ (2021)
Hoegh-Guldbergs Gade 2
DK-8000 Arhus C
geologi@au.dk
http://geo.au.dk
Programs: Geology
Geophysics

Geological Survey of Denmark and Greenland (GEUS)

Geological Survey of Denmark and Greenland (GEUS) ☒ (2021)
Oester Voldgade 10
Copenhagen DK-1350
p. +45 38 20 00
geus@geus.dk
http://www.geus.dk/
Programs: As a research institute affiliated to the Danish Ministry of Climate, Energy and Utilities we do not offer degree programs but some of our researchers act as co-supervisors with university colleagues for both master- and PhD-students, and in some cases, PhD-students are employed at GEUS .

Roskilde University

QuadLab, ENSPAC (2015)
Universitetsvej 1
Roskilde DK-4000
p. 45 46743097
storey@ruc.dk
http://www.quadlab.dk/bcms-ui-base/

Technical University of Denmark

Dept of Earth Sciences (2015)
Anker Engelunsved
DK-2800 Lyngby
thho@env.dtu.dk
http://www.igg.dtu.dk/index_z.htm

University of Copenhagen

Inst for Geography and Geology (2015)
Oster Voldgage 5-7
DK-1350 Copenhagen K
p. +4535322400
pab@ign.ku.dk
http://geo.ku.dk/

Dept of Geophysics ☒ (2017)
Juliane Maries Vej 30
Copenhagen 2100 Copenhagen
p. +45 353 20605
losos@sci.muni.cz
http://www.nbi.ku.dk/theinstitute/page52794.htm

Geological Museum ☒ (2021)
Oster Voldgade 5-7
Copenhagen K DK-1350
p. +45 35322345
rcp@snm.ku.dk
http://geologi.snm.ku.dk/english/

Djibouti

Insitut de Physique du Globe de Paris, (IPGP)

Dept of Volcanic Systems (B) (2015)
Observatoire Géophysique d'Arta, BP 1888
p. (253) 42 21 92
komorow@ipgp.fr
http://volcano.ipgp.jussieu.fr/djibouti/stationdj.html

Universite de Djibouti

Dept de Geologie/Biologie (B) (2015)
BP 1904
p. +253-250459
webmaster@univ.edu.dj
http://www.univ.edu.dj/facultes.fsti.bg.html

Dominican Republic

Mineterio de Energie y Minas Republica Dominica

Servicio Geologico Nacional Republica Dominica (2016)
Ave Winston Churchill No 75
Edificio J.F. Martinez 3er Piso
Santa Domingo
p. (809) 732 0363
smunoz@sgn.gov.do
http://www.sgn.gov.do

Ecuador

Escuela Politecnica Nacional

Facultad de Geologia, Minas y Petroleos (2015)
Ladron de Guevara E11
253 Quito
p. (593-02) 2-507 - 126
deparamento.geologia@epn.edu.ec
http://www.epn.edu.ec/index.php?option=com_content&view=article&id=1202%3Adepartamento-de-geologia-dg&catid=163&Itemid=342

Escuela Superior Politecnica Del Litoral

Facultad de Ciencias de la Tierra (2015)
Km 30.5, Via Perimentral
Guayaquil EC090150

Universidad de Guayaquil

Facultad de Ciencias Naturales (2015)
Av Raul Gomez Lynx s / n Av Juan Tanca Marengo
Guayaquil
p. 3080777 to 3080758
carmenbonifaz@hotmail.com
http://fccnnugye.com/

Egypt

Ain Shams University

Dept of Geology (B) (2015)
Abbassia 11566
Cairo 11566
p. +20(2)6830963
deans@asunet.shams.edu.eg
http://sci.shams.edu.eg/Departments_Geology_Index.ASP

Dept of Geophysics (B) (2015)
Abbassia 11566
Cairo 11566
p. +20(2)6830963
deans@asunet.shams.edu.eg
http://sci.shams.edu.eg/Departments_Geophysics_Index.ASP

Al Azhar University

Dept of Geology (B) (2015)
Yosief Abbas Street

Cairo 11787
p. +20 (2) 262 3274
k.ubeid@alazhar.edu.ps
http://www.uazhar.edu.eg/bfac/sci/jiolojy.htm

Alexandria University

Dept of Environmental Sciences (B) (2015)
22 Al-Guish Avenue
Alexandria
p. +20 (3) 591 1152
anwar_elfiky@hotmail.com
http://www.alex.edu.eg/dept.jsp?FC=4&CODE=09

Dept of Geology (A,B,M,D) O (2015)
Baghdad Street
Qism Moharram Bek
Alexandria 21511
p. (+203) 3921595
sc-dean@alexu.edu.eg
http://www.sci.alexu.edu.eg/en/Departments/Default.aspx?Dept=4
f: https://www.facebook.com/groups/GSAU.alex/
Enrollment (2014): B: 26 (0)
Professor:
Galal Mohamed I Galal, (D), Germany, 1994, GgPeGe
Khalil I. Khalil Ebeid, (D), Germany, 1995, GgEmm
Kadry Nasser Sediek, (D), USSR Acad of Sci, 1991, GgsGd
Mohamad Nasser Shaaban, (D), 1992, GgsGd
Assistant Lecturer:
Ahmed Ibrahim Dyab, (M), Egypt, 2013, Gg
Assistant Professor:
Hossam EL-Din Ahmed EL-S Helba, (D), Germany, 1994, GgZm
Ahmed Sadek Mansour, (D), Egypt, 1999, Ggs
Instructor:
Sara Akram M. Mahmoud, (B), Egypt, 2006, Gg
Emeritus Professor:
Mohamed Waguih El Dakkak, (D), Egypt, 1971, GgsGd
Galal Abd EL-Ham Ewas, (D), Norway, 1969, GgNr
Hanafy M. Holail, (D), 1988, Ggs
Rousine Tanios Toni, (D), Egypt, 1967, GgPg
Emeritus Lecturer:
Mohamed M. Tamish, (D), W Germany, 1988, GgsCg
Emeritus Professor:
Mohamed Ahmed Rashed, (D), Moscow (Russia), 1984, GgSo

Oceanography Dept (B) (2015)
22 Al-Guish Avenue
Alexandria
p. +20 (3) 591 1152
h_mitwally@sci.alex.edu.eg
http://www.alex.edu.eg/dept.jsp?FC=4&CODE=07

American University of Cairo

Dept of Petroleum and Energy Engineering (B) (2015)
New Cairo Campus: AUC Avenue
PO Box 74
New Cairo 11835
p. +20.2.2615.1000
amrserag@aucegypt.edu
http://www.aucegypt.edu/academics/dept/peng/Pages/

Assiut University

Dept of Geology (B) (2015)
Assiut Governorate
Assiut City
PO Box 71515
Assiut 71515
p. +20 (88) 235 7007
sci@aun.edu.eg
http://www.aun.edu.eg/fac_sci/depart/ge1.htm

Mining & Metallurgical Engineering Dept (B) (2015)
Assiut Governorate
Assiut City
PO Box 71515
Assiut 71515
p. +20 (88) 235 7007
mamoah@aun.edu.eg
http://www.aun.edu.eg/fac_eng?Dpart/Mining/Mining.htm

Beni Suef University

Geology Dept (B) (2015)
Salah Salem Street
Beni Suef 62511
p. +(20) 822324879, +(20) 2082232
elsherif_zakaria@yahoo.com
http://193.227.1.224/sci/

British University in Egypt

Petroleum Engineering (B) (2015)
Misr Ismalia Road
El Sherouk City 11837
enas.sabry@bue.edu.eg
http://www.bue.edu.eg/

Cairo University

Dept of Geophysics (B) (2015)
University Avenue - Univeristy Square
Giza
p. +20 (2) 572 9584
http://www.freewebtown.com/geophysics2/

Mining, Petroleum, and Metallurgical Engineering (B) (2015)
Univerisity Avenue - University Square
Giza
p. +20 (2) 572 9584
nahed_ecae2003@yahoo.com
http://www.eng.cu.edu.eg/dept/en/mpm

Dept of Geology (B) (2015)
University Avenue - University Square
Giza, Cairo
p. +20 (2) 572 9584
portal@cu.edu.eg
http://www.cu.edu.eg/english/

Egyptian Geological Survey and Mining Authority

egov@ad.gov.eg
http://www.egsma.gov.eg/

El Mansoura University

Dept of Geology (B,M,D) (2015)
Faculty of Science
at Mansoura
Department of Geology
Mansoura, Dakahliya governorat 35516
p. +20 050 2242388 Ext. 582
ghazala@mans.edu.eg
http://scifac.mans.edu.eg/en/scientific-dept/geology-department
Enrollment (2012): B: 250 (230) M: 25 (13) D: 15 (7)
Head:
Hosni H. Ghazala, (D), Mansoura, 1990, Ygx

El Zagazig University

Dept of Geology (B,M,D) ●⃠ (2021)
Zagazig
p. +20 (55) 324 577
Khaledgemail@zu.edu.eg
http://www.zu.edu.eg/science
Programs: Geophysics (B.sc.), Geology (B.sc.), Petroleum and water geology (B.sc.), Geology and chemistry (B.sc.)
Enrollment (2020): B: 78 (78) M: 11 (9) D: 7 (3)
Professor:
Khaled Said Gemail, (D), Zagazig, 2003, YuRcYe

Fayoum University

Geology Dept (B,M,D) (2016)
fayoum-Egypt University Zone
ags00@fayoum.edu.eg
Fayoum 63514
p. +20 01005856505

ags00@fayoum.edu.eg
http://www.fayoum.edu.eg/English/Science/Geology/About-Board.aspx
Enrollment (2016): B: 20 (18) M: 4 (0) D: 2 (0)
Professor:
ahmad gaber shedied, (D), Cairo, 1995, GgHww

Minia University
Geology & Chemistry Dept (B) (2015)
Minia
p. +(208-6) 324 420 #321 443
minia@frcu.eun.rg
http://www.minia.edu.eg

Sohag University
Geology Dept (B) (2015)
EL Kawaser
PO Box 82524
Sohag 82524
p. +(20) 93 4605745
a_abudeif@yahoo.com
http://www.sohag-univ.edu.eg/

South Valley University
Dept of Geology (Aswan Campus) (B) (2015)
Qena 83523
p. +20 (96) 339 756
mohammedsm2003@yahoo.com
http://www.svu.edu.eg/arabic/aswan/sci/en/depart/Geology/Geology.htm

Tanta University
Dept of Geology (B) (2015)
El-Geish Street
Tanta 31527
p. +20 (40) 337 7929
president@tainta.edu.eg
http://www.tanta.edu.eg/ar/Tanta/3elom/geology.html

Zagazig University
Dept of Geology (B,M,D) (2015)
Sharkia Governorate
Zagazig City
geology@zu.edu.eg
http://www.zu.edu.eg/

Eritrea

University of Asmara
Dept of Marine Sciences (B) (2015)
PO Box 1220
Asmara
p. 291 1 161926 (Ext. 259)
zekeria@marine.uoa.edu.er
http://www.uoa.edu.er/academics/dmarine

Estonia

Geological Survey of Estonia
Eesti Geoloogiakeskus OU (2015)
Juniper tee 82
Tallinn 12618
p. 672 0094
egk@egk.ee
http://www.egk.ee/

University of Tartu
Inst of Geology (B,M,D) ● ☒ (2019)
Ravila 14a
Tartu 50411
p. +372 7 375 891
geol@ut.ee
http://www.geoloogia.ut.ee/et
Programs: Geology (B, M, D); Environmental Technology (B)
Enrollment (2017): B: 3 (0) M: 4 (0) D: 2 (0)

Ethiopia

Addis Ababa University
Dept of Planetary and Earth Sciences (2015)
PO Box 1176
Addis Ababa
p. 251-111239462
balem@geo.aau.edu.at
http://www.aau.edu.et/index.php/earth-sciences

School of Civil & Environmental Engineering (B) (2015)
PO Box 1176
Addis Ababa
youngkyunkim@aait.edu.et
http://www.aau.edu.et/index.php/earth-sciences

Arba Minch University
Dept of Geology (B) (2015)
PO Box 21
Arba Minch
p. 251-468814972
yoditayalew@fastmail.fm
http://www.arbaminch-univ.com/

College of Natural Sciences (B) (2015)
PO Box 21
Arba Minch
p. +251-46-8810070
alemayehu.hailemicael@amu.edu.et
http://www.arbamich-univ.com/WTIMeteorlogy.html#

Water & Environmental Engineering (B) (2015)
PO Box 21
Arba Minch
p. +251-46-8810070
nigussie_tg@yahoo.com
http://www.arbaminch-univ.com/WTIWEE.html

Mekelle University
Dept of Earth Science (B) (2015)
P.O.Box: 231
Management Building, Main Campus
Mekelle
p. (+251) 344 40 40 05
cciad.mu@gmail.com
http://www.mu.edu.et/index.php/department-of-earth-science

Institute of Geo-information and Earth Observation Sciences (B) (2015)
P.O.Box: 231
Management Building, Main Campus
Makelle
p. +251 914 720398
meseleagw@yahoo.com
http://www.mu.edu.et/index.php/programs/ethiopia-institute-of-technology-mekelle/institute-of-geo-information-and-earth-observat

Semera University
Dept of Geology (B) (2015)
PO Box 132
Semera
p. 251-336660603
semerauniversity@ethionet.et

Wollega University
Dept of Geology (B) (2015)
PO Box 395 Nekemte
Nekemte
p. 251-576615038
wu@ethionet.et
http://www.wuni.edu.et/

Fiji

Ministry of Lands and Mineral Resources

Mineral Resources Dept of Fiji (2015)
Private Mail Bag, GPO
Suva
p. (679) 338 1611
director@mrd.gov.fj
http://www.mrd.gov.fj/

University of the South Pacific

Div of Earth and Environment Science (2015)
Private Mail Bag
GPO Suva
Suva, Fiji Islands
kahsai_k@usp.ac.fj
http://www.sidsnet.org/pacific/usp/earth/

Finland

Aalto University

Dept of civil engineering (B,M,D) ⦸ (2019)
Rakentajanaukio 4
Espoo
SF-02150 Espoo 00076 AALTO
leena.korkiala-tanttu@aalto.fi
https://www.aalto.fi/en/department-of-civil-engineering
Programs: Geoengineering
European Mining and Mineral Education Programme
Certificates: No
Associate Professor:
Leena Korkiala-Tanttu, (D), Helsinki Univ of Tech, 2009
Leena Korkiala-Tanttu, (D), Helsinki Univ of Tech, 2009

Abo Akademi University

Geology and Mineralogy (B,M,D) O (2016)
Domkyrkotorget 1
Turku Fi-20500
p. (+)358442956429
geologi@abo.fi
http://www.abo.fi/fakultet/geologi
Enrollment (2015): B: 26 (8) M: 50 (4) D: 9 (2)
Professor:
Olav Eklund, (D), Abo Akademi, 1993, GxeGz

Geological Survey of Finland

Geologian tutkimuskeskus ⊠ (2020)
P.O.Box 96
Espoo FI-02151
p. +358 29 503 0000
gtk@gtk.fi
https://www.gtk.fi/
f: https://www.facebook.com/GTK.FI
t: @GTK_FI
Director, Strategy and Operational Support:
Mikko Eklund, (M)
Director, Science and Innovation:
Saku Vuori, (D)
Director, Operative Units:
Olli Breilin, (M), Oulu, 1988, GmlGs
Director, Human Resources, Talent Management and Working Env:
Hannu Sivula, (M)
Director General:
Mika Nykänen, (M)

University of Helsinki

Dept of Geosciences and Geography (B,M,D) (2015)
Gustaf Hällströmink 2
P.O. BOX 68
Helsinki 00014
p. 358-294150827
Mia.Kotilainen@helsinki.fi
http://www.helsinki.fi/geology/
Enrollment (2007): B: 0 (6) M: 26 (15) D: 6 (0)
Head:
Juha A. Karhu, (D), Helsinki, 1993, Csg

University of Oulu

Dept of Geology (B,M,D) O (2015)
Linnanmaa
FIN-90014
Oulu
vesa.peuraniemi@oulu.fi
http://cc.oulu.fi/~geolwww/Geology.htm

Dept of Geophysics (2015)
Pertti.Kaikkonen@oulu.fi
http://www.gh.oulu.fi/

France

Bureau de Recherches Geologiques et Minieres

BRGM-Orleans (2015)
3 avenue Claude-Guillemin
BP 36009
Orleans 45060 Cedex 2
p. +33 (0)2 38 64 34 34
http://www.brgm.fr/

Catholic University of the West

Environmental Management (2015)
3, place Andre Leroy
BP 808
49008 Anger
sciences@uco.fr

Centre de Recheches Petrographiques et geochimiques

Center of Petrographic and Geochemical Research (CRPG du CNRS) (2015)
15, rue Notre Dame des Pauvres
BP 20
54501 Vandoeuvre Les Nancy Cedex
p. + 33 (0)3 83 59 42 02
rpik@crpg.cnrs-nancy.fr
http://www.crpg.cnrs-nancy.fr

Ecole des Mines de Paris

Ecole des Mines de Paris (2015)
60-62, Boulevard Saint Michel
75272 PARIS cedex 06
Paris, France 75272
xavier.caillard@mines-paristech.fr
http://www.ensmp.fr/Eng/ENSMP/aboutENSMP.html

Ecole Nationale Supérieure de Géologie (ENSG)

ENSG Géologie (M,D) O⊠ (2020)
2 Rue du Doyen Marcel Roubault
BP 10162
VANDOEUVRE-LES-NANCY, Lorraine F-54505
p. 33 (0)3 72 74 46 00
ensg-contact@univ-lorraine.fr
http://www.ensg.univ-lorraine.fr/
Programs: Geology, Earth Science
Director:
Sausse Judith, (D), GgeGq

Ecole Nationale Superieure des Mines de Nancy

Ecole des Mines de Nancy (M,D) ●⊠ (2018)
Campus ARTEM
92 rue du Sergent Blandan
CS14234
NANCY 54042
p. +33 0355662600
mines-nancy-scolarite-ficm@univ-lorraine.fr
http://www.mines-nancy.univ-lorraine.fr/content/g%C3%A9oing%C3%A9nierie
f: https://www.facebook.com/groups/geoingenierie/
t: @minesnancy

Professor:
Olivier DECK

Ecole Nationale Superieure des Mines de Saint Etiene

(2015)
158 Cours Fauriel
CS 62362
Saint Etienne 42023
p. (+33) (0)4 77 420 278
accueil@ccsti-larotonde.com
http://www.mines-stetienne.fr/fr

Ecole Normale Superieure de Paris

Dept of Geosciences (M,D) ● (2015)
24 rue Lhomond
Paris 75005
p. (+33) (0)1 44 32 22 11
delescluse@geologie.ens.fr
http://www.geosciences.ens.fr
Enrollment (2015): M: 20 (10) D: 29 (6)

ENSPM - Institut Francais du Petrole

Centre Exploration (2015)
1-4 avenue de Bois Preau
BP 311
92506 Rueil Malmaison
vincent.richard@ifpen.fr

French Institute for Research Exploitation of the Sea (IFREMER)

Dept of Marine Geosciences (2015)
BP 70
29263 Plouzane

Higher National School of Mines in Paris (ENSMP)

Center of Geosciences and Geoengineering (M,D) O☒ (2020)
35, rue Saint-Honore
77305 Fontainebleau Cedex
contact@geosciences.mines-paristech.fr
https://www.geosciences.minesparis.psl.eu/en/home/
Programs: Master's Degree in Science and Executive Engineering, Master in earth and planetary science, environment - PSL university, Master Recherche Sciences de l'Univers, Environnement, Écologie (SDUEE), Doctorat of PSL university at MINES ParisTech

Higher Natl School of Mines at Saint-Etienne (ENSME)

Departement Geosciences et environnement (A,M,D) ☒ (2020)
158, cours Fauriel
42023 Saint-Etienne Cedex 02
steve.peuble@emse.fr
https://www.mines-stetienne.fr/formation/master-geospheres/#new_tab
Programs: Geology, Earth Science Education

Inst of Physics of the Globe-Paris VII

Lab de Geochimie, Geomateriaux, Geomag, Sismo, Tech, Obser Volcanologiques ☒ (2019)
Tour 14/24 - 2e etage, 4, place Jussieu
75252 Paris Cedex 05
cartigny@ipgp.fr

Institut de Physique Du Globe De Paris

Institut de Physique Du Globe De Paris (M,D) (2016)
1 rue Jussieu
Paris 75005
p. 01 83 95 74 00
accueil@ipgp.fr
http://www.ipgp.fr/

Institut Polytechnique LaSalle Beauvais (ex-IGAL)

Dept of Geosciences (B,M,D) (2015)
19 Rue Pierre WAGUET - BP 30313
Beauvais 60026 cedex
p. +33 (0) 3 44 06 89 91
yannick.vautier@lasalle-beauvais.fr
http://www.lasalle-beauvais.fr/
Administrative Assistant: Nathalie Lermurier
Director of the Geosciences Department:
Yannick Vautier, Inst Géologique Albert-de-Laparent, 1999, GodCo
Director of the Education Program in Geosciences:
Hervé Leyrit, (D), Gv
Director of School/Companies relations:
Pascal Barrier, (D), Inst Géologique Albert-de-Laparent, PmGsPs
Professor:
Olivier Pourret, (D), Rennes I (France), 2006, CgaGe
Lahcen Zouhri, (D), Lille (France), 2000, HwgGe
Geotechnics:
Bassam Barakat, (D), Ecole Centrale Paris (France), 1991, NrgGq
Engineer in Mining & Quarry:
Lucien Corbineau, Inst Géologique Albert-de-Laparent, 2007, EgGgNm
Engineer in Marine Geology:
Olivier Bain, Inst Géologique Albert-de-Laparent, 2000, OuGgZi
Engineer in Geotechnics:
Jean-David Vernhes, Polytech Paris UPMC (France), 1998, YgNgr
Engineer in Geology:
Benoit Proudhon, Inst Géologique Albert-de-Laparent, 1997, GgcGt
Associate Professor:
Jessica Bonhoure, (D), CREGU-Nancy, 2007, GziCc
Sadek Brahmi, (D), UPMC Paris VI (France), 1991, Nr
Claudia Cherubini, (D), Bari (Italia), 2007, HwGe
Cyril Gagnaison, (D), Sorbonne (France), 2006, PgGsa
Sébastien Laurent-Charvet, (D), Orléans (France), 2001, GctZe
Pascale Lutz, (D), Pau (France), 2002, YgxYd
Mohamed Nasraoui, (D), ENSMP, 1996, EgGzEm
Elsa Ottavi-Pupier, (D), CRPG-CNRS Nancy, 1996, GvzGi
Sébastien Potel, (D), Bâle, 2001, GpzGi
Elodie Saillet, (D), Glasgow, 2009, GctGo
Renaud Toullec, (D), Bordeaux, 2006, GsoEo
Ghislain Trullenque, (D), Basel (Switzerland), 2005, GcNrGg

Laboratoire d'Hydrologie et de Geochimie de Strasbourg

1, rue Blessing
67084 Strasbourg Cedex
p. (+33) (0)3 68 85 04 02
marie-claie.pierret@unistra.fr
http://lhyges.unistra.fr/PIERRET-Marie-Claire,250?lang=fr

National Institute of Applied Science

Lab de Mineralogie et Geotechnique (2015)
20, avenue des Buttes de Coesmes
35043 Rennes Cedex 7
p. (+33) (0)2 23 23 82 00
olivier.guillou@insa-rennes.fr
http://www.insa-rennes.fr/insa-rennes.html

National Polytechnic Inst. of Grenoble

Ecole Doctorale Terre, Univers, Environnement (2015)
Domaine Univ de Grnoble - BP 95
46 avenue Félix Viallet
Cedex 1
Grenoble 38031

Pytheas Institute - Earth Sciences and Astronomy Observatory (PYTHEAS)

Faculte des Sciences de Luminy (2015)
Laboratoires de Geologie Marine et Sedimentologie
70 avenue Leon Lachamp
13288 Marseille
secretariat-direction@osupytheas.fr

FRANCE

Toulouse University

Satellite Geophysics and Oceanography Laboratory (M,D) (2015)
14, Avenue Edouard Belin
31400 Toulouse
p. (+33) (0)5 61 33 29 02
directeur@legos.obs-mip.fr
http://www.legos.obs-mip.fr/Presentation-generale?set_language=en&cl=en

Universite Blaise Pascal (Clermont Ferrand II)

Dept des Sciences de la Terra (2015)
34 Avenue Carnot
63038 Clermont Ferrand Cedex
p. (+33) 04 73 34 67 22
cecile.sergere@univ-bpclermont.fr
http://wwwobs.univ-bpclermont.fr/lmv/cursus/

Université Claude Bernard Lyon 1

Laboratoire de Géologie de Lyon: Terre, Planètes, Environnement (B,M,D) (2016)
Bd du 11 Novembre
Campus de La Doua
Bâtiment Géode
Villeurbanne 69622
p. 0033 (0)472445800
emanuela.mattioli@univ-lyon1.fr
http://lgltpe.ens-lyon.fr/
Administrative Assistant: Marie-Jeanne Barrière
Enrollment (2012): B: 36 (30) M: 16 (16) D: 10 (10)

Professor:
Pascal Allemand
Nicolas Coltice
Fabrice Cordey
Gilles Cuny
Isabelle Daniel
Gilles Dromart
philippe Gillet
Stephane Labrosse
Christophe Lécuyer
Emanuela Mattioli
Guillemette Ménot
Cathy Quantin
Pierre Thomas

Senior Scientist:
Thierry Alboussiere
Vincent Balter
janne Blichert toft
Bernard Bourdon
Razvan Caracas
Eric Debayle
Vincent Grossi
Serge Légendre
Philippe Herve Leloup
Bruno Reynard
yanick Ricard
Jean Vannier
Ricard Yanick

Associate Professor:
Muriel Andréani
Anne-Marie Aucourt
Frederic Chambat
Regis Chirat
Claude Colombié
Véronique Daviéro-Gomez
Renaud Deguen
Véronique Gardien
Bernard Gomez
Vincent Langlois
Gweltaz Mahéo
Matthew Makou
Jean-Emmanuel Martelat
Davide Olivero
Vincent Perrier
Jean-Philippe Perrillat
Sylvain Pichat
Bernard Pittet
Frédéric Quillévéré
Stéphane Reboulet
Philippe Sorrel
Guillaume Suan
Benoît Tauzin

Associate Scientist:
Romain Amiot
Thomas Bodin
caroline Fitoussi
Bertrand Lefebvre
Laurence Lemelle
Jérémy Martin
Jan Matas

Emeritus:
francis Albarede

Related Staff:
Emmanuelle Albalat
Ingrid Antheaume
Florent Arnaud-Godet
Brigitte Barchasz
Ghislaine Broillet
Herve Cardon
Fabien Dubuffet
Philippe Fortin
François Fourel
Philippe Grandjean
Naïma Khrouz
Aline Lamboux
Gilles Montagnac
Sophie Passot
Emmanuel Robert
Magali Seris
Philippe Telouk

Universite d'Orleans

Dept des Sciences de la Terre (2015)
BP. 6759
45067 Orleans
scolarite-osuc@univ-orleans.fr

Universite de Bordeaux I

Dept des Sciences de la Terra et de la Mer (2015)
341 Cours de la Liberation
Talence 33400
p. (+33) 05 40 00 88 79
termer@adm.u-bordeaux1.fr
http://www.u-bordeaux1.fr/universite/organisation/composantes-ufr-instituts/ufr-des-sciences-de-la-terre-et-de-la-mer.html

Universite de Bourgogne

UFR Sciences Vie, Terre & Environnement (B,M,D) (2015)
6 boulevard Gabriel
21100 Dijon
direction-ufrsvte@u-bourgogne.fr
http://ufr-svte.u-bourgogne.fr/

Universite de Bretagne Occidentale

Departement des Sciences de la Terre (2015)
3 Rue des Archives
Brest 29287
p. (+33) 02 98 01 61 88
alain.cottignies@univ-brest.fr
http://www.univ-brest.fr/ufr-sciences/menu/Les_departements/Sciences_de_la_Terre

Universite de Caen

Dept des Sciences de la Terre (2015)
Esplanade de la Paix
Caen 14000
p. (+33) 02 31 56 55 87
isabelle.villette@unicagen.fr
http://ufrsciences.unicaen.fr/departements/departement-des-sciences-de-la-terre/

Universite de Lorraine - Faculte des Sciences et Technologies

Dept Geosciences (B,M) ● ☒ (2018)
Boulevard des Aiguillettes

BP 239
Vandoeuvre Les Nancy, 54506
p. (+33) (0)3 83 68 47 18
cecile.fabre@univ-lorraine.fr
http://www.geologie.uhp-nancy.fr/Php
Enrollment (2014): B: 31 (0) M: 51 (0)
Head:
Cecile FABRE, (D), 2000, Gg

Universite de Montpellier

Geosciences Montpellier (M,D) ☒ (2019)
Campus Triolet
CC 060
Montpellier cedex 5 34095
p. (+33) (0)4 67 14 36 43
dirgm@gm.univ-montp2.fr
http://www.gm.univ-montp2.fr/

Universite de Paris Sud (Orsay)

Dept Sciences de la Terre (B,M,D) ● ☒ (2019)
15 Rue Georges Clemenceau
Orsay 91400
p. (+33) (0)1 69 15 49 09
cecile.quantin@u-psud.fr
http://geosciences.geol.u-psud.fr/
f: https://www.facebook.com/geosciences.paris.sud/
t: @GEOPS_Orsay
Programs: Hydro(geo)logy; Ressources; Sedimentary Basins; Planetology; Paleoclimate; Engineering Geology
Enrollment (2019): B: 31 (27) M: 68 (63) D: 56 (20)

Universite de Paris VI

Lab of Sub-Marine Geodynamics (CEROV) (2015)
Port de la Darse - BP 48
06230 Villefranche-Sur-Mer

Center of Geosynamics Research (2015)
4 Place Jussieu
Paris 75005
p. (+33) 01 44 27 46 98
licence.sciterre@upmc.fr
http://www.upmc.fr/en/education/diplomas/sciences_and_technologies/bachelor_s_degrees/department_of_earth_sciences.html

Universite de Paris VII

Dept des Sciences Physiques de la Terre (2015)
4 place Jussieu
75251 Paris
p. (+33) (0)1 57 27 57 27
zarie.rouas@univ-paris-diderot.fr

Universite de Pau

Dept of Geology (A,B,M,D) (2015)
I.P.R.A. - Geologie
Avenue de L'Universite
Pau 64230
anne-sophie.laloge@univ-pau.fr
http://www.univ-pau.fr/RECHERCHE/GEOPHY/

Universite de Pau et des Pays de l'Adour

Faculte des Sciences (2015)
Avenue de l'Universite
64000 Pau

Universite de Rennes I

Dept. de Geosciences (2015)
2 Rue du Thabot
35065 Rennes Cedex
p. (+33) (0)2 23 23 60 76
olivier.dauteuil@univ-rennes1.fr
http://www.geosciences.univ-rennes1.fr/?lang=en

Universite de Strasbourg

Ecole et Observatoire des Sciences de la Terre (B,M,D) ● (2015)
5 rue Descartes
67084 Strasbourg cedex F
p. (+33) (0)3 68 85 03 53
eost-contact@unistra.fr
http://eost.unistra.fr/nouveautes-du-site/
Director:
Frederic Masson, (D)
Laboratory Director:
Ulrich Achauer, (D), Karlsruhe, 1990, Ysg

Université Jean Monnet, Saint-Etienne

Département de Géologie - Faculte des Sciences et Techiques (B,M,D) ● (2015)
23 rue du Dr. Paul Michelon
Saint-Etienne Cedex F-42023
p. (+33) (0)4 77 48 15 85
veronique.lavastre@univ-st-etienne.fr
http://portail.univ-st-etienne.fr/bienvenue/presentation/ufr-des-sciences-dpt-geologie-327810.kjsp
Head:
Bertrand N. MOINE, (D), Macquarie, 2000, CgtGx
Professor:
Jean-Yves COTTIN, (D), Mus Nat d'Histoire Nat (Paris), 1978
Damien GUILLAUME, (D)
Jean-François MOYEN, (D), 2000, GiCtGp
Assistant Professor:
Marie-Christine GERBE, (D), GisZe

Universite Paul Sabatier (Toulouse III)

Dept Biologie & Geosciences (B,M) ● ☒ (2018)
118 Route de Narbonne
31062 Toulouse
p. (+33) (0)5 82 52 57 21
fsi.sec@univ-tlse3.fr
http://www.univ-tlse3.fr/04628859/0/fiche___pagelibre/&RH=ACCUEIL&RF=1237305837890

Université de Franche-Comté

Faculte des Sciences et Techniques (2015)
16, route de Gray
25030 Besancon Cedex
p. (+33) (0)3 81 66 62 09
scolarite.ufr-2t@univ-fcomte.fr
http://sciences.univ-fcomte.fr/pages/fr/menu3795/formations/licence--sciences-de-la-vie-16862-15340.html

University of Caen

Dept des Sciences de la Terre (2015)
Lab de Geologie structurals
Esplanadde de la Paix
14032 Caen Cedex

University of Franche-Comte

Lab de Geol Strucurale et appliquee (2015)
Faculte des Sci et Techniques
Place Leclerc
25030 Besancon
master.geologie@univ-fcomte.fr

Sciences environnementales (2015)
Sciences et techniques
Service Scolarité
16, route de Gray
25030 Besançon cedex
p. 03 81 66 62 09 / 62 11
Scolarite.UFR-ST@univ-fcomte.fr
http://sciences.univ-fcomte.fr/formations/listedesformations.htm

University of Francois Rabelais

Laboratoire de Geologie (2015)
Parc de Grandmot
37200 Tours

University of Lille

Dept of Geology and Laboratory of Oceanology and Geosci-

ences (LOG) (B,M,D) ● ☒ (2019)
Cite Scientifique
Batiment SN-5
Villeneuve D'Ascq 59655
bruno.vendeville@univ-lille.fr
http://log.cnrs.fr
Programs: Geology (B,M,D)

University of Louis Pasteur (Strasbourg 1)

School and Observatory of Earth Sciences (2015)
1, rue Blessing
67084 Strasbourg Cedex

University of Maine

Faculte des Sci - Lab de Geologie ☒ (2017)
Avenue Olivier Messiasen
72085 Le Mans
p. (+33) (0)2 43 83 30 00
http://sciences.univ-lemans.fr/Biologie-Geosciences

University of Montpellier II

Observatoire des sciences de l'univers OREME (2015)
2, place Eugene Bataillon
34095 Montpellier Cedex 05
eric.servat@msem.univ-montp2.fr

University of Nantes

Departement des Sci de la Terre (2015)
2, rue de la Houssiniere
44072 Nantes Cedex 03
Christophe.Monnier@univ-nantes.fr

University of Nice

Dept of Earth Science (2015)
Faculte des Sciences
28, avenue Valrose
06034 Nice Cedex
secretariat-master-PPA@unice.fr

University of Nice-Sopia Antipollis-1

Laboratoire des Sciences de la Terre (2017)
Rue A. Einstein
06560 Valbonne
dir.recherche@unice.fr
http://www-geoazur.unice.fr/

University of Orleans

Dept des Sciences de la Terre (2015)
Domaine de la Source
BP 6759
45067 Orleans Cedex 02

University of Perpignan

Centre de Sed et Geochimie marines (2015)
52 Avenue Paul Alduy
66100 Perpignan
p. (+33) (0)4 68 66 21 39
facscien@univ-perp.fr

University of Picardy

Dept de Geologie (2015)
Chemin du Thil
80000 Amiens
p. (+33) (0)4 22 82 76 65
mohamed.benlahsen@u-picardie.fr
http://www.u-picardie.fr/jsp/fiche_structure.jsp?STNAV=US&RUBNAV=&CODE=US&LANGUE=0

University of Pierre & Marie Curie (Paris VI)

Dept de Geotectonique (2015)
Tour 26 - ler etage (Boite 219)
4, place Jussieu
75252 Paris Cedex 05

Dept of Living Earth and Environment (2015)
Tour 15 - 4e etage
4, place Jussieu
75252 Paris Cedex 05
chrystele.sanloup@upmc.fr
http://www.ipgp.jussieu.fr/

University of Poitiers

Dept des Sciences de la Terre (2015)
40, ave du Recteur Pineau
86022 Poitiers Cedex

University of Provence (Aix-Marseille I)

Lab de Geol Structurale et appliquee (2015)
Centre Saint Charles
3, place Victor Hugo - Case 28
13331 Marseille Cedex 3
bertrand.martin-garin@univ-amu.fr

University of Reims-Champagne

Dept des Sciences de la Terre (2015)
Moulin de la Housse - BP 1039
51687 Reims Cedex
p. (+33) (0)3 26 91 34 19
scolarite.sceiences@univ-reims.fr
http://www.univ-reims.fr/formation/ufr-instituts-et-ecoles/ufr-sciences-exactes-et-naturelles/presentation,8370.html?

University of Rouen-Upper Normandy

Dept de Geologie (2015)
1 Rue Thomas Becket
76821 Mont-Saint-Aignan
p. (+33) (0)2 35 14 68 26
francoise.baillot@univ-rouen.fr

University of Savoy

Laborotoire de Geologie (2015)
Faculte des Sci et Techniques
Campus de Technolac, BP 1104
73011 Chambery Cedex
Directeur.SceM@univ-smb.fr

University of Science & Technology of Lille

Inst Des Sciences De La Terre (2015)
Flandres - Artois, Cite Scientifique
Bat SN5, BP 36
59655 Villeneuve D'Ascq Cedex
alain.trentesaux@univ-lille1.fr

University of West Brittany

Earth Sciences (2015)
Groupement de Recherche: GEDO
6, avenue Le Gorgeu
29287 Brest

Gabon

Universite des Sciences et Techniques de Masuku

Dept de Geologie (B) (2015)
BP 901
Franceville
p. (+241) 01 67 75 78
http://www.labogabon.net/ustm/facscience

Universite Omar Bongo

Dept de Geologie (B) (2015)
BP 13 131
Boulevard Leon Mba
Libreville
p. +241 73 20 45, (241-72) 69 10
uob@internetgabon.com
http://www.uob.ga/

Germany

Aachen University of Technology

Inst of Structural Geology, Tectonics and Geomechanics (2015)
Lochnerstr 4-20
D-52056
ged@ged.rwth-aachen.de
http://www.ged.rwth-aachen.de

Baden-Wuerttemberg - Landesamt fuer Geologie, Rohstoffe und Bergbau (LGRB)

Regional Government of Freiburg State Office of Geology, Raw Materials and Mining ☒ (2021)
Albertstrasse 5
Freiburg, Baden-Wuerttemberg 79104
p. ++49 9761 208 3000
abteilung9@rpf.bwl.de
http://www.lgrb-bw.de/

Bavarian Environment Agency

Department Geological Survey ☒ (2018)
Buergermeister-Ulrich-Strasse
160
Augsburg , Bavaria 86179
poststelle@lfu.bayern.de
https://www.lfu.bayern.de/geologie/
Programs: None
Certificates: None

Brandenburg - Landesamt fuer Geowissenschaften und Rohstoffe (LGRB)

State Office for Mining , Geology and Minerals of Brandenburg (2015)
Inselstrabe 26
03046 Cottbus
info@lbgr.brandenburg.de
http://www.lbgr.brandenburg.de

Bundesanstalt fur Geowissenschaften und Rohstoffe (BGR)

Federal Institute for Geosciences and Natural Resources ☒ (2018)
Stilleweg 2
Hannover 30655
poststelle@bgr.de
http://www.bgr.bund.de

Christian-Albrechts-Universitaet

Geology Dept (2015)
Olshausenstrasse 40/60
2300 Kiel 1

Ernst-Moritz-Arndt Universitaet

Institut fur Geographie und Geologie (2015)
Domstrabe 11
17489 Griesswald
p. (+49) (0) 3834 86-4502
geogra@uni-greifswald.de
http://www.mnf.uni-greifswald.de/institute/geo.html

Freie Universitaet Berlin

Institute of Geological Sciences, Planetary Sciences and Remote Sensing ☒ (2021)
Malteserstr. 74-100
12249 Berlin
p. (030) 838-70 575
plansec@zedat.fu-berlin.de
http://www.geo.fu-berlin.de/geol/fachrichtungen/planet

Inst fuer Palaontologie (2015)
Maltese-Strasse
74-100, Haus D
D-12249 Berlin
palaeont@zedat.fu-berlin.de
http://userpage.fu-berlin.de/~palaeont/WELCOME.HTM

Friedrich-Schiller-University Jena

Institute for Geosciences (B,M,D) ● (2015)
Burgweg 11
Jena 07749
p. 0049(0)3641/948600
geowissenschaften@uni-jena.de
http://www.geo.uni-jena.de
Enrollment (2014): B: 17 (43) M: 16 (22) D: 69 (12)

Univ.-Prof. Dr.:
Sabine Attinger, (D), Hy
Georg Büchel, (D), Gg
Christoph Heubeck, (D), Stanford, 1994, GsdPg
Nina Kukowski, (D), Ygx
Falko H. Langenhorst, (D), Gz
Juraj Majzlan, (D), Gz
Kai U. Totsche, (D), Bayreuth, 1994, HwClSo
Lothar Viereck, (D)

Jun.-Prof. Dr.:
Anke Hildebrandt, (D), MIT, 2005, HgSpf

Univ.-Prof. Dr.:
Kamil M. Ustaszewski, (D), 2004, Gct

Garching Technical University

Inst fur Geologie und Mineralogie (2015)
Lichtenbergergstrasse 4
0-8046 Garching
rieder@tum.de

Geologischer Dienst Nordrhein-Westfalen

NRW Geological Survey (2015)
Postfach 10 07 63
De-Greiff-Strasse 195
Krefeld D-47707
p. +49-2151-897-0
geoinfo@gd.nrw.de
http://www.gd.nrw.de/home.php

Geologisches Institut der Universitaet

Dept of Geology (2015)
Plelcherwael 1
87 Wuerzburg

Georg-August University of Goettingen

Dept of Geobiology (B,M,D) ☒ (2020)
Goldschmidstr. 3
Goettingen, Lower Saxony 37077
p. +49 551 397951
jreitne@gwdg.de
http://www.geobiologie.uni-goettingen.de/
Programs: Bachelor & Master Geosciences/Geobiology
Enrollment (2018): B: 2 (2) M: 4 (1) D: 10 (4)

Prof.Dr.:
Joachim Reitner, (D), PggPg

Professor:
Volker Thiel, Dr., (D), CooCo

Dr.:
Gernot Arp, Dr., (D), PggPg
Andreas Reimer, (D), OcCmm
Jan-Peter Duda, (D), 2014, PgCoGs

Goethe Universitaet

Fachbereich Geowissenschaften (2015)
Altenhoferallee 1
60438 Frankfurt
p. (+49) (0)69 798 40208
dekanat-geowiss@em.uni-frankfurt.de
http://www.uni-frankfurt.de/fb/fb11

Hamburg - Geological Survey

Ministry of Urban Development and Environmental Protec-

tion Agency for the Environment (2015)
Neuenfelder Straße 19
21109 Hamburg
gla@bue.hamburg.de
http://www.geologie.hamburg.de

Helmholtz-Zentrum Potsdam Deutsches GeoForschungsZentrum

GeoForschungs Zentrum GFZ (2015)
Telegrafenberg 14473
14473 Potsdam
p. (+49) 331 288-1045
presse@gfz-potsdam.de
http://www.gfz-potsdam.de/startseite/

Hessen - Landesamt fuer Umwelt und Geologie

65203 Wiesbaden, Rheingaustraße 186
p. 0611-6939-0
http://www.hlug.de/

Humboldt Universitaet zu Berlin

Palaontologisches Museum (2015)
Invaliden Strasse 43
0-4010 Berlin

Institut fur Palaontologie

Dept of Geology (2015)
O. Weidlich, Fohrenweg 19
W-8504 Stein
palsek@univie.ac.at

Karlsruhe Institute of Technology

Geophysical Institut (B,M,D) (2015)
Hertzstr. 16
Karlsruhe 76187
p. +49-721-6084431
geophysics@gpi.kit.edu
http://www-gpi.physik.uni-karlsruhe.de/
Enrollment (2010): B: 15 (0) D: 10 (0)

Professor:
Thomas Bohlen, (D), Yx

Senior Scientist:
Thomas Forbriger, (D), Ys

Associate Professor:
Joachim R.R. Ritter, (D), Universit, 1996, YsGtv

Research Associate:
Rebecca Harrington, (D), Ys

Dept of Geology (2015)
Kaiserstrasse 12
76131 Karlsruhe
p. (+49) 721 608 4219 2/43651
geophysik@gpi.kit.edu
http://www.bgu.kit.edu

Institute for Applied Geosciences (2015)
Hertzstr. 16
Karlsruhe
susanne.winter@kit.edu
http://www.agw.kit.edu/

Institute for Mineralogy and Geochemistry (2015)
Adenauerring 20b
Karlsruhe D-76131
p. +49 721 608- 43323
img@img.uka.de
http://www.img.kit.edu/

Ludwig-Maximilians-Universitaet Muenchen

Dept of Earth & Enviromental Sciences (B,M,D) (2015)
Theresienstr. 41/III
Munich 80333
p. 0049/89/21804250
dingwell@lmu.de
http://min.geo.uni-muenchen.de/
Enrollment (2007): B: 173 (28) M: 12 (0) D: 24 (0)

Director:
Donald Bruce Dingwell, Giv

Professor:
Alexander Altenbach, Pg
Wladyslaw Altermann, Gg
Michael Amler, Pg
Valerian Bachtadse, Yg
Hans-Peter Bunge, Yg
Christina De Campos, Gz
Karl Thomas Fehr, Gz
Friedrich Frey, Gz
Anke Friedrich, (D)
Anke Friedrich, (D), MIT, 1998, GgtCc
Helmut Gebrande, (D), LMU Munich, 1975, YgsEo
Stuart Gilder, (D), Ym
Peter Gille, (D), Humboldt (Germany), 1984, GzZm
Wolfgang Heckel, Gz
Ernst Hegner, Gg
Soraya Heuss-Aßbichler, Gz
Heiner Igel, Yg
Harald Immel, Pg
Bernd L. Lammerer, (D), LMU Munich, 1972, GgtGc
Reinhold Leinfelder, Pg
Rocco Malservisi, Yg
Robert Marschik, (D), EgmCg
Ludwig Masch, Gz
Wolfgang Moritz, Gz
Bettina Reichenbacher, (D), Johann Wolfgang Goethe, 1992, PgvPe
Wolfgang Schmahl, Gz
Klaus Weber-Diefenbach, Gg
Christian Wolkersdorfer, Gg

Adjunct Professor:
Frank Trixler, (D), GzZmXc

Emeritus:
Nikolai Petersen, (D), 1964, Ygm

Other:
Kirill Aldushin, Gz
Greta Barbi, Yg
Robert Barsch, Yg
Johannes Birner, Gg
Florian Bleibinhaus, Yg
Hans Boysen, Gz
Gilbert Britzke, Yg
Benoit Cordonnier, Gz
Alexander Dorfman, Gz
Thomas Dorfner, Gz
Barbara Emmer, Yg
Werner Ertel-Ingrisch, Gz
Andreas Fichtner, Yg
Michaela Frei, Gg
Frantisek Gallovic, Yg
Alexander Gigler, Gz
Stefan Grießl, Gz
Hagen Göttlich, Gz
Marc Hennemeyer, Gz
Katja Henßel, Pg
Kai-Uwe Hess, Gz
Maria Linda Iaccheri, Gg
Giampiero Iaffaldano, Yg
Guntram Jordan, Gz
Ines Kaiser-Bischoff, Gz
Thorsten Kowalke, Pg
Thomas Kunzmann, Gz
Martin Käser, Yg
Markus Lackinger, Gz
Yan Lavallee, Yg
Maike Lübbe, Gz
Götz Meisterernst, Gz
Timo Casjen Merkel, Gz
Marcus Mohr, Yg
Lena Müller, Gz
Dieter Müller-Sohnius, Gz
Malik Naumann, Pg
Jens Oeser, (D), Yg
Sohyun Park, Gz
Karin Paschert, Gg
Rossitza Pentcheva, Gz

Helen Pfuhl, Yg
Antonio Sebastian Piazzoni, Yg
Christina Plattner, Yg
Josep Puente Alvarez de la
Oliver Riedel, Gz
Alexander Rocholl, Gz
Javier Rubio-Sierra, Gz
Gertrud Rößner, Pg
Dieter Schmid, Pg
Julius Schneider, Gz
Bernhard Schuberth, Yg
Oliver Spieler, Gz
Robert Stark, Gz
Katja Steffens, Gg
Stefan Strasser, Gz
Marco Stupazzini, Yg
Frank Söllner, Gg
Ferdinand Walther, Gz
Joachim Wassermann, Yg
Laura Wehrmann, Pg
Michael Winklhofer, Yg
Ayhan Yurtsever, Gz
Matthias Zeitlhöfler, Gg
Albert Zink, Gz

Palaeontology & Geobiology, Dept of Earth and Env Sci (B,M,D) O☒ (2020)
Richard-Wagner-Strasse 10
Muenchen, Bavaria 80333
geobiologie@geo.lmu.de
http://www.palmuc.de
Programs: Geobiology & Paleobiology (M)
Prof. Dr.:
Gert Woerheide, (D), Pgi
Prof. Dr.:
William Orsi, (D), PgZn
Bettina Reichenbacher, (D), PggPv

Marburg Chome University

Geology Dept (2015)
Deutschhausstrabe 10
35032 Marburg
p. (+49) 06421/28-24257
edda.walz@geo.uni-marburg.de
https://www.uni-marburg.de/fb19_alt

Martin-Luther-Universitaet Halle-Wittenberg

Inst for Geosciences and Geography (A,B,M,D) ●⊘ (2019)
Von-Seckendorff-Platz 3
D-06120 Halle
p. ++49-045-55 26010
direktor@geo.uni-halle.de
http://www.geo.uni-halle.de
Programs: Geography (B,M); Geosciences (B,M); Natural Resource Management (B,M); Intl Area Studies (M); Geography Education
Director:
Christine Fürst, (D), Bonn, 2013, ZucZi

Mecklenburg-Vorpommern - Landesamt fuer Umwelt, Naturschutz und Geologie

State office for the Environment, Nature Conservation and Geology ☒ (2018)
Goldberger Strasse 12
18273 Gustrow
p. ++49-3843-777 0
poststelle@lung.mv-regierung.de
http://www.lung.mv-regierung.de/

Niedersachsen - Landesamt fuer Bodenforschung

p. +49 (0)511-643-0
poststelle-hannover@lbeg.niedersachsen.de
http://www.lbeg.niedersachsen.de

Rheinisch-Westfaelische Technische Hochschule Aachen

Fachgruppe fuer Geowissenschaften und Geographie (2015)
Lochnerstr. 4-20 (Haus B)
Aachen 52056
p. 0241 80 96219
geowiss@rwth-aachen.de
http://www.fgeo.rwth-aachen.de/

Rheinland-Pfalz - Landesamt fuer Geologie und Bergbau

State Office for Geology and Mining (2015)
Emy-Roeder-Strabe 5
PO Box 100 255
Mainz-Hechtsheim D-55129
office@lgb-rlp.de
http://www.lgb-rlp.de/

RWTH Aachen University

Institute of Geology and Palaeontology (B,M,D) ☒ (2019)
Faculty Georessources and
Materials Engineering
Wuellnerstr. 2
52062 Aachen 52062
geo.sek@emr.rwth-aachen.de
Programs: Applied Geosciences, Applied Geophysics, Georessources Management

Sachsen - Landesamt fuer Umwelt und Geologie (LfUG)

Saxon State Agency for Environment, Agriculture and Geology (2015)
Postfach 54 01 37
Dresden 01 311
lfulg@smul.sachsen.de
http://www.smul.sachsen.de/

State Survey for Geology and Mining of Sachsen-Anhalt

State Survey for Geology and Mining of Sachsen-Anhalt ☒ (2019)
Halle, Saxony-Anhalt D-06035
p. +49 345 52 12 0
poststelle@lagb.mw.sachsen-anhalt.de
http://www.lagb.sachsen-anhalt.de

Technical University of Munich

Engineering Geology (B,M,D) ●☒ (2018)
Arcisstr. 21
Munich, Bavaria 80333
p. +498928925850
geologie@tum.de
http://www.eng.geo.tum.de/
Programs: Geosciences (B); Engineering Geology & Hydrogeology (M); Geothermal Energy (M)
Enrollment (2017): B: 0 (1) M: 0 (3) D: 11 (0)
Chair-Prof.:
Kurosch Thuro, (D), Tech (Munich), 1995, NgrGg
Senior Scientist:
Gerhard Lehrberger, (D), TUM, EgGxg
Bernhard Lempe, (D), TUM, 2012, GlgNg
Associate Professor:
Hans Albert Gilg, (D), TUM, 1995, CsEgn
Associate Scientist:
Katja R. Lokau, (D), TUM, 1999, Ng
Marion Nickmann, (D), TUM, 2006, Ng
Bettina Sellmeier, (M), Tech (Munich), Ngr
Research Associate:
Tamara Breuninger, (M), TUM, 2018, Ngx
Matthias Brugger, (M), TUM, 2015, NgGg
Martin Potten, (M), Erlangen (Germany), 2016, NxGg
Margreta Sonnenwald, (M), TUM, 2016, Ng
Georg Maximilian Stockinger, (M), TUM, 2015, NrtNx
Laboratory Director:
Heiko Käsling, (D), TUM, 2009, NrmNg

Technische Hochschule

Institute of Applied Geoscience (2015)
Karolinenplatz 5
64289 Darmstadt
p. (+49) 6151 16-2171
herrmann@geo.tu-darmstadt.de
http://www.geo.tu-darmstadt.de/iag/index.de.jsp

Technische Universitaet Bergakademie Freiberg

Faculty for Geosciences, Geoengineering and Mining (A,B,M,D) ☒ (2021)
Dekanat Fak. 3
Postfach 47/Bernhard-Cotta Strasse
Freiberg 09599
p. +49 (0)3731 / 39 - 3249
Andrea.Thuemmel@geort.tu-freiberg.de
https://tu-freiberg.de/fakultaet3
Programs: Geology, Mineralogy, Mining, Geotechnics, Petroleum Engineering, Geophysics, ...

Technische Universitaet Berlin

Applied Geosciences (2015)
Str. Des 17 Juni 135
W-1000 Berlin 12
p. +49 30314-7260 5
http://www.geo.tu-berlin.de/

Technische Universitaet C.W. Braunschweig

Institute of Environmental Geology (2015)
Postfach 3329
Braunschweig D-38023
geosecret@tu-bs.de
http://www.tu-braunschweig.de/iug

Inst fuer Geologie und Palaontologie (2015)
Fachbereich fur Physik und Geowissenschaften
Pockelstrasse 14
D-3300 Braunschweig DEN

Inst fuer Geophysik und Meteorologie (2015)
Mendelssohnstr 2-3
D-3300 Braunschweig

Technische Universitaet Clausthal

Institut fuer Geologie und Palaeontologie (2015)
LeibnizstraBe 10
D-38678
Clausthal-Zellerfeld 38678
Office@geologie.tu-clausthal.de
http://www.geologie.tu-clausthal.de/

Inst for Petroleum Engineering (2015)
Agricolastrasse 10
38678 Clausthal-Zellerfeld
p. +49-5323-72-2239
marion.bischof@tu-clausthal.de
http://www.ite.tu-clausthal.de/

Technische Universitaet Darmstadt

Institute of Applied Geosciences (B,M,D) (2015)
Schnittspahnstr. 9
Darmstadt D-64287
p. +49 6151 16 2171
iag@geo.tu-darmstadt.de
http://www.geo.tu-darmstadt.de/
Enrollment (2011): B: 280 (3) M: 54 (0) D: 29 (2)

Acting head:
Hans-Joachim Kleebe, GzZm

Professor:
Rafael Ferreiro Maehlmann, Gxp
Matthias Hinderer, Gs
Andreas Hoppe, GgZui
Stephan Kempe, GgCgHs
Ingo Sass, Ng
Christoph Schueth, Hw
Stephan Weinbruch, GzAmZm

Technische Universitat Dresden

Dept of Geosciences (2015)
Mommsenstr 13
0-8027 Dresden
p. +49 351 463-32863
doris.salomon@tu-dresden.de
http://tu-dresden.de/die_tu_dresden/fakultaeten/fakultaet_forst_geo_und_hydrowissenschaften/fachrichtung_geowissenschaften

Thuringen - Landesanstalt fuer Umwelt und Geologie

Thuringen State Institute for Environment and Geology (2015)
Goeschwitzer Str forty-one
07745 Jena
Poststelle@tlug.thueringen.de
http://www.tlug-jena.de/de/tlug/

Universitaet Bochum

Institut fuer Geologie, Mineralogie und Geophysik (B,M,D) (2015)
Universitaetsstr. 150
Bochum 44780
p. +49 234 32 23233
sabine.sitter@ruhr-uni-bochum.de
http://www.ruhr-uni-bochum.de/gmg/

Universitaet Bonn

Steinmann-Institut für Geologie, Mineralogie und Paläontologie (B,M,D) ● (2015)
Nussallee 8
Bonn 53115
p. +49 228 73 4803
tmartin@uni-bonn.de
http://www.steinmann.uni-bonn.de/

Universitaet Erlangen-Nuernberg

Geozentrum Nordbayern (2015)
Schlossgarten 5
91054 Erlangen
p. 09131/85-22615
geologie@geol.uni-erlangen.de
http://www.geol.uni-erlangen.de

Institut fur Geographie (2015)
Kochstr. 4/4
91054 Erlangen
p. 09131/85-22633
common@geographie.uni-erlangen.de
http://www.geographie.uni-erlangen.de/

Universitaet Frankfurt

Institut fur Geowissenschaften (2015)
Fachbereisch 17
Senckenberganlage 32-34
6000 Frankfurt
geowissenschaften@em.uni-frankfurt.de
http://www.geo.uni-frankfurt.de/ifg/

Universitaet Freiburg

Institut fur Geo- und Umweltnaturwissenschaften - Geologie (B,M,D) ☒ (2019)
Albertstr. 23-B
Freiburg i. Br., Baden-Wuerttemberg 79104
ulmer@uni-freiburg.de
http://portal.uni-freiburg.de/geowissenschaften
Programs: Geowissenschaften, Geology, Sustainable Materials
Enrollment (2017): B: 140 (50) M: 52 (19) D: 2 (1)

Universitaet Giessen

Inst fuer Geowissenschaften und LithosphSrenforshung (2015)
Senckenbergstrasse 3
35390 Giessen
p. (+49) 641 990

brigitte.becker-lins@geolo.uni-giessen.de
http://www.uni-giessen.de/fbr08/geolith/

Universitaet Goettingen

Geowissenschaftliches Zentrum (2015)
Goldschmidstr. 3
Lower Saxony
Gottingen D-37077
p. +49 551 397951
bhinz@gwdg.de
http://www.uni-goettingen.de/de/125309.html

Universitaet Greifswald

Institute for Geography and Geology (2015)
F.L. Jahn Strasse 17
Greifswald
p. +49 (0)3834 86-4570
geologie@uni-greifswald.de
http://www.mnf.uni-greifswald.de/institute/geo.html

Universitaet Halle-Wittenberg

Institute for Geosciences and Geographie (A,B,M,D) ●☒ (2018)
Von-Seckendorff-Platz 3/4
Halle D-06120
p. +49-0345-55 26055
direktor@geo.uni-halle.de
http://www.geo.uni-halle.de/
Programs: Geography, Geology, International Area Studies, Natural Resource Management, Teachers
Certificates: great variety

Universitaet Hamburg

Center for Earth System Research and Sustainability (M,D) ☒ (2019)
Bundesstrasse 53
Hamburg 20146
anke.allner@uni-hamburg.de
http://www.cen.uni-hamburg.de/

Institute of Geophysics (B,M,D) ●☒ (2019)
Bundesstrasse 55
Hamburg 20146
p. +4940428382973
dirk.gajewski@uni-hamburg.de
http://www.geo.uni-hamburg.de/de/geophysik.html
Programs: BSc Geophysics/Oceanography
MSc Geophysics
Certificates: none
Enrollment (2016): B: 47 (23) M: 14 (11) D: 12 (8)
Professor:
Dirk J. Gajewski, (D), Karlsruhe, 1987, YesYg

Universitaet Hannover

Institut fur Geologie (2015)
Fachbeleich Erdwissenschaften
Callinstrasse 30
D-30167 Hannover
p. +49-(0)511-762 2343
sekretariat@geowi.uni-hannover.de
http://www.geologie.uni-hannover.de

Universitaet Heidelberg

Insitut fuer Geowissenschaften (2015)
Im Neuenheimer Feld 236
Heidelberg D-69120
p. 06221-54-8291
Elfriede.Hofmann@geow.uni-heidelberg.de
http://www.geow.uni-heidelberg.de/

Facultat fur Chemie und Geowissenschaften (2015)
Im Neuenheimer Feld 234
69120 Heidelberg
p. (+49) 06221/544 844
dcg@urz.uni-heidelberd.de
http://www.chemgeo.uni-hd.de/

Universitaet Leipzig

Institut fur Geophysik und Geologie (2015)
Talstrasse 35
04103 Leipzig
geologie@rz.uni-leipzig.de
http://www.uni-leipzig.de/~geo/

Universitaet Marburg

Inst fuer Geologie und Palaontologie (2015)
Biergenstrasse 12
Lahnberge
D-3550 Marburg-Lahn

Universitaet Muenster

Institut fuer Mineralogie ☒ (2019)
Correnstrasse 24
Muenster 48149
p. +49 251 83-33472
minsek@uni-muenster.de
http://www.uni-muenster.de/Mineralogie/

Institut fuer Geologie und Palaeontologie (B,M,D) ●☒ (2019)
Correnstr. 24
D-48149 Muenster
p. +49 251-83 33974
sklaus@uni-muenster.de
http://www.uni-muenster.de/GeoPalaeontologie/en
Programs: BSc Geosciences, MSc Geosciences, MSc Water Sciences
Enrollment (2016): B: 270 (41) M: 46 (21) D: 25 (3)
Professor:
Christine Achten, (D), Frankfurt (Germany), 2002, CloEg
Heinrich Bahlburg, (D), Tech (Berlin), 1986, GsgCc
Ralph Thomas Becker, (D), Ruhr (Germany), 1990, PisPm
Ralf Hetzel, (D), Gcm
Hans Kerp, (D), Utrecht, 1986, PblGg
Harald Strauss, (D), Goettingen (Germany), 1985, CsGg

Universitaet of Kiel

Institute of Geoscience (2015)
Christian-Albrechts-Platz 4
24118 Kiel
p. (+49) 431 880 3900
wussow@geophysik.uni-kiel.de
http://www.ifg.uni-kiel.de/6+M52087573ab0.html

Universitaet Oldenburg

Institute for Chemistry and Biology of the Marine Environment (2015)
Carl-von-Ossietzky-Str. 9-11
Box 2503
Oldenburg 26111
p. +49-0441-798-5342
director@icbm.de
http://www.icbm.uni-oldenburg.de/

Universitaet Potsdam

Institute for Earth and Environmental Sciences (B,M,D) (2015)
Karl-Liebknecht-Str. 24-25
Potsdam 14476
p. +49 331 977 2116
sekretariat@geo.uni-potsdam.de
http://www.geo.uni-potsdam.de/
Enrollment (2013): B: 319 (14) M: 79 (11) D: 122 (16)

Universitaet Stuttgart

Inst fuer Geol und Palaontogisch (2015)
Fakultaet-7-Geo. und Biowissenschaften
Boblinger Str. 72
D-7000 Stuttgart 10

Universitaet Trier

Regional and Environmental Science (2015)
Behringstrabe 21

D-54296 Trier
p. (+49) (0) 651-201-4528
dekanatfb6@uni-trier.de
http://www.uni-trier.de/index.php?id=2220

Lehrstuhl fuer Geologie (B,M,D) ☒ (2020)
Geowissenschaften (FB VI)
Trier 54286
p. 0651 201 4647
ensch@uni-trier.de
http://www.uni-trier.de/index.php?id=2632
Programs: Geography; Environmental Sciences; Geoarchaeology
Enrollment (2020): B: 14 (4) M: 12 (3) D: 3 (1)

Universitaet Tuebingen

Institute for Geoscience (2015)
72076 Tuebingen
Sigwartstr. 10
Christophe.Pascal@rub.de
http://www.ifg.uni-tuebingen.de/

Universitaet Würzburg

Institut für Paläontologie (2015)
Pleicherwall 1
D-97070 Würzburg
p. 49 0931- 31 25 97
i-palaeontologie@mail.uni-wuerzburg.de
http://www.palaeontologie.uni-wuerzburg.de

Institut für Geographie und Geologie (2015)
Am Hubland
97074 Würzburg
p. +49 (0) 931 / 31-85555
http://www.geographie.uni-wuerzburg.de

Universitaet zu Koeln

Institute for Geology and Mineralogy (2015)
Cologne
p. +49 221 470-5619
ellen.stefan@uni-koeln.de
http://www.geologie.uni-koeln.de/

University of Bayreuth

Bayerisches Geoinstitut (M,D) (2015)
Bayreuth 95440
p. +49(0)921 55-3700
bayerisches.geoinstitut@uni-bayreuth.de
http://www.bgi.uni-bayreuth.de/

University of Bremen

Geosciences (A,B,M,D) ●☒ (2019)
Klagenfurter Strasse 2-4
Bremen, Bremen 28359
p. +49 421 218 - 65010
info@geo.uni-bremen.de
http://www.geo.uni-bremen.de
Programs: Geosciences (BSc,MSc); Marine Geosciences (MSc); Materials Chemistry and Mineralogy (MSc)
Enrollment (2019): B: 199 (0) M: 289 (0)

University of Cologne

Dept of Geology and Mineralogy (B,M,D) ● (2015)
Zuelpicherstr. 49a
50674 Koeln
p. +49-221-470-5619
ellen.stefan@uni-koeln.de
http://www.uni-koeln.de/math-nat-fak/geologie

Institute of Geophysics and Meteorology (B,M,D) (2015)
Pohligstraße 3
D-50969 Köln
p. +49 (0)221 470 2552
sekretar@geo.uni-koeln.de
http://www.geomet.uni-koeln.de/en/general/home/

Universität Mainz

Institut für Geowissenschaften (B,M,D) ●☒ (2017)
Joh.-J.-Becher-Weg 21
55128 Mainz
p. +49 6131 39 24373
igw@uni-mainz.de
http://www.geowiss.uni-mainz.de/
Head:
Boris PJ Kaus, (D), Yg
Associate Professor:
Roman Botcharnikov, (D), Gx
Jonathan M. Castro, (D), Gv
Michael Kersten, (D), Ca
Cees W. Passchier, (D), Gt
Denis Scholz, (D), Cl
Bernd R. Schöne, (D), PegPi
Frank Sirocko, (D), Gs
Adjunct Professor:
Kirsten I. Grimm, (D), Pm
Dieter Mertz, (D), Cc
Thomas Tütken, (D), Pv

West Wilhelms Universitat

Dept of Applied Geology (2015)
Schlossplatz 2
4400 Muenster

Westfälische Wilhelms-Universität Münster

Fachbereich Geowissenschaften (B,M,D) (2016)
Heisenbergstrasse 2
Münster D-48149
p. +49 251 83-30002
dekangeo@uni-muenster.de
http://www.uni-muenster.de/Geowissenschaften/

Ghana

Kwame Nkrumah University of Science and Technology

Petroleum Engineering (B) (2015)
http://www.knust.edu.gh/ceng/faculties.php

Dept of Geomatic Engineering (B,M,D) O (2017)
geomaticeng@knust.edu.gh
head.geomatic@knust.edu.gh
Kumasi PMB KNUST
p. +233 (0)3220 60227
geomaticeng@knust.edu.gh
http://www.knust.edu.gh/ceng/faculties.php

Geological Engineering (B,M,D) ● (2015)
Geological Engineering Department
College of Engineering
KNUST
Kumasi PMB
geologicaleng@knust.edu.gh
https://coe.knust.edu.gh/
Senior Scientist:
Emmanuel K. Appiah-Adjei, (D), Hohai, 2013, HwgGg
Associate Professor:
Simon K. Gawu, (D), Witwatersrand, 2004, GgEgZn
Lecturer:
Bukari Ali, (D), Birmingham (UK), 1996, HwNgYg
Godfrey C. Amedjoe, (M), Ghana, 2005, GidGc
Samuel Banash, (M)
Gordon Foli, (M), 2004
Solomon S. Gidigasu, (M), Sci & Tech (China), 2013, GeZrNr
Emmanuel Mensah, (M), Sci & Tech (China), 1998, EgGg

University of Development Studies

Earth and Environmental Science (B) (2015)
PO Box 1350
Tamale
p. +233 (71) 22422
edambayi@uds.edu.gh
http://www.uds.edu.gh/

University of Ghana

Dept of Earth Science (B,M,D) ● (2015)
PO Box LG 58
Legon
Accra
p. +233-244-116-879
pmnude@ug.edu.gh
http://www.ug.edu.gh/index1.php?linkid=185&sublinkid=40&subsublinkid=36
Enrollment (2013): B: 336 (104) M: 105 (33) D: 2 (1)
Dean of Science:
Daniel K. Asiedu, (D), GsCgGd
Professor:
Bruce K. Banoeng-Yakubo, (D), Ghana, GcHw
Senior Scientist:
Thomas K. Armah, (D), YgeYe
Jacob M. Kutu, (D), GctGc
Patrick Asamoah Sakyi, (D), Cg
Head of Department:
Prosper M. NUDE, (D), Ghana, GipGx
Associate Professor:
Thomas M. Akabzaa, (D), Ghana, 2004, EgGeNm
David Atta-Peters, (D), Ghana, Pl
Johnson Manu, (D), GzEgGz
Frank K. Nyame, (D), Cg
Sandow M. Yidana, (D), Hwq
Lecturer:
Francis Achampong, (D), Ngr
Chris Y. Anani, (D), Gsd
Larry-Pax CHEGBELEH, (D), Ng
Yvonne A.S Loh, (M), Hw
Issac A. Oppong, (D), Np

University of Mines and Technology

Dept of Geological Engineering (B) (2015)
PO Box 237
Tarkwa
p. +233 3123 20935
sps@umat.edu.gh
http://www2.umat.edu.gh/dept/gl/

Dept of Geomatic Engineering (B) (2015)
PO Box 237
Tarkwa
p. +233(0)362 20324
gm@umat.edu.gh
http://www.umat.edu.gh/UndergraduatePrograms/geomatic.html

Dept of Mineral Engineering (B) (2015)
PO Box 237
Tarkwa
p. +233(0)362 21136
mr@umat.edu.gh
http://www.umat.edu.gh/UndergraduatePrograms/mineral.html

Dept of Mining Engineering (B) (2015)
PO Box 237
Tarkwa
p. +233 3123 20935
mn@umat.edu.gh
http://www.umat.edu.gh/UndergraduatePrograms/Mining.html

Greece

Aristotle University of Thessaloniki

School of Geology (2015)
GR-541 24
Thessaloniki 54124
p. (+30) 2310 99.8450
info@geo.auth.gr
http://www.geo.auth.gr/index_en.htm

Greek Institute of Geology & Mineral Exploration

Greek Institute of Geology & Mineral Exploration ☒ (2018)
1, Spirou Louis St.,
Olympic Village
Acharnae P.C. 13677
dirgen@igme.gr
http://www.igme.gr

National Technical University of Athens

Dept of Mining Engineering and Metallurgy (2015)
Zographou Campus
15 780 Athens
secretary@metal.ntua.gr
http://www.metal.ntua.gr/div-geology

University of Athens

Faculty of Geology and Geoenvironment (2015)
National & Capodistran Univ. of Athens
Panepistimioupolis, Ilistra
Athens
secr@geol.uoa.gr
http://www.geol.uoa.gr/engindex.htm

University of Patras

Dept of Geology (2015)
26110 Patras

Guatemala

Universidad sde San Carlos de Guatemala

Centro de Estudios Superiores de Energia y Minas (2015)
Ciudad Universitaria Zona 12, Guatemala City 01012
p. (502) 2418-9139 ex. 86211
usacesem@ing.usac.edu.gt
http://cesem.ingenieria.usac.edu.gt/

Guinea

Univerité Gamal Abdel Nasser de Conakry

Faculty of Geology and Mining (M,D) ●☒ (2019)
BP 1147
Conakry, Guinée
p. +224 631 54 48 38
sekoumoussa@gmail.com
http://www.uganc.org/index.php/2013-01-12-06-22-44/cere
Enrollment (2018): M: 30 (0)

Guyana

Guyana Geology and Mines Commission

Guyana Geology and Mines Commission (2015)
Upper Brickdam
Georgetown
p. 226-5591, 225-2862
http://www.ggmc.gov.gy/

Haiti

Ecole Nacionale de Geologie Appliquee

Ecole Nacionale de Geologie Appliquee (2015)
B.P. 1560-Varreux, Port-au-Prince

Hungary

Eotvos Lorand University

Insitute of Geography and Earth Sciences (B,M,D) ● (2018)
Pazmany Peter setany 1/C
Budapest H-1117
p. (+36 1) 381 2191
altfoldtan@ttk.elte.hu
http://geosci.elte.hu/en_index.htm
Enrollment (2014): B: 900 (360) M: 300 (120) D: 40 (18)
Professor:
Judit Bartholy, (D), Eotvos Lorand, 1978, Am

Associate Professor:
Gábor Timár, (D), Eotvos Lorand, 2003, YgdZi
Research Professor:
János Lichtenberger, (D), Hungarian Acad of Sci, 1996, AsZrXy
Professor:
Kristof Petrovay, (D), Eotvos Lorand, 1992, Xy
Miklos Kazmer, (D), Eotvos Lorand, 1982, PggRh
Associate Professor:
Agnes Gorog, (D), Eotvos Lorand, Pmi
László Lenkey, (D), Vrije (Amsterdam), 1999, YhHwGa
Balázs Székely, (D), Tubingen, 2001, GmZri
Associate Scientist:
Orsolya Ferencz, (D), Budapest, 2001, XyZr
Anikó Kern, (D), Eotvos Lorand, 2012, ZrAms
Gábor Molnár, (D), Eotvos Lorand, 2004, ZrYgZi
Assistant Professor:
László Balázs, (D), Eotvos Lorand, 2009, EoYeg
Attila Galsa, (D), Eotvos Lorand, 2004, YgHwYe
Attila Osi, (D), Eotvos Lorand, PviPe
Emoke Toth, (D), Eotvos Lorand, PmsPb
Research Associate:
Istvan Szente, (D), Eotvos Lorand, Pig
Professor:
Ferenc Horváth, (D), Eotvos Lorand, 1971, YgRhGc
Péter Márton, (D), Eotvos Lorand, 1971, YmgYs

Hungarian Geological Survey

Hungarian Geological Institute (2021)
Stefánia út 14
Budapest HU-1143
p. 36 1267 1433
muzeum@mbfsz.gov.hu

Jozsef Attila University

Dept of Mineralogy, Geochem & Petrology (2015)
P O Box 651
H-6701 Szeged

Dept of Geology & Paleontology (2015)
Egyetum u. 2-6
H-6722 Szeged

Mining and Geological Survey of Hungary

Mining and Geological Survey of Hungary (2015)
PO Box 95
1590 Budapest 1145
p. (+36-1) 301-2900
hivatal@mbfh.hu
https://mbfsz.gov.hu/en

Univesity of Szeged

Dept of Physical Geography and Geoinformatics (B,M,D) (2017)
SZTE Termeszeti Foldrajzi Tanszek
Szeged, 6722 Egyetem utca 2. PF:653
Szeged
p. 0036 62544158
mezosi@geo.u-szeged.hu
http://www.geo.u-szeged.hu/ANG/HPfirst.html
Enrollment (2012): D: 20 (0)
Professor:
Janos Rakonczai, (D), 1978, Ze
dean of faculty:
lászló Mucsi, (D), Szeged, 1996, ZirZy
Associate Professor:
Andrea Farsang, (D), Szeged, 2016, SdZe
Timea Kiss, (D), Debrecen, 2001, GmZy
György Sipos, (D), Szeged, 2007, HqYm
József Szatmári, (D), Szeged, 2007, ZriZy

Iceland

Landmælingar Íslands

National Land Survey of Iceland ☒ (2017)
Stillholt 16-18 300 Akranes
Akranes 300
p. 4309000
lmi@lmi.is
http://www.lmi.is/

University of Iceland

Faculty of Earth Science (2015)
Öskju, Sturlugötu 7
101 Reykjavik
p. (+354) 5254600
dagrun@hi.is
http://english.hi.is/sens/faculty_of_earth_sciences/about_faculty

India

Aligarh Muslim University

Dept of Geology (B,M,D) ● (2015)
Aligarh - U.P.
Aligarh, Uttar Pradesh 202002
p. 0571-2700615
lakrao@yahoo.com
http://www.amu.ac.in/fsc/no4.html

Andhra University

Dept of Geology (2015)
Vishakha-patnam-530 003
College of Science and Technology
Andhra Pradesh
p. 91-891-2844888
principal_science@andhrauniversity.info
http://www.andhrauniversity.info/

Anna University

Dept of Geology (2015)
Guindy, Chennai-600 025,
Tamil Nadu
p. 044-22358442 / 8444 / 8452
geonag@gmail.com
http://www.annauniv.edu

Annamalai University

Faculty of Marine Sciences (2015)
Annamalainagar-608 025
Tamil Nadu
p. 91 - 4144 - 238248
info@annamalaiuniversity.ac.in
http://annamalaiuniversity.ac.in/marinesciences.htm

Banaras Hindu University

Dept of Geology (B,M,D) ☒ (2017)
Varanasi
U.P. 221005
hbsrivastava@gmail.com
http://www.bhu.ac.in/Geology
Programs: Geology
Enrollment (2017): B: 150 (0) M: 56 (0) D: 50 (0)
Professor:
HARI BAHADUR SRIVASTAVA, (D), Banaras Hindu, 1980, GctGp

Bharathidasan University

Dept of Geology (2015)
School of Geosciences
Tiruchirapalli 620 024
p. +91 431 2407034
drmm_bdu@yahoo.co.uk
http://www.bdu.ac.in/schools/geo_sciences/geology/

Cochin University of Science & Technology

Dept of Geology (2015)
Kochi
p. +91(484)2577550
akv@cusat.ac.in
http://www.cusat.ac.in/

Geological Survey of India

Geological Survey of India O☒ (2021)
27, J.L.Nehru Road
Kolkata
Kolkata, West Bengal 700016
dg.gsi@gov.in
http://www.gsi.gov.in
f: https://www.facebook.com/gsipage/
t: @GeologyIndia
Certificates: Advanced GIS, Digital Cartography, Geological Mapping, Mineral Exploration, Geophysical Survey, etc

Goa University

School of Earth, Ocean and Atmospheric Sciences (M,D) O☒ (2021)
Taleigao Plateau
Goa University P.O.
Taleigao Plateau
Panaji, Goa 403 206
p. +91-8669609193
mkotha@unigoa.ac.in
http://www.unigoa.ac.in/department.php?adepid=11&mdepid=3
Programs: Applied Geology
Certificates: GIS
Enrollment (2018): M: 22 (22) D: 1 (1)
Professor:
Mahender Kotha, (D), IIT (Bombay), 1987, GsoZi
Associate Professor:
Anthony V. Viegas, (D), Goa, 1997, GiEmGx
On Contract:
Poornima Dhavaskar, (M), Geology, 2013, Gge
Purushottam Verlekar, (M), GrmGg
Assistant Professor:
Niyati Kalangutkar, (D), Goa, GugGe
Cooperating Faculty:
Sohini Ganguly, (D), Gi

Guru Nanak Dev University

Dept of Geology (2015)
Amritsar
http://www.gndu.ac.in/

Indian Institute of Science Education and Research, Kolkata

Dept of Earth Science (B,M,D) ●☒ (2017)
Main Campus
Nadia
Mohanpur (Kolkata) , West Bengal 741246
des.chair@iiserkol.ac.in
http://earth.iiserkol.ac.in/
Programs: Geological Sciences

Indian Institute of Technology

Dept of Applied Geology (2015)
Bombay, Powai
Bombay
ayaz@iitb.ac.in
http://www.geos.iitb.ac.in/

Indian Institute of Technology, Kharagpur

Dept of Geology & Geophysics (B,M,D) (2015)
Kharagpur, Kharagpur
West Bengal 721302
Kharagpur, West Bengal 721302
p. +91-3222-282268
head@gg.iitkgp.ernet.in
http://www.iitkgp.ac.in/departments/home.php?deptcode=MG

Indian Institute of Technology, Roorkee

Dept of Earth Sciences (M,D) (2015)
Department of Earth Sciences
IITRoorkee
Roorkee, Uttrakhand 247667
p. +911332285532
dpkesfes@iitr.ac.in
http://members.tripod.com/rurkiu/acd-earth

Indian School of Mines

Dept of Applied Geology (2015)
Dhanbad
West Bengal 826 004
p. +91-326-2296616
agl@ismdhanbad.ac.in
http://www.ismdhanbad.ac.in/depart/geology

Institute of Science

Dept of Geology (2015)
Aurangabad 431004
Aurangabad , Maharashtra
p. +91 (0240) 2400586
director@inosca.org
http://www.inosca.org

Jadavpur University

Dept of Applied Geology (B,M,D) (2015)
Jadavpur
Calcutta
p. +913324572268
hod@geology.jdvu.ac.in
http://www.jaduniv.edu.in/view_department.php?deptid=76

Jmia Millia Islamia

Dept of Geography (2015)
Jamia Nagar
New Delhi-25
rocketibrahim@yahoo.com
http://jmi.ac.in/aboutjamia/departments/geography/introduction

Lucknow University

Dept of Geology (2015)
Lucknow 226007 U.P.
info@lkouniv.ac.in
http://www.lkouniv.ac.in/dept_geology.htm

Maharaja Sayajirao University of Baroda

Dept of Geology (2015)
Baroda - Gujarat
p. (919) 426721547
ischamyal@yahoo.com
http://www.msubaroda.ac.in/science

Nagpur University

Dept of Geology (2015)
Rao Bahadur D. Laxminarayan Educational Campus
Law College Square
Amravati Road
Nagpur 440 001
p. +91-712-253241
geodeptplacecell@gmail.com
http://www.nagpuruniversity.org/links/FacultyofScience.htm

Osmania University

Dept of Geology (2015)
Hyderabad 500007 A.P.
http://www.osmania.ac.in/

Centre of Exploration Geophysics (M,D) O☒ (2019)
Department of Geophysics
Osmania University Campus
Hyderabad, Telengana 500007
p. (+91) 40-27097116
head.geophysics@osmania.ac.in
http://www.osmania.ac.in/
Programs: Geophysics (M.Sc.)
Enrollment (2019): M: 32 (27) D: 11 (11)
Chairman, Board of Studies in Geophysics:
Veeraiah B, (D), Osmania, 2005, YexYg
Head, Department of Geophysics:
Ram Raj Mathur, (D), Osmania, 1989, YeuYm

Assistant Professor:
Manjula Dharmasoth, (M), Osmania (India), 2012, YmeYg
Vijay Kumar Dubba, (D), Osmania (India), 2015, YevYs
Udaya Laxm Gakka, (D), Osmania, 2009, HwYge

Panjab University

Dept of Geology (B,M,D) ●☒ (2020)
Sector-14
Chandigarh, Punjab 160014
p. (+91) 1722534250
chairperson_geology@pu.ac.in
http://geology.puchd.ac.in/
Programs: Geology

Centre for Petroleum and Applied Geology (U.I.E.A.S.T.) (2015)
Chandigarh 160014
rpatnaik@pu.ac.in
http://pu.ac.in/

Pondicherry University

Dept of Earth Science (B,M,D) (2015)
The Head
Department of Earth Sciences
Pondicherry University
Pondicherry 605 014
p. +914132656741
head.esc@pondiuni.edu.in
http://www.pondiuni.edu.in/department/department-earth-sciences
Professor:
Balakrishnan Srinivasan, (D), Jawaharlal Nehru (India), 1986, CcGiz

Presidency College

Dept of Geology (2015)
College Street
Calcutta
hnb.geol@presidencycollegekolkata.ac.in
http://www.concentric.net/~slahiri/pc/Department/Geology/geo

Pt. Ravishankar Shukla University

School of Studies in Geology and Water Resource Management (M,D) (2015)
SOS Geology
Pt. Ravishankar Shukla UNiversity
Raipur, Chhattisgarh 492010
geology@prsu.com
http://www.prsu.ac.in/
Enrollment (2013): M: 15 (0) D: 4 (1)
Professor:
Srikant k. Pande, (D), Nagoya, 1986, GgHyg
Professor:
Ninad Bodhankar, (D), Raipur, 1992, GcNm
Kosiyath Rghavan Na Hari, (D), Vikram Univ Ujjain, 1992, GiiCp
Mohammad Wahdat Yar Khan, (D), AMU, Aligarh, 1979, GdEgCl

Savitribai Phule Pune University,

Dept of Geology (M,D) ☒ (2019)
Ganeshkhind Road
Pune, Maharashtra 411 007
p. +91-020-25601360
geology@unipune.ac.in
http://www.unipune.ac.in/dept/science/geology/
Programs: M.Sc. Geology, Ph.D Geology
Professor:
Makarand Ganesh Kale, (D), 1992, Gso

University of Baroda

Dept of Geology (2015)
Baroda , Vadodara 390 002
swanikhil@yahoo.co.in
http://www.msubaroda.ac.in/deptindex.php?ffac_code=2&fdept_code=6

University of Delhi

Dept of Geology (B,M,D) O⊘ (2020)
Department of Geology
University of Delhi
Delhi
New Delhi 110 007
p. 27667073
csdubey@gmail.com
http://www.geology.du.ac.in/
Programs: Geology
Enrollment (2014): B: 105 (1200) M: 60 (600) D: 30 (130)
Director COL:
C S. Dubey, (D), Delhi, 1993, GexGt

University of Madras

Dept of Geology (2015)
Madras, 600 025
Maraimalai Adigalar Campus
spmohan50@hotmail.com
http://www.unom.ac.in/departments/geology/geology.html

Dept of Geology (2015)
Maraimalai Adigalar Campus
Chennai 600 005
p. 044 - 22202790
spmohan50@hotmail.com
http://www.unom.ac.in/departments/geology/geology.html

University of Mysore

Dept of Geology (2015)
Mysore 570 005
p. +91 821 2419724
bb@geology.uni-mysore.ac.in
http://www.uni-mysore.ac.in/geology/#A

Vijayanagara SriKrishnaDevaraya University

Dept of Applied Geology (M,D) O☒ (2021)
Dr.C.Venkataiah
Professor of Geology
Vijayanagara SriKrishnaDevaraya University
Bellary, Karnataka 583 104
p. (937) 909-0588
venkataiah.c@gmail.com
http://www.vskub.ac.in
Programs: M.Sc two years Applied Geology

Indonesia

Direktorat Vulkanologi

Volcanological Survey of Indonesia (2015)
Jl. Diponegoro 57
Bandung , West Java
http://portal.vsi.esdm.go.id/

Gadjah Mada University

Dept of Geology (2015)
Jalan Bulaksmur
Yogzakarta 55281
p. (+62) 274 6492340
geografi@geo.ugm.ac.id
http://geo.ugm.ac.id/main/

Indonesian Directorate General of Geology and Mineral Resources

Ministry of Mines and Energy (2015)
pengaduan@esdm.go.id
http://www.esdm.go.id

Institut Teknologi Bandung

Dept of Geology (2015)
Jalan Ganesa, No. 10
Bandung 40132, Jawa Barat
p. 022 2514990
sisfo@fitb.ac.id
http://www.fitb.itb.ac.id/en/

Dept of Geological Engineering (2015)
Jl. Ganesha 10
Bandung, 40135
geologi@gc.itb.ac.id

Trisakti University

Faculty of Earth and Energy Technologies (2015)
Jl. Kiai Tapa, Grogel
Jakarta 11440
p. 5663232 Ext. 8510

Universitas Hasanudin

Dept of Geological Engineering (2015)
Jl. Perintis Kemerdekaan
Ujung Pandang 90245

Universitas Padjadjaran

Dept of Geological Engineering
(2015)
Jl. Raya Bandung-Sumedang km.21,
Jatinangor

Universitas Pakuan

Dept of Geological Engineering (2015)
Jl. Pakuan, PO Box 452
Bogor 16143, Jawa Barat
p. 0251-8312206
rektorat@unpak.ac.id
http://www.unpak.ac.id/

Ireland

Geological Survey of Ireland

Geological Survey of Ireland (2015)
Beggars Bush
Haddington Road
Dublin 4
john.butler@gsi.ie
http://www.gsi.ie/

Geological Survey of Northern Ireland

Geological Survey of Northern Ireland (2015)
Colby House
Stranmillis Court
Belfast BT9 5BF
gsni@economy-ni.gov.uk
https://www2.bgs.ac.uk/gsni/

National University of Ireland Galway

Earth and Ocean Sciences (B,D) (2015)
Earth & Ocean Sciences
National University of Ireland
University Road
Galway
p. + 353 (0)91 492 126
lorna.larkin@nuigalway.ie
http://www.nuigalway.ie/eos/

Professor:
Peter Croot, (D), Otago (NZ), Ct

Lecturer:
Rachel R. Cave, (D), Southampton (UK), Cm
Eve Daly, (D), National (Ireland), Ygu
Tiernan Henry, (D), National (Ireland), 2014, HwyEg
John Murray, (D), Trinity Coll (Cambridge), PgGs
Robin Raine, (D), National (Ireland), Yg
Tyrrell Shane, (D), Univ Coll (Dublin), Gs
Martin White, (D), Southampton (UK), Op

Emeritus:
Martin Feely, (D), National (Ireland), 1982, GzxEg

Trinity College

Dept of Geology (2018)
Department of Geology
Museum Building
Trinity College-Dublin
Dublin 2
p. +353 01 896 1074
earth@tcd.ie
http://www.tcd.ie/Geology/

Chair:
Balz S. Kamber, (D), CgGgp

Associate Professor:
David Chew, (D), Univ Coll (Dublin), 2001, CcGgt
Catherine Coxon, GeOu
Robin Edwards, Ge
Patrick N. Wyse Jackson, (D), Dublin, 1992, PiRh

Assistant Professor:
Quentin G. Crowley, Cc
Seán h. mcClenaghan, Eg
Chris Nicholas, Eo
Juan Diego Rodriguez-Blanco, (D), 2006, GzClZm
Catherine V. Rose, Cg
Emma L. Tomlinson, Cc

University College Cork

Dept of Geology (B,M,D) (2015)
Donovans Road
Cork
p. +353 21 4902657
s.culloty@ucc.ie
http://www.ucc.ie/ucc/depts/geology/
Administrative Assistant: Patricia Hegarty

Head:
John Gamble, Gi

Chair:
Andy J. Wheeler, (D), Cambridge, 1994, GusGg

Professor:
Ken Higgs, Pl

Research Associate:
Tara Davis, Yg
Jim Smith, Pl

Lecturer:
Bettie M. Higgs, (D), Sheffield, 1977, YgGqRh
Ed Jarvis, Pl
Ivor MacCarthy, (D), 1974, Gs
Pat Meere, (D), National (Ireland), 1992, Gc
John Reavy, (D), GicGt

Other:
Mary Lehane, Zn
Mick O'Callaghan, Zn
Dan Rose, Zn

University College Dublin

School of Earth Sciences (2015)
Science Centre West
University College Dublin
Belfield, Dublin 4
p. +353 1 716 2331
geology@ucd.ie
http://www.ucd.ie/geology/

Head:
J. Stephen Daly

Professor:
Peter D. W. Haughton
Frank McDermott, (D), Open (UK), 1987, GgCgZg
Patrick M. Shannon
John J. Walsh

Associate Professor:
Christopher J. Bean
Julian F. Menuge, (D), Cambridge, 1983, EmCcs
Ian D. Somerville

Lecturer:
Conrad Childs
Aggeliki Georgiopopoulou, (D), Southampton (UK), 2006, GusOg
Ivan Lokmer
Patrick J. Orr

Adjunct Professor:
Tom Manzocchi, (D), Goc

Israel

Ben Gurion University of the Negev

Dept of Geological and Env Sciences (B,M,D) ●☒ (2021)
P.O. Box 653
84105 Beer Sheva
Beer-Sheva 84105
p. +972-8-6461290
katzir@bgu.ac.il
http://www.bgu.ac.il/geol/

Geological Survey of Israel

Geological Survey of Israel (2015)
30 Malkhe Israel St.
Jerusalem, 95501
ask_gsi@gsi.gov.il
http://www.gsi.gov.il/

Hebrew University of Jerusalem

Faculty of Advanced Environmental Studies (2015)
Givat Ram
Jerusalem 91904
msfeitel@mscc.huji.ac.il

Institute of Earth Sciences (B,M,D) ●☒ (2017)
Jerusalem 91904
Jerusalem 91904
p. 97226584686
arimatmon@mail.huji.ac.il
http://earth.huji.ac.il/
f: https://www.facebook.com/earthhuji/
Programs: Geology (B,M); Atmosphere, Oceanography & Climate (B); Environmental Studies (B); Atmospheric Sciences (M); Oceanography (M); Hydrology (M); Environmental Studies (M)
Enrollment (2017): B: 70 (0)

Tel Aviv University

Dept of Geophysical, Atmospheric and Planetary Sciences (B,M,D) ● (2016)
Ramat Aviv
P O Box 30940
Tel Aviv 69978 69978
p. 972-3-6408633
batshevc@tauex.tau.ac.il
http://geophysics.tau.ac.il/
Full Professor:
Shmuel Marco, (D), Gg

Geosciences (B,M,D) ● (2015)
Levanon Road
Ramat Aviv
Tel Aviv 6997801
p. 972-3-6408633
shmulikm@tau.ac.il
http://geophysics.tau.ac.il/
Professor:
Pinhas Alpert, (D), Hebrew, 1980, AsZrAm
Zvi Ben-Avraham, (D), MIT/WHOI, 1973, YrGt
Shmulik Marco, (D), Hebrew, 1997, Ggc
Morris Podolak, (D), Yeshiva, 1974, ZnnZn
Colin G. Price, (D), Columbia, 1993, As
Moshe Reshef, (D), Tel Aviv, 1985, Yeg
Senior Scientist:
Pavel Kishcha, (D), Russian Acad of Sci, 1985, As
Dr:
Nili Harnik, (D), MIT, 2000, As
Lecturer:
Gilles Hillel Wust-Bloch, (D), 1990, Ys
Alon Ziv, (D), Ys
Principal Research Assoc. (Assoc. Professor):
Lev Eppelbaum, (D), Inst of Geophysics of Georgia, 1989, YvmGt

Italy

Alma Mater Studiorum Università di Bologna

Dipartimento di Scienze Biologiche, Geologiche e Ambientali (B,M,D) ○ (2016)
Piazza di Porta San Donato 1
Bologna 40126
p. ++39 - 051 - 2094238
alessandro.gargini@unibo.it
http://www.bigea.unibo.it/it
Enrollment (2016): B: 120 (30) M: 120 (30) D: 28 (7)

Alma Mater Studiorum University of Bologna

Dept. of Biological, Geological and Environmental Sciences (B,M,D) ○⃠ (2020)
Piazza di Porta San Donato, 1
Bologna 40126
p. +39 051 2094238
bigea.direttore@unibo.it
https://bigea.unibo.it/en/
Programs: Geological Sciences, Geology and Land for the Protection of Environment, Raw Materials
Enrollment (2020): B: 40 (10) M: 20 (9) D: 6 (3)
Head:
Alessandro Gargini, (D), HwRwZc

Servizio Geologico d'Italia

Servizio Geologico d'Italia (2015)
Via Vitaliano Brancati
Roma 48-00144
p. (+39) 0650071
emergenzeambientali@isprambiente.it
http://www.isprambiente.gov.it/it/servizi-per-lambiente/il-servizio-geologico-ditalia

Università degli Studi di Padova

Department of Geosciences (B,M,D) ●☒ (2019)
Via G. Gradenigo 6
Padova 35131
p. +390498279110
geoscienze.direzione@unipd.it
http://www.geoscienze.unipd.it/
Programs: Geological Sciences (Bachelor), Geology and Technical Geology (Master), Earth Sciences (Doctorate)
Enrollment (2017): B: 259 (49) M: 112 (38) D: 17 (7)
Full Professor:
Fabrizio Nestola, (D), Modena & Reggio Emilia, 2003, Gz
Full Professor:
Gilberto Artioli, (D), Chicago, 1985, GzyZm
Alessandro Caporali, (D), Ludwig-Maximilian (Germany), 1979, YdsZr
Alberto Carton, (M), Gm
Giorgio Cassiani, (D), YgHs
Bernardo Cesare, (D), Gp
Giulio Di Toro, (D), Gc
Silvana Martin, Gc
Giorgio Pennacchioni, Gc
Cristina Stefani, Gd
Nicola Surian, Gm
Massimiliano Zattin, (D), Gs
Professor:
Francesca Da Porto
Associate Professor:
Claudia Agnini, (D), Padua, 2007, PmeGu
Lapo Boschi, Yg
Luca Capraro, (D), Padua, 2002, PelGg
Andrea D'Alpaos, (D), Hs
Maria Chiara Dalconi, (D), Gz
Paolo Fabbri, Hw
Manuele Faccenda, (D), Gq
Mario Floris, (D), NgZr
Alessandro Fontana, (D), Gm
Eliana Fornaciari, (D), Pgm
Massimiliano Ghinassi, (D), Gs
Luca Giusberti, (D), Pm
Lara Maritan, (D), Gx
Andrea Marzoli, (D), Cg
Matteo Massironi, (D), XgZr
Claudio Mazzoli, Gx
Stefano Monari, Pg
Paolo Mozzi, (D), Gm
Paolo Nimis, Eg

Nereo Preto, (D), Gs
Manuel Rigo, (D), Gs
Gabriella Salviulo, Gz
Raffaele Sassi, Ggx
Paolo Scotton, Hg
Luciano Secco, Gz
Alberta Silvestri, (D), Gz
Richard Spiess, Gp
Annalisa Zaja, Yg
Dario Zampieri, Gc
Assistant Professor:
Omar Bartoli, Gp
Jacopo Boaga, Yg
Anna Breda, (D), Padua, 2003, GsrGg
Antonio Galgaro, Ng
Roberto Gatto, Pg
Christine Marie Meyzen, (D), Cg
Leonardo Piccinini, (D), Hg
Telemaco Tesei
Luca Valentini

Università degli Studi di Pavia

Dept of Earth and Environmental Sciences (A,B,M,D) ○ (2015)
via Ferrata, 1
Pavia 27100
p. +30 0382 985754
dvagnini@unipv.it
http://sciter.unipv.eu/site/home.html
Enrollment (2014): B: 45 (25) M: 25 (14) D: 15 (5)

Universita Degli Studi di Siena

Centro di GeoTecnologie (2015)
Via Vetri Vecchi 34
San Giovanni Valdarno 52027
p. +390559119400
bottacchi@unisi.it
http://www.geotecnologie.unisi.it

Universita di Bari

Department of Earth and Geo-environmental Sciences (2015)
Via E. Orabona
4-70125 Bari
scandale@geomin.uniba.it
http://www.geomin.uniba.it/

Universita di Cagliari

Dept di Geoingegneria e Tecnologie Ambientali (2015)
Via Marengo,3
09124 Cagliari
p. +39 70 675 52/29
mazzella@unica.it
http://geoing.unica.it/digita.htm
Professor:
Antonio AM MAZZELLA, Gq

Universita di Calabria

Dept of Biology Ecology and Earth Science (DIBEST) (D) (2015)
87036 Arcavacata di Rende
Calabria
crisci@unical.it
http://www.unical.it

Universita di Camerino

Dept Scienze della Terra (B,M,D) ○☒ (2017)
Via Gentile III da Varano
Camerino, MC 62032
p. (+39) 737402126
sst@pec.unicam.it
http://www.sst.unicam.it/SST/en/course-of-degree
Programs: Geology (B); Natural Science (B); Geoenvironmental Resources and Risks (M)

Universita di Catania

Inst Scienze della Terra (2015)
Corso Italia 57
95129 Catania
p. (+39) 095-7195730
giovali@unict.it
http://www3.unict.it/idgeg/

Universita di Firenze

Dept Scienze della Terra (B,M,D) ● (2015)
via La Pira 4
50121 Firenze
direttore@geo.unifi.it
http://www.dst.unifi.it/

Universita di Genova

Dept Scienze della Terra Ambiente e Vita - DISTAV (B,D) (2015)
Corso Europa 26
16132 Genoa
p. +39 010 353 8311
direttore@dipteris.unige.it
http://www.distav.unige.it/drupalint
Professor:
Egidio Armadillo, (D), Ye
Research Associate:
Donato Belmonte, (D), Cg

Università di Modena e Reggio Emilia

Dept di Scienze Chimiche e Geologiche (B,M,D) (2015)
Largo S. Eufemia, 19
Modena, Italy 41121
p. 390592055885
direttore.chimgeo@unimore.it
http://www.dscg.unimore.it/
Enrollment (2013): B: 23 (13) M: 14 (4) D: 10 (9)

Universita di Napoli FEDERICO II

Dipartimento di Scienze della Terra, dell'Ambiente e delle Risorse (B,M,D) ● (2016)
L.go S. Marcellino, 10
Naples 80138
p. +390812538112
domenico.calcaterra@unina.it
http://www.distar.unina.it

Universita di Perrugia

Dept Scienze della Terra (2015)
Piazza Università, 1
06100 Perugia
cclgeol@unipg.it
http://cclgeol.unipg.it/cclgeol/

Università di Torino

Dept Scienze della Terra (B,M,D) ●☒ (2021)
via Valperga Caluso 35
Torino 10125
p. 011.6705184
direzione.scienzeterra@unito.it
http://www.dst.unito.it/do/home.pl
Programs: Geological Sciences, Science in applied Geology, Environmental monitoring, protection and remediation
Enrollment (2020): B: 25 (25) M: 15 (15)
Professor:
Elena Belluso, (D), Gz
Giorgio Carnevale, (D), Pg
Rodolfo Carosi, (D), Gc
Daniele Castelli, (D), Gx
Anna Maria Ferrero, (D), Nr
Alessandro Pavese, Gz
Associate Professor:
Piera Benna, (M), Gz
Alessandro Borghi, (D), Gx
Marco Bruno, (D), Gz
Paola Cadoppi, (D), Gc
Cesare Comina, (D), Yx
Diego Coppola, Gv

Domenico Antonio De Luca, (D), Hy
Francesco dela Pierre, (D), Gd
Massimo Delfino, (D), Pg
Andrea Festa, (D), Gc
Maria Gabriella Forno, (M), Gg
Giandomenico Fubelli, (D), Gm
Marco Gattiglio, (D), Gc
Rocco Gennari, Gn
Marco Giardino, (D), Gm
Roberto Giustetto, (D), Gz
Chiara Teresa Groppo, (D), Gx
Luca Martire, (D), Gd
Michele Motta, (M), Zy
Pierluigi Pieruccini, Gm
Mauro Prencipe, (D), Gz
Franco Rolfo, (D), Gx
Sergio Carmelo Vinciguerra, (D), Nr

Assistant Professor:
Gianni Balestro, (D), Gc
Carlo Bertok, (D), Gd
Sabrina Maria Rita Bonetto, (D), Ng
Corrado Cigolini, (M), Gv
Emanuele Costa, (D), Gz
Anna d'Atri, (D), Gr
Simona Ferrando, (D), Gx
Franco Gianotti, (D), Gg
Daniele Giordano, (D), Gv
Salvatore Iaccarino, Gc
Francesca Lozar, (D), Pg
Edoardo Martinetto, (D), Pb
Luciano Masciocco, (M), Ge
Luigi Motta, (M), Zy
Marcello Natalicchio, Gs
Marco Davide Tonon, (M), Ze
Elena Zanella, (D), Ym

Emeritus:
Emiliano Bruno, (M), Gz
Ezio Callegari, (M), Gx
Roberto Compagnoni, (M), Gx
Giovanni Ferraris, (M), Gz
Giulio Pavia, (M), Pg

Università di Trieste

Dipartimento di Matematica e Geoscienze (B,M,D) ☒ (2021)
via Weiss 2
Trieste , Italy I-34128
p. +39 040 5582055
dmg@pec.units.it
https://dmg.units.it/
Programs: bachelor in Geology, master in Geosciences, master in Geophysics and Geodata
Certificates: GIS

Università di Udine

Dipartimento di Georisorse e Territorio (2015)
Dipartimento di Georisorse e Territorio
Via Cotonificio 114
33100 Udine
ta.tempoindeterminato@uniud.it
http://udgtls.dgt.uniud.it/

Universita di Urbino

Inst di Geologia Applicata (2015)
Via Muzio Oddi 14
61029 Urbino

Universita Pisa

Dept of Geosciences (D) (2015)
via S. Maria 53
56126 Pisa
p. +39050847260
martinelli@dst.unipi.it
http://www.dst.unipi.it/

University of Ferrara

Department of Physics and Earth Sciences ☒ (2021)
Via G. Saragat 1
44122 Ferrara
p. (+39) 0532 974211
dip.fisicascienzeterra@unife.it
http://fst.unife.it/it

University of Milano

Dept of Geology (2015)
Via Festa Del Perdono 7
20126 Milano
p. (+39) 02 6448 1
welcome.desk@unimib.it
http://www.unimib.it/go/46204/Home/English/Academic-Programs/Mathematics-Physics-and-Natural-Sciences/Geological-Sciences-and-Te

University of Siena

Dept of Physical Science, Earth, and Environment (B,M,D) ●☒ (2020)
Strada Laterina, 8
Siena 53100
p. (+39) 0577 233938
pec.dsfta@pec.unisipec.it
http://www.dsfta.unisi.it/it
f: https://www.facebook.com/dsfta.siena

Professor:
Mauro Coltorti, (M), GmYg

Associate Professor:
Luca Maria Foresi, (D), PmGs
Cecilia Viti, Gz

Jamaica

University of the West Indies Mona Campus

Dept of Geography and Geology (B,M,D) (2015)
University of the West Indies
Mona
Kingston KGN7
p. 876-927-2728
geoggeol@uwimona.edu.jm
http://myspot.mona.uwi.edu/dogg/

Head:
Simon F. Mitchell, (D), Liverpool (UK), 1993, GsgGs

Japan

Akita University

Deparment of Earth Science and Technology (2015)
1-1 Tagata Gakuen-cho, Akita-shi
Akita

Ehime University

Department of Earth Sciences (B,M) ○⃠ (2021)
Bunkyo-cho
2-5
Matsuyama City, Ehime Prefecture 790-8577
p. +81-89-927-9623
hori.rie.mm@ehime-u.ac.jp
http://www.ehime-u.ac.jp/~cutie
Programs: Geoscience, Earth Science
Certificates: field surveying, Paleontology
Enrollment (2020): B: 30 (5) M: 18 (6)

Geological Survey of Japan

Geological Survey of Japan (2015)
http://www.gsj.jp/

Hirosaki University

Dept of Earth Science (2015)
wata@cc.hirosaki-u.ac.jp
http://sci.hirosaki-u.ac.jp/~earth

Hiroshima University

Dept of Earth and Planetary Systems Science (2015)
Kagami-yama 1-3-1
Higashi-Hiroshima
Hiroshima 739
toiawase@geol.sci.hiroshima-u.ac.jp
http://www.geol.sci.hiroshima-u.ac.jp/index_e.html

Kagoshima University

Faculty of Science (2015)
koko@sci.kagoshima-u.ac.jp
http://earth.sci.kagoshima-u.ac.jp

Kanazawa University

Dept of Earth Sciences (2015)
Kakuma-machi
Kanazawa 920-1192
fsci-pla-director@edu.kobe-u.ac.jp
http://earth.s.kanazawa-u.ac.jp/

Kobe University

Earth & Planetary Sciences (2015)
fsci-pla-director@edu.kobe-u.ac.jp
http://shidahara1.earth.s.kobe-u.ac.jp

Kumamoto University

Dept of Earth and Environment (B,M,D) (2015)
2-39-1, Kurokami
Kumamoto City 860-8555
p. 81-96-342-3411
tadao@sci.kumamoto-u.ac.jp
http://www.sci.kumamoto-u.ac.jp/earthsci
Professor:
Shiro Hasegawa, (D), Pm
Toshiaki Hasenaka, (D), Gv
Hiroki Matsuda, (D), Gs
Tadao Nishiyama, (D), Gp
Hidetoshi Shibuya, (D), Ymg
Jun Shimada, (D), Hw
Akira Yoshiasa, (D), Gz

Nagoya University

Dept of Earth and Planetary Sciences (2015)
env@post.jimu.nagoya-u.ac.jp
http://www.eps.nagoya-u.ac.jp/

Shizuoka University

Inst of Geosciences (2015)
Shizuoka 422-8529
setmasu@ipc.shizuoka.ac.jp
http://www.sci.shizuoka.ac.jp/~geo/Welcome.html

Tohoku University

Dept of Mineralogy, Petrology and Economic Geology (2015)
Sendai 980-8578
kaiho@m.tohoku.ac.jp
http://www.ganko.tohoku.ac.jp/

Tsukuba University

College of Geoscience (2015)
kankyojoho@ynu.ac.jp
http://www.geo.tsukuba.ac.jp/

University of Tokyo

Deparment of earth and Planetary Science (2016)
3-1, Hongo 7chome, Bunkyo-ku
Tokyo
Hirata@eri.u-tokyo.ac.jp
http://www.eri.u-tokyo.ac.jp/

University of Toyama

Deptt of Earth Sciences (B,M,D) (2015)
3190 Gofuku
Toyama City, Toyama Prefecture 930-8555
p. 81-76-445-6654
takeuchi@sci.u-toyama.ac.jp
http://www.sci.u-toyama.ac.jp/earth/index-en.html
Enrollment (2015): B: 208 (0) M: 36 (0) D: 7 (0)
Professor:
Akira Takeuchi, (D), Osaka, 1979, GtcYe
Tohru Watanabe, (D), Tokyo, 1991, YxsGv
Associate Professor:
Shigekazu Kusumoto, (D), Kyoto, 1999, YvdGt

Yokohama National University

Dept of Environment and Natural Sciences (2015)
kankyojoho@ynu.ac.jp
http://chigaku.ed.ynu.ac.jp/geology-e.html

Kenya

Jomo Kenyatta University of Agriculture & Technology

Geomatic Engineering and Geospatial Information Systems (B,M,D) ☒ (2017)
PO Box 62000
-00200 Nairobi
Nairobi
p. +254-67-5352391
gegis@eng.jkuat.ac.ke
http://www.jkuat.ac.ke/departments/gegis/
t: @JKUAT_GEGIS
Programs: Geomatic Engineering; Geospatial Information Sciences
Enrollment (2014): B: 175 (35) M: 45 (19) D: 8 (0)
Chair:
Thomas G. Ngigi, (D), Chiba (Japan), 2007, ZriZr
Lecturer:
Nathan O. Agutu, Jomo Kenyatta, ZgiZr
Mark Boitt, (M), Stuttgart, 2010, ZgrZi
George W. Chege, (M), Jomo Kenyatta, 2014, ZgrZi
Charles Gaya, (M), Stuttgart, 2002, ZrgZi
Andrew Imwati, (D), Nairobi, ZggZi
Benson K. Kenduiywo, (D), Tech (Darmstadt), 2016, ZriYd
Fridah K. Kirimi, (M), Jomo Kenyatta, 2010, ZiiZr
Moffat G. Magondu, (M), Jomo Kenyatta, 2014, ZirZg
Felix N. Mutua, (D), Tokyo, 2012, ZigZr
Nancy Mwangi, (M), Jomo Kenyatta, 2008, ZiiZr
Mercy W. Mwaniki, (M), Jomo Kenyatta, 2010, ZiiZr
Eunice W. Nduati, (M), Jomo Kenyatta, 2014, ZrrZi
Patroba A. Odera, (D), Kyoto, 2012, YdZge
Hunja Waithaka, (D), Hokkaido, YdZgi
Charles B. Wasomi, (M), Stuttgart, ZrrZi

Dept of Environmental Studies (B) (2021)
P.O. Box 62000 00200
Nairobi
pro@jkuat.ac.ke
http://www.jkuat.ac.ke/

Kenyatta University

School of Environmental Sciences (B,M,D) (2015)
Maseno
p. +254-057-351620/2
dean-envs@ku.ac.ke
http://www.maseno.ac.ke/index3.php?section=schools&page=school-encironment

University of Nairobi

Dept of Geology (B) (2016)
PO Box 30197
Nairobi
p. +254 20 4449856
geology@uonbi.ac.ke
http://geology.uonbi.ac.ke/

Dept of Geography (B) (2015)
PO Box 30917
Nairobi
p. +254 (020) 318262 (28400)

samowuor@uonbi.ac.ke
http://uonbi.ac.ke/departments/?dept_code=HF&&face_code=32

Dept of Meteorology (B,M,D) (2015)
PO Box 30197
Nairobi 00100
p. 254 020-4449004 (2070)
dept-meteo@uonbi.ac.ke
http://www.uonbi.ac.ke

Latvia

Latvija Valst Geologijas Dienests

Latvia State Geological Survey (2015)
Moscow street 165
Riga, LV-1019
lvgma@lvgma.gov.lv
http://mapx.map.vgd.gov.lv/geo3/

University of Latvia

Faculty of Geographical and Earth Sciences (2015)
10 Alberta Str.
202-203 Room
Riga
zeme@lu.lv
http://www.lu.lv/e_strukt/fakult/geog/info/

Lebanon

American University of Beirut

Dept of Geology (2015)
Faculty of Arts and Sciences
P.O.Box 11-0236
Riad El-Solh
Beirut 1107 2020
p. (961)-1-340460/ext. 4160
arahman@aub.edu.lb

Lesotho

National University of Lesotho

Dept of Geology & Mines (B) (2015)
P.O. Box 750, Maseru
p. (266) 34 0601
registrar@nul.ls
http://www.nul.ls/

Dept of Geography and Environmental Science (B) (2015)
P.O. Roma 180
Maseru 100
p. +266 2234 0601
registrar@nul.ls
http://www.nul.ls/faculties/fost/geography

Liberia

University of Liberia

Dept of Geology (B) (2015)
Capitol Hill
PO Box 9020
Monrovia 9020
p. 231-6-422-304
weekso@fiu.edu
http://www.universityliberia.org/ul_course_master_list_biology.htm#geology

Dept of Mining Engineering (B) (2015)
Captiol Hill
PO Box 9020
Monrovia 9020
p. +231 6422304
weekso@fiu.edu
http://www.universityliberia.org/ul_course_master_list_mining.htm#mine

Libya

Oil Companies School

Oil Companies School (B) (2015)
info@ocslibya.com
http://www.geocites.com/chatalaine/OCS.html

Petroleum Training and Qualifying Institute (PTQI)

(B) (2015)
Gergarish Road 9KM - Asiahia
Tripoli
p. +218 21 4833771-5
info@ptqi.edu.ly
http://www.ptqi.edu.ly/online/en_home.php#

University of Garyounis

Dept of Geology (B) (2015)
PO Box 1308
Benghazi
p. +218-61-86304
uni.office@uob.edu.ly
http://www.garyounis.edu/

Lithuania

Lithuanian Geological Survey under the Ministry of Environment

Lithuanian Geological Survey (2015)
S. Konarskio St. 35
LT-03123 Vilnius
indre.virbickiene@lgt.lt
http://www.lgt.lt/

Vilniaus Pedagoginis Universitetas

Dept of Geology (2015)
Studentu 39, 2034 Vilnius
p. (8 5) 275 89 35
gmtf.dekanatas@leu.lt
http://www.leu.lt/lt/gmtf/gmtf_apie_mus/all.html

Vilniaus Universitetas

Dept of Hydrogeology & Engin Geol (2015)
Giurlionio 21/27, 2009, Vilnius
p. 239 8278
robert.mokrik@gf.vu.lt
http://www.vu.lt/en/scientific-report-2012/faculties-and-institutes/faculty-of-natural-sciences#DEPARTMENT_OF_HYDROGEOLOGY_AND_E

Dept of Geology and Mineralogy (B,M,D) ● (2015)
Ciurlionio str. 21/27
LT03101
Vilnius LT03101
p. +370 5 2398272
eugenija.rudnickaite@gf.vu.lt
http://www.geol.gf.vu.lt/lt
Enrollment (2015): B: 8 (8) M: 11 (11) D: 10 (3)

Luxembourg

Administration des ponts et chaussées

Service Geologique du Luxembourg ☒ (2021)
23, rue du Chemin de Fer
L-8057 Bertrange
geologie@pch.etat.lu
http://www.geology.lu

Madagascar

Universite d' Antananarivo

Dept of Chemistry (B) (2015)
BP 566
Antananarivo 101
p. +261 20 22 326 39
rtianasoa.manoelson@gmail.com
http://www.univ-antananarivo.mg/

Dept of Biology (B) (2015)
BP 566
Antananarivo 101
p. +261 20 22 329 39
arovonjy@yahoo.fr
http://www.univ-antananarivo.mg/

Dept des Sciences de la Terre (A,B,M,D) (2017)
BP 906
Antananarivo 101 , Madagascar
p. 00261324205328
saphirzzf@gmail.com
http://www.univ-antananarivo.mg/
Enrollment (2016): A: 144 (138) B: 127 (111) M: 63 (14) D: 1 (0)

Malawi

Mzuzu University

Faculty of Environmental Sciences (B) (2015)
Private Bag 201
Mzuzu
p. +(265) 1 320 722/ 320 575
ur@mzuni.ac.mw
http://www.mzuni.ac.mw/index.php?option=com_content&view=article&id=21&Itemid=15

University of Malawi

Dept of Natural Resources Management (B) (2015)
PO Box 219
Lilongwe
p. (265) 01 277 260
david.mkwambisi@bunda.luanar.mw
http://www.bunda.unima.mw/nrm.thm

Chancellor College, Natural Resources and Environment Centre (B) (2015)
PO Box 280
Zomba
p. +(265) 1 524 685
geo@chanco.unima.mw
http://www.chanco.unima.mw/department/department.php?DepartmentID=4&Source=Department_of_Geography_and_Earth_Sciences

Malaysia

Minerals and Geoscience Department Malaysia

Minerals and Geoscience Dept Malaysia (2015)
20th Floor, Bangunan Tabung Haji
Jalan Tun Razak
50658 Kuala Lumpur
jmgkll@jmg.gov.my
http://www.jmg.gov.my/

National University of Malaysia

Geology Dept (2015)
43600 Bangi
Selangor
dftsm@ftsm.ukm.my

Universiti Putra Malaysia

Dept of Environmental Sciences (2015)
43400 UPM Serdang
puziah@env.upm.edu.my
http://fsas.upm.edu.my/~sas/envpage/Dept.html

University of Malaya

Dept of Geology (B,M,D) (2015)
Dept. of Geology
University of Malaya
50603 Kuala Lumpur, Malaysia.
Kuala Lumpur, Selangor 50603
p. 03-79674203
ketua_geologi@um.edu.my
http://www.um.edu.my

Head:
Wan Hasiah Abdullah, (D), Newcastle upon Tyne, 1994, Ec

Professor:
Teh Guan Hoe, (D), Heidelberg, Ca
Lee Chai Peng, (D), Liverpool (UK), Pg
John Kuna Raj, (D), Malaya, 1983, Ng
Denis N.K Tan, (M), Malaya, Go

Associate Professor:
Abd Rashid Ahmad, (D), Oxford, Sc
Azman Abdul Ghani, (D), Liverpool (UK), Gi
Mohamed Ali Hasan, (M), Ulster, Hg
Azhar Hj Hussin, (D), London (UK), Gs
Tajul Anuar Jamaluddin, (D), Wales, 1997, Ng
Mustaffa Kamal Shuib, (M), London (UK), 1986, Gc
Samsudin Hj. Taib, (D), Durham (UK), Yg

Lecturer:
Nuraiteng Tee Abdullah, (D), London (UK), Gr
Ahmad Tajuddin Hj Ibrahim, (D), Newcastle upon Tyne, Ng
Che Noorliza Lat, (M), Nevada (Reno), 1989, Yg
Mat Ruzlin Maulud, (B), Malaya, Zn
Nur Iskandar Taib, (D), Indiana, Gi
Ismail Yusoff, (D), Norwich, Hg

Mali

Universite de Bamako

Sciences de la Terre (B) (2015)
BP 3206
Bamako
p. (223) 222 32 44
phine.romagnoli@unige.ch
http://www.ml.refer.org/u-bamako/spip.php?article.137

Malta

University of Malta

Dept of Geosciences (B,M,D) ☒ (2020)
Department of Geosciences
University of Malta
Msida Campus
Msida MSD2080
p. (+356) 2340 2362
geo.sci@um.edu.mt
http://www.um.edu.mt/science/geosciences
f: https://www.facebook.com/um.geosciences/
Programs: Geoscience and Physics (B); Geoscience and Mathematics (B); Geoscience and Statistics and Operations Research (B); Geoscience (M); Applied Oceanography (M); Geosciences(D)
Enrollment (2018): M: 5 (8) D: 8 (0)

Dr:
Pierre-Sandre Farrugia, (D), Malta

Professor:
Raymond Ellul, (D), As
Alfred Micallef, (D), Ap

Associate Professor:
Alan Deidun, (D)
Aldo Drago, (D), Southampton (UK), Opg
Pauline Galea, (D), Victoria (NZ), 1993, YsgZg
Aaron Micallef, (D), Southampton (UK), 2008, GumOu

Dr:
Noel Aquilina, (D), Birmingham (UK), Asm
Sebastiano D'Amico, (D), YsgZg
Anthony Galea, (D), Trieste, Opg

Lecturer:
Adam Gauci, (D), Malta, 2018, Op

Mauritania

Universite de Nouakchott

Dept de Geologie (B) (2015)
BP 5026
Nouakchott
p. (222) 25 13 82
awa@univ-nkc.mr
http://www.univ-nkc.mr/spip.php?rubrique34

Mauritius

University of Mauritius

Mauritius Radio Telescope (B) (2015)
Reduit
p. (230) 454 1041
nalini@uom.ac.mu
http://www.uom.ac.mu/mrt/mrt2.html

Dept of Chemical and Environmental Engineering (B) (2015)
Reduit
p. (230) 454 1041
d.surroop@uom.ac.mu
http://www.uom.ac.mu/Faculties/FOE/CEE

Mexico

Centro de Investigación Científica y de Educación Superior de Ensenada

Earth Sciences Division (M,D) (2016)
Carretera Tijuana-Ensenada # 3918
Zona Playitas
Ensenada, Baja California 22860
p. (01152-664)1750500
dir-ct@cicese.mx
http://www.cicese.mx
Enrollment (2010): M: 44 (8) D: 20 (2)

Titular researcher:
Edgardo Canon-Tapia, (D), Hawaii, 1996, GvYmGt

Research Associate:
Jose G. Acosta, (M), CICESE (Ensenada), 1980, Ne
Jesus M. Brassea, (M), Cinvestav, 1986, Ye
Juan M. Espinosa, (M), CICESE (Ensenada), 1983, Ye
Jose J. Gonzalez, (M), CICESE (Ensenada), 1986, Yd
Alejandro Hinojosa, (M), CICESE (Ensenada), 1988, Zr
Luis H. Mendoza, (M), CICESE (Ensenada), 1982, Ne
Alfonso Reyes, (B), UNAM, Ne

Titular researcher:
Raul Castro, (D), Nevada (Reno), 1991, Ys
Juan Contreras, (D), Columbus, 1999, Gt
Luis A. Delgado-Argote, (D), UNAM, 2000, GitGu
Francisco Esparza, (D), CICESE (Ensenada), 1991, Ye
John Fletcher, (D), Utah, 1994, Gpt
Carlos Flores, (D), Toronto, 1986, Ye
Jose Frez, (M), California (Los Angeles), 1980, Ys
Juan Garcia, (D), Oregon State, 1990, Yv
Ewa Glowacka, (D), Polish Acad of Sci, 1991, Ys
Enrique Gomez, (D), Toronto, 1981, Ye

Titular Researcher:
Mario Gonzalez-Escobar, (D), CICESE (Ensenada), 2002, YesYs

Titular researcher:
Antonio Gonzalez-Fernandez, (D), Complutense (Madrid), 1996, Gu
Javier Helenes, (D), Stanford, 1980, Gr
Thomas Kretzschmar, (D), Tubingen, 1995, Ge
Margarita Lopez, (D), Toronto, 1985, Cc
Arturo Martin, (D), Paris XI Orsay, 1988, Gd
Luis Munguia, (D), California (San Diego), 1982, Ys
Alejandro Nava, (D), California (San Diego), 1980, Ys
Marco A. Perez, (D), CICESE (Ensenada), 1995, Ye
Jose M. Romo, (D), CICESE (Ensenada), 2002, Ye
Pratap Sahay, (D), Alberta, 1986, Ys
Rogelio Vazquez, (D), CICESE (Ensenada), 2002, Ye
Antonio Vidal, (D), CICESE (Ensenada), 2001, Ys
Bodo Weber, (D), Gp

Ciudad Universitaria

Facultad de Ingenieria (2015)
C.P. 04510
p. 56 22 08 66
fainge@servidor.unam.mx
http://www.ingenieria.unam.mx/

SGM

Servicio Geológico Mexicano (2016)
Blvd. F. Angeles 93.50-4 km.
Hidalgo 42080, Pachuca 42083
gciadoctec@sgm.gob.mx
http://www.sgm.gob.mx/

Universidad Autonoma de Baja California Sur

Dept of Marine Geology (B) (2015)
Carretera al Sur km 5.5, Box 19-B
La Paz, BS 23000
p. 682/2-47-55/2-01-40/2-45-69
oceanologia.fcm@uabc.edu.mx

Chair:
Alejandro Alvarez-Arellano, (M), Nac Auton, 1984, Gs

Professor:
Rodolfo Cruz-Orozco, (D), Louisiana State, 1974, Gu
Javier Gaitan-Moran, (M), Intl Inst-Aerospace Sur & Earth Sci, 1986, Zr
Carlos A. Galli-Olivier, (D), Utah, 1968, Gd
Jose I. Peredo-Jaime, (B), Auto de Baja California, 1978, Og
Luis R. Segura-Vernis, (D), Nac Auton, 1977, Pi

Associate Professor:
Alejandro J. Carillo-Chavez, (M), Cincinnati, 1981, Gp
Efrain Cornejo-Luna, (B), Nac Auton, 1969, Gq
Genaro Martinez-Gutierrez, (B), Inst Politecnico Nac, 1982, Gr
Cesar Martinez-Noriega, (B), Nac Auton, Ou
Jaime I. Monroy-Sanchez, (M), 1987, Ge
Miriam Nunez-Velazco, (B), Tech (Madero), 1980, Go
Jose A. Perez-Venzor, (B), Autonoma (SLP), 1978, Gi
Ramon Pimentel-Hernandez, (B), Inst Politecnico Nac, 1980, Yg
Humberto Rojas-Soriano, (B), Nac Auton, 1983, Gz
Paulino Rojo-Garcia, (B), Inst Politecnico Nac, 1983, Gc

Assistant Professor:
Luis A. Herrera-Gil, (B), Nac Auton, 1980, Pg

Lecturer:
Cesar A. Lopez-Ferreira, (B), Nac Auton, 1979, Hw

Cooperating Faculty:
Oscar Rodriguez-Plasencia, (B), Escuela Militar de Met, 1959, Am

Universidad Autonoma de Chihuahua

Facultad de Ingenieria (B,M) (2015)
Circuito Universitario Campus 2
Chihuahua, CH 31170
p. (614) 442-9500
ancorral@uach.mx

Director:
Arturo Leal-Bejarano, (B), Auto de Chihuahua, 1976, Zn

Head:
Arturo Lujan-Lopez, (M), Essex (UK), 1975, Zn

Chair:
Socorro I. Aguirre-Moriel, (B), ITR (Switzerland), 1979, Nx
Hector M. Mendoza-Aguilar, (B), Auto de Chihuahua, 1980, Nx

Professor:
Rafael Chavez-Aguirre, (M), Auto de Chihuahua, 1993, Hw
Adolfo Chavez-Rodriguez, (D), Arizona, 1987, Hy
Miguel Franco-Rubio, (M), Nac Auton, 1978, Eg
Rafael Madrigal-Rubio, (B), Nac Auton, 1969, Ng
Teodulo Mena-Zambrano, (B), Inst Politecnico Nac, 1964, Ng
Hector Minor-Velazquez, (B), Auto de Chihuahua, 1978, Nx
Ignacio A. Reyes-Cortes, (B), Texas (El Paso), 1997, Gx
Manuel Reyes-Cortes, (B), Nac Auton, 1970, Gi
Miguel Royo-Ochoa, (M), Auto de Chihuahua, 1997, Hw
David H. Ruiz-Cisneros, (B), Auto de Chihuahua, 1974, Nx
Luis M. Trevizo-Cano, (B), Auto de Chihuahua, 1978, Nx

Universidad Autonoma de Nuevo Leon

Facultad de Ciencias de la Tiera (2015)
Hacienda Guadalupe Km. 8 Camino a Cerro Prieto. - Linares, N 67700
p. (81) 8329 4170 Ext. 4170
fmedina@fct.uanl.mx
http://www.fct.uanl.mx/portal

Universidad Autonoma de San Luis Potosi

Area de Ciencias de la Terra (B,M) (2015)
Facultad de Ingenieri#2.a
Av. Dr. Manuel Nava No. 8
San Luis Potosi#2., SL 78290
p. (48) 13-82-22
aaguillonr@uaslp.mx
Department Secretary: Juan Manuel Torres Aguilera
Director:
Hector David Atisha-Castillo, (M), Texas, 1978, Zn
Head:
Joel Milan-Navarro, (M), Nancy (France), 1979, Zr
Professor:
Jose Refugio Acevedo-Arroyo, (B), Nac Auton, 1957, Ng
Luis Garcia-Gutierrez, (M), Stanford, 1951, Eg
Panfilo R. Martinez-Macias, (M), Nac Auton, 1995, Gc
Francisco Javier Orozco-Villasenor, (M), Colorado State, 1983, Eg
Ramon Ortiz-Aguirre, (M), Madrid, 1979, Hg
Carlos Francisco Puente-Muniz, (B), Autonoma (SLP), 1979, Hw
Delfino C. Ruvalcaba-Ruiz, (D), Colorado State, 1982, Em
Juan Manuel Torres-Agulera, (B), Autonoma (SLP), 1980, Gx
Librarian:
Panfilo R. Martinez-Macias, Zn

Universidad Autonoma de Sonora

Ejecutivo de la Unidad Regional Norte (2015)
Av. Universidad e Irigoyen
Col. Ortiz
Hermosillo

Universidad de Guanajuato

Departamento de Ingeniería en Minas, Metalurgia y Geología (B) O (2016)
Sede San Matias
Ex Hda. de San Matías s/n
Col. San Javier
Guanajuato, Guanajuato C.P. 36025
p. ((+473) 73 2 2291 (Ext. 5304)
juancho@ugto.mx
http://www.di.ugto.mx/minas/index.php/antecedentes
Enrollment (2015): B: 7 (7)

Universidad Estatal de Sonora

Escuela Superior de Geociencias (B) O☒ (2021)
Col. Apolo
Hermosillo, SO 83240
p. (662) 6890100
maricela.lopez@ues.mx
https://www.ues.mx/?p=especiales/ofertaeducativa/malla.aspx&cid=0&sid=13&smid=0&latder=0&params=pa=007_pe=14_tipopa=l
f: https://www.facebook.com/ues.mx/
Programs: minning, metallurgy and geology
Enrollment (2020): B: 450 (23)
Director:
Maricela López, (M), Sonora, 2015, NxGg
Associate Professor:
Gustavo E. Durazo-Tapia, (B), Sonora, 1981, Em
David García-Martínez, (D), 2017, GzEmNx
Gonzalo de Jesus Ibarra-Dessens, (M), Sonora, 2019, Nm
Rafael Jordan-Hernandez, (D), La Habana, 2005, Zn
Veronica Moreno-Rodriguez, (D), Madrid, Eg
Christian A. Murguía-Romero, (M), Sonora, 2018, Nx
Hector O. Murillo-Valenzuela, (B), CESUES, 1989, Nx
Paula C. Santos-Munguia, (D), CINVESTAV, 2019, Nx

Universidad Nacional Autonoma de Mexico

Ciencias de la Tierra (B) ☒ (2018)
Ciudad Universitaria,CDMX
Facultad de Ciencias
Ciudad de Mexico 04510
tierra.coord@ciencias.unam.mx
Programs: Earth Sciences
Enrollment (2017): B: 700 (84)
Dr.:
Blanca Mendoza, (D), Oxford, 1985, Zn

Facultad de Ingeniería (B) (2015)
Av. Universidad 3000, Ciudad Universitaria
Coyoacán, CP 4510
p. 56 22 08 66
fainge@servidor.unam.mx
http://www.ingenieria.unam.mx/paginas/Carreras/ingenieriaMinas/ingMinas_Desc.php
Director:
Antonio Nieto Antunez, (M), Stanford, 1970, Nm
Professor:
Angelica Casillas, (B), Inst Politecnico Nac, 1976, Hw
Esteban Cedillo, (D), Heidelberg, 1988, Em
Juventino Martinez, (D), Paris VI, 1980, Gt
Edgardo Meave, (B), Guanajuato, 1947, Gg
Francisco Medina, (B), Guanajuato, 1982, Zg
Ricardo Navarro, (B), Inst Politecnico Nac, 1973, Nm
Salvador Ulloa, (B), Guanajuato, 1947, Eg
Fernando Vasallo, (D), Lomonosov (USSR), 1982, Em
Carlos Yanez, (B), Inst Politecnico Nac, 1976, Ce

Inst de Geologia (M,D) (2015)
Apdo. postal 70-296
Ciudad Universitaria
Delegacion Coyoacan, DF 04510
p. (52) 5622 4314
academicaigl@geologia.unam.mx
https://www.geologia.unam.mx/
Administrative Assistant: Ana María Rodriguez Simental
Director:
Dante J. Moran-Zenteno, (D), Nac Auton, 1992, Cc
Head:
Susana A. Alaniz Alvarez, (D), Nac Auton, 1995, Gc
Luca Ferrari Pedraglio, (D), Milan, 1992, Gt
Sergio Cevallos Ferriz, (D), Alberta, 1990, Pg
Carlos M. Gonzalez Leon, (D), Arizona, 1992, Gr
Klavdia Oleschko Loutkova, (D), Lomosov (Moscow), 1984, So
Maria S. Lozano Garcia, (D), d'Aix (Marseilles), 1979, Pe
Francisco J. Vega Vera, (D), Nac Auton, 1988, Pg
Chair:
Gustavo Tolson Jones, (D), Nac Auton, 1998, Gc
Senior Scientist:
Shelton Applegate-Pleasants, (D), Chicago, 1961, Pv
Jorge Aranda, (D), Oregon, 1982, Gi
Blanca E. Buitron-Sanchez, (D), Nac Auton, 1974, Pi
Oscar Carranza-Castaneda, (D), Nac Auton, 1989, Pv
Gerardo Carrasco-Nunez, (D), Michigan Tech, 1993, Gv
Ana L. Carreno, (D), d'Orsay (Paris), 1979, Pm
Miguel Carrillo Martinez, (D), Paris VI, 1976, Pb
Liberto De Pablo, (D), Ohio State, 1958, Gz
Rodolfo Del Arenal-Capetillo, (B), Nac Auton, 1960, Hw
Ismael Ferrusquia, (D), Houston, 1971, Gr
David Flores-Roman, (D), Nac Auton, 1981, So
Celestina Gonzalez-Arreola, (D), Nac Auton, 1989, Pi
Jose C. Guerrero-Garcia, (D), Texas (Dallas), 1975, Ym
John D. Keppie, (D), Glasgow, 1964, Gt
Victor M. Malpica-Cruz, (D), Bordeaux, 1980, Gs
Enrique Martinez Hernandez, (D), Michigan State, 1979, Pl
Juventino Martinez-Reyes, (D), Paris VI, 1980, Gt
Luis M. Mitre-Salazar, (D), Paris IV, 1978, Ge
Adrian Ortega, (D), Waterloo, 1993, Hw
Fernando Ortega-Gutierrez, (D), Leeds (UK), 1975, Gp
Sergio Palacios-Mayorga, (M), Nac Auton, 1972, So
Jerjes Pantoja-Alor, (M), Arizona, 1963, Gg
Maria del Carmen Perrilliat-Montoya, (D), Nac Auton, 1969, Pi
Angel Nieto Samaniego, (D), Nac Auton, 1994, Gc
Christina D. Siebe Grabach, (D), Hohenheim (Germany), 1993, Sc
Alicia Silva-Pineda, (D), Nac Auton, 1980, Pg
Max Suter-Cargnelutti, (D), Basel (Switzerland), 1978, Gt

Jordi Tritlla, (D), Barcelona, 1994, Eg
Ana B. Villasenor-Martinez, (D), Nac Auton, 1991, Pi
Reinhard Weber-Gobel, (D), Tubingen, 1967, Pg

Associate Scientist:
Gerardo J. Aguirre Diaz, (D), Texas, 1993, Gv
Thierry Calmus, (D), Paris VI, 1983, Gu
Antoni Camprubi, (D), Barcelona, 1998, Eg
Alejandro J. Carillo Chavez, (D), Wyoming, 1996, Hg
Elena Centeno Garcia, (D), Arizona, 1994, Gt
Rodolfo Corona-Esquivel, (M), Nac Auton, 1985, Em
Mariano Elias-Herrera, (M), Nac Auton, 1982, Gp
Maria L. Flores-Delgadillo, (M), Nac Auton, 1987, So
Gilberto Hernandez-Silva, (D), Nac Auton, 1983, So
Rafael Huizar-Alvarez, (D), Franche Comte, 1989, Hw
Cesar Jacques Ayala, (D), Cincinnati, 1983, Gr
Marisol Montellano-Ballesteros, (D), California (Berkeley), 1986, Pv
Amabel M. Oretega Rivera, (D), Queens, 1997, Cc
Odranoel Quintero, (D), Sorbonne (France), 1995, Gc
Jose L. Rodriguez-Castaneda, (M), Pittsburgh, 1984, Gg
Jaime Roldan Quintana, (M), Iowa, 1976, Gv
Gerardo Sanchez-Rubio, (M), Imperial Coll (UK), 1984, Gv
Jesu Sole, (D), Barcelona, 1996, Cc
Luis F. Vassallo-Morales, (D), Lomonosov (USSR), 1981, Em
Maria G. Villasenor-Cabral, (M), Leeds (UK), 1974, Ca

Research Associate:
Irma Aguilera-Ortiz, (B), Iberoameric, 1971, Ca
Victor M. Davila-Alcocer, (M), Texas (Dallas), 1986, Ps
Jose G. Solorio-Munguia, (B), Nac Auton, 1958, Gz

Adjunct Professor:
J. Duncan Keppie, (D), Glasgow, 1967, Gt
Luis Silva-Mora, (D), d'Aix (Marseilles), 1979, Gi

Emeritus:
Gloria Alencaster-Ybarra, (D), Nac Auton, 1969, Pi
Zoltan De Cserna, (D), Columbia, 1955, Gt

Geology Librarian:
Teresa Soledad Medina Malagon, (B), Zn

Inst de Geofisica (2015)
losos@sci.muni.cz
http://tlacaelel.igeofcu.unam.mx/index.eng.html

Mongolia

Gazarchin Institute

Gazarchin Institute (2015)
Bayanzurkh District
Ulaanbaatar 46
marketing.gazarchin@gmail.com
http://www.gazarchin.edu.mn/

Mineral Resources Authority of Mongolia

Mineral Resources Authority of Mongolia (2015)
info@mram.gov.mn
http://www.mram.gov.mn/

Mongolian University of Science and Technology

School of Geology and Petroleum Engineering (2015)
Bagatoiruu-46, P. O. Box-520
Ulaanbaatar 46
p. 976-11-312291
jepces@must.edu.mn
http://www.gs.edu.mn

National University of Mongolia

Geology and Geography Faculty (2015)
Ikh Surguuliin gudamj - 1, Baga Toiruu,
Sukhbaatar district,
Ulaanbaatar
p. 976-11-311890
geo@num.edu.mn
http://geo.num.edu.mn

Morocco

Ecole Nationale de l' Industrie Minerale

Dept de Sciences de la Terre (B) (2015)
Avenue Hadj Ahmed Cherkaoui
BP 753
Agdal, Rabat
p. (+212) 037 68 02 30
zaydi@enim.ac.ma
http://www.enim.ac.ma/formation/sciences_de_la_terre/

Dept de Mines (B) (2015)
Avenue Hadj Ahmed Cherkaoui
BP 753
Adgal, Rabat
p. (+212) 037 68 02 30
zaydi@enim.ac.ma
http://www.enim.ac.ma/formation/mines

Dept de Sciences des Materiaux (B) (2015)
Avenue Hadj Ahmed Cherkaoui
BP 753
Agdal, Rabat
p. (+212) 037 68 02 30
zaydi@enim.ac.ma
http://www.enim.ac.ma/formation/materiaux/

ONAREP - Naional Office of Petroleum Research

ONAREP - Naional Office of Petroleum Research (B) (2015)
PO Box 8030
Rabat 10050
p. +212 37 28-1616

ONHYM

National Office of Hydrocarbons and Mines (2015)
rh@onhym.com
http://www.onhym.com/

School of Mines of Marrakech

School of Mines (B,M,D) (2015)
Rue Machaar, El Harm Quartier Issil-B.P. 38
Marrakech
p. 212-30-97-79

Universite Abdelmalek Essaadi

Dept de Sciences de la Terre (B) (2015)
p. +212 539 97 93 16
presidence@uae.ma
http://www.uae.ma/portail/FR/

Faculte de Sciences de Tetouen (B) (2015)
BP 2121
Tetouan 93002
p. +212 (0) 39 97 24 23
vdap.fs@gmail.com
http://www.fst.ac.ma/stu.html

Universite Cadi Ayyad

Dept of Geology (2015)
Prince Moulay Abdellah
BP 515
Marakech
p. +212 (0)5 24 43 46 49
http://www.fssm.ucam.ac.ma/pages/geologie.php

Universite Hassan 1er - Settat

Dept de Geologie Apliquee (B) (2015)
BP 577
Settat 26000
p. 05.23.40.07.36
http://www.fsts.ac.ma/fsts/index/php?option=com_content&task=view&id=37&Itemid=12

Universite Hassan II

Dept of Geology (B) (2015)
9, Rue Tarik Bnou Zia
Anfa Casablanca
p. 0522 23 06 80
z.hilmi@fsac.ac.ma
http://www.fsac.ac.ma/depart/geo

Universite Hassan II - Mohammedia

Dept de Sciences de la Terre (B) (2015)
279 Cite Yassmina
Mohammedia, Casablanca
p. +212(33)314635
presidence@univh2m.ac.ma

Universite Ibn Tofail

Dept de Geologie (B,M,D) ●☒ (2020)
Abdelhakboua@Yahoo.com
Kenitra 14 000
p. +212 061984449
abdelhakboua@yahoo.com
http://www.univ-ibntofail.ac.ma/fre/departments.php?esp=4&rub=14&srub=36&srub_=96
Enrollment (2020): B: 11 (0) M: 35 (0) D: 20 (0)

Universite Ibn Zohr, Agadir

Dept de Sciences de la Terre (B) (2015)
BP 32/S
Agadir 80000
p. +212 (28) 22 71 25
acma2008@esta.ac.ma
http://www.esta.ac.ma/

Universite Mohammed 1er (Oujda)

Ecole Nationale des Sciences Appliquees d'Al Hoceima (ENSAH) (B) (2015)
BP 724
Oujda 60000
p. +212(56)500612
presidence@ump.ma
http://webserver1.ump.ma/ecoles_facultes/ensah

Dept des Sciences de la Terre (B,M,D) (2015)
BP 717
60000 Oujda
p. (212)536500601/02
fso@fso.ump.ma
http://sciences1.univ-oujda.ac.ma

Universite Mohammed V

Dept of Geology (2015)
BP 554
Rue Michlifen Agdal
Rbat-Chellah
p. +212 05 37 77 54 71
http://www.fsr.ac.ma/ancien/index.php/departement/giologie.html

Universite Mohammed V (Agdal)

Dept de Genie Minerale (B) (2015)
Avenue Ibnsina
BP 765
Adgal Raba
p. (212 - 537) 77.26.47 - 77.19.0
contact@um5a.ac.ma
http://www.emi.ac.ma

Universite Moulay Ismail, Meknes

Dept de Sciences de la Terre (B) (2015)
Marjane II BP 298
Meknes 5003
p. +212 5 35 53 78 96
doyen@fs-umi.ac.ma
http://ww.umi.ac.ma/

Universite Sidi Mohammed Ben Abdallah

Dept of Geology (2015)
Dhar El Mahraz
BP 42
Atlas-Fes
p. 06 61 35 04 81
dept_geo@fsdmfes.ac.ma
http://www.fsdmfes.ac.ma/Presentation/Departements/Geologie.php

University Mohammed I

Dept of Geology (B,M,D) (2015)
Faculté des Sciences Bd. Mohammed VI
BP 717
Oujda, Oujda-Angad 60000
p. (212)667772215
mbouabdellah2002@yahoo.fr
http://webserver1.ump.ma/

Mozambique

Universidade Eduardo Mondlane

Escola Superior de Ciencias Marinhas e Costeiras (B) (2015)
CP 128
Avenida 1 de Julho
Bairro Chuabo Dembe
Didad de Quelimane, Zambezia
p. +258 24900500/1
valera.dias@uem.mz
http://www.marine.uem.mz/

Laboratorio de Gemologia (B,M) ☒ (2019)
Av. Julius Nyerere 3453, Departamento de Física
Campus Universitário
Maputo
p. (+258) 21 497003
uthui@zebra.uem.mz
http://www.fisica.uem.mz/index.php?option=com_content&view=article&id=51&Itemid=57
Programs: Geology
Certificates: None
Associate Professor:
Akil Askharhodjaev, (D), URSS, 1985
Rogério J. Uthui, (D), Sweden, 1996

Universidade Lurio

Faculdade de Engenharia e Ciencias Naturais (B) (2015)
Av. 25 de Setembro
N. 958
Pemba, Cabo Delgado
p. (+258) 27 221238
fecn@unilurio.ac.mz
http://www.unilurio.ac.mz/faculdades_pmb_pt.htm

Namibia

Geological Survey of Namibia in Windhoek

Geological Survey of Namibia in Windhoek (2015)
Private Bag 13297
Windhoek
p. +264-61-2848111
gschneider@mme.gov.na
http://www.mme.gov.na/gsn/

University of Namibia

Dept of Geology (B,M,D) ●☒ (2020)
P.O. Box 1727
Gordon Street,
Kronlein,
Keetmanshoop 9000
p. (+264 63) 2202038
ttjipura@unam.na
http://www.unam.na/faculties/science/departments.html
Programs: Geology (B); Applied Geology in Exploration (M);

Hydrogeology (D)
Enrollment (2020): B: 47 (7) M: 10 (2) D: 4 (0)
Senior Lecturer:
Innocent Muchingami, (D), W Cape, 2014, Ye
Associate Professor:
Holgar Sommer , (D), Mainz, 2004, Gp
Akah Tses, (D), Nigeria, , Gec
Lecturer:
Gilbert Chongwain, (D), Pan Africa, 2017, Go
Josephine Hamutoko, (D), Namibia, 2017, Hw
Martin Harris, (M), Geosciences (Beijing), 2013
Albertina Nakwafila, (M), Stellenbosch, 2014
Ester Shalimba, (M), China Geosciences, 2014, GgpEz
Collen Uahengo, (D), China Geosciences, 2020, PgGoEg
Shoopala Uugulu, (M), France, 2012
Absai Vatuva, (D), China Geosciences, 2016, EgGtc

Nepal

Tribhuvan University

Central Dept of Geology (2015)
Gandhi Bhavan, Kirtipur, Kathmandu
info@geology.edu.np
http://www.geology.edu.np/

Netherlands

Delft University of Technology

Department of Geoscience & Engineering (B,M,D) O (2016)
Stevinweg 1
2628 Delft
p. +31 15 2781328
J.D.Jansen@tudelft.nl
http://www.tudelft.nl

Dept of Geoscience & Engineering (A,B,M,D) ●☒ (2019)
Stevinweg 1
2628 CN Delft
The Netherlands
Delft 2628 CN
p. +31 15 27 81423
m.j.m.ammerlaan@tudelft.nl
https://www.tudelft.nl/citg/over-faculteit/afdelingen/geoscience-engineering/
f: https://www.facebook.com/AppliedEarthSciencesTUDelft/
Programs: Applied Geophysics, Environmental Engineering, Geo-Engineering, Geo-Energy Engineering, Geo-Resource Engineering
Certificates: -

National Geological Survey of the Netherlands

National Geological Survey of the Netherlands (2015)
Princetonlaan 6
3584 CB Utrecht
p. (+31)30-2564256
http://www.en.geologicalsurvey.nl/

Royal NIOZ

Jaap Sinninghe Damste (D) ☒ (2017)
PO Box 59
Den Burg, Texel 1790 AB
p. +31222369550
Jaap.Damste@nioz.nl
https://www.nioz.nl/en/about/mmb
Programs: Organic Biogeochemistry; Marine Microbiology; Marine Microbial Ecology (w/ Utrecht Univ)

Physical Oceanography ☒ (2021)
Landsdiep 4
't Horntje 1797 SZ
secretary@nioz.nl
http://www.nioz.nl

State University of Groningen

Faculty of Spatial Sciences (B,M) ☒ (2019)
P.O. Box 800
Groningen 9700 AV
p. +31 50 363 8891
i.l.veen@rug.nl
http://www.rug.nl/frw
f: http://www.facebook.com/FRWRUG
t: @FRW_RUG
Programs: Geography, urban planning, demography, real estate, education, environment, infrastructure, sustainability
Enrollment (2014): B: 190 (0) M: 60 (0)

State University of Utrecht

Faculty of Geoscience (B,M,D) (2015)
P.O. Box 80.115
Utrecht 3508 TA
p. (+31) (0)30 253 2044
info@geo.uu.nl
http://www.uu.nl/faculty/geosciences/EN/Contact/Pages/

Universiteit Utrecht

Faculty of Geosciences (B,M) (2016)
Budapestlaan 4b
Utrecht 3584 CD
p. +31 30 253 7890
mscinfo.geo@uu.nl
http://www.geo.uu.nl/

University of Amsterdam

Dept of Geology (2015)
Science Park 904
1098 XH Amsterdam
p. +31 (0)20525 8626
info-science@uva.nl

University of Twente

Faculty of Geo-Information Sciences and Earth Observation (ITC) (M,D) ● (2020)
P.O. Box 217
Enschede 7500 AE
p. +31 (0)53 487 44 44
info-itc@utwente.nl
https://www.itc.nl
f: https://www.facebook.com/ITC.UTwente
Programs: Master's Geo-information Science and Earth Observation with specialisations in Applied Remote Sensing; Natural Hazards and Disaster Risk Reduction; Geoinformatics; Land Administration; Natural Resources Management; Urban Planning and Management; Water Resources and Environmental Management, Master's Spatial Engineering
Certificates: See: https://www.itc.nl/studyfinder

University of Utrecht

Dept of Earth Sciences ☒ (2017)
Heidelberglaan 2
P.O. Box 80115
Utrecht
C.L.M.Marcelis@uu.nl

Vrije Universiteit Amsterdam

Faculty of Beta Science, Dep. of Earth Sciences (B,M,D) ●☒ (2021)
De Boelelaan 1085-1087
1081 HV Amsterdam 1081 HV
p. +31 (0)20 59 87310
f.bosse@vu.nl
https://science.vu.nl/en/research/earth-sciences
Enrollment (2015): B: 248 (56) M: 67 (45)
Professor:
Gareth R. Davies, (D), GiCcGf
Han J. Dolman, (D), CbAmHg
Sander Houweling, (D), AscAp
Klaudia Kuiper, (D), Cc
Wouter Schellart, (D), Gt
Ronald R.T. van Balen, (D), GgmGt

Guido R. van der Werf, (D), Zr
Wim van Westrenen, (D), CpGz
Jan Wijbrans, (D), CcGtv

Associate Professor:
Fraukje M. Brouwer, (D), Utrecht, 2000, GptGc
Gerald M. Ganssen, (D), ObPe
Kees Kasse, (D), GmsSd
Janne Koornneef, (D), GvCa
Frank J.C. Peeters, (D), PmOg
Didier Roche, (D), AsZn
Sander Veraverbeke, (D), Zr
Jorien Vonk, (D), Hg
Pieter Vroon, (D), GvCcl

Assistant Professor:
Kay J. Beets, Cg
Anouk Beniest, (D), ZyGcg
Wouter Berghuijs , (D), Hq
Kim Naudts, (D), HgPe
Maarten A. Prins, (D), GsOg
Monica Sanchez Roman, (D), GdsGg
Marlies ter Voorde, (D), YgGt
Jeroen van der Lubbe, (D), Gs
Nathalie Van der Putten, (D), PecZy
Ype van der Velde, (D), Hw

Research Associate:
Antoon Meesters, (D), AmGq

Dr:
Bernd Andeweg, (D), 2002, GtcGg
Ron Kaandorp, (D), Gg
Els Ufkes, (D), PmZgGu

Netherlands Antilles

Royal NIOZ

Marine Geology (2015)
Landsdiep 4
Den Burg 1797 SZ
p. +31(0)222 369 300
Jens.Greinert@nioz.nl
http://www.nioz.nl

New Zealand

Institute of Geological and Nuclear Sciences Ltd (New Zealand)

Institute of Geological and Nuclear Sciences Ltd (New Zealand) (2015)
1 Fairway Drive, Avalon 5010. PO Box 30-368, 5040.
Lower Hutt
p. +64-4-570-1444
G.Alderwick@gns.cri.nz
http://www.gns.cri.nz/
f: https://www.facebook.com/gnsscience

Massey University

Soil and Earth Sciences Group (2015)
Private Bag
Palmerston North
p. 0800 MASSEY (0800 627 739)
contact@massey.ac.nz
http://www.massey.ac.nz/massey/learning/programme-course-paper/programme.cfm?major_code=2044&prog_id=92431

University of Auckland

School of Environment (B,M,D) ☒ (2017)
Private Bag 92019
Auckland Mail Center
Auckland 1142
p. 64 9 3737599
p.kench@auckland.ac.nz
http://www.env.auckland.ac.nz
Programs: Geography; Earth Sciences; Environmental Science; Environmental Management; Geophysics; Geology

University of Canterbury

Dept of Geological Sciences (B,M,D) ●☒ (2018)
Private Bag 4800
Christchurch 8140
p. (643) 3694384
geology@canterbury.ac.nz
http://www.geol.canterbury.ac.nz/title.html
Enrollment (2014): B: 28 (0) M: 0 (35) D: 0 (20)

Professor Hazard & Disaster Management:
Timothy R H Davies, (D)

Professor:
James W. Cole, (D), Wellington, 1966, Gv
Andy Nicol, (D), Canterbury (NZ), 1991, GctGo
Jarg R. Pettinga, (D), Auckland, 1981, Gtc

Senior Lecturer Hazard & Disaster Management:
Thomas Wilson, (D), Canterbury (NZ), Gv

Senior Lecturer:
Kari N. Bassett, (D), Minnesota, 1995, GstGd
Catherine Reid, (D), Pg

Associate Professor:
Ben Kennedy, (D), Gv

Lecturer:
Darren Gravley, (D), Gv
Samuel J. Hampton, (D), Canterbury (NZ), 2010, GvZe
Alex Nichols, (D)

University of Otago

Dept of Geology (B,M,D) O☒ (2017)
P. O. Box 56
360 Leith Walk
Dunedin 9054
p. +64 3 479-7519
geology@otago.ac.nz
http://www.otago.ac.nz/geology/

Head of Department:
James D. L. White, (D), California (Santa Barbara), 1989, Gvs

Professor:
Dave Craw, (D), Otago (NZ), 1981, Eg
R. Ewan Fordyce, (D), Canterbury (NZ), 1981, Pv
David J. Prior, (D), Leeds (UK), 1988, Gct

Senior Lecturer:
Candace E. Martin, (D), Yale, 1990, ClcGz
Virginia G. Toy, (D), Otago (NZ), 2008, Gct

Dr:
Christopher M. Moy, (D), Gus

Associate Professor:
Andrew R. Gorman, (D), British Columbia, 2001, YrgYe
Daphne E. Lee, (D), Otago (NZ), 1980, Pib

Senior Lecturer:
J. Michael Palin, (D), Yale, 1992, CcGip

Lecturer:
Christina R. Riesselman, (D), Stanford, 2011, Ou
James M. Scott, (D), Otago (NZ), 2008, Gp
Steven AF Smith, (D)

Emeritus:
Douglas S. Coombs, (D), Gi
Alan F. Cooper, (D), Otago (NZ), 1970, GpiGt
Rick H. Sibson, (D), Imperial Coll (UK), 1977, Gc

University of Waikato

Dept of Earth Sciences (2015)
Private Bag 3105
Hamilton 3240
p. +64 7 838 4625
science@waikato.ac.nz
http://sci.waikato.ac.nz/study/subjects/earth-sciences

Victoria University of Wellington

School of Geography, Environment and Earth Sciences (A,B,M,D) O⊘ (2020)
P. O. Box 600
Wellington 6140
p. +6444635337
geo-enquiries@vuw.ac.nz
http://www.wgtn.ac.nz/sgees
Programs: Earth Sciences, Geology, Development Studies, Environmental Studies, Human Geography, Physical Geography,

Geophysics, Meteorology, Environmental Science, GIS, Climate Change and Science Policy
Enrollment (2012): B: 153 (107) M: 51 (22)
Emeritus:
Tim Little, (D), Stanford, 1988, Gct

Dept of Geology (2015)
P. O. Box 600
Wellington
p. +64 4 463 5337
geo-enquiries@vuw.ac.nz
http://www.victoria.ac.nz/sgees/study/postgraduate-study/geology/

Nicaragua

University of Managua

Centro de Investigaciones Geocientificas (2015)
Colonia Miguel Bonilla No. 165, P.O. Box A-131 Cc. Managua, Managua

Niger

Institut de Recherche pour le Developpement au Niger

Institut de Recherche pour le Developpement au Niger (B) (2015)
Avenue de Maradi
Niamey BP 11 416
p. (227) 20 75 38 27
irdniger@ird.fr
http://www.ird.ne/

Universite Abdou Moumouni de Niamey

Dept de Geologie (2015)
B.P. 10662
Niamey
p. (227) 20 31 50 72
http://www.secheresse.info/article.php3?id_article=1664
Doyen:
Abdoulaye M. Alassane

Nigeria

Adekunle Ajasin University

Dept of Earth Sciences (B) (2015)
Akungba Akoko, Ikare Akoko 23401
p. +234 (34) 246444
iosazuwa@yahoo.com
http://www.ajasin.edu.ng/academics

African University of Science & Technology

Petroleum Engineering (B,M) (2015)
PMB 681
Abuja F.C.T.
Km 10 Airport Road
Garki
p. +234 9 7800680
http://aust.edu.ng/

Ahmadu Bello University

Dept of Geology (2015)
Sokoto Road
Samaru-Zaria
Zaria 2222, Kaduna
p. +234 (69) 50 691
ybijimi@yahoo.com
http://www.abu.edu.ng/

American University of Nigeria

School of Arts and Sciences (B) (2015)
Lamido Zubairu Way
PMB 2250, Yola 23455
p. +234 (805) 5485 702
dsas@aun.edu.ng
http://www.abti-american.edu.ng

Caleb University

Dept of Surveying and Geoinformatics (B) (2015)
PMB 21238
Ikeja GPO, Lagos
p. +234-1-764-7312
info@calebuniversity.edu.ng
http://calebuniversity.edu.ng/courses.php?collUid=4

Dept of Environmental Protection and Management (B) (2015)
PMB 21238
Ikeja GPO, Lagos
p. +234-1-764-7312
info@calebuniversity.edu.ng
http://calebuniversity.edu.ng/courses.php?coll_id=4

Crawford University

Dept of Mathematics and Physical Sciences (B) O☒ (2019)
PMB 2001
Faith City, Ogun 112102
p. +2348023003436
info@crawforduniversity.edu.ng
http://www.crawforduniversity.edu.ng
f: https://www.facebook.com/CrawfordCRU/
t: @unicrawford
Programs: Geology and Mineral Sciences

Delta State University

Dept of Geology (B) (2015)
PMB 1
Abraka
p. +234 (54) 66009
delsu03@yahoo.com
http://www.delsunigeria.net/
Director:
S. H. O. Egboh, (D)
Chair:
E. Adaikpoh, (D)

Enugu State University of Science and Technology

Dept of Geology and Mining (B) (2015)
MB 01660, Enugu
p. +234 (42) 451319
dean.fans@esut.edu.ng
http://www.esut.edu.ng/

Dept of Geography and Meteorology (B) (2015)
MB 01660, Enugu
p. +234 (42) 451319
dean.fans@esut.edu.ng
http://www.esut.edu.ng/

Federal Polytechnic, Bida

Dept of Survey and Geoinformatics (B) (2015)
http://www.fedpolybidaportal.com/

Dept of Quantitative Surveying (B) (2015)
http://www.fedpolybidaportal.com/

Federal Polytechnic, Offa

School of Environmental Studies (B) (2015)
http://www.fedpoffa.edu.ng/

Federal University of Technology, Akure

Earth & Mineral Sciences (B) (2015)
PMB 704
Akure
p. +234 (34) 243744
sems@futa.edu.ng
http://www.futa.edu.ng/sems/

Dept of Applied Geophysics (B,M,D) (2015)
PMB 704
Akure, Ondo
p. +234 803-595-9029
joamigun@futa.edu.ng
http://agp.futa.edu.ng/page.php?pageid=179

Applied Geology (B,M,D) ● ☒ (2019)
PMB 704
Akure, Ondo
p. +234 8036672708
agy@futa.edu.ng
http://www.futa.edu.ng/agy/
Programs: Bachelor of Technology, Master of Technology and Doctor of Philosophy degree programs in Applied Geology
Certificates: Post Graduate Diploma program in Applied Geology
Enrollment (2019): B: 96 (96) M: 8 (8) D: 1 (1)

Professor:
Saka Adelayo Opeloye, (D), Bauchi, 2003, GsPgGo

Professor:
Yinusa Ayodele Asiwaju-Bello, (D), Leeds (UK), 1991, HwNgGu
Idowu Bolofinde Odeyemi, (D), Ibadan, 1976, GgxZr
Chukwuemeka Tony Okonkwo, (D), Keele, 1991, GcxGg

Dr:
Anthony Odunyemi Ademeso, (D), Akure, 2011, NgrNt
Peter Sunday Ola, (D), Akure, 2002, GosGg

Mr:
Blessing Adeoti, (M), Akure, 2015, GcxGg
Adeshina Luqman Adisa, (M), Akure, 2012, CgeGc
Isaac Ominyi Ajigo, (M), Jos, 2013, GgCgGx
Sunday Olabisi Daramola, (M), Akure, 2012, GeNtHw
Oladimeji Rilwan Egbeyemi, (M), Ibadan, 2004, GgCeEg
Simeon O. Idowu, (M), Ago-Iwoye, 2007, NgHwGg
Emmanuel Eghietseme Igonor, (M), Ibadan, 2007, GgCeGi
Osazuwa Abifade Ogbahon, (M), Akure, 2011, PlGsPm
Franklin Oluwaseun Olabode, (M), Akure, 2016, HwNgGg

Dr Mrs:
Oluwaseyi Adunola Bamisaiye, (D), Pretoria, 2018, GcZrRn

Dr:
Mohammed Olatoye Adepoju, (D), Akure, 2017, CeEgGg
Stephen O. Ariyo, (D), Ibadan, 2014, YegYx
Timothy Iyobosa Asowata, (D), Ibadan, 2017, GeiGg
Olusiji Samuel Ayodele, (D), Ago-Iwoye, 2015, CeGcZr
Oladotun Afolabi Oluwajana, (D), Ibadan, 2017, GsPgGo
Joshua Oluwasanmi Owoseni, (D), Akure, 2019, HwNgRn

Federal University of Technology, Yola

Dept of Surveying & Geoinformatics (B) (2015)
PMB 2076
Yola
p. +234 (803) 6065646
survey@futy.edu.ng
http://www.futy.edu.ng/academic/dsurvey.htm

Dept of Soil Science (B) (2015)
PMB 2076
Yola
p. +234 805 3372 784
soilscience@futy.edu.ng
http://www.futy.edu.ng/academic/dsoil.htm

Dept of Geography (B) (2015)
PMB 2076
Yola
p. +234 (803) 6065646
geography@futy.edu.ng
http://www.futy.edu.ng/academic/dgeography.htm

Dept of Geology (B) (2015)
PMB 2076
Yola
p. +234 (803) 6065646
geology@futy.edu.ng
http://www.futy.edu.ng/academic/dgeology.htm

Gombe State University

Dept of Geography (B) (2015)
contact@gsu.edu.ng
http://www.gomsu.org/

Dept of Geology (B) (2015)
contact@gsu.edu.ng
http://www.gomsu.org/

Ladoke Akintola University of Technology

Dept of Earth Sciences (B) ☒ (2020)
PMB 4000
Ogbomoso, Oyo 4000
p. +234 8137400195
contact@lautech.edu.ng
http://www.lautech.edu.ng/Academics/undergraduates/FPAS
t: @lautechinfo
Enrollment (2015): B: 13 (13)

Dr:
Oyelowo Gabriel Bayowa, (D), Obafemi Awolowo, 2013, GggGg
Abosede Olufunmi Adewoye, (D), Ladoke Akintola, 2014, GeeGe
Moruffdeen Adedapo Adabanija, (D), Ibadan, 2009, GggGg

Mr:
Olukayode Adegoke Afolabi, (M), Ibadan, 2000, GxxGx
Ismaila Abiodun Akinlabi, (M), Ibadan, 2011, GggGg
Mustapha Taiwo Jimoh, (M), Ibadan, 2006, GxxGx
Lanre Lateef Kolawole, (M), Newcastle, 1985, GeeGe

Lagos State Polytechnic

School of Environmental Studies (Quantity Surveying) (B) (2015)
info@mylaspotech.edu.ng
http://mylaspotech.net/

National Open University of Nigeria

School of Science & Technology (B) (2015)
PO Box 1866
Bauchi
p. +234 1-8188849, +234 1-4820720
sst@noun.edu.ng
http://www.nou.edu.ng/noun/

Nnamdi Azikiwe University

Dept of Geology/Meteorology and Env Management (B) (2015)
PMB 5025
Awka, Nnewi 5025
p. +234 (46) 550018
emmaojukwu@unizik.edu.ng
http://www.unizikeduportal.org/

Dept of Geological Sciences (B,M,D) ● ☒ (2017)
Awka Campus
PMB 5025
Awka, Anambra 5025
p. +234 (46) 550018
ne.ajaegwu@unizik.edu.ng
http://www.unizikeduportal.org/
Programs: Geology

Dr.:
Norbert E. Ajaegwu, (D), Nnamdi Azikiwe (Nigeria), 2014, GorGg

Obafemi Awolowo University

Dept of Geology (B,M,D) ● (2015)
Ile-Ife, Osun State 220002
p. 08128181062
geoife@oauife.edu.ng
http://gly.oauife.edu.ng/
Enrollment (2014): B: 213 (0) M: 24 (0) D: 12 (0)

Head:
A. A. Adepelumi, (D), YgsNe

Professor:
S. A. Adekola, (D), GdoCg
O. Afolabi, Yg
J. O. Ajayi, No
T. R. Ajayi, CgEgGe
O. A. Alao, (D), Yg
U. K. Benjamin, GoCg
S. L. Fadiya, (D), God
A. O. Ige, Cg

A. O. Ige, Cg
E. James-Aworeni, Hg
J. I. Nwachukwu, GoCg
O. O. Ocan, GtzGp
S. B. Ojo, Yg
V. O. Olarewaju, GozCg
A. O. Olorunfemi, Go
M. O. Olorunfemi, Yg
A. A. Oyawale, GeoCg
M. A. Rahaman, GpcGi
B. M. Salami, Hg
I. A. Tubosun
Associate Professor:
A Adetunji, (D), EgGi
Assistant Professor:
Dele E. Falebita, (D), Obafemi Awolowo, YeRnZg
Research Associate:
M. A. Olayiwola, GugPi
O. M. Oyebanjo

Dept of Soil Science and Land Resources Management (B,M,D) O⊘ (2021)
Department of Soil Science and Land Resources Management
Faculty of Agriculture
Ile-Ife, Osun 220005
p. (803) 827-2331
midowu@oauife.edu.ng
http://www.oauife.edu.ng/faculties/agric/soil_sci.html
Programs: B.Agric., M.Sc. and Ph.D. D. (Soil Science)

Department of Geography (B,M,D) O (2018)
Ile-Ife
p. +234 (70) 37772355
sinaayanlade@yahoo.co.uk
http://www.oauife.edu.ng/faculties/soc_sciences/departments/geo/home.htm
Programs: Geography and GIS
Certificates: GIS
Assistant Professor:
Ayansina Ayanlade, (D), AtZir

Rivers State University of Science & Technology

Inst of Geoscience & Space Technology (IGST) (2015)
P.M.B. 5080
Nkpolu - Oroworukwo
Port Harcourt, Rivers State
info@ust.edu.ng
http://www.ust.edu.ng/

University of Ado - Ekiti

Dept of Agricultural Sciences
(B) (2015)
PMB 5363
Ado-Ekiti
p. +234 (30) 250026
http://www.unadportal.com/

Geology Dept (B) (2015)
PMB 5363
Ado-Ekiti
p. +234 (30) 250026
info@eksu.edu.ng
http://www.unadportal.com/

University of Benin

Dept of Petroleum Engineering (B) (2015)
PMB 115
Benin City, Edo State
p. 234 0802 345 5681
deanengineering@uniben.edu
http://www.uniben.edu/UniversityOfBenin-PetroleumEngineering.html

Dept of Geology (B,M,D) ● (2015)
P. M. B. 1155
Benin City, Edo State
p. 234 0802 345 5681
registrar@uniben.edu
http://www.uniben.edu/physicalscielcdfaculty.html
Professor:
Godwin Osarenkhoe Asuen, (D), EcGsg
Professor:
Christopher Nnaemeka Akujieze, (D), GgHwGe
Williams Ogbevire Emofurieta, (D), GzCeGe
Tony Uzozili Onyeobi, (D), NrgGq
Associate Professor:
Isaac Okpeseyi Imasuen, (D), W Ontario, CgGee
Senior Lecturer:
Ben Obelenwa Ezenabor, (M), HgZrGe
Franklin A. Lucas, (D), PmlGr
Lecturer II:
Aitalokhai Joel Edegbai, (M), GosPi
Efetobore Gladys Maju-Oyovwikowhe, (M), GszGo
Sikiru Adeoye Salami, (D), YgeGg
Lecturer I:
Ovie Odokuma-Alonge, (M), CgGip
Graduate Assistant:
Tomilola Andre-Obayanju, (B), NgHgGe
Assistant Lecturer:
Aiyevbekpen Helen Akenzua-Adamcyzk, (M), GeHgGg
Nosa Samuel Igbinigie, (M), GorGg
Alexander Ogbamikhumi, (M), YsgGg
Sunday Erapkpower Okunuwadje, (M), GsoGd
Edoseghe Edwin Osagiede, (M), GctGx

University of Calabar

Dept of Geology (B) (2015)
PMB 1115 Eta Agbo Road,
Calabar Municipal, Cross River State
p. (+234) 8173740083
general@unical.edu.ng
http://www.unical.edu.ng/pages/programs_courses/sciences.php?nav=departments
Head:
Nse U. Essien

University of Ibadan

Dept of Geology (B,M,D) (2015)
Ibadan, Oyo 200284
p. 02-8101100-8101104
uigeology@yahoo.com
http://sci.ui.edu.ng/geowelcome
Professor:
I. M. Akaegbobi, Cg
A. A. Elueze, Eg
Ougbenga. Akindeji. Okunlola, (D), Ibadan, 2001, EgCgGe
A. I. Olayinka, Yg
Moshood N. Tijani, (D), Muenster (Germany), 1997, HwCgGe
Lecturer:
A. E. Abimbola, Cg
O. C. Adeigbe, (D), Ibadan, 2009, GosGe
G. O. Adeyemi, NgHg
O. A. Boboye, Go
A. T. Bolarinwa, EgGz
M. E. Nton, Go
M. A. Oladunjoye, Yg
O. O. Osinowo, Yg
I. A. Oyediran, Ng

Dept of Geology (B,M,D) O⊘ (2021)
Ibadan
Ibadan, Oyo 200284
p. +234-8033819066
ehinola01@yahoo.com
http://www.ui.edu.ng/?q=departmentofgeology
Programs: Geology
Certificates: Training Certificate, COMEG
Enrollment (2020): B: 200 (0) M: 35 (0) D: 35 (0)
Professor:
Olugbenga A. Ehinola, (D), Ibadan, 2002, GoeCo
Olugbenga Ajayi Ehinola, (D), Ibadan, 2002, GoeGs
Associate Professor:
A. S. Olatunji, (D), Ibadan, 2006, CgGeCt

Dept of Petroleum Engineering (B,M,D) ☒ (2021)
Oyo Road
Ibadan
p. +234-2-813-004-968
falodelias@gmail.com
http://www.ui.edu.ng/?q=petengine
Programs: Petroleum Engineering
Enrollment (2016): B: 223 (43) M: 17 (17) D: 10 (2)
Professor:
Olugbenga Falode, (D), NpZa

University of Ilorin

Dept of Geology and Mineral Sciences (B) (2015)
PMB 1515
p. +234 (31) 221691
deanfacsci@unilorin.edu.ng
http://www.unilorin.edu.ng/unilorin/index.php/sciences-dept/geology-mineral-sciences
Head:
J.I. D. Adekeye, (D), GoCg
Professor:
S. O. Akande, (D), EgCg
O. Ogunsanwo, Ng
Lecturer:
A. Abdurrahman, (M), CeEg
A. D. Adedcyin, (M), Eg
O. A. Adekeye, (D), Pm
S.M. A. Adelana, (M), HgYgGe
D. A. Alao, NgGz
O. O. Ige, (M), Ng
Kehinde A. Olawuyi, (D), Fed Univ Tech (Nigeria), 2015, YeGge
O. A. Omotoso, (M), Ge
W. O. Raji, (M), Ye

University of Jos

Dept of Geosciences and Mining (B) (2015)
PMB 2084
Jos 930001
p. +234 (73) 559 52
vc@unijos.edu.ng
http://www.unijos.edu.ng/

University of Lagos

Dept of Metalurgical and Materials Engineering (B) (2015)
Akoka
Yaba, Lagos
p. +234 (1) 493 2600 3
informationunit@unilag.edu.ng
http://www.unilag.edu.ng/index.php?page=home

Dept of Civil and Environmental Engineering (B) (2015)
Akoka
Yaba, Lagos
p. +234 (1) 493 2660 3
informationunit@unilag.edu.ng
http://www.unilag.edu.ng/index.php?page=about_departmentdetail&sno=11

Dept of Petroleum and Gas Engineering (B) (2015)
Akoka
Yaba, Lagos
p. +234 (1) 493 2660 3
informationunit@unilag.edu.ng
http://www.unilag.edu.ng/index.php?page=home

Dept Surveying and Geoinformatics (B) (2015)
Akoka
Yaba, Lagos
p. +234 (1) 493 2660 3
informationunit@unilag.edu.ng
http://www.unilag.edu.ng/index.php?page=about_departmentdetail&sno=16

University of Maiduguri

Dept of Geology (2015)
PMB 1069 FEA
Maiduguri
info@unimaid.edu.ng
http://www.unimaid.edu.ng/root/faculty_of_sciences/dept_geology.html

University of Maiduguri, Borno State

Dept of Geology (B,M,D) (2015)
Bama Road
PMB 1069
Maiduguri
p. +234 (76) 231730
info@unimaid.edu.ng
http://www.unimaid.edu.ng/home.php
Professor:
I. B. Goni
Assistant Professor:
Saidu Baba
Lecturer:
Sani Adamu
Kyari M. Ajar
Musa Malana Aji
Fati Bukar
Shettima Bukar
Jalo M. El-Nafaty
Millitus V. Joseph
Samaila C. Kali
Yakubu B. Mohd
Mohammed Poukar
Aishatu Sani
Manaja Mijinyawa Uba
Sidi M. Waru
Asabe Kuku Yahaya
Soloman N. Yusuf
A. Adam Zarma

University of Nigeria

Dept of Geology (B) (2015)
Nsukka
micah.osilike@unn.edu.ng
http://www.unn.edu.ng/physicalsciences/content/view/700/601/

University of Nigeria Nsukka

Dept of Geology (B) (2015)
anthony.okonta@unn.edu.ng
http://unn.edu.ng/department/geology
Lecturer:
Alloysuis Okwudili Anyiam
Luke I. Manah
Smart Chicka Obiora

Dept of Geoinformatics and Surveying (B) (2015)
batho.okolo@unn.edu.ng
http://www.unn.edu.ng/environmentalstudies/content/view/27/44/

University of Port Harcourt

Dept of Geography & Environmental Management (B) (2015)
East/ West Road
PMB 5323
Choba, Port Harcourt 500001
p. +234 (84) 230890-99
edulms@chimpgroup.com
http://uniport.edu.ng/

Dept of Geology (B) (2015)
East/ West Road
P.M.B. 5323
Choba, Port Harcourt 500001
p. +234 (0)84 817 941
uniport@uniport.edu.ng
http://www.uniport.edu.ng/faculties/science.html

Dept of Petroleum and Gas Engineering (B) (2015)
East/ West Road
PMB 5323
Choba, Port Harcourt 500001
p. +234 (84) 230890-99
dean@eng.uniport.edu.ng

http://uniport.edu.ng/

University of Uyo

Faculty of Science Education (B,M,D) (2015)
PMB 1017
Uyo
p. +234 (85) 200303
vc@uniuyo.edu.ng
http://www.uniuyo.edu.ng

Faculty of Social Science (B,M,D) (2015)
PMB 1017
Uyo
p. +234 (85) 200303
vc@uniuyo.edu.ng
http://www.uniuyo.edu.ng

Faculty of Engineering (B,M,D) (2016)
PMB 1017
Uyo
p. +234 (85) 200303
vc@uniuyo.edu.ng
http://www.uniuyo.edu.ng

Faculty of Agriculture (B,M,D) (2015)
PMB 1017
Uyo, Akwa Ibom State 520001
p. +234 (85) 200303
vc@uniuyo.edu.ng
http://www.uniuyo.edu.ng

Faculty of Environmental Studies (B,M,D) (2015)
PMB 1017
Uyo
p. +234 (85) 200303
vc@uniuyo.edu.ng
http://www.uniuyo.edu.ng

Western Delta University

Geology and Petroleum Studies (B) (2015)
PMB 10
Oghara
p. +234 (70) 35400531
info@wdu.edu.ngg

http://www.wduniversity.org/

Wukari Jubilee University

Dept of Geography and Environmental Conservation (B) (2015)
PMB 1019
Wukari, Taraba State
p. +234 (080) 80329138
wukari_jubilee@yahoo.com
http://wukarijubileeuniversity.org/

Norway

Norges Geologiske Undersokelse

Geological Survey of Norway ☒ (2019)
Postboks 6315 Torgarden
7491 Trondheim
ngu@ngu.no
http://www.ngu.no/no/

Norwegian University of Life Sciences (NMBU)

Section of Soil and Water Sciences, Favulty of Environmental Sciences and NAtural Resource Management (B,M,D) O☒ (2017)
P.O. Box 5003
1432 AS
Ås 1432
p. +47 67 23 00 00
post-mina@nmbu.no
https://www.nmbu.no/en/faculty/mina
Programs: Environmental Sciences (B, M); Ecology and Natural Resource Management; Renewable Energy; Sustainable Tourism; Forestry

Professor:
Trond Børresen, Sp
Petter Jenssen, Zu
Tore Krogstad, Sc
Jan Mulder, Cb
Gunnhild Riise, Hs
Trine Sogn, Sb
Rohrlack Thomas, Hs

Norwegian University of Science and Technology

Dept of Geology and Mineral Resources Engineering (2015)
N-7034 Trondheim
mai.britt.mork@ntnu.no

Faculty of Engineering Science and Technology (2015)
S. P. Andersens vei 15A
N7034 Trondheim
p. 73594779
ingvald.strommen@ntnu.no

NTNU Norwegian University of Science and Technology

Dept of Geology and Mineral Resources Engineering (B,M,D) (2015)
Sem Sælands vei 1
7491 Trondheim
Trondheim
p. (+47) 73 59 48 00
iigb-info@ivt.ntnu.no
http://www.ntnu.no/igb
f: https://www.facebook.com/geologibergNTNU

University of Bergen

Dept of Earth Science (B,M,D) O☒ (2017)
Allegaten 41
N-5007 Bergen
p. +47 55583600
post@geo.uib.no
http://www.geo.uib.no/
f: https://www.facebook.com/earthscienceuib
t: @uibgeo

University of Oslo

Deptartment of Geosciences (B,M,D) ☒ (2019)
Post Box 1047, Blindern
N-0316 Oslo
p. +47 22856656
geosciences@geo.uio.no
http://www.mn.uio.no/geo/english/
f: https://www.facebook.com/uiogeo/
Programs: Two BSc programmes in Geosciences (in Norwegian)

Masterprogramme in Geosciences (master's two years)

Mineralogical-Geological Museum (2015)
Sars gate 1
P.O. Box 1172
Blindern, Oslo 0318
p. +47 228 55050
postmottak@nhm.uio.no
http://www.nhm.uio.no/english/

University of Tromso

Geology Dept (2015)
N-9037 Tromso
matthias.forwick@uit.no
http://www.ibg.uit.no/geologi/geo_eng_end.html

Oman

Sultan Qaboos University

Dept of Earth Science (B,M,D) ● (2015)
123 Al-Khod
P.O. Box 36
Muscat
p. +968 2414 6832
khirbash@squ.edu.om
http://www.squ.edu.om/earth-sci/tabid/11718/language/en-US/
Enrollment (2013): B: 85 (60) M: 5 (25) D: 2 (1)
Head:
Salah Al-Khirbash, (D)

Pakistan

COMSATS

Institute of Information Technology (2015)
Park Road, Chak Shahzad
Islamabad
p. +92-51-9247000-2
info@ciit.edu.pk
http://www.comsats.edu.pk/

Geological Survey of Pakistan

p. (+958) 9211032
qta@gsp.gov.pk
http://www.gsp.gov.pk/

Institute of Space Technology

Institute of Space Technology (B,M,D) (2015)
P.O. Box 2750
Islamabad 44000
p. 92.51.9075100
info@ist.edu.pk
http://www.ist.edu.pk/

National University of Sciences and Technology

Institute of Geographic Information System (2015)
RIMMS building, NUST H-12 Campus
Islamabad
p. +92-51-90854400
info@igis.nust.edu.pk
http://igis.nust.edu.pk/

Sind University Pakistan

Dept of Geology (2015)
University of Sindh, Allama I.I. Kazi Campus
Jamshoro
Sindh 76080
p. 92-22-9213172-9213181-90 Ext:
dean.science@usindh.edu.pk

University of Engineering and Technology

Geological Engineering (B,M,D) ●☒ (2019)
Lahore, Punjab 54890
p. 0092-42-99029487
mzubairab1977@gmail.com
http://www.uet.edu.pk/faculties/facultiesinfo/geological/index.html?RID=introduction
Programs: B.Sc. Geological Engineering
M.Sc. Geological Engineering
M.Sc. Geological Sciences
Ph.D. Geological Engineering
Ph.D. Geological Sciences
Enrollment (2018): B: 50 (50)
Chair:
Muhammad Zubair Abu Bakar, (D), 2012, NrmNg
Associate Professor:
Muhammad Farooq Ahmed, (D), Missouri (Rolla), 2013, NgxNt

University of Karachi

Dept of Geology (2015)
KARACHI-75270
p. 99261300-06 Ext: 2295
vc@uok.edu.pk
http://uok.edu.pk/faculties/geology/

University of Sargodha

Dept of Earth Science (B,M,D) ●☒ (2019)
Department of Earth Sciences
University of Sargodha-
Sargodha-Pakistan.
Sargodha , Punjab 40100
p. +92-48-9230591
earthscience@uos.edu.pk
http://www.uos.edu.pk
Programs: BS Geology 4 Year, MS Geology 2 Year, BS Geography 4 Year, M.Sc. Geography 2 Year

College of Agriculture (2015)
Sargodha
agri@uos.edu.pk
http://www.uos.edu.pk

University of the Punjab

Department of Geography (A,B,M,D) ●☒ (2020)
New Campus
Lahore 54590
shirazi.geog@pu.edu.pk
http://pu.edu.pk/home/department/46/Department-of-Geography
Programs: Geography,Remote Sensing and GIS
Enrollment (2019): A: 50 (50) B: 200 (175) M: 30 (26) D: 14 (8)

Panama

Universidad de Panama

Facultad de Ciencias Naturales, Exactas y Technologia (2015)
Urbanizacion El Cangrejo, Estafeta Universitaria
ciencias@ancon.up.ac.pa

Paraguay

Universidad Nacional se Asuncion

Dept de Geologia (2015)
University Campus Km. 11, Asuncion
facen@facen.una.py

Peru

Geological Survey of Peru

Instituto Geologico Minero y Metalurgico - INGEMMET (2015)
Av. Canada 1470 San Borja
Lima
p. 051-1-6189800
webmaster@ingemmet.gob.pe
http://www.ingemmet.gob.pe/

San Agustin's Natl University

Escuela Academico Profesional de Ingenieria Geologica y Geofisica (2015)
Av. Indraendencia #1015
Arequipa
p. (054) 244498
geologia@unsa.edu.pe
http://www.unsa.edu.pe

Univ Nacional de Ingeneiria

Escuela Academico Profesional de Ingenieria Geologica (2015)
Av. Tupac Amaru S/N
Rimac, Lima
esanchez@uingemmet.gob.pe
http://www.uni.edu.pe/sitio/academico/facultades/geologica/

Univ Nacional Mayor San Marcos

Escuela Academico Profesional de Ingenieria Geologica (2016)
Av. Venezuela S/N
Lima

j_jacay@yahoo.com
http://www.unmsm.edu.pe

Philippines

University of the Philippines

National Institute of Geological Sciences (B,M,D) ● (2015)
C.P. Garcia corner Velasquez Street
Diliman, Quezon City 1101
p. (+632) 9296046
inquire@nigs.org
http://nigs.org

Poland

AGH University of Science and Technology

Faculty of Geology, Geophysics, and Environmental Protection (2015)
A. Mickiewicza 30 Ave.
30-059 Krakow
p. +48 12 633 29 36
aglown@geol.agh.edu.pl
http://www.wggios.agh.edu.pl/

Dept of Mining and Geoengineering (2015)
Inst. of Drilling & Oil Exploration
Krakow
p. +48 12 617 21 15
wgig@agh.edu.pl
https://www.agh.edu.pl/en/wydzialy/faculty-of-mining-and-geoengineering/

Faculty of Mining and Geoengineering (2015)
Al. Mickiewicza 30
PL-30059 Krakow
p. +48 12 617 21 15
gorn@agh.edu.pl

Jagiellonian University

Institute of Geological Sciences (2015)
Oleandry 2a Str.
30-063 Krakow
sekretariat.ing@uj.edu.pl
http://www.ing.uj.edu.pl

Ministry of Environmental Protection, Natural Resources and Forestry

Dept of Geology (2016)
st. Wawelska 52/54
Warsaw 00-922
p. +48 22 3692449
Departament.Geologii.i.Koncesji.Geologicznych@mos.gov.pl
http://www.mos.gov.pl/dg/dga1.htm

Panstwowy Instytut Geologiczny

Polish Geological Institute (2015)
Ul. Rakowiecka 4 ,
PL-00-975 Warszawa
sekretariat@pgi.gov.pl
http://www.pgi.gov.pl/

Polish Academy of Sciences

Institute of Geological Sciences
(2015)
Al Zwirki i Wigury 93
02-089 Warsaw
p. (+48 22) 620 33 46, 656 60 63
ingpanhard@pan.pl

Silesian University of Technology

Faculty of Mining and Geology (B,M,D) ● (2015)
Wydzial Gornictwa i Geologii
Politechnika Slaska
ul.Akademicka 2
Gliwice 44-100
p. +48 32 2371283
rg@polsl.pl
http://www.polsl.pl/Wydzialy/RG/Strony/Witamy.aspx
Enrollment (2014): B: 2556 (615) M: 327 (283) D: 98 (5)

University of Wroclaw

Inst of Geological Sciences (B,M,D) (2017)
Pl. Maksa Borna 9
50-205 Wroclaw
p. (+4871) 321-10-76
sekretariat.ing@uwr.edu.pl
http://www.ing.uni.wroc.pl/home-page
Enrollment (2016): D: 14 (8)

Director:
Krystyna Choma-Moryl, (D), 1983, Ng

Professor:
Pawel Aleksandrowski, (D), Polish Acad of Sci, 1985, GctYe
Marek Awdankiewicz, (D), 1997, Gvi
Piotr Gunia, (D), 1983, Gaz
Jacek Gurwin, (D), 1997, HwyZf
Henryk Marszalek, (D), 1994, Hy
Jacek Puziewicz, (D), 1985, Gix
Jerzy Sobotka, (D), AGH (Poland), 1992, YeuEo
Andrzej Solecki, (D), 1987, Eg
Stanislaw Stasko, (D), 1986, Hg
Jacek Szczepanski, (D), 1999, Ggc

Adjunct Professor:
Anna Gorecka-Nowak, (D), 1992, Pg
Maciej Gorka, (D), 2007, AsCa
Jakub Kierczak, (D), 2007, GeSc
Antoni Muszer, (D), 1994, Eg
Anna Pietranik, (D), Wroclaw, 2006, CgGie
Marta Rauch, (D), 2002, Gc
Robert Tarka, (D), 1995, Hg
Jurand Wojewoda, (D), 1989, Gs

Portugal

Istituto Geologico e Mineiro (IGM)

Geological and Mining Institute of Portugal (2015)
Estrada da Portela
Zambujal
atendimento@ineti.pt
http://www.ineti.pt/

Oporto University

Dept of Geology (2015)
Faculdade de Ciencias do Porto
Praca de Gomes Teixeira
4099-002 PORTO
dg.sec@fc.up.pt
http://www.fc.up.pt/depts/geo/

Universidade da Madeira

Dept de Biologia (B) (2015)
Campus Universitario da Penteada
9000-390 Funchal
p. +251 291 705 380
mgouveia@uma.pt
http://www.uma.pt/Unidades/Biologia/

Universidade de Aveiro

Dept de Geociencias (B,M,D) ☒ (2020)
Campo Universitario Santiago
Aveiro 3810-193
p. +351 234 370 357
eafsilva@ua.pt
http://www.ua.pt/geo
Programs: Geology BSc, Geological Engineering MSc, Geosciences PhD

Professor:
Eduardo Ferreira da Silva, (D), CeGbCl
Fernando Rocha, (D), Aveiro, 1994, EnGzb

Universidade de Coimbra

Dept de Ciencias da Terra (A,B,M,D) O☒ (2017)
Rua Silvio Lima, Univ. Coimbra, Pólo II Coimbra
Coimbra 3030-790 Coimbra
p. +351-239 860 514
cgeo@ci.uc.pt
http://www.dct.uc.pt
Programs: Geology
Professor:
Rui Pena dos Reis, (D), GorGs
Associate Professor:
Alcides Castilho Pereira, (D), Coimbra, 1992, GebZr

Universidade de Lisboa

Dept of Geology (A,B,M,D) ●☒ (2020)
Ed. C6, Campo Grande
Campo Grande
Lisboa 1749-016
p. +35121 750 00 66 / + 351 21 75
dgeologia@fc.ul.pt
http://www.fc.ul.pt/en/dg?refer=1
f: https://www.facebook.com/Departamento-de-Geologia-FCUL-192772970763173
Programs: Geology
Certificates: Applied Geology, Petroleum Geosciences
Enrollment (2018): B: 314 (51) M: 87 (13) D: 30 (2)
Professor:
Maria da Conceição Pombo Freitas, (D), Lisbon, 1996, GusGe
Professor:
César Andrade, (D), Gu
Ana Azerêdo, (D), Gd
Maria da Conceiç Freitas, (D), GseGu
António Mateus, (D), Em
Associate Professor:
Mário Cachão, (D), PgeGg
Nuno Pimentel, (D), GrsGo
Assistant Professor:
Maria do Rosário Carvalho, (D), HwyZn
Telmo Bento dos Santos, (D), GptGi
Carla Kullberg, (D), Gt
Carlos Marques Silva, (D), Pg
Catrina Silva, (D), Hg
António Brum Silveira, (D), Zf

Universidade de Trás-os-Montes e Alto Douro

Departamento de Geologia (B,M,D) ⊘ (2020)
Apartado 1013
Vila Real 5001-801
p. +351259350224
geologia@utad.pt
http://www.geologia.utad.pt
Enrollment (2020): B: 7 (0) M: 3 (0) D: 2 (0)
Professor:
Maria E.P. Gomes, (D), UTAD, 1996, GiCgGz
Associate Professor:
Ana M.P. Alencoão, (D), UTAD, 1998, HgGgm
Artur A.A. Sá, (D), UTAD, 2005, PgiPs
Assistant Professor:
Maria E.P.S. Abreu, (D), UTAD, 2012, GaaGa
João C.C.V. Baptista, (D), UTAD, 1998, GmmGa
Maria R.M. Costa, (D), UTAD, 2000, Hw
Paulo J.C. Favas, (D), UTAD, 2008, GeCtGg
José M.M. Lourenço, (D), UTAD, 2006, YeZin
Alcino S. Oliveira, (D), UTAD, 2002, Hww
Anabela R.R.C. Oliveira, (D), UTAD, 2011, Gss
Fernando A.L. Pacheco, (D), UTAD, 2001, Hq
Luís M.O. Sousa, (D), 2001, EnGgNg
Rui J.S. Teixeira, (D), UTAD, 2008
Nuno M.O.C.M. Vaz, (D), UTAD, 2010, PmlYg

Universidade do Minho

Dept de Ciencias da Terra (B,M,D) (2015)
Campus de Gualtar
Braga 4710-057
p. 351 253 604 300
sec@dct.uminho.pt
http://www.dct.uminho.pt/

Universidade Nova de Lisboa

Dept de Ciencias da Terra (2015)
Qta. da Torre
2829-516 Caparica
p. (351) 212 948 573
dct.secretariado@fct.unl.pt
http://www.dct.fct.unl.pt/

Qatar

University of Qatar

Dept of Geology (B) (2015)
PO Box 2713
Doha
hamadsaad@qu.edu.qa
http://www.angelfire.com/ms/GeoQU/
Professor:
Sobhi J. Nasir, (D), Germany, 1986, Gx
Associate Professor:
Hamad A. Al-Saad, (D), Egypt, 1996, PsGsu
Abdulali A. Sadiq, (D), Southampton (UK), 1995, Zr
Assistant Professor:
Latifa B. AL-Nouimy, (D), Egypt, 1994, Hgw
Sief A. Alhajari, (D), North Carolina, 1992, Hgw

Reunion

Universite de la Reunion

Faculte de Sciences et Technologie - Sciences de la Terre (B) (2015)
15, avenue Rene Cassin
CS 92003
Saint-Denis, Cedex 9 97744
p. (262) 0262 938697
jean-lambert.join@univ-reunion.fr
http://sciences.univ-reunion.fr/rubrique.php3?id_rubrique=72
Professor:
Jean-Lambert Join, (D), Hw
Associate Professor:
Fabrice R. Fontaine, (D), Yg

Laboratoire GeoSciences Reunion (B,M,D) (2015)
15 avenue Rene Cassin
BP 7151
Saint Denis, Messag Cedex 9 97744
vfamin@univ-reunion.fr
http://www.geosciencesreunion.fr/
Professor:
Laurent Michon, (D), GtvGg
Professor:
Jean-Lambert Join, HwGsHg
Associate Professor:
Vincent Famin, (D), GcCgGg
Fabrice R. Fontaine, (D), Ysg
Claude Smutek, NrZrg

Romania

Alexandru Ioan Cuza

Department of Geology (B,M,D) ☒ (2019)
geology@uaic.ro
Bulevardul Carol I nr. 20A
Iai 700505
geology@uaic.ro
http://geology.uaic.ro
Enrollment (2015): B: 59 (26) M: 40 (18) D: 11 (5)
Head:
Nicolae Buzgar, (D), A I Cuza Univ of Iasi, 1998, GziGd
Professor:
Sorin Dorin Baciu, (D), A I Cuza Univ of Iasi, 2001, GcPv
Dumitru Bulgariu, (D), Cga
Ovidiu Gabriel Iancu, (D), A I Cuza Univ of Iasi, 1998, GpeCg
Crina Genoveva Miclaus, (D), A I Cuza Univ of Iasi, 2001, Gsr
Dan Stumbea, (D), Bolyai Univ of Cluj, 1998, Gez

Associate Professor:
Andrei Ionut Apopei, (D), A I Cuza Univ of Iasi, 2014, GziGg
Andrei Buzatu, (D), A I Cuza Univ of Iasi, 2014, GziGg
Viorel Ionesi, (D), A I Cuza Univ of Iasi, 2005, PmGgHg
Daniel Tabara, (D), A I Cuza Univ of Iasi, 2000, Pl
Paul Tibuleac, (D), A I Cuza Univ of Iasi, 1999, Pgs
Assistant Professor:
Iuliana Buliga, (D), A I Cuza Univ of Iasi, 2014, Gep
Traian Gavriloaiei, (D), A I Cuza Univ of Iasi, 1999, CaAsCg
Florentina Pascariu, (D), A I Cuza Univ of Iasi, Nt
Anca Maria Seserman, (D), A I Cuza Univ of Iasi, 2015, Gs
Lecturer:
Laviniu Apostoae, (D), A I Cuza Univ of Iasi, 1999, Eg
Ciprian Chelariu, (D), A I Cuza Univ of Iasi, 2013, Go
Claudia Cirimpei, (D), A I Cuza Univ of Iasi, 2010, PgGr
Tony Cristian Dumitriu, (D), A I Cuza Univ of Iasi, 2015, GcZir
Dan Bogdan Hanu, (D), Yge
Mitica Pintilei, (D), A I Cuza Univ of Iasi, 2010, CgeCt
Bogdan Gabriel Ratoi, (D), A I Cuza Univ of Iasi, 2013, PvGr
Smaranda Doina Sîrbu, (D), A I Cuza Univ of Iasi, 2002, Ge
Oana Stan, (D), A I Cuza Univ of Iasi, 2009, GedCb
Dan Ttefanei, (D), A I Cuza Univ of Iasi, 2012, Cga
Visiting Professor:
Mihai Brânzila, (D), A I Cuza Univ of Iasi, 1998, GgrPg
Mihai Remus Saramet, (D), A I Cuza Univ of Iasi, 2004, NpGo

Babes-Bolyai University

Department of Geology (B,M,D) ⦸ (2020)
Str. M. Kogalniceanu nr.1
RO - 400084 Cluj-Napoca
Cluj-Napoca 400084
p. +40-264-405371
nicolae.har@ubbcluj.ro
http://bioge.ubbcluj.ro/pages/geologie/
Programs: Geology; Applied Geology
Professor:
Ioan Bucur, (D), Babes-Bolyai, 1991, PgmGs
Vlad Codrea, (D), Babes-Bolyai, 1995, PvGo
Sorin Filipescu, (D), Babes-Bolyai, 1996, GrPm

Institul Geologic al Romaniei

Geological Institute of Romania ☒ (2019)
1 Caransebes St, Sector 1
Bucuresti 012271
p. +40314933400
office@igr.ro
http://www.igr.ro/

University of Bucharest

Department of Geophysics - Faculty of Geology and Geophysics (B,M,D) ●☒ (2021)
6 Traian Vuia Street
Sector 2
Bucharest, Bucharest 020956
p. +40-21-3125024
bogdan.niculescu@g.unibuc.ro
https://gg.unibuc.ro/organizare/departamentul-geofizica/
Programs: Geophysics; Geological Engineering
Enrollment (2017): B: 30 (30) M: 20 (20)
Associate Professor:
Bogdan Mihai NICULESCU, (D), Bucharest, 2002, YgeYu

Rwanda

Universite Nationale du Rwanda

Dept of Geology (B) (2015)
Faculty of Science
PO Box 56
Butare
p. +250 (0) 252 530 122
info@nur.ac.rw
http://www.nur.ac.rw/

Dept of Geography (B) (2015)
PO Box 56
Butare
p. +250 (0) 252 530 122
info@nur.ac.rw
http://ww.nur.ac.rw/

Saudi Arabia

King Abdulaziz University

Dept of Geology (2015)
P. O. Box 1744
Building No 55
Jeddah 21441
jha25@hotmail.com
http://earthscience.kau.edu.sa/Default.aspx?Site_ID=145&Lng=EN

King Fahd University of Petroleum and Minerals

Geosciences Department (B,M,D) ●☒ (2018)
P. O. Box 5070
KFUPM
Dhahran, Easter Provience 31261
p. +96638602620
c-es@kfupm.edu.sa
https://cpg.kfupm.edu.sa/academics/departments/department-of-geosciences/
Enrollment (2018): B: 60 (0) M: 53 (0) D: 11 (0)
Chair Professor:
Luis Gonzalez, (D), Michigan, 1989, CgGn
Stewart Alan Greenhalgh, (D), Minnesota, 1979, Yse
John Reijmer, (D), Vrije (Amsterdam), 1991, Gsg
Professor:
Abdullatif Al-Shuhail, (D), Texas A&M, 1998, Ygs
Michael A. Kaminski, (D), MIT/WHOI, 1988, GuPm
Panteleimon Soupios, (D), Aristotle, 2000, Yg
Associate Professor:
Osman Abdullatif, (D), Khartoum, 1993, Gso
Khalid Al-Ramadan, (D), Uppsala, 2006, GodGs
Abdulaziz Al-Shaibani, (D), Texas A&M, 1999, HwGeg
Sherif Hanafy, (D), Kiel, 2002, Yg
John Dean Humphrey, (D), Brown, 1987, Gdo
Mohammad Makkawi, (D), Colorado State, 1998, HwGoq
Bassam S. Tawabini, (D), King Fahd, 2002, GeHsCa
Scot Whattam, (D), Hong Kong, GxXc
Assistant Professor:
Waleed Abdulghani, (D), Go
Abdullah Al-Shuhail, (D), Calgary, 2011, Ye
Ammar Elhusseiny, Stanford, Yg
Ismail Kaka, (D), Carleton, 2006, Ys
Mohammed Qurban, (D)
Umair Bin Waheed, (D), Kaust, 2015, Yg
Lecturer:
Ayman Al-Lehyani, (M), King Fahd, Yg
Mutasim Sami Osman, (M), King Fahd, 2014, GosGc

Saudi Geological Survey

Saudi Geological Survey (2015)
P.O. Box: 54141
21514
p. 966-2-619-5000
sgs@sgs.org.sa
http://www.sgs.org.sa/Arabic/Pages/

Senegal

Universite Cheikh Anta Diop

Dept de Geologie (B) (2015)
Faculte Des Sciences
BP 5005
Dakar-Fann
p. +221 869.27.66
fst@ucad.edu.sn
http://fst.ucad.sn/index.php?option=com_content&task=view&id=19&Itemid=35

Institut des Sciences de l' Environnement (ISE) (B) ☒ (2019)
BP 5005

Dakar-Fann
p. +221 869.27.66
diengdiomaye@yahoo.fr

Sierra Leone

Njala University

Dept of Mining and Metallurgy (B) (2015)
Freetown
p. +232-22-228788, +232-22-226851
nuc@sierratel.sl
http://www.nu-online.com/

Dept of Soil Science (A,B,M,D) (2015)
Freetown
p. +232-22-228788, +232-22-226851
nuc@sierratel.sl
http://ww.nu-online.com/

Dept of Geography & Rural Development (B) (2015)
Freetown
p. +232-22-228788, +232-22-226851
nuc@sierratel.sl
http://www.nu-online.com/

Institute of Environmental Management and Quality Control (B) (2015)
Freetown
p. +232-22-228788, +232-22-226851
nuc@sierratel.sl
http://www.nu-online.com/

University of Sierra Leone

Dept of Geology (2015)
PO Box 87
Freetown
aiah_gbakima2000@yahoo.com
http://www.tusol.org/programmes

Slovakia

Comenius University in Bratislava

Department of Geology and Palaeontology (A,B,M,D) O☒ (2019)
Faculty of Natural Sciences
Ilkovičova 6
Mlynska dolina G
Bratislava 842 15
p. 00421260296529
kgp@fns.uniba.sk
http://geopaleo.fns.uniba.sk/
Programs: Geology (B); Palaeobiology (B); Dynamic Geology (M); Palaeontology (M,D); Tectonics (D); Sedimentology (D)
Enrollment (2016): B: 12 (0) M: 1 (0) D: 5 (0)
Professor:
Michal Kovac, (D), Gsg
Dusan Plasienka, (D), Gt
Daniela Rehakova, (D), Pms
Aubrecht Roman, (D), Gdr
Associate Professor:
Jozef Hok, (A), Ggt
Natalia H. Hudackova, (A), PimPg
Marianna Kovácová, (A), PlcPe
Martin Sabol, (D), Comenius Univ (Slovakia), 2000, PvgPs
Rastislav Vojtko, (D), GctGm
Associate Scientist:
Matus Hyzny, Pi
Jan Schlogl, (D), Pig
Assistant Professor:
Peter Joniak, (D), Pv

Dionyz Stur Institute of Geology

Geology Dept (2015)
Mlynska Dolina 1
81704 Bratislava 11
p. 02 / 59375111
secretary@geology.sk
http://www.geology.sk/new/en

Geologicka Sluzba Slovenskej Republiky

Geological Survey of Slovak Republic (2015)
Mill Valley 1
817 04 Bratislava 11
secretary@geology.sk
http://www.sguds.sk

Kosice Technical University

Faculty of Mining, Ecology, Process Control and Geotechnology (2015)
Fakulta BERG
Park Komenskeho 12
040 01 Kosice
p. +421-55-602 1111
sekrd.fberg@tuke.sk
http://www.fberg.tuke.sk/bergweb/index.php?IdLang=0&Selection=4

Slovenia

Geoloski zavod Slovenije

Geological Survey of Slovenia (M,D) (2015)
Dimiceva ulica 14
Ljubljana SI - 1000
p. +386 1 2809702
www@geo-zs.si
http://www.geo-zs.si

University of Ljubljana

Faculty of natural science and engineering (2015)
Aškerčeva c. 12
Ljubljana 1000
p. 01/470-45-00
tanja.kocevar@ntf.uni-lj.si
http://www.uni-lj.si/academies_and_faculties/faculties/2013071111502957/

Oddelek za Geologijo (2015)
Askerceva 12
Ljubljana
spela.turic@ntf.uni-lj.si
http://www.ntf.uni-lj.si/og

Somalia

Burao University

Dept of Community Development (B) (2015)
p. +252 7126481
info@universityofburao.com
http://www.buraouniversity.com/rural_and_environmental_studies.htm

Mogadishu University

Somali Centre for Water and Environment (B) (2021)
p. (252)-5-932454/ 223433/ 658479
info@mu.edu.so
https://mu.edu.so/somali-center-for-water-environment/

Nugaal University

Institute of Geology (B,M) ● (2016)
Lasanod
p. +252 275 4063 / 7412619
nugaaluniversity@gmail.com
http://www.nugaaluniversity.com

South Africa

Cape Peninsula University of Technology

Dept of Environmental and Occupational Studies (B) (2015)
Cape Town
p. (+27) 021 959 6230
vanderwesthuizenh@cput.ac.za
http://www.cput.ac.za/

Geological Survey of South Africa

Council for Geoscience ● (2015)
Private Bag X112
Pretoria 0001
p. 0027128411911
info@geoscience.org.za
http://www.geoscience.org.za/
Executive Manager:
Fhatuwani L. Ramagwede, (M), 2011, EgGzEg

Nelson Mandela Metropolitan University

Dept of Geoscience (B,M,D) (2015)
PO Box 77000
Summerstrand, Port Elizabeth 6031
p. 041 504 2325
sheila.entress@nmmu.ac.za
http://geosci.nmmu.ac.za/
Administrative Assistant: Sheila Entress
Head:
Nigel Webb, (D)
Professor:
Vincent Kakembo, Sp
Associate Professor:
Moctar Doucoure, (D)
Daniel Mikes, (D)
Post-Doctoral Fellowship:
Bastien Linol, (D), NMMU, 2013, Gs
Lecturer:
Callum Anderson, (M), Port Elizabeth, Gzs
Wilma Britz, (D)
Gideon Brunsdon, (M)
Anton de Wit, (D)
Pakama Syongwana, (D)
Nicolas Tonnelier, (D)
Leizel Williams-Bruinders, (M), Zn
Emeritus:
Peter Booth, (D)
Anthony Christopher
Related Staff:
Paul Baldwin
Willie Deysel

Coastal and Marine Research Institute (B) (2015)
Summerstand Campus (South)
PO Box 77000
Port Elizabeth 6031
p. +27 41 5042877
cmr@nmmu.ac.za
http://www.nmmu.ac.za/default.asp?id=380&bhcp=1

Centre for African Conservation Ecology (M,D) O (2015)
Summerstand Campus (South)
PO Box 77000
Port Elizabeth 6031
p. +27 41 504 2308
Graham.Kerley@nmmu.ac.za
http://ace.nmmu.ac.za/

North-West University

School of Environmental and Health Sciences (B) (2015)
Private Bag x 1290
Potchefstroom 2520
p. (27) 18 299 2528
monica.mosala@nwu.ac.za
http://www.puk.ac.za/opencms/export/PUK/html/fakulteite/natur/geol/index_e.html

Rhodes University

Dept of Geography (B) (2015)
PO Box 94
Grahamstwon 6140
p. +27 (0)46 603 8111
registrar@ru.ac.za
http://oldwww.ru.ac.za/academic/departments/geography/

Institute for Water Research (M,D) (2015)
PO Box 94
Grahamstown 6140
p. +27 46 62224014 / 6222428 / 62
registrar@ru.ac.za
http://www.ru.ac.za/static/institutes/iwr//?request=institutes/iwr/
Professor:
Denis Hughes, (D), Wales, 1978, Hqs

Dept of Geology (B,M,D) (2015)
PO Box 94
Grahamstown , Eastern Cape Provinc 6140
p. +27 (0)46 603 8309
geolsec@ru.ac.za
http://www.ru.ac.za/geology/
Administrative Assistant: Ashley Goddard, Vuyokazi Nkayi
Head:
Steve Prevec, Cg
Professor:
Annette Gotz, Gs
Peter Horvath, (D), Gp
Bantubonke Izwe Ntsaluba, Gi
Briony Proctor
Hari Tsikos, CgEg
Yon Yao, Eg
Associate Professor:
Steffen Buttner, (D), Frankfurt (Germany), 1997, Gcp
Associate Scientist:
Billy De Klerk, Pg
Robert Gess, Pg
Rose Prevec
Mike Skinner
Emeritus:
Roger Jacobs
Julian S. Marsh, (D), Cape Town, 1973, GiCgGv
Laboratory Director:
Gelu Costin, Gp
Cooperating Faculty:
John Hepple

Stellenbosch University

Dept of Process Engineering (Chemical and Mineral Processing) (B,M,D) (2015)
Private Bag X1
Matieland 7602
p. +27 21 808-4485
chemeng@sun.ac.za
http://www.chemeng.sun.ac.za/

Centre for Geographical Analysis ☒ (2019)
Private Bag X1
Matieland 7602
p. (27) 21 808 3218
garth@sun.ac.za
http://www0.sun.ac.za/cga/
f: https://www.facebook.com/cga.sun/
Certificates: Introduction to Geographic Information Systems (GIS), Introduction to Earth Observation (EO), Introduction to Geospatial Object-based Image Analysis (GEOBIA)
Director:
Adriaan van Niekerk, (D), Stellenbosch, Zri
Manager:
Garth Stephenson, (M), Stellenbosch, 2010, Zri

Dept of Earth Sciences (B,M,D) (2015)
Private Bag X1
Matieland, Western Cape 7602
p. +27 (0)21 808 3219
lcon@sun.ac.za
http://www.sun.ac.za/earthSci/

Professor:
Alakendra N. Roychoudhury, (D), Georgia Tech, 1999, ClmOc

Tshwane University of Technology

Dept of Environmental, Water & Earth Sciences (B,M,D) (2015)
Private Bag x680
Pretoria 0001
p. 012 382 6232
gerberme@tut.ac.za
http://www.tut.ac.za/Students/facultiesdepartments/science/departments/environscience/Pages/
Administrative Assistant: Sarah Galebies, Retha Gerber
Enrollment (2015): B: 59 (37) M: 1 (0)
Lecturer:
Chamunorwa Kambewa, (M), 1998, CgeZe
Thando Majodina, (M), GgzGe
Skhumbuzo Sibeko, (B), GggGg
Other:
Mlindelwa Lupankwa, (D), HywGg

Dept of Environmental Health (B) (2015)
Private Bag X680
Staatsartillerie Road
Pretoria West 0001
p. +27 (0)12 382 5911
vanrooyenps@tut.ac.za
http://www.tut.ac.za/Pages/

University of Cape Town

Dept of Oceanography (B) (2015)
Private Bag X3
Rhondebosch 7701
p. +27 (0) 21 650-3277
isabelle.ansorge@uct.ac.za
http://www.sea.uct.ac.za

Dept of Environmental and Geographical Science (B) (2015)
Shell Environmental & Geographical Science Building
South Lane, Upper Campus
Private Bad X3
Rondebosch 7701
p. (27) 21 - 6502873 / 4
michael.meadows@uct.ac.za
http://www.egs.uct.ac.za/

Dept of Geological Sciences (B,M,D) ● (2016)
Private Bag X3
Rondebosch 7701, Western Cape
p. +27 (0)21-650-2931 
head.geologicalsciences@uct.ac.za
http://www.geology.uct.ac.za/
Administrative Assistant: Lynn Evon, Denise Lesch
Enrollment (2014): B: 30 (30) M: 30 (8) D: 10 (0)
Head:
Chris Harris, GiCsGg
Professor:
Steve Richardson, Cg
Senior Scientist:
Nicholas Laidler
Petrus J. Le Roux, (D), Cape Town, 2000, CaGia
Christel Tinguely
Associate Professor:
John Compton, (D), Harvard, 1986, CmGa
Associate Scientist:
Fayrooza Rawoot
Assistant Professor:
Emese M. Bordy, (D), Rhodes, 2001, GsPes
Lecturer:
Johann Diener, Gp
Lynnette N. Greyling, (D), Witwatersrand, 2009, EgmCe
Phillip Janney, (D), California (San Diego), 1996, GiCaXc
Beth Kahle, YgEoYg
Laboratory Director:
Kerryn Gray, (M)

University of Fort Hare

Dept of Geology (2015)
Sobukwe Walk 8
Livingstone Hall
Alice, Eastern Cape 5700
p. +27 (0)40 602 2011
wkoll@ufh.ac.za
http://wvw.ufh.ac.za/departments/geology/
Head:
Oswald Gwavava
Lecturer:
CJ Gunter
Vuyokazi Mazomba
Related Staff:
Luzuko Sigabi

Dept of Geographic Information Systems (B) (2015)
Private Bag X1314
Alice 5700
p. +27 (0)40 602 2011
wkoll@ufh.ac.za
http://www.ufh.ac.za/departments/gis/gishome.html

Dept of Geography, Land Use, and Environmental Sciences (B) (2015)
Private Bag X1314
Alice 5700
p. +27 (0)40 602 2011
wkoll@ufh.ac.za
http://www.ufh.ac.za/

University of Johannesburg

Dept of Geology (B) (2015)
PO Box 524
Kingsway & University (APK Campus)
Auckland Park 2006
p. +27 (11) 559-4701
mdekock@uj.ac.za
http://www.uj.ac.za/Default.aspx?alias=www.uj.ac.za/geology

Dept of Geography, Environmental Management & Energy Studies (B,M,D) (2015)
PO Box 524
Auckland Park, Gauteng 2006
p. +27 (0)11 559 2433
science@uj.ac.za
http://www.uj.ac.za/Default.aspx?alias=www.uj.ac.za/geography
Dr:
Isaac T. Rampedi, (D), South Africa, 2010, PgSdHg

Dept of Mining Engineering and Mine Surveying (B) ☒ (2017)
PO Box 17011
Doornfontein 2028
p. +27 (0)11 559-6628
hgrobler@uj.ac.za
http://www.uj.ac.za/Default.aspx?alias=www.uj.ac.za/mining
Programs: Mine Surveying; Mineral Resource Management; Mining Engineering
Certificates: Gyroscope Surveying

Dept of Mine Surveying (B) ●☒ (2019)
P.O. Box 17011
Doornforntein
Johannesburg, Gauteng 2028
p. +27 (0)11 559-6186
hgrobler@uj.ac.za
http://www.uj.ac.za/Default.aspx?alias=www.uj.ac.za/minesurv
Programs: Bachelor of Mine Surveying, Bachelor of Mine Surveying (Honours), Masters of Sustainable Mining
Certificates: Gyroscopic surveying techniques
Enrollment (2019): B: 10 (10)
Associate Professor:
Hendrik Christoffe Grobler, (D), Witwatersrand, 2015, ZnNm

University of KwaZulu-Natal

School of Civil Engineering Surveying & Construction (B)

(2015)
Centenary Building
King George V Avenue
Durban 4041
p. (+27) 2603065
troisc@ukzn.ac.za
http://engineering.ukzn.ac.za/Home.aspx

Centre for Water Resources Research (B,M,D) ☒ (2017)
Room 203
Rabie Saunders Building
Pietermaritzburg, KwaZulu-Natal 3201
p. +27-(0)33-260 5490
smithers@ukzn.ac.za
http://cwrr.ukzn.ac.za/
Programs: Hydrology; Water Resources; Agricultural Engineering
Enrollment (2017): B: 55 (0) M: 30 (0) D: 14 (0)

School of Environmental Sciences (B,M,D) ☒ (2019)
Discipline of Geography
King Edward Avenue
Pietermaritzburg Campus
Pietermaritzburg, KwaZulu-Natal 3209
p. + 27 (0)33 260 5346
gijsbertsen@ukzn.ac.za
http://saees.ukzn.ac.za/Homepage.aspx
f: https://www.facebook.com/FriendsOfUkznAgriculture

Discipline of Geological Sciences, School of Agricultural, Earth and Environmental Sciences (B,M,D) ●☒ (2018)
Private Bag X 54001
Durban, KwaZulu-Natal 4000
p. +27 (0)31 260 2516
mccoshp@ukzn.ac.za
http://www.geology.ukzn.ac.za/
Programs: Environmental and Engineering Geology (B); Geology and Ore Deposits (B)
Enrollment (2018): B: 195 (51) M: 14 (1) D: 6 (2)
Professor:
Tesfaye K. Birke, (D), France, 1999, GcYmGg
Emmanuel John Carranza, (D), Tech (Delft), 2002, EdCeZr
Associate Professor:
Andrew Green, (D), KwaZulu-Natal, 2009, GuYgGs
Senior Lecturer:
Molla Demlie, (D), Ruhr (Germany), 2007, HwGeg
Jeremy Woodard, (D), Turku (Finland), 2010, CcGiz
Developmental Lecturer:
Nonkululeko Dladla, (M), KwaZulu-Natal, 2013, GusGr
Palesa Leuta-Madondo, (M), W Cape, 2010, CgGig
Lecturer:
Warwick William Hastie, (D), KwaZulu-Natal, 2013, NrgGc
Egerton Hingston, (D), Leeds (UK), 2008, NtxNg
Lauren Hoyer, (D), KwaZulu-Natal, 2016, EgGc
Philani Mavimbela, (M), Pretoria, 2013, GpzEg
Saumitra Misra, (D), Calcutta, 1993, GiCgu

University of Limpopo

Dept of Soil Sciences (B) (2015)
Turfloop Campus
Private Bag X1106
Sovenga 0727
p. +27 (0)15 268 9111
Funso.Kutu@ul.ac.za
http://www.ul.ac.za/index.php?Entity=agri_soil_scie

Geography & Environmental Studies Dept (B) (2018)
Turfloop Campus
Private Bag X1106
Sovenga 0727
p. (+27) (0)15 268 3756
salphy.ramokolo@ul.ac.za
http://www.ul.ac.za/index.php?Entity=agri_geo_environ

School of Physical and Mineral Science (B) (2015)
Turfloop Campus
Private Bag X1106
Sovenga 0727
p. +27(0) 15 268 3492
SPMS@ul.ac.za
https://www.ul.ac.za/index.php?Entity=phy_geo
Administrative Assistant: M. D.. Ramusi
Head:
K. E. Rammutia
Professor:
John Dunlevey, (D), Stellenbosch, 1985, GzxEg
M. Khanyi
M. A. Letsoalo
M. A. Mahladisa
R. M. Makwela
T, Mobakazi
T. E. Mosuang
J. M. T. Mphahlele
T. T. Netshisaulu
M. Netsianda
P. Ntoahee
O. O. Nubi
M. Phala
M. J. Ramusi
L. Wilsenach
Other:
J. P. T. Crafford, (N), ZnNgZn

University of Pretoria

Centre of Environmental Studies (M,D) (2015)
Pretora 0002
p. +27 (0)12 420-3111
willemferguson@zoology.up.ac.za
http://www.up.ac.za/centre-environmental-studies

University of Pretoria Natural Hazards Centre, Department of Geology (M,D) ☒ (2020)
Department of Geology
University of Pretoria, Private Bag X20, Hatfield, PRETORIA, 0028
Pretoria 0028
p. +27 (0)12 420 3613
andrzej.kijko@up.ac.za
http://www.up.ac.za/university-of-pretoria-natural-hazard-centre-africa
Programs: The Centre liaise with various academic departments at the University of Pretoria to serve a primary or co-supervisor for Masters and Doctoral students in the respective departments.
Professor:
Andrzej Kijko, (D), AGH (Poland), 1979, YsgNe
Dr.:
Ansie Smit, (D), Mathematical Statistics, 2019, Rn

Dept of Mining Engineering (B,M,D) (2015)
Pretoria 0002
p. +27 0 12 420-3111
ssc@up.ac.za
https://www.up.ac.za/mining-engineering

Department of Geography, Geoinformatics and Meteorology (B,M,D) ☒ (2020)
Room 1-3
Geography Building
Cnr Lynnwood and University Roads
Hatfield, Pretoria 0083
p. +27 (0)12 420 3536
ggm.support@up.ac.za
https://www.up.ac.za/ggm
Programs: Geography, Environmental Science, Geoinformatics & Meteorology
Certificates: GIS, GIS professional practice, Introductory remote sensing
Administrative Assistant: Lunga Ngcongo, Martha C. van Aardt
Enrollment (2020): B: 266 (77) M: 65 (10) D: 32 (5)
Professor:
Serena Coetzee, (D), Pretoria, 2009, Zi
Associate Professor:
Emma Archer, (D), Clark, At
Greg Breetzke, (D), Pretoria
Liesl Dyson, (D), Pretoria, Am
Willem A. Landman, (D), Witwatersrand, Ams

Lecturer:
Adedayo Adeleke, (D), Cape Town, YdZf
Nerhene Davis, (D), W Cape
Joos Esterhuizen, (M), Pretoria
Christel D. Hansen, (D), Rhodes, 2018, ZiGmZy
Natalie S. Haussmann, (D), Stellenbosch, Gm
Michael J. Loubser, (M), Pretoria, GmZy
Thando Ndarana, (D), Johns Hopkins, Ams
Victoria J. Rautenbach, (D), Pretoria, Zif
Philemon L. Tsele, (D), Pretoria, Zfr
Barend van der Merwe, (M), Pretoria, Gm
Francis Wasswa Nsubuga, (D), Pretoria
Support Staff:
Popi Mahlangu
Erika Pretorius, (M), Pretoria, Zi
Senior Cartographer:
Lourens Snyman, (M), Pretoria, Zi

Dept of Geology (B,M,D) ● (2017)
Pretoria 0002
p. +27 (0)12 420 2454
wlady.Altermann@up.ac.za
https://www.up.ac.za/geology

University of the Free State

Department of Geology (B,M,D) ●☒ (2021)
PO Box 339
Bloemfontein, Free State Province 9300
p. +27 (0)51 401 2515
yibasbabsob@ufs.ac.za
https://www.ufs.ac.za/natagri/departments-and-divisions/geol-ogy-home
Programs: Geology; Environmental Geology; Geochemistry; Mineral Resource Management
Enrollment (2020): B: 140 (7) M: 6 (10) D: 8 (1)
Head:
Bisrat Yibas, (D), Witwatersrand, 2000, GegEg
Prof:
Frederick Roelofse, (D), Witwatersrand, 2010, Gip
Ms:
Jarlen J. Beukes, (M), Free State, Gi
Justine Magson, (M), Free State, 2016, CgGi
Thendo Mapholi, (B), Free State, Ggp
Makhadi Rinae, (B), Free State, Gge
Mr:
Justin Nel, (B), Free State, Gc
Adriaan Odendaal, (B), Free State, 2010, GgsGr
Dr:
Martin D. Clark, Austria, ZriGc
Robert N. Hansen, (D), Stellenbosch, 2014, CgGe
Matthew Huber, (D), Vienna, EgXm
Hendrik Minnaar, (D), Free State, Gc
Ms:
Megan Purchase, (M), Free State, Gx
Mr:
Pelele Lehloenya, (M), Free State, Cg

Institute for Groundwater Studies (B,M,D) (2016)
PO Box 339
Internal Bus 56
Bloemfontein 9300
p. +27(0)51-4019111
vermeulend@ufs.ac.za
http://www.ufs.ac.za/igs

Centre for Environmental Management (B) (2015)
Po Box 338
Bloemfontein 9300
p. +27(0)51-4019111
avenantmf@ufs.ac.za

http://www.ufs.ac.za/faculties/index.php?FCode=04&DCode=106

University of the Western Cape

International Ocean Institute of Southern Africa (B) (2015)
Private Bag X17
Bellville 7535
p. +27 21 959 3088
ioi-sa@uwc.ac.za
http://www.ioisa.org.za/

Dept of Earth Science (B) (2015)
Modderdam Road
Private Bag X17
Bellville, Cape Town 7530
p. +27 (0)21 959 2223
wdavids@uwc.ac.za
http://www.uwc.ac.za/Faculties/NS/EarthScience/Pages/
Administrative Assistant: Caroline Barnard, Wasielah Davids, Chantal Johannes, Mandy Naidoo
Head:
Charles Okujeni, (D), Berlin
Chair:
Jacqueline Goldin, (D), UCT
Yongxin Xu
Professor:
Dominic Mazvimavi, (D), Wageningen (Neth), 2003
Jan M. van Bever Donker, (D), Cape Town, 1979, GcpGt
Associate Professor:
Ebernard Braune
Lecturer:
Marcelene Andrews
James Ayuk Ayuk, (M), W Cape
Lewis Jonkey, (M)
Thokozani Kanyerere
Mimonitu Opuwari, (D), W Cape
Henok Solomon, (M), W Cape
VLIR Coordinator:
Shauib Dustay
HIVE Manager:
Yafah Hoosain, (M), W Cape
Deputy Head:
Theo Scheepers, (M), Stellenbosch
Related Staff:
Janine Becorney
Shamiel Davids
Peter Meyer

University of the Witwatersrand

School of Geography, Archaeology and Environmental Studies (B,M,D) ☒ (2017)
Private Bag 32050
Wits, Johannesburg
p. +27 11 717 6503
donna.koch@wits.ac.za
http://web.wits.ac.za/Academic/Science/Geography/Home.htm
Programs: Geography

School of Mining Engineering (B,M,D) ● (2015)
Private Bag 3
WITS, Johannesburg 2050
p. +27 11-717-7003
bekir.genc@wits.ac.za
http://web.wits.ac.za/Academic/EBE/MiningEng/

School of Geosciences (B,M,D) ● (2016)
Faculty of Science
Private Bag 3
Wits, Johannesburg 2050
p. 27 11 717 6547
sharon.ellis@wits.ac.za
http://web.wits.ac.za/Academic/Science/GeoSciences/Home.htm
Professor:
Lewis D. Ashwal, (D), Princeton, 1979, GxCgGt
Roger L. Gibson, (D), Cambridge, 1990, GcpGg
Kim AA Hein, (D), Tasmania, 1995, GgEmGc
Judith A. Kinnaird, (D), St Andrews, 1987, EmGi
Associate Professor:
Paul A.M. Nex, (D), Univ Coll (Cork), 1997, Eg
Dr:
Michael QW Jones, (D), Witwatersrand, 1981, YhGtYg
Electron Microprobe Scientist:
Peter Horvath, (D), Eotvos Lorand, 2002, GpCpGz

Dr:
Grant M. Bybee, (D), Witwatersrand, 2013, Gi
Katie A. Smart, (D), Alberta, 2011, CsGx
Doctor:
Zubair A. Jinnah, (D), Witwatersrand, 2011, GsPg
Emeritus:
Carl R. Anhaeusser, (D), Witwatersrand, 1983, GgEgZg

University of Venda

Dept of Geography and Geo-Information Sciences (B) (2015)
University of Venda
Private Bag X5050
Thohoyandou, Limpopo 0950
p. +27 15 962 8593
nthaduleni.nethengwe@univen.ac.za
http://www.univen.ac.za/enviornmental_sciences/dep_geography_geo_sciences.html
Head:
Nthaduleni S. Nethengwe, (D), West Virginia, RnZiRw
Acting Head:
T. M. Nelwamondo, (D), UP, 2010, GeZuy
Lecturer:
E. Kori, (M), Univen, GmZgAt
M. J. Mokgoebo, (M), Univen
N. V. Mudau, (D), Univen, 2015, Rm
A. Muyoki, (D), Howard
M. Nembudani, (M), Stellenbosch
Related Staff:
K. H. Mathivha, (M), Univen

Mining and Environmental Geology (A,B,M,D) ☒ (2019)
School of Environmental Science
Private Bag X5050
Thohoyandou , Limpopo Province 0950
p. +27 159628580
mkataka@univen.ac.za
http://www.univen.ac.za/environmental_sciences/dep_mining_environmental.html
Programs: Geology and Earth Sciences
Certificates: None
Enrollment (2019): B: 288 (46) M: 26 (6) D: 6 (1)
Dr.:
Milton Kataka, (D), Witwatersrand, 2003

University of Venda for Science & Technology

GIS Resource Centre (B,M,D) ⊘ (2021)
GIS Resource Centre
Private Bag x5050
Thohoyandou, Limpopo 0950
p. +27 15 962 8044
farai.dondofema@univen.ac.za
http://www.univen.ac.za/environmental_sciences/gis_centre.html
t: @chinomukutu3
Programs: GIS, Geography, Remote sensing, Geology, Mining, Hydrology, Environmental Science, Ecology, Urban and Rural planning
Certificates: GIS, Ecology
Enrollment (2018): B: 46 (35) M: 13 (9) D: 4 (1)
Chief Technician:
Farai Dondofema, (M), Zimbabwe, 2007, ZrHgZi

Institute of Semi-Arid Environment and Disaster Management (B) (2015)
p. (+27) 015 962 8513
ndidzum@univen.ac.za
http://www.univen.ac.za/index.php?Entity=Institute%20of%20Semi-Arid%20Environment&Sch=3

Dept of Hydrology and Water Resources (B) (2015)
University of Venda
Private Bag X5050
Thohoyandou, Limpopo 0950
p. +27 015 962 8513
environmental@univen.ac.za
http://www.univen.ac.za/environmental_sciences/dep_hydrology_water.html
Head:
J. O. Odiyo, (D)
Lecturer:
J. R. Gumbo, (D)
P. M. Kundu, (D)
R. Makungo, (M), Venda, 2010, HzqHw
Tinyiko Rivers Nkuna, (M), Venda, 2012, HgwAs

University of Zululand

Dept of Geography and Environmental Studies (B) (2015)
Private Bag X1001
KwaDlangezwa 3886
p. +27 (035) 902 6282
kamwendog@unizulu.ac.za
http://www.uzulu.ac.za/scie_geo_env.php

Dept of Hydrology (B,M,D) O☒ (2020)
Private Bag X1001
KwaDlangezwa 3886
p. +27 (035) 902 6282
SimonisJ@unizulu.ac.za
http://www.uzulu.ac.za/scie_hydro.php
Programs: Hydrology, Geohydrology, Geology
Certificates: GIS
Enrollment (2016): B: 332 (79) M: 15 (2) D: 2 (0)
Prof:
Jean Simonis, (D), UNIZULU, 2009, HyGgHg

Spain

Coruna University

University Institute of Geology (D) (2016)
Edificio Servicios Centrales de Investigación
Campus de Elviña s/n
La Coruna 15071
p. 0034 981167000
xeoloxia@udc.es
http://www.udc.es/iux
Enrollment (2015): D: 8 (80)
Director:
Juan Ramon Vidal Romani, (D), Complutense (Madrid), 1983, GmlGc
Professor:
Antonio Paz Gonzalez, (D), Santiago de Compostela, 1982, Sd
Paleontologist:
Aurora Grandal d'Anglade, (D), Coruña, 1993, Pv
Associate Professor:
Elena Pilar de Uña Alvarez, (D), Santiago de Compostela, 1986, Zy
Cruz Iglesias, (D), Corunna, 2001, GaZmNr
Jorge Sanjurjo, (D), Corunna, 2005, GeCcGa
María Teresa Taboada Castro, (D), Santiago de Compostela, 1990, Sd
Associate Scientist:
Marcos Vaqueiro Rodriguez, (M), Vigo (Spain), GcmYd

Institute of Marine Sciences (CSIC)

Marine Geosciences Departmen ☒ (2021)
Passeig Maritim de la Barceloneta
37-49
Barcelona 08003
p. (+34) 63 230 95 00
secredir@icm.csic.es
https://www.icm.csic.es/en/department/marine-geosciences

Instituto Geologico y Minero de Espana

Instituto Geologico y Minero de Espana (2015)
Rios Rosas, 23
28003 Madrid
igme@igme.es
http://www.igme.es

Univ Complutense de Madrid

Facultad de Ciencias Geologicas (B,M,D) O🖰 (2019)
C/ Jose Antonio Novais 12
Cuidad Universitaria
Madrid E-28040
p. 34 91394 4837

secre.adm@geo.ucm.es
https://geologicas.ucm.es
t: @geologicasUCM
Programs: Geology (Bachelor)
Engineering Geology (Bachelor)
Environmental Geology (Master)
Engineering Geology (Master)
Advanced Paleontology (Master)
Oil and Ore deposits exploration (Master)
Certificates: Paleontology (on line)
Mineral deposits (on line)
Enrollment (2019): B: 514 (3) M: 73 (27) D: 75 (64)

Vicedean for Research:
Javier Martín Chivelet, (D), PcGs

Professor:
Ana María Alonso, (D), Gd
Eumenio Ancochea, (D), Gv
Ricardo Arenas, (D), Gp
Juan Luis Arsuaga, (D), Zn
César Casquet, (D), Gip
Lourdes Fernández, (D), Gz
Sixto Fernández, (D), Pg
Sol López, (D), Gz
Sergio Rodríguez, (D), PgGg
Carlos Villaseca, (D), Gi

Vicedean for quality:
María de la Luz García Lorenzo, (D), Cl

Vicedean for Master programs and international affairs:
María Luisa Canales, (D), PmgGg

Vicedean for Bachelor programs :
Eugenia Arribas, (D), Gd

Vicedean for academic issues:
Alfonso Muñoz, (D), Ygr

Dean:
Lorena Ortega, (D), 1993, EmgGg

Associate Professor:
Jacobo Abati, (D), Gp
Saturnino Alba, (D), Gm
José Antonio Alvarez, (D), Gc
Pilar Andonaegui, (D), Gg
Carmen Arias, (D), Gg
José Manuel Astilleros, (D), Gz
María Isabel Benito, (D), Gs
Manuel Bustillo, (D), Eg
Pedro Castiñeiras, (D), Gp
María José Comas, (D), Pi
Elena Crespo, (D), EnGz
Cristina de Ignacio, (D), Cg
Raúl de la Horra, (D), Gs
Lucia de Stefano, (D), Hw
Gerardo de Vicente, (D), Gt
Javier Fernández Suárez, (D), Cc
José María Fernández-Barrenechea, (D), Gz
María Antonia Fregenal, (D), Gsg
Fernando Gacía Joral, (D), Pi
Nuria García, (D), Pv
Alejandra García Frank, (D), Gg
Emilia García Romero, (D), Gz
Laura González, (D), Gr
José Luis Granja, (D), Yg
Manuel Hernández, (D), Pv
Concepción Herrero, (D), Pm
María Josefa Herrero, (D), Gs
María José Huertas, (D), Gi
Juan Miguel Insua, (D), NtGc
María del Pilar Llanes, (D), Yr
Francisco Javier Luque, (D), Gz
José Francisco Martín Duque, (D), Gm
Gemma Martínez, (D), Pg
José Jesús Martínez, (D), GcRn
Pedro Martínez, (D), Hw
Nieves Meléndez, (D), Ggs
Esperanza Montero, (D), Hw
Belén Muñoz, (D), Gr
David Orejana, (D), Gig
Cecilia Pérez-Soba, (D), Gi
Rubén Piña, (D), EmGz
Marta Rodríguez, (D), Ggs
Martín Jesús Rodríguez, (D), Ng
Ignacio Romeo, (D), GcXg
Carlos Rossi, (D), GdEo
Javier Ruiz, (D), Xg
Nuria Sánchez, (D), Gz
Sonia Sánchez, (D), Gp
Yolanda Sánchez, (D), Gs
Juan Ignacio Santisteban, (D), Gr
Esther Sanz, (D), Gd
Miguel Angel Sanz, (D), Zi
Paloma Sevilla, (D), Pi
Meaza Tsige, (D), Ng
David Uribelarrea, (D), Ga
María Josefa Varas, (D), Gd
Cristóbal Viedma, (D), Gz
Elena Vindel, (D), Gz

Assistant Professor:
Laura Domingo, (D), PveCs
Julio Garrote, (D), Gm

Adjunct Professor:
Enrique Aracil, (B), Yu
Sonia Bautista, (M), Ng
María Druet, (D), Yr
Alejandro Faúndez, (B), Ng
Luis Ramón Fernández, (M), Nt
David Jiménez, (B), GcNt
Cristina Martin, (D), Gm
Svetlana Melentijevic, (D), Nx
Luis Eugenio Suárez, (B), Zn

Emeritus:
José Arribas, (D), Gd

Universidad Autonoma de Madrid

Departamento de Geologia y Geoquimica (M,D) O☒ (2017)
Faculdad de ciencias
Campus de Cantoblanco, C/ Francisco Tomás y Valiente, 7
Módulo 06, 6ª planta
Madrid 28049
p. 91 497 48 00
directora.geologia@uam.es
http://www.uam.es/GyG
Programs: Earth Science; Biology; Chemistry
Certificates: GIS
Enrollment (2017): M: 9 (0) D: 8 (0)

Universidad de Alicante

Environment and Earth Sciences Dept (B,M,D) (2015)
Facultad de Ciencia
San Vicente de Raspeig
Alicante E-03080
p. (+34) 96 590 3552
dctma@ua.es
http://dctma.ua.es/en/environment-and-earth-sciences-department.html

Universidad de Granada

Dept de Geologia (2015)
Andalusian Institute of Geophysics
Campus Universitario de la Cartuja
18071 Granada
jaguirre@ugr.es
http://www.ugr.es/iag/iagpds.html

Universidad de Huelva

Geologia (B,M,D) (2015)
Huelva
p. 959219809
secgeo@uhu.es
http://www.uhu.es/dgeo/

Universidad de Jaen

Departamento de Geologia (B,M,D) O☒ (2021)
Edificio B-3
Campus Universitario
Jaen 23071
p. +34-953-212295
jmmolina@ujaen.es
http://geologia.ujaen.es/

SPAIN

Universidad de Las Palmas de Gran Canaria

Dept de Fisica (B) (2015)
C/Juan de Quesada, nº 30
Las Palmas de Gran C 35001
p. (+34) 928 451 000/023
universidad@ulpgc.es
http://www.dfis.ulpgc.es/

Facultad de Ciencias del Mar (B,M,D) (2015)
Edificio de Ciencias Básicas
Campus Universitario de Tafira
Las Palmas de Gran Canaria, Las Palmas 35017
p. +34 928 452 900
sec_dec_fcm@ulpgc.es
http://www.fcm.ulpgc.es

Universidad de Murcia

Dept of Geography and Regional Planning (2015)
Facultad de Sciencia
Calle Santo Cristo 1
Murcia 30100
p. (868) 88-7446
jagb@um.es

Universidad de Oviedo

Dept de Geologia (2015)
Campus de Llamaquique
Jesus Arias de Velasco, s/n
33005 Oviedo E-33005
geodir@geol.uniovi.es
http://www.geol.uniovi.es/

Universidad de Pais Vascu

Dept de Geologia (2015)
Facultad de Sciencia
37008 Salamanca
p. 946015491
sec-centro.fct@ehu.es

Universidad de Palma de Mallorca

Dept de Geologia/Geofisica (2015)
Facultad de Sciencia
07012 Palma

Universidad de Sevilla

Applied Geology to Civil Engineering (D) (2016)
Departamento de Cristalografía y Mineralogía
calle Profesor García González 1
Seville 410012
p. +34954556318
igonza@us.es
http://www.departamento.us.es/dcmqa/
Professor:
Isabel González, (D), GzeSc

Universidad de Valencia

Dept de Geologia (M,D) (2015)
Faculty of Biological Sciences
Building A (2nd and 3rd floor)
C/ Dr. Moliner, 50
Burjassot- (Valencia) 46100
p. (+34) 96 354 46 02
dep.geologia@uv.es
http://www.uv.es/geologia

Universidad de Valladolid

Dept of Geography (2015)
Facultad de Faculty of Philosophy and Arts
Palacio Santa Cruz/Plaza Santa Cruz B
Valladolid
p. +34 983 423 005
belart@fyl.uva.es

Universidad de Zaragoza

Facultad de Ciencias (2015)
50.009 Zaragoza
seccienz@unizar.es
http://wzar.unizar.es/acad/fac/geolo/adepo.html

Museo de Ciencias Naturales (D) ○☒ (2018)
Museo de Ciencias Naturales
Universidad de Zaragoza
Edificio Paraninfo. Plaza Basilio Paraiso
Zaragoza, Aragón 50005
p. +34 976762096
museonat@unizar.es
http://museonat.unizar.es/
f: https://www.facebook.com/museopaleounizar
t: @museonat
Professor:
José Ignacio Canudo, (D), Pv

Universitat Autonoma de Barcelona

Geologia (B,M,D) ●☒ (2019)
Facultat de Ciencies, Edifici C
Campus UAB
Bellaterra, Catalunya 08193
p. +34 93 581 3022
d.geologia@uab.es
http://departaments.uab.cat/geologia/
Programs: B.S. Geology, B.S. Environmental Science, MSc. Reservoir Geology and Geophysics, MSc. Paleobiology and Fossil Record, MSc. Resources and Risks, PhD Geology
Enrollment (2018): B: 284 (46) M: 47 (47) D: 14 (7)
Chair:
Antoni Teixell Cácharo, (D), 1992, GtcYx
Professor:
María Luísa Arboleya Cimadevilla, (D), Gc
Joan Bach Plaza, (D), Gg
Esteve Cardellach López, (D), GzeCs
David Gómez Gras, (D), Gd
Juan Francesc Piniella Febrer, (D), Gz
Eduard Remacha Grau, (D), Univ Aut, 1983, Gso
Antonio Teixell, (D), 1992, Gtc
Associate Professor:
Lluís Casas Duocastella, (D), GzaYm
Mercè Corbella Cordomí, (D), GzCl
Elena Druguet Tantiña, (D), Gc
Joan Estalrich López, (D), HgGe
Gúmer Galán garcía, (D), GiCg
Rogelio Linares, (D), NgYx
Oriol Oms Llobet, (D), GrsYm
Joan Reche Estrada, (D), GpCp
Enric Vicens Batet, (D), Pg
Assistant Professor:
Carme Boix, (D), Pm
Isaac Corral, (D), Gx
Victor Fondevilla, (D), PgGr
Marc Furió, (D), Pv
Ona Margalef, (D), Ge
Didac Navarro, (D), Gz
Joan Poch Serra, (B), Auto Univ Barcelona, 2003, GrsZe
Felix Sacristan, (M), Ge
Eduard Saura, (D), Gc
Bernat Vila, (D), Pv
Lecturer:
Albert Griera Artigas, (D), GcCl
Mario Zarroca Hernández, (D), YgNg
Emeritus:
Francisco Martínez Fernández, (D), GpCp

Universitat de Barcelona

Estratigrafia, Paleontologia i Geociencies marines (2015)
c/Marti Franques, s/n
08028
Barcelona
p. +33 934021384
secretaria-geologia@ub.edu
http://www.ub.es/dpep/1welcom3.htm

Dept de Geoquimica, Petrologia I Prospeccio Geologica

(2015)
Marti Franques, s/n
Barcelona
8028
dept-geoquimica@ub.edu
http://www.ub.es/geoquimi

Facultat de Ciències de la Terra (Earth Sciences Faculty) (B,M,D) O (2016)
Martí Franqués s/n
Barcelona 08028
p. +34 934 021 335
deganat-geologia@ub.edu
http://www.ub.edu/geologia/en/

Universitat de les Illes Balears

Dept de Ciencies de la Terra (B,M,D) (2015)
Carretera de Valldemossa, km 7.5
Palma, Balearic Islands 07122
p. +34 971172362
dct@uib.es
http://www.uib.es/depart/dctweb/home.htm

University of the Basque Country UPV/EHU

Departamento de Geodinamica (B,M,D) O☒ (2019)
Facultad de Ciencia y Tecnología
Barrio Sarriena, s/n
Leioa, Vizcaya 48940 Leioa
p. + 34. 94 601 2563
julia.cuevas@ehu.eus
http://www.geodinamica.ehu.es/s0001-home1/es/
Programs: Geology, Environmental Sciences
Enrollment (2017): B: 45 (0) D: 2 (0)

Professor:
Julia Cuevas, (D), 1988, GctGg

Professor:
Benito Abalos, (D), Basque (Spain), 1990, GctGp
Iñaki Antigüedad, (D), Hw
Luis Eguiluz, (D), 1988, Ggt
Jose M. Tubia, (D), 1985, GctYg

Senior Scientist:
Aitor Aranguren, (D), GcYm
Nestor Vegas, (D), Pais Vasco UPV/EHU, 2002, GctYm

Associate Professor:
Jose Julian Esteban, (D), GtCcYg
Tomas Morales, (D), NgHg
Pablo Puelles, (D), Gct
Jesus Angel Uriarte, (D), NgHg

Assistant Professor:
Arturo Apraiz, (D), Gpt
Vicente Iribar, (D), HwGm
Luis Miguel Martinez Torres, (D), Ggt
Fernando Sarrionandia, (D), Basque (Spain), 2006, GigGv

Emeritus:
Hilario Llanos, (D), Hgy

Univesidad de Malaga

Dept de Geography (2015)
El Ejido
29071 Malaga
ocana@uma.es

Sri Lanka

Sabaragamuwa University of Sri Lanka

Dept of Natural Resources (2015)
P.O Box 02
Belihuloya , Sabaragamuwa Provinc
p. 0094-45-2280293
head_nr@sab.ac.lk
http://www.sab.ac.lk

Sri Lanka Geological Survey & Mines Bureau

Sri Lanka Geological Survey & Mines Bureau (2015)
Senanayake Building, No 4, Galle Road,
Dehiwala
info@gsmb.gov.lk
http://www.gsmb.gov.lk/

University of Moratuwa

Dept of Earth Resources Engineering (2015)
Katubedda, Moratuwa
Western Province
Moratuwa
p. 0094-11-2650353
shiromi@earth.mrt.ac.lk
http://www.ere.mrt.ac.lk/

University of Peradeniya

Dept of Geology (2015)
Central Province
Peradeniya 22000
p. 0094-81 2394 200/201
geology@pdn.ac.lk
http://www.pdn.ac.lk/sci/geology/

Uwa Wellassa University of Sri Lanka

Dept Mineral Resources & Technology (2015)
2nd Mile Post Passara Road
Badulla , Uwa province
p. 0094-55-2226400
info@uwu.ac.lk
http://www.uwu.ac.lk/

Sudan

Cairo University

Dept of Geology (2015)
Khartoum Branch
PO Box 1055
Khartoum

El-Neelain University

Dept of Geology (B) (2015)
Gamhuria Street
Khartoum
p. +249 (183) 77-441
salihsas@gmail.com
https://www.neelain.edu.sd/sites/colleges/14/dept/79

Gama'at El Khartoum

Dept of Geology (2015)
PO Box 321
Khartoum
dc.itna@uofk.edu
http://staffpages.uofk.edu/department-of-geology/

International University of Africa

Faculty of Minerals and Petroleum (B) (2015)
PO Box 2469
Khartoum
p. (+249) 183 223211
minerals@iua.edu.sd
https://metals.iua.edu.sd/

Sudan University of Science and Technology

Surveying Engineering Dept (B) (2015)
Southern and Northern Campus
Khartoum
p. +249183468622
bama_my@sustech.edu
http://engineering.sustech.edu/index.php/College_of_Engineering/Surveying_Engineering_Department/en/sections

College of Water & Environmental Engineering (B) (2015)
p. +24985200512 / 985200511 / 918
m.ginaya@sustech.edu
http://www.sustech.edu/faculty_en/index.php?coll_no=13&chk=cdf8953eb5124fa6f08f046043be8bf

College of Petroleum Engineering and Technology (B) (2015)
Southern Campus
Khartoum
zeinabkhaleel@sustech.edu
http://www.sustech.edu/faculty_en/index.php?coll_no=23&chk=1d4f14cee52598202e0fc32a12b2dfc2

University of Dongola
Dept of Geology (B) (2015)
PO Box 47
Northern Province, Dongola
p. +249-241-821-516, +249-241-821
http://www.uofd.edu.sd/index.php/ar/

University of Gezira
Dept of Geology (2015)
Faculty of Science and Technology
PO Box 20
Wad Medani
p. (002) 49511825724
webinfo@uofg.edu.sd
http://snc.uofg.edu.sd/EN/Department.aspx?dep=6

University of Juba
Dept of Geology and Mining (B) (2015)
PO Box 321/1
Khartoum Center, Juba
p. +249 (83) 222125
info@juba.edu.sd
http://www.juba.edu.sd/

Dept of Environmental Studies (B) (2015)
PO Box 321/1
Khartoum Center, Juba
p. +249 (83) 222125
info@juba.edu.sd
http://www.juba.edu.sd/

University of Khartoum
Dept of Geology (B,M,D) (2015)
PO Box 321
Khartoum 11115
geology@uofk.edu
http://www.uofk.edu/
Head:
Ibahim Abdu Mohamed
Professor:
Saad Eldin Hamad Moha Ali
Abdelhalim Hassan Elnadi, Goz
Associate Professor:
Abdelwahab Yousif Abbas
Salah Bashir Abdalla, Ng
Osman Mahmoud Abdelatif
Samia Abdelrahman
Badr Eldin Khal Agmed
Fath Elrahman ali Birair
Omar Elbadri ali Elmaki
Abdelhafiz Gad Almula
Mohamed Zaid Awad
Insaf Sanhoory Babiker
Almed Sulaiman Daood
Abdalla Guma Farwa
Instructor:
Eltayeb Elasha Abdalia
Sami Osman Ibrahim
Amro Shaikh Idris Ahmed
Waleed Elmahdi Siddig
Saif Eldin Sir Elkhatim
Lecturer:
Amany Ali Badi
Related Staff:
Walaa Elnasir Ibrahim

Marine Research Laboratory in Suakin (B) (2015)
PO Box 321
Khartoum 11115
sbabdalla@hotmail.com
https://www.fkm.utm.my/marine/mtl/?Album:Visitor

University of Kordofan
Dept of Soil and Water Sciences (B) (2015)
p. 860008-611-00249
hadiaabdelatif@kordofan.edu.sd
http://science.kordofan.edu.sd/

University of Neelain
Dept of Geology (B) (2015)
science_dean@neelain.edu.sd
http://www.neelain.edu.sd/

University of the Red Sea
Dept of Geology (B) (2015)
PO Box 24
Red Sea, Port Sudan
p. +249-311-219-28
redseauniv44@hotmail.com

Wad El Magbout
Training Centre for Earth Science Technicians (B) (2015)

Suriname
Anton de Kom University of Suriname
Dept of Geology & Mining (2015)
Leysweg, P.O. Box 9212, Universiteits Complex, Gebouw VI

Environmental Sciences Dept (B) O (2016)
Universiteitscomplex Leysweg
P.O.B. 9212
Gebouw 17
Paramaribo
p. 597465558 (Ext. 308)
s.carilho@uvs.edu
http://adekus.uvs.edu/section/sectSection.php?secID=5304&lb=Onderwijs%20.%20Technologie%20.%20Milieu
f: https://www.facebook.com/AdeKUS.official/

Swaziland
University of Swaziland
Dept of Geography, Environmental Science and Planning (B,M,D) (2015)
Private Bag 4
Kwaluseni M201
p. (+268) 2517-0000
kwaluseni@uniswa.sz
http://www.uniswa.sz/academics/science/gep

Sweden
Chalmers University of Technology
Dept of Geology (2015)
S-412 96 Goteborg
Gothenburg
sofie.hallden@chalmers.se
http://geo.chalmers.se

Karlstad University
Department of Risk and Environmental Studies (B,M,D) ● (2020)
Karlstad University
Karlstad 65188
p. +46547001000
Magnus.Johansson@kau.se
https://www.kau.se/en/risk-and-environmental-studies
Programs: Bachelor: Risk and environmental studies
Master: Risk management in Society

Lund University
Dept of Geology (B,M,D) ● ☒ (2021)
Solvegatan 12
223 62 Lund
p. (+46) 462221424
anders.schersten@geol.lu.se
https://www.geology.lu.se/
Programs: Geology with specialities in Quaternary geology, Palaeontology and Mineralogy & petrology

Stockholm University
Dept of Geological Sciences (B,M,D) ● (2016)
Svante Arrheniusväg 8
106 91 Stockholm
office@geo.su.se
http://www.geo.su.se

Sveriges geologiska Undersokning
Geological Survey of Sweden (2016)
Box 670
751 28 Uppsala
sgu@sgu.se
http://www.sgu.se/

Umea Universitet
Dept of Ecology and Environmental Science (2015)
Natural Sciences, Johan Bures Road 14, Umeå
S-901 87 Umea
p. +46 90 786 50 00
jolina.orrell@emg.umu.se
http://www.emg.umu.se

University of Gothenberg
Master of Earth Science (2015)
Box 100
S-405 30 Gothenburg
p. +46 31-786 0000

University of Stockholm
Dept of Geology and Geochemistry (2015)
106 91 Stockholm
Barbara@geo.su.se
http://www.geo.su.se/

Uppsala Universitet
Dept of Earth Sciences (B,M,D) ● (2015)
Villavagen 16
UPPSALA SE-752 36
p. +46-18-4710000
PREFEKT@geo.uu.se
http://www.geo.uu.se/default.asp?pageid=1&lan=1

Switzerland

ETH Hoenggerberg
Geophysical Inst ETH (2015)
Sonneggstrasse 5
8092 Zurich
p. +41 44 633 26 05
christoph.baerlocher@erdw.ethz.ch
http://www.geophysics.ethz.ch/

ETH Zurich
Department of Earth Sciences (B,M,D) ☒ (2020)
Sonneggstrasse 5
CH-8092 Zurich
department@erdw.ethz.ch
https://erdw.ethz.ch/en/
Programs: Earth Sciences, Climate Sciences, Applied Geophysics

Federal Office for the Environment (FOEN)
Federal Office for the Environment (FOEN) (2015)
info@bafu.admin.ch
Bern 3003
p. 0041313229311
info@bafu.admin.ch
http://www.bafu.admin.ch/
t: @bafuCH

Université de Lausanne
Dept of Geosciences and Environment (B,M,D) ☒ (2018)
Décanat FGSE
Quartier Mouline
Géopolis
Lausanne, Vaud 1015
p. 0041216923500
doyen.gse@unil.ch
http://www.unil.ch/gse
Programs: Master of Science in Geology, Master of Science in Environmental Geosciences, Master of Science in Geography, Master of Science in Biogeosciences, Master in Tourism Studies, Master in foundations and practices of sustainability

University of Basel
Geol & Palaeontological Inst (2015)
Bernouillistrasse 32
CH-4056 Basale
joelle.glanzmann@unibas.ch
http://www.unibas.ch/earth/GPI/paleo

Inst of Earth Sciences (2015)
Bernoullistrasse 30
Basel 4056
eberhard.parlow@unibas.ch
http://therion.minpet.unibas.ch/minpet

Dept of Earth Sciences (2015)
Bernoullistr.32
CH-4056 Basel
Joelle.Glanzmann@unibas.ch
http://duw.unibas.ch/

University of Fribourg
Div of Earth Sciences (2017)
Chemin du Musee 6
Perolles
CH-1700 Fribourg
nicole.bruegger@unifr.ch
http://www.unifr.ch/geology/

University of Geneva
Section of Earth Sciences and Environment (2015)
13, rue des Maraichers
Geneva CH-1205
p. 0041223796628
elisabeth.lagut@unige.ch
http://www.unige.ch/sciences/terre/

University of Lausanne
Faculty of Geosciences and Environment (B,M,D) ● ☒ (2019)
Geopolis
Lausanne CH-1015
p. +41 21 692 35 00
doyen.gse@unil.ch
http://www.unil.ch/gse/home.html
Programs: geography, environmental sciences, geology, biogeosciences, tourism studies, foundations and practices of sustainability
Enrollment (2018): B: 388 (0) M: 345 (98) D: 144 (24)

University of Neuchatel
Centre for Hydrogeology and Geothermics (B,M,D) (2016)
Rue Emile-Argand 11
CH-2000 Neuchatel
secretariat.chyn@unine.ch
http://www.unine.ch/chyn

Universität Bern

Institut für Geologie (B,M,D) (2017)
Baltzerstrasse 1+3
Bern CH-3012
p. +41 (0) 31 631 87 61
info@geo.unibe.ch
http://www.geo.unibe.ch

Syria

Damascus University

Dept of Geology (2015)
Jammah Dimasq
Damscus

Taiwan

Academia Sinica

Institute of Earth Sciences (D) ☒ (2020)
128, Section 2, Academia Road, Nangang
Taipei 11529
p. 886-2-2783-9910
jhwang@earth.sinica.edu.tw
http://www.earth.sinica.edu.tw/index_e.php

Distinguished Researcg Fellow:
Jeen-Hwa Wang, (D), SUNY, 1982, Ysn

Associate Research Fellow:
Wu-Cheng Chi, (D), California (Berkeley), GtYrs

Assistant Research Fellow:
Wen-che Yu, (D), SUNY (Stony Brook), 2007, Ys

Central Geological Survey (MOEA) of Taiwan

Central Geological Survey (MOEA) of Taiwan (2015)
District No. 2, Lane 109
Taipei 235
cgs@moeacgs.gov.tw
http://www.moeacgs.gov.tw/main.jsp

Chinese Culture University

Dept of Geology (2015)
Hanaoka Yangmingshan
Taipei 1111455
p. (02) 2861-0511 rpm 26105
crssge@staff.pccu.edu.tw

National Cheng-Kung University

Dept Earth Sciences (2015)
Tainan
wong56@mail.ncku.edu.tw

National Chung Cheng University

Inst of Seismology (2015)
168 University Rd
Min-Hsiung Chia-Yi
p. (886) -5--2720 x 9 ext: 61201?61209)
seismo@ccu.edu.tw
http://www.eq.ccu.edu.tw

National Taiwan University

Inst of Geology (2015)
245 Choushan Road, Taipei 106-17

Tanzania

ARDHI University

School of Geospatial Sciences and Technolgy (B,M,D) (2015)
P.O.Box 35176
Dar es Salaam
hagai@aru.ac.tz
http://www.aru.ac.tz/page.php?id=63
Enrollment (2012): B: 120 (112) M: 10 (2) D: 6 (0)

Geological Survey of Tanzania

Geological Survey of Tanzania (2015)
P .O Box 903
Dodoma
madini-do@gst.go.tz
http://www.gst.go.tz/

University of Dar es Salaam

Dept of Geology (B,M,D) ● (2015)
PO Box 35052
Dar es Salaam
p. +255 22 2410013
geology@udsm.ac.tz
http://www.conas.udsm.ac.tz/geology/
Enrollment (2015): B: 65 (53) M: 17 (0)

Head:
Nelson Boniface, (D), Kiel, GcpGz

Professor:
Makenya A. Maboko, (D), Australian Nat, 1991, GpCgGx

Senior Lecturer:
Charles Z. Kaaya, (D), Cologne, 1993, GrsGu
Isaac Muneji Marobhe, (D), Helsinki Univ of Tech, 1990, YegYx

Associate Professor:
Shukrani Manya, (D), Dar Es Salaam, 2008, CgGzg
Hudson H. Nkotagu, (D), Tech (Berlin), 1994, HwgGe

Lecturer:
Kasanzu Charles, (D), 2014, GgRh
Emmanuel O. Kazimoto, (D), Kiel, 2014, EgGpCg
Elisante E. Mshiu, (D), Martin Luther (Germany), 2014, ZrCgZi
Elisante E. Mshiu, (D), Martin Luther (Germany), 2014, GgCeZr
Gabriel D. Mulibo, (D), Penn State, 2013, Ysg
Ferdinand W. Richard, (D), Uppsala, 1999, YsGt

Institute of Marine Sciences (B) (2015)
Mizingani Road
PO Box 35091
Zanzibar
p. 255-24-2232128/2230741
director@ims.udsm.ac.tz
http://www.ims.udsm.ac.tz

University of Dodoma

Dept of Geology and Petroleum Studies (2015)
P.O Box 259
Dodoma
p. +255 26 2310000
vc@udom.ac.tz
http://www.udom.ac.tz/

School of Mines and Petroleum Engineering (2015)
PO Box 259
Dodoma
p. +255 22 2410013
vc@udom.ac.tz
http://www.udom.ac.tz

Thailand

Asian Institute of Technology

Dept of Geology (2015)
P.O. Box 4
Klong Luang
Pathumthani 12120
Bangkok 10501
p. +66 (0) 2524 6057
supamas@ait.ac.th
http://www.set.ait.ac.th/page.php?fol=gte&page=gte

Dept of Mineral Resources

75/10 Rama 6 Road, Phayathai
Bangkok 10400
pornthip@dmr.go.th
http://www.dmr.go.th/

Togo

Universite de Lome

Dept de Geologie (B) (2015)
BP 1515
Lomé
p. (+228) 22-25-50-93

Tunisia

Birzeit University

Dept of Geology (2015)
Faculty of Science
P. O. Box 14
7021 Jarzouna Tunis
Bizerte
p. 216590717
fsb@fsb.rnu.tn
http://www.fsb.rnu.tn/index_fr/contact.html

Universite de Carthage

Dept de Geologie (B) (2015)
Jarzouna 7021
p. +21671841353
fsb@fsb.rnu.tn
http://www.fsb.rnu.tn/fsbindex.htm

Universite de Gabes

Dept de Sciences de la Terre (B) (2015)
Cite Riadh
Zerig, Gabes 6072
p. +216 75 394 800
mail@fsg.rnu.tn
http://www/fsg.rnu.tn/PRESENTATION.htm

Inst Superieur des Sciences et Techniques des Eaux de Gabes (B) (2015)
Cite Riadh
Zerig, Gabes 6072
p. +216 75 394 800
samir.kamal@isstegb.rnu.tn
http://www.isstegb.rnu.tn/francais

Universite de Sfax

Dept de Sciences de la Terre (B) (2015)
Route de l Aeroport km 0.5
Sfax 3029
p. 216 74 276 400
fss@www.fss.rnu.tn
http://www.fss.rnu.tn

Dept de Genie Materiaux (B) (2015)
B.P:w.3038
Sfax
p. (216) 74 274 088
enis@enis.rnu.tn
http://www.enis.rnu.tn/content/enis00003.htm

Dept de Genie Georessources et Environnement (B) (2015)
B.P:w.3038
Sfax
p. (216) 74 274 088
enis@enis.rnu.tn
http://www.enis.rnu.tn/content/enis00003.htm

Universite de Tunis

Dept of Geology (2015)
Faculty of Science
1 Rue de Beja
Tunis 2092
p. 21671872600
http://www.fst.rnu.tn/fr

Turkey

Canakkale Onsekiz Mart University

Jeoloji Bolumu (2015)
Terzioglu Campus
Canakkale 17020
sztutkun@comu.edu.tr
http://jeoloji.comu.edu.tr/

Cukurova Universitesi

Jeoloji Muhendisligi Bolumu (B,M,D) ● (2015)
Faculty of Engineering and Architecture, Department of Geological Engineering
01330 Adana
Balcali
p. (+ 90 322) 338 67 15
parlak@cu.edu.tr
http://jeoloji.cu.edu.tr
Professor:
Osman Parlak, (D), Geneva, 1996, GipCc

Eskisehir Universitesi

Maden Muhendisligi Bolumu (2015)
Muhendislik Fakultesi
Yunus Emre Kampusu
Eskisehir

Firat University

Dept of Geological Engineering (A,B,M,D) O☒ (2021)
Fırat University, Department of Geological Engineering
23119 Elazıg Turkey
Elazig 23100
p. 424-2370000-5979
asasmaz@firat.edu.tr
http://jeo.muh.firat.edu.tr/tr/node/104
f: https://www.facebook.com/groups/firatjeoloji/
Programs: Geological Engineering
Enrollment (2018): A: 1 (1) B: 10 (10) M: 4 (4) D: 2 (2)
Chair:
Ahmet Sasmaz, (D), Firat, 2006, EgGeCe
Professor:
Ercan Aksoy, (A), Ggt
Melahat Beyarslan, (D), GipGx
Ahmet Feyzi Bingol, (A), GipGv
Bahattin Cetindag, (A), NgYv
Zulfu Gurocak, (A), Nrg
Leyla Kalender, (A), CgcCs
Ahmet Sagiroglu, (A), Egm
Associate Professor:
Bunyamin Akgul, (D), GzyGi
Dicle Bal Akkoca, (D), EnCo
Hasan Celik, (A), GscEo
Calibe Koc Tasgin, (A), GsdGg
Sevcan Kurum, (A), GivGx
Assistant Professor:
Ayse Didem Kilic, (D), GxpGy
Esra Ozel Yildirim, (D), Gxi
Ozlem Oztekin Okan, (D), HgwHs
Melek Ural, (D), GivCc
Research Assistant:
Mehmet Kokum, (D), Firat, 2017, GtcGg
Research Assistant:
Hatice Kara, (M), Cg
Nevin Ozturk, (D), Firat, 2017, Cg
Research Asistant:
Elif Akgun, (M), GgcGt
Onur Alkac, GgsGu
Gizem Arslan, (M), GxiGp
Yasemin Aslan, Nr
Serap Colak Erol, (D), 2014, GgcGt
Mehmet Ali Erturk, (D), 2016, GiCc
Mustafa Kanik, (D), 2015, NrSo
Sibel Kaygili, (D), 2016, GgPgs
Mahmut Palutoglu, (D), YgsGc
Mustafa Eren Rizeli, (M), Gxi
Abdullah Sar, (M), GviGp
Ismail Yildirim, ScGix

Hacettepe University

Geological Engineering Dept (2015)
Muhendislik Fakultesi
Beytepe Kampusu
tunay@hacettepe.edu.tr
http://www.jeo.hun.edu.tr/800x600.htm
Assistant Professor:
Turker Kurttas, (D), Hacettepe, 1997, HwgZr

Hydrogeological Engineering Programme (B,M,D) ● (2015)
Beytepe Campus
Ankara 06800
p. +90 (312) 297730
ekmekci@hacettepe.edu.tr
http://www.hacettepe.edu.tr/
Enrollment (2015): B: 235 (42) M: 12 (0) D: 11 (3)
Professor:
Serdar Bayari, (D), Hacettepe, 1991, Hw
Mehmet Ekmekci, (D), HwyCs
Sakir Simsek, (D), Istanbul, 1982, Hw
Galip Yüce, (D), Hw
Nur Naciye Özyurt, (D), Hacettepe, Hw
Assistant Professor:
Levent Tezcan, (D), Hacettepe, 1993, Hw

Istanbul Universitesi

Jeoloji Bolumu (2015)
Muhendislik Fakultesi
Beyazit
p. 0 (212) 473 70 70 ex. 17600
koral@istanbul.edu.tr
http://muhendislik.istanbul.edu.tr/jeoloji/?p=6909

ITU

Jeoloji Bolumu (2015)
Maden Fakultesi
80394, Macka
Istanbul

Middle East Technical University

Inst of Marine Science (2015)
Div. of Marine Geology & Geophysics
P.O. Box 28
33731 Erdemli-Mersin
p. +90-324 521 3434
adminims@metu.edu.tr
http://www.ims.metu.edu.tr/

Dept of Geological Engineering (B,M,D) (2015)
Inonu Bulvari
ODTU
Ankara TR-06531
p. +90-312-2102682
gesin@metu.edu.tr
http://www.geoe.metu.edu.tr/

Mineral Research and Exploration General Directorate of Turkey

p. +90 312 201 11 51
mta@mta.gov.tr
http://www.mta.gov.tr/

Selcuk Universitesi

Faculty of Sciences (2015)
Muhendislik Fakultesi
42040 Konya
p. (+)903322412484
fen@selcuk.edu.tr

Uganda

Gulu University

Faculty of Agriculture and Environment (B,M,D) (2016)
P.O. Box 166
Gulu
p. +256782673491
d.ongeng@gu.ac.ug
http://www.gu.ac.ug

Dept of Geography (B) ● (2015)
P.O. Box 166
Gulu
p. +256772517488
charles.okumu52@gmail.com
http://www.gu.ac.ug/index.php?option=com_content&view=category&layout=blog&id=48&Itemid=66
Lecturer:
Expedito Nuwategeka, (D), Gulu, 2015, ZyyGv

Kabale University

Dept of Environmental Science and Natural Resources (B) (2015)
PO Box 317
Kabale
p. 256-4864-22803
akampabf@gmail.com

http://www.kabaleuniversity.ac.ag/

Makerere University

Dept of Geology and Petroleum Studies (2015)
P. O. Box 7062
Kampala 041
p. +256 41 532631-4
http://mak.ac.ug/
Instructor:
Kevin Aanyu, (M), Mak
Wycliff Kawule, (M), ITC
Robert Mamgbi, (M), CT-Prague
Lecturer:
Erasmus Barifajio, (D), Mak
John Mary Kiberu, (D), Tubingen
Agnes Alaba Kuterama, (M), ITC
Andrew Muwanga, (D), Braunschweig (Germany)
Immaculate Nakimera Ssemanda, (D), Mak

Dept of Geography, Geoinformatics & Climatic Sciences (B) (2015)
PO Box 7062
Kampala
p. +256-41-53126 1
geog@caes.mak.ac.ug
http://www.geography.mak.ac.ug/

Institute of Environment and Natural Resources (B) (2015)
PO Box 7062
Kampala 041
p. 256 414 530134
fkansiime@muienr.mak.ac.ug
http://muienr.mak.ac.ug/

Ndejje University

Faculty of Forest Science & Environmental Management (B) (2015)
PO Box 7088
Kampala, Ndejje Hill
p. +256-0392-730326
forest@ndejjeuniversity.ac.ug
http://www.ndejjeuinversity.ac.ug/academics.htm

Ukraine

National Mining University (in Ukraine)

State Mining University of Ukraine (2015)
19 Karl Marx Avenue
Dnepropetrovsk
320600
dfr@nmuu.dp.ua
http://www.apex.dp.ua/english/uageo/ukraine.html

United Arab Emirates

United Arab Emirates University

Dept of Geology (B,M,D) ● (2015)
P.O. Box 15551
College of Science, UAE University
Jamma Street
Al-Ain, Abu Dhabi 9713
p. +971-3-7136380
Ahmed.murad@uaeu.ac.ae

United Kingdom

Aberystwyth University

Dept of Geography & Earth Sciences (B,M,D) ☒ (2018)
Llandinam Building
Penglais
Aberystwyth SY23 3DB
p. 01970 622606
gesstaff@aber.ac.uk
http://www.aber.ac.uk/en/iges

Professor:
Ron Fuge, (D), Wales, GbCgGe

Emeritus:
Michael M J Hambrey, (D), Manchester (UK), 1974, GlsGm

Anglia Ruskin University

Dept of Life Sciences (2015)
Cambridge Campus
East Road
Cambridge CB1 1PT
p. +44 845 271 3333
michael.cole@anglia.ac.uk
http://www.anglia-ruskin.ac.uk/ruskin/en/home/faculties/fst/departments/lifesciences.html

Bangor University

School of Ocean Sciences (B,M,D) (2015)
Menai Bridge,
Isle of Anglesey
LL59 5AB
p. +44-1248-382854
oss011@bangor.ac.uk
http://www.sos.bangor.ac.uk/

Associate Professor:
Andrew J. Davies, (D), Queen's (Ireland), 2004, ObZir

Birkbeck College

Dept of Earth and Planetary Sciences (2015)
Department of Earth and Planetary Sciences
University of London - Birkbeck
Malet Street
Bloomsbury, London WC1E 7HX
p. +44 (0)20 7631 6665
p.gaunt@bbk.ac.uk
http://www.bbk.ac.uk/geology/
Administrative Assistant: Peter Gaunt

Head:
Gerald Roberts, (D), Durham (UK), 1991, Gct

Professor:
Charlie Bristow, (D), Leeds (UK), 1987, Gs
Andy Carter, Zg
Ian Crawford, Zn
Hilary Downes, Cg

Instructor:
Karen Hudson-Edwards, Gez

Lecturer:
Andy Beard
Simon Drake, Gv
Dominic Fortes, Zg
Steve Hirons, Cl
Philip Hopley, Pe
Phillip Pogge von Strandmann, (D), Csl
Vincent C. H. Tong, Yg
Charlie Underwood, c.un, Pg

British Antarctic Survey

British Antarctic Survey ☒ (2020)
High Cross, Madingley Road
Cambridge CB3 0ET
p. +44 (0)1223 221400
trr@bas.ac.uk
https://www.bas.ac.uk/team/science-teams/geosciences/
t: @BAS_News

British Geological Survey

British Geological Survey (2015)
Environmental Science Centre
Nicker Hill
Keyworth
Nottingham NG12 5GG
p. 0115 936 3100
enquiries@bgs.ac.uk
http://www.bgs.ac.uk/

Cardiff University

School of Earth and Ocean Sciences (B,M,D) (2015)
Main Building
Park Place
Cardiff, Wales CF10 3YE
p. +44 (0)29 2087 4830
earth-ug@cf.ac.uk
http://www.cardiff.ac.uk/earth/

Head:
Ian R. Hall, (D), GuCsGs
R J. Parkes

Professor:
J A. Cartwright, (D), Ys
Dianne Edwards, (D), Pb
Dianne Edwards, (D), Pb
I Hall, Zn
A Harris
C Harris, Ge
A C. Kerr, (D), Durham (UK), 1994, Gxi
Bernard Elgey Leake, (D), Bristol, 1974, GipGz
R J. Lisle, Gc
C MacLeod, Gu
J A. Pearce, Cg
P N. Pearson, Pe
D Rickard, Cg
V P. Wright, Gs

Associate Professor:
Tiago Alves, (D), Manchester (UK), 2002, GouGt

Commander:
N Rodgers, (D), Am

Lecturer:
Rhoda Ballinger, (D), Zn
Stephen Barker, Pe
C M. Berry, (D), Pb
P J. Brabham, (D), Ye
L C. Cherns, Pg
Jose Constantine, (D), Hy
J H. Davies, Yg
I Fryett, Zn
TC Hales, (D), Gm
A Hemsley, Pl
T Jones, Ge
C Lear, Ou
Johan Lissenberg
Sergio Lourenco, (D), Sp
R Perkins, Zn
J Pike, Zn
H M. Prichard, Gx
H Sass
H D. Smith, Zn
S J. Wakefield, Cm
C F. Wooldridge, Zn
Y Yang, Hg

Durham University

Dept of Earth Sciences (B,M,D) ☒ (2018)
Science Laboratories

South Road
Durham DH1 3LE
p. +44 0191 3342300
earth.sciences@durham.ac.uk
http://www.dur.ac.uk/earthsciences/
f: https://www.facebook.com/DurUniEarthSci/
t: @DurUniEarthSci
Programs: Geology
Geophysics with Geology
Geoscience
Environmental Geoscience
Earth Science

Professor:
Mark Allen, Gt
Andrew Aplin, Go
Kevin Burton, Cg
Jon Gluyas, Eo
Chris Greenwell, (D), CqEoCg
David Harper, Pg
Richard Hobbs, Ys
Robert E. Holdsworth, (D), Leeds (UK), Gc
Colin G. Macpherson, (D), London (UK), 1994, CgGiCs
Simon Mathias, Hy
Kenneth J. McCaffrey, (D), Durham (UK), Gc
Stefan Nielsen
Yaoling Niu, (D), Hawaii, 1992, Git
Christine Peirce, (D), Cambridge, Yg
Dave Selby, Cc
Peter Talling, Rn
Fred Worrall, (D), Cambridge, Cg

Associate Professor:
James Baldini, Pc
Richard James Brown, Gv
Nicola De Paola, Gc
Darren Grocke, Cs
Claire Horwell, Rn
Stuart Jones, Gs
Ed Llewellin, Gv
Julie Prytulak, Cg
Jeroen van Hunen, (D), 2001, Gt

Assistant Professor:
Martin Smith, Pe
Fabian Wadsworth, Gv
Richard Walters, Yd

Edinburgh University

School of Geosciences (B,M,D) ●⦸ (2019)
Kings Buildings
West Mains Road
Edinburgh EH9 3JW
p. +44 (0) 131 651 7068
Susan.Orr@ed.ac.uk
http://www.geos.ed.ac.uk/
f: https://www.facebook.com/geosciences/
t: @geosciencesed
Programs: Geology; Geology and Physical Geography; Geophysics; Environmental GeoSciences; Geoenergy; GIS; Earth Observation; Geoinformation Management
Enrollment (2019): B: 1000 (1000) M: 450 (450) D: 250 (250)

Director:
Bruce M. Gittings, (M), Edinburgh, Zi

Head:
Alexander W. Tudhope, (D), Cs

Chair:
Chris Dibben, Zn
Mark D. A. Rounsevell, (D), Zu
Charles W. J. Withers, (D)

Professor:
Rob Bingham, (D), Zc
Tim Cresswell, (D), Zn
Andrew Curtis, Ys
Andrew J. Dugmore, (D), ZycGa
J. Godfrey Fitton, Gi
Simon L. Harley, Gt
R. Stuart Haszeldine, (D), Strathclyde, GoRmZo
Gabriele C. Hegerl, (D), As
Simon Kelley, (D), London (UK), 1985, CcsZg
Dick Kroon, Gg
Hayden Lorimer, (D), Zn
Ian G. Main, (D), Ys
John B. Moncrieff, As
Peter W. Neinow, (D), Cantab, Gl
Paul Palmer, As
Jamie R. Pearce, (D), Ge
Alastair H. F. Robertson, (D), Leicester (UK), 1975, GtgGs
Hugh D. Sinclair, (D), So
David Stevenson, (D), As
Simon F. B. Tett, Am
Kathryn A. Whaler, (D), Cambridge, 1981, YmRn
Mathew Williams, (D), E Anglia (UK), 1994, ZcrZu
Wyn Williams, Ym
Iain H. Woodhouse, (D), Zi
Rachel A. Woods, (D), Open, Gs
Anton M. Ziolkowski, (D), Cambridge, 1971, YesYg

Senior Scientist:
Nicola Cayzer, (D), Edinburgh, Yg
Richard Hinton, Cg

Associate Professor:
Stuart M. V. Gilfillan, (D), Manchester (UK), 2006, CgsCe

Assistant Professor:
Massimo A. Bollasina, (D), Maryland, 2010, Asp
Steve Brusatte, (D), Pv

Research Associate:
Andrew Bell, Gt
Ian B. Butler, (D), Cg
John Craven, Yg
Jan C. de Hoog, (D), Utrecht, 2001, GxzGv
Chris L. Hayward, Ga
Sian F. Henley, (D), Edinburgh, 2013, CmOcCs
Mark Naylor, (D), Edinburgh, Gt
Anthony J. Newton, (D), Edinburgh, Zn
Laetitia Pichevin, (D), Bordeaux, Cg

Instructor:
Richard L. H. Essery, As
Raja Ganeshram, Pg
Bryne T. Ngwenya, (D), Reed, Co
David Reay, (D), As
Tom Slater, (D), London (UK), Zn
Samantha Staddon

Lecturer:
Peter Alexander, (D), Zc
Mikael Attal, (D), Joseph Fourier, 2003, GmtZy
Clare Barnes, (D), Zn
Geoffrey Bromily, (D), Ge
Eliza Calder, Gv
Mark Chapman, (D), Yg
Murray Collins, (D), Zi
Gregory L. Cowie, Co
Kate Crowley, (D), Zc
Julie Cupples, Zn
Kyle Dexter
Ruth Doherty, (D), Edinburgh, As
Zhiqiang Feng, (D), Zn
Janet Fisher, (D), Zn
Florian Fusseis, Gc
Alfy Gathorne-Hardy, (D), Zc
Daniel Goldberg
Noel Gourmelen
Margaret C. Graham, Ge
Steven Hancock, (D), Zi
Kate V. Heal, Co
Sebastian Hennige, (D), Zc
Lea-Anne Henry, Zn
Rachel Hunt, Zn
Gail D. Jackson, PbGe
Simon Jung, Og
Hamish Kallin, (D), Zn
Aidan Keane, (D), Zc
Linda Kirstein, Gt
sukanya Krishnamurthy, (D), Zn
Eric Laurier, Zn
Fraser MacDonald
William A. Mackaness, Zi
Ondrej Masek, (D), Ng
Christopher I. McDermott, Hg
Marc J. Metzger, (D), Wageningen (Neth), Ge
Nina J. Morris

Simon N. Mudd, (D), Hg
Caroline Nichol
Eva Panagiotakopulu, Pe
Genevieve Patenaude, (D), Ge
Hugh C. Pumphrey, (D), Mississippi, AscYv
Kanchana Ruwanpura
Casey Ryan
Simon J. Shackley, Eg
Niamh K. Shortt, Eg
Sran P. Sohi, (D), London (UK), So
Neil Stuart, Zi
Daniel Swanton, (D), Durham (UK)
Alexander Thomas
Dan van der Horst, (D), Eg
Mark Wilkinson, (D)
Merwether Wilson, Ob

Teaching Fellow:
Thomas Challads, Hg

Other:
Andrew S. Hein, (D), Edinburgh
Tetsuya Komabayashi, (D), Gz
Isla Myers-Smith
Jan Penrose, (D), Toronto
Marisa Wilson, (D), Oxcon

Exeter University

Camborne School of Mines (2015)
College of Engineering, Mathematics and Physical Sciences
University of Exeter
Penryn Campus
Penryn, Cornwall TR10 9FE
p. (+44) 1392 661000
cornwall@exeter.ac.uk
http://emps.exeter.ac.uk/geology/contact/

Director:
John Coggan, (D), Newcastle, Nx
Charlie Moon, (D), Imperial Coll (UK), 1983, CeEmZi
Neill Wood, (B), Imperial Coll (UK), 1983, YuZen

Professor:
Hylke J. Glass, (D), NxmEm
Stephen Hasselbo, Gs
Kip Jeffrey, Nx
Bernd Lottermoser, Ca

Lecturer:
Jens C. Andersen, (D), Copenhagen, GiEmCa
Ian Bailey, (D), Univ Coll (UK), Zn
Robert Barley
Christopher Bryan, Nx
Patrick Foster, Nm
Sam Hughes, Gt
Gareth Kennedy, Nm
Kate L. Littler, (D), Univ Coll (UK), 2011, PeCl
John Macadam, Ge
Lewis Meyer, (D), Exeter (UK), 2001, Nmr
Kathryn Moore, (D), Bristol, 1999, Ge
Kim Moreton, (D), Exeter (UK), 2008, EnZur
Richard Pascoe, (D), Gz
Duncan Pirrie
Robin Shail, (D), Keele, 1992, GtcEm
Ross Stickland
David Watkins, Hg
Andrew Wetherelt, Nm
Paul Wheeler, Nx
Ben Williamson, (D), London (UK), 1991, EmGv

Heriot-Watt University

Institute of Petroleum Engineering (M,D) O✓🏛 (2019)
Research Park, Riccarton
Heriot-Watt University
Edinburgh Campus
Edinburgh EH14 4AS
p. +44 (0) 131 451 3543
egis-staff@hw.ac.uk
https://www.hw.ac.uk/schools/energy-geoscience-infrastructure-society/research/ige.htm
f: https://www.facebook.com/hwu.egis
t: @HWUPetroleum
Programs: Petroleum Engineering
Applied Petroleum Geoscience
Reservoir Evaluation and Management
Subsurface Energy Systems
Mature Field Management
Enrollment (2019): M: 83 (0) D: 121 (0)

Director:
Andy Gardiner
Mahmoud Jamiolahmady, (D), Ins Pet Eng, 2001, Zn
Eric Mackay
Uisdean Nicholson
Asghar Shams, Yg
Rink van Dijke

Head:
Sebastian Geiger, (D), ETH (Switzerland), 2004, NpEoYh

Chair:
John Underhill

Professor:
Patrick Corbett, Np
Gary Couples, Np
David Davies, Ng
Colin MacBeth
Ken Sorbie
Dorrik Stow

Associate Professor:
Andreas Busch
Babak Jafarizadeh, (D), Eo
Jingsheng Ma, (D), Np
Kamaljit Singh, (D), Np

Assistant Professor:
Elli-Maria (Elma) Charalampidou
Morteza Haghighat Sefat

Research Associate:
Ross Anderson, Eo
Lorraine Boak
Matthew Booth
Rachel Brackenridge
Rod Burgass
Antonio Carvalho
Antonin Chapoy
Romain Chassagne
Ilya Fursov
Alexader Graham
Sally Hamilton, Gs
Oleg Ishkov
Rachel Jamieson
Marco Lorusso
Maria-Daphne Mangriotis, Ys
Pedro Martinez Garcia
Robin Shields, Cg
Mike Singleton
Oscar Vazquez
Francesca Watson
Jinhai Yang
Zhen Yin
Zhao Zhang
Zhao Zhang, (D)
Stephanie Zihms

Instructor:
Steve McDougall

Lecturer:
Vasily Demyanov, Zi
Florian Doster, Hg
Ahmed H. Elsheikh
Zeyun Jiang
Helen Lever, (D), James Cook, 2003, Go
Helen Lewis, (D), Gc
Khafiz Muradov, (D)
Gillian E. Pickup, (D), Np
Karl D. Stephen

Laboratory Director:
Jim Buckman
Mike Christie

Other:
Bahman Tohidi

Imperial College

Earth Science and Engineering (2018)
Imperial College London

South Kensington Campus
London SW7 2AZ
p. +44 (0)20 7589 5111
philip.allen@imperial.ac.uk
http://www3.imperial.ac.uk/earthscienceandengineering
Director:
Nigel Brandon, Ge
Head:
Johannes Cilliers, (D), Cape Town, 1994, Gz
Chair:
Alastair Fraser, (D), Glasgow, 1995, Go
Matthew Jackson, (D), Liverpool (UK), 1997
Howard Johnson, Go
Peter King, (D), Cambridge, 1982, Np
Ann H. Muggeridge, (D), Oxford, 1986, NpHwEo
Yanghua Wang, (D), Imperial Coll (UK), 1997, Yg
Professor:
Martin J. Blunt, (D), Cambridge, 1988, NpHw
John Cosgrove, (D), Imperial Coll, 1972, Gc
Sevket Durucan, (D), Nottingham (UK), 1981, NmEcNr
Sanjeev Gupta, Gs
Joanna Morgan, (D), Cambridge, 1988, Yg
Jane Plant, Ge
Mark Rehkamper, (D), Mainz, 1995, CsaCc
Mark Sephton, (D), Open, 1996, Xm
Velisa Vesovic, (D), Imperial Coll (UK), 1998, Np
Michael Warner, (D), York, 1979, Ys
Dominik Weiss, (D), Bern, 1998, ClaCq
Robert W. Zimmerman, (D), California (Berkeley), 1984, NrHwNp
Associate Professor:
Gerard Gorman, (D), Imperial Coll, 2005, Yg
Samuel Krevor, (D), Eo
Lidia Lonergan, (D), Oxford, 1991, GtcGs
Research Associate:
Rebecca Bell, (D), Southampton (UK), 2008, Gt
Branko Bijeljic, (D), Imperial Coll (UK), 2000, Np
Raphael Blumenfeld, (D), Cambridge, Zn
Rhordri Davies, (D), Cardiff, 2007, Yg
Zita Martins, (D), Leiden (Neth), 2007, Xm
Christopher Pain, Yg
Randall Perry, Zg
Instructor:
Jenny Collier, (D), Cambridge, 1989, Yr
Saskia Goes, (D), California (Santa Cruz), 1995, Yg
Gary Hampson, (D), Liverpool (UK), 1995, Gd
Christopher Jackson, (D), Manchester (UK), 2002, Gt
Anna Korre, Ng
Jian Guo Liu, (D), Imperial Coll (UK), 2002, Zr
Stephen Neethling, (D), UMIST, 1999, Gz
Emma Passmore
Matthew Piggot, Bath, 2001, Hg
Lecturer:
Ian Bastow, (D), Leeds (UK), 2005, Yg
Gareth Collins, (D), Imperial Coll, 2002, Xm
Matthew Genge, (D), Univ Coll (UK), 1993, Xm
Kathryn Hadler, (D), Manchester (UK), 2006, Gz
Cedric John, (D), Potsdam, 2003, Gs
John-Paul Latham, (D), Imperial Coll (UK), 2003
Philippa J. Mason, Zr
Adrian Muxworthy, (D), Oxford, 1998, Ym
Julie Prytulak, (D), Bristol, 2008, Gg
Mark Sutton, (D), Wales, 1996, Pg
Tina van de Flierdt, (D), ETH (Switzerland), 2003, Cs
Alex Whittaker, (D), Edinburgh, 2007, Gt
Visiting Professor:
Rosalind Coogon, Cs
Emeritus:
Alain Gringarten, (D), Stanford, 1971, Np
John Woods, (D), Imperial Coll (UK), 1964

Keele University

Geography, Geology and the Environment (B,M,D) ☒ (2018)
William Smith Building,
Keele University
Keele, Staffordshire ST5 5BG
p. (+44) 01782 733615
gge@keele.ac.uk
http://www.keele.ac.uk/gge/
f: https://www.facebook.com/KeeleGeology
t: @KeeleGeology
Programs: BSc Geology (single & combined honours)
M. Geology
MSc Geoscience Research
Certificates: None
Enrollment (2014): B: 149 (45) M: 29 (15) D: 10 (2)
Dr:
Stuart Egan, (D), Keele, Gtc
Jamie K. Pringle, (D), Heriot-Watt, YuGfa
Associate Professor:
Ralf Gertisser, (D), Freiburg (Germany), 2001, GivGz
Ian G. Stimpson, (D), Wales, 1987, YeuRc
Dr:
Glenda Jones, (D), Keele, NgYg
Stu Clarke, (D), Keele, GsoGd
Ralf Halama, (D), Tubingen, GpiCa
Guido Meinhold, (D), Mainz, GdCa
Michael Montenari, Tubingen, PmgPs
Steven L. Rogers, (D), Keele, PgGs

Kingston University

School of Geography, Geology and Environment (2015)
Penrhyn Road Centre
Penrhyn Road
Kingston upon Thames
Surrey KT1 2EE
p. +44 (0)20 8417 9000
G.Gillmore@kingston.ac.uk
http://www.kingston.ac.uk/geolsci/
Director:
Stuart Downward
Head:
Gavin Gillmore, (D), Univ Coll (UK), Gb
Professor:
Ian Jarvis, (D), Oxon, 1980, CgGsr
Peter Treloar, (D), Glasgow, 1978, Gc
Nigel Walford, (D), London (UK), 1981, Zi
Instructor:
Peter Hooda, (D), London (UK), 1992, Em
Annie Hughes, (D), Bristol, 1997, Zi
Mike Smith, (D), Sheffield, 1999, Zr
Lecturer:
Andy Adam-Bredford
Alistair Baird
Douglas Brown, Zi
Kerry Brown, (D), SUNY (Stony Brook), 2004, Ge
Norman Cheun, Ge
Tracey Coates
Hadrian Cook, (D), E Anglia (UK), 1986, Ge
Peter Garside, (D), Liverpool (UK)
Paul Grant
Ian Greatbatch, (D), 2008, Zi
Frances Harris, (D), Kingston, 1995
Mary Kelly
David Kidd, (D), St Andrews, 2005, Ziy
James Lambert-Smith, (D), Kingston, 2014, Gg
Andrew Miles, (D), Edinburgh, 2012, Gz
Stephanie Mills, (D), Witwatersrand, 2006, Gl
Pamela Murphy
Colin Ryall
Neil Thomas
Visiting Professor:
Rosalind Taylor
Emeritus:
Richard Moody
Andy Rankin
Other:
Andrew Swan

Leicester University

School of Geography, Geology and the Environment (B,M) ☒ (2021)
University Road
Leicester LE1 7RH
p. +44 (0)116 252 3933
geology@le.ac.uk
http://www2.le.ac.uk/departments/geology

Programs: Geology, Applied & Environmental Geology, Geology with Geophysics, Geology with Palaeontology.
Geography, Human Geography
Environmental Science

Head:
Stewart Fishwick, Yg

Professor:
Mike Branney, Gv
Sarah Davies, (D), Gs
Richard England, Yg
Sarah Gabbott, Pg
Gawen Jenkin
Mike Lovell, Yg
Mark Purnell, Pg
Mark Williams, Pg
Jens Zinke, (D)

Lecturer:
Tiff Barry
Tom Harvey, Pg
Dave Holwell, Ge
Sarah Lee
Andrew Miles
Marc Reichow
Dan Smith, Ge

Emeritus:
Andy D. Saunders, (D), Birmingham (UK), 1976, GiCgGe

Liverpool John Moores University

School of Natural Sciences and Psychology (B,M,D) (2016)
Byrom Street
Liverpool L3 3AF
p. (+44) 0151 904 6300
j.r.kirby@ljmu.ac.uk
https://www.ljmu.ac.uk/research/centres-and-institutes/environment-research-group
f: https://www.facebook.com/groups/LJMU.geography.env.sci/
t: @ljmugeog
Enrollment (2016): B: 72 (0) M: 3 (0)

Professor:
Andy Tattersall

Dr:
Jason Kirby

Nottingham Trent University

Dept of Animal, Rural, and Environmental S ciences (2015)
Burton Street
Nottingham NG1 4BU
p. +44 (0)115 941 8418
robert.mortimer@ntu.ac.uk
http://www.ntu.ac.uk

Open University

Dept of Environment, Earth & Ecosystems (B,M,D) (2015)
Faculty of Science
The Open University
Walton Hall
Milton Keynes MK7 6AA
p. +44 (0) 1908 652886
Env-Earth-Ecosystems-Enquiries@open.ac.uk
http://www.open.ac.uk/science/environment-earth-ecosystems/
f: https://www.facebook.com/pages/OU-Environment-Earth-Ecosystems/234968859948707
t: @OU_EEE

Head:
Arlene G. Hunter, (D), Open, 1993, ZeGiCg

Professor:
Fabrizio Ferrucci, Yg
David Gowing, (D), Lancaster (UK), 1991, Pb
Nigel B.W. Harris, (D), Cambridge, 1973, GtiGp
Walter Oechel, As

Associate Professor:
Mark A. Brandon, (D), Cambridge, 1995, OgGlOp
Angela L. Coe, (D), Oxford, GsrCg
Dave McGarvie, (D), Lancaster (UK), 1985, GviCt

Associate Scientist:
Peter Sheldon

Research Associate:
Marie-Laure Bagard
Gareth Davies, (D), Cranfield, Ze

Reader:
Neil Edwards, (D)

Instructor:
Stephen Blake, (D), Lancaster (UK), 1982, Gv

Lecturer:
Pallavi Anand, (D), Cambridge, 2002, ClPe
Tom Argles, (D), Oxon, Zi
Anthony Cohen, (D), Cambridge, 1988, Cs
Sarah Davies, (D), Sheffield, Ze
Miranda Dyson, (D), Witwatersrand, 1989, Pg
Tamsin Edwards, (D)
Richard Holliman, (D), Open, Ze
Philip Sexton, (D), Southampton (UK), 2000, Ge
Carlton Wood

Visiting Professor:
Stephen Self, (D)
Edward Youngs, (D), Cambridge, 1972, Sp

Emeritus:
Phil Potts
Robert Spicer, (D), Imperial Coll, 1975

Polytechnic Southwest

Dept of Earth Sciences (2015)
Drake Circus
Plymouth, Devon PL4 8AA
p. (+44) (0)1752 584584
science.environment@plymouth.ac.uk
http://www5.plymouth.ac.uk/schools/school-of-geography-earth-and-environmental-sciences/earth-sciences

Queen's University Belfast

School of Natural and Built Environment (Geography) (B,M,D) ●☒ (2017)
University Road
Belfast BT7 1NN
p. + 44 (0) 28 90973186
p.warke@qub.ac.uk
http://www.qub.ac.uk/schools/NBE/
f: https://www.facebook.com/QUBGeography/
Programs: Geography (B); Geography with a Language (French or Spanish) (B)
Enrollment (2016): B: 320 (106) M: 6 (6) D: 40 (5)

Head:
Patricia Warke, (D), Queen's (Ireland), 1994, GmZym

Professor:
Keith Lilley, (D)
David Livingstone, (D)

Dr:
Andrew Newton, (D), 2017, GmlGs

Associate Professor:
Merav Amir, (D)
Oliver Dunnett, (D)
Paul Ell, (D)
Diarmd Finnegan, (D)
Nuala Johnson, (D)
M. Satish Kumar, (D), Jawaharlal Nehru (India), 1991, ZnnZn
Jennifer McKinley, (D)
Donal Mullan, (D)
Helen Roe, (D)
Alastair Ruffell, (D)
Ian Shuttleworth, (D)
Tristan Sturm, (D)

Lecturer:
Niall Majury, (D), Toronto, 1999

Royal Holloway University of London

Department of Earth Sciences (B,M,D) ●⦸ (2021)
Department of Earth Sciences
Royal Holloway University of London
Egham Hill
Egham , Surrey TW20 0EX
p. +44 (0) 1784 443 581
info@es.rhul.ac.uk
https://www.royalholloway.ac.uk/earthsciences/home.aspx

f: https://www.facebook.com/RhulEarthSci
t: @RHULEarthSci
Programs: BSc/MSci Geology; Environmental Geology; Petroleum Geology; Geoscience; Digital Geoscience; Environmental Geoscience; Geosciences & Sustainable Energy; Earth, Climate & Environmental Change
MSc Environmental Diagnosis & Management; Energy Geosciences; Petroleum Geosciences

Head of Department:
Jurgen Adam, (D), Gc

Emeritus:
Robert Hall, (D), Univ Coll (UK), 1974, Gt
Dave Mattey, (D), Cs
Ken R. McClay, (D), Imperial Coll (UK), 1978, GctGo
Andrew Cunningham Scott, (D), Pb

Professor:
Margaret Collinson, (D), Pg
Howard Falcon-Lang, (D), Pg
Richard Ghail, (D), Gt
Agust Gudmundsson, (D), Gc
F. Javier Hernandez Molina, (D), Granada (Spain), 1993, GsuOu
Martin King, (D), As
Euan G. Nisbet, (D), Cambridge, 1974, ZgAcGi
Matthew Thirlwall, Cs
Dave Waltham, (D), Yg

Senior Lecturer:
Anirban Basu, (D), Illinois (Urbana), CglCs
Christina Manning, (D), Cg
Nicola Scarselli, (D), Go
Giulio Solferino, (D), Gg
Ian M. Watkinson, (D), 2009, GtcRn

Reader:
Kevin C. Clemitshaw, (D), E Anglia (UK), AsZg
Alex Dickson, (D), Cas
David Lowry, (D), CsZg

Associate Professor:
Domenico Chiarella, (D), Basilicata (Italy), 2011, Gs

Research Fellow:
Paula Koellemeijer, (D), Ys

Leturer:
Jonathan Paul, (D), Hw

Lecturer:
Queenie Chan, (D), XmCa
Rebecca Fisher, (D), As
Amy Gough, (D), Gs
Nathalie Grassineau, (D), Cs

Honorary Lecturer:
Dave Alderton, (D), Gz

Staffordshire Polytechnic

Geography and the Environment (2015)
j.w.wheeler@staffs.ac.uk
http://www.staffs.ac.uk/sands/scis/geology/geology.html#

Dept of Applied Sciences (2015)
College Road, Stroke-on-Trent
Staffordshire ST4 2DE
p. (+44) 1782 294000
r.boast@staffs.ac.uk
http://www.staffs.ac.uk/academic_depts/sciences/subjects/environment/

Swansea University Prifysgol Abertawe

Dept of Earth Sciences (2015)
Wallace Building
Swansea University
Singleton Park
Swansea, Wales SA2 8PP
p. +44 (0) 1792 205678 ext 8112
geography@swansea.ac.uk
http://www.swansea.ac.uk/geography/

Teesside University

School of Science and Engineering (B,M) (2016)
Tees Valley
Middlesborough TS1 3BA
p. 01642 738800
sse-admissions@tees.ac.uk
http://www.tees.ac.uk/schools/sse

Ulster University, Coleraine

School of Geography and Environmental Sciences (A,B,M,D) O✓ (2019)
Cromore Road
Coleraine BT521SA
p. 0044(0)2870124401
a.moore@ulster.ac.uk
https://www.ulster.ac.uk/faculties/life-and-health-sciences/schools/geography-and-environmental-sciences
t: @UlsterUniGES
Programs: MSc Geographic Information Systems; MScCoastal Zone Management; MScEnvironmental Management; MScEnvironmental Management and MSc Geographic Information Systems; MSc Environmental Management with Geographic Information Systems; MScEnvironmental Pollution and Ecotoxicology;
Certificates: Geographic Information Systems; Coastal Zone Management; Environmental Management; Environmental Management and Geographic Information Systems; Environmental Management with Geographic Information Systems; Environmental Pollution and Ecotoxicology;
Enrollment (2019): B: 320 (100) M: 170 (25) D: 30 (8)

University College London

Dept of Earth Sciences (B,M,D) ☒ (2020)
Gower Street
London WC1E 6BT
p. +44 (0)20 3108 6339
earthsci@ucl.ac.uk
http://www.ucl.ac.uk/es
Programs: Earth Sciences
Geology
Geophysics
Environmental Geoscience
Natural Sciences

Professor:
Dario Alfe, (D), Intl Sch for Adv Studies (Italy), 1997, ZmGyYh
Tim Atkinson, (D), Bristol, 1971, PcHwGm
Paul Bown, (D), Univ Coll (UK), 1986, Pm
John Brodholt, (D), Bristol, 1992, Yg
William Graham Burgess, (D), Birmingham (UK), 1987, Hwy
David Dobson, (D), Univ Coll (UK), 1995, Gz
Adrian P. Jones, (D), Durham (UK), 1980, GiCgGg
Chris Kilburn, (D), Univ Coll (UK), 1984, Yx
John M. McArthur, (D), Imperial Coll (UK), 1974, ClHwPs
Philip Meredith, (D), Imperial Coll (UK), 1983, Nr
Eric Oelkers, (D), California (Berkeley), 1988, ClGze
Kevin Pickering, (D), Oxford, 1979, Gs
Chris Rapley, (D), London (UK), 1976, ZgrGl
Graham Shields-Zhou, (D), Eidgenössische Tech Hochschule Zürich, 1997, Cg
Julienne Stroeve, (D), Colorado, 1996, GlZr
Juergen Thurow, (D), Eberhard-Karls, 1987, Gs
Paul Upchurch, (D), Cambridge, 1993, Pg
Lidunka Vocadlo, (D), Univ Coll (UK), 1993, Gy
Bridget S. Wade, (D), Edinburgh, PmeCl
Ian Wood, (D), Univ Coll (UK), 1977, Gz

Associate Professor:
Anna Ferreira, (D), Oxford, 1005, Ys
Tom Mitchell, Gc
Phillip Pogge von Strandmann, (D), Open (UK), 2006, Csl
Alex Song, (D), Caltech, Ysg
Pieter Vermeesch, (D), Stanford, 2005, Cc

Lecturer:
Dominic Papineau, (D), Colorado, 2006, Cg

University College of Swansea

Dept of Geography (2015)
Singleton Park
Swansea SA2 8PP

University of Aberdeen

Dept of Geology and Petroleum Geology (B,M) (2016)
Meston Building

King's College
Aberdeen AB24 3UE
geology@abdn.ac.uk
http://www.abdn.ac.uk/geology/
Head:
David Jolley, (D), PlsGv
Chair:
Ian Alsop, (D)
Rob Butler
Adrian Hartley
John Howell, (D), Birmingham (UK), 1992, GsoGc
Andrew Hurst
Ben Kneller
David MacDonald
Randell A. Stephenson, (D), Dalhousie, 1981, YgGtZg
Associate Professor:
Clare Bond, (D), Gct
Research Associate:
Steven Andrews
Robert Daly
Jyldz Tabyldy Kyzy
Sam Spinks
Christian Vallejo
Instructor:
David Muirhead
Lecturer:
Stephen Bowden, (D), Newcastle upon Tyne, CoGoCb
David G. Cornwell, (D), Leicester (UK), 2008, YsGtYe
Dave Healy
Malcolm J. Hole
David Iacopini
Joyce Neilson
Colin North
Nick Schofield

University of Bedfordshire

Dept of Life Sciences (2015)
Park Square
Luton, Bedfordshire LU1 3JU
p. +44 1234 400400
international@beds.ac.uk
http://www.beds.ac.uk/howtoapply/departments/science

University of Birmingham

School of Geography, Earth & Environmental Sciences
(B,M,D) ☒ (2021)
School of Geography, Earth and Environmental Sciences
University of Birmingham
Edgbaston, Birmingham B15 2TT
p. +44 (0)121 414 5531
j.d.oldfield@bham.ac.uk
http://www.birmingham.ac.uk/schools/gees
Director:
Rob MacKenzie
Head:
David Hannah, Hg
Chair:
Eugenia Valsami-Jones, (D), ClGeCa
Professor:
Stuart Harrad
Roy M. Harrison, (D), Birmingham (UK), 1989, As
Alexander Milner
Tim Reston
Jon Sadler
John H. Tellam, (D), Birmingham (UK), 1983, Hw
Associate Professor:
Bridin Carroll
Rosie Day, (D), Univ Coll (UK), Zn
Lloyd Jenkins
Stephen M. Jones, (D), Cambridge, 2000, Zg
Jonathan Oldfield, (D), Zy
Research Associate:
Mohamed A. Abdallah
Salim Alam
Mohammed Baalousha
David Beddows
Ian Boomer
Leigh R. Crilley, (D), 2013, As
Mark Cuthbert
Simon J. Dixon, (D), Gms
Jonathan Eden
Sophie Hadfield-Hill
James Hale
Stephanie Handley-Sidhu
Marie Hutton
Kieran Khamis
Marcus Kohler
James Levine
Yuning Ma
Paul Martin
Sara Martinez-Loriente
Mauro Masiol
Heiko Moossen
Catherine L. Muller
Martin Müller
Irina Nikolova
Irina Nikolova
Matt O'Callaghan
Isabella Romer Roche
Zongbo Shi
Shei Sia Su
Rick Thomas
Amey S. Tilak
Sarah Jane Veevers
Saskia Warren
Sebastian Watt
Jianxin Yin
Deputy Head of School:
William Bloss
Instructor:
James Bendle
Lee Chapman
Jason Hilton
Dominique Moran
Ian Phillips
Jo Southworth
Lecturer:
Austin Barber
Nicholas Barrand
Rebecca Bartlett
Lesley Batty
Mike Beazley
Chris Bradley, (D), Leicester (UK), 1994, Hg
Julian Clark
Juana Maria Delgado-Saborit
Steven Emery
Sara Fregonese
Guy Harrington
Phil Jones
Nick Kettridge
Stephen Krause
Mark Ledger
Peter Lee
Iseult Lynch
Zena Lynch
Patricia Noxolo
Francis Pope
Jessica Pykett
Adam Ramadan
Joanna Renshaw
Michael Riley
Michael Rivett
John Round
Ivan Sansom
Greg Sambrook Smith
Carl Stevenson
James Wheeley
Martin Widman
Emeritus:
Ian Fairchild, (D), Nottingham (UK), 1978, GsClGm
Birmingham Fellow & Academic Keeper, Lapworth Museum of Geology:
Richard Butler
Other:
Tom Dunkley Jones
Related Staff:
Melanie Bickerton

University of Bristol

School of Earth Sciences (B,M,D) ☒ (2017)
Wills Memorial Building
Queens Road
Bristol BS8 1RJ
p. +44 117 954 5400
m.j.walter@bristol.ac.uk
http://www.bristol.ac.uk/earthsciences/
f: https://www.facebook.com/School-of-Earth-Sciences-Bristol-University-146277648746662/
t: @UOBEarthscience
Programs: Geology; Environmental Geoscience; Geophysics; Palaeobiology
Enrollment (2013): B: 25 (9) M: 44 (5)

Professor:
Michael Walter , (D), 1991, GiCpg

University of Cambridge

Dept of Earth Sciences (B,M,D) ●☒ (2018)
Downing Street
Cambridge , Cambridgeshire CB2 3EQ
p. +44 (0)1223 333400
satr@cam.ac.uk
http://www.esc.cam.ac.uk
f: https://www.facebook.com/pages/Department-of-Earth-Sciences-University-of-Cambridge/131259610400860
t: @EarthSciCam
Programs: Earth Sciences

Head:
Simon Redfern, (D), Cambridge, 1989, Gzy

Professor:
Michael Bickle, (D), Oxford, 1973, GtYgGo
Nicholas J. Butterfield, Pg
Michael Carpenter, Gy
David Hodell, Ge
Tim Holland, (D), Oxford, GptGz
Marian Holness, Gi
James A. Jackson, (D), Cambridge, 1980, YgGt
Simon Conway Morris, Pg
Keith Priestley, YgGt
Nick Rawlinson, Ygg
Ekhard Salje, Gy
Nicky White, YgGt
Robert White, YgGt
Eric W. Wolff, (D), Cambridge, 1992, GlPe
Andy Woods, YgGt

Lecturer:
David Al-Attar, YdGt
Alex Copley, YgGt
Sanne Cottaar, Ys
Neil Davies, Gs
Marie Edmonds, Gv
Ian Farnan, Gz
Sally Gibson, Gi
Richard Harrison, Gz
John Maclennan, Gi
Kenneth McNamara, Pg
Jerome Anthony Neufeld, GoYgGt
David Norman, Pg
John Rudge, YgGt
Luke C. Skinner, (D), Cambridge, 2005, GeCmOg
Ed Tipper, Cl
Alexandra Turchyn, Ge

Emeritus:
Nigel H. Woodcock, (D), Imperial Coll (UK), 1973, GcsGt

University of Derby

Geographical, Earth and Environmental Sciences (B,M) (2015)
Kedleston Road
Derby DE22 1GAB
p. +44 (0) 1332 591703
fehs@derby.ac.uk
http://www.derby.ac.uk/science/gees/
Enrollment (2013): B: 120 (30) M: 9 (10)

Head:
Hugh Rollinson, Cg

Professor:
Aradhana Mehra, Co

Instructor:
Jacob Adentunji, Ge

Lecturer:
Martin Whiteley, Go

University of East Anglia

School of Env Sciences (2015)
Norwich Research Park
Norwich NR4 7TJ
p. +44 (0)1603 592542
env.enquiries@uea.ac.uk
http://www.uea.ac.uk/environmental-sciences

Director:
Corinne Le Qu, (D), Zg

Professor:
Jan Alexander, (D), Leeds (UK), GseGd
Julian E. Andrews, (D), Leicester (UK), 1984, CsGsCl
Simon Clegg, (D), E Anglia (UK), 1986, AsOcCg
Brett Day, (D), UEA, 2004, Ge
Alastair Grant, (D), Wales, 1983, GeObCt
Karen Heywood, Op
Kevin Hiscock, (D), Birmingham (UK), 1987, Hwg
Tim Jickells, (D), Southampton (UK), Ob
Phillip D. Jones, (D), Newcastle upon Tyne, 1977, AsPeHg
Andy Jordan, Ge
Andrew A. Lovett, (D), Wales, 1990, Ziu
Coling Murrell, As
Timothy J. Osborn, (D), E Anglia (UK), 1996, At
Carlos Peres, Sf
Ian Renfrew, Am
Ian Renfrew, Am
Bill Sturges, As
Roland von Glasow, (D), Max Planck, Yg
Andrew Watkinson, Ge
Sir Robert Watson

Assistant Professor:
Gill Malin, (D), Liverpool (UK), 1983, ObcCb

Research Associate:
Amy Binner

Instructor:
Alex Baker, (D), Plymouth (UK), On
Jenni Barclay, (D), Bristol, Gv
Paul Burton, (D), Cambridge, Ys
Mark Chapman, (D), E Anglia (UK), Pm
Paul Dolman, Zu
Jan Kaiser, Cs
Adrian Matthews, (D), Reading (UK), Am
Claire Reeves, (D), UEA, Cg
Carol Robinson, Ob
Parvadha Suntharalingam, Oc
Cock von Oosterhout, (D), Leiden (Neth)
Rachel Warren, Eg

Lecturer:
Annela Anger-Kraavi, EgGe
Annela Anger-Kraavi, Eg
Victor Bense, Hg
Alan Bond, (D), Lancaster (UK), Ge
Jason Chilvers, (D), Univ Coll (UK), Ge
Pietro Cosentino, Yg
Stephen Dorling, Am
Aldina Franco, (D), UEA, Ge
Robert Hall, (D), Proudman Ocean Lab, On
Tom Hargreaves, Ge
Richard Herd, (D), Lancaster (UK), Gv
Martin Johnson, Cm
Manoj Joshi, (D), Oxford, Zi
Iain Lake, Ge
Irene Lorenzoni, Eg
Nikolai Pedentchouk, (D), Penn State, 2004, Cs
Jane Powell, Ge
Brian Reid, GeCg
Gill Seyfang, Og
Congxiao Shang, (D), Queen Mary (London), Hw
Peter Simmons, Eg
Trevor Tolhurst, Sb
Jenni Turner, (D), 2008, Gt
Naomi Vaughan, (D), UEA, Am
Charlie Wilson, (D), British Columbia, Ge

Xiaoming Zhai, (D), Dalhousie, Og
Emeritus:
Peter S. Liss, (D), OcCbAc
Professorial Fellow:
Kerry Turner, GeEg

University of Exeter

Camborne School of Mines (2015)
Redruth, Cornwall
TR15 3SE
C.Jeffrey@exeter.ac.uk
http://www.ex.ac.uk/CSM/

University of Glasgow

School of Geographical and Earth Sciences (2015)
The Gregory Building
East Quadrangle
University Avenue
Glasgow G12 8QQ
p. +44 (0) 141 330 5436
GES-General@glasgow.ac.uk
http://www.gla.ac.uk/schools/ges/
Head:
Maggie Cusack, Gz
Professor:
Paul Bishop, (D)
John Briggs, Zu
Roderick Brown, Cc
Gordon Curry, (D), Imperial Coll (UK), 1979, GegPg
Deborah Dixon
Jim Hansom, (D), Aberdeen, 1979, OnGmZy
Trevor Hoey, Gs
Martin Lee, Gz
Christopher Philo
Senior Scientist:
Nicolas Beaudoin
Associate Professor:
David Forrest, (D), Glasgow, 1996, Zi
Research Associate:
Enateri Alakpa
Susan Fitzer, Ob
Michael Gallagher
Lydia Hallis
Ulrich Kelka
Angela Last
Paula Lindgren, As
Alistair Mcgowan, Pg
Larissa Naylor
Alan W. Owen, (D), Glasgow, 1977, PgsPg
Instructor:
Anne Dunlop
Mhairi Harvey
Hayden Lorimer
Rhian Meara
Hester Parr
Vernon Phoenix
Daisy Rood
Lecturer:
Brian Bell, So
David Brown, Gvs
Seamus Coveney, Zi
Tim Dempster, Gz
Jane Drummond, Zi
Derek Fabel, Xg
David Featherstone
Nick Kamenos
Ozan Karaman
Daniel Koehn, Gt
Hannah Mathers, (D), GmlGg
Cheryl Mcgeachan
Simon Naylor
Cristina Persano

University of Leeds

School of Earth and Environment (B,M,D) ☒ (2018)
Maths/Earth and Environment Building
The University of Leeds
Leeds LS2 9JT
p. +44 113 343 2846
enquiries@see.leeds.ac.uk
https://environment.leeds.ac.uk/see
f: https://www.facebook.com/SchoolofEarthandEnvironment/
t: @SEELeeds
Director:
Piers M. Forster, (D), Reading (UK), 1994, As
Head:
Simon Bottrell
Chair:
Christopher Collier
Simon Poulton, (D), Cls
Peter Taylor, Ge
Professor:
John Barrett, Ge
Alan Blyth, As
Ian Brooks, (D), UMIST, Zn
Ken Carslaw, (D), E Anglia (UK), 1994, As
Andy Challinor, (D), Leeds, 1999, Am
Martyn P. Chipperfield, (D), Cambridge, 1990, AscAp
Surage Dessai, (D), E Anglia (UK)
Andy Dougil, (D), Sheffield, So
Paul Field
Quentin Fisher, Np
Paul W.J. Glover, (D), E Anglia (UK), 1989, YxGoa
Andy Gouldson, Ge
Alan Haywood, Pe
Steve Hencher, Ng
Andy Hooper, Ydg
Greg Houseman, (D), Cambridge, Yg
Bill McCaffrey, Gs
Jurgen Neuberg, (D), Colorado, Gv
Jouni Paavola, Ge
Doug Parker, (D), Reading (UK), Am
Jeff Peakall, Gs
Andrew Shepherd
Lindsay C. Stinger, (D), Zn
Graham Stuart, Ys
Paul Wignall, PgGs
Tim Wright, Yd
Bruce W.D. Yardley, (D), Bristol, 1974, CgEgGg
William Young, (D), Ge
Associate Professor:
Doug Angus, Ys
Stephen Arnold, (D), Leeds (UK), As
Wolfgang Buermann, (D), Boston, 2012, Zu
Ian Burke, (D), Southampton (UK), Ge
Robert J. Chapman, (D), Leeds (UK), 1990, EmCe
Steven Dobbie, (D), Dalhousie, As
Luuk Flesken, (D), Wageningen (Neth), Ge
Phil Livermore, Ym
Christian Maerz, (D), Bremen, 2008, CmOuEm
Jim McQuaid, (D), Leeds (UK), 1999, As
Daniel Morgan, (D), Open (UK), 2003, Giv
Jon Mound, (D), Toronto, 2001, Gt
Noelle Odling, (D), Queens, Hg
Caroline Peacock, (D), Bristol, Sb
Sebastian Rost, (D), Universit, 2000, Ysg
Sally Russell, (D), Queensland, Ge
Dominick Spracklen, (D), Leeds (UK), 1999, Zn
Julia Steinberger, Zu
Jared West, Hg
Research Associate:
David Banks, Cg
Lauren Gregoire, (D), Bristol
Ruza Ivanovic, (D), Bristol, 2013, OgAsPe
John Marsham, (D), Edinburgh, 2003, As
Instructor:
Nick Dixon, (D), Leeds (UK), 2002, Zu
Tim Foxon, Ge
Chris Green
Dave Hodgson
Jacqueline Houghton
Damian Howells
Geoff Lloyd, (D), Birmingham (UK), 1984
Lecturer:
Emma Bramham, Ym
Roger A. Clark, (D), Leeds (UK), 1982, YseYs

Martin Dallimer, (D), Edinburgh, 2001, Ge
Monica Di Gregorio, (D), London Schl of Econ, Eg
Jen Dyer, (D), Leeds (UK), Ge
Alan Gadian
Fiona Gill, (D), PgCa
Clare E. Gordon, (B), Zi
Dabo Guan, Eg
Jason Harvey, (D), 2005, Cg
Mark Hildyard
George Holmes, Ge
Andrea Jackson, (D), Lancaster (UK), As
Julia Leventon, (D), Cent, Ge
Crispin Little, (D), Bristol, 1995, Pg
Piroska Lorinczi, (D), Leeds (UK), 2006, Np
Vernon Manville
Andrew McCair, (D), Cambridge, 1983, Gc
Lucie Middlemiss, (D), Leeds (UK), 2009, Zn
Nigel Mountney, Gs
Rob Newton, (D), Leeds (UK), Ge
Alice OWen, (D), Leeds (UK)
Douglas Paton, Gc
Richard Phillips, (D), Oxford, Gt
Claire Quinn, (D), King's Coll (UK), Ge
Andrew Ross, (D), Cambridge, Am
Susannah Sallu, Ga
Ivan Savov, (D), S Florida, 2004, Cg
Anne Tallontire
Mark Thomas, (D), Ng
Taija Torvela, (D), Abo Akademi, 2007, GctEg
James van Alstine, Ge
Xianyun Wen, (D), Sichuan (China), 1982, NoAsm

Visiting Professor:
Jane Francis, Pe
Tim Needham, Gc

University of Liverpool

School of Environmental Sciences (B,M,D) ☒ (2019)
Jane Herdman Building
4 Brownlow Street
Liverpool, Merseyside L69 3GP
p. +44 151 794 5146
envsci@liv.ac.uk
http://www.liv.ac.uk/environmental-sciences

Dept of Earth, Ocean, and Ecological Sciences (2015)
Jane Herdman Building
4 Brownlow Street
Liverpool L69 3GP
p. +44 (0)151 795 4642
faulkner@liverpool.ac.uk
http://www.liv.ac.uk/earth-ocean-and-ecological-sciences/

Head:
Andreas Rietbrock, YsGv

Professor:
Daniel Faulkner, Ys
Richard Holme, Ym
Nick Kusznir, Yd
Yan Lavallee, Gv
Rob Marrs, So
Jim Marshall, Cs
Jonathan Sharples, Ocp
Stan van der Berg, Em
John Wheeler, (D), GpcGz
Richard Worden, Gs

Research Associate:
Katherine Allen, Zi
James Ball
Helen Bloomfield, Ob
Stephen Crowley, Gs
Jonathan Lauderdale, Og
Claire Melet
Andreas Nilsson, Ym
Vassil M. Roussenov, (D), Sofia (Bulgaria), 1987, OpZo
Anu Thompson, Oc
Xiao Wang
Tsuyuko Yamanaka, Ob

Lecturer:
Charlotte Jeffrey Abt, Zn
Andy Biggin, Ym
Alan P. Boyle, (D), Univ Coll (UK), 1982, GzEmZe
Bryony Caswell, Ob
Silvio De Angelis, Ys
Rob Duller, Gvs
Liz Fisher, Co
Jonathan Green, Ob
Mimi Hill, Ym
Janine Kavanagh, Gv
Helen Kinvig, Gs
Harry Leach, (D), Leeds (UK), 1975, Og
Claire Mahaffey, Oc
Elisabeth Mariani, Nr
Kate Parr, Pe
John Piper, YmGt
Leonie Robinson, Ob
Isabelle Ryder, Gt
Matthew Spencer, Og
Neil Suttie
Alessandro Tagliabue, Oc
Jack Thomson, Ob

Visiting Professor:
Peter Kokelaar, (D), Wales, 1977, GstGv

Other:
Sara Henton De Angelis
Jackie Kendrick
Rachel Salaun, Oc
Felix von Aulock

University of Manchester

School of Earth and Environmental Sciences (2015)
Williamson Building
Oxford Road
Manchester M13 9PL
p. +44 (0) 161 306 9360
earth.support@manchester.ac.uk
Administrative Assistant: Steven Olivier

Director:
Stephen Boult, Hg

Chair:
Jonathan Redfern, (D), Bristol, 1990, GsoGl

Professor:
Mike Bowman, (D), Wales, Go
Andrew T. Chamberlain, (D), Liverpool (UK), 1987, GaSaPv
Thomas Choularton, (D), Manchester (UK), 1987, As
Hue Coe, (D), UMIST, 1993, As
Stephen Flint, (D), Leeds (UK), 1985, GrsGo
Martin Gallagher, (D), UMIDST, 1986, As
Jamie Gilmour, (D), Sheffield
Colin Hughes, (D), Open, 1992, Go
Francis Livens, Cg
Jonathan Lloyd, (D), Canterbury (NZ), 1993, Ge
Ian Lyon, (D), 1993, Xc
Gordon McFiggans, (D), UEA, 2000, As
Carl Percival, (D), Oxford, 1995, As
David Poyla, (D), Manchester (UK), 1987, Cm
Ernest H. Rutter, (D), Imperial Coll (UK), 1970, NrGct
David Schultz, Am
Kevin Taylor, Go
David Vaughan, (D), Oxford, 1971, GzClGe
Geraint Vaughan, (D), Oxford, 1982, As
Roy Wogelius, (D), Northwestern, 1990, Cg

Associate Professor:
Neil C. Mitchell, (D), Oxford, 1989, GumYg

Research Associate:
Alastair Booth, As
Gerard Capes, As
Deborah Chavrit, (D), Nantes (France), 2010, Gi
Patricia L. Clay, (D), Open (UK), 2010, CgaGg
Filipa Cox
Ian Crawford, As
Sarah Crowther, (D), Oxford, 2003, As
Christopher Dearden, As
Patrick Dowey
Helen Downie, Ge
Nicholas Edwards, Pg
Christopher Emersic, (D)
Torsten Henkel, Cs

Hazel Jones, As
Richard Kift, As
Kimberly Leather, As
Dantong Liu, As
Douglas Lowe, As
William Morgan, As
Miquel Poyatos-More
Laura Richards, Ge
Hugo Ricketts, As
Athanasios Rizoulis, Ge
Andrew Smedley, As
Robert Sparkes, (D), Cambridge, 2012
Jonathan Taylor, (D), Manchester (UK)
Karen Theis, (D), Manchester (UK), 2008, Zn
Paul Williams, As

Lecturer:
Grant Allen, (D), Leicester (UK), 2005, As
Simon Brocklehurst, (D), MIT, 2002, Gm
Kate Brodie, (D), Imperial Coll (UK), 1979, Gc
Rufus Brunt, (D), Leeds (UK), Gs
Michael Buckley, (D), York, 2008, Ga
Ray Burgess, (D), Open, Cs
Victoria Coker, (D), Manchester (UK), 2007, Gz
Paul Connolly, (D), Manchester (UK), 2006, As
Stephen Covery-Crump, (D), Univ Coll (UK), 1992
Giles Droop, (D), Oxford, 1979, Gp
Victoria Egerton, Pg
David Hodgetts, (D), Keele, 1995, Gsc
Cathy Hollis, (D), Aberdeen, 1995, Gs
Merren Jones, (D), Wyoming, 1997, Gst
Julian Mecklenburgh, Gc
John Nudds, (D), Dunhelm, 1975, Pg
Clare Robinson, (D), Lancaster (UK), 1990, Co
Stefan Schroeder, (D), Bern, 2000, Go
Bart van Dongen, Utrecht, 2003, Co

Emeritus:
Christopher Henderson
Peter Jonas
Grenville Turner, (D), Oxford, 1962, XcCc

University of Newcastle Upon Tyne

School of Civil Engineering and Geosciences (2016)
Newcastle University
Newcastle upon Tyne
NE1 7RU
p. +44 (0)191 208 6323
ceg@ncl.ac.uk
http://www.ncl.ac.uk/ceg/

Professor of Soil Science / Head of School :
David Manning

Professor:
Margaret Carol Bell, Ge
Andras Bordossy, Zg
Peter J. Clarke, (D), Oxford, 1997, YdZri
Stephen Larter, Gg
Zhenhong Li, Yd
Phillip Moore, Yd

Research Associate:
David Alderson, Zi
Joana Baptista, Ng
Stephen Blenkinson, Zn
Bernard Bowler, Go
Aidan Burton
Allistair Ford, Gq
Kirill Palamartchouk, Yd

Instructor:
James Barhurst, Gs
Neil Gray, Pg
Helen Talbot, Co

Lecturer:
Jamie Amezaga, Ge
Stuart Barr, Zi
Colin Davie, (D), Glasgow, 2002, Ngr
Stuart Edwards, Gq
Gaetano Elia, gaet, Ng
David Fairbairn, Gq
Rachel Gaulton, Zr
Jean Hall, Ng
Geoffrey Parkin, Hg
Nigel Penna, Gq
Paul Quinn, Hg

Visiting Professor:
Rick Brassington, Hg

Related Staff:
Peter Cunningham, Hg

University of Nottingham

Dept of Mineral Resources (2015)
University Park
Nottingham HG7 2RD
wpadmin@nottingham.ac.uk

University of Oxford

Dept of Earth Sciences (2015)
Department of Earth Sciences
South Parks Road
Oxford, Oxfordshire OX1 3AN
p. +44 1865 272000
reception@earth.ox.ac.uk
http://www.earth.ox.ac.uk/

Head:
Alex Halliday, Cs

Chair:
Christopher Ballentine, Xg
Phillip England, Gt

Professor:
Martin Brasier, Pg
Joe Cartwright, Gs
Shamita Das, Gtv
Donalf G. Fraser, Cg
Gideon Henderson, Cg
Hugh C. Jenkyns, (D), Leicester (UK), 1970, GrsCs
Samar Khatiwala
Conall Mac Niocaill, (D), GtgYm
Tamsin A. Mather, (D), Gv
Barry Parsons, Yd
David M. Pyle, (D), Cambridge, 1990, GviRh
Ros Rickaby, Gz
Mike Searle, Gt
Anthony B. Watts, (D), Durham (UK), 1970, GutYv
Bernard Wood, Gz
John Woodhouse, Yg

Associate Professor:
Stuart Robinson, (D), Oxford, 2002, PeGr
Karin Sigloch, (D), Princeton, 2008, YgsGt

Lecturer:
Roger Benson, Pg
Heather Bouman, Cg
Matt Friedman, Pg
Lars Hansen, Gz
Helen Johnson, Og
Richard Katz, Cg
Graeme Lloyd, Gs
Don Porcelli, Cg
Richard Walker, Zr

Emeritus:
Dave Waters, (D), Oxford, 1976, GpzGc

University of Plymouth

Dept of Earth Sciences (2018)
Drake Circus
Plymouth, Devon PL4 8AA
p. +44 (0)1752 584584
science.technology@plymouth.ac.uk
http://www.plymouth.ac.uk/schools/sogees

Head:
Mark Anderson, (D), Wales, Gct

Professor:
Antony Morris, (D), Edinburgh, 1990, YmGtu
Greogry Price, (D), Reading (UK), 1994, Gsr

Associate Professor:
Paul D. Cole, (D), 1990, Gvg
Stephen Grimes, (D), Cardiff, 1998, Cs
Martin Stokes, (D), Plymouth (UK), 1997, Gm
Graeme Taylor, Yg

Matthew Watkinson, (D), Open, 1989, Gs
Lecturer:
Sarah Boulton, (D), Edinburgh, 2005, Zr
Arjan Dijkstra, (D), Utrecht, 2001, Gi
Meriel E.J. FitzPatrick, (D), Plymouth (UK), 1992, PlgGr
Luca Menegon, (D), Padua, 2006, Gct
Andrew Merritt, (D), Leeds (UK), 2010, Ng
Kevin Page, (D), Univ Coll (UK), 1988, Gr
Christopher Smart, (D), Southampton (UK), 1993, Pg
Colin Wilkins, (D), James Cook, 1991, Eg
Emeritus:
Malcolm B. Hart, (D), London (UK), 1993, PmGur

University of Portsmouth

School of Earth and Environmental Sciences (2015)
Burnaby Road
Portsmouth, Hampshire PO1 3QL
p. +44 (0)23 9284 2257
sees.enquiries@port.ac.uk
http://www.sci.port.ac.uk/departments/academic/sees
Head:
Rob Strachan, (D), Keele, 1982, Cc
Professor:
Andrew Gale, (D), King's Coll (UK), 1984, PgGrCl
Jim Smith, (D), Ge
Craig D. Storey, (D), Leicester (UK), 2002, GptCc
Associate Professor:
David Giles, (D), NzGlm
Research Associate:
Emilie Braund, (D), Graz, 2011, Gz
Fay Couceiro, (D), On
Penny Lancaster, (D), Bristol, 2011, Gz
Robert Loveridge
Darren Naish
David Ray, (D)
Alan Raybould, (D)
Steve Sweetman, (D), Pg
Mark Whitton, (D), Portsmouth, 2008, Pg
Instructor:
Chris Dewdney, (D), Birkbeck, 1983, Yg
Gary Fones, (D), C Lancashire, Cm
Lecturer:
John Allen, (D), Southampton (UK), 1996, Og
Hooshyar Assadullahi
Philip Benson, (D)
Michelle Bloor, (D), Hg
Dean Bullen, (D), Gt
Anthony Butcher, (D), PlmZe
James Darling, (D), Bristol, 2009, Cs
Mike Fowler, (D), Imperial Coll, Gi
David Franklin, (D), Ym
Martyn Gardiner, (D)
Andy Gibson, (D), Eg
Michelle Hale, (D), Flinders, Og
Nick Koor
David K. Loydell, (D), Aberystwyth, 1989, GrPg
Nicholas Minter, (D), Bristol, 2007, Gs
Derek Rust, (D), Gt
Camen Solana, (D), Gv
Richard Teeuw, (D), Stirring (UK), 1985, AsGmZi
Melvin M. Vopson, (D), C Lancashire, 2002, Yg
Nick Walton, Hw
John Whalley, (D), Gc
Malcolm Whitworth, (D)
Adjunct Professor:
David Martill, (D), PvgPe

University of Reading

Soil Research Centre (B,M,D) (2015)
Department of Geography and Environmental Science
School of Human and Environmental Sciences
Whiteknights
Reading RG6 6AB
p. +44 (0)118 378 8911
shes@reading.ac.uk
http://www.reading.ac.uk/soil-research-centre
Professor:
Chris Collins, (D), Sb
Associate Professor:
Stuart Black, (D), Lancaster (UK), Cc
Chris Collins, (D), Sc
McGoff Hazel, (D), Liverpool (UK), Pg
Steve Robinson, (D), Sf
Liz Shaw, (D), Sb
Dr:
Joanna Clark, (D), Leeds (UK), Sc

University of South Wales

Geology Section (2015)
Department of Science
Pontypridd

University of Southampton

School of Ocean and Earth Science (B,M,D) ●☒ (2018)
University of Southampton Waterfront Campus
National Oceanography Centre Southampton
European Way
Southampton, Hampshire SO14 3ZH
p. +44 (0)23 8059 2011
soes@soton.ac.uk
http://www.southampton.ac.uk/oes
f: https://www.facebook.com/UoSOceanography
t: @OceanEarthUoS
Programs: Geology with Physical Geography (B); Geophysical Sciences (B); Oceanography (B); Oceanography with Physical Geography (B); Marine Biology with Oceanography (B); Geology (B,M), Geology with Study Abroad (M); Geophysics (M); Geophysics with study abroad (M); Engineering/Physics/Maths/Geophysics (M); Biology and Marine Biology (M); Marine Biology (M); Marine Biology with study abroad (M); Oceanography (M); Oceanography with French (M); Oceanography with study abroad (M); Foundation Year in Science
Professor:
Stephen Roberts, (D), Open (UK), 1986, Cg
Head of Physical Oceanography Research Group:
Alberto Naveira Garabato, (D), Liverpool (UK), 1999, Op
Head of Palaeoceanography and Palaeoclimate Research Group:
Paul A. Wilson, (D), Cambridge, 1995, GsCg
Head of NOCS Graduate School and Inspire:
Martin R. Palmer, (D), Leeds (UK), 1984, Cg
Head of Marine Biology & Ecology Research Group:
Jorg Wiedenmann, (D), Ulm (Germany), 2000, Ob
Head of Marine Biogeochemistry Research Group:
Christopher Mark Moore, (D), Southampton (UK), 2002, Ob
Head of Geology and Geophysics Research Group:
Justin Dix, (D), St Andrews, 1994, GuYuNx
Faculty Director of Graduate School:
Timothy A. Minshull, (D), Cambridge, 1990, Yr
Director, GAU-Radioanalytical, Professorial Fellow:
Phillip Warwick, (D), Southampton (UK), 1999, CaGe
Deputy Head of School Research and Enterprise:
Rachael James, (D), Cambridge, 1995, Oc
Deputy Head of School International:
Andy Cundy, (D), Southampton (UK), 1994
Deputy Head of School Education:
Chris Hauton, (D), Southampton (UK), 1995, Ob
Dean, Faculty of Environmental and Life Sciences:
Rachel A. Mills, (D), Cambridge, 1992, Cm
Professor:
Nicholas R. Bates, (D), Southampton (UK), 1995, Oc
Thomas Bibby, (D), Imperial Coll, 2003, Ob
Colin Brownlee, (D), Newcastle upon Tyne, Ob
Jonathan M. Bull, (D), Edinburgh, 1990, YrGct
Sybren Drijfhout, (D), Urtecht, 1992, Op
Gavin Foster, (D), Open, 2000, Csg
Tim Henstock, (D), Cambridge, 1994, YgrYe
Alan Kemp, (D), Edinburgh, 1985, Pe
Maeve Lohan, (D), Southampton (UK), 2003, Ob
Robert Marsh, (D), Southampton (UK), 2000, Op
John E.A Marshall, (D), Bristol, 1981, PlGro
Lisa McNeill, (D), Oregon State, 1998, GtYr
Duncan A. Purdie, (D), Wales, 1982, Ob
David Sims, (D), Plymouth (UK), 1994, Ob
Martin Solan, (D), National (Ireland), 2000, Ob
Damon A.H Teagle, (D), Cambridge, 1993, CgEmGp
Toby Tyrrell, (D), Edinburgh, 1993, OgPe

Head of Geochemistry Research Group:
Juerg M. Matter, (D), Swiss Fed Inst Tech, 2001, Ng
Associate Professor:
Jonathan Copley, (D), Southampton (UK), 1998, Ob
Thomas M. Gernon, (D), Bristol, 2007, ZgGvi
Ivan D. Haigh, (D), Southampton (UK), 2009, On
Ian C. Harding, (D), Cambridge, 1986, PmlPc
Antony Jensen, (D), Southampton (UK), 1982, Ob
Derek Keir, (D), Royal Holloway (UK), 2006, Gtv
Phyllis Lam, (D), Hawaii, 2004, Ob
Cathy Lucas, (D), Southampton (UK), 1993, Ob
Catherine A. Rychert, (D), Brown, 2007, Yg
Rex N. Taylor, (D), Southampton (UK), 1987, GvCa
Sven Thatje, (D), Bremen, 2003, Ob
Clive Trueman, (D), Bristol, 1997, Cg
Jessica H. Whiteside, (D), Columbia, 2006, Pe
Teaching and Research Fellow :
Hachem Kassem, (D), Southampton (UK), 2016, OnGsZi
SMMI Lecturer:
Steven Bohaty, (D), California (Santa Cruz), 2006, Og
Senior Tutor, Principle Teaching Fellow:
Simon R. Boxall, (D), Liverpool (UK), 1985, Op
Senior Tutor:
Andy J. Barker, (D), Wales, 1983, Gg
Senior Research Fellow:
Kenneth Collins, (D), Southampton (UK), 1979, Ob
NERC Advanced Senior Research Fellow:
Tom H.G Ezard, (D), Imperial Coll, 2007
Lecturer:
Maria C. D'Angelo, Ob
Phillip Fenberg, (D), California (San Diego), 2008, Ob
Jasmin A. Godbold, (D), Aberdeen, 2009, Ob
Phillip A. Goodwin, (D), Liverpool (UK), 2007, Pe
Nicholas Harmon, (D), Brown, 2007, Yg
Anna Hickman, (D), Southampton (UK), 2007, Og
Kevin Oliver, (D), E Anglia (UK), 2003, Op
Marc Rius, (D), Barcelona, 2008, Znn
Esther Sumner, (D), Bristol, 2009, Gs
Chuang Xuan, (D), Florida, 2010, Ym
Visiting Professor:
Ian Townend, (B), ETH (Switzerland), 1975
Emeritus Fellow:
Lawrence Hawkins, (D), Southampton (UK), 1985, Ob
Visiting Fellow:
Claudie Beaulieu, (D), Quebec, 2009, Op
Laura Grange, (D), Southampton (UK), 2005
Mathis P. Hain, Princeton, 2013
Torben Stichel, (D), Christian-Albrechts (Germany), 2011
Teaching Fellow, Project Manager for Oman Drilling Project:
Jude A. Coggon, (D), Durham (UK), 2010, Cg
Senior Research Fellow:
Matthew Cooper, (D), Cambridge, 1999, Oc
Royal Society University Research Fellow:
Rosalind M. Coggon, (D), Southampton (UK), 2006, Ce
Samantha J. Gibbs, (D), Cambridge, 2002, Zg
Ben A. Ward, (D), Southampton (UK), 2009, Ob

University of St. Andrews

School of Geography & Geosciences (2015)
Division of Geology
St. Andrews
Fife KY16 9ST
Emeritus:
Colin K. Ballantyne, (D), Edinburgh, 1981, ZyGml

Dept of Earth and Environmental Science (B,M,D) (2015)
Irvine Building
North St.
Fife, Scotland KY16 9AL
p. (+44) (0)1334 463940
earthsci@st-andrews.ac.uk
http://earthsci.st-andrews.ac.uk/
f: https://www.facebook.com/EarthSciStA/
t: @EarthSciStA
Director:
Richard Bates, (D), Wales, Yx
Ruth Robinson, (D), Penn State, 1997, Gs
Head:
Tony Prave, (D), Penn State, 1986, GgrGs
Associate Professor:
Andrea Burke, (D), MIT/WHOI, 2011, ClPc
Assistant Professor:
Timothy D. Raub, (D), Yale, 2008, YmGgPc
Research Associate:
Nicky Allison, (D), Edinburgh, 1994, Oc
Mark Claire, (D), Washington, As
Catherine Cole, (D), Southampton (UK), 2013, Cm
Ruth Hindshaw, (D), ETH (Switzerland), 2011, Cs
Gareth Izon, (D), Cg
Coralie Mills
James Rae, (D), Bristol, Cg
Vincent Rinterknecht, (D), CcGma
Lecturer:
Adriam Finch, Gz
Timothy Hill, (D), Edinburgh, 2003, Ge
Michael Singer, (D), California (Santa Barbara), 2003, Hg
John Walden, (D), Wolverhampton Poly, 1990, Ym
Robert Wilson, (D), W Ontario, 2003, Zn
Aubrey Zerkle, (D), Penn State, 2006, Co

University of Sunderland

Faculty of Applied Science (2015)
Edinburgh Building
City Campus
Chester Rd.
Sunderland SR1 3SD
p. (+44) 191 515 2000
john.macintyre@sunderland.ac.uk
http://www.sunderland.ac.uk/faculties/apsc/ourdepartments/cet/

University of Ulster

Dept of Environmental Sustainability (2015)
Jordanstown Campus
Shore Road
Newtown Abbey
environment@ulster.ac.uk
http://www.ulster.ac.uk/sustainability

University of Wales

Dept of Earth and Ocean Sciences (2015)
College of Cardiff
Main Building
Park Place
Cardiff CF1 3YE
p. +44 (0)29 208 74830
earth-ug@cf.ac.uk
http://www.cardiff.ac.uk/earth/
Professor:
Thomas Blenkinspo
Ian R. Hall
Richard Lisle
Chris MacLeod, Og
Wolfgang Maier
Paul Pearson, PmCg
Instructor:
Stephen Barker
Huw Davies
Andrew Kerr, Og
Jenny Pike, Og
Lecturer:
Tiego Alves, Og
Liz Bagshaw
Rhoda Ballinger, On
Peter Brabham, Ng
David Buchs
Alan Channing, Gd
Jose Constantine
T. C. Hales, Gt
Alan Hemsley, Pl
Tim Jones
C. Johan Lissenberg
Iain MacDonald, Ca
Rupert Perkins
Phil Renforth

David Reynolds
Henrik Sass, Co
Simon Wakefield
Emeritus:
Hazel Prichard, (D), EgGze
Laboratory Director:
Caroline Lear, Og
Tutorial Fellow:
Ian Fryett
Nick Rodgers, Xm

School of Ocean Sciences (2015)
Bangor University
Menai Bridge
Anglesey, Bangor LL59 5AB
p. (01248) 382851
oss011@bangor.ac.uk
http://www.bangor.ac.uk/oceansciences/
Director:
Colin Jago
Professor:
David Bowers
Alan Davies
Michel Kaiser
Hilary Kennedy
Chris Richardson
Tom Rippeth
James Scourse
John Simpson
David Thomas
Associate Professor:
Simon P. Neill, (D), Strathclyde, 2001, OnpOg
Instructor:
Jan Geert Hiddink
Stuart Jenkins
Lecturer:
Martin Austin
Jaco H. Baas
Paul Butler
Lui Gimenez
Mattias Green
Cara Hughes
Dei G. Huws, (D), Wales, 1992, YruNt
Suzanna Jackson
Lewis LeVay
Shelagh Malham
Irene Martins
Ian McCarthy
Gay Mitchelson-Jacob
Anna Pienkowski
Martin Skov
John Russel Turner
Katrien van Landeghem
Stephanie Wilson
Related Staff:
Timothy Whitton

Geography and Earth Sciences (2015)
Llandinam Building
Penglais Campus
Aberystwyth SY23 3DB
p. +44(0) 1970 622 606
dges@aber.ac.uk
http://www.aber.ac.uk/en/iges/
Director:
Neil Glasser
Head:
Rhys Jones
Professor:
Paul A. Brewer, (D), Gm
John Grattan
Matthew Hannah
Alun Hubbard
Bryn Hubbard
David Kay
Henry Lamb
Richard Lucas
Mark Macklin
Alex Maltman, (D), Illinois, 1973
Nick Pearce
Andrew D. Thomas, (D), Swansea, 1996, SbGmSf
Mark Whitehead
Michael Woods
Instructor:
Peter Abrahams
Peter Merriman
Andrew Mitchell
Helen Roberts
Stephen Tooth
Lecturer:
Charlie Bendall
Peter Bunting
Rachel Carr
Rhys Dafydd Jones
Sarah Davies
Carina Fearnley
Elizabeth Gagen
Hywel Griffiths
Kevin Grove
Andrew Hardy
Jesse Heley
Tom Holt
Gareth Hoskins
Tristram Irvine-Fynn
Cerys Jones
Bill Perkings
Kimberly Peters
George Petropoulos
Mitch Rose
Richard Williams
Sophie Wynne-Jones
Teaching Fellow:
Stefania Amici

Uruguay

Direccion Nacional de Mineria y Geologia de Uruguay

Direccion Nacional de Mineria y Geologia de Uruguay (2015)
Hervidero 2861
Montevideo, Montevideo 11800
p. + 5982 2001951
infomiem@miem.gub.uy
http://www.dinamige.gub.uy/

Universidad de la Republica Montevideo

Dept de Geologia (2015)
Avenida 18 de Julio 1968, Montevideo

Universidad de la Republica Oriental del Uruguay (UDELAR)

Instituto de Geología y Paleontología (2015)
Avenida 18 de Julio 1968, Montevideo
CP11 400
Montevideo 10773
http://www.fcien.edu.uy/menu2/estructura2/ingepa2.html

Deptartamento de Geografia (B) ☒ (2017)
Iguá 4225 Piso 14 Sur C.P: 11400
Montevideo, Montevideo 11400
p. (598-2) 525 15 52
geotecno@fcien.edu.uy
http://geografia.fcien.edu.uy/
Professor:
Virginia Fernández, (M), Girona, 2001, ZirZn
Assistant Professor:
Yuri Resnichenko, (M), la República, 2010, ZirZn
Related Staff:
Carlos Miguel, (B), Valladolid, 4, ZirSf
Virginia Pedemonte, (B), Fac de Arquitectura, 5, ZirZu

Dept de Suelos y Aguas (2015)
p. (598 2) 359 82 72
suelosyaguas@fagro.edu.uy
http://suelosyaguas.fagro.edu.uy/

Uzbekistan

Institute of Geology and Geophysics

http://www.ingeo.uz/

Institute of Mineral Resources

gpniimr@evo.uz
http://www.gpniimr.uz/

National University of Uzbekistan

Faculty of Geology (2015)
Tashkent
University City 100095
p. +998712460224
geology@nuu.uz
http://nuu.uz/geolog

State Committee for Nature Protection

100 159, Tashkent, pl. Independence, 5
info@uznature.uz
http://www.uznature.uz

State Committee of the Republic of Uzbekistan on Geology and Mineral Resources

11, T.Shevchenko str., Tashkent, Republic of Uzbekistan 100060
p. +998 (71) 256-8653
geolcom@bcc.com.uz
http://www.uzgeolcom.uz

Tashkent State Technical University

Faculty of Geology (2015)
Uzbekistan, Tashkent, 10095 Universitetskaya street, 2
p. +998712464600
TFTU_info@mail.ru

Uzbekistan National Oil and Gas Company - Uzbekneftegaz (UNG)

100047, city Street, Tashkent.
Istiqbol, 21
p. +998 (71) 233-5757
kans@uzneftegaz.uz
http://www.uzneftegaz.uz

Venezuela

Universidad Central de Venezuela

Inst de Ciencias de la Tierra (2015)
Los Chaguaramos, Apdo. 3895, 1010-A Caracas
p. 0212 6366236
coordinv@ciens.ucv.ve
http://www.coordinv.ciens.ucv.ve/investigacion/genci/sitios/35

Escuela de Geologia, Minas y Geofisica (2015)
Ciudad Universitaria, 47028 Caracas 1041 A

Universidad de la Este, Cumana

Dept de Geologia y Minas (2015)
Apartado Postal 245, Cumana (Estado Sucre)

Universidad de Los Andes

Dept de Geologia y Minas (2015)
Avenida 3, Independencia, La Hechlcera, Merida
ocamacho@ula.ve
http://llama.adm.ula.ve/pingenieria/index.php?option=com_content&view=article&id=313&Itemid=215

Escuela de Ingenieria Geologica (2015)
Av. Tulio Febres C., Merida 5101

Universidad de Oriente, Nucleo Bolivar

Escuela de Ciencias de la Tierra (2015)
Av. Universidad, Campus Universitario La Sabanita, Ciudad Bolivar

Universidad Simon Bolivar

Coordinacion de Ingenieria Geofisica (2015)
Valle de Sarteneja, Baruta, Edo. Miranda 80659, Caracas 1080
p. 9063545
coord-geo@usb.ve
http://www.gc.usb.ve/geocoordweb

Vietnam

Hanoi University of Mining & Geology

Faculty of Geology (A,B,M,D) O (2015)
Duc Thang Ward - North Tu Liem Distr.
Hanoi
p. +84-4-38387567
diachat@humg.edu.vn
http://khoadiachat.edu.vn
Enrollment (2015): B: 2800 (420) M: 205 (50) D: 24 (6)
Dean of Faculty:
Lam Van Nguyen, (D), Hanoi Univ of Mining and Geology, 2002, HwGeHg
Deputy Dean of Faculty:
Thanh Xuan Ngo, (D), Okayama, 2009, GtcGi

Hanoi University of Science

Dept of Environmental Science (2015)
334 Nguyen Trai St, Dist Thanh Xuan
Hanoi
p. 04-8584615/8581419
huse@vnu.edu.vn
http://www.huse.edu.vn

Institute for Environment Science and Technology (INEST) (2015)
1 Dai Co Viet Road
Hanoi
p. (844) 38681686
inest@mail.hut.edu.vn
http://inest.hut.edu.vn/trang-chu

Ho Chi Minh City University of Technology

Geology and Petroleum Engineering (2015)
268 Ly Thuong Kiet Street
District 10
Ho Chi Minh City
webmaster@hcmut.edu.vn
http://www.hcmut.edu.vn/en/

Ho Chi Minh University

Dept of Geology (2015)
227 Nguyen Van Cu St., Dist 5
Ho Chi Minh City, City S1
p. 84.08.8 355 271
khoadiachat@hcmuns.edu.vn
http://www.geology.hcmus.edu.vn/english

Vietnam Maritime University

Vietnam Maritime University (2015)
484 Lach Tray Road
Hai Phong City
p. 84.031.3735931
info@vimaru.edu.vn
http://www.vimaru.edu.vn

Water Resource University

Faculty of Water Resources Engineering & Environment (2015)
175 Tay Son Road, Dist Dong Da
Hanoi
p. 844 3852 2201
wru@wru.edu.vn

http://www.wru.edu.vn/en/web/ department-of-geoinformatics-and-surveying

Zambia

Copperbelt University

Mining Dept (B) (2015)
Kitwe
deansot@cbu.ac.zm
http://www.cbu.edu.zm/technology

University of Zambia

Dept of Metallurgy and Mineral Processing (B) (2015)
PO Box 32379
Lusaka
p. +360-21-1-250871
registrar@unza.zm
http://www.unza.zm/index.php?option=com_content&task=view&id=479&Itemid=574

Zimbabwe

Africa University

Faculty of Agriculture and Natural Sciences (B) (2015)
Fairview Rd (Off- Nyanga Rd)
PO Box 1320
Old Mutare, Mutare
p. +2632060075
info@africau.edu
http://www.africau.edu/academic/

University of Zimbabwe

Dept of Geology (B,M,D) (2015)
Building B047
University of Zimbabwe
P.O. Box MP167
Mount Pleasant, Harare
p. 303211 Ext. 15032
gchipari@science.uz.ac.zw
http://www.uz.ac.zw/index.php/2013-07-09-08-51-40/the-department-of-geology/226-sci/dept-sci/geology-dpt/826-dr-lrm-nhamo
Enrollment (2012): B: 27 (17) M: 1 (0) D: 3 (1)
Chair:
LRM Nhamo
Lecturer:
Trendai Jnila, (D)
Isidro Rafael Vit Manuel, (D)
Maideyi Lydia Meck, (D)

Dept of Geography & Environmental Science (B,M,D) (2015)
PO Box MP167
Mount Pleasant, Harare
p. +263-04-303211
geography@arts.uz.ac.zw
http://www.uz.ac.zw/science/geography/

Institute of Mining Research (B) (2015)
PO Box MP167
Mount Pleasant, Harare
p. +263-4-336418
speka@science.uz.ac.zw
http://www.uz.ac.zw/

Dept of Mining Engineering (B) (2015)
PO Box MP167
Mount Pleasant, Harare
p. (263) 4 -3335 x ext: 17089)
kudzie@eng.uz.ac.zw
http://www.uz.ac.zw/index.php/mining-about

Dept of Geoinformatics and Surveying (B) (2015)
PO Box MP167
Mount Pleasant, Harare
p. +263 772 318 473
bukalt@eng.uz.ac.zw
http://www.uz.ac.zw/index.php/fac-of-eng/

THESES AND DISSERTATIONS, 2018

The following section documents all of the 2018 geoscience dissertations and theses from U.S. and Canadian institutions that were reported to GeoRef Information Services. If you have questions about the data or to make sure your institution's data is included in the future, please contact Monika Long at ml@americangeosciences.org.

Auburn University

Cartwright, Jennifer H., *Volatile and Sr isotope analysis of melt inclusions from the Bandelier Tuff, Valles Caldera, New Mexico; insights into pre-eruptive magma conditions*

De Marchi, Leticia Pacetta, *Marine resurge sequences at Flynn Creek impact structure, Tennessee, USA*

Eckes, Samantha Waverley, *Exploring the use of ground penetrating radar for determining floodplain function of restored streams in the Gulf Coastal Plain, Alabama*

Griffin, Kayla M., *$^{40}Ar/^{39}Ar$ diffusion and age constraints in muscovite from the Ruby Mountains, northeastern Nevada*

Salisbury, Michael Evan, *Analysis of the D'Olive Creek watershed; identifying the local drivers that have led to stream degradation*

Siddique, Sumaiya Tul, *Social vulnerability and earthquake impact modeling in Federal Emergency Management Agency (FEMA) Region IV (Southeast U.S.)*

Speetjens, Sara, *Magma evolution and processes of the Ashi Volcano, NW Tibet, China; Sr isotope studies of plagioclase crystals*

Wilson, Theodore Jeffrey, *Pyrite biomineralization and arsenic sequestration at a Florida industrial site; imaging and geochemical analysis*

Australian National University

Sieber, Melanie Jutta, *Experimental investigation of the fluid driven carbonation of serpentinites and spinel-peridotites; implications for the carbon and trace element cycle in the forearc region of the mantle wedge*

Timmerman, Suzette, *Diamonds; time capsules of volatiles and the key to dynamic Earth evolution*

Bowling Green State University

Kanters, Christopher James, *The nature of gold mineralization in the unoxidized zone of the Mesquite Mine, CA*

Ramanayaka Mudiyanselage, Asanga, *Analyzing vertical crustal deformation induced by hydrological loadings in the US using integrated Hadoop/GIS framework*

Saalfield, Megan A., *Petrology of the 1877 eruption of Cotopaxi Volcano, Ecuador; insight on magma evolution and storage*

Smeltz, Jonathan Brett, *Dedolomitization and alkali-silica reactions in Ohio-sourced dolostone aggregates*

Brigham Young University

Checketts, Hannah Nicole, *Dissolved organic carbon and dissolved metal pulses during snowmelt runoff in the upper Provo River watershed, Utah, USA*

Deng, Han, *Assessing tsunami risk in southwest Java, Indonesia; paleotsunami deposits and inundation modeling*

Gunnell, Evan R., *Lithofacies and sequence architecture of the upper Desert Creek Sequence (Middle Pennsylvanian, Paradox Formation) in the Greater Aneth Field, southern Paradox Basin, Utah*

Hale, Colin Andrus, *Strontium isotopes; a tracer for dust and flow processes in an alpine catchment*

Lewis, Robert Corbin, *Linear dune morphometrics in Titan's Belet sand sea and a comparison with the Namib sand sea*

Northrup, Dustin Shawn, *A geomorphological study of yardangs in China, the Altiplano/Puna of Argentina, and Iran as analogs for yardangs on Titan*

Packer, Brian Noel, *Mercury and dissolved organic matter dynamics during snowmelt in a montane watershed, upper Provo River, Utah*

Ritter, Geoffrey William, *Lithofacies and sequence architecture of the upper Paradox Formation (Middle Pennsylvanian) in the subsurface northern Blanding Subbasin, Paradox Basin, Utah*

Smith, Katelynn Marie, *A geophysical and geological analysis of a regressive-phase Lake Bonneville deposit, Pilot Valley, NV*

Spilker, Braxton Clark, *Writing and designing a chapter on Mercury and Pluto for the textbook Exploring the Planets (explanet.info)*

Stuart, Kevin L., *Discovery of possible paleotsunami deposits in Pangandaran and Adipala, Java, Indonesia using grain size, XRD, and ^{14}C analyses*

Sulaeman, Hanif Ibadurrahman, *Discovery of paleotsunami deposits along eastern Sunda Arc; potential for megathrust earthquakes in Bali*

Tuttle, Trevor Robinson, *Paleo-environmental interpretations and weathering effects of the Mowry Shale from geochemical analysis of outcrop samples in the western margin of the Wind River basin near Lander, Wyoming*

Washburn, Alex M., *Constraining Kura and south Caspian Basin Maikop source rock stratigraphy, deposition, and timing using chemostratigraphy of redox-sensitive trace metals and Re-Os geochronology*

California State University at Fresno

Liu, Christine, *Near-surface geophysical imaging of the internal structure of El Capitan Meadow rock avalanche in Yosemite National Park, California*

Perez, Magaly, *Taphonomy of brachiopods from Devonian carbonate records*

Pytlak, Alexandra, *Petrogenesis of the Pine Flat Complex of the Sierra Nevada; a geochemical investigation of differentiation within the crust*

Rarick, John Carleton, *Variation in exoplanetary structure and mineralogy from observed stellar metallicities, and related geophysical implications*

California State University at Long Beach

Cole, Matthew C., *Periodic hydraulic tests in a fractured crystalline bedrock*

Davidson, Benjamin P., *Deformation of the tectonic erratics at Henderson Summit, Vinini Creek, Mineral Hill, and Lone Mountain in Eureka County, Nevada*

Davis, Maia C., *Spatial and geochemical characterization of an anomalous, map-scale dolomite breccia in the Monterey Formation, Santa Maria Basin, California*

De Baun, Derik K., *Silica replacement in the southern White Pine Range, east central Nevada; a stable isotope study*

Ellis, Weston, *Determining spatial and temporal variability of percolation rates from a riverside recharge basin using fiber optic distributed temperature sensing*

Faulkner, Kirsten E., *A recharge analysis of the Indian Wells Basin, California using geochemical analysis of tritium and radiocarbon*

Florence, Meghan M., *Lithology of the Alamos Canyon Siltstone Member of the Peace Valley Formation and the formation of dolomite, Ridge Basin, California*

Harlow, Jeanette, *Assessing spatial and temporal patterns of groundwater recharge on Catalina Island, California, from soil water balance modeling*

Santana, Roman, *Integrating inquiry-based physical science lessons with English language development*

Shimer, Peter A., *Rifting and inversion along the Palos Verdes fault zone, San Pedro Shelf, offshore Southern California*

Vasquez, Elizabeth E., *Potentially active faults in north central Mongolia*

Weller, Ryan M., *Compositional and diagenetic controls of hardness in siliceous mudstones of the Monterey Formation, Belridge oil field, CA; implications for fracture development*

California State University at Northridge

Burkert, Alexander, *Identifying changes in the active, dead, and dormant microbial community structure across a chronosequence of ancient Alaskan permafrost*

California State University, East Bay

McEvilly, Adrian Thomas, *Seismic imaging of a portion of the West Chabot Fault at California State University, East Bay*

Veale, Nathan, *Nitrate in California; isotopic composition and spatial trends in groundwater*

Carleton University

Craig, Andrew Thomas, *Using heated column experiments to investigate the effects of in-situ thermal recovery operations on groundwater geochemistry in Cold Lake, Alberta*

Greenman, Wilder, *Characterization of a ~1 billion year old carbonate ramp in the Brock Inlier, Arctic Canada*

Harris, Kyle D., *The use of distributed acoustic sensing for 4D monitoring using vertical seismic profiles; results from the Aquistore CO2 storage project*

Kang, He, *Stratigraphy, sedimentology, and diagenesis of Ordovician outliers, northern Ottawa-Bonnechere Graben, central Ontario*

Roussel, Stephanie Ann, *Metal transport near a tailings facility in the Alberta Oil Sands*

Thompson, Michael Glen Wenstob, *A multidisciplinary palaeoenvironmental reconstruction of the Campanian Foremost Formation of southern Alberta*

College of William and Mary

Clyne, Elisabeth Rose, *Assessment of the high-resolution sediment gravity flow record in Prince William Sound, Alaska*

Mitchell, Molly, *Impacts of sea level rise on tidal wetland extent and distribution*

Williams, Bethany Lynn, *The role of ecological interactions in saltmarsh geomorphic processes*

Colorado School of Mines

Abbuhl, Brittany M., *An analysis of the stratigraphy, sedimentology and reservoir quality of the Dean sandstone within Borden and Dawson Counties,*

Midland Basin, West Texas
Akarapatima, Thanyanat, *Model comparisons of multivariate statistics with theoretical predictions of elastic properties in sandstones*
Alford, Lee, *Hydrothermal evolution of Au-bearing pyrite-quartz veins and their association to base metal veins in Central City, Colorado*
Alrashed, Ahmed Ali, *Lateral reservoir heterogeneities and their impacts on stress shadowing in the Eagle Ford reservoir*
Azizian, Mitra, *Stochastic inversion of seismic data by implementing image quilting to build a litho-facies model for reservoir characterization of Delhi Field, LA*
Bane, Lauren T., *Integrated analysis, reservoir characterization, and resource potential of the Niobrara Formation; Lowry Bombing Range, Arapahoe and Adams County, CO*
Batbayar, Kherlen, *Source rock quality, depositional and geochemical characterization of the Khoot Basin in Mongolia*
Beisman, James Joseph, *Hydrogeochemical model development and advanced numerical simulation of alpine hillslope geochemical response to temperature-induced hydrologic changes*
Berger, Michael Lee, *Geology and mineralization of the Pajarita Mountain layered peralkaline syenitic pluton-hosted REE-Zr prospect, Mescalero Apache Reservation, New Mexico*
Bratton, Tom, *Stress induced changes in elastic wave attributes in the Wattenberg Field, Colorado, USA*
Bray, Matthew P., *Velocity, attenuation, and microseismic uncertainty analysis of the Niobrara and Montney reservoirs*
Bulguroglu, Muhammed Emin, *Influence of dolerites on coal rank, maturity and total gas content in coal bed methane play, Botswana*
Chen, Tingting, *Integrated reservoir characterization in Delhi Field, Louisiana; a continuous CO_2 injection EOR project*
Cheney, Alexander King, *Controls on deposition, lithologic variability, and reservoir heterogeneity of prolific Western Interior shelf sandstone reservoirs; Tocito and El Vado Sandstones, San Juan Basin, NM*
Coleman, Robert D., *The tectonic evolution of Taranaki Basin, offshore New Zealand*
Copley, Matthew Kupecz, *Seismic characterization of Niobrara fluid and rock properties; a 4D study and multicomponent (3C) analysis*
Do, Mimi, *Nature and distribution of clay minerals in high net-to-gross deepwater fans; Taranaki Basin outcrops, New Zealand case study*
Dunnington, Lucila, *Geothermal heat for remote acid mine drainage remediation; a laboratory and modelling study*
Eker, Ilkay, *Mass transport within the fracture-matrix systems of unconventional shale reservoirs; application to primary production and EOR in Eagle Ford*
El Khoury, Paul, *Integration of rock physics and facies-based seismic inversion for reservoir characterization of the Ordovician Red River Formation at Cedar Creek Anticline, Williston Basin, USA*
Foiles, Lauren C., *R-mode factor analysis of stream sediment data in the Fairbanks mining district, east-central Alaska*
Foster, Lauren, *Modeling climate change impacts to Rocky Mountain headwater hydrology*
Frieman, Ben M., *U-Pb and Lu-Hf LA-ICP-MS detrital zircon and structural investigations in the Abitibi Subprovince, Canada, with implications for Archean geodynamic processes and deformation behavior along goldbearing, crustal-scale faults*
Fryer, Rosemarie C., *Quantification of the bed-scale architecture of submarine depositional environments and application to lobe deposits of the Point Loma Formation, California*
Gentry, Emilie, *Characterizing the southwestern extent of the Norumbega fault system, a mid-Paleozoic crustal-scale strike-slip fault system in the New England Appalachians*
Gordon, Andrew, *Rock property characteristics and correlation from outcrop to wireline logs of the Green River Formation, Red Wash Field, eastern Uinta Basin*
Halford, Daniel Thomas, *Isotopic analyses of helium from wells location in the Four Corners area, Southwestern US*
Hein, Annette, *Drought on the North American High Plains; modeling effects of vegetation, temperature and rainfall perturbations on regional hydrology*
Henry, Richard L., *Low temperature aqueous solubility of fluorite at temperatures of 5, 25, and 50°C and ionic strengths up to 0.72M*
Huels, Matthew L., *New opportunities in the mature fields of the central Illinois Basin; a case study of the Mode Field, Shelby County, IL, USA*
Joewondo, Nerine, *Pore structure of micro- and mesoporous mudrocks based on nitrogen and carbon dioxide sorption*
Johnson, Andrew Charles, *Constructing a Niobrara reservoir model using outcrop and downhole data*
Karasozen, Ezgi, *Seismotectonics of Turkey and Iran from calibrated earthquake relocations*
Keator, Allison Elizabeth, *Geologic characterization and reservoir properties of the upper Smackover Formation, Haynesville Shale, and lower Bossier Shale, Thorn Lake Field, Red River Parish, Louisiana, USA*
Khademian, Zoheir, *Computational framework for studying seismicity induced by rock engineering activities*
Kramer, Shawn P., *Structural analysis and tectonostratigraphic evolution of the Reinga Basin, offshore northwestern New Zealand*
LaPorte, David, *Evaluating landslide risk management in Guatemala City through a study of risk perception and behavior changes*
Levon, Taylor, *Workflow development and sensitivity investigation of offset well-to-well interference through 3D fracture modeling and reservoir simulation in the Denver-Julesburg Basin*
Li, Xun, *A unified interpretation of nonlinear elasticity in granular solids*
Liu, Zhuangxiaoxue, *Seismic geomorphology of continental margin evolution in the Late Cretaceous to Neogene of the Browse Basin, northwest Australia*
Lopez, Shawn, *Peloid characterization and diagenesis of the A chalk, Niobrara Formation, Denver Basin, CO*
Malenda, Helen Fitzgerald, *From grain to floodplain; evaluating heterogeneity of floodplain hydrostratigraphy using sedimentology, geophysics, and remote sensing*
McDowell, Bryan Patrick, *Application of a custom-built, 400 MHz NMR probe on Eagle Ford Shale core plug samples, Gonzales and La Salle Counties, Texas*
Melo, Aline Tavares, *Integrated quantitative interpretation of multiple geophysical data for geology differentiation*
Minnick, Matthew, *Multi-agent simulation and geospatial infrastructure for oil shale production and water resource utilization in the Piceance Basin*
Nandy, Dipanwita, *Dolomitization and porosity evolution of middle Bakken Member, Elm Coulee Field and facies characterization, chemostratigraphy and organic-richness of upper Bakken Shale, Williston Basin*
Ou, Liwei, *Experimental study on the anisotropy of unconventional tight reservoirs; joint ultrasonic and electrical measurements under pressure*
Podzorski, Hannah L., *Expression of geochemical controls on water quality in Loch Vale, Rocky Mountain National Park*
Pommer, Maxwell, *Biochemical and chemical controls on sedimentation, sequence stratigraphy, and diagenesis, in the Phosphoria rock complex (Permian), Rocky Mountain region, USA*
Rodriguez Jeangros, Nicolas, *Development of a high-resolution land cover product of the Rocky Mountains with application to carbon concentrations in its streams; assessing anthropogenic, climatological, and morphological contributions*
Ruybal, Christopher J., *Spatio-temporal assessment of groundwater resources in the Denver Basin aquifer system*
Safipour, Roxana G., *Electrical and electromagnetic methods for submarine massive sulfide exploration; a case study of the Palinuro Seamount, Tyrrhenian Sea*
Sams, Bonnie C., *Contact metamorphism of the Mancos Shale; impacts on solute release and weatherability in the East River valley, Gothic, CO*
Schindler, Mandy, *On pore-scale imaging and elasticity of unconsolidated sediments*
Smith, Alyssa, *Tracing the magmatic to hydrothermal evolution of the Mount Rosa Complex, Colorado; textural and chemical evidence using zircon*
Swift Bird, Kenneth, *Hydrogeological controls of uranium and arsenic mobility in groundwater of the Pine Ridge Reservation, South Dakota*
Thatch, Lauren M., *Untangling water management and groundwater extraction signals in the California Central Valley; an integrated hydrologic model and remote sensing synthesis approach*
Timm, Kira K., *Geological and geochemical assessment of the Sharon Springs Member of the Pierre Shale and the Niobrara Formation within the Canon City Embayment, south-central Colorado*
Vazquez-Garcia, Oscar, *Tectonic synthesis of the deepwater Lamprea thrust and fold belt, offshore Burgos Basin, western Gulf of Mexico*
Wang, Cong, *A multi-scale, multi-continuum and multi-physics model to simulate coupled fluid flow and geomechanics in shale gas reservoirs*
Wang, Jianqiao, *Fluvial fan architecture, facies, and interaction with lake; lessons learned from the Sunnyside Delta interval of the Green River Formation, Uinta Basin, Utah*
Wibowo, Noor C., *Seismic reservoir characterization of the Najmah Formation, Raudhatain Field, north Kuwait*
Zeeck, Lauren R., *The role of flashing in the formation of high-grade, low-sulfidation epithermal deposits; a case study from the Omu Camp in Hokkaido, Japan*
Zhao, Haochen, *A new image processing algorithm for geological structure identification of rock slopes based on drone-captured images*

Columbia University

Rabinowitz, Hannah, *The seismogenic potential of subducting sediments*

Cornell University

Anderson, Brendan Matthew, *The evolution of unusual shell morphologies in fossil and living Turritellidae (Gastropoda)*

Root, Jonathan, *Petrological and isotopic evidence for diagenetic evolution in the Cherry Valley carbonates and adjacent mudrocks of the Marcellus "Shale" from West Virginia, Pennsylvania, and New York*

Dalhousie University

Campbell, Taylor Jane, *Seismic stratigraphy and architecture of the Jurassic Abenaki Margin, at Cohasset-Migrant, and potential for distal organic-rich facies*

Ellis, Ben, *Geochronology of the Chicoutimi gneiss belt, St. Fulgence, Quebec*

Evangelatos, John, *The genesis and evolution of Makarov Basin, Arctic Ocean*

Frail-Gauthier, Jennifer Lena, *Ecological interactions and geological implications of Foraminifera and associated meiofauna in temperate salt marshes of Eastern Canada*

Keltie, Erin E., *An experimental study of the role of contamination in the formation of chromitites in the Ring of Fire Intrusive Suite*

Kerford, Graham, *Structure of the Mohorovicic discontinuity (MOHO) at the East Pacific Rise from 3D multichannel seismic reflection data*

McLeod, Sarah, *Shortening of southern Tibet*

Soukup, Maya, *Testing a muogenic isotope method to monitor relief generation over millions of years*

Thomsen, Dana, *Investigating fluid exchange between granitic hosts, dykes and enclaves in the South Mountain Batholith*

VanderWal, Jacob, *Calcite fracture-filling; a proxy for geothermal energy systems, and implications for the tectonic history of the northeastern Midland Valley, Scotland*

Wong, Juan Carlos, *Petroleum system modelling of potential Lower Jurassic source rocks along the Scotian Margin*

Woods, Kate, *An experimental study of the effect of water on chromite solubility in komatiite*

Drake University

Wayne, Kimberly S., *Keeping them in the STEM pipeline; a phenomenology exploring the experiences of young women and underrepresented minorities in a long-term STEM enrichment program*

Emporia State University

Rice, James Robert, *Development of a new, direct-push-based, geophysical and geochemical approach for groundwater tracer tests*

Florida International University

Burke, Brandon, *The sedimentation and diagenesis of a Miocene-Pliocene mixed-system; Cibao Basin, Dominican Republic*

George Mason University

LaCivita, Lisa Frances, *Amphibian monitoring for ecosystem services, citizen engagement and public policy*

George Washington University

Green, Matthew J., *Clarence King & his friends; on mountaineering in the American West*

Idaho State University

Shebala, Rudy R., *Horses and grazing on the Navajo Indian Reservation*

Illinois State University

Harris, Frances Claire, *Understanding 1-D vertical flux dynamics in a low-gradient stream; an assessment of stage as a control of vertical hyporheic exchange*

Honings, Joseph, *Modeling climate change impacts on water balance components of the Mackinaw River watershed, central Illinois*

Rutte, Monique M., *Analysis of short-term erosion of the St. Peter Sandstone in Lasalle County, Illinois*

Lakehead University

Beardy, Ethan, *Pyrite characterization at Musselwhite Mine*

Dolega, Simon, *Geochemistry of shallow and deep water Archean meta-iron formations and their post-depositional alteration in western Superior Province, Canada*

Gelinas, Brigitte Rachel, *Geology and geochemistry of the Laird Lake property and associated gold mineralization, Red Lake greenstone belt, northwestern Ontario*

Hietala, Jeremy, *Bar formation on the sub-aqueous sand sheet of the gravel river delta, Lake Superior*

Hinz, Sheree Laina Kirsten, *Geochemistry and petrography of the ultramafic metavolcanic rocks in the eastern portion of the Shebandowen greenstone belt, northwestern Ontario*

Jedemann, Andrew, *The geochemistry and petrology of the Boyer showing within the Coldwell alkaline complex*

Killins, Spencer, *Kimberlite indicator mineral analysis above kimberlite pipe DO18, Northwest Territories*

Leale, Carina, *The effects of fire, harvest and compound disturbance on soil carbon and nitrogen stores in a boreal mixed wood forest*

O'Brien, Sean, *Petrology of the Crystal Lake Gabbro and the Mount Mollie Dyke, Midcontinent Rift, northwest Ontario*

Ojala, Teegan, *Sequence stratigraphic and architectural analysis of a 1.83 Ga turbidite system; the Rove Formation, northwestern Ontario*

Veneruz, Dominique, *Biotite characterization at Musselwhite Mine*

Louisiana State University

Dailey, Sarah, *The sedimentology and origins of a giant mass transport complex; the Nataraja Slide, Arabian Sea*

Massachusetts Institute of Technology

Flaspohler, Genevieve Elaine, *Statistical models and decision making for robotic scientific information gathering*

Gruen, Danielle S., *Biogeochemical and phylogenetic signals of Proterozoic and Phanerozoic microbial metabolisms*

Kipp, Lauren, *Radium isotopes as tracers of boundary inputs of nutrients and trace elements to the coastal and open ocean*

Lerner, Paul, *Scavenging and transport of thorium radioisotopes in the North Atlantic Ocean*

Mississippi State University

Dubois, Kalli Alyse, *Regional stratigraphy and lithologic characterization of the Tuscaloosa marine shale in southwest Mississippi*

Gjyshja, Zhaneta, *Petrographic and chemical analysis of grinding stones collected by the Shkodra Archaeological Project*

Lomago, Brendan Michael, *Subsurface framework and fault timing in the Missourian Granite Wash interval, Stiles Ranch and Mills Ranch Fields, Wheeler County, Texas*

Missouri University of Science and Technology

Akturk, Onur, *Reprocessing of the 2 Hz P-P data from the Blackfoot 3C-2D survey with special reference to multicomponent seismic processing*

Al-Hakeem, Aamer, *3D seismic attribute analysis and machine learning for reservoir characterization in Taranaki Basin, New Zealand*

Alfarge, Dheiaa Khafief Khashan, *Integrated study on the applicability of CO_2-EOR in unconventional liquids rich reservoirs*

Alkhamis, Mohammed Mousa M., *New wellbore-integrity classification for gas migration problems and new cement formulations using graphene nano platelets to prevent gas migration through cement*

Ariani, Nadia, *Data analysis of low-salinity waterflooding to enhance the oil recovery in sandstone reservoirs*

Awad, Walaa K., *Paleogene-early Neogene palynomorphs from the eastern Equatorial Atlantic and southeastern Florida, USA; biostratigraphy and paleoenvironmental implications*

Bashir, Nathainail, *The utility of geophysical techniques to image the shallow subsurface in karst areas in Missouri*

Cinar, Yusuf Alper, *The importance of chemical grouting materials for optimum mechanical performance with different soil conditions*

Demir, Yasin, *Reprocessing of 3C-2D seismic reflection data from the Spring Coulee Field, Alberta*

Ellafi, Abdulaziz Mustafa E., *An integrated method for understanding the fluid flow behavior and forecasting well deliverability in gas condensate reservoirs with water aquifer drive*

Hadi, Farqad Ali, *Geomechanical characterizations and correlations to reduce uncertainties of carbonate reservoir analysis*

Kidanu, Shishay T., *GIS-based spatial analysis coupled with geophysical imaging to identify and evaluate factors that control the formation of karst sinkholes in southwestern Missouri*

Liu, Lin, *Lithospheric layering and thickness beneath the contiguous United States*

Unkaracalar, Ersin Erdem, *3D seismic imaging of submarine stratovolcanic and salt structures beneath the Taranaki Basin, New Zealand and the Gulf of Mexico*

Wu, Yuxing, *The role of flexural slip in the development of chevron folds*

Montana State University

Bartos, Jeffrey Michael, *Mining for empire; gold, American engineers, and transnational extractive capitalism, 1889-1914*

Murray State University

Roberson, Philip, *A quantitative analysis of intermediate forms within Astarte from the Atlantic Coastal Plain*

North Dakota State University

Bohn, Meyer Patrick, *Predicting soil health and function of the Barnes catena using evapotranspiration, vegetative, geologic, and terrain attributes in the eastern glaciated plains of North Dakota*

Northern Arizona University

Benson, Christopher Warren, *16,000 years of paleoenvironmental change from the Lake Peters-Schrader area, northeastern Brooks Range, Alaska*

Gerber, Creighton C., *Digital recording and interpretation of rock art at Walnut Canyon National Monument*

Northern Illinois University

Engler, Ty M., *Upper Miocene history of the West Antarctic ice sheet inferred* *from sequence stratigraphy, clay mineralogy, and paleoecology of the Andrill 1B core*

Kerwin, Sean Patrick, *Sodic alteration in magmatic-hydrothermal systems*

Lohani, Garima, *Investigating the effect of magma viscosity changes on the eruption style of Masaya caldera complex, Nicaragua*

Moore, Justin Wayne, *Spatial feedback as a mechanism to improve topographic map literacy using the augmented reality sandbox*

Olson, Elizabeth Joy, *Hydrogen, carbon, and oxygen isotopes in Prosopis sp. trees; a new climate proxy for Holocene paleoclimate in the Atacama Desert, Chile*

Perdziola, Stephen, *Late Holocene oxygen isotope record of hydroclimate variability in Nicaragua from Lake Asososca*

Reddick, Angela D., *Assessing the Jurassic Cleveland-Lloyd bone bed predator trap hypothesis by statistical comparison of Allosaurus fragilis and Pleistocene La Brea Canis dirus femora*

Rock, Marlena Joyce, *An experimental study of lead and zinc solubility in a hydrothermal fluid*

Ohio State University

Aaron, Fransiscus X., *Comparing mud volcano characteristics and association with oil and gas*

Ahmad Zulkifli, Siti Faizura, *Carbon export at Shatsky Rise during Maastrichtian from 67.776 to 67.704 million years ago using marine barite accumulation rate as proxy*

Amooie, Mohammad Amin, *Fluid mixing in multiphase and hydrodynamically unstable porous-media flows*

Bell, Matthew J., *Interactive presentations as accessories to museum exhibits*

Bonin, Clay, *Development of water-based fracturing fluids*

Bradley, Cole E., *Measurement of anthropogenic gadolinium in the Scioto and Olentangy river system using inductively coupled plasma mass spectrometry (ICP-MS)*

Brady, Allyson, *Subsurface conditions promoting groundwater contamination at Elkhart, Indiana*

Brooks, Zuri M., *Stable isotopes 18O and D in the Olentangy River*

Clark, Casey, *The geology and hydrogeology of the Teays-Mahomet aquifer system in east-central Illinois*

Fuad, Mohamad Irfan, *A comparison of high and low resolution two-dimensional seismic data at Integrated Ocean Drilling Program Expedition 308 Site U1320, Brazos-Trinity Basin IV, northwestern Gulf of Mexico*

Gilbert, Daniel, *Estimating relative surface ages and wetting histories in ice-free Antarctic regions using geochemical analysis of soils*

Green, Adam, *Constraining magma evolution mechanisms along the Galapagos spreading center between 102°W and 82°W through trace element geochemistry*

Hishammudin, Anis Hidayah, *Paleoproductivity from barite in Maastrichtian samples from the southern high of Shatsky Rise (ODP Site 1209)*

Keister, Laura E., *Rock properties of Silurian Niagaran reef carbonates in Michigan after CO2 injection*

Keister, Laura E., *Rock properties of Silurian Niagaran reef carbonates in Michigan after CO_2 injection*

Kessler, Cody M., *Changes in gastropod ecology in response to the formation of the Isthmus of Panama*

Kinash, Nicole M., *Recovery and lithologic analysis of sediment from Holes UT-GOM2-1-H002 and H005, in Green Canyon 955, northern Gulf of Mexico*

Lamantia, Kara A., *Comparison of glacier loss on Qori Kalis, Peru and Mt. Kilimanjaro, Tanzania over the last decade using digital photogrammetry and stereo analysis*

Lary, Brent, *Use of noble gas and hydrocarbon geochemistry to determine the source of hydrocarbons in Gulf of Mexico gas hydrates*

Majumdar, Urmi, *Gas hydrate occurrence and volume estimate in the northern Gulf of Mexico*

Mason, Keith, *An analysis of shallow sediment overlying gas hydrate, Green Canyon Block 955 (GC-955), Gulf of Mexico, USA*

Mitchin, Jasper I., *Modeling pressure-temperature conditions of garnet amphibolite from the Himalaya of northwestern Bhutan*

Mohd Amin, Ariff Izzuddin, *Modelling evolution of parental magma in the Siqueiros transform for the East Pacific Rise 4° to 14°*

Mohd, Ahmad Farhan, *A comparative study of the mineralogy and petrology of the Mazraeh Cu-Fe skarn deposit, Iran and the Cu-Fe skarn deposit in the Edong ore district, China*

Morgal, Louis P., *Ground water contamination of the old O-field site Aberdeen Proving Ground MD*

O'Malley, Michael D., *A multi-channel seismic interpretation of the Canterbury Basin offshore New Zealand and potential hydrocarbon sources*

Oborn, Collin A., *Examination of a method; testing the Kelley-Barton method on the Herdubreid Tuya, northern volcanic zone, Iceland*

Ross, James J., *A literature survey of noble gas solubility measurements in formation brines to interpret tracer experiments*

Russell, Paul, *Tsunami stratigraphy in a salt pond on St. Croix, US Virgin Islands*

Sazali, Nurnadira, *Modelling of fractional crystallization of basalts along the Galapagos spreading center*

Schlessman, Sydney, *Was there an increase in export productivity of the biological pump during the Eocene Thermal Maximum three?*

Sudilovsky, Stas, *Gravity and magnetic investigation of the Surtsey Volcano of Iceland's Vestmannaeyjar Archipelago*

Trotter, Bennett, *Pore pressure prediction in the Point Pleasant Formation in the Appalachian Basin, in parts of Ohio, Pennsylvania, and West Virginia*

Vennemeyer, William D., *Principal component analysis of the geochemistry of sediments from boreholes CRP-2 and CRP-3, McMurdo Sound, Antarctica*

Wu, Qingting, *Distribution and mapping of high-magnesium calcite vs. aragonite in stromatolites of Storr's Lake, San Salvador, Bahamas*

Yang, Zhe, *Origin of pyrite concretions from the Dunkirk Shale Member of the Canadaway Formation (Devonian), western New York*

Oklahoma State University

Missi, Charles, *Physical, chemical and isotopic characteristics of groundwater and surface water in the Lake Chilwa Basin, Malawi*

Nyalugwe, Victor, *Lithospheric structure beneath the Mesozoic (~140-~110 Ma) Chilwa alkaline province (CAP) in southern Malawi and northeastern Mozambique*

Pennsylvania State University at University Park

Pourpoint, Maeva, *Lithospheric and glacial structures from seismic wave analysis in Greenland and Antarctica*

Valdez, Robert Dennis, *Mechanical behavior of major plate boundary fault systems; insights into the stress state of the Nankai subduction-accretion complex offshore SW Japan and slip stability of the Alpine fault zone in New Zealand*

Portland State University

McCarley, Justin Craig, *Using repeat terrestrial laser scanning and photogrammetry to monitor reactivation of the Silt Creek landslide in the western Cascade Mountains, Linn County, Oregon*

Prescott College

Boyle, Kaitlyn, *Expeditionary place-based environmental education; a field semester curriculum on the Colorado Plateau*

Rice University

Lin, Pei-Hsuan, *Lattice-Boltzmann modeling of potential fluid flow impairment caused by asphaltene deposition in porous media*

Prothro, Lindsay O'Neal, *Glacial retreat patterns and processes on Antarctic continental margins*

San Jose State University

Hutcherson, Alex Jon, *Rock strength; a main control of Yosemite's topography?*

Scudder, Christopher, *Structure and emplacement of the Eocene Golden Horn Batholith, north Cascades, Washington*

South Dakota School of Mines and Technology

A Elahi, Md Manjur, *Performance studies on Portland-Limestone cement in sulfate environments*

Southern Illinois University at Edwardsville

Davis, Mickey, *Heavy metal residues in soils related to former coal mines and railways*

Okalanwa, Chima Ezeakachi, *Evaluation of total mercury, zinc, lead, and arsenic concentration in fish fillets, water and sediments from Dunlap Lake in Edwardsville, Illinois*

Southern Methodist University

Andrzejewski, Kate, *Cretaceous dinosaurs and the world they lived in; a new species of ornithischian dinosaur from the Early Cretaceous (Aptian) of Texas, reconstruction of the brain endocast and inner ear of Malawisaurus dixeyi, and reconstruction of the paleoclimate and paleoenvironment of Cretaceous terrestrial formations in Texas and Oklahoma using pedogenic minerals*

Clemens, Matt, *An early Late Cretaceous nodosaur from marine Eagle Ford Group of north central Texas, a test of the endothermy in the mosasaurs from the Late Cretaceous of Angola, and the ontogeny of a new pipid frog from the Miocene of Ethiopia*

Cloos, Marlee, *Palynology of the Cenomanian Woodbine Group*

Friesenhahn, Brody, *The transition from Sevier to Laramide orogeny captured in upper-plate magmatic structures, eastern Transverse Ranges, CA*

Hu, Xie, *Characterization of ground deformation associated with shallow groundwater processes using satellite radar interferometry*

MacPhail, Mason, *Detection, containment and scaling relations of near source explosions in granite through moment tensor representations*

McIntosh, Julia A., *An analysis of a mixed-layer clay minerals and major element geochemical trends in Middle-Upper Pennsylvanian-aged paleosols as a proxy for characterizing basin-wide diagenetic patterns and the paleoenvironment of the Illinois Basin, U.S.A.*

Quinones, Louis, *Determining principal stress orientations and magnitudes in the Fort Worth Basin, Texas*

State University of New York, University at Buffalo

Adetokunbo, Rasheed Peter, *ERTh; electrical resistivity monitoring of heat tracer to characterize aquifer heterogeneities*
Awatey, Michael Teye, *Hydrologic process parameterization of electrical resistivity imaging of solute plumes using POD MCMC*
Cowling, Owen, *Contrasting hydroclimate response of coastal Norway and Arctic Russia during late-glacial and Holocene climate change*
Cramer, Jennifer, *A low-altitude remote sensing approach to monitoring groundwater-surface water interaction using large-scale particle image velocimetry*
Doody, Erica, *A latest Pleistocene palynologic record from western New York*
Frederiks, Ryan, *Predicting permeability and water quantity in fractured rock aquifers of northwestern Uganda with applications for refugee populations*
Frieman, Richard A., *Geochemical constraints on the distribution of Climacograptus? rugosus within the late Sandbian-aged basal Utica Shale; implications on Taconic foreland basin development and graptolite community turnover*
Green, Evan, *Forecasting changes to groundwater and surface water flow regimes in western New York under a changing climate*
Harp, Andrew Gary, *The impacts of local stress fields and host rocks heterogeneity on magma transport and extrusion at stratovolcanoes*
Hyman, David Matthew, *Pressurization-induced failure of deforming lava domes; theory, experiment, and application*
Johnson, Peter Jacob, *Fluid flow in disrupted porous media; volcanological and radiological waste applications*
Kiekhaefer, Rebecca, *Evaluation of a field method for monitoring the diffusion of trichloroethene (TCE) and its degradation products in fractured sedimentary rock*
Schweigel, Tayler Cathryn, *Structural analysis of the Utica Group in four unoriented cores from the Mohawk Valley, New York State; implications for tectonics, burial history, timing of vein formation and hydrocarbon migration*
Schweinsberg, Avriel D., *Centennial-scale reconstructions of mountain glacier fluctuations during the Holocene, West Greenland*
Sweeney, Matthew Ryan, *Multiphase flow in explosive volcanic eruptions; field and numerical results*
Younger, Zachary Paul, *Basaltic 'a'a lava field emplacement of the intraplate Marcath Volcano (central Nevada) from field and LiDAR data*

Stephen F. Austin State University

Ellison, Cory Dean, *Regional stress regime study of East Texas based on orientation of fractures in the Weches Formation*
Kantala, Talban, *An outcrop based study of the Weches Formation in Sabine County, Texas; investigating its unconventional resource potential through the study of stratigraphy, sedimentology, petrology, and geochemistry*
Meinerts, Jacob Allan, *Depositional environment and facies analyses of the Owl Mountain Province, Fort Hood Military Installation, Bell and Coryell Counties, Texas*
Messmer, Martin Lee, *Structural geology of the Caddo Gap area, Ouachita Mountains, Arkansas*
Minteer, Danielle Renee, *A geophysical delineation of a normal fault within the Gulf Coastal Plain, Montgomery County, Texas*
Morris, Jonah, *Physical and chemical controls on suffosion development in gypsic soil, Culberson County, Texas*
Reece, Colby, *Delineation of karst potential using LiDAR and GIS analyses, Fort Hood Military Installation, Texas*
Shields, Jessica Marie, *Speleogenetic evolution and geological remote sensing of the Gypsum Plain, Eddy County, New Mexico*
Watkins, Joseph Daniel, *Mercury in Big Cypress Bayou and Caddo Lake watersheds in Marion and Harrison Counties Texas*
Wilkerson, Austin Conner, *Petrographic and stratigraphic analysis along the Lower Cretaceous strata, in Kimble County Texas*

SUNY, Binghamton University

Aguirre Maturana, Ramon A., *Geology of the iron ore deposits of the Pleito-Melon District, Coastal Cordillera, Atacama region, Chile*
Bourke, James R., *Origin of the Klyuchevskoy upper mantle anomaly; asthenospheric flow or lithospheric artifact?*
Cheng, Nanfei, *Experimental investigation of reactions relevant to the blueschist-eclogite transition*
Haddad, James R., *Order and chaos in the olivine underworld; two mechanisms for the formation of basal olivine layers*
Martone, Patricia M., *Induced seismicity in northeastern Pennsylvania*
Saba, David J., *Quantifying factors that influence road deicer retention and export in a multi-landuse upstate New York watershed*
Starbuck, Nicholas C., *Detoxification and isotopic fractionation of antimony (V) by a novel bacterium isolated from sediments collected from an alkaline lake in Warner Valley, OR*

SUNY, Stony Brook University

Hantz, Catherine, *Early history of Earth science education in New York State (1865-1910)*
Lashley, Justin Michael, *Reassessment of geomorphic features on the continental shelf off of Watch Hill, Fire Island National Sea Shore, NY*
Shirley, Katherine Anne, *The effects of particle size and albedo on mid-infrared spectroscopy for the Moon*

SUNY, University at Buffalo

Dunning, Ian Thomas, *Mapping the previous extent of the Medusae Fossae Formation, Mars*
Grenier, Michael Richard, *A phylogenetic analysis of Darriwilian graptolites, suborder Axonophora*
O'Hara, Alex P., *Defining the width and average fracture frequency of fracture intensification domains using a partial least squares analysis, linear piecewise regression, and the Akaike information criterion; implications for the evolution of fracture-dominated fault damage zones*
Pugnetti, Michele, *TCE-TCFE equilibrium competitive sorption for sedimentary rock from the Newark Basin (NJ)*

Tulane University

Bridgeman, Jonathan G., *Understanding Mississippi Delta subsidence through stratigraphic and geotechnical analysis of a continuous Holocene core at a subsidence superstation*
Jankowkswi, Krista L., *Implications of environmental change for wetland vulnerability and carbon storage in coastal Louisiana*

University of Alaska at Fairbanks

Khalaj-Teimoury, Masoud, *Environmental impacts on Guam's water security and sustainable management of the resource*
Li, Shanshan, *Spatial and temporal variations in slip behavior beneath Alaska-Aleutian subduction zone*
McPherson, Amanda Michelle, *Shear wave splitting and mantle flow in Alaska*
Raymond, Luke M., *Gold and base metal mineralization of the Dolphin intrusion-related gold deposit, Fairbanks Mining District, Alaska*

University of Arizona

Soza, Danielle R., *Points of view; landscape persistence in northeastern, AZ*

University of Arkansas at Fayetteville

Barker, Abram Max, *An integrated well log and 3D seismic interpretation of Missourian clinoforms, Osage County, Oklahoma*
Liner, Thomas, *Subsurface analysis of Mississippian tripolitic chert in northwest Arkansas*
Sanks, Kelly, *Keeping pace with relative sea level rise; marsh platform monitoring shows minimal sediment deficit along the Louisiana coast*

University of British Columbia

Adinata, James, *Impact of bidirectional seismic shearing on volumetric response of sand deposits*
Aubry, Thomas J., *Interactions between climate and the rise of explosive volcanic plumes; a new feedback in the Earth system*
Bigdeli, Amin, *Evaluation and control of collapsible soils in Okanagan-Thompson region*
Booker, William, *The controls of morphodynamics in steep, aggrading channels; a flume investigation*
Brown, Alexandra E., *Geochemical sampling strategies for discovering buried copper porphyries, Atacama Desert, Chile*
Brubacher, Alex, *Cooling and exhumation in the footwall of the Dangardzong fault, Thakkhola graben, west central Nepal*
Capraro, Ilaria, *Damage, collapse potential and long duration effects of subduction ground motions on structural systems*
Chouinard, Rachel L. M., *Surficial geochemical tools for Cu-Mo porphyry exploration in till-covered terrain*
Chuang, Yuling, *Plateau subduction, intraslab seismicity, and the Denali (Alaska) volcanic gap*
De Rego, Kathryn Grace, *Decadal-scale evolution of Elwha River downstream of Glines Canyon Dam; perspectives from numerical modeling*
Dinsdale, Daniel, *Methods for preferential sampling in geostatistics*
Elgueta Astaburuaga, Maria A., *Effects of episodic sediment supply on channel adjustment of an experimental gravel bed*
Emo, Robert Bernard, *Archean crustal evolution constrained by strontium isotopes in apatite and uranium-lead geochronology and trace element geochemistry of zircon*
Evans, Elana, *Effects of weathering on chemical and mineralogical properties of the Mount Polley mine tailings; preliminary implications for long-term ecosystem health*
Eyster, Theodore, *Modeling dam removal in a mountain meadow with MODFLOW-NWT*
Fagan, Andrew Jeffrey, *The ruby and pink sapphire deposits of SW*

Greenland; geological setting, genesis, and exploration techniques
Fang, Zhilong, *Source estimation and uncertainty quantification for wave-equation based seismic imaging and inversion*
Fitzpatrick, Noel, *An investigation of surface energy balance and turbulent heat flux on mountain glaciers*
Fourny, Anais, *Radiogenic isotopic systematics of layered intrusions; application to the Mesoproterozoic Kiglapait Intrusion of coastal Labrador, Canada, and to mafic-ultramafic rock reference materials*
Gallagher, Tanya Louise, *Linking landscape indicators to groundwater nitrate concentrations in a transboundary aquifer*
Grau Galofre, Anna, *Insights on the origin and evolution of the Martian valley networks from erosion models; reconciling climate modeling and geomorphological observations*
Heagy, Lindsey J., *Electromagnetic methods for imaging subsurface injections*
Herron, Christopher Stephen, *Mapping the carbonate alteration footprint of the Cortez Hills carlin-type gold deposit, Nevada using carbon-oxygen isotopes, and geochemistry as a vectoring tool*
Hund, Silja Verena, *Community-based stream and groundwater monitoring and future change impact modelling of a socio-ecohydrological system to inform drought adaptation in the seasonally-dry tropics*
Kang, Seogi, *On recovering distributed induced polarization information from time-domain electromagnetic data*
King, Leonora Adele, *Identifying and characterizing the spatial variability of supraglacial hydrological features on the western Greenland ice sheet*
Kovacs, Nikolett, *Genesis and post-ore modification of the migmatized Carmacks copper Cu-Au-Ag porphyry deposit, Yukon, Canada*
Letham, Eric, *New insights into pore structure characterization and permeability measurement of fine-grained sedimentary reservoir rocks in the laboratory at reservoir stress states*
MacWilliam, Kathryn R. G., *The geology and genesis of the Coffee gold deposit in west-central Yukon, Canada; implications for the structural, magmatic, and metallogenic evolution of the Dawson Range, and gold deposit models*
Maia, Fabricio, *A diagnostic assessment of operational, environmental and safety procedures in the onshore cassiterite artisanal mining sector in Indonesia*
Miyoshi, Takako, *Influence of data characterization process on the kinematic stability analysis of engineered rock slopes using discrete fracture network models and its implications for rock mass classification system*
Nadolski, Stefan, *Cave-to-mill; mine and mill integration for block cave mines*
Patsa, Eleni, *The use of geothermal energy in mining; a decision-making framework*
Rabayrol, Fabien, *Late Cenozoic post-subduction tectonic, magmatic and metallogenic evolution of the Anatolide-Tauride orogenic belt, Turkey*
Rego, Alan Joseph, *Atmospheric alkaline pre-oxidation of refractory sulphide gold ores*
Rouse, Pascale C., *Numerical modeling and analysis of pullout tests of sheet and geogrid inclusions in sand*
Savard, Genevieve, *Seismic velocity structure under Vancouver Island from travel time inversion; insight from low frequency earthquakes*
Schmidt, Erika Susan, *Experimental and numerical investigation of hydraulic stimulation as a risk mitigation technique for fault slip rockburst hazards in deep underground mining*
Seidalinov, Gaziz, *Constitutive and numerical modeling of clay subjected to cyclic loading*
Sim, Nari, *Biogeochemical cycling of dissolved and particulate manganese in the Northeast Pacific and Canadian western Arctic*
Skierszkan, Elliott Karl, *Application of molybdenum (and zinc) stable isotopes to trace geochemical attenuation in mine waste*
Tessema, Mekdes Ayalew, *Evaluation of dynamically downscaled near-surface meteorological variables and energy fluxes at three mountain glaciers in British Columbia*
Turnbull, Marie, *The glaciovolcanic origin of Kima'Kho Mountain, northern British Columbia*
Whiteford, Arran, *Pattern-forming instabilities in the coupling of ice sheets and subglacial drainage systems*
Williams, Haley, *Paraglacial landscape evolution in a rapidly deglaciating environment; a case study of Taan Fjord, southeast Alaska, USA*
Yin, Ziming, *Noise induced tipping in ocean circulation based on the Stommel model*
Zhang, Yiming, *Large-scale seismic data compression; application to full waveform inversion and extended image volume*

University of California at Berkeley

Chowdhury, Khaled Hossain, *Evaluation of the state of practice regarding nonlinear seismic deformation ayalyses of embankment dams subject to soil liquefaction based on case histories*

University of California at San Diego

DeSanto, John B., *Measuring seafloor displacement using repeated sidescan sonar surveys*

University of California at Santa Barbara

Meerdink, Susan Kay, *Remote sensing of plant species using airborne hyperspectral visible-shortwave infrared and thermal infrared imagery*
Reynolds, Laura Conners, *The late Quaternary evolution of the Southern California coast; sea-level change, storms, and subsidence*

University of Colorado at Boulder

Lovelle, Taylor Patterson, *From Holocene to anthropocene and back again; a deep ecological critique of three apocalyptic eco-narratives in the long nineteenth century*

University of Colorado at Denver

McPherson, Rachel, *Walking with Lucy; modeling mobility patterns of Australopithecus afarensis using GIS*

University of Hawaii at Manoa

Dores, Daniel E., *Stable isotope and geochemical source-tracking of groundwater and surface water pollution to Kane'ohe Bay, Hawaii*
Hudson, Catherine Y., *The source and magnitude of submarine groundwater discharge along the Kona coast of the Big Island, Hawaii*
Mathioudakis, Michael R., *Hydrology of contaminant flow regimes to groundwater, streams, and the ocean waters of Kane'ohe Bay, O'ahu*

University of Louisiana at Lafayette

Alekhue, Jude E., *Investigation of the Miocene Moki Formation within the Parahaki 3D survey; Taranaki Basin, offshore New Zealand using some geophysical tools*
Allen, Carson B., *Lithological influences on the synthetic precipitation leaching procedure test and implications to assessment and remediation at the Southwest Foods Site in Lafayette, Louisiana (LDEQ Agency interest no. 69569)*
Bennett, Randall, *Gravity investigation of a normal fault in southern St. Landry Parish, Louisiana*
Bennett, Randall P., *Gravity investigation of a normal fault in southern St. Landry Parish, Louisiana*
Berry, Hunter D., *Dissolution of Permian salt, Las Animas Arch, Colorado*
Borel, Megan E., *A microstructural and geochronological investigation of the Coyote Mountain metamorphic core complex (AZ)*
Brennan, Anne C., *Depositional environment of the Carrizo Sandstone in central Louisiana, implications for future oil discoveries*
Broussard, Kevin Tyler, *Regional subsurface investigation of the Uppermost Cretaceous and the James Limestone in the eastern region of Texas*
Cai, Xiao, *Numerical simulation of deposition and piling of particles in fractures*
Canezaro, Morgan Elise, *Magnetic susceptibility and XRF analysis of soils from Baton Rouge, Louisiana; correlation and implications for heavy metal pollution*
Clark, Cameron Wilhite, *Investigation into the Niobrara Formation and missing section associated with pre-lithification faults, Wattenberg Field (CO)*
Dorn, Taylor C., *Channel morphology, streamflow patterns, and sediment transport of two intermittent rivers along the Balcones Escarpment*
Dye, Brian Christopher, *Identifying Strombolian eruptions through cross-correlation of seismic data and machine learning of infrared, lava-lake images on Mount Erebus, Antarctica*
Furrh, Marshall, *Subsurface and geophysical investigation of the Oligocene Frio Formation, South Elton Field, Jefferson Davis Parish, Louisiana*
Furrh, Marshall A., *Subsurface and geophysical investigation of the Oligocene Frio Formation, South Elton Field, Jefferson Davis Parish, Louisiana*
Gaiennie, Edward Wilson, Jr., *An investigation into secondary migration of hydrocarbons in the San Joaquin Basin near Fresno, California*
Ghalayini, Zachary T., *Geophysical investigation of Carrizo Formation by using two-dimensional seismic surveys in the Tullos-Urania oilfield in La Salle Parish, LA*
Jensen, Sean Ross, *Paleomagnetic analysis of Quaternary sediments from Baffin Bay, western Greenland*
Jiang, Shuxian, *Comparative study of petrophysical and elastic properties of marl and interbedded limestone layers within Eagle Ford Formation*
Leglue, Parker C., *Investigating the origin of the Sierra Quemada structure, Big Bend National Park, Texas through geochemical analyses of related igneous rocks*
Locci-Lopez, Daniel Eduardo, *Permian Basin reservoir quantitative interpretation applying the multi-scale boxcar transform spectral decomposition*
Loundagin, Nicholas R., *Geophysical characterization of the structural configuration and tectonic evolution along the northern margin of the Gulf of Mexico Basin, northwestern Mississippi*
Miller, Madison, *Investigation of fluid migration in the Austin Chalk and Eagle Ford Formations*

Muchiri, Eric, *Optical inspections and scanning electron microscopy across the Cretaceous-Paleogene boundary deposit in well-core IPNH no. 2 from La Salle Parish, central Louisiana*
O'Leary, Matthew Covington, *Relationship between growth faults and subsidence; impact on coastal erosion, an example from Cameron Parish, southwestern Louisiana, USA*
Parrish, Alexis Fay, *The application of SAR analysis to measure relative permeability to specific ions in the Eagle Ford Shale*
Pasley, James, *Evaluating petrophysical variations of turbidite depositional systems with implications for enhanced reservoir modelling in Ewing Bank 873 (Lobster Field), Gulf of Mexico*
Quick, Nathan, *Subsurface mapping and seismic modeling from resistivity data to tie locally productive formations of the Wilcox Group in La Salle Parish, Louisiana to a high-resolution shallow imaging seismic dataset*
Song, Jinze, *Special problems and solutions in development of shale gas/oil reservoirs*
Teter, David, *Understanding potential controls on production in the Louisiana Austin Chalk Formation*
Udeogu, Henry E., *Quantitative micro-PIXE analysis using the GEOPIXE software*
Vaught-Mijares, Roxanna, *Tying hydrologic balance and human settlement through stable isotope analysis of lacustrine sediments (Titicaca Basin, Peru)*
Workman, Sydne, *Batch leaching of hydrocarbon source rocks at 150°C under variable concentrations of chloride and organic acids*
Yun, Samuel, *Mechanical analysis of a detachment shear zone, Picacho Mountain metamorphic core complex (AZ)*

University of Massachusetts at Amherst

Smith, Rebecca, *Mid-Pliocene to early Pleistocene sea surface and land temperature history in NW Australia based on organic geochemical proxies from Site U1463*

University of Memphis

Ahamed, Sabber, *Computational journey across multiphysics and multitemporal scales; from slow tectonic movement to fast earthquake slip*
Azizzadeh-Roodpish, S., *Statistical analysis of seismicity catalog of Alaska; the mysteries of the time series*
DePriest, Thomas Arlanda, Jr., *Urbanization in Jackson, Madison County, TN and the environmental impact of urbanization on the region*
Gilmour, Elizabeth Ann, *Dynamic rupture modeling of induced earthquakes in Oklahoma*
Jambo, Eric, *Lg Q of northern, eastern and southeastern Alaska and crustal Q variations*
Ogweno, Luke Philip, *Earthquake early warning system (EEWs) for the New Madrid seismic zone*
Schoefernacker, Scott, *Evaluation and evolution of a groundwater contaminant plume at the former Shelby County landfill, Memphis, Tennessee*
Simco, William A., *Recharge of the Memphis Aquifer in an incised urban watershed*
Smith, Michael Ryan, *Evaluating modern recharge to the Memphis Aquifer at the Lichterman well field, Memphis, Tennessee*

University of Miami (Florida)

Billings, William, *An exploration of the two-dimensional poroelastic properties of oceanic crust at the formation scale*
Cabrera, Talib Oliver, *InSAR applications for environmental and hazard monitoring*
Giri, Sharmila Joy, *The influence of seawater chemistry on the geochemistry of scleractinian corals*
Havazli, Emre, *Quantifying the effect of tropospheric delay on interferometric synthetic aperture radar and its application to crustal deformation*
Mehterian, Sevag, *Holocene-Pleistocene climate variability through stalagmites*
Morales Rivera, Anieri M., *Geophysical characterization and modeling of volcanic systems; multiparameter approach from geodetic and seismic signals*
Rivera, Anieri Morales, *Geophysical characterization and modeling of volcanic systems; multi-parameter approach from geodetic and seismic signals*
Schnyder, Jara, *Submarine mass wasting in carbonate environment; preconditions, triggers, and consequences*
Solano-Rojas, Dario Emannuel, *Geological hazard assessments for Mexico City and its surroundings based on synthetic aperture radar interferometry (InSAR) observations*
Staudigel, Philip Tauxe, *The application of clumped isotopes in the study of marine diagenesis*
Yuksek, Mustafa Kamil, *Acoustic velocity characterization of the Vaca Muerta Formation, Neuquen Basin, Argentina*

University of Missouri at Columbia

Broce, Jesse S., *Taphonomic characteristics of fossils on the Burgess-Shale-type spectrum*

University of Montana

Florentine, Caitlyn Elizabeth, *Understanding changes to glacier and ice sheet geometry; the roles of climate and ice dynamics*

University of Nevada at Reno

Claypoole, Micah N., *Mineral Ridge; a Late Cretaceous orogenic gold system in the Miocene Silver Peak-Lone Mountain metamorphic core complex*
Freedman, David J., *Igneous and hydrothermal geology of the central Cherry Creek Range, White Pine County, Nevada*
McLachlan, Holly S., *stratigraphy, structure, and fluid flow at the Soda Lake geothermal field, western Nevada, USA*

University of New Mexico

Carrier, Agathe E., *Investigation of molluscan survivorship across the Cenomanian-Turonian boundary event using ecological niche modeling*
Decker, David, *New geochemical and isotopic approaches to shallow crust landform evolution*
Finlay, Tori S., *Dense-array teleseismic imaging of the southern Albuquerque Basin*
Lewis, Jonathan A., *Microtextural studies of feldspar in ordinary chondrites*
Peinado, Justin G., *A speleothem record of climate variability in southwestern North America during Marine Isotope Stage 3*
Singerling, Sheryl A., *Primary pristine and altered iron sulfides in CM and CR carbonaceous chondrites; insights into nebular and parent body processes*
Thomas, Nicole, *Magma mixing at Oldoinyo Lengai; a mineralogical and trace element analysis of the 2007-8 eruption*
Walk, Cory J., *Birth and evolution of the Virgin River; 1 km of post-5 Ma uplift of the western Colorado Plateau*
White, David Allen, *Global seawater redox trends during the Late Devonian mass extinction detected using U isotopes of marine carbonates*
Zhang, Han, *Application of Ps scattering kernels to imaging the mantle transition zone with receiver functions*

University of North Carolina at Charlotte

Arey, Jordan Vincent, *Stratigraphy and soils of fluvial terraces on the Catawba River, NC and SC; landscape evolution of the southeastern US*
Ching, Suzanne Sadler, *Acoustic emission and environmental monitoring of two natural granite boulders; semi-arid vs. temperate environment*

University of North Carolina at Wilmington

Knowlton, Aaron, *Causeway influence on sedimentation and vegetation of Bradley and Hewletts Creeks, North Carolina*

University of Oklahoma

Adams, Steven, *Evaluating desert silt production using field, experimental, and remote-sensing methods*
Adams, Steven Michael, *Evaluating desert silt production using field, experimental, and remote-sensing methods*
AlAli, Abdulmohsen, *Seismic data conditioning and analysis for fractured reservoirs*
AlShafei, Ali, *3D quantitative seismic stratigraphy of Jurassic carbonate strata on the Arabian platform*
Armstrong, Madison, *Trilobites from a Cambrian extinction interval at the base of the Steptoean, Riley Formation, central Texas*
Armstrong, Madison Layne, *Trilobites from a Cambrian extinction interval at the base of the Steptoean Stage, Riley Formation, central Texas*
Cassel, Murphy, *Machine learning and the construction of a seismic attribute-seismic facies analysis data base*
Castro Manrique, Brian J., *Structural geology of the Woodford Shale in the southeastern Anadarko Basin, Grady County, Oklahoma*
Clark, Sarah, *Fluvial architecture of the Burro Canyon Formation using UAV-based photogrammetry; implications for reservoir performance, Escalante Canyon, southwestern Piceance Basin, Colorado*
Drummond, Katherine, *Regional stratigraphy and proximal to distal variation of lithology and porosity within a mixed carbonate-siliciclastic system, Meramec and Osage series (Mississippian), central Oklahoma*
Duarte Coronado, Davis, *Rock characterization and stratigraphy of the Mississippian strata, Meramec / Sycamore merge play, central Oklahoma*
Hardwick, Jeffrey, *Reservoir quality evaluation of the Meramec and upper Osage units in the Anadarko Basin*
Heij, Gerhard, *Magnetic fabrics and paleomagnetism of North American mudrocks; relics of complex burial histories*
Henglai, Puntira, *Sequence-stratigraphic and facies controls on reservoir quality and productivity of early to middle Miocene fluvial and tide-dominated deltaic deposits, Formation 2, Gulf of Thailand*
Hickman, Garrett, *Parasequence-scale stratigraphic variability of lithology and porosity of Mississippian Meramec reservoirs and the relationships to production characteristics, STACK trend, Oklahoma*
Horton, Ashley, *Baseline concentrations of contaminants of emerging concern in the Lake Thunderbird watershed, planning for indirect potable reuse in Oklahoma*

Infante-Paez, Lennon, *Seismic expression of igneous bodies in sedimentary basins and their impact on hydrocarbon exploration; examples from a compressive tectonic setting, Taranaki Basin, New Zealand*
Kushner, Baylee Elizabeth, *Heterogeneity of clastic provenance to the Anadarko Basin and implications for paleogeography*
Lewis, Kelsey, *Fluvial architecture of the Burro Canyon Formation using UAV-based photogrammetry and outcrop-based modeling; implications for reservoir performance, Rattlesnake Canyon, southwestern Piceance Basin, Colorado*
Li, Peiyao, *Towards the usage of quarry blasts as active seismic source*
Lubo-Robles, David, *Development of independent component analysis for reservoir geomorphology and unsupervised seismic facies classification in the Taranaki Basin, New Zealand*
Marsh, Stephen, *Development of a state-wide velocity profile in Oklahoma using ambient noise seismic tomography*
Matemilola, Muizz, *Reservoir characterization of the Brae Formation, South Brae Field, UK North Sea*
McConville, Marlena, *Subsurface pressure modeling of saltwater disposal for the Arbuckle and Timbered Hills-basement system, Anadarko Shelf, Oklahoma*
Miller, Joshua, *Regional stratigraphy and organic richness of the Mississippian Meramec and associated strata, Anadarko Basin, central Oklahoma*
Moreland, Travis, *Catastrophic process event stratigraphy of the Rader Member in the Delaware Basin*
Oordt, Andrew, *A record of mid-latitude dustiness in a Carboniferous-Permian carbonate ramp on central Spitsbergen*
Qi, Xuan, *Seismic attributes assisted quantitative unconventional reservoirs characterization*
Ryan, Emily, *Variation in time averaging and taphonomic character of shell beds in Lake Tanganyika, Africa; paleoenvironmental and stratigraphic implications of shell beds in rift lakes*
Sanchez Flores, Laura Beatriz, *Structural analysis of a naturally fractured carbonate field in the south-east Gulf of Mexico*
Sumer Gorenekli, Yagmur, *Geochemical characterization of the Lower Pennsylvanian Morrow Shale in the Anadarko Basin of Oklahoma*
Wang, Zhuobo, *Forward seismic model of Permian Guadalupian shelf-to-basin sedimentation through novel integration of LiDAR and Schmidt Hammer, McKittrick Canyon, West Texas*
Xu, Chenxi, *High-resolution XRF-LiDAR sequence stratigraphy of the late Guadalupian Capitan Slope at McKittrick Canyon, Texas; process-response of oscillating Delaware Basin sea level*

University of Oregon

Colon, Dylan Patrick, *Understanding the origins of Yellowstone Hot Spot magmas through isotope geochemistry, high-precision geochronology, and magmatic-thermomechanical computer modeling*
Jarrett, Corey Brantley, *Analysis of an exposed portion of the Badwater Turtleback shear-zone, Death Valley, California, USA*
McLaughlin, Win Nadia Francis, *Landscape and biotic evolution of the Kochkor Basin, Kyrgyzstan*
Ozimek, Constance, *Mass cycling through crustal magma chambers and the influence of thermo-mechanical state on magma compositions through time*
Perdue, Genevieve Violet, *The evolution of cranial modularity and integration in the Caviomorpha lineage (Mammalia, Rodentia)*
Schachtman, Nathan, *Climate regulates stable weathering fluxes over interglacial-glacial cycles*
Sexton, Emily, *Characterization of aftershock sequences from large strike-slip earthquakes along geometrically complex faults*

University of Pittsburgh

Fu, Wei, *Hydraulic fracture interacting with partially-cemented and non-persistent natural fracture*
Tavakkoli, Sakineh, *A systems-level approach for integrated shale gas wastewater management*

University of Rhode Island

McAleer, Christopher James, *Environmental factors affecting methane cycling in Narragansett Bay*
Sauvage, Justine Flore, *Sedimentary catalysis of radiolytic hydrogen production*

University of Shippensburg

Shaffer, Corry L., *Intrinsic organisms and fluorescent dye traces locate recharge and measure discharge from a submerged karst spring, Cumberland Valley Pennsylvania*

University of South Florida at Tampa

Gray, John Willis, *The stability of sand waves in a tidally-influenced shipping channel, Tampa Bay, Florida*
Karegar, Makan A., *Theory and application of geophysical geodesy for studying Earth surface deformation*
Parmenter, Dylan S., *Ice and guano in El Malpais lava tubes; potential paleoclimate archives for the Southwest United States*

University of Southern Mississippi

Epps, Sarah A., *The feasibility of using inherent optical properties and the apparent optical property remote sensing reflectance to estimate suspended particulate matter, particularly for use in airborne hydrographic surveys*
Griffis, Anne, *Identifying overwash deposits in arid environments; towards a millennial-scale record of cyclones and Makran Trench tsunamis from Sur Lagoon, Oman*

University of Texas at Austin

Abalkhail, Nassir, *Chemical enhanced oil recovery application in a high-temperature, high-salinity carbonate reservoir*
Al Tammar, Murtadha Jawad, *Experimental studies in hydraulic fracture growth; fundamental insights and validation experiments for geomechanical models*
Alrubaie, Naif Mohammed, *Dynamic petrophysical properties of laminated rocks; an experimental investigation*
Anand, Neha, *Review of asphaltene properties and precipitation modeling*
Aydin, Erdi, *Numerical simulation and history matching of steam-foam process to enhance heavy oil recovery*
Barut, Kahraman, *Investigation of chemically bonded phosphate ceramics/cements and applicability of magnesium potassium phosphate cements as wellbore sealants in the oil & gas industry*
Chang, Leonard Yulya, *Prediction of microemulsion phase behavior from surfactant and co-solvent structures*
Estrada Santos, Javier Andres, *Lattice-Boltzmann modeling of multiphase flow through rough heterogeneously wet fractures*
Hanson, Katy Lynn, *Isogeometric analysis; applications for torque and drag models, drillstring and bottom-hole assembly design*
Jiang, Han, *Characterization of petrophysical properties of organic-rich shales by experiments, lab measurements and machine learning analysis*
Jung, Hojung, *Investigation of coupled thermo-chemo-mechanical processes for safe carbon geological storage*
Lee, Hyungjoo, *Estimation of in-situ properties from the combined interpretation of nuclear, dielectric, optical, and magnetic resonance measurements*
Li, Tianyu, *Modeling of hydraulic fracture propagation and height growth in layered formations*
Liu, Wendi, *Reservoir fluid characterization and optimization of condensate banking treatment with dimethyl ether in the shale gas condensate reservoir*
Mejia, Lucas, *Experimental investigation of low interfacial tension displacements in oil-wet, fractured micromodels*
Mejia, Miguel, *Experimental investigation of surfactant flooding in fractured limestones*
Murphy, Zachary Walter, *Three-phase relative permeability of hydrate-bearing sediments*
Nasir, Yusuf, *Derivative-free techniques for optimal development of conventional and unconventional reservoirs*
Nwachukwu, Chiazor, *Machine learning solutions for reservoir characterization, management, and optimization*
Oszowe, Williams Osagie, *Capillary pressure curve and liquid permeability estimation in tight oil reservoirs using pressure decline versus time data*
Qi, Pengpeng, *The effect of polymer viscoelasticity on residual oil saturation*
Ruiz Maraggi, Leopoldo Matias, *Mechanistic and probablistic rate-time analysis of unconventional reservoirs*
Ryu, Jenny, *Fault reactivation and CO_2 migration in carbon storage*
Salazar Neira, Jose Julian, *Heterogeneity study of the Little Creek Field from petrophysical data*
Shiriyev, Javid, *A tri-axial electromagnetic induction tool for hydraulic fracture diagnostics*
Shovkun, Igor, *Coupled chemo-mechanical processes in reservoir geomechanics*
Suresh Kumar, Adithya, *A study of a novel down-hole gas-liquid separator/connector*
Tang, Brandon Chok-Yie, *Application of dynamic optimization methods for foam floods in stratified reservoirs*
Verma, Rahul, *Pore scale modeling of multiphase flow in heterogeneously wet media*
Wang, Denning, *Surfactant retention in limestones*
Wang, Haotian, *A general poro-elasto-plastic model for poorly consolidated sands*
Wu, Chu-Hsiang, *Modeling particulate flows in conduits and porous media*
Xu, Ke, *Construction and validation of microfluidic platforms for investigation of multiphase flow and nanofluid in porous media*
Yang, Hongtao, *Pore-scale modeling of particle filtration in porous media*
Yi, Sophie, *Development of computationally efficient 2D and pseudo-3D multi-fracture models with applications to fracturing and refracturing*
York, Jason, *Advanced hydraulic fracture modelling; peridynamics, inelasticity, and coupling to FEM*
Zhang, Peng, *Low frequency downhole electrical measurements for mapping proppant distribution in hydraulic fractures in cased-hole wells*

Zhou, Jimin Daniel, *Gas injection and mobility control in fracture, oil-wet carbonate reservoirs*

University of Texas at San Antonio

Allen, Jena J., *A new family of Arcestaceae from East Timor, Indonesia*
Knight, John, *Quantifying climate change over the Early Cretaceous Ruby Ranch Member of the Cedar Mountain Formation, east-central Utah*
Ortiz, Michelle, *A method to estimate water depth of the Pennsylvanian late Paleozoic Midcontinent Seaway in north-central Texas using stable isotope stratigraphy*
Sitler, Owen, *Channel bar development in a poorly sorted sand-bed river*

University of Tulsa

Daniele, John, *Sequence stratigraphy analysis of Google Earth images of the San Bois Mountains of southeastern Oklahoma*
Liu, Xiaobo, *Seismic wave propagation and Q-compensated imaging in viscoelastic media with an irregular free surface*
Marti, Nicklos, *Sequence stratigraphy of the Boggy Formation in the Sans Bois Mountains, southeast Oklahoma*
Ye, Shan, *Finite element method analysis of multi-layer buckling systems with heterogeneous matrices*

University of Western Ontario

Langford, Joelle E., *Modelling the thermal transport of a thawing permafrost plateau*

University of Wisconsin at Green Bay

Ashauer, Zachary Michael, *Textural analysis of classical rapakivi granites*
Hamby, Amanda L., *The effects of faults and changing water levels on confined deep aquifer water chemistry in northeastern Wisconsin*

University of Wisconsin at Madison

Batchelor, Cameron J., *A high-precision U-Th chronology of calcite deposition at Cave of the Mounds, Wisconsin, and its implications for climate and permafrost in the late Pleistocene*
Becker, Richard A., *Glacial geology and geomorphology of the west-central Sierra Nevada, USA*
Bremmer, Sarah E., *Three-dimensional structural interpretation and analysis of spatial and temporal accretionary wedge evolution, Nankai subduction zone, Kii-Kumano region, Japan*
Cronin, Reagan A., *Three dimensional velocity structure and earthquake locations at Yellowstone*
Fortney, Nathaniel W., *Microbial and geochemical iron redox cycling in Chocolate Pots hot springs, Yellowstone National Park*
Hart, Laney, *Earthquake detection, relocation, and body-wave tomography at Okmok Volcano, Alaska*
Kahn, Maureen J., *Exhumation across the Idaho-Oregon border; implications for the arc-continent suture and Hells Canyon extensional province*
Miller, David J., *Ambient noise tomography of Okmok Caldera, Alaska*
Patterson, Jeremy R., *Understanding constraints on geothermal sustainability through reservoir characterization at Brady geothermal field, Nevada*
Schaen, Allen J., *Petrochronology and crystal-melt dynamics of a late Miocene upper crustal Andean pluton*

University of Wyoming

Han, Guang, *In-situ stress inversion based on circular and elliptical borehole model*
Hoppes, Kara L., *Sediment flux and sand thickness mass conservation analysis of the Parkman Sandstone Member, Mesaverde Formation, Powder River basin, Wyoming, USA*
Javanbakht, Gina, *Impact of asphaltene and surfactant molecular structures on pore-scale displacement mechanisms of nonaqueous-phase liquids in heterogeneous rocks*
King, Matthew S., *Hydromorphology of Calcareous soils in western Wyoming*
Laker, Rachel Marie, *Quantifying mineral and organic alteration of young fossil specimens using Raman spectroscopy*
McPeak, Andrew J., *Constraints on oceanic detachment fault formation; a macro- and microstructural study of fault rocks from Atlantis Massif (MAR 30°N)*
Meyers, Kelly, *Temperature-dependence of crude oil-brine interfacial rheological properties*
Mirchi, Vahideh, *Multi-scale investigations of the impact of surfactant structure on oil recovery from natural porous media*
Pankau, Marcin, *Three-dimensional petroleum system modeling in the Bighorn Basin, Wyoming*
Perlinski, Anthony T., *Semiarid rangeland watersheds; quantifying ecohydrologic processes across scales*
Sabti, Mohammad J., *Three-phase flow in fractured porous media; experimental investigation of matrix-fracture interactions using X-ray microtomography*
Scott, Sean R., *Geological applications of isotope geochemistry and the role of water in geologic processes*

Utah State University

Bullard, Abigail R., *New CA-ID-TIMS detrital zircon constraints on middle Neoproterozoic sedimentary successions, Southwestern United States*
Hill, Brianna V., *Analysis of the Parkway Drive landslide, North Salt Lake, UT*
Lathrop, Erin C., *Understanding the late Mesoproterozoic Earth system from the oldest strata in Grand Canyon; C-isotope stratigraphy and facies analysis of the 1254 Ma Bass Formation, Grand Canyon Supergroup, AZ, USA*
Mauch, James P., *Quaternary incision, salt tectonism, and landscape evolution of Moab-Spanish Valley, Utah*
Wigginton, Sarah S., *The influence of mechanical stratigraphy on thrust-ramp nucleation and propagation of thrust faults*

Villanova University

Carambelas, Emily Elizabeth, *Monitoring the effectiveness of stormwater control measures on reversing deteriorated stream functions in an urban setting*

Washington University

Powell, Kathryn Elizabeth, *Spectral and stratigraphic mapping of layered sulfate deposits on Mars using advanced CRISM data processing techniques*

West Virginia University

Reed, Miles, *How will anthropogenic valley fills in Appalachian headwaters erode?*

Western Michigan University

Aldiney, Muthanna Yousif Yaqoob, *Detection of bedrock fractures and joints beneath cover; geophysical approaches to an engineering geology problem*
Backhaus, Karl John, *Geologic mapping of the Bronson North and Bronson South 7.5-minute quadrangles, Branch County, Michigan*
Gebremichael, Esayas Gebrekidan, *Assessing land deformation and sea encroachment in the Nile Delta; a radar interferometric and modeling approach*
Koerber, Alexander J., *Geochemical and petrological investigation of the prospective Ni-Cu-PGE mineralization at the Echo Lake Intrusion in the Upper Peninsula of Michigan, USA*
Seiderman, Benjamin B., *Mapping bedrock topography of the Portage and Schoolcraft NW 7.5' quadrangles, Kalamazoo Co. MI, using the HVSR passive seismic method*
VanderMeer, Sarah M., *Mapping and interpreting the glacial geology of Pictured Rocks National Lakeshore, Michigan*

Wilfrid Laurier University

Haughton, Emily, *Permafrost thaw-induced forest to wetland conversion; potential impacts on snowmelt and basin runoff in northwestern Canada*

Woods Hole Oceanographic Institution

Black, Erin E., *An investigation of basin-scale controls on upper ocean export and remineralization*
Grozeva, Niya G., *Carbon and mineral transformations in seafloor serpentinization systems*
Jones, Katie R., *Measurements and dynamics of multiple scale bedforms in tidally energetic environments*
Moos, Simone, *The marine biogeochemistry of chromium isotopes*
Sarafian, Adam Robert, *Water and volatile element accretion to the inner planets*

Yale University

Bellefroid, Eric John, *Deciphering the boring billion; a combined sedimentological and geochemical study of mid-Proterozoic carbonates*

Alabama

Geological Survey of Alabama

Geological Survey of Alabama ☒ (2021)
420 Hackberry Lane
P.O. Box 869999
Tuscaloosa, AL 35486-6999
p. (205) 349-2852
ntew@gsa.state.al.us
http://www.gsa.state.al.us/
Programs: None. Research agency.
Certificates: None. Research agency.
State Geologist:
Berry H (Nick) Tew , (D), Alabama, 1999, GroGs
Division Manager, Geologic Investigations Division:
Sandy M. Ebersole, (D), Alabama, 2009, Zi
Division Manager, Energy Investigations Program:
Denise J. Hills, (M), Delaware, 1998, EoZfYe
Division Manager, Ecosystems Investigations :
Stuart W. McGregor, (M), Tennessee Tech, 1987, Hs
Division Manager, Coastal Resources:
Stephen C. Jones, (M), Alabama, 1996, HyGeCg
Manager, Geologic Mapping:
Gene Daniel Irvin, (M), Alabama, 1994, Gg
Manager, Petroleum Systems & Technology:
David C. Kopaska-Merkel, (D), Kansas, 1983, GsPiZe
Visiting Professor:
William A. Thomas, (D), Virginia Tech, 1960, GtcGr
Geologist & Paleontology Curator:
T. Lynn Harrell, Jr., (D), Alabama, 2016, PvGg
Geologist:
Guohai Jin, (M), Zhejiang, 1989, Np
Mac McKinney, (B), Alabama, 2007, Hws
Neil E. Moss, (M), Alabama, 1987, Hw
Marcella Redden, (M), Alabama, 2004, Gg
David Tidwell, (M), S Florida, 2005, Gm
Dane S. VanDervoort, (M), Auburn, 2016, GcpZi
Chemist:
Rick Wagner, (B), Texas (San Antonio), 1982, Cg
Biologist:
Rebecca A. Bearden, (B), Auburn, 2007, Hs
Chief of Staff, Asst. State Geologist:
Bennett L. Bearden, (D), McGeorge Law, 2011, HgEo

Alaska

Alaska Division of Geological & Geophysical Surveys

Department of Natural Resources (2017)
3354 College Road
Fairbanks, AK 99709-3707
p. (907) 451-5010
dggspubs@alaska.gov
http://www.dggs.alaska.gov
f: http://www.facebook.com/pages/Fairbanks-AK/Alaska-DGGS/346699054500
t: @akdggs
Director & State Geologist:
Steven S. Masterman, (M), Alaska (Fairbanks), 1990, EgNg
Petroleum Geologist I:
David Lepain, (D), Alaska, 1993, EoGos
GeoScientist I:
Melanie B. Werdon, (D), Alaska (Fairbanks), Eg
Geologist V:
Janet R. G. Schaefer, (M), Alaska (Fairbanks), Gv
De Anne S.P. Stevens, (M), Alaska (Fairbanks), Ng
Geologist IV:
Marwan A. Wartes, (M), Wisconsin, GsoGt
Gabriel J. Wolken, (D), Gm
Geohydrologist-Geologist IV:
Ronald P. Daanen, (D), Minnesota, 2004, HyGme
Division Operation Manager:
Kenneth R. Papp, (M), Alaska (Fairbanks), Gg

Alberta

Alberta Geological Survey

Alberta Geological Survey ☒ (2018)
402, Twin Atria Building
4999 - 98 Avenue
Edmonton, AB T6B 2X3
p. (780) 638-4491
AGS-Info@aer.ca
https://ags.aer.ca/

Arizona

University of Arizona

Arizona Geological Survey ☒ (2021)
1955 E 6th St.
PO Box 210184
Tucson, AZ 85721
p. (520) 621-2352
fmconway@email.arizona.edu
http://www.azgs.arizona.edu
f: https://www.facebook.com/AZ.Geological.Survey
t: @AZGeology
Programs: Not applicable
Certificates: Not applicable
Director & State Geologist:
Philip A. Pearthree, (D), Arizona, Ge
Senior Research Scientist:
Michael F. Conway, (D), Michigan Tech, 1993, RcGvg
Chief, Environmental Geology:
Ann Youberg, (D), Arizona, Ge
Senior Scientist:
Andrew A. Zaffos, (D), Cincinnati, 2014, Zf
Research Scientist:
Victor H. Garcia, (D), Texas (El Paso)
Thompson A. Lisa, (M), N Arizona, 2005
Research Geologist:
Joseph P. Cook, (M), Arizona, 2006, Gm
Senior Research Scientist:
Carson A. Richardson, (D), Arizona, 2019, Emg
Research Geologist:
Charles A. Ferguson, (D), Calgary, Gcv
Brian F. Gootee, (M), Arizona State, Gm
Brad Johnson, (D), Carleton, 1994, Gc
Jeri J. Young, (D), Arizona State, Ys

Arkansas

Arkansas Geological Survey

Arkansas Geological Survey (2015)
Vardelle Parham Geology Center
3815 West Roosevelt Road
Little Rock, AR 72204
p. (501) 296-1877
ags@arkansas.gov
http://www.geology.ar.gov
Administrative Assistant: Laure Hinze
Director & State Geologist:
Bekki C. White, (M), Centenary, 1993, GoEoGg
Geology Supervisor:
William D. Hanson, (M), Memphis State, 1991, EgnGs
Geologist Supervisor:
William L. Prior, (M), Memphis State, 1979, GggEc
Information Systems Analyst:
James K. Curry, (M), S Methodist, 1978, Zn
Geologist:
Sandra Chandler, Ze
Andrew Haner, Zi
David Johnston, Gg
Lea Nondorf, Cg
Senior Petroleum Geologist:
Peng Li, (D), Alabama, 2007, GoEoCo
M. Ed Ratchford, (D), Idaho, 1994, GocEo
Professional Geologist:
Richard S. Hutto, (B), Arkansas Tech, 1994, Gg

GIS Analyst:
Nathan H. Taylor, (B), 2007, ZiyGe
Geology Supervisor:
Scott Ausbrooks, (B), Arkansas, 2001, YsGeg
Angela Chandler, (M), Arkansas, 1996, GgrGs
Geologist:
Ty Johnson, (M), Arkansas, 2008, GgZiGr
Daniel S. Rains, (M), Arkansas, 2009, GgZi
Deputy Director & Asst State Geologist:
Mac B. Woodward, (B), Sacramento State, 1957, Gog

British Columbia

British Columbia Geological Survey

British Columbia Geological Survey ☒ (2019)
PO Box 9333 Stn Prov Govt
Victoria, BC V8W 9N3
Geological.Survey@gov.bc.ca
https://www2.gov.bc.ca/gov/content/industry/mineral-exploration-mining/british-columbia-geological-survey

California

California Geological Survey

California Geological Survey ☒ (2019)
801 K Street
Suite 1200
Sacramento, CA 95814
p. (916) 445-1825
cgshq@consrv.ca.gov
http://www.consrv.ca.gov/CGS/Pages
State Geologist:
John G. Parrish, (D)
Supervising Engineering Geologist:
John Clinkenbeared, (B), Eg
Supervising Engineering Geologist:
Timothy P. McCrink, (M), New Mexico Tech, 1982, Ng
William Short, (M), Ng
Senior Sesimologist:
Hamid Haddidi, (D), Ys
Senior Geologist:
Chris T. Higgins, (M), California (Davis), 1977, Gg
Senior Engineering Geologist (Specialist):
Jennifer Thornburg, (M), California (Santa Cruz), Ng
Senior Engineering Geologist:
David Branum, (B), Ng
Rui Chen, (D), Edmonton, Nr
Ron C. Churchill, (D), Minnesota, 1980, Cg
Tim Dawson, (M), Ng
Marc Delattre, (M), Ng
Fred Gius, (M), Gz
Will Harris, (B), Ng
Jeremy Lancaster, (M), Ng
Jeremy Lancaster, (B), Gg
Donald Lindsay, (M), Ng
David Longstreth, (M), Ng
Anne Rosinski, (M), Ng
Michael A. Silva, (B), California (Davis), 1978, Ng
Senior Engineer:
Moh J. Huang, (D), Caltech, 1983, Ne
Materials Engineer:
Badie Rowshandel, (D), Ne
Senior Scientist:
Badie Rowshandel, (D), Ys
Geologist:
Lawrence Busch, (A), Eg
Engineering Geologist:
Jackie Bott, (D), Gc
Patrick Brand, (M), Ng
Kevin Doherty, (M), Ng
Michael Fuller, (B), Ng
Joshua Goodwin, (M), Gg
Carlos Guiterrez, (B), Sacramento State, Ng
Wayne Haydon, (M), Ng
Cheryl Hayhurst, (B), Ng
Janis Hernandez, (M), Ng
Peter Holland, (M), Ng
Maxime Mareschal, (M), Ng
Michael McKinney, (M), Gg
Ante Mlinarevic, (M), Ng
Matt O'Neal, (B), Gi
Brian Olson, (M), Ng
John Oswald, (B), Ng
Florante Perez, Ng
Cindy L. Pridmore, (M), San Diego State, 1983, Ng
Pete Roffers, (M), Ng
Ron Rubin, (M), Ng
Gordon Seitz, (D), Ng
Eleanor Spangler, (M), Ng
Ellie Spangler, (M), Gc
Brian Swanson, (M), Ng
Mark Weigers, (M), Ng
Chase White, (M), Ng
Judy Zachariasen, (D), Gg
Civil Engineer:
Daniel Swensen, (D), Ne
Engineering Geologist:
Rick I. Wilson, (B), Fresno State, 1987, Ge
Associate Scientist:
Lijam Hagos, (D), Ys
Carla Rosa, (M), Ng

Colorado

Colorado Geological Survey

Colorado Geological Survey ☒ (2019)
1801 Moly Rd.
Golden, CO 80401
p. 303-384-2655
cgs_pubs@mines.edu
http://www.coloradogeologicalsurvey.org/
f: https://www.facebook.com/ColoradoGeologicalSurvey
State Geologist:
Karen Berry, (B), Colorado Mines, NgZu
Senior Mapping Geologist:
Matt Morgan, (M), Colorado Mines, 2006, GgmXm
Senior Hydrogeologist:
Peter Barkmann, (M), Montana, 1984, HwGcg
Senior Geothermal Geologist:
Paul Morgan, (D), Imperial Coll (UK), 2003, YhGtYg
Senior Engineering Geologist:
Jonathan Lovekin, (M), Colorado Mines, 2007, NgZuGs
Engineering Geologist:
Jill Carlson, (B), Wesleyan, 1987, NgZu
Senior Engineering Geologist:
Jonathan White, (B), E Illinois, 1983, NgZuGg
Hydrogeologist:
Lesley Sebol, (D), Waterloo, 2005, HwGeZg
GIS Hazard Analyst:
Francis Scot Fitzgerald, (M), Denver, 2011, ZirGg
Geologist:
Kassandra Lindsey, (M), Portland State, 2015, NgGmZi
Mike O'Keeffe, (M), New Mexico Tech, 1994, GgeEg
Engineering Geologist:
Kevin McCoy, (D), Colorado Mines, 2015, NgZiHw
Scientific & Technical Graphic Designer:
Larry Scott, (B), Univ Arts, 1985, Zy

Connecticut

Dept of Energy and Environmental Protection

Connecticut Geological Survey ☒ (2019)
Office of Information Management
79 Elm Street, 6th floor
Hartford, CT 06106-5127
p. (860) 424-3540
deep.ctgeosurvey@ct.gov
http://www.ct.gov/deep/geology
State Geologist:
Margaret A. Thomas, (M), Connecticut, 1983, Gg
Senior Research Associate:
Randolph P. Steinen, (D), Brown, 1973, Gsg
Civil Engineer:
Thomas E. Nosal, (M), C Connecticut, 1992, Zn
Research Associate:
Lindsey Belliveau, (M), Connecticut, 2016, Gmt

Teresa K. Gagnon, (M), Boston Coll, 1992, Gg
Resource Assistant:
James M. Bogart, (B), S Connecticut State, 2015, Ge

Delaware

University of Delaware

Delaware Geological Survey ☒ (2020)
Delaware Geological Survey
257 Academy Street
Newark, DE 19716-7501
p. (302) 831-2833
delgeosurvey@udel.edu
http://www.dgs.udel.edu
Administrative Assistant: Denise T. Heldorfer, Laura K. Wisk
State Geologist:
David R. Wunsch, (D), Kentucky, 1992, ClHwNg
Hydrogeologist:
A. Scott Andres, (M), Lehigh, 1984, Hg
Senior Scientist:
Peter P. McLaughlin, (D), Louisiana State, 1989, HgPm
Hydrogeologist:
Thomas E. McKenna, (D), Texas, 1997, Hg
Hydrogeologist:
Changming He, (D), Nevada (Reno), 2004, GqHg
Associate Scientist:
Stefanie J. Baxter, (M), Delaware, 1994, On
Research Associate:
John A. Callahan, (M), Delaware, 2014, Zri
Jaime L. Tomlinson, (M), Delaware, 2006, Zn
Emeritus:
John H. Talley, (M), Franklin and Marshall, 1974, As
Scientist:
Kelvin W. Ramsey, (D), Delaware, 1988, As
William S. Schenck, (M), Delaware, 1997, ZiGi
GIS Specialist:
Lillian T. Wang, (M), Delaware, 2005, Zi

Florida

Florida Geological Survey

Florida Dept of Environmental Protection ☒ (2021)
Commonwealth Building
3000 Commonwealth Blvd, Suite 1
Tallahassee, FL 32303
p. (850) 617-0300
jonathan.arthur@FloridaDEP.gov
https://floridadep.gov/fgs
State Geologist:
Jonathan D. Arthur, (D), Florida State, 1994, HwCgGe
Assistant State Geologist:
Guy H. Means, (M), Florida State, 2009, PgGe

Georgia

Georgia Dept of Natural Resources

Georgia Environmental Protection Div (2016)
Environmental Protection Division
2 Martin Luther King Jr. Dr., Suite 1152
East Tower
Atlanta, GA 30334-9004
p. (404) 657-5947
askepd@gaepd.org
http://epd.georgia.gov/
Senior Scientist:
James Kennedy, (D), Texas A&M, 1981

Hawaii

Dept of Land & Natural Resources

Commission on Water Resource Management ☒ (2018)
Kalanimoku Building
P.O. Box 621
1151 Punchbowl Street, #227
Honolulu, HI 96809
p. (808) 587-0214
dlnr.cwrm@hawaii.gov
http://dlnr.hawaii.gov/cwrm

Idaho

University of Idaho

Idaho Geological Survey ☒ (2019)
875 Perimeter Dr. MS 3014
University of Idaho
Moscow, ID 83844-3014
p. (208) 885-7991
igs@uidaho.edu
http://www.idahogeology.org/
f: https://www.facebook.com/IDGeoSurvey/
t: @IDGeoSurvey
Director:
Claudio Berti, (D), Chieti (Italy), 2009, GgmGc
Research Geologist:
Virginia S. Gillerman, (D), California (Berkeley), 1982, Eg
Reed S. Lewis, (D), Oregon State, 1990, GgiEg
Senior Petroleum Geologist:
Mark Barton
Senior Geologist:
Dennis M. Feeney, (M), W Washington, 2008, GgiYg
Hydrogeologist:
Alexandra Clark, (M)
Hazard Geologist:
Zachary Lifton, (D)

Illinois

Illinois State Geological Survey

Energy & Earth Resource Center (2015)
615 E. Peabody Drive.
Champaign, IL 61820-6964
p. (217) 244-2430
finley@isgs.uiuc.edu
Center Director:
Robert J. Finley, (D), South Carolina, 1975, Eo
Scientist:
Latif A. Khan, (D), Tech, 1971, Nx
Senior Scientist:
Scott M. Frailey, (D), Missouri (Rolla), 1989, Np
Massoud Rostam-Abadi, (D), Wayne State, 1982, Zn
Scientist:
Mei-In (Melissa) Chou, (D), Michigan State, 1977, Co
Sheng-Fu Joseph Chou, (D), Michigan State, 1977, Co
Joseph A. Devera, (M), S Illinois, 1985, Gr
Ivan G. Krapac, (M), Illinois, 1987, Ca
Zakaria Lasemi, (D), Miami, 1990, En
Hannes E. Leetaru, (D), Illinois, 1997, Eo
Donald G. Mikulic, (D), Oregon State, 1979, Ps
Beverly Seyler, (M), SUNY, 1978, Eo
Associate Scientist:
Cheri A. Chenoweth, (B), Illinois, 1979, Ec
Joan E. Crockett, (B), Illinois, 1983, EoZg
John P. Grube, (M), Colorado Mines, 1984, Eo
Bryan G. Huff, (M), Illinois, 1984, Eo
Rex A. Knepp, (M), Go
Assistant Scientist:
F. Brett Denny, (B), Missouri (Rolla), 1985, Gr
Christopher P. Korose, (B), Illinois, 1995, Ec
Vinodkumar A. Patel, (B), Inst of Tech, 1973, Zn
Emeritus:
Pam Cookus, Zn
Assistant Scientist:
Kathleen M. Henry, (B), Illinois State, 1982, Gg

Illinois State Geological Survey ☒ (2017)
615 East Peabody Drive
Champaign, IL 61820-6964
p. 217-333-4747
info@isgs.illinois.edu
https://www.isgs.illinois.edu/
f: https://www.facebook.com/ILGeoSurvey
t: @ILGeoSurvey
Administrative Assistant: Tamra S. Montgomery
Director:
Richard C. Berg, (D), Illinois, 1979, GleGm

Senior Geologist:
Anne L. Ellison, (M), Ge
Geoscience Information Stewardship:
Mark Yacucci, (M), Illinois State
Associate Geologist:
Scott D. Elrick, (M), California (Riverside), 1999, EcGsPg
Senior Geologist:
Zakaria Lasemi, (D), Illinois, Eg
Senior Geochemist:
Samuel V. Panno, (M), S Illinois, 1978, ClGgHw
Head Geochemistry:
Randall Locke, (M), Cl
Chief Scientist:
Steven E. Brown, (M), Wisconsin, 1990, Glm
Associate Quaternary Geologist:
David A. Grimley, (D), Illinois, 1996, GmlSc
Senior Scientist:
Richard A. Cahill, (M), Maryland, 1974, CaGeCt
Associate Quaternary Geologist:
Andrew C. Phillips, (D), Illinois (Chicago), 1993, GsmZi
Adjunct Assistant Professor:
Ethan Theuerkauf, (D), North Carolina, 2016, GmuGs
Assistant Petroleum Geologist:
Nathan D. Webb, (M), Illinois (Urbana), 2009, EoGo
Illinois State Geologist:
E. Donald McKay III, (D), Illinois, 1977, GlsGr
Wetlands Geology Specialist:
Colleen Long, (M), North Carolina, 2012, Gg
Jessica Monson, (M), Gg
Wetlands Geologist and Head:
James J. Miner, (M), Gg
Wetlands Geologist:
Jessica R. Ackerman, Zn
Team Leader/Associate Geologist:
Dale R. Schmidt, (M), Ge
Team Leader:
D. Adomaitis, Ge
Senior Petroleum Geologist:
Hannes E. Leetaru, (D), Illinois, 1997, Gor
Senior Paleontologist:
Joseph A. Devera, (M), Pg
Senior Geophysicist:
Timothy H. Larson, (D)
Remote Sensing Data Manager:
Janet Carmarca
Program Manager, Illinois Height Modernization Project:
Sheena K. Beaverson, Zr
Principal Engineering Geologist:
R. A. Bauer, (M), Ng
Media and Information Technology Administrator:
Daniel Byers
Map Standards Coordinator:
Jennifer Carrell, Zg
Hydrogeologist and Assistant Section Head:
Yu-Feng Forrest Lin, (D), Wisconsin, 2002, Hg
Geospatial Applications Developer/GIS Specialist:
Melony Barrett, Zi
Geologic Specialist:
Zohreh Askari, (M), Azad, 1997, Gsc
Alan R. Myers, (B), EcGo
Jennifer M. Obrad, (M), EcGo
Enviromental Data Coordinator:
Clint Beccue, Ge
Associate Wetlands Geologist:
Steven Benton, Gg
Keith W. Carr, (M), Gg
Eric T. Plankell, (M), Hg
Geoff Pociask, (M), Hw
Associate Quaternary Geologist:
Olivier J. Caron, (D), Québec (Montréal), Ng
Associate Geologist:
Cheri Chenoweth, GoEc
Christopher P. Korose, (M), EcGo
Associate Geohydrologist:
Jason F. Thomason, (D), Hw
Associate Geochemist:
Shari E. Effert-Fanta, (M), Cas
Associate Engineering Geologist:
Andrew Anderson, Ng
Greg A. Kientop, (M), Ge
Associate Economic Geologist:
F. Brett Denny, (M), GzEg
Associate Director Advanced Energy Technology Initiative:
Sallie Greenberg, (D), Illinois (Urbana), 2013, ClZg
Assistant Wetlands Geologist:
Kathleen E. Bryant, (M), Gg
Assistant Section Head, Environmental Assessments:
Mark Collier, Ge
Assistant Section Head:
B. Brandon Curry, (D), Illinois (Urbana), 1995, Gel
Assistant Geologist:
James Damico, (M)
Craig R. Decker, (B)
Scott R. Ellis, (B), Ge
Bradley Ettlie, (B), Ge
Jared Freiburg, (M), GgzGx
James W. Geiger, (B), Ge
Nathan P. Grigsby, (B)
Matthew P. Spaeth, (M), Ge
Assistant Geochemist:
Peter M. Berger, (M), Illinois (Urbana), 2008, Cg
Other:
Hong Wang, Illinois (Urbana), 1996, Cg

University of Illinois

Illinois State Geological Survey/Prairie Research Institute ☒ (2018)
615 E. Peabody Dr.
Champaign, IL 61820-6964
p. (217) 333-4747
info@isgs.illinois.edu
http://www.isgs.edu
f: https://www.facebook.com/ILGeoSurvey/
t: @ILGeoSurvey
State Geologist:
Richard Berg, (D), Illinois (Urbana), 1979, GlRwZu
Energy & Minerals Group:
Steven Whittaker, (D), Saskatchewan
Principle Geologist:
B. Brandon Curry, Illinois, Gl
Principal Scientist:
Randall A. Locke II, (M), CgHw
Principal Geologist:
Scott D. Elrick, (M), California (Riverside), 1998, EcGgs
Assoociate Geologist:
Geoffrey Pociask, (M), Wisconsin, Hs
Head:
Anne L. Ellison, (M), Ge
Hannes Leetaru, (D), Illinois, Go
Jason Thomason, (D), Iowa State, Gl
Mark A. Yacucci, (M), Zi
Senior Scientist:
Yongqi Lu, (D), Zm
Chief Scientist:
Steven E. Brown, (M), Gl

Illinois State Water Survey ☒ (2020)
2204 Griffith Drive
Champaign, IL 61820
p. (217) 244-5459
info@isws.illinois.edu
http://www.isws.illinois.edu/
Programs: N/A
Certificates: N/A
Head, Groundwater Science Section:
Walton R. Kelly, (D), Virginia, 1993, Hw
Senior Scientist:
Steven D. Wilson, (M), Illinois, 1988, Hw
Associate Scientist:
Daniel Abrams, (D), Indiana, 2013, Hw
Daniel Hadley, (M), N Arizona, 2014, Hw
Devin Mannix, (M), S Illinois, 2013, Hw

Indiana

Indiana University

Indiana Geological and Water Survey (2017)
611 North Walnut Grove Avenue
Bloomington, IN 47405
p. (812) 855-7636
igsinfo@indiana.edu
http://igws.indiana.edu/

State Geologist & Director:
Todd A. Thompson, (D), Indiana, 1987, GsmGu
Senior Scientist:
Maria Mastalerz, (D), Silesian Tech, 1988, Ec
Assitant Director for Research:
Lee J. Florea, (D), S Florida, 2006, HqGeCl
Associate Scientist:
Sally L. Letsinger, (D), Indiana, 2001, HqZir
Research Associate:
Patrick I. McLaughlin, (D), Cincinnati, 2006, GrClGs
Reservoir Geologist:
Cristian R. Medina, (M), Indiana, 2007, GoeHw
Research Geophysicist/Hydrologist:
Kevin M. Ellett, (M), California (Davis), 2002, YeHw
Research Geologist:
José Luis Antinao, (D), Dalhousie, 2009, CcGlr
Robert J. Autio, (M), Indiana, 1992, HgGle
Alyssa M. Bancroft, (D), Ohio State, 2014, PmGr
Tracy D. Branam, (M), Indiana, 1991, CasEm
Christopher Dintaman, (M), Indiana, 1997, Hw
Agnieszka Drobniak, (D), Sci Tech (Krakow), 2002, Ec
Jayson Eldridge, (B), California (Davis), 2012, EoGr
Nancy R. Hasenmueller, (M), Ohio State, 1969, Gre
Rebecca A. Meyer, Ec
Gary J. Motz, (M), Akron, 2010, PqgPi
Shawn C. Naylor, (M), Montana, 2006, Hw
John A. Rupp, (M), E Washington, 1980, Go
Quaternary Geologist:
Henry M. Loope, (D), Wisconsin, 2013, Gls

Iowa

Iowa Dept of Natural Resources

Iowa Geological and Water Survey (2015)
109 Trowbridge Hall
Iowa City, IA 52242-1319
p. (319) 335-1575
MaryPat.Heitman@dnr.iowa.gov
http://www.igsb.uiowa.edu
Administrative Assistant: Mary Pat. Heitman

Research Geologist:
Richard A. Langel, (M), Iowa, 1996, Gg
State Geologist:
Robert D. Libra, Gg
Section Supervisor, Geology and Groundwater Studies:
J. Michael Gannon, (M), Arizona, Gg
Section Supervisor, Geographic Information:
Chris Ensminger
Research Geologist:
Mary R. Howes, Gg
Lynette S. Seigley, (M), Iowa, Gg
Natural Resource Biologist:
Jacklyn Gautsch, (B), Wisconsin, Zn
GIS Technician:
Chris Kahle, (M), Kansas, Zi
Geologist 3, Research Geologist:
Paul Hiaibao Liu, (D), Nebraska, Gg
Robert M. McKay, (B), Tulane, Gg
Deborah J. Quade, (M), Iowa, 1992, GleGm
Robert Rowden, (M), Iowa, Gg
Keith Schilling, (M), Iowa State, Gg
Stephanie Tassier-Surine, (M), Massachusetts, Gg
Paul E. VanDorpe, (M), Wayne State, Gg
Geologist 3, Remote Sensing Analyst:
James D. Giglierano, (M), Purdue, GgZri
Pete Kollasch, (M), Iowa, GgZri
Geologist 3, GIS Analyst:
Kathryne Clark, (M), New Mexico, GgZi
Geologist 3, Geographic Information System Analyst:
Calvin Wolter, (B), Arizona, GgZi
Geologist 2, Research Geologist:
Michael Bounk, (M), Iowa, Gg
Chad Fields, (M), N Iowa, Gg
Geologist 3, NRGIS Library Manager and GIS Analyst:
Casey Kohrt, (B), Iowa State, GgZi

Kansas

University of Kansas

Kansas Geological Survey ☒ (2021)
1930 Constant Avenue
West Campus
Lawrence, KS 66047-3724
p. (785) 864-3965
http://www.kgs.ku.edu/
f: www.facebook.com/KansasGeologicalSurvey
t: @ksgeology

Director:
Rolfe D. Mandel, (D), Kansas, 1991, Ga
Section Chief, Senior Scientist:
Richard D. Miller, (D), Leoben, 2007, Ye
Research Project Director:
Kenneth A. Nelson, (B), Kansas, 1993, Zy
Manager, Wichita Well Sample Library:
Mike Dealy, (B), Fort Hays State, 1979, Gg
Manager, Geohydrology Support Services:
Blake Brownie Wilson, (M), Kansas State, 1993, Zi
Senior Scientific Fellow:
Evan K. Franseen, (D), Wisconsin, 1989, Gs
Section Chief, Senior Scientist:
Greg A. Ludvigson, (D), Iowa, 1988, GrCsPc
Senior Scientist:
James J. Butler, Jr., (D), Stanford, 1987, Hw
Associate Scientist:
Geoffrey C. Bohling, (D), Kansas, 1999, Hw
Gaisheng Liu, (D), Alabama, 2004, Hy
Kerry D. Newell, (D), Kansas, 1996, Go
Petroleum Engineer:
Yehven I. Holubnyak, (M), North Dakota, 2008, Np
Assistant Researcher Senior:
Edward Reboulet, (M), Boise State, 2003, Hy
Assistant Research Professor:
Julian Ivanov, (D), Kansas, 2002, Yg
Research Engineer Senior:
Brett Bennet, (B), Kansas, 1982, Ng
Outreach Manager:
Blair Schneider, Gg
DASC Manager:
Eileen Battles, (B), Kansas, 1993, Zy
Assistant Scientist:
Jon J. Smith, (D), Kansas, 2007, Gg

Kentucky

University of Kentucky

Kentucky Geological Survey ☒ (2020)
228 Mining & Minerals Resources Building
504 Rose Street
Lexington, KY 40506-0107
p. (859) 257-5500
KGSmail@uky.edu
http://www.uky.edu/KGS
f: www.uky.edu/KGS

State Geologist and Director:
William C. Haneberg, (D), Cincinnati, 1989, NgRnNp
Head, Water Resources Section:
Charles J. Taylor, (M), Kentucky, 1992, HwgCl
Head, Geoscience Information Management:
Doug C. Curl, (M), Tennessee, 1998, ZfGgc
Head, Geologic Mapping Section:
William M. Andrews, (D), Kentucky, 2004, GmZiEc
Head, Geologic Hazards Section:
Zhenming Wang, (D), Kentucky, 1998, Ys
Head, Energy & Minerals:
David C. Harris, (M), SUNY (Stony Brook), 1982, Go

Head, Administration:
Kathryn E. Ellis, (M), Kentucky, 2012, Zn

Louisiana

Louisiana State University

Basin Research Energy Section (2015)
Louisiana Geological Survey/LSU
208 Howe Russell Geoscience Complex
Baton Rouge, LA 70803-4101
p. (225) 578-8328
bharde1@lsu.edu
http://www.bri.lsu.edu
Office Coordinator: Cherri B. Webre

Associate Professor:
Ronald K. Zimmerman, (D), Louisiana State, 1966, Go
Assistant Professor:
Clayton F. Breland, (D), Tennessee, 1980, Ye
John B. Echols, (D), Louisiana State, 1966, Go
Research Associate:
Brian J. Harder, (B), Louisiana State, 1981, Eo
Bobby L. Jones, (B), Louisiana State, 1953, Go
Phillip W. Lemay, (B), Centenary, 1999, Gg
Michael B. Miller, (M), North Carolina, 1982, Go
Lloyd R. Milner, (B), Louisiana State, 1985, Gg
Patrick M. O'Neill, (B), Louisiana State, 1985, Sf
Computer Analyst:
Reed J. Bourgeois, (B), Louisiana State, 1983, Zn
Accountant Technician:
Carla Domingue, Zn

Louisiana Geological Survey (2015)
3079-Energy,
Coast and Environment Bldg.
Baton Rouge, LA 70803
p. (225) 578-5320
hammer@lsu.edu
http://www.lgs.lsu.edu

State Geologist and Professor:
Chacko J. John, (D), Delaware, 1977, GosGe
Assistant Professor:
Douglas A. Carlson, (D), Wisconsin (Milwaukee), 2001, Hw
Marty R. Horn, (D), Texas (Arlington), 1996, EoGgr
GIS Coordinator:
R Hampton Peele, (M), Louisiana State, 2000, ZirZg
Computer Analyst:
Reed J. Bourgeois, (B), Nicholls State, 1985, Zn
Research Associate:
Brian J. Harder, (B), Louisiana State, 1981, Eo
Paul V. Heinrich, (M), Illinois, 1982, GsaGm
Bobby Jones
Richard P. McCulloh, (M), Texas, 1977, Gg
Lloyd R. Milner, (B), Louisiana State, 1985, Gg
Patrick M. O'Neill, (B), Louisiana State, 1985, Sf
Robert L. Paulsell, (B), Louisiana State, 1987, ZyGg
Lisa G. Pond, (B), Louisiana State, 1987, Zg
Arren Schulingkamp, Gg
Cartographic Manager:
John I. Snead, (B), Louisiana State, 1978, Gm
Assistant Director:
John E. Johnston, III, (M), Texas, 1977, EoGe
Office Coordinator:
Melissa H. Esnault, (B), Louisiana Tech, Zn

Maine

Dept of Agriculture, Conservation, and Forestry

Maine Geological Survey ☒ (2020)
93 State House Station
Augusta, ME 04333-0093
p. (207) 287-2801
mgs@maine.gov
http://www.maine.gov/dacf/mgs/
Administrative Assistant: Tammara Roberts

State Geologist:
Robert G. Marvinney, (D), Syracuse, 1986, Gg
Senior Geologist:
Lindsay Spigel, (D), Wisconsin, 2006, Gm
Amber Whittaker, (M), New Mexico, 2006, GcZiCg
Physical Geologist:
Henry N. Berry IV, (D), Massachusetts, 1989, Gg
Marine Geologist:
Stephen M. Dickson, (D), Maine, 1999, OnGuOu
Peter Slovinsky, (M), South Carolina, 2001, Gu
Hydrogeologist:
Ryan Gordon, (D), Syracuse, 2014, HwGm
Daniel B. Locke, (B), Maine, 1982, Hw
Director, Earth Resources Information:
Christian Halsted, (M), Wisconsin, 2020, Zi

Manitoba

Manitoba Geological Survey

Manitoba Agriculture and Resource Development ☒ (2020)
360-1395 Ellice Avenue
Winnipeg, MB R3G 3P2
p. 1-800-223-5215
michelle.nicolas@gov.mb.ca
http://www.manitoba.ca/iem

Director:
Michelle P.B. Nicolas, (M), Manitoba, 1997, GrsGo
Senior Scientist:
Christian Bohm, (D), ETH (Switzerland), 1996, GgCgEg

Maryland

Maryland Department of Natural Resources

Maryland Geological Survey ☒ (2020)
2300 St. Paul Street
Baltimore, MD 21218-5210
p. (410) 554-5500
mgsinfo.dnr@maryland.gov
http://www.mgs.md.gov/

State Geologist:
Richard A. Ortt, Jr., (B), Johns Hopkins, 1991, NtGeYr
Hydrogeologist, Program Chief:
David C. Andreasen, (B), Maryland, 1985, Hw
Geologist/Program Chief:
Stephen Van Ryswick, (B), Maryland, 2002, Ge
Senior Scientist:
David K. Brezinski, (D), Pittsburgh, 1984, Gr
Hydrogeologist:
Emelia Furlong, (D), Caltech, HwCqSp
Andrew W. Staley, (M), Wisconsin, 1992, Hw
Tiffany J. VanDerwerker, (M), Virginia Tech, Hw
Geologist:
Christopher B. Connallon, (M), Michigan State, 2015, GmZi
William D. Junkin, (M), California (Santa Barbara), 2018, GvrGg
Rebecca H. Kavage Adams, (M), Virginia Tech, 2002, GmZiGe
Heather A. Quinn, (M), Florida, 1988, GgHwg
Elizabeth R. Sylvia, (M), Towson, 2013, Ge
Education Specialist:
Dale W. Shelton, (B), Towson, 1986, ZeGg

Massachusetts

Massachusetts Geological Survey

Dept of Geosciences ☒ (2020)
Univ of Massachusetts (Amherst)
627 North Pleasant Street
Amherst, MA 01003
p. (413) 545-4814
sbmabee@geo.umass.edu
Programs: N/A
Certificates: N/A

State Geologist:
Stephen B. Mabee, (D), Massachusetts, 1992, Hw

Minnesota

University of Minnesota

Minnesota Geological Survey ☒ (2021)
2609 West Territorial Road
Saint Paul, MN 55114-1009
p. 612-626-2969
mgs@umn.edu

https://cse.umn.edu/mgs
f: https://www.facebook.com/UMNMGS
Director:
Harvey Thorleifson, (D), Colorado, 1989, Gl
Geologist:
Emily Bauer, (B), Wisconsin (River Falls), 1989, Zi
Terrence Boerboom, (M), Minnesota (Duluth), 1987, GivGc
Angela S. Gowan, (M), Minnesota (Duluth), 1993, Gl
Mark Jirsa, (M), Minnesota (Duluth), 1980, Gc
Alan Knaeble, (B), Minnesota, 1982, Gl
Rich Lively, (M), Michigan State, 1977, Cc
Gary Meyer, (M), North Dakota, 1979, Gl
Julia Steenberg, (M), Idaho State, 2008, Gs
Chief Geologist:
Anthony Runkel, (D), Texas, 1988, Gs
Associate Director:
Barb Lusardi, (M), Maine, 1992, Gl
Geologist:
Angela Berthold, (M), Minnesota (Duluth), 2014, Gl
Maximiliano Bezada Diaz, (D), Venezuelan Inst Sci Inv, 1989, Gl
Amy Block, (M), Minnesota (Duluth), 2013, Gp
Jarrod Cicha, (M), Maine, 2015, Zi
Daniel Conrad, (M), N Arizona, 2018, Gl
Jacqueline Hamilton, (M), Minnesota, 2007, ZiGe
Jordan Mayer, (M), Michigan Tech, 2016, Zi
Jennifer McDonald, (M), Toledo, 2015, Gl
Maurice Nguyen, (M), W Ontario, 2014, Gl
Andrew J. Retzler, (M), Idaho State, 2013, GrsPi
Allison Severson, (D), Colorado Mines, 2020, Gp
Kaleb Wagner, (M), Brock, 2014, Gl
Technical Editor:
Lori Robinson, (M), Alaska (Fairbanks), 1999, Zi
Information Science:
Corey Betchwars, (M), Minnesota, 2014, Zi

Mississippi

Mississippi Office of Geology

Geospatial Resources Div (2015)
P.O. Box 2279
700 N. State St
Jackson, MS 39225-2279
p. (601) 961-5500
barbara_yassin@deq.state.ms.us
http://www.deq.state.ms.us
Geologist:
Steven D. Champlin, (B), Alabama, 1976, Go
GIS Analyst:
Barbara E. Yassin, (B), Illinois State, 1989, ZyiGm
Geologist:
Peter S. Hutchins, (B), Millsaps, 1990, Zn

Mississippi Dept of Environmental Quality (2016)
P.O. Box 2279
Jackson, MS 39225-2279
p. (601) 961-5500
mbograd@mdeq.ms.gov
http://www.deq.state.ms.us/
State Geologist:
Michael B. E. Bograd, (M), Mississippi, 2002, Gg

Missouri

Missouri Dept of Natural Resources

Dam & Reservoir Safety (2015)
PO Box 250
Buehler Bldg/111 Fairgrounds Rd
Rolla, MO 65402
p. (573) 368-2175
bob.clay@dnr.mo.gov
Professional Staff:
Robert Clay, (M), Oklahoma State, 1977, Zn
Professional Staff:
Glenn D. Lloyd, (B), Zn
Other:
Paul Simon, (B), Missouri Tech
Ryan Stack, (B), Missouri Tech

Div of Geology and Land Survey (2015)
PO Box 250
111 Fairgrounds Road
Rolla, MO 65402-0250
p. (573) 368-2100
joe.gillman@dnr.mo.gov
http://www.dnr.state.mo.us/geology.htm
Administrative Assistant: Tami L.. Allison
State Geologist & Division Director:
Mimi R. Garstang, (B), SW Missouri State, Ge
Deputy Director & Assistant State Geologist:
James W. Duley, (B), C Missouri, 1975, Hy

Geological Survey Program ☒ (2019)
PO Box 250
111 Fairgrounds Rd
Rolla, MO 65402-0250
p. (573) 368-2100
gspgeol@dnr.mo.gov
http://www.dnr.mo.gov/geology
State Geologist:
Joe Gillman, (B), Missouri State, 1992, Gg
Senior Scientist:
Pat Mulvany, (D), Missouri S&T, 1996
Unit Chief:
Justin Davis, (M), Missouri S&T, 2012
Jeremiah Jackson, (M), Missouri State, 2011, Gg
Brenna McDonald, (B), SE Missouri State, 1997, Ge
Cheryl M. Seeger, (D), Missouri S&T, 2003, Gig
Vicki Voigt, (B), Missouri S&T, 2010, Gg
Section Chief:
Larry Pierce, (M), Zn
Kyle Rollins, (B), Missouri State, 1986, ZyGg
Sherri Stoner, (B), Missouri State, 1991
Program Director:
Amber Steele, (M), Missouri, 2011, Sd
Geologist:
Peter Bachle, (B), Missouri S&T, 1997, Gg
Fletcher Bone, (B), C Missouri, 2007, Gg
David L. Bridges, (D), Missouri S&T, 2011, GgiPg
Kyle Brown, Mizzou, 2015, Gg
John H. Corley, (M), Missouri, 2014, Geg
Jeff Crews, (M), Missouri S&T, 2004, Hy
Trevor Ellis, (B), Missouri S&T, 2010, Gg
Kyle Ganz, (M), Missouri S&T, 2013
Airin J. Haselwander, (B), Missouri S&T, 2011, Gg
Terry Hawkins, (B), Brigham Young, 1988, Geg
Katelyn Kane-DeVries, (M), N Illinois, 2016, Gg
Lisa Lori, (M), Missouri S&T, 2016, Gp
Brad Mitchell, (M), Missouri S&T, 2010
Matt Parker, (B), Missouri S&T, 1993
Kirsten Schaefer, (B), Illinois State, 2016
Michael A. Siemens, (M), Wichita State, 1985, GgHgZi
Molly Starkey, (M), Missouri State, 2011
Chris Vierrether, (M), Missouri S&T, 1988, GgoGe
Geological Tech:
Cecil Boswell, Zn
Karen Loveland, Zn
Dan Nordwald, Zn
Patrick Scheel, Zn
Fred Shaw, Zn
Environmental Specialist:
Andrew Combs
Michelle Oglesby
Deputy Director:
Jerry L. Prewett, (B), Missouri State, 1992, GgHw

Water Resources Program ☒ (2020)
PO Box 250
111 Fairgrounds Rd
Rolla, MO 65401-0250
p. (573) 368-2175
mowaters@dnr.mo.gov
http://www.dnr.state.mo.us/mgs/
Geologist:
Scott Kaden, Hw
Associate Scientist:
Robert Bacon, Hs

Professional Staff:
Charles Du Charme, (B), Hs

Montana

Montana Tech of The University of Montana

Montana Bureau of Mines & Geology (A,B,M,D) ☒ (2018)
1300 West Park Street
Butte, MT 59701-8997
p. (406) 496-4180
jmetesh@mtech.edu
http://www.mbmg.mtech.edu
f: https://www.facebook.com/MontanaGeology/
Administrative Assistant: Margaret Delaney

State Geologist:
John J. Metesh, (D), Montana, 2003, HwCa
Assistant Director RET:
Marvin R. Miller, (M), Indiana, 1965, Hw
Research Division Chief:
Thomas W. Patton, (M), Montana Tech, 1987, Hw
Program Manager Geologist:
Catherine McDonald, (M), California (Davis), 1992, Grs
Assistant Research Geologist:
Jeff Lonn, (M), Montana, 1985, GgtGc
Senior Hydrogeologist:
Jon C. Reiten, (M), North Dakota, 1983, Hw
Geologist:
Susan M. Vuke, (M), Montana, 1982, GgrGs
Professor:
Colleen G. Elliott, (D), New Brunswick, 1988, GctGg
Senior Research Hydrogeologist:
John R. Wheaton, (M), Montana, 1987, HwEc
Program Manager Hydrogeologist:
Ginette Abdo, (M), Penn State, 1989, Hw
John I. La Fave, (M), Texas, 1987, Hw
Hydrogeologist:
Andrew L. Bobst, (M), SUNY (Binghamton), 2000, HwCgEo
Gary Icopini, (D), Michigan State, 2000, ClHwCb
Geologist:
Michael C. Stickney, (M), Montana, 1980, YsGtm
Publications Editor:
Susan A. Barth, (M), Montana Tech, 2009, Zn
Assistant Research Hydrogeologist:
Camela Carstarphen, (M), Oregon State, 1991, Hw
Assistant Research Geologist:
Phyllis Hargrave, (M), Montana Tech, 1990, Gg
Sr. Hydrogeologist:
Kirk B. Waren, (M), Wright State, 1988, HwsZe
Hydrogeologist:
Terence E. Duaime, (B), Montana Tech, 1978, Hws
Senior Research Geologist, Museum Curator:
Richard B. Berg, (D), Montana, 1964, EnGz
Seismic Analyst:
Deborah Smith
Research Assistant III:
Jaqueline R. Timmer, (B), Montana Tech, 1990, Ca
Hydrogeologist:
Daniel D. Blythe, (B), Montana State, 2006, Hws
GIS Specialist:
Ken L. Sandau, (A), Montana Tech, 1999, Zi
Paul R. Thale, (M), Montana State, 1994, Zi
Geologic Cartographer:
Susan M. Smith, (B), Montana State, 1970, Zn
Director of Sponsored Programs:
Joanne Lee
Chemist:
Ashley Huft, (B), Montana Tech, 2008, Ca
Associate Research Professor:
Steve F. McGrath, (M), Montana Tech, 1992, CaEgCe
Assistant Hydrogeologist:
Mary K. Sutherland, (M), Montana, 2009, Hws
Computer Software Eng/Applications:
Luke Buckley, (B), Montana Tech, 1995, Zn

Nebraska

University of Nebraska, Lincoln

Conservation & Survey Div (D) (2015)
Conservation & Survey Division
3310 Holdrege Street
616 Hardin Hall
Lincoln, NE 68583-0996
p. (402) 472-3471
rjoeckel3@unl.edu
http://snr.unl.edu/csd/

Director:
Mark S. Kuzila, (D), Nebraska, 1988, Sd
Professor:
Xun-Hong Chen, (D), Wyoming, 1994, Hq
David C. Gosselin, (D), SD Mines, 1987, CgHw
James W. Merchant, (D), Kansas, 1984, Zru
Jozsef Szilagyi, (D), California (Davis), 1997, HqAs
Senior Scientist:
Susan Olafsen-Lackey, (B), SD Mines, 1982, Hw
Steven S. Sibray, (M), New Mexico, 1977, HwGg
Associate Professor:
Paul Hanson, (D), Nebraska, 2005, Gm
Matt Joeckel, (D), Iowa, 1993, GsrGg
Research Associate:
Leslie M. Howard, (M), Nebraska, 1989, Zyi
Emeritus:
Marvin P. Carlson, (D), Nebraska, 1969, Gt
Robert F. Diffendal, Jr., (D), Nebraska, 1971, GrPiRh
Duane A. Eversoll, (M), Nebraska, 1977, Ng
Anatoly Gitelson, (D), Inst Radio Tech (Russia), 1972, Zn
James W. Goeke, (M), Colorado State, 1970, HwGmYe
Donald C. Rundquist, (D), Nebraska, 1977, Zri
James Swinehart, (D), Gg

Nevada

University of Nevada, Reno

Nevada Bureau of Mines and Geology ☒ (2018)
Mail Stop 178
University of Nevada
Reno, NV 89557-0088
p. (775) 682-8766
jfaulds@unr.edu
http://www.nbmg.unr.edu/
f: https://www.facebook.com/Nevada-Bureau-of-Mines-and-Geology-106397989390636/
Administrative Assistant: Alex Nesbitt

State Geologist/Professor:
James E. Faulds, (D), New Mexico, 1989, Gc
Professor:
Geoffrey Blewitt, (D), Caltech, 1996, Yd
William C. Hammond, (D), Oregon, 2000, Yd
Christopher D. Henry, (D), Texas, 1975, GtvCc
Corne Kreemer, (D), SUNY (Stony Brook), 2001, YdRn
Geologic Mapping Specialist:
Seth Dee, (M), Oregon, 2006, Gg
Director, Center for Research in Economic Geology:
John Muntean, (D), Stanford, 1998, Eg
Associate Professor:
Bridget Ayling, (D), Australian Nat, 2006, CgYhGo
Craig M. dePolo, (D), Nevada (Reno), 1998, Ng
Assistant Professor:
Rich Koehler, (D), Nevada (Reno), 2009, GmtNg
Mike Ressel, (D), Nevada (Reno), 2005, EgGiCc
Andrew V. Zuza, (D), California (Los Angeles), 2016, Gct
Adjunct Professor:
Mark F. Coolbaugh, (D), Nevada (Reno), 2003, Eg
Emeritus:
John W. Bell, (M), Arizona State, 1974, NgGm
Stephen B. Castor, (D), Nevada (Reno), 1972, Eg
Larry J. Garside, (M), Nevada (Reno), 1968, Gg
Liang-Chi Hsu, (D), California (Los Angeles), 1966, Cp
Daphne D. LaPointe, (M), Montana, 1977, Gg
Paul J. Lechler, (D), Nevada (Reno), 1995, Cg
Jonathan G. Price, (D), California (Berkeley), 1977, Gg
Alan R. Ramelli, (M), Nevada (Reno), 1988, Ng
Lisa Shevenell, (D), Nevada, 1990, Cg

Joseph V. Tingley, (M), Nevada (Reno), 1963, Em
Geologic Information Specialist:
David A. Davis, (M), Nevada (Reno), 1990, Gg

New Hampshire

New Hampshire Geological Survey

New Hampshire Dept of Environmental Services ☒ (2020)
29 Hazen Drive
P.O.Box 95
Concord, NH 03302-0095
p. (603) 271-1975
geology@des.nh.gov
http://des.nh.gov/organization/commissioner/gsu/
State Geologist:
Frederick H. Chormann, Jr., (M), New Hampshire, 1985, HyZiGm
Geoscience Program Specialist:
Gregory A. Barker, (B), Rhode Island, 1985, GglZi
Program Hydrogeologist:
Joshua A. Keeley, (M), Idaho State, 2011, GgHyZi
Assistant Flood Hazards Geoscientist:
Kyle W. Hacker, (B), New Hampshire, 2018
Administrator, Flood Hazards Program:
Shane Csiki, (D), Illinois (Urbana), 2014, ZyGm

New Jersey

New Jersey Geological and Water Survey

New Jersey Geological and Water Survey ☒ (2018)
PO Box 420, Mail Code:29-01
Trenton, NJ 08625-0420
p. (609) 292-1185
njgsweb@dep.nj.gov
http://www.njgeology.org
Administrative Assistant: Tenika Jacobs
State Geologist:
Jeffrey L. Hoffman, (M), Princeton, 1981, HqwRw
Bureau Chief:
David L. Pasicznyk, (B), Temple, 1979, Yg
Research Scientist 1:
Steven E. Spayd, (M), UMD New Jersey, 2004, HwGb
Peter J. Sugarman, (D), Rutgers, 1995, Gr
Supervising Geologist:
Eric W. Roman, (M), Temple, 1999, Hw
Supervising Env Specialist:
Helen L. Rancan, (M), Stevens, 1995, Hs
Supervising Env Engineer:
Richard Shim-Chim, (B), Toronto, 1973, Hw
Research Scientist 2:
James T. Boyle, (M), New Mexico Tech, 1984, Hw
Donald H. Monteverde, (D), Rutgers, 2008, Grg
Research Scientist 1:
Scott D. Stanford, (D), Rutgers, 2001, Gml
GIS Specialist 1:
Zehdreh Allen-Lafayette, (M), Syracuse, 1994, Zi
Mark A. French, (B), Rutgers, 1989, Hq
Ted J. Pallis, (M), Montclair State, 1994, Zi
Ronald Pristas, (B), Penn State, 1990, Zi
Principal Environmental Specialist:
Raymond T. Bousenberry, (M), New Jersey Inst Tech, 2007, Ge
Steven E. Domber, (M), Wisconsin, 2000, Hw
Gregg M. Steidl, (B), Rutgers, 1995, Ge
Research Scientist 2:
John H. Dooley, (M), New Mexico Tech, 1983, CgGfe
GIS Specialist 2:
Michael W. Girard, (B), Bloomsburg, 1996, Zi
Section Chief:
William P. Graff, (B), Clark, 1979, Zn
Investigator:
Walter Marzulli, Zy

New Mexico

New Mexico Institute of Mining and Technology

New Mexico Bureau of Geology & Mineral Resources ☒ (2020)
801 Leroy Place
Socorro, NM 87801-4796
p. (575) 835-5302
Nelia.Dunbar@nmt.edu
http://geoinfo.nmt.edu/
Director and State Geologist:
Nelia W. Dunbar, (D), New Mexico Tech, 1989, GivCa
Economic Geologist:
Alexander Gysi, (D), Iceland, 2011, EgCpGz
Research Scientist II:
Nels Iverson, (D), New Mexico Tech, 2017, GvCga
Adjunct Associate Research Professor of Geology:
Dana Ulmer-Scholle, (D), S Methodist, 1992, Gsd
Karst Hydrogeologist:
Lewis A. Land, (D), North Carolina (Chapel Hill), 1999, Hg
Sr. Principal Environmental Geologist Emeritus:
David W. Love, (D), New Mexico, 1980, Ge
Sr. Industrial Mineralogist Emeritus:
George S. Austin, (D), Iowa, 1971, Gz
Sr. Geologist, Head of Archives & Collections Emeritus:
Maureen Wilks, (D), New Mexico Tech, 1991, Gp
Sr. Field Geologist Emeritus:
Steven Cather, (D), Texas, 1986, Gg
Sr. Extractive Metallurgist Emeritus:
Ibrahim H. Gundiler, (D), New Mexico Tech, 1975, Nx
Senior Volcanologist, Geochronologist Emeritus:
William C. McIntosh, (D), New Mexico Tech, 1990, CcGv
Senior Mining Engineer Emeritus:
Robert W. Eveleth, (B), New Mexico Tech, 1969, Nm
Senior Field Geologist Emeritus:
Richard M. Chamberlin, (D), Colorado Mines, 1980, Gg
Senior Environmental Geologist Emeritus:
John W. Hawley, (D), Illinois (Urbana), 1962, Ge
Senior Chemist Emeritus:
Lynn A. Brandvold, (M), North Dakota State, 1964, Ca
Principal Senior Petroleum Geologist:
Ronald F. Broadhead, (M), Cincinnati, 1979, Go
Principal Senior Geophysicist Emeritus:
Marshall A. Reiter, (D), Virginia Tech, 1969, Yh
Principal Geologist Emeritus:
Paul W. Bauer, (D), New Mexico Tech, 1988, Gp
Industrial Mineralogist Emeritus:
James M. Barker, (M), California (Santa Barbara), 1972, En
Director and State Geologist Emeritus:
Charles E. Chapin, (D), Colorado Mines, 1966, Gt
L Greer Price, (M), Washington, 1974, Gg
Peter Scholle, (D), Princeton, 1970, Gd
Sr. Field Geologist:
Daniel Koning, (M), New Mexico, 1999, GsRnGm
Specialist/Water Data Engagement:
Jeri Sullivan Graham, (D), New Mexico Tech, 1997, Hw
Specialist/Publications Resource:
Elena Taylor, (B), New Mexico State, 2010
Specialist GIS TechnicianCartographer:
Andi Knight, (M), New Mexico State, 2007, Zi
Senior Field Geologist:
Bruce D. Allen, (D), New Mexico, 1993, Gm
Senior Data/GIS specialist:
Richard Kelley, (M), S Methodist, 1982, ZiGg
Seismic analyst:
Erica . Doerr, (M), Arkansas, 2004, YsGgZe
Amy Record, (M), Utah, 2020, Ys
Research Scientist II:
Jake Ross, (D), New Mexico Tech, 2014, Cc
Research Scientist:
Kristin Pearthree, (M), New Mexico, 2019, Gge
Production Editor:
Belinda Harrison, (B), New Mexico Tech, 1998
Petroleum Information Coordinator:
Annabelle Lopez, Go
Petroleum Geologist:
Joseph Grigg, (M), New Mexico Tech, 2016, Go
Luke Martin, (M), N Arizona, 2005, GorGd
Network Systems Administrator:
David Kasefang, (M), Bowling Green, 1986
Museum Curator & X-Ray Diffraction Lab Manager:
Kelsey McNamara, (M), Montana State, 2010, Gz
Mechanic II:
Brian Wheeler
Manager, Publications Sales Office:
Kelly Luster, (B), New Mexico Tech, 2009

Manager, Publications Program:
Brigitte Felix-Kludt
Manager, NMT Seismological Observatory:
Mairi Litherland, (D), Stanford, 2018, Ys
Manager, Education Outreach:
Cynthia Connolly, (M), New Mexico Tech, 2003, Ze
Lead Maintenance Carpenter:
Onesimo (Albert) Baca
Hydrogeologist/GIS Specialist:
Amanda Doherty, (M), Colorado State, 2019, HwCg
Hydrogeologist:
Marissa Fichera, (M), Colorado State, 2019, Hwq
Ethan Mamer, (M), SUNY (Buffalo), 2013, Hw
Brad Talon Newton, (D), Queens, 2013, HwCgs
Hydrogeological Lab Technician:
Cathryn Pokorny, (B), Arizona, 2004
Hydrogeological Field Technician:
Scott Christenson, (M), Missouri, 1977, Hw
Hydrogeologic Lab Associate:
Trevor Kludt, (D), New Mexico, 2006, Hw
GIS Technician/Cartographer:
Amy Dunn, (B), Michigan Tech, 2010, Zi
GIS Specialist/Cartographer:
Justine Nicolette, Zi
GIS Analyst I:
Mark Mansell, (B), New Mexico Tech, 2001, Zif
Geological Archives Coordinator:
Amy Trivitt-Kracke, (B), New Mexico Tech, 1999, ZfGg
Geochemist/Chemistry Lab Manager:
Bonnie A. Frey, (M), New Mexico Tech, 2002, Cg
Field Geologist – Surficial Mapper:
Kevin Hobbs, (D), New Mexico, 2016, GsrSd
Field Geologist II:
Matthew Zimmerer, (D), New Mexico Tech, 2011, Gvg
Field Geologist:
Snir Attia, (D), S California, 2020, GcgGi
Jacob Thacker, (D), New Mexico, 2020, GtcGr
Electron Microprobe Lab Manager/Geochemist:
Lynn Heizler, (B), Minnesota, 1983, Ca
Database Manager:
Jeanine McGann, (M), New Mexico, 2006
Coordinator/Map Production:
Phillip Miller, (B), New Mexico Tech, 2014, Zi
Computer Systems Administrator:
Christopher Armijo
Chemistry Lab Tech.:
Dustin Baca, Cag
Cartographer II:
Stephanie Chavez, (B), Southwest Univ of Visual Arts, 2010
Associate Director for Hydrogeology Programs:
Stacy Timmons, (M), Oregon State, 2002, Hwg
Associate Director for Finance:
Valentina Avramidi, (B), Rostov State (Russia), 1984
Aquifer Mapping Program Manager:
Laila Sturgis, (M), New Mexico Tech, 2003, Hw
Administrative Services Coordinator:
Connie Apache
Sr. Mineralogist/Economic Geologist/Museum Director:
Virgil W. Lueth, (D), Texas (El Paso), 1988, Gg
Sr. Geochronologist/Associate Director for Labs:
Matthew T. Heizler, (D), California (Los Angeles), 1993, Cc
Sr. Field Geologist:
Geoffrey Rawling, (D), New Mexico Tech, 2002, Gg
Senior Lab Associate:
Lisa Peters, (M), Texas (El Paso), 1986, Gg
Senior Geophysicist, Field Geologist:
Shari Kelley, (D), S Methodist, 1984, Yg
Principal Sr. Coal Geologist Emeritus:
Gretchen K. Hoffman, (M), Arizona, 1979, Ec
Principal Sr. Economic Geologist:
Virginia McLemore, (D), Texas (El Paso), 1993, Em
Geologist, Webmaster, ABQ Office Manager:
Adam S. Read, (M), New Mexico, 1997, Gg
Education Outreach Advisor-Retired:
Susan Welch, (B), New Mexico State, 1980, Ze
Associate Director for Map Program, Deputy Director:
J. Michael Timmons, (D), New Mexico, 2004, Gg

New York

New York State Geological Survey

New York State Geological Survey (2015)
3000 Cultural Education Center
Madison Avenue
Albany, NY 12230
p. (518) 473-6262
djornov@mail.nysed.gov
http://www.nysm.nysed.gov/research-collections/geology
Administrative Assistant: Donna Jornov
Curator of Sedimentary Geology:
Charles Ver Straeten, (D), Rochester, 1996, Grs
Curator of Geology:
Marian V. Lupulescu, (D), IASI (Romania), 1987, GzxEm
Senior Scientist:
Andrew Kozlowski, (D), W Michigan, 2002, Gl
Langhorne Smith, (D), Virginia Tech, 1996, Go
Museum Scientist 1:
Brian Bird, (D), GlZi
Project Geologist:
James Leone, (B), SUNY (Albany), 2006, EoGoCg
Brian Slater, (M), SUNY (Albany), 2007, GoEoGr
Education Specialist:
Kathleen Bonk, (B), SUNY (Albany), 2009, GoCg
Brandon L. Graham
State Paleontologist and Paleontology Curator:
Ed Landing, (D), Michigan, 1979, PscCc
Emeritus:
Michael A. Hawkins, (B), USNY Regents, 1972, Gz
Paleontology Collections Technician:
Frank Mannolini
Technician:
Michael Pascussi, (A), Schenectady Comm Coll, 1999, Eo
Related Staff:
Linda A. VanAller-Hernick, (B), St Rose, 1974, Pgb
Cooperating Faculty:
Barry Floyd, (M), Rensselaer, 1987, Zn

North Carolina

N.C. Department of Environmental Quality

North Carolina Geological Survey ☒ (2020)
1612 Mail Service Center
Raleigh, NC 27699-1612
p. 919-707-9210
kenneth.b.taylor@ncdenr.gov
http://portal.ncdenr.org/lr/geological_home
Administrative Assistant: Joyce Sanford
State Geologist:
Kenneth B. Taylor, (D), Saint Louis, 1991, YsGgEo
Senior Geologist:
Philip Bradley, (M), North Carolina State, 1996, Gcg
Senior Geologist :
Bart Cattanach, (M), North Carolina State, 1998, Gc
Senior Geologist:
Kathleen M. Farrell, (D), Louisiana State, 1989, Gs
Engineering Geologist:
Richard M. Wooten, (M), Georgia, 1980, RnGc
Senior Scientist:
Dwain Veach
Associate Scientist:
William Blocker, (M), Ohio State
Geologist I:
Nick Bozdog, (B), W Carolina, 2005, Gg
Kenny Gay, (M), E Carolina, 1980, GzsPi
Sierra J. Isard, (M), Iowa, 2014, Gcg

North Dakota

North Dakota Geological Survey

North Dakota Geological Survey ☒ (2019)
1016 E. Calgary Ave.
600 East Boulevard Avenue
Bismarck, ND 58505-0840
p. (701) 328-8000
emurphy@nd.gov
https://www.dmr.nd.gov/ndgs/

State Geologist:
Edward C. Murphy, (M), North Dakota, 1983, Zn
Paleontologist:
Jeff Person, Pg
Geologist:
Ned Kruger, Gg
Lorraine A. Manz, (D), London (UK), 1982, GmlGg

Northern Territory

Northern Territory Government Minerals and Energy

Northern Territory Government Minerals and Energy (2015)
48-50 Smith St
Paspalis Centrepoint Building
GPO Box 3000
Darwin, NT 0800
p. +61 8 8999 5511
minerals@nt.gov.au
http://www.minerals.nt.gov.au

Nortwest Territories

Northwest Territories Geological Survey

Industry Tourism and Investment - Government of the Northwest Territories ☒ (2020)
P.O. Box 1320
Yellowknife, NT X1A 2L9
p. (867) 767-9211
ntgs@gov.nt.ca
http://www.nwtgeoscience.ca/

Nova Scotia

Geological Survey of Canada

Atlantic Div (2015)
Bedford Institute of Oceanography
1 Challenger Drive
P.O. Box 1006
Dartmouth, NS B2Y 4A2
p. (902) 426-4386
Pat.Dennis@NRCan-RNCan.gc.ca
http://gsc.nrcan.gc.ca/org/atlantic/index_e.php
Senior Scientist:
Kumiko Azetsu-Scott, (D), Dalhousie, 1992, Ocp

Nova Scotia Natural Resources

Nova Scotia Natural Resources (2015)
P.O. Box 698
Founders Square
Halifax, NS B3J 3M8
p. (902) 424-5935
http://www.gov.ns.ca/natr/

Ohio

Ohio Dept of Natural Resources

Div of Geological Survey ☒ (2018)
2045 Morse Road Bldg. C-1
Columbus, OH 43229
p. (614) 265-6576
geo.survey@dnr.state.oh.us
http://www.ohiodnr.com/geosurvey/
Programs: N/A
Certificates: N/A
Geologist:
Michael P. Solis, (M), Kentucky, 2010, GgcGt
Senior Scientist:
Frank Fugitt, (B), Ohio, GrHw
Geologist:
Daniel R. Blake, (M), Wright State, 2013, Ysg
Geologic Assistant:
Madge R. Fitak, (B), Mt Union, 1972, Gg

Oklahoma

University of Oklahoma

Oklahoma Geological Survey (2015)
100 East Boyd
Energy Center
Suite N-131
Norman, OK 73019-0628
p. (405) 325-3031
ogs@ou.edu
http://www.ogs.ou.edu/homepage.php
Geologist:
Thomas M. Stanley, (D), Kansas, 2000, PiGsc
Adjunct Professor:
Kyle E. Murray, (D), Colorado Mines, 2003, HwZiGo
Seismologist:
Amberlee Darold, (M), Oregon, 2012, Ys
Geologist:
Julie M. Chang, (D), Texas (El Paso), 2006, GgZnn
Brittany Pritchett, Go

Ontario

Ontario Geological Survey

Ontario Geological Survey ☒ (2021)
933 Ramsey Lake Road
Sudbury, ON P3E6B5
p. (705) 670-5614
mines.library.ndm@ontario.ca
http://www.mndm.gov.on.ca/en/mines-and-minerals
f: www.facebook.com/OGSgeology
t: @OGSgeology
Director:
Steve . Beneteau
Senior Manager, Earth Resources & Geoscience Mapping Section:
John Hechler, (M), Laurentian
Senior Manager, OGS Geoservices Section:
John Beals

Oregon

Oregon Dept of Geology & Mineral Industries

Coastal Field Office (2015)
PO Box 1033
Newport, OR 97365
p. (541) 574-6658
Jonathan.Allan@dogami.state.or.us
Regional Geologist:
Rob Witter, (D), Oregon, 1999, Zg
Geologist:
George R. Priest, (D), Oregon State, 1980, Gg
Coastal Section Supervisor:
Jonathan C. Allan, (D), Canterbury (NZ), 1998, Gm

Oregon Dept of Geology and Mineral Industries

Oregon Dept of Geology and Mineral Industries ☒ (2017)
800 NE Oregon Street
Suite 965
Portland, OR 97232-2162
p. (971) 673-1555
dogami-info@oregon.gov
http://www.oregongeology.org
State Geologist:
Brad Avy, (M), Alaska
Chief Scientist, Deputy Director:
Ian P. Madin, (M), Oregon State, Gg
Reclamationist:
Ben Mundie, Ge
Industrial Minerals Geologist:
Clark Niewendorp, (M), Eg
Hydrogeologist:
Robert Brinkmann, (B), Colorado State, 1983, HwGoEm
Hydrocarbon and Metallic Ore Geologist:
Robert Houston, (M), Oregon, Ge
Geotechnical Engineer:
Yumei Wang, (M), California (Berkeley), 1988, Ne
Engineering Gelogist:
Bill Burns, (M), Portland State, 1999, Ng

Eastern Oregon Regional Geologist:
Jason McClaughry, (M), WSU, 2003, Gg
Coastal Geomorphologist:
Jonathan C. Allan, (D), Canterbury (NZ), 1998, Gm

Pennsylvania

DCNR- Pennsylvania Bureau of Geological Survey

Pennsylvania Geological Survey ☒ (2020)
3240 Schoolhouse Road
Middletown, PA 17057-3534
p. (717) 702-2017
http://www.dcnr.pa.gov/Geology/Pages
f: https://www.facebook.com/padcnr
Programs: none
Certificates: none
Administrative Assistant: Connie Cross, Audrey Kissinger
State Geologist and Bureau Director:
Gale C. Blackmer, (D), Penn State, 1992, Gc
Geologist Manager:
Kristin M. Carter, (M), Lehigh, 1993, EoCqEg
Michael E. Moore, (B), Penn State, 1975, HwZi
Stuart O. Reese, (M), Tennessee, 1986, Hw
Senior Geologic Scientist:
Robin Anthony, (B), Case Western, Ego
Rose-Anna Behr, (M), New Mexico Tech, 1999, Gcr
Aaron D. Bierly, (B), Pitt (Johnstown), GgZn
Helen L. Delano, (M), SUNY (Binghamton), 1979, GgmNg
Clifford H. Dodge, (M), Northwestern, 1976, GrEcRh
Craig Ebersole, (B), Juniata, ZiHw
Ellen R. Fehrs, (M), Colorado Mines, 2019, Zir
Antonette K. Markowski, (M), S Illinois, 1990, Eo
Victoria V. Neboga, (M), Kiev, 1985, GgHwNx
Caron E. Pawlicki, (M), Pittsburgh, 1986, ZiGgc
Katherine W. Schmid, (M), Pittsburgh, 2005, GoCcXb
James R. Shaulis, (M), Penn State, 1985, EcZe
Geologist Supervisor:
Kristen Hand, (B), Nicholls State, HwGg
Stephen G. Shank, (D), Penn State, 1993, GziGp
Simeon Suter, (B), Millersville, 1982, HwGg
Geologic Scientist:
Leonard J. Lentz, (M), North Carolina State, 1983, Ec
John C. Neubaum, (M), American Military Univ, 2001, EcnGg
Librarian:
Jody L. Smale, (M), Clarion, 2010, Zn
IT Technician:
Mark A. Dornes
IT Generalist:
David Fletcher
IT Adminstrator:
Sandipkumar P. Patel, (B)
Clerk Typist:
Jody L. Rebuck, (B), Messiah
Renee Speicher

Puerto Rico

Puerto Rico Bureau of Geology

Dept of Natural & Environmental Resources (2015)
Apartado 9066600
Puerta de Tierra Station
San Juan, PR 00906-6600
p. (787) 722-2526
Director:
Vanessa del S. Rodriguez, Zn

Quebec

Ministère de l'Énergie et des Ressources naturelles Québec

Ministère de l'Énergie et des Ressources naturelles Québec (2017)
5700 4eme avenue ouest
local A-409
Quebec, QC G1H 6R1
p. 1-866-248-6936
services.clientele@mern.gouv.qc.ca
http://www.mern.gouv.qc.ca/

Queensland

Queensland Environment and Resource Management

Queensland Environment and Resource Management (2015)
GPO Box 2454
Brisbane, QLD 4001
info@derm.qld.gov.au
http://www.derm.qld.gov.au/

Rhode Island

University of Rhode Island

Rhode Island Geological Survey (D) (2015)
9 East Alumni Ave.
314 Woodward Hall
University of Rhode Island
Kingston, RI 02881
p. 401.874.2191
rigsurv@etal.uri.edu
http://www.uri.edu/cels/geo/GEO_risurvey.html
State Geologist (Research Professor Emeritus):
Jon C. Boothroyd, (D), South Carolina, 1974, GslOn
Professor:
Thomas Boving, (D), Arizona, 1999, Hg
David Fastovsky, (D), Wisconsin, 1986, PvGsPs
Assistant Professor:
Dawn Cardace, (D), Washington (St Louis), 2006, Pg
Simon Engelhard, (D), Pennsylvania, 2010, Gg
Brian Savage, (D), Caltech, 2004, Ys
Lecturer:
Elizabeth Laliberte, (D), Rhode Island, 1997, Og
Research Associate:
Bryan A. Oakley, (D), Rhode Island, 2012, Gsl

Saskatchewan

Saskatchewan Ministry Energy and Resources

Saskatchewan Ministry Energy and Resources ☒ (2020)
1000 - 2103 - 11th Avenue
Regina, SK S4P 3Z8
p. (306) 787-9580
dmoadmin.er@gov.sk.ca
http://www.saskatchewan.ca/

South Carolina

South Carolina Dept of Natural Resources

Geological Survey ☒ (2017)
5 Geology Road
Columbia, SC 29212
p. 803.896.7931
scgs@dnr.sc.gov
http://www.dnr.sc.gov/geology/
Director:
Charles W. Clendenin, Jr., (D), Witwatersrand, 1989, Eg
Geologist III:
William R. Doar, III, (D), South Carolina, 2014, GrdGp
Chief Geologist:
C. Scott Howard, (D), Delaware
Research Associate:
Andy Wykel, (B), S California, 2017, Gg
Geologist II:
Katherine E. Luciano, (M), Coll of Charleston, GusGm
Program Manager-Drilling:
Joe Koch, Zg
Digitizer II:
Matt Henderson, (B), South Carolina, Zi

South Dakota

South Dakota Dept of Environment and Natural Resources

Geological Survey Program ☒ (2017)
Akeley-Lawrence Science Center

University of South Dakota
414 East Clark Street
Vermillion, SD 57069-2390
p. (605) 677-5227
tim.cowman@usd.edu
http://www.sdgs.usd.edu/
State Geologist:
Derric L. Iles, (M), Iowa State, 1977, HwGg
Geologist:
Darren J. Johnson, (M), Washington, 2009, GgEo
Geologist:
Nicholas J. Krohe, (M), Idaho State, 2016, Gg

Tennessee

Tennessee Geological Survey

Dept of Environment & Conservation ☒ (2021)
William R. Snodgrass TN Tower
312 Rosa L. Parks Ave., 12th Floor
Nashville, TN 37243
p. (615) 532-1502
Ronald.Zurawski@tn.gov
https://www.tn.gov/environment/program-areas/tennessee-geological-survey.html
State Geologist:
Ronald P. Zurawski, (M), Vanderbilt, 1973, GgPzEg
Environmental Consultant:
Albert B. Horton, (M), Vanderbilt, 1981, GgZi
Peter J. Lemiszki, (D), Tennessee, 1992, GcZiGg
Barry W. Miller, (M), Tennessee, 1989, EcZiGg
Environmental Scientist:
Vince Antonacci, (M), Ball State, 1987, GgZi
Ronald J. Clendening, (B), Tennessee Tech, 1986, GgcGm
Admin. Services Asst. 2 :
Carolyn A. Patton

Texas

University of Texas at Austin, Jackson School of Geosciences

Bureau of Economic Geology (2015)
University Station, Box X
Austin, TX 78713-8924
p. (512) 471-1534
begmail@beg.utexas.edu
http://www.beg.utexas.edu
Director:
Scott W. Tinker, (D), Colorado, 1996, Gor
Associate Director:
Jay P. Kipper, (M), Trinity (San Antonio), 1983, Zn
Eric C. Potter, (M), Oregon State, 1975, Eo
Senior Research Scientist:
Shirley P. Dutton, (D), Texas, 1986, Gd
Bob A. Hardage, (D), Oklahoma State, 1967, Yg
Susan D. Hovorka, (D), Texas, 1990, Gse
Michael R. Hudec, (D), Wyoming, 1990, GcEo
Martin P. A. Jackson, (D), Cape Town, 1976, Gc
Stephen E. Laubach, (D), Illinois, 1986, GcNrGz
Bob Loucks, (D), Texas, 1976, Go
Bridget R. Scanlon, (D), Kentucky, 1985, Hw
Research Scientist Associate V:
Tucker F. Hentz, (M), Kansas, 1982, GrsGo
Research Scientist:
William A. Ambrose, (M), Texas, 1983, Gs
Peter Eichhubl, (D), California (Santa Barbara), 1997, GcCgNr
Jean-Philippe Nicot, (D), Texas, 1998, HwCg
Senior Scientist:
Ian Duncan, (D), British Columbia, 1982, Gg
F. Jerry Lucia, (M), Minnesota, 1954, Go
Stephen C. Ruppel, (D), Tennessee, 1979, Gd
Senior Research Scientist:
Kitty L. Milliken
Research Scientist:
Sergey Fomel, (D), Stanford, 2002, Yx
Jeffrey G. Paine, (D), Washington, 1991, Gr
Julia Stowell Gale, (D), Exeter (UK), 1987, Gc
Hongliu Zeng, (D), Texas, 1994, Gs
Associate Professor:
Charles Kerans, (D), Carleton, 1982, Gd
Research Scientist:
Tim Dooley, (D), London (UK), 1994, Gc
Associate Scientist:
Katherine D. Romanak, (D), Texas, 1997, CgScGe
Research Scientist Associate IV:
Robert C. Reedy, (M), New Mexico Tech, 1996, Hgw
Research Scientist Associate:
John R. Andrews, (B), North Carolina, 1990, Zi
Research Associate:
Bruce Cutright
Qilong Fu, (D), Regina, 2005, Gso
H, Scott Hamlin, (D), Texas, Gr
Ursula Hammes, (D), Colorado, 1992, Gg
Farzam Javadpour, (D)
Timothy A. Meckel, (D)
Osareni C. Ogiesoba, (D)
Katherine D. Romanak, (D)
Diana Sava, (D), Stanford, 2004, Yg
Changbing Yang, (D)
Christopher K. Zahm, (D)
Beverly Blakeney DeJarnett, (M), Penn State, 1986, GrsGx
Edward W. Collins, (M), Stephen F. Austin, 1978, Ge
Micheal V. DeAngelo, (M), Texas (El Paso), 1988, Ye
Xavier Janson, (D), Miami, 2002, Gr
Research Scientist Associate:
Seay Nance, (D), Texas, 1988, Gg
Research Scientist Associate IV:
Robert M. Reed, (D), Texas, 1999, GxoGc
IT Manager:
Ron Russell, (M), Oklahoma, 1993, Zn
Associate Director:
Michael H. Young, Arizona, 1995, Ge
512-471-7135:
George Bush, (B), Texas Tech
Research Scientist Associate IV:
Thomas A. Tremblay, (M), Texas, 1992, Zy
Research Scientist Associate:
Caroline Breton, (B), Texas, 2001, Zi
Dallas B. Dunlap, (B), Texas, 1997, Ye
Tiffany Hepner, (M), S Florida, 2000, Og
Project Manager:
Rebecca C. Smyth, (M), Texas, 1995, Hg
Ramon H. Trevino, (M), Texas (Arlington), 1988, GsoGe
Related Staff:
Joseph S. Yeh, (B), Fu-Jen Catholic, 1977, Gm

Utah

Utah Geological Survey

Dept of Natural Resources ☒ (2020)
1594 West North Temple, Ste 3110
Box 146100
Salt Lake City, UT 84114-6100
p. (801) 537-3300
https://geology.utah.gov
f: https://www.facebook.com/UTGeologicalSurvey/
t: @utahgeological
Director/State Geologist:
Bill Keach, (M), Cornell, 1986, YegZg
Program Manager:
Steve D. Bowman, (D), Nevada (Reno), 2002, NgGe
Hugh Hurlow, (D), Washington, 1992, Hw
Mark Milligan, (M), Utah, 1994, Ze
Michael Vanden Berg, (M), Utah, 2003, Eo
Grant C. Willis, (M), Brigham Young, 1983, Gg
Librarian:
Suzanne Sawyer, (M), N Texas, 2012, Zn
GIS Manager:
Gordon Douglass, (M), Utah, 1986, Zi
Financial Manager:
Jodi T. Patterson, (M), Weber State, 2002, Zn
Deputy Director:
Michael D. Hylland, (M), Oregon State, 1990, Gg
Curator Core Research Center:
Peter J. Nielsen, (M), Brigham Young, 1992, Eo

Environmental Sciences Program (2015)
1594 West North Temple, Ste 3110
PO Box 146100
Salt Lake City, UT 84114-6100
p. (801) 537-3389
pamperri@utah.gov
http://geology.utah.gov
Manager:
Mike Lowe, (M), Utah State, 1985, Hw
Geologist:
Charles E. Bishop, (B), Utah, 1986, Hw
Hugh A. Hurlow, (D), Washington, 1982, Hw
Janae Wallace, (M), N Arizona, 1993, Hw
Senior Geologist:
James I. Kirkland, (D), Colorado, 1990, Pg
Senior Scientist:
David B. Madsen, (D), Missouri, 1973, Ga
Research Associate:
Martha C. Hayden, (B), Utah, 1978, Pv
Geotechnician:
Alison Corey, Zn

Geologic Hazards Program (2015)
1594 West North Temple
P O Box 146100
Salt Lake City, UT 84114-6100
p. (801) 537-3300
rickallis@utah.gov
http://geology.utah.gov/ghp/
Program Manager:
Steve D. Bowman, (D), Nevada (Reno), 2002, NgZn
Senior Scientist:
William R. Lund, (B), Idaho, 1970, Ng
Paleoseismologist:
Christopher B. DuRoss, (M), Utah, 2004, Ng
Landslide Geologist:
Gregg S. Beukelman, (M), Boise State, 1997, NgZi
Hazards Mapping Geologist:
Jessica Castleton, (B), Weber State, 2005, Ng
Adam McKean, (M), Brigham Young, 2011, Gmg
Hazards Geologist:
Tyler R. Knudsen, (M), Nevada, 2005, Ng
Gregory N. McDonald, (B), Utah, 1992, Ng
Hazard Mapping Geologist:
Ben A. Erickson, (M), Utah, 2011, Ng
Debris Flow/Landslide Geologist:
Richard E. Giraud, (M), Idaho, 1986, Ng
Geologist:
Mike Hylland, (M), Oregon State, 1990, PgYs
GIS Analyst:
Corey Unger, (B), Weber State, 2001, Zi

Geologic Mapping Program (2015)
1594 West North Temple, Ste 3110
PO Box 146100
Salt Lake City, UT 84114-6100
p. (801) 537-3355
grantwillis@utah.gov
http://geology.utah.gov
Senior Scientist:
Robert Biek, (M), N Illinois, 1988, Gg
Adjunct Associate Professor:
James I. Kirkland, (D), Colorado, 1990, PvsPi
Senior Geologist:
Donald Clark, (M), N Illinois, 1987, Gg
Jonathan K. King, (M), Wyoming, 1984, Gg
Douglas A. Sprinkel, (M), Utah State, 1977, GosGg
Manager:
Grant C. Willis, (M), Brigham Young, 1983, Gg
GIS Analyst:
Basia Matyjasik, (B), Warsaw, 1988, Gg
Senior GIS Analyst:
Kent D. Brown, Zn

Vermont

Agency of Natural Resources, Dept of Environmental Conservation

Vermont Geological Survey ☒ (2018)
1 National Life Drive
Main 2
Montpelier, VT 05620-3902
p. (802) 522-5210
marjorie.gale@vermont.gov
https://dec.vermont.gov/geological-survey
State Geologist:
Marjorie H. Gale, (M), Vermont, 1980, GgcGe
Geologist -Environmental Scientist:
Jonathan Kim, (D), Buffalo, 1995, GetCg

Victoria

Geological Survey of Victoria, Australia

Victoria - Dept of Economic Development, Jobs, Transport and Resources (2016)
GPO Box 2392
Melbourne, VIC 3001
p. +61 3 94528906
gsv.info@ecodev.vic.gov.au
http://www.earthresources.vic.gov.au/earth-resources

Victoria - Dept of Sustainability and Environment

Dept of Sustainability and Environment (2015)
8 Nicholson Street
East Melbourne, VIC 3002
p. +61 3 5332 5000
peter.walsh@parliament.vic.gov.au
http://www.dse.vic.gov.au/

Virginia

Division of Geology and Mineral Resources

Virginia Dept of Mines, Minerals & Energy ☒ (2019)
Fontaine Research Park
900 Natural Resources Drive
Suite 500
Charlottesville, VA 22903
p. (434) 951-6341
DGMRInfo@dmme.virginia.gov
http://dmme.virginia.gov/DGMR/divisiongeologymineralresources.shtml
State Geologist:
David B. Spears, (M), Virginia Tech, 1983, GcEg
Manager, Geologic Mapping:
Matthew J. Heller, (M), North Carolina State, 1996, GgRnGe
Manager, Economic Geology:
William L. Lassetter, (M), Nevada (Reno), 1996, EgHg

University of Virginia

Virginia State Climatology Office (2015)
291 McCormick Road
P.O. Box 400123
Charlottesville, VA 22904-4123
p. 434-924-0548
pjs2i@virginia.edu
http://climate.virginia.edu/home.htm
Director:
Patrick J. Michaels, (D), Wisconsin, 1979, As

Washington

Geological Survey of Western Australia

Geological Survey of Western Australia (2016)
Mineral House
100 Plain Street
East Perth , WA 6004
p. +61 8 9222 3333
geological.survey@dmp.wa.gov.au
http://www.dmp.wa.gov.au/Geological-Survey/Geological-Survey-262.aspx

Washington Geological Survey

Washington Dept of Natural Resources ☒ (2021)
1111 Washington Street, SE, MS 47007
Olympia, WA 98504-7007
p. (360) 902-1450
geology@dnr.wa.gov
http://www.dnr.wa.gov/geology/

State Geologist:
Casey R. Hanell, (M), W Washington, 2011, Gg
Geology Librarian:
Stephanie Earls, (M), Washington, 2010, Gge

West Virginia

West Virginia Geological & Economic Survey

West Virginia Geological & Economic Survey (2016)
Mont Chateau Research Center
1 Mont Chateau Road
Morgantown, WV 26508-8079
p. (304) 594-2331
info@geosrv.wvnet.edu
http://www.wvgs.wvnet.edu
f: https://www.facebook.com/WVGeoSurvey

State Geologist:
Michael Ed. Hohn, (D), Indiana, 1976, Eg
Adjunct Professor:
Paula J. Hunt, (M), Purdue, 1988, GgHw

Wisconsin

University of Wisconsin, Madison, Division of Extension

Wisconsin Geological and Natural History Survey ☒ (2020)
3817 Mineral Point Road
Madison, WI 53705-5100
p. (608) 262-1705
jill.pongetti@wisc.edu
https://wgnhs.wisc.edu
f: https://www.facebook.com/WGNHS
t: @WGNHS

Director and State Geologist:
Kenneth R. Bradbury, (D), Wisconsin, 1982, Hw
Hydrogeologist:
David J. Hart, (D), Wisconsin, 2000, HwYg
Geologist:
J. Elmo Rawling, (D), Wisconsin (Milwaukee), 2002, Gml
Geologist:
Eric C. Carson, (D), Wisconsin, 2003, Gl
State Geologist and Director:
James M. Robertson, (D), Michigan, 1972, Eg
Professor:
John W. Attig, (D), Wisconsin, 1984, Gl
Thomas J. Evans, (D), Wisconsin, 1994, Eg
Emeritus:
Bruce A. Brown, (D), Manitoba, 1984, GcEg
Ron G. Hennings, (M), Wisconsin, 1977
M. Carol L. McCartney, (D), Wisconsin, 1979, RcGee
Roger M. Peters, (B), Wisconsin, 1969, Gg
Web Developer:
David Sibley, (B), Wisconsin, 2009
Samples Coordinator:
Carsyn Ames, (M), Iowa State, 2018
Project Quaternary Geologist:
Kacie Stolzman, (B), Winona State, 2019, Gm
Project Geoscientist:
Sarah Bremmer, (M), Wisconsin, 2018, Ggt
William Fitzpatrick, (M), Arizona, 2020, EgGi
Project Geologist:
Stefanie Dodge, (B), Wisconsin (Milwaukee), Gg
Hydrogeologist:
Maureen Muldoon, (D), Wisconsin, 1999, GeHw
Mike J. Parsen, (M), Hw
GIS Specialist:
Steve Mauel
Matthew Rehwald, (M), Wisconsin, 2005, Zi
Caroline Rose, (M), Wisconsin, 2015, Zi
Kathy Roushar, (B), Iowa, 1979, Zi
Geotechnician:
Peter M. Chase, (B), Wisconsin (Milwaukee), 1985, HwYgRw
Geoscience Program Coordinator:
Ian Orland, (D), Wisconsin, 2012, PcCls
Geologist:
Irene D. Lippelt, (B), Manitoba, 1978, Gg
Eric Stewart, (D), Texas A&M, 2015, GgcGi
Esther K. Stewart, (M), Idaho State, 2008, Gg
Front Office Administrator:
Jill Pongetti, (B), Florida, 1997
Editor:
Linda Deith, (B), Illinois (Urbana-Champaign), 1984
Assistant Director for Administration:
Sushmita Lotlikar, (M), Wisconsin, 2014
Assistant Director:
Peter Schoephoester, (M), Indiana, 2003, Zi
Archivist:
Bradford Gottschalk, (M), Wisconsin, 2007, Rh
Related Staff:
Amber Boudreau
Grace E. Graham, (B), Beloit, 2013, Hw

Wyoming

Wyoming State Geological Survey

Wyoming State Geological Survey ☒ (2019)
P.O. Box 1347
Laramie, WY 82073
p. (307) 766-2286
wsgs-info@wyo.gov
http://www.wsgs.wyo.gov/
Administrative Assistant: Christina George, Austin Heller, Shari Williamson

Director:
Erin A. Campbell, (D), Wyoming, 1997, Gc
Geologist:
Robert Gregory, (M), En
Ranie Lynds, (D), EoGro
Wayne Sutherland, (M), Eng
Technical Analysis & Data Management Manager:
David Lucke
General Geology & Minerals:
Patty Webber, (M), Iowa, 2018, CcGct
General Geology & Geologic Hazards:
James Mauch, (M), Utah State, 2018, GmRnGg

Yukon

Yukon Geological Survey

Yukon Geological Survey (2015)
Whitehorse, YT
suzanne.roy@gov.yk.ca
http://www.geology.gov.yk.ca/

Agencies and Intl Organizations

United Nations Education, Scientific, and Cultural Organization

International Geoscience Programme (2015)
Division of Ecological and Earth Sciences
1 rue Miollis
Paris, Cedex 15 F-75732
p. +33 (0)1 45 68 10 00
m.alaawah@unesco.org
http://www.unesco.org/new/en/natural-sciences/environment/earth-sciences/international-geoscience-programme/
IGCP Chairperson:
Patricia Vickers-Rich, (D), Columbia, 1972
Team Leader, Hydrogeology:
Gil Mahe
Team Leader, Global Change and Evolution of Life:
Guy Narbonne
Team Leader, Geohazards:
Andrej Gosar
Team Leader, Geodynamic:
George Gibson
Team Leader, Earth Resources:
Robert Moritz
IGCP/SIDA Representative:
Vivi Vajda, (D), Lund (Sweden), 1998

Geological Survey of India

Geological Survey of India O☒ (2021)
27, J.L.Nehru Road
Kolkata
Kolkata, West Bengal 700016
dg.gsi@gov.in
http://www.gsi.gov.in
f: https://www.facebook.com/gsipage/
t: @GeologyIndia
Certificates: Advanced GIS, Digital Cartography, Geological Mapping, Mineral Exploration, Geophysical Survey, etc

Ministry of Environmental Protection, Natural Resources and Forestry

Dept of Geology (2016)
st. Wawelska 52/54
Warsaw 00-922
p. +48 22 3692449
Departament.Geologii.i.Koncesji.Geologicznych@mos.gov.pl
http://www.mos.gov.pl/dg/dga1.htm

Sveriges geologiska Undersokning

Geological Survey of Sweden (2016)
Box 670
751 28 Uppsala
sgu@sgu.se
http://www.sgu.se/

Argonne National Laboratory

Chemical Technology Div (2015)
9700 South Cass Avenue
Building 205
Argonne, IL 60439
p. (630) 252-4383
ebunel@anl.gov
Senior Scientist:
Milton Blander, (D), Yale, 1953, Xc
Paul A. Fenter, (D), Pennsylvania, 1990, ClZm
Associate Scientist:
Allen J. Bakel, (D), Oklahoma, 1990, Co
Ronald P. Chiarello, (D), Northeastern, 1990, Zm
Donald G. Graczyk, (D), Wisconsin, 1975, Cs
Ben D. Holt, (D), Illinois Inst Tech, 1969, Ca
James J. Mazer, (D), Northwestern, 1987, Cl
David J. Wronkiewicz, (D), New Mexico Tech, 1989, Cg
Adjunct Professor:
Neil C. Sturchio, (D), Washington (St Louis), 1983, Cg
Related Staff:
Alice M. Essling, (B), St Xavier, 1956, Ca
Edmund A. Huff, (M), Chicago, 1957, Ca
Francis J. Markun, (B), Lewis, 1961, Cc
Florence P. Smith, (B), Southern, 1968, Ca

Geosciences & Information Technology Section (2015)
9700 South Cass Avenue
Argonne, IL 60439
p. (630) 252-6034
djmiller@anl.gov
Department Secretary: Sue Baumann
Manager, Geosciences & Information Tech:
Lisa A. Durham, (M), Purdue, 1989, Hw
Assistant System Engineer:
Cheong-yip R. Yuen, (D), Wisconsin (Milwaukee), 1986, Ge
Associate Scientist:
Robert L. Johnson, (D), Cornell, 1991, Zn
Research Associate:
John Ditmars, (D), Caltech, 1971, Zn
Jennifer Herbert, (B), N Illinois, 1997, Gg
Zhenhua Jiang, (D), Duke, 1992, Zn
David S. Miller, (D), Johns Hopkins, 1995, Ge
Terri L. Patton, (M), NE Illinois, 1989, Cl
John J. Quinn, (M), Minnesota, 1992, Hq
Geology Librarian:
Swati Wagh, Zn

Environmental Research Div (2015)
9700 South Cass Avenue
Argonne, IL 60439
p. (630) 252-3879
bmlesht@anl.gov
http://www.evs.anl.gov/
Senior Scientist:
Jeffrey S. Gaffney, (D), California (Riverside), 1975, As
Raymond M. Miller, (D), Illinois State, 1975, Sb
Marvin L. Wesely, (D), Wisconsin, 1970, As
Associate Scientist:
Jacqueline C. Burton, (D), Tennessee, 1978, Cg
Richard L. Coulter, (D), Penn State, 1976, As
Paul V. Doskey, (D), Wisconsin, 1982, As
Julie D. Jastrow, (D), Chicago, 1994, Sb
Lorraine M. LaFreniere, (D), Wisconsin, 1980, Zn
In Young Lee, (D), California (Los Angeles), 1975, As
Barry M. Lesht, (D), Chicago, 1977, Op
Nancy A. Marley, (D), Florida State, 1984, As
William T. Meyer, (D), Imperial Coll (UK), 1973, Cg
Robert A. Sedivy, (M), Georgia Tech, 1979, Hw
Jack D. Shannon, (D), Oklahoma, 1975, Am
Douglas L. Sisterson, (M), Wyoming, 1975, As
Mohamed Sultan, (D), Washington (St Louis), 1984, Cg
John L. Walker, (D), Imperial Coll (UK), 1964, Cg
Y Eugene Yan, (D), Ohio State, 1998, Gg
Research Associate:
Richard H. Becker, (M), Washington (St Louis), Zr
Clyde B. Dennis, (M), Florida, 1979, Zn
Richard L. Hart, (B), Illinois Inst Tech, 1970, As
Timothy J. Martin, (B), Beloit, 1974, As
Barney W. Nashold, (M), Illinois (Chicago Circle), 1976, Zn
Kent A. Orlandini, (B), Illinois, 1957, Cc
Candace M. Rose, (B), Benedictine Coll, 1985, Zn

Energy Systems Div (2015)
9700 South Cass Avenue
Bldg 362 E-340
Argonne, IL 60439-4815
p. (630) 252-3392
energy_systems@anl.gov
Administrative Assistant: Barbara Sullivan
Head:
Donald O. Johnson, (D), Illinois, 1972, Gr
Senior Scientist:
Lyle D. McGinnis, (D), Illinois, 1965, Yg
Scientist:
Kenneth L. Brubaker, (D), Wisconsin, 1972, As

Dorland E. Edgar, (D), Purdue, 1976, Gm
Steven F. Miller, (B), Knox, 1984, Gg
R. Eric Zimmerman, (D), Northwestern, 1972, Ng
Research Associate:
Paul C. Heigold, (D), Illinois, 1969, Yg
Theresa C. Scholtz, (B), N Illinois, 1985, Ge
Michael D. Thompson, (M), N Illinois, 1989, Yg
Related Staff:
John F. Schneider, (M), N Illinois, 1977, Ca
Linda M. Shem, (M), Northwestern, 1991, Ge
Patrick L. Wilkey, (M), Illinois, 1976, Ng

Bureau of Land Management

National Operations Center (2015)
PO Box 25047
Denver, CO 80225
p. (303) 236-8857
lgraham@blm.gov

National Training Center (2015)
9828 North 31st Avenue
Phoenix, AZ 85051
p. (602) 906-5500
dwilkins@blm.gov

Alaska State Office (2015)
222 West Seventh Ave
#13
Anchorage, AK 99513
p. (907) 271-3212
dlassuy@blm.gov

Arizona State Office (2015)
One North Central Ave
Suite 800
Phoenix, AZ 85004
p. (602) 417-9500
egomez@blm.gov

California State Office ☒ (2021)
2800 Cottage Way
Suite W-1623
Sacramento, CA 95825
p. (916) 978-4400
nml_ca_web_so@blm.gov
https://www.blm.gov/office/california-state-office
f: https://www.blm.gov/media/social-media

Colorado State Office (2015)
2850 Youngfield Street
Lakewood, CO 80215
p. (303) 239-3600
hhankins@blm.gov

Headquarters Directorate (2015)
1849 C Street NW
Rm 5665
Washington, DC 20240
p. (202) 208-3801
director@blm.gov

Eastern States Office (2015)
7450 Boston Boulevard
Springfield, VA 22153
p. (703) 440-1600
es_general_web@blm.gov

Idaho State Office (2015)
1387 South Vinnell Way
Boise, ID 83709
p. (208) 373-4000
sellis@blm.gov

Wyoming State Office (2015)
PO Box 1828
Cheyenne, WY 82003
p. (307) 775-6256
jcamargo@blm.gov

Utah State Office (2015)
440 West 200 South
Suite 500
Salt Lake City, UT 84101
p. (801) 539-4001
utsomail@blm.gov

Oregon State Office (2015)
333 SW 1st Avenue
Portland, OR 97204
p. (503) 808-6001
b2jackso@blm.gov

New Mexico State Office (2015)
301 Dinosaur Trail
Santa Fe, NM 87502
p. (505) 954-2098
jjuen@blm.gov

Nevada State Office (2015)
1340 Financial Blvd
Reno, NV 89502
p. (775) 861-6400
jswickard@blm.gov

Montana State Office (2015)
5001 Southgate Drive
Billings, MT 59101
p. (406) 896-5012
kiszler@blm.gov

Department of Commerce

National Institute of Standards & Technology ☒ (2021)
100 Bureau Drive
Stop 1070
Gaithersburg, MD 20899-3460
p. (301) 975-2000
inquiries@nist.gov
https://www.nist.gov/

Department of Interior Office of Surface Mining Reclamation and Enforcement

OSMRE Geospatial Information Services ☒ (2019)
OSMRE Attn: David Carter
1999 Broadway, Suite 3320
Denver, CO 80225
p. (303) 293-5019
dcarter@osmre.gov
https://www.tips.osmre.gov/geospatial.shtm
Branch Manager:
David Carter, (M), Denver, 1999, Zir
Physical Scientist:
Carrie A. Middleton, (M), Colorado Mines, 2008, ZrGfZi

Dept of Agriculture

Natural Resources Conservation Service (2016)
14th and Independence Ave., SW
Washington, DC 20250
p. (202) 720-7246
jason.weller@wdc.usda.gov
http://www.nrcs.usda.gov

Dept of Commerce

National Oceanic & Atmospheric Administration (2015)
Silver Spring Metro Center 3
1315 East-West Highway
Silver Spring, MD 20910-3282
p. (202) 482-3436
edward.horton@noaa.gov
http://www.noaa.gov

Dept of Defense

Space & Naval Warfare Systems Command (2015)
4301 Pacific Highway
San Diego, CA 92110-3127

p. (619) 524-7053
http://www.spawar.navy.mil/

Naval Oceanography Command (2015)
U.S. Naval Observatory
34th Street & Massachusetts Avenue, NW
Washington, DC 20007
p. (202) 762-1020
http://www.oceanographer.navy.mil

Air Weather Service (2015)
106 Peacekeeper Drive
Offutt Air Force Base, NE 68113-4039
p. (402) 294-5749

Air Force Center for Environmental Excellence (2015)
3207 North Road
Brooks Air Force Base, TX 78235-5363
p. (210) 536-2162

U.S. Army Corps of Engineers (2015)
441 G Street, NW
Washington, DC 20314
p. (202) 761-0001
http://www.usace.army.mil/working.html

U.S. Army Research Laboratory Command (2015)
The Pentagon
Washington, DC 20310
p. (703) 695-0363
http://www.army.mil/csa/

Defense Threat Reduction Agency (2015)
8725 John T. Kingman Road
MS 6201
Ft. Belvoir, VA 22060-6201
p. (703) 767-4883
dtra.publicaffairs@dtra.mil
http://www.dtra.mil

Office of Naval Research (2015)
Ballston Towers #1
800 North Quincy Street
Arlington, VA 22203
p. (703) 696-4767
http://www.onr.navy.mil/

Naval Intelligence Command (2015)
4251 Suitland Road
Washington, DC 20395-5720
p. (301) 669-4000
http://www.nmic.navy.mil/

U.S. Army Chemical & Biological Defense Command (2015)
The Pentagon
Washington, DC 20310
p. (703) 695-0363
http://www.army.mil/csa/

U.S. Special Operations Command (Air Force) (2015)
100 Bartley Street
Hurlburt Field, FL 32544-5273
p. (850) 884-2323
http://www.af.mil/sites/afsoc.html

Space Command (2015)
150 Vandenberg Street
Peterson Air Force Base, CO 80914-4020
p. (719) 554-3001
http://www.af.mil/sites/afspc.shtml

Dept of Energy

Office of Nuclear Energy, Science & Technology (2015)
Forrestal Building
1000 Independence Avenue, SW
Washington, DC 20585-0117
p. (202) 586-6630
http://www.ne.doe.gov/

Assistant Secretary for Fossil Energy (2015)
Forrestal Building
1000 Independence Avenue, SW
Washington, DC 20585-0301
p. (202) 586-6660
FECommunications@hq.doe.gov
http://www.fe.doe.gov/

Assistant Secretary for Energy Efficiency & Renewable Energy (2015)
Forrestal Building
1000 Independence Avenue, SW
Washington, DC 20585-0121
p. (202) 586-9220
http://www.eren.doe.gov/

Office of Resource Management (2015)
Forrestal Building
1000 Independence Avenue, SW
Washington, DC 20585-0620
p. (202) 586-3521

Assistant Secretary for Environmental Management (2017)
Forrestal Building
1000 Independence Avenue, SW
Washington, DC 20585-0113
p. (202) 586-7709
EM.WebContentManager@em.doe.gov
http://www.em.doe.gov/

Assistant Secretary for Environment, Safety & Health (2015)
Forrestal Building
1000 Independence Avenue, SW
Washington, DC 20585-0119
p. (202) 586-6151
http://www.eh.doe.gov/

Energy Information Administration (2015)
Forrestal Building
1000 Independence Avenue, SW
Washington, DC 20585-0601
p. (202) 586-8800
howard.gruenspecht@eia.gov
http://www.eia.doe.gov/

Office of Coal, Nuclear, Electric & Alternate Fuels (2015)
COMSAT Building
950 L'Enfant Plaza, SW
Washington, DC 20024
p. (202) 287-7990

Coal & Power Systems (2015)
Forrestal Building
1000 Independence Avenue, SW
Washington, DC 20585-0320
p. (202) 586-1650

Office of Energy Projects (2015)
Federal Energy Regulatory Commission
888 First Street, NE
Washington, DC 20426
p. (202) 219-2700

Office of Oil & Gas (2015)
Forrestal Building
1000 Independence Avenue, SW
Washington, DC 20585-0640
p. (202) 586-6012

Dept of Health & Human Services

Agency for Toxic Substances & Disease Registry (2015)
1600 Clifton Road
Atlanta, GA 30333
p. (404) 639-7000
http://www.atsdr.cdc.gov/atsdrhome.html

Centers for Disease Control & Prevention (2015)
1600 Clifton Rd.
Atlanta, GA 30333
p. (404) 639-3535
http://www.cdc.gov

Dept of Labor

Mine Safety & Health Administration (2015)
Balston Tower #3
4015 Wilson Boulevard
Arlington, VA 22203
p. (703) 235-1385
http://www.msha.gov

Dept of State

Intl Boundary & Water Commission, US & Mexico (2015)
The Commons
4171 North Mesa, Suite C-310
El Paso, TX 79902-1441
p. 1-800-262-8857
john.merino@ibwc.state.gov

Dept of the Interior

National Park Service (2015)
1849 C. Street N.W.
Washington, DC 20240
p. (202) 208-4621
http://www.nps.gov

U.S. Fish & Wildlife Service (2015)
1849 C. Street N.W.
Washington, DC 20240
p. (202) 208-4545
http://www.fws.gov/

Bureau of Reclamation (2015)
1849 C. Street N.W.
Washington, DC 20240
p. (202) 513-0501
http://www.usbr.gov

Office of Surface Mining, Reclamation & Enforcement (2015)
1951 Constitution Ave. N.W.
Washington, DC 20240
p. (202) 208-2565
osm-getinfo@osmre.gov
http://www.osmre.gov/

Bureau of Indian Affairs (2015)
1849 C. Street N.W.
Washington, DC 20240
p. (202) 208-7163
http://www.doi.gov/bureau-indian-affairs.html

Office of the Secretary (2015)
1849 C. Street N.W.
Washington, DC 20240
p. (202) 208-3100
feedback@ios.doi.gov
http://www.doi.gov

Bureau of Land Management (2015)
Office of Public Affairs
1849 C Street, Room 406-LS
Washington, DC 20240
p. (202) 208-3801
director@blm.gov
http://www.blm.gov

Dept of the Treasury

Internal Revenue Service (2015)
1111 Constitution Avenue, NW
Washington, DC 20224
p. (202) 622-9511
http://www.irs.ustreas.gov

Dept of Transportation

U.S. Coast Guard (2015)
2100 Second Street, SW
Washington, DC 20593
p. (202) 366-4000
http://www.uscg.mil

Federal Aviation Administration (2015)
800 Independence Avenue, SW
Washington, DC 20591
p. (202) 267-3484
http://www.faa.gov

Environmental Protection Agency

Office of Wetlands, Oceans & Watersheds (2015)
Fairchild Building
499 South Capitol Street, SW
Washington, DC 20003
p. (202) 260-7166
best-wong.benita@epa.gov

Assistant Administrator for Water Programs ☒ (2017)
1200 Pennsylvania Avenue, NW
Washington, DC 20460
p. (202) 260-5700
Beauvais.joel@Epa.gov
https://www.epa.gov/aboutepa/about-office-water

Office of Wastewater Management (2015)
1200 Pennsylvania Avenue, NW
Washington, DC 20460
p. (202) 564-0748
ow-general@epa.gov

Office of Emergency & Remedial Response (Superfund/Oil Programs) (2015)
Crystal Gateway One
1235 Jefferson Davis Highway
Arlington, VA 22202
p. (703) 603-8960
oilinfo@epamail.epa.gov
http://www.epa.gov/superfund

Office of Solid Waste (2015)
1301 Constitutiion Ave. NW
Arlington, VA 22202
p. (202) 566-0200
aastanislaus@epa.gov
http://www2.epa.gov/aboutepa/about-office-solid-waste-and-emergency-response-oswer

Office of Science Policy (2019)
1200 Pennsylvania Ave., NW
MC-8104R
Washington, DC 20460
p. (202) 564-6705
hauchman.fred@epa.gov

Office of Science & Technology (2015)
1200 Pennsylvania Avenue, NW
Washington, DC 20460
p. (202) 260-5400
Southerland.elizabeth@Epa.gov

Office of Underground Storage Tanks (2015)
Crystal Gateway One
1235 Jefferson Davis Highway
Arlington, VA 22202
p. (703) 603-9900
hoskinson.carolyn@epa.gov

Office of Atmospheric Programs (2015)
501 Third Street, NW
Washington, DC 20001
p. (202) 564-9140
McCabe.janet@Epa.gov

Office of Ground Water & Drinking Water (2015)
1200 Pennsylvania Avenue, NW
Washington, DC 20460
p. (202) 260-5400
grevatt.peter@epa.gov

Assistant Administrator for Environmental Information (2015)
1200 Pennsylvania Avenue, NW
Washington, DC 20460
p. (202) 564-6665
Nelson.kimberly@Epa.gov

Safety, Health & Environmental Management Div (2015)
1200 Pennsylvania Avenue, NW
Washington, DC 20460
p. (202) 564-1640
dfe@epa.gov

National Air & Radiation Environmental Laboratory (2015)
540 South Morris Avenue
Montgomery, AL 36115-2601
p. (334) 270-3404
griggs.john@epa.gov

Office of Research and Development ☒ (2020)
USEPA-ORD-8101R
1200 Pennsylvania Avenue, NW
Washington, DC 20460
p. 202-564-3512
frithsen.jeff@epa.gov
http://www.epa.gov/research

National Center for Environmental Research (2015)
Ronald Reagan Building
1300 Pennsylvania Avenue, NW
Washington, DC 20004
p. (202) 564-6825
johnson.jim@epa.gov

Federal Emergency Management Agency

Office of the Director (2015)
500 C Street, SW
Washington, DC 20472
p. (202) 646-4600
http://www.fema.gov/

Jet Propulsion Laboratory

Earth & Space Sciences Div (2015)
Geology & Planetology Section
Pasadena, CA 91109
p. (818) 354-3440
daniel.j.mccleese@jpl.nasa.gov
Department Administrative Manager: Murray Geller

Lead Scientist:
Bruce E. Banerdt, (D), S California, 1983, Xy

Section Manager:
Ronald G. Blom, (D), California (Santa Barbara), 1987, Zr

Section Member:
Michael J. Abrams, (M), Caltech, 1973, Zr
Ronald E. Alley, (M), Northwestern, 1972, Zr
Diana L. Blaney, (D), Hawaii, 1990, Xg
Bonnie J. Buratti, (D), Cornell, 1983, Zr
Robert E. Crippen, (D), California (Santa Barbara), 1989, Zr
Joy A. Crisp, (D), Princeton, 1984, Gv
Thomas C. Duxbury, (M), Purdue, 1966, Zn
Diane L. Evans, (D), Washington, 1981, Gm
Tom G. Farr, (D), Washington, 1981, Gm
Ken E. Herkenhoff, (D), Caltech, 1989, Xg
Simon J. Hook, (D), Durham (UK), 1989, Zr
Erik R. Ivins, (M), California (Los Angeles), 1976, Gt
Anne B. Kahle, (D), California (Los Angeles), 1975, Zr
Harold R. Lang, (D), Calgary, 1983, Gr
Kyle C. McDonald, (D), Michigan, 1991, Zn
Robert M. Nelson, (D), Pittsburgh, 1978, Xg
Eni G. Njoku, (D), MIT, 1976, Zr
Frank D. Palluconi, (M), Penn State, 1963, Zr
David C. Pieri, (D), Cornell, 1979, Gt
Jeffrey J. Plant, (D), Washington (St Louis), 1991, Zn
Jeffrey Plescia, (D), S California, 1985, Zn
Carol A. Raymond, (D), Columbia, 1989, Yr
Suzanne E. Smrekar, (D), S Methodist, 1990, Xy
Linda J. Spilker, (D), California (Los Angeles), 1992, XyZr
Ellen R. Stofan, (D), Brown, 1989, Xg
Glenn J. Veeder, (D), Caltech, 1974, Zn

Section Member:
Matthew P. Golombek, (D), Massachusetts, 1981, XgyGt

Senior Scientist:
Ronald S. Sanders, (D), Brown, 1970, Gr

Lawrence Livermore National Laboratory

Atmospheric, Earth and Energy (2015)
7000 East Avenue
L-203
Livermore, CA 94550
p. (925) 423-1848
antoun1@llnl.gov
https://www-pls.llnl.gov/?url=about_pls-atmospheric_earth_and_energy_division
Administrative Assistant: Laura Long

Head:
Kenneth J. Jackson, (D), California (Berkeley), 1983, Cl

Senior Scientist:
Roger D. Aines, (D), Caltech, 1984, Cg
Bill L. Bourcier, (D), Oregon State, 1983, Cg
Thomas A. Buscheck, (D), California (Berkeley), 1984, Ng
Steven Carle, (D), California (Davis), 1996, Hw
Charles R. Carrigan, (D), California (Los Angeles), 1977, Yg
Susan A. Carroll, (D), Northwestern, 1988, Cl
M Lee Davisson, (M), California (Davis), 1992, Cg
Quingyun Duan, (D), Arizona, 1991, Hg
Robert C. Finkel, (D), California (San Diego), 1974, Cg
Samuel (Julio) J. Friedmann, (D), MIT, Gg
Richard B. Knapp, (D), Arizona, 1978, Ng
Gayle A. Pawloski, (B), Cal State (Hayward), 1979, Gg
Abelardo L. Ramirez, (M), Purdue, 1979, Ng
Sarah K. Roberts, (M), Arizona State, 1990, Cl
Andrew F B Tompson, (D), Princeton, 1985, HwSpCc
Jeffrey L. Wagoner, (M), California (Riverside), 1977, Gs
Ananda M. Wijesinghe, (D), MIT, 1978, Nr
Sun Yunwei, (D), Israel Inst of Tech, 1995, Ng
Mavrik Zavarin, Yr

Los Alamos National Laboratory

Chemistry Div (B,M,D) (2015)
P.O. Box 1663
Los Alamos, NM 87545
p. (505) 667-4457
chemistry@lanl.gov
http://pearl1.lanl.gov/external/

Division Leader:
Alexander J. Gancarz, (D), Caltech, 1976, Cc

Staff:
Kent D. Abney, (D), Colorado State, 1987, Zn
Stephen F. Agnew, (D), Washington State, 1981, Zn
Moses Attrep, (D), Arkansas, 1965, Ze
Timothy M. Benjamin, (D), Caltech, 1979, Ca
Scott M. Bowen, (D), New Mexico, 1983, Ca
James R. Brainard, (D), Indiana, 1979, Zn
Jeffrey C. Bryan, (D), Washington, 1988, Zn
Carol J. Burns, (D), California (Berkeley), 1987, Zn
Timothy P. Burns, (D), Nebraska, 1986, Co
Gilbert W. Butler, (D), California (Berkeley), 1967, Cc
Edwin P. Chamberlain, (D), Texas A&M, 1971, Cc
David L. Clark, (D), Indiana, 1986, Zn
Dean A. Cole, (D), Iowa, 1985, Co
David B. Curtis, (D), Oregon State, 1974, Cc
Paul R. Dixon, (D), Yale, 1989, Zn
Robert J. Donahoe, (D), North Carolina State, 1985, Zn
Stephen K. Doorn, (D), Northwestern, 1989, Zn
Clarence J. Duffy, (D), British Columbia, 1977, Cg
Deward W. Efurd, (D), Arkansas, 1975, Ct
Phillip G. Eller, (D), Ohio State, 1971, Zn
June T. Fabryka-Martin, (D), Arizona, 1988, Hg
Bryan L. Fearey, (D), Iowa State, 1986, Cc
David L. Finnegan, (D), Maryland, 1984, As
John R. Fitzpatrick, (M), New Mexico, 1983, Zn

Malcolm M. Fowler, (D), Washington (St Louis), 1972, As
Sammy R. Garcia, (B), New Mexico Highlands, 1972, Ca
Russell E. Gritzo, (B), New Mexico State, 1983, Zn
Richard C. Heaton, (D), Illinois, 1973, Zn
Sara B. Helmick, (B), Southwestern, 1955, Zn
David R. Janecky, (D), Minnesota, 1982, Cl
Kung King-Hsi, (D), Cornell, 1989, Zn
Scott Kinkead, (D), Idaho, 1983, Zn
Gregory J. Kubas, (D), Northwestern, 1970, As
Pat J. Langston-Unkefer, (D), Texas A&M, 1978, Co
Patrick A. Longmire, (D), New Mexico, 1991, Zn
Michael MacInnes, (M), Wisconsin, 1969, Zn
Allen S. Mason, (D), Miami, 1974, As
Charles M. Miller, (D), Stanford, 1980, Cc
Geoffrey G. Miller, (D), Rensselaer, 1984, Cc
Terrance L. Morgan, (M), Colorado State, 1984, Ng
David Morris, (D), North Carolina State, 1984, Cc
Eugene J. Mroz, (D), Maryland, 1976, As
Michael T. Murrell, (D), California (San Diego), 1980, Cc
Allen E. Ogard, (D), Chicago, 1957, Hw
Jose A. Olivares, (D), Iowa State, 1985, Cs
Hain Oona, (D), Arizona, 1979, Zn
Kevin C. Ott, (D), Caltech, 1983, Zn
Edward S. Patera, (D), Arizona State, 1982, Cg
Richard E. Perrin, (B), Denver, 1952, Cc
Eugene J. Peterson, (D), Arizona State, 1976, Ct
Dennis Phillips, (D), Hawaii, 1976, Co
Jane Poths, (D), Chicago, 1982, Cc
Pamela Z. Rogers, (D), California (Berkeley), 1981, Cl
Donald J. Rokop, (D), Lake Forest, 1985, Cc
Robert S. Rundberg, (D), CUNY, 1978, Gq
Nancy N. S. Sauer, (D), Iowa State, 1986, Zn
Norman C. Schroeder, (D), Iowa State, 1985, Cc
Louis A. Silks, (B), Suffolk, 1978, Zn
Paul H. Smith, (D), California (Berkeley), 1987, Zn
Zita V. Svitra, (B), Roosevelt, 1967, Zn
Basil I. Swanson, (D), Northwestern, 1969, Zn
C. Drew Tait, (D), North Carolina State, 1984, Cp
Wayne A. Taylor, (B), New Mexico, 1978, Cl
Kimberly W. Thomas, (D), California (Berkeley), 1978, Ct
Joseph L. Thompson, (D), Penn State, 1963, Ct
Ines Triay, (D), Miami, 1985, Hg
Clifford J. Unkefer, (D), Minnesota, 1981, Zn
David J. Vieira, (D), California (Berkeley), 1978, Zn
Jerry B. Wilhelmy, (D), California (Berkeley), 1969, Zn
Kurt Wolfsberg, (D), Washington (St Louis), 1959, Cc
William H. Woodruff, (D), Purdue, 1972, Zn
Mary Anne Yates, (D), Carnegie Mellon, 1976, Zn

Emeritus:
Ernest A. Bryant, (D), Washington (St Louis), 1956, Cg
Merle E. Bunker, (D), Indiana, 1950, Zn
William R. Daniels, (D), New Mexico, 1965, Ct
Donald L. Hull, (M), Iowa State, 1974, Zn

Earth & Environmental Sciences Div (2016)
P.O. Box 1663
Los Alamos, NM 87545
p. (505) 667-3644
wallacet@lanl.gov

Technical Staff:
James E. Bossert, (D), Colorado State, 1990, As

Director:
Terry C. Wallace, Jr., (D), Caltech, 1983, Ys

Technical Staff:
Kay H. Birdsell, (M), Colorado, 1985, Hqy
James W. Carey, (D), Harvard, 1990, CpYxNr
Lianjie Huang, (D), Paris, 1994, Yg
Kenneth H. Wohletz, (D), Arizona State, 1980, YxGvRm

Technical Staff:
Paul Aamodt, (M), Nevada, 1991, Zn
Douglas Alde, (D), Illinois, 1979, Zn
M. James Aldrich, (D), New Mexico, 1972, Gc
Fairley J. Barnes, (D), New Mexico State, 1986, Zn
Naomi M. Becker, (D), Wisconsin, 1991, Hg
James D. Blacic, (D), California (Los Angeles), 1971, Nr
Rainer Bleck, (D), Penn State, 1968, Am
Christopher R. Bradley, (D), MIT, 1993, Yg
Thomas L. Brake, (M), New Mexico State, 1985, Nr
David E. Broxton, (M), New Mexico, 1976, Gx
Wendee M. Brunish, (D), Illinois, 1981, Zn
Gilles Y. Bussod, (D), California (Los Angeles), 1988, Yx
Katherine Campbell, (D), New Mexico, 1979, Gq
Theodore C. Carney, (M), Colorado State, 1981, Ng
Gregory L. Cole, (D), Arizona, 1990, Zg
Steffanie Coonley, (M), New Mexico, 1984, Zn
Keeley R. Costigan, (D), Colorado State, 1992, As
William Cottingame, (D), Texas, 1984, As
James L. Craig, (B), Nevada, 1974, Gg
Bruce M. Crowe, (D), California (Santa Barbara), 1974, Gv
Zora V. Dash, (M), New Mexico, 1988, Zn
Deborah J. Daymon, (M), Idaho, 1994, Zn
Kalpak Dighe, (D), Clemson, 1994, Zn
John C. Dinsmoor, (B), Colorado Mines, 1989, Nm
Alison M. Dorries, (D), Harvard, 1986, Zn
Donald S. Dreesen, (B), New Mexico, 1968, Np
David V. Duchane, (D), Michigan, 1978, Zn
Michael H. Ebinger, (D), Purdue, 1988, So
C L Edwards, (D), New Mexico Tech, 1975, Yg
C. James Elliott, (D), Yale, Zn
Scott M. Elliott, (D), California, 1983, As
Perry D. Farley, (D), Oklahoma, 1981, Zn
George T. Farmer, (D), Cincinnati, 1968, Hw
David N. Fogel, (M), Cal State, 1997, Zn
Carl W. Gable, (D), Harvard, 1989, Gt
Edward S. Gaffney, (D), Caltech, 1973, Yg
Anthony F. Gallegos, (D), Colorado State, 1970, Pg
Jamie N. Gardner, (D), California (Davis), 1985, Gg
Fraser Goff, (D), California (Santa Cruz), 1977, Cg
Jeffrey C. Hansen, (B), Weber State, 1971, Zn
Charles D. Harrington, (D), Indiana, 1970, Gm
Hans E. Hartse, (D), New Mexico Tech, 1991, Ys
Ward L. Hawkins, (B), Nevada (Reno), 1977, Zg
Grant Heiken, (D), California (Santa Barbara), 1972, Gv
Donald D. Hickmott, (D), MIT, 1988, Gp
Steve T. Hildebrand, (D), Texas (Dallas), 1993, Ys
Emil F. Homuth, (D), Washington, 1974, Ye
Paul A. Johnson, (M), Arizona, 1984, Yg
Eric M. Jones, (D), Wisconsin, 1970, As
Hemendra N. Kalia, (D), Missouri Sch of Mines, 1970, Nm
Jim C. Kao, (D), Illinois, 1985, As
Danny Katzman, (M), New Mexico, 1991, HyGem
Elizabeth Keating, (D), Wisconsin, 1995, Gg
Sharad Kelkar, (M), Texas, 1979, Np
C. F. Keller, Jr., (D), Indiana, 1969, As
Richard G. Kovach, (M), Naval Postgrad Sch, 1979, Nm
Donathon J. Krier, (M), New Mexico, 1980, Gv
Thomas D. Kunkle, (D), Hawaii, 1978, Xy
Edward M. Kwicklis, (M), Colorado, 1987, Gg
Chung Chieng A. Lai, (D), Texas A&M, 1984, Am
Schon S. Levy, (M), Texas, 1975, Gi
Peter C. Lichtner, (D), Mainz, 1974, Zn
Rodman Linn, (D), New Mexico State, 1997, Ng
Lynn McDonald, (M), Cal State, Zn
Maureen A. McGraw, (D), California (Berkeley), 1996, Zn
Laurie A. McNair, (D), Carnegie Mellon, 1995, Zn
Wayne R. Meadows, (B), Cal State (Bakersfield), 1974, Yg
Theodore Mockler, (M), Carnegie Mellon, 1986, Zn
Orrin B. Myers, (D), Colorado State, 1992, Pg
Balu Nadiga, (D), Caltech, 1992, Zn
Brent D. Newman, (D), New Mexico Tech, 1996, Gg
John W. Nyhan, (D), Colorado State, 1972, So
Ronald D. Oliver, (B), Oregon Inst of Tech, 1972, Yg
Howard J. Patton, (D), MIT, 1978, Yg
Frank V. Perry, (D), California, 1988, Gv
William S. Phillips, (D), MIT, 1985, Yg
Eugene W. Pokorny, (B), Missouri, 1979, Nm
William M. Porch, (D), Washington, 1971, Yg
Allyn R. Pratt, (M), Boise State, 1977, Ge
George Randall, (D), SUNY (Binghamton), Yg
Steen Rasmussen, (D), Tech (Denmark), 1985, Yg
Jon M. Reisner, (D), Iowa State, As
Steven L. Reneau, (D), California (Berkeley), 1988, Gm
Douglas O. Revelle, (D), Michigan, 1974, As
Peter Roberts, (D), MIT, 1989, Ys
Bruce A. Robinson, (D), MIT, 1985, Zn
R. Roussel-Dupre, (D), Colorado, 1979, Zn
Thomas J. Shankland, (D), Harvard, 1966, Yx
Catherine H. Smith, (D), New Mexico State, 1995, Ca

Wendy E. Soll, (D), MIT, 1991, Hw
Everett P. Springer, (D), Utah State, 1983, Hq
Lee Steck, (D), California, Gg
Robert P. Swift, (D), Washington, 1969, Nr
E.M.D. Symbalisty, (D), Chicago, 1984, Zn
Steven R. Taylor, (D), MIT, 1980, Ys
James Tencate, (D), Texas, 1992, Zn
Bryan J. Travis, (D), Florida State, 1974, Hq
David T. Vaniman, (D), California (Santa Cruz), 1976, Gx
Richard G. Warren, (M), New Mexico, 1972, Gi
Douglas J. Weaver, (M), Nevada, 1995, Zn
Thomas A. Weaver, (D), Chicago, 1973, Yg
Rodney W. Whitaker, (D), Indiana, 1976, As
Earl M. Whitney, (D), Utah, Zn
Judith L. Winterkamp, (B), Texas, 1977, Zn
Giday WoldeGabriel, (D), Case Western, 1987, Gx
Andrew V. Wolfsberg, (D), Stanford, 1993, Hw
George A. Zyvoloski, (D), California (Santa Barbara), 1975, Ng

Project Leader:
Mark T. Peters, (D), Chicago, 1992, Yg

Technical Staff:
James N. Albright, (D), Chicago, 1969, Yg
Donald W. Brown, (M), California (Los Angeles), 1961, Nr
Leigh S. House, (D), Columbia, 1982, Ys
Larry Allan Jones, (B), Nebraska, 1972, Ng

Technical Staff:
W. Scott Baldridge, (D), Caltech, 1979, GicGt

Other:
Christina "Tina" Behr-Andres, (D), Michigan Tech, 1992, Zn

National Aeronautics & Space Administration

NASA Headquarters (2015)
Washington, DC 20546-0001
p. (202) 358-2345
info-center@hq.nasa.gov
http://www.hq.nasa.gov/

Ames Research Center (2015)
Building BN200
Moffett Field, CA 94035-1000
p. (650) 604-5111
michael.s.mewhinney@nasa.gov

Chair:
Penelope Boston, (D), Colorado, 1985, Zg

Goddard Space Flight Center (2015)
Greenbelt Road
Greenbelt, MD 20771-0001
p. (301) 286-5121
stephanie.s.keene@nasa.gov

Lyndon B. Johnson Space Center (2015)
Houston, TX 77058-3696
p. (281) 483-5309
ellen.ochoa-1@nasa.gov

George C. Marshall Space Flight Center (2015)
Marshall Space Flight Center, AL 35812-0001
p. (256) 544-1910
patrick.e.scheuermann@nasa.gov

National Oceanic and Atmospheric Administration

National Centers for Environmental Information ☒ (2018)
David Skaggs Research Center
325 Broadway
Boulder, CO 80303
p. (303) 497-6826
ncei.info@noaa.gov
http://www.ngdc.noaa.gov/
f: http://www.facebook.com/NOAANCEIoceangeo
t: @NOAANCEIocngeo

National Science Foundation

Earth Sciences Div ☒ (2017)
4201 Wilson Boulevard
Arlington, VA 22230
p. (703) 292-8550
cfrost@nsf.gov
http://www.nsf.gov/div/index.jsp?div=EAR
t: @NSF_EAR

Program Director for Hydrologic Sciences:
Thomas Torgersen

Program Director for Instrumentation and Facilities:
David Lambert

Section Head:
Gregory J. Anderson

Section Head :
Lina Patino, (D)

Section for Antarctic Sciences:
Scott G. Borg, (D), Arizona State, 1984, Git

Program Director for Tectonics Program:
David M. Fountain
Stephen S. Harlan

Program Director for Petrology and Geochemistry Program:
Sonia Esperanca
Jennifer Wade

Program Director for Integrated Earth Systems:
Leonard E. Johnson

Program Director for Instrumentation and Facilities:
Russell C. Kelz

Program Director for Geophysics Program:
Robin Reichlin

Program Director for Geobiology and low-T Geochemistry:
Jonathan Wynn

Program Director for Geobiology and Low Temp Geochemistry:
Enriqueta C. Barrera

Program Director for Earthscope:
Margaret Benoit

Ocean Sciences Division (2016)
4201 Wilson Boulevard
Arlington, VA 22230
p. (703) 292-8580
rwmurray@nsf.gov
http://www.nsf.gov/div/index.jsp?div=OCE

Division Director:
Richard W. Murray

Section Head for Integrative Programs Section:
Bauke Houtman

Program Director for Ship Operations Program:
Rose Dufour

Program Director for Physical Oceanography Program:
Eric C. Itsweire
Baris Mete Uz

Program Director for Oceanographic Instrumentation and Technical Service Programs:
James Holik

Program Director for Ocean Observatories Initiative:
Jean M. McGovern

Program Director for Ocean Education Programs:
Elizabeth L. Rom

Program Director for Ocean Drilling Programs:
James F. Allan

Program Director for Marine Geology and Geophysics Program:
Candace O. Major
Barbara Ransom

Program Director for Chemical Oceanography Program:
Donald Rice

Program Director for Biological Oceanography Program:
David L. Garrison

Program Director:
John Walter

Program Directof for Ocean Drilling Programs:
Thomas Janacek

Associate Program Director for Oceanographic Technology and Interdisciplinary Coordination Program:
Kandace S. Binkley

Office of Polar Programs ☒ (2019)
2415 Eisenhower Avenue
Alexandria, VA 22314
p. (703) 292-8030
kfalkner@nsf.gov
https://www.nsf.gov/div/index.jsp?div=opp
f: https://www.facebook.com/NSFOPP/

Office of Polar Programs:
Kelly K. Falkner, (D)
Arctic Sciences Section:
Simon Stephenson, (M)
Antarctic Sciences Section:
Alexandra Isern, (D)
Antarctic Infrastructure and Logistics Section:
Stephanie A. Short, (M)
Polar Environment, Safety and Health Section:
Renee Crain
Technical Information Specialist, Office of Polar Programs:
David Friscic
Senior Advisor, Environment, Polar Environment, Safety and Health Section:
Polly A. Penhale, (D)
Senior Advisor, Business Analyst, Office of Polar Programs:
Scot Arnold, (D)
Science Assistant, Office of Polar Programs:
Beverly Walker
Science Assistant, Antarctic Sciences Section:
Wilson Sauthoff
Safety & Occupational Health Manager, Polar Environment, Safety and Health Section:
Gwendolyn Adams
Safety & Health Officer, Polar Environment, Safety and Health Section:
Jon Fentress
Program Support Contract Specialist, Arctic Sciences Section:
Randall V. Sisco
Program Support Contract Specialist, Antarctic Infrastructure & Logistics Section:
Russell McElyea
Program Specialist, Polar Environment, Safety and Health Section:
Karen Sloane
Program Specialist, Office of Polar Programs:
Erika N. Davis
Angela Lyons
Program Manager, Techology Development, Antarctic Infrastructure & Logistics Section:
Patrick D. Smith
Program Manager, Organisms & Ecosystems, Antarctic Sciences Section:
Karla Heidelberg, (D)
Program Manager, Operations, Antarctic Infrastructure & Logistics Section:
Margaret A. Knuth
Program Manager, Office of Polar Programs:
Erica Sahler
Program Manager, Ocean Projects, Antarctic Infrastructure & Logistics Section:
Timothy M. McGovern, (M), Hawaii, 2011
Program Manager, IT Support & USAP Info Security, Antarctic Infrastructure & Logistics Section:
Tim Howard
Program Manager, Facilities Engineering Projects, Antarctic Infrastructure & Logistics Section:
Ben D. Roth
Program Manager, Facilities Construction & Maintenance, Antarctic Infrastructure & Logistics Section:
Michael Gencarelli
Program Manager, Capital Planning, Antarctic Infrastructure & Logistics Section:
Brian MacDonald
Program Manager, Aviation, Antarctic Infrastructure & Logistics Section:
Gary James
Program Manager, Arctic Research Support and Logistics, Arctic Sciences Section:
Frank Rack, (B)
Program Manager, Arctic Research Support and Logistics, Acrtic Sciences Section:
Jennifer Mercer, (D)
Program Manager, Arctic Research Support & Logistics, Arctic Sciences Section:
Patrick R. Haggerty
Program Manager, Antarctic Research Support, Antarctic Infrastructure & Logistics Section:
Jessie L. Crain
Program Manager, Antarctic Integrated System Sciences, Antarctic Sciences Section:
Jennifer Burns, (D)
Program Manager Polar Outreach, Office of Polar Programs:
Peter West, (B)
Program Director, Ocean & Atmospheric Sciences, Antarctic Sciences Section:
Peter Milne, (D)
Program Director, Glaciology, Antarctic Sciences Section:
Paul Cutler, (D)
Program Director, Earth Sciences, Antarctic Sciences Section:
Michael Jackson, (D)
Program Director, Astrophysics & Geospace, Antarctic Sciences Section:
Robert Moore, (D)
Program Director, Arctic System Sciences, Arctic Sciences Section:
Gregory J. Anderson, (D)
Program Director, Arctic Observing Networks, Arctic Sciences Section:
Roberto Delgado, (D)
Program Director, Arctic Natural Sciences, Arctic Sciences Section:
Xujing Davis, (D)
Cynthia Suchman, (D)
Program Director, Arctic Natural Resources, Arctic Sciences Section:
Marc Stieglitz, (D)
Program Director, Antarctic Research Facilities & Special Projects, Antarctic Sciences Section:
Vladimir O. Papitashvili, (D), Russian Acad of Sci, 1981, YmXpa
Program Coordination Specialist, Arctic Sciences Section:
Linda Izzard
Program Coordination Specialist, Antarctic Sciences Section:
Desiree Marshall
Program Coordination Specialist, Antarctic Infrastructure & Logistics Section:
Carlena Fooks
Program Analyst, Office of Polar Programs:
Kimiko S. Bowens-Knox
Management & Program Analyst, Office of Polar Programs:
Andrew Backe, (D)
IT Specialist:
Dan King
Environmental Policy Specialist, Polar Environment, Safety and Health Section:
Nature McGinn, (D)
Communications Specialist, Office of Polar Programs:
Terri Edillon
Chief Program Manager, Antarctic Infrastructure & Logistics Section:
Paul Sheppard
Associate Program Director, Arctic System Sciences, Arctic Sciences Section:
Colleen Strawhacker, (D)
Administrative Officer, Office of Polar Programs:
Pawnee Maiden
AAAS Sciences and Technology Fellow, Arctic Sciences Section:
Yekaterina Kontar, (D)

Directorate for Geosciences ☒ (2018)
2415 Eisenhower Avenue
Room C8000
Alexandria, VA 22314
p. (703) 292-8500
sborg@nsf.gov
https://www.nsf.gov/dir/index.jsp?org=GEO
f: https://www.facebook.com/US.NSF
t: @NSF
Program Director for International Activities:
Maria Uhle

Office of the Director (2015)
4201 Wilson Boulevard
Arlington, VA 22230
p. (703) 292-5111
fcordova@nsf.gov
http://www.nsf.gov
f: https://www.facebook.com/US.NSF
t: @NSF

Atmospheric and Geospace Sciences Div (2015)
4201 Wilson Boulevard
Arlington, VA 22230
p. (703) 292-8520
pshepson@nsf.gov
http://www.nsf.gov/div/index.jsp?div=AGS

Division Director:
Paul B. Shepson
Section Head for NCAR/Facilities Section:
Stephan P. Nelson
Section Head for Geospace Section:
Richard A. Behnke
Section Head for Atmosphere Section:
David J. Verardo
Program Director for Solar Terrestrial Research Program:
Therese M. Jorgensen
Program Director for Physical and Dynamic Meteorology Program:
A. Gannet Hallar
Chungu Lu
Bradley F. Smull
Program Director for Paleoclimate Program:
Candace O. Major
Program Director for Magnetospheric Physics Program:
Raymond J. Walker
Program Director for Geospace Facilities:
Robert M. Robinson
Program Director for Education and Cross Disciplinary Activities Program:
Linda George
Program Director for Climate and Large Scale Dynamics Program & Carbon and Water in Earth Systems Program:
Eric T. DeWeaver
Program Director for Climate and Large Scale Dynamics Program:
Anjuli Bamzai
Program Director for Atmospheric Chemistry Program:
Peter Milne
Anne-Marie Schmoltner
Program Director for Aeronomy Program:
Anja Stromme
Program Coodinator for NCAR/Facilities Section:
Sarah L. Ruth
Facilities Program Manager for NCAR/Facilities Section:
Linnea M. Avallone
Assistant Program Director for Atmosphere Section:
Nicholas F. Anderson

Nuclear Regulatory Commission

NRC Headquarters (2015)
One White Flint North Building
11555 Rockville Pike
Rockville, MD 20852
p. (301) 415-8200
http://www.nrc.gov/

Oak Ridge National Laboratory

Environmental Sciences Div (2015)
P.O. Box 2008
Mail Stop 6035
Oak Ridge, TN 37831
p. (865) 574-7374
envsci@ornl.gov
http://www.esd.ornl.gov
Director:
Stephen G. Hildebrand, (D), Michigan, 1973, Zn
Professor:
Baohua Gu, (D), California (Berkeley), 1991, CbqSb
Senior Scientist:
Marshall Adams, (D), North Carolina, 1974, Ob
Jeff Amthor, (D), Yale, 1987, Sf
Tom Ashwood, (M), Murray State, 1975, Ge
Mark Bevelhimer, (D), Tennessee, 1990, Hs
Terence J. Blasing, (D), Wisconsin, 1975, As
Thomas Boden, (M), Miami, 1985, As
Craig Brandt, (M), Tennessee, 1988, Ge
Scott C. Brooks, (D), Virginia, 1994, Cl
Robert S. Burlage, (D), Tennessee, 1990, Sb
Meng-Dawn Cheng, (D), Illinois, 1986, As
Robert B. Cook, (D), Columbia, 1981, Cg
William E. Doll, (D), Wisconsin, 1983, Yg
Thomas O. Early, (D), Washington (St Louis), 1969, Cl
Philip M. Jardine, (D), Virginia Tech, 1985, Sc
Liyuan Liang, (D), Caltech, 1988, Cl
Steven E. Lindberg, (D), Florida State, 1979, Cl
John F. McCarthy, (D), Rhode Island, 1975, Co
Gerilynn R. Moline, (D), Wisconsin, 1992, Hw
Tony V. Palumbo, (D), North Carolina State, 1980, Sb
Tommy J. Phelps, (D), Wisconsin, 1985, Sb
Ellen D. Smith, (M), Wisconsin, 1979, Hg
Brian P. Spalding, (D), Cornell, 1976, Sc
Robert S. Turner, (D), Pennsylvania, 1983, Cl
David B. Watson, (M), New Mexico Tech, 1983, Hw
Olivia M. West, (D), MIT, 1991, Ng
Associate Scientist:
Tammy Beaty, Zi
Mary Anna Bogle, (M), Miami, 1975, Ge
Norman D. Farrow, (B), Oregon State, 1974, Hg
Deputy Director:
Gary K. Jacobs, (D), Penn State, 1981, Cg

Energy Div (2015)
P.O. Box 2008
Oak Ridge, TN 37831-6187
p. (615) 574-5510
wullschlegsd@ornl.gov
Administrative Assistant: Teresa D. Ferguson
Director:
Robert B. Shelton, (D), S Illinois, 1970, Zn
Chair:
Donald W. Lee, (D), Michigan, 1977, Hw
Senior Scientist:
Richard H. Ketelle, (M), Tennessee, 1977, Ge
Russell Lee, (D), McMaster, 1978, Zy
William P. Staub, (D), Iowa State, 1969, Ng
Research Associate:
Arthur C. Curtis, (M), Colorado State, 1993, Ge
Robert O. Johnson, (D), Tennessee, 1984, Hg
Richard R. Lee, (M), Temple, 1982, Gr
John D. Tauxe, (D), Texas, 1994, Hw

Pacific Northwest National Laboratory

Applied Geology & Geochemistry (2015)
Environmental Technology Div
Wayne J. Martin, Manager
PO Box 999 MSIN K6-81
Richland, WA 99352
p. (509) 376-5952
Christopher.Brown@pnnl.gov
http://www.pnl.gov/agg
Administrative Assistant: Charissa J. Chou
Head:
George R. Holdren, (D), Johns Hopkins, 1977, Cl
Staff Scientist:
Christopher J. Murray, (D), Stanford, 1992, Gq
Senior Research Engineer:
Mark D. White, (D), Colorado State, 1986, Hy
Lab Fellow:
Bernard P. McGrail, (D), Columbia S, 1996, Cg
Senior Scientist:
Douglas B. Barnett, (M), E Washington, 1985, Em
Bruce N. Bjornstad, (M), E Washington, 1980, Gs
Kirk J. Cantrell, (D), Georgia Tech, 1989, Cl
Amy P. Gamerdinger, (D), Cornell, 1989, Cl
Tyler J. Gilmore, (M), Idaho, 1987, Hg
Floyd N. Hodges, (D), Texas, 1975, Cg
Duane G. Horton, (D), Illinois, 1983, Gz
Kenneth M. Krupka, (D), Penn State, 1984, Cl
George V. Last, (M), Washington State, 1997, Ge
Jonathan W. Lindberg, (M), Washington State, 1995, Ec
Shas V. Mattigod, (D), Washington State, 1976, Cl
Alan C. Rohay, (D), Washington, 1982, Ys
Herbert T. Schaef, (M), Texas Tech, 1991, Cg
R. Jeffrey Serne, (B), Washington, 1969, CgSoCl
Mark D. Sweeney, (B), C Washington, 1985, Yg
Bruce A. Williams, (B), Colorado Mines, 1980, Ng
Associate Scientist:
Yi-Ju Chien, (M), Stanford, 1998, Gq
Jonathan P. Icenhower, (D), Oklahoma, 1995, Cl
David C. Lanigan, (B), Michigan Tech, 1980, Hg
Virginia L. Legore, (B), Oregon State, 1974, Cg
Clark W. Lindenmeier, (M), E Washington, 1995, Cg
Paul F. Martin, (B), Pacific Lutheran, 1982, Cg
Kent E. Parker, (M), Washington State, 1995, Cg

Research Associate:
Alexandra B. Amonette, (M), CUNY, 1976, Cg
Deborah S. Burke, (B), E Washington, 1992, Sc
Elsa A. Camacho, (B), Heritage, 1996, Cg
Matthew J. O'Hara, (B), Montana, 1996, Cg
Robert D. Orr, (B), N State, 1994, Ca

Sandia National Laboratory

Geoscience and Environment (2015)
1515 Eubank SE
P.O. Box 5800
Albuquerque, NM 87185
gobrela@sandia.gov
http://www.sandia.gov/
Research Scientist:
Thomas Dewers, (D), Indiana, 1990, Yx

Smithsonian Institution

Smithsonian Astrophysical Observatory ☒ (2017)
60 Garden Street
Cambridge, MA 02138
p. (617) 495-7100
calcock@cfa.harvard.edu
https://www.cfa.harvard.edu/sao
f: https://www.facebook.com/HarvardSmithsonianCenterFo-rAstrophysics

U.S. Geological Survey

Regional Director, Northeast (2015)
12201 Sunrise Valley Drive, MS 953
Reston, VA 20192
p. (703) 648-6660
druss@usgs.gov
http://www.usgs.gov

Regional Director, Southeast (2015)
1770 Corporate Drive, Suite 500
Norcross, GA 30093
p. (770) 409-7701
jdweaver@usgs.gov
http://www.usgs.gov

Regional Director, Midwest (2015)
1451 Green Road
Ann Arbor, MI 48105
p. (737) 214-7207
lcarl@usgs.gov
http://www.usgs.gov

Regional Director, Northwest (2015)
909 1st Avenue
Seattle, WA 98104
p. (206) 220-4600
ddlynch@usgs.gov
http://www.usgs.gov

Associate Director, Office of Comm & Publishing (2015)
12201 Sunrise Valley Drive, MS 119
Reston, VA 20192
p. (703) 648-5750
bwainman@usgs.gov
http://www.usgs.gov

Associate Director, Human Capital (2015)
12201 Sunrise Valley Drive, MS 201
Reston, VA 20192
p. (703) 648-7261
dwade@usgs.gov
http://www.usgs.gov

Associate Director, Office of Budget, Planning, & Integration (2015)
12201 Sunrise Valley Drive, MS 105
Reston, VA 20192
p. (703) 648-4443
cburzyk@usgs.gov
http://www.usgs.gov

Associate Director, Climate and Land-Use Change (2015)
12201 Sunrise Valley Drive, MD 409
Reston, VA 20192
p. (703) 648-5215
sryker@usgs.gov
http://www.usgs.gov

Associate Director, Administration & Enterprise Information (2019)
12201 Sunrise Valley Drive, MS 201
Reston, VA 20192
p. (703) 648-7261
timothy_quinn@ios.doi.gov
http://www.usgs.gov

Associate Director, Core Science Systems (M) (2017)
12201 Sunrise Valley Drive, MD 108
Reston, VA 20192
p. (703) 648-5747
kgallagher@usgs.gov
http://www.usgs.gov

Natural Hazards Mission Area ☒ (2021)
12201 Sunrise Valley Drive, MS 111
Reston, VA 20192
p. (703) 648-6600
applegate@usgs.gov
http://www.usgs.gov/natural_hazards/

Regional Safety Manager ☒ (2018)
PO Box 596
Brightwood, OR 97011
p. (503) 622-4432
wsimonds@usgs.gov
http://www.usgs.gov

Office of the Director (2015)
12201 Sunrise Valley Drive, MS 100
Reston, VA 20192
p. (703) 648-7411
abwade@usgs.gov
http://www.usgs.gov

Associate Director, Ecosystems (M) (2016)
12201 Sunrise Valley Drive, MS 300
Reston, VA 20192
p. (703) 648-4050
akinsinger@usgs.gov
http://www.usgs.gov

Director, Office of Science Quality & Integrity (2015)
12201 Sunrise Valley Drive, MS 911
Reston, VA 20192
p. (703) 648-6601
athornhill@usgs.gov
http://www.usgs.gov

SPECIALTY CODES

Specialty codes are used to indicate the research or teaching specialties of faculty members listed in the directory. Bold numbers are total number of individuals for each major category. Numbers in parentheses are individual specialty totals.

GEOLOGY **6610**

Gg General Geology (1360)
Ga Archaeological Geology (138)
Ge Environmental Geology (755)
Gm Geomorphology (648)
Gl Glaciology and Glacial Geology (333)
Gu Marine Geology (260)
Gz Mineralogy & Crystallography (562)
Gn Paleolimnology (72)
Go Petroleum Geology (311)
Gx General Petrology (225)
Gi Igneous Petrology (574)
Gp Metamorphic Petrology (296)
Gd Sedimentary Petrology (192)
Gs Sedimentology (882)
Gr Physical Stratigraphy (350)
Gc Structural Geology (800)
Gt Tectonics (762)
Gv Volcanology (376)
Gq Mathematical Geology (69)
Gy Mineral Physics (73)
Gb Medical Geology (22)
Gf Forensic Geology (12)

ECONOMIC GEOLOGY **622**

Eg General Economic Geology (280)
Ec Coal (53)
Em Metallic Ore Deposits (159)
En Industrial Minerals (30)
Eo Oil and Gas (124)
Es Construction Materials (SSG) (2)
Ed Ore Deposits (Other) (12)

GEOCHEMISTRY **2326**

Cg General Geochemistry (655)
Ca Analytical Geochemistry (200)
Cp Experimental Petrology/Phase Equilibria (102)
Ce Exploration Geochemistry (69)
Cc Geochronology & Radioisotopes (357)
Cl Low-temperature Geochemistry (392)
Cm Marine Geochemistry (206)
Co Organic Geochemistry (138)
Cs Stable Isotopes (361)
Ct Trace Element Distribution (84)
Cb Biogeochemistry (107)
Cu High-temperature Geochemistry (34)
Cq Aqueous Geochemistry (47)

GEOPHYSICS **1735**

Yg General Geophysics (629)
Yx Experimental Geophysics (100)
Ye Exploration Geophysics (246)
Yd Geodesy (115)
Ym Geomagnetism & Paleomagnetism (156)
Yv Gravity (33)
Yh Heat Flow (27)
Ys Seismology (563)
Yr Marine Geophysics (164)
Yn Nonlinear Geophysics (6)
Yu Near-surface Geophysics (50)

PALEONTOLOGY **1593**

Pg General Paleontology (528)
Ps Paleostratigraphy (117)
Pm Micropaleontology (173)
Pb Paleobotany (66)
Pl Palynology (64)
Pq Quantitative Paleontology (25)
Pv Vertebrate Paleontology (256)
Pi Invertebrate Paleontology (251)
Pe Paleoecology (334)
Po Geomicrobiology (27)
Pc Paleoclimatology (95)

HYDROLOGY **1485**

Hg General Hydrology (346)
Hw Ground Water/Hydrogeology (716)
Hq Quantitative Hydrology (125)
Hs Surface Waters (179)
Hy Geohydrology (113)
Ht Materials Transport (6)

SOIL SCIENCE **818**

Sp Soil Physics/Hydrology (107)
Sc Soil Chemistry/Mineralogy (184)
Sd Pedology/Classification/Morphology (85)
Sf Forest Soils/Rangelands/Wetlands (59)
Sb Soil Biology/Biochemistry (120)
Sa Paleopedology/Archeology (31)
So Other Soil Science (232)

ENGINEERING GEOLOGY **704**

Ng General Engineering Geology (286)
Ne Earthquake Engineering (22)
Nx Mining Tech/Extractive Metallurgy (45)
Nm Mining Engineering (89)
Np Petroleum Engineering (80)
Nr Rock Mechanics (117)
No Ocean Engineering/Mining (29)
Nt Geotechnical Engineering (16)
Nx Geological Engineering (20)

OCEANOGRAPHY **1544**

Og General Oceanography (226)
Ob Biological Oceanography (453)
Oc Chemical Oceanography (257)
Ou Geological Oceanography (153)
Op Physical Oceanography (406)
On Shore and Nearshore Processes (124)
Oo Paleooceanography (23)

ASTRONOMICAL SCIENCES **416**

Xs Astronomy (3)
Xc Cosmochemistry (69)
Xg Extraterrestrial Geology (169)
Xy Extraterrestrial Geophysics (93)
Xm Meteorites & Tektites (77)
Xa Astrophysics (45)
Xp Heliophysics (2)
Xb Astrobiology (12)

ATMOSPHERIC SCIENCES **1197**

As Atmospheric Sciences (897)
Am Meteorology (324)
Ac Atmospheric Chemistry (30)
Ap Atmospheric Physics (25)
At Climatology (65)

GEOSCIENCE & SOCIETY **198**

Rn Natural Hazards (78)
Rm Manmade Hazards (11)
Rw Water Quality/Use (48)
Rc Geoscience Communication (22)
Rh History of Geoscience (46)

OTHER **3344**

Zg General Earth Sciences (401)
Ze Earth Science Education (365)
Zy Physical Geography (336)
Zr Remote Sensing (475)
Zm Material Science (56)
Zu Land Use/Urban Geology (122)
Zi Geographic Information Systems (573)
Zf Geoinformatics (46)
Zc Global Change (100)
Za Nanogeoscience (11)
Zo Climate Modeling (36)
Zn Not Elsewhere Classified (1289)

Total **23,656**

FACULTY SPECIALTY INDEX

GEOLOGY

General Geology

Abbott, Lon, University of Colorado
Abousleiman, Younane N., University of Oklahoma
Abreu, Vitor, Rice University
Abushagur, Sulaiman, El Paso Community College
Adabanija, Moruffdeen A., Ladoke Akintola University of Technology
Adinolfi, Bryan, Southern Connecticut State University
Agbogun, Henry, Fort Hays State University
Ahmed, Samir, Graduate School of the City University of New York
Ahola, John, Bristol Community College
Ajigo, Isaac O., Federal University of Technology, Akure
Akgun, Elif , Firat University
Akinlabi, Ismaila A., Ladoke Akintola University of Technology
Aksoy, Ercan, Firat University
Akujieze, Christopher N., University of Benin
Alexander, Dane, Western Michigan University
Alexander, Elaine, McLennan Community College
Alfsen, Sheila, Portland State University
Alkac, Onur, Firat University
Allison, Alivia J., Emporia State University
Altermann, Wladyslaw, Ludwig-Maximilians-Universitaet Muenchen
Amaach, Noureddin, College of Staten Island/CUNY
Amato, James A., University of Wisconsin, Oshkosh
Anderson, Paula, University of Arkansas, Fayetteville
Andonaegui, Pilar, Univ Complutense de Madrid
Andronicos, Chris, Purdue University
Anhaeusser, Carl R., University of the Witwatersrand
Antonacci, Vince, Tennessee Geological Survey
Arias, Carmen, Univ Complutense de Madrid
Ashe, Douglas, Tulsa Community College
Athaide, Dileep, University of British Columbia
Athaide, Dileep J., Capilano University
Athey, Jennifer E., Alaska Division of Geological & Geophysical Surveys
Bach Plaza, Joan, Universitat Autonoma de Barcelona
Bachle, Peter, Missouri Dept of Natural Resources
Baer, Eric M., Highline College
Bagley, Evan, University of Southern Mississippi
Baker, Cathy, Arkansas Tech University
Balakrishnan, Meena, Tarrant County College, Northeast Campus
Ballero, Deniz Z., Georgia State University, Perimeter College, Online
Bally, Albert W., Rice University
Balmat, Jennifer L., Chadron State College
Balsley, Christopher, Southern Connecticut State University
Banda, Anna F., El Centro College - Dallas Community College District
Bandosz, Teresa, Graduate School of the City University of New York
Barcena, Homar S., Graduate School of the City University of New York
Barclay, Julie L., SUNY, Cortland
Barker, Andy J., University of Southampton
Barker, Gregory A., New Hampshire Geological Survey
Barminski, Robert, Hartnell College
Barnes, Brenda, El Paso Community College
Bassett, Damon, Missouri State University
Baxter, P.G., James E., Harrisburg Area Community College
Bayowa, Oyelowo G., Ladoke Akintola University of Technology
Beatty, Lynne, Johnson County Community College
Beausoleil, Denis, Douglas College
Beltz, John F., University of Akron
Bender, Hallock J., Mt. San Antonio College
Bennett, Sara, Western Illinois University
Benson, Donna M., Mesa Community College
Bentley, Callan, Northern Virginia Community College - Annandale
Benton, Steven, Illinois State Geological Survey
Beranek, Luke, Memorial University of Newfoundland
Berry IV, Henry N., Dept of Agriculture, Conservation, and Forestry
Berti, Claudio, University of Idaho
Best, Myron G., Brigham Young University
Beyer, Adam, Nicholls State University
Bice, David M., Pennsylvania State University, University Park
Biek, Robert, Utah Geological Survey
Bierly, Aaron D., DCNR- Pennsylvania Bureau of Geological Survey
Birner, Johannes, Ludwig-Maximilians-Universitaet Muenchen
Blaylock, Glenn W., Laredo College
Blome, Margaret, East Carolina University
Boehm, David A., SUNY, The College at Brockport
Bograd, Michael B., Mississippi Office of Geology
Bohm, Christian, Manitoba Geological Survey
Bolze, Claude E., Tulsa Community College
Bone, Fletcher, Missouri Dept of Natural Resources
Booth, James, Graduate School of the City University of New York
Boroughs, Terry J., American River College
Bouker, Polly A., Georgia State University, Perimeter College, Newton Campus
Bounk, Michael, Iowa Dept of Natural Resources
Bour, William, Northern Virginia Community College - Loudoun Campus
Bouse, Robin, El Camino College
Bowen, Esther E., Argonne National Laboratory
Bowles, Zack, Mesa Community College
Bozdog, Nick, N.C. Department of Environmental Quality
Bradshaw, Lanna K., Brookhaven College
Branciforte, Chloe, Mesa Community College
Branco, Brett, Graduate School of the City University of New York
Brânzila, Mihai, Alexandru Ioan Cuza
Bremmer, Sarah, University of Wisconsin, Madison, Division of Extension
Bridges, David L., Missouri Dept of Natural Resources
Bries Korpik, Jill, Inver Hills Community College
Brill, Jr., Richard C., Honolulu Community College
Brock, Patrick W. G., Queens College (CUNY)
Brown, Alan, Middle Tennessee State University
Brown, Kyle, Missouri Dept of Natural Resources
Brown, Summer, University of Kentucky
Browning, James M., Texas Tech University
Browning, James V., Rutgers, The State University of New Jersey
Browning, Sharon, Baylor University
Broze, Elliot, Whitman College
Brueckner, Hannes K., Queens College (CUNY)
Brunengo, Matthew , Portland State University
Bruschke, Freddi Jo, California State University, Fullerton
Bryan, Sean, Colorado State University
Bryant, Kathleen E., Illinois State Geological Survey
Bryant, Marita, Bates College
Buchanan, Paul C., Kilgore College
Buchwald, Caryl E., Carleton College
Bucke, David P., University of Vermont
Bultman, John, Asheville-Buncombe Technical Community College
Burd, Aurora, Antelope Valley College
Burns, Emily, Community College of Rhode Island
Burris, John H., San Juan College
Burtis, Erik, Northern Virginia Community College - Woodbridge
Butcher, William, Bowling Green State University
Butkos, Darryl J., Suffolk County Community College, Ammerman Campus
Büchel, Georg, Friedrich-Schiller-University Jena
Caldwell, Andy, Front Range Community College - Larimer
Caldwell, Marianne O., Hillsborough Community College
Callahan, Caitlin N., Grand Valley State University
Cameron, Kevin, Simon Fraser University
Canalda, Sabrina, El Paso Community College
Caputi, Samantha , Tarrant County College, Southeast Campus
Carpi, Anthony, Graduate School of the City University of New York
Carr, Keith W., Illinois State Geological Survey
Case, Jeanne, Eastern Washington University
Cather, Steven, New Mexico Institute of Mining and Technology
Cervato, Cinzia C., Iowa State University of Science & Technology
Chadima, Sarah A., South Dakota Dept of Env and Natural Resources
Chamberlin, Richard M., New Mexico Institute of Mining and Technology
Chandler, Angela, Arkansas Geological Survey
Chang, Julie M., University of Oklahoma
Charles, Kasanzu, University of Dar es Salaam
Chasteen, Hayden R., Tarrant County College, Northeast Campus
Cherukupalli, Nehru, Hofstra University
Cholnoky, Jennifer, Skidmore College
Christensen, Wesley P., South Dakota Dept of Env and Natural Resources
Ciciarelli, John A., Pennsylvania State University, Monaca
Clark, Donald, Utah Geological Survey
Clark, Kathryne, Iowa Dept of Natural Resources
Clark, Ken P., University of Puget Sound

Clayton, Rodney L., Tidewater Community College
Clendening, Ronald J., Tennessee Geological Survey
Coffman, David, El Centro College - Dallas Community College District
Coffman, Stephanie, El Centro College - Dallas Community College District
Colak Erol, Serap, Firat University
Coleman, Alvin L., Cape Fear Community College
Collins, Laura R., Middle Tennessee State University
Colosimo, Amanda, Monroe Community College
Conquy, Xenia, Broward College
Cooper, Jonathon L., Carleton College
Cornell, Kristie, University of Louisiana at Lafayette
Cornell, Sean R., Shippensburg University
Cornell , William , University of Texas, El Paso
Couroux, Emile, El Paso Community College
Coutand, Isabelle, Dalhousie University
Craig, James L., Los Alamos National Laboratory
Crain, John R., College of the Sequoias
Crawford, Vernon J., Southern Oregon University
Creveling, Jessica, Oregon State University
Criswell, James, Cape Fear Community College
Cron, Mitch, Drexel University
Cronoble, James M., Metropolitan State College of Denver
Cummings, Michael L., Portland State University
Curtis, Lynn A., Broward College
Cvetko Tešoviæ, Blanka, University of Zagreb
Damir, Buckoviæ, University of Zagreb
Davarpanah, Armita, Georgia State University
Davis, David A., University of Nevada, Reno
Davis, Timothy, Temple University
Dawes, Ralph, Wenatchee Valley College
Day, Damon P., Mt. San Antonio College
Day, Mackenzie, University of California, Los Angeles
Deakin, Joann, Cochise College
Dealy, Mike, University of Kansas
Dee, Seth, University of Nevada, Reno
Deering, Chad, Michigan Technological University
Delano, Helen L., DCNR- Pennsylvania Bureau of Geological Survey
Devaney, Kathleen, El Paso Community College
Devlahovich, Vincent A., College of the Canyons
DeVries-Zimmerman, Suzanne, Hope College
Dhavaskar, Poornima, Goa University
Di Fiori, Sara, El Camino College
Dinklage, William, Santa Barbara City College
Dittmer, Eric, Southern Oregon University
Dodge, Stefanie, University of Wisconsin, Madison, Division of Extension
Doelling, Helmut H., University of Utah
Doherty, David J., Wayne State University
Donnelly, Thomas W., Binghamton University
Dooley, Brett, Patrick Henry Community College
Dougan, Bernie, Whatcom Community College
Doyle, Joseph, Bridgewater State University
Drobny, Gerry, Cosumnes River College
Dudley, Jutta S., SUNY, The College at Brockport
Duncan, Ian, University of Texas at Austin, Jackson School of Geosciences
Dushman, Beth, American River College
Dyab, Ahmed I., Alexandria University
Earls, Stephanie, Washington Geological Survey
Easterday, Cary, Bellevue College
Eaton, Timothy, Graduate School of the City University of New York
Ebel, Denton, Graduate School of the City University of New York
Edson, Carol, Las Positas College
Egbeyemi, Oladimeji R., Federal University of Technology, Akure
Eguiluz, Luis, University of the Basque Country UPV/EHU
Eide, Elizabeth A., National Academies of Sciences, Engineering, and Medicine
Eisenhart, Ralph, York College of Pennsylvania
El Dakkak, Mohamed W., Alexandria University
Ellis, Trevor, Missouri Dept of Natural Resources
Emerson, Norlene, University of Wisconsin Colleges
Engelhard, Simon, University of Rhode Island
Erlandsson, Viktor, University Leoben
Escartin, Javier, Woods Hole Oceanographic Institution
Escuer, Joan, Universitat Autonoma de Barcelona
Evans, Thomas J., University of Wisconsin, Extension
Ewas, Galal A., Alexandria University
Faatz, Renee M., Snow College
FABRE, Cecile, Universite de Lorraine - Faculte des Sciences et Technologies
Fagnan, Brian A., South Dakota Dept of Env and Natural Resources
Fahrenbach, Mark D., South Dakota Dept of Env and Natural Resources
Farquharson, Phil, MiraCosta College
Farrell, Michael, Cuyamaca College
Farris, David, East Carolina University
Feeney, Dennis M., University of Idaho
Fengler, Keegan , Central Washington University
Fields, Chad, Iowa Dept of Natural Resources
Figg, Sean, Palomar College
Filkorn, Harry, Los Angeles Pierce College
Finley, Mark, Heartland Community College
Fitak, Madge R., Ohio Dept of Natural Resources
Fitchett, Rebekah, Northeastern Illinois University
Fitz, Thomas J., Northland College
Fleck, Michelle C., Utah State University Eastern
Flower, Hilary, Saint Petersburg College, Clearwater
Flowers Falls, Emily, Washington & Lee University
Flynn, John T., Graduate School of the City University of New York
Forno, Maria Gabriella, Università di Torino
Forsman, Nels F., University of North Dakota
Frail, Pam, Acadia University
Frederick, Bruce, Johnson County Community College
Fredrick, Kyle, California University of Pennsylvania
Freed, Andrew M., Purdue University
Frei, Allan, Graduate School of the City University of New York
Frei, Michaela, Ludwig-Maximilians-Universitaet Muenchen
Freiburg, Jared, Illinois State Geological Survey
Friedmann, Samuel (Julio) J., Lawrence Livermore National Laboratory
Friedrich, Anke, Ludwig-Maximilians-Universitaet Muenchen
Frieman, Richard, SUNY, Oswego
Fromm, Jeanne M., University of South Dakota
Frost, Gina M., San Joaquin Delta College
Fuerst, Alice, Metropolitan Community College-Kansas City
Gagnon, Teresa K., Dept of Energy and Environmental Protection
Galal, Galal M., Alexandria University
Gale, Marjorie H., Agency of Natural Resources, Dept of Env Conservation
Gannon, J. Michael, Iowa Dept of Natural Resources
García Frank, Alejandra, Univ Complutense de Madrid
Gardner, Eleanor E., University of Tennessee, Martin
Gardner, Jamie N., Los Alamos National Laboratory
Garrett, Maureen, Arizona Western College
Garside, Larry J., University of Nevada, Reno
Garwood, Phil, Cape Fear Community College
Gawloski, Joan, Midland College
Gawu, Simon K., Kwame Nkrumah University of Science and Technology
Gentry, Amanda L., Weber State University
Gianotti, Franco, Università di Torino
Giegengack, Jr., Robert F., University of Pennsylvania
Giglierano, James D., Iowa Dept of Natural Resources
Giles, Antony, Midland College
Gillman, Joe, Missouri Dept of Natural Resources
Glynn, William G., SUNY, The College at Brockport
González-Juarez, Marco, Univ Estatal de Sonora
Goodkin, Nathalie , Graduate School of the City University of New York
Goodwin, Joshua, California Geological Survey
Gorokhovich, Yuri, Graduate School of the City University of New York
Gould, Joseph C., Saint Petersburg College, Clearwater
Grace, Cathy A., University of Mississippi
Grassman, Jean, Graduate School of the City University of New York
Greenaway, Darren, Tarrant County College, Southeast Campus
Greene, Mott, University of Washington
Griffin, William R., University of Texas, Dallas
Griffing, Corinne, Douglas College
Gross, Amy, University of North Carolina, Pembroke
Grover, Jeffrey A., Cuesta College
Grupp, Steve, Everett Community College
Guggino, Steve N., Georgia Southern University
Gušiæ, Ivan, University of Zagreb
Hagadorn, James W., Denver Museum of Nature & Science
Hakimian, Adina, Hofstra University
Hale, Leslie J., Smithsonian Institution / National Museum of Natural History
Haley, John C., Virginia Wesleyan College
Hall, Clarence A., University of California, Los Angeles
Hall, Tracy, Georgia Highlands College
Hamdan, Abeer, Phoenix College
Hamecher, Emily A., California State University, Fullerton

Hammes, Ursula, University of Texas at Austin, Jackson School of Geosciences
Hams, Jacquelyn E., Los Angeles Valley College
Hand, Linda M., College of San Mateo
Hanell, Casey R., Washington Geological Survey
Hanger, Brendan, Oklahoma State University
Hanna, Ruth L., Las Positas College
Hanson, Gilbert N., Stony Brook University
Harder, Vicki, University of Texas, El Paso
Hargrave, Phyllis, Montana Tech of The University of Montana
Harma, Roberta L., Moorpark College
Harone, Imad, College of Staten Island/CUNY
Harrell, Michael, Seattle Central College
Harris, Ann, Eastern Kentucky University
Harris, Michelle, Centralia College
Harrison, Linda , Western Michigan University
Hart, George, Louisiana State University
Hart, Roger M., Community College of Rhode Island
Hartley, Susan, Lake Superior College
Haselwander, Airin J., Missouri Dept of Natural Resources
Hauer, Kendall L., Miami University
Hayes, Garry F., California State University, Stanislaus
Hayes, Garry F., Modesto Junior College
Heck, Frederick R., Ferris State University
Heerschap, Lauren, Fort Lewis College
Hegner, Ernst, Ludwig-Maximilians-Universitaet Muenchen
Heidlauf, Lisa, Wheaton College
Hein, Kim A., University of the Witwatersrand
Helba, Hossam EL-Din A., Alexandria University
Heller, Matthew J., Division of Geology and Mineral Resources
Helmke, Vicky, West Chester University
Hendrey, George, Graduate School of the City University of New York
Henley, Barbara D., Mercer University
Henry, Kathleen M., Illinois State Geological Survey
Hepburn, J. Christopher, Boston College
Herbert, Jennifer, Argonne National Laboratory
Hernandez, Larry, MiraCosta College
Herring Mayo, Lisa L., Motlow State Community College
Herzig, Chuck, El Camino College
Hetherington, Jean, Diablo Valley College
Hickcox, Charles W., Emory University
Higgins, Chris T., California Geological Survey
Hill, Catherine R., Arizona Western College
Hill, Chris, Grossmont College
Hinthorne, James R., University of Texas, Rio Grande Valley
Hinz, Nicholas, University of Nevada, Reno
Ho, Anita, Flathead Valley Community College
Hobbs, Thomas M., Lonestar College - North Harris
Hochstaedter, Alfred, Monterey Peninsula College
Hodder, Donald R., SUNY, New Paltz
Hok, Jozef, Comenius University in Bratislava
Holail, Hanafy M., Alexandria University
Holmes, Stevie L., South Dakota Dept of Env and Natural Resources
Hood, Teresa A., University of Miami
Hood, William C., Colorado Mesa University
Hopkins, David M., University of Alaska, Fairbanks
Hoppe, Andreas, Technische Universitaet Darmstadt
Horn, John, Metropolitan Community College-Kansas City
Horton, Albert B., Tennessee Geological Survey
House, Martha, Pasadena City College
Howard, Katie, Olympic College
Howard, Kieren, Graduate School of the City University of New York
Howes, Mary R., Iowa Dept of Natural Resources
Hunt, Paula J., West Virginia Geological & Economic Survey
Hural, Kirsten, Dickinson College
Hutto, Richard S., Arkansas Geological Survey
Huxta, Stephen, Drexel University
Huycke, David, Yakima Valley College
Hylland, Michael D., Utah Geological Survey
Hylton, Alisa, Central Piedmont Community College
Hynes, Joanna , California State University, Fullerton
Iaccheri, Maria Linda, Ludwig-Maximilians-Universitaet Muenchen
Ianno, Adam J., Juniata College
Idstein, Peter J., University of Kentucky
Igonor, Emmanuel E., Federal University of Technology, Akure
Ikwuazorm, Okia, Northern Virginia Community College - Loudoun Campus
Irvin, Gene D., Geological Survey of Alabama
Isenor, Fenton M., Cape Breton University
Jackson, Hiram, Cosumnes River College
Jackson, Jeremiah, Missouri Dept of Natural Resources
Jacobs, Jon, Western University
Jaecks, Glenn, American River College
Jammes, Suzon, Texas State University
Jans, Urs, Graduate School of the City University of New York
Janusz, Robert, San Antonio Community College
Jellinek, Mark, University of British Columbia
Jensen, Ann R., South Dakota Dept of Env and Natural Resources
Jessee, Anna, Indiana University - Purdue University Indianapolis
Jiang, James Xinxia, Mount Allison University
Jiron, Rebecca, William & Mary
Johnson, Darren J., South Dakota Dept of Env and Natural Resources
Johnson, Edward, College of Staten Island/CUNY
Johnson, Kurt, Alaska Division of Geological & Geophysical Surveys
Johnson, Ty, Arkansas Geological Survey
Johnston, David, Arkansas Geological Survey
Johnston, Paul L., Emporia State University
Jones, Charles E., University of Pittsburgh
Jones, Gwyn, Bellevue College
Jordan, Bradley C., Bucknell University
Judith, Sausse, Ecole Nationale Supérieure de Géologie (ENSG)
Jurena, Dwight, Alamo Colleges, San Antonio College
Kaandorp, Ron, Vrije Universiteit Amsterdam
Kaldor, Michael, Miami-Dade College (Wolfson Campus)
Kane-DeVries, Katelyn, Missouri Dept of Natural Resources
Kapp, Jessica, University of Arizona
Karwoski, Todd, University of Maryland
Kaye, John M., Mississippi State University
Kaygili, Sibel, Firat University
Keane, Christopher M., American Geosciences Institute
Keating, Elizabeth, Los Alamos National Laboratory
Keattch, Sharen , Eastern Washington University
Keeley, Joshua A., New Hampshire Geological Survey
Keene, Deborah A., University of Alabama
Kelley, Neil P., Vanderbilt University
Kempe, Stephan, Technische Universitaet Darmstadt
Kerwin, Charles M., Keene State College
Kerwin, Michael W., University of Denver
Kessler, Carsten, Graduate School of the City University of New York
Ketcham, Richard A., University of Texas, Austin
Khalil Ebeid, Khalil I., Alexandria University
Khandaker, Nazul, Graduate School of the City University of New York
Kiesel, Diann, University of Wisconsin Colleges
Kim, Keonho, Midland College
King, Jonathan K., Utah Geological Survey
Kirkby, Kent C., University of Minnesota, Twin Cities
Klaus, James S., University of Miami
Klee, Thomas M., Hillsborough Community College
Klosterman, Sue, University of Dayton
Knowlton, Kelly, Northwestern State University
Kodosky, Larry, Oakland Community College
Koenig, Brian, College of the Desert
Kohrt, Casey, Iowa Dept of Natural Resources
Kolkas, Mosbah, College of Staten Island/CUNY
Kollasch, Pete, Iowa Dept of Natural Resources
Koutavas, Athanasios, Graduate School of the City University of New York
Kowallis, Bart J., Brigham Young University
Kraft, Kaatje, Mesa Community College
Kraft, Kaatje, Whatcom Community College
Krakauer, Nir, Graduate School of the City University of New York
Kramer, J. Curtis, University of the Pacific
Kramer, Kate, McHenry County College
Kramer, Walter V., Del Mar College
Kranz, Dwight S., Houston Community College System
Krohe, Nicholas J., South Dakota Dept of Env and Natural Resources
Kroon, Dick, Edinburgh University
Kruger, Ned , North Dakota Geological Survey
Kuehner, Scott, University of Washington
Kuhlman, Robert, Montgomery County Community College
Kuhnhenn, Gary L., Eastern Kentucky University
Kukoè, Duje, University of Zagreb
Kumpf, Amber C., Muskegon Community College
Kuntz, Mark R., Elgin Community College
Kutis, Michael, Ball State University

Kwicklis, Edward M., Los Alamos National Laboratory
lacy, tor b., Cerritos College
Lambert-Smith, James, Kingston University
Lammerer, Bernd L., Ludwig-Maximilians-Universitaet Muenchen
Lancaster, Jeremy, California Geological Survey
Langel, Richard A., Iowa Dept of Natural Resources
Langille, Amanda, Memorial University of Newfoundland
LaPointe, Daphne D., University of Nevada, Reno
Larsen, David, Weber State University
Larter, Stephen, University of Newcastle Upon Tyne
Lauziere, Kathleen, Universite du Quebec
Leite, Michael B., Chadron State College
Lemay, Phillip W., Louisiana State University
Leszczynski, Raymond F., Cayuga Community College
Levy, Melissa H., American River College
Lewis, Chris, City College of San Francisco
Lewis, Mary, Contra Costa College
Lewis, Reed S., University of Idaho
Lewis, Tammy, Graduate School of the City University of New York
Liauw, Henri L., Broward College
Libra, Robert D., Iowa Dept of Natural Resources
Liebling, Richard, Hofstra University
Lippelt, Irene D., University of Wisconsin, Madison, Division of Extension
Liu, Paul Hiaibao, Iowa Dept of Natural Resources
Locke, Erika, Texas A&M University, Corpus Christi
Lombard, Armand J., Mesa Community College
Long, Colleen, Illinois State Geological Survey
Lonn, Jeff, Montana Tech of The University of Montana
Lovett, Cole, Lake Michigan College
Lu, Yuehan, University of Alabama
Ludman, Allan, Graduate School of the City University of New York
Ludman, Allan, Queens College (CUNY)
Lueth, Virgil W., New Mexico Institute of Mining and Technology
Lužar-Oberiter, Borna, University of Zagreb
Lyle, Mike, Tidewater Community College
Lyle, Mitchell, Oregon State University
Lyman, John C., Bakersfield College
Mabee, Stephen B., University of Massachusetts, Amherst
Macdonald, Francis, University of California, Santa Barbara
Macias, Steve E., Olympic College
MacLachlan, James, Metropolitan State College of Denver
Madin, Ian P., Oregon Dept of Geology and Mineral Industries
Magee, Robert, Virginia Wesleyan College
Mahaffee, Tina, Middle Georgia College
Mahlen, Nancy J., SUNY, Geneseo
Mahmoud, Sara A., Alexandria University
Majodina, Thando, Tshwane University of Technology
Major, Penni, Lonestar College - North Harris
Major, Ruth H., Hudson Valley Community College
Malone, Shawn, University of Wisconsin, Green Bay
Mandziuk, William S., University of Manitoba
Mansour, Ahmed S., Alexandria University
Mapholi, Thendo, University of the Free State
Marchand, Gerard, Mount Holyoke College
Marchisin, John, New Jersey City University
Marco, Shmuel, Tel Aviv University
Marco, Shmulik, Tel Aviv University
Marshall, Thomas R., South Dakota Dept of Env and Natural Resources
Martin, Gale D., College of Southern Nevada - West Charleston Campus
Martinez Torres, Luis Miguel, University of the Basque Country UPV/EHU
Martinuš, Maja, University of Zagreb
Martz, Todd, University of California, San Diego
Marvinney, Robert G., Dept of Agriculture, Conservation, and Forestry
Mata, Scott, California State University, Fullerton
Mattox, Tari, Grand Rapids Community College
Matyjasik, Basia, Utah Geological Survey
May, S J., Collin College - Preston Ridge Campus
Mayer, Larry, Woods Hole Oceanographic Institution
McCall, Rosemary, College of Staten Island/CUNY
McCauley, Steven, El Centro College - Dallas Community College District
McClaughry, Jason, Oregon Dept of Geology and Mineral Industries
McCoy, Floyd W., Windward Community College
McCulloh, Richard P., Louisiana State University
McCutchen, William T., University of Tennessee, Martin
McDermott, Frank, University College Dublin
McDowell, Robin J., Georgia State Univ, Perimeter Coll, Dunwoody Campus
McDowell, Ronald, Fairmont State University
McIlrath, Judy, University of South Florida
McIlroy, Duncan, Memorial University of Newfoundland
McKay, Robert M., Iowa Dept of Natural Resources
McKinney, Michael, California Geological Survey
McMonagle, Julie, Wilkes University
Meave, Edgardo, Univ Nacional Autonoma de Mexico
Meister, Paul A., Illinois State University
Melcher, Frank, University Leoben
Meldahl, Keith H., MiraCosta College
Meléndez, Nieves, Univ Complutense de Madrid
Metz, Cheyl L., Blinn College
Metzler, Christopher V., MiraCosta College
Mey, Jacob, Graduate School of the City University of New York
Meyer, Jeffrey W., Santa Barbara City College
Michel, Suzanne, Cuyamaca College
Millan, Christina, Ohio State University
Millen, Timothy M., Elgin Community College
Miller, Steven F., Argonne National Laboratory
Miller-Hicks, Bryan, Cuyamaca College
Milner, Lloyd R., Louisiana State University
Milner, Lloyd R., Louisiana State University
Miner, James J., Illinois State Geological Survey
Minium, Deborah, Bellevue College
Mitzman, Stephanie, Tarrant County College, Southeast Campus
Moll, Nancy E., College of the Desert
Monet, Julie, California State University, Chico
Monson, Jessica, Illinois State Geological Survey
Montayne, Simone, Alaska Division of Geological & Geophysical Surveys
Montwill, Gail F., Santiago Canyon College
Mora, Claudia, University of Texas, Austin
Morand, Vincent J., La Trobe University
Morealli, Sarah A., University of Mary Washington
Morgan, Matt, Colorado Geological Survey
Morris, Billy, Georgia Highlands College
Moshary, Fred , Graduate School of the City University of New York
Mosteller, Joey D., Appalachian State University
Mshiu, Elisante E., University of Dar es Salaam
Muhlbauer, Jason , University of Tennessee, Chattanooga
Munn, Barbara J., Sacramento State University
Murphy, Cindy, Saint Francis Xavier University
Murphy, Dan, Asheville-Buncombe Technical Community College
Muskatt, Herman, Utica College
Mutti, Laurel, SUNY, New Paltz
Nagorski, Sonia, University of Alaska, Southeast
Nagy-Shadman, Elizabeth, Pasadena City College
Nance, Seay, University of Texas at Austin, Jackson School of Geosciences
Neboga, Victoria V., DCNR- Pennsylvania Bureau of Geological Survey
Nelson, Jennifer, Indiana University - Purdue University Indianapolis
Newman, Brent D., Los Alamos National Laboratory
Newman, Jamie, American Museum of Natural History
Ni-Meister, Wenge, Graduate School of the City University of New York
Nielsen, Gregory B., Weber State University
Norouzi, Hamidreza, Graduate School of the City University of New York
Norrish, Winston, Central Washington University
Nugent, Barnes, Fairmont State University
O'Brien, Lawrence E., Orange County Community College
O'Brien, Philip, Alvin Community College
O'Keeffe, Mike, Colorado Geological Survey
Oakes-Miller, Hollie, Portland Community College - Sylvania Campus
Odendaal, Adriaan, University of the Free State
Odeyemi, Idowu B., Federal University of Technology, Akure
Oldfield, Bruce K., Broome Community College
Oldham, Richard L., American River College
Opfer, Christina, Tulsa Community College
Opperman, William, Broward College
Orr, William , Portland State University
Oswald, Peter J., University of Alaska, Anchorage
Pande, Srikant k., Pt. Ravishankar Shukla University
Pantoja-Alor, Jerjes, Univ Nacional Autonoma de Mexico
Papp, Kenneth R., Alaska Division of Geological & Geophysical Surveys
Parish, Cynthia L., Lamar University
Parker, Richard M., Texas A&M University, Kingsville
Parnella, Bill, University of Delaware
Parrick, Brittany, Ohio Dept of Natural Resources
Parsons, Michael, Dalhousie University

Paschert, Karin, Ludwig-Maximilians-Universitaet Muenchen
Patterson, Gary, University of Memphis
Patton, Jason A., Arkansas Tech University
Patton, Terri, Argonne National Laboratory
Patwardhan, Kaustubh, SUNY, New Paltz
Pawloski, Gayle A., Lawrence Livermore National Laboratory
Pearthree, Kristin, New Mexico Institute of Mining and Technology
Pellowski, Christopher J., South Dakota School of Mines & Technology
Perez, Adriana, University of Texas, El Paso
Perez, Adriana, El Paso Community College
Perkis, Bill, Gogebic Community College
Pesavento, Jim, Palomar College
Peters, Lisa, New Mexico Institute of Mining and Technology
Peters, Roger M., University of Wisconsin, Madison, Division of Extension
Peterson, Joseph E., Elgin Community College
Phillips, Michael, Illinois Valley Community College
Piasecki, Michael, Graduate School of the City University of New York
Pierce, David, Lakeland Community College
Pirie, Diane H., Florida International University
Polissar, Pratigya J., Columbia University
Poole, T. Craig, Fresno City College
Posiloviæ, Hrvoje, University of Zagreb
Pound, Kate S., Saint Cloud State University
Powers, Elizabeth, California State University, Bakersfield
Prave, Tony, University of St. Andrews
Prewett, Jerry L., Missouri Dept of Natural Resources
Price, Jonathan G., University of Nevada, Reno
Price, L G., New Mexico Institute of Mining and Technology
Prichystal, Antonín, Masaryk University
Priesendorf, Carl, Metropolitan Community College-Kansas City
Priest, George R., Oregon Dept of Geology & Mineral Industries
Priewisch, Alexandra, Fresno City College
Prior, William L., Arkansas Geological Survey
Prothero, Donald, Los Angeles Pierce College
Proudhon, Benoit, Institut Polytechnique LaSalle Beauvais (ex-IGAL)
Prytulak, Julie, Imperial College
Purkiss, Robert, Angelo State University
Quick, Thomas J., University of Akron
Quinn, Heather A., Maryland Department of Natural Resources
Ragland, Deborah, University of New Mexico, Taos
Rahman, Ata U., Austin Community College District
Rains, Daniel S., Arkansas Geological Survey
Ranhofer, Melissa, Furman University
Rantitsch, Gerd, University Leoben
Rashall, Jenny M., Stephen F. Austin State University
Rashed, Mohamed A., Alexandria University
Rath, Carolyn, California State University, Fullerton
Rathburn, Sara L., Colorado State University
Ratschbacher, Barbara C., University of California, Davis
Rawling, Geoffrey, New Mexico Institute of Mining and Technology
Ray, Waverly, Cuyamaca College
Raymer, Janet, Metropolitan Community College-Kansas City
Read, Adam S., New Mexico Institute of Mining and Technology
Redden, Marcella, Geological Survey of Alabama
Reesman, Arthur L., Vanderbilt University
Reif, Samantha, Lincoln Land Community College
Reinmann, Andrew , Graduate School of the City University of New York
Rennie, Colette, Saint Francis Xavier University
Repka, James, Saddleback Community College
Richards, Bill, North Idaho College
Riegel, Hannah B., Appalachian State University
Riker-Coleman, Kristin E., University of Wisconsin, Superior
Rinae, Makhadi, University of the Free State
Riordan, Jean, Alaska Division of Geological & Geophysical Surveys
Rivera, Mark, University of Alaska, Anchorage
Roberson, Randal P., Austin Peay State University
Robert, Sanborn, University of Wisconsin Colleges
Robinson, Sarah, United States Air Force Academy
Rocha, Guillermo, Brooklyn College (CUNY)
Roche, James E., Louisiana State University
Rodgers, Jim, Wyoming State Geological Survey
Rodríguez, Marta, Univ Complutense de Madrid
Rodriguez-Castaneda, Jose L., Univ Nacional Autonoma de Mexico
Rohbaugh, Robert, El Paso Community College
Ross, Theodore W., Lawrence University
Rossbach, Thomas, Indiana University - Purdue University Indianapolis
Rothemund, Kirk, El Paso Community College
Rounds, Steven W., Sacramento State University
Rowden, Robert, Iowa Dept of Natural Resources
Ruffel, Alice, El Centro College - Dallas Community College District
Rumrill, Julie, Southern Connecticut State University
Ruppert, Kelly R., California State University, Fullerton
Rutberg, Randye, Graduate School of the City University of New York
Rygel, Michael C., Indiana University, Bloomington
Sacramentogrilo, Isabelle, San Diego State University
Salle, Bethan, El Centro College - Dallas Community College District
Salmun, Haydee, Graduate School of the City University of New York
Samimi, Naser, University of Tabriz
Sassi, Raffaele, Università degli Studi di Padova
Sato, Yoko, Montclair State University
Schafer, Carl M., Macomb Community College, Center Campus
Scheffler, Joanna, Mesa Community College
Schenck, William S., University of Delaware
Schilling, Keith, Iowa Dept of Natural Resources
Schimmrich, Steven, SUNY, Ulster County Community College
Schmidt, Bennetta, Lamar University
Schneider, Blair, University of Kansas
Schulingkamp, Arren, Louisiana State University
Schulte, Kimberly D., Georgia State University, Perimeter College, Online
Schultz, Jan, Santa Barbara City College
Sediek, Kadry N., Alexandria University
Seigley, Lynette S., Iowa Dept of Natural Resources
Severs, Matthew , Stockton University
Shaaban, Mohamad N., Alexandria University
Shade, Harry, West Valley College
Shafer, Erik, Portland State University
Shakun, Jeremy D., Boston College
Shalimba, Ester, University of Namibia
Shannon, Jeremy, Michigan Technological University
shedied, ahmad g., Fayoum University
Shields, Stephen, Angelo State University
Shiels, Christine, Douglas College
Shimizu, Melinda, Mesa Community College
Shinn, Eugene, University of South Florida
Shorey, Christian V., Colorado School of Mines
Shroba, Cynthia S., College of Southern Nevada - West Charleston Campus
Sibeko, Skhumbuzo, Tshwane University of Technology
Sicard, Karri, Alaska Division of Geological & Geophysical Surveys
Siegelberg, Alan, Long Island University, Brooklyn Campus
Siemens, Michael A., Missouri Dept of Natural Resources
Sipola, Maija, Miami University
Skinner, Randall, Brigham Young University
Sledzinski, Grazyna, Wayne State University
Sloan, Heather , Graduate School of the City University of New York
Smaglik, Suzanne M., Central Wyoming College
Smith, Jason J., Broome Community College
Smith, Jon J., University of Kansas
Smith, Mike, Front Range Community College - Larimer
Smithson, Jayne, Contra Costa College
Snyder, Daniel, Middle Georgia College
Snyder, Noah, Boston College
Solferino, Giulio, Royal Holloway University of London
Solis, Michael P., Ohio Dept of Natural Resources
Speed, Don, Phoenix College
Sperone, Felice, Wayne State University
Stakes, Debra, Cuesta College
Stanton, Kathryn, Sacramento City College
Stanton, Kelsay, Wenatchee Valley College
Steart, David, La Trobe University
Steck, Lee, Los Alamos National Laboratory
Steffens, Katja, Ludwig-Maximilians-Universitaet Muenchen
Steinberg, Roger T., Del Mar College
Stewart, Eric, University of Wisconsin, Madison, Division of Extension
Stewart, Esther K., University of Wisconsin, Madison, Division of Extension
Straight, William, Northern Virginia Community College - Loudoun Campus
Straub, Kyle M., Tulane University
Stumpf, Andrew , Illinois State University
Summers, Sara, Weber State University
Sumrall, Jonathan B., Fort Hays State University
Sundell, Ander, College of Western Idaho
Sundell, Kent A., Casper College
Sunderlin, David, Lafayette College

Suszek, Thomas J., University of Wisconsin, Oshkosh
Szczepanski, Jacek, University of Wroclaw
Söllner, Frank, Ludwig-Maximilians-Universitaet Muenchen
Tajik, Atieh, Georgia State University
Tamish, Mohamed M., Alexandria University
Tassier-Surine, Stephanie, Iowa Dept of Natural Resources
Taylor, Carolyn, Mesa Community College
Taylor, Penny M., Mount Holyoke College
Taylor, Sid, Saint Francis Xavier University
Teklay, Mengist, Georgia State University, Perimeter College, Decatur Campus
Tetrault, Denis, University of Windsor
Thole, Jeffrey T., Macalester College
Thomas, Margaret A., Dept of Energy and Env Protection
Thompson, Todd, Indiana University, Bloomington
Thorleifson, Harvey, University of Minnesota, Twin Cities
Thornberry-Ehrlich, Trista L., Colorado State University
Thul, David, University of Utah
Tibbits, Matthew, Chadron State College
Tibbits, Tawny, Chadron State College
Timmons, J. Michael, New Mexico Institute of Mining and Technology
Tolley, William, Southern Connecticut State University
Tomiæ, Vladimir, University of Zagreb
Toni, Rousine T., Alexandria University
Towery, Brooke L., Pensacola State College
Tucker, Eva, Pennsylvania State University, Erie
Turbeville, John, MiraCosta College
Turner, Wesley L., Stephen F. Austin State University
Turner, III, Henry, University of Arkansas, Fayetteville
Tvelia, Sean, Suffolk County Community College, Ammerman Campus
Ugland, Richard, Southern Oregon University
Ullrich, Alexander D., Georgia State Univ, Perimeter Coll, Dunwoody Campus
Urquhart, Joanne, Bowdoin College
Valenti, Christine D., Georgia State University, Perimeter College, Online
Valenti, Christine, Montclair State University
van Balen, Ronald R., Vrije Universiteit Amsterdam
Van Brocklin, Matthew F., St. Lawrence University
VanDorpe, Paul E., Iowa Dept of Natural Resources
Vickery, Nancy, University of New England
Vidoviæ, Jelena, University of Zagreb
Viens, Rob, Bellevue College
Vierrether, Chris, Missouri Dept of Natural Resources
Vig, Pradeep K., Kaskaskia College
Vinton, Bonita L., Slippery Rock University
Voigt, Vicki, Missouri Dept of Natural Resources
Vuke, Susan M., Montana Tech of The University of Montana
Wacker, Michael, Florida International University
Wadleigh, Hank, Cypress College
Waggoner, Karen, Midland College
Wakefield, Kelli, Mesa Community College
Wang, Zhengrong, Graduate School of the City University of New York
Waugh, John, Tidewater Community College
Weatherford, Jonathan, Portland Community College - Sylvania Campus
Webber, Jeffrey, Stockton University
Weber, Diane, Illinois Central College
Weber-Diefenbach, Klaus, Ludwig-Maximilians-Universitaet Muenchen
Weborg-Benson, Kimberly, SUNY, Fredonia
Weeden, Lori, University of Massachusetts, Lowell
Wein, Agatha, Cuyamaca College
Werhner, Matthew J., Hillsborough Community College
West, Robert, East Los Angeles College
Wheeler, Richard F., Austin Peay State University
White, Paul, Community College of Rhode Island
Whitehead, James, University of New Brunswick
Whitehead, Peter W., James Cook University
Whitehill, Matthew, Lake Superior College
Whittier, Michael, California State University, Stanislaus
Whittington, Carla, Highline College
Wilbur, Bryan, Pasadena City College
Willahan, Duane, Gavilan College
Williams, Curtis J., Cypress College
Willis, Grant C., Utah Geological Survey
Willis, Marc, Fullerton College
Willsey, Shawn P., College of Southern Idaho
Wilson, Jeffrey A., University of Michigan
Wolfe, Ben, Metropolitan Community College-Kansas City
Wolkersdorfer, Christian, Ludwig-Maximilians-Universitaet Muenchen
Wolter, Calvin, Iowa Dept of Natural Resources
Wood, Jacqueline, Delgado Community College
Woodall, Debra W., Daytona State College
Worcester, Peter, Eastern Kentucky University
Wortmann, Ulrich B., University of Toronto
Wykel, Andy, South Carolina Dept of Natural Resources
Wypych, Alicja, Alaska Division of Geological & Geophysical Surveys
Yalcin, Kaplan, Oregon State University
Yalcin, Rebecca, Oregon State University
Yan, Y E., Argonne National Laboratory
Yoshida, Glenn, Los Angeles Southwest College
Young, Mike, Dalhousie University
Zabel, Garrett E., Colorado Mountain College
Zabielski, Victor, Northern Virginia Community College - Alexandria
Zachariasen, Judy, California Geological Survey
Zanetti, Kathleen, University of Nevada, Las Vegas
Zawiskie, John M., Wayne State University
Zayac, John M., Los Angeles Pierce College
Zeitlhöfler, Matthias, Ludwig-Maximilians-Universitaet Muenchen
Zentner, Nick, Central Washington University
Zimmer, Brian W., Appalachian State University
Zurawski, Ronald P., Tennessee Geological Survey

Archaeological Geology

Abreu, Maria E., Unive de Trás-os-Montes e Alto Douro
Adams, Kenneth, University of Nevada, Reno
Adovasio, James M., Mercyhurst University
Ballard, Robert D., University of Rhode Island
Bowers, Peter, University of Alaska, Fairbanks
Buckley, Michael, University of Manchester
Chamberlain, Andrew T., University of Manchester
Degryse, Patrick, Katholieke Universiteit Leuven
Dunn, Richard K., Norwich University
Dye, David H., University of Memphis
Elkins, Nichole, Bowling Green State University
Fadem, Cynthia M., Earlham College
Farrand, William, University of Michigan
Ferguson, Terry A., Wofford College
Ferring, C. Reid, University of North Texas
Garrison, Ervan G., University of Georgia
Greenlee, Diana M., University of Louisiana, Monroe
Gundersen, James N., Wichita State University
Gunia, Piotr, University of Wroclaw
Haynes, Jr., C. Vance, University of Arizona
Hayward, Chris L., Edinburgh University
Holliday, Vance, University of Arizona
Holliday, Vance T., University of Arizona
Iglesias, Cruz, Coruna University
Jones, Jeri L., York College of Pennsylvania
Kelley, Alice R., University of Maine
Kvamme, Kenneth L., Boston University
Lee-Gorishti, Yolanda, Southern Connecticut State University
Madsen, David B., Utah Geological Survey
Mandel, Rolfe, University of Kansas
Mandel, Rolfe D., University of Kansas
Manning, Sturt W., Cornell University
Mason, Owen, University of Alaska, Fairbanks
Mickelson, Andrew M., University of Memphis
Milne, Brooke, University of Manitoba
Nagaoka, Lisa A., University of North Texas
Ortmann, Anthony L., Murray State University
Page, David, Desert Research Institute
Parish, Ryan M., University of Memphis
Pike, Scott, Willamette University
Pope, Richard, University of Derby
Pournelle, Jennifer R., University of South Carolina
Powell, Wayne G., Brooklyn College (CUNY)
Reitz, Elizabeth J., University of Georgia
Rogers, Joe D., West Texas A&M University
Sallu, Susannah, University of Leeds
Schiffman, Robert A., Bakersfield College
Smith, Jen R., Washington University in St. Louis
Smith, Jennifer R., Washington University in St. Louis
Stafford, C. Russell, Indiana State University
Swyrtek, Sheila, Charles Stewart Mott Community College
Thieme, Donald, Valdosta State University

Tomaso, Matthew S., Montclair State University
Towner, Ronald, University of Arizona
Uribelarrea, David, Univ Complutense de Madrid
Venter, Marcie, Murray State University
Vento, Frank, Mercyhurst University
Waters, Michael R., Texas A&M University
Whitney , Sandra , University of Georgia
Wilson, Lucy A., University of New Brunswick Saint John
Wilson, Michael C., Douglas College
Wolverton, Steve, University of North Texas
Wygal, Brian, Adelphi University

Environmental Geology

Abbasnejad, Ahmad, Shahid Bahonar University of Kerman
Aden, Douglas J., Ohio Dept of Natural Resources
Adentunji, Jacob, University of Derby
Adewoye, Abosede O., Ladoke Akintola University of Technology
Adomaitis, D., Illinois State Geological Survey
Akenzua-Adamcyzk, Aiyevbekpen H., University of Benin
Albee-Scott, Steven R., Jackson College
Amezaga, Jamie, University of Newcastle Upon Tyne
Apotsos, Alex, Williams College
Argyilan, Erin, Indiana University Northwest
Aristilde, Ludmilla, Cornell University
Ashwood, Tom, Oak Ridge National Laboratory
Asowata, Timothy I., Federal University of Technology, Akure
Babcock, Daphne H., Collin College - Spring Creek Campus
Baker-Treloar, Elizabeth, University of San Diego
Bang, John, North Carolina Central University
Barber, Donald C., Bryn Mawr College
Barone, Jessica, Monroe Community College
Barrett, John, University of Leeds
Bartholemew, Paul, University of New Haven
Bartolucci, Valerio, Broward College
Beccue, Clint, Illinois State Geological Survey
Bechtel, Timothy D., Franklin and Marshall College
Beebe, Alex, University of South Alabama
Bell, Margaret C., University of Newcastle Upon Tyne
Bernstein, Neil P., University of Iowa
Bhattacharya, Tripti, Syracuse University
Bilanovic, Dragoljub D., Bemidji State University
Binda, Pier L., University of Regina
Bircher, Harry, Youngstown State University
Bogart, James M., Dept of Energy and Env Protection
Bogle, Mary Anna, Oak Ridge National Laboratory
Bond, Alan, University of East Anglia
Bousenberry, Raymond T., New Jersey Geological and Water Survey
Brake, Sandra S., Indiana State University
Brandon, Nigel, Imperial College
Brandt, Craig, Oak Ridge National Laboratory
Branfireun, Brian, Western University
Brodie, Gregory, University of Tennessee, Chattanooga
Bromily, Geoffrey, Edinburgh University
Brown, Huntting (Hunt), Wright State University
Brown, Kerry, Kingston University
Brown, Thomas W., Austin Community College District
Bryan, Mark, Wayland Baptist University
Budkewitsch, Paul, Brock University
Buliga, Iuliana, Alexandru Ioan Cuza
Burke, Ian, University of Leeds
Cadet, Eddy, Utah Valley University
Callison, James, Utah Valley University
Cathcart, Eric, University of San Diego
Caudill, Kimberly S., Hocking College
Chapman, LeeAnna Y., University of San Diego
Chappell, James R., Colorado State University
Chaput, Julien, University of Texas, El Paso
Chaudhuri, Sambhudas, Kansas State University
Chernoff, Barry, Wesleyan University
Cheun, Norman, Kingston University
Chhetri, Parveen, California State University, Dominguez Hills
Chilvers, Jason, University of East Anglia
Chipman, Melissa, Syracuse University
Cloutier, Danielle, Universite Laval
Colegial Gutierrez, Juan D., Univ Industrial de Santander
Collier, Mark, Illinois State Geological Survey
Collins, Edward W., Univ of Texas at Austin, Jackson Sch of Geosciences
Congleton, John D., University of West Georgia
Constantopoulos, James T., Eastern New Mexico University
Cook, Hadrian, Kingston University
Corley, John H., Missouri Dept of Natural Resources
Cowart, Richard, Coastal Bend College
Cox, Christena, Ohio State University
Coxon, Catherine, Trinity College
Cummins, R. Hays, Miami University
Curry, B. B., Northern Illinois University
Curry, B. B., Illinois State Geological Survey
Curry, Gordon, University of Glasgow
Curtis, Arthur C., Oak Ridge National Laboratory
Dallimer, Martin, University of Leeds
Daramola, Sunday O., Federal University of Technology, Akure
Davis, R. Laurence, University of New Haven
Davis, Steven J., University of California, Irvine
Day, Brett, University of East Anglia
Denniston, Rhawn F., Cornell College
deWet, Andrew P., Franklin and Marshall College
Dimmick, Charles W., Central Connecticut State University
Diochon, Amanda, Lakehead University
Downie, Helen, University of Manchester
Dubey, C S., University of Delhi
Duncan, Ian J., University of Texas, Austin
Durrant, Jeffrey O., Brigham Young University
Dyer, Jen, University of Leeds
Eastler, Thomas E., University of Maine, Farmington
Edwards, Robin, Trinity College
Elliott, Susan J., McMaster University
Ellis, Scott R., Illinois State Geological Survey
Ellison, Anne L., Illinois State Geological Survey
Ellison, Anne L., University of Illinois
Ettlie, Bradley, Illinois State Geological Survey
Eyles, John D., McMaster University
Faulkner, Melinda S., Stephen F. Austin State University
Favas, Paulo J., Unive de Trás-os-Montes e Alto Douro
Fehn, Udo, University of Rochester
Field, Cathryn K., Bowdoin College
Flesken, Luuk, University of Leeds
Foley, Duncan, Pacific Lutheran University
Foret, Jim, University of Louisiana at Lafayette
Foxon, Tim, University of Leeds
Franco, Aldina, University of East Anglia
Frappier, Amy, Skidmore College
Galicki, Stan, Millsaps College
Gallen, Sean, Colorado State University
Garrison, Trent, Northern Kentucky University
Garstang, Mimi R., Missouri Dept of Natural Resources
Geary, Lindsey, Utica College
Geiger, James W., Illinois State Geological Survey
Gerald, Carresse, North Carolina Central University
Geršlová, Eva, Masaryk University
Gidigasu, Solomon S., Kwame Nkrumah University of Science and Technology
Glenn, Craig R., University of Hawai'i, Manoa
Goetz, Heinrich, Collin College - Preston Ridge Campus
Gomes, Nuno N., Unive Independente de Angola
Gomezdelcampo, Enrique, Bowling Green State University
Gouldson, Andy, University of Leeds
Graham, Margaret C., Edinburgh University
Grant, Alastair, University of East Anglia
Halfman, John D., Hobart & William Smith Colleges
Hanes, Daniel M., Saint Louis University
Hargreaves, Tom, University of East Anglia
Harris, Ann G., Youngstown State University
Harris, C, Cardiff University
Harris, Jr., Stanley E., Southern Illinois University Carbondale
Harvey, Omar R., Texas Christian University
Havenith, Hans-Balder, Universite de Liege
Hawkins, Terry, Missouri Dept of Natural Resources
Hawley, John W., New Mexico Institute of Mining and Technology
Hawley, John W., New Mexico Institute of Mining and Technology
Helgers, Karen, SUNY, Ulster County Community College
Herbert, Bruce, Texas A&M University
Hickey, James, Northwest Missouri State University
Hill, Nicole, Bentley University

FACULTY BY SPECIALTY

Hill, Timothy, University of St. Andrews
Hodell, David, University of Cambridge
Holmes, George, University of Leeds
Holwell, Dave, Leicester University
Hoppie, Bryce W., Minnesota State University
Houston, Robert, Oregon Dept of Geology and Mineral Industries
Hubeny, J B., Salem State University
Hudson-Edwards, Karen, Birkbeck College
Humphreys, Robin, College of Charleston
Isaacson, Carl, Bemidji State University
Jackman, Toni K., Wichita State University
Jacobs, Alan M., Youngstown State University
Jamieson, Heather E., Queen's University
Jin, Lixin, University of Texas, El Paso
Jones, T, Cardiff University
Jordan, Andy, University of East Anglia
Jovanovic, Vladimir, College of Staten Island/CUNY
Kairies-Beatty, Candace L., Winona State University
Keller, John E., College of Southern Nevada - West Charleston Campus
Kertes, Randy, Rider University
Ketelle, Richard H., Oak Ridge National Laboratory
Kientop, Greg A., Illinois State Geological Survey
Kierczak, Jakub, University of Wroclaw
Kim, Jonathan, Agency of Natural Resources, Dept of Env Conservation
Kirchner, James W., University of California, Berkeley
Kolawole, Lanre L., Ladoke Akintola University of Technology
Krekeler, Mark, Miami University
Kretzschmar, Thomas, Ctr de Invest Científica y de Ed Superior de Ensenada
Lake, Iain, University of East Anglia
Last, George V., Pacific Northwest National Laboratory
Lawry-Berkins, Cynthia, Lonestar College - Montgomery
Lee, Arthur C., Roane State Community College - Oak Ridge
Lee, Cindy M., Clemson University
Lee-Cullin, Joe, Albion College
Lene, Gene W., Saint Mary's University
Leventon, Julia, University of Leeds
Lloyd, Jonathan, University of Manchester
Love, David W., New Mexico Institute of Mining and Technology
Lundgren, Lawrence W., University of Rochester
Macadam, John, Exeter University
Maher, Damien, Southern Cross University
Manser, Nathan, Michigan Technological University
Margalef, Ona, Universitat Autonoma de Barcelona
Martin, Scott C., Youngstown State University
Masciocco, Luciano, Università di Torino
Matthews, Robert A., University of California, Davis
May, Michael, Western Kentucky University
Mayer, Margaret, Dine' College
McCullough, Jr., Edgar J., University of Arizona
McDonald, Brenna, Missouri Dept of Natural Resources
McGivern, Tiffany, Utica College
McKinney, Michael L., University of Tennessee, Knoxville
Metzger, Marc J., Edinburgh University
Meyer, Brian, Georgia State University
Meyer, W. Craig, Los Angeles Pierce College
Miller, David S., Argonne National Laboratory
Mitre-Salazar, Luis M., Univ Nacional Autonoma de Mexico
Moloney, Marguerite M., Nicholls State University
Monroy-Sanchez, Jaime I., Univ Autonoma de Baja California Sur
Moore, Kathryn, Exeter University
Morse, Linda D., William & Mary
Mouat, David A., Desert Research Institute
Muldoon, Maureen, University of Wisconsin, Madison, Division of Extension
Mundie, Ben, Oregon Dept of Geology and Mineral Industries
Nelwamondo, T. M., University of Venda
Newbold, K. B., McMaster University
Newton, Rob, University of Leeds
Null, E. Jan, San Francisco State University
O'Connor, Yuet-Ling, Pasadena City College
Omotoso, O. A., University of Ilorin
Orndorff, Richard L., Eastern Washington University
Oyawale, A. A., Obafemi Awolowo University
Paavola, Jouni, University of Leeds
Paltseva, Anna, University of Louisiana at Lafayette
Panko, Andrew W., Brock University
Patenaude, Genevieve, Edinburgh University
Pearce, Jamie R., Edinburgh University
Pearthree, Philip A., University of Arizona
Penzo, Michael A., Bridgewater State University
Perault, David R., University of Lynchburg
Perdrial, Nicolas, University of Vermont
Pereira, Alcides C., Unive de Coimbra
Perkons, Eriks, Towson University
Peterson, Jon W., Hope College
Piotrowski, Alexander, University of Cambridge
Pisani-Gareau, Tara, Boston College
Plant, Jane, Imperial College
Pohopien, Kazimierz M., Mt. San Antonio College
Pope, Jeanette K., DePauw University
Pospelova, Vera, University of Minnesota, Twin Cities
Poudel, Durga, University of Louisiana at Lafayette
Powell, Jane, University of East Anglia
Pratt, Allyn R., Los Alamos National Laboratory
Quinn, Claire, University of Leeds
Radko, Nicholas, Georgia Southern University
Rasmussen, Pat E., University of Ottawa
Reeves, Donald Matt, University of Alaska, Anchorage
Reid, Brian, University of East Anglia
Rezaie-Boroon, Mohammad H., California State University, Los Angeles
Rice, Thomas L., Cedarville University
Richards, Laura, University of Manchester
Rizoulis, Athanasios, University of Manchester
Roberts, Ray L., Hill College
Roberts, Sheila M., University of Montana Western
Roberts-Semple, Dawn, York College (CUNY)
Rocheford, MaryKathryn (Kat), Lake Superior State University
Rogers, William C., West Texas A&M University
Rucklidge, John C., University of Toronto
Ruhl, Laura S., University of Arkansas at Little Rock
Russell, Sally, University of Leeds
Rutter, Nathaniel W., University of Alberta
Ryan, Anne-Marie, Dalhousie University
Sacristan, Felix, Universitat Autonoma de Barcelona
Sanjurjo, Jorge, Coruna University
Sarah, Willig B., University of Pennsylvania
Satkoski, Alina A., Austin Community College District
Schleifer, Stanley, York College (CUNY)
Schmidt, Dale R., Illinois State Geological Survey
Schoenemann, Spruce W., University of Montana Western
Scholtz, Theresa C., Argonne National Laboratory
Scott, Robert B., University of Texas, Austin
Segall, Marylin, University of Utah
Sewall, Jacob, Kutztown University of Pennsylvania
Sexton, Philip, Open University
Sharma, Mukul, Dartmouth College
Shem, Linda M., Argonne National Laboratory
Sims, Douglas , College of Southern Nevada - West Charleston Campus
Sîrbu, Smaranda D., Alexandru Ioan Cuza
Skinner, Luke C., University of Cambridge
Slobodnik, Marek, Masaryk University
Smith, Dan, Leicester University
Smith, Jim, University of Portsmouth
Snider, Henry I., Eastern Connecticut State University
Snow, Daniel, University of Nebraska, Lincoln
Spaeth, Matthew P., Illinois State Geological Survey
Spahr, Paul, Ohio Dept of Natural Resources
Spooner, Ian S., Acadia University
Stahle, David W., University of Arkansas, Fayetteville
Stan, Oana, Alexandru Ioan Cuza
Stearman, Will, Queensland University of Technology
Steidl, Gregg M., New Jersey Geological and Water Survey
Stevens, Anthony, Montgomery County Community College
Stinchcomb, Gary E., Murray State University
Stumbea, Dan, Alexandru Ioan Cuza
Sturm, Diana, University of South Alabama
Sublette, Kerry, University of Tulsa
Sylvia, Elizabeth R., Maryland Department of Natural Resources
Tank, Ronald W., Lawrence University
Tawabini, Bassam S., King Fahd University of Petroleum and Minerals
Taylor, Eric, Kent State University at Stark
Taylor, Peter, University of Leeds
Thorpe, Mary S., Del Mar College

Triplett, Laura, Gustavus Adolphus College
Tses, Akah, University of Namibia
Turchyn, Alexandra, University of Cambridge
Turner, Derek, Douglas College
Turner, Kerry, University of East Anglia
Tuttle, Samuel, Syracuse University
Vaezi, Reza, University of Tabriz
van Alstine, James, University of Leeds
Van Horn, Stephen R., Muskingum University
Van Ryswick, Stephen, Maryland Department of Natural Resources
VanGundy, Robert D., University of Virginia's College at Wise
Vann, David R., University of Pennsylvania
Villa, Jorge, University of Louisiana at Lafayette
Walsh, Maud M., Louisiana State University
Watkinson, Andrew, University of East Anglia
Webb, John A., La Trobe University
Welling, Tim, Dutchess Community College
Wen, Tao, Syracuse University
Wilson, Charlie, University of East Anglia
Wilson, Rick I., California Geological Survey
Wunsch, David R., University of Delaware
Yiannakoulias, Niko, McMaster University
Yibas, Bisrat, University of the Free State
Youberg, Ann, University of Arizona
Young, Michael H., Univ of Texas at Austin, Jackson Sch of Geosciences
Young, William, University of Leeds
Yuen, Cheong-yip R., Argonne National Laboratory

Geomorphology

Aalto, Rolf E., University of Washington
Adams, Kenneth D., Desert Research Institute
Adams, Peter N., University of Florida
Alba, Saturnino, Univ Complutense de Madrid
Allan, Jonathan C., Oregon Dept of Geology and Mineral Industries
Allan, Jonathan C., Oregon Dept of Geology & Mineral Industries
Allen, Bruce D., New Mexico Institute of Mining and Technology
Allen, Phillip, Frostburg State University
Anders, Alison M., University of Illinois, Urbana-Champaign
Anderson, Robert S., University of California, Santa Cruz
Anderson, Robert, University of Colorado
Andrews, William M., University of Kentucky
Antinao, JoseLuis, Desert Research Institute
Applegarth, Michael T., Shippensburg University
Armour, Jake, University of North Carolina, Charlotte
Aslan, Andres, Colorado Mesa University
Attal, Mikael, Edinburgh University
Bacon, Steven N., Desert Research Institute
Baker, Sophie, Desert Research Institute
Baker, Victor R., University of Arizona
Baptista, João C., Unive de Trás-os-Montes e Alto Douro
Barendregt, Rene W., University of Lethbridge
Bauer, Bernard O., University of British Columbia, Okanagan Campus
Beget, James E., University of Alaska, Fairbanks
Belliveau, Lindsey, Dept of Energy and Environmental Protection
Benedetti, Michael M., University of North Carolina, Wilmington
Bergeron, Normand, Universite du Quebec
Berta, Susan, Indiana State University
Bierman, Paul R., University of Vermont
Bird, Broxton, Indiana University - Purdue University Indianapolis
Blisniuk, Kimberly, San Jose State University
Booth, Adam M., Portland State University
Booth, Derek, University of Washington
Bradley, William C., University of Colorado
Breilin, Olli, Geological Survey of Finland
Brewer, Paul A., University of Wales
Brock-Hon, Amy, University of Tennessee, Chattanooga
Brocklehurst, Simon, University of Manchester
Brush, Nigel, Ashland University
Bull, William B., University of Arizona
Bullard, Thomas F., Desert Research Institute
Bullard, Tom, University of Nevada, Reno
Burbank, Doug, University of California, Santa Barbara
Burke, Raymond M., Humboldt State University
Buynevich, Ilya, Temple University
Campbell, Ian A., University of Alberta
Carson, Robert J., Whitman College
Carton, Alberto, Università degli Studi di Padova
Carver, Gary A., Humboldt State University
Castillon, David A., Missouri State University
Chenoweth, M. S., University of Louisiana, Monroe
Chin, Anne, Texas A&M University
Clark, James A., Wheaton College
Clark, Jeffrey J., Lawrence University
Clark, Marin, University of Michigan
Coates, Donald R., Binghamton University
Colgan, Patrick M., Grand Valley State University
Collins, Brian, University of Washington
Collins, Charles W., University of Wisconsin, Platteville
Collins, Joe D., Middle Tennessee State University
Coltorti, Mauro, University of Siena
Connallon, Christopher B., Maryland Department of Natural Resources
Constantine, Jose A., Williams College
Cook, Joseph P., University of Arizona
Cooke, M. J., Austin Community College District
Cornwell, Kevin J., Sacramento State University
Cotter, Edward, Bucknell University
Crosby, Benjamin T., Idaho State University
Currey, Donald R., University of Utah
Dale, Janis, University of Regina
Daly, Julia F., University of Maine, Farmington
Daniels, J. Michael, University of Denver
Day, Stephanie S., North Dakota State University
Dethier, David P., Williams College
DiBiase, Roman , Pennsylvania State University, University Park
Dietrich, William E., University of California, Berkeley
Dixon, Jean, Montana State University
Dixon, John C., University of Arkansas, Fayetteville
Dixon, Simon J., University of Birmingham
Dogwiler, Toby J., Illinois State University
Dolliver, Holly A., University of Wisconsin, River Falls
Dort, Jr., Wakefield, University of Kansas
Durbin, James, University of Southern Indiana
Duvall, Alison, University of Washington
Eaton, Lewis S., James Madison University
Edgar, Dorland E., Argonne National Laboratory
Ely, Lisa L., Central Washington University
England, John, University of Alberta
Evans, Diane L., Jet Propulsion Laboratory
Fagherazzi, Sergio, Boston University
Farr, Tom G., Jet Propulsion Laboratory
Ferrier, Ken, University of Wisconsin, Madison
Finnegan, Noah J., University of California, Santa Cruz
Fontana, Alessandro, Università degli Studi di Padova
Ford, Derek C., McMaster University
Ford, Richard L., Weber State University
Fubelli, Giandomenico, Università di Torino
Furbish, David J., Vanderbilt University
Gabet, Emmanuel, San Jose State University
Garcia, Antonio F., California Polytechnic State University
Garcia, Marcelo H., University of Illinois, Urbana-Champaign
Gardner, Thomas W., Trinity University
Garrote, Julio, Univ Complutense de Madrid
Gartner, John, Norwich University
Gasparini, Nicole, Tulane University
Germanoski, Dru, Lafayette College
Ghoneim, Eman, Boston University
Giardino, John R., Texas A&M University
Giardino, Marco, Università di Torino
Gill, Thomas E., University of Texas, El Paso
Gillam, Mary L., Fort Lewis College
Gillespie, Alan R., University of Washington
Gonzalez, Juan L., University of Texas, Rio Grande Valley
Gootee, Brian F., University of Arizona
Gordon, Steven J., United States Air Force Academy
Gosse, John, University of Kansas
Gran, Karen B., University of Minnesota Duluth
Greenberg, Harvey, University of Washington
Grimley, David A., Illinois State Geological Survey
Guccione, Margaret J., University of Arkansas, Fayetteville
Hales, TC, Cardiff University
Hallet, Bernard, University of Washington
Hancock, Gregory S., William & Mary

Hansen, Edward C., Hope College
Hanson, Lindley S., Salem State University
Hanson, Paul, University of Nebraska, Lincoln
Hanson, Paul, Unversity of Nebraska, Lincoln
Harbor, David J., Washington & Lee University
Harbor, Jon M., Purdue University
Hardage, Sarah M., University of Texas, Rio Grande Valley
Harrington, Charles D., Los Alamos National Laboratory
Harrison, Bruce I., New Mexico Institute of Mining and Technology
Hasbargen, Leslie E., SUNY, Oneonta
Haussmann, Natalie S., University of Pretoria
Heinzel, Chad E., University of Northern Iowa
Heitmuller, Franklin, University of Southern Mississippi
Hesp, Patrick, Flinders University
Hesp, Patrick A., Louisiana State University
Higgins, Charles G., University of California, Davis
Hooke, Roger L., University of Maine
Hooks, W. Gary, University of Alabama
Hopkins, Kenneth D., University of Northern Colorado
Howard, Alan D., University of Virginia
Hubbard, Trent, Alaska Division of Geological & Geophysical Surveys
Hungr, Oldrich, University of British Columbia
Hyatt, James A., Eastern Connecticut State University
Isacks, Bryan L., Cornell University
Jerolmack, Douglas, University of Pennsylvania
Jewell, Paul W., University of Utah
Johnson, Sarah E., Northern Kentucky University
Kasse, Kees, Vrije Universiteit Amsterdam
Kavage Adams, Rebecca H., Maryland Department of Natural Resources
Kehew, Alan E., Western Michigan University
Keller, Edward A., University of California, Santa Barbara
Kelsey, Harvey M., Humboldt State University
Kemmerly, Phillip R., Austin Peay State University
Kendrick, Katherine J., University of California, Riverside
Kenny, Ray, Fort Lewis College
Kirwan, Matthew L., William & Mary
Kiss, Timea, Univesity of Szeged
Kite, J. Steven, West Virginia University
Knott, Jeffrey R., California State University, Fullerton
Kochel, R. Craig, Bucknell University
Koehler, Rich, University of Nevada, Reno
Kori, E., University of Venda
Kowalewski, Douglas E., Worcester State University
Laabs, Benjamin J., SUNY, Geneseo
Lamb, Michael P., California Institute of Technology
Lancaster, Nick, University of Nevada, Reno
Larsen, Isaac J., University of Massachusetts, Amherst
Larson, Erik B., Shawnee State University
Lasca, Norman P., University of Wisconsin, Milwaukee
Lehre, Andre K., Humboldt State University
Leverington, David W., Texas Tech University
Levine, Rebekah, University of Montana Western
Li, Junran, University of Tulsa
Li, Yanan, Texas State University
Lifton, Nathaniel A., Purdue University
Lininger, Katherine, University of Colorado
Linneman, Scott R., Western Washington University
Lips, Elliott W., University of Utah
Lisenby, Peyton E., Midwestern State University
Long, Ann D., University of Illinois, Urbana-Champaign
Loring, Arthur P., York College (CUNY)
Loubser, Michael J., University of Pretoria
MacGregor, Kelly, Macalester College
Madej, Mary Ann, U.S. Geological Survey
Manz, Lorraine A., North Dakota Geological Survey
Marchant, David R., Boston University
Marchetti, David W., Western Colorado University
Marshall, Jeffrey S., California State Polytechnic University, Pomona
Marshall, Jill A., University of Arkansas, Fayetteville
Martín, Cristina, Univ Complutense de Madrid
Martín Duque, José Francisco, Univ Complutense de Madrid
Mason, Joseph, University of Wisconsin, Madison
Mathers, Hannah, University of Glasgow
Mauch, James, Wyoming State Geological Survey
McCoy, Scott W., University of Nevada, Reno
McDermott, Jeni, University of Saint Thomas
McDowell, Patricia, University of Oregon
McKean, Adam, Utah Geological Survey
McKenney, Rosemary, Pacific Lutheran University
McKenzie, Garry D., Ohio State University
McMillan, Margaret E., University of Arkansas at Little Rock
Menking, Kirsten M., Vassar College
Merritts, Dorothy J., Franklin and Marshall College
Meyer, Grant A., University of New Mexico
Michaud, Yves, Universite du Quebec
Miller, Jerry R., Western Carolina University
Misner, Tamara, Edinboro University of Pennsylvania
Montgomery, David R., University of Washington
Moon, Seulgi, University of California, Los Angeles
Moore, Andrew, Earlham College
Moore, Laura J., University of North Carolina, Chapel Hill
Morgan, Daniel J., Vanderbilt University
Mount, Jeffrey F., University of California, Davis
Mozzi, Paolo, Università degli Studi di Padova
Murray, A. Bradshaw, Duke University
Musselman, Zachary A., Millsaps College
Mylroie, John E., Mississippi State University
Namikas, Steven, Louisiana State University
Napieralski, Jacob A., University of Michigan, Dearborn
Nash, David, University of Cincinnati
Nelson, Robert S., Illinois State University
Neubeck, William S., Union College
Newton, Andrew, Queen's University Belfast
Newton, Robert M., Smith College
Nichols, Kyle K., Skidmore College
Nielsen, Dennis N., Winona State University
Nikitina, Daria L., West Chester University
Nittrouer, Jeffrey A., Rice University
Okunade, Samuel, Central State University
Olsen, Paul E., Columbia University
ONeal, Michael, University of Delaware
Orme, Amalie, California State University, Northridge
Ortiz, Alejandra C., Colby College
Osborn, Gerald D., University of Calgary
Oskin, Michael, University of California, Davis
Ouimet, William, University of Connecticut
Oviatt, Charles G., Kansas State University
Owen, Lewis, University of Washington
Owen, Lewis, University of Cincinnati
Owen, Lewis A., North Carolina State University
Paradise, Thomas R., University of Arkansas, Fayetteville
Parker, Gary, University of Illinois, Urbana-Champaign
Pasternack, Gregory B., University of California, Davis
Patton, Peter C., Wesleyan University
Pavlowsky, Robert T., Missouri State University
Pazzaglia, Frank J., Lehigh University
Pearson, Adam, SUNY Potsdam
Pederson, Joel L., Utah State University
Pelletier, Jon D., University of Arizona
Perron, Taylor, Massachusetts Institute of Technology
Persico, Lyman P., Whitman College
Pierce, Jennifer L., Boise State University
Pieruccini, Pierluigi, Università di Torino
Pinter, Nicholas, University of California, Davis
Pitlick, John, University of Colorado
Pizzuto, James E., University of Delaware
Plug, Lawrence, Dalhousie University
Polk, Jason, Western Kentucky University
Pope, Gregory A., Montclair State University
Potter, Jr., Noel, Dickinson College
Putkonen, Jaakko, University of North Dakota
Rawling, J. E., University of Wisconsin, Madison, Division of Extension
Rayburn, John A., SUNY, New Paltz
Rech, Jason, Miami University
Reed, Denise J., University of New Orleans
Refsnider, Kurt, Prescott College
Reneau, Steven L., Los Alamos National Laboratory
Rhoads, Bruce, University of Illinois, Urbana-Champaign
Rhodes, Dallas D., Georgia Southern University
Rice-Snow, R. Scott, Ball State University
Rittenour, Tammy M., Utah State University
Ritter, John B., Wittenberg University

Robinson, Cordula, Boston University
Rockwell, Thomas K., San Diego State University
Roering, Joshua J., University of Oregon
Rogerson, Robert J., University of Lethbridge
Roth, Danica, Colorado School of Mines
Savina, Mary E., Carleton College
Sawyer, Carol F., University of South Alabama
Schaller, Mirjam, University of Michigan
Schiefer, Erik, Northern Arizona University
Schmidt, Amanda H., Oberlin College
Schmutz, Phillip P., University of West Florida
Scuderi, Louis A., University of New Mexico
Shepherd, Stephanie L., Auburn University
Shreve, Ronald L., University of California, Los Angeles
Shroder, Jr., John F., University of Nebraska, Omaha
Sklar, Leonard, San Francisco State University
Smith, Richard, University of Arkansas, Fayetteville
Snead, John I., Louisiana State University
Snyder, Jeffrey A., Bowling Green State University
Souch, Catherine J., Indiana University, Indianapolis
Spigel, Lindsay, Dept of Agriculture, Conservation, and Forestry
Springer, Gregory S., Ohio University
Springston, George E., Norwich University
Stanford, Scott D., New Jersey Geological and Water Survey
Stewart, USA (ret), Alexander K., St. Lawrence University
Stine, Scott W., California State University, East Bay
Stokes, Martin, University of Plymouth
Stolzman, Kacie, University of Wisconsin, Madison, Division of Extension
Straffin, Eric, Edinboro University of Pennsylvania
Strasser, Jeffrey C., Augustana College
Stroup, Justin, SUNY, Oswego
Surian, Nicola, Università degli Studi di Padova
Swanson, Benjamin, University of Iowa
Sweeney, Mark R., University of South Dakota
Székely, Balázs, Eotvos Lorand University
Taylor, Stephen B., Western Oregon University
Tchakerian, Vatche P., Texas A&M University
Ten Brink, Norman W., Grand Valley State University
Theuerkauf, Ethan, Illinois State Geological Survey
Thomas, Paul, Western Washington University
Thorson, Robert M., University of Connecticut
Tidwell, David, Geological Survey of Alabama
Tomkin, Jonathan H., University of Illinois, Urbana-Champaign
Toy, Terrence J., University of Denver
Tranel, Lisa M., Illinois State University
Trenhaile, Alan S., University of Windsor
Tucker, Gregory E., University of Colorado
van der Merwe, Barend, University of Pretoria
van Dijk, Deanna, Calvin College
Vandeberg, Gregory S., University of North Dakota
Vidal Romaní, Juan Ramon, Coruna University
Vitek, John D., Texas A&M University
Vitek, John D., Oklahoma State University
Wakabayashi, John, Fresno State University
Walker, Ian , Arizona State University
Walters, James C., University of Northern Iowa
Walther, Suzanne, University of San Diego
Ward, Dylan, University of Cincinnati
Warke, Patricia, Queen's University Belfast
Webb, Robert H., University of Arizona
Wegmann, Karl, North Carolina State University
Weirich, Frank H., University of Iowa
Werner, Bradley T., University of California, San Diego
West, Nicole, Central Michigan University
Whipple, Kelin, Arizona State University
Whisner, Jennifer B., Bloomsburg University
White, Susan Q., La Trobe University
Whiting, Peter J., Case Western Reserve University
Whittecar, Jr., G. Richard, Old Dominion University
Wickert, Andrew D., University of Minnesota, Twin Cities
Wilcock, Peter W., Johns Hopkins University
Wilcox, Andrew, University of Montana
Williams, Harry F. L., University of North Texas
Williams, Kevin K., Buffalo State College
Wilson, Fred L., Angelo State University
Wilson, Greg C., Grand Valley State University
Wilson, Monte D., Boise State University
Wohl, Ellen E., Colorado State University
Wolken, Gabriel J., Alaska Division of Geological & Geophysical Surveys
Wood, Spencer H., Boise State University
Yanites, Brian, Indiana University, Bloomington
Yeh, Joseph S., University of Texas at Austin, Jackson School of Geosciences
Young, Richard A., SUNY, Geneseo

Glaciology and Glacial Geology

Aber, James S., Emporia State University
Aizen, Vladimir, University of Idaho
Alley, Richard B., Pennsylvania State University, University Park
Andrews, John T., University of Colorado
Angle, Michael P., Ohio Dept of Natural Resources
Armstrong, William H., Appalachian State University
Arnaud, Emmanuelle, University of Guelph
Attig, John W., University of Wisconsin, Madison, Division of Extension
Attig, John W., University of Wisconsin, Extension
Barclay, David J., SUNY, Cortland
Bartholomaus, Timothy, University of Idaho
Bassis, Jeremy, University of Michigan
Berg, Richard C., Illinois State Geological Survey
Berg, Richard, University of Illinois
Berthold, Angela, University of Minnesota
Bevis, Kenneth A., Hanover College
Bezada Diaz, Maximiliano, University of Minnesota
Bird, Brian, New York State Geological Survey
Birkel, Sean, University of Maine
Blake, Kevin, Eastern Michigan University
Blankenship, Donald D., University of Texas, Austin
Booth, Adam, Imperial College
Borns, Jr., Harold W., University of Maine
Breckenridge, Andy, University of Wisconsin, Superior
Brigham-Grette, Julie, University of Massachusetts, Amherst
Briner, Jason P., SUNY, Buffalo
Broster, Bruce E., University of New Brunswick
Brown, Steven E., Illinois State Geological Survey
Brown, Steven E., University of Illinois
Brugger, Keith A., University of Minnesota, Morris
Campbell, Seth W., University of Maine
Carlson, Anders, Oregon State University
Carson, Eric C., University of Wisconsin, Extension
Carson, Eric C., University of Wisconsin, Madison, Division of Extension
Catania, Ginny A., University of Texas, Austin
Christianson, Knut, University of Washington
Clague, John J., Simon Fraser University
Clark, Douglas H., Western Washington University
Clark, Peter U., Oregon State University
Clayton, Lee, University of Wisconsin, Extension
Clebnik, Sherman M., Eastern Connecticut State University
Conrad, Daniel, University of Minnesota
Conway, Howard B., University of Washington
Cotter, James F., University of Minnesota, Morris
Creyts, Timothy T., Columbia University
Crossen, Kristine J., University of Alaska, Anchorage
Csatho, Beata M., SUNY, Buffalo
Curry, B. B., University of Illinois
Das, Sarah B., Woods Hole Oceanographic Institution
Davis, P. Thompson, Bentley University
Denton, George H., University of Maine
Doughty, Alice, Bates College
Douglass, Daniel C., Northeastern University
Dupont, Todd, University of California, Irvine
Dupont, Todd, Miami University
Easterbrook, Don J., Western Washington University
Enderlin, Ellyn, Boise State University
Evenson, Edward B., Lehigh University
Eyles, Nicholas, University of Toronto
Fahnestock, Mark A., University of New Hampshire
Fisher, David A., University of Ottawa
Fisher, Timothy G., University of Toledo
Fleisher, P. Jay, SUNY, Oneonta
Flowers, Gwenn, Simon Fraser University
Fountain, Andrew G., Portland State University
Franzi, David A., SUNY, Plattsburgh
Froese, Duane, University of Alberta

Fudge, T.J., University of Washington
Goldstein, Barry, University of Puget Sound
Gowan, Angela S., University of Minnesota
Hall, Brenda L., University of Maine
Ham, Nelson R., Saint Norbert College
Hambrey, Michael M., Aberystwyth University
Harper, Joel, University of Montana
Hawley, Bob, University of Washington
Hawley, Robert L., Dartmouth College
Headley, Rachel, University of Wisconsin, Parkside
Hicock, Stephen R., Western University
Hock, Regine M., University of Alaska, Fairbanks
Holschuh, Nicholas D., Amherst College
Hooke, Roger L., University of Minnesota, Twin Cities
Howat, Ian M., Ohio State University
Hughes, Terence J., University of Maine
Hughes III, Richard O., Crafton Hills College
Hulbe, Christina L., Portland State University
Humphrey, Neil F., University of Wyoming
Hutchings, Jennifer, Oregon State University
Iverson, Neal R., Iowa State University of Science & Technology
Jiskoot, Hester, University of Lethbridge
Johnson, Beth , University of Wisconsin Colleges
Johnson, James B., Colorado Mesa University
Joughin, Ian, University of Washington
Kaplan, Michael, Columbia University
Karrow, Paul, University of Waterloo
Kelly, Meredith, Dartmouth College
Kiver, Eugene P., Eastern Washington University
Knaeble, Alan, University of Minnesota
Koutnik, Michelle, University of Washington
Kozlowski, Andrew, New York State Geological Survey
Laabs, Benjamin J., North Dakota State University
Lamothe, Michel, Universite du Quebec a Montreal
Lampkin, Derrick, University of Maryland
Langway, Chester C., SUNY, Buffalo
Lea, Peter D., Bowdoin College
Lempe, Bernhard, Technical University of Munich
Leonard, Eric M., Colorado College
Levson, Victor M., University of Victoria
Levy, Joseph, Colgate University
Licciardi, Joseph M., University of New Hampshire
Licciardi, Joseph M., University of New Hampshire
Licht, Kathy J., Indiana University - Purdue University Indianapolis
Loope, Henry M., Indiana University
Lowell, Thomas V., University of Cincinnati
Lusardi, Barb, University of Minnesota
Malone, Andrew, University of Illinois at Chicago
Marcott, Shaun, University of Wisconsin, Madison
Matsuoka, Kenichi, University of Washington
McCarthy, Daniel P., Brock University
McDonald, Jennifer, University of Minnesota
McKay III, E. Donald, Illinois State Geological Survey
Menzies, John, Brock University
Meyer, Gary, University of Minnesota
Mickelson, David M., University of Wisconsin, Madison
Miller, Gifford H., University of Colorado
Mills, Stephanie, Kingston University
Mode, William N., University of Wisconsin, Oshkosh
Mooers, Howard D., University of Minnesota Duluth
Morgan, Alan V., University of Waterloo
Munroe, Jeffrey S., Middlebury College
Muto, Atsuhiro, Temple University
Nash, Thomas A., Ohio Dept of Natural Resources
Neinow, Peter W., Edinburgh University
Neumann, Tom, University of Washington
Nguyen, Maurice, University of Minnesota
Nowicki, Sophie, SUNY, Buffalo
Pair, Donald, University of Dayton
Parent, Michel, Universite du Quebec
Poinar, Kristin, SUNY, Buffalo
Prothro, Lindsay O., Texas A&M University, Corpus Christi
Putnam, Aaron E., University of Maine
Quade, Deborah J., Iowa Dept of Natural Resources
Radic, Valentina, University of British Columbia
Raymond, Charles F., University of Washington
Retelle, Michael J., Bates College
Rexius, James E., Schoolcraft College
Ridge, John C., Tufts University
Rignot, Eric, University of California, Irvine
Rodbell, Donald T., Union College
Roy, Martin, Universite du Quebec a Montreal
Rutford, Robert H., University of Texas, Dallas
Rysgaard, Soren, University of Manitoba
Schneider, Allan F., University of Wisconsin, Parkside
Schoof, Christian, University of British Columbia
Schroeder, Dustin M., Stanford University
Schulz, Layne D., South Dakota Dept of Env and Natural Resources
Sharp, Martin J., University of Alberta
Shaw, John, University of Alberta
Smith, Ben , University of Washington
Spencer, Matt, Lake Superior State University
Stansell, Nathan D., Northern Illinois University
Starr, Paepin K., Austin Community College District
Stearns, Leigh, University of Kansas
Stroeve, Julienne, University College London
Swanger, Kate, University of Massachusetts, Lowell
Syverson, Kent M., University of Wisconsin, Eau Claire
Szymanski, Jason, Monroe Community College
Taylor, Lawrence D., Albion College
Tedesco, Marco, Columbia University
Thackray, Glenn D., Idaho State University
Thomason, Jason, University of Illinois
Thompson, Lonnie G., Ohio State University
Thorleifson, Harvey, University of Minnesota
Todd, Claire E., Pacific Lutheran University
Totten, Stanley M., Hanover College
Tulaczyk, Slawek, University of California, Santa Cruz
Ullman, David J., Northland College
Waddington, Edwin D., University of Washington
Wagner, Kaleb, University of Minnesota
Wake, Cameron P., University of New Hampshire
Ward, Brent C., Simon Fraser University
Werner, Alan, Mount Holyoke College
Westgate, John A., University of Toronto
Wilch, Thomas I., Albion College
Wiles, Gregory C., College of Wooster
Winebrenner, Dale P., University of Washington
Wolff, Eric W., University of Cambridge
Wright, Stephen F., University of Vermont
Young, Robert R., University of British Columbia, Okanagan Campus
Zoet, Lucas, University of Wisconsin, Madison

Marine Geology

Abrams, Lewis J., University of North Carolina, Wilmington
Aksu, Ali E., Memorial University of Newfoundland
Allen, Katherine A., University of Maine
Aluwihare, Lihini I., University of California, San Diego
Anderson, John B., Rice University
Andrade, César, Unive de Lisboa
Austin, Jr., James A., University of Texas, Austin
Bacchus, Tania S., Northern Vermont University-Lyndon
Bangs, Nathan L., University of Texas, Austin
Barclay, Andrew, University of Washington
Barrie, Vaughn, University of Victoria
Becel, Anne, Columbia University
Belknap, Daniel F., University of Maine
Benoit-Bird, Kelly, Oregon State University
Bentley, Samuel J., Louisiana State University
Brooks, Gregg R., Eckerd College
Brown, Kevin M., University of California, San Diego
Browne, Kathleen M., Rider University
Calmus, Thierry, Univ Nacional Autonoma de Mexico
Carlin, Joe, California State University, Fullerton
Carson, Bobb, Lehigh University
Chase, Richard L., University of British Columbia
Cleary, William J., University of North Carolina, Wilmington
Coffroth, Mary Alice, SUNY, Buffalo
Conway, Flaxen D., Oregon State University
Cook, Ann, Ohio State University
Crone, Timothy, Columbia University
Cruz-Orozco, Rodolfo, Univ Autonoma de Baja California Sur

Curray, Joseph R., University of California, San Diego
Damuth, John E., University of Texas, Arlington
Daniell, James J., James Cook University
Das, Indrani, Columbia University
De Deckker, Patrick, Australian National University
Delaney, John R., University of Washington
Dix, Justin, University of Southampton
Dladla, Nonkululeko, University of KwaZulu-Natal
Dobson, David M., Guilford College
Donnelly, Jeffrey, Woods Hole Oceanographic Institution
Driscoll, Neal W., University of California, San Diego
Dugan, Brandon, Colorado School of Mines
Eberli, Gregor P., University of Miami
Edwards, Margo H., University of Hawai'i, Manoa
Fornari, Daniel J., Woods Hole Oceanographic Institution
Freeman-Lynde, Raymond, University of Georgia
Freitas, Maria da Conceição P., Unive de Lisboa
Fryer, Patricia B., University of Hawai'i, Manoa
Fulthorpe, Craig S., University of Texas, Austin
Gee, Jeffrey S., University of California, San Diego
Georgen, Jennifer, Florida State University
Georgen, Jennifer, Old Dominion University
Georgiopopoulou, Aggeliki, University College Dublin
Gilerson, Alexander, Graduate School of the City University of New York
Giosan, Liviu, Woods Hole Oceanographic Institution
Glickson, Deborah, National Academies of Sciences, Engineering, and Medicine
Goes, Joaquim, Columbia University
Goff, John A., University of Texas, Austin
Goni, Miguel A., Oregon State University
Gonzalez-Fernandez, Antonio, Ctr de Invest Cien y de Ed Superior de Ensenada
Grabowski, Jonathan, Northeastern University
Green, Andrew, University of KwaZulu-Natal
Greene, H. Gary, Moss Landing Marine Laboratories
Greenfield, Dianne I., Graduate School of the City University of New York
Grossman, Eric, Western Washington University
Guerin, Gilles, Columbia University
Haggerty, Janet A., University of Tulsa
Hall, Ian R., Cardiff University
Harte, Michael, Oregon State University
Hine, Albert C., University of South Florida
Humphris, Susan E., Woods Hole Oceanographic Institution
Jacobson, Gary L., Grossmont College
Jamieson, John, Memorial University of Newfoundland
Johnson, Harlan P., University of Washington
Johnson, Joel E., University of New Hampshire
Juraèiæ, Mladen, University of Zagreb
Kalangutkar, Niyati, Goa University
Kaminski, Michael A., King Fahd University of Petroleum and Minerals
Katuna, Michael P., College of Charleston
Kearney, Micheal S., University of Maryland
Keller, Randall A., Oregon State University
Kelley, Joseph T., University of Maine
Kidd, Karen, McMaster University
Kienast, Stephanie, Dalhousie University
Klasik, John A., California State Polytechnic University, Pomona
Klaus, Adam, Texas A&M University
Laine, Edward P., Bowdoin College
Lasker, Howard R., SUNY, Buffalo
Leonard, Lynn A., University of North Carolina, Wilmington
Liu, Jingpu P., North Carolina State University
Lonsdale, Peter F., University of California, San Diego
Luciano, Katherine E., South Carolina Dept of Natural Resources
MacLeod, C, Cardiff University
Malinverno, Alberto , Columbia University
Mallinson, David, East Carolina University
Manfrino, Carrie M., Kean University
Marinelli, Roberta, Oregon State University
Mayer, Larry A., University of New Hampshire
McCoy, Jr., Floyd W., University of Hawai'i, Manoa
Meadows, Guy A., Michigan Technological University
Mekik, Figen A., Grand Valley State University
Meylan, Maurice A., University of Southern Mississippi
Micallef, Aaron, University of Malta
Miller, Kenneth G., Rutgers, The State University of New Jersey
Miot da Silva, Graziela, Flinders University
Mitchell, Neil C., University of Manchester
Moberly, Ralph, University of Hawai'i, Manoa
Mountain, Gregory S., Rutgers, The State University of New Jersey
Moy, Christopher M., University of Otago
Naehr, Thomas H., Texas A&M University, Corpus Christi
Neitzke Adamo, Lauren, Rutgers, The State University of New Jersey
Nicholson, David, Woods Hole Oceanographic Institution
Nitsche, Frank, Columbia University
Nittrouer, Charles A., University of Washington
Norris, Richard D., University of California, San Diego
Oehlert, Amanda M., University of Miami
Olayiwola, M. A., Obafemi Awolowo University
Patton, Jason R., Humboldt State University
Peterson, Larry C., University of Miami
Phipps, James B., Grays Harbor College
Pietro, Kathryn R., Woods Hole Oceanographic Institution
Piper, David J., Dalhousie University
Pratt, Thomas, University of Washington
Purkis, Sam J., University of Miami
Ramirez, Wilson R., University of Puerto Rico
Raphael, Constantine N., Eastern Michigan University
Rasmussen, Kenneth, Northern Virginia Community College - Annandale
Rea, David K., University of Michigan
Reed, Donald L., San Jose State University
Richardson, Mary Jo, Texas A&M University
Richaud, Mathieu, Fresno State University
Riggs, Stanley R., East Carolina University
Rodolfo, Kelvin S., University of Illinois at Chicago
Ross, David A., Woods Hole Oceanographic Institution
Ruddiman, William F., University of Virginia
Saffer, Demian, University of Texas, Austin
Scher, Howie, University of South Carolina
Schwartz, David, Cabrillo College
Scott, Steven D., University of Toronto
Skarke, Adam, Mississippi State University
Slagle, Angela, Columbia University
Slovinsky, Peter, Dept of Agriculture, Conservation, and Forestry
Tinto, Kirsteen, Columbia University
Tucholke, Brian E., Woods Hole Oceanographic Institution
Ward, Larry G., University of New Hampshire
Watts, Anthony B., University of Oxford
Wehmiller, John F., University of Delaware
Wheeler, Andy J., University College Cork
Wilcock, William S., University of Washington
Winguth, Cornelia, University of Texas, Arlington
Ziervogel, Kai, University of New Hampshire

Mineralogy & Crystallography

Abdu, Yassir, University of Manitoba
Ague, Jay J., Yale University
Akgul, Bunyamin, Firat University
Alderton, Dave, Royal Holloway University of London
Aldushin, Kirill, Ludwig-Maximilians-Universitaet Muenchen
Altaner, Stephen P., University of Illinois, Urbana-Champaign
Anderson, Callum, Nelson Mandela Metropolitan University
Antao, Sytle, University of Calgary
Apopei, Andrei I., Alexandru Ioan Cuza
Artioli, Gilberto, Università degli Studi di Padova
Astilleros, José Manuel, Univ Complutense de Madrid
Austin, George S., New Mexico Institute of Mining and Technology
Ball, Neil, University of Manitoba
Bassett, William A., Cornell University
Beane, Rachel J., Bowdoin College
Belluso, Elena, Università di Torino
Benna, Piera, Università di Torino
Bermanec, Vladimir, University of Zagreb
Bish, David L., Indiana University, Bloomington
Bladh, Kenneth W., Wittenberg University
Bloss, F. D., Virginia Polytechnic Institute & State University
Bonhoure, Jessica, Institut Polytechnique LaSalle Beauvais (ex-IGAL)
Boyle, Alan P., University of Liverpool
Boysen, Hans, Ludwig-Maximilians-Universitaet Muenchen
Braund, Emilie, University of Portsmouth
Brearley, Adrian J., University of New Mexico
Brown, Jr., Gordon E., Stanford University
Bruno, Emiliano, Università di Torino
Bruno, Marco, Università di Torino

Burnham, Charles W., Harvard University
Burnham, Charles, Fort Lewis College
Burns, Peter C., University of Notre Dame
Buzatu, Andrei, Alexandru Ioan Cuza
Buzgar, Nicolae, Alexandru Ioan Cuza
Cardellach López, Esteve, Universitat Autonoma de Barcelona
Carrigan, Charles W., Olivet Nazarene University
Cartier, Laurent E., University of Delaware
Casas Duocastella, Lluís, Universitat Autonoma de Barcelona
Catlos, Elizabeth J., University of Texas, Austin
Cavosie, Aaron, Curtin University
Cenpírek, Jan, Masaryk University
Chakhmouradian, Anton, University of Manitoba
Chen, Ning, University of Saskatchewan
Chiarenzelli, Jeffrey R., St. Lawrence University
Choi, Seon-Gyu, Korea University
Cilliers, Johannes, Imperial College
Clement, Stephen C., William & Mary
Cody, Robert, Iowa State University of Science & Technology
Cofer, Harland E., Georgia Southwestern State University
Coker, Victoria, University of Manchester
Cole, Kevin C., Grand Valley State University
Collins, Lorence G., California State University, Northridge
Cooper, Mark, University of Manitoba
Copjakova, Renata, Masaryk University
Corbella Cordomí, Mercè, Universitat Autonoma de Barcelona
Cordonnier, Benoit, Ludwig-Maximilians-Universitaet Muenchen
Costa, Emanuele, Università di Torino
Cox, Richard, Dalhousie University
Crandall, Jake R., Eastern Illinois University
Cusack, Maggie, University of Glasgow
Dalconi, Maria C., Università degli Studi di Padova
Darling, Robert S., SUNY, Cortland
De Campos, Christina, Ludwig-Maximilians-Universitaet Muenchen
De Nault, Kenneth J., University of Northern Iowa
De Pablo, Liberto, Univ Nacional Autonoma de Mexico
Dehon, Rene, Texas State University
Dempster, Tim, University of Glasgow
Deng, Youjun, Texas A&M University
Denny, F. B., Illinois State Geological Survey
Dobson, David, University College London
Dollase, Wayne A., University of California, Los Angeles
Dorfman, Alexander, Ludwig-Maximilians-Universitaet Muenchen
Dorfner, Thomas, Ludwig-Maximilians-Universitaet Muenchen
Downs, James W., Ohio State University
Duchesne, Josee, Universite Laval
Dunlevey, John, University of Limpopo
Dutrow, Barbara L., Louisiana State University
Ehm, Lars, Stony Brook University
Elsen, Jan, Katholieke Universiteit Leuven
Emofurieta, Williams O., University of Benin
Ercit, T. Scott, Carleton University
Ertel-Ingrisch, Werner, Ludwig-Maximilians-Universitaet Muenchen
Ewing, Rodney E., University of New Mexico
Ewing, Rodney C., Stanford University
Farnan, Ian, University of Cambridge
Farthing, Dori J., SUNY, Geneseo
Farzaneh, Akbar, University of Tabriz
Feather, Russell, Smithsonian Institution / National Museum of Natural History
Feely, Martin, National University of Ireland Galway
Fehr, Karl Thomas, Ludwig-Maximilians-Universitaet Muenchen
Feinglos, Mark N., Duke University
Ferguson, Robert B., University of Manitoba
Fernández, Lourdes, Univ Complutense de Madrid
Fernández-Barrenechea, José María, Univ Complutense de Madrid
Ferraris, Giovanni, Università di Torino
Field, Stephen W., Tarleton State University
Finch, Adriam, University of St. Andrews
Flemming, Roberta L., Western University
Foit, Jr., Franklin F., Washington State University
Fransolet, Andre-Mathieu, Universite de Liege
Freed, Robert L., Trinity University
Frenette, Jean, Universite Laval
Frey, Friedrich, Ludwig-Maximilians-Universitaet Muenchen
Frueh, Alfred J., University of Connecticut
Gadikota, Greeshma, University of Wisconsin, Madison
Gait, Robert I., Royal Ontario Museum
Gann, Delbert E., Millsaps College
Garapic, Gordana, SUNY, New Paltz
García Romero, Emilia, Univ Complutense de Madrid
García-Martínez, David, Univ Estatal de Sonora
Garvie, Laurence, Arizona State University
Gay, Kenny, N.C. Department of Environmental Quality
Gibbs, Jerry, Virginia Polytechnic Institute & State University
Gieré, Reto, University of Pennsylvania
Gigler, Alexander, Ludwig-Maximilians-Universitaet Muenchen
Gille, Peter, Ludwig-Maximilians-Universitaet Muenchen
Gius, Fred, California Geological Survey
Giustetto, Roberto, Università di Torino
Gollmer, Steven, Cedarville University
González, Isabel , Univ de Sevilla
Grießl, Stefan, Ludwig-Maximilians-Universitaet Muenchen
Griffen, Dana T., Brigham Young University
Groat, Lee A., University of British Columbia
Grover, John E., University of Cincinnati
Guggenheim, Stephen J., University of Illinois at Chicago
Guillemette, Renald, Texas A&M University
Gunter, Mickey E., University of Idaho
Göttlich, Hagen, Ludwig-Maximilians-Universitaet Muenchen
Hadler, Kathryn, Imperial College
Hall, Anne M., Emory University
Hansen, Lars, University of Oxford
Harlow, George E., Graduate School of the City University of New York
Harlow, George E., American Museum of Natural History
Harrison, Richard, University of Cambridge
Hawkins, David, Wellesley College
Hawkins, Michael A., New York State Geological Survey
Hawthorne, Frank C., University of Manitoba
Hazen, Robert M., Carnegie Institution for Science
Heaney, Peter J., Pennsylvania State University, University Park
Heckel, Wolfgang, Ludwig-Maximilians-Universitaet Muenchen
Heimann, Adriana, East Carolina University
Henderson, Grant S., University of Toronto
Hennemeyer, Marc, Ludwig-Maximilians-Universitaet Muenchen
Hess, Kai-Uwe, Ludwig-Maximilians-Universitaet Muenchen
Heuss-Aßbichler, Soraya, Ludwig-Maximilians-Universitaet Muenchen
Hollabaugh, Curtis L., University of West Georgia
Hooper, Robert L., University of Wisconsin, Eau Claire
Horton, Duane G., Pacific Northwest National Laboratory
Hovis, Guy L., Lafayette College
Huff, Warren D., University of Cincinnati
Hughes, John M., Miami University
Hughes, John M., University of Vermont
Hummer, Daniel R., Southern Illinois University Carbondale
Izawa, Matt, Western University
Joesten, Raymond, University of Connecticut
Johanesen, Katharine, Juniata College
Johnson, Neil E., Virginia Polytechnic Institute & State University
Jones, Rhian, University of New Mexico
Jordan, Guntram, Ludwig-Maximilians-Universitaet Muenchen
Kaiser, Jason, Southern Utah University
Kaiser-Bischoff, Ines, Ludwig-Maximilians-Universitaet Muenchen
Kamhi, Samuel R., Long Island University, Brooklyn Campus
Kampf, Anthony R., Los Angeles County Museum of Natural History
Kearns, Lance E., James Madison University
Keller, Dianne M., Colgate University
Kerestedjian, Thomas N., Bulgarian Academy of Sciences
Kim, Bojeong, Temple University
Kleebe, Hans-Joachim, Technische Universitaet Darmstadt
Komabayashi, Tetsuya, Edinburgh University
Krol, Michael A., Bridgewater State University
Kunzmann, Thomas, Ludwig-Maximilians-Universitaet Muenchen
Lackinger, Markus, Ludwig-Maximilians-Universitaet Muenchen
Lancaster, Penny, University of Portsmouth
Langenhorst, Falko H., Friedrich-Schiller-University Jena
Lapen, Thomas, University of Houston
Leavens, Peter B., University of Delaware
Lee, Martin, University of Glasgow
Leimer, H. Wayne, Tennessee Tech University
Leitz, Robert E., Metropolitan State College of Denver
Leung, Irene S., Lehman College (CUNY)
Levesque, Andre, Universite Laval

Levine, Jamie S., Appalachian State University
Lian, Jie, University of Michigan
López, Sol, Univ Complutense de Madrid
Losh, Steven, Minnesota State University
Losos, Zdenek, Masaryk University
Lueth, Virgil L., New Mexico Institute of Mining and Technology
Lupulescu, Marian V., New York State Geological Survey
Luque, Francisco Javier, Univ Complutense de Madrid
Lübbe, Maike, Ludwig-Maximilians-Universitaet Muenchen
Macris, Catherine, Indiana University - Purdue University Indianapolis
Majzlan, Juraj, Friedrich-Schiller-University Jena
Manu, Johnson, University of Ghana
Marshall, Craig, University of Kansas
Martin, Robert F., McGill University
Masch, Ludwig, Ludwig-Maximilians-Universitaet Muenchen
McCausland, Phil, Brock University
McCormack, John K., University of Nevada, Reno
McCormick, George R., University of Iowa
McCurry, Michael O., Idaho State University
McDonald, Andrew M., Laurentian University, Sudbury
McHenry, Lindsay J., University of Wisconsin, Milwaukee
McNamara, Kelsey, New Mexico Institute of Mining and Technology
McNamee, Brittani D., University of North Carolina, Asheville
Meisterernst, Götz, Ludwig-Maximilians-Universitaet Muenchen
Merkel, Timo Casjen, Ludwig-Maximilians-Universitaet Muenchen
Miles, Andrew, Kingston University
Miyagi, Lowell, University of Utah
Moritz, Wolfgang, Ludwig-Maximilians-Universitaet Muenchen
Myers, George, Temple University
Müller, Lena, Ludwig-Maximilians-Universitaet Muenchen
Müller-Sohnius, Dieter, Ludwig-Maximilians-Universitaet Muenchen
Navarro, Didac, Universitat Autonoma de Barcelona
Neethling, Stephen, Imperial College
Nestola, Fabrizio, Università degli Studi di Padova
Nord, Julia, George Mason University
Novak, Milan , Masaryk University
Nusbaum, Robert L., College of Charleston
Paktunc, Dogan, University of Ottawa
Paquette, Jeanne, McGill University
Parise, John B., Stony Brook University
Park, Sohyun, Ludwig-Maximilians-Universitaet Muenchen
Pascoe, Richard, Exeter University
Pavese, Alessandro, Università di Torino
Peacor, Donald R., University of Michigan
Pentcheva, Rossitza, Ludwig-Maximilians-Universitaet Muenchen
Peterson, Ronald C., Queen's University
Phillips, Brian L., Stony Brook University
Phillips, William R., Brigham Young University
Piniella Febrer, Juan Francesc, Universitat Autonoma de Barcelona
Post, Jeffrey E., Smithsonian Institution / National Museum of Natural History
Prencipe, Mauro, Università di Torino
Price, Nancy A., SUNY, Plattsburgh
Putnis, Andrew, Curtin University
Radcliffe, Dennis, Hofstra University
Rakovan, John F., Miami University
Raudsepp, Mati, University of British Columbia
Redfern, Simon, University of Cambridge
Regan, Sean, University of Alaska, Fairbanks
Reinthal, William A., Ashland University
Reuss, Robert L., Tufts University
Ribbe, Paul H., Virginia Polytechnic Institute & State University
Rickaby, Ros, University of Oxford
Riedel, Oliver, Ludwig-Maximilians-Universitaet Muenchen
Robinson, George W., St. Lawrence University
Robinson, Paul D., Southern Illinois University Carbondale
Rocholl, Alexander, Ludwig-Maximilians-Universitaet Muenchen
Rodriguez-Blanco, Juan Diego, Trinity College
Rojas-Soriano, Humberto, Univ Autonoma de Baja California Sur
Rosenberg, Philip E., Washington State University
Ross, Nancy L., Virginia Polytechnic Institute & State University
Rossman, George R., California Institute of Technology
Rouse, Roland C., University of Michigan
Rubio-Sierra, Javier, Ludwig-Maximilians-Universitaet Muenchen
Rutstein, Martin S., SUNY, New Paltz
Salviulo, Gabriella, Università degli Studi di Padova
Sánchez, Nuria, Univ Complutense de Madrid
Schindler, Michael, Laurentian University, Sudbury
Schmahl, Wolfgang, Ludwig-Maximilians-Universitaet Muenchen
Schneider, Julius, Ludwig-Maximilians-Universitaet Muenchen
Schroeder, Paul A., University of Georgia
Scott Smith, Barbara H., University of British Columbia
Secco, Luciano, Università degli Studi di Padova
Sethi, Parvinder S., Radford University
Shank, Stephen G., DCNR- Pennsylvania Bureau of Geological Survey
Sharp, Thomas G., Arizona State University
Sharp, W. Edwin, University of South Carolina
Sheets, Julie, Ohio State University
Sherriff, Barbara L., University of Manitoba
Shim, Sang-Heon, Arizona State University
Shuller-Nickles, Lindsay C., Clemson University
Silvestri, Alberta, Università degli Studi di Padova
Simmons, William B., University of Michigan
Simmons, William B., University of New Orleans
Singer, David M., Kent State University
Skoda, Radek, Masaryk University
Smith, Michael S., University of North Carolina, Wilmington
Smyth, Joseph R., University of Colorado
Sokolova, Elena, University of Manitoba
Solorio-Munguia, Jose G., Univ Nacional Autonoma de Mexico
Spieler, Oliver, Ludwig-Maximilians-Universitaet Muenchen
Spilde, Michael N., University of New Mexico
Stark, Robert, Ludwig-Maximilians-Universitaet Muenchen
Stefano, Christopher J., Michigan Technological University
Stewart, Dion C., Georgia State Univ, Perimeter College, Alpharetta Campus
Strasser, Stefan, Ludwig-Maximilians-Universitaet Muenchen
Tait, Kimberly T., Royal Ontario Museum
Tettenhorst, Rodney T., Ohio State University
Thibault, Yves, Western University
Tibljaš, Darko, University of Zagreb
Timms, Nick, Curtin University
Tomašiæ, Nenad, University of Zagreb
Trixler, Frank, Ludwig-Maximilians-Universitaet Muenchen
Uzochukwu, Godfrey A., North Carolina Agricultural & Tech State University
Vassiliou, Andreas H., Rutgers, The State University of New Jersey, Newark
Vaughan, David, University of Manchester
Viedma, Cristóbal, Univ Complutense de Madrid
Vindel, Elena, Univ Complutense de Madrid
Viti, Cecilia, University of Siena
Walker, Jeffrey R., Vassar College
Walther, Ferdinand, Ludwig-Maximilians-Universitaet Muenchen
Warner, Richard D., Clemson University
Webb, Christine R., Smithsonian Inst/Nat Mus of Nat History
Weinbruch, Stephan, Technische Universitaet Darmstadt
Wenk, Hans-Rudolf, University of California, Berkeley
Wicks, Frederick J., University of Toronto
Wicks, Frederick J., Royal Ontario Museum
Wilson, James R., Weber State University
Winchell, Robert E., California State University, Long Beach
Wise, Michael A., University of New Orleans
Wise, Michael A., Smithsonian Institution / National Museum of Natural History
Witter-Shelleman, Molly, University of Akron
Wood, Bernard, University of Oxford
Wood, Ian, University College London
Wylie, Ann G., University of Maryland
Xu, Huifang, University of Wisconsin, Madison
Yoshiasa, Akira, Kumamoto University
Yurtsever, Ayhan, Ludwig-Maximilians-Universitaet Muenchen
Zimmerman, Brian S., Edinboro University of Pennsylvania
Zink, Albert, Ludwig-Maximilians-Universitaet Muenchen
Zurevinski, Shannon, Lakehead University
Šæavnièar, Stjepan, University of Zagreb
Žigoveèki Gobac, Željka, University of Zagreb

Paleolimnology

Anderson, Roger Y., University of New Mexico
Axford, Yarrow L., Northwestern University
Brady, Kristina, University of Minnesota, Twin Cities
Brant, Lynn A., University of Northern Iowa
Brenner, Mark, University of Florida
Buchheim, Paul, Loma Linda University
Davies, Caroline P., University of Missouri, Kansas City
De Batist, Marc, Ghent University

Ferris, Grant F., University of Toronto
Gennari, Rocco, Università di Torino
Glaser, Paul H., University of Minnesota, Twin Cities
Heyvaert, Alan, University of Nevada, Reno
Hillman, Aubrey, University of Louisiana at Lafayette
Kaplan, Samantha W., University of Wisconsin, Stevens Point
Kirby, Matthew E., California State University, Fullerton
Lisiecki, Lorraine, University of California, Santa Barbara
McGlue, Michael M., University of Kentucky
Noren, Anders, University of Minnesota, Twin Cities
Porter, Susannah, University of California, Santa Barbara
Rosen, Michael R., University of Nevada, Reno
Russell, James M., Brown University
Shapley, Mark, University of Minnesota, Twin Cities
Smith, Alison J., Kent State University
Steinman, Byron A., University of Minnesota Duluth
Stevens (Landon), Lora R., California State University, Long Beach
Stone, Alexander, University of Minnesota, Twin Cities
Theissen, Kevin, University of Saint Thomas
Waters, Matthew N., Auburn University

Petroleum Geology

Abdulghani, Waleed, King Fahd University of Petroleum and Minerals
Adeigbe, O. C., University of Ibadan
Adekeye, J.I. D., University of Ilorin
Aden, Leon, University of Iowa
Ajaegwu, Norbert E., Nnamdi Azikiwe University
Al-Ramadan, Khalid, King Fahd University of Petroleum and Minerals
Ali, Hendratta N., Fort Hays State University
Alves, Tiago, Cardiff University
Andrews, Richard D., University of Oklahoma
Aplin, Andrew, Durham University
Arnold, Dan, Heriot-Watt University
Asquith, George B., Texas Tech University
Avary, Katherine L., West Virginia University
Bartlett, Wendy, Marietta College
Bartok, Peter, University of Houston
Bellian, Jerome, Miami University
Bend, Stephen L., University of Regina
Benjamin, U. K., Obafemi Awolowo University
Bible, Gary G., University of Tennessee, Knoxville
Bissell, Clinton R., Texas A&M University, Corpus Christi
Bloxson, Julie M., Stephen F. Austin State University
Boboye, O. A., University of Ibadan
Bonk, Kathleen, New York State Geological Survey
Bowersox, John R., University of Kentucky
Bowler, Bernard, University of Newcastle Upon Tyne
Bowman, Mike, University of Manchester
Broadhead, Ronald F., New Mexico Institute of Mining and Technology
Burton, Bradford R., Western Colorado University
Carr, Timothy R., West Virginia University
Carr, Timothy R., University of Kansas
Cassidy, Martin, University of Houston
Champlin, Steven D., Mississippi Office of Geology
Cheadle, Burns A., Western University
Chelariu, Ciprian, Alexandru Ioan Cuza
Chenoweth, Cheri, Illinois State Geological Survey
Chongwain, Gilbert, University of Namibia
Cochrane, Claudia, Western University
Cranganu, Constantin, Brooklyn College (CUNY)
Curtis, John B., Colorado School of Mines
Dallegge, Todd A., University of Northern Colorado
Denne, Richard A., Texas Christian University
Echols, John B., Louisiana State University
Edegbai, Aitalokhai J., University of Benin
Ehinola, Olugbenga A., University of Ibadan
Ehinola, Olugbenga A., University of Ibadan
Elnadi, Abdelhalim H., University of Khartoum
Fadiya, S. L., Obafemi Awolowo University
Fakhari, Mohammad D., Ohio Dept of Natural Resources
Finley, Robert J., University of Illinois, Urbana-Champaign
Folorunso, I. O., University of Ilorin
Fraser, Alastair, Imperial College
Giles, Katherine A., University of Texas, El Paso
Gillespie, Janice, California State University, Bakersfield
Gingras, Murray, University of Alberta
Graham, Stephan A., Stanford University
Grender, Gordon C., Virginia Polytechnic Institute & State University
Grigg, Joseph, New Mexico Institute of Mining and Technology
Hanks, Catherine L., University of Alaska, Fairbanks
Harris, David C., University of Kentucky
Harun, Nina, Alaska Division of Geological & Geophysical Surveys
Haszeldine, R. S., Edinburgh University
Henk, Jr., Floyd, Texas Christian University
Herrmann, Leo A., Louisiana Tech University
Hileman, Mary E., Oklahoma State University
Hofmann, Michael, University of Montana
Holford, Simon, University of Adelaide
Hu, Qinhong (Max), University of Texas, Arlington
Hudson, Samuel M., Brigham Young University
Hughes, Colin, University of Manchester
Igbinigie, Nosa S., University of Benin
Jiang , Shu, University of Utah
John, Chacko J., Louisiana State University
Johnson, Howard, Imperial College
Jones, Bobby L., Louisiana State University
Kaldi, John, University of Adelaide
Kavousi Ghahfarohki, Payam, West Virginia University
Keach, William, University of Utah
Knepp, Rex A., Illinois State Geological Survey
Leetaru, Hannes E., Illinois State Geological Survey
Leetaru, Hannes, University of Illinois
Leetaru, Hannes E., University of Illinois, Urbana-Champaign
Lever, Helen, Heriot-Watt University
Li, Peng, Arkansas Geological Survey
Lopez, Annabelle, New Mexico Institute of Mining and Technology
Loucks, Bob, University of Texas at Austin, Jackson School of Geosciences
Lucia, F. Jerry, University of Texas at Austin, Jackson School of Geosciences
Machel, Hans G., University of Alberta
Malinverno, Alberto, Columbia University
Manzocchi, Tom, University College Dublin
Martin, Luke, New Mexico Institute of Mining and Technology
Mazzullo, Salvatore J., Wichita State University
Mc Mahon, Michelle, Lonestar College - North Harris
McCabe, Peter, University of Adelaide
Meddaugh, W. S., Midwestern State University
Medina, Cristian R., Indiana University
Miller, Michael B., Louisiana State University
Minzoni, Marcello, University of Alabama
Neufeld, Jerome A., University of Cambridge
Newell, Kerry D., University of Kansas
Nixon, R. Paul, Brigham Young University
Nordeng, Stephan, University of North Dakota
North, F. K., Carleton University
Nton, M. E., University of Ibadan
Nunez-Velazco, Miriam, Univ Autonoma de Baja California Sur
Nwachukwu, J. I., Obafemi Awolowo University
Ola, Peter S., Federal University of Technology, Akure
Olarewaju, V. O., Obafemi Awolowo University
Olorunfemi, A. O., Obafemi Awolowo University
Osman, Mutasim S., King Fahd University of Petroleum and Minerals
Panah, Assad I., University of Pittsburgh, Bradford
Pashin, Jack C., Mississippi State University
Pedersen, Per, University of Calgary
Pena dos Reis, Rui, Unive de Coimbra
Pertl, David, Amarillo College
Pigott, John D., University of Oklahoma
Pranter, Matthew J., University of Oklahoma
Pritchett, Brittany, University of Oklahoma
Puckette, James, Oklahoma State University
Ratchford, M. E., Arkansas Geological Survey
Resnic, Victor S., Lonestar College - North Harris
Richards-McClung, Bryony, University of Utah
Riess, Carolyn M., Austin Community College District
Ronck, Catherine, Tarleton State University
Rupp, John A., Indiana University
Scarselli, Nicola, Royal Holloway University of London
Schmid, Katherine W., DCNR- Pennsylvania Bureau of Geological Survey
Schneider, Robert V., Texas A&M University, Kingsville
Schroeder, Stefan, University of Manchester
Sharman, Glenn R., University of Arkansas, Fayetteville
Shumaker, Robert C., West Virginia University

Simpson, Altus, Cypress College
Slater, Brian, New York State Geological Survey
Smith, Greg, Curtin University
Smith, Langhorne, New York State Geological Survey
Song, Liaosha, California State University, Bakersfield
Sonnenberg, Stephen A., Colorado School of Mines
Sprinkel, Douglas A., Utah Geological Survey
Stewart, Gary, Oklahoma State University
Stright, Lisa, Colorado State University
Sullivan, Raymond, San Francisco State University
Sun, Yuefeng, Texas A&M University
Tan, Denis N., University of Malaya
Taylor, Kevin, University of Manchester
Temples, Tommy, Clemson University
Tinker, Scott W., University of Texas at Austin, Jackson School of Geosciences
Toner, Rachel, Wyoming State Geological Survey
Trentham, Robert C., University of Texas Permian Basin
Van Kooten, Gerald K., Calvin College
Vautier, Yannick, Institut Polytechnique LaSalle Beauvais (ex-IGAL)
Wach, Grant D., Dalhousie University
Wardlaw, Norman C., University of Calgary
Weimer, Paul, University of Colorado
White, Bekki C., Arkansas Geological Survey
Whiteley, Martin, University of Derby
Woodward, Mac B., Arkansas Geological Survey
Xie, Xiangyang, Texas Christian University
Zimmerman, Ronald K., Louisiana State University
Zonneveld, John-Paul, University of Alberta

General Petrology

Afolabi, Olukayode A., Ladoke Akintola University of Technology
Ague, Jay J., Yale University
Aird, Hannah M., California State University, Chico
Anderson, Alan J., Saint Francis Xavier University
Arslan, Gizem, Firat University
Ashwal, Lewis D., University of the Witwatersrand
Balen, Dražen, University of Zagreb
Barr, Sandra, Dalhousie University
Basu, Asish, University of Texas, Arlington
Bickel, Charles E., San Francisco State University
Biševac, Vanja, University of Zagreb
Blackburn, William H., University of Kentucky
Bonamici, Chloe, University of Wisconsin, Madison
Borghi, Alessandro, Università di Torino
Botcharnikov, Roman, Universität Mainz
Brady, John B., Smith College
Brandriss, Mark E., Smith College
Brown, Michael, University of Maryland
BrownLee, Sarah J., Wayne State University
Broxton, David E., Los Alamos National Laboratory
Cain, J. Allan, University of Rhode Island
Callegari, Ezio, Università di Torino
Carmichael, Sarah, Appalachian State University
Castelli, Daniele, Università di Torino
Chaumba, Jeff B., University of North Carolina, Pembroke
Cherniak, Daniele J., Rensselaer Polytechnic Institute
Chu, Xu, University of Toronto
Compagnoni, Roberto, Università di Torino
Compton, Robert R., Stanford University
Cordell, Ann S., University of Florida
Corral, Isaac, Universitat Autonoma de Barcelona
Crawford, Maria Luisa B., Bryn Mawr College
Dasgupta, Rajdeep, Rice University
Day, Howard W., University of California, Davis
de Hoog, Jan C., Edinburgh University
DeBari, Susan M., Western Washington University
Deininger, Robert W., University of Memphis
Dobrzhinetskaya, Larissa F., University of California, Riverside
Doolan, Barry L., University of Vermont
Eklund, Olav, Abo Akademi University
Elliot, David H., Ohio State University
Encarnacion, John, Saint Louis University
Erickson, Rolfe C., Sonoma State University
Ferrando, Simona, Università di Torino
Ferreiro Maehlmann, Rafael, Technische Universitaet Darmstadt
Finn, Gregory C., Brock University
Flynn, Natalie, Temple University
Ford, Mark T., Texas A&M University, Kingsville
Frank, Charles O., Southern Illinois University Carbondale
Ganguly, Jiba, University of Arizona
Goble, Ronald G., University of Nebraska, Lincoln
Gonzales, David A., Fort Lewis College
Graham, Ian, University of New South Wales
Gray, Norman H., University of Connecticut
Groppo, Chiara Teresa, Università di Torino
Haileab, Bereket, Carleton College
Hanson, Richard E., Texas Christian University
Hatheway, Richard B., SUNY, Geneseo
Hayob, Jodie, University of Mary Washington
Hetherington, Callum J., Texas Tech University
Hollocher, Kurt T., Union College
Hutchison, David, Hartwick College
Ihinger, Phillip D., University of Wisconsin, Eau Claire
Jercinovic, Michael J., University of Massachusetts, Amherst
Jimoh, Mustapha T., Ladoke Akintola University of Technology
Johnson, Julie, University of Memphis
Jolliff, Bradley L., Washington University in St. Louis
Kerr, A C., Cardiff University
Keskinen, Mary J., University of Alaska, Fairbanks
Kilic, Ayse Didem, Firat University
Leichmann, Jaromir, Masaryk University
Lewy, Robert, Bakersfield College
Malcuit, Robert J., Denison University
Mallik, Ananya, University of Rhode Island
Manning, Craig E., University of California, Los Angeles
Maritan, Lara, Università degli Studi di Padova
Martin, Barton S., Ohio Wesleyan University
Mathez, Edmond A., American Museum of Natural History
Mazza, Sarah, Smith College
Mazzoli, Claudio, Università degli Studi di Padova
McFadden, Rory, Gustavus Adolphus College
McLeod, Claire, Miami University
Mirnejad, Hassan, Miami University
Moecher, David P., University of Kentucky
Moore, Daniel K., Brigham Young University - Idaho
Murphy, J. Brendan, Dalhousie University
Mutti, Laurence J., Juniata College
Nasir, Sobhi J., University of Qatar
Nesse, William D., University of Northern Colorado
Nielsen, Peter A., Keene State College
Noblett, Jeffrey B., Colorado College
Owens, Brent E., William & Mary
Ozel Yildirim, Esra , Firat University
Pan, Yuanming, University of Saskatchewan
Peterson, Virginia L., Grand Valley State University
Plank, Terry A., Columbia University
Plymate, Thomas G., Missouri State University
Prichard, H M., Cardiff University
Ptacek, Anton D., San Diego State University
Purchase, Megan, University of the Free State
Purdom, William B., Southern Oregon University
Ranson, William A., Furman University
Reed, Robert M., University of Texas at Austin, Jackson School of Geosciences
Reyes-Cortes, Ignacio A., Univ Autonoma de Chihuahua
Rizeli, Mustafa Eren, Firat University
Roadifer, Jack E., Colorado Mesa University
Rolfo, Franco, Università di Torino
Rougvie, James R., Beloit College
Saini-Eidukat, Bernhardt, North Dakota State University
Severs, Matthew R., Stockton University
Sharma, Shiv K., University of Hawai'i, Manoa
Shoemaker, Kurt A., Shawnee State University
Snyder, Lori D., University of Wisconsin, Eau Claire
Spandler, Carl, James Cook University
Stelling, Pete, Western Washington University
Sun, Chenguang, University of Texas, Austin
Thy, Peter, University of California, Davis
Torres-Agulera, Juan Manuel, Univ Autonoma de San Luis Potosi
Van Buer, Nicholas J., California State Polytechnic University, Pomona
van Kranendonk, Martin, University of New South Wales
Van Rythoven, Adrian, Bloomsburg University
Vaniman, David T., Los Alamos National Laboratory

Vanko, David A., Towson University
Walker, David, Columbia University
Warren, Jessica, University of Delaware
Weaver, Stephen G., Colorado College
Welsh, James L., Gustavus Adolphus College
Westerman, David S., Norwich University
Whattam, Scot , King Fahd University of Petroleum and Minerals
Whelan, Peter M., University of Minnesota, Morris
WoldeGabriel, Giday, Los Alamos National Laboratory
Wortel, Matthew J., University of Iowa
Yurkovich, Steven P., Western Carolina University

Igneous Petrology

Albee, Arden L., California Institute of Technology
Allen, Jack C., Bucknell University
Amedjoe, Godfrey C., Kwame Nkrumah University of Science and Technology
Amel, Nasir, University of Tabriz
Andersen, Jens C., Exeter University
Anderson, James Lawford, Boston University
Annesley, Irvine, University of Saskatchewan
Anthony, Elizabeth Y., University of Texas, El Paso
Aranda, Jorge, Univ Nacional Autonoma de Mexico
Atlas, Zachary, University of South Florida
Badger, Robert L., SUNY Potsdam
Bailey, David G., Hamilton College
Baldridge, W. Scott, Los Alamos National Laboratory
Barboni, Melanie, Arizona State University
Barnes, Calvin G., Texas Tech University
Barr, Sandra M., Acadia University
Barth, Andrew P., Indiana University - Purdue University Indianapolis
Barton, Michael, Ohio State University
Beard, James S., Virginia Polytechnic Institute & State University
Bedard, Jean H., Universite du Quebec
Bender, E. E., Orange Coast College
Bender, John F., University of North Carolina, Charlotte
Benimoff, Alan I., College of Staten Island/CUNY
Bentley, Robert, Central Washington University
Bergantz, George W., University of Washington
Beswick, Anthony E., Laurentian University, Sudbury
Beukes, Jarlen J., University of the Free State
Beyarslan, Melahat, Firat University
Bingol, Ahmet Feyzi, Firat University
Bizimis, Michael, University of South Carolina
Blackerby, Bruce A., Fresno State University
Bladh, Katherine L., Wittenberg University
Bloomer, Sherman H., Oregon State University
Boerboom, Terrence, University of Minnesota
Bohrson, Wendy A., Central Washington University
Borg, Scott G., National Science Foundation
Boroughs, Scott, Washington State University
Boudreau, Alan E., Duke University
Brandon, Alan, University of Houston
Brandriss, Mark E., Williams College
Brophy, James G., Indiana University, Bloomington
Brown, Kenneth L., DePauw University
Browne, Brandon L., Humboldt State University
Brueseke, Matthew E., Kansas State University
Bryan, Scott E., Queensland University of Technology
Bybee, Grant M., University of the Witwatersrand
Byerly, Gary R., Louisiana State University
Canil, Dante, University of Victoria
Carmichael, Ian S., University of California, Berkeley
Casquet, César, Univ Complutense de Madrid
Castillo, Paterno R., University of California, San Diego
Cathey, Henrietta, Queensland University of Technology
Cecil, M. R., California State University, Northridge
Cepeda, Joseph C., West Texas A&M University
Chadwick, John, College of Charleston
Chavrit, Deborah, University of Manchester
Cheney, John T., Amherst College
Chesner, Craig A., Eastern Illinois University
Christiansen, Eric H., Brigham Young University
Claiborne, Lily L., Vanderbilt University
Clark, Russell G., Albion College
Clarke, D B., Dalhousie University
Clausen, Benjamin L., Loma Linda University
Clemens-Knott, Diane, California State University, Fullerton
Coleman, Robert G., Stanford University
Collins, Bill, Curtin University
Condit, Christopher D., University of Massachusetts, Amherst
Constantin, Marc, Universite Laval
Coogan, Laurence, University of Victoria
Coombs, Douglas S., University of Otago
Cooper, Kari M., University of California, Davis
Cooper, Roger W., Lamar University
Cornell, Winton, University of Tulsa
Cote, Denis, Universite du Quebec a Chicoutimi
Cottle, John, University of California, Santa Barbara
Cousens, Brian L., Carleton University
Crawford, Anthony J., University of Tasmania
Cribb, Warner, Middle Tennessee State University
Davies, Gareth R., Vrije Universiteit Amsterdam
Dean, Robert, Dickinson College
Delgado-Argote, Luis A., Ctr de Invest Científica y de Ed Superior de Ensenada
Dick, Henry J B., Woods Hole Oceanographic Institution
Dickson, Loretta D., Lock Haven University
Dijkstra, Arjan, University of Plymouth
Dingwell, Donald Bruce, Ludwig-Maximilians-Universitaet Muenchen
Dolejs, David, Charles University
Dorais, Michael J., Brigham Young University
Doucet, Luc, Curtin University
Downs, Robert T., University of Arizona
Dunbar, Nelia W., New Mexico Institute of Mining and Technology
Duncan, Megan S., Virginia Polytechnic Institute & State University
Dunn, John Todd, University of New Brunswick
Dygert, Nick, University of Tennessee, Knoxville
Dymek, Robert F., Washington University in St. Louis
Edwards, Benjamin R., Dickinson College
Elardo, Stephen, University of Florida
Elders, Wilfred A., University of California, Riverside
Elkins, Lynne J., University of Nebraska, Lincoln
Erturk, Mehmet Ali, Firat University
Fagan, Amy, Western Carolina University
Fernandez, Louis A., California State University, San Bernardino
Fiesinger, Donald W., Utah State University
Fitton, J. G., Edinburgh University
Fleming, Thomas H., Southern Connecticut State University
Flower, Martin F., University of Illinois at Chicago
Fodor, Ronald V., North Carolina State University
Fournelle, John, University of Wisconsin, Madison
Fowler, Mike, University of Portsmouth
Fowler, Sarah, Katholieke Universiteit Leuven
Fox, Lydia K., University of the Pacific
Francis, Don, McGill University
Furman, Tanya, Pennsylvania State University, University Park
Gaetani, Glenn A., Woods Hole Oceanographic Institution
Galán garcía, Gúmer, Universitat Autonoma de Barcelona
Gamble, John, University College Cork
Ganguly, Sohini, Goa University
Garcia, Michael O., University of Hawai'i, Manoa
Garrison, Jennifer M., California State University, Los Angeles
Geist, Dennis J., University of Idaho
GERBE, Marie-Christine, Université Jean Monnet, Saint-Etienne
Gertisser, Ralf, Keele University
Ghani, Azman Abdul, University of Malaya
Gibson, David, University of Maine, Farmington
Gibson, Sally, University of Cambridge
Gill, James B., University of California, Santa Cruz
Gittins, John, University of Toronto
Glazner, Allen F., University of North Carolina, Chapel Hill
Gomes, Maria E., Unive de Trás-os-Montes e Alto Douro
Gonzalez, Maria M., Central Michigan University
Gorring, Matthew L., Montclair State University
Green, John C., University of Minnesota Duluth
Greenberg, Jeffrey K., Wheaton College
Greenough, John D., University of British Columbia, Okanagan Campus
Grove, Timothy L., Massachusetts Institute of Technology
Grunder, Anita L., Oregon State University
Gualda, Guilherme, Vanderbilt University
Gust, David A., Queensland University of Technology
Haggerty, Stephen E., Florida International University
Halsor, Sid P., Wilkes University

Hammer, Julia E., University of Hawai'i, Manoa
Hammersley, Lisa, Sacramento State University
Hammond, Paul E., Portland State University
Hannah, Judith L., Colorado State University
Hanson, Sarah L., Adrian College
Hari, Kosiyath R., Pt. Ravishankar Shukla University
Harris, Chris, University of Cape Town
Hart, William K., Miami University
Hearn Jr, B. Carter, Smithsonian Inst/Nat Mus of Nat History
Hebert, Rejean J., Universite Laval
Hermes, O D., University of Rhode Island
Hess, Paul C., Brown University
Hidalgo, Paulo J., Georgia State University
Higgins, Michael D., Universite du Quebec a Chicoutimi
Hirschmann, Marc M., University of Minnesota, Twin Cities
Hirt, William H., College of the Siskiyous
Holness, Marian, University of Cambridge
Hudgins, Thomas, University of Puerto Rico
Huertas, María José, Univ Complutense de Madrid
Husch, Jonathan M., Rider University
Huysken, Kristin, Indiana University Northwest
Irvine, T. Neil, Carnegie Institution for Science
Jagoutz, Oliver, Massachusetts Institute of Technology
Jahangiri, Ahmad, University of Tabriz
Janney, Phillip, University of Cape Town
Jaye, Shelley, Northern Virginia Community College - Annandale
Johnson, Kenneth, University of Houston Downtown
Johnson, Kevin T. M., University of Hawai'i, Manoa
Jones, Adrian P., University College London
Jones, Norris W., University of Wisconsin, Oshkosh
Jordan, Brennan T., University of South Dakota
Kay, Robert W., Cornell University
Kay, Suzanne M., Cornell University
Kelemen, Peter, Columbia University
Kelemen, Peter B., Columbia University
Kelemen, Peter B., Woods Hole Oceanographic Institution
Kempton, Pamela D., Kansas State University
Kent, Adam J., Oregon State University
Klein, Emily M., Duke University
Kopylova, Maya G., University of British Columbia
Koteas, G. Christopher, Norwich University
Kreiger, William (Bill), York College of Pennsylvania
Kurum, Sevcan, Firat University
Kyle, Philip R., New Mexico Institute of Mining and Technology
Kysar Mattietti, Giuseppina, George Mason University
Lackey, Jade Star, Pomona College
Landenberger, Bill, University of Newcastle
Lange, Rebecca A., University of Michigan
Le Roux, Veronique, Woods Hole Oceanographic Institution
Leake, Bernard E., Cardiff University
Leeman, William P., Rice University
Lehnert, Kerstin, Columbia University
Lesher, Charles E., University of California, Davis
Levy, Schon S., Los Alamos National Laboratory
Lidiak, Edward G., University of Pittsburgh
Lindline, Jennifer, New Mexico Highlands University
Luth, Robert W., University of Alberta
Lynn, Kendra J., University of Delaware
Lytwyn, Jennifer N., University of Houston
MacDonald, James H., Florida Gulf Coast University
Maclennan, John, University of Cambridge
Mahood, Gail A., Stanford University
Manduca, Cathryn A., Carleton College
Marsh, Julian S., Rhodes University
Mattioli, Glen, University of Texas, Arlington
Matty, David J., Weber State University
Mayborn, Kyle R., Western Illinois University
McCanta, Molly, University of Tennessee, Knoxville
McClellan, Elizabeth, Radford University
McMillan, Nancy J., New Mexico State University, Las Cruces
Medaris, Jr., Levi G., University of Wisconsin, Madison
Memeti, Valbone, California State University, Fullerton
Mertzman, Stanley A., Franklin and Marshall College
Michael, Peter J., University of Tulsa
Miller, Calvin F., Vanderbilt University
Miller, James D., University of Minnesota Duluth
Miller, Jonathan S., San Jose State University
Mills, James G., DePauw University
Misra, Saumitra, University of KwaZulu-Natal
Mitchell, Roger H., Lakehead University
Moayyed, Mohsen -., University of Tabriz
Morgan, Daniel, University of Leeds
Morse, Stearns A., University of Massachusetts, Amherst
MOYEN, Jean-François, Université Jean Monnet, Saint-Etienne
Mungall, James E., Carleton University
Mustart, David A., San Francisco State University
Myers, James D., University of Wyoming
Nabelek, Peter I., University of Missouri
Nash, Barbara P., University of Utah
Naslund, H. Richard, Binghamton University
Naumann, Terry R., University of Alaska, Anchorage
Neal, Clive R., University of Notre Dame
Nelson, Stephen A., Tulane University
Nelson, Wendy, Towson University
Nicholls, James W., University of Calgary
Nicholson, Kirsten N., Ball State University
Nicolaysen, Kirsten P., Whitman College
Nielsen, Roger L., Oregon State University
Niu, Yaoling, Durham University
Ntsaluba, Bantubonke I., Rhodes University
NUDE, Prosper M., University of Ghana
O'Neal, Matt, California Geological Survey
Orejana, David, Univ Complutense de Madrid
Ouimette, Mark A., Hardin-Simmons University
Page, Philippe, Universite du Quebec a Chicoutimi
Panter, Kurt S., Bowling Green State University
Parker, Don, Wayland Baptist University
Parker, Don F., Baylor University
Parlak, Osman, Cukurova Universitesi
Patino-Douce, Marta, University of Georgia
Peate, David W., University of Iowa
Pérez-Soba, Cecilia, Univ Complutense de Madrid
Perez-Venzor, Jose A., Univ Autonoma de Baja California Sur
Perfit, Michael R., University of Florida
Petrinec, Zorica, University of Zagreb
Philpotts, Anthony R., University of Connecticut
Polat, Ali, University of Windsor
Potter, Katherine E., Utah State University
Price, Jonathan D., Midwestern State University
Puffer, John H., Rutgers, The State University of New Jersey, Newark
Puziewicz, Jacek, University of Wroclaw
Raia, Federica, City College (CUNY)
Ratajeski, Kent, University of Kentucky
Reagan, Mark K., University of Iowa
Reavy, John, University College Cork
Reid, Arch M., University of Houston
Reidel, Stephen P., Washington State University
Reyes-Cortes, Manuel, Univ Autonoma de Chihuahua
Roden, Michael F., University of Georgia
Roelofse, Frederick, University of the Free State
Rooney, Tyrone, Michigan State University
Ross, Martin E., Northeastern University
Ruprecht, Philipp P., University of Nevada, Reno
Sarrionandia, Fernando, University of the Basque Country UPV/EHU
Saunders, Andy D., Leicester University
Schmidt, Mariek, Brock University
Schrader, Christian M., SUNY Potsdam
Schulze, Daniel J., University of Toronto
Schwab, Brandon E., Western Carolina University
Schwartz, Joshua J., California State University, Northridge
Scoates, James S., University of British Columbia
Seaman, Sheila J., University of Massachusetts, Amherst
Seeger, Cheryl M., Missouri Dept of Natural Resources
Sen, Gautam, Florida International University
Shaw, Cliff S., University of New Brunswick
Shearer, Jr., Charles K., University of New Mexico
Shervais, John W., Utah State University
Shuster, Robert D., University of Nebraska, Omaha
Sigurdson, David, California State University, Dominguez Hills
Silva-Mora, Luis, Univ Nacional Autonoma de Mexico
Sinton, John M., University of Hawai'i, Manoa
Sirbescu, Mona, Central Michigan University

Size, William B., Emory University
Sjoblom, Megan, Brigham Young University - Idaho
Smedes, Harry W., Southern Oregon University
Smith, Diane R., Trinity University
Smith, Douglas, University of Texas, Austin
Smith, Eugene I., University of Nevada, Las Vegas
Smith, Matthew C., University of Florida
Smith, Terence E., University of Windsor
Somarin, Alireza, Brandon University
Spera, Frank J., University of California, Santa Barbara
Springer, Robert K., Brandon University
Stachel, Thomas, University of Alberta
Stearns, Michael, Utah Valley University
Stern, Charles R., University of Colorado
Stewart, Michael A., University of Illinois, Urbana-Champaign
Stork, Allen L., Western Colorado University
Stormer, Jr., John C., Rice University
Streck, Martin J., Portland State University
Stull, Robert J., California State University, Los Angeles
Swanson , Sam , University of Georgia
Szymanski, David, Bentley University
Tacinelli, John C., Rochester Community & Technical College
Taib, Nur Iskandar, University of Malaya
Templeton, Jeffrey H., Western Oregon University
Tepley, III, Frank J., Oregon State University
Tepper, Jeffrey H., University of Puget Sound
Thakurta, Joyashish, Western Michigan University
Thomas, Jay, Syracuse University
Till, Christy, Arizona State University
Turner, Stephen, University of Massachusetts, Amherst
Ural, Melek, Firat University
Urbanczyk, Kevin, Sul Ross State University
Van Tongeren, Jill A., Rutgers, The State University of New Jersey
Vance, Joseph A., University of Washington
Vance, Robert K., Georgia Southern University
Vander Auwera, Jacqueline, Universite de Liege
VanTongeren, Jill, Tufts University
Vetter, Scott K., Centenary College of Louisiana
Viegas, Anthony V., Goa University
Villaseca, Carlos, Univ Complutense de Madrid
von der Handt, Anette, University of Minnesota, Twin Cities
Wadsworth, William B., Whittier College
Walker, Barry , Portland State University
Walowski, Kristina J., Middlebury College
Walter , Michael , University of Bristol
Wanless, Dorsey, Boise State University
Warren, Richard G., Los Alamos National Laboratory
Webster, John R., Minot State University
Wehner, Peter J., Austin Community College District
Weiblen, Paul W., University of Minnesota, Twin Cities
Weiland, Thomas J., Georgia Southwestern State University
Wendlandt, Richard F., Colorado School of Mines
Wenner, Jennifer M., University of Wisconsin, Oshkosh
Whattam, Scott A., Korea University
White, Craig M., Boise State University
White, John C., Eastern Kentucky University
Whitney, James A., University of Georgia
Whittington, Alan, University of Missouri
Wiese, Katryn, City College of San Francisco
Wirth, Karl R., Macalester College
Wittke, James, Northern Arizona University
Wobus, Reinhard A., Williams College
Wolf, Michael B., Augustana College
Wolff, John A., Washington State University
Wolff, John A., Washington State University
Worcester, Peter A., Hanover College
Wulff, Andrew H., Whittier College
Yogodzinkski, Gene M., University of South Carolina
Young, Davis A., Calvin College
Zamzow, Craig E., Clarion University
Zieg, Michael J., Slippery Rock University

Metamorphic Petrology

Abati, Jacobo, Univ Complutense de Madrid
Allen, Gary C., University of New Orleans
Appleyard, Edward C., University of Waterloo
Apraiz, Arturo, University of the Basque Country UPV/EHU
Arenas, Ricardo, Univ Complutense de Madrid
Ashton, Kenneth E., University of Regina
Baldwin, Julia, University of Montana
Bartoli, Omar, Università degli Studi di Padova
Bauer, Paul W., New Mexico Institute of Mining and Technology
Bebout, Gray E., Lehigh University
Berg, Christopher A., Orange Coast College
Berg, Christopher A., University of West Georgia
Berman, Robert, Carleton University
Blake, David E., University of North Carolina, Wilmington
Block, Amy, University of Minnesota
Brouwer, Fraukje M., Vrije Universiteit Amsterdam
Brown, Edwin H., Western Washington University
Burnley, Pamela C., University of Nevada, Las Vegas
Burwash, Ronald A., University of Alberta
Caddick, Mark, Virginia Polytechnic Institute & State University
Cardace, Dawn, University of Rhode Island
Carillo-Chavez, Alejandro J., Univ Autonoma de Baja California Sur
Carlson, William D., University of Texas, Austin
Castiñeiras, Pedro, Univ Complutense de Madrid
Castro, Adrian, Wellesley College
Cesare, Bernardo, Università degli Studi di Padova
Chacko, Thomas, University of Alberta
Clark, Chris, Curtin University
Clarke, Geoffrey L., University of Sydney
Cooper, Alan F., University of Otago
Costin, Gelu, Rhodes University
Cruz-Uribe, Alicia M., University of Maine
Daniel, Christopher G., Bucknell University
Davidson, Cameron, Carleton College
Dawson, Jane P., Iowa State University of Science & Technology
DeAngelis, Michael T., University of Arkansas at Little Rock
DesOrmeau, Joel, University of Nevada, Reno
Devore, George W., Florida State University
Diener, Johann, University of Cape Town
Dietsch, Craig, University of Cincinnati
Dipple, Gregory M., University of British Columbia
dos Santos, Telmo B., Unive de Lisboa
Droop, Giles, University of Manchester
Duke, Edward F., South Dakota School of Mines & Technology
Dunn, Steven R., Mount Holyoke College
Dymek, Robert F., Washington University in St. Louis
Eckert, James O., Yale University
El Shazly, Aley, Marshall University
Elias-Herrera, Mariano, Univ Nacional Autonoma de Mexico
Evans, Bernard W., University of Washington
Evans, Katy, Curtin University
Faryad, Shah Wali, Charles University
Fawcett, J. J., University of Toronto
Fitzsimons, Ian, Curtin University
Fletcher, John, Ctr de Invest Científica y de Ed Superior de Ensenada
Flores, Kennet, Brooklyn College (CUNY)
Foster Jr., Charles T., University of Iowa
Frost, B. Ronald, University of Wyoming
Ghent, Edward D., University of Calgary
Giaramita, Mario J., California State University, Stanislaus
Gillis, Kathryn, University of Victoria
Goodge, John W., University of Minnesota Duluth
Gordon, Stacia M., University of Nevada, Reno
Grew, Edward S., University of Maine
Grew, Priscilla C., University of Nebraska, Lincoln
Grover, Timothy W., University of Northern Colorado
Grover, Timothy W., Castleton University
Guevara, Victor E., Amherst College
Guevara, Victor, Skidmore College
Hacker, Bradley R., University of California, Santa Barbara
Hajialioghli, Robab, University of Tabriz
Halama, Ralf, Keele University
Hallett, Benjamin W., University of Wisconsin, Oshkosh
Henry, Darrell J., Louisiana State University
Hepburn, J. Christopher, Boston College
Hickmott, Donald D., Los Alamos National Laboratory
Hoisch, Thomas D., Northern Arizona University
Holdaway, Michael J., Southern Methodist University
Holland, Tim, University of Cambridge

Hollister, Lincoln S., Princeton University
Horvath, Peter, University of the Witwatersrand
Horvath, Peter, Rhodes University
Huizenga, Jan Marten, James Cook University
Iancu, Ovidiu G., Alexandru Ioan Cuza
Indares, Aphrodite D., Memorial University of Newfoundland
James, Richard, Laurentian University, Sudbury
Johnson, Eric L., Hartwick College
Johnson, Tim, Curtin University
Jones, Jon W., University of Calgary
Kamber, Balz, Queensland University of Technology
Kays, Marvin A., University of Oregon
Kerrick, Derrill M., Pennsylvania State University, University Park
Labotka, Theodore C., University of Tennessee, Knoxville
Laird, Jo, University of New Hampshire
Lamb, Will, Texas A&M University
Law, Eric W., Muskingum University
Leech, Mary L., San Francisco State University
Liou, Juhn G., Stanford University
Lori, Lisa, Missouri Dept of Natural Resources
Maboko, Makenya A., University of Dar es Salaam
Magloughlin, Jerry F., Colorado State University
Mahan, Kevin H., University of Colorado
Manecan, Teodosia, Hunter College (CUNY)
Manon, Matthew R., Union College
Martínez Fernández, Francisco, Universitat Autonoma de Barcelona
Mattinson, Chris, Central Washington University
Mavimbela, Philani, University of KwaZulu-Natal
McLelland, James, Colgate University
Menold, Carrie A., Albion College
Metcalf, Rodney V., University of Nevada, Las Vegas
Metzger, Ellen P., San Jose State University
Moazzen, Mohssen -., University of Tabriz
Mogk, David W., Montana State University
Morton, Douglas M., University of California, Riverside
Mulcahy, Sean R., Western Washington University
Nishiyama, Tadao, Kumamoto University
Ortega-Gutierrez, Fernando, Univ Nacional Autonoma de Mexico
Page, F Zeb, Oberlin College
Panish, Peter T., University of Massachusetts, Amherst
Parkinson, Christopher D., University of New Orleans
Pattison, David R., University of Calgary
Peck, William H., Colgate University
Penniston-Dorland, Sarah, University of Maryland
Perkins, III, Dexter, University of North Dakota
Pervunina, Aelita, Institute of Geology (Karelia, Russia)
Plummer, Charles C., Sacramento State University
Potel, Sébastien, Institut Polytechnique LaSalle Beauvais (ex-IGAL)
Raeside, Robert P., Acadia University
Rahaman, M. A., Obafemi Awolowo University
Reche Estrada, Joan, Universitat Autonoma de Barcelona
Rietmeijer, Frans J., University of New Mexico
Rivers, Toby C. J. S., Memorial University of Newfoundland
Roberts, Frank, Montgomery County Community College
Roselle, Gregory T., Brigham Young University - Idaho
Rumble, III, Douglas, Carnegie Institution for Science
Sánchez, Sonia, Univ Complutense de Madrid
Sawyer, Edward W., Universite du Quebec a Chicoutimi
Schiffman, Peter, University of California, Davis
Scott, James M., University of Otago
Selverstone, Jane E., University of New Mexico
Severson, Allison, University of Minnesota
Sisson, Virginia, University of Houston
Sommer , Holgar, University of Namibia
Sorensen, Sorena S., Smithsonian Inst/Nat Mus of Nat History
Spear, Frank S., Rensselaer Polytechnic Institute
Spiess, Richard, Università degli Studi di Padova
Spray, John G., University of New Brunswick
Srogi, LeeAnn, West Chester University
Staples, Reid, Douglas College
Stevens, Liane M., Stephen F. Austin State University
Stoddard, Edward F., North Carolina State University
Storey, Craig D., University of Portsmouth
Stout, James H., University of Minnesota, Twin Cities
Stowell, Harold H., University of Alabama
Swapp, Susan M., University of Wyoming
Thomson, Jennifer A., Eastern Washington University
Tinkham, Doug, Laurentian University, Sudbury
Toraman, Erkan, Salem State University
Turnock, Allan C., University of Manitoba
Walsh, Emily O., University of Iowa
Walsh, Emily O., Cornell College
Waters, Dave, University of Oxford
Weber, Bodo, Ctr de Invest Científica y de Ed Superior de Ensenada
Wheeler, John, University of Liverpool
Whitney, Donna L., University of Minnesota, Twin Cities
Wilks, Maureen, New Mexico Institute of Mining and Technology
Wintsch, Robert P., Indiana University, Bloomington
Woodland, Bertram G., Field Museum of Natural History
Zhai, Xiaoming, College of Lake County

Sedimentary Petrology

Adekola, S. A., Obafemi Awolowo University
Al-Aasm, Ihsan S., University of Windsor
Alberstadt, Leonard P., Vanderbilt University
Alonso, Ana María, Univ Complutense de Madrid
Arribas, Eugenia, Univ Complutense de Madrid
Arribas, José, Univ Complutense de Madrid
Azerêdo, Ana , Unive de Lisboa
Babek, Ondrej, Masaryk University
Basu, Abhijit, Indiana University, Bloomington
Benson, Donald J., University of Alabama
Bertog, Janet, Northern Kentucky University
Bertok, Carlo, Università di Torino
Boulvain, Frederic P., Universite de Liege
Brengman, Latisha A., University of Minnesota Duluth
Bruner, Katherine R., West Virginia University
Budd, David A., University of Colorado
Chafetz, Henry S., University of Houston
Channing, Alan, University of Wales
Choh, Suk-Joo, Korea University
Corcoran, Patricia, Western University
Cousineau, Pierre, Universite du Quebec a Chicoutimi
dela Pierre, Francesco, Università di Torino
Dockal, James A., University of North Carolina, Wilmington
Donovan, R N., Texas Christian University
Dutton, Shirley P., University of Texas at Austin, Jackson School of Geosciences
Elmore, R. Douglas, University of Oklahoma
Fitzgerald, David, Saint Mary's University
Folk, Robert L., University of Texas, Austin
Franseen, Evan K., University of Kansas
Galli-Olivier, Carlos A., Univ Autonoma de Baja California Sur
Gómez Gras, David, Universitat Autonoma de Barcelona
Griffing, David H., Hartwick College
Grigsby, Jeffry D., Ball State University
Hampson, Gary , Imperial College
Horton, Jr., Robert A., California State University, Bakersfield
Humphrey, John D., King Fahd University of Petroleum and Minerals
James, Noel P., Queen's University
Kaczmarek, Stephen E., Western Michigan University
Kerans, Charles, University of Texas at Austin, Jackson School of Geosciences
Khan, Mohammad Wahdat Y., Pt. Ravishankar Shukla University
Khandaker, Nazrul I., York College (CUNY)
Kirkland, Brenda L., Mississippi State University
Laury, Robert L., Southern Methodist University
Liutkus-Pierce, Cynthia M., Appalachian State University
Lowe, Donald R., Stanford University
Lumsden, David N., University of Memphis
Mackey, Tyler, University of New Mexico
Martin, Arturo, Ctr de Invest Científica y de Ed Superior de Ensenada
Martire, Luca, Università di Torino
McBride, Earle F., University of Texas, Austin
McKean , Rebecca, Saint Norbert College
McKnight, Brian K., University of Wisconsin, Oshkosh
Measures, Elizabeth A., Sul Ross State University
Meinhold, Guido, Keele University
Melim, Leslie A., Western Illinois University
Milliken, Kitty L., University of Texas, Austin
Montañez, Isabel P., University of California, Davis
Moore, Bruce R., University of Kentucky
Moshier, Stephen O., Wheaton College
Muntean, Thomas, Adrian College

Nothdurft, Luke, Queensland University of Technology
Pedone, Vicki A., California State University, Northridge
Perkins, Ronald D., Duke University
Portner, Ryan, San Jose State University
Richardson, Darlene S., Indiana University of Pennsylvania
Roman, Aubrecht, Comenius University in Bratislava
Rossi, Carlos, Univ Complutense de Madrid
Ruppel, Stephen C., Univ of Texas at Austin, Jackson Sch of Geosciences
Saja, David, Cleveland Museum of Natural History
Sanchez Roman, Monica, Vrije Universiteit Amsterdam
Sandberg, Philip A., University of Illinois, Urbana-Champaign
Sanz, Esther, Univ Complutense de Madrid
Savrda, Charles E., Auburn University
Schacht, Ulrike, University of Adelaide
Scholle, Peter, New Mexico Institute of Mining and Technology
Schreiber, B. Charlotte, Queens College (CUNY)
Schwab, Frederick L., Washington & Lee University
Siegrist, jr, Henry G., University of Guam
Stefani, Cristina, Università degli Studi di Padova
Sutterlin, Peter G., Wichita State University
Suttner, Lee J., Indiana University, Bloomington
Sutton, Sally J., Colorado State University
Teixeira, Bernardo, University of Louisiana at Lafayette
Textoris, Daniel A., University of North Carolina, Chapel Hill
Thayer, Paul A., University of North Carolina, Wilmington
Uddin, Ashraf, Auburn University
Varas, María Josefa, Univ Complutense de Madrid
Vice, Mari A., University of Wisconsin, Platteville
Videtich, Patricia E., Grand Valley State University
Walker, Theodore R., University of Colorado
Young, Harvey R., Brandon University
Zeigler, E. Lynn, Georgia State Univ, Perimeter College, Clarkston Campus

Sedimentology

Abbott, Mark B., University of Pittsburgh
Abbott, Patrick L., San Diego State University
Abdullatif, Osman, King Fahd University of Petroleum and Minerals
Adams, Robert W., SUNY, The College at Brockport
Alexander, Jan, University of East Anglia
Alexander, Jane L., College of Staten Island/CUNY
Algeo, Thomas J., University of Cincinnati
Allison, Mead A., Tulane University
Alvarez-Arellano, Alejandro, Univ Autonoma de Baja California Sur
Ambrose, William A., Univ of Texas at Austin, Jackson Sch of Geosciences
Amos, Kathryn, University of Adelaide
Anani, Chris Y., University of Ghana
Andersen, David W., San Jose State University
Anderson, Thomas B., Sonoma State University
Anderson-Folnagy, Heidi, University of Montana Western
Anfinson, Owen, Sonoma State University
Anglen, Jeff, Fresno State University
Arnott, R. William C., University of Ottawa
Ashley, Gail M., Rutgers, The State University of New Jersey
Asiedu, Daniel K., University of Ghana
Askari, Zohreh, Illinois State Geological Survey
Austin, Steve A., Cedarville University
Autin, Whitney J., SUNY, The College at Brockport
Bahlburg, Heinrich, Universitaet Muenster
Balog-Szabo, Anna, Virginia Western Community College
Barbeau, Jr., David, University of South Carolina
Barham, Milo, Curtin University
Barhurst, James, University of Newcastle Upon Tyne
Bartley, Julie K., Gustavus Adolphus College
Bassett, Kari N., University of Canterbury
Beck, Catherine C., Hamilton College
Behl, Richard J., California State University, Long Beach
Bekker, Andrey, University of California, Riverside
Benito, María Isabel, Univ Complutense de Madrid
Bergmann, Kristin, Massachusetts Institute of Technology
Bershaw, John T., Portland State University
Best, James L., University of Illinois, Urbana-Champaign
Bestland, Erick, Flinders University
Bhattacharya, Janok, University of Houston
Birgenheier, Lauren, University of Utah
Bjornstad, Bruce N., Pacific Northwest National Laboratory
Blake, Bascombe (Mitch), West Virginia University
Blum, Michael D., University of Kansas
Bodenbender, Brian E., Hope College
Boothroyd, Jon C., University of Rhode Island
Bordy, Emese M., University of Cape Town
Borowski, Walter S., Eastern Kentucky University
Bourgeois, Joanne (Jody), University of Washington
Bowen, Brenda , University of Utah
Brand, Brittany, Boise State University
Brandon, Christine M., Bridgewater State University
Breda, Anna, Università degli Studi di Padova
Breyer, John, Texas Christian University
Bristow, Charlie, Birkbeck College
Broda, James E., Woods Hole Oceanographic Institution
Brunt, Rufus, University of Manchester
Burns, Diane M., Eastern Illinois University
Buyce, M. Raymond, Mercyhurst University
Caputo, Mario V., San Diego State University
Carrapa, Barbara, University of Arizona
Carroll, Alan R., University of Wisconsin, Madison
Cartwright, Joe, University of Oxford
Caruthers, Andrew, Western Michigan University
Cassel, Elizabeth J., University of Idaho
Castle, James W., Clemson University
Catuneanu, Octavian, University of Alberta
Caudill, Michael R., Hocking College
Celik, Hasan, Firat University
Chan, Marjorie A., University of Utah
Cheel, Richard J., Brock University
Chiarella, Domenico, Royal Holloway University of London
Chow, Nancy, University of Manitoba
Chowns, Timothy M., University of West Georgia
Christie-Blick, Nicholas, Columbia University
Clarke, Stu, Keele University
Clift, Peter, Louisiana State University
Coch, Nicholas K., Queens College (CUNY)
Coe, Angela L., Open University
Colburn, Ivan P., California State University, Los Angeles
Cole, Rex D., Colorado Mesa University
Connely, Melissa, Casper College
Conrad, Susan H., Dutchess Community College
Cope, Tim D., DePauw University
Corsetti, Frank A., University of Southern California
Cowan, Clinton A., Carleton College
Cowan, Ellen A., Appalachian State University
Cox, Ronadh, Williams College
Crowley, Stephen, University of Liverpool
Cullen, James L., Salem State University
Cuneen, Jane, Curtin University
Currie, Brian S., Miami University
Dade, William B., Dartmouth College
Dalrymple, Robert W., Queen's University
Dansereau, Pauline, Universite Laval
Davatzes, Alexandra K., Temple University
Davies, Neil, University of Cambridge
Davies, Sarah, Leicester University
de la Horra, Raúl, Univ Complutense de Madrid
de Wet, Carol B., Franklin and Marshall College
Dehler, Carol M., Utah State University
Deibert, Jack, Austin Peay State University
Demicco, Robert V., Binghamton University
Deocampo, Daniel M., Georgia State University
Desrochers, Andre, University of Ottawa
Diemer, John A., University of North Carolina, Charlotte
Dix, George R., Carleton University
Dominic, David F., Wright State University
Donald, Roberta, Simon Fraser University
Donaldson, J. Allan, Carleton University
Dravis, Jeffrey J., Rice University
Droxler, Andre W., Rice University
Dumas, Simone, University of Ottawa
Dunagan, Stan P., University of Tennessee, Martin
Dutta, Prodip K., Indiana State University
Dutton, Shirley P., University of Texas, Austin
Dwyer, Gary S., Duke University
Eberth, David A., Royal Tyrrell Museum of Palaeontology
Edmonds, Douglas A., Indiana University, Bloomington

Edwards, Cole T., Appalachian State University
Egenhoff, Sven O., Colorado State University
Elliott, Jr., William S., University of Southern Indiana
Elrick, Maya, University of New Mexico
Enos, Paul, University of Kansas
Eriksson, Kenneth A., Virginia Polytechnic Institute & State University
Ethridge, Frank G., Colorado State University
Evans, James E., Bowling Green State University
Eyles, Carolyn H., McMaster University
Fagel, Nathalie, Universite de Liege
Fairchild, Ian, University of Birmingham
Fan, Majie, University of Texas, Arlington
Farkas, Steven, Central Washington University
Farrell, Kathleen M., N.C. Department of Environmental Quality
Fedo, Christopher, University of Tennessee, Knoxville
Fedorchuk, Nicholas D., Southern Connecticut State University
Fielding, Christopher R., University of Nebraska, Lincoln
Fillmore, Robert P., Western Colorado University
Finkenbinder, Matthew S., Wilkes University
Finzel, Emily, University of Iowa
Fischer, Alfred G., University of Southern California
Fisher, William L., University of Texas, Austin
Flaig, Peter P., University of Texas, Austin
Fletcher, Charles H., University of Hawai'i, Manoa
Fouke, Bruce W., University of Illinois, Urbana-Champaign
Fox, James E., South Dakota School of Mines & Technology
Fralick, Philip W., Lakehead University
Frank, Tracy D., University of Nebraska, Lincoln
Franseen, Evan K., University of Kansas
Fregenal, María Antonia, Univ Complutense de Madrid
Freile, Deborah, New Jersey City University
Freitas, Maria d., Unive de Lisboa
Fu, Qilong, University of Texas at Austin, Jackson School of Geosciences
Gabel, Sharon, Lee College
Gaines, Robert R., Pomona College
Gall, Quentin, University of Ottawa
Galli, Kenneth G., Boston College
Galloway, William E., University of Texas, Austin
Galloway, William E., University of Texas, Austin
Gani, M. Royhan, Western Kentucky University
Gannaway Dalton, Evelyn, Utah State University
Garrison, Robert E., University of California, Santa Cruz
Garzione, Carmala N., University of Rochester
Gaylord, David R., Washington State University
Gerhard, Lee C., University of Kansas
Ghinassi, Massimiliano, Università degli Studi di Padova
Gianniny, Gary, Fort Lewis College
Gibling, Martin R., Dalhousie University
Gilleaudeau, Geoff, George Mason University
Gillespie, Robb, Western Michigan University
Gilley, Brett H., University of British Columbia
Glumac, Bosiljka, Smith College
Goff, James, University of New South Wales
Goldstein, Robert H., University of Kansas
Goodbred, Jr., Steven L., Vanderbilt University
Gore, Pamela J. W., Georgia State Univ, Perimeter College, Clarkston Campus
Gore, Pamela J. W., Emory University
Gorte, Mary C., Delta College
Gotz, Annette, Rhodes University
Goudge, Timothy, University of Texas, Austin
Gough, Amy, Royal Holloway University of London
Grammer, Michael, Oklahoma State University
Greb, Stephen F., University of Kentucky
Greene, Todd, California State University, Chico
Greer, Lisa, Washington & Lee University
Gregg, Jay M., Oklahoma State University
Gregor, C. B., Wright State University
Grimm, Kurt A., University of British Columbia
Grippo, Alessandro, Santa Monica College
Grothe, Pamela, University of Mary Washington
Grotzinger, John P., California Institute of Technology
Grove, Karen, San Francisco State University
Guo, Junhua, California State University, Bakersfield
Gupta, Sanjeev, Imperial College
Hajek, Elizabeth, Pennsylvania State University, University Park
Hall, Mary Jo, Rider University
Halverson, Galen, McGill University
Hamilton, Sally, Heriot-Watt University
Hampton, Brian A., New Mexico State University, Las Cruces
Harris, Clay D., Middle Tennessee State University
Harris, Mark T., University of Wisconsin, Milwaukee
Harris, Nicholas, University of Alberta
Harrison, III, William B., Western Michigan University
Hasselbo, Stephen, Exeter University
Havholm, Karen G., University of Wisconsin, Eau Claire
Hayes, Miles O., University of New Orleans
Haywick, Douglas W., University of South Alabama
Hazel, Jr., Joseph E., Northern Arizona University
Heinrich, Paul V., Louisiana State University
Henderson, Miles, University of Texas Permian Basin
Hendrix, Marc S., University of Montana
Hernandez Molina, F. J., Royal Holloway University of London
Herrero, María Josefa, Univ Complutense de Madrid
Hess-Tanguay, Lillian, Long Island University, C.W. Post Campus
Hesse, Reinhard, McGill University
Heubeck, Christoph, Friedrich-Schiller-University Jena
Hiatt, Eric E., University of Wisconsin, Oshkosh
Hickson, Thomas A., University of Saint Thomas
Higgins, Sean M., Columbia University
Hilbert-Wolf, Hannah L., James Cook University
Hill, Paul S., Dalhousie University
Hill, Philip R., University of Victoria
Hinderer, Matthias, Technische Universitaet Darmstadt
Hiscott, Richard N., Memorial University of Newfoundland
Hobbs, Kevin, New Mexico Institute of Mining and Technology
Hodgetts, David, University of Manchester
Hoey, Trevor, University of Glasgow
Holbrook, John M., Texas Christian University
Hollis, Cathy, University of Manchester
Holmes, Mary Anne, University of Nebraska, Lincoln
Horton, Brian, University of Texas, Austin
Houston, William (Bill), Lake Superior State University
Hovorka, Susan D., Univ of Texas at Austin, Jackson Sch of Geosciences
Howard, Jeffrey L., Wayne State University
Howell, John, University of Aberdeen
Hubbard, Dennis K., Oberlin College
Hubbard, Stephen M., University of Calgary
Huntoon, Jacqueline E., Michigan Technological University
Hurtgen, Matthew T., Northwestern University
Husinec, Antun, St. Lawrence University
Hussin, Azhar Hj, University of Malaya
Ielpi, Alessandro, Laurentian University, Sudbury
Ingersoll, Raymond V., University of California, Los Angeles
Isbell, John L., University of Wisconsin, Milwaukee
Jackson, Chester W., Georgia Southern University
Jackson, William T., University of South Alabama
Jaeger, John M., University of Florida
Janson, Xavier, University of Texas, Austin
Jiang, Ganqing, University of Nevada, Las Vegas
Jinnah, Zubair A., University of the Witwatersrand
Joeckel, Matt, Unversity of Nebraska, Lincoln
John, Cedric, Imperial College
Johnson, Cari, University of Utah
Johnson, Joel P., University of Texas, Austin
Jones, David S., Amherst College
Jones, Lawrence S., Colorado Mesa University
Jones, Merren, University of Manchester
Jones, Stuart, Durham University
Jordan, William M., Millersville University
Kah, Linda, University of Tennessee, Knoxville
Kale, Makarand G., Savitribai Phule Pune University,
Kamola, Diane, University of Kansas
Kanfoush, Sharon L., Utica College
Kendall, Christopher G., University of South Carolina
Kent, Donald M., University of Regina
Kerans, Charles, University of Texas, Austin
Kerr, Dennis R., University of Tulsa
Kidwell, Susan M., University of Chicago
Kilibarda, Zoran, Indiana University Northwest
Kinvig, Helen, University of Liverpool
Koc Tasgin, Calibe, Firat University
Kocurek, Gary A., University of Texas, Austin

Kocurko, John, Midwestern State University
Kokelaar, Peter, University of Liverpool
Koning, Daniel, New Mexico Institute of Mining and Technology
Kopaska-Merkel, David C., Geological Survey of Alabama
Korus, Jesse, University of Nebraska, Lincoln
Kotha, Mahender, Goa University
Kovac, Michal, Comenius University in Bratislava
Kovaèiæ, Marijan, University of Zagreb
Krantz, David E., University of Toledo
Kraus, Mary J., University of Colorado
Krause, Federico F., University of Calgary
Krissek, Lawrence A., Ohio State University
Kurtanjek, Dražen, University of Zagreb
Langford, Richard P., University of Texas, El Paso
Last, William M., University of Manitoba
Lavoie, Denis, Universite du Quebec
Leary, Ryan, New Mexico Institute of Mining and Technology
Leckie, Dale A., Carleton University
LeFever, Richard D., University of North Dakota
Lehman, Thomas M., Texas Tech University
Leier, Andrew L., University of South Carolina
Leithold, Elana L., North Carolina State University
Leorri, Eduardo, East Carolina University
Levin, Naomi, Johns Hopkins University
Levy, Laura B., Humboldt State University
Licht, Alexis, University of Washington
Liddell, W. David, Utah State University
Link, Paul K., Idaho State University
Linn, Anne M., National Academies of Sciences, Engineering, and Medicine
Linol, Bastien, Nelson Mandela Metropolitan University
Little, William W., Brigham Young University - Idaho
Lloyd, Graeme, University of Oxford
Lock, Brian E., University of Louisiana at Lafayette
Long, Darrel, Laurentian University, Sudbury
Loope, David B., University of Nebraska, Lincoln
Loucks, Robert G., University of Texas, Austin
Ludvigson, Gregory A., University of Kansas
Lynds, Ranie, University of Wyoming
Mac Eachern, James A., Simon Fraser University
MacCarthy, Ivor, University College Cork
Macdonald, R. Heather, William & Mary
MacInnes, Breanyn, Central Washington University
Macintyre, Ian G., Smithsonian Institution / National Museum of Natural History
MacLachlan, John, McMaster University
Mahoney, J. Brian, University of Wisconsin, Eau Claire
Maju-Oyovwikowhe, Efetobore G., University of Benin
Malpica-Cruz, Victor M., Univ Nacional Autonoma de Mexico
Manker, John P., Georgia Southwestern State University
Mankiewicz, Carol, Beloit College
Manning-Berg, Ashley, University of Tennessee, Chattanooga
Manos, Constantine, SUNY, New Paltz
Marjanac, Tihomir, University of Zagreb
Marsaglia, Kathleen M., California State University, Northridge
Marshall, Madeline, Albion College
Martini, I. Peter, University of Guelph
Martino, Ronald L., Marshall University
Marzolf, John E., Southern Illinois University Carbondale
Matsuda, Hiroki, Kumamoto University
McCaffrey, Bill, University of Leeds
McCarthy, Paul, University of Alaska, Fairbanks
McCrone, Alistair W., Humboldt State University
McDowell, Ronald, West Virginia University
McElroy, Brandon, University of Wyoming
McNeill, Donald F., University of Miami
Mehrtens, Charlotte J., University of Vermont
Melas, Faye, Hunter College (CUNY)
Merrill, Robert D., Fresno State University
Meyers, Jamie A., Winona State University
Miall, Andrew D., University of Toronto
Miclaus, Crina G., Alexandru Ioan Cuza
Middleton, Larry T., Northern Arizona University
Milligan, Timothy, Dalhousie University
Minter, Nicholas, University of Portsmouth
Minzoni, Rebecca T., University of Alabama
Mitchell, Simon F., University of the West Indies Mona Campus
Mohrig, David, University of Texas, Austin
Monecke, Katrin, Wellesley College
Moskalski, Susanne, Stockton University
Mount, Jeffrey F., University of California, Davis
Mountney, Nigel, University of Leeds
Mozley, Peter S., New Mexico Institute of Mining and Technology
Mrinjek, Ervin, University of Zagreb
Munoz, Samuel, Northeastern University
Murray, Bryan P., California State Polytechnic University, Pomona
Myers, Jeffrey A., Western Oregon University
Myrow, Paul M., Colorado College
Nadon, Gregory C., Ohio University
Nalin, Ronald, Loma Linda University
Natalicchio, Marcello, Università di Torino
Neal, William J., Grand Valley State University
Nehyba, Slavomír, Masaryk University
Nelson, Bruce W., University of Virginia
Neuweiler, Fritz, Universite Laval
Nick, Kevin, Loma Linda University
Noffke, Nora K., Old Dominion University
O'Brien, John M., New Jersey City University
Oakley, Bryan A., University of Rhode Island
Oaks, Jr., Robert Q., Utah State University
OConnell, Suzanne B., Wesleyan University
Okunuwadje, Sunday E., University of Benin
Oliveira, Anabela R., Unive de Trás-os-Montes e Alto Douro
Oluwajana, Oladotun A., Federal University of Technology, Akure
Opeloye, Saka A., Federal University of Technology, Akure
Oppo, Davide, University of Louisiana at Lafayette
Ortiz, Joseph D., Kent State University
Paola, Christopher, University of Minnesota, Twin Cities
Pattison, Simon A., Brandon University
Peakall, Jeff, University of Leeds
Pearson, Eugene F., University of the Pacific
Peck, John A., University of Akron
Penman, Donald E., Utah State University
Perscio, Lyman, Mercyhurst University
Peters, Shanan, University of Wisconsin, Madison
Petersen, Morris S., Brigham Young University
Phillips, Andrew C., Illinois State Geological Survey
Pickering, Kevin, University College London
Pietras, Jeff, Binghamton University
Pikelj, Kristina, University of Zagreb
Piper, David, Dalhousie University
Platt, Brian F., University of Mississippi
Plink-Bjorklund, Piret, Colorado School of Mines
Plint, A G., Western University
Potter, Paul E., University of Cincinnati
Potter-McIntyre, Sally, Southern Illinois University Carbondale
Powell, Ross D., Northern Illinois University
Pratson, Lincoln F., Duke University
Preto, Nereo, Università degli Studi di Padova
Price, Greogry, University of Plymouth
Price, Jason R., Millersville University
Prins, Maarten A., Vrije Universiteit Amsterdam
Qing, Hairuo, University of Regina
Rainbird, R. R., Carleton University
Ramirez, Pedro C., California State University, Los Angeles
Ramsey, Kelvin W., University of Delaware
Rankey, Gene, University of Kansas
Read, J. Fred, Virginia Polytechnic Institute & State University
Reams, Max W., Olivet Nazarene University
Redfern, Jonathan, University of Manchester
Redmond, Brian T., Wilkes University
Rees, Margaret N., University of Nevada, Las Vegas
Reid, Pam, University of Miami
Reid, Steven K., Morehead State University
Reijmer, John, King Fahd University of Petroleum and Minerals
Remacha Grau, Eduard, Universitat Autonoma de Barcelona
Renaut, Robin W., University of Saskatchewan
Ridgway, Kenneth D., Purdue University
Rigo, Manuel, Università degli Studi di Padova
Rigsby, Catherine A., East Carolina University
Ritts, Malinda, University of Idaho
Roberts, Eric M., James Cook University
Roberts, Harry H., Louisiana State University
Robinson, Ruth, University of St. Andrews

Rogers, Raymond R., Macalester College
Romans, Brian W., Virginia Polytechnic Institute & State University
Runkel, Anthony, University of Minnesota, Twin Cities
Runkel, Anthony, University of Minnesota
Ruppel, Stephen C., University of Texas, Austin
Rygel, Michael C., SUNY Potsdam
Saltzman, Matthew R., Ohio State University
Sánchez, Yolanda, Univ Complutense de Madrid
Sawyer, J. F., South Dakota School of Mines & Technology
Saylor, Beverly Z., Case Western Reserve University
Scheingross, Joel S., University of Nevada, Reno
Schieber, Juergen, Indiana University, Bloomington
Schneiderman, Jill S., Vassar College
Scholz, Christopher A., Syracuse University
Schreiber, Charlotte, University of Washington
Schwartz, Robert K., Allegheny College
Schwimmer, Reed A., Rider University
Scott, Robert W., University of Tulsa
Self, Robert P., University of Tennessee, Martin
Seserman, Anca M., Alexandru Ioan Cuza
Shane, Tyrrell, National University of Ireland Galway
Shanmugam, Ganapathy, University of Tennessee, Knoxville
Shaw, John B., University of Arkansas, Fayetteville
Shea, James H., University of Wisconsin, Parkside
Shimer, Grant, Southern Utah University
Siewers, Fredrick D., Western Kentucky University
Simms, Alexander, University of California, Santa Barbara
Simonson, Bruce M., Oberlin College
Simpson, Edward L., Kutztown University of Pennsylvania
Simpson, Frank -., University of Windsor
Singer, Jill K., Buffalo State College
Singler, Charles R., Youngstown State University
Sirocko, Frank, Universität Mainz
Slingerland, Rudy L., Pennsylvania State University, University Park
Sloss, Craig, Queensland University of Technology
Smith, Jon, University of Kansas
Smith, Larry N., Montana Tech of the University of Montana
Smith, Michael E., Northern Arizona University
Smith, Norman D., University of Nebraska, Lincoln
Smith, Shane V., Youngstown State University
Smith-Engle, Jennifer M., Texas A&M University, Corpus Christi
Soreghan, Gerilyn S., University of Oklahoma
Soreghan, Michael J., University of Oklahoma
Soster, Frederick M., DePauw University
Southard, John B., Massachusetts Institute of Technology
Staub, James R., University of Montana
Steel, Ronald J., University of Texas, Austin
Steenberg, Julia, University of Minnesota
Steinen, Randolph P., Dept of Energy and Environmental Protection
Stoner, Joseph, Oregon State University
Strauss, Justin V., Dartmouth College
Sumner, Dawn Y., University of California, Davis
Sumner, Esther, University of Southampton
Surpless, Kathleen D., Trinity University
Swanson, Travis, Georgia Southern University
Sweet, Alisan C., Texas Tech University
Sweet, Dustin E., Texas Tech University
Swennen, Rudy, Katholieke Universiteit Leuven
Tamulonis, Kathryn L., Allegheny College
Teller, James T., University of Manitoba
Thomas, Robert C., University of Montana Western
Thomka, James R., SUNY, Plattsburgh
Thompson, Todd A., Indiana University
Thornburg, Jesse, Temple University
Thurow, Juergen, University College London
Totten, Matthew W., Kansas State University
Toullec, Renaud, Institut Polytechnique LaSalle Beauvais (ex-IGAL)
Trevino, Ramon H., Univ of Texas at Austin, Jackson Sch of Geosciences
Triplehorn, Donald M., University of Alaska, Fairbanks
Trofimovs, Jessica, Queensland University of Technology
Trop, Jeffrey M., Bucknell University
Törnqvist, Torbjörn E., Tulane University
Ulmer-Scholle, Dana, New Mexico Institute of Mining and Technology
Ulmer-Scholle, Dana S., New Mexico Institute of Mining and Technology
Underwood, Michael B., University of Missouri
Van Daele, Maarten, Ghent University
Van De Poll, Henk W., University of New Brunswick
van der Lubbe, Jeroen, Vrije Universiteit Amsterdam
Villegas, Monica B., Univ Nacional de Rio Cuarto
Voice, Peter J., Western Michigan University
Wagoner, Jeffrey L., Lawrence Livermore National Laboratory
Walsh, Tim R., Wayland Baptist University
Walton, Anthony W., University of Kansas
Wang, Ping, University of South Florida
Wanless, Harold R., University of Miami
Warme, John E., Colorado School of Mines
Wartes, Marwan A., Alaska Division of Geological & Geophysical Surveys
Washburn, Robert H., Juniata College
Watkinson, Matthew, University of Plymouth
Weislogel, Amy L., West Virginia University
Wellner, Julia, University of Houston
Wells, Neil A., Kent State University
Whalen, Michael T., University of Alaska, Fairbanks
Whisonant, Robert C., Radford University
Whiteaker, Timothy, University of Texas, Austin
Wilkinson, Bruce H., University of Michigan
Wilkinson, Bruce, Syracuse University
Wilson, Carol A., Louisiana State University
Wilson, Paul A., University of Southampton
Winkelstern, Ian Z., Grand Valley State University
Wittkop, Chad, Minnesota State University
Wizevich, Michael, Central Connecticut State University
Wojewoda, Jurand, University of Wroclaw
Wolak, Jeannette, Tennessee Tech University
Wood, Lesli, Colorado School of Mines
Woodruff, Jonathan D., University of Massachusetts, Amherst
Woods, Adam D., Santiago Canyon College
Woods, Adam D., California State University, Fullerton
Woods, Rachel A., Edinburgh University
Worden, Richard, University of Liverpool
Wright, V P., Cardiff University
Wynn, Thomas C., Lock Haven University
Yang, Wan, Wichita State University
Yang, Wan, Missouri University of Science and Technology
Yeager, Kevin M., University of Kentucky
Yellen, Brian, University of Massachusetts, Amherst
Young, Robert S., Western Carolina University
Zaleha, Michael J., Wittenberg University
Zattin, Massimiliano, Università degli Studi di Padova
Zeng, Hongliu, University of Texas at Austin, Jackson School of Geosciences

Physical Stratigraphy

Abdullah, Nuraiteng Tee, University of Malaya
Aitchison, Jonathan, University of Sydney
Alvarez, Walter, University of California, Berkeley
Anderson, Raymond R., University of Iowa
Archer, Allen W., Kansas State University
Aschoff, Jennifer, University of Alaska, Anchorage
Atchley, Stacy C., Baylor University
Baird, Gordon C., SUNY, Fredonia
Balgord, Elizabeth A., Weber State University
Bart, Philip J., Louisiana State University
Bartholomew, Alexander J., SUNY, New Paltz
Benison, Kathleen , West Virginia University
Bhattacharya, Janok, McMaster University
Blakeney DeJarnett, Beverly, Univ of Texas at Austin, Jackson Sch of Geosci
Blakey, Ronald C., Northern Arizona University
Boone, Peter A., Austin Community College District
Bowen, David W., Montana State University
Brezinski, David K., Maryland Department of Natural Resources
Busch, Richard M., West Chester University
Byers, Charles W., University of Wisconsin, Madison
Catacosinos, Paul A., Delta College
Chipping, David H., California Polytechnic State University
Clark, Joseph C., Indiana University of Pennsylvania
Colombi, Carina, Miami University
Coniglio, Mario, University of Waterloo
Cramer, Bradley D., University of Iowa
d'Atri, Anna, Università di Torino
Dalton, Richard F., New Jersey Geological and Water Survey
Denny, F. Brett, Illinois State Geological Survey
Devera, Joseph A., Illinois State Geological Survey

Diecchio, Richard J., George Mason University
Diffendal, Jr., Robert F., University of Nebraska, Lincoln
Doar, III, William R., South Carolina Dept of Natural Resources
Dodge, Clifford H., DCNR- Pennsylvania Bureau of Geological Survey
Dorsey, Rebecca J., University of Oregon
Drzewiecki, Peter A., Eastern Connecticut State University
Ebert, James R., SUNY, Oneonta
Elliott, Monty A., Southern Oregon University
Evanoff, Emmett, University of Northern Colorado
Evans, Kevin R., Missouri State University
Feibel, Craig S., Rutgers, The State University of New Jersey
Ferrusquia, Ismael, Univ Nacional Autonoma de Mexico
Fichter, Lynn S., James Madison University
Filipescu, Sorin, Babes-Bolyai University
Flemings, Peter B., University of Texas, Austin
Flint, Stephen, University of Manchester
Foreman, Brady Z., Western Washington University
Freeman, Rebecca, University of Kentucky
Fritz, William J., College of Staten Island/CUNY
Fugitt, Frank, Ohio Dept of Natural Resources
Gardulski, Anne F., Tufts University
Gentile, Richard J., University of Missouri, Kansas City
González, Laura, Univ Complutense de Madrid
Gonzalez Leon, Carlos M., Univ Nacional Autonoma de Mexico
Hamlin, H, Scott, University of Texas at Austin, Jackson School of Geosciences
Harris, W. Burleigh, University of North Carolina, Wilmington
Harvey, Cyril H., Guilford College
Hasenmueller, Nancy R., Indiana University
Heckel, Philip H., University of Iowa
Heermance, Richard V., California State University, Northridge
Helenes, Javier, Ctr de Invest Científica y de Ed Superior de Ensenada
Hentz, Tucker F., University of Texas at Austin, Jackson School of Geosciences
Heron, Duncan, Duke University
Hinnov, Linda, George Mason University
Hippensteel, Scott P., University of North Carolina, Charlotte
Holland, Steven M., University of Georgia
Hyland, Ethan, North Carolina State University
Jacques Ayala, Cesar, Univ Nacional Autonoma de Mexico
Janson, Xavier, University of Texas at Austin, Jackson School of Geosciences
Jenkyns, Hugh C., University of Oxford
Joeckel, R. M., University of Nebraska, Lincoln
Joeckel, R.M., University of Nebraska, Lincoln
Johnson, Donald O., Argonne National Laboratory
Johnson, Gary D., Dartmouth College
Johnson, William C., University of Kansas
Jordan, Robert R., University of Delaware
Jordan, Teresa E., Cornell University
Kaaya, Charles Z., University of Dar es Salaam
King, Norman R., University of Southern Indiana
King, Jr., David T., Auburn University
Kulp, Mark A., University of New Orleans
Lang, Harold R., Jet Propulsion Laboratory
Lash, Gary G., SUNY, Fredonia
Lee, Richard R., Oak Ridge National Laboratory
Lincoln, Jonathan M., Montclair State University
Loydell, David K., University of Portsmouth
Lozinsky, Richard P., Fullerton College
Ludvigson, Greg A., University of Kansas
Lundblad, Steven P., University of Hawai'i, Hilo
Mancini, Ernest A., University of Alabama
Manger, Walter, University of Arkansas, Fayetteville
Manspeizer, Warren, Rutgers, The State University of New Jersey, Newark
Martinez-Gutierrez, Genaro, Univ Autonoma de Baja California Sur
Maytorena-Silva, Jesus F., Univ Estatal de Sonora
McDonald, Catherine, Montana Tech of The University of Montana
McKee, James W., University of Wisconsin, Oshkosh
McLaughlin, Patrick I., Indiana University
McLaughlin, Patrick I., University of Wisconsin, Extension
McLaughlin, Jr., Peter P., University of Delaware
McLaurin, Brett T., Bloomsburg University
Meckel, Timothy A., University of Texas, Austin
Merriam, Daniel F., Wichita State University
Metz, Robert, Kean University
Monreal-Saavedra, Rogelio, Univ Estatal de Sonora
Monteverde, Don, Rutgers, The State University of New Jersey
Monteverde, Donald H., New Jersey Geological and Water Survey
Morris, Thomas H., Brigham Young University
Muñoz, Belén, Univ Complutense de Madrid
Nance, Hardie S., University of Texas, Austin
Nicolas, Michelle P., Manitoba Geological Survey
Nielson, R. LaRell, Stephen F. Austin State University
Obrist Farner, Jonathan, Missouri University of Science and Technology
Olariu, Cornel, University of Texas, Austin
Olariu, Mariana, University of Texas, Austin
Oms Llobet, Oriol, Universitat Autonoma de Barcelona
Owen, Donald E., Lamar University
Page, Kevin, University of Plymouth
Paine, Jeffrey G., University of Texas at Austin, Jackson School of Geosciences
Parcell, William C., Wichita State University
Pashin, Jack C., Oklahoma State University
Peterson, Gary L., San Diego State University
Peterson, Larry C., University of Miami
Pimentel, Nuno , Unive de Lisboa
Poch Serra, Joan, Universitat Autonoma de Barcelona
Pope, Michael , Texas A&M University
Retzler, Andrew J., University of Minnesota
Sadler, Peter M., University of California, Riverside
Sanders, Ronald S., Jet Propulsion Laboratory
Santisteban, Juan Ignacio, Univ Complutense de Madrid
Simmons, Lizanne V., Santiago Canyon College
Snyder, Walter S., Boise State University
Stieglitz, Ronald D., University of Wisconsin, Green Bay
Sugarman, Peter P., Rutgers, The State University of New Jersey
Sugarman, Peter J., New Jersey Geological and Water Survey
Swenson, John B., University of Minnesota Duluth
Tew , Berry H., Geological Survey of Alabama
Tierney, Kate, University of Iowa
Turner, Elizabeth C., Laurentian University, Sudbury
Vail, Peter R., Rice University
Valenzuela-Renteria, Manuel, Univ Estatal de Sonora
Van de Water, Peter, Fresno State University
Ver Straeten, Charles, New York State Geological Survey
Verlekar, Purushottam, Goa University
Vondra, Carl F., Iowa State University of Science & Technology
Wainman, Carmine, University of Adelaide
Watney, W. Lynn, University of Kansas
Weimer, Robert J., Colorado School of Mines
Witzke, Brian J., University of Iowa
Young, Grant M., Western University
Zachry, Doy L., University of Arkansas, Fayetteville

Structural Geology

Abalos, Benito, University of the Basque Country UPV/EHU
Abdelsalam, Mohamed G., Oklahoma State University
Abolins, Mark J., Middle Tennessee State University
Adam, Jurgen, Royal Holloway University of London
Adams, John B., University of Washington
Adeoti, Blessing, Federal University of Technology, Akure
Akciz, Sinan, California State University, Fullerton
Alaniz Alvarez, Susana A., Univ Nacional Autonoma de Mexico
Aldrich, M. James, Los Alamos National Laboratory
Aleksandrowski, Pawel, University of Wroclaw
Allard, Stephen T., Winona State University
Allen, Joseph L., Concord University
Allen, Richardson B., University of Utah
Allison, David T., University of South Alabama
Allmendinger, Richard W., Cornell University
Alsleben, Helge, Texas Christian University
Alvarez, José Antonio, Univ Complutense de Madrid
Amato, Jeffrey M., New Mexico State University, Las Cruces
Amenta, Roddy V., James Madison University
Amos, Colin B., Western Washington University
Amrouch, Khalid, University of Adelaide
Anastasio, David J., Lehigh University
Anderson, James L., University of Hawai'i, Hilo
Anderson, Mark, University of Plymouth
Anderson, Ryan, Idaho State University
Andrew, Joseph E., Youngstown State University
Aranguren, Aitor, University of the Basque Country UPV/EHU
Arboleya Cimadevilla, María Luísa, Universitat Autonoma de Barcelona
Armstrong, Phillip A., California State University, Fullerton
Aronoff, Ruth F., Furman University

FACULTY BY SPECIALTY

Arrowsmith, Ramon, Arizona State University
Attia, Snir, New Mexico Institute of Mining and Technology
Axen, Gary, New Mexico Institute of Mining and Technology
Aydin, Atilla, Stanford University
Babaie, Hassan A., Georgia State University
Baciu, Sorin D., Alexandru Ioan Cuza
Bailey, Christopher M., William & Mary
Baird, Graham, University of Northern Colorado
Balestro, Gianni, Università di Torino
Bamisaiye, Oluwaseyi A., Federal University of Technology, Akure
Bangs, Nathan L., University of Texas, Austin
Banoeng-Yakubo, Bruce K., University of Ghana
Baran, Zeynep O., South Dakota School of Mines & Technology
Barineau, Clinton I., Columbus State University
Barnes, Charles W., Northern Arizona University
Barquero-Molina, Miriam, University of Missouri
Bartley, John M., University of Utah
Bauer, Paul W., New Mexico Institute of Mining and Technology
Beaucamp-Stout, Celine, University of Montana Western
Behr, Rose-Anna, DCNR- Pennsylvania Bureau of Geological Survey
Bernard, Rachael E., Amherst College
Berry, Ron F., University of Tasmania
Bethune, Kathryn, University of Regina
Betka, Paul, George Mason University
Beutel, Erin K., College of Charleston
Bhattacharyya, Prajukti, University of Wisconsin, Whitewater
Bidgoli, Tandis, University of Kansas
Bier, Sara E., SUNY Potsdam
Bilodeau, William L., California Lutheran University
Birke, Tesfaye K., University of KwaZulu-Natal
Bishop, Kim, California State University, Los Angeles
Bjorklund, Tom, University of Houston
Bjornerud, Marcia, Lawrence University
Blackmer, Gale C., DCNR- Pennsylvania Bureau of Geological Survey
Bobyarchick, Andy R., University of North Carolina, Charlotte
Bodhankar, Ninad, Pt. Ravishankar Shukla University
Bond, Clare, University of Aberdeen
Boniface, Nelson, University of Dar es Salaam
Bosbyshell, Howell, West Chester University
Bothner, Wallace A., University of New Hampshire
Bott, Jackie, California Geological Survey
Bradbury, Kelly K., Utah State University
Bradley, Michael, Eastern Michigan University
Bradley, Philip, N.C. Department of Environmental Quality
Brandon, Mark T., Yale University
Brennan, William J., SUNY, Geneseo
Brisbin, William C., University of Manitoba
Brodie, Kate, University of Manchester
Brown, Bruce A., University of Wisconsin, Madison, Division of Extension
Bunds, Michael, Utah Valley University
Burberry, Caroline M., University of Nebraska, Lincoln
Burchfiel, B. C., Massachusetts Institute of Technology
Burger, H. Robert, Smith College
Burks, Rachel J., Towson University
Burtis, Erik W., Plymouth State University
Buttner, Steffen, Rhodes University
Bykerk-Kauffman, Ann, California State University, Chico
Byrne, Timothy, University of Connecticut
Cadoppi, Paola, Università di Torino
Camilleri, Phyllis A., Austin Peay State University
Campbell, Erin A., Wyoming State Geological Survey
Campbell, Patricia A., Slippery Rock University
Carlson, Diane H., Sacramento State University
Carosi, Rodolfo, Università di Torino
Carpenter, Brett, University of Oklahoma
Carter, Matthew J., Allegheny College
Casale, Gabriele M., Appalachian State University
Cashman, Susan M., Humboldt State University
Caskey, John, San Francisco State University
Cather, Steven M., New Mexico Institute of Mining and Technology
Cattanach, Bart, N.C. Department of Environmental Quality
Çemen, Ibrahim, University of Alabama
Chamberlin, Richard, New Mexico Institute of Mining and Technology
Chapman, Alan, Macalester College
Chapman, James, University of Wyoming
Chester, Frederick M., Texas A&M University
Chester, Frederick, Texas A&M University
Chester, Judith, Texas A&M University
Cladouhos, Trenton, University of Washington
Clayton, Robert W., Brigham Young University - Idaho
Cloos, Mark P., University of Texas, Austin
Coleman, Jr., Paul J., University of California, Los Angeles
Connelly, Jeffrey B., University of Arkansas at Little Rock
Connors, Christopher, Washington & Lee University
Cooke, Michele L., University of Massachusetts, Amherst
Cooper-Boemmels, Jennifer, Southern Connecticut State University
Coppinger, Walter, Trinity University
Cosgrove, John, Imperial College
Cowan, Darrel S., University of Washington
Cox, Randel T., University of Memphis
Crespi, Jean M., University of Connecticut
Crider, Juliet G., University of Washington
Cronin, Vincent S., Baylor University
Crowley, Peter D., Amherst College
Cruikshank, Kenneth M., Portland State University
Cuevas, Julia, University of the Basque Country UPV/EHU
Culshaw, Nicholas, Dalhousie University
Czeck, Dyanna M., University of Wisconsin, Milwaukee
D'Allura, Jad A., Southern Oregon University
Daigneault, Real, Universite du Quebec a Chicoutimi
Darin, Mike, University of Nevada, Reno
Davatzes, Nicholas, Temple University
Davis, George H., University of Arizona
Davis, Peter B., Pacific Lutheran University
Dawers, Nancye H., Tulane University
De Paola, Nicola, Durham University
Dean, Sarah L., Hope College
Di Toro, Giulio, Università degli Studi di Padova
DiPietro, Joseph A., University of Southern Indiana
Dixon, John M., Queen's University
Dooley, Tim, University of Texas at Austin, Jackson School of Geosciences
Douglas, Bruce, Indiana University, Bloomington
Draper, Grenville, Florida International University
Druguet Tantiña, Elena, Universitat Autonoma de Barcelona
Duebendorfer, Ernest M., Northern Arizona University
Dumitriu, Tony C., Alexandru Ioan Cuza
Dunne, George C., California State University, Northridge
Dunne, William M., University of Tennessee, Knoxville
Dutch, Steven I., University of Wisconsin, Green Bay
Eichhubl, Peter, University of Texas, Austin
Eichhubl, Peter, University of Texas at Austin, Jackson School of Geosciences
Elders, Chris, Curtin University
Elliott, Colleen G., Montana Tech of The University of Montana
Erdmer, Philippe, University of Alberta
Erslev, Eric A., University of Wyoming
Erslev, Eric A., Colorado State University
Eusden, J. Dykstra, Bates College
Evans, James P., Utah State University
Evans, Mark, Central Connecticut State University
Famin, Vincent, Universite de la Reunion
Faulds, James, University of Nevada, Reno
Faulds, James E., University of Nevada, Reno
Faure, Stephane, Universite du Quebec a Montreal
Fayon, Annia K., University of Minnesota, Twin Cities
Ferguson, Charles A., University of Arizona
Festa, Andrea, Università di Torino
Fischer, Mark P., Northern Illinois University
Fisher, Donald M., Pennsylvania State University, University Park
Forte, Adam, Louisiana State University
Fraser, Alastair, University of Utah
French, Melodie E., Rice University
Fryer, Karen H., Ohio Wesleyan University
Fryxell, Joan E., California State University, San Bernardino
Fueten, Frank, Brock University
Fusseis, Florian, Edinburgh University
Fyson, William K., University of Ottawa
Gale, Julia F., University of Texas, Austin
Gani, Nahid, Western Kentucky University
Garihan, John M., Furman University
Gates, Alexander E., Rutgers, The State University of New Jersey, Newark
Gattiglio, Marco, Università di Torino
Gibson, H. Daniel (Dan), Simon Fraser University

Gibson, Roger L., University of the Witwatersrand
Gibson, Ronald C., Golden West College
Gillespie, Thomas, College of New Jersey
Gilotti, Jane A., University of Iowa
Giorgis, Scott D., SUNY, Geneseo
Girty, Gary H., San Diego State University
Gleason, Gayle C., SUNY, Cortland
Godin, Laurent, Queen's University
Gold, David (Duff) P., Pennsylvania State University, University Park
Goodwin, Laurel B., University of Wisconsin, Madison
Gottardi, Raphael, University of Louisiana at Lafayette
Goulet, Normand, Universite du Quebec a Montreal
Gray, Mary Beth, Bucknell University
Greene, David C., Denison University
Griera Artigas, Albert, Universitat Autonoma de Barcelona
Griffith, Ashley, University of Texas, Arlington
Griffith, William A., Ohio State University
Groshong, Jr., Richard H., University of Alabama
Gross, Michael, Florida International University
Groszos, Mark S., Valdosta State University
Gudmundsson, Agust, Royal Holloway University of London
Guitierrez-Alonso, Gabriel, Florida International University
Gulick, Sean S., University of Texas, Austin
Guth, Peter L., United States Naval Academy
Hack, Alistair, University of Newcastle
Hacker, David B., Kent State University
Halfpenny, Angela, Central Washington University
Hall, Frank W., Indiana University of Pennsylvania
Hanley, Thomas B., Columbus State University
Hanmer, Simon, Carleton University
Hannula, Kimberly, Fort Lewis College
Harrap, Rob, Queen's University
Harris, Lyal B., Universite du Quebec
Harris, Ron, Brigham Young University
Harrison, Michael J., Tennessee Tech University
Hatcher Jr., Robert D., University of Tennessee, Knoxville
Hawkins, John F., Auburn University
Heimsath, Arjun, Arizona State University
Helmstaedt, Herwart, Queen's University
Helper, Mark A., University of Texas, Austin
Hendrix, Thomas E., Grand Valley State University
Hennings, Peter H., University of Wyoming
Hetherington, Eric D., College of the Sequoias
Hetzel, Ralf, Universitaet Muenster
Hibbard, James P., North Carolina State University
Hill, Mary Louise, Lakehead University
Hinz, Nick, University of Nevada, Reno
Hirth, Greg, Brown University
Hirth, Gregory, Woods Hole Oceanographic Institution
Hoffman, Paul F., Harvard University
Hogan, John, Missouri University of Science and Technology
Holdsworth, Robert E., Durham University
Holm, Daniel K., Kent State University
Holst, Timothy, University of Minnesota Duluth
Holyoke, Caleb, University of Akron
Hooks, Benjamin P., University of Tennessee, Martin
Horsman, Eric M., East Carolina University
Horst, Andrew J., Oberlin College
Horst, Andrew J., Marshall University
Hozik, Michael J., Stockton University
Hudec, Michael R., University of Texas at Austin, Jackson School of Geosciences
Hudec, Michael R., University of Texas, Austin
Hudleston, Peter J., University of Minnesota, Twin Cities
Hughes, Kenneth S., University of Puerto Rico
Hull, Joseph M., Seattle Central College
Hynes, Andrew J., McGill University
Iaccarino, Salvatore, Università di Torino
Isard, Sierra J., N.C. Department of Environmental Quality
Ismat, Zeshan, Franklin and Marshall College
Jackson, Martin P. A., Univ of Texas at Austin, Jackson Sch of Geosciences
Jackson, Richard A., Long Island University, Brooklyn Campus
Jacobi, Robert D., SUNY, Buffalo
Jessup, Micah, University of Tennessee, Knoxville
Jiang, Dazhi, Western University
Jiménez, David, Univ Complutense de Madrid
Jirsa, Mark, University of Minnesota
John, Barbara E., University of Wyoming
Johnson, Arvid M., Purdue University
Johnson, Brad, University of Arizona
Johnson, Scott E., University of Maine
Johnston, Scott, California Polytechnic State University
Johnston, Stephen T., University of Victoria
Johnston, Stephen T., University of Alberta
Jones, Gustavo Tolson, Univ Nacional Autonoma de Mexico
Kalakay, Thomas J., Rocky Mountain College
Karabinos, Paul, Williams College
Karimi, Bobak, Wilkes University
Kath, Randal L., University of West Georgia
Kehlenbeck, Manfred M., Lakehead University
Kelsch, Jesse, Sul Ross State University
Kelty, Thomas, California State University, Long Beach
Kennedy, Lori, University of British Columbia
Kirkpatrick, James, McGill University
Klepeis, Keith A., University of Vermont
Klimczak, Christian, University of Georgia
Knapp, James, Oklahoma State University
Kopf, Christopher F., Mansfield University
Kruckenberg, Seth C., Boston College
Kruckenberg, Seth, Boston College
Krugh, W C., California State University, Bakersfield
Kuiper, Yvette D., Colorado School of Mines
Kulander, Byron, Wright State University
Kutu, Jacob M., University of Ghana
Lafrance, Bruno, Laurentian University, Sudbury
Lageson, David R., Montana State University
Langille, Jackie M., University of North Carolina, Asheville
Lao, Daniel A., Oklahoma State University
Lapusta, Nadia, California Institute of Technology
Laubach, Stephen E., Univ of Texas at Austin, Jackson Sch of Geosciences
Laurent-Charvet, Sébastien, Institut Polytechnique LaSalle Beauvais (ex-IGAL)
Law, Richard D., Virginia Polytechnic Institute & State University
Lee, Jeffrey, Central Washington University
Lemiszki, Peter J., Pellissippi State Community College
Lemiszki, Peter J., Tennessee Geological Survey
Lemiszki, Peter J., University of Tennessee, Knoxville
Lenardic, Adrian, Rice University
Lennox, Paul G., University of New South Wales
Lewis, Helen, Heriot-Watt University
Lewis, Jon C., Indiana University of Pennsylvania
Lincoln, Beth Z., Albion College
Lisle, R J., Cardiff University
Little, Tim, Victoria University of Wellington
Livaccari, Richard F., Colorado Mesa University
Long , Sean P., Washington State University
Loveland, Andrea M., Wyoming State Geological Survey
Lowry, Wallace D., Virginia Polytechnic Institute & State University
Luther, Amy, Louisiana State University
MacDonald, William D., Binghamton University
MacLean, John S., Southern Utah University
Maher, Jr., Harmon D., University of Nebraska, Omaha
Mali, Heinrich, University Leoben
Malone, David H., Illinois State University
Mana, Sara, Salem State University
Markley, Michelle J., Mount Holyoke College
Marrett, Randall A., University of Texas, Austin
Marshak, Stephen, University of Illinois, Urbana-Champaign
Martin, Silvana, Università degli Studi di Padova
Martínez, José Jesús, Univ Complutense de Madrid
Martinez-Macias, Panfilo R., Univ Autonoma de San Luis Potosi
Mattson, Peter H., Queens College (CUNY)
McCaffrey, Kenneth J., Durham University
McCair, Andrew, University of Leeds
McClay, Ken R., Royal Holloway University of London
McGill, George E., University of Massachusetts, Amherst
McKay, Matthew P., Missouri State University
McNaught, Mark A., Mount Union College
McNulty, Brendan A., California State University, Dominguez Hills
McQuarrie, Nadine, University of Pittsburgh
Mecklenburgh, Julian, University of Manchester
Meere, Pat, University College Cork
Meigs, Andrew J., Oregon State University
Menegon, Luca, University of Plymouth

Merguerian, Charles M., Hofstra University
Metcalf, Kathryn, SUNY, Oneonta
Mezger, Jochen E., University of Alaska, Fairbanks
Mies, Jonathan W., University of Tennessee, Chattanooga
Miller, Elizabeth L., Stanford University
Miller, Marli G., University of Oregon
Miller, Robert B., San Jose State University
Milligan, G. Clinton, Dalhousie University
Minnaar, Hendrik, University of the Free State
Miranda, Elena A., California State University, Northridge
Mitchell, Tom, University College London
Mitra, Gautam, University of Rochester
Mitra, Shankar, University of Oklahoma
Mookerjee, Matty, Sonoma State University
Moore, J. Casey, University of California, Santa Cruz
Morgan, Julia K., Rice University
Morgan, Julia K., Rice University
Morgan, Sven S., Iowa State University of Science & Technology
Morrow, Robert H., South Carolina Dept of Natural Resources
Mosher, Sharon, University of Texas, Austin
Muller, Otto H., Alfred University
Murphy, Michael, University of Houston
Needham, Tim, University of Leeds
Nel, Justin, University of the Free State
Nemcok, Michal, University of Utah
Neuhauser, Kenneth R., Fort Hays State University
Newman, Julie, Texas A&M University
Nicol, Andy, University of Canterbury
Northrup, Clyde J., Boise State University
Nourse, Jonathan A., California State Polytechnic University, Pomona
O'Hara, Kieran D., University of Kentucky
O'Meara, Stephanie A., Colorado State University
Okonkwo, Chukwuemeka T., Federal University of Technology, Akure
Onasch, Charles M., Bowling Green State University
Osagiede, Edoseghe E., University of Benin
Palmquist, John C., Lawrence University
Paterson, Scott R., University of Southern California
Paton, Douglas, University of Leeds
Patton, Regan L., Washington State University
Paulsen, Timothy S., University of Wisconsin, Oshkosh
Pavlis, Terry L., University of Texas, El Paso
Pawley, Alison, University of Manchester
Pearson, David M., Idaho State University
Pennacchioni, Giorgio, Università degli Studi di Padova
Perry, Bruce, California State University, Long Beach
Petrie, Elizabeth S., Western Colorado University
Phipps, Stephen P., University of Pennsylvania
Pirouz, Mortaza X., University of Texas, Dallas
Platt, John P., University of Southern California
Pogue, Kevin R., Whitman College
Pollard, David D., Stanford University
Potter, Jr., Donald B., Sewanee: University of the South
Prior, David J., University of Otago
Pritchard, Chad, Eastern Washington University
Puelles, Pablo, University of the Basque Country UPV/EHU
Quintero, Odranoel, Univ Nacional Autonoma de Mexico
Raffini, Sylvain, Universite du Quebec a Chicoutimi
Rafini, Silvain, Universite du Quebec a Chicoutimi
Rauch, Marta, University of Wroclaw
Reber, Jacqueline, Iowa State University of Science & Technology
Ree, Jin-Han, Korea University
Reese, Joseph F., Edinboro University of Pennsylvania
Reinen, Linda A., Pomona College
Resor, Phillip G., Wesleyan University
Reynolds, Stephen J., Arizona State University
Ricketts, Jason, University of Texas, El Paso
Ritchie, Alexander W., College of Charleston
Roberts, Gerald, Birkbeck College
Robin, Pierre-Yves F., University of Toronto
Robinson, Alexander, University of Houston
Robinson, Delores, University of Alabama
Robinson, Kevin, San Diego State University
Robinson, Peter, University of Massachusetts, Amherst
Rodgers, David W., Idaho State University
Rogers, Robert D., California State University, Stanislaus
Rojo-Garcia, Paulino, Univ Autonoma de Baja California Sur
Romeo, Ignacio, Univ Complutense de Madrid
Rousell, Don H., Laurentian University, Sudbury
Rowe, Christie, McGill University
Roy, Denis W., Universite du Quebec a Chicoutimi
Rusmore, Margaret E., Occidental College
Saillet, Elodie, Institut Polytechnique LaSalle Beauvais (ex-IGAL)
Saja, David, Case Western Reserve University
Sak, Peter B., Dickinson College
Saleeby, Jason B., California Institute of Technology
Samaniego, Angel Nieto, Univ Nacional Autonoma de Mexico
Sanchez, Veronica I., Texas A&M University, Kingsville
Sanislav, Ioan, James Cook University
Satterfield, Joseph I., Angelo State University
Saura, Eduard, Universitat Autonoma de Barcelona
Saxon, Christopher, Tarleton State University
Scharnberger, Charles K., Millersville University
Schlische, Roy W., Rutgers, The State University of New Jersey
Schmidt, Keegan L., Lewis-Clark State College
Schoonmaker, Adam, Utica College
Schrank, Christoph, Queensland University of Technology
Schwerdtner, Walfried M., University of Toronto
Sears, James W., University of Montana
Shami, Malek, York College (CUNY)
Shaw, Colin, Montana State University
Shuib, Mustaffa Kamal, University of Malaya
Sibson, Rick H., University of Otago
Siddoway, Christine S., Colorado College
Simony, Philip S., University of Calgary
Singleton, John, Colorado State University
Skehan, James W., Boston College
Skemer, Philip, Washington University in St. Louis
Snyder, Morgan E., Acadia University
Solar, Gary S., Buffalo State College
Sorkhabi, Rasoul, University of Utah
Soucy de la Roche, Renaud, Universite du Quebec
Spangler, Ellie, California Geological Survey
Spratt, Deborah A., University of Calgary
SRIVASTAVA, HARI B., Banaras Hindu University
Stauffer, Mel R., University of Saskatchewan
Stearns, David W., University of Oklahoma
Stewart, Kevin G., University of North Carolina, Chapel Hill
Stinson, Amy L., Santiago Canyon College
Stinson, Amy L., Irvine Valley College
Stowell Gale, Julia, Univ of Texas at Austin, Jackson Sch of Geosciences
Strayer, Luther M., California State University, East Bay
Sullivan, Walter, Colby College
Suneson, Neil H., University of Oklahoma
Surpless, Benjamin E., Trinity University
Talbot, James L., Western Washington University
Tapp, J. B., University of Tulsa
Taylor, Lansing, University of Utah
Taylor, Wanda J., University of Nevada, Las Vegas
Tewksbury, Barbara J., Hamilton College
Teyssier, Christian P., University of Minnesota, Twin Cities
Thompson, Margaret D., Wellesley College
Tikoff, Basil, University of Wisconsin, Madison
Timmons, J M., New Mexico Institute of Mining and Technology
Tindall, Sarah E., Kutztown University of Pennsylvania
Titus, Sarah J., Carleton College
Tobisch, Othmar T., University of California, Santa Cruz
Toro, Jaime, West Virginia University
Torvela, Taija, University of Leeds
Toy, Virginia G., University of Otago
Treloar, Peter, Kingston University
Tremblay, Alain, Universite du Quebec a Montreal
Trexler, Charles C., Ohio Wesleyan University
Trudgill, Bruce D., Colorado School of Mines
Trullenque, Ghislain, Institut Polytechnique LaSalle Beauvais (ex-IGAL)
Tso, Jonathan L., Radford University
Tubía, Jose M., University of the Basque Country UPV/EHU
Tull, James F., Florida State University
Tullis, Jan A., Brown University
Twiss, Robert J., University of California, Davis
Ustaszewski, Kamil M., Friedrich-Schiller-University Jena
Van Arsdale, Roy B., University of Memphis
van Bever Donker, Jan M., University of the Western Cape

van der Kolk, Dolores, Texas State University
van der Pluijm, Ben, University of Michigan
VanDervoort, Dane S., Geological Survey of Alabama
Vaqueiro Rodriguez, Marcos, Coruna University
Vegas, Nestor, University of the Basque Country UPV/EHU
Vogl, Jim, University of Florida
Voicu, Gabriel-Constantin, Universite du Quebec a Montreal
Vojtko, Rastislav , Comenius University in Bratislava
Vollmer, Frederick W., SUNY, New Paltz
Waag, Charles J., Boise State University
Waldron, John W., University of Alberta
Walker, J. Douglas, University of Kansas
Washington, Paul A., Marietta College
Waters-Tormey, Cheryl, Western Carolina University
Waterworth, Lauren H., Appalachian State University
Watkinson, A. John, Washington State University
Waugh, Richard A., University of Wisconsin, Platteville
Webber, Jeffrey R., Stockton University
Weber, John C., Grand Valley State University
Weil, Arlo B., Bryn Mawr College
Weldon, Ray J., University of Oregon
Wells, Michael L., University of Nevada, Las Vegas
West, David P., Middlebury College
Wetmore, Paul, University of South Florida
Whalley, John, University of Portsmouth
Whisner, S. Christopher, Bloomsburg University
White, Joseph C., University of New Brunswick
Whitmeyer, Steven J., James Madison University
Whittaker, Amber, Dept of Agriculture, Conservation, and Forestry
Wickham, John S., University of Texas, Arlington
Wilkerson, M. S., University of Illinois, Urbana-Champaign
Wilkerson, M. Scott, DePauw University
Williams, Michael L., University of Massachusetts, Amherst
Williams, Paul F., University of New Brunswick
Wilson, Terry J., Ohio State University
Winslow, Margaret A., City College (CUNY)
Withjack, Martha O., Rutgers, The State University of New Jersey
Wojtal, Steven F., Oberlin College
Woodcock, Nigel H., University of Cambridge
Woodward, Lee A., University of New Mexico
Woodwell, Grant R., University of Mary Washington
Workman-Ford, Kerry, Fresno State University
Yikilmaz, Burak, University of California, Davis
Yonkee, W. A., Weber State University
Yoshinobu, Aaron S., Texas Tech University
Young, David, Ohio State University
Young, Jeffrey, University of Manitoba
Zampieri, Dario, Università degli Studi di Padova
Zimmerman, Jr., Jay, Southern Illinois University Carbondale
Zuza, Andrew V., University of Nevada, Reno
Zuza, Andrew , University of Nevada, Reno

Tectonics

Abercrombie, Rachel, Boston University
Allen, Mark, Durham University
Anderson, Robert G., University of British Columbia
Andeweg, Bernd , Vrije Universiteit Amsterdam
Arkle, Jenny C., Augustana College
Ault, Alexis K., Utah State University
Avouac, Jean-Philippe, California Institute of Technology
Barth, Nicolas, University of California, Riverside
Bartholomew, Mervin J., University of Memphis
Bell, Andrew, Edinburgh University
Bell, Rebecca, Imperial College
Bemis, Sean P., Virginia Polytechnic Institute & State University
Bennett, Scott E., U.S. Geological Survey
Bickle, Michael, University of Cambridge
Bieler, David B., Centenary College of Louisiana
Bird, G. Peter, University of California, Los Angeles
Boggs, Katherine, Mount Royal University
Boland, Irene B., Winthrop University
Boutelier, David, University of Newcastle
Bradshaw, John, University of Canterbury
Bullen, Dean, University of Portsmouth
Burgette, Reed J., New Mexico State University, Las Cruces
Burgmann, Roland, University of California, Berkeley
Busby, Cathy J., University of California, Davis
Camacho, Alfredo, University of Manitoba
Cao, Wenrong, University of Nevada, Reno
Carlson, Marvin P., Unversity of Nebraska, Lincoln
Carr, Sharon D., Carleton University
Casey, John F., University of Houston
Cawood, Peter A., Monash University
Centeno Garcia, Elena, Univ Nacional Autonoma de Mexico
Chapin, Charles E., New Mexico Institute of Mining and Technology
Chi, Wu-Cheng, Academia Sinica
Choi, Eunseo, University of Memphis
Church, William R., Western University
Cole, Ron B., Allegheny College
Contreras, Juan, Ctr de Invest Científica y de Ed Superior de Ensenada
Corrigan, David, University of Manitoba
Cottle, John M., University of Tennessee, Knoxville
Cowgill, Eric S., University of California, Davis
Cox, Randel T., University of Memphis
Cunningham, Dickson, Eastern Connecticut State University
Dallmeyer, R. David, University of Georgia
Dalziel, Ian W. D., University of Texas, Austin
Das, Shamita, University of Oxford
Davis, Gregory A., University of Southern California
De Cserna, Zoltan, Univ Nacional Autonoma de Mexico
de Vicente, Gerardo, Univ Complutense de Madrid
DeCelles, Peter G., University of Arizona
Derakhshani, Reza, Shahid Bahonar University of Kerman
DeVecchio, Duane, Arizona State University
Dewey, John, University of California, Davis
Dickinson, William R., University of Arizona
Dilek, Yildirm, Miami University
Dinter, David A., University of Utah
Dolan, James F., University of Southern California
Dong, Yunpeng, Western University
Dooley, Tim P., University of Texas, Austin
Driscoll, Peter E., Carnegie Institution for Science
Ducea, Mihai N., University of Arizona
Dumond, Gregory, University of Arkansas, Fayetteville
Egan, Stuart, Keele University
Egger, Anne E., Central Washington University
Engebretson, David C., Western Washington University
England, Phillip, University of Oxford
Esteban, Jose Julian, University of the Basque Country UPV/EHU
Feigl, Kurt L., University of Wisconsin, Madison
Ferrari Pedraglio, Luca, Univ Nacional Autonoma de Mexico
Fitzgerald, Paul G., Syracuse University
Foster, David A., University of Florida
Furlong, Kevin P., Pennsylvania State University, University Park
Gable, Carl W., Los Alamos National Laboratory
Gans, Phillip B., University of California, Santa Barbara
Garver, John I., Union College
Gehrels, George E., University of Arizona
Geissman, John D., University of Texas, Dallas
Gerbi, Christopher C., University of Maine
German, Chris, Woods Hole Oceanographic Institution
Ghail, Richard, Royal Holloway University of London
Gifford, Jennifer N., University of Mississippi
Gomez, Francisco, University of Missouri
Gries, John C., Wichita State University
Grujic, Djordje, Dalhousie University
Guenthner, Willy, University of Illinois, Urbana-Champaign
Hales, T. C., University of Wales
Haley, J C., Miami University
Hall, Robert, Royal Holloway University of London
Hansen, Vicki L., University of Minnesota Duluth
Haq, Saad, Purdue University
Harley, Simon L., Edinburgh University
Harms, Tekla A., Amherst College
Harris, Nigel B., Open University
Hatcher, Jr., Robert D., Washington University in St. Louis
Hemphill-Haley, Mark, Humboldt State University
Henderson, Robert, James Cook University
Henry, Christopher D., University of Nevada, Reno
Herman, Mathew, California State University, Bakersfield
Hughes, Sam, Exeter University
Huntington, Katharine W., University of Washington

Hurtado, Jose M., University of Texas, El Paso
Insel, Nadja, Northeastern Illinois University
Isacks, Bryan L., Cornell University
Ivins, Erik R., Jet Propulsion Laboratory
Jackson, Christopher, Imperial College
Jacobson, Carl E., Iowa State University of Science & Technology
Jadamec, Margarete, SUNY, Buffalo
Janecke, Susanne U., Utah State University
John, Hickman B., University of Kentucky
Judge, Shelley, College of Wooster
Kapp, Paul A., University of Arizona
Karlstrom, Karl E., University of New Mexico
Karson, Jeffrey, Syracuse University
Kato, Terence T., California State University, Chico
Keir, Derek, University of Southampton
Kelley, Shari A., New Mexico Institute of Mining and Technology
Keppie, J. Duncan, Univ Nacional Autonoma de Mexico
Keppie, John D., Univ Nacional Autonoma de Mexico
Kirby, Eric, Oregon State University
Kirstein, Linda, Edinburgh University
Kleinspehn, Karen L., University of Minnesota, Twin Cities
Klemperer, Simon L., Stanford University
Knapp, Camelia, Oklahoma State University
Knuepfer, Peter L. K., Binghamton University
Koehn, Daniel, University of Glasgow
Kokum, Mehmet, Firat University
Koons, Peter O., University of Maine
Kronenberg, Andreas, Texas A&M University
Kullberg, Carla , Unive de Lisboa
Lamb, Melissa A., University of Saint Thomas
Larson, Kyle, University of British Columbia, Okanagan Campus
Lavier, Luc L., University of Texas, Austin
Lin, Jian, Woods Hole Oceanographic Institution
Lonergan, Lidia, Imperial College
Loveless, Jack, Smith College
Luo, Gang, University of Texas, Austin
Lynner, Colton, University of Delaware
Mac Niocaill, Conall, University of Oxford
Mallard, Laura D., Appalachian State University
Malone, Shawn J., Ball State University
Mann, Paul, University of Texas, Austin
Marsellos, Antonios, Hofstra University
Martinez, Juventino, Univ Nacional Autonoma de Mexico
Martinez-Reyes, Juventino, Univ Nacional Autonoma de Mexico
May, Daniel J., University of New Haven
McClelland, William C., University of Iowa
McGill, Sally F., California State University, San Bernardino
McGrew, Allen J., University of Dayton
McNeill, Lisa, University of Southampton
McPherson, Robert C., Humboldt State University
McRivette, Michael, Albion College
Melichar, Rostislav, Masaryk University
Melosh, Henry J., University of Arizona
Mesbahi, Fatemeh, University of Tabriz
Michon, Laurent, Universite de la Reunion
Mickus, Kevin L., Missouri State University
Milan, Luke, University of New England
Molnar, Peter, University of Colorado
Moore, Gregory F., University of Hawai'i, Manoa
Moores, Eldridge M., University of California, Davis
Moser, Desmond, Western University
Moucha, Robert, Syracuse University
Mound, Jon, University of Leeds
Mueller, Karl J., University of Colorado
Murphy, J. Brendan, Saint Francis Xavier University
Möller, Andreas, University of Kansas
Nabelek, John L., Oregon State University
Nadin, Elisabeth S., University of Alaska, Fairbanks
Nakov, Radoslav A., Bulgarian Academy of Sciences
Nance, R. Damian, Ohio University
Nash, Greg, University of Utah
Naylor, Mark, Edinburgh University
Ngo, Thanh X., Hanoi University of Mining & Geology
Niemi, Nathan A., University of Michigan
Niemi, Tina M., University of Missouri, Kansas City
Ocan, O. O., Obafemi Awolowo University
Onderdonk, Nate, California State University, Long Beach
Partin, Camille, University of Saskatchewan
Passchier, Cees W., Universität Mainz
Pavlis, Terry L., University of New Orleans
Peacock, Simon M., University of British Columbia
Peterman, Emily M., Bowdoin College
Pettinga, Jarg R., University of Canterbury
Phillips, Richard, University of Leeds
Pieri, David C., Jet Propulsion Laboratory
Plasienka, Dusan, Comenius University in Bratislava
Pluhar, Christopher J., Fresno State University
Price, Raymond A., Queen's University
Rahl, Jeffrey, Washington & Lee University
Regalla, Christine, Boston University
Reusch, Douglas N., University of Maine, Farmington
Richter, Frank M., University of Chicago
Robertson, Alastair H., Edinburgh University
Roeske, Sarah M., University of California, Davis
Rowan, Christopher J., Kent State University
Rowley, David B., University of Chicago
Royden, Leigh H., Massachusetts Institute of Technology
Rubin, Charles M., Central Washington University
Rust, Derek, University of Portsmouth
Ryder, Isabelle, University of Liverpool
Sager, William W., University of Houston
Sample, James C., Northern Arizona University
Schellart, Wouter , Vrije Universiteit Amsterdam
Schermer, Elizabeth R., Western Washington University
Schmidt, David , University of Washington
Schneider, David, University of Ottawa
Scotese, Christopher R., University of Texas, Arlington
Searle, Mike, University of Oxford
Shail, Robin, Exeter University
Shaw, John, Harvard University
Sinha, A. Krishna, Virginia Polytechnic Institute & State University
Sintubin, Manuel, Katholieke Universiteit Leuven
Spotila, James A., Virginia Polytechnic Institute & State University
Srimal, Neptune, Florida International University
Stanley, Jessica, University of Idaho
Steltenpohl, Mark G., Auburn University
Stern, Robert J., University of Texas, Dallas
Stock, Joann M., California Institute of Technology
Strecker, Manfred, Cornell University
Streepey Smith, Meg, Earlham College
Stump, Edmund, Arizona State University
Suppe, John, University of Houston
Suter-Cargnelutti, Max, Univ Nacional Autonoma de Mexico
Takeuchi, Akira, University of Toyama
Taylor, Brian, University of Hawai'i, Manoa
Taylor, Frederick W., University of Texas, Austin
Taylor, Michael H., University of Kansas
Teixell, Antonio, Universitat Autonoma de Barcelona
Teixell Cácharo, Antoni, Universitat Autonoma de Barcelona
Thacker, Jacob, New Mexico Institute of Mining and Technology
Thigpen, Ryan, University of Kentucky
Thomas, William A., Geological Survey of Alabama
Thorkelson, Derek J., Simon Fraser University
Toke', Nathan, Utah Valley University
Turner, Jenni, University of East Anglia
Umhoefer, Paul J., Northern Arizona University
Unsworth, Martyn, University of Alberta
Valentine, Michael , Highline College
Valentino, David W., SUNY, Oswego
van Hunen, Jeroen, Durham University
Van Wijk, Jolante, New Mexico Institute of Mining and Technology
vanKeken, Peter E., Carnegie Institution for Science
Wallace, Laura, University of Texas, Austin
Watkinson, Ian M., Royal Holloway University of London
Webb, Laura E., University of Vermont
Wernicke, Brian P., California Institute of Technology
Whittaker, Alex, Imperial College
Willis, Julie B., Brigham Young University - Idaho
Wong, Martin, Colgate University
Wright, James (Jim) E., University of Georgia
Wu, Jonny, University of Houston
Yeats, Robert S., Oregon State University

Yin, An, University of California, Los Angeles
Yule, J. Douglas, California State University, Northridge
Zamani, Behzad, University of Tabriz

Volcanology

Aguirre Diaz, Gerardo J., Univ Nacional Autonoma de Mexico
Ancochea, Eumenio, Univ Complutense de Madrid
Anderson, Steven W., University of Northern Colorado
Anderson, Jr., Alfred T., University of Chicago
Andrews, Benjamin, Smithsonian Inst/Nat Mus of Nat History
Andrews, Graham D., West Virginia University
Awdankiewicz, Marek, University of Wroclaw
Banik, Tenley, Illinois State University
Barclay, Jenni, University of East Anglia
Befus, Kenneth S., Baylor University
Blake, Stephen, Open University
Bohrson, Wendy, Colorado School of Mines
Boroughs, Scott, Washington State University
Branan, Yvonne K., Indiana University of Pennsylvania
Branney, Mike, Leicester University
Brown, David, University of Glasgow
Brown, Richard J., Durham University
Brunstad, Keith A., SUNY, Oneonta
Burkett, Brett, Collin College - Central Park Campus
Burkett, Shannon, Collin College - Central Park Campus
Bursik, Marcus I., SUNY, Buffalo
Calder, Eliza, Edinburgh University
Cameron, Barry I., University of Wisconsin, Milwaukee
Cameron, Cheryl, Alaska Division of Geological & Geophysical Surveys
Camp, Victor E., San Diego State University
Canon-Tapia, Edgardo, Ctr de Invest Científica y de Ed Superior de Ensenada
Carley, Tamara, Lafayette College
Carr, Michael J., Rutgers, The State University of New Jersey
Carrasco-Nunez, Gerardo, Univ Nacional Autonoma de Mexico
Casares, Heather, Arizona Western College
Castro, Jonathan M., Universität Mainz
Chapin, Charles E., New Mexico Institute of Mining and Technology
Chapman, Marshall, Morehead State University
Charbonnier, Sylvain, University of South Florida
Cigolini, Corrado, Università di Torino
Clarke, Amanda, Arizona State University
Cole, James W., University of Canterbury
Cole, Paul D., University of Plymouth
Connor, Charles B., University of South Florida
Coppola, Diego, Università di Torino
Coulson, Ian, University of Regina
Crisp, Joy A., Jet Propulsion Laboratory
Crowe, Bruce M., Los Alamos National Laboratory
de Silva, Shanika, Oregon State University
de' Michieli Vitturi, Mattia, SUNY, Buffalo
Deardorff, Nicholas, Indiana University of Pennsylvania
Domagall, Abigail M., Black Hills State University
Drake, Simon, Birkbeck College
Dufek, Josef, University of Oregon
Dufek, Josef, Georgia Institute of Technology
Duffield, Wendell A., Northern Arizona University
Duller, Rob, University of Liverpool
Edmonds, Marie, University of Cambridge
Eggers, Albert A., University of Puget Sound
Escobar-Wolf, Rudiger, Michigan Technological University
Fagents, Sarah, University of Hawai'i, Manoa
Fauria, Kristen, Vanderbilt University
Fischer, Tobias, University of New Mexico
Flood, Tim P., Saint Norbert College
Frey, Holli M., Union College
Gansecki, Cheryl A., University of Hawai'i, Hilo
Gardner, James E., University of Texas, Austin
Genareau, Kimberly, University of Alabama
Genna, Dominique, Universite du Quebec a Chicoutimi
Germa, Aurelie, University of South Florida
Giachetti, Thomas, University of Oregon
Giordano, Daniele, Università di Torino
Girard, Guillaume, Northern Illinois University
Godchaux, Martha M., Mount Holyoke College
Gonnermann, Helge, Rice University
Graettinger, Alison, University of Missouri, Kansas City
Grapenthin, Ronni, New Mexico Institute of Mining and Technology
Gravley, Darren, University of Canterbury
Green, Jack, California State University, Long Beach
Gregg, Tracy K. P., SUNY, Buffalo
Gutmann, James T., Wesleyan University
Hampton, Samuel J., University of Canterbury
Harpp, Karen, Colgate University
Hasenaka, Toshiaki, Kumamoto University
Hausback, Brian, Sacramento State University
Head, Elisabet M., Northeastern Illinois University
Heiken, Grant, Los Alamos National Laboratory
Heliker, Christina C., University of Hawai'i, Hilo
Herd, Richard, University of East Anglia
Holm, Richard F., Northern Arizona University
Hon, Ken, University of Hawai'i, Hilo
Houghton, Bruce F., University of Hawai'i, Manoa
Houle, Michel, University of Manitoba
Huber, Christian, Brown University
Hughes, Scott S., Idaho State University
Iverson, Nels, New Mexico Institute of Mining and Technology
Jackson, Marie D., University of Utah
Johnson, Emily R., New Mexico State University, Las Cruces
Junkin, William D., Maryland Department of Natural Resources
Kavanagh, Janine, University of Liverpool
Kennedy, Ben, University of Canterbury
Kieffer, Susan W., University of Illinois, Urbana-Champaign
Klemetti, Erik, Denison University
Knesel, Kurt, Trinity University
Kobs-Nawotniak, Shannon E., Idaho State University
Koleszar, Alison, Colgate University
Kolzenburg, Stephan, SUNY, Buffalo
Koornneef, Janne, Vrije Universiteit Amsterdam
Krier, Donathon J., Los Alamos National Laboratory
Lang, Nicholas, Mercyhurst University
Larsen, Jessica F., University of Alaska, Fairbanks
Lavallee, Yan, University of Liverpool
Le Mevel, Helene, Carnegie Institution for Science
Lee, Rachel J., SUNY, Oswego
Lehto, Heather L., Angelo State University
LeMasurier, Wesley E., University of Colorado, Denver
Lev, Einat , Columbia University
LeVeque, Randy, University of Washington
Leyrit, Hervé, Institut Polytechnique LaSalle Beauvais (ex-IGAL)
Llewellin, Ed, Durham University
Lockwood, John P., University of Hawai'i, Hilo
Magsino, Sammantha L., Nat Acad of Sciences, Eng, and Medicine
Manga, Michael, University of California, Berkeley
Maria, Tony, University of Southern Indiana
Mather, Tamsin A., University of Oxford
Matoza, Robin, University of California, Santa Barbara
McGarvie, Dave, Open University
McPhie, Jocelyn, University of Tasmania
Michelfelder, Gary, Missouri State University
Moore, Joseph N., University of Utah
Moran, Seth, University of Washington
Morton, Ronald L., University of Minnesota Duluth
Neuberg, Jurgen, University of Leeds
O'Sullivan, Katie, California State University, Bakersfield
Ort, Michael H., Northern Arizona University
Ottavi-Pupier, Elsa, Institut Polytechnique LaSalle Beauvais (ex-IGAL)
Pallister, John S., University of Pittsburgh
Perry, Frank V., Los Alamos National Laboratory
Phipps Morgan, Jason, Cornell University
Pistone , Mattia , University of Georgia
Putirka, Keith D., Fresno State University
Pyle, David M., University of Oxford
Quick, James E., Southern Methodist University
Reynolds, Robert W., Central Oregon Community College
Rhodes, J. Michael, University of Massachusetts, Amherst
Riggs, Nancy, Northern Arizona University
Rodgers, Mel, University of South Florida
Rodriguez, Lizzette A., University of Puerto Rico
Roldan Quintana, Jaime, Univ Nacional Autonoma de Mexico
Roman, Diana C., Carnegie Institution for Science
Rose, William I., Michigan Technological University
Ross, Pierre-Simon, Universite du Quebec

Ruiz Cubillo, Paulo, Univ de Costa Rica
Russell, James K., University of British Columbia
Sanchez-Rubio, Gerardo, Univ Nacional Autonoma de Mexico
Sar, Abdullah, Firat University
Schaefer, Janet R. G., Alaska Division of Geological & Geophysical Surveys
Sennert, Sally K., Smithsonian Institution / National Museum of Natural History
Shea, Thomas, University of Hawai'i, Manoa
Sheridan, Michael F., SUNY, Buffalo
Smith, Alan L., California State University, San Bernardino
Solana, Camen, University of Portsmouth
Soldati, Arianna, North Carolina State University
Sonder, Ingo, SUNY, Buffalo
Soule, S. Adam, Woods Hole Oceanographic Institution
Stix, John, McGill University
Straub, Susanne, Columbia University
Swanson, Donald A., University of Hawai'i, Manoa
Taylor, Rex N., University of Southampton
Teasdale, Rachel, California State University, Chico
Townsend, Meredith, University of Oregon
Ukstins, Ingrid, University of Iowa
Valentine, Gregory, SUNY, Buffalo
Van Ry, Michael, Orange Coast College
Vanderkluysen, Loyc, Drexel University
Venzke, Edward, Smithsonian Institution / National Museum of Natural History
Vigouroux-Caillibot, Nathalie, Douglas College
Voight, Barry, Pennsylvania State University, University Park
Vroon, Pieter, Vrije Universiteit Amsterdam
Wadsworth, Fabian, Durham University
Wallace, Paul, University of Oregon
Waters, Laura E., Sonoma State University
Webber, Karen L., University of Michigan
Webber, Karen L., University of New Orleans
White, James D., University of Otago
Williams, Stanley N., Arizona State University
Williams-Jones, Glyn, Simon Fraser University
Wilson, Thomas, University of Canterbury
Wulff, Andrew, Western Kentucky University
Zimmerer, Matthew, New Mexico Institute of Mining and Technology

Mathematical Geology

Barton, Christopher C., Wright State University
Bolton, Edward W., Yale University
Campbell, Katherine, Los Alamos National Laboratory
Cathles, Lawrence M., Cornell University
Chien, Yi-Ju, Pacific Northwest National Laboratory
Chou, Charissa J., Pacific Northwest National Laboratory
Cornejo-Luna, Efrain, Univ Autonoma de Baja California Sur
de Hoop, Maarten, Purdue University
Doveton, John H., University of Kansas
Edwards, Stuart, University of Newcastle Upon Tyne
Faccenda, Manuele, Università degli Studi di Padova
Fairbairn, David, University of Newcastle Upon Tyne
Ford, Allistair, University of Newcastle Upon Tyne
Ford, Arianne, James Cook University
Fox, Peter A., Rensselaer Polytechnic Institute
Gordon, Terence M., University of Calgary
Harbaugh, John W., Stanford University
Harding, Chris, Iowa State University of Science & Technology
He, Changming, University of Delaware
Hesse, Marc A., University of Texas, Austin
Hunt, Allen G., Wright State University
Johnson, Glenn W., University of Utah
Journel, Andre G., Stanford University
Lee, Jejung, University of Missouri, Kansas City
Lutz, Timothy M., West Chester University
MAZZELLA, Antonio A., Universita di Cagliari
Murray, Christopher J., Pacific Northwest National Laboratory
Penna, Nigel, University of Newcastle Upon Tyne
Rogova, Galina L., SUNY, Buffalo
Rundberg, Robert S., Los Alamos National Laboratory
Sonder, Leslie J., Dartmouth College
Spiegelman, Marc W., Columbia University
Sun, Alexander, University of Texas, Austin
Therrien, Pierre, Universite Laval
Tuttle, Samuel , Mount Holyoke College
Walton, Ian, University of Utah

Mineral Physics

Abramson, Evan H., University of Washington
Bass, Jay D., University of Illinois, Urbana-Champaign
Brown, J. Michael, University of Washington
Bukowinski, Mark S., University of California, Berkeley
Carpenter, Michael, University of Cambridge
Chen, Jiuhua, Florida International University
Cohen, Ronald E., Carnegie Institution for Science
Cooper, Reid F., Brown University
Duffy, Thomas S., Princeton University
Farver, John R., Bowling Green State University
Fenter, Paul, University of Illinois at Chicago
Fischer, Rebecca A., Harvard University
Goncharov, Alexander F., Carnegie Institution for Science
Heinz, Dion L., University of Chicago
Hugo, Richard, Portland State University
Jackson, Jennifer M., California Institute of Technology
Jacobsen, Steven D., Northwestern University
Jeanloz, Raymond, University of California, Berkeley
Karato, Shun-ichiro, Yale University
Kavner, Abby, University of California, Los Angeles
Knittle, Elise, University of California, Santa Cruz
Kronenberg, Andreas, Texas A&M University
Lieberman, Robert C., Stony Brook University
Lin, Jung-Fu, University of Texas, Austin
Militzer, Burkhard, University of California, Berkeley
Riggs, Eric, Texas A&M University
Rucks, Melinda, Princeton University
Salje, Ekhard, University of Cambridge
Saxena, Surendra K., Florida International University
Secco, Richard A., Western University
Stracher, Glenn B., East Georgia State College
Struzhkin, Viktor V., Carnegie Institution for Science
Tschauner, Oliver, University of Nevada, Las Vegas
Tyburczy, James A., Arizona State University
Vocadlo, Lidunka, University College London
Weidner, Donald J., Stony Brook University
Williams, Quentin, University of California, Santa Cruz
Zhang, Jin, University of New Mexico

Medical Geology

Buck, Brenda J., University of Nevada, Las Vegas
Finkelman, Robert B., University of Texas, Dallas
Fuge, Ron, Aberystwyth University
Gillmore, Gavin, Kingston University
Hunt, Andrew, University of Texas, Arlington
Markowitz, Steven, Queens College (CUNY)
Morabia, Alfredo, Queens College (CUNY)
Pasteris, Jill D., Washington University in St. Louis
Williams, Lynda, Arizona State University

Forensic Geology

Williams, Thomas, University of Idaho

ECONOMIC GEOLOGY

General Economic Geology

Adedcyin, A. D., University of Ilorin
Adetunji, A, Obafemi Awolowo University
Akabzaa, Thomas M., University of Ghana
Akande, S. O., University of Ilorin
Alavi, Ghafour, University of Tabriz
Alexandre, Paul, Brandon University
Alexandrov, Eugene A., Queens College (CUNY)
Allard, Gilles O., University of Georgia
Anger-Kraavi, Annela, University of East Anglia
Ansdell, Kevin M., University of Saskatchewan
Anthony, Robin, DCNR- Pennsylvania Bureau of Geological Survey
Apostoae, Laviniu, Alexandru Ioan Cuza
Ashley, Paul, University of New England
Atkinson, Jr., William W., University of Colorado
Banerjee, Neil, Western University
Barnes, Sarah- J., Universite du Quebec a Chicoutimi
Barton, Mark D., University of Arizona
Beaudoin, Georges, Universite Laval
Bolarinwa, A. T., University of Ibadan

Bornhorst, Theodore J., Michigan Technological University
Bouzari, Farhad, University of British Columbia
Bradshaw, Peter M., University of British Columbia
Brimhall, George H., University of California, Berkeley
Burt, Donald M., Arizona State University
Busch, Lawrence, California Geological Survey
Bustillo, Manuel, Univ Complutense de Madrid
Calagari, Ali Asghar, University of Tabriz
Camprubi, Antoni, Univ Nacional Autonoma de Mexico
Castor, Stephen B., University of Nevada, Reno
Chang, Zhaoshan, Colorado School of Mines
Cheney, Eric S., University of Washington
Cheng, Yanbo, James Cook University
Chi, Guoxiang, University of Regina
Clark, Kenneth F., University of Texas, El Paso
Clendenin, Jr., Charles W., South Carolina Dept of Natural Resources
Clinkenbeared, John, California Geological Survey
Conly, Andrew G., Lakehead University
Cook, Robert B., Auburn University
Cooke, David R., University of Tasmania
Coolbaugh, Mark F., University of Nevada, Reno
Corbineau, Lucien, Institut Polytechnique LaSalle Beauvais (ex-IGAL)
Coron, Cynthia R., Southern Connecticut State University
Corral, Isaac, James Cook University
Coveney Jr, Raymond M., University of Missouri, Kansas City
Craig, James R., Virginia Polytechnic Institute & State University
Craw, Dave, University of Otago
Crawford, Thomas J., University of West Georgia
Dewaele, Stijn, Ghent University
Di Gregorio, Monica, University of Leeds
Donovan, John F., Winona State University
Duke, Norman A., Western University
Elueze, A. A., University of Ibadan
Evans, Thomas J., University of Wisconsin, Madison, Division of Extension
Fitzpatrick, William, University of Wisconsin, Madison, Division of Extension
Flawn, Peter T., University of Texas, Austin
Franco-Rubio, Miguel, Univ Autonoma de Chihuahua
Garcia-Gutierrez, Luis, Univ Autonoma de San Luis Potosi
Gauthier, Michel, Universite du Quebec a Montreal
Gemmell, J B., University of Tasmania
Gibson, Andy, University of Portsmouth
Gillerman, Virginia S., University of Idaho
Gillerman, Virginia S., Boise State University
Greyling, Lynnette N., University of Cape Town
Guan, Dabo, University of Leeds
Guha, Jayanta, Universite du Quebec a Chicoutimi
Gulen, Gurcan, University of Texas, Austin
Gysi, Alexander, New Mexico Institute of Mining and Technology
Hannington, Mark, University of Ottawa
Hanson, William D., Arkansas Geological Survey
Harris, DeVerle P., University of Arizona
Hayman, Patrick C., Queensland University of Technology
Hedenquist, Jeffrey W., University of Ottawa
Hickey, Kenneth A., University of British Columbia
Hickson, Catherine J., University of British Columbia
Hohn, Michael E., West Virginia Geological & Economic Survey
Hollenbaugh, Kenneth M., Boise State University
Holley, Elizabeth, Colorado School of Mines
Hollings, Peter N., Lakehead University
Hoyer, Lauren, University of KwaZulu-Natal
Huber, Matthew, University of the Free State
Ikonnikova, Svetlana, University of Texas, Austin
Jago, Bruce C., Laurentian University, Sudbury
Jebrak, Michel, Universite du Quebec a Montreal
Jugo, Pedro J., Laurentian University, Sudbury
Kamilli, Robert J., University of Arizona
Karginoglu, Yusuf, Firat University
Kazimoto, Emmanuel O., University of Dar es Salaam
Keith, Jeffrey D., Brigham Young University
Kelly, William C., University of Michigan
Kesler, Stephen E., University of Michigan
Kish, Stephen A., Florida State University
Kontak, Daniel J., Laurentian University, Sudbury
La Berge, Gene L., University of Wisconsin, Oshkosh
Laki, Sam, Central State University
Large, Ross R., University of Tasmania
Lasemi, Zakaria, Illinois State Geological Survey
Lassetter, William L., Division of Geology and Mineral Resources
Layton-Matthews, Daniel, Queen's University
Lehrberger, Gerhard, Technical University of Munich
Li, Chusi, Indiana University, Bloomington
Linnen, Robert, University of Waterloo
Locmelis, Marek, Missouri University of Science and Technology
Lorenzoni, Irene, University of East Anglia
Maher, Kierran, New Mexico Institute of Mining and Technology
Mantilla Figueroa, Luis C., Univ Industrial de Santander
Marschik, Robert, Ludwig-Maximilians-Universitaet Muenchen
Masterman, Steven S., Alaska Division of Geological & Geophysical Surveys
Mattieu, Lucie, Universite du Quebec a Chicoutimi
mcClenaghan, Seán h., Trinity College
McLemore, Virginia T., New Mexico Institute of Mining and Technology
Mensah, Emmanuel, Kwame Nkrumah University of Science and Technology
Misra, Kula C., University of Tennessee, Knoxville
Mohammad Reza, Hosseinzadeh, University of Tabriz
Moreno-Rodriguez, Veronica, Univ Estatal de Sonora
Morton, Penelope C., University of Minnesota Duluth
Mumin, A. Hamid, Brandon University
Muntean, John, University of Nevada, Reno
Murphy, Sean C., Austin Community College District
Muszer, Antoni, University of Wroclaw
Nasraoui, Mohamed, Institut Polytechnique LaSalle Beauvais (ex-IGAL)
Nex, Paul A., University of the Witwatersrand
Niewendorp, Clark, Oregon Dept of Geology and Mineral Industries
Nimis, Paolo, Università degli Studi di Padova
Okunlola, Ougbenga. A., University of Ibadan
Olivo, Gema, Queen's University
Orozco-Villasenor, Francisco Javier, Univ Autonoma de San Luis Potosi
Paez, H. A., McMaster University
Paterson, Colin J., South Dakota School of Mines & Technology
Pietrzak-Renaud, Natalie, Western University
Potra, Adriana, University of Arkansas, Fayetteville
Prichard, Hazel, University of Wales
Pride, Douglas E., Ohio State University
Ramagwede, Fhatuwani L., Geological Survey of South Africa
Rambaud, Fabienne M., Austin Community College District
Ressel, Mike, University of Nevada, Reno
Ridley, John R., Colorado State University
Robertson, Daniel E., Monroe Community College
Robertson, James M., University of Wisconsin, Madison
Robertson, James M., University of Wisconsin, Madison, Division of Extension
Robertson, James M., University of Wisconsin, Extension
Sagiroglu, Ahmet, Firat University
Sasmaz, Ahmet, Firat University
Seedorff, Eric, University of Arizona
Shackley, Simon J., Edinburgh University
Shaver, Stephen A., Sewanee: University of the South
Shortt, Niamh K., Edinburgh University
Siahcheshm, Kamal, University of Tabriz
Simmons, Peter, University of East Anglia
Solecki, Andrzej, University of Wroclaw
Stucker, James D., Ohio Dept of Natural Resources
Talley, John H., University of Delaware
Thompson, Tommy, Colorado State University
Titley, Spencer R., University of Arizona
Tribe, Selina, Douglas College
Tritlla, Jordi, Univ Nacional Autonoma de Mexico
Twelker, Evan, Alaska Division of Geological & Geophysical Surveys
Ulloa, Salvador, Univ Nacional Autonoma de Mexico
van der Horst, Dan, Edinburgh University
van Hinsberg, Vincent, McGill University
Vatuva, Absai , University of Namibia
Warren, Rachel, University of East Anglia
Werdon, Melanie B., Alaska Division of Geological & Geophysical Surveys
Wilkins, Colin, University of Plymouth
Wolfgram, Diane, Montana Tech of the University of Montana
Yao, Yon, Rhodes University
Yates, Martin G., University of Maine
Yellich, John, Western Michigan University
Zentilli, Marcos, Dalhousie University

Coal

Abdullah, Wan Hasiah, University of Malaya
Asuen, Godwin O., University of Benin
Bailey, Judy, University of Newcastle
Bustin, R. Marc, University of British Columbia
Calder, John, Dalhousie University
Cardott, Brian J., University of Oklahoma
Chenoweth, Cheri A., Illinois State Geological Survey
Drobniak, Agnieszka, Indiana University
Elrick, Scott D., University of Illinois
Elrick, Scott D., Illinois State Geological Survey
Flood, Peter, University of New England
Hoffman, Gretchen K., New Mexico Institute of Mining and Technology
Hower, James C., University of Kentucky
Huggett, William, Southern Illinois University Carbondale
Kehoe, Kelsey, Wyoming State Geological Survey
Khawaja, Ikram U., Youngstown State University
Korose, Christopher P., Illinois State Geological Survey
Korose, Christopher P., Illinois State Geological Survey
Lentz, Leonard J., DCNR- Pennsylvania Bureau of Geological Survey
Lindberg, Jonathan W., Pacific Northwest National Laboratory
Mastalerz, Maria, Indiana University
Mastalerz, Maria D., Indiana University, Bloomington
Meyer, Rebecca A., Indiana University
Miller, Barry W., Tennessee Geological Survey
Mukhopadhyay, Prasanta, Dalhousie University
Myers, Alan R., Illinois State Geological Survey
Neubaum, John C., DCNR- Pennsylvania Bureau of Geological Survey
Obrad, Jennifer M., Illinois State Geological Survey
Renton, John J., West Virginia University
Rimmer, Susan M., Southern Illinois University Carbondale
Shaulis, James R., DCNR- Pennsylvania Bureau of Geological Survey
Ward, Colin R., University of New South Wales
Wright, Chris, Ohio Dept of Natural Resources

Metallic Ore Deposits

Barnett, Douglas B., Pacific Northwest National Laboratory
Bissig, Thomas, University of British Columbia
Broughton, William A., University of Wisconsin, Platteville
Brown, Philip E., University of Wisconsin, Madison
Cedillo, Esteban, Univ Nacional Autonoma de Mexico
Chang, Zhaoshan, James Cook University
Chapman, Robert J., University of Leeds
Chavez, Jr., William X., New Mexico Institute of Mining and Technology
Chen, Yuan, University of British Columbia, Okanagan Campus
Clark, Alan H., Queen's University
Cline, Jean S., University of Nevada, Las Vegas
Corona-Esquivel, Rodolfo, Univ Nacional Autonoma de Mexico
Corriveau, Louise, Universite du Quebec
Crowe, Douglas E., University of Georgia
Dilles, John H., Oregon State University
Dube, Benoit, Universite du Quebec
Dugdale, Allison, Curtin University
Durazo-Tapia, Gustavo E., Univ Estatal de Sonora
Fifarek, Richard, Southern Illinois University Carbondale
Friehauf, Kurt, Kutztown University of Pennsylvania
Gaboury, Damien, Universite du Quebec a Chicoutimi
Gibson, Harold L., Laurentian University, Sudbury
Gibson, Harold, Carleton University
Good, David, Western University
Graf, Jr., Joseph L., Southern Oregon University
Guilbert, John M., University of Arizona
Hagni, Richard D., Missouri University of Science and Technology
Hannington, Mark D., Carleton University
Harlaux, Matthieu, University of Nevada, Reno
Hart, Craig J., University of British Columbia
Hooda, Peter, Kingston University
Keays, Reid R., Laurentian University, Sudbury
Kinnaird, Judith A., University of the Witwatersrand
Kissin, Stephen A., Lakehead University
Koestel, Mark, Mt. San Antonio College
Kyle, J. Richard, University of Texas, Austin
Lesher, Michael, Laurentian University, Sudbury
Linnen, Robert, Western University
Lodge, Robert, University of Wisconsin, Eau Claire
Macfarlane, Andrew W., Florida International University
Mateus, António, Unive de Lisboa
McAllister, Arnold L., University of New Brunswick
McLemore, Virginia, New Mexico Institute of Mining and Technology
Melchiorre, Erik, California State University, San Bernardino
Menuge, Julian F., University College Dublin
Monecke, Thomas, Colorado School of Mines
Morel-Kraepiel, Anne, Princeton University
Morton, Roger D., University of Alberta
Mossman, David J., Mount Allison University
Muchez, Philippe, Katholieke Universiteit Leuven
Muntean, John L., University of Nevada, Reno
Naldrett, Anthony J., University of Toronto
Newberry, Rainer J., University of Alaska, Fairbanks
Ortega, Lorena, Univ Complutense de Madrid
Petersen, Erich U., University of Utah
Piña, Rubén, Univ Complutense de Madrid
Powell, Wayne G., Graduate School of the City University of New York
Richards, Jeremy P., Laurentian University, Sudbury
Richardson, Carson A., University of Arizona
Romberger, Samuel B., Colorado School of Mines
Ruvalcaba-Ruiz, Delfino C., Univ Autonoma de San Luis Potosi
Salaun, Pascal, University of Liverpool
Shelton, Kevin L., University of Missouri
Simmons, Stuart, University of Utah
Sinclair, Alastair J., University of British Columbia
Spry, Paul G., Iowa State University of Science & Technology
Thompson, John F., Cornell University
Thompson, John F. H., University of British Columbia
Tingley, Joseph V., University of Nevada, Reno
Tosdal, Richard, University of British Columbia
Uzunlar, Nuri, South Dakota School of Mines & Technology
van der Berg, Stan, University of Liverpool
Vasallo, Fernando, Univ Nacional Autonoma de Mexico
Vassallo-Morales, Luis F., Univ Nacional Autonoma de Mexico
Walker, Alex, Curtin University
Watkinson, David H., Carleton University
Wheeler, Greg, Sacramento State University
Williamson, Ben, Exeter University

Industrial Minerals

Bal Akkoca, Dicle, Firat University
Barker, James M., New Mexico Institute of Mining and Technology
Berg, Richard B., Montana Tech of The University of Montana
Calengas, Peter L., Western Illinois University
Crespo, Elena, Univ Complutense de Madrid
Gregory, Robert, Wyoming State Geological Survey
Krukowski, Stanley T., University of Oklahoma
Lasemi, Zakaria, Illinois State Geological Survey
Moreton, Kim, Exeter University
Power, W. Robert, Georgia State University
Rocha, Fernando, Unive de Aveiro
Simandl, George J., University of Victoria
Sousa, Luís M., Unive de Trás-os-Montes e Alto Douro
Spooner, Edward T. C., University of Toronto
Sutherland, Wayne, Wyoming State Geological Survey
Van Straaten, H. Peter, University of Guelph

Oil and Gas

Anderson, Ross, Heriot-Watt University
Balázs, László, Eotvos Lorand University
Begg, Stephen, University of Adelaide
Brown, Alan, West Virginia University
C., Jeffrey C., Youngstown State University
Carter, Kristin M., DCNR- Pennsylvania Bureau of Geological Survey
Clarkson, Christopher , University of Calgary
Cox, John, Mount Royal University
Crockett, Joan E., Illinois State Geological Survey
Deisher, Jeffrey , Ohio Dept of Natural Resources
Eldridge, Jayson, Indiana University
Evans, Martin J., Cornell University
Finley, Robert J., Illinois State Geological Survey
Gillis, Robert, Alaska Division of Geological & Geophysical Surveys
Gluyas, Jon, Durham University
Grube, John P., Illinois State Geological Survey
Harder, Brian J., Louisiana State University
Herriott, Trystan, Alaska Division of Geological & Geophysical Surveys
Hills, Denise J., Geological Survey of Alabama
Hooks, Chris H., Geological Survey of Alabama

Horn, Marty R., Louisiana State University
Hosseini, Seyyed Abolfazi, University of Texas, Austin
Huff, Bryan G., Illinois State Geological Survey
Hulett, Sam, Ohio Dept of Natural Resources
Jafarizadeh, Babak, Heriot-Watt University
Johnston, III, John E., Louisiana State University
King, Carey, University of Texas, Austin
Krevor, Samuel, Imperial College
Leetaru, Hannes E., Illinois State Geological Survey
Leighton, Morris W., University of Illinois, Urbana-Champaign
Leone, James, New York State Geological Survey
Lepain, David, Alaska Division of Geological & Geophysical Surveys
Levey, Raymond A., University of Utah
Lucia, F. J., University of Texas, Austin
Lynds, Ranie, Wyoming State Geological Survey
Malinconico, Mary Ann, Lafayette College
Markowski, Antonette K., DCNR- Pennsylvania Bureau of Geological Survey
Nicholas, Chris, Trinity College
Nielsen, Peter J., Utah Geological Survey
Oldershaw, Michael, Bakersfield College
Pascussi, Michael, New York State Geological Survey
Potter, Eric C., University of Texas at Austin, Jackson School of Geosciences
Seyler, Beverly, Illinois State Geological Survey
Shew, Roger D., University of North Carolina, Wilmington
Tew, Nick, University of Alabama
Vanden Berg, Michael, Utah Geological Survey
Vigrass, Laurence W., University of Regina
Waid, Christopher, Ohio Dept of Natural Resources
Webb, Nathan D., Illinois State Geological Survey
Zeidouni, Mehdi, University of Texas, Austin

Construction Materials (SSG)

Cnudde, Veerle, Ghent University

Ore Deposits (Other)

Baig, Ayat, Brandon University
Carranza, Emmanuel John, University of KwaZulu-Natal
Haroldson, Erik L., Austin Peay State University
Mantei, Erwin J., Missouri State University
Runyon, Simone, University of Wyoming

GEOCHEMISTRY

General Geochemistry

Abimbola, A. E., University of Ibadan
Adisa, Adeshina L., Federal University of Technology, Akure
Aines, Roger D., Lawrence Livermore National Laboratory
Ajayi, T. R., Obafemi Awolowo University
Akaegbobi, I. M., University of Ibadan
Allen, Douglas, Salem State University
Allen-King, Richelle, SUNY, Buffalo
Amonette, Alexandra B., Pacific Northwest National Laboratory
Anderson, Robert F., Columbia University
April, Richard, Colgate University
Atekwana, Eliot A., University of Delaware
Ayers, John C., Vanderbilt University
Ayling, Bridget, University of Nevada, Reno
Babcock, R. S., Western Washington University
Bales, Roger C., University of Arizona
Banks, David, University of Leeds
Barnes, Hubert L., Pennsylvania State University, University Park
Barnes, Jaime D., University of Texas, Austin
Basu, Anirban, Royal Holloway University of London
Beets, Kay J., Vrije Universiteit Amsterdam
Beiersdorfer, Raymond E., Youngstown State University
Belmonte, Donato, Universita di Genova
Bender, Michael L., Princeton University
Berger, Peter M., Illinois State Geological Survey
Bergquist, Bridget, University of Toronto
Berkelhammer, Max, University of Illinois at Chicago
Bernhard, Joan M., Woods Hole Oceanographic Institution
Bernier, Luc, McMaster University
Bird, Dennis K., Stanford University
Bissada, K. K., Rice University
Blake, Ruth E., Yale University
Blowes, David W., University of Waterloo
Bodnar, Robert J., Virginia Polytechnic Institute & State University
Boger, Phillip D., SUNY, Geneseo
Bohm, Christian, University of Manitoba
Bolge, Louise, Columbia University
Bouman, Heather, University of Oxford
Bourcier, Bill L., Lawrence Livermore National Laboratory
Brantley, Susan L., Pennsylvania State University, University Park
Broecker, Wallace S., Columbia University
Brooks, Paul D., University of Arizona
Brounce, Maryjo, University of California, Riverside
Brown, Cathe, Smithsonian Institution / National Museum of Natural History
Bryant, Ernest A., Los Alamos National Laboratory
Bryce, Julia G., University of New Hampshire
Bulgariu, Dumitru, Alexandru Ioan Cuza
Burton, Jacqueline C., Argonne National Laboratory
Burton, Kevin, Durham University
Buseck, Peter R., Arizona State University
Butler, Ian B., Edinburgh University
Cai, Yue, Columbia University
Camacho, Elsa A., Pacific Northwest National Laboratory
Catling, David C., University of Washington
Centorbi, Tracey, University of Maryland
Chague-Goff, Catherine, University of New South Wales
Chatterjee, Nilanjan, Massachusetts Institute of Technology
Chen, Chu-Yung, University of Illinois, Urbana-Champaign
Chillrud, Steven, Columbia University
Chorover, Jonathan D., University of Arizona
Churchill, Ron C., California Geological Survey
Claeys, Philippe, Vrije University Brussel
Class, Connie, Columbia University
Clay, Patricia L., University of Manchester
Coe, Douglas A., Montana Tech of the University of Montana
Coggon, Jude A., University of Southampton
Cole, David R., Ohio State University
Collier, James D., Fort Lewis College
Cook, Robert B., Oak Ridge National Laboratory
Cowman, Tim C., South Dakota Dept of Env and Natural Resources
Darrah, Thomas, Ohio State University
Davisson, M L., Lawrence Livermore National Laboratory
Dawson, M. Robert, Iowa State University of Science & Technology
Day, James, University of California, San Diego
de Ignacio, Cristina, Univ Complutense de Madrid
Deng, Baolin, New Mexico Institute of Mining and Technology
Derry, Louis A., Cornell University
Ding, Kang, University of Minnesota, Twin Cities
Dong, Hailiang, Miami University
Dooley, John H., New Jersey Geological and Water Survey
Dostal, Jarda, Dalhousie University
Downes, Hilary, Birkbeck College
Drew, Douglas A., Montana Tech of the University of Montana
Duffy, Clarence J., Los Alamos National Laboratory
Dunbar, Nelia W., New Mexico Institute of Mining and Technology
Durham, William, Massachusetts Institute of Technology
Eby, G. Nelson, University of Massachusetts, Lowell
Eiler, John M., California Institute of Technology
Erhardt, Andrea M., University of Kentucky
Evans, Owen C., Stony Brook University
Eves, Robert L., Southern Utah University
Fajkoviæ, Hana, University of Zagreb
Fall, Andras, University of Texas, Austin
Farley, Kenneth A., California Institute of Technology
Farmer, G. Lang, University of Colorado
Faure, Gunter, Ohio State University
Feigenson, Mark D., Rutgers, The State University of New Jersey
Fernandez, Diego, University of Utah
Finkel, Robert C., Lawrence Livermore National Laboratory
Finkelstein, David, Hobart & William Smith Colleges
Flegal, Russell, University of California, Santa Cruz
Flowers, Rebecca M., University of Colorado
Foustoukos, Dionysis, Carnegie Institution for Science
Fraser, Donalf G., University of Oxford
Frey, Bonnie A., New Mexico Institute of Mining and Technology
Gambrell, Robert P., Louisiana State University
Gammons, Christopher H., Montana Tech of the University of Montana
Garbesi, Karina, California State University, East Bay
George, Graham, University of Saskatchewan
Ghiorso, Mark , University of Washington

Gilfillan, Stuart M., Edinburgh University
Gili, Stefania, Princeton University
Gleason, James D., University of Michigan
Goff, Fraser, Los Alamos National Laboratory
Goff, Fraser, University of New Mexico
Goldstein, Steven, Columbia University
Gonzalez, Luis , King Fahd University of Petroleum and Minerals
Gosselin, David C., Unversity of Nebraska, Lincoln
Gouldey, Jeremy C., Grand Valley State University
Goulet, Richard, University of Ottawa
Grant, Willard H., Emory University
Gurlea, Lawrence P., Youngstown State University
Gustin, Mae, University of Nevada, Reno
Gutierrez, Melida, Missouri State University
Halden, Norman M., University of Manitoba
Hall, Cynthia V., West Chester University
Hanchar, John, Memorial University of Newfoundland
Hansen, Robert N., University of the Free State
Hart, Stanley R., Woods Hole Oceanographic Institution
Harvey, Jason, University of Leeds
Hattori, Keiko, University of Ottawa
Hausrath, Elisabeth M., University of Nevada, Las Vegas
Hemming, Sidney, Columbia University
Henderson, Gideon, University of Oxford
Herndon, Elizabeth M., University of Tennessee, Knoxville
Hervig, Richard, Arizona State University
Hickey-Vargas, Rosemary, Florida International University
Hinman, Nancy W., University of Montana
Hinton, Richard, Edinburgh University
Hodges, Floyd N., Pacific Northwest National Laboratory
Hudson, Robert J. M., University of Illinois, Urbana-Champaign
Ige, A. O., Obafemi Awolowo University
Imasuen, Isaac O., University of Benin
Irving, Tony, University of Washington
Izon, Gareth, University of St. Andrews
Jacobs, Gary K., Oak Ridge National Laboratory
Jacobson, Roger, University of Nevada, Reno
Jarvis, Ian, Kingston University
Jerde, Eric, Morehead State University
Jin, Qusheng, University of Oregon
John, Bratton F., Wayne State University
Johnson, Clark M., University of Wisconsin, Madison
Johnston, David T., Harvard University
Kalender, Leyla, Firat University
Kallemeyn, Gregory, University of California, Los Angeles
Kamber, Balz S., Trinity College
Kambewa, Chamunorwa , Tshwane University of Technology
Kamenov, George D., University of Florida
Kaplan, Isaac R., University of California, Los Angeles
Kara, Hatice, Firat University
Kaszuba, John P., University of Wyoming
Katz, Richard, University of Oxford
Kellman, Lisa M., Dalhousie University
Kenna, Timothy, Columbia University
Kim, Sang-Tae, McMaster University
Kiro Feldman, Yael, Columbia University
Kirste, Dirk, Simon Fraser University
Knudsen, Andrew, Lawrence University
Koeman-Shields, Elizabeth, Angelo State University
Kolesar, Peter T., Utah State University
Koppers, Anthony, Oregon State University
Koretsky, Carla, Western Michigan University
Kotzer, Tom, University of Saskatchewan
Krawczynski, Michael J., Washington University in St. Louis
Ku, Teh-Lung, University of Southern California
Kuzyk, Zou Zou, University of Manitoba
Labidi, Jabrane, University of Maryland
Lange, Eric, Ball State University
Langmuir, Charles H., Harvard University
Layne, Graham, Memorial University of Newfoundland
Le Roex, Anton, University of Cape Town
Lechler, Paul J., University of Nevada, Reno
Lee, Cin-Ty A., Rice University
Legore, Virginia L., Pacific Northwest National Laboratory
Lehloenya, Pelele, University of the Free State
Lentz, David R., University of New Brunswick
Lerman, Abraham, Northwestern University
Leuta-Madondo, Palesa, University of KwaZulu-Natal
Léveillé, Richard, McGill University
Leybourne, Matthew I., Laurentian University, Sudbury
Lindenmeier, Clark W., Pacific Northwest National Laboratory
Liu, Xiaolei , University of Oklahoma
Liu, Xiaoming, University of North Carolina, Chapel Hill
Livens, Francis, University of Manchester
Locke II, Randall A., University of Illinois
Longerich, Henry, Memorial University of Newfoundland
Lopez, Dina L., Ohio University
Loyd, Sean, California State University, Fullerton
Lu, Zunli, Syracuse University
Luttge, Andreas, Rice University
Lyons, Timothy W., University of California, Riverside
Macdougall, J. Douglas, University of California, San Diego
Macpherson, Colin G., Durham University
Magson, Justine, University of the Free State
Mango, Helen N., Castleton University
Manning, Christina, Royal Holloway University of London
Manya, Shukrani, University of Dar es Salaam
Marquez, L. Lynn, Millersville University
Martin, Paul F., Pacific Northwest National Laboratory
Martin, Scot T., Harvard University
Marzoli, Andrea, Università degli Studi di Padova
McClelland, James W., University of Texas, Austin
McDonough, William F., University of Maryland
McGrail, Bernard P., Pacific Northwest National Laboratory
McIntosh, Jennifer C., University of Arizona
McKibben, Michael A., University of California, Riverside
McKinley, Galen, Columbia University
McLennan, Scott M., Stony Brook University
McNicol, Gavin, University of Illinois at Chicago
Meduniæ, Gordana, University of Zagreb
Meixner, Thomas, University of Arizona
Mensing, Teresa, Ohio State University
Mercy, Edward L., Lakehead University
Meyer, William T., Argonne National Laboratory
Meyzen, Christine M., Università degli Studi di Padova
Michel, Jacqueline, University of New Orleans
Milkov, Alexei, Colorado School of Mines
MOINE, Bertrand N., Université Jean Monnet, Saint-Etienne
Moldovan, Brett, University of Saskatchewan
Morrill, Penny, Memorial University of Newfoundland
Mortlock, Richard , Rutgers, The State University of New Jersey
Mukasa, Samuel, University of Minnesota, Twin Cities
Mukhopadhyay, Sujoy, University of California, Davis
Murgulet, Valeriu, Texas A&M University, Corpus Christi
Murowchick, James B., University of Missouri, Kansas City
Murphy, David T., Queensland University of Technology
Nagy, Kathryn L., University of Illinois at Chicago
Naranjo, Ramon, University of Nevada, Reno
Nondorf, Lea, Arkansas Geological Survey
Nyame, Frank K., University of Ghana
O'Driscoll, Nelson, Acadia University
O'Hara, Matthew J., Pacific Northwest National Laboratory
O'Neil, Jonathan, University of Ottawa
Odokuma-Alonge, Ovie, University of Benin
Odom, LeRoy A., Florida State University
Okulewicz, Steven C., Hofstra University
Olanrewaju, Johnson, Gannon University
Olatunji, A. S., University of Ibadan
Olsen, Khris B., Pacific Northwest National Laboratory
Olszewski, Kathy, SUNY, Maritime College
Omelon, Christopher, University of Texas, Austin
Otamendi, Juan E., Univ Nacional de Rio Cuarto
Ozturk, Nevin, Firat University
Palinkaš, Ladislav, University of Zagreb
Palmer, Martin R., University of Southampton
Pant, Hari, Lehman College (CUNY)
Papineau, Dominic, University College London
Parker, Kent E., Pacific Northwest National Laboratory
Parris, Thomas M., University of Kentucky
Patera, Edward S., Los Alamos National Laboratory
Pearce, J A., Cardiff University
Peng, Yongbo, Louisiana State University

Philben, Michael , Hope College
Piccoli, Philip M., University of Maryland
Pichevin, Laetitia, Edinburgh University
Pickering, Ingrid J., University of Saskatchewan
Pietranik, Anna, University of Wroclaw
Pintilei, Mitica, Alexandru Ioan Cuza
Plank, Terry, Columbia University
Plante, Martin, Universite Laval
Pommier, Anne, University of California, San Diego
Porcelli, Don, University of Oxford
Pourmand, Ali, University of Miami
Pourret, Olivier, Institut Polytechnique LaSalle Beauvais (ex-IGAL)
Powell, Brian A., Clemson University
Pracny, Pavel, Masaryk University
Prevec, Steve, Rhodes University
Price, Douglas M., Youngstown State University
Prohiæ, Esad, University of Zagreb
Prowse, Terry D., University of Waterloo
Prytulak, Julie, Durham University
Ptacek, Carol J., University of Waterloo
Rae, James, University of St. Andrews
Reed, Mark H., University of Oregon
Reeves, Claire, University of East Anglia
Reiners, Peter, University of Arizona
Richardson, Steve, University of Cape Town
Rickard, D, Cardiff University
Riedinger, Natascha, Oklahoma State University
Roberts, Stephen, University of Southampton
Rohs, C. Renee, Northwest Missouri State University
Rollinson, Hugh, University of Derby
Romanak, Katherine D., Univ of Texas at Austin, Jackson Sch of Geosciences
Romaniello, Stephen J., University of Tennessee, Knoxville
Rose, Arthur W., Pennsylvania State University, University Park
Rose, Catherine V., Trinity College
Rudnick, Roberta L., University of Maryland
Ruiz, Joaquin, University of Arizona
Ruttenberg, Kathleen C., University of Hawai'i, Manoa
Ruttenberg, Kathleen, University of Hawai'i, Manoa
Saal, Alberto E., Brown University
Sack, Richard, University of Washington
Sakyi, Patrick A., University of Ghana
Salters, Vincent J., Florida State University
Samson, Iain M., University of Windsor
Savov, Ivan, University of Leeds
Schaef, Herbert T., Pacific Northwest National Laboratory
Schaefer, Joerg, Columbia University
Schlosser, Peter, Columbia University
Schrag, Daniel P., Harvard University
Schubert, Brian, University of Louisiana at Lafayette
Seitz, Jeffery C., California State University, East Bay
Senko, John M., University of Akron
Serne, R. Jeffrey, Pacific Northwest National Laboratory
Shahar, Anat, Carnegie Institution for Science
Shevenell, Lisa, University of Nevada, Reno
Shields, Robin, Heriot-Watt University
Shields-Zhou, Graham, University College London
Shock, Everett, Arizona State University
Sims, Kenneth W., University of Wyoming
Skippen, George B., Carleton University
Slater, Gregory F., McMaster University
Smethie, William, Columbia University
Speidel, David H., Queens College (CUNY)
Spencer, Ronald J., University of Calgary
Sprain, Courtney, University of Florida
Stack, Andrew, Georgia Institute of Technology
Stebbins, Jonathan F., Stanford University
Steele, Kenneth F., University of Arkansas, Fayetteville
Stevenson, Ross, Universite du Quebec a Montreal
Strmiæ Palinkaš, Sabina, University of Zagreb
Stubbins, Aron, Northeastern University
Sturchio, Neil C., Argonne National Laboratory
Sultan, Mohamed, Argonne National Laboratory
Susak, Nicholas J., University of New Brunswick
Taylor, Richard P., Carleton University
Teagle, Damon A., University of Southampton
Tefend, Karen S., University of West Georgia
Teng, Fangzhen, University of Washington
Thomas, Jim, University of Nevada, Reno
Tierney, Kate E., Denison University
Tomascak, Paul B., SUNY, Oswego
Trueman, Clive, University of Southampton
Tsikos, Hari, Rhodes University
Ttefanei, Dan, Alexandru Ioan Cuza
Van Geen, Alexander, Columbia University
Van Orman, James A., Case Western Reserve University
Vann, Jamie, West Chester University
Varekamp, Johan C., Wesleyan University
Vulava, Vijay M., College of Charleston
Wagner, Rick, Geological Survey of Alabama
Walker, John L., Argonne National Laboratory
Walther, John V., Southern Methodist University
Wang, Hong, Illinois State Geological Survey
Wang, Yang, Florida State University
Warburton, David L., Florida Atlantic University
Warren, Lesley A., McMaster University
Watkins, James, University of Oregon
Whipkey, Charles, University of Mary Washington
White, William B., Pennsylvania State University, University Park
Wigley, Rochelle, University of New Hampshire
Williams, Jeremy C., Kent State University
Wilson, Emily, Franklin and Marshall College
Winckler, Gisela, Columbia University
Wogelius, Roy, University of Manchester
Worrall, Fred, Durham University
Wronkiewicz, David J., Argonne National Laboratory
Wyman, Derek A., University of Saskatchewan
Yan, Beizhan, Columbia University
Yang, Qiang, Columbia University
Yardley, Bruce W., University of Leeds
Young, Edward, University of California, Los Angeles
Young, Nicolas, Columbia University
Zanazzi, Alessandro, Utah Valley University
Zeman, Josef, Masaryk University
Zhang, Tongwei, University of Texas, Austin
Zheng, Yan, Queens College (CUNY)
Zhu, Chen, Indiana University, Bloomington
Zolotov, Mikhail Y., Arizona State University

Analytical Geochemistry

Aguilera-Ortiz, Irma, Univ Nacional Autonoma de Mexico
Ash, Richard, University of Maryland
Baca, Dustin, New Mexico Institute of Mining and Technology
Barnes, Melanie A., Texas Tech University
Beauchamp, Marc, Western University
Bedard, Paul, Universite du Quebec a Chicoutimi
Benjamin, Timothy M., Los Alamos National Laboratory
Bhattacharyya, Sidhartha, University of Alabama
Blamey, Nigel J., New Mexico Institute of Mining and Technology
Bowen, Scott M., Los Alamos National Laboratory
Branam, Tracy D., Indiana University
Brandvold, Lynn A., New Mexico Institute of Mining and Technology
Burton, Edward, Southern Cross University
Cahill, Richard A., Illinois State Geological Survey
Castañeda, Isla, University of Massachusetts, Amherst
Catalano, Jeff, Washington University in St. Louis
Chappaz, Anthony, Central Michigan University
Cheng, Zhongqi, Brooklyn College (CUNY)
Dewey, Janet, University of Wyoming
Dickson, Alex, Royal Holloway University of London
Dore, John, Montana State University
Effert-Fanta, Shari E., Illinois State Geological Survey
Elam, Tim, University of Washington
Essling, Alice M., Argonne National Laboratory
Evans, Noreen, Curtin University
Frew, Nelson M., Woods Hole Oceanographic Institution
Gabitov, Rinat, Mississippi State University
Gagnon, Joel E., University of Windsor
Garcia, Sammy R., Los Alamos National Laboratory
Gavriloaiei, Traian, Alexandru Ioan Cuza
Greenwood, Paul, Curtin University
Halbig, Joseph B., University of Hawai'i, Hilo
Hart, Brian R., Western University

Heizler, Lynn, New Mexico Institute of Mining and Technology
Hemming, N. G., Queens College (CUNY)
Hinthorne, James R., Central Washington University
Hoe, Teh Guan, University of Malaya
Holman, Alex, Curtin University
Holt, Ben D., Argonne National Laboratory
Hopper, Peter, Curtin University
Hu, Wan-Ping (Sunny), Queensland University of Technology
Huff, Edmund A., Argonne National Laboratory
Huft, Ashley, Montana Tech of The University of Montana
Jackson, Brian P., Dartmouth College
Jedrysek, Mariusz O., University of Wroclaw
Johnson, Carl G., Woods Hole Oceanographic Institution
Johnston, Scott, Southern Cross University
Jones, Graham, Southern Cross University
Kersten, Michael, Universität Mainz
Klinkhammer, Gary P., Oregon State University
Knaack, Charles, Washington State University
Knudstrup, Renee, Salem State University
Krapac, Ivan G., Illinois State Geological Survey
Kuehn, Stephen C., Concord University
Kuentz, David C., Miami University
Landry, Peter B., Woods Hole Oceanographic Institution
Le Roux, Petrus J., University of Cape Town
Lottermoser, Bernd, Exeter University
MacDonald, Iain, University of Wales
Marshall, Dan D., Simon Fraser University
McGrath, Steve F., Montana Tech of The University of Montana
McMurtry, Gary M., University of Hawai'i, Manoa
Messo, Charles W., University of Dar es Salaam
Mock, R. Stephen, University of Montana Western
Moore, Lowell P., Virginia Polytechnic Institute & State University
Mora-Klepeis, Gabriela, University of Vermont
Mujumba, Jean K., University of Dar es Salaam
Navarre-Sitchler, Alexis, Colorado School of Mines
Neill, Owen K., Washington State University
Nelsen, Lori, Furman University
Olesik, John W., Ohio State University
Olmsted, Wayne, Montana Tech of the University of Montana
Orouji, Maqsood, University of Tabriz
Orr, Robert D., Pacific Northwest National Laboratory
Papike, James J., University of New Mexico
Pietruszka, Aaron, University of Hawai'i, Manoa
Pike, Steven M., Woods Hole Oceanographic Institution
Pun, Aurora, University of New Mexico
Ragland, Paul C., Florida State University
Ranville, James, Colorado School of Mines
Rose, Timothy, Smithsonian Institution / National Museum of Natural History
Rouff, Ashaki, Queens College (CUNY)
Savard, Dany, Universite du Quebec a Chicoutimi
Schneider, John F., Argonne National Laboratory
Shen, Linhan, Princeton University
Shimizu, Nobumichi, Woods Hole Oceanographic Institution
Smith, Catherine H., Los Alamos National Laboratory
Smith, Florence P., Argonne National Laboratory
Snow, Jonathan, University of Houston
Student, James J., Central Michigan University
Thomas, Donald M., University of Hawai'i, Manoa
Thompson, Christopher J., Pacific Northwest National Laboratory
Timmer, Jaqueline R., Montana Tech of The University of Montana
Van Loon, Lisa, Western University
Villasenor-Cabral, Maria G., Univ Nacional Autonoma de Mexico
Voelker, Bettina, Colorado School of Mines
Volborth, Alexis, Montana Tech of the University of Montana
Wang, Alian, Washington University in St. Louis
Warwick, Phillip, University of Southampton
Weis, Dominique A., University of British Columbia
Williams, Kim R., Colorado School of Mines
Yang, Panseok, University of Manitoba

Experimental Petrology/Phase Equilibria

Agee, Carl A., University of New Mexico
Anderson, G M., University of Toronto
Asimow, Paul D., California Institute of Technology
Brenan, James M., Dalhousie University
Candela, Philip A., University of Maryland
Carey, James W., Los Alamos National Laboratory
Cottrell, Elizabeth, University of Maryland
Cottrell, Elizabeth, Smithsonian Inst/Nat Mus of Nat History
Davis, Fred A., University of Minnesota Duluth
Eggler, David H., Pennsylvania State University, University Park
Ernst, W. Gary, Stanford University
Fedortchouk, Yana, Dalhousie University
Fei, Yingwei, University of Maryland
Fei, Yingwei, Carnegie Institution for Science
Feineman, Maureen D., Pennsylvania State University, University Park
Frank, Mark R., Northern Illinois University
Gilbert, M. Charles, University of Oklahoma
Hajash, Andrew, Texas A&M University
Herzberg, Claude T., Rutgers, The State University of New Jersey
Hewitt, David A., Virginia Polytechnic Institute & State University
Hsu, Liang-Chi, University of Nevada, Reno
Jenkins, David M., Binghamton University
Johnston, A. Dana, University of Oregon
Kilinc, Attila I., University of Cincinnati
Koster Van Groos, August F., University of Illinois at Chicago
Koziol, Andrea M., University of Dayton
Lambart, Sarah, University of Utah
Lazar, Codi, California State University, San Bernardino
Liang, Yan, Brown University
Lindsley, Donald H., Stony Brook University
London, David, University of Oklahoma
Lundstrom, Craig C., University of Illinois, Urbana-Champaign
McCauley, Marlene, Guilford College
Minarik, William G., McGill University
Mosenfelder, Jed, University of Minnesota, Twin Cities
Munoz, James L., University of Colorado
Mysen, Bjorn O., Carnegie Institution for Science
Nekvasil, Hanna, Stony Brook University
Newton, Robert C., University of California, Los Angeles
Parman, Stephen, Brown University
Presnall, Dean C., University of Texas, Dallas
Robert, Genevieve, Bates College
Rutherford, Malcolm J., Brown University
Seewald, Jeffrey S., Woods Hole Oceanographic Institution
Simmons, Craig, Colorado School of Mines
Steiner, Jeffrey, City College (CUNY)
Stolper, Edward M., California Institute of Technology
Tait, C. Drew, Los Alamos National Laboratory
Trail, Dustin, University of Rochester
Ustunisik, Gokce K., South Dakota School of Mines & Technology
van Westrenen, Wim, Vrije Universiteit Amsterdam
Walker, David, Columbia University
Watson, E. Bruce, Rensselaer Polytechnic Institute
Windom, Kenneth E., Iowa State University of Science & Technology
Withers, Tony, Western University
Wyllie, Peter J., California Institute of Technology

Exploration Geochemistry

Abdurrahman, A., University of Ilorin
Adepoju, Mohammed O., Federal University of Technology, Akure
Aspandiar, Mehrooz, Curtin University
Ayling, Bridget F., University of Nevada, Reno
Ayodele, Olusiji S., Federal University of Technology, Akure
Borojeviæ Šoštariæ, Sibila, University of Zagreb
Closs, L. Graham, Colorado School of Mines
Coggon, Rosalind M., University of Southampton
Cohen, David R., University of New South Wales
da Silva, Eduardo F., Unive de Aveiro
Dreschoff, Gisela, University of Kansas
Fletcher, William K., University of British Columbia
Gazel, Esteban, Cornell University
Goodell, Philip C., University of Texas, El Paso
Mathur, Ryan, Juniata College
McGoldrick, Peter J., University of Tasmania
Moon, Charlie, Exeter University
Pearson, Graham, University of Alberta
Price, Vaneaton, Clemson University
Stanley, Clifford R., Acadia University
White, William M., Cornell University
Whitehead, Robert E., Laurentian University, Sudbury
Williams-Jones, Anthony E., McGill University

Yanez, Carlos, Univ Nacional Autonoma de Mexico

Geochronology & Radioisotopes

Allen, Charlotte M., Queensland University of Technology
Amidon, Will, Middlebury College
Anderson, Alyssa, Princeton University
Ankney, Meagan, Northwestern University
Antinao, José Luis , Indiana University
Archibald, Doug A., Queen's University
Asmerom, Yemane, University of New Mexico
Baksi, Ajoy K., Louisiana State University
Baldwin, Suzanne L., Syracuse University
Bauer, Annie, University of Wisconsin, Madison
Baxter, Ethan, Boston College
Beard, Brian L., University of Wisconsin, Madison
Bell, Keith, Carleton University
Bickford, M. E., Syracuse University
Black, Stuart, University of Reading
Blackburn, Terrence, University of California, Santa Cruz
Blenkinsop, John, Carleton University
Blusztajn, Jurek, Woods Hole Oceanographic Institution
Blythe, Ann, Occidental College
Brown, Roderick, University of Glasgow
Brown, Tom, University of Washington
Butler, Gilbert W., Los Alamos National Laboratory
Carlson, Richard W., Carnegie Institution for Science
Chamberlain, Edwin P., Los Alamos National Laboratory
Chamberlain, Kevin R., University of Wyoming
Cheng, Hai, University of Minnesota, Twin Cities
Chew, David, Trinity College
Clark, George S., University of Manitoba
Coleman, Drew S., University of North Carolina, Chapel Hill
Copeland, Peter, University of Houston
Cowart, James B., Florida State University
Creaser, Robert A., University of Alberta
Crowley, Jim, Boise State University
Crowley, Quentin G., Trinity College
Curtice, Joshua M., Woods Hole Oceanographic Institution
Curtis, David B., Los Alamos National Laboratory
Curtis, Garniss H., University of California, Berkeley
Davis, Donald W., University of Toronto
De Grave, Johan, Ghent University
DePaolo, Donald J., University of California, Berkeley
Dickin, Alan P., McMaster University
Dulai, Henrietta, University of Hawai'i, Manoa
Dunning, Gregory R., Memorial University of Newfoundland
Edwards, R. Lawrence, University of Minnesota, Twin Cities
Enkelmann, Eva, University of Calgary
Fearey, Bryan L., Los Alamos National Laboratory
Fenton, Cassandra, Colorado Mesa University
Fernández Suárez, Javier, Univ Complutense de Madrid
Foland, Kenneth A., Ohio State University
Forman, Stephen, Baylor University
Frost, Carol D., University of Wyoming
Fullagar, Paul D., University of North Carolina, Chapel Hill
Gallup, Christina D., University of Minnesota Duluth
Gancarz, Alexander J., Los Alamos National Laboratory
Gaschnig, Richard M., University of Massachusetts, Lowell
Gaudette, Henri E., University of New Hampshire
Georgiev, Svetoslav, Colorado State University
Gillespie, Jack, Curtin University
Goehring, Brent M., Tulane University
Gosse, John C., Dalhousie University
Gromet, L. P., Brown University
Hall, Chris, University of Michigan
Hames, Willis E., Auburn University
Hamilton, Michael A., University of Toronto
Hanan, Barry B., San Diego State University
Hanes, John A., Queen's University
Harrison, T. Mark, University of California, Los Angeles
Hartnady, Michael, Curtin University
Hayatsu, Akio, Western University
Heaman, Larry M., University of Alberta
Heatherington, Ann L., University of Florida
Heizler, Matthew T., New Mexico Institute of Mining and Technology
Hodges, Kip V., Arizona State University
Horan, Mary F., Carnegie Institution for Science
Hourigan, Jeremy, University of California, Santa Cruz
Hughen, Konrad A., Woods Hole Oceanographic Institution
Idleman, Bruce D., Lehigh University
Jacobsen, Stein B., Harvard University
Joannes-Boyau, Renaud, Southern Cross University
Jourdan, Fred, Curtin University
Jull, A. J. Timothy, University of Arizona
Karner, Daniel B., Sonoma State University
Kelley, Simon, Edinburgh University
Kimbrough, David L., San Diego State University
Kinny, Pete, Curtin University
Kirkland, Chris, Curtin University
Konter, Jasper G., University of Hawai'i, Manoa
Krummenacher, Daniel, San Diego State University
Kuiper, Klaudia, Vrije Universiteit Amsterdam
Kurz, Mark D., Woods Hole Oceanographic Institution
Lakatos, Stephen, York College (CUNY)
Lassiter, John, University of Texas, Austin
Lepper, Kenneth, North Dakota State University
Lively, Rich, University of Minnesota
Long, Leon E., University of Texas, Austin
Lopez, Margarita, Ctr de Invest Científica y de Ed Superior de Ensenada
Maneiro, Kathryn A., Wheaton College
Manton, William I., University of Texas, Dallas
Markun, Francis J., Argonne National Laboratory
McDowell, Fred W., University of Texas, Austin
McIntosh, William C., New Mexico Institute of Mining and Technology
McIntosh, William C., New Mexico Institute of Mining and Technology
McLean, Noah, University of Kansas
Menninga, Clarence, Calvin College
Mertz, Dieter, Universität Mainz
Miller, Brent, Texas A&M University
Miller, Charles M., Los Alamos National Laboratory
Miller, Geoffrey G., Los Alamos National Laboratory
Min, Kyoungwon, University of Florida
Mock, Timothy D., Carnegie Institution for Science
Monteleone, Brian D., Woods Hole Oceanographic Institution
Moore, Willard S., University of South Carolina
Moran-Zenteno, Dante J., Univ Nacional Autonoma de Mexico
Morris, David, Los Alamos National Laboratory
Mortensen, James K., University of British Columbia
Mueller, Paul A., University of Florida
Mukasa, Samuel B., University of Michigan
Murrell, Michael T., Los Alamos National Laboratory
Nelson, Bruce K., University of Washington
Nemchin, Alexander, Curtin University
Olierook, Hugo, Curtin University
Omar, Gomaa I., University of Pennsylvania
Oretega Rivera, Amabel M., Univ Nacional Autonoma de Mexico
Orlandini, Kent A., Argonne National Laboratory
Osmond, John K., Florida State University
Palin, J. Michael, University of Otago
Pardi, Richard R., William Paterson University
Perrin, Richard E., Los Alamos National Laboratory
Pidgeon, Bob, Curtin University
Placzek, Christa, James Cook University
Polyak, Victor J., University of New Mexico
Poths, Jane, Los Alamos National Laboratory
Puchtel, Igor, University of Maryland
Ramos, Frank C., New Mexico State University, Las Cruces
Rasbury, E. Troy, Stony Brook University
Renne, Paul, University of California, Berkeley
Rhodes, Edward J., University of California, Los Angeles
Rink, W. J., McMaster University
Rinterknecht, Vincent, University of St. Andrews
Rioux, Matt, University of California, Santa Barbara
Rokop, Donald J., Los Alamos National Laboratory
Rooney, Alan, Yale University
Ross, Jake, New Mexico Institute of Mining and Technology
Rubin, Kenneth H., University of Hawai'i, Manoa
Samson, Scott D., Syracuse University
Schmitz, Mark D., Boise State University
Schneider, Robert J., Woods Hole Oceanographic Institution
Schoene, Blair, Princeton University
Schroeder, Norman C., Los Alamos National Laboratory

Seidemann, David E., Graduate School of the City University of New York
Seidemann, David E., Brooklyn College (CUNY)
Selby, Dave, Durham University
Shea, Erin, University of Alaska, Anchorage
Shirey, Steven B., Carnegie Institution for Science
Shumlyanskyy, Leonid, Curtin University
Silver, Leon T., California Institute of Technology
Singer, Bradley S., University of Wisconsin, Madison
Sole, Jesu, Univ Nacional Autonoma de Mexico
Southon, John, University of California, Irvine
Spell, Terry L., University of Nevada, Las Vegas
Spencer, Chris, Curtin University
Spencer, Joel Q., Kansas State University
Srinivasan, Balakrishnan, Pondicherry University
Stein, Holly, Colorado State University
Stevens-Goddard, Andrea L., Indiana University, Bloomington
Stewart, Brian W., University of Pittsburgh
Stockli, Daniel, University of Texas, Austin
Stone, John O., University of Washington
Strachan, Rob, University of Portsmouth
Stuiver, Minze, University of Washington
Swanson, Karen, William Paterson University
Swanson, Terry W., University of Washington
Swisher III, Carl C., Rutgers, The State University of New Jersey
Szymanowski, Dawid, Princeton University
Tera, Fouad, Carnegie Institution for Science
Thibodeau, Alyson M., Dickinson College
Tomlinson, Emma L., Trinity College
Turek, Andrew, University of Windsor
Turrin, Brent D., Rutgers, The State University of New Jersey
Van Schmus, W. Randall, University of Kansas
Vermeesch, Pieter, University College London
Vervoort, Jeffrey D., Washington State University
Walker, Richard J., University of Maryland
Walter, Robert C., Franklin and Marshall College
Wampler, J. Marion, Georgia State University
Webber, Patty, Wyoming State Geological Survey
White, William M., Cornell University
Widom, Elisabeth, Miami University
Wielicki, Matthew, University of Alabama
Wielicki, Michelle, University of Alabama
Wijbrans, Jan, Vrije Universiteit Amsterdam
Wilde, Simon, Curtin University
Wolfsberg, Kurt, Los Alamos National Laboratory
Woodard, Jeremy, University of KwaZulu-Natal
Yang, Gang, Colorado State University
Yin, Qing-zhu, University of California, Davis
Zeitler, Peter K., Lehigh University
Zimmerman, Aaron, Colorado State University
Zou, Haibo, Auburn University
Zreda, Marek, University of Arizona

Low-temperature Geochemistry

Achten, Christine, Universitaet Muenster
Agrawal, Abinash, Wright State University
Aharon, Paul, University of Alabama
Ahm, Anne-Sofie, Princeton University
Aja, Stephen U., Graduate School of the City University of New York
Aja, Stephen U., Brooklyn College (CUNY)
Alessi, Daniel S., University of Alberta
Alexander, Clark R., Georgia Institute of Technology
Amend, Jan, University of Southern California
Anand, Pallavi, Open University
Andersen, C. B., Clemson University
Andersen, C. Brannon, Furman University
Angino, Ernest E., University of Kansas
Azmy, Karem, Memorial University of Newfoundland
Baker, Leslie L., University of Idaho
Balogh-Brunstad, Zsuzsanna, Hartwick College
Banner, Jay L., University of Texas, Austin
Basak, Chandranath, University of Delaware
Bataille, Clement, University of Ottawa
Beckingham, Barbara, College of Charleston
Benner, Shawn, Boise State University
Bergslien, Elisa T., Buffalo State College
Bertine, Kathe K., San Diego State University
Bickmore, Barry R., Brigham Young University
Bird, MIchael I., James Cook University
Bischoff, William D., Wichita State University
Blanton, Jackson O., Georgia Institute of Technology
Bogner, Jean E., University of Illinois at Chicago
Borrok, David, Missouri University of Science and Technology
Bowser, Carl J., University of Wisconsin, Madison
Brabander, Daniel J., Wellesley College
Brand, Uwe, Brock University
Breecker, Daniel O., University of Texas, Austin
Brook, Edward J., Oregon State University
Brooks, Scott C., Oak Ridge National Laboratory
Burke, Andrea, University of St. Andrews
Cantrell, Kirk J., Pacific Northwest National Laboratory
Cao, Hongsheng, Wichita State University
Capo, Rosemary C., University of Pittsburgh
Carroll, Susan A., Lawrence Livermore National Laboratory
Casey, William H., University of California, Davis
Catalano, Jeffrey G., Washington University in St. Louis
Cerling, Thure E., University of Utah
Chermak, John A., Virginia Polytechnic Institute & State University
Chesworth, Ward, University of Guelph
Christina, Thomas D., Georgia Institute of Technology
Clark, Jordan F., University of California, Santa Barbara
Cody, Anita M., Iowa State University of Science & Technology
Crossey, Laura J., University of New Mexico
Datta, Saugata, Kansas State University
Derry, Louis A., Cornell University
Diebold, Frank E., Montana Tech of the University of Montana
Donahoe, Rona J., University of Alabama
Dostie, Philip, Bates College
Dove, Patricia M., Virginia Polytechnic Institute & State University
Drake, John C., University of Vermont
Druschel, Greg, Indiana University - Purdue University Indianapolis
Dworkin, Stephen I., Baylor University
Early, Thomas O., Oak Ridge National Laboratory
Eggleston, Carrick M., University of Wyoming
Elliott, W. Crawford, Georgia State University
Elswick, Erika R., Indiana University, Bloomington
Elwood Madden, Andrew S., University of Oklahoma
Elwood Madden, Megan E., University of Oklahoma
Engel, Annette S., University of Tennessee, Knoxville
Evans, Les J., University of Guelph
Fein, Jeremy B., University of Notre Dame
Fenter, Paul A., Argonne National Laboratory
Ferrell, Jr., Ray E., Louisiana State University
Fortner, Sarah K., Wittenberg University
Frape, Shaun K., University of Waterloo
Frisia, Silvia, University of Newcastle
Fryer, Brian J., University of Windsor
Gamerdinger, Amy P., Pacific Northwest National Laboratory
García Lorenzo, María de la Luz, Univ Complutense de Madrid
Gerke, Tammie, Miami University
Gilhooly, William, Indiana University - Purdue University Indianapolis
Graf, Donald L., University of Illinois, Urbana-Champaign
Grandstaff, David E., Temple University
Graney, Joseph R., Binghamton University
Graustein, William C., Yale University
Greenberg, Sallie, Illinois State Geological Survey
Haas, Johnson R., Western Michigan University
Hannigan, Robyn, University of Massachusetts, Boston
Hanor, Jeffrey S., Louisiana State University
Harrison, Wendy J., Colorado School of Mines
Hasenmueller, Elizabeth, Saint Louis University
Herman, Janet S., University of Virginia
Higgins, John A., Princeton University
Hirons, Steve, Birkbeck College
Hixon, Amy E., University of Notre Dame
Hluchy, Michele M., Alfred University
Hochella, Jr., Michael F., Virginia Polytechnic Institute & State University
Holdren, George R., Pacific Northwest National Laboratory
Hounslow, Arthur, Oklahoma State University
Hutcheon, Ian E., University of Calgary
Icenhower, Jonathan P., Pacific Northwest National Laboratory
Icopini, Gary, Montana Tech of The University of Montana
Ito, Emi, University of Minnesota, Twin Cities

Jacinthe, Pierre-Andre, Indiana University - Purdue University Indianapolis
Jackson, Kenneth J., Lawrence Livermore National Laboratory
Jacobson, Andrew D., Northwestern University
Jahnke, Richard, Georgia Institute of Technology
Janecky, David R., Los Alamos National Laboratory
Karlsson, Haraldur R., Texas Tech University
Kaste, James, William & Mary
Kelly, Jacque L., Georgia Southern University
Kettler, Richard M., University of Nebraska, Lincoln
Kirby, Carl S., Bucknell University
Knapp, Elizabeth P., Washington & Lee University
Kneeshaw, Tara A., Grand Valley State University
Krabbenhoft, David, University of Wisconsin, Madison
Kramer, James R., McMaster University
Krupka, Kenneth M., Pacific Northwest National Laboratory
Ku, Timothy C., Wesleyan University
Kubicki, James D., University of Texas, El Paso
Kump, Lee R., Pennsylvania State University, University Park
Kurtz, Andrew, Boston University
Langman, Jeffrey, University of Idaho
Larsen, Daniel, University of Memphis
Lawrence, James, University of Houston
Leckie, James O., Stanford University
Liang, Liyuan, Oak Ridge National Laboratory
Lindberg, Steven E., Oak Ridge National Laboratory
Lindsay, Matthew B., University of Saskatchewan
Locke, Randall, Illinois State Geological Survey
Long, Austin, University of Arizona
Long, David T., Michigan State University
Lowenstein, Tim K., Binghamton University
Macalady, Donald L., Colorado School of Mines
Martin, Candace E., University of Otago
Martin, Ellen E., University of Florida
Martin, Jonathan B., University of Florida
Martini, Anna M., Amherst College
Mattigod, Shas V., Pacific Northwest National Laboratory
Mayes, Melanie A., University of Tennessee, Knoxville
Maynard, J. Barry, University of Cincinnati
Mazer, James J., Argonne National Laboratory
McArthur, John M., University College London
McGee, David, Massachusetts Institute of Technology
McGehee, Thomas L., Texas A&M University, Kingsville
Merino, Enrique, Indiana University, Bloomington
Moore, Joel, Towson University
Morel, Francois M M., Princeton University
Munk, LeeAnn, University of Alaska, Anchorage
Murray, Kendra, Idaho State University
Nelson, Marc A., University of Arkansas, Fayetteville
Nesbitt, H W., Western University
Neumann, Klaus, Ball State University
Newell, Dennis L., Utah State University
Nezat, Carmen A., Eastern Washington University
Niemitz, Jeffery W., Dickinson College
Noll, Mark R., SUNY, The College at Brockport
Norton, Stephen A., University of Maine
Nzengung, Valentine A., University of Georgia
Oelkers, Eric, University College London
Olsen, Amanda A., University of Maine
Oster, Jessica L., Vanderbilt University
Panno, Samuel V., Illinois State Geological Survey
Parnell, Roderic A., Northern Arizona University
Patton, Terri L., Argonne National Laboratory
Perdrial, Julia, University of Vermont
Peters, Stephen C., Lehigh University
Pingitore, Jr., Nicholas E., University of Texas, El Paso
Poulson, Simon, University of Nevada, Reno
Poulton, Simon, University of Leeds
Rademacher, Laura K., University of the Pacific
Raven, Morgan, University of California, Santa Barbara
Reardon, Eric J., University of Waterloo
Reeder, Richard J., Stony Brook University
Rhodes, Amy L., Smith College
Riebe, Clifford S., University of Wyoming
Roberts, Sarah K., Lawrence Livermore National Laboratory
Rogers, Pamela Z., Los Alamos National Laboratory
Romanek, Christopher, Furman University
Rouff, Ashaki, Rutgers, The State University of New Jersey, Newark
Roychoudhury, Alakendra N., Stellenbosch University
Runnells, Donald D., University of Colorado
Rustad, James R., University of California, Davis
Ryan, Peter C., Middlebury College
Schlautman, Mark, Clemson University
Scholz, Denis, Universität Mainz
Schoonen, Martin A., Stony Brook University
Schroth, Andrew W., University of Vermont
Shiel, Alyssa E., Oregon State University
Sigman, Daniel M., Princeton University
Sjostrom, Derek, Rocky Mountain College
Skidmore, Mark L., Montana State University
Stillings, Lisa L., University of Nevada, Reno
Stoessell, Ronald K., University of New Orleans
Stone, Alan T., Johns Hopkins University
Sturchio, Neil C., University of Delaware
Suarez, Celina, University of Arkansas, Fayetteville
Sverjensky, Dimitri A., Johns Hopkins University
Swart, Peter K., University of Miami
Taillefert, Martial, Georgia Institute of Technology
Taylor, Wayne A., Los Alamos National Laboratory
Telmer, Kevin, University of Victoria
Templeton, Alexis, University of Colorado
Thurber, David L., Queens College (CUNY)
Tipper, Ed, University of Cambridge
Toner, Brandy M., University of Minnesota, Twin Cities
Turner, Robert S., Oak Ridge National Laboratory
Valsami-Jones, Eugenia, University of Birmingham
Van Der Flier-Keller, Eileen, University of Victoria
Varner, Ruth K., University of New Hampshire
Veizer, Jan, University of Ottawa
Velbel, Michael A., Michigan State University
Voglesonger, Kenneth M., Northeastern Illinois University
Walder, Ingar F., New Mexico Institute of Mining and Technology
Walker, Charles T., California State University, Long Beach
Wallace, Adam F., University of Delaware
Walter, Lynn M., University of Michigan
Wang, Jianwei, Louisiana State University
Wasylenki, Laura, Northern Arizona University
Wehmiller, John F., University of Delaware
Weiss, Dominik, Imperial College
Welch, Susan A., Ohio State University
West, A. Joshua (Josh), University of Southern California
Whittemore, Donald O., University of Kansas
Widanagamage, Inoka, University of Mississippi
Wood, James R., Michigan Technological University
Wronkiewicz, David, Missouri University of Science and Technology
Wunsch, David R., University of Delaware
Xu, Jie, University of Texas, El Paso
Yuretich, Richard F., University of Massachusetts, Amherst
Zhaohui, Li, University of Wisconsin, Parkside

Marine Geochemistry

Adkins, Jess F., California Institute of Technology
Aller, Robert C., Stony Brook University
Aller, Robert C., SUNY, Stony Brook
Barry, Peter, Woods Hole Oceanographic Institution
Berelson, William M., University of Southern California
Betzer, Peter R., University of South Florida
Biscaye, Pierre E., Columbia University
Bollinger, Marsha S., Winthrop University
Breier, John, University of Texas, Rio Grande Valley
Broecker, Wallace S., Columbia University
Byrne, Robert H., University of South Florida
Cahill, Kevin, Woods Hole Oceanographic Institution
Calvert, Stephen E., University of British Columbia
Cave, Rachel R., National University of Ireland Galway
Charette, Matthew A., Woods Hole Oceanographic Institution
Church, Thomas M., University of Delaware
Coble, Paula G., University of South Florida
Cole, Catherine, University of St. Andrews
Compton, John, University of Cape Town
Cuomo, Carmela, University of New Haven
Dai, Minhan, Woods Hole Oceanographic Institution
De Carlo, Eric H., University of Hawai'i, Manoa

Dickson, Andrew G., University of California, San Diego
Doney, Scott C., Woods Hole Oceanographic Institution
Dunlea, Ann, Woods Hole Oceanographic Institution
Dutkiewicz, Stephanie, Massachusetts Institute of Technology
Farmer, Jesse, Princeton University
Fehrenbacher, Jennifer, Oregon State University
Feng, Huan E., Montclair State University
Filippelli, Gabriel M., Indiana University - Purdue University Indianapolis
Fones, Gary, University of Portsmouth
Francois, Roger, University of British Columbia
Fulweiler, Robinson, Boston University
Galy, Valier, Woods Hole Oceanographic Institution
Gerwick, William H., University of California, San Diego
Glazer, Brian, University of Hawai'i, Manoa
Godfrey, Linda, Rutgers, The State University of New Jersey
Gospodinova, Kalina D., Woods Hole Oceanographic Institution
Goudreau, Joanne, Woods Hole Oceanographic Institution
Graham, David W., Oregon State University
Grassian, Vicki, University of California, San Diego
Hammerschmidt, Chad, Wright State University
Hammond, Douglas E., University of Southern California
Hansel, Colleen, Woods Hole Oceanographic Institution
Hardison, Amber, William & Mary
Hardison, Amber K., University of Texas, Austin
Harrison, Peter, Southern Cross University
Heath, G. Ross, University of Washington
Henderson, Paul, Woods Hole Oceanographic Institution
Henley, Sian F., Edinburgh University
Hoenisch, Baerbel, Columbia University
Horner, Tristan, Woods Hole Oceanographic Institution
Hu, Xinping, Texas A&M University, Corpus Christi
Huber, Julie, Woods Hole Oceanographic Institution
Ingall, Ellery D., Georgia Institute of Technology
Jayakumar, Amal, Princeton University
Johnson, Martin, University of East Anglia
Juranek, Lauren W., Oregon State University
Kastner, Miriam, University of California, San Diego
Kim, Hyewon (Heather), Woods Hole Oceanographic Institution
Klein, Frieder, Woods Hole Oceanographic Institution
Latimer, Jennifer C., Indiana State University
Levas, Stephen J., University of Wisconsin, Whitewater
Li, Yuan-Hui, University of Hawai'i, Manoa
Long, Matthew, Woods Hole Oceanographic Institution
Lueders-Dumont, Jessica, Princeton University
Luther, III, George W., University of Delaware
Mackenzie, Fred T., University of Hawai'i, Manoa
Maerz, Christian, University of Leeds
Malahoff, Alexander, University of Hawai'i, Manoa
Marconi, Dario, Princeton University
McCorkle, Daniel C., Woods Hole Oceanographic Institution
McDermott, Jill I., Lehigh University
McGillis, Wade, Columbia University
McKay, Jennifer L., Oregon State University
McManus, Jerry, Columbia University
Mills, Rachel A., University of Southampton
Montoya, Joseph, Georgia Institute of Technology
Moore, Bradley S., University of California, San Diego
Mucci, Alfonso, McGill University
Murray, Richard, Boston University
Nuester, Jochen, California State University, Chico
Orians, Kristin J., University of British Columbia
Osburn, Chris, North Carolina State University
Owen, Robert M., University of Michigan
Patterson, Molly , Binghamton University
Pedersen, Thomas F., University of Victoria
Peucker-Ehrenbrink, Bernhard, Woods Hole Oceanographic Institution
Popp, Brian N., University of Hawai'i, Manoa
Poyla, David, University of Manchester
Ravizza, Gregory, University of Hawai'i, Manoa
Ries, Justin, Northeastern University
Rosenthal, Yair, Rutgers, The State University of New Jersey
Russell, Ann D., University of California, Davis
Rutberg, Randye L., Hunter College (CUNY)
Sansone, Francis J., University of Hawai'i, Manoa
Schoonmaker, Jane E., University of Hawai'i, Manoa
Sericano, Jose L., Texas A&M University
Seyfried, Jr., William E., University of Minnesota, Twin Cities
Sherrell, Robert M., Rutgers, The State University of New Jersey
Simpson, Jr., H. James, Columbia University
Smith, Joseph P., United States Naval Academy
Soares Cruz, Anna Paula ., California State University, Bakersfield
Spero, Howard J., University of California, Davis
Stillings, Lisa, University of Nevada, Reno
Sulanowska, Margaret, Woods Hole Oceanographic Institution
Sundby, Bjorn, McGill University
Sutherland, Bruce, University of Alberta
Takahashi, Taro, Columbia University
Tan, Chunyang, University of Minnesota, Twin Cities
Them, II, Theodore R., College of Charleston
Thompson, Geoffrey, Woods Hole Oceanographic Institution
Tivey, Margaret K., Woods Hole Oceanographic Institution
Torres, Marta E., Oregon State University
Tripati, Aradhna, University of California, Los Angeles
Ullman, William J., University of Delaware
Valentine, David, University of California, Santa Barbara
Wakefield, S J., Cardiff University
Wan, Xianhui S., Princeton University
Wang, Weihong, Utah Valley University
Wang, Z. Aleck, Woods Hole Oceanographic Institution
Wankel, Scott, Woods Hole Oceanographic Institution
Ward, Collin, Woods Hole Oceanographic Institution
Weiss, Ray F., University of California, San Diego
Winckler, Gisela, Columbia University
Windom, Herbert L., Georgia Institute of Technology
Wong, Chi S., University of British Columbia

Organic Geochemistry

Abdulla, Hussain, Texas A&M University, Corpus Christi
Amend, Jan P., Washington University in St. Louis
Anderson, Ken B., Southern Illinois University Carbondale
Aravena, Ramon, University of Waterloo
Bada, Jeffrey L., University of California, San Diego
Bakel, Allen J., Argonne National Laboratory
Banfield, Jillian, University of California, Berkeley
Barker, James F., University of Waterloo
Bianchi, Thomas S., University of Florida
Bissada, Adry, University of Houston
Blair, Neal E., Northwestern University
Bowden, Stephen, University of Aberdeen
Brassell, Simon C., Indiana University, Bloomington
Burns, Timothy P., Los Alamos National Laboratory
Chen, Bob, University of Massachusetts, Boston
Chou, Mei-In (Melissa), Illinois State Geological Survey
Chou, Sheng-Fu Joseph, Illinois State Geological Survey
Cody, George D., Carnegie Institution for Science
Cole, Dean A., Los Alamos National Laboratory
Cowie, Gregory L., Edinburgh University
Diefendorf, Aaron, University of Cincinnati
Engel, Michael H., University of Oklahoma
Eyre, Bradley, Southern Cross University
Farrington, John W., Woods Hole Oceanographic Institution
Feakins, Sarah, University of Southern California
Fernandez, Loretta, Northeastern University
Filley, Timothy R., Purdue University
Fisher, Liz, University of Liverpool
Francis, Robert D., California State University, Long Beach
Freeman, Katherine H., Pennsylvania State University, University Park
Fu, Qi, University of Houston
Grice, Kliti, Curtin University
Hanson, Andrew D., University of Nevada, Las Vegas
Hartnett, Hilairy E., Arizona State University
Harvey, H. Rodger, Old Dominion University
Heal, Kate V., Edinburgh University
Hernes, Peter J., University of California, Davis
Hites, Ronald A., Indiana University, Bloomington
Hockaday, William C., Baylor University
Huang, Yongsong, Brown University
Kenig, Fabien, University of Illinois at Chicago
Kotulova, Julia, University of Utah
Kruge, Michael A., Montclair State University
Langston-Unkefer, Pat J., Los Alamos National Laboratory
Love, Gordon D., University of California, Riverside

MacCarthy, Patrick, Colorado School of Mines
Macko, Stephen A., University of Virginia
McCarthy, John F., Oak Ridge National Laboratory
Mehra, Aradhana, University of Derby
Meyers, Philip A., University of Michigan
Mitra, Siddhartha, East Carolina University
Mitterer, Richard M., University of Texas, Dallas
Moslow, Thomas F., University of Calgary
Nelson, Robert K., Woods Hole Oceanographic Institution
Ngwenya, Bryne T., Edinburgh University
Nolan, Robert P., Graduate School of the City University of New York
Perdue, Edward Michael, Georgia Institute of Technology
Petsch, Steven, University of Massachusetts, Amherst
Phillips, Dennis, Los Alamos National Laboratory
Philp, R. Paul, University of Oklahoma
Pratt, Lisa M., Indiana University, Bloomington
Pruell, Richard J., University of Rhode Island
Reddy, Christopher M., Woods Hole Oceanographic Institution
Repeta, Daniel J., Woods Hole Oceanographic Institution
Robinson, Clare, University of Manchester
Rohrssen, Megan, Central Michigan University
Sass, Henrik, University of Wales
Sepúlveda, Julio C., University of Colorado
Sessions, Alex L., California Institute of Technology
Silliman, James, Texas A&M University, Corpus Christi
Spongberg, Alison L., University of Toledo
Steen, Andrew, University of Tennessee, Knoxville
Stierle, Donald, Montana Tech of the University of Montana
Summons, Roger, Massachusetts Institute of Technology
Talbot, Helen, University of Newcastle Upon Tyne
Tanner, Benjamin R., Western Carolina University
Thiel, Dr., Volker, Georg-August University of Goettingen
Thomas, Elizabeth K., SUNY, Buffalo
Tierney, Jessica, University of Arizona
Townsend-Small, Amy, University of Cincinnati
van Dongen, Bart, University of Manchester
Van Vleet, Edward S., University of South Florida
Venkatesan, M I., University of California, Los Angeles
Visscher, Pieter T., University of Connecticut
Visscher, Pieter, University of Connecticut
Voorhees, Kent J., Colorado School of Mines
Wagner, Sasha, Rensselaer Polytechnic Institute
Wakeham, Stuart G., Georgia Institute of Technology
Weisener, Christopher, University of Windsor
Werne, Josef, University of Pittsburgh
Whelan, Jean K., Woods Hole Oceanographic Institution
Whiticar, Michael J., University of Victoria
Williams, Amy, University of Florida
Zerkle, Aubrey, University of St. Andrews
Zhang, Yige, Texas A&M University
Zhuang, Guangsheng, Louisiana State University
Zimmerman, Andrew, University of Florida
Ziolkowski, Lori A., University of South Carolina

Stable Isotopes

Anderson, Thomas F., University of Illinois, Urbana-Champaign
Anderson, William T., Florida International University
Andrews, Julian E., University of East Anglia
Atudorei, Nieu-Viorel, University of New Mexico
Bao, Huiming, Louisiana State University
Bedaso, Zelalem, University of Dayton
Berke, Melissa, University of Notre Dame
Bindeman, Ilya N., University of Oregon
Blum, Joel D., University of Michigan
Bowen, Gabriel, University of Utah
Bowman, John R., University of Utah
Bray, Colin, University of Toronto
Brunner, Benjamin, University of Texas, El Paso
Buczynska, Anna, Northern Illinois University
Burgess, Ray, University of Manchester
Burns, Stephen J., University of Massachusetts, Amherst
Campbell, Andrew R., New Mexico Institute of Mining and Technology
Cao, Xiaobin, Louisiana State University
Clayton, Robert N., University of Chicago
Cohen, Anthony, Open University
Conroy, Jessica, University of Illinois, Urbana-Champaign
Coogon, Rosalind, Imperial College
Criss, Robert E., Washington University in St. Louis
Criss, Robert E., Washington University in St. Louis
Crowley, Brooke E., University of Cincinnati
Darling, James, University of Portsmouth
Davidson, Garry J., University of Tasmania
Denniston, Rhawn F., University of Iowa
Dettman, David, University of Arizona
Deuser, Werner G., Woods Hole Oceanographic Institution
Dodd, Justin P., Northern Illinois University
Dorale, Jeffrey A., University of Iowa
Douglas, Peter, McGill University
Eastoe, Chris J., University of Arizona
Economos, Rita C., Southern Methodist University
Edwards, Thomas W. D., University of Waterloo
Elder, Kathryn L., Woods Hole Oceanographic Institution
Fantle, Matthew S., Pennsylvania State University, University Park
Farquhar, James, University of Maryland
Fayek, Mostafa, University of Manitoba
Feng, Xiahong, Dartmouth College
Fike, David A., Washington University in St. Louis
Fisher, David E., University of Miami
Foster, Gavin, University of Southampton
Fricke, Henry C., Colorado College
Gagnon, Alan R., Woods Hole Oceanographic Institution
Gao, Yongjun, University of Houston
Gazis, Carey A., Central Washington University
Gibson, John J., University of Waterloo
Gilbert, Kathleen W., Wellesley College
Gilg, Hans A., Technical University of Munich
Gill, Benjamin, Virginia Polytechnic Institute & State University
Gillikin, David P., Union College
Goldstein, Steven L., Columbia University
Gonzalez, Luis A., University of Kansas
Graczyk, Donald G., Argonne National Laboratory
Grassineau, Nathalie, Royal Holloway University of London
Gregory, Robert T., Southern Methodist University
Griffith, Elizabeth, Ohio State University
Griffith, Liz, University of Texas, Arlington
Grimes, Stephen, University of Plymouth
Grocke, Darren, Durham University
Grossman, Ethan L., Texas A&M University
Guo, Weifu, Woods Hole Oceanographic Institution
Haley, Brian, Oregon State University
Halliday, Alex, University of Oxford
Haynes, Shannon, Princeton University
Helie, Jean-François, Universite du Quebec a Montreal
Hemming, Sidney R., Columbia University
Henkel, Torsten, University of Manchester
Henkes, Gregory, Stony Brook University
Hillaire-Marcel, Claude, Universite du Quebec a Montreal
Hindshaw, Ruth, University of St. Andrews
Holk, Gregory J., California State University, Long Beach
Holmden, Chris, University of Saskatchewan
Horton, Travis, University of Canterbury
Howe, Stephen S., SUNY, Albany
Hren, Michael, University of Connecticut
Ingram, B. Lynn, University of California, Berkeley
Johnson, Beverly J., Bates College
Junium, Christopher, Syracuse University
Kaiser, Jan, University of East Anglia
Kaplan, Isaac R., University of California, Los Angeles
Karhu, Juha A., University of Helsinki
Kaufman, Alan J., University of Maryland
Keigwin, Lloyd D., Woods Hole Oceanographic Institution
Kellman, Lisa M., Saint Francis Xavier University
Kieffer, Bruno, University of British Columbia
Kienast, Markus, Dalhousie University
Kirtland Turner, Sandra, University of California, Riverside
Knauth, L. Paul, Arizona State University
Kohn, Matthew, Boise State University
Krantz, David E., University of Delaware
Kreutz, Karl J., University of Maine
Krishnamurthy, R. V., Western Michigan University
Lambert, W. J., University of Alabama
Larson, Peter B., Washington State University

Law, Kim, Western University
Leavitt, Steven W., University of Arizona
Lefticariu, Liliana, Southern Illinois University Carbondale
Li, Long, University of Alberta
Lini, Andrea, University of Vermont
Lohmann, Kyger C., University of Michigan
Longstaffe, Frederick J., Western University
Lowry, David, Royal Holloway University of London
Luzincourt, Marc R., Universite du Quebec
Marshall, Jim, University of Liverpool
Masterson, Andrew, Northwestern University
Matheney, Ronald K., University of North Dakota
Mattey, Dave, Royal Holloway University of London
Mayer, Bernhard, University of Calgary
Menicucci, Anthony, University of South Florida
Michalski, Greg, Purdue University
Mix, Alan C., Oregon State University
Mora, Claudia I., University of Tennessee, Knoxville
Muehlenbachs, Karlis, University of Alberta
Munizzi, Jordan S., University of Kentucky
Nelson, Stephen T., Brigham Young University
Nielsen, Sune G., Woods Hole Oceanographic Institution
O'Neil, James, University of Michigan
Ohmoto, Hiroshi, Pennsylvania State University, University Park
Oleynik, Sergey, Princeton University
Olivares, Jose A., Los Alamos National Laboratory
Padden, Maureen, McMaster University
Parai, Rita, Washington University in St. Louis
Passey, Benjamin, University of Michigan
Patterson, William P., University of Saskatchewan
Pedentchouk, Nikolai, University of East Anglia
Pinti, Daniele Luigi, Universite du Quebec a Montreal
Planavsky, Noah, Yale University
Pogge von Strandmann, Phillip, University College London
Pogge von Strandmann, Phillip, Birkbeck College
Poirier, Andre, Universite du Quebec a Montreal
Ponton, Camilo, Western Washington University
Popp, Brian N., University of Hawai'i, Manoa
Poulson, Simon R., University of Nevada, Reno
Ravelo, Christina, University of California, Santa Cruz
Rehkamper, Mark, Imperial College
Reid, Rachel E., Virginia Polytechnic Institute & State University
Richards, Ian J., Southern Methodist University
Rye, Danny M., Yale University
Savin, Samuel M., Case Western Reserve University
Schaller, Morgan F., Rensselaer Polytechnic Institute
Schauble, Edwin A., University of California, Los Angeles
Schimmelmann, Arndt, Indiana University, Bloomington
Schwarcz, Henry P., McMaster University
Sedlacek, Alexa, University of Northern Iowa
Shahar, Anat, University of Maryland
Sharma, Shikha, West Virginia University
Sharp, Zachary D., University of New Mexico
Sherwood, Owen, Dalhousie University
Sherwood Lollar, Barbara, University of Toronto
Shieh, Yuch-Ning, Purdue University
Showers, William J., North Carolina State University
Smart, Katie A., University of the Witwatersrand
Smirnov, Anna, Universite du Quebec
Sowers, Todd, Pennsylvania State University, University Park
Steig, Eric J., University of Washington
Steig, Eric J., University of Washington
Strauss, Harald, Universitaet Muenster
Stute, Martin, Columbia University
Syrup, Krista A., Moraine Valley Community College
Szynkiewicz, Anna, University of Tennessee, Knoxville
Taylor, Hugh P., California Institute of Technology
Theiling, Bethany P., University of Tulsa
Thirlwall, Matthew, Royal Holloway University of London
Tudhope, Alexander W., Edinburgh University
Valley, John W., University of Wisconsin, Madison
van de Flierdt, Tina, Imperial College
Wanamaker, Alan D., Iowa State University of Science & Technology
Wang, Jianhua, Carnegie Institution for Science
Webb, Elizabeth A., Western University
Welp, Lisa, Purdue University
Wenner, David B., University of Georgia
White, James W. C., University of Colorado
Widory, David, Universite du Quebec a Montreal
Wright, James D., Rutgers, The State University of New Jersey
Yapp, Crayton J., Southern Methodist University
Yeung, Laurence Y., Rice University
Young, Edward D., University of California, Los Angeles
Yun, Misuk, University of Manitoba
Zhang, Lin, Texas A&M University, Corpus Christi
Zhang, Ren, Baylor University
Zheng, Xinyuan, University of Minnesota, Twin Cities
Ziegler, Karen, University of New Mexico
Zierenberg, Robert A., University of California, Davis

Trace Element Distribution

Coale, Kenneth H., Moss Landing Marine Laboratories
Condie, Kent C., New Mexico Institute of Mining and Technology
Croot, Peter, National University of Ireland Galway
Cullers, Robert L., Kansas State University
Daniels, William R., Los Alamos National Laboratory
Efurd, Deward W., Los Alamos National Laboratory
Frey, Frederick A., Massachusetts Institute of Technology
Gabrielli, Paolo, Ohio State University
Hale, Beverley A., University of Guelph
Kar, Aditya, Fort Valley State University
Kyte, Frank T., University of California, Los Angeles
LaFleche, Marc R., Universite du Quebec
Liese, Homer C., University of Connecticut
Marcantonio, Franco, Texas A&M University
McGowan, Nicole M., Western Washington University
Newton, Robert, Columbia University
Nicolescu, Stefan, Yale University
Peterson, Eugene J., Los Alamos National Laboratory
Rader, Shelby, Indiana University, Bloomington
Ritter, Charles J., University of Dayton
Ryan, Jeffrey G., University of South Florida
Seifert, Karl E., Iowa State University of Science & Technology
Simonetti, Tony, University of Notre Dame
Thomas, Kimberly W., Los Alamos National Laboratory
Thompson, Joseph L., Los Alamos National Laboratory
Von Reden, Karl F., Woods Hole Oceanographic Institution
Weaver, Barry L., University of Oklahoma
Wildeman, Thomas R., Colorado School of Mines

Biogeochemistry

Abou Najm, Majdi, University of California, Davis
Amon, Rainier M., Texas A&M University
Anbar, Ariel D., Arizona State University
Babbin, Andrew, Massachusetts Institute of Technology
Barker, Joel D., Ohio State University
Bradley, Alexander S., Washington University in St. Louis
Buick, Roger, University of Washington
Cassar, Nicolas, Duke University
Costa, Jr, Ozeas S., Ohio State University
Curtis, P. J., University of British Columbia, Okanagan Campus
Darnajoux, Romain, Princeton University
Dolman, Han J., Vrije Universiteit Amsterdam
Elliott, Emily M., University of Pittsburgh
Fortin, Danielle, University of Ottawa
Fowle, David A., University of Kansas
Gu, Baohua, Oak Ridge National Laboratory
Hornibrook, Edward R., University of British Columbia, Okanagan Campus
Jaisi, Deb, University of Delaware
Jones, Daniel, New Mexico Institute of Mining and Technology
Kavanaugh, Maria, Oregon State University
Lau, Kimberly, University of Wyoming
Lazcano, Cristina, University of California, Davis
Liang, Liyuan, University of Tennessee, Knoxville
Mahmoudi, Nagissa, McGill University
Marin-Spiotta, Erika, University of Wisconsin, Madison
Matisoff, Gerald, Case Western Reserve University
McCormick, Michael L., Hamilton College
Mellinger, David, Oregon State University
Mulder, Jan, Norwegian University of Life Sciences (NMBU)
Okie, Jordan, Arizona State University
Pearson, Ann, Harvard University
Phelps, Tommy J., University of Tennessee, Knoxville

Reddy, K R., University of Florida
Reji, Linta, Princeton University
Richardson, Justin, University of Massachusetts, Amherst
Richey, Jeffrey E., University of Washington
Riding, Robert, University of Tennessee, Knoxville
Roberts, Jennifer A., University of Kansas
Sanford, Robert A., University of Illinois, Urbana-Champaign
Scarlett, Alan, Curtin University
Smith, Robert, University of Idaho
Steenwerth, Kerri, University of California, Davis
Tang, Weiyi, Princeton University
Throop, Heather, Arizona State University
Thurber, Andrew, Oregon State University
Torres, Mark, Rice University
Trembath-Reichert, Elizabeth, Arizona State University
Tufillaro, Nicholas, Oregon State University
Wang, Xinchen, Boston College
Winnick, Matthew, University of Massachusetts, Amherst
Xu, Tingying, Oklahoma State University
Zhang, Xinning, Princeton University

High-temperature Geochemistry

Babechuk, Michael, Memorial University of Newfoundland
Baker, Don, McGill University
Chin, Emily J., University of Tennessee, Knoxville
Jackson, Matt, University of California, Santa Barbara
Le Voyer, Marion, Smithsonian Institution / National Museum of Natural History
Pollock, Meagen, College of Wooster
Reid, Mary R., Northern Arizona University
Zajacz, Zoltan, University of Toronto
Zhang, Youxue, University of Michigan

Aqueous Geochemistry

Chin, Yu-Ping, Ohio State University
Clark, Elyse, Fitchburg State University
Cox, Alysia, Montana Tech of the University of Montana
Greenwell, Chris, Durham University
Hasan, M A., University of Dhaka
Hinkle, Margaret A., Washington & Lee University
Hon, Rudolph, Boston College
Kurz, Marie J., Drexel University
MacKay, Allison A., Ohio State University
Matiasek, Sandrine, California State University, Chico
O'Shea, Bethany, University of San Diego
Pasek, Matthew, University of South Florida
Pincus, Lauren N., Princeton University
Polizzotto, Matthew, University of Oregon
Ridley, Moira K., Texas Tech University
Saccocia, Peter J., Bridgewater State University
Wolff-Boenisch, Dom, Curtin University
Wood, Scott A., North Dakota State University
Yun, Seong-Taek, Korea University

GEOPHYSICS

General Geophysics

Adams, Aubreya, Colgate University
Adepelumi, A. A., Obafemi Awolowo University
Afolabi, O., Obafemi Awolowo University
Ahern, Judson L., University of Oklahoma
Ahmed, Mohamed, Texas A&M University, Corpus Christi
Al-Lehyani, Ayman, King Fahd University of Petroleum and Minerals
Al-Shuhail, Abdullatif, King Fahd University of Petroleum and Minerals
Alao, O. A., Obafemi Awolowo University
Albright, James N., Los Alamos National Laboratory
Angelopoulos, Vassilis, University of California, Los Angeles
Armah, Thomas K., University of Ghana
Audet, Pascal, University of Ottawa
Aurnou, Jonathan M., University of California, Los Angeles
Bachtadse, Valerian, Ludwig-Maximilians-Universitaet Muenchen
Bailey, Richard C., University of Toronto
Barbi, Greta, Ludwig-Maximilians-Universitaet Muenchen
Barklage, Mitchell, Northwestern University
Barsch, Robert, Ludwig-Maximilians-Universitaet Muenchen
Bastow, Ian, Imperial College
Beaumont, Christopher, Dalhousie University
Becker, Alex, University of California, Berkeley
Becker, Thorsten, University of Texas, Austin
Bedle, Heather, University of Oklahoma
Behn, Mark, Boston College
Bendick, Rebecca, University of Montana
Bercovici, David, Yale University
Beresnev, Igor A., Iowa State University of Science & Technology
Billen, Magali I., University of California, Davis
Billings, Stephen, University of British Columbia
Bina, Craig R., Northwestern University
Blankenship, Donald D., University of Texas, Austin
Bleibinhaus, Florian, Ludwig-Maximilians-Universitaet Muenchen
Bloxham, Jeremy, Harvard University
Boaga, Jacopo, Università degli Studi di Padova
Bokelmann, Goetz, University of Vienna
Boschi, Lapo, Università degli Studi di Padova
Bradley, Christopher R., Los Alamos National Laboratory
Braun, Alexander, Queen's University
Bregman, Martin, Tulsa Community College
Briggs, Derek E., Yale University
Britzke, Gilbert, Ludwig-Maximilians-Universitaet Muenchen
Brodholt, John, University College London
Brooks, Debra A., Santiago Canyon College
Brown, Wesley A., Stephen F. Austin State University
Buck, IV, W. R., Columbia University
Bunge, Hans-Peter, Ludwig-Maximilians-Universitaet Muenchen
Bustin, Amanda, University of British Columbia
Butler, Karl, University of New Brunswick
Butler, Sam, University of Saskatchewan
Calvin, Wendy, University of Nevada, Reno
Carlson, Barry A., Delta College
Carpenter, Philip J., Northern Illinois University
Carrigan, Charles R., Lawrence Livermore National Laboratory
Cassiani, Giorgio, Università degli Studi di Padova
Cayzer, Nicola, Edinburgh University
Chapman, Mark, Edinburgh University
Chase, Clement G., University of Arizona
Cheadle, Michael J., University of Wyoming
Clark, H. C., Rice University
Clarke, Garry K. C., University of British Columbia
Coakley, Bernard, University of Alaska, Fairbanks
Colgan, William, York University
Colin, Farquharson, Memorial University of Newfoundland
Comas, Xavier, Florida Atlantic University
Cooper, Catherine , Washington State University
Copley, Alex, University of Cambridge
Cosentino, Pietro, University of East Anglia
Couture, Gilles, Universite du Quebec a Montreal
Craig, Mitchell S., California State University, East Bay
Craven, John, Edinburgh University
Daly, Eve, National University of Ireland Galway
Daniels, Jeffrey J., Ohio State University
Davies, Gregory, Princeton University
Davies, J H., Cardiff University
Davies, Rhordri, Imperial College
Davis, Daniel M., Stony Brook University
Davis, Tara, University College Cork
Dengler, Lorinda, Humboldt State University
Dewdney, Chris, University of Portsmouth
Dickman, Steven R., Binghamton University
Dieterich, James H., University of California, Riverside
Dmochowski, Jane, University of Pennsylvania
Doll, William E., Oak Ridge National Laboratory
Dorman, Leroy M., University of California, San Diego
Dunbar, John A., Baylor University
Dunning, Jeremy D., Indiana University, Bloomington
Durland, Theodore, Oregon State University
Dzunic, Aleksandar, Curtin University
Ebel, John E., Boston College
Eckert, Andreas, Missouri University of Science and Technology
Edwards, C L, Los Alamos National Laboratory
Ehlers, Todd A., University of Michigan
Ekstrom, Goran, Columbia University
Elhusseiny, Ammar , King Fahd University of Petroleum and Minerals
Ellwood, Brooks, University of Texas, Arlington
Emmer, Barbara, Ludwig-Maximilians-Universitaet Muenchen
England, Richard, Leicester University

Erickson, Brittany, University of Oregon
Fehler, Michael, Massachusetts Institute of Technology
Ferguson, John F., University of Texas, Dallas
Ferrucci, Fabrizio, Open University
Fialko, Yuri A., University of California, San Diego
Fichtner, Andreas, Ludwig-Maximilians-Universitaet Muenchen
Filina, Irina, University of Nebraska, Lincoln
Fishwick, Stewart, Leicester University
Flesch, Lucy M., Purdue University
Foley, Bradford, Pennsylvania State University, University Park
Fontaine, Fabrice R., Universite de la Reunion
Forte, Alessandro Marco, Universite du Quebec a Montreal
Fortier, Richard, Universite Laval
Gaffney, Edward S., Los Alamos National Laboratory
Gaidos, Eric J., University of Hawai'i, Manoa
Gallovic, Frantisek, Ludwig-Maximilians-Universitaet Muenchen
Galsa, Attila, Eotvos Lorand University
Gao, Stephen , Missouri University of Science and Technology
Gebrande, Helmut, Ludwig-Maximilians-Universitaet Muenchen
Ghazala, Hosni H., El Mansoura University
Goes, Saskia, Imperial College
Goforth, Thomas T., Baylor University
Goldsby, David, University of Pennsylvania
Goodliffe, Andrew, University of Alabama
Gorman, Gerard, Imperial College
Gosnold, William D., University of North Dakota
Graham, Gina R., Alaska Division of Geological & Geophysical Surveys
Grand, Stephen P., University of Texas, Austin
Granja, José Luis, Univ Complutense de Madrid
Greenfield, Roy J., Pennsylvania State University, University Park
Gregg, Patricia, University of Illinois, Urbana-Champaign
Gribenko, Alex, University of Utah
Grindlay, Nancy R., University of North Carolina, Wilmington
Haas, Christian, York University
Haber, Eldad, University of British Columbia
Hamzaoui, Cherif, Universite du Quebec a Montreal
Hanafy, Sherif , King Fahd University of Petroleum and Minerals
Hanu, Dan B., Alexandru Ioan Cuza
Hardage, Bob A., University of Texas at Austin, Jackson School of Geosciences
Harder, Steven H., University of Texas, El Paso
Harmon, Nicholas, University of Southampton
Harry, Dennis L., Colorado State University
Hayes, Jorden L., Dickinson College
Heigold, Paul C., Argonne National Laboratory
Hellio, Gabrielle, University of Southampton
Henson, Harvey, Southern Illinois University Carbondale
Henstock, Tim, University of Southampton
Henyey, Thomas L., University of Southern California
Higgs, Bettie M., University College Cork
Hofmeister, Anne M., Washington University in St. Louis
Hornbach, Matthew, University of Texas, Austin
Horowitz, Franklin G., Cornell University
Horváth, Ferenc, Eotvos Lorand University
Houseman, Greg, University of Leeds
Huang, Lianjie, Los Alamos National Laboratory
Huerta, Audrey, Central Washington University
Hussein, Musa, University of Texas, El Paso
Iaffaldano, Giampiero, Ludwig-Maximilians-Universitaet Muenchen
Igel, Heiner, Ludwig-Maximilians-Universitaet Muenchen
Ishii, Miaki, Harvard University
Ito, Garrett T., University of Hawai'i, Manoa
Ivanov, Julian, University of Kansas
Jackson, James A., University of Cambridge
Jacob, Robert W., Bucknell University
Jaiswal, Priyank, Oklahoma State University
James, Peter B., Baylor University
Jarvis, Gary T., York University
Jayawickreme, Dushmantha, Southern Connecticut State University
Jensen, Olivia G., McGill University
Jezek, Kenneth, Ohio State University
Jiang, Junle , University of Oklahoma
Johnson, Kaj, Indiana University, Bloomington
Johnson, Paul A., Los Alamos National Laboratory
Johnson, Verner C., Colorado Mesa University
Jomeiri, Rahim, University of Tabriz
Jurdy, Donna M., Northwestern University
Kafka, Alan L., Boston College
Kahle, Beth, University of Cape Town
Kaplinski, Matthew A., Northern Arizona University
Kaus, Boris P., Universität Mainz
Kavner, Abby, University of California, Los Angeles
Keller, G. Randy, University of Oklahoma
Keller , George R., University of Texas, El Paso
Kelley, Shari, New Mexico Institute of Mining and Technology
Kellogg, James N., University of South Carolina
Kenyon, Patricia M., Graduate School of the City University of New York
Kenyon, Patricia M., City College (CUNY)
King, Scott D., Virginia Polytechnic Institute & State University
Kingdon, Kevin, University of British Columbia
Kinsland, Gary L., University of Louisiana at Lafayette
Korenaga, Jun, Yale University
Kroeger, Glenn C., Trinity University
Kruger, Joseph M., Lamar University
Kruse, Sarah E., University of South Florida
Kukowski, Nina, Friedrich-Schiller-University Jena
Kuo, John T., Columbia University
Käser, Martin, Ludwig-Maximilians-Universitaet Muenchen
Lai, Ching-Yao, Princeton University
Lat, Che Noorliza, University of Malaya
Lathrop, Daniel, University of Maryland
Lavallee, Yan, Ludwig-Maximilians-Universitaet Muenchen
Lavier, Luc L., University of Texas, Austin
Leitch, Alison, Memorial University of Newfoundland
Lenardic, Adrian, Rice University
Leonard, Lucinda, University of Victoria
Lewis, Stephen D., Fresno State University
Li, Mingming, Arizona State University
Lin, Fan-Chi, University of Utah
Lin, Guoqing, University of Miami
Lithgow-Bertelloni, Carolina, University of California, Los Angeles
Liu, Lanbo, University of Connecticut
Liu, Lijun, University of Illinois, Urbana-Champaign
Liu, Mian, University of Missouri
Liu, Qiangcheng, Princeton University
Liu, Qinya, University of Toronto
Liu, Yajing, McGill University
Liu, Zhaolun, Princeton University
Lohman, Rowena B., Cornell University
López-Pineda, Leobardo, Univ Estatal de Sonora
Louie, John, University of Nevada, Reno
Lovell, Mike, Leicester University
Lozos, Julian, California State University, Northridge
Luttrell, Karen, Louisiana State University
Lutz, Pascale, Institut Polytechnique LaSalle Beauvais (ex-IGAL)
Mackwell, Stephen J., Rice University
Malcolm, Alison, Memorial University of Newfoundland
Malinconico, Lawrence L., Lafayette College
Malservisi, Rocco, Ludwig-Maximilians-Universitaet Muenchen
Mareschal, Jean-Claude, Universite du Quebec a Montreal
Martens, Hilary R., University of Montana
Mavko, Gerald M., Stanford University
Maxwell, Michael, University of British Columbia
McElwaine, Jim, Durham University
McGinnis, Lyle D., Argonne National Laboratory
Meade, Brendan, Harvard University
Meadows, Wayne R., Los Alamos National Laboratory
Meert, Joseph G., University of Florida
Merriam, James B., University of Saskatchewan
Merrill, Ronald T., University of Washington
Milne, Glenn A., University of Ottawa
Minchew, Brent, Massachusetts Institute of Technology
Mitrovica, Jerry X., Harvard University
Mohr, Marcus, Ludwig-Maximilians-Universitaet Muenchen
Montesi, Laurent G., University of Maryland
Morgan, F D., Massachusetts Institute of Technology
Morgan, Joanna, Imperial College
Morris, William A., McMaster University
Morrison, H. Frank, University of California, Berkeley
Morse, David L., University of Texas, Austin
Muñoz, Alfonso, Univ Complutense de Madrid
Murphy, Vincent, Boston College
NICULESCU, Bogdan M., University of Bucharest

Niu, Qifei i., Boise State University
Nunn, Jeffrey A., Louisiana State University
Nur, Amos M., Stanford University
Nyblade, Andrew A., Pennsylvania State University, University Park
Nyquist, Jonathan, Temple University
O'Farrell, Keely A., University of Kentucky
Oeser, Jens, Ludwig-Maximilians-Universitaet Muenchen
Ojo, S. B., Obafemi Awolowo University
Oladunjoye, M. A., University of Ibadan
Olayinka, A. I., University of Ibadan
Oldenburg, Douglas W., University of British Columbia
Olgaard, David L., Rice University
Oliver, Ronald D., Los Alamos National Laboratory
Olorunfemi, M. O., Obafemi Awolowo University
Olson, Peter L., Johns Hopkins University
Osinowo, O. O., University of Ibadan
Oware, Erasmus K., SUNY, Buffalo
Paillet, Fred, University of Arkansas, Fayetteville
Pain, Christopher, Imperial College
Palmer, Donald F., Kent State University
Palutoglu, Mahmut, Firat University
Panero, Wendy R., Ohio State University
Parmentier, E. Marc, Brown University
Parsekian, Andrew D., University of Wyoming
Pasicznyk, David L., New Jersey Geological and Water Survey
Patton, Howard J., Los Alamos National Laboratory
Peavy, Samuel T., Georgia Southwestern State University
Peirce, Christine, Durham University
Pelton, John R., Boise State University
Peters, Mark T., Los Alamos National Laboratory
Petersen, Nikolai, Ludwig-Maximilians-Universitaet Muenchen
Pfuhl, Helen, Ludwig-Maximilians-Universitaet Muenchen
Phillips, William S., Los Alamos National Laboratory
Piazzoni, Antonio Sebastian, Ludwig-Maximilians-Universitaet Muenchen
Pimentel-Hernandez, Ramon, Univ Autonoma de Baja California Sur
Plattner, Christina, Ludwig-Maximilians-Universitaet Muenchen
Pollack, Henry N., University of Michigan
Porch, William M., Los Alamos National Laboratory
Porter, Ryan, Northern Arizona University
Priestley, Keith, University of Cambridge
Pysklywec, Russell N., University of Toronto
Raine, Robin, National University of Ireland Galway
Ranalli, Giorgio, Carleton University
Randall, George, Los Alamos National Laboratory
Rasmussen, Steen, Los Alamos National Laboratory
Ravat, Dhananjay, University of Kentucky
Rawlinson, Nick, University of Cambridge
Rempel, Alan W., University of Oregon
Revetta, Frank A., SUNY Potsdam
Rice, James R., Harvard University
Richard, Robert, University of California, Los Angeles
Richards, Mark A., University of California, Berkeley
Richardson, Randall M., University of Arizona
Roach, Michael, University of Tasmania
Roberts, Mark L., Woods Hole Oceanographic Institution
Robinson, Judith, Rutgers, The State University of New Jersey, Newark
Rochester, Michael G., Memorial University of Newfoundland
Roecker, Steven W., Rensselaer Polytechnic Institute
Romanovsky, Vladimir, University of Alaska, Fairbanks
Rothman, Daniel H., Massachusetts Institute of Technology
Rubin, Allan M., Princeton University
Rudge, John, University of Cambridge
Rudolph, Maxwell L., University of California, Davis
Russell, Christopher T., University of California, Los Angeles
Russell, R. Doncaster, University of British Columbia
Russo, Raymond, University of Florida
Ryall, Patrick J., Dalhousie University
Rychert, Catherine A., University of Southampton
Sabra, Karim, Georgia Institute of Technology
Sahakian, Valerie J., University of Oregon
Salami, Sikiru A., University of Benin
Sammis, Charles G., University of Southern California
Sauck, William A., Western Michigan University
Sava, Diana, University of Texas at Austin, Jackson School of Geosciences
Sava, Diana C., University of Texas, Austin
Sawyer, Derek, Ohio State University
Schmandt, Brandon, University of New Mexico
Schriver, David, University of California, Los Angeles
Schubert, Gerald, University of California, Los Angeles
Schuberth, Bernhard, Ludwig-Maximilians-Universitaet Muenchen
Schultz, Adam, Oregon State University
Searls, Mindi L., University of Nebraska, Lincoln
Segall, Paul, Stanford University
Serzu, Mulu, University of Manitoba
Shams, Asghar, Heriot-Watt University
Shcherbakov, Robert, Western University
Sherrod, Laura, Kutztown University of Pennsylvania
Siegler, Matthew, Southern Methodist University
Sigloch, Karin, University of Oxford
Simila, Gerald W., California State University, Northridge
Simmons, M. G., Massachusetts Institute of Technology
Simms, Janet E., Mississippi State University
Sit, Stefany , University of Illinois at Chicago
Sleep, Norman H., Stanford University
Smylie, Douglas E., York University
Solomatov, Viatcheslav S., Washington University in St. Louis
Sonett, Charles P., University of Arizona
Soupios, Panteleimon , King Fahd University of Petroleum and Minerals
Spanos, T.J.T (Tim), University of Alberta
Sparks, David, Texas A&M University
Stein, Carol A., University of Illinois at Chicago
Stephenson, Randell A., University of Aberdeen
Stidham, Christiane W., Stony Brook University
Stixrude, Lars, University of California, Los Angeles
Stupazzini, Marco, Ludwig-Maximilians-Universitaet Muenchen
Suckale, Jenny, Stanford University
Swain, Chris, Curtin University
Sweeney, Mark D., Pacific Northwest National Laboratory
Szeliga, Walter, Central Washington University
Szeto, Anthony M. K., York University
Taib, Samsudin Hj., University of Malaya
Tatham, Robert H., University of Texas, Austin
Taylor, Graeme, University of Plymouth
ten Brink, Uri S., Woods Hole Oceanographic Institution
ter Voorde, Marlies, Vrije Universiteit Amsterdam
Thiruvathukal, John V., Montclair State University
Thompson, Michael D., Argonne National Laboratory
Timár, Gábor, Eotvos Lorand University
Tisato, Nicola, University of Texas, Austin
Tobin, Harold, University of Wisconsin, Madison
Tong, Vincent C., Birkbeck College
Trugman, Daniel, University of Texas, Austin
Tsai, Victor, California Institute of Technology
Tsoflias, George P., University of Kansas
Turcotte, Donald L., University of California, Davis
Utgard, Russell O., Ohio State University
Van Avendonk, Harm, University of Texas, Austin
van Keken, Peter J., University of Michigan
Velli, Marco, University of California, Los Angeles
Vernhes, Jean-David, Institut Polytechnique LaSalle Beauvais (ex-IGAL)
Versteeg, Roelof, Columbia University
Vincent, Robert K., Bowling Green State University
von Glasow, Roland, University of East Anglia
Vopson, Melvin M., University of Portsmouth
Waheed, Umair B., King Fahd University of Petroleum and Minerals
Waltham, Dave, Royal Holloway University of London
Wang, Chi-Yuen, University of California, Berkeley
Wang, Herbert F., University of Wisconsin, Madison
Wang, Kelin, University of Victoria
Wang, Yanghua, Imperial College
Warren, Linda M., Saint Louis University
Wassermann, Joachim, Ludwig-Maximilians-Universitaet Muenchen
Weaver, Thomas A., Los Alamos National Laboratory
Weeraratne, Dayanthie, California State University, Northridge
Wettlaufer, John S., Yale University
White, Nicky, University of Cambridge
White, Robert, University of Cambridge
Whitman, Dean, Florida International University
Williams, Ian S., University of Wisconsin, River Falls
Wilson, Clark R., University of Texas, Austin
Winberry, Paul, Central Washington University
Winklhofer, Michael, Ludwig-Maximilians-Universitaet Muenchen

Wisely, Beth , Casper College
Wishart, De Bonne N., Central State University
Woodhouse, John, University of Oxford
Woods, Andy, University of Cambridge
Worthington, Lindsay L., University of New Mexico
Yelisetti, Subbarao, Texas A&M University, Kingsville
Zahm, Christopher K., University of Texas, Austin
Zaja, Annalisa, Università degli Studi di Padova
Zakharova, Natalia, Central Michigan University
Zarroca Hernández, Mario, Universitat Autonoma de Barcelona
Zaspel, Craig E., University of Montana Western
Zelt, Colin A., Rice University
Zha, Changsheng, Carnegie Institution for Science
Zhang, Chi, University of Kansas
Zhang, Zhendong, Princeton University
Zoback, Mark D., Stanford University

Experimental Geophysics

Anderson, Orson L., University of California, Los Angeles
Askari, Roohollah, Michigan Technological University
Bates, Richard, University of St. Andrews
Bevis, Michael G., Ohio State University
Bohlen, Thomas, Karlsruhe Institute of Technology
Bona, Andrej, Curtin University
Bridges, Frank, University of California, Santa Cruz
Bussod, Gilles Y., Los Alamos National Laboratory
Carson, Michael, Curtin University
Christensen, Nikolas I., University of Wisconsin, Madison
Comina, Cesare, Università di Torino
Dewers, Thomas, Sandia National Laboratory
Dillman, Amanda, University of Minnesota, Twin Cities
Dyaur, Nikolay, University of Houston
Evans, J. B., Massachusetts Institute of Technology
Fomel, Sergey, University of Texas at Austin, Jackson School of Geosciences
Fratta, Dante, University of Wisconsin, Madison
Glover, Paul W., University of Leeds
Glover, Paul W., Universite Laval
Glubokovskikh, Stanislav, Curtin University
Goebel, Thomas H., University of Memphis
Graham, Jr., Earl K., Pennsylvania State University, University Park
Gross, Gerardo W., New Mexico Institute of Mining and Technology
Hansen, Lars N., University of Minnesota, Twin Cities
Kaip, Galen M., University of Texas, El Paso
Karlstrom, Leif, University of Oregon
Kilburn, Chris, University College London
Kitajima, Hiroko, Texas A&M University
Kohlstedt, David L., University of Minnesota, Twin Cities
Lebedev, Maxim, Curtin University
Li, Baosheng, Stony Brook University
Manghnani, Murli H., University of Hawai'i, Manoa
Mao, Ho-kwang, Carnegie Institution for Science
Marone, Chris, Pennsylvania State University, University Park
Marshall, Hans-Peter, Boise State University
Marshall, Scott T., Appalachian State University
Mei, Shenghua, University of Minnesota, Twin Cities
Narod, Barry, University of British Columbia
Parks, George K., University of Washington
Pevzner, Roman, Curtin University
Ruina, Andy L., Cornell University
Schmitt, Douglas R., Purdue University
Scholz, Christopher H., Columbia University
Shankland, Thomas J., Los Alamos National Laboratory
Shaw, George H., Union College
Shieh, Sean R., Western University
Shu, Jinfu, Carnegie Institution for Science
Tullis, Terry E., Brown University
Vanorio, Tiziana, Stanford University
Vaughan, Michael T., Stony Brook University
Velasco, Aaron A., University of Texas, El Paso
Vialle, Stephanie, Curtin University
Watanabe, Tohru, University of Toyama
Wohletz, Kenneth H., Los Alamos National Laboratory
Wong, Teng-fong, Stony Brook University
Yong, Wenjun, Western University
Zebker, Howard A., Stanford University
Zimmerman, Mark, University of Minnesota, Twin Cities

Exploration Geophysics

Al-Shuhail, Abdullah, King Fahd University of Petroleum and Minerals
Alumbaugh, David L., University of California, Berkeley
Ariyo, Stephen O., Federal University of Technology, Akure
Armadillo, Egidio, Universita di Genova
B, Veeraiah, Osmania University
Backus, Milo M., University of Texas, Austin
Becker, Alex, University of California, Berkeley
Biondi, Biondo L., Stanford University
Black, Ross A., University of Kansas
Brabham, P J., Cardiff University
Brassea, Jesus M., Ctr de Invest Científica y de Ed Superior de Ensenada
Breland, Clayton F., Louisiana State University
Brown, Larry D., Cornell University
Bunch, Mark, University of Adelaide
Carmichael, Robert S., University of Iowa
Castagna, John P., University of Houston
Chandler, Val W., University of Minnesota, Twin Cities
Chen, Jingyi, University of Tulsa
Claerbout, Jon F., Stanford University
Cook, Frederick A., University of Calgary
Corbato, Charles E., Ohio State University
Coruh, Cahit, Virginia Polytechnic Institute & State University
DeAngelo, Micheal V., Univ of Texas at Austin, Jackson Sch of Geosciences
Donaldson, Paul R., Boise State University
Dubba, Vijay K., Osmania University
Dunlap, Dallas B., University of Texas at Austin, Jackson School of Geosciences
Dunn, Bernie, Western University
Ellett, Kevin M., Indiana University
Esparza, Francisco, Ctr de Invest Científica y de Ed Superior de Ensenada
Espinosa, Juan M., Ctr de Invest Científica y de Ed Superior de Ensenada
Falebita, Dele E., Obafemi Awolowo University
Ferguson, Ian J., University of Manitoba
Ferguson, Robert, University of Calgary
Flores, Carlos, Ctr de Invest Científica y de Ed Superior de Ensenada
Fomel, Sergey B., University of Texas, Austin
Gaede, Oliver M., Queensland University of Technology
Gajewski, Dirk J., Universitaet Hamburg
Galvin, Robert, Curtin University
Gao, Dengliang, West Virginia University
Gendzwill, Donald J., University of Saskatchewan
Giroux, Bernard, Universite du Quebec
Gloaguen, Erwan, Universite du Quebec
Gomez, Enrique, Ctr de Invest Científica y de Ed Superior de Ensenada
Gonzalez-Escobar, Mario, Ctr de Invest Científica y de Ed Superior de Ensenada
Grana, Dario, University of Wyoming
Gurevich, Boris, Curtin University
Han, De-hua, University of Houston
Hardage, Bob A., University of Texas, Austin
Harris, James B., Millsaps College
Hauser, Ernest C., Wright State University
Herrmann, Felix J., Georgia Institute of Technology
Hilterman, Fred, University of Houston
Hinze, William J., Purdue University
Hole, John A., Virginia Polytechnic Institute & State University
Holt, John W., University of Texas, Austin
Homuth, Emil F., Los Alamos National Laboratory
Howman, Dominic J., Curtin University
Hu, Hao, University of Houston
Innanen, Kristopher, University of Calgary
Jin, Ge, Colorado School of Mines
Jiracek, George R., San Diego State University
Johnson, Ansel G., Portland State University
Jones, Francis H., University of British Columbia
Keach, Bill, Utah Geological Survey
Keach II, R. William, Brigham Young University
Kepic, Anton W., Curtin University
Khalil, Mohamed, Montana Tech of the University of Montana
Lawton, Donald C., University of Calgary
Lee, Ki Ha, University of California, Berkeley
Levander, Alan R., Rice University
Li, Yaoguo, Colorado School of Mines
Link, Curtis A., Montana Tech of the University of Montana
Liu, Kelly, Missouri University of Science and Technology
Louie, John N., University of Nevada, Reno
Lourenço, José M., Unive de Trás-os-Montes e Alto Douro

Madadi, Mahyar, Curtin University
Margrave, Gary F., University of Calgary
Marobhe, Isaac M., University of Dar es Salaam
Mathur, Ram Raj, Osmania University
McBride, John H., Brigham Young University
McPherson, Brian, University of Utah
Mikhaltsevitch, Vassily, Curtin University
Milkereit, Bernd, University of Toronto
Miller, Richard D., University of Kansas
Morrison, Huntly Frank, University of California, Berkeley
Muchingami, Innocent , University of Namibia
Olawuyi, Kehinde A., University of Ilorin
Olsen, Kim B., San Diego State University
Palmer, Derecke, University of New South Wales
Perez, Marco A., Ctr de Invest Científica y de Ed Superior de Ensenada
Pethick, Andrew, Curtin University
Potter, David, University of Alberta
Pratt, R. Gerhard, Western University
Pujol, Jose, University of Memphis
Puzyrev, Vladimir, Curtin University
Raef, Abdelmoneam E., Kansas State University
Raji, W. O., University of Ilorin
Rector, James W., University of California, Berkeley
Reshef, Moshe, Tel Aviv University
Richard, Benjamin H., Wright State University
Roche, Steven L., University of Tulsa
Romo, Jose M., Ctr de Invest Científica y de Ed Superior de Ensenada
Sarwar, A. K. Mostofa, University of New Orleans
Sava, Paul, Colorado School of Mines
Sbar, Marc, University of Arizona
Scanlin, Michael A., Elizabethtown College
Seifoullaev, Roustam K., University of Texas, Austin
Sen, Mrinal K., University of Texas, Austin
Serpa, Laura F., University of Texas, El Paso
Sexton, John L., Southern Illinois University Carbondale
Shaw, Kenneth L., University of Utah
Slater, Lee S., Rutgers, The State University of New Jersey, Newark
Smith, Richard S., Laurentian University, Sudbury
Smithyman, Brenden, Western University
Snieder, Roel, Colorado School of Mines
Sobotka, Jerzy, University of Wroclaw
Speece, Marvin A., Montana Tech of the University of Montana
Spikes, Kyle T., University of Texas, Austin
Sprenke, Kenneth F., University of Idaho
Steer, David N., University of Akron
Sternberg, Ben K., University of Arizona
Stewart, Robert, University of Houston
Stewart, Robert R., University of Houston
Stimpson, Ian G., Keele University
Stoffa, Paul L., University of Texas, Austin
Sturmer, Daniel M., University of Cincinnati
Swidinsky, Andrei, Colorado School of Mines
Tertyshnikov, Konstantin, Curtin University
Thomsen, Leon, University of Houston
Tsvankin, Ilya D., Colorado School of Mines
Turpening, Roger M., Michigan Technological University
Unsworth, Martyn, Cornell University
Urosevic, Milovan, Curtin University
Vazquez, Rogelio, Ctr de Invest Científica y de Ed Superior de Ensenada
Verma, Sumit, University of Texas Permian Basin
von Frese, Ralph R., Ohio State University
Wannamaker, Phillip E., University of Utah
Watts, Doyle, Wright State University
Weglein, Arthur B., University of Houston
Weiss, Chester J., University of New Mexico
Wilson, Thomas H., West Virginia University
Wolfe, Paul J., Wright State University
Zhang, Bo, University of Alabama
Zhang, Rui, University of Louisiana at Lafayette
Zhdanov, Michael S., University of Utah
Ziolkowski, Anton M., Edinburgh University
Ziramov, Sasha, Curtin University

Geodesy

Adeleke, Adedayo, University of Pretoria
Al-Attar, David, University of Cambridge
Araya , María C., Univ de Costa Rica
Barnhart, William, University of Iowa
Bennett, Richard, University of Arizona
Blewitt, Geoffrey, University of Nevada, Reno
Caporali, Alessandro, Università degli Studi di Padova
Chaussard, Estelle, University of Oregon
Claessens, Sten, Curtin University
Clarke, Peter J., University of Newcastle Upon Tyne
Crossley, David J., Saint Louis University
Davis, James , Columbia University
Dixon, Tim, University of South Florida
El-Mowafy, Ahmed, Curtin University
Elliott, Julie, Purdue University
Evans, Eileen L., California State University, Northridge
Featherstone, Will, Curtin University
Feigl, Kurt, University of Wisconsin, Madison
Filmer, Mick, Curtin University
Flake, Rex , Central Washington University
Fotopoulos, Georgia, Queen's University
Funning, Gareth J., University of California, Riverside
Gonzalez, Jose J., Ctr de Invest Científica y de Ed Superior de Ensenada
Grapenthin, Ronni, University of Alaska, Fairbanks
Hammond, William C., University of Nevada, Reno
Herring, Thomas A., Massachusetts Institute of Technology
Hiroji, Anand D., University of Southern Mississippi
Hooper, Andy, University of Leeds
James, Thomas S., University of Victoria
Jekeli, Christopher, Ohio State University
Johnston, Paul, Curtin University
Kirby, Jon, Curtin University
Kogan, Mikhail, Columbia University
Kreemer, Corne, University of Nevada, Reno
Kuhn, Michael, Curtin University
Kusznir, Nick, University of Liverpool
Kyriakopoulos, Christodoulos, University of Memphis
LaFemina, Peter C., Pennsylvania State University, University Park
Li, Zhenhong, University of Newcastle Upon Tyne
Lopez, Alberto, University of Puerto Rico
Lowry, Anthony R., Utah State University
Malservisi, Rocco, University of South Florida
Masterlark, Timothy L., South Dakota School of Mines & Technology
Melbourne, Timothy I., Central Washington University
Melgar, Diego, University of Oregon
Miller, M. Meghan, Central Washington University
Moore, Phillip, University of Newcastle Upon Tyne
Mueller, Ivan, Ohio State University
Murray, Mark, New Mexico Institute of Mining and Technology
Newman, Andrew V., Georgia Institute of Technology
Odera, Patroba A., Jomo Kenyatta University of Agriculture & Technology
Pagiatakis, Spiros, York University
Palamartchouk, Kirill, University of Newcastle Upon Tyne
Parker, Amy, Curtin University
Parsons, Barry, University of Oxford
Pritchard, Matthew E., Cornell University
Rapp, Richard H., Ohio State University
Rundle, John, University of California, Davis
Samsonov, Sergey V., Natural Resources Canada
Santillan, Marcelo, Central Washington University
Schaffrin, Burkhard A., Ohio State University
Shirzaei, Manoochehr, Arizona State University
Shum, CK, Ohio State University
Smalley, Jr., Robert, University of Memphis
Smith-Konter, Bridget R., University of Hawai'i, Manoa
Sparks, David, Texas A&M University
Spinler, Joshua C., University of Arkansas at Little Rock
Stamps, D. S., Virginia Polytechnic Institute & State University
Stegman, Dave, University of California, San Diego
Teunissen, Peter, Curtin University
Tiampo, Kristy F., Western University
van Dam, Tonie, University of Utah
Waithaka, Hunja, Jomo Kenyatta University of Agriculture & Technology
Walters, Richard, Durham University
Wang, Kan, Curtin University
Wdowinski, Shimon, Florida International University
Wells, David E., University of Southern Mississippi

Wright, Tim, University of Leeds
Yi, Yuchan, Ohio State University

Geomagnetism & Paleomagnetism

Aldridge, Keith D., York University
Backus, George E., University of California, San Diego
Banerjee, Subir K., University of Minnesota, Twin Cities
Beardmore, Josh, Curtin University
Biggin, Andy, University of Liverpool
Bilardello, Dario, University of Minnesota, Twin Cities
Bogue, Scott W., Occidental College
Booker, John, University of Washington
Bowles, Julie, University of Wisconsin, Milwaukee
Braginsky, Stanislav I., University of California, Los Angeles
Bramham, Emma , University of Leeds
Brown, Laurie L., University of Massachusetts, Amherst
Burmester, Russell F., Western Washington University
Channell, James E., University of Florida
Cioppa, Maria T., University of Windsor
Clough, Gene A., Bates College
Coe, Robert S., University of California, Santa Cruz
Constable, Catherine G., University of California, San Diego
Cottrell, Rory D., University of Rochester
DeMets, D. Charles, University of Wisconsin, Madison
Dharmasoth, Manjula, Osmania University
Doh, Seong-Jae, Korea University
Dulin, Shannon, University of Oklahoma
Ellwood, Brooks B., Louisiana State University
Evans, David A., Yale University
Evans, Michael E., University of Alberta
Everett, Mark, Texas A&M University
Feinberg, Joshua, University of Minnesota, Twin Cities
Ferre', Eric C., University of Louisiana at Lafayette
Franklin, David, University of Portsmouth
Fraser-Smith, Antony C., Stanford University
Fu, Roger, Harvard University
Garcia Lasanta, Cristina, Western Washington University
Geissman, John W., University of New Mexico
Geissman, John W., University of Michigan
Gilder, Stuart, Ludwig-Maximilians-Universitaet Muenchen
Gordon, Richard G., Rice University
Guerrero-Garcia, Jose C., Univ Nacional Autonoma de Mexico
Hall, Stuart A., University of Houston
Halls, Henry C., University of Toronto
Harbert, William P., University of Pittsburgh
Hill, Mimi, University of Liverpool
Hodych, Joseph P., Memorial University of Newfoundland
Holme, Richard, University of Liverpool
Housen, Bernard A., Western Washington University
Jackson, Michael, University of Minnesota, Twin Cities
Jones, F. Walter, University of Alberta
Kean, Jr., William F., University of Wisconsin, Milwaukee
Kelso, Paul R., Lake Superior State University
Kent, Dennis V., Rutgers, The State University of New Jersey
Kodama, Kenneth P., Lehigh University
Kravchinsky, Vadim, University of Alberta
Larson, Edwin E., University of Colorado
Lepre, Christopher H., Rutgers, The State University of New Jersey
Li, Zheng-Xiang, Curtin University
Lima, Eduardo A., Massachusetts Institute of Technology
Lippert, Peter C., University of Utah
Liu, Yebo, Curtin University
Livermore, Phil, University of Leeds
Lund, Steven P., University of Southern California
Maloof, Adam C., Princeton University
Marshall, Monte, San Diego State University
Márton, Péter, Eotvos Lorand University
McCausland, Phil J., Western University
Merrill, Ronald T., University of Washington
Morris, Antony, University of Plymouth
Moskowitz, Bruce M., University of Minnesota, Twin Cities
Muxworthy, Adrian, Imperial College
Negrini, Robert M., California State University, Bakersfield
Nilsson, Andreas, University of Liverpool
Noltimier, Hallan C., Ohio State University
Palmer, H. C., Western University
Panzik, Joeseph, University of South Florida
Papitashvili, Vladimir O., National Science Foundation
Pares, Josep M., University of Michigan
Park, Stephen K., University of California, Riverside
Parker, Robert L., University of California, San Diego
Paty, Carol M., Georgia Institute of Technology
Petronis, Michael S., New Mexico Highlands University
Piper, John, University of Liverpool
Pisarevskiy, Sergei, Curtin University
Plattner, Alain, University of Alabama
Rankin, David, University of Alberta
Raub, Timothy D., University of St. Andrews
Richter, Carl, University of Louisiana at Lafayette
Roberts, Paul H., University of California, Los Angeles
Shibuya, Hidetoshi, Kumamoto University
Smirnov, Aleksey V., Michigan Technological University
Srnka, Len, University of California, San Diego
Sternberg, Robert S., Franklin and Marshall College
Stone, David B., University of Alaska, Fairbanks
Symons, David T., University of Windsor
Tarduno, John A., University of Rochester
Tauxe, Lisa, University of California, San Diego
Tikoo, Sonia M., Rutgers, The State University of New Jersey
Valentine, Michael J., University of Puget Sound
Van der Voo, Rob, University of Michigan
Verosub, Kenneth L., University of California, Davis
Walden, John, University of St. Andrews
Weaver, John T., University of Victoria
Whaler, Kathryn A., Edinburgh University
Williams, Wyn, Edinburgh University
Xuan, Chuang, University of Southampton
Zanella, Elena, Università di Torino

Gravity

Aiken, Carlos L., University of Texas, Dallas
Eppelbaum, Lev, Tel Aviv University
Garcia, Juan, Ctr de Invest Científica y de Ed Superior de Ensenada
Grannell, Roswitha B., California State University, Long Beach
Kusumoto, Shigekazu, University of Toyama
Steckler, Michael, Columbia University

Heat Flow

Beltrami, Hugo, Saint Francis Xavier University
Blackwell, David D., Southern Methodist University
Fulton, Patrick M., Texas A&M University
Harris, Robert N., Oregon State University
Hsieh, Wen-Pin, Academia Sinica
Huang, Shaopeng, University of Michigan
Jones, Michael Q., University of the Witwatersrand
Lenkey, László, Eotvos Lorand University
Morgan, Paul, Colorado Geological Survey
Morgan, Paul, Northern Arizona University
Reiter, Marshall A., New Mexico Institute of Mining and Technology
Sclater, John G., University of California, San Diego

Seismology

Abers, Geoffrey A., Cornell University
Achauer, Ulrich, Universite de Strasbourg
Agnew, Duncan C., University of California, San Diego
Alexander, Shelton S., Pennsylvania State University, University Park
Allen, Clarence R., California Institute of Technology
Allen, Richard M., University of California, Berkeley
Ammon, Charles J., Pennsylvania State University, University Park
Ampuero, Jean-Paul, California Institute of Technology
Anandakrishnan, Sridhar, Pennsylvania State University, University Park
Anderson, John G., University of Nevada, Reno
Angus, Doug, University of Leeds
Archuleta, Ralph J., University of California, Santa Barbara
Arrowsmith, Stephen J., Southern Methodist University
Assatourians, Karen, Western University
Aster, Richard C., Colorado State University
Atkinson, Gail M., Western University
Ausbrooks, Scott, Arkansas Geological Survey
Austermann, Jacqueline, Columbia University
Bachmann, Etienne, Princeton University
Bagley, Brian, University of Minnesota, Twin Cities
Balch, Robert S., New Mexico Institute of Mining and Technology

Barazangi, Muawia, Cornell University
Barclay, Andrew, Columbia University
Barker, Jeffrey S., Binghamton University
Beaumont, Christopher, Dalhousie University
Beck, Susan L., University of Arizona
Beghein, Caroline, University of California, Los Angeles
Beller, Stephen, Princeton University
Ben-Zion, Yehuda, University of Southern California
Benavides-Iglesias, Alfonso, Texas A&M University
Bennett, Scott, University of Washington
Benoit, Margaret, College of New Jersey
Beroza, Gregory C., Stanford University
Bezada, Max, University of Minnesota, Twin Cities
Biasi, Glenn P., University of Nevada, Reno
Bilek, Susan L., New Mexico Institute of Mining and Technology
Biundo, Marc, University of Washington
Blake, Daniel R., Ohio Dept of Natural Resources
Bodin, Paul A., University of Washington
Bollinger, G. A., Virginia Polytechnic Institute & State University
Bostock, Michael G., University of British Columbia
Bozdag, Ebru, Colorado School of Mines
Braile, Lawrence W., Purdue University
Braunmiller, Jochen, University of South Florida
Brodsky, Emily, University of California, Santa Cruz
Brudzinski, Michael, Miami University
Brumbaugh, David S., Northern Arizona University
Brune, James N., University of Nevada, Reno
Burdick, Scott, Wayne State University
Burton, Paul, University of East Anglia
Byrnes, Joseph, University of Minnesota, Twin Cities
Calvert, Andrew J., Simon Fraser University
Cann, Johnson R., Woods Hole Oceanographic Institution
Caplan-Auerbach, Jackie, Western Washington University
Cardimona, Steve, Mendocino College
Cartwright, J A., Cardiff University
Cassidy, John, University of Victoria
Castro, Raul, Ctr de Invest Científica y de Ed Superior de Ensenada
Cattania, Camilla, Massachusetts Institute of Technology
Chapman, Martin C., Virginia Polytechnic Institute & State University
Chen, Po, University of Wyoming
Chen, Wang-Ping, University of Illinois, Urbana-Champaign
Chen, Xiaowei, University of Oklahoma
Chesnokov, Evgeny, University of Houston
Chiu, Jer-Ming, University of Memphis
Christensen, Douglas, University of Alaska, Fairbanks
Cicerone, Robert D., Bridgewater State University
Cipar, John J., Boston College
Clark, Roger A., University of Leeds
Clayton, Robert W., California Institute of Technology
Clowes, Ronald M., University of British Columbia
Cochran, Elizabeth, University of California, Riverside
Collins, John A., Woods Hole Oceanographic Institution
Conder, James A., Southern Illinois University Carbondale
Cormier, Vernon F., University of Connecticut
Cornwell, David G., University of Aberdeen
Cottaar, Sanne , University of Cambridge
Cramer, Chris, University of Memphis
Creager, Kenneth C., University of Washington
Crosson, Robert S., University of Washington
Curtis, Andrew, Edinburgh University
D'Amico, Sebastiano, University of Malta
Dalton, Colleen, Brown University
Darbyshire, Fiona Ann, Universite du Quebec a Montreal
Darold, Amberlee, University of Oklahoma
Davis, Paul M., University of California, Los Angeles
Day, Steven M., San Diego State University
De Angelis, Silvio, University of Liverpool
Denolle, Marine, Harvard University
dePolo, Diane, University of Nevada, Reno
DeShon, Heather R., Southern Methodist University
Dettmer, Jan, University of Calgary
Doerr, Erica ., New Mexico Institute of Mining and Technology
Doll, William E., University of Tennessee, Knoxville
Dongmo Wamba, Mathurin, Princeton University
Dorman, James, University of Memphis
Doser, Diane I., University of Texas, El Paso
Douilly, Roby, University of California, Riverside
Dreger, Douglas S., University of California, Berkeley
Duan, Benchuan, Texas A&M University
Duan, Benchun, Texas A&M University
Dueker, Kenneth G., University of Wyoming
Dunham, Eric M., Stanford University
Eaton, David, University of Calgary
Ebel, John E., Boston College
Eilon, Zach, University of California, Santa Barbara
Ekstrom, Goran, Columbia University
Ellis, Robert M., University of British Columbia
Ellsworth, William L., Stanford University
Farrell, Jamie, University of Utah
Faulkner, Daniel, University of Liverpool
Ferreira, Anna, University College London
Finley, William R., University of Louisiana at Lafayette
Fischer, Karen M., Brown University
Fontaine, Fabrice R., Universite de la Reunion
Forbriger, Thomas, Karlsruhe Institute of Technology
Ford, Heather, University of California, Riverside
Fox, Jeff, Ohio Dept of Natural Resources
Frankel, Arthur, University of Washington
Frazer, L. N., University of Hawai'i, Manoa
Frederiksen, Andrew, University of Manitoba
Frez, Jose, Ctr de Invest Científica y de Ed Superior de Ensenada
Frohlich, Cliff, University of Texas, Austin
Frohlich, Clifford A., University of Texas, Austin
Fujita, Kazuya, Michigan State University
Gabrielov, Andrei, Purdue University
Gaherty, James, Columbia University
Galea, Pauline, University of Malta
Gao, Haiying, University of Massachusetts, Amherst
Garces, Milton A., University of Hawai'i, Manoa
Garnero, Edward, Arizona State University
Gharti, Hom Nath, Princeton University
Ghosh, Abhijit, University of California, Riverside
Gibson, Jr., Richard L., Texas A&M University
Gilbert, Hersh, University of Calgary
Gilbert, Hersh, Purdue University
Gilpin, Bernard J., Golden West College
Glowacka, Ewa, Ctr de Invest Científica y de Ed Superior de Ensenada
Gomberg, Joan, University of Washington
Grand, Stephen P., University of Texas, Austin
Greenhalgh, Stewart A., King Fahd University of Petroleum and Minerals
Gu, Jeff, University of Alberta
Gurnis, Michael C., California Institute of Technology
Gurrola, Harold, Texas Tech University
Haddidi, Hamid, California Geological Survey
Hager, Bradford H., Massachusetts Institute of Technology
Hagerty, Michael, Boston College
Hagos, Lijam, California Geological Survey
Hajnal, Zoltan, University of Saskatchewan
Hall, Jeremy, Memorial University of Newfoundland
Hamburger, Michael W., Indiana University, Bloomington
Hammer, Philip T., University of British Columbia
Hansen, Samantha E., University of Alabama
Harrington, Rebecca, Karlsruhe Institute of Technology
Harris, Jerry M., Stanford University
Hartog, Renate, University of Washington
Hartse, Hans E., Los Alamos National Laboratory
Hassanpour Sedghi, Mohammad, University of Tabriz
Hauksson, Egill, California Institute of Technology
Hawman, Robert B., University of Georgia
Hayward, Christopher T., Southern Methodist University
Hearn, Thomas M., New Mexico State University, Las Cruces
Helmberger, Donald V., California Institute of Technology
Herrmann, Robert B., Saint Louis University
Hildebrand, Steve T., Los Alamos National Laboratory
Hobbs, Richard, Durham University
Holland, Austin A., University of Oklahoma
Holt, William E., Stony Brook University
Holtzman, Benjamin, Columbia University
Honjas, Bill, University of Nevada, Reno
Horton, Stephen P., University of Memphis
House, Leigh S., Los Alamos National Laboratory
Houston, Heidi B., University of Southern California

Howell, Jr., Benjamin F., Pennsylvania State University, University Park
Huerfano, Victor, University of Puerto Rico
Humphreys, Eugene D., University of Oregon
Hurich, Charles A., Memorial University of Newfoundland
Hyndman, Roy D., University of Victoria
Ismail, Ahmed, Oklahoma State University
Jackson, David D., University of California, Los Angeles
Jacob, Klaus H., Columbia University
Janiszewski, Helen, University of Hawai'i, Manoa
Jasbinsek, John J., California Polytechnic State University
Jaumé, Steven C., College of Charleston
Ji, Chen, University of California, Santa Barbara
Johnson, Jeffrey , Boise State University
Johnson, Lane R., University of California, Berkeley
Johnson, Roy A., University of Arizona
Johnston, Archibald C., University of Memphis
Jones, Alan, Binghamton University
Jones, Craig H., University of Colorado
Jordan, Thomas H., University of Southern California
Kafka, Alan L., Boston College
Kaka, Ismail, King Fahd University of Petroleum and Minerals
Kanamori, Hiroo, California Institute of Technology
Karplus, Marianne, University of Texas, El Paso
Kent, Graham, University of Nevada, Reno
Keranen, Katie M., Cornell University
Kijko, Andrzej, University of Pretoria
Kim, Won-Young, Columbia University
Knopoff, Leon, University of California, Los Angeles
Koellemeijer, Paula, Royal Holloway University of London
Kovach, Robert L., Stanford University
Krebes, Edward S., University of Calgary
Langston, Charles A., University of Memphis
Laske, Gabi, University of California, San Diego
Lay, Thorne, University of California, Santa Cruz
Lees, Jonathan M., University of North Carolina, Chapel Hill
Lei, Wenjie, Princeton University
Lekic, Vedran, University of Maryland
Lerner-Lam, Arthur L., Columbia University
Lerner-Lam, Arthur L., Columbia University
Levander, Alan, Rice University
Levin, Vadim, Rutgers, The State University of New Jersey
Li, Aibing, University of Houston
Li, Yong-Gang, University of Southern California
Liberty, Lee M., Boise State University
Linde, Alan T., Carnegie Institution for Science
Liner, Christopher, University of Arkansas, Fayetteville
Litherland, Mairi, New Mexico Institute of Mining and Technology
Lizarralde, Daniel, Woods Hole Oceanographic Institution
Lohman, Rowena B., Cornell University
Long, Maureen D., Yale University
Lorenzo, Juan M., Louisiana State University
Lough, Amanda, Drexel University
Louie, John N., University of Nevada, Reno
Louie, John, University of Nevada, Reno
Lumley, David, University of Texas, Dallas
Ma, Shuo, San Diego State University
Magnani, M. Beatrice, Southern Methodist University
Main, Ian G., Edinburgh University
Malin, Peter E., Duke University
Mallick, Subhashis, University of Wyoming
Malone, Stephen D., University of Washington
Mangriotis, Maria-Daphne , Heriot-Watt University
Marfurt, Kurt J., University of Oklahoma
Masters, T. Guy, University of California, San Diego
McCarthy, Christine, Columbia University
McClelland, Lori, University of Nevada, Reno
McGuire, Jeffrey J., Woods Hole Oceanographic Institution
McLaskey, Greg C., Cornell University
McLaskey, Greg C., Cornell University
McMechan, George A., University of Texas, Dallas
McNutt, Steve, University of South Florida
Meltzer, Anne S., Lehigh University
Meng, Lingsen, University of California, Los Angeles
Menke, William H., Columbia University
Mereu, Robert F., Western University
Michel, Gero, Western University
Mikesell, Dylan, Boise State University
Miller, Kate, Texas A&M University
Minster, J. Bernard H., University of California, San Diego
Molnar, Sheri, Western University
Morozov, Igor B., University of Saskatchewan
Moulis, Anastasia, Boston College
Mulibo, Gabriel D., University of Dar es Salaam
Munguia, Luis, Ctr de Invest Científica y de Ed Superior de Ensenada
Nakamura, Yosio n., University of Texas, Austin
Nakamura, Yosio, University of Texas, Austin
Nava, Alejandro, Ctr de Invest Científica y de Ed Superior de Ensenada
Nedimovic, Mladen, Dalhousie University
Neighbors, Corrie, Western New Mexico University
Nettles, Meredith, Columbia University
Ni, James F., New Mexico State University, Las Cruces
Nikulin, Alex, Binghamton University
Nissen-Meyer, Targe, University of Oxford
Niu, Fenglin, Rice University
Nowack, Robert L., Purdue University
Nyland, Edo, University of Alberta
Ogbamikhumi, Alexander, University of Benin
Oglesby, David D., University of California, Riverside
Okal, Emile A., Northwestern University
Okaya, David A., University of Southern California
Oliver, Adolph A., Chabot College
Olson, Ted L., Snow College
Olugboji, Tolulope, University of Rochester
Owens, Thomas J., University of South Carolina
Pancha, Aasha, University of Nevada, Reno
Pankow, Kristine L., University of Utah
Park, Jeffrey J., Yale University
Pavlis, Gary L., Indiana University, Bloomington
Pechmann, James C., University of Utah
Peng, Zhigang, Georgia Institute of Technology
Pennington, Wayne D., Michigan Technological University
Persaud, Patricia, Louisiana State University
Phinney, Robert A., Princeton University
Plank, Gabriel, University of Nevada, Reno
Polet, Jascha, California State Polytechnic University, Pomona
Powell, Christine A., University of Memphis
Pride, Steven, University of California, Berkeley
Pulliam, Jay, Baylor University
Pulliam, Robert J., University of Texas, Austin
Pulliam, Robert J., Baylor University
Reading, Anya, University of Tasmania
Record, Amy, New Mexico Institute of Mining and Technology
Rector, III, James W., University of California, Berkeley
Rennie, Tom, University of Nevada, Reno
Revenaugh, Justin, University of Minnesota, Twin Cities
Richard, Ferdinand W., University of Dar es Salaam
Richards, Paul G., Columbia University
Richardson, Eliza, Pennsylvania State University, University Park
Rieger, Duayne, Community College of Rhode Island
Rietbrock, Andreas, University of Liverpool
Ritsema, Jeroen, University of Michigan
Ritter, Joachim R., Karlsruhe Institute of Technology
Roberts, Peter, Los Alamos National Laboratory
Rogers, Garry C., University of Victoria
Rohay, Alan C., Pacific Northwest National Laboratory
Romanowicz, Barbara A., University of California, Berkeley
Rost, Sebastian, University of Leeds
Rowe, Charlotte A., New Mexico Institute of Mining and Technology
Rowshandel, Badie, California Geological Survey
Ruff, Larry J., University of Michigan
Ruffman, Alan, Dalhousie University
Ruhl, Christine J., University of Tulsa
Sacchi, Mauricio D., University of Alberta
Sacks, I. Selwyn, Carnegie Institution for Science
Sahay, Pratap, Ctr de Invest Científica y de Ed Superior de Ensenada
Sandvol, Eric A., University of Missouri
Savage, Brian K., University of Rhode Island
Savage, Brian, University of Rhode Island
Savage, Heather M., Columbia University
Sawyer, Dale S., Rice University
Schaff, David, Columbia University
Schlue, John W., New Mexico Institute of Mining and Technology

Scholz, Christopher H., Columbia University
Schutt, Derek L., Colorado State University
Schwab, Fred, University of California, Los Angeles
Schwartz, Susan, University of California, Santa Cruz
Seeber, Leonardo, Columbia University
Serpa, Laura F., University of New Orleans
Shaw, Bruce, Columbia University
Shearer, Peter M., University of California, San Diego
Sheehan, Anne F., University of Colorado
Shen, Weisen, Stony Brook University
Sherrod, Brian L., University of Washington
Shipley, Thomas H., University of Texas, Austin
Shragge, Jeffrey, Colorado School of Mines
Simon, Joel D., Princeton University
Simons, Frederik J., Princeton University
Simons, Mark, California Institute of Technology
Slater, David, University of Nevada, Reno
Slawinski, Michael A., Memorial University of Newfoundland
Smith, Ken D., University of Nevada, Reno
Smith, Stewart W., University of Washington
Smythe, William, University of California, Los Angeles
Snoke, J. Arthur, Virginia Polytechnic Institute & State University
Song, Alex, University College London
Song, Xiaodong, University of Illinois, Urbana-Champaign
Spence, George D., University of Victoria
Spetzler, Hartmut A., University of Colorado
Spiegelman, Marc, Columbia University
Stachnik, Joshua, Lehigh University
Steele, Bill, University of Washington
Steeples, Don W., University of Kansas
Stein, Seth, Northwestern University
Stephen, Ralph A., Woods Hole Oceanographic Institution
Stickney, Michael C., Montana Tech of The University of Montana
Street, Ronald L., University of Kentucky
Streig, Ashley, Portland State University
Stuart, Graham, University of Leeds
Stump, Brian W., Southern Methodist University
Sverdrup, Keith A., University of Wisconsin, Milwaukee
Sykes, Lynn R., Columbia University
Talwani, Pradeep, University of South Carolina
Tanimoto, Toshiro, University of California, Santa Barbara
Tape, Carl, University of Alaska, Fairbanks
Taylor, Kenneth B., N.C. Department of Environmental Quality
Taylor, Steven R., Los Alamos National Laboratory
Teng, Ta-liang, University of Southern California
Thomas, Amanda, University of Oregon
Thompson, zglenn, University of South Florida
Thorne, Michael S., University of Utah
Thurber, Clifford, University of Wisconsin, Madison
Thurber, Clifford H., University of Wisconsin, Madison
Tibuleac, Ileana, University of Nevada, Reno
Toksoz, M N., Massachusetts Institute of Technology
Toomey, Douglas R., University of Oregon
Tromp, Jeroen, Princeton University
Tsai, Victor, Brown University
Tura, Ali, Colorado School of Mines
Van Avendonk, Harm J., University of Texas, Austin
van der Hilst, Robert, Massachusetts Institute of Technology
van der Lee, Suzan, Northwestern University
Vanacore, Elizabeth A., University of Puerto Rico
Vidal, Antonio, Ctr de Invest Científica y de Ed Superior de Ensenada
Vidale, John E., University of Southern California
Vlahovic, Gordana, North Carolina Central University
von Seggern, David H., University of Nevada, Reno
Wagner, Lara S., Carnegie Institution for Science
Waite, Gregory P., Michigan Technological University
Waldhauser, Felix, Columbia University
Wallace, Jr., Terry C., Los Alamos National Laboratory
Wang, Jeen-Hwa, Academia Sinica
Wang, Zhenming, University of Kentucky
Ward, Kevin M., South Dakota School of Mines & Technology
Warner, Michael, Imperial College
Waszek, Lauren, New Mexico State University, Las Cruces
Wen, Lianxing, Stony Brook University
Wentzcovitch, Renata, Columbia University
Wesnousky, Steve, University of Nevada, Reno
Wesnousky, Steven G., University of Nevada, Reno
Wesnousky, Steven, University of Nevada, Reno
Wiens, Douglas A., Washington University in St. Louis
Williams, Erik, University of Nevada, Reno
Wirth, Erin, University of Washington
Withers, Mitchell M., University of Memphis
Wolf, Lorraine W., Auburn University
Wolny, Dave, Colorado Mesa University
Woolery, Edward W., University of Kentucky
Wu, Francis T., Binghamton University
Wust-Bloch, Gilles H., Tel Aviv University
Wysession, Michael E., Washington University in St. Louis
Young, Jeri J., University of Arizona
Yu, Wen-che, Academia Sinica
Zandt, George, University of Arizona
Zelt, Colin A., Rice University
Zeng, Hongliu, University of Texas, Austin
Zhan, Zhongwen, California Institute of Technology
Zhou, Hua-Wei, University of Houston
Zhou, Ying, Virginia Polytechnic Institute & State University
Zhu, Hejun, University of Texas, Dallas
Zhu, Lupei, Saint Louis University
Ziv, Alon, Tel Aviv University

Marine Geophysics

Anderson, Franz E., University of New Hampshire
Archer, David, University of Chicago
Austin, Jr., James A., University of Texas, Austin
Becker, Keir, University of Miami
Behn, Mark D., Woods Hole Oceanographic Institution
Bell, Robin E., Columbia University
Ben-Avraham, Zvi, Tel Aviv University
Bohnenstiehl, DelWayne, North Carolina State University
Bokuniewicz, Henry J., SUNY, Stony Brook
Bokuniewicz, Henry J., Stony Brook University
Bonatti, Enrico, Columbia University
Bowin, Carl O., Woods Hole Oceanographic Institution
Buck, Roger W., Columbia University
Buizert, Christo, Oregon State University
Bull, Jonathan M., University of Southampton
Butterfield, David A., University of Washington
Canales Cisneros, Juan Pablo, Woods Hole Oceanographic Institution
Carbotte, Suzanne, Columbia University
Carlson, Richard L., Texas A&M University
Chamberlain, C. Page, Stanford University
Christeson, Gail L., University of Texas, Austin
Cochran, James R., Columbia University
Collier, Jenny, Imperial College
Commane, Roisin, Columbia University
Constable, Steven C., University of California, San Diego
Deans, Jeremy, University of Southern Mississippi
Delaney, John R., University of Washington
Druet, María, Univ Complutense de Madrid
Duncan, Alec, Curtin University
Dunn, Robert A., University of Hawai'i, Manoa
Edwards, Richard N., University of Toronto
Egbert, Gary D., Oregon State University
Eloranta, Edwin W., University of Wisconsin, Madison
Evans, Robert L., Woods Hole Oceanographic Institution
Forsyth, Donald W., Brown University
Fricker, Helen A., University of California, San Diego
Gavrilov, Alexander, Curtin University
Goff, John A., University of Texas, Austin
Goldberg, David S., Columbia University
Goldfinger, Chris, Oregon State University
Gorelick, Steven, Stanford University
Gorman, Andrew R., University of Otago
Gulick, Sean S., University of Texas, Austin
Harris, Paul M., Rice University
Harrison, Christopher G., University of Miami
Henderson, Naomi, Columbia University
Hildebrand, John A., University of California, San Diego
Hooft, Emilie E., University of Oregon
Hornbach, Matthew J., Southern Methodist University
Huang, Li, Western University
Huws, Dei G., University of Wales

Ji, Peng, Columbia University
Johnson, H. Paul, University of Washington
Karig, Daniel E., Cornell University
Kingslake, Jonathan, Columbia University
Krastel, Sebastian , Dalhousie University
Kummerow, Christian D., Colorado State University
Kurapov, Alexander, Oregon State University
Lawver, Lawrence A., University of Texas, Austin
Lewis, Brian T. R., University of Washington
Llanes, María del Pilar, Univ Complutense de Madrid
Louden, Keith E., Dalhousie University
MacAyeal, Douglas R., University of Chicago
Macelloni, Leonardo, University of Southern Mississippi
Mack, Seymour, Fresno State University
Madsen, John A., University of Delaware
Manley, Patricia L., Middlebury College
Martinez, Fernando, University of Hawai'i, Manoa
McClain, James S., University of California, Davis
McIntosh, Kirk D., University of Texas, Austin
Minshull, Timothy A., University of Southampton
Mittelstaedt, Eric L., University of Idaho
Muller, Dietmar, University of Sydney
Mutter, John C., Columbia University
Oakley, Adrienne, Kutztown University of Pennsylvania
Odom, Robert I., University of Washington
Ollerhead, Jeffery W., Mount Allison University
Orcutt, John A., University of California, San Diego
Parnum, Iain, Curtin University
Penrose, John, Curtin University
Purdy, G. Michael, Columbia University
Raymond, Carol A., Jet Propulsion Laboratory
Rodriguez Simental, Ana María, Univ Nacional Autonoma de Mexico
Ryan, William B. F., Columbia University
Sandwell, David T., University of California, San Diego
Sawyer, Dale S., Rice University
Schouten, Hans, Woods Hole Oceanographic Institution
Sheridan, Robert E., Rutgers, The State University of New Jersey
Shillington, Donna, Columbia University
Shipley, Thomas H., University of Texas, Austin
Shreve, Ronald L., University of Washington
Silver, Eli A., University of California, Santa Cruz
Sloan, Heather, Lehman College (CUNY)
Sohn, Robert A., Woods Hole Oceanographic Institution
Spitz, Yvette H., Oregon State University
Stephens, Jason H., Austin Community College District
Swift, Stephen A., Woods Hole Oceanographic Institution
Talwani, Manik, Rice University
Thompson, David W. J., Colorado State University
Tivey, Maurice A., Woods Hole Oceanographic Institution
Tolstoy, Maria, Columbia University
Trehu, Anne M., Oregon State University
Van Rooij, David, Ghent University
Wattrus, Nigel J., University of Minnesota Duluth
Webb, Spahr, Columbia University
Webb, Spahr C., Columbia University
Wessel, Paul, University of Hawai'i, Manoa
Wetzel, Laura R., Eckerd College
White, Scott M., University of South Carolina
Wilkes, Daniel, Curtin University
Wooding, Frank B., Woods Hole Oceanographic Institution
Xu, Li, Woods Hole Oceanographic Institution
Zavarin, Mavrik, Lawrence Livermore National Laboratory
Zhu, Wenlu, University of Maryland

Near-surface Geophysics

Alam, Md Iftekhar, University of Tennessee, Knoxville
Aracil, Enrique, Univ Complutense de Madrid
Bradford, John, Colorado School of Mines
Clement, William P., University of Massachusetts, Amherst
Ferdowsi, Behrooz, Princeton University
Gemail, Khaled S., El Zagazig University
Herman, Rhett B., Radford University
Holbrook, W. S., Virginia Polytechnic Institute & State University
Irons, Trevor , Montana Tech of the University of Montana
Katumwehe, Andrew, Midwestern State University
Keating, Kristina M., Rutgers, The State University of New Jersey, Newark
Lamb, Andrew P., University of Arkansas, Fayetteville
McGrath, Daniel, Colorado State University
Ntarlagiannis, Dimitrios, Rutgers, The State University of New Jersey, Newark
Pringle, Jamie K., Keele University
Wood, Neill, Exeter University

PALEONTOLOGY

General Paleontology

Adrain, Tiffany S., University of Iowa
Allmon, Warren D., Cornell University
Allmon, Warren D., Paleontological Research Institution
Altenbach, Alexander, Ludwig-Maximilians-Universitaet Muenchen
Amler, Michael, Ludwig-Maximilians-Universitaet Muenchen
Anderson, Wayne I., University of Northern Iowa
Arens, Nan Crystal, Hobart & William Smith Colleges
Arnone, John, Desert Research Institute
Arp, Dr., Gernot, Georg-August University of Goettingen
Ausich, William I., Ohio State University
Awramik, Stanley M., University of California, Santa Barbara
Babcock, Loren E., Ohio State University
Bailey, Jack B., Western Illinois University
Bailey, Jake, University of Minnesota, Twin Cities
Bajraktareviæ, Zlatan, University of Zagreb
Baumiller, Tomasz K., University of Michigan
Beatty, William L., Winona State University
Beck, Charles, University of Michigan
Belasky, Paul, Ohlone College
Bell, Phil R., University of New England
Benson, Roger, University of Oxford
Bergstrom, Stig M., Ohio State University
Berman, David S., Carnegie Museum of Natural History
Bill, Steven D., Keene State College
Blackwelder, Patricia L., University of Miami
Bordeaux, Yvette, University of Pennsylvania
Bosak, Tanja, Massachusetts Institute of Technology
Branstrator, Jon W., Earlham College
Brasier, Martin, University of Oxford
Bray, Emily, University of Colorado
Brink, Alyson, University of Southern Mississippi
Britt, Brooks B., Brigham Young University
Brzobohaty, Rostislav, Masaryk University
Bucur, Ioan, Babes-Bolyai University
Budd, Ann F., University of Iowa
Busbey, Arthur B., Texas Christian University
Bush, Andrew M., University of Connecticut
Butterfield, Nicholas J., University of Cambridge
Cachão, Mário, Unive de Lisboa
Caldwell, Roy, University of California, Berkeley
Cardace, Dawn, University of Rhode Island
Carew, James L., College of Charleston
Carlson, Sandra J., University of California, Davis
Carnevale, Giorgio, Università di Torino
Caron, Jean-Bernard, Royal Ontario Museum
Carter, Burchard D., Georgia Southwestern State University
Chamberlain, John A., Graduate School of the City University of New York
Chamberlain, John A., Brooklyn College (CUNY)
Cheetham, Alan H., Smithsonian Inst/Nat Mus of Nat History
Cherns, L C., Cardiff University
Chin, Karen, University of Colorado
Christie, Max L., University of Illinois, Urbana-Champaign
Cirimpei, Claudia, Alexandru Ioan Cuza
Cisne, John L., Cornell University
Clementz, Mark T., University of Wyoming
Clyde, William C., University of New Hampshire
Cohen, Phoebe A., Williams College
Collette, Joseph, Minot State University
Collins, Laurel S., Florida International University
Collinson, James W., Ohio State University
Collinson, Margaret, Royal Holloway University of London
Conley, Catharine A., New Mexico Institute of Mining and Technology
Coorough Burke, Patricia J., Milwaukee Public Museum
Coulson, Alan B., Clemson University
Cowen, Richard, University of California, Davis
Cramer, Howard R., Emory University
Curran, H. Allen, Smith College

Darroch, Simon A., Vanderbilt University
De Klerk, Billy, Rhodes University
Deboo, Phili B., University of Memphis
Delfino, Massimo, Università di Torino
Derstler, Kraig L., University of New Orleans
Devera, Joseph A., Illinois State Geological Survey
Dietl, Gregory, Paleontological Research Institution
Dietz, Anne D., San Antonio Community College
Diggins, Thomas P., Youngstown State University
Domack, Cynthia R., Hamilton College
Droser, Mary L., University of California, Riverside
Drumheller-Horton, Stephanie K., University of Tennessee, Knoxville
Duda, Jan-Peter, Georg-August University of Goettingen
Dupraz, Christophe, University of Connecticut
Dyson, Miranda, Open University
Edwards, Nicholas, University of Manchester
Egerton, Victoria, University of Manchester
Erickson, J. Mark, St. Lawrence University
Falcon-Lang, Howard, Royal Holloway University of London
Fall, Leigh M., SUNY, Oneonta
Farmer, Jack D., Arizona State University
Felton, Richard M., Northwest Missouri State University
Fernández, Sixto, Univ Complutense de Madrid
Ferriz, Sergio Cevallos, Univ Nacional Autonoma de Mexico
Fio, Karmen, University of Zagreb
Fisher, Frank, University of Colorado
Flessa, Karl W., University of Arizona
Flood, Beverly, University of Minnesota, Twin Cities
Fondevilla, Victor, Universitat Autonoma de Barcelona
Foote, Michael J., University of Chicago
Forcino, Frank, Western Carolina University
Fornaciari, Eliana, Università degli Studi di Padova
Fournier, Gregory, Massachusetts Institute of Technology
Fowler, Gerald A., University of Wisconsin, Parkside
Fox, David L., University of Minnesota, Twin Cities
Fox, Nathaniel, South Dakota School of Mines & Technology
Fox-Dobbs, Kena L., University of Puget Sound
Frederick, Daniel L., Austin Peay State University
Freeman, Veronica, Marietta College
Friedman, Matt, University of Oxford
Fritsen, Christian H., Desert Research Institute
Gabbott, Sarah, Leicester University
Gagnaison, Cyril, Institut Polytechnique LaSalle Beauvais (ex-IGAL)
Gahn, Forest J., Brigham Young University - Idaho
Gaidos, Eric J., University of Hawai'i, Manoa
Gale, Andrew, University of Portsmouth
Gallegos, Anthony F., Los Alamos National Laboratory
Ganeshram, Raja, Edinburgh University
Garb, Matt, Brooklyn College (CUNY)
Gatto, Roberto, Università degli Studi di Padova
Geary, Dana H., University of Wisconsin, Madison
Gess, Robert, Rhodes University
Gibson, Michael A., University of Tennessee, Martin
Gill, Fiona, University of Leeds
Glamoclija, Mihaela, Rutgers, The State University of New Jersey, Newark
Glasauer, Susan, University of Guelph
Gold, David, University of California, Davis
Goldman, Daniel, University of Dayton
Gorecka-Nowak, Anna, University of Wroclaw
Gorman-Lewis, Drew J., University of Washington
Gray, Lee M., Mount Union College
Gray, Neil, University of Newcastle Upon Tyne
Green, Keith E., Cypress College
Greenwood, David , University of Saskatchewan
Haggart, James, University of British Columbia
Haiar, Brooke, University of Lynchburg
Hansen, Thor A., Western Washington University
Harper, David, Durham University
Harvey, Tom, Leicester University
Hawkins, Andrew, Towson University
Hazel, McGoff, University of Reading
Heaney, Michael , Texas A&M University
Heim, Noel A., Tufts University
Henderson, Wayne G., California State University, Fullerton
Hendy, Ingrid, University of Michigan
Henßel, Katja, Ludwig-Maximilians-Universitaet Muenchen
Herrera-Gil, Luis A., Univ Autonoma de Baja California Sur
Hickman, Carole S., University of California, Berkeley
Hintze, Lehi F., Brigham Young University
Hlusko, Leslea, University of California, Berkeley
Hopkins, Samantha, University of Oregon
House, Christopher H., Pennsylvania State University, University Park
Hughes, Nigel C., University of California, Riverside
Hylland, Mike, Utah Geological Survey
Immel, Harald, Ludwig-Maximilians-Universitaet Muenchen
Ivanov, Martin, Masaryk University
Jackson, Jeremy B. C., University of California, San Diego
Johnson, Gerald H., William & Mary
Johnson, Kayleigh, South Dakota School of Mines & Technology
Johnston, Carl G., Youngstown State University
Jones, Douglas S., University of Florida
Jorge, Maria Luisa, Vanderbilt University
Kazmer, Miklos, Eotvos Lorand University
Kelley, Patricia H., University of North Carolina, Wilmington
Kendrick, David C., Hobart & William Smith Colleges
Kern, J. Philip, San Diego State University
Khaleel, Tasneem, Montana State University, Billings
Kirkland, James I., Utah Geological Survey
Kirschvink, Joseph L., California Institute of Technology
Kleffner, Mark A., Ohio State University
Klemow, Kenneth M., Wilkes University
Koehl, Mimi A. R., University of California, Berkeley
Konhauser, Kurt, University of Alberta
Kowalke, Thorsten, Ludwig-Maximilians-Universitaet Muenchen
Kozdon, Reinhard, Columbia University
Kulp, Thomas, Binghamton University
Laporte, Leo F., University of California, Santa Cruz
Leinfelder, Reinhold, Ludwig-Maximilians-Universitaet Muenchen
Lenhart, Stephen W., Radford University
Li, Rong-Yu, Brandon University
Lieberman, Bruce S., University of Kansas
Lindberg, David R., University of California, Berkeley
Little, Crispin, University of Leeds
Lockwood, Rowan, William & Mary
Love, Renee, University of Idaho
Lozar, Francesca, Università di Torino
Macalady, Jennifer L., Pennsylvania State University, University Park
MacLeod, Kenneth A., University of Missouri
Macomber, Richard, Long Island University, Brooklyn Campus
Mandra, York T., San Francisco State University
Marenco, Pedro J., Bryn Mawr College
Martindale, Rowan, University of Texas, Austin
Martínez, Gemma, Univ Complutense de Madrid
McBeth, Joyce M., University of Saskatchewan
McCall, Peter L., Case Western Reserve University
McCollum, Linda B., Eastern Washington University
McGhee, Jr., George R., Rutgers, The State University of New Jersey
Mcgowan, Alistair, University of Glasgow
McHugh, Julia, Colorado Mesa University
McKenzie, Scott C., Mercyhurst University
McMenamin, Mark, Mount Holyoke College
McNamara, Kenneth, University of Cambridge
McRoberts, Christopher A., SUNY, Cortland
Mead, James I., Northern Arizona University
Means, Guy H., Florida Geological Survey
Melchin, Michael, Dalhousie University
Meyer Dombard, DArcy, University of Illinois at Chicago
Mezga, Aleksandar, University of Zagreb
Miller, Joshua H., University of Cincinnati
Miller, Randall F., University of New Brunswick
Mitchell, Charles E., SUNY, Buffalo
Mock, Thomas, University of East Anglia
Moe-Hoffman, Amy P., Mississippi State University
Monaco, Pat, University of Colorado
Monari, Stefano, Università degli Studi di Padova
Montgomery, Homer A., University of Texas, Dallas
Moro, Alan, University of Zagreb
Morris, Simon C., University of Cambridge
Munro, Ildi, Carleton University
Murray, Alison E., Desert Research Institute
Murray, John, National University of Ireland Galway
Muscente, Drew, Cornell College

Musil, Rudolf, Masaryk University
Myers, Orrin B., Los Alamos National Laboratory
Naumann, Malik, Ludwig-Maximilians-Universitaet Muenchen
Nealson, Kenneth, University of Southern California
Newman, Dianne K., California Institute of Technology
Newton, Cathryn R., Syracuse University
Norman, David, University of Cambridge
Nudds, John, University of Manchester
O'Mullan, Gregory, Queens College (CUNY)
Oboh-Ikuneobe, Francisca, Missouri University of Science and Technology
Olcott Marshall, Alison, University of Kansas
Ono, Shuhei, Massachusetts Institute of Technology
Onstott, Tullis C., Princeton University
Orchard, Michael, University of British Columbia
Orphan, Victoria, California Institute of Technology
Orsi, William, Ludwig-Maximilians-Universitaet Muenchen
Owen, Alan W., University of Glasgow
Parsons-Hubbard, Karla M., Oberlin College
Patzkowsky, Mark E., Pennsylvania State University, University Park
Pavia, Giulio, Università di Torino
Peng, Lee Chai, University of Malaya
Perez-Huerta, Alberto, University of Alabama
Person, Jeff, North Dakota Geological Survey
Peter, Mark, Ohio Dept of Natural Resources
Peterson, Joseph E., University of Wisconsin, Oshkosh
Petuch, Edward J., Florida Atlantic University
Pezelj, Đurđica, University of Zagreb
Plotnick, Roy E., University of Illinois at Chicago
Porter, Susannah, University of California, Santa Barbara
Poteet, Mary F., University of Texas, Austin
Pratt, Brian R., University of Saskatchewan
Pruss, Sara B., Smith College
Puchalski, Stephaney, Highline College
Purnell, Mark, Leicester University
Rampedi, Isaac T., University of Johannesburg
Read, Michael T., Stephen F. Austin State University
Reichenbacher, Bettina, Ludwig-Maximilians-Universitaet Muenchen
Reid, Catherine, University of Canterbury
Reitner, Joachim, Georg-August University of Goettingen
Rhenberg, Elizabeth, University of Memphis
Risk, Michael J., McMaster University
Roden, Eric E., University of Wisconsin, Madison
Rodríguez, Sergio, Univ Complutense de Madrid
Rogers, Karyn L., Rensselaer Polytechnic Institute
Rogers, Kristina C., University of Minnesota, Twin Cities
Rogers, Raymond, University of Minnesota, Twin Cities
Rogers, Steven L., Keele University
Ross, Robert M., Paleontological Research Institution
Ross, Robert M., Cornell University
Runnegar, Bruce, University of California, Los Angeles
Rößner, Gertrud, Ludwig-Maximilians-Universitaet Muenchen
Sá, Artur A., Unive de Trás-os-Montes e Alto Douro
Santelli, Cara M., University of Minnesota, Twin Cities
Sanudo, Sergio, University of Southern California
Scatterday, James W., SUNY, Geneseo
Schiffbauer, James, University of Missouri
Schmid, Dieter, Ludwig-Maximilians-Universitaet Muenchen
Schopf, J. William, University of California, Los Angeles
Schrenk, Matt, Michigan State University
Scudder, Sylvia J., University of Florida
Seibt, Ulrike, University of California, Los Angeles
Shapiro, Russell S., California State University, Chico
Shropshire, K. Lee, University of Northern Colorado
Silva, Carlos M., Unive de Lisboa
Silva-Pineda, Alicia, Univ Nacional Autonoma de Mexico
Slatkin, Montgomery, University of California, Berkeley
Slaughter, Richard, University of Wisconsin, Madison
Smart, Christopher, University of Plymouth
Smith, Dena M., University of Colorado
Smith, Paul L., University of British Columbia
Southam, Gordon, Western University
Spencer, Patrick K., Whitman College
Stafford, Emily, Western Carolina University
Steele, Michael A., Wilkes University
Steinker, Don C., Bowling Green State University
Steinker, Paula J., Bowling Green State University
Stetter, Karl O., University of California, Los Angeles
Stifel, Peter B., University of Maryland
Stigall, Alycia L., Ohio University
Stratton, James F., Eastern Illinois University
Superchi-Culver, Tonia, University of Colorado
Sutherland, Stuart, University of British Columbia
Sutton, Mark, Imperial College
Sweetman, Steve, University of Portsmouth
Tesmer, Irving, Buffalo State College
Thomas, Roger D. K., Franklin and Marshall College
Thompson, Jann W. M., Smithsonian Inst/Nat Mus of Nat History
Thompson, Joel B., Eckerd College
Thuy, Ben, University of Tennessee, Knoxville
Tibuleac, Paul, Alexandru Ioan Cuza
Tice, Mike, Texas A&M University
Toots, Heinrich, Long Island University, C.W. Post Campus
Toth, Natalie, Denver Museum of Nature & Science
Uahengo, Collen, University of Namibia
Underwood, Charlie, Birkbeck College
Upchurch, Paul, University College London
Valentine, James W., University of California, Berkeley
Van Alstine, James B., University of Minnesota, Morris
Van Iten, Heyo, Hanover College
VanAller-Hernick, Linda A., New York State Geological Survey
Vega Vera, Francisco J., Univ Nacional Autonoma de Mexico
Vicens Batet, Enric, Universitat Autonoma de Barcelona
Wake, David B., University of California, Berkeley
Wake, Marvalee H., University of California, Berkeley
Wallace, Steve, University of Colorado
Ward, Peter D., University of Washington
Weber, Karrie A., University of Nebraska, Lincoln
Weber-Gobel, Reinhard, Univ Nacional Autonoma de Mexico
Wehrmann, Laura, Ludwig-Maximilians-Universitaet Muenchen
West, Ronald R., Kansas State University
White, Lisa D., San Francisco State University
Whitmore, John H., Cedarville University
Whitton, Mark, University of Portsmouth
Wignall, Paul, University of Leeds
Wilf, Peter D., Pennsylvania State University, University Park
Williams, Mark, Leicester University
Woerheide, Gert, Ludwig-Maximilians-Universitaet Muenchen
Yacobucci, Peg M., Bowling Green State University
Yancey, Thomas E., Texas A&M University
Yee, Nathan, Rutgers, The State University of New Jersey
Zalasiewicz, Jan, Leicester University
Zelenitsky, Darla, University of Calgary

Paleostratigraphy

Al-Saad, Hamad A., University of Qatar
Arden, Daniel D., Georgia Southwestern State University
Baarli, B. Gudveig, Williams College
Baird, Gordon C., SUNY, Fredonia
Barrick, James E., Texas Tech University
Bauer, Jeffrey A., Shawnee State University
Berggren, William A., Woods Hole Oceanographic Institution
Buatois, Luis, University of Saskatchewan
Caldwell, William G. E., University of Saskatchewan
Cohen, Andrew S., University of Arizona
Davila-Alcocer, Victor M., Univ Nacional Autonoma de Mexico
Eaton, Jeffrey G., Weber State University
Ettensohn, Frank R., University of Kentucky
Finney, Stanley C., California State University, Long Beach
Grubb, Barbara, Mt. San Antonio College
Isaacson, Peter E., University of Idaho
Jeffery, David L., Marietta College
Johnson, David B., New Mexico Institute of Mining and Technology
Johnson, Markes E., Williams College
Jones, Brian, University of Alberta
Kalvoda, Jiri, Masaryk University
Kumpan, Tomas, Masaryk University
Kurtz, Vincent E., Missouri State University
Landing, Ed, New York State Geological Survey
Landman, Neil H., Graduate School of the City University of New York
Le Mone, David V., University of Texas, El Paso
Leatham, W. Britt, California State University, San Bernardino
Lewis, Gerald L., Pasadena City College

Liebe, Richard M., SUNY, The College at Brockport
Mangano, Gabriela, University of Saskatchewan
Martin, James E., South Dakota School of Mines & Technology
Maurrasse, Florentin J., Florida International University
McLaughlin, Patrick, Indiana University, Bloomington
McWilliams, Robert G., Miami University
Mikulic, Donald G., Illinois State Geological Survey
Miller, James F., Missouri State University
Miller, Richard H., San Diego State University
Murphy, Michael A., University of California, Riverside
Ogg, James G., Purdue University
Olson, Hillary C., University of Texas, Austin
Over, D. Jeffrey, SUNY, Geneseo
Ritter, Scott M., Brigham Young University
Rosario, Jose, California State University, East Bay
Sageman, Bradley B., Northwestern University
Shaw, Frederick C., Lehman College (CUNY)
Smith, Gerald R., University of Michigan
Stearn, Colin, McGill University
Stevens, Calvin H., San Jose State University
Taylor, John F., Indiana University of Pennsylvania
Thoms, Richard E., Portland State University
Titus, Robert C., Hartwick College
Tobin, Tom S., University of Alabama
Trexler, J. Peter, Juniata College
Van Niewenhuise, Donald, University of Houston
Vandenbroucke, Thijs, Ghent University
Zinsmeister, William J., Purdue University

Micropaleontology

Adekeye, O. A., University of Ilorin
Agnini, Claudia, Università degli Studi di Padova
Arnold, Anthony J., Florida State University
Aubry, Marie-Pierre, Rutgers, The State University of New Jersey
Bancroft, Alyssa M., Indiana University
Barnes, Christopher R., University of Victoria
Barrier, Pascal, Institut Polytechnique LaSalle Beauvais (ex-IGAL)
Beauchamp, Benoit, University of Calgary
Berggren, William A., Rutgers, The State University of New Jersey
Boix, Carme, Universitat Autonoma de Barcelona
Bollmann, Jörg, University of Toronto
Borrelli, Chiara, University of Rochester
Bown, Paul, University College London
Burke, Collette D., Wichita State University
Burkett, Ashley, Oklahoma State University
Buzas, Martin A., Smithsonian Institution / National Museum of Natural History
Caldwell, W. Glen E., Western University
Canales, María Luisa, Univ Complutense de Madrid
Carreno, Ana L., Univ Nacional Autonoma de Mexico
Chapman, Mark, University of East Anglia
Clark, David L., University of Wisconsin, Madison
Corliss, Bruce H., Duke University
Culver, Stephen J., East Carolina University
Curry, William B., Woods Hole Oceanographic Institution
Czaja, Andrew D., University of Cincinnati
de Vernal, Anne, Universite du Quebec a Montreal
Eicher, Don L., University of Colorado
Eicher, Donald, University of Colorado
Finger, Ken, University of California, Berkeley
Fluegeman, Richard H., Ball State University
Foresi, Luca Maria, University of Siena
Frankel, Larry, University of Connecticut
Fritts, Paul J., California State University, Long Beach
Giusberti, Luca, Università degli Studi di Padova
Goldstein, Susan T., University of Georgia
Gorog, Agnes, Eotvos Lorand University
Grimm, Kirsten I., Universität Mainz
Harding, Ian C., University of Southampton
Hart, Malcolm B., University of Plymouth
Harwood, David M., University of Nebraska, Lincoln
Hasegawa, Shiro, Kumamoto University
Hemphill-Haley, Eileen, Humboldt State University
Henderson, Charles M., University of Calgary
Herrero, Concepción, Univ Complutense de Madrid
Huber, Brian T., Smithsonian Institution / National Museum of Natural History
Hunt, Gene, Smithsonian Institution / National Museum of Natural History
Ingle, Jr., James C., Stanford University
Ionesi, Viorel, Alexandru Ioan Cuza
Ishman, Scott E., Southern Illinois University Carbondale
Kanungo, Sudeep, University of Utah
Katz, Miriam E., Rensselaer Polytechnic Institute
Keller, Gerta, Princeton University
Kelly, D. Clay, University of Wisconsin, Madison
Klapper, Gilbert, Northwestern University
Knox, Larry W., Tennessee Tech University
Leadbetter, Jared R., California Institute of Technology
Leckie, R. Mark, University of Massachusetts, Amherst
Lewandowski, Katherine, Eastern Illinois University
Lobegeier, Melissa, Middle Tennessee State University
Louwye, Stephen, Ghent University
Lucas, Franklin A., University of Benin
Lundin, Robert F., Arizona State University
Lupia, Richard, University of Oklahoma
Maddocks, Rosalie F., University of Houston
Martin, Ronald E., University of Delaware
McCarthy, Francine G., Brock University
McCartney, Kevin, University of Maine, Presque Isle
Mendelson, Carl V., Beloit College
Metcalfe, Ian, University of New England
Metzger, Ronald A., Southwestern Oregon Community College
Montenari, Michael, Keele University
Nathan , Stephen, Eastern Connecticut State University
Nestell, Galina P., University of Texas, Arlington
Nestell, Merlynd K., University of Texas, Arlington
Noble, Paula J., University of Nevada, Reno
Olsson, Richard K., Rutgers, The State University of New Jersey
Oppo, Delia W., Woods Hole Oceanographic Institution
Orr, William N., University of Oregon
Patterson, R. Timothy, Carleton University
Pearson, Paul, University of Wales
Peeters, Frank J., Vrije Universiteit Amsterdam
Pessagno, Jr., Emile A., University of Texas, Dallas
Puckett, Mark, University of Southern Mississippi
Pujana, Ignacio, University of Texas, Dallas
Rathburn, Anthony E., California State University, Bakersfield
Rehakova, Daniela, Comenius University in Bratislava
Reinhardt, Edward G., McMaster University
Roberts, Charles, Mt. San Antonio College
Robinson, Edward, Florida International University
Rodrigues, Cyril G., University of Windsor
Ross, Charles A., Western Washington University
Rosscoe, Steven, Hardin-Simmons University
Sartipzadeh, Siavosh, University of Tabriz
Scherer, Reed P., Northern Illinois University
Schroder-Adams, Claudia, Carleton University
Scott, David B., Dalhousie University
Sen Gupta, Barun K., Louisiana State University
Siesser, William G., Vanderbilt University
Sloan, Doris, University of California, Berkeley
Sloan, Jon R., California State University, Northridge
Speijer, Robert, Katholieke Universiteit Leuven
Stott, Lowell D., University of Southern California
Thomas, Ellen, Wesleyan University
Thomas, Ellen, Yale University
Toth, Emoke, Eotvos Lorand University
Ufkes, Els , Vrije Universiteit Amsterdam
Vaz, Nuno M., Unive de Trás-os-Montes e Alto Douro
von Bitter, Peter H., University of Toronto
Wade, Bridget S., University College London
Walker, Sally E., University of Georgia
Watkins, David K., University of Nebraska, Lincoln
Webb, Peter N., Ohio State University
Wise, Jr, Sherwood W., Florida State University

Paleobotany

Basinger, James F., University of Saskatchewan
Beck, John H., Boston College
Berry, C M., Cardiff University
Burnham, Robyn J., University of Michigan
Carrillo Martinez, Miguel, Univ Nacional Autonoma de Mexico
Currano, Ellen, University of Wyoming
Dilcher, David L., University of Florida

DiMichele, William A., Smithsonian Inst/National Museum of Natural History
Donoghue, Michael J., Yale University
Doyle, James A., University of California, Davis
Edwards, Dianne, Cardiff University
Erwin, Diane, University of California, Berkeley
Gabel, Mark, Black Hills State University
Gastaldo, Robert A., Colby College
Gowing, David, Open University
Griffin, Kevin L., Columbia University
Heath, Kathleen M., Indiana State University
Hu, Shusheng, Yale University
Jackson, Gail D., Edinburgh University
Jarzen, David M., University of Florida
Kerp, Hans, Universitaet Muenster
Knoll, Andrew H., Harvard University
Looy, Cynthia, University of California, Berkeley
Manchester, Steven R., University of Florida
Martinetto, Edoardo, Università di Torino
McCoy, Victoria, University of Wisconsin, Milwaukee
McElwain, Jenny, Field Museum of Natural History
Miller, Ian, Denver Museum of Nature & Science
Mustoe, George, Western Washington University
Peppe, Daniel J., Baylor University
Pfefferkorn, Hermann W., University of Pennsylvania
Punyasena, Surangi W., University of Illinois, Urbana-Champaign
Raymond, Anne, Texas A&M University
Retallack, Gregory J., University of Oregon
Rigby, John, Queensland University of Technology
Scott, Andrew C., Royal Holloway University of London
Stromberg, Caroline, University of Washington
Taggart, Ralph E., Michigan State University
Taylor, Edith, University of Kansas
Thomasson, Joseph R., Fort Hays State University
Tiffney, Bruce H., University of California, Santa Barbara
Tyler, Carrie, Miami University
Wing, Scott L., Smithsonian Institution / National Museum of Natural History

Palynology

Anderson, Patricia M., University of Washington
Asselin, Esther, Natural Resources Canada
Atta-Peters, David, University of Ghana
Brenner, Gilbert J., SUNY, New Paltz
Brush, Grace S., Johns Hopkins University
Burden, Elliott T., Memorial University of Newfoundland
Butcher, Anthony, University of Portsmouth
Calcote, Randy, University of Minnesota, Twin Cities
Darrell, James H., Georgia Southern University
Davis, Owen K., University of Arizona
Dolakova, Nela, Masaryk University
Eble, Cortland F., University of Kentucky
Farley, Martin B., University of North Carolina, Pembroke
FitzPatrick, Meriel E., University of Plymouth
Fowell, Sarah J., University of Alaska, Fairbanks
Habib, Daniel, Queens College (CUNY)
Head, Martin J., Brock University
Hebda, Richard J., University of Victoria
Hemsley, A, Cardiff University
Hemsley, Alan, University of Wales
Higgs, Ken, University College Cork
Ivory, Sarah, Pennsylvania State University, University Park
Jacobs, Bonnie F., Southern Methodist University
Jarvis, Ed, University College Cork
Javaux, Emmanuelle, Universite de Liege
Jolley, David, University of Aberdeen
Kovácová, Marianna, Comenius University in Bratislava
Maher, Jr., Louis J., University of Wisconsin, Madison
Marshall, John E., University of Southampton
Martinez Hernandez, Enrique, Univ Nacional Autonoma de Mexico
McAndrews, John H., University of Toronto
Milne, Lynne, Curtin University
Mudie, Peta J., Dalhousie University
Norris, Geoffrey, University of Toronto
O'Keefe, Jennifer, Morehead State University
Ogbahon, Osazuwa A., Federal University of Technology, Akure
Rich, Fredrick J., Georgia Southern University
Rueger, Bruce F., Colby College
Smith, Jim, University College Cork
Stefanova, Ivanka, University of Minnesota, Twin Cities
Strother, Paul K., Boston College
Strother, Paul L., Boston College
Tabara, Daniel, Alexandru Ioan Cuza
Warny, Sophie, Louisiana State University
Zobaa, Mohamed, University of Texas Permian Basin

Quantitative Paleontology

Daley, Gwen M., Winthrop University
Huntley, John, University of Missouri
Marshall, Charles R., University of California, Berkeley
Miller, Arnold I., Cincinnati Museum Center
Motz, Gary J., Indiana University
Parker, William C., Florida State University
Sallan, Lauren, University of Pennsylvania

Vertebrate Paleontology

Adams, Thomas, San Antonio Community College
Applegate-Pleasants, Shelton, Univ Nacional Autonoma de Mexico
Archer, Michael, University of New South Wales
Baltensperger, David D., Texas A&M University
Barnosky, Anthony D., University of California, Berkeley
Bartels, William S., Albion College
Beard, K. Christopher, Carnegie Museum of Natural History
Behrensmeyer, Anna K., Smithsonian Inst/Nat Mus of Nat History
Bell, Christopher J., University of Texas, Austin
Bhullar, Bhart-Anjan, Yale University
Bloch, Jonathan, University of Florida
Bolt, John R., Field Museum of Natural History
Brand, Leonard R., Loma Linda University
Brinkman, Donald B., Royal Tyrrell Museum of Palaeontology
Brochu, Christopher A., University of Iowa
Brown, Caleb, Royal Tyrrell Museum of Palaeontology
Brusatte, Steve, Edinburgh University
Burger, Benjamin J., Utah State University
Caldwell, Michael W., University of Alberta
Campbell, Kenneth E., Los Angeles County Museum of Natural History
Canudo, José Ignacio, Univ de Zaragoza
Carpenter, Kenneth, University of Colorado
Carrano, Matthew T., Smithsonian Inst/Nat Mus of Nat History
Carranza-Castaneda, Oscar, Univ Nacional Autonoma de Mexico
Chatterjee, Sankar, Texas Tech University
Chiappe, Luis M., Los Angeles County Museum of Natural History
Cicimurri, Christian M., Clemson University
Cicimurri, Christian M., Clemson University
Cicimurri, David J., Clemson University
Clarke, Julia A., University of Texas, Austin
Clemens, William A., University of California, Berkeley
Codrea, Vlad, Babes-Bolyai University
Cooke, H.B. S., Dalhousie University
Coombs, Margery C., Amherst College
Covert, Herbert, University of Colorado
Cumbaa, Steve L., Carleton University
Curry Rogers, Kristina A., Macalester College
Daeschler, Ted, Drexel University
Davis, Edward B., University of Oregon
Dawson, Mary, University of Colorado
Dawson, Mary R., Carnegie Museum of Natural History
Delson, Eric, Graduate School of the City University of New York
DeSantis, Larisa R., Vanderbilt University
Domingo, Laura, Univ Complutense de Madrid
Druckenmiller, Patrick S., University of Alaska, Fairbanks
Druckenmiller, Patrick S., University of Alaska, Fairbanks
Dundas, Robert G., Fresno State University
Dzanh, Trihn, University of Colorado
Eberle, Jaelyn J., University of Colorado
Eberle, Jaelyn J., University of Colorado
Elliott, David K., Northern Arizona University
Emry, Robert, Smithsonian Institution / National Museum of Natural History
Engelmann, George F., University of Nebraska, Omaha
Esperante, Raul, Loma Linda University
Evans, David C., Royal Ontario Museum
Fastovsky, David E., University of Rhode Island
Fastovsky, David, University of Rhode Island
Fiorillo, Anthony R., Southern Methodist University
Flynn, John J., American Museum of Natural History

Flynn, John J., Columbia University
Fordyce, R. Ewan, University of Otago
Froehlich, David J., Austin Community College District
Furió, Marc, Universitat Autonoma de Barcelona
Gaffney, Eugene S., American Museum of Natural History
Gallagher, William B., Rider University
García, Nuria, Univ Complutense de Madrid
Garcia, William, University of North Carolina, Charlotte
Gardner, James D., Royal Tyrrell Museum of Palaeontology
Gauthier, Jacques A., Yale University
Gauthier, Jacques, Yale University
Gillette, David D., Northern Arizona University
Gnidovec, Dale M., Ohio State University
Goodwin, Mark B., University of California, Berkeley
Gottfried, Michael D., Michigan State University
Graham, Russell W., Pennsylvania State University, University Park
Grandal d'Anglade, Aurora, Coruna University
Grande, Lance, Field Museum of Natural History
Gray, Robert S., Santa Barbara City College
Green, Harry W., University of California, Berkeley
Hammer, William R., Augustana College
Hand, Suzanne J., University of New South Wales
Hargrave, Jennifer E., University of Louisiana at Lafayette
Harrell, Jr., T. L., Geological Survey of Alabama
Harris, Judith A., University of Colorado
Hayden, Martha C., Utah Geological Survey
Heaton, Timothy H., University of South Dakota
Heckert, Andrew B., Appalachian State University
Henderson, Donald, Royal Tyrrell Museum of Palaeontology
Henrici, Amy C., Carnegie Museum of Natural History
Hernández, Manuel, Univ Complutense de Madrid
Hitz, Ralph B., Tacoma Community College
Holroyd, Pat, University of California, Berkeley
Holtz, Jr., Thomas R., University of Maryland
Horner, John R., Montana State University
Hungerbuehler, Axel, Mesalands Community College
Hunt, Robert M., University of Nebraska, Lincoln
Indeck, Jeff, University of Colorado
Jackson, Frankie, Montana State University
Jacobs, Louis L., Southern Methodist University
Jasinski, Steven E., State Museum of Pennsylvania
Johnson, Ned K., University of California, Berkeley
Joniak, Peter , Comenius University in Bratislava
Keenan, Sarah W., South Dakota School of Mines & Technology
Kirkland, James I., Utah Geological Survey
Koch, Paul L., University of California, Santa Cruz
Konishi, Takuya, Cincinnati Museum Center
Krishtalka, Leonard, University of Kansas
Lamanna, Matthew C., Carnegie Museum of Natural History
Lamanna, Matthew C., University of Pittsburgh
Lamb, James P., University of West Alabama
Lidicker, Jr., William Z., University of California, Berkeley
Lindsay, Everett H., University of Arizona
Loewen, Mark, University of Utah
Luo, Zhexi, Carnegie Museum of Natural History
Lyson, Tyler, Denver Museum of Nature & Science
MacFadden, Bruce J., University of Florida
Maisey, John G., American Museum of Natural History
Makovicky, Peter, University of Minnesota, Twin Cities
Makovicky, Peter J., Field Museum of Natural History
Marcot, Jonathan, University of Colorado
Martill, David, University of Portsmouth
Martin, James E., University of Louisiana at Lafayette
Massare, Judy A., SUNY, The College at Brockport
McDonald, Greg, University of Colorado
McFadden, Bruce J., University of Florida
McLeod, Samuel A., Los Angeles County Museum of Natural History
Meng, Jin, American Museum of Natural History
Meng, Jin, Graduate School of the City University of New York
Merck, Jr., John W., University of Maryland
Miller, Wade E., Brigham Young University
Miller-Camp, Jessica, Indiana University, Bloomington
Montellano-Ballesteros, Marisol, Univ Nacional Autonoma de Mexico
Morales, Michael A., Emporia State University
Motani, Ryosuke, University of California, Davis
Naples, Virginia, Northern Illinois University
Nesbitt, Sterling J., Virginia Polytechnic Institute & State University
Neuman, Andrew G., Royal Tyrrell Museum of Palaeontology
Njau, Jackson K., Indiana University, Bloomington
Norell, Mark A., American Museum of Natural History
Norell, Mark A., Columbia University
Novacek, Michael J., American Museum of Natural History
O'Leary, Maureen, Stony Brook University
Olsen, Paul E., Columbia University
Osi, Attila, Eotvos Lorand University
Padian, Kevin, University of California, Berkeley
Pagnac, Darrin C., South Dakota School of Mines & Technology
Parham, James, California State University, Fullerton
Patton, James L., University of California, Berkeley
Pol, Diego, Cornell University
Polly, P. David, Indiana University, Bloomington
Ratoi, Bogdan G., Alexandru Ioan Cuza
Ray, Clayton E., Smithsonian Institution / National Museum of Natural History
Rensberger, John M., University of Washington
Rieppel, Olivier C., Field Museum of Natural History
Robinson, Peter, University of Colorado
Rowe, Timothy B., University of Texas, Austin
Russell, Dale A., North Carolina State University
Sabol, Martin, Comenius University in Bratislava
Sagebiel, J. C., San Bernardino County Museum
Samonds, Karen, Northern Illinois University
Sankey, Julia, California State University, Stanislaus
Schiebout, Judith A., Louisiana State University
Schultz, Gerald E., West Texas A&M University
Schwartz, Hilde, University of California, Santa Cruz
Schwimmer, David R., Columbus State University
Scott, Craig, Royal Tyrrell Museum of Palaeontology
Sears, Karen, University of Colorado
Secord, Ross, University of Nebraska, Lincoln
Semken, Jr., Holmes A., University of Iowa
Sertich, Joseph, Denver Museum of Nature & Science
Shaw, Christopher A., Los Angeles County Museum of Natural History
Shiller, Thomas, Sul Ross State University
Sidor, Christian A., University of Washington
Smith, Kathlyn M., Georgia Southern University
Steadman, David W., University of Florida
Stearley, Ralph F., Calvin College
Stocker, Michelle, Virginia Polytechnic Institute & State University
Storrs, Glenn W., Cincinnati Museum Center
Storrs, Glenn W., University of Cincinnati
Sumida, Stuart S., California State University, San Bernardino
Tabrum, Alan R., Carnegie Museum of Natural History
Tedford, Richard H., American Museum of Natural History
Therrien, Francois, Royal Tyrrell Museum of Palaeontology
Tumarkin-Deratzian, Allison, Temple University
Tütken, Thomas, Universität Mainz
Uhen, Mark, George Mason University
VanRegenmorter, John M., Grand Valley State University
Varricchio, David J., Montana State University
Vietti, Laura, University of Wyoming
Vila, Bernat, Universitat Autonoma de Barcelona
Voorhies, Michael R., University of Nebraska, Lincoln
Vrba, Elisabeth S., Yale University
Wilkins, Kenneth, Baylor University
Williamson, Thomas E., University of New Mexico
Wilson, Gregory, University of Washington
Wilson, Laura E., Fort Hays State University
Winkler, Alisa, Southern Methodist University
Winkler, Dale A., Southern Methodist University
Wood, Aaron R., Iowa State University of Science & Technology
Woodburne, Michael O., University of California, Riverside
Wuerthele, Norman, Carnegie Museum of Natural History
Wyss, Andre R., University of California, Santa Barbara
Yarborough, Vicki, Virginia Polytechnic Institute & State University
Zakrzewski, Richard J., Fort Hays State University

Invertebrate Paleontology

Adrain, Jonathan M., University of Iowa
Alencaster-Ybarra, Gloria, Univ Nacional Autonoma de Mexico
Anderson, Laurie C., South Dakota School of Mines & Technology
Bailey, Richard H., Northeastern University
Batten, Roger L., American Museum of Natural History

Becker, Ralph Thomas, Universitaet Muenster
Bishop, Gale A., Georgia Southern University
Blake, Daniel B., University of Illinois, Urbana-Champaign
Bonem, Rena M., Baylor University
Bonuso, Nicole, California State University, Fullerton
Bork, Kennard B., Denison University
Brandt, Danita S., Michigan State University
Briggs, Derek E., Yale University
Broadhead, Thomas W., University of Tennessee, Knoxville
Brown, Lewis M., Lake Superior State University
Buitron-Sanchez, Blanca E., Univ Nacional Autonoma de Mexico
Buss, Leo W., Yale University
Butts, Susan H., Yale University
Cairns, Stephen, Smithsonian Institution / National Museum of Natural History
Caldwell, Roy L., University of California, Berkeley
Camp, Mark J., University of Toledo
Caron, Jean-Bernard, University of Toronto
Chatelain, Edward E., Valdosta State University
Chatterton, Brian D., University of Alberta
Cintra-Buenrostro, Carlos, University of Texas, Rio Grande Valley
Clark, Murlene W., University of South Alabama
Comas, María José, Univ Complutense de Madrid
Copper, Paul, Laurentian University, Sudbury
Cuffey, Roger J., Pennsylvania State University, University Park
Dahl, Robyn, Western Washington University
Day, James E., Illinois State University
Deline, Brad, University of West Georgia
Dutro, Thomas, Smithsonian Institution / National Museum of Natural History
Eldredge, Niles, American Museum of Natural History
Elias, Robert J., University of Manitoba
Erwin, Douglas H., Smithsonian Inst/Nat Mus of Nat History
Evanoff, Emmett, University of Colorado
Feldmann, Rodney M., Kent State University
Ferguson, Laing, Mount Allison University
Finks, Robert M., Queens College (CUNY)
Finnegan, Seth, University of California, Berkeley
Fisher, Daniel C., University of Michigan
Fraiser, Margaret L., University of Wisconsin, Milwaukee
Full, Robert J., University of California, Berkeley
Gacía Joral, Fernando, Univ Complutense de Madrid
Gilmour, Ernest H., Eastern Washington University
Glass, Alexander, Duke University
Gonzalez-Arreola, Celestina, Univ Nacional Autonoma de Mexico
Goodwin, David H., Denison University
Hageman, Steven J., Appalachian State University
Hanger, Rex, University of Wisconsin, Whitewater
Hannibal, Joseph T., Cleveland Museum of Natural History
Hannibal, Joseph T., Case Western Reserve University
Harnik, Paul, Colgate University
Harper, Jr., Charles W., University of Oklahoma
Hartman, Joseph H., University of North Dakota
Hegna, Thomas A., Western Illinois University
Hembree, Daniel, Ohio University
Hendricks, Jonathan R., Paleontological Research Institution
Hudackova, Natalia H., Comenius University in Bratislava
Hughes, Nigel C., Cincinnati Museum Center
Hunda, Brenda R., University of Cincinnati
Hunda, Brenda, Cincinnati Museum Center
Hyzny, Matus, Comenius University in Bratislava
Jablonski, David, University of Chicago
James, Matthew J., Sonoma State University
Jin, Jisuo, Western University
Johns, Ronald A., Austin Community College District
Johnston, Paul, Mount Royal University
Kammer, Thomas W., West Virginia University
Key, Jr., Marcus M., Dickinson College
Kosloski, Mary, University of Iowa
Kues, Barry S., University of New Mexico
Kukalova-Peck, Jarmila, Carleton University
Labandeira, Conrad C., Smithsonian Inst/Nat Mus of Nat History
Landman, Neil H., American Museum of Natural History
Lee, Daphne E., University of Otago
Leggitt, Leroy, Loma Linda University
Lehrmann, Daniel J., Trinity University
Leighton, Lindsey, University of Alberta
Lenz, Alfred C., Western University
Leonard-Pingel, Jill, Ohio State University
Lewis, Ronald D., Auburn University
Lidgard, Scott H., Field Museum of Natural History
Lindberg, David R., University of California, Berkeley
Lockley, Martin G., University of Colorado, Denver
LoDuca, Steven T., Eastern Michigan University
Mann, Keith O., Ohio Wesleyan University
Marenco, Katherine N., Bryn Mawr College
Mason, Charles E., Morehead State University
McAfee, Gerald B., Odessa College
Melchin, Michael J., Saint Francis Xavier University
Merrill, Glen K., University of Houston Downtown
Meyer, David L., University of Cincinnati
Miller, Arnold I., University of Cincinnati
Miller, William C., Humboldt State University
Morris, Robert W., Wittenberg University
Nagel-Myers, Judith, St. Lawrence University
Narbonne, Guy M., Queen's University
Nitecki, Matthew H., Field Museum of Natural History
Oleinik, Anton, Florida Atlantic University
Paterson, John R., University of New England
Perrilliat-Montoya, Maria del Carmen, Univ Nacional Autonoma de Mexico
Petsios, Elizabeth, Baylor University
Pietsch, Carlie, San Jose State University
Pojeta, John, Smithsonian Institution / National Museum of Natural History
Pope, John K., Miami University
Portell, Roger W., University of Florida
Poty, Edouard, Universite de Liege
Powell, Matthew G., Juniata College
Prichonnet, Gilbert P., Universite du Quebec a Montreal
Rhodes, Frank H. T., Cornell University
Ritterbush, Linda A., California Lutheran University
Robison, Richard A., University of Kansas
Rodland, David L., Muskingum University
Rohr, David M., Sul Ross State University
Rosenberg, Gary, Drexel University
Rowell, Albert J., University of Kansas
Rowland, Stephen, University of Nevada, Las Vegas
Sandy, Michael R., University of Dayton
Santos, Hernan, University of Puerto Rico
Savage, Norman M., University of Oregon
Schiappa, Tamra A., Slippery Rock University
Schlogl, Jan , Comenius University in Bratislava
Schmidt, David, Wright State University
Schweitzer, Carrie E., Kent State University
Schweitzer, Carrie E., Kent State University at Stark
Segura-Vernis, Luis R., Univ Autonoma de Baja California Sur
Selden, Paul A., University of Kansas
Sevilla, Paloma, Univ Complutense de Madrid
Sheehan, Peter M., Milwaukee Public Museum
Sheehan, Peter M., University of Wisconsin, Milwaukee
Shubak, Kenneth A., University of Wisconsin, Platteville
Soja, Constance M., Colgate University
Sorauf, James E., Binghamton University
Spinosa, Claude, Boise State University
Sprinkle, James T., University of Texas, Austin
Squires, Richard L., California State University, Northridge
Stanley, Thomas M., University of Oklahoma
Stanley, Jr., George D., University of Montana
Stephen, Daniel, Utah Valley University
Stock, Carl W., University of Alabama
Sumrall, Colin, University of Tennessee, Knoxville
Szente, Istvan, Eotvos Lorand University
Szlavecz, Katalin, Johns Hopkins University
Tapanila, Leif, Idaho State University
Tarhan, Lidya, Yale University
Tshudy, Dale, Edinboro University of Pennsylvania
Tsujita, Cameron J., Western University
Villasenor-Martinez, Ana B., Univ Nacional Autonoma de Mexico
Visaggi, Christy, Georgia State University
Votaw, Robert, Indiana University Northwest
Wagner, Peter J., University of Nebraska, Lincoln
Wagner, Peter J., Field Museum of Natural History
Waller, Thomas R., Smithsonian Inst/Nat Mus of Nat History
Webber, Andrew, Cincinnati Museum Center
Webster, Gary D., Washington State University

Webster, Mark, University of Chicago
Westrop, Stephen R., University of Oklahoma
Wilson, Mark A., College of Wooster
Wyse Jackson, Patrick N., Trinity College
Xiao, Shuhai, Virginia Polytechnic Institute & State University
Young, Graham A., University of Manitoba
Young, Graham A., Manitoba Museum
Zachos, Louis G., University of Mississippi
Zodrow, Erwin L., Cape Breton University
Zumwalt, Gary S., Louisiana Tech University

Paleoecology

Allabush, Kathleen, University of Utah
Almendinger, James E., University of Minnesota, Twin Cities
Andreu-Hayles, Laia, Columbia University
Arkle, Kelsey M., Augustana College
Ashworth, Allan C., North Dakota State University
Baker, Richard G., University of Iowa
Balescu, Sanda, Universite du Quebec a Montreal
Barker, Stephen, Cardiff University
Bartlein, Patrick, University of Oregon
Begin, Christian, Universite du Quebec
Bennington, J Bret, Hofstra University
Billups, Katharina, University of Delaware
Blanchet, Jean-Pierre, Universite du Quebec a Montreal
Blyth, Alison, Curtin University
Bottjer, David J., University of Southern California
Boyd, Bill, Southern Cross University
Bralower, Timothy J., Pennsylvania State University, University Park
Brett, Carlton E., University of Cincinnati
Briskin, Madeleine, University of Cincinnati
Buckley, Brendon, Columbia University
Caissie, Beth E., Iowa State University of Science & Technology
Camill III, Philip, Bowdoin College
Capraro, Luca, Università degli Studi di Padova
Casey, Michelle , Towson University
Chapin, F. Stuart, University of California, Berkeley
Charles, Christopher D., University of California, San Diego
Cobb, Kim M., Georgia Institute of Technology
Cohen, Anne L., Woods Hole Oceanographic Institution
Cole, Julia E., University of Arizona
Colgan, Mitchell W., College of Charleston
Curtin, Tara M., Hobart & William Smith Colleges
Curtis, Jason H., University of Florida
D'Andrea, William J., Columbia University
de Menocal, Peter B., Columbia University
Dekens, Petra, San Francisco State University
deMenocal, Peter B., Columbia University
Dietl, Gregory P., Cornell University
Dornbos, Stephen Q., University of Wisconsin, Milwaukee
Duhamel, Solange, Columbia University
Edlund, Mark B., University of Minnesota, Twin Cities
Elick, Jennifer M., Susquehanna University
Endres, Anthony E., University of Waterloo
Engstrom, Daniel R., University of Minnesota, Twin Cities
Evans, Michael N., University of Maryland
Fariduddin, Mohammad, Northeastern Illinois University
Fawcett, Peter J., University of New Mexico
Francis, Jane, University of Leeds
Francus, Pierre, Universite du Quebec
Fritz, Sherilyn C., University of Nebraska, Lincoln
Gabler, Christopher, University of Texas, Rio Grande Valley
Goodwin, Phillip A., University of Southampton
Grigg, Laurie, Norwich University
Guber, Albert L., Pennsylvania State University, University Park
Halfar, Jochen, University of Toronto
Hasiotis, Stephen T., University of Kansas
Hays, James D., Columbia University
Haywood, Alan, University of Leeds
He, Helen, University of East Anglia
Herbert, Gregory, University of South Florida
Herbert, Timothy D., Brown University
Herrmann, Achim, Louisiana State University
Hill, Tessa M., University of California, Davis
Hopley, Philip, Birkbeck College
Hu, Feng-Sheng, University of Illinois, Urbana-Champaign
Hughes, Malcolm K., University of Arizona
Huybers, Peter, Harvard University
Ivany, Linda C., Syracuse University
Johnson, Claudia C., Indiana University, Bloomington
Johnson, Robert G., University of Minnesota, Twin Cities
Jones, Douglas S., University of Florida
Kemp, Alan, University of Southampton
Kennedy, Lisa M., Virginia Polytechnic Institute & State University
Knight, Tiffany, Washington University in St. Louis
Koutavas, Athanasios, College of Staten Island/CUNY
Kutzbach, John E., University of Wisconsin, Madison
Lachniet, Matthew S., University of Nevada, Las Vegas
Lea, David W., University of California, Santa Barbara
Lebold, Joe, West Virginia University
Linsley, Braddock, Columbia University
Littler, Kate L., Exeter University
Livingstone, Daniel A., Duke University
Lohmann, George P., Woods Hole Oceanographic Institution
Long, Colin, University of Wisconsin Oshkosh
Lozano Garcia, Maria S., Univ Nacional Autonoma de Mexico
Mann, Daniel H., University of Alaska, Fairbanks
Marchal, Olivier, Woods Hole Oceanographic Institution
Martin, Anthony J., Emory University
Mayewski, Paul A., University of Maine
McIntyre, Andrew, Queens College (CUNY)
McManus, Jerry F., Columbia University
McManus, Jerry F., Woods Hole Oceanographic Institution
McWethy, David B., Montana State University
Medina Elizalde, Martin A., Auburn University
Meehan, Kimberly, SUNY, Buffalo
Miller, Joshua H., Cincinnati Museum Center
Miller, Keith B., Kansas State University
Miller, Molly F., Vanderbilt University
Mishler, Brent, University of California, Berkeley
Morgan, Ryan, Tarleton State University
Myers, Corinne E., University of New Mexico
Nichols, Jonathan E., Columbia University
Olszewski, Thomas, Texas A&M University
Ortegren, Jason, University of West Florida
Panagiotakopulu, Eva, Edinburgh University
Parr, Kate, University of Liverpool
Pearson, P N., Cardiff University
Pekar, Stephen, Queens College (CUNY)
Peteet, Dorothy M., Columbia University
Phelps, William, Riverside City College
Poli, Maria-Serena, Eastern Michigan University
Pospelova, Vera, University of Victoria
Poulsen, Christopher J., University of Michigan
Power, Mary E., University of California, Berkeley
Quinn, Terry, University of Texas, Austin
Raymo, Maureen, Columbia University
Rhode, David E., Desert Research Institute
Rindsberg, Andrew K., University of West Alabama
Robinson, Stuart, University of Oxford
Royer, Dana, Wesleyan University
Sahagian, Dork, Lehigh University
Salzer, Matthew W., University of Arizona
Sauer, Peter, Indiana University, Bloomington
Schaefer, Joerg, Columbia University
Schellenberg, Stephen A., San Diego State University
Schwert, Donald P., North Dakota State University
Schöne, Bernd R., Universität Mainz
Sessa, Jocelyn A., Drexel University
Severinghaus, Jeffrey P., University of California, San Diego
Shaak, Graig D., University of Florida
Shanahan, Timothy M., University of Texas, Austin
Sheffield, Sarah, University of South Florida
Shroat-Lewis, Rene A., University of Arkansas at Little Rock
Shuman, Bryan N., University of Wyoming
Sinha, Ashish, California State University, Dominguez Hills
Sloan, Lisa C., University of California, Santa Cruz
Smerdon, Jason, Columbia University
Smiley, Tara M., Indiana University, Bloomington
Smith, Dena M., University of Colorado
Smith, Martin, Durham University
Speer, James, Indiana State University

Sremac, Jasenka, University of Zagreb
Stoykova, Kristalina C., Bulgarian Academy of Sciences
Surge, Donna M., University of North Carolina, Chapel Hill
Swetnam, Thomas W., University of Arizona
Tackett, Lydia S., North Dakota State University
Talyor, Frederick W., University of Texas, Austin
Thompson, William G., Woods Hole Oceanographic Institution
Trouet, Valerie, University of Arizona
Uno, Kevin, Columbia University
Van der Putten, Nathalie, Vrije Universiteit Amsterdam
Verardo, Stacey, George Mason University
Vermeij, Geerat J., University of California, Davis
Waddington, J. M., McMaster University
Walker, Ian R., University of British Columbia, Okanagan Campus
Warnock, Jonathan P., Indiana University of Pennsylvania
Webb, III, Thompson, Brown University
Weldeab, Syee, University of California, Santa Barbara
Westgate, James W., Lamar University
Whiteside, Jessica H., University of Southampton
Whitlock, Cathy, Montana State University
Williams, Christopher J., Franklin and Marshall College
Williams, John W., University of Wisconsin, Madison
Woodhouse, Connie, University of Arizona
Yanes, Yurena, University of Cincinnati
Yu, Zicheng, Lehigh University
Æosoviæ, Vlasta, University of Zagreb

Geomicrobiology
Ashbolt, Nicholas J., Southern Cross University
Chan, Clara S., University of Delaware
Coolen, Marco, Curtin University
Flannery, David, Queensland University of Technology
Frantz, Carie M., Weber State University
Hazen, Terry C., University of Tennessee, Knoxville
Liang, Renxing, Princeton University
Lower, Steven K., Ohio State University
McDermott, Timothy, Montana State University
McKay, Luke, Montana State University
Osburn, Magdalena , Northwestern University
Pérez-Rodríguez, Ileana, University of Pennsylvania
Priscu, John, Montana State University
Ward, David M., Montana State University
Wilhelm, Steven W., University of Tennessee, Knoxville

Paleoclimatology
Andrus, C. Fred T., University of Alabama
Atkinson, Tim, University College London
Baker, Paul A., Duke University
Baldini, James, Durham University
Cleaveland, Malcolm K., University of Arkansas, Fayetteville
Cook, Tim, University of Massachusetts, Amherst
Cotton, Jennifer, California State University, Northridge
Doner, Lisa A., Plymouth State University
Hoenisch, Baerbel, Columbia University
Johnson, Thomas C., University of Minnesota Duluth
Kaspari, Susan, Central Washington University
Keegan, Kaitlin M., University of Nevada, Reno
Koffman, Bess, Colby College
Konecky, Bronwen L., Washington University in St. Louis
Martín Chivelet, Javier, Univ Complutense de Madrid
Maxbauer, Dan, Carleton College
McKay, Nicholas, Northern Arizona University
Meyers, Stephen R., University of Wisconsin, Madison
Michel, Lauren, Tennessee Tech University
Onac, Petroniu (Bogdan), University of South Florida
Orland, Ian, University of Wisconsin, Madison, Division of Extension
Osleger, David A., University of California, Davis
Quinton, Page, Indiana University, Bloomington
Quinton, Page C., SUNY Potsdam
Railsback, L. Bruce, University of Georgia
Salacup, Jeff, University of Massachusetts, Amherst
Shackelton, Sarah, Princeton University
Sullivan, Donald G., University of Denver
Touchan, Ramzi, University of Arizona
van Beynen, Phil, University of South Florida
Weiss, Anna M., Midwestern State University
Williams, Alton P., Columbia University
Winsor, Kelsey, Northern Arizona University
Zachos, James, University of California, Santa Cruz
Zambito, James J., Beloit College

HYDROLOGY

General Hydrology
Adelana, S.M. A., University of Ilorin
AL-Nouimy, Latifa B., University of Qatar
Alencoão, Ana M., Unive de Trás-os-Montes e Alto Douro
Alhajari, Sief A., University of Qatar
Allan, Craig J., University of North Carolina, Charlotte
Allen, Peter M., Baylor University
Alsdorf, Douglas E., Ohio State University
Andres, A. S., University of Delaware
Arain, M. A., McMaster University
Autio, Robert J., Indiana University
Bain, Daniel J., University of Pittsburgh
Barnard, Holly R., University of Colorado
Baron, Dirk, California State University, Bakersfield
Bearden, Bennett L., Geological Survey of Alabama
Becker, Naomi M., Los Alamos National Laboratory
Bennett, Philip, University of Texas, Austin
Bense, Victor, University of East Anglia
Bloor, Michelle, University of Portsmouth
Borsa, Adrian, University of California, San Diego
Boult, Stephen, University of Manchester
Boving, Thomas, University of Rhode Island
Bowman, Jean A., Texas A&M University
Boyle, Douglas, University of Nevada, Reno
Bradley, Chris, University of Birmingham
Brassington, Rick, University of Newcastle Upon Tyne
Brooks, Paul D., University of Utah
Brown, David L., California State University, Chico
Burkhart, Patrick A., Slippery Rock University
Byrne, James M., University of Lethbridge
Campana, Michael E., Oregon State University
Cardenas, Bayani, University of Texas, Austin
Carey, Sean, McMaster University
Carillo Chavez, Alejandro J., Univ Nacional Autonoma de Mexico
Carman, Cary D., Angelo State University
Caylor, Kelly, University of California, Santa Barbara
Challads, Thomas, Edinburgh University
Chaubey, Indrajeet, Purdue University
Cheng, Chu-Lin, University of Texas, Rio Grande Valley
Cianfrani, Christina, Hampshire College
Cirmo, Christopher P., SUNY, Cortland
Coombes, Peter J., Southern Cross University
Coulibaly, Paulin, McMaster University
Crawford, Nicholas, Western Kentucky University
Cunningham, Peter, University of Newcastle Upon Tyne
Dahlke, Helen E., University of California, Davis
Darby, Jeannie, University of California, Davis
Dee, Kato , University of Oklahoma
DeVries, Stephanie, University of Tennessee, Chattanooga
Doster, Florian, Heriot-Watt University
Dowling, Carolyn B., Ball State University
Duan, Quingyun, Lawrence Livermore National Laboratory
Duex, Timothy W., University of Louisiana at Lafayette
Dymond, Salli F., University of Minnesota Duluth
Eaton, Timothy, Queens College (CUNY)
El Kadiri, Racha, Middle Tennessee State University
Enright, Richard L., Bridgewater State University
Entekhabi, Dara, Massachusetts Institute of Technology
Eshleman, Keith N., University of Maryland
Estalrich López, Joan, Universitat Autonoma de Barcelona
Ezenabor, Ben O., University of Benin
Fabryka-Martin, June T., Los Alamos National Laboratory
Faramarzi, Monireh, University of Alberta
Farrow, Norman D., Oak Ridge National Laboratory
Fedele, Juan J., Saint Cloud State University
Florea, Lee, Indiana University, Bloomington
Foufoula-Georgiou, Efi, University of Minnesota, Twin Cities
Fox, Haydn A., Texas A&M University, Commerce
Frasson, Renato , Ohio State University
Gannon, John P., Western Carolina University

Gary, Marcus, University of Texas, Austin
Gilmore, Tyler J., Pacific Northwest National Laboratory
Godsey, Sarah E., Idaho State University
Grieneisen, Michael L., University of California, Davis
Groves, Christopher, Western Kentucky University
Guan, Huade, Flinders University
Gutierrez-Jurado, Hugo A., University of Texas, El Paso
Hamann, Hillary, University of Denver
Hannah, David, University of Birmingham
Hart, David J., University of Wisconsin, Madison
Harter, Thomas, University of California, Davis
Hasan, Mohamed Ali, University of Malaya
Hauswirth, Scott, California State University, Northridge
Heimann, William H., Fort Hays State University
Heitz, Leroy F., University of Guam
Heo, Joon, University of Texas Permian Basin
Hernes, Peter J., University of California, Davis
Hildebrandt, Anke, Friedrich-Schiller-University Jena
Hill, Mary C., University of Kansas
Hooyer, Thomas S., University of Wisconsin, Madison
Hornberger, George, Vanderbilt University
Hubbard, John E., SUNY, The College at Brockport
Huntington, Justin, University of Nevada, Reno
Ibaraki, Motomu, Ohio State University
Inamdar, Shreeram, University of Delaware
Jacobs, Katharine L., University of Arizona
James-Aworeni, E., Obafemi Awolowo University
Jefferson, Anne, University of North Carolina, Charlotte
Jefferson, Anne J., Kent State University
Johannesson, Karen H., Tulane University
Johnson, Robert O., Oak Ridge National Laboratory
Johnson, Robert L., Argonne National Laboratory
Kandel, Hari, Lake Superior State University
Kang, Peter, University of Minnesota, Twin Cities
Kasenow, Michael, Eastern Michigan University
Kelly, Walton R., Illinois State University
Kesel, Richard H., Louisiana State University
Keyantash, John, California State University, Dominguez Hills
Kilroy, Kathyrn, Minot State University
Kinner, David A., Western Carolina University
Kuchovsky, Tomas, Masaryk University
Land, Lewis A., New Mexico Institute of Mining and Technology
Lane, Charles L., Southern Oregon University
Lanigan, David C., Pacific Northwest National Laboratory
Lavanchy, G. Thomas, University of Denver
Laycock, Arleigh H., University of Alberta
Lee, Michael D., California State University, East Bay
Lightbody, Anne F., University of New Hampshire
Lin, Yu-Feng F., Illinois State Geological Survey
Liu, Gaisheng, University of Kansas
Llanos, Hilario, University of the Basque Country UPV/EHU
Ma, Lin, University of Texas, El Paso
Masteller, Claire C., Washington University in St. Louis
Matheny, Ashley, University of Texas, Austin
McColl, Kaighin, Harvard University
McDermott, Christopher I., Edinburgh University
McDowell, William H., University of New Hampshire
McElwee, Carl D., University of Kansas
McKenna, Thomas E., University of Delaware
McLaughlin, Peter P., University of Delaware
McNamara, James P., Boise State University
Megdal, Sharon B., University of Arizona
Mehnert, Edward, Illinois State University
Meindl, Christopher, University of South Florida
Molotch, Noah, University of Colorado
Monohan, Carrie, California State University, Chico
Moysey, Stephen, East Carolina University
Mudd, Simon N., Edinburgh University
Naudts, Kim, Vrije Universiteit Amsterdam
Nkuna, Tinyiko R., University of Venda for Science & Technology
Nolin, Anne , University of Nevada, Reno
O'Reilly, Catherine M., Illinois State University
Odling, Noelle, University of Leeds
Ortiz-Aguirre, Ramon, Univ Autonoma de San Luis Potosi
Oztekin Okan, Ozlem, Firat University
Palmer, Arthur N., SUNY, Oneonta
Papuga, Shirley, Wayne State University
Parkin, Geoffrey, University of Newcastle Upon Tyne
Pavelsky, Tamlin M., University of North Carolina, Chapel Hill
Payn, Robert, Montana State University
Pettijohn, J. C., University of Illinois, Urbana-Champaign
Piccinini, Leonardo, Università degli Studi di Padova
Piggot, Matthew, Imperial College
Plankell, Eric T., Illinois State Geological Survey
Poole, Geoff, Montana State University
Prestegaard, Karen L., University of Maryland
Puente, Carlos E., University of California, Davis
Quinn, Paul, University of Newcastle Upon Tyne
Rakovan, Monica, Miami University
Reay, William G., William & Mary
Reedy, Robert C., University of Texas at Austin, Jackson School of Geosciences
Reidenbach, Matthew A., University of Virginia
Reinfelder, Ying Fan, Rutgers, The State University of New Jersey
Rempe, Daniella, University of Texas, Austin
Renshaw, Carl E., Dartmouth College
Rice, Karen C., University of Virginia
Richards, Paul L., SUNY, The College at Brockport
Ricka, Adam, Masaryk University
Root, Tara L., Florida Atlantic University
Saar, Martin O., University of Minnesota, Twin Cities
Salami, B. M., Obafemi Awolowo University
Sandoval, Samuel, University of California, Davis
Sandoval Solis, Samuel, University of California, Davis
Scanlon, Bridget R., University of Texas, Austin
Scanlon, Todd M., University of Virginia
Scanlon, Todd M., University of Virginia
Schilling, Keith E., University of Iowa
Scotton, Paolo, Università degli Studi di Padova
Screaton, Elizabeth J., University of Florida
Silva, Catrina, Unive de Lisboa
Singer, Michael, University of St. Andrews
Slade, Jr., Raymond M., Austin Community College District
Smith, Ellen D., Oak Ridge National Laboratory
Smith, James A., Princeton University
Smith, Michael, Geological Survey of Alabama
Smith, Ronald M., Pacific Northwest National Laboratory
Smyth, Rebecca C., Univ of Texas at Austin, Jackson Sch of Geosciences
Sorooshian, Soroosh, University of California, Irvine
Sorooshian, Soroosh, University of Arizona
Spane, Frank A., Pacific Northwest National Laboratory
Sritharan, Subramania I., Central State University
Stafford, James, Wyoming State Geological Survey
Stasko, Stanislaw, University of Wroclaw
Steenhuis, Tammo S., Cornell University
Sterling, Shannon, Dalhousie University
Tarka, Robert, University of Wroclaw
Thorne, Paul D., Pacific Northwest National Laboratory
Triay, Ines, Los Alamos National Laboratory
Turek, Marni, University of British Columbia, Okanagan Campus
Turner, Anne, Austin Community College District
Tyler, Scott, University of Nevada, Reno
Van Stan, John, Georgia Southern University
Vermeul, Vincent R., Pacific Northwest National Laboratory
Vivoni, Enrique, Arizona State University
Vonk, Jorien, Vrije Universiteit Amsterdam
Wallender, Wes W., University of California, Davis
Watkins, David, Exeter University
West, Jared, University of Leeds
White, Jeffrey R., Indiana University, Bloomington
Witt, Emma, Stockton University
Wolf, Aaron T., Oregon State University
Woltemade, Christopher J., Shippensburg University
Woo, Ming-Ko, McMaster University
Wood, Eric F., Princeton University
Wymore, Adam, University of New Hampshire
Xu, Shangping, University of Wisconsin, Milwaukee
Yan, Eugene, University of Illinois at Chicago
Yang, Y, Cardiff University
Ye, Ming, Florida State University
Yusoff, Ismail, University of Malaya
Zaccaria, Daniele, University of California, Davis
Zhang, Minghua , University of California, Davis

Ziemkiewicz, , Paul F., West Virginia University
Zume, Joseph T., Shippensburg University

Ground Water/Hydrogeology
Abdo, Ginette, Montana Tech of The University of Montana
Abrams, Daniel, University of Illinois
Ahmed, Kazi M., University of Dhaka
Al, Tom A., University of Ottawa
Al-Shaibani, Abdulaziz, King Fahd University of Petroleum and Minerals
Alexander, Scott, University of Minnesota, Twin Cities
Alexander, Jr., E. Calvin, University of Minnesota, Twin Cities
Ali, Bukari, Kwame Nkrumah University of Science and Technology
Ali, Genevieve, University of Manitoba
Amin, Isam E., Youngstown State University
Anderson, Mary P., University of Wisconsin, Madison
Anderson, William P., Appalachian State University
Andreasen, David C., Maryland Department of Natural Resources
Andres, A. S., University of Delaware
Antigüedad, Iñaki, University of the Basque Country UPV/EHU
Appiah-Adjei, Emmanuel K., Kwame Nkrumah University of Science and Technology
Appold, Martin S., University of Missouri
Arthur, Jonathan D., Florida Geological Survey
Asante, Joseph, Tennessee Tech University
Asghari Moghadam, Asghar, University of Tabriz
Asiwaju-Bello, Yinusa A., Federal University of Technology, Akure
Bagtzoglou, Ross, Columbia University
Bahr, Jean M., University of Wisconsin, Madison
Bair, E. Scott, Ohio State University
Bajjali, William, University of Wisconsin, Superior
Baker, Andy, University of New South Wales
Baldwin, Jr., A. Dwight, Miami University
Banks, Eddie, Flinders University
Barbecot, Florent, Universite du Quebec a Montreal
Barbee, Gary C., West Texas A&M University
Barkmann, Peter, Colorado Geological Survey
Barrash, Warren, Boise State University
Batelaan, Okke, Katholieke Universiteit Leuven
Batelaan, Okke, Flinders University
Bayari, Serdar, Hacettepe University
Becker, Matthew, California State University, Long Beach
Beckie, Roger D., University of British Columbia
Bennett, Steven W., Western Illinois University
Bentley, Laurence R., University of Calgary
Bergamaschi, Brian, Sacramento State University
Besancon, James, Wellesley College
Bethke, Craig M., University of Illinois, Urbana-Champaign
Bishop, Charles E., Utah Geological Survey
BlackEagle, Cory, Eastern Kentucky University
Blythe, Daniel D., Montana Tech of The University of Montana
Bobst, Andrew L., Montana Tech of The University of Montana
Bohling, Geoff, University of Kansas
Bohling, Geoffrey C., University of Kansas
Bolster, Diogo, University of Notre Dame
Bordeleau, Geneviève, Universite du Quebec
Boutt, David, University of Massachusetts, Amherst
Boving, Thomas B., University of Rhode Island
Boyle, James T., New Jersey Geological and Water Survey
Bradbury, Kenneth R., University of Wisconsin, Madison
Bradbury, Kenneth R., University of Wisconsin, Madison, Division of Extension
Brahana, John V., University of Arkansas, Fayetteville
Brame, Scott E., Clemson University
Bratcher, Susan, Fresno State University
Breitmeyer, Ronald, University of Nevada, Reno
Brikowski, Tom H., University of Texas, Dallas
Brinkmann, Robert, Oregon Dept of Geology and Mineral Industries
Brookfield, Andrea, University of Kansas
Brown, Megan R., Northern Illinois University
Brusseau, Mark L., University of Arizona
Buchanan, John P., Eastern Washington University
Burbey, Thomas J., Virginia Polytechnic Institute & State University
Burgess, William G., University College London
Burnett, Joree, Tarleton State University
Butler, Jr., James J., University of Kansas
Callahan, Timothy J., College of Charleston
Capuano, Regina M., University of Houston
Cardiff, Michael A., University of Wisconsin, Madison
Cardiff, Mike, University of Wisconsin, Madison
Carey, Anne E., Ohio State University
Carle, Steven, Lawrence Livermore National Laboratory
Carling, Gregory T., Brigham Young University
Carlson, Catherine A., Eastern Connecticut State University
Carlson, Douglas A., Louisiana State University
Carstarphen, Camela, Montana Tech of The University of Montana
Carvalho, Maria d., Unive de Lisboa
Casillas, Angelica, Univ Nacional Autonoma de Mexico
Cassidy, Daniel P., Western Michigan University
Celia, Michael A., Princeton University
Chase, Peter M., University of Wisconsin, Madison, Division of Extension
Chavez-Aguirre, Rafael, Univ Autonoma de Chihuahua
Cheng, Songlin, Wright State University
Cheng, Tao, Memorial University of Newfoundland
Cherkauer, Douglas S., University of Wisconsin, Milwaukee
Cherry, John A., University of Waterloo
Cherubini, Claudia, Institut Polytechnique LaSalle Beauvais (ex-IGAL)
Chesnaux, Romain, Universite du Quebec a Chicoutimi
Chowdhury, Shafiul H., SUNY, New Paltz
Christenson, Scott, New Mexico Institute of Mining and Technology
Clarey, Timothy L., Delta College
Clark, Ian D., University of Ottawa
Conant, Brewster, University of Waterloo
Cook, Edward R., Columbia University
Cook, Peter, Flinders University
Costa, Maria R., Unive de Trás-os-Montes e Alto Douro
Crewdson, Robert, California State University, Bakersfield
Croxen III, Fred W., Arizona Western College
Davidson, Gregg R., University of Mississippi
Davis, Arden D., South Dakota School of Mines & Technology
Davis, J. Matthew, University of New Hampshire
de Stefano, Lucia, Univ Complutense de Madrid
Decker, Dave, University of Nevada, Reno
Del Arenal-Capetillo, Rodolfo, Univ Nacional Autonoma de Mexico
Demlie, Molla, University of KwaZulu-Natal
Denizman, Can, Valdosta State University
Devlin, J. F., University of Kansas
Dhar, Ratan K., York College (CUNY)
Dimova, Natasha T., University of Alabama
Dintaman, Christopher, Indiana University
Doherty, Amanda, New Mexico Institute of Mining and Technology
Domber, Steven E., New Jersey Geological and Water Survey
Doran, Peter, Louisiana State University
Doss, Paul K., University of Southern Indiana
Douglas, Ellen, University of Massachusetts, Boston
Dripps, Weston R., Furman University
Druhan, Jennifer, University of Illinois, Urbana-Champaign
Duaime, Terence E., Montana Tech of The University of Montana
Dunkle, Kallina M., Austin Peay State University
Durham, Lisa, Argonne National Laboratory
Durham, Lisa A., Argonne National Laboratory
Earman, Sam, Millersville University
Ekmekci, Mehmet, Hacettepe University
El-Kadi, Aly I., University of Hawai'i, Manoa
Ellis, Andre, California State University, Los Angeles
Erickson, Melinda L., University of Minnesota, Twin Cities
Esling, Steven P., Southern Illinois University Carbondale
Evans, Sarah G., Appalachian State University
Fabbri, Paolo, Università degli Studi di Padova
Fairley, Jerry P., University of Idaho
Famiglietti, James, University of California, Irvine
Farmer, George T., Los Alamos National Laboratory
Feinstein, Daniel T., University of Wisconsin, Milwaukee
Ferre, Paul A., University of Arizona
Fichera, Marissa, New Mexico Institute of Mining and Technology
Fisher, Andrew T., University of California, Santa Cruz
Fitzpatrick, Stephan D., Georgia State Univ, Perimeter Coll, Clarkston Campus
Flowers, George C., Tulane University
Fogg, Graham E., University of California, Davis
Foglia, Laura, University of California, Davis
Fountain, John C., North Carolina State University
Frisbee, Marty, Purdue University
Fryar, Alan E., University of Kentucky
Furlong, Emelia, Maryland Department of Natural Resources

Gakka, Udaya Laxm, Osmania University
Gardner, Payton, University of Montana
Gargini, Alessandro, Alma Mater Studiorum University of Bologna
Garing, Charlotte , University of Georgia
Garven, Grant, Tufts University
Ge, Shemin, University of Colorado
Geary, Phil, University of Newcastle
Geidel, Gwendelyn, University of South Carolina
Gemperline, Johanna M., Maryland Department of Natural Resources
Gerla, Philip J., University of North Dakota
Gilmore, Troy, University of Nebraska, Lincoln
Goeke, James W., Unversity of Nebraska, Lincoln
Gordon, Ryan, Dept of Agriculture, Conservation, and Forestry
Gotkowitz, Madeline B., University of Wisconsin, Extension
Gouzie, Douglas R., Missouri State University
Graham, Grace E., University of Wisconsin, Madison, Division of Extension
Grasby, Stephen E., University of Calgary
Grismer, Mark E., University of California, Davis
Grundl, Timothy J., University of Wisconsin, Milwaukee
Gulley, Jason, University of South Florida
Gurdak, Jason, San Francisco State University
Gurwin, Jacek, University of Wroclaw
Haacker, Erin, University of Nebraska, Lincoln
Habana, Nathan C., University of Guam
Hadley, Daniel, University of Illinois
Haggerty, Roy D., Oregon State University
Halihan, Todd, Oklahoma State University
Hampton, Duane R., Western Michigan University
Hamutoko, Josephine, University of Namibia
Hand, Kristen, DCNR- Pennsylvania Bureau of Geological Survey
Hargis, David, University of Arizona
Harrington, Glenn, Flinders University
Harris, Brett D., Curtin University
Hart, David J., University of Wisconsin, Madison, Division of Extension
Hart, David J., University of Wisconsin, Extension
Harter, Thomas L., University of California, Davis
Harter, Thomas, University of California, Davis
Hatch, Christine, University of Massachusetts, Amherst
Hayashi, Masaki, University of Calgary
Hays, Phillip D., University of Arkansas, Fayetteville
Heiss, James, University of Massachusetts, Lowell
Helmke, Martin F., West Chester University
Hendrickx, Jan M., New Mexico Institute of Mining and Technology
Hendry, Jim, University of Saskatchewan
Henry, Eric J., University of North Carolina, Wilmington
Henry, Tiernan, National University of Ireland Galway
Herman, Ellen K., Bucknell University
Hermans, Thomas, Ghent University
Hershey, Ronald L., University of Nevada, Reno
Hibbs, Barry, California State University, Los Angeles
Hiscock, Kevin, University of East Anglia
Hoff, Jean L., Saint Cloud State University
Hoover, Karin A., California State University, Chico
Horner, Tim C., Sacramento State University
Howard, Kenneth W., University of Toronto
Howe III, Thomas R., Western Michigan University
Hu, Bill X., Florida State University
Hudak, Paul F., University of North Texas
Huizar-Alvarez, Rafael, Univ Nacional Autonoma de Mexico
Hurlow, Hugh A., Utah Geological Survey
Hurlow, Hugh, Utah Geological Survey
Huysmans, Marijke, Katholieke Universiteit Leuven
Iles, Derric L., South Dakota Dept of Env and Natural Resources
Iqbal, Mohammad Z., University of Northern Iowa
Iribar, Vicente , University of the Basque Country UPV/EHU
Irvine, Dylan, Flinders University
James, Scott C., Baylor University
Jannik, Nancy O., Winona State University
Jarvis, W. T., Oregon State University
Jenson, John W., University of Guam
Johnson, Thomas M., University of Illinois, Urbana-Champaign
Join, Jean-Lambert, Universite de la Reunion
Juster, Thomas C., University of South Florida
Kaden, Scott, Missouri Dept of Natural Resources
Keen, Kerry L., University of Wisconsin, River Falls
Keller, C. Kent, Washington State University
Kelly, Bryce, University of New South Wales
Kelly, Walton R., University of Illinois
Kent, Douglas, Oklahoma State University
Khalequzzaman, Md., Lock Haven University
Kim, Yongsang (Barry), University of Guam
Kirk, Scott, Ohio Dept of Natural Resources
Kludt, Trevor, New Mexico Institute of Mining and Technology
Knoll, Martin A., Sewanee: University of the South
Kreamer, David K., University of Nevada, Las Vegas
Kreamer, David, University of Nevada, Reno
Kurttas, Turker, Hacettepe University
La Fave, John I., Montana Tech of The University of Montana
Lachhab, Ahmed, Susquehanna University
Lachmar, Thomas E., Utah State University
LaFreniere, Lorraine, Argonne National Laboratory
Lahiri, Chayan, Adams State University
Lambert, Carolyn D., University of Northern Colorado
Larocque, Marie, Universite du Quebec a Montreal
Laton, W. R., California State University, Fullerton
Lee, David R., University of Waterloo
Lee, Donald W., Oak Ridge National Laboratory
Lee, Eung Seok, Ohio University
Lee, Ming-Kuo, Auburn University
Lefebvre, Rene, Universite du Quebec
Lemke, Lawrence D., Central Michigan University
Lenczewski, Melissa E., Northern Illinois University
Leonhart, Leo S., University of Arizona
Leslie, Deborah, University of Memphis
Levy, Jonathan, Miami University
Li, Liangping, South Dakota School of Mines & Technology
Locke, Daniel B., Dept of Agriculture, Conservation, and Forestry
Loh, Yvonne A., University of Ghana
Loheide, Steven P., University of Wisconsin, Madison
Lopez-Ferreira, Cesar A., Univ Autonoma de Baja California Sur
Lord, Mark L., Western Carolina University
Love, Andew, Flinders University
Lowe, Mike, Utah Geological Survey
Lowry, Christopher S., SUNY, Buffalo
Luczaj, John A., University of Wisconsin, Green Bay
Luhmann, Andrew J., Wheaton College
Lutz, Alexandra, University of Nevada, Reno
Lyons, William B., Ohio State University
Mabee, Stephen B., Massachusetts Geological Survey
Mace, Robert, Texas State University
MacNish, Robert, University of Arizona
Macpherson, Gwendolyn L., University of Kansas
Maharjan, Madan, University of North Carolina, Pembroke
Makkawi, Mohammad, King Fahd University of Petroleum and Minerals
Malzone, Jonathan, Eastern Kentucky University
Mamer, Ethan, New Mexico Institute of Mining and Technology
Manda, Alex K., East Carolina University
Mannix, Devin, University of Illinois
Marino, M. A., University of California, Davis
Martel, Richard, Universite du Quebec
Martínez, Pedro, Univ Complutense de Madrid
Mastropaolo, Carl, Drexel University
Matyjasik, Marek, Weber State University
May, James, Mississippi State University
Mayer, James R., University of West Georgia
Mayo, Alan L., Brigham Young University
McCurdy, Maureen, Louisiana Tech University
McKenzie, Jeffrey M., McGill University
McKinney, Mac, Geological Survey of Alabama
Mendoza, Carl, University of Alberta
Mendoza, Carl A., University of Alberta
Metesh, John J., Montana Tech of The University of Montana
Meyer, Jessica R., University of Iowa
Michael, Holly A., University of Delaware
Michel, Fred A., Carleton University
Milewski, Adam, University of Georgia
Miller, Marvin R., Montana Tech of The University of Montana
Misra, Debsmita, University of Alaska, Fairbanks
Mitchell, Robert J., Western Washington University
Moline, Gerilynn R., Oak Ridge National Laboratory
Montero, Esperanza, Univ Complutense de Madrid
Montgomery, William W., New Jersey City University

Moore, Michael E., DCNR- Pennsylvania Bureau of Geological Survey
Moortgat, Joachim, Ohio State University
Moran, Jean E., California State University, East Bay
Moss, Neil E., Geological Survey of Alabama
Moysey, Stephen M., Clemson University
Muldoon, Maureen A., University of Wisconsin, Oshkosh
Murdoch, Lawrence C., Clemson University
Murgulet, Dorina, Texas A&M University, Corpus Christi
Murray, Kent S., University of Michigan, Dearborn
Murray, Kyle E., University of Oklahoma
Nadiri, Ata Allah, University of Tabriz
Narasimhan, T. N., University of California, Berkeley
Naylor, Shawn C., Indiana University
Naymik, Thomas G., Ohio State University
Nedunuri, Krishna K., Central State University
Nelson, Craig, Ohio Dept of Natural Resources
Neuman, Shlomo P., University of Arizona
Newcomer, Darrell R., Pacific Northwest National Laboratory
Newton, Brad T., New Mexico Institute of Mining and Technology
Nguyen, Lam V., Hanoi University of Mining & Geology
Nichol, Craig F., University of British Columbia, Okanagan Campus
Nicot, Jean-Philippe, Univ of Texas at Austin, Jackson Sch of Geosciences
Nkotagu, Hudson H., University of Dar es Salaam
Noonan, Mathew T., South Dakota Dept of Env and Natural Resources
O'Brien, Arnold L., University of Massachusetts, Lowell
O'Brien, Rachel, Allegheny College
O'Reilly, Andrew M., University of Mississippi
Oberdorfer, June A., San Jose State University
Ogard, Allen E., Los Alamos National Laboratory
Olabode, Franklin O., Federal University of Technology, Akure
Olafsen-Lackey, Susan, Unversity of Nebraska, Lincoln
Oliveira, Alcino S., Unive de Trás-os-Montes e Alto Douro
Olyphant, Greg A., Indiana University, Bloomington
Ophori, Duke U., Montclair State University
Opper, Carl, Saint Petersburg College, Clearwater
Ortega, Adrian, Univ Nacional Autonoma de Mexico
Osborn, Stephen G., California State Polytechnic University, Pomona
Owoseni, Joshua O., Federal University of Technology, Akure
Ozsvath, David L., University of Wisconsin, Stevens Point
Pan, Feifei, University of North Texas
Paniconi, Claudio, Universite du Quebec
Paradis, Charles, University of Wisconsin, Milwaukee
Parizek, Richard R., Pennsylvania State University, University Park
Parkin, Gary, University of Guelph
Parsen, Mike J., University of Wisconsin, Madison, Division of Extension
Patton, Thomas W., Montana Tech of The University of Montana
Paul, Jonathan, Royal Holloway University of London
Pederson, Darryll T., University of Nebraska, Lincoln
Peters, Catherine A., Princeton University
Peterson, Eric W., Illinois State University
Peterson, Holly, Guilford College
Pfannkuch, Hans O., University of Minnesota, Twin Cities
Phillips, Fred M., New Mexico Institute of Mining and Technology
Pleasants, Mark S., Ohio Dept of Natural Resources
Pociask, Geoff, Illinois State Geological Survey
Pohll, Greg, University of Nevada, Reno
Post, Vincent , Flinders University
Prestegaard, Karen L., University of Maryland
Price, Rene, Florida International University
Puente-Muniz, Carlos Francisco, Univ Autonoma de San Luis Potosi
Puleo, Jack, University of Delaware
Quinn, John, Argonne National Laboratory
Raab, James, Ohio Dept of Natural Resources
Rains, Mark C., University of South Florida
Rauch, Henry W., West Virginia University
Reese, Stuart O., DCNR- Pennsylvania Bureau of Geological Survey
Reeve, Andrew S., University of Maine
Reeves, Donald Matthew M., Western Michigan University
Reichard, James S., Georgia Southern University
Reiten, Jon C., Montana Tech of The University of Montana
Remenda, Victoria H., Queen's University
Remson, Irwin, Stanford University
Riemersma, Peter E., Grand Valley State University
Rios-Sanchez, Miriam, Bemidji State University
Ritzi, Jr., Robert W., Wright State University
Robbins, Gary A., University of Connecticut
Robertson, Wendy, Central Michigan University
Robertson, Will, University of Waterloo
Roman, Eric W., New Jersey Geological and Water Survey
Romanowicz, Edwin A., SUNY, Plattsburgh
Ronayne, Michael J., Colorado State University
Rose, Seth E., Georgia State University
Rostron, Benjamin J., University of Alberta
Rotz, Rachel, Florida Gulf Coast University
Rouleau, Alain, Universite du Quebec a Chicoutimi
Royo-Ochoa, Miguel, Univ Autonoma de Chihuahua
Russo, Tess A., Pennsylvania State University, University Park
Ryan, Cathy, University of Calgary
Saffer, Demian M., Pennsylvania State University, University Park
Saint, Prem K., California State University, Fullerton
Salvage, Karen M., Binghamton University
Samuelson, Alan C., Ball State University
Sanders, Laura L., Northeastern Illinois University
Sanford, William E., Colorado State University
Sasowsky, Ira D., University of Akron
Sawyer, Audrey , Ohio State University
Scanlon, Bridget R., Univ of Texas at Austin, Jackson Sch of Geosciences
Scheidt, Brian, Mineral Area College
Schincariol, Robert A., Western University
Schlosser, Peter, Columbia University
Schmitz, Darrel W., Mississippi State University
Schreiber, Madeline E., Virginia Polytechnic Institute & State University
Schueth, Christoph, Technische Universitaet Darmstadt
Schulmeister, Marcia K., Emporia State University
Schulze-Makuch, Dirk, Washington State University
Schwartz, Frank W., Ohio State University
Scott, Christopher A., University of Arizona
Sebol, Lesley, Colorado Geological Survey
Sedivy, Robert A., Argonne National Laboratory
Sedivy, Robert, Argonne National Laboratory
Sendlein, Lyle V. A., University of Kentucky
Seyoum, Wondwosen M., Illinois State University
Shanafield, Margaret, Flinders University
Shang, Congxiao, University of East Anglia
Shaw, Glenn D., Montana Tech of the University of Montana
Sheldon, Amy L., SUNY, Geneseo
Shevenell, Lisa, University of Nevada, Reno
Shim-Chim, Richard, New Jersey Geological and Water Survey
Shimada, Jun, Kumamoto University
Sibray, Steven S., Unversity of Nebraska, Lincoln
Siegel, Donald I., Syracuse University
Simmons, Craig, Flinders University
Simpkins, William W., Iowa State University of Science & Technology
Simsek, Sakir, Hacettepe University
Singha, Kamini, Colorado School of Mines
Skalbeck, John D., University of Wisconsin, Parkside
Smith, J. Leslie, University of British Columbia
Smith, James E., McMaster University
Smith, James E., University of Arizona
Smith, Karen, Argonne National Laboratory
Soll, Wendy E., Los Alamos National Laboratory
Solomon, Douglas K., University of Utah
Soltanian, Reza, University of Cincinnati
Spayd, Steven E., New Jersey Geological and Water Survey
Spinelli, Glenn, New Mexico Institute of Mining and Technology
Springer, Abraham E., Northern Arizona University
Stafford, Kevin W., Stephen F. Austin State University
Staley, Andrew W., Maryland Department of Natural Resources
Stotler, Randy, University of Kansas
Strack, Otto D., University of Minnesota, Twin Cities
Sturgis, Laila, New Mexico Institute of Mining and Technology
Sudicky, Edward A., University of Waterloo
Suen, C. J., Fresno State University
Sukop, Michael C., Florida International University
Sullivan Graham, Jeri, New Mexico Institute of Mining and Technology
Sun, Hongbing, Rider University
Suter, Simeon, DCNR- Pennsylvania Bureau of Geological Survey
Sutherland, Mary K., Montana Tech of The University of Montana
Swanson, Susan K., Beloit College
Szilagyi, Jozsef, University of Nebraska, Lincoln
Tabidian, M. Ali, California State University, Northridge
Taboga, Karl, Wyoming State Geological Survey

Tagne, Gilles V., Wheaton College
Tauxe, John D., Oak Ridge National Laboratory
Taylor, Charles J., University of Kentucky
Tellam, John H., University of Birmingham
Tezcan, Levent, Hacettepe University
Therrien, Rene, Universite Laval
Thomason, Jason F., Illinois State Geological Survey
Tick, Geoffrey, University of Alabama
Tidwell, Vincent C., New Mexico Institute of Mining and Technology
Tijani, Moshood N., University of Ibadan
Tilton, Eric E., University of Colorado
Timmons, Stacy, New Mexico Institute of Mining and Technology
Tompson, Andrew F., Lawrence Livermore National Laboratory
Toran, Laura, Temple University
Tóth, József, University of Alberta
Totsche, Kai U., Friedrich-Schiller-University Jena
Tucker, Carla M., Lamar University
Tyler, Scott W., University of Nevada, Reno
Unger, Andre, University of Waterloo
Valerio, Mitch, Ohio Dept of Natural Resources
Van Der Hoven, Steve, Illinois State University
Van der Kamp, Garth, University of Waterloo
van der Velde, Ype, Vrije Universiteit Amsterdam
VanDerwerker, Tiffany J., Maryland Department of Natural Resources
Veeger, Anne I., University of Rhode Island
Veeger, Anne, University of Rhode Island
Vengosh, Avner, Duke University
Vesper, Dorothy, West Virginia University
Wallace, Janae, Utah Geological Survey
Walraevens, Kristine E., Ghent University
Walter, Julien, Universite du Quebec a Chicoutimi
Walton, Nick, University of Portsmouth
Wang, Dong, Fresno State University
Waren, Kirk B., Montana Tech of The University of Montana
Wassenaar, Len, University of Saskatchewan
Watson, David B., Oak Ridge National Laboratory
Weissmann, Gary S., University of New Mexico
Welby, Charles W., North Carolina State University
Werner, Adrian , Flinders University
Wheatcraft, Steve, University of Nevada, Reno
Wheaton, John R., Montana Tech of The University of Montana
Whiting, Duane L., University of Utah
Wicks, Carol M., Louisiana State University
Widdowson, Mark A., Virginia Polytechnic Institute & State University
Wilcox, Jeffrey D., University of North Carolina, Asheville
Wilson, Alicia M., University of South Carolina
Wilson, John L., New Mexico Institute of Mining and Technology
Wilson, Lorne G., University of Arizona
Wilson, Steven D., University of Illinois
Wolaver, Brad, University of Texas, Austin
Wolfsberg, Andrew V., Los Alamos National Laboratory
Woods, Juliette, University of South Australia
Yan, Eugene, Argonne National Laboratory
Yang, Changbing, University of Texas, Austin
Yang, Jianwen, University of Windsor
Yelderman, Jr., Joe C., Baylor University
YEO, MYEONG-HO (CHRIS), University of Guam
Yidana, Sandow M., University of Ghana
Yüce, Galip, Hacettepe University
Zarnetske, Jay, Michigan State University
Zhan, Hongbin, Texas A&M University
Zhang, Pengfei, City College (CUNY)
Zhang, You-Kuan, University of Iowa
Zheng, Chunmiao, University of Alabama
Ziegler, Brady A., Trinity University
Zimmer, Margaret, University of California, Santa Cruz
Zlotnik, Vitaly A., University of Nebraska, Lincoln
Zouhri, Lahcen, Institut Polytechnique LaSalle Beauvais (ex-IGAL)
Zreda, Marek G., University of Arizona
Özyurt, Nur N., Hacettepe University

Quantitative Hydrology

Benson, David A., Colorado School of Mines
Berghuijs , Wouter, Vrije Universiteit Amsterdam
Birdsell, Kay H., Los Alamos National Laboratory
Bywater-Reyes, Sharon, University of Northern Colorado
Carroll, Rosemary, University of Nevada, Reno
Chebana, Fateh, Universite du Quebec
Chen, Xun-Hong, Unversity of Nebraska, Lincoln
Covington, Matthew, University of Arkansas, Fayetteville
Danko, George, University of Nevada, Reno
Dingman, S. Lawrence, University of New Hampshire
Donovan, Joseph J., West Virginia University
Duckstein, Lucien, University of Arizona
Dymond, Randel, Virginia Polytechnic Institute & State University
Evans, David G., Sacramento State University
Falta, Ronald W., Clemson University
Florea, Lee J., Indiana University
Flores, Alejandro N., Boise State University
French, Mark A., New Jersey Geological and Water Survey
Frind, Emil O., University of Waterloo
Gillham, Robert W., University of Waterloo
Gupta, Hoshin V., University of Arizona
Harpold, Adrian, University of Nevada, Reno
Hermance, John F., Brown University
Hoffman, Jeffrey L., New Jersey Geological and Water Survey
Holt, Robert M., University of Mississippi
Hubbart, Jason A., West Virginia University
Hughes, Denis, Rhodes University
Kandiah, Ramanitharan, Central State University
Kiem, Anthony, University of Newcastle
Letsinger, Sally L., Indiana University
Li, Dan, Boston University
Looney, Brian, Clemson University
Maddock, III, Thomas, University of Arizona
Martin-Hayden, James, University of Toledo
Meko, David M., University of Arizona
Michaud, Jene D., University of Hawai'i, Hilo
Pacheco, Fernando A., Unive de Trás-os-Montes e Alto Douro
Pangle, Luke, Georgia State University
Parashar, Rishi, University of Nevada, Reno
Park, Young-Jin, University of Waterloo
Perkins, Robert B., Portland State University
Pollyea, Ryan M., Virginia Polytechnic Institute & State University
Puente, Carlos E., University of California, Davis
Quinn, John J., Argonne National Laboratory
Ravi, Sujith, Temple University
Reinhold, Ann Marie, Montana State University
Restrepo, Jorge I., Florida Atlantic University
Rudolph, David L., University of Waterloo
Salvucci, Guido D., Boston University
Schumer, Rina, University of Nevada, Reno
Sharp, Jr., John M., University of Texas, Austin
Sipos, György, Univesity of Szeged
Spellman, Patricia, University of South Florida
Springer, Everett P., Los Alamos National Laboratory
Stockton, Charles W., University of Arizona
Szilagyi, Jozsef, Unversity of Nebraska, Lincoln
Telyakovskiy, Aleksey S., University of Nevada, Reno
Thorbjarnarson, Kathryn W., San Diego State University
Travis, Bryan J., Los Alamos National Laboratory
Verdon-Kidd, Danielle, University of Newcastle
Vitale, Sarah A., University of Wisconsin, Eau Claire
Wallis, Ilka, Flinders University
Wei, Xiaohua (Adam), University of British Columbia, Okanagan Campus
Whitman, Brian E., Wilkes University
Yeh, Tian-Chyi J., University of Arizona
Zhang, Yong, University of Alabama

Surface Waters

Acharya, Kumud, University of Nevada, Reno
Aitkenhead-Peterson, Jacqueline A., Texas A&M University
Aryal, Niroj, North Carolina Agricultural & Tech State University
Bacon, Robert, Missouri Dept of Natural Resources
Bauer, Carl J., University of Arizona
Bearden, Rebecca A., Geological Survey of Alabama
Benavides, Jude, University of Texas, Rio Grande Valley
Bevelhimer, Mark, Oak Ridge National Laboratory
Beyer, Patricia J., Bloomsburg University
Blanken, Peter D., University of Colorado
Blersch, Stacey S., Columbus State University
Blumentritt, Dylan, Winona State University

Cadol, Daniel, New Mexico Institute of Mining and Technology
Chandra, Sudeep, University of Nevada, Reno
Christian, Alan D., University of Massachusetts, Boston
Clark, Robert A., University of Arizona
D'Alpaos, Andrea, Università degli Studi di Padova
Demchak, Jennifer, Mansfield University
Dennett, Keith E., University of Nevada, Reno
Doran, Peter T., University of Illinois at Chicago
Du Charme, Charles, Missouri Dept of Natural Resources
Duan, Shuiwang, University of Maryland
Durand, Michael T., Ohio State University
Franek, Benjamin, Bloomsburg University
Franz, Kristie, Iowa State University of Science & Technology
Goodrich, David C., University of Arizona
Grable, Judy, Valdosta State University
Grant, Stanley, Virginia Polytechnic Institute & State University
Gulliver, John S., University of Minnesota, Twin Cities
Hamlet, Alan, University of Notre Dame
Harris, Randa R., University of West Georgia
Hasan, Khaled W., Austin Community College District
Hawkins, R. B., University of Arizona
Helz, George, University of Maryland
Hester, Erich, Virginia Polytechnic Institute & State University
Ince, Simon, University of Arizona
Julian, Jason, Texas State University
Kindelman, Julie, University of Wisconsin, Parkside
Kisila, Ben O., University of Mary Washington
Kunza, Lisa, South Dakota School of Mines & Technology
Lancaster, Stephen, Oregon State University
Lansey, Kevin E., University of Arizona
Ledford, Sarah, Georgia State University
Lund, Jay R., University of California, Davis
Maneta, Marco, University of Montana
Mayfield, Michael W., Appalachian State University
McGregor, Stuart W., Geological Survey of Alabama
McIsaac, Gregory F., University of Illinois, Urbana-Champaign
Meitzen, Kimberly, Texas State University
Neukrug, Howard, University of Pennsylvania
Noe, Garry, Virginia Wesleyan College
Pociask, Geoffrey , University of Illinois
Pradhanang, Soni M., University of Rhode Island
Rancan, Helen L., New Jersey Geological and Water Survey
Reichelt-Brushett, Amanda, Southern Cross University
Richard, Gigi A., Colorado Mesa University
Ridenour, Gregory D., Austin Peay State University
Riise, Gunnhild, Norwegian University of Life Sciences (NMBU)
Royer, Todd, Indiana University, Bloomington
Shuttleworth, W. James, University of Arizona
Smerdon, Ernest T., University of Arizona
Smith, Brianne, Brooklyn College (CUNY)
Smith, Erik, University of South Carolina
Smith, Laurence C., University of California, Los Angeles
Smith, Sean, University of Maine
Splinter, Dale, University of Wisconsin, Whitewater
Stieglitz, Marc, Georgia Institute of Technology
Strom, Kyle, Virginia Polytechnic Institute & State University
Swanson, Sherman, University of Nevada, Reno
Thomas, Rohrlack, Norwegian University of Life Sciences (NMBU)
Troch, Peter A., University of Arizona
Valdes, Juan B., University of Arizona
Van Meter, Kimberly, University of Illinois at Chicago
Wampler, Peter J., Grand Valley State University
Ward, Adam, Indiana University, Bloomington
Wilderman, Candie, Dickinson College
Zollweg, James A., SUNY, The College at Brockport

Geohydrology

Allen, Diana M., Simon Fraser University
Attinger, Sabine, Friedrich-Schiller-University Jena
Baedke, Steven J., James Madison University
Beddows, Patricia A., Northwestern University
Burkart, Michael R., Iowa State University of Science & Technology
Castro, Maria Clara, University of Michigan
Chavez-Rodriguez, Adolfo, Univ Autonoma de Chihuahua
Chormann, Jr., Frederick H., New Hampshire Geological Survey
Clair, Thomas A., Mount Allison University
Constantine, Jose, Cardiff University
Cooper, Clay A., University of Nevada, Reno
Crews, Jeff, Missouri Dept of Natural Resources
Daanen, Ronald P., Alaska Division of Geological & Geophysical Surveys
De Luca, Domenico Antonio, Università di Torino
Deuerling, Kelly, University of Wisconsin, Green Bay
Dowd, John F., University of Georgia
Drake, Lon D., University of Iowa
Duley, James W., Missouri Dept of Natural Resources
Fogg, Graham E., University of California, Davis
Gamage, Kusali R., Austin Community College District
Gartner, Janette, Bentley University
Gierke, John S., Michigan Technological University
Haile, Estifanos, University of Tennessee, Knoxville
Hong, Sung-ho, Murray State University
Hyndman, David W., Michigan State University
Jones, Stephen C., Geological Survey of Alabama
Katzman, Danny, Los Alamos National Laboratory
Khanbilvardi, Reza M., Graduate School of the City University of New York
Knight, Rosemary J., Stanford University
Koch, Magaly, Boston University
Land, Lewis, New Mexico Institute of Mining and Technology
Lauer, Rachel, University of Calgary
Leap, Darrell I., Purdue University
Liu, Gaisheng, University of Kansas
Lovell, Mark D., Brigham Young University - Idaho
Lupankwa, Mlindelwa , Tshwane University of Technology
Marszalek, Henryk, University of Wroclaw
Mathias, Simon, Durham University
Mayer, Alex S., Michigan Technological University
McIntosh, Jennifer, University of Arizona
McKay, Larry D., University of Tennessee, Knoxville
McKenna, Thomas E., University of Delaware
Mount, Gregory, Indiana University of Pennsylvania
Ng, Crystal, University of Minnesota, Twin Cities
Noyes, Joanne M., South Dakota Dept of Env and Natural Resources
Oshun, Jasper, Humboldt State University
Person, Mark A., New Mexico Institute of Mining and Technology
Raymond, Jasmin, Universite du Quebec
Rayne, Todd W., Hamilton College
Reboulet, Edward, University of Kansas
Rovey, Charles W., Missouri State University
Sargent, Kenneth A., Furman University
Simonis, Jean, University of Zululand
Sushama, Laxmi, Universite du Quebec a Montreal
Torres, Raymond, University of South Carolina
Wang, Lixin, Indiana University - Purdue University Indianapolis
White, Mark D., Pacific Northwest National Laboratory
Zhang, Ye, University of Wyoming

Materials Transport

Pham van Bang, Damien, Universite du Quebec
Troy, Marleen, Wilkes University

SOIL SCIENCE

Soil Physics/Hydrology

Amoozegar, Aziz, North Carolina State University
Anderson, Stephen H., University of Missouri
Arnone, John J., University of Nevada, Reno
Baker, John M., University of Minnesota, Twin Cities
Berli, Marcus, University of Nevada, Reno
Black, T. Andrew, University of British Columbia
Bland, William L., University of Wisconsin, Madison
Boast, Charles W., University of Illinois, Urbana-Champaign
Brown, Sandra, University of British Columbia
Børresen, Trond , Norwegian University of Life Sciences (NMBU)
Caldwell, Todd, University of Texas, Austin
Casey, Francis, North Dakota State University
Cassel, Donald K., North Carolina State University
Cushman, John, Purdue University
Ellsworth, Timothy R., University of Illinois, Urbana-Champaign
Fermanich, Kevin J., University of Wisconsin, Green Bay
Feyereisen, Gary, University of Minnesota, Twin Cities
Flury, Markus, Washington State University
Fritton, Daniel D., Pennsylvania State University, University Park

Galbraith, John M., Virginia Polytechnic Institute & State University
Grattan, Stephen R., University of California, Davis
Groenevelt, Pieter H., University of Guelph
Gupta, Satish C., University of Minnesota, Twin Cities
Hook, James E., University of Georgia
Horton, Robert, Iowa State University of Science & Technology
Hutson, John , Flinders University
Jawitz, James W., University of Florida
Johnson, Mark S., University of British Columbia
Jones, Tim L., New Mexico State University, Las Cruces
Kakembo, Vincent, Nelson Mandela Metropolitan University
Kanemasu, Edward T., University of Georgia
Kang, James, University of Texas, Rio Grande Valley
Kirkham, Mary Beth, Kansas State University
Kluitenberg, Gerard J., Kansas State University
Knappenberger, Thorsten J., Auburn University
Kung, King-Jau S., University of Wisconsin, Madison
Lal, Rattan, Ohio State University
Lourenco, Sergio, Cardiff University
Lowery, Birl, University of Wisconsin, Madison
McCoy, Edward L., Ohio State University
McDonald, Eric, University of Nevada, Reno
McInnes, Kevin J., Texas A&M University
Molz, Fred, Clemson University
Moncrief, John F., University of Minnesota, Twin Cities
Morgan, Cristine L., Texas A&M University
Mulla, David J., University of Minnesota, Twin Cities
Neely, Haly L., Texas A&M University
Nkedi-Kizza, Peter, University of Florida
Nocco, Mallika, University of California, Davis
Norman, John M., University of Wisconsin, Madison
Papendick, Robert I., Washington State University
Perfect, Edmund, University of Tennessee, Knoxville
Persaud, Naraine, Virginia Polytechnic Institute & State University
Radcliffe, David E., University of Georgia
Reece, Julia S., Texas A&M University
Ressler, Daniel E., Susquehanna University
Rogowski, Andrew S., Pennsylvania State University, University Park
Sammis, Theodore W., New Mexico State University, Las Cruces
Scott, David F., University of British Columbia, Okanagan Campus
Selim, Hussein M., Louisiana State University
Sharma, Vasudha, University of Minnesota, Twin Cities
Simmons, F. William, University of Illinois, Urbana-Champaign
Spokas, Kurt, University of Minnesota, Twin Cities
Stone, Loyd, Kansas State University
Thomas, John, University of Florida
Venterea, Rodney T., University of Minnesota, Twin Cities
Wang, Zhi (Luke), Fresno State University
Warrick, Arthur W., University of Arizona
Welch, Steve M., Kansas State University
Wierenga, Peter J., University of Arizona
Wierenga, Peter J., University of Arizona
Yeh, Jim, University of Arizona
Young, Michael H., University of Texas, Austin
Youngs, Edward, Open University

Soil Chemistry/Mineralogy

Adriano, Domy C., Virginia Polytechnic Institute & State University
Adriano, Domy C., University of Georgia
Ahmad, Abd Rashid, University of Malaya
Alley, Marcus M., Virginia Polytechnic Institute & State University
Appel, Christopher (Chip) S., California Polytechnic State University
Artiola, Janick F., University of Arizona
Baligar, V. C., Virginia Polytechnic Institute & State University
Barak, Phillip W., University of Wisconsin, Madison
Basta, Nicholas T., Ohio State University
Bertsch, Paul M., University of Georgia
Blanchar, Robert W., University of Missouri
Bleam, William F., University of Wisconsin, Madison
Bloom, Paul R., University of Minnesota, Twin Cities
Bomke, Arthur A., University of British Columbia
Bostick, Benjamin C., Columbia University
Burke, Deborah S., Pacific Northwest National Laboratory
Callanan, Jennifer R., William Paterson University
Chirenje, Tait, Stockton University
Chorover, Jon, University of Arizona
Chorover, Jonathan, University of Arizona
Clark, Joanna, University of Reading
Collins, Chris, University of Reading
Crouse, David A., North Carolina State University
Curry, Joan E., University of Arizona
Donohue, Stephen J., Virginia Polytechnic Institute & State University
Dowdy, Robert H., University of Minnesota, Twin Cities
Dudley, Lynn M., Florida State University
Eckert, Donald J., Ohio State University
Eick, Matthew J., Virginia Polytechnic Institute & State University
Eivazi, Frieda, University of Missouri
Elzinga, Evert J., Rutgers, The State University of New Jersey, Newark
Engel, Richard E., Montana State University
Evangelou, V. P., Iowa State University of Science & Technology
Evanylo, Gregory K., Virginia Polytechnic Institute & State University
Fernandez, Fabian G., University of Minnesota, Twin Cities
Gamble, Audrey V., Auburn University
Gascho, Gary J., University of Georgia
Gaston, Lewis A., Louisiana State University
Ginder-Vogel, Matt, University of Wisconsin, Madison
Goos, Robert J., North Dakota State University
Goyne, Keith W., University of Missouri
Grandy, Stuart, University of New Hampshire
Guertal, Elizabeth A., Auburn University
Han, Nizhou, Virginia Polytechnic Institute & State University
Harris, Jr., Willie G., University of Florida
Harsh, James B., Washington State University
Hassett, John J., University of Illinois, Urbana-Champaign
Havlin, John L., North Carolina State University
He, Zhenli, University of Florida
Heil, Dean, New Mexico State University, Las Cruces
Helmke, Philip A., University of Wisconsin, Madison
Hemzacek Laukant, Jean M., Northeastern Illinois University
Hesterberg, Dean L., North Carolina State University
Hettiarachchi, Ganga, Kansas State University
Horwath, William R., University of California, Davis
Howe, Julie, Texas A&M University
Huluka, Gobena E., Auburn University
Inskeep, William P., Montana State University
Jaouich, Alfred, Universite du Quebec a Montreal
Jardine, Philip M., Oak Ridge National Laboratory
Jones, Robert L., University of Illinois, Urbana-Champaign
Kabengi, Nadine, Georgia State University
Kaiser, Daniel E., University of Minnesota, Twin Cities
Kissel, David E., University of Georgia
Komarneni, Sridhar, Pennsylvania State University, University Park
Koskinen, William C., University of Minnesota, Twin Cities
Krause, Samantha, Texas State University
Krogstad, Tore, Norwegian University of Life Sciences (NMBU)
Kuo, Shiou, Washington State University
Laird, David A., Iowa State University of Science & Technology
Lamb, John A., University of Minnesota, Twin Cities
Lee, Young Jae, Korea University
Lewis, Katie, Texas A&M University
Li, Yuncong, University of Florida
Ma, Lena Q., University of Florida
Malzer, Gary L., University of Minnesota, Twin Cities
Marinos, Richard, SUNY, Buffalo
Marion, Giles, Desert Research Institute
Massey, Michael S., California State University, East Bay
McCaslin, Bobby D., New Mexico State University, Las Cruces
McLaughlin, Richard A., North Carolina State University
Miao, Yuxin, University of Minnesota, Twin Cities
Miller, William P., University of Georgia
Moore, Duane M., University of New Mexico
Mowrer, Jake, Texas A&M University
Mullins, Gregory L., Virginia Polytechnic Institute & State University
Mulvaney, Richard L., University of Illinois, Urbana-Champaign
Mylavarapu, S R., University of Florida
Myneni, Satish C B., Princeton University
Nair, Vimala D., University of Florida
O'Connor, George A., University of Florida
Olson, Kenneth R., University of Illinois, Urbana-Champaign
Pagliari, Paulo H., University of Minnesota, Twin Cities
Parikh, Sanjai, University of California, Davis
Peck, Theodore R., University of Illinois, Urbana-Champaign

Peryea, Frank J., Washington State University
Pierzynski, Gary M., Kansas State University
Plank, Owen C., University of Georgia
Provin, Tony L., Texas A&M University
Quade, Jay, University of Arizona
Rehm, George W., University of Minnesota, Twin Cities
Reneau, Raymond B., Virginia Polytechnic Institute & State University
Robarge, Wayne P., North Carolina State University
Rosen, Carl J., University of Minnesota, Twin Cities
Russelle, Michael P., University of Minnesota, Twin Cities
Schmitt, Michael A., University of Minnesota, Twin Cities
Schwab, Paul, Texas A&M University
Segars, William P., University of Georgia
Seyfferth, Angelia L., University of Delaware
Shuman, Larry M., University of Georgia
Siebe Grabach, Christina D., Univ Nacional Autonoma de Mexico
Sims, Albert L., University of Minnesota, Twin Cities
Smyth, Thomas J., North Carolina State University
Spalding, Brian P., Oak Ridge National Laboratory
Strawn, Daniel G., University of Idaho
Stucki, Joseph W., University of Illinois, Urbana-Champaign
Szulczewski, Melanie, University of Mary Washington
Thien, Steve J., Kansas State University
Thompson, Michael L., Iowa State University of Science & Technology
Toor, Gurpal, University of Florida
Trumbore, Susan E., University of California, Irvine
Werts, Scott P., Winthrop University
Wilson, Melissa L., University of Minnesota, Twin Cities
Wright, Alan, University of Florida
Yildirim, Ismail, Firat University
Zelazny, Lucian W., Virginia Polytechnic Institute & State University

Pedology/Classification/Morphology

Anderson, James L., University of Minnesota, Twin Cities
Baker, James C., Virginia Polytechnic Institute & State University
Bell, James C., University of Minnesota, Twin Cities
Bettis III, E. A., University of Iowa
Bigham, Jerry M., Ohio State University
Birkeland, Peter W., University of Colorado
Burras, Lee, Iowa State University of Science & Technology
Calhoun, Frank G., Ohio State University
Ciolkosz, Edward J., Pennsylvania State University, University Park
Collins, Mary E., University of Florida
Cooper, Terence H., University of Minnesota, Twin Cities
Daniels, Walter L., Virginia Polytechnic Institute & State University
Darmody, Robert G., University of Illinois, Urbana-Champaign
Daugherty, LeRoy A., New Mexico State University, Las Cruces
Dere, Ashlee L., University of Nebraska, Omaha
Evans, Barry M., Pennsylvania State University, University Park
Ewing, Stephanie, Montana State University
Farsang, Andrea, Univesity of Szeged
Frederick, Holly, Wilkes University
Heck, Richard, University of Guelph
Hoover, Michael T., North Carolina State University
Hopkins, David G., North Dakota State University
Jacobs, Peter, University of Wisconsin, Whitewater
Jelinski, Nicolas, University of Minnesota, Twin Cities
Johnson-Maynard, Jodi, University of Idaho
Kleiss, Harold J., North Carolina State University
Kuzila, Mark S., Unversity of Nebraska, Lincoln
Lavkulich, Leslie M., University of British Columbia
Lindbo, David, North Carolina State University
Madison, Frederick W., University of Wisconsin, Madison
Mbila, Monday O., Alabama A&M University
McDaniel, Paul A., University of Idaho
McDonald, Eric, Desert Research Institute
McFadden, Leslie M., University of New Mexico
McGahan, Donald, Texas A&M University
McSweeney, Kevin, University of Wisconsin, Madison
Miles, Randall J., University of Missouri
Miller, Gerald A., Iowa State University of Science & Technology
Montagne, Cliff, Montana State University
Nater, Edward A., University of Minnesota, Twin Cities
Nielsen, Gerald A., Montana State University
Nordt, Lee C., Baylor University
Paz Gonzalez, Antonio, Coruna University
Petersen, Gary W., Pennsylvania State University, University Park
Post, Donald F., University of Arizona
Ransom, Michel D., Kansas State University
Ryder, Roy, University of South Alabama
Sandor, Jonathan A., Iowa State University of Science & Technology
Shaw, Joey N., Auburn University
Slater, Brian K., Ohio State University
Steele, Amber , Missouri Dept of Natural Resources
Taboada Castro, María T., Coruna University
Tabor, Neil J., Southern Methodist University
Thomas, Pamela J., Virginia Polytechnic Institute & State University
Turk, Judith, University of Nebraska, Lincoln
Tyler, E. Jerry, University of Wisconsin, Madison
Vepraskas, Michael J., North Carolina State University
Verburg, Paul, University of Nevada, Reno
West, Larry T., University of Georgia
Yoo, Kyungsoo, University of Minnesota, Twin Cities

Forest Soils/Rangelands/Wetlands

Amthor, Jeff, Oak Ridge National Laboratory
Andrus, Richard E., Binghamton University
Balster, Nick J., University of Wisconsin, Madison
Bauder, James W., Montana State University
Bockheim, James G., University of Wisconsin, Madison
Broome, Stephen W., North Carolina State University
Chambers, Jeanne, University of Nevada, Reno
Clark, Mark W., University of Florida
Clark, Melissa, Indiana University, Bloomington
Comerford, Nicholas B., University of Florida
David, Mark B., University of Illinois, Urbana-Champaign
Dietze, Michael, Boston University
Ferris, Dawn, Ohio State University
Fick, Walter H., Kansas State University
Franz, Eldon H., Washington State University
Gunderson, Lance, Emory University
Hallock, Brent G., California Polytechnic State University
Hook, Paul B., Montana State University
Inglett, Patrick, University of Florida
Kleindl, William, Montana State University
Krzic, Maja, University of British Columbia
Laingen, Christopher R., Eastern Illinois University
Meretsky, Vicky J., Indiana University, Bloomington
O'Neill, Patrick M., Louisiana State University
Osborne, Todd, University of Florida
Owensby, Clenton E., Kansas State University
Peres, Carlos, University of East Anglia
Posler, Gerry L., Kansas State University
Rains, Kai, University of South Florida
Riha, Susan, Cornell University
Robinson, Steve, University of Reading
Smalley, Glendon W., Sewanee: University of the South
Smith, C. Ken, Sewanee: University of the South
Smoak, Joseph (Donny), University of South Florida
Taskey, Ronald D., California Polytechnic State University
Torreano, Scott, Sewanee: University of the South
Wegner, John, Emory University

Soil Biology/Biochemistry

Allan, Deborah L., University of Minnesota, Twin Cities
Armstrong, Felicia P., Youngstown State University
Balser, Teri C., University of Wisconsin, Madison
Berry, Duane F., Virginia Polytechnic Institute & State University
Bezdicek, David F., Washington State University
Bird, Jeffrey, Queens College (CUNY)
Bird, Jeffrey, Graduate School of the City University of New York
Blum, Linda K., University of Virginia
Bollag, Jean-Marc, Pennsylvania State University, University Park
Burlage, Robert S., Oak Ridge National Laboratory
Cates, Anna, University of Minnesota, Twin Cities
Chanway, Christopher, University of British Columbia
Cheng, H. H., University of Minnesota, Twin Cities
Collins, Chris, University of Reading
Crozier, Carl, North Carolina State University
Davenport, Joan R., Washington State University
Dick, Richard P., Ohio State University
Dick, Warren A., Ohio State University
Dunfield, Kari, University of Guelph

Feng, Yucheng, Auburn University
Frey, Serita, University of New Hampshire
Fultz, Lisa M., Louisiana State University
Geisseler, Daniel, University of California, Davis
Gentry, Terry, Texas A&M University
Gerba, Charles P., University of Arizona
Gilliam, James W., North Carolina State University
Graham, Jr., James H., University of Florida
Graves, Alexandria, North Carolina State University
Grayston, Sue, University of British Columbia
Groffman, Peter, Brooklyn College (CUNY)
Gutknecht, Jessica L., University of Minnesota, Twin Cities
Hagedorn, Charles, Virginia Polytechnic Institute & State University
Hagedorn, Jake, University of North Carolina, Asheville
Harris, Glendon H., University of Georgia
Harris, Robin F., University of Wisconsin, Madison
Hartel, Peter G., University of Georgia
Hickey, William J., University of Wisconsin, Madison
Hladik, Christine, Georgia Southern University
Hoyt, Greg D., North Carolina State University
Ishii, Satoshi, University of Minnesota, Twin Cities
Israel, Daniel W., North Carolina State University
Jaffe, Peter R., Princeton University
Jastrow, Julie D., Argonne National Laboratory
Kennedy, Ann C., Washington State University
Knudsen, Guy, University of Idaho
Kremer, Robert J., University of Missouri
Lindemann, William C., New Mexico State University, Las Cruces
Lybrand, Rebecca A., University of California, Davis
Miller, Raymond M., Argonne National Laboratory
Molina, Jean-Alex E., University of Minnesota, Twin Cities
Morra, Matthew J., University of Idaho
Ogram, Andrew V., University of Florida
Oikawa, Patricia, California State University, East Bay
Osmond, Deanna L., North Carolina State University
Palumbo, Tony V., Oak Ridge National Laboratory
Pan, William L., Washington State University
Parker, David B., West Texas A&M University
Peacock, Caroline, University of Leeds
Pereira, Engil I., University of Texas, Rio Grande Valley
Phelps, Tommy J., Oak Ridge National Laboratory
Plante, Alain F., University of Pennsylvania
Prasad, Rishi, Auburn University
Prescott, Cindy, University of British Columbia
Ribbons, Relena R., Lawrence University
Rice, Chuck W., Kansas State University
Rodrigues, Jorge, University of California, Davis
Ruehr, Thomas A., California Polytechnic State University
Sadowsky, Michael J., University of Minnesota, Twin Cities
Scow, Kate M., University of California, Davis
Shaw, Liz, University of Reading
Shi, Wei, North Carolina State University
Silva, Lucas C., University of California, Davis
Simard, Suzanne, University of British Columbia
Smith, Jeffery L., Washington State University
Sogn, Trine, Norwegian University of Life Sciences (NMBU)
Somenhally, Anil, Texas A&M University
Stevens, Robert G., Washington State University
Thomas, Andrew D., University of Wales
Tolhurst, Trevor, University of East Anglia
Torrents, Alba, University of Maryland
Voroney, R. Paul, University of Guelph
Wagger, Michael G., North Carolina State University
Wenzel, Christopher, Eastern Wyoming College
Wilkie, Ann C., University of Florida

Paleopedology/Archeology

Beck, Colleen M., Desert Research Institute
Busacca, Alan J., Washington State University
Driese, Steven G., Baylor University
Driese, Steven G., University of Tennessee, Knoxville
Follmer, Leon R., University of Illinois, Urbana-Champaign
Herrmann, Edward W., Indiana University, Bloomington
Irmis, Randall B., University of Utah
Monger, H. C., New Mexico State University, Las Cruces
Terry, Dennis O., Temple University

Other Soil Science

Adamsen, Floyd, University of Arizona
Adee, Eric, Kansas State University
Bader, Nicholas E., Whitman College
Balser, Teri , University of Florida
Bell, Brian, University of Glasgow
Berg, Peter, University of Virginia
Bonczek, James, University of Florida
Brown, James R., University of Missouri
Budke, William, Ventura College
Bundy, Larry G., University of Wisconsin, Madison
Cabrera, Miguel L., University of Georgia
Cambardella, Cynthia, Iowa State University of Science & Technology
Ciampitti, Ignacio, Kansas State University
Claassen, Mark, Kansas State University
Claassen, Victor P., University of California, Davis
Coleman, Tommy L., Alabama A&M University
Contosta, Alexandra, University of New Hampshire
Cramer, Gary, Kansas State University
Cruse, Richard M., Iowa State University of Science & Technology
Dahlgren, Randy A., University of California, Davis
Daroub, Samira H., University of Florida
DeLaune, Paul, Texas A&M University
DeSutter, Tom, North Dakota State University
Dingus, Delmar D., California Polytechnic State University
Dormaar, John, University of Lethbridge
Dou, Fugen, Texas A&M University
Dougil, Andy, University of Leeds
Drescher, Andrew, University of Minnesota, Twin Cities
Duncan, Stewart, Kansas State University
Eberle, Bill, Kansas State University
Ebinger, Michael H., Los Alamos National Laboratory
Ehler, Stan, Kansas State University
Eppes, Martha C., University of North Carolina, Charlotte
Favorito, Jessica, Stockton University
Ferre, Paul (Ty), University of Arizona
Fjell, Dale, Kansas State University
Flores-Delgadillo, Maria L., Univ Nacional Autonoma de Mexico
Flores-Roman, David, Univ Nacional Autonoma de Mexico
Fritz, Allan, Kansas State University
Gale, Paula M., University of Tennessee, Martin
Gantzer, Clark J., University of Missouri
Geisseler, Daniel, University of California, Davis
Gerber, Stefan, University of Florida
Gordon, Barney, Kansas State University
Goss, Michael J., University of Guelph
Haag, Lucas, Kansas State University
Hall, III, John R., Virginia Polytechnic Institute & State University
Halverson, Larry, Iowa State University of Science & Technology
Hartshorn, Tony, Montana State University
Henning, Stanley J., Iowa State University of Science & Technology
Hernandez-Silva, Gilberto, Univ Nacional Autonoma de Mexico
Hochmuth, George J., University of Florida
Holman, John, Kansas State University
Hopmans, Jan W., University of California, Davis
Horwath, William R., University of California, Davis
Houlton, Ben, University of California, Davis
Inglett, Kanika Sharma, University of Florida
Jackson, Louise E., University of California, Davis
Jacobsen, Jeffrey, Montana State University
Janssen, Keith, Kansas State University
Jasoni, Richard, Desert Research Institute
Johnson, Arthur H., University of Pennsylvania
Johnson, Jane M., University of Minnesota, Twin Cities
Jones, Clain, Montana State University
Jones, Julia A., Oregon State University
Jugulam, Mithila, Kansas State University
Karkanis, Pano G., University of Lethbridge
Karlen, Douglas L., Iowa State University of Science & Technology
Kaspar, Thomas A., Iowa State University of Science & Technology
Keeney, Dennis R., Iowa State University of Science & Technology
Kelling, Keith A., University of Wisconsin, Madison
Killorn, Randy J., Iowa State University of Science & Technology
Kitchen, Newell R., University of Missouri
Kolka, Randall K., University of Minnesota, Twin Cities
Kramer, Marc, University of Florida

Kusssow, Wayne R., University of Wisconsin, Madison
Laboski, Carrie A., University of Wisconsin, Madison
Landschoot, Peter J., Pennsylvania State University, University Park
Lauzon, John, University of Guelph
Lerch, Robert N., University of Missouri
Liang, George, Kansas State University
Liebens, Johan, University of West Florida
Loutkova, Klavdia Oleschko, Univ Nacional Autonoma de Mexico
Loynachan, Thomas E., Iowa State University of Science & Technology
Mackowiak, Cheryl, University of Florida
Mallarino, Antonio W., Iowa State University of Science & Technology
Marrs, Rob, University of Liverpool
McBride, Raymond G., University of Guelph
Mengel, David, Kansas State University
Miller, Murray H., University of Guelph
Mills, Aaron L., University of Virginia
Min, Doo-Hong, Kansas State University
Mishra, Umakant, Argonne National Laboratory
Moorberg, Colby, Kansas State University
Moorman, Thomas B., Iowa State University of Science & Technology
Morgan, Kelly, University of Florida
Morris, Geoffrey, Kansas State University
Motavalli, Peter P., University of Missouri
Nelson, Nathan, Kansas State University
Norman, John M., University of Wisconsin, Madison
Nyhan, John W., Los Alamos National Laboratory
O'Geen, Toby A., University of California, Davis
O'Geen, Toby, University of California, Davis
O'Halloran, Ivan, University of Guelph
Obour, Augustine, Kansas State University
Obreza, Thomas A., University of Florida
Palacios-Mayorga, Sergio, Univ Nacional Autonoma de Mexico
Parikh, Sanjai, University of California, Davis
Pedersen, Joel A., University of Wisconsin, Madison
Perumal, Ram, Kansas State University
Peterson, Dallas, Kansas State University
Picardal, Flynn W., Indiana University, Bloomington
Polito, Thomas A., Iowa State University of Science & Technology
Powell, J. Mark, University of Wisconsin, Madison
Prasad, Vara , Kansas State University
Presley, DeAnn, Kansas State University
Qualls, Robert G., University of Nevada, Reno
Randall, Gyles W., University of Minnesota, Twin Cities
Rechcigl, John E., University of Florida
Reganold, John P., Washington State University
Regehr, David, Kansas State University
Rice, Pamela J., University of Minnesota, Twin Cities
Richards, James H., University of California, Davis
Richter, Daniel D., Duke University
Risk, Dave A., Saint Francis Xavier University
Rolston, Dennis E., University of California, Davis
Roozeboom, Kraig, Kansas State University
Roth, Gregory W., Pennsylvania State University, University Park
Ruark, Matthew D., University of Wisconsin, Madison
Ruiz-Diaz, Dorivar, Kansas State University
Santos, Eduardo, Kansas State University
Sartain, Jerry B., University of Florida
Sassenrath, Gretchen, Kansas State University
Schaap, Marcel, University of Arizona
Schapaugh, Bill T., Kansas State University
Schardt, Lawrence A., Pennsylvania State University, University Park
Schlegel, Alan, Kansas State University
Schumann, Arnold W., University of Florida
Scow, Kate, University of California, Davis
Sherwood, William C., James Madison University
Shoup, Doug, Kansas State University
Shroyer, Jim, Kansas State University
Shuford, James W., Alabama A&M University
Silveira, Maria, University of Florida
Silvertooth, Jeffrey C., University of Arizona
Sinclair, Hugh D., Edinburgh University
Sletten, Ronald S., University of Washington
Smith, Terry L., California Polytechnic State University
Smukler, Sean, University of British Columbia
Sohi, Sran P., Edinburgh University
Soldat, Douglas J., University of Wisconsin, Madison
Southard, Randal J., University of California, Davis
Stahlman, Phillip, Kansas State University
Stapleton, Michael G., Slippery Rock University
Stevens, W. G., University of Missouri
Strock, Jeffrey S., University of Minnesota, Twin Cities
Stubler, Craig, California Polytechnic State University
Szecsody, James E., Pacific Northwest National Laboratory
Tesso, Tesfaye, Kansas State University
Thompson, Curtis, Kansas State University
Tomlinson, Peter, Kansas State University
Tubana, Brenda S., Louisiana State University
Vanderlip, Richard, Kansas State University
Voss, Regis D., Iowa State University of Science & Technology
Walworth, James, University of Arizona
Wesley Wood, Charley, University of Florida
White, Jeffrey G., North Carolina State University
Whitney, D.A., Kansas State University
Wilson, P. Christopher, University of Florida
Woida, Kathleen, University of Iowa
Zhang, Guorong, Kansas State University

ENGINEERING GEOLOGY

General Engineering Geology

Abdalla, Salah B., University of Khartoum
Acevedo-Arroyo, Jose Refugio, Univ Autonoma de San Luis Potosi
Achampong, Francis, University of Ghana
Adams, Herbert G., California State University, Northridge
Ademeso, Anthony O., Federal University of Technology, Akure
Adeyemi, G. O., University of Ibadan
Ahmed, Muhammad F., University of Engineering and Technology
Aimone-Martin, Cathrine T., New Mexico Institute of Mining and Technology
Alao, D. A., University of Ilorin
Anderson, Andrew, Illinois State Geological Survey
Andre-Obayanju, Tomilola, University of Benin
Axelbaum, Richard, Washington University in St. Louis
Aydin, Adnan, University of Mississippi
Baptista, Joana, University of Newcastle Upon Tyne
Bauer, R. A., Illinois State Geological Survey
Bautista, Sonia, Univ Complutense de Madrid
Bell, David, University of Canterbury
Bell, John W., University of Nevada, Reno
Bennet, Brett, University of Kansas
Berry, Karen, Colorado Geological Survey
Beukelman, Gregg S., Utah Geological Survey
Biswas, Pratim, Washington University in St. Louis
Bonetto, Sabrina Maria Rita, Università di Torino
Bowman, Steve D., Utah Geological Survey
Brabham, Peter, University of Wales
Brady, Roland H., Fresno State University
Brand, Patrick, California Geological Survey
Branum, David, California Geological Survey
Breuninger, Tamara, Technical University of Munich
Brugger, Matthias, Technical University of Munich
Brunkal, Holly, Western Colorado University
Buchanan, George, Montgomery County Community College
Burns, Bill, Oregon Dept of Geology and Mineral Industries
Burns, Scott F., Portland State University
Buscheck, Thomas A., Lawrence Livermore National Laboratory
Carlson, Jill, Colorado Geological Survey
Carney, Theodore C., Los Alamos National Laboratory
Caron, Olivier J., Illinois State Geological Survey
Castleton, Jessica, Utah Geological Survey
Cato, Kerry, California State University, San Bernardino
Cetindag, Bahattin, Firat University
CHEGBELEH, Larry-Pax, University of Ghana
Choma-Moryl, Krystyna, University of Wroclaw
Davie, Colin, University of Newcastle Upon Tyne
Davies, David, Heriot-Watt University
Dawson, Tim, California Geological Survey
Delattre, Marc, California Geological Survey
dePolo, Craig M., University of Nevada, Reno
Doherty, Kevin, California Geological Survey
DuRoss, Christopher B., Utah Geological Survey
Dusseault, Maurice B., University of Waterloo
Eberhardt, Erik, University of British Columbia

Edil, Tuncer B., University of Wisconsin, Madison
Elia, Gaetano, University of Newcastle Upon Tyne
Erickson, Ben A., Utah Geological Survey
Evans, Stephen G., University of Waterloo
Eversoll, Duane A., Unversity of Nebraska, Lincoln
Faúndez, Alejandro, Univ Complutense de Madrid
Ferriz, Horacio, California State University, Stanislaus
Floris, Mario, Università degli Studi di Padova
Fournier, Benoit, Universite Laval
Fratta, Dante, University of Wisconsin, Madison
Fuller, Michael, California Geological Survey
Galgaro, Antonio, Università degli Studi di Padova
Gautam, Tej P., Marietta College
Giraud, Richard E., Utah Geological Survey
Greene, Brian M., Youngstown State University
Guiterrez, Carlos, California Geological Survey
Hall, Jean, University of Newcastle Upon Tyne
Haneberg, William, New Mexico Institute of Mining and Technology
Haneberg, William C., University of Kentucky
Harris, Will, California Geological Survey
Hasan, Syed E., University of Missouri, Kansas City
Haydon, Wayne, California Geological Survey
Hayhurst, Cheryl, California Geological Survey
Hencher, Steve, University of Leeds
Henika, William S., Virginia Polytechnic Institute & State University
Hernandez, Janis, California Geological Survey
Ho, I-Hsuan, University of North Dakota
Holland, Peter, California Geological Survey
Horns, Daniel, Utah Valley University
Hudec, Peter P., University of Windsor
Ibrahim, Ahmad Tajuddin Hj, University of Malaya
Idowu, Simeon O., Federal University of Technology, Akure
Ige, O. O., University of Ilorin
Jamaluddin, Tajul Anuar, University of Malaya
Jo, Ho Young, Korea University
Johnson, William P., University of Utah
Jones, Glenda, Keele University
Jones, Larry Allan, Los Alamos National Laboratory
Joyce, James, University of Puerto Rico
Karanfil, Tanju, Clemson University
Kavanaugh, Jeffrey, University of Alberta
Knapp, Richard B., Lawrence Livermore National Laboratory
Knizek, Martin, Masaryk University
Knudsen, Tyler R., Utah Geological Survey
Korre, Anna, Imperial College
Kreylos, Oliver, University of California, Davis
Krohn, James P., Los Angeles Pierce College
Kudlac, John J., Point Park University
Lancaster, Jeremy, California Geological Survey
Likos, William J., University of Wisconsin, Madison
Linares, Rogelio, Universitat Autonoma de Barcelona
Lindsay, Donald, California Geological Survey
Lindsey, Kassandra, Colorado Geological Survey
Linn, Rodman, Los Alamos National Laboratory
Locat, Jacques E., Universite Laval
Lokau, Katja R., Technical University of Munich
Longstreth, David, California Geological Survey
Lovekin, Jonathan, Colorado Geological Survey
Lund, William R., Utah Geological Survey
Lupogo, Keneth, University of Dar es Salaam
Madrigal-Rubio, Rafael, Univ Autonoma de Chihuahua
Mareschal, Maxime, California Geological Survey
Martel, Stephen J., University of Hawai'i, Manoa
Martin, Beth, Washington University in St. Louis
Masek, Ondrej, Edinburgh University
Mathewson, Christopher C., Texas A&M University
Matter, Juerg M., University of Southampton
McCoy, Kevin, Colorado Geological Survey
McCrink, Timothy P., California Geological Survey
McDonald, Gregory N., Utah Geological Survey
McMahon, Katherine, University of Wisconsin, Madison
Mena-Zambrano, Teodulo, Univ Autonoma de Chihuahua
Merifield, Paul M., University of California, Los Angeles
Merritt, Andrew, University of Plymouth
Mlinarevic, Ante, California Geological Survey
Moeglin, Thomas D., Missouri State University
Mogilevskaya, Sonia, University of Minnesota, Twin Cities
Moore, Jeffrey, University of Utah
Morales, Tomas, University of the Basque Country UPV/EHU
Morgan, Terrance L., Los Alamos National Laboratory
Nickmann, Marion, Technical University of Munich
Niemann, William L., Marshall University
Nieto, Alberto S., University of Illinois, Urbana-Champaign
O'Rourke, Thomas D., Cornell University
Ogunsanwo, O., University of Ilorin
Olson, Brian , California Geological Survey
Origlia, Hector D., Univ Nacional de Rio Cuarto
Oswald, John, California Geological Survey
Oyediran, I. A., University of Ibadan
Patrick, David M., University of Southern Mississippi
Perez, Florante, California Geological Survey
Perret, Didier H., Universite du Quebec
Pestrong, Raymond, San Francisco State University
Pipkin, Bernard W., University of Southern California
Poeter, Eileen P., Colorado School of Mines
Potter, Kenneth, University of Wisconsin, Madison
Poulton, Mary, University of Arizona
Pridmore, Cindy L., California Geological Survey
Rahn, Perry H., South Dakota School of Mines & Technology
Raj, John K., University of Malaya
Ramelli, Alan R., University of Nevada, Reno
Ramirez, Abelardo L., Lawrence Livermore National Laboratory
Rockaway, John D., Northern Kentucky University
Rodríguez, Martín Jesús, Univ Complutense de Madrid
Roffers, Pete, California Geological Survey
Roggenthen, William M., South Dakota School of Mines & Technology
Rosa, Carla, California Geological Survey
Rosinski, Anne, California Geological Survey
Rubin, Ron, California Geological Survey
Santi, Paul M., Colorado School of Mines
Sass, Ingo, Technische Universitaet Darmstadt
Savigny, K. Wayne, University of British Columbia
Schiff, Sherry L., University of Waterloo
Seitz, Gordon, California Geological Survey
Sellmeier, Bettina, Technical University of Munich
Shakoor, Abdul, Kent State University
Short, William, California Geological Survey
Silva, Michael A., California Geological Survey
Song, Lin-Ping, University of British Columbia
Sonnenwald, Margreta, Technical University of Munich
Spangler, Eleanor, California Geological Survey
Staub, William P., Oak Ridge National Laboratory
Stead, Douglas, Simon Fraser University
Stevens, De Anne S., Alaska Division of Geological & Geophysical Surveys
Swanson, Brian, California Geological Survey
Tester, Jefferson W., Cornell University
Thomas, Mark, University of Leeds
Thornburg, Jennifer, California Geological Survey
Thuro, Kurosch, Technical University of Munich
Tinjum, James M., University of Wisconsin, Madison
Tsige, Meaza, Univ Complutense de Madrid
Turner, A. Keith, Colorado School of Mines
Uriarte, Jesus Angel, University of the Basque Country UPV/EHU
Urzua, Alfredo, Boston College
Villeneuve, Marlene C., University of Canterbury
Vorosmarty, Charles, Graduate School of the City University of New York
Walton, Gabriel, Colorado School of Mines
Wang, Dongmei, University of North Dakota
Watts, Chester F., Radford University
Weigers, Mark, California Geological Survey
West, Olivia M., Oak Ridge National Laboratory
West, Terry R., Purdue University
White, Chase, California Geological Survey
White, Jonathan, Colorado Geological Survey
White, Owen L., University of Waterloo
Wilkey, Patrick L., Argonne National Laboratory
Williams, Bruce A., Pacific Northwest National Laboratory
Williams, John W., San Jose State University
Wu, Chin, University of Wisconsin, Madison
Yarbrough, Lance D., University of Mississippi
Yunwei, Sun, Lawrence Livermore National Laboratory
Zhou, Wendy W., Colorado School of Mines

Zimmerman, R. Eric, Argonne National Laboratory
Zyvoloski, George A., Los Alamos National Laboratory

Earthquake Engineering

Acosta, Jose G., Ctr de Invest Científica y de Ed Superior de Ensenada
Atkinson, Gail M., Carleton University
Heaton, Thomas H., California Institute of Technology
Huang, Moh J., California Geological Survey
Kutter, Bruce, University of California, Davis
Mendoza, Luis H., Ctr de Invest Científica y de Ed Superior de Ensenada
Michaels, Paul, Boise State University
Oommen, Thomas, Michigan Technological University
Reyes, Alfonso, Ctr de Invest Científica y de Ed Superior de Ensenada
Rowshandel, Badie, California Geological Survey
Swensen, Daniel, California Geological Survey
Wang, Yumei, Oregon Dept of Geology and Mineral Industries

Mining Tech/Extractive Metallurgy

Aguirre-Moriel, Socorro I., Univ Autonoma de Chihuahua
Bryan, Christopher, Exeter University
Coggan, John, Exeter University
Demopoulos, George, McGill University
Doyle, Fiona M., University of California, Berkeley
Duby, Paul F., Columbia University
Evans, James W., University of California, Berkeley
Feunstenau, Maurice, University of Nevada, Reno
Fuerstenau, Douglas W., University of California, Berkeley
Glass, Hylke J., Exeter University
Griswold, George B., New Mexico Institute of Mining and Technology
Gundiler, Ibrahim H., New Mexico Institute of Mining and Technology
Guthrie, Roderick I., McGill University
Hasan, Mainul, McGill University
Hiskey, J. Brent, University of Arizona
Hurtado de La Ree, Maria B B., Univ Estatal de Sonora
Jeffrey, Kip, Exeter University
Jonas, John J., McGill University
Khan, Latif A., Illinois State Geological Survey
Kinabo, Crispin P., University of Dar es Salaam
Lee, Jaeheon, University of Arizona
López, Maricela , Univ Estatal de Sonora
Mendoza-Aguilar, Hector M., Univ Autonoma de Chihuahua
Minor-Velazquez, Hector, Univ Autonoma de Chihuahua
Murguía-Romero, Christian A., Univ Estatal de Sonora
Murillo-Valenzuela, Hector O., Univ Estatal de Sonora
Nesbitt, Carl, University of Nevada, Reno
Ruiz-Cisneros, David H., Univ Autonoma de Chihuahua
Salazar- Avila, Arnulfo , Univ Estatal de Sonora
Santos-Munguia, Paula C., Univ Estatal de Sonora
Sastry, Kalanadh V. S., University of California, Berkeley
Seal, Thom, University of Nevada, Reno
Smith, Karl A., University of Minnesota, Twin Cities
Somasundaran, Ponisseril, Columbia University
Themelis, Nickolas J., Columbia University
Trevizo-Cano, Luis M., Univ Autonoma de Chihuahua
Wheeler, Paul, Exeter University
Yue, Stephen, McGill University

Mining Engineering

Bandopadhyay, Sukumar, University of Alaska, Fairbanks
Bessinger, Stephen, University of Utah
Boshkov, Stefan H., Columbia University
Brune, Jürgen F., Colorado School of Mines
Calizaya, Felipe, University of Utah
Chatterjee, Snehamoy, Michigan Technological University
Chen, Gang, University of Alaska, Fairbanks
Dagdelen, Kadri, Colorado School of Mines
Danko, George, University of Nevada, Reno
Dimitrakopoulos, Roussos, McGill University
Dinsmoor, John C., Los Alamos National Laboratory
Donovan, James, University of Utah
Durucan, Sevket, Imperial College
Eveleth, Robert W., New Mexico Institute of Mining and Technology
Foster, Patrick, Exeter University
Ganguli, Rajive, University of Alaska, Fairbanks
Hafez, Sabry ., University of Alaska, Fairbanks
Hassani, Ferri, McGill University
Honkaer, Rick, University of Kentucky
Ibarra-Dessens, Gonzalo de Jesus, Univ Estatal de Sonora
Kalia, Hemendra N., Los Alamos National Laboratory
Kaunda, Rennie, Colorado School of Mines
Kennedy, Gareth, Exeter University
Kim, Kwangmin, University of Arizona
Kohler, Jeffery L., Pennsylvania State University, University Park
Kovach, Richard G., Los Alamos National Laboratory
Kuchta, Mark, Colorado School of Mines
Liu, Shimin, Pennsylvania State University, University Park
Lusk, Braden , University of Kentucky
MANCA, Pierpaolo P., Universita di Cagliari
MASSACCI, Giorgio, Universita di Cagliari
Mayer, Ulrich, University of British Columbia
McCarter, Michael K., University of Utah
Meyer, Lewis, Exeter University
Miller, Hugh, Colorado School of Mines
Mitri, Hani, McGill University
Momayez, Moe, University of Arizona
Monteverde- Gutierrez, Gerardo, Univ Estatal de Sonora
Mousset-Jones, Pierre, University of Nevada, Reno
Navarro, Ricardo, Univ Nacional Autonoma de Mexico
Nelson, Michael G., University of Utah
Nieto Antunez, Antonio, Univ Nacional Autonoma de Mexico
Novak, Thomas, University of Kentucky
Petr, Vilem, Colorado School of Mines
Pokorny, Eugene W., Los Alamos National Laboratory
Silva-Castro, Jhon, University of Kentucky
Slistan- Grijalva, Angel, Univ Estatal de Sonora
Sottile, Jr., Joseph, University of Kentucky
Squelch, Andrew P., Curtin University
Taylor, Danny L., University of Nevada, Reno
Tenorio, Victor O., University of Arizona
Tharp, Thomas M., Purdue University
Vite-Picazo, Luis G., Univ Estatal de Sonora
Wala, Andrew M., University of Kentucky
Wane, Malcolm T., Columbia University
Wedding, William C., University of Kentucky
Wetherelt, Andrew, Exeter University
Whyatt, Jeffrey, University of Utah
Yegulalp, Tuncel M., Columbia University
Zavodni, Zavis, University of Utah
Zhang, Jinhong, University of Arizona
Zipf, Karl, Colorado School of Mines

Petroleum Engineering

Ahmed, Ramadan, University of Oklahoma
Alvarado, Vladimir, University of Wyoming
Badalyan, Alex, University of Adelaide
Bedrikovetski, Pavel, University of Adelaide
Bijeljic, Branko, Imperial College
Blasingame, Tom, Texas A&M University
Blunt, Martin J., Imperial College
Borazjani, Sara, University of Adelaide
Callard, Jeff, University of Oklahoma
Carageorgos, Themis, University of Adelaide
Civan, Faruk, University of Oklahoma
Cooper, George A., University of California, Berkeley
Corbett, Patrick, Heriot-Watt University
Couples, Gary, Heriot-Watt University
Devegowda, Deepak, University of Oklahoma
Dreesen, Donald S., Los Alamos National Laboratory
El-Monier, Ilham, University of Oklahoma
Fahes, Mashhad, University of Oklahoma
Falode, Olugbenga, University of Ibadan
Fisher, Quentin , University of Leeds
Frailey, Scott M., Illinois State Geological Survey
Geiger, Sebastian, Heriot-Watt University
Gonzalez-Perdomo, Maria, University of Adelaide
Gringarten, Alain, Imperial College
Haghighi, Manouchehr, University of Adelaide
Holubnyak, Yehven I., University of Kansas
Jamili, Ahmad, University of Oklahoma
Javadpour, Farzam, University of Texas, Austin
Jin, Guohai, Geological Survey of Alabama
Kadkhodai Ilkhchi, Ali, University of Tabriz
Kelkar, Sharad, Los Alamos National Laboratory

King, Peter, Imperial College
Knapp, Roy M., University of Oklahoma
Lorinczi, Piroska, University of Leeds
Ma, Jingsheng, Heriot-Watt University
Misra, Siddharth, University of Oklahoma
Moghanloo, Rouzbeh, University of Oklahoma
Muggeridge, Ann H., Imperial College
Nikolinakou, Maria-Aikaterini, University of Texas, Austin
Oppong, Issac A., University of Ghana
Patzek, Tad W., University of California, Berkeley
Pickup, Gillian E., Heriot-Watt University
Pournik, Maysam, University of Oklahoma
Rai, Chandra S., University of Oklahoma
Rose, Peter E., University of Utah
Sakhaee-Pour, Ahmad, University of Oklahoma
Salmachi, Alireza, University of Adelaide
Saramet, Mihai R., Alexandru Ioan Cuza
Sayyafzadeh, Mohammad, University of Adelaide
Shah, Subhash N., University of Oklahoma
Sharma, Suresh, University of Oklahoma
Singh, Kamaljit, Heriot-Watt University
Sondergeld, Carl H., University of Oklahoma
Teodoriu, Catalin, University of Oklahoma
Vesovic, Velisa, Imperial College
Wu, Xingru, University of Oklahoma
Zaman, Musharraf, University of Oklahoma
Zeinijahromi, Abbas, University of Adelaide

Rock Mechanics

Abousleiman, Younane, University of Oklahoma
Abu Bakar, Muhammad Z., University of Engineering and Technology
Agioutantis, Zach, University of Kentucky
Archambault, Guy, Universite du Quebec a Chicoutimi
Asbury, Brian, Colorado School of Mines
Aslan, Yasemin, Firat University
Barakat, Bassam, Institut Polytechnique LaSalle Beauvais (ex-IGAL)
Barzegari, Ghodrat, University of Tabriz
Blacic, James D., Los Alamos National Laboratory
Brahmi, Sadek, Institut Polytechnique LaSalle Beauvais (ex-IGAL)
Brake, Thomas L., Los Alamos National Laboratory
Brown, Donald W., Los Alamos National Laboratory
Chen, Rui, California Geological Survey
Cruden, David M., University of Alberta
Cundall, Peter A., University of Minnesota, Twin Cities
Daemen, Jaak, University of Nevada, Reno
Detournay, Emmanuel M., University of Minnesota, Twin Cities
Diederichs, Mark, Queen's University
Enderlin, Milton, Texas Christian University
Engelder, Terry, Pennsylvania State University, University Park
Ferrero, Anna Maria, Università di Torino
Germanovich, Leonid, Georgia Institute of Technology
Ghassemi, Ahmed, University of Oklahoma
Gordon, Robert B., Yale University
Gurocak, Zulfu, Firat University
Guzina, Bojan B., University of Minnesota, Twin Cities
Haimson, Bezalel C., University of Wisconsin, Madison
Hastie, Warwick W., University of KwaZulu-Natal
Jung, SJ, University of Idaho
Kanik, Mustafa, Firat University
Kemeny, John M., University of Arizona
Kim, Eunhye, Colorado School of Mines
Käsling, Heiko, Technical University of Munich
Labuz, Joseph F., University of Minnesota, Twin Cities
MacLaughlin, Mary M., Montana Tech of the University of Montana
Mariani, Elisabeth, University of Liverpool
Meredith, Philip, University College London
Mojtabai, Navid, New Mexico Institute of Mining and Technology
Nelson, Priscilla P., Colorado School of Mines
Onyeobi, Tony U., University of Benin
Oravecz, Kalman I., New Mexico Institute of Mining and Technology
Ozbay, M. Ugur, Colorado School of Mines
Pariseau, William G., University of Utah
Pec, Matej, Massachusetts Institute of Technology
Perry , Kyle, University of Kentucky
Persson, Per-Anders, New Mexico Institute of Mining and Technology
Prasad, Manika, Colorado School of Mines
Roegiers, Jean-Claude, University of Oklahoma
Rojas Hernandez, Sergio, Curtin University
Rutter, Ernest H., University of Manchester
Saeidi, Ali, Universite du Quebec a Chicoutimi
Sinha, Krishna P., University of Utah
Smutek, Claude, Universite de la Reunion
Sone, Hiroki, University of Wisconsin, Madison
Stockinger, Georg M., Technical University of Munich
Swift, Robert P., Los Alamos National Laboratory
Unrug, Kot F., University of Kentucky
Vinciguerra, Sergio Carmelo, Università di Torino
Watters, Robert J., University of Nevada, Reno
Wijesinghe, Ananda M., Lawrence Livermore National Laboratory
Zimmerman, Robert W., Imperial College

Ocean Engineering/Mining

Ajayi, J. O., Obafemi Awolowo University
Cambazoglu, Mustafa K., University of Southern Mississippi
Carpenter, Roy, University of Washington
Gibson, Carl H., University of California, San Diego
Hodgkiss, Jr., William S., University of California, San Diego
Hoopes, John A., University of Wisconsin, Madison
Irish, Jennifer, Virginia Polytechnic Institute & State University
Nootz, Gero, University of Southern Mississippi
Wen, Xianyun, University of Leeds

Geotechnical Engineering

Fernández, Luis Ramón, Univ Complutense de Madrid
Hingston, Egerton, University of KwaZulu-Natal
Insua, Juan Miguel, Univ Complutense de Madrid
Ortt, Jr., Richard A., Maryland Department of Natural Resources
Pascariu, Florentina, Alexandru Ioan Cuza
Sanchez, Marcelo J., Texas A&M University

Geological Engineering

Gardner, Michael H., University of Nevada, Reno
Garnier Villareal, Maximiliano, Univ de Costa Rica
Higgins, Jerry D., Colorado School of Mines
Katzenstein, Kurt W., South Dakota School of Mines & Technology
Melentijevic, Svetlana, Univ Complutense de Madrid
Potten, Martin, Technical University of Munich
Stetler, Larry D., South Dakota School of Mines & Technology

OCEANOGRAPHY

General Oceanography

Abernathy, Ryan, Columbia University
Allen, John, University of Portsmouth
Alves, Tiego, University of Wales
Asper, Vernon, University of Southern Mississippi
Barros, Tony, Miami-Dade College (Wolfson Campus)
Becker, Janet M., University of Hawai'i, Manoa
Bohaty, Steven, University of Southampton
Brandes, Jay, Georgia Institute of Technology
Brandon, Mark A., Open University
Brown, Erik T., University of Minnesota Duluth
Buchanan, Donald G., San Bernardino Valley College
Calder, Brian, University of New Hampshire
Chamberlin, William S., Fullerton College
Chandler, Cyndy, Woods Hole Oceanographic Institution
Ciannelli, Lorenzo, Oregon State University
Cooney, Michael, University of Hawai'i, Manoa
Curewitz, Daniel, Syracuse University
DeJesus, Roman, Fullerton College
Denton, George, University of South Florida
Dickens, Gerald R., Rice University
Dijkstra, Semme, University of New Hampshire
Dong, Charles, El Camino College
Falkowski, Paul G., University of Hawai'i, Manoa
Field, Richard T., University of Delaware
Florie, Joshua, Tulsa Community College
Fritsen, Christian H., University of Nevada, Reno
Froelich, Philip, Florida State University
Gomez, Natalya, McGill University
Gordon, Elizabeth S., Fitchburg State University
Grossman, Walter, San Bernardino Valley College
Hale, Michelle, University of Portsmouth

Heimbach, Patrick, University of Texas, Austin
Hepner, Tiffany, University of Texas at Austin, Jackson School of Geosciences
Herdendorf, Charles E., Ohio State University
Hickman, Anna, University of Southampton
Holland, Christina, University of Texas, Austin
Holliday, Joseph W., El Camino College
Horton, Radley, Columbia University
Hoyt, William H., University of Northern Colorado
Hughes-Clarke, John E., University of New Hampshire
Ivanovic, Ruza, University of Leeds
Johnson, Ashanti, University of Texas, Arlington
Johnson, Helen, University of Oxford
Judkins, Heather L., Saint Petersburg College, Clearwater
Jung, Simon, Edinburgh University
Keller, Klaus, Pennsylvania State University, University Park
Kerr, Andrew, University of Wales
Kim, Yong Hoon, West Chester University
King, Andrew, University of Illinois at Chicago
Kustka, Adam B., Rutgers, The State University of New Jersey, Newark
Laliberte, Elizabeth, University of Rhode Island
Lauderdale, Jonathan, University of Liverpool
Leach, Harry, University of Liverpool
Lear, Caroline, University of Wales
Ledbetter, Michael T., University of Arkansas at Little Rock
Lee, Alyce, Concord University
Lee, Dong, Columbia University
Lee, Stephen C., Los Angeles Pierce College
Leinen, Margaret, University of California, San Diego
Lenz, Petra H., University of Hawai'i, Manoa
Lindo Atachati, David, Graduate School of the City University of New York
Liu, Zhanfei, University of Texas, Austin
Ma, Yanxia, Louisiana State University
MacLeod, Chris, University of Wales
Maxwell, Arthur E., University of Texas, Austin
McPhaden, Michael J., University of Washington
McWilliams, James, University of California, Los Angeles
Min, Dong-Ha, University of Texas, Austin
Montenegro, Alvaro, Ohio State University
Moore, Dennis, University of Hawai'i, Manoa
Mosher, David C., University of New Hampshire
Muir, William, San Bernardino Valley College
Myers, Paul, University of Alberta
Noyes, Jim, El Camino College
Ogston, Andrea, University of Washington
Pearson, Jenna L., Princeton University
Peredo-Jaime, Jose I., Univ Autonoma de Baja California Sur
Perry, Malcolm, Curtin University
Pike, Jenny, University of Wales
Porter, Dwayne E., University of South Carolina
Quan, Tracy, Oklahoma State University
Radulski, Robert, Southern Connecticut State University
Rappe, Michael S., University of Hawai'i, Manoa
Roesler, Collin, Bowdoin College
Salisbury, Joseph, University of New Hampshire
Schlegel, Mary A., Millersville University
Schneider, Niklas, University of Hawai'i, Manoa
Schroeder, William W., Dauphin Island Sea Lab
Scott, Robert B., University of Texas, Austin
Seyfang, Gill, University of East Anglia
Spencer, Matthew, University of Liverpool
Steger, John M., Miami Dade College (Kendall Campus)
Sullivan-Watts, Barbara K., University of Rhode Island
Swanson, R. L., SUNY, Stony Brook
Thompson, LuAnne, University of Washington
Thomson, Richard, University of Victoria
Thurman, Harold V., Mt. San Antonio College
Tyrrell, Toby, University of Southampton
Ulanski, Stanley L., James Madison University
Veeramony, Jayaram, Mississippi State University
Venn, Cynthia, Bloomsburg University
Walker, Brett, University of Ottawa
Walker, Nan D., Louisiana State University
Wallace, William G., Graduate School of the City University of New York
Wang, Lei, Columbia University
Westervelt, Daniel, Columbia University
Wheatcroft, Rob, Oregon State University
Wiberg, Patricia L., University of Virginia
Wiesenburg, Denis A., University of Southern Mississippi
Williams, Ric, University of Liverpool
Wiltshire, John C., University of Hawai'i, Manoa
Wolcott, Ray, Cuyamaca College
Wolff, George, University of Liverpool
Wu, Yutian, Columbia University
Yeager, Lauren A., University of Texas, Austin
Yin, Jianjun, University of Arizona
Yon, Lisa, Palomar College
Zhai, Xiaoming, University of East Anglia

Biological Oceanography

Adams, Marshall, Oak Ridge National Laboratory
Adams, Michael S., University of Wisconsin, Madison
Algar, Christopher, Dalhousie University
Allam, Bassem, SUNY, Stony Brook
Allen, Eric E., University of California, San Diego
Aller, Josephine Y., SUNY, Stony Brook
Anderson, George C., University of Washington
Antoine, David, Curtin University
Apprill, Amy, Woods Hole Oceanographic Institution
Armbrust, Virginia E., University of Washington
Atkinson, Marlin J., University of Hawai'i, Manoa
Audet, Celine, Universite du Quebec a Rimouski
Auster, Peter, University of Connecticut
Azam, Farooq, University of California, San Diego
Baltz, Donald M., Louisiana State University
Banse, Karl, University of Washington
Barber, Bruce, University of South Florida
Barber, Richard T., Duke University
Barlow, Jay P., University of California, San Diego
Baross, John A., University of Washington
Bartlett, Douglas H., University of California, San Diego
Baumann, Hannes, University of Connecticut
Baumann, Zofia, University of Connecticut
Baumgartner, Mark, Dalhousie University
Benfield, Mark C., Louisiana State University
Benner, Ron, University of South Carolina
Bibby, Thomas, University of Southampton
Bienfang, Paul K., University of Hawai'i, Manoa
Biggs, Douglas C., Texas A&M University
Blake, Norman J., University of South Florida
Bloomfield, Helen, University of Liverpool
Boar, Rosalind, University of East Anglia
Bochdansky, Alexander, Old Dominion University
Bollens, Stephen, Washington State University
Boudrias, Michel A., University of San Diego
Bowen, Jennifer, University of Massachusetts, Boston
Bowser, Paul, SUNY, Stony Brook
Breitbart, Mya, University of South Florida
Brethes, Jean-Claude, Universite du Quebec a Rimouski
Briggs, John C., University of South Florida
Brownlee, Colin, University of Southampton
Bruno, Barbara, University of Hawai'i, Manoa
Bucklin, Ann, University of Connecticut
Burton, Ronald S., University of California, San Diego
Buskey, Edward J., University of Texas, Austin
Campbell, Lisa, Texas A&M University
Carlile, Amy L., University of New Haven
Carney, Robert S., Louisiana State University
Carpenter, Steve, University of Wisconsin, Madison
Carr, Mark, University of California, Santa Cruz
Case, James M., Wilkes University
Caswell, Bryony, University of Liverpool
Cerrato, Robert M., SUNY, Stony Brook
Checkley, David M., University of California, San Diego
Christian, James R., University of Victoria
Church, Matthew, University of Hawai'i, Manoa
Collie, Jeremy S., University of Rhode Island
Collier, Jackie, SUNY, Stony Brook
Collins, Kenneth, University of Southampton
Conover, David O., SUNY, Stony Brook
Copley, Jonathan, University of Southampton
Coull, Bruce, University of South Carolina
Cranford, Peter, Dalhousie University

Croll, Don, University of California, Santa Cruz
Cuba, Thomas, University of South Florida
Cuker, Benjamin E., Hampton University
Cullen, John J., Dalhousie University
D'Angelo, Maria C., University of Southampton
D'Elia, Christopher, University of South Florida
Daly, Kendra L., University of South Florida
Dam, Hans G., University of Connecticut
Davies, Andrew J., Bangor University
Dayton, Paul K., University of California, San Diego
Dean, John Mark, University of South Carolina
Demers, Serge, Universite du Quebec a Rimouski
Deming, Jody W., University of Washington
Denton, Gary R. W., University of Guam
DeWitt, Calvin B., University of Wisconsin, Madison
DiBacco, Claudio, Dalhousie University
Dieterle, Dwight A., University of South Florida
Dobbs, Fred C., Old Dominion University
Donaghay, Percy, University of Rhode Island
Doty, Thomas, Roger Williams University
Dower, John, University of Victoria
Drazen, Jeffrey C., University of Hawai'i, Manoa
Ducklow, Hugh, Columbia University
Duffy, Tara , Northeastern University
Dunton, Kenneth H., University of Texas, Austin
Durbin, Edward G., University of Rhode Island
Dyhrman, Sonya, Columbia University
Edgcomb, Virginia, Woods Hole Oceanographic Institution
Eggleston, David B., North Carolina State University
Epp, Leonard G., Mount Union College
Erbe, Christine, Curtin University
Erdner, Deana L., University of Texas, Austin
Erisman, Brad, University of Texas, Austin
Esbaugh, Andrew J., University of Texas, Austin
Falkowski, Paul G., Rutgers, The State University of New Jersey
Fast, Mark, SUNY, Stony Brook
Felbeck, Horst, University of California, San Diego
Feller, Robert, University of South Carolina
Fenberg, Phillip, University of Southampton
Fennel, Katja, Dalhousie University
Fisher, Jr., Thomas R., University of Maryland
Fisk, Aaron, University of Windsor
Fitzer, Susan, University of Glasgow
Fletcher, Madilyn, University of South Carolina
Fournier, Robert O., Dalhousie University
Francis, Robert, University of Washington
Frank, Kenneth, Dalhousie University
Franks, Peter J. S., University of California, San Diego
Frost, Bruce W., University of Washington
Fuiman, Lee A., University of Texas, Austin
Gaasterland, Terry, University of California, San Diego
Gallagher, Eugene, University of Massachusetts, Boston
Ganssen, Gerald M., Vrije Universiteit Amsterdam
Gardner, Wayne S., University of Texas, Austin
Gates, Ruth D., University of Hawai'i, Manoa
Gibson, Deidre M., Hampton University
Gifford, Dian J., University of Rhode Island
Gilbert, Patricia M., University of Maryland
Gobler, Christopher, SUNY, Stony Brook
Godbold, Jasmin A., University of Southampton
Goetze, Erica, University of Hawai'i, Manoa
Gomes, Helga, Columbia University
Gosselin, Michel, Universite du Quebec a Rimouski
Gould, Mark D., Roger Williams University
Graham, Linda K., University of Wisconsin, Madison
Graham, Michael, Moss Landing Marine Laboratories
Grant, Jonathan, Dalhousie University
Green, Jonathan, University of Liverpool
Greene, Charles H., Cornell University
Grigg, Richard W., University of Hawai'i, Manoa
Grottoli, Andrea G., Ohio State University
Grunbaum, Daniel, University of Washington
Hargraves, Paul E., University of Rhode Island
Hargreaves, Bruce R., Lehigh University
Harvey, James T., Moss Landing Marine Laboratories
Hastings, Philip A., University of California, San Diego
Hauton, Chris, University of Southampton
Hawkins, Lawrence, University of Southampton
Healey, Michael, University of British Columbia
Heil, Cynthia, University of South Florida
Hicks, David, University of Texas, Rio Grande Valley
Holland, Nicholas D., University of California, San Diego
Holt, Gloria J., University of Texas, Austin
Hood, Raleigh, University of Maryland
Hopkins, Thomas S., Dauphin Island Sea Lab
Hopkins, Thomas L., University of South Florida
Hotchkiss, Sarah, University of Wisconsin, Madison
Humm, Harold J., University of South Florida
Hunsucker, Kelli, Florida Institute of Technology
Hunt, Brian, University of British Columbia
Jeffries, H. Perry, University of Rhode Island
Jensen, Antony, University of Southampton
Jickells, Tim, University of East Anglia
Johnson, Kevin, Florida Institute of Technology
Jordan, Robert A., Hampton University
Juhl, Andrew, Columbia University
Jumars, Peter A., University of Washington
Juniper, Kim, University of Victoria
Kamykowski, Daniel, North Carolina State University
Kana, Todd M., University of Maryland
Karl, David M., University of Hawai'i, Manoa
Kaufmann, Ronald S., University of San Diego
Kelley, Christopher, University of Hawai'i, Manoa
Kelly, John, University of New Haven
Kemp, Paul, University of Hawai'i, Manoa
Kenney, Robert D., University of Rhode Island
Kimball, Matthew, University of South Carolina
Kirschenfeld, Taylor, University of West Florida
Kitchell, James F., University of Wisconsin, Madison
Kooyman, Gerald L., University of California, San Diego
Kraemer, George P., SUNY, Purchase
Krieger-Brockett, Barbara B., University of Washington
Lam, Phyllis, University of Southampton
Landry, Michael R., University of California, San Diego
LaRock, Paul A., Louisiana State University
Lee, Carol, University of Wisconsin, Madison
Leichter, James J., University of California, San Diego
Lessard, Evelyn J., University of Washington
Letelier, Ricardo, Oregon State University
Levin, Lisa A., University of California, San Diego
Levinton, Jeffrey, SUNY, Stony Brook
Lewin, Joyce C., University of Washington
Lewis, Alan G., University of British Columbia
Lewis, Marlon R., Dalhousie University
Li, William K., Dalhousie University
Lilley, Marvin D., University of Washington
Lin, Senjie, University of Connecticut
Logan, Alan, University of New Brunswick Saint John
Lohan, Maeve, University of Southampton
Longoria, Lorena, University of Texas, Rio Grande Valley
Lonsdale, Darcy J., SUNY, Stony Brook
Lopez, Glenn R., SUNY, Stony Brook
Lucas, Cathy, University of Southampton
MacIntyre, Hugh, Dalhousie University
Mackas, David L., University of Victoria
Mahegan, Mairead, Woods Hole Oceanographic Institution
Maldonado, Maria, University of British Columbia
Malin, Gill, University of East Anglia
Marra, John, Brooklyn College (CUNY)
Martiny, Adam, University of California, Irvine
Matassa, Catherine, University of Connecticut
McCarthy, James T., Harvard University
McCauley, Rob, Curtin University
McElroy, Anne E., SUNY, Stony Brook
McGlathery, Karen J., University of Virginia
McGlathery, Karen, University of Virginia
McGowan, John A., University of California, San Diego
McManus, George B., University of Connecticut
Mendelssohn, Irving A., Louisiana State University
Metaxas, Anna, Dalhousie University
Meylan, Anne, University of South Florida
Miller, Douglas C., University of Delaware

Mills, Eric L., Dalhousie University
Milroy, Scott P., University of Southern Mississippi
Mobley, Curtis D., University of Washington
Mojica, Kristina, University of Southern Mississippi
Monger, Bruce, Cornell University
Montagna, Paul, Texas A&M University, Corpus Christi
Moore, Christopher M., University of Southampton
Moran, Dawn, Woods Hole Oceanographic Institution
Mueller, Erich M., University of South Alabama
Mulholland, Margaret, Old Dominion University
Munch, Stephan, SUNY, Stony Brook
Murray, Alison, University of Nevada, Reno
Murtugudde, Raghuram G., University of Maryland
Napora, Theodore A., University of Rhode Island
Napp, Jeffrey, University of Washington
Newman, William A., University of California, San Diego
Newton, Jan, University of Washington
Nixon, Scott W., University of Rhode Island
Nosal, Andrew, University of San Diego
Nye, Janet, SUNY, Stony Brook
Ohman, Mark D., University of California, San Diego
Oliver, John S., Moss Landing Marine Laboratories
Oliver, Matthew J., University of Delaware
Oschlies, Andreas, Dalhousie University
Oviatt, Candace, University of Rhode Island
Padilla, Dianna K., SUNY, Stony Brook
Pakhomov, Evgeny, University of British Columbia
Palenik, Brian, University of California, San Diego
Paul, John H., University of South Florida
Peebles, Ernst B., University of South Florida
Pellerin, Jocelyne, Universite du Quebec a Rimouski
Perry, Mary Jane, University of Washington
Peterson, Bradley, SUNY, Stony Brook
Pikitch, Ellen K., SUNY, Stony Brook
Pinckney, James, University of South Carolina
Plotkin, Pamela, Texas A&M University
Pollack, Jennifer, Texas A&M University, Corpus Christi
Potts, Donald C., University of California, Santa Cruz
Powers, Sean, University of South Alabama
Prairie, Jennifer, University of San Diego
Purdie, Duncan A., University of Southampton
Quattro, Joseph, University of South Carolina
Rabalais, Nancy N., Louisiana State University
Ragotzkie, Robert A., University of Wisconsin, Madison
Ray, G. Carleton, University of Virginia
Redalje, Donald G., University of Southern Mississippi
Reese, Brandi K., Texas A&M University, Corpus Christi
Resplandy, Laure, Princeton University
Richardson, Tammi, University of South Carolina
Robinson, Carol, University of East Anglia
Robinson, Charlotte, Curtin University
Robinson, Leonie, University of Liverpool
Rocap, Gabrielle L., University of Washington
Roman, Charles T., University of Rhode Island
Roughgarden, Joan, Stanford University
Rouse, Gregory W., University of California, San Diego
Rowe, Gilbert T., Texas A&M University
Roy, Suzanne, Universite du Quebec a Rimouski
Ruttan, Lore, Emory University
Saila, Saul B., University of Rhode Island
Sambrotto, Raymond N., Columbia University
Sautter, Leslie R., College of Charleston
Schnetzer, Astrid, North Carolina State University
Schulze, Anja, Texas A&M University
Scott, Tim, Roger Williams University
Searcy, Steven, University of San Diego
Selph, Karen E., University of Hawai'i, Manoa
Shaw, Richard F., Louisiana State University
Shuman, Randy, University of Washington
Shumway, Sandra, University of Connecticut
Sibert, John R., University of Hawai'i, Manoa
Sieburth, John M., University of Rhode Island
Silver, Mary W., University of California, Santa Cruz
Sims, David, University of Southampton
Smalley, Gabriela W., Rider University
Smayda, Theodore J., University of Rhode Island
Smith, Craig R., University of Hawai'i, Manoa
Smith, David E., University of Virginia
Smith, David C., University of Rhode Island
Smith, Jennifer E., University of California, San Diego
Solan, Martin, University of Southampton
Sommer, Ulrich , Dalhousie University
Sousa, Wayne P., University of California, Berkeley
Specker, Jennifer, University of Rhode Island
Stanley, Emily, University of Wisconsin, Madison
Steppe, Cecily N., United States Naval Academy
Steward, Grieg F., University of Hawai'i, Manoa
Stickney, Robert R., Texas A&M University
Stoecker, Diane, University of Maryland
Stoner, Betsy, Bentley University
Strickland, Richard M., University of Washington
Subramaniam, Ajit, Columbia University
Sugihara, George, University of California, San Diego
Suttle, Curtis, University of British Columbia
Swain, Geoffrey, Florida Institute of Technology
Swift, Elijah V., University of Rhode Island
Sylvan, Jason B., Texas A&M University
Taggart, Christopher T., Dalhousie University
Talley, Drew, University of San Diego
Taylor, Frank J. R., University of British Columbia
Taylor, Gordon T., SUNY, Stony Brook
Thatje, Sven, University of Southampton
Thomas, Florence, University of Hawai'i, Manoa
Thomas, Peter, University of Texas, Austin
Thompson, Diane, Boston University
Thomsen, Laurenz A., University of Washington
Thomson, Jack, University of Liverpool
Thornton, Daniel C., Texas A&M University
Tlusty, Michael, University of Massachusetts, Boston
Toonen, Robert, University of Hawai'i, Manoa
Torres, Joseph J., University of South Florida
Tortell, Philippe, University of British Columbia
Treude, Tina, University of California, Los Angeles
Tunnicliffe, Verena, University of Victoria
Turner, Robert E., Louisiana State University
Tynan, Cynthia T., University of Washington
Urban-Rich, Juanita, University of Massachusetts, Boston
Vacquier, Victor D., University of California, San Diego
Vaillancourt, Robert, Millersville University
Varela, Diana, University of Victoria
Vargo, Gabriel A., University of South Florida
Vaudrey, Jamie, University of Connecticut
Villalard-Bohnsack, Martine, Roger Williams University
Villareal, Tracy A., University of Texas, Austin
Waldbusser, George, Oregon State University
Waldman, John, Graduate School of the City University of New York
Walsh, John J., University of South Florida
Ward, Ben A., University of Southampton
Ward, Bess B., Princeton University
Ward, J. Evan, University of Connecticut
Warren, Joseph, SUNY, Stony Brook
Weber, Thomas, University of Rochester
Wei, Chong, Curtin University
Wells, Randy, University of South Florida
Welschmeyer, Nicholas A., Moss Landing Marine Laboratories
Weng, Kevin, University of Hawai'i, Manoa
Wetz, Michael, Texas A&M University, Corpus Christi
Wiedenmann, Jorg, University of Southampton
Wilson, Merwether, Edinburgh University
Wishner, Karen, University of Rhode Island
Wolcott, Donna L., North Carolina State University
Wolcott, Thomas G., North Carolina State University
Woodin, Sarah A., University of South Carolina
Yamanaka, Tsuyuko, University of Liverpool
Yandle, Tracy, Emory University
Young, Richard E., University of Hawai'i, Manoa
Zakardjian, Bruno, Universite du Quebec a Rimouski
Zedler, Joy, University of Wisconsin, Madison
Zehr, Jonathan P., University of California, Santa Cruz
Zhang, Huan, University of Connecticut

Chemical Oceanography

Allison, Nicky, University of St. Andrews
Andersen, Raymond J., University of British Columbia
Anderson, Robert F., Columbia University
Andersson, Andreas, University of California, San Diego
Andren, Anders W., University of Wisconsin, Madison
Andrews, Allen H., University of Hawai'i, Manoa
Annett, Amber, University of Southampton
Armstrong, David E., University of Wisconsin, Madison
Armstrong, Robert A., SUNY, Stony Brook
Azetsu-Scott, Kumiko, Geological Survey of Canada
Bacon, Michael P., Woods Hole Oceanographic Institution
Balistrieri, Laurie, University of Washington
Barbeau, Katherine A., University of California, San Diego
Bates, Nicholas R., University of Southampton
Benitez-Nelson, Claudia R., University of South Carolina
Benway, Heather, Woods Hole Oceanographic Institution
Bishop, James K., University of California, Berkeley
Boudreau, Bernard P., Dalhousie University
Bourbonnais, Annie, University of South Carolina
Boyle, Edward A., Massachusetts Institute of Technology
Brownawell, Bruce J., SUNY, Stony Brook
Bruland, Kenneth W., University of California, Santa Cruz
Buchwald, Carolyn, Dalhousie University
Buckley, Lawrence J., University of Rhode Island
Buesseler, Ken O., Woods Hole Oceanographic Institution
Bullister, John, University of Washington
Burdige, David J., Old Dominion University
Canuel, Elizabeth A., William & Mary
Chan, Kwan M., California State University, Long Beach
Chapman, Piers, Texas A&M University
Chappell, P. D., Old Dominion University
Cherrier, Jennifer, Brooklyn College (CUNY)
Cochran, J. K., Stony Brook University
Cochran, J. Kirk, SUNY, Stony Brook
Coffin, Richard, Texas A&M University, Corpus Christi
Cooper, Matthew, University of Southampton
Cornwell, Jeffery C., University of Maryland
Crutzen, Paul, University of California, San Diego
Culberson, Charles H., University of Delaware
Cullen, Jay, University of Victoria
Cutter, Gregory A., Old Dominion University
deAngelis, Marie, SUNY, Maritime College
Delaney, Margaret L., University of California, Santa Cruz
DeMaster, David J., North Carolina State University
Devol, Allan H., University of Washington
Doney, Scott, University of Virginia
Druffel, Ellen R. M., University of California, Irvine
Drysdale, Jessica, Woods Hole Oceanographic Institution
Duce, Robert A., Texas A&M University
Eglinton, Tim, Woods Hole Oceanographic Institution
Emerson, Steven R., University of Washington
Emile-Geay, Julien, University of Southern California
Engel, Anga, SUNY, Stony Brook
Estapa, Margaret, Woods Hole Oceanographic Institution
Estapa, Margaret, Skidmore College
Fanning, Kent A., University of South Florida
Feely, Richard A., University of Washington
Fenical, William H., University of California, San Diego
Fisher, Nicholas S., SUNY, Stony Brook
Fitzgerald, William F., University of Connecticut
Fitzsimmons, Jessica N., Texas A&M University
Fogel, Marilyn L., University of Delaware
Fox, Austin, Florida Institute of Technology
Fox, Lewis, Broward College
Fredricks, Helen, Woods Hole Oceanographic Institution
Gagne, Jean-Pierre, Universite du Quebec a Rimouski
Gammon, Richard H., University of Washington
Garcia-Rubio, Luis H., University of South Florida
Gieskes, Joris M., University of California, San Diego
Glover, David M., Woods Hole Oceanographic Institution
Gold-Bouchot, Gerardo, Texas A&M University
Granger, Julie, University of Connecticut
Hales, Burke R., Oregon State University
Hamme, Roberta C., University of Victoria
Hanson, Jr., Alfred K., University of Rhode Island
Hayes, Christopher T., University of Southern Mississippi
Haymet, Anthony D., University of California, San Diego
Ho, David, University of Hawai'i, Manoa
Hollander, David J., University of South Florida
Hong, Gi-Hoon, Wayne State University
Hu, Xinping, Texas A&M University, Corpus Christi
Huebert, Barry J., University of Hawai'i, Manoa
Ingalls, Anitra E., University of Washington
James, Rachael, University of Southampton
Johnson, Bruce D., Dalhousie University
Keil, Richard G., University of Washington
Kessler, John , University of Rochester
Kiene, Ronald P., University of South Alabama
Knap, Anthony, Texas A&M University
Kujawinski, Elizabeth B., Woods Hole Oceanographic Institution
Lang, Susan Q., University of South Carolina
LaVigne, Michéle, Bowdoin College
Lee, Cindy, SUNY, Stony Brook
Letscher, Robert T., University of New Hampshire
Lima, Ivan D., Woods Hole Oceanographic Institution
Liss, Peter S., University of East Anglia
Loder, Theodore C., University of New Hampshire
Longnecker, Krista, Woods Hole Oceanographic Institution
Lott, Dempsey E., Woods Hole Oceanographic Institution
Lucotte, Marc Michel, Universite du Quebec a Montreal
Lund, David, University of Connecticut
Lwiza, Kamazima M., SUNY, Stony Brook
Mahaffey, Claire, University of Liverpool
Maloney, Ashley, Princeton University
Marchitto, Thomas M., University of Colorado
Martin, William R., Woods Hole Oceanographic Institution
Mason, Robert P., University of Connecticut
Matsumoto, Katsumi, University of Minnesota, Twin Cities
McDuff, Russell E., University of Washington
McIlvin, Matt, Woods Hole Oceanographic Institution
McKinley, Galen, University of Wisconsin, Madison
McNichol, Ann P., Woods Hole Oceanographic Institution
Measures, Christopher, University of Hawai'i, Manoa
Merrill, John T., University of Rhode Island
Moffett, James W., University of Southern California
Moore, Robert M., Dalhousie University
Moran, S. Bradley, University of Rhode Island
Murray, James W., University of Washington
Najjar, Raymond G., Pennsylvania State University, University Park
Nuzzio, Donald B., University of Delaware
Palevsky, Hilary I., Boston College
Pellenbarg, Robert, College of the Desert
Pelletier, Emilien, Universite du Quebec a Rimouski
Pennock, Jonathan R., Dauphin Island Sea Lab
Pilson, Michael E., University of Rhode Island
Precedo, Laura, Broward College
Presley, Bobby J., Texas A&M University
Pyrtle, Ashanti J., University of South Florida
Quay, Paul D., University of Washington
Quinn, James G., University of Rhode Island
Rahn, Kenneth A., University of Rhode Island
Ravelo, Ana C., University of California, Santa Cruz
Reimer, Andreas, Georg-August University of Goettingen
Reimers, Clare, Oregon State University
Resing, Joseph A., University of Washington
Rheuban, Jennie, Woods Hole Oceanographic Institution
Roethel, Frank J., SUNY, Stony Brook
Russell, Joellen, University of Arizona
Sabine, Christopher L., University of Washington
Saito, Mak A., Woods Hole Oceanographic Institution
Salaun, Rachel, University of Liverpool
Santschi, Peter H., Texas A&M University
Sarmiento, Jorge L., Princeton University
Sayles, Frederick L., Woods Hole Oceanographic Institution
Schwartz, Matthew C., University of West Florida
Scranton, Mary I., SUNY, Stony Brook
Shamberger, Kathryn E., Texas A&M University
Sharp, Jonathan H., University of Delaware
Sharples, Jonathan, University of Liverpool
Shiller, Alan M., University of Southern Mississippi
Sholkovitz, Edward R., Woods Hole Oceanographic Institution
Simjouw, Jean-Paul, University of New Haven

Skoog, Annelie, University of Connecticut
Sonzogni, William C., University of Wisconsin, Madison
Stewart, Gillian, Queens College (CUNY)
Stewart, Gillian, Graduate School of the City University of New York
Sundby, Bjorn, Universite du Quebec a Rimouski
Suntharalingam, Parvadha, University of East Anglia
Swarr, Gretchen, Woods Hole Oceanographic Institution
Sylva, Sean, Woods Hole Oceanographic Institution
Tagliabue, Alessandro, University of Liverpool
Takahashi, Taro, Columbia University
Tanhua, Toste, Dalhousie University
Thomas, Helmuth, Dalhousie University
Thompson, Anu, University of Liverpool
Timmermans, Mary-Louise, Yale University
Tobias, Craig, University of Connecticut
Ullman, William J., University of Delaware
Van Mooy, Benjamin, Woods Hole Oceanographic Institution
Velinsky, David, Drexel University
Veron, Alain J., University of Delaware
Vlahos, Penny, University of Connecticut
Wade, Terry L., Texas A&M University
Wallace, Douglas, Dalhousie University
Wallace, Douglas W. R., SUNY, Stony Brook
Williams, Dave E., University of British Columbia
Windsor, Jr., John G., Florida Institute of Technology
Yao, Wensheng, University of South Florida
Yvon-Lewis, Shari A., Texas A&M University
Zafiriou, Oliver C., Woods Hole Oceanographic Institution
Zhu, Qingzhi, SUNY, Stony Brook

Geological Oceanography

Agardy, Rachael, Central Michigan University
Aiello, Ivano, Moss Landing Marine Laboratories
Alexander, Clark R., Georgia Southern University
Alt, Jeffrey C., University of Michigan
Arthur, Michael A., Pennsylvania State University, University Park
Bain, Olivier, Institut Polytechnique LaSalle Beauvais (ex-IGAL)
Baker, Edward T., University of Washington
Baldauf, Jack G., Texas A&M University
Berquist, Jr., Carl R., William & Mary
Billups, Katharina, University of Delaware
Black, David, SUNY, Stony Brook
Busch, William H., University of New Orleans
Bush, David M., University of West Georgia
Byrne, Timothy, University of Connecticut
Carey, Steven N., University of Rhode Island
Clemens, Steven C., Brown University
Coffin, Richard, Texas A&M University, Corpus Christi
Cook, Mea S., Williams College
Creager, Joe S., University of Washington
D'Hondt, Steven L., University of Rhode Island
Darby, Dennis A., Old Dominion University
Dellapenna, Timothy M., Texas A&M University
Diercks, Arne R., University of Southern Mississippi
Dudley, Walter, University of Hawai'i, Manoa
Emerick, Christina M., University of Washington
Farmer, Emma C., Hofstra University
Farrell, John, University of Rhode Island
Ferrini, Victoria, Columbia University
Finney, Bruce P., University of Alaska, Fairbanks
Flood, Roger D., SUNY, Stony Brook
Gagnon, Katie, Seattle Central College
Gardner, Wilford D., Texas A&M University
Hallock-Muller, Pamela, University of South Florida
Harris, Sara, University of British Columbia
Hawkins, James W., University of California, San Diego
Hayman, Nicholas W., University of Texas, Austin
Hein, Christopher J., William & Mary
Holcomb, Robin T., University of Washington
Holcombe, Troy L., Texas A&M University
Holmes, Mark L., University of Washington
Honjo, Susumu, Woods Hole Oceanographic Institution
Hovan, Steven A., Indiana University of Pennsylvania
Kelley, Deborah S., University of Washington
Kincaid, Christopher, University of Rhode Island
King, John, University of Rhode Island
Kominz, Michelle A., Western Michigan University
Kuehl, Steven A., William & Mary
Larson, Roger, University of Rhode Island
Lear, C, Cardiff University
Leinen, Margaret, University of Rhode Island
Leventer, Amy, Colgate University
Locker, Stanley D., University of South Florida
Longworth, Brett, Woods Hole Oceanographic Institution
Manganini, Steven J., Woods Hole Oceanographic Institution
Martinez-Noriega, Cesar, Univ Autonoma de Baja California Sur
McHugh, Cecilia M., Graduate School of the City University of New York
McHugh, Cecilia, Queens College (CUNY)
McManus, Dean A., University of Washington
Moore, Theodore C., University of Michigan
Mosher, David C., Dalhousie University
Mottl, Michael J., University of Hawai'i, Manoa
Murray, David, Brown University
Muza, Jay P., Broward College
Naar, David F., University of South Florida
Nittrouer, Charles A., University of Washington
Nowell, Arthur R. M., University of Washington
Ogston, Andrea S., University of Washington
Oostdam, Bernard L., Millersville University
Parsons, Jeffrey D., University of Washington
Pilkey, Jr., Orrin H., Duke University
Pinet, Paul, Colgate University
Prell, Warren L., Brown University
Quinn, Terrence, University of South Florida
Riesselman, Christina R., University of Otago
Sager, William W., Texas A&M University
Schilling, Jean-Guy E., University of Rhode Island
Schmidt, Matthew, Old Dominion University
Shen, Yang, University of Rhode Island
Sigurdsson, Haraldur, University of Rhode Island
Slowey, Niall C., Texas A&M University
Smith, Stephen V., University of Hawai'i, Manoa
Smythe, Wendy F., University of Minnesota Duluth
Snoeckx, Hilde, University of West Florida
Sommerfield, Christopher K., University of Delaware
St. John, Kristen E., James Madison University
Stanley, Daniel J., Smithsonian Institution / National Museum of Natural History
Sternberg, Richard W., University of Washington
Thomas, Debbie, Texas A&M University
Trembanis, Art, University of Delaware
Tyce, Robert, University of Rhode Island
Uchupi, Elazar, Woods Hole Oceanographic Institution
Wallace, Davin, University of Southern Mississippi
Whitman, Jill M., Pacific Lutheran University
Wilcock, William S., University of Washington
Zarillo, Gary , Florida Institute of Technology
Zeebe, Richard E., University of Hawai'i, Manoa

Physical Oceanography

Aagaard, Knut, University of Washington
Abernathey, Ryan P., Columbia University
Alford, Matthew H., University of Washington
Allen, Susan E., University of British Columbia
Andrefouet, Serge, University of South Florida
Anis, Ayal, Texas A&M University
Armi, Laurence, University of California, San Diego
Atkinson, Larry P., Old Dominion University
Barclay, David R., Dalhousie University
Baum, Steven K., Texas A&M University
Beaulieu, Claudie, University of Southampton
Bishop, Stuart P., North Carolina State University
Bogucki, Darek, Texas A&M University, Corpus Christi
Bohlen, Walter F., University of Connecticut
Boicourt, William, University of Maryland
Bordoni, Simona, California Institute of Technology
Bostater, Charles, Florida Institute of Technology
Bourke, Robert H., Naval Postgraduate School
Bowman, Malcolm J., SUNY, Stony Brook
Boxall, Simon R., University of Southampton
Boyd, John, University of Michigan
Bracco, Annalisa, Georgia Institute of Technology
Breaker, Laurence, Moss Landing Marine Laboratories

Brooks, David A., Texas A&M University
Buckingham, Michael J., University of California, San Diego
Buijsman, Maarten, University of Southern Mississippi
Bulusu, Subrahmanyam, University of South Carolina
Cane, Mark A., Columbia University
Cannon, Glenn A., University of Washington
Carder, Kendall L., University of South Florida
Carmack, Edward, University of British Columbia
Carter, Glenn, University of Hawai'i, Manoa
Carton, James, University of Maryland
Cessi, Paola, University of California, San Diego
Chang, Ping, Texas A&M University
Chao, Shenn-Yu, University of Maryland
Chapman, Ross N., University of Victoria
Chen, Dake, Columbia University
Chiu, Ching-Sang, Naval Postgraduate School
Chu, Peter C., Naval Postgraduate School
Cole, Rick, University of South Florida
Collins, Curtis A., Naval Postgraduate School
Cornillon, Peter, University of Rhode Island
Craig, Susanne , Dalhousie University
Crease, James, University of Delaware
Criminale, Jr., William O., University of Washington
Cronin, Meghan F., University of Washington
D'Asaro, Eric A., University of Washington
Davis, Leslie M., Austin Community College District
de Szoeke, Simon P., Oregon State University
Denman, Kenneth L., University of Victoria
Dever, Edward P., Oregon State University
Dewey, Richard K., University of Victoria
Di Lorenzo, Emanuele, Georgia Institute of Technology
Dierssen, Heidi, University of Connecticut
DiMarco, Steven F., Texas A&M University
Donohue, Kathleen, University of Rhode Island
Donovan, Jeff C., University of South Florida
Dorman, Clive E., San Diego State University
Dosso, Stanley E., University of Victoria
Drago, Aldo, University of Malta
Drijfhout, Sybren, University of Southampton
Dushaw, Brian D., University of Washington
Dutrieux, Pierre, Columbia University
Edson, James, University of Connecticut
Ellis, Dale, Dalhousie University
English, David C., University of South Florida
Eriksen, Charles C., University of Washington
Ewart, Terry E., University of Washington
Fedorov, Alexey V., Yale University
Ferrari, Raffaele, Massachusetts Institute of Technology
Firing, Eric, University of Hawai'i, Manoa
Flagg, Charles, SUNY, Stony Brook
Flament, Pierre J., University of Hawai'i, Manoa
Flierl, Glenn R., Massachusetts Institute of Technology
Flynn, Russell L., Cypress College
Follows, Michael, Massachusetts Institute of Technology
Foreman, Michael G., University of Victoria
Foreman, Michael G. G., University of British Columbia
Fox-Kemper, Baylor, Brown University
Fram, Jonathan, Oregon State University
Galea, Anthony, University of Malta
Galperin, Boris, University of South Florida
Garfield, Newell (Toby), San Francisco State University
Garrett, Christopher J. R., University of Victoria
Garwood, Roland W., Naval Postgraduate School
Gauci, Adam, University of Malta
Gerbi, Greg, Skidmore College
Giese, Benjamin S., Texas A&M University
Gille, Sarah T., University of California, San Diego
Ginis, Isaac, University of Rhode Island
Gnanadesikan, Anand, Johns Hopkins University
Gong, Donglai, William & Mary
Gonzalez, Frank I., University of Washington
Gordon, Arnold L., Columbia University
Greatbatch, Richard , Dalhousie University
Greenberg, David, Dalhousie University
Gregg, Michael C., University of Washington
Guinasso, Norman L., Texas A&M University
Haine, Thomas W., Johns Hopkins University
Hara, Tetsu, University of Rhode Island
Harrison, Cheryl, University of Texas, Rio Grande Valley
Harrison, Don E., University of Washington
Hautala, Susan L., University of Washington
Hay, Alex E., Dalhousie University
He, Ruoying, North Carolina State University
Heavers, Richard, Roger Williams University
Hebert, David, Dalhousie University
Hebert, David L., University of Rhode Island
Heimbach, Patrick, University of Texas, Austin
Hendershott, Myrl C., University of California, San Diego
Herbers, Thomas H., Naval Postgraduate School
Hermann, Albert, University of Washington
Hetland, Robert D., Texas A&M University
Heywood, Karen, University of East Anglia
Hickey, Barbara M., University of Washington
Hines, Paul, Dalhousie University
Hofmann, Eileen E., Old Dominion University
Howard, Matthew K., Texas A&M University
Howden, Stephan, University of Southern Mississippi
Howe, Bruce M., University of Washington
Hsieh, William W., University of British Columbia
Huang, Bohua, George Mason University
Jackson, George A., Texas A&M University
Jacobs, Stanley, Columbia University
Jochens, Ann E., Texas A&M University
Johnson, Gregory C., University of Washington
Justic, Dubravko, Louisiana State University
Kaplan, Alexey, Columbia University
Kawase, Mitsuhiro, University of Washington
Kelley, Dan, Dalhousie University
Kelly, Kathryn A., University of Washington
Kessler, William S., University of Washington
Klinck, John M., Old Dominion University
Klinger, Barry, George Mason University
Kloosterziel, Rudolf C., University of Hawai'i, Manoa
Klymak, Jody, University of Victoria
Knauss, John A., University of Rhode Island
Knowles, Charles E., North Carolina State University
Kosro, Michael, Oregon State University
Koutitonsky, Vladimir G., Universite du Quebec a Rimouski
Kumar, Ajoy, Millersville University
Kuperman, William A., University of California, San Diego
Lebow, Ruth Y., Los Angeles Pierce College
Lee, Craig M., University of Washington
Lerczak, Jim, Oregon State University
Lesht, Barry, University of Illinois at Chicago
Lesht, Barry M., Argonne National Laboratory
Liao, Enhui, Princeton University
Liu, Zheng-yu, University of Wisconsin, Madison
Liu, Zhengyu, University of Wisconsin, Madison
Lozier, M. Susan, Duke University
Lu, Youyu, Dalhousie University
Lukas, Roger, University of Hawai'i, Manoa
Luther, Douglas S., University of Hawai'i, Manoa
Luther, Mark E., University of South Florida
MacCready, Parker, University of Washington
Magaard, Lorenz, University of Hawai'i, Manoa
Malanotte-Rizzoli, Paola M., Massachusetts Institute of Technology
Manley, Thomas O., Middlebury College
Marsh, Robert, University of Southampton
Marshall, John C., Massachusetts Institute of Technology
Martin, Seelye, University of Washington
Martinson, Douglas G., Columbia University
Martinson, Douglas G., Columbia University
Maslowski, Wieslaw, Naval Postgraduate School
Matano, Ricardo P., Oregon State University
Maul, George A., Florida Institute of Technology
Mazzini, Pierro, William & Mary
McCreary, Julian P., University of Hawai'i, Manoa
McManus, Margaret Anne, University of Hawai'i, Manoa
Mellor, George, Princeton University
Melville, W. Kendall, University of California, San Diego
Merrifield, Mark A., University of Hawai'i, Manoa
Mitchum, Gary T., University of South Florida

Mofjeld, Harold O., University of Washington
Moore, Dennis W., University of Washington
Moore, Jefferson K., University of California, Irvine
Morison, James H., University of Washington
Moum, James N., Oregon State University
Muller, Andrew C., United States Naval Academy
Muller, Peter, University of Hawai'i, Manoa
Munk, Walter H., University of California, San Diego
Myers, Paul, University of Alberta
Mysak, Lawrence A., McGill University
Nash, Jonathan, Oregon State University
Naveira Garabato, Alberto, University of Southampton
Nechaev, Dmitri, University of Southern Mississippi
Nowlin, Jr., Worth D., Texas A&M University
Nystuen, Jeffrey A., University of Washington
O'Donnell, James, University of Connecticut
Oliver, Eric, Dalhousie University
Oliver, Kevin, University of Southampton
Oltman-Shay, Joan M., University of Washington
Orsi, Alejandro H., Texas A&M University
Paduan, Jeffrey D., Naval Postgraduate School
Pawlowicz, Richard A., University of British Columbia
Perrie, William, Dalhousie University
Perry, David J., Chabot College
Philander, S. George H., Princeton University
Pieters, Roger, University of British Columbia
Pinkel, Robert, University of California, San Diego
Pond, Stephen G., University of British Columbia
Potter, Henry, Texas A&M University
Powell, Brian, University of Hawai'i, Manoa
Powell, Thomas M., University of California, Berkeley
Primeau, Francois, University of California, Irvine
Pringle, James M., University of New Hampshire
Qiu, Bo, University of Hawai'i, Manoa
Radko, Timour, Naval Postgraduate School
Rhines, Peter B., University of Washington
Richards, Kelvin J., University of Hawai'i, Manoa
Richardson, Mary J., Texas A&M University
Riser, Stephen C., University of Washington
Rocha, Cesar, University of Connecticut
Roden, Gunnar I., University of Washington
Roemmich, Dean H., University of California, San Diego
Romero, Leonel, University of Connecticut
Ross, Tetjana, Dalhousie University
Rossby, Hans T., University of Rhode Island
Rothrock, David A., University of Washington
Rothstein, Lewis, University of Rhode Island
Rouse, Jr., Lawrence J., Louisiana State University
Roussenov, Vassil M., University of Liverpool
Ruddick, Barry R., Dalhousie University
Rudnick, Daniel L., University of California, San Diego
Salmon, Richard L., University of California, San Diego
Salmun, Haydee, Hunter College (CUNY)
Samelson, Roger, Oregon State University
Sanford, Lawrence P., University of Maryland
Sanford, Thomas B., University of Washington
Schopf, Paul S., George Mason University
Send, Uwe, University of California, San Diego
Shaw, Ping-Tung, North Carolina State University
Shearman, Kipp, Oregon State University
Shen, Jian, William & Mary
Sheng, Jinyu, Dalhousie University
Smith, Peter C., Dalhousie University
Smith, Robert L., Oregon State University
Smyth, William D., Oregon State University
Southam, John R., University of Miami
Spindel, Robert C., University of Washington
Spinrad, Richard, Oregon State University
Stanton, Timothy P., Naval Postgraduate School
Stewart, Robert H., Texas A&M University
Stoessel, Achim, Texas A&M University
Stoessel, Marion, Texas A&M University
Stramski, Dariusz, University of California, San Diego
Straub, David, McGill University
Sutherland, Dave, University of Oregon
Swaters, Gordon E., University of Alberta
Talley, Lynne D., University of California, San Diego
Thompson, Andrew F., California Institute of Technology
Thompson, Keith R., Dalhousie University
Thompson, LuAnne, University of Washington
Thomson, Richard E., University of British Columbia
Thurnherr, Andreas M., Columbia University
Thurnherr, Andreas, Columbia University
Timmermann, Axel, University of Hawai'i, Manoa
Tokmakian, Robin T., Naval Postgraduate School
Tremblay, Bruno, McGill University
Tziperman, Eli, Harvard University
Von Schwind, Joseph J., Naval Postgraduate School
Wang, Harry, William & Mary
Wang, Zhankun, Texas A&M University
Warner, Mark J., University of Washington
Watts, D. Randolph, University of Rhode Island
Weaver, Andrew J., University of Victoria
Webster, Ferris, University of Delaware
Weisberg, Robert H., University of South Florida
Wells, Neil C., University of Southampton
White, Martin, National University of Ireland Galway
Whitney, Michael, University of Connecticut
Wiederwohl, Chrissy, Texas A&M University
Wiggert, Jerry, University of Southern Mississippi
Williams, Kevin L., University of Washington
Wilson, Robert E., SUNY, Stony Brook
Wimbush, Mark, University of Rhode Island
Winguth, Arne M., University of Texas, Arlington
Wolfe, Christopher, SUNY, Stony Brook
Woodgate, Rebecca A., University of Washington
Wu, Jin, University of Delaware
Wunsch, Carl I., Massachusetts Institute of Technology
Wunsch, Carl, Harvard University
Yankovsky, Alexander E., University of South Carolina
Young, William R., University of California, San Diego
Yuan, Xiaojun, Columbia University
Zappa, Christopher, Columbia University
Zappa, Christopher J., Columbia University
Zhang, Rong, Princeton University
Zhang, Xiaodong, University of Southern Mississippi
Zhang, Y. J., William & Mary

Shore and Nearshore Processes

Ashton, Andrew, Woods Hole Oceanographic Institution
Baker, Alex, University of East Anglia
Ballinger, Rhoda, University of Wales
Barth, Jack A., Oregon State University
Baxter, Stefanie J., University of Delaware
Blomberg, Brittany N., Austin Community College District
Boardman, Mark R., Miami University
Bowen, Anthony J., Dalhousie University
Branco, Brett, Brooklyn College (CUNY)
Briggs, Tiffany Roberts M., Florida Atlantic University
Buonaiuto, Frank, Hunter College (CUNY)
Burbanck, George P., Hampton University
Camann, Eleanor J., Red Rocks Community College
Couceiro, Fay, University of Portsmouth
Dickson, Stephen M., Dept of Agriculture, Conservation, and Forestry
Dunbar, Robert B., Stanford University
Dupre, William R., University of Houston
Dura, Christina, Virginia Polytechnic Institute & State University
Duxbury, Alyn C., University of Washington
Engelhart, Simon E., University of Rhode Island
Farnsworth, Katie, Indiana University of Pennsylvania
Farrell, Stewart C., Stockton University
Fenster, Michael S., Randolph-Macon College
FitzGerald, Duncan M., Boston University
Friedrichs, Carl T., William & Mary
Gibeaut, James, Texas A&M University, Corpus Christi
Giese, Graham S., Woods Hole Oceanographic Institution
Griggs, Garry, University of California, Santa Cruz
Guza, Robert T., University of California, San Diego
Haigh, Ivan D., University of Southampton
Hall, Robert, University of East Anglia
Haller, Merrick C., Oregon State University
Hansom, Jim, University of Glasgow

Harris, Courtney K., William & Mary
Harris, M. Scott, College of Charleston
Heise, Elizabeth, University of Texas, Rio Grande Valley
Helmuth, Brian, Northeastern University
Jackson, Chester M., Georgia Southern University
Kassem, Hachem, University of Southampton
Kemp, Andrew, Tufts University
Kennedy, Andrew, University of Notre Dame
Kineke, Gail C., Boston College
Koppelman, Lee K., SUNY, Stony Brook
Lippmann, Thomas C., University of New Hampshire
MacMahan, Jamie, Naval Postgraduate School
McBride, Randolph, George Mason University
McManus, Margaret A., University of California, Santa Cruz
Neill, Simon P., University of Wales
Oakley, Bryan, Eastern Connecticut State University
Oxner-Jones, D. M., Ohio Dept of Natural Resources
Ozkan-Haller, Tuba, Oregon State University
Paine, Jeffrey G., University of Texas, Austin
Rosen, Peter S., Northeastern University
Ruggiero, Peter, Oregon State University
Seibel, Erwin, San Francisco State University
Shroyer, Emily L., Oregon State University
Siedlecki , Samantha, University of Connecticut
Thornton, Edward B., Naval Postgraduate School
Vander Zanden, Jake, University of Wisconsin, Madison
Voulgaris, George, University of South Carolina
Westerink, Joannes J., University of Notre Dame
Wilson, Greg, Oregon State University
Winant, Clinton D., University of California, San Diego
Wu, Chin, University of Wisconsin, Madison

Paleooceanography
Came, Rosemarie E., University of New Hampshire
Ivanochko, Tara, University of British Columbia
Lawrence, Kira, Lafayette College
Lynch-Stieglitz, Jean, Georgia Institute of Technology
Tems, Caitlin E., Weber State University

ASTRONOMICAL SCIENCES

Astronomy
Malhotra, Renu, University of Arizona
Wood, David A., San Antonio Community College

Cosmochemistry
Agee, Carl B., University of New Mexico
Alexander, Conel M., Carnegie Institution for Science
Bermingham, Katherine R., University of Maryland
Blake, Geoffrey A., California Institute of Technology
Bland, Phil, Curtin University
Blander, Milton, Argonne National Laboratory
Bodenheimer, Peter, University of California, Santa Cruz
Bose, Maitrayee, Arizona State University
Bouvier, Audrey, Western University
Boynton, William V., University of Arizona
Brown, Robert H., University of Arizona
Burnett, Donald S., California Institute of Technology
Ciesla, Fred, University of Chicago
Dauphas, Nicolas, University of Chicago
Davis, Andrew, University of Chicago
Drake, Michael J., University of Arizona
Fegley, Bruce, Washington University in St. Louis
Fegley, M. Bruce, Washington University in St. Louis
Greenwood, James P., Wesleyan University
Gross, Juliane, Rutgers, The State University of New Jersey
Herd, Christopher D., University of Alberta
Humayun, Munir, Florida State University
Huntress, Jr., Wesley T., Carnegie Institution for Science
Jordan, Jim L., Lamar University
Korycansky, Don, University of California, Santa Cruz
Kring, David, University of Arizona
Lauretta, Dante, University of Arizona
Lewis, John S., University of Arizona
Lin, Douglas, University of California, Santa Cruz
Lodders-Fegley, Katharina, Washington University in St. Louis
Lunine, Jonathan I., Cornell University
Lunine, Jonathan I., University of Arizona
Lyon, Ian, University of Manchester
MacPherson, Glenn J., Smithsonian Inst/Nat Mus of Nat History
McKeegan, Kevin D., University of California, Los Angeles
McSween, Jr., Harry Y., University of Tennessee, Knoxville
Mojzsis, Stephen J., University of Colorado
Nittler, Larry R., Carnegie Institution for Science
Smith, William H., Washington University in St. Louis
Swindle, Timothy, University of Arizona
Telus, Myriam, University of California, Santa Cruz
Turner, Grenville, University of Manchester
Vogt, Steven, University of California, Santa Cruz
Wadhwa, Meenakshi, Arizona State University
Wang, Kun, Washington University in St. Louis

Extraterrestrial Geology
Adams, Mark, Lamar University
Anderson, Jennifer L., Winona State University
Arvidson, Raymond E., Washington University in St. Louis
Asphaug, Erik, University of California, Santa Cruz
Baker, Victor R., University of Arizona
Ballentine, Christopher, University of Oxford
Batygin, Konstantin, California Institute of Technology
Bell, James, Arizona State University
Benedix, Gretchen, Curtin University
Blaney, Diana L., Jet Propulsion Laboratory
Bleamaster III, Leslie F., Trinity University
Bourassa, Matthew, Western University
Burr, Devon M., University of Tennessee, Knoxville
Byrne, Paul K., North Carolina State University
Calvin, Wendy M., University of Nevada, Reno
Christensen, Philip R., Arizona State University
Coles, Kenneth S., Indiana University of Pennsylvania
Craddock, Robert A., Smithsonian Institution / National Air & Space Museum
Cull-Hearth, Selby, Bryn Mawr College
Delaney, Jeremy S., Rutgers, The State University of New Jersey
Dietz, Richard D., University of Northern Colorado
Ehlmann, Bethany L., California Institute of Technology
Elachi, Charles, California Institute of Technology
Elkins-Tanton, Linda, Arizona State University
Fabel, Derek, University of Glasgow
Fishman, George , Bentley University
Forman, Lucy, Curtin University
Gilmore, Martha S., Wesleyan University
Glotch, Timothy, Stony Brook University
Golombek, Matthew P., Jet Propulsion Laboratory
Grant, John A., Smithsonian Institution / National Air & Space Museum
Grieve, Richard, Western University
Grieve, Richard A. F., University of New Brunswick
Grosfils, Eric B., Pomona College
Hardgrove, Craig, Arizona State University
Hardgrove, Craig J., University of Tennessee, Knoxville
Hayes, Alexander G., Cornell University
Head, III, James W., Brown University
Herkenhoff, Ken E., Jet Propulsion Laboratory
Horgan, Briony, Purdue University
Howell, Robert R., University of Wyoming
Hurowitz, Joel A., Stony Brook University
Hynek, Brian M., University of Colorado
Jacobsen, Abram, University of Washington
Jakosky, Bruce M., University of Colorado
Jurena, Dwight J., San Antonio Community College
Karuntillake, Suniti, Louisiana State University
Klimczak, Christian, University of Tennessee, Knoxville
Knutson, Heather, California Institute of Technology
Korotev, Randy L., Washington University in St. Louis
Kraal, Erin, Kutztown University of Pennsylvania
Lagain, Anthony, Curtin University
Landa, Keith, SUNY, Purchase
Leake, Martha A., Valdosta State University
Lorenz, Ralph, University of Arizona
Mack, John E., Buffalo State College
Massironi, Matteo, Università degli Studi di Padova
Maxwell, Ted A., Smithsonian Institution / National Air & Space Museum
McEwen, Alfred, University of Arizona
McEwen, Alfred S., University of Arizona

McGowan, Eileen, University of Massachusetts, Amherst
McKinnon, William B., Washington University in St. Louis
Milam, Keith A., Ohio University
Minton, David, Purdue University
Moersch, Jeffery E., University of Tennessee, Knoxville
Mouginis-Mark, Peter J., University of Hawai'i, Manoa
Neish, Catherine, Western University
Nelson, Robert M., Jet Propulsion Laboratory
Newsom, Horton E., University of New Mexico
Osinski, Gordon R., Western University
Parsons, Reid A., Fitchburg State University
Piatex, Jennifer L., Central Connecticut State University
Prockter, Louise M., University of Tennessee, Knoxville
Radebaugh, Jani, Brigham Young University
Rice, Melissa S., Western Washington University
Robinson, Mark, Arizona State University
Rogers, A. D., Stony Brook University
Ruff, Steven, Arizona State University
Ruiz, Javier , Univ Complutense de Madrid
Runyon, Cassandra R., College of Charleston
Schultz, Peter H., Brown University
Shepard, Michael K., Bloomsburg University
Siebach, Kirsten L., Rice University
Solomon, Sean C., Columbia University
Squyres, Steven W., Cornell University
Stofan, Ellen R., Jet Propulsion Laboratory
Strom, Robert G., University of Arizona
Thomson, Bradley J., University of Tennessee, Knoxville
Tornabene, Livio, Western University
Towner, Martin, Curtin University
Turtle, Elizabeth, University of Arizona
Viviano-Beck, Christina E., University of Tennessee, Knoxville
Warner, Nicholas H., SUNY, Geneseo
Watters, Thomas R., Smithsonian Institution / National Air & Space Museum
Williams, David, Arizona State University
Williams, Kevin K., Buffalo State College
Wordsworth, Robin, Harvard University
Zimbelman, James R., Smithsonian Institution / National Air & Space Museum

Extraterrestrial Geophysics

Angelopoulos, Vassilis, University of California, Los Angeles
Arkani-Hamed, Jafar, McGill University
Asphaug, Erik I., University of Arizona
Banerdt, Bruce E., Jet Propulsion Laboratory
Benacquista, Matt, Montana State University, Billings
Bord, Don, University of Michigan, Dearborn
Brown, Michael E., California Institute of Technology
Brown, Peter, Western University
Dombard, Andrew J., University of Illinois at Chicago
Dombard, Andrew, Case Western Reserve University
Emery, Joshua P., University of Tennessee, Knoxville
Fenrich, Francis, University of Alberta
Ferencz, Orsolya, Eotvos Lorand University
Garrick-Bethell, Ian, University of California, Santa Cruz
Giacalone, Joe, University of Arizona
Goldreich, Peter M., California Institute of Technology
Greenberg, Richard J., University of Arizona
Hapke, Bruce W., University of Pittsburgh
Harnett, Erika M., University of Washington
Hauck, II, Steven A., Case Western Reserve University
Holzworth, Robert H., University of Washington
Hood, Lonnie L., University of Arizona
Hubbard, William B., University of Arizona
Jewitt, David, University of California, Los Angeles
Jokipii, Jack R., University of Arizona
Kivelson, Margaret G., University of California, Los Angeles
Kunkle, Thomas D., Los Alamos National Laboratory
Larsen, Kristine, Central Connecticut State University
Line, Michael, Arizona State University
Lucey, Paul G., University of Hawai'i, Manoa
Margot, Jean-Luc, University of California, Los Angeles
Matzke, David, University of Michigan, Dearborn
McCarthy, Michael P., University of Washington
McGovern, Patrick J., Rice University
McPherron, Robert L., University of California, Los Angeles
Miljkovic, Katarina, Curtin University
Muhleman, Duane O., California Institute of Technology
Newman, William I., University of California, Los Angeles
Nimmo, Francis, University of California, Santa Cruz
O'Rourke, Joseph, Arizona State University
Paige, David A., University of California, Los Angeles
Petrovay, Kristof, Eotvos Lorand University
Rankin, Robert, University of Alberta
Robinson, R. Craig, Central Connecticut State University
Rostoker, Gordon, University of Alberta
Russell, Christopher T., University of California, Los Angeles
Samson, John C., University of Alberta
Schlichting, Hilke, University of California, Los Angeles
Schmerr, Nicholas C., University of Maryland
Seager, Sara, Massachusetts Institute of Technology
Smrekar, Suzanne E., Jet Propulsion Laboratory
Solomon, Sean , Columbia University
Spilker, Linda J., Jet Propulsion Laboratory
Steele, Andrew, Carnegie Institution for Science
Stevenson, David J., California Institute of Technology
Sydora, Richard D., University of Alberta
Terzian, Yervant, Cornell University
Urquhart, Mary, University of Texas, Dallas
Walker, Raymond J., University of California, Los Angeles
Winglee, Robert M., University of Washington
Zuber, Maria T., Massachusetts Institute of Technology

Meteorites & Tektites

Albin, Edward, Georgia State University, Perimeter College, Online
Alpert, Sam, American Museum of Natural History
Binzel, Richard P., Massachusetts Institute of Technology
Cartwright, Julia, University of Alabama
Chan, Queenie, Royal Holloway University of London
Collins, Gareth, Imperial College
Corrigan, Catherine, Smithsonian Inst/Nat Mus of Nat History
Dunn, Tasha L., Colby College
Ebel, Denton S., American Museum of Natural History
French, Bevan, Smithsonian Institution / National Museum of Natural History
Genge, Matthew, Imperial College
Glass, Billy P., University of Delaware
Hartman, Ron N., Mt. San Antonio College
Harvey, Ralph P., Case Western Reserve University
Heymann, Dieter, Rice University
Hildebrand, Alan R., University of Calgary
Howie, Robert, Curtin University
Hutson, Melinda, Portland Community College - Sylvania Campus
Hutson, Melinda, Portland State University
Jurewicz, Amy , Arizona State University
Karner, James M., University of Utah
Krot, Alexander N., University of Hawai'i, Manoa
Martins, Zita, Imperial College
McCoy, Timothy J., Smithsonian Inst/Nat Mus of Nat History
Melosh, H. J., Purdue University
Park, Jisun, Graduate School of the City University of New York
Rodgers, Nick, University of Wales
Rubin, Alan E., University of California, Los Angeles
Ruzicka, Alexander (Alex) M., Portland State University
Sansom, Ellie, Curtin University
Schrader, Devin, Arizona State University
Sephton, Mark, Imperial College
Simon, Steven B., University of New Mexico
Sipiera, Paul P., Mercer University
Swindle, Timothy D., University of Arizona
Tait, Kim, Western University
Taylor, G. Jeffrey, University of Hawai'i, Manoa
Wadhwa, Meenakshi, Field Museum of Natural History
Warren, Paul, University of California, Los Angeles
Wasson, John T., University of California, Los Angeles

Astrophysics

Borthakur, Sanchayeeta, Arizona State University
Boss, Alan P., Carnegie Institution for Science
Bowman, Judd, Arizona State University
Butler, Nathaniel, Arizona State University
Butler, R. Paul, Carnegie Institution for Science
Chambers, John E., Carnegie Institution for Science
Cruzen, Shawn, Columbus State University
Desch, Steven, Arizona State University

Devillepoix, Hadrien, Curtin University
Gagne, Marc R., West Chester University
Groppi, Christopher, Arizona State University
Hawthorne Allen, Alice M., Concord University
Horst, Sarah, Johns Hopkins University
Jacobs, Daniel, Arizona State University
Kulkarni, Shrinivas R., California Institute of Technology
MacIssac, Daniel E., Buffalo State College
Mauskopf, Philip, Arizona State University
Morgan, Siobahn M., University of Northern Iowa
Noble, Allison, Arizona State University
Paglione, Timothy, York College (CUNY)
Patience, Jennifer, Arizona State University
Puckett, Andrew, Columbus State University
Scannapieco, Evan, Arizona State University
Schwarz, Karen, West Chester University
Scowen, Paul, Arizona State University
Sheppard, Scott S., Carnegie Institution for Science
Shkolnik, Evgenya, Arizona State University
Starrfield, Sumner, Arizona State University
Timmes, Francis, Arizona State University
Van Engelen, Alexander, Arizona State University
Weinberger, Alycia J., Carnegie Institution for Science
Williams, Rosa, Columbus State University
Windhorst, Rogier, Arizona State University
Young, Patrick, Arizona State University
Ziemba, Tim, University of Washington

Heliophysics
Moldwin, Mark B., University of Michigan

Astrobiology
Walker, Sara, Arizona State University

ATMOSPHERIC SCIENCES

Atmospheric Sciences
Ackerman, Thomas P., University of Washington
Adames-Corraliza, Angel F., University of Michigan
Adegoke, Jimmy, University of Missouri, Kansas City
Agee, Ernest M., Purdue University
Aiyyer, Anantha, North Carolina State University
Aldrich, Eric A., University of Missouri
Alexander, Becky, University of Washington
Allan, Andrea, Oregon State University
Allard, Jason, Valdosta State University
Allen, Grant, University of Manchester
Allen, Robert J., University of California, Riverside
Alpert, Pinhas, Tel Aviv University
Anastasio, Cort, University of California, Davis
Ancell, Brian C., Texas Tech University
Anderson, Bruce, Boston University
Anderson, James G., Harvard University
Anderson, Mark R., University of Nebraska, Lincoln
Antonescu, Adrian, University of Manchester
Aquilina, Noel , University of Malta
Arakawa, Akio, University of California, Los Angeles
Ariya, Parisa A., McGill University
Arnfield, A. John, Ohio State University
Arnold, David L., Frostburg State University
Arnold, Stephen, University of Leeds
Arritt, Raymond W., Iowa State University of Science & Technology
Arya, Satyapal S., North Carolina State University
Atkinson, Christopher, University of North Dakota
Austin, Philip, University of British Columbia
Back, Larissa E., University of Wisconsin, Madison
Baker, Marcia B., University of Washington
Baldwin, Michael, Purdue University
Balmforth, Neil, University of British Columbia
Barlow, Mathew, University of Massachusetts, Lowell
Barnes, Elizabeth A., Colorado State University
Barnes, Jeffrey R., Oregon State University
Barrett, Bradford S., United States Naval Academy
Barrett, Kevin M., Tarrant County College, Northeast Campus
Bartello, Peter, McGill University
Barthelmie, Rebecca J., Cornell University
Bates, Timothy S., University of Washington
Bathke, Deborah J., University of Nebraska, Lincoln
Battisti, David S., University of Washington
Beard, Kenneth V., University of Illinois, Urbana-Champaign
Bell, Michael M., Colorado State University
Bennartz, Ralf, Vanderbilt University
Bergin, Michael H., Georgia Institute of Technology
Bierly, Gregory, Indiana State University
Bitz, Cecilia M., University of Washington
Black, Benjamin, Graduate School of the City University of New York
Black, Robert X., Georgia Institute of Technology
Blanchard, Edward, University of Washington
Blasing, Terence J., Oak Ridge National Laboratory
Blechman, Jerome B., SUNY, Oneonta
Blyth, Alan, University of Leeds
Boden, Thomas, Oak Ridge National Laboratory
Boering, Kristie, University of California, Berkeley
Bollasina, Massimo A., Edinburgh University
Bond, Nicholas A., University of Washington
Booth, Alastair, University of Manchester
Bosart, Lance F., SUNY, Albany
Bossert, James E., Los Alamos National Laboratory
Bou-Zeid, Elie, Princeton University
Boybeyi, Zafer, George Mason University
Bradley, Raymond S., University of Massachusetts, Amherst
Bretherton, Christopher S., University of Washington
Bromwich, David H., Ohio State University
Brooks, Sarah D., Texas A&M University
Brown, Robert A., University of Washington
Brubaker, Kenneth L., Argonne National Laboratory
Bruning, Eric C., Texas Tech University
Budikova, Dagmar, Illinois State University
Burls, Natalie, George Mason University
Bush, Andrew B., University of Alberta
Bush, Andrew B. G., University of Alberta
Businger, Joost A., University of Washington
Calhoun, Joseph, Millersville University
Camargo, Suzana, Columbia University
Cannon, Alex, University of British Columbia
Capehart, William J., South Dakota School of Mines & Technology
Capes, Gerard, University of Manchester
Carslaw, Ken, University of Leeds
Case Hanks, Anne T., University of Louisiana, Monroe
Castro, Mark S., University of Maryland
Cess, Robert D., SUNY, Stony Brook
Chameides, William L., Duke University
Chang, Edmund K., SUNY, Stony Brook
Chang, Hai-ru, Georgia Institute of Technology
Chang, Young-Soo, Argonne National Laboratory
Charlevoix, Donna J., University of Illinois, Urbana-Champaign
Charlson, Bob, University of Washington
Charlson, Robert J., University of Washington
Chen, Shuyi S., University of Washington
Chen, Tsing-Chang, Iowa State University of Science & Technology
Chen, Yi-Leng, University of Hawai'i, Manoa
Chen, Yongsheng, York University
Cheng, Meng-Dawn, Oak Ridge National Laboratory
Chipperfield, Martyn P., University of Leeds
Chiu, Christine, Colorado State University
Chiu, Long S., George Mason University
Choate, Jessica (Jessie), University of Illinois, Urbana-Champaign
Choularton, Thomas, University of Manchester
Chu, Pao-Shin, University of Hawai'i, Manoa
Chuang, Patrick Y., University of California, Santa Cruz
Clabo, Darren R., South Dakota School of Mines & Technology
Claire, Mark, University of St. Andrews
Clark, Richard D., Millersville University
Clarke, Antony D., University of Hawai'i, Manoa
Clegg, Simon, University of East Anglia
Clemitshaw, Kevin C., Royal Holloway University of London
Cobb, Steven R., Texas Tech University
Coe, Hue, University of Manchester
Colle, Brian, SUNY, Stony Brook
Collett, Jr., Jeffrey L., Colorado State University
Collins, Jennifer, University of South Florida
Collins, William D., University of California, Berkeley
Collis, Scott, Argonne National Laboratory

Colman, Bradley R., University of Washington
Colucci, Stephen J., Cornell University
Connolly, Paul, University of Manchester
Cook, Kerry H., University of Texas, Austin
Corcoran, William, Missouri State University
Costigan, Keeley R., Los Alamos National Laboratory
Côté, Jean, Universite du Quebec a Montreal
Cottingame, William, Los Alamos National Laboratory
Coulter, Richard L., Argonne National Laboratory
Covert, David S., University of Washington
Cowan, Nicolas B., McGill University
Crawford, Ian, University of Manchester
Crawford, James, Georgia Institute of Technology
Crilley, Leigh R., University of Birmingham
Cronin, Timothy W., Massachusetts Institute of Technology
Crowther, Sarah, University of Manchester
Curry, Judith A., Georgia Institute of Technology
Davis, Robert, University of Virginia
de Foy, Benjamin, Saint Louis University
Dearden, Christopher, University of Manchester
DeCaria, Alex J., Millersville University
DeConto, Robert, University of Massachusetts, Amherst
DeGaetano, Arthur, Cornell University
Delcambre, Sharon, Portland Community College - Sylvania Campus
DelSole, Timothy, George Mason University
Dempsey, David P., San Francisco State University
Deng, Yi, Georgia Institute of Technology
Denning, A. Scott, Colorado State University
Derome, Jacques F., McGill University
Desai, Ankur R., University of Wisconsin, Madison
Dessler, Alex, Texas A&M University
Dessler, Andrew E., Texas A&M University
Detwiler, Andrew G., South Dakota School of Mines & Technology
DeWekker, Stephan F., University of Virginia
Didlake, Jr., Anthony, Pennsylvania State University, University Park
Dirmeyer, Paul A., George Mason University
Dixon, Richard, Texas State University
Dobbie, Steven, University of Leeds
Dobler, Scott, Western Kentucky University
Doherty, Ruth, Edinburgh University
Dominguez, Francina, University of Illinois, Urbana-Champaign
Doskey, Paul V., Argonne National Laboratory
Dugas, Bernard, Universite du Quebec a Montreal
Dunn, Allison L., Worcester State University
Durkee, Josh, Western Kentucky University
Durran, Dale R., University of Washington
Edgell, Dennis J., University of North Carolina, Pembroke
Elliott, Scott M., Los Alamos National Laboratory
Ellul, Raymond , University of Malta
Epifanio, Craig, Texas A&M University
Essery, Richard L., Edinburgh University
Esslinger, Kelly L., Arizona Western College
Fabry, Frederic, McGill University
Faloona, Ian C., University of California, Davis
Fan, Xingang, Western Kentucky University
Faraji, Maedeh, Austin Community College District
Feng, Song, University of Arkansas, Fayetteville
Feng, Yan, Argonne National Laboratory
Fernando, Joe, University of Notre Dame
Ferruzza, David, Elizabethtown College
Fink, Uwe, University of Arizona
Finnegan, David L., Los Alamos National Laboratory
Fiore, Arlene M., Columbia University
Fiore, Arlene, Columbia University
Fischer, Emily, Colorado State University
Fisher, Rebecca, Royal Holloway University of London
Fishman, Jack, Saint Louis University
Fitzjarrald, David R., SUNY, Albany
Flato, Gregory M., University of Victoria
Fletcher, Roy J., University of Lethbridge
Forster, Piers M., University of Leeds
Fovell, Robert, University of California, Los Angeles
Fowler, Malcolm M., Los Alamos National Laboratory
Fox, Neil I., University of Missouri
Frame, Jeffrey, University of Illinois, Urbana-Champaign
Frederick, John E., University of Chicago
French, Adam, South Dakota School of Mines & Technology
Frierson, Dargan M., University of Washington
Frolking, Stephen E., University of New Hampshire
Fthenakis, Vasilis M., Columbia University
Fu, Qiang, University of Washington
Fu, Rong, University of Texas, Austin
Fueglistaler, Stephan A., Princeton University
Fuentes, Jose D., Pennsylvania State University, University Park
Fuhrmann, Christopher, Mississippi State University
Fung, Inez, University of California, Berkeley
Fyfe, John C., University of Victoria
Gachon, Philippe, Universite du Quebec a Montreal
Gaffney, Jeffrey S., Argonne National Laboratory
Gallagher, Martin, University of Manchester
Galloway, James N., University of Virginia
Gallus, William A., Iowa State University of Science & Technology
Gao, Yuan, Rutgers, The State University of New Jersey, Newark
Garcia, Oswaldo, San Francisco State University
Garrett, Timothy J., University of Utah
Gedzelman, Stanley, City College (CUNY)
Geller, Marvin A., SUNY, Stony Brook
Gervais, Melissa, Pennsylvania State University, University Park
Ghate, Virendra P., Argonne National Laboratory
Ghil, Michael, University of California, Los Angeles
Giannini, Alessandra, Columbia University
Gill, Swarndeep S., California University of Pennsylvania
Gluhovsky, Alexander, Purdue University
Goddard, Lisa M., Columbia University
Godfrey, Christopher, University of North Carolina, Asheville
Goldblatt, Colin, University of Victoria
Gonzalez, Alex, Iowa State University of Science & Technology
Goodman, Paul, University of Arizona
Goodrich, Greg, Western Kentucky University
Gordon, Mark, York University
Gordon, Rob J., University of Guelph
Gorka, Maciej, University of Wroclaw
Granger, Darryl E., Purdue University
Graves, Charles E., Saint Louis University
Grenfell, Thomas C., University of Washington
Griffis, Timothy J., University of Minnesota, Twin Cities
Grise, Kevin M., University of Virginia
Grotjahn, Richard , University of California, Davis
Guinan, Patrick E., University of Missouri
Gutzler, David J., University of New Mexico
Hage, Keith D., University of Alberta
Hakim, Gregory J., University of Washington
Hallar, Anna G., University of Utah
Hameed, Sultan, SUNY, Stony Brook
Hanrahan, Janel, Northern Vermont University-Lyndon
Hansen, William, Pace University, New York Campus
Hanson, Howard, Florida Atlantic University
Harnik, Nili, Tel Aviv University
Harrison, Halstead, University of Washington
Harrison, Roy M., University of Birmingham
Harshvardhan, Purdue University
Hart, Richard L., Argonne National Laboratory
Hartmann, Dennis L., University of Washington
Hastenrath, Stefan L., University of Wisconsin, Madison
Hastings, Meredith, Brown University
Hawkins, Timothy W., Shippensburg University
Hayes, Michael J., University of Nebraska, Lincoln
Heald, Colette, Massachusetts Institute of Technology
Hegerl, Gabriele C., Edinburgh University
Hegg, Dean A., University of Washington
Heikes, Brian G., University of Rhode Island
Helsdon, John H., South Dakota School of Mines & Technology
Hence, Deanna A., University of Illinois, Urbana-Champaign
Henderson, Gina R., United States Naval Academy
Hennon, Chris, University of North Carolina, Asheville
Hickmon, Nicki, Argonne National Laboratory
Hindman, Edward E., City College (CUNY)
Hirschboeck, Katherine K., University of Arizona
Hitchman, Matthew H., University of Wisconsin, Madison
Hjelmfelt, Mark R., South Dakota School of Mines & Technology
Holberg, Jay B., University of Arizona
Holgood, Jay S., Ohio State University

Holloway, Tracey, University of Wisconsin, Madison
Holzer, Mark, University of British Columbia
Horel, John, University of Utah
Horton, Daniel E., Northwestern University
Houston, Adam L., University of Nebraska, Lincoln
Houweling, Sander, Vrije Universiteit Amsterdam
Houze, Robert A., University of Washington
Hoyos, Carlos, Georgia Institute of Technology
Hu, Qi S., University of Nebraska, Lincoln
Hu, Qi (Steve), University of Nebraska, Lincoln
Huang, Alex, University of North Carolina, Asheville
Huey, Gregory L., Georgia Institute of Technology
Hugli, Wilbur G., University of West Florida
Hunten, Donald M., University of Arizona
Hurrell, James, Colorado State University
Hutyra, Lucy, Boston University
Idone, Vincent P., SUNY, Albany
Igel, Adele, University of California, Davis
Igel, Matthew, University of California, Davis
Ingersoll, Andrew P., California Institute of Technology
Jablonowski, Christiane, University of Michigan
Jackson, Andrea, University of Leeds
Jacob, Daniel J., Harvard University
Jaegle, Lyatt, University of Washington
Jaffe, Daniel A., University of Washington
Jain, Atul K., University of Illinois, Urbana-Champaign
Jenkins, Mary Ann, York University
Jewett, Brian, University of Illinois, Urbana-Champaign
Johnson, Donald R., University of Wisconsin, Madison
Johnson, Graham, Queensland University of Technology
Jones, Eric M., Los Alamos National Laboratory
Jones, Hazel, University of Manchester
Jones, Phillip D., University of East Anglia
Kaiser, Jason, Northern Vermont University-Lyndon
Kalidindi, Sirisha, Princeton University
Kang, Song-Lak, Texas Tech University
Kao, Jim C., Los Alamos National Laboratory
Karamperidou, Christina, University of Hawai'i, Manoa
Karmalkar, Ambarish, University of Massachusetts, Amherst
Kasting, James F., Pennsylvania State University, University Park
Kauffman, Chad, California University of Pennsylvania
Keables, Michael J., University of Denver
Keeling, Ralph F., University of California, San Diego
Keene, William, University of Virginia
Keesee, Robert G., SUNY, Albany
Keller, Linda M., University of Wisconsin, Madison
Keller, Jr., C. F., Los Alamos National Laboratory
Kennel, Charles F., University of California, San Diego
Keyser, Daniel, SUNY, Albany
Khairoutdinov, Marat, SUNY, Stony Brook
Kidder, Steven, Graduate School of the City University of New York
Kieu, Chanh Q., Indiana University, Bloomington
Kift, Richard, University of Manchester
Kim, Daehyun, University of Washington
Kim, Hyemi, Georgia Institute of Technology
Kim, Saewung, University of California, Irvine
King, Kenneth M., University of Guelph
King, Martin, Royal Holloway University of London
Kinter, Jim, George Mason University
Kirkpatrick, Cody, Indiana University, Bloomington
Kirlin, R. Lynn, University of British Columbia
Kirshbaum, Daniel, McGill University
Kishcha, Pavel, Tel Aviv University
Klaassen, Gary P., York University
Klees, Alicia, University of Illinois, Urbana-Champaign
Kliche, Donna V., South Dakota School of Mines & Technology
Kluver, Daria, Central Michigan University
Knapp, Warren, Cornell University
Knight, David, SUNY, Albany
Knopf, Daniel A., SUNY, Stony Brook
Koehler, Thomas , United States Air Force Academy
Konigsberg, Alvin S., SUNY, New Paltz
Kopacz, Dawn, University of Nebraska, Lincoln
Korty, Robert, Texas A&M University
Kossin, James, University of Wisconsin, Madison
Kota, Jozsef, University of Arizona
Kotamarthi, Rao, Argonne National Laboratory
Kreidenweis, Sonia M., Colorado State University
Krueger, Steven, University of Utah
Kuang, Zhiming, Harvard University
Kubas, Gregory J., Los Alamos National Laboratory
Kucharik, Chris, University of Wisconsin, Madison
Kung, Ernest C., University of Missouri
Kursinski, Robert, University of Arizona
Kushnir, Yochanan, Columbia University
Kutzbach, John E., University of Wisconsin, Madison
L'Ecuyer, Tristan S., University of Wisconsin, Madison
Lackmann, Gary M., North Carolina State University
Laird, Neil, Hobart & William Smith Colleges
Laprise, Rene, Universite du Quebec a Montreal
Lasher-Trapp, Sonia, University of Illinois, Urbana-Champaign
Lazarus, Steven M., Florida Institute of Technology
Leather, Kimberly, University of Manchester
Lee, In Young, Argonne National Laboratory
Lee, Meehye, Korea University
Leibensperger, Eric, SUNY, Plattsburgh
Leighton, Henry G., McGill University
Leppert, Ken, University of Louisiana, Monroe
Lew, Jeffrey, University of California, Los Angeles
Li, Laifang, Pennsylvania State University, University Park
Li, Tim, University of Hawai'i, Manoa
Li, Xiangshan, University of Houston
Lichtenberger, János, Eotvos Lorand University
Light, Bonnie, University of Washington
Lin, Hai, McGill University
Lin, Jialin, Ohio State University
Lin, John C., University of Utah
Lin, Wuyin, SUNY, Stony Brook
Lindgren, Paula, University of Glasgow
Liou, Kuo Nan, University of California, Los Angeles
Liu, Chuntao, Texas A&M University, Corpus Christi
Liu, Dantong, University of Manchester
Liu, Jiping, Georgia Institute of Technology
Liu, Ping, SUNY, Stony Brook
Lombardo, Kelly A., Pennsylvania State University, University Park
Lora, Juan, Yale University
Loriot, George, Northern Vermont University-Lyndon
Lowe, Douglas, University of Manchester
Lozowski, Edward P., University of Alberta
Lundquist, Jessica D., University of Washington
Luo, Chao, Georgia Institute of Technology
Lupo, Anthony R., University of Missouri
Lynch, Amanda H., Brown University
Lyons, Lawrence, University of California, Los Angeles
Lyons, Walter A., University of Northern Colorado
Maasch, Kirk A., University of Maine
Mace, Gerald, University of Utah
Magee, Nathan, College of New Jersey
Magnusdottir, Gudrun, University of California, Irvine
Mahowald, Natalie M., Cornell University
Mak, John E., SUNY, Stony Brook
Mak, Mankin, University of Illinois, Urbana-Champaign
Malcolm, Elizabeth, Virginia Wesleyan College
Maloney, Eric, Colorado State University
Manabe, Syukuro, Princeton University
Mann, Michael E., Pennsylvania State University, University Park
Mann, Michael E., Pennsylvania State University, University Park
Manning, Andrew, University of East Anglia
Marchand, Roger T., University of Washington
Mark, Bryan G., Ohio State University
Market, Patrick S., University of Missouri
Marley, Nancy A., Argonne National Laboratory
Marsham, John, University of Leeds
Martin, Randal S., New Mexico Institute of Mining and Technology
Martin, Timothy J., Argonne National Laboratory
Martin, Walter, University of North Carolina, Charlotte
Mason, Allen S., Los Alamos National Laboratory
Mass, Clifford F., University of Washington
Mauzerall, Denise L., Princeton University
Mawalagedara, Rachindra, Iowa State University of Science & Technology
Maykut, Gary A., University of Washington
Mayor, Shane D., California State University, Chico

Mazzocco, Elizabeth, Ashland University
McCollor, Doug, University of British Columbia
McDonald, Kyle, Graduate School of the City University of New York
McElroy, Michael B., Harvard University
McElroy, Tom, York University
McFarlane, Norman, University of Victoria
McFiggans, Gordon, University of Manchester
McGregor, Kent M., University of North Texas
McMurdie, Lynn A., University of Washington
McQuaid, Jim, University of Leeds
McWilliams, James C., University of California, Los Angeles
Mechoso, Carlos R., University of California, Los Angeles
Merlis, Timothy, McGill University
Meskhidze, Nicholas, North Carolina State University
Metz, Nicholas, Hobart & William Smith Colleges
Meyer, Steven J., University of Wisconsin, Green Bay
Michaels, Patrick J., University of Virginia
Miller, Doug, University of North Carolina, Asheville
Miller, Ronald L., Columbia University
Millet, Dylan B., University of Minnesota, Twin Cities
Mitchell, Jonathan, University of California, Los Angeles
Modzelewski, Henryk, University of British Columbia
Molina, Mario J., University of California, San Diego
Molinari, John E., SUNY, Albany
Monahan, Edward C., University of Connecticut
Moncrieff, John B., Edinburgh University
Montenegro, Alvaro, Ohio State University
Monteverdi, John P., San Francisco State University
Moody, Jennie L., University of Virginia
Morawska, Lidia, Queensland University of Technology
Morgan, William, University of Manchester
Mosley-Thompson, Ellen E., Ohio State University
Mote, Philip W., University of Washington
Mote, Philip, Oregon State University
Moyer, Elisabeth, University of Chicago
Moyer, Kerry A., Edinboro University of Pennsylvania
Mroz, Eugene J., Los Alamos National Laboratory
Mudrick, Stephen E., University of Missouri
Mullen, Steven L., University of Arizona
Murphy, Todd, University of Louisiana, Monroe
Murrell, Coling, University of East Anglia
Murthy, Prahlad N., Wilkes University
Nakamura, Noboru, University of Chicago
Nappo, Carmen, Georgia Institute of Technology
Nathan, Terrence R., University of California, Davis
Nathan, Terry, University of California, Davis
Neelin, J. David, University of California, Los Angeles
Nenes, Athanasios, Georgia Institute of Technology
Nesbitt, Stephen W., University of Illinois, Urbana-Champaign
Newman, Steven B., Central Connecticut State University
Nielsen-Gammon, John, Texas A&M University
Niyogi, Dev, Purdue University
Niyogi, Dev, University of Texas, Austin
Nogueira, Ricardo, Georgia State University
Norris, Joel R., University of California, San Diego
North, Gerald, Texas A&M University
Nugent, Alison D., University of Hawai'i, Manoa
O'Brien, Travis A., University of California, Davis
O'Brien, Travis, Indiana University, Bloomington
O'Gorman, Paul, Massachusetts Institute of Technology
Obrist, Daniel, University of Massachusetts, Lowell
Oechel, Walter, Open University
Ojala, Carl F., Eastern Michigan University
Okumura, Yuko, University of Texas, Austin
Oppenheimer, Michael, Princeton University
Orlanski, Isidoro, Princeton University
Orlove, Benjamin S., Columbia University
Orville, Richard E., Texas A&M University
Osterberg, Erich C., Dartmouth College
Overland, James E., University of Washington
Overpeck, Jonathan T., University of Arizona
Palmer, Paul, Edinburgh University
Pan, Ying, Pennsylvania State University, University Park
Pan, Zaitao, Saint Louis University
Pani, Eric A., University of Louisiana, Monroe
Paulson, Suzanne, University of California, Los Angeles
Paw U, Kyaw Tha, University of California, Davis
Pegion, Kathy, George Mason University
Percell, Peter, University of Houston
Percival, Carl, University of Manchester
Perez, Richard R., SUNY, Albany
Perry, Kevin D., University of Utah
Persad, Geeta, University of Texas, Austin
Peterson, Richard E., Texas Tech University
Petters, Markus, North Carolina State University
Petty, Grant W., University of Wisconsin, Madison
Pierce, Jeff, Colorado State University
Plumb, Raymond A., Massachusetts Institute of Technology
Polzin, Dierk T., University of Wisconsin, Madison
Powell, Mark L., Los Angeles Pierce College
Prather, Kimberly A., University of California, San Diego
Prather, Michael J., University of California, Irvine
Preston, Aaron, Northern Vermont University-Lyndon
Preston, Thomas C., McGill University
Previdi, Michael, Columbia University
Price, Colin G., Tel Aviv University
Prinn, Ronald G., Massachusetts Institute of Technology
Proistosescu, Cristian (Cristi), University of Illinois, Urbana-Champaign
Pryor, Sara C., Cornell University
Pu, Zhaoxia, University of Utah
Pumphrey, Hugh C., Edinburgh University
Pusede, Sally, University of Virginia
Radke, Lawrence F., University of Washington
Raman, Sethu S., North Carolina State University
Ramanathan, V., University of California, San Diego
Ramsey, Kelvin W., University of Delaware
Randall, David A., Colorado State University
Rappenglueck, Bernhard, University of Houston
Rasmussen, Kristen L., Colorado State University
Rauber, Robert M., University of Illinois, Urbana-Champaign
Ravishankara, A.R., Colorado State University
Rawlins, Michael, University of Massachusetts, Amherst
Ray, Pallav, Florida Institute of Technology
Rayner, John N., Ohio State University
Raysoni, Amit , University of Texas, Rio Grande Valley
Reay, David, Edinburgh University
Reichler, Thomas, University of Utah
Reisner, Jon M., Los Alamos National Laboratory
Reiss, Nathan, Pace University, New York Campus
Reuter, Gerhard W., University of Alberta
Revelle, Douglas O., Los Alamos National Laboratory
Richter, David, University of Notre Dame
Ricketts, Hugo, University of Manchester
Riemer, Nicole, University of Illinois, Urbana-Champaign
Riordan, Allen J., North Carolina State University
Ristovski, Zoran, Queensland University of Technology
Ritsche, Michael, Argonne National Laboratory
Robertson, Andrew W., Columbia University
Robinson, Walter A., University of Illinois, Urbana-Champaign
Robinson, Walter, North Carolina State University
Roche, Didier, Vrije Universiteit Amsterdam
Roe, Gerard H., University of Washington
Rogers, Jeffrey C., Ohio State University
Ross, Robert S., Millersville University
Rowe, Clinton M., University of Nebraska, Lincoln
Rupp, David, Oregon State University
Russell, Armistead G., Georgia Institute of Technology
Russell, Lynn M., University of California, San Diego
Rutledge, Steven A., Colorado State University
Saltzman, Eric S., University of California, Irvine
Samson, Perry, University of Michigan
Sandel, Bill R., University of Arizona
Sarachik, Edward, University of Washington
Sarachik, Edward S., University of Washington
Saravanan, R., Texas A&M University
Schade, Gunnar, Texas A&M University
Schlosser, C. Adam, Massachusetts Institute of Technology
Schmittner, Andreas, Oregon State University
Schneider, Edwin K., George Mason University
Schneider, Tapio, California Institute of Technology
Schroeder, John L., Texas Tech University
Schumacher, Courtney, Texas A&M University

Schumacher, Russ, Colorado State University
Seeley, Mark W., University of Minnesota, Twin Cities
Selin, Noelle, Massachusetts Institute of Technology
Semazzi, Fred H. M., North Carolina State University
Serreze, Mark, University of Colorado
Shafer, Jason, Northern Vermont University-Lyndon
Shell, Karen M., Oregon State University
Shellito, Lucinda, University of Northern Colorado
Shen, Samuel S., University of Alberta
Shen, Xinhua, University of Northern Iowa
Shepherd, Gordon G., York University
Shepherd, Mark A., Austin Community College District
Shepson, Paul B., Purdue University
Sherman-Morris, Kathleen M., Mississippi State University
Shinoda, Toshiaki, Texas A&M University, Corpus Christi
Shirley, Terry, University of North Carolina, Charlotte
Shukla, Jagadish, George Mason University
Shulski, Martha D., University of Nebraska, Lincoln
Sikora, Todd D., Millersville University
Simpson, Robert M., University of Tennessee, Martin
Sisterson, Doug, Argonne National Laboratory
Sisterson, Douglas L., Argonne National Laboratory
Siuta, David, Northern Vermont University-Lyndon
Smedley, Andrew, University of Manchester
Smith, Paul L., South Dakota School of Mines & Technology
Smith, Phillip J., Purdue University
Smith, Ronald B., Yale University
Snow, Julie A., Slippery Rock University
Snyder, Peter K., University of Minnesota, Twin Cities
Snyder, Richard L., University of California, Davis
Sobel, Adam H., Columbia University
Sobel, Adam, Columbia University
Sokolik, Irina, Georgia Institute of Technology
Solomon, Susan, Massachusetts Institute of Technology
Somerville, Richard C., University of California, San Diego
Soule, Peter T., Appalachian State University
Srivastava, Ramesh C., University of Chicago
Sriver, Ryan, University of Illinois, Urbana-Champaign
St. John, James C., Georgia Institute of Technology
Stan, Cristiana, George Mason University
Staten, Paul W., Indiana University, Bloomington
Steenburgh, Jim, University of Utah
Stevens, Philip S., Indiana University, Bloomington
Stevenson, David, Edinburgh University
Steyn, Douw G., University of British Columbia
Stickel, Robert, Georgia Institute of Technology
Stoelinga, Mark T., University of Washington
Stone, Peter H., Massachusetts Institute of Technology
Straub, Derek J., Susquehanna University
Straus, David M., George Mason University
Strobel, Darrell F., Johns Hopkins University
Strong, Courtenay, University of Utah
Stull, Roland B., University of British Columbia
Sturges, Bill, University of East Anglia
Stutz, Jochen P., University of California, Los Angeles
Sun, Jingru, Princeton University
Sun, Wen-Yih, Purdue University
Suvocarev, Kosana, University of California, Davis
Suyker, Andrew E., University of Nebraska, Lincoln
Swann, Abigail L., University of Washington
Swanson, Brian, University of Washington
Szunyogh, Istvan, Texas A&M University
Takle, Eugene S., Iowa State University of Science & Technology
Talley, John H., University of Delaware
Tatarskii, Viatcheslav, Georgia Institute of Technology
Taylor, Elwynn, Iowa State University of Science & Technology
Taylor, Peter A., York University
Teeuw, Richard, University of Portsmouth
Thorncroft, Christopher D., SUNY, Albany
Thorne, Richard M., University of California, Los Angeles
Thornton, Joel A., University of Washington
Thurtell, George W., University of Guelph
Tillman, James E., University of Washington
Ting, Mingfang, Columbia University
Tomasko, Martin G., University of Arizona
Tongue, Jeffrey, SUNY, Stony Brook
Trapp, Robert J., University of Illinois, Urbana-Champaign
Tung, Ka-Kit, University of Washington
Tung, Wen-wen, Purdue University
Turco, Richard, University of California, Los Angeles
Twine, Tracy E., University of Minnesota, Twin Cities
Tzortziou, Maria, Graduate School of the City University of New York
Ullrich, Paul, University of California, Davis
Van Den Broeke, Matthew S., University of Nebraska, Lincoln
van den Heever, Sue, Colorado State University
van Leeuwen, Peter Jan, Colorado State University
Vaughan, Geraint, University of Manchester
Veres, Michael, SUNY, Oswego
Vimont, Daniel J., University of Wisconsin, Madison
Vincent, Dayton G., Purdue University
Vogelmann, Andrew, SUNY, Stony Brook
von Salzen, Knut, University of Victoria
von Salzen, Knut, University of British Columbia
Vukovich, George, York University
Wagner, Timothy J., Creighton University
Walcek, Christopher J., SUNY, Albany
Waliser, Duane E., SUNY, Stony Brook
Wallace, John M., University of Washington
Walter-Shea, Elizabeth A., University of Nebraska, Lincoln
Wang, Hsiang-Jui, Georgia Institute of Technology
Wang, Jian, SUNY, Stony Brook
Wang, Pao-Kuan, University of Wisconsin, Madison
Wang, Wei-Chyung, SUNY, Albany
Wang, Yuhang, Georgia Institute of Technology
Wang, Yuqing, University of Hawai'i, Manoa
Wang, Yuxuan, University of Houston
Wang, Zhuo, University of Illinois, Urbana-Champaign
Warland, Jon, University of Guelph
Warren, Stephen G., University of Washington
Waugh, Darryn W., Johns Hopkins University
Wax, Charles L., Mississippi State University
Weare, B. C., University of California, Davis
Weaver, Justin E., Texas Tech University
Weber, Rodney J., Georgia Institute of Technology
Webster, Peter J., Georgia Institute of Technology
Weinbeck, Robert S., SUNY, The College at Brockport
Weiss, Christopher C., Texas Tech University
Wennberg, Paul O., California Institute of Technology
Wesely, Marvin L., Argonne National Laboratory
Wettstein, Justin, Oregon State University
Whitaker, Rodney W., Los Alamos National Laboratory
Whiteway, James, York University
Wikle, Christopher K., University of Missouri
Wilhelmson, Robert B., University of Illinois, Urbana-Champaign
Wilks, Daniel, Cornell University
Williams, John M., SUNY, The College at Brockport
Williams, Paul, University of Manchester
Willoughby, Hugh E., Florida International University
Wilson, John D., University of Alberta
Wine, Paul H., Georgia Institute of Technology
Wofsy, Steven C., Harvard University
Wood, Kim, Mississippi State University
Wood, Robert, University of Washington
Wu, Shiliang, Michigan Technological University
Wu, Xiaoqing, Iowa State University of Science & Technology
Wu, Yutian, Purdue University
Wuebbles, Donald J., University of Illinois, Urbana-Champaign
Wysocki, Mark, Cornell University
Xie, Lian, North Carolina State University
Yalda, Sepideh, Millersville University
Yang, Da, University of California, Davis
Yang, Ping, Texas A&M University
Yang, Wenchang, Princeton University
Yarger, Douglas N., Iowa State University of Science & Technology
Yau, Man Kong, McGill University
Yi, Chuixiang, Queens College (CUNY)
Young, John A., University of Wisconsin, Madison
Yu, Jin-Yi, University of California, Irvine
Yung, Yuk L., California Institute of Technology
Yuter, Sandra, North Carolina State University
Zaitchik, Benjamin, Johns Hopkins University
Zarzycki, Colin, Pennsylvania State University, University Park

Zawadzki, Isztar, McGill University
Zehnder, Joseph A., Creighton University
Zender, Charles, University of California, Irvine
Zeng, Ning, University of Maryland
Zhang, Chidong, University of Washington
Zhang, Henian, Georgia Institute of Technology
Zhang, Minghua, SUNY, Stony Brook
Zhang, Renyi, Texas A&M University
Zhang, Xi, University of California, Santa Cruz
Zhu, Ping, Florida International University
Zhuang, Qianlai, Purdue University
Zipser, Edward, University of Utah
Zuend, Andreas, McGill University

Meteorology

Adams, Manda S., University of North Carolina, Charlotte
Allen, John, Central Michigan University
Ault, Toby R., Cornell University
Babb, David M., Pennsylvania State University, University Park
Bahrmann, Chad, Pennsylvania State University, University Park
Bannon, Peter R., Pennsylvania State University, University Park
Bartholy, Judit, Eotvos Lorand University
Baxter, Martin, Central Michigan University
Bernhardt, Jase, Hofstra University
Biasutti, Michela, Columbia University
Billings, Brian J., Saint Cloud State University
Blackwell, Keith G., University of South Alabama
Bleck, Rainer, Los Alamos National Laboratory
Bohren, Craig F., Pennsylvania State University, University Park
Bowman, Kenneth P., Texas A&M University
Brown, Michael E., Mississippi State University
Brown, Paul W., University of Arizona
Brune, William H., Pennsylvania State University, University Park
Brunet, Gilbert, McGill University
Businger, Joost, University of Washington
Businger, Steven, University of Hawai'i, Manoa
Cahir, John J., Pennsylvania State University, University Park
Carlson, Richard E., Iowa State University of Science & Technology
Carlson, Toby N., Pennsylvania State University, University Park
Carroll, David, Virginia Polytechnic Institute & State University
Challinor, Andy, University of Leeds
Chang, Chih-Pei, Naval Postgraduate School
Chen, Hway-Jen, Naval Postgraduate School
Chen, Jing, McMaster University
Clark, John H., Pennsylvania State University, University Park
Clothiaux, Eugene E., Pennsylvania State University, University Park
Colby, Frank P., University of Massachusetts, Lowell
Cook, David R., Argonne National Laboratory
Corona, Thomas J., Metropolitan State College of Denver
Crafts, Christine, SUNY, The College at Brockport
Creasey, Robert L., Naval Postgraduate School
Croft, Paul J., Mississippi State University
Croft, Paul J., Kean University
Cullen, Heidi, Georgia Institute of Technology
Czarnetzki, Alan C., University of Northern Iowa
Dahl, Johannes M., Texas Tech University
Davidson, Kenneth L., Naval Postgraduate School
Davis, Kenneth J., Pennsylvania State University, University Park
Dixon, P. Grady, Fort Hays State University
Dorling, Stephen, University of East Anglia
Duncan Tabb, Neva, Saint Petersburg College, Clearwater
Durkee, Philip A., Naval Postgraduate School
Dutton, John A., Pennsylvania State University, University Park
Dyer, Jamie, Mississippi State University
Dyson, Liesl, University of Pretoria
Eastin, Matt, University of North Carolina, Charlotte
Ellingson, Don, Western Oregon University
Elsberry, Russell L., Naval Postgraduate School
Emanuel, Kerry A., Massachusetts Institute of Technology
Evans, Jenni L., Pennsylvania State University, University Park
Fairchild, Jane, University of Wisconsin Colleges
Farrell, Brian F., Harvard University
Ferger, Marisa, Pennsylvania State University, University Park
Fillion, Luc, McGill University
Finley, Jason P., Los Angeles Pierce College
Fitzpatrick, Patrick J., Mississippi State University
Flory, David M., Iowa State University of Science & Technology
Flynn, Wendilyn, University of Northern Colorado
Frank, William M., Pennsylvania State University, University Park
Fraser, Alistair B., Pennsylvania State University, University Park
Frederickson, Paul A., Naval Postgraduate School
Fritsch, J. Michael, Pennsylvania State University, University Park
Fullmer, James W., Southern Connecticut State University
Galewsky, Joseph, University of New Mexico
Garza, Jessica, Angelo State University
Gauthier, Pierre, Universite du Quebec a Montreal
Gillespie, Terry J., University of Guelph
Girard, Eric, Universite du Quebec a Montreal
Godek, Melissa, SUNY, Oneonta
Greybush, Steven J., Pennsylvania State University, University Park
Griswold, Jennifer S., University of Hawai'i, Manoa
Guest, Peter S., Naval Postgraduate School
Gutowski, William J., Iowa State University of Science & Technology
Gyakum, John R., McGill University
Hacker, Joshua P., Naval Postgraduate School
Haimberger, Leopold, University of Vienna
Hamill, Paul, McHenry County College
Haney, Christa M., Mississippi State University
Haney, Robert, Naval Postgraduate School
Hansen, Anthony R., Saint Cloud State University
Harlim, John, Pennsylvania State University, University Park
Harr, Patrick A., Naval Postgraduate School
Harrington, Jerry Y., Pennsylvania State University, University Park
Heyniger, William C., Kean University
Hilliker, Joby, West Chester University
Hoffman, Eric G., Plymouth State University
Hosler, Charles L., Pennsylvania State University, University Park
Illari, Lodovica, Massachusetts Institute of Technology
Jenkins, Gregory S., Pennsylvania State University, University Park
Jin, Fei Fei, University of Hawai'i, Manoa
Jordan, Mary S., Naval Postgraduate School
Karmosky, Christopher, SUNY, Oneonta
Kaster, Mark A., Wilkes University
Keeler, Jason, Central Michigan University
Kimball, Sytske K., University of South Alabama
Kubesh, Rodney, Saint Cloud State University
Kumjian, Matthew R., Pennsylvania State University, University Park
Lai, Chung Chieng A., Los Alamos National Laboratory
Lamb, Dennis, Pennsylvania State University, University Park
Lander, Mark A., University of Guam
Landman, Willem A., University of Pretoria
Lawson, Merlin P., University of Nebraska, Lincoln
Lee, Sukyoung, Pennsylvania State University, University Park
Leonard, Meredith L., Los Angeles Valley College
Lerach, David G., University of Northern Colorado
Lindzen, Richard S., Massachusetts Institute of Technology
Liu, Yongqiang, Georgia Institute of Technology
Lyons, Steven, Angelo State University
Mandia, Scott A., Suffolk County Community College, Ammerman Campus
Manzi, Anthony, SUNY, Maritime College
Martin, Jonathan E., University of Wisconsin, Madison
Matthews, Adrian, University of East Anglia
McGauley, Michael G., Miami Dade College (Kendall Campus)
Meesters, Antoon, Vrije Universiteit Amsterdam
Mendenhall, Larry, Mt. San Antonio College
Mercer, Andrew, Mississippi State University
Montgomery, Michael T., Naval Postgraduate School
Moore, Richard W., Naval Postgraduate School
Morgan, Michael C., University of Wisconsin, Madison
Morschauser, Lindsey, Mississippi State University
Mower, Richard, Central Michigan University
Murphree, James Thomas, Naval Postgraduate School
Murray, Andrew, University of South Alabama
Ndarana, Thando, University of Pretoria
Nese, Jon, Pennsylvania State University, University Park
Nielsen, Kurt E., Naval Postgraduate School
Nietfeld, Daniel, Creighton University
Noone, David, Oregon State University
Nordstrom, Greg, Mississippi State University
North, Gerald R., Texas A&M University
Nowotarski, Christopher J., Texas A&M University
Nuss, Wendell A., Naval Postgraduate School

O'Neill, Larry, Oregon State University
Panetta, Richard L., Texas A&M University
Park, Myung-Sook, Naval Postgraduate School
Parker, Doug, University of Leeds
Parker, Matthew, North Carolina State University
Pasken, Robert W., Saint Louis University
Penny, Andrew, Naval Postgraduate School
Person, Arthur, Pennsylvania State University, University Park
Polvani, Lorenzo M., Columbia University
Priest, Eric, College of Lake County
Renard, Robert J., Naval Postgraduate School
Renfrew, Ian, University of East Anglia
Reuter, Gerhard, University of Alberta
Richardson, Yvette P., Pennsylvania State University, University Park
Ritchie, Harold C., Dalhousie University
Ritz, Richard, Creighton University
Rochette, Scott M., SUNY, The College at Brockport
Rockwood, Anthony A., Metropolitan State College of Denver
Rodgers, N, Cardiff University
Rodriguez-Plasencia, Oscar, Univ Autonoma de Baja California Sur
Ross, Andrew, University of Leeds
Russell, William H., Los Angeles Pierce College
Ryan, William F., Pennsylvania State University, University Park
Sanabia, Elizabeth R., United States Naval Academy
Scarnato, Barbara V., Naval Postgraduate School
Schaffer, David L., Wichita State University
Schrage, Jon M., Creighton University
Schultz, David, University of Manchester
Seager, Richard, Columbia University
Seaman, Nelson L., Pennsylvania State University, University Park
Shannon, Jack D., Argonne National Laboratory
Shirer, Hampton N., Pennsylvania State University, University Park
Skubis, Steven T., SUNY, Oswego
Skyllingstad, Eric, Oregon State University
Stamm, Alfred J., SUNY, Oswego
Stauffer, David R., Pennsylvania State University, University Park
Steiger, Scott, SUNY, Oswego
Stensrud, David J., Pennsylvania State University, University Park
Straub, Katherine H., Susquehanna University
Syrett, William, Pennsylvania State University, University Park
Terwey, Wes, University of South Alabama
Tett, Simon F., Edinburgh University
Thomson, Dennis W., Pennsylvania State University, University Park
Todd, Steve, Portland Community College - Sylvania Campus
Torlaschi, Enrico, Universite du Quebec a Montreal
Tripoli, Gregory J., University of Wisconsin, Madison
Vaughan, Naomi, University of East Anglia
Verlinde, Johannes, Pennsylvania State University, University Park
Vernon, James Y., Los Angeles Pierce College
Wagner Riddle, Claudia, University of Guelph
Wallace, Tim, Mississippi State University
Wang, Bin, University of Hawai'i, Manoa
Wang, Qing, Naval Postgraduate School
Wash, Carlyle H., Naval Postgraduate School
Weisman, Robert A., Saint Cloud State University
Williams, Aaron, University of South Alabama
Williams, Forrest, Naval Postgraduate School
Williams, Roger T., Naval Postgraduate School
Wilson, John D., University of Alberta
Wyngaard, John C., Pennsylvania State University, University Park
Wysong, Jr., James F., Hillsborough Community College
Yang, Zong-Liang, University of Texas, Austin
Yoh, Shing, Kean University
Young, George S., Pennsylvania State University, University Park
Zhao, Jingxia, University of Hawai'i, Manoa
Zois, Constantine S., Kean University
Zunkel, Paul, Emporia State University

Atmospheric Chemistry

Anastasio, Cort, University of California, Davis
Aneja, Viney P., North Carolina State University
Dibb, Jack E., University of New Hampshire
Elshorbany, Yasin, University of South Florida
Faloona, Ian, University of California, Davis
Francisco, Joseph, University of Pennsylvania
Hess, Peter G., Cornell University
Miljevic, Branka, Queensland University of Technology
Murray, Lee, University of Rochester
Schwab, James J., SUNY, Albany
Talbot, Robert, University of Houston
Tong, Daniel, George Mason University

Atmospheric Physics

Atreya, Sushil, University of Michigan
Chen, Shu-Hua, University of California, Davis
Kok, Jasper F., University of Tennessee, Knoxville
Malakar, Nabin, Worcester State University
Micallef, Alfred, University of Malta
Paget, Aaron C., Concord University
Torri , Giuseppe, University of Hawai'i, Manoa
Warren, Stephen G., University of Washington

Climatology

Archer, Emma, University of Pretoria
Ayanlade, Ayansina, Obafemi Awolowo University
Bradley, Alice, Williams College
Burakowski, Elizabeth, University of New Hampshire
Burnette, Dorian, University of Memphis
Daoust, Mario, Missouri State University
DeCosmo, Janice, University of Washington
Diem, Jeremy E., Georgia State University
Druckenbrod, Daniel L., Rider University
Feldl, Nicole, University of California, Santa Cruz
Foster, Stuart A., Western Kentucky University
Frei, Allan, Hunter College (CUNY)
Frye, John , University of Wisconsin, Whitewater
Hass, Alisa L., Middle Tennessee State University
Hirschboeck, Katherine K., University of Arizona
Kelsey, Eric, Plymouth State University
Kravitz, Ben, Indiana University, Bloomington
Monier, Erwan, University of California, Davis
Osborn, Timothy J., University of East Anglia
Payne, Ashley E., University of Michigan
Pidwirny, Michael, University of British Columbia, Okanagan Campus
Saunders, Ian , University of British Columbia, Okanagan Campus
Schultze, Steven R., University of South Alabama
Skinner, Christopher , University of Massachusetts, Lowell
Stine, Alexander, San Francisco State University
Suriano, Zac, University of Nebraska, Omaha
Tian, Di, Auburn University
Tudhope, Alexander, University of Washington
Vega, Anthony J., Clarion University
Yow, Donald M., Eastern Kentucky University
Zarzar, Christopher, North Carolina Central University

GEOSCIENCE & SOCIETY

Natural Hazards

Aranda, Angela, California State University, Fullerton
Atwater, Brian, University of Washington
Blanchard, R. Denise, Texas State University
Blodgett, Robert H., Austin Community College District
Cullen, Cheila, Graduate School of the City University of New York
De Scally, Fes, University of British Columbia, Okanagan Campus
Dewan, Ashraf, Curtin University
Goda, Katsu, Western University
Hagelman III, Ronald, Texas State University
Haney, Jennifer, Bloomsburg University
Hill, Arleen A., University of Memphis
Holloway, Tess, Ashland University
Horwell, Claire, Durham University
Johanson, Erik, Florida Atlantic University
Koehler, Rich D., University of Nevada, Reno
Kozak, Amanda L., Ashland University
Nethengwe, Nthaduleni S., University of Venda
Smit, Ansie, University of Pretoria
Talling, Peter, Durham University
Taylor, Mackenzie, Ashland University
Tiefenbacher, John, Texas State University
Vidale, Jon , University of Washington
Weiss, Robert, Virginia Polytechnic Institute & State University
Wittke, Seth, Wyoming State Geological Survey
Wooten, Richard M., N.C. Department of Environmental Quality

Manmade Hazards
Keil, Chris, Wheaton College

Water Quality/Use
Alsharif, Kamal, University of South Florida
Bouwer, Edward, Johns Hopkins University
Bradford, Joel, Utah Valley University
Crootof, Arica, University of Montana Western
Frankel, Tyler E., University of Mary Washington
Keller, Troy, Columbus State University
Korths, Patrick, SUNY, Plattsburgh
Kuwabara, James, City College of San Francisco
Loftus, Timothy, Texas State University
Martin, Zackary E., Austin Community College District
Muller, Marc, University of Notre Dame
Rippy, Megan, Virginia Polytechnic Institute & State University
Sigler, Adam, Montana State University
Steinschneider, Scott, Cornell University
Zhang, Ning, Central State University

Geoscience Communication
Boss, Stephen K., University of Arkansas, Fayetteville
Conway, Michael F., University of Arizona
McCartney, M. Carol L., University of Wisconsin, Madison, Div of Extension

History of Geoscience
Case, Stephen, Olivet Nazarene University
Dezzani, Raymond, University of Idaho
Drobnyk, John W., Southern Connecticut State University
Gottschalk, Bradford, University of Wisconsin, Madison, Division of Extension
Graber, Anna, University of Minnesota, Twin Cities
Kohlstedt, Sally G., University of Minnesota, Twin Cities
Oreskes, Naomi, Harvard University
Rosenberg, Gary D., Milwaukee Public Museum
Strick, James E., Franklin and Marshall College

OTHER

General Earth Sciences
Admire, Amanda R., Humboldt State University
Agutu, Nathan O., Jomo Kenyatta University of Agriculture & Technology
Antipova, Anzhelika, University of Memphis
Balch, Jennifer K., University of Colorado
Bank, Carl-Georg, University of Toronto
Barron, Robert, Michigan Technological University
Beach Davis, Janet, Heartland Community College
Benjamin, Patricia A., Worcester State University
Berry, Leonard, Florida Atlantic University
Boger, Rebecca, Graduate School of the City University of New York
Boitt, Mark, Jomo Kenyatta University of Agriculture & Technology
Booher, Gary, El Camino College
Boorstein, Margaret F., Long Island University, C.W. Post Campus
Bordossy, Andras, University of Newcastle Upon Tyne
Boston, Penelope, National Aeronautics & Space Administration
Boyce, Joseph I., McMaster University
Bradley, Jeffrey, Northwest Missouri State University
Branlund, Joy, Southwestern Illinois College - Sam Wolf Granite City Campus
Bretherton, Francis P., University of Wisconsin, Madison
Bries-Korpik, Jill, Century College
Britton, Gloria C., Cuyahoga Community College - Western Campus
Brod, Joseph D., Hillsborough Community College
Burns, Danny, Coastal Bend College
Busa, Mark, Middlesex Community College
Carlson, Galen R., California State University, Fullerton
Carlson, Heath, Eastern Connecticut State University
Carrell, Jennifer, Illinois State Geological Survey
Carter, Andy, Birkbeck College
Champion, Kyle M., Hillsborough Community College
Chapa, Laura E., Austin Community College District
Chege, George W., Jomo Kenyatta University of Agriculture & Technology
Chen, jiquan, Michigan State University
Cheng, Zhongqi (Joshua), Graduate School of the City University of New York
Cherrier, Jennifer, Graduate School of the City University of New York
Childers, Daniel, Delaware County Community College
Cihacek, Larry J., North Dakota State University
Clark, Michael, Mount Royal University
Cleveland, Natasha, Frederick Community College
Clift, Sigrid, University of Texas, Austin
Cole, Gregory L., Los Alamos National Laboratory
Condreay, Denise, Central Community College
Cordero, David I., Lower Columbia College
Cornebise, Michael W., Eastern Illinois University
Craig, Cameron D., Eastern Illinois University
Cranganu, Constantin, Graduate School of the City University of New York
Davis, James A., Eastern Illinois University
de Wit, Cary, University of Alaska, Fairbanks
Deka, Jennifer, Cuyahoga Community College - Western Campus
DeLima, Lynn-Ann, Eastern Connecticut State University
Dennison, Robert, Heartland Community College
Dod, Bruce D., Mercer University
Dolgoff, Anatole, Pace University, New York Campus
Douglas, Arthur V., Creighton University
Douthat, Jr., James R., Hillsborough Community College
Dutton, Jessica, Suffolk County Community College, Ammerman Campus
Erski, Theodore, McHenry County College
Ezerskis, John L., Cuyahoga Community College - Western Campus
Falk, Lisa, North Carolina State University
Fatherree, James W., Hillsborough Community College
Fielding, Lynn, El Camino College
Fields, Nancy, El Centro College - Dallas Community College District
Flanagan, Michael, Suffolk County Community College, Ammerman Campus
Flores, Kennet, Graduate School of the City University of New York
Fondran, Carol, Cuyahoga Community College - Western Campus
Fortes, Dominic, Birkbeck College
Foss, Donald J., College of Marin
Fritz, William, Graduate School of the City University of New York
Gernon, Thomas M., University of Southampton
Gibbs, Samantha J., University of Southampton
Goetz, Andrew R., University of Denver
Goulden, Michael L., University of California, Irvine
Groffman, Peter , Graduate School of the City University of New York
Hamilton, Thomas, Edmonds Community College
Harrington, Philip, Suffolk County Community College, Ammerman Campus
Haverluk, Terry W., United States Air Force Academy
Hawkins, Ward L., Los Alamos National Laboratory
Hayes, Van E., Hillsborough Community College
Hendrey, George, Queens College (CUNY)
Hillier, John, Grays Harbor College
Hobbs, Chasidy, University of West Florida
Hoke, Gregory, Syracuse University
Hoppe, Kathryn A., Green River Community College
Hughes, Noah C., Modesto Junior College
Hurd, David, Edinboro University of Pennsylvania
Ibrahim, Mohamed, Hunter College (CUNY)
Ide, Kayo, University of California, Los Angeles
Imwati, Andrew, Jomo Kenyatta University of Agriculture & Technology
Inglis, Michael, Suffolk County Community College, Ammerman Campus
Jackson, Allyson K., SUNY, Purchase
Johnson, Jean M., Dalton State Community College
Johnson, Kathleen, University of California, Irvine
Jones, Stephen M., University of Birmingham
Kane, Mustapha, Florida Gateway College
Keefover-Ring, Ken, University of Wisconsin, Madison
Keeling, David J., Western Kentucky University
Kellner, Patricia, Los Angeles Harbor College
Kelly, Maria, Edmonds Community College
Khade, Vishnu R., Eastern Connecticut State University
Koch, Joe, South Carolina Dept of Natural Resources
Lane, Joseph M., Cuyahoga Community College - Western Campus
Le Qu, Corinne, University of East Anglia
Leighty, Robert S., Mesa Community College
Lerch, Derek, Feather River College
Levasseur, Emile , Eastern Connecticut State University
Lew, Alan A., Northern Arizona University
Locke, James L., College of Marin
Lofthouse, Stephen T., Pace University, New York Campus
Lomaga, Margaret, Suffolk County Community College, Ammerman Campus
Longpre, Marc-Antoine, Graduate School of the City University of New York
Luo, Johnny, Graduate School of the City University of New York
Mack, John, Los Angeles Harbor College
Mackenzie, Kristen, Denver Museum of Nature & Science
MacNeil, James E., Hillsborough Community College
Marchisin, John, Pace University, New York Campus

Marlowe, Brian W., Hillsborough Community College
Marra, John, Graduate School of the City University of New York
Martek, Lynnette F., University of South Carolina, Lancaster
Mason, Sherri A., SUNY, Fredonia
McConnaughhay, Mark, Dutchess Community College
McDougall, Jim, Tacoma Community College
McGinn, Chris, North Carolina Central University
McNicol, Barbara, Mount Royal University
Meador, Cindy D., West Texas A&M University
Medina, Francisco, Univ Nacional Autonoma de Mexico
Meisner, Caroline B., Great Basin College
Mignery, Jill, Miami University
Mitra, Chandana, Auburn University
Moreland, Amy L., Austin Community College District
Moreno, Rafael, Metropolitan State College of Denver
Morton, Bruce, Eastern Connecticut State University
Motyka, James, Eastern Connecticut State University
Munasinghe, Tissa, Los Angeles Harbor College
Nagel, Athena, Mississippi State University
Narey, Martha A., University of Denver
Neumann, Patricia, El Camino College
Neves, Douglas, El Camino College
Newlon, Charles F. J., William Jewell College
Nisbet, Euan G., Royal Holloway University of London
North, Leslie, Western Kentucky University
Norton-Krane, Abby N., Cuyahoga Community College - Western Campus
O'Brien, Suzanne R., Bridgewater State University
O'Mullan, Gregory, Graduate School of the City University of New York
Olney, Jessica L., Hillsborough Community College
Olney, Matthew P., Hillsborough Community College
Osborn, Joe, Century College
Oxford, Jeremiah, Western Oregon University
Oymayan, Avo, Florida Gateway College
Pant, Hari, Graduate School of the City University of New York
Pappas, Matthew, Suffolk County Community College, Ammerman Campus
Parrot, Lael, University of British Columbia, Okanagan Campus
Pedley, Kate, University of Canterbury
Pekar, Stephen , Graduate School of the City University of New York
Peprah, Ebenezer, El Camino College
Perry, Baker, Appalachian State University
Perry, Randall, Imperial College
Pettengill, Gordon H., Massachusetts Institute of Technology
Phillippi, Nathan E., University of North Carolina, Pembroke
Pittman, Jason, Folsom Lake College
Pond, Lisa G., Louisiana State University
Potess, Marla, Hardin-Simmons University
Pringle, Patrick T., Centralia College
Rapley, Chris, University College London
Renfrew, Melanie, Los Angeles Harbor College
Ritter, Paul, Heartland Community College
Rock, Jessie L., North Dakota State University
Rosa, Lynn C., West Texas A&M University
Roth, Leonard T., Hillsborough Community College
Ryan, Susan, California University of Pennsylvania
Sasowsky, Kathryn, Cuyahoga Community College - Western Campus
Saunders, Charles, Randolph-Macon College
Saunders, Ralph, California State University, Dominguez Hills
Schreier, Hans D., University of British Columbia
Schulze, Karl, Waubonsee Community College
Schumacher, Matthew, Saint Francis Xavier University
Shaw, Katy, Green River Community College
Shugart, Jr., Herman H., University of Virginia
Smilnak, Roberta A., Metropolitan State College of Denver
Smith, Grant, Western Oregon University
Smith, H. Dixon, Metropolitan State College of Denver
Smith, Steven J., University of Northern Iowa
Smith, Thomas M., University of Virginia
Snyder, Jennifer L., Delaware County Community College
Soash, Norman E., Hillsborough Community College
Spooner, Alecia, Everett Community College
Springer, Kathleen B., San Bernardino County Museum
Stermer, Ed, Illinois Central College
Stone, Jim, Aims Community College
Sumrall, Jeanne L., Fort Hays State University
Tarr, Alexander, Worcester State University
Thomas, Ray G., University of Florida
Thurston, Phillips C., Laurentian University, Sudbury
Tidwell, Allan, Chipola College
Tinsley, Mark, Central Virginia Community College
Tongdee, Poetchanaporn, Hillsborough Community College
Travers, Steven, Heartland Community College
Valencia, Victor A., Washington State University
Valentine, Michael, Tacoma Community College
Van Cleave, Kevan A., Hillsborough Community College
van de Gevel, Saskia, Appalachian State University
Veblen, Thomas T., University of Colorado
Voorhees, David H., Waubonsee Community College
Vorwald, Brian, Suffolk County Community College, Ammerman Campus
Waddington, David C., Douglas College
Wade, Phillip, Western Oregon University
Walter, Nathan A., University of West Georgia
Wang, Enru, University of North Dakota
Ward, Sarah, Princeton University
Warger, Jane, Chaffey College
Webb, Craig A., Mt. San Antonio College
White, Susan, Los Angeles Harbor College
Williams, Mark W., University of Colorado
Wills, William V., Hillsborough Community College
Winterbottom, Wesley, Eastern Connecticut State University
Witter, Rob, Oregon Dept of Geology & Mineral Industries
Woods, Karen M., Lamar University
XU, Yingfeng, University of Louisiana at Lafayette
Yacucci, Mark, Heartland Community College
Yi, Chuixiang, Graduate School of the City University of New York
Zaleha, Robert, Cuyahoga Community College - Western Campus
Zhang, Pengfei, Graduate School of the City University of New York

Earth Science Education

Albach, Suzanne M., Washtenaw Community College
Atchison, Christopher L., University of Cincinnati
Attrep, Moses, Los Alamos National Laboratory
Aylward, Linda, Illinois Central College
Baker, Brett, University of Texas, Austin
Barnett, Michael, Boston College
Bednarski, Marsha, Central Connecticut State University
Bednarz, Robert S., Texas A&M University
Bednarz, Sarah W., Texas A&M University
Benner, Jake, University of Tennessee, Knoxville
Bergwerff, Kenneth A., Calvin College
Bernard-Kingsley, Noell, University of Washington
Black, Alice (Jill), Missouri State University
Blanford, William , Graduate School of the City University of New York
Block, Karin, Graduate School of the City University of New York
Bowman, Cassandra, Arizona State University
Buonaiuto Jr., Frank S., Graduate School of the City University of New York
Burns, Sandra, Central Connecticut State University
Butcher, Patricia M., California State University, Fullerton
Cadieux, Sarah, Rensselaer Polytechnic Institute
Carden-Jessen, Melanie E., Missouri State University
Carrick, Tina L., El Paso Community College
Cercone, Karen Rose, Indiana University of Pennsylvania
Chandler, Sandra, Arkansas Geological Survey
Clark, Scott K., University of Wisconsin, Eau Claire
Clary, Renee M., Mississippi State University
Clepper, Marta L., SUNY, Oneonta
Coburn, Daniel, Southern Connecticut State University
Coleman, Catherine, Arizona State University
Connolly, Cynthia, New Mexico Institute of Mining and Technology
Cooney, Timothy M., University of Northern Iowa
Crowder, Margaret, Western Kentucky University
d'Alessio, Matthew, California State University, Northridge
Dakin, Susan, University of Lethbridge
Dalman, Michael, Blinn College
Davies, Gareth, Open University
Davies, Sarah, Open University
De Kock, Walter E., University of Northern Iowa
de Ritter, Samantha, Flinders University
Dehne, Kevin T., Delta College
DeKraker, Dan, Cerritos College
Denton-Hedrick, Meredith Y., Austin Community College District
DePriest, Thomas A., University of Tennessee, Martin
Dieckmann, Melissa S., Eastern Kentucky University

Douglass, David N., Pasadena City College
Elkins, Joe T., University of Northern Colorado
Emerson, Cheryl R., Illinois Central College
Ensign, Todd I., Fairmont State University
Falkena, Lee, University of Illinois at Chicago
Faust, Megan, Portland State University
Ferguson, Julie , University of California, Irvine
Flanagan, Timothy, Berkshire Community College
Frankic, Anamarija, University of Massachusetts, Boston
Geraghty Ward, Emily, Rocky Mountain College
Gibbons, Doug, University of Washington
Glesener, Gary, Virginia Polytechnic Institute & State University
Godsey, Holly, University of Utah
Goodell, Laurel P., Princeton University
Gosselin, David C., University of Nebraska, Lincoln
Gray, Kyle R., University of Northern Iowa
Hamane, Angel, California State University, Los Angeles
Hammond, Amie C., Austin Community College District
Harrell, Michael, University of Washington
Heid, Kelly L., Grand Valley State University
Hemler, Deb, Fairmont State University
Hepple, Alex, Queensland University of Technology
Herman, Theodore C., West Valley College
Holliman, Richard, Open University
Hubenthal, Michael, Binghamton University
Hunter, Arlene G., Open University
Jahanyar, Alireza, University of Tabriz
Jo, Injeong, Texas State University
Johnston, Thomas, University of Lethbridge
Kornreich Wolf, Susan, Augustana College
Kortz, Karen M., Community College of Rhode Island
Krause, Lois B., Clemson University
Krockover, Gerald H., Purdue University
Kusnick, Judith E., Sacramento State University
LaDue, Nicole D., Northern Illinois University
Libarkin, Julie C., Michigan State University
Longoria, Jose F., Florida International University
Ludwikoski, David J., Community College of Baltimore County, Catonsville
MacKinnon, Stuart J., University of British Columbia, Okanagan Campus
MacLachlan, Ian R., University of Lethbridge
Maltese, Adam V., Indiana University, Bloomington
Martin-Vermilyea, Laurie, Montgomery County Community College
Mattox, Stephen R., Grand Valley State University
Maxwell, James "Sandy", West Chester University
McCollough, Cherie, Texas A&M University, Corpus Christi
McConnell, David A., North Carolina State University
McEvoy, Jamie , Montana State University
McGeary, Susan, University of Delaware
McMullin, David W., Acadia University
McNeal, Karen S., Auburn University
Messina, Paula, San Jose State University
Miller, Heather R., Austin Community College District
Milligan, Mark, Utah Geological Survey
Miyares, Ines, Hunter College (CUNY)
Morgan, Emory, Hampton University
Morton, Allan E., Central Arizona College
Mulkey, Sean, Illinois Central College
Muniz-Solari, Oswaldo, Texas State University
Munski, Douglas C., University of North Dakota
Murray, Daniel P., University of Rhode Island
Nakagawa, Masami, Colorado School of Mines
O'Neal, Claire J., University of Delaware
Oxley, Meghan, University of Washington
Papcun, George, New Jersey City University
Pepple, Christopher, Bowling Green State University
Petit, Martin A., Illinois Central College
Phillips, Paul, Fort Hays State University
Preston, William L., California Polytechnic State University
Pyle, Eric J., James Madison University
Rakonczai, Janos, Univesity of Szeged
Refenes, James L., Concordia University
Revels, Josh, Fairmont State University
Ricchezza, Victor J., Georgia State Univ, Perimeter College, Clarkston Campus
Roemmele, Christopher, West Chester University
Russ, Jean M., College of Southern Maryland
Ryker, Katherine, University of South Carolina
Schaffer, Linda J., SUNY, The College at Brockport
Schmitt, Danielle M., Princeton University
Scott, Vernon, Oklahoma State University
Semken, Steven, Arizona State University
Shelton, Dale W., Maryland Department of Natural Resources
Shepardson, Daniel P., Purdue University
Shipp, Stephanie S., Rice University
Skinner, Lisa, Northern Arizona University
Slattery, William, Wright State University
Smay, Jessica J., San Jose City College
Spurr, Aaron, University of Northern Iowa
Straw, Byron, University of Northern Colorado
Sundareshwar, P. V., South Dakota School of Mines & Technology
Sutton, Connie J., Indiana University of Pennsylvania
Swyrtek, Sheila M., Mott Community College
Taylor, Ta-Shana A., University of Miami
Teed, Rebecca, Wright State University
Thompson, Kenneth W., Emporia State University
Tonon, Marco Davide, Università di Torino
Villalobos, Joshua, El Paso Community College
Viskupic, Karen, Boise State University
Wagner, John R., Clemson University
Welch, Susan, New Mexico Institute of Mining and Technology
White, Lisa D., University of California, Berkeley
Wood, Howard, Texas A&M University, Corpus Christi
Wright, Carrie L., University of Southern Indiana
Yuan, Yihong, Texas State University
Zafian, Holly, Austin Community College District
Zipper, Carl E., Virginia Polytechnic Institute & State University
Zlotkin, Howard, New Jersey City University
Zwick, Thomas T., Montana State University, Billings

Physical Geography

Aay, Henry, Calvin College
Abend, Martin, New Jersey City University
Aber, Jeremy, Middle Tennessee State University
Adam, Iddrisu, University of Wisconsin Colleges
Akiwumi, Fenda, University of South Florida
Albright, Thomas , University of Nevada, Reno
Allen, Kelly E., Tulsa Community College
Amador, Nathanael S., Ohio Wesleyan University
Andresen, Christian, University of Wisconsin, Madison
Applegate, Toby, University of Massachusetts, Amherst
Aubert, John E., American River College
Balascio, Nicholas, William & Mary
Ballantyne, Colin K., University of St. Andrews
Barnett, Roger T., University of the Pacific
Barton, James H., Thiel College
Bascom, Johnathan, Calvin College
Bass, David, Flinders University
Bates, Mary, College of the Canyons
Battles, Eileen, University of Kansas
Bein, F. L., Indiana University, Indianapolis
Bekker, Matthew F., Brigham Young University
Beniest, Anouk, Vrije Universiteit Amsterdam
Berry, Kate, University of Nevada, Reno
Bitner, Thomas, University of Wisconsin Colleges
Black, Kathryn, Montclair State University
Blackburn, William, Western Kentucky University
Boester, Michael, Monroe Community College
Brothen, Jerry, El Camino College
Brothers, Timothy S., Indiana University, Indianapolis
Butzow, Dean G., Lincoln Land Community College
Cairns, David M., Texas A&M University
Camille, Michael A., University of Louisiana, Monroe
Campbell, Glenn A., Eastern Kentucky University
Carter, Greg, University of Southern Mississippi
Chacko, Elizabeth, George Washington University
Chaddock, Lisa, Cuyamaca College
Chatterjee, Meera, University of Akron
Clarke, Beverley, Flinders University
Clennan, Patrick D., College of Southern Nevada - West Charleston Campus
Coburn, Craig, University of Lethbridge
Comrie, Andrew, University of Arizona
Coveney, Eamonn, Fort Hays State University
Croft, Gary M., San Bernardino Valley College

Cross, John A., University of Wisconsin Oshkosh
Csank, Adam, University of Nevada, Reno
Csiki, Shane, New Hampshire Geological Survey
Curry, Janel M., Calvin College
Davidson, Fiona M., University of Arkansas, Fayetteville
Dawsey, Cyrus B., Auburn University
de Uña Alvarez, Elena P., Coruna University
Deckert, Garret, University of Wisconsin Colleges
DeWeese, Georgina G., University of West Georgia
Dexter, Leland R., Northern Arizona University
Dixon, Richard W., Texas State University
Dommissee, Edwin, University of Wisconsin Colleges
Dubsky, Scott , United States Air Force Academy
Dugmore, Andrew J., Edinburgh University
Duncan, Ian, City College of San Francisco
Ebiner, Matt, El Camino College
Eisenhart, Karen, Edinboro University of Pennsylvania
Engstrom, Vanessa, San Bernardino Valley College
Feeney, Thomas P., Shippensburg University
Fonstad, Mark, University of Oregon
Frolking, Tod A., Denison University
Gamble, Douglas W., University of North Carolina, Wilmington
Gaubatz, Piper, University of Massachusetts, Amherst
Gavin, Dan, University of Oregon
Girhard, T S., San Antonio Community College
Goudge, Theodore L., Northwest Missouri State University
Graham, Barbara, College of Southern Nevada - West Charleston Campus
Greene, Don M., Baylor University
Gripshover, Margaret , Western Kentucky University
Hall, Luke D., Ventura College
Hampson, Arthur, University of Utah
Harley, Grant, University of Idaho
Harrison, Robert S., Long Island University, C.W. Post Campus
Hart, Evan A., Tennessee Tech University
Harty, John P., Johnson County Community College
Hay, Iain, Flinders University
Hazen, Helen, University of Denver
Hedquist, Brent, Texas A&M University, Kingsville
Heibel, Todd, San Bernardino Valley College
Hepner, George F., University of Utah
Hess, Darrel E., City College of San Francisco
Heywood, Neil C., University of Wisconsin, Stevens Point
Hickcox, David H., Ohio Wesleyan University
Hindle, Tobin, Florida Atlantic University
Holland, Edward C., University of Arkansas, Fayetteville
Holt, David, University of Southern Mississippi
Houston, Serin D., Mount Holyoke College
Howard, Leslie M., Unversity of Nebraska, Lincoln
Ivey, James, University of South Florida
Jarvis, Richard S., University of Texas, El Paso
Jeon, Sung Bae, Eastern Kentucky University
Johnson, Mark O., Worcester State University
Jones, Alice, Eastern Kentucky University
Jordan, Karen J., University of South Alabama
Karpilo, Jr, Ronald J., Colorado State University
Kavanagh, Trudy A., University of British Columbia, Okanagan Campus
Kay, Jonathan, William & Mary
Kebbede, Girma, Mount Holyoke College
Kennedy, Linda, Mansfield University
Key, Doug, Palomar College
Khan, Belayet H., Eastern Illinois University
Kiage, Lawrence M., Georgia State University
Kilcoyne, John R., Metropolitan State College of Denver
Kimber, Clarissa T., Texas A&M University
Kung, Hsiang-Te, University of Memphis
Kuzera, Kristopher , University of Denver
Laity, Julie E., California State University, Northridge
Lambert, Dean P., San Antonio Community College
Lambert, Dean, Alamo Colleges, San Antonio College
League, Larry D., Dickinson State University
Lee, Jeffrey A., Texas Tech University
Lee, Russell, Oak Ridge National Laboratory
Little, Jonathan, Monroe Community College
Liu, Jing, Santa Monica College
LoVetere, Crystal, Cerritos College
Lynn, Resler M., Virginia Polytechnic Institute & State University
MacQuarrie, Pamela, Mount Royal University
Maher, John, Johnson County Community College
Maio, Chris, University of Alaska, Fairbanks
Mann, Dan, University of Alaska, Fairbanks
Manos, Leah D., Northwest Missouri State University
Markwith, Scott H., Florida Atlantic University
Marzulli, Walter, New Jersey Geological and Water Survey
Mbatu, Richard, University of South Florida
McAfee, Stephanie , University of Nevada, Reno
McCallister, Robert, University of Wisconsin Colleges
McCoy, William D., University of Massachusetts, Amherst
McGwire, Kenneth C., Desert Research Institute
Mensing, Scott A., University of Nevada, Reno
Minnich, Richard A., University of California, Riverside
Mizak, Connie, University of South Florida
Montgomery, Keith, University of Wisconsin Colleges
Montoya, Judith, Northern Arizona University
Morris, Pete, Santa Monica College
Motta, Luigi, Università di Torino
Motta, Michele, Università di Torino
Musolf, Gene E., University of Wisconsin Colleges
Nelson, Kenneth A., University of Kansas
Ngoy, Kikombo, Kean University
Nicholas, Joseph W., Mary Washington College
Nuwategeka, Expedito, Gulu University
Ogbuchiekwe, Edmund Jekwu, San Bernardino Valley College
Oldfield, Jonathan, University of Birmingham
Olson, Kimberly, American River College
Paulsell, Robert L., Louisiana State University
Peake, Jeffrey S., University of Nebraska, Omaha
Pennington, Deana, University of Texas, El Paso
Pesses, Michael, Antelope Valley College
Phillips, Nathan, Boston University
Pierce, Heather, Monroe Community College
Pinnt, Todd, Arizona Western College
Ponette-Gonzalez, Alexandra, University of North Texas
Precht, Francis L., Frostburg State University
Price, Alan P., University of Wisconsin Colleges
Price, Marie D., George Washington University
Privette, David, Central Piedmont Community College
Rahman, Abu, Antelope Valley College
Reese, Andy, University of Southern Mississippi
Rettig, Andrew, University of Dayton
Riley, James D., Eastern Illinois University
Robinson, Michael A., Santa Barbara City College
Rodgers, John C., Mississippi State University
Rohe, Randall, University of Wisconsin Colleges
Rollins, Kyle, Missouri Dept of Natural Resources
Rose, Leanna S., University of West Georgia
Ross, Thomas E., University of North Carolina, Pembroke
Rudnicki, Ryan E., Alamo Colleges, San Antonio College
Rudnicki, Ryan E., San Antonio Community College
Saladyga, Thomas, Concord University
Sandlin, Stephen H., San Bernardino Valley College
Santelmann, Mary V., Oregon State University
Schafer, Tom, Fort Hays State University
Schmidt, Lisa, San Bernardino Valley College
Scott, Larry, Colorado Geological Survey
Scott, Thomas A., University of California, Riverside
Sharkey, Debra, Cosumnes River College
Smith, C. K., San Antonio Community College
Smith, Charles K., Alamo Colleges, San Antonio College
Smith, Steven C., American River College
Stampone, Mary D., University of New Hampshire
Stern, Herschel I., MiraCosta College
Stevens, Stan, University of Massachusetts, Amherst
Stocks, Lee, Mansfield University
Swarts, Stanley W., Northern Arizona University
Thomsen, Charles E., American River College
Todhunter, Paul, University of North Dakota
Townsend, Christi, Texas State University
Tremblay, Thomas A., Univ of Texas at Austin, Jackson Sch of Geosciences
van Leeuwen, Willem, University of Arizona
Veverka, Laura, Metropolitan Community College-Kansas City
Vogel, Eve, University of Massachusetts, Amherst
Walter, Thomas, Hunter College (CUNY)

Watson, James R., Oregon State University
Webb, Craig, Eastern Kentucky University
Weisberg, Michael, Graduate School of the City University of New York
West, Keith, University of Wisconsin Colleges
White, Justin, Utah Valley University
Wilkie, Richard W., University of Massachusetts, Amherst
Wilkins, David E., Boise State University
Wilson, Jeffey S., Indiana University, Indianapolis
Wu, Shuang-Ye, University of Dayton
Wyckoff, John W., University of Colorado, Denver
Yassin, Barbara E., Mississippi Office of Geology
Ye, Hengchun, California State University, Los Angeles
Zhou, Yuyu, Iowa State University of Science & Technology

Remote Sensing

Aanstoos, James V., Iowa State University of Science & Technology
Abdalati, Waleed, University of Colorado
Abrams, Michael J., Jet Propulsion Laboratory
Ackerman, Steven A., University of Wisconsin, Madison
Ali, K. Adem, College of Charleston
Alley, Ronald E., Jet Propulsion Laboratory
Asner, Gregory, Arizona State University
Barros, Jose Antonio, Florida International University
Beaverson, Sheena K., Illinois State Geological Survey
Becker, Richard H., University of Toledo
Becker, Richard H., Argonne National Laboratory
Berlin, Graydon L., Northern Arizona University
Bernier, Monique, Universite du Quebec
Blom, Ronald G., Jet Propulsion Laboratory
Boulton, Sarah, University of Plymouth
Broadfoot, Lyle A., University of Arizona
Buratti, Bonnie J., Jet Propulsion Laboratory
Cablk, Mary, Desert Research Institute
Callahan, John A., University of Delaware
Calvin, Wendy, University of Nevada, Reno
Campbell, Bruce A., Smithsonian Institution / National Air & Space Museum
Campbell, James B., Virginia Polytechnic Institute & State University
Carn, Simon, Michigan Technological University
Cetin, Haluk, Murray State University
Chen, Shu-Hua, University of California, Davis
Chen, Xianfeng, Slippery Rock University
Chopping, Mark J., Montclair State University
Clark, Martin D., University of the Free State
Crippen, Robert E., Jet Propulsion Laboratory
Currit, Nathan, Texas State University
Dai, Chunli, Ohio State University
Dana, Gayle L., University of Nevada, Reno
Dash, Padmanava, Mississippi State University
Delahunty, Tina, Bloomsburg University
Di Girolamo, Larry, University of Illinois, Urbana-Champaign
Dodge, Rebecca L., Midwestern State University
Dondofema, Farai, University of Venda for Science & Technology
Duchesne, Rocio, University of Wisconsin, Whitewater
Easson, Gregory L., University of Mississippi
El-Baz, Farouk, Boston University
Engstrom, Ryan, George Washington University
Fenstermaker, Lynn, Desert Research Institute
Ferris, Michael H., California State University, Dominguez Hills
Fildes, Stephen , Flinders University
Fletcher, Andrew, Queensland University of Technology
Flynn, Luke P., University of Hawai'i, Manoa
Forster, Richard R., University of Utah
Frankenberg, Christian, California Institute of Technology
Frazier, Ryan J., Weber State University
Friedl, Mark, Boston University
Friedl, Mark A., Boston University
Frost, Eric G., San Diego State University
Gaitan-Moran, Javier, Univ Autonoma de Baja California Sur
Gammack-Clark, James, Florida Atlantic University
Gamon, John, University of Alberta
Gaulton, Rachel, University of Newcastle Upon Tyne
Gaya, Charles , Jomo Kenyatta University of Agriculture & Technology
Ghent, Rebecca, University of Toronto
Gibson, Glen, United States Air Force Academy
Gilbes, Fernando, University of Puerto Rico
Gimmestad, Gary G., Georgia Institute of Technology
Giraldo, Mario A., California State University, Northridge
Glenn, Nancy, Boise State University
Goetz, Alexander, University of Colorado
Hacker, Jorg, Flinders University
Hanna, Stephen P., Mary Washington College
Hardin, Perry J., Brigham Young University
Haritashya, Umesh, University of Dayton
Hay, Rodrick, California State University, Dominguez Hills
Heidinger, Andrew, University of Wisconsin, Madison
Hinojosa, Alejandro, Ctr de Invest Científica y de Ed Superior de Ensenada
Hobbs, Richard D., Amarillo College
Homayouni, Saied, Universite du Quebec
Hook, Simon J., Jet Propulsion Laboratory
Hossain, A K M Azad, University of Tennessee, Chattanooga
Hu, Baoxin, York University
Hu, Zhiyong, University of West Florida
Huang, Yi, McGill University
Humes, Karen, University of Idaho
Hung, Ming-Chih, Northwest Missouri State University
Hutchinson, Charles F., University of Arizona
Jaworski, Eugene, Eastern Michigan University
Jensen, Jennifer, Texas State University
Ji, Wei, University of Missouri, Kansas City
Jin, Yufang, University of California, Davis
Johnson, Elias, Missouri State University
Kahle, Anne B., Jet Propulsion Laboratory
Kasar, Sheila , Clarion University
Kenduiywo, Benson K., Jomo Kenyatta University of Agriculture & Technology
Kennedy, Robert, Oregon State University
Kern, Anikó, Eotvos Lorand University
Kessler, Fritz, Frostburg State University
Key, Jeffrey R., University of Wisconsin, Madison
Khan, Shuhab D., University of Houston
Klein, Andrew G., Texas A&M University
Klemas, Victor, University of Delaware
Kollias, Pavlos, McGill University
Kudela, Raphael M., University of California, Santa Cruz
Lakhan, V. Chris, University of Windsor
Larson, Eric J., University of Wisconsin, Stevens Point
Lawrence, Rick L., Montana State University
Lee, Keenan, Colorado School of Mines
Lee, Zhongping, University of Massachusetts, Boston
Li, Lin, Indiana University - Purdue University Indianapolis
Liu, Jian G., Imperial College
Lu, Zhong, Southern Methodist University
Lulla, Kamlesh, University of Delaware
Lynch, Merv, Curtin University
Lyon, Ronald J. P., Stanford University
Malhotra, Rakesh, North Carolina Central University
Mason, Philippa J., Imperial College
Mbuh, Mbongowo J., University of North Dakota
Mccoy, Roger M., University of Utah
McDade, Ian C., York University
McGrath, Andrew, Flinders University
McGwire, Kenneth, University of Nevada, Reno
Merchant, James W., Unversity of Nebraska, Lincoln
Meyer, Franz J., University of Alaska, Fairbanks
Miao, Xin, Missouri State University
Middleton, Carrie A., Dept of Int Off of Surface Mining Recl and Enforcement
Milan-Navarro, Joel, Univ Autonoma de San Luis Potosi
Miller, John, York University
Millette, Thomas L., Mount Holyoke College
Minor, Timothy B., Desert Research Institute
Molnár, Gábor, Eotvos Lorand University
Molnia, Bruce F., Duke University
Moon, Wooil M., University of Manitoba
Mshiu, Elisante E., University of Dar es Salaam
Muller-Karger, Frank E., University of South Florida
Mushkin, Amit, University of Washington
Mustard, John F., Brown University
Myneni, Ranga , Boston University
Nduati, Eunice W., Jomo Kenyatta University of Agriculture & Technology
Newland, Franz, York University
Ngigi, Thomas G., Jomo Kenyatta University of Agriculture & Technology
Ni-Meister, Wenge, Hunter College (CUNY)
Njoku, Eni G., Jet Propulsion Laboratory

Noh, Myoung-Jong, Ohio State University
O'Banion, Matthew S., United States Military Academy
Oubelkheir, Kadija, Curtin University
Palluconi, Frank D., Jet Propulsion Laboratory
Palmer, Richard, Curtin University
Parrish, Christopher E., University of New Hampshire
Pathirana, Sumith, Southern Cross University
Peddle, Derek R., University of Lethbridge
Peltzer, Gilles, University of California, Los Angeles
Petrie, Gregg, University of Washington
Pieters, Carle M., Brown University
Platnick, Steven, University of Wisconsin, Madison
Powell, Rebecca , University of Denver
Powell, Scott, Montana State University
Price, Kevin, Kansas State University
Pu, Ruiliang, University of South Florida
Qin, Rongjun, Ohio State University
Quisenberry, Dan R., Mercer University
Rahman, Abdullah F., University of Texas, Rio Grande Valley
Ramage, Joan, Lehigh University
Ramsey, Michael S., University of Pittsburgh
Ramspott, Matthew E., Frostburg State University
Rapp, Anita, Texas A&M University
Reed, Wallace E., University of Virginia
Ridd, Merrill K., University of Utah
Rivard, Benoit, University of Alberta
Roberts, Charles E., Florida Atlantic University
Rundquist, Bradley C., University of North Dakota
Rundquist, Donald C., Unversity of Nebraska, Lincoln
Sadiq, Abdulali A., University of Qatar
Sahr, John D., University of Washington
Schaaf, Crystal, Boston University
Schaaf, Crystal, University of Massachusetts, Boston
Schenk, Anton, SUNY, Buffalo
Seirer, Jami J., Fort Hays State University
Shirzaei, Manoochehr, Virginia Polytechnic Institute & State University
Siegfried, Matthew, Colorado School of Mines
Slivkoff, Matthew, Curtin University
Small, Christopher, Columbia University
Smith, Mike, Kingston University
Smith, Peter, University of Arizona
Stephenson, Garth, Stellenbosch University
Strahler, Alan, Boston University
Strain, Priscilla L., Smithsonian Institution / National Air & Space Museum
Sui, Daniel Z., Texas A&M University
Sultan, Mohamed, Western Michigan University
Szatmári, József, Univesity of Szeged
Thomas, Jeremy, University of Washington
Torres Parisian, Cathleen, University of Minnesota, Twin Cities
Toth, Charles K., Ohio State University
Tullis, Jason A., University of Arkansas, Fayetteville
Ustin, Susan L., University of California, Davis
van der Werf, Guido R., Vrije Universiteit Amsterdam
van Niekerk, Adriaan, Stellenbosch University
Vandemark, Douglas C., University of New Hampshire
Velicogna, Isabella, University of California, Irvine
Ventura, Stephen J., University of Wisconsin, Madison
Veraverbeke, Sander, Vrije Universiteit Amsterdam
Viertel, David C., Eastern Illinois University
Walker, Richard, University of Oxford
Wang, Lei, Ohio State University
Warner, Timothy A., West Virginia University
Wasomi, Charles B., Jomo Kenyatta University of Agriculture & Technology
Watson, Kelly, Eastern Kentucky University
Wei, Xiaofang, Central State University
Weng, Qihao, Indiana State University
Werth, Susanna, Virginia Polytechnic Institute & State University
White, Joseph D., Baylor University
Woo, David, California State University, East Bay
Woodcock, Curtis, Boston University
Woodcock, Curtis E., Boston University
Wright, William C., United States Military Academy
Yan, Xiao-Hai, University of Delaware
Yang, Zhiming, North Carolina Central University
Yool, Stephen R., University of Arizona
Yu, Qian, University of Massachusetts, Amherst
Zhang, Caiyun, Florida Atlantic University
Zhou, Xiaobing, Montana Tech of the University of Montana

Material Science

Alfe, Dario, University College London
Calaway, Wallis F., Argonne National Laboratory
Chiarello, Ronald P., Argonne National Laboratory
Chrzan, Daryl, University of California, Berkeley
Cook, Jane, Pennsylvania State University, University Park
deFontaine, Didier, University of California, Berkeley
DeJonghe, Lutgard, University of California, Berkeley
Devine, Thomas M., University of California, Berkeley
Eberhart, Mark E., Colorado School of Mines
Ferrari, Mauro, University of California, Berkeley
Glaeser, Andreas, University of California, Berkeley
Gronsky, Ronald, University of California, Berkeley
Gruen, Dieter M., Argonne National Laboratory
Haller, Eugene, University of California, Berkeley
Hayden, Geoffrey W., Mercer University
Hojjatie, Barry, Valdosta State University
Lu, Yongqi, University of Illinois
Morris, Jr., J. W., University of California, Berkeley
Nakote, Heinz, New Mexico State University, Las Cruces
Navrotsky, Alexandra, University of California, Davis
Pellin, Michael J., Argonne National Laboratory
Pylypenko, Svitlana, Colorado School of Mines
Ritchie, Robert O., University of California, Berkeley
Sands, Timothy, University of California, Berkeley
Strobel, Timothy A., Carnegie Institution for Science
Valiunas, Jonas K., Lakehead University
Voller, Vaughan R., University of Minnesota, Twin Cities
Weber, Eicke, University of California, Berkeley

Land Use/Urban Geology

Agrawal, Sandeep , University of Alberta
Bassett, Scott, University of Nevada, Reno
Bedore, Melanie, McMaster University
Bereitschaft, Bradley, University of Nebraska, Omaha
Birchall, Jeff, University of Alberta
Bodenman, John E., Bloomsburg University
Bonine, Michael E., University of Arizona
Bremer, Keith A., Fort Hays State University
Briggs, John, University of Glasgow
Buermann, Wolfgang, University of Leeds
Clark, Jessie , University of Nevada, Reno
Day, Rick L., Pennsylvania State University, University Park
Dixon, Nick, University of Leeds
Dolman, Paul, University of East Anglia
Emmi, Philip C., University of Utah
Ford, Andrew, Washington State University
Fusch, Richard D., Ohio Wesleyan University
Fürst, Christine, Martin-Luther-Universitaet Halle-Wittenberg
Godfrey, Brian J., Vassar College
Gosnell, Hannah, Oregon State University
Haggerty, Julia H., Montana State University
Harris, Richard S., McMaster University
Hines, Mary E., University of North Carolina, Wilmington
Hintz, Rashauna, University of Arkansas, Fayetteville
Holl, Karen D., University of California, Santa Cruz
Hungerford, Hilary, Utah Valley University
James, Valentine U., Clarion University
Jantz, Claire A., Shippensburg University
Jenssen, Petter, Norwegian University of Life Sciences (NMBU)
Kaushal, Sujay, University of Maryland
Kisekka, Isaya, University of California, Davis
Larson, David J., California State University, East Bay
Lee, Chung M., University of Utah
Liao, Haifeng (Felix), University of Idaho
Marston, Sallie A., University of Arizona
Mercier, Michael , McMaster University
Millington, Andrew, Flinders University
Moscovici, Daniel, Stockton University
Nevins, Joseph, Vassar College
Odogba, Ismaila, University of Wisconsin, Stevens Point
Ormerod, Kerri Jean , University of Nevada, Reno
Otterstrom, Samuel M., Brigham Young University
Platt, Rutherford H., University of Massachusetts, Amherst

Pomeroy, George M., Shippensburg University
Ptak, Tom, University of Idaho
Riebesell, John, University of Michigan, Dearborn
Rounsevell, Mark D., Edinburgh University
Shirgaokar, Manish, University of Alberta
Singh, Amrita, University of Alberta
Skillen, James, Calvin College
Smith, Betty E., Eastern Illinois University
Solecki, William, Montclair State University
Solecki, William, Hunter College (CUNY)
Steinberger, Julia, University of Leeds
Sullivan, Jack B., University of Maryland
Thomas, Valerie, Georgia Institute of Technology
Tilt, Jenna, Oregon State University
Troost, Kathy G., University of Washington
Van Den Hoek, Jamon, Oregon State University
Wickham, Thomas, California University of Pennsylvania
Wollheim, Wil, University of New Hampshire
Zhou, Yu, Vassar College

Geographic Information Systems

Adhikari, Sanchayeeta, California State University, Northridge
Ahearn, Sean C., Hunter College (CUNY)
Albrecht, Jochen, Hunter College (CUNY)
Alderson, David, University of Newcastle Upon Tyne
Algeo, Catherine, Western Kentucky University
Allen, Katherine, University of Liverpool
Allen-Lafayette, Zehdreh, New Jersey Geological and Water Survey
Ambinakudige, Shrinidhi, Mississippi State University
Amer, Reda, Tulane University
Andrews, John R., University of Texas at Austin, Jackson School of Geosciences
Argles, Tom, Open University
Artigas, Francisco, Rutgers, The State University of New Jersey, Newark
Ayad, Yasser M., Clarion University
Badruddin, Abu Z., Cayuga Community College
Bailey, Keiron D., University of Arizona
Barr, Stuart, University of Newcastle Upon Tyne
Barrett, Melony, Illinois State Geological Survey
Bauer, Emily, University of Minnesota
Beaty, Tammy, Oak Ridge National Laboratory
Becker, Lorene Y., Oregon State University
Benger, Simon, Flinders University
Benson, Jane L., Murray State University
Betchwars, Corey, University of Minnesota
Bloechle, Amber, University of West Florida
Boger, Rebecca, Brooklyn College (CUNY)
Boroushaki, Soheil, California State University, Northridge
Bottenberg, H. Carrie, Idaho State University
Bourbonnais, Mathieu L., University of British Columbia, Okanagan Campus
Bowlick, Forrest J., University of Massachusetts, Amherst
Breton, Caroline, University of Texas at Austin, Jackson School of Geosciences
Brown, Douglas, Kingston University
Bruns, Dale A., Wilkes University
Brunskill, Jeffrey C., Bloomsburg University
Burton, Christopher G., Auburn University
Busby, Michael R., Murray State University
Cao, Guofeng, Texas Tech University
Carstensen, Laurence W., Virginia Polytechnic Institute & State University
Carter, David, Dept of Int Off of Surface Mining Reclamation and Enforcement
Cary, Kevin, Western Kentucky University
Cheng, Qiuming, York University
Cheung, Wing, Palomar College
Cheung, Wing H., Palomar College
Chokmani, Karem, Universite du Quebec
Chow, Edwin, Texas State University
Christopherson, Gary, University of Arizona
Cicha, Jarrod, University of Minnesota
Cloutis, Ed, Western University
Coetzee, Serena, University of Pretoria
Colby, Jeff, Appalachian State University
Collins, Murray, Edinburgh University
Compas, Eric, University of Wisconsin, Whitewater
Congalton, Russell, University of New Hampshire
Cothren, Jackson D., University of Arkansas, Fayetteville
Coulibaly, Mamadou, University of Wisconsin Oshkosh
Cova, Thomas J., University of Utah
Coveney, Seamus, University of Glasgow
Crook, Steven, Palomar College
Cunningham, Mary A., Vassar College
Curri, Neil, Vassar College
Curry, Susan, University of Florida
Dai, Dajun, Georgia State University
Davis, Trevor J., University of Utah
De Kemp, Eric, University of Ottawa
Deakin, Ann K., SUNY, Fredonia
Deal, Richard, Edinboro University of Pennsylvania
Delparte, Donna M., Idaho State University
Demyanov, Vasily, Heriot-Watt University
Diver, Kim, Wesleyan University
Dixon, Barnali, University of South Florida
Dogwiler, Toby, Missouri State University
Dong, Pinliang, University of North Texas
Douglass, Gordon, Utah Geological Survey
Downs, Joni, University of South Florida
Drake, Luke, California State University, Northridge
Drummond, Jane, University of Glasgow
Drzyzga, Scott A., Shippensburg University
Duke, Jason E., Tennessee Tech University
Dunn, Amy, New Mexico Institute of Mining and Technology
Earle, Robert, American River College
Ebersole, Craig, DCNR- Pennsylvania Bureau of Geological Survey
Eichenbaum, Jack, Hunter College (CUNY)
Fan, Chao, University of Idaho
Fan, Weihong, Stockton University
Feeney, Alison E., Shippensburg University
Fehrs, Ellen R., DCNR- Pennsylvania Bureau of Geological Survey
Feng, Jia , University of Nevada, Reno
Fernández, Virginia, Univ de la Republica Oriental del Uruguay (UDELAR)
Fitzgerald, Francis S., Colorado Geological Survey
Forrest, David, University of Glasgow
Fox, Nicholas, Montana State University
Garren, Sandra J., Hofstra University
Gathany, Mark, Cedarville University
Gatrell, Jay, Eastern Illinois University
Gauthier, Donald J., Los Angeles Valley College
Gentry, Christopher, Austin Peay State University
Giordano, Alberto, Texas State University
Girard, Michael W., New Jersey Geological and Water Survey
Gittings, Bruce M., Edinburgh University
Gopal, Sucharita, Boston University
Gordon, Clare E., University of Leeds
Gorsevski, Peter, Bowling Green State University
Grala, Katarzynz, Mississippi State University
Graniero, Phil A., University of Windsor
Greatbatch, Ian, Kingston University
Greene, Chris, Dalhousie University
Grunwald, Sabine -., University of Florida
Haddock, Gregory D., Northwest Missouri State University
Halls, Joanne N., University of North Carolina, Wilmington
Halsted, Christian, Dept of Agriculture, Conservation, and Forestry
Hamilton, Jacqueline, University of Minnesota
Hancock, Gregory, University of Newcastle
Hancock, Steven, Edinburgh University
Haner, Andrew, Arkansas Geological Survey
Hansen, Christel D., University of Pretoria
Hansen, William J., Worcester State University
Haugerud, Ralph, University of Washington
Hedberg, Russell, Shippensburg University
Henderson, Matt, South Carolina Dept of Natural Resources
Hernandez, Michael W., Weber State University
Hick, Steven R., University of Denver
Hill, Malcolm D., Northeastern University
Hintz, John G., Bloomsburg University
Hong, Jessie, University of West Georgia
Hotz, Helenmary, University of Massachusetts, Boston
Howard, Hugh H., American River College
Huang, Jane, Fitchburg State University
Huffman, F. T., Eastern Kentucky University
Hughes, Annie, Kingston University
Humagain, Kamal, SUNY Potsdam
Ivanova, Ivana, Curtin University
Jennings, Nathan, American River College

Jensen, Ryan R., Brigham Young University
Jeu, Amy, Hunter College (CUNY)
Jin, He (Hannah), University of South Florida
Joshi, Manoj, University of East Anglia
Kahle, Chris, Iowa Dept of Natural Resources
Kambesis, Patricia, Western Kentucky University
Kar, Bandana, University of Southern Mississippi
Kelleher, Cole, University of Minnesota, Twin Cities
Kelley, Richard, New Mexico Institute of Mining and Technology
Kelley, Scott , University of Nevada, Reno
Kidd, David, Kingston University
Kienzle, Stefan, University of Lethbridge
Kimerling, A. Jon, Oregon State University
Kirimi, Fridah K., Jomo Kenyatta University of Agriculture & Technology
Klancher, Jacki, Central Wyoming College
Knight, Andi, New Mexico Institute of Mining and Technology
Kobara, Shinichi, Texas A&M University
Kohler, Nicholas, University of Oregon
Kostelnick, John, Illinois State University
Krizek, Jeffrey, San Bernardino Valley College
Kronenfeld, Barry J., Eastern Illinois University
Krygier, John B., Ohio Wesleyan University
Kwon, Youngsang, University of Memphis
Laffan, Shawn, University of New South Wales
lalap-Ayça, Seda, University of Massachusetts, Amherst
Landry, Shawn, University of South Florida
LaRue, Michelle, University of Minnesota, Twin Cities
Law, Zada, Middle Tennessee State University
Le, Yanfen, Northwest Missouri State University
Lee, Wook, Edinboro University of Pennsylvania
Lethbridge, Mark, Flinders University
Levine, Norman S., College of Charleston
Li, Gary, California State University, East Bay
Li, Jing, University of Denver
Li, Ping-Chi, Tennessee Tech University
Liang, Lu, University of North Texas
Lin, Meimei, Georgia Southern University
Lisichenko, Richard, Fort Hays State University
Liu, Weibo, Florida Atlantic University
Lobben, Amy, University of Oregon
Logsdon, Miles G., University of Washington
Longbrake, David, University of Denver
Lovett, Andrew A., University of East Anglia
Lu, Yongmei, Texas State University
Lukinbeal, Christopher, University of Arizona
Luo, Jun, Missouri State University
Lupo, Tom, American River College
Maantay, Juliana, Lehman College (CUNY)
Maas, Regan, California State University, Northridge
Machovina, Brett , United States Air Force Academy
Mackaness, William A., Edinburgh University
Magondu, Moffat G., Jomo Kenyatta University of Agriculture & Technology
Mansell, Mark, New Mexico Institute of Mining and Technology
Marcano, Eugenio J., Mount Holyoke College
Marin, Liliana, Baylor University
Marsan, Yvonne, University of North Carolina, Wilmington
Marzen, Luke J., Auburn University
May, Cynthia, Northland College
Mayer, Jordan, University of Minnesota
Mazariegos, Ruben, University of Texas, Rio Grande Valley
McCluskey, James, University of Wisconsin Colleges
Meentemeyer, Ross, University of North Carolina, Charlotte
Meng, Qingmin, Mississippi State University
Metcalf, Meredith, Eastern Connecticut State University
Micander, Rachel, University of Nevada, Reno
Miguel, Carlos, Univ de la Republica Oriental del Uruguay (UDELAR)
Miller, Harvey J., Ohio State University
Miller, Phillip, New Mexico Institute of Mining and Technology
Mitasova, Helena, North Carolina State University
Morgan, John D., University of West Florida
Morgan, Tamie, Texas Christian University
Morris, John A., Mississippi State University
Mucsi, lászló, University of Szeged
Mueller, Thomas, California University of Pennsylvania
Mukherjee, Falguni, Sam Houston State University
Mulligan, Kevin R., Texas Tech University
Mulrooney, Timothy, North Carolina Central University
Muthukrishnan, Suresh, Furman University
Mutua, Felix N., Jomo Kenyatta University of Agriculture & Technology
Mwangi, Nancy , Jomo Kenyatta University of Agriculture & Technology
Mwaniki, Mercy W., Jomo Kenyatta University of Agriculture & Technology
Nagihara, Seiichi, Texas Tech University
Nemon, Amy, Western Kentucky University
Nicolette, Justine, New Mexico Institute of Mining and Technology
Nimako, Solomon Nana Kwaku, San Bernardino Valley College
Obermeyer, Nancy J., Indiana State University
Oduor, Peter, North Dakota State University
Olson, Jeff, University of Wisconsin, Whitewater
Oxendine, Christopher E., United States Military Academy
Ozdenerol, Esra, University of Memphis
Palladino, Steve D., Ventura College
Pallis, Ted J., New Jersey Geological and Water Survey
Palmer, Evan, United States Air Force Academy
Pavlovskaya, Marianna, Hunter College (CUNY)
Pawlicki, Caron E., DCNR- Pennsylvania Bureau of Geological Survey
Pedemonte, Virginia, Univ de la Republica Oriental del Uruguay (UDELAR)
Peele, R Hampton, Louisiana State University
Percy, David, Portland State University
Porter, Claire, University of Minnesota, Twin Cities
Porter, John H., University of Virginia
Portillo, Danny, United States Air Force Academy
Pretorius, Erika, University of Pretoria
Price, Curtis V., South Dakota School of Mines & Technology
Price, Maribeth H., South Dakota School of Mines & Technology
Price, Peter E., Lonestar College - North Harris
Pristas, Ronald, New Jersey Geological and Water Survey
Proctor, Elizabeth, City College of San Francisco
Qi, Feng, Kean University
Qiang, Yi, University of South Florida
Qiu, Xiaomin, Missouri State University
Raber, George, University of Southern Mississippi
Rautenbach, Victoria J., University of Pretoria
Reader, Steven , University of South Florida
Rehwald, Matthew, University of Wisconsin, Madison, Division of Extension
Resnichenko, Yuri, Univ de la Republica Oriental del Uruguay (UDELAR)
Rice, Keith W., University of Wisconsin, Stevens Point
Riney, Kaylin, South Carolina Dept of Natural Resources
Robinson, Lori, University of Minnesota
Robinson, Michael, Georgia Southern University
Roof, Steven, Hampshire College
Rose, Caroline, University of Wisconsin, Madison, Division of Extension
Roushar, Kathy, University of Wisconsin, Madison, Division of Extension
Rowley, Rex J., Illinois State University
Saalfeld, Alan J., Ohio State University
Sadd, James L., Occidental College
Sagan, Vasit, Saint Louis University
Sanchez-Azofeifa, G. Arturo, University of Alberta
Sandau, Ken L., Montana Tech of The University of Montana
Sanz, Miguel Angel, Univ Complutense de Madrid
Schenck, William S., University of Delaware
Schoephoester, Peter, University of Wisconsin, Madison, Division of Extension
Scott, Darren M., McMaster University
Seong, Jeong C., University of West Georgia
Shears, Andrew, University of Wisconsin Colleges
Sleezer, Richard O., Emporia State University
Smith, Janet S., Shippensburg University
Snyman, Lourens, University of Pretoria
Starek, Michael , Texas A&M University, Corpus Christi
Stuart, Neil, Edinburgh University
Su, Haibin, Texas A&M University, Kingsville
Sun, Jeff, Casper College
Sun, Yifei, California State University, Northridge
Tadesse, Tsegaye, University of Nebraska, Lincoln
Tao, Ran, University of South Florida
Taylor, Nathan H., Arkansas Geological Survey
Taylor, Ryan W., SUNY, Purchase
Templeton, Alan R., Washington University in St. Louis
Thale, Paul R., Montana Tech of The University of Montana
Thayn, Jonathan B., Illinois State University
Tinkler, Dorothy, Treasure Valley Community College
Tiwari, Chetan, University of North Texas
Tong, Daoqin, University of Arizona

Tran, Linda C., Lonestar College - North Harris
Trotter, Lewis, Curtin University
Tu, Wei, Georgia Southern University
Unger, Corey, Utah Geological Survey
VanHorn, Jason E., Calvin College
Veisze, Paul M., American River College
Vincent, Paul C., Valdosta State University
Vlcan, Jennifer, University of Nevada, Reno
Walford, Nigel, Kingston University
Walls, Charles C., Dalhousie University
Walters, Steven, University of Washington
Wang, Lillian T., University of Delaware
Weber, Keith, Idaho State University
Weiss, Alfred W., Waubonsee Community College
Wen, Yuming, University of Guam
White, Scott, Fort Lewis College
Whiteaker, Timothy L., University of Texas, Austin
Williamson, Douglas, Hunter College (CUNY)
Wilson, Blake B., University of Kansas
Wilson, John R., Lafayette College
Wilson, Roy R., Eastern Connecticut State University
Woodhouse, Iain H., Edinburgh University
Xia, Jianhong (Cecilia), Curtin University
Xiao, Dana, Bloomsburg University
Xie, Zhixiao, Florida Atlantic University
Xu, Wei, University of Lethbridge
Yacucci, Mark A., University of Illinois
Yan, Jun, Western Kentucky University
Ye, Gordon, City College of San Francisco
Yin, Zhi-Yong, University of San Diego
Zhan, F Benjamin, Texas State University
Zhang, Guiming, University of Denver
Zhang, Qiaofeng (Robin), Murray State University
Zhao, Bo, Oregon State University

Geoinformatics

Awange, Joseph, Curtin University
Belton, Dave, Curtin University
Bhaskaran, Sunil, Graduate School of the City University of New York
Connor, Laura, University of South Florida
Curl, Doug C., University of Kentucky
Helmholz, Petra, Curtin University
Limp, William (., University of Arkansas, Fayetteville
Mansur, Adam, Smithsonian Institution / National Museum of Natural History
Marr, Paul G., Shippensburg University
Momm, Henrique G., Middle Tennessee State University
O'Dean, Emily, University of Nevada, Reno
Robinson, Todd, Curtin University
Savelyev, Alexander, Texas State University
Silveira, António B., Unive de Lisboa
Sui, Daniel, University of Arkansas, Fayetteville
Trivitt-Kracke, Amy, New Mexico Institute of Mining and Technology
Tsele, Philemon L., University of Pretoria
West, Geoff, Curtin University
Yilmaz, Alper, Ohio State University
Zaffos, Andrew A., University of Arizona

Global Change

Alexander, Peter, Edinburgh University
Bingham, Rob, Edinburgh University
Boschmann, E. Eric, University of Denver
Brookshire, Jack, Montana State University
Crimmins, Michael A., University of Arizona
Crowley, Kate, Edinburgh University
Ducey, Mark, University of New Hampshire
El Masri, Bassil, Murray State University
Ernakovich, Jessica, University of New Hampshire
Felzer, Benjamin S., Lehigh University
Ficken, Cari, SUNY, Buffalo
Gathorne-Hardy, Alfy, Edinburgh University
Giefer, Madeline M., Austin Peay State University
Gilligan, Jonathan M., Vanderbilt University
Goode, Ryan , Cerritos College
Hennige, Sebastian, Edinburgh University
Hernandez, Rebecca, University of California, Davis
Hicke, Jeffrey, University of Idaho
Kaufman, Darrell S., Northern Arizona University
Kopp, Robert E., Rutgers, The State University of New Jersey
Lawrence, Deborah, University of Virginia
Mathenge, Christine, Austin Peay State University
Nyantakyi-Frimpong, Hanson, University of Denver
Oches, Rick, Bentley University
Ollinger, Scott, University of New Hampshire
Rood, Richard B., University of Michigan
Rooney-Varga, Juliette, University of Massachusetts, Lowell
Sutton, Paul C., University of Denver
Taylor, Matthew, University of Denver
Tierney, Sean, University of Denver
Trigoso, Erika, University of Denver
Watson, Elizabeth, Drexel University
Wexler, Anthony S., University of California, Davis
Williams, Mathew, Edinburgh University
Wood, Gillen D., University of Illinois, Urbana-Champaign

Nanogeoscience

Fougerouse, Denis, Curtin University
Michel, F. M., Virginia Polytechnic Institute & State University
Reddy, Steve, Curtin University

Climate Modeling

Abatzoglou, John, University of Idaho
Cheng, Linyin, University of Arkansas, Fayetteville
Coats, Sloan, University of Hawai'i, Manoa
Dee, Sylvia G., Rice University
Galbraith, Eric, McGill University
Gutowski, William J., Iowa State University of Science & Technology
Hegewisch, Katherine, University of Idaho
Jackson, Charles S., University of Texas, Austin
Jackson, Charles, University of Texas, Austin
Lora, Juan, Yale University
Marinov, Irina, University of Pennsylvania
Sun, Fengpeng, University of Missouri, Kansas City
Vecchi, Gabriel, Princeton University

Not Elsewhere Classified

(Deep) McGregor, Mary, Montgomery College
Aamodt, Paul, Los Alamos National Laboratory
Abney, Kent D., Los Alamos National Laboratory
Abt, Charlotte J., University of Liverpool
Ackerman, Jessica R., Illinois State Geological Survey
Acosta, Patricia E., Williams College
Adams, Debi, West Texas A&M University
Agnew, Stephen F., Los Alamos National Laboratory
Aguilera, Juan Manuel Torres, Univ Autonoma de San Luis Potosi
Ahmed, Waquar, University of North Texas
Alavi, Hedy, Johns Hopkins University
Alberts, Heike C., University of Wisconsin Oshkosh
Albrecht, Lorraine, University of Waterloo
Albright, Katia, University of Nevada, Reno
Alde, Douglas, Los Alamos National Laboratory
Algin, Barbara, Columbia University
Ali-Bray, Julie, Mt. San Antonio College
Allen, Ashley L., Ohio Wesleyan University
Allen, Karen, Furman University
Allison, Tami L., Missouri Dept of Natural Resources
Ambruster, W. Scott, University of Alaska, Fairbanks
Amelung, Falk, University of Miami
Amor, John, University of British Columbia
Anand, Madhur, University of Guelph
Antar, Ali A., Central Connecticut State University
Anthony, Nina, Furman University
Appel, Heidi, University of Toledo
Arabas, Karen, Willamette University
Argenbright, Robert T., University of North Carolina, Wilmington
Armstrong, Andrew, University of New Hampshire
Arsuaga, Juan Luis, Univ Complutense de Madrid
Arundale, Wendy H., University of Alaska, Fairbanks
Arvidson, Raymond E., Washington University in St. Louis
Ashour-Abdalla, Maha, University of California, Los Angeles
Atisha-Castillo, Hector David, Univ Autonoma de San Luis Potosi
Au, Whitlow W L., University of Hawai'i, Manoa
Aufrecht, Walter E., University of Lethbridge
Ayers, Joseph , Northeastern University
Bailey, Ian, Exeter University

Baldizon, Ileana, Miami-Dade College (Wolfson Campus)
Ball, Elizabeth, University of Nevada, Reno
Ball, William P., Johns Hopkins University
Ballinger, Rhoda, Cardiff University
Bannon, Ann, Dalhousie University
Barmore, Garrett, University of Nevada, Reno
Barnbaum, Cecilia S., Valdosta State University
Barnes, Clare, Edinburgh University
Barnes, Fairley J., Los Alamos National Laboratory
Barnes, Jessica, University of South Carolina
Barnes, Philip, University of South Carolina
Barnes, Randal J., University of Minnesota, Twin Cities
Barra, Monica, University of South Carolina
Barron, Elizabeth, University of Wisconsin Oshkosh
Barron, George, University of Guelph
Barth, Susan A., Montana Tech of The University of Montana
Bartl, Simona, Moss Landing Marine Laboratories
Baskin, Perry A., Valdosta State University
Bass, Jerry, University of Southern Mississippi
Basso, Bruno, Michigan State University
Baumann, Sue, Argonne National Laboratory
Beatty, Merrill Ann, University of New Brunswick
Beck, Alan, Western University
Becker, Laurence, Oregon State University
Becker, Udo, University of Michigan
Bederman, Sanford H., Georgia State University
Behr-Andres, Christina "Tina", Los Alamos National Laboratory
Bellew, Angela, University of Iowa
Berchem, Jean, University of California, Los Angeles
Betancourt, Julio, University of Arizona
Bezdecny, Kris, California State University, Los Angeles
Bienvenu, Nadean S., University of Louisiana at Lafayette
Billiot, Fereshteh, Texas A&M University, Corpus Christi
Black, Annjeannette , Community College of Baltimore County, Catonsville
Blankenship, Robert, Washington University in St. Louis
Blatner , Keith , Washington State University
Blenkinson, Stephen, University of Newcastle Upon Tyne
Blumenfeld, Raphael, Imperial College
Boelman, Natalie, Columbia University
Boggs, Carol, University of South Carolina
Boisvert, Eric, Universite du Quebec
Boland, Greg J., University of Guelph
Boland, John J., Johns Hopkins University
Booth, Robert K., Lehigh University
Bosman, Martin, University of South Florida
Bossenbroek, Jonathon , University of Toledo
Boswell, Cecil, Missouri Dept of Natural Resources
Bourgeois, Reed J., Louisiana State University
Bourgeois, Reed J., Louisiana State University
Bowen, Dawn S., Mary Washington College
Bowen, Jennifer, Northeastern University
Bowen, Robert, University of Massachusetts, Boston
Bowersox, Joe, Willamette University
Bozzato, Edda, Laurentian University, Sudbury
Bradley, Michael D., University of Arizona
Brainard, James R., Los Alamos National Laboratory
Bratman, Eve, Franklin and Marshall College
Braught, Patricia, Dickinson College
Brewer, Margene, Calvin College
Bridgeman, Thomas, University of Toledo
Brooks, Ian, University of Leeds
Brown, Bradford D., University of Idaho
Brown, Kent D., Utah Geological Survey
Brown, Rob, Appalachian State University
Brunetto, Eileen, Middlebury College
Brunish, Wendee M., Los Alamos National Laboratory
Bryan, Jeffrey C., Los Alamos National Laboratory
Bryant, Anita M., University of West Georgia
Buck, Daniel, University of Oregon
Buck, Gregory, Texas A&M University, Corpus Christi
Buckley, Luke, Montana Tech of The University of Montana
Bullamore, Henry W., Frostburg State University
Bunker, Merle E., Los Alamos National Laboratory
Burk, Sue, University of Maryland
Burns, Carol J., Los Alamos National Laboratory
Burns, John W., Mt. San Antonio College
Busse, Friedrich H., University of California, Los Angeles
Butts, Thomas R., University of Texas, Dallas
Byrand, Karl, University of Wisconsin Colleges
Cahill, Michael J., SUNY, Stony Brook
Cahoy, Kerri, Massachusetts Institute of Technology
Cailliet, Gregor M., Moss Landing Marine Laboratories
Calegari, Pat, Pace University, New York Campus
Cammerata, Kirk , Texas A&M University, Corpus Christi
Campana, Michael E., University of New Mexico
Cannon, Kevin, Colorado School of Mines
Cantarero, Debra A., Pasadena City College
Capoccia, Mary, Ohio State University
Carey, Kristine M., Lakehead University
Carlin, Scott, Long Island University, C.W. Post Campus
Carr, David E., University of Virginia
Carroll, Matt, Washington State University
Carroll, Tracy, Missouri State University
Catalano, Valerie, Roger Williams University
Catau, John C., Missouri State University
Cattolico, Rose Ann, University of Washington
Caupp, Craig L., Frostburg State University
Cavello, Seth, University of South Florida
Chan, Selene, University of British Columbia
Chaney, Phil L., Auburn University
Chase, Anne, University of Arizona
Chase, Jon M., Washington University in St. Louis
Chatterjee, Ipsita, University of North Texas
Cheek, William H., Missouri State University
Chen, Kai Loon, Johns Hopkins University
Cheney, Donald, Northeastern University
Chief, Karletta, University of Arizona
Childs, Geoff, Washington University in St. Louis
Choquette, Marc, Universite Laval
Chouinard, Vera, McMaster University
Christopher, Micol, Mt. San Antonio College
Church, Warren, Columbus State University
Clark, David L., Los Alamos National Laboratory
Clark, James S., Duke University
Clark, Robert O., Northern Arizona University
Clark, Shannon, University of New Mexico
Clay, Robert, Missouri Dept of Natural Resources
Cleek, Richard, University of Wisconsin Colleges
Cochran, David, University of Southern Mississippi
Coffin, Richard B., University of Delaware
Cohen, Alice, Acadia University
Cohen, Joel E., Columbia University
Cohen, Matt, Furman University
Cohen, Shaul, University of Oregon
Colby, Bonnie C., University of Arizona
Colby, Sarah, Northern Arizona University
Coleman, Gary D., University of Maryland
Collins, Damian, University of Alberta
Collins, Lisa J., Northwestern University
Colwell, Frederick (Rick), Oregon State University
Confer, John, California University of Pennsylvania
Conkle, Jeremy, Texas A&M University, Corpus Christi
Cook, Stanton, University of Oregon
Cook, Steve, Oregon State University
Cookus, Pam, Illinois State Geological Survey
Coonley, Steffanie, Los Alamos National Laboratory
Copeman, Louise A., Oregon State University
Corcoran, Deborah, Missouri State University
Corey, Alison, Utah Geological Survey
Costea, Lidia, Northeastern Illinois University
Costello, Margaret, California State University, Long Beach
Couch, Libby, Denver Museum of Nature & Science
Cox, Shelah, Temple University
Crafford, J. P., University of Limpopo
Crail, Todd, University of Toledo
Crawford, Ian, Birkbeck College
Crepeau, Richard J., Appalachian State University
Cresswell, Tim, Edinburgh University
Cromar, Nancy, Flinders University
Crumbly, Isaac J., Fort Valley State University
Cupak, Martin, Curtin University
Cupples, Julie, Edinburgh University

Curry, Barbara, University of Texas, Dallas
Curry, James K., Arkansas Geological Survey
D'Arrigo, Rosanne, Columbia University
Damschen, Ellen, Washington University in St. Louis
Dash, Zora V., Los Alamos National Laboratory
Dasvarma, Gour, Flinders University
Daugherty, Carolyn M., Northern Arizona University
Davey, Patricia M., Brown University
Davis, James A., Brigham Young University
Dawson, Sarah, Franklin and Marshall College
Day, Rosie, University of Birmingham
Daymon, Deborah J., Los Alamos National Laboratory
De Beus, Barbara, Montclair State University
De Santo, Eilzabeth, Franklin and Marshall College
de Wit, Julien, Massachusetts Institute of Technology
Dean, Jeffrey S., University of Arizona
Deaton, Tami, University of North Texas
DeGraff, Jerry, Fresno State University
Delawder, Sandra, James Madison University
Demanet, Laurent, Massachusetts Institute of Technology
Deming, Jody, University of Manitoba
Dennis, Clyde B., Argonne National Laboratory
Dennis, Pam, University of Florida
Derrick, Sharon, Texas A&M University, Corpus Christi
Deschaine, Sylvia, Bates College
Dessler, Alexander, University of Arizona
Detrich, William, Northeastern University
Dibben, Chris, Edinburgh University
Dickerson, Richard E., University of California, Los Angeles
Dickhoff, Willem H., Washington University in St. Louis
Dighe, Kalpak, Los Alamos National Laboratory
Dill, Carilee, Bucknell University
Dingman, Steve, San Antonio Community College
Ditmars, John, Argonne National Laboratory
Divine, Aaron, Northern Arizona University
Dixon, Clifton, University of Southern Mississippi
Dixon, Michael, University of Guelph
Dixon, Paul R., Los Alamos National Laboratory
Domingue, Carla, Louisiana State University
Donahoe, Robert J., Los Alamos National Laboratory
Doorn, Stephen K., Los Alamos National Laboratory
Doro, Kennedy, University of Toledo
Dorries, Alison M., Los Alamos National Laboratory
Driever, Steven L., University of Missouri, Kansas City
Driscoll, John R., SUNY, Cortland
Duchane, David V., Los Alamos National Laboratory
Dudukovic, Mike, Washington University in St. Louis
Duff, John, University of Massachusetts, Boston
Duffey, Patricia, Fort Hays State University
Dunton, Karen K., Illinois State University
Duxbury, Thomas C., Jet Propulsion Laboratory
Dvorzak, Marie, University of Wisconsin, Madison
Dwyer, Daryl F., University of Toledo
Earls, Sandy, Oklahoma State University
Ebert, David, Moss Landing Marine Laboratories
Eby, Stephanie, Northeastern University
Edwards, John , Flinders University
Eggers, Delores M., University of North Carolina, Asheville
Eisenberger, Peter M., Columbia University
Eller, Phillip G., Los Alamos National Laboratory
Ellins, Katherine K., University of Texas, Austin
Elliott, C. James, Los Alamos National Laboratory
Ellis, Hugh, Johns Hopkins University
Ellis, Kathryn E., University of Kentucky
Emmett, Chad, Brigham Young University
Epstein, Howard E., University of Virginia
Esnault, Melissa H., Louisiana State University
Esser, Corinne, University of California, Davis
Evans, Claude, Washington University in St. Louis
Evans, Krista M., Missouri State University
Fadiman, Maria, Florida Atlantic University
Fallowfield, Howard, Flinders University
Fares, Mary A., Valdosta State University
Farley, Perry D., Los Alamos National Laboratory
Farrell, Mark O., Point Park University
Favor, Michael, University of Michigan, Dearborn
Felix, Joseph D., Texas A&M University, Corpus Christi
Feng, Zhiqiang, Edinburgh University
Ferguson, Teresa D., Oak Ridge National Laboratory
Ferreira, Maryanne F., Woods Hole Oceanographic Institution
Ferren, Richard L., Berkshire Community College
Fifer, Fred L., University of Texas, Dallas
Fish, Jennifer M., University of California, Santa Cruz
Fisher, Janet, Edinburgh University
Fitzpatrick, John R., Los Alamos National Laboratory
Fitzsimmons, Kevin, University of Arizona
Flaherty, Frank A., Valdosta State University
Fletcher, Austin, University of Guelph
Flores-Garcia, Mari C., California State University, Northridge
Floyd, Barry, New York State Geological Survey
Fogel, David N., Los Alamos National Laboratory
Foley, John P., Montana Tech of The University of Montana
Foster, Michael, Moss Landing Marine Laboratories
Foti, Pamela, Northern Arizona University
Fox, Laurel R., University of California, Santa Cruz
Freiermuth, Sue, University of Wisconsin, River Falls
Frisk, DeAnn M., Iowa State University of Science & Technology
Fry, Matthew, University of North Texas
Fryett, I, Cardiff University
Fuellhart, Kurtis G., Shippensburg University
Fuente, David E., University of South Carolina
Fuentes, Edna L., University of Illinois at Chicago
Gagosian, Carol, Wellesley College
Gallick, Roberta T., Point Park University
Ganey-Curry, Patricia E., University of Texas, Austin
Gao, Mengsheng, University of Florida
Gao, Oliver H., Cornell University
Garcia, Jan, Occidental College
Gartner, John F., University of Waterloo
Garvin, Theresa D., University of Alberta
Gautsch, Jacklyn, Iowa Dept of Natural Resources
Gehrels, Tom, University of Arizona
Geller, Jonathan, Moss Landing Marine Laboratories
Geller, Murray, Jet Propulsion Laboratory
Gemignani, Robert, Washington University in St. Louis
Gerhardt, Hannes, University of West Georgia
Gerry, Janelle, University of Nebraska, Lincoln
Ghattas, Omar, University of Texas, Austin
Ghosheh, Baher A., Edinboro University of Pennsylvania
Giammar, Daniel, Washington University in St. Louis
Gibbs, Gaynell, Louisiana State University
Gibson, Deana, Missouri State University
Gifford-Gonzalez, Dianne, University of California, Santa Cruz
Gilbert, Co'Quesie, Columbia University
Gillespie, Thomas, Emory University
Gillette, David P., University of North Carolina, Asheville
Gitelson, Anatoly, Unversity of Nebraska, Lincoln
Glenn, Ed, University of Arizona
Gong, Hongmian, Hunter College (CUNY)
Good, Daniel B., Georgia Southern University
Goodin, Ruth, University of Miami
Goodwin, Paul, University of Guelph
Gordon, Andrew, University of Guelph
Gouhier, Tarik, Northeastern University
Grace, Shannon M., Austin Community College District
Graff, William P., New Jersey Geological and Water Survey
Grande, Anthony, Hunter College (CUNY)
Granshaw, Frank D., Portland State University
Gravely, Cynthia Rae, Clemson University
Gray, Sarah, University of San Diego
Green, Brittany, Kansas State University
Griffin, Kevin, Columbia University
Griffith, Caitlin, University of Arizona
Gritzo, Russell E., Los Alamos National Laboratory
Grobler, Hendrik C., University of Johannesburg
Grossman, Lawrence S., Virginia Polytechnic Institute & State University
Guerra, Oralia, Austin Community College District
Guerrieri, Mary, University of Arizona
Guikema, Seth, Johns Hopkins University
Guzman, Ernesto, University of Guelph
Habash, Marc, University of Guelph
Habron, Geoffrey, Furman University

Haddad, Brent, University of California, Santa Cruz
Haff, Peter K., Duke University
Hafner, James A., University of Massachusetts, Amherst
Haggart, Renee, University of British Columbia
Halfman, Barbara, Hobart & William Smith Colleges
Hall, Christopher C., University of Guelph
Hall, I, Cardiff University
Hall, Jude, Denison University
Hall, Robert, University of Guelph
Hall, Ron, University of Lethbridge
Halladay, Sylvia R., Ohio Dept of Natural Resources
Hallett, Rebecca, University of Guelph
Hamilton, George, Berkshire Community College
Hammersley, Charles, Northern Arizona University
Hammond, Anne, Lakehead University
Hanke, Steve H., Johns Hopkins University
Hankins, Katherine B., Georgia State University
Hanna, Kevin, University of British Columbia, Okanagan Campus
Hansen, Jeffrey C., Los Alamos National Laboratory
Hardy, Shaun J., Carnegie Institution for Science
Harris, Virginia M., Wesleyan University
Harrison, Conor, University of South Carolina
Hartig, Ben, Curtin University
Hawley, Rebecca D., Northern Arizona University
Haynes, Kyle J., University of Virginia
Haynes, Kyle J., University of Virginia
Heaton, Jill, University of Nevada, Reno
Heaton, Richard C., Los Alamos National Laboratory
Heatwole, Charles A., Hunter College (CUNY)
Heckathorn, Scott, University of Toledo
Heenan, Cleo J., South Dakota School of Mines & Technology
Hegarty, Patricia, University College Cork
Heidt, James, University of Wisconsin Colleges
Heimpel, Moritz, University of Alberta
Heitman, Mary P., Iowa Dept of Natural Resources
Helmick, Sara B., Los Alamos National Laboratory
Hendrikx, Jordy, Montana State University
Henry, Lea-Anne, Edinburgh University
Henshel, Diane S., Indiana University, Bloomington
Herr, Larry, University of Lethbridge
Hicks, Andrea, University of Wisconsin, Madison
Higinbotham, Pamela, California University of Pennsylvania
Hildebrand, Stephen G., Oak Ridge National Laboratory
Hill, Christopher, Massachusetts Institute of Technology
Hill, Julie, University of Nevada, Reno
Hilpert, Markus, Johns Hopkins University
Hilts, Stewart G., University of Guelph
Hinderaker, Pam, Iowa State University of Science & Technology
Hintz, William, University of Toledo
Hirsch, Eric, Franklin and Marshall College
Hiser, Susan, Marietta College
Hobbs, Benjamin F., Johns Hopkins University
Hobbs, John D., Montana Tech of the University of Montana
Hockey, Thomas A., University of Northern Iowa
Hodges, Jackie, Fort Valley State University
Holbrook, Amanda, Morehead State University
Holdren, John P., Harvard University
Hollenbeck, Diane, Metropolitan State College of Denver
Holstein, Thomas J., Roger Williams University
Holt, Caecilia, Kutztown University of Pennsylvania
Homan, Amy L., Pennsylvania State University, University Park
Hommel, Demian, Oregon State University
Horne, Sharon, University of Windsor
Hrepic, Zdeslav, Columbus State University
Hsiang, Tom, University of Guelph
Hsiao, Theodore C., University of California, Davis
Huang, Norden E., University of Delaware
Huckabey, Marsha, University of Missouri
Huffman, Debra E., University of South Florida
Huffman, Robert L., Mercer University
Hughes, Randall, Northeastern University
Hull, Donald L., Los Alamos National Laboratory
Hunt, Kathy, University of Maryland
Hunt, Rachel, Edinburgh University
Hunt, Shelley, University of Guelph
Huntoon, Laura, University of Arizona
Hutchins, Peter S., Mississippi Office of Geology
Hysell, David, Cornell University
Hysell, David L., Cornell University
Iantria, Linnea, Missouri State University
Immonen, Wilma, Montana Tech of the University of Montana
Ioannides, Dimitri, Missouri State University
Ivy, Russell L., Florida Atlantic University
Jackson, Robert B., Duke University
Jacobs, Tenika, New Jersey Geological and Water Survey
Jamiolahmady, Mahmoud, Heriot-Watt University
Janetos, Tony, Boston University
Jarcho, Kari A., University of Minnesota, Twin Cities
Jensen, Scott W., South Dakota Dept of Env and Natural Resources
Jiang, Zhenhua, Argonne National Laboratory
Joanna, Lucero, New Mexico Institute of Mining and Technology
Johns, Rebecca, University of South Florida
Johnson, Daniel L., University of Lethbridge
Johnson, Emily P., Boston University
Johnson, Jeanne L., Louisiana State University
Johnson, Judy L., University of Alaska, Fairbanks
Johnson, Robert L., Argonne National Laboratory
Jones, Gwilym, Northeastern University
Jones, Minnie O., University of Illinois at Chicago
Jones, III, John P., University of Arizona
Jordan-Hernandez, Rafael, Univ Estatal de Sonora
Jornov, Donna, New York State Geological Survey
Joseph, Miranda, University of Arizona
Juanes, Ruben, Massachusetts Institute of Technology
Jun, Young-Shin, Washington University in St. Louis
Jurmanovich, Barb, Delta College
Juszczyk , Carmen , University of Colorado
Jutla, Rajinder S., Missouri State University
Kaczynski, Kristen M., California State University, Chico
Kallin, Hamish, Edinburgh University
Karl, Tami S., Florida State University
Kastrisios, Christos , University of New Hampshire
Kay, Richard F., Duke University
Keala, Lori, Pomona College
Keaton, Jeffrey R., University of Utah
Keatts, Merida, Kent State University
Kehoe-Forutan, Sandra J., Bloomsburg University
Keller, Jean, United States Military Academy
Kelly, Kimberly, Montgomery College
Kelly, Sherrie, St. Lawrence University
Kennedy, Christina B., Northern Arizona University
Kennel, Charles F., University of California, Los Angeles
Kevan, Peter, University of Guelph
Keyser, Jan, University of South Alabama
Khurana, Krishan, University of California, Los Angeles
Kidder, T.R., Washington University in St. Louis
Kidwell, Jen, Stanford University
Kifer, Lauri A., SUNY, The College at Brockport
Kile, Susan, Eastern Illinois University
Kim, Stacy, Moss Landing Marine Laboratories
Kim, Wan, Carnegie Institution for Science
Kimberly, Shaw, Columbus State University
Kimbro, David, Northeastern University
King-Hsi, Kung, Los Alamos National Laboratory
Kinkead, Scott, Los Alamos National Laboratory
Kipper, Jay P., University of Texas at Austin, Jackson School of Geosciences
Kneas, David, University of South Carolina
Komoto, Cary, Normandale Community College
Kontuly, Thomas M., University of Utah
Koralek, Susan, Southern Oregon University
Kosinski, Leszek A., University of Alberta
Kostov, Svilen, Georgia Southwestern State University
Kressler, Sharon J., University of Minnesota, Twin Cities
Krieble, Kelly, Moravian College
Krishnamurthy, sukanya, Edinburgh University
Kruse, Jennifer, Gustavus Adolphus College
Kumar, M. Satish, Queen's University Belfast
Kuntz, Kara, Fort Hays State University
LaBella, Joel, Wesleyan University
LaDochy, Steve, California State University, Los Angeles
LaFreniere, Lorraine M., Argonne National Laboratory
Lagowski, Alison A., SUNY, Buffalo

Lam, Anita, University of British Columbia
Lane, Mark, Palomar College
Larkin, Patrick, Texas A&M University, Corpus Christi
Larock, B. E., University of California, Davis
Larson, Harold P., University of Arizona
Laughlin, Andrew, University of North Carolina, Asheville
Laurier, Eric, Edinburgh University
Leal-Bejarano, Arturo, Univ Autonoma de Chihuahua
Lebofsky, Larry A., University of Arizona
Ledbetter, Cynthia E., University of Texas, Dallas
Lee, Alexis, University of North Carolina, Wilmington
Lee, Hung, University of Guelph
Lehane, Mary, University College Cork
Lekan, Thomas, University of South Carolina
Leland, John, University of Nevada, Reno
Lemmond, Peter C., Woods Hole Oceanographic Institution
Lener, Edward, Virginia Polytechnic Institute & State University
Lerdau, Manuel, University of Virginia
Lermurier, Nathalie, Institut Polytechnique LaSalle Beauvais (ex-IGAL)
Leveque, Connie, University of Maine, Presque Isle
Li, Wenhong, Duke University
Lichtner, Peter C., Los Alamos National Laboratory
Lin, Hsing K., University of Alaska, Fairbanks
Lin, Shoufa, University of Waterloo
Lin, Xiaomao, Kansas State University
Lindley, Stacy, Sacramento State University
Linky, Edward, Hunter College (CUNY)
Lipeles, Maxine I., Washington University in St. Louis
Lippert, Sarah, University of Chicago
Lloyd, Glenn D., Missouri Dept of Natural Resources
Loeb, Valerie, Moss Landing Marine Laboratories
Long, Laura, Lawrence Livermore National Laboratory
Long, Lisa, Ohio Dept of Natural Resources
Longmire, Patrick A., Los Alamos National Laboratory
Lorimer, Hayden, Edinburgh University
Lotterhos, Kathleen, Northeastern University
Lounsbury, Diane E., SUNY, Geneseo
Loveland, Karen, Missouri Dept of Natural Resources
Lovseth, John, Principia College
Lowry, William R., Washington University in St. Louis
Loxsom, Fred, Eastern Connecticut State University
Lucas, Beth, Virginia Polytechnic Institute & State University
Lujan-Lopez, Arturo, Univ Autonoma de Chihuahua
Lumpkin, Thomas A., Washington State University
Lynch, Casey, University of Nevada, Reno
Maciha, Mark J., Northern Arizona University
MacInnes, Michael, Los Alamos National Laboratory
Magee, Elizabeth, Northeastern University
Mahler, Robert L., University of Idaho
Maier, Raina M., University of Arizona
Maksoudian, Michell, California Polytechnic State University
Malagon, Teresa Soledad Medina, Univ Nacional Autonoma de Mexico
Malega, Ron, Missouri State University
Mangel, Mark S., University of California, Santa Cruz
Marks, Dennis W., Valdosta State University
Marshall, Stephen, University of Guelph
Martinez-Macias, Panfilo R., Univ Autonoma de San Luis Potosi
Masiello, Caroline A., Rice University
Maulud, Mat Ruzlin, University of Malaya
May, Diane M., Missouri State University
May, Fred E., University of Utah
Mayer, Christine M., University of Toledo
Maynard, David, California State University, San Bernardino
McArthur, Russell, San Francisco State University
McConnell, Joseph, University of Nevada, Reno
McCoy, Sue, Cosumnes River College
McDermott, Thomas M., SUNY, The College at Brockport
McDonald, Kyle C., Jet Propulsion Laboratory
McDonald, Lynn, Los Alamos National Laboratory
McFadden, Jennifer, Elizabethtown College
McGee, Tara, University of Alberta
McGraw, Maureen A., Los Alamos National Laboratory
McKenzie, Connie, Louisiana Tech University
McKenzie, Phyllis, Smithsonian Inst/Nat Mus of Nat History
McKenzie, Ross, University of Lethbridge
McLaughlin, Richard, Texas A&M University, Corpus Christi
McLeod, Clara, Washington University in St. Louis
McMillan, Robert S., University of Arizona
McNair, Laurie A., Los Alamos National Laboratory
Medlin, Peggy, Tennessee Tech University
Mehes, Roxane J., Laurentian University, Sudbury
Mendoza, Blanca, Univ Nacional Autonoma de Mexico
Meyer, Christopher, Smithsonian Inst/Nat Mus of Nat History
Meyer, Judith, Missouri State University
Meyerson, Rohana, Lafayette College
Michel, Shirley, University of Toledo
Middlemiss, Lucie, University of Leeds
Miller, Judy, Monroe Community College
Miller, Mark, University of Southern Mississippi
Miller, Ted R., South Dakota Dept of Env and Natural Resources
Milligan, Richard, Georgia State University
Mills, Suzanne, McMaster University
Milner, Jennifer, Augustana College
Mitchneck, Beth A., University of Arizona
Mittleider, Stacy, Chadron State College
Mockler, Theodore, Los Alamos National Laboratory
Moe-Hoffman, Amy P., Mississippi State University
Mollner, Daniel, Gustavus Adolphus College
Momen, Nasim, Boston University
Monahan, Adam, University of Victoria
Montgomery, Tamra S., Illinois State Geological Survey
Moodie, T. Bryant, University of Alberta
Moody, Eva, Tarleton State University
Mooney, Phillip, Sonoma State University
Moore, Clyde, Louisiana State University
Moorhead, Daryl L., University of Toledo
Moran-Taylor, Michelle, University of Denver
Morehouse, Barbara, University of Arizona
Morgan, Gary, Hampton University
Morin, Paul, University of Minnesota, Twin Cities
Morris, Donald P., Lehigh University
Morrison, Lauren, East Carolina University
Moss, Patti, Whitman College
Mozzachiodi, Riccardo, Texas A&M University, Corpus Christi
Mueller, Amy, Northeastern University
Murphy, Alexander, University of Oregon
Murphy, Edward C., North Dakota Geological Survey
Myers, Clifford D., Berkshire Community College
Myers, Tammy, Shippensburg University
Nadiga, Balu, Los Alamos National Laboratory
Nakatsuka, James, University of California, Los Angeles
Narinder, Kaushik, University of Guelph
Nashold, Barney W., Argonne National Laboratory
Nesbitt, Alex, University of Nevada, Reno
Nevins, Susan K., SUNY, Cortland
Newman, Jonathan, University of Guelph
Newton, Anthony J., Edinburgh University
Newton, Seth A., Geological Survey of Alabama
Nichols, Terry E., University of Arkansas, Fayetteville
Nicholson, Nanette, American Museum of Natural History
Nielsen, Mary, University of South Dakota
Niemiller, Matthew L., University of Tennessee, Knoxville
njoh, Ambe, University of South Florida
Noll, Michael G., Valdosta State University
Nordwald, Dan, Missouri Dept of Natural Resources
Norman, Catherine, Johns Hopkins University
Nosal, Thomas E., Dept of Energy and Environmental Protection
Nussear, Kenneth , University of Nevada, Reno
O'Callaghan, Mick, University College Cork
O'Day, Sandra, Central Connecticut State University
O'Melia, Charles R., Johns Hopkins University
O'Neil, Jennifer, University of Nevada, Reno
Occhiuzzi, Tony, Mesa Community College
Odland, Sarah K., Columbia University
Oglesby, Elizabeth, University of Arizona
Okafor, Florence A., Alabama A&M University
Olson, Derek, Naval Postgraduate School
Olson, James R., South Dakota Dept of Env and Natural Resources
Oona, Hain, Los Alamos National Laboratory
Oppong, Joseph R., University of North Texas
Ormsby, Alison, University of North Carolina, Asheville
Orrock, John, Washington University in St. Louis

Otis, Gard, University of Guelph
Ott, Kevin C., Los Alamos National Laboratory
Owens, Tamera, Muskegon Community College
Oza, Rupal, Hunter College (CUNY)
Pace, Michael L., University of Virginia
Pacia, Christina, Kean University
Palace, Michael W., University of New Hampshire
Palma, Miclelle, University of Wisconsin Colleges
Palmer, Christina, California State University, San Bernardino
Palmer, Clare, Washington University in St. Louis
Papaleo, Silvanna, University of Toronto
Parendes, Laurie A., Edinboro University of Pennsylvania
Parker, Jim, University of Houston
Parker, Joan, Moss Landing Marine Laboratories
Parker, Marjorie, Bowdoin College
Parker, Stephen R., Montana Tech of the University of Montana
Parrish, Pia, San Diego State University
Pasteris, Jill D., Washington University in St. Louis
Patel, Vinodkumar A., Illinois State Geological Survey
Patino-Douce, Alberto E., University of Georgia
Patronas, Dennis, Dauphin Island Sea Lab
Patterson, Jodi T., Utah Geological Survey
Patterson, Mark, Northeastern University
Penney, Paulette, Baylor University
Pepper, Ian L., University of Arizona
Peri, Francesco, University of Massachusetts, Boston
Perkins, R, Cardiff University
Petersen, Bruce, Washington University in St. Louis
Peterson, Peter A., Iowa State University of Science & Technology
Pickering, Dan, Carnegie Museum of Natural History
Pickett, Nicki, Broward College
Pierce, Larry, Missouri Dept of Natural Resources
Pike, J, Cardiff University
Plane, David A., University of Arizona
Plant, Jeffrey J., Jet Propulsion Laboratory
Plescia, Jeffrey, Jet Propulsion Laboratory
Pociask, Walter, Wayne State University
Podolak, Morris, Tel Aviv University
Pollak, Robert, Washington University in St. Louis
Polovina, Jeffrey J., University of Hawai'i, Manoa
Polsky, Colin, Florida Atlantic University
Potter, Amy E., Georgia Southern University
Powers, Roger W., University of Alaska, Fairbanks
Poynton, Helen, University of Massachusetts, Boston
Prewitt, Charles, University of Arizona
Pulkkinen, Tuija, University of Michigan
Pundsack, Jonathan, University of Minnesota, Twin Cities
Purtle, Jennifer M., University of Arkansas, Fayetteville
Qian, Song, University of Toledo
Quinn, Courtney, Furman University
Quintero, Sylvia, University of Arizona
Radil, Steven, University of Idaho
Rallis, Donald N., Mary Washington College
Rankin, Seth, University of Wisconsin Colleges
Rasmussen, Tab, Washington University in St. Louis
Rauber, Carolyn, University of Minnesota, Twin Cities
Ravela, Sai, Massachusetts Institute of Technology
Reaven, Sheldon, SUNY, Stony Brook
Refsnider-Streby, Jeanine, University of Toledo
Rennie, Tim, University of Guelph
Reusch, David B., New Mexico Institute of Mining and Technology
Rice, Murray, University of North Texas
Ricker, Alison, Oberlin College
Ridgwell, Andy, University of California, Riverside
Ridky, Alice M., Colby College
Rieke, George H., University of Arizona
Riley, James, University of Arizona
Riley, Rhonda, Southern Utah University
Ritter, Leonard, University of Guelph
Rius, Marc, University of Southampton
Robas, Sheryl A., Princeton University
Roberts, A. Lynn, Johns Hopkins University
Robinson, Bruce A., Los Alamos National Laboratory
Robinson, David, Open University
Robinson, William, University of Massachusetts, Boston
Rodriguez, Vanessa del S., Puerto Rico Bureau of Geology
Roe, Carol, William & Mary
Roemer, Elizabeth, University of Arizona
Rogers, Jefferson S., University of Tennessee, Martin
Rogers, William J., West Texas A&M University
Roinstad, Lori L., South Dakota Dept of Env and Natural Resources
Rojas, Adena, Johns Hopkins University
Rollinson, Paul A., Missouri State University
Rooney, Neil, University of Guelph
Rose, Candace M., Argonne National Laboratory
Rose, Dan, University College Cork
Rosengaus, Rebeca, Northeastern University
Ross, Kirstin, Flinders University
Ross, Paula, New Mexico State University, Las Cruces
Rossell, Irene M., University of North Carolina, Asheville
Rostam-Abadi, Massoud, Illinois State Geological Survey
Rostron, Ben, University of Alberta
Rouhani, Farhang, Mary Washington College
Rouse, Jesse, University of North Carolina, Pembroke
Roussel-Dupre, R., Los Alamos National Laboratory
Rowland, Scott K., University of Hawai'i, Manoa
Rozmus, Wojciech, University of Alberta
Rumstay, Kenneth S., Valdosta State University
Rupert, Denise, Lock Haven University
Russell, Ron, University of Texas at Austin, Jackson School of Geosciences
Russell, Terry P., University of Victoria
Russell, Theresa J., University of Arkansas, Fayetteville
Russo, Mary Rose, Princeton University
Ruzicka, Jaromir, University of Hawai'i, Manoa
Saikia, Udoy, Flinders University
Saito, Heather, University of Hawai'i, Manoa
Saku, James C., Frostburg State University
Sammarco, Paul W., Louisiana State University
Sanchez, Charles, University of Arizona
Sandhu, Harpinder, Flinders University
Santander, Erma, University of Arizona
Sapigao, Gladys, Queens College (CUNY)
Sarin, Manmohan, University of Delaware
Sarmiento, Jorge L., Princeton University
Sauer, Nancy N. S., Los Alamos National Laboratory
Sawyer, Suzanne, Utah Geological Survey
Scapelli, Krista, Texas Christian University
Scarpino, Samuel, Northeastern University
Schaal, Barbara, Washington University in St. Louis
Schauss, Kim E., University of Southern Indiana
Scheel, Patrick, Missouri Dept of Natural Resources
Scheidemen, Kathy J., University of California, Santa Barbara
Schlesinger, William H., Duke University
Schlumpberger, Debbie, Saint Cloud State University
Schmidt, Jonathan, University of Guelph
Schoenberger, Erica, Johns Hopkins University
Schroeder, Kathleen, Appalachian State University
Schwenke, Eszter, University of New Brunswick
Schwob, Stephanie L., Southern Methodist University
Scott, Kathy, University of British Columbia
Scott-Dupree, Cynthia, University of Guelph
Scyphers, Steven, Northeastern University
Seifu, Abiye, Columbus State University
Seymour, Dorie, Montana State University
Shade, Janet, University of Pittsburgh, Bradford
Shah, Ashru, North Carolina State University
Sharma, Govind, Alabama A&M University
Shaw, Fred, Missouri Dept of Natural Resources
Shchukin, Eugene D., Johns Hopkins University
Sheley, Christina, Indiana University, Bloomington
Shelton, Robert B., Oak Ridge National Laboratory
Shields, Nancy, Virginia Polytechnic Institute & State University
Showman, Adam, University of Arizona
Shumway, Matthew J., Brigham Young University
Sibley, Paul, University of Guelph
Sigler, William V., University of Toledo
Silks, Louis A., Los Alamos National Laboratory
Simonetti, Stephanie, University of Notre Dame
Singh, Hanumant, Northeastern University
Singh, Harbans, Montclair State University
Sissom, David , West Texas A&M University
Sitwell, O.F. George, University of Alberta

Skeel, Loreene, University of Montana
Slater, Tom, Edinburgh University
Slavetskas, Carol, Binghamton University
Smale, Jody L., DCNR- Pennsylvania Bureau of Geological Survey
Smith, Derald, University of Lethbridge
Smith, Donald R., University of California, Santa Cruz
Smith, Elizabeth Y., University of Nevada, Las Vegas
Smith, H D., Cardiff University
Smith, Jim, Flinders University
Smith, K. L., Wichita State University
Smith, Paul H., Los Alamos National Laboratory
Smith, Peter J., University of Alberta
Smith, Susan M., Montana Tech of The University of Montana
Smout, Brooklyn, Weber State University
Snow, Tony, Curtin University
Solomon, Keith, University of Guelph
Somers, Jr., Arnold E., Valdosta State University
Southwell, Benjamin, Lake Superior State University
Spanbauer, Trisha, University of Toledo
Sperazza, Michael, Stony Brook University
Spracklen, Dominick, University of Leeds
Stadnyk, Leona, Mount Royal University
Standridge, Debbie, Georgia Southwestern State University
Starr, Richard, Moss Landing Marine Laboratories
Steadman, Todd A., Clemson University
Stechmann, Samuel, University of Wisconsin, Madison
Steller, Diana, Moss Landing Marine Laboratories
Stephenson, Gerry, University of Guelph
Sterling, Tracy M., Montana State University
Sternberg, Rolf, Montclair State University
Stevens, Joan M., California Polytechnic State University
Stierle, Andrea, Montana Tech of the University of Montana
Stimer, Debra, Kent State University at Stark
Stinger, Lindsay C., University of Leeds
Stone, Glenn D., Washington University in St. Louis
Strangeway, Robert J., University of California, Los Angeles
Streby, Henry, University of Toledo
Strong, Ellen, Smithsonian Institution / National Museum of Natural History
Stunz, Greg, Texas A&M University, Corpus Christi
Su, Xiaobo, University of Oregon
Suárez, Luis Eugenio, Univ Complutense de Madrid
Subulwa, Angela G., University of Wisconsin Oshkosh
Sullivan, Barbara, Argonne National Laboratory
Summers, Robert, University of Alberta
Sussman, Robert W., Washington University in St. Louis
Sutherland, Bruce R., University of Alberta
Svitra, Zita V., Los Alamos National Laboratory
Swanson, Basil I., Los Alamos National Laboratory
Swetnam, Thomas W., University of Arizona
Swindall, Diane, University of California, Davis
Symbalisty, E.M.D., Los Alamos National Laboratory
Sywensky, Ann, Moravian College
Taney, R. Marieke, Northern Arizona University
Tanji, K. K., University of California, Davis
Tavener, Kristi, Lakehead University
Taylor, Michael, Flinders University
Taylor, Robert W., Montclair State University
Tencate, James, Los Alamos National Laboratory
Teplitski, Max, University of Florida
Ter-Simonian, Vardui, University of Southern California
Thacker, Heather, Shawnee State University
Theis, Karen, University of Manchester
Thériault, Julie Mireille, Universite du Quebec a Montreal
Thompson, Glennis, University of California, Berkeley
Thomson, Cary, University of British Columbia
Thomson, Cynthia, Columbia University
Thomson, Vivian E., University of Virginia
Tingey, David G., Brigham Young University
Tippett, John, University of Mary Washington
Tissot, Philippe , Texas A&M University, Corpus Christi
Todd, Brenda, University of Nebraska, Omaha
Tomlinson, Jaime L., University of Delaware
Townshend, Ivan, University of Lethbridge
Tracy, Matthew, United States Air Force Academy
Trevors, Jack, University of Guelph
Triplehorn, Judy, University of Alaska, Fairbanks
Trost, G K., University of Arkansas, Fayetteville
Trout, Jennifer, Western Michigan University
Trussell, Geoffrey, Northeastern University
Tuller, Markus, University of Arizona
Turner, Jay, Washington University in St. Louis
Tyning, Thomas F., Berkshire Community College
Unkefer, Clifford J., Los Alamos National Laboratory
Unsworth, Martyn, University of Alberta
Urquhart, Alvin, University of Oregon
van den Akker, Ben, Flinders University
Van Eerd, Laura, University of Guelph
Van Otten, George A., Northern Arizona University
Van Roosendaal, Susan, University of Utah
Varadi, Ferenc D., University of California, Los Angeles
Varady, Robert G., University of Arizona
Veeder, Glenn J., Jet Propulsion Laboratory
Vieira, David J., Los Alamos National Laboratory
Vollmer, Steve, Northeastern University
Wada, Ikuko, University of Minnesota, Twin Cities
Wagh, Swati, Argonne National Laboratory
Waite, Cynthia H., University of Southern California
Walker, Mark, University of Nevada, Reno
Walker, Peter, University of Oregon
Walker, Raymond J., University of California, Los Angeles
Walraven, Brenda, Mercer University
Walrod, Amanda G., University of Arkansas, Fayetteville
Walsh, Christopher, University of Maryland
Walsh, Daniel E., University of Alaska, Fairbanks
Walsh, Ellen c., Lawrence University
Warburg, Helena F., Williams College
Ward, Landon, University of North Carolina, Asheville
Warhaft, Zellman, Cornell University
Warkentin, Alicia, University of British Columbia
Waterstone, Marvin, University of Arizona
Watson, Alan, University of Guelph
Wauthier, Christelle, Pennsylvania State University, University Park
Weaver, Douglas J., Los Alamos National Laboratory
Webre, Cherri B., Louisiana State University
Weinstein, Charles E., Berkshire Community College
Weintraub, Michael N., University of Toledo
Wells, Steve G., University of Nevada, Reno
Welton, Leicha, University of Alaska, Fairbanks
Wenz, Helmut C., University of Tennessee, Martin
West, Alan, University of Virginia's College at Wise
Wetzel, Dan L., University of Alaska, Fairbanks
Whiley, Harriet, Flinders University
White, George W., Frostburg State University
White, Paul , University of Nevada, Reno
Whitney, Earl M., Los Alamos National Laboratory
Wiederspahn, Mark, University of Texas, Austin
Wilder, Margaret, University of Arizona
Wilhelmy, Jerry B., Los Alamos National Laboratory
Wille, Frank, California State Polytechnic University, Pomona
William, Nancy, Kansas State University
Williams, Allison M., McMaster University
Williams-Bruinders, Leizel, Nelson Mandela Metropolitan University
Willson, Lee, Rice University
Wilmut, Michael, University of Victoria
Wilson, Robert, University of St. Andrews
Wilson, Sarah B., Washington & Lee University
Wilson, Thomas B., University of Arizona
Wilton, Robert D., McMaster University
Winston, Barbara, Washington University in St. Louis
Winterkamp, Judith L., Los Alamos National Laboratory
Winton, Alison, Texas Tech University
Wisdom, Jack, Massachusetts Institute of Technology
Wise, Dana, Southern Illinois University Carbondale
Withers, Kim, Texas A&M University, Corpus Christi
Wixman, Ronald, University of Oregon
Wolfe, Karen M., Middle Tennessee State University
Wollan, Jacinda, North Dakota State University
Wong, Cindy, Buffalo State College
Wood, Carolyn F., Dauphin Island Sea Lab
Woodard, Gary C., University of Arizona
Woodley, Teresa, University of British Columbia
Woodruff, William H., Los Alamos National Laboratory

Woods, Neal, University of South Carolina
Wooldridge, C F., Cardiff University
Wright, Kathyrn, Western Michigan University
Wu, David T., Colorado School of Mines
Wyckoff, William K., Montana State University
Yarbrough, Robert A., Georgia Southern University
Yates, Mary Anne, Los Alamos National Laboratory
Yelle, Roger, University of Arizona
Yoskowitz, David , Texas A&M University, Corpus Christi
Young, Donald W., University of Arizona
Young, Priscilla E., South Dakota Dept of Env and Natural Resources
Yutzy, Gale, Frostburg State University
Zajac, Roman N., University of New Haven
Zamstein, Lavi, Columbus State University
Zaniewski, Kazimierz J., University of Wisconsin Oshkosh
Zeiger, Elaine, Field Museum of Natural History
Zelizer, Nora, Princeton University
Zhang, Max, Cornell University
Zimba, Paul, Texas A&M University, Corpus Christi
Zotti, Maria, Flinders University
Zurick, David, Eastern Kentucky University
Zwiefelhofer, Luke, Winona State University

FACULTY INDEX

A

Aagaard, Knut, (206) 543-8942 aagaard@apl.washington.edu, Univ of Washington; Op
Aalto, Rolf E., +44 (0) 1392-26-3344 aalto@uw.edu, Univ of Washington; Gms
Aamodt, Paul, (505) 665-1331 plaamod@lanl.gov, Los Alamos; Zn
Aanstoos, James V., 515-294-1032 aanstoos@iastate.edu, Iowa State Univ of Sci & Tech; ZrAs
Aay, Henry, (616) 526-7033 aay@calvin.edu, Calvin Coll; Zyu
Abalos, Benito, benito.abalos@ehu.eus, Univ of the Basque Country UPV/EHU; GctGp
Abati, Jacobo, abati@ucm.es, Univ Complutense de Madrid; Gp
Abatzoglou, John, 208-885-6239 jabatzoglou@uidaho.edu, Univ of Idaho; ZoyZc
Abbasnejad, Ahmad, abbasnejadahmad@yahoo.com, Shahid Bahonar Univ of Kerman ; GemHg
Abbott, Lon, (303) 492-6172 lon.abbott@colorado.edu, Univ of Colorado; GgtGm
Abbott, Mark B., (412) 624-1408 mabbott1@pitt.edu, Univ of Pittsburgh; Gs
Abbott, Patrick L., (619) 594-5591 pabbott@mail.sdsu.edu, San Diego State Univ; Gs
Abdalati, Waleed, waleed.abdalati@colorado.edu, Univ of Colorado; Zr
Abdalla, Salah B., geology@uofk.edu, Univ of Khartoum; Ng
Abdelsalam, Mohamed G., 405-744-6358 mohamed.abdel_salam@okstate.edu, Oklahoma State Univ; GctYg
Abdo, Ginette, 406-496-4152 gabdo@mtech.edu, Montana Tech of The Univ of Montana; Hw
Abdu, Yassir, (204) 474-7356 abdu@cc.umanitoba.ca, Univ of Manitoba; Gz
Abdulghani, Waleed, +96638602848 wmaghani@kfupm.edu.sa, King Fahd Univ of Petroleum and Minerals; Go
Abdulla, Hussain, 361-825-6050 hussain.abdulla@tamucc.edu, Texas A&M Univ, Corpus Christi; Co
Abdullah, Nuraiteng Tee, 03-79674229 naiteng@um.edu.my, Univ of Malaya; Gr
Abdullah, Wan Hasiah, 03-79674232 wanhasia@um.edu.my, Univ of Malaya; Ec
Abdullatif, Osman, +96638601479 osmanabd@kfupm.edu.sa, King Fahd Univ of Petroleum and Minerals; Gso
Abdurrahman, A., aabdrrahman@unilorin.edu.ng, Univ of Ilorin; CeEg
Abend, Martin, (201) 200-3161 mabend@njcu.edu, New Jersey City Univ; Zy
Aber, James S., jaber@emporia.edu, Emporia State Univ; Gl
Aber, Jeremy, jeremy.aber@mtsu.edu, Middle Tennessee State Univ; Zyi
Abercrombie, Rachel, rea@bu.edu, Boston Univ; Gt
Abernathey, Ryan P., 845-365-8185 rpa@ldeo.columbia.edu, Columbia Univ; Op
Abernathy, Ryan, rpa@ldeo.columbia.edu, Columbia Univ; Og
Abers, Geoffrey A., 607-255-3879 abers@cornell.edu, Cornell Univ; YsGt
Abimbola, A. E., af.abimbola@mail.ui.edu.ng, Univ of Ibadan; Cg
Abney, Kent D., (505) 665-3894 Los Alamos; Zn
Abolins, Mark J., (615)904-8372 mark.abolins@mtsu.edu, Middle Tennessee State Univ; Gc
Abou Najm, Majdi, mabounajm@ucdavis.edu, Univ of California, Davis; CbSb
Abousleiman, Younane, 405-325-2900 yabousle@ou.edu, Univ of Oklahoma; Nr
Abrams, Daniel, (217) 244-1520 dbabrams@illinois.edu, Univ of Illinois; Hw
Abrams, Lewis J., 910-962-2350 abramsl@uncw.edu, Univ of North Carolina, Wilmington; Gu
Abrams, Michael J., (818) 354-0937 Jet Propulsion Lab; Zr
Abramson, Evan H., 206-616-4388 evana@uw.edu, Univ of Washington; Gy
Abreu, Maria E., msabreu@utad.pt, Unive de Trás-os-Montes e Alto Douro; GaaGa
Abt, Charlotte J., +440151 794 5178 chj@liverpool.ac.uk, Univ of Liverpool; Zn
Abu Bakar, Muhammad Z., 0092-42-99029487 mzubairab1977@gmail.com, Univ of Eng and Tech; NrmNg
Abushagur, Sulaiman, 915-831-2539 sulaiman@epcc.edu, El Paso Comm Coll; Gg
Acharya, Kumud, (702) 862-5371 kumud.acharya@dri.edu, Univ of Nevada, Reno; HsGeHq
Achauer, Ulrich, ulrich.achauer@unistra.fr, Universite de Strasbourg; Ysg
Achten, Christine, +49-251-83-33941 achten@uni-muenster.de, Univ Muenster; CloEg
Ackerman, Jessica R., 217-333-4258 jracker@illinois.edu, Illinois State Geological Survey; Zn
Ackerman, Steven A., (608)263-3647 stevea@ssec.wisc.edu, Univ of Wisconsin, Madison; Zr
Ackerman, Thomas P., (206) 221-2767 ackerman@atmos.washington.edu, Univ of Washington; As
Acosta, Jose G., jchang@cicese.mx, Centro de Investigación Científica y de Educación Superior de Ensenada; Ne
Acosta, Patricia E., (413) 597-2221 patricia.e.acosta@williams.edu, Williams Coll; Zn
Adabanija, Moruffdeen A., +2348037786592 maadabanija@lautech.edu.ng, Ladoke Akintola Univ of Tech; GggGg
Adam, Iddrisu, iddrisu.adam@uwc.edu, Univ of Wisconsin Colls; ZynZn
Adam, Jurgen, +44 1784 414258 jurgen.adam@rhul.ac.uk, Royal Holloway Univ of London; Gc
Adames-Corraliza, Angel F., afadames@umich.edu, Univ of Michigan; Ast
Adams, Aubreya, 315-228-7202 aadams@colgate.edu, Colgate Univ; Yg
Adams, Debi, 806-651-2570 dadams@wtamu.edu, West Texas A&M Univ; Zn
Adams, Herbert G., (818) 677-2575 herb.adams@csun.edu, California State Univ, Northridge; Ng
Adams, John B., adams@ess.washington.edu, Univ of Washington; GcXgZr
Adams, Kenneth, 775.673.7345 ken.adams@dri.edu, Univ of Nevada, Reno; Gam
Adams, Manda S., 704-687-5984 manda.adams@uncc.edu, Univ of North Carolina, Charlotte; Am
Adams, Mark, capt.mark.adams@gmail.com, Lamar Univ; Xg
Adams, Marshall, (865) 574-7335 sma@ornl.gov, Oak Ridge; Ob
Adams, Michael S., (608) 263-5994 Univ of Wisconsin, Madison; Ob
Adams, Peter N., (352) 846-0825 adamsp@ufl.edu, Univ of Florida; Gm
Adams, Thomas, 210-486-0045 tadams67@alamo.edu, San Antonio Comm Coll; PvGg
Adamsen, Floyd, (602) 437-1702 f.j.adamsen@gmail.com, Univ of Arizona; So
Adedcyin, A. D., deloadedoyin@yahoo.com, Univ of Ilorin; Eg
Adee, Eric, (785) 354-7236 eadee@ksu.edu, Kansas State Univ; So
Adegoke, Jimmy, (816) 235-2978 adegokej@umkc.edu, Univ of Missouri, Kansas City; AsZyr
Adeigbe, O. C., oc.adeigbe@mail.ui.edu.ng, Univ of Ibadan; GosGe
Adekeye, J.I. D., adekeye2001@yahoo.com, Univ of Ilorin; GoCg
Adekeye, O. A., geologistolabisi@yahoo.com, Univ of Ilorin; Pm
Adekola, S. A., 234-708-928-5170 adekoladsolo@gmail.com, Obafemi Awolowo Univ; GdoCg
Adelana, S.M. A., adelana@gmx.net, Univ of Ilorin; HgYgGe
Adeleke, Adedayo, +27 (0) 12 420 3536 adedayo.adeleke@up.ac.za, Univ of Pretoria; YdZf
Ademeso, Anthony O., +2348034738470 aoademeso@futa.edu.ng, Federal Univ of Tech, Akure; NgrNt
Aden, Douglas J., (614) 265-6579 douglas.aden@dnr.ohio.gov, Ohio Dept of Natural Resources; GeRnGl
Aden, Leon, leon-aden@uiowa.edu, Univ of Iowa; Go
Adentunji, Jacob, j.adetunji@derby.ac.uk, Univ of Derby; Ge
Adeoti, Blessing, +2347065810638 badeoti@futa.edu.ng, Federal Univ of Tech, Akure; GcxGg
Adepelumi, A. A., 234-8128181062 aadepelu@oauife.edu.ng, Obafemi Awolowo Univ; YgsNe
Adepoju, Mohammed O., +2348034722855 moadepoju@futa.edu.ng, Federal Univ of Tech, Akure; CeEgGg
Adetunji, A, 234-8137433622 Obafemi Awolowo Univ; EgGi
Adewoye, Abosede O., +2347032045714, +2347036602812 aoadewoye55@lautech.edu.ng, Ladoke Akintola Univ of Tech; GeeGe
Adeyemi, G. O., go.adeyemi@mail.ui.edu.ng, Univ of Ibadan; NgHg
Adhikari, Sanchayeeta, 818-677-5630 sadhikari@csun.edu, California State Univ, Northridge; Zi
Adinolfi, Bryan, adinolfib1@southernct.edu, Southern Connecticut State Univ; GgZg
Adisa, Adeshina L., +2348029458886 aladisa@futa.edu.ng, Federal Univ of Tech, Akure; CgeGc
Adkins, Jess F., (626) 395-8550 jess@gps.caltech.edu, California Inst of Tech; Cm
Admire, Amanda R., 707-826-3111 ara11@humboldt.edu, Humboldt State Univ; Zg
Adomaitis, D., 217-244-8872 dadomait@illinois.edu, Illinois State Geological Survey; Ge
Adovasio, James M., 814-824-2581 adovasio@mercyhurst.edu, Mercyhurst Univ; GafGs
Adrain, Jonathan M., (319) 335-1539 jonathan-adrain@uiowa.edu, Univ of Iowa; Pi

Adrain, Tiffany S., (319) 335-1822 tiffany-adrain@uiowa.edu, Univ of Iowa; Pg
Adriano, Domy C., (803) 725-2752 Univ of Georgia; Sc
Afolabi, O., 234-803-512-4838 toltobi@yahoo.com, Obafemi Awolowo Univ; Yg
Afolabi, Olukayode A., +2348052158722 oaafolabi@lautech.edu.ng, Ladoke Akintola Univ of Tech; GxxGx
Agardy, Rachael, 989-774-7596 agard1rv@cmich.edu, Central Michigan Univ; OuGrs
Agbogun, Henry, 785-628-4574 hmagobogun@fhsu.edu, Fort Hays State Univ; GgYg
Agee, Carl A., (505) 277-1644 agee@unm.edu, Univ of New Mexico; Cp
Agee, Ernest M., (765) 494-3282 eagee@purdue.edu, Purdue Univ; As
Agioutantis, Zach, 859-257-953 zach.agioutantis@uky.edu, Univ of Kentucky; NrmEc
Agnew, Duncan C., (858) 534-2590 dagnew@ucsd.edu, Univ of California, San Diego; Ys
Agnew, Stephen F., (505) 665-1764 Los Alamos; Zn
Agnini, Claudia, 39-049-827918 claudia.agnini@unipd.it, Univ degli Studi di Padova; PmeGu
Agrawal, Abinash, (937) 775-3455 abinash.agrawal@wright.edu, Wright State Univ; ClHwPg
Agrawal, Sandeep , 780-492-1230 sagrawal@ualberta.ca, Univ of Alberta; Zu
Ague, Jay J., 203-432-3171 jay.ague@yale.edu, Yale Univ; Gzx
Agutu, Nathan O., nagutu@jkuat.ac.ke, Jomo Kenyatta Univ of Agriculture & Tech; ZgiZr
Aharon, Paul, (205) 348-2528 paharon@ua.edu, Univ of Alabama; ClmCq
Ahearn, Sean C., (212) 772-5327 sahearn@hunter.cuny.edu, Hunter Coll (CUNY); Zi
Ahern, Judson L., (405) 325-4480 jahern@ou.edu, Univ of Oklahoma; Yg
Ahm, Anne-Sofie, 609-258-4101 aahm@princeton.edu, Princeton Univ; ClsPc
Ahmad, Abd Rashid, 03-79674156 abrashid@um.edu.my, Univ of Malaya; Sc
Ahmed, Kazi M., +880 1711846840 kmahmed@du.ac.bd, Univ of Dhaka ; HwGgHg
Ahmed, Mohamed, 361-825-3278 mohamed.ahmed@tamucc.edu, Texas A&M Univ, Corpus Christi; YgZri
Ahmed, Muhammad F., mfanr5@mst.edu, Univ of Eng and Tech; NgxNt
Ahmed, Ramadan, r.ahmed@ou.edu, Univ of Oklahoma; Np
Ahmed, Samir, 212-650-7250 ahmed@ccny.cuny.edu, Graduate Sch of the City Univ of New York; Gg
Ahmed, Waquar, 940-565-2721 waquar.ahmed@unt.edu, Univ of North Texas; Zn
Ahola, John, john.ahola@bristolcc.edu, Bristol Comm Coll; Gg
Aiello, Ivano, (831) 771-4400 iaiello@mlml.calstate.edu, Moss Landing Marine Lab; OuGmu
Aiken, Carlos L., (972) 883-2450 aiken@utdallas.edu, Univ of Texas, Dallas; Yv
Aines, Roger D., (925) 423-7184 aines1@llnl.gov, Lawrence Livermore; Cg
Aird, Hannah M., 530-898-6369 haird@csuchico.edu, California State Univ, Chico; GxEg
Aitchison, Jonathan, geoscience.headofschool@sydney.edu.au, Univ of Sydney; GrtPm
Aitkenhead-Peterson, Jacqueline A., (979) 845-3682 jacqui_a-p@tamu.edu, Texas A&M Univ; HsSoGf
Aiyyer, Anantha, 919-515-7973 aaiyyer@ncsu.edu, North Carolina State Univ; As
Aizen, Vladimir, 208-885-5888 aizen@uidaho.edu, Univ of Idaho; GlHg
Aja, Stephen U., (718) 951-5405 Graduate Sch of the City Univ of New York; Cl
Ajaegwu, Norbert E., (+234) 8023649729 ne.ajaegwu@unizik.edu.ng, Nnamdi Azikiwe Univ; GorGg
Ajayi, J. O., 234-803-401-4357 owoajayi@oauife.edu.ng, Obafemi Awolowo Univ; No
Ajayi, T. R., 234-803-725-8924 traajayi@oauife.edu.ng, Obafemi Awolowo Univ; CgEgGe
Ajigo, Isaac O., +2348032107038 ioajigo@futa.edu.ng, Federal Univ of Tech, Akure; GgCgGx
Akabzaa, Thomas M., 233-246325685 akabzaa@ug.edu.gh, Univ of Ghana; EgGeNm
Akaegbobi, I. M., izumike2002@yahoo.com, Univ of Ibadan; Cg
Akande, S. O., samoakande2004@yahoo.com, Univ of Ilorin; EgCg
Akciz, Sinan, (657) 278-4371 sakciz@fullerton.edu, California State Univ, Fullerton; GcRn
Akenzua-Adamcyzk, Aiyevbekpen H., aiyevbekpen.akenzua@uniben.edu, Univ of Benin; GeHgGg
Akgul, Bunyamin, 00904242370000-5988 bakgul@firat.edu.tr, Firat Univ; GzyGi
Akgun, Elif , 00904242370000-5972 efiratligil@firat.edu.tr, Firat Univ; GgcGt
Akinlabi, Ismaila A., +2348050225113 iaakinlabi@lautech.edu.ng, Ladoke Akintola Univ of Tech; GggGg
Akiwumi, Fenda, fakiwumi@usf.edu, Univ of South Florida; Zy
Aksoy, Ercan, 00904242370000-5974 Firat Univ; Ggt
Aksu, Ali E., (709) 737-8385 aaksu@mun.ca, Memorial Univ of Newfoundland; Gu
Akujieze, Christopher N., krisjiaku@yahoo.com, Univ of Benin; GgHwGe
Al, Tom A., tom.al@uottawa.ca, Univ of Ottawa; HwCgZg
Al-Aasm, Ihsan S., (519) 253-3000 ext 2494 alaasm@uwindsor.ca, Univ of Windsor; GdClGo
Al-Attar, David, +44 (0) 1223 348935 da380@cam.ac.uk, Univ of Cambridge; YdGt
Al-Lehyani, Ayman, +96638601661 allehyani@kfupm.edu.sa, King Fahd Univ of Petroleum and Minerals; Yg
Al-Ramadan, Khalid, +96638607175 ramadank@kfupm.edu.sa, King Fahd Univ of Petroleum and Minerals; GodGs
Al-Saad, Hamad A., hamadsaad@qu.edu.qa, Univ of Qatar; PsGsu
Al-Shaibani, Abdulaziz, +96638604002 shaibani@kfupm.edu.sa, King Fahd Univ of Petroleum and Minerals; HwGeg
Al-Shuhail, Abdullah, +966138602538 shuhail@kfupm.edu.sa, King Fahd Univ of Petroleum and Minerals; Ye
Al-Shuhail, Abdullatif, +96638603584 ashuhail@kfupm.edu.sa, King Fahd Univ of Petroleum and Minerals; Ygs
Alam, Md Iftekhar, 865-974-3665 malam11@utk.edu, Univ of Tennessee, Knoxville; Yu
Alao, D. A., lomalao@yahoo.com, Univ of Ilorin; NgGz
Alao, O. A., 234-805-466-7314 olade77@yahoo.com, Obafemi Awolowo Univ; Yg
Alavi, Hedy, (410) 516-7091 alavi@jhu.edu, Johns Hopkins Univ; Zn
Alba, Saturnino, sdeal@baucm.es, Univ Complutense de Madrid; Gm
Albach, Suzanne M., 734-677-5111 salbach@wccnet.edu, Washtenaw Comm Coll; ZegGe
Albee, Arden L., 626.395.6260 aalbee@caltech.edu, California Inst of Tech; GizXg
Albee-Scott, Steven R., (517) 796-8526 albeescsteven@jccmi.edu, Jackson Coll; GePeSf
Alberstadt, Leonard P., 615-322-2160 leonard.p.alberstadt@vanderbilt.edu, Vanderbilt Univ; Gd
Alberts, Heike C., (920) 424-4105 alberts@uwosh.edu, Univ of Wisconsin Oshkosh; Zn
Albin, Edward, ealbin@gsu.edu, Georgia State Univ, Perimeter Coll, Online; Xm
Albrecht, Jochen, (212) 772-5221 jochen@hunter.cuny.edu, Hunter Coll (CUNY); ZiyZu
Albrecht, Lorraine, klalbrec@uwaterloo.ca, Univ of Waterloo; Zn
Albright, James N., (505) 667-4318 j_albright@lanl.gov, Los Alamos; Yg
Albright, Katia, (775) 682-8370 kalbright@unr.edu, Univ of Nevada, Reno; Zn
Albright, Thomas , (775) 784-6673 talbright@unr.edu, Univ of Nevada, Reno; Zy
Alde, Douglas, (505) 667-0488 dxa@lanl.gov, Los Alamos; Zn
Alderson, David, +44 (0) 191 208 7121 david.alderson@ncl.ac.uk, Univ of Newcastle Upon Tyne; Zi
Alderton, Dave, +44 1784 443585 d.alderton@rhul.ac.uk, Royal Holloway Univ of London; Gz
Aldrich, Eric A., 573-882-6301 aldriche@missouri.edu, Univ of Missouri; As
Aldrich, M. James, (505) 667-1495 jaldrich@lanl.gov, Los Alamos; Gc
Aldridge, Keith D., (416) 399-0124 keith@yorku.ca, York Univ; YmdYh
Aldushin, Kirill, 089/2180 4337 kirill.aldushin@lrz.uni-muenchen.de, Ludwig-Maximilians-Univ Muenchen; Gz
Aleksandrowski, Pawel, pawel.aleksandrowski@uwr.edu.pl, Univ of Wroclaw; GctYe
Alencoão, Ana M., alencoao@utad.pt, Unive de Trás-os-Montes e Alto Douro; HgGgm
Alessi, Daniel S., (780) 492-8019 alessi@ualberta.ca, Univ of Alberta; ClGeHw
Alexander, Becky, (206) 543-0164 beckya@atmos.washington.edu, Univ of Washington; AsCsPe
Alexander, Clark R., 912-598-2329 clark.alexander@skio.usg.edu, Georgia Southern Univ; OuGsOn
Alexander, Conel M., (202) 478-8478 calexander@carnegiescience.edu, Carnegie Inst for Sci; Xc
Alexander, Dane, (269) 387-5486 dane.alexander@wmich.edu, Western Michigan Univ; GgZnn
Alexander, Elaine, (254) 299-8442 ealexander@mclennan.edu, McLennan Comm Coll; Gg

Alexander, Jan, +44 (0)1603 59 3759 j.alexander@uea.ac.uk, Univ of East Anglia; GseGd
Alexander, Jane L., 718-982-3013 jane.alexander@csi.cuny.edu, Coll of Staten Island/CUNY; GsClt
Alexander, Peter, peter.alexander@ed.ac.uk, Edinburgh Univ; Zc
Alexander, Scott, 612-626-4164 alexa107@umn.edu, Univ of Minnesota, Twin Cities; Hw
Alexander, Shelton S., (814) 863-7246 shel@geosc.psu.edu, Pennsylvania State Univ, Univ Park; Ys
Alexander, Jr., E. Calvin, (612) 624-3517 alexa001@umn.edu, Univ of Minnesota, Twin Cities; HwCcl
Alexandre, Paul, 204-727-9693 alexandrep@brandonu.ca, Brandon Univ; EgCgGz
Alfe, Dario, +44 202 7679 32361 d.alfe@ucl.ac.uk, Univ Coll London; ZmGyYh
Alford, Matthew H., 206-221-3257 malford@apl.washington.edu, Univ of Washington; Op
Alfsen, Sheila, sheila.alfsen@pdx.edu, Portland State Univ; GgPgOu
Algar, Christopher, (902) 494-7192 calgar@dal.ca, Dalhousie Univ; Obc
Algeo, Catherine, (270) 745-5922 katie.algeo@wku.edu, Western Kentucky Univ; Zi
Algeo, Thomas J., (513) 556-4195 thomas.algeo@uc.edu, Univ of Cincinnati; Gs
Algin, Barbara, (212) 854-2905 ba110@columbia.edu, Columbia Univ; Zn
Ali, Bukari, +233 20 330 7976 bukariali@yahoo.co.uk, Kwame Nkrumah Univ of Sci and Tech; HwNgYg
Ali, Genevieve, 204-474-7266 genevieve.ali@umanitoba.ca, Univ of Manitoba; Hw
Ali, Hendratta N., (785) 628-4608 hnali@fhsu.edu, Fort Hays State Univ; GogYs
Ali, K. Adem, (843) 953-0877 alika@cofc.edu, Coll of Charleston; ZrHwNg
Alkac, Onur, 00904242370000-5970 oalkac@firat.edu.tr, Firat Univ; GgsGu
Allabush, Kathleen, 801-581-7062 k.ritterbush@utah.edu, Univ of Utah; Pe
Allam, Bassem, (632) 632-8745 bassem.allam@stonybrook.edu, SUNY, Stony Brook; Ob
Allan, Andrea, (541) 737-3427 aallan@coas.oregonstate.edu, Oregon State Univ; As
Allan, Craig J., 704-687-5999 cjallan@email.uncc.edu, Univ of North Carolina, Charlotte; Hg
Allan, Deborah L., (612) 625-3158 dallan@soils.umn.edu, Univ of Minnesota, Twin Cities; Sb
Allan, Jonathan C., (541) 574-6658 Oregon Dept of Geology and Mineral Industries; Gm
Allard, Gilles O., (706) 542-2420 goallar@uga.edu, Univ of Georgia; Eg
Allard, Jason, (229) 333-5752 jmallard@valdosta.edu, Valdosta State Univ; AsZg
Allard, Stephen T., 507-457-2739 sallard@winona.edu, Winona State Univ; GctGx
Allen, Ashley L., (740) 368-3624 alallen@owu.edu, Ohio Wesleyan Univ; Znu
Allen, Bruce D., 575-366-2531 bruce.allen@nmt.edu, New Mexico Inst of Mining and Tech; Gm
Allen, Charlotte M., +61 7 3138 0177 cm.allen@qut.edu.au, Queensland Univ of Tech; CcaGi
Allen, Clarence R., (626) 395-6904 allen@gps.caltech.edu, California Inst of Tech; Ys
Allen, Diana M., (778) 782-3967 dallen@sfu.ca, Simon Fraser Univ; Hy
Allen, Douglas, dallen@salemstate.edu, Salem State Univ; CgHsCt
Allen, Eric E., (858) 534-2570 eallen@ucsd.edu, Univ of California, San Diego; Ob
Allen, Gary C., 828-747-7818 gallen@uno.edu, Univ of New Orleans; Gp
Allen, Grant, +44 0161 306-6851 grant.allen@manchester.ac.uk, Univ of Manchester; As
Allen, John, 989-774-1923 allen4jt@cmich.edu, Central Michigan Univ; Ams
Allen, Joseph L., 304-384-5238 allenj@concord.edu, Concord Univ; Gct
Allen, Karen, (864)294-2504 karen.allen@furman.edu, Furman Univ; Zn
Allen, Katherine, +44 0151 795 4646 k.a.allen@liverpool.ac.uk, Univ of Liverpool; Zi
Allen, Kelly E., 918-595-7085 kely.e.allen@tulsacc.edu, Tulsa Comm Coll; ZyiZe
Allen, Mark, +44 191 33 42344 m.b.allen@durham.ac.uk, Durham Univ; Gt
Allen, Peter M., (254)710-2189 peter_allen@baylor.edu, Baylor Univ; HgNg
Allen, Phillip, 301/687-4891 ppallen@frostburg.edu, Frostburg State Univ; GmePe
Allen, Richard M., (510) 642-1275 rallen@seismo.berkeley.edu, Univ of California, Berkeley; Ys
Allen, Richardson B., (801) 581-7574 pallen@egi.utah.edu, Univ of Utah; GctZi
Allen, Robert J., (951) 827-4870 robert.allen@ucr.edu, Univ of California, Riverside; As
Allen, Susan E., (604) 822-2828 sallen@eos.ubc.ca, Univ of British Columbia; Op
Allen-King, Richelle, (716) 645-4287 richelle@buffalo.edu, SUNY, Buffalo; Cg
Allen-Lafayette, Zehdreh, (609) 292-2576 zehdreh.allen-lafayette@dep.nj.gov, New Jersey Geological and Water Survey; Zi
Aller, Josephine Y., (631) 632-8655 josephine.aller@stonybrook.edu, SUNY, Stony Brook; ObAs
Aller, Robert C., (631) 632-8746 robert.aller@stonybrook.edu, SUNY, Stony Brook; Cm
Alley, Marcus M., (540) 231-9777 malley@vt.edu, Virginia Polytechnic Inst & State Univ; Sc
Alley, Richard B., (814) 863-1700 rba6@psu.edu, Pennsylvania State Univ, Univ Park; Gl
Alley, Ronald E., (818) 354-0751 ron@lithos.jpl.nasa.gov, Jet Propulsion Lab; Zr
Allison, Alivia J., 620-341-5984 aalliso2@emporia.edu, Emporia State Univ; GgaGm
Allison, David T., 251-460-6381 dallison@southalabama.edu, Univ of South Alabama; Gc
Allison, Mead A., (504) 862-3270 meadallison@tulane.edu, Tulane Univ; Gs
Allison, Nicky, +44 01334 463952 na9@st-andrews.ac.uk, Univ of St. Andrews; Oc
Allison, Tami L., tami.allison@dnr.mo.gov, Missouri Dept of Natural Resources; Zn
Allmendinger, Richard W., rwa1@cornell.edu, Cornell Univ; Gc
Allmon, Warren D., (607) 273-6623 (Ext. 14) wda1@cornell.edu, Paleontological Research Inst; Pg
Almendinger, James E., 651-433-5953 dinger@smm.org, Univ of Minnesota, Twin Cities; Pe
Alonso, Ana María, alonsoza@ucm.es, Univ Complutense de Madrid; Gd
Alpert, Pinhas, pinhas@post.tau.ac.il, Tel Aviv Univ; AsZrAm
Alpert, Sam, 212-769-5383 salpert@amnh.org, American Mus of Natural History; Xm
Alsdorf, Douglas E., 614 247-6908 alsdorf.1@osu.edu, Ohio State Univ; HgYg
Alsharif, Kamal, kalshari@usf.edu, Univ of South Florida; Rw
Alsleben, Helge, (817) 257-5455 h.alsleben@tcu.edu, Texas Christian Univ; GctGg
Alt, Jeffrey C., (734) 764-8380 jalt@umich.edu, Univ of Michigan; Ou
Altaner, Stephen P., (217) 244-1244 altaner@illinois.edu, Univ of Illinois, Urbana-Champaign; Gz
Altenbach, Alexander, 089/2180 6598 a.altenbach@lrz.uni-muenchen.de, Ludwig-Maximilians-Univ Muenchen; Pg
Altermann, Wladyslaw, 089/2180 6552 wlady.altermann@iaag.geo.uni-muenchen.de, Ludwig-Maximilians-Univ Muenchen; Gg
Alumbaugh, David L., (510) 215-4227 dalumbaugh@berkeley.edu, Univ of California, Berkeley; Ye
Aluwihare, Lihini I., (858) 822-4886 laluwihare@ucsd.edu, Univ of California, San Diego; Gu
Alvarado, Vladimir, 307-766-6464 valvarad@uwyo.edu, Univ of Wyoming; Np
Alvarez, José Antonio, jaalvare@ucm.es, Univ Complutense de Madrid; Gc
Alvarez, Walter, 510-642-2602 platetec@berkeley.edu, Univ of California, Berkeley; GrRh
Alves, Tiago, alvest@cf.ac.uk, Cardiff Univ; GouGt
Alves, Tiego, +44(0)29 208 76754 alvest@cf.ac.uk, Univ of Wales; Og
Amador, Nathanael S., 740-368-3619 nsamador@owu.edu, Ohio Wesleyan Univ; ZyGlZr
Amato, James A., (920) 424-2268 amatoj@uwosh.edu, Univ of Wisconsin, Oshkosh; GgZi
Amato, Jeffrey M., (575) 646-3017 amato@nmsu.edu, New Mexico State Univ, Las Cruces; GcCc
Ambinakudige, Shrinidhi, (662) 268-1032 x210 shrinidhi@geosci.msstate.edu, Mississippi State Univ; ZiyZr
Ambrose, William, 512-471-0258 william.ambrose@beg.utexas.edu, Univ of Texas, Austin; GsrEo
Ambruster, W. Scott, (907) 474-7161 ffwsa@aurora.alaska.edu, Univ of Alaska, Fairbanks; Zn
Amedjoe, Godfrey C., +233 24 5961 073 chiri.amedjoe@gmail.com, Kwame Nkrumah Univ of Sci and Tech; GidGc
Amel, Nasir, +98 (411) 339 2696 amel@tabrizu.ac.ir, Univ of Tabriz; GivGg
Amelung, Falk, 305 421-4949 famelung@rsmas.miami.edu, Univ of Miami; Zn
Amend, Jan, (213) 740-0652 janamend@usc.edu, Univ of Southern California; ClmCo
Amenta, Roddy V., (540) 568-6674 amentarv@jmu.edu, James Madison

FACULTY INDEX – A

Univ; Gc
Amer, Reda, 504-862-3220 ramer1@tulane.edu, Tulane Univ; ZirGe
Amezaga, Jamie, +44 (0) 191 208 4876 jaime.amezaga@ncl.ac.uk, Univ of Newcastle Upon Tyne; Ge
Amidon, Will, 802-443-5980 wamidon@middlebury.edu, Middlebury Coll; CcGmt
Amin, Isam E., (330) 941-2293 ieamin@ysu.edu, Youngstown State Univ; Hw
Amler, Michael, 089/2180 6602 amler@lrz.uni-muenchen.de, Ludwig-Maximilians-Univ Muenchen; Pg
Ammon, Charles J., (814) 865-2310 cammon@geosc.psu.edu, Pennsylvania State Univ, Univ Park; Ys
Amon, Rainier M., 409 740 4719 amonr@tamug.edu, Texas A&M Univ; CbOcb
Amonette, Alexandra B., (509) 376-5019 Pacific Northwest; Cg
Amoozegar, Aziz, (919) 515-3967 North Carolina State Univ; Sp
Amor, John, (604) 822-6933 jamor@eos.ubc.ca, Univ of British Columbia; Zn
Amos, Colin B., 360-650-3587 colin.amos@wwu.edu, Western Washington Univ; Gc
Amos, Kathryn, kathryn.amos@adelaide.edu.au, Univ of Adelaide; Gs
Ampuero, Jean-Paul, 626.395.6958 ampuero@gps.caltech.edu, California Inst of Tech; Ys
Amrouch, Khalid, khalid.amrouch@adelaide.edu.au, Univ of Adelaide; Gc
Amthor, Jeff, (865) 576-2773 Oak Ridge; Sf
Anand, Madhur, (519) 824-4120 Ext.56254 manand@uoguelph.ca, Univ of Guelph; Zn
Anand, Pallavi, +44 (0) 1908 652225 x 52225 pallavi.anand@open.ac.uk, Open Univ; ClPe
Anandakrishnan, Sridhar, (814) 863-6742 sak@essc.psu.edu, Pennsylvania State Univ, Univ Park; Ys
Anastasio, Cort, 530-754-6095 canastasio@ucdavis.edu, Univ of California, Davis; As
Anastasio, David J., (610) 758-5117 dja2@lehigh.edu, Lehigh Univ; Gca
Anbar, Ariel D., (480) 965-0767 anbar@asu.edu, Arizona State Univ; CbsXb
Ancell, Brian C., 806-834-3143 brian.ancell@ttu.edu, Texas Tech Univ; As
Ancochea, Eumenio, anco@ucm.es, Univ Complutense de Madrid; Gv
Anders, Alison M., 217-244-3917 amanders@illinois.edu, Univ of Illinois, Urbana-Champaign; Gm
Andersen, C. B., brannon.andersen@furman.edu, Clemson Univ; Cl
Andersen, C. Brannon, (864) 294-3366 brannon.andersen@furman.edu, Furman Univ; ClGe
Andersen, David W., (408) 924-5014 david.andersen@sjsu.edu, San Jose State Univ; GsCl
Andersen, Jens C., +44 01326 371836 j.c.andersen@exeter.ac.uk, Exeter Univ; GiEmCa
Andersen, Raymond J., (604) 822-4511 randersn@eos.ubc.ca, Univ of British Columbia; Oc
Anderson, Alan J., (902) 867-2309 aanderso@stfx.ca, Saint Francis Xavier Univ; Gx
Anderson, Alyssa, 609-258-4101 alyssaa@princeton.edu, Princeton Univ; CcgGz
Anderson, Andrew, 217-244-0995 acandrsn@illinois.edu, Illinois State Geological Survey; Ng
Anderson, Bruce, brucea@bu.edu, Boston Univ; AsOp
Anderson, Callum, 27 41 504 2811 callum.anderson@nmmu.ac.za, Nelson Mandela Metropolitan Univ; Gzs
Anderson, G M., (416) 978-2062 Univ of Toronto; Cp
Anderson, James G., (617) 495-5922 anderson@huarp.harvard.edu, Harvard Univ; As
Anderson, James Lawford, lawford@bu.edu, Boston Univ; Gi
Anderson, Jennifer L., 507-457-2457 jlanderson@winona.edu, Winona State Univ; XgYgZe
Anderson, John B., (713) 348-4652 johna@rice.edu, Rice Univ; Gu
Anderson, Ken B., 618-453-7389 kanderson@geo.siu.edu, Southern Illinois Univ Carbondale; Co
Anderson, Laurie C., (605) 394-1290 laurie.anderson@sdsmt.edu, South Dakota Sch of Mines & Tech; PiePq
Anderson, Mark, +44 1752 584768 m.anderson@plymouth.ac.uk, Univ of Plymouth; Gct
Anderson, Mary P., (914) 365-8335 andy@geology.wisc.edu, Univ of Wisconsin, Madison; Hw
Anderson, Orson L., (310) 825-2386 Univ of California, Los Angeles; Yx
Anderson, Patricia M., pata@uw.edu, Univ of Washington; Ple
Anderson, Paula, 479-575-3355 pea001@uark.edu, Univ of Arkansas, Fayetteville; Gg
Anderson, Raymond R., (319) 335-1589 raymond.anderson@dnr.iowa.gov, Univ of Iowa; Gr
Anderson, Robert, 303-735-4684 robert.s.anderson@colorado.edu, Univ of Colorado; Gm
Anderson, Ross, +44 (0) 131 451 3798 r.anderson@hw.ac.uk, Heriot-Watt Univ; Eo
Anderson, Ryan, (208) 282-5024 ryananderson@isu.edu, Idaho State Univ; GcCaZe
Anderson, Stephen H., 573-882-6303 andersons@missouri.edu, Univ of Missouri; Sp
Anderson, Steven W., (970) 351-2973 steven.anderson@unco.edu, Univ of Northern Colorado; GvZeXg
Anderson, Thomas B., (775) 747-1438 tom.anderson@sonoma.edu, Sonoma State Univ; GsrGd
Anderson, Wayne I., (319) 273-3125 wayne.anderson@uni.edu, Univ of Northern Iowa; Pg
Anderson, William P., (828) 262-7540 andersonwp@appstate.edu, Appalachian State Univ; HwqHs
Anderson, Jr., Alfred T., (773) 702-8138 Univ of Chicago; Gv
Anderson-Folnagy, Heidi, (406) 683-7134 heidi.anderson@umwestern.edu, Univ of Montana Western; Gs
Andersson, Andreas, (858) 822-2486 aandersson@ucsd.edu, Univ of California, San Diego; Oc
Andeweg, Bernd , 31 20 5987339 bernd.andeweg@vu.nl, Vrije Universiteit Amsterdam; GtcGg
Andonaegui, Pilar, andonaeg@ucm.es, Univ Complutense de Madrid; Gg
Andrade, César, candrade@fc.ul.pt, Unive de Lisboa; Gu
Andre-Obayanju, Tomilola, tomilola.obayanju@uniben.edu, Univ of Benin; NgHgGe
Andreasen, David C., (410) 260-8814 david.andreasen@maryland.gov, Maryland Department of Natural Resources; Hw
Andres, A. S., (302) 831-2833 asandres@udel.edu, Univ of Delaware; HwZi
Andresen, Christian, candresen@wisc.edu, Univ of Wisconsin, Madison; Zy
Andreu-Hayles, Laia, lah@ldeo.columbia.edu, Columbia Univ; Pe
Andrews, Allen H., allen.andrews@noaa.gov, Univ of Hawai'i, Manoa; Oc
Andrews, Benjamin, (202) 633-1818 andrewsb@si.edu, Smithsonian Inst / Nat Mus of Natural History; Gv
Andrews, Graham D., (304) 293-2192 graham.andrews@mail.wvu.edu, West Virginia Univ; GvtGx
Andrews, John R., 512-471-1534 john.andrews@beg.utexas.edu, Univ of Texas at Austin, Jackson Sch of Geosciences; Zi
Andrews, Julian E., +44 (0)1603 59 2536 j.andrews@uea.ac.uk, Univ of East Anglia; CsGsCl
Andrews, Richard D., 405-325-3991 rdandrews@ou.edu, Univ of Oklahoma; Go
Andrews, William M., 859-323-0506 wandrews@uky.edu, Univ of Kentucky; GmZiEc
Andronicos, Chris, (765) 494-5982 candroni@purdue.edu, Purdue Univ; Gg
Andrus, C. Fred T., (205) 348-5177 fandrus@ua.edu, Univ of Alabama; PcGaCs
Andrus, Richard E., (607) 777-2453 Binghamton Univ; Sf
Aneja, Viney P., 91951557808 viney_aneja@ncsu.edu, North Carolina State Univ; Ac
Anfinson, Owen, anfinson@sonoma.edu, Sonoma State Univ; GsdGg
Angelopoulos, Vassilis, (310) 794-7090 vassilis@ucla.edu, Univ of California, Los Angeles; XyAsYm
Anger-Kraavi, Annela, +44 (0)1603 59 2633 a.anger-kraavi@uea.ac.uk, Univ of East Anglia; Eg
Angino, Ernest E., (785) 843-7503 Univ of Kansas; Cl
Angle, Michael P., 614 265 6602 mike.angle@dnr.state.oh.us, Ohio Dept of Natural Resources; GlgHw
Angus, Doug, +4401133431326 d.angus@leeds.ac.uk, Univ of Leeds; Ys
Anhaeusser, Carl R., 011-7176581 carl.anhaeusser@wits.ac.za, Univ of the Witwatersrand; GgEgZg
Anis, Ayal, (409) 740-4987 anisa@tamug.tamu.edu, Texas A&M Univ; Opn
Ankney, Meagan, meagan@earth.northwestern.edu, Northwestern Univ; CcqCa
Annett, Amber, +44 023 80596041 a.l.annett@soton.ac.uk, Univ of Southampton; Oc
Ansdell, Kevin M., (306) 966-5698 kevin.ansdell@usask.ca, Univ of Saskatchewan; EgCgGt
Antao, Sytle, 403 220-3083 antao@ucalgary.ca, Univ of Calgary; Gz
Antar, Ali A., (860) 832-2931 antar@ccsu.edu, Central Connecticut State Univ; Zn
Anthony, Elizabeth Y., (915) 747-5483 eanthony@utep.edu, Univ of Texas, El Paso; GiCcGv
Anthony, Nina, 864-294-2052 nina.anthony@furman.edu, Furman Univ; Zn
Anthony, Robin, 412-442-4295 robanthony@pa.gov, DCNR- Pennsylvania Bureau of Geological Survey; Ego
Antigüedad, Iñaki, inaki.antiguedad@ehu.eus, Univ of the Basque Country UPV/EHU; Hw
Antinao, José Luis , (812) 855-1366 jantinao@indiana.edu, Indiana Univ;

CcGlr
Antinao, JoseLuis, 775-673-7450 joseluis.antinao@dri.edu, Desert Research Inst; Gm
Antipova, Anzhelika, 901-678-2178 antipova@memphis.edu, Univ of Memphis; Zg
Antonacci, Vince, (615) 532-1507 vince.antonacci@tn.gov, Tennessee Geological Survey; GgZi
Antonescu, Adrian, +44 0161 306-3911 bogdan.antonescu@manchester.ac.uk, Univ of Manchester; As
Aplin, Andrew, +44 191 33 42332 Durham Univ; Go
Apopei, Andrei I., 0040747760718 andrei.apopei@uaic.ro, Alexandru Ioan Cuza; GziGg
Apostoae, Laviniu, 00400232201463 laviniu@uaic.ro, Alexandru Ioan Cuza; Eg
Apotsos, Alex, 413-597-5082 alex.apotsos@williams.edu, Williams Coll; Ge
Appel, Christopher (Chip) S., (805) 756-1691 cappel@calpoly.edu, California Polytechnic State Univ; Sc
Appel, Heidi, (419) 530-2812 heidi.appel@utoledo.edu, Univ of Toledo; Zn
Appiah-Adjei, Emmanuel K., +233 20 7934 556 ekappiah-adjei.soe@knust.edu.gh, Kwame Nkrumah Univ of Sci and Tech; HwgGg
Applegarth, Michael T., (717) 477-1712 mtappl@ship.edu, Shippensburg Univ; GmZrSo
Applegate, Toby, 413-545-1535 tapplega@geo.umass.edu, Univ of Massachusetts, Amherst; Zy
Appold, Martin S., (573) 882-0701 appoldm@missouri.edu, Univ of Missouri; HwEm
Apprill, Amy, (505) 289-2649 aapprill@whoi.edu, Woods Hole Oceanographic Inst; Ob
Apraiz, Arturo, arturo.apraiz@ehu.eus, Univ of the Basque Country UPV/EHU; Gpt
April, Richard, (315) 228-7212 rapril@colgate.edu, Colgate Univ; CgGze
Aquilina, Noel , noel.aquilina@um.edu.mt, Univ of Malta; Asm
Arabas, Karen, 503-370-6666 karabas@willamette.edu, Willamette Univ; Zn
Aracil, Enrique, earacil@ucm.es, Univ Complutense de Madrid; Yu
Arain, M. A., (905) 525-9140 (Ext. 27941)) arainm@mcmaster.ca, McMaster Univ; Hg
Arakawa, Akio, (310) 825-9874 aar@atmos.ucla.edu, Univ of California, Los Angeles; As
Aranda, Angela, (657) 278-3551 angperez@fullerton.edu, California State Univ, Fullerton; Rn
Aranguren, Aitor, aitor.aranguren@ehu.eus, Univ of the Basque Country UPV/EHU; GcYm
Araya , María C., mariacristina.araya@ucr.ac.cr, Univ de Costa Rica; YdGtYs
Arboleya Cimadevilla, María Luísa, ++935811951 marialuisa.arboleya@uab.cat, Universitat Autonoma de Barcelona; Gc
Archambault, Guy, garchambault@uqac.ca, Universite du Quebec a Chicoutimi; Nr
Archer, Allen W., (785) 532-2244 aarcher@ksu.edu, Kansas State Univ; Gr
Archer, David, (773) 702-0823 Univ of Chicago; Yr
Archer, Emma, +27 (0) 12 420 2881 emma.archer@up.ac.za, Univ of Pretoria; At
Archer, Michael, m.archer@unsw.edu.au, Univ of New South Wales; Pv
Archibald, Doug A., (613) 545-6594 Queen's Univ; Cc
Archuleta, Ralph J., (805) 893-8441 archuleta@geol.ucsb.edu, Univ of California, Santa Barbara; Ys
Arenas, Ricardo, rarenas@ucm.es, Univ Complutense de Madrid; Gp
Arens, Nan Crystal, 315-781-3930 arens@hws.edu, Hobart & William Smith Colls; Pg
Argenbright, Robert T., (910) 962-3498 argenbrightr@uncw.edu, Univ of North Carolina, Wilmington; Zn
Argles, Tom, tom.argles@open.ac.uk, Open Univ; Zi
Argyilan, Erin, 219-980-7124 eargyila@iun.edu, Indiana Univ Northwest; GeHwAm
Arias, Carmen, cariasf@ucm.es, Univ Complutense de Madrid; Gg
Aristilde, Ludmilla, la31@cornell.edu, Cornell Univ; GeSb
Ariya, Parisa A., (514) 398-3615 parisa.ariya@mcgill.ca, McGill Univ; As
Ariyo, Stephen O., +234-8038047475 Federal Univ of Tech, Akure; YegYx
Arkani-Hamed, Jafar, 514-398-6767 jafar@physics.utoronto.ca, McGill Univ; Xy
Arkle, Jenny C., 309-794-7844 jennyarkle@augustana.edu, Augustana Coll; GtmCc
Arkle, Kelsey M., 309-794-7487 kelseyarkle@augustana.edu, Augustana Coll; PeGsg
Armadillo, Egidio, +390103538085 egidio@dipteris.unige.it, Universita di Genova; Ye
Armbrust, Virginia E., (206) 616-1783 armbrust@ocean.washington.edu, Univ of Washington; Ob
Armi, Laurence, (858) 534-6843 larmi@ucsd.edu, Univ of California, San Diego; Op
Armour, Jake, 704-687-5968 jarmour@uncc.edu, Univ of North Carolina, Charlotte; GmlGg
Armstrong, Andrew, 603-862-4559 andya@ccom.unh.edu, Univ of New Hampshire; Zn
Armstrong, David E., (608) 262-2470 Univ of Wisconsin, Madison; Oc
Armstrong, Felicia P., 330-941-1385 fparmstrong@ysu.edu, Youngstown State Univ; Sb
Armstrong, Phillip A., (657) 278-3169 parmstrong@fullerton.edu, California State Univ, Fullerton; GcYg
Armstrong, Robert A., (609) 258-5260 robert.armstrong@stonybrook.edu, SUNY, Stony Brook; Ocb
Armstrong, William H., armstrongwh@appstate.edu, Appalachian State Univ; Glm
Arnaud, Emmanuelle, 519-824-4120 x58087 earnaud@uoguelph.ca, Univ of Guelph; Gls
Arnold, Anthony J., (850) 644-4228 arnold@gly.fsu.edu, Florida State Univ; Pm
Arnold, Dan, +44 (0) 131 451 8298 d.arnold@hw.ac.uk, Heriot-Watt Univ; Go
Arnold, David L., 301/687-4053 dlarnold@frostburg.edu, Frostburg State Univ; As
Arnold, Stephen, +44(0) 113 34 37245 s.arnold@leeds.ac.uk, Univ of Leeds; As
Arnone, John, (775) 673-7445 jarnone@dri.edu, Desert Research Inst; Pg
Arnott, R. William C., warnott@uottawa.ca, Univ of Ottawa; GsSo
Aronoff, Ruth F., (864)294-3363 ruth.aronoff@furman.edu, Furman Univ; Gc
Arp, Dr., Gernot, +49 (0)551 397986 garp@gwdg.de, Georg-August Univ of Goettingen; PggPg
Arribas, Eugenia, earribas@ucm.es, Univ Complutense de Madrid; Gd
Arribas, José, arribas@ucm.es, Univ Complutense de Madrid; Gd
Arritt, Raymond W., (515) 294-9870 rwarritt@iastate.edu, Iowa State Univ of Sci & Tech; As
Arrowsmith, Ramon, (480) 965-3541 ramon.arrowsmith@asu.edu, Arizona State Univ; GcmGt
Arrowsmith, Stephen J., sarrowsmith@smu.edu, Southern Methodist Univ; Ys
Arslan, Gizem, 00904242370000-5972 gturus@firat.edu.tr, Firat Univ; GxiGp
Arsuaga, Juan Luis, azara@ucm.es, Univ Complutense de Madrid; Zn
Arthur, Jonathan D., (850) 617-0320 jonathan.arthur@floridadep.gov, Florida Geological Survey; HwCgGe
Arthur, Michael A., (814) 863-6054 maa6@psu.edu, Pennsylvania State Univ, Univ Park; OuClGs
Artigas, Francisco, 201-460-2801 francisco.artigas@rutgers.edu, Rutgers, The State Univ of New Jersey, Newark; Zi
Artiola, Janick F., (520) 621-3516 jartiola@email.arizona.edu, Univ of Arizona; ScHsCa
Artioli, Gilberto, 39-049-8279162 gilberto.artioli@unipd.it, Univ degli Studi di Padova; GzyZm
Arundale, Wendy H., (907) 474-7039 Univ of Alaska, Fairbanks; Zn
Arvidson, Raymond E., (314) 935-5679 arvidson@wunder.wustl.edu, Washington Univ in St. Louis; Xg
Arya, Satyapal S., (919) 515-7002 pal_arya@ncsu.edu, North Carolina State Univ; As
Aryal, Niroj, (336) 285-3832 naryal@ncat.edu, North Carolina Agricultural & Tech State Univ; HsgZi
Asante, Joseph, (931) 372-3576 jasante@tntech.edu, Tennessee Tech Univ; HwZrGe
Asbury, Brian, 303-273-3123 basbury@mines.edu, Colorado Sch of Mines; Nr
Aschoff, Jennifer, (907) 786-1442 jaschoff@uaa.alaska.edu, Univ of Alaska, Anchorage; GrdGo
Asghari Moghadam, Asghar, +98 (411) 339 2703 moghadam@tabrizu.ac.ir, Univ of Tabriz; HwqHy
Ash, Richard, (301) 405-7504 rdash@umd.edu, Univ of Maryland; Ca
Ashbolt, Nicholas J., nick.ashbolt@scu.edu.au, Southern Cross Univ; PoCb
Ashe, Douglas, douglas.ashe@tulsacc.edu, Tulsa Comm Coll; GgZe
Ashley, Gail M., (848) 445-2221 gmashley@eps.rutgers.edu, Rutgers, The State Univ of New Jersey; GsmSa
Ashley, Paul, +61-2-67732348 pashley@une.edu.au, Univ of New England; EgGeEm
Ashour-Abdalla, Maha, (310) 825-8881 mabdalla@igpp.ucla.edu, Univ of California, Los Angeles; Zn
Ashton, Andrew, 508-289-3751 aashton@whoi.edu, Woods Hole Oceanographic Inst; On
Ashwal, Lewis D., +27 11 717 6652 lewis.ashwal@wits.ac.za, Univ of the Witwatersrand; GxCgGt

Ashwood, Tom, (865) 574-7542 Oak Ridge; Ge
Ashworth, Allan C., 701-231-7919 allan.ashworth@ndsu.edu, North Dakota State Univ; Pe
Asimow, Paul D., (626) 395-4133 asimow@gps.caltech.edu, California Inst of Tech; CpGzy
Asiwaju-Bello, Yinusa A., +2348036672708 ayoasiwajubello@futa.edu.ng, Federal Univ of Tech, Akure; HwNgGu
Askari, Roohollah, (906) 487-2029 raskari@mtu.edu, Michigan Technological Univ; YxxNp
Askari, Zohreh, (217) 300-1819 askari@illinois.edu, Illinois State Geological Survey; Gsc
Aslan, Andres, (970) 248-1614 aaslan@coloradomesa.edu, Colorado Mesa Univ; Gm
Aslan, Yasemin, 00904242370000-5959 yaslan@hotmail.com, Firat Univ; Nr
Asmerom, Yemane, (505) 277-4204 asmerom@unm.edu, Univ of New Mexico; CcPeCg
Asner, Gregory, gregasner@asu.edu, Arizona State Univ; ZrGmSb
Asowata, Timothy I., +2348065348350 tiasowata@futa.edu.ng, Federal Univ of Tech, Akure; GeiGg
Asper, Vernon, (228) 688-3178 Univ of Southern Mississippi; Og
Asphaug, Erik, (831) 459-2260 easphaug@pmc.ucsc.edu, Univ of California, Santa Cruz; Xg
Asquith, George B., 806-834-0497 george.asquith@ttu.edu, Texas Tech Univ; Go
Assatourians, Karen, 519-661-2111, ext. 84715 kassatou@uwo.ca, Western Univ; Ys
Asselin, Esther, (418) 654-2612 esther.asselin@canada.ca, Natural Resources Canada; PlGuRh
Aster, Richard C., (970) 491-7606 rick.aster@colostate.edu, Colorado State Univ; YsGv
Astilleros, José Manuel, jmastill@ucm.es, Univ Complutense de Madrid; Gz
Asuen, Godwin O., godwin.asuen@uniben.edu, Univ of Benin; EcGsg
Atchison, Christopher L., (513) 556-3613 christopher.atchison@uc.edu, Univ of Cincinnati; Ze
Atchley, Stacy C., (254) 710-2196 stacy_atchley@baylor.edu, Baylor Univ; GroGo
Atekwana, Eliot A., 302-8312569 eatekwan@udel.edu, Univ of Delaware; CgsCq
Athaide, Dileep, (604) 984-1771 dathaide@eos.ubc.ca, Univ of British Columbia; Gg
Athey, Jennifer E., (907) 451-5028 jennifer.athey@alaska.gov, Alaska Division of Geological & Geophysical Surveys; Gg
Atkinson, Christopher, christopher.atkinson@und.edu, Univ of North Dakota; AsZi
Atkinson, Gail M., 519-661-2111 x.84207 gatkins6@uwo.ca, Western Univ; YssYs
Atkinson, Larry P., (757) 683-4926 latkinso@odu.edu, Old Dominion Univ; Op
Atkinson, Marlin J., 235-2224 mja@hawaii.edu, Univ of Hawai'i, Manoa; Ob
Atkinson, Tim, +44 020 7679 37711 t.atkinson@ucl.ac.uk, Univ Coll London; PcHwGm
Atkinson, Jr., William W., (303) 492-6103 william.atkinson@colorado.edu, Univ of Colorado; EgmCg
Atlas, Zachary, zatlas@usf.edu, Univ of South Florida; Gi
Atreya, Sushil, (734) 936-0489 atreya@umich.edu, Univ of Michigan; ApZy
Attal, Mikael, +44 (0) 131 650 8533 mikael.attal@ed.ac.uk, Edinburgh Univ; GmtZy
Attia, Snir, 575-835-5290 snir.attia@nmt.edu, New Mexico Inst of Mining and Tech; GcgGi
Attig, John W., john.w.attig@wisc.edu, Univ of Wisconsin, Madison, Division of Extension; Gl
Attinger, Sabine, 0049(0)3641/948651 sabine.attinger@ufz.de, Friedrich-Schiller-Univ Jena; Hy
Attrep, Moses, (505) 667-0088 Los Alamos; Ze
Atudorei, Nieu-Viorel, atudorei@unm.edu, Univ of New Mexico; Cs
Atwater, Brian, 206-553-2927 atwater@uw.edu, Univ of Washington; RnGr
Au, Whitlow W L., 808-247-5026 wau@hawaii.edu, Univ of Hawai'i, Manoa; Zn
Aubert, John E., (916) 484-8637 aubertj@arc.losrios.edu, American River Coll; Zy
Aubry, Marie-Pierre, (732) 445-0822 aubry@eps.rutgers.edu, Rutgers, The State Univ of New Jersey; Pms
Audet, Celine, (418) 723-1986 (Ext. 1744) celine_audet@uqar.qc.ca, Universite du Quebec a Rimouski; Ob
Audet, Pascal, pascal.audet@uottawa.ca, Univ of Ottawa; YgGc
Aufrecht, Walter E., (403) 329-2485 aufrecht@uleth.ca, Univ of Lethbridge; Zn
Ault, Alexis K., aault@email.arizona.edu, Utah State Univ; GtCc
Ault, Toby R., 607-255-1509 tra38@cornell.edu, Cornell Univ; Am
Aurnou, Jonathan M., (310) 825-2054 aurnou@epss.ucla.edu, Univ of California, Los Angeles; YgmYx
Ausbrooks, Scott, 501 683-0119 scott.ausbrooks@arkansas.gov, Arkansas Geological Survey; YsGeg
Ausich, William I., (614) 292-3353 ausich.1@osu.edu, Ohio State Univ; PgGs
Auster, Peter, 860-405-9118 peter.auster@uconn.edu, Univ of Connecticut; Ob
Austermann, Jacqueline, jackya@ldeo.columbia.edu, Columbia Univ; Ys
Austin, George S., gaustin@sdc.org, New Mexico Inst of Mining and Tech; Gz
Austin, Philip, (604) 822-2175 paustin@eos.ubc.ca, Univ of British Columbia; As
Austin, Jr., James A., (512) 471-0450 jamie@ig.utexas.edu, Univ of Texas, Austin; Gut
Autin, Whitney J., 585-395-5738 dirtguy@esc.brockport.edu, SUNY, The Coll at Brockport; Gs
Autio, Robert J., (812) 856-9104 rjautio@indiana.edu, Indiana Univ; HgGle
Avary, Katherine L., 304 594 2331 avarygeo@gmail.com, West Virginia Univ; Go
Avouac, Jean-Philippe, 626.395.2350 avouac@gps.caltech.edu, California Inst of Tech; GtYs
Awdankiewicz, Marek, marek.awdankiewicz@uwr.edu.pl, Univ of Wroclaw; Gvi
Awramik, Stanley M., (805) 893-3830 awramik@geol.ucsb.edu, Univ of California, Santa Barbara; Pg
Axelbaum, Richard, rla@me.wustl.edu, Washington Univ in St. Louis; Ng
Axen, Gary, 575.835.5178 gaxen@ees.nmt.edu, New Mexico Inst of Mining and Tech; Gct
Axford, Yarrow L., 847.467.2268 yarrow@earth.northwestern.edu, Northwestern Univ; GnPmi
Ayad, Yasser M., yayad@clarion.edu, Clarion Univ; Zi
Ayanlade, Ayansina, (803) 777-2355 sinaayanlade@yahoo.co.uk, Obafemi Awolowo Univ; AtZir
Aydin, Adnan, (662) 915-1342 aaydin@olemiss.edu, Univ of Mississippi; NgrYe
Aydin, Atilla, (650) 725-8708 aydin@pangea.stanford.edu, Stanford Univ; Gc
Ayers, John C., 615-322-2158 john.c.ayers@vanderbilt.edu, Vanderbilt Univ; CgGx
Ayers, Joseph , 7815817370 x309 lobster@neu.edu, Northeastern Univ; Zn
Ayling, Bridget, (775) 682-8768 bayling@unr.edu, Univ of Nevada, Reno; CgYhGo
Aylward, Linda, (309) 694-5256 Illinois Central Coll; Ze
Ayodele, Olusiji S., +2347060566760 osayodele@futa.edu.ng, Federal Univ of Tech, Akure; CeGcZr
Azam, Farooq, (858) 534-6850 fazam@ucsd.edu, Univ of California, San Diego; Ob
Azerêdo, Ana , acazeredo@fc.ul.pt, Unive de Lisboa; Gd
Azetsu-Scott, Kumiko, (902) 426-8572 kumiko.azetsu-scott@mar.dfo-mpo.gc.ca, Geological Survey of Canada; Ocp
Azmy, Karem, 709 864 6731 kazmy@mun.ca, Memorial Univ of Newfoundland; Cl

B

Baarli, B. Gudveig, (413) 597-2329 gudveig.baarli@williams.edu, Williams Coll; PssPi
Babaie, Hassan A., (404) 413-5766 hbabaie@gsu.edu, Georgia State Univ; GcZf
Babb, David M., (814) 863-3918 dmb16@psu.edu, Pennsylvania State Univ, Univ Park; Am
Babbin, Andrew, (617) 253-2181 babbin@mit.edu, Massachusetts Inst of Tech; Cb
Babcock, Daphne H., (972) 578-5518 dbabcock@collin.edu, Collin Coll - Spring Creek Campus; Geg
Babcock, Loren E., (614) 292-2103 babcock.5@osu.edu, Ohio State Univ; Pg
Babcock, R. S., (360) 650-3592 babcock@wwu.edu, Western Washington Univ; Cg
Babechuk, Michael, 709 864 6095 mbabechuk@mun.ca, Memorial Univ of Newfoundland; Cu
Babek, Ondrej, +420 549 49 3163 Masaryk Univ; Gds
Baca, Dustin, 575-835-5416 dustin.baca@nmt.edu, New Mexico Inst of Mining and Tech; Cag
Bacchus, Tania S., (802) 635-1329 tania.bacchus@jsc.edu, Northern Vermont Univ-Lyndon; GuAm
Bach Plaza, Joan, ++935811272 joan.bach@uab.cat, Universitat Autonoma

de Barcelona; Gg
Bachle, Peter, (573) 368-2472 peter.bachle@dnr.mo.gov, Missouri Dept of Natural Resources; Gg
Bachmann, Etienne, 609-258-4101 etienneb@princeton.edu, Princeton Univ; Ys
Bachtadse, Valerian, 089/2180 4237 valerian@geophysik.uni-muenchen.de, Ludwig-Maximilians-Univ Muenchen; Yg
Baciu, Sorin D., 0040740404546 dsbaciu@gmail.com, Alexandru Ioan Cuza; GcPv
Back, Larissa E., 608-262-0776 lback@wisc.edu, Univ of Wisconsin, Madison; As
Backus, George E., (858) 534-2468 gebackus@ucsd.edu, Univ of California, San Diego; YmsOp
Bacon, Robert, (573) 526-0807 Missouri Dept of Natural Resources; Hs
Bacon, Steven N., 775-673-7473 steve.bacon@dri.edu, Desert Research Inst; Gm
Bada, Jeffrey L., (858) 534-4258 jbada@ucsd.edu, Univ of California, San Diego; Co
Badalyan, Alex, alex.badalyan@adelaide.edu.au, Univ of Adelaide; Np
Bader, Nicholas E., (509) 527-5113 baderne@whitman.edu, Whitman Coll; SoHgZi
Badger, Robert L., badgerrl@potsdam.edu, SUNY Potsdam; GipGc
Badruddin, Abu Z., 315 2948610 ext.231 badruddin@cayuga-cc.edu, Cayuga Comm Coll; Zi
Baedke, Steven J., (540) 568-6156 baedkesj@jmu.edu, James Madison Univ; Hy
Baer, Eric M., (206) 592-3513 ebaer@highline.edu, Highline Coll; GgvZg
Bagley, Brian, 612-624-8539 bagl0025@umn.edu, Univ of Minnesota, Twin Cities; YsZn
Bagley, Evan, 601-266-4729 evan.bagley@usm.edu, Univ of Southern Mississippi; GgEo
Bagtzoglou, Ross, (212) 854-3154 Columbia Univ; Hw
Bahlburg, Heinrich, +49-251-83-33935 bahlbur@uni-muenster.de, Univ Muenster; GsgCc
Bahr, Jean M., (608) 262-2396 jmbahr@geology.wisc.edu, Univ of Wisconsin, Madison; Hw
Bahrmann, Chad, 814-865-9500 cbahrmann@psu.edu, Pennsylvania State Univ, Univ Park; Am
Baig, Ayat, 204-227-7499 baiga@branedonu.ca, Brandon Univ; EdmEg
Bailey, Christopher M., (757) 221-2445 cmbail@wm.edu, William & Mary; Gc
Bailey, David G., (315) 859-4142 dbailey@hamilton.edu, Hamilton Coll; GizGa
Bailey, Ian, +4401326 259322 i.bailey@exeter.ac.uk, Exeter Univ; Zn
Bailey, Jack B., (309) 298-1481 jb-bailey@wiu.edu, Western Illinois Univ; Pg
Bailey, Jake, (612) 624-1603 baileyj@umn.edu, Univ of Minnesota, Twin Cities; Pg
Bailey, Judy, 61 02 4921 5415 judy.bailey@newcastle.edu.au, Univ of Newcastle; Ec
Bailey, Keiron D., kbailey@email.arizona.edu, Univ of Arizona; Zi
Bailey, Richard C., (416) 978-3231 bailey@physics.utoronto.ca, Univ of Toronto; Yg
Bain, Daniel J., (412) 624-8780 dbain@pitt.edu, Univ of Pittsburgh; HgGmZu
Bain, Olivier, +33(0)3 44069304 olivier.bain@lasalle-beauvais.fr, Institut Polytechnique LaSalle Beauvais (ex-IGAL); OuGgZi
Bair, E. Scott, 614-592-3900 bair.1@osu.edu, Ohio State Univ; HwGe
Baird, Gordon C., (716) 673-3840 baird@fredonia.edu, SUNY, Fredonia; GrPgGs
Baird, Graham, 970-351-2830 graham.baird@unco.edu, Univ of Northern Colorado; GcgGz
Bajjali, William, (715) 394 8056 wbajjali@uwsuper.edu, Univ of Wisconsin, Superior; HwCsg
Bajraktareviæ, Zlatan, +38514606098 zbajrak@geol.pmf.hr, Univ of Zagreb; PgvPm
Bakel, Allen J., (630) 252-5486 Argonne; Co
Baker, Alex, +44 (0)1603 59 1529 alex.baker@uea.ac.uk, Univ of East Anglia; On
Baker, Andy, a.baker@unsw.edu.au, Univ of New South Wales; HwCs
Baker, Brett, 361-749-6774 brett_baker@utexas.edu, Univ of Texas, Austin; Ze
Baker, Cathy, (479) 968-0661 cbaker@atu.edu, Arkansas Tech Univ; Gg
Baker, Don, 514-398-7485 don.baker@mcgill.ca, McGill Univ; CuGvCp
Baker, Edward T., (206) 526-6251 baker@pmel.noaa.gov, Univ of Washington; Ou
Baker, James C., (540) 231-9785 suebrown@vt.edu, Virginia Polytechnic Inst & State Univ; Sd
Baker, John M., (612) 625-4249 jbaker@soils.umn.edu, Univ of Minnesota, Twin Cities; Sp
Baker, Leslie L., 885-6192 lbaker@uidaho.edu, Univ of Idaho; ClXgGe
Baker, Marcia B., mbbaker@u.washington.edu, Univ of Washington; As
Baker, Paul A., (919) 684-6450 pbaker@duke.edu, Duke Univ; PcCgGg
Baker, Richard G., (319) 335-1827 dick-baker@uiowa.edu, Univ of Iowa; PebPc
Baker, Sophie, 775-673-7434 sophie.baker@dri.edu, Desert Research Inst; Gm
Baker, Victor R., (520) 621-7875 baker@email.arizona.edu, Univ of Arizona; XgGmRh
Baker-Treloar, Elizabeth, (619) 260-6822 ebaker@sandiego.edu, Univ of San Diego; Geu
Baksi, Ajoy K., (225) 388-3422 abaksi@geol.lsu.edu, Louisiana State Univ; Cc
Bal Akkoca, Dicle, 00904242370000-5982 dbal@firat.edu.tr, Firat Univ; EnCo
Balakrishnan, Meena, 817-515-6360 meena.balakrishnan@tccd.edu, Tarrant County Coll, Northeast Campus; GggGg
Balascio, Nicholas, 757-221-2880 nbalascio@wm.edu, William & Mary; ZyGnl
Balázs, László, balazslaszlo@windowslive.com, Eotvos Lorand Univ; EoYeg
Balch, Jennifer K., jennifer.balch@colorado.edu, Univ of Colorado; Zg
Balch, Robert S., 575-835-5305 balch@prrc.nmt.edu, New Mexico Inst of Mining and Tech; Yse
Baldauf, Jack G., (979) 845-3651 jbaldauf@tamu.edu, Texas A&M Univ; Ou
Baldini, James, +44 191 33 42334 james.baldini@durham.ac.uk, Durham Univ; Pc
Baldizon, Ileana, (305) 237-3658 ileana.baldizo@mdc.edu, Miami-Dade Coll (Wolfson Campus); Zn
Baldridge, W. Scott, (505) 667-4338 sbaldridge@lanl.gov, Los Alamos; GicGt
Baldwin, Julia, 406-243-5778 jbaldwin@mso.umt.edu, Univ of Montana; Gp
Baldwin, Michael, baldwin@purdue.edu, Purdue Univ; As
Baldwin, Suzanne L., (315) 443-2672 sbaldwin@syr.edu, Syracuse Univ; Cc
Baldwin, Jr., A. Dwight, dbbaldwin@comcast.net, Miami Univ; Hw
Balen, Dražen, +38514605967 drbalen@geol.pmf.hr, Univ of Zagreb; GxpGi
Bales, Roger C., rbales@eng.ucmerced.edu, Univ of Arizona; Cg
Balescu, Sanda, 514-987-3000 #3126 sanda.balescu@club-internet.fr, Universite du Quebec a Montreal; Pe
Balestro, Gianni, gianni.balestro@unito.it, Univ di Torino; Gc
Balgord, Elizabeth A., (801) 626-6225 balgord@email.arizona.edu, Weber State Univ; Grt
Balistrieri, Laurie, (206) 543-8966 balistri@ocean.washington.edu, Univ of Washington; Oc
Ball, Elizabeth, (775) 682-7351 ball@mines.unr.edu, Univ of Nevada, Reno; Zn
Ball, Neil, (204) 474-8075 na_ball@umanitoba.ca, Univ of Manitoba; Gz
Ball, William P., (410) 516-5434 bball@jhu.edu, Johns Hopkins Univ; Zn
Ballantyne, Colin K., ckb@st-andrews.ac.uk, Univ of St. Andrews; ZyGml
Ballard, Robert D., (401) 874-6115 bballard@gso.uri.edu, Univ of Rhode Island; Ga
Ballentine, Christopher, +44 (1865) 272000 (72938) chrisb@earth.ox.ac.uk, Univ of Oxford; Xg
Ballero, Deniz Z., 678-212-7567 dballero@gsu.edu, Georgia State Univ, Perimeter Coll, Online; GgPm
Ballinger, Rhoda, ballingerrc@cf.ac.uk, Cardiff Univ; Zn
Bally, Albert W., (713) 348-6063 geol@rice.edu, Rice Univ; Gg
Balmat, Jennifer L., (308) 432-6483 jbalmat@csc.edu, Chadron State Coll; GgZe
Balmforth, Neil, (604) 822-9835 njb@math.ubc.ca, Univ of British Columbia; As
Balog-Szabo, Anna, 540-857-7222 abalog-szabo@virginiawestern.edu, Virginia Western Comm Coll; Gs
Balogh-Brunstad, Zsuzsanna, (607) 431-4734 balogh_brunz@hartwick.edu, Hartwick Coll; ClHgSo
Balser, Teri , 352-294-3157 tcbalser@ufl.edu, Univ of Florida; Soo
Balser, Teri C., (608) 262-0132 tcbalser@wisc.edu, Univ of Wisconsin, Madison; Sb
Balsley, Christopher, 203-392-6647 balsleyc1@southernct.edu, Southern Connecticut State Univ; Gg
Balster, Nick J., (608) 263-5719 njbalster@wisc.edu, Univ of Wisconsin, Madison; Sf
Baltensperger, David D., (979) 845-3041 dbaltensperger@tamu.edu, Texas A&M Univ; PvCbSb
Baltz, Donald M., (225) 388-6512 Louisiana State Univ; Ob
Bamisaiye, Oluwaseyi A., +2347031533939 oabamisaye@futa.edu.ng, Federal Univ of Tech, Akure; GcZrRn
Bancroft, Alyssa M., (812) 856-5313 ambancro@indiana.edu, Indiana Univ;

PmGr
Banda, Anna F., (903) 802-0186 aperry@dcccd.edu, El Centro Coll - Dallas Comm Coll District; GgeGv
Bandopadhyay, Sukumar, (907) 474-6876 sbandopadhyay@alaska.edu, Univ of Alaska, Fairbanks; Nm
Bandosz, Teresa, 212-650-6017 tbandosz@ccny.cuny.edu, Graduate Sch of the City Univ of New York; Gge
Banerdt, Bruce E., (818) 354-5413 Jet Propulsion Lab; Xy
Banerjee, Neil, (519) 661-2111 x.83727 nbanerj3@uwo.ca, Western Univ; EgCgGx
Banerjee, Subir K., (612) 624-5722 banerjee@tc.umn.edu, Univ of Minnesota, Twin Cities; Ym
Banfield, Jillian, 510-642-9488 jill@seismo.berkeley.edu, Univ of California, Berkeley; CoGz
Bang, John, (919) 530-6569 jjbang@nccu.edu, North Carolina Central Univ; GeZa
Bangs, Nathan L., (512) 471-0424 nathan@ig.utexas.edu, Univ of Texas, Austin; Gu
Banik, Tenley, 309-438-8922 tjbanik@ilstu.edu, Illinois State Univ; GviCc
Bank, Carl-Georg, (416) 978-4381 bank@geology.utoronto.ca, Univ of Toronto; Zg
Banks, David, +44(0) 113 34 35244 d.banks@see.leeds.ac.uk, Univ of Leeds; Cg
Banks, Eddie, eddie.banks@flinders.edu.au, Flinders Univ; Hw
Banner, Jay L., (512) 471-5016 banner@mail.utexas.edu, Univ of Texas, Austin; Cl
Bannon, Ann, ann.bannon@dal.ca, Dalhousie Univ; Zn
Bannon, Peter R., (814) 863-1309 bannon@ems.psu.edu, Pennsylvania State Univ, Univ Park; Am
Banse, Karl, (206) 543-5079 banse@ocean.washington.edu, Univ of Washington; Ob
Bao, Huiming, (225) 578-3419 bao@lsu.edu, Louisiana State Univ; CsAcCu
Baptista, Joana, +44 (0) 191 208 5899 joana.baptista@ncl.ac.uk, Univ of Newcastle Upon Tyne; Ng
Baptista, João C., jbaptist@utad.pt, Unive de Trás-os-Montes e Alto Douro; GmmGa
Barak, Phillip W., (608) 890-0689 phillip.barak@wisc.edu, Univ of Wisconsin, Madison; ScGzRw
Barakat, Bassam, +33(0)3 44068973 bassam.barakat@lasalle-beauvais.fr, Institut Polytechnique LaSalle Beauvais (ex-IGAL); NrgGq
Baran, Zeynep O., (605) 394-2461 zeynep.baran@sdsmt.edu, South Dakota Sch of Mines & Tech; GcoGt
Barazangi, Muawia, (607) 255-6411 mb44@cornell.edu, Cornell Univ; Ys
Barbeau, Katherine A., (858) 822-4339 kbarbeau@ucsd.edu, Univ of California, San Diego; Oc
Barbeau, Jr., David, dbarbeau@geol.sc.edu, Univ of South Carolina; Gs
Barbecot, Florent, 514-987-3000 #7786 barbecot.florent@uqam.ca, Universite du Quebec a Montreal; Hw
Barbee, Gary C., (806) 651-2294 gbarbee@wtamu.edu, West Texas A&M Univ; HwSoZi
Barber, Donald C., (610) 526-5110 dbarber@brynmawr.edu, Bryn Mawr Coll; GesOn
Barber, Richard T., (919) 728-2111 rbarber@duke.edu, Duke Univ; Ob
Barbi, Greta, 089/2180 4234 barbi@gophysik.uni-muenchen.de, Ludwig-Maximilians-Univ Muenchen; Yg
Barboni, Melanie, (480) 965-0612 melanie.barboni@asu.edu, Arizona State Univ; Gi
Barcena, Homar S., 718-368-5758 homar.barcena@kingsborough.edu, Graduate Sch of the City Univ of New York; Gg
Barclay, Andrew, barclay@ldeo.columbia.edu, Columbia Univ; Ys
Barclay, David J., (607) 753-2921 david.barclay@cortland.edu, SUNY, Cortland; Glm
Barclay, Jenni, +44 (0)1603 59 3887 j.barclay@uea.ac.uk, Univ of East Anglia; Gv
Barclay, Julie L., julie.barclay@cortland.edu, SUNY, Cortland; Ggm
Barendregt, Rene W., (403) 329-2530 barendregt@uleth.ca, Univ of Lethbridge; Gm
Barhurst, James, +44 (0) 191 208 5431 james.bathurst@ncl.ac.uk, Univ of Newcastle Upon Tyne; Gs
Barineau, Clinton I., 706-507-8092 barineau_clinton@columbusstate.edu, Columbus State Univ; GctGg
Barker, Andy J., +44 (0)23 80593641 a.j.barker@soton.ac.uk, Univ of Southampton; Gg
Barker, Gregory A., (603) 271-7332 gbarker@des.state.nh.us, New Hampshire Geological Survey; GglZi
Barker, James M., 575-835-5322 james.barker@nmt.edu, New Mexico Inst of Mining and Tech; En
Barker, Jeffrey S., (607) 777-2522 jbarker@binghamton.edu, Binghamton Univ; Ys
Barker, Joel D., (740) 725-6097 barker.246@osu.edu, Ohio State Univ; CblPe
Barker, Stephen, barkers3@cardiff.ac.uk, Cardiff Univ; Pe
Barklage, Mitchell, mitch@earth.northwestern.edu, Northwestern Univ; YgeYs
Barkmann, Peter, 303-384-2642 barkmann@mines.edu, Colorado Geological Survey; HwGcg
Barlow, Jay P., (858) 546-7178 jbarlow@ucsd.edu, Univ of California, San Diego; Ob
Barlow, Mathew, (978) 934-3908 mathew_barlow@uml.edu, Univ of Massachusetts, Lowell; As
Barminski, Robert, 831-770-7056 rbarminski@aol.com, Hartnell Coll; GgOg
Barmore, Garrett, 775-784-4528 gbarmore@unr.edu, Univ of Nevada, Reno; Zn
Barnard, Holly R., holly.barnard@colorado.edu, Univ of Colorado; Hg
Barnbaum, Cecilia S., (229) 249-2645 cbarnbau@valdosta.edu, Valdosta State Univ; Zn
Barnes, Calvin G., 806-834-7389 cal.barnes@ttu.edu, Texas Tech Univ; Gi
Barnes, Charles W., (928) 774-6079 chuck.barnes@nau.edu, Northern Arizona Univ; GcXg
Barnes, Christopher R., (250) 721-8847 crbarnes@uvic.ca, Univ of Victoria; PmOgPe
Barnes, Clare, c.barnes@ed.ac.uk, Edinburgh Univ; Zn
Barnes, Elizabeth A., eabarnes@atmos.colostate.edu, Colorado State Univ; As
Barnes, Fairley J., (505) 667-4933 fyb@lanl.gov, Los Alamos; Zn
Barnes, Hubert L., (814) 865-7573 barnes@psu.edu, Pennsylvania State Univ, Univ Park; CgEmCe
Barnes, Jaime D., jdbarnes@jsg.utexas.edu, Univ of Texas, Austin; CgsCc
Barnes, Jeffrey R., (541) 737-5685 barnes@coas.oregonstate.edu, Oregon State Univ; As
Barnes, Jessica, jebarnes@mailbox.sc.edu, Univ of South Carolina; Zn
Barnes, Melanie A., (806) 834-7965 melanie.barnes@ttu.edu, Texas Tech Univ; CaGie
Barnes, Philip, pbarnes@environ.sc.edu, Univ of South Carolina; Zn
Barnes, Randal J., (612) 625-5828 Univ of Minnesota, Twin Cities; Zn
Barnes, Sarah- J., 418 545 5011 sjbarnes@uqac.ca, Universite du Quebec a Chicoutimi; EgGiCt
Barnett, Douglas B., (509) 376-3416 brent.barnett@pnl.gov, Pacific Northwest; Em
Barnett, Michael, 617-552-8300 barnetge@bc.edu, Boston Coll; Ze
Barnett, Roger T., rbarnett@pacific.edu, Univ of the Pacific; Zy
Barnhart, William, william-barnhart-1@uiowa.edu, Univ of Iowa; YdsGt
Barnosky, Anthony D., barnosky@berkeley.edu, Univ of California, Berkeley; Pv
Barone, Jessica, 585-292-2448 jbarone@monroecc.edu, Monroe Comm Coll; Ge
Baross, John A., (206) 543-0833 Univ of Washington; Ob
Barquero-Molina, Miriam, (573) 882-9557 barqueromolinam@missouri.edu, Univ of Missouri; Gct
Barr, Sandra M., (902) 585-1340 sandra.barr@acadiau.ca, Acadia Univ; GitGg
Barr, Stuart, +44 (0) 191 208 6449 stuart.barr@ncl.ac.uk, Univ of Newcastle Upon Tyne; Zi
Barra, Monica, (803) 576-8340 mbarra@seie.sc.edu, Univ of South Carolina; Zn
Barrash, Warren, (208) 426-1229 wbarrash@boisestate.edu, Boise State Univ; HwYxGe
Barrett, Bradford S., 410-293-6567 bbarrett@usna.edu, United States Naval Academy; As
Barrett, John, +44(0) 113 34 32394 j.r.barrett@leeds.ac.uk, Univ of Leeds; Ge
Barrett, Kevin M., (817) 515-6352 kevin.barrett@tccd.edu, Tarrant County Coll, Northeast Campus; AsZgr
Barrett, Melony, 217-333-7917 mebarret@illinois.edu, Illinois State Geological Survey; Zi
Barrick, James E., (806) 834-2717 jim.barrick@ttu.edu, Texas Tech Univ; Psm
Barrie, Vaughn, (250) 363-6424 Univ of Victoria; Gu
Barrier, Pascal, +33(0)3 44068975 pascal.barrier@lasalle-beauvais.fr, Institut Polytechnique LaSalle Beauvais (ex-IGAL); PmGsPs
Barron, Elizabeth, (920) 424-4105 barrone@uwosh.edu, Univ of Wisconsin Oshkosh; Zn
Barron, George, gbarron@uoguelph.ca, Univ of Guelph; Zn
Barron, Robert, (906) 487-2096 rjbarron@mtu.edu, Michigan Technological Univ; ZgGzi
Barros, Tony, (305) 237-3754 tbarros@mdc.edu, Miami-Dade Coll (Wolfson Campus); Og
Barry, Peter, pbarry@whoi.edu, Woods Hole Oceanographic Inst; Cm

Barsch, Robert, 089/2180 4201 barsch@geophysik.uni-muenchen.de, Ludwig-Maximilians-Univ Muenchen; Yg
Bart, Philip J., (225) 388-3109 pbart@geol.lsu.edu, Louisiana State Univ; Gr
Bartello, Peter, (514) 398-8075 peter.bartello@mcgill.ca, McGill Univ; As
Bartels, William S., (517) 629-0313 wbartels@albion.edu, Albion Coll; Pv
Barth, Andrew P., (317) 274-1243 ibsz100@iupui.edu, Indiana Univ - Purdue Univ Indianapolis; Gi
Barth, Jack A., (541) 737-1607 barth@coas.oregonstate.edu, Oregon State Univ; On
Barth, Nicolas, (951) 827-3138 nic.barth@ucr.edu, Univ of California, Riverside; Gt
Barth, Susan A., (406) 496-4687 sbarth@mtech.edu, Montana Tech of The Univ of Montana; Zn
Barthelmie, Rebecca J., rb737@cornell.edu, Cornell Univ; Ass
Bartholemew, Paul, pbartholomew@newhaven.edupbartholomew@newhaven.edu, Univ of New Haven; GeZiGz
Bartholomaus, Timothy, (208) 885-6217 tbartholomaus@uidaho.edu, Univ of Idaho; Gl
Bartholomew, Alexander J., 845-257-3765 barthola@newpaltz.edu, SUNY, New Paltz; GrPi
Bartholomew, Mervin J., (901) 678-1613 jbrthlm1@memphis.edu, Univ of Memphis; Gtc
Bartholy, Judit, +36 20 3722945 bartholy@caesar.elte.hu, Eotvos Lorand Univ; Am
Bartl, Simona, 831-771-4400 sbartl@mlml.calstate.edu, Moss Landing Marine Lab; Zn
Bartlein, Patrick, (541) 346-4967 bartlein@uoregon.edu, Univ of Oregon; Pe
Bartlett, Douglas H., (858) 534-5233 dbartlett@ucsd.edu, Univ of California, San Diego; Ob
Bartlett, Wendy, 740-376-4782 bartletw@marietta.edu, Marietta Coll; Goe
Bartley, John M., (801) 58--7162 john.bartley@utah.edu, Univ of Utah; GciCc
Bartley, Julie K., 507-933-7541 jbartley@gustavus.edu, Gustavus Adolphus Coll; GsPgo
Bartok, Peter, 713-444-7751 peter@bartokinc.com, Univ of Houston; GoYeNr
Bartolucci, Valerio, (954) 201-6678 vbartolu@broward.edu, Broward Coll; Ge
Barton, Christopher C., (727) 215-5538 chris.barton@wright.edu, Wright State Univ; GqYgHq
Barton, James H., (412) 589-2821 Thiel Coll; Zy
Barton, Mark D., (520) 621-8529 mdbarton@email.arizona.edu, Univ of Arizona; Eg
Barton, Michael, (614) 292-3132 barton.2@osu.edu, Ohio State Univ; GiCpt
Barzegari, Ghodrat, gbarzegari@gmail.com, Univ of Tabriz; Nr
Basak, Chandranath, 302-831-8230 cbasak, Univ of Delaware; ClOcCs
Bascom, Johnathan, (616) 526-7053 jbascom@calvin.edu, Calvin Coll; Zy
Basinger, James F., (306) 966-5684 jim.basinger@usask.ca, Univ of Saskatchewan; Pb
Baskin, Perry A., (229) 259-5052 pbaskin@valdosta.edu, Valdosta State Univ; Zn
Bass, David, david.bass@flinders.edu.au, Flinders Univ; Zy
Bass, Jay D., (217) 333-1018 jaybass@illinois.edu, Univ of Illinois, Urbana-Champaign; Gy
Bass, Jerry, 601 266-4732 joby@usm.edu, Univ of Southern Mississippi; Zn
Bassett, Damon, (417) 836-4897 dbassett@missouristate.edu, Missouri State Univ; Gg
Bassett, Kari N., (03) 369-4495 kari.bassett@canterbury.ac.nz, Univ of Canterbury; GstGd
Bassett, Scott, (775) 784-1434 sbassett@unr.edu, Univ of Nevada, Reno; Zu
Bassett, William A., wab7@cornell.edu, Cornell Univ; Gz
Bassis, Jeremy, (734) 615-3606 jbassis@umich.edu, Univ of Michigan; GlOgZg
Basta, Nicholas T., 614-292-6282 basta.4@osu.edu, Ohio State Univ; Sc
Bastow, Ian, +44 20 759 42974 i.bastow@imperial.ac.uk, Imperial Coll; Yg
Basu, Abhijit, 8128556654/5581 basu@indiana.edu, Indiana Univ, Bloomington; Gd
Basu, Anirban, +44 1784 414083 anirban.basu@rhul.ac.uk, Royal Holloway Univ of London; CglCs
Basu, Asish, (817) 272-2987 abasu@uta.edu, Univ of Texas, Arlington; GxCcs
Bataille, Clement, (613)562-6800 x6736 clement.bataille@uottawa.ca, Univ of Ottawa; ClGeCs
Batelaan, Okke, okke.batelaan@ees.kuleuven.be, Katholieke Universiteit Leuven; Hw
Bates, Mary, (661) 362-5054 mary.bates@canyons.edu, Coll of the Canyons; Zyg
Bates, Nicholas R., n.r.bates@soton.ac.uk, Univ of Southampton; Oc
Bates, Richard, +44 01334 463997 crb@st-andrews.ac.uk, Univ of St. Andrews; Yx
Bates, Timothy S., (206) 526-6248 tim.bates@noaa.gov, Univ of Washington; As
Bathke, Deborah J., dbathke2@unl.edu, Univ of Nebraska, Lincoln; AsZe
Battisti, David S., (206) 543-2019 battisti@uw.edu, Univ of Washington; As
Battles, Eileen, (785) 864-2129 battles@kgs.ku.edu, Univ of Kansas; Zy
Batygin, Konstantin, 626-395-2920 kbatygin@gps.caltech.edu, California Inst of Tech; Xg
Bauder, James W., (406) 994-5685 jbauder@montana.edu, Montana State Univ; Sf
Bauer, Annie, annie.bauer@wisc.edu, Univ of Wisconsin, Madison; Cca
Bauer, Bernard O., 250-807-9595 bernard.bauer@ubc.ca, Univ of British Columbia, Okanagan Campus; GmOnZy
Bauer, Carl J., cjbauer@email.arizona.edu, Univ of Arizona; Hs
Bauer, Emily, (612) 626-0909 bauer010@umn.edu, Univ of Minnesota; Zi
Bauer, Jeffrey A., jbauer@shawnee.edu, Shawnee State Univ; Ps
Bauer, Paul W., (575) 835-5106 bauer@nmt.edu, New Mexico Inst of Mining and Tech; Gc
Bauer, R. A., 217-244-2394 rabauer@illinois.edu, Illinois State Geological Survey; Ng
Baum, Steven K., (979) 845-0793 sbaum@ocean.tamu.edu, Texas A&M Univ; Op
Baumann, Hannes, 860-405-9297 hannes.baumann@uconn.edu, Univ of Connecticut; Ob
Baumann, Zofia, (860) 405-9281 zofia.baumann@uconn.edu, Univ of Connecticut; ObcCm
Baumgartner, Mark, mbaumgartner@whoi.edu, Dalhousie Univ; Ob
Baumiller, Tomasz K., (734) 764-7543 tomaszb@umich.edu, Univ of Michigan; Pg
Bautista, Sonia, sbautist@ucm.es, Univ Complutense de Madrid; Ng
Baxter, Ethan, 617-552-3640 ethan.baxter@bc.edu, Boston Coll; Ccg
Baxter, Martin, 989-774-2055 baxte1ma@cmich.edu, Central Michigan Univ; Ams
Baxter, Stefanie J., 302-831-1576 steff@udel.edu, Univ of Delaware; On
Baxter, P.G., James E., 717-780-2377 jebaxter@hacc.edu, Harrisburg Area Comm Coll; GgHwGm
Bayari, Serdar, +90 (312) 2977740 serdar@hacettepe.edu.tr, Hacettepe Univ; Hw
Bayowa, Oyelowo G., +2348030820291 obayowa@lautech.edu.ng, Ladoke Akintola Univ of Tech; GggGg
Beach Davis, Janet, (309) 268-8513 janet.beach-davis@heartland.edu, Heartland Comm Coll; Zg
Beane, Rachel J., (207) 725-3160 rbeane@bowdoin.edu, Bowdoin Coll; GzxZe
Beard, Brian L., 608-262-1806 beardb@geology.wisc.edu, Univ of Wisconsin, Madison; Cc
Beard, James S., (276) 634-4170 jim.beard@vmnh.virginia.gov, Virginia Polytechnic Inst & State Univ; GiClg
Beard, K. Christopher, (412) 622-5782 beardc@carnegiemnh.org, Carnegie Mus of Natural History; Pv
Beard, Kenneth V., (217) 333-1676 k-beard@uiuc.edu, Univ of Illinois, Urbana-Champaign; As
Bearden, Bennett L., 205-247-3683 bbearden@gsa.state.al.us, Geological Survey of Alabama; HgEo
Bearden, Rebecca A., 205-247-3623 rbearden@gsa.state.al.us, Geological Survey of Alabama; Hs
Beatty, Lynne, 9134698500 x3785 lbeatty@jccc.edu, Johnson County Comm Coll; GgZy
Beatty, Merrill Ann, (506) 453-4803 mbeatty@unb.ca, Univ of New Brunswick; Zn
Beatty, William L., 507-474-5789 wbeatty@winona.edu, Winona State Univ; PgiGs
Beaty, Tammy, (865) 574-0119 taw@ornl.gov, Oak Ridge; Zi
Beaucamp-Stout, Celine, 775-397-2775 celine.beaucampstout@umwestern.edu, Univ of Montana Western; GctEm
Beauchamp, Marc, 519-661-2111 ext 88104 mbeauch6@uwo.ca, Western Univ; Ca
Beaudoin, Georges, (418) 656-3141 beaudoin@ggl.ulaval.ca, Universite Laval; EgGzCa
Beaulieu, Claudie, clbeauli@ucsc.edu, Univ of Southampton; Op
Beaumont, Christopher, (902) 494-3779 chris.beaumont@dal.ca, Dalhousie Univ; Yg
Beausoleil, Denis, 604-777-6019 beausoleild@douglascollege.ca, Douglas Coll; GgZg
Beaverson, Sheena K., 217-244-9306 sbeavers@illinois.edu, Illinois State Geological Survey; Zr
Bebout, Gray E., (610) 758-5831 geb0@lehigh.edu, Lehigh Univ; Gp
Beccue, Clint, 217-265-5161 cbeccue@illinois.edu, Illinois State Geological Survey; Ge

Becel, Anne, annebcl@ldeo.columbia.edu, Columbia Univ; Gu
Bechtel, Timothy D., 717 358--4750 timothy.bechtel@fandm.edu, Franklin and Marshall Coll; GeYg
Beck, Catherine C., 315-859-4847 ccbeck@hamilton.edu, Hamilton Coll; GsnGr
Beck, Charles, (734) 763-5089 chbeck@umich.edu, Univ of Michigan; Pg
Beck, Colleen M., (702) 795-8077 colleen@dri.edu, Desert Research Inst; Sa
Beck, John H., 617-552-8300 john.beck@bc.edu, Boston Coll; Pb
Beck, Susan L., (520) 621-8628 slbeck@email.arizona.edu, Univ of Arizona; YsGt
Becker, Alex, (510) 643-9181 Univ of California, Berkeley; Yg
Becker, Janet M., (808) 956-6514 jbecker@soest.hawaii.edu, Univ of Hawai'i, Manoa; Og
Becker, Keir, (305) 421-4661 kbecker@rsmas.miami.edu, Univ of Miami; YrGu
Becker, Laurence, (541) 737-9504 beckerla@geo.oregonstate.edu, Oregon State Univ; Zn
Becker, Lorene Y., 541-737-6993 beckelo@geo.oregonstate.edu, Oregon State Univ; Zi
Becker, Matthew, 562-985-8983 mbecker3@csulb.edu, California State Univ, Long Beach; Hwg
Becker, Naomi M., (505) 667-2165 nmb@lanl.gov, Los Alamos; Hg
Becker, Ralph Thomas, +49-251-83-33951 rbecker@uni-muenster.de, Univ Muenster; PisPm
Becker, Richard H., (630) 252-7595 Argonne; Zr
Becker, Thorsten, twb@ig.utexas.edu, Univ of Texas, Austin; Yg
Becker, Udo, (734) 615-6894 ubecker@umich.edu, Univ of Michigan; Zn
Beckie, Roger D., (604) 822-6462 rbeckie@eos.ubc.ca, Univ of British Columbia; HwCl
Beckingham, Barbara, (843) 953-0483 beckinghamba@cofc.edu, Coll of Charleston; Cl
Bedard, Jean H., (418) 654-2671 jbedard@nrcan.gc.ca, Universite du Quebec; Gi
Bedard, Paul, 4185455011, 2276 pbedard@uqac.ca, Universite du Quebec a Chicoutimi; CaGzEg
Bedaso, Zelalem, (937) 229-2393 zbedaso1@udayton.edu, Univ of Dayton; CslGs
Beddows, Patricia A., (847) 491-7460 patricia@earth.northwestern.edu, Northwestern Univ; HyGma
Bedle, Heather, hbedle@ou.edu, Univ of Oklahoma; Yg
Bednarski, Marsha, (860) 832-2943 bednarskim@ccsu.edu, Central Connecticut State Univ; Ze
Bednarz, Robert S., r-bednarz@tamu.edu, Texas A&M Univ; Zeu
Bednarz, Sarah W., (979) 845-1579 s-bednarz@tamu.edu, Texas A&M Univ; Ze
Bedore, Melanie, (905) 525-9140 (Ext. 23525)) bedorem@mcmaster.ca, McMaster Univ; Zu
Bedrikovetski, Pavel, pavel.bedrikovetski@adelaide.edu.au, Univ of Adelaide; Np
Beebe, Alex, dbeebe@southalabama.edu, Univ of South Alabama; Ge
Beets, Kay J., +31 20 59 87357 c.j.beets@vu.nl, Vrije Universiteit Amsterdam; Cg
Befus, Kenneth S., (254)710-2192 kenneth_befus@baylor.edu, Baylor Univ; GviGv
Beget, James E., ffjeb1@uaf.edu, Univ of Alaska, Fairbanks; Gm
Begg, Stephen, steve.begg@adelaide.edu.au, Univ of Adelaide; Eo
Beghein, Caroline, (310) 825-0742 cbeghein@ucla.edu, Univ of California, Los Angeles; Ysg
Begin, Christian, (418) 654-2648 christian.begin@canada.ca, Universite du Quebec; PeGmSo
Behl, Richard J., (562) 985-5850 behl@csulb.edu, California State Univ, Long Beach; GsPeGd
Behn, Mark, 617 552-2180 mark.behn@bc.edu, Boston Coll; YgrGt
Behr, Rose-Anna, 717-702-2035 rosbehr@pa.gov, DCNR- Pennsylvania Bureau of Geological Survey; Gcr
Behr-Andres, Christina "Tina", (505) 667-3644 behr-andres@lanl.gov, Los Alamos; Zn
Behrensmeyer, Anna K., (202) 633-1307 Smithsonian Inst / Nat Mus of Natural History; Pv
Beiersdorfer, Raymond E., (330) 941-1753 rebeiersdorfer@ysu.edu, Youngstown State Univ; Cg
Bein, F. L., (317) 274-1100 Indiana Univ, Indianapolis; Zy
Bekker, Andrey, (951) 827-4611 andrey.bekker@ucr.edu, Univ of California, Riverside; GsrCg
Bekker, Matthew F., (801) 422-1961 matthew_bekker@byu.edu, Brigham Young Univ; Zy
Belasky, Paul, 510-676-0945 pbelasky@ohlone.edu, Ohlone Coll; PgqGs
Belknap, Daniel F., (207) 581-2159 belknap@maine.edu, Univ of Maine; GusGa
Bell, Andrew, +44 (0) 131 650 4918 a.bell@ed.ac.uk, Edinburgh Univ; Gt
Bell, Brian, +44 01413306898 brian.bell@glasgow.ac.uk, Univ of Glasgow; So
Bell, Christopher J., (512) 471-7301 cjbell@mail.utexas.edu, Univ of Texas, Austin; Pv
Bell, David, (03) 3642-717 david.bell@canterbury.ac.nz, Univ of Canterbury; Ng
Bell, James, (480) 965-1044 jim.bell@asu.edu, Arizona State Univ; Xg
Bell, John W., (775) 784-1939 jbell@unr.edu, Univ of Nevada, Reno; NgGm
Bell, Keith, keith_bell@carleton.ca, Carleton Univ; Cc
Bell, Margaret C., +44 (0) 191 208 7936 margaret.bell@ncl.ac.uk, Univ of Newcastle Upon Tyne; Ge
Bell, Michael M., mmbell@colostate.edu, Colorado State Univ; As
Bell, Phil R., pbell23@une.edu.au, Univ of New England; PgvPg
Bell, Rebecca, +44 20 759 40903 rebecca.bell@imperial.ac.uk, Imperial Coll; Gt
Bell, Robin E., robinb@ldeo.columbia.edu, Columbia Univ; Yr
Beller, Stephen, 609-258-4101 sbeller@princeton.edu, Princeton Univ; Ysg
Bellew, Angela, (319) 335-1819 angela-bellew@uiowa.edu, Univ of Iowa; Zn
Bellian, Jerome, jerry.bellian@whiting.com, Miami Univ; Go
Belliveau, Lindsey, 860-424-3581 lindsey.belliveau@ct.gov, Dept of Energy and Environmental Protection; Gmt
Belluso, Elena, elena.belluso@unito.it, Univ di Torino; Gz
Belmonte, Donato, +39 010 353 8136 Universita di Genova; Cg
Beltrami, Hugo, 902-867-2326 hbeltram@stfx.ca, Saint Francis Xavier Univ; YhAs
Beltz, John F., 330 972-6687 jfb4@uakron.edu, Univ of Akron; GgRh
Bemis, Sean P., sbemis@vt.edu, Virginia Polytechnic Inst & State Univ; Gt
Ben-Avraham, Zvi, zviba@tau.ac.il, Tel Aviv Univ; YrGt
Ben-Zion, Yehuda, (213) 740-6734 ybz@earth.usc.edu, Univ of Southern California; Ys
Benacquista, Matt, (406) 657-2341 Montana State Univ, Billings; Xy
Benavides, Jude, 956 883-5938 jude.benavides@utrgv.edu, Univ of Texas, Rio Grande Valley; Hsq
Benavides-Iglesias, Alfonso, a.benavides@geos.tamu.edu, Texas A&M Univ; Ys
Bender, E. E., (714) 432-5681 ebender@occ.cccd.edu, Orange Coast Coll; GitGz
Bender, John F., 704-687- 5956 jfbender@email.uncc.edu, Univ of North Carolina, Charlotte; GiCtOu
Bender, Michael L., 609-258-5807 bender@princeton.edu, Princeton Univ; Cg
Bendick, Rebecca, 406-243-5774 bendick@mso.umt.edu, Univ of Montana; Yg
Benedetti, Michael M., (910) 962-7650 benedettim@uncw.edu, Univ of North Carolina, Wilmington; GmSaZy
Benfield, Mark C., (225) 388-6372 mbenfie@lsu.edu, Louisiana State Univ; Ob
Benger, Simon, simon.benger@flinders.edu.au, Flinders Univ; Ziy
Benimoff, Alan I., 718-982-2835 alan.benimoff@csi.cuny.edu, Coll of Staten Island/CUNY; GizGp
Benison, Kathleen , 304-293-5603 West Virginia Univ; GrsCm
Benitez-Nelson, Claudia R., 777-0018 cbnelson@geol.sc.edu, Univ of South Carolina; OcGe
Benito, María Isabel, mibenito@ucm.es, Univ Complutense de Madrid; Gs
Benjamin, Patricia A., 508-929-8606 pbenjamin@worcester.edu, Worcester State Univ; Zg
Benjamin, Timothy M., (505) 667-5154 Los Alamos; Ca
Benjamin, U. K., 234-8038312732 uzochukwu.benjamin@oauife.edu.ng, Obafemi Awolowo Univ; GoCg
Benna, Piera, piera.benna@unito.it, Univ di Torino; Gz
Bennartz, Ralf, ralf.bennartz@vanderbilt.edu, Vanderbilt Univ; AsZr
Benner, Jake, 865-974-6013 jbenner@utk.edu, Univ of Tennessee, Knoxville; ZePg
Benner, Ron, benner@mailbox.sc.edu, Univ of South Carolina; Ob
Benner, Shawn, shawnbenner@gmail.com, Boise State Univ; Clt
Bennet, Brett, 785-864-2117 bb@kgs.ku.edu, Univ of Kansas; Ng
Bennett, Philip, (512) 471-3587 pbennett@mail.utexas.edu, Univ of Texas, Austin; Hg
Bennett, Richard, (520) 621-2324 rab@geo.arizona.edu, Univ of Arizona; YdGt
Bennett, Sara, 309/298-1905 sc-bennett@wiu.edu, Western Illinois Univ; Gg
Bennett, Scott, scottekb@uw.edu, Univ of Washington; YsGtm
Bennett, Steven W., (309) 298-1256 sw-bennett1@wiu.edu, Western Illinois Univ; Hw
Bennington, J Bret, 516 463-5568 geojbb@hofstra.edu, Hofstra Univ; PeGs
Benoit-Bird, Kelly, 541-737-2063 kbenoit@coas.oregonstate.edu, Oregon

FACULTY INDEX – B

State Univ; Gu
Bense, Victor, +44 (0)1603 59 1297 v.bense@uea.ac.uk, Univ of East Anglia; Hg
Benson, David A., 303-273-3806 dbenson@mines.edu, Colorado Sch of Mines; Hq
Benson, Donna M., (480) 461-7247 donnabenson@mesacc.edu, Mesa Comm Coll; Gg
Benson, Jane L., (270) 809-3106 jbenson1@murraystate.edu, Murray State Univ; Zi
Benson, Roger, +44 (1865) 272000 roger.benson@earth.ox.ac.uk, Univ of Oxford; Pg
Bentley, Callan, (703) 323-3276 cbentley@nvcc.edu, Northern Virginia Comm Coll - Annandale; Gg
Bentley, Laurence R., (403) 220-4512 Univ of Calgary; Hw
Bentley, Samuel J., 225-578-5735 sjb@lsu.edu, Louisiana State Univ; Gu
Benton, Steven, 217-244-0082 s-benton@illinois.edu, Illinois State Geological Survey; Gg
Benway, Heather, (508) 289-2838 hbenway@whoi.edu, Woods Hole Oceanographic Inst; OcCmOo
Beranek, Luke, 709 864 4588 lberanek@mun.ca, Memorial Univ of Newfoundland; GgsCc
Berchem, Jean, (310) 206-6484 jberchem@igpp.ucla.edu, Univ of California, Los Angeles; Zn
Bercovici, David, (203) 432-3168 david.bercovici@yale.edu, Yale Univ; Yg
Bereitschaft, Bradley, 402-554-2674 bbereitschaft@unomaha.edu, Univ of Nebraska, Omaha; Zuy
Berelson, William M., (213) 740-5828 berelson@usc.edu, Univ of Southern California; Cm
Beresnev, Igor A., (515) 294-7529 beresnev@iastate.edu, Iowa State Univ of Sci & Tech; YgsYe
Berg, Christopher A., (714)432-0202 x21229 cberg5@occ.cccd.edu, Orange Coast Coll; GpZeGt
Berg, Peter, (804) 924-1318 pb8n@virginia.edu, Univ of Virginia; So
Berg, Richard, 217-244-2776 rberg@illinois.edu, Univ of Illinois; GlRwZu
Bergantz, George W., 206-685-4972 bergantz@uw.edu, Univ of Washington; Gi
Berger, Peter M., 217-333-7078 pmberger@illinois.edu, Illinois State Geological Survey; Cg
Bergeron, Normand, (418) 654-3703 normand.bergeron@ete.inrs.ca, Universite du Quebec; Gm
Berggren, William A., (508) 289-2593 wberggren@whoi.edu, Woods Hole Oceanographic Inst; Ps
Bergin, Michael H., (404) 894-9723 mike.bergin@ce.gatech.edu, Georgia Inst of Tech; As
Bergmann, Kristin, (617) 253-9852 kdberg@mit.edu, Massachusetts Inst of Tech; GsCl
Bergquist, Bridget, bergquist@es.utoronto.ca, Univ of Toronto; Cgb
Bergslien, Elisa T., 716-878-3793 bergslet@buffalostate.edu, Buffalo State Coll; ClHw
Bergstrom, Stig M., (614) 292-4473 bergstrom.1@osu.edu, Ohio State Univ; Pg
Bergwerff, Kenneth A., (616) 526-6371 kbergwer@calvin.edu, Calvin Coll; Ze
Berke, Melissa, melissa.berke.1@nd.edu, Univ of Notre Dame; Cs
Berkelhammer, Max, 312-413-8271 berkelha@uic.edu, Univ of Illinois at Chicago; Cg
Berli, Marcus, 702.862.5452 markus.berli@dri.edu, Univ of Nevada, Reno; Sp
Berlin, Graydon L., lenn.berlin@nau.edu, Northern Arizona Univ; Zr
Berman, David S., (412) 622-3248 bermand@carnegiemnh.org, Carnegie Mus of Natural History; PggPv
Bermanec, Vladimir, +38514605972 vberman@public.carnet.hr, Univ of Zagreb; GzEnGi
Bermingham, Katherine R., (301) 405-2707 kberming@umd.edu, Univ of Maryland; XcCcg
Bernard, Rachael E., rbernard@amherst.edu, Amherst Coll; Gc
Bernard-Kingsley, Noell, 206-616-8511 noelleon@uw.edu, Univ of Washington; Ze
Bernhard, Joan M., 508-289-3480 jbernhard@whoi.edu, Woods Hole Oceanographic Inst; Cg
Bernhardt, Jase, 516-463-5731 jase.e.bernhardt@hofstra.edu, Hofstra Univ; Ams
Bernier, Luc, (905) 525-9140 (Ext. 26364) berniejm@mcmaster.ca, McMaster Univ; Cg
Bernier, Monique, 418 654-2585 monique.bernier@ete.inrs.ca, Universite du Quebec; Zr
Bernstein, Neil P., neil-bernstein@uiowa.edu, Univ of Iowa; Ge
Beroza, Gregory C., (650) 723-4958 beroza@stanford.edu, Stanford Univ; Ys
Berquist, Jr., Carl R., (757) 221-2448 crberq@wm.edu, William & Mary; Ou
Berry, C M., chris.berry@earth.cf.ac.uk, Cardiff Univ; Pb
Berry, Duane F., (540) 231-9792 duberry@vt.edu, Virginia Polytechnic Inst & State Univ; Sb
Berry, Karen, 303-384-2640 kaberry@mines.edu, Colorado Geological Survey; NgZu
Berry, Kate, (775) 784-6344 kberry@unr.edu, Univ of Nevada, Reno; Zy
Berry, Leonard, 561 297-2935 berry@fau.edu, Florida Atlantic Univ; Zg
Berry, Ron F., 61 3 6226 2456 ron.berry@utas.edu.au, Univ of Tasmania; Gc
Berry IV, Henry N., 207-287-7179 henry.n.berry@maine.gov, Dept of Agriculture, Conservation, and Forestry; Gg
Bershaw, John T., (503) 725-3778 bershaw@pdx.edu, Portland State Univ; GsCsHy
Berta, Susan, 812-237-2260 sberta@indstate.edu, Indiana State Univ; GmZr
Berthold, Angela, (612) 626-6744 berth084@d.umn.edu, Univ of Minnesota; Gl
Berti, Claudio, (208) 885-7479 cberti@uidaho.edu, Univ of Idaho; GgmGc
Bertine, Kathe K., (619) 594-6369 kbertine@geology.sdsu.edu, San Diego State Univ; Cl
Bertog, Janet, 859-572-1523 bertogj@nku.edu, Northern Kentucky Univ; Gd
Bertok, Carlo, carlo.bertok@unito.it, Univ di Torino; Gd
Bertsch, Paul M., (803) 725-2752 Univ of Georgia; Sc
Besancon, James, (781) 283-3030 jbesancon@wellesley.edu, Wellesley Coll; Hww
Best, James L., 217-244-1839 jimbest@illinois.edu, Univ of Illinois, Urbana-Champaign; Gs
Best, Myron G., best_myron_g@byu.edu, Brigham Young Univ; Gg
Bestland, Erick, erick.bestland@flinders.edu.au, Flinders Univ; GsSa
Beswick, Anthony E., (705) 675-1151 Laurentian Univ, Sudbury; Gi
Betancourt, Julio, jlbetanc@usgs.gov, Univ of Arizona; Zn
Betchwars, Corey, (612) 625-3507 betch038@umn.edu, Univ of Minnesota; Zi
Betka, Paul, pbetka@gmu.edu, George Mason Univ; GctGg
Bettis III, E. A., (319) 335-1831 art-bettis@uiowa.edu, Univ of Iowa; SdGmSa
Betzer, Peter R., (727) 553-1130 pbetzer@marine.usf.edu, Univ of South Florida; Cm
Beukelman, Gregg S., (801) 903-8138 greggbeukelman@msn.com, Utah Geological Survey; Ng
Beukes, Jarlen J., (051) 401-2318 beukesj@ufs.ac.za, Univ of the Free State; Gi
Beutel, Erin K., (843) 953-5591 beutele@cofc.edu, Coll of Charleston; Gct
Bevelhimer, Mark, (865) 576-0266 mb2@ornl.gov, Oak Ridge; Hs
Bevis, Kenneth A., (812) 866-7307 bevis@hanover.edu, Hanover Coll; GlmGe
Bevis, Michael G., 614 247 5071 bevis.6@osu.edu, Ohio State Univ; Yx
Beyarslan, Melahat, 00904242370000-5985 mbeyarslan@firat.edu.tr, Firat Univ; GipGx
Beyer, Adam, adam.beyer@nicholls.edu, Nicholls State Univ; Gg
Beyer, Patricia J., (570) 389-4570 pbeyer@bloomu.edu, Bloomsburg Univ; HsZyGm
Bezada, Max, 614-624-3280 mbezada@umn.edu, Univ of Minnesota, Twin Cities; Ys
Bezada Diaz, Maximiliano, 612-625-3507 mbezadad@umn.edu, Univ of Minnesota; Gl
Bezdecny, Kris, (323) 343-2400 kbezdec@calstatela.edu, California State Univ, Los Angeles; ZniZn
Bezdicek, David F., (509) 335-3644 bezdicek@wsu.edu, Washington State Univ; Sb
Bhaskaran, Sunil, 718-289-5566 sunil.bhaskaran@bcc.cuny.edu, Graduate Sch of the City Univ of New York; ZfrZi
Bhattacharya, Janok, (905) 525-9140 (Ext. 23528) bhattaj@mcmaster.ca, McMaster Univ; Gr
Bhattacharya, Tripti, 315-443-1348 trbhatta@syr.edu, Syracuse Univ; Ge
Bhattacharyya, Prajukti, (262) 472-5257 bhattacj@uww.edu, Univ of Wisconsin, Whitewater; Gce
Bhattacharyya, Sidhartha, 205-348-6427 bhatt001@crimson.ua.edu, Univ of Alabama; CatGe
Bhullar, Bhart-Anjan, 402-689-5998 Yale Univ; Pv
Bianchi, Thomas S., 352-392-6138 tbianchi@ufl.edu, Univ of Florida; Co
Biasi, Glenn P., (775) 784-4576 glenn@seismo.unr.edu, Univ of Nevada, Reno; Ys
Biasutti, Michela, biasutti@ldeo.columbia.edu, Columbia Univ; Am
Bibby, Thomas, +44 (0)23 8059 6446 tsb@noc.soton.ac.uk, Univ of Southampton; Ob
Bible, Gary G., garybible11@gmail.com, Univ of Tennessee, Knoxville; Go
Bice, David M., 814-865-4477 dbice@geosc.psu.edu, Pennsylvania State Univ, Univ Park; Gg

Bickel, Charles E., (415) 338-1963 bickel@sfsu.edu, San Francisco State Univ; Gx
Bickford, M. E., (315) 443-2672 mebickfo@syr.edu, Syracuse Univ; CcGiz
Bickle, Michael, +44 (0) 1223 333484 mb72@esc.cam.ac.uk, Univ of Cambridge; GtYgGo
Bickmore, Barry R., (801) 422-4680 barry_bickmore@byu.edu, Brigham Young Univ; ClGz
Bidgoli, Tandis, (785) 864-3315 bidgoli@kgs.ku.edu, Univ of Kansas; GcoCc
Biek, Robert, (801) 537-3356 bobbiek@utah.gov, Utah Geological Survey; Gg
Bieler, David B., (318) 869-5234 dbieler@centenary.edu, Centenary Coll of Louisiana; GtrYe
Bienfang, Paul K., 808-956-7402 bienfang@soest.hawaii.edu, Univ of Hawai'i, Manoa; Ob
Bienvenu, Nadean S., (337) 482-6647 nadean@louisiana.edu, Univ of Louisiana at Lafayette; Zn
Bier, Sara E., (315) 267-3482 bierse@potsdam.edu, SUNY Potsdam; GctGg
Bierly, Aaron D., 717-702-2034 aabierly@pa.gov, DCNR- Pennsylvania Bureau of Geological Survey; GgZn
Bierly, Gregory, 812-237-3225 gregory.bierly@indstate.edu, Indiana State Univ; Asm
Bierman, Paul R., (802) 656-4411 pbierman@uvm.edu, Univ of Vermont; GmeCc
Biggin, Andy, +440151 794 3460 a.biggin@liverpool.ac.uk, Univ of Liverpool; Ym
Biggs, Douglas C., (979) 845-3423 d-biggs@tamu.edu, Texas A&M Univ; Ob
Bigham, Jerry M., (614) 292-9066 bigham.1@osu.edu, Ohio State Univ; Sd
Bijeljic, Branko, +44 20 759 46420 b.bijeljic@imperial.ac.uk, Imperial Coll; Np
Bilanovic, Dragoljub D., 218-755-2801 dbilanovic@bemidjistate.edu, Bemidji State Univ; GePgCa
Bilardello, Dario, (612) 624-5049 dario@umn.edu, Univ of Minnesota, Twin Cities; Ym
Bilek, Susan L., 575.835.6510 sbilek@nmt.edu, New Mexico Inst of Mining and Tech; Ys
Bill, Steven D., sbill@keene.edu, Keene State Coll; Pg
Billen, Magali I., (530) 752-4169 mibillen@ucdavis.edu, Univ of California, Davis; Yg
Billings, Brian J., 320-308-3298 bjbillings@stcloudstate.edu, Saint Cloud State Univ; Am
Billings, Stephen, sbillings@skyri.com, Univ of British Columbia; Yg
Billiot, Fereshteh, 361-825-6067 fereshteh.billiot@tamucc.edu, Texas A&M Univ, Corpus Christi; Zn
Billups, Katharina, 302-645-4249 kbillups@udel.edu, Univ of Delaware; Ou
Bilodeau, William L., (805) 493-3264 bilodeau@callutheran.edu, California Lutheran Univ; GcsGg
Bina, Craig R., (847) 491-5097 craig@earth.northwestern.edu, Northwestern Univ; YgZmGy
Bindeman, Ilya N., 541-346-3817 bindeman@uoregon.edu, Univ of Oregon; CsGvCl
Bingham, Rob, r.bingham@ed.ac.uk, Edinburgh Univ; Zc
Bingol, Ahmet Feyzi, 00904242370000-5973 fbingol@firat.edu.tr, Firat Univ; GipGv
Binzel, Richard P., (617) 253-6486 rpb@mit.edu, Massachusetts Inst of Tech; Xm
Biondi, Biondo L., (650) 723-9831 biondo@sep.stanford.edu, Stanford Univ; Ye
Birchall, Jeff, (780) 248-5758 jeff.birchall@ualberta.ca, Univ of Alberta; ZuyZg
Bircher, Harry, 330-549-9051 harrybircher@buckeyecivildesign.com, Youngstown State Univ; Ge
Bird, Brian, bbird@mail.nysed.gov, New York State Geological Survey; GlZi
Bird, Broxton, bwbird@iupui.edu, Indiana Univ - Purdue Univ Indianapolis; Gmn
Bird, Dennis K., (650) 723-1664 bird@pangea.stanford.edu, Stanford Univ; Cg
Bird, G. Peter, (310) 825-1126 pbird@epss.ucla.edu, Univ of California, Los Angeles; GtYsRn
Bird, Jeffrey, 718-997-3332 jeffrey.bird@qc.cuny.edu, Graduate Sch of the City Univ of New York; Sbf
Bird, MIchael I., 61742421137 michael.bird@jcu.edu.au, James Cook Univ; ClsSa
Birdsell, Kay H., (505) 665-0260 khb@lanl.gov, Los Alamos; Hqy
Birgenheier, Lauren, (801) 585-3158 lauren.birgenheier@utah.edu, Univ of Utah; Gso
Birke, Tesfaye K., (031) 260-8781 birket@ukzn.ac.za, Univ of KwaZulu-Natal; GcYmGg
Birkel, Sean, sean.birkel@maine.edu, Univ of Maine; Gl
Birkeland, Peter W., (303) 492-6985 birkelap@stripe.colorado.edu, Univ of Colorado; Sd
Birner, Johannes, 089/2180 6565 johannes.birner@web.de, Ludwig-Maximilians-Univ Muenchen; Gg
Biscaye, Pierre E., biscaye@ldeo.columbia.edu, Columbia Univ; Cm
Bischoff, William D., (316) 978-6659 Wichita State Univ; Cl
Bish, David L., (812) 855-2039 bish@indiana.edu, Indiana Univ, Bloomington; Gz
Bishop, Charles E., (801) 537-3361 nrugs.cbishop@state.ut.us, Utah Geological Survey; Hw
Bishop, Gale A., (912) 681-5361 Georgia Southern Univ; Pi
Bishop, James K., (510) 495-2457 bishop@atmos.berkeley.edu, Univ of California, Berkeley; Oc
Bishop, Kim, 323 343-2409 kbishop@calstatela.edu, California State Univ, Los Angeles; Gc
Bishop, Stuart P., 919-515-7894 spbishop@ncsu.edu, North Carolina State Univ; OpGq
Bissada, Adry, 713-743-4026 kbissada@uh.edu, Univ of Houston; Co
Bissell, Clinton R., randy.bissell@tamucc.edu, Texas A&M Univ, Corpus Christi; GosGr
Bissig, Thomas, 604-822-5503 tbissig@eos.ubc.ca, Univ of British Columbia; EmCg
Biswas, Pratim, pratim.biswas@seas.wustl.edu, Washington Univ in St. Louis; Ng
Bitz, Cecilia M., (206) 543-1339 bitz@atmos.washington.edu, Univ of Washington; As
Biundo, Marc, mbiundo@uw.edu, Univ of Washington; Ys
Bizimis, Michael, 803-777-5565 mbizimis@geol.sc.edu, Univ of South Carolina; GiCg
Biševac, Vanja, +38514605969 vabisevac@geol.pmf.hr, Univ of Zagreb; GxpGz
Bjorklund, Tom, 281-589-6846 tbjorklund@uh.edu, Univ of Houston; Gco
Bjornerud, Marcia, (920) 832-7015 marcia.bjornerud@lawrence.edu, Lawrence Univ; GctRc
Bjornstad, Bruce N., (509) 373-6948 bruce.bjornstad@pnl.gov, Pacific Northwest; Gs
Blacic, James D., (505) 667-6815 jblacic@lanl.gov, Los Alamos; Nr
Black, Alice (Jill), (417) 836-5300 ablack@missouristate.edu, Missouri State Univ; ZeAsHw
Black, Annjeannette , 443-840-4560 ablack@ccbcmd.edu, Comm Coll of Baltimore County, Catonsville; Zn
Black, Benjamin, 212-650-7027 bblack@ccny.cuny.edu, Graduate Sch of the City Univ of New York; As
Black, David, (631) 632-8676 david.black@stonybrook.edu, SUNY, Stony Brook; Ou
Black, Kathryn, (973) 655-4448 Montclair State Univ; Zy
Black, Robert X., (404) 894-1756 rob.black@eas.gatech.edu, Georgia Inst of Tech; As
Black, Ross A., (785) 864-2740 black@ku.edu, Univ of Kansas; Ye
Black, Stuart, s.black@rdg.ac.uk, Univ of Reading; Cc
Black, T. Andrew, (604) 822-2730 Univ of British Columbia; Sp
Blackburn, Terrence, terryb@ucsc.edu, Univ of California, Santa Cruz; Cc
Blackburn, William, (270) 745-8849 will.blackburn@wku.edu, Western Kentucky Univ; Zy
BlackEagle, Cory, cory.blackeagle@eku.edu, Eastern Kentucky Univ; HwZg
Blackmer, Gale C., 717-702-2032 gblackmer@pa.gov, DCNR- Pennsylvania Bureau of Geological Survey; Gc
Blackwelder, Patricia L., 305 421-4677 pblackwelder@rsmas.miami.edu, Univ of Miami; Pg
Blackwell, Keith G., 251-460-6302 kblackwell@southalabama.edu, Univ of South Alabama; Am
Bladh, Katherine L., klbladh@wittenberg.edu, Wittenberg Univ; Gi
Bladh, Kenneth W., kbladh@wittenberg.edu, Wittenberg Univ; GzEm
Blair, Neal E., (847) 491-8790 n-blair@northwestern.edu, Northwestern Univ; CoSbOc
Blake, Bascombe (Mitch), (304) 594-2331 blake@geosrv.wvnet.edu, West Virginia Univ; GsEcPb
Blake, Daniel B., (217) 333-3833 dblake@illinois.edu, Univ of Illinois, Urbana-Champaign; Pi
Blake, David E., (910) 962-3387 blaked@uncw.edu, Univ of North Carolina, Wilmington; Gp
Blake, Geoffrey A., (626) 395-6296 gab@gps.caltech.edu, California Inst of Tech; Xc
Blake, Norman J., (727) 553-1521 nblake@marine.usf.edu, Univ of South Florida; Ob
Blake, Ruth E., (203) 432-3191 ruth.blake@yale.edu, Yale Univ; Cg
Blake, Stephen, stephen.blake@open.ac.uk, Open Univ; Gv
Blakeney DeJarnett, Beverly, 713-896-6740 bev.dejarnett@beg.utexas.edu,

Univ of Texas at Austin, Jackson Sch of Geosciences; GrsGx

Blakey, Ronald C., (928) 523-2740 ronald.blakey@nau.edu, Northern Arizona Univ; Gr

Blamey, Nigel J., 905-688-3365 nblamey@brocku.ca, New Mexico Inst of Mining and Tech; CaeCl

Blanchard, Edward, (206) 543-5219 ed@atmos.washington.edu, Univ of Washington; As

Blanchard, R. Denise, (512) 245-2170 Texas State Univ; RnmRc

Blanchet, Jean-Pierre, 514-987-3000 #3316 blanchet.jean-pierre@uqam.ca, Universite du Quebec a Montreal; Pe

Bland, William L., (608) 262-0221 wlbland@wisc.edu, Univ of Wisconsin, Madison; Sp

Blander, Milton, (630) 252-4548 Argonne; Xc

Blaney, Diana L., (818) 354-5419 Jet Propulsion Lab; Xg

Blanford, William , 718-997-3303 william.blanford!qc.cuny.edu, Graduate Sch of the City Univ of New York; Ze

Blanken, Peter D., blanken@colorado.edu, Univ of Colorado; HsAsm

Blankenship, Donald D., (512) 471-0489 blank@ig.utexas.edu, Univ of Texas, Austin; Yg

Blankenship, Robert, blankship@wustl.edu, Washington Univ in St. Louis; Zn

Blasing, Terence J., (865) 574-7368 blasingtj@ornl.gov, Oak Ridge; As

Blasingame, Tom, (979) 845-2292 t-blasingame@spindletop.tamu.edu, Texas A&M Univ; Np

Blatner , Keith , 509-335-4499 blatner@wsu.edu, Washington State Univ; Zn

Blaylock, Glenn W., 956-764-5715 glenn.blaylock@laredo.edu, Laredo Coll; Ggv

Bleam, William F., (608) 262-9956 wfbleam@wisc.edu, Univ of Wisconsin, Madison; Sc

Bleamaster III, Leslie F., (210) 999-7740 lbleamas@trinity.edu, Trinity Univ; Xg

Blechman, Jerome B., (607) 436-3322 jerome.blechman@oneonta.edu, SUNY, Oneonta; As

Bleck, Rainer, (505) 665-9150 bleck@lanl.gov, Los Alamos; Am

Bleibinhaus, Florian, 089/2180 4202 bleibi@geophysik.uni-muenchen.de, Ludwig-Maximilians-Univ Muenchen; Yg

Blenkinson, Stephen, +44 (0)191 208 7933 stephen.blenkinsop@ncl.ac.uk, Univ of Newcastle Upon Tyne; Zn

Blenkinsop, John, jblenkin@ccs.carleton.ca, Carleton Univ; Cc

Blersch, Stacey S., 706-507-8068 blersch_stacey@columbusstate.edu, Columbus State Univ; HsgRw

Blewitt, Geoffrey, (775) 682-8778 gblewitt@unr.edu, Univ of Nevada, Reno; Yd

Blisniuk, Kimberly, 408 924-5045 kimberly.blisniuk@sjsu.edu, San Jose State Univ; Gmt

Bloch, Jonathan, jbloch@flmnh.ufl.edu, Univ of Florida; Pv

Block, Amy, (612) 626-4434 rada0042@d.umn.edu, Univ of Minnesota; Gp

Block, Karin, 212-650-8543 kblock@ccny.cuny.edu, Graduate Sch of the City Univ of New York; Ze

Blodgett, Robert H., (512) 964-3351 rblodget@austincc.edu, Austin Comm Coll District; RnGsZe

Bloechle, Amber, (850) 857-6121 abloechle@uwf.edu, Univ of West Florida; Zi

Blom, Ronald G., (818) 354-4681 Jet Propulsion Lab; Zr

Blomberg, Brittany N., brittany.blomberg@austincc.edu, Austin Comm Coll District; OnbRn

Blome, Margaret, 252 328 6360 blome19@ecu.edu, East Carolina Univ; Ggn

Bloom, Paul R., (612) 625-4711 pbloom@soils.umn.edu, Univ of Minnesota, Twin Cities; Sc

Bloomer, Sherman H., (541) 737-4811 sherman.bloomer@oregonstate.edu, Oregon State Univ; Gi

Bloomfield, Helen, +440151 795 4652 h.j.bloomfield@liverpool.ac.uk, Univ of Liverpool; Ob

Bloor, Michelle, +44 023 92 842295 michelle.bloor@port.ac.uk, Univ of Portsmouth; Hg

Bloxham, Jeremy, (617) 495-9517 jeremy_bloxham@harvard.edu, Harvard Univ; Yg

Bloxson, Julie M., 936-468-3701 bloxsonjm@sfasu.edu, Stephen F. Austin State Univ; Go

Blum, Joel D., (734) 764-1435 jdblum@umich.edu, Univ of Michigan; CsaCl

Blum, Linda K., (434) 924-0560 lkb2e@virginia.edu, Univ of Virginia; Sb

Blum, Michael D., 785-864-4974 Univ of Kansas; GsrGm

Blumenfeld, Raphael, r.blumenfeld@imperial.ac.uk, Imperial Coll; Zn

Blumentritt, Dylan, 507.457.5234 dblumentritt@winona.edu, Winona State Univ; HsGm

Blunt, Martin J., 442075946500 m.blunt@imperial.ac.uk, Imperial Coll; NpHw

Blusztajn, Jurek, (508) 289-2692 jblusztajn@whoi.edu, Woods Hole Oceanographic Inst; CcGi

Blyth, Alan, +44(0) 113 34 31632 a.m.blyth@leeds.ac.uk, Univ of Leeds; As

Blythe, Ann, 323 259-2553 ablythe@oxy.edu, Occidental Coll; Cc

Blythe, Daniel D., 406.496.4379 dblythe@mtech.edu, Montana Tech of The Univ of Montana; Hws

Boaga, Jacopo, jacopo.boaga@unipd.it, Univ degli Studi di Padova; Yg

Boar, Rosalind, +44 (0)1603 59 3103 r.boar@uea.ac.uk, Univ of East Anglia; Ob

Boardman, Mark R., (513) 529-3230 boardman@miamioh.edu, Miami Univ; On

Boast, Charles W., (217) 333-1278 Univ of Illinois, Urbana-Champaign; Sp

Boboye, O. A., oa.boboye@mail.ui.edu.ng, Univ of Ibadan; Go

Bobst, Andrew L., 406.496.4409 abobst@mtech.edu, Montana Tech of The Univ of Montana; HwCgEo

Bobyarchick, Andy R., 704-687-5998 arbobyar@email.uncc.edu, Univ of North Carolina, Charlotte; Gc

Bochdansky, Alexander, 757-6834933 abochdan@odu.edu, Old Dominion Univ; Ob

Bockheim, James G., (608) 263-5903 bockheim@wisc.edu, Univ of Wisconsin, Madison; Sf

Boden, Thomas, (865) 241-4842 tab@ornl.gov, Oak Ridge; As

Bodenbender, Brian E., (616) 395-7541 bodenbender@hope.edu, Hope Coll; GsPiGe

Bodenheimer, Peter, (831) 459-2064 peter@ucolick.org, Univ of California, Santa Cruz; Xc

Bodenman, John E., (570) 389-4697 boden@bloomu.edu, Bloomsburg Univ; Zu

Bodin, Paul A., 206-616-7315 bodin@uw.edu, Univ of Washington; Ys

Bodnar, Robert J., (540) 231-7455 rjb@vt.edu, Virginia Polytechnic Inst & State Univ; CgEmGv

Boehm, David A., dirtboy@rochester.rr.com, SUNY, The Coll at Brockport; Gg

Boelman, Natalie, nboelman@ldeo.columbia.edu, Columbia Univ; Zn

Boerboom, Terrence, (612) 626-3369 boerb001@umn.edu, Univ of Minnesota; GivGc

Boering, Kristie, (510) 642-3472 boering@cchem.berkeley.edu, Univ of California, Berkeley; As

Boester, Michael, mboester@monroecc.edu, Monroe Comm Coll; Zy

Bogart, James M., james.bogart@ct.gov, Dept of Energy and Environmental Protection; Ge

Boger, Rebecca, 718-951-5000 x2159 rboger@brooklyn.cuny.edu, Brooklyn Coll (CUNY); ZiHs

Boggs, Carol, boggscl@mailbox.sc.edu, Univ of South Carolina; Zn

Boggs, Katherine, (403) 440-6645 kboggs@mtroyal.ca, Mount Royal Univ; Gt

Bogle, Mary Anna, (865) 574-7824 amb@ornl.gov, Oak Ridge; Ge

Bogner, Jean E., jbogner@uic.edu, Univ of Illinois at Chicago; ClSbHy

Bograd, Michael B., (601) 961-5528 mbograd@mdeq.ms.gov, Mississippi Office of Geology; Gg

Bogucki, Darek, 361-825-825-2836 darek.bogucki@tamucc.edu, Texas A&M Univ, Corpus Christi; Op

Bogue, Scott W., (323) 259-2563 bogue@oxy.edu, Occidental Coll; Ym

Bohaty, Steven, +44 (0)23 8059 3040 s.bohaty@noc.soton.ac.uk, Univ of Southampton; Og

Bohlen, Thomas, +49-721-6084416 thomas.bohlen@kit.edu, Karlsruhe Inst of Tech; Yx

Bohlen, Walter F., 860-405-9176 walter.bohlen@uconn.edu, Univ of Connecticut; Op

Bohling, Geoff, 785-864-2093 geoff@kgs.ku.edu, Univ of Kansas; Hw

Bohling, Geoffrey C., (785) 864-2093 geoff@kgs.ku.edu, Univ of Kansas; Hw

Bohm, Christian, 204-945-6549 christian.bohm@gov.mb.ca, Univ of Manitoba; Cg

Bohnenstiehl, DelWayne, (919) 515-7449 drbohnen@ncsu.edu, North Carolina State Univ; YrsGt

Bohren, Craig F., (814) 865-2951 bohren@ems.psu.edu, Pennsylvania State Univ, Univ Park; Am

Bohrson, Wendy, (303) 273-3066 bohrson@mines.edu, Colorado Sch of Mines; Gv

Boicourt, William, (410) 221-8426 boicourt@hpl.umces.edu, Univ of Maryland; Op

Boisvert, Eric, (418) 654-3705 eboisvert@nrcan.gc.ca, Universite du Quebec; Zn

Boitt, Mark, mboitt@jkuat.ac.ke, Jomo Kenyatta Univ of Agriculture & Tech; ZgrZi

Boix, Carme, carme.boix@uab.cat, Universitat Autonoma de Barcelona; Pm

Bokelmann, Goetz, goetz.bokelmann@univie.ac.at, Univ of Vienna; Ygs

Bokuniewicz, Henry J., (631) 632-8674 henry.bokuniewicz@stonybrook.

edu, SUNY, Stony Brook; Yr
Boland, Greg J., (519) 824-4120 x52755 gboland@uoguelph.ca, Univ of Guelph; Zn
Boland, Irene B., 803-323-4949 bolandi@winthrop.edu, Winthrop Univ; GtgZe
Boland, John J., (410) 516-7103 jboland@jhu.edu, Johns Hopkins Univ; Zn
Bolarinwa, A. T., at.bolarinwa@mail.ui.edu.ng, Univ of Ibadan; EgGz
Bolge, Louise, bolge@ldeo.columbia.edu, Columbia Univ; Cg
Bollag, Jean-Marc, (814) 863-0843 jmbollag@psu.edu, Pennsylvania State Univ, Univ Park; Sb
Bollasina, Massimo A., +44 (0) 131 651 3464 massimo.bollasina@ed.ac.uk, Edinburgh Univ; Asp
Bollens, Stephen, 360-546-9116 sbollens@vancouver.wsu.edu, Washington State Univ; Ob
Bollinger, G. A., (540) 231-6521 Virginia Polytechnic Inst & State Univ; Ys
Bollinger, Marsha S., 803-323-4944 bollingerm@winthrop.edu, Winthrop Univ; CmOcCc
Bollmann, Jörg, (416) 978-2061 bollmann@geology.utoronto.ca, Univ of Toronto; Pm
Bolster, Diogo, diogo.bolster.5@nd.edu, Univ of Notre Dame; Hw
Bolt, John R., (312) 665-7629 jbolt@fieldmuseum.org, Field Mus of Natural History; Pv
Bolton, Edward W., (203) 432-3149 edward.bolton@yale.edu, Yale Univ; GqHqCq
Bolze, Claude E., claude.bolze@tulsacc.edu, Tulsa Comm Coll; GgoZe
Bomke, Arthur A., (604) 822-6534 Univ of British Columbia; Sc
Bona, Andrej, +61 8 9266 7194 a.bona@curtin.edu.au, Curtin Univ; Yx
Bonamici, Chloe, bonamici@wisc.edu, Univ of Wisconsin, Madison; GxCa
Bonatti, Enrico, bonatti@ldeo.columbia.edu, Columbia Univ; Yr
Bonczek, James, 352-294-3112 bonczek@ufl.edu, Univ of Florida; SoHsg
Bond, Alan, +44 (0)1603 59 3402 alan.bond@uea.ac.uk, Univ of East Anglia; Ge
Bond, Clare, +44 (0)1224 273492 clare.bond@abdn.ac.uk, Univ of Aberdeen; Gct
Bond, Nicholas A., (206) 526-6459 nicholas.bond@noaa.gov, Univ of Washington; As
Bone, Fletcher, (573) 368-2183 fletcher.bone@dnr.mo.gov, Missouri Dept of Natural Resources; Gg
Bonem, Rena M., (254) 710-2187 rena_bonem@baylor.edu, Baylor Univ; PieOb
Bonetto, Sabrina Maria Rita, sabrina.bonetto@unito.it, Univ di Torino; Ng
Bonhoure, Jessica, +33(0)3 44068994 jessica.bonhoure@lasalle-beauvais.fr, Institut Polytechnique LaSalle Beauvais (ex-IGAL); GziCc
Boniface, Nelson, +255222410013 nelson.boniface@udsm.ac.tz, Univ of Dar es Salaam; GcpGz
Bonine, Michael E., kebonine@u.arizona.edu, Univ of Arizona; Zu
Bonk, Kathleen, 518-473-9988 kbonk@mail.nysed.gov, New York State Geological Survey; GoCg
Bonuso, Nicole, (657) 278-8451 nbonuso@fullerton.edu, California State Univ, Fullerton; Pie
Booher, Gary, (310) 660-3593 gbooher@elcamino.edu, El Camino Coll; Zg
Booker, John, 206-543-0489 jrbooker@uw.edu, Univ of Washington; YmGct
Boone, Peter A., pboone@austincc.edu, Austin Comm Coll District; Gro
Boorstein, Margaret F., (516) 299-3058 maboorst@liu.edu, Long Island Univ, C.W. Post Campus; Zg
Booth, Adam, +44 20 759 46528 a.booth@imperial.ac.uk, Imperial Coll; Gl
Booth, Alastair, murray.booth@manchester.ac.uk, Univ of Manchester; As
Booth, Derek, 206-914-5031 dbooth@uw.edu, Univ of Washington; Gm
Booth, James, 212-650-6471 jbooth@ccny.cuny.edu, Graduate Sch of the City Univ of New York; Gge
Booth, Robert K., rkb205@lehigh.edu, Lehigh Univ; ZnnPc
Boothroyd, Jon C., (401) 874-2265 jon_boothroyd@uri.edu, Univ of Rhode Island; GslOn
Borazjani, Sara, sara.borazjani@adelaide.edu.au, Univ of Adelaide; Np
Bord, Don, (313) 593-5483 dbord@umich.edu, Univ of Michigan, Dearborn; Xy
Bordeaux, Yvette, (215) 898-9191 bordeaux@sas.upenn.edu, Univ of Pennsylvania; Pg
Bordeleau, Geneviève, 418 654-2543 genevieve.bordeleau@ete.inrs.ca, Universite du Quebec; Hw
Bordoni, Simona, 626.395.2672 bordoni@gps.caltech.edu, California Inst of Tech; Op
Bordossy, Andras, +44 (0) 191 208 6319 andras.bardossy@ncl.ac.uk, Univ of Newcastle Upon Tyne; Zg
Bordy, Emese M., 021-650-2901 emese.bordy@uct.ac.za, Univ of Cape Town; GsPes
Borg, Scott G., 703-292-8500 sborg@nsf.gov, Nat Sci Foundation; Git
Borghi, Alessandro, alessandro.borghi@unito.it, Univ di Torino; Gx
Bork, Kennard B., (928) 554-4942 bork@denison.edu, Denison Univ; PiRhGs
Bornhorst, Theodore J., 906-487-2721 tjb@mtu.edu, Michigan Technological Univ; EgCgGx
Borns, Jr., Harold W., (207) 581-2196 borns@maine.edu, Univ of Maine; Gl
Borojeviæ Šoštariæ, Sibila, +38514605961 sborojsost@geol.pmf.hr, Univ of Zagreb; CegCc
Boroughs, Scott, geoentoptics@wsu.edu, Washington State Univ; Gv
Boroughs, Terry J., (916) 331-8596 borougt@arc.losrios.edu, American River Coll; GgXgCg
Boroushaki, Soheil, 818-677-4715 soheil.boroushaki@csun.edu, California State Univ, Northridge; Zi
Borowski, Walter S., (859) 622-1277 w.borowski@eku.edu, Eastern Kentucky Univ; GsrOu
Borrelli, Chiara, (585) 275-7884 cborrelli@ur.rochester.edu, Univ of Rochester; PmcCb
Borrok, David, 573-341-6784 borrokd@mst.edu, Missouri Univ of Sci and Tech; Cl
Borsa, Adrian, (858) 534-6895 aborsa@ucsd.edu, Univ of California, San Diego; Hg
Borthakur, Sanchayeeta, (480) 965-3171 sanchayeeta.borthakur@asu.edu, Arizona State Univ; Xa
Bosak, Tanja, 617-324-3959 tbosak@mit.edu, Massachusetts Inst of Tech; Pg
Bosart, Lance F., (518) 442-4564 bosart@atmos.albany.edu, SUNY, Albany; As
Bosbyshell, Howell, (610) 436-2805 hbosbyshell@wcupa.edu, West Chester Univ; GcpGt
Boschmann, E. Eric, 303-871-4387 eric.boschmann@du.edu, Univ of Denver; Zc
Bose, Maitrayee, (480) 965-4244 maitrayee.bose@asu.edu, Arizona State Univ; Xc
Bosman, Martin, bosman@usf.edu, Univ of South Florida; Zn
Boss, Alan P., (202) 478-8858 aboss@carnegiescience.edu, Carnegie Inst for Sci; Xa
Boss, Stephen K., (479) 575-7134 sboss@uark.edu, Univ of Arkansas, Fayetteville; RcYgGg
Bossenbroek, Jonathon , 419-530-4595 jonathon.bossenbroek@utoledo.edu, Univ of Toledo; Zn
Bossert, James E., (505) 667-6268 bossert@lanl.gov, Los Alamos; As
Bostater, Charles, (321) 674-8096 bostater@fit.edu, Florida Inst of Tech; Op
Bostick, Benjamin C., bostick@ldeo.columbia.edu, Columbia Univ; Sc
Bostock, Michael G., (604) 822-2082 bostock@eos.ubc.ca, Univ of British Columbia; YsGt
Boston, Penelope, 604 224 1141 penelope.j.boston@nasa.gov, Nat Aeronautics & Space Administration; Zg
Boswell, Cecil, 573-368-2146 cecil.boswell@dnr.mo.gov, Missouri Dept of Natural Resources; Zn
Bothner, Wallace A., (603) 862-1718 wally.bothner@unh.edu, Univ of New Hampshire; Gc
Bottenberg, H. Carrie, 208-282-3538 bottcarr@isu.edu, Idaho State Univ; ZiGtc
Bottjer, David J., (213) 740-6100 dbottjer@usc.edu, Univ of Southern California; Pe
Bou-Zeid, Elie, (609) 258-5429 ebouzeid@princeton.edu, Princeton Univ; As
Boudreau, Alan E., (919) 684-5646 boudreau@duke.edu, Duke Univ; Gi
Boudreau, Bernard P., (902) 494-8895 bernie.boudreau@dal.ca, Dalhousie Univ; OcCml
Boudrias, Michel A., (619) 260-4794 boum@sandiego.edu, Univ of San Diego; Ob
Bouker, Polly A., (770) 278-1320 pbouker@gsu.edu, Georgia State Univ, Perimeter Coll, Newton Campus; Gg
Boult, Stephen, +44 0161 275-3867 s.boult@manchester.ac.uk, Univ of Manchester; Hg
Boulton, Sarah, +44 1752 584762 sarah.boulton@plymouth.ac.uk, Univ of Plymouth; Zr
Boulvain, Frederic P., 32 4 366 22 52 fboulvain@ulg.ac.be, Universite de Liege; GdgGs
Bouman, Heather, +44 (1865) 272019 heather.bouman@earth.ox.ac.uk, Univ of Oxford; Cg
Bounk, Michael, michael.bounk@dnr.iowa.gov, Iowa Dept of Natural Resources; Gg
Bour, William, (703) 450-2612 wbour@nvcc.edu, Northern Virginia Comm Coll - Loudoun Campus; Gge
Bourassa, Matthew, 519-661-2111 ext 80370 mbouras@uwo.ca, Western Univ; Xg
Bourbonnais, Annie, (803) 777-7042 abourbonnais@seoe.sc.edu, Univ of South Carolina; Oc
Bourbonnais, Mathieu L., 250-807-8186 mathieu.bourbonnais@ubc.ca, Univ of British Columbia, Okanagan Campus; ZifRn

Bourcier, Bill L., (925) 423-3745 bourcier1@llnl.gov, Lawrence Livermore; Cg
Bourgeois, Joanne (Jody), (206) 685-2443 jbourgeo@uw.edu, Univ of Washington; GsrRh
Bourgeois, Reed J., (225) 388-8879 reed@lgs.bri.lsu.edu, Louisiana State Univ; Zn
Bourke, Robert H., (831) 656-2673 rbourke@nps.edu, Naval Postgraduate Sch; Op
Bouse, Robin, (310) 660-3593 rbouse@elcamino.edu, El Camino Coll; Gg
Bousenberry, Raymond T., (609) 984-6587 raymond.bousenberry@dep.nj.gov, New Jersey Geological and Water Survey; Ge
Boutt, David, (413) 545-2724 dboutt@geo.umass.edu, Univ of Massachusetts, Amherst; HwqHy
Bouvier, Audrey, 519-661-2111 x.88516 audrey.bouvier@uwo.ca, Western Univ; Xc
Bouwer, Edward, (410) 516-7437 bouwer@jhu.edu, Johns Hopkins Univ; RwHws
Bouzari, Farhad, (604) 822-1874 fbouzari@eos.ubc.ca, Univ of British Columbia; Eg
Boving, Thomas, (401) 874-7053 boving@uri.edu, Univ of Rhode Island; Hg
Bowden, Stephen, +44 (0)1224 273467 s.a.bowden@abdn.ac.uk, Univ of Aberdeen; CoGoCb
Bowen, Anthony J., (902) 494-7082 tony.bowen@dal.ca, Dalhousie Univ; On
Bowen, Brenda , (801) 585-5326 brenda.bowen@utah.edu, Univ of Utah; Gse
Bowen, David W., dbowen@montana.edu, Montana State Univ; GroGs
Bowen, Dawn S., (540) 654-1491 dbowen@mwc.edu, Mary Washington Coll; Zn
Bowen, Esther E., (630) 252-7553 ebowen@anl.gov, Argonne; Gg
Bowen, Gabriel, (801) 585-7925 gabe.bowen@utah.edu, Univ of Utah; Cs
Bowen, Jennifer, 7815817370 x346 je.bowen@northeastern.edu, Northeastern Univ; Zn
Bowen, Robert, bob.bowen@umb.edu, Univ of Massachusetts, Boston; ZnnZn
Bowen, Scott M., (505) 667-4313 Los Alamos; Ca
Bowersox, Joe, 503-370-6220 jbowerso@willamette.edu, Willamette Univ; Zn
Bowersox, John R., (859) 257-1147 j.r.bowersox@uky.edu, Univ of Kentucky; God
Bowin, Carl O., (508) 289-2572 cbowin@whoi.edu, Woods Hole Oceanographic Inst; YrGtg
Bowler, Bernard, +44 (0) 191 208 5931 bernard.bowler@ncl.ac.uk, Univ of Newcastle Upon Tyne; Go
Bowles, Julie, 414-229-6110 bowlesj@uwm.edu, Univ of Wisconsin, Milwaukee; Ym
Bowles, Zack, zbowles@mesacc.edu, Mesa Comm Coll; Gg
Bowlick, Forrest J., (413)-577-3816 fbowlick@umass.edu, Univ of Massachusetts, Amherst; ZieZg
Bowman, Cassandra, c.bowman@asu.edu, Arizona State Univ; Ze
Bowman, Jean A., (409) 862-6544 jbowman@tamu.edu, Texas A&M Univ; Hg
Bowman, John R., (801) 581-7250 john.bowman@utah.edu, Univ of Utah; Cs
Bowman, Judd, (480) 965-8880 judd.bowman@asu.edu, Arizona State Univ; Xa
Bowman, Kenneth P., (979) 845-4060 k-bowman@tamu.edu, Texas A&M Univ; Am
Bowman, Malcolm J., (631) 632-8669 malcolm.bowman@stonybrook.edu, SUNY, Stony Brook; Op
Bowman, Mike, michael.bowman@manchester.ac.uk, Univ of Manchester; Go
Bowman, Steve D., (801) 537-3304 stevebowman@utah.gov, Utah Geological Survey; NgGe
Bown, Paul, +44 020 7679 32431 p.bown@ucl.ac.uk, Univ Coll London; Pm
Bowser, Carl J., (608) 262-8955 bowser@geology.wisc.edu, Univ of Wisconsin, Madison; Cl
Bowser, Paul, prb4@cornell.edu, SUNY, Stony Brook; Ob
Boxall, Simon R., +44 (0)23 80592744 simon.boxall@soton.ac.uk, Univ of Southampton; Op
Boybeyi, Zafer, (703) 993-1560 zboybeyi@gmu.edu, George Mason Univ; As
Boyce, Joseph I., (905) 525-9140 (Ext. 24188) boycej@mcmaster.ca, McMaster Univ; Zg
Boyd, Bill, william.boyd@scu.edu.au, Southern Cross Univ; Pe
Boyd, John, (734) 764-3338 jpboyd@umich.edu, Univ of Michigan; OpAs
Boyle, Alan P., +44 0151 794 5154 apboyle@liverpool.ac.uk, Univ of Liverpool; GzEmZe
Boyle, Douglas, 775-784-6995 geography@unr.edu, Univ of Nevada, Reno; Hg
Boyle, Edward A., (617) 253-3388 eaboyle@mit.edu, Massachusetts Inst of Tech; Oc
Boyle, James T., (609) 984-6587 jim.boyle@dep.nj.gov, New Jersey Geological and Water Survey; Hw
Boynton, William V., (520) 621-6941 wboynton@lpl.arizona.edu, Univ of Arizona; XcZr
Boysen, Hans, 089/2180 4333 boysen@lmu.de, Ludwig-Maximilians-Univ Muenchen; Gz
Bozdag, Ebru, 303-273-3578 bozdag@mines.edu, Colorado Sch of Mines; Ys
Bozdog, Nick, 828-296-4635 nick.bozdog@ncdenr.gov , N.C. Department of Environmental Quality; Gg
Bozzato, Edda, 7056751151, ext. 2272 ebozzato@laurentian.ca, Laurentian Univ, Sudbury; ZnnZn
Brabander, Daniel J., 781-283-3056 dbraband@wellesley.edu, Wellesley Coll; Cl
Brabham, P J., brabham@cf.ac.uk, Cardiff Univ; Ye
Brabham, Peter, +44(0)29 208 74334 brabham@cardiff.ac.uk, Univ of Wales; Ng
Bracco, Annalisa, (404) 894-1749 annalisa@eas.gatech.edu, Georgia Inst of Tech; OpZnn
Bradbury, Kelly K., kellykbradbury@gmail.com, Utah State Univ; Gc
Bradbury, Kenneth R., (608) 263-7921 ken.bradbury@uwex.edu, Univ of Wisconsin, Madison; Hw
Bradford, Joel, (801) 863-7263 bradfojo@uvu.edu, Utah Valley Univ; RwGe
Bradford, John, 303-273-3938 jbradford@mines.edu, Colorado Sch of Mines; Yue
Bradley, Alexander S., (314) 935-6333 abradley@levee.wustl.edu, Washington Univ in St. Louis; CboGg
Bradley, Alice, (413) 597-4649 alice.c.bradley@williams.edu, Williams Coll; AtOn
Bradley, Chris, +44 (0)121 414 8097 c.bradley@bham.ac.uk, Univ of Birmingham; Hg
Bradley, Christopher R., (505) 665-6713 cbradley@lanl.gov, Los Alamos; Yg
Bradley, Jeffrey, (660) 562-1818 jbradle@nwmissouri.edu, Northwest Missouri State Univ; Zg
Bradley, Michael, (313) 487-0218 Eastern Michigan Univ; Gc
Bradley, Philip, 919-707-9241 pbradley@ncdenr.gov, N.C. Department of Environmental Quality; Gcg
Bradley, Raymond S., (413) 545-2120 rbradley@geo.umass.edu, Univ of Massachusetts, Amherst; As
Bradshaw, John, (03) 3667-001 x7487 john.bradshaw@canterbury.ac.nz, Univ of Canterbury; Gt
Bradshaw, Lanna K., 972/860-4713 lannabradshaw@dcccd.edu, Brookhaven Coll; GgZg
Bradshaw, Peter M., (604) 681-8600 pbradshaw@firstpointminerals.com, Univ of British Columbia; EgCeGe
Brady, John B., (413) 585-3953 jbrady@smith.edu, Smith Coll; GxzZe
Brady, Kristina, 612-626-7889 brad0311@umn.edu, Univ of Minnesota, Twin Cities; Gn
Brady, Roland H., (559) 278-2391 roland_brady@csufresno.edu, Fresno State Univ; NgZuGa
Braginsky, Stanislav I., (310) 794-1331 jbragin@ucla.edu, Univ of California, Los Angeles; Ym
Brahana, John V., 479-575-3355 brahana@uark.edu, Univ of Arkansas, Fayetteville; HwGe
Brahmi, Sadek, +33(0)3 44068978 sadek.brahmi@lasalle-beauvais.fr, Institut Polytechnique LaSalle Beauvais (ex-IGAL); Nr
Braile, Lawrence W., (765) 494-5979 braile@purdue.edu, Purdue Univ; Ys
Brainard, James R., (505) 667-0150 Los Alamos; Zn
Brake, Sandra S., (812) 237-2270 sandra.brake@indstate.edu, Indiana State Univ; GeEm
Brake, Thomas L., (702) 794-7828 brake_thomas_l@lanl.gov, Los Alamos; Nr
Bralower, Timothy J., 814-863-1240 bralower@psu.edu, Pennsylvania State Univ, Univ Park; Pe
Brame, Scott E., (864) 656-7167 scott@clemson.edu, Clemson Univ; Hw
Bramham, Emma , +44(0) 113 34 35595 e.k.bramham@leeds.ac.uk, Univ of Leeds; Ym
Branam, Tracy D., (812) 855-8390 tbranam@indiana.edu, Indiana Univ; CasEm
Branan, Yvonne K., ykbranan@iup.edu, Indiana Univ of Pennsylvania; Gv
Branciforte, Chloe, cbranciforte@mesacc.edu, Mesa Comm Coll; Gg
Branco, Brett, 718-951-5000, ext. 6441 bbranco@brooklyn.cuny.edu, Graduate Sch of the City Univ of New York; Gg
Brand, Brittany, 208-426-4154 brittanybrand@boisestate.edu, Boise State Univ; Gsv
Brand, Leonard R., (909) 558-4530 lbrand@llu.edu, Loma Linda Univ; Pv

Bromwich, David H., (614) 688-5314 bromwich.1@osu.edu, Ohio State Univ; As
Brook, Edward J., (541) 737-8197 brooke@geo.oregonstate.edu, Oregon State Univ; ClPeGl
Brookfield, Andrea, 785-864-2199 andrea@ku.edu, Univ of Kansas; Hw
Brooks, David A., (979) 845-5527 dbrooks@ocean.tamu.edu, Texas A&M Univ; Op
Brooks, Debra A., (714) 564-4788 Santiago Canyon Coll; Yg
Brooks, Gregg R., (727) 864-8992 brooksgr@eckerd.edu, Eckerd Coll; Gu
Brooks, Ian, +44(0) 113 34 36743 i.m.brooks@leeds.ac.uk, Univ of Leeds; Zn
Brooks, Paul D., (520) 621-3424 brooks@hwr.arizona.edu, Univ of Arizona; Cg
Brooks, Sarah D., (979) 845-5632 sbrooks@tamu.edu, Texas A&M Univ; AsZc
Brooks, Scott C., (865) 574-6398 3sb@ornl.gov, Oak Ridge; Cl
Brookshire, Jack, jbrookshire@montana.ede, Montana State Univ; Zc
Broome, Stephen W., (919) 515-2643 North Carolina State Univ; Sf
Brophy, James G., (812) 855-6417 brophy@indiana.edu, Indiana Univ, Bloomington; Gi
Broster, Bruce E., (506) 453-4804 broster@unb.ca, Univ of New Brunswick; Gl
Brothen, Jerry, (310) 660-3593 jbrothen@elcamino.edu, El Camino Coll; Zy
Brothers, Timothy S., (317) 274-1101 tbrother@iupui.edu, Indiana Univ, Indianapolis; Zy
Brounce, Maryjo, (951) 827-3151 maryjo.brounce@ucr.edu, Univ of California, Riverside; Cg
Brouwer, Fraukje M., +31-20-598 7335 fraukje.brouwer@vu.nl, Vrije Universiteit Amsterdam; GptGc
Brown, Alan, abrown11@houston.oilfield.slb.com, West Virginia Univ; EoYe
Brown, Bradford D., (208) 722-6701 Univ of Idaho; Zn
Brown, Bruce A., (608) 263-3201 babrown1@wisc.edu, Univ of Wisconsin, Madison, Division of Extension; GcEg
Brown, Caleb, (403) 823-7707 Royal Tyrrell Mus of Palaeontology; Pv
Brown, Cathe, (202) 633-1788 brownc@si.edu, Smithsonian Inst / Nat Mus of Natural History; CgGzi
Brown, David, +44 01413307410 david.brown@glasgow.ac.uk, Univ of Glasgow; Gvs
Brown, Donald W., (505) 667-1926 dwb@lanl.gov, Los Alamos; Nr
Brown, Douglas, +44 208 417 2245 doug.brown@kingston.ac.uk, Kingston Univ; Zi
Brown, Edwin H., (360) 650-3597 ehbrown@wwu.edu, Western Washington Univ; Gp
Brown, Erik T., (218) 726-8891 etbrown@d.umn.edu, Univ of Minnesota Duluth; Og
Brown, Huntting (Hunt), 937 775-4996 hunt.brown@wright.edu, Wright State Univ; Ge
Brown, J. Michael, 206-616-6058 jmbrown5@uw.edu, Univ of Washington; Gy
Brown, Kenneth L., (765) 658-6767 kennethbrown@depauw.edu, DePauw Univ; GizGe
Brown, Kent D., 801-537-3350 kentbrown@utah.gov, Utah Geological Survey; Zn
Brown, Kerry, k.brown@kingston.ac.uk, Kingston Univ; Ge
Brown, Kevin M., (858) 534-5368 kmbrown@ucsd.edu, Univ of California, San Diego; Gu
Brown, Kyle, 573-368-2168 kyle.brown@dnr.mo.gov, Missouri Dept of Natural Resources; Gg
Brown, Larry D., (607) 255-6346 ldb7@cornell.edu, Cornell Univ; Ye
Brown, Laurie L., (413) 545-0245 lbrown@geo.umass.edu, Univ of Massachusetts, Amherst; Ymg
Brown, Lewis M., (906) 635-2155 lbrown@lssu.edu, Lake Superior State Univ; PiZe
Brown, Megan R., 815753-1778 mbrown18@niu.edu, Northern Illinois Univ; HwRw
Brown, Michael, (301) 405-4080 mbrown@umd.edu, Univ of Maryland; GxpGt
Brown, Paul W., (520) 621-1319 pbrown@ag.arizona.edu, Univ of Arizona; Am
Brown, Peter, 5196612111 ext.86458 pbrown@uwo.ca, Western Univ; Xym
Brown, Philip E., (608) 262-5954 pebrown@wisc.edu, Univ of Wisconsin, Madison; EmGzp
Brown, Richard J., +44 (0) 191 33 42303 richard.brown3@durham.ac.uk, Durham Univ; Gv
Brown, Rob, (828) 262-7222 brownrn@appstate.edu, Appalachian State Univ; Zn
Brown, Robert A., rabrown@atmos.washington.edu, Univ of Washington; As
Brown, Roderick, +44 01413305460 roderick.brown@glasgow.ac.uk, Univ of Glasgow; Cc
Brown, Sandra, 604-822-5965 Univ of British Columbia; Sp
Brown, Steven E., 217-333-5143 steebrow@illinois.edu, Univ of Illinois; Gl
Brown, Summer, 859-218-0873 summer.brown@uky.edu, Univ of Kentucky; GgZei
Brown, Thomas W., tbrown1@austincc.edu, Austin Comm Coll District; Ges
Brown, Tom, (925) 423-8507 tabrown@llnl.gov, Univ of Washington; CcAt
Brown, Wesley A., (936) 468-2422 brownwa1@sfasu.edu, Stephen F. Austin State Univ; YgsGt
Brown, Jr., Gordon E., (650) 723-9168 gordon@pangea.stanford.edu, Stanford Univ; Gz
Brownawell, Bruce J., (631) 632-8658 bruce.brownawell@stonybrook.edu, SUNY, Stony Brook; Oc
Browne, Brandon L., (707) 826-3950 brandon.browne@humboldt.edu, Humboldt State Univ; GivZe
Browne, Kathleen M., (609) 896-5408 browne@rider.edu, Rider Univ; GuZe
Browning, James M., 806-834-7782 james.browning@ttu.edu, Texas Tech Univ; Ggx
Browning, Sharon, (254)710-2159 sharon_browning@baylor.edu, Baylor Univ; Gg
Brownlee, Colin, +44 (0)1752 633347 cb1e11@soton.ac.uk, Univ of Southampton; Ob
BrownLee, Sarah J., (313) 577-6223 sarah.brownlee@wayne.edu, Wayne State Univ; GxcGy
Broxton, David E., 505-667-2492 broxton@lanl.gov, Los Alamos; Gx
Broze, Elliot, brozeea@whitman.edu, Whitman Coll; Gg
Brubaker, Kenneth L., (630) 252-7630 Argonne; As
Brudzinski, Michael, 513-529-9758 brudzimr@miamioh.edu, Miami Univ; Ys
Brueckner, Hannes K., (845) 521-4637 hannes@ldeo.columbia.edu, Queens Coll (CUNY); GgtCg
Brueseke, Matthew E., (785) 532-6724 brueseke@ksu.edu, Kansas State Univ; GitGv
Brugger, Keith A., (320) 589-6310 bruggeka@mrs.umn.edu, Univ of Minnesota, Morris; GllGm
Brugger, Matthias, +49 89 289 - 25886 m.brugger@tum.de, Technical Univ of Munich; NgGg
Bruland, Kenneth W., (831) 459-4587 bruland@cats.ucsc.edu, Univ of California, Santa Cruz; OcCtm
Brumbaugh, David S., (928) 523-7191 david.brumbaugh@nau.edu, Northern Arizona Univ; Ys
Brune, James N., (775) 784-4974 brune@seismo.unr.edu, Univ of Nevada, Reno; Ys
Brune, Jürgen F., 303.273.3704 jbrune@mines.edu, Colorado Sch of Mines; Nm
Brune, William H., (814) 865-3286 whb2@psu.edu, Pennsylvania State Univ, Univ Park; Am
Brunengo, Matthew , 503-725-3391 mbruneng@pdx.edu, Portland State Univ; GgNgGm
Bruner, Katherine R., (304) 293-5603 bruner@geo.wvu.edu, West Virginia Univ; Gd
Brunet, Gilbert, 514 421-4617 gilbert.brunet@canada.ca, McGill Univ; Am
Brunetto, Eileen, (802) 443-5970 efahey@middlebury.edu, Middlebury Coll; Zn
Bruning, Eric C., 806-834-3120 eric.bruning@ttu.edu, Texas Tech Univ; As
Brunish, Wendee M., (505) 667-5724 wb@lanl.gov, Los Alamos; Zn
Brunkal, Holly, 970.943.2180 hbrunkal@western.edu, Western Colorado Univ; NgGm
Brunner, Benjamin, 915-747-5507 bbrunner@utep.edu, Univ of Texas, El Paso; Cs
Bruno, Barbara, (808) 956-0901 barb@hawaii.edu, Univ of Hawai'i, Manoa; Ob
Bruno, Emiliano, emiliano.bruno@unito.it, Univ di Torino; Gz
Bruno, Marco, marco.bruno@unito.it, Univ di Torino; Gz
Bruns, Dale A., 570-408-4603 dale.bruns@wilkes.edu, Wilkes Univ; ZirSf
Brunskill, Jeffrey C., 570-389-4355 jbrunski@bloomu.edu, Bloomsburg Univ; ZiAmZy
Brunstad, Keith A., (607) 436-3066 keith.brunstad@oneonta.edu, SUNY, Oneonta; GviEg
Brunt, Rufus, +44 0161 306-6816 rufus.brunt@manchester.ac.uk, Univ of Manchester; Gs
Brusatte, Steve, stephen.brusatte@ed.ac.uk, Edinburgh Univ; Pv
Bruschke, Freddi Jo, 657-278-3551 fbruschke@fullerton.edu, California State Univ, Fullerton; Gg
Brush, Grace S., (410) 516-7107 gbrush@jhu.edu, Johns Hopkins Univ; PleGn
Brush, Nigel, (419) 289-5271 nbrush@ashland.edu, Ashland Univ; GmdGa
Brusseau, Mark L., (520) 621-3244 brusseau@ag.arizona.edu, Univ of Arizona; Hw
Bryan, Christopher, +44 01326 259482 c.g.bryan@exeter.ac.uk, Exeter Univ;

Nx
Bryan, Scott E., +61 7 3138 4827 scott.bryan@qut.edu.au, Queensland Univ of Tech; GitGs
Bryant, Anita M., (678) 839-4051 abryant@westga.edu, Univ of West Georgia; Zn
Bryant, Ernest A., (505) 667-2422 Los Alamos; Cg
Bryant, Kathleen E., 217-244-9045 kebryant@illinois.edu, Illinois State Geological Survey; Gg
Bryant, Marita, (207) 786-6452 mbryant@bates.edu, Bates Coll; Gg
Bryce, Julia G., (603) 862-3139 julie.bryce@unh.edu, Univ of New Hampshire; CgcCb
Brzobohaty, Rostislav, +420 549 49 3326 rosta@sci.muni.cz, Masaryk Univ; PgsPe
Buatois, Luis, luis.buatois@usask.ca, Univ of Saskatchewan; Ps
Buchanan, Donald G., 9093844399 ext. 5467 dbuchanan@sbccd.cc.ca.us, San Bernardino Valley Coll; Og
Buchanan, George, gbuchana@mc3.edu, Montgomery County Comm Coll; Ng
Buchanan, John P., (509) 359-7493 jbuchanan@ewu.edu, Eastern Washington Univ; Hw
Buchanan, Paul C., (903) 983-8253 pbuchanan@kilgore.edu, Kilgore Coll; GgiXm
Buchheim, Paul, (909) 558-4530 pbuchheim@llu.edu, Loma Linda Univ; GnsPe
Buchwald, Carolyn, (902) 494-3666 cbuchwald@dal.ca, Dalhousie Univ; Oc
Buck, Brenda J., (702) 895-1694 buckb@unlv.nevada.edu, Univ of Nevada, Las Vegas; GbSd
Buck, Daniel, (541) 346-2353 danielb@uoregon.edu, Univ of Oregon; Zn
Buck, Gregory, 361-825-3717 gregory.buck@tamucc.edu, Texas A&M Univ, Corpus Christi; Zn
Buck, Roger W., buck@ldeo.columbia.edu, Columbia Univ; Yr
Buck, IV, W. R., (845) 365-8592 buck@ldeo.columbia.edu, Columbia Univ; YgGt
Bucke, David P., (802) 899-3584 david.bucke@uvm.edu, Univ of Vermont; GgdGs
Buckingham, Michael J., (858) 534-7977 mbuckingham@ucsd.edu, Univ of California, San Diego; Op
Buckley, Brendon, bmb@ldeo.columbia.edu, Columbia Univ; Pe
Buckley, Lawrence J., (401) 874-6671 lbuckley@gso.uri.edu, Univ of Rhode Island; Oc
Buckley, Luke, (406) 496-4677 lbuckley@mtech.edu, Montana Tech of The Univ of Montana; Zn
Buckley, Michael, +44(0)161 306 5175 m.buckley@manchester.ac.uk, Univ of Manchester; Ga
Bucklin, Ann, 860-405-9260 ann.bucklin@uconn.edu, Univ of Connecticut; Ob
Bucur, Ioan, +40-264-405371 ibucur@bioge.ubbcluj.ro, Babes-Bolyai Univ; PgmGs
Buczynska, Anna, 815-753-7945 abuczynska@niu.edu, Northern Illinois Univ; Csa
Budd, Ann F., (319) 335-1818 ann-budd@uiowa.edu, Univ of Iowa; Pgi
Budd, David A., (303) 492-3988 david.budd@colorado.edu, Univ of Colorado; GdsEo
Budikova, Dagmar, (309) 438-2546 dbudiko@ilstu.edu, Illinois State Univ; AsZyi
Buermann, Wolfgang, +44(0) 113 34 34958 w.buermann@leeds.ac.uk, Univ of Leeds; Zu
Buesseler, Ken O., (508) 289-2309 kbuesseler@whoi.edu, Woods Hole Oceanographic Inst; Oc
Buick, Roger, 206-543-1913 buick@uw.edu, Univ of Washington; CbXbPm
Buijsman, Maarten, (228) 688-2385 maarten.buijsman@usm.edu, Univ of Southern Mississippi; Op
Buizert, Christo, 541-737-1572 buizertc@science.oregonstate.edu, Oregon State Univ; Yr
Bukowinski, Mark S., (510) 642-0977 Univ of California, Berkeley; Gy
Bulgariu, Dumitru, 0040232201656 dbulgariu@yahoo.com, Alexandru Ioan Cuza; Cga
Buliga, Iuliana, 0040744297849 iuliana.buliga@uaic.ro, Alexandru Ioan Cuza; Gep
Bull, Jonathan M., +44 (0)23 8059 3078 bull@soton.ac.uk, Univ of Southampton; YrGct
Bull, William B., (520) 621-6024 Univ of Arizona; Gm
Bullamore, Henry W., (301) 687-4413 hbullamore@frostburg.edu, Frostburg State Univ; Zn
Bullard, Thomas F., (775) 673-7420 tbullard@dri.edu, Desert Research Inst; Gm
Bullard, Tom, (775) 673-7420 tbullard@dri.edu, Univ of Nevada, Reno; Gm
Bullen, Dean, +44 023 92 842289 dean.bullen@port.ac.uk, Univ of Portsmouth; Gt
Bullister, John, (206) 526-6741 bullister@pmel.noaa.gov, Univ of Washington; Oc
Bultman, John, (828) 254-1921 ext 319 jbultman@abtech.edu, Asheville-Buncombe Technical Comm Coll; Gg
Bulusu, Subrahmanyam, 803-777-2572 sbulusu@geol.sc.edu, Univ of South Carolina; Op
Bunch, Mark, mark.bunch@adelaide.edu.au, Univ of Adelaide; Ye
Bunds, Michael, (801) 863-6306 michael.bunds@uvu.edu, Utah Valley Univ; GctRn
Bundy, Larry G., (608) 263-2889 lgbundy@wisc.edu, Univ of Wisconsin, Madison; So
Bunge, Hans-Peter, 089/2180 4225 bunge@lmu.de, Ludwig-Maximilians-Univ Muenchen; Yg
Buonaiuto, Frank, 212-650-3092 frank.buonaiuto@hunter.cuny.edu, Hunter Coll (CUNY); On
Buonaiuto Jr., Frank S., 212-650-3092 jbuonaiu@hunter.cuny.edu, Graduate Sch of the City Univ of New York; Ze
Burakowski, Elizabeth, elizabeth.burakowski@unh.edu, Univ of New Hampshire; At
Buratti, Bonnie J., (818) 354-7427 Jet Propulsion Lab; Zr
Burbanck, George P., (757) 727-5783 george.burbanck@hamptonu.edu, Hampton Univ; On
Burbank, Doug, (805) 893-7858 burbank@ucsb.edu, Univ of California, Santa Barbara; GmtGs
Burberry, Caroline M., (402) 472-7157 cburberry2@unl.edu, Univ of Nebraska, Lincoln; Gct
Burbey, Thomas J., (540) 231-6696 tjburbey@vt.edu, Virginia Polytechnic Inst & State Univ; HwyZr
Burchfiel, B. C., bcburch@mit.edu, Massachusetts Inst of Tech; Gc
Burd, Aurora, aburd@avc.edu, Antelope Valley Coll; GgZgYm
Burden, Elliott T., (709) 864-8388 etburden@mun.ca, Memorial Univ of Newfoundland; PlGso
Burdick, Scott, (313) 577-6412 sburdick@wayne.edu, Wayne State Univ; Ysg
Burdige, David J., (757) 683-4930 dburdige@odu.edu, Old Dominion Univ; OcCbo
Burger, Benjamin J., 435.722.1778 benjamin.burger@usu.edu, Utah State Univ; PvGs
Burger, H. Robert, rburger@smith.edu, Smith Coll; GcYeZi
Burgess, Ray, +44 0161 275-3958 ray.burgess@manchester.ac.uk, Univ of Manchester; Cs
Burgess, William G., +44 020 7679 37820 william.burgess@ucl.ac.uk, Univ Coll London; Hwy
Burgette, Reed J., 575-646-3782 burgette@nmsu.edu, New Mexico State Univ, Las Cruces; Gtc
Burgmann, Roland, (510) 643-9545 burgmann@seismo.berkeley.edu, Univ of California, Berkeley; GtYd
Burk, Sue, 301-405-6244 Univ of Maryland; Zn
Burkart, Michael R., mburkart@iastate.edu, Iowa State Univ of Sci & Tech; Hy
Burke, Andrea, +44 01334 463910 ab276@st-andrews.ac.uk, Univ of St. Andrews; ClPc
Burke, Collette D., (316) 978-3140 Wichita State Univ; Pm
Burke, Deborah S., (509) 372-2483 deborah.burke@pnl.gov, Pacific Northwest; Sc
Burke, Ian, +44(0) 113 34 37532 lab 33965 i.t.burke@leeds.ac.uk, Univ of Leeds; Ge
Burke, Raymond M., (707) 826-4292 rmb2@humboldt.edu, Humboldt State Univ; Gm
Burkett, Ashley, 405-744-6358 ashley.burkett@okstate.edu, Oklahoma State Univ; Pme
Burkett, Brett, (976) 548-6510 bburkett@collin.edu, Collin Coll - Central Park Campus; Gvg
Burkett, Shannon, (972) 548-6611 sburkett@collin.edu, Collin Coll - Central Park Campus; Gv
Burkhart, Patrick A., (724) 738-2502 patrick.burkhart@sru.edu, Slippery Rock Univ; Hg
Burks, Rachel J., (410) 704-3005 rburks@towson.edu, Towson Univ; Gc
Burlage, Robert S., (865) 574-7321 Oak Ridge; Sb
Burls, Natalie, 703-993-5756 nburls@gmu.edu, George Mason Univ; AsOp
Burmester, Russell F., (360) 650-3654 russ.burmester@wwu.edu, Western Washington Univ; Ym
Burnett, Donald S., (626) 395-6117 burnett@gps.caltech.edu, California Inst of Tech; Xc
Burnett, Joree, 254-968-1868 jburnett@tarleton.edu, Tarleton State Univ; HwGe
Burnette, Dorian, 901-678-4452 djbrntte@memphis.edu, Univ of Memphis; Atm
Burnham, Charles, burnham_c@fortlewis.edu, Fort Lewis Coll; Gz

Burnham, Robyn J., (734) 764-0489 rburnham@umich.edu, Univ of Michigan; Pb
Burnley, Pamela C., 702-895-2536 pamela.burnley@unlv.edu, Univ of Nevada, Las Vegas; GpyGg
Burns, Bill, (971) 673-1555 Oregon Dept of Geology and Mineral Industries; Ng
Burns, Carol J., (505) 665-1765 Los Alamos; Zn
Burns, Danny, 361-354-2405 deburns@coastalbend.edu, Coastal Bend Coll; Zgn
Burns, Diane M., (217) 581-2626 dmburns@eiu.edu, Eastern Illinois Univ; GsrGe
Burns, Emily, eburns@ccri.edu, Comm Coll of Rhode Island; GgOgZi
Burns, Peter C., (574) 631-5380 peter.burns.50@nd.edu, Univ of Notre Dame; Gz
Burns, Sandra, (860) 832-2934 burns@ccsu.edu, Central Connecticut State Univ; Ze
Burns, Scott F., (503) 725-3389 burnss@pdx.edu, Portland State Univ; Ng
Burns, Stephen J., (413) 545-0142 sburns@geo.umass.edu, Univ of Massachusetts, Amherst; Cs
Burns, Timothy P., (505) 667-4600 Los Alamos; Co
Burr, Devon M., devon.burr@nau.edu, Univ of Tennessee, Knoxville; Xg
Burras, Lee, (515) 294-0559 lburras@iastate.edu, Iowa State Univ of Sci & Tech; Sd
Burris, John H., (505) 566-3325 burrisj@sanjuancollege.edu, San Juan Coll; GgRhGz
Bursik, Marcus I., (716) 645-4265 mib@buffalo.edu, SUNY, Buffalo; Gv
Burt, Donald M., (480) 965-6180 donald.burt@asu.edu, Arizona State Univ; EgCgGz
Burtis, Erik, (703) 878-5614 eburtis@nvcc.edu, Northern Virginia Comm Coll - Woodbridge; GgcGi
Burton, Bradford R., 970.943.2252 bburton@western.edu, Western Colorado Univ; GocGt
Burton, Christopher G., 334-844-3418 cgb0038@abuurn.edu, Auburn Univ; Zi
Burton, Edward, ed.burton@scu.edu.au, Southern Cross Univ; CaHy
Burton, Jacqueline C., (630) 252-8795 jcburton@anl.gov, Argonne; Cg
Burton, Kevin, +44 (0) 191 33 44298 kevin.burton@durham.ac.uk, Durham Univ; Cg
Burton, Paul, +44 (0)1603 59 2982 p.burton@uea.ac.uk, Univ of East Anglia; Ys
Burton, Ronald S., (858) 822-5784 rburton@ucsd.edu, Univ of California, San Diego; Ob
Burwash, Ronald A., (780) 492-3085 ronald.burwash@telus.net, Univ of Alberta; Gp
Busa, Mark, 860-343-5779 mbusa@mxcc.commnet.edu, Middlesex Comm Coll; ZgEgYg
Busacca, Alan J., (509) 335-1859 busacca@wsu.edu, Washington State Univ; Sa
Busbey, Arthur B., (817) 257-7301 a.busbey@tcu.edu, Texas Christian Univ; PgvGr
Busby, Cathy J., cjbusby@ucdavis.edu, Univ of California, Davis; Gt
Busby, Michael R., (270) 809-3370 mbusby@murraystate.edu, Murray State Univ; Zi
Busch, Richard M., (610) 436-2716 rbusch@wcupa.edu, West Chester Univ; GrPgZe
Busch, William H., (503) 392-3341 whbusch@gmail.com, Univ of New Orleans; Ou
Buscheck, Thomas A., (925) 423-9390 buscheck1@llnl.gov, Lawrence Livermore; Ng
Buseck, Peter R., (480) 965-3945 pbuseck@asu.edu, Arizona State Univ; Cg
Bush, Andrew B., (780) 492-0351 andrew.bush@ualberta.ca, Univ of Alberta; AsOpPe
Bush, Andrew B. G., (780) 492-0351 andrew.bush@ualberta.ca, Univ of Alberta; As
Bush, David M., (678) 839-4057 dbush@westga.edu, Univ of West Georgia; Ou
Businger, Joost, 206-543-4250 Univ of Washington; Am
Businger, Steven, businger@hawaii.edu, Univ of Hawai'i, Manoa; Am
Buskey, Edward J., (361) 749-3102 ed.buskey@utexas.edu, Univ of Texas, Austin; Ob
Buss, Leo W., 203-432-3869 leo.buss@yale.edu, Yale Univ; Pi
Busse, Friedrich H., (310) 825-7698 Univ of California, Los Angeles; Zn
Bussod, Gilles Y., (505) 667-7220 gbussod@lanl.gov, Los Alamos; Yx
Bustillo, Manuel, bustillo@ucm.es, Univ Complutense de Madrid; Eg
Bustin, Amanda, abustin@eos.ubc.ca, Univ of British Columbia; YgNg
Bustin, R. Marc, (604) 822-6179 mbustin@eos.ubc.ca, Univ of British Columbia; Ec
Butcher, Anthony, +44 023 92 842486 anthony.butcher@port.ac.uk, Univ of Portsmouth; PlmZe
Butcher, Patricia M., (657) 278-3561 pbutcher@fullerton.edu, California State Univ, Fullerton; Zeg
Butkos, Darryl J., (631) 451-4354 butkosd@sunysuffolk.edu, Suffolk County Comm Coll, Ammerman Campus; GgHw
Butler, Gilbert W., (505) 667-6005 Los Alamos; Cc
Butler, Ian B., +44 (0) 131 650 5885 ian.butler@ed.ac.uk, Edinburgh Univ; Cg
Butler, Karl, (506) 453-4804 Univ of New Brunswick; Yg
Butler, Nathaniel, (480) 965-8207 nathaniel.butler@asu.edu, Arizona State Univ; Xa
Butler, R. Paul, (202) 478-8866 pbutler@carnegiescience.edu, Carnegie Inst for Sci; Xa
Butler, Sam, (306) 966-5702 sam.butler@usask.ca, Univ of Saskatchewan; Yg
Butler, Jr., James J., (785) 864-2116 jbutler@kgs.ku.edu, Univ of Kansas; Hw
Butterfield, David A., (206) 526-6722 dab3@u.washington.edu, Univ of Washington; Yr
Butterfield, Nicholas J., +44 (0) 1223 333379 njb1005@esc.cam.ac.uk, Univ of Cambridge; Pg
Buttner, Steffen, +27 (0)46-603-8775 s.buettner@ru.ac.za, Rhodes Univ; Gcp
Butts, Susan H., (203) 432-3037 susan.butts@yale.edu, Yale Univ; PiGsPe
Butzow, Dean G., 217-786-4923 dean.butzow@llcc.edu, Lincoln Land Comm Coll; Zy
Buyce, M. Raymond, rbuyce@mercyhurst.edu, Mercyhurst Univ; GsaOn
Buynevich, Ilya, (215) 204-3635 coast@temple.edu, Temple Univ; GmPeOn
Buzas, Martin A., (202) 633-1313 Smithsonian Inst / Nat Mus of Natural History; Pm
Buzatu, Andrei, 0040232201463 andrei.buzatu@uaic.ro, Alexandru Ioan Cuza; GziGg
Buzgar, Nicolae, 0040232201462 nicolae.buzgar@uaic.ro, Alexandru Ioan Cuza; GziGd
Bybee, Grant M., 011 717 6633 grant.bybee@wits.ac.za, Univ of the Witwatersrand; Gi
Büchel, Georg, +49(0)3641 948640 georg.buechel@uni-jena.de, Friedrich-Schiller-Univ Jena; Gg
Byerly, Gary R., (225) 578-5318 glbyer@lsu.edu, Louisiana State Univ; Gi
Byers, Charles W., cwbyers@wisc.edu, Univ of Wisconsin, Madison; Grs
Bykerk-Kauffman, Ann, 530-898-6305 abykerk-kauffman@csuchico.edu, California State Univ, Chico; GcZe
Byrand, Karl, (920) 459-6619 karl.byrand@uwc.edu, Univ of Wisconsin Colls; Zny
Byrne, James M., (403) 329-2002 byrne@uleth.ca, Univ of Lethbridge; Hg
Byrne, Paul K., 919-513-2578 paul.byrne@ncsu.edu, North Carolina State Univ; XgGcZr
Byrne, Robert H., (727) 553-1508 byrne@marine.usf.edu, Univ of South Florida; Cm
Byrne, Timothy, 860-486-8144 tim.byrne@uconn.edu, Univ of Connecticut; Ou
Byrnes, Joseph, jsbyrnes@umn.edu, Univ of Minnesota, Twin Cities; Ys
Bywater-Reyes, Sharon, 970-351-1086 sharon.bywaterreyes@unco.edu, Univ of Northern Colorado; HqsHt

C

C., Jeffrey C., (330) 941-3612 jcdick@ysu.edu, Youngstown State Univ; EoNgHy
Cablk, Mary, (775) 673-7371 mcablk@dri.edu, Desert Research Inst; Zr
Cabrera, Miguel L., (706) 542-1242 Univ of Georgia; So
Cachão, Mário, mcachao@fc.ul.pt, Unive de Lisboa; PgeGg
Caddick, Mark, 540-231-9919 caddick@vt.edu, Virginia Polytechnic Inst & State Univ; GpCa
Cadet, Eddy, (801) 863-8881 cadeted@uvu.edu, Utah Valley Univ; Ge
Cadieux, Sarah, (518) 276-6474 cadies@rpi.edu, Rensselaer Polytechnic Inst; ZeCb
Cadol, Daniel, 575-835-5645 dcadol@ees.nmt.edu, New Mexico Inst of Mining and Tech; HsGe
Cadoppi, Paola, paola.cadoppi@unito.it, Univ di Torino; Gc
Cahill, Kevin, (508) 289-2925 kcahill@whoi.edu, Woods Hole Oceanographic Inst; Cm
Cahill, Michael J., (631) 588-8778 mjc@germanocahill.com, SUNY, Stony Brook; Zn
Cahill, Richard A., 217-244-2532 racahill49@gmail.com, Illinois State Geological Survey; CaGeCt
Cahir, John J., (814) 863-8358 cahir@ems.psu.edu, Pennsylvania State Univ, Univ Park; Am
Cahoy, Kerri, 617-324-6005 kcahoy@mit.edu, Massachusetts Inst of Tech; Zn
Cai, Yue, cai@ldeo.columbia.edu, Columbia Univ; Cg
Cairns, David M., (979) 845-2783 cairns@geog.tamu.edu, Texas A&M

Univ; Zy
Cairns, Stephen, cairnss@si.edu, Smithsonian Inst / Nat Mus of Natural History; Pi
Caissie, Beth E., 515-294-7528 bethc@iastate.edu, Iowa State Univ of Sci & Tech; Pe
Calagari, Ali Asghar, +98 (411) 339 2699 calagari@tabrizu.ac.ir, Univ of Tabriz; EgmCg
Calaway, Wallis F., (630) 972-3586 Argonne; Zm
Calcote, Randy, calco001@umn.edu, Univ of Minnesota, Twin Cities; Ple
Calder, Brian, 603-862-0526 brc@ccom.unh.edu, Univ of New Hampshire; Og
Calder, Eliza, +44 (0) 131 650 4910 ecalder@staffmail.ed.ac.uk, Edinburgh Univ; Gv
Calder, John, (902) 424-2778 Dalhousie Univ; Ec
Caldwell, Andy, 970-204-8228 andrew.caldwell@frontrange.edu, Front Range Comm Coll - Larimer; Gg
Caldwell, Marianne O., mcaldwell@hccfl.edu, Hillsborough Comm Coll; Ggs
Caldwell, Michael W., 780-492-3458 mw.caldwell@ualberta.ca, Univ of Alberta; Pv
Caldwell, Roy, (510) 642-1391 rlcaldwell@berkeley.edu, Univ of California, Berkeley; Pg
Caldwell, Todd, 512-471-2003 todd.caldwell@beg.utexas.edu, Univ of Texas, Austin; Sp
Caldwell, W. Glen E., 519-661-3187 gcaldwel@uwo.ca, Western Univ; Pm
Caldwell, William G. E., (519) 661-3857 Univ of Saskatchewan; Ps
Calegari, Pat, (212) 346-1502 Pace Univ, New York Campus; Zn
Calengas, Peter L., (309) 298-1151 pl-calengas@wiu.edu, Western Illinois Univ; En
Calhoun, Frank G., (330) 263-3722 scalhoun@coas.oregonstate.edu, Ohio State Univ; Sd
Calhoun, Joseph, 717-872-3289 jcalhoun@hearst.com, Millersville Univ; As
Calizaya, Felipe, (801) 581-5422 felipe.calizaya@utah.edu, Univ of Utah; Nm
Callahan, Caitlin N., 616-331-3601 callahac@gvsu.edu, Grand Valley State Univ; GgZg
Callahan, John A., 302-831-3584 john.callahan@udel.edu, Univ of Delaware; Zri
Callahan, Timothy J., (843) 953-8278 callahant@cofc.edu, Coll of Charleston; Hwq
Callanan, Jennifer R., (973) 720-3979 callananj@wpunj.edu, William Paterson Univ; ScGmSz
Callard, Jeff, callard@ou.edu, Univ of Oklahoma; Np
Callegari, Ezio, ezio.callegari@unito.it, Univ di Torino; Gx
Callison, James, (801) 863-8679 jcallison@uvu.edu, Utah Valley Univ; GeSfo
Calvert, Andrew J., (778) 782-5511 acalvert@sfu.ca, Simon Fraser Univ; Ys
Calvert, Stephen E., (604) 822-5210 calvert@eos.ubc.ca, Univ of British Columbia; Cm
Calvin, Wendy, 775.784.1785 wcalvin@unr.edu, Univ of Nevada, Reno; YgZr
Camacho, Alfredo, (204) 474-7413 camacho@cc.umanitoba.ca, Univ of Manitoba; Gt
Camacho, Elsa A., (509) 376-5473 elsa.camacho@pnl.gov, Pacific Northwest; Cg
Camann, Eleanor J., 303-914-6290 eleanor.camann@rrcc.edu, Red Rocks Comm Coll; OnZeGs
Camargo, Suzana, suzana@ldeo.columbia.edu, Columbia Univ; As
Cambardella, Cynthia, (515) 294-2921 cindy.cambardella@ars.usda.gov, Iowa State Univ of Sci & Tech; So
Cambazoglu, Mustafa K., 228.688.3009 kemal.cambazoglu@usm.edu, Univ of Southern Mississippi; No
Came, Rosemarie E., 603-862-1720 rosemarie.came@unh.edu, Univ of New Hampshire; OoZnn
Cameron, Barry I., 414-229-3136 bcameron@uwm.edu, Univ of Wisconsin, Milwaukee; Gvi
Cameron, Cheryl, (907) 451-5012 cheryl.cameron@alaska.gov, Alaska Division of Geological & Geophysical Surveys; Gv
Cameron, Kevin, (778) 782-4703 kjc@sfu.ca, Simon Fraser Univ; Gg
Camill III, Philip, 207-721-5149 pcamill@bowdoin.edu, Bowdoin Coll; PebSb
Camille, Michael A., (318) 342-1750 Univ of Louisiana, Monroe; Zy
Camilleri, Phyllis A., (931) 221-7317 camillerip@apsu.edu, Austin Peay State Univ; Gct
Cammerata, Kirk , 361-825-2468 kirk.cammerata@tamucc.edu, Texas A&M Univ, Corpus Christi; Zn
Camp, Mark J., (419) 530-2398 mark.camp@utoledo.edu, Univ of Toledo; PiRhEs
Camp, Victor E., (619) 594-7170 vcamp@mail.sdsu.edu, San Diego State Univ; Gv
Campana, Michael E., (541) 737-2413 michael.campana@oregonstate.edu, Oregon State Univ; Hg
Campbell, Andrew R., (575) 835-5327 campbell@nmt.edu, New Mexico Inst of Mining and Tech; CsEmGz
Campbell, Bruce A., 202-633-2472 Smithsonian Inst / Nat Air & Space Mus; Zr
Campbell, Erin A., 307-766-2286 erin.campbell@wyo.gov, Wyoming State Geological Survey; Gc
Campbell, Glenn A., (859) 622-6474 glenn.campbell@eku.edu, Eastern Kentucky Univ; Zy
Campbell, Ian A., ian.campbell@ualberta.ca, Univ of Alberta; Gm
Campbell, James B., (540) 231-5841 Virginia Polytechnic Inst & State Univ; Zr
Campbell, Katherine, (505) 667-2799 ksc@lanl.gov, Los Alamos; Gq
Campbell, Kenneth E., (213) 763-3425 kcampbell@nhm.org, Los Angeles County Mus of Natural History; PvGgr
Campbell, Lisa, (979) 845-5706 lisacampbell@tamu.edu, Texas A&M Univ; Ob
Campbell, Patricia A., (724) 738-4405 patricia.campbell@sru.edu, Slippery Rock Univ; Gc
Campbell, Seth W., seth.campbell@maine.edu, Univ of Maine; Gl
Canalda, Sabrina, 915-831- 2617 mren@epcc.edu, El Paso Comm Coll; Gg
Canales, María Luisa, 34 913944819 mcanales@ucm.es, Univ Complutense de Madrid; PmgGg
Canales Cisneros, Juan Pablo, (508) 289-2893 jpcanales@whoi.edu, Woods Hole Oceanographic Inst; Yr
Candela, Philip A., (301) 405-2783 candela@geol.umd.edu, Univ of Maryland; CpgEg
Cane, Mark A., mcane@ldeo.columbia.edu, Columbia Univ; Op
Canil, Dante, (250) 472-4180 dcanil@uvic.ca, Univ of Victoria; Gi
Cannon, Alex, acannon@eoas.ubc.ca, Univ of British Columbia; As
Cannon, Kevin, 303-273-3819 cannon@mines.edu, Colorado Sch of Mines; ZnnZr
Canon-Tapia, Edgardo, ecanon@cicese.mx, Centro de Investigación Científica y de Educación Superior de Ensenada; GvYmGt
Cantarero, Debra A., (626) 585-7138 dacantarero@pasadena.edu, Pasadena City Coll; Zn
Cantrell, Kirk J., (509) 376-2136 kirk.cantrell@pnl.gov, Pacific Northwest; Cl
Canudo, José Ignacio, jicanudo@unizar.es, Univ de Zaragoza; Pv
Canuel, Elizabeth A., (804) 684-7134 ecanuel@vims.edu, William & Mary; Oc
Cao, Guofeng, 806-834-8920 guofeng.cao@ttu.edu, Texas Tech Univ; Zi
Cao, Hongsheng, 316-978-3140 Wichita State Univ; Cl
Cao, Wenrong, 775-784-1770 wenrongc@unr.edu, Univ of Nevada, Reno; Gtc
Cao, Xiaobin, xcao@lsu.edu, Louisiana State Univ; Cs
Capehart, William J., (605) 394-2291 william.capehart@sdsmt.edu, South Dakota Sch of Mines & Tech; AsZoHq
Capes, Gerard, gerard.capes@manchester.ac.uk, Univ of Manchester; As
Caplan-Auerbach, Jackie, 360-650-4153 caplanj@wwu.edu, Western Washington Univ; Ys
Capo, Rosemary C., (412) 624-8873 rcapo@pitt.edu, Univ of Pittsburgh; Cl
Capoccia, Mary, (614) 292-8522 capoccia.6@osu.edu, Ohio State Univ; Zn
Caporali, Alessandro, 39-049-8279122 alessandro.caporali@unipd.it, Univ degli Studi di Padova; YdsZr
Capraro, Luca, 39-049-8279182 luca.capraro@unipd.it, Univ degli Studi di Padova; PelGg
Capuano, Regina M., 713-743-2957 capuano@uh.edu, Univ of Houston; HwCqs
Caputi, Samantha , samantha.caputi@tccd.edu, Tarrant County Coll, Southeast Campus; Gg
Caputo, Mario V., (909) 214-7742 mvcaputo@earthlink.net, San Diego State Univ; GsdOn
Carageorgos, Themis, themis.carageorgos@adelaide.edu.au, Univ of Adelaide; Np
Carbotte, Suzanne, carbotte@ldeo.columbia.edu, Columbia Univ; Yr
Cardace, Dawn, 401-874-9384 cardace@uri.edu, Univ of Rhode Island; GpPg
Cardellach López, Esteve, ++34935813091 esteve.cardellach@uab.cat, Universitat Autonoma de Barcelona; GzeCs
Carden-Jessen, Melanie E., (417) 836-3231 mcardenjessen@missouristate.edu, Missouri State Univ; Ze
Cardenas, Bayani, cardenas@jsg.utexas.edu, Univ of Texas, Austin; Hg
Cardiff, Michael A., (608) 262-8960 cardiff@wisc.edu, Univ of Wisconsin, Madison; HwYg
Cardiff, Mike, cardiff@wisc.edu, Univ of Wisconsin, Madison; Hw
Cardimona, Steve, (707) 468-3219 scardimo@mendocino.edu, Mendocino

Coll; Ys
Cardott, Brian J., (405) 325-8065 bcardott@ou.edu, Univ of Oklahoma; EcoGg
Carew, James L., (843) 953-5592 carewj@cofc.edu, Coll of Charleston; PgGd
Carey, Anne E., (614) 292-2375 carey.145@osu.edu, Ohio State Univ; HwCg
Carey, James W., (505) 667-5540 bcarey@lanl.gov, Los Alamos; CpYxNr
Carey, Kristine M., (807) 343-8461 kristine.carey@lakeheadu.ca, Lakehead Univ; Zn
Carey, Sean, 905-525-9140 (Ext. 20134) careysk@mcmaster.ca, McMaster Univ; Hg
Carey, Steven N., (401) 874-6209 scarey@gso.uri.edu, Univ of Rhode Island; Ou
Carle, Steven, (925) 423-5039 carle1@llnl.gov, Lawrence Livermore; Hw
Carley, Tamara, 610-330-5199 carleyt@lafayette.edu, Lafayette Coll; GviCg
Carlile, Amy L., 203-479-4257 acarlile@newhaven.edu, Univ of New Haven; ObZn
Carlin, Joe, (657) 278-3054 jcarlin@fullerton.edu, California State Univ, Fullerton; GuOuGs
Carlin, Scott, 516-299-2318 scott.carlin@liu.edu, Long Island Univ, C.W. Post Campus; Zn
Carling, Gregory T., (801) 422-2622 greg.carling@byu.edu, Brigham Young Univ; HwCts
Carlson, Anders, 541-737-3625 acarlson@coas.oregonstate.edu, Oregon State Univ; GlCt
Carlson, Barry A., bacarlso@delta.edu, Delta Coll; Yg
Carlson, Catherine A., 860-465-5218 carlsonc@easternct.edu, Eastern Connecticut State Univ; Hwg
Carlson, Diane H., carlsondh@csus.edu, Sacramento State Univ; Gc
Carlson, Douglas A., 225/578-3671 dcarlson@lsu.edu, Louisiana State Univ; Hw
Carlson, Galen R., 657-278-3882 gcarlson@exchange.fullerton.edu, California State Univ, Fullerton; Zg
Carlson, Heath, carlsonh@easternct.edu, Eastern Connecticut State Univ; Zg
Carlson, Jill, 303-384-2643 carlson@mines.edu, Colorado Geological Survey; NgZu
Carlson, Marvin P., (402) 472-3471 rockdrmpc@hotmail.com, Unversity of Nebraska, Lincoln; Gt
Carlson, Richard E., (515) 294-9868 richard@iastate.edu, Iowa State Univ of Sci & Tech; Am
Carlson, Sandra J., (530) 752-2834 sjcarlson@ucdavis.edu, Univ of California, Davis; Pg
Carlson, Toby N., (814) 863-1582 tnc@psu.edu, Pennsylvania State Univ, Univ Park; Am
Carlson, William D., (512) 471-4770 wcarlson@jsg.utexas.edu, Univ of Texas, Austin; GpzCp
Carmack, Edward, (250) 363-6585 carmack@dfo-mpo.gc.ca, Univ of British Columbia; Op
Carman, Cary D., 325-944-4600 cdcarman@usgs.gov, Angelo State Univ; Hg
Carmichael, Ian S., (510) 642-2577 ian@eps.berkeley.edu, Univ of California, Berkeley; Gi
Carmichael, Robert S., (319) 337-6499 robert-carmichael@uiowa.edu, Univ of Iowa; YexGg
Carmichael, Sarah, (828) 262-8471 carmichaelsk@appstate.edu, Appalachian State Univ; GxCgGd
Carn, Simon, 906/487-1756 scarn@mtu.edu, Michigan Technological Univ; ZrGv
Carnevale, Giorgio, giorgio.carnevale@unito.it, Univ di Torino; Pg
Carney, Robert S., (225) 388-6511 Louisiana State Univ; Ob
Carney, Theodore C., (505) 667-3415 tedc@lanl.gov, Los Alamos; Ng
Caron, Jean-Bernard, (416) 586-5753 jcaron@rom.on.ca, Univ of Toronto; Pi
Caron, Olivier J., 217-300-0198 caron@illinois.edu, Illinois State Geological Survey; Ng
Carosi, Rodolfo, rodolfo.carosi@unito.it, Univ di Torino; Gc
Carpenter, Brett, brett.carpenter@ou.edu, Univ of Oklahoma; Gc
Carpenter, Michael, +44 (0) 1223 333483 mc43@esc.cam.ac.uk, Univ of Cambridge; Gy
Carpenter, Philip J., (815) 753-1523 pjcarpenter@niu.edu, Northern Illinois Univ; YgHwNg
Carpenter, Roy, (206) 543-8535 rcarp@u.washington.edu, Univ of Washington; No
Carpi, Anthony, 212-237-8195 acarpi@jjay.cuny.edu, Graduate Sch of the City Univ of New York; Gg
Carr, David E., 540-837-1758 blandy@virginia.edu, Univ of Virginia; Zn
Carr, Keith W., 217-265-0267 kw-carr@illinois.edu, Illinois State Geological Survey; Gg
Carr, Mark, (831) 459-3958 carr@biology.ucsc.edu, Univ of California, Santa Cruz; Ob
Carr, Michael J., carr@rutgers.edu, Rutgers, The State Univ of New Jersey; Gv
Carr, Sharon D., scarr@ccs.carleton.ca, Carleton Univ; Gt
Carr, Timothy R., (785) 864-2135 tcarr@kgs.ku.edu, Univ of Kansas; Go
Carrano, Matthew T., (202) 633-1506 Smithsonian Inst / Nat Mus of Natural History; Pv
Carranza, Emmanuel John, (031) 260-2803 carranzae@ukzn.ac.za, Univ of KwaZulu-Natal; EdCeZr
Carrapa, Barbara, 520-621-4910 bcarrapa@email.arizona.edu, Univ of Arizona; Gs
Carrell, Jennifer, 217-244-2764 jcarrell@illinois.edu, Illinois State Geological Survey; Zg
Carrick, Tina L., 915-831-8905 tcarrick@epcc.edu, El Paso Comm Coll; ZeGgYg
Carrigan, Charles R., (925) 422-3941 carrigan1@llnl.gov, Lawrence Livermore; Yg
Carroll, Alan R., (608) 262-2368 acarroll@geology.wisc.edu, Univ of Wisconsin, Madison; Gs
Carroll, David, (540) 231-5469 carrolld@vt.edu, Virginia Polytechnic Inst & State Univ; Am
Carroll, Matt, 509-335-2235 carroll@wsu.edu, Washington State Univ; Zn
Carroll, Rosemary, rosemary.carroll@dri.edu, Univ of Nevada, Reno; Hq
Carroll, Susan A., (925) 423-7552 Lawrence Livermore; Cl
Carroll, Tracy, (417) 836-5800 tracycarroll@missouristate.edu, Missouri State Univ; Zn
Carslaw, Ken, +44(0) 113 34 31597 k.s.carslaw@leeds.ac.uk, Univ of Leeds; As
Carson, Bobb, bc00@lehigh.edu, Lehigh Univ; GusGt
Carson, Eric C., 608-890-1998 eccarson@wisc.edu, Univ of Wisconsin, Extension; Gl
Carson, Michael, +618 9266-4973 michael.carson@curtin.edu.au, Curtin Univ; Yx
Carson, Robert J., (509) 527-5224 carsonrj@whitman.edu, Whitman Coll; GmeGl
Carstarphen, Camela, 406-496-4633 ccarstarphen@mtech.edu, Montana Tech of The Univ of Montana; Hw
Carstensen, Laurence W., (540) 231-2600 Virginia Polytechnic Inst & State Univ; Zi
Carter, Andy, +44 020 7679 2418 a.carter@ucl.ac.uk, Birkbeck Coll; Zg
Carter, Burchard D., (229) 931-2325 burchard.carter@gsw.edu, Georgia Southwestern State Univ; Pg
Carter, David, (303) 293-5014 dcarter@osmre.gov, Department of Interior Office of Surface Mining Reclamation and Enforcement; Zir
Carter, Glenn, (808) 956-9267 gscarter@hawaii.edu, Univ of Hawai'i, Manoa; Op
Carter, Greg, (228) 214-3305 greg.carter@usm.edu, Univ of Southern Mississippi; Zyi
Carter, Kristin M., 412.442.4234 krcarter@pa.gov, DCNR- Pennsylvania Bureau of Geological Survey; EoCqEg
Carter, Matthew J., 814-332-2876 mcarter@allegheny.edu, Allegheny Coll; Gct
Cartier, Laurent E., laurent.cartier@unil.ch, Univ of Delaware; Gz
Carton, Alberto, +390498279141 alberto.carton@unipd.it, Univ degli Studi di Padova; Gm
Carton, James, (301) 405-5365 Univ of Maryland; Op
Cartwright, J A., cartwrightja@cf.ac.uk, Cardiff Univ; Ys
Cartwright, Joe, +44 (1865) 272000 joe.cartwright@earth.ox.ac.uk, Univ of Oxford; Gs
Caruthers, Andrew, (269) 387-8633 andrew.caruthers@wmich.edu, Western Michigan Univ; GsCsGr
Carvalho, Maria d., mdrcarvalho@fc.ul.pt, Unive de Lisboa; HwyZn
Carver, Gary A., (907) 487-4551 Humboldt State Univ; Gmt
Cary, Kevin, (270) 745-2981 kevin.cary@wku.edu, Western Kentucky Univ; Zi
Casale, Gabriele M., casalegm@appstate.edu, Appalachian State Univ; Gct
Casares, Heather, heather.casares@azwestern.edu, Arizona Western Coll; Gvi
Casas Duocastella, Lluís, ++34935868365 lluis.casas@uab.cat, Universitat Autonoma de Barcelona; GzaYm
Case, James M., james.case@wilkes.edu, Wilkes Univ; Ob
Case, Jeanne, 509-359-4288 jdcase@ewu.edu, Eastern Washington Univ; Gg
Case, Stephen, (815) 939-5681 scase@olivet.edu, Olivet Nazarene Univ; RhXg
Case Hanks, Anne T., (318) 342-1822 casehanks@ulm.edu, Univ of Louisiana, Monroe; AsZe
Casey, Francis, francis.casey@ndsu.edu, North Dakota State Univ; SpHq
Casey, John F., 713-743-2824 jfcasey@uh.edu, Univ of Houston; GtiGu
Casey, Michelle , (410) 704-2744 mcasey@towson.edu, Towson Univ; Pe
Casey, William H., (916) 752-3211 Univ of California, Davis; Cl

Cashman, Susan M., (707) 826-3114 smc1@humboldt.edu, Humboldt State Univ; Gc
Caskey, John, (415) 405-0353 caskey@sfsu.edu, San Francisco State Univ; Gc
Casquet, César, casquet@ucm.es, Univ Complutense de Madrid; Gip
Cassar, Nicolas, 919 681-8865 nicolas.cassar@duke.edu, Duke Univ; CbOcb
Cassel, Donald K., (919) 515-1457 North Carolina State Univ; Sp
Cassel, Elizabeth J., (208) 885-4289 ecassel@uidaho.edu, Univ of Idaho; Gs
Cassiani, Giorgio, +390498279189 giorgio.cassiani@unipd.it, Univ degli Studi di Padova; YgHs
Cassidy, Daniel P., (269) 387-5324 daniel.cassidy@wmich.edu, Western Michigan Univ; Hw
Cassidy, John, cassidy@pgc.nrcan.gc.ca, Univ of Victoria; Ys
Cassidy, Martin, 713-616-5853 mcassidy@uh.edu, Univ of Houston; GoCo
Castagna, John P., 713-743-8699 jpcastagna@uh.edu, Univ of Houston; Ye
Castañeda, Isla, 413 577-1124 isla@geo.umass.edu, Univ of Massachusetts, Amherst; Ca
Castelli, Daniele, daniele.castelli@unito.it, Univ di Torino; Gx
Castillo, Paterno R., (858) 534-0383 pcastillo@ucsd.edu, Univ of California, San Diego; Giu
Castillon, David A., (417) 836-5801 davidcastillon@missouristate.edu, Missouri State Univ; Gm
Castiñeiras, Pedro, castigar@ucm.es, Univ Complutense de Madrid; Gp
Castle, James W., (864) 656-5015 jcastle@clemson.edu, Clemson Univ; GseHw
Castleton, Jessica, (801) 537-3381 jessicacastleton@utah.gov, Utah Geological Survey; Ng
Castor, Stephen B., 775-682-8766 scastor@unr.edu, Univ of Nevada, Reno; Eg
Castro, Adrian, ac114@wellesley.edu, Wellesley Coll; Gp
Castro, Maria Clara, 734-615-3812 mccastro@umich.edu, Univ of Michigan; Hy
Castro, Mark S., (301) 689-3115 castro@al.umces.edu, Univ of Maryland; As
Castro, Raul, raul@cicese.mx, Centro de Investigación Científica y de Educación Superior de Ensenada; Ys
Caswell, Bryony, +440151 795 4390 b.a.caswell@liverpool.ac.uk, Univ of Liverpool; Ob
Catalano, Jeff, 314-935-6015 catalano@levee.wustl.edu, Washington Univ in St. Louis; Ca
Catalano, Jeffrey G., 314-935-6015 catalano@levee.wustl.edu, Washington Univ in St. Louis; Cl
Catania, Ginny A., (512) 471-0403 gcatania@utig.ig.utexas.edu, Univ of Texas, Austin; Gl
Catau, John C., (417) 836-5801 johncatau@missouristate.edu, Missouri State Univ; Zn
Cates, Anna, 612-625-3135 catesa@umn.edu, Univ of Minnesota, Twin Cities; Sb
Cathcart, Eric, (619) 260-4099 cathcart@sandiego.edu, Univ of San Diego; Geg
Cather, Steven, 575-835-5153 steven.cather@nmt.edu, New Mexico Inst of Mining and Tech; Gg
Cathey, Henrietta, +61 7 3138 0416 henrietta.cathey@qut.edu.au, Queensland Univ of Tech; Giv
Cathles, Lawrence M., (607) 255-2844 lmc19@cornell.edu, Cornell Univ; GqYgEg
Catling, David C., (206) 543-8653 dcatling@uw.edu, Univ of Washington; CgAsXb
Catlos, Elizabeth J., 512-471-4762 ejcatlos@gmail.com, Univ of Texas, Austin; GzCg
Cato, Kerry, (909) 537-5409 kerry.cato@csusb.edu, California State Univ, San Bernardino; Ng
Cattanach, Bart, 828-296-4634 bart.cattanach@ncdenr.gov, N.C. Department of Environmental Quality; Gc
Cattania, Camilla, camcat@mit.edu, Massachusetts Inst of Tech; Ys
Cattolico, Rose Ann, (206) 543-9363 racat@u.washington.edu, Univ of Washington; Zn
Catuneanu, Octavian, (780) 492-6569 octavian.catuneanu@ualberta.ca, Univ of Alberta; Gs
Caudill, Kimberly S., 740-753-6289 caudillk7007@hocking.edu, Hocking Coll; GeZuHw
Caudill, Michael R., 740-753-6277 caudillm@hocking.edu, Hocking Coll; GsSaHw
Caupp, Craig L., (301) 687-4755 ccaupp@frostburg.edu, Frostburg State Univ; ZnHs
Cave, Rachel R., +353 (0)91 492 351 rachel.cave@nuigalway.ie, Nat Univ of Ireland Galway; Cm
Cavello, Seth, cavello@usf.edu, Univ of South Florida; Zn
Cawood, Peter A., (+44) (0)1334 463911 peter.cawood@monash.edu, Monash Univ; GtcGg
Caylor, Kelly, caylor@ucsb.edu, Univ of California, Santa Barbara; HgZcy
Cayzer, Nicola, +44 (0) 131 650 8527 nicola.cayzer@ed.ac.uk, Edinburgh Univ; Yg
Cecil, M. R., (818) 677-7009 robinson.cecil@csun.edu, California State Univ, Northridge; GiCcGz
Celia, Michael A., (609) 258-5425 Princeton Univ; Hw
Celik, Hasan, 00904242370000-5980 hasancelik@firat.edu.tr, Firat Univ; GscEo
Çemen, Ibrahim, 205-348-8019 icemen@ua.edu, Univ of Alabama; Gct
Cenpírek, Jan, +420 549 49 6450 jcemp@sci.muni.cz, Masaryk Univ; Gz
Centorbi, Tracey, (301) 405-6965 tlcento@umd.edu, Univ of Maryland; Cg
Cepeda, Joseph C., 806-651-2272 jcepeda@mail.wtamu.edu, West Texas A&M Univ; GiHw
Cercone, Karen Rose, (724) 357-5623 kcercone@iup.edu, Indiana Univ of Pennsylvania; Zeg
Cerling, Thure E., (801) 581-5558 thure.cerling@utah.edu, Univ of Utah; ClsZc
Cerrato, Robert M., (631) 632-8666 robert.cerrato@stonybrook.edu, SUNY, Stony Brook; Ob
Cervato, Cinzia C., (515) 294-7583 cinzia@iastate.edu, Iowa State Univ of Sci & Tech; GgZe
Cesare, Bernardo, +390498279148 bernardo.cesare@unipd.it, Univ degli Studi di Padova; Gp
Cessi, Paola, (858) 534-0622 pcessi@ucsd.edu, Univ of California, San Diego; Op
Cetin, Haluk, (270) 809-2085 hcetin@murraystate.edu, Murray State Univ; ZrGe
Cetindag, Bahattin, 00904242370000-5957 bcetindag@firat.edu.tr, Firat Univ; NgYv
Chacko, Elizabeth, (202) 994-6185 echack@gwu.edu, George Washington Univ; Zy
Chacko, Thomas, (780) 492-5395 tom.chacko@ualberta.ca, Univ of Alberta; Gp
Chaddock, Lisa, 6196604000 x3033 lisa.chaddock@gcccd.edu, Cuyamaca Coll; Zy
Chadima, Sarah A., 605-677-6166 sarah.chadima@usd.edu, South Dakota Dept of Environment and Natural Resources; Gg
Chadwick, John, (843) 953-5950 chadwickj@cofc.edu, Coll of Charleston; GiZrGt
Chafetz, Henry S., (713) 743-3227 hchafetz@uh.edu, Univ of Houston; Gds
Chague-Goff, Catherine, c.chague-goff@unsw.edu.au, Univ of New South Wales; CgGs
Chakhmouradian, Anton, (204) 474-7278 anton.chakhmouradian@umanitoba.ca, Univ of Manitoba; GziCg
Challads, Thomas, +44 (0) 131 650 8543 tchallan@staffmail.ed.ac.uk, Edinburgh Univ; Hg
Challinor, Andy, +44(0) 113 34 33194 a.j.challinor@leeds.ac.uk, Univ of Leeds; Am
Chamberlain, Andrew T., +44 (0)161 306 4176 andrew.chamberlain@manchester.ac.uk, Univ of Manchester; GaSaPv
Chamberlain, Edwin P., (718) 951-5416 Los Alamos; Cc
Chamberlain, John A., (718) 951-5926 johnc@brooklyn.cuny.edu, Graduate Sch of the City Univ of New York; Pg
Chamberlain, Kevin R., (307) 766-2914 kchamber@uwyo.edu, Univ of Wyoming; CcGt
Chamberlin, Richard, (575) 835-5310 richard@nmbg.nmt.edu, New Mexico Inst of Mining and Tech; GcvGg
Chamberlin, William S., (714) 992-7443 schamberlin@fullcoll.edu, Fullerton Coll; OgbZe
Chambers, Jeanne, 775-784-5329 chambers@unr.edu, Univ of Nevada, Reno; SfHg
Chambers, John E., (202) 478-8855 jchambers@carnegiescience.edu, Carnegie Inst for Sci; Xa
Chameides, William L., 613-8004 bill.chameides@duke.edu, Duke Univ; AsGe
Champion, Kyle M., 813-253-7326 Hillsborough Comm Coll; Zg
Champlin, Steven D., (601) 961-5506 stephen_champlin@deq.state.ms.us, Mississippi Office of Geology; Go
Chan, Clara S., 302-831-1819 cschan@udel.edu, Univ of Delaware; PoObGz
Chan, Kwan M., (562) 985-4817 kmchan@csulb.edu, California State Univ, Long Beach; Oc
Chan, Marjorie A., (801) 581-6551 marjorie.chan@utah.edu, Univ of Utah; Gs
Chan, Queenie, +44 1784 443896 queenie.chan@rhul.ac.uk, Royal Holloway Univ of London; XmCa
Chan, Selene, (604) 822-2034 schan@eos.ubc.ca, Univ of British Columbia; Zn
Chandler, Angela, (501) 683-0111 angela.chandler@arkansas.gov, Arkansas

Geological Survey; GgrGs
Chandler, Cyndy, (508) 289-2765 cchandler@whoi.edu, Woods Hole Oceanographic Inst; Og
Chandler, Sandra, (501) 683-0125 sandra.chandler@arkansas.gov, Arkansas Geological Survey; Ze
Chandler, Val W., 612-627-4780 (Ext. 203) chand004@umn.edu, Univ of Minnesota, Twin Cities; Ye
Chandra, Sudeep, 775.784.6221 sudeep@unr.edu, Univ of Nevada, Reno; Hs
Chaney, Phil L., (334) 844-3420 chanepl@auburn.edu, Auburn Univ; ZnnZn
Chang, Chih-Pei, 831-656-2840 cpchang@nps.edu, Naval Postgraduate Sch; Am
Chang, Edmund K., (631) 632-6170 kar.chang@stonybrook.edu, SUNY, Stony Brook; As
Chang, Hai-ru, hrc@eas.gatech.edu, Georgia Inst of Tech; As
Chang, Julie M., 405-325-7055 jmchang@ou.edu, Univ of Oklahoma; GgZnn
Chang, Ping, (979) 845-8196 pchang@ocean.tamu.edu, Texas A&M Univ; Op
Chang, Young-Soo, (630) 252-4076 changy@anl.gov, Argonne; As
Chang, Zhaoshan, 303-384-2127 chang@mines.edu, Colorado Sch of Mines; Eg
Channell, James E., 352-392-3658 jetc@ufl.edu, Univ of Florida; YmGt
Channing, Alan, +44(0)29 208 76213 channinga@cardiff.ac.uk, Univ of Wales; Gd
Chanway, Christopher, 604–822–3716 christopher.chanway@ubc.ca, Univ of British Columbia; Sb
Chao, Shenn-Yu, (410) 221-8427 chao@hpl.umces.edu, Univ of Maryland; Op
Chapa, Laura E., (512) 820-9079 laura.chapa@austincc.edu, Austin Comm Coll District; ZgeZr
Chapin, Charles E., cechapin2@comcast.net, New Mexico Inst of Mining and Tech; Gt
Chapin, F. Stuart, (510) 642-1003 Univ of California, Berkeley; Pe
Chapman, Alan, chapman@macalester.edu, Macalester Coll; GctCc
Chapman, James, jay.chapman@uwyo.edu, Univ of Wyoming; Gct
Chapman, LeeAnna Y., 6192604600x2441 leeannachapman@sandiego.edu, Univ of San Diego; GeZe
Chapman, Mark, +44 (0)1603 59 3114 mark.chapman@uea.ac.uk, Univ of East Anglia; Pm
Chapman, Marshall, (606) 783-5397 m.chapman@moreheadstate.edu, Morehead State Univ; Gv
Chapman, Martin C., (540) 231-5036 mcc@vt.edu, Virginia Polytechnic Inst & State Univ; Ys
Chapman, Piers, (979) 845-9399 piers.chapman@tamu.edu, Texas A&M Univ; OcCm
Chapman, Robert J., +44(0) 113 34 33190 r.j.chapman@leeds.ac.uk, Univ of Leeds; EmCe
Chapman, Ross N., (250) 472-4340 chapman@uvic.ca, Univ of Victoria; Op
Chappaz, Anthony, 989-774-4388 chapp1a@cmich.edu, Central Michigan Univ; Cat
Chappell, James R., (970) 491-5147 jim_chappell@partner.nps.gov, Colorado State Univ; Ge
Chappell, P. D., 757-683-4937 pdchappe@odu.edu, Old Dominion Univ; Oc
Chaput, Julien, 915-747-7003 jachaput@utep.edu, Univ of Texas, El Paso; GeYes
Charbonnier, Sylvain, sylvain@usf.edu, Univ of South Florida; Gv
Charette, Matthew A., (508) 289-3205 mcharette@whoi.edu, Woods Hole Oceanographic Inst; Cm
Charles, Christopher D., (858) 534-5911 ccharles@ucsd.edu, Univ of California, San Diego; Pe
Charles, Kasanzu, kcharls16@yahoo.com, Univ of Dar es Salaam; GgRh
Charlevoix, Donna J., (217) 244-9575 charlevo@atmos.uiuc.edu, Univ of Illinois, Urbana-Champaign; As
Charlson, Bob, 206-543-2537 Univ of Washington; As
Charlson, Robert J., charlson@chem.washington.edu, Univ of Washington; As
Chase, Anne, (520) 621-6004 achase@email.arizona.edu, Univ of Arizona; Zn
Chase, Clement G., (520) 621-2417 cgchase@email.arizona.edu, Univ of Arizona; Yg
Chase, Jon M., jchase@biology2.wustl.edu, Washington Univ in St. Louis; Zn
Chase, Peter M., (608) 265.6003 pete.chase@wisc.edu, Univ of Wisconsin, Madison, Division of Extension; HwYgRw
Chase, Richard L., (604) 822-3086 rchase@eos.ubc.ca, Univ of British Columbia; Gu
Chasteen, Hayden R., 817-515-6694 hayden.chasteen@tccd.edu, Tarrant County Coll, Northeast Campus; GgeGg
Chatelain, Edward E., (229) 333-5758 echatela@valdosta.edu, Valdosta State Univ; PiGlPv
Chatterjee, Ipsita, 940-565-2372 ipsita.chatterjee@unt.edu, Univ of North Texas; Zn
Chatterjee, Meera, 330 972-2394 meera@uakron.edu, Univ of Akron; Zy
Chatterjee, Nilanjan, (617) 253-1995 nchat@mit.edu, Massachusetts Inst of Tech; Cg
Chatterjee, Sankar, 806-834-4590 sankar.chatterjee@ttu.edu, Texas Tech Univ; PvGct
Chatterjee, Snehamoy, 906-487-2516 schatte1@mtu.edu, Michigan Technological Univ; NmGqNx
Chatterton, Brian D., (780) 492-3085 brian.chatterton@ualberta.ca, Univ of Alberta; Pi
Chaubey, Indrajeet, (765) 494-3258 ichaubey@purdue.edu, Purdue Univ; Hg
Chaudhuri, Sambhudas, (785) 532-2246 ksuncsc@ksu.edu, Kansas State Univ; GeoCc
Chaumba, Jeff B., (910) 522-5787 jeff.chaumba@uncp.edu, Univ of North Carolina, Pembroke; GxEgGz
Chaussard, Estelle, 541-346-4573 estelle@uoregon.edu, Univ of Oregon; Yd
Chavrit, Deborah, +44 0161 275-0760 deborah.chavrit@manchester.ac.uk, Univ of Manchester; Gi
Cheadle, Burns A., 519-661-2111 x.89009 bcheadle@uwo.ca, Western Univ; Go
Cheadle, Michael J., (307) 766-3206 cheadle@uwyo.edu, Univ of Wyoming; Yg
Chebana, Fateh, fateh.chebana@ete.inrs.ca, Universite du Quebec; Hq
Checkley, David M., (858) 534-4228 dcheckley@ucsd.edu, Univ of California, San Diego; Ob
Cheek, William H., (417) 836-5801 billcheek@missouristate.edu, Missouri State Univ; Zn
Cheel, Richard J., (905) 688-5550 (Ext. 3512) rcheel@brocku.ca, Brock Univ; Gs
Chege, George W., gchege@jkuat.ac.ke, Jomo Kenyatta Univ of Agriculture & Tech; ZgrZi
Chelariu, Ciprian, 0040232201486 ciprian.chelariu@uaic.ro, Alexandru Ioan Cuza; Go
Chen, Bob, bob.chen@umb.edu, Univ of Massachusetts, Boston; CoOc
Chen, Chu-Yung, cychen7@illinois.edu, Univ of Illinois, Urbana-Champaign; Cg
Chen, Dake, dchen@ldeo.columbia.edu, Columbia Univ; Op
Chen, Gang, (907)474-6875 gchen@alaska.edu, Univ of Alaska, Fairbanks; Nm
Chen, Hway-Jen, 831-656-3788 hjchen@nps.edu, Naval Postgraduate Sch; Am
Chen, Jing, chenj@geog.utoronto.ca, McMaster Univ; AmZry
Chen, Jingyi, 918-631-3014 jingyi-chen@utulsa.edu, Univ of Tulsa; Yes
Chen, jiquan, (419) 932-1517 jqchen@msu.edu, Michigan State Univ; Zg
Chen, Jiuhua, 305-348-3030 chenj@fiu.edu, Florida International Univ; Gyz
Chen, Ning, ning.chen@lightsource.ca, Univ of Saskatchewan; Gz
Chen, Po, 307-766-3086 pchen@uwyo.edu, Univ of Wyoming; YseYg
Chen, Shu-Hua, 530-752-1822 shachen@ucdavis.edu, Univ of California, Davis; ZrAsm
Chen, Shuyi S., (206) 685-1736 shuyic@uw.edu, Univ of Washington; As
Chen, Tsing-Chang, (515) 294-9874 tmchen@iastate.edu, Iowa State Univ of Sci & Tech; As
Chen, Wang-Ping, wpchen@illinois.edu, Univ of Illinois, Urbana-Champaign; YsGt
Chen, Xianfeng, (724) 738-2385 xianfeng.chen@sru.edu, Slippery Rock Univ; Zr
Chen, Xiaowei, 508-289-3820 xiaowei.fengr@gmail.com, Univ of Oklahoma; YsGt
Chen, Xun-Hong, (402) 472-0772 xchen2@unl.edu, Unversity of Nebraska, Lincoln; Hq
Chen, Yi-Leng, (808) 956-2570 yileng@hawaii.edu, Univ of Hawai'i, Manoa; Asm
Chen, Yongsheng, (416)736-2100 #40124 yochen@yorku.ca, York Univ; As
Chen, Yuan, 250-807-9594 yuan.chen@ubc.ca, Univ of British Columbia, Okanagan Campus; EmCeGz
Cheney, Donald, d.cheney@neu.edu, Northeastern Univ; Zn
Cheney, Eric S., 206-543-1163 vaalbara@uw.edu, Univ of Washington; Eg
Cheney, John T., (413) 542-2311 jtcheney@amherst.edu, Amherst Coll; Gi
Cheng, Chu-Lin, 956 665-2464 chulin.cheng@utrgv.edu, Univ of Texas, Rio Grande Valley; HgwHq
Cheng, H. H., (612) 625-1793 hcheng@soils.umn.edu, Univ of Minnesota, Twin Cities; Sb
Cheng, Hai, 86-29-83395119 cheng021@xjtu.edu.cn, Univ of Minnesota, Twin Cities; CcPe
Cheng, Linyin, 479-575-5569 lc032@uark.edu, Univ of Arkansas, Fayetteville; Zo
Cheng, Meng-Dawn, (423) 241-5918 ucn@ornl.gov, Oak Ridge; As

Cheng, Qiuming, (416)736-2100 #22842 qiuming@yorku.ca, York Univ; Zi
Cheng, Songlin, 937 775-3455 songlin.cheng@wright.edu, Wright State Univ; Hw
Cheng, Tao, 709 864 8924 tcheng@mun.ca, Memorial Univ of Newfoundland; Hw
Cheng, Yanbo, 07 47816808 yanbo.cheng1@jcu.edu.au, James Cook Univ; EgGgEm
Cheng, Zhongqi, 7189515000 x2647 zcheng@brooklyn.cuny.edu, Brooklyn Coll (CUNY); CaScGe
Cheng, Zhongqi (Joshua), 718-951-5000, ext. 2647 zcheng@brooklyn.cuny.edu, Graduate Sch of the City Univ of New York; Zg
Chenoweth, Cheri, 217-244-4610 cchenowe@illinois.edu, Illinois State Geological Survey; GoEc
Chenoweth, M. S., (318) 342-1887 chenoweth@ulm.edu, Univ of Louisiana, Monroe; GmZir
Cherkauer, Douglas S., (262) 628-3672 aquadoc@uwm.edu, Univ of Wisconsin, Milwaukee; HwGe
Chermak, John A., 540-239-4504 jchermak@vt.edu, Virginia Polytechnic Inst & State Univ; ClGeEd
Cherniak, Daniele J., (518) 276-3358 chernd@rpi.edu, Rensselaer Polytechnic Inst; Gx
Chernoff, Barry, 860 6852452 bchernoff@wesleyan.edu, Wesleyan Univ; Ge
Cherns, L C., cherns@cf.ac.uk, Cardiff Univ; Pg
Cherrier, Jennifer, 718-951-5000 x2927 jennifer.cherrier18@brooklyn.cuny.edu, Brooklyn Coll (CUNY); OcCmRw
Cherubini, Claudia, +33(0)3 44068977 claudia.cherubini@lasalle-beauvais.fr, Institut Polytechnique LaSalle Beauvais (ex-IGAL); HwGe
Cherukupalli, Nehru, 516 463-6545 geonec@hofstra.edu, Hofstra Univ; Gg
Chesnaux, Romain, 418-545-5011 ext: 5426 rchesnaux@uqac.ca, Universite du Quebec a Chicoutimi; Hw
Chesner, Craig A., (217) 581-2626 cachesner@eiu.edu, Eastern Illinois Univ; GivGz
Chesnokov, Evgeny, 713-743-2579 emchesnokov@uh.edu, Univ of Houston; YseYx
Chester, Frederick, (979) 845-3296 chesterf@tamu.edu, Texas A&M Univ; GcNrYx
Chester, Judith, (979) 845-1380 chesterj@geo.tamu.edu, Texas A&M Univ; GcNr
Chesworth, Ward, (519) 824-4120 (Ext. 52457) wcheswor@uoguelph.ca, Univ of Guelph; ClGe
Cheun, Norman, +44 020 8417 2811 k.w.cheung@kingston.ac.uk, Kingston Univ; Ge
Cheung, Wing, 7607441150 x3652 wcheung@palomar.edu, Palomar Coll; ZirZy
Chew, David, + 353 1 8963481 chewd@tcd.ie, Trinity Coll; CcGgt
Chhetri, Parveen, (310) 243-3377 pchhetri@csudh.edu, California State Univ, Dominguez Hills; Geg
Chi, Wu-Cheng, 886-2-2783-9910 ext 510 wchi@sinica.edu.tw, Academia Sinica; GtYrs
Chiappe, Luis M., (213) 863-3323 lchiappe@nhm.org, Los Angeles County Mus of Natural History; Pv
Chiarella, Domenico, +44 1784 443890 domenico.chiarella@rhul.ac.uk, Royal Holloway Univ of London; Gs
Chiarello, Ronald P., (630) 252-9327 Argonne; Zm
Chiarenzelli, Jeffrey R., 315-229-5202 jchiarenzelli@stlawu.edu, St. Lawrence Univ; GzCg
Chief, Karletta, (520) 626-5598 kchief@email.arizona.edu, Univ of Arizona; Zn
Chien, Yi-Ju, (509) 373-4822 yi-hu.chien@pnl.gov, Pacific Northwest; Gq
Childers, Daniel, (610) 359-5242 dchilder@dccc.edu, Delaware County Comm Coll; ZgOuZi
Childs, Geoff, gchilds@wustl.edu, Washington Univ in St. Louis; Zn
Chillrud, Steven, chilli@ldeo.columbia.edu, Columbia Univ; Cg
Chilvers, Jason, +44 (0)1603 59 3130 jason.chilvers@uea.ac.uk, Univ of East Anglia; Ge
Chin, Anne, (409) 845-7141 Texas A&M Univ; Gm
Chin, Emily J., e8chin@ucsd.edu, Univ of Tennessee, Knoxville; Cu
Chin, Karen, 303-735-3074 karen.chin@colorado.edu, Univ of Colorado; Pg
Chin, Yu-Ping, (614) 292-6953 chin.15@osu.edu, Ohio State Univ; CqHw
Chipman, Melissa, 315-443-2489 mlchipma@syr.edu, Syracuse Univ; GelGn
Chipperfield, Martyn P., +44(0) 113 34 36459 m.chipperfield@leeds.ac.uk, Univ of Leeds; AscAp
Chipping, David H., (805) 528-0914 dchippin@calpoly.edu, California Polytechnic State Univ; Grt
Chirenje, Tait, 609-652-4588 tait.chirenje@stockton.edu, Stockton Univ; Sc
Chiu, Ching-Sang, (831) 656-3239 chiu@nps.edu, Naval Postgraduate Sch; Op
Chiu, Christine, christine.chiu@colostate.edu, Colorado State Univ; As
Chiu, Jer-Ming, (901) 678-2007 jerchiu@memphis.edu, Univ of Memphis; Ys
Chiu, Long S., (703) 993-1984 lchiu@gmu.edu, George Mason Univ; AsZrAm
Choate, Jessica (Jessie), choate2@illinois.edu, Univ of Illinois, Urbana-Champaign; Asm
Choh, Suk-Joo, 82-2-3290-3180 sjchoh@korea.ac.kr, Korea Univ; GdsPe
Choi, Eunseo, (901) 678-4923 echoi2@memphis.edu, Univ of Memphis; Gtq
Choi, Seon-Gyu, 82-2-3290-3174 seongyu@korea.ac.kr, Korea Univ; GzEmg
Chokmani, Karem, karem.chokmani@ete.inrs.ca, Universite du Quebec; Zi
Cholnoky, Jennifer, (518) 580-8127 jcholnok@skidmore.edu, Skidmore Coll; Gg
Choma-Moryl, Krystyna, krystyna.choma-moryl@uwr.edu.pl, Univ of Wroclaw; Ng
Chongwain, Gilbert, gchongwai@unam.na, Univ of Namibia; Go
Chopping, Mark J., 973-655-4448 choppingm@mail.montclair.edu, Montclair State Univ; ZriZe
Choquette, Marc, choquette@ggl.ulaval.ca, Universite Laval; Zn
Chormann, Jr., Frederick H., (603) 271-1975 frederick.chormann@des.nh.gov, New Hampshire Geological Survey; HyZiGm
Chorover, Jon, 520-626-5635 chorover@cals.arizona.edu, Univ of Arizona; Sc
Chorover, Jonathan, (520) 621-7228 chorover@cals.arizona.edu, Univ of Arizona; ScClo
Chou, Charissa J., (509) 372-3804 charissa.chou@pnl.gov, Pacific Northwest; Gq
Chou, Mei-In (Melissa), 217-244-0312 chou@isgs.uiuc.edu, Illinois State Geological Survey; Co
Chou, Sheng-Fu Joseph, 217-244-2744 jchou@isgs.uiuc.edu, Illinois State Geological Survey; Co
Chouinard, Vera, (905) 525-9140 (Ext. 23518) chouinar@mcmaster.ca, McMaster Univ; Zn
Choularton, Thomas, +44 0161 306-3950 choularton@manchester.ac.uk, Univ of Manchester; As
Chow, Edwin, (512) 245-2170 Texas State Univ; ZiRn
Chow, Nancy, (204) 474-6451 n_chow@umanitoba.ca, Univ of Manitoba; Gs
Chowdhury, Shafiul H., chowdhus@newpaltz.edu, SUNY, New Paltz; HwGe
Chowns, Timothy M., (678) 839-4052 tchowns@westga.edu, Univ of West Georgia; GsrGg
Christensen, Douglas, doug@giseis.alaska.edu, Univ of Alaska, Fairbanks; Ys
Christensen, Nikolas I., (608) 265-4469 chris@geology.wisc.edu, Univ of Wisconsin, Madison; Yx
Christensen, Philip R., (480) 965-7105 phil.christensen@asu.edu, Arizona State Univ; Xg
Christensen, Wesley P., 605-677-6149 wes.christensen@usd.edu, South Dakota Dept of Environment and Natural Resources; Gg
Christenson, Scott, scott.christenson@nmt.edu, New Mexico Inst of Mining and Tech; Hw
Christeson, Gail L., (512) 471-0463 gail@ig.utexas.edu, Univ of Texas, Austin; YrsGt
Christian, Alan D., 617-287-6639 alan.christian@umb.edu, Univ of Massachusetts, Boston; HsGmCs
Christian, James R., jim.christian@canada.ca, Univ of Victoria; Obc
Christiansen, Eric H., 801422 2113 eric_christiansen@byu.edu, Brigham Young Univ; GiXgGv
Christianson, Knut, knut@uw.edu, Univ of Washington; GlZr
Christie, Max L., 217-333-3540 mlc7@illinois.edu, Univ of Illinois, Urbana-Champaign; PgGr
Christie-Blick, Nicholas, ncb@ldeo.columbia.edu, Columbia Univ; Gs
Christopherson, Gary, garych@casa.arizona.edu, Univ of Arizona; Zi
Chrzan, Daryl, (510) 643-1624 dcchrzan@berkeley.edu, Univ of California, Berkeley; Zm
Chu, Pao-Shin, chu@hawaii.edu, Univ of Hawai'i, Manoa; As
Chu, Peter C., (831) 656-3688 pcchu@nps.edu, Naval Postgraduate Sch; OpZr
Chuang, Patrick Y., (831) 459-1501 pchuang@pmc.ucsc.edu, Univ of California, Santa Cruz; As
Church, Matthew, (808) 956-8779 mjchurch@hawaii.edu, Univ of Hawai'i, Manoa; Ob
Church, Thomas M., (302) 831-2558 tchurch@udel.edu, Univ of Delaware; Cm
Church, Warren, 706-507-8093 church_warren@columbusstate.edu, Columbus State Univ; ZnPcZc
Church, William R., (519) 661-3192 wrchurch@uwo.ca, Western Univ; Gt
Churchill, Ron C., (916) 327-0745 California Geological Survey; Cg
Ciampitti, Ignacio, (785) 532-6940 ciampitti@ksu.edu, Kansas State Univ;

FACULTY INDEX – C

So
Cianfrani, Christina, ccns@hampshire.edu, Hampshire Coll; Hg
Ciannelli, Lorenzo, 541-737-3142 lciannelli@coas.oregonstate.edu, Oregon State Univ; Og
Cicerone, Robert D., (508) 531-2713 rcicerone@bridgew.edu, Bridgewater State Univ; YsgXy
Cicha, Jarrod, 612-626-4468 cich0060@morris.umn.edu, Univ of Minnesota; Zi
Ciciarelli, John A., (412) 773-3867 jac7@psu.edu, Pennsylvania State Univ, Monaca; Gg
Cicimurri, Christian M., (864)656-4602 cmcici@clemson.edu, Clemson Univ; Pv
Cicimurri, David J., (864) 656-4601 dcheech@clemson.edu, Clemson Univ; Pv
Ciesla, Fred, (773) 702-8169 Univ of Chicago; Xcg
Cigolini, Corrado, corrado.cigolini@unito.it, Univ di Torino; Gv
Cihacek, Larry J., (701) 231-8572 North Dakota State Univ; Zg
Cilliers, Johannes, +44 20 759 47360 j.j.cilliers@imperial.ac.uk, Imperial Coll; Gz
Cintra-Buenrostro, Carlos, 956 882-5746 carlos.cntra@utrgv.edu, Univ of Texas, Rio Grande Valley; PiCsPe
Ciolkosz, Edward J., (814) 865-1530 f8i@psu.edu, Pennsylvania State Univ, Univ Park; Sd
Cioppa, Maria T., 519-253-3000 ext. 2502 mcioppa@uwindsor.ca, Univ of Windsor; Ym
Cipar, John J., 617-552-8300 cipar@bc.edu, Boston Coll; Ys
Cirimpei, Claudia, (023) 220-1496 claudia.cirimpei@yahoo.com, Alexandru Ioan Cuza; PgGr
Cirmo, Christopher P., (607) 753-2924 cirmoc@cortland.edu, SUNY, Cortland; Hg
Cisne, John L., john.cisne@cornell.edu, Cornell Univ; PgsPe
Civan, Faruk, (405) 325-6778 fcivan@ou.edu, Univ of Oklahoma; Np
Claassen, Mark, (785) 532-6101 mclaasse@ksu.edu, Kansas State Univ; So
Claassen, Victor P., vpclaassen@ucdavis.edu, Univ of California, Davis; So
Clabo, Darren R., 605-394-1996 darren.clabo@sdsmt.edu, South Dakota Sch of Mines & Tech; AssAs
Cladouhos, Trenton, 206 729-2400 ttcladouhos@gmail.com, Univ of Washington; Gcg
Claerbout, Jon F., (650) 723-3717 Stanford Univ; Ye
Claeys, Philippe, (322) 629-3391 phclaeys@vub.be, Vrije Univ Brussel; CgaXc
Clague, John J., (778) 782-4657 Simon Fraser Univ; Gl
Claiborne, Lily L., (615) 343-4515 lily.claiborne@vanderbilt.edu, Vanderbilt Univ; GivCg
Claire, Mark, +44 01334 463688 mc229@st-andrews.ac.uk, Univ of St. Andrews; As
Clarey, Timothy L., (989) 686-9252 tlclarey@delta.edu, Delta Coll; HwGcPv
Clark, Alan H., (613) 533-6187 Queen's Univ; Em
Clark, David L., (505) 665-0005 Los Alamos; Zn
Clark, Donald, (801) 537-3344 donclark@utah.gov, Utah Geological Survey; Gg
Clark, Douglas H., (360) 650-7939 doug.clark@wwu.edu, Western Washington Univ; Gl
Clark, George S., (204) 474-7343 gs_clark@umanitoba.ca, Univ of Manitoba; Cc
Clark, H. C., (713) 527-4887 hcclark@owlnet.rice.edu, Rice Univ; YgGeYu
Clark, Ian D., idclark@uottawa.ca, Univ of Ottawa; HwGel
Clark, James A., james.clark@wheaton.edu, Wheaton Coll; GmYgZi
Clark, Jeffrey J., (920) 832-6733 Lawrence Univ; Gm
Clark, Jessie , (775) 784-6345 jessieclark@unr.edu, Univ of Nevada, Reno; Zu
Clark, Joanna, j.m.clark@reading.ac.uk, Univ of Reading; Sc
Clark, John H., 814-863-1581 clark@ems.psu.edu, Pennsylvania State Univ, Univ Park; Am
Clark, Jordan F., (805) 893-7838 jfclark@geol.ucsb.edu, Univ of California, Santa Barbara; ClHg
Clark, Joseph C., (724) 357 5622 Indiana Univ of Pennsylvania; Gr
Clark, Kathryne, kathryne.clark@dnr.iowa.gov, Iowa Dept of Natural Resources; GgZi
Clark, Ken P., (253) 879-3138 kclark@pugetsound.edu, Univ of Puget Sound; GgcGi
Clark, Kenneth F., 915-581-8371 clark@utep.edu, Univ of Texas, El Paso; Eg
Clark, Marin, 734-615-0484 marinkc@umich.edu, Univ of Michigan; Gm
Clark, Mark W., (352) 392-1803 (Ext. 316) clarkmw@ufl.edu, Univ of Florida; Sf
Clark, Martin D., 051 401 3892 Univ of the Free State; ZriGc
Clark, Melissa, (812) 855-4556 Indiana Univ, Bloomington; SfZg
Clark, Michael, (403) 440-8944 mdclark@mtroyal.ca, Mount Royal Univ; Zg
Clark, Murlene W., 251-460-6381 mclark@southalabama.edu, Univ of South Alabama; PiGrg
Clark, Peter U., (541) 737-1247 clarkp@geo.oregonstate.edu, Oregon State Univ; Gl
Clark, Richard D., 717-872-3930 richard.clark@millersville.edu, Millersville Univ; As
Clark, Robert A., (520) 621-3842 clark@hwr.arizona.edu, Univ of Arizona; Hs
Clark, Roger A., +44(0) 113 34 35221 r.a.clark@leeds.ac.uk, Univ of Leeds; YseYs
Clark, Russell G., (517) 629-0312 rgclark@albion.edu, Albion Coll; GiZi
Clark, Scott K., (715) 836-2958 clarksco@uwec.edu, Univ of Wisconsin, Eau Claire; Ze
Clark, Shannon, (505) 277-1644 skclark@unm.edu, Univ of New Mexico; Zn
Clarke, Amanda, 480-965-6590 amanda.clarke@asu.edu, Arizona State Univ; Gv
Clarke, Antony D., (808) 956-6215 tclarke@soest.hawaii.edu, Univ of Hawai'i, Manoa; As
Clarke, Beverley, beverley.clarke@flinders.edu.au, Flinders Univ; Zy
Clarke, Garry K. C., (604) 822-3602 gclarke@eos.ubc.ca, Univ of British Columbia; Yg
Clarke, Geoffrey L., +61293512919 geoffrey.clarke@usyd.edu.au, Univ of Sydney; Gp
Clarke, Julia A., (512) 232-7563 julia_clarke@jsg.utexas.edu, Univ of Texas, Austin; PvgPq
Clarke, Peter J., +44 (0) 191 208 6351 peter.clarke@ncl.ac.uk, Univ of Newcastle Upon Tyne; YdZri
Clarke, Stu, (+44) 01782 733171 s.m.clarke@keele.ac.uk, Keele Univ; GsoGd
Clarkson, Christopher , 403 220-6445 clarksoc@ucalgary.ca, Univ of Calgary; Eo
Clary, Renee M., (662) 268-1032 x215 rclary@geosci.msstate.edu, Mississippi State Univ; ZePgGe
Class, Connie, class@ldeo.columbia.edu, Columbia Univ; Cg
Clausen, Benjamin L., (909) 558-4548 bclausen@llu.edu, Loma Linda Univ; GiCtYg
Clay, Patricia L., +44 0161 275-0407 patricia.clay@manchester.ac.uk, Univ of Manchester; CgaGg
Clay, Robert, 573/368-2177 bob.clay@dnr.mo.gov, Missouri Dept of Natural Resources; Zn
Clayton, Lee, (608) 263-6839 lclayton@wisc.edu, Univ of Wisconsin, Extension; Gl
Clayton, Robert N., (773) 702-7777 Univ of Chicago; Cs
Clayton, Rodney L., 757-822-7089 rclayton@tcc.edu, Tidewater Comm Coll; GgOg
Cleary, William J., 910-962-2320 clearyw@uncw.edu, Univ of North Carolina, Wilmington; Gu
Cleaveland, Malcolm K., (479) 575-3355 mcleavel@uark.edu, Univ of Arkansas, Fayetteville; PcZc
Clebnik, Sherman M., (860) 465-4323 clebniks@easternct.edu, Eastern Connecticut State Univ; Gl
Clegg, Simon, +44 (0)1603 59 3185 s.clegg@uea.ac.uk, Univ of East Anglia; AsOcCg
Clemens, Steven C., (401) 863-1964 steven_clemens@brown.edu, Brown Univ; Ou
Clemens, William A., (510) 642-6675 Univ of California, Berkeley; Pv
Clemens-Knott, Diane, (657) 278-2369 dclemensknott@fullerton.edu, California State Univ, Fullerton; Gig
Clement, William P., (413) 545-5910 wclement@geo.umass.edu, Univ of Massachusetts, Amherst; Yue
Clementz, Mark T., (307) 766-6048 mclement1@uwyo.edu, Univ of Wyoming; Pg
Clemitshaw, Kevin C., +44 1784 414026 k.clemitshaw@rhul.ac.uk, Royal Holloway Univ of London; AsZg
Clendenin, Jr., Charles W., (803) 896-7702 clendeninb@dnr.sc.gov, South Carolina Dept of Natural Resources; Eg
Clendening, Ronald J., (615) 532-1504 ron.clendening@tn.gov, Tennessee Geological Survey; GgcGm
Clennan, Patrick D., 702-651-7501 patrick.clennan@csn.edu, Coll of Southern Nevada - West Charleston Campus; ZyGe
Clepper, Marta L., 607-436-3736 marta.clepper@oneonta.edu, SUNY, Oneonta; ZeGgs
Cleveland, Natasha, 301-846-2563 ncleveland@frederick.edu, Frederick Comm Coll; Zge
Clift, Peter, 225-578-2153 pclift@lsu.edu, Louisiana State Univ; GsuGo
Clift, Sigrid, 512-471-0320 sigrid.clift@beg.utexas.edu, Univ of Texas, Austin; Zg

Cline, Jean S., (702) 575-9968 jean.cline@unlv.edu, Univ of Nevada, Las Vegas; EmCe

Cloos, Mark P., (512) 471-4170 cloos@jsg.utexas.edu, Univ of Texas, Austin; Gcx

Closs, L. Graham, (303) 273-3856 lcloss@mines.edu, Colorado Sch of Mines; Ce

Clothiaux, Eugene E., 814-865-2915 eec3@psu.edu, Pennsylvania State Univ, Univ Park; Am

Clough, Gene A., (207) 786-6396 gclough@bates.edu, Bates Coll; Ym

Cloutier, Danielle, (418) 656-7679 danielle.cloutier@ggl.ulaval.ca, Universite Laval; GeOg

Cloutis, Ed, 204-786-9386 e.cloutis@uwinnipeg.ca, Western Univ; Zi

Clowes, Ronald M., (604) 822-4138 clowes@eos.ubc.ca, Univ of British Columbia; Ys

Clyde, William C., 603-862-3148 will.clyde@unh.edu, Univ of New Hampshire; PgYmGs

Cnudde, Veerle, veerle.cnudde@ugent.be, Ghent Univ; EsHt

Coakley, Bernard, 907-474-5385 bernard.coakley@gi.alaska.edu, Univ of Alaska, Fairbanks; Yg

Coale, Kenneth H., (831) 771-4400 coale@mlml.calstate.edu, Moss Landing Marine Lab; CtcOc

Coats, Sloan, scoats@hawaii.edu, Univ of Hawai'i, Manoa; Zo

Cobb, Kim M., (404) 894-3895 kcobb@eas.gatech.edu, Georgia Inst of Tech; PeCsOg

Cobb, Steven R., 806-834-1395 steve.cobb@ttu.edu, Texas Tech Univ; As

Coble, Paula G., (727) 553-1631 pcoble@marine.usf.edu, Univ of South Florida; Cm

Coburn, Craig, (403) 317-2818 craig.coburn@uleth.ca, Univ of Lethbridge; Zy

Coburn, Daniel, 203-392-5835 coburnd1@southernct.edu, Southern Connecticut State Univ; Ze

Coch, Nicholas K., (718) 997-3326 nicholas.coch@qc.cuny.edu, Queens Coll (CUNY); GseOu

Cochran, David, 601-266-6014 david.cochran@usm.edu, Univ of Southern Mississippi; Zn

Cochran, Elizabeth, cochran@ucr.edu, Univ of California, Riverside; Ys

Cochran, J. K., (631) 632-8746 kcochran@notes.cc.sunysb.edu, Stony Brook Univ; Oc

Cochran, J. Kirk, (631) 632-8733 kirk.cochran@stonybrook.edu, SUNY, Stony Brook; Oc

Cochran, James R., jrc@ldeo.columbia.edu, Columbia Univ; Yr

Cochrane, Claudia, ccochra3@uwo.ca, Western Univ; Go

Codrea, Vlad, +40-264-405300 ext 5205 vcodrea@bioge.ubbcluj.ro, Babes-Bolyai Univ; PvGo

Cody, Anita M., amcody@iastate.edu, Iowa State Univ of Sci & Tech; Cl

Cody, George D., 202-478-8980 gcody@carnegiescience.edu, Carnegie Inst for Sci; Co

Cody, Robert, rdcody@iastate.edu, Iowa State Univ of Sci & Tech; Gz

Coe, Angela L., angela.coe@open.ac.uk, Open Univ; GsrCg

Coe, Douglas A., (406) 496-4207 dcoe@mtech.edu, Montana Tech of the Univ of Montana; Cg

Coe, Hue, +44 0161 306-9362 hugh.coe@manchester.ac.uk, Univ of Manchester; As

Coe, Robert S., (831) 459-2393 rcoe@pmc.ucsc.edu, Univ of California, Santa Cruz; Ym

Coetzee, Serena, +27 (0)12 420 3823 serena.coetzee@up.ac.za, Univ of Pretoria; Zi

Coffin, Richard, 361-825-2814 richard.coffin@tamucc.edu, Texas A&M Univ, Corpus Christi; Ouc

Coffman, David, david.coffman@dcccd.edu, El Centro Coll - Dallas Comm Coll District; Gg

Coffman, Stephanie, svcoffman@dcccd.edu, El Centro Coll - Dallas Comm Coll District; Gg

Coffroth, Mary Alice, 716-645-4871 coffroth@buffalo.edu, SUNY, Buffalo; Gu

Coggan, John, +44 01326 371824 j.coggan@exeter.ac.uk, Exeter Univ; Nx

Coggon, Jude A., +44 (0)23 80596539 jude.coggon@soton.ac.uk, Univ of Southampton; Cg

Coggon, Rosalind M., 023 80596539 r.m.coggon@soton.ac.uk, Univ of Southampton; Ce

Cohen, Alice, 902-585-1126 alice.cohen@acadiau.ca, Acadia Univ; ZnnZn

Cohen, Andrew S., (520) 621-4691 cohen@email.arizona.edu, Univ of Arizona; Ps

Cohen, Anne L., (508) 289-2958 acohen@whoi.edu, Woods Hole Oceanographic Inst; PecOo

Cohen, Anthony, anthony.cohen@open.ac.uk, Open Univ; Cs

Cohen, David R., 612 9385 8084 d.cohen@unsw.edu.au, Univ of New South Wales; Cet

Cohen, Joel E., (212) 327-8883 cohen@rockvax.rockefeller.edu, Columbia Univ; Zn

Cohen, Matt, (864) 294 - 2505 matthew.cohen@furman.edu, Furman Univ; Zn

Cohen, Phoebe A., 413-597-2358 phoebe.a.cohen@williams.edu, Williams Coll; Pgg

Cohen, Ronald E., 202-478-8937 rcohen@carnegiescience.edu, Carnegie Inst for Sci; Gy

Cohen, Shaul, (541) 346-4500 scohen@uoregon.edu, Univ of Oregon; Zn

Coker, Victoria, +44 0161 275-3803 vicky.coker@manchester.ac.uk, Univ of Manchester; Gz

Colak Erol, Serap, 00904242370000-5995 serapcolak@firat.edu.tr, Firat Univ; GgcGt

Colburn, Ivan P., (323) 343-2413 California State Univ, Los Angeles; Gs

Colby, Bonnie C., (520) 621-4775 bcolby@email.arizona.edu, Univ of Arizona; Zn

Colby, Frank P., (978) 934-3906 frank_colby@uml.edu, Univ of Massachusetts, Lowell; Am

Colby, Jeff, (828) 262-7126 colbyj@appstate.edu, Appalachian State Univ; Zi

Colby, Sarah, (928) 523-4561 Northern Arizona Univ; Zn

Cole, Catherine, +44 01334 464018 csc5@st-andrews.ac.uk, Univ of St. Andrews; Cm

Cole, David R., (614) 688-7407 cole.618@osu.edu, Ohio State Univ; CgsZa

Cole, Dean A., (505) 665-0832 Los Alamos; Co

Cole, Gregory L., (505) 667-1858 gcole@lanl.gov, Los Alamos; Zg

Cole, James W., (03) 3642-766 jim.cole@canterbury.ac.nz, Univ of Canterbury; Gv

Cole, Julia E., (520) 626-2341 jecole@email.arizona.edu, Univ of Arizona; PeCsAs

Cole, Kevin C., 616-331-3791 colek@gvsu.edu, Grand Valley State Univ; Gz

Cole, Paul D., +44 1752 585985 paul.cole@plymouth.ac.uk, Univ of Plymouth; Gvg

Cole, Rex D., (970) 248-1599 rcole@coloradomesa.edu, Colorado Mesa Univ; GsrGo

Cole, Rick, (727) 553-1522 rickcole@rdsea.com, Univ of South Florida; Op

Cole, Ron B., (814) 332-3393 rcole@allegheny.edu, Allegheny Coll; Gt

Colegial Gutierrez, Juan D., (316) 237-2685 colegial@uis.edu.co, Univ Industrial de Santander; GeNgZr

Coleman, Alvin L., (910) 362-7365 acoleman@cfcc.edu, Cape Fear Comm Coll; Gg

Coleman, Catherine, cady-coleman@asu.edu, Arizona State Univ; Ze

Coleman, Drew S., 919-962-0705 dcoleman@email.unc.edu, Univ of North Carolina, Chapel Hill; CcGit

Coleman, Robert G., (650) 723-9205 coleman@pangea.stanford.edu, Stanford Univ; Gi

Coleman, Tommy L., (205) 851-5462 tcoleman@aamu.edu, Alabama A&M Univ; So

Coleman, Jr., Paul J., (310) 825-1776 Univ of California, Los Angeles; Gc

Coles, Kenneth S., (724) 357-5626 kcoles@iup.edu, Indiana Univ of Pennsylvania; XgZeYg

Colgan, Mitchell W., (843) 953-7171 colganm@cofc.edu, Coll of Charleston; PeGe

Colgan, Patrick M., (616) 313-3201 colganp@gvsu.edu, Grand Valley State Univ; GmlPe

Colgan, William, (416)736-2100 #77703 colgan@yorku.ca, York Univ; Yg

Colin, Farquharson, 709 864 6890 cgfarquh@mun.ca, Memorial Univ of Newfoundland; Yg

Colle, Brian, (631) 632-3174 brian.colle@stonybrook.edu, SUNY, Stony Brook; As

Collett, Jr., Jeffrey L., collett@atmos.colostate.edu, Colorado State Univ; As

Collette, Joseph, 701-858-4142 joseph.collette@minotstateu.edu, Minot State Univ; PgGsr

Collie, Jeremy S., (401) 874-6859 jcollie@gso.uri.edu, Univ of Rhode Island; Ob

Collier, Jackie, (631) 632-8696 jackie.collier@stonybrook.edu, SUNY, Stony Brook; Ob

Collier, James D., (970) 247-7129 collier_j@fortlewis.edu, Fort Lewis Coll; Cg

Collier, Jenny, +44 20 759 46547 r.coggon@imperial.ac.uk, Imperial Coll; Yr

Collier, Mark, 217-300-1171 mcollier@illinois.edu, Illinois State Geological Survey; Ge

Collins, Brian, 206-685-1910 bcollins@uw.edu, Univ of Washington; Gm

Collins, Chris, c.d.collins@reading.ac.uk, Univ of Reading; Sc

Collins, Curtis A., (831) 656-3271 collins@nps.edu, Naval Postgraduate Sch; Op

Collins, Damian, 780-492-3197 damian.collins@ualberta.ca, Univ of Alberta; Zn

Collins, Edward W., (512) 471-6247 eddie.collins@beg.utexas.edu, Univ of Texas at Austin, Jackson Sch of Geosciences; Ge

Collins, Gareth, +44 20 759 41518 g.collins@imperial.ac.uk, Imperial Coll;

Xm
Collins, Jennifer, collinsjm@usf.edu, Univ of South Florida; As
Collins, Joe D., (615) 898-2376 joe.collins@mtsu.edu, Middle Tennessee State Univ; Gms
Collins, John A., (508) 289-2733 jcollins@whoi.edu, Woods Hole Oceanographic Inst; Ys
Collins, Kenneth, +44 (0)23 8059 6010 kjc@noc.soton.ac.uk, Univ of Southampton; Ob
Collins, Laura R., (615) 494-8635 laura.collins@mtsu.edu, Middle Tennessee State Univ; Gg
Collins, Laurel S., (305) 348-1732 collinsl@fiu.edu, Florida International Univ; Pg
Collins, Lisa J., (847) 491-3238 earth@northwestern.edu, Northwestern Univ; ZnnZn
Collins, Lorence G., lorencec@sysmatrix.net, California State Univ, Northridge; Gzx
Collins, Mary E., (352) 392-1951 mec@ufl.edu, Univ of Florida; Sd
Collins, Murray, murray.collins@ed.ac.uk, Edinburgh Univ; Zi
Collins, William D., (510) 495-2407 wdcollins@berkeley.edu, Univ of California, Berkeley; As
Collinson, James W., collinson.1@osu.edu, Ohio State Univ; PgGsg
Collinson, Margaret, +44 1784 443607 m.collinson@rhul.ac.uk, Royal Holloway Univ of London; Pg
Collis, Scott, 630-252-0550 scollis@anl.gov, Argonne; As
Colman, Bradley R., brad.colman@noaa.gov, Univ of Washington; As
Colosimo, Amanda, (585) 292-2421 acolosimo@monroecc.edu, Monroe Comm Coll; Gg
Coltorti, Mauro, +390577233814 mauro.coltorti@unisi.it, Univ of Siena; GmYg
Colucci, Stephen J., (607) 255-1752 sjc25@cornell.edu, Cornell Univ; As
Colwell, Frederick (Rick), (541) 737-5220 rcolwell@coas.oregonstate.edu, Oregon State Univ; Zn
Comas, María José, mjcomas@ucm.es, Univ Complutense de Madrid; Pi
Comas, Xavier, 561 297-3256 xcomas@fau.edu, Florida Atlantic Univ; Yg
Comerford, Nicholas B., (850) 875-7100 nbc@ufl.edu, Univ of Florida; Sf
Comina, Cesare, cesare.comina@unito.it, Univ di Torino; Yx
Commane, Roisin, rcommane@ldeo.columbia.edu, Columbia Univ; Yr
Compagnoni, Roberto, roberto.compagnoni@unito.it, Univ di Torino; Gx
Compas, Eric, compase@uww.edu, Univ of Wisconsin, Whitewater; ZiRw
Compton, John, (021) 650-2927 john.compton@uct.ac.za, Univ of Cape Town; CmGa
Comrie, Andrew, (520) 621-1585 comrie@email.arizona.edu, Univ of Arizona; Zy
Conder, James A., (618) 453-7352 conder@geo.siu.edu, Southern Illinois Univ Carbondale; Ysr
Condie, Kent C., (575) 835-5531 kcondie@nmt.edu, New Mexico Inst of Mining and Tech; Ct
Condit, Christopher D., (413) 545-0272 ccondit@geo.umass.edu, Univ of Massachusetts, Amherst; Gi
Condreay, Denise, 402-562-1216 dcondreay@cccneb.edu, Central Comm Coll; Zg
Confer, John, 724-938-4211 confer@calu.edu, California Univ of Pennsylvania; Zn
Congalton, Russell, russ.congalton@unh.edu, Univ of New Hampshire; Zi
Congleton, John D., (678) 839-4066 jconglet@westga.edu, Univ of West Georgia; GeZiHs
Conkle, Jeremy, 361-825-2682 jeremy.conkle@tamucc.edu, Texas A&M Univ, Corpus Christi; Zn
Conley, Catharine A., 202-358-3912 cassie.conley@nasa.gov, New Mexico Inst of Mining and Tech; Pg
Conly, Andrew G., (807) 343-8463 andrew.conly@lakeheadu.ca, Lakehead Univ; EgCgGz
Connallon, Christopher B., (410) 554 5545 christopher.connallon@maryland.gov, Maryland Department of Natural Resources; GmZi
Connelly, Jeffrey B., (501) 569-3546 jbconnelly@ualr.edu, Univ of Arkansas at Little Rock; GcNg
Connely, Melissa, 307-268-2017 mconnely@caspercollege.edu, Casper Coll; GsPev
Connolly, Cynthia, 575-835-5264 cynthia.connolly@nmt.edu, New Mexico Inst of Mining and Tech; Ze
Connolly, Paul, paul.connolly@manchester.ac.uk, Univ of Manchester; As
Connor, Charles B., cconnor@cas.usf.edu, Univ of South Florida; Gv
Connor, Laura, lconnor@usf.edu, Univ of South Florida; Zf
Connors, Christopher, (540) 458-8514 connorsc@wlu.edu, Washington & Lee Univ; GcYeGo
Conover, David O., david.conover@stonybrook.edu, SUNY, Stony Brook; Ob
Conquy, Xenia, xconquy@broward.edu, Broward Coll; Gg
Conrad, Daniel, 612-626-4819 dconrad@umn.edu, Univ of Minnesota; Gl
Conrad, Susan H., 845-431- 8534 conrad@sunydutchess.edu, Dutchess Comm Coll; GsmHs
Conroy, Jessica, 217-244-4855 jconro@illinois.edu, Univ of Illinois, Urbana-Champaign; Cs
Constable, Catherine G., (858) 534-3183 cconstable@ucsd.edu, Univ of California, San Diego; Ymg
Constable, Steven C., (858) 534-2409 sconstable@ucsd.edu, Univ of California, San Diego; Yr
Constantin, Marc, (418) 656-3139 marc.constantin@ggl.ulaval.ca, Universite Laval; Gi
Constantine, Jose, constantineja@cf.ac.uk, Cardiff Univ; Hy
Constantopoulos, James T., (575) 562-2651 jim.constantopoulos@enmu.edu, Eastern New Mexico Univ; GezGx
Contosta, Alexandra, alix.contosta@unh.edu, Univ of New Hampshire; So
Contreras, Juan, juanc@cicese.mx, Centro de Investigación Científica y de Educación Superior de Ensenada; Gt
Conway, Flaxen D., (541) 737-1339 fconway@coas.oregonstate.edu, Oregon State Univ; Gu
Conway, Howard B., (206) 685-8085 hcon@uw.edu, Univ of Washington; Gl
Conway, Michael F., 520.621.2352 fmconway@email.arizona.edu, Univ of Arizona; RcGvg
Coogan, Laurence, lacoogan@uvic.ca, Univ of Victoria; Gi
Coogon, Rosalind, +44 20 759 46547 r.coggon@imperial.ac.uk, Imperial Coll; Cs
Cook, Ann, (614) 247-6085 cook.1129@osu.edu, Ohio State Univ; GuYg
Cook, David R., (630) 252-5840 drcook@anl.gov, Argonne; AmsSo
Cook, Edward R., drdendro@ldeo.columbia.edu, Columbia Univ; Hw
Cook, Frederick A., (250) 537-8892 fcook@ucalgary.ca, Univ of Calgary; YeGtYs
Cook, Hadrian, +44 020 8417 67756 h.cook@kingston.ac.uk, Kingston Univ; Ge
Cook, Jane, 814-863-8554 jbc6075@psu.edu, Pennsylvania State Univ, Univ Park; ZmeZn
Cook, Joseph P., 520-621-2470 joecook@email.arizona.edu, Univ of Arizona; Gm
Cook, Kerry H., 512-232-7931 kc@jsg.utexas.edu, Univ of Texas, Austin; AsPe
Cook, Mea S., 413-597-4541 mea.s.cook@williams.edu, Williams Coll; OuGe
Cook, Peter, peter.cook@flinders.edu.au, Flinders Univ; Hw
Cook, Robert B., cookrb@ornl.gov, Oak Ridge; Cg
Cook, Steve, (541) 737-0962 cooks@geo.oregonstate.edu, Oregon State Univ; Zn
Cook, Tim, 413-545-1831 tcook@geo.umass.edu, Univ of Massachusetts, Amherst; Pc
Cooke, David R., 61 3 6226 7605 d.cooke@utas.edu.au, Univ of Tasmania; Eg
Cooke, M. J., mary.cooke@austincc.edu, Austin Comm Coll District; GmCl
Cooke, Michele L., (413) 547-3142 cooke@geo.umass.edu, Univ of Massachusetts, Amherst; Gc
Cookus, Pam, 217-244-2486 cookus@isgs.uiuc.edu, Illinois State Geological Survey; Zn
Coolbaugh, Mark F., mfc@unr.edu, Univ of Nevada, Reno; Eg
Coombes, Peter J., peter.coombes@scu.edu.au, Southern Cross Univ; Hgs
Coombs, Douglas S., +64 3 479-7505 doug.coombs@otago.ac.nz, Univ of Otago; Gi
Coombs, Margery C., mcoombs@amherst.edu, Amherst Coll; Pv
Cooney, Michael, (808) 956-7337 mcooney@hawaii.edu, Univ of Hawai'i, Manoa; Og
Cooney, Timothy M., (319) 273-2918 timothy.cooney@uni.edu, Univ of Northern Iowa; Ze
Coonley, Steffanie, (505) 665-2330 scoonley@lanl.gov, Los Alamos; Zn
Cooper, Alan F., +64 3 479-7515 alan.cooper@stonebow.otago.ac.nz, Univ of Otago; GpiGt
Cooper, Catherine , 509-335-1501 cmcooper@wsu.edu, Washington State Univ; Yg
Cooper, Clay A., (775) 673-7372 clay.cooper@dri.edu, Univ of Nevada, Reno; HySpHq
Cooper, Jonathon L., (507) 222-4401 jlcooper@carleton.edu, Carleton Coll; Gg
Cooper, Kari M., (530) 754-8826 kmcooper@ucdavis.edu, Univ of California, Davis; Gi
Cooper, Mark, (204) 474-8075 mark_cooper@umanitoba.ca, Univ of Manitoba; Gz
Cooper, Matthew, +44 (0)23 80592062 matthew.cooper@noc.soton.ac.uk, Univ of Southampton; Oc
Cooper, Reid F., (401) 863-2160 reid_cooper@brown.edu, Brown Univ; Gy
Cooper, Roger W., (409) 880-8239 roger.cooper@lamar.edu, Lamar Univ; Gi

Cox, Randel T., (901) 678-4361 randycox@memphis.edu, Univ of Memphis; GcmGt
Cox, Richard, 902 494 3362 richard.cox@dal.ca, Dalhousie Univ; GzEdGg
Cox, Ronadh, (413) 597-2297 ronadh.cox@williams.edu, Williams Coll; GsXg
Cox, Shelah, 215 204-8227 scox@temple.edu, Temple Univ; Zn
Coxon, Catherine, + 353 1 8962235 cecoxon@tcd.ie, Trinity Coll; GeOu
Craddock, Robert A., 202-633-2473 Smithsonian Inst / Nat Air & Space Mus; Xg
Crafford, J. P., +27 (0)15 268 2217 krappie.crafford@ul.ac.za, Univ of Limpopo; ZnNgZn
Craig, Cameron D., (217) 581-2626 cdcraig@eiu.edu, Eastern Illinois Univ; ZgAm
Craig, James L., (505) 665-7996 jlcraig@lanl.gov, Los Alamos; Gg
Craig, Mitchell S., (510) 885-3425 mitchell.craig@csueastbay.edu, California State Univ, East Bay; Yg
Craig, Susanne , (902) 494-4381 susanne.craig@dal.ca, Dalhousie Univ; Op
Crail, Todd, 419-530-4583 todd.crail@utoledo.edu, Univ of Toledo; Zn
Crain, John R., (209) 730-3812 Coll of the Sequoias; Gg
Cramer, Bradley D., (319) 335-0704 bradley-cramer@uiowa.edu, Univ of Iowa; GrPsGs
Cramer, Chris, (901) 678-2007 ccramer@memphis.edu, Univ of Memphis; Ys
Cramer, Gary, (620) 662-9021 gcramer@ksu.edu, Kansas State Univ; So
Crandall, Jake R., (217) 581-6245 jrcrandall@eiu.edu, Eastern Illinois Univ; GzXgEd
Cranford, Peter, (902) 426-3277 cranfordp@mar.dfo-mpo.gc.ca, Dalhousie Univ; Ob
Cranganu, Constantin, 7189515000 x2878 cranganu@brooklyn.cuny.edu, Brooklyn Coll (CUNY); GoYhHw
Craven, John, +44 (0) 131 650 7887 john.craven@ed.ac.uk, Edinburgh Univ; Yg
Craw, Dave, +64 3 479-7529 dave.craw@otago.ac.nz, Univ of Otago; Eg
Crawford, Anthony J., tony.crawford@utas.edu.au, Univ of Tasmania; Git
Crawford, Ian, +44 020 3073 8026 i.crawford@bbk.ac.uk, Birkbeck Coll; Zn
Crawford, James, 757-864-7231 j.h.crawford@larc.nasa.gov, Georgia Inst of Tech; As
Crawford, Maria Luisa B., (610) 526-5111 mcrawfor@brynmawr.edu, Bryn Mawr Coll; GxzGp
Crawford, Nicholas, (270) 745-5889 nicholas.crawford@wku.edu, Western Kentucky Univ; Hg
Crawford, Thomas J., (678) 839-4062 Univ of West Georgia; Eg
Crawford, Vernon J., (541) 552-6479 crawford@sou.edu, Southern Oregon Univ; Gg
Creager, Kenneth C., 206-685-2803 kcc@uw.edu, Univ of Washington; Ys
Crease, James, (302) 645-4240 Univ of Delaware; Op
Creaser, Robert A., (780) 492-2942 robert.creaser@ualberta.ca, Univ of Alberta; Cc
Creasey, Robert L., 831-656-3178 creasey@nps.edu, Naval Postgraduate Sch; Am
Crepeau, Richard J., (828) 262-7052 crepeaurj@appstate.edu, Appalachian State Univ; Zn
Crespi, Jean M., (860) 486-0601 crespi@geol.uconn.edu, Univ of Connecticut; Gc
Crespo, Elena, ecrespo@ucm.es, Univ Complutense de Madrid; EnGz
Cresswell, Tim, tim.cresswell@ed.ac.uk, Edinburgh Univ; Zn
Creveling, Jessica, 541-737-2112 crevelij@oregonstate.edu, Oregon State Univ; GgsGr
Crewdson, Robert, rcrewdson1@csub.edu, California State Univ, Bakersfield; HwYgCg
Crews, Jeff, (573) 368-2356 jeff.crews@dnr.mo.gov, Missouri Dept of Natural Resources; Hy
Creyts, Timothy T., tcreyts@ldeo.columbia.edu, Columbia Univ; Gl
Cribb, Warner, (615) 898-2379 warner.cribb@mtsu.edu, Middle Tennessee State Univ; GipGz
Crider, Juliet G., 206-543-8715 criderj@uw.edu, Univ of Washington; GcmNr
Crilley, Leigh R., +44 (0)121 414 5523 l.crilley@bham.ac.uk, Univ of Birmingham; As
Criminale, Jr., William O., (206) 543-9506 Univ of Washington; Op
Crimmins, Michael A., (520) 626-4244 crimmins@email.arizona.edu, Univ of Arizona; Zc
Crippen, Robert E., (818) 354-2475 robert.e.crippen@jpl.nasa.gov, Jet Propulsion Lab; Zr
Crisp, Joy A., (818) 354-9036 Jet Propulsion Lab; Gv
Criss, Robert E., (314) 935-7441 criss@levee.wustl.edu, Washington Univ in St. Louis; Cs
Criswell, James, (910) 392-7536 jcriswell@cfcc.edu, Cape Fear Comm Coll; Gg
Crockett, Joan E., (217) 244-2388 crockett@illinois.edu, Illinois State Geological Survey; EoZg
Croft, Gary M., gcroft@valleycollege.edu, San Bernardino Valley Coll; Zy
Croft, Paul J., (908) 737-3737 pcroft@kean.edu, Kean Univ; AmsZe
Croll, Don, (831) 459-3610 dcroll@cats.ucsc.edu, Univ of California, Santa Cruz; Ob
Cromar, Nancy, nancy.cromar@flinders.edu.au, Flinders Univ; Zn
Cron, Mitch, mitch.cron@gmail.com, Drexel Univ; Gge
Crone, Timothy, tjc@ldeo.columbia.edu, Columbia Univ; Gu
Cronin, Meghan F., (206) 526-6449 meghan.f.cronin@noaa.gov, Univ of Washington; Op
Cronin, Timothy W., twcronin@mit.edu, Massachusetts Inst of Tech; As
Cronin, Vincent S., (254) 710-2174 vince_cronin@baylor.edu, Baylor Univ; GctNg
Cronoble, James M., (303) 556-3070 Metropolitan State Coll of Denver; Gg
Croot, Peter, + 353 (0)91 492 194 peter.croot@nuigalway.ie, Nat Univ of Ireland Galway; Ct
Crootof, Arica, 406-683-7075 arica.crootof@umwestern.edu, Univ of Montana Western; RwcZi
Crosby, Benjamin T., (208) 282-2949 crosby@isu.edu, Idaho State Univ; GmHsRn
Cross, John A., (920) 424-4105 cross@uwosh.edu, Univ of Wisconsin Oshkosh; ZyAst
Crossen, Kristine J., (907) 786-6838 kjcrossen@uaa.alaska.edu, Univ of Alaska, Anchorage; Gl
Crossey, Laura J., (505) 277-4204 lcrossey@unm.edu, Univ of New Mexico; Cl
Crossley, David J., (314) 977-3153 david.crossley@slu.edu, Saint Louis Univ; YdsXy
Crosson, Robert S., crosson@uw.edu, Univ of Washington; YsGct
Crouse, David A., (919) 515-7302 North Carolina State Univ; Sc
Crowder, Margaret, (270) 745-5973 margaret.crowder@wku.edu, Western Kentucky Univ; Ze
Crowe, Bruce M., (702) 794-7206 bmc@lanl.gov, Los Alamos; Gv
Crowe, Douglas E., 706-542-2382 crowe@gly.uga.edu, Univ of Georgia; Em
Crowley, Brooke E., (513) 556-7181 brooke.crowley@uc.edu, Univ of Cincinnati; CsPev
Crowley, Jim, jimcrowley@boisestate.edu, Boise State Univ; Ccg
Crowley, Kate, kate.crowley@ed.ac.uk, Edinburgh Univ; Zc
Crowley, Peter D., (413) 542-2715 pdcrowley@amherst.edu, Amherst Coll; Gc
Crowley, Quentin G., + 353 1 8962403 crowleyq@tcd.ie, Trinity Coll; Cc
Crowley, Stephen, +44 0151 794 5163 sfcrow@liverpool.ac.uk, Univ of Liverpool; Gs
Crowther, Sarah, +44 0161 275-0407 sarah.crowther@manchester.ac.uk, Univ of Manchester; As
Croxen III, Fred W., 928-344-7586 fred.croxen@azwestern.edu, Arizona Western Coll; HwPvZi
Crozier, Carl, (919) 793-4428 North Carolina State Univ; Sb
Cruden, David M., (780) 492-3085 dave.cruden@ualberta.ca, Univ of Alberta; Nr
Cruikshank, Kenneth M., (503) 725-3383 cruikshankk@pdx.edu, Portland State Univ; Gc
Crumbly, Isaac J., (912) 825-6454 Fort Valley State Univ; Zn
Cruse, Richard M., (515) 294-7850 rmc@iastate.edu, Iowa State Univ of Sci & Tech; So
Crutzen, Paul, pcrutzen@ucsd.edu, Univ of California, San Diego; Oc
Cruz-Uribe, Alicia M., (207) 581-4494 alicia.cruzuribe@maine.edu, Univ of Maine; GpCpt
Cruzen, Shawn, 706-649-1785 cruzen_shawn@columbusstate.edu, Columbus State Univ; Xa
Csank, Adam, 775-784-6663 acsank@unr.edu, Univ of Nevada, Reno; Zy
Csatho, Beata M., (716) 645-4325 bcsatho@buffalo.edu, SUNY, Buffalo; GlZrYg
Csiki, Shane, (603) 271-2876 shane.csiki@des.nh.gov, New Hampshire Geological Survey; ZyGm
Cuevas, Julia, julia.cuevas@ehu.eus, Univ of the Basque Country UPV/EHU; GctGg
Cuffey, Roger J., (814) 865-1293 rcuffey@psu.edu, Pennsylvania State Univ, Univ Park; PiePv
Cuker, Benjamin E., (757) 727-5783 benjamin.cuker@hamptonu.edu, Hampton Univ; Ob
Cull-Hearth, Selby, scull@brynmawr.edu, Bryn Mawr Coll; XgGzx
Cullen, Cheila, 718-289-5558 cheila.cullen@bcc.cuny.edu, Graduate Sch of the City Univ of New York; Rn
Cullen, Heidi, hcullen@weather.com, Georgia Inst of Tech; Am
Cullen, James L., jcullen@salemstate.edu, Salem State Univ; GsPmOu
Cullen, Jay, 250-721-6120 jcullen@uvic.ca, Univ of Victoria; Oc

D

Daoust, Mario, 417-836-5301 mariodaoust@missouristate.edu, Missouri State Univ; AtZy
Daramola, Sunday O., +2348060256588 sunday.daramola@gmail.com, Federal Univ of Tech, Akure; GeNtHw
Darby, Dennis A., (757) 683-4701 ddarby@odu.edu, Old Dominion Univ; Ou
Darby, Jeannie, (916) 752-5670 Univ of California, Davis; Hg
Darbyshire, Fiona Ann, 514-987-3000 #5054 darbyshire.fiona_ann@uqam.ca, Universite du Quebec a Montreal; Ys
Darin, Mike, (775) 682-8751 mdarin@unr.edu, Univ of Nevada, Reno; Gct
Darling, James, +44 023 92 842247 james.darling@port.ac.uk, Univ of Portsmouth; Cs
Darling, Robert S., (607) 753-2923 darlingr@cortland.edu, SUNY, Cortland; GzpCp
Darmody, Robert G., (217) 333-9489 Univ of Illinois, Urbana-Champaign; Sd
Darnajoux, Romain, 609-258-4101 romaind@princeton.edu, Princeton Univ; Cb
Darold, Amberlee, 405/325-8611 amberlee.p.darold-1@ou.edu, Univ of Oklahoma; Ys
Daroub, Samira H., (561) 993-1500 sdaroub@ufl.edu, Univ of Florida; So
Darrah, Thomas, (614) 688-2132 darrah.24@osu.edu, Ohio State Univ; Cg
Darrell, James H., (912) 478-5361 jdarrell@georgiasouthern.edu, Georgia Southern Univ; Pl
Darroch, Simon A., simon.a.darroch@vanderbilt.edu, Vanderbilt Univ; PgiPe
Das, Indrani, indrani@ldeo.columbia.edu, Columbia Univ; Gu
Das, Sarah B., 508-289-2464 sdas@whoi.edu, Woods Hole Oceanographic Inst; GlAtZg
Dasgupta, Rajdeep, 713.348.2664 rajdeep.dasgupta@rice.edu, Rice Univ; GxCg
Dash, Padmanava, 662-325-3915 pd175@msstate.edu, Mississippi State Univ; ZrHg
Dash, Zora V., (505) 667-1923 zvd@lanl.gov, Los Alamos; Zn
Dasvarma, Gour, gour.dasvarma@flinders.edu.au, Flinders Univ; Zn
Datta, Saugata, (785) 532-2241 sdatta@ksu.edu, Kansas State Univ; ClHwGe
Daugherty, Carolyn M., carolyn.daugherty@nau.edu, Northern Arizona Univ; Zn
Daugherty, LeRoy A., (505) 646-3406 New Mexico State Univ, Las Cruces; Sd
Dauphas, Nicolas, (773) 702-2930 Univ of Chicago; Xc
Davatzes, Alexandra K., (215) 204-3907 alix@temple.edu, Temple Univ; GsXgZe
Davatzes, Nicholas, (215) 204-2837 davatzes@temple.edu, Temple Univ; GcNrZn
Davenport, Joan R., (509) 786-9384 jdavenp@tricity.wsu.edu, Washington State Univ; Sb
Davey, Patricia M., 863-2449 patricia_davey@brown.edu, Brown Univ; Zn
David, Mark B., (217) 333-4308 dmnicol@illinois.edu, Univ of Illinois, Urbana-Champaign; Sf
Davidson, Cameron, (507) 222-7144 cdavidso@carleton.edu, Carleton Coll; GptCc
Davidson, Fiona M., (479) 575-3879 fdavidso@comp.uark.edu, Univ of Arkansas, Fayetteville; Zy
Davidson, Garry J., 61 3 6226 2815 garry.davidson@utas.edu.au, Univ of Tasmania; Cs
Davidson, Gregg R., (662) 915-5824 davidson@olemiss.edu, Univ of Mississippi; Hw
Davidson, Kenneth L., 831-656-2309 kldavids@nps.edu, Naval Postgraduate Sch; Am
Davie, Colin, +44 (0) 191 208 6458 colin.davie@ncl.ac.uk, Univ of Newcastle Upon Tyne; Ngr
Davies, Andrew J., andrew.j.davies@bangor.ac.uk, Bangor Univ; ObZir
Davies, Caroline P., daviesc@umkc.edu, Univ of Missouri, Kansas City; GnZce
Davies, David, +44 (0) 131 451 3569 d.davies@hw.ac.uk, Heriot-Watt Univ; Ng
Davies, Gareth, +44(0)7780864555 gareth.davies@open.ac.uk, Open Univ; Ze
Davies, Gregory, 609-258-4101 gd3@princeton.edu, Princeton Univ; Yg
Davies, J H., huw@earth.cf.ac.uk, Cardiff Univ; Yg
Davies, Neil, +44 (0) 1223 333453 nsd27@cam.ac.uk, Univ of Cambridge; Gs
Davies, Rhordri, +44 20 759 45722 rhodri.davies@imperial.ac.uk, Imperial Coll; Yg
Davies, Sarah, sarah.davies@open.ac.uk, Open Univ; Ze
Davis, Andrew, (773) 702-8164 Univ of Chicago; Xc
Davis, Arden D., (605) 394-2527 arden.davis@sdsmt.edu, South Dakota Sch of Mines & Tech; HwNx
Davis, Daniel M., 631-632-8217 daniel.davis@sunysb.edu, Stony Brook Univ; Yg
Davis, David A., (775) 682-8767 ddavis@unr.edu, Univ of Nevada, Reno; Gg
Davis, Donald W., (416) 946-0365 dond@geology.utoronto.ca, Univ of Toronto; Cc
Davis, Edward B., 541-346-3461 edavis@uoregon.edu, Univ of Oregon; PvePq
Davis, Fred A., (218) 726-8331 fdavis@d.umn.edu, Univ of Minnesota Duluth; CpGi
Davis, George H., (520) 621-1856 gdavis@u.arizona.edu, Univ of Arizona; Gc
Davis, Gregory A., (213) 740-6726 gdavis@usc.edu, Univ of Southern California; GtcGe
Davis, J. Matthew, (603) 862-1718 matt.davis@unh.edu, Univ of New Hampshire; HwYh
Davis, James , jdavis@ldeo.columbia.edu, Columbia Univ; Yd
Davis, James A., (217) 581-5528 jadavis2@eiu.edu, Eastern Illinois Univ; Zg
Davis, Kenneth J., (814) 863-8601 kjd10@psu.edu, Pennsylvania State Univ, Univ Park; Am
Davis, Leslie M., ldavis1@austincc.edu, Austin Comm Coll District; Op
Davis, Owen K., (520) 621-7953 odavis@email.arizona.edu, Univ of Arizona; Pl
Davis, P. Thompson, (781) 891-3479 pdavis@bentley.edu, Bentley Univ; GlmZc
Davis, Paul M., (310) 825-1343 pdavis@epss.ucla.edu, Univ of California, Los Angeles; YsmYg
Davis, Peter B., 253-538-5770 davispb@plu.edu, Pacific Lutheran Univ; GcpGz
Davis, R. Laurence, (203) 932-7108 rldavis@newhaven.edu, Univ of New Haven; GemHg
Davis, Robert, (804) 924-0579 red3u@virginia.edu, Univ of Virginia; AsmZy
Davis, Steven J., (949) 824-1821 sjdavis@uci.edu, Univ of California, Irvine; GeCsZu
Davis, Tara, +353 21 4903696 t.davis@ucc.ie, Univ Coll Cork; Yg
Davis, Trevor J., (801) 587-9019 Univ of Utah; Zi
Davisson, M L., (925) 423-5993 davisson2@llnl.gov, Lawrence Livermore; Cg
Dawers, Nancye H., (504) 865-5198 ndawers@tulane.edu, Tulane Univ; GcoGm
Dawes, Ralph, 509-682-6754 rdawes@wvc.edu, Wenatchee Valley Coll; GgeAm
Dawsey, Cyrus B., (334) 844-3418 dawsecb@auburn.edu, Auburn Univ; Zy
Dawson, Jane P., (515) 294-6302 jpdawson@iastate.edu, Iowa State Univ of Sci & Tech; Gp
Dawson, Mary R., (412) 622-3246 dawsonm@carnegiemnh.org, Carnegie Mus of Natural History; Pv
Dawson, Sarah, (717)358-5870 sarah.dawson@fandm.edu, Franklin and Marshall Coll; Zn
Day, Brett, +44 (0)1603 59 1413 brett.day@uea.ac.uk, Univ of East Anglia; Ge
Day, Howard W., (530) 752-2882 hwday@ucdavis.edu, Univ of California, Davis; Gx
Day, James, (858) 534-5431 jmdday@ucsd.edu, Univ of California, San Diego; Cg
Day, Mackenzie, daym@epss.ucla.edu, Univ of California, Los Angeles; Ggs
Day, Rick L., (814) 863-1615 r4d@psu.edu, Pennsylvania State Univ, Univ Park; Zu
Day, Rosie, +44 (0)121 41 48096 r.j.day@bham.ac.uk, Univ of Birmingham; Zn
Day, Stephanie S., 701-231-8837 stephanie.day@ndsu.edu, North Dakota State Univ; GmZiu
Day, Steven M., (619) 594-2663 sday@mail.sdsu.edu, San Diego State Univ; Ys
Daymon, Deborah J., (505) 667-9021 deba@lanl.gov, Los Alamos; Zn
Dayton, Paul K., (858) 534-6740 pdayton@ucsd.edu, Univ of California, San Diego; Ob
De Angelis, Silvio, +44-151-794-5161 s.de-angelis@liverpool.ac.uk, Univ of Liverpool; Ys
De Batist, Marc, marc.debatist@ugent.be, Ghent Univ; GnuGs
De Beus, Barbara, (973) 655-4448 debeusb@mail.montclair.edu, Montclair State Univ; Zn
De Campos, Christina, 089/2180 4264 campos@min.uni-muenchen.de, Ludwig-Maximilians-Univ Muenchen; Gz
De Carlo, Eric H., (808) 956-5924 edecarlo@soest.hawaii.edu, Univ of Hawai'i, Manoa; Cm
De Deckker, Patrick, +61-2-6125 2070 patrick.dedeckker@anu.edu.au, Australian Nat Univ; GuPmGn
de Foy, Benjamin, (314) 977-3122 bdefoy@slu.edu, Saint Louis Univ; As

De Grave, Johan, johan.degrave@ugent.be, Ghent Univ; Cc
de Hoog, Jan C., +44 (0) 131 650 8525 ceesjan.dehoog@ed.ac.uk, Edinburgh Univ; GxzGv
de Hoop, Maarten, (765) 496-6439 mdehoop@math.purdue.edu, Purdue Univ; Gq
de Ignacio, Cristina, cris@ucm.es, Univ Complutense de Madrid; Cg
De Kemp, Eric, 613-947-3738 edekemp@nrcan.gc.ca, Univ of Ottawa; ZirZg
De Klerk, Billy, +27 (0)46-622-2312 b.deklerk@ru.ac.za, Rhodes Univ; Pg
De Kock, Walter E., (319) 266-6577 Univ of Northern Iowa; Ze
de la Horra, Raúl, rhorraba@ucm.es, Univ Complutense de Madrid; Gs
De Luca, Domenico Antonio, domenico.deluca@unito.it, Univ di Torino; Hy
de Menocal, Peter B., (845) 365-8483 peter@ldeo.columbia.edu, Columbia Univ; PeOuCg
De Paola, Nicola, nicola.de-paola@durham.ac.uk, Durham Univ; Gc
De Santo, Eilzabeth, (717) 358-4555 edesanto@fandm.edu, Franklin and Marshall Coll; Zn
De Scally, Fes, 250-807-9361 fes.descally@ubc.ca, Univ of British Columbia, Okanagan Campus; RnZyRm
de Silva, Shanika, (541) 737-1212 desilvsh@geo.oregonstate.edu, Oregon State Univ; Gv
de Stefano, Lucia, luciads@ucm.es, Univ Complutense de Madrid; Hw
de Szoeke, Simon P., 541-737-8391 sdeszoek@coas.oregonstate.edu, Oregon State Univ; OpAs
de Uña Alvarez, Elena P., 00 34 988387137 edeuna@uvigo.es, Coruna Univ; Zy
de Vernal, Anne, 514-987-3000 #8599 devernal.anne@uqam.ca, Universite du Quebec a Montreal; Pm
de Vicente, Gerardo, gdv@ucm.es, Univ Complutense de Madrid; Gt
de Wet, Carol B., 717-358-4388 cdewet@fandm.edu, Franklin and Marshall Coll; GsdGn
de Wit, Cary, (907) 474-7141 cwdewit@alaska.edu, Univ of Alaska, Fairbanks; Zg
de Wit, Julien, (617) 258-0209 jdewit@mit.edu, Massachusetts Inst of Tech; Zn
de' Michieli Vitturi, Mattia, (716) 645-3489 mattiade@buffalo.edu, SUNY, Buffalo; Gv
Deakin, Ann K., (716) 673-3303 deakin@fredonia.edu, SUNY, Fredonia; ZiGgZr
Deakin, Joann, 520-249-9042 deakinj@cochise.edu, Cochise Coll; Ggg
Deal, Richard, (814) 732-1733 rdeal@edinboro.edu, Edinboro Univ of Pennsylvania; Zi
Dealy, Mike, (316) 943-2343 mdealy@kgs.ku.edu, Univ of Kansas; Gg
Dean, Jeffrey S., (520) 621-2320 jdean@ltrr.arizona.edu, Univ of Arizona; Zn
Dean, John Mark, jmdean36@gmail.com, Univ of South Carolina; Ob
Dean, Robert, 717-245-1109 deanr@dickinson.edu, Dickinson Coll; Gi
Dean, Sarah L., 616 395 7306 deansl@hope.edu, Hope Coll; Gc
deAngelis, Marie, 718-409-7380 mdeangelis@sunymaritime.edu, SUNY, Maritime Coll; Oc
DeAngelis, Michael T., 569-3542 mtdeangelis@ualr.edu, Univ of Arkansas at Little Rock; GpCp
DeAngelo, Micheal V., (512) 232-3373 michael.deangelo@beg.utexas.edu, Univ of Texas at Austin, Jackson Sch of Geosciences; Ye
Deans, Jeremy, 601-266-4729 jeremy.deans@usm.edu, Univ of Southern Mississippi; YrGc
Dearden, Christopher, +44 0161 306-3911 christopher.dearden@manchester.ac.uk, Univ of Manchester; As
Deardorff, Nicholas, 724-357-2379 n.deardorff@iup.edu, Indiana Univ of Pennsylvania; Gv
Deaton, Tami, (940) 565-2091 tami.deaton@unt.edu, Univ of North Texas; Zn
DeBari, Susan M., (360) 650-3588 debari@wwu.edu, Western Washington Univ; GxZe
Deboo, Phili B., (901) 678-4424 pdeboo@memphis.edu, Univ of Memphis; Pg
DeCaria, Alex J., (717) 871-4739 alex.decaria@millersville.edu, Millersville Univ; As
DeCelles, Peter G., (520) 621-4910 decelles@email.arizona.edu, Univ of Arizona; GtsGc
Decker, Dave, 775.673.7353 dave.decker@dri.edu, Univ of Nevada, Reno; Hw
DeConto, Robert, (413) 545-3426 deconto@geo.umass.edu, Univ of Massachusetts, Amherst; As
DeCosmo, Janice, 206-221-6178 jdecosmo@uw.edu, Univ of Washington; AtZe
Dee, Kato , kdee@ou.edu, Univ of Oklahoma; HgCg
Dee, Seth, (775) 682-7704 sdee@unr.edu, Univ of Nevada, Reno; Gg
Dee, Sylvia G., 713.348.4889 sylvia.dee@rice.edu, Rice Univ; Zo
Deering, Chad, 906/487-1187 cddeerin@mtu.edu, Michigan Technological Univ; Ggi
DeGaetano, Arthur, (607) 255-0385 atd2@cornell.edu, Cornell Univ; As
Degryse, Patrick, patrick.degryse@ees.kuleuven.be, Katholieke Universiteit Leuven; GaCeGf
Dehler, Carol M., (435) 797-0764 carol.dehler@usu.edu, Utah State Univ; Gs
Dehne, Kevin T., (989) 686-9326 ktdehne@delta.edu, Delta Coll; Ze
Dehon, Rene, (512) 245-2170 Texas State Univ; GzxGg
Deibert, Jack, (931) 221-6318 deibertj@apsu.edu, Austin Peay State Univ; GsrGo
Deininger, Robert W., (901) 678-2177 Univ of Memphis; Gx
Deisher, Jeffrey , 740 2012765 jeffrey.deischer@dnr.state.oh.us, Ohio Dept of Natural Resources; Eo
DeJesus, Roman, 714-992-7462 rdejesus@fullcoll.edu, Fullerton Coll; Og
Deka, Jennifer, (216) 987-5827 jennifer.deka@tri-c.edu, Cuyahoga Comm Coll - Western Campus; Zg
Dekens, Petra, (415) 338-6015 dekens@sfsu.edu, San Francisco State Univ; Pe
DeKraker, Dan, (562) 860-2451 x2668 ddekraker@cerritos.edu, Cerritos Coll; ZeOpGg
dela Pierre, Francesco, francescodelapierre@unito.it, Univ di Torino; Gd
Delahunty, Tina, (570) 389-5181 tdelahun@bloomu.edu, Bloomsburg Univ; Zri
Delaney, Jeremy S., jsd@eps.rutgers.edu, Rutgers, The State Univ of New Jersey; XgmGx
Delaney, John R., 206-543-4830 jdelaney@ocean.washington.edu, Univ of Washington; GuYr
Delaney, Margaret L., (831) 459-4736 delaney@cats.ucsc.edu, Univ of California, Santa Cruz; Oc
Delano, Helen L., 717.702.2031 hdelano@pa.gov, DCNR- Pennsylvania Bureau of Geological Survey; GgmNg
DeLaune, Paul, 940-552-9941x207 pbdelaune@ag.tamu.edu, Texas A&M Univ; So
Delawder, Sandra, delawdsa@jmu.edu, James Madison Univ; Zn
Delcambre, Sharon, sharon.delcambre@pcc.edu, Portland Comm Coll - Sylvania Campus; AsOg
Delfino, Massimo, massimo.delfino@unito.it, Univ di Torino; Pg
Delgado-Argote, Luis A., ldelgado@cicese.mx, Centro de Investigación Científica y de Educación Superior de Ensenada; GitGu
DeLima, Lynn-Ann, delimal@easternct.edu, Eastern Connecticut State Univ; Zg
Deline, Brad, (678) 839-4061 bdeline@westga.edu, Univ of West Georgia; Pi
Dellapenna, Timothy M., (409) 740-4952 dellapet@tamug.tamu.edu, Texas A&M Univ; Ou
Delparte, Donna M., 208-282-4419 delparte@isu.edu, Idaho State Univ; Zir
DelSole, Timothy, (703) 993-5715 tdelsole@gmu.edu, George Mason Univ; As
Delson, Eric, (718) 960-8405 eric.delson@lehman.cuny.edu, Graduate Sch of the City Univ of New York; PvqPs
Demanet, Laurent, (617) 253-2614 laurent@math.mit.edu, Massachusetts Inst of Tech; Zn
DeMaster, David J., (919) 515-7026 david_demaster@ncsu.edu, North Carolina State Univ; OcCbc
Demchak, Jennifer, 570-662-4613 jdemchak@mansfield.edu, Mansfield Univ; Hs
deMenocal, Peter B., peter@ldeo.columbia.edu, Columbia Univ; Pe
Demers, Serge, (418) 723-1986 (Ext. 1483) Universite du Quebec a Rimouski; Ob
DeMets, D. Charles, (608) 262-8598 chuck@geology.wisc.edu, Univ of Wisconsin, Madison; Ym
Demicco, Robert V., (607) 777-2604 demicco@binghamton.edu, Binghamton Univ; Gs
Deming, Jody, jdeming@u.washington.edu, Univ of Manitoba; Zn
Demlie, Molla, (031) 260-7380 demliem@ukzn.ac.za, Univ of KwaZulu-Natal; HwGeg
Demopoulos, George, (514) 398-4755 McGill Univ; Nx
Dempsey, David P., (415) 338-7716 ddempsey@norte.sfsu.edu, San Francisco State Univ; As
Dempster, Tim, +4401413305445 tim.dempster@glasgow.ac.uk, Univ of Glasgow; Gz
Demyanov, Vasily, +44 (0) 131 451 8298 v.demyanov@hw.ac.uk, Heriot-Watt Univ; Zi
Deng, Baolin, (505) 835-5505 New Mexico Inst of Mining and Tech; Cg
Deng, Yi, 404-385-1821 yi.deng@eas.gatech.edu, Georgia Inst of Tech; AsZoAm
Deng, Youjun, 979-862-8476 yjd@tamu.edu, Texas A&M Univ; GzSc
Dengler, Lorinda, (707) 826-3115 lad1@humboldt.edu, Humboldt State Univ; Yg
Denizman, Can, (229) 333-5752 Valdosta State Univ; Hw
Denman, Kenneth L., (250) 363-8230 denmank@ec.gc.ca, Univ of Victoria;

Dieckmann, Melissa S., (859) 622-1274 melissa.dieckmann@eku.edu, Eastern Kentucky Univ; ZeCl
Diederichs, Mark, 613-533-6504 diederim@queensu.ca, Queen's Univ; Nr
Diefendorf, Aaron, (513) 556-3787 aaron.diefendorf@uc.edu, Univ of Cincinnati; Co
Diem, Jeremy E., (404) 413-5770 jdiem@gsu.edu, Georgia State Univ; At
Diemer, John A., 704-687-5994 jadiemer@email.uncc.edu, Univ of North Carolina, Charlotte; Gs
Diener, Johann, 021-650-2925 johann.diener@uct.ac.za, Univ of Cape Town; Gp
Diercks, Arne R., 662.915.2301 arne.diercks@usm.edu, Univ of Southern Mississippi; Ou
Dierssen, Heidi, 860-405-9239 heidi.dierssen@uconn.edu, Univ of Connecticut; Op
Dieterich, James H., (951) 827-2976 james.dieterich@ucr.edu, Univ of California, Riverside; Yg
Dieterle, Dwight A., (727) 553-1114 ddieterle@marine.usf.edu, Univ of South Florida; Ob
Dietl, Gregory, 607-273-6623 gpd3@cornell.edu, Paleontological Research Inst; Pg
Dietrich, William E., (510) 642-2633 bill@geomorph.berkeley.edu, Univ of California, Berkeley; Gm
Dietsch, Craig, (513) 556-2547 craig.dietsch@uc.edu, Univ of Cincinnati; Gp
Dietz, Anne D., 210-486-0470 adietz@alamo.edu, San Antonio Comm Coll; PgZg
Dietz, Richard D., (970) 351-2950 richard.dietz@unco.edu, Univ of Northern Colorado; Xg
Dietze, Michael, dietze@bu.edu, Boston Univ; SfZr
Diffendal, Jr., Robert F., 402-472-7546 rfd@unl.edu, Unversity of Nebraska, Lincoln; GrPiRh
Diggins, Thomas P., 330-941-3605 tpdiggins@ysu.edu, Youngstown State Univ; Pg
Dighe, Kalpak, (505) 665-1701 kdighe@lanl.gov, Los Alamos; Zn
Dijkstra, Arjan, +44 1752 584774 arjan.dijkstra@plymouth.ac.uk, Univ of Plymouth; Gi
Dijkstra, Semme, 603-862-0525 semmed@ccom.unh.edu, Univ of New Hampshire; Og
Dilcher, David L., 3523921721 x460 dilcher@flmnh.ufl.edu, Univ of Florida; Pb
Dilek, Yildirım, (513) 529-2212 dileky@miamioh.edu, Miami Univ; Gt
Dilles, John H., (541) 737-1245 dillesj@geo.oregonstate.edu, Oregon State Univ; Em
Dillman, Amanda, dillm004@umn.edu, Univ of Minnesota, Twin Cities; Yx
DiMarco, Steven F., (979) 862-4168 sdimarco@tamu.edu, Texas A&M Univ; OpnOg
DiMichele, William A., (202) 633-1319 Smithsonian Inst / Nat Mus of Natural History; Pb
Dimmick, Charles W., (860) 832-2936 dimmick@ccsu.edu, Central Connecticut State Univ; Ge
Dimova, Natasha T., 205-348-0256 ntdimova@ua.edu, Univ of Alabama; HwCcm
Ding, Kang, 612-626-1860 mlcd@umn.edu, Univ of Minnesota, Twin Cities; Cg
Dingman, S. Lawrence, (603) 862-1718 Univ of New Hampshire; Hq
Dingus, Delmar D., (805) 756-2753 ddingus@calpoly.edu, California Polytechnic State Univ; So
Dingwell, Donald Bruce, 089/21804136 dingwell@min.uni-muenchen.de, Ludwig-Maximilians-Univ Muenchen; Giv
Dinklage, William, 805-730-4114 wsdinklage@sbcc.edu, Santa Barbara City Coll; Gge
Dinsmoor, John C., (702) 295-6189 john_dinsmoor@lanl.gov, Los Alamos; Nm
Dintaman, Christopher, (812) 856-5654 cdintama@indiana.edu, Indiana Univ; Hw
Dinter, David A., (801) 581-7937 david.dinter@utah.edu, Univ of Utah; GtcGu
Diochon, Amanda, (807) 343-8444 adiochon@lakeheadu.ca, Lakehead Univ; Ge
DiPietro, Joseph A., (812) 465-7041 dipietro@usi.edu, Univ of Southern Indiana; GcpGm
Dipple, Gregory M., (604) 827-0653 gdipple@eoas.ubc.ca, Univ of British Columbia; Gp
Dirmeyer, Paul A., (703) 993-5363 pdirmeye@gmu.edu, George Mason Univ; As
Ditmars, John, (630) 252-5953 Argonne; Zn
Dittmer, Eric, (541) 552-6496 dittmer@sou.edu, Southern Oregon Univ; Gg
Diver, Kim, 860-685-2610 kdiver@wesleyan.edu, Wesleyan Univ; ZiyZg
Divine, Aaron, (928) 523-7835 aaron.divine@nau.edu, Northern Arizona Univ; ZnnZn
Dix, George R., (613) 520-2600 george.dix@carleton.ca, Carleton Univ; Gsd
Dix, Justin, +44 (0)23 8059 3057 j.k.dix@soton.ac.uk, Univ of Southampton; GuYuNx
Dixon, Barnali, bdixon@usf.edu, Univ of South Florida; Zi
Dixon, Clifton, 601-266-4731 c.dixon@usm.edu, Univ of Southern Mississippi; Zn
Dixon, Jean, (406) 994-3342 jean.dixon@montana.edu, Montana State Univ; GmScZg
Dixon, John C., (479) 422-2115 jcdixon@uark.edu, Univ of Arkansas, Fayetteville; GmXgSo
Dixon, Michael, (519) 824-4120 Ext.52555 dixon@ces.uoguelph.ca, Univ of Guelph; Zn
Dixon, Nick, +44(0) 113 34 34931 fuensd@leeds.ac.uk, Univ of Leeds; Zu
Dixon, P. Grady, (785) 628-4536 pgdixon@fhsu.edu, Fort Hays State Univ; AmZyAs
Dixon, Richard, (512) 245-2170 Texas State Univ; AsOpRn
Dixon, Simon J., s.j.dixon@bham.ac.uk, Univ of Birmingham; Gms
Dixon, Tim, thd@usf.edu, Univ of South Florida; Yd
Dladla, Nonkululeko, (031) 260-2801 dladlan2@ukzn.ac.za, Univ of KwaZulu-Natal; GusGr
Dmochowski, Jane, 215-5735388 janeed@sas.upenn.edu, Univ of Pennsylvania; Yg
Doar, III, William R., (803) 609-7065 doarw@dnr.sc.gov, South Carolina Dept of Natural Resources; GrdGp
Dobbie, Steven, +44(0) 113 34 36725 j.s.e.dobbie@leeds.ac.uk, Univ of Leeds; As
Dobbs, Fred C., (757) 683-4301 fdobbs@odu.edu, Old Dominion Univ; Ob
Dobler, Scott, (270) 745-7078 scott.dobler@wku.edu, Western Kentucky Univ; As
Dobrzhinetskaya, Larissa F., (951) 827-2028 larissa@ucrac1.ucr.edu, Univ of California, Riverside; Gx
Dobson, David, +44 020 7679 32398 d.dobson@ucl.ac.uk, Univ Coll London; Gz
Dockal, James A., (563) 845-1034 dockal@uncw.edu, Univ of North Carolina, Wilmington; GdcEm
Dodd, Justin P., 815-753-7949 jdodd@niu.edu, Northern Illinois Univ; Cs
Dodge, Clifford H., 717.702.2036 cdodge@pa.gov, DCNR- Pennsylvania Bureau of Geological Survey; GrEcRh
Dodge, Rebecca L., rebecca.dodge@msutexas.edu, Midwestern State Univ; Zre
Dodge, Stefanie, (414) 324-5676 stefanie.dodge@wisc.edu, Univ of Wisconsin, Madison, Division of Extension; Gg
Doerr, Erica ., erica.doerr@nmt.edu, New Mexico Inst of Mining and Tech; YsGgZe
Dogwiler, Toby, tdogwiler@missouristate.edu, Missouri State Univ; ZiGmZy
Doh, Seong-Jae, 82-2-3290-3173 sjdoh@korea.ac.kr, Korea Univ; YmgYe
Doherty, Amanda, 575-835-5038 amanda.doherty@nmt.edu, New Mexico Inst of Mining and Tech; HwCg
Doherty, David J., (313) 577-2506 ah0654@wayne.edu, Wayne State Univ; GgEoGx
Doherty, Ruth, +44 (0) 131 650 6759 ruth.doherty@ed.ac.uk, Edinburgh Univ; As
Dolakova, Nela, +420 549 49 3542 nela@sci.muni.cz, Masaryk Univ; Plg
Dolan, James F., (213) 740-8599 dolan@usc.edu, Univ of Southern California; Gt
Dolejs, David, +420-221951525 Charles Univ; GiCpg
Dolgoff, Anatole, (212) 346-1502 Pace Univ, New York Campus; Zg
Doll, William E., d8e@ornl.gov, Oak Ridge; Yg
Dollase, Wayne A., (310) 825-3823 dollase@ucla.edu, Univ of California, Los Angeles; Gz
Dolliver, Holly A., holly.dolliver@uwrf.edu, Univ of Wisconsin, River Falls; GmSd
Dolman, Han J., +31 20 5987358 han.dolman@vu.nl, Vrije Universiteit Amsterdam; CbAmHg
Dolman, Paul, +44 (0)1603 59 3175 p.dolman@uea.ac.uk, Univ of East Anglia; Zu
Domack, Cynthia R., (315) 859-4710 cdomack@hamilton.edu, Hamilton Coll; Pg
Domagall, Abigail M., (605) 642-6506 abigail.domagall@bhsu.edu, Black Hills State Univ; GveZe
Dombard, Andrew J., (312) 996-9206 adombard@uic.edu, Univ of Illinois at Chicago; Xy
Domber, Steven E., (609) 984-6587 steven.domber@dep.nj.gov, New Jersey Geological and Water Survey; Hw
Domingo, Laura, ldomingo@ucm.es, Univ Complutense de Madrid; PveCs
Domingue, Carla, (225) 388-8407 carla@lgs.bri.lsu.edu, Louisiana State Univ; Zn
Dominguez, Francina, 217-265-5483 francina@illinois.edu, Univ of Illinois, Urbana-Champaign; AsHg

Dominic, David F., 937 775-2201 david.dominic@wright.edu, Wright State Univ; GsrRc
Donaghay, Percy, (401) 874-6944 donaghay@gso.uri.edu, Univ of Rhode Island; Ob
Donahoe, Robert J., (505) 667-7603 Los Alamos; Zn
Donahoe, Rona J., 205-348-1879 rdonahoe@geo.ua.edu, Univ of Alabama; Cl
Donald, Roberta, (778) 782-4925 robbie_donald@sfu.ca, Simon Fraser Univ; GsZe
Donaldson, Paul R., (208) 426-3639 pdonalds@boisestate.edu, Boise State Univ; Ye
Dondofema, Farai, +27 15 962 80044 farai.dondofema@univen.ac.za, Univ of Venda for Sci & Tech; ZrHgZi
Doner, Lisa A., 603-535-2245 ladoner@plymouth.edu, Plymouth State Univ; PcGes
Doney, Scott, 434-924-0570 scd5c@virginiae.edu, Univ of Virginia; Oc
Dong, Charles, (310) 660-3593 El Camino Coll; Og
Dong, Hailiang, (513) 529-2517 dongh@miamioh.edu, Miami Univ; Cg
Dong, Pinliang, (940) 565-2377 pinliang.dong@unt.edu, Univ of North Texas; Zir
Dong, Yunpeng, ydong265@uwo.ca, Western Univ; GtcCg
Dongmo Wamba, Mathurin, 609-258-4101 mw1685@princeton.edu, Princeton Univ; YsnYg
Donnelly, Jeffrey, 508-289-2994 jdonnelly@whoi.edu, Woods Hole Oceanographic Inst; Gu
Donoghue, Michael J., 203-432-1935 michael.donoghue@yale.edu, Yale Univ; Pbg
Donohue, Kathleen, (401) 874-6615 kdonohue@gso.uri.edu, Univ of Rhode Island; Op
Donohue, Stephen J., (540) 231-9740 donohue@vt.edu, Virginia Polytechnic Inst & State Univ; Sc
Donovan, James, (801) 585-3029 james.donovan@utah.edu, Univ of Utah; NmrZr
Donovan, Jeff C., (727) 553-1116 jdonovan@marine.usf.edu, Univ of South Florida; Op
Donovan, Joseph J., (304) 293-5603 donovan@geo.wvu.edu, West Virginia Univ; Hq
Donovan, R N., (817) 257-7214 r.donovan@tcu.edu, Texas Christian Univ; GdcGt
Doolan, Barry L., (802) 656-0248 bdoolan@uvm.edu, Univ of Vermont; Gx
Dooley, Brett, bdooley@ph.vccs.edu, Patrick Henry Comm Coll; Gg
Dooley, John H., (609) 292-2576 john.dooley@dep.state.nj.us, New Jersey Geological and Water Survey; CgGfe
Dooley, Tim, 512-471-8261 tim.dooley@beg.utexas.edu, Univ of Texas at Austin, Jackson Sch of Geosciences; Gc
Dorais, Michael J., (801) 422-1347 dorais@byu.edu, Brigham Young Univ; Gi
Dorale, Jeffrey A., (319) 335-0822 jeffrey-dorale@uiowa.edu, Univ of Iowa; CsPc
Doran, Peter, pdoran@lsu.edu, Louisiana State Univ; Hws
Dore, John, (406) 600-5932 jdore@montana.edu, Montana State Univ; Ca
Dorfman, Alexander, 089/2180 4275 Ludwig-Maximilians-Univ Muenchen; Gz
Dorfner, Thomas, 089/2180 4278 dorfner@min.uni-muenchen.de, Ludwig-Maximilians-Univ Muenchen; Gz
Dorling, Stephen, +44 (0)1603 59 2533 s.dorling@uea.ac.uk, Univ of East Anglia; Am
Dormaar, John, (403) 327-4561 Univ of Lethbridge; So
Dorman, Clive E., (619) 594-5707 cdorman@mail.sdsu.edu, San Diego State Univ; OpAmt
Dorman, James, (901) 678-4753 dorman@comcast.net, Univ of Memphis; Ys
Dorman, Leroy M., (858) 534-2406 ldorman@ucsd.edu, Univ of California, San Diego; Yg
Dornbos, Stephen Q., sdornbos@uwm.edu, Univ of Wisconsin, Milwaukee; PeiPo
Doro, Kennedy, (419) 530-2811 kennedy.doro@utoledo.edu, Univ of Toledo; Zn
Dorries, Alison M., (505) 665-6952 adorries@lanl.gov, Los Alamos; Zn
Dorsey, Rebecca J., (541) 346-4431 rdorsey@uoregon.edu, Univ of Oregon; Gr
Dort, Jr., Wakefield, (785) 864-4974 Univ of Kansas; Gm
dos Santos, Telmo B., tmsantos@fc.ul.pt, Unive de Lisboa; GptGi
Doser, Diane I., 915-747-5851 doser@utep.edu, Univ of Texas, El Paso; Ys
Doskey, Paul V., (630) 252-7662 pvdoskey@anl.gov, Argonne; As
Doss, Paul K., (812) 465-7132 pdoss@usi.edu, Univ of Southern Indiana; HwGeZu
Dosso, Stanley E., (250) 472-4341 sdosso@uvic.ca, Univ of Victoria; Op
Dostal, Jarda, (902) 420-5747 Dalhousie Univ; Cg
Doster, Florian, +44 (0)131 451 3171 f.doster@hw.ac.uk, Heriot-Watt Univ; Hg
Dostie, Philip, (207) 786-6485 pdostie@bates.edu, Bates Coll; Cl
Doty, Thomas, (401) 254-3066 Roger Williams Univ; Ob
Dou, Fugen, (409) 752-2741 ext. 2223 f-dou@aesrg.tamu.edu, Texas A&M Univ; So
Dougan, Bernie, (360) 383-3877 bdougan@whatcom.ctc.edu, Whatcom Comm Coll; Gg
Doughty, Alice, 207-786-6113 adoughty@bates.edu, Bates Coll; Gl
Dougil, Andy, +44(0) 113 34 36782 a.j.dougill@leeds.ac.uk, Univ of Leeds; So
Douglas, Arthur V., (402) 280-2464 sonora@creighton.edu, Creighton Univ; Zg
Douglas, Bruce, 812-855-3848 douglasb@indiana.edu, Indiana Univ, Bloomington; Gcg
Douglas, Ellen, ellen.douglas@umb.edu, Univ of Massachusetts, Boston; HwqHy
Douglas, Peter, 514-398-6772 peter.douglas@mcgill.ca, McGill Univ; Cs
Douglass, Daniel C., (617) 373-4381 d.douglass@northeastern.edu, Northeastern Univ; GlSdPc
Douglass, David N., (626) 585-7036 dndouglass@pasadena.edu, Pasadena City Coll; Ze
Douglass, Gordon, (801) 538-4810 gdouglass@utah.gov, Utah Geological Survey; Zi
Douilly, Roby, (951) 827-3180 roby.douilly@ucr.edu, Univ of California, Riverside; YsGtYg
Dove, Patricia M., (540) 231-2444 pdove@vt.edu, Virginia Polytechnic Inst & State Univ; Cl
Doveton, John H., 785-864-3965 doveton@kgs.ku.edu, Univ of Kansas; Gq
Dowd, John F., (706) 542-2383 jdowd@uga.edu, Univ of Georgia; Hy
Dowdy, Robert H., (612) 625-7058 bdowdy@soils.umn.edu, Univ of Minnesota, Twin Cities; Sc
Dower, John, 250-721-6120 dower@uvic.ca, Univ of Victoria; Ob
Dowling, Carolyn B., 765-285-8274 cbdowling@bsu.edu, Ball State Univ; HgGeCg
Downes, Hilary, +44 020 3073 8027 h.downes@ucl.ac.uk, Birkbeck Coll; Cg
Downie, Helen, helen.downie@manchester.ac.uk, Univ of Manchester; Ge
Downs, James W., downs.1@osu.edu, Ohio State Univ; Gz
Downs, Joni, downs@usf.edu, Univ of South Florida; Zi
Downs, Robert T., (520) 626-8092 rdowns@email.arizona.edu, Univ of Arizona; Gi
Doyle, James A., (530) 752-7591 jadoyle@ucdavis.edu, Univ of California, Davis; Pb
Doyle, Joseph, j6doyle@bridgew.edu, Bridgewater State Univ; Gg
Drago, Aldo, aldo.drago@um.edu.mt, Univ of Malta; Opg
Drake, John C., (802) 656-0244 jdrake@uvm.edu, Univ of Vermont; Cl
Drake, Lon D., (319) 335-1826 Univ of Iowa; Hy
Drake, Luke, 818-677-3508 luke.drake@csun.edu, California State Univ, Northridge; Zi
Drake, Michael J., (520) 621-6962 drake@lpl.arizona.edu, Univ of Arizona; Xc
Drake, Simon, +440203 073 8024 drakesimon1@gmail.com, Birkbeck Coll; Gv
Draper, Grenville, (305) 348-3087 draper@fiu.edu, Florida International Univ; GctRh
Drazen, Jeffrey C., (808) 956-6567 jdrazen@hawaii.edu, Univ of Hawai'i, Manoa; Ob
Dreesen, Donald S., (505) 667-1913 dreesen@lanl.gov, Los Alamos; Np
Dreger, Douglas S., (510) 643-1719 dreger@seismo.berkeley.edu, Univ of California, Berkeley; Ys
Drescher, Andrew, (612) 625-2374 Univ of Minnesota, Twin Cities; So
Dreschoff, Gisela, (785) 864-4517 Univ of Kansas; Ce
Drew, Douglas A., (404) 496-4202 ddrew@mtech.edu, Montana Tech of the Univ of Montana; Cg
Driese, Steven G., 254-710-2361 steven_driese@baylor.edu, Univ of Tennessee, Knoxville; SaClGs
Driever, Steven L., (816) 235-2971 drievers@umkc.edu, Univ of Missouri, Kansas City; ZnnZn
Drijfhout, Sybren, +44 (0)23 8059 6202 s.s.drijfhout@soton.ac.uk, Univ of Southampton; Op
Dripps, Weston R., (864) 294-3392 weston.dripps@furman.edu, Furman Univ; HwsGe
Driscoll, John R., (607) 753-2926 driscollj@cortland.edu, SUNY, Cortland; Zn
Driscoll, Neal W., (858) 822-5026 ndriscoll@ucsd.edu, Univ of California, San Diego; Gu
Driscoll, Peter E., 202-478-8827 pdriscoll@carnegiescience.edu, Carnegie Inst for Sci; GtYm
Drobniak, Agnieszka, (812) 855-2687 agdrobni@indiana.edu, Indiana Univ;

Dupre, William R., 713-743-4987 wdupre@uh.edu, Univ of Houston; On
Dura, Christina, (540) 231-3785 tinadura@vt.edu, Virginia Polytechnic Inst & State Univ; OnRnPm
Durand, Michael T., (614)247-4835 durand.8@osu.edu, Ohio State Univ; HsZr
Durazo-Tapia, Gustavo E., gustavo.durazo@ues.mx, Univ Estatal de Sonora; Em
Durbin, Edward G., (401) 874-6850 edurbin@gso.uri.edu, Univ of Rhode Island; Ob
Durbin, James, 812-465-1208 jdurbin@usi.edu, Univ of Southern Indiana; Gm
Durham, Lisa, 630-252-3170 ladurham@anl.gov, Argonne; Hw
Durham, William, 617-253-5810 wbdurham@mit.edu, Massachusetts Inst of Tech; Cg
Durkee, Josh, joshua.durkee@wku.edu, Western Kentucky Univ; AsZy
Durkee, Philip A., 831-656-2517 durkee@nps.edu, Naval Postgraduate Sch; AmZr
Durland, Theodore, 541-737-5058 tdurland@coas.oregonstate.edu, Oregon State Univ; Yg
DuRoss, Christopher B., (801) 537-3348 christopherduross@utah.gov, Utah Geological Survey; Ng
Durran, Dale R., (206) 543-7440 drdee@uw.edu, Univ of Washington; As
Durrant, Jeffrey O., (801) 422-4116 jodurrant@byu.edu, Brigham Young Univ; Ge
Durucan, Sevket, +44 20 759 47354 s.durucan@imperial.ac.uk, Imperial Coll; NmEcNr
Dushaw, Brian D., (206) 685-4198 dushaw@apl.washington.edu, Univ of Washington; Op
Dutch, Steven I., (920) 465-2371 dutchs@uwgb.edu, Univ of Wisconsin, Green Bay; GcgGe
Dutkiewicz, Stephanie, 617-253-8039 stephd@mit.edu, Massachusetts Inst of Tech; Cm
Dutrieux, Pierre, pierred@ldeo.columbia.edu, Columbia Univ; Op
Dutro, Thomas, (202) 633-1322 Smithsonian Inst / Nat Mus of Natural History; Pi
Dutrow, Barbara L., (225) 388-2525 dutrow@geol.lsu.edu, Louisiana State Univ; Gz
Dutta, Prodip K., (812) 237-2268 prodip.dutta@indstate.edu, Indiana State Univ; Gs
Dutton, Jessica, duttonj@sunysuffolk.edu, Suffolk County Comm Coll, Ammerman Campus; Zg
Dutton, John A., 814-865-1534 dutton@ems.psu.edu, Pennsylvania State Univ, Univ Park; Am
Dutton, Shirley P., 512-471-0329 shirley.dutton@beg.utexas.edu, Univ of Texas, Austin; Gs
Duvall, Alison, 206-211-8311 aduvall@uw.edu, Univ of Washington; GmcGt
Duxbury, Thomas C., (818) 354-4301 Jet Propulsion Lab; Zn
Dvorzak, Marie, (608) 262-8956 mdvorzak@geology.wisc.edu, Univ of Wisconsin, Madison; Zn
Dworkin, Stephen I., (254) 710-2186 steve_dworkin@baylor.edu, Baylor Univ; ClGd
Dwyer, Daryl F., 419-5302661 daryl.dwyer@utoledo.edu, Univ of Toledo; Zn
Dwyer, Gary S., (919) 681-8164 gsd3@duke.edu, Duke Univ; Gs
Dyab, Ahmed I., 002-03-3921595 seawolf_5000@yahoo.com, Alexandria Univ; Gg
Dyaur, Nikolay, 713-743-6539 ndyaur@uh.edu, Univ of Houston; Yxs
Dye, David H., 901-678-3330 daviddye@memphis.edu, Univ of Memphis; Ga
Dyer, Jamie, (662) 268-1032 Ext 220 jamie.dyer@msstate.edu, Mississippi State Univ; Am
Dyer, Jen, +44(0) 113 34 39086 j.dyer@leeds.ac.uk, Univ of Leeds; Ge
Dygert, Nick, 865-974-6022 ndygert1@utk.edu, Univ of Tennessee, Knoxville; Giz
Dyhrman, Sonya, 845-365-8165 sdyhrman@ldeo.columbia.edu, Columbia Univ; Ob
Dymek, Robert F., (314) 935-5344 bob_d@levee.wustl.edu, Washington Univ in St. Louis; GpiGa
Dymond, Randel, (540) 231-9962 dymond@vt.edu, Virginia Polytechnic Inst & State Univ; HqsZi
Dymond, Salli F., (218) 726-6582 dymon003@umn.edu, Univ of Minnesota Duluth; Hg
Dyson, Liesl, +27 (0)12 420 2469 liesl.dyson@up.ac.za, Univ of Pretoria; Am
Dyson, Miranda, +44 (0)1908 653398 x 53398 miranda.dyson@open.ac.uk, Open Univ; Pg
Dzunic, Aleksandar, +61 8 9266 2297 a.dzunic@curtin.edu.au, Curtin Univ; YgsYe

E

Earls, Sandy, 405-744-6358 sandy.earls@okstate.edu, Oklahoma State Univ; Zn
Earls, Stephanie, (360) 902-1473 stephanie.earls@dnr.wa.gov, Washington Geological Survey; Gge
Early, Thomas O., eot@ornl.gov, Oak Ridge; Cl
Earman, Sam, (717) 871-4336 searman@millersville.edu, Millersville Univ; HwCsl
Easson, Gregory L., (662) 915-5995 geasson@olemiss.edu, Univ of Mississippi; Zr
Easterbrook, Don J., 360 319-5389 don.easterbrook@wwu.edu, Western Washington Univ; GlmGe
Easterday, Cary, cary.easterday@bellevuecollege.edu, Bellevue Coll; GgPg
Eastin, Matt, 704-687-5914 mdeastin@uncc.edu, Univ of North Carolina, Charlotte; Am
Eastler, Thomas E., 207-778-7401 eastler@maine.edu, Univ of Maine, Farmington; GeZrGg
Eastoe, Chris J., (520) 791-7430 eastoe@email.arizona.edu, Univ of Arizona; CsGg
Eaton, David, 403 220-4233 eatond@ucalgary.ca, Univ of Calgary; Ys
Eaton, Jeffrey G., jeaton@weber.edu, Weber State Univ; PsGs
Eaton, Lewis S., (540) 568-3339 eatonls@jmu.edu, James Madison Univ; Gm
Eaton, Timothy, 718-997-3327 timothy.eaton@qc.cuny.edu, Queens Coll (CUNY); HgwGg
Ebel, Denton, 212-769-5381 debel@amnh.org, Graduate Sch of the City Univ of New York; Gg
Ebel, John E., (617) 552-3399 ebel@bc.edu, Boston Coll; Ys
Eberhardt, Erik, (604) 827-5573 eeberhardt@eos.ubc.ca, Univ of British Columbia; Ng
Eberhart, Mark E., (303) 273-3726 meberhar@mines.edu, Colorado Sch of Mines; Zm
Eberle, Bill, (785) 532-6101 weberle@ksu.edu, Kansas State Univ; SoZu
Eberle, Jaelyn J., 303-492-8069 jaelyn.eberle@colorado.edu, Univ of Colorado; Pv
Eberli, Gregor P., (305) 421-4678 geberli@rsmas.miami.edu, Univ of Miami; GusYx
Ebersole, Craig, 717-702-2023 craebersol@pa.gov, DCNR- Pennsylvania Bureau of Geological Survey; ZiHw
Ebert, David, 831-771-4400 debert@mlml.calstate.edu, Moss Landing Marine Lab; Zn
Ebert, James R., (607) 436-3065 james.ebert@oneonta.edu, SUNY, Oneonta; GrsZe
Eberth, David A., 403-823-7707 Royal Tyrrell Mus of Palaeontology; Gs
Ebiner, Matt, (310) 660-3593 mebiner@elcamino.edu, El Camino Coll; Zy
Ebinger, Michael H., (505) 667-3147 mhe@lanl.gov, Los Alamos; So
Eble, Cortland F., 8592575500 x 149 eble@uky.edu, Univ of Kentucky; Pl
Eby, G. Nelson, (978) 934-3907 nelson_eby@uml.edu, Univ of Massachusetts, Lowell; CgGiCt
Eby, Stephanie, (617) 373-4380 s.eby@neu.edu, Northeastern Univ; Zn
Echols, John B., (225) 388-8573 john@lgs.bri.lsu.edu, Louisiana State Univ; Go
Eckert, Andreas, 573-341-4876 eckertan@mst.edu, Missouri Univ of Sci and Tech; Yg
Eckert, Donald J., (614) 292-9048 eckert.1@osu.edu, Ohio State Univ; Sc
Eckert, James O., (203) 432-3181 xwn6w3i02@sneakemail.com, Yale Univ; Gp
Economos, Rita C., 214-768-3313 reconomos@smu.edu, Southern Methodist Univ; CsGc
Edegbai, Aitalokhai J., aitalokhai.edegbai@uniben.edu, Univ of Benin; GosPi
Edgar, Dorland E., (630) 252-7596 Argonne; Gm
Edgcomb, Virginia, 508-289-3734 vedgcomb@whoi.edu, Woods Hole Oceanographic Inst; ObZc
Edgell, Dennis J., (910) 521-6479 dennis.edgell@uncp.edu, Univ of North Carolina, Pembroke; As
Edil, Tuncer B., (608) 262-3225 edil@engr.wisc.edu, Univ of Wisconsin, Madison; Ng
Edlund, Mark B., mbedlund@smm.org, Univ of Minnesota, Twin Cities; Pe
Edmonds, Douglas A., (812) 855-4512 edmondsd@indiana.edu, Indiana Univ, Bloomington; Gsm
Edmonds, Marie, +44 (0) 1223 333463 medm06@esc.cam.ac.uk, Univ of Cambridge; Gv
Edson, Carol, 925-424-1336 cedson@laspositascollege.edu, Las Positas Coll; Gg
Edson, James, james.edson@uconn.edu, Univ of Connecticut; Op
Edwards, Benjamin R., (717) 254-8934 edwardsb@dickinson.edu, Dickinson Coll; GivCg
Edwards, C L, (505) 667-8464 cledwards@lanl.gov, Los Alamos; Yg

Edwards, Cole T., edwardsct4@appstate.edu, Appalachian State Univ; GsCs
Edwards, Dianne, +44(0)29 208 74264 edwardsd2@cardiff.ac.uk, Cardiff Univ; Pb
Edwards, John , john.edwards@flinders.edu.au, Flinders Univ; Zn
Edwards, Margo H., (808) 956-5232 margo@soest.hawaii.edu, Univ of Hawai'i, Manoa; Gu
Edwards, Nicholas, +44 0161 275-3810 nicholas.edwards@manchester.ac.uk, Univ of Manchester; Pg
Edwards, R. Lawrence, 612-626-0207 edwar001@umn.edu, Univ of Minnesota, Twin Cities; Cc
Edwards, Richard N., (416) 978-2267 edwards@core.physics.utoronto.ca, Univ of Toronto; Yr
Edwards, Robin, robin.edwards@tcd.ie, Trinity Coll; Ge
Edwards, Stuart, +44 (0) 191 208 3986 stuart.edwards@ncl.ac.uk, Univ of Newcastle Upon Tyne; Gq
Effert-Fanta, Shari E., 217-244-2192 sfanta@illinois.edu, Illinois State Geological Survey; Cas
Efurd, Deward W., (505) 667-2437 Los Alamos; Ct
Egan, Stuart, (+44) 01782 733174 s.s.egan@keele.ac.uk, Keele Univ; Gtc
Egbert, Gary D., (541) 737-2947 egbert@coas.oregonstate.edu, Oregon State Univ; Yr
Egbeyemi, Oladimeji R., +2348167781509 oregbeyemi@futa.edu.ng, Federal Univ of Tech, Akure; GgCeEg
Egenhoff, Sven O., (970) 491-0749 sven@warnercnr.colostate.edu, Colorado State Univ; Gsu
Egerton, Victoria, victoria.egerton@manchester.ac.uk, Univ of Manchester; Pg
Egger, Anne E., annegger@geology.cwu.edu, Central Washington Univ; GtZeRn
Eggers, Delores M., (828) 251-6654 eggers@unca.edu, Univ of North Carolina, Asheville; Zn
Eggler, David H., (814) 571-1960 dhe1@psu.eu, Pennsylvania State Univ, Univ Park; CpGiv
Eggleston, Carrick M., (307) 766-6769 carrick@uwyo.edu, Univ of Wyoming; ClqCb
Eggleston, David B., (919) 515-7840 eggleston@ncsu.edu, North Carolina State Univ; Ob
Eguiluz, Luis, luis.eguiluz@ehu.eus, Univ of the Basque Country UPV/EHU; Ggt
Ehinola, Olugbenga A., +2348033819066 oa.ehinola@mail.ui.edu.ng, Univ of Ibadan; GoeCo
Ehler, Stan, (785) 532-6101 swehler@ksu.edu, Kansas State Univ; So
Ehlers, Todd A., (734) 763-5112 tehlers@umich.edu, Univ of Michigan; Yg
Ehlmann, Bethany L., 626.395.6720 ehlmann@caltech.edu, California Inst of Tech; XgZrGz
Ehm, Lars, 631-632-8058 lars.ehm@stonybrook.edu, Stony Brook Univ; Gz
Eichenbaum, Jack, (718) 961-8406 jaconet@aol.com, Hunter Coll (CUNY); Zie
Eicher, Don L., (303) 492-6187 Univ of Colorado; Pm
Eichhubl, Peter, (512) 475-8829 peter.eichhubl@beg.utexas.edu, Univ of Texas, Austin; GcCgNr
Eick, Matthew J., (540) 231-8943 eick@vt.edu, Virginia Polytechnic Inst & State Univ; Sc
Eide, Elizabeth A., (202) 334-2392 eeide@nas.edu, Nat Academies of Scis, Eng, and Medicine; GgoGt
Eiler, John M., (626) 395-6239 eiler@gps.caltech.edu, California Inst of Tech; Cg
Eilon, Zach, eilon@geol.ucsb.edu, Univ of California, Santa Barbara; Ys
Eisenberger, Peter M., (917) 568-6915 petere@ldeo.columbia.edu, Columbia Univ; Zn
Eisenhart, Karen, (814) 732-2398 keisenhart@edinboro.edu, Edinboro Univ of Pennsylvania; Zy
Eisenhart, Ralph, (717) 846-7788 York Coll of Pennsylvania; Gg
Eivazi, Frieda, 573-681-5459 Univ of Missouri; Sc
Eklund, Olav, +358442956429 olav.eklund@abo.fi, Abo Akademi Univ; GxeGz
Ekmekci, Mehmet, +90 312 2977730 ekmekci@hacettepe.edu.tr, Hacettepe Univ; HwyCs
Ekstrom, Goran, (845) 365-8427 ekstrom@ldeo.columbia.edu, Columbia Univ; Ys
El Dakkak, Mohamed W., 002-03-3921595 waguihm@yahoo.com, Alexandria Univ; GgsGd
El Kadiri, Racha, 615-484-7641 racha.elkadiri@mtsu.edu, Middle Tennessee State Univ; Hg
El Masri, Bassil, (270) 809-3110 belmasri@murraystate.edu, Murray State Univ; Zc
El Shazly, Aley, (304) 696-6756 elshazly@marshall.edu, Marshall Univ; GpiCg
El-Baz, Farouk, (617) 353-5081 farouk@bu.edu, Boston Univ; Zr
El-Kadi, Aly I., (808) 956-6331 elkadi@hawaii.edu, Univ of Hawai'i, Manoa; Hw
El-Monier, Ilham, ilham.el-monier@ou.edu, Univ of Oklahoma; Np
Elachi, Charles, 626.395.8858 charles.elachi@jpl.nasa.gov, California Inst of Tech; Xg
Elam, Tim, 206-685-3092 wtelam@apl.uw.edu, Univ of Washington; Cag
Elardo, Stephen, 352-392-2634 selardo@ufl.edu, Univ of Florida; GiXgCp
Elder, Kathryn L., (508) 289-2513 kelder@whoi.edu, Woods Hole Oceanographic Inst; Cs
Elders, Wilfred A., wilfred.elders@ucr.edu, Univ of California, Riverside; Gi
Eldredge, Niles, (212) 769-5723 American Mus of Natural History; Pi
Eldridge, Jayson, (812) 856-2382 jayeldri@indiana.edu, Indiana Univ; EoGr
Elhusseiny, Ammar , +966138602625 ammar.elhusseiny@kfupm.edu.sa, King Fahd Univ of Petroleum and Minerals; Yg
Elia, Gaetano, +44 (0) 191 208 7934 Univ of Newcastle Upon Tyne; Ng
Elias, Robert J., (204) 474-8862 eliasrj@ms.umanitoba.ca, Univ of Manitoba; Pi
Elick, Jennifer M., 570-372-4214 elick@susqu.edu, Susquehanna Univ; Pe
Elkins, Joe T., 970-351-3060 joe.elkins@unco.edu, Univ of Northern Colorado; ZeGgCl
Elkins, Lynne J., (402) 472-7563 lelkins@unl.edu, Univ of Nebraska, Lincoln; GivCt
Elkins-Tanton, Linda, (480) 727-2451 ltelkins@asu.edu, Arizona State Univ; Xg
Eller, Phillip G., (505) 667-5830 Los Alamos; Zn
Ellett, Kevin M., 812-856-3671 kmellett@indiana.edu, Indiana Univ; YeHw
Ellingson, Don, 503-838-8865 ellingd@wou.edu, Western Oregon Univ; AmZgXg
Ellins, Katherine K., (512) 232-3251 kellins@ig.utexas.edu, Univ of Texas, Austin; Zn
Elliot, David H., (614) 292-5076 elliot.1@osu.edu, Ohio State Univ; GxtGv
Elliott, C. James, (505) 667-9517 cje@lanl.gov, Los Alamos; Zn
Elliott, Colleen G., (406) 496-4143 celliott@mtech.edu, Montana Tech of The Univ of Montana; GctGg
Elliott, David K., (928) 523-7188 david.elliott@nau.edu, Northern Arizona Univ; Pv
Elliott, Emily M., (412) 624-8780 eelliott@pitt.edu, Univ of Pittsburgh; Cbs
Elliott, Julie, (765) 496-7206 julieelliott@purdue.edu, Purdue Univ; Yd
Elliott, Monty A., (541) 552-6482 Southern Oregon Univ; Gr
Elliott, Scott M., (505) 667-0949 sme@lanl.gov, Los Alamos; As
Elliott, Susan J., (519) 888-4567 (Ext. 33923) elliotts@uwaterloo.ca, McMaster Univ; Ge
Elliott, W. Crawford, (404) 413-5756 wcelliott@gsu.edu, Georgia State Univ; Clc
Elliott, Jr., William S., (812) 228-5053 wselliott@usi.edu, Univ of Southern Indiana; GsrCl
Ellis, Andre, aellis3@calstatela.edu, California State Univ, Los Angeles; HwCg
Ellis, Dale, daledellis@gmail.com, Dalhousie Univ; Op
Ellis, Hugh, (901) 678-2007 hugh.ellis@jhu.edu, Johns Hopkins Univ; Zn
Ellis, Kathryn E., (859) 323-0504 kathryn.ellis@uky.edu, Univ of Kentucky; Zn
Ellis, Robert M., (604) 822-6574 rellis@eos.ubc.ca, Univ of British Columbia; Ys
Ellis, Scott R., 217-265-5105 ellis3@illinois.edu, Illinois State Geological Survey; Ge
Ellis, Trevor, 573-368-2153 trevor.ellis@dnr.mo.gov, Missouri Dept of Natural Resources; Gg
Ellison, Anne L., 217-244-2502 aerdmann@illinois.edu, Univ of Illinois; Ge
Ellsworth, Timothy R., (217) 333-2055 Univ of Illinois, Urbana-Champaign; Sp
Ellsworth, William L., (650) 723-9390 wellsworth@stanford.edu, Stanford Univ; Ys
Ellwood, Brooks B., (225) 578-3416 ellwood@lsu.edu, Louisiana State Univ; Ym
Elmore, R. Douglas, delmore@ou.edu, Univ of Oklahoma; GdYm
Elnadi, Abdelhalim H., geology@uofk.edu, Univ of Khartoum; Goz
Eloranta, Edwin W., (608)262-7327 eloranta@lidar.ssec.wisc.edu, Univ of Wisconsin, Madison; Yr
Elrick, Maya, (505) 277-5077 dolomite@unm.edu, Univ of New Mexico; Gs
Elrick, Scott D., (217) 333-3222 elrick@illinois.edu, Univ of Illinois; EcGgs
Elsberry, Russell L., 831-656-2373 elsberry@nps.edu, Naval Postgraduate Sch; Am
Elsen, Jan, jan.elsen@ees.kuleuven.be, Katholieke Universiteit Leuven; Gz
Elshorbany, Yasin, elshorbany@usf.edu, Univ of South Florida; Ac
Elswick, Erika R., (812) 855-2493 eelswick@indiana.edu, Indiana Univ, Bloomington; Cl
Elueze, A. A., aa.elueze@mail.ui.edu.ng, Univ of Ibadan; Eg

Elwood Madden, Andrew S., (405) 325-3253 amadden@ou.edu, Univ of Oklahoma; ClZaCb
Elwood Madden, Megan E., (405) 325-3253 melwood@ou.edu, Univ of Oklahoma; ClXgCg
Ely, Lisa L., (509) 963-2177 ely@cwu.edu, Central Washington Univ; Gm
Elzinga, Evert J., 973-353-5238 elzinga@newark.rutgers.edu, Rutgers, The State Univ of New Jersey, Newark; Sc
Emanuel, Kerry A., (617) 253-2462 emanuel@mit.edu, Massachusetts Inst of Tech; AmRn
Emerick, Christina M., (206) 543-2491 tina@ocean.washington.edu, Univ of Washington; Ou
Emerson, Cheryl R., (309) 694-5373 Illinois Central Coll; Ze
Emerson, Norlene, (608) 647-6186 x109 norlene.emerson@uwc.edu, Univ of Wisconsin Colls; GgPiGs
Emerson, Steven R., (206) 543-0428 emerson@u.washington.edu, Univ of Washington; OcCmOg
Emery, Joshua P., joshua.emery@nau.edu, Univ of Tennessee, Knoxville; Xy
Emile-Geay, Julien, 213-740-2945 julieneg@usc.edu, Univ of Southern California; Oc
Emmer, Barbara, 089/2180 4231 Ludwig-Maximilians-Univ Muenchen; Yg
Emmett, Chad, (801) 422-7886 chad_emmett@byu.edu, Brigham Young Univ; Zn
Emmi, Philip C., (801) 581-5562 pcemmi@geog.utah.edu, Univ of Utah; Zu
Emofurieta, Williams O., wemofu@uniben.edu, Univ of Benin; GzCeGe
Emry, Robert, (202) 633-1323 Smithsonian Inst / Nat Mus of Natural History; Pv
Encarnacion, John, (314) 977-3119 john.encarnacion@slu.edu, Saint Louis Univ; Gx
Enderlin, Milton, 817 257 5318 m.enderlin@tcu.edu, Texas Christian Univ; Nr
Endres, Anthony E., (519) 888-4567 (Ext. 3552) Univ of Waterloo; Pe
Engebretson, David C., (360) 650-3595 david.engebretson@wwu.edu, Western Washington Univ; Gt
Engel, Anga, mpeschke@geomar.de, SUNY, Stony Brook; Oc
Engel, Annette S., 865-974-0402 aengel1@utk.edu, Univ of Tennessee, Knoxville; Cl
Engel, Michael H., (405) 325-4435 ab1635@ou.edu, Univ of Oklahoma; Co
Engel, Richard E., (406) 994-5295 rengel@montana.edu, Montana State Univ; Sc
Engelder, Terry, (814) 865-3620 engelder@geosc.psu.edu, Pennsylvania State Univ, Univ Park; Nr
Engelhard, Simon, (401) 874-2187 engelhart@uri.edu, Univ of Rhode Island; Gg
Engelhart, Simon E., 401-874-2187 engelhart@uri.edu, Univ of Rhode Island; OnGmYs
Engelmann, George F., 402-554-4804 gengelmann@unomaha.edu, Univ of Nebraska, Omaha; PvGdr
England, John, (780) 492-5673 john.england@ualberta.ca, Univ of Alberta; Gml
England, Phillip, +44 (1865) 272000 philip@earth.ox.ac.uk, Univ of Oxford; Gt
England, Richard, +440116 252 3522 rwe5@le.ac.uk, Leicester Univ; Yg
English, David C., (727) 553-1503 denglish@marine.usf.edu, Univ of South Florida; Op
Engstrom, Daniel R., (612) 433-5953 (Ext. 18) dre@umn.edu, Univ of Minnesota, Twin Cities; Pe
Engstrom, Ryan, rengstro@gwu.edu, George Washington Univ; Zr
Engstrom, Vanessa, vengstrom@valleycollege.edu, San Bernardino Valley Coll; Zy
Enkelmann, Eva, eva.enkelmann@ucalgary.ca, Univ of Calgary; CcGmt
Enos, Paul, (785) 864-9714 enos@ku.edu, Univ of Kansas; GsdGu
Enright, Richard L., (508) 531-1390 enright@bridgew.edu, Bridgewater State Univ; HgZrEg
Ensign, Todd I., 304-367-8438 tensign@fairmontstate.edu, Fairmont State Univ; Ze
Entekhabi, Dara, (617) 253-9698 darae@mit.edu, Massachusetts Inst of Tech; Hg
Epifanio, Craig, cepi@tamu.edu, Texas A&M Univ; As
Eppelbaum, Lev, +97236405086 levap@post.tau.ac.il, Tel Aviv Univ; YvmGt
Eppes, Martha C., 704-687-5993 meppes@uncc.edu, Univ of North Carolina, Charlotte; So
Epstein, Howard E., (434) 924-4308 hee2b@virginia.edu, Univ of Virginia; Zn
Erdmer, Philippe, (403) 492-2676 philippe.erdmer@ualberta.ca, Univ of Alberta; Gc
Erdner, Deana L., (361) 749-6719 derdner@utexas.edu, Univ of Texas, Austin; Ob
Erhardt, Andrea M., 859-257-6931 andrea.erhardt@uky.edu, Univ of Kentucky; CgsCm
Erickson, Ben A., (801) 537-3379 benerickson@utah.gov, Utah Geological Survey; Ng
Erickson, Brittany, 541-346-1350 bae@cs.uoregon.edu, Univ of Oregon; Ygs
Erickson, J. Mark, (315) 379-5198 St. Lawrence Univ; Pgi
Erickson, Melinda L., 763-783-3231 merickso@usgs.gov, Univ of Minnesota, Twin Cities; Hw
Erickson, Rolfe C., (707) 664-2334 rolfe.erickson@sonoma.edu, Sonoma State Univ; Gx
Eriksen, Charles C., (206) 543-6528 eriksen@u.washington.edu, Univ of Washington; Op
Eriksson, Kenneth A., (540) 231-4680 kaeson@vt.edu, Virginia Polytechnic Inst & State Univ; Gs
Erisman, Brad, 361-749-6833 berisman@utexas.edu, Univ of Texas, Austin; Ob
Ernst, W. Gary, (650) 723-2750 ernst@pangea.stanford.edu, Stanford Univ; Cp
Erski, Theodore, (815) 455-8992 tederski@gmail.com, McHenry County Coll; ZgEg
Erslev, Eric A., (970) 231-2654 eric.erslev@colostate.edu, Colorado State Univ; GctGg
Ertel-Ingrisch, Werner, 089/2180 4275 ertel@min.uni-muenchen.de, Ludwig-Maximilians-Univ Muenchen; Gz
Erturk, Mehmet Ali, 00904242370000-5981 maerturk@firat.edu.tr, Firat Univ; GiCc
Erwin, Diane, (510) 642-3921 dmerwin@berkeley.edu, Univ of California, Berkeley; Pb
Erwin, Douglas H., (202) 633-1324 Smithsonian Inst / Nat Mus of Natural History; Pi
Esbaugh, Andrew J., (361) 749-6835 a.esbaugh@austin.utexas.edu, Univ of Texas, Austin; Ob
Escobar-Wolf, Rudiger, 906/487-2128 rpescoba@mtu.edu, Michigan Technological Univ; Gv
Escuer, Joan, joan.escuer@uab.cat, Universitat Autonoma de Barcelona; Gg
Eshleman, Keith N., (301) 689-7170 eshleman@al.umces.edu, Univ of Maryland; Hg
Esling, Steven P., (618) 453-7376 esling@siu.edu, Southern Illinois Univ Carbondale; HwGl
Esnault, Melissa H., (225) 578-5320 mesnau1@lsu.edu, Louisiana State Univ; Zn
Esparza, Francisco, fesparz@cicese.mx, Centro de Investigación Científica y de Educación Superior de Ensenada; Ye
Esperante, Raul, resperante@llu.edu, Loma Linda Univ; Pv
Espinosa, Juan M., jespinos@cicese.mx, Centro de Investigación Científica y de Educación Superior de Ensenada; Ye
Esser, Corinne, (530) 752-3668 caesser@ucdavis.edu, Univ of California, Davis; Zn
Essery, Richard L., +44 (0) 131 651 9093 richard.essery@ed.ac.uk, Edinburgh Univ; As
Essling, Alice M., (630) 252-3493 Argonne; Ca
Esslinger, Kelly L., kelly.esslinger@azwestern.edu, Arizona Western Coll; AsOpGg
Estalrich López, Joan, ++935811270 joan.estalrich@uab.cat, Universitat Autonoma de Barcelona; HgGe
Estapa, Margaret, 518-589-5477 mestapa@skidmore.edu, Skidmore Coll; Oc
Esteban, Jose Julian, jj.esteban@ehu.es, Univ of the Basque Country UPV/EHU; GtCcYg
Ethridge, Frank G., (970) 491-6195 fredpet@cnr.colostate.edu, Colorado State Univ; Gs
Ettensohn, Frank R., (859) 257-1401 f.ettensohn@uky.edu, Univ of Kentucky; PsGdPi
Ettlie, Bradley, 217-265-6543 ettlie76@illinois.edu, Illinois State Geological Survey; Ge
Eusden, J. Dykstra, (207) 786-6015 deusden@bates.edu, Bates Coll; Gc
Evangelou, V. P., (515) 294-9237 Iowa State Univ of Sci & Tech; Sc
Evanoff, Emmett, 970-351-2647 emmett.evanoff@unco.edu, Univ of Northern Colorado; GrPgGs
Evans, Barry M., (814) 863-3531 bmel@psu.edu, Pennsylvania State Univ, Univ Park; Sd
Evans, Bernard W., 206-543-1163 bwevans@uw.edu, Univ of Washington; GpzGi
Evans, Claude, (314) 935-6684 Washington Univ in St. Louis; Zn
Evans, David A., (203) 432-3127 david.evans@yale.edu, Yale Univ; YmGt
Evans, Diane L., (818) 354-2418 Jet Propulsion Lab; Gm
Evans, Eileen L., (818) 677-5026 eileen.evans@csun.edu, California State Univ, Northridge; YdGtYg
Evans, J. B., (617) 253-2856 brievans@mit.edu, Massachusetts Inst of Tech; Yx
Evans, James E., (419) 372-2414 evansje@bgsu.edu, Bowling Green State Univ; GsHsGe

Evans, Jenni L., (814) 865-3240 jle7@psu.edu, Pennsylvania State Univ, Univ Park; Am
Evans, Kevin R., (417) 836-5590 kevinevans@missouristate.edu, Missouri State Univ; GrsGt
Evans, Krista M., (417) 836-5688 kristaevans@missouristate.edu, Missouri State Univ; Zn
Evans, Les J., (519) 824-4120 (Ext. 53017) levans@lrs.uoguelph.ca, Univ of Guelph; Cl
Evans, Mark, evansmaa@ccsu.edu, Central Connecticut State Univ; GciGz
Evans, Martin J., mje72@cornell.edu, Cornell Univ; Eo
Evans, Michael E., (780) 492-5517 evans@phys.ualberta.ca, Univ of Alberta; Ym
Evans, Owen C., (631) 632-8061 owen.evans@sunysb.edu, Stony Brook Univ; Cg
Evans, Robert L., (508) 289-2673 revans@whoi.edu, Woods Hole Oceanographic Inst; Yrr
Evans, Sarah G., evanssg@appstate.edu, Appalachian State Univ; Hwq
Evans, Thomas J., (608) 263-4125 tevans@wisc.edu, Univ of Wisconsin, Extension; Gg
Evanylo, Gregory K., (540) 231-9739 gevanylo@vt.edu, Virginia Polytechnic Inst & State Univ; Sc
Eveleth, Robert W., 575-835-5325 bob.eveleth@nmt.edu, New Mexico Inst of Mining and Tech; Nm
Evenson, Edward B., (610) 758-3659 ebe0@lehigh.edu, Lehigh Univ; Gl
Everett, Mark, (979) 862-2129 everett@geo.tamu.edu, Texas A&M Univ; Ym
Eversoll, Duane A., (402) 472-7524 deversoll2@unl.edu, Unversity of Nebraska, Lincoln; Ng
Eves, Robert L., (435) 586-1934 eves@suu.edu, Southern Utah Univ; CgZeCa
Ewart, Terry E., (206) 543-1327 ewart@apl.washington.edu, Univ of Washington; Op
Ewas, Galal A., 002-03-3921595 goueiss@gmail.com, Alexandria Univ; GgNr
Ewing, Rodney C., (650) 497-6203 rewing1@stanford.edu, Stanford Univ; GzeCl
Ewing, Stephanie, stephanie.ewing@montana.edu, Montana State Univ; Sd
Eyles, Carolyn H., (905) 525-9140 (Ext. 24077) eylesc@mcmaster.ca, McMaster Univ; GslGm
Eyles, John D., (905) 525-9140 (Ext. 23152) eyles@mcmaster.ca, McMaster Univ; Ge
Eyles, Nicholas, 416-287-7195 eyles@utsc.utoronto.ca, Univ of Toronto; Gl
Eyre, Bradley, bradley.eyre@scu.edu.au, Southern Cross Univ; CoGeCs
Ezenabor, Ben O., benedict.ezenabor@uniben.edu, Univ of Benin; HgZrGe
Ezerskis, John L., (216) 268-0493 john.ezerskis@tri-c.edu, Cuyahoga Comm Coll - Western Campus; ZgGcHw

F

Faatz, Renee M., (435) 283-7519 renee.faatz@snow.edu, Snow Coll; Gg
Fabbri, Paolo, +390498279124 paolo.fabbri@unipd.it, Univ degli Studi di Padova; Hw
Fabel, Derek, +4401413305473 derek.fabel@glasgow.ac.uk, Univ of Glasgow; Xg
FABRE, Cecile, cecile.fabre@univ-lorraine.fr, Universite de Lorraine - Faculte des Scis et Technologies; Gg
Fabry, Frederic, (514) 398-7733 frederic.fabry@staff.mcgill.ca, McGill Univ; As
Fabryka-Martin, June T., (505) 665-2300 Los Alamos; Hg
Faccenda, Manuele, +390498279159 manuele.faccenda@unipd.it, Univ degli Studi di Padova; Gq
Fadem, Cynthia M., (765) 983-1231 fademcy@earlham.edu, Earlham Coll; GaSoCs
Fadiman, Maria, 561 297-3314 mfadiman@fau.edu, Florida Atlantic Univ; Zn
Fadiya, S. L., 234-803-332-0230 fadiyalawrence@yahoo.co.uk, Obafemi Awolowo Univ; God
Fagan, Amy, 828 227 3820 alfagan@wcu.edu, Western Carolina Univ; GiXg
Fagel, Nathalie, +32 4 3662209 nathalie.fagel@ulg.ac.be, Universite de Liege; GsuGe
Fagents, Sarah, 808-956-3163 fagents@higp.hawaii.edu, Univ of Hawai'i, Manoa; Gv
Fagherazzi, Sergio, (617) 353-2092 sergio@bu.edu, Boston Univ; GmOnGs
Fagnan, Brian A., 605-394-6652 brian.fagnan@state.sd.us, South Dakota Dept of Environment and Natural Resources; Gg
Fahes, Mashhad, mashhad.fahes@ou.edu, Univ of Oklahoma; Np
Fahnestock, Mark A., 603-862-0322 mark.fahnestock@unh.edu, Univ of New Hampshire; Gl
Fahrenbach, Mark D., 605-394-6830 mark.fahrenbach@state.sd.us, South Dakota Dept of Environment and Natural Resources; Gg
Fairbairn, David, +44 (0) 191 208 6353 david.fairbairn@ncl.ac.uk, Univ of Newcastle Upon Tyne; Gq
Fairchild, Ian, +44 (0)121 414 4181 i.j.fairchild@bham.ac.uk, Univ of Birmingham; GsClGm
Fairchild, Jane, jane.fairchild@uwc.edu, Univ of Wisconsin Colls; Am
Fairley, Jerry P., (208) 885-9259 jfairley@uidaho.edu, Univ of Idaho; HwGv
Fajkoviæ, Hana, +38514605969 hanaf@geol.pmf.hr, Univ of Zagreb; CgGeCm
Fakhari, Mohammad D., 614 6584 mohammad.fakhari@dnr.state.oh.us, Ohio Dept of Natural Resources; GocNx
Falcon-Lang, Howard, +44 1784 414039 howard.falcon-lang@rhul.ac.uk, Royal Holloway Univ of London; Pg
Falebita, Dele E., 234-703-298-7836 delefale@oauife.edu.ng, Obafemi Awolowo Univ; YeRnZg
Falk, Lisa, 919-515-8458 esfalk@ncsu.edu, North Carolina State Univ; Zg
Falkena, Lee, 312-996-4499 lfalkena@uic.edu, Univ of Illinois at Chicago; ZeGig
Falkowski, Paul G., falco@imcs.rutgers.edu, Univ of Hawai'i, Manoa; Og
Fall, Andras, (512) 471-8334 andras.fall@beg.utexas.edu, Univ of Texas, Austin; CgGcEg
Fall, Leigh M., 607 436-2615 leigh.fall@oneonta.edu, SUNY, Oneonta; Pgq
Fallowfield, Howard, howard.fallowfield@flinders.edu.au, Flinders Univ; Zn
Falode, Olugbenga, 08130049657 falodelias@gmail.com, Univ of Ibadan; NpZa
Faloona, Ian, 530-752-2044 icfaloona@ucdavis.edu, Univ of California, Davis; AcpAm
Falta, Ronald W., (864) 656-0125 faltar@clemson.edu, Clemson Univ; Hq
Famiglietti, James, (949)824-9434 jfamigli@uci.edu, Univ of California, Irvine; Hw
Fan, Chao, 208-885-0949 cfan@uidaho.edu, Univ of Idaho; Zir
Fan, Majie, (817) 272-2987 mfan@uta.edu, Univ of Texas, Arlington; GstCs
Fan, Weihong, weihong.fan@stockton.edu, Stockton Univ; Zi
Fan, Xingang, xingang.fan@wku.edu, Western Kentucky Univ; As
Fanning, Kent A., (727) 553-1594 kaf@marine.usf.edu, Univ of South Florida; OcGu
Fantle, Matthew S., 814-863-9968 mfantle@geosc.psu.edu, Pennsylvania State Univ, Univ Park; Cs
Faraji, Maedeh, maedeh.faraji@austincc.edu, Austin Comm Coll District; AsZge
Faramarzi, Monireh, monireh.faramarzi@ualberta.ca, Univ of Alberta; HgwHq
Fares, Mary A., (229) 333-5755 mfares@valdosta.edu, Valdosta State Univ; Zn
Fariduddin, Mohammad, 773/442-6059 m-fariduddin@neiu.edu, Northeastern Illinois Univ; Pe
Farley, Kenneth A., (626) 395-6005 farley@gps.caltech.edu, California Inst of Tech; Cg
Farley, Martin B., 910-521-6478 martin.farley@uncp.edu, Univ of North Carolina, Pembroke; PlZe
Farley, Perry D., (505) 667-2415 dfarley@lanl.gov, Los Alamos; Zn
Farmer, Emma C., 516 463-5568 geoecf@hofstra.edu, Hofstra Univ; Ou
Farmer, G. Lang, 303-492-6534 farmer@colorado.edu, Univ of Colorado; Cg
Farmer, George T., (505) 665-0225 gfarmer@lanl.gov, Los Alamos; Hw
Farmer, Jack D., (480) 965-6748 jfarmer@asu.edu, Arizona State Univ; Pg
Farmer, Jesse, 609-258-4101 jess.farmer@princeton.edu, Princeton Univ; Cm
Farnan, Ian, +44 (0) 1223 333431 ifarnan@esc.cam.ac.uk, Univ of Cambridge; Gz
Farnsworth, Katie, 724-357-3406 katie.farnsworth@iup.edu, Indiana Univ of Pennsylvania; Ong
Farquhar, James, (301) 405-5034 jfarquha@umd.edu, Univ of Maryland; Cs
Farquharson, Phil, pfarquharson@miracosta.edu, MiraCosta Coll; Gg
Farr, Tom G., (818) 354-9057 tom.farr@jpl.nasa.gov, Jet Propulsion Lab; Gm
Farrand, William, (734) 764-1435 wfarrand@umich.edu, Univ of Michigan; Ga
Farrell, Brian F., (617) 495-2998 farrell@seas.harvard.edu, Harvard Univ; Am
Farrell, Jamie, 801-581-7856 jamie.farrell@utah.edu, Univ of Utah; Ys
Farrell, John, (401) 874-6561 jfarrell@gso.uri.edu, Univ of Rhode Island; Ou
Farrell, Kathleen M., (919) 733-7353 kathleen.farrell@ncdenr.gov, N.C. Department of Environmental Quality; Gs
Farrell, Mark O., (412) 392-3879 Point Park Univ; Zn
Farrell, Michael, michaelfarrell@myefolio.com, Cuyamaca Coll; Gg
Farrell, Stewart C., (609) 652-4245 Stockton Univ; On
Farrington, John W., 5082741926 (cell Phone) jfarrington@whoi.edu, Woods Hole Oceanographic Inst; ComOc
Farris, David, 252 328 6773 farrisd19@ecu.edu, East Carolina Univ; Ggc

Farrow, Norman D., ndf@ornl.gov, Oak Ridge; Hg
Farsang, Andrea, +3662544156 farsang@geo.u-szeged.hu, Univesity of Szeged; SdZe
Farthing, Dori J., 585-245-5298 farthing@geneseo.edu, SUNY, Geneseo; Gz
Farver, John R., (419) 372-7203 jfarver@bgnet.bgsu.edu, Bowling Green State Univ; Gy
Faryad, Shah Wali, +420221951521 faryad@natur.cuni.cz, Charles Univ; GpzGi
Fastovsky, David, (401) 874-2185 defastov@uri.edu, Univ of Rhode Island; PvGsPs
Fatherree, James W., 813-253-7906 jfatherree@hccfl.edu, Hillsborough Comm Coll; Zg
Faulds, James, (775) 682-8751 jfaulds@unr.edu, Univ of Nevada, Reno; Gc
Faulkner, Daniel, +440151 794 5169 faulkner@liverpool.ac.uk, Univ of Liverpool; Ys
Faulkner, Melinda S., (936) 468-2236 mgshaw@sfasu.edu, Stephen F. Austin State Univ; GeClEg
Faúndez, Alejandro, afaundez@ucm.es, Univ Complutense de Madrid; Ng
Faure, Gunter, faure.1@osu.edu, Ohio State Univ; CgHw
Faure, Stephane, 514-987-3000 #2369 faure.stephane@uqam.ca, Universite du Quebec a Montreal; Gc
Fauria, Kristen, (615) 322-2976 kristen.fauria@vanderbilt.edu, Vanderbilt Univ; GvqYu
Faust, Megan, megfaust@pdx.edu, Portland State Univ; ZeGr
Favas, Paulo J., 351259350220 pjcf@utad.pt, Unive de Trás-os-Montes e Alto Douro; GeCtGg
Favor, Michael, (313) 593-5235 Univ of Michigan, Dearborn; Zn
Favorito, Jessica, jessica.favorito@stockton.edu, Stockton Univ; So
Fawcett, J. J., (416) 978-3027 fawcett@quartz.geology.utoronto.ca, Univ of Toronto; Gp
Fawcett, Peter J., (505) 277-3867 fawcett@unm.edu, Univ of New Mexico; Pe
Fayek, Mostafa, (204) 474-7982 fayek@cc.umanitoba.ca, Univ of Manitoba; Cs
Fayon, Annia K., 612-626-9805 fayon001@umn.edu, Univ of Minnesota, Twin Cities; Gc
Feakins, Sarah, (213) 740-7168 feakins@usc.edu, Univ of Southern California; CoGuCs
Fearey, Bryan L., (505) 665-2423 Los Alamos; Cc
Feather, Russell, (202) 633-1793 featherr@si.edu, Smithsonian Inst / Nat Mus of Natural History; Gz
Fedele, Juan J., 320-308-1049 jjfedele@stcloudstate.edu, Saint Cloud State Univ; Hg
Fedo, Christopher, (865) 974-6002 cfedo@utk.edu, Univ of Tennessee, Knoxville; GsXgCg
Fedorchuk, Nicholas D., (203) 392-2586 fedorchukn1@southernct.edu, Southern Connecticut State Univ; GslGg
Fedorov, Alexey V., (203) 432-3153 alexey.fedorov@yale.edu, Yale Univ; Op
Fedortchouk, Yana, 902 494 8432 yana@dal.ca, Dalhousie Univ; CpEdGi
Feely, Martin, +353 (0)91 492 129 martin.feely@nuigalway.ie, Nat Univ of Ireland Galway; GzxEg
Feely, Richard A., (206) 526-6214 feely@pmel.noaa.gov, Univ of Washington; Oc
Feeney, Alison E., (717) 477-1319 aefeen@ship.edu, Shippensburg Univ; ZinZn
Feeney, Dennis M., (208) 885-5203 dmfeeney@uidaho.edu, Univ of Idaho; GgiYg
Feeney, Thomas P., (717) 477-1297 tpfeen@ship.edu, Shippensburg Univ; ZyGeHw
Fegley, Bruce, (314) 935-4852 bfegley@levee.wustl.edu, Washington Univ in St. Louis; Xc
Fegley, M. Bruce, (314) 935-4852 bfegley@levee.wustl.edu, Washington Univ in St. Louis; Xc
Fehler, Michael, 617-253-3589 fehler@mit.edu, Massachusetts Inst of Tech; Yg
Fehn, Udo, (585) 244-4868 udo.fehn@rochester.edu, Univ of Rochester; GeCgOu
Fehr, Karl Thomas, 089/2180 4256 fehr@min.uni-muenchen.de, Ludwig-Maximilians-Univ Muenchen; Gz
Fehrenbacher, Jennifer, 541-737-6285 fehrenje@coas.oregonstate.edu, Oregon State Univ; Cm
Fehrs, Ellen R., efehrs@pa.gov, DCNR- Pennsylvania Bureau of Geological Survey; Zir
Fei, Yingwei, fei@gl.ciw.edu, Univ of Maryland; CpGxCg
Feibel, Craig S., (848) 445-2721 feibel@eps.rutgers.edu, Rutgers, The State Univ of New Jersey; GrsGa
Feigenson, Mark D., (848) 445-3149 feigy@eps.rutgers.edu, Rutgers, The State Univ of New Jersey; CgGiv
Feigl, Kurt, 608-262-0176 feigl@wisc.edu, Univ of Wisconsin, Madison; Yd
Fein, Jeremy B., (574) 631-6101 fein.1@nd.edu, Univ of Notre Dame; Cl
Feinberg, Joshua, (612) 624-8429 feinberg@umn.edu, Univ of Minnesota, Twin Cities; YmGze
Feineman, Maureen D., 814) 863-6649 mdf12@psu.edu, Pennsylvania State Univ, Univ Park; Cp
Feinglos, Mark N., (919) 668-1367 mark.feinglos@duke.edu, Duke Univ; Gz
Feinstein, Daniel T., (414) 962-2582 dtfeinst@usgs.gov, Univ of Wisconsin, Milwaukee; Hw
Felbeck, Horst, (858) 534-6647 hfelbeck@ucsd.edu, Univ of California, San Diego; Ob
Feldl, Nicole, 831-459-3693 nfeldl@ucsc.edu, Univ of California, Santa Cruz; At
Feldmann, Rodney M., (330) 672-2506 rfeldman@kent.edu, Kent State Univ; Pi
Felix, Joseph D., 361-825-4180 joseph.felix@tamucc.edu, Texas A&M Univ, Corpus Christi; Zn
Feller, Robert, feller@biol.sc.edu, Univ of South Carolina; Ob
Felton, Richard M., (660) 562-1569 rfelton@nwmissouri.edu, Northwest Missouri State Univ; Pg
Felzer, Benjamin S., (610) 758-3536 bsf208@lehigh.edu, Lehigh Univ; ZcoZn
Fenberg, Phillip, +44 (0)23 80592729 p.b.fenberg@soton.ac.uk, Univ of Southampton; Ob
Feng, Huan E., (973) 655-7549 fengh@mail.montclair.edu, Montclair State Univ; Cm
Feng, Jia , (775)682-7251 jiaf@unr.edu, Univ of Nevada, Reno; Zi
Feng, Song, (479) 575-4748 songfeng@uark.edu, Univ of Arkansas, Fayetteville; AsZyAm
Feng, Xiahong, 603-646-1712 xiahong.feng@dartmouth.edu, Dartmouth Coll; Cs
Feng, Yan, 630-252-2550 yfeng@anl.gov, Argonne; As
Feng, Yucheng, (334) 844-3967 yfeng@auburn.edu, Auburn Univ; SbCb
Feng, Zhiqiang, zhiqiang.feng@ed.ac.uk, Edinburgh Univ; Zn
Fengler, Keegan , 509.963.2719 keegan@geology.cwu.edu, Central Washington Univ; Gg
Fenical, William H., (858) 534-2133 wfenical@ucsd.edu, Univ of California, San Diego; Oc
Fennel, Katja, (902) 494-4526 katja.fennel@dal.ca, Dalhousie Univ; Ob
Fenrich, Francis, (780) 492-2149 frances@space.ualberta.ca, Univ of Alberta; Xy
Fenster, Michael S., (804)752-3745 mfenster@rmc.edu, Randolph-Macon Coll; OnGue
Fenstermaker, Lynn, (702) 862-5412 lynn@dri.edu, Desert Research Inst; Zr
Fenter, Paul, (630) 252-7053 fenter@anl.gov, Univ of Illinois at Chicago; Gy
Fenton, Cassandra, 970-248-1077 cfenton@coloradomesa.edu, Colorado Mesa Univ; CcGmCl
Ferdowsi, Behrooz, 609-258-4101 behrooz@princeton.edu, Princeton Univ; Yu
Ferencz, Orsolya, orsi@sas.elte.hu, Eotvos Lorand Univ; XyZr
Ferger, Marisa, (814) 863-4229 mferger@psu.edu, Pennsylvania State Univ, Univ Park; Am
Ferguson, Charles A., 520.621.2470 caf@email.arizona.edu, Univ of Arizona; Gcv
Ferguson, Ian J., (204) 474-9154 ij_ferguson@umanitoba.ca, Univ of Manitoba; YemYu
Ferguson, John F., (972) 883-2410 ferguson@utdallas.edu, Univ of Texas, Dallas; Yg
Ferguson, Julie , (949)824-9411 julie.ferguson@uci.edu, Univ of California, Irvine; Ze
Ferguson, Robert, 403 220-3269 rjfergus@ucalgary.ca, Univ of Calgary; Ye
Ferguson, Terry A., (864) 597-4527 fergusonta@wofford.edu, Wofford Coll; Ga
Fermanich, Kevin J., (920) 465-2240 fermanik@uwgb.edu, Univ of Wisconsin, Green Bay; SpRwHt
Fernandez, Diego, (801) 587-9366 diego.fernandez@utah.edu, Univ of Utah; Cg
Fernandez, Fabian G., 612-625-7460 fabiangf@umn.edu, Univ of Minnesota, Twin Cities; ScbSo
Fernandez, Loretta, 617.373.5461 l.fernandez@neu.edu, Northeastern Univ; Co
Fernandez, Louis A., (909) 537-5024 California State Univ, San Bernardino; Gi
Fernández, Lourdes, lfdiaz@ucm.es, Univ Complutense de Madrid; Gz
Fernández, Luis Ramón, lrfernandez@ucm.es, Univ Complutense de Madrid; Nt
Fernández, Sixto, sixto@ucm.es, Univ Complutense de Madrid; Pg
Fernández, Virginia, (598) 2525 1552 vivi@fcien.edu.uy, Univ de la Republica Oriental del Uruguay (UDELAR); ZirZn
Fernández Suárez, Javier, jfsuarez@ucm.es, Univ Complutense de Madrid;

Cc
Fernández-Barrenechea, José María, barrene@ucm.es, Univ Complutense de Madrid; Gz
Fernando, Joe, harindra.j.fernando.10@nd.edu, Univ of Notre Dame; As
Ferrando, Simona, simona.ferrando@unito.it, Univ di Torino; Gx
Ferrari, Raffaele, (617) 253-1291 raffaele@mit.edu, Massachusetts Inst of Tech; OpAsOb
Ferraris, Giovanni, giovanni.ferraris@unito.it, Univ di Torino; Gz
Ferre, Paul A., (520) 621-2952 ty@hwr.arizona.edu, Univ of Arizona; Hw
Ferre, Paul (Ty), (520) 621-6082 ty@hwr.arizona.edu, Univ of Arizona; So
Ferre', Eric C., 337-482-2228 eric.ferre@louisiana.edu, Univ of Louisiana at Lafayette; YmGc
Ferreira, Anna, +44 020 7679 37704 a.ferreira@ucl.ac.uk, Univ Coll London; Ys
Ferreira, Maryanne F., (508) 289-2266 mferreira@whoi.edu, Woods Hole Oceanographic Inst; Zn
Ferrell, Jr., Ray E., (225) 388-5306 rferrell@lsu.edu, Louisiana State Univ; Cl
Ferren, Richard L., (413) 236-4553 rferren@berkshirecc.edu, Berkshire Comm Coll; Zn
Ferrero, Anna Maria, anna.ferrero@unito.it, Univ di Torino; Nr
Ferrier, Ken, kferrier@wisc.edu, Univ of Wisconsin, Madison; GmZo
Ferring, C. Reid, (940) 565-2993 reid.ferring@unt.edu, Univ of North Texas; Ga
Ferrini, Victoria, ferrini@ldeo.columbia.edu, Columbia Univ; Ou
Ferris, Dawn, 419-755-3909 dferris@sciencesocieties.org, Ohio State Univ; Sf
Ferris, Grant F., 416-978-0526 ferris@quartz.geology.utoronto.ca, Univ of Toronto; Gn
Ferris, Michael H., 310 243-3405 mferris@csudh.edu, California State Univ, Dominguez Hills; Zr
Ferriz, Horacio, 209 667-3874 hferriz@csustan.edu, California State Univ, Stanislaus; NgHgYe
Ferrucci, Fabrizio, fabrizio.ferrucci@open.ac.uk, Open Univ; Yg
Ferruzza, David, (not) li-sted ferruzzad@etown.edu, Elizabethtown Coll; AsZn
Festa, Andrea, andrea.festa@unito.it, Univ di Torino; Gc
Feunstenau, Maurice, mcf@unr.edu, Univ of Nevada, Reno; Nx
Feyereisen, Gary, 612-625-0968 gfeyer@umn.edu, Univ of Minnesota, Twin Cities; Sp
Fialko, Yuri A., (858) 822-5028 yfialko@ucsd.edu, Univ of California, San Diego; YgdGt
Fichera, Marissa, 575-835-5308 marissa.fichera@nmt.edu, New Mexico Inst of Mining and Tech; Hwq
Fichter, Lynn S., (540) 568-6531 fichtels@jmu.edu, James Madison Univ; Gr
Fichtner, Andreas, 089/2180 4230 andreas.fichtner@geophysik.uni-muenchen.de, Ludwig-Maximilians-Univ Muenchen; Yg
Fick, Walter H., (785) 532-7223 whfick@ksu.edu, Kansas State Univ; Sf
Ficken, Cari, (716) 645-3489 carifick@buffalo.edu, SUNY, Buffalo; Zc
Field, Cathryn K., cfield@bowdoin.edu, Bowdoin Coll; Ge
Field, Richard T., 302-831-2695 Univ of Delaware; Og
Field, Stephen W., (254) 968-9887 field@tarleton.edu, Tarleton State Univ; Gz
Fielding, Christopher R., (402) 472-9801 cfielding2@unl.edu, Univ of Nebraska, Lincoln; Gs
Fielding, Lynn, (310) 660-3593 lfielding@elcamino.edu, El Camino Coll; Zg
Fields, Chad, chad.fields@dnr.iowa.gov, Iowa Dept of Natural Resources; Gg
Fields, Nancy, 214-860-2429 nfields@dcccd.edu, El Centro Coll - Dallas Comm Coll District; Zg
Fiesinger, Donald W., don.fiesinger@usu.edu, Utah State Univ; Gi
Fifarek, Richard, fifarek@geo.siu.edu, Southern Illinois Univ Carbondale; Em
Figg, Sean, (760)744-1150 ext 2513 sfigg@palomar.edu, Palomar Coll; Gg
Fike, David A., (314) 935-6607 dfike@levee.wustl.edu, Washington Univ in St. Louis; CsmPg
Fildes, Stephen , stephen.fildes@flinders.edu.au, Flinders Univ; Zri
Filina, Irina, (402) 472-2077 ifilina2@unl.edu, Univ of Nebraska, Lincoln; YgGtYe
Filipescu, Sorin, +40-264-405300 ext 5206 sorin.filipescu@ubbcluj.ro, Babes-Bolyai Univ; GrPm
Filippelli, Gabriel M., (317) 274-3795 gfilippe@iupui.edu, Indiana Univ - Purdue Univ Indianapolis; CmGb
Filkorn, Harry, filkornh@piercecollege.edu, Los Angeles Pierce Coll; GgPi
Filley, Timothy R., (765) 494-6581 filley@purdue.edu, Purdue Univ; Co
Fillion, Luc, 514-421-4770 luc.fillion@ec.gc.ca, McGill Univ; Ams
Fillmore, Robert P., (970) 943-2650 rfillmore@western.edu, Western Colorado Univ; Gs
Finch, Adriam, +44 (0) 1334 462384 aaf1@st-and.ac.uk, Univ of St. Andrews; Gz
Finger, Ken, 510-6432559 kfinger@berkeley.edu, Univ of California, Berkeley; PmZnn
Fink, Uwe, (520) 2736 uwefink@lpl.arizona.edu, Univ of Arizona; As
Finkel, Robert C., (925) 422-2044 finkel1@llnl.gov, Lawrence Livermore; Cg
Finkelman, Robert B., (972) 883-2459 bobf@utdallas.edu, Univ of Texas, Dallas; GbEcCa
Finkelstein, David, (315) 781-4443 finkelstein@hws.edu, Hobart & William Smith Colls; CgbCs
Finkenbinder, Matthew S., (570) 408-3871 matthew.finkenbinder@wilkes.edu, Wilkes Univ; GsmGl
Finks, Robert M., (718) 997-3305 Queens Coll (CUNY); Pi
Finley, Jason P., finleyjp@piercecollege.edu, Los Angeles Pierce Coll; Am
Finley, Mark, (309) 268-8642 mark.finley@heartland.edu, Heartland Comm Coll; Gg
Finley, Robert J., 217-244-8389 finley@isgs.uiuc.edu, Illinois State Geological Survey; Eo
Finley, William R., 337-482-6468 wfinley@rocmando.com, Univ of Louisiana at Lafayette; YsZi
Finn, Gregory C., (905) 688-5550 x3528 greg.finn@brocku.ca, Brock Univ; Gx
Finnegan, David L., (505) 667-6548 Los Alamos; As
Finnegan, Noah J., 831-459-5110 nfinnegan@pmc.ucsc.edu, Univ of California, Santa Cruz; Gm
Finnegan, Seth, sethf@berkeley.edu, Univ of California, Berkeley; Pig
Finney, Bruce P., (907) 474-7724 Univ of Alaska, Fairbanks; Ou
Finney, Stanley C., (562) 985-8637 scfinney@csulb.edu, California State Univ, Long Beach; Psi
Finzel, Emily, (319) 335-0405 emily-finzel@uiowa.edu, Univ of Iowa; GstEo
Fio, Karmen, +38514606088 karmen.fio@gmail.com, Univ of Zagreb; PgGg
Fiore, Arlene, amfiore@ldeo.columbia.edu, Columbia Univ; As
Fiorillo, Anthony R., (214) 421-3466 Southern Methodist Univ; Pv
Firing, Eric, (808) 956-7894 efiring@hawaii.edu, Univ of Hawai'i, Manoa; Op
Fischer, Alfred G., (213) 740-5821 fisher@usc.edu, Univ of Southern California; Gs
Fischer, Emily, evf@rams.colostate.edu, Colorado State Univ; As
Fischer, Karen M., (401) 863-1360 karen_fischer@brown.edu, Brown Univ; Ys
Fischer, Mark P., (815) 753-0523 mfischer@niu.edu, Northern Illinois Univ; GcoHy
Fischer, Rebecca A., 617-384-6992 rebeccafischer@fas.harvard.edu, Harvard Univ; Gy
Fischer, Tobias, (505) 277-0683 fischer@unm.edu, Univ of New Mexico; Gv
Fish, Jennifer M., 831-459-1235 jmsfish@ucsc.edu, Univ of California, Santa Cruz; Zn
Fisher, Andrew T., (831) 459-5598 afisher@ucsc.edu, Univ of California, Santa Cruz; Hw
Fisher, Daniel C., (734) 764-0488 dcfisher@umich.edu, Univ of Michigan; Pi
Fisher, David A., 613-996-7623 fisher@nrcan-rncan.gc.ca, Univ of Ottawa; Gl
Fisher, Donald M., (814) 865-3206 fisher@geosc.psu.edu, Pennsylvania State Univ, Univ Park; GctZm
Fisher, Janet, janet.fisher@ed.ac.uk, Edinburgh Univ; Zn
Fisher, Liz, +440151 795 4390 e.h.fisher@liverpool.ac.uk, Univ of Liverpool; Co
Fisher, Nicholas S., (631) 632-8649 nicholas.fisher@stonybrook.edu, SUNY, Stony Brook; Oc
Fisher, Quentin , +44(0) 113 34 31920 q.j.fisher@leeds.ac.uk, Univ of Leeds; Np
Fisher, Rebecca, +44 1784 443628 r.e.fisher@rhul.ac.uk, Royal Holloway Univ of London; As
Fisher, Timothy G., (419) 530-2009 timothy.fisher@utoledo.edu, Univ of Toledo; GlmGn
Fisher, William L., (512) 471-5600 wfisher@mail.utexas.edu, Univ of Texas, Austin; GsrGo
Fisher, Jr., Thomas R., (410) 221-8432 fisher@hpl.umces.edu, Univ of Maryland; ObZiCl
Fishman, George , (781) 891-2721 gfishman@bentley.edu, Bentley Univ; XgbXc
Fishman, Jack, (314) 977-3132 jfishma2@slu.edu, Saint Louis Univ; As
Fishwick, Stewart, +44 0116 252 3810 hos-geoggeolenv@leicester.ac.uk, Leicester Univ; Yg
Fisk, Aaron, 519-253-3000 x4740 afisk@uwindsor.ca, Univ of Windsor; ObCs
Fitak, Madge R., 614-265-6585 madge.fitak@dnr.state.oh.us, Ohio Dept of Natural Resources; Gg
Fitchett, Rebekah, 773-442-6052 r-fitchett@neiu.edu, Northeastern Illinois

Univ; GgCg
Fitton, J. G., +44 (0) 131 650 8529 godfrey.fitton@ed.ac.uk, Edinburgh Univ; Gi
Fitz, Thomas J., (715) 682-1852 tfitz@northland.edu, Northland Coll; GgxGc
Fitzer, Susan, +44 01413305442 susan.fitzer@glasgow.ac.uk, Univ of Glasgow; Ob
Fitzgerald, David, (210) 436-3235 Saint Mary's Univ; Gd
FitzGerald, Duncan M., (617) 353-2530 dunc@bu.edu, Boston Univ; OnGsu
Fitzgerald, Francis S., 303-384-2644 ffitzger@mines.edu, Colorado Geological Survey; ZirGg
Fitzgerald, Paul G., (315) 443-2672 pgfitzge@syr.edu, Syracuse Univ; GtCc
Fitzgerald, William F., (860) 405-9158 william.fitzgerald@uconn.edu, Univ of Connecticut; Oc
Fitzjarrald, David R., (518) 437-8735 dfitzjarrald@albany.edu, SUNY, Albany; Asm
Fitzpatrick, John R., (505) 667-4761 Los Alamos; Zn
FitzPatrick, Meriel E., +44 1752 584769 m.e.fitzpatrick@plymouth.ac.uk, Univ of Plymouth; PlgGr
Fitzpatrick, Patrick J., (228) 688-1157 fitz@gri.msstate.edu, Mississippi State Univ; Am
Fitzpatrick, Stephan D., (678) 891-3773 sfitzpatrick1@gsu.edu, Georgia State Univ, Perimeter Coll, Clarkston Campus; HwCgSo
Fitzpatrick, William, (608) 263-0972 wfitzpatric3@wisc.edu, Univ of Wisconsin, Madison, Division of Extension; EgGi
Fitzsimmons, Jessica N., 979-845-5137 jessfitz@tamu.edu, Texas A&M Univ; OcCta
Fitzsimmons, Kevin, (520) 626-3324 kevfitz@ag.arizona.edu, Univ of Arizona; Zn
Fjell, Dale, (785) 532-5833 dfjell@ksu.edu, Kansas State Univ; So
Flagg, Charles, (631) 632-3184 charles.flagg@stonybrook.edu, SUNY, Stony Brook; Op
Flaherty, Frank A., (229) 333-5665 flaherty@valdosta.edu, Valdosta State Univ; Zn
Flaig, Peter P., peter.flaig@beg.utexas.edu, Univ of Texas, Austin; GsrEo
Flake, Rex , 509.963.1114 rex@geology.cwu.edu, Central Washington Univ; Yd
Flament, Pierre J., (808) 956-6663 pflament@hawaii.edu, Univ of Hawai'i, Manoa; Op
Flanagan, Michael, flanagam@sunysuffolk.edu, Suffolk County Comm Coll, Ammerman Campus; Zg
Flanagan, Timothy, (413) 236-4503 tflanaga@berkshirecc.edu, Berkshire Comm Coll; Zei
Flannery, David, +61 7 3138-1615 david.flannery@qut.edu.au, Queensland Univ of Tech; PoCaXg
Flato, Gregory M., (250) 363-8223 greg.flato@ec.gc.ca, Univ of Victoria; As
Flawn, Peter T., (512) 471-1825 pflawn@po.utexas.edu, Univ of Texas, Austin; Eg
Fleck, Michelle C., (435) 613-5232 michelle.fleck@usu.edu, Utah State Univ Eastern; GgZy
Flegal, Russell, (831) 459-2093 rflegal@es.ucsc.edu, Univ of California, Santa Cruz; Cg
Fleisher, P. Jay, (607) 286-7541 fleishpj@oneonta.edu, SUNY, Oneonta; GlmGe
Fleming, Thomas H., 203-392-5837 flemingt1@southernct.edu, Southern Connecticut State Univ; GiCgc
Flemings, Peter B., 512-471-6156 flemings@ig.utexas.edu, Univ of Texas, Austin; Gr
Flemming, Roberta L., (519) 661-3143 rflemmin@uwo.ca, Western Univ; GzXmZm
Flesch, Lucy M., (765) 494-0263 lmflesch@purdue.edu, Purdue Univ; Yg
Flesken, Luuk, +31(0) 317 485467 l.fleskens@leeds.ac.uk, Univ of Leeds; Ge
Flessa, Karl W., (520) 621-7336 kflessa@email.arizona.edu, Univ of Arizona; PgeGe
Fletcher, Andrew, +61 7 3138 5362 a20.fletcher@qut.edu.au, Queensland Univ of Tech; Zri
Fletcher, Austin, rfletche@uoguelph.ca, Univ of Guelph; Zn
Fletcher, Charles H., (808) 956-2582 fletcher@soest.hawaii.edu, Univ of Hawai'i, Manoa; GsOnZu
Fletcher, John, jfletche@cicese.mx, Centro de Investigación Científica y de Educación Superior de Ensenada; Gpt
Fletcher, Madilyn, fletcher@sc.edu, Univ of South Carolina; Ob
Fletcher, William K., (604) 822-2392 wfletcher@eos.ubc.ca, Univ of British Columbia; Ce
Flierl, Glenn R., (617) 253-4692 glenn@lake.mit.edu, Massachusetts Inst of Tech; Op
Flint, Stephen, +44 0161 306-6971 stephen.flint@manchester.ac.uk, Univ of Manchester; GrsGo
Flood, Beverly, 612-624-1603 floo0017@umn.edu, Univ of Minnesota, Twin Cities; Pg
Flood, Peter, +61-2-67732329 pflood@une.edu.au, Univ of New England; EcGt
Flood, Roger D., (631) 632-6971 roger.flood@stonybrook.edu, SUNY, Stony Brook; Ou
Flood, Tim P., (920) 403-1356 tim.flood@snc.edu, Saint Norbert Coll; GvZe
Florea, Lee, (812) 855-1376 lflorea@indiana.edu, Indiana Univ, Bloomington; Hg
Flores, Alejandro N., lejoflores@boisestate.edu, Boise State Univ; HqAs
Flores, Carlos, cflores@cicese.mx, Centro de Investigación Científica y de Educación Superior de Ensenada; Ye
Flores, Kennet, 718-951-5000 x3253 keflores@brooklyn.cuny.edu, Brooklyn Coll (CUNY); Gpc
Flores-Garcia, Mari C., (818) 677-3541 mari.flores@csun.edu, California State Univ, Northridge; Zn
Florie, Joshua, joshua.florie@tulsacc.edu, Tulsa Comm Coll; OgGg
Floris, Mario, +390498279121 mario.floris@unipd.it, Univ degli Studi di Padova; NgZr
Flory, David M., (515) 294-0264 flory@iastate.edu, Iowa State Univ of Sci & Tech; AmsZn
Flower, Hilary, flower.hilary@spcollege.edu, Saint Petersburg Coll, Clearwater; Gg
Flower, Martin F., +1 312 391-7632 flower@uic.edu, Univ of Illinois at Chicago; GiCuGt
Flowers, George C., (504) 862-3192 flowers@tulane.edu, Tulane Univ; Hw
Flowers, Gwenn, (778)782-6638 gflowers@sfu.ca, Simon Fraser Univ; Gl
Flowers, Rebecca M., (303) 492-5135 rebecca.flowers@colorado.edu, Univ of Colorado; CgcGt
Flowers Falls, Emily, (540) 458-8868 fallse@wlu.edu, Washington & Lee Univ; Gg
Floyd, Barry, 518-473-9988 esogis@mail.nysed.gov, New York State Geological Survey; Zn
Fluegeman, Richard H., (765) 285-8267 rfluegem@bsu.edu, Ball State Univ; PmGro
Flynn, John J., (212) 769-5806 American Mus of Natural History; Pv
Flynn, Luke P., (808) 956-3154 flynn@higp.hawaii.edu, Univ of Hawai'i, Manoa; Zr
Flynn, Wendilyn, 970-351-1071 wendilyn.flynn@unco.edu, Univ of Northern Colorado; Ams
Fodor, Ronald V., (919) 515-7177 ron_fodor@ncsu.edu, North Carolina State Univ; Gi
Fogel, David N., (505) 665-3305 fogel@lanl.gov, Los Alamos; Zn
Fogg, Graham E., (916) 752-6810 Univ of California, Davis; Hy
Foglia, Laura, lfoglia@ucdavis.edu, Univ of California, Davis; HwZc
Foit, Jr., Franklin F., (509) 335-3093 Washington State Univ; Gz
Foland, Kenneth A., foland.1@osu.edu, Ohio State Univ; CcgCs
Foley, Bradford, (814) 863-3591 bjf5382@psu.edu, Pennsylvania State Univ, Univ Park; YgXyGt
Foley, Duncan, (253) 535-7568 foleyd@plu.edu, Pacific Lutheran Univ; GeHyZe
Foley, John P., (406) 496-4414 jfoley@mtech.edu, Montana Tech of The Univ of Montana; Zn
Folk, Robert L., (512) 471-5294 rlfolk@mail.utexas.edu, Univ of Texas, Austin; Gd
Follmer, Leon R., (217) 359-2090 lfollmer@illinois.edu, Univ of Illinois, Urbana-Champaign; SaGlm
Follows, Michael, (617) 253-5939 mick@mit.edu, Massachusetts Inst of Tech; Op
Folorunso, I. O., foloisgood@yahoo.com, Univ of Ilorin; GoCg
Fomel, Sergey, 512-475-9573 sergey.fomel@beg.utexas.edu, Univ of Texas at Austin, Jackson Sch of Geosciences; Yx
Fondevilla, Victor, victor.fondevilla@uab.cat, Universitat Autonoma de Barcelona; PgGr
Fondran, Carol, (216) 987-5227 carol.fondran@tri-c.edu, Cuyahoga Comm Coll - Western Campus; Zg
Fones, Gary, +44 023 92 842252 gary.fones@port.ac.uk, Univ of Portsmouth; Cm
Fonstad, Mark, fonstad@uoregon.edu, Univ of Oregon; Zy
Fontaine, Fabrice R., +262262938207 fabrice.fontaine@univ-reunion.fr, Universite de la Reunion; Yg
Fontana, Alessandro, +390498279118 alessandro.fontana@unipd.it, Univ degli Studi di Padova; Gm
Foote, Michael J., (773) 702-4320 mfoote@midway.uchicago.edu, Univ of Chicago; Pg
Forbriger, Thomas, +49-721-6084593 thomas.forbriger@kit.edu, Karlsruhe Inst of Tech; Ys
Forcino, Frank, (828) 227-2888 flforcino@wcu.edu, Western Carolina Univ; PgZeGr
Ford, Allistair, +44 (0) 191 208 7121 alistair.ford@ncl.ac.uk, Univ of

Newcastle Upon Tyne; Gq
Ford, Andrew, 509-335-7846 forda@wsu.edu, Washington State Univ; Zu
Ford, Arianne, arianne.ford@jcu.edu.au, James Cook Univ; GqZiEg
Ford, Derek C., (905) 525-9140 x20132 dford@mcmaster.ca, McMaster Univ; GmHwCc
Ford, Heather, (951) 827-3194 heather.ford@ucr.edu, Univ of California, Riverside; Ys
Ford, Mark T., 361-593-2767 mark.ford@tamuk.edu, Texas A&M Univ, Kingsville; GxzCg
Ford, Richard L., (801) 626-6942 rford@weber.edu, Weber State Univ; GmZeEo
Fordyce, R. Ewan, +64 3 479-7510/7535 ewan.fordyce@otago.ac.nz, Univ of Otago; Pv
Foreman, Brady Z., 360-650-2546 brady.foreman@wwu.edu, Western Washington Univ; Grs
Foreman, Michael G., 250-363-6306 mike.foreman@dfo-mpo.gc.ca, Univ of Victoria; OpZo
Foreman, Michael G. G., (250) 363-6306 foremanm@pac.dfo-mpo.gc.ca, Univ of British Columbia; Op
Foresi, Luca Maria, luca.foresi@unisi.it, Univ of Siena; PmGs
Foret, Jim, 337-482-6064 jaf3663@louisiana.edu, Univ of Louisiana at Lafayette; Ge
Forman, Stephen, (254)710-2495 steve_forman@baylor.edu, Baylor Univ; CcPc
Fornaciari, Eliana, +390498279185 eliana.fornaciari@unipd.it, Univ degli Studi di Padova; Pgm
Fornari, Daniel J., (508) 289-2857 dfornari@whoi.edu, Woods Hole Oceanographic Inst; Gu
Forno, Maria Gabriella, gabriella.forno@unito.it, Univ di Torino; Gg
Forrest, David, +4401413305401 david.forrest@glasgow.ac.uk, Univ of Glasgow; Zi
Forsman, Nels F., (701) 777-4349 nels.forsman@engr.und.edu, Univ of North Dakota; GgXgRh
Forster, Piers M., +44(0) 113 34 36476 p.m.forster@leeds.ac.uk, Univ of Leeds; As
Forster, Richard R., (801) 581-3611 rick.forster@geog.utah.edu, Univ of Utah; Zr
Forsyth, Donald W., (401) 863-1699 donald_forsyth@brown.edu, Brown Univ; YrsGt
Forte, Adam, aforte8@lsu.edu, Louisiana State Univ; Gcm
Forte, Alessandro Marco, 514-987-3000 #5607 forte.alessandro@uqam.ca, Universite du Quebec a Montreal; Yg
Fortes, Dominic, andrew.fortes@ucl.ac.uk, Birkbeck Coll; Zg
Fortier, Richard, (418) 656-2746 richard.fortier@ggl.ulaval.ca, Universite Laval; Yg
Fortin, Danielle, dfortin@uottawa.ca, Univ of Ottawa; CblGe
Fortner, Sarah K., (937) 327-7328 sfortner@wittenberg.edu, Wittenberg Univ; ClZeHg
Foss, Donald J., (415) 485-9523 jcprice@metro.net, Coll of Marin; Zg
Foster, David A., (352) 392-2231 dafoster@ufl.edu, Univ of Florida; GtCc
Foster, Gavin, +44 (0)23 8059 3786 gavin.foster@noc.soton.ac.uk, Univ of Southampton; Csg
Foster, Patrick, +44 01326 371828 p.j.foster@exeter.ac.uk, Exeter Univ; Nm
Foster, Stuart A., (270) 745-5983 stuart.foster@wku.edu, Western Kentucky Univ; At
Foster Jr., Charles T., (319) 335-1801 tom-foster@uiowa.edu, Univ of Iowa; GptGg
Foti, Pamela, (928) 523-6196 pam.foti@nau.edu, Northern Arizona Univ; Zn
Fotopoulos, Georgia, (613) 533-6639 georgia.fotopoulos@queensu.ca, Queen's Univ; Yd
Foufoula-Georgiou, Efi, (612) 626-0369 Univ of Minnesota, Twin Cities; Hg
Fouke, Bruce W., (217) 244-5431 fouke@illinois.edu, Univ of Illinois, Urbana-Champaign; GsdGb
Fountain, Andrew G., (503) 725-3386 andrew@pdx.edu, Portland State Univ; Gl
Fountain, John C., 919-515-3717 fountain@ncsu.edu, North Carolina State Univ; Hw
Fournelle, John, (608) 438-7480 johnf@geology.wisc.edu, Univ of Wisconsin, Madison; GiZn
Fournier, Benoit, (418) 656-3930 benoit.fournier@ggl.ulaval.ca, Universite Laval; NgZmGg
Fournier, Gregory, 617-324-6164 g4nier@mit.edu, Massachusetts Inst of Tech; Pg
Fournier, Robert O., (902) 494-3666 robert.fournier@dal.ca, Dalhousie Univ; Ob
Foustoukos, Dionysis, dfoustoukos@carnegiescience.edu, Carnegie Inst for Sci; Cg
Fovell, Robert, (310) 206-9956 fovell@atmos.ucla.edu, Univ of California, Los Angeles; As
Fowell, Sarah J., (907) 474-7810 sjfowell@alaska.edu, Univ of Alaska, Fairbanks; Pl
Fowle, David A., (785) 864-1955 fowle@ku.edu, Univ of Kansas; Cb
Fowler, Gerald A., fowler@uwp.edu, Univ of Wisconsin, Parkside; PgGg
Fowler, Malcolm M., (505) 667-5439 Los Alamos; As
Fowler, Mike, +44 023 92 842293 mike.fowler@port.ac.uk, Univ of Portsmouth; Gi
Fowler, Sarah, sarah.fowler@ees.kuleuven.be, Katholieke Universiteit Leuven; Gip
Fox, Austin, (321) 674-7463 afox@fit.edu, Florida Inst of Tech; Oc
Fox, David L., 612-624-6361 dlfox@umn.edu, Univ of Minnesota, Twin Cities; Pg
Fox, James E., (605) 394-2461 james.fox@sdsmt.edu, South Dakota Sch of Mines & Tech; Gs
Fox, Jeff, 740 2012762 jeff.fox@dnr.state.oh.us, Ohio Dept of Natural Resources; YsmZe
Fox, Laurel R., (831) 459-2533 fox@biology.ucsc.edu, Univ of California, Santa Cruz; Zn
Fox, Lewis, 954-201-6674 lfox@broward.edu, Broward Coll; Oc
Fox, Lydia K., (209) 946-2481 lkfox@pacific.edu, Univ of the Pacific; GizZe
Fox, Nathaniel, 605-394-2487 nathaniel.fox@sdsmt.edu, South Dakota Sch of Mines & Tech; Pgv
Fox, Neil I., 573-882-2144 foxn@missouri.edu, Univ of Missouri; As
Fox, Nicholas, nicholas.fox3@montana.edu, Montana State Univ; Zi
Fox, Peter A., (518) 727-4862 pfox@cs.rpi.edu, Rensselaer Polytechnic Inst; GqZig
Fox-Dobbs, Kena L., 253-879-2458 kena@pugetsound.edu, Univ of Puget Sound; PgCsGe
Fox-Kemper, Baylor, 401-863-3979 baylor@brown.edu, Brown Univ; OpYnAt
Foxon, Tim, +44(0) 113 34 37910 t.j.foxon@leeds.ac.uk, Univ of Leeds; Ge
Frail, Pam, (902) 585-1513 pam.frail@acadiau.ca, Acadia Univ; Gg
Frailey, Scott M., 217-244-2430 sfrailey@illinois.edu, Illinois State Geological Survey; Np
Fraiser, Margaret L., mfraiser@uwm.edu, Univ of Wisconsin, Milwaukee; PiePg
Fralick, Philip W., (807) 343-8288 philip.fralick@lakeheadu.ca, Lakehead Univ; Gs
Fram, Jonathan, 541-737-3966 jfram@coas.oregonstate.edu, Oregon State Univ; Op
Frame, Jeffrey, 217-244-9575 frame@illinois.edu, Univ of Illinois, Urbana-Champaign; Asm
Francis, Don, donald.francis@mcgill.ca, McGill Univ; Gi
Francis, Jane, j.e.francis@leeds.ac.uk, Univ of Leeds; Pe
Francis, Robert, (206) 543-7345 Univ of Washington; Ob
Francisco, Joseph, frjoseph@sas.upenn.edu, Univ of Pennsylvania; Ac
Franco, Aldina, +44 (0)1603 59 2721 a.franco@uea.ac.uk, Univ of East Anglia; Ge
Francois, Roger, rfrancois@eos.ubc.ca, Univ of British Columbia; Cm
Francus, Pierre, pierre.francus@ete.inrs.ca, Universite du Quebec; PeGse
Franek, Benjamin, (570) 389-4567 bfranek@bloomu.edu, Bloomsburg Univ; HsZy
Frank, Charles O., (618) 453-7365 frank@geo.siu.edu, Southern Illinois Univ Carbondale; Gx
Frank, Kenneth, (902) 426-3498 frankk@mar.dfo-mpo.gc.ca, Dalhousie Univ; Ob
Frank, Mark R., (815) 753-8395 mfrank@niu.edu, Northern Illinois Univ; Cp
Frank, Tracy D., (402) 472-9799 tfrank2@unl.edu, Univ of Nebraska, Lincoln; GssCs
Frank, William M., frank@ems.psu.edu, Pennsylvania State Univ, Univ Park; Am
Frankel, Arthur, 206-553-0626 afrankel@uw.edu, Univ of Washington; Ys
Frankel, Tyler E., tfrankel@umw.edu, Univ of Mary Washington; Rw
Frankenberg, Christian, 626-395-6143 cfranken@caltech.edu, California Inst of Tech; Zr
Frankic, Anamarija, anamarija.frankic@umb.edu, Univ of Massachusetts, Boston; Ze
Franklin, David, +44 023 92 843540 david.franklin@port.ac.uk, Univ of Portsmouth; Ym
Franks, Peter J. S., (858) 534-7528 pfranks@ucsd.edu, Univ of California, San Diego; Ob
Franseen, Evan K., (785) 864-2072 evanf@kgs.ku.edu, Univ of Kansas; Gd
Fransolet, Andre-Mathieu, 32 4 366 22 06 amfransolet@ulg.ac.be, Universite de Liege; Gz
Frantz, Carie M., (801) 626-6181 cariefrantz@weber.edu, Weber State Univ; PoCbZn
Franz, Eldon H., (206) 300-9259 franz@wsu.edu, Washington State Univ; Sf
Franz, Kristie, (515) 294-7454 kfranz@iastate.edu, Iowa State Univ of Sci

& Tech; Hs
Franzi, David A., (518) 564-4033 franzida@plattsburgh.edu, SUNY, Plattsburgh; Gl
Frappier, Amy, 518-580-8371 afrappie@skidmore.edu, Skidmore Coll; GePe
Fraser, Alastair, 44-20-7594-6530 afraser@egi.utah.edu, Univ of Utah; Gco
Fraser, Alistair B., abf1@psu.edu, Pennsylvania State Univ, Univ Park; Am
Fraser, Donalf G., +44 (1865) 272033 don@earth.ox.ac.uk, Univ of Oxford; Cg
Fraser-Smith, Antony C., (650) 723-3684 Stanford Univ; Ym
Frasson, Renato , frasson.1@osu.edu, Ohio State Univ; Hg
Fratta, Dante, 608-265-5644 fratta@wisc.edu, Univ of Wisconsin, Madison; Yx
Frazer, L. N., (808) 956-3724 neil@soest.hawaii.edu, Univ of Hawai'i, Manoa; Ys
Frazier, Ryan J., (801) 626-7435 ryanfrazier@weber.edu, Weber State Univ; ZriZc
Frederick, Bruce, bfreder6@jccc.edu, Johnson County Comm Coll; Gg
Frederick, Daniel L., (931) 221-7455 frederickd@apsu.edu, Austin Peay State Univ; PgGsr
Frederick, Holly, 570-408-4880 holly.frederick@wilkes.edi, Wilkes Univ; Sdb
Frederick, John E., (773) 702-3237 Univ of Chicago; As
Frederickson, Paul A., 831-595-5212 pafreder@nps.edu, Naval Postgraduate Sch; Am
Frederiksen, Andrew, (204) 474-9460 andrew_frederiksen@umanitoba.ca, Univ of Manitoba; YsGt
Fredrick, Kyle, (724) 938-4180 fredrick@calu.edu, California Univ of Pennsylvania; GgHgGm
Fredricks, Helen, 508-289-3678 hfredricks@whoi.edu, Woods Hole Oceanographic Inst; Oc
Freed, Andrew M., freed@purdue.edu, Purdue Univ; Gg
Freed, Robert L., (210) 999-7092 bfreed@trinity.edu, Trinity Univ; Gz
Freeman, Katherine H., (814) 863-8177 khf4@psu.edu, Pennsylvania State Univ, Univ Park; Cos
Freeman, Rebecca, (859) 257-3758 rebecca.freeman@uky.edu, Univ of Kentucky; GrPi
Freeman, Veronica, 740-376-4779 freemanv@marietta.edu, Marietta Coll; Pg
Freeman-Lynde, Raymond, rfreeman@uga.edu, Univ of Georgia; Gu
Fregenal, María Antonia, mariana@ucm.es, Univ Complutense de Madrid; Gsg
Frei, Allan, 212-772-5322 afrei@hunter.cuny.edu, Graduate Sch of the City Univ of New York; Gg
Frei, Michaela, 089/2180 6590 michaela.frei@iaag.geo.uni-muenchen.de, Ludwig-Maximilians-Univ Muenchen; Gg
Freiburg, Jared, 217-244-2495 freiburg@illinois.edu, Illinois State Geological Survey; GgzGx
Freiermuth, Sue, (715) 425-3345 susan.m.freiermuth@uwrf.edu, Univ of Wisconsin, River Falls; Zn
Freile, Deborah, (201) 200-3161 dfreile@njcu.edu, New Jersey City Univ; GseGg
Freitas, Maria d., cfreitas@fc.ul.pt, Unive de Lisboa; GseGu
Freitas, Maria da Conceição P., +351217500352 cfreitas@fc.ul.pt, Unive de Lisboa; GusGe
French, Adam, (605) 394-1649 adam.french@sdsmt.edu, South Dakota Sch of Mines & Tech; Asm
French, Bevan, (202) 633-1326 Smithsonian Inst / Nat Mus of Natural History; Xm
French, Mark A., (609) 984-6587 mark.french@dep.state.nj.us, New Jersey Geological and Water Survey; Hq
French, Melodie E., 713.348.5088 mefrench@rice.edu, Rice Univ; Gc
Frenette, Jean, 418-656-8123 frenette@ggl.ulaval.ca, Universite Laval; Gz
Frew, Nelson M., (508) 289-2489 nfrew@whoi.edu, Woods Hole Oceanographic Inst; Ca
Frey, Bonnie A., 575-835-5160 bonnie.frey@nmt.edu, New Mexico Inst of Mining and Tech; Cg
Frey, Frederick A., (617) 253-2818 fafrey@mit.edu, Massachusetts Inst of Tech; CtGvi
Frey, Friedrich, 089/21804332 f.frey@lmu.de, Ludwig-Maximilians-Univ Muenchen; Gz
Frey, Holli M., 518-388-6418 freyh@union.edu, Union Coll; GvCag
Frey, Serita, serita.frey@unh.edu, Univ of New Hampshire; Sb
Frez, Jose, jofrez@cicese.mx, Centro de Investigación Científica y de Educación Superior de Ensenada; Ys
Fricke, Henry C., (719) 389-6514 hfricke@coloradocollege.edu, Colorado Coll; Cs
Fricker, Helen A., (858) 534-6145 hafricker@ucsd.edu, Univ of California, San Diego; Yr
Friedl, Mark, friell@bu.edu, Boston Univ; Zr
Friedman, Matt, +44 (1865) 272035 matt.friedman@earth.ox.ac.uk, Univ of Oxford; Pg
Friedmann, Samuel (Julio) J., (925) 423-0585 friedmann2@llnl.gov, Lawrence Livermore; Gg
Friedrich, Anke, friedrich@iaag.geo.uni-muenchen.de, Ludwig-Maximilians-Univ Muenchen; GgtCc
Friedrichs, Carl T., (804) 684-7303 cfried@vims.edu, William & Mary; On
Friehauf, Kurt, (610) 683-4446 friehauf@kutztown.edu, Kutztown Univ of Pennsylvania; EmCgGx
Frieman, Richard, richard.frieman@oswego.edu, SUNY, Oswego; Gg
Frierson, Dargan M., (206) 685-7364 dargan@atmos.washington.edu, Univ of Washington; As
Frind, Emil O., (519) 888-4567 (Ext. 3959) Univ of Waterloo; Hq
Frisbee, Marty, (765) 494-8678 mfrisbee@purdue.edu, Purdue Univ; Hws
Frisia, Silvia, +61 2 4921 5402 silvia.frisia@newcastle.edu.au, Univ of Newcastle; ClPeGd
Frisk, DeAnn M., (515) 294-4477 dfrisk@iastate.edu, Iowa State Univ of Sci & Tech; Zn
Fritsch, J. Michael, (814) 863-1842 fritsch@ems.psu.edu, Pennsylvania State Univ, Univ Park; Am
Fritsen, Christian H., (775) 673-7487 cfritsen@dri.edu, Desert Research Inst; Pg
Fritton, Daniel D., (814) 865-1143 ddf@psu.edu, Pennsylvania State Univ, Univ Park; Sp
Fritz, Allan, (785) 532-7245 akf@ksu.edu, Kansas State Univ; So
Fritz, Sherilyn C., (402) 472-6431 sfritz2@unl.edu, Univ of Nebraska, Lincoln; Pem
Fritz, William, 718-982-2400 william.fritz@csi.cuny.edu, Graduate Sch of the City Univ of New York; Zg
Froehlich, David J., (512) 223-4894 eohippus@austincc.edu, Austin Comm Coll District; PvZn
Froelich, Philip, 850-644-4331 froelich@ocean.fsu.edu, Florida State Univ; Og
Froese, Duane, (780) 492-1968 duane.froese@ualberta.ca, Univ of Alberta; GlmPe
Frohlich, Cliff, (512) 471-0460 cliff@ig.utexas.edu, Univ of Texas, Austin; Ys
Frohlich, Clifford A., 512-471-0460 cliff@ig.utexas.edu, Univ of Texas, Austin; YsGt
Frolking, Stephen E., (603) 862-0244 steve.frolking@unh.edu, Univ of New Hampshire; As
Frolking, Tod A., (740) 587-6222 frolking@denison.edu, Denison Univ; Zy
Fromm, Jeanne M., (605) 582-3416 jeanne.fromm@usd.edu, Univ of South Dakota; GgHs
Frost, B. Ronald, (307) 399-5585 rfrost@uwyo.edu, Univ of Wyoming; GpiEd
Frost, Bruce W., 206-543-7186 frost@ocean.washington.edu, Univ of Washington; Ob
Frost, Carol D., frost@uwyo.edu, Univ of Wyoming; CcGit
Frost, Eric G., (619) 594-5003 eric.frost@sdsu.edu, San Diego State Univ; Zr
Frost, Gina M., 209 954 5380 gfrost@deltacollege.edu, San Joaquin Delta Coll; Gg
Fry, Matthew, 940-369-7576 mfry@unt.edu, Univ of North Texas; Zn
Fryar, Alan E., (859) 257-4392 alan.fryar@uky.edu, Univ of Kentucky; HwGeCl
Frye, John , fryej@uww.edu, Univ of Wisconsin, Whitewater; AtZr
Fryer, Brian J., 519-253-3000 ext, 3750 bfryer@uwindsor.ca, Univ of Windsor; Cla
Fryer, Karen H., khfryer@owu.edu, Ohio Wesleyan Univ; GcpGt
Fryer, Patricia B., (808) 956-3146 pfryer@soest.hawaii.edu, Univ of Hawai'i, Manoa; GuiGt
Fryett, I, fryetti@cf.ac.uk, Cardiff Univ; Zn
Fryxell, Joan E., (909) 537-5311 jfryxell@csusb.edu, California State Univ, San Bernardino; Gct
Fthenakis, Vasilis M., (516) 282-2830 Columbia Univ; As
Fu, Qi, (713) 743-3660 qfu3@uh.edu, Univ of Houston; CosCa
Fu, Qiang, (206) 685-2070 qfu@atmos.washington.edu, Univ of Washington; As
Fu, Qilong, (512) 232-9372 qilong.fu@beg.utexas.edu, Univ of Texas at Austin, Jackson Sch of Geosciences; Gso
Fu, Roger, 617-384-6991 rogerfu@fas.harvard.edu, Harvard Univ; YmXym
Fu, Rong, 512-232-7932 rongfu@jsg.utexas.edu, Univ of Texas, Austin; As
Fubelli, Giandomenico, giandomenico.fubelli@unito.it, Univ di Torino; Gm
Fudge, T.J., 206-543-0162 tjfudge@uw.edu, Univ of Washington; Gl
Fueglistaler, Stephan A., 609-258-8238 stf@princeton.edu, Princeton Univ; As
Fuellhart, Kurtis G., (717) 477-1309 kgfuel@ship.edu, Shippensburg Univ; ZnnZn
Fuente, David E., 803 777-2757 fuente@seoe.sc.edu, Univ of South Carolina; Zn

Fuentes, Edna L., (312) 996-6123 eriver15@uic.edu, Univ of Illinois at Chicago; Zn
Fuentes, Jose D., jdfuentes@psu.edu, Pennsylvania State Univ, Univ Park; As
Fueten, Frank, (905) 688-5550 (Ext. 3856) ffueten@brocku.ca, Brock Univ; Gc
Fuge, Ron, +44 (0)1970 622 642 rrf@aber.ac.uk, Aberystwyth Univ; GbCgGe
Fugitt, Frank, (614) 265-6759 frank.fugitt@dnr.state.oh.us, Ohio Dept of Natural Resources; GrHw
Fuhrmann, Christopher, (662) 268-1032 Ext 219 cmf396@msstate.edu, Mississippi State Univ; As
Fuiman, Lee A., (361) 749-6775 lee.fuiman@utexas.edu, Univ of Texas, Austin; Ob
Fujita, Kazuya, 517-355-0142 fujita@msu.edu, Michigan State Univ; Ys
Full, Robert J., (510) 642-9896 rjfull@garnet.berkeley.edu, Univ of California, Berkeley; Pi
Fullagar, Paul D., fullagar@unc.edu, Univ of North Carolina, Chapel Hill; CcGaZe
Fullmer, James W., fullmerj1@southernct.edu, Southern Connecticut State Univ; AmXa
Fulthorpe, Craig S., (512) 471-0459 craig@ig.utexas.edu, Univ of Texas, Austin; Gu
Fulton, Patrick M., (979) 862-2493 pfulton@tamu.edu, Texas A&M Univ; YhHyRn
Fultz, Lisa M., 225-578-1344 lfutz@agcenter.lsu.edu, Louisiana State Univ; Sb
Fulweiler, Robinson, 617-358-5466 rwf@bu.edu, Boston Univ; Cm
Fung, Inez, (510) 643-9367 inez@atmos.berkeley.edu, Univ of California, Berkeley; As
Funning, Gareth J., gareth.funning@ucr.edu, Univ of California, Riverside; YdgYs
Furbish, David J., 615-322-2137 david.j.furbish@vanderbilt.edu, Vanderbilt Univ; GmHg
Furió, Marc, marc.furio@uab.cat, Universitat Autonoma de Barcelona; Pv
Furlong, Emelia, emeliaa.furlong@maryland.gov, Maryland Department of Natural Resources; HwCqSp
Furlong, Kevin P., (814) 863-0567 kevin@geodyn.psu.edu, Pennsylvania State Univ, Univ Park; Gt
Furman, Tanya, (814) 865-5782 furman@psu.edu, Pennsylvania State Univ, Univ Park; GiCu
Fusch, Richard D., (740) 368-3616 rdfusch@owu.edu, Ohio Wesleyan Univ; Zu
Fusseis, Florian, +44 (0) 131 650 6755 ffusseis@staffmail.ed.ac.uk, Edinburgh Univ; Gc
Fyfe, John C., (250) 363-8236 john.fyfe@ec.gc.ca, Univ of Victoria; As
Fürst, Christine, +345 5526017 christine.fuerst@geo.uni-halle.de, Martin-Luther-Univ Halle-Wittenberg; ZucZi
Fyson, William K., 613-745-6645 wfyson@uottawa.ca, Univ of Ottawa; Gc

G

Gaasterland, Terry, (858) 822-4600 tgaasterland@ucsd.edu, Univ of California, San Diego; Ob
Gabbott, Sarah, +440116 252 3636 sg21@le.ac.uk, Leicester Univ; Pg
Gabel, Mark, (605) 642-9035 Black Hills State Univ; Pb
Gabel, Sharon, 281-425-6335 sgabel@lee.edu, Lee Coll; GseGg
Gabet, Emmanuel, 408 924-5035 manny.gabet@sjsu.edu, San Jose State Univ; Gm
Gabitov, Rinat, (662) 268-1032 Ext 218 rg850@msstate.edu, Mississippi State Univ; Cas
Gable, Carl W., (505) 665-3533 gable@lanl.gov, Los Alamos; Gt
Gabler, Christopher, 956 882 7656 christopher.gabler@utrgv.edu, Univ of Texas, Rio Grande Valley; PeSf
Gaboury, Damien, 418-545-5011 dgaboury@uqac.ca, Universite du Quebec a Chicoutimi; EmCe
Gabrielli, Paolo, 614 292 6664 gabrielli.1@osu.edu, Ohio State Univ; CtPeGl
Gabrielov, Andrei, (765) 496-2868 gabriea@purdue.edu, Purdue Univ; Ys
Gachon, Philippe, 514-987-3000 #2601 gachon.philippe@uqam.ca, Universite du Quebec a Montreal; As
Gacía Joral, Fernando, fgjoral@ucm.es, Univ Complutense de Madrid; Pi
Gadikota, Greeshma, gadikota@wisc.edu, Univ of Wisconsin, Madison; GzCqu
Gaede, Oliver M., +61 7 3138 2535 oliver.gaede@qut.edu.au, Queensland Univ of Tech; YeNrYs
Gaetani, Glenn A., (508) 289-3724 ggaetani@whoi.edu, Woods Hole Oceanographic Inst; Gi
Gaffney, Edward S., (505) 665-6387 gaffney@lanl.gov, Los Alamos; Yg
Gaffney, Eugene S., (212) 769-5801 American Mus of Natural History; Pv
Gaffney, Jeffrey S., (630) 252-5178 gaffney@anl.gov, Argonne; As
Gagnaison, Cyril, +33(0)3 44068997 cyril.gagnaison@lasalle-beauvais.fr, Institut Polytechnique LaSalle Beauvais (ex-IGAL); PgGsa
Gagne, Jean-Pierre, 418-723-1986 ext 1870 jean-pierre_gagne@uqar.ca, Universite du Quebec a Rimouski; OcCmo
Gagne, Marc R., (610) 436-3014 mgagne@wcupa.edu, West Chester Univ; Xa
Gagnon, Alan R., (508) 289-2961 agagnon@whoi.edu, Woods Hole Oceanographic Inst; Cs
Gagnon, Joel E., (519) 253-3000 x2496 jgagnon@uwindsor.ca, Univ of Windsor; CaqEg
Gagnon, Katie, 206-516-3161 kgagnon@sccd.ctc.edu, Seattle Central Coll; OuZg
Gagnon, Teresa K., (860) 424-3680 teresa.gagnon@ct.gov, Dept of Energy and Environmental Protection; Gg
Gagosian, Carol, 781-283-3151 cgagosian@wellesley.edu, Wellesley Coll; Zn
Gaherty, James, gaherty@ldeo.columbia.edu, Columbia Univ; Ys
Gahn, Forest J., (208) 496-7677 gahnf@byui.edu, Brigham Young Univ - Idaho; PggGs
Gaidos, Eric J., (808) 956-7897 gaidos@hawaii.edu, Univ of Hawai'i, Manoa; Yg
Gaines, Robert R., (909) 621-8674 robert.gaines@pomona.edu, Pomona Coll; GsClPi
Gajewski, Dirk J., +4940428382975 dirk.gajewski@uni-hamburg.de, Univ Hamburg; YesYg
Gakka, Udaya Laxm, +914027097116 udayalaxmi.g@gmail.com, Osmania Univ; HwYge
Galal, Galal M., 002-03-3921595 galalgalal2004@yahoo.com, Alexandria Univ; GgPeGe
Galán garcía, Gúmer, ++935812835 gumer.galan@uab.cat, Universitat Autonoma de Barcelona; GiCg
Galbraith, Eric, (514) 398-3677 eric.galbraith@mcgill.ca, McGill Univ; Zo
Galbraith, John M., (540) 231-9784 ttcf@vt.edu, Virginia Polytechnic Inst & State Univ; Sp
Gale, Andrew, +44 023 92 846127 andy.gale@port.ac.uk, Univ of Portsmouth; PgGrCl
Gale, Julia F., (512) 232-7957 julia.gale@beg.utexas.edu, Univ of Texas, Austin; GctGo
Gale, Marjorie H., (802) 522-5210 marjorie.gale@vermont.gov, Agency of Natural Resources, Dept of Environmental Conservation; GgcGe
Gale, Paula M., (731) 881-7326 pgale@utm.edu, Univ of Tennessee, Martin; SodSc
Galea, Anthony, anthony.galea@um.edu.mt, Univ of Malta; Opg
Galea, Pauline, +356 2340 3034 pauline.galea@um.edu.mt, Univ of Malta; YsgZg
Galewsky, Joseph, 505-277-4204 galewsky@unm.edu, Univ of New Mexico; Am
Galgaro, Antonio, +390498279123 antonio.galgaro@unipd.it, Univ degli Studi di Padova; Ng
Galicki, Stan, (601) 974-1340 galics@millsaps.edu, Millsaps Coll; Ged
Gall, Quentin, (613) 234-0188 qgall@rogers.com, Univ of Ottawa; GsEmGe
Gallagher, Eugene, eugene.gallagher@umb.edu, Univ of Massachusetts, Boston; Ob
Gallagher, Martin, +44 0161 306-3937 martin.gallagher@manchester.ac.uk, Univ of Manchester; As
Gallagher, William B., 609-896-5000 ext. 7784 wgallagher@rider.edu, Rider Univ; PvgGr
Gallegos, Anthony F., (505) 665-0862 agallegos@lanl.gov, Los Alamos; Pg
Gallen, Sean, sean.gallen@colostate.edu, Colorado State Univ; GemGt
Galli, Kenneth G., (617) 552-4504 kenneth.galli@bc.edu, Boston Coll; GsdGg
Gallovic, Frantisek, 089/2180 4209 frantisek.gallovic@geophysik.uni-muenchen.de, Ludwig-Maximilians-Univ Muenchen; Yg
Galloway, James N., (804) 924-1303 jng@virginia.edu, Univ of Virginia; As
Galloway, William E., (512) 471-5673 galloway@austin.utexas.edu, Univ of Texas, Austin; GsoGr
Gallup, Christina D., (218) 726-8984 cgallup@d.umn.edu, Univ of Minnesota Duluth; Cct
Gallus, William A., (515) 294-2270 wgallus@iastate.edu, Iowa State Univ of Sci & Tech; As
Galperin, Boris, (727) 553-1101 bgalperin@marine.usf.edu, Univ of South Florida; Op
Galsa, Attila, gali@pangea.elte.hu, Eotvos Lorand Univ; YgHwYe
Galvin, Robert, r.galvin@curtin.edu.au, Curtin Univ; Ye
Galy, Valier, (508) 289-2340 vgaly@whoi.edu, Woods Hole Oceanographic Inst; Cm
Gamage, Kusali R., kgamage@austincc.edu, Austin Comm Coll District; HyOuPm
Gamble, Audrey V., (334) 844-4100 avg0001@auburn.edu, Auburn Univ; Sc
Gamble, Douglas W., (910) 962-3778 gambled@uncw.edu, Univ of North

Gattiglio, Marco, marco.gattiglio@unito.it, Univ di Torino; Gc
Gatto, Roberto, +390498279172 roberto.gatto@unipd.it, Univ degli Studi di Padova; Pg
Gaubatz, Piper, (413) 545-0768 gaubatz@geo.umass.edu, Univ of Massachusetts, Amherst; Zy
Gauci, Adam, adam.gauci@um.edu.mt, Univ of Malta; Op
Gaudette, Henri E., (603) 862-1718 Univ of New Hampshire; Cc
Gaulton, Rachel, +44 (0) 191 208 6577 rachel.gaulton@ncl.ac.uk, Univ of Newcastle Upon Tyne; Zr
Gautam, Tej P., 740-376-4371 tej.gautam@marietta.edu, Marietta Coll; NgGeZi
Gauthier, Donald J., (818) 778-5514 gauthidj@lavc.edu, Los Angeles Valley Coll; ZiyAm
Gauthier, Jacques, (203) 432-3150 jacques.gauthier@yale.edu, Yale Univ; Pv
Gauthier, Michel, 514-987-3000 #4560 gauthier.michel@uqam.ca, Universite du Quebec a Montreal; Eg
Gauthier, Pierre, 514-987-3000 #3304 gauthier.pierre@uqam.ca, Universite du Quebec a Montreal; Am
Gautsch, Jacklyn, 319-335-1761 jackie.gautsch@dnr.iowa.gov, Iowa Dept of Natural Resources; Zn
Gavin, Dan, (541) 346-5787 dgavin@uoregon.edu, Univ of Oregon; ZyPle
Gavriloaiei, Traian, 0040232201462 tgavrilo@uaic.ro, Alexandru Ioan Cuza; CaAsCg
Gawloski, Joan, 432-685-4630 jgawloski@midland.edu, Midland Coll; GgzGe
Gawu, Simon K., +233 244 067804 skygawu@yahoo.com, Kwame Nkrumah Univ of Sci and Tech; GgEgZn
Gay, Kenny, 9197337353 x28 kenny.gay@ncdenr.gov, N.C. Department of Environmental Quality; GzsPi
Gaya, Charles , cogaya@jkuat.ac.ke, Jomo Kenyatta Univ of Agriculture & Tech; ZrgZi
Gaylord, David R., (509) 335-8127 gaylordd@wsu.edu, Washington State Univ; Gs
Gazel, Esteban, egazel@cornell.edu, Cornell Univ; CeGiv
Gazis, Carey A., 509.963-2820 cgazis@geology.cwu.edu, Central Washington Univ; CsHw
Ge, Shemin, (303) 492-8323 ges@colorado.edu, Univ of Colorado; HwEoYg
Geary, Dana H., dana@geology.wisc.edu, Univ of Wisconsin, Madison; Pg
Geary, Lindsey, (315)792-3134 Utica Coll; Geg
Geary, Phil, 61 02 4921 6726 phil.geary@newcastle.edu.au, Univ of Newcastle; HwSoHw
Gebrande, Helmut, 089/2180 4325 gebrande@geophysik.uni-muenchen.de, Ludwig-Maximilians-Univ Muenchen; YgsEo
Gedzelman, Stanley, (212) 650-6470 City Coll (CUNY); As
Gee, Jeffrey S., (858) 534-4707 jsgee@ucsd.edu, Univ of California, San Diego; Gu
Gehrels, George E., (520) 349-4702 ggehrels@email.arizona.edu, Univ of Arizona; Gt
Gehrels, Tom, (520) 621-6970 tgehrels@lpl.arizona.edu, Univ of Arizona; Zn
Geidel, Gwendelyn, (803) 777-7171 geidel@environ.sc.edu, Univ of South Carolina; HwGeCg
Geiger, James W., 217-265-8989 jgeiger@illinois.edu, Illinois State Geological Survey; Ge
Geiger, Sebastian, s.geiger@hw.ac.uk, Heriot-Watt Univ; NpEoYh
Geisseler, Daniel, djgeisseler@ucdavis.edu, Univ of California, Davis; So
Geissman, John D., 972-883-2403 geissman@utdallas.edu, Univ of Texas, Dallas; GtYm
Geist, Dennis J., (208) 885-6491 dgeist@uidaho.edu, Univ of Idaho; Giv
Geller, Jonathan, 831-771-4400 geller@mlml.calstate.edu, Moss Landing Marine Lab; Zn
Geller, Marvin A., (631) 632-8701 marvin.geller@stonybrook.edu, SUNY, Stony Brook; As
Gemail, Khaled S., 01145031722 khaledgemail@zu.edu.eg, El Zagazig Univ; YuRcYe
Gemignani, Robert, (314) 935-4614 rgemigna@levee.wustl.edu, Washington Univ in St. Louis; Zn
Gemmell, J B., 61 3 6226 2893 bruce.gemmell@utas.edu.au, Univ of Tasmania; Eg
Gemperline, Johanna M., (410) 554-5552 johanna.gemperline@maryland.gov, Maryland Department of Natural Resources; Hw
Genareau, Kimberly, 205-348-1878 kdg@ua.edu, Univ of Alabama; Gvi
Gendzwill, Donald J., don.gendzwill@usask.ca, Univ of Saskatchewan; Ye
Genge, Matthew, +44 20 759 46499 m.genge@imperial.ac.uk, Imperial Coll; Xm
Genna, Dominique, gennadomi@hotmail.com, Universite du Quebec a Chicoutimi; GvEn
Gennari, Rocco, rocco.gennari@unito.it, Univ di Torino; Gn
Gentile, Richard J., (816) 235-2974 gentiler@umkc.edu, Univ of Missouri, Kansas City; GrsNx
Gentry, Amanda L., (303) 319-0695 amandagentry@weber.edu, Weber State Univ; GgsGg
Gentry, Christopher, 931-221-7478 gentryc@apsu.edu, Austin Peay State Univ; Ziy
Gentry, Terry, 979-845-5323 tjgentry@tamu.edu, Texas A&M Univ; Sb
George, Graham, 306-966-5722 g.george@usask.ca, Univ of Saskatchewan; Cg
Georgen, Jennifer, 850-645-4987 georgen@gly.fsu.edu, Florida State Univ; Gu
Georgiev, Svetoslav, (970)-491-3789 svetoslav.georgiev@colostate.edu, Colorado State Univ; CcGo
Georgiopopoulou, Aggeliki, (+353) 1 716 2062 aggie.georg@ucd.ie, Univ Coll Dublin; GusOg
Geraghty Ward, Emily, emily.ward@rocky.edu, Rocky Mountain Coll; ZeGc
Gerald, Carresse, (919) 530-7117 cgerald6@nccu.edu, North Carolina Central Univ; GeZg
Gerba, Charles P., (520) 621-6906 gerba@ag.arizona.edu, Univ of Arizona; Sb
GERBE, Marie-Christine, 33-477485123 gerbe@univ-st-etienne.fr, Université Jean Monnet, Saint-Etienne; GisZe
Gerber, Stefan, 352294-3174 sgerber@ufl.edu, Univ of Florida; So
Gerbi, Christopher C., 207 581-2153 Univ of Maine; Gt
Gerbi, Greg, 518-580-5127 ggerbi@skidmore.edu, Skidmore Coll; OpYg
Gerhard, Lee C., 78538643965 leegtn37@gmail.com, Univ of Kansas; GsoGd
Gerhardt, Hannes, (678) 839-4064 hgerhard@westga.edu, Univ of West Georgia; Zn
Gerke, Tammie, 513-727-3268 gerketl@miamioh.edu, Miami Univ; ClGea
Gerla, Philip J., (701) 777-3305 phil.gerla@engr.und.edu, Univ of North Dakota; Hw
Germa, Aurelie, agerma@usf.edu, Univ of South Florida; Gv
German, Chris, 508-289-2853 cgerman@whoi.edu, Woods Hole Oceanographic Inst; Gt
Germanoski, Dru, (610) 330-5196 germanod@lafayette.edu, Lafayette Coll; Gm
Germanovich, Leonid, (404) 894-2284 leonid@ce.gatech.edu, Georgia Inst of Tech; NrYg
Gernon, Thomas M., +44 (0)23 8059 2670 thomas.gernon@noc.soton.ac.uk, Univ of Southampton; ZgGvi
Gerry, Janelle, 402-472-2663 Univ of Nebraska, Lincoln; Zn
Gertisser, Ralf, (+44) 01782 733181 r.gertisser@keele.ac.uk, Keele Univ; GivGz
Gervais, Melissa, mmg62@psu.edu, Pennsylvania State Univ, Univ Park; As
Gerwick, William H., (858) 534-0578 wgerwick@ucsd.edu, Univ of California, San Diego; Cm
Geršlová, Eva, +420 549 49 4027 gerslova@sci.muni.cz, Masaryk Univ; Ge
Gess, Robert, +27 (0)82-7595848 robg@imaginet.co.za, Rhodes Univ; Pg
Ghail, Richard, +44 1784 276766 richard.ghail@rhul.ac.uk, Royal Holloway Univ of London; Gt
Ghani, Azman Abdul, 03-79674234 azmangeo@um.edu.my, Univ of Malaya; Gi
Gharti, Hom Nath, 609-258-2605 hgharti@princeton.edu, Princeton Univ; YsdYg
Ghassemi, Ahmed, ahmad.ghassemi@ou.edu, Univ of Oklahoma; Nr
Ghate, Virendra P., (630) 252-1609 vghate@anl.gov, Argonne; AsmZr
Ghattas, Omar, (512) 232-4304 omar@ices.utexas.edu, Univ of Texas, Austin; ZnYg
Ghazala, Hosni H., (109) 688-7904 ghazala@mans.edu.eg, El Mansoura Univ; Ygx
Ghent, Edward D., (403) 220-5847 ghent@geo.ucalgary.ca, Univ of Calgary; Gp
Ghent, Rebecca, (416) 978-0597 ghentr@geology.utoronto.ca, Univ of Toronto; Zr
Ghil, Michael, (310) 206-2285 ghil@atmos.ucla.edu, Univ of California, Los Angeles; AsYdOp
Ghinassi, Massimiliano, +390498279181 massimiliano.ghinassi@unipd.it, Univ degli Studi di Padova; Gs
Ghiorso, Mark , 206-550-1850 ghiorso@uw.edu, Univ of Washington; CgGx
Ghoneim, Eman, ghoneime@uncw.edu, Boston Univ; Gm
Ghosh, Abhijit, (951) 827-4493 aghosh@ucr.edu, Univ of California, Riverside; YsGt
Ghosheh, Baher A., (814) 732-2207 ghosheh@edinboro.edu, Edinboro Univ of Pennsylvania; Zn
Giacalone, Joe, 520-626-8365 giacalone@lpl.arizona.edu, Univ of Arizona; Xy
Giachetti, Thomas, tgiachet@uoregon.edu, Univ of Oregon; Gvu
Giammar, Daniel, degiammar@seas.wustl.edu, Washington Univ in St. Louis; Zn

Giannini, Alessandra, (845) 680-4473 alesall@iri.columbia.edu, Columbia Univ; AsOpZc
Gianniny, Gary, (970) 247-7254 gianniny_g@fortlewis.edu, Fort Lewis Coll; Gs
Gianotti, Franco, franco.gianotti@unito.it, Univ di Torino; Gg
Giaramita, Mario J., (209) 667-3558 mgiaramita@csustan.edu, California State Univ, Stanislaus; Gpz
Giardino, John R., (979) 845-3224 giardino@geo.tamu.edu, Texas A&M Univ; GmNg
Giardino, Marco, marco.giardino@unito.it, Univ di Torino; Gm
Gibbons, Doug, 206-685-8180 dgibbons@uw.edu, Univ of Washington; ZeYs
Gibbs, Gaynell, ocean@lsu.edu, Louisiana State Univ; Zn
Gibbs, Samantha J., +44 (0)23 80592003 samantha.gibbs@noc.soton.ac.uk, Univ of Southampton; Zg
Gibeaut, James, 361-825-2060 james.gibeaut@tamucc.edu, Texas A&M Univ, Corpus Christi; OnZi
Gibling, Martin R., mgibling@is.dal.ca, Dalhousie Univ; Gs
Gibson, Andy, +44 023 92 842654 andy.gibson@port.ac.uk, Univ of Portsmouth; Eg
Gibson, Carl H., (858) 534-3184 cgibson@ucsd.edu, Univ of California, San Diego; No
Gibson, David, (207) 778-7402 dgibson@maine.edu, Univ of Maine, Farmington; GigGz
Gibson, Deana, (417) 836-5801 deanagibson@missouristate.edu, Missouri State Univ; Zn
Gibson, Deidre M., 757.727.5883 deidre.gibson@hamptonu.edu, Hampton Univ; Ob
Gibson, Glen, 719-333-3080 glen.gibson@usafa.edu, United States Air Force Academy; Zri
Gibson, H. Daniel (Dan), (778) 782-7057 hdgibson@sfu.ca, Simon Fraser Univ; GcCcGp
Gibson, Harold L., 7056751151 x2371 hgibson@laurentian.ca, Laurentian Univ, Sudbury; EmGv
Gibson, Michael A., (731) 881-7435 mgibson@utm.edu, Univ of Tennessee, Martin; PgiZe
Gibson, Roger L., 011 717 6553 roger.gibson@wits.ac.za, Univ of the Witwatersrand; GcpGg
Gibson, Ronald C., (714) 895-8194 rgibson@gwc.cccd.edu, Golden West Coll; Gc
Gibson, Sally, +44 (0) 1223 333401 sally@esc.cam.ac.uk, Univ of Cambridge; Gi
Gibson, Jr., Richard L., (979) 862-8653 gibson@tamu.edu, Texas A&M Univ; Yse
Gidigasu, Solomon S., +233 27 7807 707 ssrgidigasu.soe@knust.edu.gh, Kwame Nkrumah Univ of Sci and Tech; GeZrNr
Giefer, Madeline M., 931-221-7473 gieferm@apsu.edu, Austin Peay State Univ; ZcrZi
Giegengack, Jr., Robert F., (215) 898-5191 gieg@sas.upenn.edu, Univ of Pennsylvania; Gg
Gieré, Reto, giere@sas.upenn.edu, Univ of Pennsylvania; GzCgGe
Gierke, John S., (906) 487-2535 jsgierke@mtu.edu, Michigan Technological Univ; Hy
Giese, Benjamin S., (979) 845-2306 bgiese@ocean.tamu.edu, Texas A&M Univ; Op
Giese, Graham S., (508) 289-2297 ggiese@whoi.edu, Woods Hole Oceanographic Inst; On
Gieskes, Joris M., (858) 534-4257 jgieskes@ucsd.edu, Univ of California, San Diego; Oc
Gifford, Dian J., (401) 874-6690 dgifford@uri.edu, Univ of Rhode Island; Ob
Gifford, Jennifer N., 662-915-2079 jngiffor@olemiss.edu, Univ of Mississippi; GtxCg
Gifford-Gonzalez, Dianne, (831) 459-2633 Univ of California, Santa Cruz; Zn
Gigler, Alexander, 089/2180 4185 Ludwig-Maximilians-Univ Muenchen; Gz
Giglierano, James D., james.giglierano@dnr.iowa.gov, Iowa Dept of Natural Resources; GgZri
Gilbert, Co'Quesie, (619) 534-2470 cag65@columbia.edu, Columbia Univ; Zn
Gilbert, Hersh, 403 220-6446 hersh.gilbert@ucalgary.ca, Univ of Calgary; Ys
Gilbert, Kathleen W., 781-283-3086 kgilbert@wellesley.edu, Wellesley Coll; Cs
Gilbert, M. Charles, (405) 325-3253 mcgilbert@ou.edu, Univ of Oklahoma; Cp
Gilbert, Patricia M., (410) 221-8422 Univ of Maryland; Ob
Gilbes, Fernando, 787 2653845 fernando.gilbes@upr.edu, Univ of Puerto Rico; ZrGuZi
Gilder, Stuart, 089/2180 4239 stuart.gilder@geophysik.uni-muenchen.de, Ludwig-Maximilians-Univ Muenchen; Ym
Gilerson, Alexander, gilerson@ccny.cuny.edu, Graduate Sch of the City Univ of New York; Gu
Giles, Antony, (432) 685-5580 agiles@midland.edu, Midland Coll; GgvGi
Giles, David, +44 023 92 842248 david.giles@port.ac.uk, Univ of Portsmouth; NzGlm
Giles, Katherine A., 915-747-7075 kagiles@utep.edu, Univ of Texas, El Paso; Go
Gilfillan, Stuart M., +44 (0) 131 651 3462 stuart.gilfillan@ed.ac.uk, Edinburgh Univ; CgsCe
Gilg, Hans A., +49 89 289 - 25855 agilg@tum.de, Technical Univ of Munich; CsEgn
Gilhooly, William, wgilhool@iupui.edu, Indiana Univ - Purdue Univ Indianapolis; ClOc
Gili, Stefania, 609-258-4101 sgili@princeton.edu, Princeton Univ; CgGgCo
Gill, Benjamin, 540-231-7485 bcgill@vt.edu, Virginia Polytechnic Inst & State Univ; CsPcGs
Gill, Fiona, +44(0) 113 34 35190 f.gill@leeds.ac.uk, Univ of Leeds; PgCa
Gill, James B., (831) 459-3842 jgill@pmc.ucsc.edu, Univ of California, Santa Cruz; Gi
Gill, Swarndeep S., (724) 938-1677 gill@calu.edu, California Univ of Pennsylvania; As
Gill, Thomas E., (915) 747-5168 tegill@utep.edu, Univ of Texas, El Paso; GmAsCl
Gillam, Mary L., gillam@rmi.net, Fort Lewis Coll; Gm
Gille, Peter, 089/2180 4355 peter.gille@lrz.uni-muenchen.de, Ludwig-Maximilians-Univ Muenchen; GzZm
Gille, Sarah T., (858) 822-4425 sgille@ucsd.edu, Univ of California, San Diego; Op
Gilleaudeau, Geoff, (703) 993-3289 ggilleau@gmu.edu, George Mason Univ; Gs
Gillerman, Virginia S., (208) 426-4002 vgillerm@boisestate.edu, Boise State Univ; Eg
Gillespie, Alan R., arg3@uw.edu, Univ of Washington; GmlZr
Gillespie, Janice, jgillespie@csub.edu, California State Univ, Bakersfield; GorZi
Gillespie, Robb, (269) 387-5364 robb.gillespie@wmich.edu, Western Michigan Univ; GsoGm
Gillespie, Terry J., (519) 824-4120 (Ext. 54276) tgillesp@uoguelph.ca, Univ of Guelph; Am
Gillespie, Thomas, (609) 771-2569 Coll of New Jersey; Gc
Gillette, David D., david.gillette@nau.edu, Northern Arizona Univ; Pv
Gilley, Brett H., bgilley@eoas.ubc.ca, Univ of British Columbia; GsZeRn
Gilliam, James W., (919) 515-2040 North Carolina State Univ; Sb
Gilligan, Jonathan M., (615) 322-2420 jonathan.gilligan@vanderbilt.edu, Vanderbilt Univ; ZcRwZu
Gillikin, David P., (518) 388-6679 gillikid@union.edu, Union Coll; CsmCl
Gillis, Kathryn, 250-721-6120 kgillis@uvic.ca, Univ of Victoria; Gp
Gillis, Robert, (907) 451-5024 robert.gillis@alaska.gov, Alaska Division of Geological & Geophysical Surveys; Eo
Gillman, Joe, (573) 368-2101 joe.gillman@dnr.mo.gov, Missouri Dept of Natural Resources; Gg
Gillmore, Gavin, +44 020 8417 2518 g.gillmore@kingston.ac.uk, Kingston Univ; Gb
Gilmore, Martha S., (860) 685-3129 mgilmore@wesleyan.edu, Wesleyan Univ; XgGmZr
Gilmore, Tyler J., (509) 376-2370 tyler.gilmore@pnl.gov, Pacific Northwest; Hg
Gilmour, Ernest H., (509) 359-7480 egilmour@ewu.edu, Eastern Washington Univ; Pi
Gilotti, Jane A., (319) 335-1097 jane-gilotti@uiowa.edu, Univ of Iowa; GctGp
Gilpin, Bernard J., (714) 895-8233 bgilpin@gwc.cccd.edu, Golden West Coll; Ys
Gimmestad, Gary G., (404) 493-1331 gary.gimmestad@gmail.com, Georgia Inst of Tech; ZrAs
Ginder-Vogel, Matt, 608-262-0768 mgindervogel@wisc.edu, Univ of Wisconsin, Madison; Sc
Gingras, Murray, 780-492-1963 mgringras@ualberta.ca, Univ of Alberta; Go
Ginis, Isaac, (401) 874-6484 iginis@gso.uri.edu, Univ of Rhode Island; Op
Giordano, Alberto, (512) 245-2170 Texas State Univ; Zi
Giordano, Daniele, daniele.giordano@unito.it, Univ di Torino; Gv
Giorgis, Scott D., (585) 245-5293 giorgis@geneseo.edu, SUNY, Geneseo; GctYm
Giosan, Liviu, 508-289-2257 lgiosan@whoi.edu, Woods Hole Oceanographic Inst; GusPc
Giraldo, Mario A., (818) 677-4431 mario.giraldo@csun.edu, California State Univ, Northridge; ZriZg
Girard, Eric, 514-987-3000 #3325 girard.eric@uqam.ca, Universite du Quebec a Montreal; Am

Girard, Guillaume, 815-753-1778 ggirard@niu.edu, Northern Illinois Univ; GviCu
Girard, Michael W., (609) 292-2576 mike.girard@dep.state.nj.us, New Jersey Geological and Water Survey; Zi
Giraud, Richard E., (801) 537-3351 richardgiraud@utah.gov, Utah Geological Survey; Ng
Girhard, T S., 486-0045 tgirhard@alamo.edu, San Antonio Comm Coll; ZyAm
Giroux, Bernard, bernard.giroux@ete.inrs.ca, Universite du Quebec; Yeg
Girty, Gary H., (619) 594-2552 ggirty@mail.sdsu.edu, San Diego State Univ; Gc
Gitelson, Anatoly, gitelson@calmit.unl.edu, Unversity of Nebraska, Lincoln; Zn
Gittings, Bruce M., +44 (0) 131 650 2558 bruce@ed.ac.uk, Edinburgh Univ; Zi
Gittins, John, (416) 483-9345 j.gittins@utoronto.ca, Univ of Toronto; GipGz
Giusberti, Luca, +390498279183 Univ degli Studi di Padova; Pm
Giustetto, Roberto, roberto.giustetto@unito.it, Univ di Torino; Gz
Glamoclija, Mihaela, (973) 353-2509 m.glamoclija@rutgers.edu, Rutgers, The State Univ of New Jersey, Newark; PgXgGe
Glasauer, Susan, (519) 824-4120 xt52453 glasauer@uoguelph.ca, Univ of Guelph; Pg
Glaser, Paul H., 612-624-8395 glase001@umn.edu, Univ of Minnesota, Twin Cities; Gn
Glass, Alexander, (919) 684-6167 alex.glass@duke.edu, Duke Univ; PiGgZe
Glass, Billy P., (302) 449-2464 bglass@udel.edu, Univ of Delaware; XmcGz
Glass, Hylke J., +44 01326 371823 h.j.glass@exeter.ac.uk, Exeter Univ; NxmEm
Glazer, Brian, 808-956-6658 glazer@hawaii.edu, Univ of Hawai'i, Manoa; Cm
Glazner, Allen F., (919) 962-0689 afg@unc.edu, Univ of North Carolina, Chapel Hill; GitZf
Gleason, Gayle C., (607) 753-2816 gleasong@cortland.edu, SUNY, Cortland; Gct
Gleason, James D., 734-764-9523 jdgleaso@umich.edu, Univ of Michigan; Cg
Glenn, Craig R., (808) 956-2200 glenn@soest.hawaii.edu, Univ of Hawai'i, Manoa; GeCmGs
Glenn, Ed, (520) 626-2664 eglenn@ag.arizona.edu, Univ of Arizona; Zn
Glenn, Nancy, 208.221.1245 nancyglenn@boisestate.edu, Boise State Univ; ZrNgZi
Glickson, Deborah, (202) 334-2024 dglickson@nas.edu, Nat Academies of Scis, Eng, and Medicine; GutGg
Gloaguen, Erwan, erwan.gloaguen@ete.inrs.ca, Universite du Quebec; Ye
Glotch, Timothy, (631) 632-1168 timothy.glotch@stonybrook.edu, Stony Brook Univ; XgGz
Glover, David M., (508) 289-2656 dglover@whoi.edu, Woods Hole Oceanographic Inst; Oc
Glover, Paul W., 418-656-5180 paul.glover@ggl.ulaval.ca, Universite Laval; Yx
Glowacka, Ewa, glowacka@cicese.mx, Centro de Investigación Científica y de Educación Superior de Ensenada; Ys
Glubokovskikh, Stanislav, +618 9266-7190 stanislav.glubokovskikh@curtin.edu.au, Curtin Univ; Yxe
Gluhovsky, Alexander, (765) 494-0670 aglu@purdue.edu, Purdue Univ; As
Glumac, Bosiljka, (413) 585-3680 bglumac@smith.edu, Smith Coll; Gs
Gluyas, Jon, +44 (0) 191 33 42302 j.g.gluyas@durham.ac.uk, Durham Univ; Eo
Glynn, William G., wglynn@brockport.edu, SUNY, The Coll at Brockport; Gg
Gnanadesikan, Anand, (410) 516-0722 gnanades@jhu.edu, Johns Hopkins Univ; OpcAs
Gnidovec, Dale M., (614) 292-6896 gnidovec.1@osu.edu, Ohio State Univ; PvGr
Gobler, Christopher, (631) 632-5043 christopher.gobler@stonybrook.edu, SUNY, Stony Brook; Ob
Goda, Katsu, kgoda2@uwo.ca, Western Univ; Rn
Godbold, Jasmin A., +44 (0)23 80593639 j.a.goldbold@soton.ac.uk, Univ of Southampton; Ob
Godchaux, Martha M., (208) 882-9062 Mount Holyoke Coll; Gv
Goddard, Lisa M., (845) 680-4430 goddard@iri.columbia.edu, Columbia Univ; AstZc
Godek, Melissa, (607) 436-3375 melissa.godek@oneonta.edu, SUNY, Oneonta; AmsZg
Godfrey, Brian J., 845-437-5544 godfrey@vassar.edu, Vassar Coll; Zu
Godfrey, Christopher, 828-232-5160 cgodfrey@unca.edu, Univ of North Carolina, Asheville; AsZnn
Godfrey, Linda, godfrey@marine.rutgers.edu, Rutgers, The State Univ of New Jersey; CmlCq
Godin, Laurent, (613) 533-3223 godinl@queensu.ca, Queen's Univ; Gct
Godsey, Holly, (801) 587-7865 holly.godsey@utah.edu, Univ of Utah; Ze
Godsey, Sarah E., 208-282-3170 godsey@isu.edu, Idaho State Univ; HgsHq
Goebel, Thomas H., (901) 678-4885 thgoebel@memphis.edu, Univ of Memphis; Yxs
Goehring, Brent M., (504) 862-3196 bgoehrin@tulane.edu, Tulane Univ; CcGlm
Goeke, James W., (308) 530-4437 jgoeke@unl.edu, Unversity of Nebraska, Lincoln; HwGmYe
Goes, Joaquim, jig@ldeo.columbia.edu, Columbia Univ; Gu
Goes, Saskia, +44 20 759 46434 s.goes@imperial.ac.uk, Imperial Coll; Yg
Goetz, Alexander, 303-492-5086 goetz@cses.colorado.edu, Univ of Colorado; Zr
Goetz, Andrew R., (303) 871-2674 agoetz@du.edu, Univ of Denver; Zgu
Goetz, Heinrich, (972) 377-1079 hgoetz@collin.edu, Collin Coll - Preston Ridge Campus; Ge
Goetze, Erica, (808) 956-7156 egoetze@hawaii.edu, Univ of Hawai'i, Manoa; Ob
Goff, Fraser, (505) 667-8060 fraser@lanl.gov, Los Alamos; Cg
Goff, James, j.goff@unsw.edu.au, Univ of New South Wales; Gsm
Goff, John A., (512) 471-0476 goff@ig.utexas.edu, Univ of Texas, Austin; Yr
Goforth, Thomas T., (254) 710-2183 tom_goforth@baylor.edu, Baylor Univ; Yg
Golabi, Mohammad H., 671-735-2143 mgolabi@triton.uog.edu, Univ of Guam; SzpSc
Gold, David, 530 754-5361 dgold@ucdavis.edu, Univ of California, Davis; Pg
Gold, David (Duff) P., (814) 865-9993 gold@ems.psu.edu, Pennsylvania State Univ, Univ Park; GcgGx
Gold-Bouchot, Gerardo, (979) 845-9826 ggold@tamu.edu, Texas A&M Univ; OcCm
Goldberg, David S., goldberg@ldeo.columbia.edu, Columbia Univ; Yr
Goldblatt, Colin, 250-721-6120 czg@uvic.ca, Univ of Victoria; As
Goldfinger, Chris, (541) 737-9622 gold@coas.oregonstate.edu, Oregon State Univ; Yr
Goldman, Daniel, (937) 229-5637 dgoldman1@udayton.edu, Univ of Dayton; PgqGr
Goldreich, Peter M., (626) 395-6193 pmg@gps.caltech.edu, California Inst of Tech; Xy
Goldsby, David, 215-746-0090 dgoldsby@sas.upenn.edu, Univ of Pennsylvania; Yg
Goldstein, Barry, (253) 879-3822 goldstein@pugetsound.edu, Univ of Puget Sound; GlmGs
Goldstein, Robert H., (785) 864-2738 gold@ku.edu, Univ of Kansas; Gs
Goldstein, Steven, steveg@ldeo.columbia.edu, Columbia Univ; Cg
Goldstein, Susan T., (706) 542-2397 sgoldst@uga.edu, Univ of Georgia; Pm
Gollmer, Steven, 937-766-7764 gollmers@cedarville.edu, Cedarville Univ; GzAmOg
Golombek, Matthew P., (818) 393-7948 mgolombek@jpl.nasa.gov, Jet Propulsion Lab; XgyGt
Gomberg, Joan, 206-616-5581 gomberg@usgs.gov, Univ of Washington; YsGt
Gomes, Helga, helga@ldeo.columbia.edu, Columbia Univ; Ob
Gomes, Maria E., 351259350261 mgomes@utad.pt, Unive de Trás-os-Montes e Alto Douro; GiCgGz
Gomes, Nuno N., +244924987900 ngomes999@gmail.com, Unive Independente de Angola; GesGu
Gomez, Enrique, egomez@cicese.mx, Centro de Investigación Científica y de Educación Superior de Ensenada; Ye
Gomez, Francisco, (573) 882-9744 fgomez@missouri.edu, Univ of Missouri; Gt
Gomez, Natalya, 514-398-4885 natalya.gomez@mcgill.ca, McGill Univ; Og
Gómez Gras, David, ++935813093 david.gomez@uab.cat, Universitat Autonoma de Barcelona; Gd
Gomezdelcampo, Enrique, 419 372 2886 egomezd@bgsu.edu, Bowling Green State Univ; Ge
Goncharov, Alexander F., 202-478-8947 agoncharov@carnegiescience.edu, Carnegie Inst for Sci; GyYxh
Gong, Donglai, 804-684-7529 gong@vims.edu, William & Mary; Op
Gong, Hongmian, (212) 772-4658 gong@hunter.cuny.edu, Hunter Coll (CUNY); Zn
Goni, Miguel A., (541) 737-0578 mgoni@coas.oregonstate.edu, Oregon State Univ; Gu
Gonnermann, Helge, (713) 348-6263 helge.m.gonnermann@rice.edu, Rice Univ; Gv
Gonzales, David A., (970) 247-7378 gonzales_d@fortlewis.edu, Fort Lewis Coll; Gx
Gonzalez, Alex, (515) 294-8729 agon@iastate.edu, Iowa State Univ of Sci & Tech; As

Gonzalez, Frank I., 206-290-0903 figonzal@uw.edu, Univ of Washington; OpRn
González, Isabel , +34954556317 igonza@us.es, Univ de Sevilla; GzeSc
Gonzalez, Jose J., javier@cicese.mx, Centro de Investigación Científica y de Educación Superior de Ensenada; Yd
Gonzalez, Juan L., (956) 665-3523 juan.l.gonzalez@utrgv.edu, Univ of Texas, Rio Grande Valley; GmsGa
González, Laura, lgacebron@ucm.es, Univ Complutense de Madrid; Gr
Gonzalez, Luis , +966138607981 gonzalez@kfupm.edu.sa, King Fahd Univ of Petroleum and Minerals; CgGn
Gonzalez, Luis A., 785-864-2743 lgonzlez@ku.edu, Univ of Kansas; CsGd
Gonzalez, Maria M., 989-774-2295 gonza1mm@cmich.edu, Central Michigan Univ; Gig
Gonzalez Leon, Carlos M., cmgleon@servidor.unam.mx, Univ Nacional Autonoma de Mexico; Gr
Gonzalez-Escobar, Mario, mgonzale@cicese.mx, Centro de Investigación Científica y de Educación Superior de Ensenada; YesYs
Gonzalez-Fernandez, Antonio, mindundi@cicese.mx, Centro de Investigación Científica y de Educación Superior de Ensenada; Gu
Gonzalez-Perdomo, Maria, maria.gonzalezperdomo@adelaide.edu.au, Univ of Adelaide; Np
Good, Daniel B., (912) 478-5361 dangood@georgiasouthern.edu, Georgia Southern Univ; Zn
Good, David, dgood3@uwo.ca, Western Univ; Em
Goodbred, Jr., Steven L., (615) 343-6424 steven.goodbred@vanderbilt.edu, Vanderbilt Univ; GsOn
Goode, Ryan , rgoode@cerritos.edu, Cerritos Coll; Zc
Goodell, Laurel P., 609-258-1043 laurel@princeton.edu, Princeton Univ; ZeGgc
Goodell, Philip C., 915-747-5593 goodell@utep.edu, Univ of Texas, El Paso; Ce
Goodge, John W., (218) 726-7491 jgoodge@d.umn.edu, Univ of Minnesota Duluth; Gp
Goodin, Ruth, 305-284-4253 ruthgoodin@miami.edu, Univ of Miami; Zn
Goodkin, Nathalie , 212-769-5379 ngoodkin@amnh.org, Graduate Sch of the City Univ of New York; Gg
Goodliffe, Andrew, amg@ua.edu, Univ of Alabama; YgeGt
Goodman, Paul, 520-621-8484 pgoodman@email.arizona.edu, Univ of Arizona; As
Goodrich, David C., (520) 670-6380 goodrich@tucson.ars.ag.gov, Univ of Arizona; Hs
Goodrich, Greg, gregory.goodrich@wku.edu, Western Kentucky Univ; Ast
Goodwin, David H., (740) 587-5621 goodwind@denison.edu, Denison Univ; PiCs
Goodwin, Laurel B., (608) 265-4234 laurel@geology.wisc.edu, Univ of Wisconsin, Madison; Gc
Goodwin, Mark B., (505) 835-5178 mark@berkeley.edu, Univ of California, Berkeley; Pv
Goodwin, Paul, (519) 824-4120 Ext.52754 pgoodwin@uoguelph.ca, Univ of Guelph; Zn
Goodwin, Phillip A., +44 (0)23 80596161 p.a.goodwin@soton.ac.uk, Univ of Southampton; Pe
Goos, Robert J., (701) 231-8581 North Dakota State Univ; Sc
Gootee, Brian F., 602.708.8846 bgootee@email.arizona.edu, Univ of Arizona; Gm
Gopal, Sucharita, suchi@bu.edu, Boston Univ; Zi
Gordon, Andrew, (519) 824-4120 ext 52415 agordon@uoguelph.ca, Univ of Guelph; Zn
Gordon, Arnold L., (845) 365-8325 agordon@ldeo.columbia.edu, Columbia Univ; Op
Gordon, Barney, (785) 532-6101 bgordon@ksu.edu, Kansas State Univ; So
Gordon, Clare E., +44(0) 113 34 35210 c.e.gordon@leeds.ac.uk, Univ of Leeds; Zi
Gordon, Mark, (416)736-2100 mgordon@yorku.ca, York Univ; As
Gordon, Richard G., (713) 348-5279 rgg@rice.edu, Rice Univ; YmGtYd
Gordon, Rob J., (519) 824-4120 Ext.52285 rjgordon@uoguelph.ca, Univ of Guelph; As
Gordon, Robert B., (203) 432-3125 robert.gordon@yale.edu, Yale Univ; Nr
Gordon, Ryan, 207-287-7178 ryan.gordon@maine.gov, Dept of Agriculture, Conservation, and Forestry; HwGm
Gordon, Stacia M., 775-784-6476 staciag@unr.edu, Univ of Nevada, Reno; Gpz
Gordon, Steven J., (719) 333-3067 usafa.dfeg@usafa.edu, United States Air Force Academy; Gm
Gordon, Terence M., (403) 220-8301 tmg@geo.ucalgary.ca, Univ of Calgary; Gq
Gore, Pamela J. W., 678-891-3754 pgore@gsu.edu, Georgia State Univ, Perimeter Coll, Clarkston Campus; GsZeGn
Gorecka-Nowak, Anna, anna.gorecka-nowak@uwr.edu.pl, Univ of Wroclaw; Pg
Gorelick, Steven, (650) 725-2950 gorelick@geo.stanford.edu, Stanford Univ; Yr
Gorka, Maciej, maciej.gorka@uwr.edu.pl, Univ of Wroclaw; AsCa
Gorman, Andrew R., +64 3 479-7516 andrew.gorman@otago.ac.nz, Univ of Otago; YrgYe
Gorman, Gerard, +44 20 759 49985 g.gorman@imperial.ac.uk, Imperial Coll; Yg
Gorman-Lewis, Drew J., 206-543-3541 dgormanl@uw.edu, Univ of Washington; PgCl
Gorog, Agnes, gorog@ludens.elte.hu, Eotvos Lorand Univ; Pmi
Gorokhovich, Yuri, 718-960-1981 yuri.gorokhovich@lehman.cuny.edu, Graduate Sch of the City Univ of New York; Gg
Gorring, Matthew L., (973) 655-5409 gorringm@mail.montclair.edu, Montclair State Univ; Gi
Gorsevski, Peter, (419) 372-7201 peterg@bgsu.edu, Bowling Green State Univ; ZirGm
Gosnell, Hannah, (541) 737-1222 gosnell@colorado.edu, Oregon State Univ; Zu
Gosnold, William D., (701) 777-2631 will.gosnold@engr.und.edu, Univ of North Dakota; YghCt
Gospodinova, Kalina D., 508-289-3212 kgospodinova@whoi.edu, Woods Hole Oceanographic Inst; Cm
Goss, Michael J., (519) 824-4120 (Ext. 2491) mgoss@uoguelph.ca, Univ of Guelph; So
Gosse, John, 902-494-6632 jcgosse@is.dal.ca, Univ of Kansas; Gm
Gosselin, David C., 402-472-8919 dgosselin2@unl.edu, Univ of Nebraska, Lincoln; Ze
Gosselin, Michel, 4187241761 x1284 michel_gosselin@uqar.ca, Universite du Quebec a Rimouski; Ob
Gotkowitz, Madeline B., (608) 262-1580 mbgotkow@wisc.edu, Univ of Wisconsin, Extension; Hw
Gottardi, Raphael, 337-482-6177 rxg0121@louisiana.edu, Univ of Louisiana at Lafayette; Gcp
Gottfried, Michael D., 517-432-5480 gottfrie@msu.edu, Michigan State Univ; Pv
Gottschalk, Bradford, (608) 263-7389 bradford.gottschalk@wisc.edu, Univ of Wisconsin, Madison, Division of Extension; Rh
Gotz, Annette, +27 (0)46-603-8313 a.gotz@ru.ac.za, Rhodes Univ; Gs
Goudge, Theodore L., (660) 562-1798 tgoudge@nwmissouri.edu, Northwest Missouri State Univ; Zy
Goudge, Timothy, tgoudge@jsg.utexas.edu, Univ of Texas, Austin; Gs
Goudreau, Joanne, (508) 289-2560 jgoudreau@whoi.edu, Woods Hole Oceanographic Inst; Cm
Gough, Amy, +44 1784 44 amy.gough@rhul.ac.uk, Royal Holloway Univ of London; Gs
Gouhier, Tarik, 7815817370 x302 t.gouhier@neu.edu, Northeastern Univ; Zn
Gould, Joseph C., gould.joe@spcollege.edu, Saint Petersburg Coll, Clearwater; Gg
Gould, Mark D., (401) 254-3087 Roger Williams Univ; Ob
Goulden, Michael L., (949) 824-1983 mgoulden@uci.edu, Univ of California, Irvine; Zg
Gouldey, Jeremy C., 616-331-2995 gouldjer@gvsu.edu, Grand Valley State Univ; CgPeCg
Gouldson, Andy, +44(0) 113 34 36417 a.gouldson@leeds.ac.uk, Univ of Leeds; Ge
Goulet, Normand, (514) 987-3375 r27254@er.uqam.ca, Universite du Quebec a Montreal; Gc
Goulet, Richard, 613-943-9922 richard.goulet@cnsc-ccsn.gc.ca, Univ of Ottawa; CgPgGe
Gouzie, Douglas R., (417) 836-5228 douglasgouzie@missouristate.edu, Missouri State Univ; HwGeCl
Gowan, Angela S., (612) 626-6451 gowa0001@umn.edu, Univ of Minnesota; Gl
Gowing, David, +44 (0)1908 659468 x 59468 david.gowing@open.ac.uk, Open Univ; Pb
Goyne, Keith W., 573-882-0090 Univ of Missouri; Sc
Graber, Anna, agraber@umn.edu, Univ of Minnesota, Twin Cities; Rh
Grable, Judy, (229) 333-5752 Valdosta State Univ; Hs
Grabowski, Jonathan, 7815817370 x337 j.grabowski@neu.edu, Northeastern Univ; GuEg
Grace, Cathy A., (662)915-1799 cag@olemiss.edu, Univ of Mississippi; Gg
Grace, Shannon M., (512) 223-4891 sgrace@austincc.edu, Austin Comm Coll District; Zn
Graczyk, Donald G., (630) 252-3489 Argonne; Cs
Graettinger, Alison, 816-235-6701 graettingera@umkc.edu, Univ of Missouri, Kansas City; Gv
Graf, Jr., Joseph L., (541) 552-6861 graf@sou.edu, Southern Oregon Univ; Em

Graff, William P., (609) 292-2576 bill.graff@dep.nj.gov, New Jersey Geological and Water Survey; Zn
Graham, Barbara, 702-651-4173 barbara.graham@csn.edu, Coll of Southern Nevada - West Charleston Campus; ZyAm
Graham, David W., (541) 737-4140 dgraham@coas.oregonstate.edu, Oregon State Univ; Cm
Graham, Gina R., 907-451-5031 gina.graham@alaska.gov, Alaska Division of Geological & Geophysical Surveys; Yg
Graham, Grace E., (608) 263-4125 grace.graham@wisc.edu, Univ of Wisconsin, Madison, Division of Extension; Hw
Graham, Ian, i.graham@unsw.edu.au, Univ of New South Wales; GxEg
Graham, Margaret C., +44 (0) 131 650 4767 margaret.graham@ed.ac.uk, Edinburgh Univ; Ge
Graham, Michael, (831) 771-4400 mgraham@mlml.calstate.edu, Moss Landing Marine Lab; Ob
Graham, Russell W., (814) 865-6336 graham@ems.psu.edu, Pennsylvania State Univ, Univ Park; Pv
Graham, Stephan A., (650) 723-0507 graham@pangea.stanford.edu, Stanford Univ; Go
Graham, Jr., Earl K., (814) 865-2273 graham@ems.psu.edu, Pennsylvania State Univ, Univ Park; Yx
Graham, Jr., James H., (863) 956-1151 jhgraham@ufl.edu, Univ of Florida; Sb
Grala, Katarzynz, (662) 268-1032 Ext 222 kg160@msstate.edu, Mississippi State Univ; Zi
Grammer, Michael, 405-744-6358 michael.grammer@okstate.edu, Oklahoma State Univ; GsEoGr
Gran, Karen B., (218) 726-7406 kgran@d.umn.edu, Univ of Minnesota Duluth; Gms
Grana, Dario, 307-766-3449 dgrana@uwyo.edu, Univ of Wyoming; Ye
Grand, Stephen P., (512) 471-3005 steveg@maestro.geo.utexas.edu, Univ of Texas, Austin; Yg
Grandal d'Anglade, Aurora, 00 34 981 167000 xeaurora@udc.es, Coruna Univ; Pv
Grande, Anthony, 212-772-5265 agrande@hunter.cuny.edu, Hunter Coll (CUNY); Zn
Grande, Lance, (312) 665-7632 lgrande@fieldmuseum.org, Field Mus of Natural History; Pv
Grandstaff, David E., (215) 204-8228 grand@temple.edu, Temple Univ; Cl
Grandy, Stuart, stuart.grandy@unh.edu, Univ of New Hampshire; Sc
Graney, Joseph R., (607) 777-6347 jgraney@binghamton.edu, Binghamton Univ; ClGeHs
Granger, Darryl E., (765) 494-0043 dgranger@purdue.edu, Purdue Univ; As
Granger, Julie, 860-405-9094 julie.granger@uconn.edu, Univ of Connecticut; Oc
Graniero, Phil A., (519) 253-3000 x2485 graniero@uwindsor.ca, Univ of Windsor; ZinZy
Granja, José Luis, jlgranja@ucm.es, Univ Complutense de Madrid; Yg
Grannell, Roswitha B., (562) 985-4927 grannell@csulb.edu, California State Univ, Long Beach; Yv
Granshaw, Frank D., (503) 725-3391 fgransha@pdx.edu, Portland State Univ; ZnGl
Grant, Alastair, +44 (0)1603 59 2537 a.grant@uea.ac.uk, Univ of East Anglia; GeObCt
Grant, John A., 202-633-2474 Smithsonian Inst / Nat Air & Space Mus; Xg
Grant, Jonathan, (902) 494-2021 jon.grant@dal.ca, Dalhousie Univ; Ob
Grant, Stanley, 703-361-5606 stanleyg@vt.edu, Virginia Polytechnic Inst & State Univ; Hs
Grapenthin, Ronni, 575-835-5924 rg@nmt.edu, New Mexico Inst of Mining and Tech; Gv
Grassian, Vicki, (858) 534-2499 vhgrassian@ucsd.edu, Univ of California, San Diego; Cm
Grassineau, Nathalie, +44 1784 443810 nathalie.grassineau@rhul.ac.uk, Royal Holloway Univ of London; Cs
Grassman, Jean, 718-951-5000 ext 2752 Graduate Sch of the City Univ of New York; Gg
Grattan, Stephen R., 530-752-4618 srgrattan@ucdavis.edu, Univ of California, Davis; Sp
Graustein, William C., (203) 287-2853 william.graustein@yale.edu, Yale Univ; Cl
Gravely, Cynthia Rae, (864) 656-3438 gravelc@clemson.edu, Clemson Univ; Zn
Graves, Alexandria, 919-513-0635 alexandria_graves@ncsu.edu, North Carolina State Univ; Sb
Graves, Charles E., (314) 977-3121 gravesce@slu.edu, Saint Louis Univ; As
Gravley, Darren, +64 3 3667001 Ext 45683 darren.gravley@canterbury.ac.nz, Univ of Canterbury; Gv
Gray, Kyle R., 319-273-2809 kyle.gray@uni.edu, Univ of Northern Iowa; ZeGg
Gray, Lee M., (330) 823-3605 graylm@mountunion.edu, Mount Union Coll; PgGg
Gray, Mary Beth, (570) 577-1146 mbgray@bucknell.edu, Bucknell Univ; Gc
Gray, Neil, +44 (0) 191 208 4887 neil.gray@ncl.ac.uk, Univ of Newcastle Upon Tyne; Pg
Gray, Norman H., dlfox@umn.edu, Univ of Connecticut; Gx
Gray, Robert S., (805) 965-0581 gray@sbcc.net, Santa Barbara City Coll; PvGzx
Gray, Sarah, (619) 260-4098 sgray@sandiego.edu, Univ of San Diego; Zn
Grayston, Sue, 604–822–5928 sue.grayston@ubc.ca, Univ of British Columbia; Sb
Greatbatch, Ian, +44 020 8417 2879 i.greatbatch@kingston.ac.uk, Kingston Univ; Zi
Greatbatch, Richard , rgreatbatch@geomar.de, Dalhousie Univ; Op
Greb, Stephen F., 8592575500 x136 greb@uky.edu, Univ of Kentucky; GsEcGr
Green, Andrew, (031) 260-2516 greena1@ukzn.ac.za, Univ of KwaZulu-Natal; GuYgGs
Green, Brittany, (785) 532-6101 bdgreen@ksu.edu, Kansas State Univ; Zn
Green, Harry W., (510) 642-3059 Univ of California, Berkeley; Pv
Green, Jack, (562) 985-4198 jgreen3@csulb.edu, California State Univ, Long Beach; Gv
Green, John C., (218) 726-7208 jgreen@d.umn.edu, Univ of Minnesota Duluth; GieGv
Green, Jonathan, +44 0151 795 4385 jonathan.green@liverpool.ac.uk, Univ of Liverpool; Ob
Greenaway, Darren, 817-515-3606 darren.greenaway@tccd.edu, Tarrant County Coll, Southeast Campus; Gg
Greenberg, David, (902) 426-2431 greenbergd@mar.dfo-mpo.gc.ca, Dalhousie Univ; Op
Greenberg, Harvey, (206) 685-7981 hgreen@uw.edu, Univ of Washington; Gml
Greenberg, Jeffrey K., jeffrey.greenberg@wheaton.edu, Wheaton Coll; GicGe
Greenberg, Richard J., (520) 621-6940 greenberg@lpl.arizona.edu, Univ of Arizona; Xy
Greenberg, Sallie, (217) 244-4068 sallieg@illinois.edu, Illinois State Geological Survey; ClZg
Greene, Brian M., 412-395-7323 brian.greene@usace.army.mil, Youngstown State Univ; Ng
Greene, Charles H., chg2@cornell.edu, Cornell Univ; Ob
Greene, Chris, 902-494-7018 csgreene@dal.ca, Dalhousie Univ; Zi
Greene, David C., (740) 587-6476 greened@denison.edu, Denison Univ; GctGe
Greene, Don M., (254) 710-2193 don_greene@baylor.edu, Baylor Univ; ZyAm
Greene, Mott, 206-713-0917 mgreene@uw.edu, Univ of Washington; GgAmOg
Greene, Todd, 530-898-5546 tjgreene@csuchico.edu, California State Univ, Chico; Gsr
Greenfield, Dianne I., 212-413-3154 dianne.greenfield@asrc.cuny.edu, Graduate Sch of the City Univ of New York; Gu
Greenfield, Roy J., (814) 237-1810 rkg4@psu.edu, Pennsylvania State Univ, Univ Park; YgsYu
Greenhalgh, Stewart A., +966138608716 greenhalgh@kfupm.edu.sa, King Fahd Univ of Petroleum and Minerals; Yse
Greenlee, Diana M., (318) 926-3314 greenlee@ulm.edu, Univ of Louisiana, Monroe; GaCo
Greenough, John D., 250-807-9520 john.greenough@ubc.ca, Univ of British Columbia, Okanagan Campus; GiCtGa
Greenwell, Chris, +44 (0) 191 33 42324 chris.greenwell@durham.ac.uk, Durham Univ; CqEoCg
Greenwood, James P., 860 685-2545 jgreenwood@wesleyan.edu, Wesleyan Univ; Xc
Greer, Lisa, 540-458-8870 greerl@wlu.edu, Washington & Lee Univ; GsPe
Gregg, Jay M., 405-744-6358 jay.gregg@okstate.edu, Oklahoma State Univ; Gs
Gregg, Michael C., (206) 543-1353 gregg@apl.washington.edu, Univ of Washington; Op
Gregg, Patricia, 217-333-3540 pgregg@illinois.edu, Univ of Illinois, Urbana-Champaign; YgCg
Gregg, Tracy K. P., (716) 645-4328 tgregg@buffalo.edu, SUNY, Buffalo; Gv
Gregor, C. B., 937 775-3455 Wright State Univ; Gs
Gregory, Robert, (307) 766-2286 Ext. 237 robert.gregory@wyo.gov, Wyoming State Geological Survey; En
Grender, Gordon C., (540) 231-6521 Virginia Polytechnic Inst & State Univ; Go
Grenfell, Thomas C., tcg@atmos.washington.edu, Univ of Washington; As
Grew, Edward S., (207) 581-2169 esgrew@maine.edu, Univ of Maine; Gpz

Grew, Priscilla C., (402) 472-2095 pgrew1@unl.edu, Univ of Nebraska, Lincoln; GpeZe
Greybush, Steven J., 814-867-4926 sjg213@psu.edu, Pennsylvania State Univ, Univ Park; Am
Greyling, Lynnette N., 021-650-294886 l.greyling@uct.ac.za, Univ of Cape Town; EgmCe
Gribenko, Alex, (801) 585-6484 alex.gribenko@utah.edu, Univ of Utah; Yg
Grieneisen, Michael L., mgrien@ucdavis.edu, Univ of California, Davis; Hg
Griera Artigas, Albert, ++935811035 albert.griera@uab.cat, Universitat Autonoma de Barcelona; GcCl
Gries, John C., (316) 978-3140 Wichita State Univ; Gt
Grieve, Richard, rgrieve2@uwo.ca, Western Univ; Xg
Grieve, Richard A. F., (613) 995-5372 geology@unb.ca, Univ of New Brunswick; Xg
Grießl, Stefan, 089/2180 4188 stefan.griessl@uni.muenchen.de, Ludwig-Maximilians-Univ Muenchen; Gz
Griffen, Dana T., 801-422-2305 dana_griffen@byu.edu, Brigham Young Univ; Gz
Griffin, Kevin, griff@ldeo.columbia.edu, Columbia Univ; Zn
Griffin, William R., (972) 883-2430 griffin@utdallas.edu, Univ of Texas, Dallas; Gg
Griffing, Corinne, 604-527-5217 griffingc@douglascollege.ca, Douglas Coll; GgeGm
Griffing, David H., 607-431-4629 griffingd@hartwick.edu, Hartwick Coll; GduGm
Griffis, Timothy J., (612) 625-3117 tgriffis@soils.umn.edu, Univ of Minnesota, Twin Cities; As
Griffith, Ashley, (817) 272-2987 wagriff@uta.edu, Univ of Texas, Arlington; Gct
Griffith, Caitlin, (520) 626-3806 griffith@lpl.arizona.edu, Univ of Arizona; Zn
Griffith, Elizabeth, griffith.906@osu.edu, Ohio State Univ; CsOoCb
Griffith, Liz, (817) 272-2987 lgriff@uta.edu, Univ of Texas, Arlington; CslCm
Griffith, William A., griffith.233@osu.edu, Ohio State Univ; GcNr
Grigg, Joseph, 575-835-5336 joseph.grigg, New Mexico Inst of Mining and Tech; Go
Grigg, Laurie, 802 485 3323 lgrigg@norwich.edu, Norwich Univ; PeGnZi
Grigg, Richard W., (808) 956-7186 rgrigg@soest.hawaii.edu, Univ of Hawai'i, Manoa; Ob
Griggs, Garry, 831-459-5006 griggs@ucsc.edu, Univ of California, Santa Cruz; On
Grigsby, Jeffry D., (765) 285-8270 jgrigsby@bsu.edu, Ball State Univ; GdClGo
Grimes, Stephen, +44 1752 584759 stephen.grimes@plymouth.ac.uk, Univ of Plymouth; Cs
Grimley, David A., 217-244-7324 dgrimley@illinois.edu, Illinois State Geological Survey; GmlSc
Grimm, Kurt A., (604) 822-9258 kgrimm@eos.ubc.ca, Univ of British Columbia; Gs
Grindlay, Nancy R., (910) 962-2352 grindlayn@uncw.edu, Univ of North Carolina, Wilmington; Yg
Gringarten, Alain, +44 20 759 47440 a.gringarten@imperial.ac.uk, Imperial Coll; Np
Grippo, Alessandro, grippo_alessandro@smc.edu, Santa Monica Coll; Gs
Gripshover, Margaret , margaret.gripshover@wku.edu, Western Kentucky Univ; Zy
Grise, Kevin M., (434) 924-0433 kmg3r@virginia.edu, Univ of Virginia; As
Grismer, Mark E., (530) 752-3245 megrismer@ucdavis.edu, Univ of California, Davis; Hw
Griswold, George B., (505) 299-6192 New Mexico Inst of Mining and Tech; Nx
Griswold, Jennifer S., smalljen@hawaii.edu, Univ of Hawai'i, Manoa; AmZr
Gritzo, Russell E., (505) 667-0481 Los Alamos; Zn
Groat, Lee A., (604) 822-1289 groat@mail.ubc.ca, Univ of British Columbia; GzEg
Grobler, Hendrik C., +27115596838 hgrobler@uj.ac.za, Univ of Johannesburg; ZnNm
Grocke, Darren, +44 (0) 191 33 42282 Durham Univ; Cs
Groenevelt, Pieter H., (519) 824-4120 (Ext. 53585) pgroenev@lrs.uoguelph.ca, Univ of Guelph; Sp
Groffman, Peter , 719-951-5000, ext. 5416 peter.groffman@brooklyn.cuny.edu, Graduate Sch of the City Univ of New York; Zg
Groffman, Peter, 212-413-3143 peter.groffman@brooklyn.cuny.edu, Brooklyn Coll (CUNY); SbCl
Gromet, L. P., 401-863-1920 peter_gromet@brown.edu, Brown Univ; Cc
Groppi, Christopher, (480) 965-6436 cgroppi@asu.edu, Arizona State Univ; XaZm
Groppo, Chiara Teresa, chiara.groppo@unito.it, Univ di Torino; Gx
Grosfils, Eric B., (909) 621-8673 egrosfils@pomona.edu, Pomona Coll; XgGvq
Groshong, Jr., Richard H., 205-348-1882 rhgroshon@cs.com, Univ of Alabama; Gc
Gross, Amy, 910-521-6588 amy.gross@uncp.edu, Univ of North Carolina, Pembroke; Gg
Gross, Gerardo W., grossgw@nmt.edu, New Mexico Inst of Mining and Tech; Yx
Gross, Juliane, (848) 445-3619 jgross@eps.rutgers.edu, Rutgers, The State Univ of New Jersey; Xcm
Gross, Michael, (305) 348-3932 grossm@fiu.edu, Florida International Univ; Gc
Grossman, Eric, (360) 650-4697 eric.grossman@wwu.edu, Western Washington Univ; GusGm
Grossman, Ethan L., (979) 845-0637 e-grossman@tamu.edu, Texas A&M Univ; Csl
Grossman, Lawrence S., (540) 231-5116 Virginia Polytechnic Inst & State Univ; Zn
Grossman, Walter, wgrossman@yahoo.com, San Bernardino Valley Coll; Og
Groszos, Mark S., (229) 333-5664 msgroszo@valdosta.edu, Valdosta State Univ; GctEg
Grothe, Pamela, pgrothe@umw.edu, Univ of Mary Washington; GsOgZc
Grotjahn, Richard , 530-752-2246 grotjahn@ucdavis.edu, Univ of California, Davis; As
Grottoli, Andrea G., 614 292 5782 grottoli.1@osu.edu, Ohio State Univ; ObCbOo
Grotzinger, John P., 626.395.6785 grotz@gps.caltech.edu, California Inst of Tech; GsPeXg
Grove, Karen, (415) 338-2617 kgrove@sfsu.edu, San Francisco State Univ; Gs
Grove, Timothy L., (617) 253-2878 tlgrove@mit.edu, Massachusetts Inst of Tech; Gi
Grover, Jeffrey A., 8055463100 x2759 jgrover@cuesta.edu, Cuesta Coll; Gg
Grover, John E., john.grover@uc.edu, Univ of Cincinnati; Gz
Grover, Timothy W., (802) 468-1289 tim.grover@castleton.edu, Castleton Univ; GptGc
Groves, Christopher, (270) 745-5974 chris.groves@wku.edu, Western Kentucky Univ; Hg
Grube, John P., 217-244-1716 grube@isgs.uiuc.edu, Illinois State Geological Survey; Eo
Gruen, Dieter M., (630) 972-3513 Argonne; Zm
Grujic, Djordje, (902) 494-2208 dgrujic@is.dal.ca, Dalhousie Univ; Gt
Grunbaum, Daniel, (206) 221-6594 grunbaum@ocean.washington.edu, Univ of Washington; Ob
Grunder, Anita L., (541) 737-5189 grundera@geo.oregonstate.edu, Oregon State Univ; Gi
Grundl, Timothy J., 414-229-4765 grundl@uwm.edu, Univ of Wisconsin, Milwaukee; HwCl
Grunwald, Sabine -., (352) 294-3145 sabgru@ufl.edu, Univ of Florida; ZiSoZr
Grupp, Steve, 425-388-9450 sgrupp@everettcc.edu, Everett Comm Coll; GgOg
Gu, Baohua, 865-574-7286 gub1@ornl.gov, Oak Ridge; CbqSb
Gu, Jeff, (780) 492-2292 jgu@phys.ualberta.ca, Univ of Alberta; Ys
Gualda, Guilherme, 615-322-2976 g.gualda@vanderbilt.edu, Vanderbilt Univ; GivGz
Guan, Dabo, +44(0) 113 34 37432 d.guan@leeds.ac.uk, Univ of Leeds; Eg
Guan, Huade, huade.guan@flinders.edu.au, Flinders Univ; HgsHg
Guber, Albert L., guber@ems.psu.edu, Pennsylvania State Univ, Univ Park; Pe
Guccione, Margaret J., (479) 575-3354 guccione@comp.uark.edu, Univ of Arkansas, Fayetteville; GmaGg
Gudmundsson, Agust, +44 1784 276345 agust.gudmundsson@rhul.ac.uk, Royal Holloway Univ of London; Gc
Guenthner, Willy, wrg@illinois.edu, Univ of Illinois, Urbana-Champaign; GtzCg
Guerin, Gilles, guerin@ldeo.columbia.edu, Columbia Univ; Gu
Guerra, Oralia, (512) 223-7483 oguerra1@austincc.edu, Austin Comm Coll District; Zn
Guerrieri, Mary, (520) 621-2828 mary@lpl.arizona.edu, Univ of Arizona; Zn
Guertal, Elizabeth A., eguertal@acesag.auburn.edu, Auburn Univ; Sc
Guest, Peter S., 831-656-2451 pguest@nps.edu, Naval Postgraduate Sch; Am
Guevara, Victor, vguevara@skidmore.edu, Skidmore Coll; Gp
Guggenheim, Stephen J., (312) 996-3263 xtal@uic.edu, Univ of Illinois at Chicago; Gz
Guggino, Steve N., (912) 478-5361 sguggino@georgiasouthern.edu, Georgia Southern Univ; GgCg
Guha, Jayanta, 418 545 5222 jguha@uqac.c, Universite du Quebec a Chicoutimi; Eg
Guilbert, John M., (520) 621-6024 j.guilbert@comcast.net, Univ of Arizona;

Em
Guillemette, Renald, (979) 845-6301 guillemette@geo.tamu.edu, Texas A&M Univ; Gz
Guinan, Patrick E., 573-882-5909 guinanp@missouri.edu, Univ of Missouri; As
Guinasso, Norman L., (979) 862-2323 norman@geos.tamu.edu, Texas A&M Univ; Opc
Guitierrez-Alonso, Gabriel, gabi@gugu.usal.es, Florida International Univ; Gc
Gulen, Gurcan, (713) 654-5404 gurcan.gulen@beg.utexas.edu, Univ of Texas, Austin; Ego
Gulick, Sean S., 512-471-0483 sean@ig.utexas.edu, Univ of Texas, Austin; Gc
Gulley, Jason, jdgulley@usf.edu, Univ of South Florida; Hw
Gulliver, John S., (612) 625-4080 gulli003@tc.umn.edu, Univ of Minnesota, Twin Cities; Hs
Gundersen, James N., (316) 978-3140 Wichita State Univ; Ga
Gunderson, Lance, 404 727 8108 lgunder@emory.edu, Emory Univ; Sf
Gundiler, Ibrahim H., 575-835-5730 ibrahim.gundiler@nmt.edu, New Mexico Inst of Mining and Tech; Nx
Gunia, Piotr, piotr.gunia@uwr.edu.pl, Univ of Wroclaw; Gaz
Gunter, Mickey E., (208) 885-6015 mgunter@uidaho.edu, Univ of Idaho; GzEnGb
Guo, Junhua, jguo1@csub.edu, California State Univ, Bakersfield; Gs
Guo, Weifu, (508) 289-3380 wguo@whoi.edu, Woods Hole Oceanographic Inst; CslPe
Gupta, Hoshin V., (520) 275-5534 hoshin.gupta@hwr.arizona.edu, Univ of Arizona; HqZgAs
Gupta, Sanjeev, +44 20 759 46527 s.gupta@imperial.ac.uk, Imperial Coll; Gs
Gupta, Satish C., (612) 625-1241 sgupta@soils.umn.edu, Univ of Minnesota, Twin Cities; Sp
Gurdak, Jason, (415) 338-6869 jgurdak@sfsu.edu, San Francisco State Univ; HwCqAt
Gurevich, Boris, +61 8 9266-7359 b.gurevich@curtin.edu.au, Curtin Univ; Ye
Gurlea, Lawrence P., lisobar@aol.com, Youngstown State Univ; Cg
Gurnis, Michael C., (626) 395-6979 gurnis@gps.caltech.edu, California Inst of Tech; Ys
Gurocak, Zulfu, 00904242370000-5991 zgurocak@firat.edu.tr, Firat Univ; Nrg
Gurrola, Harold, 806-834-8625 harold.gurrola@ttu.edu, Texas Tech Univ; Ys
Gurwin, Jacek, jacek.gurwin@uwr.edu.pl, Univ of Wroclaw; HwyZf
Gust, David A., 61 7 3138 2217 d.gust@qut.edu.au, Queensland Univ of Tech; GiCpGt
Gustin, Mae, 775.784.4203 mgustin@cabnr.unr.edu, Univ of Nevada, Reno; Cg
Guth, Peter L., (410) 293-6560 pguth@usna.edu, United States Naval Academy; GcZiy
Guthrie, Roderick I., (514) 398-4755 McGill Univ; Nx
Gutierrez, Melida, (417) 836-5967 mgutierrez@missouristate.edu, Missouri State Univ; CgHy
Gutierrez-Jurado, Hugo A., 915-747-5159 hagutierrez@utep.edu, Univ of Texas, El Paso; HgsHw
Gutknecht, Jessica L., 612-626-8435 jgutknec@umn.edu, Univ of Minnesota, Twin Cities; Sb
Gutmann, James T., (860) 685-2258 jgutmann@wesleyan.edu, Wesleyan Univ; GviGz
Gutowski, William J., (515) 294-5632 gutowski@iastate.edu, Iowa State Univ of Sci & Tech; Am
Gutzler, David J., (505) 277-3328 gutzler@unm.edu, Univ of New Mexico; As
Guza, Robert T., (858) 534-0585 rguza@ucsd.edu, Univ of California, San Diego; On
Guzina, Bojan B., (612) 626-0789 guzina@wave.ce.umn.edu, Univ of Minnesota, Twin Cities; Nr
Guzman, Ernesto, (519) 824-4120 Ext.53609 eguzman@uoguelph.ca, Univ of Guelph; Zn
Gušiæ, Ivan, +38514606102 ivangusic@yahoo.com, Univ of Zagreb; GgPsm
Gyakum, John R., (514) 398-6076 john.gyakum@mcgill.ca, McGill Univ; Am
Gysi, Alexander, 575-835-5754 alexander.gysi@nmt.edu, New Mexico Inst of Mining and Tech; EgCpGz
Göttlich, Hagen, 089/2180 5615 goettlich@ennab.de, Ludwig-Maximilians-Univ Muenchen; Gz

H

Haag, Lucas, (785) 462-6281 lhaag@ksu.edu, Kansas State Univ; So
Haas, Christian, (416)736-2100 #77705 haasc@yorku.ca, York Univ; Yg
Haas, Johnson R., (269) 387-2878 johnson.haas@wmich.edu, Western Michigan Univ; Cl
Habana, Nathan C., (671) 735-2693 nhabana@triton.uog.edu, Univ of Guam; Hw
Habash, Marc, (519) 824-4120 Ext.52748 mhabash@uoguelph.ca, Univ of Guelph; Zn
Haber, Eldad, (604) 822-4525 haber@eos.ubc.ca, Univ of British Columbia; YgZn
Habib, Daniel, (718) 997-3333 daniel.habib@qc.cuny.edu, Queens Coll (CUNY); Pl
Habron, Geoffrey, 864-294-3413 geoffrey.habron@furman.edu, Furman Univ; Zn
Hacker, Bradley R., (805) 893-7952 hacker@geol.ucsb.edu, Univ of California, Santa Barbara; Gp
Hacker, David B., 330-672-8831 dhacker@kent.edu, Kent State Univ; GcHw
Hacker, Jorg, jorg.hacker@flinders.edu.au, Flinders Univ; ZrAs
Hacker, Joshua P., 831-656-2722 jphacker@nps.edu, Naval Postgraduate Sch; Am
Haddad, Brent, (831) 459-4149 bhaddad@cats.ucsc.edu, Univ of California, Santa Cruz; Zn
Haddock, Gregory D., (660) 562-1719 haddock@nwmissouri.edu, Northwest Missouri State Univ; Zi
Hadler, Kathryn, +44 20 759 47198 k.hadler@imperial.ac.uk, Imperial Coll; Gz
Hadley, Daniel, drhadley@illinois.edu, Univ of Illinois; Hw
Hafez, Sabry ., (907) 474- 6917 ssabour@alaska.edu, Univ of Alaska, Fairbanks; Nm
Haff, Peter K., (919) 684-5902 haff@duke.edu, Duke Univ; Zn
Hafner, James A., (413) 545-0778 hafner@geo.umass.edu, Univ of Massachusetts, Amherst; Zn
Hagadorn, James W., (303) 370-6058 james.hagadorn@dmns.org, Denver Mus of Nature & Sci; GgsPg
Hagedorn, Charles, (540) 231-4895 chagedor@vt.edu, Virginia Polytechnic Inst & State Univ; Sb
Hagedorn, Jake, 828-232-5183 jghagedo@unca.edu, Univ of North Carolina, Asheville; SbZun
Hagelman III, Ronald, 51422452170 Texas State Univ; Rnm
Hageman, Steven J., (828) 262-6609 hagemansj@appstate.edu, Appalachian State Univ; PieGg
Hager, Bradford H., (617) 253-0126 bhhager@mit.edu, Massachusetts Inst of Tech; Ys
Hagerty, Michael, 617-552-8300 hagertmb@bc.edu, Boston Coll; Ys
Haggart, James, jim.haggart@canada.ca, Univ of British Columbia; PgGr
Haggart, Renee, (604) 822-2789 rhaggart@eos.ubc.ca, Univ of British Columbia; Zn
Haggerty, Janet A., 918-631-2304 janet-haggerty@utulsa.edu, Univ of Tulsa; GudGs
Haggerty, Julia H., (406) 994-6904 julia.haggerty@montana.edu, Montana State Univ; Zu
Haggerty, Roy D., (541) 737-0663 roy.haggerty@oregonstate.edu, Oregon State Univ; Hw
Haggerty, Stephen E., (305) 348-7338 haggerty@fiu.edu, Florida International Univ; GiEgGz
Haghighi, Manouchehr, manouchehr.haghighi@adelaide.edu.au, Univ of Adelaide; Np
Haiar, Brooke, haiar@lynchburg.edu, Univ of Lynchburg; PgGeg
Haigh, Ivan D., +44 (023) 80596501 i.d.haigh@soton.ac.uk, Univ of Southampton; On
Haile, Estifanos, 865-974-8340 ehaile1@utk.edu, Univ of Tennessee, Knoxville; Hy
Haileab, Bereket, (507) 222-5746 bhaileab@carleton.edu, Carleton Coll; GxzGi
Haimberger, Leopold, 0043 1 4277 53712 leopold.haimberger@univie.ac.at, Univ of Vienna; Ams
Haimson, Bezalel C., (608) 262-2563 bhaimson@wisc.edu, Univ of Wisconsin, Madison; Nr
Haine, Thomas W., (410) 516-7048 thomas.haine@jhu.edu, Johns Hopkins Univ; OpgAs
Hajash, Andrew, (979) 845-0642 hajash@geo.tamu.edu, Texas A&M Univ; Cp
Hajek, Elizabeth, hajek@psu.edu, Pennsylvania State Univ, Univ Park; Gs
Hajnal, Zoltan, (306) 966-5694 zoltan.hajnal@usask.ca, Univ of Saskatchewan; YsGtc
Hakim, Gregory J., (206) 685-2439 hakim@atmos.washington.edu, Univ of Washington; As
Hakimian, Adina, 516-463-6545 adina.i.hakimian@hofstra.edu, Hofstra Univ; Gg
Halama, Ralf, +44 (0) 1782 7 34960 r.halama@keele.ac.uk, Keele Univ; GpiCa
Halbig, Joseph B., halbig@wazoo.com, Univ of Hawai'i, Hilo; Ca
Halden, Norman M., (204) 474-6910 nm_halden@umanitoba.ca, Univ of Manitoba; Cg
Hale, Beverley A., (519) 824-4120 (Ext. 53434) bhale@uoguelph.ca, Univ

of Guelph; Ct
Hale, Leslie J., (202) 633-1796 halel@si.edu, Smithsonian Inst / Nat Mus of Natural History; GgZnRh
Hale, Michelle, +44 023 92 842290 michelle.hale@port.ac.uk, Univ of Portsmouth; Og
Hales, Burke R., (541) 737-8121 bhales@coas.oregonstate.edu, Oregon State Univ; Oc
Hales, T. C., +44(0)29 208 74329 halest@cardiff.ac.uk, Univ of Wales; Gt
Hales, TC, halest@cf.ac.uk, Cardiff Univ; Gm
Haley, Brian, 541-737-2649 bhaley@coas.oregonstate.edu, Oregon State Univ; Cs
Haley, J C., jachaley@vwc.edu, Miami Univ; Gts
Haley, John C., 757-455-3407 jchaley@vwc.edu, Virginia Wesleyan Coll; GgeZi
Halfar, Jochen, (905) 828-5419 jochen.halfar@utoronto.ca, Univ of Toronto; Pe
Halfman, John D., (315) 781-3918 halfman@hws.edu, Hobart & William Smith Colls; GeHsGn
Halfpenny, Angela, 509-963-2826 angela.halfpenny@cwu.edu, Central Washington Univ; Gcz
Halihan, Todd, 405-744-6358 todd.halihan@okstate.edu, Oklahoma State Univ; HwYuRc
Hall, Anne M., (404) 727-2863 ahall04@emory.edu, Emory Univ; Gz
Hall, Brenda L., (207) 581-2191 brendah@maine.edu, Univ of Maine; Gl
Hall, Chris, (734) 764-6391 cmhall@umich.edu, Univ of Michigan; Cc
Hall, Christopher C., (519) 824-4120 Ext.52740 jchall@uoguelph.ca, Univ of Guelph; Zn
Hall, Clarence A., (310) 825-1010 hall@epss.ucla.edu, Univ of California, Los Angeles; GgtGe
Hall, Cynthia V., (610) 436-1003 chall@wcupa.edu, West Chester Univ; Cg
Hall, I, hall@cf.ac.uk, Cardiff Univ; Zn
Hall, Ian R., +44(0)29 208 75612 hall@cardiff.ac.uk, Cardiff Univ; GuCsGs
Hall, Jean, +44 (0) 191 208 8783 jean.hall@ncl.ac.uk, Univ of Newcastle Upon Tyne; Ng
Hall, Jeremy, (709) 864-7569 jeremyh@mun.ca, Memorial Univ of Newfoundland; YsGtYr
Hall, Jude, (740) 587-6217 hall@denison.edu, Denison Univ; Zn
Hall, Luke D., (805) 642-3211 lhall@vcccd.net, Ventura Coll; Zy
Hall, Robert, rhall@uoguelph.ca, Univ of Guelph; Zn
Hall, Stuart A., 713-743-3416 sahgeo@uh.edu, Univ of Houston; Ym
Hall, Tracy, 678-872-8415 thall@highlands.edu, Georgia Highlands Coll; Gg
Hall, III, John R., (504) 231-6305 jrhall3@vt.edu, Virginia Polytechnic Inst & State Univ; So
Halladay, Sylvia R., 614 265 6624 sylvia.halladay@dnr.state.oh.us, Ohio Dept of Natural Resources; Zn
Hallar, Anna G., (801) 587-7238 gannet.hallar@utah.edu, Univ of Utah; AspAc
Haller, Merrick C., (541) 737-9141 merrick.haller@oregonstate.edu, Oregon State Univ; OnZrOp
Hallet, Bernard, 206-685-2409 hallet@uw.edu, Univ of Washington; Gml
Hallett, Benjamin W., 920-424-0868 hallettb@uwosh.edu, Univ of Wisconsin, Oshkosh; Gpx
Hallett, Rebecca, (519) 824-4120 Ext.54488 rhallett@uoguelph.ca, Univ of Guelph; Zn
Halliday, Alex, +44 (1865) 272969 alex.halliday@earth.ox.ac.uk, Univ of Oxford; Cs
Hallock, Brent G., (805)756-2436 bhallock@calpoly.edu, California Polytechnic State Univ; Sf
Hallock-Muller, Pamela, (727) 553-1567 pmuller@usf.edu, Univ of South Florida; OuGsPm
Halls, Henry C., 905-828-5363 hlhalls@utm.utoronto.ca, Univ of Toronto; Ym
Halls, Joanne N., (910) 962-7614 hallsj@uncw.edu, Univ of North Carolina, Wilmington; Zi
Halsor, Sid P., (570) 408-4611 sid.halsor@wilkes.edu, Wilkes Univ; Giv
Halsted, Christian, (207) 287-7175 christian.h.halsted@maine.gov, Dept of Agriculture, Conservation, and Forestry; Zi
Halverson, Galen, 514-398-4894 galen.halverson@mcgill.ca, McGill Univ; GsrCs
Halverson, Larry, (515) 294-0495 larryh@iastate.edu, Iowa State Univ of Sci & Tech; So
Ham, Nelson R., (920) 403-3977 nelson.ham@snc.edu, Saint Norbert Coll; Gl
Hamane, Angel, ahamane2@calstatela.edu, California State Univ, Los Angeles; Ze
Hamann, Hillary, (303) 871-3977 hillary.hamann@du.edu, Univ of Denver; HgZy
Hambrey, Michael M., +44 (0)1970 621 860 mjh@aber.ac.uk, Aberystwyth Univ; GlsGm
Hamburger, Michael W., (812) 855-2934 hamburg@indiana.edu, Indiana Univ, Bloomington; YsGtv
Hamdan, Abeer, abeer.hamdan@phoenixcollege.edu, Phoenix Coll; Gg
Hamecher, Emily A., 626-660-8314 ehamecher@fullerton.edu, California State Univ, Fullerton; GgzGi
Hameed, Sultan, (631) 632-8319 sultan.hameed@stonybrook.edu, SUNY, Stony Brook; As
Hames, Willis E., (334) 844-4881 hameswe@auburn.edu, Auburn Univ; CcGpt
Hamill, Paul, (815) 455-8698 phamill@mchenry.edu, McHenry County Coll; AmZg
Hamilton, George, (413) 499-4660 bhamilton@berkshirecc.edu, Berkshire Comm Coll; Zn
Hamilton, Jacqueline, (612) 626-8292 stub0035@umn.edu, Univ of Minnesota; ZiGe
Hamilton, Michael A., (416) 946-7424 mahamilton@es.utoronto.ca, Univ of Toronto; CcGiCu
Hamilton, Sally, +44 (0)131 451 3198 s.hamilton@hw.ac.uk, Heriot-Watt Univ; Gs
Hamilton, Thomas, 4256401339x7067 thomas.hamilton@edcc.edu, Edmonds Comm Coll; Zg
Hamlet, Alan, alan.hamlet.1@nd.edu, Univ of Notre Dame; Hs
Hamlin, H, Scott, 512-4759527 scott.hamlin@beg.utexas.edu, Univ of Texas at Austin, Jackson Sch of Geosciences; Gr
Hamme, Roberta C., (250) 472-4014 rhamme@uvic.ca, Univ of Victoria; Oc
Hammer, Julia E., 808-956-5996 jhammer@hawaii.edu, Univ of Hawai'i, Manoa; GiCpGv
Hammer, Philip T., (604) 822-5703 phammer@eos.ubc.ca, Univ of British Columbia; Ys
Hammer, William R., (309) 794-7487 williamhammer@augustana.edu, Augustana Coll; Pv
Hammerschmidt, Chad, 937 775-3457 chad.hammerschmidt@wright.edu, Wright State Univ; CmOcCb
Hammersley, Charles, (928) 523-6655 charles.hammersley@nau.edu, Northern Arizona Univ; Zn
Hammersley, Lisa, 916-278-7200 hammersley@csus.edu, Sacramento State Univ; Gig
Hammes, Ursula, 512-471-1891 ursula.hammes@beg.utexas.edu, Univ of Texas at Austin, Jackson Sch of Geosciences; Gg
Hammond, Amie C., ahammond@austincc.edu, Austin Comm Coll District; ZeGg
Hammond, Anne, (807) 343-8677 anne.hammond@lakeheadu.ca, Lakehead Univ; Zn
Hammond, Douglas E., (213) 740-5837 dhammond@usc.edu, Univ of Southern California; Cm
Hammond, Paul E., (503) 725-3387 hammondp@pdx.edu, Portland State Univ; Gi
Hammond, William C., (775) 784-6436 whammond@unr.edu, Univ of Nevada, Reno; Yd
Hampson, Arthur, (801) 585-5698 spike.hampson@geog.utah.edu, Univ of Utah; Zy
Hampson, Gary , +44 20 759 46475 g.j.hampson@imperial.ac.uk, Imperial Coll; Gd
Hampton, Brian A., 575-646-2997 bhampton@nmsu.edu, New Mexico State Univ, Las Cruces; Gst
Hampton, Duane R., (269) 387-5496 duane.hampton@wmich.edu, Western Michigan Univ; HwSpHg
Hampton, Samuel J., +64 3 3667001 Ext 6770 samuel.hampton@canterbury.ac.nz, Univ of Canterbury; GvZe
Hams, Jacquelyn E., (818) 778-5566 hamsje@lavc.edu, Los Angeles Valley Coll; GgOuZe
Hamutoko, Josephine, jhamutoko@unam.na, Univ of Namibia; Hw
Hamzaoui, Cherif, 514-987-3000 #6837 hamzaoui.cherif@uqam.ca, Universite du Quebec a Montreal; Yg
Han, De-hua, 713-743-9293 dhan@uh.edu, Univ of Houston; Ye
Han, Nizhou, (540) 231-2403 nhan@vt.edu, Virginia Polytechnic Inst & State Univ; Sc
Hanafy, Sherif , +9661368603765 sherif.mahmoud@kfupm.edu.sa, King Fahd Univ of Petroleum and Minerals; Yg
Hanan, Barry B., (619) 594-6710 bhanan@mail.sdsu.edu, San Diego State Univ; Cc
Hanchar, John, 709 864 6785 jhanchar@mun.ca, Memorial Univ of Newfoundland; Cg
Hancock, Gregory, 61 02 4921 5090 greg.hancock@newcastle.edu.au, Univ of Newcastle; ZiGmm
Hancock, Steven, steven.hancock@ed.ac.uk, Edinburgh Univ; Zi
Hand, Kristen, 717–702–2046 khand@pa.gov, DCNR- Pennsylvania Bureau of Geological Survey; HwGg
Hand, Linda M., 650 574-6633 hand@smccd.edu, Coll of San Mateo; GgPgOg
Hand, Suzanne J., s.hand@unsw.edu.au, Univ of New South Wales; Pv

Haneberg, William, (505) 255-8005 New Mexico Inst of Mining and Tech; Ng
Hanell, Casey R., (360) 902-1439 casey.hanell@dnr.wa.gov, Washington Geological Survey; Gg
Haner, Andrew, (501) 683-0153 andrew.haner@arkansas.gov, Arkansas Geological Survey; Zi
Hanes, Daniel M., (314) 977-3703 dan.hanes@slu.edu, Saint Louis Univ; GesGm
Hanes, John A., (613) 533-6188 hanes@queensu.ca, Queen's Univ; Cc
Haney, Christa M., 662-268-1032 Ext 224 meloche@geosci.msstate.edu, Mississippi State Univ; Am
Haney, Jennifer, (570) 389-5305 jhaney@bloomu.edu, Bloomsburg Univ; Rn
Haney, Robert, rlhaney@nps.edu, Naval Postgraduate Sch; Am
Hanger, Brendan, 405-744-6358 brendan.hanger@okstate.edu, Oklahoma State Univ; Ggz
Hanger, Rex, hangerr@uww.edu, Univ of Wisconsin, Whitewater; PigGs
Hanke, Steve H., (410) 516-7183 hanke@jhu.edu, Johns Hopkins Univ; Zn
Hankins, Katherine B., 404 413-5775 khankins@gsu.edu, Georgia State Univ; Zn
Hanks, Catherine L., 907-474-5562 chanks@gi.alaska.edu, Univ of Alaska, Fairbanks; Go
Hanna, Kevin, 250-807-9265 kevin.hanna@ubc.ca, Univ of British Columbia, Okanagan Campus; ZnRcZu
Hanna, Ruth L., 925-424-1319 rhanna@laspositascollege.edu, Las Positas Coll; Gg
Hanna, Stephen P., (540) 654-1490 shanna@umw.edu, Mary Washington Coll; Zr
Hannah, David, +44 (0)121 41 46925 d.m.hannah@bham.ac.uk, Univ of Birmingham; Hg
Hannah, Judith L., (970) 491-1329 jhannah@warnercnr.colostate.edu, Colorado State Univ; GiCc
Hannibal, Joseph T., (216) 231-4600 jhanniba@cmnh.org, Case Western Reserve Univ; Pi
Hannigan, Robyn, robyn.hannigan@umb.edu, Univ of Massachusetts, Boston; ClmCt
Hannington, Mark, mark.hannington@uottawa.ca, Univ of Ottawa; Eg
Hannula, Kimberly, (970) 247-7463 hannula_k@fortlewis.edu, Fort Lewis Coll; GctGp
Hanor, Jeffrey S., (225) 388-3418 hanor@geol.lsu.edu, Louisiana State Univ; Cl
Hanrahan, Janel, 802-626-6370 janel.hanrahan@northernvermont.edu, Northern Vermont Univ-Lyndon; AsZoRc
Hansel, Colleen, (508) 289-3738 chansel@whoi.edu, Woods Hole Oceanographic Inst; Cm
Hansen, Anthony R., 320-308-2009 arhansen@stcloudstate.edu, Saint Cloud State Univ; Am
Hansen, Christel D., +27 (0)12 420 4255 christel.hansen@up.ac.z, Univ of Pretoria; ZiGmZy
Hansen, Edward C., hansen@hope.edu, Hope Coll; GmpGc
Hansen, Jeffrey C., (505) 667-5043 jchansen@lanl.gov, Los Alamos; Zn
Hansen, Lars, +44 (1865) 272000 lars.hansen@earth.ox.ac.uk, Univ of Oxford; Gz
Hansen, Robert N., +27 (0)51 401 2712 hansenr@ufs.ac.za, Univ of the Free State; CgGe
Hansen, Samantha E., (205) 348-7089 shansen@ua.edu, Univ of Alabama; YsGt
Hansen, Thor A., thor.hansen@wwu.edu, Western Washington Univ; Pg
Hansen, Vicki L., (218) 726-8628 vhansen@d.umn.edu, Univ of Minnesota Duluth; GtXgGc
Hansen, William, (212) 346-1502 Pace Univ, New York Campus; As
Hansom, Jim, +4401413305406 jim.hansom@glasgow.ac.uk, Univ of Glasgow; OnGmZy
Hanson, Andrew D., (702) 895-1092 Univ of Nevada, Las Vegas; Co
Hanson, Gilbert N., (631) 632-8210 gilbert.hanson@stonybrook.edu, Stony Brook Univ; GgZe
Hanson, Howard, 561 297 2460 hphanson@fau.edu, Florida Atlantic Univ; AsOg
Hanson, Lindley S., lhanson@salemstate.edu, Salem State Univ; GmgOn
Hanson, Paul, (402)472-7762 phanson2@unl.edu, Univ of Nebraska, Lincoln; Gm
Hanson, Richard E., (817) 257-7996 r.hanson@tcu.edu, Texas Christian Univ; GxvGt
Hanson, Sarah L., 517-264-3944 slhanson@adrian.edu, Adrian Coll; Giz
Hanson, William D., 501 683-0115 doug.hanson@arkansas.gov, Arkansas Geological Survey; EgnGs
Hanson, Jr., Alfred K., (401) 874-6899 akhanson@gso.uri.edu, Univ of Rhode Island; Oc
Hanu, Dan B., 0040232201464 bogdan.hanu@gmail.com, Alexandru Ioan Cuza; Yge
Hapke, Bruce W., (412) 624-8876 hapke@pitt.edu, Univ of Pittsburgh; Xy
Haq, Saad, (765) 496-7206 haq@purdue.edu, Purdue Univ; Gt
Hara, Tetsu, (401) 874-6509 thara@uri.edu, Univ of Rhode Island; Op
Harbaugh, John W., (650) 723-3365 harbaugh@pangea.stanford.edu, Stanford Univ; Gq
Harbert, William P., (412) 624-8874 harbert@pitt.edu, Univ of Pittsburgh; Ym
Harbor, David J., 540 458 8871 harbord@wlu.edu, Washington & Lee Univ; Gm
Harbor, Jon M., (765) 494-4753 jharbor@purdue.edu, Purdue Univ; GmlGe
Hardage, Bob A., (512) 471-0300 bob.hardage@beg.utexas.edu, Univ of Texas at Austin, Jackson Sch of Geosciences; Yg
Hardage, Sarah M., 956 665 3023 sarah.fearnleyhardage@utrgv.edu, Univ of Texas, Rio Grande Valley; GmZiGg
Harder, Brian J., (225) 578-8533 bharde1@lsu.edu, Louisiana State Univ; Eo
Harder, Steven H., (915) 747-5746 harder@utep.edu, Univ of Texas, El Paso; Yg
Harder, Vicki, 915-747-5501 vmharder@utep.edu, Univ of Texas, El Paso; Gg
Hardgrove, Craig, (480) 727-2170 craig.hardgrove@asu.edu, Arizona State Univ; Xg
Hardin, Perry J., (801) 378-6062 perry_hardin@byu.edu, Brigham Young Univ; Zr
Harding, Chris, (515) 294-7521 charding@iastate.edu, Iowa State Univ of Sci & Tech; Gq
Harding, Ian C., +44 (0)23 80592071 ich@noc.soton.ac.uk, Univ of Southampton; PmlPc
Hardison, Amber, akhardison@vims.edu, William & Mary; Cm
Hardy, Shaun J., (202) 478-7960 shardy@carnegiescience.edu, Carnegie Inst for Sci; Zn
Hargis, David, 619-521-0165 dhargis@hargis.com, Univ of Arizona; Hwq
Hargrave, Jennifer E., 337-482-0678 jhargrave@louisiana.edu, Univ of Louisiana at Lafayette; PvGrZe
Hargrave, Phyllis, 406-496-4606 phargrave@mtech.edu, Montana Tech of The Univ of Montana; Gg
Hargraves, Paul E., (401) 874-6241 pharg@gso.uri.edu, Univ of Rhode Island; Ob
Hargreaves, Bruce R., (610) 758-3683 brh0@lehigh.edu, Lehigh Univ; Ob
Hargreaves, Tom, +44 (0)1603 59 3116 tom.hargreaves@uea.ac.uk, Univ of East Anglia; Ge
Hari, Kosiyath R., krharigeology@gmail.com, Pt. Ravishankar Shukla Univ; GiiCp
Haritashya, Umesh, 937-229-2939 umesh.haritashya@notes.udayton.edu, Univ of Dayton; ZrGm
Harlaux, Matthieu, (775) 682-8752 mharlaux@unr.edu, Univ of Nevada, Reno; Em
Harley, Grant, 208-885-0950 gharley@uidaho.edu, Univ of Idaho; ZynZn
Harley, Simon L., +44 (0) 131 650 4839 simon.harley@ed.ac.uk, Edinburgh Univ; Gt
Harlim, John, jharlim@psu.edu, Pennsylvania State Univ, Univ Park; Am
Harlow, George E., (212) 769-5378 gharlow@amnh.org, Graduate Sch of the City Univ of New York; Gz
Harmon, Nicholas, +44 (0)23 80594783 n.harmon@noc.soton.ac.uk, Univ of Southampton; Yg
Harms, Tekla A., (413) 542-2711 taharms@amherst.edu, Amherst Coll; Gt
Harnett, Erika M., 206-543-0212 eharnett@uw.edu, Univ of Washington; XyGev
Harnik, Nili, 03-640-6359 harnik@tau.ac.il, Tel Aviv Univ; As
Harnik, Paul, (315) 228-6802 pharnik@colgate.edu, Colgate Univ; PieOb
Haroldson, Erik L., 931-221-7449 haroldsone@apsu.edu, Austin Peay State Univ; EdGzCg
Harper, David, +44 (0) 191 33 47143 david.harper@durham.ac.uk, Durham Univ; Pg
Harper, Joel, (406) 243-2341 joel.harper@umontana.edu, Univ of Montana; GlZc
Harper, Jr., Charles W., (405) 325-7725 charper@gcn.ou.edu, Univ of Oklahoma; Pi
Harpold, Adrian, (775) 784-6759 aharpold@cabnr.unr.edu, Univ of Nevada, Reno; HqsZr
Harpp, Karen, (315) 228-7211 kharpp@colgate.edu, Colgate Univ; GvCgGi
Harr, Patrick A., 831-656-3787 paharr@nps.edu, Naval Postgraduate Sch; Am
Harrap, Rob, 613-533-2553 harrap@queensu.ca, Queen's Univ; Gc
Harrell, Michael, 206-543-0367 mdh666@uw.edu, Univ of Washington; Ze
Harrell, Jr., T. L., 205-247-3559 tlharrell@gsa.sate.al.us, Geological Survey of Alabama; PvGg
Harrington, Charles D., (505) 667-0078 charrington@lanl.gov, Los Alamos; Gm
Harrington, Glenn, glenn.harrington@flinders.edu.au, Flinders Univ; Hw
Harrington, Jerry Y., harring@meteo.psu.edu, Pennsylvania State Univ, Univ Park; Am

Hebda, Richard J., (250) 387-5493 Univ of Victoria; Pl
Hebert, David, (902) 426-1216 david.hebert@dfo-mpo.gc.ca, Dalhousie Univ; Op
Hebert, Rejean J., 418-656-3137 herbert@ggl.ulaval.ca, Universite Laval; Gi
Heck, Frederick R., (231) 591-2588 heckf@ferris.edu, Ferris State Univ; GgZg
Heck, Richard, (519) 824-4120 (Ext. 52450) rheck@uoguelph.ca, Univ of Guelph; Sd
Heckathorn, Scott, 419-530-4328 scott.heckathorn@utoledo.edu, Univ of Toledo; Zn
Heckel, Philip H., (319) 335-1804 philip-heckel@uiowa.edu, Univ of Iowa; GrPsGd
Heckel, Wolfgang, 089/2180 4331 heckl@lmu.de, Ludwig-Maximilians-Univ Muenchen; Gz
Heckert, Andrew B., (828) 262-7609 heckertab@appstate.edu, Appalachian State Univ; PvgZe
Hedberg, Russell, 717-477-1515 rchedberg@ship.edu, Shippensburg Univ; ZiSoZc
Hedquist, Brent, 361-593-3586 brent.hedquist@tamuk.edu, Texas A&M Univ, Kingsville; ZyAtZi
Heenan, Cleo J., (605) 394-2461 cleo.heenan@sdsmt.edu, South Dakota Sch of Mines & Tech; Zn
Heermance, Richard V., (818) 677-4357 richard.heermance@csun.edu, California State Univ, Northridge; GrCc
Heerschap, Lauren, 970-247-7620 heerschap_l@fortlewis.edu, Fort Lewis Coll; GgEgGt
Hegarty, Patricia, +353 21 4902533 p.hegarty@ucc.ie, Univ Coll Cork; Zn
Hegerl, Gabriele C., +44 (0) 131 651 9092 gabi.hegerl@ed.ac.uk, Edinburgh Univ; As
Hegewisch, Katherine, 208-885-6622 khegewisch@uidaho.edu, Univ of Idaho; Zo
Hegg, Dean A., (206) 543-1984 deanhegg@atmos.washington.edu, Univ of Washington; As
Hegna, Thomas A., (309) 298-1366 ta-hegna@wiu.edu, Western Illinois Univ; PigPg
Hegner, Ernst, 089/2180 4274 hegner@lmu.de, Ludwig-Maximilians-Univ Muenchen; Gg
Heibel, Todd, 909-384-8638 theibel@sbccd.cc.ca.us, San Bernardino Valley Coll; Zyi
Heid, Kelly L., 616-331-3783 heidke@gvsu.edu, Grand Valley State Univ; Ze
Heidinger, Andrew, 608-263-6757 heidinger@ssec.wisc.edu, Univ of Wisconsin, Madison; Zr
Heidlauf, Lisa, lisa.heidlauf@wheaton.edu, Wheaton Coll; Gg
Heigold, Paul C., (630) 252-7861 Argonne; Yg
Heiken, Grant, (505) 667-8477 heiken@lanl.gov, Los Alamos; Gv
Heikes, Brian G., (401) 874-6810 zagar@notos.gso.uri.edu, Univ of Rhode Island; As
Heil, Dean, (505) 646-3405 New Mexico State Univ, Las Cruces; Sc
Heim, Noel A., 617-627-2207 noel.heim@tufts.edu, Tufts Univ; PgiPs
Heimann, Adriana, 252 328 5206 heimanna@ecu.edu, East Carolina Univ; GzpGi
Heimann, William H., (785) 625-5663 whheimann@fhsu.edu, Fort Hays State Univ; HgwGm
Heimbach, Patrick, (512) 232-7694 heimbach@utexas.edu, Univ of Texas, Austin; OpGlAs
Heimpel, Moritz, (780) 492-3519 mheimpel@phys.ualberta.ca, Univ of Alberta; Zn
Heimsath, Arjun, 480-965-5585 arjun.heimsath@asu.edu, Arizona State Univ; Gc
Hein, Christopher J., 804-684-7533 hein@vims.edu, William & Mary; Ou
Hein, Kim A., 011 717 6623 kim.ncube0hein@wits.ac.za, Univ of the Witwatersrand; GgEmGc
Heinrich, Paul V., 225-578-4398 heinric@lsu.edu, Louisiana State Univ; GsaGm
Heinz, Dion L., (773) 702-3046 heinz@uchicago.edu, Univ of Chicago; GyzYx
Heinzel, Chad E., (319) 273-6168 chad.heinzel@uni.edu, Univ of Northern Iowa; GmaSa
Heise, Elizabeth, 956 882-6769 elizabeth.heise@utrgv.edu, Univ of Texas, Rio Grande Valley; OnZeGg
Heiss, James, (978) 934-6304 james_heiss@uml.edu, Univ of Massachusetts, Lowell; Hw
Heitman, Mary P., marypat.heitman@dnr.iowa.gov, Iowa Dept of Natural Resources; Zn
Heitmuller, Franklin, 601-266-5423 franklin.heitmuller@usm.edu, Univ of Southern Mississippi; GmsGe
Heitz, Leroy F., lheitz@triton.uog.edu, Univ of Guam; Hg
Heizler, Lynn, 575-835-5166 lynn.heizler@nmt.edu, New Mexico Inst of Mining and Tech; Ca
Heizler, Matthew T., (575) 835-5244 matt@nmt.edu, New Mexico Inst of Mining and Tech; Cc
Helba, Hossam EL-Din A., 002-03-3921595 kahralran2009@yahoo.com, Alexandria Univ; GgZm
Helenes, Javier, jhelenes@cicese.mx, Centro de Investigación Científica y de Educación Superior de Ensenada; Gr
Helgers, Karen, (845) 687-5224 helgersk@sunyulster.edu, SUNY, Ulster County Comm Coll; GeZgy
Helie, Jean-François, 514-987-3000 #2413 helie.jean-francois@uqam.ca, Universite du Quebec a Montreal; Cs
Heliker, Christina C., (808) 967-8807 cheliker@usgs.gov, Univ of Hawai'i, Hilo; Gv
Heller, Matthew J., (434) 951-6351 matt.heller@dmme.virginia.gov, Division of Geology and Mineral Resources; GgRnGe
Hellio, Gabrielle, +44 023 80599258 g.c.hellio@soton.ac.uk, Univ of Southampton; Yg
Helmberger, Donald V., (626) 395-6998 helm@gps.caltech.edu, California Inst of Tech; Ys
Helmick, Sara B., (505) 667-9583 Los Alamos; Zn
Helmke, Martin F., 610-436-3565 mhelmke@wcupa.edu, West Chester Univ; HwSdZg
Helmke, Philip A., (608) 263-4947 pahelmke@wisc.edu, Univ of Wisconsin, Madison; Sc
Helmke, Vicky, (610) 738-0308 vhelmke@wcupa.edu, West Chester Univ; Gg
Helmstaedt, Herwart, (613) 533-6175 Queen's Univ; Gc
Helmuth, Brian, 7815817370 x307 b.helmuth@northeastern.edu, Northeastern Univ; OnZcRc
Helper, Mark A., (512) 471-1009 helper@jsg.utexas.edu, Univ of Texas, Austin; GctXg
Helsdon, John H., (605) 394-2291 john.helsdon@sdsmt.edu, South Dakota Sch of Mines & Tech; As
Hembree, Daniel, (740) 597-1495 hembree@ohio.edu, Ohio Univ; Pi
Hemler, Deb, (304) 367-4393 dhemler@fairmontstate.edu, Fairmont State Univ; Ze
Hemming, N. G., 718-997-3335 Queens Coll (CUNY); CaOcGg
Hemming, Sidney, sidney@ldeo.columbia.edu, Columbia Univ; Cg
Hemphill-Haley, Eileen, emh21@humboldt.edu, Humboldt State Univ; Pm
Hemphill-Haley, Mark, (707) 826-3933 mah54@humboldt.edu, Humboldt State Univ; Gt
Hemsley, A, hemsleyar@cf.ac.uk, Cardiff Univ; Pl
Hemsley, Alan, +44(0)29 208 75367 hemsleyar@cardiff.ac.uk, Univ of Wales; Pl
Hemzacek Laukant, Jean M., 773/442-6056 j-hemzacek@neiu.edu, Northeastern Illinois Univ; Sc
Hence, Deanna A., 217-244-6014 dhence@illinois.edu, Univ of Illinois, Urbana-Champaign; AsmAp
Hencher, Steve, s.r.hencher@leeds.ac.uk, Univ of Leeds; Ng
Hendershott, Myrl C., (858) 534-5705 mhendershott@ucsd.edu, Univ of California, San Diego; Op
Henderson, Charles M., (403) 220-6170 henderson@geo.ucalgary.ca, Univ of Calgary; Pm
Henderson, Donald, (403) 823-7707 Royal Tyrrell Mus of Palaeontology; Pv
Henderson, Gideon, gideon.henderson@earth.ox.ac.uk, Univ of Oxford; Cg
Henderson, Gina R., 410-293-6555 ghenders@usna.edu, United States Naval Academy; As
Henderson, Grant S., (416) 978-6041 henders@geology.utoronto.ca, Univ of Toronto; Gz
Henderson, Matt, (803) 896-7931 hendersonm@dnr.sc.gov, South Carolina Dept of Natural Resources; Zi
Henderson, Miles, (432) 552-2245 henderson_m@utpb.edu, Univ of Texas Permian Basin; GsdGg
Henderson, Naomi, naomi@ldeo.columbia.edu, Columbia Univ; Yr
Henderson, Paul, (508) 289-3466 phenderson@whoi.edu, Woods Hole Oceanographic Inst; Cm
Henderson, Robert, 747814746 bob.henderson@jcu.edu.au, James Cook Univ; GtPiGg
Henderson, Wayne G., (657) 278-3561 whenderson@fullerton.edu, California State Univ, Fullerton; PgGg
Hendrey, George, 718-997-3325 george.hendrey@qc.cuny.edu, Graduate Sch of the City Univ of New York; Gg
Hendricks, Jonathan R., 6072736623 (Ext. 20) jrh42@cornell.edu, Paleontological Research Inst; Pig
Hendrickx, Jan M., (575) 835-5892 hendrick@nmt.edu, New Mexico Inst of Mining and Tech; Hw
Hendrikx, Jordy, (406) 994-6918 jordy.hendrikx@montana.edu, Montana State Univ; ZnHsAs
Hendrix, Marc S., 406-243-5867 marc.hendrix@umontana.edu, Univ of

Montana; Gs
Hendrix, Thomas E., 616-331-3728 Grand Valley State Univ; Gc
Hendry, Jim, (306) 966-5720 jim.hendry@usask.ca, Univ of Saskatchewan; HwClHy
Hendy, Ingrid, 734615-6892 ihendy@umich.edu, Univ of Michigan; Pg
Henika, William S., (540) 231-4298 bhenika@vt.edu, Virginia Polytechnic Inst & State Univ; Ng
Henkel, Torsten, +44 0161 275-3810 torsten.henkel@manchester.ac.uk, Univ of Manchester; Cs
Henkes, Gregory, 631-632-2905 gregory.henkes@stonybrook.edu, Stony Brook Univ; Cs
Henley, Sian F., +44 (0) 131 650 7010 s.f.henley@ed.ac.uk, Edinburgh Univ; CmOcCs
Hennemeyer, Marc, 089/2180 4340 marc@hennemeyer.de, Ludwig-Maximilians-Univ Muenchen; Gz
Hennige, Sebastian, s.hennige@ed.ac.uk, Edinburgh Univ; Zc
Henning, Stanley J., (515) 294-7846 sjhennin@iastate.edu, Iowa State Univ of Sci & Tech; So
Hennings, Peter H., (307) 766-3386 Univ of Wyoming; Gc
Hennon, Chris, (828) 232-5159 chennon@unca.edu, Univ of North Carolina, Asheville; AstZn
Henrici, Amy C., (412) 622-3265 henricia@carnegiemnh.org, Carnegie Mus of Natural History; Pv
Henry, Christopher D., (775) 682-8753) chenry@unr.edu, Univ of Nevada, Reno; GtvCc
Henry, Darrell J., (225) 388-2693 dhenry@geol.lsu.edu, Louisiana State Univ; Gp
Henry, Eric J., 910-962-7622 henrye@uncw.edu, Univ of North Carolina, Wilmington; Hw
Henry, Kathleen M., (217) 244-8994 kmhenry@illinois.edu, Illinois State Geological Survey; Gg
Henry, Lea-Anne, l.henry@ed.ac.uk, Edinburgh Univ; Zn
Henry, Tiernan, +353 (0)91 495 096 tiernan.henry@nuigalway.ie, Nat Univ of Ireland Galway; HwyEg
Henshel, Diane S., (812) 855-4556 dhenshel@indiana.edu, Indiana Univ, Bloomington; Zn
Henson, Harvey, 618-536-6666 henson@geo.siu.edu, Southern Illinois Univ Carbondale; Yg
Henstock, Tim, +44 (0)23 80596491 then@noc.soton.ac.uk, Univ of Southampton; YgrYe
Hentz, Tucker F., (512) 471-7281 tucker.hentz@beg.utexas.edu, Univ of Texas at Austin, Jackson Sch of Geosciences; GrsGo
Henyey, Thomas L., (213) 740-5832 henyey@usc.edu, Univ of Southern California; Yg
Henßel, Katja, 089/2180 6624 k.henssel@lrz.uni-muenchen.de, Ludwig-Maximilians-Univ Muenchen; Pg
Heo, Joon, heo_j@utpb.edu, Univ of Texas Permian Basin; Hg
Hepburn, J. Christopher, 617-552-3642 john.hepburn@bc.edu, Boston Coll; Gg
Hepner, George F., (801) 581-6021 george.hepner@geog.utah.edu, Univ of Utah; Zy
Hepner, Tiffany, (512) 475-9572 tiffany.hepner@beg.utexas.edu, Univ of Texas at Austin, Jackson Sch of Geosciences; Og
Hepple, Alex, 3138 5051 a.hepple@qut.edu.au, Queensland Univ of Tech; ZerGg
Herbers, Thomas H., (831) 656-2917 herbers@nps.edu, Naval Postgraduate Sch; Op
Herbert, Bruce, (979) 845-2405 herbert@geo.tamu.edu, Texas A&M Univ; Ge
Herbert, Gregory, gherbert@usf.edu, Univ of South Florida; Pe
Herbert, Jennifer, (630) 252-0493 Argonne; Gg
Herbert, Timothy D., (401) 863-1207 timothy_herbert@brown.edu, Brown Univ; Pe
Herd, Christopher D., (780) 492-5798 herd@ualberta.ca, Univ of Alberta; XcGiCp
Herd, Richard, +44 (0)1603 59 3667 r.herd@uea.ac.uk, Univ of East Anglia; Gv
Herdendorf, Charles E., 440-934-1514 herdendorf.1@osu.edu, Ohio State Univ; OgGuOn
Herkenhoff, Ken E., (818) 354-3539 ken.e.herkenhoff@jpl.nasa.gov, Jet Propulsion Lab; Xg
Herman, Ellen K., (570) 577-3088 ekh008@bucknell.edu, Bucknell Univ; Hw
Herman, Janet S., (434) 924-0553 jsh5w@virginia.edu, Univ of Virginia; ClHw
Herman, Mathew, mherman2@csub.edu, California State Univ, Bakersfield; GtYsRn
Herman, Rhett B., 540 831-5441 rherman@radford.edu, Radford Univ; YuXaGa
Hermance, John F., (508) 252-3116 john_hermance@brown.edu, Brown Univ; HqZrHw
Hermann, Albert, 206-526-6495 albert.j.hermann@noaa.gov, Univ of Washington; Opb
Hermans, Thomas, thomas.hermans@ugent.be, Ghent Univ; HwYeu
Hermes, O D., dhermes@uri.edu, Univ of Rhode Island; Gi
Hernandez, Larry, (760) 757-2121, x6329 lhernandez@miracosta.edu, MiraCosta Coll; Gg
Hernández, Manuel, hdezfdez@ucm.es, Univ Complutense de Madrid; Pv
Hernandez, Michael W., (801) 626-8186 mhernandez@weber.edu, Weber State Univ; Zir
Hernandez, Rebecca, 530-752-5471 rrhernandez@ucdavis.edu, Univ of California, Davis; Zcn
Hernandez Molina, F. J., javier.hernandez-molina@rhul.ac.uk, Royal Holloway Univ of London; GsuOu
Herndon, Elizabeth M., 865-974-2366 eherndo4@utk.edu, Univ of Tennessee, Knoxville; Cg
Hernes, Peter J., 530-754-4327 pjhernes@ucdavis.edu, Univ of California, Davis; CoHg
Heron, Duncan, (919) 684-5321 duncan.heron@duke.edu, Duke Univ; Grg
Herrero, Concepción, cherrero@ucm.es, Univ Complutense de Madrid; Pm
Herrero, María Josefa, mjherrero@ucm.es, Univ Complutense de Madrid; Gs
Herring, Thomas A., (617) 253-5941 tah@mit.edu, Massachusetts Inst of Tech; Yd
Herring Mayo, Lisa L., 931-393-2136 lmayo@mscc.edu, Motlow State Comm Coll; GgZge
Herriott, Trystan, (907) 451-5011 trystan.herriott@alaska.gov, Alaska Division of Geological & Geophysical Surveys; Eo
Herrmann, Achim, 225-578-3016 aherrmann@lsu.edu, Louisiana State Univ; PeGd
Herrmann, Edward W., (812) 856-0587 edherrma@indiana.edu, Indiana Univ, Bloomington; Sa
Herrmann, Felix J., +1 (404) 385-7069 felix.herrmann@gatech.edu, Georgia Inst of Tech; YesZn
Herrmann, Robert B., (314) 977-3120 robert.herrmann@slu.edu, Saint Louis Univ; Ys
Hershey, Ronald L., (775) 673-7393 ron.hershey@dri.edu, Univ of Nevada, Reno; HwCls
Hervig, Richard, (480) 965-8427 hervig@asu.edu, Arizona State Univ; Cg
Herzberg, Claude T., (848) 445-3154 herzberg@eps.rutgers.edu, Rutgers, The State Univ of New Jersey; CpGi
Herzig, Chuck, (310) 660-3593 cherzig@elcamino.edu, El Camino Coll; GgOg
Hesp, Patrick, patrick.hesp@flinders.edu.au, Flinders Univ; GmZy
Hess, Darrel E., (415) 239-3104 dhess@ccsf.edu, City Coll of San Francisco; Zy
Hess, Kai-Uwe, 089/2180 4275 hess@min.uni-muenchen.de, Ludwig-Maximilians-Univ Muenchen; Gz
Hess, Paul C., (401) 863-1929 paul_hess@brown.edu, Brown Univ; Gi
Hess, Peter G., 607-255-2495 peter.hess@cornell.edu, Cornell Univ; Acs
Hess-Tanguay, Lillian, (516) 299-2318 lhess@liu.edu, Long Island Univ, C.W. Post Campus; Gs
Hesse, Marc A., (512) 471-0768 mhesse@jsg.utexas.edu, Univ of Texas, Austin; GqoYg
Hesse, Reinhard, 514-398-3627 reinhard.hesse@mcgill.ca, McGill Univ; Gs
Hester, Erich, (540) 231-9758 ehester@vt.edu, Virginia Polytechnic Inst & State Univ; Hsw
Hesterberg, Dean L., (919) 515-2636 North Carolina State Univ; Sc
Hetherington, Callum J., (806) 834-3110 callum.hetherington@ttu.edu, Texas Tech Univ; GxzCg
Hetherington, Eric D., (209) 730-3812 Coll of the Sequoias; Gc
Hetherington, Jean, (925) 685-1230 (Ext. 462) jhetheri@dvc.edu, Diablo Valley Coll; Gg
Hetland, Robert D., (979) 458-0096 rhetland@ocean.tamu.edu, Texas A&M Univ; Op
Hettiarachchi, Ganga, (785) 532-7209 ganga@ksu.edu, Kansas State Univ; Sc
Hetzel, Ralf, +49-251-83-33908 rahetzel@uni-muenster.de, Univ Muenster; Gcm
Heubeck, Christoph, 0049(0)3641/948620 christoph.heubeck@uni-jena.de, Friedrich-Schiller-Univ Jena; GsdPg
Heuss-Aßbichler, Soraya, 089/21804252 soraya@min.uni-muenchen.de, Ludwig-Maximilians-Univ Muenchen; Gz
Hewitt, David A., (540) 231-6521 dhewitt@vt.edu, Virginia Polytechnic Inst & State Univ; Cp
Heymann, Dieter, (713) 348-4890 dieter@owlnet.rice.edu, Rice Univ; Xm
Heyniger, William C., (908) 737-3660 wheynige@kean.edu, Kean Univ; Am
Heyvaert, Alan, 775.673.7322 alan.heyvaert@dri.edu, Univ of Nevada, Reno; GnHs
Heywood, Karen, +44 (0)1603 59 2555 k.heywood@uea.ac.uk, Univ of East Anglia; Op

Heywood, Neil C., (715) 346-4452 nheywood@uwsp.edu, Univ of Wisconsin, Stevens Point; Zy
Hiatt, Eric E., (920) 424-7001 hiatt@uwosh.edu, Univ of Wisconsin, Oshkosh; GsOcGu
Hibbard, James P., (919) 515-7242 jphibbar@ncsu.edu, North Carolina State Univ; GctZn
Hibbs, Barry, (323) 343-2414 bhibbs@calstatela.edu, California State Univ, Los Angeles; Hw
Hick, Steven R., 303-871-2535 shick@du.edu, Univ of Denver; Zi
Hickcox, Charles W., (404) 727-0118 geocwh@emory.edu, Emory Univ; Gg
Hicke, Jeffrey, 208-885-6240 jhicke@uidaho.edu, Univ of Idaho; ZcyZn
Hickey, Barbara M., (206) 543-4737 bhickey@u.washington.edu, Univ of Washington; Op
Hickey, James, (660) 562-1817 jhickey@nwmissouri.edu, Northwest Missouri State Univ; Ge
Hickey, Kenneth A., (778) 384-7074 khickey@eos.ubc.ca, Univ of British Columbia; EgGcg
Hickey, William J., (608) 262-9018 wjhickey@wisc.edu, Univ of Wisconsin, Madison; Sb
Hickey-Vargas, Rosemary, (305) 348-3471 hickey@fiu.edu, Florida International Univ; Cg
Hickman, Anna, +44 (0)23 80592132 a.hickman@noc.soton.ac.uk, Univ of Southampton; Og
Hickman, Carole S., (510) 642-3429 Univ of California, Berkeley; Pg
Hickmon, Nicki, 630-252-7662 nhickmon@anl.gov, Argonne; As
Hickmott, Donald D., (505) 667-8753 dhickmott@lanl.gov, Los Alamos; Gp
Hicks, Andrea, hicks5@wisc.edu, Univ of Wisconsin, Madison; Zn
Hicks, David, 956 882 5055 david.hicks@utrgv.edu, Univ of Texas, Rio Grande Valley; Ob
Hickson, Catherine J., (604) 761-5573 ttgeo@telus.net, Univ of British Columbia; EgGvZe
Hickson, Thomas A., (651) 962-5241 tahickson@stthomas.edu, Univ of Saint Thomas; GsmGe
Hicock, Stephen R., shicock@uwo.ca, Western Univ; Gl
Hidalgo, Paulo J., (404) 413-5789 phidalgo@gsu.edu, Georgia State Univ; GivGz
Higgins, Charles G., paulah88@hotmail.com , Univ of California, Davis; Gm
Higgins, Chris T., (916) 322-9997 California Geological Survey; Gg
Higgins, Jerry D., (303) 273-3817 jhiggins@mines.edu, Colorado Sch of Mines; NxgNt
Higgins, John A., 609-258-2756 jahiggin@princeton.edu, Princeton Univ; ClPcCs
Higgins, Michael D., 4185455011 x 5052 mhiggins@uqac.ca, Universite du Quebec a Chicoutimi; Gi
Higgins, Sean M., sean@ldeo.columbia.edu, Columbia Univ; Gs
Higgs, Bettie M., +353 860476789 b.higgs@ucc.ie, Univ Coll Cork; YgGqRh
Higgs, Ken, +353 21 4902290 k.higgs@ucc.ie, Univ Coll Cork; Pl
Higinbotham, Pamela, 724-938-4180 higinbotham@calu.edu, California Univ of Pennsylvania; Zn
Hilbert-Wolf, Hannah L., hannah.hilbertwolf@my.jcu.edu.au, James Cook Univ; GsCc
Hildebrand, Alan R., 403-220-2291 ahildebr@ucalgary.ca, Univ of Calgary; XmgXc
Hildebrand, John A., (858) 534-4069 jhildebrand@ucsd.edu, Univ of California, San Diego; Yr
Hildebrand, Stephen G., hildebrandsg@ornl.gov, Oak Ridge; Zn
Hildebrand, Steve T., (505) 667-4318 hildebrand@lanl.gov, Los Alamos; Ys
Hildebrandt, Anke, 349-3641-948651 hildebrandt.a@uni-jena.de, Friedrich-Schiller-Univ Jena; HgSpf
Hileman, Mary E., (405) 744-4341 mary.hileman@okstate.edu, Oklahoma State Univ; GorGd
Hill, Arleen A., 901-678-2589 aahill@memphis.edu, Univ of Memphis; Rn
Hill, Catherine R., 928344-7719 catherine.hill@azwestern.edu, Arizona Western Coll; GgOgHw
Hill, Chris, chris.hill@gcccd.edu, Grossmont Coll; GgOg
Hill, Christopher, 617-253-6430 cnh@mit.edu, Massachusetts Inst of Tech; Zn
Hill, Julie, (775) 784-6987 juliehill@unr.edu, Univ of Nevada, Reno; Zn
Hill, Malcolm D., (617) 373-4377 m.hill@neu.edu, Northeastern Univ; ZiGze
Hill, Mary C., 785-864-2728 mchill@ku.edu, Univ of Kansas; HgqHw
Hill, Mary Louise, (807) 343-8319 mary.louise.hill@lakeheadu.ca, Lakehead Univ; Gc
Hill, Mimi, +44 0151 794 3462 m.hill@liverpool.ac.uk, Univ of Liverpool; Ym
Hill, Nicole, nhill@bentley.edu, Bentley Univ; Ge
Hill, Paul S., (902) 494-2266 paul.hill@dal.ca, Dalhousie Univ; Gs
Hill, Philip R., philip.hill@canada.ca, Univ of Victoria; Gsu
Hill, Tessa M., (530) 752-0179 tmhill@ucdavis.edu, Univ of California, Davis; Pe
Hill, Timothy, +44 01334 464013 tch2@st-andrews.ac.uk, Univ of St. Andrews; Ge
Hillaire-Marcel, Claude, 514-987-3000 #3376 hillaire-marcel.claude@uqam.ca, Universite du Quebec a Montreal; Cs
Hillier, John, jhillier@ghc.edu, Grays Harbor Coll; ZgCa
Hilliker, Joby, (610) 436-2213 jhilliker@wcupa.edu, West Chester Univ; Am
Hillman, Aubrey, (337) 482-5162 aubrey.hillman@louisiana.edu, Univ of Louisiana at Lafayette; GneGa
Hills, Denise J., (205) 247-3694 dhills@gsa.state.al.us, Geological Survey of Alabama; EoZfYe
Hilterman, Fred, 713-850-7600 x3318 fhilterman@uh.edu, Univ of Houston; Ye
Hilts, Stewart G., (519) 824-4120 (Ext. 52448) shilts@uoguelph.ca, Univ of Guelph; Zn
Hindle, Tobin, 561 297-2846 thindle@fau.edu, Florida Atlantic Univ; ZyiZc
Hindman, Edward E., (212) 650-6469 City Coll (CUNY); As
Hindshaw, Ruth, +44 01334 463936 rh71@st-andrews.ac.uk, Univ of St. Andrews; Cs
Hine, Albert C., (727) 553-1161 hine@usf.edu, Univ of South Florida; Gus
Hines, Mary E., (910) 962-3012 hinese@uncw.edu, Univ of North Carolina, Wilmington; Zu
Hines, Paul, phines50@gmail.com, Dalhousie Univ; Op
Hingston, Egerton, (031) 260-2805 hingstone@ukzn.ac.za, Univ of KwaZulu-Natal; NtxNg
Hinkle, Margaret A., (540) 458-8271 hinklem@wlu.edu, Washington & Lee Univ; Cqb
Hinman, Nancy W., (406) 243-5277 nancy.hinman@umontana.edu, Univ of Montana; Cgl
Hinnov, Linda, 703-993-3082 lhinnov@gmu.edu, George Mason Univ; GrYg
Hinojosa, Alejandro, alhinc@cicese.mx, Centro de Investigación Científica y de Educación Superior de Ensenada; Zr
Hinthorne, James R., james.hinthorne@utrgv.edu, Univ of Texas, Rio Grande Valley; GgzCa
Hinton, Richard, +44 (0) 131 650 8548 richard.hinton@ed.ac.uk, Edinburgh Univ; Cg
Hintz, John G., (570)389-4140 jhintz@bloomu.edu, Bloomsburg Univ; Zin
Hintz, Rashauna, 479-575-3355 rmicken@uark.edu, Univ of Arkansas, Fayetteville; Zu
Hintz, William, (419) 530-5079 william.hintz@utoledo.edu, Univ of Toledo; Zn
Hintze, Lehi F., 801 422-6361 lehi.hintze@gmail.com, Brigham Young Univ; Pg
Hinz, Nicholas, (775)784-1446 nhinz@unr.edu, Univ of Nevada, Reno; Gg
Hinz, Nick, 775-784-1446 nhinz@unr.edu, Univ of Nevada, Reno; Gcg
Hinze, William J., wjh730@comcast.net, Purdue Univ; YevGt
Hippensteel, Scott P., 704-687-5992 shippens@email.uncc.edu, Univ of North Carolina, Charlotte; Gr
Hiroji, Anand D., (228) 688-1510 anand.hiroji@usm.edu, Univ of Southern Mississippi; Yd
Hirons, Steve, +44 020 3073 8028 s.hirons@ucl.ac.uk, Birkbeck Coll; Cl
Hirsch, Eric, eric.hirsch@fandm.edu, Franklin and Marshall Coll; Zn
Hirschboeck, Katherine K., (520) 621-6466 katie@ltrr.arizona.edu, Univ of Arizona; AtHsRn
Hirschmann, Marc M., 612-625-6698 hirsc022@umn.edu, Univ of Minnesota, Twin Cities; Gi
Hirt, William H., (530) 938-5255 hirt@siskiyous.edu, Coll of the Siskiyous; Gi
Hirth, Greg, (401) 863-7063 greg_hirth@brown.edu, Brown Univ; GcyYg
Hirth, Gregory, 508-289-2776 greg_hirth@brown.edu, Woods Hole Oceanographic Inst; Gc
Hiscock, Kevin, +44 (0)1603 59 3104 k.hiscock@uea.ac.uk, Univ of East Anglia; Hwg
Hiscott, Richard N., (709) 737-8394 rhiscott@mun.ca, Memorial Univ of Newfoundland; Gs
Hiser, Susan, 740-376-4775 sch030@marietta.edu, Marietta Coll; Zn
Hiskey, J. Brent, (520) 621-6185 jbh@engr.arizona.edu, Univ of Arizona; Nx
Hitchman, Matthew H., (608)262-4653 matt@aos.wisc.edu, Univ of Wisconsin, Madison; As
Hites, Ronald A., (812) 855-0193 hitesr@indiana.edu, Indiana Univ, Bloomington; Co
Hitz, Ralph B., (253) 566-5299 rhitz@tacomacc.edu, Tacoma Comm Coll; PvSaZi
Hixon, Amy E., (574) 631-1872 ahixon@nd.edu, Univ of Notre Dame; ClqCc
Hjelmfelt, Mark R., (605) 394-2291 mark.hjelmfelt@sdsmt.edu, South Dakota Sch of Mines & Tech; As

Hladik, Christine, (912) 478-0338 chladik@georgiasouthern.edu, Georgia Southern Univ; SbZr
Hluchy, Michele M., (607) 871-2838 Alfred Univ; Cl
Hlusko, Leslea, (510) 643-8838 hlusko@berkeley.edu, Univ of California, Berkeley; PgZnn
Ho, Anita, (406) 756-3873 aho@fvcc.edu, Flathead Valley Comm Coll; Gg
Ho, David, (808) 956-3311 ho@hawaii.edu, Univ of Hawai'i, Manoa; OcCb
Ho, I-Hsuan, (701) 777-6156 ihsuan.ho@engr.und.edu, Univ of North Dakota; Ng
Hobbs, Benjamin F., (410) 516-4681 bhobbs@jhu.edu, Johns Hopkins Univ; Zn
Hobbs, Chasidy, (850) 474-2735 chobbs@uwf.edu, Univ of West Florida; ZgeZy
Hobbs, John D., dhobbs@mtech.edu, Montana Tech of the Univ of Montana; Zn
Hobbs, Kevin, 575-835-6213 kevin.hobbs@nmt.edu, New Mexico Inst of Mining and Tech; GsrSd
Hobbs, Richard, +44 (0) 191 33 44295 r.w.hobbs@durham.ac.uk, Durham Univ; Ys
Hobbs, Thomas M., 281-618-5796 tom.hobbs@nhmccd.edu, Lonestar Coll - North Harris; Gg
Hochella, Jr., Michael F., (540) 231-6227 hochella@vt.edu, Virginia Polytechnic Inst & State Univ; ClGze
Hochmuth, George J., 352-392-1803 318 hoch@ufl.edu, Univ of Florida; So
Hochstaedter, Alfred, (831) 646-4149 ahochstaedter@mpc.edu, Monterey Peninsula Coll; GgOgZg
Hock, Regine M., 907-474-7691 regine.hock@gi.alaska.edu, Univ of Alaska, Fairbanks; Gl
Hockaday, William C., (254)7102639 william_hockaday@baylor.edu, Baylor Univ; CoaSb
Hockey, Thomas A., (319) 273-2065 thomas.hockey@uni.edu, Univ of Northern Iowa; Zn
Hodder, Donald R., (914) 257-3757 SUNY, New Paltz; Gg
Hodell, David, +44 (0) 1223 330270 dhod07@esc.cam.ac.uk, Univ of Cambridge; Ge
Hodges, Floyd N., (509) 376-4627 floyd.hodges@pnl.gov, Pacific Northwest; Cg
Hodges, Kip V., 480-965-5331 kvhodges@asu.edu, Arizona State Univ; CcGtXg
Hodgetts, David, david.hodgetts@manchester.ac.uk, Univ of Manchester; Gsc
Hodgkiss, Jr., William S., (858) 534-1798 whodgkiss@ucsd.edu, Univ of California, San Diego; No
Hodych, Joseph P., (709) 864-7567 jhodych@mun.ca, Memorial Univ of Newfoundland; Ym
Hoe, Teh Guan, 03-79674231 tehgh@um.edu.my, Univ of Malaya; Ca
Hoenisch, Baerbel, (845) 365-8828 hoenisch@ldeo.columbia.edu, Columbia Univ; PcClm
Hoey, Trevor, +4401413307736 trevor.hoey@glasgow.ac.uk, Univ of Glasgow; Gs
Hoff, Jean L., (320) 308-5914 jhoff@stcloudstate.edu, Saint Cloud State Univ; HwZeGg
Hoffman, Eric G., 603-535-2321 ehoffman@plymouth.edu, Plymouth State Univ; Am
Hoffman, Gretchen K., 575-835-6105 gretchen.hoffman@nmt.edu, New Mexico Inst of Mining and Tech; Ec
Hoffman, Jeffrey L., (609) 292-1185 jeffrey.l.hoffman@dep.nj.gov, New Jersey Geological and Water Survey; HqwRw
Hoffman, Paul F., (617) 496-6380 paulfhoffman@gmail.com, Harvard Univ; Gc
Hofmann, Eileen E., (757) 683-5334 ehofmann@odu.edu, Old Dominion Univ; Op
Hofmann, Michael, (406) 243-5855 michael.hofmann@umontana.edu, Univ of Montana; GosGr
Hofmeister, Anne M., (314) 935-7440 hofmeist@levee.wustl.edu, Washington Univ in St. Louis; YghXa
Hogan, John, 573-341-4618 jhogan@mst.edu, Missouri Univ of Sci and Tech; Gc
Hohn, Michael E., 304 594-2331 hohn@geosrv.wvnet.edu, West Virginia Geological & Economic Survey; Eg
Hoisch, Thomas D., (928) 523-1904 thomas.hoisch@nau.edu, Northern Arizona Univ; Gp
Hojjatie, Barry, (229) 333-5753 bhojjati@valdosta.edu, Valdosta State Univ; Zm
Hok, Jozef, jozef.hok@uniba.sk, Comenius Univ in Bratislava; Ggt
Hoke, Gregory, (315) 443-1903 gdhoke@syr.edu, Syracuse Univ; ZgGmt
Holail, Hanafy M., 002-03-3921595 hanafyholail@hotmail.com, Alexandria Univ; Ggs
Holberg, Jay B., (520) 621-4571 holberg@vega.lpl.arizona.edu, Univ of Arizona; As
Holbrook, Amanda, (606) 783-2381 a.holbrook@moreheadstate.edu, Morehead State Univ; Zn
Holbrook, John M., 817-257-6275 john.holbrook@tcu.edu, Texas Christian Univ; Gsr
Holbrook, W. S., 540-231-6521 wstevenh@vt.edu, Virginia Polytechnic Inst & State Univ; Yur
Holcomb, Robin T., (206) 543-5274 rholcomb@ocean.washington.edu, Univ of Washington; Ou
Holcombe, Troy L., 979 845-3528 or 979 690-7398 tholcombe@ocean.tamu.edu, Texas A&M Univ; OuGcg
Holdaway, Michael J., (214) 692-2750 Southern Methodist Univ; Gp
Holdren, George R., (509) 376-2242 rich.holdren@pnl.gov, Pacific Northwest; Cl
Holdren, John P., 617-495-1498 john_holdren@hks.harvard.edu, Harvard Univ; Zn
Holdsworth, Robert E., 0191 3742529 r.e.holdsworth@durham.ac.uk, Durham Univ; Gc
Hole, John A., (540) 231-3858 hole@vt.edu, Virginia Polytechnic Inst & State Univ; Ye
Holford, Simon, simon.holford@adelaide.edu.au, Univ of Adelaide; Go
Holgood, Jay S., (614) 292-3999 hobgood.1@osu.edu, Ohio State Univ; As
Holk, Gregory J., 562-985-5006 gholk@csulb.edu, California State Univ, Long Beach; CsGxEm
Holl, Karen D., (831) 459-3668 kholl@cats.ucsc.edu, Univ of California, Santa Cruz; Zu
Hollabaugh, Curtis L., (678) 839-4050 chollaba@westga.edu, Univ of West Georgia; GzCg
Holland, Austin A., 405-325-8497 austin.holland@ou.edu, Univ of Oklahoma; YsZnn
Holland, Edward C., 479-575-6635 echollan@uark.edu, Univ of Arkansas, Fayetteville; Zy
Holland, Nicholas D., (858) 534-2085 nholland@ucsd.edu, Univ of California, San Diego; Ob
Holland, Steven M., (706) 542-0424 stratum@gly.uga.edu, Univ of Georgia; Gr
Holland, Tim, +44 (0) 1223 333466 tjbh@esc.cam.ac.uk, Univ of Cambridge; GptGz
Hollander, David J., (727) 553-1019 davidh@usf.edu, Univ of South Florida; Oc
Hollenbaugh, Kenneth M., (208) 426-3700 khollenb@boisestate.edu, Boise State Univ; Eg
Holley, Elizabeth, 303-273-3409 eholley@mines.edu, Colorado Sch of Mines; Eg
Holliday, Joseph W., 3106603593 xt. 3371 jholliday@elcamino.edu, El Camino Coll; Og
Holliday, Vance, vthollid@email.arizona.edu, Univ of Arizona; Ga
Holliman, Richard, +44(0) 1908 654 646 x 54646 richard.holliman@open.ac.uk, Open Univ; Ze
Hollings, Peter N., (807) 343-8329 peter.hollings@lakeheadu.ca, Lakehead Univ; Eg
Hollis, Cathy, +44 0161 306-6583 cathy.hollis@manchester.ac.uk, Univ of Manchester; Gs
Hollister, Lincoln S., 609-258-4106 linc@princeton.edu, Princeton Univ; GptGz
Hollocher, Kurt T., (518) 388-6518 hollochk@union.edu, Union Coll; GxCga
Holloway, Tess, thollow2@ashland.edu, Ashland Univ; Rn
Holloway, Tracey, (608) 262-5356 taholloway@wisc.edu, Univ of Wisconsin, Madison; AscZn
Holm, Daniel K., (330) 672-4094 dholm@kent.edu, Kent State Univ; Gc
Holm, Richard F., richard.holm@nau.edu, Northern Arizona Univ; Gv
Holman, John, (620) 276-8286 jholman@ksu.edu, Kansas State Univ; So
Holmden, Chris, (306) 966-5697 chris.holmden@usask.ca, Univ of Saskatchewan; Csc
Holme, Richard, +44 0151 794 5254 r.t.holme@liverpool.ac.uk, Univ of Liverpool; Ym
Holmes, George, +44(0) 113 34 31163 g.holmes@leeds.ac.uk, Univ of Leeds; Ge
Holmes, Mark L., 425 487-2639 mholmes@uw.edu, Univ of Washington; OuGl
Holmes, Mary Anne, 402-588-2492 mholmes2@unl.edu, Univ of Nebraska, Lincoln; GsOuZn
Holmes, Stevie L., 605-677-6147 stevie.holmes@usd.edu, South Dakota Dept of Environment and Natural Resources; Gg
Holness, Marian, +44 (0) 1223 333434 marian@esc.cam.ac.uk, Univ of Cambridge; Gi
Holroyd, Pat, (510) 642-3733 pholroyd@berkeley.edu, Univ of California, Berkeley; Pv
Holschuh, Nicholas D., nholschuh, Amherst Coll; GlYg

Holst, Timothy, tholst@d.umn.edu, Univ of Minnesota Duluth; GcYnGt
Holstein, Thomas J., (401) 254-3097 Roger Williams Univ; Zn
Holt, Ben D., (630) 252-4347 Argonne; Ca
Holt, Caecilia, 610 683-4445 holt@kutztown.edu, Kutztown Univ of Pennsylvania; Zn
Holt, David, 228-214-3255 david.h.holt@usm.edu, Univ of Southern Mississippi; Zyi
Holt, Gloria J., (361) 749-6716 joanholt@utexas.edu, Univ of Texas, Austin; Ob
Holt, John W., 512-471-0487 jack@ig.utexas.edu, Univ of Texas, Austin; Ye
Holt, Robert M., (662) 915-6687 rmholt@olemiss.edu, Univ of Mississippi; Hq
Holt, William E., 631-632-8215 william.holt@sunysb.edu, Stony Brook Univ; Ys
Holtz, Jr., Thomas R., (301) 405-4084 tholtz@umd.edu, Univ of Maryland; PvgPg
Holtzman, Benjamin, benh@ldeo.columbia.edu, Columbia Univ; Ys
Holubnyak, Yehven I., (785) 864-2070 eugene@kgs.ku.edu, Univ of Kansas; Np
Holwell, Dave, +440116 252 3804 dah29@le.ac.uk, Leicester Univ; Ge
Holyoke, Caleb, (330) 972-7635 cholyoke@uakron.edu, Univ of Akron; GcNrYx
Holzer, Mark, (604) 822-0531 mholzer@langara.bc.ca, Univ of British Columbia; As
Holzworth, Robert H., (206) 685-7410 bobholz@uw.edu, Univ of Washington; XyAsZg
Homan, Amy L., (814) 865-2622 aqs3@psu.edu, Pennsylvania State Univ, Univ Park; Zn
Homayouni, Saied, 418 654-2687 saeid.homayouni@ete.inrs.ca, Universite du Quebec; Zrf
Hommel, Demian, 541-737-5070 hommeld@geo.oregonstate.edu, Oregon State Univ; Zn
Homuth, Emil F., (702) 794-7351 fred_homuth@notes.ymp.gov, Los Alamos; Ye
Hon, Ken, (808) 974-7302 kenhon@hawaii.edu, Univ of Hawai'i, Hilo; Gvi
Hon, Rudolph, (617) 552-3656 hon@bc.edu, Boston Coll; Cq
Hong, Gi-Hoon, (313) 577-2506 gihoonh@gmail.com, Wayne State Univ; OcCcm
Hong, Jessie, (678) 839-5466 jhong@westga.edu, Univ of West Georgia; ZieZy
Hong, Sung-ho, 270-809-6319 shong4@murraystate.edu, Murray State Univ; HyGe
Honjas, Bill, (775) 784-6613 bhonjas@optimsoftware.com , Univ of Nevada, Reno; Ys
Honjo, Susumu, (508) 289-2589 shonjo@whoi.edu, Woods Hole Oceanographic Inst; Ou
Honkaer, Rick, 859-257-1108 rick.honaker@uky.edu, Univ of Kentucky; Nm
Hood, Lonnie L., (520) 621-6936 lon@lpl.arizona.edu, Univ of Arizona; XyAs
Hood, Raleigh, (305) 361-4668 rhood@umces.edu, Univ of Maryland; Ob
Hood, Teresa A., 305-284-8647 t.hood@miami.edu, Univ of Miami; Gg
Hood, William C., (970) 241-8020 Colorado Mesa Univ; Gg
Hooda, Peter, +44 020 8417 2155 p.hooda@kingston.ac.uk, Kingston Univ; Em
Hooft, Emilie E., (541) 346-4762 emilie@uoregon.edu, Univ of Oregon; Yr
Hook, James E., (912) 386-3182 Univ of Georgia; Sp
Hook, Paul B., paul@intermountainaquatics.com, Montana State Univ; Sf
Hook, Simon J., (818) 354-0974 simon@lithos.jpl.nasa.gov, Jet Propulsion Lab; Zr
Hooke, Roger L., (207) 581-2203 rhooke@acadia.net, Univ of Maine; Gm
Hooks, Benjamin P., (731) 881-7430 bhooks@utm.edu, Univ of Tennessee, Martin; GciNr
Hooks, Chris H., (205) 247-3721 chooks@gsa.state.al.us, Geological Survey of Alabama; EoGxo
Hooks, W. Gary, (205) 348-1877 Univ of Alabama; Gm
Hooper, Andy, +44(0) 113 34 37723 a.hooper@leeds.ac.uk, Univ of Leeds; Ydg
Hooper, Robert L., (715) 836-4932 hooperrl@uwec.edu, Univ of Wisconsin, Eau Claire; Gz
Hoover, Karin A., 530-898-6269 khoover@csuchico.edu, California State Univ, Chico; Hw
Hoover, Michael T., (919) 515-7305 North Carolina State Univ; Sd
Hooyer, Thomas S., 608-263-4175 hooyer@uwm.edu, Univ of Wisconsin, Madison; Hg
Hopkins, David G., (701) 231-8948 North Dakota State Univ; Sd
Hopkins, Kenneth D., (970) 351-2853 kenneth.hopkins@unco.edu, Univ of Northern Colorado; Gml
Hopkins, Samantha, 541-346-5976 shopkins@uoregon.edu, Univ of Oregon; Pg
Hopkins, Thomas S., (205) 348-1791 Dauphin Island Sea Lab; Ob
Hopley, Philip, +44 020 3073 8029 p.hopley@ucl.ac.uk, Birkbeck Coll; Pe
Hopmans, Jan W., (916) 752-3060 Univ of California, Davis; So
Hoppe, Kathryn A., 2538339111 x 4323 khoppe@greenriver.edu, Green River Comm Coll; ZgOgPg
Hoppie, Bryce W., (507) 389-2315 bryce.hoppie@mnsu.edu, Minnesota State Univ; GeHw
Horan, Mary F., 202-478-8481 mhoran@carnegiescience.edu, Carnegie Inst for Sci; Cc
Horel, John, 801-581-7091 john.horel@utah.edu, Univ of Utah; AsZf
Horgan, Briony, (765) 496-2290 briony@purdue.edu, Purdue Univ; XgZr
Horn, John, (816) 604-3132 john.horn@mcckc.edu, Metropolitan Comm Coll-Kansas City; GgZy
Horn, Marty R., 225-578-2681 mhorn@lsu.edu, Louisiana State Univ; EoGgr
Hornbach, Matthew J., 214-768-2389 mhornbach@smu.edu, Southern Methodist Univ; YrhYe
Hornberger, George, (615) 343-1144 george.m.hornberger@vanderbilt.edu, Vanderbilt Univ; HgwHs
Horne, Sharon, (519) 253-3000 ext, 2528 shorne@uwindsor.ca, Univ of Windsor; Zn
Horner, John R., (406) 994-3982 jhorner@montana.edu, Montana State Univ; Pv
Horner, Tim C., (916) 278-5635 hornertc@csus.edu, Sacramento State Univ; HwGs
Horner, Tristan, (508) 289-3825 thorner@whoi.edu, Woods Hole Oceanographic Inst; Cm
Hornibrook, Edward R., 250-807-8059 ed.hornibrook@ubc.ca, Univ of British Columbia, Okanagan Campus; CbsSc
Horns, Daniel, (801) 863-8582 hornsda@uvu.edu, Utah Valley Univ; NgGeRn
Horowitz, Franklin G., +16072754955 frank.horowitz@cornell.edu, Cornell Univ; YgZnYe
Horsman, Eric M., 252 3285265 horsmane@ecu.edu, East Carolina Univ; GcYgGt
Horst, Andrew J., 440-775-8714 ahirst@oberlin.edu, Oberlin Coll; Gcg
Horst, Sarah, 410-516-5286 sarah.horst@jhu.edu, Johns Hopkins Univ; XaAcXb
Horton, Albert B., (615) 532-1509 albert.horton@tn.gov, Tennessee Geological Survey; GgZi
Horton, Brian, 512-471-5172 horton@mail.utexas.edu, Univ of Texas, Austin; Gs
Horton, Daniel E., 847-467-6185 danethan@earth.northwestern.edu, Northwestern Univ; AsPeZn
Horton, Duane G., (509) 376-6868 duane.horton@pnl.gov, Pacific Northwest; Gz
Horton, Radley, hortonr@ldeo.columbia.edu, Columbia Univ; Og
Horton, Robert, (515) 294-7843 rhorton@iastate.edu, Iowa State Univ of Sci & Tech; Sp
Horton, Stephen P., (901) 678-2007 shorton@memphis.edu, Univ of Memphis; Ys
Horton, Travis, +64 3 3667001 Ext 7734 travis.horton@canterbury.ac.nz, Univ of Canterbury; Cs
Horton, Jr., Robert A., 661-654-3059 rhorton@csub.edu, California State Univ, Bakersfield; GdsGo
Horváth, Ferenc, frankh@ludens.elte.hu, Eotvos Lorand Univ; YgRhGc
Horvath, Peter, +27 (0)46-603-8312 p.horvath@ru.ac.za, Rhodes Univ; Gp
Horwath, William R., (530) 754-6029 wrhorwath@ucdavis.edu, Univ of California, Davis; Sob
Horwath, William R., 530-754-6029 wrhorwath@ucdavis.edu, Univ of California, Davis; ScCo
Horwell, Claire, +44 (0) 191 33 42253 claire.horwell@durham.ac.uk, Durham Univ; Rn
Hosler, Charles L., (814) 863-8358 hosler@ems.psu.edu, Pennsylvania State Univ, Univ Park; Am
Hossain, A K M Azad, 423-425-4404 azad-hossain@utc.edu, Univ of Tennessee, Chattanooga; ZriZg
Hosseini, Seyyed Abolfazi, 512-471-1534 seyyed.hosseini@beg.utexas.edu, Univ of Texas, Austin; Eo
Hotz, Helenmary, helenmary.hotz@umb.edu, Univ of Massachusetts, Boston; Zi
Houghton, Bruce F., (808) 956-2561 bhought@soest.hawaii.edu, Univ of Hawai'i, Manoa; Gv
Houlton, Ben, bzhoulton@ucdavis.edu, Univ of California, Davis; So
Hounslow, Arthur, 405-372-2328 Oklahoma State Univ; Cl
Hourigan, Jeremy, 831-459-2879 hourigan@ucsc.edu, Univ of California, Santa Cruz; Cc
House, Christopher H., (814) 865-8802 chouse@geosc.psu.edu, Pennsylvania State Univ, Univ Park; Pg

House, Leigh S., house@lanl.gov, Los Alamos; Ys
House, Martha, mahouse@pasadena.edu, Pasadena City Coll; Gg
Houseman, Greg, +44(0) 113 34 35206 g.a.houseman@leeds.ac.uk, Univ of Leeds; Yg
Housen, Bernard A., (360) 650-3588 bernieh@wwu.edu, Western Washington Univ; Ym
Houston, Adam L., ahouston2@unl.edu, Univ of Nebraska, Lincoln; Asm
Houston, Heidi B., 310 691 9152 houstonh@usc.edu, Univ of Southern California; YsGt
Houston, Robert, (541) 967-2039 Oregon Dept of Geology and Mineral Industries; Ge
Houston, Serin D., 413-538-2055 shouston@mtholyoke.edu, Mount Holyoke Coll; Zyn
Houston, William (Bill), 906-635-2155 whouston1@lssu.edu, Lake Superior State Univ; Gsg
Houweling, Sander, +31 20 59 83687 s.houweling@vu.nl, Vrije Universiteit Amsterdam; AscAp
Houze, Robert A., (206) 543-6922 houze@atmos.washington.edu, Univ of Washington; As
Hovan, Steven A., (724) 357-5625 hovan@iup.edu, Indiana Univ of Pennsylvania; Ou
Hovis, Guy L., (610) 258-3907 hovisguy@lafayette.edu, Lafayette Coll; GzxCg
Hovorka, Susan D., 512-471-4863 susan.hovorka@beg.utexas.edu, Univ of Texas, Austin; Gs
Howard, Alan D., (804) 924-0563 ah6p@virginia.edu, Univ of Virginia; GmXg
Howard, Hugh H., 916 484-8805 howardh@arc.losrios.edu, American River Coll; Zi
Howard, Jeffrey L., 313-577-3258 jhoward@wayne.edu, Wayne State Univ; GsScGa
Howard, Katie, 360-475-7700 khoward@llion.org, Olympic Coll; Gg
Howard, Kenneth W., 416-287-7233 Univ of Toronto; Hw
Howard, Kieren, 917-974-6168 khoward@amnh.org, Graduate Sch of the City Univ of New York; Ggz
Howard, Leslie M., (402) 472-9192 thoward@unl.edu, Unversity of Nebraska, Lincoln; Zyi
Howard, Matthew K., (979) 862-4169 mkhoward@tamu.edu, Texas A&M Univ; Op
Howat, Ian M., (614) 292-4839 howat.4@osu.edu, Ohio State Univ; GlZr
Howden, Stephan, (228) 688-5284 stephan.howden@usm.edu, Univ of Southern Mississippi; Op
Howe, Bruce M., (206) 543-9141 billhowe@cs.washington.edu, Univ of Washington; Op
Howe, Julie, jhowe@tamu.edu, Texas A&M Univ; Sc
Howe, Stephen S., (518) 442-5053 showe@albany.edu, SUNY, Albany; Cs
Howe III, Thomas R., (269) 387-5492 thomas.r.howe@wmich.edu, Western Michigan Univ; HwGem
Howell, John, +44 (0)1224 272606 john.howell@abdn.ac.uk, Univ of Aberdeen; GsoGc
Howell, Robert R., (307) 766-6296 rhowell@uwyo.edu, Univ of Wyoming; XgZr
Howell, Jr., Benjamin F., (814) 863-0886 howellbf@aol.com, Pennsylvania State Univ, Univ Park; Ys
Hower, James C., (859) 257-0261 james.hower@uky.edu, Univ of Kentucky; Ec
Howes, Mary R., mary.howes@dnr.iowa.gov, Iowa Dept of Natural Resources; Gg
Howman, Dominic J., +61 8 9266-2329 d.howman@curtin.edu.au, Curtin Univ; Ye
Hoyer, Lauren, 031-2601613 hoyerl@ukzn.ac.za, Univ of KwaZulu-Natal; EgGc
Hoyos, Carlos, carlos.hoyos@eas.gatech.edu, Georgia Inst of Tech; As
Hoyt, Greg D., (919) 684-3562 North Carolina State Univ; Sb
Hoyt, William H., (970) 351-2487 william.hoyt@unco.edu, Univ of Northern Colorado; OgGsZe
Hozik, Michael J., 609 652-4277 hozikm@stockton.edu, Stockton Univ; GcYmg
Hren, Michael, 860-486-9511 michael.hren@uconn.edu, Univ of Connecticut; CslCo
Hrepic, Zdeslav, 706-569-3052 hrepic_zdeslav@columbusstate.edu, Columbus State Univ; Zn
Hsiang, Tom, (519) 824-4120 Ext.52753 thsiang@uoguelph.ca, Univ of Guelph; Zn
Hsieh, Wen-Pin, 886-227839910-509 wphsieh@earth.sinica.edu.tw, Academia Sinica; YhGy
Hsieh, William W., (250) 388-0508 whsieh@eos.ubc.ca, Univ of British Columbia; OpAs
Hsu, Liang-Chi, (775) 682-8746 lihsu@unr.edu, Univ of Nevada, Reno; Cp
Hu, Baoxin, (416)736-2100 #20557 baoxin@yorku.ca, York Univ; Zr
Hu, Bill X., 850-644-3943 hu@gly.fsu.edu, Florida State Univ; Hw
Hu, Feng-Sheng, (217) 244-2982 fhu@illinois.edu, Univ of Illinois, Urbana-Champaign; Pe
Hu, Hao, hhu5@central.uh.edu, Univ of Houston; Ye
Hu, Qi S., 402-472-6642 qhu2@unl.edu, Univ of Nebraska, Lincoln; As
Hu, Qi (Steve), qhu2@unl.edu, Univ of Nebraska, Lincoln; As
Hu, Qinhong (Max), (817) 272-5398 maxhu@uta.edu, Univ of Texas, Arlington; GoHwNg
Hu, Shusheng, 203-432-3790 shusheng.hu@yale.edu, Yale Univ; PblGs
Hu, Wan-Ping (Sunny), +61 7 3138 7314 sunny.hu@qut.edu.au, Queensland Univ of Tech; Ca
Hu, Xinping, 361-825-3395 xinping.hu@tamucc.edu, Texas A&M Univ, Corpus Christi; Cms
Hu, Zhiyong, 850-474-3494 zhu@uwf.edu, Univ of West Florida; Zr
Huang, Alex, (828) 232-5157 Univ of North Carolina, Asheville; As
Huang, Bohua, (703) 993-6084 bhuang@gmu.edu, George Mason Univ; Op
Huang, Li, (519) 661-3188 lhuang3@uwo.ca, Western Univ; Yr
Huang, Lianjie, (505) 665-1108 ljh@lanl.gov, Los Alamos; Yg
Huang, Moh J., (916) 322-9304 California Geological Survey; Ne
Huang, Norden E., (301) 286-8879 Univ of Delaware; Zn
Huang, Shaopeng, (734) 763-3169 shaopeng@umich.edu, Univ of Michigan; YhZcGt
Huang, Yi, 514-398-8217 yi.huang@mcgill.ca, McGill Univ; ZrYgAs
Huang, Yongsong, yongsong_huang@brown.edu, Brown Univ; Co
Hubbard, Dennis K., 440-775-8346 dennis.hubbard@oberlin.edu, Oberlin Coll; Gsu
Hubbard, Stephen M., 403 220-6236 shubbard@ucalgary.ca, Univ of Calgary; Gs
Hubbard, Trent, (907) 451-5009 trent.hubbard@alaska.gov, Alaska Division of Geological & Geophysical Surveys; GmNgZi
Hubbard, William B., (520) 621-6942 hubbard@lpl.arizona.edu, Univ of Arizona; XyYvAs
Hubbart, Jason A., (304) 293-2472 jason.hubbart@mail.wvu.edu, West Virginia Univ; HqgHs
Hubenthal, Michael, (607) 777-4612 hubenth@iris.edu, Binghamton Univ; ZeYg
Hubeny, J B., bhubeny@salemstate.edu, Salem State Univ; GeOnCs
Huber, Brian T., (202) 633-1328 Smithsonian Inst / Nat Mus of Natural History; Pm
Huber, Christian, christian_huber@brown.edu, Brown Univ; Gv
Huber, Julie, 508-289-2556 jhuber@whoi.edu, Woods Hole Oceanographic Inst; Cm
Huber, Matthew, +27 (0)51 401 3944 huberms@ufs.ac.za, Univ of the Free State; EgXm
Huckabey, Marsha, (573) 882-2040 huckabeym@missouri.edu, Univ of Missouri; Zn
Hudackova, Natalia H., natalia.hudackova@uniba.sk, Comenius Univ in Bratislava; PimPg
Hudak, Paul F., (940) 565-4312 paul.hudak@unt.edu, Univ of North Texas; Hw
Hudec, Michael R., 512-471-1428 michael.hudec@beg.utexas.edu, Univ of Texas, Austin; Gc
Hudec, Peter P., (519) 253-3000 x2491 hudec@uwindsor.ca, Univ of Windsor; NgEmGe
Hudgins, Thomas, (787) 265-3845 thomas.hudgins@upr.edu, Univ of Puerto Rico; GiCpGv
Hudleston, Peter J., 612-625-0046 hudle001@umn.edu, Univ of Minnesota, Twin Cities; Gc
Hudson, Robert J. M., (217) 333-7641 rjhudson@uiuc.edu, Univ of Illinois, Urbana-Champaign; Cg
Hudson, Samuel M., sam.hudson@byu.edu, Brigham Young Univ; GosGr
Hudson-Edwards, Karen, +44 0203 073 8030 k.hudson-edwards@bbk.ac.uk, Birkbeck Coll; Gez
Huebert, Barry J., (808) 258-4673 huebert@hawaii.edu, Univ of Hawai'i, Manoa; OcCg
Huerfano, Victor, (787) 265-3845 victor.huerfano@upr.edu, Univ of Puerto Rico; YsgGt
Huerta, Audrey, 509.963.2718 huerta@geology.cwu.edu, Central Washington Univ; Ygd
Huertas, María José, huertas@ucm.es, Univ Complutense de Madrid; Gi
Huey, Gregory L., (404) 894-5541 greg.huey@eas.gatech.edu, Georgia Inst of Tech; As
Huff, Bryan G., 217-244-2509 huff@isgs.uiuc.edu, Illinois State Geological Survey; Eo
Huff, Edmund A., (630) 252-3633 Argonne; Ca
Huff, Warren D., (513) 556-3731 warren.huff@uc.edu, Univ of Cincinnati; GzvGr

Huffman, Debra E., (727) 553-3930 debrah@usf.edu, Univ of South Florida; Zn
Huffman, F. T., (859) 622-6968 tyler.huffman@eku.edu, Eastern Kentucky Univ; Zi
Huffman, Robert L., (912) 752-2704 Mercer Univ; Zn
Huft, Ashley, (406) 496-4789 ahuft@mtech.edu, Montana Tech of The Univ of Montana; Ca
Huggett, William, 618-453-7392 huggett@geo.siu.edu, Southern Illinois Univ Carbondale; Ec
Hughen, Konrad A., (508) 289-3353 khughen@whoi.edu, Woods Hole Oceanographic Inst; Cc
Hughes, Annie, +44 020 8417 2603 ku08925@kingston.ac.uk, Kingston Univ; Zi
Hughes, Colin, colin.hughes@manchester.ac.uk, Univ of Manchester; Go
Hughes, Denis, +27 46 6224014 d.hughes@ru.ac.za, Rhodes Univ; Hqs
Hughes, John M., (802) 656-9443 jmhughes@uvm.edu, Univ of Vermont; Gz
Hughes, Kenneth S., (787) 265-3845 kenneth.hughes@upr.edu, Univ of Puerto Rico; Gcm
Hughes, Malcolm K., (520) 621-6470 mhughes@ltrr.arizona.edu, Univ of Arizona; Pe
Hughes, Nigel C., nigel.hughes@ucr.edu, Cincinnati Mus Center; Pi
Hughes, Noah C., (209) 575-6172 hughesn@yosemite.edu, Modesto Junior Coll; ZgAs
Hughes, Randall, 7815817370 x314 rhughes@neu.edu, Northeastern Univ; Zn
Hughes, Sam, +44 07727 096492 s.p.hughes@exeter.ac.uk, Exeter Univ; Gt
Hughes, Scott S., (530) 533-1933 hughscot@isu.edu, Idaho State Univ; GvXgGi
Hughes III, Richard O., 909-389-3237 rihughes@craftonhills.edu, Crafton Hills Coll; GlZe
Hughes-Clarke, John E., 603-862-5505 jhc@ccom.unh.edu, Univ of New Hampshire; Og
Hugli, Wilbur G., 850-474-3470 whugli@uwf.edu, Univ of West Florida; As
Hugo, Richard, 503-725-3356 hugo@pdx.edu, Portland State Univ; Gy
Huizenga, Jan Marten, (074) 781-4597 jan.huizenga@jcu.edu.au, James Cook Univ; GpCgGc
Hulbe, Christina L., chulbe@pdx.edu, Portland State Univ; Gl
Hulett, Sam, 614 265 6573 sam.hulett@dnr.state.oh.us, Ohio Dept of Natural Resources; Eo
Hull, Donald L., (505) 667-4151 Los Alamos; Zn
Hull, Joseph M., jhull@sccd.ctc.edu, Seattle Central Coll; Gc
Huluka, Gobena E., (334) 844-4100 hulukgo@auburn.edu, Auburn Univ; Sc
Humagain, Kamal, (315) 267-3356 humagak@potsdam.edu, SUNY Potsdam; Zir
Humayun, Munir, 850-644-5860 humayun@magnet.fsu.edu, Florida State Univ; XcCgGi
Humes, Karen, 208-885-6506 khumes@uidaho.edu, Univ of Idaho; ZriZn
Hummer, Daniel R., 618-453-7386 daniel.hummer@siu.edu, Southern Illinois Univ Carbondale; GzyCu
Humphrey, John D., +966 13 860 7982 humphrey@kfupm.edu.sa, King Fahd Univ of Petroleum and Minerals; Gdo
Humphrey, Neil F., (307) 314-2332 neil@uwyo.edu, Univ of Wyoming; GlmYh
Humphreys, Eugene D., (541) 852-0091 genehumphreys@gmail.com, Univ of Oregon; YsGt
Humphreys, Robin, (843) 953-7424 humphreysr@cofc.edu, Coll of Charleston; Ge
Humphris, Susan E., (508) 289-3451 shumphris@whoi.edu, Woods Hole Oceanographic Inst; GuCm
Hunda, Brenda, (513) 455-7160 bhunda@cincymuseum.org, Cincinnati Mus Center; Pi
Hung, Ming-Chih, (660) 562-1797 mhung@nwmissouri.edu, Northwest Missouri State Univ; Zr
Hungerbuehler, Axel, (575) 461-3466 axelh@mesalands.edu, Mesalands Comm Coll; PvgGg
Hungerford, Hilary, (801) 863-7160 hilary.hungerford@uvu.edu, Utah Valley Univ; ZuRw
Hungr, Oldrich, (604) 822-8471 ohungr@eos.ubc.ca, Univ of British Columbia; Gm
Hunsucker, Kelli, (321) 674-8437 khunsucker@fit.edu, Florida Inst of Tech; Ob
Hunt, Allen G., (937) 775-3116 allen.hunt@wright.edu, Wright State Univ; GqSpCl
Hunt, Andrew, 817 272 2987 hunt@uta.edu, Univ of Texas, Arlington; GbCg
Hunt, Brian, (604) 822-9135 bhunt@eos.ubc.ca, Univ of British Columbia; Ob
Hunt, Gene, (202) 633-1331 Smithsonian Inst / Nat Mus of Natural History; Pm
Hunt, Kathy, bhunt@ipst.umd.edu, Univ of Maryland; Zn
Hunt, Paula J., (304) 594-2331 phunt@geosrv.wvnet.edu, West Virginia Geological & Economic Survey; GgHw
Hunt, Rachel, rachel.hunt@ed.ac.uk, Edinburgh Univ; Zn
Hunt, Robert M., (402) 472-4604 rhunt2@unl.edu, Univ of Nebraska, Lincoln; Pv
Hunt, Shelley, (519) 824-420 Ext.53065 shunt@uoguelph.ca, Univ of Guelph; Zn
Hunten, Donald M., (520) 621-4002 dhunten@lpl.arizona.edu, Univ of Arizona; As
Hunter, Arlene G., +44 (0) 1908 655400 x55400 a.g.hunter@open.ac.uk, Open Univ; ZeGiCg
Huntington, Justin, 775.673.7670 justin.huntington@dri.edu, Univ of Nevada, Reno; HgZr
Huntington, Katharine W., 206-543-1750 kate1@uw.edu, Univ of Washington; Gt
Huntley, John, (573) 884-8083 Univ of Missouri; PqgPe
Huntoon, Jacqueline E., (906) 487-2440 jeh@mtu.edu, Michigan Technological Univ; GsZe
Huntoon, Laura, huntoon@email.arizona.edu, Univ of Arizona; Zn
Huntress, Jr., Wesley T., (202) 478-8910 whuntress@carnegiescience.edu, Carnegie Inst for Sci; Xc
Hural, Kirsten, (717) 245-1632 Dickinson Coll; Gg
Hurd, David, (814) 732-2493 dhurd@edinboro.edu, Edinboro Univ of Pennsylvania; Zg
Hurich, Charles A., (709) 737-2384 churich@mun.ca, Memorial Univ of Newfoundland; Ys
Hurlow, Hugh, (801) 537-3385 hughhurlow@utah.gov, Utah Geological Survey; Hw
Hurowitz, Joel A., 631-632-5355 joel.hurowitz@stonybrook.edu, Stony Brook Univ; Xg
Hurrell, James, james.hurrell@colostate.edu, Colorado State Univ; As
Hurtado, Jose M., (915) 747-5669 jhurtado@utep.edu, Univ of Texas, El Paso; Gt
Hurtgen, Matthew T., (847) 491-7539 matt@earth.northwestern.edu, Northwestern Univ; GsPgGr
Husch, Jonathan M., (609) 896-5330 husch@rider.edu, Rider Univ; GieXg
Husinec, Antun, (315) 229-5248 ahusinec@stlawu.edu, St. Lawrence Univ; GsCsGo
Hussein, Musa, (915) 747-5424 mjhussein@utep.edu, Univ of Texas, El Paso; YgeYm
Hussin, Azhar Hj, 03-79674203 azharhh@um.edu.my, Univ of Malaya; Gs
Hutcheon, Ian E., (403) 220-6744 ian@earth.geo.ucalgary.ca, Univ of Calgary; Cl
Hutchings, Jennifer, (541) 737-4453 jhutchings@coas.oregonstate.edu, Oregon State Univ; Gl
Hutchins, Peter S., (601) 961-5505 peter_hutchins@deq.state.ms.us, Mississippi Office of Geology; Zn
Hutchinson, Charles F., chuck@ag.arizona.edu, Univ of Arizona; Zr
Hutchison, David, 607-431-4730 hutchisond@hartwick.edu, Hartwick Coll; GxgGi
Hutson, John , john.hutson@flinders.edu.au, Flinders Univ; Spc
Hutson, Melinda, 971-722-4146 mhutson@pcc.edu, Portland Comm Coll - Sylvania Campus; Xm
Hutto, Richard S., (501) 683-0151 richard.hutto@arkansas.gov, Arkansas Geological Survey; Gg
Hutyra, Lucy, lrhutyra@bu.edu, Boston Univ; AsZr
Huws, Dei G., 01248 382523 oss082@bangor.ac.uk, Univ of Wales; YruNt
Huybers, Peter, 617-495-8391 phuybers@fas.harvard.edu, Harvard Univ; Pe
Huycke, David, 509-574-4817 dhuycke@yvcc.edu, Yakima Valley Coll; Gg
Huysken, Kristin, (219) 980-6739 khuysken@iun.edu, Indiana Univ Northwest; GizGc
Huysmans, Marijke, marijke.huysmans@ees.kuleuven.be, Katholieke Universiteit Leuven; Hw
Hyatt, James A., (860) 465-5789 hyattj@easternct.edu, Eastern Connecticut State Univ; Gml
Hyland, Ethan, 207-999-9047 ehyland@unity.ncsu.edu, North Carolina State Univ; GrCsPe
Hylland, Michael D., (801) 537-3382 mikehylland@utah.gov, Utah Geological Survey; Gg
Hylland, Mike, 801.537.3382 mikehylland@utah.gov, Utah Geological Survey; PgYs
Hylton, Alisa, (704)330-6297 alisa.hylton@cpcc.edu, Central Piedmont Comm Coll; Gg
Hyndman, David W., 517-353-4442 hyndman@msu.edu, Michigan State Univ; Hy
Hyndman, Roy D., (250) 363-6428 Univ of Victoria; Ys
Hynek, Brian M., 303-735-4312 brian.hynek@colorado.edu, Univ of Colorado; Xg

Hynes, Andrew J., andrew.hynes@mcgill.ca, McGill Univ; Gc
Hynes, Joanna , (657) 278-5464 jfantozzi@fullerton.edu, California State Univ, Fullerton; Gg
Hysell, David, dlh37@cornell.edu, Cornell Univ; Znr
Hyzny, Matus, hyzny@fns.uniba.sk, Comenius Univ in Bratislava; Pi

I

Iaccarino, Salvatore, salvatore.iaccarino@unito.it, Univ di Torino; Gc
Iaccheri, Maria Linda, 089/2180 4274 Ludwig-Maximilians-Univ Muenchen; Gg
Iaffaldano, Giampiero, 089/2180 4220 giampiero@geophysik.uni-muenchen.de, Ludwig-Maximilians-Univ Muenchen; Yg
Iancu, Ovidiu G., 0040232201455 ogiancu@uaic.ro, Alexandru Ioan Cuza; GpeCg
Ianno, Adam J., (814) 641-6662 iannoa@juniata.edu, Juniata Coll; GgiCu
Iantria, Linnea, (417) 836-4486 liantria@missouristate.edu, Missouri State Univ; Zn
Ibaraki, Motomu, (614) 292-7528 ibaraki.1@osu.edu, Ohio State Univ; Hg
Ibrahim, Ahmad Tajuddin Hj, 03-79674230 ahmadt@um.edu.my, Univ of Malaya; Ng
Ibrahim, Mohamed, 212-772-5267 mibrahim@hunter.cuny.edu, Hunter Coll (CUNY); ZgRwZc
Icenhower, Jonathan P., (509) 372-0078 jon.icenhower@pnl.gov, Pacific Northwest; Cl
Icopini, Gary, 406-496-4841 gicopini@mtech.edu, Montana Tech of The Univ of Montana; ClHwCb
Ide, Kayo, (310) 206-6484 Univ of California, Los Angeles; Zg
Idleman, Bruce D., bdi2@lehigh.edu, Lehigh Univ; Cc
Idone, Vincent P., (518) 442-4577 vpi@atmos.albany.edu, SUNY, Albany; As
Idowu, Simeon O., +234-8060227871 Federal Univ of Tech, Akure; NgHwGg
Idstein, Peter J., 859-257-2770 peter.idstein@uky.edu, Univ of Kentucky; Gg
Ielpi, Alessandro, (705) 675-1151 aielpi@laurentian.ca, Laurentian Univ, Sudbury; GsmGr
Igbinigie, Nosa S., nosa.igbinigie@uniben.edu, Univ of Benin; GorGg
Ige, A. O., aige@oauife.edu.ng, Obafemi Awolowo Univ; Cg
Ige, O. O., vickeyeg2002@yahoo.com, Univ of Ilorin; Ng
Igel, Adele, (530)752-1018 aigel@ucdavis.edu, Univ of California, Davis; Asp
Igel, Heiner, 089/2180 4204 heiner.igel@lmu.de, Ludwig-Maximilians-Univ Muenchen; Yg
Igel, Matthew, (530) 752-6280 migel@ucdavis.edu, Univ of California, Davis; Asm
Iglesias, Cruz, 0034981167000 cruzi@udc.es, Coruna Univ; GaZmNr
Igonor, Emmanuel E., +2348066943346 eeigonor@futa.edu.ng, Federal Univ of Tech, Akure; GgCeGi
Ihinger, Phillip D., (715) 836-2158 ihinger@uwec.edu, Univ of Wisconsin, Eau Claire; Gx
Ikonnikova, Svetlana, 512-232-9464 s.ikonnikova@mail.utexas.edu, Univ of Texas, Austin; Ego
Iles, Derric L., (605) 677-6148 derric.iles@usd.edu, South Dakota Dept of Environment and Natural Resources; HwGg
Illari, Lodovica, (617) 253-2286 illari@mit.edu, Massachusetts Inst of Tech; Am
Imasuen, Isaac O., okpeseyi.imasuen@uniben.edu, Univ of Benin; CgGee
Immel, Harald, 089/2180 6615 h.immel@lrz.uni-muenchen.de, Ludwig-Maximilians-Univ Muenchen; Pg
Immonen, Wilma, (406) 496-4182 wimmonen@mtech.edu, Montana Tech of the Univ of Montana; Zn
Inamdar, Shreeram, 302-831-8877 inamdar@udel.edu, Univ of Delaware; Hg
Ince, Simon, (520) 621-5082 Univ of Arizona; Hs
Indares, Aphrodite D., (709) 737-2456 aindares@mun.ca, Memorial Univ of Newfoundland; Gp
Ingall, Ellery D., (404) 894-3883 ellery.ingall@eas.gatech.edu, Georgia Inst of Tech; CmlOc
Ingalls, Anitra E., 206-221-6748 aingalls@u.washington.edu, Univ of Washington; Oc
Ingersoll, Andrew P., 626 395-6167 api@gps.caltech.edu, California Inst of Tech; As
Ingersoll, Raymond V., (310) 825-8634 ringer@epss.ucla.edu, Univ of California, Los Angeles; Gst
Ingle, Jr., James C., (650) 723-3366 ingle@pangea.stanford.edu, Stanford Univ; Pm
Inglett, Kanika Sharma, 352-294-3164 Univ of Florida; So
Inglett, Patrick, 352-392-1803 pinglett@ufl.edu, Univ of Florida; Sf
Inglis, Michael, 631-451-4120 ingism@sunysuffolk.edu, Suffolk County Comm Coll, Ammerman Campus; Zg
Ingram, B. Lynn, (510) 643-1474 ingram@eps.berkeley.edu, Univ of California, Berkeley; Cs
Innanen, Kristopher, 403 210-6837 k.innanen@ucalgary.ca, Univ of Calgary; Ye
Insel, Nadja, 773-442-6058 n-insel@neiu.edu, Northeastern Illinois Univ; Gt
Inskeep, William P., (406) 994-5077 binskeep@montana.edu, Montana State Univ; Sc
Insua, Juan Miguel, insuarev@ucm.es, Univ Complutense de Madrid; NtGc
Ioannides, Dimitri, 417-836-5801 dioannides@missouristate.edu, Missouri State Univ; Zn
Ionesi, Viorel, vioion@uaic.ro, Alexandru Ioan Cuza; PmGgHg
Iqbal, Mohammad Z., (319) 273-2998 m.iqbal@uni.edu, Univ of Northern Iowa; Hw
Iribar, Vicente , vicente.iribar@ehu.eus, Univ of the Basque Country UPV/EHU; HwGm
Irish, Jennifer, (540) 231-2298 jirish@vt.edu, Virginia Polytechnic Inst & State Univ; NoOg
Irmis, Randall B., (801) 581-6555 irmis@umnh.utah.edu, Univ of Utah; Sa
Irons, Trevor , 406-496-4144 tirons@mtech.edu, Montana Tech of the Univ of Montana; Yue
Irvin, Gene D., 205/247-3542 dirvin@gsa.state.al.us, Geological Survey of Alabama; Gg
Irvine, Dylan, dylan.irvine@flinders.edu.au, Flinders Univ; Hw
Irvine, T. Neil, 202-478-8950 nirvine@carnegiescience.edu, Carnegie Inst for Sci; Gi
Irving, Tony, irvingaj@uw.edu, Univ of Washington; CgXmGi
Isaacson, Carl, 218-755-4104 cisaacson@bemidjistate.edu, Bemidji State Univ; Ge
Isaacson, Peter E., (208) 885-7969 isaacson@uidaho.edu, Univ of Idaho; Psi
Isacks, Bryan L., bli1@cornell.edu, Cornell Univ; Gmt
Isard, Sierra J., 828-296-4629 sierra.isard@ncdenr.gov, N.C. Department of Environmental Quality; Gcg
Isbell, John L., 414-229-2877 jisbell@uwm.edu, Univ of Wisconsin, Milwaukee; Gs
Isenor, Fenton M., fenton_isenor@cbu.ca, Cape Breton Univ; GgNgGm
Ishii, Miaki, 617-384-8066 ishii@eps.harvard.edu, Harvard Univ; Yg
Ishii, Satoshi, 612-624-7902 ishi0040@umn.edu, Univ of Minnesota, Twin Cities; SbPg
Ishman, Scott E., (618) 453-7377 sishman@siu.edu, Southern Illinois Univ Carbondale; Pmc
Ismail, Ahmed, 405-744-6358 ahmed.ismail@okstate.edu, Oklahoma State Univ; Ysu
Ismat, Zeshan, 717-358-4485 zeshan.ismat@fandm.edu, Franklin and Marshall Coll; Gc
Israel, Daniel W., (919) 515-2388 North Carolina State Univ; Sb
Ito, Emi, 612-624-7881 eito@umn.edu, Univ of Minnesota, Twin Cities; ClGnCs
Ito, Garrett T., (808) 956-9717 gito@hawaii.edu, Univ of Hawai'i, Manoa; YgrGt
Ivanochko, Tara, (604) 827-3179 tivanochko@eos.ubc.ca, Univ of British Columbia; OoZce
Ivanov, Julian, (785) 864-2089 jivanov@kgs.ku.edu, Univ of Kansas; Yg
Ivanov, Martin, +420 549 49 4600 mivanov@sci.muni.cz, Masaryk Univ; PgiPe
Ivanovic, Ruza, +44(0) 113 34 34945 r.ivanovic@leeds.ac.uk, Univ of Leeds; OgAsPe
Ivany, Linda C., (315) 443-3626 lcivany@syr.edu, Syracuse Univ; PegCs
Iverson, Neal R., (515) 294-8048 niverson@iastate.edu, Iowa State Univ of Sci & Tech; Gl
Iverson, Nels, 575-835-5319 nels.iverson@nmt.edu, New Mexico Inst of Mining and Tech; GvCga
Ivey, James, jivey@usf.edu, Univ of South Florida; Zy
Ivins, Erik R., (818) 354-4785 Jet Propulsion Lab; Gt
Ivory, Sarah, sarah_ivory@psu.edu, Pennsylvania State Univ, Univ Park; Pl
Ivy, Russell L., ivy@fau.edu, Florida Atlantic Univ; Zn
Izawa, Matt, mizawa2@uwo.ca, Western Univ; Gz
Izon, Gareth, +44 01334 463936 gji3@st-andrews.ac.uk, Univ of St. Andrews; Cg

J

Jablonowski, Christiane, (734) 763-6238 cjablono@umich.edu, Univ of Michigan; AsmZo
Jablonski, David, (773) 702-8163 djablons@midway.uchicago.edu, Univ of Chicago; Pi
Jacinthe, Pierre-Andre, pjacinth@iupui.edu, Indiana Univ - Purdue Univ Indianapolis; Cl
Jackson, Allyson K., (914) 251-6646 allyson.jackson@purchase.edu, SUNY, Purchase; ZgcZe
Jackson, Andrea, +44(0) 113 34 36728 a.v.jackson@leeds.ac.uk, Univ of Leeds; As

Jackson, Brian P., (603) 646-1272 brian.jackson@dartmouth.edu, Dartmouth Coll; CaGeCt
Jackson, Charles, (512) 471-0401 charles@ig.utexas.edu, Univ of Texas, Austin; ZoOoAt
Jackson, Chester M., (912) 598-2328 cjackson@georgiasouthern.edu, Georgia Southern Univ; OnGs
Jackson, Christopher, +44 20 759 47450v c.jackson@imperial.ac.uk, Imperial Coll; Gt
Jackson, David D., (310) 825-0421 djackson@ucla.edu, Univ of California, Los Angeles; YsdYg
Jackson, Frankie, (406) 994-6642 frankiej@montana.edu, Montana State Univ; Pv
Jackson, Gail D., +44 (0) 131 650 5436 g.jackson@ed.ac.uk, Edinburgh Univ; PbGe
Jackson, George A., (979) 845-0405 gjackson@ocean.tamu.edu, Texas A&M Univ; Op
Jackson, Hiram, (916) 691-7605 Cosumnes River Coll; Gg
Jackson, James A., +44 (0) 1223 337197 jaj2@cam.ac.uk, Univ of Cambridge; YgGt
Jackson, Jennifer M., (626) 395-6780 jackson@gps.caltech.edu, California Inst of Tech; Gy
Jackson, Jeremiah, 573-368-2182 jeremiah.jackson@dnr.mo.gov, Missouri Dept of Natural Resources; Gg
Jackson, Jeremy B. C., (858) 518-7613 jbjackson@ucsd.edu, Univ of California, San Diego; PgePi
Jackson, Kenneth J., (925) 422-6053 jackson8@llnl.gov, Lawrence Livermore; Cl
Jackson, Louise E., 530-754-9116 lejackson@ucdavis.edu, Univ of California, Davis; So
Jackson, Marie D., 801-581-7062 m.d.jackson@utah.edu, Univ of Utah; Gv
Jackson, Martin P. A., (512) 475-9548 martin.jackson@beg.utexas.edu, Univ of Texas at Austin, Jackson Sch of Geosciences; Gc
Jackson, Matt, jackson@geol.ucsb.edu, Univ of California, Santa Barbara; Cu
Jackson, Michael, 612-624-5274 jacks057@umn.edu, Univ of Minnesota, Twin Cities; Ym
Jackson, Richard A., (718) 460-1476 Long Island Univ, Brooklyn Campus; Gc
Jackson, Robert B., 919 660 7408 jackson@duke.edu, Duke Univ; Zn
Jackson, William T., wjackson@southalabama.edu, Univ of South Alabama; GsCc
Jacob, Daniel J., (617) 495-1794 djj@io.harvard.edu, Harvard Univ; As
Jacob, Klaus H., jacob@ldeo.columbia.edu, Columbia Univ; Ys
Jacob, Robert W., (570) 577-1791 rwj003@bucknell.edu, Bucknell Univ; Yg
Jacobi, Robert D., (716) 645-3489 rdjacobi@buffalo.edu, SUNY, Buffalo; GctGs
Jacobs, Alan M., 330-941-2933 amjacobs@ysu.edu, Youngstown State Univ; Ge
Jacobs, Bonnie F., bjacobs@smu.edu, Southern Methodist Univ; Pl
Jacobs, Daniel, (480) 727-2227 daniel.c.jacobs@asu.edu, Arizona State Univ; Xa
Jacobs, Gary K., jacobsgk@gmail.com, Oak Ridge; Cg
Jacobs, Jon, 519-661-2111 ext 86752 jjacobs@uwo.ca, Western Univ; Gg
Jacobs, Katharine L., (520) 626-0684 jacobsk@email.arizona.edu, Univ of Arizona; Hg
Jacobs, Louis L., (214) 768-2773 Southern Methodist Univ; Pv
Jacobs, Peter, jacobsp@uww.edu, Univ of Wisconsin, Whitewater; SdaGm
Jacobs, Stanley, sjacobs@ldeo.columbia.edu, Columbia Univ; Op
Jacobs, Tenika, (609) 984-6587 tenika.jacobs@dep.state.nj.us, New Jersey Geological and Water Survey; Zn
Jacobsen, Abram, 360-734-5019 abramj@uw.edu, Univ of Washington; Xg
Jacobsen, Stein B., (617) 495-5233 jacobsen@neodymium.harvard.edu, Harvard Univ; Cc
Jacobsen, Steven D., 847-467-1825 s-jacobsen@northwestern.edu, Northwestern Univ; GyzZm
Jacobson, Andrew D., (847) 491-3132 adj@earth.northwestern.edu, Northwestern Univ; ClPeCa
Jacobson, Carl E., cejac@iastate.edu, Iowa State Univ of Sci & Tech; GtcGp
Jacobson, Gary L., gary.jacobson@gcccd.edu, Grossmont Coll; GucEm
Jacobson, Roger, (775) 673-7364 roger@dri.edu, Univ of Nevada, Reno; Cg
Jadamec, Margarete, 716-645-4262 mjadamec@buffalo.edu, SUNY, Buffalo; GtYgZf
Jaecks, Glenn, jaecksg@arc.losrios.edu, American River Coll; GgOgPg
Jaeger, John M., (352) 846-1381 jmjaeger@ufl.edu, Univ of Florida; Gs
Jaegle, Lyatt, (206) 685-2679 jaegle@atmos.washington.edu, Univ of Washington; As
Jafarizadeh, Babak, b.jafarizadeh@hw.ac.uk, Heriot-Watt Univ; Eo
Jaffe, Daniel A., (425) 352-5357 djaffe@u.washington.edu, Univ of Washington; As
Jaffe, Peter R., (609) 258-4653 jaffe@princeton.edu, Princeton Univ; SbHgw
Jago, Bruce C., (705) 675-1151 x7227 bjago@laurentian.ca, Laurentian Univ, Sudbury; EgCe
Jagoutz, Oliver, (617) 324-5514 jagoutz@mit.edu, Massachusetts Inst of Tech; GitGc
Jahangiri, Ahmad, +98 (411) 339 2695 jahangiri@tabriu.ac.ir, Univ of Tabriz; GivGg
Jain, Atul K., (217) 333-2128 jain1@illinois.edu, Univ of Illinois, Urbana-Champaign; As
Jaisi, Deb, 302-831-1376 jaisi@udel.edu, Univ of Delaware; Cb
Jaiswal, Priyank, 405-744-6358 priyank.jaiswal@okstate.edu, Oklahoma State Univ; Yg
Jakosky, Bruce M., 303-492-8004 bruce.jakosky@colorado.edu, Univ of Colorado; Xg
Jamaluddin, Tajul Anuar, 03-79674152 taj@um.edu.my, Univ of Malaya; Ng
James, Matthew J., (707) 664-2301 james@sonoma.edu, Sonoma State Univ; PiRhPg
James, Noel P., (613) 533-6170 jamesn@queensu.ca, Queen's Univ; Gd
James, Peter B., (254)710-2351 p_james@baylor.edu, Baylor Univ; Ygg
James, Rachael, +44 (0)23 80599005 r.h.james@soton.ac.uk, Univ of Southampton; Oc
James, Richard, 7056751151 x2271 rjames@laurentian.ca, Laurentian Univ, Sudbury; GpiEm
James, Scott C., (254) 710-2534 sc_james@baylor.edu, Baylor Univ; HwGeEo
James, Thomas S., (250) 363-6403 thomas.james@canada.ca, Univ of Victoria; YdvYg
James, Valentine U., (814) 393-1938 vjames@clarion.edu, Clarion Univ; ZuRwZn
James-Aworeni, E., 234-705-326-6216 dawnjames@gmail.com, Obafemi Awolowo Univ; Hg
Jamieson, Heather E., (613) 545-6181 Queen's Univ; Ge
Jamieson, John, 709 864 2273 jjamieson@mun.ca, Memorial Univ of Newfoundland; Gu
Jamili, Ahmad, ahmad.jamili@ou.edu, Univ of Oklahoma; Np
Jamiolahmady, Mahmoud, +44 (0) 131 451 3122 m.jamiolahmady@pet.hw.ac.uk, Heriot-Watt Univ; Zn
Jammes, Suzon, (512) 245-2170 Texas State Univ; GgYg
Janecke, Susanne U., (435) 797-3877 susanne.janecke@usu.edu, Utah State Univ; Gt
Janecky, David R., (505) 667-7603 Los Alamos; Cl
Janetos, Tony, ajanetos@bu.edu, Boston Univ; Zn
Janiszewski, Helen, hajanisz@hawaii.edu, Univ of Hawai'i, Manoa; Ys
Janney, Phillip, +27-21-650-2929 phil.janney@uct.ac.za, Univ of Cape Town; GiCaXc
Jans, Urs, 212-650-8369 ujans@ccny.cuny.edu, Graduate Sch of the City Univ of New York; Gg
Janson, Xavier, 512-475-9524 xavier.janson@beg.utexas.edu, Univ of Texas at Austin, Jackson Sch of Geosciences; Gr
Janssen, Keith, (785) 532-6101 kjanssen@ksu.edu, Kansas State Univ; So
Jantz, Claire A., (717) 477-1399 cajant@ship.edu, Shippensburg Univ; ZuiZc
Janusz, Robert, 210-486-0045 San Antonio Comm Coll; Gg
Jaouich, Alfred, 514-987-3000 #3378 jaouich.alfred@uqam.ca, Universite du Quebec a Montreal; Sc
Jarcho, Kari A., (612) 625-5251 kjarcho@umn.edu, Univ of Minnesota, Twin Cities; Zn
Jardine, Philip M., ipj@ornl.gov, Oak Ridge; Sc
Jarvis, Ed, +353 21 4902698 e.jarvis@ucc.ie, Univ Coll Cork; Pl
Jarvis, Gary T., (416)736-2100 #77710 jarvis@yorku.ca, York Univ; Yg
Jarvis, Ian, +44 020 8417 2526 i.jarvis@kingston.ac.uk, Kingston Univ; CgGsr
Jarvis, Richard S., (915) 747-5263 rsjarvis@utep.edu, Univ of Texas, El Paso; ZyGmAs
Jarvis, W. T., 541-737-4032 todd.jarvis@oregonstate.edu, Oregon State Univ; Hw
Jarzen, David M., 3523921721 x 245 dilcher@flmnh.ufl.edu, Univ of Florida; Pb
Jasbinsek, John J., (805) 756-2013 jjasbins@calpoly.edu, California Polytechnic State Univ; YsuHw
Jasinski, Steven E., (717) 783-9897 c-sjasinsk@pa.gov, State Mus of Pennsylvania; PvgPg
Jasoni, Richard, 775-673-7472 richard.jasoni@dri.edu, Desert Research Inst; So
Jastrow, Julie D., (630) 252-3226 jdjastrow@anl.gov, Argonne; Sb
Jaumé, Steven C., (843) 953-1802 jaumes@cofc.edu, Coll of Charleston; Ys
Javadpour, Farzam, (512) 232-8068 farzam.javadpour@beg.utexas.edu, Univ of Texas, Austin; NpEo
Javaux, Emmanuelle, 32 4 366 54 22 ej.javaux@ulg.ac.be, Universite de Liege; Pl

Jawitz, James W., 352-392-1951 (203) jawitz@ufl.edu, Univ of Florida; SpHsw
Jayakumar, Amal, 609-258-6294 ajayakum@princeton.edu, Princeton Univ; Cm
Jayawickreme, Dushmantha, (203) 392-7286 jayawickred1@southernct.edu, Southern Connecticut State Univ; YgSpNg
Jaye, Shelley, (703) 425-5180 sjaye@nvcc.edu, Northern Virginia Comm Coll - Annandale; Giy
Jeanloz, Raymond, (510) 642-2639 jeanloz@uclink.berkeley.edu, Univ of California, Berkeley; Gy
Jebrak, Michel, 514-987-3000 #3986 jebrak.michel@uqam.ca, Universite du Quebec a Montreal; Eg
Jedrysek, Mariusz O., mariusz.jedrysek@uwr.edu.pl, Univ of Wroclaw; CaGe
Jefferson, Anne, 704-687-5977 ajefferson@uncc.edu, Univ of North Carolina, Charlotte; HgGm
Jeffery, David L., 740-376-4844 jefferyd@marietta.edu, Marietta Coll; PsGo
Jeffrey, Kip, +4401326259442 c.jeffrey@exeter.ac.uk, Exeter Univ; Nx
Jeffries, H. Perry, (401) 874-6222 jeffries@uri.edu, Univ of Rhode Island; Ob
Jekeli, Christopher, 614 292 7117 jekeli.1@osu.edu, Ohio State Univ; Ydv
Jelinski, Nicolas, 612-626-9936 jeli0026@umn.edu, Univ of Minnesota, Twin Cities; SdCs
Jellinek, Mark, mjellinek@eos.ubc.ca, Univ of British Columbia; Gg
Jenkins, David M., (607) 777-2736 dmjenks@binghamton.edu, Binghamton Univ; CpGzp
Jenkins, Gregory S., 814-865-0479 gsj1@psu.edu, Pennsylvania State Univ, Univ Park; Am
Jenkins, Mary Ann, (416)736-2100 #22992 maj@yorku.ca, York Univ; As
Jenkyns, Hugh C., +44 (1865) 272023 hugh.jenkyns@earth.ox.ac.uk, Univ of Oxford; GrsCs
Jensen, Ann R., 605-677-6159 ann.jensen@usd.edu, South Dakota Dept of Environment and Natural Resources; Gg
Jensen, Antony, +44 (0)23 80593428 acj@noc.soton.ac.uk, Univ of Southampton; Ob
Jensen, Jennifer, (512) 245-2170 Texas State Univ; Zru
Jensen, Olivia G., 514-398-3587 olivia.jensen@mcgill.ca, McGill Univ; Yg
Jensen, Ryan R., (801) 422-5386 rjensen@byu.edu, Brigham Young Univ; Zii
Jensen, Scott W., 605-677-6869 scott.jensen@usd.edu, South Dakota Dept of Environment and Natural Resources; Zn
Jenson, John W., (671) 735-2689 jjenson@triton.uog.edu, Univ of Guam; HwGel
Jeon, Sung Bae, sungbae.jeon@eku.edu, Eastern Kentucky Univ; Zy
Jercinovic, Michael J., (413) 545-2431 mjj@geo.umass.edu, Univ of Massachusetts, Amherst; Gx
Jerde, Eric, (606) 783-5406 e.jerde@moreheadstate.edu, Morehead State Univ; Cg
Jerolmack, Douglas, 215-746-2823 sediment@sas.upenn.edu, Univ of Pennsylvania; GmYxHq
Jessee, Anna, manowick@iu.edu, Indiana Univ - Purdue Univ Indianapolis; GgYg
Jessup, Micah, (865) 974-2366 mjessup@utk.edu, Univ of Tennessee, Knoxville; Gc
Jeu, Amy, (212) 772-4019 ajeu@hunter.cuny.edu, Hunter Coll (CUNY); Zi
Jewell, Paul W., (801) 581-6636 paul.jewell@utah.edu, Univ of Utah; GmHg
Jewett, Brian, 217-333-3957 bjewett@illinois.edu, Univ of Illinois, Urbana-Champaign; As
Jewitt, David, (310) 825-3880 jewitt@epss.ucla.edu, Univ of California, Los Angeles; XyZnn
Jezek, Kenneth, 614-292-7973 jezek.1@osu.edu, Ohio State Univ; YgPcGl
Ji, Chen, (805) 893-2923 ji@geol.ucsb.edu, Univ of California, Santa Barbara; Ys
Ji, Peng, pengji@ldeo.columbia.edu, Columbia Univ; Yr
Ji, Wei, (816) 235-1334 jiwei@umkc.edu, Univ of Missouri, Kansas City; ZriZy
Jiang, Dazhi, 519-661-3192 djiang3@uwo.ca, Western Univ; GcgGg
Jiang, Ganqing, (702) 895-2708 ganqing.jiang@unlv.edu, Univ of Nevada, Las Vegas; GsClGr
Jiang, James Xinxia, (506) 364-2326 Mount Allison Univ; Gg
Jiang, Junle , jiang@ou.edu, Univ of Oklahoma; Yg
Jiang , Shu, 801-585-9816 sjiang@egi.utah.edu, Univ of Utah; GoYsNp
Jiang, Zhenhua, (410) 436-6864 Argonne; Zn
Jickells, Tim, +44 (0)1603 59 3117 t.jickells@uea.ac.uk, Univ of East Anglia; Ob
Jiménez, David, davidj03@ucm.es, Univ Complutense de Madrid; GcNt
Jimoh, Mustapha T., +2348052472942 mtjimoh@lautech.edu.ng, Ladoke Akintola Univ of Tech; GxxGx
Jin, Fei Fei, 808-956-4645 jff@hawaii.edu, Univ of Hawai'i, Manoa; AmsZo
Jin, Ge, 303-273-3455 gjin@mines.edu, Colorado Sch of Mines; Ye
Jin, Guohai, 205-247-3560 gjin@gsa.state.al.us, Geological Survey of Alabama; Np
Jin, He (Hannah), hjin1@usf.edu, Univ of South Florida; Zi
Jin, Jisuo, (519) 661-4061 jjin@uwo.ca, Western Univ; Pi
Jin, Lixin, (915) 747-5559 ljin2@utep.edu, Univ of Texas, El Paso; Ge
Jin, Qusheng, 541-346-4999 qjin@uoregon.edu, Univ of Oregon; Cg
Jin, Yufang, (530) 601 9805 jin.yufang@gmail.com, Univ of California, Davis; Zr
Jinnah, Zubair A., (011) 717-6554 zubair.jinnah@wits.ac.za, Univ of the Witwatersrand; GsPg
Jiracek, George R., (619) 594-5160 gjiracek@mail.sdsu.edu, San Diego State Univ; Ye
Jiron, Rebecca, 757-221-2484 rljiron@wm.edu, William & Mary; GgsZi
Jirsa, Mark, (612) 626-4028 jirsa001@umn.edu, Univ of Minnesota; Gc
Jiskoot, Hester, (403) 329-2739 hester.jiskoot@uleth.ca, Univ of Lethbridge; GlmZy
Jo, Ho Young, 82-2-3290-3179 hyjo@korea.ac.kr, Korea Univ; NgCaGe
Jo, Injeong, (512) 245-2170 Texas State Univ; Ze
Joannes-Boyau, Renaud, renaud.joannes-boyau@scu.edu.au, Southern Cross Univ; CcaCs
Jochens, Ann E., (979) 845-6714 ajochens@ocean.tamu.edu, Texas A&M Univ; Op
Joeckel, Matt, (402) 472-7520 rjoeckel3@unl.edu, Unversity of Nebraska, Lincoln; GsrGg
Joeckel, R. M., 402-472-7520 rjoeckel3@unl.edu, Univ of Nebraska, Lincoln; GrsGm
Joeckel, R.M., (402)472-7520 rjoeckel3@unl.edu, Univ of Nebraska, Lincoln; Grs
Joesten, Raymond, raymond.joesten@uconn.edu, Univ of Connecticut; GzZmGp
Johanesen, Katharine, (814) 641-3601 johanesen@juniata.edu, Juniata Coll; GzxGc
Johannesson, Karen H., 504-862-3193 kjohanne@tulane.edu, Tulane Univ; HgCg
Johanson, Erik, (561) 297-4153 ejohanson@fau.edu, Florida Atlantic Univ; RnZy
John, Barbara E., (307) 223-1951 bjohn@uwyo.edu, Univ of Wyoming; Gci
John, Bratton F., (313) 577-2506 jbratton@limno.com, Wayne State Univ; Cg
John, Cedric, +44 20 759 46461 cedric.john@imperial.ac.uk, Imperial Coll; Gs
John, Chacko J., (225) 578-8681 cjohn@lsu.edu, Louisiana State Univ; GosGe
John, Hickman B., 859-323-0541 jhickman@uky.edu, Univ of Kentucky; Gto
Johns, Rebecca, rjohns@usf.edu, Univ of South Florida; Zn
Johns, Ronald A., (512) 223-7491 rjohns@austincc.edu, Austin Comm Coll District; Pi
Johnson, Ansel G., (503) 725-3381 Portland State Univ; Ye
Johnson, Arthur H., ahj@sas.upenn.edu, Univ of Pennsylvania; So
Johnson, Ashanti, (817) 272-2987 ashanti@uta.edu, Univ of Texas, Arlington; OgGe
Johnson, Beth , beth.johnson@uwc.edu, Univ of Wisconsin Colls; GlRh
Johnson, Beverly J., 207 786-6062 bjohnso3@bates.edu, Bates Coll; CsbCl
Johnson, Brad, 520-621-2470 bradjohnson@email.arizona.edu, Univ of Arizona; Gc
Johnson, Bruce D., (902) 494-3259 bruce.johnson@dal.ca, Dalhousie Univ; Oc
Johnson, Cari, (801) 585-3782 cari.johnson@utah.edu, Univ of Utah; Gs
Johnson, Carl G., (508) 289-2304 cjohnson@whoi.edu, Woods Hole Oceanographic Inst; Ca
Johnson, Clark M., (828) 265-8680 clarkj@geology.wisc.edu, Univ of Wisconsin, Madison; CgcCs
Johnson, Claudia C., 812-855-0646 claudia@indiana.edu, Indiana Univ, Bloomington; Peg
Johnson, Daniel L., (403) 327-4561 Univ of Lethbridge; Zn
Johnson, Darren J., 605-677-6162 darren.j.johnson@usd.edu, South Dakota Dept of Environment and Natural Resources; GgEo
Johnson, David B., (575) 835-5635 djohnson@nmt.edu, New Mexico Inst of Mining and Tech; Ps
Johnson, Donald O., (630) 252-3392 Argonne; Gr
Johnson, Elias, (417) 836-5801 Missouri State Univ; Zr
Johnson, Emily P., (617) 353-9709 Boston Univ; Zn
Johnson, Eric L., 1-607-4314658 johnsone@hartwick.edu, Hartwick Coll; GpcGi
Johnson, Gary D., (603) 636-2371 gary.d.johnson@dartmouth.edu, Dartmouth Coll; GrdYm

FACULTY INDEX – J

Johnson, Glenn W., (801) 581-6151 gjohnson@egi.utah.edu, Univ of Utah; Gq
Johnson, Graham, +61 7 3138 4371 g.johnson@qut.edu.au, Queensland Univ of Tech; Asp
Johnson, Gregory C., (206) 526-6806 Univ of Washington; Op
Johnson, H. Paul, (206) 543-8474 johnson@ocean.washington.edu, Univ of Washington; Yr
Johnson, Harlan P., 206-543-8474 johnson@ocean.washington.edu, Univ of Washington; Gu
Johnson, Helen, +44 01865 272142 helen.johnson@earth.ox.ac.uk, Univ of Oxford; Og
Johnson, Howard, +44 20 759 46461 h.d.johnson@imperial.ac.uk, Imperial Coll; Go
Johnson, Jane M., (320) 589-3411 Univ of Minnesota, Twin Cities; So
Johnson, Jean M., (706) 272-2666 jmjohnson@daltonstate.edu, Dalton State Comm Coll; Zg
Johnson, Jeanne L., (225) 354-9562 jeannej@lsu.edu, Louisiana State Univ; Zn
Johnson, Jeffrey , 208-426-2959 jeffrey.b.johnson@gmail.com, Boise State Univ; YsGv
Johnson, Joel E., 603-862-1718 joel.johnson@unh.edu, Univ of New Hampshire; Gus
Johnson, Judy L., (907) 474-7388 jljohnson21@alaska.edu, Univ of Alaska, Fairbanks; ZnnZn
Johnson, Julie, 901-678-4217 jjhnsn79@memphis.edu, Univ of Memphis; Gx
Johnson, Kaj, 812-855-3612 kajjohns@indiana.edu, Indiana Univ, Bloomington; Yg
Johnson, Kathleen, 949-824-6174 kathleen.johnson@uci.edu, Univ of California, Irvine; Zg
Johnson, Kayleigh, kayleigh.johnson@sdsmt.edu, South Dakota Sch of Mines & Tech; Pgv
Johnson, Kenneth, (713) 222-5375 johnsonk@uhd.edu, Univ of Houston Downtown; GiCac
Johnson, Kevin, 321-674-7186 johnson@fit.edu, Florida Inst of Tech; Ob
Johnson, Kevin T. M., 808-956-3444 kjohnso2@hawaii.edu, Univ of Hawai'i, Manoa; Gi
Johnson, Kurt, (907) 696-0079 kurt.johnson@alaska.gov, Alaska Division of Geological & Geophysical Surveys; Gg
Johnson, Lane R., lrjohnson@lbl.gov, Univ of California, Berkeley; Ys
Johnson, Mark O., mjohnson15@worcester.edu, Worcester State Univ; Zy
Johnson, Markes E., 413-597-2329 markes.e.johnson@williams.edu, Williams Coll; PseGm
Johnson, Martin, +44 (0)1603 59 1299 martin.johnson@uea.ac.uk, Univ of East Anglia; Cm
Johnson, Ned K., (510) 642-3059 Univ of California, Berkeley; Pv
Johnson, Neil E., 540-231-1785 johnsonne@vt.edu, Virginia Polytechnic Inst & State Univ; GzEg
Johnson, Paul A., (507) 933-7442 Los Alamos; Yg
Johnson, Robert G., 612-626-0853 johns088@umn.edu, Univ of Minnesota, Twin Cities; Pe
Johnson, Roy A., (520) 621-4890 johnson6@email.arizona.edu, Univ of Arizona; Ys
Johnson, Sarah E., 859-572-6907 johnsonsa@nku.edu, Northern Kentucky Univ; GmNgZi
Johnson, Scott E., (207) 581-2142 johnsons@maine.edu, Univ of Maine; Gc
Johnson, Thomas C., tcj@d.umn.edu, Univ of Minnesota Duluth; PcGn
Johnson, Ty, (501) 683-0153 ty.johnson@arkansas.gov, Arkansas Geological Survey; GgZiGr
Johnson, Verner C., (970) 248-1672 vjohnson@coloradomesa.edu, Colorado Mesa Univ; Yg
Johnson, William C., 785-864-5548 wcj@ku.edu, Univ of Kansas; Grm
Johnson, William P., (801) 581-5033 william.johnson@utah.edu, Univ of Utah; Ng
Johnston, A. Dana, (541) 346-5588 adjohn@uoregon.edu, Univ of Oregon; Cp
Johnston, Archibald C., (901) 678-2007 ajohnstn@memphis.edu, Univ of Memphis; Ys
Johnston, Carl G., 330-941-7151 cgjohnston@ysu.edu, Youngstown State Univ; Pg
Johnston, David, (501) 683-0126 david.johnston@arkansas.gov, Arkansas Geological Survey; Gg
Johnston, Paul, (403) 440-6174 pajohnston@mtroyal.ca, Mount Royal Univ; Pi
Johnston, Scott, 805-756-1650 scjohnst@calpoly.edu, California Polytechnic State Univ; GcpCc
Johnston, Stephen T., (780) 492-5249 stjohnst@ualberta.ca, Univ of Alberta; GctGg
Johnston, Thomas, (403) 329-2534 johnston@uleth.ca, Univ of Lethbridge; Ze
Johnston, III, John E., (225) 578-8657 hammer@lsu.edu, Louisiana State Univ; EoGe
Join, Jean-Lambert, +262262938697 jean-lambert.join@univ-reunion.fr, Universite de la Reunion; Hw
Jokipii, Jack R., (520) 621-4256 jokipii@lpl.arizona.edu, Univ of Arizona; Xy
Jolley, David, +44 (0)1224 273450 d.jolley@abdn.ac.uk, Univ of Aberdeen; PlsGv
Jolliff, Bradley L., (314) 935-5622 blj@levee.wustl.edu, Washington Univ in St. Louis; GxzGi
Jomeiri, Rahim, +98 (411) 339 2704 Univ of Tabriz; Yg
Jonas, John J., (514) 398-4755 McGill Univ; Nx
Jones, Adrian P., +44 020 7679 32415 adrian.jones@ucl.ac.uk, Univ Coll London; GiCgGg
Jones, Alan, (607) 777-2518 Binghamton Univ; Ys
Jones, Alice, (859) 622-1424 alice.jones@eku.edu, Eastern Kentucky Univ; Zyn
Jones, Bobby L., (225) 388-8328 Louisiana State Univ; Go
Jones, Brian, (780) 492-3074 brian.jones@ualberta.ca, Univ of Alberta; Ps
Jones, Charles E., (412) 624-6347 cejones@pitt.edu, Univ of Pittsburgh; GgsPg
Jones, Clain, clainj@montana.edu, Montana State Univ; So
Jones, Craig H., (303) 492-6994 craig.jones@colorado.edu, Univ of Colorado; YsGtYg
Jones, Daniel, daniel.s.jones@nmt.edu, New Mexico Inst of Mining and Tech; Cb
Jones, David S., (413) 542-2714 djones@amherst.edu, Amherst Coll; GsClGr
Jones, Douglas S., 3523921721 x485 dsjones@flmnh.ufl.edu, Univ of Florida; Pg
Jones, Eric M., (505) 667-6386 honais@lanl.gov, Los Alamos; As
Jones, F. Walter, (780) 492-0667 wjones@phys.ualberta.ca, Univ of Alberta; Ym
Jones, Francis H., (604) 822-2138 fjones@eoas.ubc.ca, Univ of British Columbia; YeZe
Jones, Glenda, +44 1782 734309 g.m.jones@keele.ac.uk, Keele Univ; NgYg
Jones, Gwilym, g.jones@neu.edu, Northeastern Univ; Zn
Jones, Gwyn, gwjones@bellevuecollege.edu, Bellevue Coll; Gg
Jones, Hazel, hazel.jones@manchester.ac.uk, Univ of Manchester; As
Jones, Jon W., (403) 220-5024 Univ of Calgary; Gp
Jones, Julia A., (541) 737-1224 jonesj@geo.oregonstate.edu, Oregon State Univ; So
Jones, Larry Allan, (505) 667-0142 ljones@lanl.gov, Los Alamos; Ng
Jones, Lawrence S., (970) 248-1708 lajones@coloradomesa.edu, Colorado Mesa Univ; GsmGr
Jones, Merren, merren.a.jones@manchester.ac.uk, Univ of Manchester; Gst
Jones, Michael Q., (011) 717-6628 michael.jones@wits.ac.za, Univ of the Witwatersrand; YhGtYg
Jones, Minnie O., (312) 996-3154 mojones@uic.edu, Univ of Illinois at Chicago; Zn
Jones, Norris W., (920) 424-4460 jonesnw@uwosh.edu, Univ of Wisconsin, Oshkosh; Gi
Jones, Phillip D., +44 (0)1603 59 2090 p.jones@uea.ac.uk, Univ of East Anglia; AsPeHg
Jones, Rhian, 505-277-4204 rjones@unm.edu, Univ of New Mexico; Gz
Jones, Robert L., (217) 333-9490 Univ of Illinois, Urbana-Champaign; Sc
Jones, Stephen C., (205) 247-3601 sjones@gsa.state.al.us, Geological Survey of Alabama; HyGeCg
Jones, Stuart, +44 (0) 191 33 42319 stuart.jones@durham.ac.uk, Durham Univ; Gs
Jones, T, jonestp@cf.ac.uk, Cardiff Univ; Ge
Jones, Tim L., (505) 646-3405 New Mexico State Univ, Las Cruces; Sp
Jones, III, John P., jpjones@email.arizona.edu, Univ of Arizona; Zn
Joniak, Peter , joniak@fns.uniba.sk, Comenius Univ in Bratislava; Pv
Jordan, Andy, +44 (0)1603 59 2552 a.jordan@uea.ac.uk, Univ of East Anglia; Ge
Jordan, Bradley C., (570) 577-3024 jordan@bucknell.edu, Bucknell Univ; Gg
Jordan, Brennan T., (605) 677-6143 brennan.jordan@usd.edu, Univ of South Dakota; GiAm
Jordan, Guntram, 089/2180 4353 guntram.jodan@lrz.uni-muenchen.de, Ludwig-Maximilians-Univ Muenchen; Gz
Jordan, Jim L., (409) 880-8211 jim.jordan@lamar.edu, Lamar Univ; XcgXm
Jordan, Karen J., 251-460-6381 kjordan@southalabama.edu, Univ of South Alabama; Zyr
Jordan, Mary S., 831-656-7571 jordan@nps.edu, Naval Postgraduate Sch; Am

K

Kapp, Jessica, 520-626-5701 jkapp@email.arizona.edu, Univ of Arizona; Gg
Kapp, Paul A., (520) 626-8763 pkapp@email.arizona.edu, Univ of Arizona; GtcGm
Kar, Aditya, (912) 825-6844 Fort Valley State Univ; Ct
Kar, Bandana, 601-266-5786 bandana.kar@usm.edu, Univ of Southern Mississippi; Zi
Kara, Hatice, 00904242370000-5965 haticekara@firat.edu.tr, Firat Univ; Cg
Karabinos, Paul, (413) 597-2079 paul.m.karabinos@williams.edu, Williams Coll; Gc
Karamperidou, Christina, 808-956-2565 ckaramp@hawaii.edu, Univ of Hawai'i, Manoa; AsZoc
Karanfil, Tanju, (864) 656-1005 tkaranf@clemson.edu, Clemson Univ; NgZnn
Karato, Shun-ichiro, (203) 432-3147 shun-ichiro.karato@yale.edu, Yale Univ; Gy
Karginoglu, Yusuf, 00904242370000-5989 Firat Univ; Eg
Karhu, Juha A., 358-294150834 juha.karhu@helsinki.fi, Univ of Helsinki; Csg
Karig, Daniel E., dek9@cornell.edu, Cornell Univ; YrGl
Karimi, Bobak, 570-408-4698 bobak.karimi@wilkes.edu, Wilkes Univ; GctYg
Karkanis, Pano G., (403) 317-0156 Res. (403) 330-9445 Cel. karkanis@telusplanet.net, Univ of Lethbridge; So
Karl, David M., (808) 956-8964 dkarl@soest.hawaii.edu, Univ of Hawai'i, Manoa; Ob
Karl, Tami S., (850) 644-5861 karl@gly.fsu.edu, Florida State Univ; Zn
Karlen, Douglas L., (515) 294-3336 doug.karlen@ars.usda.gov, Iowa State Univ of Sci & Tech; So
Karlsson, Haraldur R., 806-834-7978 hal.karlsson@ttu.edu, Texas Tech Univ; Cl
Karlstrom, Karl E., (505) 277-4346 kek1@unm.edu, Univ of New Mexico; Gt
Karlstrom, Leif, (541) 346-4323 leif@uoregon.edu, Univ of Oregon; Yx
Karmalkar, Ambarish, akarmalkar@geo.umass.edu, Univ of Massachusetts, Amherst; As
Karmosky, Christopher, christopher.karmosky@oneonta.edu, SUNY, Oneonta; AmsZy
Karner, Daniel B., (707) 664-2854 karner@sonoma.edu, Sonoma State Univ; Cc
Karner, James M., 801-585-5976 j.karner@utah.edu, Univ of Utah; Xm
Karpilo, Jr, Ronald J., (970) 225-3500 ron_karpilo@partner.nps.gov, Colorado State Univ; Zy
Karplus, Marianne, (915) 747-5413 mkarplus@utep.edu, Univ of Texas, El Paso; Ysg
Karson, Jeffrey, 315-443-7976 jakarson@syr.edu, Syracuse Univ; GtcGv
Karuntillake, Suniti, 225-578-2337 sunitiw@lsu.edu, Louisiana State Univ; Xg
Karwoski, Todd, (301) 405-0084 karwoski@geol.umd.edu, Univ of Maryland; Gg
Kasar, Sheila , 814-393-2718 skazar@clarion.edu, Clarion Univ; ZreGe
Kaspar, Thomas A., (515) 294-8873 tom.kaspar@ars.usda.gov, Iowa State Univ of Sci & Tech; So
Kaspari, Susan, kaspari@geology.cwu.edu, Central Washington Univ; PcAtGl
Kasse, Kees, +31 20 59 87381 c.kasse@vu.nl, Vrije Universiteit Amsterdam; GmsSd
Kassem, Hachem, +44 (0)23 8059 6205 hachem.kassem@soton.ac.uk, Univ of Southampton; OnGsZi
Kaste, James, 757-221-2591 jmkaste@wm.edu, William & Mary; ClcSc
Kaster, Mark A., 570-408-5046 mark.kaster@wilkes.edu, Wilkes Univ; Am
Kasting, James F., (814) 865-3207 jfk4@psu.edu, Pennsylvania State Univ, Univ Park; As
Kastner, Miriam, (858) 534-2065 mkastner@ucsd.edu, Univ of California, San Diego; CmlCm
Kastrisios, Christos , (603) 862-0618 mailto:christos.kastrisios@unh.edu, Univ of New Hampshire; Zn
Kaszuba, John P., 307-766-3392 jkaszub1@uwyo.edu, Univ of Wyoming; CgGze
Kath, Randal L., (678) 839-4063 rkath@westga.edu, Univ of West Georgia; GcNgHg
Kato, Terence T., 530-898-5262 tkato@csuchico.edu, California State Univ, Chico; GtcGp
Katumwehe, Andrew, (940) 397-4031 andrew.katumwehe@msutexas.edu, Midwestern State Univ; YuvYe
Katuna, Michael P., katunam@cofc.edu, Coll of Charleston; Gus
Katz, Miriam E., (518) 276-8521 katzm@rpi.edu, Rensselaer Polytechnic Inst; PmeGu
Katz, Richard, +44-1865-282122 richard.katz@earth.ox.ac.uk, Univ of Oxford; Cg
Katzenstein, Kurt W., (605) 394-2461 kurt.katzenstein@sdsmt.edu, South Dakota Sch of Mines & Tech; NxtZr
Katzman, Danny, (505) 667-0599 katzman@lanl.gov, Los Alamos; HyGem
Kauffman, Chad, 724 938-5760 kauffman@cup.edu, California Univ of Pennsylvania; As
Kaufman, Alan J., (301) 405-0395 kaufman@geol.umd.edu, Univ of Maryland; Csg
Kaufman, Darrell S., (928) 523-7192 darrell.kaufman@nau.edu, Northern Arizona Univ; Zc
Kaufmann, Ronald S., (619) 260-5904 kaufmann@sandiego.edu, Univ of San Diego; Ob
Kaunda, Rennie, 303-273-3772 rkaunda@mines.edu, Colorado Sch of Mines; Nm
Kaushal, Sujay, (301) 405-0454 skaushal@umd.edu, Univ of Maryland; ZuGeHs
Kavage Adams, Rebecca H., (410) 554-5553 rebecca.adams@maryland.gov, Maryland Department of Natural Resources; GmZiGe
Kavanagh, Janine, +44-151-794-5150 janine.kavanagh@liverpool.ac.uk, Univ of Liverpool; Gv
Kavanagh, Trudy A., 250-807-8564 trudy.kavanagh, Univ of British Columbia, Okanagan Campus; ZyRcZg
Kavanaugh, Jeffrey, 780-492-1740 jeff.kavanaugh@ualberta.ca, Univ of Alberta; Ng
Kavanaugh, Maria, mkavanau@coas.oregonstate.edu, Oregon State Univ; Cb
Kavner, Abby, (310) 206-3675 akavner@ucla.edu, Univ of California, Los Angeles; GyYg
Kavousi Ghahfarohki, Payam, 304-293-5603 pkavousi@mail.wvu.edu, West Virginia Univ; Gog
Kawase, Mitsuhiro, (206) 543-0766 kawase@ocean.washington.edu, Univ of Washington; Op
Kay, Jonathan, 757-221-2106 jpkay@wm.edu, William & Mary; ZyiGc
Kay, Richard F., (919) 684-2143 richard.kay@duke.edu, Duke Univ; Zn
Kay, Robert W., (607) 255-3461 rwk6@cornell.edu, Cornell Univ; Giz
Kay, Suzanne M., (607) 255-4701 smk16@cornell.edu, Cornell Univ; GiCuGt
Kaye, John M., (662) 325-3915 Mississippi State Univ; Gg
Kaygili, Sibel, 00904242370000-5962 skaygili@firat.edu.tr, Firat Univ; GgPgs
Kays, Marvin A., (541) 346-4578 makays@oregon.uoregon.edu, Univ of Oregon; GpcGt
Kazimoto, Emmanuel O., +255222410013 ekazimoto@udsm.ac.tz, Univ of Dar es Salaam; EgGpCg
Kazmer, Miklos, +36-1-372-2500 ext. 8627 mkazmer@gmail.com, Eotvos Lorand Univ; PggRh
Keables, Michael J., (303) 871-2653 michael.keables@du.edu, Univ of Denver; AstAm
Keach, Bill, (801) 537-3301 billkeach@utah.gov, Utah Geological Survey; YegZg
Keach, William, 801-585-1717 bkeach@egi.utah.edu, Univ of Utah; GoYes
Keach II, R. William, 801-857-7728 bkeach@byu.edu, Brigham Young Univ; YeEoGg
Keala, Lori, (909) 621-8675 lkeala@pomona.edu, Pomona Coll; Zn
Kean, Jr., William F., 414-229-5231 wkean@uwm.edu, Univ of Wisconsin, Milwaukee; Ym
Keane, Christopher M., (703) 379-2480 keane@americangeosciences.org, American Geosciences Inst; GgmZf
Kearney, Micheal S., (301) 405-4057 kearneym@umd.edu, Univ of Maryland; Gu
Kearns, Lance E., 540-568-6130 kearnsle@jmu.edu, James Madison Univ; Gz
Keating, Elizabeth, (505) 665-6714 ekeating@lanl.gov, Los Alamos; Gg
Keating, Kristina M., 973-353-1263 kmkeat@newark.rutgers.edu, Rutgers, The State Univ of New Jersey, Newark; Yug
Keaton, Jeffrey R., (801) 581-8218 Univ of Utah; Zn
Keattch, Sharen , 509-359-7358 skeattch@ewu.edu, Eastern Washington Univ; Gg
Keatts, Merida, 330-672-2897 mkeatts@kent.edu, Kent State Univ; Zn
Keays, Reid R., (705) 675-1151 Laurentian Univ, Sudbury; Em
Kebbede, Girma, 413-538-2004 gkebbede@mtholyoke.edu, Mount Holyoke Coll; Zy
Keegan, Kaitlin M., 775-682-6049 kkeegan@unr.edu, Univ of Nevada, Reno; PcNg
Keeler, Jason, 989-774-3179 keele1j@cmich.edu, Central Michigan Univ; Am
Keeley, Joshua A., 603-271-2875 joshua.a.keeley@des.nh.gov, New Hampshire Geological Survey; GgHyZi
Keeling, David J., (270) 745-4555 david.keeling@wku.edu, Western Kentucky Univ; Zg
Keeling, Ralph F., (858) 534-7582 rkeeling@ucsd.edu, Univ of California,

San Diego; As
Keen, Kerry L., (715) 425-3729 kerry.l.keen@uwrf.edu, Univ of Wisconsin, River Falls; HwGse
Keenan, Sarah W., (605) 394-2461 sarah.keenan@sdsmt.edu, South Dakota Sch of Mines & Tech; PvClb
Keene, Deborah A., 205-348-3334 dakeene@ua.edu, Univ of Alabama; Gga
Keene, William, (804) 924-0586 wck@virginia.edu, Univ of Virginia; As
Keeney, Dennis R., (515) 294-8066 drkeeney@iastate.edu, Iowa State Univ of Sci & Tech; So
Keesee, Robert G., (518) 442-4566 rgk@atmos.albany.edu, SUNY, Albany; As
Kehew, Alan E., (269) 387-5495 alan.kehew@wmich.edu, Western Michigan Univ; GmlHw
Kehoe, Kelsey, (307) 766-2286 Ext. 233 kelsey.kehoe@wyo.gov, Wyoming State Geological Survey; EcGo
Kehoe-Forutan, Sandra J., (570) 389-4106 skehoe@bloomu.edu, Bloomsburg Univ; Znu
Keigwin, Lloyd D., (508) 289-2784 lkeigwin@whoi.edu, Woods Hole Oceanographic Inst; CsGul
Keil, Chris, (630) 752-7271 chris.keil@wheaton.edu, Wheaton Coll; Rm
Keil, Richard G., (206) 616-1947 rickkeil@ocean.washington.edu, Univ of Washington; Oc
Keir, Derek, +44 (023) 8059 6614 d.keir@soton.ac.uk, Univ of Southampton; Gtv
Keith, Jeffrey D., 801-422-2189 jeff_keith@byu.edu, Brigham Young Univ; Eg
Kelemen, Peter, peterk@ldeo.columbia.edu, Columbia Univ; Gi
Kelkar, Sharad, (505) 667-4639 kelkar@vega.lanl.gov, Los Alamos; Np
Kelleher, Cole, 612-626-0505 Univ of Minnesota, Twin Cities; Zi
Keller, C. Kent, (509) 335-3040 ckkeller@wsu.edu, Washington State Univ; Hw
Keller, Dianne M., (315) 228-7893 dkeller@colgate.edu, Colgate Univ; Gz
Keller, Edward A., (805) 893-4207 keller@geol.ucsb.edu, Univ of California, Santa Barbara; Gm
Keller, G. Randy, (405) 255-0608 grkeller@ou.edu, Univ of Oklahoma; YgGtEo
Keller , George R., keller@utep.edu, Univ of Texas, El Paso; Yg
Keller, Gerta, 609-258-4117 gkeller@princeton.edu, Princeton Univ; Pm
Keller, Jean, (845) 938-4185 United States Military Academy; Zn
Keller, John E., 702-651-5887 john.keller@csn.edu, Coll of Southern Nevada - West Charleston Campus; GeHw
Keller, Klaus, (814) 865-6718 kkeller@geosc.psu.edu, Pennsylvania State Univ, Univ Park; Og
Keller, Linda M., (608) 265-2209 lmkeller@wisc.edu, Univ of Wisconsin, Madison; As
Keller, Randall A., 541-737-7648 kellerr@geo.oregonstate.edu, Oregon State Univ; Gu
Keller, Troy, 706-507-8099 keller_troy@columbusstate.edu, Columbus State Univ; RwZc
Keller, Jr., C. F., (505) 667-0920 cfk@lanl.gov, Los Alamos; As
Kelley, Alice R., (207) 581-2056 akelley@maine.edu, Univ of Maine; GalGm
Kelley, Christopher, (808) 956-7437 ckelley@hawaii.edu, Univ of Hawai'i, Manoa; Ob
Kelley, Dan, (902) 494-1694 dan.kelley@dal.ca, Dalhousie Univ; Op
Kelley, Deborah S., (206) 685-9556 dskelley@uw.edu, Univ of Washington; OuGvp
Kelley, Joseph T., (207) 581-2162 jtkelley@maine.edu, Univ of Maine; Gua
Kelley, Neil P., neil.p.kelley@vanderbilt.edu, Vanderbilt Univ; GgOgPg
Kelley, Patricia H., (910) 448-0526 kelleyp@uncw.edu, Univ of North Carolina, Wilmington; Pgi
Kelley, Richard, 505-412-2967 richard.kelley@nmt.edu, New Mexico Inst of Mining and Tech; ZiGg
Kelley, Scott , 775-784-6705 scottkelley@unr.edu, Univ of Nevada, Reno; Zi
Kelley, Shari, 575-835-5306 shari.kelley@nmt.edu, New Mexico Inst of Mining and Tech; Yg
Kelley, Simon, +44 (0)131 650 2537 simon.kelley@ed.ac.uk, Edinburgh Univ; CcsZg
Kelling, Keith A., (608) 263-2795 kkelling@wisc.edu, Univ of Wisconsin, Madison; So
Kellman, Lisa M., (902) 867-5086 lkellman@stfx.ca, Saint Francis Xavier Univ; CsSo
Kellner, Patricia, pakellner@socal.rr.com, Los Angeles Harbor Coll; Zg
Kellogg, James N., (803) 777-4501 kellogg@geol.sc.edu, Univ of South Carolina; Yg
Kelly, Bryce, bryce.kelly@unsw.edu.au, Univ of New South Wales; HwAcGe
Kelly, D. Clay, (608) 262-1698 ckelly@geology.wisc.edu, Univ of Wisconsin, Madison; Pm
Kelly, Jacque L., (912) 478-8677 jkelly@georgiasouthern.edu, Georgia Southern Univ; Cl
Kelly, John, 203-479-4822 jkelly@newhaven.edu, Univ of New Haven; ObZn
Kelly, Kathryn A., (206) 543-9810 kkelly@apl.washington.edu, Univ of Washington; Op
Kelly, Kimberly, (240) 567-5227 kimberly.kelly@montgomerycollege.edu, Montgomery Coll; Zn
Kelly, Maria, (425) 640-1918 mkelly@edcc.edu, Edmonds Comm Coll; Zg
Kelly, Meredith, 603-646-9647 meredith.kelly@dartmouth.edu, Dartmouth Coll; Gl
Kelly, Sherrie, 315-229-5851 skelly@stlawu.edu, St. Lawrence Univ; Zn
Kelly, Walton R., (217) 898-0657 wkelly@illinois.edu, Univ of Illinois; Hw
Kelly, William C., (734) 764-1435 billkell@umich.edu, Univ of Michigan; Eg
Kelsch, Jesse, (432) 837-8657 jkelsch@sulross.edu, Sul Ross State Univ; Gct
Kelsey, Eric, ekelsey2@plymouth.edu, Plymouth State Univ; AtsGl
Kelsey, Harvey M., (707) 826-3991 hmk1@humboldt.edu, Humboldt State Univ; Gmt
Kelso, Paul R., (906) 635-2158 pkelso@lssu.edu, Lake Superior State Univ; YmGct
Kelty, Thomas, (562) 985-4589 t.kelty@csulb.edu, California State Univ, Long Beach; Gc
Kemeny, John M., (520) 621-4448 kemeny@email.arizona.edu, Univ of Arizona; Nr
Kemmerly, Phillip R., (931) 221-7471 kemmerlyp@apsu.edu, Austin Peay State Univ; GmeHg
Kemp, Alan, +44 (0)23 80592788 aesk@noc.soton.ac.uk, Univ of Southampton; Pe
Kemp, Andrew, (617) 627-0869 andrew.kemp@tufts.edu, Tufts Univ; OnPmOg
Kemp, Paul, (808) 956-6220 paulkemp@hawaii.edu, Univ of Hawai'i, Manoa; Ob
Kempton, Pamela D., (785) 532-6724 pkempton@ksu.edu, Kansas State Univ; GiCtc
Kendrick, David C., 315-781-3929 kendrick@hws.edu, Hobart & William Smith Colls; PgGg
Kendrick, Katherine J., (951) 276-4418 kendrick@gps.caltech.edu, Univ of California, Riverside; Gm
Kenduiywo, Benson K., bkenduiywo@jkuat.ac.ke, Jomo Kenyatta Univ of Agriculture & Tech; ZriYd
Kenig, Fabien, (312) 996-3020 fkenig@uic.edu, Univ of Illinois at Chicago; CobOo
Kenna, Timothy, tkenna@ldeo.columbia.edu, Columbia Univ; Cg
Kennedy, Andrew, andrew.b.kennedy.117@nd.edu, Univ of Notre Dame; On
Kennedy, Ann C., (509) 335-1554 akennedy@wsu.edu, Washington State Univ; Sb
Kennedy, Ben, +64 3 3667001 Ext 7775 ben.kennedy@canterbury.ac.nz, Univ of Canterbury; Gv
Kennedy, Christina B., tina.kennedy@nau.edu, Northern Arizona Univ; Zn
Kennedy, Gareth, +44 01326 371876 g.a.kennedy@exeter.ac.uk, Exeter Univ; Nm
Kennedy, Linda, 570-662-4609 lkennedy@mansfield.edu, Mansfield Univ; Zy
Kennedy, Lisa M., (540) 231-1422 kennedy1@vt.edu, Virginia Polytechnic Inst & State Univ; Pe
Kennedy, Lori, (604) 822-1811 lkennedy@eos.ubc.ca, Univ of British Columbia; Gc
Kennedy, Robert, (541) 737-6332 rkennedy@coas.oregonstate.edu, Oregon State Univ; Zri
Kennel, Charles F., (310) 825-4018 Univ of California, Los Angeles; Zn
Kenney, Robert D., (401) 874-6664 rkenney@uri.edu, Univ of Rhode Island; Ob
Kenny, Ray, (970) 247-7462 kenny_r@fortlewis.edu, Fort Lewis Coll; Gm
Kent, Adam J., (541) 737-1205 adam.kent@geo.oregonstate.edu, Oregon State Univ; GiCga
Kent, Dennis V., 848-445-7049 dvk@rutgers.edu, Rutgers, The State Univ of New Jersey; YmZcGr
Kent, Douglas, 405-377-0166 Oklahoma State Univ; Hw
Kent, Graham, (775) 784-4977 gkent@seismo.unr.edu, Univ of Nevada, Reno; Ys
Kenyon, Patricia M., (212) 650-6472 City Coll (CUNY); Yg
Kepic, Anton W., +61 8 9266-7503 a.kepic@curtin.edu.au, Curtin Univ; YexYg
Keppie, J. Duncan, 56224303 duncan@servidor.unam.mx, Univ Nacional Autonoma de Mexico; Gt
Keranen, Katie M., kmk299@cornell.edu, Cornell Univ; Ys
Kerans, Charles, (512) 471-1368 charles.kerans@beg.utexas.edu, Univ of Texas at Austin, Jackson Sch of Geosciences; Gd

Kerestedjian, Thomas N., +359 2 979 2244 thomas@geology.bas.bg, Bulgarian Academy of Scis; GzeEg
Kern, Anikó, anikoc@nimbus.elte.hu, Eotvos Lorand Univ; ZrAms
Kern, J. Philip, jphilipkern@gmail.com, San Diego State Univ; Pg
Kerp, Hans, +49-251-83-23966 kerp@uni-muenster.de, Univ Muenster; PblGg
Kerr, A C., kerra@cf.ac.uk, Cardiff Univ; Gxi
Kerr, Andrew, +44(0)29 208 74578 kerra@cardiff.ac.uk, Univ of Wales; Og
Kerr, Dennis R., 918 631 3020 dennis-kerr@utulsa.edu, Univ of Tulsa; GsrGt
Kerrick, Derrill M., (814) 865-7574 kerrick@geosc.psu.edu, Pennsylvania State Univ, Univ Park; Gp
Kertes, Randy, rkertes@rider.edu, Rider Univ; Ge
Kerwin, Charles M., 603.358.2405 ckerwin@keene.edu, Keene State Coll; Gg
Kerwin, Michael W., 303-871-3998 mkerwin@du.edu, Univ of Denver; GgeZc
Kesel, Richard H., (225) 578-5880 gakesel@lsu.edu, Louisiana State Univ; Hg
Keskinen, Mary J., (907) 474-7769 mjkeskinen@alaska.edu, Univ of Alaska, Fairbanks; Gxz
Kesler, Stephen E., (734) 763-5057 skesler@umich.edu, Univ of Michigan; Eg
Kessler, Carsten, hello@carsten.io, Graduate Sch of the City Univ of New York; Gg
Kessler, Fritz, (301) 687-4266 fkessler@frostburg.edu, Frostburg State Univ; Zr
Kessler, John , 585-273-4572 john.kessler@rochester.edu, Univ of Rochester; Oc
Kessler, William S., (206) 526-6221 kessler@pmel.noaa.gov, Univ of Washington; Op
Ketcham, Richard A., (512) 471-6942 ketcham@jsg.utexas.edu, Univ of Texas, Austin; GgCc
Kettler, Richard M., (402) 472-0882 rkettler1@unl.edu, Univ of Nebraska, Lincoln; Cl
Kevan, Peter, pkevan@uoguelph.ca, Univ of Guelph; Zn
Key, Doug, 7607441150 ext.2515 dkey@palomar.edu, Palomar Coll; Zy
Key, Jeffrey R., (608) 263-2605 jkey@ssec.wisc.edu, Univ of Wisconsin, Madison; ZrAs
Key, Jr., Marcus M., (717) 245-1448 key@dickinson.edu, Dickinson Coll; PiGsa
Keyantash, John, (310) 243-2363 jkeyantash@csudh.edu, California State Univ, Dominguez Hills; HgAsZe
Keyser, Daniel, (518) 442-4559 dkeyser@albany.edu, SUNY, Albany; As
Khade, Vishnu R., khadev@easternct.edu, Eastern Connecticut State Univ; Zg
Khairoutdinov, Marat, (631) 632-6339 marat.khairoutdinov@stonybrook.edu, SUNY, Stony Brook; As
Khalequzzaman, Md., (570) 484-2075 mkhalequ@lockhaven.edu, Lock Haven Univ; HwOnZi
Khalil, Mohamed, 406-496-4716 mkhalil@mtech.edu, Montana Tech of the Univ of Montana; YeuGe
Khalil Ebeid, Khalil I., 01227431425 kebeid@yahoo.com, Alexandria Univ; GgEmm
Khan, Belayet H., 217-581-2626 bhkhan@eiu.edu, Eastern Illinois Univ; Zy
Khan, Latif A., 217-244-2383 info@isgs.illinois.edu, Illinois State Geological Survey; Nx
Khan, Mohammad Wahdat Y., (982) 719-7331 mwykhan@rediffmail.com, Pt. Ravishankar Shukla Univ; GdEgCl
Khan, Shuhab D., (713) 743-5404 sdkhan@uh.edu, Univ of Houston; ZrGtYg
Khanbilvardi, Reza M., 212-650-8009 khanbilvardi@ccny.cuny.edu, Graduate Sch of the City Univ of New York; Hy
Khandaker, Nazrul I., (718) 262-2079 nkhandaker@york.cuny.edu, York Coll (CUNY); GdeZe
Khandaker, Nazul, 781-262-2079 nkhandaker@york.cuny.edu, Graduate Sch of the City Univ of New York; Gg
Khawaja, Ikram U., john@cis.ysu.edu, Youngstown State Univ; Ec
Khurana, Krishan, (310) 825-8240 Univ of California, Los Angeles; Zn
Kiage, Lawrence M., (404) 413-5777 geolkk@langate.gsu.edu, Georgia State Univ; ZyPlZr
Kidd, David, +44 020 8417 62541 david.kidd@kingston.ac.uk, Kingston Univ; Ziy
Kidd, Karen, 905-525-9140 (Ext. 23550) karenkidd@mcmaster.ca, McMaster Univ; Gu
Kidder, Steven, 212-650-8431 skidder@ccny.cuny.edu, Graduate Sch of the City Univ of New York; As
Kidder, T.R., trkidder@wustl.edu, Washington Univ in St. Louis; Zn
Kidwell, Jen, (650) 723-0891 jparis@stanford.edu, Stanford Univ; Zn
Kidwell, Susan M., (773) 702-3008 skidwell@uchicago.edu, Univ of Chicago; GsPe
Kieffer, Bruno, bkieffer@eos.ubc.ca, Univ of British Columbia; Cs
Kieffer, Susan W., (217) 244-6206 skieffer@illinois.edu, Univ of Illinois, Urbana-Champaign; Gv
Kienast, Markus, (902) 494-8338 markus.kienast@dal.ca, Dalhousie Univ; Cs
Kienast, Stephanie, (902) 494-2203 stephanie.kienast@dal.ca, Dalhousie Univ; Gu
Kiene, Ronald P., (251) 861-7526 rkiene@jaguar1.usouthal.edu, Univ of South Alabama; Oc
Kientop, Greg A., 217-265-6581 gkientop@illinois.edu, Illinois State Geological Survey; Ge
Kienzle, Stefan, stefan.kienzle@uleth.ca, Univ of Lethbridge; Zi
Kierczak, Jakub, jakub.kierczak@uwr.edu.pl, Univ of Wroclaw; GeSc
Kiesel, Diann, (608) 355-5223 diann.kiesel@uwc.edu, Univ of Wisconsin Colls; GgZyGg
Kieu, Chanh Q., (812) 856-5704 ckieu@indiana.edu, Indiana Univ, Bloomington; As
Kifer, Lauri A., (585) 395-2636 lmulley@brockport.edu, SUNY, The Coll at Brockport; Zn
Kift, Richard, +44 0161 306-8770 richard.kift@manchester.ac.uk, Univ of Manchester; As
Kijko, Andrzej, +27 12 420 3613 andrzej.kijko@up.ac.za, Univ of Pretoria; YsgNe
Kilburn, Chris, +44 020 7679 37194 c.kilburn@ucl.ac.uk, Univ Coll London; Yx
Kilcoyne, John R., (303) 556-4258 Metropolitan State Coll of Denver; Zy
Kile, Susan, 217-581-2626 skkile@eiu.edu, Eastern Illinois Univ; Zn
Kilibarda, Zoran, (219) 980-6753 zkilibar@iun.edu, Indiana Univ Northwest; GsmGd
Kilic, Ayse Didem, 00904242370000-5969 adkilic@firat.edu.tr, Firat Univ; GxpGy
Kilinc, Attila I., (513) 556-5967 attila.kilinc@uc.edu, Univ of Cincinnati; CpGvCu
Killorn, Randy J., (515) 294-1923 rkillorn@iastate.edu, Iowa State Univ of Sci & Tech; So
Kilroy, Kathyrn, 701-858-3114 kathryn.kilroy@minotstateu.edu, Minot State Univ; Hg
Kim, Bojeong, 215-204-3304 bkim@temple.edu, Temple Univ; GzZa
Kim, Daehyun, (206) 221-8935 daehyun@atmos.washington.edu, Univ of Washington; As
Kim, Eunhye, 303-273-3428 ekim1@mines.edu, Colorado Sch of Mines; NrnNt
Kim, Hyemi, (404) 894-1738 hyemi.kim@eas.gatech.edu, Georgia Inst of Tech; As
Kim, Hyewon (Heather), hkim@whoi.edu, Woods Hole Oceanographic Inst; Cm
Kim, Jonathan, (802) 522-5401 jon.kim@vermont.gov, Agency of Natural Resources, Dept of Environmental Conservation; GetCg
Kim, Keonho, 432-685-4739 kkim@midland.edu, Midland Coll; GgAmPi
Kim, Kwangmin, kimkm@email.arizona.edu, Univ of Arizona; NmrNx
Kim, Saewung, (949)824-4531 saewungk@uci.edu, Univ of California, Irvine; As
Kim, Sang-Tae, (905) 525-9140 (Ext. 26494) sangtae@mcmaster.ca, McMaster Univ; Cg
Kim, Stacy, 831-771-4400 skim@mlml.calstate.edu, Moss Landing Marine Lab; Zn
Kim, Wan, (202) 478-8871 wkim@carnegiescience.edu, Carnegie Inst for Sci; Zn
Kim, Won-Young, wykim@ldeo.columbia.edu, Columbia Univ; Ys
Kim, Yong Hoon, (610) 436-2203 ykim@wcupa.edu, West Chester Univ; OgZr
Kim, Yongsang (Barry), (671) 735-1223 kimys@triton.uog.edu, Univ of Guam; Hw
Kimball, Matthew, matt@belle.baruch.sc.edu, Univ of South Carolina; Ob
Kimball, Sytske K., skimball@southalabama.edu, Univ of South Alabama; Am
Kimber, Clarissa T., (409) 845-7141 Texas A&M Univ; Zy
Kimberly, Shaw, 706-507-8344 Columbus State Univ; Zn
Kimbro, David, 7815817370 x310 d.kimbro@neu.edu, Northeastern Univ; Zn
Kimbrough, David L., (619) 594-1385 dkimbrough@mail.sdsu.edu, San Diego State Univ; Cc
Kimerling, A. Jon, kimerlia@geo.oregonstate.edu, Oregon State Univ; Zir
Kinabo, Crispin P., kinabo_2003@yahoo.co.uk, Univ of Dar es Salaam; NxGe
Kincaid, Christopher, (401) 874-6571 kincaid@gso.uri.edu, Univ of Rhode Island; Ou
Kineke, Gail C., (617) 552-3655 gail.kineke.1@bc.edu, Boston Coll; On

Knepp, Rex A., 217-244-2422 knepp@isgs.uiuc.edu, Illinois State Geological Survey; Go
Knesel, Kurt, 210-999-7606 kknesel@trinity.edu, Trinity Univ; Gvi
Knight, Andi, 575-835-5594 andi.knight@nmt.edu, New Mexico Inst of Mining and Tech; Zi
Knight, David, (518) 442-4204 knight@atmos.albany.edu, SUNY, Albany; As
Knight, Rosemary J., (650) 723-4746 Stanford Univ; Hy
Knight, Tiffany, tknight@biology2.wustl.edu, Washington Univ in St. Louis; Pe
Knittle, Elise, (831) 459-4949 eknittle@pmc.ucsc.edu, Univ of California, Santa Cruz; Gy
Knizek, Martin, +420 549 49 6298 kniza@sci.muni.cz, Masaryk Univ; NgmNr
Knoll, Andrew H., (617) 495-9306 aknoll@harvard.edu, Harvard Univ; Pb
Knoll, Martin A., (931) 598-1713 mknoll@sewanee.edu, Sewanee: Univ of the South; Hw
Knopf, Daniel A., (631) 632-3092 daniel.knopf@stonybrook.edu, SUNY, Stony Brook; As
Knopoff, Leon, (310) 825-1885 knopoff@physics.ucla.edu, Univ of California, Los Angeles; Ys
Knott, Jeffrey R., (657) 278-5547 jknott@fullerton.edu, California State Univ, Fullerton; Gmg
Knowles, Charles E., (919) 515-3700 ernie_knowles@ncsu.edu, North Carolina State Univ; Op
Knox, Larry W., (931) 372-3523 lknox@tntech.edu, Tennessee Tech Univ; Pmg
Knudsen, Andrew, (920) 832-6731 knudsena@lawrence.edu, Lawrence Univ; CgGez
Knudsen, Guy, gknudsen@uidaho.edu, Univ of Idaho; Sb
Knudsen, Tyler R., (435) 865-9036 tylerknudsen@utah.gov, Utah Geological Survey; Ng
Knudstrup, Renee, rknudstrup@salemstate.edu, Salem State Univ; Ca
Knuepfer, Peter L. K., (607) 777-2389 Binghamton Univ; Gt
Knutson, Heather, 626.395.4268 hknutson@caltech.edu, California Inst of Tech; Xg
Kobara, Shinichi, 979 845 4089 shinichi@tamu.edu, Texas A&M Univ; Zi
Kobs-Nawotniak, Shannon E., (208) 282-3365 kobsshan@isu.edu, Idaho State Univ; Gv
Koc Tasgin, Calibe, 00904242370000-5976 calibekoc@firat.edu.tr, Firat Univ; GsdGg
Koch, Joe, (803) 896-4167 kochj@dnr.sc.gov, South Carolina Dept of Natural Resources; Zg
Koch, Magaly, mkoch@bu.edu, Boston Univ; HyZri
Koch, Paul L., (831) 459-5861 pkoch@pmc.ucsc.edu, Univ of California, Santa Cruz; Pv
Kochel, R. Craig, (570) 577-3032 kochel@bucknell.edu, Bucknell Univ; Gm
Kocurek, Gary A., (512) 471-5855 garyk@mail.utexas.edu, Univ of Texas, Austin; Gs
Kocurko, John, 940-397-4250 Midwestern State Univ; Gs
Kodama, Kenneth P., (610) 758-3663 kpk0@lehigh.edu, Lehigh Univ; Ym
Kodosky, Larry, 248-232-4538 lgkodosk@oaklandcc.edu, Oakland Comm Coll; GgvEg
Koehl, Mimi A. R., (510) 642-8103 Univ of California, Berkeley; Pg
Koehler, Rich, (775) 682-8763 rkoehler@unr.edu, Univ of Nevada, Reno; GmtNg
Koehler, Thomas , (719) 333-8712 thomas.koehler@usafa.edu, United States Air Force Academy; As
Koehn, Daniel, daniel.koehn@glasgow.ac.uk, Univ of Glasgow; Gt
Koellemeijer, Paula, paula.koelemeijer@rhul.ac.uk, Royal Holloway Univ of London; Ys
Koeman-Shields, Elizabeth, 325-486-6767 elizabeth.koeman-shields@angelo.edu, Angelo State Univ; CgXg
Koenig, Brian, bkoenig@collegeofthedesert.edu, Coll of the Desert; Gge
Koffman, Bess, bkoffman@colby.edu, Colby Coll; PcClZc
Kogan, Mikhail, (845) 365-8882 kogan@ldeo.columbia.edu, Columbia Univ; Yd
Kohler, Jeffery L., 814-865-9834 jk9@psu.edu, Pennsylvania State Univ, Univ Park; Nm
Kohler, Nicholas, (541) 346-4160 nicholas@uoregon.edu, Univ of Oregon; Zi
Kohlstedt, David L., (612) 626-1544 dlkohl@umn.edu, Univ of Minnesota, Twin Cities; YxGzi
Kohlstedt, Sally G., 612-624-9368 sgk@umn.edu, Univ of Minnesota, Twin Cities; Rh
Kohn, Matthew, mattkohn@boisestate.edu, Boise State Univ; CsGpPv
Kohrt, Casey, casey.kohrt@dnr.iowa.gov, Iowa Dept of Natural Resources; GgZi
Kok, Jasper F., jfkok@ucla.edu, Univ of Tennessee, Knoxville; Ap
Kokelaar, Peter, p.kokelaar@liverpool.ac.uk, Univ of Liverpool; GstGv
Kokum, Mehmet, 00904242370000-5963 mkokum@firat.edu.tr, Firat Univ; GtcGg
Kolawole, Lanre L., +2348032277598 llkolawole@lautech.edu.ng, Ladoke Akintola Univ of Tech; GeeGe
Kolesar, Peter T., peter.t.kolesar@gmail.com, Utah State Univ; Cg
Koleszar, Alison, (315) 228-7835 Colgate Univ; GviCu
Kolka, Randall K., (218) 326-7100 Univ of Minnesota, Twin Cities; So
Kolkas, Mosbah, mossbah.kolkas@csi.cuny.edu, Coll of Staten Island/CUNY; Gg
Kollasch, Pete, pete.kollasch@dnr.iowa.gov, Iowa Dept of Natural Resources; GgZri
Kollias, Pavlos, 514-398-1500 pavlos.kollias@stonybrook.edu, McGill Univ; ZrAs
Kolzenburg, Stephan, (716) 645-3489 stephank@buffalo.edu, SUNY, Buffalo; Gv
Komabayashi, Tetsuya, +44 (0) 131 650 8518 tetsuya.komabayashi@ed.ac.uk, Edinburgh Univ; Gz
Komarneni, Sridhar, (814) 865-1542 komarneni@psu.edu, Pennsylvania State Univ, Univ Park; Sc
Kominz, Michelle A., (269) 387-5340 michelle.kominz@wmich.edu, Western Michigan Univ; OuYgGu
Komoto, Cary, 952-358-9007 cary.komoto@normandale.edu, Normandale Comm Coll; ZnnZn
Konecky, Bronwen L., (415) 420-8083 bronwen.konecky@colorado.edu, Washington Univ in St. Louis; PcGn
Konhauser, Kurt, 780-492-2571 kurtk@ualberta.ca, Univ of Alberta; Pg
Koning, Daniel, 575-835-6950 dan.koning@nmt.edu, New Mexico Inst of Mining and Tech; GsRnGm
Konishi, Takuya, 513-556-9726 konishta@ucmail.uc.edu, Cincinnati Mus Center; Pv
Kontak, Daniel J., 7056751151 x2352 dkontak@laurentian.ca, Laurentian Univ, Sudbury; Eg
Konter, Jasper G., 808-956-8705 jkonter@hawaii.edu, Univ of Hawai'i, Manoa; CcGiCt
Kontuly, Thomas M., (801) 581-8218 thomas.kontuly@geog.utah.edu, Univ of Utah; Zn
Koons, Peter O., (207)-581-2158 peter.koons@maine.edu, Univ of Maine; Gt
Koornneef, Janne, +31 20 59 81824 j.m.koornneef@vu.nl, Vrije Universiteit Amsterdam; GvCa
Kooyman, Gerald L., (858) 534-2091 gkooyman@ucsd.edu, Univ of California, San Diego; Ob
Kopaska-Merkel, David C., (205) 247-3695 davidkm@gsa.state.al.us, Geological Survey of Alabama; GsPiZe
Kopf, Christopher F., (570) 662-4615 ckopf@mansfield.edu, Mansfield Univ; Gcp
Kopp, Robert E., (732) 200-2705 robert.kopp@rutgers.edu, Rutgers, The State Univ of New Jersey; ZcOoZg
Koppers, Anthony, 541-737-5425 akoppers@coas.oregonstate.edu, Oregon State Univ; CgGv
Kopylova, Maya G., (604) 822-0865 mkopylova@eos.ubc.ca, Univ of British Columbia; Gi
Koralek, Susan, koralek@sou.edu, Southern Oregon Univ; Zn
Korenaga, Jun, (203) 432-7381 jun.korenaga@yale.edu, Yale Univ; YgsCg
Koretsky, Carla, (269) 387-4372 carla.koretsky@wmich.edu, Western Michigan Univ; CglHs
Kori, E., +27 15 962 8565 edmore.kori@univen.ac.za, Univ of Venda; GmZgAt
Kornreich Wolf, Susan, (309) 794-7369 susanwolf@augustana.edu, Augustana Coll; Ze
Korose, Christopher P., 217-333-7256 korose@illinois.edu, Illinois State Geological Survey; Ec
Korotev, Randy L., (314) 935-5637 korotev@wustl.edu, Washington Univ in St. Louis; XgCtXm
Korre, Anna, +44 20 759 47372 a.korre@imperial.ac.uk, Imperial Coll; Ng
Korths, Patrick, 518-564-2028 pkort001@plattsburgh.edu, SUNY, Plattsburgh; RwGg
Korty, Robert, 979-847-9090 korty@tamu.edu, Texas A&M Univ; As
Kortz, Karen M., kkortz@ccri.edu, Comm Coll of Rhode Island; ZeGg
Korus, Jesse, (402)472-7561 jkorus3@unl.edu, Univ of Nebraska, Lincoln; Gs
Korycansky, Don, (831) 459-5843 Univ of California, Santa Cruz; Xc
Koskinen, William C., (612) 625-4276 koskinen@soils.umn.edu, Univ of Minnesota, Twin Cities; Sc
Kosloski, Mary, (319) 335-0893 mary-kosloski@uiowa.edu, Univ of Iowa; Pig
Kosro, Michael, (541) 737-3079 kosro@coas.oregonstate.edu, Oregon State Univ; OpZrOn
Kossin, James, 608-265-5356 kossin@ssec.wisc.edu, Univ of Wisconsin,

Madison; As
Kostelnick, John, 309-438-7679 jckoste@ilstu.edu, Illinois State Univ; Zi
Koster Van Groos, August F., (312) 996-8678 kvg@uic.edu, Univ of Illinois at Chicago; Cp
Kostov, Svilen, 229-931-2321 skostov@gsw.edu, Georgia Southwestern State Univ; Zn
Kota, Jozsef, (520) 621-4396 kota@lpl.arizona.edu, Univ of Arizona; As
Kotamarthi, Rao, 630-252-7164 vrkotamarthi@anl.gov, Argonne; As
Koteas, G. Christopher, 802 485 3321 gkoteas@norwich.edu, Norwich Univ; GitYh
Kotha, Mahender, +91-832-6519329 mkotha@unigoa.ac.in, Goa Univ; GsoZi
Kotulova, Julia, jkotulova@egi.utah.edu, Univ of Utah; CoGo
Koutavas, Athanasios, 718-932-2524 koutavas@mail.csi.cuny.edu, Graduate Sch of the City Univ of New York; Gg
Koutitonsky, Vladimir G., (418) 724-1986 (Ext. 1763) vgk@uqar.qc.ca, Universite du Quebec a Rimouski; Op
Koutnik, Michelle, 206-221-5041 mkoutnik@uw.edu, Univ of Washington; Gll
Kovac, Michal, +421260296555 kovacm@uniba.sk, Comenius Univ in Bratislava; Gsg
Kovach, Richard G., (702) 295-6180 rkovach@lanl.gov, Los Alamos; Nm
Kovach, Robert L., (650) 723-4827 Stanford Univ; Ys
Kovácová, Marianna, marianna.kovacova@uniba.sk, Comenius Univ in Bratislava; PlcPe
Kovaèiæ, Marijan, +38514605963 mkovacic@geol.pmf.hr, Univ of Zagreb; GsdGx
Kowalewski, Douglas E., 508-929-8646 douglas.kowalewski@worcester.edu, Worcester State Univ; GmlZy
Kowalke, Thorsten, 089/2180 6733 t.kowalke@lrz.uni-muenchen.de, Ludwig-Maximilians-Univ Muenchen; Pg
Kowallis, Bart J., (801) 422-2467 bkowallis@byu.edu, Brigham Young Univ; GgCcGz
Kozak, Amanda L., akozak@ashland.edu, Ashland Univ; Rn
Kozdon, Reinhard, rkozdon@ldeo.columbia.edu, Columbia Univ; PgGg
Koziol, Andrea M., (937) 229-2954 andrea.koziol@notes.udayton.edu, Univ of Dayton; Cp
Kozlowski, Andrew, 518 486-2012 akozlows@mail.nysed.gov, New York State Geological Survey; Gl
Kraal, Erin, 484-646-5859 kraal@kutztown.edu, Kutztown Univ of Pennsylvania; XgGm
Krabbenhoft, David, (608) 821-3843 dpkrabbe@usgs.gov, Univ of Wisconsin, Madison; ClGeHw
Kraemer, George P., 914-251-6640 george.kraemer@purchase.edu, SUNY, Purchase; ObnCm
Kraft, Kaatje, (360) 383-3539 kkraft@whatcom.ctc.edu, Whatcom Comm Coll; Gg
Krakauer, Nir, 212-650-8009 nir@sci.ccny.cuny.edu, Graduate Sch of the City Univ of New York; Gg
Kramer, J. Curtis, (209) 946-2482 ckramer@pacific.edu, Univ of the Pacific; Gg
Kramer, James R., kramer@mcmaster.ca, McMaster Univ; Cl
Kramer, Kate, (815) 479-7877 kkramer@mchenry.edu, McHenry County Coll; GgZg
Kramer, Marc, 352-294-3165 mgkramer@ufl.edu, Univ of Florida; So
Kramer, Walter V., (361) 698-1385 wkramer@delmar.edu, Del Mar Coll; GgoGx
Krantz, David E., (419) 530-2662 david.krantz@utoledo.edu, Univ of Toledo; Gs
Kranz, Dwight S., (713) 718-5641 dwight.kranz@hccs.edu, Houston Comm Coll System; Gg
Krapac, Ivan G., 217-333-6442 krapac@isgs.uiuc.edu, Illinois State Geological Survey; Ca
Krastel, Sebastian , skrastel@geophysik.uni-kiel.de, Dalhousie Univ; Yr
Kraus, Mary J., 303-492-7251 mary.kraus@colorado.edu, Univ of Colorado; GsSa
Krause, Federico F., (403) 220-5845 fkrause@ucalgary.ca, Univ of Calgary; GsdGo
Krause, Lois B., (864) 656-7653 Clemson Univ; Ze
Krause, Samantha, (512) 245-2170 Texas State Univ; ScHyZc
Kravchinsky, Vadim, (780) 492-5591 vkrav@phys.ualberta.ca, Univ of Alberta; Ym
Kravitz, Ben, (812) 855-4334 bkravitz@iu.edu, Indiana Univ, Bloomington; At
Krawczynski, Michael J., 314-935-6328 mikekraw@levee.wustl.edu, Washington Univ in St. Louis; Cg
Kreamer, David, 702.895.3553 dave.kreamer@unlv.edu, Univ of Nevada, Reno; HwGn
Krebes, Edward S., (403) 220-5028 Univ of Calgary; Ys
Kreemer, Corne, (775) 682-8780 kreemer@unr.edu, Univ of Nevada, Reno; Yd
Kreidenweis, Sonia M., sonia@atmos.colostate.edu, Colorado State Univ; As
Kreiger, William (Bill), (717) 815-1379 wkreiger@ycp.edu, York Coll of Pennsylvania; GisZg
Krekeler, Mark, 513-785-3106 krekelmp@miamioh.edu, Miami Univ; Ge
Kremer, Robert J., 573-882-6408 Univ of Missouri; Sb
Kressler, Sharon J., 612-625-5068 kress004@umn.edu, Univ of Minnesota, Twin Cities; Zn
Kretzschmar, Thomas, tkretzsc@cicese.mx, Centro de Investigación Científica y de Educación Superior de Ensenada; Ge
Kreutz, Karl J., (207)-581-3011 karl.kreutz@maine.edu, Univ of Maine; Cs
Krevor, Samuel, s.krevor@imperial.ac.uk, Imperial Coll; Eo
Kreylos, Oliver, okreylos@ucdavis.edu, Univ of California, Davis; Ng
Krieble, Kelly, (610) 861-1437 krieblek@moravian.edu, Moravian Coll; ZnnZn
Krieger-Brockett, Barbara B., (206) 543-2216 krieger@cheme.washington.edu, Univ of Washington; Ob
Krier, Donathon J., (505) 665-7834 krier@lanl.gov, Los Alamos; Gv
Kring, David, (281) 486-2119 kring@lpi.usra.edu, Univ of Arizona; XcGiXg
Krishnamurthy, R. V., (269) 387-5501 r.v.krishnamurthy@wmich.edu, Western Michigan Univ; Cs
Krishnamurthy, sukanya, sukanya.krishnamurthy@ed.ac.uk, Edinburgh Univ; Zn
Krishtalka, Leonard, (785) 864-4540 krishtalka@ku.edu, Univ of Kansas; Pv
Krissek, Lawrence A., (614) 292-1924 krissek.1@osu.edu, Ohio State Univ; Gsu
Krockover, Gerald H., (765) 494-5795 hawk1@purdue.edu, Purdue Univ; Ze
Kroeger, Glenn C., (210) 999-7607 gkroeger@trinity.edu, Trinity Univ; Yg
Krohe, Nicholas J., 605-677-3923 nick.krohe@usd.edu, South Dakota Dept of Environment and Natural Resources; Gg
Krohn, James P., krohnjp@piercecollege.edu, Los Angeles Pierce Coll; NgGg
Krol, Michael A., mkrol@bridgew.edu, Bridgewater State Univ; GzxGt
Kronenberg, Andreas, (979) 845-0132 a-kronenberg@geos.tamu.edu, Texas A&M Univ; GtyGc
Kronenfeld, Barry J., (217) 581-7014 bjkronenfeld@eiu.edu, Eastern Illinois Univ; Zi
Kroon, Dick, +44 (0) 131 651 7089 d.kroon@ed.ac.uk, Edinburgh Univ; Gg
Krot, Alexander N., 808-956-3900 sasha@higp.hawaii.edu, Univ of Hawai'i, Manoa; Xm
Kruckenberg, Seth, 617-552-8300 seth.kruckenberg@bc.edu, Boston Coll; Gc
Krueger, Steven, 801-581-3903 steve.krueger@utah.edu, Univ of Utah; As
Kruge, Michael A., 973-655-7668 krugem@mail.montclair.edu, Montclair State Univ; Co
Kruger, Joseph M., (409) 880-8233 joseph.kruger@lamar.edu, Lamar Univ; YgGgZi
Kruger, Ned , ekadrmas@nd.gov, North Dakota Geological Survey; Gg
Krugh, W C., 661-654-3126 wkrugh@csub.edu, California State Univ, Bakersfield; GcmCc
Krukowski, Stanley T., 405-325-3031 skrukowski@ou.edu, Univ of Oklahoma; En
Krupka, Kenneth M., (509) 376-4412 ken.krupka@pnl.gov, Pacific Northwest; Cl
Kruse, Jennifer, (507) 933-7333 jkruse@gustavus.edu, Gustavus Adolphus Coll; Zn
Kruse, Sarah E., skruse@usf.edu, Univ of South Florida; Yg
Krygier, John B., (740) 368-3622 jbkrygie@owu.edu, Ohio Wesleyan Univ; Zi
Krzic, Maja, 604-822-0252 maja.krzic@ubc.ca, Univ of British Columbia; Sf
Ku, Teh-Lung, (213) 740-5826 rku@usc.edu, Univ of Southern California; CgcGn
Ku, Timothy C., (860)685-2265 tcku@wesleyan.edu, Wesleyan Univ; Cl
Kuang, Zhiming, 617-495-2354 kuang@eps.harvard.edu, Harvard Univ; As
Kubas, Gregory J., (505) 667-5846 Los Alamos; As
Kubesh, Rodney, 320-308-4217 rjkubesh@stcloudstate.edu, Saint Cloud State Univ; Am
Kubicki, James D., 915-747-5501 Univ of Texas, El Paso; ClGe
Kucharik, Chris, 608-890-3021 kucharik@wisc.edu, Univ of Wisconsin, Madison; As
Kuchovsky, Tomas, +420 549 49 5452 tomas@sci.muni.cz, Masaryk Univ; Hgy
Kuchta, Mark, (303) 273-3306 mkuchta@mines.edu, Colorado Sch of Mines; Nm
Kudela, Raphael M., (831) 459-3290 kudela@cats.ucsc.edu, Univ of California, Santa Cruz; Zr
Kudlac, John J., (412) 392-3423 Point Park Univ; Ng

Kuehl, Steven A., (804) 684-7118 kuehl@vims.edu, William & Mary; Ou
Kuehn, Stephen C., 304-384-6322 sckuehn@concord.edu, Concord Univ; CaGv
Kuehner, Scott, 206-543-8393 kuehner@uw.edu, Univ of Washington; Ggz
Kuentz, David C., (513) 529-5992 kuentzdc@miamioh.edu, Miami Univ; Ca
Kues, Barry S., (505) 277-3626 bkues@unm.edu, Univ of New Mexico; Pi
Kuhlman, Robert, rkuhlman@mc3.edu, Montgomery County Comm Coll; Gg
Kuhnhenn, Gary L., (859) 622-8140 gary.kuhnhenn@eku.edu, Eastern Kentucky Univ; GgZe
Kuiper, Klaudia, k.f.kuiper@vu.nl, Vrije Universiteit Amsterdam; Cc
Kuiper, Yvette D., 303-273-3105 ykuiper@mines.edu, Colorado Sch of Mines; Gc
Kujawinski, Elizabeth B., (508) 289-3493 ekujawinski@whoi.edu, Woods Hole Oceanographic Inst; Oc
Kukoè, Duje, +38514606111 duje.kukoc@geol.pmf.hr, Univ of Zagreb; Gg
Kukowski, Nina, 0049(0)3641/948680 nina.kukowski@uni-jena.de, Friedrich-Schiller-Univ Jena; Ygx
Kulander, Byron, byron.kulander@wright.edu, Wright State Univ; Gc
Kulkarni, Shrinivas R., (626) 395-4010 srk@astro.caltech.edu, California Inst of Tech; Xa
Kullberg, Carla , ckullberg@fc.ul.pt, Unive de Lisboa; Gt
Kulp, Mark A., (504) 280-1170 mkulp@uno.edu, Univ of New Orleans; GrmGs
Kulp, Thomas, tkulp@binghamton.edu, Binghamton Univ; Pg
Kumar, Ajoy, (717) 871-2432 ajoy.kumar@millersville.edu, Millersville Univ; OpZr
Kumar, M. Satish, +442890973479 s.kumar@qub.ac.uk, Queen's Univ Belfast; ZnnZn
Kumjian, Matthew R., 814-863-1581 kumjian@psu.edu, Pennsylvania State Univ, Univ Park; Am
Kummerow, Christian D., kummerow@atmos.colostate.edu, Colorado State Univ; Yr
Kump, Lee R., (814) 863-1274 lkump@psu.edu, Pennsylvania State Univ, Univ Park; ClPeCm
Kumpan, Tomas, +420 549 49 3314 kumpan@sci.muni.cz, Masaryk Univ; Ps
Kumpf, Amber C., (231) 777-0289 amber.kumpf@muskegoncc.edu, Muskegon Comm Coll; GgYrOu
Kung, Ernest C., 573-882-5909 Univ of Missouri; As
Kung, Hsiang-Te, (901) 678-4538 hkung@memphis.edu, Univ of Memphis; Zy
Kung, King-Jau S., (608) 262-6530 kskung@wisc.edu, Univ of Wisconsin, Madison; Sp
Kunkle, Thomas D., (505) 667-1259 Los Alamos; Xy
Kuntz, Kara, (785) 628-5804 kkuntz@fhsu.edu, Fort Hays State Univ; Zn
Kuntz, Mark R., (847) 697-1000 mkuntz@elgin.edu, Elgin Comm Coll; Gg
Kunza, Lisa, (605) 394-2449 lisa.kunza@sdsmt.edu, South Dakota Sch of Mines & Tech; HsZe
Kunzmann, Thomas, 089/2180 4292 kunzmann@min.uni-muenchen.de, Ludwig-Maximilians-Univ Muenchen; Gz
Kuo, Shiou, (206) 840-4573 skuo@wsu.edu, Washington State Univ; Sc
Kuperman, William A., (858) 534-3158 wkuperman@ucsd.edu, Univ of California, San Diego; Op
Kurapov, Alexander, 541-737-2865 kurapov@coas.oregonstate.edu, Oregon State Univ; Yr
Kursinski, Robert, (520) 626-3338 kursinsk@atmo.arizona.edu, Univ of Arizona; As
Kurtanjek, Dražen, +38514605965 dkurtan@inet.hr, Univ of Zagreb; GsdGg
Kurttas, Turker, +90-312-2977760 kurttast@gmail.com, Hacettepe Univ; HwgZr
Kurtz, Andrew, kurtz@bu.edu, Boston Univ; Clg
Kurtz, Vincent E., (417) 836-5801 Missouri State Univ; Ps
Kurum, Sevcan, 00904242370000-5992 skurum@firat.edu.tr, Firat Univ; GivGx
Kurz, Marie J., mk3483@drexel.edu, Drexel Univ; CqbHw
Kurz, Mark D., (508) 289-2888 mkurz@whoi.edu, Woods Hole Oceanographic Inst; Cc
Kushnir, Yochanan, kushnir@ldeo.columbia.edu, Columbia Univ; As
Kusnick, Judith E., (916) 278-4692 Sacramento State Univ; Ze
Kusssow, Wayne R., (608) 263-3631 wrkussow@wisc.edu, Univ of Wisconsin, Madison; So
Kustka, Adam B., 973-353-5509 kustka@newark.rutgers.edu, Rutgers, The State Univ of New Jersey, Newark; OgCmHs
Kusumoto, Shigekazu, 81-76-445-6653 kusu@sci.u-toyama.ac.jp, Univ of Toyama; YvdGt
Kusznir, Nick, +44-151-794-5182 n.kusznir@liverpool.ac.uk, Univ of Liverpool; Yd
Kutis, Michael, 765-285-2487 mkutis@bsu.edu, Ball State Univ; Gg
Kutzbach, John E., (608)262-0392 jek@facstaff.wisc.edu, Univ of Wisconsin, Madison; As
Kuwabara, James, 415-452-7776 kuwabara@usgs.gov, City Coll of San Francisco; RwOgCg
Kuzera, Kristopher , 303-871-3378 kristopher.kuzera@du.edu, Univ of Denver; ZyHg
Kuzila, Mark S., (402) 472-7537 mkuzila@unl.edu, Unversity of Nebraska, Lincoln; Sd
Kuzyk, Zou Zou, 204-272-1535 umkuzyk@cc.umanitoba.ca, Univ of Manitoba; Cg
Kvamme, Kenneth L., (617) 353-3415 Boston Univ; Ga
Kwicklis, Edward M., (505) 665-7408 kwicklis@lanl.gov, Los Alamos; Gg
Kwon, Youngsang, 901-678-2979 ykwon@memphis.edu, Univ of Memphis; Zi
Kyle, J. Richard, (512) 471-4351 rkyle@jsg.utexas.edu, Univ of Texas, Austin; EmnCe
Kyle, Philip R., (575) 835-5995 kyle@nmt.edu, New Mexico Inst of Mining and Tech; Giv
Kyriakopoulos, Christodoulos, (901) 678-4830 ckyrkpls@memphis.edu, Univ of Memphis; Yd
Kysar Mattietti, Giuseppina, (703) 993-9269 gkysar@gmu.edu, George Mason Univ; GiZeGa
Kyte, Frank T., (310) 825-2015 kyte@igpp.ucla.edu, Univ of California, Los Angeles; Ct
Käser, Martin, 089/2180 4138 martin.kaeser@geophysik.uni-muenchen.de, Ludwig-Maximilians-Univ Muenchen; Yg
Käsling, Heiko, +49 89 289 25831 heiko.kaesling@tum.de, Technical Univ of Munich; NrmNg

L

L'Ecuyer, Tristan S., 608-262-2828 Univ of Wisconsin, Madison; As
La Berge, Gene L., (920) 424-4460 laberge@uwosh.edu, Univ of Wisconsin, Oshkosh; Eg
La Fave, John I., 406-496-4306 jlafave@mtech.edu, Montana Tech of The Univ of Montana; Hw
Laabs, Benjamin J., (701) 231-6197 benjamin.laabs@ndsu.edu, North Dakota State Univ; GlPcGm
Labandeira, Conrad C., (202) 633-1336 Smithsonian Inst / Nat Mus of Natural History; Pi
LaBella, Joel, (860)685-2242 jlabella@wesleyan.edu, Wesleyan Univ; Zn
Laboski, Carrie A., (608) 263-2795 laboski@wisc.edu, Univ of Wisconsin, Madison; So
Labotka, Theodore C., (865) 974-2366 tlabotka@utk.edu, Univ of Tennessee, Knoxville; GpCg
Labuz, Joseph F., (612) 625-9060 jlabuz@umn.edu, Univ of Minnesota, Twin Cities; Nr
Lachhab, Ahmed, 570-374-4215 lachhab@susqu.edu, Susquehanna Univ; Hw
Lachmar, Thomas E., (435) 797-1247 tom.lachmar@gmail.com, Utah State Univ; Hw
Lachniet, Matthew S., 702-895-4388 matthew.lachniet@unlv.edu, Univ of Nevada, Las Vegas; PeCs
Lackey, Jade Star, (909) 621-8677 jadestar.lackey@pomona.edu, Pomona Coll; GipCs
Lackinger, Markus, 089/2180 Ludwig-Maximilians-Univ Muenchen; Gz
Lackmann, Gary M., 919-515-1439 gary@ncsu.edu, North Carolina State Univ; As
lacy, tor b., (657) 464-0409 torlacy@yahoo.com, Cerritos Coll; GgcGc
LaDochy, Steve, (323) 343-3222 sladoch@calstatela.edu, California State Univ, Los Angeles; Zn
LaDue, Nicole D., (815) 753-7935 nladue@niu.edu, Northern Illinois Univ; Ze
LaFemina, Peter C., 814-865-7326 pfemina@geosc.psu.edu, Pennsylvania State Univ, Univ Park; Yd
Laffan, Shawn, shawn.laffan@unsw.edu.au, Univ of New South Wales; Ziy
LaFleche, Marc R., (418) 654-2670 marc.richer-lafleche@ete.inrs.ca, Universite du Quebec; Ct
Lafrance, Bruno, 7056751151 x2264 blafrance@laurentian.ca, Laurentian Univ, Sudbury; GcEmGt
LaFreniere, Lorraine, (630) 252-7969 lafreniere@anl.gov, Argonne; HwGoPs
Lageson, David R., (406) 994-6913 lageson@montana.edu, Montana State Univ; GctGs
Lagowski, Alison A., (716) 645-4856 aal@buffalo.edu, SUNY, Buffalo; Zn
Lahiri, Chayan, (719) 587-7357 chayanlahiri@adams.edu, Adams State Univ; HwZr
Lai, Ching-Yao, 609-258-4101 cylai@princeton.edu, Princeton Univ; YgZoGl
Lai, Chung Chieng A., (505) 665-6635 cal@lanl.gov, Los Alamos; Am

Lasemi, Zakaria, 217-244-6944 lasemi@isgs.uiuc.edu, Illinois State Geological Survey; En
Lash, Gary G., (716) 673-3842 lash@fredonia.edu, SUNY, Fredonia; Gr
Lasher-Trapp, Sonia, 217-244-4250 slasher@illinois.edu, Univ of Illinois, Urbana-Champaign; As
Laske, Gabi, (858) 534-8774 glaske@ucsd.edu, Univ of California, San Diego; Ys
Lasker, Howard R., 716-645-4870 hlasker@buffalo.edu, SUNY, Buffalo; Gu
Lassetter, William L., (434) 951-6361 william.lassetter@dmme.virginia.gov, Division of Geology and Mineral Resources; EgHg
Lassiter, John, (512) 471-4002 lassiter1@mail.utexas.edu, Univ of Texas, Austin; Cc
Last, George V., (509) 376-3961 george.last@pnl.gov, Pacific Northwest; Ge
Last, William M., (204) 474-8361 wm_last@umanitoba.ca, Univ of Manitoba; GsnGo
Lat, Che Noorliza, 03-79674157 noorliza@um.edu.my, Univ of Malaya; Yg
Lathrop, Daniel, (301) 405-1594 lathrop@umd.edu, Univ of Maryland; Yg
Latimer, Jennifer C., (812) 237-2254 jen.latimer@indstate.edu, Indiana State Univ; CmGeb
Laton, W. R., (657) 278-7514 wlaton@fullerton.edu, California State Univ, Fullerton; HwGeHy
Lau, Kimberly, kimberly.lau@uwyo.edu, Univ of Wyoming; Cb
Laubach, Stephen E., 512-471-6303 steve.laubach@beg.utexas.edu, Univ of Texas, Austin; GcoNp
Lauderdale, Jonathan, j.lauderdale@liverpool.ac.uk, Univ of Liverpool; Og
Lauer, Rachel, 403 220-7923 rachel.lauer@ucalgary.ca, Univ of Calgary; Hy
Laughlin, Andrew, 828-250-3993 alaughli@unca.edu, Univ of North Carolina, Asheville; Zn
Laurent-Charvet, Sébastien, +33(0)3 44068995 sebastien.laurent-charvet@lasalle-beauvais.fr, Institut Polytechnique LaSalle Beauvais (ex-IGAL); GctZe
Lauretta, Dante, (520) 626-1138 lauretta@lpl.arizona.edu, Univ of Arizona; XcmXg
Laurier, Eric, +44 (0) 131 651 4303 eric.laurier@ed.ac.uk, Edinburgh Univ; Zn
Lauziere, Kathleen, (418) 654-2658 klauzier@nrcan.gc.ca, Universite du Quebec; Gg
Lauzon, John, (519) 824-4120 (Ext. 52459) lauzonj@uoguelph.ca, Univ of Guelph; So
Lavallee, Yan, +440151 794 5183 yan.lavallee@liverpool.ac.uk, Univ of Liverpool; Gv
Lavanchy, G. Thomas, 303-871-7521 thomas.lavanchy@du.edu, Univ of Denver; Hg
Lavier, Luc L., 512-471-0455 luc@ig.utexas.edu, Univ of Texas, Austin; Gt
LaVigne, Michéle, 207-798-4283 mlavign@bowdoin.edu, Bowdoin Coll; OcPe
Lavkulich, Leslie M., (604) 822-3477 Univ of British Columbia; Sd
Lavoie, Denis, (418) 654-2571 delavoie@nrcan.gc.ca, Universite du Quebec; Gs
Law, Eric W., (740) 826-8242 ericlaw@muskingum.edu, Muskingum Univ; Gp
Law, Kim, 519-661-2111 ext 83881 krlaw@uwo.ca, Western Univ; Cs
Law, Richard D., (540) 231-6685 rdlaw@vt.edu, Virginia Polytechnic Inst & State Univ; Gc
Law, Zada, (615) 494-8805 zada.law@mtsu.edu, Middle Tennessee State Univ; Zin
Lawrence, Deborah, (434) 924-0581 dl3c@virginia.edu, Univ of Virginia; ZcoZg
Lawrence, James, jimrslawrence@gmail.com, Univ of Houston; Cl
Lawrence, Kira, (610) 330-5194 lawrenck@lafayette.edu, Lafayette Coll; Oo
Lawrence, Rick L., (406) 994-5409 rickl@montana.edu, Montana State Univ; Zr
Lawry-Berkins, Cynthia, 936-273-7407 cynthia.lawryberkins@lonestar.edu, Lonestar Coll - Montgomery; Ges
Lawson, Merlin P., (402) 202-5392 mlawson1@unl.edu, Univ of Nebraska, Lincoln; AmtZr
Lawton, Donald C., (403) 220-5718 lawton@ucalgary.ca, Univ of Calgary; Ye
Lawver, Lawrence A., (512) 471-0433 lawver@ig.utexas.edu, Univ of Texas, Austin; YrGt
Lay, Thorne, (831) 459-3164 tlay@pmc.ucsc.edu, Univ of California, Santa Cruz; Ys
Layne, Graham, 709 864 3766 gdlayne@mun.ca, Memorial Univ of Newfoundland; Cg
Layton-Matthews, Daniel, (613) 533-6338 dlayton@queensu.ca, Queen's Univ; EgCte
Lazar, Codi, 909-537-5586 clazar@csusb.edu, California State Univ, San Bernardino; Cp
Lazarus, Steven M., 321-674-2160 slazarus@fit.edu, Florida Inst of Tech; As
Lazcano, Cristina, clazcano@ucdavis.edu, Univ of California, Davis; CbSb
Le, Yanfen, 660-562-1525 le@nwmissouri.edu, Northwest Missouri State Univ; Zi
Le Mevel, Helene, 202-478-8842 hlemevel@carnegiescience.edu, Carnegie Inst for Sci; Gv
Le Mone, David V., 915-747-5501 lemone@utep.edu, Univ of Texas, El Paso; Ps
Le Qu, Corinne, +44 (0)1603 59 2840 c.lequere@uea.ac.uk, Univ of East Anglia; Zg
Le Roex, Anton, 021-650-2902 anton.leroex@uct.ac.za, Univ of Cape Town; Cg
Le Roux, Petrus J., 021-650-4139 petrus.leroux@uct.ac.za, Univ of Cape Town; CaGia
Le Roux, Veronique, (508) 289-3549 vleroux@whoi.edu, Woods Hole Oceanographic Inst; Gi
Le Voyer, Marion, (626) 786-3716 levoyermarion@gmail.com, Smithsonian Inst / Nat Mus of Natural History; Cu
Lea, David W., (805) 893-8665 lea@geol.ucsb.edu, Univ of California, Santa Barbara; PeCm
Lea, Peter D., (207) 725-3439 plea@bowdoin.edu, Bowdoin Coll; Gl
Leach, Harry, +44 0151 794 4097 leach@liverpool.ac.uk, Univ of Liverpool; Og
Leadbetter, Jared R., 626.395.4182 jleadbetter@caltech.edu, California Inst of Tech; Pm
Leake, Bernard E., 00442920876421 leakeb@cf.ac.uk, Cardiff Univ; GipGz
Leake, Martha A., (229) 333-5756 mleake@valdosta.edu, Valdosta State Univ; Xg
Leap, Darrell I., (765) 494-3699 mountains2oceans@comcast.net, Purdue Univ; Hy
Lear, C, carrie@earth.cf.ac.uk, Cardiff Univ; Ou
Lear, Caroline, +44(0)29 208 79004 learc@cardiff.ac.uk, Univ of Wales; Og
Leary, Ryan, ryan.leary@nmt.edu, New Mexico Inst of Mining and Tech; Gs
Leatham, W. Britt, (909) 537-5322 bleatham@csusb.edu, California State Univ, San Bernardino; PsmOg
Leather, Kimberly, kimberley.leather@manchester.ac.uk, Univ of Manchester; As
Leavens, Peter B., 302-831-8106 pbl@udel.edu, Univ of Delaware; Gz
Leavitt, Steven W., (520) 621-6468 sleavitt@ltrr.arizona.edu, Univ of Arizona; Csc
Lebedev, Maxim, +61 8 9266 3519 m.lebedev@curtin.edu.au, Curtin Univ; YxNr
Lebofsky, Larry A., (520) 621-6947 lebofsky@lpl.arizona.edu, Univ of Arizona; ZngXm
Lebold, Joe, (304) 293-0749 joe.lebold@mail.wvu.edu, West Virginia Univ; PeGrg
Lechler, Paul J., (775) 682-8773 plechler@unr.edu, Univ of Nevada, Reno; Cg
Leckie, James O., leckie@cive.stanford.edu, Stanford Univ; Cl
Leckie, R. Mark, (413) 545-1948 mleckie@geo.umass.edu, Univ of Massachusetts, Amherst; PmGru
Ledbetter, Michael T., mtledbetter@ualr.edu, Univ of Arkansas at Little Rock; Og
Ledford, Sarah, 404-413-5780 sledford@gsu.edu, Georgia State Univ; HsRw
Lee, Alexis, (910) 962-3736 leea@uncw.edu, Univ of North Carolina, Wilmington; Zn
Lee, Alyce, 304-256-0270 alee@concord.edu, Concord Univ; Og
Lee, Arthur C., (865) 220-9145 leea@roanestate.edu, Roane State Comm Coll - Oak Ridge; Ges
Lee, Chung M., (801) 581-8218 chunglee@geog.utah.edu, Univ of Utah; Zu
Lee, Cin-Ty A., 713.348.5084 ctlee@rice.edu, Rice Univ; CgGiv
Lee, Cindy, (632) 220-2101 cindy.lee@stonybrook.edu, SUNY, Stony Brook; OcCo
Lee, Craig M., (206) 685-7656 craig@apl.washington.edu, Univ of Washington; Op
Lee, Daphne E., +64 3 479-7525 daphne.lee@otago.ac.nz, Univ of Otago; Pib
Lee, Dong, dlee@ldeo.columbia.edu, Columbia Univ; Og
Lee, Eung Seok, (740) 593-1101 leee1@ohio.edu, Ohio Univ; Hw
Lee, Hung, (519) 824-4120 Ext.53828 hlee@uoguelph.ca, Univ of Guelph; Zn
Lee, In Young, (630) 252-8724 Argonne; As
Lee, Jaeheon, 520-626-4967 jaeheon@email.arizona.edu, Univ of Arizona; Nx
Lee, Jeffrey, jeff@geology.cwu.edu, Central Washington Univ; Gct
Lee, Jejung, leej@umkc.edu, Univ of Missouri, Kansas City; GqHw
Lee, Keenan, (303) 273-3808 klee@mines.edu, Colorado Sch of Mines; Zr
Lee, Martin, +4401413302634 martin.lee@glasgow.ac.uk, Univ of Glasgow; Gz
Lee, Meehye, 82-2-3290-3178 meehye@korea.ac.kr, Korea Univ; AsOgCm

FACULTY INDEX – L

Leventon, Julia, +44(0) 113 34 31635 j.leventon@leeds.ac.uk, Univ of Leeds; Ge
LeVeque, Randy, 206.685.3037 rjl@uw.edu, Univ of Washington; GvYs
Lever, Helen, +44 (0) 131 451 4057 h.lever@hw.ac.uk, Heriot-Watt Univ; Go
Leverington, David W., 806-834-5310 david.leverington@ttu.edu, Texas Tech Univ; GmZrXg
Levesque, Andre, levesque.andre@ggl.ulaval.ca, Universite Laval; Gz
Levey, Raymond A., (801) 585-3826 rlevey@egi.utah.edu, Univ of Utah; Eo
Levin, Lisa A., (858) 534-3579 llevin@ucsd.edu, Univ of California, San Diego; Ob
Levin, Naomi, 410-516-4317 nlevin3@jhu.edu, Johns Hopkins Univ; Gs
Levin, Vadim, 848-445-5415 vlevin@eps.rutgers.edu, Rutgers, The State Univ of New Jersey; Ysg
Levine, Jamie S., levinejs@appstate.edu, Appalachian State Univ; Gzp
Levine, Norman S., (843) 953-5308 levinen@cofc.edu, Coll of Charleston; ZiGeNg
Levine, Rebekah, 406-683-7134 rebekah.levine@umwestern.edu, Univ of Montana Western; GmHsSd
Levinton, Jeffrey, (631) 632-8602 jeffrey.levinton@stonybrook.edu, SUNY, Stony Brook; Ob
Levson, Victor M., (250) 952-0391 vic.levson@gems9.gov.bc.ca, Univ of Victoria; Gl
Levy, Jonathan, (513) 529-1947 levyj@miamioh.edu, Miami Univ; Hw
Levy, Joseph, (315) 228-7834 jlevy@colgate.edu, Colgate Univ; GlsGm
Levy, Laura B., 707-826-3165 laura.levy@humboldt.edu, Humboldt State Univ; GslPc
Levy, Melissa H., (916) 484-8684 levym@arc.losrios.edu, American River Coll; GgZgy
Levy, Schon S., (505) 667-9504 sslevy@lanl.gov, Los Alamos; Gi
Lew, Alan A., (928) 523-6567 alan.lew@nau.edu, Northern Arizona Univ; Zgn
Lew, Jeffrey, (310) 825-3023 lew@atmos.ucla.edu, Univ of California, Los Angeles; As
Lewandowski, Katherine, (217) 581-7270 kjlewandowski@eiu.edu, Eastern Illinois Univ; PmcZe
Lewis, Alan G., (604) 822-3626 alewis@eos.ubc.ca, Univ of British Columbia; Ob
Lewis, Brian T. R., (206) 543-7419 blewis@u.washington.edu, Univ of Washington; Yr
Lewis, Chris, cjlewis@ccsf.edu, City Coll of San Francisco; GgEmSo
Lewis, Gerald L., (626) 585-7137 gllewis@pasadena.edu, Pasadena City Coll; Ps
Lewis, Helen, +44 (0) 131 451 3691 h.lewis@hw.ac.uk, Heriot-Watt Univ; Gc
Lewis, John S., (360) 873-8781 jsl@u.arizona.edu, Univ of Arizona; Xcm
Lewis, Jon C., (724) 357-5624 jclewis@iup.edu, Indiana Univ of Pennsylvania; Gc
Lewis, Katie, 806-746-6101 krothlisberger@tamu.edu, Texas A&M Univ; Sco
Lewis, Marlon R., (902) 494-3513 marlon.lewis@dal.ca, Dalhousie Univ; Ob
Lewis, Mary, 5102357800 x.4284 mlewis@contracosta.edu, Contra Costa Coll; Gg
Lewis, Reed S., (208) 885-7472 reedl@uidaho.edu, Univ of Idaho; GgiEg
Lewis, Ronald D., (334) 844-4886 lewisrd@auburn.edu, Auburn Univ; Pi
Lewis, Stephen D., (559) 278-6956 slewis@csufresno.edu, Fresno State Univ; Yg
Lewis, Tammy, 718-951-5000 tlewis@brooklyn.cuny.edu, Graduate Sch of the City Univ of New York; Gg
Leybourne, Matthew I., 7056751151 x2263 mleybourne@laurentian.ca, Laurentian Univ, Sudbury; Cg
Leyrit, Hervé, +33(0)3 44068998 herve.leyrit@lasalle-beauvais.fr, Institut Polytechnique LaSalle Beauvais (ex-IGAL); Gv
Li, Aibing, 713-743-2878 ali2@uh.edu, Univ of Houston; Ys
Li, Baosheng, 631-632-9642 baosheng.li@stonybrook.edu, Stony Brook Univ; Yx
Li, Chusi, (812) 855-1558 cli@indiana.edu, Indiana Univ, Bloomington; EgGiEm
Li, Dan, lidan@bu.edu, Boston Univ; HqAs
Li, Gary, 510-885-3165 gary.li@csueastbay.edu, California State Univ, East Bay; Zi
Li, Jing, 303-871-4687 jing.li145@du.edu, Univ of Denver; Zi
Li, Junran, 918-631-3013 junran-li@utulsa.edu, Univ of Tulsa; Gme
Li, Laifang, lfl5240@psu.edu, Pennsylvania State Univ, Univ Park; AsZo
Li, Liangping, (605) 394-2461 liangping.li@sdsmt.edu, South Dakota Sch of Mines & Tech; HwqHt
Li, Lin, ll3@iupui.edu, Indiana Univ - Purdue Univ Indianapolis; ZrXgZg
Li, Long, 780-492-9288 long4@ualberta.ca, Univ of Alberta; CsGpv
Li, Mingming, (480) 965-1733 mingming.li@asu.edu, Arizona State Univ; Yg
Li, Peng, (501) 683-0118 peng.li@arkansas.gov, Arkansas Geological Survey; GoEoCo
Li, Ping-Chi, (931) 372-3752 pli@tntech.edu, Tennessee Tech Univ; Zi
Li, Rong-Yu, 204-727-9684 lir@brandonu.ca, Brandon Univ; PgmGg
Li, Tim, 808-956-9427 timli@hawaii.edu, Univ of Hawai'i, Manoa; Asm
Li, Wenhong, 919 684-5015 wl66@duke.edu, Duke Univ; Zn
Li, William K., (902) 426-6349 lib@mar.dfo-mpo.gc.ca, Dalhousie Univ; Ob
Li, Xiangshan, 713-743-0742 xli10@uh.edu, Univ of Houston; Asm
Li, Yanan, (512) 245-2170 Texas State Univ; GmCcPc
Li, Yaoguo, 303-273-3510 ygli@mines.edu, Colorado Sch of Mines; Yev
Li, Yong-Gang, (213) 740-3556 hylirenko@marshall.usc.edu, Univ of Southern California; Ys
Li, Yuan-Hui, 808-956-6297 yhli@soest.hawaii.edu, Univ of Hawai'i, Manoa; Cm
Li, Yuncong, (305) 246-7000 yunli@ufl.edu, Univ of Florida; Sco
Li, Zhenhong, +44 (0) 191 208 5704 zhenhong.li@ncl.ac.uk, Univ of Newcastle Upon Tyne; Yd
Lian, Jie, 734-647-5704 jlian@umich.edu, Univ of Michigan; Gz
Liang, George, (785) 532-6101 gliang@ksu.edu, Kansas State Univ; So
Liang, Liyuan, 865-241-3933 2ll@ornl.gov, Oak Ridge; Cl
Liang, Lu, 940.369.5198 lu.liang@unt.edu, Univ of North Texas; Zi
Liang, Renxing, 609-258-4101 Princeton Univ; Po
Liang, Yan, (401) 863-9477 yan_liang@brown.edu, Brown Univ; Cp
Liao, Enhui, 609-258-4101 enhui.liao@princeton.edu, Princeton Univ; Op
Liao, Haifeng (Felix), 208-885-6452 hliao@uidaho.edu, Univ of Idaho; ZuiZn
Liauw, Henri L., hliauwap@broward.edu, Broward Coll; Gg
Libarkin, Julie C., (517) 355-8369 libarkin@msu.edu, Michigan State Univ; Zen
Liberty, Lee M., (208) 426-1166 lml@cgiss.boisestate.edu, Boise State Univ; Ys
Libra, Robert D., robert.libra@dnr.iowa.gov, Iowa Dept of Natural Resources; Gg
Licciardi, Joseph M., 603-862-1718 joe.licciardi@unh.edu, Univ of New Hampshire; Gl
Licht, Alexis, licht@uw.edu, Univ of Washington; Gsn
Licht, Kathy J., (317) 278-1343 klicht@iupui.edu, Indiana Univ - Purdue Univ Indianapolis; Gl
Lichtenberger, János, lityi@sas.elte.hu, Eotvos Lorand Univ; AsZrXy
Lichtner, Peter C., (505) 667-3420 lichtner@lanl.gov, Los Alamos; Zn
Liddell, W. David, (435) 797-1261 dave.liddell@usu.edu, Utah State Univ; GsPg
Lidgard, Scott H., (312) 665-7625 slidgard@fieldmuseum.org, Field Mus of Natural History; Pi
Lidiak, Edward G., (412) 624-8871 egl@pitt.edu, Univ of Pittsburgh; Gi
Lidicker, Jr., William Z., (510) 642-3059 Univ of California, Berkeley; Pv
Liebe, Richard M., (585) 395-5100 (Ext. 7524) rliebe@weather.brockport.edu, SUNY, The Coll at Brockport; Ps
Liebens, Johan, 850-474-2065 liebens@uwf.edu, Univ of West Florida; So
Lieberman, Bruce S., (785) 864-2741 blieber@ku.edu, Univ of Kansas; Pgi
Lieberman, Robert C., (631) 632-8214 robert.liebermann@sunysb.edu, Stony Brook Univ; GyYsx
Liebling, Richard, 516 463-6545 georsl@hofstra.edu, Hofstra Univ; Gg
Lifton, Nathaniel A., (765) 494-0754 nlifton@purdue.edu, Purdue Univ; GmCc
Light, Bonnie, (206) 543-9824 bonnie@apl.washington.edu, Univ of Washington; As
Lightbody, Anne F., 603-862--0711 anne.lightbody@unh.edu, Univ of New Hampshire; HgsZn
Likos, William J., 608-890-2662 likos@wisc.edu, Univ of Wisconsin, Madison; NgSp
Lilley, Marvin D., (206) 543-0859 lilley@ocean.washington.edu, Univ of Washington; Ob
Lima, Eduardo A., 617-324-2829 limaea@mit.edu, Massachusetts Inst of Tech; Ym
Lima, Ivan D., ilima@whoi.edu, Woods Hole Oceanographic Inst; Oc
Limp, William (., (479) 575-7909 flimp@uark.edu, Univ of Arkansas, Fayetteville; Zfi
Lin, Douglas, (831) 459-2732 lin@lick.ucsc.edu, Univ of California, Santa Cruz; Xc
Lin, Fan-Chi, (801) 581-4373 fanchi.lin@utah.edu, Univ of Utah; Ygs
Lin, Guoqing, glin@rsmas.miami.edu, Univ of Miami; Yg
Lin, Hai, hai.lin@ec.gc.ca, McGill Univ; As
Lin, Hsing K., (907) 474-6347 hklin@alaska.edu, Univ of Alaska, Fairbanks; Zn
Lin, Jialin, (614) 292-6634 lin.789@osu.edu, Ohio State Univ; As
Lin, Jian, (508) 289-2576 jlin@whoi.edu, Woods Hole Oceanographic Inst;

Gt
Lin, John C., 801-581-7530 john.lin@utah.edu, Univ of Utah; As
Lin, Jung-Fu, 512-471-8054 afu@jsg.utexas.edu, Univ of Texas, Austin; GyYm
Lin, Meimei, (912) 344-2974 meimeilin@georgiasouthern.edu, Georgia Southern Univ; Zi
Lin, Senjie, (860) 405-9168 senjie.lin@uconn.edu, Univ of Connecticut; Ob
Lin, Shoufa, (519) 888-4567 (Ext. 6557) shoufa@uwaterloo.ca, Univ of Waterloo; Zn
Lin, Wuyin, (631) 632-3141 wuyin.lin@stonybrook.edu, SUNY, Stony Brook; As
Lin, Xiaomao, (785) 532-6816 xlin@ksu.edu, Kansas State Univ; Zn
Lin, Yu-Feng F., 217-333-0235 yflin@illinois.edu, Illinois State Geological Survey; Hg
Linares, Rogelio, ++935811259 rogelio.linares@uab.cat, Universitat Autonoma de Barcelona; NgYx
Lincoln, Beth Z., (517) 629-0331 blincoln@albion.edu, Albion Coll; Gc
Lincoln, Jonathan M., (973) 655-7273 lincolnj@mail.montclair.edu, Montclair State Univ; Gr
Lindberg, David R., (510) 642-3926 Univ of California, Berkeley; Pi
Lindberg, Jonathan W., (509) 376-5005 jon.lindberg@pnl.gov, Pacific Northwest; Ec
Lindberg, Steven E., partnerships@ornl.gov, Oak Ridge; Cl
Lindbo, David, (919) 793-4428 North Carolina State Univ; Sd
Linde, Alan T., alinde@carnegiescience.edu, Carnegie Inst for Sci; Ys
Lindemann, William C., (505) 646-3405 New Mexico State Univ, Las Cruces; Sb
Lindenmeier, Clark W., (509) 376-8419 clark.lindenmeier@pnl.gov, Pacific Northwest; Cg
Lindgren, Paula, 441413305442 paula.lindgren@glasgow.ac.uk, Univ of Glasgow; As
Lindley, Stacy, (916) 278-6337 stacy.lindley@csus.edu, Sacramento State Univ; Zn
Lindline, Jennifer, (505) 426-2046 lindlinej@nmhu.edu, New Mexico Highlands Univ; GizZe
Lindo Atachati, David, 718-982-2919 david.lindo@csi.cuny.edu, Graduate Sch of the City Univ of New York; Og
Lindsay, Everett H., (520) 621-6024 ehlind@geo.arizona.edu, Univ of Arizona; Pv
Lindsay, Matthew B., (306) 966-5693 matt.lindsay@usask.ca, Univ of Saskatchewan; ClGg
Lindsey, Kassandra, 303-384-2660 kolindsey@mines.edu, Colorado Geological Survey; NgGmZi
Lindsley, Donald H., (631) 632-8195 donald.lindsley@stonybrook.edu, Stony Brook Univ; Cp
Lindzen, Richard S., (617) 253-2432 rlindzen@mit.edu, Massachusetts Inst of Tech; Am
Line, Michael, (480) 965-3971 michael.line@asu.edu, Arizona State Univ; Xy
Liner, Christopher, 479-575-5667 liner@uark.edu, Univ of Arkansas, Fayetteville; YseGg
Lini, Andrea, (802) 656-0245 andrea.lini@uvm.edu, Univ of Vermont; CsGn
Lininger, Katherine, katherine.lininger@colorado.edu, Univ of Colorado; Gm
Link, Curtis A., (406) 496-4165 clink@mtech.edu, Montana Tech of the Univ of Montana; Ye
Link, Paul K., (208) 282-3365 linkpaul@isu.edu, Idaho State Univ; GsgGr
Linky, Edward, (212) 772-5265 linky.edward@epamail.epa.gov, Hunter Coll (CUNY); Zn
Linn, Anne M., (202) 334-2744 alinn@nas.edu, Nat Academies of Scis, Eng, and Medicine; Gs
Linn, Rodman, (505) 665-6254 rrl@lanl.gov, Los Alamos; Ng
Linneman, Scott R., (360) 650-3446 scott.linneman@wwu.edu, Western Washington Univ; GmZe
Linnen, Robert, 519-661-2111 x89207 rlinnen@uwo.ca, Western Univ; EmCe
Linol, Bastien, bastien.aeon@gmail.com, Nelson Mandela Metropolitan Univ; Gs
Linsley, Braddock, blinsley@ldeo.columbia.edu, Columbia Univ; Pe
Liou, Juhn G., (650) 723-2716 liou@pangea.stanford.edu, Stanford Univ; Gp
Liou, Kuo Nan, (415) 723-2716 knliou@atmos.ucla.edu, Univ of California, Los Angeles; As
Lipeles, Maxine I., (314) 935-5482 milipeles@seas.wustl.edu, Washington Univ in St. Louis; Zn
Lippelt, Irene D., (608) 262-7430 irene.lippelt@wisc.edu, Univ of Wisconsin, Madison, Division of Extension; Gg
Lippert, Peter C., (801) 581-4599 pete.lippert@utah.edu, Univ of Utah; YmGtPe
Lippmann, Thomas C., 603-862-4450 lippmann@ccom.unh.edu, Univ of New Hampshire; Onp
Lips, Elliott W., (801) 581-8218 elliott.lips@geog.utah.edu, Univ of Utah; Gm
Lisenby, Peyton E., (940) 397-4475 peyton.lisenby@msutexas.edu, Midwestern State Univ; GmeZi
Lisichenko, Richard, 785-628-4159 rlisiche@fhsu.edu, Fort Hays State Univ; Zie
Lisiecki, Lorraine, (805) 893-4437 lisiecki@geol.ucsb.edu, Univ of California, Santa Barbara; Gn
Lisle, R J., lisle@cf.ac.uk, Cardiff Univ; Gc
Liss, Peter S., +44 (0)1603 59 2563 p.liss@uea.ac.uk, Univ of East Anglia; OcCbAc
Litherland, Mairi, 575-835-5921 mairi.litherland@nmt.edu, New Mexico Inst of Mining and Tech; Ys
Lithgow-Bertelloni, Carolina, 310-267-4719 clb@epss.ucla.edu, Univ of California, Los Angeles; Yg
Little, Crispin, +44(0) 113 34 36621 earctsl@leeds.ac.uk, Univ of Leeds; Pg
Little, Jonathan, jlittle@monroecc.edu, Monroe Comm Coll; ZyGlZi
Little, Tim, +64 4 463 6198 tim.little@vuw.ac.nz, Victoria Univ of Wellington; Gct
Little, William W., (208) 496-7679 littlew@byui.edu, Brigham Young Univ - Idaho; GsdGm
Littler, Kate L., 01326255725 k.littler@exeter.ac.uk, Exeter Univ; PeCl
Liu, Chuntao, 361-825-3845 chuntao.liu@tamucc.edu, Texas A&M Univ, Corpus Christi; As
Liu, Dantong, dantong.liu@manchester.ac.uk, Univ of Manchester; As
Liu, Gaisheng, 785-864-2115 gliu@kgs.ku.edu, Univ of Kansas; Hy
Liu, Jian G., +44 20 759 46418 j.g.liu@imperial.ac.uk, Imperial Coll; Zr
Liu, Jing, liu_jing@smc.edu, Santa Monica Coll; ZyiZr
Liu, Jingpu P., 919-515-3711 jpliu@ncsu.edu, North Carolina State Univ; Gu
Liu, Jiping, jiping.liu@eas.gatech.edu, Georgia Inst of Tech; As
Liu, Kelly, 573-341-6724 liukh@mst.edu, Missouri Univ of Sci and Tech; Ye
Liu, Lanbo, (860) 486-1388 lanbo.liu@uconn.edu, Univ of Connecticut; Yg
Liu, Lijun, (217) 300-0378 ljliu@illinois.edu, Univ of Illinois, Urbana-Champaign; YgGtm
Liu, Mian, (573) 882-3784 lium@missouri.edu, Univ of Missouri; Yg
Liu, Paul Hiaibao, paul.liu@dnr.iowa.gov, Iowa Dept of Natural Resources; Gg
Liu, Ping, (631) 632-3195 ping.liu@stonybrook.edu, SUNY, Stony Brook; As
Liu, Qiangcheng, 609-258-4101 q.liu@princeton.edu, Princeton Univ; Yg
Liu, Qinya, 416-978-5434 Univ of Toronto; Ygx
Liu, Shimin, (814) 863-4491 szl3@psu.edu, Pennsylvania State Univ, Univ Park; Nm
Liu, Weibo, 561 297-4965 liuw@fau.edu, Florida Atlantic Univ; Zi
Liu, Xiaolei , xlliu@ou.edu, Univ of Oklahoma; Cg
Liu, Xiaoming, (919) 962-0675 xiaomliu@unc.edu, Univ of North Carolina, Chapel Hill; Cgl
Liu, Yajing, 514-398-4085 yajing.liu@mcgill.ca, McGill Univ; Ygs
Liu, Yongqiang, (706) 559-4240 yliu@fs.fed.us, Georgia Inst of Tech; Am
Liu, Zhanfei, 361-749-6772 zhanfei.liu@utexas.edu, Univ of Texas, Austin; Og
Liu, Zhaolun, 609-258-4101 zhaolunl@princeton.edu, Princeton Univ; Yg
Liu, Zhengyu, (608)262-0777 zliu3@wisc.edu, Univ of Wisconsin, Madison; Op
Liutkus-Pierce, Cynthia M., 828-262-6933 liutkuscm@appstate.edu, Appalachian State Univ; Gd
Livaccari, Richard F., (970) 248-1081 rlivacca@coloradomesa.edu, Colorado Mesa Univ; Gc
Lively, Rich, (612) 626-3103 lively@umn.edu, Univ of Minnesota; Cc
Livens, Francis, +44 0161 275-4647 francis.livens@manchester.ac.uk, Univ of Manchester; Cg
Livermore, Phil, +44(0) 113 34 30379 p.w.livermore@leeds.ac.uk, Univ of Leeds; Ym
Livingstone, Daniel A., (919) 684-3264 livingst@duke.edu, Duke Univ; Pe
Lizarralde, Daniel, 508-289-2942 dlizarralde@whoi.edu, Woods Hole Oceanographic Inst; Ys
Llanes, María del Pilar, pllanes@ucm.es, Univ Complutense de Madrid; Yr
Llanos, Hilario, hilario.llanos@ehu.eus, Univ of the Basque Country UPV/EHU; Hgy
Llewellin, Ed, +44 (0) 191 33 42336 ed.llewellin@durham.ac.uk, Durham Univ; Gv
Lloyd, Glenn D., 573/368-2176 glenn.lloyd@dnr.mo.gov, Missouri Dept of Natural Resources; Zn
Lloyd, Graeme, +44 (1865) 272056 graeme.lloyd@earth.ox.ac.uk, Univ of Oxford; Gs
Lloyd, Jonathan, +44 0161 275-7155 jon.lloyd@manchester.ac.uk, Univ of Manchester; Ge
Lobben, Amy, (541) 346-4566 lobben@uoregon.edu, Univ of Oregon; ZinZn

Lobegeier, Melissa, 615-898-2403 melissa.lobegeier@mtsu.edu, Middle Tennessee State Univ; Pmg
Locat, Jacques E., (418) 656-2179 locat@ggl.ulaval.ca, Universite Laval; Ng
Lock, Brian E., (337) 482-6823 belock@louisiana.edu, Univ of Louisiana at Lafayette; Gs
Locke, Daniel B., (207) 287-7171 daniel.b.locke@maine.gov, Dept of Agriculture, Conservation, and Forestry; Hw
Locke, Erika, erika.locke@tamucc.edu, Texas A&M Univ, Corpus Christi; GgoGs
Locke, James L., (415) 485-9526 jim@marin.edu, Coll of Marin; Zg
Locke, Randall, (217) 333-3866 rlocke@illinois.edu, Illinois State Geological Survey; Cl
Locke II, Randall A., 217-333-3866 rlocke@illinois.edu, Univ of Illinois; CgHw
Locker, Stanley D., (727) 553-1502 stan@marine.usf.edu, Univ of South Florida; Ou
Lockley, Martin G., (303) 556-4884 Univ of Colorado, Denver; Pi
Lockwood, John P., (808) 967-8579 jplockwood@volcanologist.com, Univ of Hawai'i, Hilo; Gvg
Lockwood, Rowan, (757) 221-2878 rxlock@wm.edu, William & Mary; PgePi
Locmelis, Marek, 573-341-4759 locmelism@mst.edu, Missouri Univ of Sci and Tech; Eg
Lodders-Fegley, Katharina, (314) 935-4851 lodders@levee.wustl.edu, Washington Univ in St. Louis; Xc
Lodge, Robert, 715-836-4361 lodgerw@uwec.edu, Univ of Wisconsin, Eau Claire; EmCuGv
Loeb, Valerie, 831-771-4400 loeb@mlml.calstate.edu, Moss Landing Marine Lab; Zn
Lofthouse, Stephen T., (212) 346-1760 slofthouse@fsmail.pace.edu, Pace Univ, New York Campus; Zg
Loftus, Timothy, 55122452170 Texas State Univ; RwHs
Logan, Alan, (506) 648-5715 logan@unbsj.ca, Univ of New Brunswick Saint John; Ob
Logsdon, Miles G., (206) 543-5334 mlog@u.washington.edu, Univ of Washington; Zi
Lohan, Maeve, +44 (0)23 80596449 m.lohan@soton.ac.uk, Univ of Southampton; Ob
Loheide, Steven P., (608) 265-5277 loheide@wisc.edu, Univ of Wisconsin, Madison; HwSp
Lohman, Rowena B., rbl62@cornell.edu, Cornell Univ; YsZrGt
Lohmann, George P., (508) 289-2840 glohmann@whoi.edu, Woods Hole Oceanographic Inst; Pe
Lohmann, Kyger C., (734) 763-2298 kacey@umich.edu, Univ of Michigan; CsGsCl
Lokau, Katja R., +49 89 289 25857 katja.lokau@tum.de, Technical Univ of Munich; Ng
Lomaga, Margaret, lomagam@sunysuffolk.edu, Suffolk County Comm Coll, Ammerman Campus; Zg
Lombard, Armand J., ajlombard@mesacc.edu, Mesa Comm Coll; Gg
Lombardo, Kelly A., lombardo@psu.edu, Pennsylvania State Univ, Univ Park; As
London, David, (405) 325-3253 dlondon@ou.edu, Univ of Oklahoma; CpGiz
Lonergan, Lidia, +44 20 759 46465 l.lonergan@imperial.ac.uk, Imperial Coll; GtcGs
Long, Ann D., (217) 244-6172 annlong@illinois.edu, Univ of Illinois, Urbana-Champaign; Gm
Long, Austin, (520) 621-8888 along@geo.arizona.edu, Univ of Arizona; Cl
Long, Colin, (920) 424-4105 longco@uwosh.edu, Univ of Wisconsin Oshkosh; PeZyc
Long, Colleen, longcm@illinois.edu, Illinois State Geological Survey; Gg
Long, Darrel, dlong@laurentian.ca, Laurentian Univ, Sudbury; GsaGl
Long, David T., (517) 353-9618 long@msu.edu, Michigan State Univ; ClGeb
Long, Leon E., (512) 459-7838 leonlong@jsg.utexas.edu, Univ of Texas, Austin; Cc
Long, Lisa, 614 265 6590 lisa.long@dnr.state.oh.usm, Ohio Dept of Natural Resources; Zn
Long, Matthew, 508-289-2798 mlong@whoi.edu, Woods Hole Oceanographic Inst; Cm
Long, Maureen D., (203) 432-5031 maureen.long@yale.edu, Yale Univ; Ysg
Long , Sean P., 509-335-8868 sean.p.long@wsu.edu, Washington State Univ; Gc
Longbrake, David, david.longbrake@du.edu, Univ of Denver; Zi
Longerich, Henry, (709) 737-8380 henry@mun.ca, Memorial Univ of Newfoundland; Cg
Longnecker, Krista, (508) 289-2824 klongnecker@whoil.edu, Woods Hole Oceanographic Inst; Oc
Longoria, Jose F., (786) 210-0590 longoria@fiu.edu, Florida International Univ; ZeGoe
Longoria, Lorena, 956 665-5124 lorena.longoria@utrgv.edu, Univ of Texas, Rio Grande Valley; Ob
Longpre, Marc-Antoine, 718-997-3259 mlongpre@qc.cuny.edu, Graduate Sch of the City Univ of New York; Zg
Longstaffe, Frederick J., (519) 661-3177 flongsta@uwo.ca, Western Univ; Cs
Longworth, Brett, 508-289-3559 blongworth@whoi.edu, Woods Hole Oceanographic Inst; Ou
Lonn, Jeff, (406) 496-4177 jlonn@mtech.edu, Montana Tech of The Univ of Montana; GgtGc
Lonsdale, Darcy J., (631) 632-8712 darcy.lonsdale@stonybrook.edu, SUNY, Stony Brook; Ob
Lonsdale, Peter F., (858) 534-2855 plonsdale@ucsd.edu, Univ of California, San Diego; Gu
Looney, Brian, 803-725-3692 brian02.looney@srnl.doe.gov, Clemson Univ; Hq
Loope, David B., (402) 472-2647 dloope1@unl.edu, Univ of Nebraska, Lincoln; Gsg
Loope, Henry M., (812) 856-3117 hloope@indiana.edu, Indiana Univ; Gls
Looy, Cynthia, 510-642-1607 looy@berkeley.edu, Univ of California, Berkeley; Pb
Lopez, Alberto, (787) 265-3845 alberto.lopez3@upr.edu, Univ of Puerto Rico; YdGtYs
Lopez, Annabelle, 575-835-5139 annabelle.lopez@nmt.edu, New Mexico Inst of Mining and Tech; Go
Lopez, Dina L., (740) 593-9435 lopezd@ohio.edu, Ohio Univ; CgHwGv
Lopez, Glenn R., (631) 632-8660 glenn.lopez@stonybrook.edu, SUNY, Stony Brook; Ob
Lopez, Margarita, marlopez@cicese.mx, Centro de Investigación Científica y de Educación Superior de Ensenada; Cc
López, Maricela , (662) 370-6262 maricela.lopez@gmail.com, Univ Estatal de Sonora; NxGg
López, Sol, antares@ucm.es, Univ Complutense de Madrid; Gz
Lora, Juan, 203-432-2627 juan.lora@yale.edu, Yale Univ; ZoAs
Lord, Mark L., (828) 227-2271 mlord@wcu.edu, Western Carolina Univ; HwGmZe
Lorenz, Ralph, (520) 621-5585 rlorenz@lpl.arizona.edu, Univ of Arizona; Xg
Lorenzo, Juan M., (225) 388-2497 juan@geol.lsu.edu, Louisiana State Univ; Ys
Lorenzoni, Irene, +44 (0)1603 59 3173 i.lorenzoni@uea.ac.uk, Univ of East Anglia; Eg
Lori, Lisa, 573-368-2152 lisa.lori@dnr.mo.gov, Missouri Dept of Natural Resources; Gp
Lorimer, Hayden, hayden.lorimer@ed.ac.uk, Edinburgh Univ; Zn
Lorinczi, Piroska, +44(0) 113 34 39245 earpl@leeds.ac.uk, Univ of Leeds; Np
Loring, Arthur P., (718) 262-2079 York Coll (CUNY); Gm
Loriot, George, 802-626-6378 george.loriot@northernvermont.edu, Northern Vermont Univ-Lyndon; AsZn
Losh, Steven, (507) 389-6323 steven.losh@mnsu.edu, Minnesota State Univ; GzxGo
Losos, Zdenek, ++420 549 49 5623 losos@sci.muni.cz, Masaryk Univ; Gzy
Lott, Dempsey E., (508) 289-2929 dlott@whoi.edu, Woods Hole Oceanographic Inst; Oc
Lotterhos, Kathleen, (781) 581-7370 k.lotterhos@neu.edu, Northeastern Univ; Zn
Lottermoser, Bernd, +44 01326 255973 b.lottermoser@exeter.ac.uk, Exeter Univ; Ca
Loubser, Michael J., michael.loubser@up.ac.za, Univ of Pretoria; GmZy
Loucks, Bob, (512) 471-0366 bob.loucks@beg.utexas.edu, Univ of Texas at Austin, Jackson Sch of Geosciences; Go
Loucks, Robert G., (512) 471-0366 bob.loucks@beg.utexas.edu, Univ of Texas, Austin; Gso
Louden, Keith E., (902) 494-3452 keith.louden@dal.ca, Dalhousie Univ; Yr
Lough, Amanda, (215) 895 6456 amanda.c.lough@drexel.edu, Drexel Univ; Ysg
Louie, John, (775) 784-4219 louie@unr.edu, Univ of Nevada, Reno; Yse
Lounsbury, Diane E., (585) 245-5291 lounsbur@geneseo.edu, SUNY, Geneseo; Zn
Lourenço, José M., 00351259350280 martinho@utad.pt, Unive de Trás-os-Montes e Alto Douro; YeZin
Lourenco, Sergio, lourencosd@cf.ac.uk, Cardiff Univ; Sp
Louwye, Stephen, stephen.louwye@ugent.be, Ghent Univ; Pm
Love, Andew, andrew.love@flinders.edu.au, Flinders Univ; Hw
Love, David W., (575) 835-5146 dave@nmbg.nmt.edu, New Mexico Inst of Mining and Tech; Ge
Love, Gordon D., glove@ucr.edu, Univ of California, Riverside; Cog

Love, Renee, (208) 885-4079 rlove@uidaho.edu, Univ of Idaho; Pg
Lovekin, Jonathan, 303-384-2654 jlovekin@mines.edu, Colorado Geological Survey; NgZuGs
Loveland, Andrea M., (307) 766-2286 andrea.loveland@wyo.gov, Wyoming State Geological Survey; Gct
Loveland, Karen, 573-368-2142 karen.loveland@dnr.mo.gov, Missouri Dept of Natural Resources; Zn
Loveless, Jack, (413) 585-2657 jloveles@smith.edu, Smith Coll; Gtc
Lovell, Mark D., (208) 496-7680 lovellm@byui.edu, Brigham Young Univ - Idaho; HyZiGo
Lovell, Mike, +440116 252 3798 mike.lovell@le.ac.uk, Leicester Univ; Yg
LoVetere, Crystal, clovetere@cerritos.edu, Cerritos Coll; Zy
Lovett, Andrew A., +44 (0)1603 59 3126 a.lovett@uea.ac.uk, Univ of East Anglia; Ziu
Lovett, Cole, (269) 927-8744 lovett@lakemichigancollege.edu, Lake Michigan Coll; Gg
Lovseth, John, 618.374.5291 john.lovseth@principia.edu, Principia Coll; Zni
Lowe, Donald R., (650) 725-3040 lowe@pangea.stanford.edu, Stanford Univ; Gd
Lowe, Douglas, douglas.lowe@manchester.ac.uk, Univ of Manchester; As
Lowe, Mike, (801) 537-3389 nrugs.mlowe@state.ut.us, Utah Geological Survey; Hw
Lowell, Thomas V., (513) 556-4165 thomas.lowell@uc.edu, Univ of Cincinnati; Gl
Lowenstein, Tim K., (607) 777-4254 lowenst@binghamton.edu, Binghamton Univ; Cl
Lower, Steven K., 614 292-1571 lower.9@osu.edu, Ohio State Univ; PoZa
Lowery, Birl, (608) 262-2752 blowery@wisc.edu, Univ of Wisconsin, Madison; Sp
Lowry, Anthony R., (435) 797-7096 tony.lowry@usu.edu, Utah State Univ; YdsGt
Lowry, Christopher S., 716-645-4266 cslowry@buffalo.edu, SUNY, Buffalo; Hw
Lowry, David, +44 1784 443105 d.lowry@rhul.ac.uk, Royal Holloway Univ of London; CsZg
Lowry, Wallace D., (540) 231-6521 Virginia Polytechnic Inst & State Univ; Gc
Lowry, William R., (314) 935-5821 Washington Univ in St. Louis; Zn
Loxsom, Fred, loxsomf@easternct.edu, Eastern Connecticut State Univ; Zn
Loyd, Sean, 657-278-4537 sloyd@fullerton.edu, California State Univ, Fullerton; CgGe
Loydell, David K., +44 023 92 842698 david.loydell@port.ac.uk, Univ of Portsmouth; GrPg
Loynachan, Thomas E., (515) 290-7154 teloynac@iastate.edu, Iowa State Univ of Sci & Tech; So
Lozar, Francesca, francesca.lozar@unito.it, Univ di Torino; Pg
Lozier, M. Susan, (919) 681-8199 s.lozier@duke.edu, Duke Univ; Op
Lozinsky, Richard P., (714) 992-7445 rlozinsky@fullcoll.edu, Fullerton Coll; GreGm
Lozos, Julian, (818) 677-7977 julian.lozos@csun.edu, California State Univ, Northridge; YgGt
Lozowski, Edward P., (403) 492-0348 Univ of Alberta; As
Lu, Yongmei, (512) 245-2170 Texas State Univ; Zi
Lu, Yongqi, 217 244-4985 yongqilu@illinois.edu, Univ of Illinois; Zm
Lu, Youyu, (902) 426-7780 youyu.lu@ec.gc.ca, Dalhousie Univ; Op
Lu, Yuehan, 205-348-1882 yuehanlu@as.ua.edu, Univ of Alabama; GgOuGe
Lu, Zhong, 214-768-0101 zhonglu@smu.edu, Southern Methodist Univ; Zr
Lu, Zunli, 315-443-0281 zunlilu@syr.edu, Syracuse Univ; Cg
Lucas, Beth, (540) 231-4595 blucas06@vt.edu, Virginia Polytechnic Inst & State Univ; Zn
Lucas, Cathy, +44 (0)23 80596617 cathy.lucas@noc.soton.ac.uk, Univ of Southampton; Ob
Lucas, Franklin A., frank.lucas@uniben.edu, Univ of Benin; PmlGr
Lucey, Paul G., (808) 956-3137 lucey@higp.hawaii.edu, Univ of Hawai'i, Manoa; Xy
Lucia, F. J., 512-471-1534 jerry.lucia@beg.utexas.edu, Univ of Texas, Austin; Eo
Lucia, F. Jerry, (512) 471-7367 jerry.lucia@beg.utexas.edu, Univ of Texas at Austin, Jackson Sch of Geosciences; Go
Luciano, Katherine E., (843) 953-6843 lucianok@dnr.sc.gov, South Carolina Dept of Natural Resources; GusGm
Lucotte, Marc Michel, 514-987-3000 #3767 lucotte.marc_michel@uqam.ca, Universite du Quebec a Montreal; Oc
Luczaj, John A., (920) 465-5139 luczajj@uwgb.edu, Univ of Wisconsin, Green Bay; HwGsCl
Ludman, Allan, (718) 997-3271 allan.ludman@gc.cuny.edu, Graduate Sch of the City Univ of New York; Gg
Ludvigson, Greg A., (785) 864-2734 gludvigson@ku.edu, Univ of Kansas; GrCsPc
Ludvigson, Gregory A., 785-864-2734 gludvigson@kgs.ku.edu, Univ of Kansas; Gs
Ludwikoski, David J., 443-840-4216 dludwikoski@ccbcmd.edu, Comm Coll of Baltimore County, Catonsville; ZegZn
Lueders-Dumont, Jessica, 609-258-4101 jl16@princeton.edu, Princeton Univ; Cm
Lueth, Virgil L., 575-835-5140 vwlueth@nmt.edu, New Mexico Inst of Mining and Tech; GzEg
Luhmann, Andrew J., 630 752 7476 andrew.luhmann@wheaton.edu, Wheaton Coll; HwGmCl
Lukas, Roger, (808) 956-7896 rlukas@soest.hawaii.edu, Univ of Hawai'i, Manoa; Op
Lukinbeal, Christopher, clukinbe@email.arizona.edu, Univ of Arizona; Zi
Lulla, Kamlesh, kamlesh.p.lulla@jsc.nasa.gov, Univ of Delaware; Zr
Lumley, David, (972) 883-2424 david.lumley@utdallas.edu, Univ of Texas, Dallas; YsrYn
Lumpkin, Thomas A., (509) 335-2726 christie.lumpkin@wsu.edu, Washington State Univ; Zn
Lumsden, David N., (901) 678-2774 dlumsden@memphis.edu, Univ of Memphis; Gd
Lund, David, 860-405-9331 david.lund@uconn.edu, Univ of Connecticut; Oc
Lund, Jay R., (916) 752-5671 Univ of California, Davis; Hs
Lund, Steven P., (213) 740-5835 slund@usc.edu, Univ of Southern California; Ym
Lund, William R., (435) 865-9034 billlund@utah.gov, Utah Geological Survey; Ng
Lundblad, Steven P., 808-932-7548 slundbla@hawaii.edu, Univ of Hawai'i, Hilo; GraCz
Lundin, Robert F., robert.lundin@asu.edu, Arizona State Univ; Pm
Lundquist, Jessica D., (206) 685-7594 jdlund@uw.edu, Univ of Washington; As
Lundstrom, Craig C., (217) 244-6293 lundstro@illinois.edu, Univ of Illinois, Urbana-Champaign; Cpg
Lunine, Jonathan I., (520) 621-2789 jlunine@lpl.arizona.edu, Univ of Arizona; Xc
Luo, Chao, chao.luo@eas.gatech.edu, Georgia Inst of Tech; As
Luo, Gang, 512-475-6613 gangluo66@gmail.com, Univ of Texas, Austin; Gtc
Luo, Johnny, 212-650-8936 luo@sci.ccny.cuny.edu, Graduate Sch of the City Univ of New York; Zg
Luo, Jun, (417) 836-4273 junluo@missouristate.edu, Missouri State Univ; Zi
Luo, Zhexi, (412) 622-6578 calleryb@carnegiemnh.org, Carnegie Mus of Natural History; Pv
Lupankwa, Mlindelwa , 012 382 6213 lupankwam@tut.ac.za, Tshwane Univ of Tech; HywGg
Lupia, Richard, (405) 325-7229 rlupia@ou.edu, Univ of Oklahoma; Pm
Lupo, Anthony R., (573) 884-1638 lupoa@missouri.edu, Univ of Missouri; As
Lupulescu, Marian V., (518) 474-1432 marian.lupulescu@nysed.gov, New York State Geological Survey; GzxEm
Luque, Francisco Javier, jluque@ucm.es, Univ Complutense de Madrid; Gz
Lusardi, Barb, (612) 626-4791 lusar001@umn.edu, Univ of Minnesota; Gl
Lusk, Braden , 859-257-1105 braden.lusk@uky.edu, Univ of Kentucky; Nm
Luth, Robert W., (780) 492-2740 robert.luth@ualberta.ca, Univ of Alberta; Gi
Luther, Amy, (225) 578-2337 aluther@lsu.edu, Louisiana State Univ; GcZe
Luther, Douglas S., (808) 956-5875 dluther@soest.hawaii.edu, Univ of Hawai'i, Manoa; Op
Luther, Mark E., (727) 553-1528 mluther@marine.usf.edu, Univ of South Florida; Op
Luther, III, George W., (302) 645-4208 luther@udel.edu, Univ of Delaware; Cm
Luttge, Andreas, (713) 348-6304 aluttge@rice.edu, Rice Univ; Cg
Luttrell, Karen, (225) 578-5620 kluttrell@lsu.edu, Louisiana State Univ; Yg
Lutz, Alexandra, 775.673.7418 alexandra.lutz@dri.edu, Univ of Nevada, Reno; Hw
Lutz, Pascale, +33(0)3 44068990 pascale.lutz@lasalle-beauvais.fr, Institut Polytechnique LaSalle Beauvais (ex-IGAL); YgxYd
Lutz, Timothy M., (610) 436-3498 tlutz@wcupa.edu, West Chester Univ; Gq
Luzincourt, Marc R., (418) 654-3715 mluzinco@nrcan.gc.ca, Universite du Quebec; Cs
Lužar-Oberiter, Borna, +38514606115 bluzar@geol.pmf.hr, Univ of Zagreb; Gg
Lwiza, Kamazima M., (631) 632-7309 kamazima.lwiza@stonybrook.edu, SUNY, Stony Brook; Oc
Lübbe, Maike, 089/2180 4337 meike.luebbe@lrz.uni-muenchen.de, Ludwig-Maximilians-Univ Muenchen; Gz
Lybrand, Rebecca A., ralybrand@ucdavis.edu, Univ of California, Davis;

SbCb
Lyle, Mike, 757-822-7189 tclylem@tcc.edu, Tidewater Comm Coll; Gg
Lyle, Mitchell, 541-737-3427 mlyle@coas.oregonstate.edu, Oregon State Univ; GgYg
Lynch, Amanda H., amanda_lynch@brown.edu, Brown Univ; AsGe
Lynch, Casey, (775) 682-6192 caseylynch@unr.edu, Univ of Nevada, Reno; Zn
Lynch-Stieglitz, Jean, (404) 894-3944 jean@eas.gatech.edu, Georgia Inst of Tech; OoPcCs
Lynds, Ranie, (307) 766-2286 ranie.lynds@wyo.gov, Univ of Wyoming; Gsr
Lynn, Kendra J., klynn@usgs.gov, Univ of Delaware; Gi
Lynn, Resler M., (540) 231-5790 resler@vt.edu, Virginia Polytechnic Inst & State Univ; Zy
Lynner, Colton, 302-831-4558 clynner@udel.edu, Univ of Delaware; GtYsGc
Lyon, Ian, ian.lyon@manchester.ac.uk, Univ of Manchester; Xc
Lyon, Ronald J. P., (650) 725-8077 lyon@pangea.stanford.edu, Stanford Univ; Zr
Lyons, Lawrence, (310) 206-7876 larry@atmos.ucla.edu, Univ of California, Los Angeles; As
Lyons, Steven, steve.lyons@noaa.gov, Angelo State Univ; Am
Lyons, Timothy W., (951) 827-3106 timothy.lyons@ucr.edu, Univ of California, Riverside; CgOcCl
Lyons, William B., (614) 688-3241 lyons.142@osu.edu, Ohio State Univ; HwCgZg
Lyson, Tyler, 303-370-6328 tyler.lyson@dmns.org, Denver Mus of Nature & Sci; Pv
Lytwyn, Jennifer N., 713-743-3296 jlytwyn@uh.edu, Univ of Houston; Gi

M

Ma, Jingsheng, +44 (0)131 451 8296 jingsheng.ma@pet.hw.ac.uk, Heriot-Watt Univ; Np
Ma, Lena Q., (352) 392-9063 lqma@ufl.edu, Univ of Florida; Sc
Ma, Lin, 915-747-5218 lma@utep.edu, Univ of Texas, El Paso; HgCg
Ma, Shuo, 619-594-3091 sma@mail.sdsu.edu, San Diego State Univ; Ys
Ma, Yanxia, yma@lsu.edu, Louisiana State Univ; Og
Maantay, Juliana, 718-960-8574 maantay@aol.com, Lehman Coll (CUNY); Zi
Maas, Regan, 818-677-3515 regan.maas@csun.edu, California State Univ, Northridge; Zi
Maasch, Kirk A., (207) 581-2197 kirk@iceage.umeqs.maine.edu, Univ of Maine; As
Mabee, Stephen B., (413) 545-4814 sbmabee@geo.umass.edu, Massachusetts Geological Survey; Hw
Maboko, Makenya A., +255222410013 mmaboko@uccmail.co.tz, Univ of Dar es Salaam; GpCgGx
Mac Eachern, James A., 778-782-5388 jmaceach@sfu.ca, Simon Fraser Univ; Gs
Mac Niocaill, Conall, +44 (0)1865 282135 conallm@earth.ox.ac.uk, Univ of Oxford; GtgYm
Macadam, John, j.d.macadam@exeter.ac.uk, Exeter Univ; Ge
Macalady, Donald L., dmacalad@mines.edu, Colorado Sch of Mines; Cl
Macalady, Jennifer L., (814) 865-6330 jlm80@psu.edu, Pennsylvania State Univ, Univ Park; PgClSb
MacAyeal, Douglas R., (773) 702-8027 drm7@midway.uchicago.edu, Univ of Chicago; Yr
MacCarthy, Ivor, +353 21 4902152 i.maccarthy@ucc.ie, Univ Coll Cork; Gs
MacCarthy, Patrick, pmaccart@mines.edu, Colorado Sch of Mines; Co
MacCready, Parker, (206) 685-9588 parker@ocean.washington.edu, Univ of Washington; Op
Macdonald, Francis, francism@geol.ucsb.edu, Univ of California, Santa Barbara; Gg
MacDonald, Iain, +44(0)29 208 77302 mcdonaldi1@cardiff.ac.uk, Univ of Wales; Ca
MacDonald, James H., (239) 590-7429 jmacdona@fgcu.edu, Florida Gulf Coast Univ; GizGt
Macdonald, R. Heather, (757) 221-2443 rhmacd@wm.edu, William & Mary; GsZe
MacDonald, William D., (607) 777-2863 Binghamton Univ; Gc
Macdougall, J. Douglas, jdmacdougall@ucsd.edu, Univ of California, San Diego; Cg
Mace, Gerald, 801-585-9489 jay.mace@utah.edu, Univ of Utah; As
Mace, Robert, (512) 245-2170 Texas State Univ; HwgHy
Macelloni, Leonardo, (228) 688-7099 leonardo.macelloni@usm.edu, Univ of Southern Mississippi; Yr
MacFadden, Bruce J., 3523921721 x496 bmacfadd@flmnh.ufl.edu, Univ of Florida; Pv
Macfarlane, Andrew W., (305) 348-3980 macfarla@fiu.edu, Florida International Univ; Em
MacGregor, Kelly, (651) 696-6441 macgregor@macalester.edu, Macalester Coll; GmlGg
Machel, Hans G., (780) 492-5659 hans.machel@ualberta.ca, Univ of Alberta; Go
Machovina, Brett , 719-333-3080 brett.machovina@usafa.edu, United States Air Force Academy; Zir
Macias, Steve E., (360) 475-7711 smacias@olympic.edu, Olympic Coll; Gg
Maciha, Mark J., (928) 523-8242 mark.maciha@nau.edu, Northern Arizona Univ; ZnnZn
MacInnes, Breanyn, 509-963-2827 macinnes@geology.cwu.edu, Central Washington Univ; GseGu
MacInnes, Michael, (505) 665-2154 Los Alamos; Zn
MacIntyre, Hugh, (902) 494-2932 hugh.macintyre@dal.ca, Dalhousie Univ; Ob
Macintyre, Ian G., (202) 633-1339 Smithsonian Inst / Nat Mus of Natural History; Gs
MacIssac, Daniel E., (716) 878-6731 Buffalo State Coll; XaZe
Mack, John E., (716) 878-5006 mackje@buffalostate.edu, Buffalo State Coll; Xg
Mackaness, William A., +44 (0) 131 650 8163 william.mackaness@ed.ac.uk, Edinburgh Univ; Zi
Mackas, David L., (250) 363-6442 mackas@ios.bc.ca, Univ of Victoria; Ob
MacKay, Allison A., 614-247-7652 mackay.49@osu.edu, Ohio State Univ; Cq
Mackenzie, Fred T., (808) 395-7907 fredm@soest.hawaii.edu, Univ of Hawai'i, Manoa; CmGes
Mackenzie, Kristen, 303-370-8372 kristen.mackenzie@dmns.org, Denver Mus of Nature & Sci; Zg
Mackey, Tyler, tjmackey@unm.edu, Univ of New Mexico; GdPo
MacKinnon, Stuart J., 250-807-8405 stuart.mackinnon@ubc.ca, Univ of British Columbia, Okanagan Campus; ZeRcZg
Macko, Stephen A., (434) 924-6849 sam8f@virginia.edu, Univ of Virginia; CosOc
Mackowiak, Cheryl, 850-875-7126 echo13@ufl.edu, Univ of Florida; So
MacLachlan, Ian R., (403) 329-2076 maclachlan@uleth.ca, Univ of Lethbridge; Ze
MacLachlan, John, (905) 525-9140 (Ext. 24195) maclacjc@mcmaster.ca, McMaster Univ; Gs
MacLaughlin, Mary M., (406) 496-4655 mmaclaughlin@mtech.edu, Montana Tech of the Univ of Montana; NrgNt
MacLean, John S., 435.586.1937 johnmaclean@suu.edu, Southern Utah Univ; GctZe
Maclennan, John, +44 (0) 1223 761602 jmac05@esc.cam.ac.uk, Univ of Cambridge; Gi
MacLeod, C, macleod@cf.ac.uk, Cardiff Univ; Gu
MacLeod, Chris, +44(0)29 208 74332 macleod@cardiff.ac.uk, Univ of Wales; Og
MacLeod, Kenneth A., (573) 884-3118 macleodk@missouri.edu, Univ of Missouri; Pg
MacMahan, Jamie, jhmacmah@nps.edu, Naval Postgraduate Sch; Onp
MacNish, Robert, (520) 621-5082 macnish@hwr.arizona.edu, Univ of Arizona; Hw
Macomber, Richard, (718) 460-1476 Long Island Univ, Brooklyn Campus; Pg
Macpherson, Colin G., 0191 3342283 colin.macpherson@durham.ac.uk, Durham Univ; CgGiCs
MacPherson, Glenn J., (202) 633-1803 macphers@si.edu, Smithsonian Inst / Nat Mus of Natural History; XcGi
Macpherson, Gwendolyn L., (785) 864-2742 glmac@ku.edu, Univ of Kansas; Hw
MacQuarrie, Pamela, (403) 440-6176 pmacquarrie@mtroyal.ca, Mount Royal Univ; Zy
Macris, Catherine, camacris@iupui.edu, Indiana Univ - Purdue Univ Indianapolis; GzCu
Madadi, Mahyar, +61 8 9266-2324 mahyar.madadi@curtin.edu.au, Curtin Univ; Ye
Maddock, III, Thomas, (520) 621-7120 maddock@hwr.arizona.edu, Univ of Arizona; Hq
Maddocks, Rosalie F., 713-743-2772 rmaddocks@uh.edu, Univ of Houston; Pm
Madej, Mary Ann, mary_ann_madej@usgs.gov, U.S. Geological Survey; Gme
Madin, Ian P., (971) 673-1555 Oregon Dept of Geology and Mineral Industries; Gg
Madison, Frederick W., (608) 263-4004 fredmad@wisc.edu, Univ of Wisconsin, Madison; Sd
Madsen, David B., (801) 537-3314 nrugs.dmadsen@state.ut.us, Utah Geological Survey; Ga
Madsen, John A., (302) 831-1608 jmadsen@udel.edu, Univ of Delaware;

FACULTY INDEX – M

YrOuZe
Maerz, Christian, +44 (0) 1133431504 c.maerz@leeds.ac.uk, Univ of Leeds; CmOuEm
Magaard, Lorenz, 808-956-7509 lorenz@hawaii.edu, Univ of Hawai'i, Manoa; Op
Magee, Elizabeth, 7815817370 x316 e.magee@neu.edu, Northeastern Univ; Zn
Magee, Robert, rmagee@vwc.edu, Virginia Wesleyan Coll; Gge
Magloughlin, Jerry F., (970) 491-1812 jerrym@cnr.colostate.edu, Colorado State Univ; Gpz
Magnani, M. Beatrice, 214-768-1751 mmagnani@smu.edu, Southern Methodist Univ; YsGtYe
Magnusdottir, Gudrun, (949) 824-3520 gudrun@uci.edu, Univ of California, Irvine; As
Magondu, Moffat G., mmagondu@jkuat.ac.ke, Jomo Kenyatta Univ of Agriculture & Tech; ZirZg
Magsino, Sammantha L., (202) 334-2744 smagsino@nas.edu, Nat Academies of Scis, Eng, and Medicine; GvNg
Magson, Justine, +27 (0)51 401 2373 markramj1@ufs.ac.za, Univ of the Free State; CgGi
Mahaffee, Tina, 478-934-3400 tmahaffee@mgc.edu, Middle Georgia Coll; Gg
Mahaffey, Claire, +44 0151 794 4090 claire.mahaffey@liverpool.ac.uk, Univ of Liverpool; Oc
Mahan, Kevin H., kevin.mahan@colorado.edu, Univ of Colorado; Gpc
Maharjan, Madan, 910-775-4589 madan.maharjan@uncp.edu, Univ of North Carolina, Pembroke; Hw
Mahegan, Mairead, 508-289-3931 mmaheigan@whoi.edu, Woods Hole Oceanographic Inst; Ob
Maher, Damien, damien.maher@scu.edu.au, Southern Cross Univ; GeCs
Maher, John, 9134698500 x5953 jmaher1@jccc.edu, Johnson County Comm Coll; Zy
Maher, Kierran, 575-835-6354 kmaher@nmt.edu, New Mexico Inst of Mining and Tech; Eg
Maher, Jr., Harmon D., 402-554-4807 harmon_maher@unomaha.edu, Univ of Nebraska, Omaha; GcsGt
Maher, Jr., Louis J., (608) 262-9595 maher@geology.wisc.edu, Univ of Wisconsin, Madison; Pl
Mahlen, Nancy J., (585) 245-5016 mahlen@geneseo.edu, SUNY, Geneseo; GgpCc
Mahler, Robert L., (208) 885-7025 Univ of Idaho; Zn
Mahmoud, Sara A., 002-03-3921595 geo_soso2006@yahoo.com, Alexandria Univ; Gg
Mahmoudi, Nagissa, 514-398-2722 nagissa.mahmoudi@mcgill.ca, McGill Univ; Cb
Mahoney, J. Brian, (715) 836-4952 mahonej@uwec.edu, Univ of Wisconsin, Eau Claire; GstEg
Mahood, Gail A., (650) 723-1429 gail@pangea.stanford.edu, Stanford Univ; Gi
Mahowald, Natalie M., 607-255-5166 nmm63@cornell.edu, Cornell Univ; As
Maier, Raina M., (520) 621-7231 rmaier@ag.arizona.edu, Univ of Arizona; Zn
Main, Ian G., +44 (0) 131 650 4911 ian.main@ed.ac.uk, Edinburgh Univ; Ys
Maio, Chris, (907) 474-5651 cvmaio@alaska.edu, Univ of Alaska, Fairbanks; Zy
Maisey, John G., (212) 769-5811 American Mus of Natural History; Pv
Majodina, Thando, (012) 382-6283 majodinato@tut.ac.za, Tshwane Univ of Tech; GgzGe
Major, Penni, 281-765-7865 penny.westerfeld@nhmccd.edu, Lonestar Coll - North Harris; Gg
Major, Ruth H., 518-629-7131 Hudson Valley Comm Coll; GgRh
Maju-Oyovwikowhe, Efetobore G., efetobore.maju-oyovwikowhe@uniben.edu, Univ of Benin; GszGo
Majzlan, Juraj, +49(0)3641 948700 juraj.majzlan@uni-jena.de, Friedrich-Schiller-Univ Jena; Gz
Mak, John E., (631) 632-8673 john.mak@stonybrook.edu, SUNY, Stony Brook; AsCas
Mak, Mankin, (217) 333-8071 mak@atmos.uiuc.edu, Univ of Illinois, Urbana-Champaign; As
Makkawi, Mohammad, +966138602621 makkawi@kfupm.edu.sa, King Fahd Univ of Petroleum and Minerals; HwGoq
Makovicky, Peter, pmakovic@umn.edu, Univ of Minnesota, Twin Cities; Pv
Maksoudian, Michell, mmaksoud@calpoly.edu, California Polytechnic State Univ; Zn
Makungo, R., +27 15 962 8577 rachel.makungo@univen.ac.za, Univ of Venda for Sci & Tech; HzqHw
Malahoff, Alexander, (808) 956-6802 malahoff@hawaii.edu, Univ of Hawai'i, Manoa; Cm
Malakar, Nabin, nmalakar@worcester.edu, Worcester State Univ; Ap
Malanotte-Rizzoli, Paola M., (617) 253-2451 rizzoli@mit.edu, Massachusetts Inst of Tech; Op
Malcolm, Alison, (709) 864-2728 amalcolm@mun.ca, Memorial Univ of Newfoundland; Yg
Malcolm, Elizabeth, 757-233-8751 emalcolm@vwc.edu, Virginia Wesleyan Coll; AsCgOg
Malcuit, Robert J., malcuit@denison.edu, Denison Univ; Gx
Malega, Ron, 417-836-4556 rmalega@missouristate.edu, Missouri State Univ; Zn
Malhotra, Rakesh, rmalhotra@nccu.edu, North Carolina Central Univ; Zri
Malhotra, Renu, (520) 626-5899 renu@lpl.arizona.edu, Univ of Arizona; Xs
Malin, Gill, +44 (0)1603 59 2531 g.malin@uea.ac.uk, Univ of East Anglia; ObcCb
Malin, Peter E., (919) 681-8889 p.malin@auckland.ac.nz, Duke Univ; Ys
Malinconico, Lawrence L., (610) 330-5195 malincol@lafayette.edu, Lafayette Coll; YgGcv
Malinconico, Mary Ann, (610) 330-5195 Lafayette Coll; Eo
Malinverno, Alberto, alberto@ldeo.columbia.edu, Columbia Univ; Go
Malinverno, Alberto , (845) 365-8577 alberto@ldeo.columbia.edu, Columbia Univ; Gug
Mallard, Laura D., mallardl@appstate.edu, Appalachian State Univ; GtZe
Mallarino, Antonio W., (515) 294-6200 apmallar@iastate.edu, Iowa State Univ of Sci & Tech; So
Mallick, Subhashis, 307-766-2884 smallick@uwyo.edu, Univ of Wyoming; YseYg
Mallik, Ananya, 401)-874-2671 ananya_mallik@uri.edu, Univ of Rhode Island; Gx
Mallinson, David, (252) 328-1344 mallinsond@ecu.edu, East Carolina Univ; Gu
Malone, Andrew, 312-413-1868 amalone@uic.edu, Univ of Illinois at Chicago; GlAt
Malone, David H., (309) 438-7649 dhmalon@ilstu.edu, Illinois State Univ; GcsEg
Malone, Shawn, (920) 465-2349 malones@uwgb.edu, Univ of Wisconsin, Green Bay; GgpGz
Malone, Stephen D., 206-685-3811 smalone@uw.edu, Univ of Washington; YsGt
Maloney, Ashley, 609-258-4101 Princeton Univ; Oc
Maloney, Eric, emaloney@atmos.colostate.edu, Colorado State Univ; As
Maloof, Adam C., 609-258-4101 maloof@princeton.edu, Princeton Univ; Ym
Malservisi, Rocco, 089/2180 4202 malservisi@rsmas.miami.edu, Ludwig-Maximilians-Univ Muenchen; Yg
Maltese, Adam V., (812) 856-8059 amaltese@indiana.edu, Indiana Univ, Bloomington; Ze
Malzer, Gary L., (612) 625-6728 gmalzer@soils.umn.edu, Univ of Minnesota, Twin Cities; Sc
Malzone, Jonathan, (859) 622-1278 jonathan.malzone@eku.edu, Eastern Kentucky Univ; HwgGm
Mamer, Ethan, 575-835-5118 ethan.mamer@nmt.edu, New Mexico Inst of Mining and Tech; Hw
Mana, Sara, smana@salemstate.edu, Salem State Univ; GciGv
Manabe, Syukuro, (609) 258-2790 manabe@princeton.edu, Princeton Univ; AstPc
MANCA, Pierpaolo P., 070-675-5529 ppmanca@unica.it, Universita di Cagliari; Nm
Manchester, Steven R., (352) 392-1721 steven@flmnh.ufl.edu, Univ of Florida; PbGs
Mancini, Ernest A., (205) 348-4319 emancini@as.ua.edu, Univ of Alabama; Gro
Manda, Alex K., (252) 328-9403 mandaa@ecu.edu, East Carolina Univ; HwgHq
Mandel, Rolfe, (785) 864-2171 mandel@ku.edu, Univ of Kansas; Gam
Mandia, Scott A., 631-451-4104 mandias@sunysuffolk.edu, Suffolk County Comm Coll, Ammerman Campus; Amt
Mandra, York T., (415) 338-2061 ytmandra@sfsu.edu, San Francisco State Univ; Pg
Manduca, Cathryn A., (507) 222-7096 cmanduca@carleton.edu, Carleton Coll; Gi
Mandziuk, William S., (204) 474-7826 mandziu0@cc.umanitoba.ca, Univ of Manitoba; Gg
Manecan, Teodosia, (212) 772-5265 tmanecan@hunter.cuny.edu, Hunter Coll (CUNY); Gp
Maneiro, Kathryn A., 630 752 7228 kathryn.maneiro@wheaton.edu, Wheaton Coll; CcGic
Maneta, Marco, 406-243-2454 marco.maneta@mso.umt.edu, Univ of Montana; Hsg
Manfrino, Carrie M., (908) 737-3697 cmanfrin@kean.edu, Kean Univ;

Marshall, Craig, (785) 864-6029 cpmarshall@ku.edu, Univ of Kansas; GzZmXb
Marshall, Dan D., 778-782-5474 Simon Fraser Univ; Ca
Marshall, Hans-Peter, hpmarshall@boisestate.edu, Boise State Univ; YxGl
Marshall, Jeffrey S., 909-869-3461 marshall@csupomona.edu, California State Polytechnic Univ, Pomona; GmtHs
Marshall, Jill A., 479-575-2420 jillm@uark.edu, Univ of Arkansas, Fayetteville; Gm
Marshall, Jim, +44-151-794-5177 isotopes@liverpool.ac.uk, Univ of Liverpool; Cs
Marshall, John C., (617) 253-9615 jmarsh@mit.edu, Massachusetts Inst of Tech; Op
Marshall, Madeline, mmarshall@albion.edu, Albion Coll; GsPi
Marshall, Monte, mmarshall@mail.sdsu.edu, San Diego State Univ; YmGtc
Marshall, Scott T., 828-265-8680 marshallst@appstate.edu, Appalachian State Univ; YxGc
Marshall, Stephen, (519) 824-4120 Ext.52720 samarsha@uoguelph.ca, Univ of Guelph; Zn
Marshall, Thomas R., 605-677-6164 tom.marshall@usd.edu, South Dakota Dept of Environment and Natural Resources; GgEo
Marsham, John, +44(0) 113 34 36422 j.marsham@leeds.ac.uk, Univ of Leeds; As
Marston, Sallie A., marston@email.arizona.edu, Univ of Arizona; Zu
Marszalek, Henryk, henryk.marszalek@uwr.edu.pl, Univ of Wroclaw; Hy
Martek, Lynnette F., martek@mailbox.sc.edu, Univ of South Carolina, Lancaster; ZgAm
Martel, Richard, (418) 654-2683 rene.martel@ete.inrs.ca, Universite du Quebec; Hw
Martel, Stephen J., (808) 956-7797 martel@soest.hawaii.edu, Univ of Hawai'i, Manoa; Ng
Martens, Hilary R., (406) 243-6855 hilary.martens@umontana.edu, Univ of Montana; YgsYd
Martill, David, +44 023 92 842256 david.martill@port.ac.uk, Univ of Portsmouth; PvgPe
Martin, Anthony J., (740) 368-3621 geoam@learnlink.emory.edu, Emory Univ; Pe
Martin, Arturo, amartin@cicese.mx, Centro de Investigación Científica y de Educación Superior de Ensenada; Gd
Martin, Barton S., (740) 368-3621 bsmartin@owu.edu, Ohio Wesleyan Univ; GxvCg
Martin, Beth, 314-935-4136 martin@wustl.edu, Washington Univ in St. Louis; Ng
Martin, Candace E., +64 3 479-7526 candace.martin@otago.ac.nz, Univ of Otago; ClcGz
Martín, Cristina, crismartin@ucm.es, Univ Complutense de Madrid; Gm
Martin, Ellen E., (352) 392-2141 eemartin@ufl.edu, Univ of Florida; Cl
Martin, Gale D., 702-651- 3141 gale.martin@csn.edu, Coll of Southern Nevada - West Charleston Campus; Gg
Martin, James E., (337) 482-6468 geology@louisiana.edu, Univ of Louisiana at Lafayette; PvGg
Martin, Jonathan B., (352) 392-6219 jbmartin@ufl.edu, Univ of Florida; ClHg
Martin, Luke, 575-835-5283 luke.martin@nmt.edu, New Mexico Inst of Mining and Tech; GorGd
Martin, Paul F., (509) 376-2519 paul.martin@pnl.gov, Pacific Northwest; Cg
Martin, Randal S., (505) 835-5469 New Mexico Inst of Mining and Tech; As
Martin, Robert F., 514-324-2579 robert.martin@mcgill.ca, McGill Univ; GziEm
Martin, Ronald E., (302) 831-2569 daddy@udel.edu, Univ of Delaware; PmePg
Martin, Scot T., 617-495-7620 smartin@seas.harvard.edu, Harvard Univ; Cg
Martin, Scott C., 330-941-3026 scmartin@ysu.edu, Youngstown State Univ; Ge
Martin, Seelye, (206) 543-6438 seelye@ocean.washington.edu, Univ of Washington; Op
Martin, Silvana, +390498279104 silvana.martin@unipd.it, Univ degli Studi di Padova; Gc
Martin, Timothy J., (630) 252-8708 tjmartin@anl.gov, Argonne; As
Martin, Walter, 704-687-5954 wemartin@uncc.edu, Univ of North Carolina, Charlotte; As
Martin, William R., (508) 289-2836 wmartin@whoi.edu, Woods Hole Oceanographic Inst; Oc
Martin, Zackary E., zmartin@austincc.edu, Austin Comm Coll District; RwZn
Martín Chivelet, Javier, j.m.chivelet@ucm.es, Univ Complutense de Madrid; PcGs
Martín Duque, José Francisco, josefco@ucm.es, Univ Complutense de Madrid; Gm
Martin-Hayden, James, (419) 530-2634 jhayden@geology.utoledo.edu, Univ of Toledo; Hq
Martinetto, Edoardo, edoardo.martinetto@unito.it, Univ di Torino; Pb
Martinez, Fernando, (808) 956-6882 martinez@soest.hawaii.edu, Univ of Hawai'i, Manoa; Yr
Martínez, Gemma, gemmamar@ucm.es, Univ Complutense de Madrid; Pg
Martínez, José Jesús, jmdiaz@ucm.es, Univ Complutense de Madrid; GcRn
Martínez, Pedro, permatin@ucm.es, Univ Complutense de Madrid; Hw
Martínez Fernández, Francisco, ++935811513 francisco.martinez@uab.cat, Universitat Autonoma de Barcelona; GpCp
Martinez Torres, Luis Miguel, luismiguel.martinez@ehu.eus, Univ of the Basque Country UPV/EHU; Ggt
Martini, Anna M., (413) 542-2067 ammartini@amherst.edu, Amherst Coll; Cl
Martini, I. Peter, (519) 824-4120 x52488 pmartini@uoguelph.ca, Univ of Guelph; Gsl
Martino, Ronald L., (304) 696-2715 martinor@marshall.edu, Marshall Univ; GsrPe
Martins, Zita, +44 20 759 49982 z.martins@imperial.ac.uk, Imperial Coll; Xm
Martinson, Douglas G., dgm@ldeo.columbia.edu, Columbia Univ; Op
Martinuš, Maja, +38514606089 majamarti@geol.pmf.hr, Univ of Zagreb; Gg
Martiny, Adam, 949-824-9713 amartiny@uci.edu, Univ of California, Irvine; Ob
Martire, Luca, luca.martire@unito.it, Univ di Torino; Gd
Márton, Péter, martonp@ludens.elte.hu, Eotvos Lorand Univ; YmgYs
Martz, Todd, (858) 534-7466 trmartz@ucsd.edu, Univ of California, San Diego; Gg
Marvinney, Robert G., (207) 287-2804 robert.g.marvinney@maine.gov, Dept of Agriculture, Conservation, and Forestry; Gg
Marzen, Luke J., (334) 844-3462 marzelj@auburn.edu, Auburn Univ; Zir
Marzolf, John E., (618) 453-7372 marzolf@geo.siu.edu, Southern Illinois Univ Carbondale; Gs
Marzoli, Andrea, +390498279154 andrea.marzoli@unipd.it, Univ degli Studi di Padova; Cg
Marzulli, Walter, (609) 292-2576 walt.marzulli@dep.state.nj.us, New Jersey Geological and Water Survey; Zy
Masch, Ludwig, 089/2180 4273 masch@min.uni-muenchen.de, Ludwig-Maximilians-Univ Muenchen; Gz
Masciocco, Luciano, luciano.masciocco@unito.it, Univ di Torino; Ge
Masek, Ondrej, +44 (0) 131 650 5095 ondrej.masek@ed.ac.uk, Edinburgh Univ; Ng
Masiello, Caroline A., 713.348.5234 masiello@rice.edu, Rice Univ; Zn
Maslowski, Wieslaw, (831) 656-3162 maslowsk@nps.edu, Naval Postgraduate Sch; Op
Mason, Allen S., (505) 667-4140 Los Alamos; As
Mason, Charles E., (606) 783-2166 c.mason@moreheadstate.edu, Morehead State Univ; PiGrs
Mason, Owen, (907) 474-6293 Univ of Alaska, Fairbanks; Ga
Mason, Philippa J., +44 20 759 46528 p.j.mason@imperial.ac.uk, Imperial Coll; Zr
Mason, Robert P., (860) 405-9129 robert.mason@uconn.edu, Univ of Connecticut; OcCtm
Mason, Sherri A., 716.673.3292 mason@fredonia.edu, SUNY, Fredonia; ZgGe
Mass, Clifford F., cliff@atmos.washington.edu, Univ of Washington; As
MASSACCI, Giorgio, 070-675-5530 massacci@unica.it, Universita di Cagliari; Nm
Massare, Judy A., (585) 395-2419 jmassare@brockport.edu, SUNY, The Coll at Brockport; Pv
Massey, Michael S., mike.massey@csueastbay.edu, California State Univ, East Bay; ScGeCg
Massironi, Matteo, +390498279116 matteo.massironi@unipd.it, Univ degli Studi di Padova; XgZr
Mastalerz, Maria, (812) 855-5412 mmastale@indiana.edu, Indiana Univ; Ec
Masterlark, Timothy L., (605) 394-2461 timothy.masterlark@sdsmt.edu, South Dakota Sch of Mines & Tech; YdhNr
Masterman, Steven S., (907) 451-5007 steve.masterman@alaska.gov, Alaska Division of Geological & Geophysical Surveys; EgNg
Masters, T. Guy, (858) 534-4122 tmasters@ucsd.edu, Univ of California, San Diego; YsGy
Masterson, Andrew, andym@earth.northwestern.edu, Northwestern Univ; CslCa
Mata, Scott, (657) 278-7096 smata@fullerton.edu, California State Univ, Fullerton; Gg
Matano, Ricardo P., (541) 737-2212 rmatano@coas.oregonstate.edu, Oregon State Univ; OpAs
Matassa, Catherine, catherine.matassa@uconn.edu, Univ of Connecticut; Ob
Mateus, António, amateus@fc.ul.pt, Unive de Lisboa; Em
Matheney, Ronald K., (701) 777-4569 ronald.matheney@engr.und.edu, Univ

of North Dakota; Cs
Mathenge, Christine, 931-221-6434 mathengec@apsu.ecu, Austin Peay State Univ; Zcy
Matheny, Ashley, ashley.matheny@jsg.utexas.edu, Univ of Texas, Austin; Hg
Mather, Tamsin A., +44 (0)1865 282125 tamsin.mather@earth.ox.ac.uk, Univ of Oxford; Gv
Mathers, Hannah, hannah.mathers@glasgow.ac.uk, Univ of Glasgow; GmlGg
Mathewson, Christopher C., (979) 845-2488 mathewson@geo.tamu.edu, Texas A&M Univ; NgHwEg
Mathez, Edmond A., 212-769-5459 mathez@amnh.org, American Mus of Natural History; Gx
Mathias, Simon, s.a.mathias@durham.ac.uk, Durham Univ; Hy
Mathur, Ram Raj, +919347303173 ramrajmathur@gmail.com, Osmania Univ; YeuYm
Mathur, Ryan, 814-641-3725 mathur@juniata.edu, Juniata Coll; CeYgHw
Matiasek, Sandrine, 530-898-5096 smatiasek@csuchico.edu, California State Univ, Chico; CqRw
Matisoff, Gerald, (216) 368-3690 gerald.matisoff@case.edu, Case Western Reserve Univ; Cbc
Matoza, Robin, matoza@geol.ucsb.edu, Univ of California, Santa Barbara; Gv
Matsumoto, Katsumi, 612-624-0275 katsumi@umn.edu, Univ of Minnesota, Twin Cities; Oc
Matsuoka, Kenichi, +47 77 75 06 45 matsuoka@npolar.no, Univ of Washington; Gl
Matter, Juerg M., +44 (0)23 80593042 j.matter@southampton.ac.uk, Univ of Southampton; Ng
Mattey, Dave, +44 1784 443587 d.mattey@rhul.ac.uk, Royal Holloway Univ of London; Cs
Matthews, Adrian, +44 (0)1603 59 3733 a.j.matthews@uea.ac.uk, Univ of East Anglia; Am
Matthews, Robert A., (916) 752-0179 Univ of California, Davis; Ge
Mattieu, Lucie, 418-545-5011 x2538 lucie.mathieu1@uqac.ca, Universite du Quebec a Chicoutimi; EgmCe
Mattigod, Shas V., (509) 376-4311 shas.mattigod@pnl.gov, Pacific Northwest; Cl
Mattinson, Chris, 509.963.1628 mattinson@geology.cwu.edu, Central Washington Univ; GpCcGt
Mattioli, Glen, (817) 272-2987 mattioli@uta.edu, Univ of Texas, Arlington; GitYd
Mattox, Stephen R., (616) 331-3734 mattoxs@gvsu.edu, Grand Valley State Univ; ZeGv
Mattox, Tari, 616-234-2119 tmattox@grcc.edu, Grand Rapids Comm Coll; GgvCg
Mattson, Peter H., (718) 997-3335 Queens Coll (CUNY); Gc
Matty, David J., (801) 626-7195 dmatty@weber.edu, Weber State Univ; Gig
Matyjasik, Basia, (801) 537-3122 basiamatyjasik@utah.gov, Utah Geological Survey; Gg
Matyjasik, Marek, (801) 626-7726 mmatyjasik@weber.edu, Weber State Univ; HwGe
Matzke, David, (313) 593-5036 dmatzke@umich.edu, Univ of Michigan, Dearborn; Xy
Mauch, James, Ext. 236 james.mauch@wyo.gov, Wyoming State Geological Survey; GmRnGg
Maul, George A., 321-674-8096 gmaul@fit.edu, Florida Inst of Tech; Op
Maulud, Mat Ruzlin, 03-79674144 matruzlin@um.edu.my, Univ of Malaya; Zn
Maurrasse, Florentin J., (305) 348-2350 maurrass@fiu.edu, Florida International Univ; PsGsCm
Mauskopf, Philip, (480) 965-3267 philip.mauskopf@asu.edu, Arizona State Univ; Xa
Mauzerall, Denise L., (609) 258-2498 mauzeral@princeton.edu, Princeton Univ; As
Mavimbela, Philani, (031) 260-7081 mavimbelap@ukzn.ac.za, Univ of KwaZulu-Natal; GpzEg
Mavko, Gerald M., (650) 723-9438 Stanford Univ; Yg
Mawalagedara, Rachindra, 515-294-8633 rmawala@iastate.edu, Iowa State Univ of Sci & Tech; As
Maxbauer, Dan, 507-222-5787 dmaxbauer@carleton.edu, Carleton Coll; PcYm
Maxwell, Arthur E., 512-471-0411 art@ig.utexas.edu, Univ of Texas, Austin; Og
Maxwell, James "Sandy", (610) 436-2240 jmaxwell@wcupa.edu, West Chester Univ; Ze
Maxwell, Michael, (604) 296-4218 michael_maxwell@golder.com, Univ of British Columbia; Yg
May, Cynthia, (715) 682-1499 cmay@northland.edu, Northland Coll; ZiyZn
May, Daniel J., (203) 932-7262 dmay@newhaven.edu, Univ of New Haven; GtxGe
May, Diane M., dianemay@missouristate.edu, Missouri State Univ; Zn
May, Fred E., (801) 581-8218 pscem.fmay@state.ut.us, Univ of Utah; Zn
May, James, (662) 325-5806 Mississippi State Univ; Hw
May, Michael, (502) 745-4555 michael.may@wku.edu, Western Kentucky Univ; Ge
May, S J., (972) 377-1635 smay@collin.edu, Collin Coll - Preston Ridge Campus; GgoGc
Mayborn, Kyle R., (309) 298-1577 kr-mayborn@wiu.edu, Western Illinois Univ; Gic
Mayer, Alex S., (906) 487-3372 asmayer@mtu.edu, Michigan Technological Univ; Hy
Mayer, Bernhard, (403) 220-5389 bmayer@ucalgary.ca, Univ of Calgary; CslGe
Mayer, Christine M., (419) 530-8377 christine.mayer@utoledo.edu, Univ of Toledo; Zn
Mayer, James R., (678) 839-4055 jmayer@westga.edu, Univ of West Georgia; Hw
Mayer, Jordan, 612-626-2672 jmayer@umn.edu, Univ of Minnesota; Zi
Mayer, Larry A., 603-862-2615 larry.mayer@unh.edu, Univ of New Hampshire; Gu
Mayer, Margaret, 928-724-6722 Dine' Coll; GeZn
Mayer, Ulrich, (604) 822-1539 umayer@eos.ubc.ca, Univ of British Columbia; Nm
Mayes, Melanie A., 865-574-7336 mayesma@ornl.gov, Univ of Tennessee, Knoxville; ClGeHw
Mayewski, Paul A., (207) 581-3019 paul.mayewski@maine.edu, Univ of Maine; Pe
Mayfield, Michael W., (828) 262-7058 mayfldmw@appstate.edu, Appalachian State Univ; Hs
Maynard, David, (909) 537-4321 dmaynard@csusb.edu, California State Univ, San Bernardino; ZnnZn
Maynard, J. Barry, maynarjb@uc.edu, Univ of Cincinnati; Cl
Mayo, Alan L., 801-422-2338 alan_mayo@byu.edu, Brigham Young Univ; Hw
Mayor, Shane D., 530-898-6337 sdmayor@csuchico.edu, California State Univ, Chico; AsZrAp
Mazariegos, Ruben, 956-665-2154 ruben.mazariegos@utrgv.edu, Univ of Texas, Rio Grande Valley; ZiYe
Mazer, James J., (630) 252-7362 Argonne; Cl
Mazza, Sarah, (413) 558-4396 smazza@smith.edu, Smith Coll; Gx
MAZZELLA, Antonio A., 070-675-5542 mazzella@unica.it, Universita di Cagliari; Gq
Mazzini, Pierro, pmazzini@vims.edu, William & Mary; Op
Mazzocco, Elizabeth, emazzocc@ashland.edu, Ashland Univ; AsRn
Mazzoli, Claudio, +390498279144 claudio.mazzoli@unipd.it, Univ degli Studi di Padova; Gx
Mazzullo, Salvatore J., (316) 978-3140 Wichita State Univ; Go
Mbatu, Richard, mbatu@usf.edu, Univ of South Florida; Zy
Mbila, Monday O., 256-372-4185 monday.mbila@aamu.edu, Alabama A&M Univ; Sd
Mbuh, Mbongowo J., 701-777-4587 mbongowo.mbuh@und.edu, Univ of North Dakota; ZrHs
Mc Mahon, Michelle, 281-765-7865 mmckubota@aol.com, Lonestar Coll - North Harris; Go
McAfee, Gerald B., (432) 335-6558 bmcafee@odessa.edu, Odessa Coll; Pi
McAfee, Stephanie , (775) 784-6999 smcafee@unr.edu, Univ of Nevada, Reno; Zy
McAllister, Arnold L., (506) 453-4804 Univ of New Brunswick; Em
McAndrews, John H., (416) 586-5609 Univ of Toronto; Pl
McArthur, John M., +44 020 7679 2376 j.mcarthur@ucl.ac.uk, Univ Coll London; ClHwPs
McArthur, Russell, (415) 338-1755 San Francisco State Univ; Zn
McBeth, Joyce M., joyce.mcbeth@usask.ca, Univ of Saskatchewan; PgGeSb
McBride, Earle F., (512) 471-1905 efmcbride@mail.utexas.edu, Univ of Texas, Austin; Gd
McBride, John H., (801) 422-5219 john_mcbride@byu.edu, Brigham Young Univ; YeGoe
McBride, Randolph, (703) 993-1642 rmcbride@gmu.edu, George Mason Univ; On
McBride, Raymond G., (519) 824-4120 (Ext. 52492) rmcbride@uoguelph.ca, Univ of Guelph; So
McCabe, Peter, peter.mccabe@adelaide.edu.au, Univ of Adelaide; Go
McCaffrey, Bill, +44(0) 113 34 36625 w.d.mccaffrey@leeds.ac.uk, Univ of Leeds; Gs
McCaffrey, Kenneth J., 0191 3742523 k.j.mccaffrey@durham.ac.uk, Durham Univ; Gc
McCair, Andrew, +44(0) 113 34 35219 a.m.mccaig@leeds.ac.uk, Univ of Leeds; Gc

FACULTY INDEX – M

McCall, Peter L., (216) 368-3676 plm4@case.edu, Case Western Reserve Univ; Pg
McCallister, Robert, (608) 758-6556 robert.mccallister@uwc.edu, Univ of Wisconsin Colls; ZyGgZn
McCanta, Molly, 865-974-6003 mmccanta@utk.edu, Univ of Tennessee, Knoxville; GiXg
McCarter, Michael K., (801) 581-8603 k.mccarter@utah.edu, Univ of Utah; Nm
McCarthy, Christine, mccarthy@ldeo.columbia.edu, Columbia Univ; Ys
McCarthy, Daniel P., (905) 688-5550 (Ext. 3864) dmccarthy2@brocku.ca, Brock Univ; Gl
McCarthy, Francine G., (905) 688-5550 (Ext. 4286) francine@brocku.ca, Brock Univ; Pm
McCarthy, James T., 617-495-2330 jmccarthy@oeb.harvard.edu, Harvard Univ; Ob
McCarthy, Michael P., 206-685-2543 mccarthy@uw.edu, Univ of Washington; XyYx
McCarthy, Paul, (907) 474-6894 pjmccarthy@alaska.edu, Univ of Alaska, Fairbanks; GsSaPc
McCartney, Kevin, (207) 768-9482 kevin.mccartney@umpi.edu, Univ of Maine, Presque Isle; Pm
McCartney, M. Carol L., carol.mccartney@wisc.edu, Univ of Wisconsin, Madison, Division of Extension; RcGee
McCaslin, Bobby D., (505) 646-3405 New Mexico State Univ, Las Cruces; Sc
McCauley, Marlene, (336) 316-2236 mmccauley@guilford.edu, Guilford Coll; Cp
McCauley, Steven, 214-860-2398 smccauley@dcccd.edu, El Centro Coll - Dallas Comm Coll District; GgAm
McCausland, Phil, pmccausl@brocku.ca, Brock Univ; Gz
McClain, James S., (916) 752-7093 Univ of California, Davis; Yr
McClaughry, Jason, (541) 523-3133 Oregon Dept of Geology and Mineral Industries; Gg
McClay, Ken R., +44 1784 443618 k.mcclay@rhul.ac.uk, Royal Holloway Univ of London; GctGo
McClellan, Elizabeth, emcclellan@radford.edu, Radford Univ; GipGd
McClelland, James W., (361) 749-6756 jimm@utexas.edu, Univ of Texas, Austin; CgHsCs
McClelland, Lori, (775)784-4977 mcclella@unr.edu, Univ of Nevada, Reno; Ys
McClelland, William C., 319-335-1827 bill-mcclelland@uiowa.edu, Univ of Iowa; GtCcGc
mcClenaghan, Seán h., + 353 1 8961585 mcclens@tcd.ie, Trinity Coll; Eg
McCluskey, James, (715) 261-6362 jim.mccluskey@uwc.edu, Univ of Wisconsin Colls; ZinZn
McColl, Kaighin, kmccoll@seas.harvard.edu, Harvard Univ; Hg
McCollor, Doug, doug.mccollor@bchydro.com, Univ of British Columbia; Asm
McCollough, Cherie, 361-825-3166 cherie.mccollough@tamucc.edu, Texas A&M Univ, Corpus Christi; Ze
McCollum, Linda B., (509) 359-7473 lmccollum@ewu.edu, Eastern Washington Univ; Pg
McConnaughhay, Mark, 845-431-8536 mcconn@sunydutchess.edu, Dutchess Comm Coll; ZgAmEo
McConnell, David A., (919) 515-0381 damcconn@ncsu.edu, North Carolina State Univ; ZeRcGc
McConnell, Joseph, (775) 673-7348 jmcconn@dri.edu, Univ of Nevada, Reno; Zn
McCorkle, Daniel C., (508) 289-2949 dmccorkle@whoi.edu, Woods Hole Oceanographic Inst; Cm
McCormack, John K., (775) 784-4518 mccormac@mines.unr.edu, Univ of Nevada, Reno; GzEm
McCormick, George R., 419-798-4812 erie-@msn.com, Univ of Iowa; GzEmCa
McCormick, Michael L., 315-859-4832 mmccormi@hamilton.edu, Hamilton Coll; Cb
McCoy, Edward L., (330) 263-3884 mccoy.13@osu.edu, Ohio State Univ; Sp
McCoy, Floyd W., 236-9115 fmccoy@hawaii.edu, Windward Comm Coll; GgaGu
McCoy, Kevin, 303-384-2632 kemccoy@mines.edu, Colorado Geological Survey; NgZiHw
Mccoy, Roger M., (801) 581-8218 Univ of Utah; Zr
McCoy, Scott W., 775-682-7205 scottmccoy@unr.edu, Univ of Nevada, Reno; GmNg
McCoy, Timothy J., (202) 633-2206 mccoyt@si.edu, Smithsonian Inst / Nat Mus of Natural History; Xmg
McCoy, Victoria, mccoyv@uwm.edu, Univ of Wisconsin, Milwaukee; Pb
McCoy, William D., (413) 545-1535 wdmccoy@geo.umass.edu, Univ of Massachusetts, Amherst; Zy
McCoy, Jr., Floyd W., (808) 235-7318 Univ of Hawai'i, Manoa; Gu
McCreary, Julian P., (808) 956-2216 jay@soest.hawaii.edu, Univ of Hawai'i, Manoa; Op
McCrink, Timothy P., (916) 324-2549 California Geological Survey; Ng
McCulloh, Richard P., (225) 578-5327 mccullo@lsu.edu, Louisiana State Univ; Gg
McCullough, Jr., Edgar J., (520) 621-6024 Univ of Arizona; Ge
McCurdy, Maureen, (318) 257-3165 mm@coes.latech.edu, Louisiana Tech Univ; Hw
McCurry, Michael O., mccumich@isu.edu, Idaho State Univ; Gzv
McDade, Ian C., (416)736-2100 #22859 mcdade@yorku.ca, York Univ; Zr
McDaniel, Paul A., (208) 885-7012 Univ of Idaho; Sd
McDermott, Christopher I., +44 (0) 131 650 5931 cmcdermo@staffmail.ed.ac.uk, Edinburgh Univ; Hg
McDermott, Frank, (+353) 1 716 2327 frank.mcdermott@ucd.ie, Univ Coll Dublin; GgCgZg
McDermott, Jeni, jamcdermott@stthomas.edu, Univ of Saint Thomas; GmHw
McDermott, Jill I., (610) 758-3683 jill.mcdermott@lehigh.edu, Lehigh Univ; Cm
McDermott, Thomas M., (585) 395-5718 SUNY, The Coll at Brockport; Zn
McDermott, Timothy, timmcder@montana.edu, Montana State Univ; Po
McDonald, Andrew M., 7056751151 x2266 amcdonald@laurentian.ca, Laurentian Univ, Sudbury; Gz
McDonald, Brenna, (573) 368-2163 brenna.mcdonald@dnr.mo.gov, Missouri Dept of Natural Resources; Ge
McDonald, Catherine, (406) 496-4883 kmcdonald@mtech.edu, Montana Tech of The Univ of Montana; Grs
McDonald, Eric, (775) 673-7302 emcdonald@dri.edu, Univ of Nevada, Reno; Sp
McDonald, Gregory N., (801) 537-3383 gregmcdonald@utah.gov, Utah Geological Survey; Ng
McDonald, Jennifer, (612) 626-4067 jmhorton@umn.edu, Univ of Minnesota; Gl
McDonald, Kyle, 212-650-6452 kmcdonald@ccny.cuny.edu, Graduate Sch of the City Univ of New York; As
McDonald, Lynn, (505) 667-1582 lmcdonald@lanl.gov, Los Alamos; Zn
McDonough, William F., (301) 405-5561 mcdonoug@geol.umd.edu, Univ of Maryland; Cg
McDougall, Jim, 253-566-5060 jmcdougall@tacomacc.edu, Tacoma Comm Coll; Zg
McDowell, Fred W., (512) 471-1672 mcdowell@mail.utexas.edu, Univ of Texas, Austin; Cc
McDowell, Patricia, (541) 346-4567 pmcd@uoregon.edu, Univ of Oregon; Gm
McDowell, Robin J., 770-274-5466 rmcdowell@gsu.edu, Georgia State Univ, Perimeter Coll, Dunwoody Campus; Gge
McDowell, Ronald, (304) 594-2331 mcdowell@geosrv.wvnet.edu, West Virginia Univ; GsPiCe
McDowell, William H., (603) 862-2249 bill.mcdowell@unh.edu, Univ of New Hampshire; HgRw
McDuff, Russell E., (360) 453-7877 mcduff@uw.edu, Univ of Washington; OcGu
McElroy, Anne E., (631) 632-8488 anne.mcelroy@stonybrook.edu, SUNY, Stony Brook; ObCb
McElroy, Brandon, (307) 766-3601 bmcelroy@uwyo.edu, Univ of Wyoming; GsmGr
McElroy, Michael B., (617) 495-9261 mbm@io.harvard.edu, Harvard Univ; As
McElroy, Tom, (416) 736-2100 x22113 tmcelroy@yorku.ca, York Univ; As
McElwain, Jenny, (312) 665-7635 jennifer.mcelwain@gmail.com, Field Mus of Natural History; Pb
McElwaine, Jim, james.mcelwaine@durham.ac.uk, Durham Univ; Yg
McElwee, Carl D., (785) 843-4164 cmcelwee@ku.edu, Univ of Kansas; HgYg
McEvoy, Jamie , (406) 994-4069 jamie.mcevoy@montana.edu, Montana State Univ; Ze
McEwen, Alfred, (520) 621-4573 mcewen@lpl.arizona.edu, Univ of Arizona; Xg
McFadden, Bruce J., (352) 846-2000 bmacfadd@flmnh.ufl.edu, Univ of Florida; Pv
McFadden, Jennifer, 717-361-1392 mcfaddenj@etown.edu, Elizabethtown Coll; ZnnZn
McFadden, Leslie M., (505) 277-6121 lmcfadnm@unm.edu, Univ of New Mexico; Sd
McFadden, Rory, 507-933-7333 rmcfadde@gustavus.edu, Gustavus Adolphus Coll; GxcGz
McFarlane, Norman, (250) 363-8227 norm.mcfarlane@ec.gc.ca, Univ of

Victoria; As

McFiggans, Gordon, +44 0161 306-3954 gordon.b.mcfiggans@manchester.ac.uk, Univ of Manchester; As

McGahan, Donald, (254) 968-9701 mcgahan@tarleton.edu, Texas A&M Univ; Sdc

McGarvie, Dave, +44 (0) 131 549 7140 x 71140 dave.mcgarvie@open.ac.uk, Open Univ; GviCt

McGauley, Michael G., 305-237-2687 mmcgaule@mdc.edu, Miami Dade Coll (Kendall Campus); AmOp

McGeary, Susan, (302) 831-8174 smcgeary@udel.edu, Univ of Delaware; Ze

McGee, David, (617) 324-3545 davidmcg@mit.edu, Massachusetts Inst of Tech; Cl

McGee, Tara, 780-492-3042 tmcgee@ualberta.ca, Univ of Alberta; Zn

McGehee, Thomas L., (512) 595-3590 kftlm00@tamuk.edu, Texas A&M Univ, Kingsville; Cl

McGhee, Jr., George R., 848-445-8523 mcghee@eps.rutgers.edu, Rutgers, The State Univ of New Jersey; PgqPi

McGill, George E., (413) 545-0140 Univ of Massachusetts, Amherst; Gc

McGill, Sally F., (909) 537-5347 smcgill@csusb.edu, California State Univ, San Bernardino; GtYdGm

McGillis, Wade, mcgillis@ldeo.columbia.edu, Columbia Univ; Cm

McGinn, Chris, (919) 530-6269 cmcginn@nccu.edu, North Carolina Central Univ; Zgi

McGinnis, Lyle D., (630) 252-8722 Argonne; Yg

McGivern, Tiffany, (315)792-3134 Utica Coll; Geg

McGlathery, Karen, (804) 924-0558 kjm4k@virginia.edu, Univ of Virginia; Ob

McGlue, Michael M., 859-257-1952 michael.mcglue@uky.edu, Univ of Kentucky; GnrGm

McGoldrick, Peter J., 61 3 6226 7209 Univ of Tasmania; Ce

Mcgowan, Alistair, +4401413305449 alistair.mcgowan@glasgow.ac.uk, Univ of Glasgow; Pg

McGowan, Eileen, 413-586-8305 emcgowan@geo.umass.edu, Univ of Massachusetts, Amherst; Xg

McGowan, John A., (858) 534-2074 jmcgowan@ucsd.edu, Univ of California, San Diego; Ob

McGowan, Nicole M., 360-650-3835 nicole.mcgowan@wwu.edu, Western Washington Univ; CtaCg

McGrail, Bernard P., (509) 376-9193 pete.mcgrail@pnl.gov, Pacific Northwest; Cg

McGrath, Andrew, andrew.mcgrath@flinders.edu.au, Flinders Univ; ZrAs

McGrath, Daniel, daniel.mcgrath@colostate.edu, Colorado State Univ; YuGl

McGrath, Steve F., 406-496-4767 smcgrath@mtech.edu, Montana Tech of The Univ of Montana; CaEgCe

McGraw, Maureen A., (505) 665-8128 mcgraw@lanl.gov, Los Alamos; Zn

McGregor, Kent M., (940) 565-2380 kent.mcgregor@unt.edu, Univ of North Texas; AsZg

McGregor, Stuart W., 205-247-3629 smcgregor@gsa.state.al.us, Geological Survey of Alabama; Hs

McGrew, Allen J., (937) 229-5638 amcgrew1@udayton.edu, Univ of Dayton; GtcGp

McGuire, Jeffrey J., (508) 289-3290 jmcguire@whoi.edu, Woods Hole Oceanographic Inst; Ys

McGwire, Kenneth, 775.673.7324 ken.mcgwire@dri.edu, Univ of Nevada, Reno; Zr

McHenry, Lindsay J., (414) 229-3951 lmchenry@uwm.edu, Univ of Wisconsin, Milwaukee; GzaXg

McHugh, Cecilia, (718) 997-3330 cecilia.mchugh@qc.cuny.edu, Queens Coll (CUNY); Ou

McHugh, Julia, 970-248-1993 jumchugh@coloradomesa.edu, Colorado Mesa Univ; Pgv

McIlrath, Judy, jmcilrath@usf.edu, Univ of South Florida; Gg

McIlroy, Duncan, (709) 864-6722 dmcilroy@mun.ca, Memorial Univ of Newfoundland; Gg

McIlvin, Matt, 508-289-2884 mmcilvin@whoi.edu, Woods Hole Oceanographic Inst; Oc

McInnes, Kevin J., (979) 845-5986 k-mcinnes@tamu.edu, Texas A&M Univ; Sp

McIntosh, Jennifer, 520-626-2282 mcintosh@hwr.arizona.edu, Univ of Arizona; Hy

McIntosh, Kirk D., (512) 471-0480 kirk@ig.utexas.edu, Univ of Texas, Austin; Yr

McIntosh, William C., (575) 835-5324 mcintosh@nmt.edu, New Mexico Inst of Mining and Tech; Cc

McIntyre, Andrew, (718) 997-3329 Queens Coll (CUNY); Pe

McIsaac, Gregory F., (217) 333-9411 Univ of Illinois, Urbana-Champaign; Hs

McKay, Jennifer L., 541-737-4054 mckay@coas.oregonstate.edu, Oregon State Univ; Cm

McKay, Larry D., 865-974-5332 lmckay@utk.edu, Univ of Tennessee, Knoxville; HyGe

McKay, Luke, luke.mckay@montana.edu, Montana State Univ; Po

McKay, Matthew P., (417) 836-5318 matthewmckay@missouristate.edu, Missouri State Univ; Gct

McKay, Nicholas, 928-523-1918 nicholas.mckay@nau.edu, Northern Arizona Univ; PcZo

McKay, Robert M., robert.mckay@dnr.iowa.gov, Iowa Dept of Natural Resources; Gg

McKay III, E. Donald, (217) 356-7338 emckay@illinois.edu, Illinois State Geological Survey; GlsGr

McKean, Adam, (801) 537-3386 adammckean@utah.gov, Utah Geological Survey; Gmg

McKean , Rebecca, 920-403-3227 rebecca.mckean@snc.edu, Saint Norbert Coll; GdPgRh

McKee, James W., (414) 424-4460 mckee@athenet.net, Univ of Wisconsin, Oshkosh; Gr

McKeegan, Kevin D., (310) 825-3580 mckeegan@epss.ucla.edu, Univ of California, Los Angeles; XcCsc

McKenna, Thomas E., 302-831-8257 mckennat@udel.edu, Univ of Delaware; Hg

McKenney, Rosemary, 253-535-8726 mckennra@plu.edu, Pacific Lutheran Univ; Gm

McKenzie, Connie, mckenzie@coes.latech.edu, Louisiana Tech Univ; Zn

McKenzie, Garry D., mckenzie.4@osu.edu, Ohio State Univ; GmeZe

McKenzie, Jeffrey M., 514-398-6767 jeffrey.mckenzie@mcgill.ca, McGill Univ; Hw

McKenzie, Phyllis, (202) 633-1860 mckenzie@si.edu, Smithsonian Inst / Nat Mus of Natural History; Zn

McKenzie, Ross, ross.mckenzie@agric.gov.ab.ca, Univ of Lethbridge; Zn

McKenzie, Scott C., (814) 824-2382 smckenzie@mercyhurst.edu, Mercyhurst Univ; PgXmZe

McKibben, Michael A., (951) 827-3444 michael.mckibben@ucr.edu, Univ of California, Riverside; Cg

McKinley, Galen, (608) 262-4817 galen@aos.wisc.edu, Univ of Wisconsin, Madison; OcpOg

McKinney, Mac, 205-247-3549 mmckinney@gsa.state.al.us, Geological Survey of Alabama; Hws

McKinney, Michael L., (865) 974-2366 mmckinne@utk.edu, Univ of Tennessee, Knoxville; GePg

McKinnon, William B., (314) 935-5604 mckinnon@wustl.edu, Washington Univ in St. Louis; Xg

McKnight, Brian K., (920) 233-4595 briankmcknight@yahoo.com, Univ of Wisconsin, Oshkosh; Gdu

McLaskey, Greg C., gcm8@cornell.edu, Cornell Univ; YsNr

McLaughlin, Patrick, (812) 855-1350 pimclaug@iu.edu, Indiana Univ, Bloomington; Ps

McLaughlin, Peter P., 302-831-8263 ppmclau@udel.edu, Univ of Delaware; HgPm

McLaughlin, Richard, 361-825-2010 richard.mclaughlin@tamucc.edu, Texas A&M Univ, Corpus Christi; Zn

McLaughlin, Jr., Peter P., 302-831-2833 ppmclau@udel.edu, Univ of Delaware; Gr

McLaurin, Brett T., 570-389-4142 bmclauri@bloomu.edu, Bloomsburg Univ; GrsGd

McLean, Noah, noahmc@ku.edu, Univ of Kansas; CcGq

McLelland, James, jmclelland@citlink.net, Colgate Univ; Gp

McLemore, Virginia, 575-835-5521 virginia.mclemore@nmt.edu, New Mexico Inst of Mining and Tech; Em

McLennan, Scott M., (631) 632-8194 scott.mclennan@sunysb.edu, Stony Brook Univ; Cg

McLeod, Claire, 513-529-9662 mcleodcl@miamioh.edu, Miami Univ; Gx

McLeod, Clara, cpmcleod@wustl.edu, Washington Univ in St. Louis; Zn

McLeod, Samuel A., (213) 763-3325 smcleod@ref.usc.edu, Los Angeles County Mus of Natural History; Pv

McManus, Dean A., (206) 543-0587 mcmanus@u.washington.edu, Univ of Washington; Ou

McManus, George B., 860-405-9164 george.mcmanus@uconn.edu, Univ of Connecticut; Ob

McManus, Jerry, jmcmanus@ldeo.columbia.edu, Columbia Univ; Cm

McManus, Margaret A., (831) 459-4736 Univ of California, Santa Cruz; On

McManus, Margaret Anne, (808) 956-8623 mamc@hawaii.edu, Univ of Hawai'i, Manoa; Op

McMechan, George A., (972) 883-2419 mcmec@utdallas.edu, Univ of Texas, Dallas; Ys

McMenamin, Mark, 413-538-2280 mmcmenam@mtholyoke.edu, Mount Holyoke Coll; PgGst

McMillan, Margaret E., (501) 569-3024 memcmillan@ualr.edu, Univ of Arkansas at Little Rock; Gm

Mendelson, Carl V., mendelsn@beloit.edu, Beloit Coll; PmGs
Mendelssohn, Irving A., (225) 388-6425 Louisiana State Univ; Ob
Mendoza, Blanca, blanca@ciencias.unam.mx, Univ Nacional Autonoma de Mexico; Zn
Mendoza, Carl, (780) 492-2664 carl.mendoza@ualberta.ca, Univ of Alberta; Hw
Mendoza, Luis H., lmendoza@cicese.mx, Centro de Investigación Científica y de Educación Superior de Ensenada; Ne
Menegon, Luca, +44 1752 584931 luca.menegon@plymouth.ac.uk, Univ of Plymouth; Gct
Meng, Jin, (212) 496-3337 American Mus of Natural History; Pv
Meng, Lingsen, 310-825-1885 meng@epss.ucla.edu, Univ of California, Los Angeles; Ys
Meng, Qingmin, 662-268-1032 Ext 240 Mississippi State Univ; Zig
Mengel, David, (785) 532-2166 dmengel@ksu.edu, Kansas State Univ; So
Menicucci, Anthony, amenicucci@usf.edu, Univ of South Florida; Cs
Menke, William H., menke@ldeo.columbia.edu, Columbia Univ; Ys
Menking, Kirsten M., 845-437-5545 kimenking@vassar.edu, Vassar Coll; GmPeGc
Menninga, Clarence, menn@calvin.edu, Calvin Coll; CcGg
Menold, Carrie A., 517-629-0312 cmenold@albion.edu, Albion Coll; GpCsGt
Mensah, Emmanuel, +233 24 4186 193 emmamensah6@yahoo.com, Kwame Nkrumah Univ of Sci and Tech; EgGg
Mensing, Scott A., (775) 784-6346 smensing@unr.edu, Univ of Nevada, Reno; Zy
Mensing, Teresa, (740) 725-6234 mensing.1@osu.edu, Ohio State Univ; Cg
Menuge, Julian F., (+353) 1 716 2141 j.f.menuge@ucd.ie, Univ Coll Dublin; EmCcs
Menzies, John, (905) 688-5550 x3865 jmenzies@brocku.ca, Brock Univ; GlmGs
Mercer, Andrew, 662-268-1032 Ext 231 mercer@gri.msstate.edu, Mississippi State Univ; Ams
Merchant, James W., (402) 472-7531 jmerchant@unl.edu, Unversity of Nebraska, Lincoln; Zru
Mercier, Michael , (905) 525-9140 (Ext. 27597) mercieme@mcmaster.ca, McMaster Univ; Zu
Merck, Jr., John W., (301) 405-2808 jmerck@umd.edu, Univ of Maryland; Pv
Meredith, Philip, +44 020 7679 37824 p.meredith@ucl.ac.uk, Univ Coll London; Nr
Meretsky, Vicky J., (812) 855-5971 meretsky@indiana.edu, Indiana Univ, Bloomington; Sf
Mereu, Robert F., (519) 661-3605 a424@uwo.ca, Western Univ; Ys
Merguerian, Charles M., 516 463-5567 geocmm@hofstra.edu, Hofstra Univ; Gc
Merifield, Paul M., (310) 794-5019 pmerifie@ucla.edu, Univ of California, Los Angeles; Ng
Merino, Enrique, (812) 855-5088 merino@indiana.edu, Indiana Univ, Bloomington; Cl
Merkel, Timo Casjen, 089/2180 4337 casjen.merkel@lrz.uni-muenchen.de, Ludwig-Maximilians-Univ Muenchen; Gz
Merlis, Timothy, 514-398-3140 timothy.merlis@mcgill.ca, McGill Univ; Asm
Merriam, James B., (306) 966-5716 jim.merriam@usask.ca, Univ of Saskatchewan; Yg
Merrifield, Mark A., (808) 956-6161 markm@soest.hawaii.edu, Univ of Hawai'i, Manoa; Op
Merrill, Glen K., (713) 221-8168 merrillg@uhd.edu, Univ of Houston Downtown; Pi
Merrill, John T., (401) 874-6715 jmerrill@boreas.gso.uri.edu, Univ of Rhode Island; Oc
Merrill, Ronald T., (206) 543-6686 Univ of Washington; Ym
Merritt, Andrew, +44 1752 584702 andrew.merritt@plymouth.ac.uk, Univ of Plymouth; Ng
Merritts, Dorothy J., (717) 291-4398 dorothy.merritts@fandm.edu, Franklin and Marshall Coll; Gm
Mertzman, Stanley A., (717) 291-3818 stan.mertzman@fandm.edu, Franklin and Marshall Coll; GizZm
Meskhidze, Nicholas, 919-515-7243 nicholas_meskhidze@ncsu.edu, North Carolina State Univ; As
Messina, Paula, (408) 924-5027 paula.messina@sjsu.edu, San Jose State Univ; ZeGm
Metaxas, Anna, (902) 494-3021 metaxas@dal.ca, Dalhousie Univ; Ob
Metcalf, Kathryn, (607) 436-3067 kathryn.metcalf@oneonta.edu, SUNY, Oneonta; GctGg
Metcalf, Meredith, (860) 465-4370 metcalfm@easternct.edu, Eastern Connecticut State Univ; ZirHw
Metcalf, Rodney V., (702) 895-4442 kim.metcalf@unlv.edu, Univ of Nevada, Las Vegas; Gp
Metcalfe, Ian, +61-2-67726297 imetcal2@une.edu.au, Univ of New England; PmGtg
Metesh, John J., (406) 496-4159 jmetesh@mtech.edu, Montana Tech of The Univ of Montana; HwCa
Metz, Cheyl L., 979 209-7461 cl.metz@blinn.edu, Blinn Coll; GgOg
Metz, Nicholas, (315) 781-3615 metz@hws.edu, Hobart & William Smith Colls; As
Metz, Robert, (908) 737-3687 rmetz@kean.edu, Kean Univ; Gr
Metzger, Ellen P., (408) 924-5048 ellen.metzger@sjsu.edu, San Jose State Univ; GpZe
Metzger, Marc J., +44 (0) 131 651 4446 mmetzger@staffmail.ed.ac.uk, Edinburgh Univ; Ge
Metzger, Ronald A., (541) 888-7216 rmetzger@socc.edu, Southwestern Oregon Comm Coll; PmZePs
Metzler, Christopher V., (760) 944-4449, x7738 cmetzler@miracosta.edu, MiraCosta Coll; Gg
Mey, Jacob, 718-368-5770 jacob.mey@kbcc.cuny.edu, Graduate Sch of the City Univ of New York; Gg
Meyer, Brian, bmeyer2@gsu.edu, Georgia State Univ; GesHw
Meyer, Christopher, meyerc@si.edu, Smithsonian Inst / Nat Mus of Natural History; ZnPi
Meyer, David L., (513) 556-4530 david.meyer@uc.edu, Univ of Cincinnati; Pi
Meyer, Franz J., 907-474-7767 fmeyer@gi.alaska.edu, Univ of Alaska, Fairbanks; Zr
Meyer, Gary, (612) 626-1741 meyer015@umn.edu, Univ of Minnesota; Gl
Meyer, Grant A., (505) 277-4204 gmeyer@unm.edu, Univ of New Mexico; Gm
Meyer, Jeffrey W., (805) 965-0531 (Ext. 4270) meyerj@sbcc.edu, Santa Barbara City Coll; GgzGx
Meyer, Jessica R., (319) 335-1831 jessica-meyer@uiowa.edu, Univ of Iowa; Hw
Meyer, Judith, (417) 836-5604 judithmeyer@missouristate.edu, Missouri State Univ; Zn
Meyer, Lewis, +44 01326 253766 l.h.i.meyer@exeter.ac.uk, Exeter Univ; Nmr
Meyer, Rebecca A., (812) 855-2687 reameyer@indiana.edu, Indiana Univ; Ec
Meyer, Steven J., (920) 465-5022 meyers@uwgb.edu, Univ of Wisconsin, Green Bay; AsmZg
Meyer, W. Craig, (818) 710-4241 meyerwc@piercecollege.edu, Los Angeles Pierce Coll; GeuPm
Meyer, William T., (630) 969-6586 meyer@iastate.edu, Argonne; Cg
Meyer Dombard, DArcy, 312-996-2423 drmd@uic.edu, Univ of Illinois at Chicago; Pg
Meyers, Jamie A., jmeyers@winona.edu, Winona State Univ; Gsd
Meyers, Philip A., (734) 764-0597 pameyers@umich.edu, Univ of Michigan; CoGnu
Meyers, Stephen R., 608-890-2574 smeyers@geology.wisc.edu, Univ of Wisconsin, Madison; PcOoGs
Meylan, Anne, (727) 896-8626 Univ of South Florida; Ob
Meylan, Maurice A., (601) 266-4527 mmeylan@otr.usm.edu, Univ of Southern Mississippi; Gu
Meyzen, Christine M., +390498279153 christine.meyzen@unipd.it, Univ degli Studi di Padova; Cg
Mezga, Aleksandar, +38514606116 amezga@geol.pmf.hr, Univ of Zagreb; Pg
Mezger, Jochen E., (907) 474-7809 jemezger@alaska.edu, Univ of Alaska, Fairbanks; GcpCc
Miall, Andrew D., (416) 978-8841 miall@es.utoronto.ca, Univ of Toronto; Gso
Miao, Xin, (417) 836-5173 xinmiao@missouristate.edu, Missouri State Univ; Zri
Miao, Yuxin, 612-625-8101 ymiao@umn.edu, Univ of Minnesota, Twin Cities; ScZf
Micallef, Aaron, +356 23403662 aaron.micallef@um.edu.mt, Univ of Malta; GumOu
Micander, Rachel, 775-682-6351 rmicander@unr.edu, Univ of Nevada, Reno; Zie
Michael, Holly A., (302) 831-4197 hmichael@udel.edu, Univ of Delaware; Hwq
Michael, Peter J., (918) 631-3017 pjm@utulsa.edu, Univ of Tulsa; GivGz
Michaels, Patrick J., (804) 924-0549 pmichaels@cato.org, Univ of Virginia; As
Michaels, Paul, (208) 426-1929 pm@cgiss.boisestate.edu, Boise State Univ; Ne
Michalski, Greg, (765) 494-3704 gmichals@purdue.edu, Purdue Univ; CsGeAs

Michaud, Jene D., 808-974-7411 jene@hawaii.edu, Univ of Hawai'i, Hilo; HqwGm
Michaud, Yves, (418) 654-2647 Universite du Quebec; Gm
Michel, F. M., 540-231-3299 mfrede2@vt.edu, Virginia Polytechnic Inst & State Univ; ZaGz
Michel, Fred A., fmichel@ccs.carleton.ca, Carleton Univ; Hw
Michel, Gero, gmichel3@uwo.ca, Western Univ; Ys
Michel, Jacqueline, 504-280-6325 jmichel@uno.edu, Univ of New Orleans; Cg
Michel, Lauren, (931) 372-3188 lmichel@tntech.edu, Tennessee Tech Univ; PcSaCl
Michel, Shirley, 419-530-5058 shirley.michel@utoledo.edu, Univ of Toledo; Zn
Michel, Suzanne, 6196447454 x3028 suzanne.michel@gcccd.edu, Cuyamaca Coll; Gg
Michelfelder, Gary, (417) 836-3171 garymichelfelder@missouristate.edu, Missouri State Univ; GviCg
Mickelson, Andrew M., 901-678-4505 amicklsn@memphis.edu, Univ of Memphis; Ga
Mickelson, David M., (608) 262-7863 mickelson@geology.wisc.edu, Univ of Wisconsin, Madison; Glm
Mickus, Kevin L., (417) 836-6375 kevinmickus@missouristate.edu, Missouri State Univ; GtYv
Miclaus, Crina G., 00402324095 crina_miclaus@yahoo.co.uk, Alexandru Ioan Cuza; Gsr
Middlemiss, Lucie, +44(0) 113 34 35246 l.k.middlemiss@leeds.ac.uk, Univ of Leeds; Zn
Middleton, Carrie A., (303) 293-5019 cmiddleton@osmre.gov, Department of Interior Office of Surface Mining Reclamation and Enforcement; ZrGfZi
Middleton, Larry T., (928) 523-2429 larry.middleton@nau.edu, Northern Arizona Univ; Gs
Mies, Jonathan W., (423) 425-4606 jonathan-mies@utc.edu, Univ of Tennessee, Chattanooga; GctHg
Mignery, Jill, 513-529-03225 henryjm@miamioh.edu, Miami Univ; Zge
Miguel, Carlos, (598) 25251552 cmiguel@fcien.edu.uy, Univ de la Republica Oriental del Uruguay (UDELAR); ZirSf
Mikesell, Dylan, 208-426-1404 dylanmikesell@boisestate.edu, Boise State Univ; YsuYx
Mikhaltsevitch, Vassily, +61 8 9266-4976 v.mikhaltsevitch@curtin.edu.au, Curtin Univ; Ye
Mikulic, Donald G., 217-244-2518 mikulic@isgs.uiuc.edu, Illinois State Geological Survey; Ps
Milam, Keith A., (740) 593-1106 milamk@ohio.edu, Ohio Univ; Xg
Milan, Luke, +61267732019 lmilan@une.edu.au, Univ of New England; GtcGp
Miles, Andrew, andrew.miles@kingston.ac.uk, Kingston Univ; Gz
Miles, Randall J., 573-882-6607 Univ of Missouri; Sd
Milewski, Adam, (706) 542-2652 milewski@uga.edu, Univ of Georgia; Hw
Militzer, Burkhard, militzer@seismo.berkeley.edu, Univ of California, Berkeley; Gy
Miljevic, Branka, +61 7 3138 3827 b.miljevic@qut.edu.au, Queensland Univ of Tech; Acs
Milkereit, Bernd, (416) 978-2466 bm@physics.utoronto.ca, Univ of Toronto; Ye
Milkov, Alexei, 303-273-3887 amilkov@mines.edu, Colorado Sch of Mines; Cg
Millan, Christina, 614-292-0863 millan.2@osu.edu, Ohio State Univ; Ggc
Millen, Timothy M., 847-697-1000 tmillen@elgin.edu, Elgin Comm Coll; Gg
Miller, Arnold I., (513) 556-4022 arnold.miller@uc.edu, Univ of Cincinnati; Pi
Miller, Barry W., (865) 594-5599 barry.miller@tn.gov, Tennessee Geological Survey; EcZiGg
Miller, Brent, (979) 458-3671 bvmiller@geo.tamu.edu, Texas A&M Univ; Cc
Miller, Calvin F., 615-322-2232 calvin.miller@vanderbilt.edu, Vanderbilt Univ; Gi
Miller, Charles M., (505) 667-8415 Los Alamos; Cc
Miller, David S., (630) 252-7191 Argonne; Ge
Miller, Doug, 828-232-5158 dmiller@unca.edu, Univ of North Carolina, Asheville; AsZnn
Miller, Douglas C., (302) 645-4277 dmiller@udel.edu, Univ of Delaware; Ob
Miller, Elizabeth L., (650) 723-1149 miller@pangea.stanford.edu, Stanford Univ; Gc
Miller, Geoffrey G., (506) 643-2361 Los Alamos; Cc
Miller, Gerald A., (515) 291-3442 soil@iastate.edu, Iowa State Univ of Sci & Tech; SdoGm
Miller, Gifford H., 303-492-6962 gmiller@colorado.edu, Univ of Colorado; GlCc
Miller, Harvey J., (801) 585-3972 miller.81@osu.edu, Ohio State Univ; Zi
Miller, Heather R., heather.miller@austincc.edu, Austin Comm Coll District; Zeg
Miller, Hugh, (303) 273-3558 hbmiller@mines.edu, Colorado Sch of Mines; Nmg
Miller, Ian, 303-370-8351 ian.miller@dmns.org, Denver Mus of Nature & Sci; PbGg
Miller, James D., mille066@d.umn.edu, Univ of Minnesota Duluth; GiEd
Miller, Jerry R., (828) 227-2269 jmiller@wcu.edu, Western Carolina Univ; GmeGf
Miller, John, (416)736-5245 jrmiller@yorku.ca, York Univ; Zr
Miller, Jonathan S., (408) 924-5015 jonathan.miller@sjsu.edu, San Jose State Univ; GiCc
Miller, Joshua H., josh.miller@uc.edu, Cincinnati Mus Center; Pe
Miller, Judy, jmiller264@monroecc.edu, Monroe Comm Coll; Zn
Miller, Kate, (979) 845-3651 kcmiller@tamu.edu, Texas A&M Univ; Ys
Miller, Keith B., (785) 532-2250 kbmill@ksu.edu, Kansas State Univ; Pe
Miller, Kenneth G., (848) 445-3622 kgm@eps.rutgers.edu, Rutgers, The State Univ of New Jersey; GurPm
Miller, M. Meghan, (509) 963-2825 meghan@cwu.edu, Central Washington Univ; Yd
Miller, Mark, 601-266-4729 m.m.miller@usm.edu, Univ of Southern Mississippi; Zn
Miller, Marli G., (541) 346-4410 millerm@uoregon.edu, Univ of Oregon; Gc
Miller, Marvin R., (406) 496-4155 mmiller@mtech.edu, Montana Tech of The Univ of Montana; Hw
Miller, Michael B., (225) 388-3412 byron@lgs.bri.lsu.edu, Louisiana State Univ; Go
Miller, Molly F., 615-322-3528 molly.miller@vanderbilt.edu, Vanderbilt Univ; PeGs
Miller, Murray H., (519) 824-4120 (Ext. 53758) jmmiller7@sympatico.ca, Univ of Guelph; So
Miller, Phillip, 575-835-5487 phil.miller@nmt.edu, New Mexico Inst of Mining and Tech; Zi
Miller, Randall F., (506) 643-2361 Univ of New Brunswick; Pg
Miller, Raymond M., (630) 252-3395 rmmiller@anl.gov, Argonne; Sb
Miller, Richard D., (785) 864-2091 rmiller@kgs.ku.edu, Univ of Kansas; Ye
Miller, Robert B., (408) 924-5025 robert.b.miller@sjsu.edu, San Jose State Univ; Gct
Miller, Ronald L., (212) 678-5577 rmiller@giss.nasa.gov, Columbia Univ; As
Miller, Steven F., (506) 643-2361 Argonne; Gg
Miller, Ted R., 605-677-6867 ted.miller@usd.edu, South Dakota Dept of Environment and Natural Resources; Zn
Miller, Wade E., 801 422-2321 wem@geology.byu.edu, Brigham Young Univ; Pv
Miller, William C., (707) 826-3110 wm1@humboldt.edu, Humboldt State Univ; Pi
Miller-Camp, Jessica, jessmc@iu.edu, Indiana Univ, Bloomington; Pv
Miller-Hicks, Bryan, bryan.miller-hicks@gcccd.edu, Cuyamaca Coll; Gg
Millet, Dylan B., 612-626-3259 dbm@umn.edu, Univ of Minnesota, Twin Cities; As
Millette, Thomas L., (413) 538-2813 tmillett@mtholyoke.edu, Mount Holyoke Coll; ZriGm
Milligan, Mark, (801) 537-3326 markmilligan@utah.gov, Utah Geological Survey; Ze
Milligan, Richard, 404 413-5778 rmilligan@gsu.edu, Georgia State Univ; Zn
Milligan, Timothy, (902) 426-3273 milligant@dfo-mpo.gc.ca, Dalhousie Univ; Gs
Milliken, Kitty L., (512) 471-6082 kittym@mail.utexas.edu, Univ of Texas, Austin; Gd
Millington, Andrew, andrew.millington@flinders.edu.au, Flinders Univ; ZuyZr
Mills, Aaron L., (804) 924-0564 alm7d@virginia.edu, Univ of Virginia; So
Mills, Eric L., (902) 471-2016 e.mills@dal.ca, Dalhousie Univ; ObZnn
Mills, James G., (765) 658-4669 jmills@depauw.edu, DePauw Univ; Gi
Mills, Rachel A., +44 (0)23 80592678 rachel.mills@soton.ac.uk, Univ of Southampton; Cm
Mills, Stephanie, +44 020 8417 2950 s.mills@kingston.ac.uk, Kingston Univ; Gl
Mills, Suzanne, (905) 525-9140 smills@mcmaster.ca, McMaster Univ; Zn
Milne, Glenn A., gamilne@uottawa.ca, Univ of Ottawa; YgAsZg
Milner, Jennifer, (309) 794-7318 jennifermilner@augustana.edu, Augustana Coll; Zn
Milner, Lloyd R., (225) 578-3410 lmilne1@lsu.edu, Louisiana State Univ; Gg
Milroy, Scott P., (228) 688-7128 scott.milroy@usm.edu, Univ of Southern Mississippi; Ob

Min, Dong-Ha, 512-475-9290 dongha@austin.utexas.edu, Univ of Texas, Austin; Og

Min, Doo-Hong, dmin@ksu.edu, Kansas State Univ; So

Min, Kyoungwon, (352) 392-2720 kmin@ufl.edu, Univ of Florida; Cc

Minarik, William G., 514-398-2596 william.minarik@mcgill.ca, McGill Univ; Cp

Minchew, Brent, (617) 324-3704 minchew@mit.edu, Massachusetts Inst of Tech; Yg

Miner, James J., 217-244-5786 miner@illinois.edu, Illinois State Geological Survey; Gg

Minium, Deborah, (425) 564-5120 deborah.minium@bellevuecollege.edu, Bellevue Coll; Gg

Minnaar, Hendrik, +27 (0)51 401 2372 minnaarh@ufs.ac.za, Univ of the Free State; Gc

Minnich, Richard A., (951) 827-5515 richard.minnich@ucr.edu, Univ of California, Riverside; Zy

Minor, Timothy B., (775) 673-7477 tminor@dri.edu, Desert Research Inst; Zr

Minshull, Timothy A., +44 (0)23 80596569 tmin@noc.soton.ac.uk, Univ of Southampton; Yr

Minster, J. Bernard H., (858) 945-0693 jbminster@ucsd.edu, Univ of California, San Diego; Ys

Minter, Nicholas, +44 023 92 842288 nic.minter@port.ac.uk, Univ of Portsmouth; Gs

Minton, David, (765) 494-3292 daminton@purdue.edu, Purdue Univ; Xg

Minzoni, Marcello, (205)348-0768 marcello.minzoni@ua.edu, Univ of Alabama; GosEo

Minzoni, Rebecca T., (205)348-6050 rebecca.minzoni@ua.edu, Univ of Alabama; GsPme

Miot da Silva, Graziela, graziela.miotdasilva@flinders.edu.au, Flinders Univ; Gug

Miranda, Elena A., 818-677-4671 elena.miranda@csun.edu, California State Univ, Northridge; Gc

Mirnejad, Hassan, mirnejh@miamioh.edu, Miami Univ; Gx

Mirnejad, Hassan , 513-529-3216 mirnejh@miamioh.edu, Miami Univ; GxCg

Mishler, Brent, (510) 642-6810 bmishler@berkeley.edu, Univ of California, Berkeley; Pe

Mishra, Umakant, 630-252-1108 umishra@anl.gov, Argonne; So

Misner, Tamara, 814-732-1352 tmisner@edinboro.edu, Edinboro Univ of Pennsylvania; GmHs

Misra, Debsmita, (907) 474-5339 dmisra@alaska.edu, Univ of Alaska, Fairbanks; HwZrNg

Misra, Kula C., (865) 974-2366 kmisra@utk.edu, Univ of Tennessee, Knoxville; Eg

Misra, Saumitra, (031) 260-2800 misras@ukzn.ac.za, Univ of KwaZulu-Natal; GiCgu

Misra, Siddharth, 405-325-6787 misra@ou.edu, Univ of Oklahoma; Np

Mitasova, Helena, 919-513-1327 helena_mitasova@ncsu.edu, North Carolina State Univ; Zi

Mitchell, Charles E., (716) 645-4290 cem@buffalo.edu, SUNY, Buffalo; Pg

Mitchell, Jonathan, (310) 825-2970 mitch@epss.ucla.edu, Univ of California, Los Angeles; AsXg

Mitchell, Neil C., neil.mitchell@manchester.ac.uk, Univ of Manchester; GumYg

Mitchell, Robert J., (360) 650-3591 robert.mitchell@geol.wwu.edu, Western Washington Univ; Hw

Mitchell, Roger H., (807) 343-8287 roger.mitchell@lakeheadu.ca, Lakehead Univ; Gi

Mitchell, Simon F., 876-927-2728 geoggeol@uwimona.edu.jm, Univ of the West Indies Mona Campus; GsgGs

Mitchell, Tom, +44 (0)20 7679 7361 tom.mitchell@ucl.ac.uk, Univ Coll London; Gc

Mitchneck, Beth A., bethm@email.arizona.edu, Univ of Arizona; Zn

Mitchum, Gary T., (727) 553-3941 gmitchum@marine.usf.edu, Univ of South Florida; Op

Mitra, Chandana, (334) 844-4229 czm0033@auburn.edu, Auburn Univ; ZgAsZi

Mitra, Gautam, (585) 275-5816 gautam.mitra@rochester.edu, Univ of Rochester; GctNr

Mitra, Shankar, (405) 325-4462 smitra@ou.edu, Univ of Oklahoma; Gc

Mitra, Siddhartha, 252 328 6611 mitras@ecu.edu, East Carolina Univ; Co

Mitri, Hani, (514) 398-4755 McGill Univ; Nm

Mitrovica, Jerry X., 617-496-2732 jxm@eps.harvard.edu, Harvard Univ; Yg

Mittelstaedt, Eric L., (208) 885-2045 emittelstaedt@uidaho.edu, Univ of Idaho; Yr

Mitterer, Richard M., mitterer@utdallas.edu, Univ of Texas, Dallas; ColOc

Mitzman, Stephanie, stephanie.mitzman@tccd.edu, Tarrant County Coll, Southeast Campus; Gg

Mix, Alan C., 541-737-5212 amix@coas.oregonstate.edu, Oregon State Univ; Cs

Miyagi, Lowell, (801) 581-6619 lowell.miyagi@utah.edu, Univ of Utah; Gz

Miyares, Ines, (212) 772-5443 imiyares@hunter.cuny.edu, Hunter Coll (CUNY); Zen

Mizak, Connie, mizak@usf.edu, Univ of South Florida; Zy

Moayyed, Mohsen -., +98 (413) 339 2616 moayyed@tabrizu.ac.ir, Univ of Tabriz; GigEg

Moazzen, Mohssen -., +98 (411) 339 2679 moazzen@tabrizu.ac.ir, Univ of Tabriz; GpCgGz

Moberly, Ralph, (808) 956-8765 ralph@soest.hawaii.edu, Univ of Hawai'i, Manoa; GutGs

Mobley, Curtis D., (206) 230-8166 Univ of Washington; Ob

Mock, R. Stephen, (406) 683-7261 steve.mock@umwestern.edu, Univ of Montana Western; Ca

Mock, Thomas, +44 (0)1603 59 2566 t.mock@uea.ac.uk, Univ of East Anglia; Pg

Mock, Timothy D., 202-478-8466 tmock@carnegiescience.edu, Carnegie Inst for Sci; Cc

Mockler, Theodore, (505) 667-4318 mockler@lanl.gov, Los Alamos; Zn

Mode, William N., (920) 424-7004 mode@uwosh.edu, Univ of Wisconsin, Oshkosh; Gl

Modzelewski, Henryk, (604) 822-3591 hmodzelewski@eos.ubc.ca, Univ of British Columbia; As

Moe-Hoffman, Amy P., apm105@msstate.edu, Mississippi State Univ; PgZe

Moecher, David P., (859) 257-6939 moker@uky.edu, Univ of Kentucky; GxtCg

Moeglin, Thomas D., (417) 836-5800 Missouri State Univ; Ng

Moersch, Jeffery E., (865) 974-0371 jmoersch@utk.edu, Univ of Tennessee, Knoxville; XgZr

Moffett, James W., 213-740-5626 jmoffett@usc.edu, Univ of Southern California; OcCba

Mofjeld, Harold O., (206) 526-6819 mofjeld@pmel.noaa.gov, Univ of Washington; Op

Moghanloo, Rouzbeh, rouzbeh.gm@ou.edu, Univ of Oklahoma; Np

Mogilevskaya, Sonia, 612-625-4810 mogil003@umn.edu, Univ of Minnesota, Twin Cities; Ng

Mogk, David W., (406) 600-4071 mogk@montana.edu, Montana State Univ; GpZeGz

Mohammad Reza, Hosseinzadeh, +98 (411) 339 2697 Univ of Tabriz; Egm

Mohr, Marcus, 089/2180 4230 marcus.mohr@geophysik.uni-muenchen.de, Ludwig-Maximilians-Univ Muenchen; Yg

Mohrig, David, (512) 471-2282 mohrig@jsg.utexas.edu, Univ of Texas, Austin; GsmGr

MOINE, Bertrand N., 33-477481513 moineb@univ-st-etienne.fr, Université Jean Monnet, Saint-Etienne; CgtGx

Mojica, Kristina, (228) 688-3003 kristina.mojica@usm.edu, Univ of Southern Mississippi; Ob

Mojzsis, Stephen J., (303) 492-5014 stephen.mojzsis@colorado.edu, Univ of Colorado; XcCcGp

Moldwin, Mark B., (734) 647-3370 mmoldwin@umich.edu, Univ of Michigan; XpYz

Molina, Jean-Alex E., (651) 647-9865 jamolina@umn.edu, Univ of Minnesota, Twin Cities; SbCgSo

Molina, Mario J., (858) 534-1696 mjmolina@ucsd.edu, Univ of California, San Diego; As

Molinari, John E., (518) 442-4562 molinari@atmos.albany.edu, SUNY, Albany; As

Moll, Nancy E., 760-776-7272 nmoll@collegeofthedesert.edu, Coll of the Desert; Gge

Mollner, Daniel, (507) 933-7569 Gustavus Adolphus Coll; Zn

Molnár, Gábor, molnar@sas.elte.hu, Eotvos Lorand Univ; ZrYgZi

Molnar, Peter, 303-492-4936 peter.molnar@colorado.edu, Univ of Colorado; Gt

Molnar, Sheri, 519-661-2111, ext.87031 smolnar8@uwo.ca, Western Univ; Ys

Molnia, Bruce F., (703) 648-4120 bmolnia@usgs.gov, Duke Univ; ZrGlu

Moloney, Marguerite M., (985) 448-4878 marguerite.moloney@nicholls.edu, Nicholls State Univ; GeZnn

Molotch, Noah, noah.molotch@colorado.edu, Univ of Colorado; Hg

Momayez, Moe, (520) 621-6580 moe.momayez@arizona.edu, Univ of Arizona; NmYxNr

Momen, Nasim, (617) 353-5679 Boston Univ; Zn

Momm, Henrique G., (615) 904-8372 henrique.momm@mtsu.edu, Middle Tennessee State Univ; ZfHqRw

Monahan, Adam, 250-721-6120 monahana@uvic.ca, Univ of Victoria; Zn

Monahan, Edward C., (860) 405-9110 edward.monahan@uconn.edu, Univ of Connecticut; AsOp

Monari, Stefano, +390498279171 stefano.monari@unipd.it, Univ degli Studi di Padova; Pg

Moncrief, John F., (612) 625-2771 moncr001@umn.ed, Univ of Minnesota, Twin Cities; Sp
Moncrieff, John B., +44 (0) 131 650 5402 j.moncrieff@ed.ac.uk, Edinburgh Univ; As
Monecke, Katrin, kmonecke@wellesley.edu, Wellesley Coll; Gsn
Monecke, Thomas, 303-273-3841 tmonecke@mines.edu, Colorado Sch of Mines; Em
Monet, Julie, 530-898-3460 jmonet@csuchico.edu, California State Univ, Chico; GgNg
Monger, Bruce, bcm3@cornell.edu, Cornell Univ; Ob
Monger, H. C., (505) 646-3405 New Mexico State Univ, Las Cruces; Sa
Monier, Erwan, 530-754-1837 emonier@ucdavis.edu, Univ of California, Davis; Atm
Monohan, Carrie, cmonohan@csuchico.edu, California State Univ, Chico; Hg
Monson, Jessica, 217-265-6895 jlbm@illinois.edu, Illinois State Geological Survey; Gg
Montagna, Paul, 361-825-2040 paul.montagna@tamucc.edu, Texas A&M Univ, Corpus Christi; ObCmHs
Montagne, Cliff, (406) 599-7755 montagne@montana.edu, Montana State Univ; Sd
Montañez, Isabel P., (530) 754-7823 ipmontanez@ucdavis.edu, Univ of California, Davis; Gd
Montayne, Simone, (907) 451-5036 simone.montayne@alaska.gov, Alaska Division of Geological & Geophysical Surveys; Gg
Monteleone, Brian D., (508) 289-2405 bmonteleone@whoi.edu, Woods Hole Oceanographic Inst; Cc
Montenari, Michael, (+44) 01782 733162 m.montenari@keele.ac.uk, Keele Univ; PmgPs
Montenegro, Alvaro, (614) 688-5451 montenegro.8@osu.edu, Ohio State Univ; OgAsZy
Montero, Esperanza, emontero@ucm.es, Univ Complutense de Madrid; Hw
Montesi, Laurent G., (301) 405-7534 montesi@umd.edu, Univ of Maryland; YgXyGt
Monteverde, Don, dmonte@eps.rutgers.edu, Rutgers, The State Univ of New Jersey; GruGg
Monteverde, Donald H., (609) 292-2576 don.monteverde@dep.state.nj.us, New Jersey Geological and Water Survey; Grg
Monteverdi, John P., (415) 338-7728 montever@sfsu.edu, San Francisco State Univ; As
Montgomery, David R., 206-685-2560 bigdirt@uw.edu, Univ of Washington; Gm
Montgomery, Homer A., 972-883-2496 mont@utdallas.edu, Univ of Texas, Dallas; Pg
Montgomery, Keith, (715) 845-9602 keith.montgomery@uwc.edu, Univ of Wisconsin Colls; ZyGg
Montgomery, Michael T., (831) 656-2296 mtmontgo@nps.edu, Naval Postgraduate Sch; AmsZg
Montgomery, Tamra S., 217-333-5105 tmntgmry@illinois.edu, Illinois State Geological Survey; Zn
Montgomery, William W., (201) 200-3161 wmontgomery@njcu.edu, New Jersey City Univ; Hw
Montoya, Joseph, (404) 385-0479 Georgia Inst of Tech; Cm
Montoya, Judith, (928) 523-8523 judith.montoya@nau.edu, Northern Arizona Univ; Zy
Montwill, Gail F., (909) 946-1796 Santiago Canyon Coll; Gg
Moodie, T. Bryant, (780) 492-5742 bryant.moodie@ualberta.ca, Univ of Alberta; Zn
Moody, Eva, (254) 968-9143 moody@tarleton.edu, Tarleton State Univ; Zn
Moody, Jennie L., (804) 924-0592 jlm8h@virginia.edu, Univ of Virginia; As
Mooers, Howard D., (218) 726-7239 hmooers@d.umn.edu, Univ of Minnesota Duluth; GleHw
Mookerjee, Matty, (707) 664-2002 matty.mookerjee@sonoma.edu, Sonoma State Univ; GcYgZi
Moon, Charlie, +44 01326 371822 c.j.moon@exeter.ac.uk, Exeter Univ; CeEmZi
Moon, Seulgi, sgmoon@g.ucla.edu, Univ of California, Los Angeles; Gm
Moon, Wooil M., (204) 474-9833 wmoon@cc.umanitoba.ca, Univ of Manitoba; ZrYnOp
Mooney, Phillip, (707) 664-2328 mooneyp@sonoma.edu, Sonoma State Univ; ZnGc
Moorberg, Colby, (785) 532-7207 Kansas State Univ; So
Moore, Andrew, (765) 983-1672 moorean@earlham.edu, Earlham Coll; Gm
Moore, Bradley S., (858) 822-6650 bsmoore@ucsd.edu, Univ of California, San Diego; Cm
Moore, Christopher M., +44 (0)23 80594801 cmm297@noc.soton.ac.uk, Univ of Southampton; Ob
Moore, Daniel K., (208) 496-7682 moored@byui.edu, Brigham Young Univ - Idaho; GxiCp
Moore, Dennis, dmoore@pmel.noaa.gov, Univ of Hawai'i, Manoa; Og
Moore, Duane M., 505-277-4204 dewey33@unm.edu, Univ of New Mexico; Sc
Moore, Gregory F., (808) 956-6854 gmoore@hawaii.edu, Univ of Hawai'i, Manoa; Gt
Moore, J. Casey, (831) 459-2574 cmoore@pmc.ucsc.edu, Univ of California, Santa Cruz; Gc
Moore, Jefferson K., 949-824-5391 jkmoore@uci.edu, Univ of California, Irvine; Op
Moore, Jeffrey, (801) 585-0491 jeff.moore@utah.edu, Univ of Utah; NgrGm
Moore, Joel, (410) 704-4245 moore@towson.edu, Towson Univ; ClsSc
Moore, Joseph N., (801) 585-6931 jmoore@egi.utah.edu, Univ of Utah; Gv
Moore, Kathryn, +44 (0)1326 255693 k.moore@exeter.ac.uk, Exeter Univ; Ge
Moore, Laura J., (919) 962-5960 moorelj@email.unc.edu, Univ of North Carolina, Chapel Hill; Gme
Moore, Lowell P., moorelr@vt.edu, Virginia Polytechnic Inst & State Univ; Ca
Moore, Michael E., 717.702.2024 michmoore@pa.gov, DCNR- Pennsylvania Bureau of Geological Survey; HwZi
Moore, Phillip, +44 (0) 191 208 5040 philip.moore@ncl.ac.uk, Univ of Newcastle Upon Tyne; Yd
Moore, Richard W., 831-656-1041 rwmoor1@nps.edu, Naval Postgraduate Sch; Am
Moore, Robert M., (902) 494-3871 robert.moore@dal.ca, Dalhousie Univ; Oc
Moore, Theodore C., (734) 763-0202 tedmoore@umich.edu, Univ of Michigan; OuPmc
Moore, Willard S., moore@geol.sc.edu, Univ of South Carolina; Cc
Moores, Eldridge M., (916) 752-0352 Univ of California, Davis; Gt
Moorhead, Daryl L., (419) 530-2017 daryl.moorhead@utoledo.edu, Univ of Toledo; Zn
Moorman, Thomas B., (515) 294-2308 tom.moorman@ars.usda.gov, Iowa State Univ of Sci & Tech; So
Moortgat, Joachim, (614) 688-2140 moortgat.1@osu.edu, Ohio State Univ; HwNp
Mora, Claudia, claudia.mora@jsg.utexas.edu, Univ of Texas, Austin; Gg
Mora-Klepeis, Gabriela, 802-656-0246 gmora@uvm.edu, Univ of Vermont; CacGi
Morabia, Alfredo, 718-670-4180 Queens Coll (CUNY); GbZn
Morales, Michael A., (620) 794-0191 mmorales@emporia.edu, Emporia State Univ; PvGrg
Morales, Tomas, tomas.morales@ehu.eus, Univ of the Basque Country UPV/EHU; NgHg
Moran, Dawn, (508) 289-4918 dmoran@whoi.edu, Woods Hole Oceanographic Inst; Ob
Moran, Jean E., 510-885-2491 jean.moran@csueastbay.edu, California State Univ, East Bay; HwCl
Moran, S. Bradley, (401) 874-6530 moran@gso.uri.edu, Univ of Rhode Island; Oc
Moran, Seth, 360-993-8934 smoran@usgs.gov, Univ of Washington; Gv
Moran-Taylor, Michelle, 303-871-2513 michelle.moran-taylor@du.edu, Univ of Denver; Zn
Moran-Zenteno, Dante J., dante@tonatiuh.igeofcu.unam.mx, Univ Nacional Autonoma de Mexico; Cc
Morand, Vincent J., +61 3 9479 5641 v.morand@latrobe.edu.au, La Trobe Univ; GgcGt
Morawska, Lidia, +61 7 3138 2616 l.morawska@qut.edu.au, Queensland Univ of Tech; Asc
Morealli, Sarah A., 540 654-1402 smoreall@umw.edu, Univ of Mary Washington; Gg
Morehouse, Barbara, morehoub@email.arizona.edu, Univ of Arizona; Zn
Morel, Francois M M., 609-258-2416 morel@princeton.edu, Princeton Univ; Cl
Morel-Kraepiel, Anne, 609-258-7415 kraepiel@princeton.edu, Princeton Univ; Em
Moreland, Amy L., amy.moreland@austincc.edu, Austin Comm Coll District; Zge
Moreno, Rafael, (303) 556-8477 Metropolitan State Coll of Denver; Zg
Moreton, Kim, (+44) (0) 7854825368 k.moreton@exeter.ac.uk, Exeter Univ; EnZur
Morgan, Cristine L., (979) 845-3603 cmorgan@tamu.edu, Texas A&M Univ; Spd
Morgan, Daniel, +44(0) 113 34 35202 d.j.morgan@leeds.ac.uk, Univ of Leeds; Giv
Morgan, Emory, (757) 727-5783 emory.morgan@hampton.edu, Hampton Univ; Ze
Morgan, F D., (617) 253-7857 fdmorgan@mit.edu, Massachusetts Inst of Tech; Yg

Morgan, Gary, 757.727.5783 gary.morgan@hamptonu.edu, Hampton Univ; ZnnZn
Morgan, Joanna, +44 20 759 46423 j.v.morgan@imperial.ac.uk, Imperial Coll; Yg
Morgan, John D., 850-474-2224 jmorgan3@uwf.edu, Univ of West Florida; Zi
Morgan, Julia K., (713) 348-6330 morganj@rice.edu, Rice Univ; GctGv
Morgan, Kelly, 239-658-3400 conserv@ufl.edu, Univ of Florida; So
Morgan, Matt, 303-384-2632 mmorgan@mines.edu, Colorado Geological Survey; GgmXm
Morgan, Michael C., (608)265-8159 morgan@aurora.aos.wisc.edu, Univ of Wisconsin, Madison; Am
Morgan, Paul, 303-384-2648 morgan@mines.edu, Colorado Geological Survey; YhGtYg
Morgan, Ryan, 254-968-9894 rmorgan@tarleton.edu, Tarleton State Univ; Pei
Morgan, Siobahn M., (319) 273-2389 siobahn.morgan@uni.edu, Univ of Northern Iowa; Xa
Morgan, Sven S., 515-294-1837 smorgan@iastate.edu, Iowa State Univ of Sci & Tech; Gc
Morgan, Tamie, (817) 257-7743 tamie.morgan@tcu.edu, Texas Christian Univ; Zi
Morgan, Terrance L., (505) 667-0837 Los Alamos; Ng
Morgan, William, +44 0161 306-6586 will.morgan@manchester.ac.uk, Univ of Manchester; As
Morin, Paul, 612-626-0505 lpaul@umn.edu, Univ of Minnesota, Twin Cities; Zn
Morison, James H., (206) 543-1394 morison@apl.washington.edu, Univ of Washington; Op
Moritz, Wolfgang, 089/2180 4336 w.moritz@lrz.uni-muenchen.de, Ludwig-Maximilians-Univ Muenchen; Gz
Moro, Alan, +38514606093 amoro@geol.pmf.hr, Univ of Zagreb; PgsGg
Morozov, Igor B., (306) 966-2761 igor.morozov@usask.ca, Univ of Saskatchewan; YsGy
Morra, Matthew J., (208) 885-6315 Univ of Idaho; Sb
Morrill, Penny, (709) 864-6729 pmorrill@mun.ca, Memorial Univ of Newfoundland; Cg
Morris, Antony, +44 1752 584766 a.morris@plymouth.ac.uk, Univ of Plymouth; YmGtu
Morris, Billy, 706-368-7528 bmorris@highlands.edu, Georgia Highlands Coll; Gg
Morris, David, (314) 935-6926 Los Alamos; Cc
Morris, Donald P., (610) 758-5175 dpm2@lehigh.edu, Lehigh Univ; Zn
Morris, Geoffrey, (785) 532-3397 gpmorris@ksu.edu, Kansas State Univ; So
Morris, John A., 662-268-1032 Ext 235 jam16@msstate.edu, Mississippi State Univ; ZirAm
Morris, Robert W., rmorris@wittenberg.edu, Wittenberg Univ; PiGg
Morris, Simon C., +44 (0) 1223 333414 sc113@esc.cam.ac.uk, Univ of Cambridge; Pg
Morris, Thomas H., (801) 422-3761 tom_morris@byu.edu, Brigham Young Univ; Gr
Morris, William A., (905) 525-9140 (Ext. 20116) morriswa@mcmaster.ca, McMaster Univ; Yg
Morrison, Lauren, 252 328 6360 morrisonl14@ecu.edu, East Carolina Univ; Zn
Morrow, Robert H., 803.896.1214 morrowr@dnr.sc.gov, South Carolina Dept of Natural Resources; GcxGt
Morschauser, Lindsey, 662-268-1032 Ext 243 lcm193@msstate.edu, Mississippi State Univ; Am
Morse, David L., (512) 232-3241 Univ of Texas, Austin; Yg
Morse, Linda D., (757) 221-2444 ldmors@wm.edu, William & Mary; GeZg
Morse, Stearns A., (413) 545-0175 tm@geo.umass.edu, Univ of Massachusetts, Amherst; Gi
Mortensen, James K., (604) 822-6208 jmortensen@eos.ubc.ca, Univ of British Columbia; Cc
Mortlock, Richard , (848) 445-3423 rmortloc@eps.rutgers.edu, Rutgers, The State Univ of New Jersey; CgmCs
Morton, Allan E., (602) 426-4351 Central Arizona Coll; Ze
Morton, Bruce, mortonb@easternct.edu, Eastern Connecticut State Univ; Zg
Morton, Douglas M., (951) 276-6397 scamp@ucrac1.ucr.edu, Univ of California, Riverside; Gp
Morton, Penelope C., pmorton@d.umn.edu, Univ of Minnesota Duluth; EgGpCg
Morton, Roger D., (780) 492-3265 Univ of Alberta; Em
Morton, Ronald L., rmorton@d.umn.edu, Univ of Minnesota Duluth; GvEg
Moscovici, Daniel, (215) 688-2910 daniel.moscovici@stockton.edu, Stockton Univ; Zu
Mosenfelder, Jed, jmosenfe@umn.edu, Univ of Minnesota, Twin Cities; Cp
Moser, Desmond, 519-661-4214 dmoser22@uwo.ca, Western Univ; GtCcXg
Moshary, Fred , 212-684-7251 moshary@ccny.cuny.edu, Graduate Sch of the City Univ of New York; Gg
Mosher, David C., 603-862-5493 dmosher@ccom.unh.edu, Univ of New Hampshire; Og
Mosher, Sharon, (512) 471-4135 mosher@mail.utexas.edu, Univ of Texas, Austin; Gc
Moshier, Stephen O., (630) 752-5856 stephen.moshier@wheaton.edu, Wheaton Coll; Gd
Moskalski, Susanne, susanne.moskalski@stockton.edu, Stockton Univ; GsOn
Moskowitz, Bruce M., 612-624-1547 bmosk@umn.edu, Univ of Minnesota, Twin Cities; Ym
Mosley-Thompson, Ellen E., (614) 292-2580 thompson.4@osu.edu, Ohio State Univ; As
Moslow, Thomas F., (403) 269-6911 Univ of Calgary; Co
Moss, Neil E., 205-247-3557 nmoss@gsa.state.al.us, Geological Survey of Alabama; Hw
Moss, Patti, 509-527-5225 mosspm@whitman.edu, Whitman Coll; Zn
Mossman, David J., (506) 364-2326 dmossman@mta.ca, Mount Allison Univ; Em
Mosteller, Joey D., mostellerjd@appstate.edu, Appalachian State Univ; Gg
Motani, Ryosuke, 530-754-6284 rmotani@ucdavis.edu, Univ of California, Davis; Pv
Motavalli, Peter P., 573-884-3212 motavallip@missouri.edu, Univ of Missouri; So
Mote, Philip, 541-737-5694 pmote@coas.oregonstate.edu, Oregon State Univ; AsZg
Motta, Luigi, luigi.motta@unito.it, Univ di Torino; Zy
Motta, Michele, michele.motta@unito.it, Univ di Torino; Zy
Mottl, Michael J., (808) 956-7006 mmottl@soest.hawaii.edu, Univ of Hawai'i, Manoa; OuCgm
Motyka, James, motykaj@easternct.edu, Eastern Connecticut State Univ; Zg
Motz, Gary J., (812) 856-3500 garymotz@indiana.edu, Indiana Univ; PqgPi
Mouat, David A., (775) 673-7402 dmouat@dri.edu, Desert Research Inst; Ge
Moucha, Robert, 315-443-6239 rmoucha@syr.edu, Syracuse Univ; GtYeg
Mouginis-Mark, Peter J., (808) 956-3147 Univ of Hawai'i, Manoa; Xg
Moulis, Anastasia, 617-552-8300 anastasia.macherides@bc.edu, Boston Coll; Ys
Moum, James N., 541-737-2553 jmoum@coas.oregonstate.edu, Oregon State Univ; Op
Mound, Jon, +44(0) 113 34 35216 earjem@leeds.ac.uk, Univ of Leeds; Gt
Mount, Gregory, 724-357-7662 gregory.mount@iup.edu, Indiana Univ of Pennsylvania; Hy
Mount, Jeffrey F., (916) 752-7092 Univ of California, Davis; Gs
Mountain, Gregory S., 848-445-0817 gmtn@eps.rutgers.edu, Rutgers, The State Univ of New Jersey; GuYrGr
Mountney, Nigel, +44(0) 113 34 35249 n.p.mountney@leeds.ac.uk, Univ of Leeds; Gs
Mousset-Jones, Pierre, (775) 784-6959 mousset@mines.unr.edu, Univ of Nevada, Reno; Nm
Mower, Richard, 989-774-3821 mower1rn@cmich.edu, Central Michigan Univ; Am
Mowrer, Jake, 979-845-5366 jake.mowrer@tamu.edu, Texas A&M Univ; Sc
Moy, Christopher M., 64-3-479-5279 chris.moy@otago.ac.nz, Univ of Otago; Gus
MOYEN, Jean-François, (+33)477481510 jean.francois.moyen@univ-st-etienne.fr, Université Jean Monnet, Saint-Etienne; GiCtGp
Moyer, Elisabeth, (773) 834-2992 Univ of Chicago; As
Moyer, Kerry A., (814) 732-2454 kmoyer@edinboro.edu, Edinboro Univ of Pennsylvania; As
Moysey, Stephen, (864) 353-1517 moyseys18@ecu.edu, East Carolina Univ; Hg
Mozley, Peter S., (575) 835-5311 mozley@nmt.edu, New Mexico Inst of Mining and Tech; Gs
Mozzachiodi, Riccardo, 361-825-3634 riccardo.mozzachiodi@tamucc.edu, Texas A&M Univ, Corpus Christi; Zn
Mozzi, Paolo, +390498279190 paolo.mozzi@unipd.it, Univ degli Studi di Padova; Gm
Mrinjek, Ervin, +38514606057 ervin.mrinjek@zg.t-com.hr, Univ of Zagreb; GscGg
Mroz, Eugene J., (505) 667-7758 Los Alamos; As
Mshiu, Elisante E., *255768384430 mshiutz@gmail.com, Univ of Dar es Salaam; ZrCgZi
Mucci, Alfonso, 514-398-4892 alfonso.mucci@mcgill.ca, McGill Univ; CmlOc
Muchez, Philippe, 32 16 327584 philippe.muchez@kuleuven.be, Katholieke Universiteit Leuven; EmCgGd
Muchingami, Innocent , imuchingami@unam.na, Univ of Namibia; Ye
Mucsi, lászló, +3662544156 mucsi@geo.u-szeged.hu, Univesity of Szeged;

ZirZy
Mudd, Simon N., +44 (0) 131 650 2535 simon.m.mudd@ed.ac.uk, Edinburgh Univ; Hg
Mudrick, Stephen E., (573) 882-6721 Univ of Missouri; As
Muehlenbachs, Karlis, (780) 492-2827 karlis.muehlenbachs@ualberta.ca, Univ of Alberta; Cs
Mueller, Amy, 617.373.8131 a.mueller@northeastern.edu, Northeastern Univ; Zn
Mueller, Erich M., (334) 460-7136 em256@cornell.edu, Univ of South Alabama; Ob
Mueller, Ivan, 860-726-2069 mueller.3@osu.edu, Ohio State Univ; YddYv
Mueller, Karl J., (303) 492-7336 karl.mueller@colorado.edu, Univ of Colorado; GtcGm
Mueller, Paul A., (352) 392-2231 pamueller@ufl.edu, Univ of Florida; CcGit
Mueller, Thomas, (724) 938-4255 mueller@calu.edu, California Univ of Pennsylvania; Zi
Muggeridge, Ann H., +44 20 759 47379 a.muggeridge@imperial.ac.uk, Imperial Coll; NpHwEo
Muhlbauer, Jason , jason-muhlbauer@utc.edu, Univ of Tennessee, Chattanooga; Gg
Muhleman, Duane O., (626) 395-6186 dom@gps.caltech.edu, California Inst of Tech; Xy
Muir, William, 909-387-1603 wmuir@sbccd.cc.ca.us, San Bernardino Valley Coll; Og
Mukasa, Samuel, mukasa@umn.edu, Univ of Minnesota, Twin Cities; Cg
Mukherjee, Falguni, (936) 294-1073 fsm002@shsu.edu, Sam Houston State Univ; Zin
Mukhopadhyay, Sujoy, (530) 752-4711 sujoy@ucdavis.edu, Univ of California, Davis; Cg
Mulcahy, Sean R., 360-650-3645 sean.mulcahy@wwu.edu, Western Washington Univ; GpzGp
Muldoon, Maureen, (608) 265-8181 maureen.a.muldoon@wisc.edu, Univ of Wisconsin, Madison, Division of Extension; GeHw
Mulholland, Margaret, (757) 683-3972 mmulholl@odu.edu, Old Dominion Univ; Ob
Mulibo, Gabriel D., gmbelwa@yahoo.com, Univ of Dar es Salaam; Ysg
Mulla, David J., (612) 625-6721 mulla003@umn.edu, Univ of Minnesota, Twin Cities; Sp
Mullen, Steven L., (520) 621-6842 mullen@atmo.arizona.edu, Univ of Arizona; As
Muller, Andrew C., (410) 293-6569 amuller@usna.edu, United States Naval Academy; OpnOu
Muller, Dietmar, (029) 351-3244 d.muller@usyd.edu.au, Univ of Sydney; Yrg
Muller, Marc, mmuller1@nd.edu, Univ of Notre Dame; Rw
Muller, Otto H., (607) 871-2208 Alfred Univ; Gc
Muller, Peter, (808) 956-8081 pmuller@soest.hawaii.edu, Univ of Hawai'i, Manoa; Op
Muller-Karger, Frank E., (727) 553-3335 Univ of South Florida; Zr
Mulligan, Kevin R., 806-834-0391 kevin.mulligan@ttu.edu, Texas Tech Univ; ZiGmSo
Mullins, Gregory L., (540) 231-4383 gmullins@vt.edu, Virginia Polytechnic Inst & State Univ; Sc
Mulrooney, Timothy, (919) 530-6269 tmulroon@nccu.edu, North Carolina Central Univ; Zir
Mulvaney, Richard L., (217) 333-9467 Univ of Illinois, Urbana-Champaign; Sc
Mumin, A. Hamid, 204-727-9685 mumin@brandonu.ca, Brandon Univ; EgGzt
Munasinghe, Tissa, munasit@lahc.edu, Los Angeles Harbor Coll; Zg
Munch, Stephan, steve.munch@noaa.gov, SUNY, Stony Brook; Ob
Mundie, Ben, (541) 967-2039 Oregon Dept of Geology and Mineral Industries; Ge
Mungall, James E., 613 558 9337 jamesmungall@cunet.carleton.ca, Carleton Univ; GiEgCg
Munguia, Luis, lmunguia@cicese.mx, Centro de Investigación Científica y de Educación Superior de Ensenada; Ys
Muniz-Solari, Oswaldo, (512) 245-2170 Texas State Univ; Ze
Munizzi, Jordan S., (859) 257-6222 jmunizzi@uky.edu, Univ of Kentucky; Cs
Munk, LeeAnn, 907 786-6895 lamunk@uaa.alaska.edu, Univ of Alaska, Anchorage; Cle
Munk, Walter H., (858) 534-2877 wmunk@ucsd.edu, Univ of California, San Diego; Op
Munn, Barbara J., (916) 278-6811 Sacramento State Univ; Ggp
Muñoz, Alfonso, amunoz@ucm.es, Univ Complutense de Madrid; Ygr
Muñoz, Belén, mbmunoz@ucm.es, Univ Complutense de Madrid; Gr
Munoz, Samuel, s.munoz@northeastern.edu, Northeastern Univ; GsPcRn
Munro, Ildi, imunro@ccs.carleton.ca, Carleton Univ; Pg
Munroe, Jeffrey S., (802) 443-3446 jmunroe@middlebury.edu, Middlebury Coll; Gln
Munski, Douglas C., (701) 777-4591 douglas.munski@und.edu, Univ of North Dakota; ZeRhZu
Muntean, John, (775) 682-8748 munteanj@unr.edu, Univ of Nevada, Reno; Eg
Muntean, Thomas, 517-264-3943 tmuntean@adrian.edu, Adrian Coll; Gde
Murdoch, Lawrence C., (864) 656-2597 lmurdoc@clemson.edu, Clemson Univ; Hw
Murgulet, Dorina, (361) 825-2309 dorina.murgulet@tamucc.edu, Texas A&M Univ, Corpus Christi; Hw
Murgulet, Valeriu, 361-825-6023 valeriu.murgulet@tamucc.edu, Texas A&M Univ, Corpus Christi; Cg
Murowchick, James B., (816) 235-2979 murowchickj@umkc.edu, Univ of Missouri, Kansas City; CgGz
Murphree, James Thomas, 831-656-2723 murphree@nps.edu, Naval Postgraduate Sch; Am
Murphy, Alexander, (541) 346-4571 abmurphy@uoregon.edu, Univ of Oregon; Zn
Murphy, Cindy, (902) 867-2299 cmurphy@stfx.ca, Saint Francis Xavier Univ; Gg
Murphy, David T., 61 07 31382329 david.murphy@qut.edu.au, Queensland Univ of Tech; CgEgCc
Murphy, Edward C., (701) 328-8002 emurphy@nd.gov, North Dakota Geological Survey; Zn
Murphy, J. Brendan, (902) 867-2481 Dalhousie Univ; Gx
Murphy, Michael, 713-743-3564 mmurphy@central.uh.edu, Univ of Houston; Gct
Murphy, Sean C., sean.murphy@austincc.edu, Austin Comm Coll District; EgGpRc
Murphy, Todd, (318) 342-3428 murphy@ulm.edu, Univ of Louisiana, Monroe; As
Murphy, Vincent, 617-552-8300 Boston Coll; Yg
Murray, A. Bradshaw, (919) 684-5847 abmurray@duke.edu, Duke Univ; Gm
Murray, Alison, 775.673.7361 alison.murray@dri.edu, Univ of Nevada, Reno; ObCg
Murray, Andrew, 251-460-7325 amurray@southalabama.edu, Univ of South Alabama; Am
Murray, Bryan P., 909-869-3459 bpmurray@cpp.edu, California State Polytechnic Univ, Pomona; Gsg
Murray, Christopher J., (509) 376-5848 chris.murray@pnl.gov, Pacific Northwest; Gq
Murray, Daniel P., (401) 874-2265 dpmurray@uri.edu, Univ of Rhode Island; ZeGtp
Murray, David, (401) 863-3531 david_murray@brown.edu, Brown Univ; Ou
Murray, James W., (206) 543-4730 jmurray@u.washington.edu, Univ of Washington; Oc
Murray, John, + 353 (0)91 495 095 john.murray@nuigalway.ie, Nat Univ of Ireland Galway; PgGs
Murray, Kendra, (208) 282-2949 kendramurray@isu.edu, Idaho State Univ; ClGtm
Murray, Kent S., (313) 436-9129 kmurray@umich.edu, Univ of Michigan, Dearborn; Hw
Murray, Kyle E., (405) 325-7502 kyle.murray@ou.edu, Univ of Oklahoma; HwZiGo
Murray, Lee, 585-275-2077 lee.murray@rochester.edu, Univ of Rochester; Ac
Murray, Mark, 575.835.6930 murray@ees.nmt.edu, New Mexico Inst of Mining and Tech; Yds
Murray, Richard, (617) 353-6532 rickm@bu.edu, Boston Univ; Cm
Murrell, Coling, +44 (0)1603 59 2959 j.c.murrell@uea.ac.uk, Univ of East Anglia; As
Murrell, Michael T., (505) 667-0967 Los Alamos; Cc
Murthy, Prahlad N., 570-408-4617 prahlad.murthy@wilkes.edu, Wilkes Univ; AsZnn
Murtugudde, Raghuram G., (301) 314-2622 ragu@umd.edu, Univ of Maryland; ObZr
Muscente, Drew, (319) 895-4309 dmuscente@cornellcollege.edu, Cornell Coll; PgGs
Mushkin, Amit, 972(02)5314254 mushkin@uw.edu, Univ of Washington; ZrCcGm
Musil, Rudolf, +420 549 49 5997 rudolf@sci.muni.cz, Masaryk Univ; PgvGe
Muskatt, Herman, 792-3028 ewelch@utica.edu, Utica Coll; GgrPg
Musolf, Gene E., (715) 845-9602 Univ of Wisconsin Colls; Zy
Musselman, Zachary A., (601) 974-1344 musseza@millsaps.edu, Millsaps Coll; Gm
Mustard, John F., (401) 863-1264 john_mustard@brown.edu, Brown Univ; Zr

Mustart, David A., (415) 338-7729 mustart@sfsu.edu, San Francisco State Univ; GizGv
Mustoe, George, george.mustoe@wwu.edu, Western Washington Univ; PbCaPo
Muszer, Antoni, antoni.muszer@uwr.edu.pl, Univ of Wroclaw; Eg
Muthukrishnan, Suresh, (864) 294-3361 suresh.muthukrishnan@furman.edu, Furman Univ; ZiGmZr
Muto, Atsuhiro, 215-204-3699 amuto@temple.edu, Temple Univ; GlYg
Mutter, John C., (646) 269-6942 jcm7@columbia.edu, Columbia Univ; YrGtYs
Mutti, Laurel, muttil@newpaltz.edu, SUNY, New Paltz; Gg
Mutti, Laurence J., (814) 641-3067 mutti@juniata.edu, Juniata Coll; GxzSc
Mutua, Felix N., fnmutua@jkuat.ac.ke, Jomo Kenyatta Univ of Agriculture & Tech; ZigZr
Muxworthy, Adrian, +44 20 759 46442 adrian.muxworthy@imperial.ac.uk, Imperial Coll; Ym
Muza, Jay P., (954) 736-8231 jmuza@broward.edu, Broward Coll; OuPmOo
Mwangi, Nancy , nwmwangi@jkuat.ac.ke, Jomo Kenyatta Univ of Agriculture & Tech; ZiiZr
Mwaniki, Mercy W., mmwaniki@jkuat.ac.ke, Jomo Kenyatta Univ of Agriculture & Tech; ZiiZr
Myers, Alan R., 217-300-2570 amyers76@illinois.edu, Illinois State Geological Survey; EcGo
Myers, Clifford D., (413) 236-4601 cmyers@berkshirecc.edu, Berkshire Comm Coll; Zn
Myers, Corinne E., 505.277.4204 cemyers@unm.edu, Univ of New Mexico; PeqPi
Myers, James D., (307) 766-2203 magma@uwyo.edu, Univ of Wyoming; Gi
Myers, Jeffrey A., 503-838-8365 myersj@wou.edu, Western Oregon Univ; Gs
Myers, Orrin B., (505) 665-3742 obm@lanl.gov, Los Alamos; Pg
Myers, Paul, (780) 492-6706 pmyers@ualberta.ca, Univ of Alberta; Op
Myers, Tammy, (717) 477-1685 tlmyers@ship.edu, Shippensburg Univ; Zn
Mylavarapu, S R., 352-392-1951 ext 202 raom@ufl.edu, Univ of Florida; Sc
Müller, Lena, 089/2180 4340 lena-mueller@lrz.uni-muenchen.de, Ludwig-Maximilians-Univ Muenchen; Gz
Müller-Sohnius, Dieter, 089/2180 4259 mueso@min.uni-muenchen.de, Ludwig-Maximilians-Univ Muenchen; Gz
Mylroie, John E., 662-268-1032 Ext 237 mylroie@geosci.msstate.edu, Mississippi State Univ; GmHyGs
Myneni, Satish C B., 609-258-5848 smyneni@princeton.edu, Princeton Univ; Sc
Myrow, Paul M., (719) 389-6790 pmyrow@coloradocollege.edu, Colorado Coll; Gsr
Mysak, Lawrence A., (514) 398-3768 lawrence.mysak@mcgill.ca, McGill Univ; Op
Mysen, Bjorn O., (202) 478-8975 bmysen@carnegiescience.edu, Carnegie Inst for Sci; Cp
Möller, Andreas, 785864358 amoller@ku.edu, Univ of Kansas; Gt

N

Naar, David F., (727) 553-1637 dnaar@usf.edu, Univ of South Florida; Ou
Nabelek, John L., 541-737-2757 nabelek@coas.oregonstate.edu, Oregon State Univ; GtYs
Nabelek, Peter I., (573) 884-6463 nabelekp@missouri.edu, Univ of Missouri; GipCu
Nadiga, Balu, (505) 667-9466 balu@lanl.gov, Los Alamos; Zn
Nadin, Elisabeth S., (907) 474-5181 enadin@alaska.edu, Univ of Alaska, Fairbanks; Gtc
Nadiri, Ata Allah, +989143003725 nadiri@tabrizu.ac.ir, Univ of Tabriz; HwGqe
Nadon, Gregory C., (740) 593-4212 nadon@ohio.edu, Ohio Univ; Gs
Naehr, Thomas H., (361) 825-2470 thomas.naehr@tamucc.edu, Texas A&M Univ, Corpus Christi; GuCm
Nagaoka, Lisa A., (940) 565-2510 lisa.nagaoka@unt.edu, Univ of North Texas; Ga
Nagel, Athena, (662) 268-1032 ext 238 amo58@msstate.edu, Mississippi State Univ; ZgiZr
Nagel-Myers, Judith, 315-229-5239 jnagel@stlawu.edu, St. Lawrence Univ; PisPe
Nagihara, Seiichi, 806-834-4481 seiichi.nagihara@ttu.edu, Texas Tech Univ; Zi
Nagorski, Sonia, (907) 796-6580 sanagorski@alaska.edu, Univ of Alaska, Southeast; GgZcCt
Nagy, Kathryn L., 312-355-3276 klnagy@uic.edu, Univ of Illinois at Chicago; Cg
Nagy-Shadman, Elizabeth, 626 585-3369 eanagy-shadman@pasadena.edu, Pasadena City Coll; Gg
Nair, Vimala D., (352) 392-1803 Ext. 324 vdn@ufl.edu, Univ of Florida; Sc
Najjar, Raymond G., (814) 863-1586 rgn1@psu.edu, Pennsylvania State Univ, Univ Park; OcpAt
Nakagawa, Masami, 303-384-2132 mnakagaw@mines.edu, Colorado Sch of Mines; Ze
Nakamura, Noboru, (773) 702-3802 nnn@bethel.uchicago.edu, Univ of Chicago; As
Nakamura, Yosio, (512) 471-0428 yosio@ig.utexas.edu, Univ of Texas, Austin; Ys
Nakote, Heinz, (575) 646-7627 hnakotte@nmsu.edu, New Mexico State Univ, Las Cruces; Zm
Nakov, Radoslav A., +359-2-979 3472 radnac@geology.bas.bg, Bulgarian Academy of Scis; GtEgm
Naldrett, Anthony J., +441243531823 ajnaldrett@yahoo.com, Univ of Toronto; EmGiCp
Nalin, Ronald, (909) 558-7151 rnalin@llu.edu, Loma Linda Univ; Gsr
Namikas, Steven, (225) 578-6142 snamik1@lsu.edu, Louisiana State Univ; Gms
Nance, Hardie S., 512-471-6285 seay.nance@beg.utexas.edu, Univ of Texas, Austin; Grc
Nance, R. Damian, (740) 593-1107 nance@ohio.edu, Ohio Univ; Gtc
Nance, Seay, 512-471-6285 seay.nance@beg.utexas.edu, Univ of Texas at Austin, Jackson Sch of Geosciences; Gg
Napieralski, Jacob A., 313.593.5157 jnapiera@umich.edu, Univ of Michigan, Dearborn; GmlZi
Naples, Virginia, 815-753-7820 vlnaples@niu.edu, Northern Illinois Univ; Pv
Napora, Theodore A., (401) 874-6222 Univ of Rhode Island; Ob
Napp, Jeffrey, (206) 526-4148 jeff.napp@noaa.gov, Univ of Washington; Ob
Naranjo, Ramon, 775-887=7659 rnaranjo@usgs.gov, Univ of Nevada, Reno; CgHw
Narbonne, Guy M., (613) 533-6168 narbonne@queensu.ca, Queen's Univ; PigGs
Narey, Martha A., mnarey@du.edu, Univ of Denver; Zg
Narinder, Kaushik, nkaushik@uoguelph.ca, Univ of Guelph; Zn
Narod, Barry, (604) 822-2267 narod@eos.ubc.ca, Univ of British Columbia; Yx
Nash, Barbara P., (801) 581-8587 barb.nash@utah.edu, Univ of Utah; Gi
Nash, David, david.nash@uc.edu, Univ of Cincinnati; Gm
Nash, Greg, 801-585-9986 gnash@egi.utah.edu, Univ of Utah; Gt
Nash, Jonathan, 541-737-4573 nash@coas.oregonstate.edu, Oregon State Univ; Op
Nash, Thomas A., 614 265 6582 thomas.nash@dnr.state.oh.us, Ohio Dept of Natural Resources; Gl
Nashold, Barney W., (630) 252-7698 bwnashold@anl.gov, Argonne; Zn
Nasir, Sobhi J., 00974-4852207 nasir54@qu.edu.qa, Univ of Qatar; Gx
Naslund, H. Richard, (607) 777-4313 Binghamton Univ; Gi
Nasraoui, Mohamed, +33 (0)344063813 mohmed.nasraoui@lasalle-beauvais.fr, Institut Polytechnique LaSalle Beauvais (ex-IGAL); EgGzEm
Natalicchio, Marcello, marcello.natalicchio@unito.it, Univ di Torino; Gs
Nater, Edward A., (612) 625-1725 enater@umn.edu, Univ of Minnesota, Twin Cities; Sd
Nathan , Stephen, 860-465-5579 nathans@easternct.edu, Eastern Connecticut State Univ; PmEo
Nathan, Terrence R., (530) 752-1609 trnathan@ucdavis.edu, Univ of California, Davis; Asm
Nathan, Terry, 530-752-1609 trnathan@ucdavis.edu, Univ of California, Davis; AsZc
Naudts, Kim, +31 20 59 87354 Vrije Universiteit Amsterdam; HgPe
Naumann, Malik, 089/2180 6714 Ludwig-Maximilians-Univ Muenchen; Pg
Naumann, Terry R., trnaumann@uaa.alaska.edu, Univ of Alaska, Anchorage; Gi
Nava, Alejandro, fnava@cicese.mx, Centro de Investigación Científica y de Educación Superior de Ensenada; Ys
Navarre-Sitchler, Alexis, 303-384-2219 asitchle@mines.edu, Colorado Sch of Mines; Ca
Navarro, Didac, didac.navarro@uab.cat, Universitat Autonoma de Barcelona; Gz
Naveira Garabato, Alberto, +44 (0)23 80592680 acng@noc.soton.ac.uk, Univ of Southampton; Op
Navrotsky, Alexandra, (530) 752-3292 anavrotsky@ucdavis.edu, Univ of California, Davis; Zm
Naylor, Mark, +44 (0) 131 650 4918 mark.naylor@ed.ac.uk, Edinburgh Univ; Gt
Naylor, Shawn C., 812-855-2504 snaylor@indiana.edu, Indiana Univ; Hw
Naymik, Thomas G., 614-433-9280 tnaymik@geosyntec.com, Ohio State Univ; Hw
Ndarana, Thando, +27 (0) 12 420 5164 thando.ndarana@up.ac.za, Univ of Pretoria; Ams
Nduati, Eunice W., enduati@jkuat.ac.ke, Jomo Kenyatta Univ of Agriculture & Tech; ZrrZi

Neal, Clive R., (574) 631-8328 neal.1@nd.edu, Univ of Notre Dame; Gi
Neal, William J., (616) 331-3381 nealw@gvsu.edu, Grand Valley State Univ; GsdGr
Nealson, Kenneth, (213) 821-2271 knealson@usc.edu, Univ of Southern California; Pg
Neboga, Victoria V., 717–702–2026 vneboga@pa.gov, DCNR- Pennsylvania Bureau of Geological Survey; GgHwNx
Nechaev, Dmitri, (228) 688-2573 dmitri.nechaev@usm.edu, Univ of Southern Mississippi; Op
Nedimovic, Mladen, 1 902 494 4524 mladen@dal.ca, Dalhousie Univ; Ysg
Nedunuri, Krishna K., (937) 376-6455 knedunuri@centralstate.edu, Central State Univ; HwCaSo
Needham, Tim, +44(0) 113 34 39104 d.t.needham@leeds.ac.uk, Univ of Leeds; Gc
Neelin, J. David, (310) 206-3734 neelin@atmos.ucla.edu, Univ of California, Los Angeles; As
Neely, Haly L., 979-845-3041 hneely@tamu.edu, Texas A&M Univ; Spd
Neethling, Stephen, +44 20 759 49341 s.neethling@imperial.ac.uk, Imperial Coll; Gz
Negrini, Robert M., (661) 654-2185 rnegrini@csub.edu, California State Univ, Bakersfield; YmgGn
Nehyba, Slavomír, +420 549 49 6067 slavek@sci.muni.cz, Masaryk Univ; GsdGg
Neighbors, Corrie, (505) 538-6352 neighborsc@wnmu.edu, Western New Mexico Univ; Ysr
Neill, Owen K., (509) 335-6770 owen.neill@wsu.edu, Washington State Univ; Ca
Neill, Simon P., 01248 383938 s.p.neill@bangor.ac.uk, Univ of Wales; OnpOg
Neinow, Peter W., +44 (0) 131 650 9139 peter.nienow@ed.ac.uk, Edinburgh Univ; Gl
Neish, Catherine, 519-661-2111, ext.83188 cneish@uwo.ca, Western Univ; Xg
Neitzke Adamo, Lauren, (848) 932-7243 lauren.adamo@rutgers.edu, Rutgers, The State Univ of New Jersey; GuPmZe
Nekvasil, Hanna, 631-632-8201 hanna.nekvasil@sunysb.edu, Stony Brook Univ; Cp
Nel, Justin, (051) 401-3402 nelwj@ufs.ac.za, Univ of the Free State; Gc
Nelsen, Lori, (864)294-3481 lori.nelsen@furman.edu, Furman Univ; Ca
Nelson, Bruce K., (206) 543-4434 bnelson@uw.edu, Univ of Washington; CcGie
Nelson, Craig, 614 265 6603 craig.nelson@dnr.state.oh.us, Ohio Dept of Natural Resources; Hw
Nelson, Jennifer, jsembach@iupui.edu, Indiana Univ - Purdue Univ Indianapolis; Gg
Nelson, Kenneth A., (785) 864-2164 nelson@kgs.ku.edu, Univ of Kansas; Zy
Nelson, Marc A., (501) 575-3964 manelson@comp.uark.edu, Univ of Arkansas, Fayetteville; Cl
Nelson, Michael G., (801) 585-3064 nelsonelson@aol.com, Univ of Utah; Nm
Nelson, Nathan, (785) 532-5115 nonelson@ksu.edu, Kansas State Univ; So
Nelson, Priscilla P., 303-273-3700 pnelson@mines.edu, Colorado Sch of Mines; NrgNm
Nelson, Robert K., (508) 289-2656 rnelson@whoi.edu, Woods Hole Oceanographic Inst; Co
Nelson, Stephen A., (504) 862-3194 snelson@tulane.edu, Tulane Univ; GivRn
Nelson, Wendy, (410) 704-3133 wrnelson@towson.edu, Towson Univ; GiCc
Nelwamondo, T. M., +27 15 962 8582 tshililo.nelwamondo@univen.ac.za, Univ of Venda; GeZuy
Nemcok, Michal, +421-2-5463-0337 mnemcok@egi.utah.edu, Univ of Utah; GctGo
Nemon, Amy, (270) 745-6952 amy.nemon@wku.edu, Western Kentucky Univ; Zig
Nenes, Athanasios, (404) 894-9225 nenes@eas.gatech.edu, Georgia Inst of Tech; As
Nesbitt, Alex, (775) 682-8762 anesbitt@unr.edu, Univ of Nevada, Reno; Zn
Nesbitt, Carl, 775-784-8287 carln@unr.edu, Univ of Nevada, Reno; Nx
Nesbitt, H W., (519) 661-3194 hwn@uwo.ca, Western Univ; Cl
Nesbitt, Stephen W., (217) 244-3740 snesbitt@illinois.edu, Univ of Illinois, Urbana-Champaign; As
Nesbitt, Sterling J., 540-231-6330 sjn2104@vt.edu, Virginia Polytechnic Inst & State Univ; Pv
Nese, Jon, j2n@psu.edu, Pennsylvania State Univ, Univ Park; Am
Nesse, William D., (970) 351-2830 w.d.nesse@gmail.com, Univ of Northern Colorado; Gxz
Nestell, Galina P., (817) 272-2987 gnestell@uta.edu, Univ of Texas, Arlington; PmsPi
Nestell, Merlynd K., (817) 272-2987 nestell@uta.edu, Univ of Texas, Arlington; PmiPs
Nestola, Fabrizio, +390498279160 fabrizio.nestola@unipd.it, Univ degli Studi di Padova; Gz
Nethengwe, Nthaduleni S., +27 15 962 8593 nthaduleni.nethengwe2@univen.ac.za, Univ of Venda; RnZiRw
Nettles, Meredith, (845) 365-8613 nettles@ldeo.columbia.edu, Columbia Univ; YsGl
Neubaum, John C., 717-702-2039 jneubaum@pa.gov, DCNR- Pennsylvania Bureau of Geological Survey; EcnGg
Neubeck, William S., (518) 388-6519 neubeckw@union.edu, Union Coll; Gm
Neuberg, Jurgen, +44(0) 113 34 36769 j.neuberg@leeds.ac.uk, Univ of Leeds; Gv
Neufeld, Jerome A., +44 (0) 1223 765709 jn271@cam.ac.uk, Univ of Cambridge; GoYgGt
Neuhauser, Kenneth R., (785) 628-5349 kneuhaus@fhsu.edu, Fort Hays State Univ; GceGs
Neukrug, Howard, hneukrug@upenn.edu, Univ of Pennsylvania; Hs
Neuman, Andrew G., (403) 823-7707 Royal Tyrrell Mus of Palaeontology; Pv
Neuman, Shlomo P., (520) 621-7114 neuman@hwr.arizona.edu, Univ of Arizona; HwqGq
Neumann, Klaus, 765-285-8262 kneumann@bsu.edu, Ball State Univ; Cl
Neumann, Patricia, (310) 660-3593 pneumann@elcamino.edu, El Camino Coll; Zg
Neumann, Tom, 301-614-5923 thomas.neumann@nasa.gov, Univ of Washington; Gl
Neuweiler, Fritz, (418) 656-7479 fritz.neuweiler@ggl.ulaval.ca, Universite Laval; GsdPg
Neves, Douglas, (310) 660-3593 dneves@elcamino.edu, El Camino Coll; Zg
Nevins, Joseph, 845-437-7823 jonevins@vassar.edu, Vassar Coll; Zu
Nevins, Susan K., (607) 753-2815 geologydept@cortland.edu, SUNY, Cortland; Zn
Newberry, Rainer J., ffrn@uaf.edu, Univ of Alaska, Fairbanks; Em
Newbold, K. B., (905) 525-9140 (Ext. 27948) newbold@mcmaster.ca, McMaster Univ; Ge
Newcomer, Darrell R., (509) 376-1054 darrell.newcomer@pnl.gov, Pacific Northwest; Hw
Newell, Dennis L., dennis.newell@usu.edu, Utah State Univ; Cls
Newell, Kerry D., (785) 864-2183 dnewell@kgs.ku.edu, Univ of Kansas; Go
Newland, Franz, (416)736-2100 #22095 franz.newland@lassonde.yorku.ca, York Univ; Zr
Newman, Andrew V., (404) 894-3976 anewman@gatech.edu, Georgia Inst of Tech; YdsYg
Newman, Brent D., (505) 667-3021 bnewman@lanl.gov, Los Alamos; Gg
Newman, Dianne K., (636) 395-3543 dkn@caltech.edu, California Inst of Tech; Pg
Newman, Jamie, 212-769-5386 jamien@amnh.org, American Mus of Natural History; Gg
Newman, Jonathan, (519) 824-4120 Ext.52147 jnewma01@uoguelph.ca, Univ of Guelph; Zn
Newman, Julie, (979) 845-9283 newman@geo.tamu.edu, Texas A&M Univ; Gct
Newman, Steven B., (860) 832-2940 ccsuwxman@gmail.com, Central Connecticut State Univ; As
Newman, William A., (858) 534-2150 wnewman@ucsd.edu, Univ of California, San Diego; Ob
Newsom, Horton E., (505) 277-0375 newsom@unm.edu, Univ of New Mexico; XgcXm
Newton, Anthony J., +44 (0) 131 650 2546 anthony.newton@ed.ac.uk, Edinburgh Univ; Zn
Newton, Brad T., 575-835-6668 talon.newton@nmt.edu, New Mexico Inst of Mining and Tech; HwCgs
Newton, Cathryn R., 315-443-2672 crnewton@syr.edu, Syracuse Univ; Pg
Newton, Jan, (206) 616-3641 newton@ocean.washington.edu, Univ of Washington; Ob
Newton, Rob, +44(0) 113 34 31631 d.oneill@leeds.ac.uk, Univ of Leeds; Ge
Newton, Robert, bnewton@ldeo.columbia.edu, Columbia Univ; Ct
Newton, Seth A., 205-247-3708 snewton@gsa.state.al.us, Geological Survey of Alabama; ZnGg
Nex, Paul A., 011 717 6563 paul.nex@wits.ac.za, Univ of the Witwatersrand; Eg
Nezat, Carmen A., (509) 359-7959 cnezat@ewu.edu, Eastern Washington Univ; ClGeSc
Ng, Crystal, 612-624-9243 gcng@umn.edu, Univ of Minnesota, Twin Cities; Hy
Ngigi, Thomas G., tgngigi@jkuat.ac.ke, Jomo Kenyatta Univ of Agriculture & Tech; ZriZr

Ngo, Thanh X., +84-9782 24246 ngoxuanthanh@humg.edu.vn, Hanoi Univ of Mining & Geology; GtcGi
Ngoy, Kikombo, (908) 737-3718 kngoy@kean.edu, Kean Univ; Zy
Nguyen, Maurice, 612-626-8739 nguyenm@umn.edu, Univ of Minnesota; Gl
Ngwenya, Bryne T., +44 (0) 131 650 8507 bryne.ngwenya@ed.ac.uk, Edinburgh Univ; Co
Ni, James F., (505) 646-1920 jni@nmsu.edu, New Mexico State Univ, Las Cruces; YsGtYg
Ni-Meister, Wenge, 212-772-5321 wenge.ni-meister@hunter.cuny.edu, Graduate Sch of the City Univ of New York; Gg
Nichol, Craig F., 250-807-8087 craig.nichol@ubc.ca, Univ of British Columbia, Okanagan Campus; HwSpZe
Nicholas, Chris, +353 1 8962176 nicholyj@tcd.ie, Trinity Coll; Eo
Nicholas, Joseph W., (540) 654-1470 jnicola@mwc.edu, Mary Washington Coll; Zy
Nicholls, James W., (403) 220-7127 Univ of Calgary; Gi
Nichols, Jonathan E., jnichols@ldeo.columbia.edu, Columbia Univ; Pe
Nichols, Kyle K., 518-580-5194 knichols@skidmore.edu, Skidmore Coll; Gm
Nichols, Terry E., (501) 575-7317 tenichol@comp.uark.edu, Univ of Arkansas, Fayetteville; Zn
Nicholson, David, (508) 289-3547 dnicholson@whoi.edu, Woods Hole Oceanographic Inst; Gu
Nicholson, Kirsten N., 765-285-8268 knichols@bsu.edu, Ball State Univ; Gi
Nicholson, Nanette, 212-769-5390 nnicholson@amnh.org, American Mus of Natural History; Zn
Nick, Kevin, (909) 558-4530 knick@llu.edu, Loma Linda Univ; GsbGr
Nickmann, Marion, +49 89 289 25853 nickmann@tum.de, Technical Univ of Munich; Ng
Nicol, Andy, andy.nicol@canterbury.ac.nz, Univ of Canterbury; GctGo
Nicolas, Michelle P., (204) 945-6571 michelle.nicolas@gov.mb.ca, Manitoba Geological Survey; GrsGo
Nicolaysen, Kirsten P., 509-527-4934 nicolakp@whitman.edu, Whitman Coll; GiCgGa
Nicolescu, Stefan, 203-432-3141 stefan.nicolescu@yale.edu, Yale Univ; CtGpz
Nicolette, Justine, 575-835-5613 justine.nicolette@nmt.edu, New Mexico Inst of Mining and Tech; Zi
Nicot, Jean-Philippe, (512) 471-6246 jp.nicot@beg.utexas.edu, Univ of Texas at Austin, Jackson Sch of Geosciences; HwCg
NICULESCU, Bogdan M., +40-21-3125024 bogdan.niculescu@g.unibuc.ro, Univ of Bucharest; YgeYu
Nielsen, Gerald A., (406) 994-5075 nielsenmontana@aol.com, Montana State Univ; Sd
Nielsen, Gregory B., (801) 626-6394 gnielsen@weber.edu, Weber State Univ; Gg
Nielsen, Kurt E., 831-656-2295 nielsen@nps.edu, Naval Postgraduate Sch; Am
Nielsen, Mary, 605-677-5649 mary.nielsen@usd.edu, Univ of South Dakota; Zn
Nielsen, Peter A., pnielsen@keene.edu, Keene State Coll; GxzGc
Nielsen, Roger L., (541) 737-1235 nielsenr@geo.oregonstate.edu, Oregon State Univ; GizGv
Nielsen, Sune G., (508) 289-2837 snielsen@whoi.edu, Woods Hole Oceanographic Inst; Cs
Nielsen-Gammon, John, (979) 862-2248 n-g@tamu.edu, Texas A&M Univ; As
Nielson, R. LaRell, (936) 468-2248 rnielson@sfasu.edu, Stephen F. Austin State Univ; Grs
Niemann, William L., (304) 696-6721 niemann@marshall.edu, Marshall Univ; Ng
Niemi, Nathan A., 734-764-6377 naniemi@umich.edu, Univ of Michigan; Gtc
Niemi, Tina M., (816) 235-5342 niemit@umkc.edu, Univ of Missouri, Kansas City; Gt
Niemiller, Matthew L., matthew.niemiller@uah.edu, Univ of Tennessee, Knoxville; Zn
Niemitz, Jeffery W., niemitz@dickinson.edu, Dickinson Coll; ClOuGn
Nieto, Alberto S., a-nieto@illinois.edu, Univ of Illinois, Urbana-Champaign; Ng
Niewendorp, Clark, (971) 673-1555 Oregon Dept of Geology and Mineral Industries; Eg
Nikitina, Daria L., (610) 436-3103 dnikitina@wcupa.edu, West Chester Univ; Gm
Nikolinakou, Maria-Aikaterini, 512-475-6613 mariakat@austin.utexas.edu, Univ of Texas, Austin; Np
Nikulin, Alex, (607) 777-2518 anikulin@binghamton.edu, Binghamton Univ; Ys
Nilsson, Andreas, andreas.nilsson@liverpool.ac.uk, Univ of Liverpool; Ym
Nimako, Solomon Nana Kwaku, solomon.nimako@gmail.com, San Bernardino Valley Coll; Zi
Nimis, Paolo, +390498279161 paolo.nimis@unipd.it, Univ degli Studi di Padova; Eg
Nimmo, Francis, 831-459-1783 fnimmo@ucsc.edu, Univ of California, Santa Cruz; Xy
Nisbet, Euan G., +44 1784 443809 e.nisbet@rhul.ac.uk, Royal Holloway Univ of London; ZgAcGi
Nissen-Meyer, Targe, +44 (1865) 282149 tarje.nissen-meyer@earth.ox.ac.uk, Univ of Oxford; Ys
Nitecki, Matthew H., (312) 665-7093 mnitecki@fmnh.org, Field Mus of Natural History; Pi
Nitsche, Frank, fnitsche@ldeo.columbia.edu, Columbia Univ; Gu
Nittler, Larry R., (202) 478-8460 lnittler@carnegiescience.edu, Carnegie Inst for Sci; Xc
Nittrouer, Charles A., 206-543-5099 nittroue@ocean.washington.edu, Univ of Washington; GuYr
Nittrouer, Jeffrey A., 713.348.4886 nittrouer@rice.edu, Rice Univ; Gms
Niu, Fenglin, 713.348.4122 niu@rice.edu, Rice Univ; YsGt
Niu, Yaoling, +44 (0) 191 33 42311 yaoling.niu@durham.ac.uk, Durham Univ; Gi
Nixon, R. Paul, 801-422-4657 paul_nixon@byu.edu, Brigham Young Univ; Go
Nixon, Scott W., (401) 874-6803 Univ of Rhode Island; Ob
Niyogi, Dev, (765) 494-9531 climate@purdue.edu, Purdue Univ; As
Njau, Jackson K., (812) 856-3170 jknjau@indiana.edu, Indiana Univ, Bloomington; Pv
njoh, Ambe, njoh@usf.edu, Univ of South Florida; Zn
Njoku, Eni G., (818) 354-3693 eni.g.njoku@jpl.nasa.gov, Jet Propulsion Lab; Zr
Nkedi-Kizza, Peter, (352) 392-1951 kizza@ufl.edu, Univ of Florida; Sp
Nkotagu, Hudson H., nkotaguh@yahoo.com, Univ of Dar es Salaam; HwgGe
Nkuna, Tinyiko R., +27 15 962 8017 tinyiko.nkuna@univen.ac.za, Univ of Venda for Sci & Tech; HgwAs
Noble, Allison, 480-965-2552 allison.noble@asu.edu, Arizona State Univ; Xa
Noble, Paula J., 775-784-6211 noblepj@unr.edu, Univ of Nevada, Reno; PmGnPs
Noblett, Jeffrey B., (719) 389-6516 jnoblett@coloradocollege.edu, Colorado Coll; Gxv
Nocco, Mallika, manocco@ucdavis.edu, Univ of California, Davis; Sp
Noe, Garry, (757) 455-3284 gnoe@vwc.edu, Virginia Wesleyan Coll; HsZin
Noffke, Nora K., (757) 683-3313 nnoffke@odu.edu, Old Dominion Univ; GsPoGu
Nogueira, Ricardo, 404-413-5791 rnogueira@gsu.edu, Georgia State Univ; Asm
Noh, Myoung-Jong, (614) 292-5445 noh.56@osu.edu, Ohio State Univ; Zr
Nolan, Robert P., (718) 951-4242 rnolan@gc.cuny.edu, Graduate Sch of the City Univ of New York; Co
Nolin, Anne , (775) 682-8148 anolin@unr.edu, Univ of Nevada, Reno; Hg
Noll, Mark R., (585) 395-5717 mnoll@esc.brockport.edu, SUNY, The Coll at Brockport; Cl
Noll, Michael G., (229) 333-7143 mgnoll@valdosta.edu, Valdosta State Univ; Zn
Noltimier, Hallan C., (614) 292-9796 noltimier.2@osu.edu, Ohio State Univ; YmgGt
Nondorf, Lea, (501) 683-0110 lea.nondorf@arkansas.gov, Arkansas Geological Survey; Cg
Noonan, Mathew T., 605-677-6152 matthew.noonan@usd.edu, South Dakota Dept of Environment and Natural Resources; Hw
Noone, David, (541) 737-3629 dcn@coas.oregonstate.edu, Oregon State Univ; AmZg
Nootz, Gero, 228.688.3091 gero.nootz@usm.edu, Univ of Southern Mississippi; No
Nord, Julia, (703) 993-3395 jnord@gmu.edu, George Mason Univ; Gzg
Nordeng, Stephan, (701) 777-3455 stephan.nordeng@engr.und.edu, Univ of North Dakota; Go
Nordstrom, Greg, 662-268-1032 Ext 248 gjn2@msstate.edu, Mississippi State Univ; Am
Nordt, Lee C., (254) 710-4288 lee_nordt@baylor.edu, Baylor Univ; SdGa
Nordwald, Dan, 573-368-2451 dan.nordwald@dnr.mo.gov, Missouri Dept of Natural Resources; Zn
Norell, Mark A., (212) 769-5804 American Mus of Natural History; Pv
Noren, Anders, 612-626-3298 noren021@umn.edu, Univ of Minnesota, Twin Cities; Gn
Norman, David, +44 (0) 1223 333426 dn102@esc.cam.ac.uk, Univ of Cambridge; Pg

Norman, John M., (608) 262-2633 jmnorman@wisc.edu, Univ of Wisconsin, Madison; Spo
Norouzi, Hamidreza, 718-260-5410 hnorouzi@city.tech.cuny.edu, Graduate Sch of the City Univ of New York; Gg
Norris, Geoffrey, (416) 978-4851 norris@quartz.geology.utoronto.ca, Univ of Toronto; Pl
Norris, Joel R., (858) 822-4420 jnorris@ucsd.edu, Univ of California, San Diego; As
Norris, Richard D., (858) 822-1868 rnorris@ucsd.edu, Univ of California, San Diego; Gu
Norrish, Winston, 509.963.2192 norrishw@geology.cwu.edu, Central Washington Univ; GgeGo
North, Gerald, g-north@tamu.edu, Texas A&M Univ; As
North, Leslie, leslie.north@wku.edu, Western Kentucky Univ; Zg
Northrup, Clyde J., (208) 426-1581 cjnorth@boisestate.edu, Boise State Univ; Gc
Norton, Stephen A., (207) 581-2156 norton@maine.edu, Univ of Maine; Cl
Norton-Krane, Abby N., (216) 987-5227 abby.norton-krane@tri-c.edu, Cuyahoga Comm Coll - Western Campus; Zg
Nosal, Andrew, 6192604600 x2438 anosal@sandiego.edu, Univ of San Diego; Ob
Nosal, Thomas E., 86004243590 thomas.nosal@ct.gov, Dept of Energy and Environmental Protection; Zn
Nothdurft, Luke, +61 7 3138 1531 l.nothdurft@qut.edu.au, Queensland Univ of Tech; GdCmGg
Nourse, Jonathan A., 909-869-3460 janourse@cpp.edu, California State Polytechnic Univ, Pomona; GctEm
Novacek, Michael J., (212) 769-5805 American Mus of Natural History; Pv
Novak, Milan , +420 549 49 6188 mnovak@sci.muni.cz, Masaryk Univ; GzpGi
Novak, Thomas, 859-257-3818 thomas.novak@uky.edu, Univ of Kentucky; Nm
Nowack, Robert L., (765) 494-5978 nowack@purdue.edu, Purdue Univ; Ys
Nowell, Arthur R. M., (206) 543-6605 nowell@cofs.washington.edu, Univ of Washington; Ou
Nowicki, Sophie, (716) 645-3489 sophien@buffalo.edu, SUNY, Buffalo; Gl
Nowlin, Jr., Worth D., (979) 846-6747 wnowlin@tamu.edu, Texas A&M Univ; OpZn
Nowotarski, Christopher J., (979) 845-3305 cjnowotarski@tamu.edu, Texas A&M Univ; Ams
Noyes, Jim, (310) 660-3593 tnoyes@elcamino.edu, El Camino Coll; Og
Noyes, Joanne M., (605) 394-6972 joanne.noyes@state.sd.us, South Dakota Dept of Environment and Natural Resources; HyGg
Ntarlagiannis, Dimitrios, 973-353-5189 dimntar@newark.rutgers.edu, Rutgers, The State Univ of New Jersey, Newark; Yu
Nton, M. E., aa.elueze@mail.ui.edu.ng, Univ of Ibadan; Go
Ntsaluba, Bantubonke I., +27 (0)46-603-8309 b.ntsaluba@ru.ac.za, Rhodes Univ; Gi
Nudds, John, +44 0161 275-7861 john.nudds@manchester.ac.uk, Univ of Manchester; Pg
NUDE, Prosper M., +233-244-116879 pmnude@ug.edu.gh, Univ of Ghana; GipGx
Nuester, Jochen, jnuester@csuchico.edu, California State Univ, Chico; Cm
Nugent, Alison D., 808-956-2878 anugent@hawaii.edu, Univ of Hawai'i, Manoa; AsZnn
Nugent, Barnes, barnes@geosrv.wvnet.edu, Fairmont State Univ; Gg
Null, E. Jan, (415) 338-2061 San Francisco State Univ; Ge
Nunn, Jeffrey A., (225) 388-6657 jeff@geol.lsu.edu, Louisiana State Univ; Yg
Nur, Amos M., (650) 723-9526 Stanford Univ; Yg
Nusbaum, Robert L., (843) 953-5596 nusbaumr@cofc.edu, Coll of Charleston; Gz
Nuss, Wendell A., 831-656-2308 nuss@nps.edu, Naval Postgraduate Sch; Am
Nussear, Kenneth , (775) 784-6612 knussear@unr.edu, Univ of Nevada, Reno; Zn
Nuwategeka, Expedito, +256 782 889 985 nuwategeka@gmail.com, Gulu Univ; ZyyGv
Nwachukwu, J. I., 234-803-725-8122 jnwachuk@oauife.edu.ng, Obafemi Awolowo Univ; GoCg
Nyantakyi-Frimpong, Hanson, 303-871-4175 hnyanta2@du.edu, Univ of Denver; Zc
Nyblade, Andrew A., (814) 863-8341 andy@geosc.psu.edu, Pennsylvania State Univ, Univ Park; Yg
Nye, Janet, (631) 632-3187 janet.nye@stonybrook.edu, SUNY, Stony Brook; Ob
Nyhan, John W., (505) 667-3163 Los Alamos; So
Nyland, Edo, (780) 492-5502 edo@phys.ualberta.ca, Univ of Alberta; Ys
Nyquist, Jonathan, (215) 204-7484 nyq@temple.edu, Temple Univ; Ygu
Nystuen, Jeffrey A., (206) 543-1343 nystuen@apl.washington.edu, Univ of Washington; Op
Nzengung, Valentine A., (706) 202-4296 vnzengun@uga.edu, Univ of Georgia; ClGeCq

O

O'Banion, Matthew S., 845-938-2326 matthew.obanion@westpoint.edu, United States Military Academy; ZrGg
O'Brien, Arnold L., (978) 934-3902 arnold_obrien@uml.edu, Univ of Massachusetts, Lowell; Hw
O'Brien, John M., (201) 200-3161 jobrien@njcu.edu, New Jersey City Univ; Gs
O'Brien, Lawrence E., (914) 341-4570 lobrien@sunyorange.edu, Orange County Comm Coll; Gg
O'Brien, Philip, (281) 756-5670 pobrien@alvincollege.edu, Alvin Comm Coll; Gg
O'Brien, Rachel, (814) 332-2875 robrien@allegheny.edu, Allegheny Coll; HwGe
O'Brien, Suzanne R., (508) 531-1390 s6obrien@bridgew.edu, Bridgewater State Univ; Zg
O'Brien, Travis, (812) 269-2051 obrienta@iu.edu, Indiana Univ, Bloomington; As
O'Callaghan, Mick, +353 21 4902662 mick.ocallaghan@ucc.ie, Univ Coll Cork; Zn
O'Connor, George A., (352) 392-1803 (Ext. 329) gao@ufl.edu, Univ of Florida; Sc
O'Connor, Yuet-Ling, yloconnor@pasadena.edu, Pasadena City Coll; Ge
O'Dean, Emily, 775-682-9780 eodean@unr.edu, Univ of Nevada, Reno; Zf
O'Donnell, James, 860-405-9171 james.odonnell@uconn.edu, Univ of Connecticut; Op
O'Driscoll, Nelson, 902-585-1679 nelson.odriscoll@acadiau.ca, Acadia Univ; CgGgZn
O'Farrell, Keely A., 859-323-4876 k.ofarrell@uky.edu, Univ of Kentucky; Ygd
O'Geen, Toby, 530-752-2155 atogeen@ucdavis.edu, Univ of California, Davis; So
O'Gorman, Paul, (617) 452-3382 pog@mit.edu, Massachusetts Inst of Tech; As
O'Halloran, Ivan, (519) 674-1635 iohallo@ridgetownc.uoguelph.ca, Univ of Guelph; So
O'Hara, Kieran D., (859) 269-5161 geokoh@uky.edu, Univ of Kentucky; GcCg
O'Hara, Matthew J., (509) 373-1671 matt.ohara@pnl.gov, Pacific Northwest; Cg
O'Keefe, Jennifer, (606) 783-2349 j.okeefe@moreheadstate.edu, Morehead State Univ; PlEcZe
O'Keeffe, Mike, 303-384-2637 okeeffe@mines.edu, Colorado Geological Survey; GgeEg
O'Leary, Maureen, 631-444-3730 maureen.oleary@sunysb.edu, Stony Brook Univ; Pv
O'Meara, Stephanie A., (970) 491-6655 stephanie_o'meara@partner.nps.gov, Colorado State Univ; Gc
O'Melia, Charles R., (410) 516-7102 omelia@jhu.edu, Johns Hopkins Univ; Zn
O'Mullan, Gregory, 718-997-3452 gomullan@qc.cuny.edu, Queens Coll (CUNY); PgOb
O'Neal, Claire J., 302-831-8909 cjoneal@udel.edu, Univ of Delaware; Ze
O'Neil, James, (734) 764-1435 jro@umich.edu, Univ of Michigan; Cs
O'Neil, Jennifer, 775-682-8747 joneil@unr.edu, Univ of Nevada, Reno; Zn
O'Neil, Jonathan, jonathan.oneil@uottawa.ca, Univ of Ottawa; Cgc
O'Neill, Larry, (541) 737-2064 loneill@coas.oregonstate.edu, Oregon State Univ; AmOg
O'Neill, Patrick M., (504) 388-2681 pat@lgs.bri.lsu.edu, Louisiana State Univ; Sf
O'Reilly, Andrew M., 662-915-2483 aoreilly@olemiss.edu, Univ of Mississippi; Hwq
O'Reilly, Catherine M., 309-438-3493 cmoreil@ilstu.edu, Illinois State Univ; HgCgGg
O'Rourke, Joseph, jgorourk@asu.edu, Arizona State Univ; Xy
O'Rourke, Thomas D., (607) 255-6470 tdo1@cornell.edu, Cornell Univ; Nge
O'Shea, Bethany, (619) 260-4243 bethoshea@sandiego.edu, Univ of San Diego; CqGeCt
O'Sullivan, Katie, (661) 654-3991 kosullivan@csub.edu, California State Univ, Bakersfield; GviXg
Oakes-Miller, Hollie, hollie.oakesmiller@pcc.edu, Portland Comm Coll - Sylvania Campus; Gg
Oakley, Adrienne, 484-646-4334 oakley@kutztown.edu, Kutztown Univ of Pennsylvania; YrOun
Oakley, Bryan, (860) 465-0418 oakleyb@easternct.edu, Eastern Connecticut

State Univ; OnGml
Oaks, Jr., Robert Q., (435) 752-0867 boboaks@comcast.net, Utah State Univ; GsHwYv
Oberdorfer, June A., (408) 924-5026 june.oberdorfer@sjsu.edu, San Jose State Univ; HwGeHy
Obermeyer, Nancy J., 812-237-4351 njobie28@kiva.net, Indiana State Univ; Zi
Oboh-Ikuneobe, Francisca, 573-341-6946 ikuenobe@mst.edu, Missouri Univ of Sci and Tech; Pg
Obour, Augustine, (785) 625-3425 aobour@ksu.edu, Kansas State Univ; So
Obrad, Jennifer M., 217-333-8741 jobrad@illinois.edu, Illinois State Geological Survey; EcGo
Obreza, Thomas A., 352-392-1951 ext 243 obreza@ufl.edu, Univ of Florida; So
Obrist, Daniel, (978) 934-3900 daniel_obrist@uml.edu, Univ of Massachusetts, Lowell; As
Obrist Farner, Jonathan, 573-341-7879 obristj@mst.edu, Missouri Univ of Sci and Tech; Gr
Ocan, O. O., 234-803-705-8796 Obafemi Awolowo Univ; GtzGp
Occhiuzzi, Tony, 4807528888 x 81369 tocchiuzzi.cds@tuhsd.k12.az.us, Mesa Comm Coll; Zn
Oches, Rick, (781) 891-2937 roches@bentley.edu, Bentley Univ; ZcePe
OConnell, Suzanne B., (860) 685-2262 soconnell@wesleyan.edu, Wesleyan Univ; GsuGe
Odendaal, Adriaan, +27 (0)51 401 9928 odendaalai@ufs.ac.za, Univ of the Free State; GgsGr
Odera, Patroba A., podera@jkuat.ac.ke, Jomo Kenyatta Univ of Agriculture & Tech; YdZge
Odeyemi, Idowu B., +2348033436110 ibodeyemi@futa.edu.ng, Federal Univ of Tech, Akure; GgxZr
Odland, Sarah K., 845-365-8633 odland@ldeo.columbia.edu, Columbia Univ; Zn
Odling, Noelle, +44(0) 113 34 32806 n.e.odling@leeds.ac.uk, Univ of Leeds; Hg
Odogba, Ismaila, 715-346-4451 iodogba@uwsp.edu, Univ of Wisconsin, Stevens Point; Zui
Odokuma-Alonge, Ovie, ovie.odokuma-alonge@uniben.edu, Univ of Benin; CgGip
Odom, LeRoy A., (850) 644-6706 odom@magnet.fsu.edu, Florida State Univ; Cg
Odom, Robert I., 206-685-3788 odom@apl.washington.edu, Univ of Washington; YrGu
Oduor, Peter, (701) 231-7145 peter.oduor@ndsu.edu, North Dakota State Univ; ZiRwZr
Oechel, Walter, walter.oechel@open.ac.uk, Open Univ; As
Oehlert, Amanda M., 305-421-4405 aoehlert@rsmas.miami.edu, Univ of Miami; Gu
Oelkers, Eric, +44 020 7679 37870 e.oelkers@ucl.ac.uk, Univ Coll London; ClGze
Oeser, Jens, 089/21804208 jens.oeser@lmu.de, Ludwig-Maximilians-Univ Muenchen; Yg
Ogard, Allen E., (505) 667-6344 Los Alamos; Hw
Ogbahon, Osazuwa A., 08064253825 oaogbahon@futa.edu.ng, Federal Univ of Tech, Akure; PlGsPm
Ogbamikhumi, Alexander, alexander.ogbamikhumi@uniben.edu, Univ of Benin; YsgGg
Ogbuchiekwe, Edmund Jekwu, ogbuchiekwe@charter.net, San Bernardino Valley Coll; Zy
Ogg, James G., (765) 494-8681 jogg@purdue.edu, Purdue Univ; PsGsYm
Oglesby, David D., (951) 827-2036 david.oglesby@ucr.edu, Univ of California, Riverside; Ys
Oglesby, Elizabeth, eoglesby@email.arizona.edu, Univ of Arizona; Zn
Ogram, Andrew V., 3523921951 (Ext 211) aogram@ufl.edu, Univ of Florida; Sb
Ogston, Andrea, ogston@uw.edu, Univ of Washington; Og
Ogunsanwo, O., femiogunsanwo2003@yahoo.com, Univ of Ilorin; Ng
Ohman, Mark D., (858) 534-2754 mohman@ucsd.edu, Univ of California, San Diego; Ob
Ohmoto, Hiroshi, (814) 865-4074 ohmoto@geosc.psu.edu, Pennsylvania State Univ, Univ Park; Cs
Oikawa, Patricia, patty.oikawa@csueastbay.edu, California State Univ, East Bay; SbCoSf
Ojala, Carl F., (313) 487-0218 Eastern Michigan Univ; As
Ojo, S. B., 234-803-703-7226 sbojo@oauife.edu.ng, Obafemi Awolowo Univ; Yg
Okafor, Florence A., (256) 372-4926 florence.okafor@aamu.edu, Alabama A&M Univ; ZnEn
Okal, Emile A., (847) 491-3194 emile@earth.northwestern.edu, Northwestern Univ; YsgYr
Okaya, David A., (213) 740-7452 okaya@earth.usc.edu, Univ of Southern California; Ys
Okie, Jordan, jordan.okie@asu.edu, Arizona State Univ; Cb
Okonkwo, Chukwuemeka T., +2348035778090 ctokonkwo@futa.edu.ng, Federal Univ of Tech, Akure; GcxGg
Okulewicz, Steven C., (516) 463-6545 geosco@hofstra.edu, Hofstra Univ; CgGue
Okumura, Yuko, 512-471-0383 yukoo@ig.utexas.edu, Univ of Texas, Austin; AsZoOp
Okunade, Samuel, (937) 376-6455 Central State Univ; Gm
Okunlola, Ougbenga. A., +2348033814070 o.okunlola@mail.ui.edu.ng, Univ of Ibadan; EgCgGe
Okunuwadje, Sunday E., sunday.okunuwadje@uniben.edu, Univ of Benin; GsoGd
Ola, Peter S., +2348035927594 psola@futa.edu.ng, Federal Univ of Tech, Akure; GosGg
Olabode, Franklin O., +2348063139107 ofolabode@futa.edu.ng, Federal Univ of Tech, Akure; HwNgGg
Oladunjoye, M. A., ma.oladunjoye@mail.ui.edu.ng, Univ of Ibadan; Yg
Olafsen-Lackey, Susan, (402) 371-6512 slackey@unl.edu, University of Nebraska, Lincoln; Hw
Olanrewaju, Johnson, 814-871-7453 olanrewa001@gannon.edu, Gannon Univ; Cg
Olarewaju, V. O., 234-803-403-2030 volarewa@oauife.edu.ng, Obafemi Awolowo Univ; GozCg
Olariu, Cornel, 512-471-1519 cornelo@jsg.utexas.edu, Univ of Texas, Austin; Gr
Olariu, Mariana, iulialet@yahoo.com, Univ of Texas, Austin; GruGs
Olatunji, A. S., +2348055475865 as.olatunji@mail.ui.edu.ng, Univ of Ibadan; CgGeCt
Olawuyi, Kehinde A., +2348107331222 gideonola2001@yahoo.com, Univ of Ilorin; YeGge
Olayinka, A. I., aa.elueze@mail.ui.edu.ng, Univ of Ibadan; Yg
Olayiwola, M. A., 234-806-448-7416 mayiwola@oauife.edu.ng, Obafemi Awolowo Univ; GugPi
Olcott Marshall, Alison, (785) 864-1917 olcott@ku.edu, Univ of Kansas; PgCoPo
Oldenburg, Douglas W., (604) 822-5406 doldenburg@eos.ubc.ca, Univ of British Columbia; Yg
Oldfield, Jonathan, +44 (0)121 414 2943 j.d.oldfield@bham.ac.uk, Univ of Birmingham; Zy
Oldham, Richard L., 568-3100 (12147) oldhamr@arc.losrios.edu, American River Coll; Gg
Oleinik, Anton, (561) 297-3297 aoleinik@fau.edu, Florida Atlantic Univ; Pi
Olesik, John W., (614) 292-6954 olesik.2@osu.edu, Ohio State Univ; Ca
Oleynik, Sergey, 609-258-2390 soleynik@princeton.edu, Princeton Univ; Cs
Olivares, Jose A., (505) 665-2643 Los Alamos; Cs
Oliveira, Alcino S., soliveir@utad.pt, Unive de Trás-os-Montes e Alto Douro; Hww
Oliveira, Anabela R., anarreis@utad.pt, Unive de Trás-os-Montes e Alto Douro; Gss
Oliver, Adolph A., (415) 786-6865 Chabot Coll; Ys
Oliver, Kevin, +44 (0)23 80596490 k.oliver@noc.soton.ac.uk, Univ of Southampton; Op
Oliver, Matthew J., 302-645-4079 moliver@udel.edu, Univ of Delaware; ObZrOg
Oliver, Ronald D., (702) 794-7095 ron_oliver@lanl.gov, Los Alamos; Yg
Olivo, Gema, 613 533-6998 olivo@queensu.ca, Queen's Univ; Eg
Ollerhead, Jeffery W., (506) 364-2428 jollerhead@mta.ca, Mount Allison Univ; Yr
Ollinger, Scott, scott.ollinger@unh.edu, Univ of New Hampshire; Zc
Olmsted, Wayne, (406) 496-4151 Montana Tech of the Univ of Montana; Ca
Olney, Jessica L., 813-253-7647 jolney2@hccfl.edu, Hillsborough Comm Coll; ZgGg
Olney, Matthew P., molney@hccfl.edu, Hillsborough Comm Coll; ZgGg
Olorunfemi, A. O., 234-803-392-1712 akinrewa@oauife.edu.ng, Obafemi Awolowo Univ; Go
Olorunfemi, M. O., 234-903-719-2169 mlorunfe@oauife.edu.ng, Obafemi Awolowo Univ; Yg
Olsen, Amanda A., 207 581-2194 amanda.olsen@umit.maine.edu, Univ of Maine; Cl
Olsen, Khris B., (509) 376-4114 kb.olsen@pnl.gov, Pacific Northwest; Cg
Olsen, Kim B., 619-594-2649 kbolsen@mail.sdsu.edu, San Diego State Univ; Ye
Olsen, Paul E., kolsen@ldeo.columbia.edu, Columbia Univ; Gm
Olson, Derek, dolson@nps.edu, Naval Postgraduate Sch; Zn
Olson, Hillary C., (512) 653-8356 holson@austin.utexas.edu, Univ of Texas, Austin; Ps
Olson, James R., 605-677-6866 jim.olson@usd.edu, South Dakota Dept of

YgHq
Owen, Alan W., +4401413305461 alan.owen@glasgow.ac.uk, Univ of Glasgow; PgsPg
Owen, Donald E., (409) 880-8234 donald.owen@lamar.edu, Lamar Univ; Gr
Owen, Lewis, (513) 556-4203 lewis.owen@uc.edu, Univ of Cincinnati; GmlGt
Owen, Robert M., (734) 763-4593 rowen@umich.edu, Univ of Michigan; CmGu
Owens, Brent E., (757) 221-1813 beowen@wm.edu, William & Mary; Gx
Owens, Tamera, (231) 777-0289 tamera.owens@muskegoncc.edu, Muskegon Comm Coll; Zn
Owens, Thomas J., 803-777-4530 owens@seis.sc.edu, Univ of South Carolina; Ys
Owensby, Clenton E., (785) 532-7232 owensby@ksu.edu, Kansas State Univ; Sf
Owoseni, Joshua O., +2348060719411 joowoseni@futa.edu.ng, Federal Univ of Tech, Akure; HwNgRn
Oxendine, Christopher E., 845-938-4354 christopher.oxendine@westpoint.edu, United States Military Academy; ZirZf
Oxford, Jeremiah, 503-838-8680 oxfordj@wou.edu, Western Oregon Univ; Zg
Oxley, Meghan, 206-543-8904 what@uw.edu, Univ of Washington; Ze
Oxner-Jones, D. M., 740 201 2761 dalton.jones@dnr.state.oh.us, Ohio Dept of Natural Resources; OnGgZg
Oyawale, A. A., 234-803-331-2150 aoyawale@oauife.edu.ng, Obafemi Awolowo Univ; GeoCg
Oyediran, I. A., ia.oyediran@mail.ui.edu.ng, Univ of Ibadan; Ng
Oymayan, Avo, avo.oymayan@fgc.edu, Florida Gateway Coll; Zg
Oza, Rupal, 212-650-3035 rupal.oza@hunter.cuny.edu, Hunter Coll (CUNY); Zn
Ozbay, M. Ugur, (303) 273-3710 mozbay@mines.edu, Colorado Sch of Mines; Nr
Ozdenerol, Esra, 901-678-2787 eozdenrl@memphis.edu, Univ of Memphis; Zi
Ozel Yildirim, Esra , 00904242370000-5953 eozel@firat.edu.tr, Firat Univ; Gxi
Ozkan-Haller, Tuba, 541-737-9170 ozkan@coas.oregonstate.edu, Oregon State Univ; On
Ozsvath, David L., (715) 346-2287 dozsvath@uwsp.edu, Univ of Wisconsin, Stevens Point; Hw
Oztekin Okan, Ozlem, 00904242370000-5983 ooztekin@firat.edu.tr, Firat Univ; HgwHs
Ozturk, Nevin, 00904242370000-5956 nevinozturk@firat.edu.tr, Firat Univ; Cg

P

Paavola, Jouni, +44(0) 113 34 36787 j.paavola@leeds.ac.uk, Univ of Leeds; Ge
Pace, Michael L., (434) 924-6541 mlp5fy@virginia.edu, Univ of Virginia; Zn
Pacheco, Fernando A., fpacheco@utad.pt, Unive de Trás-os-Montes e Alto Douro; Hq
Pacia, Christina, (908) 737-3738 cpacia@kean.edu, Kean Univ; Zn
Padden, Maureen, (905) 525-9140 (Ext. 20118) paddenm@mcmaster.ca, McMaster Univ; CsPc
Padian, Kevin, (510) 642-7434 kpadian@berkeley.edu, Univ of California, Berkeley; Pv
Padilla, Dianna K., (631) 632-7434 dianna.padilla@stonybrook.edu, SUNY, Stony Brook; ObnZn
Paduan, Jeffrey D., (831) 656-3350 paduan@nps.edu, Naval Postgraduate Sch; Op
Paez, H. A., 905-525-9140 (Ext. 26099) paezha@mcmaster.ca, McMaster Univ; Eg
Page, David, 775-673-7110 dave.page@dri.edu, Desert Research Inst; Ga
Page, F Zeb, (440) 775-6701 zeb.page@oberlin.edu, Oberlin Coll; GpCsg
Page, Kevin, +44 1752 584750 kevin.page@plymouth.ac.uk, Univ of Plymouth; Gr
Page, Philippe, philippe_page@uqac.ca, Universite du Quebec a Chicoutimi; GiCgEm
Paget, Aaron C., 304-384-6006 apaget@concord.edu, Concord Univ; ApOpZr
Pagiatakis, Spiros, (416)736-2100 #77757 spiros@yorku.ca, York Univ; Yd
Pagliari, Paulo H., 507-752-5065 pagli005@umn.edu, Univ of Minnesota, Twin Cities; Sc
Paglione, Timothy, 718-262-2654 tpaglione@york.cuny.edu, York Coll (CUNY); Xa
Pagnac, Darrin C., 605-394-2469 darrin.pagnac@sdsmt.edu, South Dakota Sch of Mines & Tech; PvGrZe
Paige, David A., (310) 825-4268 dap@epss.ucla.edu, Univ of California, Los Angeles; Xy
Paillet, Fred, 479-575-3355 fredp@cox.net, Univ of Arkansas, Fayetteville; YgHw
Pain, Christopher, +44 20 759 49322 c.pain@imperial.ac.uk, Imperial Coll; Yg
Paine, Jeffrey G., 512-471-1260 jeff.paine@beg.utexas.edu, Univ of Texas, Austin; On
Pair, Donald, (937) 229-2936 don.pair@notes.udayton.edu, Univ of Dayton; Gl
Pakhomov, Evgeny, (604) 827-5564 epakhomov@eos.ubc.ca, Univ of British Columbia; Ob
Paktunc, Dogan, 613-947-7061 dogan.packtunc@nrcan-rncan.gc.ca, Univ of Ottawa; Gz
Palace, Michael W., 603-862-4193 mike.palace@unh.edu, Univ of New Hampshire; Zn
Palamartchouk, Kirill, +44 191 208 6421 kirill.palamartckirill.palamartchouk@ncl.ac.uk, Univ of Newcastle Upon Tyne; Yd
Palenik, Brian, (858) 534-7505 bpalenik@ucsd.edu, Univ of California, San Diego; Ob
Palevsky, Hilary I., (617) 552-4936 hilary.palevsky@bc.edu, Boston Coll; Oc
Palin, J. Michael, +64 3 479-9083 michael.palin@otago.ac.nz, Univ of Otago; CcGip
Palinkaš, Ladislav, +38514605971 lpalinka@geol.pmf.hr, Univ of Zagreb; CgeCp
Palladino, Steve D., (805) 654-6400 (Ext. 1365) Ventura Coll; Zi
Pallis, Ted J., (609) 984-6587 ted.pallis@dep.nj.gov, New Jersey Geological and Water Survey; Zi
Pallister, John S., (360) 993-8964 jpallist@usgs.gov, Univ of Pittsburgh; GviGg
Palluconi, Frank D., (818) 354-8362 frank.d.palluconi@jpl.nasa.gov, Jet Propulsion Lab; Zr
Palma, Miclelle, (262) 521-5542 michelle.palma@uwc.edu, Univ of Wisconsin Colls; ZnnZn
Palmer, Arthur N., (607) 436-3064 arthur.palmer@oneonta.edu, SUNY, Oneonta; HgqGm
Palmer, Christina, (909) 537-5336 cpalmer@csusb.edu, California State Univ, San Bernardino; Zn
Palmer, Clare, cpalmer@wustl.edu, Washington Univ in St. Louis; Zn
Palmer, Derecke, 612 9385 8719 d.palmer@unsw.edu.au, Univ of New South Wales; Ye
Palmer, Donald F., (330) 672-2680 dpalmer@kent.edu, Kent State Univ; Yg
Palmer, Evan, 719-333-3080 ronald.palmer@usafa.edu, United States Air Force Academy; Zig
Palmer, H. C., (519) 661-2111 x86749 cpalmer@uwo.ca, Western Univ; YmGv
Palmer, Martin R., +44 (0)23 80596607 pmrp@noc.soton.ac.uk, Univ of Southampton; Cg
Palmer, Paul, +44 (0) 131 650 7724 paul.palmer@ed.ac.uk, Edinburgh Univ; As
Palmquist, John C., (414) 832-6732 palmquij@lawrence.edu, Lawrence Univ; GcpGg
Paltseva, Anna, anna.paltseva@louisiana.edu, Univ of Louisiana at Lafayette; Ge
Palumbo, Tony V., (423) 576-8002 avp@ornl.gov, Oak Ridge; Sb
Palutoglu, Mahmut, 00904242370000-5954 mpalutoglu@firat.edu.tr, Firat Univ; YgsGc
Pan, Feifei, 940-369-5109 feifei/pan@unt.edu, Univ of North Texas; Hw
Pan, William L., (509) 335-3611 wlpan@wsu.edu, Washington State Univ; Sb
Pan, Ying, yyp5053@psu.edu, Pennsylvania State Univ, Univ Park; As
Pan, Yuanming, (706) 966-5699 yuanming.pan@usask.ca, Univ of Saskatchewan; Gx
Pan, Zaitao, (314) 977-3114 panz@eas.slu.edu, Saint Louis Univ; As
Panagiotakopulu, Eva, +44 (0) 131 650 2531 eva.p@ed.ac.uk, Edinburgh Univ; Pe
Panah, Assad I., (814) 362-7569 aap@pitt.edu, Univ of Pittsburgh, Bradford; GorGc
Pancha, Aasha, (775) 784-4254 pancha@seismo.unr.edu, Univ of Nevada, Reno; Ys
Panero, Wendy R., 614 292 6290 panero.1@osu.edu, Ohio State Univ; Yg
Panetta, Richard L., (979) 845-1386 r-panetta@tamu.edu, Texas A&M Univ; Am
Pangle, Luke, lpangle@gsu.edu, Georgia State Univ; HqCs
Pani, Eric A., (318) 342-1878 Univ of Louisiana, Monroe; As
Paniconi, Claudio, claudio.paniconi@ete.inrs.ca, Universite du Quebec; Hw
Panish, Peter T., (413) 545-2593 panish@geo.umass.edu, Univ of Massachusetts, Amherst; Gp
Pankow, Kristine L., 801-585-6484 pankow@seis.utah.edu, Univ of Utah; Ys
Panno, Samuel V., (217) 244-2456 s-panno@illinois.edu, Illinois State Geological Survey; ClGgHw
Pant, Hari, 718-960-5859 hari.pant@hunter.cuny.edu, Graduate Sch of the City Univ of New York; Zg
Panter, Kurt S., (419) 372-7337 kpanter@bgnet.bgsu.edu, Bowling Green State Univ; Giv
Panzik, Joeseph, jepanzik@usf.edu, Univ of South Florida; Ym

Paola, Christopher, 612-624-8025 cpaola@umn.edu, Univ of Minnesota, Twin Cities; Gs
Papaleo, Silvanna, spapaleo@zircon.geology.utoronto.ca, Univ of Toronto; Zn
Papcun, George, 12012993161 gpapcun@njcu.edu, New Jersey City Univ; Ze
Papendick, Robert I., (509) 335-1552 papendick@wsu.edu, Washington State Univ; Sp
Papike, James J., (505) 277-1633 jpapike@unm.edu, Univ of New Mexico; Ca
Papineau, Dominic, d.papineau@ucl.ac.uk, Univ Coll London; Cg
Papitashvili, Vladimir O., 703-292-8033 vpapita@nsf.gov, Nat Sci Foundation; YmXpa
Papp, Kenneth R., (907) 696-0079 kenneth.papp@alaska.gov, Alaska Division of Geological & Geophysical Surveys; Gg
Pappas, Matthew, 631-451-4301 pappasm@sunysuffolk.edu, Suffolk County Comm Coll, Ammerman Campus; Zg
Papuga, Shirley, (313) 577-9436 shirley.papuga@wayne.edu, Wayne State Univ; Hgs
Paquette, Jeanne, 514-398-4402 jeanne.paquette@mcgill.ca, McGill Univ; Gz
Paradis, Charles, paradisc@uwm.edu, Univ of Wisconsin, Milwaukee; Hw
Paradise, Thomas R., (479) 575-3159 paradise@uark.edu, Univ of Arkansas, Fayetteville; GmZyRn
Parai, Rita, 314-935-3974 rparai@levee.wustl.edu, Washington Univ in St. Louis; Cs
Parashar, Rishi, 775.673-7496 rishi.parashar@dri.edu, Univ of Nevada, Reno; Hq
Parcell, William C., (316)978- 3140 Wichita State Univ; Gr
Pardi, Richard R., (201) 595-2695 William Paterson Univ; Cc
Parendes, Laurie A., (814) 732-2840 lparendes@edinboro.edu, Edinboro Univ of Pennsylvania; Zn
Parent, Michel, (418) 654-2657 Universite du Quebec; Gl
Pares, Josep M., (734) 615-0472 jmpares@umich.edu, Univ of Michigan; Ym
Parham, James, (657) 278-2043 jparham@fullerton.edu, California State Univ, Fullerton; PvgGg
Parikh, Sanjai, 530-752-1265 sjparikh@ucdavis.edu, Univ of California, Davis; ScbCb
Parise, John B., (631) 632-8196 john.parise@sunysb.edu, Stony Brook Univ; Gz
Pariseau, William G., (801) 581-5164 w.pariseau@utah.edu, Univ of Utah; Nr
Parish, Cynthia L., cparish@gt.rr.com, Lamar Univ; Gg
Parish, Ryan M., 901-678-2606 rmparish@memphis.edu, Univ of Memphis; Ga
Parizek, Richard R., (814) 865-3012 parizek@ems.psu.edu, Pennsylvania State Univ, Univ Park; Hw
Park, Jeffrey J., (203) 432-3172 jeffrey.park@yale.edu, Yale Univ; YsZgc
Park, Jisun, 201-575-5939 jisun.park@kbcc.cuny.edu, Graduate Sch of the City Univ of New York; Xm
Park, Myung-Sook, 831-656-2858 mpark@nps.edu, Naval Postgraduate Sch; Am
Park, Sohyun, 089/2180 4333 soohyun.park@physik.uni-muenchen.de, Ludwig-Maximilians-Univ Muenchen; Gz
Park, Stephen K., (951) 827-4501 magneto@ucrmt.ucr.edu, Univ of California, Riverside; Ym
Parker, David B., 806-651-4099 dparker@wtamu.edu, West Texas A&M Univ; Sbf
Parker, Don, 806-291-1121 don.parker@wbu.edu, Wayland Baptist Univ; GivCg
Parker, Doug, +44(0) 113 34 36739 d.j.parker@leeds.ac.uk, Univ of Leeds; Am
Parker, Gary, 217-244-6161 parkerg@illinois.edu, Univ of Illinois, Urbana-Champaign; Gm
Parker, Jim, 713-743-6750 jlparker9@uh.edu, Univ of Houston; Zn
Parker, Joan, 831-771-4400 parker@mlml.calstate.edu, Moss Landing Marine Lab; Zn
Parker, Kent E., (509) 373-6337 kent.parker@pnl.gov, Pacific Northwest; Cg
Parker, Marjorie, (207) 725-3628 mparker@bowdoin.edu, Bowdoin Coll; Zn
Parker, Matthew, 919-513-4367 mdparker@ncsu.edu, North Carolina State Univ; Am
Parker, Richard M., 361-593-3590 richard.parker@tamuk.edu, Texas A&M Univ, Kingsville; GgPg
Parker, Robert L., (858) 534-2475 rlparker@ucsd.edu, Univ of California, San Diego; Ym
Parker, Stephen R., (406) 496-4185 sparker@mtech.edu, Montana Tech of the Univ of Montana; Zn
Parker, William C., (850) 644-1568 parker@gly.fsu.edu, Florida State Univ; PqeGq
Parkin, Gary, (519) 824-4120 (Ext. 52452) gparkin@uoguelph.ca, Univ of Guelph; HwSp
Parkin, Geoffrey, +44 (0) 191 208 6146 geoff.parkin@ncl.ac.uk, Univ of Newcastle Upon Tyne; Hg
Parkinson, Christopher D., 504-280-6792 cparkins@uno.edu, Univ of New Orleans; Gp
Parks, George K., (510) 643-5512 parks@ssl.berkeley.edu, Univ of Washington; YxXy
Parlak, Osman, 03223387081 parlak@cu.edu.tr, Cukurova Universitesi; GipCc
Parman, Stephen, (401) 863-3352 stephen_parman@brown.edu, Brown Univ; CpgCt
Parmentier, E. Marc, (401) 863-1700 em_parmentier@brown.edu, Brown Univ; Yg
Parnell, Roderic A., (928) 523-3329 roderic.parnell@nau.edu, Northern Arizona Univ; Cl
Parnella, Bill, 302-831-3156 parnella@udel.edu, Univ of Delaware; Gg
Parr, Kate, +44 0151 795 4640 kate.parr@liverpool.ac.uk, Univ of Liverpool; Pe
Parrick, Brittany, 614 265 6581 brittany.parrick@dnr.state.oh.us, Ohio Dept of Natural Resources; Gg
Parris, Thomas M., 859-257-1147 mparris@uky.edu, Univ of Kentucky; Cg
Parrish, Christopher E., 603-862-3438 cparrish@ccom.unh.edu, Univ of New Hampshire; Zr
Parrish, Pia, (619) 594-5587 pparrish@mail.sdsu.edu, San Diego State Univ; Zn
Parrot, Lael, 250-807-8122 lael.parrot@ubc.ca, Univ of British Columbia, Okanagan Campus; ZgiZf
Parsekian, Andrew D., (307) 766-3603 aparseki@uwyo.edu, Univ of Wyoming; Yg
Parsen, Mike J., 608629419 mike.parsen@wisc.edu, Univ of Wisconsin, Madison, Division of Extension; Hw
Parsons, Barry, +44 (1865) 272017 barry.parsons@earth.ox.ac.uk, Univ of Oxford; Yd
Parsons, Jeffrey D., (206) 221-6627 parsons@ocean.washington.edu, Univ of Washington; Ou
Parsons-Hubbard, Karla M., (440) 775-8353 karla.hubbard@oberlin.edu, Oberlin Coll; PgGu
Partin, Camille, camille.partin@usask.ca, Univ of Saskatchewan; Gtc
Pascariu, Florentina, 0040232201496 florentinavieru@yahoo.com, Alexandru Ioan Cuza; Nt
Paschert, Karin, 089/2180 6573 karin.paschert@lmu.de, Ludwig-Maximilians-Univ Muenchen; Gg
Pascoe, Richard, +4401326 371838 r.d.pascoe@exeter.ac.uk, Exeter Univ; Gz
Pascussi, Michael, (518) 486-4820 mpascucc@mail.nysed.gov, New York State Geological Survey; Eo
Pasek, Matthew, mpasek@usf.edu, Univ of South Florida; Cq
Pashin, Jack C., 405-744-6358 jack.pashin@okstate.edu, Oklahoma State Univ; GrcGo
Pasicznyk, David L., (609) 984-6587 dave.pasicznyk@dep.state.nj.us, New Jersey Geological and Water Survey; Yg
Pasken, Robert W., (314) 977-3125 paskenrw@slu.edu, Saint Louis Univ; Am
Passey, Benjamin, (410) 340-9473 passey@umich.edu, Univ of Michigan; CsaCl
Pasteris, Jill D., (314) 935-5434 pasteris@levee.wustl.edu, Washington Univ in St. Louis; GbzGe
Pasternack, Gregory B., (530) 754-9243 gpast@ucdavis.edu, Univ of California, Davis; GmHg
Patel, Vinodkumar A., 217-244-0639 patel@isgs.uiuc.edu vapatel@illinois.edu, Illinois State Geological Survey; Zn
Patenaude, Genevieve, +44 (0) 131 651 4472 genevieve.patenaude@ed.ac.uk, Edinburgh Univ; Ge
Patera, Edward S., (505) 667-4457 Los Alamos; Cg
Paterson, Colin J., (605) 394-2461 colin.paterson@sdsmt.edu, South Dakota Sch of Mines & Tech; Eg
Paterson, John R., +61-2-67732101 jpater20@une.edu.au, Univ of New England; PigPs
Paterson, Scott R., (213) 740-6103 paterson@usc.edu, Univ of Southern California; Gc
Patience, Jennifer, (480) 727-8554 jennifer.patience@asu.edu, Arizona State Univ; Xa
Patino-Douce, Alberto E., (706) 542-2394 alpatino@uga.edu, Univ of Georgia; ZnnZn
Patino-Douce, Marta, (706) 542-2399 mapatino@uga.edu, Univ of Georgia; Gi
Paton, Douglas, +44(0) 113 34 35238 d.a.paton@leeds.ac.uk, Univ of Leeds; Gc
Patrick, David M., (601) 266-4530 Univ of Southern Mississippi; Ng
Patronas, Dennis, dpatronas@disl.org, Dauphin Island Sea Lab; Zn
Patterson, Gary, (901) 678-5264 glpttrsn@memphis.edu, Univ of Memphis; Gg
Patterson, Jodi T., (801) 537-3310 jpatters@utah.gov, Utah Geological Survey; Zn
Patterson, Mark, (781) 581-7370 m.patterson@neu.edu, Northeastern Univ; Zn
Patterson, Molly , (607) 777-2831 patterso@binghamton.edu, Binghamton Univ; CmGl

FACULTY INDEX – P

Patterson, R. Timothy, tpatters@ccs.carleton.ca, Carleton Univ; Pm
Patterson, William P., (306) 966-5691 bill.patterson@usask.ca, Univ of Saskatchewan; CsPeGn
Pattison, David R., (403) 220-3263 pattison@geo.ucalgary.ca, Univ of Calgary; Gp
Pattison, Simon A., 204-727-7468 pattison@brandonu.ca, Brandon Univ; GsoGd
Patton, Howard J., (505) 667-1003 patton@lanl.gov, Los Alamos; Yg
Patton, James L., (510) 642-3059 Univ of California, Berkeley; Pv
Patton, Jason A., 479-968-0676 jpatton@atu.edu, Arkansas Tech Univ; GgeGc
Patton, Peter C., (860) 685-2268 ppatton@wesleyan.edu, Wesleyan Univ; Gm
Patton, Regan L., (509) 534-3670 rpatton@wsu.edu, Washington State Univ; Gc
Patton, Terri, 630-252-3294 tlpatton@anl.gov, Argonne; Gg
Patton, Thomas W., 406-496-4153 tpatton@mtech.edu, Montana Tech of The Univ of Montana; Hw
Patwardhan, Kaustubh, 845-257-3738 patwardk@newpaltz.edu, SUNY, New Paltz; Ggi
Paty, Carol M., (404) 894-2860 carol.paty@eas.gatech.edu, Georgia Inst of Tech; YmgZn
Patzkowsky, Mark E., (814) 863-1959 brachio@geosc.psu.edu, Pennsylvania State Univ, Univ Park; Pg
Paul, John H., (727) 553-1168 jpaul@marine.usf.edu, Univ of South Florida; Ob
Paul, Jonathan, +44 1784 44 jonathan.paul@rhul.ac.uk, Royal Holloway Univ of London; Hw
Paulsell, Robert L., (225) 578-8655 rpaulsell@lsu.edu, Louisiana State Univ; ZyGg
Paulsen, Timothy S., (920) 424-7002 paulsen@uwosh.edu, Univ of Wisconsin, Oshkosh; Gc
Paulson, Suzanne, (310) 206-4442 paulson@atmos.ucla.edu, Univ of California, Los Angeles; As
Pavelsky, Tamlin M., (919) 962-4239 pavelsky@unc.edu, Univ of North Carolina, Chapel Hill; Hg
Pavese, Alessandro, alessandro.pavese@unito.it, Univ di Torino; Gz
Pavia, Giulio, giulio.pavia@unito.it, Univ di Torino; Pg
Pavlis, Gary L., (812) 855-5141 pavlis@indiana.edu, Indiana Univ, Bloomington; YsGtYe
Pavlis, Terry L., (504) 280-6797 tpavlis@uno.edu, Univ of New Orleans; Gt
Pavlovskaya, Marianna, (212) 772-5320 mpavlov@hunter.cuny.edu, Hunter Coll (CUNY); Zi
Pavlowsky, Robert T., (417) 836-8473 robertpavlowsky@missouristate.edu, Missouri State Univ; Gm
Paw U, Kyaw Tha, 530-752-8172 ktpawu@ucdavis.edu, Univ of California, Davis; Asm
Pawley, Alison, +44 0161 275-3944 alison.pawley@manchester.ac.uk, Univ of Manchester; Gc
Pawlicki, Caron E., (717) 702-2042 coneil@pa.gov, DCNR- Pennsylvania Bureau of Geological Survey; ZiGgc
Pawloski, Gayle A., (925) 423-0437 pawloski1@llnl.gov, Lawrence Livermore; Gg
Pawlowicz, Richard A., (604) 822-1356 rpawlowicz@eos.ubc.ca, Univ of British Columbia; Op
Payn, Robert, rpayn@montana.edu, Montana State Univ; Hg
Payne, Ashley E., 734-647-1991 aepayne@umich.edu, Univ of Michigan; At
Paz Gonzalez, Antonio, 34 981167000 tucho@udc.es, Coruna Univ; Sd
Pazzaglia, Frank J., (610) 758-3667 fjp3@lehigh.edu, Lehigh Univ; Gm
Peacock, Caroline, +44(0) 113 34 37877 c.l.peacock@leeds.ac.uk, Univ of Leeds; Sb
Peacock, Simon M., simon.peacock@ubc.ca, Univ of British Columbia; GtpYs
Peacor, Donald R., (734) 764-1452 drpeacor@umich.edu, Univ of Michigan; Gz
Peakall, Jeff, +44(0) 113 34 35205 j.peakall@leeds.ac.uk, Univ of Leeds; Gs
Peake, Jeffrey S., jpeake@unomaha.edu, Univ of Nebraska, Omaha; ZyAtRm
Pearce, J A., pearceja@cf.ac.uk, Cardiff Univ; Cg
Pearce, Jamie R., +44 (0) 131 650 2294 jamie.pearce@ed.ac.uk, Edinburgh Univ; Ge
Pearson, Adam, 315 267-2951 pearsoaj@potsdam.edu, SUNY Potsdam; Gm
Pearson, Ann, (617) 384-8392 pearson@eps.harvard.edu, Harvard Univ; Cb
Pearson, David M., 208-282-3486 peardavi@isu.edu, Idaho State Univ; Gct
Pearson, Eugene F., (209) 946-2926 epearson@pacific.edu, Univ of the Pacific; GsPgZg
Pearson, Graham, (780) 492-4156 gdpearson@ualberta.ca, Univ of Alberta; Cec
Pearson, Jenna L., 609-258-4101 jennap@princeton.edu, Princeton Univ; Ogp
Pearson, P N., pearsonp@cf.ac.uk, Cardiff Univ; Pe
Pearson, Paul, +44(0)29 208 74579 pearsonp@cardiff.ac.uk, Univ of Wales; PmCg
Pearthree, Kristin, 575-835-5320 kristin.pearthree@nmt.edu, New Mexico Inst of Mining and Tech; Gge
Pearthree, Philip A., 520-621-2470 pearthre@email.arizona.edu, Univ of Arizona; Ge
Peate, David W., (319) 335-0567 david-peate@uiowa.edu, Univ of Iowa; GiCa
Peavy, Samuel T., 229-931-2330 speavy@canes.gsw.edu, Georgia Southwestern State Univ; Yg
Pec, Matej, 617-324-7279 mpec@mit.edu, Massachusetts Inst of Tech; Nr
Pechmann, James C., (801) 581-3858 pechmann@seis.utah.edu, Univ of Utah; YsGt
Peck, John A., (330) 972-7659 jpeck@uakron.edu, Univ of Akron; GseGn
Peck, Theodore R., (217) 333-9486 Univ of Illinois, Urbana-Champaign; Sc
Peck, William H., (315) 228-7698 wpeck@colgate.edu, Colgate Univ; GpiCs
Peddle, Derek R., derek.peddle@uleth.ca, Univ of Lethbridge; Zr
Pedemonte, Virginia, (598) 25251552 vpedemonte@fcien.edu.uy, Univ de la Republica Oriental del Uruguay (UDELAR); ZirZu
Pedentchouk, Nikolai, +44 (0)1603 59 3395 n.pedentchouk@uea.ac.uk, Univ of East Anglia; Cs
Pedersen, Joel A., (608) 263-4971 joelpedersen@wisc.edu, Univ of Wisconsin, Madison; So
Pedersen, Per, 403 220-8454 pkpeders@ucalgary.ca, Univ of Calgary; Go
Pedersen, Thomas F., tfp@uvic.ca, Univ of Victoria; CmOcCs
Pederson, Darryll T., (402) 472-7563 dpederson2@unl.edu, Univ of Nebraska, Lincoln; Hw
Pederson, Joel L., (435) 797-7097 joel.pederson@usu.edu, Utah State Univ; Gm
Pedley, Kate, +64 3 3667001 Ext 3892 kate.pedley@canterbury.ac.nz, Univ of Canterbury; Zg
Pedone, Vicki A., (818) 677-3541 vicki.pedone@csun.edu, California State Univ, Northridge; GdCs
Peebles, Ernst B., (727) 553-3983 epeebles@mail.usf.edu, Univ of South Florida; ObCs
Peele, R Hampton, (225) 328-6651 hampton@lsu.edu, Louisiana State Univ; ZirZg
Peeters, Frank J., +31 20 5987419 f.j.c.peeters@vu.nl, Vrije Universiteit Amsterdam; PmOg
Pegion, Kathy, 703-993-5727 kpegion@gmu.edu, George Mason Univ; AsOp
Peirce, Christine, 0191 3742515 christine.peirce@durham.ac.uk, Durham Univ; Yg
Pekar, Stephen , 718-997-3305 stephen.pekar@qc.cuny.edu, Graduate Sch of the City Univ of New York; Zg
Pekar, Stephen, (718) 997-3305 stephen.pekar@qc.cuny.edu, Queens Coll (CUNY); PeGrOu
Pellenbarg, Robert, rpellenbarg@collegeofthedesert.edu, Coll of the Desert; OcGu
Pellerin, Jocelyne, (418) 724-1704 jocelyne_pellerin@uqar.uquebec.ca, Universite du Quebec a Rimouski; Ob
Pelletier, Emilien, (418) 723-1986 (Ext. 1764) emilien_pelletier@uqar.ca, Universite du Quebec a Rimouski; Oc
Pelletier, Jon D., (520) 626-2126 jdpellet@email.arizona.edu, Univ of Arizona; Gm
Pellin, Michael J., (630) 972-3510 Argonne; Zm
Pellowski, Christopher J., (605) 394-2465 christopher.pellowski@sdsmt.edu, South Dakota Sch of Mines & Tech; Gg
Pelton, John R., (208) 426-3640 jpelton@boisestate.edu, Boise State Univ; YgeYs
Peltzer, Gilles, (310) 206-2156 peltzer@epss.ucla.edu, Univ of California, Los Angeles; ZrGt
Pena dos Reis, Rui, 965042654 penareis@dct.uc.pt, Unive de Coimbra; GorGs
Peng, Lee Chai, 03-79674233 leecp@um.edu.my, Univ of Malaya; Pg
Peng, Yongbo, 225-578-3413 ypeng@lsu.edu, Louisiana State Univ; Cg
Peng, Zhigang, 404-894-0231 zhigang.peng@eas.gatech.edu, Georgia Inst of Tech; YsgZn
Penman, Donald E., donald.penman@usu.edu, Utah State Univ; GsCbPc
Penna, Nigel, +44 (0) 191 208 8747 nigel.penna@ncl.ac.uk, Univ of Newcastle Upon Tyne; Gq
Pennacchioni, Giorgio, +390498279106 giorgio.pennacchioni@unipd.it, Univ degli Studi di Padova; Gc
Penney, Paulette, 254710-2361 paulette_penney@baylor.edu, Baylor Univ; Zn
Pennington, Deana, 915-747-5867 ddpennington@utep.edu, Univ of Texas, El Paso; ZyfZe
Pennington, Wayne D., (906) 487-2531 wayne@mtu.edu, Michigan Technological Univ; YsNe
Penniston-Dorland, Sarah, (301) 405-4087 sarahpd@geol.umd.edu, Univ of Maryland; Gp
Pennock, Jonathan R., (334) 861-7531 jonathan.pennock@unh.edu, Dauphin Island Sea Lab; Oc
Penny, Andrew, 831-656-3101 abpenny@nps.edu, Naval Postgraduate Sch; Am

Pentcheva, Rossitza, 089/2180 4352 pentcheva@lrz.uni-muenchen.de, Ludwig-Maximilians-Univ Muenchen; Gz

Penzo, Michael A., (508) 531-1390 mpenzo@bridgew.edu, Bridgewater State Univ; Ge

Peppe, Daniel J., (254) 710-2629 daniel_peppe@baylor.edu, Baylor Univ; PbcYm

Pepper, Ian L., (520) 621-7234 ipepper@ag.arizona.edu, Univ of Arizona; Zn

Peprah, Ebenezer, (310) 660-3593 epeprah@elcamino.edu, El Camino Coll; Zg

Perault, David R., (434) 544-8370 perault@lynchburg.edu, Univ of Lynchburg; Ge

Percell, Peter, 713-743-6724 ppercell@uh.edu, Univ of Houston; As

Percival, Carl, c.percival@manchester.ac.uk, Univ of Manchester; As

Percy, David, (503) 725-3373 percy@pdx.edu, Portland State Univ; Zi

Perdrial, Julia, (802) 656-0665 julia.perdrial@uvm.edu, Univ of Vermont; ClSc

Perdrial, Nicolas, nicolas.perdrial@uvm.edu, Univ of Vermont; GezCl

Perdue, Edward Michael, michael.perdue@eas.gatech.edu, Georgia Inst of Tech; Co

Pereira, Alcides C., +351-239 860 563 apereira@dct.uc.pt, Unive de Coimbra; GebZr

Pereira, Engil I., 956 665 2220 engil.pereira@utrgv.edu, Univ of Texas, Rio Grande Valley; SbZcSo

Peres, Carlos, +44 (0)1603 59 2549 c.peres@uea.ac.uk, Univ of East Anglia; Sf

Perez, Adriana, 915-747-5501 aperez13@utep.edu, Univ of Texas, El Paso; Gg

Perez, Florante, (213) 620-5026 California Geological Survey; Ng

Perez, Marco A., mperez@cicese.mx, Centro de Investigación Científica y de Educación Superior de Ensenada; Ye

Perez, Richard R., (518) 437-8751 perez@asrc.cestm.albany.edu, SUNY, Albany; As

Perez-Huerta, Alberto, (205) 348-8382 aphuerta@ua.edu, Univ of Alabama; PgClGz

Pérez-Rodríguez, Ileana, ileperez@sas.upenn.edu, Univ of Pennsylvania; Po

Pérez-Soba, Cecilia, pesoa@ucm.es, Univ Complutense de Madrid; Gi

Perfect, Edmund, (865) 974-6017 eperfect@utk.edu, Univ of Tennessee, Knoxville; SpHwGq

Perfit, Michael R., (352) 392-2128 mperfit@ufl.edu, Univ of Florida; Giu

Peri, Francesco, francesco.peri@umb.edu, Univ of Massachusetts, Boston; Zn

Perkins, R, perkinsr@cf.ac.uk, Cardiff Univ; Zn

Perkins, Robert B., rperkins@pdx.edu, Portland State Univ; Hq

Perkins, Ronald D., (919) 684-3376 rperkins@duke.edu, Duke Univ; Gdo

Perkins, III, Dexter, (701) 777-2991 dexter.perkins@engr.und.edu, Univ of North Dakota; Gp

Perkis, Bill, bill.perkis@gogebic.edu, Gogebic Comm Coll; Gg

Perkons, Eriks, (410) 704-3187 eperkons@towson.edu, Towson Univ; Ge

Perret, Didier H., (418) 654-2686 didier.perret@canada.ca, Universite du Quebec; NgeZu

Perrie, William, (902) 426-3985 william.perrie@dfo-mpo.gc.ca, Dalhousie Univ; OpAm

Perrin, Richard E., (505) 667-4755 Los Alamos; Cc

Perron, Taylor, (617) 253-5735 perron@mit.edu, Massachusetts Inst of Tech; Gm

Perry, Baker, (828) 262-7597 perrylb@appstate.edu, Appalachian State Univ; Zg

Perry, David J., (415) 786-6887 Chabot Coll; Op

Perry, Frank V., (505) 667-1033 fperry@lanl.gov, Los Alamos; Gv

Perry, Kevin D., (801) 581-6138 kevin.perry@utah.edu, Univ of Utah; As

Perry , Kyle, 859-257-0133 kyle.perry@uky.edu, Univ of Kentucky; Nr

Perry, Randall, +44 20 759 46425 r.perry@imperial.ac.uk, Imperial Coll; Zg

Persad, Geeta, geeta.persad@jsg.utexas.edu, Univ of Texas, Austin; As

Persaud, Naraine, (540) 231-3817 npers@vt.edu, Virginia Polytechnic Inst & State Univ; Sp

Persaud, Patricia, 225-578-5676 ppersaud@lsu.edu, Louisiana State Univ; Ys

Perscio, Lyman, 814-824-2076 lpersico@mercyhurst.edu, Mercyhurst Univ; GsSpHg

Persico, Lyman P., 509-527-5157 persiclp@whitman.edu, Whitman Coll; Gm

Person, Arthur, (814) 863-8568 aap1@psu.edu, Pennsylvania State Univ, Univ Park; Am

Person, Jeff, jjperson@nd.gov, North Dakota Geological Survey; Pg

Person, Mark A., (575) 835-6506 mperson@ees.nmt.edu, New Mexico Inst of Mining and Tech; HyYhg

Pertl, David, djpertl@actx.edu, Amarillo Coll; Go

Perumal, Ram, (785) 625-3425 perumal@ksu.edu, Kansas State Univ; So

Pervunina, Aelita, +78142766039 aelita@krc.karelia.ru, Inst of Geology (Karelia, Russia); GpvEm

Peryea, Frank J., (509) 663-8181 Washington State Univ; Sc

Pesavento, Jim, 7607441150 x2516 jpesavento@palomar.edu, Palomar Coll; GgZg

Pessagno, Jr., Emile A., (972) 883-2444 pessagno@utdallas.edu, Univ of Texas, Dallas; Pm

Pesses, Michael, mpesses@avc.edu, Antelope Valley Coll; Zyi

Pestrong, Raymond, (415) 338-2080 rayp@sfsu.edu, San Francisco State Univ; Ng

Peteet, Dorothy M., (845) 365-8420 peteet@ldeo.columbia.edu, Columbia Univ; PelGn

Peter, Mark, 614 265 6529 mark.peter@dnr.state.oh.us, Ohio Dept of Natural Resources; PgZe

Peterman, Emily M., 207-725-3846 epeterma@bowdoin.edu, Bowdoin Coll; Gtp

Peters, Catherine A., (609) 258-5645 cap@phoenix.princeton.edu, Princeton Univ; Hw

Peters, Lisa, 575-835-5217 lisa.peters@nmt.edu, New Mexico Inst of Mining and Tech; Gg

Peters, Mark T., (202) 586-9279 mark_peters@notes.ymp.gov, Los Alamos; Yg

Peters, Roger M., roger.peters@wisc.edu, Univ of Wisconsin, Madison, Division of Extension; Gg

Peters, Shanan, 608-262-5987 peters@geology.wisc.edu, Univ of Wisconsin, Madison; Gs

Peters, Stephen C., 610/758-3660 scp2@lehigh.edu, Lehigh Univ; Cl

Petersen, Bruce, (314) 935-5643 petersen@wustl.edu, Washington Univ in St. Louis; Zn

Petersen, Erich U., (801) 581-7238 erich.petersen@utah.edu, Univ of Utah; Em

Petersen, Gary W., (814) 865-1540 gwp2@psu.edu, Pennsylvania State Univ, Univ Park; Sd

Petersen, Nikolai, 0049/89/2180-4233 petersen@geophysik.uni-muenchen.de, Ludwig-Maximilians-Univ Muenchen; Ygm

Peterson, Bradley, bradley.peterson@stonybrook.edu, SUNY, Stony Brook; Ob

Peterson, Dallas, (785) 532-0405 Kansas State Univ; So

Peterson, Eric W., (309) 438-7865 ewpeter@ilstu.edu, Illinois State Univ; Hws

Peterson, Eugene J., (505) 667-5182 Los Alamos; Ct

Peterson, Gary L., (619) 594-5594 gpeterson@geology.sdsu.edu, San Diego State Univ; Gr

Peterson, Holly, 336-316-2263 petersonhe@guilford.edu, Guilford Coll; HwGe

Peterson, Jon W., peterson@hope.edu, Hope Coll; Ge

Peterson, Joseph E., (847) 697-1000 jpeterson@elgin.edu, Elgin Comm Coll; Gg

Peterson, Larry C., 305-284-6821 l.peterson@miami.edu, Univ of Miami; Gr

Peterson, Peter A., (515) 294-9652 pap@iastate.edu, Iowa State Univ of Sci & Tech; Zn

Peterson, Richard E., 806-834-3418 richard.peterson@ttu.edu, Texas Tech Univ; As

Peterson, Ronald C., (613) 533-6180 peterson@queensu.ca, Queen's Univ; Gz

Peterson, Virginia L., (616) 331-2811 petersvi@gvsu.edu, Grand Valley State Univ; GxcGt

Pethick, Andrew, +618 9266-2297 andrew.pethick@curtin.edu.au, Curtin Univ; YevYg

Petit, Martin A., (309) 694-5327 Illinois Central Coll; Ze

Petr, Vilem, 303-273-3222 vpetr@mines.edu, Colorado Sch of Mines; Nm

Petrie, Elizabeth S., (970) 943-2117 epetrie@western.edu, Western Colorado Univ; GcoYe

Petrie, Gregg, 206-552-6385 gregg.petrie@ieee.org, Univ of Washington; Zr

Petrinec, Zorica, +38514605969 zoricap@geol.pmf.hr, Univ of Zagreb; GipGz

Petronis, Michael S., (505) 454-3513 mspetro@nmhu.edu, New Mexico Highlands Univ; YmGcv

Petrovay, Kristof, +36 20 3722500/6621 k.petrovay@astro.elte.hu, Eotvos Lorand Univ; Xy

Petsch, Steven, (413) 545-4413 spetsch@geo.umass.edu, Univ of Massachusetts, Amherst; Col

Petsios, Elizabeth, (254)710-2388 elizabeth_petsios@baylor.edu, Baylor Univ; Pie

Pettengill, Gordon H., (617) 253-4281 ghp@space.mit.edu, Massachusetts Inst of Tech; Zg

Petters, Markus, 919-515-7144 markus_petters@ncsu.edu, North Carolina State Univ; As

Pettijohn, J. C., 217-333-3540 jcpettij@illinois.edu, Univ of Illinois, Urbana-Champaign; Hg

Pettinga, Jarg R., (03) 3667-001 x7716 jarg.pettinga@canterbury.ac.nz, Univ of Canterbury; Gtc

Petty, Grant W., (608)263-3265 gpetty@aos.wisc.edu, Univ of Wisconsin, Madison; AsZrAm

Petuch, Edward J., (561) 297-2398 epetuch@fau.edu, Florida Atlantic Univ; Pg

Peucker-Ehrenbrink, Bernhard, (508) 289-2518 bpeucker@whoi.edu, Woods Hole Oceanographic Inst; CmlHs

Pevzner, Roman, +618 9266-9805 r.pevzner@curtin.edu.au, Curtin Univ; YxxYz

Pezelj, Đurđica, +38514606117 durpezelj@yahoo.com, Univ of Zagreb; PgbPm

Pfannkuch, Hans O., (612) 624-1620 h2olafpf@umn.edu, Univ of Minnesota, Twin Cities; HwGeRh

Pfefferkorn, Hermann W., (215) 898-5156 hpfeffer@sas.upenn.edu, Univ of Pennsylvania; PbePs
Pfuhl, Helen, 089/2180 4230 helen.pfuhl@geophysik.uni-muenchen.de, Ludwig-Maximilians-Univ Muenchen; Yg
Pham van Bang, Damien, 418 654-2590 damien.pham_van_bang@ete.inrs.ca, Universite du Quebec; HtOn
Phelps, Tommy J., (423) 574-7290 partnership@ornl.gov, Oak Ridge; Sb
Phelps, William, 951-222-8350 william.phelps@rcc.edu, Riverside City Coll; PeOpPg
Philander, S. George H., 609-258-5683 gphlder@princeton.edu, Princeton Univ; Op
Philben, Michael , 616 395 6710 philben@hope.edu, Hope Coll; CgScGe
Phillippi, Nathan E., 910-521-6588 nathan.phillippi@uncp.edu, Univ of North Carolina, Pembroke; Zgi
Phillips, Andrew C., (217) 333-2513 aphillps@illinois.edu, Illinois State Geological Survey; GsmZi
Phillips, Brian L., (631) 632-6853 brian.phillips@stonybrook.edu, Stony Brook Univ; GzCl
Phillips, Dennis, (505) 667-4253 Los Alamos; Co
Phillips, Fred M., (575) 835-5540 phillips@nmt.edu, New Mexico Inst of Mining and Tech; Hw
Phillips, Michael, (815) 224-0394 mike_phillips@ivcc.edu, Illinois Valley Comm Coll; GgeGm
Phillips, Paul, (785) 628-5969 pphillip@fhsu.edu, Fort Hays State Univ; Zen
Phillips, Richard, +44(0) 113 34 31728 r.j.phillips@leeds.ac.uk, Univ of Leeds; Gt
Phillips, William R., (801) 378-4545 Brigham Young Univ; Gz
Philp, R. Paul, (405) 325-4469 pphilp@ou.edu, Univ of Oklahoma; Co
Philpotts, Anthony R., (860) 486-1394 anthony.philpotts@uconn.edu, Univ of Connecticut; Gi
Phinney, Robert A., 609-258-4118 rphinney@princeton.edu, Princeton Univ; Ys
Phipps, Stephen P., (215) 898-4602 sphipps@sas.upenn.edu, Univ of Pennsylvania; Gc
Phipps Morgan, Jason, jp369@cornell.edu, Cornell Univ; GvCmPe
Piasecki, Michael, 212-650-8000 mpiasecki@ccny.cuny.edu, Graduate Sch of the City Univ of New York; Gg
Piazzoni, Antonio Sebastian, 089/2180 4230 antonio.piazzoni@geophysik.uni-muenchen.de, Ludwig-Maximilians-Univ Muenchen; Yg
Picardal, Flynn W., (812) 855-0732 picardal@indiana.edu, Indiana Univ, Bloomington; So
Piccinini, Leonardo, +390498279124 leonardo.piccinini@unipd.it, Univ degli Studi di Padova; Hg
Piccoli, Philip M., (301) 405-6966 piccoli@umd.edu, Univ of Maryland; Cg
Pichevin, Laetitia, +44 (0) 131 650 5980 laetitia.pichevin@ed.ac.uk, Edinburgh Univ; Cg
Pickering, Ingrid J., (306) 966-5706 ingrid.pickering@usask.ca, Univ of Saskatchewan; CgtZn
Pickering, Kevin, +44 020 7679 31325 kt.pickering@ucl.ac.uk, Univ Coll London; Gs
Pickett, Nicki, 954-201-6677 npickett@broward.edu, Broward Coll; Zn
Pickup, Gillian E., +44 (0) 131 451 3168 g.pickup@hw.ac.uk, Heriot-Watt Univ; Np
Pidwirny, Michael, 250-807-8758 michael.pidwirny, Univ of British Columbia, Okanagan Campus; AtZyc
Pierce, David, 440-525-7341 dpierce@lakelandcc.edu, Lakeland Comm Coll; GgHsAm
Pierce, Heather, (585) 292-2426 hpierce@monroecc.edu, Monroe Comm Coll; Zyi
Pierce, Jeff, jeffrey.pierce@colostate.edu, Colorado State Univ; As
Pierce, Jennifer L., (208) 426-5380 jenpierce@boisestate.edu, Boise State Univ; GmRcZc
Pierce, Larry, (573) 368-2191 larry.pierce@dnr.mo.gov, Missouri Dept of Natural Resources; Zn
Pieri, David C., (818) 354-6299 Jet Propulsion Lab; Gt
Pieruccini, Pierluigi, pierluigi.pieruccini@unito.it, Univ di Torino; Gm
Pierzynski, Gary M., 785-532-6101 gmp@ksu.edu, Kansas State Univ; Sc
Pieters, Carle M., (401) 863-2417 carle_pieters@brown.edu, Brown Univ; Zr
Pieters, Roger, (604) 822-4297 rpieters@eos.ubc.ca, Univ of British Columbia; Op
Pietranik, Anna, anna.pietranik@uwr.edu.pl, Univ of Wroclaw; CgGie
Pietras, Jeff, (607) 777-3348 jpietras@binghamton.edu, Binghamton Univ; GsEo
Pietro, Kathryn R., (508) 289-3862 kpietro@whoi.edu, Woods Hole Oceanographic Inst; Gu
Pietruszka, Aaron, apietrus@hawaii.edu, Univ of Hawai'i, Manoa; Ca
Pietrzak-Renaud, Natalie, 519-473-3766 npietrz@uwo.ca, Western Univ; Eg
Pietsch, Carlie, 408 924-5279 carlie.pietsch@sjsu.edu, San Jose State Univ; PiePc
Pigott, John D., (405) 325-4498 jpigott@ou.edu, Univ of Oklahoma; GoYeGd
Pike, J, pikej@cf.ac.uk, Cardiff Univ; Zn
Pike, Jenny, +44(0)29 208 75181 pikej@cardiff.ac.uk, Univ of Wales; Og
Pike, Scott, (503) 370-6587 spike@willamette.edu, Willamette Univ; Gag
Pike, Steven M., (508) 289-2350 spike@whoi.edu, Woods Hole Oceanographic Inst; Ca
Pikelj, Kristina, +38514606113 kpikelj@geol.pmf.hr, Univ of Zagreb; Gs
Pikitch, Ellen K., (631) 632-9599 ellen.pikitch@stonybrook.edu, SUNY, Stony Brook; Ob
Pilkey, Jr., Orrin H., (919) 684-4238 opilkey@geo.duke.edu, Duke Univ; Ou
Pilson, Michael E., (401) 874-6104 pilson@gso.uri.edu, Univ of Rhode Island; Oc
Pimentel, Nuno , pimentel@fc.ul.pt, Unive de Lisboa; GrsGo
Piña, Rubén, rpinagar@ucm.es, Univ Complutense de Madrid; EmGz
Pinckney, James, 803 777 7133 pinckney@sc.edu, Univ of South Carolina; Obn
Pincus, Lauren N., 609-258-4101 lpincus@princeton.edu, Princeton Univ; CqlCg
Pinet, Paul, (315) 228-7656 ppinet@colgate.edu, Colgate Univ; Ou
Pingitore, Jr., Nicholas E., 915-747-5754 npingitore@utep.edu, Univ of Texas, El Paso; Cl
Piniella Febrer, Juan Francesc, ++34935813088 juan.piniella@uab.cat, Universitat Autonoma de Barcelona; Gz
Pinkel, Robert, (858) 534-2056 rpinkel@ucsd.edu, Univ of California, San Diego; Op
Pinnt, Todd, todd.pinnt@azwestern.edu, Arizona Western Coll; ZyiZg
Pinter, Nicholas, (530) 754-1041 npinter@ucdavis.edu, Univ of California, Davis; Gm
Pinti, Daniele Luigi, 514-987-3000 #2572 pinti.daniele@uqam.ca, Universite du Quebec a Montreal; Cs
Pintilei, Mitica, 0040232401494 mpintilei@gmail.com, Alexandru Ioan Cuza; CgeCt
Piotrowski, Alexander, +44 (0) 1223 333473 apio04@esc.cam.ac.uk, Univ of Cambridge; Ge
Piper, David J., (902) 426-6580 david.piper@canada.ca, Dalhousie Univ; GusGo
Piper, John, +44 0151 794 3461 sg04@liverpool.ac.uk, Univ of Liverpool; YmGt
Pipkin, Bernard W., (213) 740-6106 pipkin@usc.edu, Univ of Southern California; Ng
Pirie, Diane H., (305) 348-2876 Florida International Univ; Gg
Pirouz, Mortaza X., (972) 883-2406 mxp180004@utdallas.edu, Univ of Texas, Dallas; GcZiGc
Pisani-Gareau, Tara, (617) 552-0843 pisanoga@bc.edu, Boston Coll; Ge
Pistone , Mattia , mattia.pistone@uga.edu, Univ of Georgia; Gv
Pitlick, John, pitlick@colorado.edu, Univ of Colorado; Gm
Pittman, Jason, (916) 608-6668 pittmaj@flc.losrios.edu, Folsom Lake Coll; ZgiZi
Pizzuto, James E., (302) 831-2710 pizzuto@udel.edu, Univ of Delaware; Gm
Placzek, Christa, 0747 814 756 christa.placzek@jcu.edu.au, James Cook Univ; CclGe
Planavsky, Noah, 203-432-9043 noah.planavsky@yale.edu, Yale Univ; CsbCm
Plane, David A., plane@email.arizona.edu, Univ of Arizona; Zn
Plank, Gabriel, (775) 784-7039 gabe@seismo.unr.edu, Univ of Nevada, Reno; Ys
Plank, Owen C., (706) 542-9072 Univ of Georgia; Sc
Plank, Terry, tplank@ldeo.columbia.edu, Columbia Univ; Cg
Plankell, Eric T., 217-265-8029 eplankel@illinois.edu, Illinois State Geological Survey; Hg
Plant, Jane, +44 20 759 47416 jane.plant@imperial.ac.uk, Imperial Coll; Ge
Plant, Jeffrey J., (818) 393-3799 plant@jpl.nasa.gov, Jet Propulsion Lab; Zn
Plante, Alain F., (215) 898-9269 aplante@sas.upenn.edu, Univ of Pennsylvania; SboCo
Plante, Martin, (418) 656-8121 martin.plante@ggl.ulaval.ca, Universite Laval; Cg
Plasienka, Dusan, 0042160296529 plasienka@fns.uniba.sk, Comenius Univ in Bratislava; Gt
Platnick, Steven, steven.platnick@nasa.gov, Univ of Wisconsin, Madison; Zr
Platt, Brian F., 662-915-5440 bfplatt@olemiss.edu, Univ of Mississippi; GsPe
Platt, John P., (213) 821-1194 jplatt@usc.edu, Univ of Southern California; GctGp
Platt, Rutherford H., (413) 545-2499 rplatt@geo.umass.edu, Univ of Massachusetts, Amherst; Zu
Plattner, Alain, 205-348-0387 amplattner@ua.edu, Univ of Alabama; YmuYg
Plattner, Christina, 089/21804220 christina.plattner@geophysik.uni-muenchen.de, Ludwig-Maximilians-Univ Muenchen; Yg
Pleasants, Mark S., 614 265 6748 mark.pleasants@dnr.state.oh.us, Ohio Dept of Natural Resources; HwSp

Plescia, Jeffrey, (202) 358-0295 Jet Propulsion Lab; Zn
Plink-Bjorklund, Piret, (303) 384-2042 pplink@mines.edu, Colorado Sch of Mines; Gs
Plint, A G., (519) 661-3179 gplint@uwo.ca, Western Univ; Gs
Plotkin, Pamela, 979-845-3902 plotkin@tamu.edu, Texas A&M Univ; Ob
Plotnick, Roy E., (312) 996-2111 plotnick@uic.edu, Univ of Illinois at Chicago; PgiGq
Plug, Lawrence, 902-494-1200 lplug@is.dal.ca, Dalhousie Univ; Gm
Pluhar, Christopher J., (559) 278-1128 cpluhar@csufresno.edu, Fresno State Univ; GtYmNg
Plumb, Raymond A., (617) 253-6281 plumb@mit.edu, Massachusetts Inst of Tech; As
Plummer, Charles C., plummercc@csus.edu, Sacramento State Univ; Gp
Plymate, Thomas G., tomplymate@missouristate.edu, Missouri State Univ; Gx
Poch Serra, Joan, ++935811085 joan.poch@uab.cat, Universitat Autonoma de Barcelona; GrsZe
Pociask, Geoff, 217-265-8212 pociask@illinois.edu, Illinois State Geological Survey; Hw
Pociask, Geoffrey , 217 265-8029 pociask@illinois.edu, Univ of Illinois; Hs
Pociask, Walter, (313) 577-2506 wpociask@gmail.com, Wayne State Univ; Zn
Podolak, Morris, (052) 838-0976 morris@post.tau.ac.il, Tel Aviv Univ; ZnnZn
Poeter, Eileen P., epoeter@mines.edu, Colorado Sch of Mines; Ng
Pogge von Strandmann, Phillip, +44 020 7679 33637 p.strandmann@ucl.ac.uk, Univ Coll London; Csl
Pogue, Kevin R., (509) 527-5955 pogue@whitman.edu, Whitman Coll; Gc
Pohll, Greg, 775-682-6349 greg.pohll@dri.edu, Univ of Nevada, Reno; Hwq
Poinar, Kristin, (716)645-4286 kpoinar@buffalo.edu, SUNY, Buffalo; Gl
Poirier, Andre, 514-987-3000 #1718 Universite du Quebec a Montreal; Cs
Pojeta, John, (202) 633-1347 Smithsonian Inst / Nat Mus of Natural History; Pi
Pokorny, Eugene W., (702) 295-7496 eugene_pokorny@lanl.gov, Los Alamos; Nm
Pol, Diego, cacopol@gmail.com, Cornell Univ; Pv
Polat, Ali, 519-253-3000 x2495 polat@uwindsor.ca, Univ of Windsor; GixCc
Polet, Jascha, 909-869-3459 jpolet@cpp.edu, California State Polytechnic Univ, Pomona; Ysg
Polissar, Pratigya J., polissar@ldeo.columbia.edu, Columbia Univ; Gg
Polito, Thomas A., (515) 294-0513 tpolito@iastate.edu, Iowa State Univ of Sci & Tech; So
Polizzotto, Matthew, (541) 346-5217 mpolozzo@uoregon.edu, Univ of Oregon; CqSc
Polk, Jason, jason.polk@wku.edu, Western Kentucky Univ; Gm
Pollack, Henry N., (734) 763-0084 hpollack@umich.edu, Univ of Michigan; Yg
Pollack, Jennifer, 361-825-2041 jennifer.pollack@tamucc.edu, Texas A&M Univ, Corpus Christi; Ob
Pollak, Robert, pollak@wustl.edu, Washington Univ in St. Louis; Zn
Pollard, David D., (650) 723-4679 dpollard@pangea.stanford.edu, Stanford Univ; Gc
Pollock, Meagen, (330) 263-2202 mpollock@wooster.edu, Coll of Wooster; CuGiv
Polly, P. David, (812) 855-7994 pdpolly@indiana.edu, Indiana Univ, Bloomington; PvgPq
Pollyea, Ryan M., 540-231-7929 rpollyea@vt.edu, Virginia Polytechnic Inst & State Univ; Hq
Polovina, Jeffrey J., (808) 983-5390 jeffrey.polovina@noaa.gov, Univ of Hawai'i, Manoa; Zn
Polsky, Colin, (954) 236-1088 cpolsky@fau.edu, Florida Atlantic Univ; Znc
Polvani, Lorenzo M., (212) 854-7331 lmp3@columbia.edu, Columbia Univ; AmsGq
Polyak, Victor J., (505) 277-4204 polyak@unm.edu, Univ of New Mexico; CcGzm
Polzin, Dierk T., dtpolzin@wisc.edu, Univ of Wisconsin, Madison; As
Pomeroy, George M., (717) 477-1776 gmpome@ship.edu, Shippensburg Univ; ZuyZn
Pommier, Anne, (858) 822-5025 pommier@ucsd.edu, Univ of California, San Diego; Cg
Pond, Lisa G., (225) 578-0401 lgpond@lsu.edu, Louisiana State Univ; Zg
Pond, Stephen G., (604) 822-2205 spond@eos.ubc.ca, Univ of British Columbia; Op
Ponette-Gonzalez, Alexandra, 940-565-4012 alexandra.ponette@unt.edu, Univ of North Texas; Zyc
Ponton, Camilo, (360) 650-3648 camilo.ponton@wwu.edu, Western Washington Univ; CsoPc
Poole, Geoff, gpoole@montana.edu, Montana State Univ; Hg
Poole, T. Craig, (559) 442-4600 craig.poole@fresnocitycollege.edu, Fresno City Coll; Gg
Pope, Gregory A., (973) 655-7385 popeg@mail.montclair.edu, Montclair State Univ; GmaZy
Pope, Jeanette K., (765) 658-4105 jpope@depauw.edu, DePauw Univ; Ge
Pope, Michael , (979) 845-4376 mcpope@geo.tamu.edu, Texas A&M Univ; GrCc
Pope, Richard, +44 (0)1332 591751 r.j.pope@derby.ac.uk, Univ of Derby; Gam
Popp, Brian N., (808) 956-6206 popp@soest.hawaii.edu, Univ of Hawai'i, Manoa; Cm
Porcelli, Don, +44 (1865) 282121 don.porcelli@earth.ox.ac.uk, Univ of Oxford; Cg
Porch, William M., (505) 667-0971 wporch@lanl.gov, Los Alamos; Yg
Portell, Roger W., 3523921721 x258 portell@flmnh.ufl.edu, Univ of Florida; PisPv
Porter, Claire, 612-626-0505 porte254@umn.edu, Univ of Minnesota, Twin Cities; Zi
Porter, Dwayne E., 803-777-4615 porter@sc.edu, Univ of South Carolina; OgHsRw
Porter, John H., (804) 924-8999 jhp7e@virginia.edu, Univ of Virginia; Zif
Porter, Ryan, 928-523-2429 ryan.porter@nau.edu, Northern Arizona Univ; YgsGt
Porter, Susannah, (805) 893-8954 porter@geol.ucsb.edu, Univ of California, Santa Barbara; Gn
Portillo, Danny, (719) 333-3080 United States Air Force Academy; Zi
Portner, Ryan, ryan.portner@sjsu.edu, San Jose State Univ; Gdv
Posiloviæ, Hrvoje, +38514606087 posilovic@geol.pmf.hr, Univ of Zagreb; Gg
Posler, Gerry L., (785) 532-6101 gposler@ksu.edu, Kansas State Univ; Sf
Pospelova, Vera, vpospe@umn.edu, Univ of Minnesota, Twin Cities; GePl
Post, Donald F., (520) 621-1262 postdf@ag.arizona.edu, Univ of Arizona; Sd
Post, Jeffrey E., (202) 633-1814 postj@si.edu, Smithsonian Inst / Nat Mus of Natural History; Gz
Post, Vincent , vincent.post@flinders.edu.au, Flinders Univ; Hw
Poteet, Mary F., 512-471-5209 mpoteet@jsg.utexas.edu, Univ of Texas, Austin; Pg
Potel, Sébastien, +33(0)3 44068999 sebastien.potel@lasalle-beauvais.fr, Institut Polytechnique LaSalle Beauvais (ex-IGAL); GpzGi
Potess, Marla, (325) 670-1395 marla.potess@hsutx.edu, Hardin-Simmons Univ; Zgu
Poths, Jane, (505) 667-1506 Los Alamos; Cc
Potra, Adriana, 479-575-6419 potra@uark.edu, Univ of Arkansas, Fayetteville; EgCcGg
Potten, Martin, +49 89 289 - 25885 martin.potten@tum.de, Technical Univ of Munich; NxGg
Potter, Amy E., (912) 344-3612 amypotter@georgiasouthern.edu, Georgia Southern Univ; Zn
Potter, David, (780) 2481518 dkpotter@ualberta.ca, Univ of Alberta; Ye
Potter, Eric C., (512) 471-7090 eric.potter@beg.utexas.edu, Univ of Texas at Austin, Jackson Sch of Geosciences; Eo
Potter, Henry, hpotter@tamu.edu, Texas A&M Univ; Op
Potter, Katherine E., katie.potter@usu.edu, Utah State Univ; GiZeEg
Potter, Paul E., (513) 556-3732 Univ of Cincinnati; Gs
Potter, Jr., Donald B., (931) 598-1479 bpotter@sewanee.edu, Sewanee: Univ of the South; Gc
Potter, Jr., Noel, pottern@dickinson.edu, Dickinson Coll; Gmc
Potter-McIntyre, Sally, pottermcintyre@siu.edu, Southern Illinois Univ Carbondale; Gs
Potts, Donald C., (831) 459-4417 potts@biology.ucsc.edu, Univ of California, Santa Cruz; Ob
Poty, Edouard, 32 4 366 52 83 e.poty@ulg.ac.be, Universite de Liege; PiGsPe
Poudel, Durga, 337-482-6163 ddpoudel@louisiana.edu, Univ of Louisiana at Lafayette; Ge
Poulsen, Christopher J., (734) 615-2236 poulsen@umich.edu, Univ of Michigan; Pe
Poulson, Simon, 775.784.1833 poulson@mines.unr.edu, Univ of Nevada, Reno; Cls
Poulton, Mary, 520-621-8391 mpoulton@email.arizona.edu, Univ of Arizona; Ng
Poulton, Simon, +44(0) 113 34 35237 s.poulton@leeds.ac.uk, Univ of Leeds; Cls
Pound, Kate S., 320-308-2014 kspound@stcloudstate.edu, Saint Cloud State Univ; GgZeGd
Pourmand, Ali, apourmand@rsmas.miami.edu, Univ of Miami; Cga
Pournelle, Jennifer R., jpournelle@environ.sc.edu, Univ of South Carolina; GaZuSa
Pournik, Maysam, maysam.pournik@ou.edu, Univ of Oklahoma; Np
Pourret, Olivier, +33(0)3 44068979 olivier.pourret@lasalle-beauvais.fr, Institut Polytechnique LaSalle Beauvais (ex-IGAL); CgaGe
Powell, Brian, (808) 956-6724 powellb@hawaii.edu, Univ of Hawai'i, Manoa; Op
Powell, Christine A., (901) 678-8455 capowell@memphis.edu, Univ of Memphis; Ys

Powell, J. Mark, (608) 890-0070 jmpowel2@wisc.edu, Univ of Wisconsin, Madison; So
Powell, Jane, +44 (0)1603 59 2822 j.c.powell@uea.ac.uk, Univ of East Anglia; Ge
Powell, Matthew G., (814) 641-3602 powell@juniata.edu, Juniata Coll; PiqPe
Powell, Rebecca , 303-871-2667 rebecca.l.powell@du.edu, Univ of Denver; Zr
Powell, Ross D., (815) 753-7952 rpowell@niu.edu, Northern Illinois Univ; GslZc
Powell, Scott, spowell@montana.edu, Montana State Univ; Zr
Powell, Thomas M., (510) 642-7455 zackp@socrates.berkeley.edu, Univ of California, Berkeley; Op
Powell, Wayne G., (718) 951-5761 wpowell@brooklyn.cuny.edu, Graduate Sch of the City Univ of New York; EmGaCs
Power, Mary E., (510) 643-7776 Univ of California, Berkeley; Pe
Powers, Elizabeth, epowers@csub.edu, California State Univ, Bakersfield; Gg
Powers, Roger W., (907) 474-6188 Univ of Alaska, Fairbanks; Zn
Powers, Sean, spowers@southalabama.edu, Univ of South Alabama; Ob
Poyla, David, +44 0161 275-3818 david.polya@manchester.ac.uk, Univ of Manchester; Cm
Poynton, Helen, helen.poynton@umb.edu, Univ of Massachusetts, Boston; Zn
Pracny, Pavel, +420 549 49 8523 pracny@sci.muni.cz, Masaryk Univ; Cg
Pradhanang, Soni M., (401) 874-5980 spradhanang@uri.edu, Univ of Rhode Island; HsqHq
Prairie, Jennifer, (619) 260-8820 jcprairie@sandiego.edu, Univ of San Diego; Ob
Pranter, Matthew J., (405) 325-3253 matthew.pranter@ou.edu, Univ of Oklahoma; Go
Prasad, Manika, 303-273-3457 mprasad@mines.edu, Colorado Sch of Mines; NrYx
Prasad, Rishi, (334) 844-4100 rzp0050@auburn.edu, Auburn Univ; Sb
Prasad, Vara , (785) 532-3746 vara@ksu.edu, Kansas State Univ; So
Prather, Kimberly A., (858) 822-5312 kprather@ucsd.edu, Univ of California, San Diego; AsCmHg
Prather, Michael J., (949) 824-5838 mprather@uci.edu, Univ of California, Irvine; As
Pratson, Lincoln F., (919) 681-8077 lincoln.pratson@duke.edu, Duke Univ; Gs
Pratt, Allyn R., (505) 667-4308 pratt_allyn_r@lanl.gov, Los Alamos; Ge
Pratt, Brian R., (306) 966-5725 brian.pratt@usask.ca, Univ of Saskatchewan; PgGsr
Pratt, Lisa M., (812) 855-9203 prattl@indiana.edu, Indiana Univ, Bloomington; Co
Pratt, R. Gerhard, 519-661-2111 ext. 86690 gpratt2@uwo.ca, Western Univ; Yeg
Prave, Tony, +44 (0)1334462381 ap13@st-andrews.ac.uk, Univ of St. Andrews; GgrGs
Precedo, Laura, 954-201-6674 lprecedo@broward.edu, Broward Coll; Oc
Precht, Francis L., (301) 687-4440 fprecht@frostburg.edu, Frostburg State Univ; Zy
Prell, Warren L., (401) 863-3221 warren_prell@brown.edu, Brown Univ; Ou
Prencipe, Mauro, mauro.prencipe@unito.it, Univ di Torino; Gz
Prescott, Cindy, 604–822–4701 cindy.prescott@ubc.ca, Univ of British Columbia; Sb
Presley, Bobby J., (979) 845-5136 bpresley@ocean.tamu.edu, Texas A&M Univ; Oc
Presley, DeAnn, 785532128 deann@ksu.edu, Kansas State Univ; So
Presnall, Dean C., (972) 883-2444 presnall@utdallas.edu, Univ of Texas, Dallas; Cp
Prestegaard, Karen L., (301) 405-6982 kpresto@geol.umd.edu, Univ of Maryland; Hgw
Preston, Aaron, 802-626-6496 aaron.preston@northernvermont.edu, Northern Vermont Univ-Lyndon; AsZrAc
Preston, Thomas C., 514-398-3766 thomas.preston@mcgill.ca, McGill Univ; AsZnn
Preston, William L., (805) 756-2210 wpreston@calpoly.edu, California Polytechnic State Univ; Ze
Preto, Nereo, +390498279174 nereo.preto@unipd.it, Univ degli Studi di Padova; Gs
Pretorius, Erika, +27 (0)12 420 3737 erika.pretorius@up.ac.za, Univ of Pretoria; Zi
Prevec, Steve, +27 (0)46-603-8309 s.prevec@ru.ac.za, Rhodes Univ; Cg
Previdi, Michael, mprevidi@ldeo.columbia.edu, Columbia Univ; As
Prewett, Jerry L., (573) 368-2101 jerry.prewett@dnr.mo.gov, Missouri Dept of Natural Resources; GgHw
Price, Alan P., (262) 521-5498 paul.price@uwc.edu, Univ of Wisconsin Colls; ZyGmZg
Price, Colin G., +97236406029 cprice@flash.tau.ac.il, Tel Aviv Univ; As
Price, Curtis V., (605) 394-2461 curtis.price@sdsmt.edu, South Dakota Sch of Mines & Tech; ZifRw
Price, Douglas M., 330-941-3019 dmprice@ysu.edu, Youngstown State Univ; Cg
Price, Greogry, +44 1752 584771 g.price@plymouth.ac.uk, Univ of Plymouth; Gsr
Price, Jason R., 717-872-3005 jason.price@millersville.edu, Millersville Univ; Gs
Price, Jonathan D., (940) 397-4288 jonathan.price@mwsu.edu, Midwestern State Univ; GiCuGz
Price, Kevin, (785) 532-6101 kpprice@ksu.edu, Kansas State Univ; Zr
Price, L G., lloydgreer.price@nmt.edu, New Mexico Inst of Mining and Tech; Gg
Price, Maribeth H., (605) 394-2461 maribeth.price@sdsmt.edu, South Dakota Sch of Mines & Tech; Zir
Price, Marie D., (202) 994-6187 George Washington Univ; Zy
Price, Nancy A., (518)564-4032 npric002@plattsburgh.edu, SUNY, Plattsburgh; GzCgGc
Price, Peter E., 281-765-7764 peter.e.price@nhmccd.edu, Lonestar Coll - North Harris; Zi
Price, Raymond A., (613) 533-6542 pricera@queensu.ca, Queen's Univ; GtcGe
Price, Rene, (305) 348-3119 pricer@fiu.edu, Florida International Univ; HwClRw
Prichard, H M., prichard@cf.ac.uk, Cardiff Univ; Gx
Prichard, Hazel, +44(0)29 208 74323 prichard@cardiff.ac.uk, Univ of Wales; EgGze
Prichonnet, Gilbert P., 514-987-3000 #3383 prichonnet.gilbert@uqam.ca, Universite du Quebec a Montreal; Pi
Prichystal, Antonín, +420 549 49 6699 prichy@sci.muni.cz, Masaryk Univ; GgaGv
Pride, Douglas E., 614-329-0941 pride.1@osu.edu, Ohio State Univ; Eg
Pride, Steven, (510) 495-2823 srpride@lbl.gov, Univ of California, Berkeley; Ys
Pridmore, Cindy L., (916) 925-6902 California Geological Survey; Ng
Priesendorf, Carl, (816) 604-2549 carl.priesendorf@mcckc.edu, Metropolitan Comm Coll-Kansas City; GgZyGe
Priest, Eric, (847) 543-2585 epriest@clcillinois.edu, Coll of Lake County; AmZe
Priest, George R., (541) 574-6642 george.priest@dogami.state.or.us, Oregon Dept of Geology & Mineral Industries; Gg
Priestley, Keith, +44 (0) 1223 337195 Univ of Cambridge; YgGt
Priewisch, Alexandra, 505-504-3675 alexandra.priewisch@fresnocitycollege.edu, Fresno City Coll; Gg
Primeau, Francois, 949-824-9435 fprimeau@uci.edu, Univ of California, Irvine; Op
Pringle, James M., (603) 862-5000 jpringle@cisunix.unh.edu, Univ of New Hampshire; Op
Pringle, Jamie K., (+44) 01782 733163 j.k.pringle@keele.ac.uk, Keele Univ; YuGfa
Pringle, Patrick T., 360-623-8584 ppringle@centralia.edu, Centralia Coll; ZgGvZn
Prinn, Ronald G., 617-253-2452 rprinn@mit.edu, Massachusetts Inst of Tech; As
Prins, Maarten A., +31 20 59 83635 m.a.prins@vu.nl, Vrije Universiteit Amsterdam; GsOg
Prior, David J., +64 3 479-5279 david.prior@otago.ac.nz, Univ of Otago; Gct
Prior, William L., 501 683-0117 bill.prior@arkansas.gov, Arkansas Geological Survey; GggEc
Priscu, John, jpriscu@montana.edu, Montana State Univ; Po
Pristas, Ronald, (609) 984-6587 ron.pristas@dep.state.nj.us, New Jersey Geological and Water Survey; Zi
Pritchard, Chad, 509-359-7026 cpritchard@ewu.edu, Eastern Washington Univ; Gct
Pritchard, Matthew E., mp337@cornell.edu, Cornell Univ; YdGvl
Pritchett, Brittany, 405-325-7331 brittanyp@ou.edu, Univ of Oklahoma; Go
Privette, David, (704)330-6750 david.privette@cpcc.edu, Central Piedmont Comm Coll; Zy
Prockter, Louise M., prockter@lpi.usra.edu, Univ of Tennessee, Knoxville; Xg
Prohiæ, Esad, +38514605963 eprohic@geol.pmf.hr, Univ of Zagreb; CglGe
Proistosescu, Cristian (Cristi), cristi@illinois.edu, Univ of Illinois, Urbana-Champaign; AsGgAp
Prothro, Lindsay O., 361-825-4062 lindsay.prothro@tamucc.edu, Texas A&M Univ, Corpus Christi; GluGs
Proudhon, Benoit, +33(0)3 44068996 benoit.proudhon@lasalle-beauvais.fr, Institut Polytechnique LaSalle Beauvais (ex-IGAL); GgcGt
Provin, Tony L., (979) 862-4955 t-provin@tamu.edu, Texas A&M Univ; Sc
Pruell, Richard J., (401) 782-3000 Univ of Rhode Island; Co
Pruss, Sara B., (413) 585-3948 spruss@smith.edu, Smith Coll; Pg
Pryor, Sara C., 607-255-3376 sp2279@cornell.edu, Cornell Univ; AsZn
Prytulak, Julie, +44 20 759 46474 j.prytulak@imperial.ac.uk, Imperial Coll; Gg

Ptacek, Anton D., ptacek2@juno.com, San Diego State Univ; Gx
Ptak, Tom, 208-885-6238 tptak@uidaho.edu, Univ of Idaho; Zu
Pu, Ruiliang, rpu@usf.edu, Univ of South Florida; Zr
Pu, Zhaoxia, 801-585-3864 zhaoxia.pu@utah.edu, Univ of Utah; As
Puchalski, Stephaney, spuchalski@highline.edu, Highline Coll; PgGg
Puchtel, Igor, (301) 405-4054 ipuchtel@umd.edu, Univ of Maryland; CcgGi
Puckett, Andrew, 706-507-8098 puckett_andrew@columbusstate.edu, Columbus State Univ; Xa
Puckett, Mark, 601-266-4729 mark.puckett@usm.edu, Univ of Southern Mississippi; PmiGg
Puckette, James, 405-744-6358 jim.puckette@okstate.edu, Oklahoma State Univ; Go
Puelles, Pablo, pablo.puelles@ehu.eus, Univ of the Basque Country UPV/EHU; Gct
Puente, Carlos E., (916) 752-0689 Univ of California, Davis; Hg
Puffer, John H., (973) 353-5100 jpuffer@andromeda.rutgers.edu, Rutgers, The State Univ of New Jersey, Newark; GivGe
Pujana, Ignacio, (972) 883-2461 pujana@utdallas.edu, Univ of Texas, Dallas; Pm
Pujol, Jose, (901) 678-4827 jpujol@memphis.edu, Univ of Memphis; Ye
Puleo, Jack, 302-831-2440 jpuleo@udel.edu, Univ of Delaware; Hw
Pulkkinen, Tuija, 734-615-3583 tuija@umich.edu, Univ of Michigan; Zn
Pulliam, Jay, (254) 710-2183 jay_pulliam@baylor.edu, Baylor Univ; YsgYe
Pulliam, Robert J., (512) 471-6156 jay@ig.utexas.edu, Univ of Texas, Austin; Ys
Pumphrey, Hugh C., +44 (0) 131 650 6026 hugh.pumphrey@ed.ac.uk, Edinburgh Univ; AscYv
Pun, Aurora, (505) 277-5629 apun@unm.edu, Univ of New Mexico; Ca
Pundsack, Jonathan, 612-626-0505 pundsack@umn.edu, Univ of Minnesota, Twin Cities; Zn
Punyasena, Surangi W., (217) 244-8049 punyasena@life.illinois.edu, Univ of Illinois, Urbana-Champaign; PblPe
Purchase, Megan, +27 (0)51 401 7158 purchasemd@ufs.ac.za, Univ of the Free State; Gx
Purdie, Duncan A., +44 (0)23 80592263 duncan.purdie@noc.soton.ac.uk, Univ of Southampton; Ob
Purdom, William B., (541) 552-6494 purdom@sou.edu, Southern Oregon Univ; Gx
Purdy, G. Michael, (845) 365-8348 mpurdy@ldeo.columbia.edu, Columbia Univ; Yr
Purkis, Sam J., 305-421-4351 spurkis@rsmas.miami.edu, Univ of Miami; Gu
Purkiss, Robert, 325-486-6987 robert.purkiss@angelo.edu, Angelo State Univ; Gg
Purnell, Mark, +440116 252 3645 map2@le.ac.uk, Leicester Univ; Pg
Purtle, Jennifer M., (501) 575-7317 jms14@comp.uark.edu, Univ of Arkansas, Fayetteville; Zn
Pusede, Sally, (434) 924-4544 sep6a@virginia.edu, Univ of Virginia; As
Putirka, Keith D., (559) 278-4524 kputirka@csufresno.edu, Fresno State Univ; GviGp
Putkonen, Jaakko, (701) 777-3213 jaakko.putkonen@engr.und.edu, Univ of North Dakota; Gml
Putnam, Aaron E., 207-581-2186 aaron.putnam@maine.edu, Univ of Maine; Gl
Puziewicz, Jacek, jacek.puziewicz@uwr.edu.pl, Univ of Wroclaw; Gix
Pyle, David M., david.pyle@earth.ox.ac.uk, Univ of Oxford; GviRh
Pyle, Eric J., 540-568-7115 pyleej@jmu.edu, James Madison Univ; Ze
Pylypenko, Svitlana, (303) 384-2140 spylypen@mines.edu, Colorado Sch of Mines; Zmn
Pyrtle, Ashanti J., apyrtle@seas.marine.usf.edu, Univ of South Florida; Oc
Pysklywec, Russell N., (416) 978-4852 russ@geology.utoronto.ca, Univ of Toronto; Yg

Q

Qi, Feng, (908) 737-3702 fqi@kean.edu, Kean Univ; ZiyZg
Qian, Song, (419) 530-4230 song.qian@utoledo.edu, Univ of Toledo; Zn
Qiang, Yi, qiangy@usf.edu, Univ of South Florida; Zi
Qin, Rongjun, qin.324@osu.edu, Ohio State Univ; Zrf
Qiu, Bo, (808) 956-4098 bo@soest.hawaii.edu, Univ of Hawai'i, Manoa; Op
Qiu, Xiaomin, (417) 836-3219 qiu@missouristate.edu, Missouri State Univ; Zi
Quade, Deborah J., -319-337-9785 deborah.quade@dnr.iowa.gov, Iowa Dept of Natural Resources; GleGm
Quade, Jay, 520-626-3223 quadej@email.arizona.edu, Univ of Arizona; Sc
Qualls, Robert G., (775) 327-5014 qualls@unr.edu, Univ of Nevada, Reno; SoHsSf
Quan, Tracy, 405-744-6358 tracy.quan@okstate.edu, Oklahoma State Univ; Og
Quattro, Joseph, quattro@biol.sc.edu, Univ of South Carolina; Ob
Quay, Paul D., (206) 545-8061 pdquay@u.washington.edu, Univ of Washington; Oc
Quick, Thomas J., (330) 972-6935 tquick@uakron.edu, Univ of Akron; GgCaYe
Quinn, Claire, +44(0) 113 34 38700 c.h.quinn@leeds.ac.uk, Univ of Leeds; Ge
Quinn, Courtney, (864)294-3655 courtney.quinn@furman.edu, Furman Univ; Zn
Quinn, Heather A., (410) 554-5522 heather.quinn@maryland.gov, Maryland Department of Natural Resources; GgHwg
Quinn, James G., (401) 874-6219 jgquinn@gso.uri.edu, Univ of Rhode Island; Oc
Quinn, John, (630) 252-5357 quinnj@anl.gov, Argonne; Hw
Quinn, Paul, +44 (0) 191 208 5773 p.f.quinn@ncl.ac.uk, Univ of Newcastle Upon Tyne; Hg
Quinn, Terry, 512-471-0377 quinn@ig.utexas.edu, Univ of Texas, Austin; Pe
Quintero, Sylvia, (520) 621-6025 squinter@email.arizona.edu, Univ of Arizona; Zn
Quinton, Page, 315-267-2815 quintopc@potsdam.edu, Indiana Univ, Bloomington; Pc

R

Raab, James, 614 265 6747 jim.raab@dnr.state.oh.us, Ohio Dept of Natural Resources; Hw
Rabalais, Nancy N., (225) 851-2800 Louisiana State Univ; Ob
Raber, George, 601-266-5807 george.raber@usm.edu, Univ of Southern Mississippi; Zi
Radcliffe, David E., (706) 542-0897 Univ of Georgia; Sp
Radcliffe, Dennis, 516-463-6545 dennis.radcliffe@hofstra.edu, Hofstra Univ; Gzx
Radebaugh, Jani, 801 422-9127 jani.radebaugh@byu.edu, Brigham Young Univ; XgGvm
Rademacher, Laura K., (209) 946-7351 lrademacher@pacific.edu, Univ of the Pacific; ClHySo
Rader, Shelby, (812) 855-7508 shtrader@iu.edu, Indiana Univ, Bloomington; Ct
Radic, Valentina, 604-827-1446 vradic@eos.ubc.ca, Univ of British Columbia; GlAsZg
Radil, Steven, 208-885-5058 sradil@uidaho.edu, Univ of Idaho; Zn
Radke, Lawrence F., radke@ucar.edu, Univ of Washington; As
Radko, Nicholas, (912) 478-5361 nradko@georgiasouthern.edu, Georgia Southern Univ; Geg
Radko, Timour, (831) 656-3318 tradko@nps.edu, Naval Postgraduate Sch; Op
Rae, James, +44 01334 464948 jwbr@st-andrews.ac.uk, Univ of St. Andrews; Cg
Raef, Abdelmoneam E., (785) 532-2240 abraef@ksu.edu, Kansas State Univ; YesZr
Raeside, Robert P., (902) 585-1323 rob.raeside@acadiau.ca, Acadia Univ; GptGc
Rafini, Silvain, 514-987-3000 poste 2369 silvain.rafini@gmail.com, Universite du Quebec a Chicoutimi; GcHwEg
Ragland, Paul C., (850) 644-5018 ragland@magnet.fsu.edu, Florida State Univ; Ca
Ragotzkie, Robert A., ragotzkie@wisc.edu, Univ of Wisconsin, Madison; Ob
Rahaman, M. A., 234-800-337-7441 mrahaman@oauife.edu.ng, Obafemi Awolowo Univ; GpcGi
Rahl, Jeffrey, 540-458-8101 rahlj@wlu.edu, Washington & Lee Univ; Gt
Rahman, Abdullah F., 956-882-4074 abdullah.rahman@utrgv.edu, Univ of Texas, Rio Grande Valley; Zr
Rahman, Ata U., rata@austincc.edu, Austin Comm Coll District; GgdGe
Rahn, Kenneth A., (401) 874-6713 krahn@uri.edu, Univ of Rhode Island; Oc
Rahn, Perry H., (605) 394-2527 perry.rahn@sdsmt.edu, South Dakota Sch of Mines & Tech; Ng
Rai, Chandra S., (405) 325-6866 crai@ou.edu, Univ of Oklahoma; Np
Railsback, L. Bruce, (706) 542-3453 rlsbk@gly.uga.edu, Univ of Georgia; PcClGd
Raine, Robin, +353 (0)91 492271 robin.raine@nuigalway.ie, Nat Univ of Ireland Galway; Yg
Rains, Daniel S., 479-601-7521 daniel.rains@arkansas.gov, Arkansas Geological Survey; GgZi
Rains, Kai, krains@usf.edu, Univ of South Florida; Sf
Rains, Mark C., mrains@usf.edu, Univ of South Florida; Hw
Raj, John K., 03-79674225 jkraj@um.edu.my, Univ of Malaya; Ng
Raji, W. O., lanreraji24@unilorin.edu.ng, Univ of Ilorin; Ye
Rakonczai, Janos, rjanos@earth.geo.u-szeged.hu, Univesity of Szeged; Ze
Rakovan, John F., (513) 529-3245 rakovajf@miamioh.edu, Miami Univ; GzCl
Rakovan, Monica, rakovamt@miamioh.edu, Miami Univ; Hg

Rallis, Donald N., (540) 654-1492 drallis@mwcgw.mwc.edu, Mary Washington Coll; Zn
Ramage, Joan, (610) 758-6410 jmr204@lehigh.edu, Lehigh Univ; ZrGlm
Ramagwede, Fhatuwani L., 0027128411911 info@geoscience.org.za, Geological Survey of South Africa ; EgGzEg
Raman, Sethu S., (919) 515-7144 sethu_raman@ncsu.edu, North Carolina State Univ; As
Ramanathan, V., (858) 534-0219 vramanathan@ucsd.edu, Univ of California, San Diego; As
Rambaud, Fabienne M., frambaud@austincc.edu, Austin Comm Coll District; Eg
Ramelli, Alan R., (775) 784-4151 ramelli@unr.edu, Univ of Nevada, Reno; Ng
Ramirez, Abelardo L., (925) 422-6919 ramirez3@llnl.gov, Lawrence Livermore; Ng
Ramirez, Pedro C., (323) 343-2417 pramire@calstatela.edu, California State Univ, Los Angeles; Gs
Ramirez, Wilson R., (787) 265-3845 wilson.ramirez1@upr.edu, Univ of Puerto Rico; GudOu
Ramos, Frank C., 575-646-2511 framos@nmsu.edu, New Mexico State Univ, Las Cruces; CcuGi
Rampedi, Isaac T., +27115592429 isaacr@uj.ac.za, Univ of Johannesburg; PgSdHg
Ramsey, Kelvin W., (302) 831-3586 kwramsey@udel.edu, Univ of Delaware; As
Ramsey, Michael S., (412) 624-8772 ramsey@ivis.eps.pitt.edu, Univ of Pittsburgh; Zr
Ramspott, Matthew E., 301/687-4412 meramspott@frostburg.edu, Frostburg State Univ; Zr
Ranalli, Giorgio, granalli@ccs.carleton.ca, Carleton Univ; Yg
Rancan, Helen L., 609-984-6587 helen.rancan@dep.state.nj.us, New Jersey Geological and Water Survey; Hs
Randall, David A., randall@atmos.colostate.edu, Colorado State Univ; As
Randall, George, (505) 667-9483 Los Alamos; Yg
Randall, Gyles W., (507) 835-3620 Univ of Minnesota, Twin Cities; So
Ranhofer, Melissa, (864)294-3647 melissa.ranhofer@furman.edu, Furman Univ; Gg
Rankey, Gene, (785) 864-6028 grankey@ku.edu, Univ of Kansas; GsrGu
Rankin, Robert, (780) 492-5082 rankin@phys.ualberta.ca, Univ of Alberta; Xy
Ransom, Michel D., (785) 532-7203 mdransom@ksu.edu, Kansas State Univ; SdcGm
Ranson, William A., (864) 294-3364 bill.ranson@furman.edu, Furman Univ; GxzGp
Ranville, James, (303) 273-3004 jranvill@mines.edu, Colorado Sch of Mines; Ca
Rapley, Chris, +44 020 310 86320 christopher.rapley@ucl.ac.uk, Univ Coll London; ZgrGl
Rapp, Anita, arapp@tamu.edu, Texas A&M Univ; Zr
Rapp, Richard H., rapp.1@osu.edu, Ohio State Univ; Yd
Rappe, Michael S., (808) 236-7464 rappe@hawaii.edu, Univ of Hawai'i, Manoa; Og
Rappenglueck, Bernhard, 713-743-2469 brappenglueck@uh.edu, Univ of Houston; As
Rasbury, E. Troy, 631-632-1488 troy.rasbury@sunysb.edu, Stony Brook Univ; Cc
Rashall, Jenny M., 936-468-2340 jenny.rashall@sfasu.edu, Stephen F. Austin State Univ; GgPg
Rashed, Mohamed A., 002-03-3921595 rashedmohamed@yahoo.com, Alexandria Univ; GgSo
Rasmussen, Craig, (520) 621-7223 crasmuss@cals.arizona.edu, Univ of Arizona; SzGmCl
Rasmussen, Kenneth, (703) 323-2139 krasmussen@nvcc.edu, Northern Virginia Comm Coll - Annandale; Gus
Rasmussen, Kristen L., kristenr@rams.colostate.edu, Colorado State Univ; As
Rasmussen, Pat E., (613) 868-8609 pat.rasmussen@canada.gc.ca, Univ of Ottawa; GeAsGb
Rasmussen, Steen, (505) 665-0052 steen@lanl.gov, Los Alamos; Yg
Rasmussen, Tab, (314) 935-4844 dtrasmus@wustl.edu, Washington Univ in St. Louis; Zn
Ratajeski, Kent, (859) 257-4444 kent.ratajeski@email.uky.edu, Univ of Kentucky; Gi
Ratchford, M. E., (501) 683-0118 ed.ratchford@arkansas.gov, Arkansas Geological Survey; GocEo
Rath, Carolyn, (657) 278-7096 crath@fullerton.edu, California State Univ, Fullerton; Gg
Rathburn, Anthony E., (661) 654-3281 arathburn@csub.edu, California State Univ, Bakersfield; PmOoCb
Rathburn, Sara L., (970) 491-6956 sara.rathburn@colostate.edu, Colorado State Univ; Ggm
Ratoi, Bogdan G., 0040742955966 bog21rat@gmail.com, Alexandru Ioan Cuza; PvGr
Ratschbacher, Barbara C., bratschbacher@ucdavis.edu, Univ of California, Davis; GgCg
Raub, Timothy D., +44 01334 464012 timraub@st-andrews.ac.uk, Univ of St. Andrews; YmGgPc
Rauber, Carolyn, 612-625-0317 cbishoff@umn.edu, Univ of Minnesota, Twin Cities; Zn
Rauber, Robert M., (217) 333-2835 r-rauber@illinois.edu, Univ of Illinois, Urbana-Champaign; As
Rauch, Henry W., (304) 293-2187 hrauch@wvu.edu, West Virginia Univ; HwGe
Rauch, Marta, marta.rauch@uwr.edu.pl, Univ of Wroclaw; Gc
Raudsepp, Mati, (604) 822-6396 mraudsepp@eoas.ubc.ca, Univ of British Columbia; GzeZm
Rautenbach, Victoria J., +27 (0) 12 420 3489 victoria.rautenbach@up.ac.za, Univ of Pretoria; Zif
Ravat, Dhananjay, (859) 257-4726 dhananjay.ravat@uky.edu, Univ of Kentucky; YgmYv
Ravela, Sai, 617-253-0997 ravela@mit.edu, Massachusetts Inst of Tech; Zn
Ravelo, Ana C., 831-459-3722 acr@pmc.ucsc.edu, Univ of California, Santa Cruz; OcGe
Ravelo, Christina, (831) 459-3722 acr@cats.ucsc.edu, Univ of California, Santa Cruz; Cs
Raven, Morgan, raven@geol.ucsb.edu, Univ of California, Santa Barbara; Cl
Ravi, Sujith, 215-204-7122 sravi@temple.edu, Temple Univ; HqZuRw
Ravishankara, A.R., a.r.ravishankara@colostate.edu, Colorado State Univ; AsZg
Ravizza, Gregory, 808-956-2916 gravizza@soest.hawaii.edu, Univ of Hawai'i, Manoa; Cm
Rawling, Geoffrey, 575-366-2535 geoffrey.rawling@nmt.edu, New Mexico Inst of Mining and Tech; Gg
Rawling, J. E., (608) 263-6839 elmo.rawling@wisc.edu, Univ of Wisconsin, Madison, Division of Extension; Gml
Rawlins, Michael, 413 545-0659 rawlins@geo.umass.edi, Univ of Massachusetts, Amherst; As
Rawlinson, Nick, nr441@cam.ac.uk, Univ of Cambridge; Yg
Ray, G. Carleton, (804) 924-0551 cr@virginia.edu, Univ of Virginia; Ob
Ray, Pallav, 321-674-7191 pray@fit.edu, Florida Inst of Tech; AstZo
Ray, Waverly, 6196447454 x3018 waverly.ray@gcccd.edu, Cuyamaca Coll; Gg
Rayburn, John A., 845-257-3767 rayburnj@newpaltz.edu, SUNY, New Paltz; Gml
Raymo, Maureen, raymo@ldeo.columbia.edu, Columbia Univ; Pe
Raymond, Anne, (979) 845-0644 raymond@geo.tamu.edu, Texas A&M Univ; Pb
Raymond, Carol A., (818) 354-8690 Jet Propulsion Lab; Yr
Raymond, Charles F., 206-685-9697 cfr2@uw.edu, Univ of Washington; Gl
Raymond, Jasmin, 418 654-2559 jasmin.raymond@ete.inrs.ca, Universite du Quebec; Hy
Rayne, Todd W., (315) 859-4698 trayne@hamilton.edu, Hamilton Coll; Hy
Raysoni, Amit , 956-882-8835 amit.raysoni@utrgv.edu, Univ of Texas, Rio Grande Valley; Asc
Rea, David K., (734) 936-0521 davidrea@umich.edu, Univ of Michigan; Gu
Read, Adam S., 575-366-2533 adamread@gis.nmt.edu, New Mexico Inst of Mining and Tech; Gg
Read, J. Fred, (540) 231-5124 jread@vt.edu, Virginia Polytechnic Inst & State Univ; Gs
Read, Michael T., 936-468-3701 michael.read@sfasu.edu, Stephen F. Austin State Univ; PgGg
Reader, Steven , sreader@usf.edu, Univ of South Florida; Zi
Reading, Anya, 61 3 6226 2477 anya.reading@utas.edu.au, Univ of Tasmania; Ysg
Reagan, Mark K., (319) 335-1802 mark-reagan@uiowa.edu, Univ of Iowa; Gi
Reams, Max W., (815) 939-5394 mreams@olivet.edu, Olivet Nazarene Univ; GsmPg
Reaven, Sheldon, (631) 632-8765 sheldon.reaven@stonybrook.edu, SUNY, Stony Brook; Zn
Reavy, John, +353 21 4904574 j.reavy@ucc.ie, Univ Coll Cork; GicGt
Reay, David, +44 (0) 131 650 7723 david.reay@ed.ac.uk, Edinburgh Univ; As
Reay, William G., 804-684-7119 wreay@vims.edu, William & Mary; Hg
Reber, Jacqueline, (515) 294-7513 jreber@iastate.edu, Iowa State Univ of Sci & Tech; Gct
Reboulet, Edward, 785-864-2173 reboulet@kgs.ku.edu, Univ of Kansas; Hy
Rech, Jason, 513-529-1935 rechja@miamioh.edu, Miami Univ; Gm

Oceanographic Inst; Co
Repka, James, (949) 582-4694 jrepka@saddleback.edu, Saddleback Comm Coll; GgmZe
Reshef, Moshe, 972-36406880 mosher@post.tau.ac.il, Tel Aviv Univ; Yeg
Resing, Joseph A., (206) 526-6184 resing@pmel.noaa.gov, Univ of Washington; Oc
Resnic, Victor S., 281-618-5800 rvictor@mcleodusa.net, Lonestar Coll - North Harris; Go
Resnichenko, Yuri, (598) 2525 1552 yresni@fcien.edu.uy, Univ de la Republica Oriental del Uruguay (UDELAR); ZirZn
Resor, Phillip G., 860 6853139 presor@wesleyan.edu, Wesleyan Univ; Gct
Resplandy, Laure, 609-258-4101 laurer@princeton.edu, Princeton Univ; Ob
Ressel, Mike, (775) 682-7844 mressel@unr.edu, Univ of Nevada, Reno; EgGiCc
Ressler, Daniel E., 570-372-4216 resslerd@susqu.edu, Susquehanna Univ; Sp
Restrepo, Jorge I., (561) 297-2795 restrepo@fau.edu, Florida Atlantic Univ; Hqw
Retallack, Gregory J., (541) 346-4558 gregr@uoregon.edu, Univ of Oregon; PbSoGa
Retelle, Michael J., (207) 786-6155 mretelle@bates.edu, Bates Coll; Gl
Rettig, Andrew, 937-229-2261 arettig1@udayton.edu, Univ of Dayton; Zy
Retzler, Andrew J., (612) 626-3895 aretzler@umn.edu, Univ of Minnesota; GrsPi
Reusch, David B., 575-835-5404 dreusch@ees.nmt.edu, New Mexico Inst of Mining and Tech; Zn
Reusch, Douglas N., 207-778-7463 info@reuschlaw.de, Univ of Maine, Farmington; GtCgOu
Reuss, Robert L., 617-627-3494 bert.reuss@tufts.edu, Tufts Univ; Gzi
Reuter, Gerhard, (780) 492-0358 gerhard.reuter@ualberta.ca, Univ of Alberta; Am
Revelle, Douglas O., (505) 667-1256 revelle@lanl.gov, Los Alamos; As
Revenaugh, Justin, 612-624-7553 justinr@umn.edu, Univ of Minnesota, Twin Cities; Ys
Revetta, Frank A., (315) 267-3441 revettfa@potsdam.edu, SUNY Potsdam; YgGtg
Rexius, James E., 734-462-4400 jrexius@schoolcraft.edu, Schcraft Coll; Gl
Reyes, Alfonso, reyeszca@cicese.mx, Centro de Investigación Científica y de Educación Superior de Ensenada; Ne
Reynolds, Robert W., (541) 383-7557 Central Oregon Comm Coll; Gv
Reynolds, Stephen J., (480) 965-9049 sreynolds@asu.edu, Arizona State Univ; GctZe
Rezaie-Boroon, Mohammad H., (323) 343-2406 mrezaie@calstatela.edu, California State Univ, Los Angeles; GeCg
Rhenberg, Elizabeth, (901) 678-2177 erhenbrg@memphis.edu, Univ of Memphis; Pg
Rheuban, Jennie, (508) 289-3782 jrheuban@whoi.edu, Woods Hole Oceanographic Inst; Oc
Rhines, Peter B., (206) 543-0593 rhines@atmos.washington.edu, Univ of Washington; Op
Rhoads, Bruce, brhoads@illinois.edu, Univ of Illinois, Urbana-Champaign; Gm
Rhode, David E., (775) 673-7310 dave@dri.edu, Desert Research Inst; Pe
Rhodes, Amy L., (413) 585-3947 arhodes@smith.edu, Smith Coll; ClGe
Rhodes, Dallas D., (912) 478-5361 Georgia Southern Univ; Gm
Rhodes, Edward J., (310) 825-3880 erhodes@epss.ucla.edu, Univ of California, Los Angeles; CcGma
Rhodes, Frank H. T., (607) 255-6233 Cornell Univ; Pi
Rhodes, J. Michael, (413) 545-2841 jmrhodes@geo.umass.edu, Univ of Massachusetts, Amherst; GviCa
Ribbe, Paul H., (540) 231-6880 ribbe@vt.edu, Virginia Polytechnic Inst & State Univ; Gz
Ribbons, Relena R., relena.r.ribbons@lawrence.edu, Lawrence Univ; SbGe
Ricchezza, Victor J., vricchezza@gsu.edu, Georgia State Univ, Perimeter Coll, Clarkston Campus; Ze
Rice, Chuck W., (785) 532-7217 cwrice@ksu.edu, Kansas State Univ; Sb
Rice, James R., (617) 495-3445 rice@esag.harvard.edu, Harvard Univ; Ygu
Rice, Karen C., (434) 243-3429 kcr4y@virginia.edu, Univ of Virginia; HgCg
Rice, Keith W., 715-346-4454 krice@uwsp.edu, Univ of Wisconsin, Stevens Point; Zir
Rice, Melissa S., (360) 650-3592 melissa.rice@wwu.edu, Western Washington Univ; XgGsm
Rice, Murray, 940-565-3861 murray.rice@unt.edu, Univ of North Texas; Zn
Rice, Pamela J., (612) 625-1909 price@soils.umn.edu, Univ of Minnesota, Twin Cities; So
Rice, Thomas L., (937) 766-6140 trice@cedarville.edu, Cedarville Univ; GemEo
Rice-Snow, R. Scott, 765-285-8269 ricesnow@bsu.edu, Ball State Univ; Gm
Rich, Fredrick J., (912) 478-0849 frich@georgiasouthern.edu, Georgia Southern Univ; Pl
Richard, Benjamin H., benjamin.richard@wright.edu, Wright State Univ; Ye
Richard, Ferdinand W., rf@udsm.ac.tz, Univ of Dar es Salaam; YsGt
Richard, Gigi A., 970-248-1689 grichard@coloradomesa.edu, Colorado Mesa Univ; Hsg
Richard, Robert, (310) 825-6663 rrichard@igpp.ucla.edu, Univ of California, Los Angeles; Yg
Richards, Bill, (208) 769-3477 bill_richards@nic.edu, North Idaho Coll; GgzZe
Richards, Ian J., irichard@smu.edu, Southern Methodist Univ; Cs
Richards, James H., (530) 752-0170 jhrichards@ucdavis.edu, Univ of California, Davis; So
Richards, Jeremy P., (705) 675-1151 jrichards2@laurentian.ca, Laurentian Univ, Sudbury; EmGiCg
Richards, Kelvin J., 808-956-5399 rkelvin@hawaii.edu, Univ of Hawai'i, Manoa; Op
Richards, Laura, +44 0161 306-0361 laura.richards@manchester.ac.uk, Univ of Manchester; Ge
Richards, Mark A., mark_richards@berkeley.edu, Univ of California, Berkeley; Yg
Richards, Paul G., richards@ldeo.columbia.edu, Columbia Univ; Ys
Richards-McClung, Bryony, 801-585-0599 bmcclung@egi.utah.edu, Univ of Utah; Go
Richardson, Carson A., carichardson@email.arizona.edu, Univ of Arizona; Emg
Richardson, Eliza, (814) 863-2507 eliza@psu.edu, Pennsylvania State Univ, Univ Park; YsZe
Richardson, Justin, 413-545-4840 jbrichardson@umass.edu, Univ of Massachusetts, Amherst; CbSc
Richardson, Mary J., (979) 845-7966 mrichardson@ocean.tamu.edu, Texas A&M Univ; Op
Richardson, Mary Jo, (979) 845-7966 mrichardson@ocean.tamu.edu, Texas A&M Univ; Gu
Richardson, Randall M., (520) 621-4950 rmr@email.arizona.edu, Univ of Arizona; Yg
Richardson, Steve, 021-650-2921 steve.richardson@uct.ac.za, Univ of Cape Town; Cg
Richardson, Tammi, richardson@biol.sc.edu, Univ of South Carolina; Ob
Richardson, Yvette P., yrichardson@psu.edu, Pennsylvania State Univ, Univ Park; Ams
Richaud, Mathieu, (559) 278-4557 mathieu@csufresno.edu, Fresno State Univ; GusCs
Richey, Jeffrey E., (206) 543-7339 jrichey@u.washington.edu, Univ of Washington; CbHs
Richter, Carl, (337) 482-5353 richter@louisiana.edu, Univ of Louisiana at Lafayette; Ym
Richter, Daniel D., 919-613-8031 drichter@duke.edu, Duke Univ; So
Richter, David, david.richter.26@nd.edu, Univ of Notre Dame; As
Richter, Frank M., (773) 702-8118 richter@geosci.uchicago.edu, Univ of Chicago; Gt
Ricka, Adam, +420 549 49 6605 ricka@sci.muni.cz, Masaryk Univ; Hgy
Rickaby, Ros, +44 (1865) 272034 rosalind.rickaby@earth.ox.ac.uk, Univ of Oxford; Gz
Rickard, D, rickard@cf.ac.uk, Cardiff Univ; Cg
Ricketts, Hugo, +44 0161 306-3911 h.ricketts@manchester.ac.uk, Univ of Manchester; As
Ricketts, Jason, (915) 747-5599 jricketts@utep.edu, Univ of Texas, El Paso; GctGi
Ridd, Merrill K., (801) 581-7939 merrill.ridd@geog.utah.edu, Univ of Utah; Zr
Ridenour, Gregory D., (931) 221-7454 ridenourg@apsu.edu, Austin Peay State Univ; HsOgZn
Ridge, John C., (617) 627-3494 jack.ridge@tufts.edu, Tufts Univ; GlnGg
Ridgway, Kenneth D., (765) 494-3269 ridge@purdue.edu, Purdue Univ; Gs
Ridgwell, Andy, (951) 827-3186 andy@seao2.org, Univ of California, Riverside; Zn
Riding, Robert, 865-974-2366 rriding@utk.edu, Univ of Tennessee, Knoxville; Cb
Ridky, Alice M., (207) 859-5800 amridky@colby.edu, Colby Coll; Zn
Ridley, John R., (970) 491-5943 jridley@colostate.edu, Colorado State Univ; Eg
Ridley, Moira K., (806) 834-0627 moira.ridley@ttu.edu, Texas Tech Univ; CqlZm
Riebe, Clifford S., 307-766-3965 criebe@uwyo.edu, Univ of Wyoming; ClGme
Riebesell, John, (313) 593-5132 jriebese@umich.edu, Univ of Michigan, Dearborn; Zu
Riedel, Oliver, 089/2180 4335 oliver.riedl@lrz.uni-muenchen.de,

Ludwig-Maximilians-Univ Muenchen; Gz
Riedinger, Natascha, 405-744-6358 natascha.riedinger@okstate.edu, Oklahoma State Univ; CgGu
Riegel, Hannah B., riefelhb@appstate.edu, Appalachian State Univ; Ggc
Rieger, Duayne, drieger@ccri.edu, Comm Coll of Rhode Island; Ys
Rieke, George H., (520) 621-2832 grieke@as.arizona.edu, Univ of Arizona; Zn
Riemer, Nicole, 217-244-2844 nriemer@illinois.edu, Univ of Illinois, Urbana-Champaign; As
Riemersma, Peter E., 616-331-3553 riemersp@gvsu.edu, Grand Valley State Univ; Hw
Rieppel, Olivier C., (312) 665-7630 orieppel@fieldmuseum.org, Field Mus of Natural History; Pv
Ries, Justin, 7815817370 x342 j.ries@neu.edu, Northeastern Univ; Cm
Riess, Carolyn M., (512) 468-1832 criess@austincc.edu, Austin Comm Coll District; GoeGg
Riesselman, Christina R., +64 3 479-7505 christina.riesselman@otago.ac.nz, Univ of Otago; Ou
Rietbrock, Andreas, +44-151-794-5181 a.rietbrock@liverpool.ac.uk, Univ of Liverpool; YsGv
Rietmeijer, Frans J., (505) 277-5733 fransjmr@unm.edu, Univ of New Mexico; Gp
Rigby, John, 61 7 3138 1638 j.rigby@qut.edu.au, Queensland Univ of Tech; Pb
Riggs, Eric, 9798453651 emriggs@geos.tamu.edu, Texas A&M Univ; Gy
Riggs, Nancy, (928) 523-9362 nancy.riggs@nau.edu, Northern Arizona Univ; Gv
Riggs, Stanley R., (252) 328-6015 riggss@ecu.edu, East Carolina Univ; GusGe
Rignot, Eric, (949) 824-3739 erignot@uci.edu, Univ of California, Irvine; GlOpZr
Rigo, Manuel, +390498279175 manuel.rigo@unipd.it, Univ degli Studi di Padova; Gs
Rigsby, Catherine A., (252) 328-4297 rigsbyc@ecu.edu, East Carolina Univ; Gs
Riha, Susan, (607) 255-1729 sjr4@cornell.edu, Cornell Univ; Sf
Riker-Coleman, Kristin E., 715-394-8410 krikerco@uwsuper.edu, Univ of Wisconsin, Superior; Gg
Riley, James, (520) 626-6681 jjriley@ag.arizona.edu, Univ of Arizona; Zn
Riley, Rhonda, riley@suu.edu, Southern Utah Univ; Zn
Rimmer, Susan M., (618) 453-7369 srimmer@siu.edu, Southern Illinois Univ Carbondale; EcCgGo
Rinae, Makhadi, +27 (0)51 401 9008 makhadi@ufs.ac.za, Univ of the Free State; Gge
Rindsberg, Andrew K., 205 652 3416 arindsberg@uwa.edu, Univ of West Alabama; PeGePi
Riney, Kaylin, 803.896.7931 rineyk@dnr.sc.gov, South Carolina Dept of Natural Resources; Zi
Rink, W. J., 850 229-1443 rinkwj@mcmaster.ca, McMaster Univ; CcGam
Rinterknecht, Vincent, +33 (0)1 45 07 55 81 vincent.rinterknecht@lgp.cnrs.fr, Univ of St. Andrews; CcGma
Riordan, Allen J., (919) 515-7973 al_riordan@ncsu.edu, North Carolina State Univ; As
Riordan, Jean, (907) 696-0079 jean.riordan@alaska.gov, Alaska Division of Geological & Geophysical Surveys; Gg
Rios-Sanchez, Miriam, 218-755-2563 mriossanchez@bemidjistate.edu, Bemidji State Univ; HwZrGg
Rioux, Matt, rioux@geol.ucsb.edu, Univ of California, Santa Barbara; Cc
Rippy, Megan, 703-361-5606 mrippy@vt.edu, Virginia Polytechnic Inst & State Univ; Rw
Riser, Stephen C., (206) 543-1187 riser@uw.edu, Univ of Washington; Op
Risk, Dave A., drisk@stfx.ca, Saint Francis Xavier Univ; SoZr
Risk, Michael J., riskmj@mcmaster.ca, McMaster Univ; Pg
Ristovski, Zoran, +61 7 3138 1129 z.ristovski@qut.edu.au, Queensland Univ of Tech; Asp
Ritchie, Alexander W., (843) 953-5591 ritchiea@cofc.edu, Coll of Charleston; Gc
Ritchie, Harold C., (902) 494-5192 hritchie@phys.ocean.dal.ca, Dalhousie Univ; Am
Ritsche, Michael, 630-252-1554 mtritsche@anl.gov, Argonne; As
Ritsema, Jeroen, (734) 615-6405 jritsema@umich.edu, Univ of Michigan; Ysg
Rittenour, Tammy M., (435) 213-5756 tammy.rittenour@usu.edu, Utah State Univ; GmCcGa
Ritter, Charles J., (937) 229-2953 Univ of Dayton; Ct
Ritter, Joachim R., +49-721-60844539 joachim.ritter@kit.edu, Karlsruhe Inst of Tech; YsGtv
Ritter, John B., (937) 327-7332 jritter@wittenberg.edu, Wittenberg Univ; Gm
Ritter, Leonard, (519) 824-4120 Ext.52980 lritter@uoguelph.ca, Univ of Guelph; Zn
Ritter, Paul, (309) 268-8640 paul.ritter@heartland.edu, Heartland Comm Coll; Zg
Ritter, Scott M., 801-4224239 scott_ritter@byu.edu, Brigham Young Univ; Ps
Ritterbush, Linda A., ritterbu@callutheran.edu, California Lutheran Univ; Pi
Ritts, Malinda, (208) 885-1179 mritts@uidaho.edu, Univ of Idaho; GsCg
Ritz, Richard, (402) 280-2461 richard.ritz@afwa.af.mil, Creighton Univ; Am
Ritzi, Jr., Robert W., 937 775-3455 robert.ritzi@wright.edu, Wright State Univ; Hw
Rius, Marc, +44 (0)23 8059 3275 m.rius@soton.ac.uk, Univ of Southampton; Znn
Rivard, Benoit, (780) 492-0345 benoit.rivard@ualberta.ca, Univ of Alberta; Zr
Rivera, Mark, 907-786-1235 marivera@uaa.alaska.edu, Univ of Alaska, Anchorage; Gg
Rivers, Toby C. J. S., (709) 737-8392 trivers@mun.ca, Memorial Univ of Newfoundland; Gp
Rizeli, Mustafa Eren, 00904242370000-5961 merizeli@firat.edu.tr, Firat Univ; Gxi
Rizoulis, Athanasios, +44 0161 275-0311 a.rizoulis@manchester.ac.uk, Univ of Manchester; Ge
Roach, Michael, 61 3 6226 2474 Univ of Tasmania; Yg
Robarge, Wayne P., (919) 515-1454 North Carolina State Univ; Sc
Robas, Sheryl A., 609-258-6144 srobas@princeton.edu, Princeton Univ; Zn
Robbins, Gary A., (860) 486-2448 gary.robbins@uconn.edu, Univ of Connecticut; Hw
Roberson, Randal P., (931) 221-1004 robersonr@apsu.edu, Austin Peay State Univ; Gg
Robert, Genevieve, (207) 786-6105 grobert@bates.edu, Bates Coll; CpGiz
Robert, Sanborn, (262) 335-5263 robert.sanborn@uwc.edu, Univ of Wisconsin Colls; GgZyn
Roberts, A. Lynn, (410) 516-4387 lroberts@jhu.edu, Johns Hopkins Univ; Zn
Roberts, Charles E., (561) 297-3254 croberts@fau.edu, Florida Atlantic Univ; Zri
Roberts, Eric M., +61747816947 eric.roberts@jcu.edu.au, James Cook Univ; GsPvCc
Roberts, Frank, (504) 388-2964 Montgomery County Comm Coll; Gp
Roberts, Gerald, +44 020 3073 8033 gerald.roberts@ucl.ac.uk, Birkbeck Coll; Gct
Roberts, Harry H., (225) 388-2964 harry@antares.esl.lsu.edu, Louisiana State Univ; Gs
Roberts, Jennifer A., (785) 864-4997 jenrob@ku.edu, Univ of Kansas; Cbl
Roberts, Mark L., (508) 289-3654 mroberts@whoi.edu, Woods Hole Oceanographic Inst; Yg
Roberts, Paul H., (310) 206-2707 roberts@math.ucla.edu, Univ of California, Los Angeles; Ym
Roberts, Peter, (505) 667-1199 proberts@lanl.gov, Los Alamos; Ys
Roberts, Ray L., 817295-7392 rroberts@hillcollege.edu, Hill Coll; Ge
Roberts, Sarah K., (925) 423-4112 roberts28@llnl.gov, Lawrence Livermore; Cl
Roberts, Sheila M., (406) 683-7017 sheila.roberts@umwestern.edu, Univ of Montana Western; GeSo
Roberts, Stephen, +44 ()023 80593246 steve.roberts@noc.soton.ac.uk, Univ of Southampton; Cg
Roberts-Semple, Dawn, 718-262-2775 drobertssemple@york.cuny.edu, York Coll (CUNY); Gem
Robertson, Alastair H., +44 (0) 131 650 8546 alastair.robertson@ed.ac.uk, Edinburgh Univ; GtgGs
Robertson, Andrew W., 845-680-4491 awr@iri.columbia.edu, Columbia Univ; As
Robertson, Daniel E., 585-292-2422 drobertson@monroecc.edu, Monroe Comm Coll; Eg
Robertson, James M., (608) 263-7384 jmrober1@facstaff.wisc.edu, Univ of Wisconsin, Madison; Eg
Robertson, Wendy, 989-774-7517 wendy.robertson@cmich.edu, Central Michigan Univ; HwCg
Robin, Pierre-Yves F., 905 828-5419 Univ of Toronto; Gc
Robinson, Alexander, 713-743-2547 acrobinson@uh.edu, Univ of Houston; Gc
Robinson, Bruce A., (505) 667-1910 robinson@lanl.gov, Los Alamos; Zn
Robinson, Carol, +44 (0)1603 59 3174 carol.robinson@uea.ac.uk, Univ of East Anglia; Ob
Robinson, Clare, +44 0161 275-3296 a.rizoulis@manchester.ac.uk, Univ of Manchester; Co
Robinson, Cordula, cordula@crsa.bu.edu, Boston Univ; Gm
Robinson, David, +44 (0)1908 653493 x 53493 david.robinson@open.ac.uk, Open Univ; Zn
Robinson, Delores, dmr@ua.edu, Univ of Alabama; Gc

Robinson, Edward, (305) 348-3572 draper@fiu.edu, Florida International Univ; Pm
Robinson, George W., grobinson@stlawu.edu, St. Lawrence Univ; Gz
Robinson, Judith, 973-353-1976 judy.robinson@rutgers.edu, Rutgers, The State Univ of New Jersey, Newark; Yg
Robinson, Kevin, (619) 594-1386 rockrobinson@gmail.com, San Diego State Univ; Gc
Robinson, Leonie, +44 0151 795 4387 leonie.robinson@liverpool.ac.uk, Univ of Liverpool; Ob
Robinson, Lori, (612) 626-7429 robin126@umn.edu, Univ of Minnesota; Zi
Robinson, Mark, (480) 727-9691 mark.s.robinson@asu.edu, Arizona State Univ; Xg
Robinson, Michael, (912) 598-3310 mike.robinson@skio.usg.edu, Georgia Southern Univ; ZiOn
Robinson, Paul D., (618) 453-7373 robinson@geo.siu.edu, Southern Illinois Univ Carbondale; Gz
Robinson, Peter, (303) 492-5108 peter.robinson@colorado.edu, Univ of Colorado; Pv
Robinson, R. Craig, (860) 832-2950 Central Connecticut State Univ; Xy
Robinson, Ruth, +44 01334 463996 rajr@st-andrews.ac.uk, Univ of St. Andrews; Gs
Robinson, Sarah, (719) 333-9287 sarah.robinson@usafa.edu, United States Air Force Academy; GgZi
Robinson, Steve, j.s.robinson@reading.ac.uk, Univ of Reading; Sf
Robinson, Stuart, +44 (1865) 272058 stuartr@earth.ox.ac.uk, Univ of Oxford; PeGr
Robinson, Walter, 919-515-7002 walter_robinson@ncsu.edu, North Carolina State Univ; As
Robinson, William, william.robinson@umb.edu, Univ of Massachusetts, Boston; Zn
Robison, Richard A., rrobisn@ku.edu, Univ of Kansas; PiGr
Rocha, Cesar, 860-405-9153 cesar.rocha@uconn.edu, Univ of Connecticut; Op
Rocha, Fernando, tavares.rocha@ua.pt, Unive de Aveiro; EnGzb
Rocha, Guillermo, 7189515000 x2887 grocha@brooklyn.cuny.edu, Brooklyn Coll (CUNY); GgeCg
Roche, Didier, +31 20 59 83077 didier.roche@vu.nl, Vrije Universiteit Amsterdam; AsZn
Roche, James E., (225) 388-2707 jroche@geol.lsu.edu, Louisiana State Univ; Gg
Roche, Steven L., 918-631-3307 sroche@utulsa.edu, Univ of Tulsa; YesYg
Rocheford, MaryKathryn (Kat), 906-635-2140 mrocheford@lssu.edu, Lake Superior State Univ; GeZiGa
Rochester, Michael G., (709) 737-7565 mrochest@mun.ca, Memorial Univ of Newfoundland; Yg
Rochette, Scott M., (585) 395-2603 srochett@brockport.edu, SUNY, The Coll at Brockport; Am
Rocholl, Alexander, 089/2180 4293 rocholl@min.uni-muenchen.de, Ludwig-Maximilians-Univ Muenchen; Gz
Rock, Jessie L., 701-231-7951 jessie.rock@ndsu.edu, North Dakota State Univ; ZgPcg
Rockaway, John D., (859) 572-5412 rockawayj@nku.edu, Northern Kentucky Univ; Ng
Rockwell, Thomas K., (619) 594-4441 trockwell@mail.sdsu.edu, San Diego State Univ; Gm
Rockwood, Anthony A., (303) 556-8399 Metropolitan State Coll of Denver; Am
Rodbell, Donald T., (518) 388-6034 rodbelld@union.edu, Union Coll; GlmGe
Roden, Eric E., (608) 260-0724 eroden@geology.wisc.edu, Univ of Wisconsin, Madison; PgSbCl
Roden, Gunnar I., (206) 543-5627 giroden@u.washington.edu, Univ of Washington; Op
Roden, Michael F., (706) 542-2416 mroden@uga.edu, Univ of Georgia; Gi
Rodgers, David W., rodgdavi@isu.edu, Idaho State Univ; Gct
Rodgers, Jim, (307) 766-2286 Ext. 255 james.rodgers@wyo.gov, Wyoming State Geological Survey; Gg
Rodgers, John C., (662) 325-0732 jcr100@msstate.edu, Mississippi State Univ; Zy
Rodgers, Mel, melrodgers@usf.edu, Univ of South Florida; Gv
Rodgers, N, rodgersn@cf.ac.uk, Cardiff Univ; Am
Rodgers, Nick, +44(0)29 208 79064 rodgersn@cardiff.ac.uk, Univ of Wales; Xm
Rodland, David L., (740) 826-8425 drodland@muskingum.edu, Muskingum Univ; PieGr
Rodolfo, Kelvin S., krodolfo@uic.edu, Univ of Illinois at Chicago; GueGs
Rodrigues, Cyril G., 519-253-3000 ext. 2499 cgr@uwindsor.ca, Univ of Windsor; Pm
Rodrigues, Jorge, 530-341-4355 jmrodrigues@ucdavis.edu, Univ of California, Davis; SbPo
Rodriguez, Lizzette A., (787) 265-3845 lizzette.rodriguez1@upr.edu, Univ of Puerto Rico; GviZr
Rodríguez, Marta, martarm@ucm.es, Univ Complutense de Madrid; Ggs
Rodríguez, Martín Jesús, martinjr@ucm.es, Univ Complutense de Madrid; Ng
Rodríguez, Sergio, sergrodr@ucm.es, Univ Complutense de Madrid; PgGg
Rodriguez, Vanessa del S., (787) 722-2526 Puerto Rico Bureau of Geology; Zn
Rodriguez-Blanco, Juan Diego, +353 1 8961691 j.d.rodriguez-blanco@tcd.ie, Trinity Coll; GzClZm
Roe, Carol, 757-221-2440 crroex@wm.edu, William & Mary; Zn
Roe, Gerard H., (206) 543-4980 gerard@ess.washington.edu, Univ of Washington; As
Roecker, Steven W., (518) 276-6773 roecks@rpi.edu, Rensselaer Polytechnic Inst; Yg
Roegiers, Jean-Claude, (405) 255-5459 jroegiers@ou.edu, Univ of Oklahoma; Nr
Roelofse, Frederick, +27 (0)51 401 9001 roelofsef@ufs.ac.za, Univ of the Free State; Gip
Roemer, Elizabeth, (520) 621-2897 eroemer@pirlmail.lpl.arizona.edu, Univ of Arizona; Zn
Roemmele, Christopher, (610) 436-2108 croemmele@wcupa.edu, West Chester Univ; ZeGgZg
Roemmich, Dean H., (858) 534-2307 droemmich@ucsd.edu, Univ of California, San Diego; Op
Roering, Joshua J., (541) 346-5574 jroering@uoregon.edu, Univ of Oregon; Gm
Roeske, Sarah M., (530) 752-4933 smroeske@ucdavis.edu, Univ of California, Davis; GtcGp
Roesler, Collin, 207-725-3842 croesler@bowdoin.edu, Bowdoin Coll; OgpZr
Roethel, Frank J., (631) 632-8732 frank.roethel@stonybrook.edu, SUNY, Stony Brook; Oc
Rogers, A. D., 631-632-1509 deanne.rogers@stonybrook.edu, Stony Brook Univ; XgZr
Rogers, Garry C., (250) 363-6450 Univ of Victoria; Ys
Rogers, Jefferson S., (731) 881-7442 jrogers@utm.edu, Univ of Tennessee, Martin; Zn
Rogers, Jeffrey C., (614) 292-0148 rogers.21@osu.edu, Ohio State Univ; As
Rogers, Joe D., 806-651-2570 West Texas A&M Univ; Ga
Rogers, Karyn L., (518) 276-2372 rogerk5@rpi.edu, Rensselaer Polytechnic Inst; PgCl
Rogers, Pamela Z., (505) 667-1765 Los Alamos; Cl
Rogers, Raymond R., (651) 696-6434 rogers@macalester.edu, Macalester Coll; GsrPv
Rogers, Robert D., (209) 667-3466 rrogers1@csustan.edu, California State Univ, Stanislaus; GcmGt
Rogers, Steven L., (+44) 01782 733752 s.l.rogers@keele.ac.uk, Keele Univ; PgGs
Rogers, William J., 806-651-2581 West Texas A&M Univ; Zn
Rogerson, Robert J., (403) 329-5117 rogerson@uleth.ca, Univ of Lethbridge; Gm
Roggenthen, William M., (605) 394-2461 william.roggenthen@sdsmt.edu, South Dakota Sch of Mines & Tech; NgYg
Rogova, Galina L., (716)645-3489 rogova@buffalo.edu, SUNY, Buffalo; Gq
Rogowski, Andrew S., (814) 863-8758 asr@psu.edu, Pennsylvania State Univ, Univ Park; Sp
Rohay, Alan C., (509) 376-6925 alan.rohay@pnl.gov, Pacific Northwest; Ys
Rohbaugh, Robert, (915) 831-7144 rrohrba1@epcc.edu, El Paso Comm Coll; Ggt
Rohe, Randall, randall.rohe@uwc.edu, Univ of Wisconsin Colls; ZyGgZn
Rohr, David M., (432) 837-8167 drohr@sulross.edu, Sul Ross State Univ; PiGd
Rohrssen, Megan, rohrs1m@cmich.edu, Central Michigan Univ; Co
Rohs, C. Renee, (660) 562-1201 rrohs@nwmissouri.edu, Northwest Missouri State Univ; Cg
Roinstad, Lori L., 605-677-6154 lori.roinstad@usd.edu, South Dakota Dept of Environment and Natural Resources; Zn
Rokop, Donald J., (505) 667-4299 Los Alamos; Cc
Rolfo, Franco, franco.rolfo@unito.it, Univ di Torino; Gx
Rollins, Kyle, (573) 368-2171 kyle.rollins@dnr.mo.gov, Missouri Dept of Natural Resources; ZyGg
Rollinson, Hugh, +44 01332 591786 h.rollinson@derby.ac.uk, Univ of Derby; Cg
Rollinson, Paul A., paulrollinson@missouristate.edu, Missouri State Univ; Zn
Rolston, Dennis E., (916) 752-2113 Univ of California, Davis; So
Roman, Aubrecht, aubrecht@fns.uniba.sk, Comenius Univ in Bratislava; Gdr
Roman, Charles T., (401) 874-6885 croman@gso.uri.edu, Univ of Rhode Island; Ob

Roman, Diana C., 202-478-8834 droman@carnegiescience.edu, Carnegie Inst for Sci; Gv
Roman, Eric W., (609) 984-6587 eric.roman@dep.state.nj.us, New Jersey Geological and Water Survey; Hw
Romanak, Katherine D., (512) 471-6136 katherine.romanak@beg.utexas.edu, Univ of Texas at Austin, Jackson Sch of Geosciences; CgScGe
Romaniello, Stephen J., 865-974-8347 sromanie@utk.edu, Univ of Tennessee, Knoxville; Cg
Romanovsky, Vladimir, (907) 474-7459 ffver@uaf.edu, Univ of Alaska, Fairbanks; Yg
Romanowicz, Barbara A., 510-643-5690 barbara@seismo.berkeley.edu, Univ of California, Berkeley; Ys
Romanowicz, Edwin A., (518) 564-2152 romanoea@plattsburgh.edu, SUNY, Plattsburgh; HwGcYu
Romans, Brian W., 540-231-2234 romans@vt.edu, Virginia Polytechnic Inst & State Univ; GsrEo
Romberger, Samuel B., sromberg@mines.edu, Colorado Sch of Mines; Em
Romeo, Ignacio, iromerobr@ucm.es, Univ Complutense de Madrid; GcXg
Romero, Leonel, 860-405-9153 leonel.romero@uconn.edu, Univ of Connecticut; Op
Romo, Jose M., jromo@cicese.mx, Centro de Investigación Científica y de Educación Superior de Ensenada; Ye
Ronayne, Michael J., (970) 491-0666 michael.ronayne@colostate.edu, Colorado State Univ; Hwq
Ronck, Catherine, (254) 968-1862 ronck@tarleton.edu, Tarleton State Univ; God
Rood, Richard B., (734) 647-3530 rbrood@umich.edu, Univ of Michigan; ZcAsm
Rooney, Alan, 203-432-3761 alan.rooney@yale.edu, Yale Univ; Cc
Rooney, Neil, (519) 824-4120 Ext.52573 nrooney@uoguelph.ca, Univ of Guelph; Zn
Rooney, Tyrone, 517-432-5522 rooneyt@msu.edu, Michigan State Univ; Gi
Rooney-Varga, Juliette, (978) 934-4715 juliette_rooneyvarga@uml.edu, Univ of Massachusetts, Lowell; ZcRc
Root, Tara L., 561 297-3253 troot@fau.edu, Florida Atlantic Univ; Hg
Roozeboom, Kraig, (785) 532-3781 kraig@ksu.edu, Kansas State Univ; So
Rosa, Lynn C., lrosa@wtamu.edu, West Texas A&M Univ; Zge
Rosario, Jose, jose.rosario@csueastbay.edu, California State Univ, East Bay; PsSaGr
Rose, Arthur W., (814) 238-2838 awr1@psu.edu, Pennsylvania State Univ, Univ Park; Cge
Rose, Candace M., (630) 252-3499 cmrose@anl.gov, Argonne; Zn
Rose, Caroline, (608) 263-5495 caroline.rose@wisc.edu, Univ of Wisconsin, Madison, Division of Extension; Zi
Rose, Catherine V., +353 1 8961165 crose@tcd.ie, Trinity Coll; Cg
Rose, Dan, +353 21 4902189 Univ Coll Cork; Zn
Rose, Leanna S., (678) 839-4067 srose@westga.edu, Univ of West Georgia; ZyAsm
Rose, Peter E., (801) 585-7785 prose@egi.utah.edu, Univ of Utah; Np
Rose, Seth E., 404413-5750 geoser@langate.gsu.edu, Georgia State Univ; Hw
Rose, Timothy, (202) 633-1398 roset@si.edu, Smithsonian Inst / Nat Mus of Natural History; CaGv
Rose, William I., (906) 487-2367 raman@mtu.edu, Michigan Technological Univ; Gv
Roselle, Gregory T., (208) 496-7683 roselleg@byui.edu, Brigham Young Univ - Idaho; GpCaHg
Rosen, Carl J., (612) 625-8114 crosen@umn.edu, Univ of Minnesota, Twin Cities; Sc
Rosen, Michael R., 775.887.7683 mrosen@usgs.gov, Univ of Nevada, Reno; GnClHg
Rosen, Peter S., p.rosen@neu.edu, Northeastern Univ; OnZu
Rosenberg, Gary, 215.299.1033 gr347@drexel.edu, Drexel Univ; Pi
Rosenberg, Philip E., (509) 335-4368 rosenberg@wsu.edu, Washington State Univ; GzCg
Rosengaus, Rebeca, (617) 373-7032 r.rosengaus@neu.edu, Northeastern Univ; Zn
Rosenthal, Yair, 848-932-6555X227 rosentha@marine.rutgers.edu, Rutgers, The State Univ of New Jersey; CmlOc
Ross, Andrew, +44(0) 113 34 37590 a.n.ross@leeds.ac.uk, Univ of Leeds; Am
Ross, David A., (508) 289-2578 dross@whoi.edu, Woods Hole Oceanographic Inst; GuOg
Ross, Jake, 575-835-5081 jake.ross@nmt.edu, New Mexico Inst of Mining and Tech; Cc
Ross, Kirstin, kirstin.ross@flinders.edu.au, Flinders Univ; Zn
Ross, Martin E., (617) 373-3263 m.ross@neu.edu, Northeastern Univ; Gie
Ross, Nancy L., (540) 231-6356 nross@vt.edu, Virginia Polytechnic Inst & State Univ; Gz
Ross, Pierre-Simon, pierre-simon.ross@ete.inrs.ca, Universite du Quebec; GvEg
Ross, Robert M., (607) 273-6623 x18 rmr16@cornell.edu, Paleontological Research Inst; PgZePc
Ross, Tetjana, (902) 494-1327 tetjana.ross@dal.ca, Dalhousie Univ; Op
Ross, Thomas E., (910) 521-6218 tom.ross@uncp.edu, Univ of North Carolina, Pembroke; Zy
Rossbach, Thomas, trossbac@iupui.edu, Indiana Univ - Purdue Univ Indianapolis; GgPg
Rossby, Hans T., (401) 874-6521 trossby@gso.uri.edu, Univ of Rhode Island; Op
Rosscoe, Steven, (325) 670-1387 srosscoe@hsutx.edu, Hardin-Simmons Univ; PmGsPs
Rossell, Irene M., (828) 232-5185 irossell@unca.edu, Univ of North Carolina, Asheville; Zn
Rossi, Carlos, crossi@ucm.es, Univ Complutense de Madrid; GdEo
Rossman, George R., (626) 395-6471 grr@gps.caltech.edu, California Inst of Tech; GzCa
Rost, Sebastian, +44(0) 113 34 35212 s.rost@leeds.ac.uk, Univ of Leeds; Ysg
Rostam-Abadi, Massoud, 217-244-4977 massoud@isgs.uiuc.edu, Illinois State Geological Survey; Zn
Rostoker, Gordon, (780) 492-5286 rostoker@space.ualberta.ca, Univ of Alberta; Xy
Rostron, Ben, (780) 492-2178 ben.rostron@ualberta.ca, Univ of Alberta; Zn
Rostron, Benjamin J., (780) 492-2178 ben.rostron@ualberta.ca, Univ of Alberta; HwGoCg
Roth, Danica, 303-273-3802 droth@mines.edu, Colorado Sch of Mines; GmYs
Roth, Gregory W., (814) 863-1018 gwr@psu.edu, Pennsylvania State Univ, Univ Park; So
Roth, Leonard T., troth@hccfl.edu, Hillsborough Comm Coll; Zg
Rothman, Daniel H., (617) 253-7861 dhr@mit.edu, Massachusetts Inst of Tech; Yg
Rothrock, David A., (206) 545-2262 rothrock@apl.washington.edu, Univ of Washington; Op
Rothstein, Lewis, (401) 874-6517 lrothstein@gso.uri.edu, Univ of Rhode Island; Op
Rotz, Rachel, 239-745-4684 rrotz@fgcu.edu, Florida Gulf Coast Univ; HwGg
Rouff, Ashaki, 718-997-3073 ashaki.rouff@qc.cuny.edu, Queens Coll (CUNY); Cac
Roughgarden, Joan, (650) 723-3648 Stanford Univ; Ob
Rougvie, James R., (608) 363-2268 rougviej@beloit.edu, Beloit Coll; GxpGz
Rouhani, Farhang, (540) 654-1895 frouhani@mwc.edu, Mary Washington Coll; Zn
Rouleau, Alain, 4185455011x5213 arouleau@uqac.ca, Universite du Quebec a Chicoutimi; Hw
Rounds, Steven W., (916) 278-7828 rounds@csus.edu, Sacramento State Univ; Gg
Rounsevell, Mark D., +44 (0) 131 651 4468 mark.rounsevell@ed.ac.uk, Edinburgh Univ; Zu
Rouse, Gregory W., (858) 534-7943 grouse@ucsd.edu, Univ of California, San Diego; Ob
Rouse, Jesse, 910-521-6387 jesse.rouse@uncp.edu, Univ of North Carolina, Pembroke; Zni
Rouse, Roland C., (734) 763-0952 rouserc@umich.edu, Univ of Michigan; Gz
Rouse, Jr., Lawrence J., (225) 388-2953 Louisiana State Univ; Op
Rousell, Don H., 7056751151 x2265 drousell@laurentian.ca, Laurentian Univ, Sudbury; Gc
Roushar, Kathy, 608/265.4683 kathy.roushar@wisc.edu, Univ of Wisconsin, Madison, Division of Extension; Zi
Roussel-Dupre, R., (505) 667-9228 rroussel-dupre@lanl.gov, Los Alamos; Zn
Roussenov, Vassil M., +44 0151 794 4099 v.roussenov@liverpool.ac.uk, Univ of Liverpool; OpZo
Rovey, Charles W., (417) 836-6890 charlesrovey@missouristate.edu, Missouri State Univ; HyGle
Rowan, Christopher J., 330-672-7428 crowan5@kent.edu, Kent State Univ; Gt
Rowden, Robert, robert.rowden@dnr.iowa.gov, Iowa Dept of Natural Resources; Gg
Rowe, Charlotte A., 505-665-6404 char@lanl.gov, New Mexico Inst of Mining and Tech; Ys
Rowe, Christie, 514-398-2769 christie.rowe@mcgill.ca, McGill Univ; GctEm
Rowe, Clinton M., (402) 472-1946 crowe1@unl.edu, Univ of Nebraska, Lincoln; As
Rowe, Gilbert T., (409) 740-4458 roweg@tamug.edu, Texas A&M Univ; Ob

FACULTY INDEX – R

Rowe, Timothy B., (512) 471-1725 rowe@mail.utexas.edu, Univ of Texas, Austin; Pv
Rowell, Albert J., (785) 864-2747 arowell@ku.edu, Univ of Kansas; Pi
Rowland, Scott K., (808) 956-3150 Univ of Hawai'i, Manoa; Zn
Rowland, Stephen, (702) 895-3625 steve.rowland@unlv.edu, Univ of Nevada, Las Vegas; Pi
Rowley, David B., (773) 702-8146 rowley@geosci.uchicago.edu, Univ of Chicago; GtgGc
Rowley, Rex J., 309-438-7832 rjrowle@ilstu.edu, Illinois State Univ; Zi
Roy, Denis W., (418) 545-5011 dwroy@uqac.ca, Universite du Quebec a Chicoutimi; Gc
Roy, Martin, 514-987-3000 #7619 roy.matin@uqam.ca, Universite du Quebec a Montreal; Gl
Roy, Suzanne, (418) 723-1986 x1748 suzanne_roy@uqar.ca, Universite du Quebec a Rimouski; Ob
Roychoudhury, Alakendra N., +27 21 808 3124 roy@sun.ac.za, Stellenbosch Univ; ClmOc
Royden, Leigh H., (617) 253-1292 lhroyden@mit.edu, Massachusetts Inst of Tech; Gt
Royer, Dana, (860) 685-2836 droyer@wesleyan.edu, Wesleyan Univ; PegPb
Royer, Todd, 812-855-0563 Indiana Univ, Bloomington; HsZg
Rozmus, Wojciech, (780) 492-8486 rozmus@phys.ualberta.ca, Univ of Alberta; Zn
Ruark, Matthew D., (608) 263-2889 mdruark@wisc.edu, Univ of Wisconsin, Madison; So
Rubin, Alan E., (310) 825-3202 rubin@igpp.ucla.edu, Univ of California, Los Angeles; Xm
Rubin, Allan M., 609-258-1506 arubin@princeton.edu, Princeton Univ; Yg
Rubin, Charles M., (509) 963-2827 rbeling@wvu.edu, Central Washington Univ; Gt
Rubin, Kenneth H., (808) 956-8973 krubin@hawaii.edu, Univ of Hawai'i, Manoa; CcGvCg
Rubio-Sierra, Javier, 089/2180 4317 rubio@lrz.uni-muenchen.de, Ludwig-Maximilians-Univ Muenchen; Gz
Rucklidge, John C., (416) 978-2061 jcr@quartz.geology.utoronto.ca, Univ of Toronto; Ge
Rucks, Melinda, 609-258-4101 mrucks@princeton.edu, Princeton Univ; Gy
Ruddick, Barry R., (902) 494-2505 barry.ruddick@dal.ca, Dalhousie Univ; Op
Ruddiman, William F., 540-348-1963 wfr5c@virginia.edu, Univ of Virginia; Gu
Rudge, John, +44 (0) 1223 765545 jfr23@cam.ac.uk, Univ of Cambridge; YgGt
Rudnick, Daniel L., (858) 534-7669 drudnick@ucsd.edu, Univ of California, San Diego; Op
Rudnick, Roberta L., rudnick@ucsb.edu, Univ of Maryland; CgsCt
Rudnicki, Ryan E., rrudnicki@alamo.edu, Alamo Colls, San Antonio Coll; Zy
Rudolph, Maxwell L., (530) 752-3669 maxrudolph@ucdavis.edu, Univ of California, Davis; Yg
Rueger, Bruce F., (207) 859-5806 bfrueger@colby.edu, Colby Coll; PlGg
Ruehr, Thomas A., (805) 756-2552 truehr@calpoly.edu, California Polytechnic State Univ; Sb
Ruff, Larry J., (734) 763-9301 ruff@umich.edu, Univ of Michigan; Ys
Ruff, Steven, (480) 965-6089 steve.ruff@asu.edu, Arizona State Univ; Xg
Ruffel, Alice, (214) 507-9014 aruffel@dcccd.edu, El Centro Coll - Dallas Comm Coll District; Gg
Ruffman, Alan, (902) 422-6482 Dalhousie Univ; Ys
Ruggiero, Peter, (541) 737-1239 ruggierp@science.oregonstate.edu, Oregon State Univ; On
Ruhl, Christine J., 918-631-3018 cruhl@utulsa.edu, Univ of Tulsa; YsGtc
Ruhl, Laura S., 501-683-4197 lsruhl@ualr.edu, Univ of Arkansas at Little Rock; GeClGb
Ruina, Andy L., 607-255-7108 alr3@cornell.edu, Cornell Univ; Yx
Ruiz, Javier , jaruiz@ucm.es, Univ Complutense de Madrid; Xg
Ruiz, Joaquin, (520) 621-4090 jruiz@email.arizona.edu, Univ of Arizona; CgcEz
Ruiz Cubillo, Paulo, paulo.ruizcubillo@ucr.ac.cr, Univ de Costa Rica; GvmRn
Ruiz-Diaz, Dorivar, (785) 532-6183 ruizdiaz@ksu.edu, Kansas State Univ; So
Rumble, III, Douglas, 202-478-8990 drumble@carnegiescience.edu, Carnegie Inst for Sci; Gp
Rumrill, Julie, 203-392-5842 rumrillj1@southernct.edu, Southern Connecticut State Univ; GgeGl
Rumstay, Kenneth S., (229) 333-5754 krumstay@valdosta.edu, Valdosta State Univ; Znn
Rundberg, Robert S., (505) 667-4559 Los Alamos; Gq
Rundle, John, jbrundle@ucdavis.edu, Univ of California, Davis; Yd
Rundquist, Bradley C., (701) 777-4246 bradley.rundquist@und.edu, Univ of North Dakota; ZriZy
Rundquist, Donald C., (402) 472-3471 drundquist@unl.edu, Unversity of Nebraska, Lincoln; Zri
Runkel, Anthony, (612) 626-1822 runke001@umn.edu, Univ of Minnesota; Gs
Runnegar, Bruce, (310) 206-1738 Univ of California, Los Angeles; Pg
Runyon, Cassandra R., (843) 953-8279 runyonc@cofc.edu, Coll of Charleston; XgSoZe
Runyon, Simone, srunyon@uwyo.edu, Univ of Wyoming; EdGip
Rupert, Denise, (570) 484-2048 drupert@lockhaven.edu, Lock Haven Univ; Zn
Rupp, David, 541-737-5222 drupp@coas.oregonstate.edu, Oregon State Univ; AsOp
Rupp, John A., (812) 855-1323 rupp@indiana.edu, Indiana Univ; Go
Ruppel, Stephen C., 512-471-2965 stephen.ruppel@beg.utexas.edu, Univ of Texas, Austin; GsrGo
Ruppert, Kelly R., (657) 278-3561 kruppert@fullerton.edu, California State Univ, Fullerton; Gg
Ruprecht, Philipp P., 775-682-6084 pruprecht@unr.edu, Univ of Nevada, Reno; Giv
Rusmore, Margaret E., 323 259 2565 rusmore@oxy.edu, Occidental Coll; Gc
Russ, Jean M., (301) 934-7814 jruss@csmd.edu, Coll of Southern Maryland; Zey
Russell, Ann D., (530) 752-3311 adrussell@ucdavis.edu, Univ of California, Davis; Cm
Russell, Armistead G., (404) 894-3079 ted.russell@ce.gatech.edu, Georgia Inst of Tech; As
Russell, Christopher T., (310) 825-3188 ctrussell@igpp.ucla.edu, Univ of California, Los Angeles; Xy
Russell, Dale A., (919) 515-1339 dale_russell@ncsu.edu, North Carolina State Univ; Pv
Russell, James K., (604) 822-2703 krussell@eos.ubc.ca, Univ of British Columbia; GviCg
Russell, Joellen, 520-626-2194 jrussell@email.arizona.edu, Univ of Arizona; Oc
Russell, Lynn M., (858) 534-4852 lmrussell@ucsd.edu, Univ of California, San Diego; As
Russell, R. Doncaster, (604) 822-2551 drussell@eos.ubc.ca, Univ of British Columbia; Yg
Russell, Ron, (512) 471-8831 ron.russell@beg.utexas.edu, Univ of Texas at Austin, Jackson Sch of Geosciences; Zn
Russell, Sally, +44(0) 113 34 35279 s.russell@leeds.ac.uk, Univ of Leeds; Ge
Russell, Terry P., (250) 721-6184 trussell@uvic.ca, Univ of Victoria; Zn
Russell, Theresa J., (501) 575-4403 trussell@comp.uark.edu, Univ of Arkansas, Fayetteville; Zn
Russelle, Michael P., (612) 625-8145 russelle@soils.umn.edu, Univ of Minnesota, Twin Cities; Sc
Russo, Mary Rose, 609 258-4101 mrusso@princeton.edu, Princeton Univ; Zn
Russo, Raymond, 352-392-6766 rrusso@ufl.edu, Univ of Florida; Yg
Russo, Tess A., 814-865-7389 russo@psu.edu, Pennsylvania State Univ, Univ Park; Hw
Rust, Derek, +44 023 92 842298 derek.rust@port.ac.uk, Univ of Portsmouth; Gt
Rustad, James R., jrrustad@ucdavis.edu, Univ of California, Davis; Cl
Rutberg, Randye, 212-772-5326 randye.rutberg@hunter.cuny.edu, Graduate Sch of the City Univ of New York; Gg
Rutford, Robert H., (972) 883-6470 rutford@utdallas.edu, Univ of Texas, Dallas; Gl
Rutherford, Malcolm J., (401) 863-1927 malcolm_rutherford@brown.edu, Brown Univ; Cp
Rutledge, Steven A., rutledge@atmos.colostate.edu, Colorado State Univ; As
Ruttan, Lore, 404 7274217 lruttan@emory.edu, Emory Univ; Ob
Ruttenberg, Kathleen, 808-956-9371 kcr@soest.hawaii.edu, Univ of Hawai'i, Manoa; Cg
Rutter, Ernest H., +44 0161 275-3945 e.rutter@manchester.ac.uk, Univ of Manchester; NrGct
Rutter, Nathaniel W., (780) 492-3085 nat.rutter@ualberta.ca, Univ of Alberta; Ge
Ruzicka, Alexander (Alex) M., (503) 725-3372 ruzickaa@pdx.edu, Portland State Univ; Xm
Ruzicka, Jaromir, jaromirr@hawaii.edu, Univ of Hawai'i, Manoa; Zn
Ryall, Patrick J., (902) 494-3465 pryall@is.dal.ca, Dalhousie Univ; Yg
Ryan, Anne-Marie, 902 494 3184 amryan@dal.ca, Dalhousie Univ; GeZeCg
Ryan, Cathy, (403) 220-2793 ryan@geo.ucalgary.ca, Univ of Calgary; Hw
Ryan, Jeffrey G., ryan@usf.edu, Univ of South Florida; Ct

S

Univ; Zn
Scarselli, Nicola, +44 1784 443597 nicola.scarselli@rhul.ac.uk, Royal Holloway Univ of London; Go
Schaaf, Crystal, crystal.schaaf@umb.edu, Univ of Massachusetts, Boston; ZrAm
Schaal, Barbara, (314) 935-6822 schaal@wustl.edu, Washington Univ in St. Louis; Zn
Schaap, Marcel, (520) 626-4532 mschapp@cals.arizona.edu, Univ of Arizona; So
Schacht, Ulrike, ulrike.schacht@adelaide.edu.au, Univ of Adelaide; Gd
Schade, Gunnar, (979) 845-7671 schade@ariel.met.tamu.edu, Texas A&M Univ; As
Schaef, Herbert T., (509) 373-9949 todd.schaef@pnl.gov, Pacific Northwest; Cg
Schaefer, Janet R. G., (907) 451-5005 janet.schaefer@alaska.gov, Alaska Division of Geological & Geophysical Surveys; Gv
Schaefer, Joerg, 845-365-8703 schaefer@ldeo.columbia.edu, Columbia Univ; Cg
Schafer, Carl M., (586) 286-2154 schaferc@macomb.edu, Macomb Comm Coll, Center Campus; Gg
Schafer, Tom, 785-628-5969 tschafer@fhsu.edu, Fort Hays State Univ; ZyiRn
Schaff, David, dschaff@ldeo.columbia.edu, Columbia Univ; Ys
Schaffer, Linda J., schafm4@aol.com, SUNY, The Coll at Brockport; Ze
Schaffrin, Burkhard A., 614 292-0502 schaffrin.1@osu.edu, Ohio State Univ; Yd
Schaller, Mirjam, 734-615-4286 mirjam@umich.edu, Univ of Michigan; Gm
Schaller, Morgan F., (518) 276-3358 schall@rpi.edu, Rensselaer Polytechnic Inst; CsPe
Schapaugh, Bill T., (785) 532-7242 wts@ksu.edu, Kansas State Univ; So
Schardt, Lawrence A., (814) 863-7655 las233@psu.edu, Pennsylvania State Univ, Univ Park; SoHw
Schamberger, Charles K., charles.schamberger@millersville.edu, Millersville Univ; Gc
Schauble, Edwin A., (310) 825-3880 schauble@ucla.edu, Univ of California, Los Angeles; Csg
Schauss, Kim E., (812) 464-1701 keschauss@usi.edu, Univ of Southern Indiana; Zn
Scheel, Patrick, 573-368-2243 patrick.scheel@dnr.mo.gov, Missouri Dept of Natural Resources; Zn
Scheffler, Joanna, joanna.scheffler@gmail.com, Mesa Comm Coll; Gg
Scheidemen, Kathy J., (805) 893-7615 kathys@icess.ucsb.edu, Univ of California, Santa Barbara; Zn
Scheidt, Brian, 573-518-2314 bscheidt@mineralarea.edu, Mineral Area Coll; Hw
Scheingross, Joel S., (775) 682-9839 jscheingross@unr.edu, Univ of Nevada, Reno; Gsm
Schellart, Wouter , +31 20 59 8610 w.p.schellart@vu.nl, Vrije Universiteit Amsterdam; Gt
Schellenberg, Stephen A., 61959421039 saschellenberg@mail.sdsu.edu, San Diego State Univ; Pe
Schenck, William S., 302-831-8262 rockman@udel.edu, Univ of Delaware; ZiGi
Schenk, Anton, (716)645-3489 afshenko@buffalo.edu, SUNY, Buffalo; Zr
Scher, Howie, 803-777-2410 hscher@geol.sc.edu, Univ of South Carolina; GuCl
Scherer, Reed P., (815) 753-7951 reed@niu.edu, Northern Illinois Univ; Pm
Schermer, Elizabeth R., (360) 650-3658 schermer@geol.wwu.edu, Western Washington Univ; Gt
Schiappa, Tamra A., (724) 738-2829 tamra.schiappa@sru.edu, Slippery Rock Univ; PiGrZe
Schieber, Juergen, (812) 856-4740 jschiebe@indiana.edu, Indiana Univ, Bloomington; Gs
Schiebout, Judith A., (225) 578-2717 schiebout@geol.lsu.edu, Louisiana State Univ; Pv
Schiefer, Erik, (928) 523-6535 erik.schiefer@nau.edu, Northern Arizona Univ; GmZyi
Schiffbauer, James, (573) 882-9501 schiffbauerj@missouri.edu, Univ of Missouri; Pgi
Schiffman, Peter, (530) 752-3669 pschiffman@ucdavis.edu, Univ of California, Davis; Gp
Schilling, Jean-Guy E., (401) 423 1417 jgchilling@yahoo.com, Univ of Rhode Island; OuCuc
Schilling, Keith, keith.schilling@dnr.iowa.gov, Iowa Dept of Natural Resources; Gg
Schimmelmann, Arndt, (812) 855-7645 aschimme@indiana.edu, Indiana Univ, Bloomington; CsGsPe
Schimmrich, Steven, (845) 687-7683 schimmrs@sunyulster.edu, SUNY, Ulster County Comm Coll; GgZgn
Schincariol, Robert A., (519) 661-3732 schincar@uwo.ca, Western Univ; HwsNg
Schindler, Michael, 7056751151 x2368 mschindler@laurentian.ca, Laurentian Univ, Sudbury; Gz
Schlautman, Mark, (864) 656-4059 mschlau@clemson.edu, Clemson Univ; ClHgSc
Schlegel, Alan, (620) 376-4761 schlegel@ksu.edu, Kansas State Univ; So
Schleifer, Stanley, 718-262-2726 sschleifer@york.cuny.edu, York Coll (CUNY); Ge
Schlesinger, William H., (919) 613-8004 schlesin@duke.edu, Duke Univ; Zn
Schlichting, Hilke, (626) 316-3629 hilke@ucla.edu, Univ of California, Los Angeles; Xy
Schlische, Roy W., 848-445-3445 schlisch@eps.rutgers.edu, Rutgers, The State Univ of New Jersey; GctEo
Schlogl, Jan , schlogl@fns.uniba.sk, Comenius Univ in Bratislava; Pig
Schlosser, C. Adam, 617-253-3983 casch@mit.edu, Massachusetts Inst of Tech; As
Schlosser, Peter, (845) 365-8707 schlosser@ldeo.columbia.edu, Columbia Univ; Hw
Schlue, John W., jwschlue@yahoo.com, New Mexico Inst of Mining and Tech; YsgZg
Schlumpberger, Debbie, 320-308-3260 dmschlumpberger@stcloudstate.edu, Saint Cloud State Univ; Zn
Schmahl, Wolfgang, 089/2180 4311 wolfgang.schmahl@lrz.uni-muenchen.de, Ludwig-Maximilians-Univ Muenchen; Gz
Schmandt, Brandon, 505.277.4204 bschmandt@unm.edu, Univ of New Mexico; Yg
Schmerr, Nicholas C., 301-405-4385 nschmerr@umd.edu, Univ of Maryland; XyYs
Schmid, Dieter, 089/2180 6635 d.schmid@lrz.uni-muenchen.de, Ludwig-Maximilians-Univ Muenchen; Pg
Schmid, Katherine W., 412-442-4232 kschmid@pa.gov, DCNR- Pennsylvania Bureau of Geological Survey; GoCcXb
Schmidt, Amanda H., 440-775-8351 amanda.schmidt@oberlin.edu, Oberlin Coll; Gm
Schmidt, Bennetta, bennetta.schmidt@lamar.edu, Lamar Univ; Gg
Schmidt, Dale R., 217-300-1169 schmidt2@illinois.edu, Illinois State Geological Survey; Ge
Schmidt, David , 206-685-3799 dasc@uw.edu, Univ of Washington; Gt
Schmidt, David, 937 775-3539 david.schmidt@wright.edu, Wright State Univ; PiGd
Schmidt, Jonathan, (519) 824-4120 Ext.53966 jonschm@uoguelph.ca, Univ of Guelph; Zn
Schmidt, Keegan L., (208) 790-2283 klschmidt@lcsc.edu, Lewis-Clark State Coll; Gc
Schmidt, Lisa, lschmidt@sbccd.cc.ca.us, San Bernardino Valley Coll; Zy
Schmidt, Mariek, mschmidt2@brocku.ca, Brock Univ; GivXg
Schmidt, Matthew, 757-683-4285 mwschmid@odu.edu, Old Dominion Univ; Ou
Schmitt, Danielle M., 609-258-7015 dschmitt@princeton.edu, Princeton Univ; Ze
Schmitt, Douglas R., (780) 492-3985 schmitt@purdue.edu, Purdue Univ; YxNrYe
Schmitt, Michael A., (612) 625-7017 mschmitt@soils.umn.edu, Univ of Minnesota, Twin Cities; Sc
Schmittner, Andreas, 541-737-9952 aschmittner@coas.oregonstate.edu, Oregon State Univ; AsYr
Schmitz, Darrel W., 662-268-1032 Ext 241 schmitz@geosci.msstate.edu, Mississippi State Univ; Hw
Schmitz, Mark D., 208-426-5907 markschmitz@boisestate.edu, Boise State Univ; CcaCg
Schmutz, Phillip P., 850-474-3418 pschmutz@uwf.edu, Univ of West Florida; Gm
Schneider, Blair, 785-864-2063 blair.schneider@ku.edu, Univ of Kansas; Gg
Schneider, David, david.schneider@uottawa.ca, Univ of Ottawa; GtCcGg
Schneider, Edwin K., (703) 993-5364 eschnei1@gmu.edu, George Mason Univ; As
Schneider, John F., (630) 252-8923 Argonne; Ca
Schneider, Julius, 089/2180 4354 julius.schneider@lrz.uni-muenchen.de, Ludwig-Maximilians-Univ Muenchen; Gz
Schneider, Niklas, (808) 956-8383 nschneid@hawaii.edu, Univ of Hawai'i, Manoa; Og
Schneider, Robert J., 508-289-2756 rschneider@whoi.edu, Woods Hole Oceanographic Inst; Cc
Schneider, Tapio, (626) 395-6143 tapio@caltech.edu, California Inst of Tech; AsmZg
Schneiderman, Jill S., 845-437-5542 schneiderman@vassar.edu, Vassar Coll; Gs
Schnetzer, Astrid, (919) 515-7837 aschnet@ncsu.edu, North Carolina State

Univ; Ob
Schoenberger, Erica, (410) 516-6158 ericas@jhu.edu, Johns Hopkins Univ; Zn
Schoene, Blair, 609-258-5747 bschoene@princeton.edu, Princeton Univ; Cc
Schoenemann, Spruce W., 406 683-7624 spruce.schoenemann@umwestern.edu, Univ of Montana Western; GeCgs
Schoephoester, Peter, 608/262.2320 peter.schoephoester@wisc.edu, Univ of Wisconsin, Madison, Division of Extension; Zi
Scholle, Peter, peter.scholle@nmt.edu, New Mexico Inst of Mining and Tech; Gd
Scholtz, Theresa C., (630) 252-6499 Argonne; Ge
Scholz, Christopher A., 315-443-2672 cascholz@syr.edu, Syracuse Univ; Gs
Schoof, Christian, (604) 822-3063 cschoof@eos.ubc.ca, Univ of British Columbia; Gl
Schoonen, Martin A., (631) 632-8007 martin.schoonen@sunysb.edu, Stony Brook Univ; Cl
Schoonmaker, Adam, 792-2577 adschoonmaker@utica.edu, Utica Coll; GczGx
Schoonmaker, Jane E., 808-956-9935 jane@soest.hawaii.edu, Univ of Hawai'i, Manoa; Cm
Schopf, J. William, (310) 825-1170 schopf@epss.ucla.edu, Univ of California, Los Angeles; Pg
Schopf, Paul S., (703) 993-5394 pschopf@gmu.edu, George Mason Univ; OpAs
Schouten, Hans, (508) 289-2574 hschouten@whoi.edu, Woods Hole Oceanographic Inst; Yr
Schrader, Christian M., 315-267-2285 schradcm@potsdam.edu, SUNY Potsdam; GiEmGv
Schrader, Devin, (480) 965-0720 devin.schrader@asu.edu, Arizona State Univ; Xm
Schrag, Daniel P., (617) 495-7676 schrag@eps.harvard.edu, Harvard Univ; Cg
Schrage, Jon M., (402) 280-5759 schragej@gmail.com, Creighton Univ; Am
Schrank, Christoph, +61 7 3138 1583 christoph.schrank@qut.edu.au, Queensland Univ of Tech; GcqGt
Schreiber, B. Charlotte, (718) 997-3300 Queens Coll (CUNY); Gd
Schreiber, Charlotte, 206-297-1454 geologo1@uw.edu, Univ of Washington; Gsd
Schreiber, Madeline E., (540) 231-3377 Virginia Polytechnic Inst & State Univ; Hw
Schreier, Hans D., (604) 822-4401 Univ of British Columbia; Zg
Schrenk, Matt, (517) 884-7966 schrenkm@msu.edu, Michigan State Univ; Pg
Schriver, David, (310) 825-6663 dave@igpp.ucla.edu, Univ of California, Los Angeles; Yg
Schroder-Adams, Claudia, csadams@ccs.carleton.ca, Carleton Univ; Pm
Schroeder, Dustin M., (650) 725-7861 dustin.m.schroeder@stanford.edu, Stanford Univ; Gl
Schroeder, John L., 806-834-5678 john.schroeder@ttu.edu, Texas Tech Univ; As
Schroeder, Kathleen, (828) 262-7055 schroederk@appstate.edu, Appalachian State Univ; Zn
Schroeder, Norman C., (505) 667-0967 Los Alamos; Cc
Schroeder, Paul A., (706) 542-2384 schroe@uga.edu, Univ of Georgia; GzEnCl
Schroeder, Stefan, +44 0161 306-6870 stefan.schroeder@manchester.ac.uk, Univ of Manchester; Go
Schroeder, William W., (334) 861-7528 wschroeder@disl.org, Dauphin Island Sea Lab; Og
Schroth, Andrew W., (802)656 3481 aschroth@uvm.edu, Univ of Vermont; ClqCb
Schubert, Brian, 337-482-6967 bas9777@louisiana.edu, Univ of Louisiana at Lafayette; Cg
Schubert, Gerald, (310) 825-4577 Univ of California, Los Angeles; Yg
Schuberth, Bernhard, 089/2180 4220 bernhard@geophysik.uni-muenchen.de, Ludwig-Maximilians-Univ Muenchen; Yg
Schulingkamp, Arren, 225-578-3412 warrenii@lsu.edu, Louisiana State Univ; Gg
Schulmeister, Marcia K., (620) 341-5983 mschulme@emporia.edu, Emporia State Univ; HwClGe
Schulte, Kimberly D., kschulte1@gsu.edu, Georgia State Univ, Perimeter Coll, Online; Gg
Schultz, Adam, 541-737-9832 adam.schultz@oregonstate.edu, Oregon State Univ; YgmRn
Schultz, David, +44 0161 306-3909 david.schultz@manchester.ac.uk, Univ of Manchester; Am
Schultz, Gerald E., 806-651-2580 gschultz@wtamu.edu, West Texas A&M Univ; PvGzZg
Schultz, Jan, (805) 965-0581 (Ext. 2313) schultz@sbcc.edu, Santa Barbara City Coll; GgePg
Schultz, Peter H., (401) 863-2417 peter_schultz@brown.edu, Brown Univ; Xg
Schultze, Steven R., schultze@southalabama.edu, Univ of South Alabama; At
Schulz, Layne D., 605-67-76161 layne.schulz@usd.edu, South Dakota Dept of Environment and Natural Resources; Glg
Schulze, Anja, 409 740 4540 schulzea@tamug.edu, Texas A&M Univ; Ob
Schulze, Daniel J., 905-8283970 dschulze@utm.utoronto.ca, Univ of Toronto; Gi
Schulze, Karl, (630) 466-2652 kschulze@waubonsee.edu, Waubonsee Comm Coll; ZgAms
Schulze-Makuch, Dirk, 509-335-1180 dirksm@wsu.edu, Washington State Univ; Hw
Schumacher, Courtney, (979) 845-5522 cschu@tamu.edu, Texas A&M Univ; As
Schumacher, Matthew, mschumac@stfx.ca, Saint Francis Xavier Univ; Zg
Schumacher, Russ, russ.schumacher@colostate.edu, Colorado State Univ; As
Schumann, Arnold W., (863) 956-1151 schumaw@ufl.edu, Univ of Florida; So
Schumer, Rina, (775) 673-7414 rina.schumer@dri.edu, Univ of Nevada, Reno; HqwGm
Schutt, Derek L., (970) 491-5786 schutt@warnercnr.colostate.edu, Colorado State Univ; Ysg
Schwab, Brandon E., (828) 227-7495 beschwab@wcu.edu, Western Carolina Univ; GizGv
Schwab, Fred, (310) 825-3123 schwab@igpp.ucla.edu, Univ of California, Los Angeles; Ys
Schwab, Frederick L., (540) 458-5830 schwabf@wlu.edu, Washington & Lee Univ; Gdg
Schwab, James J., (518) 437-8754 jschwab@albany.edu, SUNY, Albany; Acs
Schwab, Paul, 979-845-3663 pschwab@tamu.edu, Texas A&M Univ; Sc
Schwarcz, Henry P., (905) 525-9140 (Ext. 24186) schwarcz@mcmaster.ca, McMaster Univ; Cs
Schwartz, David, (408) 479-6495 daschwar@cabrillo.edu, Cabrillo Coll; Gu
Schwartz, Frank W., (614) 292-6196 schwartz.11@osu.edu, Ohio State Univ; Hw
Schwartz, Hilde, (831) 459-5429 hschwartz@pmc.ucsc.edu, Univ of California, Santa Cruz; Pv
Schwartz, Joshua J., (818) 677-5813 joshua.schwartz@csun.edu, California State Univ, Northridge; GiCc
Schwartz, Matthew C., 850-474-3469 mschwartz@uwf.edu, Univ of West Florida; OcCl
Schwartz, Robert K., rschwartz@allegheny.edu, Allegheny Coll; GsrGt
Schwartz, Susan, 831-459-3133 syschwar@ucsc.edu, Univ of California, Santa Cruz; Ys
Schwarz, Karen, (610)436-2788 kschwarz@wcupa.edu, West Chester Univ; XaZe
Schweitzer, Carrie E., 330-244-3303 cschweit@kent.edu, Kent State Univ at Stark; PiGg
Schwerdtner, Walfried M., (416) 978-5080 fried@quartz.geology.utoronto.ca, Univ of Toronto; GctGq
Schwert, Donald P., (701) 231-7496 donald.schwert@ndsu.edu, North Dakota State Univ; PeGe
Schwimmer, David R., 706 569-3028 schwimmer_david@columbusstate.edu, Columbus State Univ; Pv
Schwimmer, Reed A., 609-896-5346 rschwimmer@rider.edu, Rider Univ; GsOgn
Schwob, Stephanie L., 214-768-2770 sschwob@smu.edu, Southern Methodist Univ; Zn
Sclater, John G., (858) 534-3051 jsclater@ucsd.edu, Univ of California, San Diego; Yh
Scoates, James S., (604) 822-3667 jscoates@eoas.ubc.ca, Univ of British Columbia; GizGv
Scotese, Christopher R., (817) 272-2987 cscotese@exchange.uta.edu, Univ of Texas, Arlington; Gt
Scott, Andrew C., +44 1784 443608 a.scott@rhul.ac.uk, Royal Holloway Univ of London; Pb
Scott, Christopher A., cascott@email.arizona.edu, Univ of Arizona; Hw
Scott, Craig, (403) 823-7707 Royal Tyrrell Mus of Palaeontology; Pv
Scott, Darren M., (905) 525-9140 (Ext. 24953) scottdm@mcmaster.ca, McMaster Univ; Zi
Scott, David B., (902) 494-3604 Dalhousie Univ; Pm
Scott, James M., +64 3 479-7520 james.scott@otago.ac.nz, Univ of Otago; Gp
Scott, Kathy, (604) 822-5606 kscott@eos.ubc.ca, Univ of British Columbia; Zn
Scott, Larry, 303-384-2631 lmscott@mines.edu, Colorado Geological Survey; Zy

Scott, Robert B., 512-471-0375 rscott@ig.utexas.edu, Univ of Texas, Austin; Ge
Scott, Steven D., (416) 978-5424 scottsd@es.utoronto.ca, Univ of Toronto; GuEmCm
Scott, Thomas A., (951) 827-5115 thomas.scott@ucr.edu, Univ of California, Riverside; Zy
Scott, Tim, (401) 254-3108 Roger Williams Univ; Ob
Scott, Vernon, 405-744-6358 vscott@okstate.edu, Oklahoma State Univ; Ze
Scott Smith, Barbara H., (604) 984-9609 bhssmith@allstream.net, Univ of British Columbia; Gz
Scott-Dupree, Cynthia, (519) 824-4120 Ext.52477 cscottdu@uoguelph.ca, Univ of Guelph; Zn
Scotton, Paolo, +390498279120 paolo.scotton@unipd.it, Univ degli Studi di Padova; Hg
Scow, Kate, (530) 752-4632 kmscow@ucdavis.edu, Univ of California, Davis; So
Scowen, Paul, (480) 965-0938 paul.scowen@asu.edu, Arizona State Univ; Xa
Scranton, Mary I., (631) 632-8735 mary.scranton@stonybrook.edu, SUNY, Stony Brook; Oc
Screaton, Elizabeth J., (352) 3924612 screaton@ufl.edu, Univ of Florida; Hg
Scudder, Sylvia J., 3523921721 x246 scudder@flmnh.ufl.edu, Univ of Florida; Pg
Scuderi, Louis A., (505) 277-4204 tree@unm.edu, Univ of New Mexico; GmPcGs
Scyphers, Steven, 781.581.7370 s.scyphers@northeastern.edu, Northeastern Univ; Zn
Seager, Richard, seager@ldeo.columbia.edu, Columbia Univ; Am
Seager, Sara, 617-253-6775 seager@mit.edu, Massachusetts Inst of Tech; Xy
Seal, Thom, 775-784-1813 tseal@unr.edu, Univ of Nevada, Reno; Nx
Seaman, Nelson L., (814) 863-1583 Pennsylvania State Univ, Univ Park; Am
Seaman, Sheila J., (413) 545-2822 sjs@geo.umass.edu, Univ of Massachusetts, Amherst; Gi
Searcy, Steven, (619) 260-2793 ssearcy@sandiego.edu, Univ of San Diego; Ob
Searle, Mike, +44 (1865) 272022 mike.searle@earth.ox.ac.uk, Univ of Oxford; Gt
Searls, Mindi L., 402-472-6934 Univ of Nebraska, Lincoln; YgGg
Sears, James W., (406) 243-5251 james.sears@umontana.edu, Univ of Montana; GctEg
Sebol, Lesley, (303) 384-2633 lsebol@mines.edu, Colorado Geological Survey; HwGeZg
Secco, Luciano, +390498279158 luciano.secco@unipd.it, Univ degli Studi di Padova; Gz
Secco, Richard A., (519) 661-4079 secco@uwo.ca, Western Univ; Gy
Secord, Ross, (402) 472-2663 rsecord2@unl.edu, Univ of Nebraska, Lincoln; PvCs
Sediek, Kadry N., 002-03-3921595 kknsed@yahoo.com, Alexandria Univ; GgsGd
Sedivy, Robert, 402-465-9021 rasedivy@anl.gov, Argonne; Hw
Sedlacek, Alexa, 319-273-3072 alexa.sedlacek@uni.edu, Univ of Northern Iowa; CsGr
Seeber, Leonardo, nano@ldeo.columbia.edu, Columbia Univ; Ys
Seedorff, Eric, (520) 626-3921 seedorff@email.arizona.edu, Univ of Arizona; Eg
Seeger, Cheryl M., (573) 368-2184 cheryl.seeger@dnr.mo.gov, Missouri Dept of Natural Resources; Gig
Seeley, Mark W., (612) 625-4724 mseeley@umn.edu, Univ of Minnesota, Twin Cities; As
Seewald, Jeffrey S., (508) 289-2966 jseewald@whoi.edu, Woods Hole Oceanographic Inst; Cp
Segall, Marylin, 801-585-5730 mpsegall@egi.utah.edu, Univ of Utah; GeOu
Segall, Paul, (650) 725-7241 Stanford Univ; Yg
Segars, William P., (706) 542-9072 Univ of Georgia; Sc
Seibel, Erwin, (415) 338-2061 San Francisco State Univ; On
Seibt, Ulrike, (310) 206-4442 useibt@ucla.edu, Univ of California, Los Angeles; PgCg
Seidemann, David E., 7189515000 x2882 dseidemann@earthlink.net, Brooklyn Coll (CUNY); Cc
Seifert, Karl E., (515) 294-5265 kseifert@iastate.edu, Iowa State Univ of Sci & Tech; Ct
Seifoullaev, Roustam K., (512) 232-3223 roustam@utig.ig.utexas.edu, Univ of Texas, Austin; Ye
Seifu, Abiye, 706-568-2187 seifu_abiye@columbusstate.edu, Columbus State Univ; Zn
Seigley, Lynette S., 319-335-1598 lynette.seigley@dnr.iowa.gov, Iowa Dept of Natural Resources; Gg
Seirer, Jami J., jjseirer2@fhsu.edu, Fort Hays State Univ; ZriZn
Seitz, Jeffery C., (510) 885-3438 jeff.seitz@csueastbay.edu, California State Univ, East Bay; CgZeGx
Selby, Dave, +44 (0) 191 33 42294 david.selby@durham.ac.uk, Durham Univ; Cc
Selden, Paul A., selden@ku.edu, Univ of Kansas; Pig
Selim, Hussein M., (504) 388-2110 Louisiana State Univ; Sp
Selin, Noelle, (617) 324-2592 selin@mit.edu, Massachusetts Inst of Tech; As
Sellmeier, Bettina, +49 (89) 289 25822 sellmeier@tum.de, Technical Univ of Munich; Ngr
Selph, Karen E., (808) 956-7941 selph@hawaii.edu, Univ of Hawai'i, Manoa; Ob
Selverstone, Jane E., selver@unm.edu, Univ of New Mexico; Gpt
Semazzi, Fred H. M., (919) 515-1434 fred_semazzi@ncsu.edu, North Carolina State Univ; As
Semken, Steven, (480) 965-7965 semken@asu.edu, Arizona State Univ; ZeGgZg
Semken, Jr., Holmes A., (319) 335-1830 holmes-semken@uiowa.edu, Univ of Iowa; Pv
Sen, Gautam, (305) 348-2299 seng@fiu.edu, Florida International Univ; Gi
Sen, Mrinal K., (512) 471-0466 Univ of Texas, Austin; Ye
Sen Gupta, Barun K., (225) 388-5984 barun@geol.lsu.edu, Louisiana State Univ; Pm
Send, Uwe, (858) 822-6710 usend@ucsd.edu, Univ of California, San Diego; Op
Senko, John M., 330 972-8047 senko@uakron.edu, Univ of Akron; Cg
Sennert, Sally K., (202) 633-1805 kuhns@si.edu, Smithsonian Inst / Nat Mus of Natural History; GvZr
Seong, Jeong C., (678) 839-4069 jseong@westga.edu, Univ of West Georgia; Zir
Sephton, Mark, +44 20 759 46542 m.a.sephton@imperial.ac.uk, Imperial Coll; Xm
Sepúlveda, Julio C., jsepulveda@colorado.edu, Univ of Colorado; Co
Sericano, Jose L., (979) 862-2323 jose@gerg.tamu.edu, Texas A&M Univ; Cm
Serne, R. Jeffrey, (360) 539-6162 jeff.serne@pnnl.gov, Pacific Northwest; CgSoCl
Serpa, Laura F., (504) 280-6801 lserpa@uno.edu, Univ of New Orleans; Ys
Serreze, Mark, mark.serreze@colorado.edu, Univ of Colorado; As
Sertich, Joseph, 303-370-6331 joe.sertich@dmns.org, Denver Mus of Nature & Sci; Pv
Seserman, Anca M., 0040232201456 anca.seserman@yahoo.com, Alexandru Ioan Cuza; Gs
Sessa, Jocelyn A., (215) 299-1149 jsessa@drexel.edu, Drexel Univ; PeCsPq
Sessions, Alex L., 626.395.6445 als@gps.caltech.edu, California Inst of Tech; CosCb
Sethi, Parvinder S., (540) 831-5619 psethi@radford.edu, Radford Univ; Gz
Severinghaus, Jeffrey P., (858) 822-2483 jseveringhaus@ucsd.edu, Univ of California, San Diego; Pe
Severs, Matthew , matthew.severs@stockton.edu, Stockton Univ; Gg
Severs, Matthew R., 609-626-6857 matthew.severs@stockton.edu, Stockton Univ; GxCgEg
Severson, Allison, 612-626-2969 sever270@d.umn.edu, Univ of Minnesota; Gp
Sevilla, Paloma, psevilla@ucm.es, Univ Complutense de Madrid; Pi
Sewall, Jacob, 484-646-5864 sewall@kutztown.edu, Kutztown Univ of Pennsylvania; GeAs
Sexton, John L., (618) 453-7374 sexton@geo.siu.edu, Southern Illinois Univ Carbondale; Ye
Sexton, Philip, philip.sexton@open.ac.uk, Open Univ; Ge
Seyfang, Gill, +44 (0)1603 59 2956 g.seyfang@uea.ac.uk, Univ of East Anglia; Og
Seyfferth, Angelia L., 302-831-4865 angelias@udel.edu, Univ of Delaware; Sc
Seyfried, Jr., William E., 612-624-1333 wes@umn.edu, Univ of Minnesota, Twin Cities; Cm
Seyler, Beverly, 217-244-2389 seyler@isgs.uiuc.edu, Illinois State Geological Survey; Eo
Seymour, Dorie, (406) 994-5718 dorie.seymour@montana.edu, Montana State Univ; Zn
Seyoum, Wondwosen M., (309) 438-2833 wmseyou@ilstu.edu, Illinois State Univ; HwqZr
Shaaban, Mohamad N., 002-03-3921595 moshaaban@yahoo.com, Alexandria Univ; GgsGd
Shaak, Graig D., 3523921721 x257 gdshaak@flmnh.ufl.edu, Univ of Florida; Pe
Shackelton, Sarah, 609-258-4101 ss77@princeton.edu, Princeton Univ; Pc
Shackley, Simon J., +44 (0) 131 650 7862 simon.shackley@ed.ac.uk, Edinburgh Univ; Eg
Shade, Harry, 4087412045 x 3678 geology1@earthlink.net, West Valley Coll; Gg

FACULTY INDEX – S

Shade, Janet, 814-362-7560 jas144@pitt.edu, Univ of Pittsburgh, Bradford; Zn
Shafer, Erik, shafere@pdx.edu, Portland State Univ; Gg
Shafer, Jason, 802-626-6225 jason.shafer@northernvermont.edu, Northern Vermont Univ-Lyndon; As
Shah, Subhash N., (405) 325-6871 subhash@ou.edu, Univ of Oklahoma; Np
Shahar, Anat, (202) 478-8929 ashahar@carnegiescience.edu, Carnegie Inst for Sci; CgYxCs
Shail, Robin, +44 01326 371826 r.k.shail@exeter.ac.uk, Exeter Univ; GtcEm
Shakoor, Abdul, (330) 672-2968 ashakoor@kent.edu, Kent State Univ; Ng
Shakun, Jeremy D., 617-552-1625 jeremy.shakun@bc.edu, Boston Coll; Gg
Shalimba, Ester, +264-61-2063839 eshalimba@unam.na, Univ of Namibia; GgpEz
Shamberger, Kathryn E., (979) 845-5752 katie.shamberger@tamu.edu, Texas A&M Univ; OcZc
Shami, Malek, (718) 262-2654 mshami2@york.cuny.edu, York Coll (CUNY); Gcg
Shams, Asghar, +44 (0)131 451 3904 a.shams@hw.ac.uk, Heriot-Watt Univ; Yg
Shanafield, Margaret, margaret.shanafield@flinders.edu.au, Flinders Univ; Hw
Shanahan, Timothy M., 512-232-7051 tshanahan@jsg.utexas.edu, Univ of Texas, Austin; PeGsCg
Shane, Tyrrell, +353 (0)91 494387 shane.tyrrell@nuigalway.ie, Nat Univ of Ireland Galway; Gs
Shang, Congxiao, +44 (0)1603 59 3123 c.shang@uea.ac.uk, Univ of East Anglia; Hw
Shank, Stephen G., 717-702-2021 stshank@pa.gov, DCNR- Pennsylvania Bureau of Geological Survey; GziGp
Shankland, Thomas J., (505) 667-4907 shanklan@lanl.gov, Los Alamos; Yx
Shanmugam, Ganapathy, shanshanmugam@aol.com, Univ of Tennessee, Knoxville; Gs
Shannon, Jack D., (630) 252-5807 jack_shannon@anl.gov, Argonne; Am
Shannon, Jeremy, (906) 487-3573 jmshanno@mtu.edu, Michigan Technological Univ; Gg
Shapiro, Russell S., (530) 898-4300 rsshapiro@csuchico.edu, California State Univ, Chico; PgGdXb
Shapley, Mark, shap0029@umn.edu, Univ of Minnesota, Twin Cities; Gn
Sharkey, Debra, (916) 691-7210 Cosumnes River Coll; Zy
Sharma, Govind, (205) 851-5462 aamaxs01@aamu.edu, Alabama A&M Univ; Zn
Sharma, Mukul, 603-646-0024 mukul.sharma@dartmouth.edu, Dartmouth Coll; Ge
Sharma, Shikha, 304-293-5603 shikha.sharma@mail.wvu.edu, West Virginia Univ; Csa
Sharma, Shiv K., (808) 956-8476 Univ of Hawai'i, Manoa; Gx
Sharma, Suresh, ssharma@ou.edu, Univ of Oklahoma; Np
Sharma, Vasudha, 612-626-4986 vasudha@umn.edu, Univ of Minnesota, Twin Cities; SpHg
Sharman, Glenn R., 479-575-4471 gsharman@uark.edu, Univ of Arkansas, Fayetteville; Go
Sharp, Jonathan H., (302) 645-4259 jsharp@udel.edu, Univ of Delaware; Oc
Sharp, Martin J., (780) 492-4156 martin.sharp@ualberta.ca, Univ of Alberta; Gl
Sharp, Thomas G., 480-965-3071 tom.sharp@asu.edu, Arizona State Univ; Gz
Sharp, Zachary D., (505) 277-4204 zsharp@unm.edu, Univ of New Mexico; Cs
Sharp, Jr., John M., (512) 471-3317 jmsharp@jsg.utexas.edu, Univ of Texas, Austin; HqwGe
Sharples, Jonathan, +44 0151 794 4093 jonathan.sharples@liverpool.ac.uk, Univ of Liverpool; Ocp
Shaulis, James R., 717.702.2037 jshaulis@pa.gov, DCNR- Pennsylvania Bureau of Geological Survey; EcZe
Shaver, Stephen A., (931) 598-1116 sshaver@sewanee.edu, Sewanee: Univ of the South; Eg
Shaw, Bruce, shaw@ldeo.columbia.edu, Columbia Univ; Ys
Shaw, Christopher A., (323) 857-6317 chrissha@bcf.usc.edu, Los Angeles County Mus of Natural History; Pv
Shaw, Cliff S., 506-447-3195 cshaw@unb.ca, Univ of New Brunswick; Giv
Shaw, Colin, 406 994 6760 colin.shaw1@montana.edu, Montana State Univ; GcEmGp
Shaw, Fred, 573-368-2479 fred.shaw@dnr.mo.gov, Missouri Dept of Natural Resources; Zn
Shaw, Frederick C., (212) 642-2202 Lehman Coll (CUNY); Ps
Shaw, George H., (518) 388-6310 shawg@union.edu, Union Coll; Yx
Shaw, Glenn D., 406-496-4809 gshaw@mtech.edu, Montana Tech of the Univ of Montana; HwCsHs
Shaw, Joey N., (334) 844-3957 shawjo1@auburn.edu, Auburn Univ; Sd
Shaw, John, (780) 492-3573 john.shaw@ualberta.ca, Univ of Alberta; Gl
Shaw, Katy, 2538339111 x 4325 kshaw@greenriver.edu, Green River Comm Coll; ZgOgGg
Shaw, Kenneth L., (212) 642-2202 kshaw@egi.utah.edu, Univ of Utah; Ye
Shaw, Liz, e.j.shaw@reading.ac.uk, Univ of Reading; Sb
Shaw, Ping-Tung, (919) 515-7276 ping-tung_shaw@ncsu.edu, North Carolina State Univ; Op
Shaw, Richard F., (225) 388-6734 Louisiana State Univ; Ob
Shcherbakov, Robert, 519-661-2111 ext.84212 rshcherb@uwo.ca, Western Univ; YgsYd
Shchukin, Eugene D., (410) 516-5079 shchukin@jhuvms.hcf.jhu.edu, Johns Hopkins Univ; Zn
Shea, Erin, 907-786-6846 eshea2@uaa.alaska.edu, Univ of Alaska, Anchorage; CcGcCg
Shea, Thomas, tshea@hawaii.edu, Univ of Hawai'i, Manoa; Gv
Shearer, Peter M., (858) 534-2260 pshearer@ucsd.edu, Univ of California, San Diego; Ysg
Shearer, Jr., Charles K., (505) 277-9159 cshearer@unm.edu, Univ of New Mexico; Gi
Shearman, Kipp, 541-737-1866 shearman@coas.oregonstate.edu, Oregon State Univ; Opn
Shears, Andrew, ashears@mansfield.edu, Univ of Wisconsin Colls; Zin
shedied, ahmad g., 01005856505 ags00@fayoum.edu.eg, Fayoum Univ; GgHww
Sheehan, Anne F., (303) 492-4597 anne.sheehan@colorado.edu, Univ of Colorado; YszYe
Sheehan, Peter M., (414) 278-2741 sheehan@mpm.edu, Milwaukee Public Mus; Pi
Sheets, Julie, (614) 406-3298 sheets.2@osu.edu, Ohio State Univ; Gz
Sheffield, Sarah, ssheffield2@usf.edu, Univ of South Florida; Pe
Sheldon, Amy L., (585) 245-5988 sheldon@geneseo.edu, SUNY, Geneseo; Hw
Shell, Karen M., (541) 737-0980 kshell@coas.oregonstate.edu, Oregon State Univ; As
Shellito, Lucinda, (970) 351-2491 lucinda.shellito@unco.edu, Univ of Northern Colorado; AsPeAm
Shelton, Dale W., (410) 554-5505 dale.shelton@maryland.gov, Maryland Department of Natural Resources; ZeGg
Shelton, Kevin L., (573) 882-1004 sheltonkl@missouri.edu, Univ of Missouri; EmCs
Shem, Linda M., (630) 252-3857 Argonne; Ge
Shen, Jian, (804) 684-7359 shen@vims.edu, William & Mary; Op
Shen, Linhan, 609-258-4101 linhans@princeton.edu, Princeton Univ; Cas
Shen, Samuel S., (780) 492-0216 shen@ualberta.ca, Univ of Alberta; As
Shen, Weisen, 631-632-8212 weisen.shen@stonybrook.edu, Stony Brook Univ; Ys
Shen, Xinhua, (319) 273-2536 xinhua.shen@uni.edu, Univ of Northern Iowa; Asm
Shen, Yang, (401) 874-6848 yshen@gso.uri.edu, Univ of Rhode Island; Ou
Sheng, Jinyu, (902) 494-2718 jinyu.sheng@dal.ca, Dalhousie Univ; Op
Shepard, Michael K., (570) 389-4568 mshepard@bloomu.edu, Bloomsburg Univ; XgYgZr
Shepardson, Daniel P., (765) 494-5284 dshep@purdue.edu, Purdue Univ; Ze
Shepherd, Gordon G., 4167362100 x33221 gordon@yorku.ca, York Univ; AsZrAp
Shepherd, Mark A., (512) 574-4227 mark.shepherd@austincc.edu, Austin Comm Coll District; AsObZn
Shepherd, Stephanie L., 334-844-4926 sls0070@auburn.edu, Auburn Univ; GmZi
Sheppard, Scott S., (202) 478-8854 ssheppard@carnegiescience.edu, Carnegie Inst for Sci; Xa
Shepson, Paul B., (765) 494-7441 pshepson@purdue.edu, Purdue Univ; As
Sheridan, Michael F., mfs@buffalo.edu, SUNY, Buffalo; Gv
Sheridan, Robert E., (848) 445-2015 rsheridan@eps.rutgers.edu, Rutgers, The State Univ of New Jersey; YrGu
Sherman-Morris, Kathleen M., (662) 268-1032 x242 kms5@geosci.msstate.edu, Mississippi State Univ; As
Sherrell, Robert M., (848) 932-6555 (Ext. 252) sherrell@ahab.rutgers.edu, Rutgers, The State Univ of New Jersey; CmOu
Sherriff, Barbara L., (204) 474-9786 bl_sherriff@umanitoba.ca, Univ of Manitoba; Gz
Sherrod, Brian L., 253-653-8358 bsherrod@uw.edu, Univ of Washington; YsGt
Sherrod, Laura, (484) 646-4113 sherrod@kutztown.edu, Kutztown Univ of Pennsylvania; YgHwGa
Shervais, John W., (435) 797-1274 john.shervais@usu.edu, Utah State Univ; Gi
Sherwood, Owen, 902 494 3604 owen.sherwood@dal.ca, Dalhousie Univ; CsOoGo

Sherwood, William C., (540) 568-6473 sherwowc@jmu.edu, James Madison Univ; So
Sherwood Lollar, Barbara, 416-978-0770 bslollar@chem.utoronto.ca, Univ of Toronto; Cs
Shevenell, Lisa, (775) 784-1779 lisaas@unr.edu, Univ of Nevada, Reno; Hw
Shew, Roger D., 910-962-7676 shewr@uncw.edu, Univ of North Carolina, Wilmington; Eo
Shi, Wei, 919-513-4641 wei_shi@ncsu.edu, North Carolina State Univ; Sb
Shieh, Sean R., 5196612111 x82467 sshieh@uwo.ca, Western Univ; YxGzZm
Shieh, Yuch-Ning, (765) 494-3272 ynshieh@purdue.edu, Purdue Univ; CsGpv
Shiel, Alyssa E., (541) 737-5209 ashiel@coas.oregonstate.edu, Oregon State Univ; ClsCt
Shields, Robin, +44 (0) 131 451 8215 robin.shields@hw.ac.uk, Heriot-Watt Univ; Cg
Shields, Stephen, 325-942-2242 stephen.shields@angelo.edu, Angelo State Univ; Ggm
Shields-Zhou, Graham, +44 020 7679 7821 g.shields@ucl.ac.uk, Univ Coll London; Cg
Shiels, Christine, 604-527-5217 shielsc@douglascollege.ca, Douglas Coll; GgxZg
Shiller, Alan M., (228) 688-1178 alan.shiller@usm.edu, Univ of Southern Mississippi; OcCtHs
Shiller, Thomas, (432) 837-8238 thomas.shiller@sulross.edu, Sul Ross State Univ; PvGrd
Shillington, Donna, djs@ldeo.columbia.edu, Columbia Univ; Yr
Shim, Sang-Heon, (480) 727-2876 shdshim@asu.edu, Arizona State Univ; Gz
Shim-Chim, Richard, (609) 984-6587 rich.shim-chim@dep.state.nj.us, New Jersey Geological and Water Survey; Hw
Shimer, Grant, 435 865 8429 grantshimer@suu.edu, Southern Utah Univ; Gs
Shimizu, Melinda, mel2066254@maricopa.edu, Mesa Comm Coll; Gg
Shimizu, Nobumichi, (508) 289-2963 Woods Hole Oceanographic Inst; Ca
Shinn, Eugene, (727) 893-3100 Univ of South Florida; Gg
Shinoda, Toshiaki, 361-825-3636 toshiaki.shinoda@tamucc.edu, Texas A&M Univ, Corpus Christi; As
Shipley, Thomas H., (512) 471-0430 tom@ig.utexas.edu, Univ of Texas, Austin; Yr
Shirer, Hampton N., (814) 863-1992 hns@psu.edu, Pennsylvania State Univ, Univ Park; Am
Shirey, Steven B., (202) 478-8473 sshirey@carnegiescience.edu, Carnegie Inst for Sci; CcGiz
Shirgaokar, Manish, 780.492.2802 shirgaokar@ualberta.ca, Univ of Alberta; Zu
Shirley, Terry, 704-687-5925 trshirle@uncc.edu, Univ of North Carolina, Charlotte; Asm
Shirzaei, Manoochehr, (480) 965-8102 shirzaei@asu.edu, Arizona State Univ; Yd
Shkolnik, Evgenya, shkolnik@asu.edu, Arizona State Univ; Xa
Shock, Everett, 480-965-0631 everett.shock@asu.edu, Arizona State Univ; Cg
Shoemaker, Kurt A., (740) 351-3395 kshoemaker@shawnee.edu, Shawnee State Univ; GxzGm
Sholkovitz, Edward R., (508) 289-2346 esholkovitz@whoi.edu, Woods Hole Oceanographic Inst; Oc
Shorey, Christian V., (303) 273-3556 cshorey@mines.edu, Colorado Sch of Mines; Gg
Shortt, Niamh K., +44 (0) 131 651 7130 niamh.shortt@ed.ac.uk, Edinburgh Univ; Eg
Shoup, Doug, (620) 421-1530 dshoup@ksu.edu, Kansas State Univ; So
Showers, William J., (919) 515-7143 w_showers@ncsu.edu, North Carolina State Univ; Cs
Showman, Adam, (520) 621-4021 showman@lpl.arizona.edu, Univ of Arizona; Zn
Shragge, Jeffrey, 303-273-3552 jshragge@mines.edu, Colorado Sch of Mines; Ys
Shreve, Ronald L., (310) 825-5273 shreve@ess.ucla.edu, Univ of California, Los Angeles; Gm
Shroat-Lewis, Rene A., 501-683-7743 rashroatlew@ualr.edu, Univ of Arkansas at Little Rock; PeZe
Shroba, Cynthia S., 702-651- 7427 cindy.shroba@csn.edu, Coll of Southern Nevada - West Charleston Campus; Gg
Shroder, Jr., John F., (402) 554-2770 jshroder@unomaha.edu, Univ of Nebraska, Omaha; GmlZy
Shropshire, K. Lee, (970) 351-2285 leeshrop@att.net, Univ of Northern Colorado; Pg
Shroyer, Emily L., 541-737-1298 eshroyer@coas.oregonstate.edu, Oregon State Univ; On
Shroyer, Jim, (785) 532-6101 jshroyer@ksu.edu, Kansas State Univ; So
Shu, Jinfu, (202) 478-8963 j.shu@gl.ciw.edu, Carnegie Inst for Sci; Yx
Shuford, James W., (205) 851-5462 jshufard@aamu.edu, Alabama A&M Univ; So
Shugart, Jr., Herman H., (804) 924-7642 hhs@virginia.edu, Univ of Virginia; Zg
Shuib, Mustaffa Kamal, 03-79674227 mustaffk@um.edu.my, Univ of Malaya; Gc
Shukla, Jagadish, (703) 993-1983 jshukla@gmu.edu, George Mason Univ; As
Shuller-Nickles, Lindsay C., 864656-1448 lshulle@clemson.edu, Clemson Univ; Gz
Shulski, Martha D., mshulski3@unl.edu, Univ of Nebraska, Lincoln; As
Shum, CK, 614 292 7118 ckshum@osu.edu, Ohio State Univ; YdHg
Shumaker, Robert C., (304) 293-5603 rshumaker@wvu.edu, West Virginia Univ; Go
Shuman, Bryan N., 307-766-6442 bshuman@uwyo.edu, Univ of Wyoming; PeGne
Shuman, Larry M., (404) 228-7276 Univ of Georgia; Sc
Shuman, Randy, (206) 296-8243 rshuman531@gmail.com, Univ of Washington; Ob
Shumway, Matthew J., (801) 422-2707 jms7@byu.edu, Brigham Young Univ; Zn
Shumway, Sandra, (860) 405-9282 sandra.shumway@uconn.edu, Univ of Connecticut; Ob
Shuster, Robert D., (402) 554-2457 rshuster@unomaha.edu, Univ of Nebraska, Omaha; GiaZe
Shuttleworth, W. James, (520) 621-8787 shuttle@hwr.arizona.edu, Univ of Arizona; Hs
Siahcheshm, Kamal, +98 (411) 339 2699 Univ of Tabriz; Egm
Sibeko, Skhumbuzo, 012 382 6271 sibekosg@tut.ac.za, Tshwane Univ of Tech; GggGg
Sibert, John R., sibert@hawaii.edu, Univ of Hawai'i, Manoa; Ob
Sibley, Paul, (519) 824-4120 Ext.52707 psibley@uoguelph.ca, Univ of Guelph; Zn
Sibray, Steven S., (308) 632-1382 ssibray@unl.edu, Unversity of Nebraska, Lincoln; HwGg
Sibson, Rick H., +64 3 479-7506 rick.sibson@otago.ac.nz, Univ of Otago; Gc
Sicard, Karri, 907-451-5040 karri.sicard@alaska.gov, Alaska Division of Geological & Geophysical Surveys; Gg
Siddoway, Christine S., (719) 389-6717 csiddoway@coloradocollege.edu, Colorado Coll; GctGg
Sidor, Christian A., 206-221-3285 casidor@uw.edu, Univ of Washington; Pv
Siebach, Kirsten L., 713.348.6751 ksiebach@rice.edu, Rice Univ; Xg
Siedlecki , Samantha, samantha.siedlecki@uconn.edu, Univ of Connecticut; On
Siegel, Donald I., 315-443-2672 disiegel@syr.edu, Syracuse Univ; Hw
Siegfried, Matthew, 303-384-2004 siegfried@mines.edu, Colorado Sch of Mines; ZrGl
Siegler, Matthew, 214-768-2745 msiegler@smu.edu, Southern Methodist Univ; YgXy
Siegrist, jr, Henry G., 410 827 8095 g.a.siegrist@gmail.com, Univ of Guam; GdzHy
Siemens, Michael A., (573) 368-2134 mike.siemens@dnr.mo.gov, Missouri Dept of Natural Resources; GgHgZi
Siesser, William G., 615-298-5659 william.g.siesser@vanderbilt.edu, Vanderbilt Univ; PmGsu
Siewers, Fredrick D., (270) 745-5988 fred.siewers@wku.edu, Western Kentucky Univ; GsPiZc
Sigler, Adam, asigler@montana.edu, Montana State Univ; Rw
Sigler, William V., (419) 530-2897 von.sigler@utoledo.edu, Univ of Toledo; Zn
Sigloch, Karin, +44 (1865) 272000 karin.sigloch@earth.ox.ac.uk, Univ of Oxford; YgsGt
Sigman, Daniel M., 609-258-2194 sigman@princeton.edu, Princeton Univ; ClsPc
Sigurdsson, Haraldur, (401) 874-6596 haraldur@gso.uri.edu, Univ of Rhode Island; Ou
Sikora, Todd D., 717-872-3292 todd.sikora@millersville.edu, Millersville Univ; As
Silliman, James, (361) 825-3718 james.silliman@tamucc.edu, Texas A&M Univ, Corpus Christi; Co
Silva, Carlos M., cmsilva@fc.ul.pt, Unive de Lisboa; Pg
Silva, Catrina, csilva@fc.ul.pt, Unive de Lisboa; Hg
Silva, Lucas C., lcsilva@ucdavis.edu, Univ of California, Davis; Sb
Silva, Michael A., (916) 324-0768 California Geological Survey; Ng
Silva-Castro, Jhon, 859-257-1173 john.silva@uky.edu, Univ of Kentucky; Nm

Silveira, António B., antonio.brum@fc.ul.pt, Unive de Lisboa; Zf
Silveira, Maria, 8637351314 x209 mlas@ufl.edu, Univ of Florida; So
Silver, Eli A., (831) 459-2266 esilver@pmc.ucsc.edu, Univ of California, Santa Cruz; Yr
Silver, Leon T., (626) 395-6490 lsilver@gps.caltech.edu, California Inst of Tech; Cc
Silver, Mary W., (831) 459-2908 msilver@cats.ucsc.edu, Univ of California, Santa Cruz; Ob
Silvertooth, Jeffrey C., (520) 621-7145 silver@ag.arizona.edu, Univ of Arizona; So
Silvestri, Alberta, +390498279142 alberta.silvestri@unipd.it, Univ degli Studi di Padova; Gz
Simandl, George J., (250) 952-0413 gsimandle@galaxy.gov.bc.ca, Univ of Victoria; En
Simard, Suzanne, 604–822–1955 suzanne.simard@ubc.ca, Univ of British Columbia; Sb
Simila, Gerald W., (818) 677-3543 gerry.simila@csun.edu, California State Univ, Northridge; Yg
Simjouw, Jean-Paul, 203-932-1253 jsimjouw@newhaven.edu, Univ of New Haven; OcCma
Simmons, Craig, craig.simmons@flinders.edu.au, Flinders Univ; Hw
Simmons, F. William, (217) 333-4424 Univ of Illinois, Urbana-Champaign; Sp
Simmons, Lizanne V., (949) 589-0562 Santiago Canyon Coll; Gr
Simmons, M. G., gene.simmons29@outlook.com, Massachusetts Inst of Tech; Yg
Simmons, Peter, +44 (0)1603 59 3122 p.simmons@uea.ac.uk, Univ of East Anglia; Eg
Simmons, Stuart, 801-581-4122 ssimmons@egi.utah.edu, Univ of Utah; EmCqHg
Simmons, William B., (504) 280-6791 wsimmons@uno.edu, Univ of New Orleans; Gz
Simms, Alexander, (805) 893-7292 asimms@geol.ucsb.edu, Univ of California, Santa Barbara; GsuGm
Simms, Janet E., (601) 634-3493 Mississippi State Univ; Yg
Simon, Joel D., 609-258-4101 jdsimon@princeton.edu, Princeton Univ; YsgYr
Simon, Steven B., sbs8@unm.edu, Univ of New Mexico; XmcGi
Simonetti, Stephanie, stefanie.simonetti.4@nd.edu, Univ of Notre Dame; Zn
Simonetti, Tony, simonetti.tony@gmail.com, Univ of Notre Dame; Ct
Simonis, Jean, +27729773994 simonismtz@yahoo.com, Univ of Zululand; HyGgHg
Simons, Frederik J., 609-258-2598 fjsimons@princeton.edu, Princeton Univ; YsdYm
Simons, Mark, (626) 395-6984 simons@caltech.edu, California Inst of Tech; Ys
Simonson, Bruce M., bruce.simonson@oberlin.edu, Oberlin Coll; GsXmHw
Simony, Philip S., (403) 220-6679 Univ of Calgary; Gc
Simpkins, William W., (515) 294-7814 bsimp@iastate.edu, Iowa State Univ of Sci & Tech; HwGlCs
Simpson, Edward L., (610) 683-4447 simpson@kutztown.edu, Kutztown Univ of Pennsylvania; Gs
Simpson, Frank -., 519-253-3000 ext. 2487 franks@uwindsor.ca, Univ of Windsor; GsrGe
Simpson, Robert M., (731) 881-7439 msimpson@utm.edu, Univ of Tennessee, Martin; AsmZi
Simpson, Jr., H. James, (703) 779-2043 simpsonj@ldeo.columbia.edu, Columbia Univ; Cm
Sims, Albert L., (218) 281-8619 simsx008@umn.edu, Univ of Minnesota, Twin Cities; Sc
Sims, David, d.w.sims@soton.ac.uk, Univ of Southampton; Ob
Sims, Douglas , 702-651-4840 douglas.sims@csn.edu, Coll of Southern Nevada - West Charleston Campus; GeSp
Sims, Kenneth W., 307-766-3386 ksims7@uwyo.edu, Univ of Wyoming; CgGvCa
Simsek, Sakir, +90 (312) 2977770 ssimsek@hacettepe.edu.tr, Hacettepe Univ; Hw
Sinclair, Alastair J., (604) 822-3086 asinclair@eos.ubc.ca, Univ of British Columbia; EmGg
Sinclair, Hugh D., +44 (0) 131 650 2518 hugh.sinclair@ed.ac.uk, Edinburgh Univ; So
Singer, Bradley S., (608) 262-6366 bsinger@geology.wisc.edu, Univ of Wisconsin, Madison; Cc
Singer, David M., 330-672-3006 dsinger4@kent.edu, Kent State Univ; Gze
Singer, Jill K., (716) 878-4724 singerjk@buffalostate.edu, Buffalo State Coll; GsOp
Singer, Michael, +44 01334 462874 michael.singer@st-andrews.ac.uk, Univ of St. Andrews; Hg
Singh, Amrita, amrita4@ualberta.ca, Univ of Alberta; Zu
Singh, Hanumant, 617.373.7286 ha.singh@neu.edu, Northeastern Univ; Zn
Singh, Harbans, (973) 655-7383 singhh@mail.montclair.edu, Montclair State Univ; Zn
Singh, Kamaljit, k.singh@hw.ac.uk, Heriot-Watt Univ; Np
Singha, Kamini, 303-273-3822 ksingha@mines.edu, Colorado Sch of Mines; Hw
Singler, Charles R., 330-941-3611 crsingler@ysu.edu, Youngstown State Univ; Gs
Singleton, John, (970) 491-0740 john.singleton@colostate.edu, Colorado State Univ; Gct
Sinha, A. Krishna, (540) 231-5580 pitlab@vt.edu, Virginia Polytechnic Inst & State Univ; Gt
Sinha, Ashish, (310) 243-3166 asinha@csudh.edu, California State Univ, Dominguez Hills; PeCs
Sinton, John M., (808) 956-7751 sinton@hawaii.edu, Univ of Hawai'i, Manoa; Gi
Sintubin, Manuel, manuel.sintubin@ees.kuleuven.be, Katholieke Universiteit Leuven; GtcGa
Sipola, Maija, 513-529-3230 sipolame@miamioh.edu, Miami Univ; Gg
Sipos, György, +3662544156 gysipos@geo.u-szeged.hu, Univesity of Szeged; HqYm
Sirbescu, Mona, 989-774-4497 sirbe1mc@cmich.edu, Central Michigan Univ; GiCup
Sîrbu, Smaranda D., doina.sirbu@uaic.ro, Alexandru Ioan Cuza; Ge
Sissom, David , dsissom@wtamu.edu, West Texas A&M Univ; Zn
Sisson, Virginia, 713-743-7634 vbsisson@uh.edu, Univ of Houston; Gpt
Sisterson, Doug, 630-252-5836 dlsisterson@anl.gov, Argonne; As
Sisterson, Douglas L., (630) 252-5836 dsisterson@anl.gov, Argonne; As
Sit, Stefany , 312-413-1868 ssit@uic.edu, Univ of Illinois at Chicago; Ygs
Sitwell, O.F. George, sitwell@telus.net, Univ of Alberta; Zn
Siuta, David, 802-626-6238 david.siuta@northernvermont.edu, Northern Vermont Univ-Lyndon; AsZn
Size, William B., (404) 727-0203 wsize@emory.edu, Emory Univ; GivGa
Sjoblom, Megan, (208) 486-7678 pickardm@byui.edu, Brigham Young Univ - Idaho; GiZeGe
Sjostrom, Derek, (406) 238-7387 derek.sjostrom@rocky.edu, Rocky Mountain Coll; ClGsHs
Skalbeck, John D., 262-595-2490 skalbeck@uwp.edu, Univ of Wisconsin, Parkside; HwYgGg
Skarke, Adam, (662) 268-1032 ext 258 adam.skarke@msstate.edu, Mississippi State Univ; GuYrOn
Skehan, James W., 617-552-8312 james.skehan@bc.edu, Boston Coll; Gc
Skemer, Philip, 314-935-3584 pskemer@levee.wustl.edu, Washington Univ in St. Louis; GcCp
Skidmore, Mark L., (406) 994-7251 skidmore@montana.edu, Montana State Univ; ClPgGl
Skillen, James, 616-526-7546 jrs39@calvin.edu, Calvin Coll; Zu
Skinner, Christopher , (978) 934-3901 christopher_skinner@uml.edu, Univ of Massachusetts, Lowell; At
Skinner, Lisa, 928-523-5814 lisa.skinner@nau.edu, Northern Arizona Univ; ZeGvZi
Skinner, Luke C., +44 (0) 1223 764912 luke00@esc.cam.ac.uk, Univ of Cambridge; GeCmOg
Skinner, Randall, 801-422-6083 randy_skinner@byu.edu, Brigham Young Univ; Gg
Skippen, George B., gskippen@ccs.carleton.ca, Carleton Univ; Cg
Sklar, Leonard, 415-338-1204 leonard@sfsu.edu, San Francisco State Univ; Gm
Skoda, Radek, +420 549 49 7392 rskoda@sci.muni.cz, Masaryk Univ; GzZmGi
Skoog, Annelie, 860-405-9220 annelie.skoog@uconn.edu, Univ of Connecticut; Oc
Skubis, Steven T., (315) 312-2799 steven.skubis@oswego.edu, SUNY, Oswego; Am
Skyllingstad, Eric, 541-737-5697 skylling@coas.oregonstate.edu, Oregon State Univ; Am
Slade, Jr., Raymond M., rslade@austincc.edu, Austin Comm Coll District; HgsHq
Slagle, Angela, aslagle@ldeo.columbia.edu, Columbia Univ; Gu
Slater, Brian, 518-473-9988 bslater@mail.nysed.gov, New York State Geological Survey; GoEoGr
Slater, David, (775) 784-4893 dslater@seismo.unr.edu, Univ of Nevada, Reno; Ys
Slater, Gregory F., (905) 525-9140 (Ext. 26388) gslater@mcmaster.ca, McMaster Univ; Cg
Slater, Lee S., 973-353-5109 lslater@newark.rutgers.edu, Rutgers, The State Univ of New Jersey, Newark; YeHw
Slater, Tom, +44 (0) 131 650 9506 tom.slater@ed.ac.uk, Edinburgh Univ; Zn
Slatkin, Montgomery, (510) 642-6300 Univ of California, Berkeley; Pg

FACULTY INDEX – S

Slattery, William, 937 775-3455 william.slattery@wright.edu, Wright State Univ; ZeGr
Slaughter, Richard, 608/262-2399 rich@geology.wisc.edu, Univ of Wisconsin, Madison; Pg
Slavetskas, Carol, cslavets@binghamton.edu, Binghamton Univ; Zn
Slawinski, Michael A., (709) 737-7541 mslawins@mun.ca, Memorial Univ of Newfoundland; Ys
Sledzinski, Grazyna, (313) 577-2506 ab4478@wayne.edu, Wayne State Univ; Gg
Sleep, Norman H., (650) 723-0882 Stanford Univ; Yg
Sleezer, Richard O., rsleezer@emporia.edu, Emporia State Univ; ZiSdHs
Sletten, Ronald S., 206-543-0571 sletten@uw.edu, Univ of Washington; Sob
Slingerland, Rudy L., (814) 865-6892 sling@geosc.psu.edu, Pennsylvania State Univ, Univ Park; Gs
Sloan, Doris, (510) 527-5710 dsloan@berkeley.edu, Univ of California, Berkeley; Pme
Sloan, Heather, 718-960-8008 heather.sloan@lehman.cuny.edu, Lehman Coll (CUNY); Yr
Sloan, Heather , 718-960-8008 heather.sloan@lehman.cuny.edu, Graduate Sch of the City Univ of New York; Gg
Sloan, Jon R., (818) 677-4880 jon.sloan@csun.edu, California State Univ, Northridge; Pm
Sloan, Lisa C., (831) 459-3693 lsloan@pmc.ucsc.edu, Univ of California, Santa Cruz; Pe
Slobodnik, Marek, +420 549 49 7055 marek@sci.muni.cz, Masaryk Univ; GeEg
Sloss, Craig, 610731382610 c.sloss@qut.edu.au, Queensland Univ of Tech; GsrGm
Slovinsky, Peter, (207) 287-7173 peter.a.slovinsky@maine.gov, Dept of Agriculture, Conservation, and Forestry; Gu
Slowey, Niall C., (979) 845-8478 nslowey@ocean.tamu.edu, Texas A&M Univ; Ou
Smaglik, Suzanne M., 307-855-2146 ssmaglik@cwc.edu, Central Wyoming Coll; GgZeCg
Smale, Jody L., 717-702-2020 jsmale@pa.gov, DCNR- Pennsylvania Bureau of Geological Survey; Zn
Small, Christopher, small@ldeo.columbia.edu, Columbia Univ; Zr
Smalley, Gabriela W., 609-896-5097 gsmalley@rider.edu, Rider Univ; ObcOp
Smalley, Glendon W., (615) 598-5714 Sewanee: Univ of the South; Sf
Smalley, Jr., Robert, (901) 678-2007 rsmalley@memphis.edu, Univ of Memphis; Yd
Smart, Christopher, +44 1752 584764 c.smart@plymouth.ac.uk, Univ of Plymouth; Pg
Smart, Katie A., 011 717 6549 katie.smart2@wits.ac.za, Univ of the Witwatersrand; CsGx
Smay, Jessica J., 4082982181 x3933 jessica.smay@sjcc.edu, San Jose City Coll; ZeGm
Smayda, Theodore J., (401) 874-6171 tsmayda@gso.uri.edu, Univ of Rhode Island; Ob
Smedes, Harry W., (541) 552-6479 Southern Oregon Univ; Gi
Smedley, Andrew, +44 0161 306-8770 andrew.smedley@manchester.ac.uk, Univ of Manchester; As
Smerdon, Jason, jsmerdon@ldeo.columbia.edu, Columbia Univ; Pe
Smethie, William, bsmeth@ldeo.columbia.edu, Columbia Univ; Cg
Smiley, Tara M., (812) 855-3728 tmsmiley@iu.edu, Indiana Univ, Bloomington; Pe
Smilnak, Roberta A., (303) 556-3144 Metropolitan State Coll of Denver; Zg
Smirnov, Aleksey V., (906) 487-2365 asmirnov@mtu.edu, Michigan Technological Univ; YmgGt
Smirnov, Anna, (418) 654-3711 asmirnov@nrcan.gc.ca, Universite du Quebec; Cs
Smit, Ansie, +27124202282 ansie.smit@up.ac.za, Univ of Pretoria; Rn
Smith, Alan L., (909) 537-5409 alsmith@csusb.edu, California State Univ, San Bernardino; GviGz
Smith, Alison J., (330) 672-3709 alisonjs@kent.edu, Kent State Univ; GnPce
Smith, Ben , 206-616-9176 bsmith@apl.washington.edu, Univ of Washington; GlZr
Smith, Betty E., (217) 581-2626 besmith@eiu.edu, Eastern Illinois Univ; Zu
Smith, Brianne, 718-951-5000 x2689 brianne.smith43@brooklyn.cuny.edu, Brooklyn Coll (CUNY); Hs
Smith, C. K., 210-486-0062 csmith55@alamo.edu, San Antonio Comm Coll; ZyzZz
Smith, C. Ken, (931) 598-3219 ksmith@sewanee.edu, Sewanee: Univ of the South; Sf
Smith, Catherine H., (505) 667-0113 chsmith@lanl.gov, Los Alamos; Ca
Smith, Charles K., csmith55@alamo.edu, Alamo Colls, San Antonio Coll; Zy
Smith, Craig R., (808) 956-7776 csmith@soest.hawaii.edu, Univ of Hawai'i, Manoa; Ob
Smith, Dan, +440116 252 5355 djs40@le.ac.uk, Leicester Univ; Ge
Smith, David C., (401) 874-6172 dcsmith@gsosun1.gso.uri.edu, Univ of Rhode Island; Ob
Smith, Dena M., 303-735-2011 dena.smith@colorado.edu, Univ of Colorado; Pg
Smith, Diane R., (210) 999-7656 dsmith@trinity.edu, Trinity Univ; Gi
Smith, Donald R., (831) 459-5041 dsmith@scipp.ucsc.edu, Univ of California, Santa Cruz; Zn
Smith, Douglas, (512) 471-4261 doug@jsg.utexas.edu, Univ of Texas, Austin; GipGz
Smith, Elizabeth Y., 702-895-4065 elizabeth.smith@unlv.edu, Univ of Nevada, Las Vegas; ZnnZn
Smith, Erik, erik@belle.baruch.sc.edu, Univ of South Carolina; HsOb
Smith, Eugene I., (702) 895-3971 gsmith@ccmail.nevada.edu, Univ of Nevada, Las Vegas; Gi
Smith, Florence P., (630) 252-7980 Argonne; Ca
Smith, Gerald R., (734) 764-0491 grsmith@umich.edu, Univ of Michigan; Ps
Smith, Grant, 503-838-8862 smithg@wou.edu, Western Oregon Univ; Zg
Smith, H D., smithhd@cf.ac.uk, Cardiff Univ; Zn
Smith, J. Leslie, (604) 822-4108 lsmith@eos.ubc.ca, Univ of British Columbia; Hw
Smith, James A., (609) 258-4615 jsmith@princeton.edu, Princeton Univ; Hg
Smith, Janet S., (717) 477-1757 jssmit@ship.edu, Shippensburg Univ; Zi
Smith, Jason J., 607-778-5116 smithjj@sunybroome.edu, Broome Comm Coll; Ggs
Smith, Jeffery L., (509) 335-7648 Washington State Univ; Sb
Smith, Jen R., jensmith@wustl.edu, Washington Univ in St. Louis; Ga
Smith, Jennifer E., (858) 246-0803 smithj@ucsd.edu, Univ of California, San Diego; Obn
Smith, Jim, j.smith@flinders.edu.au, Flinders Univ; Zn
Smith, Jon, 785-864-2179 jjsmith@kgs.ku.edu, Univ of Kansas; GsPe
Smith, Joseph P., 410-293-6568 jpsmith@usna.edu, United States Naval Academy; CmOg
Smith, K. L., (702) 895-3971 Wichita State Univ; Zn
Smith, Karen, 630-252-0136 smithk@anl.gov, Argonne; Hw
Smith, Karl A., (805) 756-2262 ksmith@tc.umn.edu, Univ of Minnesota, Twin Cities; Nx
Smith, Kathlyn M., (912) 478-5398 ksmith@georgiasouthern.edu, Georgia Southern Univ; Pv
Smith, Ken D., (775) 784-4218 ken@seismo.unr.edu, Univ of Nevada, Reno; YsGt
Smith, Langhorne, 518-473-6262 lsmith@remove@this.mail.nysed.gov, New York State Geological Survey; Go
Smith, Larry N., (406) 496-4859 lsmith@mtech.edu, Montana Tech of the Univ of Montana; GsmEo
Smith, Laurence C., (310) 825-3154 lsmith@geog.ucla.edu, Univ of California, Los Angeles; Hs
Smith, Martin, martin.smith@durham.ac.uk, Durham Univ; Pe
Smith, Matthew C., (352) 392-2106 mcsmith@ufl.edu, Univ of Florida; Gi
Smith, Michael, 205-247-3724 msmith@gsa.state.al.us, Geological Survey of Alabama; Hg
Smith, Mike, +44020 8417 2500 michael.smith@kingston.ac.uk, Kingston Univ; Zr
Smith, Norman D., (402) 472-5362 nsmith3@unl.edu, Univ of Nebraska, Lincoln; Gsm
Smith, Paul H., (505) 667-7494 Los Alamos; Zn
Smith, Peter, (520) 621-2725 psmith@lpl.arizona.edu, Univ of Arizona; Zr
Smith, Phillip J., (765) 494-3286 pjsmith@purdue.edu, Purdue Univ; As
Smith, Richard, 479-575-3355 Univ of Arkansas, Fayetteville; Gm
Smith, Robert, (208) 885-2560 smithbob@uidaho.edu, Univ of Idaho; Cb
Smith, Ronald B., (203) 432-3129 ronald.smith@yale.edu, Yale Univ; As
Smith, Sean, 207-581-2198 sean.m.smith@maine.edu, Univ of Maine; Hs
Smith, Shane V., 330-941-1752 svsmith@ysu.edu, Youngstown State Univ; Gs
Smith, Stephen V., svsmith@hawaii.edu, Univ of Hawai'i, Manoa; Ou
Smith, Steven C., 916-435-9180 smithsc@arc.losrios.edu, American River Coll; ZynZn
Smith, Stewart W., stews@uw.edu, Univ of Washington; Ys
Smith, Susan M., 406-496-4173 ssmith@mtech.edu, Montana Tech of The Univ of Montana; Zn
Smith, Terence E., tsmith@uwindsor.ca, Univ of Windsor; Gi
Smith, Terry L., (805) 756-2262 tsmith@calpoly.edu, California Polytechnic State Univ; So
Smith, Thomas M., (804) 924-3107 tms9a@virginia.edu, Univ of Virginia; Zg
Smith, William H., (314) 935-5638 whsmith@dasi.wustl.edu, Washington Univ in St. Louis; Xc
Smith-Engle, Jennifer M., (361) 825-2436 jennifer.smith-engle@tamucc.edu,

Texas A&M Univ, Corpus Christi; Gs
Smith-Konter, Bridget R., 808-956-3618 brkonter@hawaii.edu, Univ of Hawai'i, Manoa; YdXy
Smithson, Jayne, 5102357800 x.4284 jsmithson@contracosta.edu, Contra Costa Coll; Gg
Smithyman, Brenden, bsmithym@uwo.ca, Western Univ; Ye
Smoak, Joseph (Donny), smoak@usf.edu, Univ of South Florida; Sf
Smout, Brooklyn, (801) 626-7139 brooklynsmout@weber.edu, Weber State Univ; Zn
Smrekar, Suzanne E., (818) 354-4192 Jet Propulsion Lab; Xy
Smukler, Sean, 604–822–2795 sean.smukler@ubc.ca, Univ of British Columbia; So
Smylie, Douglas E., (416) 736-2100 #66438 doug@core.yorku.ca, York Univ; Yg
Smyth, Joseph R., 303-492-5521 joseph.smyth@colorado.edu, Univ of Colorado; Gz
Smyth, Rebecca C., (512) 471-0232 rebecca.smyth@beg.utexas.edu, Univ of Texas at Austin, Jackson Sch of Geosciences; Hg
Smyth, Thomas J., (919) 515-2838 North Carolina State Univ; Sc
Smyth, William D., (541) 737-3029 smyth@coas.oregonstate.edu, Oregon State Univ; Op
Smythe, Wendy F., (218) 726-7899 wsmythe@d.umn.edu, Univ of Minnesota Duluth; Ou
Smythe, William, (310) 825-2434 Univ of California, Los Angeles; Ys
Snead, John I., (225) 578-3454 snead@lsu.edu, Louisiana State Univ; Gm
Snider, Henry I., (860) 228-9815 snider@easternct.edu, Eastern Connecticut State Univ; Ge
Snieder, Roel, 303-273-3456 rsnieder@mines.edu, Colorado Sch of Mines; Ye
Snoeckx, Hilde, (850) 474-3377 snoeckx@uwf.edu, Univ of West Florida; OuZg
Snoke, J. Arthur, (540) 231-6028 snoke@vt.edu, Virginia Polytechnic Inst & State Univ; Ys
Snow, Daniel, (402)472-7539 dsnow1@unl.edu, Univ of Nebraska, Lincoln; Ge
Snow, Jonathan, 713-743-3298 jesnow@uh.edu, Univ of Houston; Ca
Snow, Julie A., (724) 738-2503 julie.snow@sru.edu, Slippery Rock Univ; As
Snyder, Daniel, 478-274-7806 dsnyder@mgc.edu, Middle Georgia Coll; Gg
Snyder, Jeffrey A., (419) 372-0533 jasnyd@bgnet.bgsu.edu, Bowling Green State Univ; Gm
Snyder, Jennifer L., (610) 359-5291 jsnyder2@dccc.edu, Delaware County Comm Coll; Zg
Snyder, Lori D., (715) 836-5086 snyderld@uwec.edu, Univ of Wisconsin, Eau Claire; Gx
Snyder, Morgan E., morgan.snyder@acadiau.ca, Acadia Univ; Gc
Snyder, Noah, 617-552-0839 snyderno@bc.edu, Boston Coll; GgHg
Snyder, Peter K., 612-625-8207 pksnyder@umn.edu, Univ of Minnesota, Twin Cities; As
Snyder, Richard L., rlsnyder@ucdavis.edu, Univ of California, Davis; As
Snyder, Walter S., (208) 426-3645 wsnyder@boisestate.edu, Boise State Univ; GrcGt
Snyman, Lourens, +27 (0) 12 420 2862 lourens.snyman@up.ac.za, Univ of Pretoria; Zi
Soares Cruz, Anna Paula ., acruz@udel.edu, California State Univ, Bakersfield; CmOoPc
Sobel, Adam, ahs129@columbia.edu, Columbia Univ; As
Sobotka, Jerzy, jerzy.sobotka@uwr.edu.pl, Univ of Wroclaw; YeuEo
Sohi, Sran P., +44 (0) 131 651 4471 saran.sohi@ed.ac.uk, Edinburgh Univ; So
Sohn, Robert A., (508) 289-3616 rsohn@whoi.edu, Woods Hole Oceanographic Inst; Yr
Soja, Constance M., (315) 228-7200 csoja@colgate.edu, Colgate Univ; PiGs
Sokolik, Irina, (404) 894-6180 isokolik@eas.gatech.edu, Georgia Inst of Tech; AsZr
Sokolova, Elena, (204) 747-8252 elena_sokolova@umanitoba.ca, Univ of Manitoba; Gz
Solan, Martin, +44 (0)23 80593755 m.solan@soton.ac.uk, Univ of Southampton; Ob
Solana, Camen, +44 023 92 842394 carmen.solana@port.ac.uk, Univ of Portsmouth; Gv
Solar, Gary S., (716) 878-4900 solargs@buffalostate.edu, Buffalo State Coll; GcpGt
Soldat, Douglas J., (608) 263-3631 djsoldat@wisc.edu, Univ of Wisconsin, Madison; So
Soldati, Arianna, asoldat@ncsu.edu, North Carolina State Univ; Gv
Solecki, Andrzej, andrzej.solecki@uwr.edu.pl, Univ of Wroclaw; Eg
Solecki, William, (973) 655-5129 soleckiw@mail.montclair.edu, Montclair State Univ; Zu
Solferino, Giulio, +44 1784 443585 giulio.solferino@rhul.ac.uk, Royal Holloway Univ of London; Gg
Solis, Michael P., 614 265 6597 michael.solis@dnr.state.oh.us, Ohio Dept of Natural Resources; GgcGt
Soll, Wendy E., (505) 665-6930 weasel@lanl.gov, Los Alamos; Hw
Solomatov, Viatcheslav S., 314-935-7882 slava@wustl.edu, Washington Univ in St. Louis; Yg
Solomon, Douglas K., (801) 581-7231 kip.solomon@utah.edu, Univ of Utah; Hw
Solomon, Keith, (519) 824-4120 Ext 58792 ksolomon@uoguelph.ca, Univ of Guelph; Zn
Solomon, Sean , 845-365-8714 solomon@ldeo.columbia.edu, Columbia Univ; Xy
Solomon, Susan, solos@mit.edu, Massachusetts Inst of Tech; As
Soltanian, Reza, mohamadreza.soltanian@uc.edu, Univ of Cincinnati; Hw
Somarin, Alireza, 204-727-9680 somarina@brandonu.ca, Brandon Univ; Gig
Somasundaran, Ponisseril, (212) 854-2926 ps24@columbia.edu, Columbia Univ; Nx
Somenhally, Anil, asomenahally@tamu.edu, Texas A&M Univ; Sb
Somers, Jr., Arnold E., (229) 333-5664 gsomers@valdosta.edu, Valdosta State Univ; Zn
Somerville, Richard C., (858) 534-4644 rsomerville@ucsd.edu, Univ of California, San Diego; As
Sommer, Ulrich , usommer@geomar.de, Dalhousie Univ; Ob
Sommerfield, Christopher K., (302) 645-4255 cs@udel.edu, Univ of Delaware; OuGsCc
Sonder, Ingo, (716)645-6366 ingomark@buffalo.edu, SUNY, Buffalo; Gv
Sonder, Leslie J., 603-646-2372 leslie.sonder@dartmouth.edu, Dartmouth Coll; Gq
Sondergeld, Carl H., (405) 325-6870 csondergeld@ou.edu, Univ of Oklahoma; NpYex
Sone, Hiroki, (608) 890-0531 hsone@wisc.edu, Univ of Wisconsin, Madison; NrYxGt
Sonett, Charles P., (520) 621-6935 sonett@dakotacom.net, Univ of Arizona; Yg
Song, Alex, +44 07472526049 alex.song@ucl.ac.uk, Univ Coll London; Ysg
Song, Liaosha, lsong1@csub.edu, California State Univ, Bakersfield; GoYeEo
Song, Xiaodong, xsong@illinois.edu, Univ of Illinois, Urbana-Champaign; Ys
Sonnenberg, Stephen A., 303-384-2182 ssonnenb@mines.edu, Colorado Sch of Mines; Go
Sonnenwald, Margreta, ‭+49 89 28925822‬ margreta.sonnenwald@tum.de, Technical Univ of Munich; Ng
Soreghan, Gerilyn S., (405) 325-4482 lsoreg@ou.edu, Univ of Oklahoma; GsPcZg
Soreghan, Michael J., (405) 325-3393 msoreg@ou.edu, Univ of Oklahoma; Gs
Sorensen, Sorena S., (202) 633-1820 sorensens@si.edu, Smithsonian Inst / Nat Mus of Natural History; Gp
Sorkhabi, Rasoul, 801-581-9070 rsorkhabi@egi.utah.edu, Univ of Utah; GctGc
Sorooshian, Soroosh, soroosh@uci.edu, Univ of Arizona; Hg
Soster, Frederick M., (765) 658-4670 fsoster@depauw.edu, DePauw Univ; Gs
Sottile, Jr., Joseph, 859-257-4616 joe.sottile@uky.edu, Univ of Kentucky; Nm
Souch, Catherine J., (317) 274-1103 Indiana Univ, Indianapolis; Gm
Soucy de la Roche, Renaud, 418-654-2609 renaud.soucy_la_roche@ete.inrs.ca, Universite du Quebec; Gc
Soule, Peter T., (828) 262-7056 soulept@appstate.edu, Appalachian State Univ; As
Soule, S. Adam, (508) 289-3213 ssoule@whoi.edu, Woods Hole Oceanographic Inst; Gvu
Soupios, Panteleimon , +966138602689 panteleimon.soupios@kfupm.edu.sa, King Fahd Univ of Petroleum and Minerals; Yg
Sousa, Luís M., lsousa@utad.pt, Unive de Trás-os-Montes e Alto Douro; EnGgNg
Sousa, Wayne P., (510) 642-2435 Univ of California, Berkeley; Ob
Southam, Gordon, (519) 661-3197 gsoutham@uwo.ca, Western Univ; Pg
Southam, John R., (305) 284-1898 jsoutham@miami.edu, Univ of Miami; Op
Southard, John B., (617) 253-3397 southard@mit.edu, Massachusetts Inst of Tech; Gs
Southard, Randal J., (530) 752-2199 rjsouthard@ucdavis.edu, Univ of California, Davis; So
Southon, John, (949) 824-3674 jsouthon@uci.edu, Univ of California, Irvine; CcOcPe
Southwell, Benjamin, (906) 635-2076 bsouthwell@lssu.edu, Lake Superior State Univ; Zn

Sowers, Todd, (814) 863-8093 sowers@geosc.psu.edu, Pennsylvania State Univ, Univ Park; Cs
Spaeth, Matthew P., 217-265-6578 spaeth@illinois.edu, Illinois State Geological Survey; Ge
Spahr, Paul, 614 265 6577 paul.spahr@dnr.state.oh.us, Ohio Dept of Natural Resources; GeHwZi
Spalding, Brian P., bps@ornl.gov, Oak Ridge; Sc
Spanbauer, Trisha, (419) 530-2823 trisha.spanbauer@utoledo.edu, Univ of Toledo; Zn
Spandler, Carl, carl.spandler@jcu.edu.au, James Cook Univ; GxEmCg
Spane, Frank A., (509) 371-7081 frank.spane@pnl.gov, Pacific Northwest; Hgw
Spanos, T.J.T (Tim), (780) 435-5245 tim@phys.ualberta.ca, Univ of Alberta; YgsEo
Sparks, David, (979) 458-1051 david-w-sparks@geos.tamu.edu, Texas A&M Univ; YdGq
Spayd, Steven E., (609) 984-6587 steve.spayd@dep.state.nj.us, New Jersey Geological and Water Survey; HwGb
Spear, Frank S., (518) 276-6103 spearf@rpi.edu, Rensselaer Polytechnic Inst; GpCpGc
Specker, Jennifer, (401) 874-6858 jspecker@gsosun1.gso.uri.edu, Univ of Rhode Island; Ob
Speece, Marvin A., (406) 496-4188 mspeece@mtech.edu, Montana Tech of the Univ of Montana; YeuYs
Speed, Don, (602) 285-7244 d.speed@phoenixcollege.edu, Phoenix Coll; Gg
Speer, James, (812) 237-2257 jim.speer@indstate.edu, Indiana State Univ; PeZyGe
Speidel, David H., (718) 261-9524 david.speidel@qc.cuny.edu, Queens Coll (CUNY); Cgp
Speijer, Robert, robert.speijer@kuleuven.be, Katholieke Universiteit Leuven; PmcOo
Spell, Terry L., (702) 895-1171 terry.spell@unlv.edu, Univ of Nevada, Las Vegas; CcGvi
Spellman, Patricia, pdspellm@usf.edu, Univ of South Florida; Hq
Spence, George D., (250) 721-6187 gspence@uvic.ca, Univ of Victoria; Ys
Spencer, Joel Q., (785) 532-2249 joelspen@ksu.edu, Kansas State Univ; CcGs
Spencer, Matt, (906) 635-2085 mspencer1@lssu.edu, Lake Superior State Univ; Gl
Spencer, Matthew, +44 0151 795 4399 m.spencer@liverpool.ac.uk, Univ of Liverpool; Og
Spencer, Patrick K., (509) 527-5222 spencerp@whitman.edu, Whitman Coll; Pg
Spencer, Ronald J., (403) 220-6447 spencer@geo.ucalgary.ca, Univ of Calgary; Cg
Spera, Frank J., (805) 893-4880 spera@geol.ucsb.edu, Univ of California, Santa Barbara; Gi
Sperazza, Michael, 631-632-1687 michael.sperazza@sunysb.edu, Stony Brook Univ; Zn
Spero, Howard J., (530) 752-3307 hjspero@ucdavis.edu, Univ of California, Davis; Cm
Sperone, Felice, (313) 577-2506 fgsperone@wayne.edu, Wayne State Univ; GgZr
Spetzler, Hartmut A., 303-492-6715 spetzler@colorado.edu, Univ of Colorado; Ys
Spiegelman, Marc, mspieg@ldeo.columbia.edu, Columbia Univ; Ys
Spieler, Oliver, 089/2180 4221 spieler@min.uni-muenchen.de, Ludwig-Maximilians-Univ Muenchen; Gz
Spiess, Richard, +390498279150 richard.spiess@unipd.it, Univ degli Studi di Padova; Gp
Spigel, Lindsay, (207) 287-7177 lindsay.spigel@maine.gov, Dept of Agriculture, Conservation, and Forestry; Gm
Spikes, Kyle T., 512-471-7674 kyle.spikes@jsg.utexas.edu, Univ of Texas, Austin; Ye
Spilde, Michael N., (505) 277-5430 mspilde@unm.edu, Univ of New Mexico; Gz
Spilker, Linda J., (818) 354-1647 linda.j.spilker@jpl.nasa.gov, Jet Propulsion Lab; XyZr
Spindel, Robert C., (206) 543-1310 spindel@apl.washington.edu, Univ of Washington; Op
Spinelli, Glenn, 575.835.6512 spinelli@nmt.edu, New Mexico Inst of Mining and Tech; Hw
Spinler, Joshua C., (501) 569-3544 jxspinler@ualr.edu, Univ of Arkansas at Little Rock; YdGt
Spinosa, Claude, (208) 426-5905 cspinosa@boisestate.edu, Boise State Univ; Pi
Spinrad, Richard, 541-220-1915 rick.spinrad@oregonstate.edu, Oregon State Univ; Op
Spitz, Yvette H., 541-737-3227 yspitz@coas.oregonstate.edu, Oregon State Univ; Yr
Splinter, Dale, splinted@uww.edu, Univ of Wisconsin, Whitewater; Hs
Spokas, Kurt, 612-626-2834 kurt.spokas@ars.usda.gov, Univ of Minnesota, Twin Cities; Spo
Spongberg, Alison L., (419) 530-4091 alison.spongberg@utoledo.edu, Univ of Toledo; Co
Spooner, Alecia, 425-388-9003 aspooner@everettcc.edu, Everett Comm Coll; Zg
Spooner, Edward T. C., (416) 978-3280 etcs@geology.utoronto.ca, Univ of Toronto; En
Spooner, Ian S., (902) 585-1312 ian.spooner@acadiau.ca, Acadia Univ; Ge
Spotila, James A., (540) 231-2109 spotila@vt.edu, Virginia Polytechnic Inst & State Univ; Gtm
Spracklen, Dominick, +44(0) 113 34 37488 d.v.spracklen@leeds.ac.uk, Univ of Leeds; Zn
Sprain, Courtney, 352-294-6319 csprain@ufl.edu, Univ of Florida; CgYg
Spratt, Deborah A., (403) 220-6446 spratt@geo.ucalgary.ca, Univ of Calgary; Gc
Spray, John G., (506) 999-3544 jgs@unb.ca, Univ of New Brunswick; GpXgGz
Sprenke, Kenneth F., (208) 885-5791 ksprenke@uidaho.edu, Univ of Idaho; Ye
Springer, Abraham E., (928) 523-7198 abe.springer@nau.edu, Northern Arizona Univ; Hw
Springer, Everett P., (505) 667-0569 everetts@lanl.gov, Los Alamos; Hq
Springer, Gregory S., (740) 593-9431 springeg@ohio.edu, Ohio Univ; GmPcGa
Springer, Kathleen B., (909) 307-2669 242 kspringer@sbcm.sbcounty.gov, San Bernardino County Mus; Zg
Springer, Robert K., springer@brandonu.ca, Brandon Univ; Gi
Springston, George E., (802) 485-2734 gsprings@norwich.edu, Norwich Univ; GmZiYg
Sprinkel, Douglas A., (801) 391-1977 douglassprinkel@utah.gov, Utah Geological Survey; GosGg
Sprinkle, James T., (512) 471-4264 echino@jsg.utexas.edu, Univ of Texas, Austin; PigGr
Spry, Paul G., (515) 294-9637 pgspry@iastate.edu, Iowa State Univ of Sci & Tech; Em
Spurr, Aaron, (319) 273-3789 aaron.spurr@uni.edu, Univ of Northern Iowa; Zeg
Squelch, Andrew P., +61 8 9266 2324 a.squelch@curtin.edu.au, Curtin Univ; NmYeZe
Squires, Richard L., (818) 677-2514 richard.squires@csun.edu, California State Univ, Northridge; Pi
Squyres, Steven W., (607) 255-3508 sws6@cornell.edu, Cornell Univ; Xg
Sremac, Jasenka, +38514606108 jsremac@yahoo.com, Univ of Zagreb; PesPb
Srimal, Neptune, (305) 919-5969 srimal@fiu.edu, Florida International Univ; Gt
Srinivasan, Balakrishnan, +914132655008 sbala.esc@pondiuni.edu.in, Pondicherry Univ; CcGiz
Sritharan, Subramania I., (937) 376-6275 sri@centralstate.edu, Central State Univ; Hg
SRIVASTAVA, HARI B., +919415353606 hbsrivastava@gmail.com, Banaras Hindu Univ; GctGp
Srivastava, Ramesh C., (312) 502-7139 srivast@geosci.uchicago.edu, Univ of Chicago; AsmAm
Sriver, Ryan, 217-300-0364 rsriver@illinois.edu, Univ of Illinois, Urbana-Champaign; As
Srnka, Len, (858) 822-1510 lsrnka@ucsd.edu, Univ of California, San Diego; Ym
Srogi, LeeAnn, (610) 436-2721 esrogi@wcupa.edu, West Chester Univ; Gp
St. John, James C., (404) 894-1754 jim.stjohn@eas.gatech.edu, Georgia Inst of Tech; As
St. John, Kristen E., 540-568-6675 stjohnke@jmu.edu, James Madison Univ; Ou
Stachel, Thomas, (780) 492-0865 thomas.stachel@ualberta.ca, Univ of Alberta; GiCs
Stachnik, Joshua, 610-758-2581 jcs612@lehigh.edu, Lehigh Univ; Ys
Stack, Andrew, (404) 894-3895 stackag@ornl.gov, Georgia Inst of Tech; Cg
Stadnyk, Leona, (403) 440-6165 lstadnyk@mtroyal.ca, Mount Royal Univ; Zn
Stafford, C. Russell, (812) 237-3989 russell.stafford@indstate.edu, Indiana State Univ; Gam
Stafford, Emily, (828) 227-7367 esstafford@wcu.edu, Western Carolina Univ; PgGg
Stafford, James, (307) 766-2286 Ext. 252 james.stafford@wyo.gov, Wyoming State Geological Survey; HgyEg
Stafford, Kevin W., (936) 468-2429 staffordk@sfasu.edu, Stephen F. Austin

State Univ; Hw
Stahle, David W., (479) 575-3703 dstahle@uark.edu, Univ of Arkansas, Fayetteville; GeZon
Stahlman, Phillip, (785) 625-3425 stahlman@ksu.edu, Kansas State Univ; So
Stakes, Debra, (805) 546-3100 dstakes@cuesta.edu, Cuesta Coll; Gg
Staley, Andrew W., (410) 260-8818 andrew.staley@maryland.gov, Maryland Department of Natural Resources; Hw
Stamm, Alfred J., (315) 312-2806 stamm@oswego.edu, SUNY, Oswego; Am
Stampone, Mary D., 603-862-3136 mary.stampone@unh.edu, Univ of New Hampshire; Zy
Stamps, D. S., 540-231-3651 dstamps@vt.edu, Virginia Polytechnic Inst & State Univ; YdGtRn
Stan, Cristiana, (703) 993-5391 cstan@gmu.edu, George Mason Univ; As
Stan, Oana, 0040232201467 cristina.stan@uaic.ro, Alexandru Ioan Cuza; GedCb
Standridge, Debbie, deborah.standridge@gsw.edu, Georgia Southwestern State Univ; Zn
Stanford, Scott D., (609) 292-2576 scott.stanford@dep.nj.gov, New Jersey Geological and Water Survey; Gml
Stanley, Clifford R., (902) 585-1344 cliff.stanley@acadiau.ca, Acadia Univ; Cea
Stanley, Daniel J., (202) 633-1354 Smithsonian Inst / Nat Mus of Natural History; Ou
Stanley, George R., (210) 486-0045 gstanley@alamo.edu, San Antonio Comm Coll; XzZgRm
Stanley, Jessica, (208) 885-4704 jessicastanley@uidaho.edu, Univ of Idaho; Gt
Stanley, Thomas M., (405) 325-7281 tmstanley@ou.edu, Univ of Oklahoma; PiGsc
Stanley, Jr., George D., (406) 243-5693 george.stanley@umontana.edu, Univ of Montana; Pi
Stansell, Nathan D., 815-753-1943 nstansell@niu.edu, Northern Illinois Univ; Gl
Stanton, Kathryn, 916-558-2343 stantok@scc.losrios.edu, Sacramento City Coll; GgPg
Stanton, Kelsay, kstanton@wvc.edu, Wenatchee Valley Coll; GgZe
Stanton, Timothy P., (831) 656-3144 stanton@nps.edu, Naval Postgraduate Sch; Op
Staples, Reid, 604-527-5226 rstaple4@douglascollege.ca, Douglas Coll; GpxGg
Stapleton, Michael G., (724) 738-2495 micheal.stapleton@sru.edu, Slippery Rock Univ; So
Starek, Michael , 361-825-3978 michael.starek@tamucc.edu, Texas A&M Univ, Corpus Christi; Zi
Stark, Robert, 089/2180 4329 stark@lrz.uni-muenchen.de, Ludwig-Maximilians-Univ Muenchen; Gz
Starr, Paepin K., paepin.starr@austincc.edu, Austin Comm Coll District; GlZrRc
Starr, Richard, 831-771-4400 starr@mlml.calstate.edu, Moss Landing Marine Lab; Zn
Starrfield, Sumner, (480) 965-7569 sumner.starrfield@asu.edu, Arizona State Univ; XaZnn
Stasko, Stanislaw, stanislaw.stasko@uwr.edu.pl, Univ of Wroclaw; Hg
Staten, Paul W., (812) 856-5135 pwstaten@indiana.edu, Indiana Univ, Bloomington; As
Staub, James R., (406) 243-4953 james.staub@umontana.edu, Univ of Montana; GsrEo
Stauffer, David R., (814) 863-3932 stauffer@essc.psu.edu, Pennsylvania State Univ, Univ Park; Am
Stauffer, Mel R., (306) 966-5708 mel.stauffer@usask.ca, Univ of Saskatchewan; Gc
Stead, Douglas, 778-782-6670 Simon Fraser Univ; Ng
Steadman, David W., (352) 273-1969 dws@flmnh.ufl.edu, Univ of Florida; PvGaPs
Steadman, Todd A., 864-656-2536 tsteadm@clemson.edu, Clemson Univ; ZnnZn
Stearley, Ralph F., (616) 526-6370 rstearle@calvin.edu, Calvin Coll; PvOgRh
Stearman, Will, +61 7 3138 4165 w.stearman@qut.edu.au, Queensland Univ of Tech; Geg
Stearns, David W., (405) 325-3253 mtdstearns@aol.com, Univ of Oklahoma; Gc
Stearns, Leigh, (785) 864-4202 stearns@ku.edu, Univ of Kansas; GlZrf
Stearns, Michael, (801) 863-8498 mstearns@uvu.edu, Utah Valley Univ; Gip
Steart, David, +61 3 9479 5641 d.steart@latrobe.edu.au, La Trobe Univ; GgPb
Stebbins, Jonathan F., (650) 723-1140 stebbins@pangea.stanford.edu, Stanford Univ; Cg
Stechmann, Samuel, 608-263-4351 stechmann@wisc.edu, Univ of Wisconsin, Madison; ZnAs
Steck, Lee, (505) 665-3528 Los Alamos; Gg
Steckler, Michael, steckler@ldeo.columbia.edu, Columbia Univ; Yv
Steel, Ronald J., (512) 471-0954 rsteel@mail.utexas.edu, Univ of Texas, Austin; Gs
Steele, Amber , 573-368-7152 amber.steele@dnr.mo.gov, Missouri Dept of Natural Resources; Sd
Steele, Andrew, 202-478-8974 asteele@carnegiescience.edu, Carnegie Inst for Sci; Xy
Steele, Bill, 206-685-5880 wsteele@uw.edu, Univ of Washington; Ys
Steele, Kenneth F., (501) 575-4403 ksteele@comp.uark.edu, Univ of Arkansas, Fayetteville; Cg
Steele, Michael A., (570) 408-4763 michael.steele@wilkes.edu, Wilkes Univ; Pg
Steen, Andrew, 865-974-0821 asteen1@utk.edu, Univ of Tennessee, Knoxville; CoOb
Steenberg, Julia, (612) 626-1830 and01006@umn.edu, Univ of Minnesota; Gs
Steenburgh, Jim, 801-581-8727 jim.steenburgh@utah.edu, Univ of Utah; As
Steenhuis, Tammo S., (607) 255-2489 tss1@cornell.edu, Cornell Univ; HgSo
Steenwerth, Kerri, ksteenwerth@ucdavis.edu, Univ of California, Davis; Cb
Steeples, Don W., (785) 737-3399 don@ku.edu, Univ of Kansas; YseGe
Steer, David N., 330 972-2099 steer@uakron.edu, Univ of Akron; Yes
Stefani, Cristina, +390498279195 cristina.stefani@unipd.it, Univ degli Studi di Padova; Gd
Stefano, Christopher J., 906-487-3028 cjstefano@mtu.edu, Michigan Technological Univ; GzxCg
Stefanova, Ivanka, 651-646-0665 stefa014@umn.edu, Univ of Minnesota, Twin Cities; Pl
Steffens, Katja, 089/2180 6533 katja.steffens@lmu.de, Ludwig-Maximilians-Univ Muenchen; Gg
Steger, John M., 305-237-2609 jsteger@mdc.edu, Miami Dade Coll (Kendall Campus); OgAmZg
Stegman, Dave, (858) 822-0767 dstegman@ucsd.edu, Univ of California, San Diego; Yd
Steidl, Gregg M., (609) 984-6587 gregg.steidl@dep.state.nj.us, New Jersey Geological and Water Survey; Ge
Steig, Eric J., (206) 685-3715 steig@uw.edu, Univ of Washington; CsGlAs
Steiger, Scott, (315) 312-2802 steiger@oswego.edu, SUNY, Oswego; Am
Stein, Carol A., (312) 996-9349 cstein@uic.edu, Univ of Illinois at Chicago; Yg
Stein, Holly, holly.stein@colostate.edu, Colorado State Univ; Cc
Stein, Seth, (847) 491-5265 seth@earth.northwestern.edu, Northwestern Univ; YsdYg
Steinberg, Roger T., (361) 698-1665 rsteinb@delmar.edu, Del Mar Coll; GgoPg
Steinberger, Julia, +44 (0)785 607 9625 j.k.steinberger@leeds.ac.uk, Univ of Leeds; Zu
Steinen, Randolph P., (860) 933-2590 randolph.steinen@ct.gov, Dept of Energy and Environmental Protection; Gsg
Steiner, Jeffrey, (212) 650-6465 City Coll (CUNY); Cp
Steinker, Don C., (419) 372-7200 Bowling Green State Univ; Pg
Steinman, Byron A., (218) 726-7435 bsteinma@d.umn.edu, Univ of Minnesota Duluth; Gn
Steinschneider, Scott, 607-255-2155 ss3378@cornell.edu, Cornell Univ; Rw
Steller, Diana, 831-771-4400 dsteller@mlml.calstate.edu, Moss Landing Marine Lab; Zn
Stelling, Pete, 360-650-4095 pete.stelling@wwu.edu, Western Washington Univ; GxEgGv
Steltenpohl, Mark G., (334) 844-4893 steltmg@auburn.edu, Auburn Univ; Gtc
Stensrud, David J., (814) 863-7714 djs78@psu.edu, Pennsylvania State Univ, Univ Park; Am
Stephen, Daniel, (801) 863-8584 daniel.stephen@uvu.edu, Utah Valley Univ; PiGsPe
Stephen, Ralph A., (508) 289-2583 rstephen@whoi.edu, Woods Hole Oceanographic Inst; Ys
Stephens, Jason H., (512) 484-0874 jason.stephens@austincc.edu, Austin Comm Coll District; YrGuYe
Stephenson, Garth, (27) 21 808 4935 garth@sun.ac.za, Stellenbosch Univ; Zri
Stephenson, Gerry, gerry.stephenson@rogers.com, Univ of Guelph; Zn
Stephenson, Randell A., +44 (0)1224 274817 r.stephenson@abdn.ac.uk, Univ of Aberdeen; YgGtZg
Steppe, Cecily N., 410-293-6552 natunewi@usna.edu, United States Naval Academy; Obp
Sterling, Shannon, 902 494 7741 shannon.sterling@dal.ca, Dalhousie Univ; HgCbHs
Sterling, Tracy M., (406) 994-4605 tracy.sterling@montana.edu, Montana

Coll; GycEc
Strack, Otto D., (612) 625-3009 strac001@tc.umn.edu, Univ of Minnesota, Twin Cities; Hw
Straffin, Eric, (814) 732-1574 estraffin@edinboro.edu, Edinboro Univ of Pennsylvania; GmsSo
Strahler, Alan, (617) 353-5984 Boston Univ; Zr
Straight, William, (703) 948-7750 wstraight@nvcc.edu, Northern Virginia Comm Coll - Loudoun Campus; GgPv
Strain, Priscilla L., 202-633-2481 Smithsonian Inst / Nat Air & Space Mus; Zr
Stramski, Dariusz, (858) 534-3353 dstramski@ucsd.edu, Univ of California, San Diego; Op
Strangeway, Robert J., (310) 206-6247 strange@igpp.ucla.edu, Univ of California, Los Angeles; Zn
Strasser, Jeffrey C., (309) 794-7218 jeffreystrasser@augustana.edu, Augustana Coll; GmlGe
Strasser, Stefan, 089/2180 4340 stefan.strasser@vr-web.de, Ludwig-Maximilians-Univ Muenchen; Gz
Stratton, James F., (217) 581-2626 jfstratton@eiu.edu, Eastern Illinois Univ; PgGu
Straub, David, (514) 398-8995 david.straub@mcgill.ca, McGill Univ; Op
Straub, Derek J., 570-372-4767 straubd@susqu.edu, Susquehanna Univ; As
Straub, Katherine H., (570) 372-4318 straubk@susqu.edu, Susquehanna Univ; Am
Straub, Kyle M., 504-862-3273 kmstraub@tulane.edu, Tulane Univ; GgCg
Straub, Susanne, smstraub@ldeo.columbia.edu, Columbia Univ; Gv
Straus, David M., (703) 993-5719 dstraus@gmu.edu, George Mason Univ; As
Strauss, Harald, +49-251-83-33932 hstrauss@uni-muenster.de, Univ Muenster; CsGg
Strauss, Justin V., (603) 646-6954 justin.v.strauss@dartmouth.edu, Dartmouth Coll; GsCgGt
Straw, Byron, (970) 351-2470 byron.straw@unco.edu, Univ of Northern Colorado; ZeGgl
Strawn, Daniel G., (208) 885-2713 dgstrawn@uidaho.edu, Univ of Idaho; Sc
Strayer, Luther M., (510) 885-3083 luther.strayer@csueastbay.edu, California State Univ, East Bay; Gc
Streby, Henry, (419) 530-8451 henry.streby@utoledo.edu, Univ of Toledo; Zn
Streck, Martin J., (503) 725-3379 streckm@pdx.edu, Portland State Univ; GivCt
Strecker, Manfred, strecker@geo.uni-potsdam.de, Cornell Univ; Gt
Streepey Smith, Meg, (765) 973-2168 streeme@earlham.edu, Earlham Coll; Gt
Streig, Ashley, 503-725-3371 streig@pdx.edu, Portland State Univ; YsGt
Strick, James E., (717) 291-3856 james.strick@fandm.edu, Franklin and Marshall Coll; RhGe
Strickland, Richard M., (206) 543-3131 strix@ocean.washington.edu, Univ of Washington; ObgZg
Stright, Lisa, (970) 491-4296 lisa.stright@colostate.edu, Colorado State Univ; GoNpYe
Strmiæ Palinkaš, Sabina, +38514605961 sabina.strmic@inet.hr, Univ of Zagreb; CgeCc
Strobel, Darrell F., (410) 516-7829 strobel@jhu.edu, Johns Hopkins Univ; AsZnn
Strobel, Timothy A., 202-478-8943 tstrobel@carnegiescience.edu, Carnegie Inst for Sci; Zm
Strock, Jeffrey S., (507) 752-7372 stroc001@umn.edu, Univ of Minnesota, Twin Cities; So
Stroeve, Julienne, j.stroeve@ucl.ac.uk, Univ Coll London; GlZr
Strom, Kyle, (540) 231-0979 strom@vt.edu, Virginia Polytechnic Inst & State Univ; HsGs
Strom, Robert G., 520- 621-2720 rstrom@lpl.arizona.edu, Univ of Arizona; Xg
Stromberg, Caroline, 206-543-1687 caestrom@uw.edu, Univ of Washington; Pbe
Strong, Courtenay, 801-585-0049 court.strong@utah.edu, Univ of Utah; As
Strong, Ellen, stronge@si.edu, Smithsonian Inst / Nat Mus of Natural History; ZnPi
Strother, Paul K., (617) 552-8395 strother@bc.edu, Boston Coll; PlbPg
Stroup, Justin, justin.stroup@oswego.edu, SUNY, Oswego; GmHwGe
Struzhkin, Viktor V., 202-478-8952 vstruzhkin@carnegiescience.edu, Carnegie Inst for Sci; Gy
Stuart, Graham, +44(0) 113 34 35217 g.w.stuart@leeds.ac.uk, Univ of Leeds; Ys
Stuart, Neil, +44 (0) 131 650 2549 n.stuart@ed.ac.uk, Edinburgh Univ; Zi
Stubbins, Aron, 617.373.5872 a.stubbins@northeastern.edu, Northeastern Univ; CgbZc
Stubler, Craig, (805) 756-2188 cstubler@calpoly.edu, California Polytechnic State Univ; So
Stucker, James D., (614) 265-6601 james.stucker@dnr.state.oh.us, Ohio Dept of Natural Resources; EgCgGl
Stucki, Joseph W., (217) 333-9636 Univ of Illinois, Urbana-Champaign; Sc
Student, James J., 989-774-2295 stude1jj@cmich.edu, Central Michigan Univ; CaGiz
Stuiver, Minze, minze@uw.edu, Univ of Washington; Cc
Stull, Robert J., (323) 343-2408 rstull@calstatela.edu, California State Univ, Los Angeles; Gi
Stull, Roland B., 604-822-5901 rstull@eos.ubc.ca, Univ of British Columbia; As
Stumbea, Dan, 0040232201464 dan.stumbea@uaic.ro, Alexandru Ioan Cuza; Gez
Stump, Brian W., (214) 768-1223 stump@smu.edu, Southern Methodist Univ; Ys
Stump, Edmund, ed.stump@asu.edu, Arizona State Univ; Gt
Stunz, Greg, 361-825-3254 greg.stunz@tamucc.edu, Texas A&M Univ, Corpus Christi; Zn
Stupazzini, Marco, 089/2180 4143 stupa@geophysik.uni-muenchen.de, Ludwig-Maximilians-Univ Muenchen; Yg
Sturchio, Neil C., (630) 252-3986 Argonne; Cg
Sturges, Bill, +44 (0)1603 59 2018 w.sturges@uea.ac.uk, Univ of East Anglia; As
Sturgis, Laila, 575-835-5327 laila.sturgis@nmt.edu, New Mexico Inst of Mining and Tech; Hw
Sturm, Diana, 251-460-6381 dsturm@southalabama.edu, Univ of South Alabama; GeZge
Sturmer, Daniel M., (513) 556-3718 daniel.sturmer@uc.edu, Univ of Cincinnati; YeGdo
Stute, Martin, (845) 365-8704 martins@ldeo.columbia.edu, Columbia Univ; CsHgGe
Stutz, Jochen P., (310) 825-1217 jochen@atmos.ucla.edu, Univ of California, Los Angeles; As
Su, Haibin, 361-593-3590 haibin.su@tamuk.edu, Texas A&M Univ, Kingsville; Zir
Su, Xiaobo, (541) 346-4568 xiaobo@uoregon.edu, Univ of Oregon; Zn
Suarez, Celina, (479) 575-4866 casuarez@uark.edu, Univ of Arkansas, Fayetteville; ClPqGg
Suárez, Luis Eugenio, luisesua@ucm.es, Univ Complutense de Madrid; Zn
Sublette, Kerry, 918-631-3085 kerry-sublette@utulsa.edu, Univ of Tulsa; Ge
Subramaniam, Ajit, ajit@ldeo.columbia.edu, Columbia Univ; ObZr
Subulwa, Angela G., (920) 424-4105 subulwaa@uwosh.edu, Univ of Wisconsin Oshkosh; Zn
Suen, C. J., (559) 278-8656 john_suen@csufresno.edu, Fresno State Univ; HwCsGe
Sugarman, Peter J., (609) 292-2576 pete.sugarman@dep.state.nj.us, New Jersey Geological and Water Survey; Gr
Sugihara, George, (858) 534-5582 gsugihara@ucsd.edu, Univ of California, San Diego; Ob
Sui, Daniel, 479-575-2470 Univ of Arkansas, Fayetteville; Zf
Sukop, Michael C., (305) 348-3117 sukopm@fiu.edu, Florida International Univ; HwqSp
Sulanowska, Margaret, (508) 289-2306 msulanowska@whoi.edu, Woods Hole Oceanographic Inst; Cm
Sullivan, Donald G., donald.sullivan@du.edu, Univ of Denver; Pc
Sullivan, Jack B., (301) 405-0106 jsull@umd.edu, Univ of Maryland; Zu
Sullivan, Raymond, (415) 338-2061 sullivan@sfsu.edu, San Francisco State Univ; Go
Sullivan, Walter, (207) 859-5800 wasulliv@colby.edu, Colby Coll; Gct
Sullivan Graham, Jeri, jeri.graham@nmt.edu, New Mexico Inst of Mining and Tech; Hw
Sullivan-Watts, Barbara K., (401) 874-6659 bsull@gso.uri.edu, Univ of Rhode Island; Og
Sultan, Mohamed, (630) 252-1929 Argonne; Cg
Sumida, Stuart S., (909) 537-5346 California State Univ, San Bernardino; Pv
Summers, Robert, 780-492-0342 robert.summers@ualberta.ca, Univ of Alberta; Zn
Summers, Sara, (801) 626-7222 sarasummers@weber.edu, Weber State Univ; Gg
Summons, Roger, (617) 452-2791 rsummons@mit.edu, Massachusetts Inst of Tech; CobCs
Sumner, Dawn Y., (530) 752-5353 dysumner@ucdavis.edu, Univ of California, Davis; Gs
Sumner, Esther, +44 (0)23 80592067 e.j.sumner@soton.ac.uk, Univ of Southampton; Gs
Sumrall, Colin, (865) 974-2366 csumrall@utk.edu, Univ of Tennessee, Knoxville; Pi
Sumrall, Jeanne L., jlsumrall@fhsu.edu, Fort Hays State Univ; Zgn
Sumrall, Jonathan B., 785-628-5348 jbsumrall@fhsu.edu, Fort Hays State

Univ; GgxZn
Sun, Alexander, 512-475-6190 alex.sun@beg.utexas.edu, Univ of Texas, Austin; Gq
Sun, Chenguang, csun@jsg.utexas.edu, Univ of Texas, Austin; Gx
Sun, Fengpeng, 816-235-2973 sunf@umkc.edu, Univ of Missouri, Kansas City; ZoiZc
Sun, Hongbing, 609-895-5185 hsun@rider.edu, Rider Univ; HwCgSc
Sun, Jeff, 307 268 3560 jsun@caspercollege.edu, Casper Coll; Zi
Sun, Jingru, 609-258-4101 jingrus@princeton.edu, Princeton Univ; As
Sun, Wen-Yih, (765) 494-7681 wysun@purdue.edu, Purdue Univ; AsZoAm
Sun, Yifei, (818) 677-3532 yifei.sun@csun.edu, California State Univ, Northridge; Zi
Sun, Yuefeng, (979) 845-0635 sun@geos.tamu.edu, Texas A&M Univ; GoYe
Sundareshwar, P. V., 605-394-2492 psundareshwar@usaid.gov, South Dakota Sch of Mines & Tech; ZeCgSb
Sundby, Bjorn, (418) 723-1986 (Ext. 1767) b.sundby@uquebec.ca, Universite du Quebec a Rimouski; Oc
Sundell, Ander, 208.562.3354 andersundell@cwidaho.cc, Coll of Western Idaho; Ggc
Sundell, Kent A., (307) 268-2498 ksundell@caspercollege.edu, Casper Coll; GgvPv
Sunderlin, David, 610-330-5198 sunderld@lafayette.edu, Lafayette Coll; Gg
Suneson, Neil H., 405-325-7315 nsuneson@ou.edu, Univ of Oklahoma; Gc
Suntharalingam, Parvadha, +44 (0)1603 59 1423 p.suntharalingam@uea.ac.uk, Univ of East Anglia; Oc
Superchi-Culver, Tonia, 303-492-5211 toni.culver@colorado.edu, Univ of Colorado; Pg
Suppe, John, jsuppe@uh.edu, Univ of Houston; Gtc
Surge, Donna M., 919-843-1994 donna64@unc.edu, Univ of North Carolina, Chapel Hill; Pe
Surian, Nicola, +390498279125 nicola.surian@unipd.it, Univ degli Studi di Padova; Gm
Suriano, Zac, 402-554-2662 zsuriano@unomaha.edu, Univ of Nebraska, Omaha; Atm
Surpless, Benjamin E., (210) 999-7110 bsurples@trinity.edu, Trinity Univ; GctGi
Surpless, Kathleen D., (210) 999-7365 ksurples@trinity.edu, Trinity Univ; Gst
Susak, Nicholas J., (506) 453-4803 nsusak@unb.ca, Univ of New Brunswick; CglEm
Sushama, Laxmi, 514-987-3000 #2414 sushama.laxmi@uqam.ca, Universite du Quebec a Montreal; Hy
Sussman, Robert W., (314) 935-5264 rwsussma@artsci.wustl.edu, Washington Univ in St. Louis; Zn
Suszek, Thomas J., suszek@uwosh.edu, Univ of Wisconsin, Oshkosh; Gg
Suter, Simeon, 717-702-2047 ssuter@pa.gov, DCNR- Pennsylvania Bureau of Geological Survey; HwGg
Sutherland, Bruce, 780-492-0573 bruce.sutherland@ualberta.ca, Univ of Alberta; Cm
Sutherland, Dave, 541-346-8753 dsuth@uoregon.edu, Univ of Oregon; Op
Sutherland, Mary K., (406) 496-4410 msutherland@mtech.edu, Montana Tech of The Univ of Montana; Hws
Sutherland, Stuart, (604) 822-0176 ssutherland@eos.ubc.ca, Univ of British Columbia; Pg
Sutherland, Wayne, (307) 766-2286 Ext. 247 wayne.sutherland@wyo.gov, Wyoming State Geological Survey; Eng
Suttle, Curtis, (604) 822-8610 csuttle@eos.ubc.ca, Univ of British Columbia; Ob
Suttner, Lee J., (812) 855-4957 suttner@indiana.edu, Indiana Univ, Bloomington; Gd
Sutton, Mark, +44 20 759 47487 m.sutton@imperial.ac.uk, Imperial Coll; Pg
Sutton, Paul C., (303) 871-2399 psutton@du.edu, Univ of Denver; Zc
Sutton, Sally J., (970) 491-5995 sallys@warnercnr.colostate.edu, Colorado State Univ; GdCl
Suvocarev, Kosana, 530-754-1929 ksuvocarev@ucdavis.edu, Univ of California, Davis; Asm
Suyker, Andrew E., asuyker@unl.edu, Univ of Nebraska, Lincoln; As
Sverdrup, Keith A., (414) 229-4017 sverdrup@uwm.edu, Univ of Wisconsin, Milwaukee; YsGt
Sverjensky, Dimitri A., (410) 516-8568 sver@jhu.edu, Johns Hopkins Univ; Cl
Svitra, Zita V., (505) 667-7616 Los Alamos; Zn
Swain, Geoffrey, (321) 674-8096 swain@fit.edu, Florida Inst of Tech; Ob
Swanger, Kate, (978) 934-2664 kate_swanger@uml.edu, Univ of Massachusetts, Lowell; Gl
Swann, Abigail L., (206) 616-0486 aswann@atmos.washington.edu, Univ of Washington; AsZn
Swanson, Basil I., (505) 667-5814 Los Alamos; Zn
Swanson, Benjamin, benjamin-swanson@uiowa.edu, Univ of Iowa; Gme
Swanson, Brian, 250-537-4330 brians@uw.edu, Univ of Washington; Asp
Swanson, Donald A., (808) 967-8863 donswan@usgs.gov, Univ of Hawai'i, Manoa; Gv
Swanson, Karen, (201) 595-2589 William Paterson Univ; Cc
Swanson, R. L., (631) 632-8704 larry.swanson@stonybrook.edu, SUNY, Stony Brook; Og
Swanson , Sam , sswanson@uga.edu, Univ of Georgia; Gi
Swanson, Sherman, (775) 784-4057 sswanson@agnt1.ag.unr.edu, Univ of Nevada, Reno; Hs
Swanson, Susan K., (608) 363-2132 swansons@beloit.edu, Beloit Coll; HwGm
Swanson, Terry W., tswanson@uw.edu, Univ of Washington; CcGe
Swanson, Travis, (912) 478-0337 tswanson@georgiasouthern.edu, Georgia Southern Univ; Gsm
Swapp, Susan M., (307) 766-2513 swapp@uwyo.edu, Univ of Wyoming; Gp
Swarr, Gretchen, (508) 289-2558 gswarr@whoi.edu, Woods Hole Oceanographic Inst; Oc
Swart, Peter K., (305) 421-4103 pswart@rsmas.miami.edu, Univ of Miami; ClPsCs
Swaters, Gordon E., (780) 492-7159 gordon.swaters@ualberta.ca, Univ of Alberta; Op
Sweeney, Mark D., (509) 373-0703 mark.sweeney@pnl.gov, Pacific Northwest; Yg
Sweet, Alisan C., 806-834-2398 alisan.sweet@ttu.edu, Texas Tech Univ; Gs
Sweet, Dustin E., (806) 834-8390 dustin.sweet@ttu.edu, Texas Tech Univ; GsdGr
Sweetman, Steve, +44 023 9284 2257 steve.sweetman@port.ac.uk, Univ of Portsmouth; Pg
Swennen, Rudy, rudy.swennen@ees.kuleuven.be, Katholieke Universiteit Leuven; Gso
Swenson, John B., (218) 726-6844 jswenso2@d.umn.edu, Univ of Minnesota Duluth; GrsGm
Swetnam, Thomas W., tswetnam@email.arizona.edu, Univ of Arizona; Zn
Swidinsky, Andrei, 303-273-3934 aswidins@mines.edu, Colorado Sch of Mines; Ye
Swift, Elijah V., (401) 874-6146 lige@gso.uri.edu, Univ of Rhode Island; Ob
Swift, Robert P., (505) 665-7871 bswift@lanl.gov, Los Alamos; Nr
Swift, Stephen A., (508) 289-2626 sswift@whoi.edu, Woods Hole Oceanographic Inst; Yr
Swindle, Timothy, 520-621-4128 tswindle@lpl.arizona.edu, Univ of Arizona; Xc
Swisher III, Carl C., 848-445-5363 cswish@eps.rutgers.edu, Rutgers, The State Univ of New Jersey; Cc
Swyrtek, Sheila, (810)232-9312 sheila.swyrtek@mcc.edu, Charles Stewart Mott Comm Coll; Ga
Sydora, Richard D., (780) 492-3624 rsydora@phys.ualberta.ca, Univ of Alberta; Xy
Sykes, Lynn R., (845) 359-7428 sykes@ldeo.columbia.edu, Columbia Univ; YsGtZn
Sylva, Sean, 508-289-3546 ssylva@whoi.edu, Woods Hole Oceanographic Inst; Oc
Sylvan, Jason B., (979) 845-5105 jasonsylvan@tamu.edu, Texas A&M Univ; ObXb
Sylvia, Elizabeth R., 410 554-5542 elizabeth.sylvia@maryland.gov, Maryland Department of Natural Resources; Ge
Symbalisty, E.M.D., (505) 667-9670 esymbalisty@lanl.gov, Los Alamos; Zn
Symons, David T., (519) 253-3000 x2493 dsymons@uwindsor.ca, Univ of Windsor; YmGtEm
Syrett, William, (814) 865-6172 wjs1@psu.edu, Pennsylvania State Univ, Univ Park; Am
Syrup, Krista A., (708) 974-5615 syrup@morainevalley.edu, Moraine Valley Comm Coll; Cs
Syverson, Kent M., (715) 836-3676 syverskm@uwec.edu, Univ of Wisconsin, Eau Claire; GlEnGe
Szatmári, József, +3662544156 szatmari@geo.u-szeged.hu, Univesity of Szeged; ZriZy
Szczepanski, Jacek, jacek.szczepanski@uwr.edu.pl, Univ of Wroclaw; Ggc
Szecsody, James E., (509) 372-6080 jim.szecsody@pnl.gov, Pacific Northwest; So
Székely, Balázs, balazs.szekely@ttk.elte.hu, Eotvos Lorand Univ; GmZri
Szeliga, Walter, 509-963-2705 walter@geology.cwu.edu, Central Washington Univ; YgsYd
Szente, Istvan, szente@ludens.elte.hu, Eotvos Lorand Univ; Pig
Szeto, Anthony M. K., (416)736-2100 #77703 szeto@yorku.ca, York Univ; Yg
Szilagyi, Jozsef, (402)472-9667 jszilagyi1@unl.edu, Univ of Nebraska, Lincoln; Hw
Szlavecz, Katalin, (410) 516-8947 szlavecz@jhu.edu, Johns Hopkins Univ; Pi

Szulczewski, Melanie, (540) 654-2345 mszulcze@umw.edu, Univ of Mary Washington; ScClZg
Szunyogh, Istvan, (979) 458-0553 szunyogh@tamu.edu, Texas A&M Univ; As
Szymanowski, Dawid, 609-258-4101 Princeton Univ; CcGiv
Szymanski, David, (781) 891-2901 dszymanski@bentley.edu, Bentley Univ; GifCg
Szymanski, Jason, 585-292-2423 jszymanski@monroecc.edu, Monroe Comm Coll; GlPe
Szynkiewicz, Anna, 865-974-6006 aszynkie@utk.edu, Univ of Tennessee, Knoxville; CslXg
Söllner, Frank, 089/2180 6519 fank.soellner@iaag.geo.uni-muenchen.de, Ludwig-Maximilians-Univ Muenchen; Gg

T

Tabara, Daniel, 0040756105973 dan.tabara@yahoo.com, Alexandru Ioan Cuza; Pl
Tabidian, M. Ali, (818) 677-2536 ali.tabidian@csun.edu, California State Univ, Northridge; Hw
Taboada Castro, María T., 00 34 981 167000 teresat@udc.es, Coruna Univ; Sd
Taboga, Karl, (307) 766-2286 Ext. 226 karl.taboga@wyo.gov, Wyoming State Geological Survey; HwGe
Tabor, Neil J., ntabor@smu.edu, Southern Methodist Univ; SdGs
Tabrum, Alan R., (412) 622-3265 tabruma@carnegiemnh.org, Carnegie Mus of Natural History; Pv
Tacinelli, John C., (507) 285-7501 john.tacinelli@rctc.edu, Rochester Comm & Technical Coll; Gig
Tackett, Lydia S., 701-231-6164 lydia.tackett@ndsu.edu, North Dakota State Univ; PeGsPi
Tadesse, Tsegaye, ttadesse2@unl.edu, Univ of Nebraska, Lincoln; ZirAs
Taggart, Christopher T., (902) 494-7144 chris.taggart@dal.ca, Dalhousie Univ; Ob
Taggart, Ralph E., 517-353-5175 taggart@msu.edu, Michigan State Univ; Pb
Tagliabue, Alessandro, +44 0151 794 4651 a.tagliabue@liverpool.ac.uk, Univ of Liverpool; Oc
Tagne, Gilles V., 630 752 7556 gilles.tagne@wheaton.edu, Wheaton Coll; HwZiGe
Taib, Samsudin Hj., 03-79674235 samsudin@um.edu.my, Univ of Malaya; Yg
Taillefert, Martial, (404) 894-6043 mtaillef@eas.gatech.edu, Georgia Inst of Tech; ClmCa
Tait, C. Drew, (505) 667-7603 Los Alamos; Cp
Tait, Kim, ktait@rom.on.ca, Western Univ; Xm
Tait, Kimberly T., (416) 586-5820 ktait@rom.on.ca, Royal Ontario Mus; GzyXm
Tajik, Atieh, 404 413 5790 geoatt@langate.gsu.edu, Georgia State Univ; Gg
Takahashi, Taro, taka@ldeo.columbia.edu, Columbia Univ; Cm
Takeuchi, Akira, 81-76-445-6654 takeuchi@sci.u-toyama.ac.jp, Univ of Toyama; GtcYe
Takle, Eugene S., (515) 294-9871 gstakle@iastate.edu, Iowa State Univ of Sci & Tech; As
Talbot, Helen, +44 (0) 191 208 6426 helen.talbot@ncl.ac.uk, Univ of Newcastle Upon Tyne; Co
Talbot, James L., (360) 733-4282 talbot@wwu.edu, Western Washington Univ; Gc
Talbot, Robert, 713-743-2725 rtalbot@uh.edu, Univ of Houston; ActAm
Talley, Drew, (619) 260-6810 dtalley@sandiego.edu, Univ of San Diego; ObZe
Talley, John H., 302-831-2833 waterman@udel.edu, Univ of Delaware; As
Talley, Lynne D., (858) 534-6610 ltalley@ucsd.edu, Univ of California, San Diego; OpZc
Talling, Peter, peter.j.talling@durham.ac.uk, Durham Univ; Rn
Talwani, Manik, (713) 348-6067 manik@rice.edu, Rice Univ; Yr
Talwani, Pradeep, talwani@geol.sc.edu, Univ of South Carolina; Ys
Talyor, Frederick W., fred@ig.utexas.edu, Univ of Texas, Austin; Pe
Tamish, Mohamed M., 002-03-3921595 mtamish@hotmail.com, Alexandria Univ; GgsCg
Tamulonis, Kathryn L., 814-332-2873 ktamulonis@allegheny.edu, Allegheny Coll; Gsr
Tan, Chunyang, tanc@umn.edu, Univ of Minnesota, Twin Cities; Cm
Tan, Denis N., denistan@um.edu.my, Univ of Malaya; Go
Taney, R. Marieke, (928) 523-2384 marieke.taney@nau.edu, Northern Arizona Univ; ZnnZn
Tang, Weiyi, 609-258-4101 weiyit@princeton.edu, Princeton Univ; CbOcb
Tanhua, Toste, ttanhua@geomar.de, Dalhousie Univ; Oc
Tanimoto, Toshiro, (805) 893-8375 toshiro@geol.ucsb.edu, Univ of California, Santa Barbara; Ys
Tanner, Benjamin R., (828) 227-3915 btanner@wcu.edu, Western Carolina Univ; Cos
Tao, Ran, rtao@usf.edu, Univ of South Florida; Zi
Tapanila, Leif, 208-282-5417 tapaleif@isu.edu, Idaho State Univ; Pig
Tape, Carl, 907-474-5456 carltape@gi.alaska.edu, Univ of Alaska, Fairbanks; Ys
Tapp, J. B., jbt@utulsa.edu, Univ of Tulsa; GceZi
Tarduno, John A., (585) 275-5713 john@earth.rochester.edu, Univ of Rochester; YmGtXm
Tarhan, Lidya, 203-432-8100 lidya.tarhan@yale.edu, Yale Univ; PiGsPe
Tarka, Robert, robert.tarka@uwr.edu.pl, Univ of Wroclaw; Hg
Tarr, Alexander, 508 929-8474 alexander.tarr@worcester.edu, Worcester State Univ; Zg
Taskey, Ronald D., (805) 756-1160 rtaskey@calpoly.edu, California Polytechnic State Univ; Sf
Tassier-Surine, Stephanie, stephanie.surine@dnr.iowa.gov, Iowa Dept of Natural Resources; Gg
Tatarskii, Viatcheslav, (404) 894-9224 vvt@eas.gatech.edu, Georgia Inst of Tech; As
Tatham, Robert H., (512) 471-9129 tatham@mail.utexas.edu, Univ of Texas, Austin; Yg
Tauxe, John D., (423) 574-5348 Oak Ridge; Hw
Tauxe, Lisa, (858) 534-6084 ltauxe@ucsd.edu, Univ of California, San Diego; Ym
Tavener, Kristi, (807) 343-8677 ktavener@lakeheadu.ca, Lakehead Univ; Zn
Tawabini, Bassam S., +96638607643 bassamst@kfupm.edu.sa, King Fahd Univ of Petroleum and Minerals; GeHsCa
Taylor, Brian, (808) 956-6182 taylorb@hawaii.edu, Univ of Hawai'i, Manoa; Gtu
Taylor, Carolyn, carolyn.taylor@mcmail.maricopa.edu, Mesa Comm Coll; Gg
Taylor, Charles J., 859-323-0523 charles.taylor@uky.edu, Univ of Kentucky; HwgCl
Taylor, Danny L., (775) 784-6922 dtaylor@mines.unr.edu, Univ of Nevada, Reno; Nm
Taylor, Edith, 785-864-3621 etaylor@ku.edu, Univ of Kansas; Pb
Taylor, Elwynn, (808) 956-3899 setaylor@iastate.edu, Iowa State Univ of Sci & Tech; As
Taylor, Frank J. R., (604) 822-4587 mtaylor@eos.ubc.ca, Univ of British Columbia; Ob
Taylor, Frederick W., (512) 471-0453 fred@ig.utexas.edu, Univ of Texas, Austin; GtmGe
Taylor, G. Jeffrey, (808) 956-3899 Univ of Hawai'i, Manoa; Xm
Taylor, Gordon T., (631) 632-8688 gordon.taylor@stonybrook.edu, SUNY, Stony Brook; Obc
Taylor, Graeme, +44 1752 584770 g.taylor@plymouth.ac.uk, Univ of Plymouth; Yg
Taylor, Hugh P., (626) 395-6116 hptaylor@gps.caltech.edu, California Inst of Tech; Cs
Taylor, John F., (724) 357-4469 jftaylor@iup.edu, Indiana Univ of Pennsylvania; PsiGs
Taylor, Kenneth B., (919) 707-9211 kenneth.b.taylor@ncdenr.gov, N.C. Department of Environmental Quality; YsGgEo
Taylor, Kevin, +44 0161 275-8557 kevin.taylor@manchester.ac.uk, Univ of Manchester; Go
Taylor, Lansing, 801-581-8430 ltaylor@egi.utah.edu, Univ of Utah; Gc
Taylor, Lawrence D., (517) 629-0308 ltaylor@albion.edu, Albion Coll; Gl
Taylor, Mackenzie, mtaylo10@ashland.edu, Ashland Univ; RnGg
Taylor, Matthew, 303-871-2656 mtaylor7@du.edu, Univ of Denver; Zc
Taylor, Michael, michael.taylor@flinders.edu.au, Flinders Univ; Zn
Taylor, Nathan H., 501 683-1085 nathan.taylor@arkansas.gov, Arkansas Geological Survey; ZiyGe
Taylor, Penny M., 413-538-3236 pmtaylor@mtholyoke.edu, Mount Holyoke Coll; Gg
Taylor, Peter, +44(0) 113 34 37169 p.g.taylor@leeds.ac.uk, Univ of Leeds; Ge
Taylor, Rex N., +44 (0)23 80592007 rex@noc.soton.ac.uk, Univ of Southampton; GvCa
Taylor, Richard P., richard_taylor@carleton.ca, Carleton Univ; Cg
Taylor, Robert W., (973) 655-4129 Montclair State Univ; Zn
Taylor, Ryan W., 914 251 6652 ryan.taylor@purchase.edu, SUNY, Purchase; ZiyZg
Taylor, Sid, (902) 867-2299 staylor@stfx.ca, Saint Francis Xavier Univ; Gg
Taylor, Stephen B., 503-838-8398 taylors@wou.edu, Western Oregon Univ; Gm
Taylor, Steven R., (505) 667-1007 taylor@lanl.gov, Los Alamos; Ys
Taylor, Ta-Shana A., (305) 284-4254 t.taylor2@miami.edu, Univ of Miami; ZePvGe
Taylor, Wanda J., (702) 895-4615 wanda.taylor@unlv.edu, Univ of Nevada, Las Vegas; Gc

Taylor, Wayne A., (505) 667-4253 Los Alamos; Cl
Tchakerian, Vatche P., (409) 845-7997 Texas A&M Univ; Gm
Teagle, Damon A., +44 (0)23 80592723 damon.teagle@southampton.ac.uk, Univ of Southampton; CgEmGp
Teasdale, Rachel, 530-898-5547 rteasdale@csuchico.edu, California State Univ, Chico; Gv
Tedford, Richard H., (212) 769-5809 American Mus of Natural History; Pv
Teed, Rebecca, 937 775-3446 rebecca.teed@wright.edu, Wright State Univ; ZePeGn
Teeuw, Richard, +44 023 92 842267 richard.teeuw@port.ac.uk, Univ of Portsmouth; AsGmZi
Tefend, Karen S., ktefend@westga.edu, Univ of West Georgia; CgGe
Teixeira, Bernardo, 337-482-1132 bernardo.teixeira@louisiana.edu, Univ of Louisiana at Lafayette; GdrGn
Teixell, Antonio, antonio.teixell@uab.cat, Universitat Autonoma de Barcelona; Gtc
Teixell Cácharo, Antoni, ++935811163 antonio.teixell@uab.cat, Universitat Autonoma de Barcelona; GtcYx
Teklay, Mengist, mteklay@gsu.edu, Georgia State Univ, Perimeter Coll, Decatur Campus; Gg
Tellam, John H., +44 (0)121 41 46138 j.h.tellam@bham.ac.uk, Univ of Birmingham; Hw
Teller, James T., (204) 474-9270 tellerjt@ms.umanitoba.ca, Univ of Manitoba; Gs
Telmer, Kevin, ktelmer@uvic.ca, Univ of Victoria; Cl
Telus, Myriam, mtelus@ucsc.edu, Univ of California, Santa Cruz; Xc
Telyakovskiy, Aleksey S., 775.784.1364 alekseyt@unr.edu, Univ of Nevada, Reno; Hqy
Temples, Tommy, (803) 348-0472 ttemples@sc.rr.com, Clemson Univ; GoYg
Templeton, Alan R., (314) 935-6868 temple_a@wustl.edu, Washington Univ in St. Louis; ZicZr
Templeton, Alexis, 303-735-6069 alexis.templeton@colorado.edu, Univ of Colorado; ClZaCq
Templeton, Jeffrey H., (503) 838-8858 templej@wou.edu, Western Oregon Univ; GivZe
Tems, Caitlin E., (801) 626-7421 caitlintems@weber.edu, Weber State Univ; OoCs
Ten Brink, Norman W., tenbrinn@gvsu.edu, Grand Valley State Univ; Gm
Tencate, James, (505) 665-6667 tencate@lanl.gov, Los Alamos; Zn
Teng, Fangzhen, 206-543-7615 fteng@uw.edu, Univ of Washington; Cg
Teng, Ta-liang, (213) 740-5838 lteng@usc.edu, Univ of Southern California; YsGtYe
Tenorio, Victor O., (520) 621-3858 vtenorio@email.arizona.edu, Univ of Arizona; Nmx
Teodoriu, Catalin, 405-325-6872 cteodoriu@ou.edu, Univ of Oklahoma; Np
Tepley, III, Frank J., 541-737-2064 ftepley@coas.oregonstate.edu, Oregon State Univ; GiCs
Teplitski, Max, 352-392-1951 maxtep@ufl.edu, Univ of Florida; Zn
Tepper, Jeffrey H., (253) 879-3820 jtepper@pugetsound.edu, Univ of Puget Sound; GiCgGv
ter Voorde, Marlies, +31 20 59 87343 m.ter.voorde@vu.nl, Vrije Universiteit Amsterdam; YgGt
Ter-Simonian, Vardui, (213) 740-6106 tersimon@usc.edu, Univ of Southern California; Zn
Tera, Fouad, (202) 478-8472 ftera@carnegiescience.edu, Carnegie Inst for Sci; CcgXm
Terry, Dennis O., (215) 204-8226 doterry@temple.edu, Temple Univ; SaPcGr
Tertyshnikov, Konstantin, +61 8 9266 2297 konstantin.tertyshnikov@curtin.edu.au, Curtin Univ; Ye
Terwey, Wes, terwey@southalabama.edu, Univ of South Alabama; Am
Terzian, Yervant, 607-255-4935 terzian@astro.cornell.edu, Cornell Univ; Xya
Tesso, Tesfaye, (785) 532-7238 ttesso@ksu.edu, Kansas State Univ; So
Tester, Jefferson W., 607-254-7211 jwt54@cornell.edu, Cornell Univ; NgCg
Tetrault, Denis, 519-253-3000 ext. 2495 deniskt@uwindsor.ca, Univ of Windsor; Gg
Tett, Simon F., +44 (0) 131 650 5341 simon.tett@ed.ac.uk, Edinburgh Univ; Am
Tettenhorst, Rodney T., 614 247-4246 tettenhorst.2@osu.edu, Ohio State Univ; Gz
Tew , Berry H., 205-247-3679 ntew@gsa.state.al.us, Geological Survey of Alabama; GroGs
Tew, Nick, 205.348.4558 bhtew@ua.edu, Univ of Alabama; EoGro
Tewksbury, Barbara J., (315) 859-4713 btewksbu@hamilton.edu, Hamilton Coll; Gc
Textoris, Daniel A., (919) 962-0690 dtextori@email.unc.edu, Univ of North Carolina, Chapel Hill; Gd
Teyssier, Christian P., (612) 624-6801 teyssier@umn.edu, Univ of Minnesota, Twin Cities; GctGg
Tezcan, Levent, +90 (312) 2977750 tezcan@hacettepe.edu.tr, Hacettepe Univ; Hw
Thacker, Heather, (740) 351-3456 hthacker@shawnee.edu, Shawnee State Univ; Zn
Thacker, Jacob, 575-835-5151 jacob.thacker@nmt.edu, New Mexico Inst of Mining and Tech; GtcGr
Thackray, Glenn D., (208) 282-3565 thacglen@isu.edu, Idaho State Univ; Glm
Thakurta, Joyashish, (269) 387-3667 joyashish.thakurta@wmich.edu, Western Michigan Univ; GiEg
Thale, Paul R., 406-496-4653 pthale@mtech.edu, Montana Tech of The Univ of Montana; Zi
Tharp, Thomas M., (765) 494-8678 ttharp1@purdue.edu, Purdue Univ; Nm
Thatje, Sven, +44 (0)23 80592009 svth@noc.soton.ac.uk, Univ of Southampton; Ob
Thayer, Paul A., (910) 520-8719 thayer@uncw.edu, Univ of North Carolina, Wilmington; GdoHg
Thayn, Jonathan B., 309-438-8112 jthayn@ilstu.edu, Illinois State Univ; Zir
Theiling, Bethany P., bethany-theiling@utulsa.edu, Univ of Tulsa; Cs
Theis, Karen, +44 0161 275-0407 karen.theis@manchester.ac.uk, Univ of Manchester; Zn
Theissen, Kevin, 651-962-5243 kmtheissen@stthomas.edu, Univ of Saint Thomas; GnOg
Them, II, Theodore R., themtr@cofc.edu, Coll of Charleston; CmOcZc
Themelis, Nickolas J., (212) 854-2138 njt1@columbia.edu, Columbia Univ; Nx
Thériault, Julie Mireille, 514 987-3000 #4276 theriault.julie@uqam.ca, Universite du Quebec a Montreal; Zn
Therrien, Francois, (403) 823-7707 Royal Tyrrell Mus of Palaeontology; Pv
Therrien, Pierre, therrien@ggl.ulaval.ca, Universite Laval; Gq
Therrien, Rene, (418) 656-5400 rene.therrien@ggl.ulaval.ca, Universite Laval; HwGe
Theuerkauf, Ethan, ejtheu@illinois.edu, Illinois State Geological Survey; GmuGs
Thibault, Yves, 613-992-1376 yves.thibault@nrcan.gc.ca, Western Univ; Gz
Thibodeau, Alyson M., (717) 245-8337 thibodea@dickinson.edu, Dickinson Coll; CcGaCs
Thiel, Dr., Volker, +49 (0)551 3914395 vthiel@gwdg.de, Georg-August Univ of Goettingen; CooCo
Thieme, Donald, (229) 333-5752 dmthieme@valdosta.edu, Valdosta State Univ; GaSdGm
Thien, Steve J., (785) 532-7207 sjthien@ksu.edu, Kansas State Univ; Sc
Thigpen, Ryan, 859-2181532 ryan.thigpen@uky.edu, Univ of Kentucky; Gtc
Thirlwall, Matthew, +44 1784 443609 m.thirlwall@rhul.ac.uk, Royal Holloway Univ of London; Cs
Thiruvathukal, John V., (973) 655-4417 Montclair State Univ; Yg
Thole, Jeffrey T., (651) 696-6426 thole@macalester.edu, Macalester Coll; GgCaHw
Thomas, Amanda, amthomas@uoregon.edu, Univ of Oregon; Ys
Thomas, Andrew D., +44 (0)1970 622 781 ant23@aber.ac.uk, Univ of Wales; SbGmSf
Thomas, Debbie, (979) 845-3651 dthomas@tamu.edu, Texas A&M Univ; Ou
Thomas, Donald M., (808) 956-6482 dthomas@soest.hawaii.edu, Univ of Hawai'i, Manoa; CaHwRn
Thomas, Elizabeth K., (716)645-4329 ekthomas@buffalo.edu, SUNY, Buffalo; Cos
Thomas, Ellen, (860) 685-2238 ellen.thomas@yale.edu, Yale Univ; Pm
Thomas, Florence, (808) 236-7418 fithomas@hawaii.edu, Univ of Hawai'i, Manoa; Ob
Thomas, Helmuth, (902) 494-7177 helmuth.thomas@dal.ca, Dalhousie Univ; Oc
Thomas, Jay, (315)443-7631 jthom102@syr.edu, Syracuse Univ; Gi
Thomas, Jeremy, 206-947-2678 jnt@uw.edu, Univ of Washington; ZrXa
Thomas, Jim, (775) 887-7648 tom_j_smith@usgs.gov, Univ of Nevada, Reno; Cg
Thomas, John, 352-392-1951 ext 216 thomas@ufl.edu, Univ of Florida; Sp
Thomas, Kimberly W., (505) 667-4379 Los Alamos; Ct
Thomas, Margaret A., (860) 424-3583 margaret.thomas@ct.gov, Dept of Energy and Environmental Protection; Gg
Thomas, Mark, +44(0) 113 34 35233 m.e.thomas@leeds.ac.uk, Univ of Leeds; Ng
Thomas, Paul, 360-650-7796 paul.thomas@wwu.edu, Western Washington Univ; Gm
Thomas, Peter, 361749-6768 peter.thomas@utexas.edu, Univ of Texas, Austin; Ob
Thomas, Ray G., (352) 392-7984 rgthomas@ufl.edu, Univ of Florida; Zg
Thomas, Robert C., (406) 683-7615 rob.thomas@umwestern.edu, Univ of

Montana Western; GseZe
Thomas, Roger D. K., (717) 358-4135 roger.thomas@fandm.edu, Franklin and Marshall Coll; PgRh
Thomas, Valerie, (404) 385-7254 valerie.thomas@isye.gatech.edu, Georgia Inst of Tech; Zu
Thomas, William A., (205) 247-3547 geowat@uky.edu, Geological Survey of Alabama; GtcGr
Thomason, Jason, 217 244-2508 jthomaso@illinois.edu, Univ of Illinois; Gl
Thomasson, Joseph R., (785) 628-5665 Fort Hays State Univ; Pb
Thomka, James R., (518)564-2227 jthom059@plattsburgh.edu, SUNY, Plattsburgh; GsPg
Thompson, Andrew F., 626.395.8345 andrewt@caltech.edu, California Inst of Tech; OpgZc
Thompson, Anu, +440151 794 4095 anu@liverpool.ac.uk, Univ of Liverpool; Oc
Thompson, Christopher J., (509) 376-6602 chris.thompson@pnl.gov, Pacific Northwest; Ca
Thompson, Curtis, (785) 532-5776 cthompso@ksu.edu, Kansas State Univ; So
Thompson, David W. J., davet@atmos.colostate.edu, Colorado State Univ; Yr
Thompson, Geoffrey, (508) 289-2397 gthompson@whoi.edu, Woods Hole Oceanographic Inst; Cm
Thompson, Glennis, (510) 642-7025 Univ of California, Berkeley; Zn
Thompson, Jann W. M., (202) 633-1357 Smithsonian Inst / Nat Mus of Natural History; Pg
Thompson, Joel B., (727) 864-8991 thompsjb@eckerd.edu, Eckerd Coll; Pg
Thompson, John F., jft66@cornell.edu, Cornell Univ; EmgNx
Thompson, John F. H., (604) 687-1117 Univ of British Columbia; Em
Thompson, Joseph L., (505) 667-4559 Los Alamos; Ct
Thompson, Keith R., (902) 494-3491 keith.thompson@dal.ca, Dalhousie Univ; Op
Thompson, Kenneth W., 620-341-5985 kthompso@emporia.edu, Emporia State Univ; Ze
Thompson, Lonnie G., (614) 292-6652 thompson.3@osu.edu, Ohio State Univ; GlZgPc
Thompson, LuAnne, (206) 543-9965 luanne@ocean.washington.edu, Univ of Washington; Op
Thompson, Margaret D., (781) 283-3029 mthompson@wellesley.edu, Wellesley Coll; Gc
Thompson, Michael D., (630) 252-9269 Argonne; Yg
Thompson, Todd, (812) 855-7428 tthomps@indiana.edu, Indiana Univ, Bloomington; Gg
Thompson, Tommy, thompsontommyt@aol.com, Colorado State Univ; Egm
Thompson, William G., (508) 289-2630 wthompson@whoi.edu, Woods Hole Oceanographic Inst; PeCc
Thompson, zglenn, thompsong@usf.edu, Univ of South Florida; Ys
Thoms, Richard E., (503) 725-3379 dick@pdx.edu, Portland State Univ; Ps
Thomsen, Charles E., (916) 484-8184 thomsec@arc.losrios.edu, American River Coll; Zy
Thomsen, Laurenz A., l.thomsen@iu-bremen.de, Univ of Washington; Ob
Thomsen, Leon, 713-743-3386 lathomsen@uh.edu, Univ of Houston; Ye
Thomson, Bradley J., 865-974-2699 bthomso1@utk.edu, Univ of Tennessee, Knoxville; Xg
Thomson, Cary, 604-822-0653 cthomson@eos.ubc.ca, Univ of British Columbia; Zn
Thomson, Cynthia, 212-854-9896 cthomson@iri.columbia.edu, Columbia Univ; Zn
Thomson, Dennis W., dwt2@psu.edu, Pennsylvania State Univ, Univ Park; Am
Thomson, Jack, +44 0151 794 3594 jack.thomson@liverpool.ac.uk, Univ of Liverpool; Ob
Thomson, Jennifer A., (509) 359-7478 jthomson@ewu.edu, Eastern Washington Univ; Gpz
Thomson, Richard E., (250) 363-6555 thomsonr@pac.dfo-mpo.gc.ca, Univ of British Columbia; Op
Thomson, Vivian E., (434) 924-3964 vet4y@virginia.edu, Univ of Virginia; Zn
Thorbjarnarson, Kathryn W., (619) 594-5586 kthorbjarnarson@mail.sdsu.edu, San Diego State Univ; Hq
Thorkelson, Derek J., 778-782-5390 dthorkel@sfu.ca, Simon Fraser Univ; Gt
Thorleifson, Harvey, (612) 626-2150 thorleif@umn.edu, Univ of Minnesota; Gl
Thornberry-Ehrlich, Trista L., (406) 420-2391 trista.thornberry@colostate.edu, Colorado State Univ; GgcGx
Thorncroft, Christopher D., (518) 442-4555 SUNY, Albany; As
Thorne, Michael S., (801) 585-9792 michael.thorne@utah.edu, Univ of Utah; YsxYv
Thorne, Paul D., (509) 372-4482 paul.thorne@pnl.gov, Pacific Northwest; HgyYg
Thorne, Richard M., (310) 614-6630 rmt@atmos.ucla.edu, Univ of California, Los Angeles; As
Thornton, Daniel C., 979 845 4092 dthornton@ocean.tamu.edu, Texas A&M Univ; Ob
Thornton, Edward B., (831) 656-2847 thornton@nps.edu, Naval Postgraduate Sch; On
Thornton, Joel A., (206) 543-4010 thornton@atmos.washington.edu, Univ of Washington; As
Thorson, Robert M., (860) 486-1396 robert.thorson@uconn.edu, Univ of Connecticut; Gm
Throop, Heather, (480) 727-2617 heather.throop@asu.edu, Arizona State Univ; Cb
Thul, David, 801-585-7013 dthul@egi.utah.edu, Univ of Utah; Gg
Thurber, Andrew, 541-737-4500 athurber@coas.oregonstate.edu, Oregon State Univ; Cb
Thurber, Clifford, (608) 262-6027 thurber@geology.wisc.edu, Univ of Wisconsin, Madison; Ysx
Thurber, David L., (718) 997-3325 dlthumper@aol.com, Queens Coll (CUNY); Cl
Thurnherr, Andreas, ant@ldeo.columbia.edu, Columbia Univ; Op
Thuro, Kurosch, +498928925850 thuro@tum.de, Technical Univ of Munich; NgrGg
Thurow, Juergen, +44 020 7679 32416 j.thurow@ucl.ac.uk, Univ Coll London; Gs
Thurston, Phillips C., 7056751151 x2372 pthurston@laurentian.ca, Laurentian Univ, Sudbury; ZgCgGr
Thurtell, George W., (519) 824-4120 (Ext. 52453) gthurtel@uoguelph.ca, Univ of Guelph; As
Thuy, Ben, ben.thuy@mnhn.lu, Univ of Tennessee, Knoxville; Pg
Thy, Peter, pthy@ucdavis.edu, Univ of California, Davis; Gx
Tiampo, Kristy F., ktiampo@uwo.ca, Western Univ; Yd
Tian, Di, (334) 844-4100 dzt0025@auburn.edu, Auburn Univ; At
Tibbits, Matthew, mtibbits@csc.edu, Chadron State Coll; Gg
Tibbits, Tawny, ttibbits@csc.edu, Chadron State Coll; Ggz
Tibljaš, Darko, +38514605970 dtibljas@geol.pmf.hr, Univ of Zagreb; GzScGx
Tibuleac, Ileana, (775) 784-6256 ileana@seismo.unr.edu, Univ of Nevada, Reno; Ys
Tibuleac, Paul, paul.tibuleac@uaic.ro, Alexandru Ioan Cuza; Pgs
Tice, Mike, 979-845-3138 tice@geo.tamu.edu, Texas A&M Univ; Pg
Tick, Geoffrey, gtick@ua.edu, Univ of Alabama; Hw
Tidwell, Allan, (850) 526-2761 tidwella@chipola.edu, Chipola Coll; Zg
Tidwell, David, 205-247-3698 dtidwell@gsa.state.al.us, Geological Survey of Alabama; Gm
Tidwell, Vincent C., (505) 844-6025 vctidwe@sandia.gov, New Mexico Inst of Mining and Tech; Hwq
Tiefenbacher, John, (512) 245-2170 Texas State Univ; Rnm
Tierney, Jessica, 520-621-5377 jesst@email.arizona.edu, Univ of Arizona; Co
Tierney, Kate, 319.335.0670 kate-tierney@uiowa.edu, Univ of Iowa; GrCsGg
Tierney, Sean, 303-871-3972 sean.tierney@du.edu, Univ of Denver; Zc
Tiffney, Bruce H., (805) 893-2959 bruce.tiffney@ccs.ucsb.edu, Univ of California, Santa Barbara; Pb
Tijani, Moshood N., +2348023252339 mn.tijani@mail.ui.edu.ng, Univ of Ibadan; HwCgGe
Tikoff, Basil, (608) 262-4678 basil@geology.wisc.edu, Univ of Wisconsin, Madison; Gc
Tikoo, Sonia M., (848) 445-3444 sonia.tikoo@rutgers.edu, Rutgers, The State Univ of New Jersey; YmXy
Till, Christy, (480) 727-2828 christy.till@asu.edu, Arizona State Univ; Gi
Tillman, James E., mars@atmos.washington.edu, Univ of Washington; As
Tilt, Jenna, 541-737-1232 tiltj@oregonstate.edu, Oregon State Univ; Zu
Tilton, Eric E., 303-735-5033 eric.small@colorado.edu, Univ of Colorado; Hw
Timár, Gábor, +36 1 3722700/1762 timar@caesar.elte.hu, Eotvos Lorand Univ; YgdZi
Timmer, Jaqueline R., 406-496-4842 jtimmer@mtech.edu, Montana Tech of The Univ of Montana; Ca
Timmermann, Axel, (808) 956-2720 axel@hawaii.edu, Univ of Hawai'i, Manoa; Op
Timmermans, Mary-Louise, 203 432-3167 mary-louise.timmermans@yale.edu, Yale Univ; Oc
Timmes, Francis, (480) 965-4274 francis.timmes@asu.edu, Arizona State Univ; Xa
Timmons, J M., 575-835-5237 mtimmons@nmbg.nmt.edu, New Mexico Inst of Mining and Tech; GctGs
Timmons, J. Michael, 575-835-5237 mike.timmons@nmt.edu, New Mexico Inst of Mining and Tech; Gg
Timmons, Stacy, 575-835-6951 stacy.timmons@nmt.edu, New Mexico Inst of Mining and Tech; Hwg
Tindall, Sarah E., (610) 683-4446 tindall@kutztown.edu, Kutztown Univ of Pennsylvania; Gc
Ting, Mingfang, (845) 365-8374 ting@ldeo.columbia.edu, Columbia Univ; As

Trentham, Robert C., 432 552-2432 trentham_r@utpb.edu, Univ of Texas Permian Basin; Go
Treude, Tina, (310) 267-5213 ttreude@g.ucla.edu, Univ of California, Los Angeles; ObPgCm
Trevino, Ramon H., (512) 471-3362 ramon.trevino@beg.utexas.edu, Univ of Texas at Austin, Jackson Sch of Geosciences; GsoGe
Trevors, Jack, (519) 824-4120 Ext.53367 jtrevors@uoguelph.ca, Univ of Guelph; Zn
Trexler, Charles C., (740) 368-3506 cctrexle@owu.edu, Ohio Wesleyan Univ; Gct
Triay, Ines, (505) 665-1755 Los Alamos; Hg
Tribe, Selina, 604-527-5471 tribes@douglascollege.ca, Douglas Coll; EgGge
Trigoso, Erika, 303-871-3936 erika.trigoso@du.edu, Univ of Denver; Zc
Tripati, Aradhna, ripple@epss.ucla.edu, Univ of California, Los Angeles; CmPeCs
Triplett, Laura, (507) 933-7442 ltriplet@gustavus.edu, Gustavus Adolphus Coll; GemCl
Tripoli, Gregory J., (608)262-3700 tripoli@aos.wisc.edu, Univ of Wisconsin, Madison; Am
Trivitt-Kracke, Amy, 575-835-5362 amy.trivitt@nmt.edu, New Mexico Inst of Mining and Tech; ZfGg
Trixler, Frank, 089/2179 509 trixler@lrz.uni-muenchen.de, Ludwig-Maximilians-Univ Muenchen; GzZmXc
Troch, Peter A., (520) 626-1277 patroch@hwr.arizona.edu, Univ of Arizona; Hs
Trofimovs, Jessica, +61 7 3138 2766 jessica.trofimovs@qut.edu.au, Queensland Univ of Tech; GsvGu
Tromp, Jeroen, 609-258-4128 jtromp@princeton.edu, Princeton Univ; Yss
Troost, Kathy G., 206-221-1770 ktroost@uw.edu, Univ of Washington; Zun
Trop, Jeffrey M., (570) 577-3027 jtrop@bucknell.edu, Bucknell Univ; Gs
Trost, G K., (501) 575-7317 garrett@dicksonstreet.com, Univ of Arkansas, Fayetteville; Zn
Trouet, Valerie, (520) 626-8004 trouet@email.arizona.edu, Univ of Arizona; PeZyAs
Trout, Jennifer, (269) 387-8633 jennifer.l.trout@wmich.edu, Western Michigan Univ; ZnnZn
Troy, Marleen, (570) 408-4615 marleen.troy@wilkes.edu, Wilkes Univ; Ht
Trudgill, Bruce D., (303) 273-3883 btrudgil@mines.edu, Colorado Sch of Mines; Gc
Trueman, Clive, +44 (0)23 80596571 trueman@noc.soton.ac.uk, Univ of Southampton; Cg
Trugman, Daniel, dtrugman@jsg.utexas.edu, Univ of Texas, Austin; Yg
Trullenque, Ghislain, +33(0)3 44069327 ghislain.trullenque@laslle-beauvais.fr, Institut Polytechnique LaSalle Beauvais (ex-IGAL); GcNrGg
Trumbore, Susan E., (949) 824-6142 setrumbo@uci.edu, Univ of California, Irvine; Sc
Trussell, Geoffrey, 7815817370 x300 g.trussell@neu.edu, Northeastern Univ; Zn
Tsai, Victor, 626.395.6993 tsai@caltech.edu, California Inst of Tech; Yg
Tsele, Philemon L., +27 (0)12 420 4939 philemon.tsele@up.ac.za, Univ of Pretoria; Zfr
Tshudy, Dale, (814) 732-2453 dtshudy@edinboro.edu, Edinboro Univ of Pennsylvania; Pi
Tsige, Meaza, meaza@ucm.es, Univ Complutense de Madrid; Ng
Tsikos, Hari, +27 (0)46-603-8511 h.tsikos@ru.ac.za, Rhodes Univ; CgEg
Tso, Jonathan L., (540) 831-5638 jtso@radford.edu, Radford Univ; Gcp
Tsoflias, George P., (785) 864-4584 tsoflias@ku.edu, Univ of Kansas; YgeGe
Tsujita, Cameron J., (519) 661-2111 (Ext. 86740) ctsujita@uwo.ca, Western Univ; Pi
Tsvankin, Ilya D., 303-273-3060 ilya@mines.edu, Colorado Sch of Mines; Ye
Ttefanei, Dan, 004023201455 astdan@uaic.ro, Alexandru Ioan Cuza; Cga
Tu, Wei, (912) 478-5233 wtu@georgiasouthern.edu, Georgia Southern Univ; Zi
Tubana, Brenda S., 225-578-9420 btubana@agcenter.lsu.edu, Louisiana State Univ; So
Tubía, Jose M., (+94) 601-5392 jm.tubia@ehu.eus, Univ of the Basque Country UPV/EHU; GctYg
Tucholke, Brian E., (508) 289-2494 btucholke@whoi.edu, Woods Hole Oceanographic Inst; Gut
Tucker, Carla M., (409) 880-8236 ctucker@lamar.edu, Lamar Univ; Hw
Tucker, Gregory E., (303) 492-6985 gregory.tucker@colorado.edu, Univ of Colorado; GmtGs
Tudhope, Alexander, +44 (0) 131 650 8508 sandy.tudhope@ed.ac.uk, Univ of Washington; AtPc
Tufillaro, Nicholas, 541-737-2064 nbt@coas.oregonstate.edu, Oregon State Univ; Cb
Tulaczyk, Slawek, (831) 459-5207 stulaczy@ucsc.edu, Univ of California, Santa Cruz; GlmNg
Tull, James F., (850) 644-1448 jtull@fsu.edu, Florida State Univ; Gct
Tuller, Markus, (520) 621-7225 mtuller@cals.arizona.edu, Univ of Arizona; Zn
Tullis, Jan A., (401) 863-1921 jan_tullis@brown.edu, Brown Univ; Gcy
Tullis, Jason A., (479) 575-8784 jatullis@uark.edu, Univ of Arkansas, Fayetteville; ZriZf
Tullis, Terry E., (401) 863-3829 terry_tullis@brown.edu, Brown Univ; Yx
Tumarkin-Deratzian, Allison, altd@temple.edu, Temple Univ; Pv
Tung, Ka-Kit, tung@amath.washington.edu, Univ of Washington; As
Tung, Wen-wen, (765) 494-0272 wwtung@purdue.edu, Purdue Univ; As
Tunnicliffe, Verena, (250) 721-7135 verenat@uvic.ca, Univ of Victoria; Ob
Tura, Ali, 303-273-3454 alitura@mines.edu, Colorado Sch of Mines; YsNr
Turbeville, John, (760) 944-4449, x6413 jturbeville@miracosta.edu, MiraCosta Coll; GgOg
Turchyn, Alexandra, +44 (0) 1223 333479 atur07@esc.cam.ac.uk, Univ of Cambridge; Ge
Turco, Richard, (310) 825-6936 turco@atmos.ucla.edu, Univ of California, Los Angeles; As
Turcotte, Donald L., (530) 752-6808 dlturcotte@ucdavis.edu, Univ of California, Davis; Yg
Turek, Andrew, (519) 969-6710 turek@uwindsor.ca, Univ of Windsor; Cc
Turek, Marni, 250-807-8284 marni.turek@ubc.ca, Univ of British Columbia, Okanagan Campus; Hg
Turk, Judith, (402)472-8024 jturk3@unl.edu, Univ of Nebraska, Lincoln; Sd
Turner, A. Keith, kturner@mines.edu, Colorado Sch of Mines; Ng
Turner, Anne, aturner@austincc.edu, Austin Comm Coll District; Hg
Turner, Derek, 604-777-6568 turnerd1@douglascollege.ca, Douglas Coll; GemGl
Turner, Elizabeth C., 7056751151 x2267 eturner@laurentian.ca, Laurentian Univ, Sudbury; GrdEm
Turner, Grenville, +44 0161 275-0401 grenville.turner@manchester.ac.uk, Univ of Manchester; XcCc
Turner, Jay, (314) 935-5480 jrturner@wustl.edu, Washington Univ in St. Louis; Zn
Turner, Jenni, +44 (0)1603 59 3109 jenni.turner@uea.ac.uk, Univ of East Anglia; Gt
Turner, Kerry, +44 (0)1603 59 2551 r.k.turner@uea.ac.uk, Univ of East Anglia; GeEg
Turner, Robert E., (225) 388-6454 Louisiana State Univ; Ob
Turner, Stephen, sjturner@umass.edu, Univ of Massachusetts, Amherst; Giv
Turner, Wesley L., (936) 468-1049 turnerwl@sfasu.edu, Stephen F. Austin State Univ; Gg
Turner, III, Henry, (479) 575-7295 hturner@uark.edu, Univ of Arkansas, Fayetteville; GgtGc
Turnock, Allan C., (204) 474-6911 ac_turnock@umanitoba.ca, Univ of Manitoba; Gp
Turpening, Roger M., (906) 487-1784 roger@mtu.edu, Michigan Technological Univ; Ye
Turrin, Brent D., 848-445-3177 bturrin@eps.rutgers.edu, Rutgers, The State Univ of New Jersey; CcGvYm
Turtle, Elizabeth, (520) 621-8284 turtle@lpl.arizona.edu, Univ of Arizona; Xg
Tuttle, Samuel, 315-443-2672 setuttle@syr.edu, Syracuse Univ; Ge
Tuttle, Samuel , stuttle@mtholyoke.edu, Mount Holyoke Coll; Gq
Tvelia, Sean, (631) 451-4303 tvelias@sunysuffolk.edu, Suffolk County Comm Coll, Ammerman Campus; Ggl
Twelker, Evan, 907-451-5086 evan.twelker@alaska.gov, Alaska Division of Geological & Geophysical Surveys; Eg
Twine, Tracy E., 612-625-7278 twine@umn.edu, Univ of Minnesota, Twin Cities; As
Twiss, Robert J., (530) 752-1860 rjtwiss@ucdavis.edu, Univ of California, Davis; Gc
Tyburczy, James A., (480) 965-2637 jim.tyburczy@asu.edu, Arizona State Univ; GyzYx
Tyce, Robert, (401) 874-6879 tyce@oce.uri.edu, Univ of Rhode Island; Ou
Tyler, Carrie, 513-529-8311 tylercl@miamioh.edu, Miami Univ; Pb
Tyler, E. Jerry, (608) 262-0853 ejtyler@wisc.edu, Univ of Wisconsin, Madison; Sd
Tyler, Scott, (775) 784-6250 styler@unr.edu, Univ of Nevada, Reno; Hg
Tynan, Cynthia T., (206) 860-6793 ctynan@coastalstudies.org, Univ of Washington; Ob
Tyning, Thomas F., (413) 236-4502 ttyning@berkshirecc.edu, Berkshire Comm Coll; Zn
Tyrrell, Toby, +44 (0)23 80596110 toby.tyrrell@soton.ac.uk, Univ of Southampton; OgPe
Tziperman, Eli, (617) 384-8381 eli@eps.harvard.edu, Harvard Univ; Op
Tzortziou, Maria, 212-650-5769 mtzortziou@ccny.cuny.edu, Graduate Sch of the City Univ of New York; As
Törnqvist, Torbjörn E., 504-314-2221 tor@tulane.edu, Tulane Univ; Gs

U

Uahengo, Collen, +8613021208022 cuahengo@unam.na, Univ of Namibia;

PgGoEg
Uchupi, Elazar, (508) 289-2830 Woods Hole Oceanographic Inst; Ou
Uddin, Ashraf, (334) 844-4885 uddinas@auburn.edu, Auburn Univ; GdoGt
Ufkes, Els , +31 20 5989953 els.ufkes@falw.vu.nl, Vrije Universiteit Amsterdam; PmZgGu
Ugland, Richard, 541-552.6479 lane@sou.edu, Southern Oregon Univ; Gg
Uhen, Mark, (703) 993-5264 muhen@gmu.edu, George Mason Univ; Pv
Ukstins, Ingrid, 319-335-1824 ingrid-peate@uiowa.edu, Univ of Iowa; GviXg
Ulanski, Stanley L., (540) 568-6130 ulanskl@jmu.edu, James Madison Univ; Og
Ullman, David J., 715.682.1312 dullman@northland.edu, Northland Coll; GlPeGm
Ullman, William J., (302) 645-4302 ullman@udel.edu, Univ of Delaware; Cm
Ullrich, Alexander D., 770-274-5083 aullrich@gsu.edu, Georgia State Univ, Perimeter Coll, Dunwoody Campus; GgZnGu
Ullrich, Paul, 530-400-9817 paullrich@ucdavis.edu, Univ of California, Davis; As
Ulmer-Scholle, Dana, dana.ulmer-scholle@nmt.edu, New Mexico Inst of Mining and Tech; Gsd
Umhoefer, Paul J., (928) 523-6464 paul.umhoefer@nau.edu, Northern Arizona Univ; Gt
Underwood, Charlie, +44 020 3073 8036 Birkbeck Coll; Pg
Underwood, Michael B., (573) 882-4685 underwoodm@missouri.edu, Univ of Missouri; GsuGt
Unger, Corey, (801) 538-4810 coreyunger@utah.gov, Utah Geological Survey; Zi
Unkefer, Clifford J., (505) 665-2560 Los Alamos; Zn
Uno, Kevin, kevinuno@ldeo.columbia.edu, Columbia Univ; Pe
Unrug, Kot F., (606) 257-1883 Univ of Kentucky; Nr
Unsworth, Martyn, (780) 492-3041 martyn.unsworth@ualberta.ca, Univ of Alberta; GtvYe
Upchurch, Paul, +44 020 7679 37947 p.upchurch@ucl.ac.uk, Univ Coll London; Pg
Ural, Melek, 00904242370000-5960 melekural@firat.edu.tr, Firat Univ; GivCc
Urban-Rich, Juanita, juanita.urban-rich@umb.edu, Univ of Massachusetts, Boston; Ob
Urbanczyk, Kevin, (432) 837-8110 kevinu@sulross.edu, Sul Ross State Univ; GiZi
Uriarte, Jesus Angel, jesusangel.uriarte@ehu.eus, Univ of the Basque Country UPV/EHU; NgHg
Uribelarrea, David, uriben@ucm.es, Univ Complutense de Madrid; Ga
Urosevic, Milovan, +61 8 9266-2296 m.urosevic@curtin.edu.au, Curtin Univ; YerYx
Urquhart, Joanne, jurquhar@bowdoin.edu, Bowdoin Coll; Gge
Urquhart, Mary, 972-883-2496 urquhart@utdallas.ede, Univ of Texas, Dallas; Xy
Urzua, Alfredo, 617-552-8339 alfredo.urzua@bc.edu, Boston Coll; Ng
Ustaszewski, Kamil M., 0049(0)3641/948623 kamil.u@uni-jena.de, Friedrich-Schiller-Univ Jena; Gct
Ustin, Susan L., (530) 752-0621 slustin@ucdavis.edu, Univ of California, Davis; Zr
Ustunisik, Gokce K., (605) 394-2461 gokce.ustunisik@sdsmt.edu, South Dakota Sch of Mines & Tech; Cp
Utgard, Russell O., 614 247-4246 utgard.1@osu.edu, Ohio State Univ; YgEnZe
Uzochukwu, Godfrey A., (336) 285-4866 uzo@ncat.edu, North Carolina Agricultural & Tech State Univ; Gz
Uzunlar, Nuri, (605) 394-2494 nuri.uzunlar@sdsmt.edu, South Dakota Sch of Mines & Tech; EmCeGc

V

Vacquier, Victor D., (858) 534-4803 vvacquier@ucsd.edu, Univ of California, San Diego; Ob
Vaezi, Reza, +98 (411) 339 2721 vaezi@tabrizu.ac.ir, Univ of Tabriz; GeHgs
Vail, Peter R., (713) 348-4888 vail@rice.edu, Rice Univ; Gr
Vaillancourt, Robert, 717-872-3294 robert.vaillancourt@millersville.edu, Millersville Univ; Obc
Valdes, Juan B., (520) 621-2266 jvaldes@email.arizona.edu, Univ of Arizona; Hs
Valencia, Victor A., (520) 300-1605 victor.valencia@wsu.edu, Washington State Univ; ZgCcEg
Valenti, Christine, (973) 655-4448 Montclair State Univ; Gg
Valentine, David, valentine@geol.ucsb.edu, Univ of California, Santa Barbara; Cm
Valentine, Gregory, (716) 645-4295 gav4@buffalo.edu, SUNY, Buffalo; Gv
Valentine, James W., (510) 643-5791 Univ of California, Berkeley; Pg
Valentine, Michael , mvalentine@highline.edu, Highline Coll; Gt
Valentine, Michael, 253-566-5060 mvalentine@tacomacc.edu, Tacoma Comm Coll; Zg
Valentino, David W., (315) 312-2798 david.valentino@oswego.edu, SUNY, Oswego; GtcYu
Valerio, Mitch, 614 265 6616 mitch.valerio@dnr.state.oh.us, Ohio Dept of Natural Resources; Hw
Valiunas, Jonas K., (807) 343-8677 jvaliuna@lakeheadu.ca, Lakehead Univ; Zm
Valley, John W., (608) 263-5659 valley@geology.wisc.edu, Univ of Wisconsin, Madison; CsGxz
Valsami-Jones, Eugenia, +44 (0)121 414 5537 e.valsamijones@bham.ac.uk, Univ of Birmingham; ClGeCa
van Alstine, James, +44(0) 113 34 37531 j.vanalstine@leeds.ac.uk, Univ of Leeds; Ge
Van Alstine, James B., (320) 589-6313 vanalstj@mrs.umn.edu, Univ of Minnesota, Morris; Pg
Van Arsdale, Roy B., (901) 678-4356 rvanrsdl@memphis.edu, Univ of Memphis; Gcm
Van Avendonk, Harm, 512-471-0429 harm@ig.utexas.edu, Univ of Texas, Austin; Yg
van Balen, Ronald R., +31 20 59 87324 r.t.van.balen@vu.nl, Vrije Universiteit Amsterdam; GgmGt
van Bever Donker, Jan M., +27 021 959 3263 jvanbeverdonker@uwc.ac.za, Univ of the Western Cape; GcpGt
van Beynen, Phil, vanbeyne@usf.edu, Univ of South Florida; Pc
Van Brocklin, Matthew F., (315) 229-5197 mvanbrocklin@stlawu.edu, St. Lawrence Univ; GgZgn
Van Buer, Nicholas J., 909-869-3457 njvanbuer@cpp.edu, California State Polytechnic Univ, Pomona; GxtGz
Van Daele, Maarten, +3292644637 maarten.vandaele@ugent.be, Ghent Univ; GsRn
van de Flierdt, Tina, +44 20 759 41290 tina.vandeflierdt@imperial.ac.uk, Imperial Coll; Cs
van de Gevel, Saskia, (828) 262-7028 gevelsv@appstate.edu, Appalachian State Univ; Zg
Van De Poll, Henk W., (506) 453-4804 Univ of New Brunswick; Gs
Van de Water, Peter, 559-278-2912 pvandewater@csufresno.edu, Fresno State Univ; GrPbGf
van den Akker, Ben, ben.vandenakker@flinders.edu.au, Flinders Univ; Zn
Van Den Broeke, Matthew S., (402) 472-2418 mvandenbroeke2@unl.edu, Univ of Nebraska, Lincoln; AsZr
van den Heever, Sue, sue@atmos.colostate.edu, Colorado State Univ; As
Van Den Hoek, Jamon, 541-737-1229 vandenhj@oregonstate.edu, Oregon State Univ; Zur
van der Berg, Stan, +440151 794 4096 vandenberg@liverpool.ac.uk, Univ of Liverpool; Em
Van Der Flier-Keller, Eileen, (250) 472-4019 fkeller@uvic.ca, Univ of Victoria; Cl
van der Hilst, Robert, (617) 253-3382 hilst@mit.edu, Massachusetts Inst of Tech; Ys
van der Horst, Dan, +44 (0) 131 651 4467 dan.vanderhorst@ed.ac.uk, Edinburgh Univ; Eg
van der Kolk, Dolores, (512) 245-2170 Texas State Univ; Gcg
van der Lee, Suzan, (847) 491-8183 suzan@earth.northwestern.edu, Northwestern Univ; YsxYg
van der Lubbe, Jeroen, +31 20 59 87366 h.j.l.vander.lubbe@vu.nl, Vrije Universiteit Amsterdam; Gs
van der Merwe, Barend, +27 (0)12 420 3699 barend.vandermerwe@up.ac.za, Univ of Pretoria; Gm
van der Pluijm, Ben, (734) 763-0373 vdpluijm@umich.edu, Univ of Michigan; GcZce
Van der Putten, Nathalie, n.n.l.vanderputten@vu.nl, Vrije Universiteit Amsterdam; PecZy
van der Velde, Ype, +31 20 59 87402 y.vander.velde@vu.nl, Vrije Universiteit Amsterdam; Hw
Van der Voo, Rob, (734) 764-8322 voo@umich.edu, Univ of Michigan; YmGtc
van der Werf, Guido R., +31 20 59 85687 guido.vander.werf@vu.nl, Vrije Universiteit Amsterdam; Zr
van Dijk, Deanna, (616) 526-6510 dvandijk@calvin.edu, Calvin Coll; GmOnZy
van Dongen, Bart, +44 0161 306-7460 bart.vandongen@manchester.ac.uk, Univ of Manchester; Co
Van Eerd, Laura, (519) 674-1644 lvaneerd@ridgetownc.uoguelph.ca, Univ of Guelph; Zn
Van Engelen, Alexander, alexander.van.engelen@asu.edu, Arizona State Univ; Xa
Van Geen, Alexander, avangeen@ldeo.columbia.edu, Columbia Univ; Cg
van Hinsberg, Vincent, 514-398-8112 vincent.vanhinsberg@mcgill.ca, McGill Univ; EgCg
Van Horn, Stephen R., (740) 826-8306 svanhorn@muskingum.edu,

Muskingum Univ; GeZiEo
van Hunen, Jeroen, +44 (0) 191 33 42293 jeroen.van-hunen@durham.ac.uk, Durham Univ; Gt
Van Iten, Heyo, (812) 866-7303 vaniten@hanover.edu, Hanover Coll; PgHgRn
van Keken, Peter J., (734) 764-1497 keken@umich.edu, Univ of Michigan; Yg
Van Kooten, Gerald K., (616) 526-6374 gvankooten1@gmail.com, Calvin Coll; GoCePi
van Leeuwen, Peter Jan, peter.vanleeuwen@colostate.edu, Colorado State Univ; As
van Leeuwen, Willem, leeuw@email.arizona.edu, Univ of Arizona; Zy
Van Loon, Lisa, 306-657-3585 lisa.vanloon@lightsource.ca, Western Univ; Ca
Van Meter, Kimberly, kvanmete@uic.edu, Univ of Illinois at Chicago; Hs
Van Mooy, Benjamin, (508) 289-2740 bvanmooy@whoi.edu, Woods Hole Oceanographic Inst; Oc
van Niekerk, Adriaan, avn@sun.ac.za, Stellenbosch Univ; Zri
Van Niewenhuise, Donald, 713-743-3423 donvann@uh.edu, Univ of Houston; PsGoPe
Van Orman, James A., jav12@case.edu, Case Western Reserve Univ; CgGyCp
Van Rooij, David, david.vanrooij@ugent.be, Ghent Univ; Yr
Van Roosendaal, Susan, (801) 581-8218 Univ of Utah; Zn
Van Ry, Michael, mvanry@occ.cccd.edu, Orange Coast Coll; Gv
Van Ryswick, Stephen, 410-554-5544 stephen.vanryswick@maryland.gov, Maryland Department of Natural Resources; Ge
Van Rythoven, Adrian, (570) 389-3912 avanrythov@bloomu.edu, Bloomsburg Univ; GxzEg
Van Schmus, W. Randall, (785) 864-2727 rvschmus@ku.edu, Univ of Kansas; Cc
Van Stan, John, (912) 478-8040 jvanstan@georgiasouthern.edu, Georgia Southern Univ; HgClSb
Van Straaten, H. Peter, (519) 824-4120 x52454 pvanstra@uoguelph.ca, Univ of Guelph; EnScCb
Van Tongeren, Jill A., (848) 445-5363 jvantongeren@eps.rutgers.edu, Rutgers, The State Univ of New Jersey; GiCgGt
Van Vleet, Edward S., (727) 553-1165 vanvleet@usf.edu, Univ of South Florida; Co
van Westrenen, Wim, w.van.westrenen@vu.nl, Vrije Universiteit Amsterdam; CpGz
Van Wijk, Jolante, (575) 835-6661 jolante.vanwijk@nmt.edu, New Mexico Inst of Mining and Tech; GtoYe
Vanacore, Elizabeth A., (787) 265-3845 elizabeth.vanacore@upr.edu, Univ of Puerto Rico; YsuYx
VanAller-Hernick, Linda A., (518) 486-3699 lhernick@mail.nysed.gov, New York State Geological Survey; Pgb
Vance, Robert K., (912) 478-5353 rkvance@georgiasouthern.edu, Georgia Southern Univ; GiEgGg
Vandeberg, Gregory S., 701-777-4588 gregory.vandeberg@und.edu, Univ of North Dakota; GmZiGl
Vandemark, Douglas C., 603-862-0195 doug.vandemark@unh.edu, Univ of New Hampshire; Zr
Vanden Berg, Michael, (801) 538-5419 michaelvandenberg@utah.gov, Utah Geological Survey; Eo
Vandenbroucke, Thijs, thijs.vandenbroucke@ugent.be, Ghent Univ; Ps
Vander Auwera, Jacqueline, 32 4 366 22 53 jvdauwera@ulg.ac.be, Universite de Liege; Giv
Vanderkluysen, Loyc, (215) 571-4673 loyc@drexel.edu, Drexel Univ; GviGz
Vanderlip, Richard, (785) 532-6101 vanderrl@ksu.edu, Kansas State Univ; So
VanDervoort, Dane S., (205) 247-3626 dvandervoort@gsa.state.al.us, Geological Survey of Alabama; GcpZi
VanDerwerker, Tiffany J., 410-554-5558 tiffany.vanderwerker@maryland.gov, Maryland Department of Natural Resources; Hw
VanDorpe, Paul E., paul.vandorpe@dnr.iowa.gov, Iowa Dept of Natural Resources; Gg
VanGundy, Robert D., (276) 376-4656 rdv4v@uvawise.edu, Univ of Virginia's Coll at Wise; GeHgZg
VanHorn, Jason E., (616) 526-7623 jev35@calvin.edu, Calvin Coll; ZirRh
Vaniman, David T., (505) 667-1863 vaniman@lanl.gov, Los Alamos; Gx
vanKeken, Peter E., pvankeken@carnegiescience.edu, Carnegie Inst for Sci; GtYsCg
Vanko, David A., (410) 704-2121 dvanko@towson.edu, Towson Univ; Gxz
Vann, David R., (215) 898-4906 drvann@sas.upenn.edu, Univ of Pennsylvania; GeSfXm
Vann, Jamie, (610) 738-0598 jvann@wcupa.edu, West Chester Univ; CgGg
VanRegenmorter, John M., 616-331-3164 vanregjo@gvsu.edu, Grand Valley State Univ; PvGsr
VanTongeren, Jill, jill.vantongeren@tufts.edu, Tufts Univ; GiCu
Vaqueiro Rodriguez, Marcos, 0034637756150 mvaqueiro@frioya.es, Coruna Univ; GcmYd
Varadi, Ferenc D., (310) 206-6484 Univ of California, Los Angeles; Zn
Varady, Robert G., (520) 626-4393 rvarady@email.arizona.edu, Univ of Arizona; Zn
Varas, María Josefa, mjvaras@ucm.es, Univ Complutense de Madrid; Gd
Varekamp, Johan C., (860) 685-2248 jvarekamp@wesleyan.edu, Wesleyan Univ; CgGzv
Varela, Diana, 250-721-6120 dvarela@uvic.ca, Univ of Victoria; Ob
Vargo, Gabriel A., (727) 864-2683 vargo@mail.usf.edu, Univ of South Florida; Ob
Varner, Ruth K., (603) 862-0853 ruth.varner@unh.edu, Univ of New Hampshire; Cl
Varricchio, David J., (406) 994-6907 djv@montana.edu, Montana State Univ; Pv
Vassiliou, Andreas H., 973-353-5100 ahvass@andromeda.rutgers.edu, Rutgers, The State Univ of New Jersey, Newark; Gz
Vatuva, Absai , avatuva@unam.na, Univ of Namibia; EgGtc
Vaudrey, Jamie, 860-405-9149 jamie.vaudrey@uconn.edu, Univ of Connecticut; Ob
Vaughan, David, +44 0161 275-3935 david.vaughan@manchester.ac.uk, Univ of Manchester; GzClGe
Vaughan, Geraint, +44 0161 306-3931 geraint.vaughan@manchester.ac.uk, Univ of Manchester; As
Vaughan, Michael T., 631 632-8030 michael.vaughan@sunysb.edu, Stony Brook Univ; Yx
Vaughan, Naomi, +44 (0)1603 59 3904 n.vaughan@uea.ac.uk, Univ of East Anglia; Am
Vautier, Yannick, +33(0)3 44068991 yannick.vautier@lasalle-beauvais.fr, Institut Polytechnique LaSalle Beauvais (ex-IGAL); GodCo
Vaz, Nuno M., nunovaz@utad.pt, Unive de Trás-os-Montes e Alto Douro; PmlYg
Vazquez, Rogelio, rvazquez@cicese.mx, Centro de Investigación Científica y de Educación Superior de Ensenada; Ye
Veblen, Thomas T., veblen@colorado.edu, Univ of Colorado; Zg
Vecchi, Gabriel, 609-258-4101 gvecchi@princeton.edu, Princeton Univ; ZoOp
Veeder, Glenn J., (818) 354-7388 Jet Propulsion Lab; Zn
Veeger, Anne, (401) 874-4184 veeger@uri.edu, Univ of Rhode Island; Hw
Vega, Anthony J., (814) 226-2023 avega@clarion.edu, Clarion Univ; AtmOp
Vegas, Nestor, 0034946015374 nestor.vegas@ehu.eus, Univ of the Basque Country UPV/EHU; GctYm
Veizer, Jan, veizer@uottawa.ca, Univ of Ottawa; Cl
Velasco, Aaron A., (915) 747-5101 aavelasco@utep.edu, Univ of Texas, El Paso; Yx
Velbel, Michael A., (517) 355-4626 velbel@msu.edu, Michigan State Univ; ClGdSc
Velicogna, Isabella, 949-824-2685 isabella.velicogna@gmail.com, Univ of California, Irvine; Zr
Velinsky, David, 215 299 1147 velinsky@drexel.edu, Drexel Univ; OcCms
Velli, Marco, 310-206-4892 mvelli@ucla.edu, Univ of California, Los Angeles; Yg
Vengosh, Avner, 919 684 5847 vengosh@duke.edu, Duke Univ; Hw
Venkatesan, M I., (310) 206-2561 Univ of California, Los Angeles; Co
Venn, Cynthia, (570) 389-4141 cvenn@bloomu.edu, Bloomsburg Univ; OgClOc
Venter, Marcie, (270) 809-3457 mventer@murraystate.edu, Murray State Univ; Ga
Venterea, Rodney T., (612) 624-7842 venterea@soils.umn.edu, Univ of Minnesota, Twin Cities; Sp
Vento, Frank, 814-824-2581 fvento@mercyhurst.edu, Mercyhurst Univ; GaSoGm
Ventura, Stephen J., (608) 262-6416 sventura@wisc.edu, Univ of Wisconsin, Madison; ZrSo
Venzke, Edward, (202) 633-1822 venzkee@si.edu, Smithsonian Inst / Nat Mus of Natural History; Gv
Vepraskas, Michael J., (919) 515-1458 North Carolina State Univ; Sd
Ver Straeten, Charles, (518) 486-2004 cverstrae@mail.nysed.gov, New York State Geological Survey; Grs
Verardo, Stacey, (703) 993-1045 sverardo@gmu.edu, George Mason Univ; Pei
Veraverbeke, Sander, +31 20 59 82975 s.n.n.veraverbeke@vu.nl, Vrije Universiteit Amsterdam; Zr
Verburg, Paul, 775-784-4511 pverburg@cabnr.unr.edu, Univ of Nevada, Reno; SdcSb
Veres, Michael, michael.veres@oswego.edu, SUNY, Oswego; As
Verlinde, Johannes, (814) 863-9711 jxv7@psu.edu, Pennsylvania State Univ, Univ Park; Am
Verma, Sumit, 432-552-2242 verma_s@utpb.edu, Univ of Texas Permian Basin; YeGo
Vermeesch, Pieter, +44 02076792418 p.vermeesch@ucl.ac.uk, Univ Coll London; Cc
Vermeij, Geerat J., (530) 752-2234 gjvermeij@ucdavis.edu, Univ of California, Davis; Pe

Vermeul, Vincent R., (509) 376-8316 vince.vermeul@pnl.gov, Pacific Northwest; Hg
Vernhes, Jean-David, +33(0)3 44062547 jean-david.vernhes@lasalle-beauvais.fr, Institut Polytechnique LaSalle Beauvais (ex-IGAL); YgNgr
Verosub, Kenneth L., (530) 752-6911 klverosub@ucdavis.edu, Univ of California, Davis; Ym
Versteeg, Roelof, versteeg@ldeo.columbia.edu, Columbia Univ; Yg
Vervoort, Jeffrey D., (509) 335-5597 vervoort@wsu.edu, Washington State Univ; CcaGt
Vesovic, Velisa, +44 20 759 47352 v.vesovic@imperial.ac.uk, Imperial Coll; Np
Vesper, Dorothy, 304 293 5603 dorothy.vesper@mail.wvu.edu, West Virginia Univ; Hw
Vetter, Scott K., (318) 869-5055 svetter@centenary.edu, Centenary Coll of Louisiana; Gi
Vialle, Stephanie, stephanie.vialle@curtin.edu.au, Curtin Univ; YxCqNp
Vice, Mari A., (608) 342-1055 vice@uwplatt.edu, Univ of Wisconsin, Platteville; Gd
Vicens Batet, Enric, ++935811783 enric.vicens@uab.cat, Universitat Autonoma de Barcelona; Pg
Vickery, Nancy, nvicker2@une.edu.au, Univ of New England; GgeYg
Vidal, Antonio, vidalv@cicese.mx, Centro de Investigación Científica y de Educación Superior de Ensenada; Ys
Vidal Romaní, Juan Ramon, 00 34 981 167000 xemoncho@udc.es, Coruna Univ; GmlGc
Vidale, John E., (206) 543-6790 vidale@uw.edu, Univ of Southern California; YsGtYg
Vidale, Jon , 310-210-2131 vidale@uw.edu, Univ of Washington; RnYs
Videtich, Patricia E., 616-331-3887 videticp@gvsu.edu, Grand Valley State Univ; Gd
Vidoviæ, Jelena, +38514606090 jelena.vidovic@geol.pmf.hr, Univ of Zagreb; Gg
Viedma, Cristóbal, viedma@ucm.es, Univ Complutense de Madrid; Gz
Viegas, Anthony V., +91-8669609198 anthonyviegas@yahoo.com, Goa Univ; GiEmGx
Vieira, David J., (505) 667-7231 Los Alamos; Zn
Viens, Rob, (425) 564-3158 rob.viens@bellevuecollege.edu, Bellevue Coll; GgZg
Vierrether, Chris, 573-368-2370 chris.vierrether@dnr.mo.gov, Missouri Dept of Natural Resources; GgoGe
Viertel, David C., 217-581-6244 dviertel@eiu.edu, Eastern Illinois Univ; Zru
Vietti, Laura, (307) 314-2024 lvietti@uwyo.edu, Univ of Wyoming; Pv
Vig, Pradeep K., 618.545.3373 pvig@kaskaskia.edu, Kaskaskia Coll; Gg
Vigouroux-Caillibot, Nathalie, 604-527-5860 vigourouxcaillibotn@douglascollege.ca, Douglas Coll; GviCg
Vila, Bernat, bernat.vila@uab.cat, Universitat Autonoma de Barcelona; Pv
Vilcaez, Javier, 405744-6358 vilcaez@okstate.edu, Oklahoma State Univ; XzNpCl
Villa, Jorge, jorge.villa@louisiana.edu, Univ of Louisiana at Lafayette; Ge
Villalard-Bohnsack, Martine, (401) 254-3243 Roger Williams Univ; Ob
Villalobos, Joshua, (915) 831-7001 jvillal6@epcc.edu, El Paso Comm Coll; ZeYgu
Villareal, Tracy A., (361) 749-6732 tracyv@austin.utexas.edu, Univ of Texas, Austin; Ob
Villaseca, Carlos, granito@ucm.es, Univ Complutense de Madrid; Gi
Villegas, Monica B., 543584676198 mvillegas@exa.unrc.edu.ar, Univ Nacional de Rio Cuarto; Gsc
Villeneuve, Marlene C., +64 3 3667001 Ext 45682 marlene.villeneuve@canterbury.ac.nz, Univ of Canterbury; Ng
Vimont, Daniel J., (608)262-2828 dvimont@wisc.edu, Univ of Wisconsin, Madison; As
Vincent, Dayton G., dvincent@purdue.edu, Purdue Univ; As
Vincent, Paul C., 229.333.5752 pvincent@valdosta.edu, Valdosta State Univ; Zig
Vincent, Robert K., (419) 372-0160 rvincen@bgnet.bgsu.edu, Bowling Green State Univ; Yg
Vinciguerra, Sergio Carmelo, sergiocarmelo.vinciguerra@unito.it, Univ di Torino; Nr
Vindel, Elena, evindel@ucm.es, Univ Complutense de Madrid; Gz
Vinton, Bonita L., (724) 738-2048 bonita.vinton@sru.edu, Slippery Rock Univ; Gg
Visaggi, Christy, cvissagi@gsu.edu, Georgia State Univ; PiZe
Viskupic, Karen, (208)426-3658 karenviskupic@boisestate.edu, Boise State Univ; ZeGc
Visscher, Pieter, (860) 486-4434 pieter.visscher@uconn.edu, Univ of Connecticut; Co
Vitale, Sarah A., 715-836-4300 vitalesa@uwec.edu, Univ of Wisconsin, Eau Claire; Hq
Vitek, John D., (405) 780-0623 jvitek@neo.tamu.edu, Texas A&M Univ; GmZe
Viti, Cecilia, cecilia.viti@unisi.it, Univ of Siena; Gz
Viviano-Beck, Christina E., christina.beck@jhuapl.edu, Univ of Tennessee, Knoxville; Xg
Vivoni, Enrique, (480) 727-3575 vivoni@asu.edu, Arizona State Univ; Hg
Vlahos, Penny, (860) 405-9269 penny.vlahos@uconn.edu, Univ of Connecticut; OcGeu
Vlahovic, Gordana, (919) 530-5172 gvlahovic@nccu.edu, North Carolina Central Univ; YsZeRn
Vlcan, Jennifer, 775-682-8759 mauldin@unr.edu, Univ of Nevada, Reno; Zi
Vocadlo, Lidunka, +44 020 7679 37919 l.vocadlo@ucl.ac.uk, Univ Coll London; Gy
Voelker, Bettina, (303) 273-3152 voelker@mines.edu, Colorado Sch of Mines; Ca
Vogel, Eve, 413-545-0778 evevogel@geo.umass.edu, Univ of Massachusetts, Amherst; Zy
Vogl, Jim, (352) 392-6987 jvogl@ufl.edu, Univ of Florida; Gct
Voglesonger, Kenneth M., 773-442-6053 k-voglesonger@neiu.edu, Northeastern Illinois Univ; ClGe
Vogt, Steven, (831) 459-2151 vogt@ucolick.org, Univ of California, Santa Cruz; Xc
Voice, Peter J., (269) 387-5446 peter.voice@wmich.edu, Western Michigan Univ; GsZn
Voicu, Gabriel-Constantin, 514-987-3000 #1648 gvoicu@videotron.ca, Universite du Quebec a Montreal; GcCg
Voight, Barry, (814) 238-4431 voight@ems.psu.edu, Pennsylvania State Univ, Univ Park; GveGg
Voigt, Vicki, 573-368-2128 vicki.voigt@dnr.mo.gov, Missouri Dept of Natural Resources; Gg
Vojtko, Rastislav , vojtko@fns.uniba.sk, Comenius Univ in Bratislava; GctGm
Volborth, Alexis, (406) 496-4134 Montana Tech of the Univ of Montana; Ca
Voller, Vaughan R., (612) 625-0764 volle001@tc.umn.edu, Univ of Minnesota, Twin Cities; Zm
Vollmer, Frederick W., 845-257-3760 vollmerf@newpaltz.edu, SUNY, New Paltz; GctGx
Vollmer, Steve, 7815817370 x312 s.vollmer@neu.edu, Northeastern Univ; Zn
von Bitter, Peter H., 416-586-5591 peterv@rom.on.ca, Univ of Toronto; Pm
von der Handt, Anette, 612-624-7370 avdhandt@umn.edu, Univ of Minnesota, Twin Cities; GiCt
von Frese, Ralph R., (614) 292-5635 von-frese.3@osu.edu, Ohio State Univ; Ye
von Glasow, Roland, +44 (0)1603 59 3204 r.von-glasow@uea.ac.uk, Univ of East Anglia; Yg
Von Reden, Karl F., (508) 289-3384 kvonreden@whoi.edu, Woods Hole Oceanographic Inst; Ct
von Salzen, Knut, (250) 363-8287 knut.vonsalzen@canada.ca, Univ of British Columbia; As
von Seggern, David H., (775) 303 8461 vonseg@seismo.unr.edu, Univ of Nevada, Reno; YsgEo
Vondra, Carl F., (515) 294-5867 cfvondra@iastate.edu, Iowa State Univ of Sci & Tech; Gr
Vonk, Jorien, +31 20 59 87336 j.e.vonk@vu.nl, Vrije Universiteit Amsterdam; Hg
Voorhees, David H., (630) 466-2783 dvoorhees@waubonsee.edu, Waubonsee Comm Coll; ZgGg
Voorhees, Kent J., kvoorhee@mines.edu, Colorado Sch of Mines; Co
Vopson, Melvin M., +44 023 92 842246 melvin.vopson@port.ac.uk, Univ of Portsmouth; Yg
Voroney, R. Paul, (519) 824-4120 (Ext. 53057) pvoroney@uoguelph.ca, Univ of Guelph; Sb
Vorosmarty, Charles, 212-650-7042 cvorosmarty@ccny.cuny.edu, Graduate Sch of the City Univ of New York; Ng
Vorwald, Brian, vorwalb@sunysuffolk.edu, Suffolk County Comm Coll, Ammerman Campus; Zg
Voss, Regis D., (515) 294-1923 Iowa State Univ of Sci & Tech; So
Votaw, Robert, rvotaw@iun.edu, Indiana Univ Northwest; PiGrs
Voulgaris, George, (803) 777-2549 gvoulgaris@geol.sc.edu, Univ of South Carolina; OnpOg
Vrba, Elisabeth S., 203-432-5008 elisabeth.vrba@yale.edu, Yale Univ; Pvg
Vroon, Pieter, p.z.vroon@vu.nl, Vrije Universiteit Amsterdam; GvCcl
Vuke, Susan M., (406) 496-4326 svuke@mtech.edu, Montana Tech of The Univ of Montana; GgrGs
Vukovich, George, (416)736-2100 #30090 vukovich@yorku.ca, York Univ; As
Vulava, Vijay M., (843) 953-1922 vulavav@cofc.edu, Coll of Charleston; CgHwSc

W

Waag, Charles J., (208) 426-3658 cwaag@boisestate.edu, Boise State Univ; Gc
Wach, Grant D., (902) 494-8019 grant.wach@dal.ca, Dalhousie Univ; GorGs

Wada, Ikuko, (612) 301-9535 iwada@umn.edu, Univ of Minnesota, Twin Cities; ZnYgGt
Waddington, David C., (604) 527-5230 waddingtond@douglascollege.ca, Douglas Coll; ZgGuEd
Waddington, Edwin D., 206-543-4585 edw@uw.edu, Univ of Washington; Gl
Waddington, J. M., (905) 525-9140 (Ext. 23217) wadding@mcmaster.ca, McMaster Univ; Pe
Wade, Bridget S., +44 020 3108 6359 b.wade@ucl.ac.uk, Univ Coll London; PmeCl
Wade, Phillip, 503-838-8225 wadep@wou.edu, Western Oregon Univ; Zge
Wade, Terry L., (979) 862-2325 t-wade@geos.tamu.edu, Texas A&M Univ; OcCao
Wadhwa, Meenakshi, (480) 965-0796 meenakshi.wadhwa@asu.edu, Arizona State Univ; Xc
Wadsworth, Fabian, fabian.b.wadsworth@durham.ac.uk, Durham Univ; Gv
Wadsworth, William B., (562) 907-4200 Whittier Coll; Gi
Wagger, Michael G., (919) 515-4269 North Carolina State Univ; Sb
Waggoner, Karen, 432-685-5540 kwaggoner@midland.edu, Midland Coll; GgRhGc
Wagner, John R., (864) 656-5024 jrwgnr@clemson.edu, Clemson Univ; ZeGm
Wagner, Kaleb, (612) 626-6901 kewagner@umn.edu, Univ of Minnesota; Gl
Wagner, Lara S., 202-478-8838 lwagner@carnegiescience.edu, Carnegie Inst for Sci; YsgGt
Wagner, Peter J., 312-665-7634 pwagner@fieldmuseum.org, Field Mus of Natural History; Pi
Wagner, Rick, 205-247-3622 rwagner@gsa.state.al.us, Geological Survey of Alabama; Cg
Wagner, Sasha, (518) 276-3075 wagnes3@rpi.edu, Rensselaer Polytechnic Inst; Cob
Wagner, Timothy J., (402) 280-2239 timothywagner@creighton.edu, Creighton Univ; As
Wagner Riddle, Claudia, (519) 824-4120 (Ext. 2787) cwagnerr@uoguelph.ca, Univ of Guelph; Am
Wagoner, Jeffrey L., (925) 422-1374 wagoner1@llnl.gov, Lawrence Livermore; Gs
Waheed, Umair B., +966138602297 umair.waheed@kfupm.edu.sa, King Fahd Univ of Petroleum and Minerals; Yg
Waid, Christopher, 614 265 6627 christopher.waid@dnr.state.oh.us, Ohio Dept of Natural Resources; Eo
Wainman, Carmine, carmine.wainman@adelaide.edu.au, Univ of Adelaide; Grs
Waite, Cynthia H., (213) 740-6109 waite@usc.edu, Univ of Southern California; Zn
Waite, Gregory P., (906) 487-3554 gpwaite@mtu.edu, Michigan Technological Univ; YsGv
Waithaka, Hunja, hunja@eng.jkuat.ac.ke, Jomo Kenyatta Univ of Agriculture & Tech; YdZgi
Wakabayashi, John, 559-278-6459 jwakabayashi@csufresno.edu, Fresno State Univ; GmcGt
Wake, Cameron P., (603) 862-2329 cameron.wake@unh.edu, Univ of New Hampshire; Gl
Wake, David B., (510) 642-3059 wakelab@uclink.berkeley.edu, Univ of California, Berkeley; Pg
Wake, Marvalee H., (510) 642-4743 Univ of California, Berkeley; Pg
Wakefield, Kelli, kelliwakefield@hotmail.com, Mesa Comm Coll; Gg
Wakefield, S J., wakefield@cf.ac.uk, Cardiff Univ; Cm
Wala, Andrew M., 859-257-2959 Univ of Kentucky; Nm
Walcek, Christopher J., (518) 437-8720 SUNY, Albany; As
Waldbusser, George, 541-737-8964 waldbuss@coas.oregonstate.edu, Oregon State Univ; Ob
Walden, John, +44 01334 463688 jw9@st-andrews.ac.uk, Univ of St. Andrews; Ym
Waldhauser, Felix, felixw@ldeo.columbia.edu, Columbia Univ; Ys
Waldman, John, 718-997-3603 john.waldman@qc.cuny.edu, Graduate Sch of the City Univ of New York; ObHsZc
Waldron, John W., john.waldron@ualberta.ca, Univ of Alberta; Gc
Walford, Nigel, +44020 8417 2512 nwalford@kingston.ac.uk, Kingston Univ; Zi
Walker, Barry , bawalker@pdx.edu, Portland State Univ; GiCgGv
Walker, Brett, brett.walker@uottawa.ca, Univ of Ottawa; OgcCc
Walker, Charles T., (562) 985-4818 California State Univ, Long Beach; Cl
Walker, David, dwalker@ldeo.columbia.edu, Columbia Univ; Gx
Walker, Ian , ianjwalker@asu.edu, Arizona State Univ; Gm
Walker, Ian R., 250-807-9559 ian.walker@ubc.ca, Univ of British Columbia, Okanagan Campus; PeGnHs
Walker, J. Douglas, (785) 864-7711 jdwalker@ku.edu, Univ of Kansas; Gc
Walker, Jeffrey R., 845-437-5546 jewalker@vassar.edu, Vassar Coll; GzScGv
Walker, John L., (630) 252-6803 jlwalker@anl.gov, Argonne; Cg
Walker, Mark, (775) 784-1938 mwalker@cabnr.unr.edu, Univ of Nevada, Reno; Zn
Walker, Nan D., (225) 388-5331 Louisiana State Univ; Og
Walker, Peter, (541) 346-4541 pwalker@oregon.uoregon.edu, Univ of Oregon; Zn
Walker, Raymond J., (310) 825-7685 rwalker@igpp.ucla.edu, Univ of California, Los Angeles; Xy
Walker, Richard, +44 (1865) 282115 richard.walker@earth.ox.ac.uk, Univ of Oxford; Zr
Walker, Sally E., (706) 542-2396 swalker@gly.uga.edu, Univ of Georgia; Pm
Walker, Sara, (480) 727-2394 sara.i.walker@asu.edu, Arizona State Univ; Xb
Wallace, Adam F., (302) 831-1950 afw@udel.edu, Univ of Delaware; ClGzZm
Wallace, Davin, (228) 688-3060 davin.wallace@usm.edu, Univ of Southern Mississippi; Ou
Wallace, Douglas, (902) 494-4132 douglas.wallace@dal.ca, Dalhousie Univ; Oc
Wallace, Douglas W. R., (631) 344-2945 wallace@notes.cc.sunysb.edu, SUNY, Stony Brook; Oc
Wallace, Janae, (801) 537-3387 nrugs.jwallace@state.ut.us, Utah Geological Survey; Hw
Wallace, John M., (206) 543-7390 wallace@atmos.washington.edu, Univ of Washington; As
Wallace, Laura, lwallace@ig.utexas.edu, Univ of Texas, Austin; GtYdZr
Wallace, Paul, (541) 346-5985 pwallace@uoregon.edu, Univ of Oregon; GviCg
Wallace, Tim, 662-268-1032 Ext 244 tjw5@msstate.edu, Mississippi State Univ; Am
Wallace, William G., (718) 982-3876 william.wallace@csi.cuny.edu, Graduate Sch of the City Univ of New York; Og
Wallace, Jr., Terry C., (505) 667-3644 wallacet@lanl.gov, Los Alamos; Ys
Wallender, Wes W., 530.752.0688 wwwallender@ucdavis.edu, Univ of California, Davis; Hg
Waller, Thomas R., (202) 357-2127 Smithsonian Inst / Nat Mus of Natural History; Pi
Wallis, Ilka, ilka.wallis@flinders.edu.au, Flinders Univ; HqCg
Walowski, Kristina J., walowski@middlebury.edu, Middlebury Coll; Gi
Walraevens, Kristine E., (329) 264-4648 kristine.walraevens@ugent.be, Ghent Univ; HwCqYu
Walrod, Amanda G., (501) 575-7317 awalrod@comp.uark.edu, Univ of Arkansas, Fayetteville; Zn
Walsh, Christopher, (301) 405-4351 cswalsh@umd.edu, Univ of Maryland; Zn
Walsh, Daniel E., (907) 474-6746 dewalsh@alaska.edu, Univ of Alaska, Fairbanks; Zn
Walsh, Ellen c., (920) 832-6739 ellen.c.walsh@lawrence.edu, Lawrence Univ; Zn
Walsh, Emily O., (319) 895-4302 ewalsh@cornellcollege.edu, Univ of Iowa; GptCc
Walsh, John J., (727) 553-1164 jwalsh@marine.usf.edu, Univ of South Florida; Ob
Walsh, Maud M., (225) 578-1211 evwals@lsu.edu, Louisiana State Univ; GeRcZe
Walsh, Tim R., 806-291-1123 Wayland Baptist Univ; GsPmGo
Walter, Julien, 41854550112680 julien_walter@uqac.ca, Universite du Quebec a Chicoutimi; HwqGm
Walter, Lynn M., (734) 763-4590 lmwalter@umich.edu, Univ of Michigan; Cl
Walter , Michael , 0117 9515007 m.j.walter@bristol.ac.uk, Univ of Bristol; GiCpg
Walter, Nathan A., (678) 839-4070 awalter@westga.edu, Univ of West Georgia; Zg
Walter, Robert C., 717 358-7198 robert.walter@fandm.edu, Franklin and Marshall Coll; Cc
Walter, Thomas, (212) 772-5457 twalter@hunter.cuny.edu, Hunter Coll (CUNY); ZyeAm
Walter-Shea, Elizabeth A., (402) 472-1553 ewalter-shea1@unl.edu, Univ of Nebraska, Lincoln; As
Walters, James C., james.walters@uni.edu, Univ of Northern Iowa; Gm
Walters, Richard, richard.walters@durham.ac.uk, Durham Univ; Yd
Walters, Steven, swalt826@uw.edu, Univ of Washington; Zir
Waltham, Dave, +44 1784 443617 d.waltham@rhul.ac.uk, Royal Holloway Univ of London; Yg
Walther, Ferdinand, 089/2180 4346 macferdi@gmx.org, Ludwig-Maximilians-Univ Muenchen; Gz
Walther, John V., (214) 768-3174 Southern Methodist Univ; Cg
Walther, Suzanne, (619) 260-4787 swalther@sandiego.edu, Univ of San Diego; GmZi
Walton, Anthony W., (785) 864-2726 twalton@ku.edu, Univ of Kansas; GsEoGv
Walton, Gabriel, (303) 273-2235 gwalton@mines.edu, Colorado Sch of Mines; NgrYg

Waters, Dave, +44 (1865) 282457 dave.waters@earth.ox.ac.uk, Univ of Oxford; GpzGc
Waters, Laura E., watersla@sonoma.edu, Sonoma State Univ; GviGz
Waters, Matthew N., (334) 844-4100 mwaters@auburn.edu, Auburn Univ; Gn
Waters, Michael R., (979) 845-5246 mwaters@tamu.edu, Texas A&M Univ; Ga
Waters-Tormey, Cheryl, (828) 227-3696 cherylwt@wcu.edu, Western Carolina Univ; Gct
Waterstone, Marvin, marvinw@email.arizona.edu, Univ of Arizona; Zn
Waterworth, Lauren H., waterworthlh@appstate.edu, Appalachian State Univ; Gcg
Watkins, David, d.c.watkins@exeter.ac.uk, Exeter Univ; Hg
Watkins, James, watkins4@uoregon.edu, Univ of Oregon; Cg
Watkinson, A. John, (509) 335-2470 watkinso@mail.wsu.edu, Washington State Univ; Gc
Watkinson, Andrew, +44 (0)1603 59 2267 a.watkinson@uea.ac.uk, Univ of East Anglia; Ge
Watkinson, David H., dwatkson@ccs.carleton.ca, Carleton Univ; Em
Watkinson, Ian M., +44 1784 414046 ian.watkinson@rhul.ac.uk, Royal Holloway Univ of London; GtcRn
Watkinson, Matthew, +44 1752 584765 m.p.watkinson@plymouth.ac.uk, Univ of Plymouth; Gs
Watney, W. Lynn, (785) 864-2184 lwatney@kgs.ku.edu, Univ of Kansas; Gr
Watson, Alan, awatson@uoguelph.ca, Univ of Guelph; Zn
Watson, David B., (865) 241-4749 v6i@ornl.gov, Oak Ridge; Hw
Watson, E. Bruce, (518) 276-8838 watsoe@rpi.edu, Rensselaer Polytechnic Inst; CpcCt
Watson, Elizabeth, 215.299.1109 elizabeth.b.watson@drexel.edu, Drexel Univ; Zc
Watson, James R., 541-737-2519 jrwatson@coas.oregonstate.edu, Oregon State Univ; Zy
Watson, Kelly, 859-622-1419 kelly.watson@eku.edu, Eastern Kentucky Univ; ZriZn
Watters, Robert J., (775) 784-6069 watters@mines.unr.edu, Univ of Nevada, Reno; Nrg
Watters, Thomas R., 202-633-2483 Smithsonian Inst / Nat Air & Space Mus; Xg
Wattrus, Nigel J., (218) 726-7154 nwattrus@d.umn.edu, Univ of Minnesota Duluth; Yr
Watts, Anthony B., +44 (1865) 272032 tony@earth.ox.ac.uk, Univ of Oxford; GutYv
Watts, Chester F., (540) 831-5637 cwatts@radford.edu, Radford Univ; NgrHw
Watts, D. Randolph, (401) 874-6507 rwatts@gso.uri.edu, Univ of Rhode Island; Op
Watts, Doyle, 937 775-3455 doyle.watts@wright.edu, Wright State Univ; YeZr
Waugh, Darryn W., (410) 516-8344 waugh@jhu.edu, Johns Hopkins Univ; As
Waugh, John, 757-822-7436 tcwaugj@tcc.edu, Tidewater Comm Coll; Gg
Waugh, Richard A., (608) 342-1386 waugh@uwplatt.edu, Univ of Wisconsin, Platteville; Gc
Wauthier, Christelle, 814-865-6711 cuw25@psu.edu, Pennsylvania State Univ, Univ Park; Zn
Wax, Charles L., (662) 325-3915 wax@geosci.msstate.edu, Mississippi State Univ; As
Wdowinski, Shimon, (305) 348-6826 shimon.wdowinski@fiu.edu, Florida International Univ; YdGt
Weatherford, Jonathan, jonathan.weatherford@pcc.edu, Portland Comm Coll - Sylvania Campus; Gg
Weaver, Andrew J., (250) 472-4001 weaver@ocean.seos.uvic.ca, Univ of Victoria; Op
Weaver, Barry L., (405) 325-4492 bweaver@ou.edu, Univ of Oklahoma; Ct
Weaver, Douglas J., (702) 295-5916 douglas_weaver@lanl.gov, Los Alamos; Zn
Weaver, John T., (250) 721-6155 weaver@phys.uvic.ca, Univ of Victoria; Ym
Weaver, Justin E., 806-834-4610 justin.e.weaver@ttu.edu, Texas Tech Univ; As
Weaver, Stephen G., (719) 389-6954 sweaver@coloradocollege.edu, Colorado Coll; Gx
Weaver, Thomas A., (505) 667-8464 tweaver@lanl.gov, Los Alamos; Yg
Webb, Christine R., (410) 507-3070 webbc@si.edu, Smithsonian Inst / Nat Mus of Natural History; GzgZn
Webb, Craig, craig.webb@eku.edu, Eastern Kentucky Univ; Zyn
Webb, Elizabeth A., 5196612111 x80208 ewebb5@uwo.ca, Western Univ; CslSa
Webb, John A., +61 3 9479 1273 john.webb@latrobe.edu.au, La Trobe Univ; GeHwGa
Webb, Laura E., (802) 656-8136 lewebb@uvm.edu, Univ of Vermont; GtCcGc
Webb, Nathan D., (217) 244-2426 ndwebb2@illinois.edu, Illinois State Geological Survey; EoGo
Webb, Peter N., (614) 292-7285 webb.3@osu.edu, Ohio State Univ; PmRhGr
Webb, Robert H., (520) 626-3293 rhwebb@usgs.gov, Univ of Arizona; Gm
Webb, Spahr, scw@ldeo.columbia.edu, Columbia Univ; Yr
Webb, III, Thompson, (401) 863-3128 thompson_webb_iii@brown.edu, Brown Univ; PelAs
Webber, Andrew, (513) 455-7160 Cincinnati Mus Center; Pi
Webber, Jeffrey, jeffrey.webber@stockton.edu, Stockton Univ; Gg
Webber, Karen L., (504) 280-7395 kwebber@uno.edu, Univ of Michigan; Gv
Webber, Patty, Ext. 243 patty.webber@wyo.gov, Wyoming State Geological Survey; CcGct
Weber, Bodo, bweber@cicese.mx, Centro de Investigación Científica y de Educación Superior de Ensenada; Gp
Weber, John C., 616-331-3191 weberj@gvsu.edu, Grand Valley State Univ; GctYd
Weber, Karrie A., (402) 472-2739 kweber@unl.edu, Univ of Nebraska, Lincoln; PgCl
Weber, Keith, (208) 282-2757 webekeit@isu.edu, Idaho State Univ; Zi
Weber, Rodney J., (404) 894-1750 rweber@eas.gatech.edu, Georgia Inst of Tech; As
Weber, Thomas, 585-275-2103 t.weber@rochester.edu, Univ of Rochester; Obu
Weber-Diefenbach, Klaus, 089/2180 6549 klaus.diefenbach@iaag.geo.uni-muenchen.de, Ludwig-Maximilians-Univ Muenchen; Gg
Weborg-Benson, Kimberly, (716) 673-3293 kim.weborg-benson@fredonia.edu, SUNY, Fredonia; GgAsPg
Webre, Cherri B., (225) 388-8328 cherri@lgs.bri.lsu.edu, Louisiana State Univ; Zn
Webster, Ferris, (302) 645-4266 Univ of Delaware; Op
Webster, Gary D., (509) 335-4369 webster@wsu.edu, Washington State Univ; Pis
Webster, John R., (701) 858-3873 john.webster@minotstateu.edu, Minot State Univ; Giz
Webster, Peter J., (404) 894-1748 pjw@eas.gatech.edu, Georgia Inst of Tech; AsOp
Wedding, William C., 859-257-1883 chad.wedding@uky.edu, Univ of Kentucky; Nm
Weeden, Lori, (978) 934-3344 lori_weeden@uml.edu, Univ of Massachusetts, Lowell; GgeGs
Weeraratne, Dayanthie, (818) 677-2046 dsw@csun.edu, California State Univ, Northridge; Yg
Weglein, Arthur B., (713) 743-3848 aweglein@uh.edu, Univ of Houston; Ye
Wegmann, Karl, 919-515-0380 karl_wegmann@ncsu.edu, North Carolina State Univ; Gm
Wegner, John, 404 727 4206 jwegner@emory.edu, Emory Univ; Sf
Wehmiller, John F., (302) 831-2926 jwehm@udel.edu, Univ of Delaware; Cl
Wehner, Peter J., (512) 223-0201 pwehner@austincc.edu, Austin Comm Coll District; GieXs
Wehrmann, Laura, 089/2180 Ludwig-Maximilians-Univ Muenchen; Pg
Wei, Xiaofang, 937 376 6193 xwei@centralstate.edu, Central State Univ; ZrOgZe
Wei, Xiaohua (Adam), 250-807-8750 adam.wei@ubc.ca, Univ of British Columbia, Okanagan Campus; HqgSf
Weiblen, Paul W., 612-625-3477 pweib@umn.edu, Univ of Minnesota, Twin Cities; Gi
Weidner, Donald J., (631) 632-8211 donald.weidner@sunysb.edu, Stony Brook Univ; Gy
Weil, Arlo B., (610) 526-5113 aweil@brynmawr.edu, Bryn Mawr Coll; GctYm
Weiland, Thomas J., tjw@canes.gsw.edu, Georgia Southwestern State Univ; Gi
Weimer, Paul, (303) 492-3809 paul.weimer@colorado.edu, Univ of Colorado; Gor
Weimer, Robert J., rweimer@mines.edu, Colorado Sch of Mines; Gr
Weinbeck, Robert S., weinbeck@ametsoc.org, SUNY, The Coll at Brockport; As
Weinberger, Alycia J., (202) 478-8820 aweinberger@carnegiescience.edu, Carnegie Inst for Sci; Xa
Weinstein, Charles E., (413) 236-4556 cweinste@berkshirecc.edu, Berkshire Comm Coll; Zn
Weintraub, Michael N., 419-530-2585 michael.weintraub@utoledo.edu, Univ of Toledo; Zn
Weirich, Frank H., (319) 335-0156 frank-weirich@uiowa.edu, Univ of Iowa; Gm
Weis, Dominique A., (604) 822-1697 dweis@eos.ubc.ca, Univ of British Columbia; CaGeCu
Weisberg, Michael, 718-997-3366 michael.weisberg@kbcc.cuny.edu, Graduate Sch of the City Univ of New York; Zy
Weisberg, Robert H., (727) 553-1568 rweisberg@marine.usf.edu, Univ of South Florida; Op
Weisener, Christopher, 5192533000 x3753 weisener@uwindsor.ca, Univ of Windsor; CoGePg
Weislogel, Amy L., 304-293-5603 amy.weislogel@mail.wvu.edu, West

Virginia Univ; Gs
Weisman, Robert A., 320-308-3247 raweisman@stcloudstate.edu, Saint Cloud State Univ; Am
Weiss, Alfred W., 630.466.2720 aweiss@waubonsee.edu, Waubonsee Comm Coll; Ziy
Weiss, Anna M., (940) 397-4448 anna.weiss@msutexas.edu, Midwestern State Univ; PcgGs
Weiss, Chester J., 540-231-6521 cjweiss@unm.edu, Univ of New Mexico; Ye
Weiss, Christopher C., 806-834-4712 chris.weiss@ttu.edu, Texas Tech Univ; AssAs
Weiss, Dominik, +44 20 759 46383 d.weiss@imperial.ac.uk, Imperial Coll; ClaCq
Weiss, Ray F., (858) 534-2598 rfweiss@ucsd.edu, Univ of California, San Diego; Cm
Weiss, Robert, 540-231-2334 weiszr@vt.edu, Virginia Polytechnic Inst & State Univ; RnOn
Weissmann, Gary S., 505-277-4204 weissman@unm.edu, Univ of New Mexico; HwGsr
Welby, Charles W., (919) 515-7158 cwwelby@unity.ncsu.edu, North Carolina State Univ; Hw
Welch, Steve M., (785) 532-7236 welchsm@ksu.edu, Kansas State Univ; Sp
Welch, Susan, 575-835-5112 susie.welch@nmt.edu, New Mexico Inst of Mining and Tech; Ze
Weldeab, Syee, 805-893-4903 weldeab@geol.ucsb.edu, Univ of California, Santa Barbara; PeCm
Weldon, Ray J., (541) 346-4584 ray@uoregon.edu, Univ of Oregon; Gc
Welling, Tim, 845-431-8536 welling@sunydutchess.edu, Dutchess Comm Coll; GeSo
Wellner, Julia, 713-743-2887 jwellner@uh.edu, Univ of Houston; GslOu
Wells, David E., (228) 688-3389 dew@unb.ca, Univ of Southern Mississippi; YdZi
Wells, Michael L., (702) 895-0828 michael.wells@unlv.edu, Univ of Nevada, Las Vegas; Gc
Wells, Neil A., (330) 672-2951 nwells@kent.edu, Kent State Univ; Gs
Wells, Randy, (941) 388-4441 Univ of South Florida; Ob
Wells, Steve G., (775) 673-7470 sgwells@dri.edu, Univ of Nevada, Reno; Zn
Welp, Lisa, (765) 496-6896 lwelp@purdue.edu, Purdue Univ; Cs
Welsh, James L., 507-933-7333 welsh@gac.edu, Gustavus Adolphus Coll; Gxc
Wen, Lianxing, (631) 632-1726 lianxing.wen@sunysb.edu, Stony Brook Univ; Ys
Wen, Tao, 315-443-2672 twen08@syr.edu, Syracuse Univ; Ge
Wen, Xianyun, +44(0) 113 34 31425 x.wen@leeds.ac.uk, Univ of Leeds; NoAsm
Wen, Yuming, 16717352685 ywen@uguam.uog.edu, Univ of Guam; Zir
Wendlandt, Richard F., (303) 273-3809 rwendlan@mines.edu, Colorado Sch of Mines; GizCp
Weng, Kevin, 808-956-4109 kevin.weng@hawaii.edu, Univ of Hawai'i, Manoa; Ob
Weng, Qihao, 812-237-2255 qweng@indstate.edu, Indiana State Univ; Zru
Wenk, Hans-Rudolf, (510) 642-7431 wenk@berkeley.edu, Univ of California, Berkeley; Gz
Wennberg, Paul O., (626) 395-2447 wennberg@gps.caltech.edu, California Inst of Tech; As
Wenner, David B., (706) 542-2393 dwenner@uga.edu, Univ of Georgia; Cs
Wenner, Jennifer M., (920) 424-7003 wenner@uwosh.edu, Univ of Wisconsin, Oshkosh; Gi
Wentzcovitch, Renata, rmw2150@columbia.edu, Columbia Univ; Ys
Wenzel, Christopher, (307) 532-8293 chris.wenzel@ewc.wy.edu, Eastern Wyoming Coll; SbfHg
Werdon, Melanie B., (907) 451-5082 melanie.werdon@alaska.gov, Alaska Division of Geological & Geophysical Surveys; Eg
Werhner, Matthew J., (813) 253-7263 mwerhner@hccfl.edu, Hillsborough Comm Coll; Gg
Werne, Josef, (412) 624-8775 jwerne@pitt.edu, Univ of Pittsburgh; CosGn
Werner, Adrian , adrian.werner@flinders.edu.au, Flinders Univ; Hw
Werner, Alan, (413) 538-2134 awerner@mtholyoke.edu, Mount Holyoke Coll; GleGm
Werner, Bradley T., (858) 534-0583 bwerner@ucsd.edu, Univ of California, San Diego; Gm
Wernicke, Brian P., (626) 395-6192 brian@gps.caltech.edu, California Inst of Tech; Gtc
Werth, Susanna, swerth@vt.edu, Virginia Polytechnic Inst & State Univ; ZrHgYv
Werts, Scott P., 803-323-4930 wertss@winthrop.edu, Winthrop Univ; ScbPg
Wesely, Marvin L., (630) 252-5827 mlwesely@anl.gov, Argonne; As
Wesley Wood, Charley, 850-9837126 woodwes@ufl.edu, Univ of Florida; So
Wesnousky, Steve, (775) 784-6067 stevew@seismo.unr.edu, Univ of Nevada, Reno; Ys
Wesnousky, Steven, (775) 784-6067 stevew@seismo.unr.edu, Univ of Nevada, Reno; Ys
Wessel, Paul, (808) 956-4778 pwessel@hawaii.edu, Univ of Hawai'i, Manoa; Yr
West, A. Joshua (Josh), (213) 740-6736 joshwest@usc.edu, Univ of Southern California; ClGmHs
West, Alan, 276-328-0203 maw4v@uvawise.edu, Univ of Virginia's Coll at Wise; Zn
West, David P., (802) 443-3476 dwest@middlebury.edu, Middlebury Coll; Gc
West, Jared, +44(0) 113 34 35253 l.j.west@leeds.ac.uk, Univ of Leeds; Hg
West, Keith, (715) 735-4352 keith.west@uwc.edu, Univ of Wisconsin Colls; ZynZn
West, Larry T., (706) 542-0906 Univ of Georgia; Sd
West, Nicole, 989-774-4475 west2n@cmich.edu, Central Michigan Univ; Gm
West, Olivia M., (615) 576-0505 qm5@ornl.gov, Oak Ridge; Ng
West, Robert, 323-260-8115 westrb@elac.edu, East Los Angeles Coll; GgmSd
West, Ronald R., (785) 532-2248 rrwest@ksu.edu, Kansas State Univ; PgeGs
West, Terry R., (765) 494-3296 trwest@purdue.edu, Purdue Univ; Ng
Westerink, Joannes J., (574) 631-6475 Univ of Notre Dame; On
Westerman, David S., (802) 485-2337 westy@norwich.edu, Norwich Univ; Gxi
Westervelt, Daniel, danielmw@ldeo.columbia.edu, Columbia Univ; Og
Westgate, James W., (409) 880-8237 james.westgate@lamar.edu, Lamar Univ; Pev
Westgate, John A., (416) 287-7235 Univ of Toronto; Gl
Westrop, Stephen R., (405) 325-0542 swestrop@ou.edu, Univ of Oklahoma; Pi
Wetherelt, Andrew, +44 01326 371827 a.wetherelt@exeter.ac.uk, Exeter Univ; Nm
Wetmore, Paul, wetmore@usf.edu, Univ of South Florida; Gc
Wettlaufer, John S., (203) 432-0892 john.wettlaufer@yale.edu, Yale Univ; Yg
Wettstein, Justin, (541) 737-5177 justinw@coas.oregonstate.edu, Oregon State Univ; As
Wetz, Michael, 361-825-2132 michael.wetz@tamucc.edu, Texas A&M Univ, Corpus Christi; Ob
Wetzel, Dan L., (907) 488-3746 Univ of Alaska, Fairbanks; Zn
Wetzel, Laura R., (727) 864-8484 wetzellr@eckerd.edu, Eckerd Coll; YrOuGg
Wexler, Anthony S., 530-754-6558 aswexler@ucdavis.edu, Univ of California, Davis; ZcAsZn
Whalen, Michael T., 907-474-5302 ffmtw@uaf.edu, Univ of Alaska, Fairbanks; Gs
Whaler, Kathryn A., +44 (0) 131 650 4904 kathy.whaler@ed.ac.uk, Edinburgh Univ; YmRn
Whalley, John, +44 023 9284 2257 john.whalley@port.ac.uk, Univ of Portsmouth; Gc
Whattam, Scot , +9661368602993 scott.whattam@kfupm.edu.sa, King Fahd Univ of Petroleum and Minerals; GxXc
Whattam, Scott A., 82-2-3290-3182 whattam@korea.ac.kr, Korea Univ; GiCtg
Wheatcraft, Steve, (775) 784-1973 steve@wheatcraftandassociates.com, Univ of Nevada, Reno; Hw
Wheatcroft, Rob, 541-737-3891 raw@coas.oregonstate.edu, Oregon State Univ; OgGg
Wheaton, John R., (406) 272-1603 jwheaton@mtech.edu, Montana Tech of The Univ of Montana; HwEc
Wheeler, Andy J., +353 21 4903951 a.wheeler@ucc.ie, Univ Coll Cork; GusGg
Wheeler, Greg, 916-278-3919 wheelergr@csus.edu, Sacramento State Univ; Em
Wheeler, John, +440151 794 5172 johnwh@liverpool.ac.uk, Univ of Liverpool; GpcGz
Wheeler, Paul, +44 01326 255778 p.wheeler@exeter.ac.uk, Exeter Univ; Nx
Wheeler, Richard F., (931) 221-1004 wheelerr@apsu.edu, Austin Peay State Univ; Ggo
Whelan, Jean K., (508) 289-2819 jwhelan@whoi.edu, Woods Hole Oceanographic Inst; Co
Whelan, Peter M., (320) 589-6315 whelan@mrs.umn.edu, Univ of Minnesota, Morris; Gx
Whiley, Harriet, harriet.whiley@flinders.edu.au, Flinders Univ; Zn
Whipkey, Charles, (540) 654-1428 cwhipkey@umw.edu, Univ of Mary Washington; Cg
Whipple, Kelin, 480-965-9508 kxw@asu.edu, Arizona State Univ; Gmt
Whisner, Jennifer B., (570) 389-4139 jwhisner@bloomu.edu, Bloomsburg Univ; GmHw
Whisner, S. Christopher, (570) 389-4746 swhisner@bloomu.edu, Bloomsburg Univ; GciGz
Whisonant, Robert C., (540) 831-5224 rwhisona@radford.edu, Radford Univ; GsaGg
Whitaker, Rodney W., (505) 667-7672 rww@lanl.gov, Los Alamos; As
White, Bekki C., 501 296-1877 bekki.white@arkansas.gov, Arkansas

Geological Survey; GoEoGg
White, Craig M., (208) 426-3633 cwhite@boisestate.edu, Boise State Univ; Giv
White, George W., (301) 687-4264 gwhite@frostburg.edu, Frostburg State Univ; Zn
White, James D., +64 3 479-9009 james.white@otago.ac.nz, Univ of Otago; Gvs
White, James W. C., 303-492-5494 jwhite@colorado.edu, Univ of Colorado; CsAt
White, Jeffrey G., (919) 515-2389 jeffrey_white@ncsu.edu, North Carolina State Univ; SoZri
White, John C., (859) 622-1276 john.white@eku.edu, Eastern Kentucky Univ; GiCgt
White, Jonathan, (303) 384-2650 jwhite@mines.edu, Colorado Geological Survey; NgZuGg
White, Joseph C., (506) 453-4804 clancy@unb.ca, Univ of New Brunswick; Gc
White, Justin, 801-863-6864 justin.white@uvu.edu, Utah Valley Univ; ZyiZu
White, Lisa D., 510-664-4966 ldwhite@berkeley.edu, Univ of California, Berkeley; ZePim
White, Mark D., (509) 372-6070 mark.white@pnl.gov, Pacific Northwest; Hy
White, Martin, +353 (0)91 493 214 martin.white@nuigalway.ie, Nat Univ of Ireland Galway; Op
White, Nicky, +44 (0) 1223 337063 njw10@cam.ac.uk, Univ of Cambridge; YgGt
White, Paul , (775) 682-6193 paulwhite@unr.edu, Univ of Nevada, Reno; Zn
White, Paul, pdwhite1@ccri.edu, Comm Coll of Rhode Island; Gg
White, Robert, +44 (0) 1223 337187 rsw1@cam.ac.uk, Univ of Cambridge; YgGt
White, Scott, (970) 247-7475 white_s@fortlewis.edu, Fort Lewis Coll; ZirZy
White, Susan, just19@earthlink.net, Los Angeles Harbor Coll; Zg
White, William B., (814) 667-2709 wbw2@psu.edu, Pennsylvania State Univ, Univ Park; CgGzy
Whiteaker, Timothy L., 512-471-0570 twhit@mail.utexas.edu, Univ of Texas, Austin; Zi
Whitehead, James, (506) 453-4593 Univ of New Brunswick; Gg
Whitehead, Peter W., +61 742321200 peter.whitehead@jcu.edu.au, James Cook Univ; Ggv
Whitehead, Robert E., rwhitehead@laurentian.ca, Laurentian Univ, Sudbury; Ce
Whitehill, Matthew, 218-733-5981 m.whitehill@lsc.edu, Lake Superior Coll; Gg
Whiteley, Martin, +44 01332 593752 m.whiteley@derby.ac.uk, Univ of Derby; Go
Whiteside, Jessica H., +44 (0)23 80593199 j.whiteside@soton.ac.uk, Univ of Southampton; Pe
Whiteway, James, (416)736-2100 #22310 whiteway@yorku.ca, York Univ; As
Whiticar, Michael J., (250) 721-6514 whiticar@uvic.ca, Univ of Victoria; CosGo
Whiting, Peter J., (216) 368-3989 peter.whiting@case.edu, Case Western Reserve Univ; Gm
Whitlock, Cathy, (406) 994-6910 whitlock@montana.edu, Montana State Univ; Peg
Whitman, Brian E., (570) 408-4882 brian.whitman@wilkes.edu, Wilkes Univ; HqwSb
Whitman, Dean, (305) 348-3089 whitmand@fiu.edu, Florida International Univ; YgGet
Whitman, Jill M., (253) 535-8720 whitmaj@plu.edu, Pacific Lutheran Univ; OuGuZe
Whitmeyer, Steven J., whitmesj@jmu.edu, James Madison Univ; GctZi
Whitmore, John H., (937) 766-7947 johnwhitmore@cedarville.edu, Cedarville Univ; PgGsg
Whitney, D.A., (785) 532-6101 whitney@ksu.edu, Kansas State Univ; So
Whitney, Donna L., (612) 626-7582 dwhitney@umn.edu, Univ of Minnesota, Twin Cities; Gpt
Whitney, Earl M., (505) 667-3595 whitney@lanl.gov, Los Alamos; Zn
Whitney, James A., (706) 548-6894 jamesawhitney@hotmail.com, Univ of Georgia; GivCg
Whitney, Michael, 860-405-9157 michael.whitney@uconn.edu, Univ of Connecticut; Op
Whitney , Sandra , swhitney@uga.edu, Univ of Georgia; Ga
Whittaker, Alex, +44 20 759 47491 a.whittaker@imperial.ac.uk, Imperial Coll; Gt
Whittaker, Amber, 207-287-2803 amber.whittaker@maine.gov, Dept of Agriculture, Conservation, and Forestry; GcZiCg
Whittecar, Jr., G. Richard, (757) 683-5197 rwhittec@odu.edu, Old Dominion Univ; GmHwZe
Whittemore, Donald O., 785-864-3965 donwhitt@kgs.ku.edu, Univ of Kansas; Cl
Whittier, Michael, mwhittier@csustan.edu, California State Univ, Stanislaus; Ggz
Whittington, Alan, (573) 884-7625 whittingtona@missouri.edu, Univ of Missouri; GivCp
Whittington, Carla, (206) 878-3710 cwhittin@highline.edu, Highline Coll; GgvZg
Whitton, Mark, +44 023 9284 2257 mark.witton@port.ac.uk, Univ of Portsmouth; Pg
Wiberg, Patricia L., (434) 924-7546 pw3c@virginia.edu, Univ of Virginia; Og
Wickert, Andrew D., (612) 625-6878 awickert@umn.edu, Univ of Minnesota, Twin Cities; Gml
Wickham, John S., (817) 272-2987 wickham@uta.edu, Univ of Texas, Arlington; Gco
Wickham, Thomas, (724) 938-4180 wickham@calu.edu, California Univ of Pennsylvania; Zu
Wicks, Carol M., (225) 578-2692 cwicks@lsu.edu, Louisiana State Univ; HwClHy
Wicks, Frederick J., (416) 978-5395 fredw@rom.on.ca, Univ of Toronto; Gz
Widanagamage, Inoka, 662-915-2154 ihwidana@olemiss.edu, Univ of Mississippi; ClGep
Widdowson, Mark A., (540) 231-7153 mwiddows@vt.edu, Virginia Polytechnic Inst & State Univ; HwSpHq
Widom, Elisabeth, (513) 529-5048 widome@miamioh.edu, Miami Univ; CcGve
Widory, David, 514-987-3000 #1968 widory.david@uqam.ca, Universite du Quebec a Montreal; Cs
Wiedenmann, Jorg, +44 (0)23 80596497 joerg.wiedenmann@noc.soton.ac.uk, Univ of Southampton; Ob
Wiederspahn, Mark, (512) 471-0406 markw@ig.utexas.edu, Univ of Texas, Austin; Zn
Wiederwohl, Chrissy, 979-845-7191 chrissyw@tamu.edu, Texas A&M Univ; Op
Wielicki, Matthew, (205) 348-0548 mmwielicki@ua.edu, Univ of Alabama; CcgGt
Wielicki, Michelle, mdwielicki@ua.edu, Univ of Alabama; CcXgGi
Wiens, Douglas A., (314) 935-6517 doug@wustl.edu, Washington Univ in St. Louis; YsrYg
Wierenga, Peter J., (520) 792-9591 wierenga@ag.arizona.edu, Univ of Arizona; Sp
Wiese, Katryn, (415) 452-5061 katryn.wiese@mail.ccsf.edu, City Coll of San Francisco; GiOg
Wiesenburg, Denis A., (601) 266-4937 denis.wiesenburg@usm.edu, Univ of Southern Mississippi; Og
Wiggert, Jerry, (228) 688-3491 jerry.wiggert@usm.edu, Univ of Southern Mississippi; Op
Wigley, Rochelle, 603-862-1135 rochelle@ccom.unh.edu, Univ of New Hampshire; CgGu
Wignall, Paul, +44(0) 113 34 35247 p.b.wignall@leeds.ac.uk, Univ of Leeds; PgGs
Wijbrans, Jan, j.r.wijbrans@vu.nl, Vrije Universiteit Amsterdam; CcGtv
Wijesinghe, Ananda M., (925) 423-0605 Lawrence Livermore; Nr
Wilbur, Bryan, 626 585-3118 bcwilbur@pasadena.edu, Pasadena City Coll; Gg
Wilch, Thomas I., (517) 629-0759 twilch@albion.edu, Albion Coll; GlvGm
Wilcock, Peter W., (410) 516-5421 Johns Hopkins Univ; Gm
Wilcock, William S., (206) 543-6043 wilcock@u.washington.edu, Univ of Washington; Ou
Wilcox, Andrew, 406-243-4761 andrew.wilcox@mso.umt.edu, Univ of Montana; Gm
Wilcox, Jeffrey D., (828) 232-5184 jwilcox@unca.edu, Univ of North Carolina, Asheville; HwClGg
Wildeman, Thomas R., twildema@mines.edu, Colorado Sch of Mines; Ct
Wilder, Margaret, mwilder@email.arizona.edu, Univ of Arizona; Zn
Wilderman, Candie, (717) 245-1573 wilderma@dickinson.edu, Dickinson Coll; Hs
Wiles, Gregory C., (330) 263-2298 gwiles@wooster.edu, Coll of Wooster; Gl
Wilf, Peter D., (814) 865-6721 pwilf@geosc.psu.edu, Pennsylvania State Univ, Univ Park; Pg
Wilhelm, Steven W., wilhelm@utk.edu, Univ of Tennessee, Knoxville; Po
Wilhelmson, Robert B., (217) 333-8651 bw@ncsa.uiuc.edu, Univ of Illinois, Urbana-Champaign; As
Wilhelmy, Jerry B., (505) 665-3188 Los Alamos; Zn
Wilkerson, M. S., (765) 658-4666 mswilke@depauw.edu, Univ of Illinois, Urbana-Champaign; Gc
Wilkerson, M. Scott, (765) 658-4666 mswilke@depauw.edu, DePauw Univ; GctZi
Wilkey, Patrick L., (630) 252-6258 Argonne; Ng
Wilkie, Ann C., (352) 392-8699 acwilkie@ifas.ufl.edu, Univ of Florida; Sb
Wilkie, Richard W., (413) 253-5752 rwilkie@geo.umass.edu, Univ of Massachusetts, Amherst; ZynZn

Wilkins, Colin, +44 1752 584773 c.wilkins@plymouth.ac.uk, Univ of Plymouth; Eg
Wilkins, David E., (208) 426-2390 dwilkins@boisestate.edu, Boise State Univ; ZyGm
Wilkinson, Bruce, 315-443-3869 eustasy@syr.edu, Syracuse Univ; Gs
Wilks, Daniel, (607) 255-1750 dsw5@cornell.edu, Cornell Univ; As
Wilks, Maureen, 575-835-5322 maureen.wilks@nmt.edu, New Mexico Inst of Mining and Tech; Gp
Willahan, Duane, (408) 848-4702 Gavilan Coll; Gg
Wille, Frank, 909-869-3648 frwille@cpp.edu, California State Polytechnic Univ, Pomona; Zn
William, Nancy, (785) 532-7257 nkw@ksu.edu, Kansas State Univ; Zn
Williams, Aaron, (251) 460-6915 bwilliams@southalabama.edu, Univ of South Alabama; Am
Williams, Allison M., (905) 525-9140 (Ext. 24334) awill@mcmaster.ca, McMaster Univ; Zn
Williams, Alton P., williams@ldeo.columbia.edu, Columbia Univ; Pc
Williams, Amy, 352-273-1287 amywilliams1@ufl.edu, Univ of Florida; Co
Williams, Bruce A., (509) 372-3799 bruce.williams@pnl.gov, Pacific Northwest; Ng
Williams, Christopher J., (717) 291-3814 chris.williams@fandm.edu, Franklin and Marshall Coll; PeSb
Williams, Curtis J., (714) 484-7000 (Ext. 48181) Cypress Coll; Gg
Williams, Dave E., williams.david@interchange.ubc.ca, Univ of British Columbia; Oc
Williams, David, (480) 965-7045 david.williams@asu.edu, Arizona State Univ; Xg
Williams, Erik, (775) 784-1396 eswilliams@unr.edu, Univ of Nevada, Reno; Ys
Williams, Forrest, 831-656-3274 fwillia@comcast.net, Naval Postgraduate Sch; Am
Williams, Harry F. L., (940) 565-3317 harryf.williams@unt.edu, Univ of North Texas; Gm
Williams, Ian S., (709) 737-8395 ian.williams@uwrf.edu, Univ of Wisconsin, River Falls; Yg
Williams, Jeremy C., (330) 672-1459 jwill243@kent.edu, Kent State Univ; Cg
Williams, John W., (408) 924-5050 john.williams@sjsu.edu, San Jose State Univ; Ng
Williams, Kevin K., 716-878-5116 williakk@buffalostate.edu, Buffalo State Coll; GmXg
Williams, Kim R., (303) 273-3245 krwillia@mines.edu, Colorado Sch of Mines; Ca
Williams, Lynda, (480) 965-0829 lynda.williams@asu.edu, Arizona State Univ; Gb
Williams, Mark, +44 0116 252 3642 mri@le.ac.uk, Leicester Univ; Pg
Williams, Mathew, +44 (0) 131 650 7776 mat.williams@ed.ac.uk, Edinburgh Univ; ZcrZu
Williams, Michael L., (413) 545-0745 mlw@geo.umass.edu, Univ of Massachusetts, Amherst; Gc
Williams, Paul, +44 0161 306-3905 paul.i.williams@manchester.ac.uk, Univ of Manchester; As
Williams, Quentin, (831) 459-3132 qwilliams@pmc.ucsc.edu, Univ of California, Santa Cruz; Gy
Williams, Ric, +44-151-794-5136 ric@liverpool.ac.uk, Univ of Liverpool; Og
Williams, Roger T., rtwillia@nps.edu, Naval Postgraduate Sch; Am
Williams, Rosa, 706-649-1474 williams_rosa@columbusstate.edu, Columbus State Univ; Xa
Williams, Stanley N., (480) 965-1438 stanley.williams@asu.edu, Arizona State Univ; Gv
Williams, Thomas, (208) 885-6656 tomw@uidaho.edu, Univ of Idaho; Gf
Williams, Wyn, +44 (0) 131 650 4909 wyn.williams@ed.ac.uk, Edinburgh Univ; Ym
Williams-Bruinders, Leizel, +27 (0)41 504 4361 leizel.williams@nmmu.ac.za, Nelson Mandela Metropolitan Univ; Zn
Williams-Jones, Anthony E., 514-398-1676 anthony.williams-jones@mcgill.ca, McGill Univ; Ce
Williams-Jones, Glyn, (778) 782-3306 glynwj@sfu.ca, Simon Fraser Univ; GvCeYe
Williamson, Ben, +44 01326 371856 b.j.williamson@exeter.ac.uk, Exeter Univ; EmGv
Williamson, Douglas, 212-772-5265 douglas.williamson@hunter.cuny.edu, Hunter Coll (CUNY); Zi
Willis, Grant C., (801) 537-3355 grantwillis@utah.gov, Utah Geological Survey; Gg
Willis, Julie B., 208-496-7681 willisj@byui.edu, Brigham Young Univ - Idaho; GtcZi
Willis, Marc, 714-992-7446 mwillis@fullcoll.edu, Fullerton Coll; Gg
Willoughby, Hugh E., 305-348-0243 hugh.willoughby@fiu.edu, Florida International Univ; As
Wills, William V., 813-253-7809 wwills@hccfl.edu, Hillsborough Comm Coll; Zg
Willsey, Shawn P., (208) 732-6421 swillsey@csi.edu, Coll of Southern Idaho; GgcGv
Willson, Lee, 713.348.6219 Rice Univ; Zn
Wilmut, Michael, (250) 472-4343 Univ of Victoria; Zn
Wilson, Alicia M., (803) 777-1240 awilson@geol.sc.edu, Univ of South Carolina; Hw
Wilson, Blake B., (785) 864-2118 bwilson@kgs.ku.edu, Univ of Kansas; Zi
Wilson, Carol A., carolw@lsu.edu, Louisiana State Univ; GsOnCc
Wilson, Charlie, +44 (0)1603 59 1386 charlie.wilson@uea.ac.uk, Univ of East Anglia; Ge
Wilson, Clark R., (512) 471-5008 crwilson@jsg.utexas.edu, Univ of Texas, Austin; Yg
Wilson, Emily, 717-358-3821 emily.wilson@fandm.edu, Franklin and Marshall Coll; CgGi
Wilson, Fred L., (325) 486-6984 fwilson@angelo.edu, Angelo State Univ; Gm
Wilson, Greg, 541-737-4015 wilsongr@coas.oregonstate.edu, Oregon State Univ; Onp
Wilson, Gregory, 206-543-8917 gpwilson@uw.edu, Univ of Washington; Pvg
Wilson, James R., jwilson@weber.edu, Weber State Univ; Gz
Wilson, Jeffey S., (317) 274-1128 jeswilso@iupui.edu, Indiana Univ, Indianapolis; Zy
Wilson, Jeffrey A., (734) 647-7461 wilsonja@umich.edu, Univ of Michigan; Gg
Wilson, John D., (780) 492-0353 Univ of Alberta; Am
Wilson, Laura E., (785) 639-6192 lewilson6@fhsu.edu, Fort Hays State Univ; PvePg
Wilson, Lorne G., (520) 621-9108 lorne@email.arizona.edu, Univ of Arizona; Hw
Wilson, Lucy A., (506) 648-5607 lwilson@unbsj.ca, Univ of New Brunswick Saint John; Ga
Wilson, Mark A., (330) 263-2247 mwilson@wooster.edu, Coll of Wooster; Pi
Wilson, Melissa L., 612-625-4276 mlw@umn.edu, Univ of Minnesota, Twin Cities; Sco
Wilson, Merwether, +44 (0) 131 650 8636 meriwether.wilson@ed.ac.uk, Edinburgh Univ; Ob
Wilson, Michael C., wilsonmi@douglascollege.ca, Douglas Coll; GaPgGs
Wilson, P. Christopher, 772-468-3922 ext 119 pcwilson@ufl.edu, Univ of Florida; So
Wilson, Paul A., +44 (0)23 80596164 paul.wilson@noc.soton.ac.uk, Univ of Southampton; GsCg
Wilson, Rick I., (709) 737-8386 California Geological Survey; Ge
Wilson, Robert, +44 01334 463914 rjsw@st-andrews.ac.uk, Univ of St. Andrews; Zn
Wilson, Roy R., (860) 465-4370 wilsonr@easternct.edu, Eastern Connecticut State Univ; Zi
Wilson, Sarah B., (540) 458-8800 wilsons@wlu.edu, Washington & Lee Univ; Zn
Wilson, Steven D., (217) 333-0956 sdwilson@illinois.edu, Univ of Illinois; Hw
Wilson, Terry J., 614-292-0723 wilson.43@osu.edu, Ohio State Univ; GctGl
Wilson, Thomas, +64 3 3667001 Ext 45511 thomas.wilson@canterbury.ac.nz, Univ of Canterbury; Gv
Wilton, Robert D., (905) 525-9140 (Ext. 24536) wiltonr@mcmaster.ca, McMaster Univ; Zn
Wiltshire, John C., (808) 956-6042 johnw@soest.hawaii.edu, Univ of Hawai'i, Manoa; Og
Wimbush, Mark, (401) 874-6515 m.wimbush@gso.uri.edu, Univ of Rhode Island; Op
Winant, Clinton D., (858) 534-2067 cwinant@ucsd.edu, Univ of California, San Diego; On
Winberry, Paul, winberry@geology.cwu.edu, Central Washington Univ; Yg
Winchell, Robert E., (562) 985-4920 California State Univ, Long Beach; Gz
Winckler, Gisela, winckler@ldeo.columbia.edu, Columbia Univ; Cg
Windhorst, Rogier, (480) 965-7143 windhorst@asu.edu, Arizona State Univ; Xa
Windom, Kenneth E., kewindom@iastate.edu, Iowa State Univ of Sci & Tech; Cp
Windsor, Jr., John G., 321-674-8096 jwindsor@fit.edu, Florida Inst of Tech; Oc
Wine, Paul H., (404) 894-3425 pw7@prism.gatech.edu, Georgia Inst of Tech; As
Winebrenner, Dale P., 206-543-1393 dpw@apl.washington.edu, Univ of Washington; GlZr
Wing, Scott L., (202) 357-2649 Smithsonian Inst / Nat Mus of Natural History; Pb
Winglee, Robert M., 206-685-8160 winglee@uw.edu, Univ of Washington; XyYx
Winguth, Arne M., 817 272 2987 awinguth@uta.edu, Univ of Texas, Arlington; OpAs

Winguth, Cornelia, 817 272 2987 cwinguth@uta.edu, Univ of Texas, Arlington; GugZm
Winkelstern, Ian Z., 616-331-9219 winkelsi@gvsu.edu, Grand Valley State Univ; GsOo
Winkler, Dale A., (214) 768-2750 dwinkler@smu.edu, Southern Methodist Univ; Pv
Winklhofer, Michael, 089/2180 4143 michael@geophysik.uni-muenchen.de, Ludwig-Maximilians-Univ Muenchen; Yg
Winnick, Matthew, 413-545-1715 mwinnick@geo.umass.edu, Univ of Massachusetts, Amherst; Cbq
Winsor, Kelsey, kelsey.winsor@nau.edu, Northern Arizona Univ; PcGm
Winston, Barbara, (314) 935-7047 Washington Univ in St. Louis; Zn
Winterbottom, Wesley, winterbottomw@easternct.edu, Eastern Connecticut State Univ; Zg
Winterkamp, Judith L., (505) 667-1264 judyw@lanl.gov, Los Alamos; Zn
Winton, Alison, (806) 834-0497 alison.winton@ttu.edu, Texas Tech Univ; ZnnZn
Wintsch, Robert P., (812) 855-4018 wintsch@indiana.edu, Indiana Univ, Bloomington; GpcGt
Wirth, Erin, ewirth@uw.edu, Univ of Washington; YsRn
Wirth, Karl R., (651) 696-6449 wirth@macalester.edu, Macalester Coll; GiZeGg
Wisdom, Jack, (617) 253-7730 wisdom@mit.edu, Massachusetts Inst of Tech; Zn
Wise, Dana, (618) 453-4362 dwise@siu.edu, Southern Illinois Univ Carbondale; Zn
Wise, Michael A., (202) 633-1826 wisem@si.edu, Smithsonian Inst / Nat Mus of Natural History; Gz
Wise, Jr, Sherwood W., (850) 644-6265 swise@fsu.edu, Florida State Univ; PmGu
Wisely, Beth , 307-268 2233 bwisely@caspercollege.edu, Casper Coll; YgHwGc
Wishart, De Bonne N., dwishart@centralstate.edu, Central State Univ; YgCa
Wishner, Karen, (401) 874-6402 kwishner@gso.uri.edu, Univ of Rhode Island; Ob
Withers, Kim, 361-825-5907 kim.withers@tamucc.edu, Texas A&M Univ, Corpus Christi; Zn
Withers, Mitchell M., (901) 678-2007 mwithers@memphis.edu, Univ of Memphis; Ys
Withers, Tony, 519-661-2111 x.88627 tony.withers@uwo.ca, Western Univ; Cp
Withjack, Martha O., (848) 445-3142 drmeow3@eps.rutgers.edu, Rutgers, The State Univ of New Jersey; GctEo
Witt, Emma, emma.witt@stockton.edu, Stockton Univ; Hgs
Witter, Rob, 541-574-7969 rwitter@usgs.gov, Oregon Dept of Geology & Mineral Industries; Zg
Witter-Shelleman, Molly, 330-972-8046 mwittershelleman@uakron.edu, Univ of Akron; Gz
Wittke, James, 9285239565/9044 james.wittke@nau.edu, Northern Arizona Univ; Gi
Wittke, Seth, (307) 766-2286 Ext. 244 seth.wittke@wyo.gov, Wyoming State Geological Survey; Rn
Wittkop, Chad, (507) 389-6929 chad.wittkop@mnsu.edu, Minnesota State Univ; GsCgGl
Witzke, Brian J., (319) 335-1590 brian-witzke@uiowa.edu, Univ of Iowa; GrPsg
Wixman, Ronald, (541) 346-4568 rwixman@uoregon.edu, Univ of Oregon; Zn
Wizevich, Michael, wizevichmic@ccsu.edu, Central Connecticut State Univ; GsdGm
Wobus, Reinhard A., (413) 597-2470 reinhard.a.wobus@williams.edu, Williams Coll; GivGz
Woerheide, Gert, geobiologie@geo.lmu.de, Ludwig-Maximilians-Univ Muenchen; Pgi
Wofsy, Steven C., (617) 495-4566 scw@io.harvard.edu, Harvard Univ; As
Wogelius, Roy, (+44)-(0)161-275 3841 roy.wogelius@manchester.ac.uk, Univ of Manchester; Cg
Wohl, Ellen E., (970) 491-5298 ellen.wohl@colostate.edu, Colorado State Univ; GmHs
Wohletz, Kenneth H., (505) 667-9202 wohletz@lanl.gov, Los Alamos; YxGvRm
Woida, Kathleen, kathleen-woida@uiowa.edu, Univ of Iowa; So
Wojewoda, Jurand, jurand.wojewoda@uwr.edu.pl, Univ of Wroclaw; Gs
Wojtal, Steven F., (440) 775-8352 steven.wojtal@oberlin.edu, Oberlin Coll; Gc
Wolak, Jeannette, (931) 372-3695 jwolak@tntech.edu, Tennessee Tech Univ; Gsr
Wolaver, Brad, (512) 471-1368 brad.wolaver@beg.utexas.edu, Univ of Texas, Austin; HwGe
Wolcott, Donna L., (919) 515-7866 donna_wolcott@ncsu.edu, North Carolina State Univ; Ob
Wolcott, Ray, 6196447454 x3099 rwolcott@palomar.edu, Cuyamaca Coll; Og
Wolcott, Thomas G., (919) 515-7866 tom_wolcott@ncsu.edu, North Carolina State Univ; Ob
WoldeGabriel, Giday, 505-667-8749 wgiday@lanl.gov, Los Alamos; Gx
Wolf, Aaron T., (541) 737-2722 wolfa@geo.oregonstate.edu, Oregon State Univ; Hg
Wolf, Lorraine W., (334) 844-4878 wolflor@auburn.edu, Auburn Univ; Ysg
Wolf, Michael B., (309) 794-7304 michaelwolf@augustana.edu, Augustana Coll; Gi
Wolfe, Ben, (816) 604-6622 ben.wolfe@mcckc.edu, Metropolitan Comm Coll-Kansas City; GgZyg
Wolfe, Christopher, christopher.wolfe@stonybrook.edu, SUNY, Stony Brook; Op
Wolfe, Karen M., (615) 898-2726 karen.wolfe@mtsu.edu, Middle Tennessee State Univ; Zn
Wolfe, Paul J., 937 775-2201 paul.wolfe@wright.edu, Wright State Univ; Ye
Wolff, Eric W., +44 (0) 1223 333486 ew428@cam.ac.uk, Univ of Cambridge; GlPe
Wolff, George, +44-151-794-4094 wolff@liverpool.ac.uk, Univ of Liverpool; Og
Wolff, John A., (509) 335-2825 jawolff@wsu.edu, Washington State Univ; Giv
Wolfgram, Diane, (406) 496-4353 dwolfgram@mtech.edu, Montana Tech of the Univ of Montana; EgoNm
Wolfsberg, Andrew V., (505) 667-3599 awolf@lanl.gov, Los Alamos; Hw
Wolfsberg, Kurt, (505) 667-4464 Los Alamos; Cc
Wolken, Gabriel J., (907) 451-5018 gabriel.wolken@alaska.gov, Alaska Division of Geological & Geophysical Surveys; Gm
Wollan, Jacinda, mandy.looser@ndsu.edu, North Dakota State Univ; Zn
Wollheim, Wil, wil.wollheim@unh.edu, Univ of New Hampshire; Zu
Wolny, Dave, (970) 248-1154 dwolmy@mesastate.edu, Colorado Mesa Univ; Ys
Woltemade, Christopher J., (717) 477-1143 cjwolt@ship.edu, Shippensburg Univ; HgRwGm
Wolter, Calvin, calvin.wolter@dnr.iowa.gov, Iowa Dept of Natural Resources; GgZi
Wolverton, Steve, 940-565-4987 steven.wolverton@unt.edu, Univ of North Texas; Ga
Wong, Chi S., (250) 363-6407 wongcs@pac.dfo-mpo.gc.ca, Univ of British Columbia; Cm
Wong, Cindy, (716) 878-6731 solargs@buffalostate.edu, Buffalo State Coll; Zn
Wong, Martin, (315) 228-7203 mswong@colgate.edu, Colgate Univ; Gtc
Wong, Teng-fong, (631) 632-8212 teng-fong.wong@stonybrook.edu, Stony Brook Univ; Yx
Woo, David, 510-885-3160 david.woo@csueastbay.edu, California State Univ, East Bay; Zr
Woo, Ming-Ko, (905) 525-9140 woo@mcmaster.ca, McMaster Univ; HgZy
Wood, Aaron R., (515) 294-8862 awood@iastate.edu, Iowa State Univ of Sci & Tech; PvGrs
Wood, Bernard, +44 (1865) 272014 bernie.wood@earth.ox.ac.uk, Univ of Oxford; Gz
Wood, David A., 210-486-0063 dwood30@alamo.edu, San Antonio Comm Coll; XsZnn
Wood, Eric F., (609) 258-4675 efwood@princeton.edu, Princeton Univ; HgZrHq
Wood, Gillen D., gdwood@illinois.edu, Univ of Illinois, Urbana-Champaign; Zc
Wood, Howard, (361) 825-3335 tony.wood@tamucc.edu, Texas A&M Univ, Corpus Christi; ZeHsZn
Wood, Ian, +44 020 7679 32405 ian.wood@ucl.ac.uk, Univ Coll London; Gz
Wood, Jacqueline, (504) 671-6485 jwood@lakelandcc.edu, Delgado Comm Coll; Gg
Wood, James R., (906) 487-2894 jrw@mtu.edu, Michigan Technological Univ; Cl
Wood, Kim, 662-268-1032 kimberly.wood@msstate.edu, Mississippi State Univ; AsmZr
Wood, Lesli, 303-273-3801 lwood@mines.edu, Colorado Sch of Mines; GsoGm
Wood, Neill, +44 01326 255163 n.a.wood@exeter.ac.uk, Exeter Univ; YuZen
Wood, Robert, (206) 543-1203 robwood@atmos.washington.edu, Univ of Washington; As
Wood, Scott A., 701-231-8552 scott.wood@ndsu.edu, North Dakota State Univ; Cq
Wood, Spencer H., (208) 426-3629 swood@boisestate.edu, Boise State Univ; Gmm
Woodall, Debra W., (386) 506-3765 woodald@daytonastate.edu, Daytona State Coll; GgOg
Woodard, Gary C., (520) 621-5399 gwoodard@sahra.arizona.edu, Univ of Arizona; Zn
Woodard, Jeremy, (031) 260-2804 woodardj@ukzn.ac.za, Univ of KwaZulu-Natal; CcGiz

Woodburne, Michael O., (909) 787-5028 michael.woodburne@ucr.edu, Univ of California, Riverside; Pv
Woodcock, Curtis, curtis@bu.edu, Boston Univ; Zr
Woodcock, Nigel H., +44 (0) 1223 333430 nhw1@esc.cam.ac.uk, Univ of Cambridge; GcsGt
Woodgate, Rebecca A., (206) 221-3268 woodgate@apl.washington.edu, Univ of Washington; Op
Woodhouse, Connie, 520-626-0235 conniew1@email.arizona.edu, Univ of Arizona; Pe
Woodhouse, Iain H., +44 (0) 131 650 2527 i.h.woodhouse@ed.ac.uk, Edinburgh Univ; Zi
Woodhouse, John, +44 (1865) 272021 john.woodhouse@earth.ox.ac.uk, Univ of Oxford; Yg
Woodin, Sarah A., (803) 782-9727 swoodin@gmail.com, Univ of South Carolina; Ob
Wooding, Frank B., (508) 289-3334 Woods Hole Oceanographic Inst; Yr
Woodland, Bertram G., (312) 665-7648 Field Mus of Natural History; Gp
Woodley, Teresa, (604) 822-3146 twoodley@eos.ubc.ca, Univ of British Columbia; Zn
Woodruff, Jonathan D., 413-577-3831 woodruff@geo.umass.edu, Univ of Massachusetts, Amherst; Gs
Woodruff, William H., (505) 665-2557 Los Alamos; Zn
Woods, Adam D., (657) 278-2921 awoods@fullerton.edu, California State Univ, Fullerton; GsPe
Woods, Andy, +44 (0) 1223 765702 andy@bpi.cam.ac.uk, Univ of Cambridge; YgGt
Woods, Juliette, juliette.woods@flinders.edu.au, Univ of South Australia; Hwq
Woods, Karen M., (409) 880-2251 karen.woods@lamar.edu, Lamar Univ; Zg
Woods, Neal, woodsn@mailbox.sc.edu, Univ of South Carolina; Zn
Woods, Rachel A., +44 (0) 131 650 6014 rachel.wood@ed.ac.uk, Edinburgh Univ; Gs
Woodward, Lee A., (505) 277-5309 Univ of New Mexico; Gc
Woodward, Mac B., 501 683-0113 mac.woodward@arkansas.gov, Arkansas Geological Survey; Gog
Woodwell, Grant R., (540) 654-1427 gwoodwel@mwc.edu, Univ of Mary Washington; Gc
Wooldridge, C F., wooldridge@cf.ac.uk, Cardiff Univ; Zn
Woolery, Edward W., (859) 257-3016 woolery@uky.edu, Univ of Kentucky; Ys
Wooten, Richard M., 828-296-4632 rick.wooten@ncdenr.gov, N.C. Department of Environmental Quality; RnGc
Worcester, Peter, peter.worcester@eku.ed, Eastern Kentucky Univ; GgOuZe
Worden, Richard, 0151 794 5184 r.worden@liverpool.ac.uk, Univ of Liverpool; Gs
Wordsworth, Robin, rwordsworth@seas.harvard.edu, Harvard Univ; Xg
Worrall, Fred, 0191 3742525 fred.worrall@durham.ac.uk, Durham Univ; Cg
Wortel, Matthew J., (319) 335-3992 matthew-wortel@uiowa.edu, Univ of Iowa; Gx
Worthington, Lindsay L., 505.277.4204 lworthington@unm.edu, Univ of New Mexico; Yg
Wortmann, Ulrich B., 416-978-2084 Univ of Toronto; Gg
Wright, Alan, 561-992-1555 alwr@ufl.edu, Univ of Florida; Sc
Wright, Carrie L., (812) 465-1145 clwright@usieagles.org, Univ of Southern Indiana; Ze
Wright, Chris, 614 265 6632 chris.wright@dnr.state.oh.us, Ohio Dept of Natural Resources; Ec
Wright, James D., (848) 445-5722 jdwright@eps.rutgers.edu, Rutgers, The State Univ of New Jersey; CsOuPm
Wright, James (Jim) E., (706) 542-4394 jwright@gly.uga.edu, Univ of Georgia; Gt
Wright, Kathyrn, (269) 387-5486 kathyrn.wright@wmich.edu, Western Michigan Univ; Zn
Wright, Stephen F., (802) 656-4479 swright@uvm.edu, Univ of Vermont; Glc
Wright, Tim, +44(0) 113 34 35258 t.j.wright@leeds.ac.uk, Univ of Leeds; Yd
Wright, V P., wrightvp@cf.ac.uk, Cardiff Univ; Gs
Wright, William C., 845-939-2063 william.wright@westpoint.edu, United States Military Academy; ZriYd
Wronkiewicz, David, 573-341-4679 wronk@mst.edu, Missouri Univ of Sci and Tech; Cl
Wu, Chin, (608) 263-3078 chinwu@engr.wisc.edu, Univ of Wisconsin, Madison; Onp
Wu, David T., (303) 273-2066 dwu@mines.edu, Colorado Sch of Mines; Zn
Wu, Francis T., (607) 777-2512 Binghamton Univ; Ys
Wu, Jonny, (713) 743-9624 jwu40@central.uh.edu, Univ of Houston; GtcGo
Wu, Shiliang, (906) 487-2590 slwu@mtu.edu, Michigan Technological Univ; AsCg
Wu, Shuang-Ye, (937) 229-1720 shuang-ye.wu@notes.udayton.edu, Univ of Dayton; Zy
Wu, Xiaoqing, (515) 294-9872 wuxq@iastate.edu, Iowa State Univ of Sci & Tech; As
Wu, Xingru, xingru.wu@ou.edu, Univ of Oklahoma; Np
Wu, Yutian, (765) 494-8677 wu640@purdue.edu, Purdue Univ; As
Wuebbles, Donald J., (217) 244-1568 wuebbles@illinois.edu, Univ of Illinois, Urbana-Champaign; As
Wuerthele, Norman, (412) 622-3265 wuerthelen@carnegiemnh.org, Carnegie Mus of Natural History; Pv
Wulff, Andrew, (270) 745-5976 andrew.wulff@wku.edu, Western Kentucky Univ; Gv
Wunsch, Carl, (617) 496-2732 cwunsch@fas.harvard.edu, Harvard Univ; Op
Wunsch, David R., (302) 831-8258 dwunsch@udel.edu, Univ of Delaware; ClHwNg
Wust-Bloch, Gilles H., (03-) 640-5475 Tel Aviv Univ; Ys
Wyckoff, John W., (303) 556-2590 john.wyckoff@ucdenver.edu, Univ of Colorado, Denver; Zy
Wyckoff, William K., (406) 994-6914 bwyckoff@montana.edu, Montana State Univ; Zn
Wygal, Brian, (516) 877-4170 bwygal@adelphi.edu, Adelphi Univ; GaRmGe
Wykel, Andy, 803.896.7703 wykelc@dnr.sc.gov, South Carolina Dept of Natural Resources; Gg
Wylie, Ann G., (301) 405-4079 awylie@umd.edu, Univ of Maryland; Gz
Wyllie, Peter J., (626) 395-6461 wyllie@gps.caltech.edu, California Inst of Tech; Cp
Wyman, Derek A., (618) 938-0117 Univ of Saskatchewan; Cg
Wymore, Adam, adam.wymore@unh.edu, Univ of New Hampshire; Hg
Wyngaard, John C., wyngaard@ems.psu.edu, Pennsylvania State Univ, Univ Park; Am
Wynn, Thomas C., (570) 484-2081 twynn@lockhaven.edu, Lock Haven Univ; GsPiEo
Wypych, Alicja, 907-451-5010 alicja.wypych@alaska.gov, Alaska Division of Geological & Geophysical Surveys; Gg
Wyse Jackson, Patrick N., + 353-1-8961477 wysjcknp@tcd.ie, Trinity Coll; PiRh
Wysession, Michael E., (314) 935-5625 michael@wucore.wustl.edu, Washington Univ in St. Louis; Ys
Wysocki, Mark, (607) 255-2568 mww3@cornell.edu, Cornell Univ; As
Wysong, Jr., James F., (813) 253-7805 jwysong@hccfl.edu, Hillsborough Comm Coll; Am
Wyss, Andre R., (805) 893-8628 wyss@geol.ucsb.edu, Univ of California, Santa Barbara; Pv

X

Xiao, Dana, (570) 389-3902 dxiao@bloomu.edu, Bloomsburg Univ; Zi
Xiao, Shuhai, 540-231-1366 xiao@vt.edu, Virginia Polytechnic Inst & State Univ; Pi
Xie, Lian, (919) 515-1435 xie@ncsu.edu, North Carolina State Univ; As
Xie, Xiangyang, (817) 257-4395 x.xie@tcu.edu, Texas Christian Univ; GoEog
Xie, Zhixiao, (561) 297-2852 xie@fau.edu, Florida Atlantic Univ; ZirZy
Xu, Huifang, 608/265-5587 hfxu@geology.wisc.edu, Univ of Wisconsin, Madison; Gz
Xu, Jie, 915-747-7556 jxu2@utep.edu, Univ of Texas, El Paso; ClPoGz
Xu, Li, (508)289-3673 lxu@whoi.edu, Woods Hole Oceanographic Inst; Yr
Xu, Shangping, 414-229-6148 xus@uwm.edu, Univ of Wisconsin, Milwaukee; Hg
Xu, Tingying, 405-744-6358 tingying.xu@okstate.edu, Oklahoma State Univ; Cbq
Xu, Wei, wei.xu@uleth.ca, Univ of Lethbridge; Zi
XU, Yingfeng, 337-482-1113 yingfeng@louisiana.edu, Univ of Louisiana at Lafayette; ZgGe
Xuan, Chuang, +44 (0)23 80596401 c.xuan@soton.ac.uk, Univ of Southampton; Ym

Y

Yacobucci, Peg M., (419) 372-7982 mmyacob@bgsu.edu, Bowling Green State Univ; Pgi
Yacucci, Mark, (309) 268-8640 mark.yacucci@heartland.edu, Heartland Comm Coll; Zg
Yalcin, Kaplan, (541) 737-1230 yalcink@geo.oregonstate.edu, Oregon State Univ; GgeZe
Yalcin, Rebecca, yalcinr@onid.orst.edu, Oregon State Univ; Gg
Yalda, Sepideh, 717-872-3293 sepi.yalda@millersville.edu, Millersville Univ; As
Yamanaka, Tsuyuko, +44 0151 795 5291 t.yamanaka@liverpool.ac.uk, Univ of Liverpool; Ob
Yan, Beizhan, yanbz@ldeo.columbia.edu, Columbia Univ; Cg
Yan, Eugene, eyan1@uic.edu, Univ of Illinois at Chicago; Hg
Yan, Jun, (270) 745-8952 jun.yan@wku.edu, Western Kentucky Univ; Zi
Yan, Xiao-Hai, (302) 831-3694 Univ of Delaware; Zr

Yan, Y E., (630) 252-6322 eyan@anl.gov, Argonne; Gg
Yancey, Thomas E., (979) 845-0643 yancey@geo.tamu.edu, Texas A&M Univ; Pg
Yandle, Tracy, 404 727 5652 tyandle@emory.edu, Emory Univ; Ob
Yanes, Yurena, yurena.yanes@uc.edu, Univ of Cincinnati; PeCsPg
Yang, Changbing, 512-471-4364 changbing.yang@beg.utexas.edu, Univ of Texas, Austin; Hw
Yang, Da, dayang@ucdavis.edu, Univ of California, Davis; Ast
Yang, Gang, (970)-491-3789 gang.yang@colostate.edu, Colorado State Univ; CcaCg
Yang, Jianwen, 519-253-3000 x2181 jianweny@uwindsor.ca, Univ of Windsor; HwYg
Yang, Panseok, (204) 474-6910 panseok.yang@umanitoba.ca, Univ of Manitoba; CaGp
Yang, Ping, (979) 845-7679 pyang@tamu.edu, Texas A&M Univ; As
Yang, Qiang, qyang@ldeo.columbia.edu, Columbia Univ; Cg
Yang, Wan, 316 -978-3140 Wichita State Univ; Gs
Yang, Wenchang, 609-258-4101 wenchang@princeton.edu, Princeton Univ; As
Yang, Y, yangy6@cf.ac.uk, Cardiff Univ; Hg
Yang, Zhiming, (919) 530-5296 zyang@nccu.edu, North Carolina Central Univ; Zry
Yang, Zong-Liang, (512) 471-3824 liang@mail.utexas.edu, Univ of Texas, Austin; AmsHq
Yanites, Brian, (812) 855-6109 byanites@indiana.edu, Indiana Univ, Bloomington; Gm
Yankovsky, Alexander E., (803) 777-3550 ayankovsky@geol.sc.edu, Univ of South Carolina; OpnAm
Yao, Wensheng, (727) 553-3922 Univ of South Florida; Oc
Yao, Yon, +27 (0)46-603-7393 y.yao@ru.ac.za, Rhodes Univ; Eg
Yapp, Crayton J., (214) 768-3897 cjyapp@smu.edu, Southern Methodist Univ; Csl
Yarborough, Vicki, vickiy3@vt.edu, Virginia Polytechnic Inst & State Univ; Pv
Yarbrough, Lance D., 662-915-7499 ldyarbro@olemiss.edu, Univ of Mississippi; Ng
Yarbrough, Robert A., 912-478-0846 ryarbrough@georgiasouthern.edu, Georgia Southern Univ; Zn
Yardley, Bruce W., b.w.d.yardley@leeds.ac.uk, Univ of Leeds; CgEgGg
Yarger, Douglas N., (515) 294-9872 doug@iastate.edu, Iowa State Univ of Sci & Tech; As
Yassin, Barbara E., (601) 961-5571 barbara_yassin@mdeq.ms.gov, Mississippi Office of Geology; ZyiGm
Yates, Martin G., (207) 581-2154 yates@maine.edu, Univ of Maine; EgGzx
Yates, Mary Anne, (505) 667-7090 Los Alamos; Zn
Yau, Man Kong, (514) 398-3719 peter.yau@mcgill.ca, McGill Univ; As
Ye, Hengchun, (323) 343-2229 hye2@calstatela.edu, California State Univ, Los Angeles; ZyHs
Ye, Ming, mingye@scs.fsu.edu, Florida State Univ; Hg
Yeager, Kevin M., (859) 257-5431 kevin.yeager@uky.edu, Univ of Kentucky; GsCmc
Yeager, Lauren A., 361-749-6776 lyeager@utexas.edu, Univ of Texas, Austin; Og
Yeats, Robert S., 541-740-3806 yeatsr@geo.oregonstate.edu, Oregon State Univ; GtYsNg
Yee, Nathan, 848-932-5714 nyee@envsci.rutgers.edu, Rutgers, The State Univ of New Jersey; PgCo
Yegulalp, Tuncel M., (212) 854-2984 yegulalp@columbia.edu, Columbia Univ; Nm
Yeh, Jim, (520) 621-5943 yeh@hwr.arizona.edu, Univ of Arizona; Sp
Yeh, Joseph S., (512) 471-3323 joseph.yeh@beg.utexas.edu, Univ of Texas at Austin, Jackson Sch of Geosciences; Gm
Yeh, Tian-Chyi J., (520) 621-5943 ybiem@hwr.arizona.edu, Univ of Arizona; Hq
Yelderman, Jr., Joe C., (254) 710-2185 joe_yelderman@baylor.edu, Baylor Univ; HwgZu
Yelisetti, Subbarao, 361-593-4894 subbarao.yelisetti@tamuk.edu, Texas A&M Univ, Kingsville; Ygs
Yelle, Roger, (520) 621-6243 yelle@lpl.arizona.edu, Univ of Arizona; Zn
Yellen, Brian, byellen@geo.umass.edu, Univ of Massachusetts, Amherst; Gs
Yellich, John, (269) 387-8649 john.a.yellich@wmich.edu, Western Michigan Univ; EgGeHw
YEO, MYEONG-HO (CHRIS), (671)735-2693 yeom@triton.uog.edu, Univ of Guam; Hwy
Yeung, Laurence Y., (713) 348-6304 ly19@rice.edu, Rice Univ; CsAsCl
Yi, Chuixiang, 718-997-3366 chuixiang.yi@qc.cuny.edu, Graduate Sch of the City Univ of New York; Zg
Yi, Yuchan, 614 292 6005 yi.3@osu.edu, Ohio State Univ; Ydv
Yiannakoulias, Niko, (905) 525-9140 (Ext. 20117) yiannan@mcmaster.ca, McMaster Univ; Ge
Yibas, Bisrat, +270514013080 yibasbabsob@ufs.ac.za, Univ of the Free State; GegEg
Yikilmaz, Burak, mbyikilmaz@ucdavis.edu, Univ of California, Davis; Gc
Yildirim, Ismail, 00904242370000-5970 iyildirim@firat.edu.tr, Firat Univ; ScGix
Yilmaz, Alper, 614-247-4323 yilmaz.15@osu.edu, Ohio State Univ; ZfrZu
Yin, An, (310) 825-8752 yin@epss.ucla.edu, Univ of California, Los Angeles; Gt
Yin, Jianjun, 520-626-7453 yin@email.arizona.edu, Univ of Arizona; Og
Yin, Qing-zhu, 530-752-0934 qyin@ucdavis.edu, Univ of California, Davis; Cc
Yin, Zhi-Yong, (619) 260-8864 zyin@sandiego.edu, Univ of San Diego; Zir
Yogodzinkski, Gene M., 803-777-9524 gyogodzin@geol.sc.edu, Univ of South Carolina; GiCuc
Yoh, Shing, (908) 737-3692 syoh@kean.edu, Kean Univ; Am
Yon, Lisa, 7607441150 x2369 lyon@palomar.edu, Palomar Coll; OgZg
Yong, Wenjun, 519-661-2111 ext 86628 wyong4@uwo.ca, Western Univ; Yx
Yonkee, W. A., (801) 626-7419 ayonkee@weber.edu, Weber State Univ; Gct
Yoo, Kyungsoo, 612-624-7784 kyoo@umn.edu, Univ of Minnesota, Twin Cities; Sd
Yool, Stephen R., yools@email.arizona.edu, Univ of Arizona; Zri
Yoshida, Glenn, (323) 241-5296 yoshidgy@lasc.edu, Los Angeles Southwest Coll; Gg
Yoshinobu, Aaron S., (806) 834-7715 aaron.yoshinobu@ttu.edu, Texas Tech Univ; GctGu
Yoskowitz, David , 361-825-2966 david.yoskowitz@tamucc.edu, Texas A&M Univ, Corpus Christi; Zn
Youberg, Ann, ayouberg@email.arizona.edu, Univ of Arizona; Ge
Young, David, young.2536@osu.edu, Ohio State Univ; GcpCc
Young, Davis A., dotndave@comcast.net, Calvin Coll; GiRhGz
Young, Donald W., (602) 542-5025 Univ of Arizona; Zn
Young, Edward D., (310) 267-4930 eyoung@epss.ucla.edu, Univ of California, Los Angeles; CsXc
Young, George S., (814) 863-4228 young@ems.psu.edu, Pennsylvania State Univ, Univ Park; Am
Young, Graham A., (204) 988-0648 gyoung@cc.umanitoba.ca, Univ of Manitoba; Pi
Young, Grant M., (519) 473-5692 gyoung@uwo.ca, Western Univ; GrCgGt
Young, Harvey R., 204-727-9798 young@brandonu.ca, Brandon Univ; Gd
Young, Jeffrey, (204) 474-8863 jeff.young@umanitoba.ca, Univ of Manitoba; GcZe
Young, Jeri J., 602.708.8558 jeribenhorin@email.arizona.edu, Univ of Arizona; Ys
Young, John A., (608)263-2374 jayoung@wisc.edu, Univ of Wisconsin, Madison; AstOp
Young, Michael H., (512) 475-8830 michael.young@beg.utexas.edu, Univ of Texas, Austin; SpHwGe
Young, Mike, 902 494 2364 mdyoung@dal.ca, Dalhousie Univ; GgcGp
Young, Nicolas, nicolasy@ldeo.columbia.edu, Columbia Univ; Cg
Young, Patrick, (480) 727-6581 patrick.young.1@asu.edu, Arizona State Univ; Xa
Young, Priscilla E., 605-677-6144 priscilla.young@usd.edu, South Dakota Dept of Environment and Natural Resources; Zn
Young, Richard A., (585) 245-5296 young@geneseo.edu, SUNY, Geneseo; GmXgZr
Young, Robert R., 250-807-9523 robert.young@ubc.ca, Univ of British Columbia, Okanagan Campus; GlmZy
Young, William, +44(0) 113 34 31640 c.w.young@leeds.ac.uk, Univ of Leeds; Ge
Youngs, Edward, edward.youngs@open.ac.uk, Open Univ; Sp
Yow, Donald M., (859) 622-1420 don.yow@eku.edu, Eastern Kentucky Univ; AtZye
Yu, Jin-Yi, (949) 824-3878 jyyu@uci.edu, Univ of California, Irvine; AsOpZc
Yu, Qian, (413) 545-2095 qyu@geo.umass.edu, Univ of Massachusetts, Amherst; Zri
Yu, Wen-che, fgsyw@earth.sinica.edu.tw, Academia Sinica; Ys
Yu, Zicheng, 610-758-6751 ziy2@lehigh.edu, Lehigh Univ; Pe
Yuan, Xiaojun, xyuan@ldeo.columbia.edu, Columbia Univ; Op
Yuan, Yihong, (512) 245-2170 Texas State Univ; Ze
Yue, Stephen, (514) 398-4755 McGill Univ; Nx
Yuen, Cheong-yip R., (630) 252-4869 yuenr@anl.gov, Argonne; Ge
Yule, J. Douglas, (818) 677-6238 j.d.yule@csun.edu, California State Univ, Northridge; Gt
Yun, Misuk, (204) 474-8870 yun@cc.umanitoba.ca, Univ of Manitoba; Cs
Yun, Seong-Taek, 82-2-3290-3176 styun@korea.ac.kr, Korea Univ; CqHyCl
Yung, Yuk L., (626) 395-6940 yly@gps.caltech.edu, California Inst of Tech; As
Yunwei, Sun, (925)422-1587 sun4@llnl.gov, Lawrence Livermore; Ng

Yuretich, Richard F., (413) 545-0538 yuretich@geo.umass.edu, Univ of Massachusetts, Amherst; Cl
Yurkovich, Steven P., (828) 227-7367 yurkovich@wcu.edu, Western Carolina Univ; Gx
Yurtsever, Ayhan, 089/2180 4346 ayhan.yurtsever@ltz.uni-uemchen.de, Ludwig-Maximilians-Univ Muenchen; Gz
Yusoff, Ismail, 03-79674153 ismaily70@um.edu.my, Univ of Malaya; Hg
Yuter, Sandra, 919-513-7963 sandra_yuter@ncsu.edu, North Carolina State Univ; As
Yutzy, Gale, (301) 687-4369 gyutzy@frostburg.edu, Frostburg State Univ; Zn
Yvon-Lewis, Shari A., 979 458 1816 syvonlewis@ocean.tamu.edu, Texas A&M Univ; Oc

Z

Zabielski, Victor, (703) 845-6507 vzabielski@nvcc.edu, Northern Virginia Comm Coll - Alexandria; GgOg
Zaccaria, Daniele, 530 219-7502 dzaccaria@ucdavis.edu, Univ of California, Davis; HgRw
Zachos, James, 831-459-4644 jzachos@ucsc.edu, Univ of California, Santa Cruz; Pc
Zachos, Louis G., (662) 915-8827 lgzachos@olemiss.edu, Univ of Mississippi; PiGeNx
Zachry, Doy L., (479) 575-2785 dzachry@uark.edu, Univ of Arkansas, Fayetteville; Gr
Zaffos, Andrew A., 520.621.3635 azafazaffos@email.arizona.edu, Univ of Arizona; Zf
Zafian, Holly, holly.zafian@austincc.edu, Austin Comm Coll District; Ze
Zafiriou, Oliver C., (508) 289-2342 ozafiriou@whoi.edu, Woods Hole Oceanographic Inst; Oc
Zahm, Christopher K., 512-471-3159 chris.zahm@beg.utexas.edu, Univ of Texas, Austin; Yg
Zaitchik, Benjamin, 410-516-7135 bzaitch1@jhu.edu, Johns Hopkins Univ; As
Zaja, Annalisa, +390498279193 annalisa.zaja@unipd.it, Univ degli Studi di Padova; Yg
Zajac, Roman N., (203) 932-7114 rzajac@newhaven.edu, Univ of New Haven; Zni
Zajacz, Zoltan, 416-946-0278 zajacz@es.utoronto.ca, Univ of Toronto; Cu
Zakardjian, Bruno, (418) 723-1986 (Ext. 1570) bruno_zakardjian@uqar.qc.ca, Universite du Quebec a Rimouski; Ob
Zakharova, Natalia, 989-774-4496 zakha1n@cmich.edu, Central Michigan Univ; YgGe
Zakrzewski, Richard J., (785) 628-5389 rzakrzew@fhsu.edu, Fort Hays State Univ; PvsPe
Zalasiewicz, Jan, +440116 252 3928 jaz1@le.ac.uk, Leicester Univ; Pg
Zaleha, Michael J., (937) 327-7331 mzaleha@wittenberg.edu, Wittenberg Univ; Gs
Zaleha, Robert, (216) 987-5278 robert.zaleha@tri-c.edu, Cuyahoga Comm Coll - Western Campus; Zg
Zaman, Musharraf, 405-325-2626 zaman@ou.edu, Univ of Oklahoma; Np
Zamani, Behzad, +98 (411) 339 2700 zamani@tabrizu.ac.ir, Univ of Tabriz; GtYs
Zambito, James J., (608) 363-2223 zambitoj@beloit.edu, Beloit Coll; PcGsPg
Zampieri, Dario, +390498279179 dario.zampieri@unipd.it, Univ degli Studi di Padova; Gc
Zamstein, Lavi, 706-507-8089 zamstein_lavi@columbusstate.edu, Columbus State Univ; Zn
Zamzow, Craig E., czamzow@clarion.edu, Clarion Univ; Gi
Zanazzi, Alessandro, (801) 863-5395 alessandro.zanazzi@uvu.edu, Utah Valley Univ; CgsPe
Zandt, George, (520) 621-2273 gzandt@email.arizona.edu, Univ of Arizona; Ys
Zanella, Elena, elena.zanella@unito.it, Univ di Torino; Ym
Zanetti, Kathleen, (702) 895-4789 Univ of Nevada, Las Vegas; Gg
Zaniewski, Kazimierz J., (920) 424-4105 zaniewsk@uwosh.edu, Univ of Wisconsin Oshkosh; Zn
Zappa, Christopher, zappa@ldeo.columbia.edu, Columbia Univ; Op
Zarillo, Gary , 321-674-7378 zarillo@fit.edu, Florida Inst of Tech; OupOn
Zarnetske, Jay, (517) 353-3249 jpz@msu.edu, Michigan State Univ; Hwg
Zarroca Hernández, Mario, ++935812033 mario.zarroca.hernandez@uab.cat, Universitat Autonoma de Barcelona; YgNg
Zarzycki, Colin, czarzycki@psu.edu, Pennsylvania State Univ, Univ Park; As
Zaspel, Craig E., (406) 683-7366 craig.zaspel@umwestern.edu, Univ of Montana Western; Yg
Zattin, Massimiliano, +390498279186 massimiliano.zattin@unipd.it, Univ degli Studi di Padova; Gs
Zawadzki, Isztar, (514) 398-1034 isztar.zawadzki@mcgill.ca, McGill Univ; AsZr
Zawiskie, John M., (313) 577-2506 jzawiskie@cranbrook.edu, Wayne State Univ; Gg
Zayac, John M., (818) 710-2218 zayacjm@piercecollege.edu, Los Angeles Pierce Coll; Ggv
Zebker, Howard A., (650) 723-8067 zebker@stanford.edu, Stanford Univ; Yx
Zeebe, Richard E., (808) 956-6473 zeebe@soest.hawaii.edu, Univ of Hawai'i, Manoa; Ou
Zehnder, Joseph A., 402-280-2448 zehnder@creighton.edu, Creighton Univ; As
Zehr, Jonathan P., (831) 459-4009 zehrj@cats.ucsc.edu, Univ of California, Santa Cruz; Ob
Zeidouni, Mehdi, mehdi.zeidouni@beg.utexas.edu, Univ of Texas, Austin; Eo
Zeiger, Elaine, (312) 665-7627 Field Mus of Natural History; Zn
Zeigler, E. Lynn, 678-891-3767 ezeigler1@gsu.edu, Georgia State Univ, Perimeter Coll, Clarkston Campus; Gdg
Zeinijahromi, Abbas, abbas.zeinijahromi@adelaide.edu.au, Univ of Adelaide; Np
Zeitler, Peter K., (610) 758-3671 pkz0@lehigh.edu, Lehigh Univ; Cc
Zeitlhöfler, Matthias, 089/2180 6570 matthias@zeitlhoefler.de, Ludwig-Maximilians-Univ Muenchen; Gg
Zelazny, Lucian W., (540) 231-9781 Virginia Polytechnic Inst & State Univ; Sc
Zelenitsky, Darla, 403 220-8016 dkzeleni@ucalgary.ca, Univ of Calgary; Pg
Zelizer, Nora, 609 258-5809 nzelizer@princeton.edu, Princeton Univ; Zn
Zelt, Colin A., (713) 348-4757 czelt@rice.edu, Rice Univ; Yg
Zeman, Josef, +420 549 49 8295 jzeman@sci.muni.cz, Masaryk Univ; CgpCe
Zender, Charles, 949-824-2987 zender@uci.edu, Univ of California, Irvine; As
Zeng, Hongliu, 512-475-6382 hongliu.zeng@beg.utexas.edu, Univ of Texas, Austin; YsGs
Zeng, Ning, (301) 405-5377 zeng@umd.edu, Univ of Maryland; AsCgGl
Zentilli, Marcos, (902) 494-3873 Dalhousie Univ; Eg
Zentner, Nick, (509) 963-2828 nick@geology.cwu.edu, Central Washington Univ; Gg
Zerkle, Aubrey, +44 01334 464949 az29@st-andrews.ac.uk, Univ of St. Andrews; Co
Zhai, Xiaoming, 847 543-2504 Coll of Lake County; Gp
Zhan, F Benjamin, (512) 245-2170 Texas State Univ; Zi
Zhan, Hongbin, (979) 862-7961 zhan@geos.tamu.edu, Texas A&M Univ; Hw
Zhan, Zhongwen, 626-395-6906 zwzhan@caltech.edu, California Inst of Tech; Ys
Zhang, Bo, 205-348-4544 bzhang33@ua.edu, Univ of Alabama; YeGoEo
Zhang, Caiyun, 561-297-2648 czhang3@fau.edu, Florida Atlantic Univ; Zr
Zhang, Chi, 785-864-4974 chizhang@ku.edu, Univ of Kansas; YgxYu
Zhang, Chidong, (206) 526-6239 chidong.zhang@noaa.gov, Univ of Washington; AsmOp
Zhang, Guiming, 303-871-7908 guiming.zhang@du.edu, Univ of Denver; Zi
Zhang, Guorong, (785) 625-3425 gzhang@ksu.edu, Kansas State Univ; So
Zhang, Henian, (404) 894-1738 henian.zhang@eas.gatech.edu, Georgia Inst of Tech; As
Zhang, Huan, 860-405-9237 huan.zhang@uconn.edu, Univ of Connecticut; Ob
Zhang, Jin , 505-277-1607 Univ of New Mexico; Gyp
Zhang, Jin, jinzhang@unm.edu, Univ of New Mexico; Gy
Zhang, Jinhong, (520) 626-9656 jhzhang@email.arizona.edu, Univ of Arizona; Nm
Zhang, Lin, 361-825-2436 lin.zhang@tamucc.edu, Texas A&M Univ, Corpus Christi; Cs
Zhang, Max, 607-254-5402 kz33@cornell.edu, Cornell Univ; Zn
Zhang, Minghua, 530-752-4953 mhzhang@ucdavis.edu, Univ of California, Davis; HgEg
Zhang, Minghua , 530-752-4953 mhzhang@ucdavis.edu, Univ of California, Davis; Hg
Zhang, Minghua, (631) 632-8318 minghua.zhang@stonybrook.edu, SUNY, Stony Brook; As
Zhang, Ning, 937 376 6043 nzhang@centralstate.edu, Central State Univ; RwEo
Zhang, Pengfei, 212-650-5609 pzhang@ccny.cuny.edu, Graduate Sch of the City Univ of New York; Zg
Zhang, Qiaofeng (Robin), (270) 809-6760 qzhang@murraystate.edu, Murray State Univ; ZirZu
Zhang, Ren, (254)7102496 ren_zhang@baylor.edu, Baylor Univ; Cs
Zhang, Renyi, (979) 845-7671 renyi-zhang@geos.tamu.edu, Texas A&M Univ; As
Zhang, Rong, (609) 987-5061 rong.zhang@noaa.gov, Princeton Univ; Op
Zhang, Rui, 337-482-6920 Univ of Louisiana at Lafayette; Ye
Zhang, Tongwei, 512-232-1496 tongwei.zhang@beg.utexas.edu, Univ of Texas, Austin; Cgs
Zhang, Xi, (831) 502-8126 xiz@ucsc.edu, Univ of California, Santa Cruz; AsXy
Zhang, Xiaodong, (228) 688-3178 xiaodong.zhang@usm.edu, Univ of Southern Mississippi; Op
Zhang, Xinning, 609-258-7438 xinningz@princeton.edu, Princeton Univ; Cb

www.ingramcontent.com/pod-product-compliance
Lightning Source LLC
Chambersburg PA
CBHW052149280326
41926CB00109B/4114
9780922152469